## KEY TO PRONUNCIATIONS

| | | | |
|---|---|---|---|
| s | see, miss | z | zeal, lazy, those |
| sh | shoe, push | zh | vision, measure |
| t | ten, bit | | |
| th | thin, path | ə | occurs only |
| ŧh | that, other | | in unaccented |
| | | | syllables and |
| ŭ | up, love | | indicates the |
| ū | use, cute | | sound of |
| û | urge, burn | | a *in* alone |
| | | | e *in* system |
| v | voice, live | | i *in* easily |
| w | west, away | | o *in* gallop |
| y | yes, young | | u *in* circus |

## TIME SCALE
### 600 B.C.–A.D. 125

**B.C.**

**600** — Ezekiel
Babylonians sack Jerusalem
Exile in Babylon

Second Isaiah
Cyrus begins Persian Empire
Haggai and Zechariah

**500** — Second temple built

Nehemiah rebuilds Jerusalem

**400** — The Pentateuch accepted
as Scripture
(or 550?)

Alexander conquers East

**300** — Egypt rules Palestine

The Prophets accepted
as Scripture

**200** — Syria rules Palestine

Maccabees
Hasmonean rulers

**100** — Romans conquer Palestine

Herod the Great
Third temple built

**A.D.** — Jesus' ministry
Paul's ministry, letters

Romans destroy Jerusalem

**100** — The Writings close OT Canon
Last NT books written

# THE INTERPRETER'S
# DICTIONARY OF THE BIBLE

# EDITORIAL BOARD

# THE INTERPRETER'S DICTIONARY OF THE BIBLE

## An Illustrated Encyclopedia

IDENTIFYING AND EXPLAINING ALL PROPER NAMES AND
SIGNIFICANT TERMS AND SUBJECTS IN
THE HOLY SCRIPTURES, INCLUDING THE APOCRYPHA
With Attention to Archaeological Discoveries and
Researches into the Life and Faith of Ancient Times

מלאה הארץ דעה את־יהוה

*The earth shall be full of the knowledge of the Lord*—ISAIAH 11:9c

NASHVILLE    *Abingdon Press*    NEW YORK

ISBN 0-687-19270-6
Library of Congress Catalog Card Number: 62-9387

Scripture quotations unless otherwise noted are from the Revised
Standard Version of the Bible and are copyright 1946 and 1952 by
the Division of Christian Education of the National Council of the
Churches of Christ in the U.S.A. Scripture quotations designated
"Moffatt" are from *The Bible, A New Translation*, by James Moffatt,
copyright in the United States, 1935, by Harper & Brothers, New
York; copyright in countries of the International Copyright Union by
Hodder & Stoughton, Ltd., London. Those designated "Amer. Trans."
or "Goodspeed" are from *The Complete Bible, An American Translation*,
by J. M. Powis Smith and Edgar J. Goodspeed, copyright 1939 by
the University of Chicago. Quotations from the Apocrypha unless
otherwise noted are from The Apocrypha: Revised Standard Version
of the Old Testament and are copyright 1957 by the Division of Education of the National Council of the Churches of Christ in the U.S.A.

**I**

MANUFACTURED BY THE PARTHENON PRESS, AT
NASHVILLE, TENNESSEE, UNITED STATES OF AMERICA

# CONSULTANTS

WILLIAM FOXWELL ALBRIGHT
Professor Emeritus of Semitic Languages, Johns Hopkins University

DAVID NOEL FREEDMAN
Professor of Hebrew and Old Testament Literature, Pittsburgh Theological Seminary

GEORGE E. MENDENHALL
Professor of Near Eastern Languages and Literature, University of Michigan

BRUCE M. METZGER
Professor of New Testament Language and Literature, Princeton Theological Seminary

JAMES MUILENBURG
Professor of Hebrew and the Cognate Languages, Union Theological Seminary, New York

JOHN C. TREVER
Professor of Religion, Baldwin-Wallace College

# CONTRIBUTORS

RAYMOND ABBA
Head of the Department of Divinity, Collegiate Faculty of the University of Wales School of Education, Swansea

ELIZABETH ACHTEMEIER
Visiting Lecturer on the Old Testament, Lancaster Theological Seminary

PAUL J. ACHTEMEIER
Professor of New Testament, Lancaster Theological Seminary

BERNHARD W. ANDERSON
Dean and Professor of Biblical Theology, The Theological School, Drew University

ELIAS ANDREWS
Principal and Professor of New Testament, Queen's Theological College, Kingston, Ontario

MICHAEL AVI-YONAH
Associate Professor of Archaeology, Hebrew University, Jerusalem

OTTO J. BAAB
Late Professor of Old Testament Interpretation, Garrett Theological Seminary

DENIS BALY
Chairman of the Department of Religion, Kenyon College

BERNARD J. BAMBERGER
Rabbi, Congregation Shaaray Tefila, New York

ALBERT E. BARNETT
Late Professor of New Testament, Candler School of Theology, Emory University

GEORGES AUGUSTIN BARROIS
Professor of the History and Theology of the Medieval Church, Princeton Theological Seminary

IRVIN W. BATDORF
Professor of New Testament Literature, United Theological Seminary, Dayton

WILLIAM A. BEARDSLEE
Professor of Bible, Emory University

FRANK W. BEARE
Professor of New Testament Studies, Trinity College, Toronto

DWIGHT MARION BECK
Professor Emeritus of Bible, Syracuse University

HARRELL F. BECK
Associate Professor of Old Testament, Boston University School of Theology

J. CHRISTIAAN BEKER
Associate Professor of New Testament Theology, Pacific School of Religion

LOUISA BELLINGER
Curator-Analyst, Textile Museum, Washington, D. C.

IMMANUEL BEN-DOR
Professor of Biblical Archaeology, Candler School of Theology, Emory University

OTTO BETZ
Associate Professor of New Testament, Chicago Theological Seminary

MATTHEW BLACK
Principal and Professor of Biblical Criticism, St. Mary's College, St. Andrews University

EDWIN CYRIL BLACKMAN
Professor of New Testament Literature and Exegesis, Emmanuel College, Victoria University, Toronto

EDWARD P. BLAIR
Professor of New Testament Interpretation, Garrett Theological Seminary

SHELDON H. BLANK
Professor of Bible, Hebrew Union College — Jewish Institute of Religion, Cincinnati

F. S. BODENHEIMER
Late Professor of Zoology, Hebrew University, Jerusalem

JOHN WICK BOWMAN
Professor of New Testament Interpretation, San Francisco Theological Seminary

RAYMOND A. BOWMAN
Professor of Oriental Languages and Literatures, Oriental Institute, University of Chicago

JAMES RODNEY BRANTON
Professor of New Testament Interpretation, Colgate Rochester Divinity School

JOHN BRIGHT
Professor of Hebrew and the Interpretation of the Old Testament, Union Theological Seminary, Richmond

WILLIAM H. BROWNLEE
Professor of Religion, Claremont Graduate School, Claremont University College

F. F. BRUCE
Professor of Biblical Criticism and Exegesis, University of Manchester

WALTER A. BRUEGGEMANN
Assistant Professor of Old Testament, Eden Theological Seminary

T. A. BURKILL
Professor of Christian Thought, Cornell University

MILLAR BURROWS
Professor Emeritus of Biblical Theology, The Divinity School, Yale University

HENRY J. CADBURY
Professor of Divinity, Emeritus, Harvard University

GEORGE B. CAIRD
Tutor, Mansfield College, Oxford

J. Y. CAMPBELL
Professor Emeritus of New Testament, Westminster College, Cambridge

SAMUEL A. CARTLEDGE
Professor of New Testament Language, Literature, and Exegesis, and Dean of the Graduate Department, Columbia Theological Seminary

BREVARD S. CHILDS
Associate Professor of Old Testament, The Divinity School, Yale University

KENNETH W. CLARK
Professor of New Testament, The Divinity School, Duke University

SIMON COHEN
Reference Librarian, Hebrew Union College—Jewish Institute of Religion, Cincinnati

ERNEST CADMAN COLWELL
President, Southern California School of Theology at Claremont

ELMER J. COOK
Late Professor of the Literature and Interpretation of the New Testament, Berkeley Divinity School, New Haven

GERALD B. COOKE
Assistant Professor of Religion, Oberlin College

RICHARD W. CORNEY
Instructor in Old Testament, General Theological Seminary

C. E. B. CRANFIELD
Lecturer in Theology, University of Durham

ABRAHAM CRONBACH
Professor Emeritus of Jewish Social Studies, Hebrew Union College—Jewish Institute of Religion, Cincinnati

OSCAR CULLMANN
Professor of New Testament and Early Christianity, University of Basel and The Sorbonne

BRUCE T. DAHLBERG
Assistant Professor of Religion and Biblical Literature, Smith College

EDWARD R. DALGLISH
Professor of Old Testament Interpretation and Hebrew, Eastern Baptist Theological Seminary

PAUL E. DAVIES
Professor of New Testament Greek and Exegesis, McCormick Theological Seminary

W. D. DAVIES
Professor of Biblical Theology, Union Theological Seminary, New York

ROBERT C. DENTAN
Professor of Old Testament Literature and Interpretation, General Theological Seminary

SIMON J. DE VRIES
Associate Professor of Religion and Bible, Hope College, and Instructor in Hebrew, Western Theological Seminary, Holland, Michigan

ERICH DINKLER
Professor of New Testament Literature, University of Bonn

GLANVILLE DOWNEY
Professor of Byzantine Literature, Dumbarton Oaks, Washington, D. C.

MARK J. DRESDEN
Professor of Iranian Studies, University of Pennsylvania

GEORGE S. DUNCAN
Former Principal and Professor of New Testament, St. Mary's College, St. Andrews University

OTTO EISSFELDT
Professor Emeritus of Old Testament and Semitic Religious History, University of Halle

KARL ELLIGER
Professor of Old Testament, University of Tübingen

WALTHER ELTESTER
Professor of Church History, University of Tübingen

DONALD M. C. ENGLERT
Professor of Hebrew and Old Testament Science, Lancaster Theological Seminary

MORTON SCOTT ENSLIN
Professor of Biblical Languages and Literature, The Theological School, St. Lawrence University

ISIDORE EPSTEIN
Principal, Jews' College, London

OWEN E. EVANS
Lecturer in New Testament, University of Manchester; Tutor, Hartley-Victoria College

WILLIAM R. FARMER
Associate Professor of New Testament, Perkins School of Theology, Southern Methodist University

S. VERNON FAWCETT
Professor of Old Testament, Union College of British Columbia

FLOYD V. FILSON
Dean and Professor of New Testament Literature and History, McCormick Theological Seminary

JACK FINEGAN
Professor of New Testament History and Archaeology, Pacific School of Religion

WILLIAM F. FLEMINGTON
Principal and Tutor in New Testament Language and Literature, Wesley House, Cambridge

JOHN W. FLIGHT
Professor Emeritus of Biblical Literature, Haverford College

DAVID NOEL FREEDMAN
Professor of Hebrew and Old Testament Literature, Pittsburgh Theological Seminary

WENDELL W. FRERICHS
Associate Professor of Old Testament, Luther Theological Seminary, St. Paul, Minnesota

CHARLES T. FRITSCH
Professor of Hebrew and Old Testament Literature, Princeton Theological Seminary

STANLEY B. FROST
Dean and Professor of Old Testament, Faculty of Divinity, McGill University

ROBERT W. FUNK
Associate Professor of New Testament, The Theological School, Drew University

KURT GALLING
Professor of Old Testament and the Archaeology of Palestine, University of Göttingen

PAUL LESLIE GARBER
Professor of Bible, Agnes Scott College

THEODOR H. GASTER
Professor of Ancient Civilizations, Fairleigh Dickinson University; Professor of Comparative Religion, Dropsie College

FRED D. GEALY
Professor of New Testament, The Methodist Theological School in Ohio

IGNACE J. GELB
Professor of Assyriology, Oriental Institute, University of Chicago

STANLEY GEVIRTZ
Assistant Professor of Palestinian History, University of Chicago

S. MacLean Gilmour
Professor of New Testament, Andover Newton Theological School

F. Wilbur Gingrich
Professor of Greek, Albright College

Victor Roland Gold
Professor of Old Testament, Pacific Lutheran Theological Seminary

Judah Goldin
Professor of Jewish Studies, Yale University

Edwin M. Good
Associate Professor of Religion and Hebrew, Stanford University

Erwin R. Goodenough
Professor Emeritus of Religion, Yale University

Cyrus H. Gordon
Professor of Near Eastern Studies, Brandeis University

Norman K. Gottwald
Professor of Old Testament, Andover Newton Theological School

Frederick C. Grant
Professor Emeritus of Biblical Theology, Union Theological Seminary, New York

Robert M. Grant
Professor of New Testament, The Divinity School, University of Chicago

John Gray
Lecturer in Hebrew and Biblical Criticism, University of Aberdeen

Kenneth Grayston
Professor of New Testament Language and Literature, Didsbury College

Moshe Greenberg
Professor of Biblical Studies, University of Pennsylvania

Jonas C. Greenfield
Associate Professor of Hebrew, University of California at Los Angeles

Kendrick Grobel
Professor of New Testament, The Divinity School, Vanderbilt University

Edward D. Grohman
Instructor in Old Testament, Pittsburgh Theological Seminary

Harvey H. Guthrie, Jr.
Associate Professor of Old Testament, Episcopal Theological School, Cambridge, Massachusetts

Moses Hadas
Professor of Greek, Columbia University

Alfred Haldar
Assistant Professor of Assyriology, University of Uppsala

Herbert Hamburger
Numismatist, Binyamina, Israel

R. W. Hamilton
Keeper of the Department of Antiquities, Ashmolean Museum, Oxford

E. John Hamlin
Principal, McGilvary Theological Seminary, Chiengmai, Thailand

Paul L. Hammer
Professor of New Testament Theology, United Theological Seminary of the Twin Cities

J. Penrose Harland
Professor of Archaeology, University of North Carolina

Walter J. Harrelson
Professor of Old Testament, The Divinity School, Vanderbilt University

R. K. Harrison
Professor of Hebrew, Wycliffe College, University of Toronto

Dorothea Ward Harvey
Assistant Professor of Religion and Philosophy, Milwaukee-Downer College

Johannes Hempel
Professor of Old Testament, University of Göttingen

GWYNNE HENTON DAVIES
Principal, Regent's Park College, Oxford University

R. LANSING HICKS
Professor of the Literature and Interpretation of the Old Testament, Berkeley Divinity School, New Haven

SIDNEY B. HOENIG
Professor of Jewish History, Yeshiva University

CARL G. HOWIE
Minister, Calvary Presbyterian Church, San Francisco

J. PHILIP HYATT
Professor of Old Testament, The Divinity School, Vanderbilt University

JARED J. JACKSON
Assistant Professor of Old Testament, Huron College

EDMOND JACOB
Professor of Old Testament, University of Strasbourg

THORKILD JACOBSEN
Professor of Social Institutions, Oriental Institute, University of Chicago

ARTHUR JEFFERY
Late Professor of Semitic Languages, Columbia University

ERNST JENNI
Professor of Old Testament, University of Basel

ROBERT FRANCIS JOHNSON
Professor of Biblical Languages and Theology, Episcopal Theological Seminary of the Southwest, Austin, Texas

SHERMAN E. JOHNSON
Dean and Professor of New Testament Literature, The Church Divinity School of the Pacific

GEORGE JOHNSTON
Professor of New Testament Language and Literature, McGill University; Prin-

cipal, United Theological College, Montreal

ARVID S. KAPELRUD
Professor of Old Testament, University of Oslo

JOSEPH KASTER
Member of Faculty, The New School for Social Research, New York

HOWARD CLARK KEE
Professor of New Testament, The Theological School, Drew University

JAMES L. KELSO
Professor of Old Testament History and Biblical Archaeology, Pittsburgh Theological Seminary

THOMAS S. KEPLER
Professor of New Testament Language and Literature, Graduate School of Theology, Oberlin College

JOHN KNOX
Professor of New Testament, Union Theological Seminary, New York

VERNON H. KOOY
Professor of Hellenistic Greek and New Testament Exegesis, New Brunswick Theological Seminary

EMIL G. KRAELING
Retired; Former Teacher of Old Testament at Union Theological Seminary, New York, and Columbia University

CHARLES F. KRAFT
Professor of Old Testament Interpretation, Garrett Theological Seminary

SAMUEL NOAH KRAMER
Curator of Tablet Collections and Research Professor of Assyriology, University of Pennsylvania

THOMAS O. LAMBDIN
Assistant Professor of Near Eastern Languages and Literature, Harvard University

# CONTRIBUTORS

G. W. H. LAMPE
Professor of Divinity, Cambridge University

GEORGE M. LANDES
Associate Professor of Old Testament, Union Theological Seminary, New York

ELMER A. LESLIE
Professor Emeritus of Hebrew and Old Testament Literature, Boston University School of Theology

HILDEGARD LEWY
Research Scholar, Cincinnati

MARC LOVELACE
Professor of Archaeology, Southeastern Baptist Theological Seminary

MARY ELY LYMAN
Professor Emerita of English Bible, Union Theological Seminary, New York

HUGH B. MACLEAN
Late Dean, New Brunswick Theological University

JOHN H. MARKS
Associate Professor of Oriental Studies, Princeton University

JOHN MARSH
Principal, Mansfield College, Oxford University

THEODOR M. MAUCH
Associate Professor of Religion, Trinity College, Hartford

HERBERT G. MAY
Professor of Old Testament Language and Literature, Graduate School of Theology, Oberlin College

HARVEY K. MCARTHUR
Professor of New Testament, The Hartford Seminary Foundation

S. VERNON MCCASLAND
Professor of Religion, University of Virginia

CHESTER C. MCCOWN
Late Professor of New Testament, Pacific School of Religion

W. STEWART MCCULLOUGH
Professor of Near Eastern Studies, University College, University of Toronto

MACHTELD J. MELLINK
Associate Professor of Classical and Near Eastern Archaeology, Bryn Mawr College

GEORGE E. MENDENHALL
Professor of Near Eastern Languages and Literature, University of Michigan

ISAAC MENDELSOHN
Professor of Semitic Languages, Columbia University

PHILIPPE H. MENOUD
Professor of New Testament, University of Neuchâtel and Montpellier Faculty of Protestant Theology

BRUCE M. METZGER
Professor of New Testament Language and Literature, Princeton Theological Seminary

JOSEPH MIHELIC
Professor of Old Testament Language and Literature, The Theological Seminary, University of Dubuque

PAUL S. MINEAR
Professor of Biblical Theology, The Divinity School, Yale University

C. LESLIE MITTON
Principal and Tutor in New Testament Studies, Handsworth College, Birmingham

DALE MOODY
Professor of Christian Theology, Southern Baptist Theological Seminary

JULIAN MORGENSTERN
President and Professor Emeritus of Bible, Hebrew Union College—Jewish Institute of Religion, Cincinnati

WILLIAM H. MORTON
Professor of Biblical Archaeology, Midwestern Baptist Theological Seminary

C. F. D. MOULE
Professor of Divinity, Cambridge University

SIGMUND MOWINCKEL
Professor Emeritus of Old Testament, University of Oslo

M. LUCETTA MOWRY
Professor of Biblical History, Wellesley College

JAMES MUILENBURG
Professor of Hebrew and the Cognate Languages, Union Theological Seminary, New York

JACOB M. MYERS
Professor of Hebrew and Old Testament Literature and Theology, Lutheran Theological Seminary, Gettysburg

B. DAVIE NAPIER
Professor of Old Testament Criticism and Interpretation, The Divinity School, Yale University

WILLIAM NEIL
Warden of Hugh Stewart Hall, University of Nottingham

MURRAY L. NEWMAN
Associate Professor of Old Testament, Protestant Episcopal Theological Seminary in Virginia

JOHN M. NORRIS
Professor of New Testament, Union Theological Seminary, Buenos Aires

CHRISTOPHER R. NORTH
Professor Emeritus of Hebrew, University College of North Wales

A. LEO OPPENHEIM
Professor of Assyriology, Oriental Institute, University of Chicago

HARRY M. ORLINSKY
Professor of Bible, Hebrew Union College—Jewish Institute of Religion, New York

YAAQOV PALMONI
Director, A. D. Gordon Agriculture and Nature Study Institute, Deganya A, Israel

PIERSON PARKER
Professor of the Literature and Interpretation of the New Testament, General Theological Seminary

MERRILL M. PARVIS
Professor of New Testament, Candler School of Theology, Emory University

DAVID C. PELLETT
Professor of Old Testament, Christian Theological Seminary, Indianapolis

ANN PERKINS
Lecturer in Archaeology, Yale University

ROBERT H. PFEIFFER
Late Curator of the Semitic Museum, Harvard University

OTTO A. PIPER
Professor of New Testament Literature and Exegesis, Princeton Theological Seminary

HAROLD H. PLATZ
Professor of Biblical Literature, United Theological Seminary, Dayton

MARVIN H. POPE
Associate Professor of Northwest Semitic Languages, The Divinity School, Yale University

NORMAN W. PORTEOUS
Professor of Hebrew and Semitic Languages, New College, Edinburgh University

JAMES B. PRITCHARD
Professor of Old Testament Literature, Church Divinity School of the Pacific

ALEXANDER C. PURDY
Dean and Professor Emeritus of New Testament, Hartford Theological Seminary

# CONTRIBUTORS

WARREN A. QUANBECK
Professor of Systematic Theology, Luther Theological Seminary, St. Paul, Minnesota

ISAAC RABINOWITZ
Professor of Biblical and Hebrew Studies, Cornell University

GERHARD VON RAD
Professor of Old Testament Exegesis, University of Heidelberg

WILLIAM L. REED
Professor of Old Testament, The College of the Bible, Lexington, Kentucky

ALAN RICHARDSON
Professor of Christian Theology, University of Nottingham

CYRIL C. RICHARDSON
Professor of Church History, Union Theological Seminary, New York

H. NEIL RICHARDSON
Associate Professor of Old Testament, Boston University School of Theology

MARTIN RIST
Professor of New Testament and Christian History, The Iliff School of Theology

BLEDDYN J. ROBERTS
Professor of Hebrew, University College of North Wales

JAMES M. ROBINSON
Professor of Theology and New Testament, Southern California School of Theology at Claremont

J. A. T. ROBINSON
Bishop Suffragan of Woolwich

JAMES F. ROSS
Assistant Professor of Old Testament, The Theological School, Drew University

H. H. ROWLEY
Emeritus Professor of Hebrew Language and Literature, University of Manchester

DONALD T. ROWLINGSON
Professor of New Testament Literature, Boston University School of Theology

J. COERT RYLAARSDAM
Professor of Old Testament Theology, The Divinity School, University of Chicago

J. ALVIN SANDERS
Professor of Old Testament Interpretation, Colgate Rochester Divinity School

J. N. SANDERS
Late Lecturer in Divinity and Dean of Peterhouse, Cambridge University

SAMUEL SANDMEL
Provost and Professor of Bible and Hellenistic Literature, Hebrew Union College—Jewish Institute of Religion, Cincinnati

ERNEST W. SAUNDERS
Professor of New Testament Interpretation, Garrett Theological Seminary

RICHARD L. SCHEEF, JR.
Associate Professor of New Testament, Eden Theological Seminary

R. F. SCHNELL
Principal and Professor of Old Testament Language and Literature, St. Andrew's College, University of Saskatchewan

FREDERICK T. SCHUMACHER
Assistant Professor of Religion, Vassar College

R. B. Y. SCOTT
Professor of Religion, Princeton University

OSCAR J. F. SEITZ
Professor of New Testament, Bexley Hall, Kenyon College

OVID R. SELLERS
Professor Emeritus of Old Testament Language and Literature, McCormick Theological Seminary

MASSEY H. SHEPHERD, JR.
Professor of Liturgics, The Church Divinity School of the Pacific

MONTGOMERY J. SHROYER
Professor Emeritus of New Testament, Wesley Theological Seminary, Washington, D. C.

JAMES D. SMART
Professor of Biblical Interpretation, Union Theological Seminary, New York

CHARLES W. F. SMITH
Professor of the Literature and Interpretation of the New Testament, Episcopal Theological School, Cambridge, Massachusetts

MORTON SMITH
Associate Professor of Ancient History, Columbia University

ISAIAH SONNE
Late Research Librarian and Lecturer on Medieval Jewish History, Emeritus, Hebrew Union College—Jewish Institute of Religion, Cincinnati

E. A. SPEISER
Professor of Hebrew and Semitic Languages and Literatures and Chairman of the Department of Oriental Studies, University of Pennsylvania

W. E. STAPLES
Professor Emeritus of Near Eastern Studies, Victoria College, University of Toronto

KRISTER STENDAHL
Professor of New Testament Studies, The Divinity School, Harvard University

W. F. STINESPRING
Professor of Old Testament and Semitics, The Divinity School, Duke University

ALBERT C. SUNDBERG, JR.
Associate Professor of New Testament, Garrett Theological Seminary

J. CARTER SWAIM
Executive Director, Department of the English Bible, National Council of the Churches of Christ in the U. S. A.

STEPHEN SZIKSZAI
Professor of Old Testament Languages and Literature, Bangor Theological Seminary

VINCENT TAYLOR
Retired Principal and Professor of New Testament Language and Literature, Wesley College, Leeds

SIDNEY S. TEDESCHE
Retired Rabbi, Union Temple, Brooklyn, New York

SAMUEL TERRIEN
Professor of Old Testament, Union Theological Seminary, New York

JOHN ALEXANDER THOMPSON
Professor of Old Testament Language and Exegesis, Evangelical Theological Seminary, Cairo, Egypt

BURTON H. THROCKMORTON, JR.
Professor of New Testament Language and Literature, Bangor Theological Seminary

LAWRENCE E. TOOMBS
Professor of Old Testament, The Theological School, Drew University

JOHN C. TREVER
Professor of Religion, Baldwin-Wallace College

OLGA TUFNELL
Archaeologist, London

NIGEL TURNER
Rector, Milton Parish, Cambridge, England

W. C. VAN UNNIK
Professor of New Testament and Early Christian Literature, University of Utrecht

GUS W. VAN BEEK
Associate Curator of Old World Archaeology, Smithsonian Institution, Washington, D. C.

A. J. VROMAN
Director, Mapping Division, Israel Geological Survey

JAMES M. WARD
Assistant Professor of Old Testament, Perkins School of Theology, Southern Methodist University

LUTHER A. WEIGLE
Dean and Professor Emeritus of Religious Education, The Divinity School, Yale University; Chairman, Standard Bible Committee

ERIC WERNER
Professor of Liturgical Music, Hebrew Union College—Jewish Institute of Religion, New York

JOHN W. WEVERS
Associate Professor of Near Eastern Studies, University College, University of Toronto

JAMES A. WHARTON
Assistant Professor of Old Testament, Austin Presbyterian Theological Seminary

CHESTER L. WICKWIRE
Lecturer in Religion, Johns Hopkins University

ALLEN WIKGREN
Chairman of the Department of New Testament and Early Christian Literature, University of Chicago

RONALD J. WILLIAMS
Professor of Near Eastern Studies, University College, University of Toronto

WALTER G. WILLIAMS
Professor of Old Testament Literature, The Iliff School of Theology

HAROLD R. WILLOUGHBY
Late Professor Emeritus of Early Christian Origins, University of Chicago

JOHN A. WILSON
Professor of Egyptology, Oriental Institute, University of Chicago

FREDERICK V. WINNETT
Head of the Department of Near Eastern Studies, University College, University of Toronto

PAUL WINTER
Research Scholar, London

ORVAL S. WINTERMUTE
Lecturer on the Old Testament, The Divinity School, Duke University

C. UMHAU WOLF
Minister, St. Paul's Lutheran Church, Toledo, Ohio

G. ERNEST WRIGHT
Professor of Old Testament, The Divinity School, Harvard University

FRANKLIN W. YOUNG
Professor of New Testament, Princeton University

MICHAEL ZOHARY
Professor of Botany, Hebrew University, Jerusalem

GÜNTHER ZUNTZ
Reader in Hellenistic Greek, University of Manchester

# EDITOR'S PREFACE

Few people would question the value of a dictionary. Those who seriously read, and still more those who seriously write, keep a dictionary at hand as an indispensable aid. Such games as crossword puzzles and scrabble have enlarged the vocabulary and *diction* of the players—through use of the *dictionary*. A comprehensive dictionary traces not only the meaning of a given word, but also its history, for words change in meaning through the generations. Let the reader thus discover why the word "cynic" meant originally both a philosopher dedicated to virtue and a snarling critic of contemporary mores; or why and when the English city of Pontefract received its name, or why the word "sincere" (*sine cera*, "without wax") came into legal and then into common use. For thoughtful people a dictionary is as necessary as hammer and chisel to a carpenter. There are deeper issues involved, for language is a vast and ever-changing symbolism which shapes a culture even while it is being shaped by its culture.

This obvious comment is enough to show the need for a dictionary of the Bible, not alone for theologians and preachers, but for anyone who would read the Bible with intelligence. Our Old Testament was not always ours: it was written originally in Hebrew, as our New Testament was originally written in Greek, which in its turn depended on an originally spoken Aramaic. Thus the first meaning of Bible words is discoverable only through a study of the language; and not of that alone, but of the language within the history and culture of the Bible people. Bible words, like words in any dictionary, are changed in their meaning through the years: our New Testament word "hypocrite" meant at first "play-actor" in no unworthy sense, and the New Testament word for "love" (*agape*) gathered a new and crucial importance through the coming of Jesus Christ. So the Bible is not well understood except by readers who trace the history, as well as the meaning, of Bible words. The deeper issues are again involved: a proper understanding and use of Bible words shapes our culture, which depends on biblical faith far more than it suspects or acknowledges.

It would hardly be true to say that no full-scale dictionary of the Bible has appeared in our language in the past fifty years—that is, since the publication of James Hastings' *Dictionary of the Bible* in five volumes between 1898 and 1904. Tempted to such a comment, I was quickly disabused when I began to canvass the extraordinary labor in this field in the last half century, in French, Hebrew, and German perhaps even more notably than in English. (For a partial list of such books, *see below.\**) But it is perhaps true to say that no work as comprehensive as these present volumes has been published in English in that time period, and that no such work included writings from as many nations and fields of scholarship; and it is certainly true that new knowledge points the need for such a work. John Robinson prophesied our time:

\* The Roman Catholic: F. Vigouroux, ed., *Dictionnaire de la Bible* (1895-1912), which maintains a supplement; the Protestant: A. Westphal, ed., *Dictionnaire Encyclopédique de la Bible* (1932). Several one-volume works, such as: M. W. Jacobus, E. C. Lane, and A. C. Zenos, eds., *New Standard Bible Dictionary* (1936); J. D. Davis, ed., *The Westminster Dictionary of the Bible* (1944; rev. H. G. Gehmann); H. Haag, ed., *Bibel-Lexikon* (1951); M. S. Miller and J. L. Miller, eds., *Harper's Bible Dictionary* (1952); *The Catholic Biblical Encyclopedia* (1956). Among multi-volumed works there is: J. Orr, ed., *The International Standard Bible Encyclopedia* (1930). There have been notable word studies, such as: G. Kittel, *Theologisches Wörterbuch zum Neuen Testament* (1932—); A. Richardson, *A Theological Word Book of the Bible* (1951); J. J. von Allmen, ed., *A Companion to the Bible* (1958).

"The Lord hath yet more truth and light to break forth from His Holy Word."

### New Knowledge

This new knowledge is so vast a treasure that the following paragraphs hardly hint its worth. As for the text of the Bible, we now have better manuscripts, such as the Chester Beatty Papyri, purchased from dealers in Egypt in 1931, and the more recently discovered Dead Sea Scrolls. These latter show, for instance, that the Septuagint (Greek) version of the Old Testament may at some points be more trustworthy than the Masoretic (continuing Hebrew) text.

As for the language of the Bible, we now know that the New Testament was written in *koine* or vernacular Greek rather than in the classical form and diction—an advance in knowledge made possible by papyri found in Egypt; and further light on the Old Testament languages has come from the Ras Shamra Texts, from many Assyrian and Babylonian cuneiform tablets and other inscriptions in cognate languages, and from a careful study of the Dead Sea Scrolls.

As for the thought-forms of the Bible, these have been illuminated by a fuller knowledge of ancient history, such as that of the life of the Fertile Crescent with which the life of Israel was closely linked, or that of the Greco-Roman world into which the Christian faith made its initial thrust.

As for the flora and fauna of the Bible, to cite but an instance, studies in this subject have brought important clarification: perhaps Jesus did not intend by "lilies of the field" the white madonna lily, but flowers in general—the reference to the robe of Solomon would seem to argue in favor of the scarlet anemone, if Jesus had in mind any specific flower. Such items find chapter and verse within this dictionary.

"Higher criticism" is a misleading term which means simply the study of the date, authorship, sources, purpose, and plan of a Bible book. New knowledge has thrown light on all these items. Study of the text, as, for instance, Greek terms in the book of Daniel, has provided added internal evidence; and historical research has brought new external evidence; and though the name or names of Bible authors may not be known for lack of sufficiently clear witness (we say "names," as well as "name," because it now becomes clear that many Bible books have corporate authorship), the manner and outlook of Bible writers now appear in sharper outline.

Form criticism, the study of the literary forms in which the units of primitive biblical tradition are cast, has helped to illuminate and to emphasize the close relation between the tradition and its social environment, and has thus provided new understanding of both Testaments.

Meanwhile archaeology moves apace: the instances known to laymen, such as the outstanding discoveries at Qumran and Jericho, are but isolated examples; and it is hardly too much to claim that this branch of study, in its scrutiny of artifacts and literary texts, has vivified both the history and the geography of the Bible world.

Overarching all these new bestowals is the revival of biblical theology which the crisis of our times has quickened and required. The judgment implicit in our apocalyptic age has taught us anew that only Bible verities about the nature and destiny of man can withstand history's stern tests, and that only God's self-disclosure in Christ can bring the solving word in our dilemma. The crux of our century has newly revealed the Bible's sharp pertinence and unplumbed depth. Thus we have "more truth and light" almost blindingly, and would be renegade were we to try to close doors and windows against its coming. Thus we confront an almost clamant need for a new, comprehensive dictionary of the Bible.

### Comprehensiveness

How comprehensive? These volumes have enlisted scholars not only from the United States, but also from Canada, Denmark, Egypt, England, France, Germany, Israel, Jordan, Norway, Scotland, Sweden,. Switzerland, Thailand, and Wales. That France and Germany should appear together in this list, or Jordan and Israel, is a sign that biblical studies overleap national boundaries. Due care has been taken to choose for each assignment the gifts of a scholar peculiarly versed in that particular field. The Editorial Board has asked repeatedly: "Who are the men who have given years of labor to this area of Bible knowledge? Who can treat most effectively this particular subject?"

This dictionary has staked out a claim wider than the words of one version of scripture. The King James Version is in the blood and tissue of our race: it is a devotional classic which has helped beyond measure to shape biblical understanding. Therefore it has been near the center of our editorial concern. But new knowledge of Bible languages, the availability of new manuscripts, and the fact that the King James Version is written in an Elizabethan English and therefore in a vocabulary which has sharply changed in meaning in three centuries, made almost mandatory our use of the Revised Standard Version. Hence this new version has had a basic importance in our labors. So all significant terms (proper names, important objects, and theological terms, for example) from this new version have been included, and the Revised Standard Version word is given as the main entry. Moreover, the important words in the Pseudepigrapha (pseudonymous writings which purport to have been written by Bible characters, and which are not without value) and in the Apocrypha and the deuterocanonical books (writings, some of considerable worth in Bible study, outside the canon of the customary Old and New Testaments) have received due attention. There are articles on such topics as form criticism and the Dead Sea Scrolls; and on subjects which may seem remote to some readers, but which have direct bearing on the understanding of scripture, such as historical backgrounds (Sumer, Babylonia and Assyria, Egypt); and on peoples of the ancient Near East (Hittites, Philistines, Horites); and on such subjects as flora, fauna, arts, cities, crafts, the calendars, archaeology, pottery, and government. The interests of theological study have been widely served: there is an introduction to each Bible book, and a thoroughgoing study of such cardinal concepts as redemption, atonement, love, and resurrection. Our title is *The Interpreter's Dictionary of the Bible,* but these volumes travel far in the direction of a Bible encyclopedia.

Comprehensiveness is evident in other regards. Cross references have been liberally used. While each article seeks to give adequate understanding—as, for instance, the article on righteousness, which discusses this term in both its Old Testament and its New Testament use—cross references here as else-

where enable the Bible reader to pursue studies in related fields. Each major article offers a bibliography, a help which standard volumes in this field have not always provided. Because it is based on two main versions, because it ranges beyond the canon and beyond a merely dictionary limitation, this work has a longer list of terms. Its major articles offer a valuable introduction to biblical and theological study, not to mention answers to inquiries in such fields as archaeology and history. Christian faith may thus be understood in clearer outline against the panorama of its world and age. These claims are made not in pride, but in gratitude: "Others have labored, and" we "are entered into their labor."

### Illustrations and Maps

If it is true, as psychologists tell us, that more than ninety per cent of people have a centrally visual imagination, pictures should have important place in a Bible dictionary. The wide reading of illustrated magazines and newspapers, which in some instances provide hardly more reading than an extended comment on the illustrations, accents this requirement. So one tenth of the space in these volumes is given to illustrations. There are maps, some in color and some black-and-white, not alone of countries, but of neighborhoods and cities. In certain instances ground plans have been provided, the temple area in successive eras being a case in point. *Charts* appear in connection with such items as archaeological "ages" and the chronology of Bible books. There are photographs or sketches, many of them new, of flowers, trees, weapons, musical instruments, household utensils, and tools. While some of the pictures have been gathered from well-known collections, others have been made expressly for this dictionary, and some are the special work of contributors.

Of particular note are the pages in color. There are five of these groups of pictures, as follows: eight pages of flora and fauna, eight pages of landscapes, four pages depicting jewels, twenty-four pages of maps, and eight pages portraying scrolls or maps including pictures of the now-famous Dead Sea Scrolls. Though we have been obliged to set some limit on visual aids, we have tried to honor specific requests from our writers, and to assure to each due occasion and each important instance its rightful illustration.

## Format

These volumes are the same in size as those of *The Interpreter's Bible,* but in different binding and color. The two, the Commentary and the Dictionary, can thus stand side by side on the shelf, each in its own right, yet as friends and companions. We hope that the two works will become for many people trusted companion-aids. The binding is in stanch cloth to withstand both wear-and-tear and microscopic enemies. The paper is like that of the Commentary, fashioned to keep both color and texture, and so processed that the type will not show through to the next page. This is not the place for an itemizing of financial costs, but it is appropriate for us to remark that the publishers have spared no pains to make a worthy book.

As to the page format, type has been chosen from many samples for attractiveness and legibility. Page headings and page numbers have been selected so as to grant the reader quickness and ease as he seeks the place. Column width has been determined so as best to serve both eye and mind. The actual printing is by the "offset" method, and the typesetting was handled by a "Fotosetter." This dictionary has pages that are clear, readable, and inviting to the eye.

As to the format of the articles, the following plan is usually utilized: first comes the word or topic in boldface type; then a suggested pronunciation, in instances in which this is necessary or helpful, though pronunciation is frequently hard to determine; then the word's original language form; and then a proposal as to its etymology. When alternative forms occur, or when the King James Version differs from the Revised Standard Version, these extra forms are noted—after the information regarding the main entry. Departures from this method are in some instances required, as with theological articles, but an attempt has been made to keep some consistency of form. Many major articles are provided with an outline and are paragraphed or set with headings to trace the course of the discussion, and to enable the reader to find quickly the writer's comment on some particular aspect of the topic. Pictures or maps are provided as the article

seems to dictate. Cross references, invaluable in serious study, are given to allied articles (assiduous care has been taken with the cross references), and finally a selected bibliography is offered. Thus a wealth of knowledge is compactly presented, with many an opening for further study.

## Function and Availability

When this dictionary was first planned, the Editorial Board asked themselves what groups of people would use it; and they tried, in the light of such questionings and the likely answers, to provide a dictionary of wide advantage. The busy preacher was at the forefront of our concern. Whatever skill he may have to communicate with his generation, his gospel is not applied surgically and healingly to men's lives unless he knows the meaning of scripture in its historical and cultural context. The reading of an older version, however devotional in mood, is not enough for an honest and effective proclamation of the Word. What does such a phrase as "considering the end of their conversation" really mean? It is not a comment on our unworthy parleys and debates. Or is the preacher's topic "truth" as the Johannine Gospel often uses the word? Then he must know the intent and derivation of the word *aletheia:* "without a veil." Thus the Bible conviction as to the nature of truth can be set with challenge and purpose over against a generation which believes truth to be a nearby land of achievable information. Too much preaching has not been preaching: it has been a web of fugitive ideas spun from the preacher's random thoughts. Preaching, by the very meaning of the word, is heralding; and no preacher can be a herald unless he knows his commissioned word.

The scholar has also been kept in a primary editorial concern. It would be easy to assume that he does not need a dictionary of the Bible, but the supposition would be a mistake. The range of Bible knowledge is now so vast that no one mind can compass more than a province—or a county. Earlier dictionaries fortified the scholar's labor. They have served us invaluably as we have planned and processed these volumes. But again and again we have been confronted by whole areas of new knowledge, and have asked ourselves how this new terrain can be fenced and cultivated. We hope this dictionary may serve the scholar well as a base from which he makes new ventures; and that here the linguist, the historian, the theologian, and the archaeologist may each be enriched by the others' labor.

The student in college and seminary has also been clearly in our mind. Seminary enrollments show a needed increase. Biblical studies in college and university spread in rapid contagion as men more and more doubt if a secular assumption is a sure base for education. We have been glad and grateful to observe that *The Interpreter's Bible* is now widely used in college studies in the biblical field, especially in its general articles and its introduction to the several Bible books. This dictionary may be, in its own way, an equally valuable resource. We hope that many a student will use it in biblical studies as readily as he turns in other studies to a competent encyclopedia.

We have been solicitous for the needs of the church-school teacher. The cruciality of his work is accented by the fact that many who espouse Christian faith are yet almost illiterate about the convictions set forth in the Bible. The church-school teacher does not wish to be spoon-fed. He craves a better help than the scanty *ad hoc* guidances which the teacher's book sometimes offers. We believe he will welcome the thoroughgoing and scholarly, yet quickly available, help offered in this dictionary.

We have not forgotten the general reader who is intent to understand the Bible. More and more people realize that the Scriptures, though a matchless book of devotion, are also a vast world of thought that speaks incisively and redeemingly to man's condition. The crisis of our age has brought mistrust of human powers. Modern man asks wistfully, skeptically, or urgently, "Is there any word from the Eternal?" Thus our age returns to the Bible, not in naïve acceptance or sentimental piety, but in resolve to know if it can give an answer to the predicament of modern man. In such a time a true understanding of scripture is of prime importance. To this end we have tried to avoid technical language in these volumes. Honesty has required reference to the original languages, but transliteration has often been used so that the general reader may not be waylaid; and the door

has been barred against erudite references and exhaustive (and exhausting) footnotes. Here may be found both up-to-date information and trustworthy guidance. We shall be disappointed if this dictionary does not find its place in the library of every sizable city and college, and on the shelves of every alert minister and Bible scholar.

## *Procedures*

Meetings of the Editorial Board began in February, 1955. The task, apart from final proofreading and correction, has occupied five years. Meetings were at first frequent: many decisions as to a ground plan were necessary before construction could begin. The scope of the work was first determined, then advisers were appointed, then a typographical format was chosen, and then a tentative plan was drawn for the main articles. These decisions were not easily made. The knotty problem of the pronunciation of Bible words took hours of discussion, and led finally to the appointment of expert help. The choice of contributors was concluded only after scores of names had been canvassed so that each topic in the Dictionary might be matched to the skill of the best-qualified scholar. 253 scholars have been enlisted in these volumes.

After some weeks members of the Board wrote sample articles, both of major and of minor length, which might serve our contributors as illustrations or examples of what the Board had in mind. These articles were submitted to rigorous criticism, then corrected, and then sent to our writers, not in any too stringent requirement, but for their guidance. Illustrations were from the first a main concern. The Board examined many sources of illustrative aid; and, when they were unable to find the desired resource, authorized new sketches and pictures. Hours were spent looking at projections on a screen, so that the best illustrations might be chosen.

Any omnibus task such as this, spread over a span of years, must meet the difficulties which sickness, sorrow, and death impose. There have been other besetments, and therefore new contributors have been sought and found in the midmost of the journey, though always with concern for their knowledge as scholars and their competence as writers. Our experience with *The Interpreter's Bible,* to which this dictionary is a companion work, has been turned to account; for by that earlier endeavor we have seen more clearly the needs of readers, the locale of available scholarship, and many a practical involvement of the task. All in all, the hazards have been fewer than we might have feared, the joys have been many, and we have found in advisers, writers, and publishers a ready and gifted co-operation.

### Acknowledgments

It is a glad and grateful task to make certain acknowledgments, and first to my fellow editors, even though against their will. Their toil has been both talented and assiduous, with a scholarship which I cannot claim. Thomas Kepler has been concerned with New Testament material, and has been responsible for all illustrative materials; and he has brought to both tasks the interest and labor of a lifetime. John Knox also has been responsible for New Testament articles, where his knowledge has long been proved; introduction and theology have been his particular charge. Herbert May has been one of the editors for Old Testament material, but in far more than routine fashion: his knowledge of languages and archaeology has been an invaluable resource. Samuel Terrien has served in the same capacity, in much the same way for the Old Testament articles as John Knox for the New: his gifts in exegesis, introduction, form criticism, and theology have been specially devoted to longer articles in the Old Testament field.

All five of us would feel renegade were this Preface to be empty of gratitude for help given by many members of the executive staff of Abingdon Press. Gifted far beyond the technical knowledge of their craft, they have established a modest custom which forbids mention by authors of co-operation given by the Press. But we cannot worthily be silent, for these volumes owe their inception, development, and completion as much to Abingdon Press as to the contributors and editors. The governing board of the Press early gave enthusiastic assent to the project, even though there was no sure prospect that the outlay of time and money could be quickly amortized. We remember with appreciation Pat Beaird, now Executive Vice-President of The Methodist Publishing House, who gave incentive and first direction to this task. Our thanks are offered also to fellow laborers at our Board meetings: to Cecil Jones, Manager of Abingdon Press, who has continued the same generous policy regarding this dictionary as was followed for *The Interpreter's Bible;* to Emory S. Bucke, Editor-in-Chief of Abingdon Press, who has brought gifts both of imagination and of fidelity; to Gordon B. Duncan for meticulous care in such items as typography, style, pronunciation, and format; to William Bosworth, especially for his knowledge and ingenuity in printing method; to Hermann Zimmermann for design and illustration; and not least to Miss Willine Hall, who has compassed with swift skill the hard day-by-day labor of preparing manuscript for the typesetter. There are also those who have been responsible for the printing and the advertising. We would have them, and the reader also, understand that we gratefully realize these volumes could not have appeared without their aid.

Thanks are offered to all our contributors. They have quickly sensed the Dictionary's purpose, and have discharged their task with scholarship and clarity of expression. To a surprising degree, in the burden of their many duties, they have met the deadline of their assignments.

We are grateful also to our gifted advisers: to Bruce M. Metzger for counsel on articles in the field of the Apocrypha; to D. Noel Freedman for similar counsel on Old Testament articles; and to George E. Mendenhall for advice in the field of archaeology and Near Eastern studies. It has been an assurance to know that we could turn to these scholars for confirmation and guidance. We are grateful also to translators, especially to Mrs. Anita C. Reichard (for German articles) and Mrs. Francisco Solinis-Herrero (for articles written in French). Our heartfelt appreciation is offered also to an unofficial consultant whose help nevertheless has been beyond compute: William Foxwell Albright. He has read many articles, and supervised others written by his students past and present, and has guided us in the selection of writers. Though no article appears under his own name, his informed mind has shaped and kindled much that others have written herein.

### In Conclusion

The nature of the material in *The Interpreter's Bible* permitted its publication two volumes each year. The required plenitude of cross references in this work dictates that it be published *in toto* on one date. We believe that it will hold its place for more than a generation. Then "the Lord hath yet more truth and light to break forth from His Holy Word." We dare to hope that these volumes will serve our crucial time under God's increasing purpose. Ignorance is no ally of the gospel. Knowledge and faith are not at odds; faith carries knowledge on strong shoulders, knowledge thus having a higher reach. Scholarship and prayer are friends, not strangers; prayer is the light in which alone scholarship can fulfil its task, and scholarship is thus prayer's harvest. Insight and practicality alike require that men shall "rightly handle the word of truth." To that end these volumes are dedicated.

Some centuries seem to be skeptic in mood: the "sea of faith" is at the ebb. Others show a return to faith: the tide comes in again on our human shore. Perhaps this dictionary appears when the tide is at the tremulous turn. Science has its own worthy witness, for man's life in the natural order is of divine ordaining; yet the word of science, if ungirded by deeper words, is but a fractional comment, for man has a stance above the natural order. That stance is the fulcrum of his freedom, and the entering in of his redemption. The Bible honors human life in its wholeness. There is no disparagement of man's body or of his daily work or of the cosmos: "The earth is the LORD's and the fulness thereof." But there is recognition of a deeper and higher dimension from which man's daily life is seen and judged. So the Bible reveals our brokenness while bringing persuasions of grace. Generation by generation men find there a lamp for their feet and a light on their path. Otherwise they stumble in darkness. Therefore this dictionary. We pray that it may quicken faith in the earth, and bear its witness to that Kingdom which was and is and is to come.

GEORGE A. BUTTRICK

# THE INTERPRETER'S DICTIONARY OF THE BIBLE
## SUPPLEMENTARY VOLUME
### PUBLISHED 1976

*Updating and supplementing information in the four-volume set*
*Based on recent archaeological discoveries and contemporary biblical studies*

**\*Cross references.** In these four volumes, an asterisk appears in front of certain entries. This indicates that a new article on this subject will be found in the supplementary volume—either under this exact title or closely related key words. For example, the cross reference from SHIPS AND SAILING, OT, and SHIPS AND SAILING, NT, will take you to a new, updated article on SHIPS AND SHIPPING. The asterisk at CITY leads to CITIES, GRECO-ROMAN.

Sometimes, in order to lead you to new information given under a totally different title, the asterisk in this four-volume set will lead to a cross reference in the supplementary volume. This, in turn, will direct you to the new article in the supplement where the information can be found.

To illustrate: the asterisk in front of CORINTHIANS, THIRD EPISTLE TO THE, leads to the same entry in the supplement, which is a dummy entry referring you to the new article on APOCRYPHA. The asterisk by QUMRAN, KHIRBET, will lead, by the way of a dummy entry in the supplement, to the definitive new article on the DEAD SEA SCROLLS.

The supplementary volume, in turn, will contain the same cross referencing system. An asterisk beside certain words refers you back to basic information in the original four-volume set.

This double system of cross referencing will provide you with the fullest and latest information on biblical themes, persons, archaeological sites, results of recent biblical studies, and the resource helps you need for better understanding of the Bible.

# EXPLANATIONS AND INSTRUCTIONS

### Range of Subjects

As indicated by the title and subtitle, this work is both a dictionary and an encyclopedia. As a dictionary it lists all the proper names and distinctive terms of the Bible, including the Apocrypha, and defines or identifies them. As an encyclopedia it presents articles summarizing the significant information known about the important names and terms and also about important subjects related to the Bible.

Terms judged distinctive enough for treatment include not merely the considerable number of words which have come into our language from the Bible—such as "apostle," "jubilee," "manna"—but all which as used in the Bible have any special meaning. Among these, e.g., are terms for plants and animals needing identification, for artifacts needing description, and for ideas needing clarification. In fact, it might be said that every biblical term has been chosen for treatment if the results of scholarly study can contribute to its understanding.

The range of subjects extends beyond terms used in the Bible to include concepts implicit therein. It extends further to cover the Bible's setting in the ancient Near East, its literary environment, its history, and the sources (including archaeology) of our knowledge about it. The latter two categories include the transmission, translation, interpretation, and study of the Bible up to the present time, but otherwise the focus is entirely within the biblical period.

So far as possible, this work is based on the Bible itself rather than any particular English version. But to the extent that versions differ in the spelling of names and in other details, a choice was made in order to avoid listing all the variants. The list of names and terms for this work, therefore, was compiled from the King James and Revised Standard Versions. The reader of either of these versions may expect to find herein every name or distinctive term that challenges his interest. Ordinarily similarities will enable the reader of any other version to readily locate a name or term. If not, he should consult one of the above versions in order to identify the entry under which his subject is treated.

### Arrangement of Subjects

Entries appear in the customary alphabetical order, except that certain pairs and series of articles beginning with the same word are arranged according to the logic of their own relationship (e.g., "Chronology of the OT" precedes "Chronology of the NT"). If an entry has two or more meanings, the definitions are numbered with boldface arabic figures, and all but the first begin new paragraphs (e.g., see "Abijah" below).

A name or term is normally defined and discussed only once, in what comprises the main entry for that subject. It is entered also in any variant forms readers would have reason to look for, but these entries merely refer to the main entry. For a name the main entry is the form most commonly used in the Revised Standard Version. For other subjects the main entry takes the form judged most likely to be sought by readers.

Related subjects can often be most effectively presented in a comprehensive article which organizes the several biblical terms and their overlapping English translations into a clear structure (e.g., see "Dress and Ornaments"). Each term treated in such an article appears also as a separate entry, where it is accorded appropriate brief treatment and a reference to the comprehensive article. If the individual entry contains more than a mere definition, a cross reference to it is included at the proper point in the comprehensive article.

The reader is advised, therefore, to seek information under whatever heading seems to him most logical. If he does not find it there, he may at least expect to find a reference to the entry where he can find it.

### Pattern of Presentation

As a typical example of the structure of the opening paragraph in the treatment of a name, observe in detail the following excerpt and comments:

**ABIJAH** ə bī′jə [אֲבִיָּהוּ, Y is (my) father]; ABIJAM —jəm [אֲבִים, *see* 5 *below*] (I Kings 14:31; 15:1, 7-8); ABI ā′bī [אֲבִי, my father] (II Kings 18:2); KJV alternately: ABIAH ə bī′ə (I Sam. 8:2; I Chr. 2:24; 6:28; 7:8); ABIA (I Chr. 3:10; Matt. 1:7; Luke 1:5). **1.** Son of Becher, of the tribe of Benjamin (I Chr. 7:8). **2.** The KJV translation of the MT אֲבִיָּה in I Chr. 2:24; the name of the wife of Hezron, of the tribe of Judah. Perhaps the correct reading is אֲבִיָּהוּ—i.e., "his

1. The entry itself is printed in boldface capital letters.

2. The name is followed immediately by its pronunciation. See the front endpaper of each volume for the key to the diacritical marks used to indicate pronunciations. For further details see the explanations below.

3. Within square brackets appear the Hebrew (or Aramaic or Greek) original and its root meaning if known (the abbreviation "Y" used in this example indicates any form of the divine name Yahweh). Textual variants, cognates in other ancient languages, or other significant information about the original word may be included within the brackets or, if discussion is needed, treated in the body of the article.

4. Variants distinguishable in the Revised Standard and King James Versions are printed in capital letters (not boldface), each accompanied by its pronunciation if different from the preceding, by its original and the etymology thereof if different, and by an indication of where the variant appears. If no version is indicated, the variant appears in the Revised Standard Version; the initials "KJV" indicate that one must turn to the King James Version to find the variant.

Derivative forms are usually presented in the same way as variants (e.g., Abiezer, Abiezrite) but may be treated separately if of sufficient importance (e.g., Aaronites).

5. Following the above data, the first sentence defines the person or place bearing the name. In the example above only the first two of the nine numbered identifications of the biblical persons named Abijah are quoted.

So far as similar information is significant for entries other than names, it is presented in an opening paragraph according to the same pattern.

In a lengthy article the discussion is organized into sections and subsections, each beginning with a numbered or lettered boldface heading. The several headings are listed in outline form as a table of contents following the opening paragraph. The reader seeking only a certain portion of such an article should ascertain the proper section from the table of contents and then locate it in the body of the article by means of the boldface heading.

### Cross References

A particular value of this work is the opportunity it affords the reader to pursue many branching paths of study according to his individual needs and interests. The signposts of such paths are cross references, which are indicated by the printing of words in SMALL CAPITAL LETTERS. Every word or phrase so printed is to be understood as if followed by "which see."

Because all biblical names appear as entries, the reader may of course consider any mention of a name an invitation to seek information about it. The printing of a name or other subject in small capitals, however, should be taken as a definite recommendation and a promise that significant information will be found under the topic so signalized.

### Quotations and Source References

Biblical quotations, unless otherwise indicated, are from the Revised Standard Version. Biblical references are punctuated as follows: a colon separates chapter from verse; a semicolon separates one reference from the next (e.g., Matt. 5:3-11; 6:9-13; 7:7-12). References to other ancient writings which are divided into chapters and verses follow the same form. The names of most such works are abbreviated in references. The abbreviations and the names for which they stand are included in the list of abbreviations on the following pages. This list is repeated at the front of each volume. The names of the books of the Bible, Apocrypha, Pseudepigrapha, and Apostolic Fathers are also printed for convenient reference on the back endpaper of each volume.

### Bibliographies

Each article on a subject to which biblical scholars have given critical study ends with a bibliography listing works where the interested reader may find further information. The bibliography also takes the place of footnotes in reporting sources of distinctive information and interpretation reported in the article. Works frequently cited in the bibliographies are abbreviated. To decode these references the reader should consult the list of abbreviations appearing at the front of each volume.

### Illustrations and Maps

The many black-and-white illustrations scattered through these volumes are identified by a code consisting of the first three letters of the subject under which the illustration appears, followed by a number (e.g., ABE 1). A reference to an illustration is indicated by an asterisk (*) at the point of reference and the code identifying the illustration at the end of the paragraph.

The four series of full-color illustrations appear in special sections, one in each volume, and are identified by roman numbers.

The full-color maps reproduced as a section in this volume are also identified by roman numbers.

Black-and-white maps are located through the text to illustrate specific articles. References to these maps in other articles identify them by the subject under which they appear.

### Pronunciations

The key to the diacritical marks used to indicate pronunciations is printed on the front endpaper of each volume. Most readers will rarely need to consult this key, however, because the marks are traditional and familiar. A possible exception is the symbol "ə"—known as "schwa." As noted in the key, this symbol may replace any of the vowels to indicate the neutral sound common in unaccented syllables of ordinary speech. The use of "schwa" or an equivalent for it has been adopted in practically all modern dictionaries as essential for accurate representation of spoken words.

Accented syllables are indicated by the usual marks following the syllables. If a word contains two or more accented syllables, a thinner mark is used to indicate lesser accent.

A dash appearing in a pronunciation indicates that the portion of the word which it replaces is the same as in the preceding pronunciation.

Proper pronunciation is determined by current usage. Certain names of the Bible are among the most frequently spoken of all names. Their pronunciation in English is well established and easy to ascertain. On the other hand, large numbers of biblical names are spoken only rarely, so that no established usage can be found for them. Most people who have needed to speak them have either guessed or consulted some authority—a Bible dictionary or "self-pronouncing" Bible. At present the pronunciations in all such authorities now available appear to be based on several lists of which the latest dates from more than half a century ago. Some of the pronunciations they show for familiar names are now clearly obsolescent. Nevertheless, as the only available guides, they must be assumed to exert considerable influence still over the pronunciation of the unfamiliar names.

To determine the pronunciations for this work, therefore, the several older lists were tabulated and compared. In addition, pronunciations were secured from the writers and editors. As a further factor, consideration was given to the likelihood that people guess at certain names because they appear to rhyme with familiar names (e.g., Asaiah and Isaiah). When all or nearly all of these are agreed, a pronunciation may perhaps be considered substantially established even though rarely confirmed in actual speech. When there is disagreement, however, one must distinguish between the situations where, on the one hand, two or more pronunciations are widely used (e.g., for Philistine) and where, on the other hand, different authorities have arbitrarily chosen pronunciations for a name no one habitually pronounces. In the first situation the alternates need to be shown; in the second, a single choice from among the possibilities seems enough. From this reasoning, therefore, the reader may gather that a pronunciation he finds here is not necessarily the only pronunciation for the name. However, he may use it with confidence that it is an acceptable pronunciation.

THE PUBLISHERS

# ABBREVIATIONS

א — Codex Sinaiticus
A — Codex Alexandrinus
*AA* — *Alttestamentliche Abhandlungen*
*AAA* — *Annals of Archaeology and Anthropology*
*AASOR* — *Annual of the American Schools of Oriental Research*
Ab. — Aboth
Add. Esth. — Additions to Esther
*AFO* — *Archiv für Orientforschung*
*AJA* — *American Journal of Archaeology*
*AJSL* — *American Journal of Semitic Languages and Literatures*
*AJT* — *American Journal of Theology*
Akkad. — Akkadian
Amer. Trans. — *The Complete Bible, an American Translation* (Smith and Goodspeed)
*ANEP* — J. B. Pritchard, ed., *The Ancient Near East in Pictures*
*ANET* — J. B. Pritchard, ed., *Ancient Near Eastern Texts*
*AO* — *Der alte Orient*
*APAW* — *Abhandlungen der Preussichen Akademie der Wissenschaften*
Apoc. — Apocrypha
Apocal. Bar. — Apocalypse of Baruch
Aq. — Aquila
'Ar. — 'Aruk
*ARAB* — D. D. Luckenbill, *Ancient Records of Assyria and Babylonia*
Arab. — Arabic
'Arak. — 'Arakin
Aram. — Aramaic
*ARE* — J. H. Breasted, *Ancient Records of Egypt*
ARN — Aboth d'Rabbi Nathan
art. — article
*ARW* — *Archiv für Religionswissenschaft*
*ASAE* — *Annales du service des antiquités de l'Égypte*
Asmp. Moses — Assumption of Moses
ASV — American Standard Version (1901)

*AT* — *Altes* or *Ancien Testament*
*ATR* — *Anglican Theological Review*
'A.Z. — 'Abodah Zarah

B — Codex Vaticanus
*BA* — *Biblical Archaeologist*
Bar. — Baruch
Barn. — The Epistle of Barnabas
*BASOR* — *Bulletin of the American Schools of Oriental Research*
B.B. — Baba Bathra
Bek. — Bekereth
Bel — Bel and the Dragon
Ber. — Berakoth
Bez. — Beẓah
B.K. — Baba Ḳamma
bk. — book
B.M. — Baba Meẓi'a
*Bibl.* — *Biblica*
*Bibl. Stud.* — *Biblische Studien*
Bik. — Bikkurim
*BS* — *Bibliotheca Sacra*
*BW* — *Biblical World*
*BWANT* — *Beiträge zur Wissenschaft vom Alten und Neuen Testament*
*BWAT* — *Beiträge zur Wissenschaft vom Alten Testament*
*BZ* — *Biblische Zeitschrift*
*BZAW* — *Beihefte zur Zeitschrift für die alttestamentliche Wissenschaft*
*BZF* — *Biblische Zeitfragen*

C — Codex Ephraemi Syri
*ca.* — *circa* (about)
CDC — Cairo Genizah Document of the Damascus Covenanters (The Zadokite Documents)
cf. — *confer* (compare)
ch. — chapter
Chr. — Chronicles
Clem. — Clement (I and II)
Clem. Misc. — Clement of Alexandria *Miscellanies*
Col. — Colossians
col. — column
Cor. — Corinthians
*CSEL* — *Corpus Scriptorum Ecclesiasticorum Latinorum*

D — Codex Bezae; Codex Claromontanus; Deuteronomist source
Dan. — Daniel
Dem. — Demai
Deut. — Deuteronomy
Did. — The Didache
div. — division
DSS — Dead Sea Scrolls

E — east; Elohist source
EB — Early Bronze Age
*EB* — *Études bibliques*
Eccl. — Ecclesiastes
Ecclus. — Ecclesiasticus
ed. — edited, edition, editor
e.g. — *exempli gratia* (for example)
Egyp. — Egyptian
*EH* — *Exegetisches Handbuch zum Alten Testament*
EI — Early Iron Age
Eph. — Ephesians
'Er. — 'Erubin
ERV — English Revised Version (1881-85)
Esd. — Esdras
esp. — especially
Esth. — Esther
*ET* — *Expository Times*
Ethio. — Ethiopian
Euseb. Hist. — Eusebius *History of the Christian Church*
Euseb. Onom. — Eusebius *Onomasticon*
Exod. — Exodus
*Exp.* — *The Expositor*
Ezek. — Ezekiel

fem. — feminine
fig. — figure (illustration)
*FRLANT* — *Forschungen zur Religion und Literatur des Alten und Neuen Testaments*

G — Greek
Gal. — Galatians
Gen. — Genesis
Giṭ. — Giṭṭin
Gordon — C. H. Gordon, *Ugaritic Manual*
Gr. — Greek
*GSAI* — *Giornale della società asiatica italiana*

GTT — *Gereformeerd theologisch Tijdschrift*

H — Hebrew; Holiness Code
Hab. — Habakkuk
Hag. — Haggai
Ḥag. — Ḥagigah
Ḥal. — Ḥallah
*HAT* — *Handbuch zum Alten Testament*
*HDB* — James Hastings, ed., *A Dictionary of the Bible*
Heb. — Hebrew; the Letter to the Hebrews
*HERE* — James Hastings, ed., *Encyclopedia of Religion and Ethics*
Herm. Mand. — The Shepherd of Hermas, Mandates
Herm. Sim. — The Shepherd of Hermas, Similitudes
Herm. Vis. — The Shepherd of Hermas, Visions
Hitt. — Hittite
*HKAT* — *Handkommentar zum Alten Testament*
Hor. — Horayoth
Hos. — Hosea
*HS* — *Die heilige Schrift des Alten Testaments*
*HTR* — *Harvard Theological Review*
*HUCA* — *Hebrew Union College Annual*

ICC — International Critical Commentary
i.e. — *id est* (that is)
*IEJ* — *Israel Exploration Journal*
Ign. Eph. — The Epistle of Ignatius to the Ephesians
Ign. Magn. — The Epistle of Ignatius to the Magnesians
Ign. Phila. — The Epistle of Ignatius to the Philadelphians
Ign. Polyc. — The Epistle of Ignatius to Polycarp
Ign. Rom. — The Epistle of Ignatius to the Romans
Ign. Smyr. — The Epistle of Ignatius to the Smyrnaeans
Ign. Trall. — The Epistle of Ignatius to the Trallians
intro. — introduction
Iren. Her. — Irenaeus *Against Heresies*
Iron — Iron Age
Isa. — Isaiah

J — Yahwist source
*JA* — *Journal asiatique*
*JAOS* — *Journal of the American Oriental Society*
Jas. — James
*JBL* — *Journal of Biblical Literature and Exegesis*
*JBR* — *Journal of Bible and Religion*

*JEA* — *Journal of Egyptian Archaeology*
Jer. — Jeremiah
*JJGL* — *Jahrbuch für jüdische Geschichte und Literatur*
*JNES* — *Journal of Near Eastern Studies*
Jos. Antiq. — Josephus *The Antiquities of the Jews*
Jos. Apion — Josephus *Against Apion*
Jos. Life — Josephus *Life*
Jos. War — Josephus *The Jewish War*
Josh. — Joshua
*JPOS* — *Journal of the Palestine Oriental Society*
*JQR* — *Jewish Quarterly Review*
*JR* — *Journal of Religion*
*JRAS* — *Journal of the Royal Asiatic Society*
*JSOR* — *Journal of the Society of Oriental Research*
J.T. — Jerusalem Talmud
Jth. — Judith
*JTS* — *Journal of Theological Studies*
Jub. — Jubilees
Judg. — Judges
Just. Apol. — Justin Martyr *Apology*
Just. Dial. — Justin Martyr *Dialogue with Trypho*

*KAT* — *Kommentar zum Alten Testament*
Kel. — Kelim
Ker. — Kerithoth
Keth. — Kethuboth
*KHC* — *Kurzer Hand-Kommentar zum Alten Testament*
Ḳid. — Ḳiddushin
Kil. — Kil'ayim
KJV — King James Version
*KUB* — *Keilschrifturkunden aus Boghazköi*

L — Lukan source
Lam. — Lamentations
Lat. — Latin
LB — Late Bronze Age
Lev. — Leviticus
LXX — Septuagint

M — Matthean source
M. — Mishna
Ma'as. — Ma'asroth
Ma'as Sh. — Ma'aser Sheni
Macc. — Maccabees
Mak. — Makkoth
Maksh. — Makshirin
Mal. — Malachi
Mart. Polyc. — *The Martyrdom of Polycarp*
masc. — masculine
Matt. — Matthew
MB — Middle Bronze Age
Meg. — Megillah

Me'il. — Me'ilah
Mek. — Mekilta
Men. — Menaḥoth
mg. — margin
*MGWJ* — *Monatsschrift für Geschichte und Wissenschaft des Judentums*
Mic. — Micah
Miḳ. — Miḳwa'oth
M.Ḳ. — Mo'ed Ḳaṭan
MS, MSS — manuscript, manuscripts
MT — Masoretic Text
*MVAG* — *Mitteilungen der vorderasiatisch-aegyptischen Gesellschaft*

N — north
n. — note
Nah. — Nahum
Naz. — Nazir
NE — northeast
Ned. — Nedarim
Neg. — Nega'im
Neh. — Nehemiah
NF — Neue Folge
Nid. — Niddah
*NKZ* — *Neue kirchliche Zeitschrift*
NS — Nova series
NT — New Testament
*NTS* — *New Testament Studies*
*NTSt* — *Nieuwe theologische Studien*
*NTT* — *Nieuw theologisch Tijdschrift*
Num. — Numbers
NW — northwest

Obad. — Obadiah
Ohol. — Oholoth
OL — Old Latin
*OLZ* — *Orientalistische Literaturzeitung*
'Or. — 'Orlah
OT — Old Testament

P — Priestly source
p., pp. — page, pages
Par. — Parah
*PEQ* — *Palestine Exploration Quarterly* (*Palestine Exploration Quarterly Fund*)
Pers. — Persian
Pes. — Pesaḥim
Pesiḳ. dRK — Pesiḳta di Rab Kahana
Pesiḳ. R. — Pesiḳtha Rabbathi
Pet. — Peter
Phil. — Philippians
Philem. — Philemon
Phoen. — Phoenicia
Pir. R. El. — Pirke di Rabbi Eliezer
*PJ* — *Palästina Jahrbuch*
pl. — plate (herein, color illustration)
Pliny Nat. Hist. — Pliny *Natural History*

Polyc. Phil. — The Epistle of Polycarp to the Philippians
Prayer Man. — The Prayer of Manasseh
Prov. — Proverbs
Ps., Pss. — Psalm, Psalms
*PSBA* — *Proceedings of the Society of Biblical Archaeology*
Pseudep. — Pseudepigrapha
Pss. Sol. — Psalms of Solomon
pt. — part
*PTR* — *Princeton Theological Review*

Q — *Quelle* ("Sayings" source in the gospels)
1QH — Thanksgiving Hymns
1QIs[a] — Isaiah Scroll (published by the American Schools of Oriental Research)
1QIs[b] — Isaiah Scroll (published by E. L. Sukenik, Hebrew University, Jerusalem, Israel)
1QM — War Scroll
1QpHab — Habakkuk Commentary
1QS — Manual of Discipline
1QSa — Rule of the Congregation

*RB* — *Revue biblique*
*REJ* — *Revue des études juives*
Rev. — Revelation
rev. — revised, revision, reviser
R. H. — Rosh Hashanah
*RHPR* — *Revue d'histoire et de philosophie religieuses*
*RHR* — *Revue de l'histoire des religions*
Rom. — Romans
*RR* — *Ricerche religiose*
*RS* — *Revue sémitique*
*RSR* — *Recherches de science religieuse*
RSV — Revised Standard Version (1946-52)
*RTP* — *Revue de théologie et de philosophie*

S — south
Sam. — Samuel
Samar. — Samaritan recension
Sanh. — Sanhedrin
SE — southeast
sec. — section
Shab. — Shabbath
Sheb. — Shebi'ith
Shebu. — Shebu'oth
Shek. — Shekalim
*SL* — *Series Latina*
Song of S. — Song of Songs
Song Thr. Ch. — Song of the Three Children (or Young Men)

Sot. — Sotah
*SPAW* — *Sitzungsberichte der Preussischen Akademie der Wissenschaften*
*STZ* — *Schweizerische theologische Zeitschrift*
Suk. — Sukkah
Sumer. — Sumerian
Sus. — Susanna
SW — southwest
*SWP* — *Survey of Western Palestine*
Symm. — Symmachus
Syr. — Syriac

Ta'an. — Ta'anith
Tac. Ann. — Tacitus *Annals*
Tac. Hist. — Tacitus *Histories*
Tam. — Tamid
Tanh. — Tanhuma
Targ. — Targum
T.B. — Babylonian Talmud
TdbK. — Tanna debe Eliyahu
Tem. — Temurah
Ter. — Terumoth
Tert. Apol. — Tertullian *Apology*
Tert. Marcion — Tertullian *Against Marcion*
Tert. Presc. Her. — Tertullian *Prescriptions Against the Heretics*
Test. Asher — Testament of Asher
Test. Benj. — Testament of Benjamin
Test. Dan — Testament of Dan
Test. Gad — Testament of Gad
Test. Iss. — Testament of Issachar
Test. Joseph — Testament of Joseph
Test. Judah — Testament of Judah
Test. Levi — Testament of Levi
Test. Naph. — Testament of Naphtali
Test. Reuben — Testament of Reuben
Test. Simeon — Testament of Simeon
Test. Zeb. — Testament of Zebulun
Theod. — Theodotion
*Theol.* — *Theology*
*Theol. Rundschau* — *Theologische Rundschau*
Thess. — Thessalonians
Tim. — Timothy
Tit. — Titus
*TLZ* — *Theologische Literaturzeitung*

Tob. — Tobit
Toh. — Tohoroth
Tosaf. — Tosafoth
Tosef. — Tosefta
*TQ* — *Theologische Quartalschrift*
trans. — translated, translation, translator
Tristram *NHB* — H. B. Tristram, *The Natural History of the Bible*
*TSBA* — *Transactions of the Society of Biblical Archaeology*
*TSK* — *Theologische Studien und Kritiken*
*TT* — *Theologisch Tijdschrift*
*TU* — *Texte und Untersuchungen zur Geschichte der altchristlichen Literatur*
*TWNT* — *Theologisches Wörterbuch zum Neuen Testament*
T.Y. — Tebul Yom

Ugar. — Ugaritic
'Uk. — 'Ukzin

vol. — volume
vs., vss. — verse, verses
*VT* — *Vetus Testamentum*
Vulg. — Vulgate

W — west
WC — Westminster Commentaries
Wisd. Sol. — Wisdom of Solomon
*WZKM* — *Wiener Zeitschrift für die Kunde des Morgenlandes*

Y — Yahweh
Yeb. — Yebamoth
Yom. — Yoma

*ZA* — *Zeitschrift für Assyriologie und verwandte Gebiete*
Zab. — Zabin
*ZAW* — *Zeitschrift für die alttestamentliche Wissenschaft*
*ZDMG* — *Zeitschrift der deutschen morgenländischen Gesellschaft*
*ZDPV* — *Zeitschrift des deutschen Palästina-Vereins*
Zeb. — Zebahim
Zech. — Zechariah
Zeph. — Zephaniah
*ZNW* — *Zeitschrift für die neutestamentliche Wissenschaft und die Kunde der älteren Kirche*
*ZS* — *Zeitschrift für Semitistik*
*ZST* — *Zeitschrift für systematische Theologie*
*ZThK* — *Zeitschrift für Theologie und Kirche*

**A.** The symbol used to designate the biblical MS ALEXANDRINUS.

**A (ALEPH** ä'lĭf) [א]. *See* SINAITICUS.

**AALAR.** KJV Apoc. form of IMMER 2.

*****AARON** âr'ən [אהרון, אהרן]. The elder brother of Moses (Exod. 6:20; 7:7). The picture of Aaron differs in various accounts. In early literary materials the data concerning Aaron is of utmost importance, although sketchy. Late materials extensively set forth his activity and significance.

In P, Chronicles, and other postexilic material, Aaron was Moses' helper in freeing the Israelites from Egyptian bondage. He was the first high priest, the ancestor of all lawful priests (cf. Ezra 7:1-5, where the ancestry of EZRA [3] is traced to Aaron; Luke 1:5; Heb. 5:4-5; 7:11). Aaron served as Moses' spokesman to Pharaoh (Exod. 7:2). God commanded both Moses and Aaron what they should do to effect deliverance (7:8; 9:8), and Moses and Aaron appeared together in the encounters with Pharaoh. At Moses' instruction Aaron with his rod performed a sign before Pharaoh (7:8-12) and brought on the first three plagues (7:19-20; 8:5-6, 16-17). God revealed to both Moses and Aaron the prescriptions for the Passover (12:1). Aaron was beside Moses in leading and organizing the people (Num. 1:3; 2:1; 4:1) and with Moses presided in judgment (15:33). The murmuring of the people was directed against both Moses and Aaron (Exod. 16:2, 6; Num. 14:2, 26; 20:2). Through anointing by Moses (Exod. 29:7; Lev. 8:5-12) Aaron became "the priest" (Exod. 31: 10; 35:19; 38:21; Lev. 13:2; Num. 18:28). God gave Moses directions for the making of glorious vestments which Aaron was to wear in the tent of meeting and in the holy place to signify the people of Israel before God (Exod. 28; Lev. 8:7-9). The tent of meeting and the ark within it were committed to Aaron's charge (Num. 4). Instructions concerning his office came to him directly from God (Num. 18). Aaron alone, once a year, entered the holy of holies (Lev. 16). Aaron was the first priest and the founder of the priesthood. His four sons, NADAB (1); ABIHU; ELEAZAR (1);

ITHAMAR, were consecrated along with him (Exod. 6:23; 28-29; Num. 3:2-3; I Chr. 24:1).

Aaron was the Levite par excellence. In two stories which set forth the cultic prerogatives of the tribe of Levi, Aaron was a leading figure: (*a*) Led by KORAH, 250 leaders of the tribes in the wilderness protested that since "all the congregation are holy," there was no need for the Levites to be specially set apart to approach God; the charge was made to Moses and Aaron; the issue was decided by a trial by ordeal; fire destroyed the rebels; Aaron with his firepan filled with incense and fire from the altar stopped a plague (the P story in Num. 16:1aα, 2b-7a, 18-24, 35, 41-50). (*b*) When a rod from each of the twelve tribes was placed in the tent of meeting before the ark, the rod of Levi with Aaron's name on it blossomed; thenceforth Aaron's rod was to be kept in the tent of meeting as a sign against rebellion (Num. 17:1-11). The pre-eminence of Aaron as the divine choice for the priesthood, over against the demand of the Levites for status as priests, was set forth in the story of Korah's rebellion as told by a P redactor (Num. 16:1aβ, 7b-11, 16-17, 35-40). Aaron and his descendants were of a higher order, full sacrificing priests; while the Levites, Aaron's brethren, were to perform subordinate duties (Num. 3-4; 18). The priesthood of Aaron and his descendants was "by a perpetual statute" (Exod. 29:9), an "everlasting covenant" (Ecclus. 45:6-22).

The priesthood of Nadab and Abihu, Aaron's first two sons, was rejected; the extant account gives little reason, but the effect of the story of this purge was that it removed any taint from the remaining Aaronites (Lev. 10:1-7; cf. Num. 3:4; I Chr. 24:2; *see* PRIESTS AND LEVITES). The priesthood is traced through Eleazar and Ithamar. Eleazar is the dominant line (Num. 25:7-13; I Chr. 6:1-15; 24:4), and ZADOK (1) is his descendant. When Aaron died on Mount Hor—like Moses, forbidden to enter the Promised Land—Moses invested Eleazar with Aaron's garments (Num. 20:23-28; 33:37-39; *see* HOR 1).

Ezekiel does not mention Aaron; the last nine chapters speak of the priests as sons of Zadok (40:46; 43:19; 44:15; 48:11). In Deuteronomy, Aaron appears in only three passages. Moses interceded for Aaron when the people had made the golden calf (Deut. 9:16, 20-21); Moses' plea for Aaron (unknown in Exod. 32; *see* JE and E *below*) indicates the stage reached in the harmonizing of the tradition concerning Moses and the tradition concerning Aaron at the time this text was written. In Deut. 10:6 (within an interpolated fragment of an old itinerary) Aaron died and was buried at MOSERAH; he was succeeded by Eleazar (a later addition). In 32:48-52 (probably a late, expanded duplicate of P in Num. 27:12-14) Yahweh's command to Moses to prepare for death retrospectively mentions the death of Aaron on Mount Hor.* Aaron appears in the books of preexilic prophets only in Mic. 6:4, where he is named with Moses and MIRIAM (1) as a leader out of bondage. Fig. HOR 31.

JE adds to J and E (*see below*). Aaron, the brother of Moses, identified as "the Levite," was the spokesman for Moses to the people (Exod. 4:14-16). Aaron met Moses at the mountain of God and, instructed by Moses, returned with him and convinced the people by words and signs (vss. 27-31). Moses and Aaron went to Pharaoh to request permission for a feast in the wilderness, but the petition was denied (5:1, 4). In the JE narrative of the plagues Aaron, named only as summoned with Moses by Pharaoh to remove the plagues, is silent and subordinate (8:8, 25; 9:27; 10:16); Moses speaks, acts, and departs as though he were alone. Aaron accompanied Moses up the mountain (19:24). His name was added to the J story of Nadab, Abihu (here not cited as sons of Aaron, cf. P), and seventy elders ascending the mountain with Moses (24:1-2, 9-11). Joshua 24:5aα is an addition: secondary E, JE, or later (cf. I Sam. 12:6, 8). Only Eleazar is named as his son (Josh. 24: 33).

In E, Aaron was an elder, a leader and judge of the people. He does not appear as the partner of Moses; indeed, according to E, sometimes Aaron acted in opposition to Moses. He was the figure by whom Miriam was identified: she was the "sister of Aaron" (Exod. 15:20). Aaron held up Moses' hands while JOSHUA (SON OF NUN) defeated the Amalekites (17:10-12). "Aaron came with all the elders" to a sacred meal presided over by JETHRO (18:12). Aaron and Hur substituted for Moses and Joshua and served as judges over the people during their absence on the mountain with God (24: 13-14). In the E story of the golden calf (32:1-4a to "hand," 4c from "and made," 6, 15-24), Aaron was the passive agent of the people's irresistible desire to commit apostasy, and he bears no responsibility: when he forged the contributed gold, "there came out this calf" (vs. 24), and he is not mentioned in the punishing trial by ordeal (vs. 20). (Another view concerning E in Exod. 32 is that E, cautiously polemical against the cult of Bethel [*see below*], employed scorn to show Aaron's guilt.) Aaron and Miriam disputed Moses' pre-eminent position in Num. 12:2-12, 14(?), the only E story in which Aaron approached the tent of meeting. In E, Aaron was not a priest: in Exod. 33:11, it was Joshua who ministered with Moses at the tent of meeting. (It should be noted that some scholars assign the above references in Exod. 33; Num. 12 to J.)

Probably nowhere in J is the name Aaron original. Concerning the original figure Aaron, two alternative suggestions may be made: (a) Behind the successively reworked narrative of the golden calf (Exod. 32) lies an ancient, independent, N Israelite saga laudatory of Aaron as the founder of the bull cult which was centered at BETHEL (*see* CALF, GOLDEN); Aaron became the eponym of the Ephraimite priesthood. (b) Some of the traditions cited in paragraphs above reflect the fact that originally Aaron was a cultic figure among the S tribes at KADESH, or among these tribes which moved northward during the conquest and formed an early cultic center at HEBRON (Josh. 21:9-19 P locates the descendants of Aaron at Hebron). If this be the case, the absence of Aaron in J may be related to the significance in J of David and to his shifting of the center of the S cult from Hebron to Jerusalem.

For the history of the sequence in which Aaron became the traditional ancestor of the priests of Yahweh in worship centered in Jerusalem, *see bibliography*. See also PRIESTS AND LEVITES § D1.

**Bibliography.** Oort, "De Aaroniden," *TT*, XVIII (1884), 289-335; R. Kennett, "The Origin of the Aaronite Priesthood," *JTS*, VI (1904-5), 161-86; Westphal, "Aaron und die Aaroniden," *ZAW*, XXVI (1906), 201-30; G. Berry, "Priests and Levites," *JBL*, XLII (1923), 227-38; T. Meek, "Aaronites and Zadokites," *AJSL*, XLV (1929), 149-66; K. Möhlenbrink, "Die levitischen Überlieferungen des ATs," *ZAW*, LII (1934), 184-231; J. Morgenstern, "A Chapter in the History of the High-Priesthood," *AJSL*, LV (1938), 1-24, 360-77; N. Snaith, "The Priesthood and the Temple," in T. Manson, ed., *A Companion to the Bible* (1939), pp. 421-27; R. Pfeiffer, *Introduction to the OT* (1941), p. 284; C. Simpson, *The Early Traditions of Israel* (1948), pp. 204-7, 319, 322, 388, 625-26, 629-30; T. Meek, *Hebrew Origins* (1950), pp. 119-47; F. North, "Aaron's Rise in Prestige," *ZAW*, LXVI (1954), 191-99.      T. M. MAUCH

*\*AARONITES âr'ǝ nīts [בְּנֵי אַהֲרֹן, sons of Aaron]. Alternately: HOUSE OF AARON (I Chr. 12:27; Ps. 115:10, 12; 118:3; 135:19); AARON (I Chr. 27: 17). A collective term for all the priests whose descent is traced from AARON as the founder and head of the priesthood. *See* PRIESTS AND LEVITES § D1.
     T. M. MAUCH

**AARON'S ROD.** In two narratives late material sets forth the significance of AARON by speaking of Aaron's rod:

In the recital of the struggle between Pharaoh's power and Yahweh's purpose to accomplish deliverance, at Moses' instruction: (a) Aaron cast down his rod, and it became a serpent, which swallowed the serpents from the rods of the Egyptian magicians; (b) Aaron used his rod to bring about the first three plagues (Exod. 7:8-13, 19-20a [to "commanded"]; 8:5-7, 16-19). These passages are part of the P portrayal of Aaron as Moses' helper in effecting deliverance; elsewhere the rod is Moses' (cf. 4:2-14 J, 16 E; 17:5 E, 9 E). The element of magic here, drawn from the folklore of the ancient Near East, is not treated as extraordinary; it is subordinate, instrumental in the narrative of God's acts in history. Two further observations concerning 7:8-13 can be suggested for inquiry: In postexilic tradition Aaron was the Levite (*see* PRIESTS AND LEVITES) par excellence (cf. the etymology of LEVI). "Serpent" (תַּנִּין; cf. נָחָשׁ [4:3]) also may be translated DRAGON.

In the P story of the confirmation of the tribe of Levi in the priesthood (Num. 17:1-11), vss. 3, 6b, 10-11, are late P amplification and accentuate Aaron. Among the representative tribal rods, the rod of Levi which blossomed had Aaron's name upon it. Moses was ordered to put back Aaron's rod "before the [ark of the?] testimony" (*see* the work of P. Wood in the *bibliography*). In Heb. 9:4 (cf. I Kings 8:9) its place was within the ark.

**Bibliography.** H. Gressmann, "Mose und seine Zeit," *FRLANT*, XLVIII (1913), 278-83; P. Wood, "Jeremiah's Figure of the Almond Rod," *JBL*, LXI (1942), 99-103; C. Simpson, *The Early Traditions of Israel* (1948), pp. 170, 242; J. Marsh, Exegesis of Numbers, *IB*, II (1953), 228.
     T. M. MAUCH

**AB** ăb [אָב]. The fifth Hebrew month (July-August). *See* CALENDAR.

**ABACUC** ăb'ə kək. KJV Apoc. form of HABAKKUK.

**ABADDON** ə băd'ən [אבדון (אבדה) *in* Prov. 27:20), from אבד, perish, be lost; LXX ἀπώλεια (τῶν μέρων *in* Job 31:12, *through fanciful combination with* בד, portion); NT ᾿Αβαδδών; Vulg. *perditio*]. A poetic name for the nether world—viz., Perdition. In the OT (Job 26:6; 28:22; 31:12; Ps. 88:11—H 88:12; Prov. 15: 11; 27:20), it denotes simply the common abode of the dead (*see* DEAD, ABODE OF THE). Similarly, in the Syr. (Peshitta) Version of Psalms the cognate אובדנא sometimes renders שחת, "the Pit"; and in Mandaean, אבחנא דחשוכה תיאתויה, "the nether Abaddon of darkness," is the grave pit. In the Dead Sea Hymns (3.19-20), the name is used figuratively to denote the "slough of despond," in contrast to the "crest of the world" (רום עולם), attained by inner vision.

In rabbinic literature, however, Abaddon comes to mean specifically the place of damnation and punishment and is regarded as a compartment of the infernal regions, situated in the third lowest stratum of the earth and reserved for the wicked. This nuance is reflected in the employment of the term (᾿Αβαδδών) in the NT (Rev. 9:11) as a designation of the angel of the Pit. It is correctly glossed by the scriptural writer as ᾿Απολλύων, "Destroyer."

T. H. GASTER

**ABADIAS** ăb'ə dī'əs. KJV Apoc. form of OBADIAH.

**ABAGTHA** ə băg'thə [אבגתא, *probably of* Middle Iranian *origin*; Syr. אגבותא]. One of the seven eunuchs sent by Ahasuerus, king of Persia (Xerxes I, 485-465 B.C.), to accompany the queen, Vashti, to the royal feast (Esth. 1:10). These chamberlains were guardians of the royal harem and ministered in the presence of the king. According to widespread custom, such eunuchs were usually foreigners, as in the case of Nehemiah. The derivation and meanings of this and the other names in the verse are uncertain; the names differ widely in the versions, and the correct text is problematical. *See also* EUNUCH.

*Bibliography.* I. Scheftelowitz, *Arisches im AT,* I (1901), 37; L. B. Paton, ICC (1916), 66-68, 147-48; J. Duchesne-Guillemin, "Les noms des Eunuques d'Assuérus," *Le Muséon,* LXVI (1953), 105-8. H. F. BECK

**ABANA** ăb'ə nə [אבנה] (II Kings 5:12). A river flowing down from Anti-Lebanon through Damascus. Its modern name is Barada (*cf.* AMANA).

The river of Abana (Barada) provides the region with water, thanks to which the oasis of Damascus is famous for its fertility. The river disappears in the steppe E of Damascus, Bahr al-Aateibe. In II Kings 5:12 Abana and PHARPAR are said to be the rivers of Damascus, which are "better than all the waters of Israel" according to the view of Naaman, captain of the host of the Aramean king. Naaman came to Elisha to be cured of his leprosy, but when the prophet ordered him to step down into the Jordan, he went his way in anger. He returned and was cured by Elisha. A. HALDAR

**ABARIM** ăb'ə rĭm [העברים, עברים, regions beyond]. A mountainous region at the W edge of the plateau of N Moab, overlooking the Dead Sea and the Jordan Valley. These mountains reach three hundred to six

hundred feet above the plateau and stand over four thousand feet above the level of the Dead Sea. The Israelites encamped in the mountains of Abarim (Num. 33:47-48) after leaving Almon-diblathaim and before reaching the plains of Moab across the Jordan from Jericho. From the principal peak of the range, Mount Nebo (*see* NEBO, MOUNT), Moses viewed the land of Canaan (Num. 27:12; Deut. 32:49). Jeremiah (22:20) figuratively summoned Jerusalem to wail from Lebanon, Bashan, and Abarim (KJV PASSAGES). E. D. GROHMAN

*ABBA ăb'ə, ä'bə [ἀββά; Aram. אבא, *emphatic form of* אב, *see below*]. A term meaning properly "the father," but used as the equivalent of "my father" or "our Father" chiefly in prayer in the later rabbinic literature (*see bibliography*). Since it is found even in Hebrew contexts, the expression is assumed to have been a common colloquial one, doubtless derived from use in the family circle. In the NT it occurs three times, all in prayers and accompanied by the Greek equivalent (ἀββά ὁ πατήρ; Mark 14:36: of Jesus; Rom. 8:15; Gal. 4:6). But the Aramaic form may lie back of many uses of the Greek in similar contexts (e.g., Matt. 6:9; Luke 11:11; 23:46; John 12:27; etc.; cf. the LXX of Ps. 88:26—H 89:26; Isa. 63:16; 64:8; Jer. 3:19; Tob. 13:4; Wisd. Sol. 14:3; Ecclus. 23:1, 4). The Greek transliteration is not found in the LXX.

In Judaism the figurative use of "father" implies the thought of a close relationship between God and Israel or God and the righteous (*see* GOD, OT). But it is rarely found in the earlier literature. Examples, in addition to those cited above, occur in I Chr. 17: 13; Ps. 68:5; Jer. 31:9; Mal. 1:6; 2:10 (cf. Deut. 14:1).

In the NT, Jesus' use of the word as a familiar name for God reflects his own emphasis on the beneficence of God as expressed in a symbolism drawn from filial relationships. Paul's usage seems also to imply a continued employment of the term as a particularly significant expression of religious faith, the double form doubtless being derived from liturgical usage and meaning "God, our Father." Those who have received "adoption as sons" and the "spirit of sonship" are able to cry "Abba! Father!" because they are spiritually the "children of God." *See* GOD, NT. *See also* RABBI.

*Bibliography.* G. F. Moore, *Judaism* (1907), II, 201-11, etc. E. D. Burton, *A Critical and Exegetical Commentary on the Epistle to the Galatians,* ICC (1920), pp. 384-92. For rabbinic examples, see: H. L. Strack and P. Billerbeck, *Kommentar zum NT aus Talmud und Midrasch,* I (1922), 392-96, 410-18, 918-19; G. Dalman, *Die Worte Jesu* (2nd ed., 1930), pp. 150-59, 296-304. S. V. McCasland, "Abba, Father," *JBL,* LXXII (1953), 79 ff. A. WIKGREN

**ABDA** ăb'də [עבדא, servant of Yahu]. **1.** The father of Adoniram, who was in charge of forced labor under Solomon (I Kings 4:6).

**2.** A Levite who lived in Jerusalem after his return from the Exile (Neh. 11:17). He is called Obadiah in I Chr. 9:16. F. T. SCHUMACHER

**ABDEEL** ăb'dĭ əl [עבדאל, servant of God] (Jer. 36:26). The father of Shelemiah, a courtier of Jehoiakim.

**ABDENAGO** ăb dĕn′ə gō. Douay Version form of Abednego. *See* SHADRACH.

**ABDI** ăb′dī [עבדי, servant of Yahu, *abbreviated form*]. 1. A Levite; father of Kishi; grandfather of Ethan, one of David's temple musicians (I Chr. 6:44—H 6: 29).

2. The father of Kish, a Levite under Hezekiah (II Chr. 29:12); possibly identical with 1 *above*.

3. One of those who married foreign wives in the time of Ezra (Ezra 10:26 = I Esd. 9:27).

F. T. SCHUMACHER

**ABDIAS** ăb dī′əs. Douay Version form of OBADIAH.

**ABDIAS, APOSTOLIC HISTORY OF** ăb′dī əs. The Latin form in which are conveniently assembled the several romances—more properly legends—purporting to describe the histories of the apostles and which in Greek circulated separately. It consists of ten books which treat respectively Peter (I), Paul (II), Andrew (III), James the Great (IV), John (V), James the Less (VI.1-6), Simon and Jude (VI.7 ff), Matthew (VII), Bartholomew (VIII), Thomas (IX), and Philip (X). The material, often widely divergent from the Greek form in which these Acts circulated, is a veritable mélange drawn from various sources, such as the canonical gospels and Acts; the Clementine literature; the earlier heretical Acts (especially the various Martyrdoms, which regularly circulated separately); the epitome of the miracles of Andrew, made by Gregory of Tours from the Greek Acts of Andrew (*see* ANDREW, ACTS OF); folklore; and wonder stories.

This collection, assembled perhaps in France, not earlier than the sixth or seventh century, became associated (with no historical warrant at all) with the name Abdias. In Book VI (Simon and Jude), after the mention of Abdias' ordination as bishop of Babylon, it is said: "For thirteen years they [Simon and Jude] traveled, and Craton his disciple recorded their acts in ten books which Africanus the historian translated into Latin, and from which we have made excerpts." In the preface to the work (purporting to be by Julius Africanus) it is said that Africanus took the material from books which Abdias had written in Hebrew about all the apostles and which his disciple Eutropius had translated into Greek. Africanus had in turn put it into Latin.

*Bibliography.* A convenient analysis of the contents of the ten books, with translation of the more interesting material not available in the other recensions, is given by M. R. James, *The Apocryphal NT* (1924), pp. 462-69. The Latin text of Abdias is printed by Fabricius, *Codex Apocryphus Novi Testamenti* (1743), II, 402-742. M. S. ENSLIN

**ABDIEL** ăb′dī əl [עבדיאל, servant of God] (I Chr. 5:15). Son of Guni and father of Ahi in the genealogy of Gad.

**ABDON** ăb′dŏn [עבדון, service(?), servile(?)]. 1. Son of Hillel; one of the so-called minor judges (Judg. 12: 13-15). The formula description tells us nothing of his exploits, which presumably took place around his home town of Pirathon in Ephraim. He "judged Israel" eight years and apparently headed a family of some wealth and prominence.

2. One of the sons of Shashak in the genealogy of Benjamin (I Chr. 8:23).

3. The first-born son of Jeiel in the twice-repeated list of Saul's ancestors (I Chr. 8:30; 9:36).

4. A courtier of King Josiah; one of the commission sent to Hulda the prophetess (II Chr. 34:20). The account in II Kings 22:12, however, lists him as Achbor. F. T. SCHUMACHER

5. A Levitical town in the territory of Asher (Josh. 21:30; I Chr. 6:74 — H 6:59). It is probably to be identified with Khirbet 'Abdeh, a site located *ca.* four miles E of Achzib. G. W. VAN BEEK

**ABEDNEGO.** *See* SHADRACH.

**ABEL** ā′bəl [הבל, *see* §1 *below*; אבל, *see* § 2 *below*; Αβελ; Syr. הביל; Vulg. *Abel*]. 1. The second son of Adam and Eve (Gen. 4:1-9).

The etymology of the name is uncertain. If originally Hebrew, הבל would most likely mean "vanity, breath, vapor," perhaps stressing the shortness of Abel's life or the weak, transitory nature of human life, similar to its use in Eccl. 2:16-17, 22-23; 3:19-21; 12:1-8. More probably it goes back to Akkadian *ablu/aplu*, "son." It could then be a generic term for "mankind," similar to ADAM and ENOSH.

A "keeper of sheep," Abel presented to Yahweh an offering "of the firstlings of his flock and of their fat portions" (Gen. 4:3-4). Because Yahweh had regard (שעה) for Abel and his offering but not for Cain, the latter plotted the murder of his innocent and unsuspecting younger brother. For discussion of this event, *see* CAIN.

Abel is memorialized as the first righteous (δί-καιος) martyr, whose death stands both as a witness to sin (Matt. 23:35; Luke 11:51; I John 3:12) and as a testimony to faith (Heb. 11:4). To this extent it is also a prototype of Christ's death (Heb. 12:24).

L. HICKS

2. In I Sam. 6:18 the MT reads "great Abel," and the KJV translators tried to make sense by interpolating "stone of." The LXX supports the view of later translators that אבן, "stone," should be read instead of, rather than in addition to, אבל.

3. *See* ABEL-BETH-MAACAH. G. W. VAN BEEK

**ABEL-BETH-MAACAH** ā′bəl bĕth mā′ə kə [אבל בית מעכה]. Alternately: ABEL OF BETH-MAACAH [אבל בית המעכה] (II Sam. 20:14-15); ABEL [אבל] (II Sam. 20:18); ABEL-MAIM ā′bəl mā′əm [אבל מים] (II Chr. 16:4); KJV ABEL . . . AND BETH MAA-CAH [אבלה ובית מעכה] (II Sam. 20:14). A fortified city in N Israel. It is to be identified with Tell Abil, a mound located approximately twelve miles N of Lake Huleh, overlooking the intersection of the route from Hazor northward and the E-W route from Tyre to Damascus.* The town is probably one of the Abels mentioned in the Thut-mose III list of conquered towns. Fig. ABE 1.

Abel-beth-maacah is the place where Sheba son of Bichri took refuge and was slain after his abortive rebellion against David (II Sam. 20:14-18). During the reign of Baasha (early ninth century), it was among the Israelite towns taken by Ben-hadad of Damascus (I Kings 15:20; II Chr. 16:4). Tiglath-pileser III also captured the city in the time of Pekah

From *Atlas of the Bible* (Thomas Nelson & Sons Limited)
1. In upper center, Tell Abil, site of Abel-beth-maacah

(*ca.* 733 B.C.), according to II Kings 15:29 and to an Assyrian text in which it is called "Abilakka." The name BALBAIM in Jth. 7:3 may possibly refer to the same place.

*Bibliography.* W. F. Albright, "The Jordan Valley in the Bronze Age," *AASOR*, VI (1926), 19; J. B. Pritchard, ed., *ANET* (2nd ed., 1955), p. 283.          G. W. VAN BEEK

**ABEL-KERAMIM** ā'bəl kĕr'ə mĭm [אבל כרמים, watercourse of vineyards] (Judg. 11:33); KJV THE PLAIN OF THE VINEYARDS. The terminal point of Jephthah's military campaign against the Ammonites (Judg. 11:29-33; *see* AMMON). The geographical situation calls for a location W and S of Rabbath-ammon (modern Amman). Some would identify it with modern Naʿur, *ca.* nine miles from Amman; others with Khirbet es-Suq, *ca.* five miles S and slightly W of Rabbath-ammon. In Eusebius' *Onomastica* (32.15-16), Abel-keramim is apparently represented by Abela, which Eusebius locates six or seven Roman miles from Philadelphia (i.e., Rabbath-ammon), although he does not specify in which direction.

*Bibliography.* F. Schulze, "Ein neuer Meilenstein und die Lage von Jaser," *PJ*, 28 (1932), 76-77; N. Glueck, *Explorations in Eastern Palestine*, III, *AASOR*, XVIII-XIX (1939), 248-49.
                                    G. M. LANDES

**ABEL-MAIM.** An alternate form of ABEL-BETH-MAACAH.

**ABEL-MEHOLAH** ā'bəl mĭ hō'lə [אבל מחלה, dance place by a perennial stream]. A city E of the Jordan; the residence of the prophet Elisha.

**1. History.** Abel-meholah is first mentioned in the time of the judges, when the Midianites, surprised in their camp in the Jezreel Valley by the night attack of Gideon, fled by way of ZERERAH and the edge of the plateau of Abel-meholah (Judg. 7:22). In the time of Solomon, Abel-meholah was at the E edge of the fifth governmental district, which stretched on both sides of the Jordan around Beth-shean (I Kings 4:12). Elijah at Horeb received the instruction to anoint Elisha of Abel-meholah as his successor; on his way back from Horeb he found Elisha and his servants plowing with twelve yoke of oxen. He cast his mantle over Elisha, who accepted this act as his call to prophecy (I Kings 19:16, 19-21).

**2. Location.** Eusebius identified Abel-meholah with Beth-maela, ten Roman miles S of Beth-shean,

apparently on the basis of a vague similarity of names. This error has been followed by most Bible students and map makers, who locate the city W of the Jordan. A careful reading of the texts involved shows that this cannot be correct. The Midianites were fleeing southeastward, and Gideon was only able to come up to them in the mountains of Gilead. Elijah was heading for Damascus, as part of his instructions from God bade him do (I Kings 19:15), and Abel-meholah must have been near the road from Horeb. Elisha, too, though he traveled extensively over the land of Israel, was evidently buried E of the Jordan (II Kings 13:20-21). The site must also have

Courtesy of Nelson Glueck
2. Tell el-Maqlub, by the Wadi Yabis, which flows into the Jordan; identified with Abel-meholah, the home of the prophet Elisha

had a precipitous slope and a place broad enough for extensive plowing, and it must have been surrounded by vineyards the harvest of which was celebrated by a festal dance. All these specifications are met by Tell el-Maqlub on the Wadi el-Yabis, which was inhabited before and during the Israelite period. Fig. ABE 2.

*Bibliography.* N. Glueck, *The River Jordan* (1946), pp. 168-72; "Explorations in Eastern Palestine, IV," *AASOR*, XXV-XXVIII (1951), pt. I, 211-23.          S. COHEN

**ABEL-MIZRAIM** ā'bəl mĭz'rĭ əm [אבל מצרים]. Alternate name of ATAD.

**ABEL-SHITTIM** ā'bəl shĭt'ĭm [אבל השטים, brook of the acacias] (Num. 33:49). Earlier name of SHITTIM.

**ABEZ.** KJV form of EBEZ.

**ABGARUS, EPISTLES OF CHRIST AND** ăb'gə rəs [Ἄβγαρος]. Two short letters, one purporting to be from Abgar (or Abgarus) Uchama, king of Edessa (7-4 B.C. and A.D. 13-50) to Jesus, and the other the latter's reply. These letters are a part of the story of the exploits of Thaddaeus, one of the seventy, sent by Thomas to Edessa after the Ascension. Euseb. Hist. I.13 translates the two letters, which Eusebius claims to have found in the archives of Edessa, from Syriac into Greek, and with them the story of the mission of Thaddaeus.

Abgar, suffering from a terrible disease and having heard of Jesus' miracles, sends a letter by a courtier Ananias to Jesus, asking Jesus to come and cure him and to share his kingdom, thus escaping the malice of the Jerusalem Jews. Jesus declines the invitation in striking Johannine phraseology, but promises after his ascension to send one of his disciples. After the Ascension, Eusebius continues, Thaddaeus arrives, heals Abgar, and converts the whole community.

A parallel, but somewhat altered, account is found in the so-called *Doctrina Addaei.* In this later version (*ca.* A.D. 400) Jesus' reply is oral—by this time the view that Jesus had written nothing was widespread. Instead of a letter, Ananias brings back a portrait of Jesus, which he himself had painted and which became the showpiece of Abgar's palace. The Greek Acts of Thaddaeus (*see* THADDAEUS, ACTS OF) repeats essentially the same legend, but with variations, notably the legend of the handkerchief given by Christ to Ananias and of the miraculous impression of his countenance.

*Bibliography.* A comprehensive bibliography of the large literature this writing has produced will be found in J. Quasten, *Patrology* (1950), I, 142-43.        M. S. ENSLIN

**ABI** ā′bī [אֲבִי, my father] (II Kings 18:2). Abbreviation of ABIJAH 7.

**ABIA, ABIAH.** KJV alternate forms of ABIJAH.

**ABI-ALBON** ā′bī ăl′bən [אֲבִי־עַלְבוֹן] (II Sam. 23:31). One of David's heroes known as the "Thirty," who probably came from BETH-ARABAH, a town on the frontier of Judah and Benjamin; called "Abi-albon the Arbathite." The name Abi-albon, however, may have suffered some corruption on account of a confusion with the name Shaalbon (II Sam. 23:32). Some propose the reading "Abiel," which has the support of the LXX (II Sam. 23:31) and the parallel passage in I Chr. 11:32 (*see* ABIEL 2); others read "Abibaal."        E. R. DALGLISH

**ABIASAPH** ə bī′ə săf [אֲבִיאָסָף, father has gathered] (Exod. 6:24). Alternately: EBIASAPH [אֶבְיָסָף, Father has added *or* increased] (I Chr. 6:23, 37; 9:19). A division of the Levites descended from KORAH. In I Chr. 9:19; 26:1 (read "Ebiasaph" for "ASAPH"), a section of this division acted as doorkeepers (*see* DOORKEEPER). The name occurs only in the genealogies of P and Chronicles.

*Bibliography.* M. Noth, *Die israelitischen Personennamen* (1928), pp. 66-75, 141-42.        T. M. MAUCH

**ABIATHAR** ə bī′ə thər [אֶבְיָתָר, the father (God) gives abundantly, *or* the father is abundant; Ἀβιάθαρ]. Son of Ahimelech and sole survivor of the slaughter of the priests of NOB. He fled to David and became his priest. He was exiled to ANATHOTH by Solomon for his support of Solomon's rival, Adonijah.

When Abiathar arrived at ADULLAM after his escape from the sword of Doeg the Edomite, whom Saul had commanded to slay the priests of Nob, he brought with him the ephod (I Sam. 23:6; omit "to Keilah"). Thus David was supplied with a sacred oracle (*see* EPHOD 2), which he consulted on various occasions (23:8-12; 30:7-8; possibly 23:2-4). It was as the interpreter of this oracle that Abiathar served David during his outlaw days.

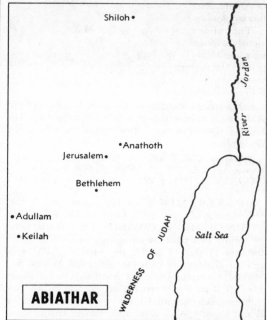

After the capture of Jerusalem, we find Abiathar coupled with Zadok as chief priests to David. It has been suggested that Zadok had charge of the ark, while Abiathar retained control of the ephod. But the account of Absalom's rebellion portrays both priests as guardians of the ark (II Sam. 15:24-36).

In the struggle over the succession during the last days of David, Abiathar supported the claims of Adonijah, while his rival Zadok backed Solomon (I Kings 1). More than professional jealousy may have been involved (*see* ZADOK 1). The party which supported Solomon came into power, and Abiathar was exiled to Anathoth, escaping death only because of his earlier association with David (2:26). Zadok was appointed in his place (vs. 35). The reference to Zadok and Abiathar as co-priests of Solomon (4:4) is probably derived from the Davidic list of II Sam. 20:25. Perhaps Jeremiah, who was "of the priests who were in Anathoth," was a descendant of the exiled Abiathar (Jer. 1:1).

The exile of Abiathar is said to have fulfilled the "word of the LORD which he had spoken concerning the house of Eli in Shiloh" (I Kings 2:27; cf. I Sam. 2:27-36). This statement implies that the Nob priesthood was descended from ELI and was therefore the guardian of the central shrine of the Israelite amphictyony. If this were so, the presence of Abiathar, the last of Eli's family, in the court of David would have been an invaluable aid in the securing and maintaining of the allegiance of the N Israelite tribes. But his identification of the Nob and

Shiloh priesthoods may be the result of later editing. *See* ELI.

Abiathar has been suggested as the author of the early source of the books of Samuel. His association with the Nob priesthood and early allegiance to David, together with the fact that if II Sam. 17:17-21 is a record of actual happenings it must rest on the reminiscences of either Jonathan son of Abiathar or Ahimaaz son of Zadok, is the ground upon which this suggestion has been made.

The reference to Abiathar in Mark 2:26 is obviously a mistake for Ahimelech. Perhaps it is a gloss, for some MSS (D W) omit "when Abiathar was high priest," or perhaps it is based on the confusion between Abiathar and Ahimelech originating in II Sam. 8:17. *See* AHIMELECH 3.

*Bibliography.* M. Noth, *Die israelitischen Personennamen* (1928), p. 193; R. H. Pfeiffer, *Introduction to the OT* (1948), pp. 356-57; W. F. Albright, *Archaeology and the Religion of Israel* (1956), pp. 138-39.                           R. W. CORNEY

**ABIB** ā'bĭb [אביב, young head of grain]. The original (Canaanite) name of the first Hebrew month (March-April), later called NISAN. *See* CALENDAR.

**ABIDA** ə bī'də [אבידע, (my) father knows (took knowledge); *cf.* Minean *personal name Abiyadi'*, Sabean *Yadi''il*, אביסף, אביתר]. The fourth son of Midian, from the line of Abraham and Keturah (Gen. 25:4 [KJV ABIDAH; LXX Αβιρα, Αβια]; I Chr. 1:33 [LXX Αβιδα, Αβειδα]. However, Gen. 25:1-4 may be a lost genealogy of Ishmaelites.

*Bibliography.* W. F. Albright, *BASOR,* 119 (1950), 15; 143 (1956), 10.                           L. HICKS

**ABIDAN** ə bī'dən [אבידן, the (divine) father judged(?), *or* my father judged(?)]. A leader of Benjamin; son of Gideoni (Num. 1:11; 2:22; 7:60, 65; 10:24). He was one of twelve tribal leaders or deputies who assisted Moses in taking a census of Israel and in other tasks in the wilderness. *See* PRINCE.                           R. F. JOHNSON

**ABIEL** ā'bĭ əl [אביאל, father is El]. **1.** A Benjaminite who appears prima facie to be the father of Kish and the grandfather of Saul, but who is more likely the father of NER, Saul's grandfather (I Sam. 9:1; 14:51). It is possible that Jeiel (KJV Jehiel), who appears in I Chr. 8:29 ( =9:35) as the father of Ner, is to be identified with Abiel.

**2.** The Arbathite who appears in I Chr. 11:32 as a member of the company of heroes of David known as the "Thirty." In II Sam. 23:31 he is called ABI-ALBON.                           E. R. DALGLISH

**ABIEZER** ăb'ĭ ē'zər [אביעזר, father is help]; **ABI-EZRITE** —ĕz'rīt [אבי העזרי]. Alternately: in Num. 26:30, IEZER ī ē'zər [איעזר]; IEZERITES —zə rīts [איעזרים]; KJV JEEZER jĭ ē'zər; —zə rīts. **1.** A family of Manasseh to whom some of the Manassite territory in Canaan was allotted (Josh. 17:2; I Chr. 7:18). In I Chr. 7:18 Abiezer appears as an individual in the Manassite genealogy and is probably to be considered the son of Gilead, although the text is obscure. "Iezer," evidently a contraction of "Abiezer," appears as a son of Gilead in Num. 26:30.

**2.** The family of Gideon (Judg. 6:11, 24, 34; 8:2, 32). Joash the Abiezrite was Gideon's father; and OPHRAH (2), the site of the theophany to Gideon and of the altar he thereafter erected, is described as belonging to the Abiezrites. It was also in Ophrah of the Abiezrites that Gideon was buried. Gideon's initial support in the campaign against the Midianites came from the Abiezrites (6:34), but when this fact aroused tribal jealousy among Ephraimites who had not been in the battle, Gideon knew how to reinstate their pride: "Is not the gleaning of the grapes of Ephraim better than the vintage of Abiezer?" (8:2).

**3.** A member of David's bodyguard; a Benjaminite from Anathoth (II Sam. 23:27; I Chr. 11:28; 27:12). According to the scheme of the Chronicler, David's army was divided into twelve divisions of 24,000 men each, and Abiezer was in charge of one of these divisions with special responsibilities in the ninth month.

*Bibliography.* M. Noth, *Die israelitischen Personennamen* (1928), pp. 16, 18, 68-71, 154.                           R. F. JOHNSON

**ABIGAIL** ăb'ə gāl [אביגיל, my father rejoices; אביגל (I Sam. 25:32; II Sam. 3:3 Kethibh; ABIGAL —gāl *in* 17:25), אבוגיל (I Sam. 25:18), אבגיל (I Sam. 25:3)]. **1.** Wife of Nabal, and later of David. Nabal the Carmelite refused to invite David to his sheepshearing. Abigail, a woman of beauty and good sense, then went to meet David and persuaded him not to take vengeance on her foolish husband (I Sam. 25). When Nabal died, Abigail became the wife of David, accompanied him to Philistia (27:3), and returned with him to Hebron. Here she bore David a son named Chileab (II Sam. 3:3), or Daniel (I Chr. 3:1), or possibly Daluiah (II Sam. 3:3 LXX).

*Bibliography.* H. Bauer, *ZAW,* XLVIII (1930), 75-76.                           D. HARVEY

**2.** A sister or half sister of David (I Chr. 2:16), and of Zeruiah, the mother of Joab (II Sam. 17:25); the mother of AMASA. According to the MT of II Sam. 17:25, Abigail's father was NAHASH, rather than Jesse. The words in II Sam. 17:25 which identify her as a daughter of Nahash (בת־נחש) are regarded by some critics as an intrusion from vs. 27 (בן־מחש, "son of Nahash").

According to I Chr. 2:16-17 Abigail married JETHER the Ishmaelite, by whom she bore Amasa; David appointed Amasa captain of his army in place of Joab (II Sam. 19:13; cf. Absalom's appointment of Amasa in 17:25). According to II Sam. 17:25, however, the father of Amasa was ITHRA the Israelite. Rabbi Kimchi suggested that the two descriptions of the father of Amasa might be reconciled by assuming that he lived among the Ishmaelites; he was known to them as an Israelite and to his own people as an Ishmaelite.                           H. F. BECK

**ABIHAIL** ăb'ə hāl [אביחיל, the Father (deity) is might; אביהיל (I Chr. 2:29; II Chr. 11:18), *probably an error for the foregoing, as attested by several MSS*]. **1.** A Levite, ancestor of the house of Merari (Num. 3:35).

**2.** Wife of Abishur, a Jerahmeelite (I Chr. 2:29).

**3.** A Gadite (I Chr. 5:14).

**4.** Apparently the wife of Jerimoth, as well as his cousin; the mother of Mahalath, wife of King Rehoboam, according to II Chr. 11:18. The reading is obscure.

5. The father of Queen Esther and uncle of Mordecai (Esth. 2:15; 9:29).

*Bibliography.* M. Noth, *Die israelitischen Personennamen* (1928), pp. 18, 69-70.                            B. T. DAHLBERG

**ABIHU** ə bī'hū [אביהוא, father is he]. One of the sons of Aaron. NADAB and Abihu are always named together. In JE they are among the chief men of Israel: Moses and Aaron, Nadab and Abihu, and seventy elders ascended the mountain to Yahweh (Exod. 24:1, 9). In P and Chronicles they are cited as the first two sons of AARON (Exod. 6:23; 28:1; Num. 3:2; 26:60; I Chr. 6:3; 24:1), who with Aaron and their two brothers, ELEAZAR and ITHAMAR were consecrated to the priesthood (Exod. 28:1; Num. 3:2-3; I Chr. 24:1). Only one story primarily speaks of Nadab and Abihu: Lev. 10:1-5 obscurely narrates their priestly sin and destruction (referred to in Num. 3:4; 26:61). According to Num. 3:4; I Chr. 24:2, they had no children.

*See also* PRIESTS AND LEVITES.

*Bibliography.* M. Noth, *Die israelitischen Personennamen* (1928), pp. 18, 66-75, 141-44; K. Möhlenbrink, "Die levitischen Überlieferungen des ATs," *ZAW*, LII (1934), 214-15.                            T. M. MAUCH

**ABIHUD** ə bī'hŭd [אביהוד, father is majesty]. A Benjaminite who appears as the third son of Bela, son of Benjamin (I Chr. 8:3). However, it seems quite probable that the text should read "Gera the father of Ehud," with which Judg. 3:15 agrees. This Ehud was a Benjaminite judge. I Chr. 8:6-28 lists the descendants of Ehud.

*Bibliography.* W. Rudolph, "Chronikbücher," *HAT* (1955). Cf. J. W. Rothstein and J. Hänel, "Das erste Buch der Chronik," *KAT* (1927).                            E. R. DALGLISH

**ABIJAH** ə bī'jə [אביה, Y is (my) father]; **ABIJAM** —jəm [אבים, *see* 5 *below*] (I Kings 14:31; 15:1, 7-8); **ABI** ā'bī [אבי, my father] (II Kings 18:2); KJV alternately: ABIAH ə bī'ə (I Sam. 8:2; I Chr. 2:24; 6:28; 7:8); ABIA (I Chr. 3:10; Matt. 1:7; Luke 1:5). 1. Son of Becher, of the tribe of Benjamin (I Chr. 7:8).

2. The KJV translation of the MT אביה in I Chr. 2:24; the name of the wife of Hezron, of the tribe of Judah. Perhaps the correct reading is אביהו—i.e., "his father" (RSV), rather than the name Abijah.

3. The younger son of Samuel. He was appointed by Samuel in his old age as a judge in Beer-sheba, along with his elder brother, Joel. But because of the wickedness and injustice of the two brothers, the people of Israel came to Samuel and demanded a king (I Sam. 8:1-9; I Chr. 6:28). This account of the founding of the monarchy comes from the later story.

4. A descendant of Aaron. David divided the priests, the sons of Aaron, into twenty-four divisions. These divisions were on duty in the temple, each in its turn. The order in which the divisions served was decided by lot. Abijah was head of the eighth division in the service of the temple (I Chr. 24:10).

Zechariah, father of John the Baptist, belonged to the division of Abijah (Luke 1:5).

5. King of Judah *ca.* 915-913 B.C.; son and successor of Rehoboam.

The spelling of the name varies in the MSS. The MT of Kings calls the king Abijam ('Αβιού in the LXX), but certain MSS and the MT of Chronicles call him Abijah (אביהו). Four explanations of the double name may be suggested: (*a*) Abijah was his throne name, Abijam his personal or given name. The practice of giving the new king a throne name when he became king seems to be clearly borne out in the case of certain of the kings of the S kingdom. Parallels have also been found in Babylonian and Egyptian literature. (*b*) The two names arose from confusion between ה ("h") and final ם ("m"), as happened frequently. (*c*) "Yam" was the name of a pagan deity (the Canaanite sea-god), and was altered for obvious reasons to that of the national God, as more suitable for a king of Judah. (*d*) The name is a hypocoristic in -*ām* (cf. Ta'annak Aḥiyami). The second of these explanations is probably correct.

Abijah is said to have reigned three years (I Kings 15:2*a;* II Chr. 13:2*a*), but it is clear that he reigned only two full years (I Kings 15:1, 9). His mother was Maacah, daughter of Abishalom (I Kings 15:2*b*). This is also in line with the evidence of II Chr. 11:20 ff, but in all probability this whole section (II Chr. 11:18-23) does not come from the hand of the Chronicler. The evidence of Chronicles is not consistent at this point, for in 13:2 we are told that Abijah's mother was Micaiah, daughter of Uriel of Gibeah. The issue is further complicated by the statement that the name of the mother of Asa son of Abijah was also Maacah, daughter of Abishalom (I Kings 15:10). It is probable that the Chronicler has preserved the true tradition in 13:2. The alternatives are that Abijah and Asa were not father and son, but brothers; or that the name of Asa's mother was soon forgotten because of the dominant position of the queen mother.

The border warfare which had gone on between Jeroboam and Rehoboam was continued in Abijah's reign. The Chronicler gives details of a great battle near Mount Zemaraim in the hill country of Ephraim (II Chr. 13:3-19). That such a battle occurred is not to be doubted, though the numbers involved are greatly exaggerated and the details given represent the Chronicler's own point of view. They cannot, therefore, be accepted as historical. Abijah's victory, in which he captured certain towns in Israel—Bethel, Jeshanah, and Ephron, each with its villages (II Chr. 13:19)—had only temporary significance in view of the much greater potential of the N kingdom. It is, however, interesting from the point of view of giving a picture of the tension which existed along the border for several years.

Abijah had fourteen wives, who bore him twenty-two sons and sixteen daughters (II Chr. 13:21)—a clear indication, from the Chronicler's point of view, of the favor of God. For this reason the Chronicler omitted the negative judgment passed on the king by the writer of Kings.

As his source of information on Abijah's reign, "his ways and his sayings," the Chronicler refers to the "midrash" of the prophet Iddo (II Chr. 13:22). His main source, however, was our present book of Kings, but in an earlier recension.

*Bibliography.* M. Noth, *Die israelitischen Personennamen* (1928), p. 234; W. F. Albright, "A Prince of Taanach in the

Fifteenth Century B.C., *BASOR*, 94 (1944), 20, note 44; G. R. Driver, "Theological and Philological Problems in the OT," *JTS*, XLVII (1946), 156; A. M. Honeyman, "The Evidence for Regnal Names Among the Hebrews," *JBL*, LXVII (1948), 16, note 17; W. F. Albright, *Alexander Marx Jubilee Volume* (1950), p. 81, note 72; C. H. Gordon, *Introduction to OT Times* (1953), pp. 77, 182; S. Yeivin, "Social, Religious and Cultural Trends in Jerusalem under the Davidic Dynasty," *Vetus Testamentum* (1953), pp. 163 ff.

**6.** Son of Jeroboam I, king of Israel (I Kings 14:1-18). As a child Abijah fell sick. Jeroboam sent his wife, whose name is not given, in disguise to the prophet Ahijah at Shiloh to find out what would happen to the child. This was the same prophet who had symbolically foretold that Jeroboam would become king of the ten N tribes (I Kings 11:29-39). Ahijah was now old, and partially blind, but the Lord had revealed to him that Jeroboam's wife was coming to see him. Thus he saw through her disguise, and pronounced doom on the house of Jeroboam because of his apostasy. He further announced that Abijah would die immediately on her return home, and that he alone of the house of Jeroboam would receive honorable burial. And so it happened. In a casual reference we learn that Jeroboam had moved his capital to Tirzah (I Kings 14:17).

The Greek supplement also tells the story with variations and assigns it to the time prior to Jeroboam's being appointed king (I Kings 14 LXX). Here there is no mention of Ahijah's earlier prophecy. He is a prophet of doom from the beginning. The Hebrew version is to be preferred.

**7.** Mother of Hezekiah, king of Judah. In II Kings 18:2 she is called simply Abi. This is a caritative form of Abijah, the name given her in II Chr. 29:1, as here also in three MSS. She was the daughter of Zechariah.

**8.** One of the priests who, probably on behalf of a father's house, set his seal on the covenant made by Nehemiah and the people to serve the Lord (Neh. 10:7).

**9.** One of the chiefs of the priests who returned with Zerubbabel from Babylon to Jerusalem (Neh. 12:4).

In the next generation Zichri is mentioned as a priest, head of the father's house of Abijah (Neh. 12:17).                    H. B. MacLean

**ABILENE** ăb'ə lē'nĭ ['Αβιληνή TR with אᵃ, or 'Αβειληνή W-H with A B; *other variations; apparently an adjectival form based on* Abila, *capital of the* "Abiline" *region*]. A small mountainous region high in the Antilebanons, NE of Mount Hermon and W of Damascus. The earliest reference to Abilene is Luke 3:1, the only occurrence in the Bible; it is referred to in literature as late as the sixth century.

Abilene had basically a Greco-Roman culture, as is shown by the ruins of Gentile temples, tombs, aqueducts, and roads. Its capital was on the highway between Damascus and the coast, E of the fork dividing for Sidon and Beirut. It was eighteen miles from Damascus, and halfway to the Roman town of Baalbek farther N. It lay on the SW bank of the upper Barada (Hebrew Amanah, Greek Chrysorrhoas, and biblical Abana) River, and the road in that vicinity passed through wild and scenic country of limestone gorge and cliff.

The tetrarchy of "Abila [Abyla] of Lysanias," as it is called by Josephus and Ptolemaeus, had been administered under Lebanon (of which it may have been a part previously) when first conquered by Pompey in 64 B.C., and continued to be governed from Chalcis by its ruler Ptolemy (often the ally of the Maccabean kings to the S). His son Lysanias ruled during successive Parthian and Roman invasions (40-38 B.C.) and was executed by Mark Antony, who gave Abilene to Cleopatra in 36 B.C. (until Actium, 31 B.C.). In turn it was included within the larger rule of his son Zenodorus until 20 B.C., but because the region became infested with robbers, Augustus assigned it to King Herod the Great. After his death in 4 B.C., Abilene was included in the province of Syria, and it is in this period that a younger Lysanias ruled as tetrarch (Luke 3:1), *ca.* A.D. 28; his existence is attested by a Greek inscription at Abila assigned to the time of Tiberius (CIG 4521). In A.D. 37 it was once again joined to Palestine under King Herod Agrippa I (37-44) and still later was made part of the northeasterly kingdom of his son Agrippa II (53-100). A Latin inscription at Abila records road-building at the expense of the Abilenians *ca.* 166. It is recorded that Abila became an episcopal seat within the Patriarchate of Antioch, that she sent Bishop Jordan to the Council of Chalcedon in 451, and Bishop Alexander to the Council in Jerusalem in 518.

Abila of Lysanias was identified *ca.* 1850 with the modern es-Suk, and should be distinguished from other Abilas located in Perea and the Decapolis region. Because the Decapolis extended from Damascus to Philadelphia (Amman), the several Abilas cited all lay within this area, but Abila of Lysanias was probably not one associated with the Decapolis. Another caution must be given, to disregard a local tradition that the tomb of Neby Habil contains the body of Cain's brother Abel, who thus gave his name to the town.

*Bibliography.* E. Robinson, *Biblical Researches in Palestine*, III (1867), 478-84, and map at back; E. Schürer, *History of the Jewish People*, div. I, vol. II (1898), Appendix I, pp. 325-44; E. Kraeling, *Bible Atlas* (1956).          K. W. CLARK

**ABIMAEL** ə bĭm'ĭ el [אבימאל]. A son of Joktan, and hence the name of an Arabian people (Gen. 10:28; I Chr. 1:22).

**ABIMELECH** ə bĭm'ə lĕk [אבימלך, Melek is father, Canaanite (Phoen.) *theophorous name*]. **1.** An ancient king of GERAR about whom we have no information except as he appears in two patriarchal narratives, variously reported (Gen. 20-21; 26). The accounts are so similar that it is impossible to avoid the conclusion that they are doublets and that therefore there is only one King Abimelech.

He is the local ruler in two of the three versions of a folk story about a patriarch's trying to pretend that his wife was only his sister, lest he be put out of the way (the third account, Gen. 12:10-20, is placed in Egypt and makes the Pharaoh the victim). ISAAC and Rebekah deceive him, but despite his anger he gives them protection (Gen. 26:6-11 J). Subsequently a more developed and sensitive version was told regarding ABRAHAM and Sarah, her apparently advanced age notwithstanding (Gen. 20 E; cf. Gen. 17:17).

The other doublet has Abimelech and his army commander, Phicol, involved in a dispute about wells with the patriarch (Isaac in Gen. 26:12-33 J; and Abraham in Gen. 21 E), but they settle it amicably and enter into a covenant together at Beer-sheba, and the patriarch prospers.

The J writer calls Abimelech "king of the Philistines" at Gerar (Gen. 26:1), which is an understandable anachronism, since the Philistines subsequently occupied the territory.

**2.** Son of Jerubbaal (GIDEON) by his Shechemite concubine (Judg. 8:31); he became king over Shechem for a brief period. The narrative (Judg. 9) seems to show the marks of antiquity, like some other stories of minor judges, and is relatively free of Deuteronomic redaction. It is a dramatic piece of ancient Israelite historiography.

Upon Gideon's death there was apparently a good deal of rivalry among his seventy sons for supremacy over their tribe of Manasseh. Abimelech won out against them all by enlisting the aid of relatives in his mother's home town of SHECHEM. Being mostly Canaanite, they naturally preferred a kinsman to achieve supremacy and therefore gave him seventy pieces of silver from the temple of BAAL-BERITH, with which he hired a band of opportunistic fellows. With this force he journeyed to his father's house at Ophrah and there slew his seventy half brothers upon one stone; only Jotham, the youngest, managed to hide himself and escape. Shechem and some surrounding territory made Abimelech "king."

JOTHAM(?), from the safety of nearby Mount Gerizim, cried out his biting parable calculated to cause dissension between Abimelech and his followers, and then fled into exile. The dissension came soon enough (vs. 22 says Abimelech ruled three years) and pitted Zebul, Abimelech's assistant, against Gaal ben Ebed (some believe he was Israelite, but he more likely became the leader of the Canaanite populace against the "half-breed" ruler; see commentaries on difficult vs. 28). Zebul called for the absent Abimelech, who, with a clever ambush, defeated the rebels. On the second day of battle (or a doublet account) he destroyed the city and sowed it with salt. Many people in the Tower of Shechem tried to hold out in the temple of El-berith, but he burned it over their heads. However, while assaulting the nearby town of Thebez, he had his skull crushed when a woman threw a millstone down on him. Rather than die so disgracefully by the hand of a woman, he asked his armor-bearer to dispatch him.

The story is significant for more than its dramatic appeal. It gives a vivid picture of the conflict between the Israelites and the resident Canaanite population during the period of the Conquest. Shechem was destroyed and subsequently became totally Israelite (cf. I Kings 12:1, 25). Despite vs. 22, Abimelech probably did not extend his control very far beyond the environs of Shechem, or at least not outside Manasseh. His "kingship" was hardly that of the subsequent hereditary monarchy, nor was he a charismatic chieftain like his father; the pattern is more like the petty ruler of a Canaanite city-state. Abimelech

is a good example of the near absorption of Israel into Canaanite ways. He is, nevertheless, sharply remembered as a soldier's object lesson (II Sam. 11: 21).

**3.** A name mentioned in the title of Ps. 34, but is certainly a copyist's error for ACHISH, king of Gath (cf. I Sam. 21:10-15). The mistake has been variously explained as: (a) substitution of a better known name for a lesser known; (b) a title for Philistine kings, comparable to "Pharaoh"; (c) confusion with the name Ahimelech in the same chapter (I Sam. 21).

**4.** According to the MT-KJV, a priest who was the son of Abiathar (I Chr. 18:16). But II Sam. 8:17; I Chr. 24:6 show that the LXX has the correct reading here: "Ahimelech." *See* AHIMELECH 3.

*Bibliography.* A. M. Honeyman, "The Salting of Shechem," *Vetus Testamentum*, III (1953), 192-95.

F. T. SCHUMACHER

**ABINADAB** ə bĭn′ə dăb [אֲבִינָדָב, father is noble].
**1.** The father of Eleazar, Ahio, and Uzzah. His residence, which was situated on a hill in Kiriath-jearim (=Baalah; cf. Josh. 15:9-10, 60; 18:14; I Chr. 13: 6), sheltered the ark for some twenty years after the disaster at Beth-shemesh (I Sam. 6:19–7:2). His son Eleazar was consecrated by the men of Kiriath-jearim to have charge over the ark. Subsequently, when David sought to bring the ark to Jerusalem, the other sons of Abinadab, Uzzah and Ahio, accompanied the new cart which was conveying the ark. When they reached the threshing floor of Nacon, the oxen stumbled, and Uzzah, attempting to brace the ark, put his hand out to take hold of it and was smitten fatally (II Sam. 6:6-7).

**2.** The second of the sons of Jesse (I Sam. 16:8; I Chr. 2:13). He appears with his brothers Eliab and Shammah as a soldier in the army of Saul when Goliath championed the Philistine cause in Ephesdammim (I Sam. 17:13).

**3.** One of the sons of Saul who perished in the Battle of Mount Gilboa (I Sam. 31:2; I Chr. 8:33; 9:39; 10:2).

**4.** For KJV "son of Abinadab" (I Kings 4:11), *see* BEN-ABINADAB.                                       E. R. DALGLISH

**ABINOAM** ə bĭn′ō əm [אֲבִינֹעַם, father is pleasantness]. A native of Kedesh in Naphtali whose son Barak, inspired by the prophetess Deborah, marshaled the N Hebrew forces and defeated the Canaanite army commanded by Sisera (Judg. 4:6, 12; 5:1, 12).

E. R. DALGLISH

**ABIRAM** ə bī′rəm [אֲבִירָם, my father is exalted; *same as* ABRAM]; KJV Apoc. ABIRON ə bī′rən.
**1.** Son of Eliab from the tribe of Reuben. Together with his brother DATHAN, Abiram was one of the leaders of the rebellion of KORAH against the leadership of Moses (Num. 16). The rebels and their households were swallowed up by a crack in the earth—an event subsequently remembered as a warning (Num. 26:9; Deut. 11:6) and extolled among the mighty acts of God's judgment (Ps. 106).

**2.** The first-born son of Hiel of Bethel. He and his brother were killed when his father rebuilt Jericho in the days of Ahab (I Kings 16:34). Many scholars see here an example of the ancient Near Eastern practice of the foundation sacrifice. The editor, in any case, attributes their deaths to a curse pronounced by Joshua when he originally destroyed the city (Josh. 6:26).                    F. T. SCHUMACHER

**ABISEI.** KJV Apoc. alternate form of ABISHUA 2.

**ABISHAG** ăb'ə shăg [אבישג, *possibly* אב *plus* שגג, my father is a wanderer, *or* Sumer. *ŠAG*, heart, interior]. A very beautiful Shunammite maiden, brought probably as a medical measure to restore David's warmth and vigor when he was old (I Kings 1:1-4, 15; cf. Jos. Antiq. VII.xiv.3). Solomon later chose to regard Abishag as David's wife, and executed Adonijah for treason when he requested her (I Kings 2:13-25).
                                              D. HARVEY

**ABISHAI** ə bī'shī [אבישי, אבשי, father exists]. The eldest son of Zeruiah, sister of David; the brother of Joab and Asahel (I Chr. 2:16).

Abishai appears first in a daring exploit in the wilderness of Ziph, when he accompanied David into the camp of Saul by night. When the two invaded the royal tent, Abishai urged the summary dispatch of Saul, but David contented himself with the removal of the royal spear and water jar (I Sam. 26:6 ff).

Abishai was present also at the Pool of Gibeon when Abner challenged Joab to let the young men arise and play before them. Twelve warriors were chosen from each side for this agonistic trial. However, when all twenty-four combatants fell, a battle ensued in which Abner and his men suffered defeat. Asahel pursued unswervingly the fleeing Abner, who, despite his warning to Asahel to desist from following him, had no other recourse than to slay him. Immediately Joab and Abishai took up the chase and were dissuaded only by the pathetic entreaty of Abner (II Sam. 2:12 ff). Subsequently, however, Joab and Abishai avenged the blood' of their brother Asahel by the treacherous murder of Abner in Hebron (II Sam. 3:26 ff).

In the first Ammonite war, which arose from the insult of King Hanun to the envoys of David, the Israelite army was apparently besieging Rabbath-ammon when the Syrian mercenaries attempted to join their confederates, the Ammonites. To prevent this union of the opposition, Joab divided his army, assigning to himself select troops which he marshaled against the Syrians, while the rest of the army he placed in charge of Abishai, who attacked the Ammonites. Both Ammonites and Syrians were routed in the conflict (II Sam. 10).

When the rebellion of Absalom forced David to flee from Jerusalem, he was met in his flight by Shimei, a member of the house of Saul. Going along the hill opposite the royal retinue, Shimei grievously cursed the king. Abishai, who had accompanied the fleeing monarch, proposed to silence with speedy death this gross impiety but was wisely restrained by David (II Sam. 16:5-14). When David returned victoriously, however, Shimei hastened to meet him at the ford of the Jordan and with profound apologies for his unworthy behavior—much to the disgust of Abishai—secured the royal pardon (II Sam. 19:16-23—H 19:17-24).

During the rebellion of Absalom, the opposing forces were preparing for battle near Transjordanic Mahanaim, with Abishai, Joab, and Ittai sharing the joint command of the Davidic troops. In the battle in the forest of Ephraim the rebellion of Absalom was effectively crushed, and the usurper was slain by Joab (II Sam. 18).

Abishai and Joab were in command also of the elite troops which successfully quelled the rebellion of Sheba the Benjaminite (II Sam. 20). It is interesting to note that when Amasa failed to return within the appointed three days, Abishai was placed in charge of the Judean troops, while Joab, the deposed commander, set out in the campaign apparently without his former military rank.

In I Chr. 18:12-13 Abishai is credited with the subjugation of Edom. However, this Edomite campaign is elsewhere attributed to David (II Sam. 8:13-14) and to Joab (Ps. 60; cf. I Kings 11:15-16). If these various ascriptions are to be taken seriously, it appears likely that Abishai shared the leadership in this Edomite campaign with David and Joab.

Abishai never attained to the rare distinction of membership among the "Three," although his name was equally as famous. However, he did have the singular honor of being the commander of the Mighty Men of David known as the "Thirty" (II Sam. 23:18-19; I Chr. 11:20-21). Among his heroic deeds were the rescue of David at Nob (*see* ISHBI-BENOB), when he was threatened by a Philistine giant (II Sam. 21:16-17), and the slaying of three hundred men (II Sam. 23:18; I Chr. 11:20-21). Abishai shared with Joab an impervious hardness, but none among the soldiers of David was ever more loyal or intrepid.
                                              E. R. DALGLISH

**ABISHALOM.** Alternative form of ABSALOM 1.

**ABISHUA** ə bĭsh'ōō ə [אבישוע, the (divine) father is salvation(?)]; KJV Apoc. ABISEI ăb'ə sē'ī; ABISUM ə bī'səm. **1.** A Benjaminite, son of Bela, the first-born of Benjamin (I Chr. 8:4).

**2.** Great-grandson of Aaron and ancestor of Ezra the scribe (I Chr. 6:4-5—H 5:30-31; 6:50—H 6:35; Ezra 7:5). Included in the genealogy of Levi, Abishua is also named among the descendants of Aaron permitted to serve at the altar, to whom Chronicles calls particular attention.

*Bibliography.* M. Noth, *Die israelitischen Personennamen* (1928), pp. 18, 68-71, 154.            R. F. JOHNSON

**ABISHUR** ə bī'shər [אבישור, my father is a wall]. One of the two sons of Shammai in the genealogy of Jerahmeel (I Chr. 2:28-29). His wife was named Abihail.

**ABISUM.** KJV Apoc. alternate form of ABISHUA 2.

**ABITAL** ə bī'təl [אביטל, Aram. *or* Heb. אב *plus* טל, my father is protection, *or* my father is dew]. A wife of David; the mother of Shephatiah (II Sam. 3:4; I Chr. 3:3).

**ABITUB** ə bī'tŭb [אביטוב, my father is good]. One of the two sons of Shaharaim, by his first wife,

Hushim; listed in the genealogy of Benjamin (I Chr. 8:11). The text is uncertain.

**ABIUD** ə bī′əd [᾽Αβιούδ, *see* ABIHUD]. An ancestor of Jesus (Matt. 1:13; also Luke 3:23 ff in MS D).

**ABLUTIONS** [βαπτισμοί]. Ceremonial washings. Ablutions are referred to three times in the NT. In Heb. 6:2 the writer bids Christians to whom he writes to progress beyond discussion of basic matters, among which he lists "teaching about ablutions." Perhaps he is alluding to the outgrown discussions about differences between Christian baptism and other ablutions. In 9:10 the author speaks scornfully of "various ablutions" (among other things) about which the Levitical code is concerned, but which are among the external rituals that have now been superseded. Cf. baptisms and lustrations in the Qumran community; *see* DEAD SEA SCROLLS.

Mark 7:4 notes that among the traditions observed by the Pharisees was the "washing" of cups and pots, etc. *See* BATHING; BAPTISM.

B. H. THROCKMORTON, JR.

**ABNER** ăb′nər [אבנר, father is Ner *or* lamp; אבינר (I Sam. 14:50)]. The commander of the Israelite army under Saul, his first cousin or, more likely, his uncle (on the problem of his genealogy, *see* NER); the dominant power in the house of Saul during the brief reign of ISH-BAAL.

The long military career of Abner in the service of Saul is passed over in comparative silence (cf. I Sam. 14:47). Abner was in charge of the Israelite army in the Philistine campaign and introduced David into the presence of the king (I Sam. 17:55-58). The importance of Abner is indicated by the protocol observed in seating him at the king's side at the banquet of the New Moon (I Sam. 20:25). Abner accompanied Saul in his frenzied persecution of David to the wilderness of Ziph and for his lack of vigilance in guarding the person of Saul was chided by David, who with Abishai had stealthily invaded the tent of the sleeping monarch (I Sam. 26:5 ff).

After the death of Saul, Abner placed Ish-baal, son of Saul, upon the throne and established the capital at Mahanaim. However, he failed to secure for the new king the allegiance of the tribe of Judah, which had defected to David (II Sam. 2:8-10). Of the prolonged warfare between the houses of Saul and David, an account of one of the skirmishes, the Battle of Gibeon, is preserved. Abner met Joab at the Pool of Gibeon and challenged him to select warriors for a trial by combat. When all the chosen twenty-four combatants fell, a battle immediately broke out in which Abner and his men were defeated. As he fled from the rout, Abner was resolutely pursued by the swift Asahel, who, heedless of Abner's warning to cease from following him, precipitated his own death. Joab and Abishai, the brothers of Asahel, took up the pursuit of Abner and were prevented from consummate blood revenge only by the pathetic pleading of Abner and by the less formidable deterrent of the reconsolidation of the Israelite forces at the hill of Ammah. Abner returned to Mahanaim with a loss of 360 men (vss. 12-31).

In the second year of Ish-baal a crisis occurred in the royal court which ultimately caused the eclipse of the house of Saul. It happened when Abner went in to Rizpah, one of the concubines of the royal harem, and was reprimanded by the king for his treasonable behavior. Greatly incensed at this censure, Abner rebuked the king for what, in view of his unquestioned loyalty to the house of Saul, he considered an unwarranted magnification of a "fault concerning a woman"; further, he boldly announced his intention of transferring the kingdom from the house of Saul to David (II Sam. 3:7-10). To effect this end, Abner immediately opened negotiation with David and complied with his prerequisite demand for the return of his wife Michal. Abner then communicated with the elders of Israel and fanned into flame their suppressed desire to have David as their king. The house of Benjamin was approached last, but even they were persuaded by this prince of Benjamin of the desirability of a united kingdom under David. Having secured the consent of Israel, Abner and his diplomatic corps arrived at Hebron to draw up final arrangements for the union of the two kingdoms. After he had been royally feted by the king, Abner set out on his mission to gather all Israel together for the purpose of making such a covenant (vss. 12-21).

Meanwhile, however, Joab, who had been absent from the capital on a foray, returned and discovered to his amazement that the king had received Abner favorably. This was too much for the stormy disposition of Joab to bear. He rebuked David for his failure to avenge the blood of his kinsman Asahel and for his credulity in receiving Abner, who, in Joab's eyes, had come for no other purpose than to spy. Secretly summoning Abner to return to Hebron, Joab—with the connivance of Abishai—foully murdered Abner (II Sam. 3:22-27).

When David learned of the tragedy, he disavowed publicly all complicity in the dastardly deed, laid a grievous curse upon Joab and his house, and proclaimed a public lamentation for Abner. In deep grief the king fasted and composed an appropriate dirge (partially preserved in II Sam. 3:33-34), which bewailed the strange fate, so unworthy of such a prince, that had befallen Abner (vss. 28-34).

In this politically crucial hour, which might easily have spelled disaster for the plan of consolidating the kingdoms, the behavior of the king convinced the people of his complete innocence and genuine regret for the unfortunate death of Abner (II Sam. 3:36-39). Abner was interred in his tomb at Hebron (vs. 32), and by a strange irony of fate the head of his murdered master, Ish-baal, was subsequently placed in his sepulchre (4:1-2, 12).

The Chronicler notices that Abner dedicated, from the spoils of war, gifts for the maintenance of the tabernacle of Yahweh (I Chr. 26:27-28) and names Abner's son Jaasiel as a leader of the house of Benjamin in the time of David (27:21).

E. R. DALGLISH

**ABOMINATION** [פגול, שקוץ, שקץ, תועבה, *see below*; βδέλυγμα (*alternately* DESOLATING SACRILEGE)]. Alternately: ABOMINABLE THING, PRACTICE, etc. Whatever is ritually or ethically loathsome and repugnant to God and men. The concept is expressed in the OT by four separate words discussed below:

*a*) תּוֹעֵבָה (from תָּעַב, "be abhorred"). This is the most frequent, especially in Deuteronomy, Proverbs, and Ezekiel, designating: offensive violation of established custom (Gen. 43:32; 46:34; Exod. 8:26); foods prohibited as unclean (*see* CLEAN AND UNCLEAN); imperfect sacrifices (Deut. 17:1; 23:18; Prov. 15:8; 21: 27; Isa. 1:13; 44:19); magic and divination (Deut. 18:12); sexual irregularities (Lev. 18:22, 26; 20:13; Deut. 24:4; I Kings 14:24; Ezek. 16:22, 43, 47, 51, 58; 22:11; 23:36; 33:26); moral and ethical faults (Deut. 25:14-16; Prov. 3:32; 6:16-19; 8:7; 11:1, 20; 12:22; 13:19; 15:9, 26; 16:5; 20:10, 23; 24:9; 26:25; 28:9; 29:27; Isa. 41:24; Jer. 6:15; 7:10; 8:12; Ezek. 18:13, 24); reversal of the natural (Deut. 22:5; Prov. 16:12; 17:15; 29:27); idolatrous practices (Lev. 18:27, 29-30; Deut. 12:31; 13:14; 17:4; 18:9; 20:18; 32:16; II Kings 16:3; 21:2, 11; II Chr. 28:3; 33:2; 34:33; 36:8, 14; Jer. 2:7; 32:35; 44:4, 22; Ezek. 5:9, 11; 6: 11; 7:3-4, 8-9; 8:6, 9, 15, 17; 9:4; 11:18; 14:6; 16:2; 18: 12; 20:4; 22:2; 36:31; 43:8; 44:6-7; Mal. 2:11); idols (Deut. 7:25-26; 27:15; II Kings 23:13; Jer. 16:18; Ezek. 14:6; 16:36). The nemesis of abominations is God's anger, judgment, and punishment without pity (Ezek. 7:3-4; 20:4).

*b*) שֶׁקֶץ, "detestation," the technical word for animal flesh which defiles if touched or eaten (Lev. 7: 21; 11:10-13, 20, 23, 41-42; Isa. 66:17; Ezek. 8:10). This word is sometimes synonymous with תּוֹעֵבָה. *See* CLEAN AND UNCLEAN.

*c*) שִׁקּוּץ (allied with שֶׁקֶץ), "detestable thing." This is employed almost exclusively for objects associated with idolatry and heathen deities (Deut. 29:17; I Kings 11:5, 7; II Kings 23:13, 24; Isa. 66:3; Jer. 4:1; 7:30; 13:27; 32:34; Ezek. 5:11; 20:7-8, 30; Hos. 9:10; Zech. 9:7). *See* ABOMINATION THAT MAKES DESOLATE; IDOL.

*d*) פִּגּוּל (from פָּגַל, "foul thing"), a technical word describing putrid, three-day-old sacrificial flesh, unlawful to eat (Lev. 7:18; 19:7; Ezek. 4:14); also flesh, possibly retaining blood, eaten in broth by heathens (Isa. 65:4). *See* SACRIFICE AND OFFERINGS.

The LXX frequently translates these four words with βδέλυγμα, which is also the NT word (Matt. 24: 15; Mark 13:14; Luke 16:15; Rev. 17:4-5; 21:27).

M. H. LOVELACE

**ABOMINATION THAT MAKES DESOLATE; KJV ABOMINATION OF DESOLATION.** An enigmatic phrase occurring in Daniel, I Maccabees (KJV), Matthew, and Mark.

**1. In Daniel.** In 9:27 we have שִׁקּוּצִים מְשֹׁמֵם; in 11:31 הַשִּׁקּוּץ מְשֹׁמֵם; in 12:11 שִׁקּוּץ שֹׁמֵם; and in 8:13 הַפֶּשַׁע שֹׁמֵם. These may for the moment be translated "desolating abominations," "the desolating abomination," "desolating abomination," and "desolating transgression." There are grammatical peculiarities, but first we must deal with the words themselves.

שִׁקּוּץ, *shiqqûs*, is a term used almost exclusively for idolatrous objects and practices, and means "a detested thing" (*see* ABOMINATION). Biblical writers normally referred to idols and Gentile deities under some byname in order to avoid pronouncing some potentially dangerous name (cf. "Old Nick" for Satan), and while *bôsheth* ("a shameful thing") was usual, *shiqqûs* was also used. Thus in the phrase

"abomination that makes desolate" the term probably indicates a foreign deity or some symbol connected with it. The root שׁמם, *sh-m-m*, has two distinct meanings: "to be appalled, overwhelmed with astonishment and dread," and "to be desolated, emptied of inhabitants." The latter two occurrences mentioned above would normally be reckoned *qal* participles, but if (as rarely happens) a preformative *mem* has dropped out, they can be taken as *po'el* participles—i.e., the same form as in the two former instances. Since an active sense is clearly required, it is presumed that the *po'el* has this force and should be translated "appalls" in the one sense and "desolates" in the other.

Before deciding between these two, we need to observe the grammatical peculiarities. Each instance exhibits a syntactical abnormality. In 9:27 we have a plural noun with a singular adjective (participle); in 11:31 the noun is definite, and the adjective, though used attributively, is indefinite, and this phenomenon reoccurs in 8:13 and so can hardly be accidental; and in both 8:13; 12:11 the participle lacks preformative *mem*. Such a string of abnormalities points to some definite cause. Nestlé's suggestion that both parts of the phrase constitute a byname has won widespread recognition. The Greek theonomic Zeus Olympios was translated into Semitic languages as *bá'al shāmēm*, as Phoenician inscriptions and the Syr. of II Macc. 6:2 testify. Literally this means "Lord of Heaven." In our phrase *shiqqûs* is substituted for the hated word *bá'al*, and *shōmēm* is a pun on *shāmēm*, the Phoenician style of *shāmáyim*. Thus for the Gentile title "Lord of Heaven" the Jew substituted "the detested thing which appalls."

But in Daniel the phrase refers to the altar of Zeus which Antiochus Epiphanes (*see* ANTIOCHUS 4) erected on Yahweh's own altar of burnt offering. This emptied the temple of true worshipers and (in Jewish thought) of Yahweh himself (cf. Ezek. 10:18; 11:22-23). Thus as used in Daniel, both senses of the root *sh-m-m* are implied: "the detested thing which appalls all good Jews and empties the temple of worshipers and Yahweh alike." Yet there is still another nuance to be glimpsed. Rowley has shown that *sh-m-m* had probably another sense of "to be mad." Antiochus called himself Epiphanes ("Divine Manifestation") and fancied he bore a facial resemblance to Zeus. But his subjects nicknamed him "Epimanes"—i.e., "Madman." Whether the altar to Zeus included (as is likely) an image of that god wearing the features of Antiochus, we do not certainly know (*see* § 2 *below*), but he was in any case the instigator of the blasphemy, so "the detested thing of the Madman" would be another implication of the phrase on which the Jews would seize. It was this desire for wordplay which caused them to be careless of grammatical niceties in its employment. Since "appall" is the primary sense of the root, Montgomery, Jeffery, and others translate thus, but tradition (*see* § 2 *below*) is on the side of "desolation" and should be respected.

We must note that in 9:27 the MT is faithfully reflected in the ASV-RSV, whereby *shiqqûsîm* is separated syntactically from *shōmēm* and the translation given is: "Upon the wing of abominations [shall come] one who makes desolate"; this is accepted by Bentzen, who thinks that "the wing" refers either to the eagle or to the winged solar disk as emblems of Zeus, and draws attention to *b'l knp* in the Ugaritic literature. Others think a wing of the temple is indicated (cf. Matt. 4:5, where "wing" is the literal translation of πτερύγιον, rendered "pinnacle"), and they translate: "On the wing [of the temple] the appalling abomination [shall appear]." Others emend כנף to כנו and translate: "In its place [i.e., instead of the proper sacrifice just mentioned] [shall be] the appalling abomination." Jeffery offers: "The wing of an appalling abomination [shall rise up]," referring to the eagle as above. The plural *shiqqûṣîm* is probably due to dittography. The value of the last three suggestions as opposed to ASV-RSV-Bentzen, etc., is that the identity of the phrase "abomination of desolation" is preserved, which is antecedently desirable.

**2. In I Maccabees.** In 1:54 we are told that a "desolating sacrilege" (KJV "abomination of desolation") was built upon the altar, and in 1:59 that "they sacrificed upon the altar [βωμός] which was upon the altar [θυσιαστήριον]." This would suggest that the object so indicated was a small altar to Zeus, placed upon Yahweh's great altar of burnt offering, rather than an idol (on this point *see* the work of Danby in the *bibliography*). The translation of our phrase שקוץ שמם is βδέλυγμα ἐρημώσεως, which shows that "desolate" rather than "appall" was the current interpretation *ca.* 135, when I Maccabees was written.

**3. In the NT.** Mark 13:14 reads: ὅταν δὲ ἴδητε τὸ βδέλυγμα τῆς ἐρημώσεως ἐστηκότα ὅπου οὐ δεῖ, which may be translated: "when you see the Abomination of Desolation standing where he ought not." The chapter is popularly called the "Little Apocalypse" (*see* MARK, GOSPEL OF), but whether Mark composed it himself or took it over from another source is in dispute. Taylor observes that the language of vss. 14-23 points to distress occasioned by military attack rather than eschatological upheaval, and says that Luke's parallel phrase: "when you see Jerusalem surrounded by armies" (Luke 21:20), is not a secondary reinterpretation, but is probably closer to the original saying of Jesus, predicting the Roman attack on the city. He suggests that this saying has been apocalypticized by Mark or his source. "What Jesus had said is seen through an apocalyptic haze." Further, he reminds us that Mark may well have been writing at a time and place which made too clear a reference to the Roman power unadvisable. Hence he falls back upon a phrase which had become standard for the forces of evil and inserts the broad hint: "Let the reader understand."

Matthew, following Mark more closely than Luke, but mindful of the Danielic origin of the phrase, draws the reader's attention to that origin, and explicates the phrase "where he ought not" in accordance therewith as "in the holy place." The phrase is anarthrous and so is properly "a holy place," and is taken by some to mean the Holy Land in general.

There remains the masculine participle ἐστηκότα. Some have taken it to be the result of Caligula's attempt to have his statue erected in the temple (A.D. 40), and suggest that a saying of Jesus was recast about that time to have reference to that incident. This suggestion is combined (e.g., by Bacon) with the personalizing influence of Paul's teaching in II Thessalonians concerning the Man of Lawlessness (*see* ANTICHRIST). This concept was itself influenced by the Caligula incident and the Antiochus tradition, as well as by the general Pauline concept of the personal nature of evil (*see* PAUL; cf. Caird [*see bibliography*], pp. 15-16, 26-27). The incident of Caligula's threat to repeat the appalling blasphemy must have given fresh currency to Daniel's phrase, and its application to Caligula was indicated by the fact that the neuter noun was treated as masculine.

Thus, while the original saying probably referred to the coming destruction of Jerusalem by Roman armies, the fact that the event was seen by the early church as one more sign that the forces of evil were loose in the world caused the original prediction to be clothed in a phrase which drew out the theological and eschatological implications of that attack. It should, however, be noted that this treatment of the phrase does not deny that there were eschatological and predictive elements in the teaching of Jesus (cf. Taylor [*see bibliography*], p. 644) and that therefore the eschatological significance of the forthcoming attack may have been perceived by Jesus himself, in which case the first use of the phrase in this connection may go back to him rather than to Mark or his source.

**Bibliography.** F. Nestlé, *ZAW* (1884), p. 248; B. W. Bacon, *The Gospel of Mark* (1925); J. A. Montgomery, *Daniel,* ICC (1927); R. H. Charles, *Commentary on Daniel* (1929); H. H. Rowley, "The Bilingual Problem of Daniel," *ZAW* (1932), p. 256; A. Bentzen, *Daniel,* HAT (2nd ed., 1952); V. Taylor, *The Gospel According to St. Mark* (1952); J. C. Dancy, *Commentary on I Maccabees* (1954); G. B. Caird, *Principalities and Powers* (1956); A. Jeffery, Introduction and Exegesis of Daniel, *IB,* VI (1956), 341-549; G. R. Beasley-Murray, *Commentary on Mark 13* (1957), pp. 59-60, note on history of interpretation.

S. B. FROST

**ABRAHAM** ā'brə hăm [אברהם, *see* § A *below;* Αβρααμ]; **ABRAM** ā'brəm [אברם; LXX Αβραμ] (Gen. 11:26–17:4). Son of Terah; husband of Sarah; and father of Isaac. Abraham was Israel's first great patriarch, and for Israel and Christianity he stands as the father of the faithful.

A. Etymology
  1. Abram
  2. Abraham
  3. Extrabiblical forms
  4. Interpretation of Gen. 17:5
B. The Genesis narrative as a whole
C. Abraham according to the individual sources
  1. According to the Yahwist
    *a.* Abraham's family
    *b.* The call of Abraham
    *c.* Wandering in Canaan
    *d.* The sojourn in Egypt
    *e.* Separation of Lot from Abraham
    *f.* The promise repeated
    *g.* The declaration of righteousness
    *h.* The covenant ceremony
    *i.* Strife at home

**A. *ETYMOLOGY.*** The OT knows two forms of the patriarch's name: "Abram" and "Abraham." The former occurs only in the Genesis narrative from 11:26 through 17:4. The latter is used elsewhere in the OT except at I Chr. 1:27; Neh. 9:7.

**1. Abram.** "Abram," perhaps a shorter form of "Abiram" (אבירם) just as "Abner" (אבנר) is of "Abiner" (אבינר), is composed of the two elements: אב, "father"; and רם (seen also in such proper names as Adoniram, Amram, Hiram/Ahiram, and Malchiram), from the verb רום, "to be high, exalted," and is best translated "exalted." It emphasizes the eminence, nobility, or loftiness of the person of whom it is predicated. Occasionally, רם has been taken as a divine name; but no support from the OT is given to this theory. It remains, rather, a descriptive adjective, stressing Yahweh's exaltation (Ps. 138:8; Isa. 6:1; 57:15). Preferably, "Abram" would mean "the (my) father is exalted" (just as the parallel form Jehoram, יהורם, would be "Yahweh is exalted"), though the rendering "exalted father" is permissible.

**2. Abraham.** The etymology and translation of "Abraham" are uncertain. The traditional etymology is given at Gen. 17:4-5: in establishing his covenant with Abram, God changed the patriarch's name to Abraham as witness to the divine promise that he should be the "father of a multitude of nations." Accordingly, *'abhrāhām* is represented as being in some way similar to *'abh hᵃmôn (gôyīm)*. But this explanation is philologically inadequate. *'Abhrāhām* cannot be derived from *'abh hᵃmôn* by any known lexicography. The biblical reference must be seen as a popular etymology (*Volksetymologie*), resting on assonance rather than sound philology—a phenomenon common in Genesis (e.g., 2:23*b;* 4:1*b,* 25*b;* 11:9*a*).

It is best to take *'abhrāhām* as an Aramaic expansion of *'abrām,* and basically identical with it in form and meaning. רהם would then be a longer, Aramaic form of the Hebrew רם, with the ה filling in the weakness in the "hollow root" רום, just as Aramaic רהט and בהת are the equivalents of Hebrew רוץ and בוש (cf. Aramaic and Syriac participles קאם from the root קום).

**3. Extrabiblical forms.** Although cuneiform parallels have occasionally been cited, neither "Abram" nor "Abraham" has yet been found in Akkadian texts. Since "Abram" is a regular Northwest Semitic formation, both by reason of its structure (as a nominal-sentence name) and of each of its components, Noth cautions against the attempt to link it with Akkadian names.

**4. Interpretation of Gen. 17:5.** Although philologically unsound, the traditional explanation of Abraham's name (17:5*b*) is nevertheless valuable; for Abraham was indeed the "father of a multitude." But the further definition "of nations" raises difficulties which can be adequately met only by viewing this element in the promise as pointing beyond Abraham to Israel's universal mission. Though most clearly articulated by the Priestly writer here and at 28:3; 35:11, this concept was also expressed earlier by the Yahwist at 12:3; 24:6; 28:14*b* (and cf. 27:29*b*). Through Abraham's seed salvation may reach the Gentiles (Isa. 42:1*b,* 4*b;* 49:6, 22-23; 60:3; Mic. 4:1-2; Zech. 8:20-22; cf. Luke 2:23; Acts 13:47; 26:23). This concept was indigenous in the Abrahamic traditions, and so formed part of Israel's heritage from the earliest days.

In the necessity of combining the two names of Israel's first patriarch, the Priestly writer found also a ready device for emphasizing this important theological affirmation. By changing Abram's name to Abraham, he has God underscore the universal mission of Israel. In accord with his covenant-centered view of Israel's history (*see* PENTATEUCH § A5), P linked this change of name with the Abrahamic covenant (Gen. 17) and editorially substituted "Abram" for all references to Abraham occurring before 17:5.

Since "Abraham" and "Sarah" are commonly preferred in the Bible, they will be used throughout this article, except in actual quotations.

**B. *THE GENESIS NARRATIVE AS A WHOLE.*** The story of Abraham (Gen. 11:27–25:11) is characterized by a wide range of movement, a dramatis personae listing many peoples of the ancient Near East, and a fine portrayal of personalities.

Starting from S Mesopotamia at UR, Abraham's family traveled up the ancient, rich Tigris-Euphrates Valley to Haran, a flourishing center in Anatolia,* where they settled. From there (*see* C1*a below*) Abraham, called by God, journeyed through Syria into Palestine. After an interlude in Egypt he returned to Palestine, the Land of Promise, and spent the rest of his life there. But before his death Abraham sent his major-domo to the city of Nahor to take a wife for Isaac. His life reached a symmetrical end, as it were, with this sweeping arc back into Upper Mesopotamia. Fig. HAR 6.

During his long life, Abraham came into contact with numerous peoples. Ur was a notable city of the Chaldeans (Babylonians); Haran, of the West Semitic Amorites and Arameans (*see also* the names of Abraham's ancestors: PELEG; SERUG; NAHOR; TERAH 1). In Palestine, Abraham moved among the Canaanites (Gen. 12:6) and Perizzites (13:7*b*) and entered into negotiations with the Hittites (ch. 23). Leaving Palestine, Abraham sojourned among the

Egyptians (12:10-20). In ch. 14 he met Amorites, Hurrians, Elamites, and Hittites, and five S kings from the Dead Sea and Transjordan area. Through Nahor's children (22:20-24) he was linked with tribes to the NE; through Keturah's children (25:1-4), to the SE. Finally, no fewer than ten groups are named in the description of the land which Yahweh promised to Abraham's descendants (15:18-21).

Circling around the central figure of Abraham is a whole galaxy of people whose keenly delineated characters cast a bright light upon the patriarch: selfish Lot (13:2-12), with the aberrated Sodomites (19:1-11), his scoffing sons-in-law (vss. 12-14), his recalcitrant wife (vs. 26), and his desperate daughters (vss. 30-38); barren, unbelieving Sarah (11:30; 16:1-2; 18:9-15); wronged Hagar (ch. 16; 21:1-21); and obedient Isaac (22:1-14). Other luminaries are the noble Pharaoh (12:10-20) and innocent Abimelech (ch. 20; cf. also 21:22-34); mysterious Melchizedek (14:17-20); formally courteous Ephron; and, in an exceptionally rich chapter (ch. 24), the trusted and faithful majordomo, avaricious Laban, and strong, lovable Rebekah.

**C. ABRAHAM ACCORDING TO THE INDIVIDUAL SOURCES.** Reading the story of Abraham as a unified narrative has distinct merit, as indicated above. Nevertheless, behind the present story are other and older stories which must be followed individually to appreciate the variety of Israel's thought about Abraham.

**1. According to the Yahwist.** The earliest written narrative of Abraham is also the fullest—that coming from the Yahwist (*see* PENTATEUCH § A3). His story is given in Gen. 11:28-30; 12:1-4a, 6-20; 13:1-5, 7-11a, 12bβ, 13-18; 15:1abβ, 2a, 3b, 4, 6-12, 17-21; 16:1b, 2, 4-8, 11-14; 18-19; 20:1a; 21:1a, 2a, 7; 22:20-24; 24; 25:1-6, 11b.

Behind the Yahwist lay, in oral and perhaps even in written form, many older traditions, whose exact age, locus, and in some cases original purpose cannot be satisfactorily determined. But in his genius the Yahwist took the extant traditions, older and younger, and articulated them into Israel's first great theological epic. Two themes run through his story of Abraham: God's promise of land and descendants,

and the patriarch's struggle for sure faith that the divine promise will be fulfilled. The resulting story must be read as neither straight biography nor pure allegory.

*a. Abraham's family (11:28-30).* Although the unified narrative, as edited by P, graphs a migration from Ur to Haran and then into Canaan (11:26-27, 31-32), the J tradition implies strongly that the original home of the Hebrews was the territory around Haran (e.g., 24:4, 7, 10; 27:43; 28:10; 29:4; *see* ISRAEL, HISTORY OF; ARAM-NAHARAIM). It seems best to consider "Ur of the Chaldeans" in 11:28; 15:7 as a harmonistic gloss and to place Abraham at home in Haran at the time of his call.

This preface ends with a terse item that serves also as an introduction to Abraham's call to faith: "Now Sarai was barren; she had no child" (11:30).

*b. The call of Abraham (12:1-3).* "Now Yahweh said to Abram, 'Go from your country and your kindred and your father's house to the land that I will show you.'" (vs. 1.) Through stringent demands Yahweh calls Abraham to forsake all, and to journey by faith (cf. Heb. 11:8).

But God's demand is completed in his promise. He will make of Abraham a great nation (גוי גדול) whose fidelity to him will be so renowned that it will be a blessing to others who have to do with him (Gen. 12:2; cf. 18:18; Isa. 51:2). All those blessing Abraham, Yahweh will bless; and the one making light of (קלל) him, Yahweh will lay under his curse (ארר; Gen. 12:3a).

Moreover, God's word of blessing is not restricted to Abraham's contemporaries. It extends to all men. Through Abraham, God reaches out to bless "all the families of the earth" (J: vs. 3b; 18:18; 28:14; E: 22:18; 26:4). The initiative lies with God, for Israel enjoys the favored position of an elect nation (Exod. 19:5-6a; cf. I Pet. 2:9; Rev. 1:6; 5:10), not because of merit (Deut. 7:6-8), but that through her God's saving grace might flow to all peoples. To this vocation Abraham—and Israel—must respond with faith.

*c. Wandering in Canaan (12:4a, 6-9).* "So Abram went, as Yahweh had told him." (vs. 4aα.) Abraham's measure of faith was sufficient for his whole

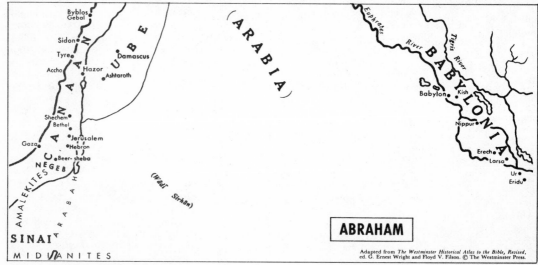

ABRAHAM

Adapted from *The Westminster Historical Atlas to the Bible, Revised,* ed. G. Ernest Wright and Floyd V. Filson. © The Westminster Press.

family, for he even took Lot with him (vs. 4aβ). In response to the promise of land and seed, Abraham set out for a land not his own, with a wife who was barren. Journeying through this foreign land by stages, he moved each time nearer the South. *See* NEGEB.

J's reminder that "at that time the Canaanites were in the land" (vs. 6b) serves as more than a historical reference. For right at Shechem, Yahweh appeared to Abraham and rewarded his obedience with the explicit promise: "To your descendants I will give this land" (vs. 7a). Looking around him at this flourishing Canaanite sanctuary (*see* SHECHEM [CITY] § 3), Abraham could acknowledge Yahweh's ownership of the land only by an act of faith. Nor did his faith consist merely of inward affirmation. He established claim to "this land" by erecting there an altar to Yahweh. Moving southward, he camped between Bethel and Ai (*see* PALESTINE, GEOGRAPHY OF, § E2d) and claimed it also by worshiping his God there (also 13:18).

These notices about Abraham's building altars to Yahweh may originally have been old cultic etiologies, legitimizing Yahweh-worship at previously non-Israelite shrines. However, they also serve now to illustrate, not only Abraham's faith, but also his piety and habit of worship, which are characteristic of his life (13:3-4, 18; cf. 18:22b; 24:40). If this is a true biographical note in proper chronological order, Abraham probably took Lot into Egypt with him (cf. 13:1; *see* LOT § 1). But since basically the same story is given twice again (ch. 20 E; ch. 26 J [concerning Isaac]), it was originally probably not a firm element in the Abrahamic tradition. Nevertheless, as it stands, it tells a great deal about Abraham. First, Abraham exhibited a surprising lack of faith by his departure from Palestine. He no sooner proved himself the faithful believer (12:1-4a, 6-9) than he deserted the Promised Land (vss. 10-20) because he did not believe that Yahweh could fulfil his promise in the face of famine. Second, the noble patriarch here sunk to the low point in his morality by deceiving the innocent Pharaoh. Third, God acted to save and bless his chosen instrument in spite of Abraham's failure of faith and deliberate prevarication. Here is the climax of the incident, which accounts for its popularity.

*e. Separation of Lot from Abraham (13:1-5, 7-11a, 12bβ, 13).* Abraham and Lot went up (עלה) from Egypt through the Negeb into the hill country of Bethel. Because strife developed between their herdsmen, Abraham invited his nephew to choose whichever section appealed to him. Lot selected the prodigiously fertile region of the Jordan Basin and settled at Sodom. *See* LOT § 1.

Abraham's magnanimity is here favorably contrasted with Lot's selfishness. But, of more significance, Abraham's faith stands in high contrast to his lack of it during the sojourn in Egypt. Here, as at 12:6b, the presence of the Canaanites created opposition to the fulfilment of Yahweh's promise. But this time Abraham exhibited firm trust by offering Lot first choice. He could deal so generously with the land because he knew that in faith it is already his.

*f. The promise repeated (13:14-18).* Abraham, having acted in faith, now received the divine promise in a form which not only was expanded in reference to his descendants but also contained an earnest of its fulfilment in reference to the land. Previously God had promised to give the land to Abraham's descendants; now he commanded the patriarch himself to look out over the land and to walk about (vs. 17 [התהלך]; Vulg. *perambula*]; cf. Josh. 18:4, 8) in it in its length and breadth so that he might know it as his own. He was no longer related to it merely as one to whose descendants it would be given but as one who received it personally.

Moreover, the "great nation" (Gen. 12:2a) to proceed from Abraham's loins would be as innumerable as the "dust of the earth" (13:16; so 28:14 [of Jacob]; and cf. 15:5; 22:17). God would perform his promise on a grand scale.

Again Abraham responded in faith to the divine word: he journeyed southward to the "oaks of Mamre, which are at Hebron"—the central sanctuary in the Abrahamic tradition—and built there also an altar to Yahweh. *See* MAMRE; HEBRON, (CITY) § 2. Figs HEB 12-13.

*g. The declaration of righteousness (15:1abβ, 2a, 3b, 4, 6).* When Abraham stood alone in the land promised to him, Yahweh assured him that he should be greatly rewarded (with countless children [for שכר, cf. Ps. 127:3; Isa. 40:10; 62:11; Jer. 31:16]) for his faithful obedience. Yet, even at this moment, Abraham could not believe it without further assurance, and he accused God of a continuing delay tantamount to impotence: "O Lord Yahweh, what wilt thou give me, for I continue childless, . . . and a slave born in my house [בן־ביתי] will be my heir" (Gen. 15:2a, 3b). Instead of a rebuke Abraham received the "word of Yahweh," which repeated the promise in its most explicit and unqualified form: "This man shall not be your heir; your own son shall be your heir" (vs. 4).

The "word" was effective. Abraham accepted it in silent faith. No further description of Abraham's response is given, and none is needed. Here, at the crucial point in his struggle between faith and doubt, Abraham believed Yahweh ("strengthened himself in, stood firm in belief in, Yahweh"; האמן ביהוה). This was enough. Yahweh reckoned this trust to him as righteousness (ויחשבה לו צדקה [vs. 6]; Rom. 4:3, 9, 22; Gal. 3:6; Jas. 2:23; cf. Exod. 14:31; Num. 14:11; 20:12; Ps. 106:31; I Macc. 2:52). God did not measure Abraham by legal prescription (as in the Priestly use of חשב; e.g., Lev. 7:18; 17:4) but counted him as worthy (cf. Gen. 18:18-19) and established between them a personal relationship of righteousness. This is the essence of Abraham's justification. *See* FAITH; RIGHTEOUSNESS IN THE OT; JUSTIFICATION.

*h. The covenant ceremony (15:7-12, 17-21).* Now Yahweh gave Abraham specific proof of his power by referring to his concrete acts in the past leading to the accomplishment of his purpose (vs. 7). But, almost unbelievably, Abraham again asked for confirmation of the divine word: "O Lord Yahweh, how am I to know that I shall possess it?" (vs. 8.) Yahweh responded by cutting with Abraham a solemn covenant (כרת ברית), which concluded with an explicit promise of the land, even enumerating its farthest borders (vss. 18-21). The covenant bound both parties together, its pledge being, on Yahweh's part, the gift of the land, and on Abraham's part, faithfulness to Yahweh and to the land (cf. Lev. 20: 22-26; Deut. 30:15-20; *see* COVENANT §§ C2-3). To this extent, Abraham now experienced partial fulfilment of the promise of the land.

Abraham, according to the Yahwistic tradition, reaches his highest level in this chapter. The God who had called and led him now declared him faithful and in the clearest, most unambiguous terms assured him of his heir and inheritance—son and land. Then he bound the two together in solemn covenant to which he, its author and arbiter, willingly submitted himself in gracious condescension.

*i. Strife at home (16:1b, 2, 4-8, 11-14).* In spite of God's promise that Abraham would have a son of his own (Gen. 15:4), Sarah remained barren. Despairing of bearing a child herself and no longer being able to believe that God would indeed accomplish his word, she proposed that Abraham go in to her maid Hagar, reasoning: "It may be that I shall obtain children ['be built up,' אבנה] by her" (vs. 2*b*). Abraham acquiesced. When Hagar conceived, hostility arose between the two women, for which Sarah blamed her husband (vss. 4-5). Further, Abraham evaded his responsibility in the situation; and Sarah dealt so harshly with ("afflicted," ענה) her maid that Hagar fled into the wilderness (vss. 6 ff). *See* SARAH; HAGAR; ISHMAEL 1.

Here again the Abraham who showed commendable faith upon one occasion fell far short upon another. By acceding to Sarah's plan, Abraham too demonstrated a grave lack of trust, in that he doubted Yahweh's power and took the matter into his own hands. Therefore Ishmael could not be the child long promised, and the fulfilment was further delayed until the birth of Isaac (chs. 18; 21). It was not a question of Hagar's servant status, for according to the prevailing custom her child would legally be considered Sarah's own (cf. 30:3, 9; *see* ADOPTION § 1). It was, rather, that God's rich blessing stored up for Abraham and Sarah could not be carried through a child begotten in such faithless impatience.

*j. God's visitation at Mamre (18:1-15).* While Abraham was sitting drowsily under the flap of his tent in the midday heat, Yahweh appeared to him, accompanied by two angels (cf. 18:22; 19:1, 13). Without recognizing their unusual nature or mission (reading *'adhōnî* for *'adhōnāy* in vs. 3, with the RSV; cf. Heb. 13:2), Abraham provided generous hospitality for his visitors. But the purpose of the divine mission was made known when Yahweh promised: "I will surely return to you in the spring, and Sarah your wife shall have a son" (vs. 10).

God tested Abraham's and Sarah's faith by coming, unexpected and unrecognized, at the time when they were past all expectation of normal procreation (vss. 12-13) and promising them a son of their own. Sarah laughed in derision, rejecting this possibility; and when confronted with the ultimate question of faith: "Is anything too hard [פלא] for Yahweh?" (vs. 14*a*), she attempted to deny her doubt.

*k. Abraham's intercession (18:16-33).* By remaining faithful in the face of such an improbable promise, Abraham was awarded further approval. He was taken into God's counsel: "Shall I hide from Abraham what I am about to do . . . ? No, for I have chosen him, . . . so that Yahweh may bring to Abraham what he has promised him" (vss. 17-19). God then revealed to Abraham his intention to destroy Sodom. At this point the Abraham of J's narrative rises to a remarkable height. Standing on his faith in Yahweh's justice, he interceded for the possible righteous citizens (צדיקים; *see* RIGHTEOUSNESS IN THE OT) of Sodom. The primary value of this scene is not that Abraham almost won an argument with God but that he assumed the role of intercessor and enunciated the possibility of a vicarious salvation— i.e., the saving of an entire city, notorious for its evil, on behalf of a mere handful of righteous people. Interceding for non-Israelites, Abraham did indeed here become a blessing to other families of the earth (cf. 12:2-3).

*l. The birth of Isaac (21:1a, 2a, 7).* "Yahweh visited Sarah as he had said, . . . and Sarah conceived, and bore Abraham a son in his old age" (vss. 1*a*, 2*a*). For Abraham and Sarah the promise of having their own son was now fulfilled in the birth of Isaac. God proved himself faithful. In his own good time he performed his word, as Sarah indirectly acknowledges in vs. 7.

*m. Abraham's last days (ch. 24; 25:1-6, 11b).* Imposing a solemn oath upon his trusted servant (cf. the deathbed scenes with Isaac [ch. 27] and Jacob [chs. 48–49]), Abraham sent him back to the city of NAHOR to obtain a wife for Isaac. Prospered in his mission, the faithful steward found Rebekah and brought her back to Canaan. *See* REBEKAH; LABAN.

Two matters are of primary importance to Abraham: that the girl be from his own kindred (24:4), and that she be willing to come to Canaan (vss. 4-9, 38-41, 54-58). By the first, Abraham sought to guard Isaac, his son of promise, from the seduction of the heathen, Canaanite religion. Nahor's family shared in the "patriarchal god" tradition; thus Rebekah could herself most easily continue the worship of the "God of Abraham" (26:24-25; cf. 28:13; 31:53; *see* NAHOR; PATRIARCHS). By the second, Abraham guarded his son from the necessity or temptation of leaving the Promised Land; for it is in "this land" (12:7; 15:7, 18; 24:7) that Yahweh would make Abraham a great nation. Here at the end of his life Abraham showed himself faithful to his call by maintaining the integrity of these two elements—land and seed.

Abraham married KETURAH and through her became the father of many peoples (25:1-5). After rewarding the "sons of his concubines" (vs. 6), he sent them away. Isaac, the witness to God's faithfulness, was left secure in the Promised Land.

**2. According to the Elohist.** Other traditions concerning Abraham circulated in Palestine. Some that were unknown to the Yahwist, or at least unused by him, were collected by the Elohist (*see* PENTATEUCH § A3*b*). These stories were at home principally in the N. They are now found in Gen. 15:1*b*α, 3*a*, 5, 13-16; 20:1*b*-18; 21:6, 8-34; 22.

Taken alone, these sections give a picture of Abraham which, though skeletal, is dominated by the question of his faithfulness to God's promise: God called him and promised the double inheritance of seed and land (ch. 15); Abraham showed lack of faith in the promise of the land by forsaking Canaan for Philistia (ch. 20), and in the promise of his own son's inheritance by driving out Ishmael (ch. 21); but Abraham finally triumphed in perfect obedience (ch. 22). If these stories represent the major portion of an independent tradition, they indicate that it also knew an Abraham who was revered as the "father of faith."

However, these stories do not now stand alone. They have been inserted in the earlier, fuller J narrative. Since they thereby acquired an even deeper dimension, they should be read as part of the larger story.

*a. The divine promise (15:1bα, 3a, 5, 13-16).* When God appeared to Abraham, he exhorted him not to be afraid, because "I am your shield" (vs. 1bα [מגן]; cf. Deut. 33:29; II Sam. 22:36; Ps. 115:9-11). If Gen. 15:2a (KJV "seeing I go childless") belongs to E, it would reflect a "call" of Abraham, probably from Mesopotamia, quite similar to J's (cf. Gen. 20:13; Josh. 24:3 E). Abraham, doubting and disappointed, charged God with failure to act (15:3a). Therefore, God brought him outside and repeated (cf. 13:14-17 J) majestically his promise of innumerable descendants (15:5) and then, after Abraham believed (vs. 6 J), his promise of the land (vss. 13-16).

*b. The sojourn in Gerar (ch. 20).* After having been assured that he would go to his fathers in peace and be buried in a good old age (15:15), Abraham nevertheless forsook the Promised Land and dwelt in GERAR. He betrayed an even greater lack of faith in God's providence by choosing to deceive ABIMELECH about Sarah. Yet the patriarch did not here appear in an unrelievedly harsh light, as in J's episode (*see* § C1*d above*); for when Abimelech was acknowledged as innocent, Abraham interceded for this heathen king and all his household. By this, Abraham appears in the role of a prophet (vs. 7; *see* PROPHET § C2), serving Israel's universal mission. *See* § A *above*.

*c. The expulsion of Hagar and Ishmael (21:6, 8-21).* Having just acknowledged God's faithfulness to his promise of a son (vs. 6), Sarah nevertheless disbelieved that he was able to maintain the child's inheritance. Fearing lest Ishmael should share along with Isaac, Sarah accosted Abraham: "Cast out this slave woman with her son; for [he] shall not be heir with my son Isaac" (vs. 10; cf. Gal. 4:30). Abraham acquiesced. This is not just another version of the earlier account (ch. 16), for here is a progression in disbelief. Isaac should have been a living testimony to God's trustworthiness, a spur to faith, for his parents. But instead, his presence made them so worried about his future that again, in total lack of trust, they took the matter into their own hands.

Yet here also Abraham was made to bear little guilt. In fact, in acquiescing he was really complying with the divine will. In clear terms God reaffirmed his promise concerning Isaac and then added that, because of Abraham, he would even make Ishmael into a nation (vss. 11-13 [גוי גדול in vs. 18]). Abraham was more than exonerated. It was on his

behalf that God saved and blessed another nation. *See* ISHMAEL 1.

*d. The treaty with Abimelech (21:22-34).* That Abraham was blessed by God was evident even to the heathen (cf. 26:28-29). Acknowledging Abraham's favored position, Abimelech petitioned the favored patriarch for a treaty. When Abraham cut a covenant (כרת ברית; 21:27b, 32a) with him, he extended, as it were, his own blessing to the heathen king and his people.

By worshiping "Yahweh, the Everlasting God" (יהוה אל עולם; vs. 33; *see* GOD, NAMES OF, § B), at Beer-sheba, Abraham again established, by implication, his claim to the land.

*e. The testing of Abraham (22:1-19).* Abraham's struggle for faith now ended victoriously. Called by God to sacrifice his only, beloved son upon "one of the mountains" in the land of Moriah (*see* MORIAH; JERUSALEM § 3c), Abraham responded in perfect obedience. To Isaac's probing question he returned an answer calculated to inspire in his son a like measure of faith: "God will provide himself the lamb . . . , my son" (vs. 8; cf. vs. 14). In this excruciating test father and son exhibit a splendid faith, each in the other and both in God (cf. Wisd. Sol. 10:15; Ecclus. 44:20).

In the face of such obedience, God now solemnly reaffirmed his promise of innumerable descendants and possession of the land (Gen. 22:15-18); and his last word to the patriarch, bringing the whole Abrahamic tradition to its climax, roots Israel's universal mission in the faith of Abraham: "By your descendants shall all the nations of the earth bless themselves, because you have obeyed my voice" (vs. 18).

**3. According to the Priestly tradition.** The Abraham of the P narrative knows very little of a tension between faith and doubt. Seen in the P passages alone (Gen. 11:26-27, 31-32; 12:4b-5; 13:6, 11b, 12abα; 14; 16:1a, 3, 15-16; 17; 19:29; 21:1b, 2b-5; 23; 25:7-11a), Abraham is a towering figure, dominating the scene around him. Ample, though sometimes confusing, statistics help delineate the length of his life, yet without adding much to its breadth. Nevertheless, the theme of promise and fulfilment is present, tying these chapters closely to the JE story.

*a. Abraham's journey to Canaan (11:26-27, 31-32; 12:4b-5; 13:6, 11b-12bα).* According to P's chronology, Abraham left Haran for Canaan sixty years before his father's death. Although no explicit reason for Abraham's journey is given, P's concentration upon this one family is not at odds with J's story of Abraham's call and election (12:1-3). When Lot and his uncle separated from each other, Abraham was left alone in the land.

*b. Abraham and Melchizedek (ch. 14).* In this unique chapter, Abraham strode out onto a vast, rich scene. When he went forth to rescue Lot, he appeared as a military hero routing a coalition of powerful Eastern kings (*see* CHEDORLAOMER; AMRAPHEL; LOT § 1). When he returned home, he was met as the savior of his people and was blessed by MELCHIZEDEK, "priest of God Most High."

*c. The birth of Ishmael (16:1a, 3, 15-16).* Judged by the standards applied earlier (*see* §§ C1*i*, C2*c above*), Abraham was here guilty of unfaith in accepting Hagar as his wife. P softens the situation considerably, however, by having Abraham agree only after having waited childless in Canaan for ten years.

*d. The divine covenant (ch. 17).* Yahweh appeared to Abraham as "God Almighty" (El Shaddai; *see* GOD, NAMES OF, § C2*a*), called him to a faultless life (תמים; cf. 6:9; Job 1:1), and promised him the blessings of his covenant for obedience (Gen. 17:1-2). The covenant entails the change of the patriarch's name, promise of multitudinous seed, possession of the land of Canaan, and a universal mission (vss. 3-8). Moreover, God promised to give a son by Sarah (vss. 15-16). Here Abraham lapsed into a moment of doubt, laughing derisively and interceding for Ishmael as his only hope (vss. 17-18); but, upon reassurance from God, hastened to indicate his obedience by observing the prescription of circumcision (vss. 9-14, 22-27). In P's story Abraham reaches both his lowest and his highest levels in this theophany.

*e. The birth of Isaac (21:1b, 2b-5).* God proved himself faithful; for in their old age Abraham and Sarah bore a son. Abraham responded in faith to the covenant by circumcising the child.

*f. The purchase of Machpelah (ch. 23).* Although the land of Canaan had been promised to Abraham from the beginning, during his life it remained the "land of [his] sojournings" (17:8; cf. 28:4; 37:1; Heb. 11:9). Now, in the purchase of MACHPELAH, he acquired a portion of it legally so that he was no longer an heir but an owner. Abraham hereby experienced partial fulfilment of this second element of the patriarchal promise of seed and land.

*g. The death of Abraham (25:7-11a).* Abraham died "in a good old age, an old man and full of years," and was buried on his own ground. At his death he —as the other fathers (35:29; 49:31; 50:13)—entered fully into the Land of Promise.

**D. ABRAHAM IN THE REST OF THE OT.** Two themes link all the early Abrahamic traditions: God's promise of innumerable seed and the land of Canaan, and Abraham's faithful response. These themes also dominate the other OT references to him. Thus, God repeated to Isaac (Gen. 26:3; cf. Ecclus. 44:22) and to Jacob (Gen. 28:13; 35:11-12) the promise made first to Abraham. Joseph expected these blessings to be shared by his brothers (50:24); and Moses was to exhort all Israel in this faith (Exod. 6:3-8; cf. Bar. 2:34).

The God who called Abraham and entered into covenant with him was the "God of Abraham" (Gen. 26:24*a;* see PATRIARCHS § 4). Israel was therefore the "people of the God of Abraham" (Ps. 47:9) or the "offspring of Abraham" (Ps. 105:6; Isa. 41:8); and Abraham was Israel's father (Isa. 51:2; 63:16). Because of Abraham's faithful obedience, he was known, not only as God's servant (Gen. 26:24*b;* Ps. 105:42), but also as his "friend" (II Chr. 20:7; Isa. 41:8).

Here the concept of Abraham as mediator and intercessor, latent in the earlier traditions (Gen. 12:3; 18:22-33), receives significant expansion. On the strength of Abraham's faith and his relationship of righteousness with God, Israel could both appeal to God to remember his holy covenant (Exod. 32:13; cf. II Macc. 1:2) and have confidence that he would hearken "for Abraham's sake" (cf. Lev. 26:42; Deut.

9:27; 29:13; II Kings 13:23; I Chr. 16:16; Ps. 105:9-11). Because of Abraham, God rescued Lot (Gen. 19:29), blessed Isaac (26:24), redeemed Israel from bondage (Exod. 2:24), and continued in faithfulness (אמן) and steadfast love (חסד; Mic. 7:20). Israel remembered Abraham as the faithful one for whose sake she was blessed.

**E. ABRAHAM IN THE NT.** The OT themes, though continued, receive significant expansion and reinterpretation in the NT. Thus, Abraham was the father of the Israelites "according to the flesh" (κατὰ σάρκα), and they are his sons and daughters. But he becomes the father of all who, after the Spirit, share in his faith (Matt. 3:9; Luke 13:16; 16:24; 19:9; Acts 13:26 [υἱοὶ γένους 'Αβραάμ]; Rom. 11:1; cf. Rom. 4:16; Gal. 3:29), while the sons themselves may be disinherited (Matt. 8:11-12; John 8:39*b*). God "swore an oath" with Abraham, sealed with promises (Luke 1:73; Acts 7:5-6), but Christians are the "children of promise" (Gal. 4:28) and its proper heirs (3:29). God is the "God of Abraham" (Mark 12:26; Acts 7:32); and Abraham, the "friend [φίλος] of God" (Jas. 2:23), lives with him in heaven (Luke 16:22; John 8:56, 58; *see* ABRAHAM'S BOSOM). But this same God "glorified his servant Jesus" and therefore acts also on behalf of Christians (Acts 3:13).

However, the strongest NT picture of Abraham portrays him as a monumental figure of faith. In his call, in his waiting upon the fulfilment of the promises, and pre-eminently in the sacrifice of Isaac, Abraham patiently endured all tests "by faith" (πίστει). This life of faith stands as a model for all Christians (Gal. 3:6-9), and, by implication, is prototypical of Christ's life of perfect obedience. *See* ALLEGORY.

**F. ABRAHAM AS THE FATHER OF THE FAITHFUL.** Abraham's faith in God is the dominant theme from the earliest OT tradition to the latest NT reference. But the fullest and most formative portrait—J's—does not show this faith as an abstract quality or easy attainment but as the hard-won result of a difficult human struggle over recurring doubt and unfaith, a victory gained through God's forgiving grace.

Abraham stands rightly, therefore, as the father of all the faithful—Jew or Gentile—who, sharing in his obedience, are blessed with him in Christ (Gal. 3:7-9, 14). Herein Abraham becomes also the "father of a multitude of nations," and Israel's universal mission is fulfilled (cf. Luke 13:28-29; John 8:56-58).

*Bibliography.* For general historical background and the contributions of archaeology, see the bibliographies under PATRIARCHS; GENESIS; also L. H. Grollenberg, *Atlas of the Bible* (1956), pp. 31-38.

For a discussion of legend, see: H. Gunkel, *The Legends of Genesis* (1901); B. D. Napier, *From Faith to Faith* (1955), pp. 60-80.

For etymology, see: M. Noth, *Die israelitischen Personennamen* (1928), pp. 52, 145; W. F. Albright, "The Names *Shaddai* and *Abram*," *JBL*, LIV (1935), 193-203.

For the Aramaic Genesis scroll from Qumran, see: N. Avigad and Y. Yadin, *A Genesis Apocryphon* (1956), pp. 22-37, 41-48.

For detailed exegesis consult the standard commentaries, among which H. Gunkel, *HKAT* (4th ed., 1917), is outstanding for form-critical analysis; S. R. Driver, *WC* (12th ed.,

1926), for portrayal of personalities; and G. von Rad, *ATD*, vol. 2 (1949); vol. 3 (1952), for theological insight.

L. Hicks

**ABRAHAM, APOCALYPSE OF.** A Jewish apocryphon which has survived only in a Slavonic version, based on a Greek translation of the original Hebrew or Aramaic. For general discussion of this type of literature, *see* APOCRYPHA; APOCALYPSES, APOCRYPHAL.

The first eight chapters deal with Abraham's youth and tell how he became convinced that there is but one God and how he fought the idolatrous follies of his time. This narrative has a general resemblance to stories of Abraham's conversion and his campaign against image-worship, found in rabbinic literature. It is followed by the apocalypse proper, which begins as a sort of midrash on Gen. 15. Escorted by a great angel, Jaoel (Hebrew Jahoel), Abraham flies up to heaven and beholds the divine throne and the attendant angels. God shows him the inhabitants of the various heavens, then bids him look down on earth, where he sees events of the past (the temptation of Adam and Eve, the murder of Abel) and of the future (the destruction of the temple, the coming of the Messiah). Abraham boldly discusses with God the problem of evil, but the outcome of the conversation is uncertain (*see below*). The final chapters of the work are obscure and contain manifestly Christian insertions.

The explicit reference to the destroyed temple and the generally gloomy character of the work are sufficient to fix its date at the end of the first or the beginning of the second Christian century—i.e., at about the same time as the apocalypses of Esdras and Baruch. Like them, the book is deeply concerned with the problem of evil and of divine justice; unlike them, however, it experiments with an extreme dualism. The devil appears under the name of Azazel; but he is not the Azazel of I Enoch, one of the ringleaders in an angelic revolt. He is a radically evil being, whose existence is not accounted for, but whose reality is vividly felt—like Belial in the Testaments of the Twelve Patriarchs. He tries to dissuade Abraham from ascending on high; he is identified with the serpent of Eden, who has hands and feet and twelve wings, and who seduces Eve with the fruit of the vine; he incites Cain to murder Abel. In Abraham's conversations with God, it is implied that Azazel has certain rights within the total world economy (cf. the NT view of Satan as the prince of this world). In addition to this radical dualism, the work contains other quasi-Gnostic touches, such as the glorification of the angel Jahoel, who actually appears by this name in some medieval Hebrew mystical writings, but usually merges with the cosmic being called Metatron.

On the other hand, many passages, both in the introductory narrative and in the apocalypse proper, present a rationalistic and thoroughgoing monism. The angels hymn God in almost philosophical terms. During the same conversation in which Abraham inquires why God tolerates Azazel, God insists that the source of evil is in man's freedom of will. The shifts between dualism and monism, determinism and voluntarism, rationalism and quasi-Gnosticism, are perhaps due in part to the various sources on which

the author drew; but even more, they seem to mirror the tragic uncertainty of the author himself, as he struggled to reconcile the massive tragedy that had befallen the nation with his faith in one righteous God.

*Bibliography.* Text, trans. G. H. Box and J. L. Landsman (1918). L. Ginzberg, "Abraham, Apocalypse of," *JE* (1901-6), I, 91 ff; *The Legends of the Jews* (1909-38), I, 209 ff; V, 217, 229-30. K. Kohler, *Heaven and Hell in Comparative Religion* (1923), pp. 74 ff; *The Origins of the Synagogue and the Church* (1929), pp. 180 ff. G. G. Scholem, *Major Trends in Jewish Mysticism* (1941), pp. 67-68.    B. J. Bamberger

**ABRAHAM, TESTAMENT OF.** A Jewish apocryphal writing, originally composed in Hebrew or Aramaic, which has survived only in a free Greek translation. (For discussion of this type of literature, *see* APOCRYPHA.) We possess a longer and a shorter version of the work; the shorter includes a few details not found in the longer.

The booklet deals chiefly with the circumstances of Abraham's death. The angel Michael is sent to take Abraham's soul; but the patriarch refuses to die, and the angel cannot summon the courage to insist. (Similar legends are found in rabbinic literature concerning the death of Moses.) Abraham pleads that he may see all created things before his death, and this request is granted. Michael takes him high in the air in a chariot. When Abraham sees men sinning with apparent impunity, he curses them, and they fall dead. A heavenly voice intervenes, and Abraham is brought up into the heavens, where he beholds the judgment of human souls. Though angels take part in their trial and punishment, it is the soul of Abel who acts as judge. When a soul whose faults and merits are equally balanced is put on trial, Abraham prays for a favorable verdict, and his prayer is efficacious. He now repents his former severity, but is reassured: the untimely death of those whom he cursed has made atonement for their sins.

Returning to earth, Abraham again refuses to yield up his soul. Death, disguised as a radiant angel, replaces Michael; but even when he reveals himself in all his terrors, so that seven thousand servants of Abraham expire (they are later revived), the patriarch will not surrender. At last, lying upon his couch, he is beguiled into giving his hand to Death, and straightway the angels bear his soul on high. (In the shorter version, God himself takes Abraham's soul as in a dream.)

The intent of the author seems to have been to create a moving story rather than to advance any particular theological interest. It is thought that the Greek texts contain some Hellenistic additions—in particular the elaborate description of the death angel—that were not in the original. This apocryphon is generally dated in the first century of the Christian era.

*Bibliography.* Text, trans. G. H. Box (1927). L. Ginzberg, "Abraham, Testament of," *JE* (1901-6), I, 93 ff; *The Legends of the Jews* (1909-38), I, 299-306; V, 266-67. K. Kohler, *Heaven and Hell in Comparative Religion* (1923), pp. 77 ff.    B. J. Bamberger

**ABRAHAM'S BOSOM** [κόλπος ʼΑβραάμ]. The place where the good go at the moment of death, and where judgment is enacted as preliminary and perhaps probationary to the Final Judgment at the end of the age. In the parable of the rich man and Lazarus, the beggar at death is carried by angels to Abraham's bosom, and is separated by a great chasm from the tormented rich man in Hades (Sheol; Luke 16:22-23). This view of a moral division among the dead who dwell in Sheol appeared in Jewish literature in the first century A.D.

**1. Location.** Older Jewish literature makes no mention of that part of Sheol reserved for the righteous dead, nor any localizing of Paradise in Sheol, though in II Esd. 7:36 the "pit of torment" and the "place of rest" are set over against each other at the Last Judgment. Interpreters are divided as to whether in this parable Hades includes both men (so Strack and Billerbeck, *Kommentar*, vol. IV, p. 1019) or only the rich man. Some believe that such figurative topographical details can be pressed no further here than in Enoch, where in ch. 22 (*ca.* 100 B.C.) the dead are separated into three groups in the underworld until the Day of Judgment. Enoch 22 bears many resemblances to Luke 16:19 ff, and may represent the popular view of Sheol in Jesus' day (cf. also Syr. Apocal. Bar. 30:2).

**2. Abraham as an eschatological figure.** Jewish literature of the NT period contains many references to Father Abraham, together with the patriarchs Isaac and Jacob, as eschatological figures. Rabbinic Judaism sometimes spoke of a rest in Abraham's bosom in relation to the meal of the blessed in the world to come, which was enjoyed by the righteous after death (Matt. 8:11; Midrash on Exod. 16:4; cf. John 13:23). But at times the rest in Abraham is unrelated to the meal and signifies the blissful fellowship enjoyed with the patriarch. In IV Macc. 13:17 the patriarchs welcome the seven martyr brothers. The bosom of Abraham as the dwelling place of the righteous is referred to in the Midrash on Lamentations and the Pesiḳ. R. 43, and in the T.B. Ḳid. 72 *a/b*. In the Lukan parable the metaphor probably indicates a blessed communion of the faithful, as of a parent and child (cf. John 1:18), apart from any reference to a heavenly banquet.

*Bibliography.* H. L. Strack and P. Billerbeck, *Kommentar zum NT aus Talmud und Midrasch*, II (1924), 226-27; IV (1928), 1018-19. R. Meyer in *TWNT*, III (1938), 825-26.

E. W. SAUNDERS

**ABRAM** ā'brəm [אברם, *see* ABRAHAM § A1; LXX Αβραμ]. The name used for ABRAHAM in Gen. 11: 26-17:4.

**ABRON** ăb'rən [ἀβρωνα (BA), χερβων (א); Vulg. *Mambre*] (Jth. 2:24); KJV ARBONAI är bō'nī. A brook (KJV "river") identified by some as the Chaboras; others conjecture a corruption of עבר הנהר.

J. C. SWAIM

**ABRONAH** ə brō'nə [עברנה, pass or passage] (Num. 33:34-35); KJV EBRONAH ĭ brō'nə. A place where the Israelites camped en route to Ezion-geber and the borders of Edom. Possibly 'Ain Defiyeh, a shallow water hole in a sandy flat *ca.* 7½ miles N of Ezion-geber.

V. R. GOLD

**ABSALOM** ăb'sə ləm [אבשלום, father in peace; Apoc. 'Αβεσσάλωμος, 'Αψάλωμος, 'Αβεσσάλωμος, *in*

*various MSS*]; ABISHALOM ə bĭsh'ə ləm [אבישלום] (I Kings 15:2, 10). **1.** The third son of David, whose regal ambitions precipitated a serious but short-lived revolt.

Absalom was born in Hebron* of Maacah the daughter of Talmai, king of Geshur in Aram (II Sam. 3:3; I Chr. 3:2). His recorded experiences commence with the pathetic story of the rape of his beautiful sister Tamar by Amnon, the first-born son of David. Absalom met the heartbroken maiden after she had been rudely ejected from the house of her abductor, and provided a sanctuary for her in his own home. After two years Absalom held a feast, as he sheared his sheep at Baal-hazar, and persuaded the somewhat reluctant king to permit the royal sons, including Amnon, to attend. During the feast the inebriated Amnon was slain by the servants of Absalom, who fled of necessity to the home of his maternal grandfather at Geshur, where he remained for three years (II Sam. 13; 15:8). Fig. HEB 12.

From this exile Absalom was finally recalled through the efforts of Joab, who, perceiving that the king's wrath had abated, was able through an astute stratagem, skilfully performed by a wise woman of Tekoa, to secure from the king permission for the prince to return to his house in Jerusalem, although he was debarred from the court. This intolerable situation continued for two years, until Absalom summoned Joab to intercede for him with the king, but for some reason—perhaps the imperiousness of Absalom—Joab refused twice to see the prince. In this virtual duress Absalom compelled Joab to put in an appearance when he set his barley field on fire. He then persuaded Joab to plead his inequitable case before David, who summoned Absalom and reinstated him in his favor (II Sam. 14).

Not long thereafter the ambitious prince began to assert publicly his prerogative as heir apparent by procuring for himself a chariot and a cortege of fifty runners. This claim was supported by the fact that at this juncture he was the eldest surviving son of David, since Amnon and presumably Chileab were now dead. This positive affirmation was complemented by a program of studied subversion, in which Absalom undermined the people's confidence in David by exaggerating the evils of the king's court and acquired for himself the allegiance of the disaffected by posing as the champion of the people. At the end of four years Absalom, abetted by the sagacious Ahithophel, planned the *coup d'état* by distributing his adherents throughout the land so that they could announce at the appointed hour his accession to the Davidic throne, while he himself, having secured permission of the king to go to Hebron, ostensibly to fulfil a vow, initiated the revolt from this erstwhile capital of David (cf. II Sam. 5:5). When the news of the conspiracy reached David, he was taken completely by surprise and had no other recourse than to flee at once from Jerusalem (II Sam. 15; cf. I Kings 2:7; Ps. 3).

While Absalom occupied Jerusalem without a struggle, the king was not devoid of loyal allies in the city. The priests Zadok and Abiathar acted as the contacts for Hushai, the friend of David who, having disarmed the suspicions of Absalom, was in a favored position to carry on his espionage and subversion of the rebel movement.

At the instance of Ahithophel the relationship between Absalom and David was irreparably breached when Absalom violated publicly the royal harem (II Sam. 16:20-23). As the next move Ahithophel counseled Absalom to place at his disposal twelve thousand troops with which to attack David immediately and to make the principal objective of the clash the liquidation of the king, so that the nation would rally to the support of its new leader. This shrewd advice was superseded, however, by the opposing counsel of Hushai, who proposed that a complete mobilization of Israel be made and a concerted attack be launched personally by Absalom in order to ensure a certain victory. Informed of these secret plans of Absalom, David crossed the Jordan and encamped at Mahanaim, while somewhat later Absalom invaded Gilead, where he took up a position with his forces under the command of Amasa (II Sam. 17).

In the ensuing conflict in the forest of Ephraim the seasoned troops of David, marshaled by Joab, Abishai, and Ittai the Gittite, attacked and utterly routed the army of Absalom. As the rebel prince fled from the battle upon his mule, his long locks of hair became entangled in the thick branches of an oak, while his mount proceeded riderless, leaving him hanging helplessly in mid-air. When the plight of Absalom was communicated to Joab, he slew him forthwith, in direct violation of the specific orders of David, and raised over his corpse a great cairn. With the death of Absalom the rebellion crumbled immediately. Upon learning of the death of his son, David was inconsolable and broke out in unrestrained grief, lamenting again and again: "O my son Absalom, my son, my son Absalom! Would I had died instead of you, O Absalom, my son, my son!" (II Sam. 18—H 18-19:1).

The victory of the Davidic troops was completely overshadowed by the sorrow of the king. This awkward situation was promptly corrected by the stern rebuke of Joab, who pointed out to the king the embarrassing incongruity of his behavior and counseled him to express at once his appreciation for the heroic efforts of his followers (II Sam. 19:1-8—H 19:2-9).

Absalom is represented to be the father of three sons and a daughter Tamar, who possessed her father's comeliness (II Sam. 14:27; cf. vss. 25-26). However, an account is elsewhere given of the erection of a monument or pillar in the King's Valley to perpetuate his name because he had no male heir (II Sam. 18:18).* The discrepancy is usually accounted for by supposing that all his sons died in infancy. MAACAH (10), the wife of Rehoboam, is called the daughter of Absalom, but was more probably his granddaughter, unless another man of the same name is intended (II Sam. 14:27 LXX; I Kings 15:2, 10; II Chr. 11:20 ff; cf. 13:2). Fig. TOM 70.

E. R. DALGLISH

2. The father of Mattathias, captain in the army of Jonathan Maccabeus. Mattathias remained faithful to his grandson when most of the rest of the army had fled in a battle against the Syrians (I Macc. 11: 70). He may also be the Absalom whose son Jona-

than was sent by Simon Maccabeus on the errand mentioned in I Macc. 13:11. Probably we should read in both places (11:70; 13:11) either "father of Jonathan" or "father of Mattathias."

3. One of two envoys sent by the Jews to LYSIAS for negotiating a peace after his defeat at BETH-ZUR in 165 B.C. (II Macc. 11:17). He may be the same as 2 above, but there is nothing corresponding in I Maccabees, and the author of II Maccabees may be mistaken about the whole incident.

N. TURNER

**ABSTINENCE.** See FASTING.

**ABUBUS** ə bōō'bŭs ["Αβουβος]. The father of Ptolemy, governor of Jericho and son-in-law and murderer of Simon the Hasmonean (I Macc. 16:15).

**ABYSS** [ἄβυσσος]; KJV and alternately RSV BOTTOMLESS PIT. The LXX rendering for תהום, "Deep" (Gen. 1:2, etc.); a bottomless, unfathomed, and unfathomable deep or underworld (Luke 8:31; Rom. 10:7; Rev. 9:1; etc.). See DEAD, ABODE OF THE.

S. TERRIEN

**ACACIA** ə kā'shə [שטה, šiṭṭâ (Isa. 41:19; KJV SHITTAH TREE shĭt'ə); otherwise plural שטים, šiṭṭîm; Arab. sanṭ, probably from Egyp. šnḏt]; KJV SHITTIM WOOD shĭt'ĭm. A tree and its wood. In all but one instance the reference is to the wood used in constructing the ARK OF THE COVENANT, the table of shewbread, altars, carrying poles, frames, and other wooden objects associated with the TABERNACLE, described in Exod. 25-27; 30; 35-38; Deut. 10:3. Ideally suited for cabinetmaking, the hard, orange-brown wood of the native Acacia seyal Del. (Arabic sayyāl) and the larger Acacia tortilis Hayne (same as Acacia raddiana Savi) is still common in the desert regions of the Negeb and Sinai. These acacias produce a very durable wood (cf. LXX ξύλων ἄσηπτον, "non-decaying wood"). שטה in Isa. 41:19 disturbs the imagery; cf. the LXX πύξον, "BOX TREE," which fits the context.

The place names SHITTIM; ABEL-SHITTIM; and BETH-SHITTIM probably developed where the acacia grew in abundance. The symbolism in Joel 3:18—H 4:18 would be clearer with the translation "valley of acacias" (LXX "torrent of rushes"), rather than "valley of Shittim."

Some have identified the BURNING BUSH (Exod. 3:2-3) with the Acacia nilotica L., a smaller species, one of the chief sources of gum arabic today. The colorful Acacia Farnesiana L., common in hedges today, is not native, but a cultivated species.

See also FLORA § A9a.

Bibliography. I. Löw, Die Flora der Juden, II (1924), 377-91; H. N. and A. L. Moldenke, Plants of the Bible (1952), pp. 24-26.

J. C. TREVER

**ACATAN.** KJV Apoc. form of HAKKATAN.

**ACCAD** ăk'ăd [אכד; Akkad. akkadî; Sumer. agadê]. A city of Shinar (Babylonia), listed along with Babel, Erech, and possibly Calneh (cf. KJV) as forming the original kingdom of Nimrod (Gen. 10:10); identified with Akkad, or Agade, of the cuneiform inscriptions. Founded to be the capital of the Dynasty of SARGON (1) of Akkad (*ca.* twenty-third–twenty-first centuries B.C.), the city seems to have been destroyed with the fall of that Akkadian dynasty, and its site has never been located. However, its name lived on in the phrase "the land of Akkad and Sumer," the usual designation for Babylonia in the inscriptions, and in the term *akkadu* for the oldest Semitic invaders of Mesopotamia and their language, of which Assyrian and Babylonian were dialects.

*See also* ASSYRIA AND BABYLONIA § B; SUMER § 2*b*.

*Bibliography.* A. Moortgat, in A. Scharff and Moortgat, *Ägypten und Vorderasien im Altertum* (1950), pp. 256-71; H. Frankfort, *The Art and Architecture of the Ancient Orient* (1954), pp. 41-46.    C. H. GORDON

**ACCARON.** Apoc. form of EKRON.

**ACCENT, GALILEAN.** Jesus and his disciples spoke Aramaic; but being Galileans, they spoke a dialect of Aramaic which had its own Galilean peculiarities. After Jesus' arrest in Judea, when Peter was denying having had any association with him, Matthew records that some bystanders identified Peter by his accent as a Galilean (Matt. 26:73). He was therefore immediately suspected of being one of Jesus' disciples; his accent betrayed him.

The Greek word translated "accent," λαλιά, commonly means "speech" or "speaking." It is used also in John 4:42; 8:43*a*. In the latter passage ("what I say") a distinction is made between Jesus' audible speaking and his "word"—i.e., his message—or Jesus himself, who is the Word.

B. H. THROCKMORTON, JR.

**ACCENTS, MUSICAL.** *See* MASORETIC ACCENTS.

**ACCEPTANCE** [ἀποδοχή; *cf.* ἀποδέχομαι, receive, accept].

**1. Men's acceptance of God or his word.** Specially notable is the phrase "worthy of full acceptance," attached to two of the "sure sayings" (KJV "faithful sayings") in the Pastoral letters—I Tim. 1:15; 4:9 (with reference to vs. 10). Here we have a stereotyped kerygmatic expression, originating in a Hellenistic environment (similar expressions are found in Hellenistic authors from Polybius onward). By acceptance of the "sure saying" men inherit the blessings of the gospel.

**2. God's acceptance of men, their worship and service.** Cf. two further passages in the Pastorals—I Tim. 2:3; 5:4—where prayer for all men and care for one's natural dependents are "acceptable" (ἀπόδεκτος) in God's sight. So acts of charity like Cornelius' (Acts 10:35), contributions to God's work (II Cor. 8:12), gifts like the Philippians' to Paul (Phil. 4:18), Paul's priestly presentation of the "offering of the Gentiles" (Rom. 15:16), and other "spiritual sacrifices" which Christians offer to God as a "holy priesthood" (I Pet. 2:5) are "acceptable" (δεκτός, εὐπρόσδεκτος) to him. The language reflects OT sacrificial terminology. See Lev. 23:11; Isa. 60:7, where the Hebrew term is רצון.

**3. Men's acceptance of one another.** The acceptance of accredited messengers of God or Christ is tantamount to acceptance of God or Christ (Matt. 10:40; cf. Mark 9:37).    F. F. BRUCE

**ACCESS** [προσαγωγή]. A term denoting the privilege of approach or of being introduced, especially to a divine or royal personage. It is used three times in the NT: in Eph. 2:18, where through Christ, Jewish and Gentile believers alike "have access in one Spirit to the Father"; in Eph. 3:12, where the sense is the same—in Christ "we have boldness and confidence of access [i.e., to God] through our faith in him"; in Rom. 5:2, where through Christ "we have obtained access to this grace in which we stand." In these places προσαγωγή probably reflects the transitive sense of the verb προσάγω, as used, e.g., in I Pet. 3:18: "Christ also died . . . that he might bring us to God."    F. F. BRUCE

*ACCO ăk'ō [עַכּוֹ; Egyp. '*Aka;* Akkad. *Akku;* Amarna *Akka;* Ἄκη, *later* πτολεμαΐς (Ptolemais); *present* Acre]; KJV ACCHO. Harbor and city-state in N Palestine, N of Carmel.

**1. Location.** Acco was founded on the small coastal plain N of the mountain of Carmel. The old town was a natural center, and the whole plain was named after it. In the N the plain is limited by Jebel el-Mushaqqah, which is the westernmost part of the N Galilean mountains. The mountain falls steeply into the sea and constitutes the N border of Palestine. The plain is *ca.* four miles wide where Acco was situated. Protected by the mountains is a natural bay, which was one of the few good harbors along the Palestinian coast. The modern Acco is only a small town, and the important harbor is now Haifa on the same plain a little farther S. Tell el-Fukhkhar, a mile E of Acre, near 'Ain es-Sitt, dug out in 1929 by Saarisalo, was supposed by some scholars to be the site of ancient Acco. It is more probable, however, that it was the citadel of Ptolemais which was once located there.

**2. History.** Acco is mentioned in an Egyptian execration, written on a figurine, from the nineteenth century B.C., and several times in the Amarna Letters from the fourteenth century B.C. The rivaling Canaanite princes accused one another of treachery in their letters to Pharaoh, and it can be seen that Egypt's domination of Acco was not very solidly founded. Acco was conquered by Thut-mose III early in the fifteenth century and by Seti I at the end of the fourteenth century. Ramses II is also reported to have "desolated Acre" in the thirteenth century. After his time new enemies came on the stage. The tribe of Asher pressed toward the coast, but as Judg. 1:31-32 notes: "Asher did not drive out the inhabitants of Acco, . . . but the Asherites dwelt among the Canaanites, the inhabitants of the land."

In 733 B.C., Acco was brought under Assyrian domination by Tiglath-pileser III. About a hundred years later Ashurbanipal deported many of the inhabitants and killed others. In Hellenistic times Acco was renamed Ptolemais, and played an important role as harbor for the Ptolemies and the Seleucids. According to the author of I Maccabees, Ptolemais was a center for the opponents of the Maccabees (I Macc. 5:15). Just after 150 B.C. the Maccabee Jonathan was ordered by Alexander Balas to meet him in Ptolemais; later Jonathan received the same order from Demetrius II (I Macc. 10:51-66; 11:21-74). A third time he was ordered to come by Trypho, and then arrested and kept in the town as prisoner (12: 39-48).

In 65 B.C., Ptolemais came under Roman domination, and it was in the Roman town that Paul landed on his third voyage (Acts 21:7). In the Middle Ages the Crusaders held the town for nearly two hundred years. It was then called St. Jean d'Acre, which has given the town its present name, Acre.

A. S. KAPELRUD

**ACCOS;** KJV alternately ACCOZ. Apoc. forms of HAKKOZ.

**ACCURSED.** Under a curse. *See also* ANATHEMA; BLESSINGS AND CURSINGS; BLASPHEMY; DEVOTED; EXCOMMUNICATION. For its use in an oath or vow, the violation of which would bring a curse, *see also* OATH.

**1. In the OT.** The noun חרם, frequently translated "accursed" or "accursed thing" in the KJV (e.g., Josh. 6:17-18; 7:1, 11-13, 15; 22:20; I Chr. 2:7), is in the RSV usually rendered "devoted" or "devoted thing" (but cf. Deut. 7:26, where the RSV uses "accursed" and the KJV "a cursed thing"). Other words rendered "accursed" in the OT are forms of the roots קלל (Deut. 21:23; Isa. 65:20), ארר (Ps. 119: 21), and זעם (Mic. 6:10). M. H. POPE

**2. In the NT.** The words so translated in the NT are usually forms or derivatives of ἀρά, ἀράομαι, or ἀνάθεμα (originally a dialectical variation of ἀνάθημα, a "votive offering," but in late Judaism and the NT always meaning "accursed"; cf. Rom. 9:3; I Cor. 12: 3; 16:22; Gal. 1:8-9). The Greek ἀρά, ἀράομαι, originally meant "prayer" and "pray" respectively, but as early as Homer are found with a bad connotation— i.e., prayer for evil upon someone, hence an imprecation or curse. Compound forms with ἐπί and κατά particularly carry this force. The meaning "accursed" or "under a curse" is found for ἐπάρατος in John 7: 49, for κατάρατος twice in the LXX (II Macc. 12: 35; IV Macc. 4:5), for ἐπικατάρατος frequently in the LXX (e.g., in Num. 5; Deut. 27, where it usually translates a form of ארר) and twice in the NT (Gal. 3:10, 13; cf. Deut. 27:26; 21:23 respectively), and for the noun κατάρα (Hebrew usually קללה), frequently in the OT and in two of its six occurrences in the NT (Gal. 3:10: "under a curse"; II Pet. 2:14: "accursed children"). Verbal forms of καταράομαι occur in Matt. 24:31; Mark 11:21; Luke 6:28; Rom. 12:14; Jas. 3:9.

*Bibliography.* See the bibliography under ANATHEMA.
A. WIKGREN

**ACCUSATION.** KJV translation of αἰτία (RSV CHARGE) in Matt. 27:37; Mark 15:26. *See* INSCRIPTION ON THE CROSS.

**ACCUSER.** *See* SATAN.

**ACELDAMA.** *See* AKELDAMA.

**ACHAB** ā'kăb. Douay Version form of AHAB.

**ACHAIA** ə kā'yə [ἡ Ἀχαία] (Acts 18:12, 27; 19:21; Rom. 15:26; I Cor. 16:15; II Cor. 1:1; 9:2; 11:10; I Thess. 1:7-8). The Roman province which comprised most of ancient Greece S of Macedonia.

See map on following page.

The Achaian land (ἡ Ἀχαιίς) appears in the Homeric poems (*Iliad* I.254; *Odyssey* XI.166; etc.) as the home of the Achaians (οἱ Ἀχαιοί). Herodotus speaks of Achaia as in the vicinity of Thessaly (VII. 173, 196-98), which may have been the oldest home of the Achaians, but he also says that "what is now called Achaia" is in the Peloponnesus (VII.94); and Strabo (VIII.383; cf. Pausanias II.5.6) likewise places the Achaians in the N coastlands of the Peloponnesus. The Achaian League was a confederation of the cities of Achaia, in which CORINTH took a leading part. In 146 B.C. the League was defeated in war by a Roman army under the consul L. Mummius. Pausanias (VII.16.9-10) speaks as if Achaia were made a Roman province at this time, and tells how Greece was assessed to pay tribute; but Plutarch (*Cimon* 2), narrating an event which took place probably in 87 B.C., states that a charge of murder against the city of Chaeronea was tried before the praetor (ὁ στρατηγός) of Macedonia, since "the Romans were not yet sending praetors to Greece." Therefore it is probable that in this period Achaia was largely under Roman control and that the supervision of its affairs was in the hands of the governor of Macedonia.

In the reorganization of the Empire by Augustus in 27 B.C., Achaia was made a senatorial province under a proconsul (ἀνθύπατος) of praetorian rank, appointed annually (Strabo XVII.840). In A.D. 15, Tiberius combined Achaia with Macedonia and Moesia in an imperial province governed by the legate of Moesia (Tac. Ann. I.76.4; 80.1; Dio LVIII. 25.5). In A.D. 44, Claudius made Achaia and Macedonia separate senatorial provinces again (Suetonius *Claudius* XXV.3; Dio LX.24.1). Upon the occasion of his visit to Achaia in A.D. 66 or 67, Nero gave freedom to the entire province (Suetonius *Nero* XXIV.2), but his successor Vespasian made Achaia once more a senatorial province (Suetonius *Vespasian* VIII.4; Pausanias VII.17.4), and it continued in this status until the time of Diocletian.

Although the text in Strabo (XVII.840) upon which our information is based is not entirely clear, the boundaries of the province of Achaia as established by Augustus seem to have extended as far as and to include (μέχρι) Thessaly, Aetolia, Akarnania, and Epirus. Within the province the land was divided into territories belonging to the various cities. The seat of administration was Corinth. At the time of Paul the proconsul of Achaia was GALLIO (Acts 18:12).

*Bibliography.* J. Toepffer and C. G. Brandis, "Achaia," *Pauly-Wissowa*, vol. I (1894), cols. 156-98; J. Keil, "The Greek Provinces: Achaea," *CAH*, XI (1936), 556-65; J. A. O. Larsen, "Roman Greece," in T. Frank, ed., *An Economic Survey of Ancient Rome*, IV (1938), 259-498. J. FINEGAN

**ACHAICUS** ə kā'ə kəs [Ἀχαϊκός]. One of the first Christians at Corinth, mentioned in I Cor. 16:17 and, in some MSS, vs. 15, as being present with Paul in Ephesus when he wrote I Corinthians. STEPHANAS and FORTUNATUS were other Corinthians with him. It is natural to suppose that these three men brought the letter mentioned in I Cor. 7:1 to Paul, and that they were also the bearers of I Corinthians, which

ADRIATIC SEA

MACEDONIA

EPIRUS

THESSALY

AEGEAN SEA

IONIAN SEA

AKARNANIA

AETOLIA

Chaeroneia

ATTICA

ACHAIA

•Athens

Corinth

N

0    50    100 mi.

**ACHAIA**

Jack Finegan

answers the questions raised in it. That they did bear it is claimed for them by the subscription to I Corinthians in the Textus Receptus. It is evident that these men were on good terms with the apostle.

F. W. GINGRICH

**ACHAN** ā'kăn [עָכָן, *see below*]. Alternately: ACHAR ā'kär (I Chr. 2:7). A Judahite who stole forbidden spoil from Jericho and, together with his family, was stoned (Josh. 7:1, 18-20, 24; 22:20). The presence of very serious sin in the Israelite community was brought to light when Joshua inquired of God the reason for Israel's lack of military success against the men of Ai. The reason disclosed was that spoil from captured Jericho, which had been DEVOTED or reserved exclusively for God, had been stolen by an Israelite and concealed in the camp. The culpability of Achan was detected by lot. When accused, he confessed his guilt and, together with the "devoted things," his family, and his property, was stoned in the valley of Achor ("trouble").

This story stands as vivid evidence of the early Israelite conception of the solidarity of the community. The guilt of one threatened the security of all, and the requisite penalty for such guilt must be inflicted upon Achan's total sphere of family and possessions. Yet the account is concerned to allow Achan to make a quite personal confession of his guilt and of the hidden motivation behind it: "Of a truth I have sinned against Yahweh God of Israel, and this is what I did: when I saw . . . , then I coveted" (Josh. 7:20-21).

The name Achan may be a euphemistic alteration of ACHAR, "man of trouble." The LXX reading, Αχαρ (cf. I Chr. 2:7), and the name of the site of Achan's stoning, "valley of Achor," lend support to the suggestion.

Bibliography. L. Koehler, "Hebräische Etymologien," *JBL*, LIX (1940), 38-39; W. Eichrodt, *Theologie des ATs*, III (2nd ed., 1948), 64, 110.      R. F. JOHNSON

**ACHAZ.** KJV NT form of AHAZ.

**ACHBOR** ăk′bôr [עכבור, mouse]. **1.** The father of Baal-hanan king of Edom (Gen. 36:38-39; I Chr. 1:49).

**2.** One of Josiah's ministers commanded to consult the Lord concerning the newly discovered law book (II Kings 22:12, 14); perhaps also the father of Elnathan, Jehoiakim's courtier (Jer. 26:22; 36:12).

*Bibliography.* W. F. Albright, *JBL*, LI (1932), 79-80.

J. M. WARD

**ACHIACHARUS.** *See* AHIKAR.

**ACHIAS.** KJV Apoc. form of AHIJAH.

**ACHIM** ā′kĭm [′Αχίμ] (Matt. 1:14). An ancestor of Jesus.

**ACHIMELECH** ə kĭm′ə lĕk. Douay Version form of AHIMELECH.

**ACHIOR** ā′kĭ ôr [′Αχιώρ=אחיאור, brother of light]. The Ammonite commander who warned Holofernes that God would defend the Israelites. When Judith showed him the head of Holofernes, Achior "believed firmly in God" (Jth. 14:10; cf. 5:5 ff; 6:1 ff; 14:6-9).

J. C. SWAIM

**ACHISH** ā′kĭsh [אכיש; Hurrian *akk sha(rur)*, the king gives]. The king of Gath with whom David found refuge. Of the two accounts of David's arrival at Gath, I Sam. 21:10-15—H 21:11-16 is probably the work of a later writer who thought ch. 27 cast doubt on David's patriotism. In the earlier account David appears as the vassal of Achish. After he had proved himself loyal to the Philistines, Achish granted him the border town of Ziklag (placing I Sam. 27:5-6 after vs. 12) and appointed him chief of his bodyguard (28:2). So sure was Achish of David's loyalty that he took David and his troops with him when he marched against Saul at GILBOA (ch. 29). It was doubtless as vassal of Achish that David began his rule at Hebron.

The reference to Achish in I Kings 2:39-40 is probably a gloss (cf. I Sam. 27:2). If he were still ruler of Gath in the time of Solomon, his reign would have been abnormally long.

The title of Ps. 34 refers to the incident in I Sam. 21:10-15—H 21:11-16, though the name Abimelech appears rather than Achish.

*Bibliography.* A. Bertholet, *Die Stellung der Israeliten und der Juden zu den Fremden* (1896), pp. 37-38. R. W. CORNEY

**ACHITOB.** KJV Apoc. form of AHITUB.

**ACHMETHA.** KJV form of ECBATANA.

*****ACHOR** ā′kôr [עכור, trouble]. A valley which formed a portion of the N boundary of Judah (Josh. 15:7); identified with the modern el-Buqe′ah ("the valley plain") SW of Jericho. Achor was the valley "up to" which Joshua took Achan, his family, and his goods to be judged and executed for transgressing the command to take no booty from Jericho (Josh. 7:24, 26).

"Achor" is also used figuratively in an eschatologi-

cal sense in Isa. 65:10; Hos. 2:15. A dry desert valley will be fruitful and provide pasturage for flocks when Israel is restored.

*Bibliography.* M. Noth, "Das Deutsche Evangelische Institut für Altertumswissenschaft des Heiligen Landes. Lehrkursus 1954," *ZDPV*, 71 (1955), 1-59; F. M. Cross and J. T. Milik, "Explorations in the Judaean Buqê′ah," *BASOR*, 142 (1956), 5-17. V. R. GOLD

**ACHSAH** ăk′sə [עכסה, *from* עכם, bangle, ankle ornament]. The daughter of Caleb. Caleb awarded her to Othniel, his brother or nephew, for the feat of capturing Debir (Tell Beit Mirsim, formerly called Kiriath-sepher). A further gift of springs of water in the Negeb was later added, as her dowry (Josh. 15: 16-19 = Judg. 1:12-13; I Chr. 2:49).

D. HARVEY

**ACHSHAPH** ăk′shăf [אכשף]. A border town in the territory of Asher (Josh. 19:25), perhaps located at Tell Kisan, a Bronze Age site approximately six miles SE of Acco, or at et-Tell *ca.* six miles NE of Acco, though the former is more probable. Achshaph was an old town when the Israelites entered Palestine under Joshua. It is mentioned in the Egyptian Execration Texts (*ca.* nineteenth-eighteenth centuries B.C.), in the Karnak list of towns conquered by Thut-mose III (1490-1435 B.C.), in the Tell el-Amarna Letters (*ca.* fourteenth century B.C.), and in Papyrus Anastasi, an Egyptian letter of the late thirteenth century. The Canaanite town was destroyed after its king, who joined a confederacy against Joshua, suffered defeat (Josh. 11:1; 12:20).

*Bibliography.* J. Garstang, *The Foundations of Bible History* (1931), pp. 98-99, 354; W. F. Albright, *The Vocalization of the Egyptian Syllabic Orthography* (1934), IIIA:18; F.-M. Abel, *Géographie de la Palestine*, II (1938), 237.

G. W. VAN BEEK

*****ACHZIB** ăk′zĭb [אכזיב]. **1.** A town on the border of the Shephelah and central Judah, according to Josh. 15:44 near Mareshah, perhaps identical with CHEZIB (Gen. 38:5). Its name, which is formed from the root כזב, "to lie," is used as a pun in Mic. 1:14:

The houses of Achzib [′akhzîbh] shall be a deceitful
  thing [′akhzābh]
to the kings of Israel.

The place is mentioned by Eusebius (Onom. 172) as Χαοβί, near Adullam, which corresponds to the now accepted identification with Tell el-Beida, three miles W of Adullam. A. Saarisalo found pottery fragments of the Israelite period on the tell (although he identifies the place with Moresheth-gath).

*Bibliography.* A. Saarisalo, *JPOS*, vol. XI (1931), no. 2, p. 98; K. Elliger, *ZDPV*, 57 (1934), 121-24; F.-M. Abel, *Géographie de la Palestine*, II (1938), 237.

**2.** A town in Galilee, on the seashore, near the border of Lebanon (ancient Phoenicia). The identification with modern ez-Zib, nine miles N of Acre, is quite certain.

According to Josh. 19:29, the town bordered on the territory of Asher, while Judg. 1:31 implies that it was assigned to that tribe. Sennacherib of Assyria mentions the conquest of the walled city Akzibi. The name occurs both as Achzib and as Chezib in Talmudic sources and as Ecdippa in Josephus and other Greek sources. In Crusader times it was known as Casal Imbert.

The ruins are at present covered by modern houses and thus cannot be excavated. Two extensive cemeteries consisting of over seventy tombs were excavated in 1941-42 by I. Ben-Dor and N. Makhouly of the Department of Antiquities of the Government of Palestine. The rock-cut tombs consist of a shaft with narrow stairs on one side and of one or more chambers. A quantity of pottery, mainly Phoenician, figurines, jewelry, and scarabs were recovered. They date mostly from the eighth-sixth centuries B.C. Also, four funerary inscriptions in Phoenicio-Hebrew characters, one reading לעבדשמש ("belonging to Ebed-shemesh") and another לעמא הנסך ("belonging to Ama, the metal founder"), were found. Some more tombs were excavated in 1958 by M. Praussnitz of the Department of Antiquities of the State of Israel.

*Bibliography.* D. D. Luckenbill, *Ancient Records of Assyria and Babylonia*, II (1927), 119; F.-M. Abel, *Géographie de la Palestine*, II (1938), 237. I. BEN-DOR

**ACIPHA.** KJV Apoc. form of HAKUPHA.

**ACITHO.** KJV Apoc. alternate form of AHITUB.

**ACRA** ăk′rə [ἄκρα, height *or* citadel]. *See* JERUSALEM.

**ACRABA** ăk′rə bə [Ἐγρεβήλ] (Jth. 7:18); KJV EKREBEL ĕk′rə bəl. A place "near CHUSI beside the brook MOCHMUR." It is probably the modern Akrabeh, some twenty-five miles N of Jerusalem in the hill country rising from the Jordan, within a few miles of Sychar's well. N. TURNER

**ACRE.** *See* WEIGHTS AND MEASURES § E3.

**ACROSTIC** ə krôs′tĭk, —krŏs—. Poetic composition in which the first letters of successive lines or strophes in the original language appear in alphabetical order. Fig. ACR 3.

---

A fish (in Greek, ΙΧΘΥΣ)

I = Ἰησοῦς = Jesus
X = Χριστός = Christ
Θ = Θεοῦ = God's
Υ = Ὑιός = Son
Σ = Σωτήρ = Savior

---

3. The Greek acrostic for "fish," which means: "Jesus Christ, God's Son, Savior." The inscribed fish, with such a hidden meaning, was frequently found in the catacombs of the early Christians.

Complete or nearly complete acrostics are found in Pss. 9–10; 25; 34; 37; 111; 112; 119 (each letter appears eight times in successive lines); 145; Prov. 31:10-31; Lam. 1–4 (*see* LAMENTATIONS, BOOK OF,

§ 1). Nah. 1:2-8 is a mutilated acrostic. There are no NT specimens.

Possible reasons for use of the acrostic form were belief in the magical power of letters (*see* ALPHABET; MAGIC), pedagogic practice in spelling and style (*see* EDUCATION; SCRIBE), aid to memory in recitation, and completeness in the expression of an idea or emotion. The latter two theories best suit the biblical examples.

*Bibliography.* M. Löhr, "Alphabetische und alphabetisierende Lieder im AT," *ZAW*, XXV (1905), 173-98; F. Dornseiff, *Das Alphabet in Mystik und Magie* (1922); P. A. Munch, "Die alphabetische Akrostichie in der jüdischen Psalmendichtung," *ZDMG*, XC (1936), 703-10; N. K. Gottwald, *Studies in the Book of Lamentations* (1954), ch. 1: "The Acrostic Form." N. K. GOTTWALD

**ACTS, APOCRYPHAL.** A long series of romances which attempt to provide the information missing in the canonical book of Acts as to the subsequent doings of the several apostles. The emphasis upon doctrine (often regarded as heretical) in the earlier of these Acts becomes less conspicuous in the later imitations, which are frankly tales of adventure in foreign lands, wonder-working by the several heroes, and detailed records of their martyrdoms (often circulated separately). The five principal writings of this sort, in the probable order of composition, are: Acts of John, Acts of Paul, Acts of Peter, Acts of Andrew, and Acts of Thomas. For a list of these and other Acts treated in separate articles in this dictionary, *see* APOCRYPHA, NT. M. S. ENSLIN

*****ACTS OF THE APOSTLES.** The fifth book in the NT. It appropriately follows the four gospels, for its narrative continues the story from where they end. Indeed, it was originally written as a sequel to one of the gospels, the Gospel "According to Luke," and refers to this "first book" in its opening words. It is a narrative, and it ends the group of five narratives —the type of literature with which the NT, like the OT, opens. Since it is unique in the period it covers —the generation following the resurrection of Jesus —it is an invaluable source for a knowledge of the apostolic age. The apocryphal Acts (*see* APOCRYPHA, NT) of individual apostles are of later date, and add little trustworthy information to the NT Acts, which, indeed, they seem to supplement rather than to parallel or to imitate.

1. Title
2. Scope
3. The story
4. Chronology and arrangement
5. Omissions
6. The materials
   *a.* Episodes
   *b.* Summaries
   *c.* Speeches
   *d.* The message of the speeches
7. Sources
   *a.* Written or oral
   *b.* Greek or Aramaic
   *c.* The itinerary and "we" passages
8. The author's contribution
   *a.* Language
   *b.* Summaries

**1. Title.** The traditional title of the book is sometimes in current English usage shortened to "Acts" or replaced by "book of Acts." The abbreviation occurs also in one of the older Greek MSS. The Greek word means "deeds," and was capable of sundry connotations, either favorable like the accomplishments of an emperor, or unfavorable like the magical tricks of charlatans. The word "apostles" is in the plural, perhaps to contrast this book with the apocryphal works about individuals—the Acts of Paul, the Acts of Peter, etc. But "the apostles" as a closed group are not all reported on, nor do they include all persons who figure in the story—e.g., Stephen and Philip (Acts 6–8), since the latter is to be distinguished from the apostle of that name (*see* PHILIP 7).

But the title of this book is no more primitive than are the titles of the other books in the NT, particularly since Acts is not an independent writing but, as already suggested, merely a second volume of a larger

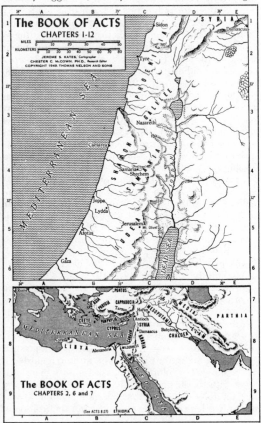

The BOOK OF ACTS
CHAPTERS 1-12

The BOOK OF ACTS
CHAPTERS 2, 6 and 7

work. If that larger work had a name, it is now lost. The term "Luke-Acts" is a quite recent formulation. Even the traditional title of Acts, unlike the titles of other NT books, does not attempt to name an author. Both volumes mention in the text itself (Luke 1:3; Acts 1:1), in accordance with ancient practice, the person to whom they were dedicated—THEOPHILUS.

**2. Scope.** The narrative begins with an account of Jesus' intercourse with his disciples after his resurrection. This is partly parallel to and partly independent of the same writer's account in Luke 24. But in Acts the intercourse is definitely concluded after some forty days by the ascension of Jesus, while Pentecost almost at once fulfils the promise which Jesus had made of the endowment with the Holy Spirit (Acts 1:8; cf. Luke 24:49). These events mark the real outset of the story, and their influence continues throughout the volume.

The narratives follow in a roughly chronological sequence and close at what seems to the modern reader a somewhat strange juncture, though not accidental to the author. The last verses tell how Paul, who had passed through various vicissitudes of legal procedure as well as an eventful journey from Palestine to Rome, spent a two-year period in custody, but not incommunicado, at Rome. The interval of time covered by the whole book seems to represent about three decades.

It would be possible, and indeed it is customary, to divide this and other books of the NT into sections. Conscious organization of this sort may not have been in the ancient author's mind. He may have wished to give an impression of unity and continuity, and what natural divisions appear may be due merely to the nature of the material available to him. Paragraphing is not part of the original form of the writings; and the chapter divisions (like the verses), no matter how convenient for modern reference, are to be used only for this convenience and without implication that these or other divisions really divide. If we were to superimpose upon the book an analytical outline in the modern manner, it might run like this:

   I. Early episodes in the Jerusalem church, 1:1–5:42
     A. Jesus' farewell and ascension, 1:1-11
     B. The first associates and the replacement for Judas, 1:12-26
     C. Pentecost and after, ch. 2
     D. A cure in Jesus' name and its sequel, 3:1-4:31
     E. The sharing of property, 4:32-5:11
     F. More cures and further arrest of the apostles, 5:12-42
   II. An early martyr and some notable conversions, 6:1-9:31
     A. The committee of seven, 6:1-7
     B. Stephen's controversy and death, 6:8-8:1
     C. Philip with the Samaritans and with an Ethiopian, 8:1-40
     D. Saul converted, 9:1-31
  III. Peter and the beginnings of Gentile conversions, 9:32–12:25
     A. Peter at Lydda and Joppa, 9:32-43
     B. Peter at Caesarea with Cornelius and reporting at Jerusalem, 10:1-11:18

C. Antioch, 11:19-30
D. Herod (Agrippa) as persecutor, 12:1-25
IV. Paul (Saul) and more Gentile conversions, 13:1-16:5
   A. To Cyprus with Barnabas, 13:1-12
   B. Antioch of Pisidia, 13:13-52
   C. Iconium, Lystra, and Derbe, ch. 14
   D. A council at Jerusalem, 15:1-29
   E. Transmitting its decisions, 15:30-16:5
V. Paul's mission extended to Macedonia, Achaia, Asia, 16:6-19:41
   A. To Philippi, 16:6-40
   B. Thessalonica to Athens, ch. 17
   C. Corinth, 18:1-17
   D. Ephesus, 18:18-19:41
VI. Paul's return both W and E, 20:1-21:26
   A. Macedonia and Achaia, 20:1-4
   B. Journey to Jerusalem and welcome there, 20:5-21:26 (visit at Miletus with Ephesian elders, 20:17-38)
VII. Paul in custody of the Roman authorities, 21:27-28:31
   A. Arrested in the temple, 21:27-36
   B. Hearings in Jerusalem, 21:37-23:11
   C. Transferred to Caesarea and hearings there, 23:12-26:32
   D. Voyage and shipwreck, ch. 27
   E. Malta, and on to Italy, 28:1-16
   F. Rome, 28:17-31

**3. The story.** It may be more useful to summarize the story as it unfolds, or rather the impression it makes of the portion of history it chooses to relate.

It begins with the friends of Jesus who had come up with him from Galilee to Jerusalem. It was there (not in Galilee) that he appeared to them after he had risen from the dead, until forty days later at the Mount of Olives, one of their earlier places of rendezvous, he was lifted up to heaven out of their sight (*see* RESURRECTION; ASCENSION). Two promises were left to them: one, that he would return in like manner from heaven; the other, that he would send the Holy Spirit upon them. The latter was fulfilled within a very few days, upon the Jewish festival called PENTECOST. The group amounted to about 120 persons, including the Twelve, among whom was Matthias, a newly elected successor to Judas; the women, presumably those who had attended in his entourage before; and of his own family, his mother and brothers.

Though both the ascension of Jesus and his gift of the Spirit were thought of as preludes to his return, the latter is told with much more emphasis because the Spirit becomes at once thereafter the energizing force in the group. The Spirit attracts new accessions, enables the apostles to work miracles, and supplies wisdom, courage, and guidance to the spokesmen. The following scenes illustrate this powerful force. The expansion is not so much humanly premeditated as incidental, or thus divinely inspired. Peter did not plan to visit Cornelius, or Philip to intercept the Ethiopian. In spite of, or even because of, criticism or persecution, the leaders are given a good chance to defend or extend their propaganda. Only when we come to the missionary work of Paul have we basis for reading deliberate human planning between the lines. The spread geographically and the

increase numerically are not so to be accounted for. Communities of Christians at Damascus and at Rome and at places in between are mentioned without the author's giving us any indication of how they came into existence. Casual and anonymous must have been many of the processes that fostered the movement. It was not that the leading Christians sought fields to conquer, but that the obscure membership were prepared to drop seed. So at least one must supplement the story actually given us.

The conversion of PAUL is one of the most dramatic events because he had been a vigorous persecutor, and one of the most important because he became such an effective and systematic promoter of the movement. The author is concerned to show thereafter both his vigorous advance and the persistence of his legal battle, once it was quite accidentally precipitated. It finally brought him to Rome, though not in the way that evangelistic campaigns usually achieve their climax.

Quite different is the story of his pioneer missionary work in Cyprus and Galatia (chs. 13-14), in Macedonia and Greece (chs. 16-18), and in the province of Asia (ch. 19). It was centered in major cities of these Roman provinces. He was accompanied by associates and/or assistants, like Barnabas and John Mark or Silas and Timothy, and he engaged in a handicraft for the support of himself and his companions (18:3; 20:34-35). He often made his first appeal at the local Jewish synagogue or place of prayer. Almost always the Jews rebuffed him, or incited hostile action against him. So he used other opportunities for public or private instruction by day or night (20:20, 31). His stay in a single city varied in length from a few weeks to years, according to circumstances. Nothing is said of touring the country around the cities. He planned to revisit old centers, including Jerusalem, and to reach new ones, including Rome itself (19:21-22).

These narratives disclose certain features of the movement. It does not acquire readily fixed names for itself, its teaching, and its members, like our modern terms "Christianity" and "Christian," though the latter is twice introduced in contexts that suggest that it was a nickname applied by others (11:26; 26:28; *see* CHRISTIAN, NAME OF). The message is "the word" of the Lord, only twice "the gospel" (15:7; 20:24), though the corresponding verb "evangelize" occurs more often, and once even the noun of agent, "evangelist" (21:8). For the rank and file are used "disciples" and "saints"—in the Pauline, not the modern, sense—or such phrases as "those who believed." Another noteworthy expression is found in "the way of the Lord [or of God]" (18:25, 26) or simply "the Way" (9:2; 19:9, 23; 24:22). "The church" is used in the wider collective sense, as well as of local groups of Christians.

Only in the most incipient and unsystematic manner does Acts disclose to us any organization and rules of the church. After all, it was a party (not a sect) in Judaism and need not have widely distinguished itself from the parent body. The author regarded it as the natural development out of Judaism in accordance with the distinctly Christian events which God had foretold and hence had made inevitable. It was not only a legitimate development but the fruition of

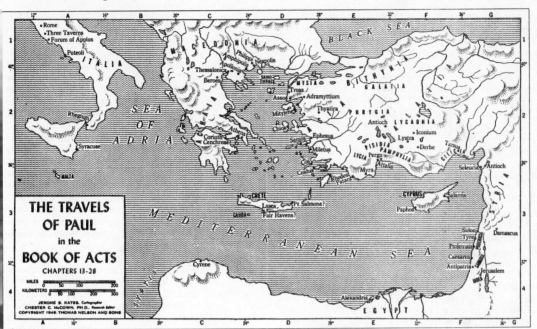

THE TRAVELS
OF PAUL
in the
BOOK OF ACTS
CHAPTERS 13-28

MILES
0    50    100    200
KILOMETERS
0    50   100   200    300

JEROME B. KATES, Cartographer
CHESTER C. McCOWN, PH.D., Research Editor
COPYRIGHT 1949, THOMAS NELSON AND SONS

God's plan. Its leaders were the apostles and/or elders. Its spokesmen were prophets and teachers (13:1). But there was also the group of the rank and file whose voice was effective when choices or decisions had to be made (1:23-26; 6:5; 15:22—"the whole church"). There was a group of elders at Jerusalem, as well as (even after others were scattered —8:1) a group of apostles. To this center innovations elsewhere were referred (8:14; 9:26-27; 11:1; 15:2). Ultimately there emerged as a leader of that church James, presumably the brother of Jesus (12:17; 15:13; 21:18), though he in no instance exercised sole authority, any more than Paul did in his churches. His introduction is as abrupt as is the exit of Peter from the narrative. In some of the other churches elders are actually mentioned (14:23 in the cities of Galatia; 20:17 at Ephesus). Of the more spontaneous leadership, we have prophets and teachers, as well as apostles. Prophets at Antioch or Caesarea are mentioned several times (11:27 ff; 13:1; 15:32). They originate from Jerusalem, as did Philip, who had four unmarried daughters who prophesied (21:9).

Just as these references do not presuppose a rigid and uniform church organization, so the book gives us no impression of uniform standards or procedures about membership or worship. The adherents in Jerusalem assembled at the temple, or in their homes, while they attended the synagogues as well. Their meetings were evidently frequent, not merely weekly. Like the rest of the NT, Acts fails to supply early evidence that meetings were held especially on Sundays. Bread is broken, but not necessarily as anything other than the usual meal. There is prayer at the gatherings and presumably extempore speaking— i.e., "preaching or prophesying." Converts are expected to repent of their past offenses and to receive the Holy Spirit. Accompanying the latter is sometimes baptism with water and/or sometimes the laying on of hands, and on at least two epoch-making

occasions (2:4; 10:46) speaking with tongues (see TONGUES, GIFT OF). There are puzzling references to the gospel contrast between baptism with water, like John's, and baptism with the Spirit (1:5; 11:16), and also evidence of the latter's accompanying as well as succeeding the former (18:25; 19:16), in the second case, associated with laying on of hands, speaking with tongues, and prophesying. Nothing is said of prior systematic instruction of converts nor of subsequent discipline, nor indeed of the private life of the convert, or of his ethical standards.

The chief exception is the group of passages suggesting mutual care and sharing, at least for those in need at Jerusalem. This took the form of the selling of pieces of real estate by those who had it to spare and of their entrusting the proceeds to the apostles to distribute to the needy (4:34-5:11; cf. 2:44-45; Luke 8:3). Evidently many of these were widows, to whom distribution was made daily (6:1), though whether in cash or in kind is not clear. Their care was transferred to a committee of seven (6:1-6). From farther afield, financial relief for the poor among the Judean believers was brought to their elders at the time of the famine under Claudius by Barnabas and Saul (Paul) from Antioch of Syria (11:27-30). But the still more elaborate and widespread collection for a like purpose, planned by Paul from Galatia, Macedonia, and Achaia, and perhaps Asia, according to accounts in his letters (Rom. 15:25-31; I Cor. 16:1-4; II Cor. 8-9; see OFFERING FOR THE SAINTS), is not separately reported in Acts (unless obscurely in 20:4; 24:17). We need scarcely doubt that Acts expects us to infer that reciprocal care and prayerful concern was felt generally by the believers for one another and especially for their leaders (4:23-31; 8:2; 9:25; 12:12-17; etc.).

From early in the book a wide geographical outlook is hinted (1:8: "end of the earth"; 2:5: "every nation under heaven"; 2:9-11), though the beginning is definitely at Jerusalem. Even Galilee is not the scene of Christ's appearances, either in Luke or in Acts (contrast Mark, Matthew, John 21, and especially Luke 24:6 with Mark 16:7). It is scarcely mentioned in the story of the church (9:31). The nucleus at the beginning is not only at Jerusalem but is also, naturally enough, exclusively Jewish. Perhaps the book is more concerned to show how the latter limitation is overcome. This is particularly true in the case of the Samaritan converts, and of Cornelius the Roman centurion at Caesarea, of the Gentile converts at Antioch (11:20), and of the converts of Paul and Barnabas in Cyprus and Asia Minor. In each case the development is consciously reviewed and approved (8:14; 11:1-18, 22; 15:1-29). Whether sheer Gentiles, apart from Jews and proselytes, are included among the foreigners living in Jerusalem and present at Pentecost, or in the Ethiopian royal minister, a visitor to Jerusalem (8:27), or among the HELLENISTS (6:1), is not clear; at least the fact is not similarly underscored. Certainly outside Jerusalem there are frequent references in the book of Acts to "God fearers" or "God worshipers," who must be understood to be Gentiles already loosely attached to Judaism though not full proselytes. They were therefore more ripe for receiving the Christian message than either the strict Jews or the completely uninitiated Gentiles. They had existed in every city for some time (15:21). They attended the synagogue services, and had presumably been attracted by the monotheism, or the ethical idealism, of Judaism. The book of Acts is, compared with much ancient writing of history, quite modern in the author's awareness of transition or development, geographical, numerical, and perhaps linguistic; but at no point is he more self-conscious than in emphasizing the transition from Jewish to Gentile Christianity. The latter was an innovation, but it occurred according to scripture (15:16-17; 22:21; 26:16-18), under the guidance of God, and with the approval of the leadership of the church. Peter had anticipated in principle this characteristic of Paul's mission (chs. 10-11; 15:7, 14). It was further justified by the general rejection of the gospel by the Jews (28:25-28).

**4. Chronology and arrangement.** The author was little concerned with chronology. References to events that would be datable to his first readers or to us are not included usually for the purpose of recording chronology (contrast Luke 3:1-2 and the discussion of it in § 10*b below*)—e.g., to Jewish feasts and fasts, or to public or political events. He is aware of the political characters, Jewish or Roman, and of the imperial, regional, and municipal governments, but they are part of his background and local color. Some scattered events that he mentions we may attempt to date from secular history, though not always with assurance (*see* CHRONOLOGY OF THE NT). The difficulty and frequent uncertainty of dates in ancient history are scarcely appreciated by the layman in this field.

Here are some events mentioned in Acts: the famine in Palestine (11:28); the death of Herod—i.e., Herod Agrippa I (12:23); the proconsulship in Cyprus of Sergius Paulus (13:7); the expulsion of Jews from Rome under the Emperor Claudius (18:2); the proconsulship in Achaia of (L. Junius) Gallio (18:12); the end of the procuratorship of (Antonius)

Felix and the beginning of that of Porcius Festus (24:27).

Another class of references in Acts is to the duration of certain situations. These are often brief and vague. Among the more definite are: "forty days" (1:3; but "many days" in 13:31); "a year and six months" (Corinth; 18:11); "three months" and "two years" (Ephesus; 19:8, 10; cf. "three years" in 20:31); "two years" (Caesarea; 24:27); "two whole years" (Rome; 28:30).

The author evidently was fully aware of sequence in the latter part of Acts, since he is pursuing the career of Paul, but in the earlier part he returns to events already mentioned—e.g., 8:1-2=11:19-20; 11:30=12:25. There is therefore less certainty of time sequence here.

In fact, the arrangement of Acts, like that of the gospels, suggests that other considerations than mere chronology have affected the grouping. Some of the grouping is about persons—e.g., the committee of seven and particularly Stephen and Philip (chs. 6-8), a later collection of episodes about Peter (9:32-11:18; 12:1-17), and finally, after earlier notices (at 7:58; 8:1, 3; 9:4-30), about Saul (Paul) in chs. 13-28. Peter assumes a leading place in much of the earlier part of the book, and it has been suggested that in several details the author is conscious of parallelism between Peter and Paul. Brief examples of topical arrangement also seem to occur.

There is a possibility, too, that the author is definitely proceeding along geographical lines. Acts 1:8 seems to propose an expanding program, which the sequel fully justifies. Paul's travels, providing as they do both time sequence and geographical sequence, are reported in such a way often as to pass lightly over his return to old scenes of his labors, or the problems arising in them (contrast the contents of many of his letters), and to move forward to new areas of conquest (an attitude also found occasionally in his own letters). The same writer's gospel also emphasizes the life of Jesus in a kind of progression (especially between chs. 9 and 18) and (to revert to the earlier point) indicates a parallelism of a kind between the birth of Jesus and that of John the Baptist and between events in the life of Jesus and some features in the lives of the characters in Acts.

**5. Omissions.** Quite as striking as what the author includes in the book is what he omits. He must have known that he was leaving much out, though not always what the events were. His omissions, like his inclusions, may be deliberate choices due to his interests, but they may also be due to the limited extent of his knowledge from the sources available to him when he wrote. The modern reader has few additional sources, and he may not share exactly the author's tastes. Hence he is unjustly critical of the author's omissions. They sometimes seem surprising. Why do we hear nothing individual about any of the TWELVE except Peter and to a slight extent John, James, and Judas? Or of any of the SEVEN except Philip and Stephen? Or of any of the five leaders at Antioch (13:1) except Barnabas and Saul? And why for the two principal characters in the book is the final reference so tantalizingly inconclusive (Peter, 12:17; 15:7 ff; Paul, 28:30-31)? Many minor persons and situations are left hanging, it seems.

In both contents and arrangement our main extant parallels are the biographical data found here and there in the letters of Paul. In spite of the relatively full outline of Paul's life given in Acts, the major part of the many vicissitudes listed in II Cor. 11:23-33 are unmentioned and unhinted in Acts up to the point when Paul was writing—the exceptions being his escape from Damascus and a stoning and one beating with rods. Many of the references to Paul's pre-Christian life in Acts are reminiscences in his speeches, just as in his letters.

The chronology of Paul's life parallel to that in Acts is deduced with difficulty from his letters. Such reminiscences as II Cor. 12:1-4; Gal. 1-2 (each of which has a reference to fourteen years), raise difficult problems of harmonizing with Acts (see CHRONOLOGY OF THE NT). If harmonizing is at any point impossible, Acts, in the nature of the case, will have to yield the preference to the firsthand words of Paul himself. Particularly in the matter of the four visits of Paul to Jerusalem after his conversion, in Acts 9:26-30; 11:30 (12:25); 15:1-29; 21:15 ff, some duplication or confusion may be suspected.

See map "The Letter to the Galatians and the Book of Acts" under GALATIANS, LETTER TO THE.

6. The materials. a. Episodes. The information offered in the early part of Acts consists of detached episodes. In this it resembles the episodes in the life of Jesus, such as healings, discussions with the authorities, parables and other teachings, interviews with individuals. The story of the Ascension and that of Pentecost are unique, though the former has some points of likeness to the gospel story of the Transfiguration. In general the narrative units are complete in themselves, and each has its own meaning. Running through them is the belief that God has revealed his power and guidance to the ongoing spread of Christianity. This he shows by the frustration of opposition and the punishment of opposers (even to death: 12:23), quite as much as by endowing adherents of the movement with the Holy Spirit, leading to miraculous power and courage (again even to death: 7:54-60). Thus the few estimates of numbers of Jewish believers in Palestine—120 (1:15); 3,000 (2:41); and 5,000 ("men"; 4:4); and more generally later, many thousands (21:20; lit. "many tens of thousands"), indicate numerical success quite as much as the geographical extension. Many of the separate stories were preserved for precisely this demonstration of the Spirit and of power.

This kind of material has had its history, much like some of the material in the gospels (see FORM CRITICISM), a history which has reduced the information to what was needed to make the episode clear. Dating is not attempted, but more than in the gospels the personal names of participants are at times retained. Thus the narrative passes on from item to item and gives a feeling of the march of events.

b. Summaries. The interstices between the episodes are sometimes filled with brief statements of a summary character. They indicate that single events of the type described were multiplied at other times and places—e.g., gifts of money from real estate sold (4:34-35; cf. 4:36–5:11); signs and wonders (5:12-16); preaching (5:42; 8:25); sufferings. Most frequently they indicate that the word of God increased and the converts were multiplied (e.g., 6:7; 9:31; 12:24), or something to that effect. They betray almost as consciously as the colophons in John 20:30; 21:25 the editor's awareness of omissions mentioned above, and they turn into a more flowing narrative what would otherwise be mere unconnected fragments. They are less necessary and, indeed, less frequent in the later part of the book, which derives its character from a continuous following of Paul on his travels, though even here a single episode is sometimes extended to a longer summary in similar fashion. But they acquire a more local or personal character—e.g., 19:8-10, 20; 28:30-31.

c. Speeches. Another feature of the contents of Acts, a more extensive and more important one, is the speeches addressed by the actors to a company of persons on a formal or impromptu occasion. These are to be distinguished from the dialogues incident to a narrative situation. They differ also from the longer collections of the sayings of Jesus, which in Matthew, and to a lesser extent in the other gospels, give an impression of continuous address. The discourses in John, though enlivened by interruption, offer perhaps the nearest parallel in composition.

These speeches occupy a substantial proportion of the book of Acts, between one third and one quarter. Among the most extended are those of Peter at Pentecost (2:14 ff); to the people in Solomon's Portico (3:12 ff); before the Sanhedrin (4:8 ff); at the house of Cornelius (10:34 ff); to the Jewish Christians at Jerusalem (11:5 ff). The speech of Stephen to his accusers (7:2 ff) is the longest of all. At a council in Jerusalem speeches are reported from both Peter (15:7-11) and James (15:13-21). The speeches of Paul are the most numerous and the most varied. At the end they are all defenses at various hearings; two of these are based on a rehearsal of his experience of conversion (22:3 ff; 26:2 ff), but there is also 24:10 ff. Earlier they include somewhat extended addresses to Jews at Antioch of Pisidia (13:16 ff); to Gentiles at Athens (17:22 ff); and to the Christian elders from Ephesus at Miletus (20:18 ff).

The above is not a complete list. Nor are we to suppose that the text as given is intended to represent more than part of what would be said on such an occasion. There is an effective injection of the speech into the narrative and often an equally effective suggestion of interruption just before the end of the speech. Sometimes we are surprised that the speech repeats what has already been said in narrative form, and sometimes we are equally surprised at items not already mentioned in the narrative but first disclosed in the course of the speech.

In any case, the speeches serve a useful purpose. They indicate the content of the movement—i.e., its ideas and claims. Without them the reader would have to depend on other writings; and except for his own first volume, there is no evidence that either the author or his readers relied on knowledge of other books, not even the letters of Paul. The gospel that the apostles preached is different from what Jesus had emphasized. Hence the author of Luke-Acts needed to indicate the former here, as he had indicated the latter in the preceding volume. The speeches interpret the narrative much as the chorus does in a Greek tragedy. They explain to the reader, quite as much as to any more immediate audience, what issues are involved, what ideas are challenged, what data need the emphasis of repetition. That they do repeat is quite evident to any careful reader. They repeat what the narratives have told, and they repeat what the Christian missionaries used as their message (*see* PREACHING). From the speeches alone in Acts the theologian finds matter for his interest. Otherwise the book belongs chiefly to the historian. Since in Christian history the theologian has tended to take precedence over the historian, the speeches in Acts have assumed a special familiarity and importance. Neither the personalities of the speakers nor the variation in their messages is the concern of the writer who reports them or, indeed, of the proper reader of them, but their total impact has been influential out of proportion to their actual scope in the book. This interest in them is shown by the fact that even the first Christians who quote much from Acts, quote most often and most extensively the speeches.

*d. The message of the speeches.* In view of the importance of the speeches the apostolic message as deduced from them may well be briefly summarized:

The preaching of repentance by Jesus following John's ministry, though interrupted by the Crucifixion, was vindicated by God's raising him from the dead. This RESURRECTION points as a divinely wrought miracle also to the future judgment for which Jesus is to return. Therefore, bearing witness to the Resurrection involves warning and a continued call to repentance. What has happened has been predicted in scripture, and also what will happen is predicted there. God has overruled the stubbornness of men, but will not sanction further disobedience.

The Jesus whom the disciples preach was designated by God as Lord and Christ (Messiah), or the prophet whose coming Moses and the prophets predicted. The Holy Spirit, who marks the experience of his messengers, also was anticipated. The God who thus vindicates himself for those who may by the Scriptures compare promise with fulfilment has "not left himself without witness" among others than Jews, but the witness is of a different kind—the inward witness of man's search for him and the outward evidence of God's provisions for mankind's welfare. But the evidence of the past and of the present throughout all the speaking in Acts is overshadowed by its futuristic appeal and warning. What their hearers may think about the past is of less importance than what it leads them to do now.

There are emphases and omissions in the context of the apostolic message in Acts which, by contrast with the gospels, with Paul, and with modern theological assumptions, deserve special attention. That Jesus was the Christ is the assertion to those who begin with a known Jesus and try to make out what to do with him. In Acts the role of a Messiah is the point of departure, at least in dealing with Jewish audiences, and the argument undertakes to prove that the expected Messiah was Jesus, rather than the reverse. In the gospels the teaching of Jesus makes explicit what acceptance of the message "Repent, for

the kingdom of heaven is at hand" means in terms of ethical conduct; in Acts the ethical implications are not spelled out in the speeches at all, and are not more than occasionally implied in the behavior of the Christians (*see* § 3 *above*). Paul's letters are in places more like the gospels in this regard, but in their emphasis on the Holy Spirit, Paul's letters and both narrative and speeches in Acts are totally different from the gospels. This could be accounted for by the fact that during Jesus' lifetime the gift of the Spirit was not yet a datum of experience, any more than was the resurrection of Jesus. On the latter also both Paul and the speeches in Acts had reason to dwell as the teaching of Jesus himself had not. Paul's interest in the death of Jesus is well known, though more by the variety than by the uniformity of his interpretation. In Acts it has little significance. It is mentioned, not as a way of God's grace, but as evidence of human sin. With slight exception Acts does not share Paul's emphasis on faith in Christ's death and its benefits in contrast with reliance upon the Law. The OT is treated in Acts for its predictive, not its prescriptive, value. While the author is clear that obedience to its laws is not properly expected of Gentile Christians, he represents the Jewish Christians, including Paul himself, as loyal to its requirements. The author of Acts, both here and in the Third Gospel, is no antilegalist. His Gentile sympathies are not associated with any inherent objection to the Jewish law, or with the discovery, as in Paul, of a substitute for it.

**7. Sources. *a. Written or oral.*** In writing the Preface to Luke-Acts the author indicates that, like writers before him, he has used what could be learned from those who were "eyewitnesses and ministers of the word" (Luke 1:1-4). This probably applies to some or all of Acts, but what he does not tell us is whether his sources were oral or written. This is a question to be answered, if at all, from the character and contents of the final volumes. He mentions earlier writers, and he also mentions what is presumably the oral tradition handed down to him and them.

Now in his gospel large parts almost certainly depend on early writings in Greek (*see* LUKE, GOSPEL OF; SYNOPTIC PROBLEM). This is evidenced by the verbal parallelism in Greek with sections in the Gospel of Mark, and with other sections common not to Mark but to the Gospel of Matthew. It has been natural to conjecture that even where no parallel narrative is extant in other parts of the Gospel of Luke and in parts of Acts, the author followed the same procedure. Whether or not this is so depends on whether prior Greek narratives were available to him here too.

Scholars have naturally given attention to this question. Some have attempted, especially in the first half of Acts, to conjecture, chiefly from slight differences of viewpoint, not one but two or more written sources. Even if no agreement is reached, the probability of some such origin is great.

Two alternatives, or rather prior stages, may also be conjectured. One of these presupposes that, even when collected and written down, the stories in Acts had circulated orally. This is almost certainly true of the Gospel of Luke or of its written sources. Before any of these sections was written down for the first time, it was part of an unwritten tradition. The sections show the marks of such currency, whether included in later collections or in earlier ones. Somewhere behind Luke or Acts the separate episodes existed in men's minds or memories, and when repeated had the earmarks of selection, of reduction, and of emphasis for some purpose. They were individually separate and self-contained. But we simply do not know which ones, as they come to us in Acts, were first arranged by its author and which ones had been gathered in writing by persons before him. In the latter case he may have simply edited, rearranged, and added to these written collections.

*b. Greek or Aramaic.* As with the gospels, so with certain parts of Acts, another question into the underlying wording of the present texts has to do with Aramaic, the language used along with Greek in Palestine at the period, and by some Jews or Christians used probably more than Greek. Paul himself wrote his letters in Greek, but he probably could write as well as speak in Aramaic (Acts 22:2: "Hebrew"). In the case of Peter and of Jesus the proportionate use of Aramaic over Greek may have been greater, and so perhaps in the case of the anonymous first reporters of their words and deeds. How about the first writings based on these reports? On the face of it, nothing prevents our supposing the written stage in the history, and certainly the oral stage, to have begun in Aramaic.

Opinions on this subject vary extensively. On the one side it has been argued that the whole first part of Acts is based upon a lost but coextensive Aramaic composition, which shows through the present Greek text by both overliteral translation and mistranslation. On the other hand, it is supposed that both the book of Acts and any written sources which it used were composed exclusively in Greek. If Semitisms appear, they then are to be attributed to the oral stage of transmission, and are echoes of the original speakers and narrators in Palestine. The last half of the book has fewer such evidences than the first part, and even in the first part some sections have more than others, perhaps owing to their different ancestry. It is, however, not to be forgotten that the final author of both volumes could vary his style and was not incapable of importing, under the influence of the Greek OT which he knew, "Septuagintisms" while composing himself in Greek.

Inconclusive as have been the scholarly debates on the lost sources of the book of Acts, they remind us that no uniform channel of information precedes the book as a whole. Its units have been somehow collected, edited, and combined to provide the present extensive writing. But this writing gives us no certain clues and few uncertain ones about the intervening process. As the author says in his Preface, it has been handed down, or, we should say, passed on. We can only conjecture what selection or alteration occurred in the process, since we have only the end product.

*c. The itinerary and "we" passages.* A degree of continuity, greater than elsewhere, appears in the part of Acts devoted to Paul. Here is detailed in sequence his travel as a missionary in Asia Minor and Europe, and then the course of his experience as a prisoner, beginning with his visit at Jerusalem leading to his arrest and continuing with his several hearings and with his transfer to Caesarea and thence to Rome. The conspicuousness of the geographical details in the former of these two sections has led to the rather inaccurate description of this material as "missionary journeys," though the original author is more aware of prolonged residence in some centers and less conscious of a home base (Antioch of Syria, or Jerusalem) than the term "missionary journeys" implies. In any case, the special nature of this section has suggested that the writer has had access to a continuous written source, which we may call the itinerary source. Though here, as in other parts of the book, there is much in the nature of separate episodes and the inclusion of speeches, one notes as well a great wealth of local detail, and an impression of eyewitness participation conveyed by the intermittent use of the first person plural.

These so-called "we" passages (16:10-17; 20:5-16; 21:1-18; 27:1–28:16) have become a famous crux of NT study. Their style and character do not differ from those of the adjacent sections, where "he" or "they" is employed. It is unlikely that they represent the exact limits of a separate, autobiographical writing; they are too closely associated with the verses that precede and follow them. They may represent the occasional lapses of the author of Acts himself into autobiographical style, in which case they would have precisely the effect of showing that here, and probably in the whole itinerary section, he was not embodying an alien written source. It is possible that in his Preface he had claimed that "for some time past" (RSV)—i.e., in the closing section of his two volumes—he had had firsthand contact (παρηκολουθηκότι) with the events, while elsewhere he had written from report. If, on the other hand, these passages and the whole surrounding material come from a written source, we shall have to assume that this source was autobiographical, written by a companion of Paul; though then too the exchange of pronouns is difficult to account for. The only distinctive trait of the passages is that they are in each case accounts of sea voyages and that the "we" disappears soon after the party has reached the land. They begin without explanation at the point of setting sail; they end in two or three instances with the separate mention of Paul and "us" (16:17; 21:18; 28:16). The peculiar and still-unexplained character of this phenomenon seems to warrant no inference as to either the presence or the absence of a written source.

**8. The author's contribution.** Whatever the form, the language, or the extent of the information that came to the author of Acts, its present form, language, and extent must have been in part his own personal contribution. To distinguish what was traditional and what is editorial is in some ways as difficult as to divide between lost sources.

*a. Language.* Most clearly attributable to the author or editor is the language in which he wrote. We fortunately have available, in the case of Mark and the substantial parts of Luke derived from Mark, evidence of how this same author revised a written source. Here the changes of factual detail are slight, but in wording the later writer has in part paraphrased his source into a less vernacular Greek and with phrasing that we may identify as his own characteristic style. A whole series of terms or turns of phrase found in these parts of his gospel recur in other parts of the work and indicate that if there were sources oral or written, Aramaic or Greek, behind any parts of the book of Acts, they would have been overlaid by the editor's style. It is safe to say that if Luke alone of our gospels had survived, the extent and editorial process in its use of sources, as actually revealed by the parallels in Mark and Matthew, could never have been guessed by us. So in Acts, for which no similar parallels survive, one can be much surer of the editor's influence than of the nature, extent, or wording of the sources.

Alongside the features of the author's style which are widely characteristic and which constantly permeate both volumes must be mentioned what seems almost contradictory—his capacity to vary style. This variety might be attributed to the influence of the sources themselves, but quite possibly it is not due to them. In this case it too must be attributed to the final author and to a sensitiveness which he had for the appropriateness of different expressions for different occasions or different settings. The early chapters of Acts, with their Palestinian setting, differ to this slight degree from the later chapters in the Gentile world. The spelling, even of some proper names of persons and places, varies in accordance perhaps with an unconscious feeling; and the same kind of variation may be suspected in less conspicuous alterations of phrase or idiom. In contrast with the biblical style of the first two chapters of Luke stands the more secular and classical Greek of the scenes in Athens (Acts 17) or elsewhere; and in more general terms a similar contrast occurs, as already noted, between the earlier and the later half of Acts.

*b. Summaries.* Besides the style or wording of the book of Acts some of its substance also may with great probability be assigned to the editor. Here first may be mentioned again the summaries. Assuming that the oral or written tradition was made up most explicitly of individual facts and of separate episodes, these summaries have every appearance of editorial composition, though not necessarily at the last stage of editing. In Luke's Gospel somewhat similar summaries occur. Those in Luke 1:80; 2:40, 52, seem to echo the LXX birth stories of Samson and Samuel; those in Luke 4:14, 37; 7:17, to be due to Mark 1:28. The creation, and especially the repetition, of summaries is thus characteristic of the last stages of editing. Those in Acts have been already listed and their serviceableness noted (§ 6b above).

*c. Speeches.* The speeches reported from sundry individuals on certain occasions also have been noted (§ 6c above) as a significant component in Acts. These may possibly have come to the author through the same channels of information as the accompanying narrative. There is, however, an alternative view of them—namely, that they are the composition of the author himself. In either case the author is responsible for much of their style and wording, but the more extreme alternatives between imaginative composition by the author and mere revising of speeches made available to him are matters of considerable debate. If we look again for illustration at Luke's Gospel, we shall find evidence that the sayings

attributed to Jesus have in many cases been taken over from the same sources as the narrative, and, indeed, with even less freedom of rewording. If, however, we look at the contemporary practice of Greek and Roman historians, we are met with the general agreement of scholars that the speeches are the dramatic elaborations of the writers and have little, if any, contact with words actually spoken on the occasion. Which analogue is applicable to the speeches in Acts?

There are aspects of the speeches which suit either alternative. Insofar as they seem to us, with our limited sources of independent judgment, to be suitable for the occasion, they can be equally well attributed to the author or to the original speakers. Insofar as they present a uniform point of view, and insofar as they show variety in expression, both the consistency and the variation can be in accord with historical facts but can also be due to the common authorship by the editor, whose ability to vary has been already noted. The concordance sometimes claimed between the speeches attributed to Peter, James, and Paul in Acts with the letters in our NT attributed to the same persons respectively is no greater than the concordance between the speech of one of the apostles and the letter of another.

The question cannot be answered by any such objective comparison. The improbability of faithful memory of what was actually said, along with the then recognized and accepted practice for historians to supply words for such occasions, has inclined many scholars to regard the speeches as a major contribution of the author himself. The traditional preservation of the sayings of Jesus may well have been due to unusual circumstances. The actual sayings of Peter or Paul may never have enjoyed like preservation. There is no unusual literary or moral irregularity if we think of the author of Acts as fashioning these speeches. Indeed, there is much about them which coincides with his practice of dramatic variation, of emphasis through repetition, and of indirect information to the reader. For it is the readers rather than the imagined audience to which the speeches seem often primarily addressed, introducing both what the reader has been told before and what he has not. It is quite as possible for such an author as for Paul himself to quote the words of scripture to Jewish audiences, the words of Greek poets to a Greek audience (17:28), and words of Jesus to a Christian audience (20:35). Like other historians, he made some effort to think through what would have been appropriate for the speakers to say.

Like other ancient writers, this author may have expended on his speeches more effort than elsewhere in his work. They were less ready-made for him than was the narrative, and sometimes he used the narrative over again in a speech. They required perhaps conscientious reconstruction of a viewpoint not necessarily quite his own, of a more primitive theology than that of his own time. They deserve our admiration, even though they are to be credited not to Peter or Paul but to their biographer.

*d. Editing of narratives.* The part played by the writer of Acts in other aspects of the book is difficult to determine, or even extensively to surmise. Certain recurrent features may be due to him, though they may instead be due to his sources, or even to the objective, original reporting of the events themselves. It is safest merely to mention some of these features here, as we have done elsewhere, and leave open the possibility that some of them, rather than all of them, represent the personal viewpoint of the author. There is the book's emphasis upon the Holy Spirit, upon the joy and triumph of the ongoing Christian movement, the inveterate opposition of Jews, the repeated vindication of the movement by supernatural protection and even by tolerance or noninterference by Roman officials. The author is certainly conscious of such features as these.

Part of the author's role may have been in the mere selection of his materials. Unfortunately we do not know whether a much larger body of information was available to him. It is quite possible that it was not, but if it was, it would be interesting to know what that was known was omitted in compiling the book and to conjecture why. This would give us some clue as to what there was in the episodes which he retained that attracted him to do so. Undoubtedly there was much in them that inherently fitted his own interests.

Substantial editorial interpretation and quite extensive adjustment in the narratives are not incompatible with the retention of much trustworthy factual detail. Because so often the historical and local color, so far as we can test it, appears to be accurate, we are tempted to regard the whole content of a passage as fully objective. Such an assumption may be quite mistaken, and the author may have bent accurate traditions in special directions of his own. The unsolved problem of the book of Acts is the difficult discrimination, section by section, between tradition and composition. Only by such analysis can we recover the underlying historical facts or give full credit to the creative effort of the author. Single narratives may have been quite differently interpreted by this author from the form in which they came to him, or by the tradition which likewise had had opportunity to revise or heighten in the retelling the congenial features in the episodes. The stories would not have been recalled at all unless they had some elements fitting the motives of the author or of his predecessors.

**9. Motive and purpose.** In this element of motive, whether originating with the author or retained in his retelling from his predecessors, we should expect some variety. Only with this proviso should one refer to the purpose of the book as a single purpose, or should one assign it to the author. Perhaps more than one audience was in prospect as readers of the book. Certainly different readers have had different impressions from it. We should like, if we could, to identify the original audience intended and the purpose with respect to this audience.

Like the gospel, this book is addressed to THEOPHILUS (1:1), called in the gospel "most excellent Theophilus" (1:3). The name was a common one in the ancient world, and was borne by Jews or Gentiles, Romans or Christians. "Most excellent" is a formal designation and doubtless fits a person of some prestige. Just who this Theophilus was is completely unknown. It would suit the book itself if one thought of him as an influential person, partially informed or misinformed (Luke 1:4) about the early

Christian movement, whom the author would like not so much to convert to Christianity as to influence to feel tolerant toward it. We must remember, however, that the addressee of an ancient book was not thought of as its sole or principal reader. The habit of writing as to an individual was really a mark of publication for a wider public of whom the addressee was not necessarily representative.

The book of Acts unmistakably is something of an apologia for the Christian movement, though if we include with it the gospel, as we should, its apologetic procedure follows rather indirect and generous lines. The gospel portrays convincingly the excellent character of the founder, as the book of Acts pursues the later movement step by step. In both volumes and perhaps particularly in the second it was possible to show that God's favor had blessed and sanctioned Christianity, whether under suspicion from Gentile authorities, or under attack from the Jews. It was a legitimate form of development in Judaism, attested by ancient Jewish prediction. For the author and his readers equally divine attestation would be found in the supernatural occurrences like the cures of the sick, the escapes of the apostles from imminent danger, or the destructive visitations on opposers (5:1-11; 12:20-23; 13:8-11).

The most immediate purpose of the volume may have been to counter possible hostility from the Roman government. If so, one can understand the emphasis on the innocence of Jesus in the opinion of Pilate (3:13; Luke 23:4, 14, 20, 22) and on the failure by later procurators or proconsuls (Acts 13:12; 18:14-15; 24:22, 26; 25:25) to convict Paul. The Herodian officials also sometimes concur (Luke 23:6-12, 15; Acts 26:32). Whenever the officials do take hostile action, it is because of Jewish pressure (Luke 23:23; Acts 12:2; 24:27). Paul was himself a Roman citizen and had been treated with respect accordingly (16:37-39; 22:25-29; 25:10-12). All this is appropriate and carries overtones of value insofar as the book first fell into the hands of a public or of individuals of influence who shared the kind of hostility that is reflected during the second half of the first century in such writings as I Peter or the Revelation to John (see REVELATION, BOOK OF) or I Clement, or in such hostile acts against Christianity as are attributed to NERO, VESPASIAN, or DOMITIAN.

It has sometimes been suggested that even with the Gentiles and their authorities, the same apologetic purpose would be served by the evidence in Acts that Christianity was the legitimate successor of Judaism. Most Gentiles were aloof from Judaism, if not positively hostile to it, but it was officially tolerated by the Roman government and was at least widely spread and well known in many of the cities. The book of Acts implies that Roman officials recognized that quarrels between Jews and Christians were family quarrels on matters not relevant to Roman jurisdiction (18:14-16; 25:19), and that Paul could claim that in preaching Christ he was using a doctrine of resurrection approved by the influential contemporary party of the Pharisees as well as promised in the Scriptures (23:6-9; 24:15; 26:6-8).

There can be no doubt that Acts presents Christianity as the legitimate fulfilment of Judaism, not only in its teaching about a general resurrection but also in the resurrection of Jesus. This is, however, only part of the way in which Jesus fulfilled or will fulfil the Scriptures. He is the promised prophet like Moses, the heir of David, the Christ, the afflicted servant of Isa. 53. These credentials are accepted by the author and by those of whom or to whom he writes, but it is improbable that they are also intended to guarantee to Christians the slight official toleration which Judaism enjoyed at the time. Compared with other religions, Judaism was not particularly favored (cf. Acts 18:2). The term *religio licita,* often used in this connection, is of later vintage, if indeed it is a Roman term at all. The legitimacy of Christianity as the true Israel might appeal to the religious response of both Jews and Gentiles, but it was hardly relevant by civil law.

We must carefully distinguish those features of Christianity which appear in the book because they were inherent in the writer's knowledge and understanding of the movement from any matters that were part of his conscious purpose. It is not likely that many of the features listed in §§ 6*d above* and 10*b below* were included for such an ulterior purpose, even though they deal with matters which either in ancient times or in modern have been controversial. The writer was neither a partisan nor a conscious conciliator. He merely reflects the picture of events as they naturally appeared to him at his later time. He may seem to promote certain theological views, or standards of church organization, to gloss over historical controversy, or to defend the legitimacy of Paul's law-free Gentile Christianity, or to equate Paul with Peter as against later claims for Peter. But if the book gives this impression, the chances are that the author is merely assuming that these various positions are all true without either polemic or apologetic intentions of his own.

The narrative contents of the book suggest that, like other histories, it was written, at least in part, out of the sheer interest of the story. Completely disinterested historiography has perhaps always been rare. In this case the writer's strong allegiance to Christianity is not likely to be questioned. The story as it is known to him and reported by him satisfies his own Christian preference and is likely to have a favorable effect on the unprejudiced reader. It would, however, be as wrong to assign this motive in some subtle form or other to each detail, as it would be to assign to each detail mere historical or factual interest. We cannot tell whether the writer was concerned to put on record these events for the benefit of the future, or for the benefit of a wider circle of his contemporaries, or out of a desire for self-expression. These, as well as other motives, may well have played some part, without having been clear to his own mind or disclosed either in the Preface to the work or elsewhere in its text. This partial inscrutability of the writer's intent fits conveniently into the traditional view of all "inspired" scriptures—that they are not explicable on purely human lines.

**10. The author.** *a. Unity of authorship.* Our most certain information about the author of the book comes from a study of the book itself and of the companion book, the Third Gospel. That both books are by the same writer is not only a traditional opinion. It is implied by the common dedication to Theophilus

and the cross reference to the gospel in Acts 1:1. It is confirmed by the general, and in some respects inimitable, similarity of style throughout, and of vocabulary. We have already noted that in different parts of Acts variations of style occur, but this is not to deny the over-all likeness of style. There may be slight variation between Acts as a whole and the gospel as a whole, but not of a kind to point to a different editor. When such a hypothesis has been proposed, re-examination of the evidence has usually disposed of it. Obviously the content of both works is not homogeneous and was not likely to be, insofar as both books were dealing with a variety of topics and rested upon different sources. This variety, however, affected contents rather than style, and could have led to contrasting motives or emphases, or even to inner contradiction. But the probability remains that a unified editorial process, a single personality and composer, is to be presumed for both books, and so at least for the second of them, with which we have to do here.

*b. Interests of the writer.* The interests of this writer have already been suggested, at least in part. In referring to them one need not assume either that they were not inherited or shared from the oral or written sources on which he depends, or that they misrepresent extensively the actual events as they would have been viewed by any sympathetic observer. Obviously the compiler is fully sympathetic with the Christian movement in its successes or its difficulties. He shares its religious positions. He admires the characters whose careers he reports.

But he may have emphasized certain things, may have glossed over others, and may have been unconcerned with some actual features of his sources or of the events they covered. If we had independent knowledge of these backgrounds, we could conjecture something of his own personal slant. We do have in Paul's letters an independent basis for judging one principal section of Acts, as in a quite different way we can compare parts of the Third Gospel with what we presume represents in Mark or Matthew its written sources. But in general any description of the author's special characteristics must be quite tentative. Some of those which are plausibly assumed from his works may be briefly given.

The writer shares the early Christian view that in its own history the predictions or unconscious hints of scripture are fulfilled. In fact, it is because they appeared in the inspired writings that they had to be fulfilled.

He freely interchanges the terms "God" and "the Lord" (and so do later scribes of Acts), using the latter not only, as does the OT, of Adonai (Yahweh), but also of Jesus. This usage occurs in his gospel also, though not in Matthew and Mark. Conspicuous too in Acts, though again not in Matthew or Mark, or even in Luke, is the Holy Spirit. Evidently "the Holy Spirit" is a theological term closely associated with God, and almost interchangeable in function. One notes the series of guidances in Acts 16:6-10 ("forbidden by the Holy Spirit. . . . The Spirit of Jesus did not allow them. . . . A vision. . . . God had called us"). But the mention of the Holy Spirit in this book is more than conventional. It is much more a part of the author's conscious view of the early church, and is represented as quite definite and datable and perceptible in experience. Its role includes the common Jewish use of the term, as the inspirer of past scriptures, but it is much wider. In early Christianity it has become, for this writer as for Paul, a vivid contemporary experience. It is for him too a presage of "the last days" (2:17).

There is, indeed, some reason to think that the Holy Spirit is one of the factors which led this writer to "play down" the more urgent features of expectancy of the last days. The apocalyptic note is not absent in Acts, but the treatment of it especially in Luke's Gospel suggests that this author, less than some other people in NT times, viewed the Lord's return as imminent.

Nevertheless, the joy of the Christian message is a feature of Luke-Acts. This is shown by the author's abundant use of the words "joy," "rejoice," "gladly," etc., and is felt in the whole tone of the narrative. There is a sense of enthusiasm conveyed even to the modern reader.

In the gospel, at least, the emphasis seems to be on the blessings that are intended for those of low degree. In contrast, the privileged persons are dispossessed, or are condemned for their relatively unsatisfactory response. In the gospel Jesus is said to show partiality to the poor, the publicans, sinners, Samaritans, and other non-Jews, and to criticize in comparison the privileged or respectable persons. The book of Acts only partly shares this description. It is, of course, throughout a vindication of Gentile Christianity and a criticism of the Jews for their stubborn rejection or even opposition. A recurrent motif in the last chapters is plots of the Jews (9:23; 13:44, 50; 14:19; 17:5, 13; 18:12; 20:3, 19; 23:12 ff). The mention of the conversion of a great many of the priests (6:7) is exceptional. There is also in Acts (8:5-25) a favorable report of the response of Samaritans.

At least in Gentile circles, the wealthy or socially elite are represented as favorable to Christianity. The author is apparently pleased to note that this was so —e.g., 17:4, 12, 34; 19:31. There are references to the attention that local officials paid to the missionaries (8:27; 13:7, 12; 28:7), as well as to the protection, already mentioned, which they extended to them.

In fact, one feature of Acts is its abundance of reference to the governmental or other local data of the several places it refers to. It knows the names of civil and military Roman officers, from centurions (10:1; 27:1; in each case with the name of the regiment or "cohort") to a military tribune (23:26), to proconsuls in Cyprus and Achaia, and up to the emperors themselves (11:28; 18:2; cf. Luke 2:1; 3:1). In Palestine there were both procurators, like Pilate, Felix, and Festus, and also Herodian princes, several of whom are mentioned in Luke-Acts; and even persons only remotely associated with them are mentioned (Luke 8:3; Acts 13:1). The author refers to the tetrarchs of Palestine (Luke 3:1), the high-priestly clique in Jerusalem (Acts 4:6), the politarchs at Thessalonica (17:6, 8: "city authorities"), the Areopagus at Athens (17:19, 22), the Asiarchs and the town clerk at Ephesus (19:31, 35), the *primus* at Malta (28:7: "chief man"). Except where a large

group of officials is involved, he gives the personal name. In fact, the general abundance of personal names is a noteworthy feature of Acts. There are nearly a hundred of them.

The allusions to officials are all involved in the story. They do not seem forced or artificially brought in. They are compatible with a substantial amount of intentional emphasis upon the author's underlying interpretive purposes. At the same time, they seem to reflect on the author's part the consciousness of the official situation. The data of secular life, the geography and local color, especially in some of the later parts of Acts, are much in evidence, as though the author or his sources of information were quite at home in places like Philippi, Athens, or Ephesus.

In another way the writer shows a secular approach, quite unlike that of the other evangelists. He is writing, not a private memorandum, nor a bit of folk literature, but a formal treatise. His dedication of his volumes to an individual, so far from making them personal, paradoxically indicates that they were to be published. His Preface accords with the customs of formal, rather than of informal, writing. He approximates, in fact, the ways of belles-lettres and of literary historians. The speeches in Acts have nearer parallels in Greek and Roman history than in biblical or other cultures, and once at least (Luke 3:1-2) he seems to announce indirectly his concern for fixing elaborately a chronological date for a key event in his narrative.

Along with these features should be mentioned certain elements of his style. Anyone expert in shades of Greek style will recognize that, without being stilted (unless possibly in the Preface of Luke 1:1-4), the style of these two volumes is more cultivated than that of most Greek biblical writings. Naturally, rather than consciously, he writes, often in accordance with the rules for correct Greek, changing the wording of his sources like Mark, both to his own personal idiom and to purer diction. This is again a sample of the evidence about the author which the books themselves give us.

None of these features, however, tells us his name or enables us to identify him. The four gospels, before they were collected and differentiated by the addition of headings, "according to . . . ," were, like Acts, anonymous. Luke and Acts go further than these writers in general by using the first person singular in the first sentence: "It seemed good to me also"; "In the first book, O Theophilus, I have dealt"; etc. The contents of these books and of others, like the Gospel of John, point to a distinctive personality behind them more creative than a mere compiler. But it is best today to rest content without expecting to identify them among the limited persons of the period known to us.

**11. Date and place of writing.** At what period were Luke and Acts written? If, as would be natural to suppose, they were written in that order, we have this much information of relative date: Mark was written before Luke, since it is used by Luke, and Acts was written after Luke, which it mentions, perhaps immediately afterward as part of the original plan rather than as an afterthought. Acts may not have known or used Paul's letters. The letters were separately written, probably in the decade before

A.D. 60. Acts relates events up to about the same year, but could have been written years later, perhaps as late as 80 or even later. Attempts to fix its date both earlier and later have been made. For example, it has been suggested that it ends with Paul's two years in Rome, so abruptly, for the simple reason that that was when it was written and there was not yet anything more to report. On the other hand, it has been argued that at Acts 5:36-37 a passage in Josephus on Theudas and Judas has been used—or, rather, misused. This is far from certain, but if it were the case, it would indicate that the author wrote later than Josephus' work (later than 93-95).

To infer dates from the record of predictions is always dangerous; it is as if the prediction were reported in such a way as to imply that the author knew already of its fulfilment. Otherwise one might venture to say that the references in Acts 20:25, 29-30, 38, show that the author knew that Paul had already died and that schism or defection had arisen in the church of Ephesus, or to say that the detailed prophecy in Luke 19:43-44 was only thus reported after the siege and destruction of Jerusalem in A.D. 70 had taken place.

It will be seen (§ 12 *below*) that our scanty knowledge of the later history of the book of Acts does not enable us to cite any use of it so soon after it was written as to limit the time of origin, as would be the case if it were known to have been used by writers like Ignatius early in the second century or by Polycarp or Papias or Justin Martyr or Marcion in the middle of that century. Some of these, and probably even the Gospel of John at an earlier date, show a knowledge of the Gospel of Luke, but not certainly of the book of Acts. Nor does the book itself give any indication of the place where it was written.

How very little we really know of the circumstances of the writing of Acts (or Luke-Acts) is shown by the number and variety of hypotheses which have been seriously proposed. One is the view that it was written at Rome as a brief for the trial of Paul before Caesar. Another is the view that Paul never was tried before Caesar but was automatically released and the case quashed because his accusers failed to appear in Rome before the statutory limit of two years (28:30) expired. Again, it has been proposed either that the author intended or even wrote a third volume to follow Acts or that he never quite finished Acts and that it was published posthumously. These hypotheses are due in part to the apparent abruptness of the end of Acts. Another view is that Acts was written prior to the writing of Luke. Again, it has been supposed that Acts was written before Paul's letters were first collected in the first century —indeed, led to that collection—and also that Luke-Acts, at least in the present form of Luke, was compiled in the second century to combat Marcionism.

**12. Subsequent history of Acts. *a. Use.*** The first clear references to the book of Acts occur *ca.* A.D. 180, and then in several different parts of Christendom. It is cited and referred to by name by Irenaeus at Lyons in Gaul (France), by an anonymous Latin fragment apparently from Rome dealing with the NT books (the Canon of Muratori), by Clement of Alexandria, by Tertullian of North Africa, and by later writers. Thus for a century, more or less, the book of Acts existed without leaving evidence in the scanty Christian literature that remains from that period. But obviously it was not forgotten or lost. Indeed, it had already been included in the select canon of the NT. It was copied and thus preserved. In fact, more than most NT books its copying was done with such freedom that by the end of the second century at least two forms of its text were in existence. By that time it had been detached from its companion, the Gospel of Luke, since that was now included in a group of four gospels in which it had acquired a distinguishing name, "According to Luke." Acts thus, left by itself, had acquired the title already mentioned and in the collection of the NT canon held a unique position, bridging in a way the two (later three) smaller collections—the four gospels, or rather the gospel according to four authorities, the letters of Paul to sundry churches and persons, and the letters supposedly of other apostles (Peter, John, James, Jude). The steps by which Acts became a part of the regular, basic NT can only be conjectured. Apparently Marcion, who one might think had reasons to like the book as well as he liked Luke and Paul's letters, did not include it in his early "canon," which consisted of merely Luke and the letters of Paul, both in a textual form different from that which the "orthodox" church has inherited (*see* MARCION, GOSPEL OF).

*b. Attribution of authorship.* By the time Luke and Acts had come to be included in the canon, while their common authorship was still properly recognized, the identification of the author had become for Christians a matter of more interest than previously. As he was one of several gospel writers, a distinctive name was needed for the author, as for each of the four, and names were forthcoming, whether from tradition going back to an earlier memory, or from inference from the data provided in the gospels or outside them. The name thus provided for Luke and Acts was LUKE. No other name is known to have been suggested in antiquity for this writer, and even today the best alternative to the view that such was his name is to let him revert to complete anonymity.

Since we cannot tell with how much authority the name Luke was assigned to this author, modern readers have sometimes tried to test its probability. If the "we" passages really belong to the author of the whole work, and if they show that a companion to Paul on various voyages, including that to Rome, wrote them, then he may be one of the many named companions mentioned in Paul's letters including letters supposed to have been written in Rome. If Colossians and Philemon were written in Rome and also II Timothy, "Luke" (Philem. 24), or "Luke the beloved physician" (Col. 4:14), is one of the candidates, and according to II Tim. 4:11—"Luke alone is with me"—the most obvious candidate. Along these lines the ancient Christians may have satisfied their curiosity about this author's name. Some modern calculations would find the same steps sound. But many scholars, noting the many ifs involved, recognize that alternatives or confirmations should be considered.

One criterion would be to inquire whether the "we" passages (*see* §7c *above*) do definitely imply a companion of Paul as writer. The "we" could be a curious literary convention used by ancient narrators in reporting voyages. Perhaps the "we" comes, not from the editor of the whole, but from his written source for some sections of it. This seems odd, since we know that the editor elsewhere shows no unnatural dependence on the wording of his sources. On this view Luke might be the author of the source of Acts, though it has also been suggested that he both wrote the source and wrote the whole book re-using the source, "we" and all, in the later parts of Acts. In favor of the "we" as referring to the author of the whole is the fact that the Preface of Luke can be understood to say in one clause in effect that the author had been in firsthand contact with the events toward the end of the story, "having followed all things closely for some time past," in distinction to having received other parts of his information second-hand from "those who from the beginning were eyewitnesses and ministers of the word."

Another criterion would be to inquire whether the two books are appropriate for a companion of Paul. Decisive answer to this question is perhaps impossible. One can point out that the author admired Paul, shared some of Paul's ideas, and knew some outward facts about him. On the other hand, Paul's behavior and some data recorded of him in Acts are hard to reconcile with parts of the Pauline letters. Trusted companions are not the only persons who in the later years could have agreed so much with Paul; and on the other hand, not all pupils exactly understand and correctly represent their master.

Still another criterion has proved indecisive. It was ingeniously suggested that if the author was a physician, his profession would show in his writings. This assumes that in his time doctors used a special vocabulary. But they did not; and the fact that many words in Luke-Acts were used also by medical writers, though laboriously proved, is made irrelevant by the fact that the same words were used by other writers who had no special medical training. The style of Luke-Acts is no more probable for a doctor than for men of other training or interests. The books could have been written by a doctor, but they need not have been.

These criteria, while not disproving that Luke wrote the books traditionally ascribed to him, do not prove it, or even confirm it. If we weigh the tradition, our judgment will depend on many quite subjective factors, especially on our understanding of the ways the Christians of the second century arrived at their views on matters not clearly disclosed by the books they inherited. An anonymous book, if popular, would be associated with an apostle. Indeed, it has been suggested that because Luke was not (like Matthew or John) one of the Twelve, his name is less likely to have been chosen without real knowledge that he was the author. But the Preface just as definitely seemed to the readers to exclude him from the Twelve, who certainly were "eyewitnesses and ministers of the word," as the "we" passages seemed to make him an associate of Paul. The kind of inference from the contents of the books themselves is the same in its procedure whether it determines which persons to include or which to exclude in considering possible authorship.

*c. Transmission of text.* During the period when the early church was developing the idea of a NT canon (*see* CANON OF THE NT) and including the book of Acts in it, the wording of the book was experiencing the variation incident to all books written and copied by hand (*see* TEXT, NT). In fact, no book of the NT gives evidence of so much verbal variation as does the Acts of the Apostles. Besides the text represented in the oldest uncial Greek MSS, beginning with Codex Vaticanus, often called the Neutral Text and dating back to the second century A.D., there is evidence either of a consistent alternative text equally old, or of a series of early miscellaneous variants, to which the name Western Text is traditionally applied. The ancient authorities for the Western Text of Acts include only one Greek (or rather bilingual Greek and Latin) uncial MS, Codex Bezae of the fifth or sixth century. But the variants often have striking content and strong early support from Latin writers and Latin NT MSS. It now appears that while both the Neutral and the Western texts were in early circulation, the former is the more likely of the two to represent the original. Actually judgment must be made between them at each individual passage. Often the two texts differ from each other simply as if one were a paraphrase of the other; at other times the variants are of the slight kind familiar in other books of the NT. Indeed, the Gospel of Luke, especially in its last chapters, has variants that suggest that the same treatment had occurred in both these books before they were separated. Thus in Luke the Western Text omits the words mentioned in the RSV margin as added by many (or some) ancient authorities in Luke 22:19-20; 24:6, 12, 40, 51-52, while the Neutral Text includes these words. Since the RSV and other English translations follow generally in Acts the Neutral Text, it will be appropriate here to mention for illustration a few of the Western readings in comparison with it. Thus at Acts 11:28 the Western Text introduces a "we" passage early at Antioch in referring to Agabus: "when we were gathered together"; at 12:8 Peter and the angel leaving the prison descend "the seven steps." Twice (15:20, 29; but not 21:25) the negative Golden Rule: "Whatever you wish that men should not do to you, do not do so to them," is added to the decree sent to Gentiles among the believers, and in all three passages (see notes in RSV) "what is strangled" is omitted from the prohibited things, reducing the list from four to three. Additions by the Western Text are indicated by the RSV margin at 15:34; 19:9; 21:1; 24:6-8.

The variety offered by the Western readings suggests that they are due to sundry causes, though some are sufficiently consistent to suggest that the Western Text is a definite recension. Until its much-debated and quite unexplained character finds a better interpretation, it remains rather an indication of the vicissitudes to which the text of Acts appears to have been especially exposed rather than as the repository of a number of substantial primitive readings. The Neutral Text is probably in most cases closer to what the author himself first wrote.

**Bibliography.** General studies: W. M. Ramsay, *St. Paul the Traveller and the Roman Citizen* (1896). A. von Harnack, *The Acts of the Apostles* (1909). E. Norden, *Agnostos Theos* (1913).

F. J. Foakes-Jackson and K. Lake, eds., *The Beginnings of Christianity*, pt. I (5 vols.; 1920-33). E. Meyer, *Ursprung und Anfänge des Christentums*, vol. III (1923). W. L. Knox, *The Acts of the Apostles* (1948). H. J. Cadbury, *The Book of Acts in History* (1954). M. Dibelius, *Studies in the Acts of the Apostles* (1956). H. J. Cadbury, *The Making of Luke-Acts* (2nd ed., 1958).

Commentaries: F. J. Foakes-Jackson and K. Lake, eds., *The Beginnings of Christianity*, vol. IV (1933). F. F. Bruce, *The Acts of the Apostles* (on the Greek text; 1951); *New London Commentary* (1954). G. H. C. Macgregor, Introduction and Exegesis of Acts, *IB*, vol. IX (1954). E. Haenchen in H. A. W. Meyer, *Kritisch-exegetischer Kommentar über das NT* (10th ed., 1956).

Special studies: A. Wikenhauser, *Die Apostelgeschichte und ihr Geschichtswert* (1921). B. S. Easton, *The Purpose of Acts* (1936; reprinted by F. C. Grant with other papers, 1954). E. Haenchen, "Tradition und Komposition in der Apostelgeschichte," *ZThK*, 52. Jahrgang (1955), pp. 205-25. On the text: T. Zahn, *Die Urausgabe der Apostelgeschichte des Lukas* (1916). J. H. Ropes, *The Beginnings of Christianity*, vol. III (1926). A. C. Clark, *The Acts of the Apostles* (1933).

H. J. CADBURY

**ACUA.** KJV Apoc. alternate form of AKKUB 3.

**ACUB.** KJV Apoc. form of BAKBUK.

**ADADAH** ăd'ə də [עֲדָעָה]. A city in the SE part of Judah, near the border of Edom (Josh. 15:22). The form of the name is unusual, and the LXX reads Ἀρουήλ, so most scholars have preferred to read the name as עֲרָעָה ('*ar'ārâ*), another form for the Judean ΑROER, to which David sent part of his spoils from he Amalekites (I Sam. 30:28).

A possible site is Khirbet 'Ar'arah, *ca.* nine miles SE of Beer-sheba. S. COHEN

**ADAH** ā'də [עָדָה, ornament; *cf.* Minaean *feminine name* עֲדָת *and* Hebrew *masculine names* עֲדוֹ, עֲדָא, עֲדָיהוּ, עֲדָיָה, *and* אֶלְעָדָה]. 1. The first of two wives of LAMECH; the mother of Jabal and Jubal (Gen. 4:19-20, 23).

2. Wife of Esau; the mother of Eliphaz (Gen. 36: 2, 4, 10, 12, 16). In Gen. 36:2 Adah is identified as the daughter of Elon the Hittite. However, her father is not named in the other passages. This notice seems to come from Gen. 26:34, where Elon is listed as the father of BASEMATH. Ethnologically the marriage between Adah and Esau points to the incorporation of Canaanite elements into Edom.

*Bibliography.* M. Noth, *Die israelitischen Personennamen* (1928), p. 182. L. HICKS

**ADAIAH** ə dā'yə [עֲדָיָה, עֲדָיָהוּ (II Chr. 23:1 *only*), Y has adorned himself]. 1. The maternal grandfather of King Josiah (II Kings 22:1).

2. A Levite; an ancestor of Asaph in the temple singers' genealogy (I Chr. 6:41—H 6:26); called Iddo in vs. 21—H vs. 6.

3. One of the sons of Shimei in the genealogy of Benjamin (I Chr. 8:21).

4. One of the priests in the list of those who returned to Jerusalem after the Exile (I Chr. 9:12); also mentioned in the parallel list (Neh. 11:12), though the genealogies do not agree.

5. The father of Maaseiah, one of the army officers who aided in the overthrow of Athaliah (II Chr. 23:1).

6. Two men listed as having married foreign wives in the time of Ezra (Ezra 10:29 = I Esd. 9:30; Ezra 10:39).

7. An ancestor of one of the Judahites living in Jerusalem (Neh. 11:5). F. T. SCHUMACHER

**ADALIA** ə dā'lĭ ə [אֲדַלְיָא, *possibly from* Pers. *ādārya*, honorable] (Esth. 9:8). The fifth son of Haman.

**ADAM** ăd'əm [אָדָם; Ἀδάμ; *see below*]. The first man, from whom all mankind is descended. He was driven from the Garden of Eden because of his disobedience. His life is greatly embellished in the later Jewish writings. The NT interprets Adam as the representative of humanity and relates all subsequent human sin to his first transgression. He appears in the NT as the antitype of Jesus Christ.

**1. In the OT. *a. Usage and etymology.*** The word אָדָם ('*ādhām*) occurs well over five hundred times in the OT with the meaning "man" or "mankind." This generic term is used only rarely as a proper name for the first man. Outside Gen. 1-5 the only unambiguous occurrence of the proper name in the OT is in I Chr. 1:1, where it appears at the head of a genealogy. There remains a difference of interpretation with several other passages (*cf.* Deut. 32:1; Job 31:33; Hos. 6:7).

The term אָדָם fluctuates between a generic usage and a proper name in Gen. 1-5. The Priestly writer (P) speaks clearly in 1:26-27 of the creation of "mankind," but in 5:1-5 the transition is made to the proper name. The Yahwist writer (J) of chs. 2-3 generally employs the generic term with the definite article. There are three exceptions to this in which the MT has pointed the word as a proper name (2:20; 3:17, 21). Most modern commentators feel that the evidence warrants the emendation of these passages to read uniformly "the man" up to 4:25. The absence of the article here shows that the writer has also made the shift to the proper name. The fluidity of the term is further indicated in the versions which frequently reflect an uncertainty in the translation.

The etymology of the root has not as yet been satisfactorily explained. The common words for "man" in the Semitic languages are not cognate with אָדָם. The traditional derivation of the word from the root אָדַם, "to be red," remains most uncertain. Various Sumerian, Akkadian, and Arabic roots have been suggested without settling the question (*see bibliography*). Gen. 2:7 presents a popular etymology in a wordplay: Yahweh God formed אָדָם ('*ādhām*), "man," from the אֲדָמָה ('*ªdhāmâh*), "earth." Adam is the "earth man." Recently some scholars have argued that this may be the scientific etymology.

***b. In the Genesis narratives.*** The Priestly writer (P) of Gen. 1:1–2:4*a* describes the creation of man on the sixth day along with the animals, but set apart by a special decree of God (vss. 26-27). God does not resolve simply to make a man, but the species of man, in two sexes. The creation of a single pair is not explicit in vss. 26-27, but is implied later in the identification of Adam with the creation of the human species (5:1-3). Man is created in the "IMAGE OF GOD." He is blessed and given dominion over the earth with the command to multiply. The creation of man, while not receiving a separate commendation, is included in the general statement: "God saw everything that he had made, and behold, it was very good" (1:31). According to 5:3, 5, Adam was 130 years old when he had a son, Seth, and he lived to the age of 930 years.

The Yahwist writer (J) of Gen. 2:4b–4:26 pictures Yahweh Elohim forming man while the earth is still in its unfruitful state. He molds him from the dust of the earth and makes him into an animated creature by breathing into him the breath of life. The man is placed in the Garden of Eden with full freedom of action except in respect to the forbidden trees (see TREE OF KNOWLEDGE, TREE OF LIFE). The man is given the task of naming the animals, but, in determining their role, he finds none suitable for his own mate. Yahweh forms Eve from the rib of the sleeping man. They live together unconscious of their nakedness until the woman is tempted by the serpent into eating from the tree (see FALL). The man follows suit, and immediately they become aware of their nakedness. Yahweh appears to punish the woman with the pain of childbirth, and to curse the ground upon which man must henceforth toil for a livelihood. The man is expelled from the garden because of the implications of his ill-won knowledge. He becomes the father of Cain, Abel, and Seth.

*c. The theological significance.* The choice of the generic term indicates the intention of the biblical writers to portray, not just the story of one man, but the universal history of mankind. The strong etiological elements in the J account reveal his basic concern to present a theological interpretation of man's plight in terms of Adam's disobedience. The shift from the generic to the proper name shows that reality finds expression in historical form for the biblical writer. His is not a philosophy about man, but the story of man's history in the light of God's revelation.

In both narratives the first man is sharply set apart from the other created beings. P indicates man's unique position with the solemn resolution preceding his creation. Only man is created in the image of God to rule the earth. J pictures Yahweh's infusing man with his spirit in a special act. In naming the animals he interprets and orders God's creation. Nevertheless, man is completely an earth-bound creature and not semidivine. He is created on the same day as the animals and likewise dependent upon the life-giving breath of God. In spite of the fresh, naïve language of J, his account offers a highly theological interpretation of God's purpose for mankind. It is a life sustained by his spirit, lived in fellowship with God, found in a created community which issues in obedient service.

**2. In the noncanonical Jewish writings.** In the Apoc. and the Pseudep. the role of Adam enters into a new and highly significant development. The hypothesis is plausible that Israel's search to understand the meaning of her political disaster in the Exile led to a rethinking of the traditions concerning man's sin and fall. Two tendencies in the expansion of the Adam tradition should be noticed especially. First, the glorification of Adam before the Fall has been greatly magnified. He enjoys a beauteous glory not shared by the rest of the human race (Ecclus.

49:16). II Enoch 30:8 ff describes the seven substances out of which Adam was formed. He was placed on the earth a "second angel, honorable, great and glorious." His name was constructed from the initials of the four quarters of the earth. The point is emphasized that the devil seduced Eve, but did not touch Adam (31:6). In the *Vita Adae* 12 ff Adam is created in the image of God to be worshiped by the angels. The climax of this development is represented in the pseudo-Clementine literature. This Jewish Christian writing rejects the idea of the Fall, and describes Adam as a heavenly figure who appears in successive incarnations.

Secondly, the malignant effect of Adam's sin on the human race receives a new emphasis which had previously never been made explicit. Apocal. Bar. 17:3 notes that Adam "brought death and cut off the years of those who were born from him." II Esd. 3:21 relates human evil directly to Adam's transgression (cf. 3:4 ff; 4:30; 7:11). The cosmological significance of Adam's sin also receives a new emphasis in the Apoc. and the Pseudep. (cf. Jub. 3:28-29).

Similarly, rabbinical literature is characterized by a tremendous growth of interest in Adam and the Fall. Adam transcended ordinary man in every way. He was created immortal with superhuman wisdom and indescribable glory which darkened the sun. His size was of such extent as to fill the entire earth. Consequently, his fall brought untold disaster. According to Rabbi Meir, his size was reduced to a hundred yards. He lost immortality and external beauty. The planetary movement was disrupted, fruit no longer ripened, and beasts became ferocious. Although the "first man" is contrasted with Abraham and the Messiah who will come to restore what Adam has lost, rabbinical Judaism did not develop the concept of the "second" or "last" Adam.

The speculation over Adam receives a most significant development in Philo, who is the best representative of Hellenistic Judaism (see PHILO JUDEUS). In commenting on the two creation accounts of Genesis (*Allegory of the Jewish Law* I.31-32), Philo distinguishes between two types of men. The first man of Gen. 1:27 is the "heavenly man," οὐράνιος ἄνθρωπος. He is not created, but formed after the image of God. He is the pure archetype of man, an idea in the mind of God. The second man of Gen. 2:7 is the "earthly man" (γήϊνος ἄνθρωπος). He is the historical Adam, who became the father of sinful mankind (cf. *On the Creation of the World* 134). Nevertheless, the earthly man receives the same glorification in Philo as was common in rabbinical Judaism.

**3. In the NT.** Adam as the first man appears twice in the NT in a historical connection. In Luke 3:38 the genealogy of Jesus is traced back to Adam, who is designated as "son of God." Jude 14 contains a reference to "Enoch in the seventh generation from Adam."

Adam appears again in I Tim. 2:13-14, in the section dealing with the proper behavior of women in the worship service. Women are to be subordinate to men on two accounts: (*a*) according to the creative order, Adam was formed before Eve (cf. I Cor. 11:12-16); (*b*) the woman was deceived into sinning, not the man. This latter reference may reflect current Jewish exegesis of the Genesis passage.

By far the most important references appear in those passages in which Adam is made a type of Christ. Paul argues in Rom. 5:12-21 that death entered the world because of the sin of Adam: "Sin came into the world through one man and death through sin, and so death spread to all men" (vs. 12). Adam is a type of the "Coming One" (τύπος τοῦ μέλλοντος), because of the similarity in the total effect of one man's action on all of humanity. But here the continuity ends. The grace of God in Jesus Christ is far superior in being able to overcome the effect of sin. Moreover, Adam's act of disobedience brought condemnation and death, while Christ's obedience leads to justification and life.

Vs. 12 has been traditionally misinterpreted by supposing the phrase "in Adam" to be implicitly included in the last clause "because all men sinned" (ἐφ' ᾧ πάντες ἥμαρτον). Nowhere does Paul state the manner by which Adam's sin is transmitted to his posterity. The concept of biological inheritance is certainly foreign. Rather, Paul is thinking historically of the initial entrance of SIN as a power over the human race.

In I Cor. 15:22 the Adam-Christ typology is used to illustrate the certainty of the resurrection. "As in Adam all die, so also in Christ shall all be made alive." Undoubtedly, the two uses of "all" are to be interpreted alike. This raises a difficulty, since participation in the resurrection is not within the context of faith which is usually so central in Pauline thought (Rom. 6:5 ff; I Cor. 15:12 ff). However, the contrast between "in Adam" (ἐν τῷ 'Αδάμ) and "in Christ" (ἐν τῷ χριστῷ) brings out Paul's intent. Adam and Christ are the "heads" of the old and the new humanity. Adam is the source of death, while Christ is the source of life. Each type of humanity joins itself in an organic solidarity to its head and thus participates in either life or death.

Finally, the certainty of the spiritual resurrection body is stressed in I Cor. 15:45-47 through the contrast between Adam and Christ. Paul cites as scriptural proof Gen. 2:7, according to the LXX and in a form which has been expanded to include specific reference to the "first man Adam" (ὁ πρῶτος ἄνθρωπος 'Αδάμ). He characterizes the "first Adam" as a "living being" (ψυχὴ ζῶσα), "from the earth" (ἐκ γῆς), a "man of dust" (χοϊκός). He is contrasted with his antitype, the "last Adam" (ὁ ἔσχατος 'Αδάμ), who is a "life-giving spirit" (πνεῦμα ζωοποιοῦν), a "man from heaven" (ἐξ οὐρανοῦ). Christians resemble the "first Adam" in respect to their earthly nature, but the "last Adam" in respect to their resurrection bodies (vs. 48).

Paul found the language of the first and the last Adam useful in delineating his position in opposition to two current misunderstandings of the resurrection. First, he stressed the necessity for a resurrection body against certain Hellenistic circles which denied the soul's need for one. Secondly, in opposing the excesses of rabbinical materialism, he made it clear that the resurrection body was not flesh and blood, but a new, spiritual body. Paul's insistence that the "spiritual man" was second in order may be a conscious polemic against Philo's teaching.

The source of the Adam-Christ typology is much debated. It has been often suggested that it stems directly from the mythical traditions of the "heavenly man" which were current in the religions of the Orient. It is possible that this complex of tradition did affect the rabbinical speculation about the first man, as well as result in the Hellenistic distinction between an earthly and a heavenly Adam (*see* MYTH, MYTHOLOGY, NT). Recently some scholars have sought for a closer source of this typology in the rabbinical doctrine of the unity of mankind in Adam. According to this teaching the body of Adam was thought to incorporate the whole of mankind. It would be easily understandable for Paul to apply this figure to Jesus Christ, who as the "last Adam" now incorporates the new humanity.

*Bibliography.* For the OT: T. C. Vriezen, *Onderzoek naar de Paradijsvoorstelling bij de oude semietische Volken* (1937), pp. 130 ff; W. Eichrodt, *Theologie des AT*, II (2 Aufl., 1948), pp. 58 ff; L. Köhler, *OT Theology* (English trans., 1957), pp. 129, 131 ff.

For rabbinical exegesis: H. L. Strack and P. Billerbeck, *Kommentar zum NT*, Index under "Adam," IV (1928), 1224; B. Murmelstein, "Adam, Ein Beitrag zur Messiaslehre," *Wiener Ztsch. f. d. Kunde d. Morgenlandes*, 35 (1928), 242 ff. For the NT: W. Manson, *Jesus the Messiah* (1943), pp. 174 ff; W. D. Davies, *Paul and Rabbinic Judaism* (1948), pp. 36 ff; M. Black, "The Pauline Doctrine of the Second Adam," *SJT*, 7 (1954), 170 ff; K. Barth, *Christ and Adam* (English trans., 1956); O. Cullmann, *Die Christologie des NT* (1957), pp. 138 ff.    B. S. CHILDS

**ADAM (CITY).** A city E of the Jordan in the Plains of Moab, not far from Jericho. It was here that the waters of the Jordan were dammed, so that Joshua and the Israelites could pass over dry-shod (Josh. 3: 9-17). Fig. JOR 28.

The site is Tell ed-Damiyeh, located on the delta of the Jabbok (Nahr ez-Zerqa) shortly before it empties into the Jordan.

*See also* ZARETHAN.

*Bibliography.* N. Glueck, *AASOR*, XXV-XXVIII (1951), 329-34.    S. COHEN

**ADAM, BOOKS OF.** A general name for extracanonical writings in which the biblical story of Adam and Eve is elaborated. The most important surviving documents of this genre are a Greek text misnamed by its first editor "The Apocalypse of Moses," and a Latin "Life of Adam and Eve." The two texts are related, though by no means identical; they are derived from Semitic originals. The theory that there was once a single Hebrew or Aramaic Adam book, the source of both these versions, can hardly be proved or disproved. For a discussion of this type of literature, *see* APOCRYPHA.

The Apocalypse of Moses begins with the expulsion from Eden, and tells of a dream in which Eve has a premonition of the murder of Abel. Following a brief account of the birth of Seth, it skips to the end of Adam's life, when, to the amazement of his children, he suffers sickness and pain for the first time. Seth and Eve return to Paradise in the hope of obtaining oil from the tree of life to relieve Adam's suffering. On the way, Seth is attacked by a beast which, since the Fall, no longer respects the "image of God." Michael notifies the suppliants that Adam cannot be healed and must die. They return; and while Adam lies dying, Eve at his bidding tells how they yielded to the blandishments of Satan, who suborned the serpent to mislead them. Adam dies, and Eve and Seth see his soul taken into the third heaven after it has been purified. Only Seth, however, is permitted to watch the angels inter Adam's body and that of Abel, which the earth had previously refused to accept. After a week, Eve too dies; Michael instructs Seth how to bury her, and enjoins him not to mourn more than six days, for on the sabbath he must be cheerful.

The Latin version traverses most of this material except Eve's narrative of the Fall, for the most part more briefly than the Apocalypse of Moses; but it includes the following elements which are missing from the Greek version:

When first expelled from Paradise, Adam and Eve are so desperate that Eve, considering herself the cause of all his misfortunes, urges her husband to slay her. He proposes instead that as a penance they shall stand for many days in water, he in the Jordan, she in the Tigris. After eighteen days, Satan appears to Eve disguised as an angel of light, and bids her leave the water, since her penitence has been accepted. Adam, however, unmasks the old enemy. Now Satan explains why he is so hostile to them. When Adam was first created, the angels were bidden to "worship" him as the image of God; Satan in his pride refused to bow down to a younger and inferior creature, and out of this rebellion came his downfall. (This account of the devil's fall was adopted by Mohammed, Koran 7.11 ff.) This version also includes a touching account of the birth of Cain, and an apocalyptic vision related by Adam to Seth.

These writings imply the existence of the temple, and probably date from about the beginning of the Christian era. Such a date fits well with the rather developed concept of Satan, a fallen angel in rebellion against God, who is not, however, identified with the serpent of Eden. The books speak repeatedly of the final judgment and the resurrection, but do not mention the Messiah. Apart from a few Hellenistic touches, some of which may be due to the translators, the Adam books are well within the traditions of the Palestinian Haggada.

Our present texts contain a few manifestly Christian insertions, and there are other passages where the translators may have imparted a certain Christian coloring to the Jewish documents. We possess, however, a number of later Adam books, derived in part from those described here, in which the Christian elements, orthodox or Gnostic, are much more extensive. The Slavonic and Armenian versions, despite such additions, are still recognizably related to the Jewish sources; the older material, however, has been completely reworked in Syriac, Ethiopic, Arabic, and Armenian Christian writings, said to date from the fourth Christian century and later. These works express a strong preference for celibacy as against marriage.

*Bibliography.* Text, trans. and ed. L. S. Wells, in R. H. Charles, *Apoc. and Pseudep. of the OT* (1913), II, 123 ff. L. Ginzberg, "Adam, Book of," *JE* (1901-6), I, 179 ff; *The Legends of the Jews* (1909-38), I, 86-107; V, 114-35.

B. J. BAMBERGER

**ADAM, SECOND.** *See* SECOND ADAM.

**ADAMAH** ăd′ə mə [אדמה]. A fortified city in the territory of Naphtali (Josh. 19:36), not to be confused with ADAM (2) or ADAMI-NEKEB. Its location is unknown; however, its place in the list of fortified cities suggests that it was situated to the NW of the Sea of Galilee. The Palestine Survey identified Adamah with Khirbet Damiyeh, but this site is better suited to the topographical requirements of Adami-nekeb.

G. W. VAN BEEK

**ADAMANT** [שמיר, šāmîr; *cf.* Akkad. *ašmur*, emery] (Ezek. 3:9; Zech. 7:12). Alternately: DIAMOND (Jer. 17:1). An imaginary stone of impenetrable hardness; formerly, a diamond; now, a poetic expression for "hardness."

The rendering "diamond" is purely interpretive. The Lord makes the forehead of Ezekiel like שמיר, harder than flint (Ezek. 3:9). The Israelites make their hearts like שמיר so as not to listen to the law (Zech. 7:12). A stylus of שמיר was required to penetrate the hardness of Judah's heart (Jer. 17:1). *See* JEWELS § 2.      W. E. STAPLES

**ADAMI-NEKEB** ăd′ə mī nĕk′ĕb [אדמי הנקב] (Josh. 19:33); KJV ADAMI, NEKEB. A border town in Naphtali, not to be confused with ADAM (2) or ADAMAH. It is probably located at Khirbet Damiyeh, a large Bronze Age site *ca.* five miles SW of the Sea of Galilee, commanding a pass on a caravan route between Hauran and the Plain of Acco. It is not to be identified with *udm* of the Keret Epic from Ugarit, or *udumu* of the Tell el-Amarna Letters.

*See also* NEKEB.

*Bibliography.* F.-M. Abel, *Géographie de la Palestine*, II (1938), 16-17, 64, 238; W. F. Albright, "Two Little Understood Amarna Letters from the Middle Jordan Valley," *BASOR*, 89 (1943), 7-17.      G. W. VAN BEEK

**ADAR** ā′där [אדר; Ἀδάρ; Akkad. *adaru*]. **1.** The twelfth month in the Hebrew CALENDAR (February-March).

**2.** KJV alternate form of ADDAR 1.

**ADASA** ăd′ə sə [Ἀδασα]. A town on the road between Beth-horon and Jerusalem where Judas intercepted and defeated the Syrian army of Nicanor; this victory was celebrated annually thereafter on the thirteenth of Adar (I Macc. 7:40, 45; Jos. Antiq. XII.x.5). The town is probably the modern Khirbet 'Addâseh, *ca.* seven miles from Beth-horon.

*Bibliography.* F.-M. Abel, *Géographie de la Palestine*, II (1938), 238.      E. W. SAUNDERS

**ADBEEL** ăd′bĭ əl [אדבאל; Akkad. *Idibi'lu*]. The third son of Ishmael, and hence the name of an Arabian tribe (Gen. 25:13; I Chr. 1:20). The latter seem to be identical with the Idiba'ileans whom Tiglath-pileser III of Assyria conquered and then appointed as guards on the Egyptian frontier. They were located in NW Arabia, close by Kedar and Nebaioth.

S. COHEN

**ADDAN** ăd′ən [אדן, strong (place)] (Ezra 2:59); **ADDON** —ŏn [אדון] (Neh. 7:61). An unidentified

Babylonian place from which came—or a leader among (I Esd. 5:36; *cf.* CHERUB)—returning exiles unable to prove their ancestry.     R. A. BOWMAN

**ADDAR** ăd'är. **1.** אדר (KJV ADAR ā'där except in I Chr. 8:3). A fortress city on the SW border of Judah, between Kadesh-barnea and Karka (Josh. 15:3). In the parallel passage in Num. 34:4, Addar and HEZRON, the next name in the Joshua list, are combined as "Hazar-addar."     S. COHEN
   **2.** Alternate translation of ארד. *See* ARD.

**ADDER** [פתן; צפע (KJV COCKATRICE); צפעוני (KJV COCKATRICE *in* Isa. 11:8; 59:5; Jer. 8:17); עכשוב (Ps. 140:3 KJV; RSV VIPER); שפיפן (Gen. 49:17 KJV; RSV VIPER)]. Alternately: ASP (Job 20:14, 16). Any of several poisonous and nonpoisonous snakes, especially the common viper, *vipera berus,* of Europe and Asia.
   The identification of the Hebrew words with specific species of snakes is very dubious. Both צפע, *sepha',* and צפעוני, *siph'ônî,* which designate a dangerous snake, may be onomatopoeic—i.e., in imitation of the hissing made by the snake. In Prov. 23:32; Isa. 14:29; Jer. 8:17, they are associated with the Hebrew word for "snake," נחש. The reference to the eggs of the צפעוני in Isa. 59:5 does not help in identifying the species of snake, for most snakes lay eggs—the chief exceptions to this are the majority of the vipers and the aquatic snakes, which generally produce living young. Wine is said to sting like a צפעוני (Prov. 23:32). The specific species of snake meant by פתן, *pethen,* and שפיפן, *shephîphôn,* are also unknown, while one scholar regards עכשוב, *'akhshôbh,* as a spider. *See* FAUNA § D.     W. S. McCULLOUGH

**ADDI** ăd'ī ['Αδδείν (B), Αδδι (A), Εδνα (Luc)]. **1.** Apparently an alternate form of the name ADNA (2). The sons of Addi in I Esd. 9:31 correspond to the sons of PAHATH-MOAB in Ezra 10:30.
   **2.** An ancestor of Jesus (Luke 3:28).
                       C. T. FRITSCH

**ADDO.** KJV Apoc. alternate form of IDDO.

**ADDON.** Alternate form of ADDAN.

**ADDUS** ăd'əs ['Αδδούς]. **1.** Head of a family of "sons of Solomon's servants" (I Esd. 5:34; omitted in Ezra 2:57; Neh. 7:59).
   **2.** KJV form of JADDUS.

**ADER.** KJV form of EDER in I Chr. 8:15.

**ADIDA** ăd'ə də [Αδιδα]. A town (probably OT HADID) on the road from Jerusalem leading NW to the coast, situated on a hill above the plains of Judea four miles E of Lydda. It was fortified by Simon (I Macc. 12:38; 13:13; cf. Jos. Antiq. XIII.vi.5; Euseb. Onom. 24:23) and by Vespasian.
   *Bibliography.* F.-M. Abel, *Géographie de la Palestine,* II (1938), 340-41.     E. W. SAUNDERS

**ADIEL** ā'dĭ əl [עדיאל, an ornament is El]. **1.** One of the Simeonite princes who enlarged their pastoral lands in the region of Gedor in the time of Hezekiah (I Chr. 4:36-43).

**2.** A priest mentioned in I Chr. 9:12 (Azarel in Neh. 11:13) whose son Maasai (Amashsai in Neh. 11:13) returned from the Babylonian exile.
   **3.** The father of Azmaveth, who was in charge of the royal treasuries in Jerusalem under David (I Chr. 27:25).     E. R. DALGLISH

**ADIN** ā'dən [עדין, voluptuous] (Ezra 2:15; 8:6; Neh. 7:20; 10:16; I Esd. 5:14; 8:32). The father and ancestor of some Jewish exiles who returned to Jerusalem with Zerubbabel or with Ezra.

**ADINA** ăd'ə nə [עדינא]. The son of Shiza; a Reubenite leader listed among the Mighty Men of David (I Chr. 11:42).

**ADINO** ăd'ə nō. A name in a KJV transliteration of an unintelligible phrase (עדינו העצנו) in II Sam. 23:8 ("Adino the Eznite"). This transliteration interprets the expression as a second name of Josheb-basshebeth, the chief of the "Three" in David's high command. However, it seems better either to adopt with the RSV the reading of the parallel passage of I Chr. 11:11; "He wielded his spear" (עורר את-חניתו), or to emend העצנו to read מעצדו or חצינו and render the whole phrase: "He brandished his axe."
   *Bibliography.* S. R. Driver, *Notes on the Hebrew Text of the Books of Samuel* (2nd ed., 1913), p. 364.     E. R. DALGLISH

**ADINUS.** KJV Apoc. form of JAMIN.

**ADITHAIM** ăd'ə thā'əm [עדיתים] (Josh. 15:36). A town in the Shephelah in the Zorah-Azekah district of the tribe of Judah. Its site is unknown.

**ADLAI** ăd'lā, —lī [עדלי] (I Chr. 27:29). The father of Shaphat, who was over the royal herds in the valleys in the time of David.

**ADMAH** ăd'mə [אדמה]. One of the "cities of the valley" which because of its wickedness was destroyed along with SODOM; GOMORRAH; and ZEBOIIM. Admah is mentioned in giving the boundaries of the Canaanites (Gen. 10:19) and as one of the five cities which were attacked by the four eastern kings (14:1-17; *see also* CHEDORLAOMER). SHINAB was the king of Admah (vs. 2). Admah's destruction is implied in Gen. 19:24-29, and its overthrow is specifically recalled in Deut. 29:23. The fate of Admah and Zeboiim is held out by Hosea (11:8) as a warning to Israel.
   Admah was situated in the Valley of Siddim (*see* SIDDIM, VALLEY OF); here it engaged in battle with the invading kings (Gen. 14:2-3, 8). Admah may be located in the area now under the water of the S embayment of the Dead Sea, on a stream, prolonged westward, between the streams Seil 'Esal and Seil en-Numeirah.
   For detailed study of location, *see* SODOM.
                       J. P. HARLAND

**ADMATHA** ăd mā'thə [אדמתא, *probably from* Pers. *admata,* untamed = ̎Αδμητος]. One of the "seven princes of Persia and Media," members of the king's council under Ahasuerus (Esth. 1:14). It was on their advice that Ahasuerus banished Queen Vashti (vs. 19). *See* ESTHER, BOOK OF.          D. HARVEY

**ADMIN** ăd'mĭn ['Αδμίν] (Luke 3:33). An ancestor of Jesus.

**ADNA** ăd'nə [עדנא, *perhaps from* Akkad.]. **1.** A priest who returned from exile with Zerubbabel (Neh. 12: 15).
**2.** One of the Israelites with foreign wives (Ezra 10:30).

**ADNAH** ăd'nə [עדנה; Akkad. *Adna*]. **1.** Judahite commander during the reign of Jehoshaphat (II Chr. 17:14).
**2.** Manassite deserter from Saul's to David's army (I Chr. 12:20).

**ADONAI** ə dō'nī [אדני, Lord]. A title of honor and majesty applied to God, and used in the late postexilic period as a substitute for the sacred name Yahweh. *See* GOD, NAMES OF, § C6; LORD.

**ADONI-BEZEK** ə dō'nī bē'zĕk [אדני בזק, *see below*] (Judg. 1:5-7). Apparently a king of Jerusalem. He was defeated and mutilated during campaigns of the tribe of Judah to conquer territory in Canaan. The invading Judahites came upon the king in company with Canaanite forces at BEZEK, a settlement of unknown location. After pursuit and capture, Adoni-bezek was subjected to the fate which he had executed on his own royal captives—the amputation of thumbs and great toes. The incapacitated king was taken to Jerusalem, presumably by his own men, and there he died.

It is probable that Adoni-bezek is identical with ADONI-ZEDEK, king of Jerusalem at the time of the Conquest (Josh. 10:1, 3). The second part of such a name as Adoni-bezek should be a divine name or designation, which "zedek" is but "bezek" evidently is not.

*Bibliography.* M. Noth, *Die israelitischen Personennamen* (1928), p. 114; G. E. Wright, "The Literary and Historical Problem of Joshua 10 and Judges 1," *JNES*, V (1946), 105-14.
                                                    R. F. JOHNSON

**ADONIJAH** ăd'ə nī'jə [אדניה, אדניהו, Yahu is the Lord]. **1.** The fourth son of David (II Sam. 3:4; I Chr. 3:1-2); his mother was Haggith. Adonijah's regal aspirations involved him in his own destruction. The right of Adonijah to consider himself the heir apparent of the Davidic throne was not without cogency. In the senile days of David, Adonijah was the eldest living prince of the dynasty, since Amnon, Absalom, and presumably Chileab were dead (I Kings 2:22). David did not discourage this kingly ambition, not even when Adonijah asserted it incontestably by procuring for himself chariots and an entourage of knights and fifty runners (I Kings 1: 5 ff). While David may have given assurance to Bathsheba, his favorite queen, that her son Solomon would succeed him—a fact that seems to find confirmation in the exclusion of Solomon from the feast of Adonijah (I Kings 1:10—this pledge does not appear to have been seriously considered, because the

nomination of Solomon came as a decided surprise to the adherents of Adonijah, who himself could later represent the situation to Bathsheba thus: "You know that the kingdom was mine, and that all Israel fully expected me to reign" (I Kings 2:15). Moreover, the cause of the very personable Adonijah elicited the support of Abiathar the priest and Joab the commander of the army (I Kings 1:7; 2:22).

Hoping to climax his hope of becoming king before his aged father died, Adonijah prepared a sacrificial feast near En-rogel and invited the royal princes and the officials of Judah, excluding Solomon and his supporters. The intent of this festal gathering was unquestionably the proclamation of Adonijah as king. However, before the actual coronation could take place, Nathan and Bathsheba secured from the aged king the succession for Solomon, who was immediately anointed by Zadok the priest at Gihon, not far from En-rogel. When the resounding acclamations from the procession that accompanied Solomon were interpreted by Jonathan the son of Abiathar to mean the ruin of the hopes of Adonijah, the adherents of the rejected prince fled from his festal gathering. Adonijah himself took sanctuary by laying hold of the horns of the altar and was persuaded to leave this asylum only by the promise of Solomon to spare his life (I Kings 1:51-53).

However, Adonijah was subsequently judged guilty of treason when he asked Bathsheba to intercede with Solomon to give him in marriage the beautiful Abishag. This former nurse of David was apparently considered part of the royal harem, and the request of Adonijah constituted in the eyes of Solomon a capital crime, whereupon Benaiah was ordered to effect Adonijah's execution (I Kings 2:19-25).
**2.** One of the Levites who in company with princes and priests instructed the people in the law during an itinerant teaching mission in the cities of Judah in the third year of Jehoshaphat (II Chr. 17:8).
**3.** One of the chiefs of the people who set his seal to the covenant of reform in the time of Ezra (Neh. 10:16—H 10:17).                 E. R. DALGLISH

**ADONIKAM** ăd'ə nī'kəm [אדניקם, my Lord has arisen]. The head of one of the families that returned to Jerusalem from Babylonia after the Exile (Ezra 2:13; 8:13; Neh. 7:18; I Esd. 5:14; 8:39). The name appears as Adonijah (אדניהו, "My Lord is Jahweh") in the list of those who set their seal to Ezra's covenant (Neh. 10:16—H 10:17).         M. NEWMAN

**ADONIRAM** ăd'ə nī'rəm [אדנירם, the Lord is exalted] (I Kings 4:6; 5:14—H 5:28). Alternately: ADORAM ə dôr'əm [אדרם] (II Sam. 20:24; I Kings 12:18); HADORAM hə dôr'əm [הדרם] (II Chr. 10: 18). The son of Abda; a high official in the courts of David, Solomon, and Rehoboam, with a long record of service in charge of the *corvée*, or forced labor (II Sam. 20:24; I Kings 4:6; 12:18; *see* SLAVERY). Adoniram was the overseer of thirty thousand laborers whom Solomon drafted from all Israel and sent in relays of ten thousand to secure in Lebanon the materials for his building projects (I Kings 5:13-14). When Rehoboam alienated the N tribes by the announcement of his tyrannical program, Adoniram, who was sent by the king to enforce immediately upon them the *corvée,* was stoned to death (I Kings 12:18; II Chr. 10:18).

*Bibliography.* I. Mendelsohn, "State Slavery in Ancient Palestine," *BASOR,* 85 (1942), 14-17.          E. R. DALGLISH

**ADONIS** ə dō'nĭs [˝Αδωνις, *from* אדון, lord]. The Syrian deity of vegetation which wilted with the summer sun. The death of the god was mourned by the women of PHOENICIA, particularly beside the River Adonis (modern Nahr Ibrahim), near Beirut. This cult was known also in Greece, where Plato mentions "Adonis gardens"—pots of herbs—which were used in rites of imitative magic during the seven-day ascendancy of the Dog Star. There is a conceivable reference to this rite in the "PLEASANT PLANTS" (נטעי נעמנים) mentioned in Isa. 17:10, the title of Adonis being "pleasant" (נעמן).

*Bibliography.* S. A. Cook, *The Religion of Ancient Palestine in the Light of Archaeology* (1930), pp. 139-40; F. Cumont, "Adonis et Canicule," *Syria,* XVI (1935), pp. 46-49; G. Contenau, *La civilisation phénicienne* (1949), pp. 94-96, 112-15.
J. GRAY

**ADONI-ZEDEK** ə dō'nĭ zē'dĕk [אדני־אדק, my lord is righteousness, *or* my lord is (the god) Zedek(?)]. King of Jerusalem, defeated by Joshua in battle at Gibeon (Josh. 10:1, 3), probably identical with ADONI-BEZEK. Adoni-zedek was the leader of a coalition of five Amorite kings from royal cities to the S and the W of Jerusalem. The defection of the city of Gibeon to the invading Israelites imperiled the position of Adoni-zedek and his confederates and led to their futile effort to penalize the city. A forced night march brought Joshua and his men to the aid of Gibeon, and the rout of the confederate forces became complete in a hailstorm as they fled along a descending route westward toward the coast. The famous poetic fragment from the book of JASHAR refers to this battle:

> Sun, stand thou still at Gibeon,
> and thou Moon in the valley of Aijalon
> (Josh. 10:12).

The five Amorite kings were captured in a cave at Makkedah, where they had taken shelter, and were put to death. Their bodies were hung on trees until sundown, when they were removed and sealed in the cave with large stones, visible in the author's day.

*Bibliography.* M. Noth, *Die israelitischen Personennamen* (1928), p. 114; G. E. Wright, "The Literary and Historical Problem of Joshua 10 and Judges 1," *JNES,* V (1946), 105-14.
R. F. JOHNSON

**ADOPTION** [υἱοθεσία]. The theological importance of this word is probably that it provides a means of describing the Christian status of sonship as a vivid reality, while at the same time pointing to its secondary and derived nature—not sonship but adoption—in contrast to the essential and inherent sonship of Christ himself. It is by God's ELECTION that Israel has been made God's son (Hos. 11:1, etc.); it is by baptism and the presence of the Holy Spirit that the Christian is enabled (Rom. 8:15; Gal. 4:6) to cry the "Abba! Father!" which first rose to the lips of Jesus (Mark 14:36) by reason of his unique status (Rom. 1:4). *See* CHRIST.

**1. OT instances.** No laws of adoption are found formulated in the OT. The Hebrews could transfer rights from one member of the family to another, a process for which the days of polygamy provided ample scope (see Gen. 48:5; 49:4, 26; Deut. 21:15-17 [correcting the practice so as to safeguard the firstborn]; I Chr. 5:1-2). But adoption is much harder to illustrate from the OT. The allusion to Abraham's servant in Gen. 15:1 ff is perhaps important in this connection, since it appears to contemplate adoption. But it is not altogether clear, especially since the crucial vs. 2 seems to be corrupt (see commentators). However, Hammurabi's Code, sections 185 ff (*see* HAMMURABI), and the documents of the fifteenth century B.C. found at Nuzi (near Kirkuk, E of the Tigris) since 1925 show that adoption was legislated for in Semitic civilizations; and adoptions, at least in special circumstances, may be illustrated by a few biblical passages. Thus, in Exod. 2:10 Moses becomes son to Pharaoh's daughter—but this is in an Egyptian setting. (In Acts 7:21 the word ἀνείλατο, in the narrating of the same incident, is translated "adopted," with some support from nonbiblical literature and papyri; but it may merely refer to the taking of Moses out of the water.) Again, Ruth 4:16 is sometimes taken to mean that Naomi adopted the son of Boaz and Ruth; but the boy is already, by the levirate law (*see* MARRIAGE), her descendant. Once more, in Esth. 2:7, 15, Mordecai adopts Esther (the words לקח־לו לבת are translated: "adopted her as his own daughter"); but again this is in a foreign milieu. Thus, while the practice is evidenced in ancient Semitic civilizations, it is seldom alluded to in the OT.

**2. Meaning in the NT.** In the NT the word υἱοθεσία occurs only at Rom. 8:15 ("sonship"), 23 ("adoption as sons"); 9:4 ("sonship"); Gal. 4:5 ("adoption as sons"); Eph. 1:5 ("to be his sons"). It may be remarked at once that in Rom. 9:4 there is applied to Israel in its relation to God precisely that technical term which, as has just been shown, Israel does not seem to have used of itself. The OT speaks of Israel as God's son (Hos. 11:1), his first-born son (Exod. 4:22; *see* CHILDREN [SONS] OF GOD); but it also shows that Israel is not such by any right of physical relationship, but only because of God's free choice (Deut. 14:2); and it is perhaps to emphasize this fact that Paul uses the word, as though to say that even the status of Israel was not something necessary and inherent, but the result of an act of graciousness on the part of God. Comparable to this (though without the actual word υἱοθεσία) is Philo's remark (*On Sobriety* 56) that one who, like Abraham, is called the friend of God has become nobly born, "for he has registered God as his father and become by adoption his only son."

It is true that the strictly contrasting word "sonship" (υἱότης) is not used of Christ, and, indeed, appears not to be extant (except just possibly in one papyrus, if it is there the correct reading) until the postbiblical Christian writers (e.g., Basil of Caesarea); and it might be argued that therefore "adoption" is not to be pressed in its distinctive sense, but is to be accepted as a slightly imprecise expression, used in default of υἱότης, for the status of a son. On the other hand, υἱοθεσία is never applied to Christ, and his unique status is made very clear in other ways (see, e.g., Phil. 2:6 ff; Col. 1:15 ff), while the position of Christians in the family of God is equally clearly derivative and secondary. Moreover, the exact meaning of υἱοθεσία is certainly not "sonship" but the "making" or "adopting" of a son. It seems best, therefore, to take it in this strict sense.

The contexts, however, in which it occurs are not in themselves altogether clear. Thus, Gal. 4:5 is somewhat perplexing. If the context were a straight contrast between servitude and υἱοθεσία, it would be simple to interpret it to mean that, though *naturally* slaves, we are *adopted* (or possibly are destined to be adopted) into the status of sons by God's graciousness. But, in fact, the argument seems to be rather that, naturally sons, we are nevertheless like slaves unless and until we "come of age." (It is not clear whether ἡ προθεσμία τοῦ πατρός in 4:2 ["the date set by the father"] is an allusion to an actual law by which the father could determine in advance when his child was to come of age, or whether it is an artificial adaptation to the theological meaning of the full arrival of the time [vs. 4] when God brought his Son into the world.) It is noteworthy that the word for "receiving" the adoption (vs. 5) is ἀπολάβωμεν, which normally refers to receiving what is a due—"duly receiving"; and vs. 7: "You are no longer a slave but a son," might, in view of vss. 1-2, only mean: "You are no longer *like* a slave [i.e., without rights, as also is a minor] but are now able to enjoy the full rights belonging to you as a son."

In the same way, it is possible to interpret Rom. 8:12-17 either way, as far as the context goes: either "You need not revert to a servile attitude," or "You need not revert to servitude itself."

Finally, Eph. 1:5 ("destined us in love to be his sons") is also, in itself, inconclusive. But our adoption as sons is here a measure of the greatness of God's love, and is through Jesus Christ, and the strict meaning of an unmerited, genuine adoption therefore fits the context well. Besides, a comparable passage in John 8:31 ff (though without the actual word) dwells on the necessity for the Son (Jesus) to set free those who otherwise are slaves.

Thus, it is reasonable to accept the strict, etymological sense in all these passages, especially since it is borne out by a few passages from secular Greek literature and by plenty of inscriptions. An instance of the latter, well illustrating the strict sense, is: Ἀντισθένης Ἰσοκλεῦς, κατὰ δὲ υἱοθεσίαν Γρίννου (Boeckh Inscription 1, n. 2448, 3, 15)—i.e., "Antisthenes (the son) of Isocles, but by adoption (the son) of Grinnus"; and Hesychius says very explicitly: υἱοθετεῖ·υἱοποιεῖ, οὐ φύσει, ἀλλὰ θέσει—i.e., the verb corresponding to υἱοθεσία means "making" a son, not by nature but by decree. The contrasting term, in the inscriptions, is κατὰ γένεσιν, "by birth."

**3. Relation with other NT ideas.** If, then, the strict sense is accepted for the NT occurrences, it may be brought into line with Paul's thought about the INHERITANCE. A slave, if adopted as a son, inherited his master's property; and it may be that in the phrase addressed to slaves in Col. 3:24: "knowing that from the Lord you will receive the inheritance as your reward," Paul is alluding to this paradox—a slave's becoming possessed of property. If

so, his use of the similar paradox of a slave's becoming a son by adoption is rendered the more probable (cf. Rom. 8:17; *see* HEIR).

Further, it has been suggested (though perhaps this is too farfetched) that in Rom. 8:16 ("It is the Spirit himself bearing witness with our spirit") there is actually a reference to the witnesses required in Roman law to the act of adoption. The Holy Spirit of God joins with the spirit of the Christian in giving evidence that an adoption has taken place. Man's spirit crying "Abba! Father!" is inspired by God's Spirit; and together they are witness to the reality of the new status. (As is well known, the word ἐπερώτημα, "appeal," in I Pet. 3:21 may be another instance of the contract language of Roman law, employed as a metaphor in Christian thinking.)

The idea of adoption, when thus linked to the idea of the Holy Spirit, carries in it the same combination of present and future tenses which is carried by the doctrine of the Spirit. Indeed, Rom. 8:23 ("We wait for adoption as sons, the redemption of our bodies") shows that, at least here if not elsewhere, adoption is regarded by Paul as a promise for the future not yet realized. Christians look forward to the future enjoyment of their inheritance, when (as appears in Rev. 21:7) "he who conquers shall have this heritage, and I will be his God and he shall be my son." That is to say, the victorious will be given the messianic status of sons of God (cf. the divine promise to David about his son: "I will be his father, and he shall be my son" [II Sam. 7:14]). In oriental law there was not, as in stricter systems, a clear, formal distinction between the proleptic guarantee of a property and the time when the recipient entered in actual fact into its enjoyment.

Thus, where the Fourth Gospel and I Peter use terms of REGENERATION, Paul uses this legal figure of adoption. Whether we may see reflected in this the dramatic suddenness of his conversion, as contrasted with terms borrowed from the natural course of things, is another matter (cf. I Cor. 15:8). After all, I John 3:1 comes near to describing adoption, even though the word is not used: "See what love the Father has given us, that we should be called children of God; and so we are." (It is a debatable question, however, whether "and so we are" is intended to describe a status even better than merely being "called," or adopted as, sons of God, or whether it is in contrast with "what we shall be" hereafter [vs. 2]). See also John 8:31 ff, cited above. *See* CHILDREN (SONS) OF GOD.

**Bibliography.** W. E. Ball, *Contemporary Review*, LX (Aug., 1891), 278-92; A. Deissmann, *Bible Studies* (English trans.; 2nd ed., 1909), p. 239; T. Whaling, *PTR*, XXI (1923), 223-35; A. Deissmann, *Light from the Ancient East* (English trans.; 2nd ed., 1927), p. 337, n. 3; L. H. Marshall, *The Challenge of NT Ethics* (1946), pp. 258-59; W. H. Russell, *JBL*, LXXI (1952), 233-34. C. F. D. MOULE

**ADORAIM** ăd'ə rā'əm [אדורים, two threshing floors(?)]; Apoc. ADORA ə dôr'ə [Ἀδωρά; *cf.* Papyrus Zeno 76 (259 B.C.) Ἀδώρεος; Josephus Δωρά]. A city of Judah identified with modern Dura, five miles W-SW of Hebron. Adoraim was among the fifteen cities fortified by Rehoboam (*ca.* 922-915; II Chr. 11:9).

Adora (Adoraim) and Marisa (MARESHAH, Tell Sandahannah) were the two major cities of Idumea. At Adora, Simon Maccabeus stopped the advance of Trypho in 142 B.C. (I Macc. 13:20-21). After the death of Antiochus VII in 129, John Hyrcanus captured Adora, and it was still in Jewish hands at the time of Alexander Janneus, ca. 79 B.C. (Jos. Antiq. XIII.ix.1; XIII.xv.4; War I.ii).

In 59 B.C., Gabinius, the proconsul of Syria, ordered the rebuilding of Adora (Jos. War I.viii.4; cf. Antiq. XIV.v.3) and designated it as the center of one of his five administrative districts (War I.viii.5; cf. Antiq. XIV.v.4).

In the book of Jubilees (38:9 ff) Adûrâm (Adora) was the scene of an attack by Esau's forces against those of Jacob which held the fortress of Hebron. In the course of the attack, Esau was killed and was buried at Adûrâm.

*Bibliography.* B. Kanael, "The Partition of Judea by Gabinius," *IEJ*, 7 (1957), 98-106.          V. R. GOLD

**ADORAM.** Alternate form of ADONIRAM.

**ADORATION.** Literally, the act of bringing the hand or fingers to the lips in praise; more generally, the giving of divine honors. *See* WORSHIP.

**ADRAMMELECH** ə drăm'ə lĕk [אדרמלך, the lordship of Melech (the king)]. **1.** A deity worshiped by the people of Sepharvaim (possibly Sabraim in Syria), settled by the Assyrians in Samaria after 722 B.C. The "Melech" element may be either the title of an unnamed local deity of Sepharvaim or that of the god Athtar, the Venus Star.

*Bibliography.* J. Gray, "The Desert God Attr in the Literature and Religion of Canaan," *JNES*, VIII (1949), 78-80; J. A. Montgomery, *Commentary on Kings*, ICC (ed. H. S. Gehman; 1951), p. 476; W. F. Albright, *Archaeology and the Religion of Israel* (1953), pp. 162-64.          J. A. GRAY

**2.** A son of Sennacherib who, according to II Kings 19:37 (=Isa. 37:38), with Sharezer murdered his father in the temple of Nisroch. The name appears as Andromachos in Jos. Antiq. X.xxiii, and in the Greek sources as Adramelos and Ardumuzan. No Assyriological interpretation of the name can be offered.          A. L. OPPENHEIM

**ADRAMYTTIUM** ăd'rə mĭt'ĭ əm [τὸ Ἀδραμύττιον] (Acts 27:2). A seaport in Mysia in the NW part of the Roman province of Asia.

Herodotus (VII.42) mentions the town of Adramyttium (Ἀδραμύττειον), and Strabo (XIII.613-14) states that it was founded by the Lydians but belonged later to the Mysians. The latter author calls it a notable city and the home of the famous orator Xenocles. The adjectival use of the name is found in Strabo (XIII.605) when he mentions the Adramyttian Gulf (ὁ Ἀδραμυττηνὸς κόλπος), and in Plutarch (*Cicero* 4) when he states that Cicero studied with Xenocles of Adramyttium (Ξενοκλεῖ τῷ Ἀδραμυττηνῷ). It is in the same form that the name occurs in Acts 27:2 when it is said that Paul embarked in an Adramyttian ship (πλοίῳ Ἀδραμυττηνῷ). The Vulg. has *navem Hadrumetinam*, and the reading of the name with a rough breathing is the basis for

a theory that the place was originally colonized by traders from Hadhramaut in South Arabia. The modern name of the city is Edremit.

*Bibliography.* J. R. Harris, "Adramyttium," *The Contemporary Review*, CXXVIII (1925), 194-202.          J. FINEGAN

**ADRIA** ā'drĭ ə [ὁ Ἀδρίας] (Acts 27:27). The sea between Italy and Greece and S of both; the Adriatic Sea.

Among towns around what is now the Gulf of Venice, Strabo (V.214) mentions Atria, a city which was at the mouth of the Po River. He says that it was once an illustrious city, and that the Adriatic Gulf got its name from it with only a slight change in spelling. Livy (V.xxxiii.8) provides the information that Hatria (as he spells the name) was an Etruscan colony, and agrees with Strabo in deriving the name of the Hadriatic or Adriatic Sea from this place. While this derivation would suggest that the name applied originally to the upper gulf, Livy also remarks that Italy was surrounded like an island by two seas—namely, those which the Italians called the Tuscan and the Hadriatic, which the Greeks knew as the Tyrrhenian and the Adriatic. Therefore, the name Adriatic belonged to the sea all the way to the S end of Italy, balancing the Tyrrhenian Sea on the W side. Strabo (II.123) also says that what was called the Adriatic Sea in his time included the Ionian Gulf, which was the sea W of Achaia; and the length of the Adriatic Sea, which he gives as six thousand stadia, or some seven hundred miles, extends this far. Ptolemy, moreover, states that Crete (*see* CAPHTOR) is surrounded on the W by the Adriatic Sea (Geography III.15), and Sicily on the E by the Adriatic Sea (Geography III.4); therefore, the Adriatic included the waters between these two islands. It must have been in this same region that Josephus suffered shipwreck on his journey to Rome in ca. A.D. 64, concerning which he writes (Life XV): "Our ship sank in the midst of the sea of Adria." The reference of Acts 27:27 to Paul's ship as being in the sea of Adria (ἐν τῷ Ἀδρίᾳ) when it was moving between Crete and MALTA is accordingly in harmony with contemporary usage. As for the danger of the passage across this sea, it is attested not only by the experience of Josephus at a time so close to that of Paul but also by literary references such as those of Horace, who speaks of the tempestuous waves and breakers of the roaring Adriatic, a sea which is restless and wanton (Odes I.xxxiii.15; II.xiv.14; III.iii.5; ix.23).

The tempestuous wind which drove Paul's ship from Crete to Melita was the Euraquilo (*see* NORTHEASTER; Acts 27:14—ὁ εὐρακύλων, Egyptian text; not εὐροκλύδων, Byzantine text), which means between the Eurus, the E wind, and the Aquilo, the NE wind. Thus it was E-NE, and this agrees with the direction the ship was driven at the outset from FAIR HAVENS to CAUDA. From Cauda on, it may be assumed that the ship was hove to on the starboard tack so that any headway would be away from the dangerous SYRTIS (Acts 27:17) off the African coast and on the course toward Italy, while the drift would be generally westward. The elapsed time from the departure from Cauda to landfall on Melita was thirteen days and a portion of the fourteenth (Acts

27:27). Under the conditions described, sea captains experienced on the run between Malta and Crete estimate a drift of one to two miles per hour. Allowing 36 miles in 24 hours for 13¼ days gives 477 miles and agrees exactly with the measured distance from Cauda to St. Paul's Bay, Malta.

*Bibliography.* Partsch, "Adria," *Pauly-Wissowa,* I (1894), cols. 417-19; E. Smith, "A Twentieth Century Sailor Reviews a First Century Shipwreck," *The Rudder,* LXIII (1947), 32 ff.

J. FINEGAN

**ADRIEL** ā'drĭ əl [עַדְרִיאֵל]. Son of Barzillai; husband of Merab, the daughter of Saul (I Sam. 18:19); called "Adriel the Meholathite." He was the father of the five sons of Merab, all of whom David delivered to the Gibeonites for execution (II Sam. 21:8, where with RSV "Merab" is read for "Michal").

E. R. DALGLISH

**ADUEL** ə dōō'əl ['Αδουήλ = אֲדִיאֵל] (Tob. 1:1). An ancestor of Tobit, listed among the "descendants of Asiel and the tribe of Naphtali."

J. C. SWAIM

**ADULLAM** ə dŭl'əm [עֲדֻלָּם, retreat, refuge]; **ADULLAMITE** —ə mīt. A Canaanite royal city in the Shephelah first referred to in Gen. 38:1, 12-20, the account of the marriage to an Adullamite woman and subsequent activities of Judah, son of Jacob, in the region of Adullam.

The ancient name of Adullam is perhaps preserved in the place name Khirbet 'Id el-Ma (or -Miyeh), a site with extensive ruins in the Wadi es-Sur just below Tell Sheikh Madhkur, the site of ancient Adullam, *ca.* 9½ miles E-NE of Beit Jibrin (Eleutheropolis).

The king of Adullam was one of the thirty-one Canaanite kings listed as defeated by Joshua in the course of the Israelite occupation (Josh. 12:15). It was one of the cities assigned to the Judean district of Zorah-Azekah in the Shephelah (15:35).

David took refuge from Saul in a cave near Adullam, where he was joined by his family and other followers (I Sam. 22:1-2). The cave became David's headquarters for a time (II Sam. 23:13 ff; I Chr. 11:15 ff; cf. Jos. Antiq. VI.xii.3).

Adullam was fortified by Rehoboam prior to Shishak's invasion of Judah (*ca.* 918 B.C.; II Chr. 11:7). It was one of the series of fortress cities forming a line of defense against possible invasion from the W and the S.

Adullam may well have been one of the forty-six fortified cities Sennacherib captured during his campaign of 701 B.C. (cf. II Kings 18:13 ff; II Chr. 32:1 ff). The lament of Micah over the cities of the Shephelah was probably in anticipation of this campaign—or possibly the campaign of Sargon II in 711, when, however, the cities of Judah were apparently spared attack (Mic. 1:8-16, especially vs. 15).

Jewish returnees from the Exile reoccupied Adullam along with other neighboring cities, including Azekah and Lachish (Neh. 11:30). In 164 Judas Maccabeus, in the course of his Idumean campaign, retired to Adullam after defeating Georgias, one of the commanders of Antiochus IV, Epiphanes (II Macc. 12:38 ff; cf. I Macc. 5:55 ff).

*Bibliography.* W. F. Albright, "Researches of the School in Western Judea," *BASOR,* 15 (1924), 3-4. V. R. GOLD

**ADULTERY** [נאף, *possibly from* Egyp. *ʾ h p;* μοιχεύω, commit adultery]. Because of the nature of marriage, adultery was not so much evidence of moral depravity as the violation of a husband's right to have sole sexual possession of his wife and to have the assurance that his children were his own. Adultery was strictly prohibited by law (Exod. 20:14; Lev. 18:20; Deut. 5:18; John 8:2-5 [RSV mg.]). Intercourse with a female slave who was betrothed to another was not a capital offense—only a guilt offering was needed (Lev. 19:22). In other cases, however, the death penalty was demanded (20:10). To determine that a woman had been adulterous, in the absence of any witnesses, she might be required to drink a special concoction (*see* JEALOUSY, ORDEAL OF). Both parties involved in adulterous intercourse were to be killed (Deut. 22:22; cf. 22:23-24; Ezek. 18:11-13; 22:11; Mal. 3:5). Job calls adultery a "heinous crime" (Job 31:11); the adulteress destroys a man (Prov. 6:26 ff). Her tactics are described in considerable detail in Prov. 7:6-23. To look lustfully at a woman is to commit adultery (Matt. 5:28); and marriage with a divorced woman is adultery (Matt. 5:32; Mark 10:11; Luke 16:18). While upholding the law against adultery, Jesus refused to condemn the woman taken in adultery (John 7:53–8:11 [RSV mg.]). Paul points out that marriage after the death of a husband is not adultery (Rom. 7:3).

"Adultery" is used of religious disloyalty and harlotry (Jer. 7:9; 23:10; cf. Ezek. 23:45; Rev. 2:22). Faithless Jews are called offspring of the adulteress and the harlot (Isa. 57:3).

For bibliography *see* MARRIAGE. O. J. BAAB

**ADUMMIM** ə dŭm'ĭm [אֲדֻמִּים, red rocks, in the phrase מַעֲלֵה אֲדֻמִּים, ascent of Adummim (KJV going up to Adummim)]. A pass leading from the Jordan Valley into the hill country. A trade route probably used this pass at a very early date to go from Jericho to the city-state of Jerusalem. In all periods, including the present, this pass was apparently a part of the road between these two cities. It formed part of Judah's N boundary (Josh. 15:7) and is a reference point establishing the location of Geliloth on Benjamin's S border (18:17).

Eusebius notes that Maledomni (from *Maʿalê-ᵃdummîm;* Jerome, Adommim) was a fortress midway between Jericho and Jerusalem. Later, a Templar stronghold was built there. Though the incident of the Good Samaritan may not have occurred there, it is referred to today as the "Inn of the Good Samaritan," following Jerome's suggestion. While perhaps reminiscent of this ancient tradition, the modern Arabic name for this pass S of the Wadi Qelt, Tal'at ed-Damm (the "ascent of blood"), is probably descriptive of the red marl on each side of the pass. V. R. GOLD

**ADVENT.** A term often used to designate the coming or the second coming of the Christ. See PAROUSIA.

**ADVENTURESS** [נכרי]; KJV STRANGE WOMAN. A woman who lives by her wits, but largely based upon sex. In Proverbs (23:27; cf. 6:24; etc.) the term is often parallel with HARLOT. Perhaps first the "harlots" were foreigners; thus the KJV translation, "strange woman," is more literal.

C. U. WOLF

**ADVERSARY.** A conventional, and literal, rendering of Hebrew SATAN.

**ADVOCATE.** The translation of παράκλητος in I John 2:1 (elsewhere COUNSELOR; COMFORTER). As the living "expiation for our sins," Christ is man's advocate with the Father. He is the representative of man to God, making intercession for man as advocate and helper. The same function is performed by the Spirit (John 14:16) as the mediator of the ascended Christ to his people.

*See also* PARACLETE; HOLY SPIRIT.

G. W. H. LAMPE

**AEDIAS.** KJV Apoc. form of ELIJAH.

**AENEAS** ĭ nē'əs [Αἰνέας]. A man at Lydda whom Peter cured of the palsy (Acts 9:33-34). He is otherwise unknown. The name appears in Homer (Αἰνείας), Thucydides, Xenophon, Pindar, and Josephus (Antiq. XIV.x.22).

H. H. PLATZ

**AENON** ē'nŏn [Αἰνών, *from* עינים עֵינַיִם, עֵינוֹן, double spring; LXX Αἰνάν] (John 3:23). A site rich in water, where John the Baptist was active. It was near a place called SALIM. The mention of Judea in the preceding verse (and the connecting ἦν δὲ καὶ introducing 3:23) supports the tradition locating this Aenon in Perea beyond the Jordan, which was part of Judea in the wider sense. This identification appears first on the Madaba Map (1.6), where to the name Aenon are added the words ἔνθα νῦν ὁ Σαπσαθάς, "there now the Sapsaphas" or "willow." The localization of the spring where John baptized is supported by Antoninus, a sixth-century pilgrim guide. A cave of Saint John is mentioned by Cyrillus Scythopolitanus; it is located beyond the Jordan by Epiphanius Monachus (*ca.* A.D. 840) and John Phocas (1177). John Moschus (*Pratum Spirituale* 1-2) mentions a cave where a monk of Saint Eustorgius saw a vision of the Baptist and where the patriarch Elias of Jerusalem (494-518) built a church. It is localized in the Wadi Kharrar, near the Jordan ford opposite Jericho.

The other tradition places Aenon S of Scythopolis (Beth-shean) in the Jordan Valley W of the river, but outside Judea as it was understood in the time of Jesus. The earliest evidence for this tradition is Eusebius (Onom. 40.1-4), who refers to an "Aenon near Salim" shown eight miles S of Scythopolis, and calls it a "spot" (τόπος) near Salim and the Jordan. He is followed by the Madaba Map (1.1); and the pilgrim Aetheria describes the site as situated in a garden with a spring or pool, the latter possibly indicated by a bluish-green row of cubes in the Madaba Map. Jerome (*Epistle* 73) also supports this location. The indications of Eusebius point to a place near Tell er-Ridgha, eight miles S of Beth-shean, a region particularly rich in water. Some travelers have noted the local Arab name Sheikh Salim in the vicinity.

*Bibliography.* P. Thomsen, *Loca Sancta* (1907), pp. 18-19. F.-M. Abel, "Exploration de la vallée du Jourdain," *RB*, XXII (1913), 220-23; "La laure de Sapsaphas," *RB*, XLI (1932), 248-52. M. Avi-Yonah, *The Madaba Mosaic Map* (1954), pp. 35-38.

M. AVI-YONAH

**AEON** ē'ŏn, —ŏn [αἰών; *related to* Lat. *aevum*, *ae(vi)ternus*]. The word used in the LXX and in the NT in the sense "long span of time," "eternity" (*see* TIME §§ 1b-c). After the first century B.C. it becomes, in the meaning of "world's age" and "world," the term for the apocalyptic doctrine of the present and the coming aeon (*see* APOCALYPTICISM; ESCHATOLOGY OF THE APOC. AND THE PSEUDEP.), which also plays a role in the NT (*see* ESCHATOLOGY OF THE NT) and in rabbinical Judaism.

E. JENNI

**AESORA** ĭ sôr'ə [Αισωρα]; KJV ESORA. A city grouped with CHOBA and the valley of Salem (Jth. 4:4), identified by some scholars with the HAZOR of Josh. 11:1, 10; Judg. 4:2, 17, the modern Tell el-Qedah N of the Sea of Galilee in Naphtali. But if the writer is referring to N Transjordan opposite Choba, it is possible that he mistakenly located Aesora there, perhaps on the basis of such texts as II Kings 15:29; Jer. 49:28-33, which relate Hazor to this NE part of Palestine. Another hypothesis is Khirbet Hazzûr, the Hazor of Neh. 11:33.

*Bibliography.* F. Stummer, *Geographie des Buches Judith* (1947), p. 17.

E. W. SAUNDERS

**AFFLICTION.** *See* SUFFERING.

**AGABA.** KJV Apoc. form of HAGAB.

**AGABUS** ăg'ə bəs [Ἄγαβος, Ἄγαβος; חגב, locust, *and a proper name* HAGAB, *or* עגב, to love]. A Christian prophet from Judea who had a charism and spoke "by the Spirit."

In Acts 11:28 it is recorded that Agabus went with other prophets from Jerusalem to Antioch and foretold a famine "over all the world"—i.e., probably Judea. There was a famine in Judea under the Emperor Claudius, apparently *ca.* A.D. 46-47. In Acts 21:10-11 Agabus predicts, by a symbolic act, that Paul will be "bound" by the Jews at Jerusalem and handed over to Gentiles—a prophecy not precisely fulfilled. The Greek church, holding him a martyr, celebrates his festival on March 8.

*Bibliography.* Jos. Antiq. XX.ii.5; v.2. Tac. Ann. XII.43. Suetonius *Claudius* 18. K. Lake, *Beginnings of Christianity*, V (1933), 452-55.

B. H. THROCKMORTON, JR.

**AGADE** ə gä'dĭ. *See* ACCAD.

**AGAG** ā'găg [אגג]. An Amalekite king, defeated by Saul, put to death by Samuel (Num. 24:7; I Sam. 15:8-9, 20, 32-33). Saul's battle against the Amalekites under Agag was the occasion for his decisive split with Samuel. Saul had disobeyed Samuel's directive that all the Amalekites and their property be destroyed (*see* DEVOTED); and when Samuel confronted him with this disobedience, he first offered a pious excuse and then attempted to shift the blame to his people. Samuel himself then executed Agag, whose "sword has made women childless" (I Sam. 15:33).

The theological description of Saul's disobedience and resultant loss of the kingship bears close resemblance to the story of man's disobedience in the Garden of Eden and his expulsion therefrom.

**Bibliography.** B. D. Napier, *From Faith to Faith* (1955), pp. 112-17.                                    R. F. JOHNSON

**AGAGITE** ā'gə gīt [אֲגָגִי, *probably* descendant of Agag]. The designation of Haman (Esth. 3:1 ff). The reference is probably to Agag king of Amalek, ancient enemy of Israel (Deut. 25:17-19); for Mordecai, the adversary of Haman, is described as a descendant of Saul, the adversary of Agag (Esth. 2:5; cf. I Sam. 15:7 ff). The LXX understood the term as "enemy" (cf. Esth. 9:24).                D. HARVEY

**AGAPE** ä gä'pā. The transliteration of ἀγάπη, one of the Greek words for "love." *See* LOVE. *See also* AGAPE, THE, for a special use of the term in the life of the early church.

**AGAPE, THE** ăg'ə pĭ [ἀγάπη, love]. The name commonly used to denote the "love feasts" of the early Christians, the meals provided by church members for religious fellowship and especially for charity to the poor and the widows of the Christian community. The custom derives from the earliest days of the church, and may well be rooted in the common meals of Jesus with his disciples, or in such instances of his ministry as the feeding of the multitude (Mark 6:34-44; 8:1-9, and parallels).

The evidence for these meals in Acts (2:42, 46; 6:1-2) is involved in the problem of distinguishing clearly between the agape and the Lord's Supper. The same ambiguity surrounds Paul's discussion of the Lord's Supper in I Cor. 11:20 ff, the breaking of bread at Paul's farewell visit to the church in Troas (Acts 20:11), and—for the early years of the second century—the directions for common meals in the Didache 9-10, the mention of the agape by Ignatius of Antioch (Smyr. 8:2), and the Christian meals reported by the pagan Pliny the Younger during his governorship of Bithynia in the year 112 (*Letters* X.97: "the custom . . . of gathering together for the taking of food—food of an innocent kind"). For a fuller discussion of the problem, *see* LORD'S SUPPER § 3.

By the middle of the second century, the agape meal for fellowship and charity, generally held in the afternoon or evening, had been definitely separated from association with the sacramental rite of the Lord's Supper or Eucharist. The only reference in the NT to the agape in this distinct sense is in Jude 12 (with which one should compare the variant reading ἀπάταις-ἀγάπαις in a parallel passage of II Pet. 2:13). The technical use of the term "agape" for these meals is attested by Clement of Alexandria (*The Instructor* II.1 ff) and in Tert. Apol. 39.16: "Our supper is called 'love' [*dilectio*] by the Greeks." Clement also applies to the agape the Pauline title "Lord's Supper" (*The Instructor* II.2.33); and the same designation for the agape occurs in the Latin and Coptic versions of Hippolytus' *Apostolic Tradition* 26.5.

The customs attending the Christian agapes stem originally from the table observances of Jewish families and associations, particularly the more formal suppers that inaugurated sabbaths and festivals. The Mishnaic and Talmudic tractates *Berakoth* ("Blessings") provide numerous details of these suppers; and despite the rabbinic disputes over the exact order of procedure at them, one may with a fair degree of accuracy reconstruct the customs obtaining in the first century A.D.

The family or group of friends would gather for supper, before sundown, at home or in a suitable house. After preliminary hors d'oeuvres, including wine when it was available, the company reclined or sat at table for the meal proper. The head of the group formally began the meal by pronouncing a benediction—i.e., a thanksgiving to God—over the bread, which was then broken and distributed. During the meal conversation, though festive and joyous, was devoted to religious topics. With the fall of night lamps were brought in and a benediction recited blessing God as the Creator of light. At the conclusion of the meal, the hands were washed, and a final benediction for food (grace after meals) was offered by the head of the company. On sabbaths and festivals, and other occasions of special solemnity, the grace after meals was said over a cup of wine mixed with water—the "cup of blessing" (cf. I Cor. 10:16) —with special remembrance before God of his providence and a prayer for the fulfilment of his purpose in the coming of his kingdom. At a later time, when these meals were observed after the conclusion of the synagogue service, and hence after sundown, the blessing over the cup was said at the beginning, rather than at the end, of the meal.

Jewish associations of a more highly organized and disciplined character made much of these meals in the promotion of their common life. They were a regular feature of the Essene communities, and are described in the Manual of Discipline discovered among the scrolls of their center at Khirbet Qumran near the Dead Sea (*see* DEAD SEA SCROLLS): "And when they prepare a table to eat, or wine to drink, the priest shall first stretch forth his hand to invoke a blessing upon the first portion of the bread and the wine." This regulation is placed in the context of rules for the gathering of the community for counsel, study of the Law, and worship. Candidates for admission to the community were not allowed to participate in these common meals until they had passed a two-year novitiate.

Similarly, Philo describes the evening assemblies of the Jewish sect of Therapeutae near Alexandria (*On the Contemplative Life* 10-11). After the exposition of the scriptures conducted by the "president" and the singing of psalms and hymns, "the younger members bring in the table, on which is set a very pure meal of leavened bread seasoned with salt mixed with hyssop." After supper, a vigil of antiphonal chanting and dancing continued until sunrise. Then; after prayer, the group dispersed.

Gatherings of early Christian disciples, as depicted in Acts and the letters of Paul, exhibit practices analogous to those of the Jewish sectaries. In conjunction with their common meals, time was devoted to the variously edifying ministries of spiritual gifts— preaching, prophesying, and speaking in tongues (cf. I Cor. 12; 14), teaching and exhortation, and the singing of "psalms and hymns and spiritual songs" (Col. 3:16-17; cf. Eph. 5:19-20). This is the case whether or not one distinguishes the blessings over the bread and wine, as the "Lord's Supper" in the strictest sense, from the rest of the meal and devotional observances. For all these devotions were related to the act of "thanksgiving"—i.e., the Eucharist (cf. I Cor. 14:16; Col. 3:17). But a peculiarly Christian emphasis was given this table fellowship by its association with charitable gifts and provisions for widows (Acts 6:1) and the poor (I Cor. 11:21).

The regulations and forms for the church's common meals given in the DIDACHE, chs. 9–10, provide: a thanksgiving over the cup and bread before the meal—and this blessed food is called "Eucharist" and denied to the unbaptized—and a thanksgiving for food after the meal, with a petition for the coming of the kingdom. There is, however, in these forms no memorial of the Lord's passion and death. This fact, plus the circumstance that these regulations were made for the guidance of lay people in churches without a settled ministry but visited from time to time by inspired prophets and teachers, lends weight to the position of those critics who interpret the Didache forms as table blessings for an agape. For later, in chs. 14–15, charge is given regarding the Sunday Eucharist, with directions for obtaining a ministry of bishops and deacons. The thanksgiving forms of the Didache show an unmistakable lineage with Jewish table blessings. It is possible, however, that the Didache preserves a primitive combination of the Eucharist with a regular meal, such as may have survived in smaller Christian communities for some time in the second century.

The most detailed accounts of the agape, once it was separated from the Eucharist, come only from the end of the second century, in the *Apology* of Tertullian (39.16) and the *Apostolic Tradition* of Hippolytus. Their descriptions show the Jewish origins of the observance: the devotions before and after the meal, and the religious conversation during the repast; the washing of the hands and lighting of the lamps. An interesting Roman feature in Hippolytus' account is the mention of an *apophoretum*, the tasty morsels and tidbits that guests were allowed to take home with them from the table of their host. Hippolytus also lays particular stress upon the provision of agapes for the benefit of widows.

A special form of agape developed in the second century and derived from pagan custom was the funerary and anniversary banquets associated with the memory of departed Christians. Near the entrance to the oldest Christian cemeteries at Rome, the catacombs of Domitilla and of Priscilla, there are chambers with benches for the celebration of these memorial repasts. Some of the earliest Christian art preserved in the catacombs provides pictorial representations of these feasts. *See* ART. *See also* WORSHIP IN THE NT, CHRISTIAN, especially §§ 3-4.

**Bibliography.** J. F. Keating, *The Agape and the Eucharist in the Early Church* (1901). F. X. Funk, "L'Agape," *Revue d'histoire ecclésiastique*, IV (1903), 5-23; V (1904), 5-15; VII (1906), 5-15. H. Leclercq, "Agape," *Dictionnaire d'archéologie chrétienne et de liturgie* (1907-53), I, 775-848. K. Völker, *Mysterium und Agape* (1927). J. M. Hanssens, "L'Agape et l'Eucharistie," *Ephemerides liturgicae*, XLI (1927), 525-48; XLII (1928), 545-71; XLIII (1929), 177-98, 520-29. F. L. Cirlot,

*The Early Eucharist* (1939), pp. 17-49. B. Reicke, *Diakonie, Festfreude und Zelos in Verbindung mit der altchristlichen Agapenfeier* (1951). *See also* the bibliography under LORD'S SUPPER.

M. H. SHEPHERD, JR.

**AGAR** ā'gär. Douay Version form of HAGAR.

**AGATE.** A chalcedony with more or less concentric bands, generally white and brown, frequent in Egypt. Three words are so translated:

*a*) שְׁבוּ, *šebhô* (cf. Akkadian *šubu*, "a stone"; LXX and Vulg. "agate"). A stone in the breastpiece of judgment (Exod. 28:19; 39:12).

*b*) כַּדְכֹּד, *kadhkōdh*. In Isa. 54:12 this is the material of the pinnacles of Jerusalem; the LXX and the Vulg. read "jasper," a red, green, or brown silica. In Ezek. 27:16 it is an article of trade between Syria and Tyre; the LXX and the Vulg. transliterate.

*c*) Χαλκηδών (Rev. 21:19). The third jewel in the foundation of the walls of the New Jerusalem.

*See also* JEWELS § 2. W. E. STAPLES

**AGE.** An expression, not always sharply defined, for a long period of time (limited or unlimited); in the NT often a translation of αἰών, "AEON" (*see also* TIME §§ 1*b-c*). For the expressions "close of the age," "age to come," etc., which presuppose the late Jewish doctrine of the two ages of the world, *cf.* APOCALYPTICISM; ESCHATOLOGY OF THE APOC. AND THE PSEUDEP.; ESCHATOLOGY OF THE NT.

E. JENNI

\*AGE, OLD. Old age in the Bible is a reward for the good life and a sign of wisdom, and the aged command respect.

1. Terms
2. Symptoms of age
3. Numerical age
4. Attitudes toward age
5. The elder
6. Old age in eschatology

**1. Terms.** Among the biblical Hebrew terms relative to old age the commonest is זָקֵן, *zāqēn*, "old man," cognate to which are the less common abstract nouns *zō'qen*, *ziqnâ*, and *zᵉqûnîm*, "old age." The word for "beard" (*zāqān*), general in Semitic languages, may be the primary form of which these other words are derivatives. Such nouns and phrases as שֵׂיבָה ("age"—i.e., gray-headedness), יָשִׁישׁ ("aged"—i.e., decrepit), בָּא בַיָּמִים ("old"—i.e., come into days), שְׂבַע יָמִים ("old," i.e., with fulness of days), occur as synonyms of *zāqēn*.

**2. Symptoms of age.** Allusions to the physical symptoms of age are frequent. The commonest terms for age, as above, allude to the beard and gray hair. Abraham and Sarah are beyond the age of begetting and bearing children, and the birth of Isaac is considered an act of providence (Gen. 18:11-14; cf. Luke 1:18). Isaac, as the end of his life approaches, and Eli the ancient priest are blind (Gen. 27:1; I Sam. 3:2; 4:15, 18). Barzillai complains of the failure of his other senses, of taste and hearing (II Sam. 19:35—H 19:36). David suffers chills, and a companion must comfort him with her warmth (I Kings 1:1-4). The classic description of the infirmities of old age is Eccl. 12:1-5; although its poetic symbols are in part obscure, the passage is distinguished for its tenderness and beauty.

**3. Numerical age.** The sources suggest the numerical age at which one might be considered "old." Irrelevant are the fantastically long lives of the quasi-immortal mythological fathers of the human race in the early chapters of Genesis (especially 5; 11) and even the heroically long lives of the semihistorical Hebrew patriarchs (Abraham: 175 years—Gen. 25:7; Isaac: 180 years—35:28; Jacob: 147 years—47:28; Joseph: 110 years—50:22) and of Moses, who according to the tradition died at the age of 120 still possessed of youthful vigor (Deut. 34:7). Such figures are symbols—theology, not vital statistics (*see* GENEALOGY; LIFE; METHUSELAH; MYTH, MYTHOLOGY, OT). The more reasonable figures on the ages attained by the kings of Israel and Judah suggest that biblical man had what we might yet call a normal life expectancy. M. Ab. 5.21 calls sixty *ziqnâ* and seventy *śêbhâ*. The psalmist says:

> The years of our life are threescore and ten,
> or even by reason of strength fourscore
> (Ps. 90:10*a*).

Ben Sirach calls a hundred a ripe old age (Ecclus. 18:9).

If normally a man attained the age of seventy or eighty, it is probable that he showed signs of age at sixty. And it is not strange, then, that the legislation concerning vows in Lev. 27:1-8 makes sixty the dividing line between what appears to be the mature and the aged. At any rate, the redemption price for a man or a woman sixty years old and upward is less than the price for one between the ages of twenty and sixty—on the ground, no doubt, of presumed diminished usefulness after sixty.

**4. Attitudes toward age.** While the legislation in Lev. 27 suggests the number of years at which old age was thought to set in, it is somewhat misleading as concerns attitudes toward the aged in biblical society. The aged commanded and enjoyed respect. A precept in the Holiness Code directs: "You shall rise up before the hoary head, and honor the face of an old man" (Lev. 19:32*a*). This respect for the aged is like the honor shown to parents (Exod. 20:12), as indeed a NT passage recognizes (I Tim. 5:1-2; cf. also Ruth 4:15; Prov. 23:22). In his description of a chaotic society Isaiah includes as a symptom:

> The youth will be insolent to the elder,
> and the base fellow to the honorable
> (Isa. 3:5*b*);

cf. Deut. 28:50; Lam. 5:12; Isa. 47:6.

The elders were esteemed as men of experience and custodians of the tradition:

> Remember the days of old,
> consider the years of many generations;
> ask your father, and he will show you;
> your elders, and they will tell you
> (Deut. 32:7).

Elihu keeps his counsel until his elders among Job's friends have finished, expecting wisdom from them:

> I said, "Let days speak,
> and many years teach wisdom"
> (Job 32:7).

There is irony in Elihu's words, but it is an accepted view which he is challenging. Ben Sirach says: "Much experience is the crown of old men, and the fear of God is their glory" (Ecclus. 25:6 KJV), and it was considered axiomatic that

> Wisdom is with the aged,
> and understanding in length of days
> (Job 12:12; cf. 15:9-10),

although a proverb likewise rejects the generalization, saying instead: "Better is a poor and wise youth than an old and foolish king" (Eccl. 4:13).

It was, accordingly, an honor to attain advanced age, and a sign of God's favor: "The beauty of old men is their gray hair" (Prov. 20:29), and

> A hoary head is a crown of glory;
> it is gained in a righteous life
> (Prov. 16:31).

**5. The elder.** The old man is not necessarily to be equated with the ELDER, who occupied an official position in biblical society, though indeed the experience and wisdom of the older man would fit him for such judicial and administrative responsibilities as the elder discharged.

**6. Old age in eschatology.** Old age is a feature also of eschatology. Going beyond the deuteronomic expectation of long life for such as keep the commandments (Deut. 30:19-20, and often), biblical eschatology contemplates a return at the end of time to the state of quasi immortality characteristic of the beginning (*see* § 3 *above*); it even speaks of an end of dying: "He will swallow up death for ever" (Isa. 25:8). On the way to this ultimate, such thoughts appear as Zech. 8:4: "Old men and old women shall again sit in the streets of Jerusalem, each with staff in hand for very age," and Isa. 65:20 (translated as in *IB*, V, 755-56):

> No more shall there be in it
> an infant that lives but a few days
> or an old man who does not fill
> out his days,
> for the child shall die a hundred years old,
> and he who comes short of a
> hundred years shall be [counted]
> accursed.

S. H. BLANK

**AGEE** ā′gē [אגא]. The father of Shammah, who is named third among the "Three" of David's high command (II Sam. 23:11); called "Agee the Hararite." The various proposals to emend the name Agee (e.g., *l.c.* G^L אלא) appear unwarranted, since the reading of the MT is supported by IQSam.

E. R. DALGLISH

**AGGEUS.** KJV Apoc. form of HAGGAI.

**AGIA** ā′gĭ ə [′Αγιά]; KJV AUGIA ô′gĭ ə. Wife of JADDUS (I Esd. 5:38), who was the ancestor of a family of unregistered pretending priests at the return from Exile. She was a Gileadite and probably an heiress, because her husband took her father's name, BARZILLAI.

N. TURNER

**AGONY.** For the general meaning, *see* SUFFERING AND EVIL. The term is used especially in connection with Jesus' suffering and struggle in GETHSEMANE.

**AGORA** ăg′ɔ rɔ [ἡ ἀγορά, *from* ἀγείρω, to bring together]. Originally, the assembly place or market place as in ATHENS and CORINTH. *See* MARKET PLACE.

**AGRAPHA** ăg′rɔ fɔ [ἄγραφα]. A term coined by J. G. Körner in the eighteenth century for sayings purporting to be by Jesus but not recorded in the canonical gospels. The use of the term, which literally means "unwritten things," is due to the view that some of these sayings are survivals of an unwritten tradition, preserved orally and essentially parallel to our written gospels.

Many collections have been made of this material, which ranges from short, aphoristic utterances to lengthy discourses and which dates from the earliest days to the present. Earlier scholars regarded many of them as genuine sayings of Jesus, and saw their source in an early oral gospel from which our canonical gospels drew heavily but not exhaustively. While far greater caution is shown today in such estimates, all judgments are bound to be subjective. Long discourses, often highly doctrinal, as in the PISTIS SOPHIA and in such romances as the Apocryphal Acts, Gnostic and Catholic alike, may be safely disregarded; but there are many terse and wholesome utterances, utterly unobjectionable and free from the bias of dubious theology or the tinsel of fantasy, which have appeared to many critics as not inappropriate to the Jesus of the canonical gospels. The fact that they are not in the canonical gospels is not in itself conclusive, but the parallel fact that so few of them are of a nature to appear to most investigators of an age and quality to make ascription to the Jesus of history probable, would suggest that the authors of the canonical gospels left very little primitive tradition out of their collections.

Many of the sayings are simply amplifications, variations, or combinations of words that are used in the canonical gospels and that appear in revised form in the later, apocryphal gospels, as in the story of the rich ruler, who scratched his head in perplexed displeasure and received a word of reproof. There are variant versions of the parable of the talents, and of Matt. 18:22—"If thy brother sin in word and give thee satisfaction, receive him seven times in the day. . . . Yea, I say unto thee, until seventy times seven; for with the prophets also, after they were anointed with the Holy Spirit, there was found sinful speech."

Several of these Agrapha occur in gospel MSS, notably the amplified parallel to Luke 14:8-11, which stands in Codex Bezae (D) at Matt. 20:28, or the famous rejoinder by Jesus to the man working on the sabbath: "Man, if thou knowest what thou art doing, blessed art thou; if thou knowest not, thou art accursed and a transgressor of the law," which is found at Luke 6:4 in the same MS. Here the problem is essentially one of textual criticism, for several of the words of Jesus, now printed in many texts of the Bible (e.g., Matt. 6:13; Mark 16:15-18; Luke 23:34) are textually of a nature to suggest that they are later additions and thus strictly as much Agrapha as some of the others regularly listed as such.

In addition to sayings that stand in individual gospel MSS are a few words attributed to Jesus in the NT but outside the gospels, notably the logion: "It is more blessed to give than to receive" (Acts 20:35), and the words quoted by Paul as Jesus' own at the institution of the Lord's Supper (I Cor. 11:24-25). As an indication of how these Agrapha grew, it may be observed that in the Apostolic Constitutions (VIII.12) Paul's next word has become a direct quotation: "For as often as ye eat this bread and drink this cup, ye do show *my* death until *I* come."

The great majority of the Agrapha come from apocryphal writings; the OXYRHYNCHUS SAYINGS OF JESUS; Christian fathers, both early and late; the so-called Gospel of Thomas, a Gnostic work discovered at Chenoboskion in 1946; the Talmud; and Mohammedan sources; with little or no certain indication, in the large majority, of their precise date or point of origin.

*Bibliography.* A fair sampling of the Agrapha is provided by M. R. James, *The Apocryphal NT* (1924), pp. 33-37, in addition to others included in other sections of the same work. The article "Agrapha" by J. H. Ropes, in the extra volume of *HDB* (pp. 343-52), may still be studied with profit, for in addition to the full bibliography of the earlier work in this field, there is there printed a lengthy and judiciously chosen list of passages (with Eng. trans.) of the various sorts, including the forty-eight Agrapha from Mohammedan sources published by D. S. Margoliouth.      M. S. ENSLIN

*AGRICULTURE. The art of arable farming, including the tools and methods used and the difficulties which the farmer faces. Agriculture is intimately related to the religion and literature of the Bible.

1. Introduction
2. Hardships faced by the Palestinian farmer
    *a.* Nature of the land
    *b.* Climate
    *c.* The problem of water
    *d.* Other factors
3. The crops
    *a.* The vine
    *b.* The olive tree
    *c.* Grains
    *d.* Flax
    *e.* Dates
    *f.* Other crops
4. Implements and their use
    *a.* Plow
    *b.* Sickle
    *c.* Threshing instruments
    *d.* Winnowing instruments
    *e.* Sieve
    *f.* Seeder
5. Storage
6. Workers
7. Agriculture and the religion of the Bible
8. Agriculture and the literature of the Bible
Bibliography

**1. Introduction.** From prehistoric times to the present day, the people of Palestine have been, in the main, agriculturists. Excavations in the Wadi el-Mughara on the W edge of the Mount Carmel range reveal clear evidence of agriculture in the Mesolithic period (*ca.* 8000-7000 B.C.). Agricultural implements, especially flint sickles, sickle edges together with curved bone handles with grooves into which the small flints were put, found in abundance at this site, suggest that the Natufian people were engaged in farming. An abundance of fragments of basalt mortars and pestles also give rise to the inference that these people made flour of the wheat or millet which they harvested. At Tell es-Sultan an advanced culture as early as 7000 B.C. is now in evidence, and although not a large number of agricultural implements have been found, the few that have appeared, together with the nature of the community itself, strongly suggest that these people were likewise food producers. In Mesopotamia at Jarmo an abundance of agricultural implements clearly attests to a highly developed stage of agricultural activity in the fifth millennium B.C.

Industry and commerce have seldom constituted the basis of a large percentage of the income of the inhabitants of Palestine. Instead, they depend upon the produce which could be grown from the land for their life and livelihood. Food, clothing, and shelter have been, to a great extent, the results of the tilling of the soil and related activities such as the raising of domesticated animals. Hence the words:

> In toil you shall eat of it [i.e., the ground] all the days
> of your life;
>
> . . . . . . . . . . . . . . . . . . . . .
>
> In the sweat of your face
> you shall eat bread (Gen. 3:17, 19)

have had real meaning for the people who have lived in this land through the centuries. It is not surprising that all facets of the life of these people have been greatly influenced by their sense of almost complete dependence upon the land and what could be produced by working it. Greatly affecting the nature and abundance of the crops were two elements over which the people had little or no control: the nature of the land itself and the climate. Thus it seemed not enough for them to plow, to sow, and to reap; they must, in addition, enter into some kind of relationship with the God who could guarantee an abundance of those things essential to life itself. Consequently, the religion of the people of Palestine was in ancient times directly related to their agricultural life.

The Israelite religious year revolved around the cultivation of the crops, so that the major fasts and feasts have both an agricultural and a religious significance. Whatever needed to be done to ensure an abundant harvest was done: fasting at the beginning and feasting at the end. In addition, many of the civil laws pertained directly to the agricultural life of the people. Hence it is important to have an appreciation of the fact that this was first and foremost an agricultural civilization, before it is possible to have an adequate understanding of the whole life of the people of the Bible.

**2. Hardships faced by the Palestinian farmer.** Nothing grows easily in Palestine. The entire year was one of unending toil, and it was literally in the sweat of his face not only that the farmer ate bread but that he was able to provide himself with most, if not all, of the basic necessities of life.

*a. Nature of the land.* Although the land was better in ancient times than it is now, with thicker layers of fertile soil overlaying the rock beneath, still there are abundant references to the stones which made the work of the farmer so difficult. "He digged it and cleared it of stones" (Isa. 5:2) is a sentence that tells of the first and constant activity of every farmer. It

was only necessary to fill a land with stones to render it useless (II Kings 3:19, 25). Hence the poet expressed what every man knew to be the truth if he was to succeed, when he wrote: "You shall be in league with the stones of the field" (Job 5:23). An Arabic story expresses well what every Israelite farmer must have felt. When Allah was creating the world, he entrusted all the stones to two angels, each with one bag full. As the angels were flying over Palestine, one of the bags broke and spilled out on this tiny land half the stones intended for the whole world!

Not only is the land stony, but it is also very hilly and was so in ancient times (*see* PALESTINE, GEOGRAPHY OF). The number of fertile valleys is limited indeed, and a high percentage of the farming has to be done on hillsides. As early as the Middle Bronze Age terracing was used in order to give the farmer a larger cultivable area. On the other hand, the soil in many parts of both the hills and the plains is very suitable for agricultural purposes, and it was possible in some areas to grow two crops of grain in one year (Amos 7:1). Even today, after a great amount of erosion has taken place in the intervening centuries, the land in many parts of Palestine will yield richly if sufficient water is available.

*b. Climate.* The Palestinian farmer not only faced the problem of tilling a land difficult at best, but he likewise found himself at the mercy of a varied climate. Palestine is a land of climatic contrasts. One of the most striking aspects of the climate is the five-month summer season without a drop of rain (although there may be exceptions). The Israelite farmer could look forward to a hot, dry season from the middle of May to the middle of October, for which he would have to prepare during the rainy winter months. But if the summer drought was certain, the rainy season was unpredictable. If there were abundant rains, then the crops would be good; but if not, then there would be famine.

*c. The problem of water.* The only safeguard for the farmer was to furnish himself with adequate storage places for WATER; hence the large number of cisterns that have been found on every major site in Palestine (II Chr. 26:10; Neh. 9:25). Even then there might be too little rain to fill the cisterns. In the Nabatean, Roman, and Byzantine periods a strong, central government was able to draft men to build dams and reservoirs such as those at Umm el-Jemal, Kurnub, and in the Wadi Dhobai, which helped materially in raising the total productivity of the land. *See* ARCHAEOLOGY.

In the earlier periods in addition to the cisterns the farmer made use of springs and perennial streams such as the Kishon, the Jabbok, and the Wadi Kufrinjeh (as it is known today) for purposes of artificial irrigation. Such water would have to be carried or, when possible, run onto the fields by means of water canals. Unfortunately there is too little evidence to furnish a clear, detailed picture of the methods of artificial irrigation employed in ancient Israel, but the numerous irrigation ditches which divert the water from the Wadi Zerqa and the Wadi Kufrinjeh (to name just two in the Jordan Valley) suggest that the same thing might well have been done in ancient times. Whether the term דלי, "bucket"

(Num. 24:7; Isa. 40:15), refers to something used for irrigation purposes is not certain; but no doubt the Israelite farmer discovered, as has the modern Arab, that when he was able to get additional water onto his land, his crops were that much more abundant.

***d. Other factors.*** In addition to the question of rainfall, other factors also materially affected the farmer and his crops. Numerous references to dew (טל) attest to the value it had for the production of good crops (Gen. 27:28; Deut. 33:28; Prov. 19:12; Hos. 14:5; Zech. 8:12). The lack of dew was taken as a sign of catastrophe or of God's disfavor (II Sam. 1:21; I Kings 17:1; Hag. 1:10). The heavy dew comes in late August and September, and the Arab farmer today eagerly awaits it. So valuable is the dew that he goes out in the light of the moon or in the early morning to hill his tomato plants or to turn the earth around his vines so as to preserve as much of the precious moisture as possible. Even in the dry summer a cool night may produce a heavy fall of dew and thus help to prevent the plants from being scorched by the next day's sun.

The hot winds from the E desert, the siroccos, could play havoc with any growing thing (Isa. 27:8; 40:6-8; Ezek. 17:10; Hos. 13:15; Luke 12:55). The siroccos occur from the middle of September to the end of October. They last from three days to a week, during which time the temperature rises as much as twenty degrees Fahrenheit above the average and the air is filled with a yellowish haze. The humidity drops sharply, and almost every drop of moisture seems to have been wrung out of the air. A prolonged sirocco is one of the farmer's most dreaded experiences.

Finally, insects and plant disease greatly increased the danger of crop failure. Of these, probably the LOCUST was the most dreaded (Deut. 28:42; I Kings 8:37; Joel 1:4). In a few days a plague of locusts could devour a whole countryside, leaving nothing but a few dry stalks. Against this disaster the ancient farmer had no protection; his only hope lay in the sudden rise of a strong, steady wind (Exod. 10:19). The Israelite farmer was also bothered by fungus growths, especially mildew (ירקון; *Puccinia graminis;* Deut. 28:22; I Kings 8:37; Amos 4:9; Hag. 2:17). It attacks the leaves of grass plants, finally destroying the plant altogether. Mildew is always mentioned along with שדפון, "blasting," "scorching," or "blight."

**3. The crops.** Three crops dominated the agricultural life of the country: the vine, the olive tree, and grain;

> wine to gladden the heart of man,
> oil to make his face shine,
> and bread to strengthen man's heart
> (Ps. 104:15);

> Behold, I am sending to you
> grain, wine, and oil
> (Joel 2:19).

These three products appear together in innumerable passages attesting both to their importance and to their widespread cultivation (Gen. 27:28; Deut. 7:13; II Kings 18:32; Neh. 5:11; Hos. 2:8; Joel 1:10; Hag. 1:11).

***a. The vine.*** The grape VINE (גפן or גפן היין; Num. 6:4; Judg. 13:4) was no doubt very widely grown throughout the whole Mediterranean world. It grew well and, once planted, required a minimum amount of care: mainly loosening the ground occasionally and pruning in the spring when the first blossoms appeared. Just as today, so in ancient times there may have been a variety of kinds. The terms שרק (Isa. 5:2; Jer. 2:21), שרקה (Gen. 49:11), and שרק (Isa. 16:8 [translate 8*b:* "The lords of the nations have struck down its choice vines]) may refer to a special kind of blood-red grape (Arabic *sharigun* is used for anything with a beautiful red color). The fruit of the vine was no doubt eaten fresh, as well as dried into raisins. For the most part, however, the grapes were turned into wine by being trampled in the wine vat located either in the vineyard or nearby. Fig. WIN 24.

***b. The olive tree.*** The OLIVE TREE (זית; ἐλαία) was particularly well suited to most areas of the land of Palestine, since it will grow in very shallow soil and is able to endure long periods of drought. It does not stand severe cold, however, and consequently does not do so well in S Judah. The olive HARVEST was the first in the year, but since the ripening process is slow, the farmer might pick his olives as his time permitted. Like the grapes, the olives could have been eaten fresh but were most valued for their oil, which served as a substitute for the scarcer animal fats. Figs. OLI 7-8.

***c. Grains.*** The third crop which has been mentioned is grain. Of the grains WHEAT (חטה) was undoubtedly the most important. The variety *Triticum sativum,* it probably grew best in Galilee. It was planted in the fall when the winter rains had started, sometime in late October or early November, and harvested in May-June. BARLEY was also widely grown but may have been at times considered a second-class food. It is a product of a drier climate and was probably grown most extensively in the S and E. It may well have been grown in fields adjoining the wheat fields where the soil was not so good, since it does not require as good a soil as wheat. Barley was planted at about the same time as the wheat but harvested about a month earlier (Ruth 2:23). A third grain was SPELT (כסמת; *Triticum spelta*), translated in the KJV as "rye" (Exod. 9:32). It was an inferior kind of wheat and was planted around the borders of the wheat and barley fields (Isa. 28:25).

***d. Flax.*** Another important crop was FLAX (פשת or פשתה; *Linum usitatissimum*), from which linen cloth and rope were made (Judg. 15:14; Hos. 2:5, 9—H 2: 7, 11). Flax was harvested a month before the barley, by being hoed off at the ground so as not to lose any of the stalk. After it was cut, it was laid out in the sun to dry (Josh. 2:6). Fig. HAR 7.

***e. Dates.*** Although there is no explicit mention in the Bible of dates as food, numerous references to the palm tree (תמר) strongly suggest that its cultivation also played an important part in the life of the farmer. The date palm was known over a large part of the ancient Near East in the S latitudes and in Palestine flourished especially in the Jordan Valley N of the Dead Sea (Deut. 34:3; Judg. 1:16). It is referred to by such writers as Pliny, Strabo, and Josephus, who speaks of the syrup made from the dates (War IV.viii.3). The Mishna also speaks of date honey (דבש תמרים). Dates may also have been made into cakes as were figs. The Talmud mentions date wine (יין תמרים), and some writers are of the opinion that the OT שכר may include wine made from dates.

*f. Other crops.* Other agricultural products included figs and pomegranates; lentils, coarse beans, chick-peas, and cucumbers; and onions, leeks, and garlic for flavoring. Of these the FIG was especially important, since it, along with the date, was the main source of sugar in the diet. Of special interest is the sycamore fig (שקמה; *Ficus sycomorus*); it was specially treated to make it grow larger and more edible (Amos 7:14). Fig. SYC 93.

Such passages as Num. 11:5; I Sam. 25:18 suggest the general nature of the diet of ancient Israel and hence the crops which were most commonly grown.

**4. Implements and their use.** Compared to the farmer today in most parts of the world, including modern Palestine, the work of the Israelite farmer was made doubly difficult by the primitive implements which he had at his disposal.

4. Stele of Esarhaddon, showing plow with seed drill, date palm, and hill or ear of grain

*a. Plow.* His PLOW (מחרשה or מחרשת) was hardly more than a wooden stick with a small metal point, drawn by oxen (I Kings 19:19). Until *ca.* the tenth century B.C. the points were made of copper or bronze, but after that they were made of iron. These were larger and harder but even then hardly more than scratched the surface, perhaps to a maximum depth of five inches. A few references to other operations, such as leveling and harrowing (Isa. 28:24-25; Hos. 10:11), suggest other processes which may have involved the use of a HOE (מעדר; Isa. 7:25). Figs. AGR 4; PLO 59-60.

*b. Sickle.* Reaping was done with a small hand SICKLE (חרמש [Deut. 16:9; 23:25]; מגל [Jer. 50:16; Joel 3:13—H 4:13]). The reaper held the stalks in his hand and cut them off close to the ground with the sickle;* this method is still commonly in use in Palestine. Until *ca.* the tenth century B.C. sickles were made of flints set in a haft; after the tenth century they were made of iron. In both cases they

more or less resembled the modern sickle. Figs. EGY 7; SIC 56.

*c. Threshing instruments.* After the grain was cut, it was taken to the THRESHING place, where the kernels were separated from the stalks. This might be done in any one of several ways: by beating it out with a stick (חבט; Judg. 6:11; Ruth 2:17); by driving the cattle around on the piled-up stalks until their hoofs gradually trampled out the grain (דוש; Deut. 25:4); by dragging some kind of instrument over the grain (עגלה [Amos 2:13]; מורג [II Sam. 24:22]). Figs. SLE 67; THR 61.

*d. Winnowing instruments.* When the grain was threshed, the next operation was WINNOWING (זרה; Isa. 41:16). Two instruments were used: מזרה (Jer. 15:7) and רחת (Isa. 30:24). The former was probably a long-handled fork with several prongs. The latter may have been a shovellike instrument (cf. Arabic *raḥatun*, or *râḥatun* according to some authors). Fig. WIN 25.

In the afternoon the wind started to blow; at this time the winnowing process began. The grain was thrown up into the air, the wind blowing the lighter materials away while the heavier kernels fell to the ground (Ps. 1:4). This was continued until there was little left but a pile of kernels.

*e. Sieve.* Even then, however, one process remained: that of sifting, since in the winnowing process not all the foreign material would be carried away. The implement used for this purpose was the sieve (כברה [Amos 9:9]; נפה [Isa. 30:28]). Whether it is possible to distinguish between the two kinds of sieves, one having a fine mesh and the other a coarse mesh, is questionable. However, it is true that both kinds are in use in Palestine today. In one case the good wheat is retained in the sieve and the fine dust passes through, while in the other case the grain falls through while larger pieces remain either to be discarded or to be thrown back and rethreshed.

*f. Seeder.* It is doubtful that the Israelite farmer had an instrument for planting seed, although such a seeder, consisting of a tube attached to the plow, did exist in Mesopotamia. Probably the seed was scattered over the land by hand, as in Egypt.

**5. Storage.** With the processes of harvesting completed, the farmer had either to store or to dispose of his produce. At certain periods apparently enough was produced for export (I Kings 5:11; Ezek. 27:17), but for the most part it was necessary to store it for their own use. The ubiquitous storage jar found in nearly every archaeological excavation attests to the manner in which grain, oil, and wine were kept, especially in homes and shops. Larger quantities of grain might be kept in dry cisterns or silos built for this purpose. Luke 12:16-18 pictures a wealthy landowner who discovered that the barns he already had were not large enough for the produce he was in the process of accumulating. *See* GRANARY.

**6. Workers.** The Gezer Calendar serves to remind us that, month in and month out, many Israelites spent their time in the fields:

His two months are (olive) harvest,
His two months are planting (grain),
His two months are late planting;
His month is hoeing up of flax,
His month is harvest of barley,

His month is harvest and feasting;
His two months are vine-tending,
His month is summer fruit

(J. B. Pritchard, ed., *Ancient Near Eastern Texts* [Princeton, N. J.: Princeton University Press, rev. 1955]).

One will quickly notice that all twelve months of the year are accounted for! We see clearly that the times and the seasons were marked by the harvests. No one in a farmer's family was exempt from the work. Owners and slaves, young men, women and children, can all be seen doing their part (Ruth 2; II Kings 4:18; Isa. 61:5). It was axiomatic that one who tilled his soil would not be in want (Prov. 12: 11). During the day the villages would be empty, as nearly every able-bodied person went out into the fields. Even at night many would be absent from their homes guarding the ripening crop or the threshed grain. Also in the fields, vineyards, and olive groves were the gleaners following behind the workers to gather up anything that had been left behind. This was their right according to the law and constituted a means whereby the widow and orphan who had no means of support of their own could get their food (Deut. 24:19-21). But it was not all drudgery. At the close of the day's work there was a freedom of spirit (Ruth 3:7), and the harvest time was marked by unrestrained gaiety (Judg. 9:27; 21:19-23).

**7. Agriculture and the religion of the Bible.** So much a part of life were the agricultural pursuits that it seemed as though God had established them from the beginning as the superior way of life (Gen. 3-4, especially 3:23). The land was the gift of Yahweh and was under his care (Deut. 11:12). It was thought by some, not only that the farmer learned the techniques of good husbandry from God (Isa. 28:26), but also that Yahweh and only Yahweh had it in his power to order the natural forces in such a way as to assure the maximum results from man's labors. On the other hand, references to what dire calamities may and do befall the man or nation who sins permeate the prophetic utterances (Isa. 5:8-10; Amos 4:1-8; Hag. 1:4-11). Much of the Torah stems from and is directly related to the agricultural life.

The three major festivals which, according to the Deuteronomist, the Israelite was required to observe in Jerusalem were strictly agricultural in nature; they were connected with the products of the earth. These in turn were the gifts of Yahweh, and therefore due reverence must be paid to him. Aside from the origin of these laws, they marked the beginning of the grain harvest, the end of that harvest, and the final ingathering of all the fruits of the year's labors (*see* FEASTS AND FASTS). The SABBATH may also have had agricultural origins, as suggested by its appearance in the old ritual decalogue (embedded in Exod. 22:29-30; 23:12-19); but if not, it certainly came to have definite agricultural overtones at a later time.

Of the thirty-five sections of the D Code, eight deal in whole or in part with matters pertaining to the agricultural life of the people (Deut. 14:22 ff; 15: 19-16:17; 19:14; 22:1-3, 9-10; 23:24-25; 25:4; 26:1-11). A tithe of the seed must be given. The first-born of the flock must be given to the Lord. Landmarks might not be moved—this law appears earlier in the original form of the anathemas (Deut. 27:17).

Grain could not be sown in a vineyard, nor was one permitted to plow with an ox and an ass yoked together (Deut. 22:9-10). It was permissible to eat of a man's grapes or grain on his property, but one was not permitted to take any with him (Deut. 23: 24-25). These few illustrations—and there are many more—suffice to show that the legislation of ancient Israel was intended to regulate many aspects of the life of the people as it related to agricultural pursuits. Since all these laws were at one time or another viewed as emanating from Yahweh, it becomes clear that this facet of life, like many others, had a strong religious tone. *See* LAW IN THE OT.

**8. Agriculture and the literature of the Bible.** Figures of speech reflecting the agricultural life may be found throughout the Bible. The glorious future of a restored Israel is expressed in agricultural terminology. Vineyards and gardens will be replanted and will flourish (Amos 9:14; Zech. 8:12). So great was the joy of a good harvest that this became the mode of expressing any great joy, and contrarily any deep sorrow was like the sorrow brought on by a poor crop (Isa. 16:10). Likewise the poets and sages found the common agricultural vocabulary pregnant with meaning and used it when they wanted to express themselves with great force (Prov. 10:5; 20:26; 24:30-34; Job 5:26; 24:2, 6, 10-11, 18-19, 24; Pss. 65:9-13; 80:8-13; 128). Especially do the words of Jesus reflect meaning which agricultural figures could convey to the man in Palestine: the parable of the sower (Mark 4:1-20); the parable of the laborers in the vineyard (Matt. 20:1-16); "From the fig tree learn its lesson: as soon as its branch becomes tender and puts forth its leaves, you know that summer is near" (Matt. 24:32); "No good tree bears bad fruit, nor again does a bad tree bear good fruit; for each tree is known by its own fruit" (Luke 6:43-44). The seed, the vine, the tree, the fruit—all these were useful metaphors when a writer or speaker wished to express the truth about God and his ways with man.

*Bibliography.* G. H. Dalman, *Arbeit und Sitte in Palästina*, vol. II (1932): "Der Ackerbau"; vol. III (1933): "Von der Ernte zum Mehle"; vol. IV (1935): "Brot, Öl und Wein." K. Galling, *Biblisches Reallexikon* (1937). W. F. Albright, *BASOR*, 92 (1943), 16-26. A. G. Barrois, *Manuel d'archéologie biblique*, vol. I (1939), chs. 5, 8; vol. II (1953), ch. 18. D. Baly, *The Geography of the Bible* (1957). G. E. Wright, *Biblical Archaeology* (1957), pp. 180-84, figs. 45, 57, 73, 130-33, 139, 178.

H. N. RICHARDSON

**AGRIPPA** ə grĭp'ə. The name of two kings of Judea.

**1.** Agrippa I, or Herod Agrippa (10 B.C.-A.D.44), was king of Judea A.D. 41-44. He was a grandson of Herod the Great.

Agrippa I spent his childhood (from before his sixth birthday) and youth in Rome, where he indulged himself in extravagant living, made possible by friendships his mother won for him in imperial circles. Particularly after his mother's death, he ran into serious debt and was obliged to leave Rome to escape the hounding of creditors. At one point he even contemplated suicide, but thanks to the initiative of his wife, his brother-in-law HEROD ANTIPAS came to his assistance and appointed him agoranome (overseer of markets) in Tiberias. The appointment, however, provided only temporary relief, for the brothers-in-law soon quarreled and Agrippa resigned his post. There was a similar outcome to his association with the Roman governor in Antioch who helped him. With considerable difficulty he eventually made his way back to Rome, once again establishing close relationships with members of the emperor's household. His lavish living continued to keep him in debt, and because of his unrestrained speech he was thrown into prison, from which he was freed after six months by the death of TIBERIUS (A.D. 37).

Agrippa's good fortune began when CALIGULA, his very close friend, succeeded Tiberius. Agrippa was not only freed immediately from prison, but also made king over the tetrarchies of Philip and Lysanias; and by the latter part of 39 he received also the territory ruled over by Herod Antipas. After the murder of Caligula in 41, Agrippa received from the new emperor, Claudius, the additional territories of Judea and Samaria. Agrippa thus became ruler of the territories which his grandfather had previously held, and in addition enjoyed a consular rank.

When he finally took over his kingdom in Palestine, either because of a genuine change in his habits or merely out of astute policy—it is impossible to determine which—his conduct was such as to win him favorable reactions from his Jewish subjects. He cultivated the good opinion of the PHARISEES; in Jewish territory he was careful to observe the laws and traditions of his countrymen; he was generous in gifts to the temple; he apparently made certain that his displays of piety were well noted. Though most scholars identify several Talmudic praises of Agrippa as references to him, it is argued, with reason, that these are not references to Agrippa I, but to his son, Agrippa II.

In those areas where there were large non-Jewish settlements Agrippa, like his grandfather, carried on a building and works program in an effort to win Gentile sympathies. According to the account in Acts 12 he persecuted some of the early Christians. The attitude of the Roman government toward his administration was a cautious one, for on two important occasions ambitious projects of his were abruptly interrupted at the instigation of the legate of Syria.

Agrippa died suddenly in Caesarea, there being two accounts of his death, one in Acts 12:19-23 and the other in Jos. Antiq. XIX.viii.2. He was survived by three daughters and one son, also named Agrippa (*see* 2 *below*).

**Bibliography.** Jos. Antiq. XVIII–XIX; J. Derenbourg, *Essaie sur l'Histoire et la Géographie de la Palestine* (1867), pp. 205-19; E. Schürer, *Geschichte des Jüdischen Volkes im Zeitalter Jesu Christi* (4th ed., 1901-9), pp. 549-64; A. H. M. Jones, *The Herods of Judaea* (1938), pp. 184-216; J. N. Epstein, *Prolegomena ad Litteras Tannaiticas* (1957), pp. 44, 399.

**2.** Agrippa II, Marcus Julius Agrippa (born A.D. 28, died after 93, probably *ca.* 100), was the son of Agrippa I.

Like his father, Agrippa II received his education in Rome. He was seventeen when his father died; and though CLAUDIUS was ready to let him succeed his father, he was advised against this by his counselors; Judea therefore was placed under procurators. In 48 Claudius gave Agrippa the small kingdom of Herod of Chalcis; somewhat later, in exchange for this, Agrippa received a much larger domain, and later still, from Nero, he had added to his territories parts of Galilee and Perea. For the most part, the population of his holdings was Gentile.

Though on a number of occasions he intervened in behalf of the Jews, principally those of the DIASPORA, his sympathies were with Roman rather than Jewish interests. He antagonized the priests of Jerusalem by some exercises of his authority in temple affairs. Throughout the great war against Rome (66-70) he was stanchly loyal to the Roman side: his conduct throughout the war and its aftermath, as well as the Thucydidean speeches put into his mouth by JOSEPHUS, reveal that Agrippa was totally subservient to the Roman powers.

His intimate relationships with his sister were a subject of widespread scandal. Despite some formal gestures, he was apparently devoid of any religious interest. He seems to have left no survivors, and after his death his kingdom was very likely made part of the province of Syria.

**Bibliography.** Jos. Antiq. XX; War II.xvi.4 ff, *et passim*. E. Schürer, *Geschichte des jüdischen Volkes im Zeitalter Jesu Christi* (4th ed., 1901-9), pp. 585-600. A. H. M. Jones, *The Herods of Judaea* (1938), pp. 217-61.　　　　　J. GOLDIN

**AGUE.** Malarial FEVER characterized by stages of chill, fever, and perspiration.

**AGUR** ā'gər [אָגוּר, *probably* hireling; Akkad. *agāru;* Aram. אגר; Arab. *'agara;* Ugar. *agr*]. An otherwise unknown author of maxims mentioned in Prov. 30:1 (*see* PROVERBS § 6); son of JAKEH. Varied witnesses suggest textual uncertainty: the Syr., the Targ., and the Greek Codex Venetus, with the MT, assume a personal name; the Vulg. translates *congregantis,* a descriptive appellative; the LXX renders φοβήθητι. Rabbinic tradition proposes an allegorical designation of Solomon. Various conjectures represent Agur as being: (*a*) the son of the Queen of Massa, and brother of LEMUEL; (*b*) from MASSA, variously placed in the Arabian Desert, Edom, Transjordan, or beyond Seir.

**Bibliography.** H. F. Mühlau, *De proverbiorum quae dicuntur Aguri et Lemuelis origine atque indole* (1869); F. Delitzsch, *Biblical Commentary on the Proverbs of Solomon,* II (1882), 260-63; M. Noth, *Die israelitischen Personennamen* (1928), p. 231; G. Ryckmans, *Les noms propres sud-sémitiques,* II (1934), 24; B. Gemser, *Sprüche Salomos* (1937), p. 81; A. Cohen, *Proverbs* (1945), p. 200.　　　　　M. H. LOVELACE

**AHAB** ā'hăb [אַחְאָב, father's brother=quite the father]. **1.** King of Israel *ca.* 869-850 B.C.; son and successor of Omri.

The name appears in Assyrian inscriptions as A-ha-ab-bu, in Akkadian as Aḥi-abi. אחואב may therefore be the full form of the word (cf. the vocalization 'Αχιαβ in the LXX of Jer. 29:21 ff, and 'Αχίαβος, a nephew of Herod [Jos. Antiq. XV.vii.8]). The name was given to Ahab presumably because of his likeness to his father.

Despite the statement that "Ahab the son of Omri reigned over Israel in Samaria twenty-two years" (I Kings 16:29), the evidence of the synchronisms makes it clear that he reigned only twenty years (I Kings 16:29; cf. 15:10; 22:51). He began to reign in the thirty-eighth year of Asa king of Judah, who reigned for forty-one years, and was succeeded by his son Ahaziah in the seventeenth year of Jehoshaphat king of Judah.

He entered into a political marriage with Jezebel, daughter of Ethbaal (Ittobaal) king of the Sidonians (I Kings 16:31) and priest of Astarte. This alliance no doubt was necessary in face of the growing power of Aram under its king, Ben-hadad. In addition, it seemed to offer other material advantages. It certainly resulted in increased trade between the two countries, with the acquisition of considerable wealth to both (cf. the notice of the "ivory house" which Ahab built [I Kings 22:39]). But this was a doubtful gain in some ways, as it produced a sharp cleavage between the new wealthy merchant class and the great mass of the people, who depended on the land for their livelihood. Further, it brought into Israel the worship of the gods of Tyre, and this finally led to the downfall of the Omride dynasty. For Jezebel was a strong-minded woman and a fanatical worshiper of the Tyrian deities Baal-Melcarth and Asherah. Her father's position as priest of Astarte may explain Jezebel's religious zeal. The cult of these deities was associated with immoral practices. Prophetic tradition remembered Jezebel as pushing her religion in Israel with ruthless vigor until finally a head-on clash occurred with the worship of the God of Israel. Probably through the influence of his wife, Ahab built a house for Baal in Samaria and erected an altar. He also made an Asherah (I Kings 16:32-33).

The summary of Ahab's reign (I Kings 22:39) makes mention of "all the cities that he built," but the only record of building in the biblical text is that of Jericho by Hiel of Bethel. Historically Jericho, which had been in ruins for centuries, was rebuilt at this time on Ahab's orders, probably as a base of operations against Moab. During the rebuilding some of the builder's children died. This seems a more likely interpretation than the suggestion that Hiel's sons were offered as foundation sacrifices. In the popular mind these deaths were regarded as the fulfilment of the curse pronounced by Joshua (Josh. 6:26).

The rest of the history of Ahab's reign consists of a series of prophet narratives (I Kings 17:1–22:38), emanating from northern circles, which center around the great figure of Elijah the Tishbite (*see* ELIJAH THE PROPHET).

Elijah as the champion of the religion of Yahweh was also the champion of the poor and the widow. This is brought out especially in the episode of Naboth's vineyard (I Kings 21).

It is certain that during Ahab's reign Israel and Aram were engaged in constant wars against each other. More often than not, Aram was the aggressor. I Kings 20; 22 furnishes background material for this period of history. Lack of evidence, however, prevents an adequate reconstruction of the historical sequence of events. The relationship between the events described in chs. 20; 22 and the Battle of Qarqar in 853 is not clear. But the reappearance of Assyria in the West was a factor of the greatest importance. It is most surprising, therefore, that the biblical record makes no mention of it. *Ca.* 970-870

Assyrian interests were confined to the area E of the Euphrates. But *ca.* 870 Asshur-nasir-apli engaged in a campaign against North Syria. The next Assyrian expedition took place in 854-853 and was a real test of strength. Shalmaneser III marched against the West and was met at Qarqar on the Orontes in the territory of Hamath by a confederacy consisting of the kings of Hamath, Aram, and Israel, together with contingents from other smaller sources, twelve in all. Shalmaneser's inscription records the presence of "Ahab the Israelite" with "two thousand chariots, ten thousand men." Ahab's contribution of two

AHAB

*Adapted from The Westminster Historical Atlas to the Bible, Revised, ed. G. Ernest Wright and Floyd V. Filson, © The Westminster Press.*

thousand chariots represented the largest contingent of chariotry among the allies. The figure given for Aram is twelve hundred chariots. This is an indication of Israel's military power at the time. The name of the king of Aram is given as Hadad-ezer. This was probably his private name. His throne name was Ben-hadad. The result of the battle was apparently indecisive, as the Assyrians withdrew and did not reappear in the West until 848. In the meantime Ahab had been killed in battle with Aram (I Kings 22). Presumably, therefore, the events described in ch. 20 belong to the period prior to the Battle of Qarqar. In general, this account gives a picture of constant war during this period, involving Aram and the neighboring states.

It is clear that the power of Aram under its King Ben-hadad I (*ca.* 880-842) was steadily increasing. This was a source of constant concern to the Omride dynasty. The Ben-hadad here mentioned is almost certainly the same king who made an attack on Israel and captured Galilee in the time of Asa (I Kings 15:20). There were only two Syrian kings of this name—not three, as has often been maintained.

Ch. 20 records two attacks on Israel by Aram; both of them were successfully beaten back. In the first, Samaria, the capital city, was besieged and Ben-hadad made exorbitant demands on King Ahab, which Ahab refused. The Syrians were routed in the ensuing battle by a surprise attack led by Ahab himself. Ben-hadad escaped from the battle. The following year he again mustered his forces and marched against Ahab. The armies met at Aphek, and again the Syrians were completely routed, although the figures of the slain (I Kings 20:29) are not historically reliable. Ben-hadad escaped, but finally surrendered and was well treated by Ahab. The terms proposed by Ben-hadad and accepted by Ahab were that the cities captured by Ben-hadad's father from Israel should be restored and bazaar facilities should be granted to Israel in Damascus (I Kings 20:34). That a covenant was actually made between the two kings seems to be borne out by their fighting together as allies at Qarqar against Assyria. The terms of the agreement cannot be established historically. Doubtless the prophetic source had in mind the reference to Asa, but Baasha was not Ahab's "father," and the Ben-hadad mentioned there and here is almost certainly the same king. If the reference to Samaria is to the Israelite capital, as is implied, the king involved must have been Omri. It seems preferable to regard this account of the treaty terms as unhistorical, although the reference to trading facilities is probably a true historical reminiscence.

Ch. 22 opens with the statement that "for three years Syria and Israel continued without war." This clearly refers, in the mind of the writer, to ch. 20, but it may also refer to the period of three years after the Battle of Qarqar. Aram and Israel were again at war, and on this occasion Ahab was the aggressor. The noteworthy feature about this war is that Jehoshaphat, the king of Judah, was Ahab's ally (I Kings 22:2-4). The two kingdoms had clearly come together in face of a threatened attack at the hands of Aram. The alliance had been strengthened by the marriage of Ahab's daughter to Jehoshaphat's eldest son (II Kings 8:18). Ahab's objective was the recovery of Ramoth-gilead (in all probability the modern Tell Ramit) on the NE frontier of Israel. Jehoshaphat king of Judah was on a visit to Ahab at the time, and Ahab persuaded him to take part in the campaign. But Jehoshaphat insisted on a divine oracle before setting out, and refused to accept the assurance of victory chanted in unison by the four hundred prophets whom Ahab assembled. The figure four hundred is open to question. These were clearly Yahweh prophets, serving in the interests of the state religion. At his insistence Micaiah the son of Imlah (*see* MICAIAH 3) was summoned. This whole section (I Kings 22:5-28) may very well be an intrusion into the story from a prophetic source. It interrupts the sequence of vss. 1-4, 29 ff.

In the ensuing battle at Ramoth-gilead, Ahab was killed, and the Israelite forces routed. The king was brought back dead to Samaria, where he was buried. The story reveals the subordinate position Judah occupied and at the same time gives an indication of the strong position Israel had attained under the leadership of Ahab.

Ahab faced difficulties, not only from Aram, but also from Moab. Despite the statements of II Kings 1:1; 3:5, it seems clear from Mesha's inscription that Moab had revolted before the death of Ahab and had attained a large measure of independence. This may serve to explain the absence of Moab from the list of allies at Qarqar, whereas Ammon is mentioned among them. Mesha declares that Israel dwelt in Medeba in the time of Omri "and half the time of his son, forty years." But perhaps "son" is to be interpreted as "grandson."

The Elijah stories present a picture of the state of religion in Israel at this time (I Kings 17–19:21). They show the queen as the dominant figure and Ahab as weak and vacillating, but his military achievements and his great building enterprises help to correct this picture.

Archaeology has verified the record of Ahab's great building achievements in Samaria. He continued the construction of the city begun by his father, Omri. The fortifications, consisting of three walls, were immensely strong. The city stood more than one siege, and finally fell after a siege lasting three years (II Kings 17:5). The workmanship has been judged to be the best yet found in Palestine. Carved ivory pieces in great numbers were found among the ruins of the city.* I Kings 22:39 tells of the "ivory house" which Ahab built. This description of Ahab's palace has been shown to be accurate, and is an indication of the wealth of the kingdom at this time.* About a century later Amos condemned those who lay on beds of ivory (Amos 6:4; cf. 3:15). Figs. INL 8; IVO 22.

*Bibliography.* L. B. Paton, "Phoenicians," *ERE* (1917), pp. 887-97; W. C. Graham and H. G. May, *Culture and Conscience* (1936), pp. 77 ff; F.-M. Abel, *Géographie de la Palestine,* II (1938), 357 ff; J. W. Crowfoot and G. M. Crowfoot, *Early Ivories from Samaria* (1938); O. Eissfeldt, "Ba' alšhamēm u. Yahwe," *ZAW,* 56 (1939); G. Loud, *The Megiddo Ivories* (1939); J. Morgenstern, *Amos Studies,* I (1941), 258-348; J. W. Crowfoot, K. Kenyon, and E. L. Sukenik, *The Buildings at Samaria* (1942), pp. 5 ff; N. Glueck, "Ramoth-Gilead," *BASOR,* 92 (1942), 10 ff; G. L. Della Vida and W. F. Albright, "Some Notes on the Stele of Ben-Hadad," *BASOR,* 90 (1943), 30 ff; R. de Vaux, "Les prophètes de Baal sur le Mont Carmel," *Bulletin du Musée de Beyrouth,* 5 (1944), 7-20; W. F. Albright, *Archaeology and the Religion of Palestine* (2nd ed., 1946), pp. 156 ff; J. B. Pritchard, ed., *ANET* (2nd ed., 1955), pp. 278-79, 320; J. A. Montgomery, *The Books of Kings,* ICC (1951), pp. 285-342.                     H. B. MacLean

**2.** Son of Kolaiah; one of the two false prophets among the Babylonian exiles, condemned by Jeremiah. Their punishment of death by fire would provide a "curse formula" for their fellow exiles (Jer. 29:21-22).                     H. B. MacLean

**AHARAH** ə hâr′ə [אחרח]. The third son of Benjamin, according to I Chr. 8:1; probably identical with AHIRAM. *See also* ROSH 1.

**AHARHEL** ə här'hĕl [אחרחל; LXX ἀδελφοῦ Ρηχαβ *presupposes* אח(י)רחב] (I Chr. 4:8). Son of Harum, of the tribe of Judah.

**AHASAI.** KJV form of AHZAI.

**AHASBAI** ə hăz'bī [אחסבי]. The father of Eliphelet (Eliphal in I Chr. 11:35), a member of the company of the Mighty Men of David known as the "Thirty" (II Sam. 23:34). Described as the "son of the Maachathite" (II Sam. 23:34 KJV), or, more correctly, "of Maacah" (RSV; cf. "the Mecherathite" (?) of I Chr. 11:36), he would appear either to be a member of the S Judean family of Maacah (I Chr. 2:48; 4:19) or to be from the city of Beth-maacah (II Sam. 20:14) or from the Aramaic city of Maacah (II Sam. 10:6, 8). The name Ahasbai of II Sam. 23:34 is read by the chronicler as ". . . Ur, Hepher" (אור חפר—I Chr. 11:35*b*-36*a*).      E. R. DALGLISH

**AHASUERUS** ə hăzh'ōō ĕr'əs, —ōō ir'— [Heb.-Aram. אחשורוש; ασυηρος (Tob. 14:15)]; KJV Apoc. **ASUERUS** ăzh'—. **1.** The Persian king who "reigned from India to Ethiopia over one hundred and twenty-seven provinces, . . . [and] sat on his royal throne in Susa the capital" (Esth. 1:1-2). He "laid tribute on the land and on the coastlands of the sea" (10:1). ESTHER became his wife. The LXX Ἀρταξερξης, Artaxerxes, has been accepted by some authorities as referring to Artaxerxes II. More likely the king referred to is XERXES (1). In Ezra 4:6 the reign of Ahasuerus is mentioned chronologically between Cyrus (vs. 5) and Artaxerxes (vs. 7). Fig. DAR 4.

**2.** The father of DARIUS THE MEDE (Dan. 9:1). *See also* ARTAXERXES; ESTHER, BOOK OF; XERXES.

     M. J. DRESDEN

**3.** According to Tob. 14:15, Nebuchadnezzar and Ahasuerus destroyed Nineveh. It was the Mede Cyaxares who was allied with Nebuchadnezzar (LXX Sinaiticus Ἀχιαχαρος; *see* AHIKAR).

**AHAVA** ə hā'və [אהוא]. A town in Babylonia located on a river or stream (to which the name Ahava was also applied; Ezra 8:15, 21, 31). It was there that Ezra assembled the Jews who were to return to Jerusalem with him.

**AHAZ** ā'hăz [אחז, he has grasped]; KJV NT **ACHAZ** ā'kăz. King of Judah *ca.* 735-715 B.C.; son and successor of Jotham. The name is a shortened form of יהואחז ("Y has grasped"). The full name Jehoahaz has been found in an Akkadian text under the form Yauḥazi. Cf. also the seal of "Ušna, minister of Ahaz." Fig. AHA 5.

Ahaz was twenty years old when he began to reign, and he reigned for sixteen years (II Kings 16:2; II Chr. 28:1*a*). This figure of sixteen years, however, can hardly be accurate. The evidence of the Assyrian inscriptions would seem to indicate that Ahaz was on the throne of Judah by *ca.* 734, and a terminal date for his reign would appear to be fixed by the year of Hezekiah's accession (*ca.* 715). Thus his reign must have lasted about twenty years. Confusion may have arisen because of his age when he became king, or perhaps on account of the sixteen years assigned to his father.

Courtesy of the American Schools of Oriental Research

5. Seal with inscription "Belonging to Ušna (Ašna?) minister (servant) of Ahaz"

No mention is made of his mother's name. This may be deliberate in view of his evil reputation (II Kings 16:2*b*-4; II Chr. 28:1*b*-4). He was remembered for his idolatrous practices (Isa. 2:8; cf. also 2:20). Ahaz "even burned his son as an offering" (II Kings 16:3; II Chr. 28:3 reads: "He . . . burned his sons as an offering"; cf. II Kings 3:27). The occasion may possibly be found in the attack on Jerusalem by Rezin of Aram and Pekah of Israel mentioned immediately thereafter (II Kings 16:5 ff). If Ahaz resorted to this last desperate measure without success, as far as raising the siege of Jerusalem was concerned, perhaps his only alternative was to appeal for help to Assyria. The datum may, however, be general, without any specific reference (cf. II Kings 21:6; 23:10; Mic. 6:7).

Rezin and Pekah were determined to annex Judah in the event of Ahaz' refusal to join them, and to set up a dynasty favorable to their policy under the "son of Tabeel" (Isa. 7:6). If the "son of Tabeel" was a prince of the royal house of Judah, whose mother was a princess of *Ṭâbh'ēl,* fresh light is thrown on this whole episode (*see* PEKAH). From the political point of view the advice of ISAIAH was based on the long view of things. Judah's hope lay, not in entangling alliances, but in faith in the power of her God (Isa. 7:9). Ahaz, however, could not see beyond the immediate situation. Gathering together the treasures of the temple and the royal house, he sent a messenger to Tiglath-pileser, asking his intervention to rescue him. Tiglath-pileser responded promptly to the request. *Ca.* 734 he marched to the W, conquered Philistia, devastated N Israel and Transjordan, and completely subdued Aram. The appeal of Ahaz had far-reaching results—not only politically, but religiously as well.

The Chronicler reports the Syro-Ephraimitic War from his own theological viewpoint as divine punishment for the idolatry of Ahaz (II Chr. 28:5-7). The details he gives are also different. It is not clear that Aram and Israel acted in conjunction as allies, nor was Jerusalem besieged, but in the invasion of her land Judah suffered considerably. The statement that "Zichri, a mighty man of Ephraim, slew Maaseiah the king's son and Azrikam the commander of the palace and Elkanah the next in authority to the king" (II Chr. 28:7) gives every appearance of historicity. Such details the Chronicler must have taken from his source. They fill in the background of the invasion. The same judgment is valid for the episode which the Chronicler relates in vss. 9-15 of the return by the Israelites of Judahite prisoners whom they had captured. The story is used to point up the faithlessness of Ahaz. Even the Israelites gave heed to a prophetic warning.

The evidence of the Chronicler enables us to see the Syro-Ephraimitic War in a wider perspective. Rezin and Pekah attacked Judah from the N. In close connection with this attack the Edomites again invaded and defeated Judah and carried away captives (II Chr. 28:17). Presumably they had already recovered Elath (II Kings 16:6). At the same time the Philistines made raids on the cities in the Shephelah and the Negeb of Judah, captured certain towns and villages in the Shephelah, and settled there (II Chr. 28:18). Uzziah had overrun certain parts of Philistia (II Chr. 26:6). Now Judah in turn was overrun by the Philistines.

In these circumstances Ahaz appealed to Tiglath-pileser for assistance. It is clear that after Aram had been overthrown, Ahaz was summoned to Damascus

(732) to appear before the Assyrian king. The contemporary Zenjirli inscription throws light on the occasion. N Ya'di also had pledged its allegiance to Assyria. Like Judah, it had won survival, but at the cost of independence.

Ahaz' visit to Damascus had other consequences as well (II Kings 16:10-16). While he was there, he saw the altar that was at Damascus, and sent details of its construction to Urijah the priest in Jerusalem. Confirmation of Urijah's position is found in Isa. 8:2. Against the king's return the priest constructed a similar altar according to the specifications sent him. Its grandeur must have made a great impression on the people. It seems more than likely that the altar was Assyrian, not Syrian, in accordance with the Assyrian practice of setting up the cult of Asshur in the conquered territories. When Ahaz returned to Jerusalem, the new altar was dedicated with royal sacrifices. It took the place of the bronze altar which had been used previously.

Vs. 15 provides an interesting contemporary picture of the ritual in the temple at this time. The old bronze altar was to be reserved for the king's use—"The bronze altar shall be for me to inquire by." The exact meaning of these words is not clear. It has been plausibly suggested that לבקר here refers to the examination of the sacrifice for omens. The following verses (17-18) present difficulties, and the details are obscure. It seems probable, however, that the sea which was set upon bronze oxen was removed and placed on a pediment of stone. The bronze was used to pay tribute to Assyria. Whatever the details of vs. 18 may be, it is probable that they refer again to changes which were made at this time in order to provide tribute. Politically and religiously Ahaz had surrendered to Assyrian domination.

The Chronicler gives a picture of complete religious chaos in the land (II Chr. 28:22-25). From the historical point of view this picture can scarcely be accurate in its details. It is clearly influenced by the Chronicler's theological viewpoint. He has taken the story in II Kings 16:10-18 and adapted it in his own way. He understood the new altar which Ahaz had caused to be erected as a Syrian altar, on which he sacrificed to the gods of Syria. Here the Chronicler followed the old belief that victory in war proved that the gods of the victors were stronger than the gods of the conquered. What he failed to see was that it was Yahweh himself who had brought destruction upon the land because of the king's apostasy. But why then did Ahaz not sacrifice to the gods of Assyria? Historically, this was what actually took place: Not only did Ahaz worship the Syrian gods. According to the Chronicler, he gathered together the vessels of the house of God and cut them in pieces so that they could no longer be used. In addition, he closed up the doors of the temple itself and made (heathen) altars in every corner of Jerusalem (vs. 24). This same policy he pursued in every city in Judah (vs. 25). From the historical point of view, it is most unlikely that this happened. The Chronicler has painted the reign of Ahaz in this way in order to provide a sharp contrast to the reforming zeal of his son Hezekiah.

As against the writer of Kings, who states that Ahaz "slept with his fathers, and was buried with his fathers in the city of David" (II Kings 16:20), the Chronicler asserts that "they buried him in the city, in Jerusalem, for they did not bring him into the tombs of the kings of Israel" (II Chr. 28:27). The use of the expression "kings of Israel" here (cf. also II Chr. 28:19) seems to indicate that the Chronicler was relying on his special source. His information may very well have been based on a sound historical tradition.

**Bibliography.** G. A. Cooke, *Text-book of North Semitic Inscriptions* (1903), pp. 171-85; S. A. Cook, *The Religion of Ancient Palestine in the Light of Archaeology* (1930), p. 103; N. Glueck, "The Third Season of Excavation at Tell el-Kheleifeh," *BASOR,* 79 (1940), 2-18; C. C. Torrey, "A Hebrew Seal from the Reign of Ahaz," *BASOR,* 79 (1940), 27-28, with note by W. F. Albright, 28-29; J. B. Pritchard, ed., *ANET* (2nd ed., 1955), p. 282; W. F. Albright, "The Son of Tabeel (Isa. 7:6)," *BASOR,* 140 (1955), 34-35.                   H. B. MacLean

**AHAZIAH** ā'ə zī'ə [(ו)אחזיה, Yahu has grasped]. **1.** King of Israel *ca.* 850-849 B.C.; son and successor of Ahab.

Ahaziah reigned for two years (I Kings 22:51). He offered to help Jehoshaphat king of Judah man a fleet based on Ezion-geber—no doubt, in an attempt to revive maritime trade with Arabia. This offer Jehoshaphat refused, clearly because he was afraid of an encroachment by Israel on this territory (I Kings 22:47-49; cf. II Chr. 20:35-37).

II Kings 1:1 states that after Ahab had died, Moab rebelled against Israel (cf. 3:5). But the Israelite king who marched against the Moabites to quell the rebellion was Jehoram, brother of Ahaziah (3:6). Presumably the revolt broke out on Ahab's death, perhaps even before it (*see* AHAB 1); but no action was taken to suppress it until Jehoram came to the throne.

The rest of Ahaziah's reign consists of a prophetic narrative which involves Elijah (II Kings 1:2-17). The picture of Elijah given here is out of keeping with the representation of his character elsewhere. Ahaziah had fallen through a lattice in the upper chamber (עליה) of his palace and was seriously injured. The reference is probably to a roof chamber with open window spaces protected by lattice work (cf. Jer. 22:14). In his sickness he sent messengers to obtain an oracle from Baal-zebub, the god of Ekron. It appears certain that the correct name of this god is Baal-zebul (as the best texts of the NT also read), and an oracle was sought from him because he was the Syrian god of life. Elijah, whose description (II Kings 1:8) gives every indication of historicity, had previously been told by the angel of the Lord that the king would die. And so it happened (vs. 17). The rest of the story is unhistorical.

Ahaziah had no son (vs. 17), so the throne passed to his brother Jehoram.

**Bibliography.** W. F. Albright, "The North-Canaanite Epic of 'Al'êyân Ba'al and Môt," *JPOS,* XII (1932), 191-92. N. Glueck, *Explorations in Eastern Palestine*, II, *AASOR,* XV (1935), 137 ff; *Explorations in Eastern Palestine*, III, *AASOR,* XVIII-XIX (1939), 242 ff.

**2.** King of Judah *ca.* 842 B.C.; son and successor of Jehoram, murdered by Jehu.

In II Chr. 21:16-17 the Chronicler reports an invasion of Judah by the Philistines and the Arabs in the reign of Jehoram. They carried off much booty, including the king's sons and his wives, "so that no son was left to him except Jehoahaz, his youngest son." In ch. 22 the new king is called Ahaziah. The two names are the same, the former having the divine names as a prefix to the verb, the latter as a suffix. The probable explanation of the two names is that the Chronicler in 21:17 is using another source than Kings. But in 22:1*b* he is relying on Kings, which used the name Ahaziah. Thus in 22:1*a* the same name was given to the king.

The Chronicler's statement that "the inhabitants of Jerusalem made Ahaziah his youngest son king in his stead" (II Chr. 22:1) seems to indicate that there was difficulty over the accession, but no details are given. Apparently, however, the initiative was taken by the inhabitants of Jerusalem. It is possible that Ahaziah was at first king only of Jerusalem, and later became king of Judah. It is also possible that because of Jehoram's illness he was incapacitated and a regent ruled for him.

Ahaziah is said to have reigned for one year (II Kings 8:26; II Chr. 22:2). He came to the throne in Joram's twelfth year (II Kings 8:25). But as both kings died at the same time at the hands of Jehu, it is clear that he could have reigned only part of a year. The alternative is to accept the statement of II Kings 9:29 that Ahaziah began to reign in the eleventh year of Joram son of Ahab. Ahaziah was twenty-two years old when he became king (II Kings 8:26). The Chronicler says he was forty-two years old (II Chr. 22:2). But this would have made him two years older than his father (II Chr. 21:5, 20). Other readings are twenty years and sixteen years. The latter number seems more reasonable for the youngest son.

His mother's name was Athaliah. She was a granddaughter of Omri king of Israel (II Kings 8:26; II Chr. 22:2). The MT reads in both cases בת ("daughter") of Omri. II Kings 8:18 makes the daughter of Ahab Ahaziah's mother. The usual explanation is to say that "daughter" is used in II Kings 8:26 in a general sense, but it is quite possible that Athaliah was not the daughter of Ahab, but his sister. She would thus be a daughter of Omri.

That Ahaziah took part in a campaign with Joram king of Israel against Hazael king of Syria at Ramoth-gilead is questionable (II Kings 8:28-29; II Chr. 22:5-6). When Joram was wounded and returned to Jezreel, nothing is said of Ahaziah. He appears later on a visit to Joram. Further, II Kings 9:14*b*, 15*a*, give a somewhat different picture. Joram and all Israel were defending Ramoth-gilead against Hazael of Syria when Joram was wounded. No mention is made of Ahaziah. He appears only in vs. 16 with the notice that he had come down to Jezreel to visit the wounded Joram. The use of the particular verb "had come down" is interesting. The implication is that he had come down from Jerusalem. These verses in ch. 9 give the impression of being original.

Meantime a revolt, under prophetic inspiration, had broken out in the army at Ramoth-gilead. Elisha gave instructions to one of the sons of the prophets to go to Ramoth-gilead; seek out JEHU son of Jehoshaphat, son of Nimshi, one of the army commanders;

and anoint him as king over Israel in the name of Yahweh. These instructions were carried out. Thereafter Jehu drove to Jezreel. Apparently Joram became suspicious when the messengers whom he had sent to meet Jehu did not return, and ordered his own chariot to be made ready. Then Joram and Ahaziah, each in his own chariot, went to meet Jehu. They met at the property of Naboth the Jezreelite. Joram turned to escape but was shot by an arrow from Jehu's bow. Ahaziah also fled, but was fatally wounded near Ibleam, S of Jezreel. He died at Megiddo. His servants brought him to Jerusalem, where he was buried with his fathers (II Kings 9:1-28).

The Chronicler clearly used here a different source from Kings (II Chr. 22:8-9). According to him, all the family of Ahaziah was killed at this time. But Ahaziah himself could not be found. He was hiding in Samaria. He was finally caught and put to death by Jehu. Then he was buried in Samaria. The Chronicler's account does not appear to be historical.

In II Chr. 22:6 the MT has "Azariah." This is clearly a scribal error for "Ahaziah."

*Bibliography.* F.-M. Abel, *Géographie de la Palestine,* II (1938), 317; M. Noth, *Geschichte Israels* (3rd ed., 1956), p. 216. Contrast J. Begrich, *ZAW*, 53 (1935), 78 ff.

H. B. MacLean

**AHBAN** ä'băn [אחבן, brother of intelligent one] (I Chr. 2:29). One of the sons of Abishur in the genealogy of Jerahmeel.

**AHER** ä'hər [אחר, another(?)]. Ostensibly a Benjaminite in the Chronicler's genealogy (I Chr. 7:12), but the text almost certainly needs revision on the basis of the LXX and of Gen. 46:23; Num. 26:42. *See* Ahiram.      F. T. Schumacher

**AHI** ä'hī [אחי, brother]. A word mentioned twice in the Chronicler's genealogies; it seems abbreviated (*see* Ahijah) and is in both cases textually suspect.

1. Son of Abdiel in the tribe of Gad (I Chr. 5:15).

2. One of the sons of Shamer in I Chr. 7:34 KJV, following the MT. The RSV "his brother" is more likely.      F. T. Schumacher

**AHIAH** ə hī'ə [אחיה, brother of Y]. English variant of the name Ahijah. It occurs once in the RSV—in the list of the leaders under Nehemiah who set their seal to the covenant (Neh. 10:26—H 10:27).

**AHIAM** ə hī'əm [אחיאם]. The son of Sharar (II Sam. 23:33) or Sachar (I Chr. 11:35) the Hararite; a member of the company of the heroes of David known as the "Thirty."

**AHIAN** ə hī'ən [אחין, brotherly(?); *variants in Greek make form somewhat uncertain*] (I Chr. 7:19). The first son of Shemida in the genealogy of Manasseh.

**AHIEZER** ä'hī ē'zər [אחיעזר, my brother is help]. 1. Son of Ammishaddai; the representative of the tribe of Dan who assisted Moses in the census (Num. 1: 12; 2:25), in the tribe's offering at the dedication of the altar (Num. 7:66, 71), and was their captain as rear guard for the line of march (Num. 10:25).

2. Leader of the Benjaminite bowmen—from Saul's own tribe—who came to David's aid while he was hiding in Ziklag (I Chr. 12:3).

F. T. Schumacher

**AHIHUD** ə hī'hŭd [אחיהוד, the (divine) brother is glorious, *or* brother of majesty(?); *in* I Chr. 8:7 אחיחד, *perhaps* the (divine) brother has ruled]. 1. An Asherite leader, son of Shelomi (Num. 34:27). He was one of those appointed, under the oversight of Eleazar and Joshua, to superintend the distribution of the W Jordanian territory among the ten tribes to be settled in that area of Canaan.

2. A Benjaminite listed in the tribal genealogy (I Chr. 8:7). The difficulties of the text make it possible to identify Ahihud as the son either of Heglam or of Gera.

*Bibliography.* M. Noth, *Die israelitischen Personennamen* (1928), pp. 18, 146, 192.      R. F. Johnson

**AHIJAH** ə hī'jə [אחיה, אחיהו, brother of Y; *cf.* Phoen. חמלך, brother of Melek = Ahimelech]; KJV alternately AHIAH ə hī'ə (I Sam. 14:3, 18; I Kings 4:3; I Chr. 8:7); KJV Apoc. ACHIAS ə kī'əs. 1. A priest in the time of Saul; son of Ahitub, grandson of Phinehas, and great-grandson of Eli (I Sam. 14:3). He was priest in Shiloh and served with Saul's army at Gibeah as the wearer of the Ephod and the one responsible for the Ark of the Covenant. Both these objects apparently were used as means of oracular consultation with God (I Sam. 14:18-19, 41-42), although the LXX reads "ephod" in vs. 18.

His name does not appear in the list of high priests in I Chr. 6:50-53; Ezra 7:2-5. Many scholars believe that his name originally was Ahimelech and that he is to be identified with the priest at Nob who is also the son of Ahitub (I Sam. 21–22). That the Canaanite deity should have been removed in favor of Yahweh is more understandable than that two brothers should have had such clashing names.

2. A Pelonite who was one of David's Mighty Men (I Chr. 11:36).

3. Son of Shisha; a secretary or scribe under Solomon (I Kings 4:3).

* 4. A prophet from Shiloh; proponent and opponent of Jeroboam, first king of Israel (I Kings 11; 14; also 12:15; 15:29; II Chr. 10:15; five times אחיהו). Representing the prophetic opposition to the syncretistic religion and despotic injustice of Solomon's reign, Ahijah met Jeroboam, a foreman over forced labor from the northern tribes, and in a dramatic scene on the road outside Jerusalem acted out a prophetic word, proclaiming the division of the kingdom and Jeroboam's accession (I Kings 11:26-40). He ripped his new garment into twelve pieces, saying: "Take for yourself ten pieces; for thus says the Lord, the God of Israel, 'Behold, I am about to tear the kingdom from the hand of Solomon, and will give you ten tribes'" (vs. 31; actually, he got all except Judah). But the prophet understood the kingship in terms of a divine commission and made his promise of God's support and a sure dynasty conditional upon Jeroboam's fidelity (vs. 38).

The king's subsequent career proved to be deficient in Yahwistic zealousness, and an incident reflecting the now blind and aged prophet's opposition is preserved in ch. 14. Jeroboam sent his disguised wife to inquire from the mentor of his youth as to the outcome of their son's illness. The prophet perceived her identity and pronounced the imminent death of the child and a violent doom upon the house of Jeroboam.

The two passages have probably been subsequently reworked by a Deuteronomic editor, but they bespeak an authentic core by which the revolt of the North originates under prophetic instigation and is subject to continuing divine critique.

In II Chr. 9:29 the "prophecy of Ahijah" is listed as a source for the history of Solomon. This might conceivably indicate a noncanonical collection of oracles but more likely simply refers to the material now preserved in I Kings 11; 14.

5. The father of Baasha, king of Israel; a member of the tribe of Issachar (I Kings 15:27, 33; 21:22; II Kings 9:9).

6. Probably the correct name for AHOAH, son of Bela (I Chr. 8:4).

7. One of the sons of Ehud who were carried captive (I Chr. 8:7); but the text is very obscure, and the names may be simply a dittograph from vs. 4.

8. One of the sons of Jerahmeel; a member of the tribe of Judah (I Chr. 2:25). The verse seems to be corrupt, and the word may not be a proper name; B and A read ἀδελφὸς αὐτοῦ; Syr has "his brothers."

9. A Levite who was in charge of treasuries in the temple (I Chr. 26:20). But the LXX is probably correct in reading "Levites, their brothers" (אחיהם).

F. T. SCHUMACHER

**AHIKAM** ə hī′kəm [אחיקם, my brother has arisen]. Josiah's minister, member of the deputation to Huldah concerning the Book of the Law (II Kings 22:12, 14), and sole protector of Jeremiah from death under Jehoiakim (Jer. 26:24). Ahikam was the father of GEDALIAH (II Kings 25:22; Jer. 39:14).

J. M. WARD

**AHIKAR** ə hī′kär [Ἀχιάχρος, Ἀχείχαρος; *perhaps* Aram. *Ah-yᵉ-qar*, precious brother]; KJV ACHIACHARUS ăk′ĭ ăk′ə rəs.

The nephew and benefactor of TOBIT (Tob. 1:21-22; 2:10). Ahikar himself was the subject of a romance much older than the book of Tobit. Though the Ahikar story had been in Western circulation through its presence in the Arabian *Thousand and One Nights,* its relationship to the book of Tobit remained unsuspected until the ELEPHANTINE PAPYRI were discovered, for among these were fragments of the Ahikar story.

The typical story (the variations are endless) relates that Ahikar was a trusted official (scribe or secretary) to Sennacherib, the king of Assyria. Childless, he had reared a nephew Nadan as his heir. The ungrateful youth composed letters, to which he forged Ahikar's signature, addressed to the kings of Egypt and Persia, and which proposed betraying Assyria's troops to them. Thereupon, the nephew had the reports of Ahikar's treason reach the king, who gullibly condemned Ahikar to death. However, the servant who was entrusted with Ahikar's execution replaced

him with a condemned criminal, and let Ahikar secretly go home, to be cared for by Ahikar's wife. It was universally believed that the noble Ahikar was dead.

Thereafter the king of Egypt presented Sennacherib with the choice of paying tribute or of helping in a project—namely, that of building a castle in the air. Sennacherib, aware that Ahikar might have helped in the latter endeavor, bemoaned having slain him. Thereupon the servant produced Ahikar.

As for building a castle in the air, Ahikar employed an eagle to carry two boys into the air; the boys kept urging the Egyptians to bring up to them bricks and mortar so that they could commence the building. Since bricks and mortar were not delivered, no fault could attach to the builders.

In gratitude to Ahikar, Sennacherib restored him to a high place, and Nadan was punished.

The incidents in the book of Ahikar are interspersed with maxims and proverbs, these being widely different in content and form in the various versions, as is to be expected in a tale known widely in many folk literatures.

There have been occasional scholars who have believed that the Ahikar story is younger than Tobit; and, they suggest, it is an amplification designed to characterize Tobit's otherwise unknown benefactor. But most scholars hold, properly, that the Ahikar story is considerably older than Tobit. This is seen most readily in Tob. 14:10, where Nadan's perfidy and punishment are alluded to as well known. The dependency of some of Tobit's maxims on Ahikar is unmistakable.

The supposition in Tobit that Ahikar was Tobit's nephew (various versions of Tobit suggest other relationships) implies that the author of Tobit conceived of Ahikar as a Jew. Such is unquestionably the case. Not only has the author of Tobit Judaized Ahikar; he has made him quite a pious Jew.

*Bibliography.* On the legend of Ahikar, see: F. C. Conybeare, J. R. Harris, and A. S. Lewis, *The Story of Ahikar* (1898); and the reworking of this book in "The Story of Ahikar," in R. H. Charles, *The Apoc. and Pseudep. of the OT* (1913), I, 191-92; II, 715-84. Of the vast bibliography which could be listed, the following brief summaries are most useful: F. Nau, *Histoire et sagesse d'Ahikar l'Assyrien* (1909); B. Meissner, "Das Märchen vom Weisen Achiqar," *Der Alte Orient* (1917), Band XVI, Heft 2; I. Abraham, "The Story of Ahikar," *By-Paths in Hebraic Bookland* (1920).

S. SANDMEL

**AHIKAR, BOOK OF.** An oriental wisdom book composed of proverbs and fables, prefaced by a narrative introduction about the sage Ahikar, who supposedly had uttered them as instruction for his son. The book had come down in Syriac, Arabic, Armenian, and other languages, but the rediscovery of portions of an Old Aramaic version of the fifth century B.C. among the ELEPHANTINE PAPYRI proved a great surprise.

Ahikar was a high official of Assyria under Sennacherib. He had no son and hence adopted a sister's son named Nadan. After educating him with the wise counsel appended to the story, he brought him to King Esarhaddon. Nadan soon was appointed Ahikar's successor, and the sage was then able to retire to his country estates. But the young man had evidently not learned all the lessons his foster father had sought to impress on him, for he defamed Ahikar as fomenting rebellion against his sovereign. The latter in anger dispatched Nabu-sum-iskun and two associates to go and execute Ahikar. They found him in his vineyard between two mountains. Apprised of their errand, Ahikar reminded Nabu-sum-iskun of how he had spared and harbored him from the wrath of Sennacherib when that ruler had ordered his execution, and how the king had been quite satisfied that he had done so when the innocence of Nabu-sum-iskun was established. Ahikar suggested a return favor of the same sort. The three executioners pledged one another to secrecy, and a slave was slain instead of Ahikar. We do not hear how the matter came out, but, no doubt, Ahikar was vindicated and the wicked Nadan punished.

There is reason to believe that the Aramaic book is derived from an Assyrian work. Some of the persons mentioned may even be historical. A high official named Nabu-sum-iskun is known to have served under Sennacherib. While the person of Ahikar has not been found as yet, his name is Assyrian (Ahi-yaqar, "the brother is precious"). The name Nadan (better, Nadin) is a short form of some name like Adad-*nadin*-shum. The supposed rebellious activity of Ahikar could well have a background in fact, for as we know from Assyrian sources, Esarhaddon's succession was achieved by a defeat of brothers who had a better claim to the throne.

It was through the Aramaic version, however, that the book of Ahikar obtained its vogue. In its present form it cannot be older than *ca.* 500 B.C., for it contains Old Persian loan words. Democritus (born *ca.* 470 B.C.) is said to have utilized the translation of a stela of Akikaros in his ethical writings. Theophrastus (born *ca.* 372 B.C.) is said to have written a book called *Akicharos*—evidently a Greek version of Ahikar. The fables of Aesop were drawn from Ahikar, and the story of Ahikar was adapted for the "life" of Aesop. The book of TOBIT, a work of the second century B.C., is familiar with the story of Ahikar (KJV Achiacharus; 1:21-22; 2:10; 11:18; 14:10-11); the name of Nadan appears in corrupted forms (KJV Aman). Strabo (born 63 B.C.) refers to Achaikaros as having been a lawgiver among the Bosporenes (no doubt, a misreading of some other word: Assyrians? Borsippenes or people of Borsippa?).

*Bibliography.* R. Smend, *Alter und Herkunft des Achikar-Romans und sein Verhältnis zu Aesop* BZAW, no. 13 (1908); F. Nau, *Histoire et Sagesse d'Ahikar l'Assyrien* (1909); E. Meyer, *Der Papyrusfund von Elephantine* (2nd ed., 1912), pp. 102-28; R. H. Charles, ed., *The Apoc. and Pseudep. of the OT,* II (1913), 715-84; F. Stummer, *Der kritische Wert der altaramäischen Achikartexte aus Elephantine, AA,* V, 5 (1914); B. Meissner, "Das Märchen vom weisen Achiqar," *Der Alte Orient,* Band XVI (1917), Heft 2; A. E. Cowley, *Aramaic Papyri of the Fifth Century B.C.* (1923), pp. 204-48 (the Aramaic text with translation and notes); J. B. Pritchard, ed., *ANET* (2nd ed., 1955), pp. 427-28.      E. G. KRAELING

**AHILUD** ə hī′ləd [אֲחִילוּד, a brother is born]. The father of David's recorder Jehoshaphat (II Sam. 8:16; I Kings 4:3; I Chr. 18:15) and, probably, of Baana, a district officer under Solomon (I Kings 4:12).

**AHIMAAZ** ə hĭm′ĭ ăz [אֲחִימַעַץ, brother is counselor (?)]. **1.** The father of Ahinoam, who was the wife of Saul (I Sam. 14:50).

**2.** A son of Zadok the high priest (II Sam. 15:27; I Chr. 6:8, 53—H 5:34; 6:38); the father of AZARIAH (I Chr. 6:9—H 5:35). Ahimaaz was in the priestly company that brought the ark to David when he had vacated Jerusalem. At the instance of the king, Zadok and Abiathar returned to the capital to await information from the spy Hushai concerning the plans of Absalom. Ahimaaz and Jonathan the son of Abiathar were stationed at En-rogel, whence they could bring David word (II Sam. 15:24 ff). In the first hours of the insurrection, when it appeared that the tactics suggested by Hushai were to be adopted, Abiathar and Zadok were so informed. These, in turn, relayed the message by an unsuspected maidservant to Ahimaaz and Jonathan, who quickly informed the king of the intentions of Absalom (II Sam. 17:1 ff). For a time this same system of espionage proved quite successful, but it was discovered. Ahimaaz and Jonathan fled for their lives and eluded the military detail of Absalom only by their effective concealment in a well at Bahurim. Subsequently, they joined the army of David at Mahanaim (II Sam. 17:17 ff).

After the battle in the forest of Ephraim in which Absalom was slain and his forces routed, Ahimaaz besought Joab to permit him to convey the news of the victory to David at Mahanaim. Joab refused at first to allow such a worthy man as Ahimaaz to undertake the unrewarding task of bearing to the king such dark tidings, for Joab knew that the death of Absalom would greatly distress the king and completely obscure the military victory. Accordingly, Joab dispatched a Cushite courier, who from a diplomatic point of view had nothing to lose, to convey the ominous news. When Ahimaaz insisted that he be allowed also to convey the news of the battle to the king, Joab finally acceded. Arriving at Mahanaim before the Cushite, Ahimaaz told the king of the military success, but when he was interrogated concerning the fate of Absalom, he professed an ignorance in the matter. However, with the arrival of the Cushite all doubt as to the fateful end of the usurper was dispelled (II Sam. 18:19-33).

Of the later career of Ahimaaz we know nothing, and there is no evidence that he succeeded his father, Zadok, in the high-priestly office.

**3.** One of the twelve officers appointed by Solomon and charged with the provision of the royal house from the revenues of his assigned district of Naphtali (I Kings 4:15). The prestige of his office is indicated by the fact that he married Basemath, a daughter of Solomon. However, some interpreters are of the opinion that Ahimaaz is the name of the father of the officer, whose own name has been accidentally destroyed like some others in the same list. In this case, it is not impossible that he may be the same as Ahimaaz the son of Zadok (2 *above*).

     E. R. DALGLISH

**AHIMAN** ə hī′mən [אֲחִימָן, *see* 1 *below*]. **1.** One of the three sons of Anak or "giants" residing in Hebron when the Israelite spies reconnoitered the land (Num. 13:22; Josh. 15:14; Judg. 1:10). The pre-Israelite inhabitants of Hebron, S of Jerusalem, were described in several slightly variant phrases as descendants of ANAK, probably meaning "sons of neck" or "tall people." Ahiman, an individual or tribal grouping among the Anakim, was defeated in Hebron, the defeat being ascribed in Judg. 1:10 to the men of Judah, in Josh. 15:14 to CALEB.

The names of the descendants of Anak, Ahiman, Sheshai, and Talmai, may point to an Aramean origin, although there are parallels to these names in other Semitic languages. The name Ahiman is probably compounded of אָח, "the (divine) brother," plus an abbreviated form of an originally complete word, no longer recoverable with certainty.

**2.** A Levite, one of the four chief gatekeepers of Jerusalem in the postexilic period (I Chr. 9:17). The somewhat confusing account in I Chr. 9:17-34 of the situation and duties of the gatekeepers appears to combine features from Mosaic and Davidic times as well as from the period contemporary with the author.

*Bibliography.* M. Noth, *Die israelitischen Personennamen* (1928), p. 40; L. Koehler and W. Baumgartner, *Lexicon in VT Libros* (1953), pp. 30-31.          R. F. JOHNSON

**AHIMELECH** ə hĭm′ə lĕk [אֲחִימֶלֶךְ, the brother (God) rules, *or* my brother is king, *or* brother of the king]. **1.** Priest of Nob, son of Ahitub. His aid to the fugitive David caused Saul to have the Nob priesthood slaughtered (I Sam. 21:1-9—H 21:2-10; 22:9-20). He appears to have been consulted by Saul on previous occasions for the result of the divine oracle (I Sam. 22:15). He has been equated with Saul's chaplain Ahijah, the son of Ahitub (I Sam. 14:3, 18). The name Ahijah is taken as a variant of Ahimelech, "Yahweh" having been substituted for "king." But this is unlikely (*see* ELI). The title of Ps. 52 places the psalm in the context of Doeg's informing Saul about the aid Ahimelech had given to David.

**2.** A Hittite in the service of David (I Sam. 26:6).
**3.** Son of Abiathar (II Sam. 8:17; I Chr. 18:16 [KJV ABIMELECH, following the MT]; I Chr. 24: 6). In II Sam. 8:17 "Ahimelech the son of Abiathar" is clearly a mistake for "Abiathar the son of Ahimelech." The other references are based on this error.

*Bibliography.* W. F. Albright, *Archaeology and the Religion of Israel* (1956), pp. 201-2.          R. W. CORNEY

**AHIMOTH** ə hī′mŏth [אֲחִימוֹת, my brother is Mot, *or* Akkad. *aḫi-miti*, my brother is my support(?), *or a hypocoristicon for* Ahimelech]. A Levite of the family of Kohath (I Chr. 6:25—H 6:10). Perhaps we should read "Ahimahath" (cf. I Chr. 6:35—H 6:20).
          R. W. CORNEY

**AHINADAB** ə hĭn′ə dăb [אֲחִינָדָב, brother is noble]. Son of Iddo; one of the twelve officers appointed by Solomon charged with the provision of the royal house from the revenues of his assigned district in S Gilead, with headquarters at Mahanaim (I Kings 4:14).          E. R. DALGLISH

**AHINOAM** ə hĭn′ō əm [אֲחִינֹעַם, *from* אָח *plus* נֹעַם, my brother is delight, joy (*cf.* Naomi, Naaman, *from*

*the same root*)]. **1.** The wife of Saul, and daughter of Ahimaaz (I Sam. 14:50).

**2.** One of David's wives, a woman from Jezreel. She, with Abigail, accompanied David's flight to Philistia, survived capture by the Amalekites, was rescued, and returned with David to Hebron. Here she became the mother of David's first-born, Amnon (I Sam. 25:43; 27:3; 30:5; II Sam. 2:2; 3:2; I Chr. 3:1).          D. HARVEY

**AHIO** ə hī′ō [אַחְיוֹ]. **1.** Son of Abinadab. He preceded the cart which carried the ark from his father's house bound for the city of David (II Sam. 6:3-4; I Chr. 13:7). To construe Ahio in these instances as a proper name seems preferable to translating it "his brother" (RSV mg.) or "his brethren" (LXX).

**2.** Considered to be a proper name in I Chr. 8:14 according to the MT, and accordingly one of the sons of Elpaal, a Benjaminite. Many scholars prefer, however, on the basis of the LXX (A L) to render the emended text as "their brethren."

**3.** One of the sons of the Benjaminite Jeiel (=ABIEL [?]); a brother of Kish (I Chr. 8:31; 9:37).
          E. R. DALGLISH

**AHIRA** ə hī′rə [אֲחִירַע; LXX Αχιρε, the (divine) brother is a friend, *or less probably* a brother is Ra]. A leader of Naphtali; son of Enan (Num. 1:15; 2:29; 7:78, 83; 10:27). He was one of twelve tribal leaders or deputies who assisted Moses in taking a census of Israel and in other tasks in the wilderness. *See* PRINCE.

*Bibliography.* Commentaries: G. B. Gray, ICC (1903), p. 9; J. Marsh, *IB*, II (1953), 144-45. See also M. Noth, *Die israelitischen Personennamen* (1928), p. 236.
          R. F. JOHNSON

**AHIRAM** ə hī′rəm [אֲחִירָם, my brother is exalted]; **AHIRAMITES** —rə mīts (Num. 26:38). The third son of Benjamin; the head of the family called Ahiramites. The Chronicler's genealogy of Benjamin —a corrupt text—lists the third son as AHARAH (I Chr. 8:1), which most scholars believe should read "Ahiram." This change in reading should probably also be made for "Aher" in I Chr. 7:12. Still another Benjaminite genealogy lists among the sons: "Ehi, Rosh, Muppim, Huppim" (Gen. 46: 21). This is probably erroneous and should read, in agreement with Num. 26: "Ahiram, and Shupham and Hupham" (change from: אחיורֹאשֹׁמֻפִּיֹחֻפִּים

to: אֲחִירָםֹשׁוּפָםֹחוּפָם).
          F. T. SCHUMACHER

**AHISAMACH** ə hĭs′ə măk [אֲחִיסָמָךְ, the (divine) brother has supported]. A Danite; father of Oholiab, who was one of those appointed to make the tabernacle and its equipment (Exod. 31:6; 35:34; 38:23).

*Bibliography.* M. Noth, *Die israelitischen Personennamen* (1928), pp. 68-70, 176.          R. F. JOHNSON

**AHISHAHAR** ə hĭsh′ə här [אֲחִישָׁחַר, brother of the dawn]. One of the sons of Bilhan ben Jediael in a dubious genealogy of Benjamin (I Chr. 7:10). The names of Bilhan and Ahishahar do not appear in a more authentic list (I Chr. 8:1-40), and many believe they are in reality part of a genealogy of ZEBULUN.                                F. T. SCHUMACHER

**AHISHAR** ə hī'shär [אחישר]. The royal chamberlain in the cabinet of Solomon (I Kings 4:6).

**AHITHOPHEL** ə hĭth'ə fĕl [אחיתפל]. A native of Giloh in the highlands of Judah who served as the royal counselor to David. He committed suicide when his advice to Absalom was rejected in favor of the plan of Hushai (I Chr. 27:33-34). Ahithophel was proverbial for his sagacity, and in the judgment of his contemporaries his counsel was tantamount to an oracle of God (II Sam. 16:23).

When Absalom revolted against his father, David, and was crowned in Hebron, Ahithophel joined the rebel cause (II Sam. 15:12). Having taken Jerusalem without a fight, Absalom complied with the first stratagem suggested by Ahithophel by violating publicly the royal harem, part of which had been left behind by the departing king, and thus giving incontestable assurance to his followers that the die was cast for all concerned (16:20-22). Ahithophel then advised that he be given twelve thousand men with whom to pursue David immediately, before his forces were consolidated, and that he concentrate his total effort on the destruction of the king only. Were this one object realized, Ahithophel prophesied, the nation would joyously receive their new king (17:1-3). While this advice seemed good at the time it was given, it was rejected by the persuasive eloquence of Hushai, the spy of David, who cast doubt upon the wisdom of such an adroit action and advocated a delay until all Israel could be mustered for battle (17:5-14). Cognizant that the plan of Hushai would involve him and all the conspirators in a speedy retribution by David, Ahithophel departed from the capital to his own house and hanged himself (17:23).

Ahithophel was the father of Eliam (II Sam. 23:34) —a garbled form of this name appears in the name of Ahijah the Pelonite (I Chr. 11:36*b*), one of the members of the illustrious company of Davidic heroes known as the "Thirty." The daughter of Eliam (or Ammiel, which is the same name with components transposed—I Chr. 3:5) was Bathsheba the wife of Uriah (II Sam. 11:3). It is not improbable that the reason for the defection of the sagacious counselor of David had its roots in the infamous incident that involved his granddaughter Bathsheba.                                E. R. DALGLISH

**AHITUB** ə hī'tŭb [אחיטוב; Akkad. *aḫu-ṭāb*, the brother (God) is good]; KJV Apoc. ACHITOB ăk'ə tŏb; ACITHO ăs'ə thō. **1.** The father of Ahimelech the priest (I Sam. 22:9, 11-12, 20). He is called the father of Saul's chaplain Ahijah in I Sam. 14:3 (probably a gloss—*see* ELI), also mistakenly the father of ZADOK THE PRIEST in II Sam. 8:17 (source of the error in I Chr. 6:8—H 5:34; 6:52-53—H 6:37-38; 18:16; Ezra 7:2; I Esd. 8:2; II Esd. 1:1).

**2.** The father (I Chr. 6:12—H 5:38) or grandfather (I Chr. 9:11; Neh. 11:11) of another priest named ZADOK (4).

**3.** An ancestor of Judith (Jth. 8:1).                                R. W. CORNEY

**AHLAB** ä'lăb [אחלב]. A town in the territory of Asher, identical with MAHALAB. It is probably located at Khirbet el-Mahalib, a site near the coast *ca.* four miles NE of Tyre. According to Judg. 1:31, Asher was unable to drive out the Canaanite inhabitants of the town.                                G. W. VAN BEEK

**AHLAI** ä'lī [אחלי, O! would that! (*cf.* II Kings 5:3; Ps. 119:5)]. **1.** A descendant (ובני), probably a daughter (see vs. 34), of Sheshan in the genealogy of Jerahmeel (I Chr. 2:31).

**2.** The father of Zabad in the list of David's Mighty Men (I Chr. 11:41). Since the name Zabad appears among the descendants of Sheshan's daughter (I Chr. 2:36), it is possible, though not likely, that this Ahlai is rather Zabad's mother and identical with 1 *above*.                                F. T. SCHUMACHER

**AHOAH** ə hō'ə [אחוח, *error for* Ahijah]. A son of Bela in the genealogy of Benjamin (I Chr. 8:4). The LXX, B, and the Syr. have the regular form (אחוה), and the apparent dittograph in vs. 7 supports the view that "Ahoah," which appears only once, is an error for "Ahijah."                                F. T. SCHUMACHER

**AHOHI** ə hō'hī [אחוחי]. If the MT is correct, the father of Dodo and grandfather of Eleazar who was second among David's three Mighty Men (II Sam. 23:9). Ahohi is not elsewhere referred to, unless it be in a patronymic, the AHOHITE, used or conferred because of the military exploits of his offspring. However, many scholars believe the MT-RSV "son of Ahohi" (בן־אחחי) should be read, with the KJV, "the Ahohite" (האחוחי) on the basis of the parallel passage in I Chr. 11:12. If the above conjecture is correct, however, one would expect the Chronicler to use the patronymic.                                F. T. SCHUMACHER

**AHOHITE, THE** ə hō'hīt [האחוחי]. A patronymic or geographic designation of uncertain reference. The most frequent suggestion has been "son of AHOAH." But *see* AHOHI as another possibility, since the term is always applied to military heroes in the time of David: (*a*) Dodo, the father of Eleazer (I Chr. 11:12; and also in I Chr. 27:4, where Dodo is spelled "Dodai" and the name Eleazer is probably to be supplied); (*b*) Zalmon, one of the Thirty (II Sam. 23:28); (*c*) Ilai, in the parallel list of David's Mighty Men (I Chr. 11:29), who should perhaps be identified with *b above*.                                F. T. SCHUMACHER

**AHOLAH.** KJV form of OHOLAH.

**AHOLIAB.** KJV form of OHOLIAB.

**AHOLIBAH.** KJV form of OHOLIBAH.

**AHOLIBAMAH.** KJV form of OHOLIBAMAH.

**AHRIMAN** ä'rĭ mən. The designation, in its Middle Persian form, of the spirit or principle of evil in Zoroastrianism; called *Angra Mainyu* (Evil Spirit) in the Avesta and Ἀρειμάνιος or Ἀριμάνης by the Greek authors. He is the counterpart and opponent of Ormuzd (Ahura-Mazda). *See* PERSIA, HISTORY AND RELIGION OF, §§ E2-3, 5.                                M. J. DRESDEN

**AHUMAI** ə hū'mī [אחומי] (I Chr. 4:2). One of the sons of Jahath in the genealogy of Judah. Some scholars follow the LXX and read "Ahimai" or "Ahiman." F. T. SCHUMACHER

**AHURA-MAZDA** ə hŏŏr'ə măz'də [Avestan *and* Old Pers. *A( h )ura-mazdā( h )*, wise lord]. Alternately: ORMUZD ôr'mŏŏzd, ORMAZD ôr'məzd, OHRMAZD [Pahlavi *Ohrmazd; cf.* 'Ωρομάσδης, 'Ωρομάζης]. The highest divine entity in Zarathushtra's teachings. In the Old Persian inscriptions Ahuramazda is the greatest of the gods, the creator of the sky and the earth, of men, and of peaceful prosperity for men. The kings claim to rule "by the favor of

Courtesy of George C. Cameron, the American Schools of Oriental Research and the University of Michigan

6. Ahura-mazda, Darius' protecting deity, is sculptured above the king's enemies at Behistun.

Ahura-mazda," who gives them also victory over their enemies. In the Pahlavi books, where the name takes the form Ohrmazd, he appears as the opponent of the evil spirit Ahriman. *See* PERSIA, HISTORY AND RELIGION OF, §§ E2-3, 5. Figs. AHU 6; PER 40.

*Bibliography.* F. B. J. Kuiper, "Avestan *mazdā-*," *Indo-Iranian Journal,* I (1957), 86-95. *See also* the bibliography under PERSIA, HISTORY AND RELIGION OF.

M. J. DRESDEN

**AHUZZAM** ə hŭz'əm [אחזם, possessor] (I Chr. 4:6); KJV AHUZAM ə hū'zəm. A son of Ashhur in the genealogy of Judah.

**AHUZZATH** ə hŭz'ăth [אחזת, seized, held fast (by God for protection and guidance?); *cf. personal names* אחז, (ו)אחזיה, אחזם, ואחז(ה)י]. The man who accompanied Abimelech from Gerar to make·a covenant with Isaac at Beersheba (Gen. 26:26-31 [J]; but *cf.* 21:22-32 [E]). He seemed to hold an official position as the king's adviser (מרעהו; KJV one of his friends). *See* FRIEND OF THE KING. L. HICKS

**AHZAI** ä'zī [אחזי, *perhaps a corruption of* אחזיה (Ahaziah), Yahu has grasped] (Neh. 11:13); KJV AHASAI ə hā'zī. A priest in Ezra's time.

*AI ī, ä'ī [העי, the ruin]. Alternately: AIATH ā'yăth [עית]; AIJA ā'jə [עיא]; KJV HAI hī, hā'ī in Gen. 12:8; 13:3. A city in Ephraim, E of Bethel.

**1. Biblical data.** Abraham is twice said to have pitched his tent between Ai and Bethel (Gen. 12:8; 13:3). According to the narrative in Josh. 7-8, Ai was the next city to be assailed by the Israelites after they had taken Jericho. Despising this city because it was small, the Israelites sent out only a few men to attack it and met with an unexpected defeat which threw them into despair. Joshua appealed to God and was told that this setback was due to someone's guilt in not destroying all the spoils of Jericho; lots were cast, and the offending individual was found to be ACHAN. As soon as justice was done, Joshua set about capturing Ai by the stratagem of a feigned retreat which would draw the defenders from the city and enable warriors set in ambuscade to walk over the deserted walls. (In Josh. 8:12, 16, "Ai," with the Qere, should probably be read instead of "the city.") The plan succeeded; Ai was taken and burned, and its remains were left as a "heap of ruins, as it is to this day" (Josh. 8:28).

While the old site remained abandoned, a new Israelite town arose nearby, with the same name. Isaiah mentions Aiath as the first of the towns occupied by the Assyrians in their march on Jerusalem (Isa. 10:28); its location was approximately the same as the ancient Ai. Among the returned exiles who came with Zerubbabel were 223 men of Bethel and Ai (Ezra 2:28; the parallel passage in Neh. 7:32 gives the number as 123). In the next century, Aija, near Bethel, is reported as having been settled by the people of Benjamin (Neh. 11:31).

**2. Archaeological evidence.** The site of ancient Ai is to be located at et-Tell, situated two miles E-SE of Bethel (modern Beïtin). This mound was excavated by Judith Krause-Marquet in 1933-35 and by Samuel Yeivin in 1936. They found extensive remains of a city of the Early and Middle Bronze periods, with an elaborate defensive system, a shrine,* and numerous vessels, some of alabaster and ivory. This city apparently arose *ca.* 3000 B.C. and was destroyed not later than *ca.* 2000. Subsequently, in the Early Iron period (after 1200), a new and smaller settlement arose, which lasted for another century. The site, however, was not occupied at all at the time of the Israelite conquest (thirteenth century B.C.). Fig. TEM 21.

This evidence shows that the narrative in Joshua is not to be taken literally, but is an example of the process by which all the Israelite conquests of several centuries were referred to the time of Joshua. One possibility is that the ancient city was taken by the HABIRU, whose name and achievements were taken over by the Israelites. Another suggestion is that the story originally referred to BETHEL, the conquest of which (by surprise) is recorded in Judg. 1:22-25 but omitted in Joshua. A third is that the story is a reminiscence of a conquest of the Early Iron city, which took place much later than the time of Joshua, but was later referred to that hero.

The latter settlements of the Israelites at Aiath and Aija are probably to be located at Khirbet Haiyan, *ca.* a mile S of et-Tell.

*Bibliography.* W. F. Albright, *AASOR*, IV (1924), 141-49; J. Marquet, *Les fouilles de 'Ay* (1949).      S. COHEN

**AIAH** ā'yɔ [איה, falcon, hawk, *perhaps as a nickname*]; KJV AJAH ā'jɔ in Gen. 36:24. **1.** The first son of clan chief (of) Zibeon; ancestor of a Horite subclan in Edom (Gen. 36:24; I Chr. 1:40).

**2.** The father of Saul's concubine Rizpah (II Sam. 3:7; 21:8, 10-11). He is perhaps related to the clan in 1 *above.*      L. HICKS

**AIATH; AIJA.** Alternate forms of AI.

**AIJALON** ā'jɔ lŏn [אילון, place of the deer; Amarna *Aialuna*]; KJV alternately AJALON ăj'ɔ lŏn. **1.** A valley which figures in the account of the defeat of the five Canaanite kings in Josh. 10 (especially vs. 12). Located on the Philistine border just below Beth-horon, it was an important pass into the mountains of Judah.

The city is identified with Yalo, near Emmaus ('Amwas), a sizable mound with remains of a fortified town of the Late Bronze, Iron I, and later periods.* Tell el-Qoqa', a small mound to the E, with Early Bronze remains, may have served first as a fortress and later as a high place for Aijalon. Fig. AIJ 7.

Aijalon was assigned to Dan on or near its border with Ephraim (Josh. 19:42). The Amorites remained, and though they resisted occupation by the Danites, Ephraim later dominated them (Judg. 1:35). Aijalon represented the W point of Jonathan's victorious pursuit of the Philistines after the Battle of Michmash (I Sam. 14:31).

In David's administrative reorganization, Aijalon became a Levitical city assigned to the Kohathites (Josh. 21:24) and was designated a city of refuge (I Chr. 6:69—H 6:54). Solomon put it in his second administrative district (read "Aijalon" for "Elon" in

From *Atlas of the Bible* (Thomas Nelson & Sons Limited)

7. Aijalon (modern Yalo), the mountains of Judah in the background

I Kings 4:9). After the division of the monarchy, it was included in Benjamin (I Chr. 8:13) and fortified by Rehoboam (*ca.* 922-915) against invasion from the W or the N (II Chr. 11:10). During the reign of Jehoahaz I (Ahaz; *ca.* 735-715), the Philistines captured the city (II Chr. 28:18).

**2.** A place in Zebulun where the judge Elon was buried (Judg. 12:12, where one may read "Elon" with LXX B); probably Tell el-Butmeh ("the terebinth") in the Sahel el-Battof (Plain of Asochis).

*Bibliography.* W. F. Albright, "Researches of the School in Western Judaea," *BASOR*, 15 (1924), 10; F.-M. Abel, *Géographie de la Palestine*, vol. II (1938); W. F. Albright, "The List of Levitic Cities," *Louis Ginsberg Jubilee Volume*, English Section (1945); M. Noth, *Das Buch Josua* (1953), *passim.*
     V. R. GOLD

**AIJELETH SHAHAR** ā'jɔ lĕth shā'här. *See* MUSIC § B1*c*.

**AIN** ān [עין, spring]. **1.** A city on the boundary of "greater Palestine," the location of which is uncertain (Num. 34:11; cf. Ezek. 47:15 ff). It may be near Riblah (modern Riblah) to the N, or it may be near the junction of the Yarmuk and the Jordan.

**2.** A city mentioned in Josh. 15:32; I Chr. 4:32 with another city, Rimmon. The two should probably be read as "Ain-rimmon." *See* EN-RIMMON.

**3.** The Levitical city assigned to the Aaronids (Josh. 21:16). "Ashan" should probably be read here (cf. the parallel lists in I Chr. 6:59—H 6:44 and the reading of Josh. 21:16 in the Codex Vaticanus).
     V. R. GOLD

**AIN (LETTER)** ā'ɔn (Heb. ä'yĭn) [ע, '(*'Ayin*)]. The sixteenth letter of the Hebrew ALPHABET as placed in the KJV at the head of the sixteenth section of the acrostic psalm, Ps. 119, where each verse of this section of the psalm begins with this letter.

**AIR, POWER OF.** The author of Ephesians refers to the "prince of the power of the air" (2:2), whom the Christians at Ephesus had once followed and who was still at work in the "sons of disobedience" —i.e., among the Gentiles.

The "air" (ἀήρ) refers to the lower atmosphere, in contrast with the sky (αἰθήρ); and, according to the astrology and demonology of the time, the air was believed to be the place where evil spirits dwelt and from which they exerted power over men. The "prince" is probably Satan. (Cf. Pythagoras in *Diogenes Laertius* VIII.32; *Test. Benj.* 3:4.) *See* DEMON.      B. H. THROCKMORTON, JR.

**AIRUS.** KJV Apoc. form of REAIAH 3.

**AJAH.** KJV form of AIAH 1 in Gen. 36:24.

**AJALON.** KJV alternate form of AIJALON.

**AKAN** ā'kăn [עקן (?)] (Gen. 36:27). A Horite. *See* JAAKAN.

**AKELDAMA** ɔ kĕl'dɔ mɔ ['Ακελδαμάχ; Aram. חקל דמא; *see below*]; KJV ACELDAMA —sĕl'—. The name of a burial ground outside the Jerusalem wall. The term is used only once in the Bible, by Luke in Acts 1:19.

The Greek term is spelled in several ways, giving rise to various possibilities of Aramaic derivation. Acts records the meaning as χωρίον αἵματος, "field of blood"; however, Klostermann and others suggest "field of sleeping."

Acts records that Judas purchased this field with the silver paid him for betraying Jesus, and implies that it was on this field that he fell and burst open —thus giving the name to the "field of blood." In a parallel account in Matt. 27:3-10, although the term Ἀκελδαμάχ is not used, there is a different explanation of how the field received its name. Here it is stated that the chief priests recognized that the silver flung back at them by a remorseful Judas, who then went out and hanged himself, was nevertheless the "price of blood" and could not be contributed to the temple treasury. So with it they bought the "potter's field" for a burial ground for foreigners, which has since been called the "field of blood" (fulfilling a prophecy of Jeremiah). It is obvious that this story also refers to the Acts' Ἀκελδαμάχ.

In these variant traditions there may be seen mingled allusions to Jer. 32:8-9, where Jeremiah bought a field from his cousin for seventeen silver shekels; to Jer. 18:2-3, where he visited the potter's house; and to Zech. 11:12-13, where the prophet was directed by the Lord to put his honest wages of thirty silver shekels into the treasury. The Hebrew term for "treasury" is easily confused with the term for "potter," which may explain the priests' alternative (in Matthew) between giving Judas' silver to the treasury or paying it for the potter's field. But in none of these OT allusions does the term "Akeldama" appear, and they throw no light upon this term.

It is probable that there existed even before the Christian era an area of caves used for burial and called by an Aramaic name similar to Akeldama. It seems more likely that this name meant "field of sleep." The meaning "field of blood" may date from the death of Judas, and the variant accounts explaining its connection with the burial area suggest that Judas' end was associated with this field, although it is not stated that it was here that he hanged himself. Luke does not describe the field as a cemetery nor offer any reason why Judas should buy it, nor does he offer information as to its future use.

In Matthew, the field becomes the place to bury "strangers"—i.e., foreigners—and it is so characterized by the pilgrim Antoninus Martyr (*ca.* A.D. 560). Since the fourth century its traditional site has been in the E end of the Valley of Hinnom, on the S slope, where deceased pilgrims have been interred at least up to the seventeenth century. In Matthew we read of the "potter's field," which may mean only that it is reported to be the potter's possession. There is no reason to conclude, as some have done, that this was where potters came (outside a "Potter's Gate") to get clay or to dump their refuse, or even where they worked. The record does not suggest that the "potter's field" was the poor man's cemetery, as a modern conception holds.

**Bibliography.** E. Robinson, *Biblical Researches in Palestine,* I (1867), 354-55; J. Sickenberger, "Judas als Stifter des Blutackers," *Biblische Zeitschrift,* 18 (1929), 69-71.    K. W. Clark

**AKH-EN-ATON** ä′kə nä′tən [Egyp. *'kh-n-itn, probably* it is well with (the sun-god) Aton]. A pharaoh (*ca.* 1369-1353 B.C.) of the Eighteenth Dynasty, pro-

In the Brooklyn Museum Collection

8. Akh-en-Aton (left) with his wife, Nefert-iti (right); sculptor's limestone model, found at Akhetaton (Tell el-Amarna)

Courtesy of the Cairo Museum, photo courtesy of the Metropolitan Museum of Art

9. King Akh-en-Aton and his wife, Nefert-iti, make their offerings to the sun-god, Aton; limestone, from Tell el-Amarna

moter of a religious and cultural revolution. First named Amen-hotep (or Amenophis) IV, a name meaning "(The god) Amon is satisfied," he changed his name, thus disavowing the old imperial god AMON and promoting a new god, the Aton, the life-giving power of the sun. Fig. AKH 8.

By 1370 B.C. the Egyptian Empire in Asia was a century old. Egypt stood at the height of wealth and power, but Egyptian culture was changing under the influences of a more complex state and of foreign cultures. E.g., the concern for peoples of other lands altered the belief that the Egyptian gods were devoted only to the interests of Egypt.

The pharaoh Amen-hotep III (ca. 1398-61 B.C.) accepted new trends in government, religion, art, and literature. His son and coregent, Amen-hotep IV, chose to make a revolution to establish new power. Akh-en-Aton soon left the old capital Thebes and moved to a new site, which he called Akhetaton, near modern TELL EL-AMARNA. There he and his queen, Nefert-iti, gave themselves over to cultivating new trends in art and worshiping the new god. His preoccupation with the Aton has been called the world's earliest monotheism. Certainly it was a close approach to this type of worship. However, there is no evidence that Moses or any other Hebrew was directly influenced by this Egyptian concentration upon a single god. Fig. AKH 9.

Letters found at this capital show that Akh-en-Aton's preoccupation with internal reforms was disastrous to the Egyptian Empire in Syria and Palestine, which broke into independent states or fell away to the Hittites. Shortly after Akh-en-Aton's death, under his son-in-law, Tut-ankh-Amon, the "Amarna revolution" collapsed, and Egypt returned

Courtesy of Foto Marburg

10. Akh-en-Aton, Nefert-iti, and their daughters; the king wears the blue crown, and the queen has a turbanlike headdress; above them is the symbol of Aton.

to the traditional forms, with the capital again at Thebes. Though the formal movement was branded as heresy, it left lasting results in the religious, intellectual, and aesthetic life in Egypt.

Fig. AKH 10.

*Bibliography.* J. H. Breasted, *Cambridge Ancient History,* II (1924), 109-30; J. D. S. Pendlebury, *Tell el-Amarna* (1935);

J. A. Wilson, *The Burden of Egypt* (1951), pp. 206-35; G. Steindorff and K. C. Seele, *When Egypt Ruled the East* (2nd ed., 1957), pp. 201-21.                    J. A. WILSON

**AKHETATON** ä'kə tä'tən [Egyp. *'kht-itn,* the place of glory of (the sun-god) Aton]. The Egyptian name of the capital founded by the heretic pharaoh Akh-en-Aton near modern Tell el-Amarna.

**AKKADIAN** ə kā'dǐ ən [Akkad. *akkadû,* of Akkad (*see* ACCAD)]. The earliest wave of Semites to settle in Mesopotamia, and their language, of which Assyrian and Babylonian were dialects. *See* ASSYRIA AND BABYLONIA § B; SUMER § 2b.

**AKKUB** ăk'ŭb [עַקּוּב]; KJV Apoc. ACUA ə kū'ə; DACOBI dā'kə bī; JACUBUS jə kū'bəs. **1.** Son of Elioenai, a remote descendant of David (I Chr. 3:24).

**2.** The head of a family of Levitical gatekeepers in the postexilic temple (Ezra 2:42; Neh. 7:45; 11: 19; 12:25; I Esd. 5:28).

**3.** The head of a family of temple servants (Ezra 2:45; I Esd. 5:30). *See* NETHINIM.

**4.** A Levitical expounder of the law (Neh. 8:7; I Esd. 9:48).                    J. M. WARD

**AKRABATTENE** ăk'rə băt'ə nǐ ['Ακραβαττήνη] (I Macc. 5:3); KJV ARABATTINE ăr'ə băt'ə nǐ. A fortress on the frontier of Judea and Idumea, near the Ascent of AKRABBIM SW of the Dead Sea, where Judas won a victory over the Idumeans. Josephus mentions a toparchy of Akrabattene SE of Shechem (War II.xii.4; IV.ix.9), and some identify the site in I Macc. 5:3 with this N Judean stronghold.

*Bibliography.* F.-M. Abel, *Géographie de la Palestine,* II (1938), 47.                    E. W. SAUNDERS

**AKRABBIM** ə krăb'ǐm [עַקְרַבִּים, scorpions; *only in the form* מַעֲלֵה עַקְרַבִּים, scorpion pass]; KJV MAALEH-ACRABBIM mā'ə lǐ— in Josh. 15:3. A mountain pass on the S border of Canaan (Num. 34:4; Josh. 15:3; Judg. 1:36). It is usually identified with Neqb es-Safa, where the road from Beer-sheba to

Courtesy of Denis Baly

11. The Ascent of the Akrabbim

the Arabah descends abruptly into the Wadi Murra. Another suggestion is Umm el-'Aqarab, on the W side of the Dead Sea, opposite the Lisan. In Hellenistic times the region was known as Akrabattene, where Judas Maccabeus defeated the Idumeans (I Macc. 5:3). Fig. AKR 11.                    S. COHEN

**ALABASTER** [שֵׁשׁ, *šēš* (Song of S. 5:15; KJV MARBLE); Egyp. *šš*]; ALABASTER JAR, FLASK, KJV

BOX [ἀλάβαστρον]. Alternately: MARBLE (Esth. 1:6). A soft stone, of light creamy color, usually veined.

The stone is known to have been imported into Palestine from Egypt in antiquity, in the form of small objects. The most frequent use was for perfume flasks (cf. Pliny the Elder, XIII.4: "Perfumes are best kept [or 'keep best'] in alabaster vases"). Accordingly, the woman of Bethany brings an alabaster container with "very expensive ointment" (Matt. 26:7; Mark 14:3; Luke 7:37). The translation "alabaster flask" is preferable archaeologically, since thousands of small perfume flasks are found in excavations of all periods.

Besides the flasks of Egyptian alabaster, which is calcium carbonate, there was a limited industry of native alabaster or gypsum, calcium sulphate, in the Jordan Valley, from the Middle Canaanite to the beginning of the Israelite period. A few examples of Palestinian vases from the Greco-Roman period are known, too. The native flasks were made under the influence of Egyptian import ware, and produced a variety of new types, some of which are based

Courtesy of the Palestine Archaeological Museum, Jerusalem, Jordan

　　12. Alabaster vases found at Beth-shan and Jericho, Middle Bronze II Age (seventeenth–early sixteenth centuries)

on Palestinian pottery forms. There is also a difference in technique: the Egyptian flasks are bored with a drill, while those made in Palestine are hollowed out with a chisel. The quarry which provided the stone for flasks made in Beth-shan during the Late Bronze Age is still used today for the quarrying of gypsum. Fig. ALA 12.

*Bibliography.* W. von Bissing, *Steingefaesse* (1907); W. M. F. Petrie, *Stone and Metal Vases* (1937); T. O. Lambdin, "Egyptian Loan Words in the OT," *JAOS*, 73 (1953), 155; I. Ben-Dor, "Palestinian Alabaster Vases," *Quarterly, Department of Antiquities of Palestine*, XI (1944), 93-112.　　I. BEN-DOR

**ALAMETH.** KJV form of ALEMETH 1.

**ALAMMELECH.** KJV form of ALLAMMELECH.

**ALAMOTH** ăl'ə mŏth. *See* MUSIC § B1.

**ALCIMUS** ăl'sĭ məs ["Αλκιμος, stout, brave= אליקים, God sets up; *cf.* 'Ιάκειμος, 'Ιάκιμος, *in* Jos.

Antiq. XII.ix.5; XX.x.3]. A renegade Jew who, in Maccabean times, schemed with Demetrius to have himself restored to the high priesthood after he had been deprived of this office.

Shortly after Demetrius began to reign, Alcimus, aspiring to his old position (II Macc. 14:7), assembled a group of malcontents and made representations to the king that Judas Maccabeus had destroyed all the king's friends and brought ruin upon the land. Demetrius appointed Alcimus to the religious post he coveted, and sent troops under Bacchides to punish Judas. Alcimus accompanied the expedition, and some Jews sued for peace, confident that the presence of the high priest guaranteed their safety. Sixty of them, however, were treacherously slain.

Judas punished some of the deserters, but Alcimus again "brought wicked charges" (I Macc. 7:25), and Nicanor was sent with a large force, whom Judas met and overcame in battle at Capharsalama. Demetrius once more sent Bacchides and Alcimus against Judas. This time Judas was himself slain in the battle of Elasa. The author of I Macc. 7:23 considered that the evil wrought by Alcimus "was more than the Gentiles had done."

Carrying his wicked work even further, Alcimus, bent on tearing down the work of the prophets, "gave orders to tear down the wall of the inner court of the sanctuary" (I Macc. 9:54). This apparently was an attempt to Hellenize the temple by leveling the barrier that separated the Court of the Gentiles from the inner court to which the Jews alone were admitted. In words suggesting those of Acts 12:23, I Macc. 9:55-56 relates that Alcimus, shortly after initiating this project, "was stricken and his work was hindered; his mouth was stopped and he was paralyzed, so that he could no longer say a word . . . . And Alcimus died at that time in great agony."

Josephus (Antiq. XII.x.6) tells a similar story regarding the death of Alcimus but places it before the death of Judas. According to Josephus, the high priesthood was then conferred upon Judas. The books of the Maccabees do not mention the latter. Josephus relates also that, after the high priesthood was bestowed upon Alcimus, "who was not of the high priest stock," Onias sought the assistance of Ptolemy in building in Egypt a "temple like to that in Jerusalem" (Antiq. XII.ix.7). He reports that, on the basis of Isa. 29:19, this aid was granted (Antiq. XIII.vi.1).

Pss. 74; 79–80 are considered by some to reflect the attitude of pious Jews during the high priesthood of Alcimus.　　　　　　　　　　　J. C. SWAIM

**ALEMA** ăl'ə mə [Αλεμα]. One of six cities in Hellenistic Gilead, where Jews had been made prisoners by the Gentile inhabitants, as reported by Nabatean tribesmen to Judas Maccabeus (I Macc. 5:26). Other Jews had escaped and were besieged in the fortress of DATHEMA. The precise location of Alema is unknown, but it has been identified with the modern 'Alma, *ca.* 8½ miles SW of Busr el-Hariri (Bosor) on the plain of Hauran; possibly identical with the HELAM of II Sam. 10:16.

*Bibliography.* F.-M. Abel, *Géographie de la Palestine*, II (1938), 103, 241, 347.　　　　　E. W. SAUNDERS

**ALEMETH** ăl'ə mĕth [עלמת]; KJV ALAMETH in
I Chr. 7:8. **1.** A son of Becher and grandson of Benjamin (I Chr. 7:8).

**2.** A descendant of Saul in the sixth generation,
through Jonathan and Meribaal (Mephibosheth).
The name of his father is given as Jehoaddah in I
Chr. 8:36 and as Jarah in 9:42.

**3.** A priestly city of Benjamin (I Chr. 6:60—H 6:
45); same as ALMON.                          S. COHEN

**ALEPH** ä'lĭf (Heb. ä'lĕf) [א, '(*Āleph*)]. **1.** The first
letter of the Hebrew ALPHABET as placed in the KJV
at the head of the first section of the acrostic psalm,
Ps. 119, where each verse of this section of the psalm
begins with this letter.

**2.** *See* SINAITICUS.

**ALEXANDER** ăl'ĭg zăn'dər, —zän— [᾽Αλέξανδρος,
man's defender]. A Greek name, given to two men in
the Apoc. and to five in the NT.

**1.** Alexander III of Macedon, a hero of the ancient world; known as Alexander the Great. He was
son of Philip II of Macedon. Born in 356 B.C., he
was taught by Aristotle, and succeeded to Philip's
throne in 336. Alexander was determined to put an
end to the Persian menace to Greece, and in 334 he
commenced the expeditions in the East for which he
is so renowned, and from which he was destined
never to return to Macedon. The victories over the
Persian emperor at Granicus (334) and Issus (333)
brought him as far as Asia Minor, and from there he
went through Syria and Palestine and conquered
Egypt (331). Subduing Darius at Gaugamela once
and for all, he advanced victoriously through Mesopotamia and the Persian Empire as far as to the Indus (326), reading Homer all the while on his travels.
Here he experienced trouble with his troops, who
after eight years away were pining for home, and he
was prevented from proceeding with the conquest of
India as he had hoped. In 323, he died from fever in
Babylon at the age of thirty-three. He did indeed defeat Darius and reign in his stead, as the author of
I Macc. 1:1 observes!

The references to Alexander the Great in the
Apoc. occur in I Macc. 1:1-8; 6:2; there is also a
veiled reference in Dan. 7; and in Dan. 11:3-4 we
read of the great king whose kingdom was broken
up after his death. Some scholars have thought that
there is also an allusion in Zech. 9:1-8 to Alexander's
conquest of Palestine.

Alexander included Palestine in a province known
as COELE-SYRIA under a governor, Andromachus,
with headquarters at Samaria. According to Josephus, the Samaritans rose against Alexander because they resented the privileges which he had
granted to the Jews; they set fire to the house of
Andromachus and burned the governor to death.
There is a persistent tradition that Alexander was
always kindly disposed toward the Jews, and they
certainly fought in his army; Josephus, supported by
the Talmud (Yoma 69*a*), describes what happened
when the great conquerer was besieging Tyre (Antiq.
IX.viii.3-6). Alexander ordered the Jews to support
him with troops and provisions. The high priest,
Simon the Just, refused on the ground that he was
bound in loyalty to Persia. But after Alexander had

taken Tyre and Gaza, the high priest was fortunate
enough to have a dream in which he was instructed
to go out with the people and welcome the victor.
He did this, and when they met, the king is said to
have bowed before the divine name on the high
priest's miter, because he said he had had a dream
in which he saw something very like it and in which
he had been promised success. Having entered Jerusalem and worshiped in the temple, he then granted
certain privileges of autonomy to the Jews in his territories. The story, if not wholly true, may contain
elements of fact; and no doubt Alexander would do
much to cultivate the loyalty of the Jews before he
ventured on the conquest of Egypt.

After this conquest, Alexander heard of the revolt
of Samaria, which he subdued; and he proceeded to
transport the population, settling his own Macedonians in the city. In Egypt he built the great city of
Alexandria in 331, and he settled many Jews there,
allowing them considerable privileges.

Courtesy of the Editions des Musées Nationaux, Paris

13. Part of a statue of Alexander the Great (in the
Louvre)

In so short a life Alexander had changed the entire map and culture and language of the world—
even the customs and dress of its peoples. Not least
among the various kinds of influence which he exerted was the Hellenization of a great many Jews,
and this had a profound effect on later Jewish and
Christian thought and culture. The OT was translated into Greek in Alexander's Alexandria by Jewish scholars who were deeply involved in the new
culture, and who were thus to wield an influence on
all later versions of the Bible and on the Greek NT
itself which is incalculable. *See* SEPTUAGINT.

Fig. ALE 13.

2. Alexander Balas, an upstart king of Syria during the Maccabean period. According to some authorities he was the son of Antiochus Epiphanes, but it is more likely that he was a lowborn Greek who made pretense of being son of Antiochus, and whose real name was Balas (meaning unknown). He assumed the name Alexander and the title Epiphanes, and with the help of the kings of Egypt, Pergamum, and Cappadocia, and encouraged by the Roman senate—which wished to weaken the Syrian state by promoting internal strife—he prepared to seize the throne from the unpopular Demetrius Soter in 153. He gained the assistance of Jonathan Maccabeus by nominating him high priest in Jerusalem in 152. Finally he defeated Demetrius in battle and married Ptolemy Philometor's daughter Cleopatra.

Having rewarded Jonathan for his help by receiving him in state at Ptolemais and granting him the governorship of Judea, Balas became the incompetent and self-indulgent ruler of the kingdom of Syria from 150 to 145 B.C. After Nicator, son of Demetrius Soter, had invaded Syria in 147, Balas was deserted by his own soldiers, though Jonathan still remained loyal. While Balas was endeavoring to crush a revolt, his father-in-law intervened from Egypt on behalf of Nicator. The authorities differ as to whether Balas was slain in battle or fled to Arabia and was there assassinated. The Jews, and particularly the historian of I Maccabees, regarded Balas with some favor, for the simple reason that under his negligent rule they achieved a measure of self-government and freedom. In the event, his reign did mark a distinct step forward on the road to Judean independence (I Macc. 10:1–11:19; Jos. Antiq. XIII.iv).

3. The son of Simon of Cyrene (see SIMON 8), and the brother of RUFUS. The brothers are referred to quite casually in Mark, in order to identify Simon, as if they were well known in the church for which Mark is writing (Mark 15:21); Matthew omits the reference to the brothers. They may have been converted Jews. Simon was probably in Jerusalem in order to keep the Feast of Passover, and the adjective "of Cyrene" does not necessarily mean that he was a Gentile. In the apocryphal Acts of Peter and Andrew, Alexander and his brother are companions and disciples of Andrew and Peter in missionary endeavor. They are also associated with Andrew and Peter in the Coptic Assumption of the Virgin by Evodius, who professes to be their kinsman, and who appears to suggest that Alexander and Rufus were among the Seventy whom Jesus sent out. After the Passion they apparently lived with the Virgin Mary, Salome, and Joanna.

4. A kinsman of the high priest Annas (Acts 4:6). Little is known of this Alexander. It has been conjectured by a few scholars that he was the "alabarch" (i.e., the governor of the Jews) of Alexandria, a brother of Philo (mentioned in Jos. Antiq. XVIII. viii.1). Another suggestion is that he was Eleasar, who we learn from Josephus was the third son of ANNAS (Antiq. XVIII.ii.2).

5. Alexander the Jew, of Ephesus (Acts 19:33). On the occasion of Paul's evangelistic work at Ephesus a riot was caused by Demetrius the silversmith, when the smiths of the city feared that their craft would suffer. The Ephesian Jews were unjustly blamed for the slight which was cast on Artemis, the city's patron, and this Alexander was put forward by them with the intention that he should address the mob in the theater and indicate the innocence of the Jews. Alexander beckoned with his hand, as if to speak, but the mob realized that he was a Jew and would not allow him to proceed. The Jews had often been accused of desecrating temples in their abhorrence of paganism. In the case of Alexander, he may have been one of the smiths themselves, and it may have been for this reason that he was put forward. If so, he may well be the same as Alexander the coppersmith described *below* (7). On the other hand, he would then be engaging in a trade which was unlawful for a Jew. He was apparently a figure known to the citizens—he does not receive the designation τις ("a certain Alexander"). Evidently it was hoped that he would convince the mob that the Jews had nothing whatever to do with Paul's activities. However, some writers have maintained that he was a Christian, endeavoring to speak on Paul's behalf, and that he was pulled down by the Jews. But there is hardly sufficient evidence for saying so much.

6. A false teacher in the church. He is coupled with HYMENAEUS in the Pastoral letters. He "made shipwreck" of his faith "by rejecting conscience," and Paul is said to have delivered him to Satan—i.e., probably excommunication (I Tim. 1:19-20). It has been conjectured by some that he was Alexander the coppersmith (*see* 7 *below*), because of the harm he did to the cause of Paul. But, far from being a personal adversary of Paul, like the coppersmith, it is probable that men like Alexander, with Hymenaeus and PHILETUS, were the earliest teachers—not necessarily as early as Paul's own day—of what became known as Gnosticism: they regarded the resurrection in a purely spiritual or intellectual way (II Tim. 2:18) and were guilty of the "disputing about words" and the "godless chatter" (2:14, 16) which seem to be part of the false gnosis—"what is falsely called knowledge" (I Tim. 6:20). If the Pastoral letters are not wholly Pauline as they stand, it would be precarious to accept the excommunicating of Alexander as having been actually carried out by Paul, rather than as a suggestion of the Paulinist as to what ought to be done with such teachers in his own day.

7. Alexander the coppersmith. He is said to have done Paul great harm (II Tim. 4:14) and to have strongly opposed his message (vs. 15). This may be a genuine Pauline fragment embodied in the Pastoral letters. The enmity against the apostle appears to be personal, and it may be that Alexander was a hostile witness at Paul's trial in Rome, as some think. Naturally, as he is described as a smith, and as Paul purports to be writing to Timothy in Ephesus, some have supposed that he was the same man as the Alexander (*see* 5 *above*) who tried to address the crowds in Ephesus when the smiths there caused a riot. But there is no real evidence for either of these views; nor for identifying him with the heretical teacher (*see* 6 *above*), although his name appears in the same group of letters.     N. TURNER

**ALEXANDRA** ăl'ĭg zăn'drə, —zăn— [Ἀλέξανδρα]. A Jewish queen. Salome Alexandra was wife of Aristobulus I (104-103 B.C.), who was the first of the

HASMONEANS to adopt the royal title. After his death, she married his brother JANNEUS. It has been thought that Ps. 2 was sung at the wedding; though this has not been proved, the psalm does express the ambition of Alexandra's husbands, to break the heathen and "dash them in pieces" (2:9) and to restore the throne of David. On the death of her second husband, Alexandra herself came to the throne (76-67 B.C.), and under her peaceful rule the Pharisees achieved considerable power, being admitted to the Sanhedrin for the first time. She was sister of the famous Pharisee, Simon ben Shetach.                    N. TURNER

**ALEXANDRIA** ăl'ĭg zăn'drĭ ə, —zän— ['Αλεξάν-δρια, Alexander's city]. The capital city of Egypt through the Hellenistic and Roman periods; next to Rome itself, the most important metropolis in the Greco-Roman world.

1. Situation and city plan
2. Edifices and institutions
3. The school of Hellenistic culture
4. The Judeo-Alexandrian school
5. The Alexandrian Christian school
6. Intertestamental and NT allusions
Bibliography

**1. Situation and city plan.** Alexandria was founded by Alexander the Great in 331 B.C., while he was on his way to the oracular oasis of Ammon at Siwa. He chose as the site an Egyptian fishing village on a somewhat narrow strip of land between the Mediterranean Sea and Lake Mareotis, *ca.* fourteen miles from the westernmost mouth of the Nile. At his direction the new city was laid out by Deinocrates of the Artemisium on an oblong plan, with main streets intersecting at right angles. A swerving island, seven stadia offshore, was connected with the mainland by a viaduct, called literally the Heptastadion. This dike divided the bay back of the island into two distinct harbors, of which the W port continues to be very importantly useful today.

Thus situated at the W angle of the Egyptian delta, Alexandria was connected with the Occident by the Mediterranean Sea itself. It was to be connected with the Orient through canals and lakes and the Red Sea. From its foundation it was in a position to become the main emporium of the Hellenistic world, the transshipment center between the West and the East.

**2. Edifices and institutions.** One of the most vivid ways to get an impression of the teeming interests and activities and institutions concentrated in Alexandria is to take a bird's-eye view of the city in the Augustan period, from the vantage point of the wonderful Pharos, the towering lighthouse at the entrance of the Great or Eastern Harbor.* In the immediate foreground the port itself formed a stage around which the royal or governmental quarter of the city extended in theaterlike fashion. At the left from the Pharos, the ample palace area—already the Roman governorate—spread over Cape Lochias and the contiguous shoreland. At the center of the unevenly curving shore were the monumental theater and the gleaming Caesareum, fresh focus of the new imperial cult (*see* EMPEROR-WORSHIP). Matching and

extending the palace precinct was the Museum with its Great Library and halls and gardens, the cultural capital of the Hellenistic world. Nearby, at almost the center of the city, was the famed Soma or Sema, where the relics of the founder himself were superbly enshrined. Towering over it all was a cone-shaped, parklike hill, the Paneum, consecrated to the god of natural life. Fig. ALE 14.

From *Atlas of the Bible* (Thomas Nelson & Sons Limited)
14. The lighthouse of Alexandria

The W and native quarter of Alexandria, locale of the original Egyptian village of Rhakotis, overlooked the Western or Eunostos Harbor. There stood the ancient acropolis, now the site of the widely revered Serapeum, with the adjunct Daughter Library. Because of its representative character, as the sanctuary of a synthetic Greco-Egyptian cult, the Serapeum continued late as a popular pilgrimage center for devout pagans. The so-called Pompey's Pillar—actually Diodetian's—signalizes the place today.

Directly back of the city, on Lake Mareotis, was the Egyptian port of Alexandria. Plain to see was the fact that this was a more busy and crowded harbor than were either of the two Mediterranean ports on the other side of the city. This was so because the Mareotis haven was also the oriental harbor, as well as specifically the Egyptian port. Thus canals had made it very important indeed.

Crowded closely together in Alexandria of the Augustan period were great institutions and buildings that monumentally represented controlling human and social concerns: Hellenistic culture, imperial government, polytheistic religion, world-wide commerce, and local industry. The spectacle could scarcely be matched in impressiveness elsewhere around the long ellipse of the Mediterranean Sea.

**3. The school of Hellenistic culture.** It is not at all strange, but altogether natural, that the ecumenical milieu of Alexandria gave rise to several religio-cultural trends that turned out to be of pre-eminent significance in the history of thought and religion. These trends were severally so specifically integrated in interest and personnel and activity that, not ineptly, they have been designated as schools. Three of them are outstanding as of special interest to modern investigators and practitioners of biblical interpretation. These are the university of Hellenistic culture that flourished in the Museum and libraries of Alexandria; and the Hellenistic Jewish school of Torah interpretation in connection with the synagogues of the city; and finally the Christian catechetical school of Alexandria.

The earliest of the Ptolemies were greatly ambitious to make their capital the cultural focus of the Greco-oriental world (*see* HELLENISM). Through the agency of the Museum and the libraries, Mother and Daughter, they succeeded in the realization of this ambition to an extent that was astonishing. At the outset the community of scholars assembled under royal patronage at the Museum concentrated on textual and philological projects, aimed to establish dependable, critical texts of standard Greek works. In elaboration their methods included textual criticism and correction, syntactical study and interpretation, and finally literary criticism. As a special point it is worth noting that the Museum school included both imaginative exponents of the allegorical method of interpretation (*see* ALLEGORY) and vigorous opponents of this technique.

As the Hellenistic period progressed, however, the initial preoccupation of Museum scholars with textual and philological matters became extensively diversified by increasing attentiveness to scientific interests as well. Intellectually the great revolution of the period was the analytical breakup of generalized philosophy into a plurality of concrete and specialized sciences (*see* SCIENCE). The particular sciences that received a large share of attention at the Museum were mathematics, astronomy, geography, botany, zoology, anatomy, and physiology. Thus to the discipline of textual and literary criticism, the Gentile scholars at Alexandria added wide-ranging and inquisitive interest in all the areas of human knowledge, and exactitude in observation and record.

**4. The Judeo-Alexandrian school.** From the time of Ptolemy I the Jews formed a singular ethnic group in the population of Alexandria. However separate from their Gentile neighbors they continued to be in race and religion, they could not remain in isolation linguistically, economically, and culturally. Almost from the outset they adopted Koine Greek as their language for everyday conversation. They translated their sacred Hebrew scriptures into the Greek of their period and place.

Notably influential on the more talented among them were the multiform Greek and Hellenistic writings available in Ptolemaic Alexandria. In response to such literary and cultural stimuli, the Diaspora Jews of the city came in time to produce the most abundant Semitic-Hellenistic literature known.

The main purposes of this literature were dual and very closely interrelated: to defend Jews and Judaism against the sharp criticisms of Gentile contemporaries; and to commend their religion and their way of life to serious-minded Gentile God-fearers. To accomplish these objectives, full use was made of the resources of Koine diction, of Hellenistic literary patterns, and of Gentile thought-forms.

The very beginning of Judeo-Hellenistic literature was the SEPTUAGINT translation of the Hebrew Pentateuch, a most concentrated project in scriptural interpretation done in straight translation. There followed historiography as fictional as II or III Maccabees, or as factual as the firsthand historical memoranda of Philo, embodied in his work *Against Flaccus* or the *Embassy to Caligula*.

There are extant several apt pieces of pseudonymous propaganda such as the Jewish moralizations of Pseudo Phocylides, the ecstatic prophecies of Jewish Sibyllines, and the Letter of Aristeas, with its traditional account of the making of the LXX.

More inclusive in perspective and more basic in concern were the writings of religio-philosophical thinkers of Jewish loyalty. PHILO JUDEUS was the most knowledgeable and eloquent of this group. Certain he was that the monotheistic God of Israel was the one God of the philosophers also, and that the teachings of Hebrew scriptures equated with the ethics and ideologies of Hellenistic schools of philosophy. Drastic techniques of interpretation were required to make plausible such equations. Philo's favorite method for the purpose was allegory. It is only factual to add that paradoxically Philo freely mixed literal and allegorical renderings in his vast interpretative writings.

**5. The Alexandrian Christian school.** Quite as deservedly famed as its Gentile or Jewish precursors was the Christian catechetical school of Alexandria. Along with its Hellenistic and Judaistic antecedents, there should also be remembered the Christian Gnostic school of Alexandria, which by a half-century preceded the emergence of the catechetical school there. Basilides and his son Isidore were the local leaders of the Gnostic enterprise. *See* GNOSTICISM.

The catechetical school was more definitely institutionalized and more closely attached to the Christian church than the Gnostic school had been. It had a succession of heads who were truly great teachers: Pantaenus, Clement, Origen, and the rest. It had an organized curriculum of which we can get an impression from the triple treatises of Clement or the writings of Origen. Student fees were not charged, but were voluntarily offered and accepted. Wealthy patrons were encouraged to support outstanding teachers in their educational and literary pursuits.

To the forwarding of methodology in scripture interpretation the catechetical school made contribution for which it will always be credited. Clement and Origen agreed in affirming that scripture exhibited distinguishably a threefold nexus of meanings: first, the literal or historical sense; second, the moral implication; and third, the spiritual meaning. Correspondingly, three lines or methods of interpretation were valid; but of the three the greatest and the most fully sufficient was the spiritual method. Here was high preference for allegorical interpretation that excelled even the great appreciation of Philo, the Hellenistic Jew.

For two full centuries, from the second to the late fourth, the catechetical school continued its intellectual discipline of E Mediterranean Christianity. When it disappeared at last, in a chaos of theological controversy, it left behind an eminent continuator in the school of Caesarea, and a rigorous rival in the school of Antioch.

**6. Intertestamental and NT allusions.** Canonical literature, Jewish and Christian, paid remarkably little attention to the city of Alexandria. The determinative circumstance was that the blooming time of Alexandrian prosperity and productivity under the earlier Ptolemies was too tardy to get canonical Jewish attention; by the same sign, it was too early to capture very much canonical Christian notice.

Noncanonical Hellenistic Jewish writings, however, in large part produced in Alexandria itself, took ample notice of the city and its life in casual and normal ways. Altogether Philo shows multitudinous local and contemporary references of this sort. The action in the Letter of Aristeas alternates between the palace of the Ptolemies and a sea-front mansion on the island of Pharos, where the LXX translation was alleged to have been made. Similarly the chief action of the second part of the melodramatic III Maccabees is set in the immense Hippodrome of Alexandria, outside the Gate of the Sun, approximately where the Sporting Club of today carries on its sports.

Within the canonical NT, the Acts of the Apostles alludes to Alexandrian Jews and to Alexandrian ships, twice over in each case. At Acts 6:9, Stephen the protomartyr is vehemently debating the issue of messianism with members of the synagogue of Alexandrians ('Αλεξανδρέων) and other Diaspora groups (*see* DISPERSION). The familiar inscription of Theodotus, found at Jerusalem, should be studied closely in reference to this passage. A cornerstone inscription, it describes in some detail just such a Jerusalem synagogue of Diaspora Jews as here mentioned.

The well-known APOLLOS, native to Alexandria ('Αλεξανδρεύς), is characterized in Acts 18:24 as an "eloquent man, well versed in the scriptures." This could be said of Philo, and of very many other Alexandrian Jews!

In a "we section" account of Paul's stormy voyage to Italy, an Alexandrian ('Αλεξανδρινόν) ship is noted at Myra in Lycia (Acts 27:6); and another Alexandrian ship, named the "Dioscuri," is indicated at Malta (28:11), as forwarding Paul and his companions on their winter-season voyage. Early in the imperial period, as through earlier centuries, Alexandrian shipping was notably conspicuous on transMediterranean runs from the provincial capital of Egypt to the imperial capital in Italy. *See* SHIPS AND SAILING.

**Bibliography.** P. Wendland, "Alexandrian Philosophy," *Jewish Encyclopedia*, I (1901), 368-71; A. von Harnack, "Alexandria, School of," *New Schaff-Herzog Encyclopedia of Religious Knowledge*, I (1908), 124-25; E. Breccia, *Alexandrea ad Aegyptum* (1922); A. Weigall, "The Alexandria of Antony," *Wonders of the Past*, II (1924), 477-90; C. M. Cobern, "Alexandria," *International Standard Bible Encyclopedia*, I (1925), 93-96; H. I. Bell, "Alexandria," *JEA*, XIII (1927), 171-84; E. Josi, "Ales-

sandria, 8. Archeologia," *Encyclopedia Cattolica*, I (1948), 773-77.                                   H. R. WILLOUGHBY

**ALEXANDRINUS** ăl'ĭg zăn drē'nǝs, —zăn—, —drī'—. An early-fifth-century Greek uncial codex MS of the Bible (symbol "A"). Originally the codex contained the whole Greek Bible plus I and II Clement and the Psalms of Solomon. It is an important witness to the text of both the LXX and the NT. *See* VERSIONS, ANCIENT; TEXT, NT.

The OT has suffered some mutilation, and the NT now lacks Matt. 1:1-25:6; John 6:50-8:52; I Cor. 4:13-12:6. The Psalms of Solomon also have been lost from the MS. The codex contains 773 vellum leaves (630 in the OT, perhaps written by two scribes; 143 in the NT, perhaps written by three scribes), each measuring 12¾ by 10¼ inches. The text is written in two columns to the page, with 46-52 lines per column. Fig. ALE 15.

15. Codex Alexandrinus (fifth century A.D.)

In 1624 the codex was given by Cyril Lucar, patriarch of Constantinople, to the British Ambassador to Turkey for presentation to James I. James died before the MS reached him, and the presentation was made to Charles I in 1627. The codex was deposited in the Royal Library. It is now housed in the British Museum, where it has been since the Royal Library was incorporated into that Museum in 1757.

**Bibliography.** A photographic reproduction of the MS was published by the trustees of the British Museum, in *Facsimile of the Codex Alexandrinus* (1879-83). See also: F. H. A. Scrivener, *Plain Introduction to the Criticism of the NT* (4th ed., rev. E. Miller; 1894), I, 97-105; C. R. Gregory, *Canon and Text of the NT* (1907), pp. 340-43; H. J. M. Milne and T. C. Skeat, *Scribes and Correctors of Codex Sinaiticus* (1938), p. 91; W. H. P. Hatch, *Principal Uncial MSS of the NT* (1939), plates XVII-XIX; I. M. Price, *Ancestry of Our English Bible* (3rd ed., rev. W. A. Irwin and A. P. Wikgren; 1956), pp. 58-60; F. G. Kenyon, *Our Bible and the Ancient MSS* (5th ed., rev. A. W. Adams; 1958), pp. 120-21, 198-202.          M. M. PARVIS

**ALGUM** ăl'gŭm [אלגומים, 'algûmîm]. A valuable wood from Lebanon (II Chr. 2:8—H 2:7) or from Ophir (9:10-11). The word is probably an error of transposition for "ALMUG." *See* FLORA § A8c.

**ALIAH.** Alternate form of ALVAH.

**ALIAN.** Alternate form of ALVAN.

**ALIEN** [גר, sojourner; זר, stranger; נכרי, foreigner; πάροικος, sojourner]. *See* FOREIGNER; SOJOURNER.

**ALLAMMELECH** ə lăm′ə lĕk [אלמלך] (Josh. 19:26); KJV ALAMMELECH. A town in Asher. The site has not yet been found, but it is perhaps located in the S part of the Plain of Acco.

**ALLEGORY.** The treatment of an ancient tradition (generally narrative in form) whereby one ignores its literal meaning and discovers new, hidden meanings in each term of the tradition. A well-known illustration is Augustine's allegorical interpretation of the parable of the Good Samaritan. In the first phrase, "A certain man was going down from Jerusalem to Jericho," Augustine equates "a certain man" with Adam, "Jerusalem" with the heavenly city of peace from which Adam was expelled, and "Jericho" with the moon, the symbol of man's mortality. None of the OT authors was an allegorist. But in NT times allegory had become an accepted exegetical procedure in certain pagan and Jewish circles. While NT authors made little use of this type of interpretation (Paul in I Cor. 5:6-8; 9:8-10; 10:1-11; Gal. 4-21-31; and the first and second evangelists in Mark 4:10-20; Matt. 13:37-43), in the post-NT period allegory was prominent in the writings of Justin Martyr, Clement, Origen, etc.

1. Terminology of allegory in the Bible
2. Nonbiblical applications of allegorical interpretation
   *a.* In Hellenism
   *b.* In Hellenistic Judaism
   *c.* In Palestinian Judaism
3. Biblical application of allegorical interpretation
   *a.* In Paul's letters
   *b.* In the Synoptic gospels
Bibliography

**1. Terminology of allegory in the Bible.** The word "allegory" does not appear in any of the OT documents and appears only once in the NT—Gal. 4:24, where Paul uses the passive form of the verb ἀλληγορεῖν. The word and its underlying concept are Greek in origin rather than Semitic, and apparently it was used by the Cynic and Stoic philosophers as a synonym for the earlier Greek word ὑπόνοια to denote allegorical exposition of mythical legends.

**2. Nonbiblical applications of allegorical interpretation.** Allegorical interpretation resulted from the efforts of certain Greek thinkers to preserve the religious values of the Homeric stories of the gods. Similarly, Jewish thinkers, particularly those who had been influenced by the Hellenistic world of thought in Alexandria, attempted to explain and defend the authority of their tradition by means of allegorical interpretation.

*a. In Hellenism.* For centuries the poems of Homer and Hesiod had nurtured the piety of the Greeks and had assumed a significance comparable to the authority of scripture for the Jews. Developments in science and philosophy, however, outstripped the mythological explanations given by these ancients for the structure and order of the universe and created a tension between the earlier and the more recent world views. The pious, wishing to save the myths and the venerated tradition represented by them, were forced to make the capricious and frequently immoral deeds of the gods intellectually respectable for Greeks trained in new schools of thought. Allegorical interpretation had its origin in ingenious etymological explanations of the names given to the deities and began to resolve the tension between myth, on the one hand, and science and philosophy, on the other, and to protect the tradition against satirical attacks. It was argued that the name Zeus must have been derived from ζῆν (zēn) and signified the life-giving power or *logos* which orders all created things. Similar explanations were given for Ares (war), Hephaestus (fire), Kronos (stream), Rhea (earth), etc. While the philosopher Thales (*ca.* 640-546 B.C.[?]) was apparently the first to initiate a moral and metaphysical interpretation of myths, Theagenes of Rhegium in his "Apology" continued to apply allegorical methods of interpretation more thoroughly to the ancient tradition, and Crates of Mallus so explained the entire text of Homer. Allegorical interpretations of Homer and Hesiod were accepted and endorsed by the Cynics and the Stoics, who established a fixed system for explaining the names and actions of the gods. Even though Plato (*Republic* 378 D) and Aristotle fought against the excesses of the allegorical method, the writings of Plutarch and others testify to the impact made by the allegorists upon the Hellenistic world. Since Greek philosophers first gave the impetus to understand a tradition allegorically, the tendency is to associate with them the attempts to find a deeper significance of a primitive tradition in terms of hidden moral and philosophical truths.

*b. In Hellenistic Judaism.* In Alexandria, Jews of the Diaspora were influenced by Greek culture and thought in general and by allegorical interpretations of traditional materials in particular. Consequently some Jews had given up their own tradition for the Greek world view, while others had isolated themselves from it that they might remain loyal to the ancient religious standards of Israel. The first representative of Hellenistic Judaism who attempted to fuse the Greek and the Jewish world views by the allegorical method of interpretation apparently was Aristobulus, who lived in Alexandria around the middle of the second century B.C. By the time of Philo (died *ca.* A.D. 50), the most prolific Jewish author to use allegory for the interpretation of OT scripture, exegetical procedures of this type had become rather fixed.

While Philo always remained a devout Jew and insisted upon reverence for the biblical text as the sacred revelation of God's word to Israel, his philosophical allegorization of texts removed him from their original meaning. Under his expert hand he transfused the ancient Hebraic tradition with Greek views on cosmology, morality, epistemology, physiology, and psychology. He tried to reconcile and to fuse two divergent world views: Judaism, with its tradition of revealed scripture; and Hellenism, with its science and philosophy. Thus Philo sought to defend Judaism against pagan criticism and to prove to his fellow Jews that Moses had already comprehended all the learning of the Greeks. By allegorical explanation of biblical texts the competent and qualified exegete could lift the veil from the riddles of scripture and enter the sacred mysteries of the hidden and more profound meaning of God's holy word. *See bibliography.*

*c. In Palestinian Judaism.* Exegetical exposition of scriptural texts among Palestinian Jews did not generally take the form of allegorization. The Mishna is a monumental work representing rabbinical skill in a juristic treatment of the Mosaic law for purposes of making specific laws applicable to contemporary situations. During the Tannaitic period Eleazer of Modiim and Akiba gave an allegorical interpretation of certain biblical texts. Palestinian Jewish allegorization and that of Hellenistic Judaism differ in that the former is less complex and adheres more closely to the literal meaning of the text.

The Dead Sea Scrolls reveal a second type of interpretation, which was used by the Qumran sect. This type stemmed from Daniel's explanation of Jeremiah's prophecy regarding the return of the Jews from Babylonian captivity. Since this type stressed the fulfilment of prophetic oracles, it can be distinguished from the juristic interpretations of the rabbis and the allegorical interpretations of the Alexandrian Jews by designating it as fulfilment exegesis of a text. This differentiation does not imply that the exegetical schools of the rabbis and of the Qumran sect did not use allegorical interpretation occasionally, but that they preferred their own types of exegesis.

**3. Biblical application of allegorical interpretation.** Of the biblical authors, Paul alone acknowledges the use of allegory (Gal. 4:24) as a means of interpreting OT texts. The preferred type of interpretation of OT passages for the authors of NT documents is fulfilment exegesis. However, in the NT it is significant that Christian authors have begun to interpret Jesus' parables allegorically (Mark 4:10-12)—a tendency apparent in their treatment of other parables *(see bibliography)*—and to allegorize parables created by them for that purpose. *See* PARABLE.

*a. In Paul's letters.* In his correspondence, Paul used allegory in four passages to bring out the force of his argument (I Cor. 5:6-8; 9:8-10; 10:1-11; Gal. 4:21-31). In his Letter to the Galatians, Paul's main theme concerns a declaration of religious independence and of freedom for all men. His development of the theme includes: a defense of his own right to be an apostle on the basis of Christ's and not of others' authorization; a repudiation of all authorities, institutions, customs, and laws which interfere with the direct access of the individual to God; and a statement setting forth the idea that true freedom can be found only in Christ. Paul explains this last affirmation by stating that true freedom gives release from fear, sin, wrath, and death. Since man cannot make himself righteous and thus escape these terrors, he must rely upon the grace of God, who has provided men with a means of acquiring a new nature of righteousness through his Son. Since God's forgiving love through Christ is the sole ground of salvation, the only access to God's eternal kingdom is by faith and by glad acceptance of his gift of grace. As a transition between this didactic section and the following hortatory section of his letter, Paul has tried

rather clumsily to support the argument by an allegory concerning two covenants (Gal. 4:21-31). Abraham had two wives: Hagar, a slave who represents Mount Sinai, the law, and the present Jerusalem; and Sarah, who was free and a representative of the Jerusalem above. Hagar's son, Ishmael, was flesh-bound, while Isaac was the child of promise. Paul has blurred the meaning of this section of his letter by leaving the allegorical interpretation of Sarah's significance incomplete and by adding a rather inappropriate quotation from Isaiah concerning barrenness and fruitfulness.

In his Corinthian correspondence (I Cor. 5:6-8; 9:8-10; 10:1-11), Paul has allegorized passages of the OT for similar purposes. The nearness of the Feast of Pentecost (I Cor. 16:8) prompted him to introduce an allegorical digression on leaven in his discussion of an incestuous situation at Corinth (I Cor. 5:6-8). Since leaven (sin) ferments the whole lump of dough (the church), the old leaven should be removed to make the dough fresh or unleavened (the righteous living of converts) for the celebration of the festival (the Christian life). The Christ who demands this moral transformation and makes possible this renewal is the paschal lamb slain before the opening of the feast. In the allegory Paul mingles affirmation with exhortation by saying that, while on the one hand the church is the unleavened dough, yet on the other it is urged to become unleavened. In an autobiographical section on his overlooking of personal privileges in order to establish Gentile churches, Paul states that, contrary to normal procedures, he feels compelled to waive certain rights (I Cor. 9). The soldier, the planter of a vineyard, the plowman, the thresher, and the priest are given just payment for services rendered. By allegorizing the law concerning the rights of oxen, Paul introduces scriptural authority as further support of his argument (I Cor. 9:8-9; cf. Deut. 25:4; also cf. the rabbinic allegorization of this same law in Yeb. 4a).

In his discussion of Christian baptismal and Eucharistic rites Paul makes use of OT analogies to rescue the Christian rites from their discredited association with comparable pagan rites (I Cor. 10:1-11). The Christian institutions were prefigured in the OT accounts of Israel's passing through the Red Sea and the cloud, and of eating manna and drinking from the water of the rock. Since Paul did not wish to deny the sacramental validity (*ex opere operato*) of pagan rites and to return to the symbolic significance of Jewish rites, he was compelled to allegorize the OT accounts. Hence Israel was "baptized into Moses" and partook of the supernatural food and water which flowed from the supernatural Rock (Christ).

Since Paul did not use allegory for philosophical interpretation, he resembles the Palestinian rather than the Alexandrian allegorists. Furthermore, his use of allegorical interpretation of OT texts is both infrequent and incidental to the main development of an argument. In comparison with his use of fulfilment exegesis, which constituted the substructure of his theological outlook, allegory was not for Paul a significant means of understanding the OT.

*b. In the Synoptic gospels.* While the record of

Jesus' parables, as reported by the Synoptic evange-lists, may imply an allegorical interpretation for a number of them, only one has been so treated; i.e., the parable of the sower (Mark 4:1-9). The parable of the tares, which has also been allegorized, is proba-bly not one of Jesus' parables (*see bibliography*). The allegorization is introduced by an explanation of the purpose of Jesus' teaching by parables. Since their hidden meaning can be understood only by those initiated into the mystery of the significance of para-bles, the true understanding of parables serves as a means of distinguishing between those inside and those outside the enlightened group (Mark 4:10-12). With this introduction, the evangelist is prepared to make allegorical equations for the separate parts of the parable. In the process of allegorization, the sets of equations have become confused: the seed is both the preached word and the people who receive it; and the people are both the soil and the plants. Also the point of the original parable has been altered. The theme in this allegory is no longer a calm ob-servation that misfortunes are unavoidable, but a warning to guard against that which brings misfor-tune.

Even though allegorical interpretation was rarely used in NT times, it had its origin in this period and became increasingly important, particularly for the Christian authors of the Alexandrian school.

**Bibliography.** L. Ginzberg, "Allegorical Interpretation," *Jewish Encyclopaedia,* I (1901), 403-11; J. Geffcken, "Alle-gory,'" in J. Hastings, *Encyclopaedia of Religion and Ethics,* I (1908), 327-31; H. A. Wolfson, *Philo* (1947), I, 115-38; F. Büchsel, "ἀλληγορέω," in G. Kittel, *TWNT,* I (1949), 260-64; J. Jeremias, *The Parables of Jesus* (English trans. S. H. Hooke; 1954), pp. 52-70.                          L. MOWRY

**ALLELUIA** ăl'ə lōō'yə. Vulg. transliteration of the shout הללוּ־יה. *See* HALLELUJAH.

**ALLIANCE** [ברית; התחברוּת (Dan. 11:23; *cf.* Ps. 94:20; Dan. 11:6); התחתן (I Kings 3:1; II Chr. 18:1); συμμαχία]. A union of interests. In the patriarchal period alliances among families, clans, and tribes were very frequent: e.g., Abraham with the Amorites (Gen. 14:13) and the Philistines; Isaac with the Phi-listines (Gen. 26:28); Jacob and Laban (Gen. 31:44); Judah's marriage to a Canaanite (Gen. 38:2). *See also* COVENANT.

In the early period such alliances were un-doubtedly commonplace; however, note Abraham's insistence that Isaac not marry a Canaanite (Gen. 24:3). Joshua made a pact with the Gibeonites (Josh. 9), and Israel frequently entered into mutual agree-ments with the Canaanites (Exod. 23:32; 34:12, 15; Deut. 7:2; Judg. 2:2; cf. I Sam. 11:1). Common dangers, however, began to draw the tribes together into a confederation or amphictyony (Judg. 4:10; 6:35), which became the foundation of the United Monarchy under Saul, David, and Solomon. Even then David entered into an alliance with Achish of Gath (I Sam. 27:2) by which he was prepared to fight Saul's own Benjaminites.

Under Solomon a formal treaty with the king of Tyre (I Kings 5:9) was established which was con-tinued with the Phoenicians by Omri and Ahab (I Kings 16:31; cf. Amos 1:9). Solomon's many mar-riages undoubtedly involved political agreements,

as with Pharaoh's daughter (I Kings 3:1; 9:16); Ahab entered an alliance with Ben-hadad of Syri (I Kings 20:34; cf. I Kings 15:19; II Chr. 16:3) Judah and Israel were allies during the reigns o Ahab and Jehoshaphat against Syria (I Kings 22 II Chr. 18). Israel and Syria joined in a commor pact directed against Judah (II Kings 16:5; cf. Isa 7:1-9).

Egypt was frequently a haven for those in Israe and Judah who sought political or legal refuge. Al liances were quite readily sought with foreign nation during the turbulent period of the rise of the As syrian and Neo-Babylonian empires of the eighth anc seventh centuries B.C. Menahem of Israel seems tc have bribed Tiglath-pileser (Pul) of Assyria to aic him against his own subjects (II Kings 15:19). Heze-kiah of Judah was the dependent party of an alliance with Egypt against Sennacherib of Assyria (II King: 18:21, 24; cf. Isa. 31:1-3). The Egyptians were agair relied on to combat the Babylonians in the last years of the kingdom of Judah under Jehoiakim, who was placed on the throne by Pharaoh Neco (II Kings 23 34), and under Zedekiah. Jehoiakim was forced tc submit to Nebuchadnezzar and became his vassal Though Egypt was decisively defeated at Carchemish in 605 B.C., there is ample evidence that Egypt offered support enough for a new alliance with Judah and was able to inflict sore losses on Nebuchadnezzar ca. 601 (*see* EXILE). Jehoiakim courted Egypt's favor and was rewarded with a thorough defeat at the hand of the Babylonians in 597. Later when Zede-kiah was put on the throne in Judah by Nebuchad-nezzar, he too was induced to put off the Babylonian yoke and make an alliance with Egypt (cf. II Kings 24:20; Ezek. 17:1-21). Because of this, Nebuchadnez-zar again laid siege to Jerusalem, destroying the city and temple, taking the people into exile.

The prophets inveighed against the practice of making foreign alliances (Isa. 20; 28:15, 18; 30:1-2; Jer. 2:18, 36; Hos. 8:9) solely for religious reasons. Israel and Judah were almost invariably the de-pendent members of such alliances and were thereby subject to influences of a cultic nature. Equally im-portant to the prophets was the false sense of security which foreign alliances aroused in the people; it was a form of apostasy and idolatry in the sense of a mis-taken trust and false commitment.

Ezra and Nehemiah vehemently opposed any al-liance which would render insecure the identity of the small state of Judah as the people of God's rev-elation, especially marriage contracts with non-Jews (Ezra 9:1-3).

During the Second Commonwealth alliances were sought and secured by the Maccabean and Has-monean leaders with both Seleucid and Roman powers in order to ensure gains made toward Jew-ish freedom and autonomy or to prosper their own personal ambitions (I Macc. 8:17; 9:70; 15:16; Jos. Antiq. XIII.i.6, vii.2, viii.3; XIV.ii.1). Antipater and Herod were particularly adept at making deals with the right Roman leader at the right time (Jos. War I.viii–II.ii; Antiq. XIV.ix-xvi).                    J. A. SANDERS

**ALLOGENES SUPREME** ă lŏj'ə nēz [ἀλλογενής]. A Gnostic work in Coptic discovered at Chenoboskion in 1946 (*see* APOCRYPHA, NT). It appears to be one of the five apocalypses which Plotinus is said by Porphyry to have combatted. It is apparently a Sethian document composed in the early third century.

M. S. ENSLIN

**ALLOM.** KJV Apoc. form of AMON 3.

**ALLON** ăl′ən [אַלּוֹן, oak]. **1.** A prince in the tribe of Simeon (I Chr. 4:37).

**2.** KJV translation in Josh. 19:33 (cf. "plain" in Judg. 4:11 KJV). The word here should be interpreted as a part of "Elon-bezaanannim" or "oak in ZAANANNIM" (so RSV).

G. W. VAN BEEK

**ALLON-BACUTH** ăl′ən băk′əth [אַלּוֹן בָּכוּת, oak of weeping] (Gen. 35:8); KJV ALLON-BACHUTH. The site of the burial of Deborah, Rebekah's nurse, in the vicinity of Bethel. If Allon-bacuth is to be identified with the site of the palm tree of the prophetess Deborah, the place was located between Bethel and Ramah (Judg. 4:5). Worship at a sacred tree may be implied in both references. Some scholars have identified Allon-bacuth with the oak of Tabor (by reading "Deborah" for "Tabor") in I Sam. 10:3.

W. L. REED

**ALLOTMENT.** In the OT this is a concept of land right, which evidently had its origin in the law of the commune. The custom of having community holdings in landed property change owners at certain intervals of time and of having them be newly distributed by lot (cf. the regulations for the sabbatical year) is in the background when the psalmist (Ps. 16:5-6) rejoices that possession of good land has been allotted to him (even though in a figurative sense his גּוֹרָל, "lot," and חֵלֶק, "portion," is here Yahweh), or when, on the other hand, the prophet (Isa. 57:6) reproves the folly of those whose absurd worship is aimed specifically at the "portion" and the "lot" which consists of the smooth stones of the stream valley. Then, too, as the communal land came to be privately owned to an increasing extent, situations resulted again and again—at the time of the dying out of a family, e.g.—which made necessary a new apportionment of this land, in the course of which the lot then played its old role. Micah hoped for such a reapportionment in the Judean communities which would be effected when the landed proprietors from the capital city, who had intruded themselves here and there in the country, had to get out after the punishment of Jerusalem:

> Therefore you will have none to cast the line by lot
> in the assembly of the LORD (Mic. 2:5).

Ezekiel foresees the time when there will no longer be such allotments in Jerusalem (Ezek. 24:6). That the lot plays such an important role in the apportionment of land is less astonishing if one considers that allotment was a sacral act, and the will of Yahweh in person was believed to be at work in the seemingly rather mechanical and random falling of the lots, according to Prov. 16:33, which seems to be of early date, judging by its inner structure:

> The lot is cast into [lit., "shaken in"] the lap,
> but the decision is wholly from the LORD.

The idea obtained from the administering of the communal land right was probably carried over very early into the conception of the process by which the tribes occupied their territory. According to this theory, which is displayed above all in Josh. 13-19, the twelve tribes came into possession of their territories for settlement by applying to the whole land of Canaan that method of allotting portions which was used on a small scale in the sphere of the rural community. In this sense—i.e., expanded almost to a sort of state law—the concept of allotment—more exactly, the word "lot" (גּוֹרָל)—originally inherent in communal right, is exemplified most frequently in the OT. In both cases it is based on the theologoumenon of Yahweh as the sole possessor of the land, who now, by lot revealing his own will, assigns portions, first of all to the individual tribes, then within each tribe to the individual clans and, finally, within each clan to the individual families. It is not impossible that the basic theologoumenon was influenced from Egypt, where, up until Ptolemaic times, the Pharaoh was considered the actual lord of the land, from whom all others had their possession only in fee. Because it is determined by lot, the individual portion of land can also be designated itself as "lot" (e.g., Judg. 1:3); because it is given in hereditary tenure, as it were, it can be called "inheritance" (נַחֲלָה); the most colorless designation is "portion" (חֵלֶק). In Num. 26:52-56, where the three terms appear alongside one another in somewhat contradictory context, the command for allotment is given in connection with the organization of the tribes. In Num. 33:54; 34:13 (cf. 36:2-3) it is repeated, here restricted to 9½ tribes, the tradition of Num. 32 being taken into account, a tradition which reports without the use of the word "lot" on the bestowal of hereditary property on Reuben, Gad, and the half-tribe of Manasseh, who were already in the land E of the Jordan. Also in Josh. 13:6 the idea of allotment does not refer to the land E of the Jordan. It becomes dominant, on the other hand, in the report on the accomplishment of the distribution of the land W of the Jordan in chs. 14-19. Not only in Josh. 14:1-2; 19:51, which frame the report, is it expressly stated that these are the territories which were distributed by "lot" as "inheritance," but the key word "lot" appears again and again in Josh. 15:1; 16:1; 17:1, 14 (along with חֶבֶל, actually "measuring line"; cf. Mic. 2:5), 17; 18:6-10 (along with חֵלֶק, "portion"); 19:1, 10, 17, 24, 32, 40. In the fact that the act of allotment is undertaken with the assistance of priests at the central sanctuary of the amphictyony in Shiloh, its sacral character distinctly emerges.

The theory of allotment of the tribal portions experienced a late readoption in the so-called constitutional draft in the supplement to the book of Ezekiel (Ezek. 45:1; 48:29). It is an elaboration of the theory when Josh. 21:4-6, 8, 10, 20, 40 (=I Chr. 6:54, 61, 63, 65—H 6:39, 46, 48, 50) also considers the Levite cities to be drawn by lot; Levi received no definite tribal territory for settlement, because Yahweh was his portion (Num. 18:20; Deut. 10:9; Josh. 13:14), and within the various tribal territories received only places of residence with pasture, but no arable fields. Once (Ps. 125:3) the whole land of Canaan appears as the "land allotted to the righteous." In Isa. 34:17, Yahweh assigns the territory of Edom to the wild beasts by lot and with the measuring line. Usually, however, in such contexts, which extend the idea of allotment beyond the scope of the individual community and the tribal assembly into the universal, the root גרל no longer appears, but rather נחל and ירש. No idea of space is bound up with the casting of lots for clothes (Ps. 22:18—H 22:19) and prisoners of war (Joel 3:3—H 4:3; Obad. 11; Nah. 3:10); or with the use of lots to resolve controversies (Prov. 18:18), or to decide in a case like that in Prov. 1:14, where also the religious significance can no longer be recognized in the proceedings, which manifests itself in the allotment of priority in executing the confederacy's decrees (Judg. 20:9), in determining the guilty (Jonah 1:7) and those who are to live in Jerusalem (Neh. 11:1) or in casting lots for the manifold cultic functions (I Chr. 24:5, 7, 31; 25:8; 26:13 ff; Neh. 10: 35; also Lev. 16:8-10). It should be noted further that the word "lot" in the OT, beyond being the instrument of decision and the allotted portion of land, can also, as in modern languages, mean "fate" (in Isa. 17:14, the overthrow of the nations; in Jer. 13:25, Jerusalem's punishment; in Dan. 12:13, the salvation of the godly who are rising from the dead).

*Bibliography.* In addition to general works on the cultural history of Israel and on biblical archaeology, see: K. Galling, "Ein Stück judäischen Bodenrechts in Jes 8," *ZDPV,* 56 (1933), 209-18; A. Alt, Micha 2, 1-3, *GES ANADASMOS* in *Juda, Interpretationes . . . S. Mowinckel* (1955), pp. 13-23= *Kleine Schriften,* III (1960), 373 ff; J. T. E. Renner, *A Study of the Word Goral in the OT* (1958), especially pp. 19 ff.

K. ELLIGER

**ALLOY.** *See* METALLURGY.

**ALMIGHTY** [שדי, *originally* the Mountain One; NT παντοκράτωρ]. For the OT word this translation has become common, under the influence of the LXX, which frequently, especially in the book of Job, renders παντοκράτωρ. Originally the word referred to the El Shaddai, "god of the mountain(s)," who was worshiped in patriarchal times. In Exod. 6:2-3 (P), the writer correctly says that the worship of Yahweh (the Lord) began with Moses, and that in the period of "the fathers" God was known as El Shaddai (Gen. 17:1; 28:3; 35:11; 43:14; 48:3; 49:25). The name was eventually reinterpreted by the content of "Yahweh" (as in Ruth 1:20-21; Pss. 68:14—H 68:15; 91:1; Ezek. 1:24; 10:5), except in the book of Job, where it is used to emphasize the power and majesty of deity.

The NT occurrences of the word παντοκράτωρ are all in the book of Revelation (e.g., 1:8; 4:8; 21: 22) with the exception of the OT quotation in II Cor. 6:18.

*See also* GOD, NAMES OF, § C2a.

B. W. ANDERSON

**ALMODAD** ăl mō′dăd [אלמודד]. The first son of Joktan, and the presumed ancestor of a South Arabian people (Gen. 10:26; I Chr. 1:20). The name is probably to be read, with the LXX, as "Elmodad," meaning "God is a friend." Other suggestions are based on the Arabic word *'al,* "tribe," and identify

the tribe either with the Gebanites or, by a change of one letter, with the tribe of Al-Murad.

S. COHEN

**ALMON** ăl′mən [עלמון]. A priestly city in Benjamin, located near Anathoth (Josh. 21:18); it is the same as Alemeth (I Chr. 6:60—H 6:45). Neither name is mentioned in the list of Benjaminite cities in Josh. 18:21-28.

On the basis of such twin forms as תחתון (*tahton*) and תחתית (*tahtith*), meaning "lower," the consonants of עלמת should be vocalized as "Almit," which would be a later form of "Almon." The name and site are preserved in Khirbet Almit, a ruined village a mile NE of Anata, on the road to 'Ain Farah.

S. COHEN

**ALMON-DIBLATHAIM** ăl′mən dĭb′lə thā′əm [עלמון דבלתימה]. The stopping place of the Israelites following Dibon-gad and preceding the mountains of Abarim (Num. 33:46-47). A possible location is Deleilat el-Gharbiyeh, a town commanding three roads, 2½ miles NE of Libb; but no identification is generally accepted. It may be the same as BETH-DIBLATHAIM.

E. D. GROHMAN

**ALMOND.** The translation of the following words: *a)* לוז, *lûz* (Gen. 30:37; KJV HAZEL). As the Aramaic and Arabic cognates (לוזא; *lawz;* see also LXX ἀμυγδάλη) show, the reference is to the almond

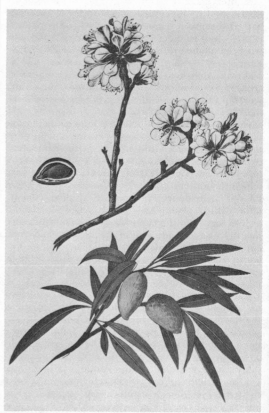

From *Plants of the Bible* (London: Crosby Lockwood & Son, Ltd.)
16. Almond

tree, *Amygdalus communis* L., common in the Near East. *See* LUZ.

b) מִשְׁקָדִים, *mᵉshuqqādhîm* (from שׁקד, "to watch, wake"; *see below*), "like almonds" (Exod. 25:33-34; 37:19-20).

c) שׁקד, *shāqēdh*, apparently a symbolic name given the almond tree because it blossoms first among the fruit trees, the pink-white flowers appearing before the leaves. It is used in Jer. 1:11 as a play on the verb "to watch, wake." The almond was among the "choice fruits of the land" (Gen. 43:11), as it is today, and was sent as a gift to Egypt by Jacob. Aaron's rod blossomed and bore almonds overnight (Num. 17:8—H 17:23). The almond blossom was an artistic feature of the Menorah (seven-branched LAMPSTAND) of the tabernacle (Exod. 25:33-34; 37:19-20). In Eccl. 12:5 the figure of the almond tree is generally likened to the white hair of the aged (but cf. *IB*, V [1956], 83-86).

*See also* FLORA § A2a; MONEY; ROD.

**Bibliography.** H. N. and A. L. Moldenke, *Plants of the Bible* (1952), pp. 35-38.                              J. C. TREVER

**ALMS** [ἐλεημοσύνη, pity, relief of the poor; Lat. *eleemosyna;* Anglo-Saxon *aelmaesse,* almsgiving]. There is apparently no Hebrew word for "alms" or "almsgiving," though the practice is attested. It is very important to note that the LXX uses ἐλεημοσύνη, of God (e.g., Ps. 103:6; Isa. 1:27; 28:17) and frequently of men (Gen. 47:29; Prov. 19:22; 20:28; 21:21; etc.), not merely for חסד, but also for the *ṣ.d.k.*, "righteousness" (e.g., Deut. 6:25; 24:13; Ps. 24:5; Isa. 1:27; 28:17; 59:16; etc.). It is open to doubt whether ἐλεημοσύνη ever means "almsgiving" in the LXX. In Matthew, Luke, and Acts the word is used of the giving and of what is given (cf. Acts 3:2-3).

References in the OT to the poor and needy and to various institutions and methods of relieving them show the practice of almsgiving to have been more widespread than the meager terminology suggests. There are a number of references to charitable practices in both Testaments.

1. In the OT
2. In Jewish writings
3. In the NT
4. Bases of almsgiving
Bibliography

**1. In the OT.** There is little direct reference to the giving of alms in the OT. Indeed, the Deuteronomist envisages that in the Promised Land "there will be no poor among you (for the LORD will bless you in the land . . .)" (Deut. 15:4; but cf. vs. 11). On the other hand, the Israelite is enjoined to be generous. He is not to shut his hand, but is to open his hand and lend to his poor brother, and give to him freely (vss. 7-11). It is difficult to decide whether the context refers to lending only (cf. vss. 8, 10) or to lending (vs. 8) and almsgiving (vs. 10; cf. Pss. 37:26; 112:5).

There are, of course, references to the poor and destitute in all branches of the literature of the OT. The psalmist has not seen the children of the righteous begging bread (37:25); rather, the righteous is a liberal giver (112:9); and Job was famed for his charity (Job 29:12-17). The prophet claims that the religious fast acceptable to the Lord includes gifts of bread to the hungry, housing for the homeless, and clothing for the naked (Isa. 58:6-8). The wise commend kindness to the poor (Prov. 14:21, 31). Noteworthy is the frequent phrase "poor and needy." The occurrences of this phrase in law, prophecy, wisdom, and psalmody show that, like the modern phrase "down and out," "poor and needy" is a colloquial, almost technical, term for the unfortunates. Beggary is a terrible fate destined to fall upon the remnants of Eli's house (I Sam. 2:36), and a curse invoked upon the children of the persecutor (Ps. 109:10). Penury and privation are abundantly attested in the OT, and where these are present, we may also assume that almsgiving and succor were not absent.

Various practices point in the same direction. Much almsgiving is concealed in hospitality which is not merely the feasting of superiors and equals but the charitable provision for the hungry. This is specially true of that hospitality connected with religious occasions and sacrifices (cf. I Sam. 9:13; 25:8; II Sam. 6:19; 15:11; Neh. 8:10). The laws prescribe provision for the poor. Arable land, the vineyard, and the olive orchard are to be left fallow every seventh year, "that the poor of your people may eat" (Exod. 23:10-11). Similarly the Deuteronomist prescribes that a tithe of the produce every third year is to be given to the Levite, the resident alien, and the poor (Deut. 14:28). Every Israelite—thus especially the poor—was allowed to pick grapes and corn to eat as he passed by (Deut. 23:24-25), and the poor would glean corn and olives and grapes (24:19-22; cf. Lev. 19:9; 23:22). The manumitted slave is to be loaded with gifts, but here the idea of reward must also be present (Deut. 15:12-15).

It may be concluded that in ancient Israel almsgiving was widely practiced, even if there are a good deal of silence and disguise concerning its terminology.

**2. In Jewish writings.** In the Damascus Document all who enter the covenant must not rob the destitute, must love the brethren and "hold fast the hand of the poor and needy." Also, the wages of at least two days per month are to be given to a central fund for organized distribution to the "poor and needy." There is no doubt, in spite of the almost complete silence of the major Dead Sea Scrolls concerning almsgiving, that this was a practice widely enjoined and performed. Elsewhere examples of precept and practice are too numerous for mention here, but three points are important:

a) In Jewish writings, generally speaking, the word "righteousness" (צדק) came to mean "almsgiving" (so in Aramaic, Syriac, and the Koran).

b) The giving of alms gained merit for the donor. This is already probably evident in such passages as Dan. 4:27; and the same is claimed for Prov. 11:4, though it is less likely, in view of the context. "Alms make atonement for sins" (Ecclus. 3:30; cf. 29:12).

c) Widely attested Jewish almsgiving is the background for the rich NT teaching.

**3. In the NT.** Almsgiving figures prominently in the Sermon on the Mount (Matt. 6:1-6, where "righteousness" [vs. 1; RSV "piety"] and "almsgiving" [vs. 2] are synonymous). The recipients of the kingdom must sell their possessions and give alms (Matt. 19:21; Luke 12:33), for to succor the poor is to succor the Savior (Matt. 25:42-46). Liberal giving is commended (Matt. 5:42; Mark 12:41-44; Luke 6:38; 14:13), as is spiritual giving (Luke 11:41). The first Christian officers were elected for almsgiving (Acts 6), and there is apostolic precept (Rom. 12:8, 13; 15:26; I Cor. 16:1-3; II Cor. 9:1; Jas. 2:16; I Tim. 5:9-16; 6:18), receipt (Phil. 4:18), and example (Acts 24:17). Hospitality is especially enjoined (e.g., Rom. 12:13; I Pet. 4:9).

**4. Bases of almsgiving.** It may be said that there is a threefold basis for almsgiving:

*a*) It is significant that in Jewish, Christian, and other writing "almsgiving" is the exercise of righteousness, and it is clear that here the original social implications of righteousness as what is fitting and normal between clan members has re-emerged. Righteousness is not merely a forensic conception but describes that loyalty between members of the same social group which has almsgiving for one of its expressions.

*b*) Thus almsgiving again is the recognition of blessedness. Israel is blessed to bless the nations (Gen. 12:3); the individual Israelite gives because he is blessed (Deut. 15:14). "You received without pay, give without pay" (Matt. 10:8), for "it is more blessed to give than to receive" (Acts 20:35).

*c*) Thirdly, almsgiving achieves rewards for those who exercise it. Daniel points out that if Nebuchadnezzar practices righteousness—i.e., almsgiving—he may be rewarded with a lengthening of tranquillity (Dan. 4:27). It is claimed that "righteousness" in Prov. 10:2; 11:4 means "almsgiving" and that it gives deliverance from (sudden) death. Though this is doubtful, nevertheless such passages (cf. Prov. 16:6; 21:3; Ecclus. 3:30; 29:12) are doubtless the basis for the later rabbinical conceptions of the atoning and sacrificial potency of almsgiving.

*Bibliography.* P. Volz, *Biblische Altertümer* (1914), p. 249; M. Weber, *Ancient Judaism* (trans. H. H. Gerth and D. Martindale; 1952), pp. 255-67.　　G. HENTON DAVIES

**ALMUG** ăl′mŭg [אלמוגים, *'almûghîm;* Ugar. *almg*]. A special kind of wood imported from Ophir by Hiram of Tyre and used in the construction of Solomon's temple and for lyres and harps (I Kings 10:11-12; LXX ξύλα ἀπελέκητα, "unhewn [rough?] wood"). The parallels in II Chr. 9:10-11 have אלגומים (ALGUM; LXX πεύκινα, "pine"), probably by transposition of two letters. Josephus (Antiq. VIII.vii.1) calls it a special pine wood. The occurrence of *almg* in an Ugaritic document (120) implies that the spelling in Kings is correct but further complicates identification. It has commonly been identified with sandalwood, particularly *Pterocarpus santalinus* L., red sandalwood, indigenous to India and Ceylon. A hard, close-grained, reddish-brown wood, it was quite suitable for musical instruments. *Santalum album,* white sandalwood, from the same countries, is still highly prized for wooden objects. Identification of the biblical wood remains uncertain.

*See also* FLORA § A8*c*.　　J. C. TREVER

**ALNATHAN.** KJV Apoc. variant of ELNATHAN.

**ALOES** ăl′ōz [אהלים, *'ăhālîm;* אהלות, *'ăhālôth;* ἀλόη, perhaps *from* Sanskrit *aghil*]. An aromatic substance used for PERFUME and probably derived from a tree. In Num. 24:6 (KJV LIGN ALOES) the word refers poetically to a kind of tree growing by a stream.

Most botanists now identify the "aloes" of the Bible with the *Aquilaria agallocha* Roxb., commonly (but mistakenly) called the eaglewood because of the similarity of the Sanskrit name *aghil* to the Latin *aquila,* "eagle." The *Santalum album* L., white sandalwood (*see* ALMUG), however, could also be intended, since both trees, native of Southeast Asia, provide the highly valued aromatic woods from the inner core of their trunks and branches. Incense and perfumes were made from them. They were a part of the imports into Bible lands in ancient times; thus specific identification with the source is more difficult.

17. Aloes

The true aloe, *Aloë succotrina* Lam. and other species, is not a tree but a succulent plant, similar in appearance to the century plant, *Agave americana,* with which it is often confused. This aloe is the source of a bitter, malodorous, purgative medicine which some botanists claim was used with MYRRH for embalming and was therefore the aloes of John 19:39. Probably all the references, except Num. 24:6, were to the eaglewood, or sandalwood. Cf. the Targ. of Job 9:30, where Aramaic *'ăhālâ* is used for Hebrew *bōr,* "lye." The poetic reference in Balaam's oracle, *'ăhālîm* (Num. 24:6), is very probably a textual error (cf. LXX "tents") for *'ēlîm,* "OAK" or "TEREBINTH," since aloes was known only as an aromatic substance and not as a tree in the Holy Land.

Fig. ALO 17.

*See also* FLORA § A7*a;* SPICES; CINNAMON; FRANKINCENSE.　　J. C. TREVER

**ALOTH.** KJV form of BEALOTH 2.

**ALPHA AND OMEGA** ăl′fə, ō mĕg′ə, ō mē′gə [A; Ω]. The first and last letters of the Greek alphabet. The basic meaning is indicated by two parallel constructions: "the first and the last, the beginning and the end" (Rev. 22:13). In the NT the two are always used together and applied to God (Rev. 1:8) or to Christ (Rev. 22:13). Alternative ways of expressing the same thought are: "he who was and he who is to come"; "from whom and to whom are all things." In Jewish thought the whole extent of a process or period is indicated by reference to its beginning and its end. That the thought does not focus simply upon the distant beginning and the distant ending of a time line, is indicated by the threefold formulations "who *is* and who was and who is to come" (Rev. 1:8); "from him and *through* him and to him are all things" (Rom. 11:36). The basic formula, which appears in Isa. 44:6; 48:12, accents the uniqueness of the one God as creator and redeemer, as the ultimate source and ground of existence. "Besides me there is no god" (Isa. 44:6). Because he is the Alpha, he alone holds supreme power over the heaven and the earth. He alone can make all things new. Because he is the Omega, the end, he alone can "tell us what is yet to be" (Isa. 44:7). He is the Life, and therefore alone can give freely "from the fountain of the water of life" (Rev. 21:6). He can banish death and Hades. His reward is final.

The application to Jesus Christ of these formulas, so expressive of unique sovereignty, is explicit and important (Rev. 22:13). He is the "first and the last, and the living one" (Rev. 1:17; cf. 2:8). In its basic meaning, this image parallels other NT assertions of Christ's primacy in creation (John 1:1 ff; Col. 1:18 ff; Heb. 1:1-3; I John 1:1), and of his role as the Coming One, the eschatological Redeemer of all things. All these assert that Christ's life and work have neither a beginning nor an end (Heb. 7:3), because he *is* the one through whom, by whom, and for whom all things are made. His firstness and lastness are validated above all by the fact of his death and resurrection (Rev. 1:17; 2:8).

The use of the alphabet to designate these attributes of God has analogy in various forms of Hellenistic speculation, but the basic symbolism is drawn from the OT. The chief contrast between the Testaments lies in the full identification of Jesus Christ as the Alpha and Omega, and in tracing his primacy and ultimacy to the Resurrection. Later Mandaean, rabbinic, and mystical thinkers develop the thought along quite different lines.

*Bibliography.* A. Schlatter, *Das AT in der johannischen Apokalypse* (1912), pp. 13-14. F. Boll, *Aus der Offenbarung Johannis* (1914), p. 27. R. H. Charles, *Revelation of St. John* (1920), I, 20; II, 220. H. F. Strack and P. Billerbeck, *Kommentar*, I (1924), 814; II (1926), 362, 546, 693. E. Lohmeyer, *Die Offenbarung des Johannes* (1926), pp. 11, 165, 176. A. Farrer, *Rebirth of Images* (1952), pp. 261-83.                     P. S. MINEAR

*ALPHABET [Lat. *alphabetum*, *from the* Greek (*originally* Semitic) *names of the first two letters*, ἄλφα *and* βῆτα]. A consonantal system of writing which was invented, probably during the first half of the second millennium B.C., by the Semitic peoples of Phoenicia or an adjacent area.

The alphabet as a system of writing is virtually unique in world history; with no certain exceptions, all comparable methods of reducing a language to written form are derived directly from, or are imitations of, the set of symbols and the system thereby represented which were first employed by the North-

western Semites during the first half of the second millennium B.C. As originally developed, the alphabet represented only the consonant sounds of the language for which it was employed. If we assume, as is highly probable, that the names of the letters were associated with their forms from the first, it would appear that each letter originally depicted, or at least represented, a specific object whose name began with the particular sound in question. Thus ' (the glottal stop) was represented by the head of an ox (Northwest Semitic *'alpu*), *b* by the plan of a house (*bêtu*), and similarly through the whole set of characters. Such a relationship between symbol and sound is termed "acrophonic." The overwhelming importance of alphabetic writing in the transmission of Western culture, as well as the unique features of this system at its inception, have led a large number of scholars to a detailed investigation of its origins and subsequent development. A summary of the more reasonable of the many suggestions concerning the origin and spread of the alphabet is presented below. But because much concerning the proto-alphabet is a matter of conjecture, our discussion will begin with a survey of the earliest undisputed forms of the alphabet as attested by Northwest Semitic, Greek, and South Semitic inscriptional material, in order to establish a foundation for the more speculative paragraphs which follow.

A. Earliest undisputed forms of the alphabet
   1. North Semitic
     *a.* Phoenician
     *b.* Hebrew
     *c.* Aramaic
   2. Greek
   3. South Semitic
     *a.* South Arabic
     *b.* North Arabic
B. Earliest, but disputed, forms of alphabetic writing
C. The order of the letters and their names
D. The origin of the alphabet
E. Epigraphy
Bibliography

**A. EARLIEST UNDISPUTED FORMS OF THE ALPHABET. 1. North Semitic. *a. Phoenician.*** Though the number of inscriptions exhibiting early forms of the Phoenician alphabet is not enormous, it is far larger and of earlier date than that of the material available from elsewhere and is accordingly taken as the norm in discussing the other branches of the North Semitic alphabet. The inscriptions, which are listed below in approximate chronological sequence, consist, in addition to the well-known royal inscriptions from Byblos, of various short inscriptions on arrowheads, spatulas (or flattened spearheads), and pottery fragments. For further information on the more important of these, *see* INSCRIPTIONS; the listing here is for their significance in tracing the early history of the alphabet: (*a*) The Ruweisah arrowhead (eleventh century); (*b*) The el-Khadr arrowheads I, II, and III (*ca.* 1100 B.C.), discovered in 1953 at el-Khadr, a village *ca.* three miles W of Bethlehem; (*c*) the Byblian spatula of Hasdrubal ('Azarba'l, 'Izriba'l; late eleventh century); (*d*) the

Table 1        Characters Used in Ancient and Modern Alphabets

| 1 (phonetic) | 2 (Hebrew) | 3 | 4 | 5 | 6 | 7 | 8 | 9 | 10 | 11 | 12 |
|---|---|---|---|---|---|---|---|---|---|---|---|
| ʾ | א | | | | | | | | | | |
| b | ב | | | | | | | | | | |
| g | ג | | | | | | | | | | |
| d | ד | | | | | | | | | | |
| h | ה | | | | | | | | | | |
| w | ו | | | | | | | | | | |
| z | ז | | | | | | | | | | |
| ḥ | ח | | | | | | | | | | |
| ṭ | ט | | | | | | | | | | |
| y | י | | | | | | | | | | |
| k | כ | | | | | | | | | | |
| l | ל | | | | | | | | | | |
| m | מ | | | | | | | | | | |
| n | נ | | | | | | | | | | |
| s | ס | | | | | | | | | | |
| ʿ | ע | | | | | | | | | | |
| p | פ | | | | | | | | | | |
| ṣ | צ | | | | | | | | | | |
| q | ק | | | | | | | | | | |
| r | ר | | | | | | | | | | |
| š | ש | | | | | | | | | | |
| t | ת | | | | | | | | | | |

*(Columns 3–12 contain hand-drawn ancient and modern alphabetic characters.)*

T. O. Lambdin

1) Phonetic value; (2) modern Hebrew; (3) Ahiram (*ca.* 1000 B.C.); (4) Shapatbaal (*ca.* 900 B.C.); (5) Gezer Calendar (tenth century B.C.); (6) Mesha (*ca.* 840 B.C.); (7) Siloam (*ca.* 700 B.C.); (8) Bir-Hadad (*ca.* 850 B.C.); (9) Sefire III (*ca.* 750 B.C.); (10) old Greek (eighth century B.C.); (11) modern Greek; (12) old S Arabic (including only those letters with a known N Semitic counterpart)

Ahiram sarcophagus inscription (*ca.* 1000); (*e*) an inscribed arrowhead from Lebanon, first published in 1956 (early tenth century); (*f*) the inscription of Yehimilk (Byblos; *ca.* 950 B.C.); (*g*) the inscription of Abibaal (Byblos; *ca.* 925); (*h*) the inscription of Elibaal (Byblos; late tenth century); (*i*) the inscription of Shapatbaal (Byblos; *ca.* 900); (*j*) a sherd with a brief inscription containing the name of 'Abda' (*ca.* 900 or slightly later).

Table I illustrates, as examples, the alphabetic forms in the inscriptions of Ahiram and Shapatbaal. All the forms in these texts show a high degree of homogeneity, with only minor variations indicating the chronological differences involved. Key letters in this instance are *k*, *m*, *n*, and to a lesser extent *b*. Study of these letters shows clearly that (*a*) the final stroke of the *m* is extended in the later inscriptions—namely, those of Shapatbaal and 'Abda'—while in the earlier ones its length is not significantly greater than those in the rest of the letter; (*b*) the lower stroke of *n* is longer in relationship to the upper in the latter two inscriptions, but not so in the earlier; (*c*) *k* is uniform throughout, but its form puts the whole group before the Mesha script (*see below*), where the common later form with the extended stroke can be recognized. The curious shape of *b*, with the bottom horizontal stroke to the right instead of the left, is found only in the Shapatbaal and 'Abda' inscriptions and serves to confirm the essential contemporaneity of the two. These details are mentioned because the chronology and sequence given above are quite different from that held just a decade or so ago.

The tenth-century dating of the Byblian material is secured mainly by the fact that the Abibaal and Elibaal inscriptions are incised on statues of Shishak and Osorkon I respectively, the first and second kings of the Libyan Dynasty (*see* LIBYA), which began *ca.* 950. Further important aid in determining the sequence is given by the genealogy of Shapatbaal, who is named explicitly as the son of Elibaal and the grandson of Yehimilk. Selected letters from the Ruweisah arrowhead and the el-Khadr arrowheads are given in Table II, where their importance as a link with even earlier forms of the alphabet is indicated; note especially that the el-Khadr ' still preserves the pupil of the eye ('*ênu*), the presumed original of the character.

*b. Hebrew.* The earliest readable inscription from the S Canaanite area is the Gezer Calendar, a small limestone tablet containing an agricultural calendar in a very archaic script. The dating of this tablet to the tenth century is primarily on the basis of the script and not on archaeological criteria of any other sort. Although quite a few other inscriptions are now available from the Palestine region, few of these are early enough to be of import in the present discussion (*see* INSCRIPTIONS). Next in order to the Gezer Calendar,* whose script, as may be seen from the accompanying table, differs little from that of the contemporary Phoenician inscriptions, there are (*a*) the Shemaiah Seal (ninth century), an oval seal with a bull and a brief inscription bearing the names *Šm'yhw* and '*Zryhw*, dated to the ninth century because of the archaic form ot *m;* (*b*) the Stele of

## Table 2

### Development of the Proto-Canaanite Alphabet
*(fifteenth-eleventh centuries B.C.)*

Courtesy of the American Schools of Oriental Research

I = fifteenth century (proto-Sinaitic)
II = thirteenth century
III = *ca.* 1200 B.C.
IV = *ca.* 1100 B.C.
V = eleventh century B.C.

Mesha king of Moab (*ca.* 835 B.C.; *see* MOABITE STONE);* (*c*) an inscribed sherd from Beth-horon (early eighth century); (*d*) the Samarian Ostraca,* a collection of sixty-three ostraca discovered during the course of the Harvard excavations at Samaria in the fall of 1910, generally attributed to the reign of Jeroboam (*ca.* 786-746), and containing records of various business transactions; (*e*) the Siloam Tunnel Inscription (*ca.* 700), discovered accidentally by a student in 1880 in the tunnel dating from the time of Hezekiah at the SE corner of Jerusalem, but now in the Museum of the Ancient Orient in Istanbul. Figs. CAL 2; MOA 66; SAM 12; INS 14.

Shown in Table I are the Gezer, Mesha, and Siloam scripts. Later than these, but illustrating the continued use of this alphabet, are the Ophel Ostracon (seventh century), stamped jar handles from various sites (seventh-sixth centuries), and various stamps and coins dating down to the second century A.D. A later form of the Hebrew alphabet was employed for writing with ink on leather, as has been demonstrated by the Qumran finds.* In general, however, this script yielded place to the Aramaic MS hand (*see below*) and survives only, in a modified form, in the MSS of the Samaritan sect. Fig. DEA 20.

*c. Aramaic.* The earliest Aramaic inscriptions are roughly contemporary with those from Phoenicia and Palestine, and the forms of the alphabets employed are little different from these except for local variations of minor significance. In Table I are two samples from the early period—namely, the script of the Bir-Hadad Stele from *ca.* 850 B.C., a dedicatory inscription to the god Milqart; and that of the Sefire III Inscription, a copy of an Aramaic treaty from approximately a century later. Of greater interest than the lapidary script, however, is the cursive variety of the Aramaic alphabet, which was quite early adapted to the use of ink on papyrus. The oldest Aramaic papyrus, found in 1942 at Saqqarah, is a letter from the king of an Asiatic state, probably Ashkelon, to the pharaoh of Egypt, requesting aid against the advancing hordes of the king of Babylon; the letter is thus a contemporary of the Lachish Letters (*see* LACHISH)* and dates to the very end of the seventh or beginning of the sixth century. A fairly straight-line sequence in the use of the cursive script may be traced from this period down into the Christian era, including the famous Elephantine Papyri* of the fifth century B.C., the Edfu Papyrus, the NASH PAPYRUS, and the majority of the texts from Qumran. This script emerges ultimately as the Hebrew square character, which is still used in modern times as the standard script for writing Hebrew. Figs. INS 15; ELE 25.

**2. Greek.** Although it is universally acknowledged that the Greeks borrowed their alphabet from the Phoenicians, opinion differs widely on the date and circumstances of this borrowing. In view of our better understanding of the development and chronology of the Semitic forms, as given above, the problem of when the borrowing took place becomes relatively simple. The earliest Greek inscriptions are generally dated to the late eighth or early seventh century, and there is no concrete reason for supposing that the alphabet had any lengthy prehistory among the Greeks. Since the forms of the letters in these early inscriptions compare most favorably with Phoenician script of the late ninth and early eighth centuries, and cannot possibly be derived from alphabetic forms from before the ninth century, the date of the Greek borrowing may be assigned confidently to this same period, with a slight preference for the early-eighth-century date.

Already in the earliest Greek inscriptions we find a regular use of certain letters to indicate vowels. This is the most striking difference between contemporary Greek and Semitic use of the script; some regard the Greek adaptation as the first real alphabet, defined as a writing system in which each symbol represents a single sound of the language, and relegate the Semitic usage of the same script to the class of syllabic writing. Although minor variations in usage occur among the epichoric, or local, varieties of the early Greek script, this universal method of representing vowels suggests a single borrowing with adaptation, rather than a double or multiple borrowing, as has been proposed by many scholars.

The stages through which the Greek alphabet

evolved into the form with which we are familiar from the later period are presumed to be the following:

*a*) Original ’, *h*, *ḥ*, *w*, *y*, and ‘ were employed to represent the vowels *a*, *e*, *ē*, *u*, *i*, and *o* respectively. The use of *ḥ* is the least uniform and poses a special problem in Greek epigraphy.

*b*) Because original *w* was employed for *u*, a new sign was developed for *w* in those areas where this sound was still used. This letter, called *digamma* after its shape, took the place of the original *w* in the alphabet, and the latter was placed at the end after *t*.

*c*) Probably on the analogy of the symbol *ṭ*, which was used to represent Greek *t*+*h*, new symbols were devised to write *p*+*h* and *k*+*h*, later φ and χ.

*d*) Likewise, on the basis of *z*=*d*+*z* in Greek usage, new symbols were chosen for *k*+*s* and *p*+*s*, later ξ and ψ.

*e*) Separate symbols came to be used to designate *ē* and *ō*, in contrast to *e* and *o*.

The Greek alphabet was borrowed by the Etruscans in Italy, probably during the seventh century B.C., and from them passed to the Romans. Subsequent spread of the Roman and Greek alphabets to nearly all parts of the civilized world make this branch of the alphabet the most prolific, rivaled only by the Aramaic branch.

**3. South Semitic. *a. South Arabic.*** The S Arabic alphabet is represented in its early phases by a large number of inscriptions and graffiti emanating from the kingdoms of Ma‘īn, Saba’, Qataban, and Hadramaut in the S part of the Arabian Peninsula.* The inscriptions, mainly votive, are usually very carefully inscribed in an alphabetic form which is not rivaled elsewhere in the Semitic world for its elegance. The successive kingdoms of S Arabia span at least a millennium, with most of the inscriptions coming from the period from the seventh century B.C. to the third A.D. Table I, col. 12, shows the standard form of this alphabet during this most important period of its use. Fig. ALP 18.

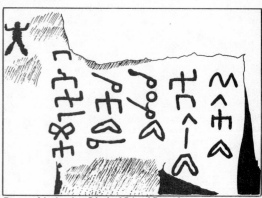

18. An archaic S Arabic rock inscription in vertical columns from Jebel Awrad

The earliest certain date in S Arabian epigraphy is that fixed by radiocarbon methods for a monograph incised on a sherd—namely, the eighth century. Older inscriptions, however, are known and may be dated on paleographical grounds to the ninth or tenth century B.C. Even in its earliest form the South Semitic alphabet, as represented on these inscriptions, has diverged greatly from its N relatives, discussed above. In the first place, there are symbols for the sounds *ḏ*, *ḫ*, *ẓ*, *ǵ*, *ś*, and *ṯ*, which we did not encounter above in the North Semitic alphabets. Secondly, a recent find makes it rather certain that the order of the alphabet in the S was quite different from that in the N. The significance of these two facts will be discussed below in connection with the order and origin of the alphabet.

Sometime during the first millennium B.C., perhaps quite early, S Arabian traders and colonizers occupied the adjacent portion of Africa, including the area now known as Ethiopia. Epigraphic remains are found antedating the Christian era, but the most important adaptation of the S Arabic script is to be found in the Ethiopic syllabary, which was used for MS writing from the fourth century A.D. on—i.e., from the introduction of Christianity. This syllabary was created by using the simple alphabetic symbols, not as simple consonants, but as the given consonant plus *a*. Other vowels were then indicated by various modifications and adjuncts to the consonant symbol; thus, *ta*, *tā*, *tī*, *t(ə)*, *tū*, and *tō* are represented by ተ,ታ,ቲ,ት,ቶ, and ት respectively. A further modified form of this alphabet-based syllabary is employed for the writing of Amharic and various other Semitic and non-Semitic languages of Ethiopia today.

*b. North Arabic.* By ancient N Arabic is meant that corpus of inscriptions from NW Arabia, from Safa in the N to al-'Ula (ancient Dedan) in the S. Unlike the fully developed monumental style of the S Arabic inscriptions, these are for the most part graffiti, and accordingly present a wider variety of alphabetic forms. The dating of the several groups involved is under dispute, but the following estimates reflect current scholarly opinion:

*a*) Dedanite, *ca.* 650-450 B.C.

*b*) Early Lihyanite, fifth century B.C.; Late Lihyanite, fourth or third century B.C.

*c*) Thamudic A, fifth-fourth century B.C.; Thamudic B, third to first century B.C.; Thamudic C, first to second century A.D.

*d*) Safaitic, first to second or third century A.D.

The subdivisions given are based on differences in the script and locale (for details, *see* the works of F. V. Winnett in the *bibliography*). Even though these inscriptions form an unbroken sequence from the end of the seventh century B.C. onward, they cannot be considered as simple stages in the evolution of a single script. Nor is it possible to derive the various early forms such as Dedanite and Thamudic A from S Arabic, since the former contain forms which, in view of the presumed parent alphabet to the N (*see below*), are more primitive. While we must reject, therefore, previous theories deriving N and S Arabic scripts from one another, the close resemblance between the two remains, and it is perhaps best to posit a Proto–South Semitic script of which both N and S Arabic are subsequent representatives.

A separate branch of this same alphabet has turned up in Mesopotamia. W. F. Albright (*see bibliography*), who has made a special study of this script, earlier termed Dedanite but called by him Proto-Arabic, places the earliest of these inscriptions in the eighth or seventh century B.C. The material includes a cylinder seal of the above-mentioned date, three brief inscriptions from Ur dating from the early years of the sixth century at the latest, and possibly two graffiti from Hamath (before 720 B.C.). According to Albright, the only possible carriers of this script were the Chaldeans, who first appear in the inscriptions of Shalmaneser III (ninth century) and who pushed steadily into Babylonia from the S. The inscriptions are accordingly called Chaldean.

The inclusion of a single example for each letter in the accompanying table would obscure the great variety exhibited by the various N Arabic scripts.

For detailed tables, *see* the works of D. Diringer and F. V. Winnett in the *bibliography*.

**B. EARLIEST, BUT DISPUTED, FORMS OF ALPHABETIC WRITING.** The earliest inscriptions generally assumed to be alphabetic belong to the Middle and Late Bronze Ages and for purpose of description may be divided into the following main groups: (*a*) the Palestinian inscriptions, (*b*) the Sinaitic inscriptions, (*c*) an isolated cylinder-seal inscription, and (*d*) the so-called enigmatic inscription from Byblos.

The Palestinian group includes, among the more important finds, the following (dates given are suggested on the basis of archaeological context and represent the mean of limits given by various scholars): (*a*) an inscribed potsherd from Gezer, *ca.* 1650 B.C.;* (*b*) an inscribed plaque from Shechem, *ca.* 1650 B.C.;* (*c*) an inscribed dagger from Lachish, *ca.* 1550 B.C.; (*d*) inscribed potsherds from Tell el-'Ajjul, Tell el-Hesi, and Beth-shemesh, all approximately of the fourteenth century or slightly later; (*e*) four pieces of inscribed pottery from Lachish, *ca.* 1250 B.C., the two most noteworthy pieces being known as the Lachish Ewer and the Lachish Bowl;* and (*f*) two sherds from Tell es-Sarem, *ca.* 1250 B.C. Figs. GEZ 26; INS 13; LAC 4.

It would be rash to assert that any of these inscriptions can be read with certainty, but the close resemblance of the signs on the Lachish Bowl and Ewer to the Sinaitic on the one hand and to the earliest Phoenician group on the other make it nearly certain that we are dealing with forms of the early alphabet. The inscriptions are generally too brief and too fragmentary to determine the accuracy of any proposed decipherment; the script is identified as alphabetic on the basis of the formal resemblance just mentioned and on the fact that the number of signs employed in any given inscription is sufficiently small to rule out the possibility of their belonging to either pictographic or syllabic systems of writing. It is quite possible, however, that some of these inscriptions belong to experimental forms of writing imitative of, but not strictly related to, the proto-alphabet. Table II, based on the research of F. M. Cross, Jr., illustrates the formal relationships which exist between several of these early scripts (including the earliest Phoenician), the main development of which is marked by a shift in the stance of various letters. This change is most probably to be attributed to the shift from vertical (columnar) writing, which is quite typical in the Sinaitic inscriptions (*see below*) and used, interestingly enough, in the earliest S Arabic inscription (*see above*), to horizontal writing and the subsequent gradual dominance of right to left as the direction of writing.

The inscriptions now known as Sinaitic were discovered first in 1905 by Flinders Petrie during his excavation at Serabit el-Khadem in the Sinai Peninsula.* New inscriptions, bringing the total number of usable ones to some twenty-five, were recovered by the Finnish expedition of 1929 and the Harvard expeditions of 1930 and 1935. The most decisive step toward their decipherment was made by the English Egyptologist Alan Gardiner in 1917, who recognized in a certain frequently occurring collocation of signs the name Ba'alat, chief goddess of Canaanite Byblos. His identification of the consonants *b'lt* is supported, not only by the relation of their forms to those of the early known inscriptions discussed above, but also by the fact that Ba'alat is known to have been identified with the Egyptian goddess Hathor, patron deity of the turquoise mines at Sinai, with which the inscriptions are associated. Although these inscriptions have not been deciphered with complete success, some real progress has been made since Gardiner's initial step, notably by Sayce, Cowley, and Albright. To Albright is due the credit for recognizing that all previous decipherments had erred in their misunderstanding of the consonantal system of the Canaanite languages contemporary with the inscriptions, which, thanks to researches into Egyptian sources on the one hand and to the recent N Canaanite material from Ugarit on the other, can now be established with a high degree of certainty. This conclusion remains valid whether one accepts the early, and now highly improbable, dating of the inscriptions to the end of the Twelfth Dynasty (*ca.* 1800 B.C.) with Gardiner or a later date in the fifteenth century, as was proposed by Petrie and is championed by W. F. Albright. Thus, the (Proto-)Sinaitic inscriptions fall most probably between the Middle Bronze Age inscriptions from Lachish, Gezer, and Shechem noted above and the later material from the thirteenth century. Fig. WRI 33.

Closely related to the Sinaitic script, but perhaps a little later in date, is the script used on a cylinder seal of unknown provenance now in a private collection in the United States. Made of steatite and containing a brief, eight-letter inscription, the seal is dated to the fourteenth century B.C. on the basis of parallels to the stylistically peripheral scene depicted thereon. A. Goetze, who has studied and published the seal and its inscription, places it between the alphabet of the Sinai texts and that of the so-called enigmatic inscription from Byblos (*see below*). Because it is hardly likely that this seal comes from the region of Sinai, it is important for showing the use of a closely related script elsewhere and increases the likelihood of there having been even at this early period a standard alphabet, barring local variation, over a large part of Palestine and Phoenicia.

The so-called enigmatic inscription of Byblos, described by Dunand as a cursive variety of the Byblian syllabary, is taken by other scholars, notably Albright, as belonging to the early alphabet and has been dated *ca.* 1200 B.C. It is best to withhold judg-

ment on this question, since the evidence is quite inconclusive. The formal objections which have been raised are certainly cogent but perhaps do not take sufficiently into consideration the possibility that this script is alphabetic, but stylistically under the influence of the pseudo-hieroglyphic forms which were possibly contemporary to some extent.

Perhaps the most important early alphabetic evidence of all comes from Ugarit. There, in 1929 French excavations turned up a quantity of tablets containing literary and other documents written in the local variety of Canaanite with a cuneiform alphabet. The possibility that this was a local invention, unrelated to the proto-alphabet, was dispelled with the publication in 1949 of an abecedary which, with the exclusion of those letters which subsequently fell into disuse in the dialects to the S, manifests the same order as we have from a much later period for the North Semitic alphabet.

**C. THE ORDER OF THE LETTERS AND THEIR NAMES.** Prior to the discovery in 1949 of the ABC from Ugarit, which shows clearly that the order of the alphabet as traditionally known from later sources was fixed as early as the fifteenth-fourteenth century B.C., our earliest material on this aspect of the system came from well into the first millennium B.C. and included (*a*) the traditional order of the Greek alphabet as reflected in the use of the alphabet for numbers and in various ABC's (including early Etruscan); (*b*) a brief inscription from Lachish, dating from the beginning of the eighth century B.C. and exhibiting in order the first five letters of the Hebrew alphabet, ' *b g d h* . . . ; (*c*) the early but not specifically datable ABC's represented in the acrostic poems of the OT, of which there are twelve in more or less complete form: Pss. 9–10; 25; 34; 37; 111; 112; 119; 145; Prov. 31:10-31; Lam. 1; 2–4; Nah. 1.

The ABC's from Ugarit, of which there are now several known, confirm the following order for the North Semitic alphabet at a stage even before we have direct evidence for the forms of some of the letters themselves:

$$' b g ḫ d h w z ḥ ṭ y k š l m d n ẓ s$$
$$' p ṣ q r t ġ t (+ 'i, 'u, and ś).$$

A comparison with the normal Hebrew order, as given in Table I, shows five intrusive signs in the alphabet from Ugarit in addition to the three at the end. These latter three are generally regarded as new creations in Ugaritic and are not taken as important for the original alphabet, which ended with *t*. There is common agreement among scholars that the five inserted letters are, in fact, part of the original Northwest Semitic alphabet and that through subsequent phonetic change in Northwest Semitic, where *ḫ* merged with *ḥ*, *š* with *ṭ*, *d* with *z*, *ẓ* with *ṣ*, and *ġ* with ', they gradually fell out of the alphabetic system.

The order of the South Semitic alphabet is known, in part, for the period *ca.* 300 B.C. from a discovery made at Hajar Kohlan in the Wadi Beihan, the site of ancient Timna, the capital of the Qatabanian kingdom of S Arabia. Here excavators found a stone gutter with rows of flat paving stones of Yemenite

imestone on both sides; some of the stones were in-
ised with masons' marks exhibiting a series, appar-
ntly originally complete, of the Qatabanian alpha-
et as follows:

l ḥ m . . š r ġ s h b k n ḫ ś p '

Comparison of this series with the Ethiopic alphabet,
:nown only from the fourth century A.D. on as far
.s its order is concerned—namely:

h l ḥ m š r s q b t ḫ n ' k w ' z y d g
ṭ p ṣ d f p—

hows a similarity too close for mere chance. Con-
idering that Ethiopic no longer used the symbols for
ʿ and ś, we can hardly regard the agreement as a
product of coincidence. Two problems arise: (a) the
relationship between the Qatabanian order and that
of Northwest Semitic, and (b) the development of the
Ethiopic order from the Qatabanian. A. M. Honeyman and J. Ryckmans (see bibliography) have offered
hypotheses to cover a; the former scholar sees in the
S Arabic order a completely independent arrangement based on the actual physical forms of the
letters, a theory which is both reasonable as pre-
ented and harmonious with the fact that S Arabian
inscriptions reflect in their careful execution a special
preoccupation with the forms of the letters and their
various symmetries. The hypothesis put forth by
J. Ryckmans involves a considerable number of complex and unfounded transpositions, beginning with
the Northwest Semitic and ending with the Qatabanian. Although the thesis of Honeyman is not without minor difficulties and uncertainties, it suits the
data well; and the same process, taken together with
known post-Qatabanian changes in the forms of the
individual letters, will account for the emergence of
the Ethiopic order.

The originality and importance of the names of
the individual letters, as preserved in the Greek and
post-Christian Jewish traditions, is disputed. There
s no reason to suppose that the Greek forms of the
names were not taken over with the alphabet itself
in the late ninth or early eighth century; these names
and those taken over by the Jews from the Aramaic
show clear evidence of N Canaanite origin. Those
who favor the acrophonic origin of the alphabet pre-
er to accept, with reservations as to the complete
accuracy of the tradition, the names of the letters as
reflecting the original situation, in which the name
of the letter was the name of the object depicted.
Others, however, rejecting the acrophonic hypothesis,
regard the names of the letters as secondary, perhaps
added at a later date for mnemonic purposes. Without more evidence, however, the problem cannot be
settled. Below are given the traditional Aramaic-
Hebrew names of the letters, the Greek counterparts,
and the accepted meanings of the names; added in a
ew cases are recent scholarly suggestions on more
original forms of the names.

'āleph (alpha), "ox"
bêth (bēta), "house"
gîmel (gamma), "camel"; perhaps originally *gamlu,
  "throw-stick"
dāleth (delta), "door"; perhaps originally *dag, "fish"
hē' (e-psilon), meaning uncertain
wāw (u-psilon), "hook"

zayin (zēta), "weapon" (?), "olive tree" (?)
ḥêth or ḥeṭ (ēta), "hedge, fence"
ṭêth (thēta), meaning uncertain
yōdh (iōta), "hand"
kaph (kappa), "palm of hand"
lāmedh (lambda), "ox-goad"
mēm (mu), "water"
nûn (nu), "fish"; cf. Ethiopian name nahās, "serpent"
sāmekh (sigma), "prop"
'ayin (o-mikron), "eye"
pēh (pi), "mouth"
ṣādhê (san), "fishhook"
qôph (koppa), "back of head" (?)
rēš (rhō), "head"; the Greek form apparently an abridgment of the more original Canaanite rôš
šîn(?), "tooth"; originally *tinnu, "composite bow"
tāw (tau), "mark"

**D. THE ORIGIN OF THE ALPHABET.** There
has certainly been no dearth of suggestions concerning the origin of the alphabet, whose supposed
sources range through Sumerian and Babylonian
cuneiform, the Cypriote syllabary, Hittite hieroglyphs, and Egyptian in all its written forms except
post-Christian Coptic. If one accepts the fact that
the Proto-Sinaitic script and its congeners are indeed
forms of the alphabet, the origin of the system cannot be put later than ca. 1500 B.C., or perhaps several
centuries earlier. This fact alone serves to rule out
many of the theories which have been advanced.

Since it is also certain that many, if not all, of the
original signs pictured a definite object, only comparisons with other hieroglyphic systems of writing
are cogent to the present discussion. It is only
natural, therefore, that Egypt, whose influence was
present in the Syro-Palestinian area from the third
millennium on, should be a prime suspect. During
the first half of the second millennium two types of
writing, hieroglyphic and its cursive variety hieratic,
were in use in Egypt; either could have been a
source of the alphabet, and there are many protagonists for each. Facts which oppose such a source,
however, are the following: (a) Egyptian had no alphabet per se which could be used as a model for
the Semitic system; (b) although correspondences in
form do occur between hieroglyphic Egyptian and
the pictorial stage of the alphabet, there are no correspondences in what these represent soundwise. As
has often been pointed out, hieroglyphic and hieratic
writing employs a combined total of well over a
thousand symbols, so that unless there is a correspondence between more than mere form, the idea
of direct borrowing is unprovable.

Much more plausible is the suggestion that the alphabet was invented under the stimulation of various
scripts, notably Egyptian, in the immediate neighborhood. Three possibilities exist: (a) hieroglyphic
Egyptian, (b) hieroglyphic Hittite, and (c) the still
undeciphered hieroglyphic-syllabic script used at
Byblos sometime during the period in question.
Many problems arise from a comparison of the early
alphabet with these scripts: the Sinaitic and still pictographic letter forms resemble Egyptian and Hittite
hieroglyphs most closely, but the Byblian signs include almost exact correspondents, formally, to the
later alphabetic forms discussed in § A above. But
these again are comparisons in form alone; and
without further evidence of systemic correspondence,

they are not too significant. The fact remains that nothing comparable to an alphabetic system of writing is known. We must accordingly see the alphabet as the invention of a single person or group of persons in Phoenicia or Palestine sometime during the first half of the second millennium B.C. The possibility of writing language by using a system of symbols corresponding to an arbitrary fragmentation of speech could have been suggested by any of the writing systems then in use, but the peculiar concept of partial representation—i.e., of consonants alone—is, so far as is known, common only to Egyptian writing, and it was perhaps from that quarter that the chief inspiration sprang. But due to the inventor's genius alone is the working out of a system, disencumbered of traditional extras, which has proved so flexible in subsequent world-wide adaptation.

E. *EPIGRAPHY.* Epigraphy is the study of written records which have survived from the ancient past. As such, epigraphy shares, and to a great extent subsumes, the data of other disciplines such as paleography and papyrology, but any narrower definition of the subject would not do justice to the divergent areas of study to which the term is currently applied.

While every facet of an inscription is of potential interest to the epigraphist, his attention is generally focused on the following categories of data, all of which are pertinent to the determination of the date and historical context of a given epigraph: (*a*) material on which the writing has survived, (*b*) tools and techniques employed in producing the original, (*c*) type of writing employed, (*d*) language in which the inscription is written, (*e*) relationship between language and writing (i.e., orthography), and (*f*) the type of inscription in regard to content and original purpose.

For further information on these subjects, *see,* in addition to the bibliography below, INSCRIPTIONS; WRITING AND WRITING MATERIALS.

*Bibliography.* General: D. Diringer, *The Alphabet* (1948). I. J. Gelb, *A Study of Writing* (1952). G. R. Driver, *Semitic Writing* (2nd ed., 1954).

Northwest Semitic: D. Diringer, *Le iscrizioni antico-ebraiche palestinesi* (1934). M. Dunand, *Byblia Grammata* (1945). F. M. Cross, Jr., and D. N. Freedman, *Early Hebrew Orthography* (1952). J. T. Milik and F. M. Cross, Jr., "Inscribed Javelin-heads from the Period of the Judges," *BASOR,* 134 (1954), 5-15. J. T. Milik, "An Unpublished Arrow-Head with Phoenician Inscription of the 11th-10th Century B.C.," *BASOR,* 143 (1956), 3-6.

Greek: R. Carpenter, "The Antiquity of the Greek Alphabet," *AJA,* 37 (1933), 8-29; "The Alphabet in Italy," *AJA,* 49 (1945), 452-64. G. Klaffenbach, *Griechische Epigraphik* (1957). R. M. Cook and A. G. Woodhead, "The Diffusion of the Greek Alphabet," *AJA,* 63 (1959), 175-78.

South Semitic: F. V. Winnett, *A Study of the Lihyanite and Thamudic Inscriptions* (1937). W. F. Albright, "The Chaldean Inscriptions in Proto-Arabic Script," *BASOR,* 128 (1952), 39-45. A. Jamme, W. F., "An Early South-Arabian Inscription in Vertical Columns," *BASOR,* 137 (1955), 32-38. G. W. Van Beek, "A Radiocarbon Date for Early South Arabic," *BASOR,* no. 143 (1956).

Earliest forms: W. F. Albright, "The Early Alphabetic Inscriptions from Sinai and Their Decipherment," *BASOR,* 110 (1948), 6-22. A. Goetze, "A Seal Cylinder with an Early Alphabetic Inscription," *BASOR,* 129 (1953), 8-11. F. M. Cross, Jr., "The Evolution of the Proto-Canaanite Alphabet," *BASOR,* 134 (1954), 15-24.

Order and names: A. M. Honeyman, "The Letter-Order of the Semitic Alphabets in Africa and the Near East," *Africa* 22 (1952), 136-47. J. Ryckmans, "L'origine et l'ordre de lettres de l'alphabet éthiopien," *Bibliotheca Orientalis,* 1 (1955), 2-8, and cf. comments by Ullendorff, pp. 217-19. W. M. Hallo, "Isaiah 28:9-13 and the Ugaritic Abecedaries," *JBL,* 77 (1958), 324-38.                    T. O. LAMBDIN

**ALPHAEUS** ăl fē'əs ['Αλφαῖος]. A purely Greek name, one of many such names used commonly by first-century Jews in Palestine. Westcott and Hort accepting the supposition that it is a transliteration of the Aramaic חלפי, give this name a rough breathing. This is, however, only an assumption, and not a necessary one. The name does not occur in the OT but it does occur five times in the NT. These divide readily into references to two separate individuals both of whom are mentioned only indirectly.

**1.** The father of Levi (Mark 2:14). If, by comparison of Matt. 9:9; Mark 2:14; Luke 5:27, it is thought that Levi and Matthew are the same individual, then this Alphaeus cannot be identified with the father of James (2 *below*), because Matt. 10:3; Mark 3:18 show an Alphaeus who is father of James but not of Matthew. Even if Levi be identified with Matthew it tells us nothing more about Alphaeus father of Levi. The NT offers no more data on this Alphaeus.

In Mark 2:14, D, Θ, and Φ read 'Ιάκωβον ("James") for "Levi," but this is probably no more than scribal effort to harmonize this passage with Mark 3:18 and parallels. The preponderant weight of MS evidence supports the reading Λευείν ("Levi").

**2.** The father of James (Matt. 10:3; Mark 3:18; Luke 6:15; Acts 1:13). The first three of these passages are Synoptic parallels and indicate nothing more than that Alphaeus is the father of the James who in the Mark and Matthew passages is clearly distinguished from James son of Zebedee. The same distinction is made in Acts 1:13.

Past efforts to identify this Alphaeus with Clopas (John 19:25) and with Cleopas (Luke 24:18) are quite arbitrary and rest upon no firm evidence. Κλεόπας (Luke 24:18) is a contraction of Κλεόπατρος, a purely Greek name, and is not to be identified with Κλωπᾶς (John 19:25), which is of Aramaic origin. Κλωπᾶς cannot be reduced to the same Hebrew original as Alphaeus; hence they cannot be identified.

J. M. NORRIS

**ALTANEUS.** KJV Apoc. form of MATTENAI 2.

\*ALTAR.

**1. Terminology.** The word מזבח, formed from the verb for "slaughter" (i.e., to cut up the animal killed according to Jewish ritual) is the most prevalent designation of the altar—independent of the sacrifice made on it. One might conclude from Gen. 22:9 that the animal to be sacrificed was given the killing blow after it had been laid down bound on the logs of the altar. But even if this may once have been a sacrificial rite (in the early days), it was soon given up especially since the jerking victim might break down the stacked-up logs of wood. The killing of the animal in front of the altar became absolutely necessary if the blood was to be collected and sprinkled on the horns of the altar. This is assumed in Lev. 1–7 and is also true of animal sacrifices on the altars without horns, as I Sam. 14:34-35; I Kings 18:23 indicate. Accordingly מזבח (with a מ location only indirectly applying) means the spot on which the pieces (and the fat) of the animal, which had already been cut up, were deposited and burned. The OT distinguishes between the following types of altars according to the material: the altar of earth (Exod. 20:24), the altar of stone (vs. 25), the bronze altar (II Kings 16:15 and repeatedly). The altar intended for the burning of incense was called "altar of incense" (מזבח קטרת; Exod. 30:27; cf. II Chr. 30:14), which is treated, along with חמנים, under INCENSE ALTAR.

**2. Descriptions in the OT.** Particulars are lacking concerning the form of the altar of earth, which is assumed in Exod. 20:24 as the normal one (in the preroyal period in Palestine?). It should probably be thought of as a relatively low cube of clods of clay, not as one out of air-dried bricks, since otherwise the expression "brick altar" would appear. In any case, in Palestine, which was rich in stones, the altar of stone (מזבח אבנים) was probably more common, not only among the Israelites, but also among the Canaanites (cf. Deut. 12:3). The rites indicate which god the worship concerned (cf. I Kings 8:22 with 18:24); the altar of Gideon (Judg. 6:24) bore the name: "Yahweh is peace."

In addition to the colorless "make," the term "build" is most commonly used for the erection of an altar (in the case of destroying, "tear down"). These terms, also used of the construction of houses, indicate that in the case of a "built" altar—even where no more particulars are given—one should imagine an altar of stone (Num. 23:1; Deut. 27:5-6; Josh. 8:31; Isa. 27:9). Understandably they used for this purpose the natural (unhewn) stones lying around on the ground just as they were found. Such stone altars could be erected in a short time (Judg. 21:4; I Sam. 14:33) and also fell to pieces if they were not taken care of for constant use. The number of stones used was of no significance. It depended on the size of the stones collected and the desired dimensions of the altar. By way of exception, there is mention in I Kings 18:31-32 of twelve stones of the Elijah altar, but this secondary statement might have developed out of the Sinai tradition in Exod. 24:4, where there is mention of an altar erected by Moses and, in addition to this, of twelve stones set up to represent the tribes of Israel (cf. Josh. 4). That the stones are to be unhewn is expressly commanded in Exod. 20:25. This could be directed against the luxury of square stones; but the idea that stone used in worship should not lose its special numinous quality by damaging hewing is probably also the basis of this practice. The Deuteronomist in Deut. 27:5-6; Josh. 8:31 (cf. later I Macc. 4:46) refers to the restriction in Exod. 20:25. Without a doubt, this prohibition did not prevail permanently. The very fact that we know of the "horns" of the altar (cf. I Kings 1:50)—Maṣṣēbôth, "pillars," once originally set at the four corners?—proves that the stones were hewn. (The incense altars which are known archaeologically in Palestine from the time of the Israelites were also hewn!) The precise statements of dimensions of certain altars (i.e., in Jerusalem) also prove it. The pro-

test (in vain) against steps in the case of monumental altars (Exod. 20:26) is based on the danger that the one who was making the sacrifice might expose his nakedness. This was prevented by a special law affecting dress (Lev. 6:10). The Jerusalem burnt-offering altar explains the fact that in Lev. 9:22 the "stepping down" of the priest is mentioned without hesitation.

Very much more infrequently than an altar built of several stones (stone heap), in the early period a large rock (in I Sam. 6:14 "a great stone") was used as an altar, for this was possible only if the stone had a sufficiently large supporting area. Of the examples mentioned for this, that of the altar of Manoah (Judg. 13:19) is pertinent. On the other hand, the rock (with holes for bowls) which bore the mealtime offerings in Judg. 6:19-21 is *not* designated as an altar (in contrast to the altar built later by Gideon in vs. 24).

We have further particulars about the burnt-offering altar in Jerusalem. It stood in front of the temple (and is not to be confused with the altar of David on the threshing floor of Ornan—in spite of I Chr. 22:1). The old archive note concerning Solomon's cycle of offerings in I Kings 9:25 designates the altar as one which Solomon had built; this indicates an altar of stones. When, in the Deuteronomic note in I Kings 8:64 (corresponding to II Kings 16:15), it is called a bronze altar, this appears to mean a grate of copper which was set on top of it (*see below*). The Deuteronomic statement of the consecration of the middle of the court before the temple by Solomon for the innumerable sacrifices (I Kings 8:63-64) does not signify that there were henceforth two altars. This statement is, on the contrary, connected with King Ahaz' regulations for worship; it was inconceivable to the Deuteronomist that the altar of Solomon, which was pushed aside by Ahaz because of its small size, could have been adequate in the beginning. The statement in II Kings 16:10 ff, taken from the original temple annals, says the following: King Ahaz, who was giving submission to Tiglath-pileser III, saw in Damascus (in the court of a temple of Ramman?) an altar which so impressed him that he passed a description on to Uriah the high priest with the command that it be copied. Uriah built this altar in Jerusalem. In order that this could take place, the bronze altar was moved aside and set up to one side. Since the dedicatory sacrifices of the king undoubtedly took place on the new (great) altar, and the direction to make *all* sacrifices for the king and the people upon the great altar can only be interpreted to mean that the Ahaz altar displaced Solomon's. No matter what II Kings 16:15 has to say about the bronze altar (which still existed in 593; cf. Ezek. 9:2), it plays only a secondary role. In any case, Ahaz wanted to preserve tradition; on the other hand, he wanted to possess a modern "Yahweh" altar. The Deuteronomist sees no reason for complaint, perhaps, since the legitimate worship of Yahweh was continued. No particulars are given concerning the appearance of the (stone) altar accessible by steps. The (supplementary) use of bronze is therefore improbable, because the king saw himself forced—because of the tribute to the Assyrian king—to have the bronze portions of the existing vessels of worship melted.

Strangely enough, nothing is said in I Kings 6 ff about the bronze altar of Solomon, which was used in its proper place for approximately two hundred years. One would expect a note about it in connection with other bronze works, and it does appear in the "parallel account" of Chronicles (II Chr. 4:1). The form of the statement of its dimensions, which deviates from the usual wording of the Chronicles, corresponds to that of the building dimensions in I Kings 6, so that one may surmise that II Chr. 4:1 was borrowed from the account in the book of Kings —between I Kings 7:22 and 7:23—and (for reasons which cannot be explained with certainty) was omitted there (it is missing already in the LXX). Unfortunately II Chr. 4:1 is put very concisely. The bronze altar made by Solomon was said to be twenty cubits long, twenty cubits wide, and ten cubits high. What on this cube was of bronze? Scarcely the sides as plates; more likely a side (and top?) grating (cf. Exod. 27:4) and probably only a large grate standing on low feet and ornamented with corner horns. The height agrees, to be sure, with the altar described in Ezek. 43:13 ff, but not the length or the breadth; and there is no mention at all in II Chr. 4:1 of the fact that the bronze altar of Solomon was tapered from bottom to top in steps or sections. Probably, after the building of the new altar of Ahaz, interest in a detailed description of the old altar (which had been put aside) dwindled. If—and this is by no means certain—the plan for the altar in Ezek. 43:13 ff is based on an actual altar in Jerusalem, it may possibly have been that of Ahaz, but not that of Solomon.

The secondary passage (Ezek. 43:13-17), attached to the Ezekiel vision of the new temple in chs. 40 ff, reads as follows (orig. tr.): "These are the measurements [better, 'dimensions'] of the altar in cubits— the cubit reckoned as one cubit plus a handbreadth— its base [read חיקו] one cubit and one cubit its breadth, and its rim at the edge one span. And this is the height [instead of MT 'mound'] of the altar from the base on the ground to the small enclosure, two cubits and a breadth of one cubit, and from the small enclosure to the large enclosure four cubits and a breadth of one cubit [thus LXX]. And up to the sacrifice socle [stage] were four cubits, and from the sacrifice socle upward were four horns [addition from vs. 16] on its four sides. And the sacrifice socle was twelve cubits long by twelve cubits broad, a square, and the [supply 'large'] enclosure was fourteen cubits long by fourteen broad on its four sides, [supply as follows: 'and the small enclosure was sixteen (cubits) in length by sixteen in breadth on its four sides,'] and the rim around it was a half cubit and the base of it, one cubit round about. And its steps face to the east." Seen as a whole, the description is consistent and clear, so that one can sketch a picture of this altar (Fig. ALT 19).* First comes the "bosom of the earth," the foundation bed (a Babylonian term) as a depression into which the altar block is placed, so that all that remains of it is a gutter. Then follow the three socles (stages), which become smaller toward the top. The two lower ones are called "enclosures," or "incasings"; this recalls the Babylonian term "cover" for the burnt brick of the outer face of the tower of Babel. The uppermost socle is called אריאל

19. Stevens-Wright reconstruction of the altar of burnt offering

("Ariel"), which one may associate with the Babylonian word *arallu* (underworld and mountain of the gods). Instead of "hearth," which is surely incorrect, we have paraphrased אריאל with "sacrifice socle." The steps of the altar might presumably have led up to the upper edge of the sacrifice socle, so that the sacrificing priest could move about on the upper surface of the socle (cf. Middoth III.1a). Since it is a question of the altar of the future in the vision, it must remain an open question as to whether the description is based on definite earlier data concerning the Ahaz altar (*see above*) or on the postexilic altar used in 515 B.C., or whether it was drawn up quite independently. The remarkable thing in the case of this altar design, indeed, is that its type is unique. To be sure, there are in the area of the ancient Orient and Egypt altar terraces reached by steps, and altars with an offset (also called stepped altars), but not square altars which taper upward uniformly in offsets like a stepped tower. On the other hand, the stepped tower (ziggurat—the best known example is that of Babylon*—*see* BABEL, TOWER OF) represents an elevated terrace (a mountain of the gods), at the very top of which is a temple (cella), and it was never—as a whole—regarded as a large altar. It is true that isolated sacrifices were made on top in front of the cella and on the roof of the chamber of the gods, also, in addition—according to the evidence of Assyrian seals—naturally, below *in front* of the tower; but the reinterpretation of a stepped tower as an altar, as it appears in Ezek. 43, is without precedent. One might reckon with the possibility of a stepped-tower altar on a late painting from Dura-Europos, though the offerings are missing in the picture. A description of the Jerusalem altar for burnt offerings, which in point of time follows the representation in the vision in Ezek. 43, stemming from the time of the Romans, differs from it. According to Josephus (War V.v.6), the altar of the Herodian temple was a block fifty by fifty by fifteen cubits, hence simpler and larger, and had a ramp approach. The Mishnah treatise Middoth (III.1 ff), which concerns the same altar, distinguishes three offsets (as Ezek. 43), but with the dimensions thirty-two by thirty-two by one cubit for the base and thirty by thirty by five cubits for the main block; the measurements of the third offset are not quite clear, but they are smaller than those of the main block, in any case. According to Middoth III, it is a matter of an extension of the pre-exilic (Solomonic) altar which had already taken place at the time of the return of the exiles from Babylon (related to Ezra 3:2). Figs. TEM 27; BAB 10.

The showbread table (the table for the bread of the Presence), which I Kings 6:20; 7:48 mention and which (with horns) measured two by two by three cubits in Ezek. 41:22, is a presentation altar. The showbread table of the wilderness sanctuary was supposed to have been half as large, according to Exod. 25:23 ff.

**3. Archaeological discoveries.** If we disregard the rock altar found at Taanach and the rock altar in the outer area of Tell el-Mutesselim ( = Megiddo; K. Galling, *Der Altar in den Kulturen des Alten Orients* [1925], plate 11, fig. 1), which are problematic in formation and also with regard to interpretation, there do, nevertheless, exist, thanks to the stratigraphic excavation in Megiddo, at other places in Palestine and in Syria, examples of altars secure enough in their dating, which can be used for comparison with the descriptions in the OT. They are arranged in chronological order below.

In stratum XIX of Megiddo (G. Loud, *Megiddo II* [1948], pp. 60-64) there was uncovered a broad-room temple (dimensions: *ca.* 5 by 8 meters), on the rear wall of which—exactly opposite the entrance—was unearthed a platform, which was enlarged in the second phase of its utilization to 1.6 by 4.1 by 0.92 meters, with a step (0.7 by 1.9 by 0.5 meters) before it.* This must probably be regarded as a table altar (deposit altar), also possibly intended for images of gods. According to Albright and Wright (cf. *ANEP* 729), the stratum, and along with it the temple, should be dated *ca.* 3000 B.C. The altar, built of stones and plastered, in an Early Bronze period shrine located close to the city wall in Ai (et-Tell), might be a scant half millennium newer. It measures 0.80 by 1.70 by 0.70 meters and should probably be regarded less as a deposit altar (table altar) than as a burnt-offering altar (Fig. TEM 42). In a temple area of stratum XV-XIII in Megiddo (G. Loud, *Megiddo II* [1948], pp. 73-84; cf. *ANEP* 734) which was constructed in the Middle Bronze period between *ca.* 2000 and 1700 B.C., and enlarged in the course of time, the oldest installation was an open courtyard. In it was erected an altar of stones and rubble—at first more elliptical, later almost round—which measured not less than 8 meters in diameter and was preserved to 1.40 meters high. At one spot four steps in a stairway cut into the stone led up to the level which was to be mounted by those making the sacrifices. One may assume that burnt offerings were also presented on this uncovered altar.* Of the (covered) temples in the immediate vicinity the main room of the W temple had at the back a flat mud-brick altar table, 4.00 by 5.00 by 0.50 meters in size. It is noteworthy that in the rebuilding of the main interior room (dated with stratum XIII) the altar of this N temple appears as the platform of a cella. This indicates that not only offerings but also images of gods were probably placed upon this altar even earlier. Figs. TEM 41; ALT 20; MEG 27.

In the temple area in Beth-shan (A. Rowe, *The Topography and History of Beth-shan* [1930], pp. 10-14; cf. *ANEP* 732), where the various strata are unclear and therefore difficult to date, in the area (fifteenth-

Courtesy of the Oriental Institute, the University of Chicago

20. Burnt-offering altar at Megiddo as rebuilt in Stratum XVI; originally built in Stratum XVII and continued in use through Stratum XIV (i.e., from perhaps *ca.* 2500-1800 B.C.)

fourteenth century B.C.) usually designated the Mekal temple after an Egyptian stela which was found there, bearing the name of the god, there is in one corner of the main courtyard an irregular structure accessible by steps, which should probably be considered a (burnt-offering) altar. Within strata VII-VIIA at Megiddo, which should be dated between the fifteenth and the twelfth centuries, there has been uncovered a long-room temple (with tower bastions, the so-called Migdol-temple type) which had been repeatedly rebuilt. In the second and third phases it had on the rear wall a platform which was intended for *deposita* (and images of gods; G. Loud, *Megiddo II* [1948], pp. 102-5; cf. *ANEP* 735). No altar (for burnt offerings) was found in the excavated area in front of the temple, although one would assume that there was such a one on the basis of the analogous temple structure in Alalakh (Atchana) in Syria (*see below*). In a section of excavation area DD in stratum VIII of Megiddo (G. Loud, *Megiddo II* [1948], pp. 113-14) in what should be regarded as the court of the temple, a partially lime-plastered mud-brick table or altar (1.10 by 1.10 by 0.55 meters) was found. It suggests the fire hearth (altar?) of Tell 'Ajjul (F. Petrie, *Ancient Gaza I* [1931], plate 6) and corresponds to the low mud-brick platform in the axis in front of the great temple at Shechem (dimensions: 2.20 by 1.30 by 0.30 meters) which must certainly be regarded as an altar (E. Sellin, "Die Ausgrabung von Sichem," *ZDPV*, 49 [1926], 312).

In the moat of the city of Lachish a long-room temple which should be dated between 1450 and 1250 was found. In addition to deposit shelves and niches on the back wall, it had an elevated "holy of holies," and in the last phase there was in front of this shrine a mud-brick altar which was approached at the side by means of steps. The altar was 0.80 by 0.80 by 1.00 meters in size. Since the temple had a roof, burnt offerings can only have been presented at this altar if the roof had a sufficiently large vent (O. Tufnell *et al.*, *Lachish II* [1940], plate 10; *cf. ANEP* 731). In stratum V (sixteenth to fifteenth century) L. Woolley discovered in Alalakh in Syria

(L. Woolley, *A Forgotten Kingdom* [1953], plate 10*a*) a temple in which there was a mud-brick altar (*ca.* 0.60 by 0.50 by 0.45 meters) next to a bench. It had a shallow depression on the top surface and was—to judge by the traces of burning—intended for burnt offerings. The stone altar in front of the Baal temple in Ugarit-Syria, which was approached by two steps, was indented on the top surface in a similar fashion (*Syria,* no. 16 [1935], plate 36). It was situated before the long-room temple, in its axis. This is also the position of the altar, which measured *ca.* 0.10 by 1.00 by 0.70 in front of the temple of stratum III (fourteenth century) in Alalakh (L. Woolley, *A Forgotten Kingdom* [1953], fig. 20).

The altar in Hazor (dimensions: *ca.* 40 by 90 by 40 inches), which consists of a single huge limestone block weighing *ca.* five tons, is unique; half of its top surface is hollowed out for solid offerings and burnt offerings; and besides that it had a rectangular basin carved out, which was probably intended to receive the blood or for liquid offerings (Fig. ALT 21). The altar block stood in a sanctuary area of the end of the Late Bronze Age.

Courtesy of Yigael Yadin: The James A. de Rothschild Expedition at Hazor, The Hebrew University, Jerusalem, Israel

21. Canaanite limestone altar from Hazor (fourteenth-thirteenth century B.C.)

In Sar'a, *ca.* 13.5 miles W of Jerusalem, there stands, even today, on the open terrain a stone block hewn from an outcropping of natural rock which was certainly used as an altar. The period when it was fashioned cannot be determined. It is probably correct to regard it as the altar on which Manoah, the father of Samson, offered a sacrifice, according to Judg. 13:19. The altar consists of an approximately rectangular block of 2.16 by 2.16 by 1.30 meters with a platform 0.27 meters high, but smaller. The unfilled gap in one corner of the platform was surely not the station of the priest, but was intended instead for the erection of an incense altar (K. Galling, *Der Altar in den Kulturen des Alten Orients* [1925], plate 12, fig. 15*f*).

In Hamath on the Orontes in open country between the castle gate and the two palaces a sharply hewn altar block (*ca.* 0.70 by 1.35 by 1.06 meters)

was found (cf. H. Ingholt, *Rapport preliminaire sur sept campagnes de fouilles a Hama en Syrie* [1940], pp. 90, 108). Like a throne, it has a low "railing" on three sides. On the upper surface two low round pedestals have been left free. Whether bowls for sacrifices or the like were set on them or whether images of gods stood here (in which case it would not be an altar) cannot be determined with certainty. The basalt block, which is called an altar by the excavators, should probably be dated to the ninth or eighth century.

The numerous places of worship at Petra, most of which also have an altar hewn out of natural rock for the sacrifices presented, stem from a very much more recent period (the Greek or Roman era) which cannot, however, be established exactly.* A large, almost level courtyard, with benches for those taking part in the ceremony, occupies the center of the "high place" of Zibb'Atuf. On the W side there was an unevenly cut-out altar for liquid offerings (*Altorientalische Bilder zum AT,* fig. 447) and immediately beside it a stepped altar (1.83 by 2.72 by 0.95 meters). The depression in the middle (0.35 by 1.08 by 0.17 meters) was presumably intended for a stone pillar (*maṣṣēbâh*). The altar could be approached by those making sacrifices by means of a stairway of four steps hewn out of the rock, which led halfway up the altar. On the top of el-Me'esara next to the ceremonial place a stepped altar was hewn out; it measured 2.43 by 3.00 by 0.95 meters (three steps in front of it). In the middle there is a small hump, reduced in size by weathering, of *ca.* 1.10 meters in diameter and 0.25 meters in height. This might well be the remaining vestige of a formerly (rectangular?) higher stone pillar (*maṣṣēbâh;* K. Galling, *Altar* . . . [1925], plate 12, fig. 12: cf. H. Gressmann, *Altorientalische Bilder zum AT* [1927], fig. 449). A similar altar at the same place is shown in *Altorientalische Bilder zum AT,* fig. 453 (K. Galling, *Altar* . . . [1925], plate 11, fig. 5*f*); in this case the stone pillar is attached to the back, so to speak. In spite of the difference in time and place, the legitimate and the illegitimate (the true and the false) "holy high places" often mentioned in the OT may be thought of as similar to the places of worship at Petra. Fig. HIG 23.

*Cf.* INCENSE ALTAR.

**Bibliography.** G. Dalman, *Petra und seine Felsheiligtümer* (1908); R. Kittel, *Studien zur hebräischen Archaeologie* (1908); J. de Groot, *Die Altäre des salomonischen Tempelhofes* (1924); K. Galling, *Der Altar in den Kulturen des Alten Orients* (1925); the same in G. Fohrer and K. Galling, *Ezechiel,* HAT, 13 (2nd ed., 1955), 237 ff. W. F. Albright, *Archeology and the Religion of Israel* (2nd ed., 1946); *Die Religion Israels im Lichte der archaeologischen Ausgrabungen* (1956).          K. GALLING

**AL TASCHITH** ăl tăs'kĭth. *See* MUSIC § B1*c.*

**ALUSH** ā'lŭsh [אלוש] (Num. 33:13). A station of Israel in their journey through the wilderness, between Dophkah and Rephidim. It has not been identified.

**ALVAH** ăl'və [עלוה; LXX Γωλα] (Gen. 36:40). Alternately: **ALIAH** ăl'ĭ ə [עליה] (I Chr. 1:51). The second of eleven clan chiefs (אלופים; KJV "dukes")

of Esauites dwelling in Edom. Perhaps this name is the same as ALVAN (עלון in Gen. 36:23; עליו [Alian] in I Chr. 1:40; note the prevalence of nunnation in the proper names in Gen. 36:20-30). L. HICKS

**ALVAN** ăl'vən [עלון; LXX Γωλων] (Gen. 36:23). Alternately: ALIAN ăl'ĭ ən [עליו] (I Chr. 1:40). Ancestor of a Horite subclan in Edom; the first son of the clan chief SHOBAL.

**AMAD** ā'măd [עמעד] (Josh. 19:26). A town in the territory of Asher. Its location is unknown.

**AMADATHA.** KJV form of HAMMEDATHA.

**AMAL** ā'məl [עמל, trouble(?)] (I Chr. 7:35). A son of Heler in the genealogy of Asher.

**AMALEK** ăm'ə lĕk [עמלק; *relationship to* Arab. *'imlâqu, 'amâliqa, strictly secondary*]; AMALEKITES ə măl'ə kīts. A nomadic tribe, descendants of Esau.

1. Origin
2. Territory
3. Early history
4. Amalek and Israel
   a. During the Exodus
   b. In the period of the judges
   c. In the period of Saul and David
Bibliography

**1. Origin.** Amalek is recorded as one of the grandsons of Esau, or, more specifically, the son of Eliphaz by his concubine Timna (Gen. 36:12; I Chr. 1:36). Amalek is also designated as one of the "clans" (אלוף; RSV "chiefs") of Eliphaz in the land of Edom (Gen. 36:16). Amalekite origins are thus traced back in biblical tradition into the early ancestry of the Edomites, and their aboriginal habitat to the land of Edom. Some scholars have identified the Amalekites with the inhabitants of the land of Melukhkha, whose name occurs in the cuneiform inscriptions of the late third millennium (*ca.* 2250-2000 B.C.). This identification is based on the false notion that Melukhkha was the Sinai Peninsula and W Arabia region, whereas it was probably located in NW India (*see bibliography*), as shown by discoveries in Babylonia, the Persian Gulf, and the W coast of India.

**2. Territory.** Throughout their entire known history, the Amalekites were primarily a nomadic desert tribe, ranging the desolate wastes from Sinai and the Negeb of S Canaan to the Arabah N of Ezion-geber and inner Arabia. The scope of Amalekite wanderings is summed up in I Sam. 15:7, which refers to the extent of Saul's conquest of this tribe as "from Havilah as far as Shur, which is east of Egypt"—i.e., from the desert interior of the N Arabian Nejd to the region N of modern Suez in Egypt. This appears to be the same territory which biblical tradition also attributed to the ISHMAELITES (cf. Gen. 25:18). On occasion the Amalekites penetrated into Palestine as far N as the hill country of Ephraim (Judg. 12:15) and as far W as the Philistine country around Ziklag (I Sam. 30:1-2).

**3. Early history.** The Amalekites were already active in the Negeb of Judah near Beer-sheba during

the early second millennium B.C. (Gen. 14:7). In this vicinity, significantly called the "country of the Amalekites," the coalition of kings under the leadership of Chedorlaomer is said to have subdued Amalek on the way homeward through Palestine. Some scholars consider the mention of Amalekites in this early context anachronistic; but according to Num. 24:20, Amalek is described as the "first of the nations," obviously attesting to their antiquity as viewed from *ca.* the thirteenth century B.C. The essential historicity of the account preserved in Gen. 14 is becoming increasingly acknowledged by recent scholarship. The appearance of the Amalekites in the patriarchal period agrees with the genealogical origin posited by the lists in Gen. 36, which were certainly compiled not later than the tenth century B.C.

**4. Amalek and Israel.** *a. During the Exodus.* Hostilities between Amalek and Israel began during the thirteenth century when the Amalekites attacked the Israelites coming out from Egypt at Rephidim (Exod. 17:8-9). Probably they were seeking to defend Kadesh from Israelite occupation, in order to protect their caravan routes linking Arabia and Egypt. The Deuteronomist informs us that the Amalekites took advantage of the weariness of the Hebrews by ruthlessly cutting down those who lagged behind (Deut. 25:17-19). Because of Amalek's merciless behavior, a special enmity developed between the two peoples, resulting in the former's being made an exception to the law of holy war (Deut. 20:10-18; 25: 19; *see* WAR, IDEAS OF). Nowhere in biblical tradition do we find Amalek and Israel on friendly terms; and throughout their history Israel preserved the memory of how Amalek had tried to oppose their entrance into Palestine (Judg. 10:12; I Sam. 15:2).

The defeat of the Amalekites gave Israel unmolested possession of Kadesh-barnea and its environs, but it by no means precluded future conflict with the same people. When the spies whom Moses sent out to survey the land of Canaan returned with their report, they expressed grave misgivings concerning the strength of the inhabitants, among whom they mentioned the Amalekites (Num. 13:29). Their formidable nature is acknowledged in a passage in which Yahweh commands the Israelites to change their direction of march from N to S because "the Amalekites and the Canaanites dwell in the valleys" (Num. 14:25). Some of the Hebrews rashly ignored the divine command and proceeded to invade the hill country of Judah, whereupon they were repulsed by both the Amalekites and the Canaanites, who pursued them as far as Hormah (Num. 14:41-45). A little later, some of the men of Judah fought successfully against the Canaanites (Judg. 1:9), and we are told that the descendants of Moses' father-in-law—i.e., the Kenites—went up with the people of Judah into the wilderness which lies in the Negeb near Arad and settled among the Amalekites (emending the text to read העמלקי instead of העם, "the people"), where they are still found in the time of Saul (I Sam. 15:6).

*b. In the period of the judges.* The first well-attested appearance of the Amalekites in Transjordan is during the early period of the judges, when they seem to assume a mercenary role in conjunction with the semisedentary Moabites and Ammonites. Eglon king of Moab had organized a coalition against Israel which invaded W Palestine as far as the CITY OF PALMS (Judg. 3:13). During this period of Moabite harassment of Israel an Amalekite enclave may have become established in the land of Ephraim near Pirathon (12:15). The MT of Judg. 5:14 (cf. KJV) would seem to relate Amalek and Ephraim, but the text is so obscure that no definite conclusion can be drawn (cf. RSV).

The Amalekites appear at the beginning of the eleventh century B.C. in company with the Midianites in the first known camel-nomad razzia to invade and pillage the settled agricultural communities of W Palestine (Judg. 6:3, 33; 7:12; see CAMEL). Although Gideon was finally able to disperse this menace to Israelite sedentary life, the Amalekites remained a constant threat to Israelite security, even after stronger political authority had been established.

*c. In the period of Saul and David.* One of the first tasks confronting Saul after he had been anointed king over Israel was to wage war against Amalek (I Sam. 15). After passing his forces in review at TELAIM, Saul advanced to the "city of Amalek" (vs. 5; its name and situation are unknown, and this is the only instance in the biblical narrative where the Amalekites are apparently associated with a sedentary occupation, although the reference may be only to a fortified village or encampment), where, after warning the Kenites to depart from among the Amalekites, he attacked Amalek, smiting them from Havilah to Shur. The latter is probably a geographical hyperbole, although the expanse of territory indicated may actually have been traversed by the Amalekites in their various wanderings. After Saul defeated them, he is reported to have slain all survivors except the king, AGAG, whose name is the only Amalekite proper name so far known.

The failure of Saul to exterminate Amalek left the latter free to continue raids against the settled communities in S Judah. While David dwelt at Gath with Achish, he is said to have made raids against the Amalekites, leaving neither man nor woman alive, and carrying off much spoil (I Sam. 27:8-9). But the Amalekites were not easily defeated. Upon returning to Ziklag, David discovered that a party of them had taken advantage of the absence of fighting men to burn the city, leading women and children away captive (30:1-2). Among the former were David's two wives, Ahinoam and Abigail. Quickly David mustered a rescue expedition, and through the help of a young Egyptian lad (described as servant of an Amalekite whom the latter had left behind because of illness), David and his host were enabled to surprise the Amalekite camp, and slay all except four hundred young men, who mounted camels and fled. David then recovered all the spoil that had been taken, and rescued his two wives (vss. 17-18).

According to one biblical tradition, Saul, at his own request, was slain by an Amalekite, who subsequently went to David bearing tidings of the king's death, presumably in hope of some reward (II Sam. 1:1-10; but cf. I Sam. 31:1-6; II Sam. 4:9-10). However, David had the Amalekite killed (or killed him himself; cf. II Sam. 4:10), because he had dared to destroy the Lord's anointed (1:14). In all probability

the Amalekite had been a mercenary in the Philistine army.

Further conflict with the Amalekites after David became king is attested in a summary of David's conquests preserved in II Sam. 8 (cf. vs. 12; I Chr. 18:11). With the firm establishment of the United Monarchy and the organization of a strong political system, it would appear that Israel effectively stopped Amalekite raids. Only once more do we hear of Amalekite hostility; Amalek is mentioned as a member of a conspiracy against Israel, although the historical context is not clear (Ps. 83:7—H 83:8). By the time of Hezekiah (late eighth century), only a "remnant of the Amalekites" remained, and they suffered defeat at the hands of five hundred Simeonites in Mount Seir—i.e., Edom (I Chr. 4:43). Thus, according to biblical tradition, Amalekite history ended where it seems to have begun: in the land of Edom.

No reliable accounts of the Amalekites are preserved outside the OT. Archaeological exploration and excavation have so far thrown no light upon them.

*Bibliography.* E. Meyer, *Die Israeliten und ihre Nachbarstämme* (1906), pp. 63, 81, 133, 164, 346-47, 389-99; A. Musil, *The Northern Heğâz* (1926), pp. 259-62; F.-M. Abel, *Géographie de la Palestine,* I (1933), 270-73, 358-59; J. Montgomery, *Arabia and the Bible* (1934), p. 20, n. 37.

On Melukhkha, see: E. Weidner, "Das Reich Sargons von Akkad," *AFO,* 16 (1952), 6-7; A. L. Oppenheim, "The Seafaring Merchants of Ur," *JAOS,* 74 (1954), 6-17 (now confirmed by recent discoveries). G. M. LANDES

**AMAM** ā′măm [אמם] (Josh. 15:26). A city in SW Judah; the site is unknown.

**AMAN** ā′mən. Douay Version form of HAMAN.

**AMANA** ə mā′nə [אמנה] (Song of S. 4:8). A mountain peak in the Anti-lebanon range, probably S of the valley of the river of Amana (or Abana).

**AMARIAH** ăm′ə rī′ə [אמריהו, אמריה, Y has spoken, promised]; KJV Apoc. AMARIAS —əs, ZAMBIS zăm′bĭs. A frequent OT name, especially in post-exilic priest lists.

**1.** One of the sons of Hebron, under the division of Kohath, in the Chronicler's listing of the Levitical houses in the time of David (I Chr. 23:19; 24:23).

**2.** Chief priest during the reign of Jehoshaphat (II Chr. 19:11). His father is not named.

**3.** Son of Hezekiah; great-grandfather of Zephaniah the prophet (Zeph. 1:1).

**4.** A subordinate Levite in the time of Hezekiah (II Chr. 31:15); one of six assistants appointed to help in the distribution of offerings.

**5.** The name appears twice in the Chronicler's list of Aaronic chief priests from Aaron to the Exile (I Chr. 6). Though a trio of names recurs as successive generations in two different places (vss. 7-8, 11-12), one hesitates to dismiss one Amariah as the mere offspring of dittography.

Amariah ben Meraioth is succeeded by Ahitub, Zadok, and Ahimaaz (I Chr. 6:7—H 5:33). This early portion of the list is repeated later in the same chapter and there stops with Ahimaaz (I Chr. 6:52

—H 6:37). This Amariah cannot be identical with 1 *above.*

Amariah ben Azariah was also chief priest—presumably during the middle monarchy—and was succeeded by Ahitub, Zadok, and Shallum (I Chr. 6:11—H 5:37). The parenthetical note (vs. 10) should probably be applied to the Azariah of vs. 9, making this Amariah approximately contemporary with Jehoshaphat and perhaps the same as 2 *above.* He appears again in the abbreviated version of this list in the Ezra genealogy (Ezra 7:3), which is in turn repeated in I Esd. 8:2; II Esd. 1:2; but each time his father or his son is different from both the Chronicles and the Ezra versions.

It would seem difficult to defend the exact accuracy of this high-priest list.

**6.** The name appears three times in closely related lists of priests in the book of Nehemiah. It is difficult to know whether they are separate individuals, priestly groups or families, or eponymous ancestors. The references are to: (*a*) one of the signers of the covenant (Neh. 10:3—H 10:4); (*b*) a priest who returned with Zerubbabel (Neh. 12:2); and (*c*) a priest group in the time of Joiakim (Neh. 12:13).

**7.** Son of Shephatiah of Judah; an ancestor of Athaiah, who volunteered to live in Jerusalem (Neh. 11:4).

**8.** One of the sons of Binnui (Hebrew adds "Bani") who had to put away a foreign wife in Ezra's reform (Ezra 10:42; cf. I Esd. 9:34).

F. T. Schumacher

**AMARNA.** *See* Tell el-Amarna.

**AMASA** ə mā′sə [עֲמָשָׂא]. **1.** A nephew of David. He served for a brief period as the commander of the Davidic troops until his treacherous murder by Joab. Amasa was the son of an Ishmaelite by the name of Ithra or Jether, while his mother was Abigail the sister of Zeruiah (II Sam. 17:25; I Chr. 2:17). He may be plausibly identified with Amasai, who made a moving assertion of loyalty in response to David's query concerning the fidelity of his followers (I Chr. 12:18—H 12:19).

When the initial success of the conspiracy of Absalom forced David to abandon the capital, Amasa was placed in command of the rebel forces (II Sam. 17:25), but in the crucial encounter in the forest of Ephraim with the seasoned troops of David, his army was ignominiously defeated. At this point history took a strange turn. Word came to the king beyond the Jordan that the northern tribes were anxious to recognize him again as sovereign (II Sam. 19:9-10—H 19:10-11). This information David forwarded to the hitherto reserved Judeans and encouraged them to effect his return to Jerusalem, significantly adding that Amasa, the defeated leader of the rebel forces, was to assume the command of the army as the replacement of Joab, who appears to have been deposed as a consequence of his disorderly conduct in the death of Absalom. This tacit amnesty to the politically culpable and the strong tribal loyalty to the royal house prompted the Judeans to invite the king to return. Without informing the northern tribes, they went down immediately to the Jordan to convey

the royal company back to Jerusalem (II Sam. 19: 11 ff). Outmaneuvered by this political move, the Israelites were indignant that they, who were the first to suggest the recall of the king, should have been so completely slighted (II Sam. 19:41 ff). The dissatisfaction crystallized into the rebellion of Sheba, a Benjaminite, who threatened the national unity by his intrigue (II Sam. 20).

This internecine strife, following in the wake of the plot of Absalom, foreboded national disaster and aroused David to direct Amasa to muster the Judean forces within the brief period of three days. When the commander failed to return in the appointed time, David placed Abishai at the head of the royal guards and charged him to quell the rebellion before the forces of Sheba could occupy the fortified cities. At Gibeon, Amasa joined his command. With calculated perfidy the redoubtable Joab murdered him, and then with Abishai continued the pursuit of Sheba while Amasa wallowed in his blood in the highway. The soldiers who paused to witness the tragic spectacle, as they hastened after the enemy, were challenged to demonstrate their loyalty to David by following Joab. The corpse was later removed from the roadway and covered with a garment when it proved a deterrent to the speedy progress of the troops who arrived at the scene. By this treachery in the removal of his rival and by the successful liquidation of the revolt by the death of its leader, Joab regained his former command of the army (II Sam. 20:23). However, the guilt involved in the assassination of Amasa and of Abner was deeply rued by the king, who subsequently instructed Solomon to render unto Joab his just desert (I Kings 2:5, 32).

**2.** Son of Hadlai. According to the Chronicler, Amasa was among the small group of Ephraimite chiefs that opposed, on moral principles, the entry into the city of Samaria of Judean captives, whom Pekah had taken in his war with Ahaz, and kindly assisted in their repatriation (II Chr. 28:12-15).

E. R. Dalglish

**AMASAI** ə mā′sī [עֲמָשַׂי]. **1.** According to the Chronicler, chief of the "Thirty" among David's soldiers (I Chr. 12:18—H 12:19). However, he is not mentioned in the military lists in II Sam. 23; I Chr. 11. Attempts have been made to equate him with either Amasa or Abishai, though we do not know that either of them ever held that rank.

**2.** The name is used several times in the Levitical lists of the Chronicler: (*a*) Amasai ben Elkanah, a Kohathite in the genealogy of Levi (I Chr. 6:25—H 6:10) who also appears in the genealogy of Heman the singer (I Chr. 6:35—H 6:20); (*b*) a priest in the time of David; appointed to blow the trumpet before the ark of God (I Chr. 15:24); (*c*) the father of Mahath, a Kohathite in the time of Hezekiah (II Chr. 29:12). Since *a* also has a son named Mahath (see I Chr. 6:35), one would identify *a* and *c*, except for the fact that the former is centuries prior to the time of Hezekiah.

F. T. Schumacher

**AMASHSAI** ə măsh′sī [עֲמַשְׁסַי, *probably a corruption of* עֲמָשַׂי, Amasai] (Neh. 11:13); KJV AMASHAI —ī. A postexilic priest, apparently to be identified with MAASAI (I Chr. 9:12).

ʿAMASIAH ăm'ə sī'ə [עמסיהו, Yahu has borne] (II Chr. 17:16). A Judahite, son of Zichri, one of the commanders in Jehoshaphat's army and a loyal servant of Yahweh.

AMATHEIS. KJV Apoc. form of ATHLAI.

AMATHIS. KJV Apoc. form of HAMATH 1.

AMAW ā'mô [עמו]. The land to which Balak king of Moab sent to call BALAAM (Num. 22:5). It included PETHOR, Balaam's city, "near the River" (i.e., the Euphrates). Pitru (Pethor) lay on the Sajur River, according to the Assyrian inscriptions. The KJV misunderstood the name and translated "the land of the children of his people."

According to the Idrimi Inscription, the king of Alalakh also ruled over the lands of Mukiskhe, Ni', and Amaw. If we date Balaam's contacts with Israel ca. 1250 B.C., Idrimi's account would be only ca. two hundred years earlier. Amaw lay W of the Euphrates. Its principle city was Emar, not over fifty miles S of Carchemish and less than that distance from Pethor.

Amaw is also mentioned in the tomb of Qen-amun, who served under Amenophis II of Egypt in the second half of the fifteenth century B.C. The land of Amaw had first been conquered by Thut-mose III, Amenophis' father, ca. 1450.

*Bibliography.* W. F. Albright, "Some Important Recent Discoveries: Alphabetic Origins and the Idrimi Statue," *BASOR,* 118 (1950), 15-20; A. Goetze, "The Syrian Town of Emar," *BASOR,* 147 (1957), 22-27.          E. D. GROHMAN

AMAZEMENT. *See* ASTONISHMENT.

AMAZIAH ăm'ə zī'ə [(ו)אמציה, Yahu is strong].
1. A Simeonite (I Chr. 4:34).
2. A Levite of the family of Merari, one of those appointed by King David to have charge of the service of song before the tabernacle of the tent of meeting (I Chr. 6:45; cf. vss. 31-32).
3. King of Judah ca. 800-783 B.C.; son and successor of Joash.

Amaziah was twenty-five years old when he began to reign, and he is said to have reigned twenty-nine years. His mother was Jehoaddin of Jerusalem (II Kings 14:2; Jehoaddan in II Chr. 25:1).

The figure of twenty-nine years for Amaziah's reign is difficult, and many suggestions have been made to explain it. None of these, however, is satisfactory. The synchronism in II Kings 14:17, that Amaziah "lived fifteen years after the death of Jehoash son of Jehoahaz, king of Israel," if historical, would seem to indicate that he was not acting as king during that period. A reign of ca. eighteen or nineteen years seems the best solution to the problem.

Amaziah faced difficulties at the outset of his rule, for his father's murderers were apparently still among the servants of the king. When he gained control, however, he put to death those who had slain his father, but he spared their sons (II Kings 14:5-6; II Chr. 25:3-4).

His reign was marked by the reconquest of Edom, which had won its independence from Judah *ca.* fifty years previously (II Kings 8:20-22). The locations of the "Valley of Salt," where ten thousand Edomites were slain, and Sela (14:7), which Amaziah took by storm and changed its name to Joktheel, have not been certainly identified. The former name may be used generally for the valley S of the Dead Sea, and the suggestion that Sela (i.e., "the Rock") is one of the heights overlooking the valley in which Petra later lay is very plausible. The figure given for the number of Edomites slain is a round figure. The addition in Chronicles of another ten thousand Edomites, who were thrown down from the top of a rock, is manifestly unhistorical (II Chr. 25:12). The further details which the chronicler adds (vss. 5-10, 13-16) by way of introduction and conclusion are of questionable historicity.

No doubt elated by his victory over Edom, Amaziah issued a challenge to Joash of Israel. No motive is given, but it may have been envy that caused him to act as he did. The result was disastrous for Judah (II Kings 14:8-14; II Chr. 25:17-24), which was reduced to the status of a vassal state of Israel.

Like his father, Amaziah was the victim of a court conspiracy. He made his escape to Lachish, but was there murdered. His body was brought back to Jerusalem in a funeral procession, and buried in the City of David.

*Bibliography.* N. Glueck, *Explorations in Eastern Palestine,* II, *AASOR,* XV (1935), 82; W. F. Albright, "Further Light on the History of Israel from Lachish and Megiddo," *BASOR,* 68 (1937), 22 ff; E. R. Thiele, *The Mysterious Numbers of the Hebrew Kings* (1951), pp. 68 ff; J. Simons, *Jerusalem in the OT* (1952), pp. 233 ff.

4. A priest of the royal sanctuary at Bethel in the time of Jeroboam II. He tried to prevent Amos from prophesying there (Amos 7:10-17).

H. B. MacLEAN

AMBASSADOR. The translation of the verb πρεσβεύω, "to be older, to act as an ambassador" (II Cor. 5:20; Eph. 6:20), and the noun πρεσβεία, "age, dignity, office of ambassador" (Luke 14:32; 19:14; KJV "AGED"); and the KJV translation of several Hebrew and Greek (Apoc.) words (*see* MESSENGER; INTERPRETER; the Hebrew word most frequently rendered "ambassador" by the KJV, מלאך, is traditionally translated "ANGEL" when referring to any supernatural messenger of God). In the Apoc., "ambassador" is the KJV translation of πρέσβυς, πρεσβύτης, and ἄγγελος. For ἄγγελος in I Macc. 1:46, *see* PRIESTS AND LEVITES.          C. U. WOLF

AMBER. The KJV translation of חשמל in Ezek. 1:4, 27; 8:2 (RSV GLEAMING BRONZE; cf. Ugaritic *trml;* Akkadian *ešmaru,* "inlay" [?]). Amber is a yellowish to brownish translucent fossil resin. It takes a good polish. Many of the examples called amber in Egyptian antiquities are other resins, not amber. The word is used in the Bible as a motif in visions. The LXX and the Vulg. suggest electrum, an amalgam of gold and silver.

*See also* JEWELS AND PRECIOUS STONES § 2.

*Bibliography.* G. G. Cameron, *Persepolis Treasury Tablets* (1948), pp. 129-30.          W. E. STAPLES

**AMBUSH** [מארב, *from* ארב; מסתרים (Ps. 64:4—H
64:5; KJV SECRET), hiding places (*cf.* Ps. 10:8);
ἔνεδρον]. A means of warfare regularly employed in
antiquity, often with great success (cf. Josh. 8; Judg.
20:29 ff). The enemies of Paul lay in ambush for him
at Jerusalem (Acts 23:16, 21) and planned an ambush on a return to Jerusalem (25:3). *See* WAR,
METHODS OF, § 5.

The Hebrew verb is usually translated "to lie in
wait," and it was often used in the OT as a symbol
for the wiles of the wicked (e.g., Pss. 10:8; 59:3—H
59:4; Prov. 1:11, 18; 24:15; Jer. 9:8).    J. W. WEVERS

**AMEN** ä′měn′, ā′ — [אמן, *from the verb* to take care,
to support (*Qal*), to be firm, true, reliable (*Niph'al*),
to trust (in), to believe (in, that; *Hiph'il*)]. An exclamation ("Truly," "Surely") by which listeners
join in an oath, a blessing, a curse, a prayer, or a
doxology they have heard, and affirm their readiness
to bear the consequences of this acknowledgment.
The LXX preserves Amen in I Chronicles and
Nehemiah and renders it by ἀληθῶς in Jer. 28:6 and
by γένοιτο in all other occurrences. The Vulg. uses
*fiat* in Ps. 41:13; 72:19; 89:52; 106:48; Jth. 13:20,
and elsewhere preserves the word untranslated. The
only occurrence of the noun Amen as a name of God
(Isa. 65:16; RSV "God of truth") is uncertain. Perhaps '*ōmēn* should be read.

**1. In the OT.** The responding Amen introduces
the answer to the words of a previous speaker: of
David ordering the enthronement of Solomon (I
Kings 1:36), of Hananiah promising the return of the
exiles (Jer. 28:6), of the town leader blessing Judith
(Jth. 13:26), or even of God cursing the disobedient
people (Jer. 11:5; or is it the aim of the prophet to
confirm the conditioned blessings of the covenant?). By
the responding Amen the speaker promises to do
what the king commands and asks God to do what
he has promised or what is prayed for.

The responding Amen is at times a part of the
liturgy. The wife accused of adultery uses the priest's
curse, so that her Amen comes near to an oath
(Num. 5:22). At an unknown feast—perhaps at the
beginning of the service—every member of the congregation, by answering Amen to the curses of the
Levites (Deut. 27:15-26), calls ill fate upon himself
in case he should be guilty, and so do the listeners
when they hear the curses of Nehemiah against the
hard-minded nobles (Neh. 5:13). "All who pass into
the covenant" of the Qumran sect have to say Amen
after the blessings uttered by the priests and the
Levites on the "men of the lot of God" and
after their curses on the "men of the lot of Belial"
(1QS 1:20; 2:10, 18).

In private life a wife hearing her husband's prayer
may join him by saying Amen with him (Tob. 8:8),
and from this use of Amen with another speaker may
derive the late custom of one's own ending prayer in
the same way (Prayer Man. 15). On solemn occasions the responding Amen becomes double (Num.
5:22; Tob. 8:8, Sinaiticus).

A special form of the responding is the doxological
Amen. In the worship in the synagogue—probably
not in the Herodian temple—the benediction
"Blessed be the Lord" of the leader in prayer—or of
the choir—was answered by the congregation with

the word Amen (I Chr. 16:36). When the book of
Psalms was divided into five books separated by
doxologies, a single (Ps. 106:48) or a double Amen
(41:13; 72:19; 89:52) was inserted, and the same was
done with III–IV Maccabees. In later times every
petition of the Amida was answered by Amen, and
this response was considered so important that when
—as in Alexandria—the synagogue was so large that
the voice of the leader in prayer could not be heard
throughout, a flag was used to notify the congregation that the doxology was being recited.

In the same manner a single Jew had to say Amen
when he heard another Jew blessing the Lord. But
if the speaker was a Samaritan or a heathen, the
Jew had to wait till the end of his benediction in
order not to join in a prayer which was not orthodox.

**2. In the NT.** The use of Amen in the NT usually
follows the OT lines. It is a response to the following: (*a*) a promise of the heavenly Christ (Rev. 22:
20), in whom "all the promises of God find their
Yes. Amen" (II Cor. 1:20, reading H), or to a vision
of the Last Judgment (Rev. 1:7); (*b*) a prayer which
has to be spoken in words understandable by all
listeners (I Cor. 14:16); (*c*) a doxology (Rev. 1:6; 5:
14), which it also may introduce (Rev. 7:12; 19:4).
It ends a prayer (Rom. 15:33; uncertain in Matt.
6:13; I Thess. 3:13), a doxology (Rom. 1:25; 9:5; 11:
36; 16:27; Gal. 1:5; Eph. 3:21; Phil. 4:20; I Tim.
1:17; 6:16; II Tim. 4:18; I Pet. 4:11; 5:11; Heb. 13:
21), or especially a blessing at the conclusion of a
letter (Gal. 6:18; Jude 25). When the custom arose
of reading from the books and the letters of the NT
in the service, Amen was added at the end of this
reading.

There are two specific NT uses of the word: (*a*)
"The Amen" becomes one of the titles of Christ as
"the faithful and true witness" (Rev. 3:14), perhaps
under the influence of Isa. 65:16 (*see above*). (*b*) Jesus
solemnly introduces his own sayings in the Synoptic
gospels by "Amen I say to you" (e.g., Matt. 5:18, 26;
6:2) and in John by "Amen, amen, I say to you"
(e.g., 1:51). This Amen comes near to an oath by
which Jesus can proclaim his exegesis of the Law,
his warnings, and his promises (Luke 23:43) to be
the true will of his Father, but he avoids pronouncing the name of God. It may be that ἀληθῶς in Luke
9:27; 12:44; 21:3 is a translation of an Amen in the
older tradition underlining the solemnity of the word
(cf. Luke 12:37; Matt. 24:47). This specific use of
Amen by Jesus is not followed by any apostle or
prophet of the early Christian church. In the service
Amen is attested at the end of a prayer (but never in
Acts!) or of a doxology looking forward to the Coming Age by Did. 10:6; I Clem. (e.g., 20:12); II Clem.
20:5; especially in the Lord's Supper by Justin
(Apol. I.65.3-4) and Eusebius (Hist. VII.9.4).

**Bibliography.** I. Elbogen, *Der jüdische Gottesdienst in seiner
geschichtlichen Entwicklung* (2nd ed., 1924); P. Glaue, *Zeitschrift für Kirchengeschichte*, 44 (1925), 184-98; L. Gillet, *ET*,
56 (1944/45), 134-36; J. C. C. van Dorssen, *De derivata van de
stam* אמן *in het hebreeusch van het Oude Testament* (1951)—
chiefly philological; A. Alt, *Kleine Schriften zur Geschichte
Israels*, II (1953), 324-27 (Deut. 27); P. Wernberg-Møller,
*The Manual of Discipline* (1957), p. 50, n. 48; E. Pfeiffer,
*Kerygma und Dogma*, 4 (1958), 129-41; A. Stuiber, *Jahrbuch
für Antike und Christentum*, 1 (1958), 153-59.    J. HEMPEL

**AMETHYST** [אחלמה; ἀμεθύστος]. A deep-purple variety of corundum known as oriental amethyst. אחלמה may be related to Egyptian *ḥnm*, red and brown jasper(?). It is a stone in the breastplate of the high priest (Exod. 28:19; 39:12). Ἀμεθύστος is the twelfth jewel in the foundation of the walls of the New Jerusalem (Rev. 21:20). Pliny notes its occurrence in Egypt.

*See also* JEWELS AND PRECIOUS STONES § 2.

W. E. STAPLES

**'AM HA'AREZ** ăm'hä är'ĕts [עַם הארץ]. Literally, "the people of the land," and so literally rendered by the versions, both ancient and modern. The LXX, e.g., translates almost exclusively ὁ λαὸς τῆς γῆς, except in Lev. 20:2; Dan. 9:6, where it has τὸ ἔθνος τὸ ἐπὶ τῆς γῆς, and in Lev. 20:4, where it has οἱ αὐτόχθονες τῆς γῆς.

On the face of it, the term seems self-explanatory as a general designation of the population of an area. In postbiblical times, however, the expression was used as a term of opprobrium for the religious illiterate, and accordingly some scholars have explained the OT terms as designating the lower strata of society—plebeians, proletariat, or the like. Several detailed studies of the term have indicated that this is not the case and that the expression was actually a technical term for a specific social class or political body. An extreme view was that the term designated a representative parliament, with both executive and judicial powers, which participated in the government of Israel throughout the period of the monarchy and survived even into the postexilic period. A sociologist understood the term to refer to a sort of squirearchy of landed gentry, a rural militia, an oligarchical army similar to that of the Hellenic cities in predemocratic times (the connection with the militia is indicated in II Kings 25:19-20).

Basic to the understanding of the term is the fact that עַם ('am), unlike the word גוי, with which it is sometimes parallel, does not properly designate the entire population, but in the strict sense includes only the responsible male citizenry, the married men who live on their own land and have full rights and duties, including the duty of serving in the army and of participating in judicial proceedings and cult festivals. They are thus the full citizens of a specific territory. Each land, accordingly, has its own *'am,* and the OT mentions that of the Egyptians (Gen. 42:6), the Canaanites (Num. 13:28), and the "Hittites" of Hebron (Gen. 23:7, 12-13). The expression may be made specific by replacing the general term "land" with the proper name of the land in question, as *'am yᵉhûdhâ* (עַם יהודה), "the people of Judah" (II Kings 14:21 = II Chr. 26:1). The word *'am* may also be replaced by the word *'anšê,* "men of," as in *'anšê yᵉhûdhâ* (אנשי יהודה), "the men of Judah" (II Sam. 2:4). Both expressions designate the same entity— the effective, responsible (male) citizenry of Judah.

The social and political importance of the *'Am Ha'arez* of Judah is indicated by the fact that in most cases where they are mentioned some matter of historic significance is involved. They first appear in connection with the coronation of Joash (II Kings 11: 12, 18-20). In 21:24 it is they who avenge the murder of Amon and make his son Josiah king. Similarly, in 23:30, after the death of Josiah, they anoint Jehoahaz king. In 23:35 the *'Am Ha'arez* are assessed to pay the tribute to Egypt. In Jeremiah and Ezekiel the *'Am Ha'arez* are several times mentioned after the king, princes, and priests (Jer. 1:18; 34:19; 37:2; 44:21; Ezek. 7:27; 22:25-29). In Jer. 34 they are said to have participated, along with the princes, eunuchs, and priests, in a covenant to liberate their slaves in the sabbatical year. Ezekiel (22:29) accuses them of oppressing the poor and the sojourner. From all this, it is patent that the *'Am Ha'arez* played an important role in the political, economic, and social life of Judah and that they must have occupied the position just below that of the priests on the social ladder. The only evidence for the view that the term comprised or included the lower strata of society is found in the expression *dallath 'am hā'āreṣ* (דלת עם הארץ), "the poorest people of the land" (II Kings 24:14), describing the people left in Jerusalem by Nebuchadnezzar. This expression, however, is unique; elsewhere the same people are called either *dallath hā'am* (דלת העם), "the poorest of the people" (Jer. 52:15), or *dallath hā'āreṣ* (דלת הארץ), "the poorest of the land" (II Kings 25:12; Jer. 40:7; 52:16). The LXX in II Kings 24:14 reads οἱ πτωχοὶ τῆς γῆς, indicating that the original reading contained no reference to the *'Am Ha'arez.*

The prisoners captured in Jerusalem by Nebuchadnezzar's forces included sixty men of the *'Am Ha'arez,* mentioned along with the chief priest, the second priest, three keepers of the threshold, a military officer, five members of the royal council, and the secretary of the commander of the army who mustered the *'Am Ha'arez.* These were taken to Nebuchadnezzar at Riblah and there executed (II Kings 25:18-21). Certainly these sixty men of the *'Am Ha'arez* were persons of social, economic, or military importance, and not merely the lower strata of society.

In the postexilic period the term *'Am Ha'arez* retained its meaning with reference to the responsible citizenry, but the situation had changed drastically. The exiles of the second, third, or fourth generation could not return and take up affairs as if nothing had happened. They had to deal with the population they found in the land; these were now the *'Am Ha'arez,* and conflict very quickly developed between them and the returnees. In Ezra 4:4 the returnees and their partisans are called "the people ['am] of Judah," and the troublesome local gentry are the *'Am Ha'arez.* In Ezra 10:2, 11; Neh. 10:30-31 the plural of the word *'am* is used to indicate the heterogeneity of this half-heathen population with whom the returning Jews had intermarried. In Ezra 9:1-2, 11, both elements of the term are plural: *'ammê hā'ᵃrāṣôth* (עמי הארצות), "the peoples of the lands"; and these are specified as Canaanites, Hittites, Perizzites, Jebusites, Ammonites, Moabites, Egyptians, and Amorites, the ancestors of the mongrel heathen with whom the Israelites, even the priests and Levites, had continued to intermarry through the centuries. In II Chr. 13:9 the same expression is used in reference to the priesthoods of the heathen cults. The RSV superfluously adds "other" ("like the peoples of other lands"). The Chronicler, who is Ezra, in a speech put in the mouth of Abijah actually aims his invective at his contemporary opponents, the indigenous people, or peoples of the land, whose origins are diverse and mixed, whose worship is impure, and with whom he wishes to have no dealings.

In rabbinic literature the term *'Am Ha'arez* appears as a contemptuous designation of those whom the rabbis regarded as immoral, irreligious, and ignorant of the law. Accordingly the general view has been that the term refers to the masses, proletariat, the common people who were too burdened with making a living to be much concerned about ritual purity. The antipathy between the common people and the Pharisaic elite is well known. Jesus took the side of the common folk in his attacks on the Pharisees (Mark 7:1-5; Luke 6:1-5; 11:37-41). The feelings of the Pharisaic elite find expression in John 7:49, where the word ὄχλος, "crowd," is applied with contempt to the ignorant masses who do not know the law. But there is no real evidence that the term in postbiblical usage has reference to social status. It has been argued that in early Tanaaitic literature the term refers to farmers, plebeians, tillers of the land, as contrasted with the *Ḥabhērîm*, the privileged class, the patricians, who regarded the former as unclean. When many of the *'Am Ha'arez* went over to Christianity, the term supposedly became a designation of Jewish Christians and then a general term of reproach and contempt. Actually the term is applied to persons of differing social positions, and always the reference is to purely religious matters, either ignorance or laxity in regard to the law. It would seem that the best explanation for the development of this sense of the term is to be found in the animosities which developed between the returning exiles and the allegedly mongrel pagan population whom they rebuffed. As Ezra used the term, it carried disapproval of their mongrel ancestry as well as their paganism. The rabbinic use of the term shows no concern with genealogy, but only contempt for ignorance or indifference in regard to the law, which could be remedied. Rabbi Aqiba was an *'Am Ha'arez* till he was forty years old.

*Bibliography.* A. Büchler, *Der Galiläische 'Am ha'Ares des zweiten Jahrhunderts* (1906). H. P. Chajes, "Am ha-Arez e Min," *Revista Israelitica*, III (1906), 83-96. M. Sulzberger, *Am Ha-aretz, The Ancient Hebrew Parliament* (1909); "The Polity of the Ancient Hebrews," *JQR*, 3 (1912-13), 1-81. N. Sloush, "Representative Government Among the Hebrews and Phoenicians," *JQR*, 4 (1913), 302. E. Gillischewski, "Der Ausdruck עם הארץ im AT," *ZAW*, 40 (1922), 137-42. S. Daiches, "The Meaning of עם הארץ in the OT," *JTS*, 30 (1928-29), 245-49. S. Zeitlin, "The am ha-arez," *JQR*, 23 (1932-33), 45 ff. L. Rost, "Die Bezeichnungen für Land und Volk im AT," *Festschrift Otto Procksch* (1934), pp. 125-48. L. Finkelstein, *The Pharisees* (1935), pp. 25-42. E. Würthwein, *Der 'amm ha'arez im AT*, BWANT, no. 17 (1936). M. Weber, *Ancient Judaism* (1952).                    M. H. POPE

**AMI.** Alternate form of AMON 3.

**AMINADAB.** KJV NT form of AMMINADAB.

**AMITTAI** ə mĭt'ī [אמתי, true] (II Kings 14:25; Jonah 1:1). The father of the prophet Jonah.

**AMMAH** ăm'ə [אמה, cubit] (II Sam. 2:24). A hill near GIAH in Benjamin, on the threshold of the wilderness descent into the Jordan Valley. Here, following the Battle of Gibeon, Abner made a stand against the pursuing forces of Joab. A truce was effected, and the opposing forces returned to their respective headquarters (II Sam. 2:24-32; Jos. Antiq. VII.i.2).                    W. H. MORTON

**AMMI** ăm'ī [עמי, my people]. The new name to be given to Israel in the day of redemption (Hos. 2:1), in contrast to LO-AMMI, "Not my people" (1:9), which signified God's decisive rejection.

**AMMIDIANS** ə mĭd'ī ənz ['Αμμίδιοι] (I Esd. 5:20); KJV AMMIDOI ăm'ə doi. A family group among those returning from exile; they and the Chadiasans numbered 422.                    J. C. SWAIM

**AMMIEL** ăm'ī əl [עמיאל, my kinsman is God]. 1. Son of Gemalli; representative of the tribe of Dan among the men Moses sent to spy out the land of Canaan (Num. 13:12).

2. The father of Machir, in whose house the son of Jonathan was hidden from David (II Sam. 9:4-5) and later befriended David (17:27).

3. The father of Bathshua (LXX Bathsheba), David's wife, according to I Chr. 3:5. In II Sam. 11: 3 he is called ELIAM.

4. Sixth son of Obed-edom; one who served among the gatekeepers in the temple (I Chr. 26:5).                    F. T. SCHUMACHER

**AMMIHUD** ə mī'hŭd [עמיהוד, my kinsman is splendor]. 1. The father of Elishama, leader of the half-tribe of Ephraim during the sojourn in the wilderness (Num. 1:10; 2:18; 7:48, 53; 10:22); great-grandfather of Joshua (I Chr. 7:26).

2. The father of Shemuel; a Simeonite in the time of Moses (Num. 34:20).

3. The father of Pedahel; a Naphtalite in the time of Moses (Num. 34:28).

4. The father of the king of Geshur to whom Absalom fled, according to *Qere* of II Sam. 13:37. The *Kethibh* of this verse reads "Ammihur" and is followed by some as the more difficult reading. But it appears nowhere else in the OT and could easily be a copyist's mistake (cf. Hebrew letters). The ancient versions all read "Ammihud," and both the KJV and the RSV accept it as the more likely.

5. Son of Omri; among the sons of Perez of Judah who returned after the Exile (I Chr. 9:4).                    F. T. SCHUMACHER

**AMMINADAB** ə mĭn'ə dăb [עמינדב, my kinsman is noble, generous; 'Αμιναδάβ]; KJV NT AMINADAB. 1. The father of Nahshon, leader of the tribe of Judah (Num. 1:7; 2:3; 7:12, 17; 10:14); father of a daughter Elisheba, the wife of Aaron (Exod. 6:23). Through the son, his name appears as an ancestor of David (Ruth 4:19-20) and thence comes also into the genealogies of the NT as an ancestor of Jesus (Matt. 1:4; Luke 3:33).

2. Chief of what was probably a Levitical group, called the sons of Uzziel (I Chr. 15:10).

**3.** Son of Kohath and father of Korah in the chronicler's genealogy of the Levites (I Chr. 6:22—H 6:7). But here, as elsewhere in this chapter, there is difficulty. The almost parallel list later in the chapter has Izhar in his place (vss. 37-38—H 22-23), as does the original genealogy in Exod. 6:18, 21. Amminadab nowhere else appears as the son of Kohath, though every list includes Izhar (I Chr. 6:2—H 5:28; Num. 3:19; in addition to the above passages). Finally, in the verse in question (I Chr. 6:22) A and L of the LXX have "Izhar"—undoubtedly the correct reading.

**4.** The father of Esther, according to the LXX of Esth. 2:15; 9:29. There is, however, no strong case for correcting the MT, which has "Abihail."

F. T. SCHUMACHER

**AMMINADIB** ə mĭn'ə dĭb. KJV translation of עמי־נדיב, wrongly understood as a personal name, in a passage of uncertain meaning (Song of S. 6:12). Conjectural translation is necessary, but little agreement has resulted. The RSV translates "my prince."

*See* SONG OF SONGS, with suggested Commentaries.

F. T. SCHUMACHER

**AMMISHADDAI** ăm'ĭ shăd'ī [עמישדי; Egyp. *Sadde'mmi,* a kinsman *or* protector is (the god) Shaddai]. The father of Ahiezer, who was the leader of Dan in the wilderness (Num. 1:12; 2:25; 7:66, 71; 10:25).

For the meaning of "Shaddai," *see* GOD, NAMES OF.

*Bibliography.* M. Noth, *Die israelitischen Personennamen* (1928), pp. 33, 129-31, 141; W. F. Albright, *The Biblical Period* (1950), p. 7.     R. F. JOHNSON

**AMMIZABAD** ə mĭz'ə băd [עמיזבד, kinsman hath bestowed]. Son of the renowned Benaiah, who was a member of the "Thirty" (II Sam. 23:20-23; I Chr. 11:22-25). According to the Chronicler, Ammizabad served David as the commander of the division for the third month (I Chr. 27:6). It is probable that when Benaiah was elevated to be head of the "Thirty," he turned over his division to his son Ammizabad.     E. R. DALGLISH

*****AMMON, AMMONITES** ăm'ən, —ə nīts [בני עמון, sons of Ammon; *also* עמוני, עמני (Deut. 23:3; Neh. 13:1), עמון (Ps. 83:7—H 83:8), עמנים (Deut. 2:20; I Kings 11:5; II Chr. 20:1; 26:8; Neh. 4:7). A Semitic people who flourished as an autonomous political state on the fringes of the Syrian Desert in central Transjordan *ca.* 1300-580 B.C. The occasional references to Ammonites after the Exile indicate an entirely different ethnic group which occupied the same geographical area but maintained no independent national existence.

1. Name
2. Origin
3. Ethnic affiliation
4. Territorial definition of the land of Ammon
5. The early Ammonite state: Ammon during Iron I
    *a.* Earliest political activity in Ammon
    *b.* Beginnings of Ammonite expansion: the war with Jephthah
    *c.* Ammonites in the Jordan Valley: war with Saul at Jabesh-gilead

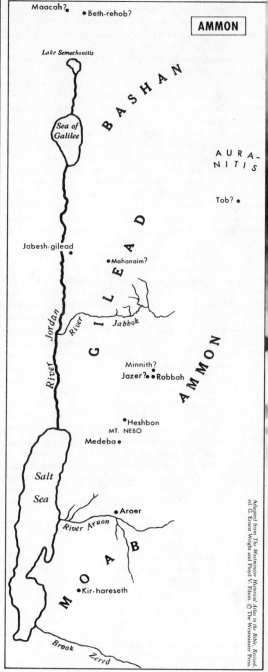

Adapted from *The Westminster Historical Atlas to the Bible, Revised,* ed. G. Ernest Wright and Floyd V. Filson. © The Westminster Press.

    *d.* Israelite conquest of Ammon: Ammon as a vassal state under David and Solomon
6. The flowering, decline, and fall of the Ammonite state
    *a.* Ammon and Israel before the resurgence of Assyrian power
    *b.* Ammon as a vassal of Assyria
    *c.* The decline and fall of Ammon
7. Postexilic Ammon
8. The culture of the Ammonites
Bibliography

**1. Name.** According to Gen. 19:38, the younger daughter of LOT gave birth to Ben-'ammi—the "father of the Ammonites to this day." At first glance, the name assigned the putative ancestor of the Ammonites appears to be merely a popular etymology to explain the origin and meaning of the common designation for the Ammonites—viz., bᵉnê 'ammôn, "sons of Ammon." In Hebrew, Ben-'ammî literally means "son of my people," or more originally, "son of my paternal clan," and thus possesses a meaning which agrees with the tradition suggesting an actual kindred relationship between Ammon and Israel. However, it is now known from guild lists of clan names preserved in Ugaritic (see UGARIT) that Ben-'ammi was a genuine name in the onomasticons of N Syria during the fifteenth century B.C. Moreover, among Alalakh and S Semitic personal names occurs what appears to be the same name. Our onomastic sources thus reveal the rather widespread use of this name in both West and South Semitic from the mid–second millennium B.C. on, and also attest to its occurrence in much the same characteristic forms. From a background study of the name in Ugaritic, one might expect the founder of the Ammonites to have been named 'Ammiya, and only his descendant(s) Ben-'ammi. It is not improbable, however, that in the oral tradition concerning the name of the original "father of the Ammonites," the patronym or clan name was remembered rather than the personal name, just as in the Ugaritic guild lists clan names, rather than personal names, were preserved for purposes of administrative record. Since the names 'my and bn 'myn, in addition to being clan names, also stand for individual persons in the Ugaritic lists, it is not difficult to see how Ben-'ammi could be identified both with the clan name of the Ammonites and with their ancestral progenitor.

In the Assyrian inscriptions the Ammonites are most frequently referred to as the Bêt Am-ma-na-aia, although in one of the recently discovered Nimrud letters occurs the unusual (mât) ba-an-am-ma-na-aia, evidently for banū Ammanaia.

**2. Origin.** According to biblical tradition, Ammonite origins were in S Transjordan in the territory later known as the land of Moab. Both the Ammonites and the Moabites were of basically Semitic stock, although, like the Hebrews, somewhat mixed, since in all probability an element of their population was composed of the HABIRU. They spoke a language closely related to Hebrew. A study of Ammonite and Moabite personal names shows that many of the names have unique parallels in Proto-Arabic. This lends some support to the hypothesis, that, if the Ammonites and Moabites did not actually originate in the S, they at least received strong influences from that direction.

An early Ammonite tradition in Deut. 3:11 suggests something with regard to Ammonite origins: a bed of iron belonging to OG, king of Bashan, resided at RABBAH. Such a bed has virtually no parallel in ancient Near Eastern temple inventories, cultic liturgies, or reports of temple excavations. In a cuneiform tablet giving a detailed description of the complex of Esagila, the temple of MARDUK at Babylon, a "bed-house" (bît irshi) is cited containing a bed nine cubits in length by four cubits in width. The precise parallel to Og's bed is most striking. It is known that a bed played some definite role in the cultic worship of Marduk, as well as in the veneration of other deities in the Babylonian pantheon. Although the deity or cult with which the bed of Og was originally linked cannot be definitely known, there are at least two instances in which the name Marduk was connected with the territory of ancient Bashan. One of these is in the name Shulum-Marduk ("welfare of Marduk"), referring to an important clan or family which controlled Ashtaroth (see ASHTAROTH 2; cf. Amarna Letter no. 256, line 20). The other is in the name Marduk (presumably contracted from Bêt-Marduk, "shrine of Marduk"), applied to a town in ancient Bashan, occurring in some early Greek inscriptions. It is probable that the Babylonian Marduk was worshiped in Bashan, and that the bed of Og may indeed have derived its original cultic significance from Marduk worship. See ZAMZUMMIM.

Thus we must look N of the land of Ammon for certain influences which contributed (at least in part) to the formation of an early Ammonite tradition, and among which are perhaps also to be sought the forces which helped create a distinctive Ammonite people. The onomastic practice of designating persons and clans by a patronym seems to find its first expression in the N. However, the problem of Ammonite origins is exceedingly complex, and no easy solution is now available. On the basis of present evidence, the tribal movement (or movements) out of which was formed the specific ethnic entity of the Ammonites was apparently associated more with a great invasion stemming from the N than with a similar phenomenon coming from the S. Although evidence for such an invasion in the fourteenth-thirteenth centuries is almost totally lacking, one such movement was the coming of the Amorites into central Transjordan to form the kingdom of SIHON. That the Ammonites were in some way connected with this invasion now seems quite possible.

**3. Ethnic affiliation.** During their early history, the West Semitic nomads were generally known to the Eastern Semites as "Amorites"—i.e., "Westerners." In the West, however, distinctions of nomenclature emerged, based on ancestral origin, tribal affiliation, or environmental characteristics. Thus, with respect to language, ethnic relationship, and physical appearance, the Ammonites may at first have been hardly distinguishable from the Amorites, but because the former traced their origin back to a common tribal ancestor, they received or assumed a corresponding distinction in name. Not impossibly the Ammonites and Amorites of Transjordan were originally closely related, and both may have entered the land at approximately the same time. We find Amorites and Ammonites settled adjacent to each other at the very beginning of Ammonite history. JAZER became the border of the Ammonites (Num. 21:24), and Amorites dwelt in the land of Jazer until Moses dispossessed them (Num. 21:21). Moreover, when the Ammonites became strong enough to engage the Israelites in battle, their first objective was recovery of the land of Gilead, which was still known as the land of the Amorites (Judg. 10:8), and the territory which the Ammonite king claimed to be rightfully his was identical with the territorial expanse once assigned to the kingdom of Sihon (Judg. 11:13, 22). The territory of Sihon definitely overlapped that known to have been Ammonite from an early period. Finally, the name Ammon itself preserves a most characteristic element in personal names of West Semitic nomadic peoples—i.e., Amorites. Thus some kind of ethnic affiliation between the Ammonites and the Amorites seems far more plausible than one between the Ammonites and the ARAMEANS, which is often suggested. The Arameans do not seem to have penetrated as far S as the land of Ammon at an early date.

**4. Territorial definition of the land of Ammon.** During the first half of the thirteenth century the Ammonites consisted of little more than a small tribal nucleus centered around their later capital, Rabbath-Ammon. Gradually, organized sedentary settlement spread, until by the eleventh century a fairly well-defined kingdom could be posited, stretching along the small, rather fertile strip of land by the S-N extension of the River Jabbok, and continuing eastward to the desert. Along this narrow strip have been discovered a number of Ammonite sites whose earliest beginnings can definitely be traced back to Iron I (1200-900). In general, the N and S extent of the original Ammonite kingdom can be judged from the N and S limits of this group of sites.

Actually, the boundaries of Ammon were never so clearly defined as those of Moab and Edom. According to biblical tradition, the main border of Ammon was on the W, formed by the E arm of the River Jabbok (Deut. 3:16; Josh. 12:2; 13:10). However, that Ammonites had settled farther W beyond the Jabbok even in the period of the early Ammonite state (i.e., before the tenth century) seems to be indicated by both archaeological and biblical evidence (cf. Num. 21:24; Deut. 2:37; Josh. 13:25).

**5. The early Ammonite state: Ammon during Iron I (1200-900).** *a. Earliest political activity in Ammon (1200-1100).* The formal organization of the Ammonite state seems to have taken place later than the kingdoms of the Amorites, Moabites, and Edomites. The earliest references to Ammon as an organized state occur in biblical literature (Judg. 3:13; 10:7). Although two biblical passages mention the presence of Ammonites when the Israelites passed through Transjordan on their way to the Promised Land (middle decades of the thirteenth century), Ammon does not appear to have reached the same level of organized sedentary life as her neighbors to the S, particularly Moab. Mention of Ammon in conjunction with Moab and Edom is significantly missing in the earliest Hebrew poems, such as the Song of Moses (Exod. 15) and the Oracles of Balaam (Num. 23-24). Unlike her S neighbors, Ammon remained in closer touch with the desert throughout her entire history, and even as late as the seventh century maintained a social organization of an essentially nomadic type.

The initial historical appearance of the Ammonites in an active military role finds them in coalition with Moabites and Amalekites (*see* AMALEK) in an effort to help Eglon, king of Moab, regain former Moabite territory in Transjordan (Judg. 3:13-14).

*b. Beginnings of Ammonite expansion: the war with Jephthah (ca. 1100-1020).* By the late eleventh century the Ammonites had strengthened themselves considerably, fortifying their borders with massive fortresses built in the "megalithic" style, and organizing an effective striking force. Soon they began to establish themselves in Gilead (Judg. 10:8). Even the tribes of Benjamin and Ephraim in W Palestine felt the effects of Ammonite aggression (Judg. 10:9). The "inhabitants of Gilead" proceeded to organize an opposition force under the command of their mighty warrior, Jephthah (Judg. 11:11), who mustered his army and defeated the Ammonites (Judg. 11:32-33). Jephthah apparently conducted no campaign in W Palestine. Josh. 18:24 records the name of a Benjaminite town, Chephar-ammoni (lit., "town of the Ammonites"), which conceivably was founded, or at least occupied, by the Ammonites during this period.

*c. Ammonites in the Jordan Valley: war with Saul at Jabesh-gilead (ca. 1020-1000).* The great Ammonite strongholds were largely untouched by Jephthah's victorious army; thus future expansion of Ammonite power was left unchecked. Sometime after the beginning of the last quarter of the eleventh century, there arose in Ammon a new king whose goal became the conquest of Israelite territory in Transjordan. This king, Nahash (*see* NAHASH 1), launched an ambitious campaign shortly after 1020, leading his army unopposed as far N as the town of JABESH-GILEAD (I Sam. 11:1-2). This military venture marked a high point in Ammon's advance to power, as may be detected in Nahash' refusal to negotiate a treaty with the men of Jabesh except upon the most humiliating terms (I Sam. 11:2). But the advent of Saul's army, which decisively defeated Ammon (I Sam. 11:8-11), preserved central Transjordan, and in particular the Jordan Valley, from Ammonite domination for several centuries. Saul apparently did not drive the Ammonites behind their original border or destroy their fortresses, for later in his reign he had to organize a punitive expedition against those Transjordan peoples who persisted in raiding and plundering the Israelite settlers (I Sam. 14:47-48).

*d. Israelite conquest of Ammon: Ammon as vassal state under David and Solomon (ca. 1000-922).* During the early years of the tenth century Israel's new king, David, became a good friend of Nahash (II Sam. 10:2). When Hanun, son of Nahash, succeeded his father on the Ammonite throne, conditions were soon created for renewed conflict between Ammon and Israel (II Sam. 10:3-5). The Ammonites sent for military assistance from the S Aramean states of Beth-rehob, Maacah, and Tob (II Sam. 10:6; I Chr. 19:6). The Aramean army quickly descended into S Gilead and encamped before the Reubenite town of Medaba. When Joab reached the vicinity of Rabbah, he discovered the Arameans already closing in (II Sam. 10:9; I Chr. 19:10). He was forced to divide his forces, sending the stronger and more capable troops against the Arameans, while leaving the rest to resist the Ammonites (II Sam. 10:9-10; I Chr. 19:10-11). Fortunately, the "picked men of Israel" were strong enough to beat back the Aramean attack, while troops under ABISHAI held the Ammonites at bay (II Sam. 10:13-14; I Chr. 19:14-15). But the victory was not decisive. David therefore launched a devastating expedition against Aram, making it a vassal (II Sam. 8:5-6; I Chr. 18:5-6). In the following year he concentrated on Ammon, sending another strong army under Joab's leadership, which ravaged the Ammonite countryside and besieged Rabbah (II Sam. 11:1, 22-24; 12:26; I Chr. 20:1). With the fall of Rabbah, Ammon became another Israelite vassal state.

Throughout the United Monarchy (*ca.* 961-922), Ammon remained subservient to Israel. It appears that David appointed a viceroy from the old Ammonite royal family to rule over the land, for when David fled to Mahanaim, among those who came to minister to him and his army was "Shobi the son of Nahash from Rabbah of the Ammonites" (II Sam. 17:27). Solomon probably continued David's policy of keeping the governorship of Ammon within the old royal family. Undoubtedly the Ammonites, while under Israelite suzerainty, shared in the wealth and prosperity of the Solomonic era. Even before their conquest by David, they must already have had a successful trading state. They were among the first of the Transjordan peoples to take full advantage of their position on the edge of the Syrian Desert to gain substantial control of the camel-caravan routes for their own profit. In such an ethnically diverse kingdom as Solomon's, it was inevitable that cultural and religious syncretism would develop, and we learn that among the foreign women Solomon loved were Ammonite women (I Kings 11:1), who eventually influenced him to build a sanctuary to their god Milcom (*see* MOLECH) on the mountain opposite Jerusalem (I Kings 11:7). The name of one of these Ammonite women, Naamah, mother of Rehoboam, is preserved by biblical tradition (I Kings 14:21, 31; II Chr. 12:13), which marks the first clear historical instance of Ammonite blood being introduced into the Israelite royal family.

**6. The flowering, decline, and fall of the Ammonite state (*ca.* 900-580).** After almost a century of subservient existence as a tributary state to Israel, political conditions again enabled the Ammonites to embark upon new conquest and expansion, initiating a period in which the fortunes of the Ammonite state were to reach their zenith.

*a. Ammon and Israel before the resurgence of Assyrian power* (ca. 922-742). The Ammonites probably took advantage of the opportunity to free themselves from Israelite control during the first half of the ninth century. Before 853 an independent king arose in Ammon whose name, Ba'sha' (Assyrian *Ba'sa*), the "son" of Ruhubi (i.e., Beth-rehob), appears in the Monolith Inscription of Shalmaneser III (col. II, line 95), in connection with an account of the famous Battle of Qarqar fought in the territory of Hamath in 853. Among the smaller contingents of troops are mentioned a thousand (or more) Ammonites, who probably joined the Aramean coalition against Assyria to protect their N commercial interests. Shortly after the successful repulsion of the Assyrian invaders, the Ammonites linked themselves with the Moabites and Meunim in a campaign presumably instigated by the Arameans to force Jehoshaphat to withdraw his army from the siege of Ramoth-gilead (II Chr. 20:1-2). This military venture was also probably directed against further expansion of Jehoshaphat's commercial enterprises (cf. I Kings 22:48). which threatened to cut off Ammonite control of the

overland caravan trade. The Ammonites and their allies were frustrated in their attempt to defeat Jehoshaphat, and finally all their armies were completely destroyed (II Chr. 20:23).

But now the upsurging Arameans overran all of Transjordan as far S as Aroer on the Arnon River (II Kings 10:32-33), and in all probability the Ammonites were either their allies or their nominal vassals in depriving Israel of her Transjordan territory. Possibly they had already begun to take advantage of Israelite preoccupation with the Arameans to enlarge their borders in Gilead (Amos 1:13). Toward the end of the ninth century Aramean power began to decline, and when Assyria resumed an aggressive policy, the Aramean states were among the first to collapse before the Assyrian onslaught. Although Adad-nirari III, the Assyrian king, claimed to have imposed tribute upon some of Aram's dependencies, Ammon appears to have remained unmolested, retaining possession of S Gilead until the middle of the eighth century.

After Uzziah became sole ruler in Judah (*ca.* 770), he firmly established Judah's hold on S Transjordan, stretching from Edom to Ammon. But a short time after Uzziah died (*ca.* 742), Jotham had to face a rebellion by the "king of the Ammonites" (II Chr. 27: 5), whom he was able to subdue and subject to large annual tribute.

*b. Ammon as a vassal of Assyria* (ca. 742-630). The resurgence of Assyrian power under Tiglath-pileser III (733) naturally affected the fortunes of Ammon. All the Transjordan states became vassals of Assyria. Each was permitted to retain its own native dynasty, which, in return for Assyrian protection, had to pay homage to the Assyrian monarch. From the Annals of Tiglath-pileser III we learn that Shanip (Assyrian *Sanipu*) was king of Ammon in 733, as he is listed among those who paid tribute to Assyria that year. He is possibly to be identified with the "king of the Ammonites" mentioned above in connection with Jotham's campaign against Ammon (II Chr. 27:5). During the remainder of the eighth century the Assyrians may have allowed the Ammonites to annex some of their former territory in the land of Gad, and this may be part of the general historical background of Ps. 83:8—H 83:9. Shortly after Sargon II died (*ca.* 705), a general rebellion forced his successor, Sennacherib, to carry out an extensive Palestine expedition (701), during which he received tribute from the Transjordan states, Ammon, Moab, and Edom. According to the Annals of Sennacherib, the king of Ammon in 701 was Bod'el (Assyrian *Bud'ilu*), who perhaps was the immediate successor of Shanip. We do not know how long Bod'el reigned in Ammon, but since his name appears again in the inscriptions of Esarhaddon (681-669) and Ashurbanipal (668-633), he probably ruled until at least 670. By *ca.* 667, he had either died or been deposed, for we have reference to a new Ammonite king in the later records of Ashurbanipal.

Throughout most of the seventh century Ammon remained a nominal Assyrian province, tributary to the Assyrian king, but still permitted to have their own native ruler. The Ammonite king Bod'el, whose name appears in a building inscription of Esarhaddon, is recorded as furnishing certain unspecified materials for the royal palace at Nineveh. From a letter apparently written to Esarhaddon himself, we learn that the Ammonites paid a tribute of two minas of gold (i.e., one thirtieth of a talent), an amount significantly larger than that exacted from either Moab or Judah. The beneficent protection of the Assyrians evidently enabled the Ammonites to keep control of a substantial part of the desert caravan trade, which contributed immensely to their prosperity.

*Ca.* 667, Bod'el died and was succeeded by (his son?) 'Ammi-nadab (Assyrian *Ammi-nadbi*). 'Ammi-nadab's name appears in the so-called Cylinder C Inscription of Ashurbanipal in a list of "twenty-two kings of the seacoast" who paid tribute to Ashurbanipal in the course of his great Egyptian campaign of 667. It is also attested on two Ammonite seals, both of which bear a representation and script which point to a seventh-century date. The reigns of 'Ammi-nadab and his immediate successors marked the *floruit* of Ammonite culture and prosperity. The rich and varied nature of archaeological finds from this era suggests that the local Ammonite officials enjoyed a higher standard of living during the seventh century than their contemporaries in Israel and Judah.

*c. The decline and fall of Ammon* (ca. *630-580*). The bloody civil war which broke out between Ashurbanipal and his brother in 652 also gave the signal for rebellion throughout the vast reaches of the Assyrian Empire. Among the peoples joining in revolt were the Arab tribes of the Syrian Desert, who now swept over the regions E of Antilibanus and Transjordan, threatening the security of the E Assyrian provinces as well as the vassal states of Ammon, Moab, and Edom. Although the Ammonites were undoubtedly affected by the razzias of the Arab hordes, it would appear that they were able to save themselves from total destruction at this time, probably because of their own stout defenses and timely Assyrian aid. However, Arab tribes continued to roam perilously close to Ammonite territory. By the beginning of the sixth century distinctive Arab influence on the Ammonites is reflected in several personal names found on Ammonite seals coming from this period, and by the special legal formula, "A maidservant of B," which was employed on certain seals to designate the relationship between a reigning prince (second name) and a particular official in his service (first name). The seals in question appear to have belonged to Ammonite officials who were women—this fact shows the superior position of women in the land of Ammon, and evidences strong influence by nomadic practice. On one Ammonite seal, however, appears the name Hananel, who probably was king of Ammon, either in the latter half of the seventh century or during the early sixth century, since his name is the same as that of the earlier Ammonite king Hanun. In the Bronze and Iron Age states of Syria, royal names tended to be repeated.

The impact of the fall of Assyria on the historical situation in Transjordan is not entirely clear, but it would appear from the biblical oracle against Ammon and Moab in Zeph. 2:8-11 and the prophecy against only Ammon in Jer. 49:1-6 (both of which seem to reflect events prior to the death of Josiah in 609/608) that the Ammonites had made boasts

against the former territory of Israel (Zeph. 2:8, 10), and had actually occupied the land and settled in the cities which once belonged to the tribe of Gad (Jer. 49:1). Thus by the beginning of the last decade of the seventh century, the Ammonites had asserted their complete independence once again, expanding as far W as the Jordan Valley, and becoming what must have been the dominant state of S Transjordan.

However, the picture soon changed. According to information from recently published tablets of the Babylonian Chronicle, in 599 Nebuchadrezzar embarked on a hitherto unknown expedition to Syria in which he sent raiding parties into the neighboring desert to plunder the Arabs. It would seem that the Ammonites and Moabites were among those induced to co-operate with the Babylonian garrison troops making raids on those disloyal to Nebuchadrezzar, including Judah (cf. II Kings 24:2). Thus in return for help and protection against the ever-threatening Arabs, the Ammonites placed themselves under Babylonian suzerainty. In a very short time, however, they became restless under the Babylonian yoke. In 593 envoys from Ammon joined others from Edom, Moab, Tyre, and Sidon in a conspiracy at Jerusalem to foment rebellion against Babylon (Jer. 27:3). The promise of Egyptian support undoubtedly stimulated the convocation of the conference.

From this point on, Ammon's revolt against Babylon was open and permanent, as is suggested by the picture the prophet Ezekiel gives of Nebuchadrezzar standing at the parting of the ways, one leading to Rabbah, the other to Judah and Jerusalem (Ezek. 21:19-22—H 21:24-27). The catastrophe that struck Judah did not immediately affect Ammon. From ensuing events, it seems the Ammonites remained in open revolt, even to the point of daring to interfere in the internal affairs of the remnant of Judah.

Among those who had taken refuge in Ammon was Ishmael (Jer. 41:1). There he fell under the influence of Baalis (for *Baal-samak* or the like), the contemporary Ammonite king, who plotted with him to assassinate GEDALIAH (Jer. 40:14). The Judean collaborationist governor underestimated the zeal of Ishmael, for Ishmael slew Gedaliah (Jer. 41:2-3) and escaped to Ammon (Jer. 41:15). The Ammonite king was apparently trying to get control over the remnant of the royal house of Judah, probably in the hope of restoring the Davidic kingdom under Ammonite rule.

Political events in Transjordan during the next few years are obscure. It is not improbable that punitive measures were exerted against the Ammonites. Josephus (Antiq. X.ix.181) supports this; he records a campaign conducted by Nebuchadrezzar in Coele-Syria, after which Nebuchadrezzar made war on Ammon and Moab. The Chaldean attack set the stage for the collapse of the Ammonite state. Archaeological explorations have shown that Transjordan was largely depopulated before the middle of the sixth century B.C., and that sedentary occupation of Ammon ceased almost completely until the third century. Nebuchadrezzar may have ordered a deportation carried out for Ammon similar to that already executed for Judah. This would explain the sudden end to extensive sedentary civilization in Ammon, which created a vacuum into which poured the *Benê Qedem* (i.e., "sons of the east," the Arab invaders; *see*

EAST, PEOPLE OF THE), who destroyed all formally organized political activity in this area (cf. Ezek. 25: 4, 8-9), bringing to an end the autonomous Ammonite state.

**7. Postexilic Ammon.** Following the destruction of sedentary civilization in Transjordan, the Arab nomads became masters of the land, tenting in the ruins of what had once been thriving walled and unwalled settlements. Political order was not restored until the coming of the Persians, whose armies gained suzerainty over the Neo-Babylonian Empire (by 530), which included N Arabia and Transjordan. How soon the Persians were able to re-establish organized political activity in the land of Ammon is not known. By the time of Nehemiah (*ca.* 440), the province of Ammon extended as far W as the Jordan Valley, bordering immediately on Judah.

During this period there lived a certain Tobiah (*see* TOBIAH 2), described as "the servant, the Ammonite" (on this title, *see below*), who appears as the *de facto* head of a Jewish enclave in Ammon (Neh. 2:10, 19; 4:3, 7, etc.). Most scholars have considered Tobiah the contemporary Persian governor of Ammon (although Nehemiah never calls him such), but a recently published early Lihyanite inscription may force revision of this opinion. According to the inscription, a certain "'Abd the governor" is mentioned next to Gashmu bin Shahru (*see* GESHEM; cf. Neh. 2:19; 6:1-2). From the context it appears that 'Abd was the contemporary Persian governor of Ammon and Dedan. The twice-mentioned formula for Tobiah (Neh. 2:10, 19) may be in reality a corruption of an original "Tobiah, and 'Abd the Ammonite" (such successive haplographies and dittographies in the Hebrew text are not uncommon). The association between 'Abd the Ammonite and Tobiah the Jew would thus be quite parallel to that between Gashmu the Arab chieftain and 'Abd the Ammonite governor, although the precise nature of this association cannot be further defined. In any event, Nehemiah does not cease to emphasize the evil intention of Tobiah (2: 19; 4:3, 7; 6:1, 12, 14; 13:4-9), who apparently became the first Jewish ancestor of a long line of Tobiads who seem to have made their home at 'Araq el-Emir in S Gilead, where tombs have been discovered bearing the family name deeply carved into their external wall, and written in an archaic Aramaic script that need not date after 400 B.C.

Following the conquest of Alexander and the subsequent division of his empire (late fourth century), effective control of the land of Ammon passed to the Egyptian Ptolemies. *Ca.* 300, mention of Ammon occurs once in a list of hierodules (male and female slaves) from Ma'in (S Arabia), indicating that Ammon was still a well-recognized territory on the fringes of Arabia. Several decades later, we again hear of an Ammonite Tobiah, cited by the Zenon (or Gerza) Papyri (260-240). His name, dwelling place, and general description confirm his relationship to the Tobiah of Nehemiah's day. According to the Zenon archive, however, this later Tobiad functioned as head of the Egyptian military colony in Ammon. His principal duty was to levy taxes and imposts, and turn over the portion due the Egyptian minister of finances in the administration of Ptolemy II Philadelphus (285-246). Thus this Tobiah was a local Jewish notable of the well-known Tobiad family chosen by Philadelphus as responsible governor of the Ammonite province (*ca.* 265).

The prosperous reign of Philadelphus continued for twenty years after the annexation of Ammon, but no record has preserved the names of the potentates of Ammon throughout this period. I Maccabees mentions a considerable dissemination of Jews still living in Ammon "among the people [RSV in the land] of Tobiah" (ἐν τοῖς Τουβίου; I Macc. 5:13) at the time of the Maccabean restoration (*ca.* 165). Between the years 183-176 (according to Jos. Antiq. XII.iv.11), one of the last known Tobiads, HYRCANUS, left the Egyptian court and took refuge in the land of Ammon (the identification of his fortress or sanctuary with 'Araq el-Emir is doubtful), where he lived in retreat, fighting the Arabs and defying the enmity of his brothers who held high offices in Jerusalem.

Arab encroachment on Ammonite territory had been constantly on the increase since the seventh century, and by the first century Ammon had become a part of the Nabatean kingdom (*see* NABATEANS). Nabatean pottery has been found in several Ammonite tombs dating from this period. Roman conquests during the first century B.C. incorporated Ammon into the Roman Empire, but apparently had little effect on the ethnic character of the land. Roman influence can be seen in the beautiful architecture still evident at Amman, and a number of Greek and Latin inscriptions coming from the Amman area bear witness to Roman culture, although personal names appearing in these inscriptions tend to show the predominance of Arabs by the second century A.D. Around the middle of this same century, the Ammonites are referred to as a contemporary ethnic group by Justin Martyr, who indicates that they were still a numerous people. In the following century, however, Origen vaguely alludes to them, along with Moabites and Edomites, as Arab tribes. With this last allusion, the Ammonites disappear from history, to "be remembered no more among the nations" (Ezek. 25:10).

**8. The culture of the Ammonites.** Most of the tomb groups, statues, and seals which have been found in Ammon date from the seventh-sixth centuries, and precisely in this period must be placed the great material prosperity of the Ammonite state. Of special interest are two statues which are among the few complete examples of native sculpture so far found in either Transjordan or W Palestine for the early periods (i.e., Iron Age or earlier). The smaller of the two statues bears an inscription in Old Aramaic characters which may be translated: "Yarachazar, chief of the horse." The appellation "chief of the horse" (not absolutely certain) would seem to indicate that Yarachazar performed an important military function as chief of the cavalry. The Ammonites probably had a well-organized cavalry division in their army under Assyrian influence. In recently cleared Iron Age tombs near Amman three small pottery horse-and-rider figurines have been found, also suggesting Ammonite cavalry.

From the tombs near Amman have come large quantities of typical Ammonite pottery, chiefly from the seventh century. Most of the pottery belongs to a homogeneous group displaying specific Transjordan types. A survey of all the pottery found shows that the ancient Ammonite potters were skilled both in design and in technique, and were not inferior to their Palestinian contemporaries.

In addition to pottery, the Ammonite tombs have yielded numerous seals, several of them inscribed. The largest group of nonpottery objects comes from the tombs at Sahab and Meqabelein, S of Amman, where iron, limestone, and alabaster utensils and glass or bead ornaments were unearthed.

The tombs have also contributed substantially to knowledge of Ammonite burial customs. At times the Ammonites buried their dead in coffins, three large specimens of which have been uncovered in the tomb of Adoni-nur at Amman. At Sahab the headpiece of a pottery anthropoid coffin was discovered, representing a crude adaptation of a type of clay coffin known from Egyptian models of the Eighteenth and Nineteenth Dynasties.

Most of the Ammonite tombs were cave tombs cut out of natural rock either below the ground surface or in the side of a hill. All tombs appear to have been of the bench variety. Unique features include cupboardlike recesses at the E end of tomb A at Amman, and a curious chimneylike construction in the middle of the SW side of a tomb at Sahab. The Iron Age Ammonite tombs disclose some of the diverse streams of cultural influence exerted on the Ammonites. As might be expected, Assyrian influence was predominant, manifest not only in pottery and seal motifs, but also in plastic art.

Architecturally, the Ammonites built in what is generally called the "megalithic" style, owing to the great size of stones used in construction. This style of building may have been adapted from the much older megalithic constructions of Neolithic Ammon, initiated by a people whom scholars sometimes refer to as the "dolmen builders" (see DOLMENS; PREHISTORY). Many dolmens have been found in the land of Ammon, especially around the ancient capital, Rabbah, and slightly to the W. Circular towers, fortresses, and other buildings the Ammonites constructed seem to have housed most of the population during the Iron Age.

Little is known about Ammonite higher culture, particularly religion. Not enough material is now available to clarify details concerning the controversial figure of the so-called national deity of Ammon, Milcom. Several individual finds from the archaeological survey of Transjordan show that many of the Iron Age settlers worshiped a pantheon of deities, including gods and goddesses of fertility. This would be expected, of course, in a largely agricultural type of civilization. Some of the Ammonites undoubtedly knew how to read and write in a dialect which must be classified as S Canaanite, which was closely related to biblical Hebrew, and in all probability could be read and understood by the Israelites. On the basis of the small amount of epigraphic material found in Ammon, it is rash to suggest that the Ammonites may have been literary artists as gifted as their contemporaries in W Palestine.

Bibliography. E. Meyer, Die Israeliten und ihre Nachbarstämme (1906). D. Mackenzie, "Megalithic Monuments of Rabbath Ammon at 'Amman," Annual of PEF (1911), pp. 1-40. H. Gressman, "Die ammonitischen Tobiaden," Sitzungs-

berichte der Preussischen Akademie der Wissenschaften (1921), pp. 663-71. D. Diringer, Le Iscrizioni Antico-Ebraiche Palestinesi (1934). M. Noth, "Die israelitischen Siedlungsgebiete im Ostjordanlande," ZDPV, 58 (1935), 230-35. F.-M. Abel, Géographie de la Palestine, vols. I-II (1933, 1938). N. Glueck, "Explorations in the Land of Ammon," BASOR, 68 (1937), 13-21; "Explorations in Eastern Palestine III," AASOR, vols. XVIII-XIX (1937-39); The Other Side of the Jordan (1940). R. de Vaux, "Notes d'histoire et de topographie Transjordaniennes," Vivre et Penser, 50 (1941), 16-47. M. Noth, "Beiträge zur Geschichte des Ostjordanlandes," PJ, 37 (1941), 56-57; "Israelitische Stämme zwischen Ammon und Moab," ZAW, 19 (1944), 11-56. Y. Aharoni, "A New Ammonite Inscription," IEJ, I (1950), 219-22. H. L. Ginsberg, "Judah and the Transjordan States from 734-582 B.C.," Alexander Marx Jubilee Volume (1950), pp. 347-68. R. Barnett, "Four Sculptures from Amman," Annual of the Department of Antiquities of Jordan, 1 (1951), 34-36. N. Avigad, "An Ammonite Seal," IEJ, II (1952), 163-64. R. O'Callaghan, "A Statue Recently Found in 'Ammān," Orientalia, 21 (1952), 184-93. G. L. Harding, "The Tomb of Adoni Nur in Amman," Annual of PEF, 6 (1953), 48-65. W. F. Albright, "Some Notes on Ammonite History," Miscellanea Biblica B. Ubach (1954), pp. 131-36; The Archaeology of Palestine (Penguin Books; 1956). D. Wiseman, Chronicles of Chaldaean Kings (1956). G. L. Harding, The Antiquities of Jordan (1959). J. Simons, The Geographical and Topographical Texts of the OT (1959).          G. M. LANDES

**AMNON** ăm'nŏn [אמנון, אמינון (II Sam. 13:20), faithful; LXX Αμνων]. 1. David's eldest son, born of Ahinoam the Jezreelitess at Hebron (II Sam. 3:2). A single incident in his life is known—namely, his rape of TAMAR (2) his half sister, which her brother Absalom avenged by slaying Amnon (ch. 13). This was the first phase of the dissolution of David's family, following his adultery with Bathsheba and the murder of Uriah.

2. A son of Shimon, and a remote descendant of Judah (I Chr. 4:20).          J. M. WARD

**AMOK** ā'mŏk [עמוק, deep, unsearchable]. A priest in the group that returned from exile with Zerubbabel (Neh. 12:7), and the ancestor of a priestly family (vs. 20).

**AMON** ăm'ən [אמון, אמן (I Kings 22:26), trustworthy, reliable, faithful; Egyp. imn; Babylonian ămănă; Assyrian ămūnû; Αμων]; KJV ALLOM ăl'əm in 3 below. Alternately: AMI ā'mī [אמי] (Ezra 2:57). 1. Governor of the city of Samaria in the reign of Ahab.

After Micaiah ben Imlah had foretold the failure of Ahab's expedition against Ramoth-gilead, he was committed to the care of Amon and Joash the king's son, to be imprisoned and fed on bread and water till the king's return (I Kings 22:26-28; II Chr. 18: 25-27).

2. King of Judah ca. 642-640 B.C.; son and successor of Manasseh.

Amon became king at the age of twenty-two and reigned for two years (II Kings 21:19; II Chr. 33:21). His mother was Meshullemeth daughter of Haruz of Jotbah. This town is probably to be located in Galilee (Assyrian Yatbatu, Greek Jotapata). The name is significant as indicating the close connection maintained with the North at this time (cf. also Rumah in II Kings 23:36). The relationship between Judah and the former kingdom is of great importance from he point of view of understanding the whole history of Judah during this period.

Amon followed in the footsteps of his father, Manasseh, and presumably owed allegiance to Assyria, whose gods he continued to worship even as his father had done. This speaks against the historicity of the Chronicler's account of Manasseh's repentance, unless it is to be assumed that Amon made new "images" (II Chr. 33:22b).

Amon was murdered by his servants after a brief reign (II Kings 21:23; II Chr. 33:24). No reason is given, but it is clear that the murder did not have popular backing, as the "people of the land" put the murderers to death and placed Josiah, Amon's son, on the throne. The assassination was probably the result of a court plot.

Bibliography. W. F. Albright, Review of Géographie de la Palestine, JBL, LVIII (1939), 184 ff. Contrast H. L. Ginsberg, Alexander Marx Jubilee Volume (1950), pp. 349 ff, especially n. 12.

**3.** One of the descendants of Solomon's servants who returned from the Babylonian exile (Neh. 7:59). In Ezra 2:57 he is called Ami.      H. B. MacLean

**4.** Amon-Ra, the imperial god of Egypt, whose chief center of worship was at the temple of Karnak in Thebes (Jer. 46:25). See EGYPT § 3a. Fig. EGY 19.

**5.** A component of the Hebrew name for THEBES.

**AMORITES** ăm'ə rīts [אמרי; Akkad. amurrū, deriving from Amurru (in Akkad. sources the name of the land W of Mesopotamia); LXX Ἀμορραῖος]. The inhabitants of the land called Amurru. Since the exact extent of the region is not known, it is not possible to mention the exact area where Amorites lived, but it may have been Syria and at least part of Palestine.

**1. OT references.** According to some passages, the Amorites are a Canaanite tribe (cf. Gen. 10:16; Exod. 3:8; I Chr. 1:14). Part of this tribe lived in the area which later was inhabited by the tribe of Judah, particularly in the mountains (Deut. 1:19 ff, 27, 44; Josh. 10:5 ff), and another part in the area E of Jordan, where two Amorite kingdoms, Heshbon and Bashan, are mentioned (Num. 21:13, etc.; Josh. 2:10; 9:10; 24:8; Judg. 10:8; 11:19 ff). In Gen. 15:16, the term "Amorite" refers to the pre-Israelite population of Palestine in general. Probably also Jerusalem was an Amorite town in pre-Israelite times (cf. Ezek. 16:3).

According to OT conceptions, the Amorites were people tall like giants (Amos 2:9). It is easy to understand that people who lived long ago, and of whom nothing was known but what popular tales had to tell, were conceived of as living in the world of myth and imagination. Myth and history were two aspects of the same thing.

**2. Extrabiblical sources.** Our knowledge of the Amorites must be gathered from extrabiblical sources, and very rich material is now available. The country of Amurru is mentioned in early Cuneiform texts. As early a ruler as the Old Akkadian king Sargon (ca. 2400 B.C.) is said to have made an expedition to Amurru in the eleventh year of his reign in order to provide material for his buildings. Gudea, king of Lagash (ca. 2000 B.C.), fetched marble from Amurru, and so on. At that time Amurru seems to have been a powerful country, the center of which

was Mari (modern Tell Hariri), at the place where the Euphrates River turns eastward.

From the region of Mari, some Amorites pushed eastward shortly after 2000; conquered the last Sumerian kingdom, the third dynasty of Ur; and founded local kingdoms, among which the first Babylonian dynasty was the most important. In Mesopotamia the Amorites merged with the people living there previously—i.e., the Sumerians and the Akkadians—but in a number of personal names it is still possible to trace them. The Amorites who remained in the W were mixed with other groups, also of Indo-European blood. Hammurabi of Babylon put an end to the Amorite Empire and conquered Mari. Because of the active policy of Hammurabi, various groups of people moved southward. Through wars with Egyptians, Hurrians, and Hittites, the Amorite world was still more divided up into small kingdoms, in which the population was of a mixed character.

In the period which is reflected in the Amarna Letters, a number of independent Amorite city-states existed. The center of one of these states was Kadesh on the Orontes, known also through Hittite sources from Boghazköy (1400-1200 B.C.). This place is known also because of the important battle between the Egyptians under Pharaoh Ramses II and the Hittites. The invasion of the Sea People and the Hittite wars made an end to the independent Amorite kingdoms in Syria.

The Amarna Letters throw light upon the Amorite kingdoms which collaborated with another ethnic group, the HABIRU, the Hebrews of the OT (see HEBREW; cf. Gen. 14). Thus the Amorites were one of the groups which played an important role in the growth of the Israelite nation. The French excavations at Mari under the direction of A. Parrot have contributed in a very important way in elucidating the earlier periods of the history of the Amorites and their language and civilization.

**3. Language and civilization.** Linguistically the Amorites were closely related to the Canaanites (see CANAAN), both being Northwest Semitic dialects. Canaanite may be said to be a branch of Amorite, if Amurru is taken to be the whole area of Syria and N Palestine. Also Aramean is to be classified as a language which developed from Amorite. The Aramean territory (Akkadian Aḥlāmē)—according to an inscription of Tiglath-pileser I (ca. 1110 B.C.)—was between Tadmar (Palmyre) in Amurru, 'Anat in Suḥi, and Rapiqu in Karduniash (Babylonia).

The Amorite language, as a consequence of what has been said, has a number of features in common with Canaanite, and Ugaritic may be regarded as one branch of Amorite, of which a number of local varieties undoubtedly existed during the second millennium. Its role in the growth of biblical Hebrew was very important. The latter fact is excellently illustrated by the occurrence of a number of words which so far occur only in the Mari Texts and in the OT.

The Mari Texts also throw light upon the civilization of the Amorites during the first half of the second millennium. In the kingdom of Mari an Amorite civilization of a high standard existed, and many fine examples of art have been unearthed at Mari. Characteristic of the cultural conditions at Mari is the role played by seminomadic tribes besides the resident population. One such group is the Benjaminites, and if this element really is the same tribe as the tribe of Benjamin of the OT, their appearing in the Mari Texts is very important. In Gen. 49:27 Benjamin is described in the following way:

> Benjamin is a ravenous wolf,
> in the morning devouring the prey,
> and at even dividing the spoil.

The picture of the Benjaminites to be found in the Mari Texts is astonishingly similar, for they are described as a people who to a great extent live upon

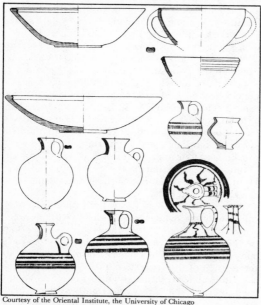

Courtesy of the Oriental Institute, the University of Chicago

22. Ceramics, probably Amorite, from Tell el-Salihiyeh (ancient Hobah?) near Damascus; Old Babylonian period

prey, because of which the king of Mari undertakes expeditions to punish them. In the region of Damascus, pieces of ceramics have been found which probably may be connected with the Amorites. Fig. AMO 22. *See* HOBAH; DAMASCENE.

**Bibliography.** F. Böhl, *Kanaanäer und Hebräer* (1911). E. Dhorme, "Les Amorrhéens," *RB*, 37 (1928), 161-80; 39 (1930), 161-78; 40 (1931), 161-84: one of the most important works on the Amorites (=*Recueil Edouard Dhorme* [1951], pp. 81 ff). W. F. Albright, "Western Asia in the 20th Century B.C.: the Archives of Mari," *BASOR*, 67 (1937), 26-30; *JBL*, 58 (1939), 91-103. A. HALDAR

\*AMOS ā′məs [עָמוֹס]. The third book of the twelve prophets in the OT canon, but the first of them in time; the work of a prophet worthy to rank with the greatest, inaugurating as he did a new period in the development of the prophetic office in Israel and Judah.

See map "Palestine: Hosea, Amos," under HOSEA, BOOK OF.

**1. A new epoch in prophecy.** The book of Amos has a unique significance in the OT, being the first collection of prophetic oracles preserved in Israel as a separate book. There were prophets in Israel for centuries before the time of Amos, but the record of their activity is embodied in the general history of the nation, and we have only fragmentary specimens of their preaching. Men such as Moses and Elijah set their mark deeply upon the soul of Israel; and others such as Nathan and Micaiah, of whom we have only a glimpse, seem to have been of a stature comparable with any of the later prophets, yet no one took in hand the collection of their oracles. Amos' scornful words (7:14) in which he disassociates himself from the official guilds of the prophets have sometimes led to a wholesale depreciation of the significance of earlier prophets. The characteristics which they shared with other schools of diviners in the Near East, such as the use of music to induce a trance condition and the temptation to adjust their oracles at the pleasure of their customers, have made them seem to belong in a totally different category from the writing prophets. But when we find in their midst a Nathan and a Micaiah (*see* NATHAN 2; MICAIAH 1), we have to recognize that, in spite of all corruptions, a genuine prophetic tradition was kept alive in these guilds. Amos condemns, not the guilds, but their corruption; the order of prophets he recognized as a divine institution in Israel (2:11). He himself became a prophet only because those whose calling this was were failing to discharge their office. It is a mistake, therefore, to exaggerate the break between the earlier prophets and the succession of writing prophets that began with Amos, as though he were the inaugurator of a totally new tradition.

There has been considerable discussion (*see* bibliography) whether or not Amos ever acknowledged himself to be a prophet. Some scholars have insisted that the relevant passage in Amos 7:14 can be translated: "I *was* no prophet," etc., so that it is a denial, not of Amos' present status as a prophet, but only of any past connection with the official prophetic profession. This translation has the support of the LXX and the Peshitta Syr., and was followed by the ERV. Others, however, hold that the absence of a verb in this clause requires the present tense, and understand Amos as denying any connection with the traditional institution of the *Nabi* in Israel, so that this passage becomes the basis for breaking completely the continuity between Amos and the earlier prophets. One unusual theory is that Amos was a *Nabi* but outside the official order, earning his living by prophesying in Israel but not belonging to a guild. Another is that he was a *Nabi*, but with two stages in his career—in the first he delivered oracles of hope like any popular prophet, but as a consequence of his visions of judgment he was transformed into a prophet of doom. Whatever may be the tense of the statement, it seems clear that Amos regarded himself as performing the function of a *Nabi*, that he respected the institution itself as a divine establishment in Israel, and that he was primarily concerned to deny any official connection between himself and the degenerate, mercenary prophets of his own day.

We must ask how the practice of collecting and preserving the oracles of a prophet in a separate book came to begin with Amos. It was to have far-reaching results, first in the raising of the prophetic office to a consistently high level, which it was to hold for two centuries, then in the consolidation and crystallization of Israel's faith in a series of prophetic books. To Amos his prophetic activity was in no way novel; he was merely doing what God had always intended a faithful prophet to do (2:11; 3:8). But it was the simplicity and thoroughness with which Amos discharged the office of prophet, combined with the swiftness with which his words were validated by disastrous historical events, that induced men to preserve his oracles and some slight record of his activity. Then, as men discovered the power of the written word to perpetuate the spirit and mission of the prophet and to inspire and train others to take up a similar mission, it became the practice for those under the influence of a prophet to record his utterances.

**2. The man and his background.** Amos, like Jesus, was, until the sudden beginning of his prophetic ministry, a layman with no professional training for a religious office. He was a shepherd and pincher of sycamore fruit (1:1; 7:14) in the region of Tekoa, some five miles S of Bethlehem and ten miles S of Jerusalem.* The sycamore fruit, which had to be pinched so that it would ripen to an edible state, was used only by the poor. The imagery of Amos' oracles reflects the shepherd life—the sound at night of the lion roaring over its prey, the plague of locusts that eat up the pasture, the seven stars and Orion that are witnesses to the creative power of God. But it is equally evident that the shepherd is familiar with the sights of the city—the overfed, callous plutocrats at ease in their expensive houses, thinking only of how to amuse themselves, the peasant burdened with debts and sold into slavery for the price of a pair of shoes, the sanctuaries crowded with confident worshipers exulting in their good fortune, prophets and priests with no word to speak to a swiftly decaying society. With eyes sharpened by the frugal, austere life of his desert regions, by the insights of faith that came to him from earlier prophets, and by his own intense consciousness of God's justice, Amos examines the life of urban Israel and can form no other conclusion than that it is ripe for judgment (8:2). Fig. TEK 7.

The fact that Amos, when he took up his prophetic task, went past the Judean city of Jerusalem and delivered his oracles at Bethel and Samaria in the N kingdom, has led to attempts to make him a northerner by origin. One theory is that Amos began as a shepherd and pincher of sycamore fruit in the N, took up his mission there, and removed to Tekoa only when the authorities expelled him from the N kingdom because of his harsh pronouncements of doom. Another is that there was a second Tekoa in the N kingdom where Amos lived, though no historic reference to such a place has been found. The absence of sycamores in the region of Tekoa, since they grow only at lower altitudes, and their presence at some

points in the N, has reinforced these attempts. The sycamore may also have grown, however, in lower parts of Judea not too far from Tekoa, so that Amos could have discharged both occupations in that region. It must also be recognized that, for Amos, Israel and Judah were one people of God, and his concern as a prophet was for the whole nation. The most forceful leadership of the nation in his time was in Samaria rather than in Jerusalem, and it was urgent that he reach with his message those who would be most able to influence national policy.

It need occasion no surprise that a Judean shepherd should have a deep appreciation of the religious heritage of his people and an ability to express his convictions in poetic language of the first order. Rudeness of occupation does not necessitate rudeness of thought and speech. It was from such peasant homes that many of Israel's greatest leaders came. Robertson Smith points out that, not only in the earlier Hebrew but also in the later Arab society of the East, knowledge and oratory were quite consistent with the simplicity and poverty of pastoral life. From Amos we learn that it was in peasant homes such as his that the true culture and faith of Israel was preserved from generation to generation.

Nor is the wide knowledge of social and political conditions evident in the book inconsistent with the life of the shepherd. His occupation would take him to the markets in the larger centers, and he may well have journeyed as far N as Damascus. He was a keen observer of life; his concern about the fulfilment of God's purpose in the world made him alert to notice what was actually happening. Because his God is Lord of the whole earth, his vision embraces all the nations with which the Hebrews had any converse, and he could interpret the advance of the Assyrians toward the Palestinian and Syrian area as a judgment of God upon the sins of the states involved. Because it was an axiom of his faith that a holy and just God could be served only by a nation that reflected in its life the holiness and justice of God, he had eyes where others were blind to see the peril in which Israel was placed by the dishonesty of its courts, the maltreatment of its poor, and the profligacy of its upper classes.

It was the silence of the professional prophets, their failure to speak into the critical situation of the time the word from God which was most needed, that forced the layman Amos to become a prophet. In his own account of his call (7:14-15) he refuses to let his name be associated in any way with the prophetic guilds in which the office was passed down from father to son. They were blind to realities which were plain to his eyes. They let themselves be dissuaded by social pressures from speaking their true message (2: 12). It was Amos' knowledge of God's will concerning Israel, his knowledge of God's mind concerning the kind of things that were happening in Israel, that compelled him to say what no one else had the vision or courage to say. God took him from following the flock and sent him as a prophet to his people.

**3. The contemporary scene.** The first half of the eighth century B.C. was singularly propitious for both Israel and Judah. In 805 B.C. the Assyrian, Adadnirari III, crushed Damascus, Israel's N neighbor, decisively. The dimensions of his booty—2,300 talents of silver, 20 talents of gold, 3,000 talents of copper, 5,000 talents of iron, plus all manner of manufactured goods—tells the story of Damascus' impoverishment. The Palestinian states had little to fear from the Syrian for many years to come. King Jehoash of Israel was not slow to grasp his opportunity, quickly recapturing the border cities that Syria had seized in its days of power (II Kings 13:25). Then, in 782 B.C., upon the death of Adad-nirari III, Assyria had a series of weak kings who no longer attempted to assert their authority as far as the Mediterranean. Not until 745 B.C. and the accession of Tiglath-pileser III was the West to be troubled by the Assyrian again.

In this period Israel was free not only to extend her borders but also to control the trade routes of the ancient world that now passed through her territory. A rich merchant class developed, sharing the nation's prosperity with the nobility and building for themselves elaborate homes. But the common people had no share in this new wealth. Earlier wars had weighed heavily on them, and now they found themselves helpless before the rapacity of power- and land-hungry upper classes. Small farmers were dispossessed to make possible the development of large estates. Israel, whose strength had been in the mass of its solid, independent citizens, was quickly becoming divided into two classes—the dissolute rich and the embittered poor. The shrines at Bethel and Gilgal were crowded continually by the prosperous citizens who interpreted the nation's prosperity as a certain sign of God's favor and who looked for yet greater days to come. Priests and prophets at the sanctuaries benefited sufficiently from the lavish offerings that they were not inclined to do or to say anything that might dampen the mood of confidence and exultation.

**4. The question of date.** Into this scene came Amos with a message of doom. The date at which he began his ministry is disputed. For some, the popular mood of confidence in the nation and the freedom from any fear of invasion points to the period *ca.* 760 B.C. or shortly afterward. For others, notably R. S. Cripps, Amos' certainty that Israel is soon to be invaded indicates that he had knowledge of Tiglath-pileser III's westward movement, which began in 745 B.C. But Amos' prediction of doom was based, not on his knowledge of developments in Assyria, but rather upon his conviction that such corruption and unfaithfulness as he saw in Israel could not long remain unpunished by Israel's God. It is significant that he never once mentions from what quarter the doom is to come. The date of his activity may therefore be placed anywhere between 760 and 745 B.C. The editor of the book (1:1) locates it merely in the reign of Uzziah (786-744 B.C.) and the reign of Jeroboam, the son of Joash (788-747 B.C.). The mention of an earthquake that occurred two years after Amos' appearance is of no assistance to us in securing a more exact date. It was still remembered in the days of Zechariah (Zech. 14:5) as having taken place in the reign of Uzziah. It may well have been interpreted as the first installment of the judgment promised by Amos. The attempt to fix a date between 745 and 740 B.C. for the earthquake is unconvincing.

How long Amos' ministry continued is uncertain. It may have been only a few months or even less.

There is no reason to assume that he did all his preaching at Bethel. In 2:9; 4:1; 6:1 he seems to be speaking to an audience in Samaria, but, of course, they could be people of Samaria worshiping in Bethel. The termination of his ministry took place in Bethel (7:10-17). Amos' sharp critique of the existing order in Israel and his announcement of an invader who would overrun the country and carry the populace into captivity had included a specific prophecy of the fall of the house of Jeroboam (7:9). This was interpreted as treason. Amos was accused to the king of conspiring against him and was ordered to return at once to Judah. The spokesman for the king was the priest of the royal sanctuary, Amaziah. His words to Amos were sharp with scorn. He assumed that all the prophet wanted to achieve was that people would be sufficiently disturbed to pay him well for a more cheerful oracle—a species of religious blackmail which apparently was not uncommon. What happened following Amos' expulsion from Bethel, we do not know.

**5. The composition of the book.** Whether or not Amos left behind him written documents containing his oracles cannot be established with certainty. At many points the freshness and force of the text suggest Amos' direct authorship. The Scandinavian traditio-historical school holds that the oracles of Amos, like those of all other prophets, were transmitted orally for a long period. The remarkably sound condition of the text, however, lends support to the view that either Amos or an amanuensis set down the oracles in writing.

The biographical passage in 7:10-17, which speaks of Amos in the third person, indicates an editor very early at work, one who was familiar with at least the closing period of Amos' mission. There is no reason why this should not be the same person who added the superscription in 1:1 and other editorial matter. The fact that the king of Judah is named before the king of Israel in 1:1 indicates that the editor was a Judean and that the work of editing was done in Judah. As might be expected after Amos' expulsion from Israel, the primary circulation of his oracles would be in Judah, and there are a number of editorial glosses which seem to have been intended to apply Amos' message more directly to Judah. Whether or not the pronouncement of doom on Judah in 2:4-5 is original to Amos may be debated. In every other instance in this extended oracle it is the inhumanity of each nation that is condemned, so that the climax is reached in the exposure of Israel's inhumanity. But the condemnation of Judah is for transgressions against the law and statutes of Yahweh. This seems to interrupt the sequence of the oracle and to show a more legalistic concern, such as one would expect from the Deuteronomic school in seventh-century Judah. On the other hand, it has been argued that for Amos to name all Israel's neighbors and leave Judah unmentioned would be strange. The denunciation of Edom in 1:11-12 has also been suspected as a Judean editorial intrusion because of the notoriousness of the enmity between Judah and Edom, particularly after Edom's ravaging of Judah in her time of helplessness in 586 B.C. But Edom may already in the eighth century have won itself a place in Amos' roster of Israel's enemies.

Another possible Judean addition may be 6:2. Calneh and Hamath are known to have fallen before the Assyrians later in the eighth century. Gath is thought by some to have been already destroyed in Amos' time, but it was taken by Sargon in 711 B.C. This verse, 6:2, in which the Israelites are asked if they think they are powerful enough to escape the fate of Calneh, Hamath, and Gath, is therefore to be interpreted as a Judean editorial addition, taking account of later events and pointing up the significance of Amos' words for Judah.

Many scholars have questioned the authenticity of the doxologies in 4:13; 5:8-9; 9:5-6 (*see bibliography*). The thesis that they were inserted at a much later date in connection with the public reading of the book has been based on the claim that they show the influence of Second Isaiah and Job. But they are not in any way inconsistent with the thought of Amos, and there seems to be no very convincing reason for denying them to him. In particular, the assumption that Amos did not yet conceive Yahweh as Creator is very questionable. In each instance the doxology breaks in as a reminder to those who are being addressed that it is the all-powerful creator of the heavens and the earth with whom they have to do, and no petty deity who can be enclosed in a manmade shrine or bound to the fortunes of Israel.

The optimistic conclusion of the book (9:8b-15) stands in such contrast to all that precedes that its attribution to Amos was questioned very early. It seems to have been written in a time when the cities of Palestine were in ruins (vss. 11, 14) and the Israelites were scattered among the nations (vss. 9, 15). The reference to the "booth of David that is fallen" (vs. 11) posits the end of the Davidic dynasty in Judah, and the anticipation of its restoration could hardly be dated earlier than the Exile. There are numerous instances of similar hopeful prophecies' being appended to oracles of doom in exilic times when it seemed impossible that any prophet should have failed to anticipate a day of restoration beyond the day of judgment. It is wrong to base the denial of these verses to Amos upon the assumption that his oracles contained only tidings of doom and had in them no hope for any future, for Amos leaves open a door to the future for a remnant. But there is in his oracles no elaboration of this hope. The commonest interpretation of the concluding verses is that a later editor who had experienced the judgment threatened by Amos provided that elaboration. Nevertheless, a vigorous defense has been made for the authenticity of the passage by a considerable number of scholars, some of whom sought to show that there was a pattern in Israelite prophecy from early times which combined oracles of blessing with oracles of doom.

R. Gordis (*see bibliography*) has tried to show that "barring minor additions, the book is the authentic work of Amos." He finds only two exceptions (7:10-17; 8:4-14) to the rule that the book manifests throughout a clear-cut organization which it received from the hand of Amos himself. He considers the epilogue to be genuine, on the ground that it is not sufficiently grandiose to be the product of later eschatology. According to Gordis there were two collections of oracles, 1:1-7:9; chs. 8-9, the former containing a hope of repentance and salvation, which

was abandoned, however, when Amos was expelled by Amaziah. Thus in the second collection the anticipated ruin is to be complete in Israel, but Judah is to be saved and the Davidic dynasty restored (9:12).

Various views have been held of the relation to each other of the two sections of the book, which may roughly be termed the oracles and the visions. Artur Weiser holds that the visions belong to a period which preceded Amos' mission to Israel and originally formed a separate document composed at the time of the earthquake, which was interpreted as a validation of the prophet's visions of doom. To this document 8:4-14 was added at a later time. The oracles in chs. 1-6 were collected at the close of the N mission and ended originally with the biographical account, 7:10-17. The two documents were not united into one until exilic or postexilic times. The theory of two collections arises largely from the presence of parallel verses in the two sections of the book. The curious heading in 1:1: "The words of Amos, . . . which he saw," is interpreted as an elision of two original headings, "The words of Amos which he heard," and "The visions of Amos which he saw." This theory, supported by Fosbrooke (*IB*, vol. VI), rests upon a very slender basis. The division into oracles and visions may well derive from Amos himself. The early dating of the visions meets a serious obstacle in the intimate connection between Amos' vision of the overthrow of the royal house in 7:9 and the immediately following narrative of his expulsion from Israel for speaking against the royal house. The idea put forward by Fosbrooke that 7:1-9 contains an account of the experience in which Amos heard himself called to become a prophet conflicts, not only with the evident location of 7:9 late in Amos' ministry, but also with the fact that in the first of the three visions Amos is already exercising the intercessory function of a prophet in pleading for God's mercy upon the nation. Also a careful comparison of the content of the visions with the content of the oracles does not disclose any essential difference.

**6. Style.** The oracles of Amos are cast in a poetic form, which is eminently suited to their content. He shows himself skilled in the use of a variety of meters. Perhaps most effective of all is his employment of the dirgelike Kinah meter, which builds up the feeling of ominous expectation, the very music of the poetry proclaiming the message of relentless doom. The poetry itself is powerful in its simplicity and is rarely surpassed by any other prophet in the beauty of its form or the vividness of its images. Its perfectly turned phrases fall like hammer blows upon the mind and heart of the nation. Never is there any touch of self-conscious artificiality in the structure of the sentences; the style is simply the man himself speaking at white heat the truth that burdens him, in phrases that he hopes may cut through the callous hide of his hearers and find lodgment in their memories.

Amos shows genius in the organization of his oracles, making particularly effective use of the repetition of certain words as a refrain. In his opening sermon (chs. 1-2) each division begins: "For three transgressions . . . , and for four," and within this framework, which remains the same while the content changes, the audience sees episodes of judgment upon neighboring nations, each one coming closer to Israel than the last. The hearer is held as under a hypnotic spell, unable to flee the steadily approaching ruin. So also the fivefold repetition of the phrase " 'Yet you did not return to me,' says the LORD," in 4:6, 8-11, and the beginning of successive oracles with "Woe" in chs. 5-6, have this same cumulative effect. We meet the same device again in the three visions of 7:1-9, where twice the prophet prevails upon God to withhold judgment, and then, the third and last time, is able to restrain the judgment no longer. Amos was a finished craftsman and no novice in his employment of poetic forms.

**7. The theology of Amos.** It is a superficial approach to the mind of Amos that makes him a prophet of God's wrath in contrast to Hosea as a prophet of God's love. Certainly in Amos the announcement of impending judgment never wavers. The unrepented sin of the nation is certain to bring doom. But in this certainty Amos and Hosea are at one. Hosea's day of hope has its beginning only on the far side of the day of doom. Amos is so engrossed in his message of doom that he has no word like Hosea's concerning the future beyond, and for this reason many scholars have concluded that he had no hope even for a remnant of Israel. This does not take account of the nature of Amos' God nor of all the words of Amos. It was the covenant of love between God and Israel that made God more severe in his dealings with Israel than with any other nation.

> You only have I known
> of all the families of the earth;
> therefore I will punish you.
> (3:2.)

God's desire was not the death of the sinful nation, but that it might turn from its sin and live.

> Seek me and live;
> . . . . . . . . . . . .
> Hate evil, and love good,
> and establish justice in the gate;
> it may be that the LORD, the God of hosts,
> will be gracious to the remnant of Joseph.
> (5:4, 15.)

The doctrine of the remnant was not fully developed by Amos, as it was later by Isaiah, but it is already present in nucleus, Amos did not close the door to repentance and restoration through repentance. He had no hope for the nation as a whole, but surely that which sent him N to brave the insults of priests and people was the hope that some might hear and live. He expected the nation to be decimated (5:3) but not to be totally destroyed.

Nowhere does Amos make mention of the covenant, but it is implicit in his conception of the relation between God and Israel. Amos rejected the popular conception which bound God to Israel by legal agreement and made the covenant relation the basis of a false security and of a self-righteousness in which Israel claimed for itself a privileged position among the nations. His sharp critique of this latter error in 9:7, where Israel is told that it has no more claim upon God than the Ethiopians, the Philistines, or the Syrians, has seemed to some scholars to constitute a rejection of the doctrine of Israel's special

relation to God. But what Amos rejects is not the covenant itself but its perversion, whereby God's grace in delivering Israel from Egypt becomes an excuse for national pride and for extravagant claims upon God. Yahweh is the God of all nations. He has had a hand in all their histories, and he holds all equally responsible for their sins against their fellow men (chs. 1-2). In Israel he has made himself known in a special way, and this knowledge is the secret of Israel's unique destiny, but far from conferring special privileges, it creates rather special responsibility (3:1-2). Because of its covenant relation with God, Israel must reflect in its life the justice and truth and mercy of God, and the absence of these in the common life of the nation is evidence that the bond with God has been broken.

Amos' primary call to Israel, like that of John the Baptist and Jesus, is: "Repent and return to God." Sometimes his emphasis upon concrete changes in conduct:

> Seek good, and not evil,
> . . . . . . . . . . . . . . .
> and so the LORD, the God of hosts, will be with you,

has seemed open to the interpretation that he was offering a way of salvation by moral reformation. But for Amos all reformation of conduct was dependent upon a radical repentance. Like Jesus he could say: "Do this, and you will live," without the possibility of being misunderstood, because the context of all "doing" was the restoration of man to his true relationship with God.

It is significant that Amos never speaks of God as "the God of Israel." This title implied too often a narrow nationalism which Amos was concerned to defeat. He speaks rather of the "Lord of hosts." Amos' God was the creator God of the J document, from whom all nations had their life, the Lord of history by whose hand the destinies of all peoples were determined. Before his dread power none could stand; he was a God who could destroy but who could also create. Let Israel persist in sin, and God will use such nations as Egypt or Assyria to punish the sinful nation. And because he is the God of the whole earth and of heaven and Sheol, there can be no place of escape from his wrath (9:2-6).

Popular expectation in Amos' time was fixed on a glorious "day of Yahweh" when Israel would triumph over all her foes. The promises of God to Israel that were recorded in the traditions of the past were expected soon to be fulfilled. The existing prosperity was interpreted as a sign of God's favor. But, where king, priests, prophets, and people saw only a culmination of national success in the near future, Amos saw only darkness and disaster. He proclaimed a day of Yahweh, but it was to be darkness and not light, fiery judgment and not deliverance (1:4, 7, 10, 12, 14; 2:2; 5:6, 18-20). Fire was to consume the filth of men not only in Israel but also among the nations.

It has sometimes been said that Amos' concern is more ethical than religious, focussed more upon righteousness of conduct than upon the issues of faith and worship. This does scant justice to the passages in which Amos directs his attention to the cult (2:7-8, 12; 3:14; 4:4-5; 5:21-27; 7:9; 8:3; 9:1). It is true that Amos nowhere condemns the bull-worship of the N kingdom, but it is unfair to suppose on this basis that he condoned the use of idols. It is closer to the truth to say that Amos rejected the cult practices of Israel *in toto.* The removal of idols from the sanctuaries would not have placated him. The evil lay, not in the idols alone, but in the delusion that God could be kept favorable toward the nation by the offering of sacrifices and by the ritual of the cult.

Whether Amos rejected the cult entirely when, in God's name, he called for the cessation of its sacrifices, songs, and ritual (5:21-23), or merely expressed in this emphatic form God's disapproval of its present perversions, is a question on which scholars are widely divided. Some hold that he envisaged a nation without a cult, in which the service of God would consist simply of obedience to him in daily life. Others consider this unrealistic and argue that Amos would know the impossibility of sustaining faith without some form of worship. Wiener holds that the way in which Amos speaks of the religious festivals of new moon and sabbath in 8:5—H 8:4 indicates a sympathetic interest in them. The picture of the cult in 2:7-8, 12, shows it to have been so utterly corrupt that Amos may well have been as hopeless concerning it as he was concerning the nation as a whole. The fact that he had nothing to say concerning a future restoration of either nation or cult dare not be used to assert that he saw no future beyond the judgment for either of them.

The heart of Amos' faith was the conviction that only a nation in which the dealings of men with one another are just can be in any true sense a people in covenant with God. For him it was axiomatic that the whole future for Israel depended upon its relationship with God. Divorced from God, the nation must quickly perish. Therefore, the dishonesty of judges, the cruelty of rapacious businessmen and landowners, and the irresponsibility of prophets were not merely blemishes upon the national life, to be exposed and reformed; they were evidences of a deeper and more serious sickness, the repudiation of its God by the nation, and thus a betrayal of the nation that must bring its ruin. It is the justice, holiness, and purity of God that calls for justice, holiness, and purity in the common life of Israel.

Amos was the inheritor of a great tradition. In him the prophetic faith of Israel came to a new focus and found expression in a way that was to inaugurate a new era. All succeeding prophets built upon the solid foundations laid by him. The collection and recording of his oracles was the first step in the growth of a vast and richly varied prophetic literature.

*Bibliography.* Commentaries: C. von Orelli, *The Twelve Minor Prophets* (in German, 1888; trans. J. S. Banks, 1893). S. R. Driver, "Joel and Amos," *Cambridge Bible* (1897). J. J. P. Valeton, Jr., *Amos en Hosea* (1894; German ed., 1898). J. Wellhausen, *Die kleinen Propheten übersetzt und erklärt* (3rd ed., 1898). H. G. Mitchell, *Amos, an Essay in Exegesis* (2nd ed., 1900). K. Marti, "Dodekapropheton," *KHC* (1903). R. F. Horton, "The Minor Prophets, Hosea-Micah," *New Century Bible* (1904). B. Duhm, *Die Zwölf Propheten* (1910). W. R. Harper, *Amos and Hosea,* ICC (1910). J. M. P. Smith, *Amos, Hosea, and Micah* (1914). L. Kohler, *Amos* (1917). H. Schmidt, *Der Prophet Amos* (1917). H. Gressmann, *Die Schriften des AT* (2nd ed., 1921), pt. II. W. Nowack, *Die kleinen Propheten übersetzt und erklärt* (1922). E. Sellin, "Die kleinen Propheten,"

*KAT* (1922). P. Volz, *Prophetengestalten* (1938). G. A. Smith, *The Book of the Twelve Prophets* (rev. ed., 1940), vol. I. N. H. Snaith, *The Book of Amos* (1945). G. Brillet, *Amos et Hosée* (1946). A. Weiser, "Die kleinen Propheten," *AT Deutsch* (1949). T. H. Robinson and F. Horst, "Die zwölf kleinen Propheten," *HAT* (1954). N. H. Snaith, *Amos, Hosea and Micah* (1956).

Special studies: E. Baumann, "Der Aufbau der Amos Reden," *ZAWB,* vol. 7 (1903). W. Baumgartner, *Kennen Amos und Hosea eine Heils-Eschatologie?* (1913). W. Caspari, "Wer hat die Aussprüche des Propheten Amos gesammelt?" *NKZ,* 25 (1914), 701-15. H. Schmidt, "Die Herkunft des Propheten Amos, Budde Festschrift," *ZAWB,* 34 (1920), 158-71. F. Horst, "Die Doxologien im Amosbuch," *ZAW,* 47 (1929), 45-54. A. Weiser, "Die Prophetie des Amos," *ZAWB,* vol. 53 (1929). W. A. Irwin, "The Thinking of Amos," *AJSL,* 49 (1932), 102-14. R. Gordis, "The Composition and Structure of Amos," *HTR,* 33 (1940), 239-51. J. Morgenstern, *Amos Studies,* vol. I (1941). H. H. Rowley, "Was Amos a Nabi?" *Eissfeldt Festschrift* (1947), pp. 191-98. A. Néher, *Amos: Contribution à l'étude du Prophétisme* (1950). E. Würthwein, "Amos Studien," *ZAW,* 62 (1950), 10-52. G. A. Danell, "War Amos wirklich ein Nabi?" *Svensk Exegetisk Arsbok,* vol. XVI (1951). W. S. McCullough, "Some Suggestions About Amos," *JBL,* LXXII (1953), 247-54. A. S. Kapelrud, *Central Ideas in Amos* (1956). J. D. Watts, *Vision and Prophecy in Amos* (1958).

J. D. SMART

**AMOZ** āʹmŏz [אָמוֹץ, strong]. The father of Isaiah (Isa. 1:1, etc.). The name, which has been found on a Palestinian seal, should not be confused with Amos.

**AMPHIPOLIS** ăm·fĭpʹə·lĭs [ἡ Ἀμφίπολις] (Acts 17:1). The capital city of the first district of Macedonia.

Amphipolis was on the River Strymon, *ca.* three miles inland from the sea. In his invasion (480 B.C.) Xerxes crossed the river by bridges at this place, which was then known as Nine Ways (Ἐννέα ὁδοί) and was a town of the Edoni, who were a Thracian tribe (Herodotus VII.114; cf. 110). Both before and after this date, attempts were made by the Greeks to establish a colony here. In 497 B.C., Aristagoras of Miletus, fleeing from King Darius, undertook to settle at the place, but was driven away and slain. Thirty-two years later the Athenians sent ten thousand colonists, but they too were cut off by the Thracians. Finally, in 437 B.C., Hagnon, son of Nikias, brought another group of Athenians, expelled the Edoni, and founded a new town. Since the Strymon curved around the site on the N, W, and S, Hagnon named the city Amphipolis ("around-city") and also built a wall across the unprotected E side (Thucydides IV.102). When MACEDONIA was divided into four districts (μερίδες) by the Romans in 167 B.C., Amphipolis was chosen as the chief city of the first district, which included the area from the Strymon River to the Nestos (Livy XLV.17-18, 29-30). The city was on the Via Egnatia *ca.* thirty miles SW of Philippi. Excavation at Amphipolis has brought to light the foundations of an early Christian basilica.

*Bibliography.* G. Hirshfeld, "Amphipolis," *Pauly-Wissowa,* vol. I (1894), cols. 1949-52; S. Pelekidēs, "Ἀνασκάφαι καὶ ἐρεῦναι ἐν Ἀμφιπόλει," Πρακτικὰ τῆς ἐν Ἀθήναις ἀρχαιολογικῆς ἑταιρείας (1920), pp. 86-87.     J. FINEGAN

**AMPLIATUS** ăm·plĭ·āʹtəs [Ἀμπλιᾶτος] (Rom. 16:8); KJV **AMPLIAS** ămʹplĭ·əs [Ἀμπλιᾶς, *shortened form of* Ἀμπλιᾶτος]. A common name, frequently given to slaves. Attempts to identify the man so named in Rom. 16 are probably futile. Paul greets Ampliatus as "my beloved in the Lord." The context indicates that Ampliatus lived in the community—probably Ephesus, according to the evidence available—to which Phoebe, a deaconess of the church at Cenchreae, was about to journey, carrying a letter of introduction from Paul. Since Ampliatus' name comes to Paul's mind early in the long list of persons greeted and since he is mentioned so warmly, it would appear that he bore some intimate and affectionate relation to Paul. J. M. NORRIS

**AMRAM** ăm′răm [עמרם, the people or kinsman is exalted(?)]; **AMRAMITES** ăm′rə mīts [עמרמי]. **1.** Son of Kohath. He married his father's sister, Jochebed, and their famous children were Aaron and Moses (Exod. 6:18, 20) and Miriam (Num. 26:58-59). He was a grandson of Levi, and his name appears frequently in genealogical and Levitical lists (Num. 3:19; I Chr. 6:2-3—H 5:28-29; 6:18—H 6:3; 23:12-13; 24:20). The Levitical family descended from him, the Amramites (Num. 3:27; I Chr. 26:23), were assigned duties in the wilderness sanctuary and possibly, at a later time, in the temple treasuries.
**2.** One of the sons of Bani who married foreign wives in the time of Ezra (Ezra 10:34=I Esd. 9:34).
**3.** KJV form (erroneous) of HAMRAN (MT-RSV) in I Chr. 1:41. The most likely reading is the well-supported LXX HEMDAN. F. T. SCHUMACHER

**AMRAPHEL** ăm′rə fĕl [אמרפל; LXX Αμαρφαλ; Syr. אמרפיל (Gen. 14:9)]. An ally of Chedorlaomer who joined a punitive campaign against five kings in S Palestine, routing them in the Valley of Siddim (Gen. 14:1, 9). Chedorlaomer's league was then defeated by "Abram the Hebrew" and his associates (vss. 13-16). *See* ABRAHAM.

Neither the man nor his territory has been identified with certainty. The MT, the Samar. (at vs. 1), the LXX, and the Syr. designate him as king of SHINAR, while the Samar. (at vs. 9), the Targ., and the Dead Sea Genesis Apocryphon specifically state BABEL. Although in the OT period "Shinar" generally referred to Mesopotamia, its exact location is still a question.

The identification of Amraphel with the Babylonian king HAMMURABI (Ḥammurapi) has often been supported. One argument sees the Hebrew אמרפל as a scribal error for עמרפי (Ammurapi; Ḥammurapi) or even עמרבי/ח (Ḥammurabi). Another sees it as a compressed transcription of *Ammurapi-ili* ("Ḥammurabi is my god"). One argument takes the final "l" as the Akkadian determinative *ilu*, "god" (though it should precede the name); another links it with the following מלך (thus *limlōkh*). However, none of these arguments is philologically convincing; and the proposed identification is best given up at this time. L. HICKS

**AMRI** ăm′rī. Douay Version form of OMRI.

**AMULETS** ăm′yə lĭts. Small objects of symbolical meaning, the purpose of which is to give protection or to ward off evil. They are nearly always pierced and worn around the neck.

**1. In the OT period.** Amulets as a general term are not mentioned in the Bible. It is, however, possible that the לחשים of Isa. 3:20 are of amuletic character, since the root denotes "to whisper, to pronounce an incantation"; the RSV consequently translates "amulets." The "crescents" worn by animals (Judg. 8:21) and by human beings (Isa. 3:20) symbolize the moon-deity. The "perfume boxes" (בתי הנפש; lit., "soul receptacles") of Isa. 3:20 are probably amulets too. And so are possibly many other ornaments listed in Isa. 3:18-23 and elsewhere. As amulets may be classified the phylacteries (Exod. 13:16; Matt. 23:5) and capsules fixed on doorposts (Deut. 6:9) both of which contained passages from the Bible. They developed in late biblical times and are used to the present day in Jewish ritual.

Although it is difficult to identify more amulets in the OT, their use must have been ubiquitous and the varieties quite numerous, to judge from the finds in all strata of excavated sites. They are made of various materials, particularly of semiprecious stones such as carnelian, of soft stones covered with glaze, or of faïence. The amulets found in Palestine are mostly of Egyptian style.* They represent figurines of Egyptian deities (Osiris, Isis, Bes, etc.), animals (as cats, baboons, and others), fruits (grapes, pomegranates [Exod. 28:34], lotus), Egyptian symbols (the sacred eye, life [*ankh*], etc.). Models of human legs and arms may solicit cure. A special type is the frequent club-shaped amulet of the Israelite period, the significance of which eludes us. Scarabs, which served primarily as seals, had an amuletic function also. *See* SEALS AND SCARABS. Fig. AMU 23.

Courtesy of the Oriental Institute, the University of Chicago

23. Amulets found at Megiddo: (1) leg amulet of clay; faïence amulets of (2) Ptah-Sokar, (3) ape, (4) Horus eye, (5) Bastet; (6) crescent amulet of gold

*Bibliography.* W. M. F. Petrie, *Amulets* (1914); E. A. Wallis Budge, *Amulets and Superstitions* (1930); A. Rowe, *A Catalogue of Scarabs . . . and Amulets in the Palestine Archaeological Museum* (1938); G. Loud, *Megiddo II* (1948), pls. 205-6, 213-16.
I. BEN-DOR

**2. In the NT period.** The OT background (*see* § 1 *above*), contemporary Jewish practices (*see* PHYLACTERIES; FRINGES), and widespread Greek and Roman customs support the use of amulets. It is striking that the NT gives so little attention to the

Courtesy of Hodder & Stoughton Ltd.

24. A charm used for "binding"; a leaden tablet from Attica (fourth century B.C.)

subject. It can be held that in the NT the effectiveness of amulets is tacitly assumed and not disapproved (Acts 19:12; *see* HANDKERCHIEF; APRON); but it is more likely, especially in light of Paul's strong confidence in the complete efficacy of the NAME and POWER of Jesus (Eph. 1:21; Phil. 2:9; 4:13), that amulets generally were regarded as among the "magic arts" (Acts 19:18-19) and that their use, along with all other MAGIC and magicians (Acts 8:9-24; 13:6-12; 19:13-16),* was opposed as sorcery (φαρμακεία) and covert idolatry (Gal. 5:20; cf. John 18:30; I Pet. 2:12; 4:15; Rev. 9:20-21). Fig. AMU 24.

*Bibliography.* E. Labatut, "Amuletum," in C. Daremberg and E. Saglio, *Dictionnaire des Antiquités Grecques et Romaines* (1877); W. M. Ramsay, *The Bearing of Recent Discovery on the Trustworthiness of the NT* (4th ed., 1920), p. 48; G. A. Deissmann, *Light From the Ancient East* (4th ed., 1927), pp. 48, 260, 284, 405.                              P. L. GARBER

**AMZI** ăm′zī [אמצי, *my strong one, or perhaps an abbreviation of* Amaziah]. **1.** An ancestor of Ethan, one of the temple singers representing the sons of Merari (I Chr. 6:46).

**2.** An ancestor of Adaiah, a postexilic priest in Jerusalem (Neh. 11:12). The parallel (I Chr. 9:12) traces a rather different genealogy, without Amzi.
                                        F. T. SCHUMACHER

**\*ANAB** ā′năb [ענב, *grape*]. A city in the hill country of Judah, near Debir, from which the Anakim were expelled by Joshua (Josh. 11:21; 15:50). It is mentioned in Egyptian texts of the Nineteenth Dynasty as *Qrt ʿnb*, which indicates that the original name of the city was Kiriath-anab.

The site must be either at the present village of ʿAnab, about fifteen miles SW of Hebron, or at the nearby Khirbet ʿAnab.                      S. COHEN

**ANAEL** ăn′ĭ əl [ʾΑναήλ] (Tob. 1:21). Brother of Tobit. Anael's son Ahikar served as Sennacherib's cupbearer, accountant, and chief administrator (Tob. 1:22).                              J. C. SWAIM

**ANAH** ā′nə [ענה; *cf.* Phoen. *bnʿn,* Ugar. *bn.ʿn,* Byblian *bʿnh*]. **1.** The father of Oholibamah and son of ZIBEON the Horite (Gen. 36:2, 14, 18, 24; I Chr. 1:40). Gen. 36:2, 14, read "daughter" (בת), although "son" (בן) is better (cf. RSV).

**2.** The fourth son of Seir; a clan chief (אלוף ענה) of native Horite inhabitants of Edom (Gen. 36:20, 25, 29; I Chr. 1:38, 41).

Textual and literary problems cloud the relation of 1 to 2. In Gen. 36:24 the LXX gives Ωναν, ὁ Ωνας, and in I Chr. 1:40 Σωναν and Ωναμ in place of its usual Ανα. Also, the Greek and Syr. versions differ about the Oholibamah in Gen. 36:25. The chapter is composed of variant family and tribal traditions which have not been harmonized.

The Anah of Gen. 36:24 is further identified as the one "who found the hot springs in the wilderness." (For "hot springs" the KJV reads "mules." The word ימם is obscure; perhaps it is an error for מים, "water." The RSV follows Vulg. *aquae calidae.*)
                                        L. HICKS

**ANAHARATH** ə nā′ə răth [אנחרת] (Josh. 19:19). A town in Issachar, also mentioned in the list of towns captured by Thut-mose III. It is located at en-Naʿurah, *ca.* two miles S of En-dor.

**ANAIAH** ə nā′yə [עניה, *Yahweh has answered*]. One of the men who stood at Ezra's right hand when he read the "book of the law of Moses" (Neh. 8:4), and who was among those who set their seal to the covenant (10:22—H 10:23).

**ANAK** ā′năk [ענק, *neck, necklace*]; **ANAKIM** ăn′ə kĭm [ענקים]; KJV **ANAKIMS.** A tribe of the pre-Israelite population of Palestine. The term was originally an appellative ("people of the neck," or "necklace") and gradually became a gentilic.

In Hebrew tradition the Anakim are described as a tall people, whose gigantic size struck terror into the hearts of the Hebrews (Num. 13:28; Deut. 2:21; 9:2). In Num. 13:33 they are described as descendants of the NEPHILIM, the offspring of the sons of God and the daughters of men (Gen. 6:4).

Most of the references connect the Anakim with the S of Palestine, especially Hebron.

According to one passage, however, the Anakim originally occupied a much wider area, and were exterminated by Joshua except for a small remnant in Gaza, Gath, and Ashdod (Josh. 11:21-22). This tradition is followed by the LXX of Jer. 47:5, the reading adopted by the RSV.

The presence in Palestine *ca.* 2000 B.C. of a tribe Anak, whose princes have Semitic names, is attested by the Egyptian Execration Texts. These are pottery fragments bearing the names of the enemies of the pharaoh, who were ritually cursed with the breaking of the jar on which the curses were inscribed.

**Bibliography.** W. F. Albright, "The Egyptian Empire in Asia in the Twenty-first Century B.C.," *JPOS,* VIII (1928), 223-56.

R. F. SCHNELL

**ANAMIM** ăn'ə mĭm [עֲנָמִים; LXX Ενεμετιειμ]. A tribe or nation listed among the descendants of Egypt in the ethnographic lists of Gen. 10:13; I Chr. 1:11.

The Anamim cannot be identified specifically with any known ethnic group. Because they are mentioned with the LUDIM; the LEHABIM; the NAPHTUHIM; the PATHRUSIM; the CASLUHIM; and the CAPHTORIM, they may quite reasonably be the people of Cyrene or thereabouts, as suggested by Albright (*see bibliography*), who equates them with a cuneiform *A-na-mi* found in a geographical text from the time of Sargon II of Assyria and parallel to *Kaptara* (=Caphtorim).

**Bibliography.** W. F. Albright, "A Colony of Cretan Mercenaries on the Coast of the Negeb," *JPOS,* 1 (1921), 191-92.

T. O. LAMBDIN

**ANAMMELECH** ə năm'ə lĕk [עֲנַמֶּלֶךְ, *probably* Anu is king]. One of the deities worshiped by the people from Sepharvaim (probably Sabraim in Syria), settled by the Assyrians in Samaria after 722 B.C. (II Kings 17:31). They are said to have burned offerings of their children to the god, but there is no specific reference to this feature of his cult in Mesopotamia. *See* MOLECH.

**Bibliography.** M. Jastrow, *The Religion of Babylonia and Assyria* (1898), pp. 88-90; E. Ebeling and B. Meissner, *Reallexikon der Assyriologie* I (1932), 115-17. On human sacrifice, *see* the bibliography under MOLECH.

J. GRAY

**ANAN** ā'năn [עָנָן] (Neh. 10:26—H 10:27). A name included in the list of signers of the Nehemiah covenant.

**ANANI** ə nā'nī [עֲנָנִי] (I Chr. 3:24). The seventh son of Elioenai, a descendant of Zerubbabel, in the list of Davidic offspring.

**ANANIAH** ăn'ə nī'ə [עֲנַנְיָה, Yahweh has manifested himself(?)]. 1. The father of Ma-aseiah, whose son, Azariah, participated in the reconstruction of the walls of Jerusalem under Nehemiah (Neh. 3:23).

2. A village of Benjamin which appears in a list of places occupied by Jews after the Exile (Neh. 11:32). It is probably to be identified with modern el-'Azirîyeh (NT BETHANY), which is located some two miles from Jerusalem. It might have received its name from the fact that members of the family of Ananiah settled there, and this could explain the NT name (בֵּית־עֲנַנְיָה, "house of Ananiah"=Βηθανία).

M. NEWMAN

**ANANIAS** ăn'ə nī'əs ['Ανανίας (WH 'Ανανίας); חֲנַנְיָה, Y is gracious]. 1. The father of Azariah, the latter being a name assumed by the angel Raphael, who thus falsely identified himself to Tobit's father (Tob. 5:12).

2. One of the ancestors of Judith (Jth. 8:1).

3. A Christian of Jerusalem; husband of Sapphira (Acts 5:1, 3, 5). This man, noting the favorable attention bestowed upon those Christians who sold their property and brought the proceeds to the apostles for distribution among the believers (Acts 4:32-37), sold a property belonging to him and—with the connivance of his wife, Sapphira—held back a portion of the price, while pretending to give the entire amount to the apostles for distribution. When Peter faced each of them separately with their duplicity, which they reaffirmed, they fell down dead. Their death is one of the punitive miracles of Luke-Acts.

4. A Christian disciple (Acts 9:10, 12-13, 17; 22:12) living in Damascus at the time of Paul's arrival there after his conversion experience on the road to Damascus. Ananias was a Jew and is described as a "disciple" (μαθητής). However, this term is used in Acts more frequently to indicate new believers than to indicate original disciples of Jesus, so we cannot be certain of Ananias' status. It is probable that he was not a direct disciple of Jesus, but it is clear that he was a Christian before Paul was. It is not clear that he was a settled resident of Damascus, and it may be that he was there as a refugee from the persecution originating in Jerusalem and of which Paul was an instrument. If so, this would well explain his alarm when in a dream he was instructed by God to go to Paul and to receive him into the Christian fellowship. Putting aside his fears, Ananias went boldly to Paul, greeting him as a Christian brother and explaining to him (Acts 22:12-16) the meaning of his experience on the Damascus road. Paul was baptized immediately and entered upon his long ministry. Ananias is not mentioned in the third account of Paul's conversion (Acts 26).

We have no further solid data concerning this Ananias, and all traditions concerning him are of late origin and small value. Though we know nothing of Ananias' previous and subsequent actions, the action here recorded places us all in his debt.

5. A Jewish high priest before whom Paul was tried after his arrest in Jerusalem at the end of his third missionary journey (Acts 23:2). He appears again among those accusing Paul at his hearing before the Roman governor Felix (Acts 24:1 ff). A son of Nebedeus, he was high priest from A.D. 48, when he was nominated by Herod Agrippa II (Jos. Antiq. XX.v.2), until 58, when he was deposed. In 52 he was sent to Rome for trial in connection with a conflict between the Jews and the Samaritans but was acquitted by Claudius Caesar through the efforts of the younger Agrippa (Jos. Antiq. XX.vi.2-3).

Ananias' arbitrary command to those standing near Paul at the trial to strike him on the mouth accords well with other indications concerning his severity and cruelty. On account of his rapacity and his long collaboration with the Roman authorities, he was hunted down and murdered by the Jewish populace at the beginning of the Jewish war of 66-70 (Jos. War II.xvii.9).

6. KJV form of HANANI 3 in I Esd. 9:21.

7. KJV Apoc. form of HANANIAH.

8. KJV form of ANAIAH 1 in I Esd. 9:43.

9. KJV form of HANAN 7 in I Esd. 9:48.

J. M. NORRIS

**ANANIEL** ə năn'ĭ əl [חֲנַנְאֵל; 'Ανανιήλ] (Tob. 1:1). Tobit's grandfather, listed among the "descendants of Asiel and the tribe of Naphtali."

J. C. SWAIM

**ANASIB** ăn'ə sĭb [Σαναβείς(B), Ανασειβ(A)]; KJV
**SANASIB** săn'—. The progenitor of a group of
priests who returned from the Exile with Zerubbabel
(I Esd. 5:24; omitted in the parallels Ezra 2:36; Neh.
7:39). The Vulg. may preserve the original form,
Eliasib. C. T. FRITSCH

**ANATH** ā'năth [עֲנָת; Ugar. 'nt]. The father of
Shamgar, one of the predynastic judges in Israel
(Judg. 3:31; 5:6). Some scholars, however, consider
that "Shamgar ben Anath" should read "Shamgar
of Beth-anath"—i.e., from the Canaanite city of
Galilee. Anath is the name of a well-known Semitic
goddess of the ancient Near East. In the Ugaritic
literature this goddess of war is the sister and consort of Baal.

*Bibliography.* W. F. Albright, "The Evolution of the West-
Semitic Divinity 'An-'Anat-'Atta," *AJSL,* XLI (1925), 73-
101; *Archaeology and the Religion of Israel* (1953), 74 ff, 111,
195, 219. E. R. DALGLISH

**ANATHEMA** ə năth'ə mə [ἀνάθεμα; חרם; cf.
ἀνάθημα and κατάθεμα]. Something set up, placed;
properly τὸ ἀνατιθέμενον, from ἀνατίθημι, "to set up,
lay by." Ἀνάθεμα is Hellenistic Greek for the
stronger classical form ἀνάθημα (e.g., Sophocles
*Antigone* 286). Both words were originally used of
something dedicated or consecrated to a divinity—
i.e., a votive offering. The etymology of the term reflects the custom of setting up or suspending such
offerings in a temple or of hanging them from a tree
or pillar outside. The form ἀνάθεμα, however, developed the special meaning of "devoted to a divinity
or to the lower world so as to be destroyed," therefore ACCURSED. While this usage is found in pagan
inscriptions (*see bibliography*), it has been regarded
as a possible Jewish Christian coinage. The two
forms were often confused by scribes and by later
writers—e.g., in II Macc. 2:13; 9:16; Luke 21:5, in
all of which the meaning is "votive offering," but
in which ἀνάθεμα is found in some MSS and critical
texts.

In the LXX the term generally represents חרם,
which has the double significance of "consecrated"
(i.e., to God) and "accursed" (i.e., devoted to destruction; cf. Lev. 27:28-29; Num. 18:14). Divine possession apparently implied the right of destruction (see
Deut. 7:26; 13:15-16; Josh. 6:17-18; etc.). With the
OT usage one may compare Rev. 22:3 (κατάθεμα,
"accursed thing"), a quotation from Zech. 14:11.

In its remaining NT occurrences the term means
"cursed," but is moving away from the ritualistic
force of the OT usage. Variant spelling is meaningless. It is found in a formula denoting the object of
a curse: "Jesus be cursed" (I Cor. 12:3); "Let him
be cursed" (I Cor. 16:22; Gal. 1:8-9). Cf. Rom. 9:3:
"I could wish myself accursed and cut off from
Christ" (ἀνάθεμα εἶναι . . . ἀπὸ τοῦ χριστοῦ). The
idea of separation as a penalty expressed here suggests the specialized development which in late
Judaism and the early church gave the term the
technical meaning of EXCOMMUNICATION. Another
special usage associates the curse with an oath or
vow, implying that the curse would fall upon the
violator (so in Acts 23:14: ἀναθέματι ἀνεθεματίσαμεν).
Cf. with the reflexive object in Acts 23:12, 21, the

LXX of Deut. 20:17; Job 6:20; and the absolute
force ("to curse") in Mark 14:71 = Matt. 26:74. In
Tannaitic thought violation of such an oath was
theoretically punishable by death (cf. CDC XX.5-6).
*See* OATH.

*Bibliography.* E. Schürer, *Geschichte des jüdischen Volkes,* II
(4th ed., 1907), 506-8; J. Mann, "Oaths and Vows in the
Synoptic Gospels," *AJT,* XXI (1917), 260-74; A. Deissmann,
*Light from the Ancient East* (2nd ed., 1927), pp. 65-66 (exam-
ples from pagan inscriptions); S. Belkin, *Philo and the Oral
Law* (1940), ch. 6: "Oaths and Vows"; G. Bornkamm, "Das
Anathema in der urchristliche Abendmals-liturgie," *TLZ,* 75
(1950), 227-30. A. WIKGREN

**ANATHOTH** ăn'ə thŏth [עֲנָתוֹת, עֲנָתֹת]; ANA-
THOTHITE —ĭt [עֲנָתוֹתִי, עַנְּתֹתִי]; KJV ANE-
THOTHITE (II Sam. 23:27); ANTOTHITE
ăn'tə thĭt (I Chr. 11:28; 12:3); ANETOTHITE
—ə tŏth ĭt (I Chr. 27:12). A priestly city in Benjamin. "Anathoth" is probably a shortened form of
"Beth-anathoth," meaning "house of the great
Anath." This would indicate that the city was the
shrine of the important Canaanite goddess Anath,
and that it was transformed by the Israelites into a
sacred city of their own. Two of David's heroes,
Jehu and Abiezer, came from the place (II Sam. 23:
27; I Chr. 11:28; 12:3). Abiathar, the last chief priest
of the line of Eli, owned property in Anathoth and
was bidden by Solomon to retire there after his
deposition (I Kings 2:26). In Isa. 10:30, Anathoth is
mentioned as one of the stages of the march of the
Assyrian hosts upon Jerusalem; the word "answer"
in this passage is a pun on the name Anathoth.

The city was the birthplace of the prophet Jeremiah (Jer. 1:1) and the scene of his first attempts at
prophecy; these met with disapproval, as the prophet
predicted an evil fate for his fellow citizens, who
silenced him and even threatened his life (11:21-23).
Nevertheless, Jeremiah retained his ties to his native
city, and was willing to redeem a plot of land which
had belonged to his cousin (32:7-9). Anathoth was
devastated by the Babylonians, but after the Exile
128 men of the city returned with Zerubbabel (Ezra
2:23; Neh. 7:27; the parallel passage in I Esd. 5:18
gives the number as 158). In the time of Nehemiah
the place was settled by Benjaminites (Neh. 11:32).

The name of Anathoth has been preserved in that
of Anata, three miles N of Jerusalem. The original
city, however, was located at the tell of Ras el-
Kharrubeh, *ca.* half a mile to the SW. S. COHEN

**ANCHOR** [ἄγκυρα; *cf.* ἀγκάλη, bent arm]. A nautical device attached to a cable and sunk in water
to hold a ship in a particular place.

The description of Paul's sea voyage to Rome informs us that the ship on which the apostle was sailing let down four anchors as it approached Malta
(Acts 27:29-30, 40). The only other biblical reference to an anchor is in Heb. 6:19, where hope is described as a "sure and steadfast anchor of the soul."
"They weighed anchor" (Acts 27:13) represents an
idiomatic nautical use of a common Greek verb
αἴρω, "lift up, hoist" (cf. KJV "loosing").

The first anchors were heavy stones let down from
the bow of a ship (cf. εὐναί, plural of εὐνή, "bed," in
Homer *Iliad* I.436; *see ANEP* 42). By 650 B.C.

wooden anchors of hook form, exhibiting the "anchor stock," and weighted by metal or stone, were in use in the E Mediterranean. A little later, anchors made wholly of metal with the familiar anchor form appeared. Pliny, in the first century A.D., was familiar with two types of anchor, the ordinary one and the double-fluked one (*bidens*), the latter being credited to Anacharsis, presumably the Hellenized Scythian sage who flourished *ca.* 600 B.C. (Nat. Hist. VII.lvi. 209). *See* SHIPS AND SAILING. W. S. MCCULLOUGH

**ANCIENT OF DAYS.** The phrase used to designate the judge in the eschatological scene in Dan. 7:9. The Aramaic עַתִּיק יוֹמִין is literally translated παλαιὸς ἡμερῶν by the LXX, and *antiquus dierum* by the Vulg., and "ancient of days" by KJV-ASV-RSV. Other translations are: "a primeval Being" (Moffatt); "a Venerable One" (Amer. Trans.); "one ... crowned with age" (Knox). The American Jewish Version retains "ancient of days."

עַתִּיק means properly "removed, passed on," and hence "old" as in I Chr. 4:22, where it is held to be an Aramaism. The phrase "old of days" is good Semitic idiom, whereby an adjective may depend in the construct state upon its noun in the absolute. Thus "fair of form" means "having a fair form," and "old of days" means simply "aged." Ugaritic has supplied a close parallel: *mlk ab shnm,* "the king, father of years"—i.e., "the aged king." For other Semitic parallels *see* Montgomery (*bibliography*). The idiom has, however, been so Anglicized (cf. Shakespeare's Lady Macbeth: "Infirm of purpose! Give me the daggers") that "ancient of days" is an intelligible translation. The figure is probably intended to be that of God himself, and the attribute of age is ascribed to convey the ideas of dignity, wisdom, and primevality (cf. Job 36:26); but some (more particularly Jewish medieval) commentators have thought the description too anthropomorphic to be that of the deity, and have explained it as referring to the Angel of Yahweh (cf. Zech. 3:1; *see* ANGEL). Some have thought it necessary to look to Iranian sources and the concept of Ahura-Mazda for the genesis of the figure, especially in its juridical aspects, but in view of I Kings 22:19-20; Ps. 50:1-6; Joel 3:2; and Zechariah as cited, it is best regarded as developed from native ideas—a process encouraged, no doubt, by the Iranian parallels.

*Bibliography.* C. H. Gordon, *Ugaritic Handbook,* II (1947), text 49:8. Commentaries on Daniel by Montgomery, ICC (1927), and Bentzen, HAT (2nd ed., 1952). S. B. FROST

**ANDREW** ăn'droͦo [Ἀνδρέας, manly]. Son of Jonah (or John), brother of Simon Peter (*see* PETER), and one of the first disciples of Jesus.

Andrew is a Greek name. It was used by Jews as well (appearing, e.g., in the Talmud as אנדראי, אנדריו). Such use indicates the extent to which Jews had become Hellenized.

The family of Jonah (Matt. 16:17) or John (John 1:42; 21:15-17) lived in BETH-SAIDA (John 1:44), the capital city of Herod Philip (4 B.C.-A.D. 34), whose realm lay to the NE of the Sea of Galilee. Philip rebuilt Beth-saida and named it Beth-saida Julias, after Julia the daughter of Augustus. This city, on the NE side of the Sea of Galilee, was inhabited by

both Jews and Gentiles. It maintained close busines and cultural relationships with Galilee, the territor of Philip's brother Herod Antipas. Simon and An drew probably spoke Greek, as well as Aramaic, and grew up in a culture more or less shaped by Gentil influences.

According to the Fourth Gospel, Andrew and ar unnamed person, before meeting Jesus, were follow ers of John the Baptist (John 1:35-40). Because o the latter's witness concerning Jesus ("Behold, the Lamb of God!"), the two disciples of John followed Jesus to his place of residence and became convinced of his messiahship (vs. 41). Andrew then brought his brother Simon to Jesus. Shortly Philip, also from Beth-saida, and Nathanael became disciples (vss. 43-51).

From this Johannine story one would conclude that Andrew was a conscientious Jew, who had re pented radically under the preaching of the Baptist had been baptized by him, and was looking eagerly for the arrival of the messianic age. He was continu ally open to new light; he was pliable and teachable. When truth broke upon him, he accepted it enthusi astically and wished others to share in it. One might say that he was the first Christian evangelist.

According to the Synoptic gospels Simon, Andrew Zebedee, and Zebedee's sons (James and John) were partners in a fishing business at the Sea of Galilee (Mark 1:16-20; Luke 5:10). Simon and Andrew at this time lived in Capernaum (Mark 1:29). Jesus' call of Zebedee's associates from their fishing opera tions appears psychologically inexplicable apart from the Johannine story concerning their association with Jesus at the Jordan, where John was baptizing, some time earlier (John 1:35-42). Though the Johannine narrative leaves no place for the "call" recorded in the Synoptics, the Synoptic narrative, if historical, can hardly do without the Johannine story. An drew's wholehearted response, and that of his com rades, testifies to the depth of their attachment to Jesus and their concern about the good news of the kingdom of God.

Andrew apparently was among the first persons named by Jesus for a place in the apostolic band. All lists of the apostles (Matt. 10:2-4; Mark 3:16-19; Luke 6:14-16; Acts 1:13) record his name among the first four, two (Matthew and Luke) as one of the first two.

Twice in the Fourth Gospel, Andrew is associated with the only other apostle who bore a Greek name —PHILIP, also from Beth-saida (John 1:44). At the feeding of the five thousand the two converse with Jesus concerning the problem of caring for the needs of the multitude. Andrew calls attention to the lad's five barley loaves and two fish, a suggestion which he feels is hardly worth making (6:5-9). Later, the two confer over the request of certain Greeks to see Jesus and decide to bring the request to the atten tion of Jesus (12:20-22).

Andrew is once more mentioned in the gospels: in connection with an inquiry addressed to Jesus by the four Galilean associates (Peter, James, John, Andrew) concerning Last Things (Mark 13:3). After this (apart from the name in the list in Acts 1:13) Andrew drops out of sight in the NT.

He reappears in a rather rank growth of church

radition. It is said in Euseb. Hist. III.1 that Scythia (the region N of the Black Sea) was allotted to Andrew as the field of his labor. He has understandably become the patron saint of Russia. The apocryphal Acts of Andrew represent him as evangelizing and suffering martyrdom by crucifixion in Achaia (Greece). Still later traditions hold that his body was carried to Constantinople and during the Crusades transferred to Amalfi, Italy. It is even claimed that his arm was transported by Regulus to Scotland, where he also became the patron saint.

*Bibliography.* M. R. James, *The Apocryphal NT* (1924), pp. 337-63, 453-60, 472-75; M. Buchberger, ed., *Lexikon für Theologie und Kirche* (2 Aufl., 1930-38), 410-11; G. Dalman, *Sacred Sites and Ways* (English trans., 1935), pp. 161 ff; E. J. Goodspeed, *The Twelve* (1957), pp. 14-17, 38-39; P. M. Peterson, *Andrew, Brother of Simon Peter—His History and His Legends* (1958). E. P. BLAIR

**ANDREW, ACTS OF.** One of a long series of early romances, commonly styled apocryphal Acts (*see* ACTS, APOCRYPHAL), and perhaps the latest of the five commonly, but mistakenly, ascribed to Leucius, adopted by the Manicheans in place of the canonical Acts, and recounting the travels, wonder-working, discourses, and martyrdom of Andrew. We have it in a shortened Latin form edited by Gregory of Tours (A.D. 538-94) and in several fragments.

Unlike the four other principal apocryphal Acts, we have no early statement as to its original length, but it may be inferred from the prolixity of our principal fragment, now preserved in a tenth-eleventh-century Greek MS in the Vatican (Gk. 808), in conjunction with the references which Gregory of Tours made to its "excessive verbosity," which "bred weariness" and which he had omitted in his Latin epitome, that it may well have been the longest of the series.

This edited and abbreviated transcript by Gregory is a long series of tales of the miracles—especially frequent are those in which the dead are raised—wrought by Andrew in Pontus, Bithynia, Thrace, and Macedonia, as well as in the province of Achaia ("his own allotted district"). In this version there is nothing heretical or even strongly ascetic. But the several episodes, such as the interrupted wedding at Philippi (ch. 11), the episode with Lesbius and his erstwhile mistress Trophima (chs. 22–24), the tale of the converted libertine Nicolaus (ch. 28), and, chief of all, the concluding story of Maximilla, the converted wife of the proconsul Egeas, suggest that the tales have been drastically edited, either by Gregory or by some earlier reviser. To what extent Gregory's epitome gives a fair view of the original content of this early apocryphon is very uncertain; his careful pruning out of the sweeping ascetic disapproval of marriage and of the prolix and tedious speeches can scarcely fail to have greatly altered the essential nature of this book, styled by Eusebius, our first witness to its existence, as one of those "forgeries of heretics" which are "not to be reckoned even among the spurious books but shunned as altogether wicked and impious" (Hist. III.25.6-7). Epiphanius too refers to it as appealed to by the Encratites, the Apostolics, and the Origenians (Heresies 47)—a circumstance hardly likely if Gregory's version had been a literal transcription. Gregory's epitome, plus a

concluding Latin martyrdom, which Gregory knew but omitted, because he "found it well done by someone else," forms the bulk of the Andrew section (Book III) of the Apostolic History of Abdias (*see* ABDIAS, APOSTOLIC HISTORY OF).

Remains of the original Greek writing, which may with probability be seen as written about the middle of the third century, perhaps in Greece or W Asia Minor, are very scanty. In the apocryphal Epistle of Titus (*see* TITUS, APOCRYPHAL EPISTLE OF) a short fragment is preserved, apparently an earlier version of the wedding at Philippi. But whereas in Gregory's version Andrew forbids the wedding because both couples are first cousins, in this certainly more original account the objection is clearly to marriage per se. So also in the fragments in the tract *De Fide*, commonly attributed to Evodius, bishop of Uzala (*ca.* A.D. 400), against the Manicheans, recounting Maximilla's attempt to escape from her husband. In the very lengthy excerpt preserved in the Vatican MS referred to above, not only are the prolixity and tedium of the earlier work clearly revealed, well meriting Gregory's strictures, but its strongly ascetic tone is constantly in evidence, as in Andrew's word to Maximilla: "I know, Maximilla, my child, that thou art moved to resist the whole attraction of nuptial union, desiring to be quit of a foul and polluted way of life."

As is true of most of the apocryphal Acts, the martyrdom circulated independently and in many forms. One form is that of a Latin letter, purporting to be from the presbyters and deacons of Achaia, containing a lengthy dialogue between Andrew and Aegeates (Egeas) and a briefer account of the actual martyrdom by crucifixion. The account is also preserved in two Greek translations. In addition are several other versions, some starting with the fatal episode of Egeas and Maximilla, others prefixing a brief account of the journeys. None of these appears to be the original conclusion of the apocryphon, but they provide the materials from which it may be conjecturally reassembled. All of them, though they differ in many details, and though some were originally written in Greek and others in Latin, agree in preserving a very prolix and stilted address by Andrew to the cross, immediately prior to his crucifixion. This is strongly reminiscent of Peter's similar oration in the Acts of Peter (*see* PETER, ACTS OF). The Acts of Andrew and Matthias (*see* ANDREW AND MATTHIAS, ACTS OF), although inserted by Gregory at the start of his version and accordingly long considered a part of the original Acts of Andrew, are now rightly considered a quite different work.

*Bibliography.* For a convenient abstract of Gregory's version and a full translation of the other principal fragments, together with a very convenient analysis of the several martyrdoms and of the work of M. Bonnet and J. Flamion in disentangling them, see M. R. James, *The Apocryphal NT* (1924), pp. 337-63. M. S. ENSLIN

**ANDREW, ACTS OF PETER AND.** *See* PETER AND ANDREW, ACTS OF.

**ANDREW, FRAGMENTARY STORY OF.** A fragment extant only in Coptic of a story from one of the Oriental Acts (*see* APOCRYPHA, NT) of the apostles. A woman in the desert killed her illegitimate child, cut it in pieces, and fed it to a dog. When Andrew, with his companion Philemon, arrives at the spot, he is told by the dog what the woman has done. In answer to his prayer, in which he alludes to a miracle Christ wrought on Mount Gebal, the fragments of the murdered child are apparently disgorged and joined together, and the restored child both weeps and laughs.     M. S. ENSLIN

## ANDREW AND MATTHIAS (MATTHEW), ACTS OF.

The most famous of the secondary apocryphal Acts (*see* ACTS, APOCRYPHAL; APOCRYPHA, NT) recounting the dramatic rescue by Andrew of Matthias, who had been taken prisoner by cannibals (*anthropophagi*), who blinded and tagged their captives, eating them on the thirtieth day. On the twenty-seventh day Jesus appears to Andrew and directs him to go to his colleague's rescue. Obediently he embarks on a vessel steered by Jesus himself. During the voyage Andrew, not knowing the identity of the pilot, recounts stories of the earlier exploits of Jesus, including his visit to the heathen temple, the talking sphinx, and the interview with Abraham, Isaac, and Jacob. Upon reaching land, Andrew rescues Matthias, performs many miracles in the wicked land, is tortured, restored by the Lord, and eventually, after nearly drowning the city by water miraculously evoked from a stone statue in the prison, restores the city in consequence of the inhabitants' repentance, draws a plan for a church, and baptizes the populace.

This tale, preserved in the Anglo-Saxon poem "Andreas," attributed to Cynewulf, is prefixed by Gregory of Tours to his Latin version of the Acts of Andrew (*see* ANDREW, ACTS OF), but is no real part of this latter. In addition to Gregory's version, the tale, probably stemming from Egypt, is extant in Greek and Syriac, and in part in Latin. To regard it as a revised or expurgated Gnostic tract is surely unwarranted; it is simply a garish congeries of wonder tales of the sort produced so lavishly in the monasteries of Egypt. The confusion of Matthias and Matthew in the several accounts may most plausibly be explained as due to the later tendency to substitute the better-known evangelist for the less-known Matthias.

*Bibliography.* A brief paraphrase is provided by M. R. James, *The Apocryphal NT* (1924), pp. 453-58.
M. S. ENSLIN

## ANDREW AND PAUL, ACTS OF.

The title commonly given to a wild tale of adventure, now extant only in Coptic, in which Andrew and Paul are joined; a fragmentary part of one of many of the lush writings commonly styled Oriental Acts (*see* APOCRYPHA, NT). Paul visits the underworld, which he has reached by diving into the sea. Upon his return, he tells Andrew of his visit with Judas, and repeats the latter's tragic story, replete with many details of his betrayal of Christ, his repentance, his seduction by Satan, a visit paid him by Christ, and his ultimate fate. The two apostles next visit some city; they cause the city's gates, which they find locked against them, to vanish into the earth, when struck by the piece of wood which Paul has brought back from the underworld; and they contest with the Jews whom they convict of fraud, and convert some twenty-seven thousand Jews.     M. S. ENSLIN

**ANDRONICUS** ăn drŏn'ə kəs ['Ανδρόνικος, conqueror of men]. **1.** An official (II Macc. 4:31-38) left in charge in Antioch by Antiochus Epiphanes while on a political mission to Cilicia. Bribed by Menelaus a usurping high priest, Andronicus executed the deposed legitimate high priest, Onias. Antiochus, returning, executed Andronicus for his treachery.

**2.** An officer (II Macc. 5:23) left in command o Gerizim by Antiochus Epiphanes after Antiochu had quelled the disorders in Judea that resulted from the false report that Antiochus had been killed in his second invasion of Egypt.

**3.** A man (Rom. 16:7) whom the recipients o Rom. 16—probably a congregation in Ephesus—are requested by Paul to greet. Andronicus, along with Junias (Julias, P[46]), is designated as a relative (συγγενής) of Paul. The plain etymological meaning of this term is "blood relative of the same generation," and this seems to be its meaning here, although some hold that Paul means only a "fellow Jew." It is possible that the second name is feminine, in which case "Junia" would be the wife or sister of Andronicus but the context indicates that both these relatives o Paul were men. At some past time both these individuals had been fellow prisoners of Paul. Both were "of note among the apostles," a term probably meaning here no more than "authorized evangelists." Both had been Christians before Paul.     J. M. NORRIS

**ANEM** ā'nəm [עֲנֵם]. A town in Issachar assigned to the sons of GERSHOM in I Chr. 6:73—H 6:58. The corresponding list (Josh. 21:29; cf. also 19:21) reads "En-gannim" (*see* EN-GANNIM 2). It is probably located at 'Olam, a site *ca.* eight miles E-SE of Moun Tabor, or perhaps at Khirbet 'Anim, *ca.* two mile NE of 'Olam.

*Bibliography.* W. F. Albright, "The Topography of the Tribe of Issachar," *ZAW* (1926), pp. 231-32; F.-M. Abel *Géographie de la Palestine*, II (1938), 244.     G. W. VAN BEEK

**ANER** ā'nər [עָנֵר]. **1.** One of three Amorite brother who were allies of Abram (Gen. 14:13, 24; LXX Αυναν; Samar. ענרם; Genesis Apocryphon ערנם). I the OT their relation to Abraham's contest with th four eastern kings is not clear, but the Genesi Apocryphon (XXII.6) states explicitly that the joined in the pursuit.

**2.** A city of refuge in Manasseh (I Chr. 6:70—H 6:55). If the text is correct, the location of Aner i unknown; but עָנֵר here may be an error for the תַּעְנַךְ (TAANACH) appearing in a similar list at Josh. 21:25     L. HICKS

**ANETHOTHITE; ANETOTHITE.** KJV alternate forms of Anathothite. *See* ANATHOTH.

**ANGEL** [מַלְאָךְ; ἄγγελος]. In common parlance, the word "angel" is used today in the twofold sense o (*a*) a messenger from God, and (*b*) a spiritual being In the earlier portions of the Bible, however, the two are nicely distinguished: while every divine messenger is regarded as a spiritual being, not every spiritual being is a divine messenger. Only in the later, postexilic books of the OT, in the Pseudep., and in the NT does this distinction break down.

A. In the OT
  1. Angels as messengers
    *a.* Ancient and modern parallels
    *b.* Stories about angels
  2. Angels as celestial beings
    *a.* Ancient Near Eastern parallels
    *b.* Stories about celestial beings
  3. Cherubim and seraphim
B. In the Apoc. and the Pseudep.
  1. Angels as spirits of phenomena
  2. The angelic hierarchy
  3. Angels as intercessors
  4. The angelic army
  5. Hostile angels
  6. Satan
  7. Specific angels
  8. Angels and the sainted dead
  9. Survivals of older concepts
  10. Folklore about angels
  11. Iranian influences
C. In the NT
Bibliography

**A. IN THE OT. 1. Angels as messengers.** The usual Hebrew word for "angel"—viz., מלאך—means simply "messenger, envoy" (cf. Ugaritic, Arabic, Ethiopic *l'k*, "send"). In the patriarchal and monarchic narratives the principal functions of such messengers are: (*a*) to convey the mandates of God to men; (*b*) to harbinger special events; (*c*) to protect the faithful, either individually or collectively, and execute condign punishment on their adversaries; and (*d*) to serve as instruments of the divine displeasure against sinners and recalcitrants within Israel itself.

It was an angel who ordered Abraham to refrain, at the last moment, from sacrificing his only son, Isaac (Gen. 22:11); who reassured Jacob against the attempts of Laban to cheat him of his wages (Gen. 31:11); and who indicated to Moses the special character of the burning bush (Exod. 3:2). An angel harbingered the birth of Ishmael (Gen. 16:11) and of Samson (Judg. 13:3-5). An angel protected Jacob from ill-hap (Gen. 48:16); escorted the Israelites through the wilderness (Exod. 23:20-23; 33:2); put a cloud between them and the Egyptians at the Red Sea (Exod. 14:19); invoked a curse on a city or village which denied them aid against the Philistines (Judg. 5:23); fed Elijah in the desert (I Kings 19:5); and inflicted disaster on the invaders of Jerusalem (II Kings 19:35; Isa. 37:36). As the later psalmists put it, angels are charged with the task of protecting the faithful in all their ways (Ps. 91:11) and of discomfiting and routing their enemies in battle (35:5-6).

Angels appear to men in human form. Abraham entertained them as guests without being aware of their true identity (Gen. 18); Joshua, at Jericho, saw the "commander of the army of Yahweh," an angelic being, in the guise of a man standing before him with a drawn sword (Josh. 5:13-14); and Manoah, the father of Samson, realized that his visitor had been an angel, only when the latter disappeared in the flame of a sacrifice (Judg. 13:20-21).

Angels possess extraordinary "goodliness" or beauty (I Sam. 29:9; II Sam. 14:17; 19:27) and know everything that happens on earth (II Sam. 14:20). They eat special food, identified as manna (Ps. 78: 24-25; cf. Wisd. Sol. 16:20; II Esd. 1:19).

*a. Ancient and modern parallels.* This conception of heavenly messengers has its roots in the earlier pagan religions of the Near East. Every major Mesopotamian and Hittite deity likewise possessed his subordinate minister (*sukkallu*) and throne-bearer (*guzalû*); while in the Canaanite mythological poems from Ras Shamra–Ugarit (fourteenth century B.C.) such prominent members of the pantheon as El, the supreme overlord; Baal, the controller of the rains; and Môt, the genius of death and aridity, communicate with one another by means of divine messengers (*ml'km*), and the goddess 'Anat has at her service a special courier and henchman (*mhr;* cf. Akkadian *mu-ár ili*, K. 3515, rev. 9). These figures are patterned after the personnel of an earthly court or administration. The *sukkallu* is mentioned as a kind of marshal or bailiff in secular documents from Mesopotamia, and the *guzalû* as a court officer in cuneiform tablets unearthed at Chagar Bazar (nos. 988, 999); while the *mhr,* or courier, has long been familiar from the famous Egyptian "satirical letter" of Hori (thirteenth century B.C.), where the term occurs (XVIII.3) as a Semitic loan word (*ANET* 477).

The particular characteristics with which angels are endowed in the earlier portions of the OT likewise derive from more ancient Near Eastern lore. Thus, the angel who interposed a cloud in order to screen the Israelites from their enemies at the Red Sea has his counterpart in the Hittite god Hasamilis, to whom a similar feat is ascribed; while the special guardian angel of Jacob echoes the common Mesopotamian belief in a "guardian of welfare" (*maṣṣar šulmi*) sent by major gods to protect their devotees.

Again, the notion that some angels are sent for good, and others for evil, finds an arresting parallel in a Hittite text which speaks of two groups of "fairies" who attend the mother-goddess. One group she dispatches to every household that is pleasing to her. They show solicitude for all its activities, assist in the cultivation of its land, weave garments for its female inmates, and get them married. The other group, however, is sent to every household with whom the goddess is displeased. They stir up quarrels, leave its female inmates to remain spinsters, and set them at odds "so that they break one another's heads." Finally, when angels are described, in Gen. 19:1, as traveling in pairs, this immediately recalls the fact that the same thing is said of the divine messengers in the Ras Shamra Texts—a notion based on an ancient practice of so dispatching couriers lest one alone meet with an accident en route.

Survivals in later Semitic folklore serve also to illustrate these more primitive concepts. Thus, the angel who accompanied the caravan of Israel on its journey through the wilderness has his counterpart in the deity Shi'a-alqum, "Accompanier (or Protector) of the people," mentioned in Nabatean inscriptions; while the fact that angels appear especially at wells (Gen. 16:7), beside oaks (Gen. 18:1-2) or broom trees (I Kings 19:4-5), and in blazing thorn bushes (Exod. 3:2) is well illustrated by modern popular beliefs concerning the presence of *welis* and *jinns* at just such places.

Further illustration is afforded by comparative folklore. The notion, e.g., that angels can screen their protégés in battle occurs also in the *Iliad* (III.381; V.776; XVIII.205; etc.) and is likewise associated with the Serbian *vily*. So too the idea of a personal guardian angel (or genius) may be readily paralleled from classical belief, from early Teutonic lore, and from many primitive cultures.

Again, the notion that angels, or heavenly beings, eat special food finds an arresting parallel in the Mesopotamian myth of Adapa, where Ea cunningly prevents the mortal hero from partaking of such fare by pretending that it is lethal (*ANET* 101-2). Similarly, according to the *Iliad* (V.341), the gods do not consume ordinary bread, but feed on ambrosia, which assures immortality (XIX.38, 347).

**b. Stories about angels.** Most of the stories told about angels in the earlier portions of the Bible belong to well-known *Märchen* types and play upon motifs familiar from the folklore of other peoples. Often, in fact, the angels take the place of such less exalted spiritual beings as demons, fairies, and even trolls in the sister versions.

Thus the story of how Abraham entertained three angels unawares and was rewarded by the promise of a son (Gen. 18:1-10) is simply a Hebrew version of the widespread tale of hospitality rewarded and has an exact parallel in the classical tale of Hyrieus of Tanagra, who entertained three gods unawares and was recompensed by the gift of a son, Orion (Ovid *Fasti* V.493-544).

To the same type, too, belongs the story of Lot's being rewarded for similar hospitality by the deliverance of himself and his family from the destruction of Sodom (Gen. 19). A good parallel to this is the tale in Grimm's collection (no. 45; *see bibliography*) relating how a couple was delivered from the general destruction of their city because, on the previous evening, they alone had given welcome to an itinerant dwarf; while a Buddhist legend tells of a man's being spared from a cataclysm which overwhelmed the city of Holaolokia because he had received an itinerant arhat whom all his neighbors had cold-shouldered.

So, too, the notion that angels "commute" between heaven and earth by means of a ladder (Gen. 28:12) finds an exact parallel both in Egyptian funerary texts and in early Greek poetry (e.g., Pindar, fragments 30, 162). Miniature ladders, it may be added, were often placed in Egyptian and Roman graves in order to facilitate the ascent of the soul to heaven, as they still are in those of the Mangars of Nepal; and the concept of the seven-runged ladder of souls played an important role in Mithraic doctrine. It survives also in medieval Christian hagiology and is introduced by Dante into his vision of the celestial realm (*Paradiso* XXI.7-10); while an Indian legend relates that Buddha once descended by ladder at Sankisa from the Trayastrinsas heavens.

Again, the troop of spiritual beings (מחנה אלהים; LXX παραβολή θεοῦ; Vulg. *castra Dei;* RSV "God's army"; but cf. Palestinian Targ. משרויין דמלאכיא קדישיא, "encampments of holy angels") which Jacob encountered at the spot subsequently named Mahanaim (Gen. 32:2) is simply a Hebrew version of the phantom host—i.e., a spectral band that rides about at night and appears occasionally to wayfarers. To be sure, in the folklore of Northern Europe this band is usually identified as a "wild hunt," but there is evidence that it was more anciently regarded as a celestial army; sometimes, indeed, it is known as the "ancient host" and thought to consist of old soldiers who "never die but simply fade away."

A familiar *Märchen* motif may be recognized also in the story (Gen. 32:24-25) of how Jacob wrestled all night, at the ford of Jabbok, with a spiritual being—variously described as a man (vs. 25); an *'elōhîm*, or "god" (vss. 28, 30; cf. Hos. 12:3—H 12:4); and a "messenger," or angel (Hos. 12:4—H 12:5)—whom he released only at daybreak, in exchange for a blessing. The motif in question is that of the traveler who has to grapple with the genius of a river or stream before he can cross it. With this, however, are combined two equally widespread secondary themes. The first is that a water spirit—like a wandering ghost, witch, fairy, or ogre—must be back in his proper abode before cockcrow. The second is that a hero who has vanquished a spirit or ogre exacts the boon of special knowledge or magical prowess as the price of the latter's release; this is familiar especially from the story of Menelaus and Proteus in the fourth book of the *Odyssey*.

Furthermore, when the angel that appeared to Manoah and his wife disappeared in the flame of a sacrifice (Judg. 13:20), it is not difficult to detect a Hebrew version of the familiar idea that a genie vanishes in smoke.

Lastly, the story of how Elijah, resting exhausted under a broom tree, was supplied by an angel with a single flask of water and a single cake of bread, which gave him strength to endure for forty days and nights (I Kings 19:5-8), connects at once with the common folk-tale motifs that languishing heroes are fed by spiritual beings or fays, and that food supplied by trolls gives mortals extraordinary strength, or that they can be sustained for a year by swallowing a single magical pill. The popular character of the biblical narrative is evident, of course, from the formulistic use of the number forty.

**2. Angels as celestial beings.** Besides messengers proper, the Hebrews recognized a wider class of celestial beings possessing the same essential nature. These are mentioned sporadically in the earlier portions of the OT, and frequent allusion is made to them also—albeit only by way of artistic conceit (like Cupid in English)—in the latter poetical books. They are called comprehensively: (*a*) "sons of God"—i.e., divine beings (בני אלהים [Gen. 6:2, 4; Job 38:7]; בני אל [Deut. 32:8; LXX, OL, and Qumran fragment in *Biblica*, XXXVI (1955), 265]; בני אלים [Pss. 29:1; 89:6]); (*b*) "holy ones" (קדושים [Deut. 33:2; Job 15: 15; Ps. 89:5, 7; Zech. 14:5]; רבבת קדש, "holy myriads" [Deut. 33:2]); and (*c*) "sons of the Most High" (בני עליון [Ps. 82:6; cf. Luke 6:35]).

*a. Ancient Near Eastern parallels.* These beings are simply folkloristic survivals of the older, pagan deities, conveniently subordinated to the hegemony of Yahweh, in much the same way that the local *numina* of the "heathen" were transmogrified, in later ages, into respectable Christian saints. Their designations hark back to this remoter Semitic antiquity. Thus, "sons of God" (*bn ilm*) is the regular term for the members of the pantheon in the Ugaritic texts (e.g., 2:16, 23, 34; 51:2-3; II AB, iii.15) and recurs on a Canaanite magical plaque from Arslan Tash, dating from the eighth century B.C. "Holy ones" (קדשם) likewise bears this meaning, both in the latter document and in an inscription of Yeḥimilk of Byblus, of the tenth century B.C., and is, indeed, actually employed in the sense of *"pagan gods"* in various passages of the OT itself (e.g., Job 5:1; Ps. 16:3; Hos. 11:12). As for the term בני עליון, usually rendered "sons of the Most High," it may be suggested that, despite the occurrence of 'Elyon as the name of a specific Phoenician (Canaanite) deity, this meant originally no more than "upper gods," in contrast to those who were believed to dwell in the subterranean realm. Such an interpretation would lend added point to passages like Ps. 82:6-7; Isa. 14:14, and the designation would find its parallel in the Mesopotamian distinction between the supernal Igigi and the infernal Anunnaki, as well as in the Hittite "upper" and "lower" gods (*šarrazēš* and *katterēš*) and the familiar Greek and Roman θεοὶ ὕπατοι καὶ νέρτεροι and *Di superi et inferi*. The divine epithet `l y` [*n m*], it may be added, has been recognized by some scholars in a Canaanite text from Ras Shamra-Ugarit (SS 3), and the word is also used in the same sense in the Talmud (Sanh. 20*b*; Keth. 104*a*).

*b. Stories about celestial beings.* A legend concerning celestial beings may be pieced together from Gen. 6:1-4; Ps. 82:6-7. This relates that in primeval times the "sons of God" (בני האלהים) impiously consorted with human women; whereupon Yahweh, outraged at the thought that the divine spirit would thus be transmitted permanently to mankind, expelled the miscreants from heaven and limited the span of human life to a maximum of 120 years. The point of the story lies in the widespread primitive notion that any intimate contact between persons—especially, sexual intercourse—communicates the qualities of the one to the other—an idea which may be detected already in the Hittite myth of the slaying of the dragon Illuyankas (*Keilschrifttexte aus Boghazköi* III.7). Accordingly, what alarmed Yahweh was the two-pronged threat that, through the action of the "angels," their own divine quality would be transmitted to men, and they themselves rendered mortal. For precisely the same reason, in Greek myth, sexual intercourse with a divine being necessarily entails the penalty of death for the presumptuous mortal.

A further piece of ancient folklore about the celestial beings is preserved in Job 38:7, where the expression "sons of God" (בני אלהים) stands parallel to "morning stars." This equivalence, which might seem at first blush to be due to Iranian influence (*see* § B11 *below*), occurs already in an Ugaritic text of the fourteenth century B.C. (IV AB, i.3-4) and reflects a far older tendency, well attested in Mesopotamian literature, to associate gods and goddesses with heavenly bodies.

**3. Cherubim and seraphim.** In addition to anthropomorphic angels, the earlier portions of the OT recognize certain celestial beings who are described as winged. These are called cherubim and seraphim. Fig. TEM 24.

The cherubim (כרובים) stand sentinel over the way to the tree of life in Eden (Gen. 3:24; cf. Ezek. 28: 14, 16) and also flank or support the throne of God (Pss. 80:1; 99:1; Isa. 37:16). Wooden images of them, overlaid with gold, and with wings outspread, were set over the ark of the covenant (Exod. 25:18-20; 37:6-9; Num. 7:89; I Sam. 4:4; I Kings 6:23-28; 8:6-7). Mounted on a cherub, Yahweh flies through the heavens (II Sam. 22:11; Ps. 18:10—H 18:11). An elaborate description of the cherubim, in which they are portrayed as four-winged and four-faced creatures, accompanied by whirling wheels (אופנים), is contained in the later visions of Ezekiel (1:4-28; 10: 3-22); but this description, combining several different concepts, is idiosyncratic rather than typical.

The seraphim (שרפים) are mentioned only in Isa. 6:2-6, where nothing further is said of them than that they are six-winged, stand beside the throne of Yahweh in heaven, and intone his praises.

Both these concepts go back, once again, to more ancient Near Eastern lore. The cherub may be identified with the winged genius who is, indeed, called *karibu* (or *kuribu*), "intercessor," in Mesopotamian texts and who is commonly portrayed in art as a sphinx, griffin, or winged human creature.* Representations of such beings, dating mostly from the ninth century B.C., have been found, e.g., at Carchemish, Nimrud, on ivories from Samaria, at Aleppo, and at Tell Halaf (*ANEP* 649-55). Several

25. Cherubim guarding the "Tree of Life," drawn by E. D. Wright; probable reconstruction of cherubim and palm-tree decoration in the temple, based on representation in Phoenician ivories

different strands, however, are interwoven in the biblical tapestry. As the guardian of the tree of life, the cherub finds his counterpart in such familiar figures of folk tale and myth as the dragons who stand sentinel over magic trees and treasures and in the winged bulls and colossi customarily placed at the entrance of Babylonian and Assyrian palaces and temples. As the supporters of the divine throne and guardians of the sacred ark, the cherubim may be compared, on the one hand, with the winged figures which flank the throne of King Hiram of Byblus* and with similar creatures on incense altars discovered at Taanach and Megiddo; and, on the other, with the draconic monsters (ζῷα) which draw the thrones and chariots of emperors in later Sassanian and Byzantine iconography. Finally, as the winged steeds of Yahweh they are perhaps to be regarded as personifications of the winds, more especially since the expression: "He rode upon a cherub and flew," stands parallel, in Ps. 18:10—H 18:11, to the words: "He came swiftly [lit., 'darted'] upon the wings of the wind." Figs. ANG 25-26; GEB 15.

Courtesy of E. G. Howland

26. The guardian cherubim, copied from a bas relief of cherubim supporting the throne of Hiram king of Byblos; from model by E. G. Howland

As for the seraphim, these may be plausibly identified with the six-winged demonic figure, holding a serpent in either hand, who is portrayed on a relief discovered at Tell Halaf. This comports especially with the fact that in Num. 21:6-8 the word "seraph" is used to describe the "fiery serpents" (cf. שרף, "burn") which assailed the Israelites in the wilderness, and the image which Moses set up as an apotropaic device against them (see NEHUSHTAN). Moreover, in Deut. 8:15; Isa. 30:6, the seraph is associated with the scorpion, and this suggests a further comparison, in point of general concept, with the demonic "scorpion-men" (aqrab-amêlu) who are described, in the Babylonian Epic of Gilgamesh (Tablet IX, col. ii) as standing sentinel at the mountains of sunrise and sunset.

Rabbinic and later exegetes have recognized a further class of angels in the "thousands of šin'ān" (אלפי שנאן; RSV "thousands upon thousands") mentioned in the MT of Ps. 68:17—H 68:18 as having accompanied Yahweh at Sinai. More probably, however, the word in question is to be connected with the ṯnnm of the Ugaritic texts (Krt A, ii 91) and the šanannu of documents from Alalaḫ (nos. 145, 183, 352, Wiseman), denoting a class of warriors—here, no doubt regarded as celestial (cf. Deut. 33:2), but not constituting a distinct order of beings. A class of angels has likewise been recognized by some in the obscure word אראלם of Isa. 33:7, but both text and interpretation are uncertain.

**B. IN THE APOC. AND THE PSEUDEP.** After the Babylonian exile, the conception of angels undergoes a profound change. This development, but faintly limned in the canonical scriptures, finds its most articulate expression in the Pseudep. and the Dead Sea Scrolls. Its principal features are:

**1. Angels as spirits of phenomena.** Angels now come to be regarded, not merely as messengers or as agents of particular situations and events, but as the controlling spirits of natural phenomena—e.g., of celestial bodies and winds (Enoch 19:1; 40:4-5; 60: 12, 16-21; 61:10; 72:1; Jub. 2:2-3; 1QH 1.10-11; 47.7-13); of the four seasons (Enoch 82:13); of countries (Dan. 10:19-21); and of such abstractions as peace (Enoch 40:8; 52:5; Test. Dan 6:5; Test. Asher 6:6; Test. Benj. 6:1; cf. Isa. 33:7), healing (Tob. 3: 17; Enoch 10:7; 40:9), and death (II Bar. 21:23; cf. Prov. 16:14). They are actually called "spirits" (רוחין) or "spirits of knowledge" (רוחות דעת; 1QH 3.23), and in one of the Dead Sea Hymns (1.10), it is said explicitly that it was only sometime after the creation of the world that these spirits were turned into angels. They are believed to be privy to the secrets of cosmos (called רזי פלא, "extraordinary mysteries," in the Dead Sea Scrolls; cf. Enoch 9:6), and are sometimes conjoined with cosmic "powers and principalities" (Enoch 41:9; 61:10)—a concept familiar especially from the NT. See § C below.

**2. The angelic hierarchy.** Angels are now pictured as a hierarchy, headed by seven (Tob. 12:15 G; Enoch 81:5; 90:21-22; II Esd. 5:20), four (Enoch 40; 87:2-3; 88:1), or three (Enoch 90:31) archangels, and including such distinct ranks as "angels of the presence" (Enoch 40:2; Jub. 1:27, 29; 2:1-2, 18; etc.; cf. Test. Levi 3:5; 13:5; 1QH 6.13; DS Order of Blessings; cf. Isa. 33:7; Ber. 51a: מלאכי פנים), and "angels of sanctification" (Jub. 2:18; 15:27; 1QH 1.11; fragment 1.1).

**3. Angels as intercessors.** Angels now serve not only as the messengers of God to man, but also of man to God. They carry men's prayers to the divine presence (Tob. 12:15; II Bar. 11 G; 1QH 6.13) and act as intercessors for them (Tobit; II Bar. 6:7; Enoch 9:10; 15:2; 40:9; 47:2; 99:3, 16; Test. Levi 3:5; 5:6-7; Dan. 6:2; 10:13, 21). In keeping with this, special emphasis is placed on their role as guardians of the righteous, both individually and collectively (Dan. 10:13, 20; 11:1; 12:1; II Macc. 11:6; III Macc. 6:18; Sus. 45; Bel 34-39; Enoch 20:5; Jub. 35:17; 1QH 5.21-22; 1QS 9.15; 1QM 9.16).

**4. The angelic army.** Angels are now conceived as an army (II Bar. 51:11; 70:7; Test. Levi 3:3), which will participate in the final war against the wicked (Zech. 14:13; 1QH 3.35-36; 10.34-35; 1QM 15.14). This idea is based partly on an interpretation of the scriptural phrase "the host of heaven" (צבא השמים), and partly on a mythopoeic projection into the celestial sphere of a common Hellenistic notion that the earthly congregation of the saints constitutes a kind of "salvation army."

**5. Hostile angels.** Under the increasing influence of Iranian dualism, a class of hostile angels, or "satans" (שטן, "obstruct"), emerges (Enoch 40:7; 54:6; 69:4, 6; 1QH fragments 4.6; 45.3; DS Order of Blessings 8). These are also called "destroyers" (משחית, 1QH; cf. II Sam. 24:16, המלאך המשחית). They are accommodated, however, to the basic premise of Judaism by being made subject to, rather than independent of, the supreme authority of Yahweh, exercising their demonic functions either as rebels defying his will or else explicitly as his agents.

In the former aspect, they are sometimes (e.g., Enoch 69:4) identified with the fallen angels of Gen. 6:1-4. In the latter, they serve as God's executioners at the Last Judgment, and are styled "angels of punishment" (Enoch 53:3; 56:1; 61:1; 62:11; 63:1; II Bar. 21:23), or "angels of destruction" [מלאכי חבל; CDC 4:12; Zadokite Document 2:6; 8:2; cf. Shab. 55a; P.T. Shebu. VI.73a [מלאכי חבלה]; and Samar. מלאכי רגוז, "angels of perturbation" [Marqeh 191a]).

**6. Satan.** SATAN himself now appears as a distinct figure, though in the OT the name is still used only as an appellative. In the book of Jubilees (49:2) and in the so-called Zadokite Document (4:3; 5:18; 6:5; 8:2), he is called by the cognate name Mastema (cf. Hos. 9:8; "hatred"), and elsewhere (e.g., Jub. 1:20; Sibylline Oracles 3:63, 73; 1QS 1.18, 23-24; Zadokite Document 4:13, 15; 5:18; 1QM, *passim*) by that of BELIAL.

**7. Specific angels.** Angels now tend to be designated by specific names—e.g., the archangels, Michael (Dan. 10:13; 12:1; Enoch 9:1; 10:11; etc.), Gabriel (Dan. 8:16; Enoch 9:1; 20:7; 40:9; 1QM 9.26), Raphael (Tob. 3:17; 12:15; Enoch 10:4; 40:9), and Uriel (Enoch 9:1; 19:1; 20:2; cf. 1QS 3.20: "the angel who is over the lights [אורים]"). In Enoch 6:7; 8:3-4; 69:2, a catalogue is given of the names of the fallen angels. Most of these are, to be sure, unintelligible in the Ethiopic and Greek texts; but with the aid of a parallel list in a medieval Hebrew version, they may be recognized as mere personifications of celestial phenomena—e.g., Baradiel, from ברד, "hail"; Ruḥiel, from רוח, "wind"; Ziqiel, from זיק, "meteor"; Kokbiel, from כוכב, "star." Similarly, in Enoch 82:13, the angels of the four seasons bear specific names—viz., Melkiel, Helemmelek, Melejal, and Narel—though the basis on which these are chosen remains obscure. Sometimes, too, the names are determined by the special functions of the angels who bear them—e.g., Raphael, the angel of healing, from רפא, "heal"; Raguel, "who takes vengeance on the world of the luminaries" (Enoch 20:4), from רעע, "disquiet." In the Talmud, names of angels are often evolved out of fanciful exegesis of a scriptural text—e.g., Lailah, the angel of conception (Nid. 16b), from Job 3:3:

> Let the day perish wherein I was born,
> and the night [לילה] which said,
> "A man-child is conceived."

The same process will probably account for at least some of the baffling names of angels in pseudepigraphic (and later magical) literature.

**8. Angels and the sainted dead.** There is a marked tendency to associate the angels with the spirits of the sainted dead—i.e., to conceive of both as forming a single congregation which stands forever in the presence of God (cf. 1QH 3.21; 6.14; 11.11-12; fragment 2.10; Enoch 104:6), and the name "holy ones" or "saints" (קדושים) comes to be applied to both.

**9. Survivals of older concepts.** Side by side with these innovations, however, the older ideas persist with remarkable tenacity. The celestial beings still bear the ancient designation "holy ones" (Dan. 4: 13, 17, 23; Ecclus. 42:17; Enoch 9:3; 71:1; Test. Levi 3:3-4; DS Genesis Apocryphon 2.1; 1QH fragments

5.3; 15.7; 24.2) and are still regarded, like the Mesopotamian gods and the Ugaritic "messenger of heaven" (RS 5.14), as clothed in light. Sometimes, too, elements of angelological folklore which are but casually introduced in the OT are elaborated in the pseudepigraphic literature in greater detail. Thus, the fall of the angels is expanded (Enoch 6:6; Jub. 4: 15) into the legend that they descended to earth in the days of the antediluvian patriarch Jared (cf. Gen. 5:15)—a legend based simply on the similarity of that name to the Hebrew word ירד, "descend"; and the miscreants are identified with the Watchers (*see* WATCHER) of Daniel (Enoch 1:5; 10:9, 15; 12:2, 4; etc.; DS Genesis Apocryphon 2.1). Again, on the strength of the idea that they encompass the Divine Glory in heaven, the angels are called "the glorified" (Test. Levi 18:5; 1QH 10.8; II Enoch 22:10; cf. Jude 8); while in Enoch 39:12, the scriptural verse (Isa. 6:3):

> Holy, holy, holy is the LORD of hosts [יהוה צבאות];
> the whole earth is full of his glory,

is paraphrased, significantly: "Holy, holy, holy, is the Lord *of Spirits*. He filleth the earth with *spirits*."

The cherubim and seraphim likewise survive (Enoch 61:10; 71:7), and in one passage (Enoch 20: 7) the latter are specifically identified as serpents. Moreover, the "whirling wheels" of Ezekiel's visions now become—as in later rabbinic literature—animate angelic beings.

**10. Folklore about angels.** This broad picture of the angels is tricked out by a number of extra touches derived from popular lore. They are said to be clothed in white garments (Dan. 10:5-6; Enoch 87:2; Test. Levi 8:1), and now for the first time appears the concept that even the anthropomorphic messengers of heaven are winged (Dan. 9:21; Enoch 61:1). The latter, however, appears still to have been something of an innovation, or not yet to have become standard and stereotyped, for in Enoch 61:1 it is said expressly that when the angels went off to measure Paradise, "they took to themselves wings," implying that they did not normally possess them. And it should be observed also that the crucial words מעף ביעף in Dan. 9:21, which mean literally, "borne in winged flight," are rendered by the LXX simply τάχει φερόμενος, "borne with speed."

Angels are said also to have their own special pathways in heaven (Enoch 18:5). This idea was probably influenced by the common Greco-Roman notion that the sainted dead ascended by a special "way of the blessed" (ὁδὸς μακάρων), often identified with the Milky Way.

Just as in the earlier scriptural narratives, so in those of the intertestamental literature, the treatment of angels draws also upon traditional folktales. The parade example of such indebtedness is to be found in the story of TOBIT, for this is simply a Jewish adaptation of the well-known motif of the grateful dead.

**11. Iranian influences.** Much of this later angelology may be attributed to the infiltration of Iranian ideas, for it runs parallel to a remarkable degree with what we find in the Gathas and other earlier portions of the Zend Avesta. Thus, the seven archangels have their counterpart in the Amesha Spentas, who attend upon the supreme Lord of Wisdom, Ahuramazda (cleverly Judaized in the Dead Sea Scrolls [1QS 3.15; 1QH 1.26; fragment 4.15] as "God of knowledge" [אל דעות]—a title borrowed from I Sam. 2:3!). The identification of the angels with the controlling spirits of natural phenomena accords strikingly with the concept of the *fravashis* and the *yazatas,* the latter of whom are said explicitly to have traced out the courses of the waters, which were originally without motion; to have shown plants how to germinate; and to have plotted the orbits of sun, moon, and stars (Yasht 13.53-57). The notion that angels intercede for men and that they will join in the final battle against the Evil One echoes the role of these same spiritual beings in the Avesta (Yasht 19.95; Yasna 30.3; 44.15; etc.). Conversely, the "satans" or hostile "angels of destruction" reproduce to a nicety the Avestan *devas.* It is to be observed in particular that, according to the Dead Sea Manual of Discipline (4.13-14), these celestial adversaries will eventually cast the unrighteous into an eternal fire; while in one of the Hymns (3.29-32), the latter is described more vividly as a stream of molten granite —a concept which adroitly blends the dire prophecy of Isaiah (34:9) with the Avestan doctrine that the wicked will be plagued by the devas, who will ultimately be thrust along with them into the "ordeal of molten metal" (*ayah khšusta;* Yasna 30.7; 31.19; 32.7; 43.4; 47.6; cf. also Bundahish 30.19, 31). As for Satan, Mastema, or Belial, this figure has its parallel in Angra Mainyu, the evil spirit opposed to Spenta Mainyu, the good spirit (Yasht 3.13; 17.19; 19.97; etc.); or in Druj, the genius of falsehood and deceit, opposed to Asha, that of truth and normalcy (represented in the Dead Sea Scrolls as אמת!). Again, the assertion in the Dead Sea Hymns (11.14) that the angels constitute a celestial choir which the pious are destined eventually to join, at once recalls the Mazdean doctrine that the righteous will be given a place in the heavenly "mansion of song" (*garomana;* Yasna 22.15; 24.61; 45.8; 50.4; cf. Bundahish 31). Finally, the role of the archangel Michael as the deliverer of the faithful (Dan. 10:21; 12:1; 1QM 17. 6-7) accords with that of the Saoshyant, or Redeemer, in the Avesta.

**C. IN THE NT.** Broadly speaking, the NT adds nothing to the traditional conception of angels. Here too they appear as harbingers of special births: Gabriel presaged that of John the Baptist (Luke 1: 11-20), and an unidentified celestial messenger that of Jesus (2:8-14). Angels likewise intervene to give succor in moments of crisis: an angel warned Joseph to flee with Mary and the infant Jesus into Egypt (Matt. 2:13); an angel encouraged Jesus on the Mount of Olives (Luke 22:43); an angel rolled away the stone from Jesus' tomb (Matt. 28:2-3); and an angel released Peter from prison (Acts 12:7-10). Angels are robed in white garments (Matt. 28:3; Rev. 15:6; 19:14) and bathed in radiance (Matt. 28: 3; Luke 2:9; Rev. 18:1). In the wake of Ezekiel's visions and of Enoch 40:2; 90:21, the book of Revelation recognizes a special order of seven spirits— evidently archangels (Rev. 1:4; 4:5)—as well as four holy creatures who wait upon the throne of God

(4:6); and to these are added, in agreement with the book of Enoch, four angels who preside over the four corners of the earth (Rev. 7:1). Moreover, in view of the parallel expression in Enoch (41:9; 61 10), where the reference is clearly to spiritual beings it may be regarded as virtually certain that the "powers" (δυνάμεις) to whom reference is made in Rom. 8:38; I Cor. 15:24; Eph. 3:10; I Pet. 3:22 are angels. Similarly, the "elemental spirits of the universe" (στοιχεῖα τοῦ κόσμου), which are mentioned in Gal. 4:3; Col. 2:8, are evidently angelic personifications of natural phenomena, since the corresponding Semitic term, יסוד, is used in precisely the same way both in the Dead Sea Scrolls and in Samaritan (Marqeh, 135a).

Angels surround the throne of God in heaven and chant his praises (Luke 2:13; Rev. 4:9; cf. Isa. 6:2-3, Enoch 39:12). They are identified as spirits (πνεύματα; Heb. 1:7), and in Jude 6 allusion is made to their primeval rebellion (cf. Enoch 6-9). They also play a major role in the eschatological picture painted in Revelation. The good angels assist Michael, and the evil angels Belial, in the final conflict (Rev. 12:7); and seven angels pour seven bowls of God's wrath on various elements of creation (ch. 16). There is, however, very little in this picture that is not to be found previously in Enoch and other apocalyptic scriptures.

In Luke 12:8-9, Jesus declares that "everyone who acknowledges me before men, the Son of man also will acknowledge before the angels of God; but he who denies me before men will be denied before the angels of God." Because in the parallel passage, Matt. 10:32-33, the words "before the angels of God" are replaced by "before my Father who is in heaven," it has been suggested that they are simply a pious circumlocution, like the Talmudic "before heaven" (קמי שמיא; Ḳid. 64c) for "before God." The fact is, however, that they refer rather to what is described explicitly in Enoch 99:3, where it is said that the prayers of the righteous will constitute a "testimony before the angels," whereas the latter will at the same time "rehearse the sin of the sinners before the Most High" (cf. 99:16; 100:10).

Lastly, it should be observed that, according to Acts 23:6-8, belief in angels, spirits, and resurrection, though acknowledged by the more plebeian Pharisees, was denied by the more aristocratic Sadducees.

*Bibliography.* General: M. A. Canney, "Sky-folk in the OT," *Journal of the Manchester Egyptian and Oriental Society,* X (1923), 53-58. J. Rybinski, *Der Mal'akh Jahwe* (1930). B. M. Bellas, *Mal'ak-Yahwe* (1931). F. Stier, *Gott und sein Engel im AT* (1934). E. Langton, *The Ministries of the Angelic Powers* (1937). O. Opham, *Die Engel* (1956). M. Ziegler, *Engel und Dämon im Lichte der Bibel* (1957).

Special Studies: J. Grimm, *Teutonic Mythology* (trans. F. Stallybrass; 1883). T. H. Gaster, *Orientalia,* XI (1942); *Thespis* (rev. ed., 1960). T. H. GASTER

**ANGELS OF THE SEVEN CHURCHES** [ἄγγελοι τῶν ἑπτὰ ἐκκλησιῶν] (Rev. 1:20). Interpreters have identified these variously with: (*a*) the messengers sent to John by the churches of Asia (vs. 4); (*b*) the churches' bishops; (*c*) their "guardian angels" (akin to those of nations and individuals; cf. Deut. 32:8 LXX; Dan. 10:13; 12:1; Ecclus. 17:17; Matt. 18:10;

Acts 12:15); (*d*) their heavenly replicas—akin to the Zoroastrian *fravashis;* and, as seems most appropriate; (*e*) the spiritual core or the ethically mature persons of the churches (cf. Paul's τέλειοι [I Cor. 2:6]), those held safe in the Lord's right hand (Rev. 1:16) and addressed in chs. 2–3, the true church of Christ in fact, to be distinguished from the "lampstands" or localized groups as a whole.

**Bibliography.** *See* the Commentaries under REVELATION, BOOK OF. J. W. BOWMAN

**ANGER.** In the biblical view there is a qualitative and theological difference between human anger on the one hand and divine anger on the other, even if the same words may often be used for either (*see* §§ 1*a*, 5, *below; see also* WRATH OF GOD). The following discussion is concerned with the concept of anger in the Bible as it relates to man. In general the notion comprehends those feelings and expressions of antipathy toward an object that have been aroused by a sense of injury or wrong and that take a variety of forms, ranging from simple resentment or pique to reactions of violence and destruction. Connoting an acute response to particular situations and acts of provocation, anger is to be distinguished from the related but relatively prolonged and lingering human affects such as HATE; JEALOUSY; and the like.

1. Terminology of anger in the Bible
   *a.* Anger in biblical Hebrew
   *b.* Anger in LXX Greek
   *c.* Anger in NT Greek
2. The biblical acknowledgment of anger
3. Anger and faith
4. Anger and sin
5. Anger and the wrath of God
Bibliography

**1. Terminology of anger in the Bible.** The word "anger" and its synonyms ("wrath," "fury," "indignation," "rage," "vexation," etc.) render into English at least eight Hebrew words and their derivatives, while they stand predominantly for two Greek words and their derivatives and occasionally for other Greek expressions.

*a. Anger in biblical Hebrew.* The commonest Hebrew expression either for divine or for human anger is the noun אַף (Gen. 27:45), which has the meaning also of "nostril" or "nose" (Num. 11:20). In ancient Hebrew psychology this organ was thought of as the seat of anger, and the phrase for "slow to anger" is literally "long of nose" (e.g., Prov. 14:29). It happens that the corresponding verb, אָנַף, "be angry," is used only of divine anger, not human, in the OT. The verb חרה, "burn," both by itself and in association with אַף (Num. 22:27; Jonah 4:1), refers nearly always to the burning or kindling of anger. The derived combination חֲרִי אַף, "burning" of anger, usually refers to man (Isa. 7:4), but the cognate expression חֲרוֹן or חֲרוֹן אַף always refers to divine wrath in the OT (Exod. 32:12). A frequently used synonym for אַף is חֵמָה, "rage" or "fury" (II Kings 5:12), used also on occasion to denote the sun's heat (Ps. 19:6), the effect of wine (Hos. 7:5), and the poison of serpents (Deut. 32:24). Synonyms only slightly less common are formed from other roots or their derivatives such as קֶצֶף, "be ill humored,

enraged" (Esth. 1:12); עֶבְרָה, "overflowing rage, fury" (Amos 1:11); זַעַם, "indignation" (Jer. 15:17); זַעַף, "be enraged, storm" (II Chr. 26:19); and כַּעַס, "vexation" (I Sam. 1:6; in Job כַּעַשׂ—e.g., 5:2). The emotion of anger can be the subject where the express terminology may be absent, the idea being implied by the language of jealousy, cursing, revenge, violence, rebellion, etc., and by descriptions of accompanying physical reactions such as heavy breathing, snorting, trembling, shouting, raving, grinding the teeth, and the like. Divine wrath is often qualitatively distinguished from human anger by expressing the former through combinations of two or even three anger termini in succession—e.g., "wrath and fierce anger" (אַף וחרון; עֶבְרָה; Isa. 13:9); "in anger and fury and great wrath" (באַף ובחמה ובקצף גדול; Deut. 29:27; *see* WRATH OF GOD).

*b. Anger in LXX Greek.* The Greek translation of the OT renders the various Hebrew expressions for anger almost entirely into either of two Greek words or their derivatives—namely, ὀργή or θυμός. Originally θυμός stood in ancient Greek for the inner affect or emotion of anger; ὀργή, for the outward effect or manifestation. But in the LXX the two expressions appear to be interchangeable, and either or both together seem to be used indifferently for any of the Hebrew terms. Two other Greek words occur only rarely in the LXX for anger—χόλος, "bile, bitter anger" (Eccl. 5:17—H 5:16; μῆνις, "wrath" (Gen. 49:7). These refer almost exclusively to human anger in the LXX, whereas in earlier ancient Greek, by contrast, they are nearly always associated with deity. *See bibliography.*

*c. Anger in NT Greek.* The terminology of anger in the NT consists mainly of the synonyms ὀργή and θυμός with their derivatives. If there is any distinction between them in the NT with regard to the human emotion, it would appear that θυμός connotes better the unreflecting passion of anger (e.g., Luke 4:28); ὀργή, the relatively more considered moral indignation (Jas. 1:19). While ὀργή is translated as either "anger" or "wrath," θυμός is always translated as "wrath."

**2. The biblical acknowledgment of anger.** Antecedent to any judgmental pronouncements on the subject in either the OT or the NT, there is the recognition and, indeed, a certain dignification of man's capacity for and exercise of anger. In the first place, it is seen simply as one of the characteristic elements of human behavior that are to be taken seriously when encountered and to be coped with prudently. The story of Cain and the Song of Lamech posit human wrath already at the very beginning of history (Gen. 4:5, 23-24). Rebekah admonishes Jacob to flee until his "brother's fury turns away" (Gen. 27:43-45). The wisdom sages, at the same time that they looked askance at displays of human anger as being alien to the well-ordered life (Ps. 37:8; Prov. 14:29; 29:22; Job 18:4; 36:18; etc.), nevertheless taught a healthy respect for anger as it might be encountered among those in authority and advised the exercise of discretion in its presence (Prov. 16:14; 20:21; Eccl. 10:4). The king in Jesus' parable, whose invited guests uniformly decline invitations to the wedding feast, is hardly expected to react otherwise than with a typical rage (Matt. 22:1-10).

While anger is appreciated in the Bible as something inherent in man's personal and social existence, it is not viewed as a thing to be treated with indifference. Jacob's blessing expresses fear and abhorrence for the fierce anger and cruel wrath of Simeon and Levi (Gen. 49:5-7). David knows his life to be endangered by the pathological outbursts of Saul (I Sam. 18:8-9; 19:9-10; 20:30-31). The collective fury of an angered crowd is invariably sinister and terrifying in the NT (cf. Matt. 27:20-23; Luke 4:28-29; Acts 7:54-58).

But beyond the fact of its destructive possibilities, it remains true for the Bible that human wrath signifies a crisis in those events where it is manifested. Thus it helps to provoke a change or turning about in subsequent human relationships with one's fellows or with the deity. The displeasure of Samuel erupts concomitantly both with the selection and with the rejection of Saul as king (I Sam. 8:6; 15:11). The Israelite monarchy is divided as a consequence, in part, of the anger of Israel against Judah (I Kings 12:1-6). The anger of Jonah answers to a reversal of divine judgment in historical events (Jonah 3:10–4:1). Jesus' anger accompanies an act of healing (Mark 3:5). His indignant zeal in the temple sharpens the conflict between him and his antagonists (John 2:13-21; cf. Luke 19:45-46), while the fury of his opponents brings closer the hour of his passion (Mark 3:6; Luke 6:11; etc.). Therefore, because of its frequent association with emphatic and even violent self-disclosures of man's will and intent at critical junctures in the biblical story, anger in the Bible seems to fall under an ambivalent judgment with regard to questions of faith and conduct.

**3. Anger and faith.** In the OT one finds a qualified justification of anger insofar as it operates in the service of faith and piety, in the defense of justice generally, or in particular in the condemnation of violations of God's claims to sovereignty. David's anger as a judge convicts him in his own eyes as he is confronted with his crime by the prophet Nathan (II Sam. 12:5-7, 13). Moses becomes furious at the faithlessness of the Israelites (Exod. 16:20). The anger of the prophets, at the same time that it is a sign of the wrath of God, is also a thoroughly human indignation with injustice and immorality (cf. Isa. 7:13; Jer. 6:11; 15:17; Amos 4:1-3; etc.). Doubtless one of the most striking—certainly one of the most blood-chilling—examples in the Bible of human wrath in the service of the divine purpose is that of Samuel, who "hewed Agag in pieces before the LORD in Gilgal" (I Sam. 15:33).

Less often do the NT writers appear to concede to human anger a positive role; however, rulers are a "terror" to bad conduct and thus serve God's wrath for man's good (Rom. 13:3-4). Indignation over wrong can become an instrument of sanctification (II Cor. 7:11). On the other hand, the prophetic anger and indignation of Jesus which he displayed on a number of occasions would seem to leave open in the NT the possibility—certainly it leaves there the memory—of the redemptive use of this human passion, where it becomes a sign and the incarnation of God's wrath (Matt. 12:34; 15:7; 23:13-36; Mark 3:5; 9:42; 10:14; John 2:15; 8:44; etc.; *see* WRATH OF GOD § 5*a*).

**4. Anger and sin.** The profession of righteous anger, nevertheless, can turn into a premature identification of the interests of man with those of God —the ministry of Jesus being both the exception to and the judgment upon such self-corruption (*see* § 3 *above*). Thus Paul proceeds to Damascus, "breathing threats and murder against the disciples of the Lord" (Acts 9:1). Intense suffering by an individual or a people seems able also to lead men into this same false identification (cf. Job 7:11; 10:1 *et passim;* Ps. 137:7-9; Mal. 1:2-5), while anger can become a purely selfish matter and the expression of a merely peevish vexation at unexpected and unwelcome misfortune or frustration (cf. Gen. 30:2; II Kings 5:12; Esth. 1:12; etc.). The wisdom sages explicitly condemn anger as antithetical to חכמה in that it stirs up trouble and has harmful consequences (Prov. 6:34; 15:1; 16:14; 19:19; 27:4), and he who is long-suffering is the genuine wise man (Prov. 14:29; Eccl. 7:8; etc.), while the man of anger is the fool (Prov. 14:17, 29; *see* WISDOM; SELF-CONTROL).

Negative judgments on human anger are not confined to the wisdom literature. In the prophetic view, the destructiveness of man's fury infects all nature with a debilitating malaise (Hos. 4:2-3). Cain is warned that in his anger "sin is couching at the door," and ultimately it drives him "away from the ground" and from the divine presence (Gen. 4:6-7, 14). Doubtless the legend of Cain lies behind the warning of Jesus in the Sermon on the Mount that the angry man shares the divine judgment on him who kills (Matt. 5:21-22; cf. vss. 23-26).

In spite of some concessions in the NT regarding human anger (*see* § 3 *above*), it seems to be the general view there that "the anger of man does not work the righteousness of God" (Jas. 1:19-20). The admonition of the writer of Ephesians to "be angry but do not sin" (4:26; cf. Ps. 4:4), is scarcely a commendation of anger to man but a warning that anger provides exceptional opportunity for sinful self-elevation and overt trespasses; moreover, the reader is immediately exhorted in the same breath: "Do not let the sun go down on your anger" (cf. Eph. 4:31; 6:4; Col. 3:8; I Tim. 2:8; Tit. 1:7).

**5. Anger and the wrath of God.** This prophetic condemnation of human wrath in the OT and the NT is not based on a rejection of anger in principle, as with the wisdom writers (*see* § 4 *above*), nor is it necessarily an appeal in behalf of pacifism. Rather, on the one hand it represents a deference to the wrath of God in the firm belief that "vengeance is mine, I will repay, says the Lord" (Rom. 12:19; Heb. 10:30; cf. Lev. 19:18; Deut. 32:35). On the other hand, there is the keen realization that the anger of man has sought to usurp the wrath of God and has for this reason become the object of that wrath. It is significant that in both the OT and NT human agents that serve as instruments of the divine anger become also its chief objects. Jehu's massacre of the house of Ahab at Jezreel is represented as divine vengeance for the blood of the LORD's prophets (II Kings 9:7; 10:11), but, paradoxically, the house of Jehu earns the divine condemnation for this very slaughter (Hos. 1:4-5). Assyria is described as the "rod" of God's anger and the "staff" of his fury against Israel (Isa. 10:5-6), but in turn becomes the object of that wrath as "the ax vaunt[s] itself over him who hews with it" (Isa. 10:15; cf. vs. 12 etc.). The state that serves as the servant of God's wrath (Rom. 13:4) becomes nevertheless the embodiment of that against which God's wrath turns in the last judgment (Rev. 18:1–19:3 *et passim*).

Although the biblical view appreciates the possibility of righteous and perhaps even redemptive anger, it is nevertheless only a vanquished human anger of which the psalmist speaks when he declares:

> Surely the wrath of men shall praise thee;
> the residue of wrath thou wilt gird upon thee
> (Ps. 76:10).

*Bibliography.* A valuable study of human anger as well as its relation to divine anger in the biblical, apocryphal, and rabbinical literature is given in J. Fichtner *et al.*, "ὀργή," *TWNT*, V (1954), 382-448. On the subject of Jesus' anger see R. V. G. Tasker, *The Biblical Doctrine of the Wrath of God* (1951), pp. 29-34. Besides the various commentaries on relevant biblical passages see also Lactantius (*ca.* A.D. 312), *A Treatise on the Anger of God* (trans. Fletcher), ch. 12: "Of the Anger of God and Man," in *The Ante-Nicene Fathers* (1886); R. C. Trench, *Exposition of the Sermon on the Mount from the Writings of St. Augustine* (3rd ed., 1869), pp. 187-92 (on Matt. 5:21-22).        B. T. DAHLBERG

**ANGLE, THE** [המקצוע]; KJV TURNING OF THE WALL. A portion of the ramparts of Jerusalem fortified by Uzziah (II Chr. 26:9) and restored under Nehemiah (Neh. 3:19-20, 24-25), in the vicinity of the palace. It is certainly not related to the CORNER GATE and probably not to "the corner" (הפנה) mentioned in Neh. 3:31.

*See also* CORNER, ASCENT OF; JERUSALEM § 7*b*.
                                        G. A. BARROIS

**ANGLO-SAXON VERSIONS** ăng'glō săk'sən. Translations of the Psalms and the gospels, with other biblical fragments. *See* VERSIONS, ENGLISH, § 1.

**ANGUISH.** *See* SUFFERING.

**ANIAM** ə nī'əm [אניעם, people's mourning, *or* I am kinsman] (I Chr. 7:19). The fourth son of Shemida in the genealogy of Manasseh.

**ANIM** ā'nĭm [ענים, springs]. A city in the SW hill-country district of Judah with Kiriath-sepher (Debir) and Eshtemoa (Josh. 15:50). It appears in the Amarna correspondence as Hawini. Anim is identified with Khirbet Ghuwein et-Tahta, eleven miles S of Hebron, three miles S of es-Semu'a (Eshtemoa). Eusebius refers to it as Anaia ('Αναιά), nine (Roman) miles S of Hebron. Khirbet Ghuwein el-Foqa, just NE of et-Tahta, represents Christian Anaia, while et-Tahta represents the Jewish village of Eusebius' day.
                                        V. R. GOLD

**ANIMAL** [*for* חיה, טבח, ζῷον, τετράπους, *see* BEAST; *for* בהמה, מקנה, κτῆνος, *see* CATTLE]; KJV BEAST; CATTLE; FOUR-FOOTED BEAST. For a full discussion of animals in the Bible, *see* FAUNA.

"Animal" seems generally to refer to quadrupeds; it designates all animals (in this restricted sense) in Jer. 27:5; II Pet. 2:12; Jude 10; clean and unclean creatures in Lev. 11:39; 27:11, 27; Deut. 14:4; wild animals in Gen. 3:14; wild and domesticated ani-

mals, excluding birds and reptiles, in Gen. 6:20; 8: 17; Acts 10:12; Rom. 1:23; all animals, excluding birds, in Gen. 7:2; all animals, except birds and fish, in I Cor. 15:39; sheep in Gen. 29:7; oxen and sheep in Lev. 27:26; horses and mules in I Kings 18:5; sacrificial victims in Lev. 7:25; 27:9; Heb. 13:11; food animals in Gen. 43:16; Lev. 7:26 (excluding birds).
                                        W. S. McCULLOUGH

**ANIMAL-WORSHIP.** *See* TOTEMISM.

27. Anise

**ANISE.** KJV translation of ἄνηθον (RSV DILL) in Matt. 23:23. The Greek for the true anise (*Pimpinella anisum* L.) is ἄννησον. Fig. ANI 27.

*See also* MINT; CUMMIN; SPICES.

**ANKLETS** [עכסים] (Isa. 3:18); KJV TINKLING ORNAMENTS ABOUT THEIR FEET. Ornamental rings worn above the ankles. They appear in Isaiah's description of the luxury articles of the daughters of Zion. Numerous anklets or ankle bracelets have been recovered in archaeological excavations all over Palestine. They were found in position in graves at Lachish. Most of them were of heavy bronze, usually flattened on the inside and measuring somewhere between 2½ and 4½ inches in diameter and from 2/25 to 2/5 inches wide.
                                        J. M. MYERS

**ANNA** ăn'ə ["Αννα *or* "Αννα; חנה, grace]. **1.** The wife of TOBIT. During his blindness she supported him. The picture of her watching for and welcoming her absent son is not unlike that of the father in the parable of the prodigal son.

**2.** An aged prophetess, long a widow, mentioned in Luke 2:36-38 as witnessing the presentation in the temple of the infant Jesus. She is apparently presented as a counterpart to Simeon; no record of her words of thanksgiving is offered.

3. The mother of Mary and the grandmother of Jesus. Unmentioned in the NT, she is prominent in the Protevangelium of James (*see* JAMES, PROTEVANGELIUM OF) and in subsequent legends of the birth of the Virgin. Anna and her husband, Joachim, have long been childless, and this fact has brought sorrow and humiliation to both. Angels appear to both parents independently, announcing that their prayers have been answered. In joy Anna promises to dedicate the child to lifelong service to God. Mary is born. Anna gives thanks, rears the child until she is three, then takes her to the temple. The story is strongly reminiscent of that of Hannah—even the name is the same—the mother of Samuel.

According to a late legend (quoted in Migne, *Dictionnaire des Légendes,* vol. II, col. 105, and found in one MS of the Gospel of Pseudo-Matthew [*see* PSEUDO-MATTHEW, GOSPEL OF]), after the death of Joachim she was married two more times, by angelic direction, first to Cleophas, to whom she bore a second Mary, subsequently the wife of Alphaeus; then to Salome (Salomas?), to whom she bore a third Mary, subsequently married to Zebedee. The legend may reflect the tendency in certain Coptic accounts to identify Mary the Virgin with all the Marys of the gospels. M. S. ENSLIN

4. Douay Version form of HANNAH.

**ANNAAS.** KJV Apoc. form of SENAAH.

**ANNAN** ăn'ən ['Avváv] (I Esd. 9:32); KJV ANNAS. Same as HARIM 2.

**ANNAS** ăn'əs [חנה, חנן; *in* 1 *below,* ῎Αννας, *cf.* Josephus ῎Ανανος; *in* 2 *below,* 'Ανάς]. **1.** A high priest as the result of his appointment by QUIRINIUS in A.D. 6/7, but deposed by Valerius Gratus in 15.

Josephus (Antiq. XVIII.ii.1) relates that Quirinius deprived Joezer of the high priesthood and appointed Annas son of Seth (*ca.* 6/7). Valerius Gratus removed Annas, first substituting for him one Ishmael son of Phabi, but shortly thereafter appointed Eleazar son of Annas. A year later Eleazar was removed in favor of Simon son of Camithus; less than a year later Joseph Caiaphas came to the office.

*See also* CAIAPHAS.

*Bibliography.* E. Schürer, *A History of the Jewish People in the Time of Jesus Christ* (English trans., 1891), div. 2, vol. I, pp. 198-99.

**2.** KJV form of ANNAN in I Esd. 9:32. *See* HARIM. S. SANDMEL

**ANNIAS** ă nī'əs ['Avveίς (B), ῎Αννιας (A)] (I Esd. 5:16; KJV ANANIAS ăn'ə nī'əs. Head of a family listed among those who returned to Jerusalem with Zerubbabel. They are omitted in the parallel passages Ezra 2:3 ff; Neh. 7:8 ff. C. T. FRITSCH

**ANNIUTH** ă nī'əth ['Avvιούθ] (I Esd. 9:48). Same as BANI 5*d*.

**ANNUNCIATION.** The announcement or declaration by the angel GABRIEL to the Virgin Mary that she would bear a son who would be called Jesus, Son of God (Luke 1:26-38). (*See* MARY, MOTHER OF JESUS; VIRGIN BIRTH.) This promise parallels one

made to Zechariah about his coming son, John the Baptist (Luke 1:5-23). In Matt. 1:18-25 an angel appears to Joseph with the forecast of Jesus' birth (cf. S-B, II, 98-100). In the apocryphal second-century Book of James, or Protevangelium (chs. 10–11), the Annunciation is retold with many added details.

"Blessed art thou among women" (Luke 1:28 Vulg.-KJV) is properly omitted in more recent versions, since the words are lacking in codices Aleph and B. They are an interpolation from vs. 42. Gabriel's entire salutation forms the scriptural part of the eleventh-century prayer called *Ave Maria.* The feast of Annunciation (Incarnation) is celebrated March 25.

*Bibliography.* O. Bardenhewer, "Maria Verkündigung," *Bibl. Stud.,* X (1905), 1-173; S. Lyonnet, "ΚΑΙΡΕ ΚΕΧΑ-ΡΙΤΩΜΕΝΗ," *Biblica,* XX (1939), 131-41. D. M. BECK

**ANNUNUS** ăn'yŏŏ nəs ['Avvouvov (A), B *omits*] (I Esd. 8:48); KJV ANNUUS ăn'yŏŏ əs. A priest. The name does not occur in Ezra 8:19; it may be a corruption of the Hebrew phrase ואתו, "and with him," in the Ezra text. C. T. FRITSCH

**ANNUUS.** KJV form of ANNUNUS.

**ANOINT.** To smear or pour oil or ointment on the head or body of a person or on an object. This custom, with secular or religious connotation, appears throughout the whole biblical period, both inside and outside Israel.

1. Terminology
   *a.* In biblical Hebrew
   *b.* In LXX Greek
   *c.* In NT Greek
2. Kinds of anointing
   *a.* Secular
   *b.* Cultic-religious
Bibliography

**1. Terminology.** The Bible uses several Hebrew and Greek words which are usually translated "anoint."

*a. In biblical Hebrew.* The OT has three words for this concept. דשן occurs only once (Ps. 23:5). Its literal meaning is "to make fat." סוך or סיך is "pour" (Deut. 28:40; Ruth 3:3; etc.) as an ointment, "anoint." משח originally meant "to smear," as a house with vermilion (Jer. 22:14), or "to spread with oil" in preparation of food, as was done with the unleavened wafers (Exod. 29:2). It also refers to cosmetics, as in Amos 6:6, or to the consecration for the office of a prophet (I Kings 19:16), a king (I Kings 1:39), or an Aaronic priest (Exod. 29:7). This verb also describes the consecration of cultic objects for exclusive use in the temple (Exod. 29:36).

*b. In LXX Greek.* The LXX renders the Hebrew דשן with λιπαίνειν (Ps. 23:5), meaning "to oil" or "to anoint." The word סוך is translated almost always with ἀλείφειν, "to anoint" (Mic. 6:15); משח is equated with χρίειν (Exod. 29:36) or ἀλείφειν (Gen. 31:13), both of which mean "to anoint."

*c. In NT Greek.* The NT Greek uses the word μυρίζειν once (Mark 14:8), but more often ἀλείφειν is used (e.g., Matt. 6:17). The verb χρίειν is used in a metaphorical sense when referring to the anointing of Christ (Luke 4:18). However, its derivatives ἐπιχρίειν (John 9:11) and ἐγχρίειν (Rev. 3:18) do not present any messianic connotation.

**2. Kinds of anointing.** *a. Secular anointing.* In the ancient Near East the daily toilet of the rich was completed by the application of scented olive oil or other perfumed ointments (*see* OINTMENT). The Hebrews anointed themselves for a festive occasion, for a joyous celebration, and for an everyday cosmetic (Deut. 28:40; Ruth 3:3; Jth. 16:8). The anointing had a connotation of gladness (Ps. 45:7—H 45:8). The head of the guest was anointed (Luke 7:46), and therefore anointing was not practiced in time of fasting (II Sam. 12:20; Matt. 6:17) or mourning (II Sam. 14:2; Dan. 10:3; Jth. 10:3). The cosmetic practice of anointing is widely attested in ancient Near Eastern literature and also by the many ointment containers and jars found by archaeologists. The cooling and pain-soothing effect of ointments, oils, and unguents prompted their frequent application in medical treatment (Isa. 1:6; Ezek. 16:9; Mark 6:13; Rev. 3:18). Jesus even applied clay upon the eyes of a blind man, according to one report on the healing of the blind (John 9:6, 11).

*b. Cultic-religious.* In the ancient Near East, as well as in Israel, both objects and persons were consecrated to cultic service by the rite of anointment. *See* CONSECRATION.

Among the objects consecrated by anointment were the sacred stones and pillars whose erection echoes ages of antiquity. The tradition centered around Jacob speaks of the anointment of the pillar of BETHEL in commemoration of the patriarch's vision (Gen. 28:18; 31:13; 35:14). Other objects connected with cultic and sacrificial worship were also anointed. Thus the altar (Exod. 29:36; Num. 7:10; etc.) with its utensils (Exod. 40:10; Num. 7:1; etc.), the tabernacle (Lev. 8:10) with its furnishings (Num. 7:1), and the ark (Exod. 30:26) were anointed. By the rite of anointment these objects were consecrated to cultic service and separated from secular use (Exod. 30:26-29). The reference in Dan. 9:24 probably alludes to the anointment of the holy of holies. It is possible that in preparation for war, the shields of the warriors were consecrated (Isa. 21:5 KJV) by anointment. However, this might merely refer to the treatment with oil of a shield made of leather and have no cultic significance, as the RSV translation:

> Arise, O princes,
> oil the shield!

would seem to indicate.

Among the persons consecrated to the service of the Lord, first must be mentioned the priests (Exod. 28:41; Lev. 6:13; Num. 3:3). According to priestly tradition, Aaron was anointed (Exod. 29:7; Lev. 8:12), and so was the high priest (Lev. 21:10). It appears that prophets were also anointed, at least in some cases, for Elijah received the command to anoint Elisha (I Kings 19:16), and a prophet, probably in a metaphorical sense, spoke of his anointment for the prophetic commission (Isa. 61:1). Further, in a poetic recounting of the sacred history of Israel, the patriarchs were referred to as "anointed prophets" (I Chr. 16:22; Ps. 105:15).

The anointing of the king was of primary impor-

tance. One of the Amarna Letters (*see* TELL EL-AMARNA) attests to the anointment of a king in Syro-Palestine during the fourteenth century B.C. The so-called Jotham's fable, which most likely had its literary conception in the premonarchic period, alludes to the anointment of kings (Judg. 9:15). The anointment of the king was not merely a part of the ceremonial of enthronement; it was of decisive importance, for it conveyed the power for the exercise of royal authority. By strength of anointment, the king became a theocratic vassal of the Lord, as texts like I Sam. 9:16; 16:3 indicate. The anointment of Saul (I Sam. 10:1), David (I Sam. 16:3), Solomon (I Kings 1:39), Jehu (II Kings 9:6), and Joash of Judah (II Kings 11:12) is reported in considerable detail. The anointment of Absalom (II Sam. 19:10) is incidentally mentioned, as is the anointment of Jehoahaz (II Kings 23:30).

The rite of the anointment of the king was originally executed by a prophet (I Sam. 10:1; I Kings 19:16; II Kings 9:6). It appears that the prophet Nathan also had an active share in the anointment of Solomon (I Kings 1:45). Later, the right to anoint the king apparently became the exclusive privilege of the priests (I Kings 1:39; II Kings 11:12). Some scholars have assumed that ancient Israel practiced, beside the theocratic anointment of the king by a priest or prophet, a democratic anointment in which the people anointed the king through its representatives, the elders. These scholars have suggested that the Hebrews of the nomadic period anointed their chieftains by stroking the head of the elected individual in the same manner as the nomadic Arabs of pre-Islamic times, and that also the anointment of the Israelite king was similar, at least in the early monarchic period. However, the biblical evidence is not sufficient for the support of this theory (cf. II Sam. 2:4; 5:3).

The theocratic character of the anointment is also exemplified by the fact that the king was the Lord's anointed (I Sam. 24:6, 10—H 24:7, 11; 26:16), and a vassal of God who reigned in God's stead over his people (I Sam. 10:1 LXX; II Sam. 6:21). The title "the LORD's anointed" was later shortened to "anointed," in Hebrew-Aramaic form *māshîaḥ*, "Messiah" (*see* MESSIAH, JEWISH), and was translated into Greek as χρίστος, or "Christ." Jesus was also anointed by God "with the Holy Spirit and with power" (Acts 10:38; cf. 4:27).

In the biblical period it was customary to use perfumed oils and ointments for the anointing of the body of the dead (Mark 14:8; Luke 23:56). The anointing of the dead could hardly have been without some religious significance, since the underlying thoughts of funeral rites in general indicate this.

**Bibliography.** H. Weinel, "מׁשׁח und seine Derivate," *ZAW*, XVIII (1898), 1-82; J. Wellhausen, "Zwei Rechtsriten bei den Hebräern," *Archiv für Religionswissenschaft*, VII (1904), 33-41; W. R. Smith, *Lectures on the Religion of the Semites* (3rd ed., 1927), pp. 233, 383-86; C. R. North, "The Religious Aspects of Hebrew Kingship," *ZAW*, L (1932), 8-38; D. Lys, "L'onction dans la Bible," *Etudes Théologiques et Religieuses*, 29 (1954), 3 ff.                                    S. SZIKSZAI

**ANOINTED, THE** [מׁשׁיח]. In the OT, the designation of the king of Israel and later of the high priest as the high official consecrated by the anointing (*see* ANOINT); in post-OT times, the title of the ultimate king, for which, however, the untranslated Aramaic or Greek forms of the word משיחא/Μεσσίας, "Messiah," and Χριστός, "Christ," are better known. *See* MESSIAH (JEWISH), § 1; CHRIST. E. JENNI

**ANOS.** KJV Apoc. form of VANIAH.

**ANT** [נמלה; Akkad. *lamattu;* Amarna *namlu;* Arab. *naml (plural)*]. An insect of the order Hymenoptera, to which bees and wasps also belong, and, more specifically, of the superfamily Formicoidea. Ants are social insects with three highly developed phases (male, female, and worker), each with specific functions which contribute to the colony's existence. One queen may serve a community of from 20,000 to 500,000 workers and males. The formicaries (nests), which are usually constructed underground in Palestine to avoid excessive heat, contain special chambers serving as nurseries, granaries, or fungus gardens.

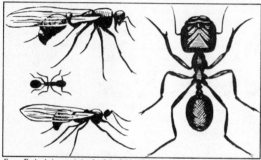

From Bodenheimer, *Animals of the Bible* (Tel Aviv: The Dvir Company Ltd.)
28. Different phases of the harvester ant (*Messor Semirufus*)

The ant is referred to only twice in scripture (Prov. 6:6; 30:25). In both cases reference is made to the wisdom, foresight, or industriousness exercised in summer by these creatures in storing up food for winter. This delineation aptly describes the *Messor semirufus,* a harvester ant, with nests near grain fields, threshing floors, or granaries.* Grain is collected from among the sown seed before it germinates, as well as from that available at harvest time. These ants are even known to bite off the radicles of kernels to prevent germination. On sunny days moist grain from their underground granaries is carried out and spread in the sun to dry. Fig. ANT 28.
*See also* FAUNA § E4a.

**Bibliography.** F. S. Bodenheimer, *Animal Life in Palestine* (1935); W. F. Albright, *BASOR,* 89 (1943), 31; A. D. Imms, *A General Textbook of Entomology* (1957).

W. W. FRERICHS

**ANTELOPE** [תאו (Deut. 14:5; KJV WILD OX), תוא (Isa. 51:20; KJV WILD BULL)]. Among the hollow-horned ruminant mammals (Bovidae) are a large number of animals which cannot be assigned to the oxen, sheep, or goats. These are generally classified as antelopes, and like all the Bovidae, and unlike the deer, their horns (sometimes absent from the female) are not shed annually but are a permanent part of their anatomy. The numerous varieties of antelope display great differences in size, but on the whole they are of more graceful build than the oxen, and they carry the head considerably above the level of the back.

It is clear that the GAZELLE, a species of antelope, was found in biblical Palestine, but whether other antelopes also lived there is uncertain. The תאו of Deut. 14:5 was presumably a wild ruminant (taken in a net; Isa. 51:20), and it must have been either an antelope or a deer, but otherwise it cannot be identified (*cf.* FAUNA § A2*fv*). The LXX in Deut. 14:5 renders it as ὄρυξ, an antelope which Herodotus (IV.192) speaks of as in Libya; the identification with the oryx (perhaps *oryx beisa* or *oryx beatrix*) is favored by Tristram (*NHB* 56-57).

*See also* FAUNA § A2*fiv,* where דישון (RSV IBEX) is identified as an antelope. W. S. McCULLOUGH

**ANTHOTHIJAH** ăn'thō thī'jə [ענתתיה] (I Chr. 8: 24). KJV ANTOTHIJAH ăn'tō thī'jə. One of the sons of Shashak in the genealogy of Benjamin.

**ANTHROPOLOGY.** *See* MAN, ETHNIC DIVISIONS OF; MAN, NATURE OF.

**ANTHROPOMORPHISM** ăn'thrə pə môr'fĭz əm. Language of analogy that portrays the personal character of God by ascribing to him human characteristics, or human feelings (anthropopathism). *See* GOD, OT VIEW OF, § 3c.

**ANTICHRIST** ăn'tĭ krīst' [ἀντίχριστος]. Strictly defined, a mythical demonic or demonic-human adversary of Christ who will appear before the Second Advent as the last oppressor and persecutor of the Christians, only in turn to be defeated and overcome by Christ in his return to earth. The term has also been used for the opponent of a Jewish messiah, but in such cases "antimessiah" is preferable. More broadly, the term is also applied to a historical or mythical potentate who wages war against the faithful. Closely associated with the concept of the Antichrist, and at times assimilated to it, is that of a pseudo Christ, who will deceive and lead many astray by his pretensions to be the Christ, by his miracles, and by his false teachings.

Origins of the Christian concept of the Antichrist as the opponent of Christ in his second advent are somewhat obscure. It should be noted that usually the Antichrist appears in an apocalyptic context insofar as Christian sources are concerned. Also, he is not the adversary of the Jesus of history; on the contrary, he is to be the opponent of the apocalyptic Christ on his return to earth. Apparently, in connection with the dualism of apocalypticism, it was but natural that this concept of an Antichrist should arise. Just as Satan, his demons, and his wicked followers were considered to be adversaries of God, his angels, and the righteous Christians, the belief in an Antichrist as the evil counterpart of Christ developed. Since Christ was considered to be God incarnate, so the Antichrist may be a kind of incarnation of Satan. Furthermore, as previously noted, he may appear as a pseudo Christ, a demonic imitation of Christ. Conceivably an attempt to provide a counterpart for the Messiah was also in part responsible for the rise of the Jewish belief in an antimessiah.

Gunkel, followed by others, has proposed that the

roots of the idea are to be found in the Babylonian chaos myth according to which Tiamat, ruler of the waters and the deeps of darkness, rebelled against the gods above, but was overcome by Marduk, the son of the god Ea. Others have found its beginnings in the dualism of the opposing supernatural forces of good and evil in Iranian beliefs.

**1. Jewish prototypes.** However, there are some Jewish prototypes—if, indeed, not antecedents and models—for the Christian concept of the Antichrist. Among these is the account of Gog of Magog in Ezek. 38–39, where Gog, either an actual or mythical adversary of the Jews, was, with his people, to be destroyed by God. In the development of this theme Gog of Magog (or GOG AND MAGOG) becomes not only a tyrannical oppressor of the Jews but also an opponent of the Messiah, who will destroy him. At times the name is omitted, but the theme is the same. A late stage is found in the neo-Hebraic Apocalypse of Elijah (see ELIJAH, APOCALYPSE OF). After the forty-year reign of the Messiah Winon with the saints in Jerusalem, Gog and Magog will gather all of the peoples of the earth to make war against the holy city, but they will be utterly defeated and slain by God and the Messiah.

In Daniel, Antiochus IV, the cruel persecutor of the Jews, depicted as a little horn, appears almost a mythical person; he will magnify himself against God, but will be brought to an inglorious end, possibly by Michael, the guardian angel of the Jews. Strictly speaking, Antiochus is not an antimessiah, for there is no messiah in Daniel; however, with some modifications he became a prototype of the Antichrist.

A somewhat different tradition is provided by the TESTAMENTS OF THE TWELVE PATRIARCHS, with Beliar, a demonic figure from the tribe of Dan, causing Israel to turn aside from the worship of God. However, the Messiah, of the tribe of Levi, will bind him and cast him into everlasting fire (cf. Test. Dan 5:10-11; Test. Levi 18:12; Test. Judah 25:3). Belial plays a prominent role in the Qumran document known as the War of the Sons of Light with the Sons of Darkness, for he is the demonic opponent of God and the leader of the Sons of Darkness in the conflict with the Sons of Light. He will finally be humbled and abased, possibly by Michael, Israel's angelic guardian (cf. chs. 1; 13; 16). This nonmessianic nonapocalyptic work throws further light on the Belial tradition.

In IV Ezra 11–12 (from the end of the first century) the Roman oppressors of the Jews are symbolized by an eagle with three heads and twelve wings. A lion, symbolizing the Messiah, condemns the eagle for its tyranny and oppression, and predicts its destruction; while he prophesies, the eagle is destroyed by fire.

This same political motif is found in II Bar. 40, where a symbolic vision is explained to mean that the last kingdom to oppress the Jews, that of the Romans, will be defeated, and their leader will be taken captive to the Messiah on Mount Zion. The Messiah will convict him and put him to death, after which the messianic kingdom will be established.

Nero, the royal matricide who committed suicide by stabbing himself in the throat, came to be both an antimessiah and an antichrist. A rumor developed that Nero had not died but had escaped across the Euphrates; it was thought by some that he had indeed died, but that he would be restored to life. In either case it was predicted that he would invade and devastate the Empire, also that he would besiege Jerusalem. Elements of this Neronic saga are found in the Sibylline Oracles. In one of several Neronic passages (5:93-110) it is predicted that Nero (referred to as the Persian) will ravage the Empire and will attempt to sack Jerusalem. God, however, will send a king (the Messiah) against him to destroy him and the kings with him, saving the holy city. Thus a mythical Nero becomes an antimessiah.

In certain neo-Hebraic sources the antimessiah is named Armilus, possibly a corruption of Romulus, the legendary founder of Rome. According to the Secrets of Rabbi Simeon ben Yohai, the wicked King Armilus will besiege Jerusalem and slay the Messiah ben Joseph, but he himself will be killed by the breath of the Messiah ben David. In the neo-Hebraic Midrash of the Ten Kings, Armilus is Satanic, for he is the offspring of sexual intercourse between Satan and the statue of a woman.

These and similar patterns of Jewish thought concerning the oppressors of the Jews and the antimessiah provided prototypes and sources, even, for the Antichrist of Christian beliefs, despite certain differences between the Jewish and Christian concepts.

**2. Early Christian examples.** One of the earliest relevant Christian passages (if not the earliest) is the Little Apocalypse of Mark 13 (taken over, with modifications, by both Matthew and Luke). Jesus is represented as predicting that before his second advent there will be many false Christs (not only one), as well as false prophets. The false Christs will perform signs and wonders and will deceive and lead people astray. At the same time there will be wars, famines, tribulations, and persecutions. It is not clear, however, that the false Christs will be responsible for these tribulations. Furthermore, nothing is said concerning their fate. Following the final tribulations, the Son of man is to come in the clouds with power and glory, and he will send his angels out to gather the elect. This passage, as it stands, is a prediction of pseudo Christs rather than of an antichrist. That it actually was a prophecy made by Jesus is open to serious question.

A second early Christian passage—how early depends upon the question of authorship—is II Thess. 2:10 (see THESSALONIANS, SECOND LETTER TO THE). First, there is to be a falling away, a defection, of the Christians, prior to the Second Coming. Then the "man of lawlessness" will appear; this "son of perdition" will oppose every god or object of worship, taking his seat in the temple of God, saying that he himself is God. Empowered by Satan, he will perform signs and wonders, deceiving those who are about to perish. When the Lord Jesus arrives, he will slay the man of lawlessness with the breath of his mouth. The readers are assured, however, that for the present the man of lawlessness is being restrained.

Whether Pauline or pseudo Pauline, this prediction is possibly the earliest Christian belief in an antichrist combined with a pseudo Christ. Some suggest that the man of lawlessness is one of the Roman emperors, and that the restraining power is the Roman Empire. The reference to the desecration of the temple may be a reflection of the desecration by Antiochus IV or the attempt by Caligula. But the man of lawlessness is more than a historical character; he is a mythical figure who is, it would seem, the embodiment of Satan; he is the adversary of Christ in his second advent. He may even be a Belial antichrist, for according to a rabbinic etymology Belial means "without a yoke" (Sanh. 111*b*)—i.e., without the yoke of the law, hence lawless.

The Testament of Hezekiah (3:13*b*–4:18 of the Ascension of Isaiah), from about the end of the first century, presents a more fully developed antichrist tradition. It is predicted that in the last days there will be a falling away and much disorder in the church. Shortly before the second advent of the Beloved (Christ), Beliar, the demonic ruler of this world, will descend from the firmament in the likeness of a man, of a lawless king who had killed his mother (Nero). He will persecute the church, putting one of the Twelve (possibly Peter is meant) to death. He will also speak and act like Christ, will call himself God, will perform wonders and miracles, and will set his image up in every city for people to worship. During his sway of 3½ years many will follow him, but others will faithfully await the Lord's return. When Christ does appear with his angels and armies of holy ones, he will drag Beliar and his armies into Gehenna. A messianic interim of indefinite duration will follow.

It is obvious that the Antichrist and the pseudo Christ are assimilated into one person in this form of the tradition. This person, moreover, is a mythical demonic-human character, for he is Beliar (the equivalent of Satan) incarnate in Nero redivivus. Symbolizing the Roman emperors, he claims to be a god; actually, the emperors are Satanic, not divine, and will soon be brought to an end by the Christ on his return in power.

The antichrist motif, it is needless to say, is present in Revelation, and in more than one form. According to Rev. 20:7-10, following his release after the millennium, Satan will cause Gog and Magog to gather the nations of the earth against Christ and the saints in Jerusalem. However, they are destroyed, not by the direct action of the Christ, but by fire from heaven, and Satan is cast into the lake of fire. Variations of this motif, but without the names Gog and Magog, are found elsewhere in Revelation (cf. 9:1-11, 13-19; 16:12-16; 17:13-14).

A theme later introduced into the antichrist pattern is that of the two witnesses from heaven (Elijah and Moses, apparently) who are slain by a beast that comes up from the abyss (Rev. 11:7 ff). They are revived and taken up into heaven. Nothing is said about the eventual fate of the beast. He is, to be sure, a persecutor, and may be a variant of the beasts in ch. 13; but in this passage he is not an antichrist.

The classical antichrist tradition in Revelation is that of the two beasts in Rev. 13; 16:12-16; 17; 19:19-21. The first beast, which is in part a combination of the four beasts of Daniel, has ten horns and seven heads, with a mortal wound that has been healed in one of the heads. He is given power and

authority by the dragon (Satan), and men worship both the dragon and the beast. This first beast is Antichrist, and is Satan incarnate. As a whole, it symbolizes the Roman Empire; its heads are various emperors who are worshiped, with one, that with the healed wound, Nero redivivus.

The second beast has two horns like a lamb, but speaks like a dragon. It not only performs miracles and deceives people, but it also enforces the worship of the first beast under penalty of death. This beast, disguised in part by its lamb's horns as the Lamb of God but actually Satanic in character, is indeed a pseudo Christ. Also, it is a persecutor of the faithful. Its role is secondary to that of the first beast.

In ch. 17 the first beast is the consort of the scarlet woman—i.e., Roma, the divine personification of Rome. The two beasts make plans and raise armies for the final conflict, which is to occur when Christ returns to earth with his heavenly armies. The two beasts are captured and thrown into the lake of fire, and Christ slays their followers with the sharp sword that issues from his mouth (19:19-21).

This depiction of Antichrist and pseudo Christ in Revelation is mysterious; but when it is realized that it is a combination of various traditional views, much of the mystery is clarified. The antichrist tradition persisted for centuries in the Christian church in one form or another, as did its Jewish equivalent in Judaism. The belief even found its way into Mohammedanism, with Al Dajjal (the Liar) as a Jewish false messiah who would be slain by Jesus.

Although the antichrist tradition was popular among the early Christians, it was not universally accepted. Quite possibly this lack of general acceptance was due in part to the rejection of CHILIASM by many Christians.

**3. Later developments.** Among the early extra-canonical references to Antichrist is the concluding chapter of the Didache, a church manual from the first part of the second century. It predicts that the deceiver will come as the Son of God, and that he will perform miracles and commit many iniquities, including persecutions. The account ends abruptly with the coming of the Lord on the clouds of heaven with his saints; we may perhaps infer that there is to be a conflict in which the Antichrist will be defeated by the Christ.

A fragmentary account is found in Barn. 4.5; the fourth kingdom of Dan. 7:7-8 is the Roman Empire, which apparently is identified with the Antichrist, who is to appear just before the last times. Polycarp, however, is in agreement with the Johannine letters that the Antichrist is the spirit of heresy, that everyone who denies the actual incarnation is, in fact, an antichrist, and that he who denies the resurrection and judgment is the first-born of Satan (Polyc. Phil. 7.1).

Irenaeus, by deciphering the Antichrist's mystical number, 666, identifies the Antichrist with Lateinos (the Roman Empire) or, preferably, with Teitan, partly because it is an ancient name of royal dignity belonging to a tyrant (Iren. Her. 5.30). His preference indicates a shift from the view of Revelation that the Empire was the Satanic Antichrist.

Hippolytus wrote an entire treatise on Christ and Antichrist, as well as a Commentary on Daniel. Victorinus, a Diocletian martyr, dealt with the antichrist tradition in his Commentary on the Apocalypse, as did Lactantius in the seventh book of his Divine Institutes. The latter predicts two antichrists; this theme is more fully developed by Commodian (middle of the fifth century) in his Apologetic Poem against Jews and Gentiles. The Goths will conquer Rome and redeem the Christians. Then the first antichrist, Nero, will appear, reconquering Rome and persecuting the Christians for 3½ years. He, in turn, will be conquered by the second and Jewish antichrist from the East, who will then go to Judea, where he will be worshiped by the Jews. At last Christ himself will come; he will defeat the second antichrist and his host, will convert the nations, and establish his kingdom in Jerusalem.

Certain popular writings of this period, such as the Apocalypse of Pseudo-John, the Apocalypse of Zephaniah, and the Greek Revelation of Esdras, depict the Antichrist as a horrendous, monstrous giant, not as a beast or a dragon. Numerous antichrist treatises or works containing the antichrist legend continued to appear, and were attributed, at times incorrectly, to writers such as Ephrem, Bede, Methodius, Adso, Nerses, Cyril of Jerusalem, Chrysostom, and others. The widespread dissemination of the belief is indicated by its appearance, not only in Greek and Latin texts, but also in Syriac, Coptic, Ethiopic, Armenian, Persian, and Arabic as well.

Attempts were made to identify the Antichrist with historical or contemporary persons. "Mohammed" was transformed to "Maometis" to conform to the number of the beast, 666. From time to time the Mohammedans, Saracens, and Turks (as well as the Jews) were considered to be the Antichrist.

Joachim of Floris (died 1202) stimulated speculation concerning the identity of the Antichrist; he believed that the Antichrist would be a pseudo pope. Persecuted Christian groups, however, such as the Waldensians and the Spiritual Franciscans, believed that there was an even closer relationship between the Antichrist and the papacy. Ubertino, a leader of the Spirituals, specifically called Boniface VIII the beast from the sea, the seven heads being his seven vices and the ten horns the Ten Commandments, which he flouted. He identified Boniface' successor, Benedict XI, with the second, lamblike beast, for his pretensions to sanctity made him more acceptable, even though he was as wicked as Boniface.

The Emperor Frederick II (whose guardian had been Pope Innocent III) was excommunicated by Pope Gregory IX in 1239, following years of dissension and quarrels between the two. Gregory termed the Emperor the beast from the sea full of words of blasphemy; Frederick replied by calling the Pope the great dragon who deceives the whole world, the Antichrist. Just how much of this name calling was rhetoric and how much was to be taken literally, is difficult to determine, as is the case with later, similar invectives.

The pre-Reformation and Reformation period, during which the political and ecclesiastical power of the papacy and church were at issue, and the corruption and immorality of many of the higher clergy were evident, the charge that the Roman church was Babylon and the papacy the Antichrist was made

with increasing frequency. Wyclif, Huss, Luther, Calvin, Zwingli, Knox, Cranmer (just before his death at the stake), and other Reformers were in general agreement in these identifications. On the other hand, the Reformers themselves were accused of being the antichrists.

These charges and countercharges have not been made so frequently in recent history. However, modern political leaders, considered by their opponents as despots and tyrants, have been called antichrists, with the wars they were engaged in being considered the final conflict. Among these may be listed Napoleon, Napoleon III, Kaiser Wilhelm, and Hitler.

The antichrist tradition has had a long and involved history. Its origins are somewhat obscure, but the use made of it through the centuries in the Christian church is fairly clear. For many Christians it is still an important belief, even if the Antichrist is not identified with any actual person, but is considered a supernatural embodiment of evil.

*Bibliography.* W. Bousset, *Der Antichrist* (1895); trans. *The Antichrist Legend* (1896). L. E. Froom, *The Prophetic Faith of Our Fathers* (4 vols.: 1950-54). M. Rist

**ANTI-LEBANON.** The E mountain range parallel to Lebanon. In antiquity several names were probably used, referring to various peaks. There does not seem to exist a general name in Hebrew or in any other ancient language, or in Arabic, though sometimes Jebel el-Sharq is used. A. Haldar

**ANTILIBANUS** ăn'tĭ lĭb'ə nəs ['Ἀντιλίβανος]. A Latinized form of the Greek name of Anti-lebanon as occurring in the LXX, Josephus, and other Greek sources. *See* Lebanon.

**ANTIMONY** ăn'tə mō'nĭ [פוך, כחל; LXX στιμμί; Vulg. *stibium*]. An element (Sb) with the appearance of tin or lead: hard, brittle, almost as heavy as iron.

To the biblical writers both Hebrew terms seem to be general terms for eye paint (*see* Cosmetics). Eye paint appears in late OT passages (II Kings 9: 30; Jer. 4:30; Ezek. 23:40), in reference to women of unworthy character. *See* Eye Paint.

In Isa. 54:11 the word פוך seems to refer to some rare black jewelers' cement which by kohl-like outlining would make precious stones appear larger and more colorful. In I Chr. 29:2, כחל appears in a list which includes precious stones. *See* Jewels and Precious Stones.

*Bibliography.* A. Lucas, *Ancient Egyptian Materials and Industries* (3rd rev. ed., 1948), pp. 99-100; C. Singer *et al.*, eds., *A History of Technology*, I (1954), 292-94, 583. P. L. Garber

**ANTINOMIANISM** ăn'tĭ nō'mĭ ə nĭz əm [ἀντί, against, *plus* νόμος, law]. The doctrine that the moral law is made void through faith, and that faith alone is necessary to salvation. The term "antinomian" is not biblical, but was used by Luther to describe the views of Johannes Agricola. In the NT, however, the *idea* of antinomianism is attacked in the book of James. The author asks: "What does it profit . . . if a man says he has faith but has not works? Can his faith save him?" (2:14)—i.e., can his faith, without works, save him? The implied answer is obviously, No. James appears to be attacking a misunderstanding of Paul's doctrine of justification by faith (cf. Rom. 3:23 ff; *see* JAMES, LETTER OF, § 2). For Paul, however, faith was impossible without works; for the justified man had received the Spirit, and where the Spirit was given, the fruits of the Spirit must appear. *See* PAUL § 8.

Antinomianism is never defended in the NT. It prevailed in some forms of Gnosticism, and has been defended periodically in the history of the church: by Johannes Agricola, in Germany, in the sixteenth century; by some Anabaptists in Germany and Holland; by Saltmarsh and some of the so-called "sectaries" during the protectorate of Cromwell in England; and later in England by some of Wesley's followers.                    B. H. THROCKMORTON, JR.

## ANTIOCH (OF PISIDIA) ăn′tĭ ŏk, pĭ sĭd′ĭ ə [′Αν- τιόχεια ἡ Πισιδία, τῆς Πισιδίας]. A city in the lake district of SW Asia Minor. Fig. ANT 29.

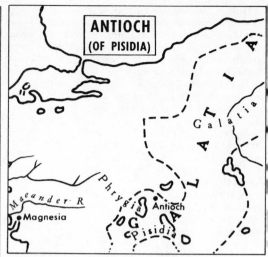

Courtesy of William Sanford LaSor

29. Ruins of aqueduct at Antioch in Pisidia

Antioch is located in the border zone between the ancient districts of Pisidia and Phrygia. It is sometimes called Pisidian Antioch (as in Acts 13:14), but Strabo refers to it as "near Pisidia" (XII.557). The ancient site has been identified some two miles to the E of modern Yalvaç (district of Isparta), SW of Aksehir. The city of Antioch lay on a plateau, its position commanding the plain of Yalvaç and well protected by natural defenses.

Although habitation in the vicinity of Antioch must date back to more ancient times, the city proper was a Hellenistic foundation of Seleucus I or Antiochus I, allegedly colonized by settlers from Magnesia on the Maeander (Strabo XII.577). Antioch served the Seleucids as a border fortress and a safeguard against the Pisidian mountaineers. After the defeat of Antiochus III by the Romans, the city was declared free (188 B.C.). In 36 B.C., Antony made it part of the domain of the Galatian king Amyntas,

after whose death the city was incorporated in the Roman province of Galatia (25 B.C.).

The Romans established Roman veterans in Antioch as colonists (*coloni*) among the natives (*incolae*). The official name of the city became Colonia Caesarea (as it appears on coins of Augustus), although the old name of Antioch was not abandoned (Antonine and later coins have "Col. Caes. Antiochea"). The Romanization of the city was undertaken seriously. The official inscription of Augustus' achievements was prominently displayed in Antioch (in Latin only as "Monumentum Antiochenum"). A cult of Augustus was established in the city during his lifetime. For practical and military purposes two new Roman roads were built, starting from Antioch, to establish communications in Pisidia around the lakes to the SW and SE (completed in 6 B.C.). Antioch was the center of enterprise in the process of the Romanization of Pisidia.

Apart from the Greek-speaking inhabitants and Roman colonists, Antioch must have contained a Phrygian element (bilingual by this time) and a large Jewish community, the latter settled in Seleucid days. Paul preached in the synagogue of Antioch (Acts 13:14-43) to a congregation of Jews and Greek-speaking Gentiles.

The ruins of Antioch were explored by many travelers and partially excavated. Some of the former magnificence of the city was reclaimed. The city walls are still prominent on three sides; the fourth (E) side is steep and overlooks the River Anthius. The main square of the city is the Augusta Platea. On its E side stood a richly decorated (tetrastyle prostyle) temple of Corinthian order, presumably the temple of Men and Augustus. Much of its sculptural elaboration is preserved. A monumental staircase of twelve steps and Propylaea with three archways connect the square of Augustus with the lower square of Tiberius (Tiberia Platea). Victory reliefs commemorating land and sea battles decorated the gate. The theater, which lies in the W part of the city, is in dilapidated condition. Farther W a triple city gate of the early third century A.D. displays pretentious decorations in a style inferior to that of the earlier buildings.

To the E of Antioch, overlooking the city from a spur of the mountains, lies the sanctuary of Men Askaios or Askaenos. An important pagan cult complex, which was active from Hellenistic into late Roman times, was identified here.

Antioch remained an important town in Byzantine times. A fourth-century basilica is noticeable for its mosaics and Byzantine graves. The city still existed as a fortress during the Crusades.

*Bibliography.* D. M. Robinson, "Roman sculptures from Colonia Caesarea (Pisidian Antioch)," *The Art Bulletin*, IX (1926-27), 5-69; D. Magie. *Roman Rule in Asia Minor* (1950), pp. 457-63.                    M. J. MELLINK

\*ANTIOCH (SYRIAN). A Hellenistic city in NW Syria (modern Antakya, Turkey), ranking with Rome and Alexandria as one of the three greatest cities of the Greco-Roman world, and an early center of Christian expansion. It was named for Antiochus, father of the founder, Seleucus.

1. Location
2. History
3. Antioch in the NT
4. Archaeology
Bibliography

Its prominence as a cultural and commercial meeting point contributed to the unique role which Antioch played in early Christian missions.
Fig. ANT 30.

From *Atlas of the Bible* (Thomas Nelson & Sons Limited)
30. Antioch on the Orontes (modern Antakya) at the foot of Mount Silpius

**1. Location.** Antioch, at the head of navigation on the Orontes River, was important throughout antiquity as a center of trade between the Mediterranean world, the Syrian hinterland, and the Eastern countries. Its seaport at the mouth of the Orontes was Seleucia Pieria, one of the principal harbors of the E Mediterranean. Antioch also lay on the best land route between Asia Minor, Syria, and Palestine.

**2. History.** The value of the site was early recognized, and it was occupied by traders from early historic times; and after the conquests of Alexander the Great had spread Hellenism through the Near East, the foundation of Antioch by Seleucus I (*see* SELEUCUS 1) in 300 B.C. played an important part in the establishment of the Greek and Macedonian control of Syria. From the first, the city had a mixed population of Macedonians, Greeks, and native Syrians, plus a colony of Jewish veterans of Seleucus' army who were given land around Antioch as a reward for their services. As the capital of the Seleucid dynasty in Syria, Antioch soon attained a political importance and a high degree of commercial prosperity which made it a wealthy and sophisticated metropolis in which Greek civilization flourished and came into close contact with oriental cultural and religious ideas. In this respect Antioch was more actively connected with both oriental and Greek interests than its sister Hellenistic capitals, ALEXANDRIA and PERGAMUM; and it was in closer touch with Rome and the W Mediterranean, as well as with Greek cities of Asia Minor and Greece. Enterprising Syrian traders from Antioch are attested everywhere throughout the Mediterranean, and the exports of Syria—wine, grain, dried fruit, and leather —passed through Antioch and were carried to Italy and Gaul.

When the development of Roman commercial and political interests in the E Mediterranean resulted in the occupation of Syria in 64 B.C., Antioch became the capital and the military headquarters of the new province of Syria, governed by a *legatus Augusti pro praetore*. The city was enlarged and beautified, along Roman lines, by a succession of benefactors, notably Julius Caesar, Augustus, and Tiberius, with the assistance of King Herod, who was anxious to show that he was a friend of the ruling power. The Romans, as was always their practice when occupy-

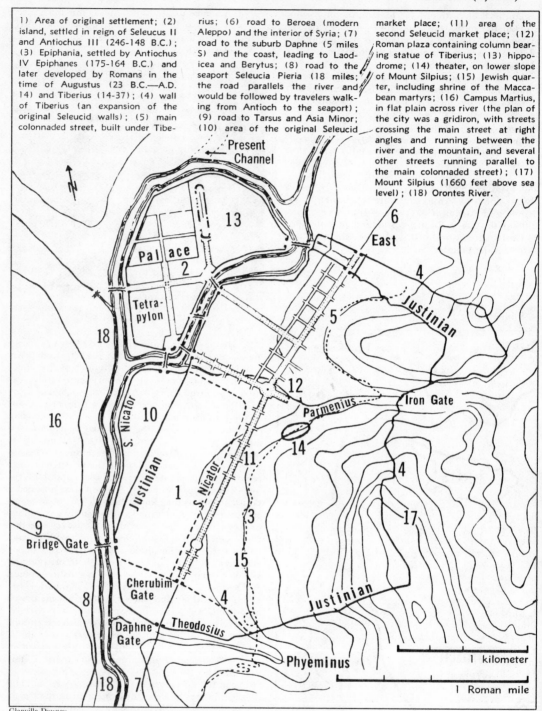

1) Area of original settlement; (2) island, settled in reign of Seleucus II and Antiochus III (246-148 B.C.); (3) Epiphania, settled by Antiochus IV Epiphanes (175-164 B.C.) and later developed by Romans in the time of Augustus (23 B.C.—A.D. 14) and Tiberius (14-37); (4) wall of Tiberius (an expansion of the original Seleucid walls); (5) main colonnaded street, built under Tibe- rius; (6) road to Beroea (modern Aleppo) and the interior of Syria; (7) road to the suburb Daphne (5 miles S) and the coast, leading to Laod- icea and Berytus; (8) road to the seaport Seleucia Pieria (18 miles; the road parallels the river and would be followed by travelers walk- ing from Antioch to the seaport); (9) road to Tarsus and Asia Minor; (10) area of the original Seleucid market place; (11) area of the second Seleucid market place; (12) Roman plaza containing column bear- ing statue of Tiberius; (13) hippo- drome; (14) theater, on lower slope of Mount Silpius; (15) Jewish quar- ter, including shrine of the Macca- bean martyrs; (16) Campus Martius, in flat plain across river (the plan of the city was a gridiron, with streets crossing the main street at right angles and running between the river and the mountain, and several other streets running parallel to the main colonnaded street); (17) Mount Silpius (1660 feet above sea level); (18) Orontes River.

Glanville Downey

31. Map of Antioch (Syria) partially restored

ing a new province, improved the road system and developed the seaport, Seleucia Pieria, so that the communications of Antioch both with Syria and Palestine and with the W Mediterranean were made more rapid and more secure; and the city began to enjoy the Pax Romana which was in time to offer a needed measure of security and police protection to the Christian missionaries.

All this time the large and ancient Jewish colony enjoyed good standing in the community and attracted to its ceremonies and teaching (in the Greek-speaking synagogues) a number of Gentiles who found Jewish monotheism and ethics more satisfying than the beliefs offered by the Greek and oriental philosophies and religions. Among the persons thus attracted to Judaism and familiar with its teaching may have been Nicolaus of Antioch, an early proselyte and one of the seven deacons of Jerusalem (Acts 6:5). We do not hear that the early Christian preachers at Antioch had to contend with Jewish fanatics as they did at Jerusalem, and in any case Antioch, as a large non-Jewish city and a major Roman administrative center, must have enjoyed a degree of public order which was not possible in a turbulent place like Jerusalem.

At the same time, the original mystery cults had made familiar in Antioch their doctrines of salvation and of death and regeneration, and their promises for the afterlife. As a result of all these developments, which had been maturing for many generations, the population of Antioch in the time of Christ was characterized by an eclectic intellectual spirit and an interest in religious inquiry which combined with the prosperous atmosphere of the city to produce an environment in which the Christian teaching, when it came, could be received in non-Jewish circles with sympathetic interest. In all these ways, Antioch differed fundamentally from the other cities outside Palestine in which the Christian mission might have found a start, and the whole history of the city, prior to the time of Christ, had given it a unique character as a place in which the followers of the Way could begin their expansion.

**3. Antioch in the NT.** When a persecution broke out in Jerusalem following the execution of STEPHEN, some followers of Jesus fled as far as Phoenicia, Cyprus, and Antioch, preaching the word only to Jews (Acts 11:19). In Antioch, however, some of the fugitives, who were Greek-speaking Jews from Cyprus and Cyrene, began to preach to "Greeks"—i.e., Greek-speaking Gentiles, not necessarily Greeks by birth (Acts 11:20). Some MSS of Acts, including the "Antiochene" textual tradition (see TEXT, NT), say that they preached to HELLENISTS—i.e., either Greek-speaking persons in general or Greek-speaking Jews; but in the case of Antioch, the writer clearly intends to distinguish between Jews and non-Jews (cf. Acts 14:1). Some of the Greeks to whom the word was preached were doubtless Gentiles who had attended the synagogues and were familiar with the background of the new teaching (cf. Acts 17:4).

Many were converted (Acts 11:21), and the missionaries had not to fear Jewish fanatics like those in Jerusalem. The Jerusalem elders sent BARNABAS— a native of Cyprus like some of the early missionaries in Antioch—to report on the novel undertaking (Acts 11:22). Seeing that the work prospered, Barnabas brought PAUL from Tarsus, and the two spent a year in Antioch teaching (Acts 11:24-26). Local tradition was that they preached in a street named Singon or Siagon ("Jawbone") near the Pantheon (Malalas 242).

It was in Antioch that the followers of Christ first came to bear the name "Christians" (Acts 11:26). The origin of the term is uncertain (see CHRISTIANS, NAME OF). It may have been a derogatory nickname invented by the Gentiles, or a title devised by the Christians themselves, or a term originated by the Roman police, who found it necessary to have an official designation for the new sect, which was becoming distinct from Judaism.

Concerning the size, composition, and administration of the Christian community, we have little evidence. It is said that "a great number . . . turned to the Lord" and that Barnabas and Paul "taught a large company of people" (Acts 11:21, 26), but we do not know what the basis of comparison was. There seem to have been no titles designating chiefs like those in Jerusalem (see MINISTRY). The only indication of how the community was led is the list of five men who, it is implied, were the most prominent and active in the local ecclesia—namely, Barnabas; Symeon NIGER; LUCIUS OF CYRENE (identified by some with the evangelist LUKE); MANAEN, "a member of the court of Herod the tetrarch"; and Paul. These are called "prophets and teachers" (Acts 13:1; see PROPHET IN NT). The ecclesia is simply the general group of the faithful in the city (Acts 11:26; 14:27), who are called the "brethren" (Acts 15:1, 32-33) and the "disciples" (Acts 11:26; 14:28).

The new converts doubtless met, as Jesus and his followers had done, in private houses for teaching and fellowship, and for prayers and breaking of bread. Jewish and Gentile Christians presumably met separately, at least insofar as orthodox Jews observed the law in the matter of eating with Gentiles. Later developments (see GNOSTICISM; NICOLAITANS) indicate that there must have been certain groups who followed their own interests in a blending of Christian teaching with other doctrines, especially the mystery cults; and different kinds of information concerning Jesus and his teaching must have been in circulation (cf. Luke 1:1).

According to Acts, when (as predicted in Antioch by AGABUS) a famine occurred ca. A.D. 46, the community at Antioch sent Barnabas and Paul to take financial aid to the brethren in Jerusalem (Acts 11:27-30). The conversion in Antioch of numbers of Gentiles had raised the question of the application of Jewish law to these converts, and it was apparently on this visit that the problem was discussed between Barnabas and Paul and the Jerusalem elders (Acts 15:1 ff; see COUNCIL OF JERUSALEM; GALATIANS, LETTER TO THE). Paul maintained that it was impracticable to apply the law to non-Jews, since, to a Gentile, CIRCUMCISION would mean that he was becoming a Jew. Some understanding seems to have been reached, to the effect that the mission to the Gentiles should not have to observe the law strictly (Acts 15:19-35; Gal. 2:1-10). This agreement is said to have been embodied in a letter addressed to the community in Antioch (Acts 15:23-29). Peter visited Antioch and ate with Gentile Christians (Gal. 2:11-12), but James sent JUDAS BARSABBAS and SILAS as emissaries who sought to win over the Jewish Christians to the view that the law must be enforced on Gentile converts (Acts 15:22-29; Gal. 2:12). Peter and Barnabas were impressed by these arguments, and, after a dispute, broke away from Paul (Gal. 2:11-13). In time, however, the Jewish Christian community in Antioch disappeared.

The date of the dispute is not known; and we do not have clear evidence as to the dates of the missionary journeys, based on Antioch, of Paul and others (*see* CHRONOLOGY OF THE NT; PAUL). According to Acts, on the first expedition Barnabas and Paul traveled together, with the blessing of the community, which presumably provided what financial aid it could (Acts 13:2-4). For the next journey (Acts 15:36-41), Paul and Barnabas, after a disagreement, separated, and Paul traveled with Silas, while Barnabas took with him JOHN MARK, who had been brought from Jerusalem. After his third journey Paul returned, not to Antioch, but to Jerusalem (Acts 18:22–21:18). This was the end of Paul's connection with the community at Antioch, where his work had been of vital importance for the future of Christianity. One problem of NT scholarship is to determine what happened in Antioch, after Paul's time, to produce the particular type of Christianity, different in certain respects from Paul's teaching, which is found in the letters of IGNATIUS, who was bishop of the city early in the second century.

In debates in post-apostolic times over Roman primacy and the rank of the "apostolic churches," Peter was sometimes spoken of as "founder" or "first bishop" of the church at Antioch. The problem of his episcopacy is obscure. However, Peter apparently was the first of the Twelve to visit Antioch (Gal. 2:11).

**4. Archaeology.** Modern Antakya is much smaller than classical Antioch, and not many ancient remains are preserved aboveground. Excavations were conducted in 1932-39, but could not be continued long enough to recover significant evidence of the apostolic period.* The "Chalice of Antioch," supposed to have been used at the Last Supper, and then taken to Antioch, dates from a later period, but is not a modern forgery, as some have claimed. Fig. ANT 31.

*Bibliography.* C. O. Müller, *Antiquitates Antiochenae* (1839); V. Schultze, *Altchristliche Städte und Landschaften*, III: *Antiochia* (1930); C. H. Kraeling, "The Jewish Community at Antioch," *JBL*, LI (1932), 130-60; W. Grundmann, "Die Apostel zwischen Jerusalem und Antiochia," *ZNTW*, XXXIX (1940), 110-37; B. M. Metzger, "Antioch-on-the-Orontes," *BA*, XI (1948), 69-88; E. J. Bickerman, "The Name of Christians," *HTR*, XLII (1949), 109-24; J. Rorimer, "The Authenticity of the Chalice of Antioch," *Studies in Art and Literature for Belle D. Greene* (1954), pp. 161-68. G. DOWNEY

**ANTIOCH, CHALICE OF.** A much-discussed example of Christian art, said to have been found in 1910 at Antioch, or at least in Syria. It consists of three parts: a plain inner cup, an outer gilded openwork shell, and a solid base, all of silver. A circle of rosettes tops the openwork shell; the framework below, consisting of vines, contains birds, animals, and twelve seated figures, divided into two groups, each with one central figure and five other persons facing him. The body of the cup has been bent out of shape slightly, and this has caused the silver to crack a little. The chalice is now in the Cloisters, New York City.

Its date has been much disputed. Each of the first six centuries has been proposed (the extreme view that the chalice is a modern forgery has been adequately refuted). G. A. Eisen has argued that the inner cup was used at Jesus' Last Supper; he dated the outer shell in the second half of the first century

Courtesy of Henry Lee Willett
32. The Chalice of Antioch

A.D., perhaps in the sixties. The figures, he held, are the youthful Jesus with the four evangelists and John's brother James, and the risen Jesus with the NT letter writers Peter, Paul, James, and Jude, and Peter's brother Andrew. Almost all students of ancient art reject this view. It assumes an interest in portraiture which the NT never reflects. It assumes that each of the NT books was written by the traditional author, and the NT canon essentially completed by *ca.* 64. These assumptions are unfounded. The chalice dates from the fourth or fifth century, and the figures probably represent Christ and ten of the NT apostles or authors. The piece is a valuable example of ancient Near Eastern Christian art. Fig. ANT 32.

*Bibliography.* G. A. Eisen, *The Great Chalice of Antioch* (2 vols.; 1923). H. H. Arnason, "The History of the Chalice of Antioch," *BA*, IV (1941), 49-64; V (1942), 10-16. F. V. Filson, "Who Are the Figures on the Chalice of Antioch?" *BA*, V (1942), 1-10. F. V. FILSON

**ANTIOCHIA** ăn′tĭ ŏk′ĭ ə. KJV Apoc. form of ANTIOCH.

**ANTIOCHIANS** ăn′tĭ ŏk′ĭ ənz ['Αντιοχεῖς]. "Citizens of Antioch," a title of honor and privilege requested for certain inhabitants of Jerusalem by the high priest Jason (*see* JASON 2) and held by his envoys to the games at Tyre (II Macc. 4:9, 19).

The privilege of registering some of the inhabitants of Jerusalem as citizens of Antioch was requested by Jason as part of his program of creating a Hellenistic community in Jerusalem (II Macc. 4:7-17; cf. I Macc. 1:11-15). Probably only a restricted number of Hellenized Jews were registered as citizens of Antioch; they formed a legal corporation which constituted the Hellenistic city of Jerusalem. It is possible, but doubtful, that Jason's program included changing the name of Jerusalem to Antioch.

Coins and inscriptions show that the inhabitants of other cities in the Seleucid Empire were given the privilege of being called citizens of ANTIOCH (e.g., Gerasa, Ptolemaïs). In many cases the legal privileges conferred included the important right to coin money; this may have been intended in Jason's request, but it is not mentioned.

*Bibliography.* I. Benzinger, in *Pauly-Wissowa*, vol. I (1894), col. 2447; E. R. Bevan, *The House of Seleucus* (1902), II, 151-54; E. Bickermann, *Der Gott der Makkabäer* (1937), pp. 59-65.
W. A. BEARDSLEE

**ANTIOCHIS** ăn tī′ə kĭs [’Αντιοχίς] (II Macc. 4:30). A concubine of Antiochus IV Epiphanes. Antiochus angered the inhabitants of Cilician Tarsus and Mallus by presenting their cities as a gift to his mistress. J. C. SWAIM

**ANTIOCHUS** ăn tī′ə kəs [’Αντίοχος, opposer]. A favorite name among the kings of the Seleucid dynasty of Syria (280 B.C. onward).

**1.** Antiochus I (280-261 B.C.), surnamed Soter ("deliverer") in accordance with the usual practice of the Seleucid kings of adding a second name. He was born in 324 B.C., the son of Seleucus Nicator (*see* SELEUCUS 1), one of the generals of Alexander the Great. The son succeeded his father in 280 B.C. and was slain in a battle against the Gauls of Asia Minor (Galatia) in 261. Much of his time had been spent in repressing them and the Celts, for which victories he acquired the name Soter, and in disputes concerning his claim to the throne of Macedon. As far as Coele-Syria (Palestine) was concerned, Antiochus was engaged in war with Ptolemy Philadelphus of Egypt, but he did not succeed in winning these territories (the First Syrian War). Otherwise little is known of this monarch.

**2.** Antiochus II (261-246 B.C.), surnamed Theos ("god"). Son of the foregoing, he married his half

sister. Unlike his father, much has been said to his discredit: that he was immoral, drunken, and ruled by favorites. His second name or title was awarded by the Milesian people when he delivered them from their tyrant Timarchus; thereby the Jews of several cities of Asia Minor also received privileges of citizenship. Shortly after his accession he was attacked by Ptolemy Philadelphus (Second Syrian War) and lost some ports in Asia Minor. Little is known of this war, but it would appear that as a condition of peace in 250 B.C., Antiochus was compelled by Ptolemy to put away his wife Laodice and take in her place Ptolemy's daughter Berenice. Bitterly resenting the slight, Laodice is said to have poisoned her former husband when he tried to reconcile her, to have put to death the baby son born to him and Berenice, and to have secured the throne for her own son Seleucus II (*see* SELEUCUS 2). These reports may have been falsifications by Egyptians on behalf of Berenice. It is a fact, however, that Antiochus II was succeeded by his eldest son by Laodice, Seleucus II.

It is usual to interpret Dan. 11:6 of this king, for it is said that an alliance is made whereby the daughter of the king of the south comes to the king of the north, but that neither she nor her child nor he who obtained her should endure. These past events are recorded in Daniel as if they were still in the future.

**3.** Antiochus III (223-187 B.C.), surnamed the Great. The younger son of Seleucus II, he succeeded his brother Seleucus III. He was only twenty years old when he came to the throne, and was at first much under the influence of Hermeas, his minister. He lost no time in declaring war on Egypt, and led his army southward. During an ensuing truce with Egypt, he was engaged in putting down the rebellion of the pretender Molon in Media. Later he returned to the task against Ptolemy IV Philopator, and,

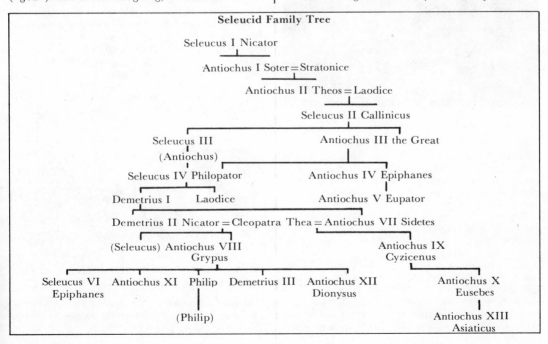

**Seleucid Family Tree**

Seleucus I Nicator

Antiochus I Soter = Stratonice

Antiochus II Theos = Laodice

Seleucus II Callinicus

Seleucus III (Antiochus) — Antiochus III the Great

Seleucus IV Philopator — Antiochus IV Epiphanes

Demetrius I — Laodice — Antiochus V Eupator

Demetrius II Nicator = Cleopatra Thea = Antiochus VII Sidetes

(Seleucus) Antiochus VIII Grypus — Antiochus IX Cyzicenus

Seleucus VI Epiphanes — Antiochus XI — Philip — Demetrius III — Antiochus XII Dionysus — Antiochus X Eusebes

(Philip)

Antiochus XIII Asiaticus

although in 218 he succeeded in establishing his position as far S as Ptolemaïs and eastward beyond Jordan, his success was short-lived, for, on emerging from winter quarters, he was severely defeated at Raphia near Gaza (217), and Egypt regained possession of Coele-Syria.

The next few years Antiochus spent in the East, as far as the Caspian Sea and India, where his successes gained for him the title "the Great." But Ptolemy Philopator died in 204, leaving behind an infant successor, and so Antiochus joined Philip V of Macedon in a scheme for partitioning Egypt

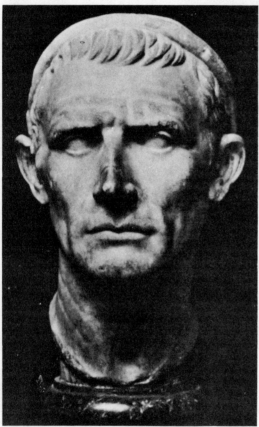

From *Atlas of the Bible* (Thomas Nelson & Sons Limited)
  33. Antiochus III

between them, while he himself pressed on to the Sinaitic Peninsula with the assistance of certain elements in Judea. However, this territory was soon lost during the absence of Antiochus, who had to give his attention to an invasion from Pergamum, the ally of Rome, in the NW.

Retiring from this task, the indomitable Antiochus, endeavoring to emulate Alexander the Great, made another attempt to dislodge the Egyptian forces from Judea and actually defeated the Egyptian general Scopas at Panium in 198, thus finally placing himself in control of all Palestine. It was an important day for the Jews, and a sad one, for this severed completely their connection with the Ptolemies and Egypt, who had treated them with considerable tolerance. It meant the beginning of a regime which

was destined to lead to fiercer persecution than the Jews had ever yet endured; and to utter tragedy. Military governors were appointed by Antiochus, taxes were imposed through tax farmers, but the temple was guaranteed inviolate and was subsidized. Josephus has much to say about these favors (Antiq. XII.iii).

In the treaty which Antiochus made with Ptolemy Epiphanes he gave the young Egyptian king the hand of his daughter Cleopatra in marriage, and he promised to grant the revenues of Coele-Syria with her. Whatever happened about this dowry, Antiochus retained sovereignty over all Palestine. His last years were busy with wars in Asia Minor and against Rome, which now virtually controlled the Mediterranean area; he was defeated by the Roman general Scipio Asiaticus at the Battle of Magnesia (190), and was killed in 187 in a rebellion.

Dan. 11:10-19 must refer to Antiochus III. The writer was contemporary with some of the events of this reign. III Macc. 1:1-7 gives what is probably a genuine account of the Battle of Raphia in 217.

Fig. ANT 33.

**4.** Antiochus IV (175-164 B.C.; or, according to some scholars, 175-163 B.C. [with an adjustment of one year in other dates listed below]), surnamed EPIPHANES ("the Manifest [God]"), which caused some of his enemies to nickname him "Epimanes" ("mad"). His coins* also include the titles νικηφόρος ("bringing victory") and θεός ("god"), and progressively represent his features as more and more like those of the Olympian Zeus. He was the younger son of Antiochus III the Great, and he followed his elder brother Seleucus Philopator (*see* SELEUCUS 4) on the throne, although Seleucus had a rightful heir, Demetrius. Antiochus had been a hostage in Rome for fourteen years after the Battle of Magnesia. Before he could take the kingdom, he had to rid himself of Heliodorus, his brother's murderer. He is known as one of the cruelest tyrants of all time, enterprising like his father, yet furious and precipitate almost to the degree of madness. His relations with Jerusalem and the Jews were particularly unfortunate. It was one of his major aims to obtain unity by spreading the movement of Hellenism throughout his dominions, and in this way he was brought into violent conflict with powerful Jewish elements. Fig. ANT 34.

  34. Antiochus IV, called Antiochus Epiphanes; from a
    silver tetradrachma

At the beginning of his reign he was asked to intervene in a dispute between the high priest ONIAS (3) and his brother JASON (1) in Jerusalem. Of course,

Antiochus, who was an ardent devotee of the Olympian Zeus and of all things Greek, supported the Hellenizer Jason, and Onias had to flee. Jason became high priest after paying a large sum of money and promising Antiochus that he would vigorously pursue the policy of Hellenization among the Jews; and he extended a lavish welcome to the king in Jerusalem. He was soon supplanted by one MENELAUS, who promised Antiochus a much larger sum, according to the writer of II Maccabees. But Jason besieged Jerusalem on hearing a rumor that Antiochus was dead. The rumor was far from true, and the enraged king returned from his successful campaign in Egypt to attack Jerusalem with savagery and spoil the temple of its treasures, leaving behind an equally tyrannical governor named Philip. His relations with the Jews and their city reached a tragic climax in 168 B.C. when he was on his way to attack Egypt for the third time. Outside Alexandria he received peremptory command from the Roman consul Gaius Popilius Laenas to desist from his projects, evacuate Egypt, and restore all Egyptian territories. Antiochus was not in the best of tempers as he retired northward; he decided that Jerusalem should be wiped out and should be colonized with Greeks. He consigned this task to Apollonius with an army of over twenty thousand men. As Apollonius entered Jerusalem on the sabbath, he met with little opposition, and most of the male inhabitants were killed, the rest rallied to Judas Maccabeus away from the city, and the women and children were enslaved. Great damage was done to the city, and a garrison was built there and occupied by Syrian troops. Though Menelaus remained as high priest, religious practices were nonexistent.

Confident that his work was almost complete, Antiochus now issued his famous edict to the effect that throughout his kingdom all peoples should be at one in religion, law, and custom. Among the Jews was the one element which would not submit, and accordingly Antiochus proceeded to sterner measures. Regulations directed against the sabbath, circumcision, and the food laws, on pain of death, were followed by the appalling scandal of the altar of Zeus which he caused to be erected over the altar of burnt offering in the temple (probably the "abomination that makes desolate" of Dan. 11:31). The Jews were compelled to take part in heathen festivities and were put to death if found in possession of the Book of the Law. There were many martyrs among the more faithful of the Jews, and at last open rebellion broke out in 167 B.C. at the hill village of MODIN, near Jerusalem. The king's representative paid a visit to see whether the edict was being observed, and he was slain by MATTATHIAS, a priest of the family destined to be known later as the Hasmoneans, who then fled to the surrounding hill country. There was a great slaughter of Mattathias' followers, many of whom were too pious to break the sabbath by defending themselves. But they were prevailed on later to defend themselves at all costs, and Mattathias was joined by large numbers of the HASIDIM, who came to see that force must be used against the heathen tyrant until Jerusalem and the temple were cleansed. So there began a guerrilla

warfare, with repeated attacks by the Hasmoneans upon the Syrian troops. Before long, however, Mattathias died (166), and his son JUDAS MACCABEUS succeeded to the leadership of the resistance movement and improved on the modest campaigns of his father. He went from one victory to another against the Syrian generals: Apollonius first, and then Seron.

Antiochus Epiphanes himself had, of course, heard of the Judean revolt and would no doubt have come in person to exterminate the Maccabeans, the followers of Judas, but he had more serious troubles elsewhere—revolts in Parthia and Armenia—which demanded his presence. He therefore left a regent named LYSIAS to be guardian of his son and at the same time to deal with the revolt of Judas Maccabeus. Lysias had orders to be quite ruthless—to depopulate the whole of Judea, make its people slaves, and lay it waste. The regent therefore dispatched three generals, PTOLEMY, NICANOR, and GORGIAS, with a large army for this task. Now the glories of Judas Maccabeus really begin. At Emmaus he routed Gorgias to such an extent that the whole Syrian army ignominiously fled from Judea. This involved the regent Lysias in a personal visit at the head of a still larger army in 165. Judas met the great man and inflicted upon him a severe defeat at Beth-zur. The only part of Judea which Judas did not now command was the Syrian citadel in Jerusalem. He restored the temple to its former glory and reintroduced the daily sacrifices on the twenty-fifth of Chislev, 165.

Judas' success served to drive the enraged Epiphanes to further madness, but he was powerless to restrain Judas. After an unsuccessful attempt to pillage the temple NANAEA in Elymais, Antiochus withdrew into the East, and it is said that he became really mad in Persia just before he died there. Josephus, I and II Maccabees (which do not agree on certain details), Polybius, and Appian are all authorities for the life of this king. The books of Maccabees and Daniel reflect the horror with which pious Jews regarded him. He is the king of fierce countenance—the little horn which challenges the host of heaven, a cunning and deceitful plotter, diabolical in the extreme.

5. Antiochus V (164-162 B.C.), surnamed Eupator ("born of a noble father"). While he was still a boy, he succeeded his father, Antiochus Epiphanes. Lysias had been appointed Eupator's guardian by his father, and with the boy-king he went up in 163 to relieve Jerusalem, which was besieged by Judas Maccabeus. Lysias was successful at Beth-zacharias, according to Josephus (but not II Macc. 13:16-17), and in turn besieged Jerusalem. He made peace, granting concessions of religious freedom to the Jews, the terms of which were soon broken when Antiochus destroyed the city's defenses and imprisoned the high priest. But he had to retire to Antioch in order to deal with Philip, who was a foster brother of the previous king, and a little later both he and Lysias were betrayed into the hands of a claimant to the throne, his cousin Demetrius Soter, who ought to have succeeded before Antiochus Epiphanes. Antiochus V and his regent were put to death in 162 B.C.

6. Antiochus VI (145-142 B.C.), surnamed on coins Epiphanes Dionysus. He was the son of Alex-

ander Balas (*see* ALEXANDER 2). He was set up as a claimant to the throne of Syria in 145, while still a boy, by TRYPHO during the reign of Demetrius Nicator.* The generals supported him, and so did

35. Antiochus VI; from a silver tetradrachma coin

Jonathan in Jerusalem. But Antiochus had not been long acknowledged king when Trypho secured his assassination and himself became king. Fig. TRY 79. Fig. ANT 35.

**7.** Antiochus VII (138-129 B.C.), surnamed Sidetes because he was brought up at Side. He took the place of his brother Demetrius and Trypho on the throne of Syria. He invaded Judea in 135 and, razing part of the walls of Jerusalem, was successful in making John Hyrcanus submit. Sidetes subdued the Parthians in 130, but the success was temporary, and he died while fighting.

**8.** Antiochus VIII (125-96 B.C.), nicknamed Grypus ("hook-nosed"). He was the second son of DEMETRIUS II. At first he reigned jointly with his mother, the notorious Cleopatra Thea. After a time his position was challenged by his half brother.

**9.** Antiochus IX (116-95 B.C.), surnamed Cyzicenus, but Philopator on his coins. He was the half brother of Antiochus Grypus; at first Grypus was victorious, when Cyzicenus challenged his power, but later the tide of fortune turned and Syria was partitioned between the half brothers. It was an opportunity for Rome to gain a footing here, and also for the Jews to make rapid progress toward complete independence under John Hyrcanus. *See* HASMONEANS § 3*b*.

**10.** Antiochus X (94-83 B.C.). The son of Cyzicenus; he expelled Seleucus VI, the son of Grypus. He was the third husband of the Egyptian princess Selene, who had married first Grypus and then Cyzicenus. Antiochus X had to meet opposition from other sons of Grypus, including Antiochus XI, and was finally expelled and killed in battle. The youngest son of Grypus was Antiochus XII, who also claimed the throne during this reign. Internal strife marked the end of the Seleucid dynasty, and in 83 Tigranes, king of Armenia, was able to master the whole of the kingdom of Syria and rule over it for fourteen years by means of a viceroy, until his own defeat by the Romans. Even then the royal house of Seleucus experienced one last spasm of life.

**11.** Antiochus XIII (69-65 B.C.), commonly called Asiaticus. The son of Antiochus X and Selene, he was permitted to reign by the Romans, until in 65 a representative of another branch of the family, Philip, staked a claim to the throne, but unsuccess-

fully. In 63 the Roman commander, Pompey, made Syria a Roman province and brought the Seleucid dynasty to its end.

**12.** The father of NUMENIUS; mentioned in I Macc. 12:16; 14:22. He is of no further importance.

*Bibliography.* E. Bevan, *The House of Seleucus* (1900, 1901); *Jerusalem Under the High Priests* (1904). "The Hellenistic Monarchies and the Rise of Rome," in *Cambridge Ancient History*, vol. 7 (1928). Histories of the Jews by Schürer and Juster. F.-M. Abel, *Les Livres des Maccabées* (1949). N. TURNER

**ANTIPAS** ăn′tə pəs ['Αντίπας, *probably a shortened* (Hebrew) *form of* 'Αντίπατρος]. **1.** An Idumean who, according to Josephus (Antiq. XIV.i.3), had been made "general of all Idumea" by "king Alexander and his wife"; father of 2 *below*.

**2.** An Idumean "who was very rich, in his nature an active and a seditious man" (Jos. Antiq. XIV.i.3). At enmity with Aristobulus, he sought in every way to calumniate him before Hyrcanus. As a result, "Hyrcanus, fearing for his life, fled to Aretas, of Arabia, who gave him refuge at Petra" (Jos. Antiq. XIV.i.4). Supported by Aretas, Antipas and Hyrcanus made an expedition against Aristobulus and gained a temporary victory. Scaurus, newly come from Pompey, however, sided with Aristobulus, and the army of Aretas and Hyrcanus was badly beaten at Papyron. This Antipas was the father of Herod the Great. *See* HEROD (FAMILY).

**3.** Son of Herod the Great by the Samaritan Malthace, one of the nine wives Herod had simultaneously. Antipas and his brother Archelaus were, according to Josephus (Antiq. XVII.i.3), "brought up with a certain private man at Rome." This Antipas was "Herod the tetrarch" of Galilee (Luke 3:1, 19), whose lust and sadism appear in his dealings with John the Baptizer and Jesus (Matt. 14:1-11; Mark 6:14; Luke 23:7-12). J. C. SWAIM

**ANTIPATER** ăn tĭp′ə tər ['Αντίπατρος]. Son of Jason, designated to accompany Numenius son of Antiochus to the Romans and the Lacedaemonians as envoys of the Jews for the purpose of renewing the "former friendship and alliance" (I Macc. 12:16; 14:22). J. C. SWAIM

**ANTIPATRIS** ăn tĭp′ə trĭs ['Αντιπατρίς]. A city *ca.* ten miles NE of Jaffa (Joppa) and ten miles N of Lydda (Ludd, Lod); named in honor of Antipater, procurator of Judea under Julius Caesar, when it was rebuilt by Antipater's son Herod the Great in 9 B.C. upon the site of Caphar Saba (S of modern Kefr Saba). Cf. Jos. Antiq. XVI.v.2.

Antipatris is mentioned only once in the Bible (Acts 23:31), as the destination of a night journey by 470 Roman soldiers conducting Paul as a prisoner from Jerusalem to Caesarea. Their mountainous descent from Jerusalem to Antipatris on the Plain of Sharon was *ca.* forty miles, while the second day's journey to the Roman capital was *ca.* twenty-five miles northward across the plain.

Antipatris served as a Roman military relay station (*mutatio*) and marked the border between Judea and Samaria. Josephus (War I.iv.7) recounts that Alexander Janneus (*ca.* 85 B.C.) constructed a moat and wall with a tower between Caphar Saba and

Joppa and that this was promptly destroyed by Antiochus of Syria.

It lay at the headwaters of the River Aujeh (the biblical Yarkon, the Greek Pegai, the medieval Nahr Abu Futrus, known also as the Jaffa River and the River of Antipatris) at Ras el-'Ain, well watered and fertile as Josephus reported. The Palestine Department of Antiquities excavated the ancient ruins in 1946, confirming the earlier identification of Alt and Albright that here was the site of OT APHEK, in existence as early as 2000 B.C., and of Hellenistic Pegai.

The Bordeaux Pilgrim *ca.* A.D. 333 made a "change" at Antipatris, and fifty years later the holy Paula is reported by Jerome to have stopped in this "small, half-ruined town." Antipatris was represented by Bishop Polychronius at the Council of Chalcedon in 451, and was then placed in the newly established Patriarchate of Jerusalem. It is mentioned as the location of massacres in 744, of Christians allied with the Ommiads. In the tenth century, Mukkadasi describes it as a "large place with a mosque, lying on the high road from Ar-Ramleh to Damascus." The ruins of the medieval Castle of Mirabel are still to be seen at Ras el-'Ain.

**Bibliography.** E. Smith, "Visit to Antipatris," *Bibliotheca Sacra* (1843), pp. 492 ff; C. R. Conder, *Survey of Western Palestine*, Memoirs, II (1882), 258-62; W. F. Albright, "A Philistine Military Base," *BASOR,* no. 11 (Oct., 1923), pp. 6-7.

K. W. CLARK

## ANTONIA, TOWER OF

ăn tō'nĭ ə ['Αντωνία]. The palatial guard tower rebuilt by Herod the Great at the NW corner of the temple court, which served as a royal residence as well as soldiers' quarters. The "Antonia" is not named in the Bible, but is referred to by the term παρεμβολή, "barracks" (KJV "castle"), only in Acts 21:34-37; 22:24; 23:10, 16, 32.

**1. History.** A tower on this site may go back to the time of Solomon, whose N wall probably made a turning at this point as it enclosed the temple mount. This point of turning is the highest rocky eminence in the neighborhood, an obvious selection for a tower (possibly the Millo, "solid tower," of David's fortifications). Such a tower must have shared the fortunes of the city walls in periodic destruction wrought by enemies, who usually attacked from the N. After the Exile, Nehemiah (2:8) speaks of rebuilding the *Birah* (Assyrian[?] "castle, fortress") on this site. Later rebuilt by Hyrcanus, it was known as the βάρις ("castle, tower") and was occupied by Maccabean rulers until the time of Herod the Great. When it was finally rebuilt by Herod in great splendor, it received the name Antonia to honor his friend and patron, Mark Antony. When in A.D. 6 Roman procurators began to rule in Jerusalem, the Antonia served as one of the official residences. The revolt of the Jews in 66 resulted in its destruction by Titus. Herodian masonry can still be seen in the lower courses of the modern barracks on the site.

**2. Structure.** The Antonia was strategically located on a rocky precipice seventy-five feet high, the rock being faced with smooth and slippery flagstones. This prominent position was more nearly impregnable because of the Tyropoeon Valley on the

W and the deep trench on the N separating it from the hill Bezetha, with a wall and moat between. Above the rock the stone walls rose another sixty feet. There were four higher corner towers, each seventy-five feet except the SE tower, facing the temple court, which was a hundred feet high.

Courtesy of J. Gabalda et Cie., Paris

36. Pavement of the court in the Tower of Antonia

Josephus, our chief source, describes the spacious and palatial grandeur of the interior, with its many apartments, cloisters, baths, and large courtyards and barracks for the accommodation of troops. It served as both palace and fortress. Stairs gave access directly to the interior temple porticoes in the Court of the Gentiles, which ran along the N wall and the W (the latter broken by four entrances from the Upper City). There was also a subterranean passage to the Court of Israel, for emergency use. The Antonia was built square and probably had a central court. In such a court a procurator might deliver legal decisions. It is possible that this court survives in the pavement found under the Convent of Our Lady of Zion and the Convent of Flagellation. Indeed, it may be identified with GABBATHA, where Jesus appeared before Pilate (John 19:13). Fig. ANT 36.

**3. Function.** From David to Antigonus, last of the Maccabean rulers, this fortress on the rock faced outward against its northern enemies. But with Herod the Great and within the vast Roman state, the Antonia faced inward as guardian over the Jews. The highest tower faced the temple courts, and the chief activity of the garrison was to police the Court of the Gentiles, where crowds of worshipers gathered. Josephus reports that a Roman cohort (between five and six hundred men) was billeted in the Antonia, besides the larger forces in the Citadel of the Upper City to the W. Herod the Great held control over the high priest by requiring that the vestments be kept in the Antonia, a practice generally followed by the procurators thereafter. The scene of Jesus' hearing before Pilate may have been at this center of Roman control.

The Antonia was the scene also of Paul's dispute with the Jewish leaders (Acts 21:37-40). The military tribune granted Paul permission to address the Jews in the temple court, as he stood on the steps leading up to the Antonia. Here also his case was later investigated by the tribune (Acts 22:23-29), after which he was confined in the Antonia for protection until the tribune spirited him off to Caesarea for further trial (Acts 23:10, 16-24).

The Tower of Antonia at the last was taken by Titus and used as a command post from which to direct his assault upon the temple mount, ending in its capitulation and burning in A.D. 70. Josephus' final comment upon the Antonia (War VI.v.4) is the recollection of an oracle that when the temple should become foursquare, Jerusalem would be captured. The removal of the Antonia at last left the temple ideally square.

*Bibliography.* Jos. Antiq. XV.xi.4; XVIII.iv.3; War V.v.8. L. H. Vincent, *Jérusalem de l'Ancien Testament,* I (1954), 193-221.      K. W. CLARK

**ANTOTHIJAH.** KJV form of ANTHOTHIJAH.

**ANTOTHITE.** KJV form of Anathothite. *See* ANATHOTH.

**ANUB** ā'nŭb [עֲנוּב] (I Chr. 4:8). A son of Koz in the genealogy of Judah.

**ANUS** ā'nəs. KJV form of ANNIUTH.

**ANVIL.** The translation of פַּעַם in Isa. 41:7, where the context and the root meaning ("to strike") suggest such an instrument. An alternative translation, "mallet" (Amer. Trans.), or a similar instrument, is supported by the parallelism in this verse and by a related term in the Ugaritic texts designating Baal's club (*p'n*).      P. L. GARBER

**ANXIETY.** In the background and the foreground of the Bible one encounters man's anxiety for his life. Anxiety is one element of the full range that extends from intent thought and interest through concern, care, worry, dread, to grief and inward pain. The biblical writers often treat anxiety as a natural part of man's existence, but anxiety also appears in its true theological context as heathenish, sinful, and a denial of God's PROVIDENCE and CARE. The opposite of anxiety is seen as the quiet, trustful mind in enjoyment of the peace of God.

    1. Terminology of anxiety in the Bible
        *a.* In biblical Hebrew
        *b.* In LXX Greek
        *c.* In NT Greek
    2. Anxiety in the OT
    3. Anxiety in the NT
    Bibliography

**1. Terminology of anxiety in the Bible.** The word "anxiety" occurs only seven times in the RSV, and other forms derived from it, "anxious" and "anxiously," appear only twenty-seven times. But the related terms such as "care," "carefulness," occur frequently and lay a broad base for the anxious mind of the man of the Bible. The review of some of these terms brings out something of the history of the English Bible, for the word "careful" in the KJV of Phil. 4:6: "Be careful for nothing," is misunderstood today, and it should read as in the RSV: "Have no anxiety about anything."

    *a. In biblical Hebrew.* The Hebrew terms are דאג, "to melt (with fear), to be afraid for, anxious about"

(I Sam. 9:5; 10:2; Isa. 57:11; Jer. 17:8); דְּאָגָה, "fear, dread, anxiety" (Prov. 12:25; Ezek. 4:16; 12:18-19); כַּעַס, "to be irritated, troubled" (I Sam. 1:6); עָצַב, "to suffer, to be afflicted, to be grieved" (Ps. 127:2). In Dan. 7:15 the Aramaic word כְּרָא, "to be pained, to grieve," is used. חֲרָדָה, "trembling, care, concern," occurs in II Kings 4:13, and the adjective form in I Sam. 4:13, חָרֵד, "trembling for, fearful for." Note also דרשׁ, "to seek out, to care for," in Deut. 11:12.

    *b. In LXX Greek.* The usual term is μέριμνα, a translation of דאגה and יחב (Ps. 55:23—G 54:23; Prov. 17:12; I Macc. 6:10). The verbal form μεριμνάω, "to be anxious, to be grieved," is used, e.g., in Ps. 37:19—H 38:18 in the sense of deep concern, "sorry for my sins." The same verb is used in Exod. 5:9 in a weaker sense: "to think thereon." Neutral thought and concern are expressed by the term φρόντις, "reflective thought, concern" (Job 11:18, where it is used in conjunction with μέριμνα; Wisd. Sol. 5:15; 6:17).

    *c. In NT Greek.* The words μέριμνα and μεριμνάω occur twenty-five times and carry the sense of anxiety and worry. Anxiety in anticipation is expressed by the verb προμεριμνάω (Mark 13:11), and freedom from anxiety by the adjective ἀμέριμνος (Matt. 28:14). Luke uses the unusual word μετεωρίζω (12:29) as a synonym for the usual μεριμνάω. Thoughtful concern is expressed by φρονέω (Phil. 4:10) and φροντίζω (Tit. 3:8). Earnest care and zeal are represented by σπουδή (II Cor. 7:11, 12; 8:16). Simple concern is the meaning of the impersonal verb μέλει, "it is a concern to" (Matt. 22:16; Mark 12:14; I Pet. 5:7).

    **2. Anxiety in the OT.** The pressure of concern, anxiety, and fear in the varied conditions of man's life can be detected throughout these writings.

Drought would bring the threat of famine (cf. Jer. 17:8). Personal anxiety is reflected in Hannah's words (because of her childlessness): "I have been speaking out of my great anxiety and vexation" (I Sam. 1:16), or in Daniel's perplexity over his dream (Dan. 7:15). The dislocations incident to war and the threat of violence were deeply disturbing to all concerned (I Chr. 17:9).

The Psalms give verbal expression to these feelings of crushing anxiety and care. The sense of sin and distance from God is a terrible burden on the consciousness of the psalmist (51). He is also conscious of the wicked oppressor and the taunts of the enemy, and his troubles keep him awake at night (102:7). His tears mingle with his drink. The waters of his anxieties are ready to overwhelm him (69:1-2). The psalmist calls on God to rescue him from the hand of the oppressor (71:4-6). In God's care he finds peace and the release from his dire condition; God cleanses and restores, God shepherds his soul (23). God, says the psalmist, "will hide me in his shelter in the day of trouble" (27:5).

> It is in vain that you rise up early, to go late to rest,
> eating the bread of anxious toil;
>     for he gives to his beloved in sleep (127:2).

In the same vein are Ps. 55:22; Isa. 26:3.

    **3. Anxiety in the NT.** The NT writings reflect many of the same concerns as have been noted in the OT.

In the NT there is seen the natural reaction to poverty, hunger, and the pressures of the common life, as in the Beatitudes. The "poor" here, as in the OT, are the righteous ones who are bereft and who must look to God for help and redress. It is interesting to note how the problems and concerns of the married state are echoed in Paul's counsels in I Cor. 7.

In the Christian life men voluntarily take over a concern for others. Paul enjoys the thoughtful provision of his friends. Paul himself is anxious about them (Phil. 2:28), and he carries on his mind the daily pressure of anxiety for all the churches.

The answer to the burdens of life is to be found in God and his care: "Cast all your anxieties on him, for he cares about you" (I Pet. 5:7). In the Beatitudes the poor and the oppressed are to find their ground of blessing in God's kingdom and its provision. Paul says that the answer to worry is prayer to God: "Have no anxiety about anything, but in everything by prayer and supplication with thanksgiving let your requests be made known to God" (Phil. 4:6).

Jesus' teaching on anxiety strikes a new and radical note, for he outlaws anxiety and brands it as pagan and worldly. He himself is deeply concerned for men, "harassed and helpless, like sheep without a shepherd" (Matt. 9:36); his disciples are as "sheep in the midst of wolves" (Matt. 10:16). The future before the city of Jerusalem brings Jesus to tears (Luke 19:41-44). But as for himself and his fortunes, he walks as one whose inward strength and peace cannot be undermined by men. He refuses to run away before Herod's threats (Luke 13:31-33). His critics detect this imperturbable quality: "Teacher, we know that you are true, and care for no man" (Mark 12:14).

Jesus' clearest teaching on anxiety is found in the Sermon on the Mount (Matt. 6:25-34; Luke 12:22-31). Jesus prohibits anxiety for the most elemental necessities, and so for all the extras that men deem necessities: "Do not be anxious about your life, what you shall eat or what you shall drink, nor about your body, what you shall put on." First of all, life properly understood is a greater thing than what sustains it, and man's concern should be centered on life's real purpose. Second, such anxiety for food and clothing ignores God's providential provision in the world. The birds are cared for, and man, made in the image of God, can count on God's provision. Third, God's sustaining providence proceeds in a way that is independent of man's anxiety. Can man by worrying add to his stature (or his span of life)? Fourth, God's care for the ephemeral flowers is perfect and complete in beauty. Man can surely depend on the minimum provision of clothing at God's hand. Fifth, such anxiety is pagan and is a direct contradiction of God's foreknowledge and care. Sixth, man's first concern should be for the cause of the kingdom of God (and treasure in heaven [Matt. 6:19], and service to one master, God [Matt. 6:24]), and this concern rules out anxiety for lesser objects.

Elsewhere Jesus couples the "cares of the world" with the "delight in riches" and the "desire for other things," and he says they choke the word (Mark 4:19). In Luke 21:34 he warns: "Take heed to your-selves lest your hearts be weighed down with dissipation and drunkenness and cares of this life." Jesus banishes all such as unfit for life in the kingdom.

The saying about anxiety for the morrow (Matt. 6:34) may be an addition from proverbial wisdom. If it comes from Jesus, he may be setting man's worried concern in a humorous, ironical light: You worry about what is yet to come. If you only knew—!

Did Jesus intend this teaching on anxiety to be taken literally, or as an interim ethic, or eschatologically? For Jesus the kingdom had broken in upon the world and was to come in full realization. The disciples who accept the rule of the kingdom have found a new orientation of life in which God's will controls all purposes and goals. Man is now to live, not in anxious self-centeredness, but in gratitude for God's great gift of the kingdom. In the kingdom all man's concerns and desires find their true place and proportion, for God's will and provision extend to the humblest needs as to the highest goals.

*Bibliography.* S. Kierkegaard, *Christian Discourses* (trans. W. Lowrie; 1939), pp. 1-93; M. Dibelius, *The Sermon on the Mount* (1940), pp. 44-52; A. M. Hunter, *A Pattern for Life* (1953), pp. 76-81; W. F. Arndt and F. W. Gingrich, *A Greek-English Lexicon of the NT and Other Early Christian Literature* (1957), trans. and adapted from W. Bauer, *Griechisch-Deutsches Wörterbuch zu den Schriften des Neuen Testaments und der übrigen urchristlichen Literatur* (1952). R. Bultmann's article in *TWNT* on μεριμνάω reflects his interest in the existential conception of man's position.                                    P. E. DAVIES

**APAME** ə pā′mĭ ['Απάμη] (I Esd. 4:29). A royal Persian concubine cited by the third page in the story of the three youths at the court of Darius (I Esd. 3: 1-4:42), as evidence of the superior power of women over men. Scholars are not agreed whether she is a fictional character or the daughter of Artabazus III and wife of Ptolemy I Soter of Egypt (305-283 B.C.).

*Bibliography.* C. C. Torrey, *Ezra Studies* (1910), pp. 39-44; R. H. Pfeiffer. *History of NT Times* (1949), p. 255.
E. W. SAUNDERS

**APE** [קוֹף (*only in plural*), קֹפִים (I Kings 10:22), קוֹפִים (II Chr. 9:21), *from* Egyp. *g′f* (*also gwf, g³f*), *a type of* small ape, *hence* Akkad. *uqūpu;* Syr. *qûpâ*]. Any of the tailless manlike animals of the Primate order, of the family Simiidae, comprising the chimpanzee, the gorilla, the orangutan, and the gibbon. The Old World monkeys and baboons belong to another family, the Cercopithecidae.

It is impossible to identify with any exactness the "apes" which the Red Sea fleet of Hiram and Solomon brought to a port on the Gulf of Aqabah; it is probable, however, that they were not apes at all, but either monkeys or baboons. The baboon was well known in Egypt, where the god Thoth was often represented by it. The commonest baboon in this area is the Arabian baboon (*papio hamadryas*), found in Arabia, Abyssinia, and the Sudan.

*See also* FAUNA § A2k.                    W. S. McCULLOUGH

**APELLES** ə pĕl′ĭz ['Απελλῆς]. Someone designated in Rom. 16:10 as one "approved in Christ," but otherwise unknown. A variant reading of Codex Sinaiticus (Acts 18:12; 19:1) identifies him as APOLLOS, but without foundation.

The name itself occurs frequently in inscriptions and is mentioned by Philo, Josephus, and Horace. It was used by both Jews and Gentiles, among the latter of whom were a famous tragic actor in the reign of Gaius and a military tribune under Vespasian.

Bibliography. W. H. P. Hatch, "Some Illustrations of NT Usage from Greek Inscriptions of Asia Minor," *JBL*, XXVII (1908), 145; J. B. Lightfoot, *St. Paul's Epistle to the Philippians* (1927), p. 174. I. W. BATDORF

**APHAIREMA** ə fâr′ə mə [Αφαιρεμα]; KJV APHEREMA —fĕr′—. One of three districts of Samaria promised to the Jews by Demetrius I in an effort to secure the support of Jonathan (I Macc. 10: 38), and later confirmed by Demetrius II (11:34), who also granted Jonathan increased power and guaranteed the Jews immunity from the crown taxes. According to Josephus, Aphairema was situated near Bethel (War IV.ix.9), undoubtedly the town identified in John 11:54 as the scene of Jesus' retirement just before his final entrance into Jerusalem. The LXX name may be a modification of an earlier form preserved by Josephus (Antiq. XIII.iv.9), *Aphereima*. Both forms represent the Aramaic place name of EPHRAIM, the earlier OPHRAH, situated on a hill five miles NE of Bethel. It is called et-Taiyibeh today.

Bibliography. F.-M. Abel, *Géographie de la Palestine*, II (1938), 247. E. W. SAUNDERS

**APHARSACHITES** ə fär′sə kīts. KJV translation of אפרסכיא (RSV GOVERNORS) in Ezra 5:6; 6:6. This is a Persian loan word, denoting a judicial official, to be connected with Old Persian *frasaka* (probably "investigator"), which appears in cuneiform texts as *iprasakku*.

See GOVERNOR.

Bibliography. W. Eilers, *Iranische Beamtennamen in der keilschriftlichen Überlieferung* (1940), pp. 5 ff, 30. A. L. OPPENHEIM

**APHARSATHCHITES** ə fär′sĭth kīts. KJV translation of אפרסתכיא (RSV GOVERNORS) in Ezra 4:9. This is a Persian loan word, denoting an official, probably to be connected with Old Persian *frēstak*, "messenger."

See GOVERNOR.

Bibliography. W. Eilers, *Iranische Beamtennamen in der keilschriftlichen Überlieferung* (1940), pp. 39-40, 100; E. Herzfeld, *Zoroaster and His World* (1947), I, 171. A. L. OPPENHEIM

**APHARSITES** ə fär′sīts. KJV translation of אפרסיא (Ezra 4:9), an undefined gentilic (RSV PERSIAN).

Bibliography. W. Eilers, *Iranische Beamtennamen in der keilschriftlichen Überlieferung* (1940), pp. 39-40.

***APHEK** ā′fĕk [אפק, bed of a brook, fortress(?)]. Alternately: APHIK ā′fĭk [אפיק] (Judg. 1:31). **1.** A city-state in the Plain of Sharon whose king was slain by Joshua and the forces of Israel during the conquest of Canaan (Josh. 12:18). It was strategically located on the Sharon section of the great trunk road through the country and on a possible access route from the coastal plain into the Ephraimite hill coun-

try. Therefore, it was a natural rallying point for Philistine forces, both on the occasion of their first full-scale engagement with Israel near Ebenezer (I Sam. 4:1), at which time the ark of the covenant was captured (*ca.* 1050 B.C.), and again in preparation for the campaign which was to result in the defeat and death of Saul (I Sam. 29:1; cf. 31:1-7).

The ancient site is represented by modern Ras el-ʿAin at the source of the Yarkon River. Here also stood the Herodian-Roman town of Antipatris (in the vicinity of which was a tower called Aphek as late as the first century A.D. [Jos. War II.xix.1]), built over the previous site of Pegae ("springs"). Middle and Late Bronze and Iron I (*ca.* 2000-900) sherds on the site testify to the presence of the earlier Canaanite settlement—its antiquity and importance being further attested by its appearance in the Memphis Stela of Amenhotep II as the first town captured during the course of his second Asiatic campaign (*ca.* 1440). It is possible, as well, that this is the Aphek which appears in the Egyptian Execration Texts of the nineteenth century B.C. It appears again (*ca.* 600) in the Aramaic letter of a Palestinian king, Adon, to his Egyptian overlord telling of the advance position of invading Babylonian forces.

**2.** A site near Canaan's N frontier with the Amorites which, though never possessed by Israel, was ideally regarded as part of her inheritance (Josh. 13:4). It is probably represented by modern Afqa (ancient Aphaca), some fifteen miles E of Jebeil (ancient Byblos) in Lebanon. Here was a shrine and center of the Astarte-Adonis cult, and its sacred spring is the source of the river now called Nahr Ibrahim but anciently known as Adonis.

**3.** One of the Canaanite cities in the inheritance apportioned to Asher (Josh. 19:30), whose inhabitants the tribe could neither expel nor render tributary. It is possibly to be identified with modern Tell Kerdanah, some six miles SE of Acco and three miles inland from the Bay of Haifa, which site was furnished with a strong spring and strategically situated on the coast road connecting Phoenicia and Egypt.

**4.** A city in the N Transjordan district of ancient Bashan and on the main highway connecting Damascus with Beth-shan and the Valley of Jezreel. On a nearby plain the Syrian Ben-hadad was defeated by the inferior forces of Ahab, and to the city itself the Syrian fled for refuge with the remnant of his routed forces, only to experience further disaster in the collapse of the city wall (I Kings 20:26-30). Here, also, Joash of Israel, according to the prophecy of Elisha, was to administer repeated defeat to the forces of Syria (II Kings 13:14-19, 25).

The ancient name survives in the modern village of Fiq (also called Afiq), overlooking the Sea of Galilee from a plateau three miles inland and a short distance to the E of Hellenistic and Roman Hippos.

Bibliography. G. A. Smith, *The Historical Geography of the Holy Land* (11th ed., 1904), pp. 427, 459, 580, 582; F.-M. Abel, *Géographie de la Palestine*, II (1938), 23, 67; J. B. Pritchard, ed., *ANET* (2nd ed., 1955), pp. 242, 246; E. G. Kraeling, *Bible Atlas* (1956), pp. 149, 173, 279; D. Baly, *The Geography of the Bible* (1957), pp. 130, 134-35, 137, 175-76; G. E. Wright, *Biblical Archaeology* (1957), p. 175; M. Noth, *The History of Israel* (1958), pp. 165, 176-77. W. H. MORTON

**APHEKAH** ə fē′kə [אֲפֵקָה] (Josh. 15:53). A city assigned to the tribe of Judah. The location is still unknown.

**APHEREMA.** KJV form of APHAIREMA.

**APHERRA** ə fĕr′ə ['Αφερρά] (I Esd. 5:34). Head of a family of Solomon's servants. His name is omitted in the parallels Ezra 2:57; Neh. 7:59.

C. T. FRITSCH

**APHIAH** ə fī′ə [אֲפִיחַ] (I Sam. 9:1). A Benjaminite who was one of the ancestors of King Saul.

**APHIK.** Alternate form of APHEK 3.

**APHRAH.** *See* BETH-LE-APHRAH.

**APHSES.** KJV form of HAPPIZZEZ.

**APIS** ā′pĭs. The translation of חַף in Jer. 46:15, resulting from a redivision of the Hebrew text, reading מדוע נס חף, "Why has Apis fled?" (RSV), instead of מדוע נסחף, "Why are [they] swept away?" (KJV). The sacred bull known as Apis was worshiped in Memphis by the Egyptians from earliest historical times as a general god of fertility. Although he was primarily a manifestation of the god Ptah, his fertility function led to his being closely associated with OSIRIS in Greco-Roman times and to his being regarded as the reincarnation of that god, under the name Osiris-Apis or Serapis. The representative bull was chosen with great care by the priests of the cult, and during its lifetime it was accorded all the honors concomitant with divine adoration. At its death it was mummified and buried in one of the several places reserved in Egypt for that purpose.

Fig. API 37.

*Bibliography.* S. A. B. Mercer, *The Religion of Ancient Egypt* 1949), pp. 233-34; J. Černý, *Ancient Egyptian Religion* (1952).

T. O. LAMBDIN

Courtesy of Ny Carlsberg Glyptotek, Copenhagen

37. The bull Apis, its body decorated with a winged scarab, a vulture, and a fringed carpet; Saïte period (*ca.* 663-525 B.C.)

**APOCALYPSE OF JOHN** ə pŏk′ə lĭps. *See* REVELATION, BOOK OF.

**APOCALYPSES, APOCRYPHAL.** A comparatively small group of apocryphal writings attributed to NT characters (Peter, Paul, Thomas, Stephen, the Virgin, etc.) and purporting to provide visions of the next world and (occasionally) prophecies of the end of this world. *See* APOCRYPHA, NT, for a further statement and a list of those apocalypses to which separate articles are devoted herein.     M. S. ENSLIN

*****APOCALYPTICISM** ə pŏk′ə lĭp′tə sĭz əm. A type of religious thought which apparently originated in Zoroastrianism, the ancient Persian religion (*see* PERSIA, HISTORY AND RELIGION OF); taken over by Judaism in the exilic and postexilic periods; and mediated by Judaism to early Christianity. Taking firm roots there, it has continued as an important element in popular Christian belief down to the present. It may be defined as the dualistic, cosmic, and eschatological belief in two opposing cosmic powers, God and Satan (or his equivalent); and in two distinct ages—the present, temporal and irretrievably evil age under Satan, who now oppresses the righteous but whose power God will soon act to overthrow; and the future, perfect and eternal age under God's own rule, when the righteous will be blessed forever. *See* ESCHATOLOGY; DUALISM.

Literary works embodying this belief, of which there are many examples both in ancient Judaism and in early Christianity, are known as apocalypses (*see* DANIEL; REVELATION, BOOK OF; ENOCH, BOOK OF; BARUCH, APOCALYPSE OF; etc.; *see also* PSEUDEPIGRAPHA). Our term has often been defined so loosely and broadly as almost to lose any distinctiveness. Thus books or portions of them as divergent as Joel, Amos, Zechariah, Daniel, Isa. 24–27, Jubilees, I Enoch, the Testament of Abraham, the Shepherd of Hermas, the Apocalypse of Paul, II Esdras, Revelation, the Psalms of Solomon, Er's vision of the next world in Plato's *Republic,* and the Apocalypse of Peter have all been termed apocalyptic by one writer or another. (*See* JOEL, BOOK OF; AMOS; ZECHARIAH, BOOK OF; JUBILEES, BOOK OF; ABRAHAM, TESTAMENT OF; HERMAS, SHEPHERD OF; PAUL, APOCALYPSE OF; ESDRAS, BOOKS OF; SOLOMON, PSALMS OF; PETER, APOCALYPSE OF.) Such vagueness of definition is due to a failure to distinguish between elements in the basic pattern of apocalypticism and various secondary features often present in apocalypses but by no means normative or constitutive.

1. The basic pattern
    *a.* Dualistic
    *b.* Eschatological
2. Secondary features
    *a.* Vision
    *b.* Pseudonymity
    *c.* A messiah
    *d.* Angelology and demonology
    *e.* Animal symbolism
    *f.* Numerology
    *g.* Predicted woes
    *h.* Astral influences
3. The relevance of apocalyptic
Bibliography

**1. The basic pattern.** *a. Dualistic.* Apocalypticism is essentially dualistic. This is not a metaphysical DUALISM of spirit and matter; instead, it is the dualism of two opposing personified forces in the universe, a good god and an evil one, hence a cosmic dualism. In ancient Persian thinking the two opposing gods of good and evil, Ormazd and Ahriman, were coequal, but were as different as light from darkness. In Jewish thinking Yahweh, of course, was the good God, whereas SATAN (or his equivalent), no longer merely Yahweh's agent as the tempter of mankind, was both God's opponent and man's oppressor. Because of the traditional monotheism of Judaism the dualism was not so marked as it was in Persian thinking. Satan was clearly inferior to God, at times was considered to be just a fallen angel. In general, God is in over-all control, with Satan ruling merely at God's good pleasure. In IV Ezra the dualism is attenuated, so that, in the main, a person's wicked deeds are attributed to the evil Yetzer; however, in the Apocalypse of Abraham, which is almost contemporaneous with IV Ezra, the dualism is much more in evidence. In Christian thinking Satan (or the Devil) is quite active as both the opponent of God and the tempter and oppressor of mankind; even so, he is inferior to God, not his equal in power.

This type of thinking may be termed cosmic dualism, since the entire cosmos, the earth, the underworld, and heaven, along with their inhabitants, are all involved in the opposition between the powers of good and evil. In Persian thinking all living creatures, both men and supernatural beings, are divided according to their allegiance to Ormazd or Ahriman. This division is also evident in Jewish and Christian apocalypses; it is most apparent, perhaps, in Revelation, where the greater number of the human and supernatural followers of God have their counterparts among Satan's human and supernatural forces.

*b. Eschatological.* The eschatological element in the apocalyptic pattern is combined with the cosmic dualism. For both time and beyond-time are involved; there are two distinct and separate ages; the second is not the outgrowth of the first, but is a new creation. The first, this present age of human history, is under the dominion of the power of evil. Consequently, it is evil and corrupt, and many of the inhabitants of earth are the evil followers of Satan, the evil power. The righteous followers of God are oppressed and persecuted and may even be put to death by their wicked contemporaries. There is no hope for them in this present age, which not only is evil but is irretrievably so. Conditions will become worse rather than better. The righteous are helpless.

Their only hope, then, is that God will soon intervene with might and power, engaging Satan in a cosmic conflict that will involve the whole of creation. After his victory God will inaugurate a new age under his immediate control. The righteous followers of God will live under his rule in an eternity of blessedness as their reward for their loyalty and faithfulness to him. Thus, the apocalyptic hope is otherworldly—pessimistic concerning this present age of history, but optimistic concerning the age to come. Frequently, but not always, in apocalypticism, this earth, as well as this age, is brought to an end, to be replaced by a newly created, incorrupt earth, or by

the descent of a heavenly city. This dualism of the two earths, however, seems to have been subordinate to, and dependent on, the dualism of the two ages.

Apocalypticism, then, provides both an explanation of the evil that is so evident in this present age and a solution of the concrete problem of the righteous. In some way or other, Satan, who is evil, has gained control of this present age, and he is responsible for its wickedness and corruption and for the evils and oppression suffered by the righteous. However, with the overthrow of Satan by God and with the end of his age, all evil disappears; and the new age, ruled over by God, will be perfectly good and righteous.

Apocalypticism, then, may readily be differentiated from prophetism, messianism, and the expectation of the kingdom of God; for these are not dualistic, cosmic in scope, and eschatological, as is the apocalyptic hope. Instead, they are based upon the belief that God is in control of this age, not Satan, and that this age will not come to an end, but is improvable. A hope of the resurrection was in time added to this belief, but even so the basic position of apocalypticism is quite different.

**2. Secondary features.** The secondary features of apocalypticism add color and interest to the basic pattern, by imparting mystery and an appearance of complexity. But they should not obscure the relatively uncomplicated and simple nature of the basic pattern, nor should they be mistaken for the primary, essential elements of the pattern.

*a. Vision.* Because the term "apocalypse" is from a Greek word meaning a disclosure, a revelation, a vision, it is often asserted that an apocalypse must be a purported vision or series of visions. True enough, apocalypses are often of this kind (e.g., Daniel, II Esdras, and Revelation). On the other hand, Isa 24–27, an apocalyptic interpolation into the book of Isaiah, does not claim to be the report of a vision; neither do the little apocalypses in Did. 16; Asmp. Moses 10. Paul, although professing to be a visionary, does not state that his apocalyptic teachings (cf I Cor. 15:20-28) are visionary in origin. Lactantius presents his lengthy apocalypse in book VII of his *Divine Institutes* without any suggestion that it came to him in a vision. Likewise, certain apocalyptic sources which are embedded in longer works proposing to be visionary, such as the Apocalypse of Weeks in Enoch 93; 91:12-17, may not originally have claimed to be visions.

Actually, instead of being primary characteristics of apocalypses, purported visions are but a vehicle of presentation, a literary technique to gain attention and authority for a writing. A careful study of these apocalyptic visions will reveal their artificial character; they are not records of actual experiences, but are literary productions, using sources and conforming to traditional patterns.

Since an apocalypse is usually considered to be a vision, a number of works that are not apocalypses, but profess to be records of visionary experiences, are at times considered to be apocalyptic. This term is applied to works like EZEKIEL; HERMAS; and JUBILEES, but it is even more frequently used in speaking of reputed visions of the next life or of the next world, such as are found in the Testament of Abraham, the Life of Adam and Eve, II Cor. 12:1-4, Er's vision of the next world as related in Plato's *Republic*, the so-called Apocalypse of Paul, and Plutarch's account of the three-day visit by the soul of a certain Thespesius to the realm of the dead, where he saw the wicked being tortured. Some of these experiences are eschatological in character, but this does not necessarily make them apocalyptic, for apocalypticism involves a distinctive type of eschatology.

**b. Pseudonymity.** It is also stated quite frequently that pseudonymity (the literary device of ascribing a work to someone other than the actual author, usually to a person of importance, like Elijah, Enoch, Abraham, or Peter) is a basic characteristic of apocalypticism. Certainly it is characteristic of quite a number of apocalypses, among them I Enoch, Daniel, Peter, II Esdras, and the Ascension of Isaiah. But Paul uses his own name in writing I Cor. 15:20-28, as does Hippolytus in his *On Christ and Antichrist* and Lactantius in book VII of his *Divine Institutes*. It is quite possible that a certain Christian named John, but not John the apostle, wrote the book of Revelation. Isa. 24–27 apparently was originally anonymous, but it gains a certain aura of pseudonymity by being interpolated into the prophecy of Isaiah. Possibly still other apocalyptic sources now found in pseudonymous works were also originally anonymous. Pseudepigraphy, like purported visionary experiences, is an old but effective literary device for obtaining sanction and authority for an apocalyptic prediction. It is not a primary element in apocalypticism.

In this connection it should be noted that the pseudonymous nature of most of the extant apocalypses has a relationship to the visionary experiences reported in these writings. All too frequently when it is admitted that a given work is pseudonymous, it is also stated that the author was a true visionary, obtaining his knowledge through his visionary experiences. Daniel (from 7:2 on) is pseudonymous according to the great majority of scholars, written during the Maccabean period by someone unknown by name to us, who attributed his work to a much earlier person named Daniel. Yet it is stated at times that the author of Daniel was a visionary, relating his own personal experiences. If so, why did he attribute his visions to someone else—to Daniel—instead of claiming them for himself? The answer is rather obvious: the author of Daniel, whoever and whatever he was, was not a visionary—otherwise he would have claimed the marvelous visions in his book for himself (rather than attributing them to an ancient worthy). Thus there may be a relationship between pseudonymity and reputed apocalyptic visions in that both are literary devices to gain sanction for the author's message.

**c. A messiah.** Strangely enough, a messiah is also a secondary feature of apocalypticism, although, to be sure, the Christian apocalypses, perforce, have a messiah—namely, Jesus Christ (in his second advent, not his first). Jewish apocalypses may or may not have a messiah. None is presented in Isa. 24–27, and none in Daniel, for the Danielic Son of man is actually the personification of the righteous remnant of Israel. There is no messiah in the source known as the Apocalypse of Weeks in Enoch, nor in Asmp. Moses 10. The Elect One (Messiah) appears in a limited role in the final chapters of the Apocalypse of Abraham, but these chapters may be later additions to the book. On the other hand, the SON OF MAN, a glorious and powerful pre-existent heavenly messiah, plays an important part in the Similitudes of Enoch (cf. chs. 46; 48; 62–63; 69). A messiah of quite a different kind, a human being, symbolized as a bull with large horns, comes after the judgment in the dream-visions of Enoch (90:37), but he has no particular function. In II Esd. 7:28-29 the messiah appears without prior announcement, and dies after playing a rather vague role during the four-hundred-year messianic interval. The relatively unimportant role of the messiah in certain apocalyptic sources, together with his absence from others, indicates that he is an addition to the Jewish apocalyptic tradition and is not a primary element of the pattern. Christianity, as we have noted, of necessity introduced the heavenly Christ into its apocalypticism; but even in Revelation various angels perform functions that might more naturally be assigned to him in the cosmic drama that is taking place. This suggests that the Messiah was missing, perhaps, from a number of the sources used in Revelation.

With the introduction of a messiah of one kind or another into apocalypticism, it was in order to balance him with a Satanic counterpart, the antimessiah or ANTICHRIST. The Antichrist was introduced into Christian apocalyptic at an early period, and became increasingly significant. Even so, he is even more a secondary characteristic of apocalypticism than the messiah is.

Strictly speaking, without a messiah there can be no messianic kingdom between the present age ruled over by Satan and God's future age. An interim "week" between these two ages, but without a messiah, is predicted in the Apocalypse of Weeks in Enoch. As stated previously, II Esd. 7:28-29 provides a messianic interval with a messiah; however, nothing is said about this period save that the messiah and the righteous who survive the first age will rejoice during the four hundred years, and then will die. This messianic interim will be followed by the new age and the general resurrection. The neo-Hebraic Apocalypse of Elijah predicts a messianic interim of forty years, which are described as years of plenty. On the other hand, there is no messianic reign in such apocalyptic sources as Isa. 24–27, Daniel, the Assumption of Moses, and the Apocalypse of Abraham. Evidently it is an addition to the apocalyptic tradition, representing the merging of the apocalyptic hope with messianism; hence, it is a secondary feature, not a primary element of the basic apocalyptic pattern. Even in Christian sources like Mark 13 and parallels; II Thess. 2:1-12; II Pet. 3:1-12; Did. 16, the Second Coming is mentioned without any specific reference to an interim kingdom of Christ. Paul allows for such a reign, but its duration is not definite (I Cor. 15:24-26). Even in Revelation, Christ's interim kingdom of a thousand years is not accorded much significance insofar as space is concerned, for it is mentioned but briefly and all too vaguely in but three verses of a total of 404 verses for the entire book. This may indicate that the author did not attach much importance to this interim period, but introduced it into the pattern to provide a special but indefinite role to Jesus Christ on his return, as well as a unique reward for the Christian martyrs. *See* MILLENNIUM.

*d. Angelology and demonology.* Apocalypticism is frequently marked by elaborate angelology and demonology, with archangels and other good angels on God's side in the cosmic drama, and fallen angels and evil spirits on the other side. There is a considerable amount of angelology, and in some cases demonology as well, in sources like Daniel, the Ascension of Isaiah, Revelation, and certain sections of Enoch. On the other hand, there is little or none in other sources, such as Isa. 24–27; the Apocalypse of Weeks; Did. 16; Asmp. Moses 10; or even in the much later book VII of Lactantius' *Divine Institutes.* Angelology and demonology were much more in evidence in Judaism following the Persian period than in earlier times, and are to be found in nonapocalyptic as well as in apocalyptic sources. Angels and evil spirits found their way into some apocalypses, but not into all. With God becoming a transcendent deity in the apocalypses, it was but natural that hosts of angels of one kind or another were assigned to do much of his work in the world. Accordingly, in Revelation the angels are very numerous and perform various functions. In order to maintain a cosmic balance, fallen angels and evil spirits were introduced as their Satanic counterparts. It need not be considered, however, that angels and demons are essential to apocalypticism; they are secondary, not primary, features.

*e. Animal symbolism.* A further secondary characteristic is that of animal and bird symbolism, at times bizarre in character, and in part mythological or astrological in origin. Such symbolism is not restricted to apocalypticism, but is provided by Ezekiel (the four living creatures); II Esd. 11 (the eagle vision, a messianic passage); II Bar. 29 (Behemoth and Leviathan); Pss. Sol. 2:29 (a dragon); and in other nonapocalyptic sources. On the other hand, this type of symbolism is present in certain apocalypses. The beasts of Daniel and Revelation are well known. Animal symbolism is also present in Isa. 24–27; in the dream-visions of Enoch 83–90; and in the Apocalypse of Abraham, e.g. But such symbolism is missing from the Similitudes and from the Apocalypse of Weeks in Enoch, from Asmp. Moses 10; from Did. 16; from the Ascension of Isaiah; and from the Apocalypse of Peter. Surely this type of symbolism, despite its frequent appearance in apocalypses, must be considered a secondary, not a primary, element of apocalypticism. Still other types of symbolism are used in apocalyptic writings, as is true of certain prophetic works as well. Indeed, some of the apocalyptic symbolism was borrowed from the prophetic books, as a comparison of Revelation, e.g., with certain of the OT prophets will readily show. On the other hand, there are other prophetic and apocalyptic writings that are practically devoid of colorful symbolism of any type.

*f. Numerology.* It is also averred that apocalypticism is characterized by numerology. This, in part, is true of Daniel, and to a considerable degree of Revelation, but the latter is by no means typical in this respect. Certainly ancient peoples, Jews and Christians among them, considered that numbers had some mystical significance. Consequently, numerology is to be found in both apocalyptic and nonapocalyptic writings. Furthermore, there are sources of both types in which no numerology is in evidence. Here, again, numerology is a popular belief that has been used in some apocalypses, disused in others.

*g. Predicted woes.* Another purportedly characteristic feature of apocalypticism is a list of stereotyped woes preceding the end of this present age. True enough, lists of this type, predicting terrestrial disasters and cosmic disturbances, are found in apocalypses, in Asmp. Moses 10, the Apocalypse of Abraham, and Revelation, e.g. But they are also present in prophetic books (as in Joel 3:14 ff) and in messianic sources (cf. II Bar. 70). There is no list of woes in Daniel, which merely states that before the end there will be a time of trouble such as there has never been before (12:1). This general statement may have been an occasion for the inclusion of specific woes in later apocalypses. However, there is an embryonic list in Isa. 24:18-20, an early source, which may have suggested later lists. Terrestrial disasters and cosmic disturbances involving irregularities in the heavenly bodies are not unrelated, for in keeping with astral thinking, what is to occur on earth has already been determined in heaven by the stars.

*h. Astral influences.* According to astral beliefs, the zodiac with its constellations was a heavenly tablet or book predetermining the deeds and fate of mankind. Judaism, and later, Christianity, appropriated this concept, so that in both apocalyptic and nonapocalyptic sources heavenly books of various types are mentioned—those that predict the future, and those that record the deeds which men have already committed. These heavenly books, when mentioned, are interesting additions to the apocalyptic tradition. In a sense, it might be noted, each apocalypse, or portion thereof, which predicts the future on the basis of a visit to heaven by the writer or a revelation made to him by an angel is a heavenly book (as are the Ten Commandments or the Koran).

The belief in a heavenly city, misnamed the New Jerusalem, which is the perfect heavenly pattern of its earthly counterpart, goes back, again, to astral thinking. Actually, the New Jerusalem is not "new," since it existed in heaven before the earthly one could come into being. Comparable to this belief in a heavenly city is that of a heavenly Garden of Eden, and a heavenly tree of life. These astral concepts appear in a few of the apocalypses, with the additional view that in the age to come the righteous would live in the heavenly Jerusalem or in the heavenly Garden of Eden, or in a combination of both (Enoch 90:29; II Esd. 7:26; 10:25-28; Apocalypse of Abraham 21; Apocalypse of Peter 15-16; Rev. 21–22; the neo-Hebraic Apocalypse of Elijah; *see* ELIJAH, APOCALYPSE OF). In some instances (e.g., Revelation and Elijah) the heavenly city and garden descend to earth.

As has been noted, determinism has been in evidence in apocalyptic thinking. In part this stems from astralism, in part from faith in the omnipotence of God. The end is predetermined; Satan is to be overcome and his age brought to an end; God's new age is to be established; those who are to be saved are predetermined; likewise, the time when the end is to take place has been set. Marked though this aspect of determinism is, it is not in order to say that it was an original and indispensable part of the apocalyptic pattern. It is possible that apocalypticism itself is a development of astralism, with its concept of the perfect heavenly pattern and the imperfect earthly copy, which could have led to a dualism in space of heaven and earth and in time of this age and the next, the first related to the earth, the second to heaven. This, however, is a surmise for which adequate evidence is lacking.

**3. The relevance of apocalyptic.** Apocalypticism is hopelessly pessimistic concerning this present age of human history, which is evil and corrupt, with no prospect whatever of betterment or improvement. Since it is irredeemable, it must be brought to a calamitous end by divine intervention. Along with this pessimism there went the related conviction that there is nothing the righteous can do to make this age a better time in which to live. Everything awaits God's expected intervention. Thus mankind is relieved of responsibility for the evils of this age. The doctrine of the kingdom of God is quite different. According to it God has not abdicated this earth to Satan; furthermore, this present (and only) age is capable of improvement if men will only learn and do God's will. Consequently, the kingdom-of-God concept is optimistic insofar as this present age is concerned, and requires that men help to improve it. The defeatism of apocalypticism may well account for the almost complete absence of ethical and social teachings from the apocalypses (II Enoch 49 ff is indeed an exception). Righteousness, for the most part, consists of loyalty and devotion to God, and is related in the main to nation or to cultus. Wickedness, on the other hand, is marked by idolatry and by the oppression of the righteous, or it may consist of being a member of a nation other than Judaism or of a religion other than Christianity.

Even so, apocalypticism has had and will continue to have a great influence, and in the main the more difficult, dismal, arduous, and perplexing the times are, the greater the influence will be. In general, it has been most widely accepted among the have-nots, the poor, the dispossessed, the oppressed, and the persecuted; this, no doubt, partly accounts for the adoption of it by the early Christians. In fact, oppression and persecution seem to have been strong incentives for the writing of apocalypses.

The strong appeal of apocalypticism down through the centuries is also in part due to its uncomplicated explanation for the existence of evil and to its strikingly dramatic solution of this age-long problem. Moreover, as the cosmic drama of the conflict between the forces of good and evil is portrayed, the reader or listener may come to think of himself as being involved in a great cosmic process; as being, indeed, not merely an interested spectator, but more a personal participant in the triumph of the forces of good over the forces of evil.

Mistaken though apocalypticism has been in its world view and in its concept of a transcendent avenging deity, it has not been without significance in the history of both Judaism and Christianity. It strengthened both Jews and Christians in times of persecution, when the former were persecuted by the Syrians and when both were persecuted by the Romans. Although it assumes that for the time being God has removed himself from the world and his people, it teaches that before long he will assume his sovereignty so that finally right will triumph over wrong. If man should believe that he, unaided, can work out his own salvation and correct the ills of the world, apocalypticism may serve as a corrective to human pride, but not necessarily the best corrective. Its emphasis upon eternal rewards for the persecuted and eternal punishments for the persecutors marks a step in the development of Christian views concerning life after death, including the resurrection, the judgment, and rewards and punishments. Revelation in particular has made its imprint upon Christian art, music, and liturgy. Much of our present theological thinking has been influenced directly or indirectly by apocalypticism. Consequently, it is essential to have an understanding of its basic features.

*See also* DANIEL § 2h.

**Bibliography.** E. Kautzsch, *Die Apokryphen und Pseudepigraphen des Alten Testaments* (1900). R. H. Charles, *The Apoc. and Pseudep. of the OT* (1913); *A Critical History of the Doctrine of a Future Life in Israel, in Judaism, and in Christianity* (1913). F. C. Burkitt, *Jewish and Christian Apocalypses* (1914). H. H. Rowley, *The Relevance of Apocalyptic* (rev. ed., 1946).

M. RIST

**APOCRYPHA** ə pŏk′rə fə. The title applied, in ordinary Protestant usage, to a collection of fourteen or fifteen books, or parts of books, which at one time stood in our English Bibles between the OT and the NT. These books are, according to the RSV, the following: I and II Esdras; Tobit; Judith; the Additions to the Book of Esther; the Wisdom of Solomon; Ecclesiasticus, or the Wisdom of Jesus the Son of Sirach; Baruch, including the Letter of Jeremiah; the Prayer of Azariah and the Song of the Three Young Men; Susanna; Bel and the Dragon; the Prayer of Manasseh; I and II Maccabees. *See* the individual entries for the discussion of each of these works. (For discussion of the NT Apoc., *see* APOCRYPHA, NT.)

These books, with one or two exceptions, came to be included in the SEPTUAGINT, or Greek translation of the OT, but not in the Hebrew scriptures as finally "canonized" by the Council of Jamnia (*ca.* A.D. 90). They were all written during the last two centuries B.C. and the first century A.D. Among the Apocrypha may be found books of history, like I and II Maccabees; romantic tales, like Tobit and Judith; a beautiful liturgical psalm in the Prayer of Manasseh; two masterpieces of the wisdom school, Ecclesiasticus and the Wisdom of Solomon; and an apocalyptic work in II Esdras. There are also additions to the canonical books of Esther, Jeremiah, and Daniel. All these books were written originally in Hebrew or Aramaic, with the exception of the Wisdom of Solomon and II Maccabees, which were composed in Greek. The fact that the Hebrew and Aramaic works were translated into Greek, and, together with the Wisdom of Solomon and II Maccabees, were circulated with the Greek OT, shows how popular this literature was in the intertestamental period. Other Jewish writings from this time include the so-called PSEUDEPIGRAPHA, hitherto unknown works discovered in the library of MSS at Qumran (*see* DEAD SEA SCROLLS), and numerous books now lost, but referred to in patristic literature. This extensive literature is not only important source material for our knowledge of the history, culture, and religion of Judaism, but it is also invaluable for our understanding of the background of the NT.

1. The term "apocrypha"
2. The Apoc. in Judaism
3. The Apoc. in Christianity
   *a.* The early church
   *b.* The Reformation view
Bibliography

**1. The term "apocrypha."** The word "apocrypha" is a Greek plural neuter adjective meaning "hidden (books)." As a literary term it was first applied to books which were to be kept from the public because of the esoteric wisdom they contained. In this sense it was a title of honor, since it referred to books whose secret doctrines imparted to them special authority. Among the esoteric works which were thus highly regarded at first were the Greek Gnostic writings and the Jewish Christian apocalyptic works. After the destruction of Jerusalem, however, in A.D. 70, the apocalyptic works were outlawed in Judaism; this may have been one reason for the deterioration of the term "apocrypha."

At any rate, the word "apocrypha" came to mean "spurious," or "heretical," since those who were not initiated into the secret lore of this literature believed that these hidden books contained heretical teachings which were especially harmful. As a result, books of this nature were put under a ban and were forbidden to be read in public or for private edification. Athanasius (died 373) and Rufinus (died 410) used the term "apocrypha" in this way.

The present usage of the word to designate certain religious books which are not canonical goes back to the time of Jerome (died 420). He held that the books found in the Greek and Latin Bibles but not in the Hebrew canon should be put among the Apoc., and used only for edification, and not for confirming the dogmas of the church. Obviously, for Jerome, "apocryphal" meant noncanonical, and not heretical, and it is this meaning of the term that has persisted in Protestant circles today.

The reason for this identification of "hidden" books with books "outside the canon," or "outside books," as the Jews called them, is probably to be found in certain passages from the apocalyptic work of II Esdras, where a clear distinction is made between works that are to be published and read openly and those that are to be kept for the wise only.

In II Esd. 14:4-6 we read that Ezra heard the voice of the Most High say: "I led him [Moses] up on Mount Sinai, where I kept him with me many days; and I told him many wondrous things, and showed him the secrets of the times and declared to him the end of the times. Then I commanded him, saying, 'These words you shall publish openly, and these you shall keep secret.' " The writer here is obviously referring to the Torah of Moses, on the one hand, which was published for all to read, and to the apocalyptic tradition on the other, which was not for public perusal. This idea of sealing up the apocalyptic teaching in a book goes back to Dan. 12:4, 9, which may well be the fundamental passage for our conception of the word "apocrypha."

In II Esd. 12:37-38 Ezra himself is instructed to "write all these things that you have seen in a book, and put it in a hidden place; and you shall teach them to the wise among your people, whose hearts you know are able to comprehend and keep these secrets."

It is 14:42-46, however, which is particularly relevant to our problem. Here we read: "The Most High gave understanding to the five men, and by turns they wrote what was dictated, in characters which they did not know. They sat forty days, and wrote during the daytime, and ate their bread at night. As for me, I spoke in the daytime and was not silent at night. So during the forty days ninety-four books were written. And when the forty days were ended, the Most High spoke to me, saying, 'Make public the twenty-four books that you wrote first and let the worthy and the unworthy read them; but keep the seventy that were written last, in order to give them to the wise among your people.' " Here is evidently the origin of the term "apocrypha" in the sense of "noncanonical." The first twenty-four books, which were written and then published, were obviously the canonical books of the Hebrew OT; the last seventy were the "hidden" books—i.e., the Apoc. —which were to be set apart for the wise among the Jews.

Around the beginning of the twentieth century F. C. Porter, following an opinion ventured by Julius Wellhausen, suggested that the origin of many of the esoteric ideas found in these "outside books" was to be sought among the Essenes, since this sect possessed secret lore and hidden books, and even took oaths not to disclose any of their doctrines to others. Today this theory seems more probable than ever with the discovery of the Essene community center at Qumran and its enormous library of MSS, which includes numerous copies of these "outside books," as well as some MSS written in cryptic scripts.

**2. The Apoc. in Judaism.** As has already been noted, the Apoc. were but a small part of a vast number of "outside books" written by the Jews between 200 B.C. and A.D. 100. These works, described in Judaism as "writings which do not defile the hands," enjoyed great popularity at first, as we see by the large number of MSS of individual works discovered at Qumran, and by the fact that both Hebrew and Aramaic copies of many of these works circulated among the people. The problem of the formal canonization of these books probably never arose at this time. At least, there does not appear any attempt to settle it by drawing up a list of the "scriptures" as such. The Law and the Prophets had acquired their "sanctity" because of their contents, which were the basis of the authoritative religious instruction and belief of the Jewish people. The Writings, which enjoyed less prestige than either the Law or the Prophets, were in a fluid state during this period, although books like the Psalms, Proverbs, and Job must have received a more or less canonical status quite early. But what about the ever-increasing stream of "outside books" which were being written during this period and were being read side by side with the Hebrew scriptures? How were these works to be collected and arranged? Which were to be considered "canonical," and which were not?

That there were different orders of books, particularly in the Prophets and the Writings, and that the number of "canonical" books varied, are well-known facts. A newly discovered witness to this fluid condition of the "canon" in Palestine before the days of Jamnia is the library at Qumran, where many MSS of works later condemned or neglected by Judaism have come to light. So far, only two fragments of Ecclesiasticus in Hebrew and three fragmentary MSS of Tobit, one in Hebrew and two in Aramaic, have turned up at Qumran of the books of the Apoc. Many more pseudepigraphical works, known and unknown, are represented among the fragments from Qumran. It is to be hoped, by the way, that the term "apocrypha" (with C. C. Torrey) or "outside books" (Jewish) will henceforth be used for this body of intertestamental literature, and that the clumsy and misleading term PSEUDEPIGRAPHA will be discarded.

As Eissfeldt remarks in the second edition of his *Einleitung* (1956), these discoveries clearly show that the indigenous Jewish community at Qumran knew a collection of sacred writings similar in extent to the Greek canon. In other words, the Alexandrian "canon," which probably never existed as such, is simply the survival of a less rigid type of "canon" which was known in Palestine before the days of Jamnia (*ca.* A.D. 90).

After the fall of Jerusalem in A.D. 70, however, these "outside books" came upon hard times in Judaism. The tragic events of the First Jewish Revolt, culminating in the downfall of Jerusalem, dealt the deathblow to the hopes and dreams of the Jewish apocalyptists, whose writings now became banned. The apocalyptic tradition, which had played such an important role in the life of Judaism since the days of Daniel, was now repudiated, and the Torah became the main rallying point of the Jews. Besides this, a rapidly growing Christian Aramaic literature and the easy possibility of Christian interpolations in the Jewish "outside books" made it necessary for the rabbis to take drastic action against these works and set up a canon of legitimate books which could be read by the pious Jew without harm. This was done at the Council of Jamnia (A.D. 90).

Fortunately for us, two contemporary sources give us the principle of selection used by the rabbis at Jamnia to distinguish between canonical and noncanonical books. One of these sources, II Esd. 14:45-46, has already been discussed (*see* § 1 *above*) in another connection. Here Ezra is described as dictating, through divine inspiration, the twenty-four books of the Hebrew Bible, as well as seventy esoteric (apocalyptic) works, in forty days. The clear meaning of this passage is that the OT canon was completely and forever closed in the time of Ezra.

The other source is Josephus, who says: "For there are not with us myriads of books, discordant and discrepant, but only two and twenty, comprising the history of all time, which are justly accredited." He then goes on to describe these books, after which he makes the important statement: "From the time of Artaxerxes up to our own everything has been recorded, but the records have not been accounted equally worthy of credit with those written before them, because the exact succession of prophets ceased" (Apion I.8). Josephus is a little more explicit

about the principle of canonicity than the author of II Esdras, for he says that the Lord no longer revealed himself to the prophets after the time of Artaxerxes—i.e., after the time of Ezra. According to this principle of selection, then, the rabbis of Jamnia automatically excluded I and II Maccabees, since they dealt with a later period of Jewish history; and Ecclesiasticus, whose author manifestly lived long after the time of Ezra. Other works were excluded on the basis of their having been written in Greek (e.g., the Wisdom of Solomon), and still others because they had ceased to be popular and so were no longer copied after their translation into Greek.

Thus the "outside books," including both the apocalypses and the Apoc., simply ceased to exist among the Jews or were systematically destroyed. The only one that seems to have escaped this fate was Ecclesiasticus, which is quoted as scripture three times in the Talmud and which survived in Hebrew until the twelfth century. According to later Jewish writings, all "outside books" were considered dangerous, as the following quotations indicate: "Whoever brings together in his house more than twenty-four books [the canonical Scriptures] brings confusion" (Midrash Qoheleth 12.12), and Rabbi Akiba's statement that among those who have no part in the world to come are "he who reads in the outside books" (J. T. Sanh. X.1, folio 28a). The survival, therefore, of this great body of literature is due entirely to the Christians who found these works especially interesting and edifying in their Greek dress, and who copied them often and translated them into other languages.

**3. The Apoc. in Christianity. *a. The early church.*** When the Christians, the "Israel of God" (Gal. 6: 16), fell heir to the OT, they found in the Greek Bible which they used a number of works which were not in the Hebrew scriptures. These favored "extracanonical" books, which were a part of a vast number of Jewish writings, had been familiar to the early Jewish Christians from childhood. There was no reason in the early days of the Christian church, therefore, to ban the Apoc., or even to disparage them, and so the early Christians continued to read them for edification and enlightenment, and even to quote from them as holy scripture.

Another important factor which led the early church to place the Apoc. on the same level with the canonical books of the OT was the introduction of the book, or codex, in Christian circles. In contrast with the Jewish custom of using the scroll for their sacred books, the Christians copied and distributed their scriptures in books or codices, where the OT canonical books and the Apoc. were side by side between the same two covers. It thus was natural for the Christians, many of whom were unfamiliar with the extent of the Hebrew canon, to treat as inspired scripture whatever was found in their OT codices.

Although there are no direct quotations from the Apoc. in the NT, the influence of these books is felt in every part of the Christian scriptures. In fact, they serve as a kind of bridge between the OT and the NT. In these books, e.g., we read for the first time about the Pharisees and Sadducees, who figure so largely in the NT story. The strong belief in demons and angels which we find in the NT can best be understood in the light of works like Tobit and II Maccabees. And above all, most of the ideas regarding the future life which are found in the NT writings had their origin in the apocalyptic writings, represented by II Esdras in the Apoc.

The NT writers, as well as their readers, were well acquainted with the Jewish "outside books." Direct quotations from the Pseudep., as well as references to unknown works, are scattered throughout the NT writings, and there are definite allusions and reminiscences which recall the phraseology of the Apoc. and the events described therein. Several sayings of Jesus are strikingly similar to certain passages from Ecclesiasticus (e.g., Matt. 11:28-30 and Ecclus. 51:23 ff; Matt. 9:16-17 and Ecclus. 9:10), and the parable of the rich fool, spoken by our Lord (Luke 12:16-20), is reminiscent of the description of the rich man in Ecclus. 11:18-19. The influence of the Wisdom of Solomon upon Paul has long been recognized in several of his letters, especially in his Letter to the Romans. Some of the significant expressions used in the sublime description of Christ found in Heb. 1:1-3 are drawn directly from Wisd. Sol. 7:25-27, where wisdom is described as a "reflection of eternal light, a spotless mirror of the working of God." Later on in the same letter (11:35-37), there is a clear reference to the terrible martyrdom of the seven brothers depicted in II Macc. 6-7. The Letter of James, commonly recognized as a "wisdom book" among the early Christian writings, contains many allusions to the wisdom literature of both the OT and the Apoc. An interesting reference to the Feast of Dedication, or Hanukkah, is found in John 10:22. This is the Maccabean celebration of the rededication of the temple in Jerusalem, referred to in I Macc. 4:59; II Macc. 10:8. These allusions, and many others not mentioned here, are convincing proof that the NT writers were well acquainted with the Apoc. and used them for religious instruction and example.

The early church fathers treated the canonical and noncanonical books much alike, for reasons already noted. They often quoted from the Apoc. in the same way as they quoted from the canonical books of scripture. I Clement, e.g., one of the earliest Christian writings outside the NT that has come down to us (*ca.* A.D. 95), includes quotations from the Wisdom of Solomon. Polycarp, bishop of Smyrna (died *ca.* 156), quotes from Tobit. The Letter of Barnabas, from the first half of the second century, quotes from the Wisdom of Solomon, Ecclesiasticus, and II Esdras. Tertullian of Carthage (died *ca.* 225) and Irenaeus of Lyons (died *ca.* 200) cite certain of the apocryphal books as part of scripture. Hippolytus of Rome (died *ca.* 236) included in his commentary on Daniel the apocryphal additions of Susanna and the Song of the Three Children. Clement and Origen of Alexandria (died *ca.* 220 and 250 respectively) and Cyprian of Carthage (died *ca.* 260) believed that the Apoc. were part of the Christian Bible. Also in the lists of "canonical books" drawn up from time to time in the various centers of Christianity the books of the Apoc. are found in varying numbers and order. In the earliest list we have of NT books, the Muratorian Fragment (*ca.* 200), the Wisdom of Solomon actually appears as a book of the NT. And finally, certain local synods, mainly in the West, confirmed the Apoc. as canonical.

All this evidence would seem to indicate that the early church accepted the Apoc. as scripture and included them in the Bible. But this was not actually the case. Origen, who, as we have noted, accepted the Apoc. as scripture, was enough of a Hebrew scholar to know that these books were not part of the Hebrew Bible. Therefore, as a churchman, Origen followed the practice of using the Apoc. for instruction and edification, but as a scholar he was compelled to limit the OT canon to the books of the Hebrew Bible. This same problem arose in the minds of Cyril of Jerusalem (died 386) and Jerome (died 420), who were more explicit in separating the Apoc. from the canonical books. In fact, it was these two scholars who used the term "Apocrypha" for the first time to designate the books in the Greek and Latin Bibles which were over and above the Hebrew OT. Jerome explicitly stated that the OT Apoc. might be read for edification, but not "for confirming the authority of Church dogmas" (Prologue to Books of Solomon). Yet, because of the practice of the church, he had to include the Apoc. in his Latin Bible, the Vulg., which became the official Roman Catholic Bible. Augustine (died 430) gave powerful support to the church view by accepting the Apoc. as canonical, although he too in his later works admitted that there was a distinct difference between the books of the Hebrew canon and the "outside books."

In the Greek Orthodox Church the Apoc., or certain books among the Apoc., have generally been recognized as canonical. In the Syriac-speaking church, which was at first under strong Jewish influence, the OT originally contained the books of the Hebrew canon (minus Chronicles, Ezra-Nehemiah, and Esther) and Ecclesiasticus. Eventually, however, the view of the Western Christian church prevailed, except among the Nestorians, and the Apoc. came to be regarded as canonical.

It is clear from this survey that there were two opposing views of the Apoc. in the early church: one which regarded these books as canonical, representing the traditional view of the church; and the other, which regarded them as uncanonical in view of the Hebrew scriptures. These two divergent attitudes, which were never resolved in the early church, continue today in the Roman Catholic Church, which accepts the Apoc. as canonical, and in the Protestant tradition, which has never regarded these "outside books" as sacred scripture.

*b. The Reformation view.* Throughout the Middle Ages, Augustine's view of the Apoc. prevailed, for the most part, over that of Jerome. For most Christians all the books in the OT of the Vulg. were on the same plane. Yet there were some scholars and theologians who never forgot the words of Jerome and claimed that the books of the Hebrew OT alone were divinely inspired. Nicholas of Lyra (died *ca.* 1340), e.g., who was a Christian of Jewish parentage, wrote a commentary on the canonical books of the Hebrew OT, and then another one on the "uncanonical" scriptures, which included the most important works of the Apoc. Later on, he published

"A Treatise on the Difference between our Version [the Vulg.] and the Hebrew Truth." This scholar had a marked influence on Luther, who was to set the Apoc. apart from the rest of the OT books in his German translation of the Bible. Wycliffe's Bible (1382) contained only the books of the Hebrew Bible, the Preface indicating on the basis of Jerome's words that those writings which stood outside the OT canon were "without authority of belief." Even Cardinal Cajetan, the foe of Luther, sensed the difference between the canonical works of the Hebrew scriptures and such works as Judith, Tobit, and I and II Maccabees, and appealed to no less an authority than Jerome himself for approval.

When the reformers broke loose from the authority of the church of Rome, they were naturally concerned with the question of the authority of the scriptures. Since the Bible now was the supreme authority in matters of faith and conduct, it became necessary and urgent to deal with the ever-present problem of the relation of the Apoc. to the canonical scriptures. With the original Hebrew text of the OT open before them, with the words of Jerome ringing in their ears, and with their dislike for some of the doctrines that the Roman church had derived from these Apoc., it did not take long for the reformers to make up their minds about the authenticity of the Apoc. Luther, following the German scholar Karlstadt, gathered the outside books together, which were scattered among the OT canonical writings in the Greek and Latin MSS, and placed them at the end of the OT in his German translation of the Bible (1534) under the following title: "Apocrypha. These books are not held equal to the sacred scriptures, and yet are useful and good for reading." This was the beginning of the end for the Apoc. in Protestant circles, for their inferior rank was now emphasized by their position between the testaments, and their being grouped together made it more easy to remove them in a body from the Bible, if and when desired.

The Roman church, not to be outdone by this vigorous reaction of Protestant leaders against the Apoc., declared in the Council of Trent (1546) that whoever did not recognize as sacred and canonical all the books contained in the Vulg. would be anathema. This decision was later confirmed by the Vatican Council of 1870. The three works, I and II Esdras and the Prayer of Manasseh, which were not included in the sacred catalogue of the Council of Trent, were later included in smaller type as an appendix to the NT in the standard Clementine edition of the Vulg. (1592). For convenience' sake, Roman Catholic scholars often refer to the Apoc. as "deutero-canonical" works—with no intention of implying, however, that they are of inferior rank or authority.

Luther's innovation of segregating the books of the Apoc. was followed in other translations of the Bible into French, the Scandinavian languages, English, etc. Most of the English editions of the Bible followed this arrangement of the books until 1626, when some copies of the KJV began to appear without the Apoc. included in them. The growing antagonism to these noncanonical books in Great Britain and on the Continent finally led the British and Foreign Bible Society, followed by the American Bible Society, to announce in 1827 that henceforth they would "exclude in their printed copies of the English Bible the circulation of those books, or parts of books, which are usually termed Apocryphal."

In Protestantism no denomination officially accepts the Apoc. as canonical scriptures, but there are various opinions regarding their value. The Anglican confession, on the one hand, recognizes that these books are instructive and edifying without being inspired. This position is best summarized in Article Six of the Thirty-nine Articles: "In the name of Holy Scripture we do understand those canonical books of the Old and New Testament, of whose authority there was never any doubt in the Church. . . . And the other Books (as Jerome saith) the Church doth read for example of life and instruction of manners; but yet doth it not apply them to establish any doctrine."

On the other hand, the Calvinistic view, followed by most Protestant churches today, is that these books should be rejected as of no authority in the church. This position is explicitly stated in the third article of the Westminster Confession (1647): "The books commonly called Apocrypha, not being of divine inspiration, are not part of the Canon of Scripture; and therefore are of no authority in the Church of God, nor to be in any otherwise approved, or made use of, than other human writings."

The long-standing controversy regarding the canonicity of the Apoc. has thus ended in a stalemate, with each side regarding its decision as final and irrevocable. The Roman church, holding that the church is authoritative in all matters of canon, has declared the Apoc. to be canonical; the Protestant view that the OT alone is canonical has led to the firm rejection of the Apoc. as divinely inspired scripture by all major Protestant bodies. There seems little hope of breaking this deadlock.

It should be added, however, that the attitude toward the Apoc. has changed considerably in recent history. All the outside books have come under the careful scrutiny of the biblical scholar, who must treat these works as part of the biblical tradition. Since the publication of R. H. Charles's *Apoc. and Pseudep.* in 1913, the scientific study of these writings has advanced rapidly. A translation of the Apoc. by E. J. Goodspeed from the best critical Greek text has been another milestone in the study of these writings; and another translation, under the auspices of the National Council of Churches, has now been published. The discovery of the MSS at Qumran has already given impetus to an even more intensive scientific investigation of the intertestamental period and its voluminous literature. Perhaps the best evaluation of the present status of the Apoc. is that found in the E. J. Goodspeed's Preface to *The Complete Bible:* "It has been truly said that no one can have the complete Bible, as a source book for the cultural study of art, literature, history, and religion, without the Apocrypha. From the earliest Christian times down to the age of the King James Version, they belonged to the Bible; and, while modern critical judgments and religious attitudes deny them a position of equality with the Old and New Testament scriptures, historically and culturally they are still an integral part of the Bible."

*Bibliography.* J. P. Lange, "Commentary on the Holy Scriptures," in E. C. Bissell, *The Apoc. of the OT with Historical Introductions, A Revised Translation, and Notes Critical and Explanatory*, vol. XV (1886). "The Speaker's Commentary," in H. Wace, ed., *Apoc.* (2 vols.; 1888). W. H. Daubney, *The Use of the Apoc. in the Christian Church* (1900). H. M. Hughes, *The Ethics of Jewish Apocryphal Literature* (1910). R. H. Charles, ed., *The Apoc. and Pseudep. in English* (2 vols.; 1913); *Religious Development Between the Old and the New Testaments* (1914). H. J. Wicks, *The Doctrine of God in the Jewish Apocryphal and Apocalyptic Literature* (1915). R. Marcus, *Law in the Apoc.* (1927). W. O. E. Oesterley, *An Introduction to the Books of the Apoc.* (1935). R. H. Malden, *The Apoc.* (1936). E. J. Goodspeed, *The Apoc.: An American Translation* (1938); *The Story of the Apoc.* (1939). C. C. Torrey, *The Apocryphal Literature: A Brief Introduction* (1945). N. B. Johnson, *Prayer in the Apoc. and Pseudep.: A Study of the Jewish Concept of God* (1948). R. H. Pfeiffer, *History of NT Times, with an Introduction to the Apoc.* (1949); "The Literature and Religion of the Apoc.," *IB*, I (1952), 391-419. R. C. Dentan, *The Apoc., Bridge of the Testaments* (1954). B. M. Metzger, *An Introduction to the Apoc.* (1957). On lost apocrypha, see: M. R. James, *The Lost Apocrypha of the OT: Their Titles and Fragments* (1920). C. T. FRITSCH

\*APOCRYPHA, NT. The NT Apoc. or, as it is often styled, the Apocryphal NT, consists of a host of books of all sorts, primarily gospels, acts, letters, and apocalypses—i.e., of books similar to, at least externally, the several kinds of writing in the canonical NT. These were composed, for the most part, to amplify and embroider matters touched on or suggested by the canonical writings, and, in part, to serve as substitutes for such among sects or groups in varying degrees remote from the main stream of catholic—i.e., orthodox—Christianity. The writings are of very different values and of very different dates, ranging from early in the second century to the present day.

The use of the term "apocrypha," meaning "hidden" or "secret," is far from happy for such writings. The word properly refers to secret or esoteric writings, regarded as having been written centuries before but supernaturally kept secret until the latter days. This was true of many writings, but hardly of these. In addition, the term suggests a parallel between these writings and those of the OT APOCRYPHA, which is quite unwarranted. The use of the term stems from the days when it had acquired the adverse meaning of "spurious" or "false." The confusion has been heightened by the publication of such volumes as William Hone's *The Apocryphal NT* (1820), which lifted bodily, and without acknowledgment, portions of nine of these writings from an earlier volume by Jeremiah Jones, and combined them with Archbishop Wake's version of the APOSTOLIC FATHERS, writings which are totally distinct and in no proper sense of the word apocryphal. The unfortunate impression, fostered by Hone's mischievous volume, that these books were suppressed by the same imaginary group who determined the Christian canon, has been heightened by the utterly unjustified claims made for other volumes of modern apocrypha, such as the so-called *Lost Books of the Bible*.

The writings properly designated by the now common term "NT Apoc." may all be styled, without the charge of oversimplification, religious. Many of them are trivial, some are highly theatrical, some are disgusting, even loathsome; nonetheless, they may properly be styled religious. Their purpose, with but few possible exceptions, was to enforce what to the particular writer seemed sound Christian beliefs. This at times takes the form of revealing new doctrines or new truths; of extolling or dilating upon some particular virtue or kind of life; of emphasizing or embroidering some spectacular doctrine, such as the virgin birth, the physical resurrection, the second coming of Christ, the future state, with especial attention to the torments and tortures of the damned; and, perhaps most conspicuous of all, of amplifying laconic and intriguing incidents and, on the authority of big names from the past, filling in certain "gaps" or "silences" or answering questions raised or at least suggested by the earlier writings.

Some of these writings were definitely the products of sects ranging all the way from reasonable orthodoxy to what was regarded the rankest and most reprehensible heresy. Many of them are scarcely more than copies—sometimes greatly expanded, sometimes drastically abridged—of earlier writings of a similar nature.

That any of them preserve authentic traditions of words or doings of their heroes—notably Jesus, the apostles, the Virgin, and other characters in the canonical NT books—is most unlikely. Occasionally it has been argued that material parallel with, but external to, that in the canonical gospels may well have stood in some of the earlier of apocryphal writings—notably the Gospel According to the Hebrews and the Gospel According to the Egyptians (*see* HEBREWS, GOSPEL ACCORDING TO THE; EGYPTIANS, GOSPEL ACCORDING TO THE), now known to us solely from occasional quotations and obscure references in the fathers; further, that were copies of these writings to be discovered, they would be found of equal, if not actually of superior, value to our canonical accounts. The nature of the quotations which are preserved and the inferences apparently to be drawn from them would not seem to warrant such conclusions, while the nature of those writings which have been preserved in whole or in sizable parts would certainly not tend to make such assumptions probable.

For the most part these writings may be styled a parasite growth—i.e., they are simply expansion, imaginative development, or dilation, of themes and incidents in the canonical writings, frequently in markedly biblical idiom and with constant irresponsible transfer of such materials (with rewriting) from one character to another. A striking example of this constant practice is to be found in the story of the birth of Mary and her upbringing in the temple, which is a greatly expanded and glamorized revision of the story of Samuel. This practice is especially conspicuous in the apocryphal Acts, notably the Acts of Thomas, but is characteristic of this whole type of writing. To deny the possibility of any historical fact or tradition's being preserved in these writings, simply because they are uncanonical, would obviously be totally unwarranted, but examination of the texts themselves fails to reveal the presence of any such fact or tradition.

This does not warrant, however, the easy assumption that they are worthless. Not only do they reveal the hopes, imaginations, likes, and dislikes of Christians of an earlier day and thus provide invaluable information to the church historian, but they also throw a light which is at times far from inconsiderable upon the canonical writings, notably the gospels. Again and again these subsequent writings do with a broad brush precisely what the later canonical gospels have done to the accounts in the earlier—e.g., the addition of the detail in John that it was *Peter* who struck off the *right* ear of *Malchus;* or Luke's adding that one of the thieves on the cross was repentant and received pardon (cf. Mark 15:32). This latter detail is illustrative of the trend of this whole style of writing: this incident in Luke, surely an expansion resulting from Christian curiosity, piqued by the terse mention in Mark of *two* thieves and the certainty that no detail was without profound significance, was in turn to result in a greatly expanded further development of the story of the two thieves, their meeting with Jesus in Egypt, his prophecy that they would be crucified with him thirty years later, and the subsequent tale of the arrival of the repentant thief (DYSMAS) in paradise to the consternation of Death and Hell. The third version of the parable of the entrusted funds (talents), now commonly ascribed to the Gospel According to the Hebrews, simply highlights the earlier development of the original parable from its version in Matthew to that in Luke, seemingly in no small part to remove from it the obvious difficulties in its earliest form.

Perhaps more important and less debatable is another sure value of these writings. They evidence unmistakably the absence of reliable historical information outside the Markan tradition. Their utter failure to provide any story having any semblance of historical probability outside the cycle of incidents included in Mark would seem to warrant the conclusion, borne out by the clear evidence that Matthean and Lukan incidents (as distinct from sayings), superficially different from Mark's, are in all probability developments and amplifications of the Markan core. In a word, the frequent assumption that Mark preserved but a portion of the stories then current about Jesus would seem in sharp contradiction to the apparent facts. Nor is it too much to say that not infrequently a thoughtful reading of an incident in one of the canonical gospels in the light of its subsequent expansion in a later apocryphon will suggest that, despite the lurid and pinchbeck rhetoric in which it is retold, the later writer occasionally saw more clearly the meaning of the earlier author than do we today. As an example of this, the treatment of the Lukan story of the twelve-year-old Jesus in the temple, by the author of the ARABIC GOSPEL OF THE INFANCY, is instructive.

As suggested in the outset, these writings superficially parallel the four types of writing in the canonical NT: gospels, acts, letters, and apocalypses. In addition to early gospels now known to us solely by occasional quotation, such as the Gospel According to the Hebrews or the Gospel According to the Egyptians, there are two special types, infancy gospels and passion gospels—i.e., accounts of purely legendary incidents, for the most part quite outside the scope of the canonical gospels, in the hidden years before the ministry and in events subsequent to the

Crucifixion. Of the infancy gospels the Protevangelium of James and the Gospel of Thomas (*see* JAMES, PROTEVANGELIUM OF; THOMAS, GOSPEL OF) were the earliest and the sources for all subsequent treatment. The former gives a totally imaginary account of the birth and upbringing of the Virgin and the story of the subsequent birth of Jesus; the latter provides a tasteless congeries of miracles wrought by Jesus as a small boy. Their total effect is to send us back to the canonical gospels with fresh approval of their chaste restraint in failing to attempt to fill in the intriguing hidden years. Of passion gospels there are two of exceptional import, the fragment of the Gospel of Peter (*see* PETER, GOSPEL OF) discovered in a tomb in Egypt in 1884, and the Acts of Pilate (*see* PILATE, ACTS OF), often styled the Gospel of Nicodemus. With them is commonly grouped the Gospel (or Questions) of Bartholomew (*see* BARTHOLOMEW, GOSPEL OF), a series of questions propounded to Jesus after his resurrection, to Mary, and to Satan, by Bartholomew.

The canonical book of Acts early proved intriguing to Christian imagination, orthodox and heretical alike. In consequence we have a long string of romances attempting to provide information absent in Acts of the doings of the several worthies. A series of five such treatments, popularly ascribed now to Leucius, were produced under the titles Acts of John, of Paul, of Peter, of Andrew, and of Thomas (*see* JOHN, ACTS OF; PAUL, ACTS OF; PETER, ACTS OF; ANDREW, ACTS OF; THOMAS, ACTS OF). All five of them, varying though they do in seeming orthodoxy or departures therefrom, came to be prized by the Manicheans and apparently were substituted by them for the canonical Acts. As is indicated in the several articles, to which the interested reader is referred, they are long and flashy romances, based on little more than vivid and uncurbed imagination, and regularly ending with the passion (martyrdom) of the apostle, which latter sections also commonly circulated as independent books. These writings set the stage for a welter of others of the most grossly legendary nature. Some of these latter, conveniently styled "secondary Acts," are extant in Greek and/or Latin. In addition there is another cycle, a veritable olla-podrida, commonly referred to as "Oriental Acts," mainly in Coptic, Arabic, and Ethiopic, of which the Acts of Andrew and Paul (*see* ANDREW AND PAUL, ACTS OF) is a not unrepresentative example.

A few letters were produced, but this type of writing never flourished as lushly as did the other types. In addition to such writings as III Corinthians (*see* PAUL, ACTS OF), the obvious Epistle to the Laodiceans (*see* LAODICEANS, EPISTLE TO THE), the turgid correspondence between Paul and Seneca, are such other apocrypha as the letters between Jesus and Abgarus, the Epistle of Lentulus, the Epistle of Titus, and the Epistle of the Apostles (*see* ABGARUS, EPISTLES OF CHRIST AND; LENTULUS, EPISTLE OF; TITUS, APOCRYPHAL EPISTLE OF; APOSTLES, EPISTLE OF).

There are several apocalypses, headed by the famous Apocalypse of Peter (*see* PETER, APOCALYPSE OF), which set the fashion for accounts of personally conducted tours of heaven and hell by the several apostles. The Apocalypse of Paul (*see* PAUL, APOCALYPSE OF) was, of course, made inevitable by Paul's intriguing reference to the experience of the "man in Christ who fourteen years ago was caught up to the third heaven" (II Cor. 12:2), which our subsequent author, understanding it, with far less hesitation than is shown by some modern commentators, to have been an experience of Paul himself, proceeded to recount at very great length. Other apocalypses followed, including those of JAMES; STEPHEN; THOMAS; and the VIRGIN herself. In addition to them are five Gnostic apocalypses, long known only by name from Porphyry's references to Plotinus' hostile opinion of them: ALLOGENES SUPREME; Apocalypse of Messos (see MESSOS, APOCALYPSE OF); Apocalypse of Zostrianus (see ZOSTRIANUS, APOCALYPSE OF); and the apocalypses of Nikotheos and Zoroaster. The first three of these have been tentatively identified among the many writings discovered at Chenoboskion, and mentioned below.

In addition to these four types of apocrypha are several having to do with the assumption of the Virgin, the Book of John the Evangelist (see JOHN THE EVANGELIST, BOOK OF), and stray sayings ascribed to Jesus found in places outside the four canonical gospels and commonly referred to by the scarcely appropriate title Agrapha. In 1946 a large collection of Gnostic writings was discovered in upper Egypt, about thirty miles N of Luxor at Chenoboskion. Thirteen codices, all in Coptic, and with some 794 pages reasonably intact, are said to contain forty-eight treatises, of which no fewer than forty-four are different. These have been provisionally dated as coming from the third and fourth centuries and are thought to be based upon Greek originals. They consist of cosmogonies, treatises of a dogmatic nature, prayers, gospels, letters, and apocalypses. (See list below.) In addition to this library, containing, as it does, so many Gnostic writings hitherto quite unknown, are several treatises, such as the PISTIS SOPHIA, the Apocryphon of John (see JOHN, APOCRYPHON OR SECRET BOOK OF), and the baffling Books of Jeu, long known to scholarship and contained in three hitherto quite unique MSS—Codex Askewianus (fourth century; British Museum), Codex Brucianus (fifth century; Bodleian Library), and Codex Berolinensis (fifth-sixth century; Berlin).

Brief mention must also be made of the long list of modern apocrypha, still appearing to perplex and excite the hopes of many uninformed readers that priceless discoveries have but recently been made available. Without exception they are worthless trash and the rankest forgeries, but a few of them—no list could be complete—may be listed as an indication that the wildfires of imagination are still burning, though with but a smoky flame: *The Unknown Life of Christ, The Aquarian Gospel, The Crucifixion of Jesus by an Eye-Witness, The Report of Pilate (Archko Volume), The Confessions of Pontius Pilate, The Letter of Benan, The Twenty-ninth Chapter of Acts, The Letter from Heaven, The Gospel of Josephus, The Book of Jasher, The Description of Christ, The Death Warrant of Jesus Christ, The Long-Lost Second Book of Acts, Oahspe, The Lost Books of the Bible,* and *The Nazarene Gospel.* None of these trivia is discussed in separate articles in this dictionary. *See bibliography.*

A list of the more important older apocrypha to which separate articles are devoted herein, including many in addition to those specifically named in the preceding paragraphs, is appended for the convenience of the reader.

### Gospels

Arabic Gospel of the Infancy
Armenian Gospel of the Infancy
Assumption of the Virgin
Bartholomew, Gospel of
Bartholomew the Apostle, Book of the Resurrection of Christ by
Basilides, Gospel of
Ebionites, Gospel of the
Egyptians, Gospel According to the
Hebrews, Gospel According to the
James, Protevangelium of
Joseph the Carpenter, History of
Marcion, Gospel of
Mary, Gospel of the Birth of
Matthias, Gospel of
Nazarenes, Gospel of the
Peter, Gospel of
Philip, Gospel of
Pseudo-Matthew, Gospel of
Thomas, Gospel of

### Acts

Abdias, Apostolic History of
Andrew, Acts of
Andrew, Fragmentary Story of
Andrew and Matthias (Matthew), Acts of
Andrew and Paul, Acts of
Barnabas, Acts of
James, Ascents of
James the Great, Acts of
John, Acts of
John, Acts of, by Prochorus
Matthew, Martyrdom of
Paul, Acts of
Paul, Passion of
Peter, Acts of
Peter, Passion of
Peter, Preaching of
Peter, Slavonic Acts of
Peter and Andrew, Acts of
Peter and Paul, Acts of
Peter and Paul, Passion of
Philip, Acts of
Pilate, Acts of
Thaddaeus, Acts of
Thomas, Acts of

### Epistles

Abgarus, Epistles of Christ and
Apostles, Epistle of the
Corinthians, Third Epistle to the
Laodiceans, Epistle to the
Lentulus, Epistle of
Paul and Seneca, Epistles of
Titus, Apocryphal Epistle of

### Apocalypses

James, Apocalypse of
Paul, Apocalypse of
Peter, Apocalypse of
Stephen, Revelation of

Thomas, Apocalypse of
Virgin, Apocalypse of the

*Gnostic Writings (Chenoboskion)*
Allogenes Supreme
Dositheus, Apocalypse of
Eugnostos, Letter of
Jesus, Wisdom of
John, Apocryphon or Secret Book of
Messos, Apocalypse of
Peter and the Twelve Apostles, Acts of
Saviour, Dialogue of the
Silvanus, Teachings of
Zostrianus, Apocalypse of

*Related Subjects*
Agrapha
Apostolic Constitutions and Canons
Cerinthus
Melkon
Oxyrhynchus Sayings of Jesus
Pistis Sophia

**Bibliography.** The literature which these writings have produced is immense. M. R. James, *The Apocryphal NT* (1924; reprinted 1950), is by far the most convenient introductory guide, since it contains, in addition to brief but lucid introductions to the several writings, complete English translations of the more important texts and full summaries of most of the others, together with a judiciously selected bibliography of the more important volumes and special studies prior to 1924. In addition to the Selected Bibliography (pp. xxix-xxxi) are very valuable additional bibliographical items, introduced in the discussion of the particular writings. Additional bibliographical material, including that subsequent to 1924, will be found in B. Altaner, *Patrologie* (2nd ed., 1950); J. Quasten, *Patrology* (1950). In both these volumes very full bibliographies are conveniently grouped at the end of each special study. In addition to the studies listed by Quasten (vol. I, p. 277) for the recently discovered Chenoboskion library of Gnostic texts, *see* V. R. Gold, "The Gnostic Library of Chenoboskion," *BA*, vol. XV, no. 4 (Dec., 1952), pp. 70-88, for an excellent (provisional) description and bibliography.

An adequate discussion of the modern apocryphal writings may be found in E. J. Goodspeed, *Modern Apoc.* (1956); *Strange New Gospels* (1931). M. S. ENSLIN

**APOLLONIA** ăp'ə lō'nĭ ə ['Απολλωνία] (Acts 17:1). A Greek city in Macedonia, distinguished as Apollonia in Mygdonis from the many other cities of this name. Apollonia lay on the Via Egnatia, thirty miles from Amphipolis and thirty-eight miles from Thessalonica, S of Lake Bolbe. Paul and Silas passed it on the way to Thessalonica. M. J. MELLINK

**APOLLONIUS** ăp'ə lō'nĭ əs ['Απολλώνιος, *from* Lat. of Apollo]. **1.** A native of Tarsus (or son of THRASEAS) who was governor of Coelesyria and Phoenicia. He conspired with Seleucus IV to raid the temple treasury in Jerusalem. Heliodorus, sent to do the actual plundering, was, according to the story in II Macc. 3:7-40, thwarted by a heavenly warrior "of frightening mien" who appeared on a "magnificently caparisoned horse." This has been a favorite theme of artists.

**2.** Governor of Coelesyria under Alexander Balas. According to Josephus, this Apollonius bore also the name Daus (i.e., "one of the Dahai"[?]; Antiq.

XIII.iv.3-4). Josephus considers this Apollonius to be the son of 1 *above*. Polyb. XXXI.21.2 identifies him as the foster brother (σύντροφος) of Demetrius I.

Without the approval of Alexander, Apollonius challenged Jonathan to battle. Jonathan took Joppa, which had been fortified by Apollonius. The latter then drew Jonathan's men into the plain and ambushed them, but Jonathan's men emerged victorious (I Macc. 10:69-85), pursuing the troops of Apollonius to Ashdod, which they burned.

**3.** General of the armies of Samaria who put together a large force of Gentiles "to fight against Israel" (I Macc. 3:10; cf. Jos. Antiq. XII.v.5); probably to be identified with the Apollonius whom Antiochus had previously sent to despoil Jerusalem (II Macc. 5:24-26; cf. I Macc. 1:29-35). He pretended to have come with peaceable intentions, but, finding the Jews not at work on the sabbath, "he ordered his men to parade under arms. He put to the sword all those who came out to see them" (II Macc. 5:25-26; cf. I Macc. 1:29-35). In the battle with Judas, Apollonius suffered the humiliation of losing his sword to the opposing commander, who "used it in battle the rest of his life" (I Macc. 3:12; cf. Jos. Antiq. XII.vii.1).

**4.** Son of Menesthius; perhaps the same as 3 *above*. He was sent by Antiochus Epiphanes to represent him at the coronation of Ptolemy Philometor (II Macc. 4:21).

**5.** Son of Gennaeus, and one of the district governors (στρατηγοί) in Palestine. He and his fellow governors "would not let [the citizens] live quietly and in peace" (II Macc. 12:2). J. C. SWAIM

**APOLLOPHANES** ăp'ə lŏf'ə nēz ['Απολλοφάνης] (II Macc. 10:37). One of three Syrians (the others being the brothers Timothy and Chaereas) slain at Gazara by "twenty young men" in the army of Judas Maccabeus. J. C. SWAIM

**APOLLOS** ə pŏl'əs ['Απολλώς, *perhaps contracted from* 'Απολλώνιος (Acts 18:24 D)] (Acts 18:24; 19:1; I Cor. 1:12; 3:4-6, 22; 4:6; 16:12; Tit. 3:13). An influential member of the early Christian church.

I Corinthians is our primary source on Apollos, for it was written by Paul after significant personal association with Apollos. In I Cor. 1:12, Apollos appears as the focus of partisan loyalty in one of the four parties into which the Corinthian church had divided, those supported by the other parties being Paul, Cephas (Peter), and Christ. This indicates a great deal of prominence for Apollos, and demonstrates also the influence of Peter in the Corinthian church, although there is nothing to suggest that Peter himself had visited Corinth.

In I Cor. 3:3-10, Paul defines the relation of Apollos to himself. Paul's work in Corinth was prior to that of Apollos, for Paul compares himself to the one who planted and Apollos to one watering that which is already planted. Paul, however, deprecates the human pettiness of partisan activity in behalf of either Apollos or himself, in the light of the overwhelming fact that it is God who gives the increase. Nevertheless, in 3:10 ff, Paul states emphatically that he was the foundation layer, and that all others—including, of course, Apollos—necessarily build on that foundation. It is probable that Paul's depreciation (I Cor. 2:1 ff; II Cor. 11:6) of the skilful use of philosophical eloquence and his bitter reference (II Cor. 11:5; 12:11) to "superlative apostles" esteemed by the Corinthian church are a reflection of adverse comparisons made by the Corinthian Christians between the eloquent Apollos and himself. Paul declares (I Cor. 4:15) to the Corinthians that, while they may well have many guides to Christ, they have but one father in Christ—namely, himself. This poignant remark seems to reflect a considerable sensitiveness concerning the Corinthian magnification of Apollos. Paul also observes (II Cor. 3:1) that he did not stand in need of letters of recommendation to them as some did, probably meaning Apollos (Acts 18:27). And although in I Cor. 3:22; 4:6 he places Apollos on a level with himself, Paul mentions himself first in each case. Nevertheless, I Cor. 16:12 shows that Apollos was with Paul and that Paul had urged him to revisit the Corinthian church. The passage implies that Apollos was declining to visit there just then, in order to avoid a resurgence of partisan tension.

All that Acts tells us about Apollos is closely interwoven with the Acts account of Paul's work in Corinth and Ephesus. Apollos in Acts seems, however, to be quite independent of Paul; and if we had no other source of information concerning Apollos, we should conclude that their paths never crossed. In Acts 18:18–19:7 it is noted that Paul, leaving Corinth with Priscilla and Aquila at the end of the second of the three missionary journeys related in Acts, proceeded to Ephesus, where, during his brief stay, he had a good reception in the synagogue. He left Priscilla and Aquila in Ephesus, and proceeded to Caesarea and Jerusalem, and then moved on to Antioch. After a brief stay there, Paul set out to revisit the churches established in Galatia and Phrygia —a journey which was to terminate in Ephesus. While Paul was thus engaged, Apollos arrived in Ephesus. Apollos was a Jew, a native of Alexandria, and the presumption is that he grew up there. He was fervent, eloquent, and well versed in the OT scriptures—certainly in the LXX Version and probably in Hebrew as well. He had been taught as a catechumen the "way of the Lord" (τὴν ὁδὸν τοῦ κυρίου; Acts 18:25) by some unnamed Christian teacher, and was accustomed already to teach accurately the "things concerning Jesus" (τὰ περὶ τοῦ Ἰησοῦ). The two expressions just cited indicate that Apollos knew not only data about Jesus but also some of Jesus' teaching. He knew, however, only the baptism of John. When Apollos arrived in Ephesus and began teaching thus in the synagogue, Prisca and Aquila took him—probably to their house (I Cor. 16:19)—and taught him "more accurately" the "way of God" (Acts 18:26), presumably instructing him in Christian baptism. When Apollos wished to move on to Greece, the brothers in Ephesus wrote letters of recommendation for him. Apollos was in Corinth vigorously refuting in public debate Jewish objections to Christian teaching, when Paul—having revisited the churches in Asia Minor—arrived in Ephesus to take up his long work there. The data already cited from I Corinthians tell all that is certainly known concerning Apollos from this point.

Tit. 3:13 tells us little, save that—to the extent that we may assume that Titus preserves fragments of a genuine letter to Titus—it accords with the general impression of Apollos derived from I Corinthians. Jerome, commenting on Tit. 3:13, says that Apollos, after a stay in Crete, returned to Corinth and was bishop there. Not much weight can be assigned to this tradition.

Luther suggests that Apollos was the writer of Hebrews (*see* HEBREWS, LETTER TO THE). This is an interesting possibility, because what we know concerning Apollos is consistent with the characteristics of the Letter to the Hebrews. It is, however, only a conjecture.                    J. M. NORRIS

**APOLLYON** ə pŏl′yən [᾿Απολλύων, destroyer]. The Greek name of the angel of the bottomless pit (the underworld—ἄβνσσος), whose Hebrew name, according to Rev. 9:11, is ABADDON. As described in Rev. 9, when the fifth angel blows his trumpet, the shaft of the bottomless pit is opened and from it arises smoke, and from the smoke come locusts (cf. Joel 1:4 ff), who have power to harm those of mankind without the seal of God on their foreheads. The king of these locusts is this angel, who is mentioned nowhere else. In Enoch 20:2 the name of the angel who is "over Tartarus" is Uriel.

B. H. THROCKMORTON, JR.

**APOSTASY** ə pŏs′tə sĭ [ἡ ἀποστασία, desertion, abandonment, rebellion, *a late form of the classical Gr. noun* ἀπόστασις, *derived from the verb* ἀφίστημι, to put away, separate]. Originally a word with political meaning; ὁ ἀποστάτης referred to a rebel; this meaning is preserved in the LXX in I Esd. 2:23. The religious understanding of the term—namely, departure from the law of God or desertion of cause, worship, temple, or synagogue, or abandonment of obedience toward God in general—appears in the LXX (Josh. 22:22; II Chr. 29:19; 33:19; Jer. 2:19; cf. especially II Macc. 5:8).

The two passages of the NT take up the religious meaning. In Acts 21:21 we are told that Paul was accused of "apostasy": "You teach all the Jews . . . to forsake Moses"—i.e., to forsake the Torah, since the apostle demanded neither to circumcise nor to "observe the customs." In II Thess. 2:3 we encounter an eschatological setting, which is often repeated throughout the history of the Christian church. The passage takes up a Jewish apocalyptic tradition, that before the return of the Lord the apostasy (rebellion) must come. This theory reflects the idea of eschatological postponement, an idea typical for II Thessalonians and II Peter.

The English word "apostasy" in Heb. 6:6 is used in translating the Greek παραπέσοντας (lit., "falling back") and refers to a denial of faith in Christ under persecution.                    E. DINKLER

**APOSTLE** ə pŏs′əl [ἀπόστολος, *adjectival noun from* ἀποστέλλειν, to send off or out]. A title denoting a commissioned messenger or ambassador. It occurs seventy-nine times in the NT, but with various shades of meaning, both of a precise and of a general character. In Christian usage the term has two distinctive connotations: (*a*) it is limited to certain men of the first generation of the church's history; and (*b*) it marks the bearer of the title, among other qualifications, as a missionary of a gospel.

1. Greek usage
2. Jewish apostles
3. Jesus and apostleship
4. The Pauline conception
5. Later Christian literature
Bibliography

**1. Greek usage.** The term "apostle" is not common in classical Greek, where it occurs as either a noun or an adjective to describe a naval expedition or a group of colonists. Only in Herodotus I.21; V.38 is it used of a personal envoy. The papyri employ the term for a dispatch given to a ship or for an export license. The Alexandrian Jew Philo does not use the word at all, and Josephus employs it once (Antiq. XVII.xi.1) in the classical sense of an embassy. Epictetus (*Discourse* III.22) speaks of the ideal Cynic teacher as one "sent by Zeus" among men to be a messenger and herald of the gods and an "overseer" of men's affairs. He does not use the noun "apostle"; but his close association of the verb "to send" and the noun "overseer" (κατάσκοπος, cognate to ἐπίσκοπος, the Christian word for "bishop") provides an interesting parallel to NT and early Christian terminology.

**2. Jewish apostles.** Jerome (commentary on Galatians I.1) first noted the similarity of Jewish and Christian apostles; and his suggestion has been much debated by modern scholars seeking an "origin" for the NT use and meaning of the term. Other fourth-century evidence, in the church fathers, Jewish inscriptions (cf. CIL, IX, 648), and the Theodosian Code (XVI.viii.14) refers to ordained Jewish emissaries of the Jerusalem patriarchate called "apostles," sent out to visit the Diaspora, especially to collect taxes for the support of the rabbinate. Usually traveling in pairs, these men sometimes preached or taught in the synagogues, but their commission ended with their return to Jerusalem and was not transferable by them to others.

The rabbinic term for such agents was *shaliaḥ* (plural *sheluḥîm*, from the root שלח, "to send"). Such persons might represent individuals or corporate bodies such as courts and synagogues, their duties depending upon the terms of their commission—to serve legal documents, collect moneys, convey instructions, particularly with regard to the calendar or festivals. In the synagogues the *shaliaḥ* might be the leader of the congregation in prayer. The rabbinic principle that "a man's *shaliaḥ* is like to himself" (**M**. Ber. 5.5) states the obvious truth that a person who follows his instructions points the responsibility for his actions to his authorizing agent. It does not define the status of the *shaliaḥ* so much as it does his function.

In the OT, *shaliaḥ* is used of four eminent figures, Moses, Elijah, Elisha, and Ezekiel, in the sense of "God's agent" by reason of power committed to them to perform miracles on God's behalf. The LXX generally translates the verb שלח by ἀποστέλλειν, but the nominal form ἀπόστολος occurs only once—in I Kings 14:6, where the prophet Ahijah announces himself thus to Jeroboam's wife as a bearer of a message from God. Some scholars have pointed particularly to the governmental agents sent on both civil and religious missions, in the literature of the Persian period (especially Ezra 7:12 ff; Neh. 2:5; Elephantine papyri [2; ed. Cowley], pp. 62-63; cf. II Chr. 17:9; Esth. 9:20; II Macc. 1:1-2, 18). But in all these cases it should be noted that the *shaliaḥ*, unlike the later Christian apostle, has no institutional status or missionary responsibility. His authority is precisely defined and given for a limited term, and the character of his commission is more juridical than religious in quality.

**3. Jesus and apostleship.** Fundamental to Jesus' conception of his person and work is his sense of being "sent" by the Father. In turn, he "sends out" his disciples with his own authority to continue and extend his mission (for references, *see* MINISTRY, CHRISTIAN § 1). Such passages as Mark 9:37 (and parallels) and John 20:21 are characteristic of his outlook and have every claim to authenticity. The idea of apostleship in these sayings is obviously comparable to the rabbinic notion of the *shaliaḥ*, but with this difference: for Jesus, apostleship, whether of himself or of his disciples, is a purely religious commission to carry out the purpose of God for man's salvation, and it is a lifelong authorization, given once for all.

The Synoptic narrative of the choice, commissioning, and naming of the Twelve as apostles (Mark 3:14 ff; cf. Matt. 10:1 ff; Luke 6:13 ff), and of their subsequent report to Jesus (Mark 6:30; Luke 9:10), raises the complicated question as to the extent to which later ecclesiastical terminology may have colored the tradition. On the face of it, the Markan and Lukan accounts present no inherent contradiction to the Jewish custom of the *shaliaḥ*; and the Matthean account, with the Lukan narrative of the sending forth of the Seventy (10:1 ff), adds verisimilar details. The Twelve are given a precise commission for a limited sphere and time, and they go out two by two for the work. But the singular use by Matthew of the word "apostle" in this instance, plus the fairly common usage of Luke to speak of the Twelve as "apostles" (cf. 17:5; 22:14; 24:10; and frequently in Acts; *see* § 5 *below*), leave some doubt as to the reliability of the term "apostle" in this connection.

In any event, church tradition ascribed to the Twelve the title of apostle, not only on the basis of this narrative, but also by reason of the postresurrection commission given to them by Jesus (cf. Matt. 28:19-20; Luke 24:48-49; John 20:21-23; Acts 1:8; and the addition to Mark, 16:15 ff). Most modern critics would certainly distinguish the peculiar character of the Christian apostle from that of the Jewish *shaliaḥ*, by emphasis upon the unique nature of the resurrection experience and commissioning.

**4. The Pauline conception.** There can be no doubt that Paul associated his own claim to be an apostle with the fact that he had seen the risen Lord and received from him a direct commission to preach the gospel (Rom. 1:1; I Cor. 9:1-2; 15:9; II Cor. 11:4-5). Though Paul again and again stressed the point that his particular commission was aimed at the conversion of the Gentiles (Rom. 11:13; Gal. 1:15-17; cf. Acts 22:15; 26:15-18; I Tim. 2:7), it is clear, both from his own testimony and from the narrative of Acts, that he did not confine his apostolic labors to the heathen, any more than Peter limited his to the Jews (cf. Gal. 2:7-8). With his claim to apostleship, Paul also insisted upon a special deference to his authority in the churches that he founded (I Cor. 4:9; 9:2). He considered apostles to be the chief and highest gift of ministry in the church (I Cor. 12:28; cf. Eph. 4:11), and its divinely given authority to be manifestly confirmed in the church by miraculous signs and wonders (II Cor. 12:12).

It is certain that Paul accounted others besides himself and the Twelve as apostles—among them James, the brother of the Lord (I Cor. 15:7; Gal. 1:19), and presumably Barnabas also (cf. I Cor. 9:6). A few critics, however, have sought an interpretation of the εἰ μή in Gal. 1:19 as excluding James from the company of apostles; but this does not seem to be the most natural reading of the text. In Rom. 16:7 Paul refers to "kinsmen and fellow prisoners" named Andronicus and Junias, who were "men of note among the apostles" and Christians of longer standing than he.

But Paul uses the word "apostle" in more than one sense. In the address of all his letters, except Philippians and Thessalonians (though note I Thess. 2:6), he describes himself as an apostle of Jesus Christ. And in the Galatian letter he makes a special point of noting that his title of apostle is "not from men nor through man, but through Jesus Christ and God the Father." There were undoubtedly opponents of Paul who contested his right to the title; but Paul, in turn, was ready to counter with his enemies by naming them "false apostles" (II Cor. 11:13; 12:11). Paul also uses the word "apostle," after the manner of the Jewish *shᵉluḥîm*, to describe the emissaries of churches (II Cor. 8:23; Phil. 2:25).

**5. Later Christian literature.** In spite of the theory of "apostolic succession" that developed in the church's doctrine of the ministry (see MINISTRY, CHRISTIAN § 9), the title and office of apostle were not transferable and died out with the passing of the original bearers of the name. Whenever it is applied to individuals in later Christian literature, the use of the term is metaphorical. The church has never had apostles in the NT sense since the first century.

Moreover, there was apparent very early in the "post-apostolic age" a tendency to limit the title to the Twelve, though without deliberate intent, by any means, to exclude Paul, James, or even Barnabas. The trend to speak of "the twelve apostles" is already evident in Matt. 10:2; Rev. 21:14. The superscription of the DIDACHE is but another indication: "The Lord's teaching to the heathen by the twelve apostles." (The reference to apostles in Did. 11.4, 6, is without doubt a conscious archaism.) That certain individuals of the second generation continued to style themselves by the title is evident from Rev. 2:2, but their claim was attacked by "orthodox" leaders as fraudulent. For it was the rise of heresy, particularly, that impelled the church to limit the final authority for its doctrine and practice to the teaching and example of the founder-apostles (cf. Eph. 2:20;

3:5). So there developed by the middle of the second century an "Apostles' Creed," a NT canon of books ascribed to apostles or to their immediate disciples, and a hierarchical ministry claiming succession from the apostles.

This process is most clearly indicated in the NT in the book of Acts. With a single exception, the word "apostles" in this book refers to the Twelve, or at least to a specified group in the Jerusalem church, who with the elders govern the church and make authoritative decisions respecting the development of its mission and organization. In 14:4, 14, however, Paul and Barnabas are called apostles in the account of their so-called first missionary journey. This circumstance may be due to a special source used by the evangelist; or it may be a survival of an older usage—perhaps of Jewish outlook, which viewed the two men in this particular instance as *shᵉluḥîm* of the church in Antioch (cf. their commissioning in Acts 13:1-3).

The author of Acts would not have denied to Paul, however, the title of an apostle; his attitude is implicit in the circumstance that he devoted half his volume to Paul's career. But the name of his book, "Acts of the Apostles," which goes back well into the second century, is testimony to the early establishment of the tradition that the apostles—mathematics notwithstanding—were twelve, but the number twelve does not exclude Paul or even a few others, such as James and Barnabas.

**Bibliography.** Fundamental is the article of K. H. Rengstorf in Kittel, *TWNT*, I, 406-46 (English trans. J. R. Coates, "Apostleship," *Bible Key Words* [1952]). J. B. Lightfoot on Galatians (rev. ed., 1896), pp. 92-101; H. Monnier, *La notion de l'apostolat des origines à Irenée* (1903); R. Schütz, *Apostel und Jünger* (1921); H. Vogelstein, "The Development of the Apostolate in Judaism and its Transformation in Christianity," *HUCA*, II (1925), 99-123; J. Wagenmann, *Die Stellung des Apostels Paulus neben den Zwölf in den ersten zwei Jahrhunderten* (Beihefte zur *ZNTW* 3; 1926); F. Gavin, "Shaliach and Apostolos," *ATR*, IX (1927), 250-59; H. F. von Campenhausen, "Der urchristliche Apostelbegriff," *Studia Theologica*, I (1947), 96-130; H. Mosbech, "Apostolos in the New Testament," *Studia Theologica*, II (1948), 166-200; T. W. Manson, *The Church's Ministry* (1948), pp. 34-46; J. Munck, "Paul, the Apostles, and the Twelve," *Studia Theologica*, III (1949), 96-110; V. Taylor, *The Gospel According to St. Mark* (1952), pp. 619-27. See also bibliography under MINISTRY, CHRISTIAN.

M. H. SHEPHERD, JR.

**APOSTLES, EPISTLE OF THE.** A second-century statement of beliefs and expectations in the form of a letter by the eleven apostles, summarizing a revelation to them by Jesus after his resurrection.

This very important apocryphon (see APOCRYPHA, NT) was utterly unknown until the discovery of a badly mutilated Coptic MS (fourth-fifth century) in Cairo. In addition, we now have a substantially complete text in Ethiopic and a fragment in Latin. No trace of the original Greek is known. A critical edition from the three available versions was produced by C. Schmidt in 1919. A translation into English was made by M. R. James, who had been the first to identify the Ethiopic "Testament of Our Lord in Galilee" as a version of the Coptic document. The epistle is commonly dated in the mid-second century. Occasional Gnostic touches have been detected by some, but its definitely non-Gnostic nature is indicated, not alone by the sharp denunciation of Simon and Cerinthus in the opening paragraph but also in the insistence upon bodily resurrection. Many of the apocryphal writings employ the fiction of detailed revelations by the resurrected Jesus to his disciples, while compositions purporting to be from several or all of the apostles are far from uncommon. The sources of the present writing are the four canonical gospels, Acts, the Apocalypse of Peter, Barnabas, Hermas, and the famous story of the youthful Jesus sent to learn his letters.

The writing opens as a letter "to the churches of the east and west, of the north and south," by the eleven apostles (among whom are Nathaniel and Cephas, the latter being distinct from Peter), and rapidly recounts the supernatural birth, miracles, and resurrection of Jesus, who had been crucified by Pontius Pilate and Archelaus. Then the epistolary form is dropped, and the writing continues as a revelation by Jesus to them in answer to their questions as to the date and nature of the Parousia, the bodily resurrection of all faithful Christians who have been baptized and faithfully observe the Lord's commands, the final judgment, portents of the end, the fate of the lost, directions for their missionary activity, the prediction of the advent of Paul, and an identification of the wise and foolish virgins. At the end of the account the Lord ascends to heaven. An especially revealing touch is Jesus' statement that he himself had appeared to Mary in the form of the angel Gabriel and had formed himself and entered her body: "For I alone was a minister unto myself in that which concerned Mary." This appears to be no esoteric speculation, although it has been so regarded by some, but a logical, if grotesque, result of the growing unwillingness to allow anyone to minister to or aid him. No longer was he regarded as empowered by the Spirit; rather, he did what he did because he was what he was.

***Bibliography.*** In M. R. James, *The Apocryphal NT* (1924), pp. 485-503, is printed the author's admirable English translation and careful comparison of the variations in the several versions. M. S. ENSLIN

## APOSTOLIC CONSTITUTIONS AND CANONS ăp'ɔ stŏl'ĭk.

A collection of ecclesiastical regulations and liturgical materials in eight books, to the last of which are appended as a final chapter the eighty-five Apostolic Canons indicating the selection, ordination, and duties of the clergy. The collection is but one of several, although the longest and most pretentious, and is heavily dependent upon the DIDACHE, the Apostolic Tradition of Hippolyptus, and the Didascalia. It is now commonly dated in the latter part of the fourth century (*ca.* A.D. 380) and regarded as coming from Syria. It purports to have been composed by the apostles and to have been transmitted by "our fellow minister Clement." In Book VIII the several apostles, beginning with Peter and including Matthias, Paul, and James of Jerusalem, speak one by one as in apostolic council ("In the first place, therefore, I Peter say . . ."), instead of jointly as in the previous books, and conclude with a final decree that "every one is to remain in that rank which is appointed him." The first six books have as their principal source the Didascalia, which is substantially reproduced even in the smallest details, although with occasional purposeful alterations and modifications. Thus the original Greek of the latter influential third-century manual, which had absorbed and expanded the earlier Didache, and which is now for its complete text extant only in Syriac— about three eighths is preserved in Latin translation in a late fourth-century palimpsest—can be substantially reconstructed.

Book VII is an expansion or adaptation of the Didache, together with prayers and prescriptions for the instruction of catechumens and for the conduct of baptism. Book VIII draws heavily upon the Apostolic Tradition of Hippolytus and provides detailed instructions for the ordination of bishops and presbyters, and contains the so-called Clementine Liturgy (5-15); then it passes on to deaconesses, subdeacons, confessors, virgins, widows, and exorcists, and concludes with sundry rules for various church observances, fasts, and prayers, all in a most practical and matter-of-fact manner. The last chapter (57) contains the eighty-five so-called Apostolic Canons, as already mentioned. The last of these is of special interest, since it contains a list of the canonical scriptures. At the end of the list are "two Epistles of Clement," "the Constitutions dedicated to you the bishops by me Clement, in eight books," and "the Acts of us the Apostles"; there is no mention of the book of Revelation.

That one man assembled this whole congeries of earlier materials would seem indicated by the similarity of style and diction throughout those sections properly to be ascribed to the editor. He is often styled an Arian or semi-Arian, but there would seem little to demand such a label. A direct connection with the spurious "Epistles of Ignatius" (*see* IGNATIUS, EPISTLES OF)—i.e., with the so-called "long recension"—is certain. Whether these latter were produced by the compiler of the Constitutions himself or whether his work was speedily employed by another is uncertain.

Among other similar writings may be mentioned the so-called Apostolic Order, a short treatise in Greek, probably to be assigned to the beginning of the fourth century and coming from Egypt. It is addressed to the "sons and daughters" and purports to be written by the Twelve at the direct command of the Lord Jesus. The first half is moralistic, embodying the gist of the "Two Ways"; the latter half is concerned with regulations for selection of bishops, presbyters, lectors, deacons, and widows. The Apostolic Tradition of Hippolytus gave rise to several other manuals, among which are: the Testament of Our Lord, in which is found, before the material common to such works, an account of the instructions which Jesus gave to the apostles prior to his ascension and his description of the signs which would prelude the end of the world; the Canons of Hippolytus, written originally in Greek but extant now only in Arabic and Ethiopic, and essentially a much reworked edition of the Apostolic Tradition; the so-called Constitutions Through Hippolytus, styled in some MSS the Epitome, and really not an epitome but a series of excerpts from Book VIII of the Apostolic Constitutions, in which at times the epitomizer has substituted the text of Hippolytus for that of the dependent work. The work long styled the Egyptian Church Order, largely because it was first known to modern scholars in a Coptic translation, is now known to be the long lost Apostolic Tradition itself.

**Bibliography.** The literature dealing with these writings is immense. The articles "Apostolical Constitutions" and "Apostolical Canons" in Smith and Cheatham's *Dictionary of Christian Antiquities*, while old, may still be studied with profit. B. Altaner, *Patrologie* (2nd ed., 1950), pp. 35-45; and J. Quasten, *Patrology* (1953), II, 119-20, 147-52, 180-90, provide full bibliographies of more recent work, as well as succinct discussions.                                        M. S. ENSLIN

\*APOSTOLIC FATHERS. The name commonly used since the seventeenth century to designate a group of writings contemporary with the later books of the NT, by authors reputed to have been associated either with the apostles or with their immediate disciples. Several of these works had a quasi-canonical authority in certain churches until the fourth or fifth century, and are preserved in ancient codices of the NT (e.g., the Epistle of Barnabas in א, and the two Epistles of Clement in A).

Though these documents are intrinsically of a quite uneven merit and authority—and in many cases their precise authorship, date, and locale of writing are uncertain—they are, by virtue of their dating prior to the formation of the NT canon, indispensable sources for the history, theology, and institutional development of Christianity in the postapostolic age. They are important, too, for the study of the vocabulary of the NT, as for tracing the process by which much of the NT came to take on canonical authority. But they are of less help, though by no means of little interest, in the study of the text of the NT. In particular, the citations and allusions to the Gospels show such divergences from the received canonical texts, that it is difficult to determine in most cases whether the authors were dependent upon oral tradition or were harmonizing or loosely quoting from written sources. There are also unmistakable instances of the use of apocryphal writings.

Since these works do not form a homogeneous group, it is best to study them individually. The first editor of the collection, J. B. Cotelier, in 1672, included the pseudo-Epistle of Barnabas; the two epistles ascribed to Clement of Rome; the epistles of Ignatius of Antioch; the single epistle and the Martyrdom of Polycarp, bishop of Smyrna; and the Shepherd of Hermas, a prophet of the Roman church. Modern editors customarily add to these the Didache, an early Church Order discovered in 1873; the fragments extant from the writing of Papias, bishop of Hierapolis; a fragment of an Apology of Quadratus, an Athenian who flourished in the reign of Hadrian (preserved in Euseb. Hist. IV.3.1-2); and an anonymous apologetic work of unknown origin and date, the Epistle to Diognetus, first published in 1592, a writing of considerable distinction of style.

*See* BARNABAS, EPISTLE OF; CLEMENT, EPISTLES OF; DIDACHE; HERMAS, SHEPHERD OF; IGNATIUS, EPISTLES OF; PAPIAS; POLYCARP, EPISTLE OF.

**Bibliography.** Texts and translations: J. B. Lightfoot and J. R. Harmer (1912); H. Lietzmann, *Handbuch zum NT, Ergänzungsband* (1923; German trans. and commentary); K. Lake (Loeb Classical Library; 1930); F. X. Glimm,

J. M. F. Marique, and G. G. Walsh (Fathers of the Church; 1947; trans. only); J. A. Kleist (Ancient Christian Writers, nos. 1, 6; 1946-48; trans. and excellent commentary); E. J. Goodspeed (1950; trans. only); C. C. Richardson, *Early Christian Fathers*, Library of Christian Classics, vol. I (1953; introduction, trans., and bibliographies; lacks Hermas and Papias); K. Bihlmeyer, *Die apostolischen Väter* (2nd ed., 1956; best text and critical introduction, but lacks Hermas).

Reference: *The NT in the Apostolic Fathers* (1905), by a Committee of the Oxford Society of Historical Theology; E. J. Goodspeed, *Index Patristicus* (1907; a concordance).

Special studies: G. Bardy, *La Théologie de l'Église de Saint Clément de Rome à Saint Irénée* (1945); T. F. Torrance, *The Doctrine of Grace in the Apostolic Fathers* (1948).

Full bibliographies may be found in: J. Quasten, *Patrology*, I (1950), 40 ff; B. Altaner, *Patrologie* (5th ed., 1958), pp. 78 ff.
                                        M. H. SHEPHERD, JR.

**APOSTOLIC HISTORY OF ABDIAS.** See ABDIAS, APOSTOLIC HISTORY OF.

**APOTHECARY** ə pŏth′ə kĕr′ĭ. KJV translation of רקח (RSV PERFUMER). *See* PERFUME §§ 1, 3c.

**APPAIM** ăp′ĭ əm [אפים, nostrils] (I Chr. 2:30-31). Son of Nadab and father of Ishi in the genealogy of Jerahmeel.

**APPAREL.** *See* DRESS AND ORNAMENTS.

**APPEAL TO CAESAR.** After Paul's arrest in Jerusalem he was taken by Roman soldiers to Caesarea to foil a Jewish plot on his life. There he was imprisoned by Felix and awaited trial. When Festus replaced Felix as governor, he had Paul brought before him for a hearing. Jews from Jerusalem brought their charges against Paul. Festus asked him whether he wished to go to Jerusalem and be tried there on the Jews' charges, presumably by the Sanhedrin (Acts 25:9). Paul answered that he did not want to be delivered to the Jews for trial—knowing they would kill him—and he appealed to Caesar (vs. 11), believing that he had "done nothing deserving death" (vs. 25) under Roman law. As Festus had no charge against Paul to send to the emperor, he had Paul brought before Agrippa II. Agrippa said that Paul could have been released if he had not appealed to Caesar (26:32); but because he had done so, he must be taken to Rome. Acts closes with Paul in prison in Rome, and says nothing about the results of Paul's appeal. *See* PAUL.

It was probably Paul's Roman citizenship (22:25 ff) which gave him the right to appeal his case to the emperor. Acts does not state this, but it appears that in cases of capital offense this right was customarily granted. In his famous *Letter to Trajan* (book X, letter 96), Pliny wrote that he had sent to Rome Christians accused of capital offenses, if they were Roman citizens. Pliny does not mention their appeals, but rather implies that he had sent them to Rome as a matter of course. On the other hand, Suetonius tells us (*Galba* IX) that Galba, while governor in Africa, ignored the claims of a Roman citizen who "invoked the law" and had him crucified in his province. The "law" which this citizen "invoked" was presumably a law allowing appeal; but, in this case, Galba did not honor it.

Paul, then, appealed to Caesar because, in the first place, he did not want to be tried under Jewish jurisdiction; and, furthermore, he apparently believed that the local Roman governors were prejudiced against him. Luke never indicates that the Romans were ever convinced that there was much to the Jews' charges against Paul; but this may reflect a Lukan coloring of the situation.

What was the result of Paul's appeal? We do not know. It is possible that the prosecuting Jews did not appear in Rome and that after two years of imprisonment there Paul was released.

*Bibliography.* H. J. Cadbury, "Roman Law and the Trial of Paul," *The Beginnings of Christianity* (1933), V, 297-338.

B. H. THROCKMORTON, JR.

**APPHIA** ăf'ĭ ə [Ἀπφία]. One of the persons addressed in the salutation of the Letter to Philemon. She is designated by Paul, the writer of the letter, as "our sister." Because her name stands next to that of Philemon in the salutation, it has sometimes been assumed that she was his wife. Some have suggested that she may have been the wife of Archippus, whose name follows hers in the salutation. There is no evidence for either position. What can be assumed with certainty is that she was a Christian, a friend of the author of the letter, and a member of the Christian community in either Colossae or Laodicea. There is no other reference to this woman in the NT. *See also* PHILEMON; ARCHIPPUS.       M. E. LYMAN

**APPHUS** ăf'əs [Ἀπφοῦς] (I Macc. 2:5). An epithet meaning "cunning," applied to Jonathan, one of the five sons of Mattathias.       J. C. SWAIM

**APPIAN WAY** ăp'ĭ ən [ἡ Ἀππία; ἡ Ἀππία ὁδός; ἡ ὁδὸς ἡ Ἀππία; *Via Appia*]. The Roman road which ran from Rome through Capua to Brundisium.

From *Atlas of the Bible* (Thomas Nelson & Sons Limited)
38. The Appian Way

The Appian Way was built in 312 B.C. by the censor Appius Claudius Caecus (Livy IX.29.5-6). It reached at first only as far as Capua, but was extended by around the middle of the next century to Brundisium. Strabo mentions the Appian Way frequently, speaking of Brundisium as its lower terminus, and of Capua as situated on it (V.233.249). Statius (*Silvae* II.2.12) calls it "the worn and well-known track of Appia, queen of the long roads." Paul, who landed (Acts 28:13) at PUTEOLI on the Bay of Naples, must have reached the Appian Way at Capua, 20 miles distant, and then proceeded on it the 132 miles to Rome, passing en route through the FORUM OF APPIUS and the THREE TAVERNS.
Fig. APP 38.

*Bibliography.* C. Hülsen, "Appia via," *Pauly-Wissowa*, vol. II (1896), cols. 238-42.       J. FINEGAN

**APPII FORUM** ăp'ĭ ĭ fôr'əm. KJV form—reproducing the original Latin name used in the Vulg. —of FORUM OF APPIUS.

**APPLE** [תַּפּוּחַ, *tappûaḥ*; Ugar. *tpḥ*(?)]. A tree (Song of S. 2:3; 8:5; Joel 1:12) and its fruit (Prov. 25:11; Song of S. 2:3, 5; 7:8—H 7:9), poetically referred to for shade, beauty, fragrance, and sweet fruit. In the Song of Songs the bride's lover is likened to this tree, which provides delightful shade and sweet fruit (2:3), its fruit is sought by the lovesick bride (vs. 5), and the breath of the bride is likened to the fragrance of its fruit (7:8—H 7:9). Prov. 25:11 implies a gold-colored fruit (unless תַּפּוּחַ is a textual error), perhaps ornamental but certainly beautiful; it is likened to apt or timely(?) speech (cf. 15:23). The tree appears in Joel 1:12 with the fig, pomegranate, and palm, trees important to the "tillers of the soil" but which wither away in the terrible "Day of the LORD."

The traditional rendering, "apple," though favored linguistically, has been challenged because of the absence of the tree from Bible lands except in remote places, where it occurs with only very poor-quality fruit. The apple (*Pyrus malus* L. or *Malus pumila* Mill.), therefore, does not fit the graphic poetic imagery of Bible times. The citron (*Citrus medica* L.—used only for preserves or candied), the golden orange (*Citrus sinensis* L., Osbeck—an important export item from the Holy Land today), the quince (*Cydonia oblonga* Mill.—the only one of the suggested fruits that is indigenous to Bible lands), and the apricot (*Prunus armeniaca* [L.]—an important fruit in Bible lands today) have been proposed. Botanists agree that the apricot best fits the biblical references (*see* FLORA § A2*b*), but the uncertainty of its origin has made biblical scholars hesitant. The apricot, apparently native to China, was brought to the Western world no earlier than the first century B.C. (Pliny tells of its introduction to Rome, apparently from Armenia, not long before his time.)

If *tpḥ* in Ugaritic tablet 121:II:11 refers to the fruit (the context is broken and uncertain), the tree was present in Syria in the fourteenth century B.C. *Tappûaḥ* in Hebrew city names (*see* BETH-TAPPUAH; TAPPUAH) in the Shephelah and the central highlands argues for the presence of these trees in these areas at least as early as the seventh century B.C. Here the apple seems most unlikely, but the apricot, citron, and orange are also botanically unsupported. Only the quince would then be left. The differing tastes of Orientals might answer the problem raised by the poetic descriptions. Similarities in appearance between the common apple and the quince could account for the linguistic confusion. The LXX use of μῆλον (any tree-borne fruit), is an indication of ancient uncertainty.

Association of the tree in the garden of Eden (Gen. 3:1-19) with the apple seems to stem from an early mistaken identification of the tree of Song of S. 8:5 with the story. The deceptive fruit described in Wisd. Sol. 10:7 (cf. Deut. 32:32; II Kings 4:39) and Josephus (War IV.viii.4) as growing near ancient Sodom is frequently called "apple of Sodom" (*see*

VINE OF SODOM). The expression "APPLE OF THE EYE" is not at all related to תפוח.

*See also* FRUIT (PRODUCTS).

*Bibliography.* I. Löw, *Die Flora der Juden,* III (1924), 155-59, 212-35, 240-44; A. L. and H. N. Moldenke, *Plants of the Bible* (1952), pp. 184-88.　　　　J. C. TREVER

**APPLE OF THE EYE.** English idiom denoting the pupil of the eye and therefore a very precious thing. "Apple" renders three Hebrew words. The first, אישון (Deut. 32:10), means literally "little man" and presumably refers to the reflected image of himself which the beholder sees in the eye of another person. The second, בת (Lam. 2:18 KJV), means "daughter," with possibly the same significance. The third is the word בבה, meaning literally "gate."

The phrase is used in its physiological meaning in Lam. 2:18 KJV. In the other passages it has a metaphorical sense, referring either to a person very dear to God (Ps. 17:8) or to a teacher's instructions (KJV "law") as very precious to his student (Prov. 7:2).
　　　　　　　　　　　　　　　　R. C. DENTAN

**APRON** [חגרה (Gen. 3:7; *elsewhere* GIRDLE); σιμικίνθιον]. Originally the inner girdle around the waist; in the NT, the girdle wrapped around the waist of the outer garment. In Gen. 3:7 aprons were made of fig leaves to cover the nakedness of Adam and Eve. In Acts 19:12 the aprons and handkerchiefs of Paul had healing powers.　　　　J. M. MYERS

**AQUEDUCT** ăk′wĭ dŭkt. *See* WATERWORKS § 4*c*.

**AQUILA AND PRISCILLA** ăk′wə lə, prĭ sĭl′ə ['Ακύλας, Πρίσκιλλα]; in Paul's letters PRISCA prĭs′kə [Πρίσκα]. Man and wife, companions of Paul in Corinth and Ephesus.

**1. Early life.** Aquila is described as a Jew, a native of the Asiatic province of Pontus (Acts 18:2) who migrated to Italy and was later expelled from Rome, along with his wife, under the act of Claudius. Since the race of Priscilla is not mentioned, it has been inferred that she was not Jewish, but Roman. However, both names are originally Latin, indicating Roman connections. Whether they were Christians at the time of expulsion, or became Christians in Corinth, is not clear. The date of their expulsion and going to Corinth has been set *ca.* A.D. 49/50, according to historical references and archaeological discoveries centering around the proconsul Gallio (Acts 18:12; *see* CHRONOLOGY, NT § B1*d*). By trade Aquila and Priscilla are described as tentmakers. This may indicate either the weaving of cloth or the making of tents from leather.

**2. Association with Paul.** Aquila and Priscilla were residents of Corinth when Paul arrived on his first visit to the city. Being of the same trade, Paul soon made contact with them. It is not unlikely that Aquila was the contractor under whom Paul worked. He had a house adequate for the accommodation of his fellow worker. The association was not only of fellow craftsmen, but Aquila and Priscilla also became partners with Paul in evangelism, possibly as "teachers" (I Cor. 12:28).

When Paul departed from Corinth after his hearing before Gallio (Acts 18:18-19), he took Aquila and Priscilla with him to Ephesus. It is possible that they also had business reasons for the change. When Paul went to Jerusalem, they were left in the city to carry on the work of evangelism. In Ephesus they came in contact with the Alexandrian Apollos, who was a brilliant man, yet uninstructed in the teaching on baptism. Priscilla and Aquila were instrumental in his enlightenment, presumably initiating him also into the meaning of such ideas as "into Christ" and the gift of the Spirit (Acts 18:25-26; 19:6). How long the two workers stayed in Ephesus is not known. They are not mentioned in the account of the riot in which Paul was involved (Acts 19:23-41). Yet there is a note in the appendix of Paul's Letter to the Romans saying that "Prisca and Aquila . . . risked their necks for my life" (Rom. 16:3-4). This note, probably not a part of the original letter, quite likely refers to an earlier persecution in Ephesus in which Aquila and Priscilla demonstrated their devotion to Paul. When Paul sent his first letter from Ephesus to the Corinthians, he included greetings from Aquila and Prisca (I Cor. 16:19). The salutation to Prisca and Aquila in II Tim. 4:19 throws no further light on the later residence of the two.

**3. Later tradition.** Since Priscilla is named first in the instruction of Apollos (Acts 18:26), the impression has grown that she was more active and more capable than her husband. Perhaps she had a cultural background both Roman and Hellenistic. Various authorities have nominated her as author of the Letter to the Hebrews.

*Bibliography.* G. S. Duncan, *St. Paul's Ephesian Ministry* (1930), pp. 26-27, 68, 156-57, 207; F. J. Foakes-Jackson, *Acts of the Apostles* (1931), pp. 168-70; J. Weiss, *The History of Primitive Christianity* (1937), pp. 186, 292, 305, 316.
　　　　　　　　　　　　　　　　M. J. SHROYER

**AQUILA'S VERSION.** A Jewish translation of the OT into Greek. Aquila was a connection of Hadrian, who brought him from his native Pontus to Jerusalem, where according to Epiphanius he was converted to Christianity but later excommunicated. Upon his excommunication he became a zealous proselyte to Judaism. According to Jerome (*Commentary on Isaiah* 7.14) he was a pupil of Rabbi Aqiba, whose exegetical principles he followed closely.

In A.D. 130 Aquila finished his new translation of the Hebrew OT, which immediately became popular with his coreligionists.

His translation was characterized by a fantastic literalism in which, in spite of his own excellence in Greek, most rules of Greek syntax were violated in order to remain as close to the Hebrew original as possible. *See* SEPTUAGINT §§ 3*a*, 4*a*.

*Bibliography.* For a bibliography of published extant fragments see J. Reider, *Prolegomena to a Greek-Hebrew and Hebrew-Greek Index to Aquila* (1916); B. J. Roberts, *The OT Text and Versions: The Hebrew Text in Transmission and the History of the Ancient Versions* (1951), p. 120.　　　　J. W. WEVERS

**AR** är [ער, city]. A Moabite place located on the S bank of the Arnon River (Num. 21:28; cf. 22:36), on the N border of Moab at the time of the Israelite exodus (Num. 21:15; Deut. 2:18). It may refer to a city (in which case Deut. 2:36: "the city that is in the valley," may refer to Ar), to a region, or both. Deut. 2:9 may use "Ar" as a synonym for "Moab." Deut. 2:29 speaks of the Moabites living in Ar and the sons of Esau in Seir. In Isa. 15:1, "Ar" is parallel to "KIR."

Ar may be the capital of Moab, although the capital would hardly be on a boundary. Ar has often been identified with a city later called Areopolis (the Greeks presumably connecting Ar with Ares, god of war) and Rabbath Moab, but this city is almost fourteen miles S of the Arnon, and so does not suit our information about Ar.                    E. D. GROHMAN

**ARA** âr'ə [ארא] (I Chr. 7:38). One of the sons of Jether in the genealogy of Asher.

**ARAB** âr'ăb [ארב, ambush] (Josh. 15:52). A village of Judah in the hill-country district of Hebron, identified with er-Rabiyeh, E of Dumah (Domeh), near Umm el-'Amad.

**ARABAH** ăr'ə bə [ערבה]. One of the main regions of the land of Israel, contrasted with the coastal plain, the Shephelah, the Negeb, and the mountain regions. It extends due S from the lower end of the Sea of Chinnereth (Sea of Galilee) on both sides of the Jordan, includes the Dead Sea, and then, veering slightly SW, continues to the head of the Gulf of Aqabah. The word is translated "plain" in most of the passages by the KJV, and once "champaign" (Deut. 11:30); but it is rather a depression between lines of higher ground and, in fact, for the greater part of its length is below sea level.

1. Terms
2. Description
   a. The Jordan Valley
   b. The Dead Sea region
   c. From the Dead Sea to the Gulf of Aqabah
3. History
4. The Arabah in later prophetic literature
Bibliography

**1. Terms.** The simple term "Arabah," almost always with the article (hā'ărābhâ), is used in the Bible to indicate any part of the depression. Thus, it refers sometimes to the part S of the Dead Sea (Deut. 2:8); and since this part was arid and sterile, the term is used by the Judean prophets and writers in the sense of "desert" or "steppe" (Job 24:5; Ps. 68:5; Isa. 33:19; Jer. 17:6). Elsewhere it is used to mean the portion E of the Jordan (Deut. 4:49), W of the Jordan (Josh. 11:16), or the entire Jordan Valley below the Sea of Chinnereth (II Sam. 4:7). The plural (ערבות) is used to indicate specific sections; thus the phrase rendered in the versions as the "plains of Moab" (ערבות מואב) means in reality the Moabite portions of the Arabah. The "plains of Jericho" (Josh. 4:13; 5:10) are that part of the Arabah which was near the city of Jericho. There is also a reference to the "plains of the wilderness" (II Sam. 15:28; 17:16 KJV), which would mean that part of the Arabah which merges into the wilderness of Judah; but the text is doubtful, and the RSV emends to read the "fords of the wilderness" (see FORD).

The term "sea of the Arabah," often qualified by the addition "the Salt Sea," is used in several places to indicate the Dead Sea; it was the boast of Jeroboam II of Israel that he had restored the boundary of his land "from the entrance of Hamath as far as the Sea of the Arabah" (II Kings 14:25)—i.e., the entire E boundary as far S as the whole of Moab. The term nahal hā'ărābhâ (Amos 6:14), rendered by the RSV as the "Brook of the Arabah" and by the KJV as the "river of the wilderness," is more difficult to locate. It may refer to some specific stream of water that flows into the Dead Sea, such as the Wadi Qelt or the brook Zered (Wadi el-Hesa), which elsewhere (Isa. 15:7) is called by the similar-sounding name nahal hā'ărābhîm, "Brook of the Willows." On the other hand, the term used by Amos is exactly paralleled by the Arabic expression Wadi el-'Arabah for the region between the S end of the Dead Sea and the Gulf of Aqabah, and it is possible that he had this in mind, with the S limit of the nation, in which he includes Judah, as the beginning of the wadi. The prophet seems to be deliberately parodying the boast of the king, as given above; for this reason it is impossible to accept the proposed emendation by some scholars to nahal miṣrayim (Brook of Egypt, Wadi el-'Arish), for Amos throughout his prophesying makes it clear that he expects the affliction of the people to come from the direction of the E.

**2. Description.** The Arabah consists of three distinct parts: the Jordan Valley, the Dead Sea region, and the stretch from the Dead Sea to the Gulf of Aqabah.

*a. The Jordan Valley.* This portion of the Arabah extends approximately fifty miles and slopes to the S from 696 feet below sea level at the Sea of Chinnereth to 1,286 feet below sea level at the Dead Sea. For the first twenty-five miles its width is about twelve miles, and the region is watered by a number of streams: the Yarmuk, 'Arab, Taiyibeh, Ziqlab, Yabis, and several smaller streams from the E, and the Nahr Jalud from the W. Here the land is comparatively fertile and well watered, and the Jordan was easily fordable. Opposite Samaria the valley becomes narrow for about five miles and changes in nature from a fertile region to a sterile one. In the last twenty miles the Jabbok (Zerqa) and Shu'aib come in from the E and the Fari'a from the W, and the aspect of the region becomes a mixed one. The Jordan has cut down about 150 feet into the soft alluvial soil and winds its way through a dense jungle. On both sides of this are stretches of very fertile land in which, according to Pliny, more than forty-nine varieties of dates were grown besides other products. On either side of these are steep scarps that rise several hundred feet; they are twelve miles apart at Jericho, after which the valley narrows until it is only six miles wide when the Jordan empties into the Dead Sea.

Because of the nature of the Arabah above the Dead Sea, it never became a highway from N to S; the main roads in Canaan run along the hills above. It is crossed by a number of E-W roads, particularly in the N half, where the tribe of Manasseh was the only one of the twelve to possess a permanent territory on both sides of the Jordan.

*b. The Dead Sea region.* The greater part of this region, about fifty miles in length and about ten in

From *Atlas of the Bible* (Thomas Nelson & Sons Limited)

39. Looking toward the Arabah; filling the foreground are the limestone hills of the Negeb; in the background beyond the depression of the Arabah are the ridges of the hill country of the Edomites in the general area of Petra.

width, is occupied by the DEAD SEA. The hills on either side are steep and barren, though there is enough room at their bases on either side for narrow roads. On the W side are the traditional sites of the cities of Sodom (Jebel Usdum) and Gomorrah (Khirbet Qumran).

*c. From the Dead Sea to the Gulf of Aqabah.* This region, the modern Wadi el-'Arabah, extends for about one hundred miles in a direction slightly SW of S. Directly S of the Dead Sea is the Sebkha, a series of mud flats into which the Wadi el-Jeib and its tributaries lose their identities, for an extent of eight miles. At this point the valley begins to slope upward, passing above sea level after thirty miles and reaching its highest point near Jebel er-Rishe some eighteen miles farther on. During this part the valley widens out to as much as twenty-five miles in places. Beyond Jebel er-Rishe it slopes downward toward the Gulf of Aqabah, becoming narrower on the way and ending at Ezion-geber. The whole region is a desert, marked only by occasional oases, but in Nabatean times a careful use of irrigation from the scanty sources of water allowed for a certain amount of agriculture. The cliffs on the W are lower and consist of a series of terraces that lead up to the Negeb; those on the E form the escarpment of the biblical kingdom of Edom. Fig. ARA 39.

Despite the sterility of its soil, this part of the Arabah possessed important advantages, which made it an object of contention between Edom and Judah. Ezion-geber, at its S extremity, was the SE gate of Canaan, and the entering point of the trade from Arabia and even India and Africa. The trade route from Ezion-geber went N along the Arabah, from which side routes connected it with the main N and S highways of Canaan: to the E, through Edom, to the King's Highway; to the NW, by way of the ascent of Akrabbim, to Beer-sheba, where it met the water-parting route, and on to Gaza, where it met the coastal route. Still more important was the fact that the Arabah contained the only mines for copper and iron that are to be found in Canaan. A number of these were discovered by F. Frank and N. Glueck, notably at Punon (modern Feinan), Mene'iyeh, Khirbet en-Nahas, and Mrashrash. It was the Arabah that the biblical writer (Deut. 8:9) had in mind when he wrote of the land promised to Israel, "whose stones are iron, and out of whose hills you can dig copper."

**3. History.** The S Arabah was one of the ways traversed by the Israelites on their journey from Egypt to Canaan. According to Deut. 2:8 they seem to have journeyed down it from a point near Kadesh-barnea to Ezion-geber, leaving it to turn N through the Wadi Yitm to skirt the borders of Edom and Moab. In the meantime the Moabite part of the Arabah had been conquered by the Amorite kingdom of Sihon; when the latter was overcome by the Israelites, they occupied it in turn, and it was the site not only of the apostasy at Abel-shittim (Num. 25) but also of the final acts of Moses (Num. 32–36; Deut. 1:1). From there Joshua crossed over into the Jericho Arabah, where he established the sanctuary at GILGAL (1) and conquered JERICHO, opening the way to the subjugation of the territory W of the Jordan. The N Arabah is mentioned occasionally in the later historical narratives. Abner fled through it after his defeat at Gibeon (II Sam. 2:29), the murderers of Ish-bosheth traversed it to bring his head to David at Hebron (II Sam. 4:7), and Zedekiah was fleeing toward it from Jerusalem when he was taken by the Babylonians (II Kings 25:4; Jer. 39:4). The S Arabah is not specifically mentioned, but it fell into the possession of Israel or Judah and was reoccupied by the Edomites in accordance with the fortunes of the wars between these countries (*see* EDOM; EZION-GEBER; ELATH). After the third century B.C. it was occupied by the NABATEANS.

**4. The Arabah in later prophetic literature.** According to the account in Gen. 13-19, the Dead Sea section of the Arabah, prior to the destruction of the five wicked cities, had been an unusually fertile plain, "like the garden of the Lord" (13:10). In the later prophetic literature, which verges on the apocalyptic, the restoration of this barren territory is one of the promises of the future restoration of Israel. Thus Ezekiel speaks of a stream that is to issue eastward from the threshold of the temple which will go down to the Arabah and make it and the Dead Sea fruitful and productive (Ezek. 47:1-12). The same promise appears in the late prophecies of Joel 3:18—H 4:18; Zech. 14:8. It is also possible that in such passages as Isa. 35:1; 51:3 the word *'arabah*, rendered as "desert," may refer to the actual Arabah.

*Bibliography.* N. Glueck, *The Other Side of the Jordan* (1940), pp. 50-88; D. Baly, *Geography of the Bible* (1957), pp. 198-216.

S. COHEN

**ARABAH, BROOK OF THE** [נחל ערבה, brook of the wilderness *or* desert]. A dry stream bed, probably S of the Dead Sea, indicating the S border of Israel (Amos 6:14; KJV "river of the wilderness"). It is perhaps the same as the Brook Zered (*see* ZERED, BROOK), or is perhaps a confusion with the Brook of Egypt (*see* EGYPT, BROOK OF), a more common indication of the S boundary. *See also* ARABAH.

E. D. GROHMAN

**ARABATTINE.** KJV Apoc. form of AKRABATTENE.

**ARABIA** ə rā′bĭ ə [ערב; Αραβία, desert, *or* steppe]. A large peninsula of Southwestern Asia. The NW portion of Arabia is the scene of some important biblical events, and its people had contacts with the Israelites.

1. Scriptural references
  *a.* In the OT
  *b.* In the Apoc.
  *c.* In the NT
2. Location, size, and boundaries
3. Divisions of Arabia
  *a.* Divisions of classical geographers
  *b.* Divisions of Arab geographers
  *c.* Modern political divisions
4. Physical features
  *a.* Geology
  *b.* Coasts
  *c.* Islands
  *d.* Mountains
  *e.* Lava fields
  *f.* Valleys
  *g.* Plains and plateaus
  *h.* Sandy deserts
  *i.* Oases
  *j.* Meteorology
  *k.* Water
5. Plants connected with Arabia in the Bible
6. Fauna connected with Arabia in the Bible
  *a.* Domestic animals
  *b.* Wild animals
  *c.* Birds
  *d.* Insects
  *e.* Marine animals
7. Caravan routes
8. Biblical places in Arabia
Bibliography

**1. Scriptural references. *a. In the OT.*** In Isa. 21:13, ערב (*'erabh*) refers to NW Arabia in the root sense of the name, "desert," or "steppe." ערב (*'arabh*) in Jer. 25:24 seems from the context to mean N Arabia, and in II Chr. 9:14; Ezek. 27:21 it includes both N and S Arabia. This latter word is really the collective name of the people, "Arabs," like Arabic *al-'arab,* and only by metonymy is translated "Arabia." Aq., Symm., Syr., Vulg., and most modern translations also have "Arabia" in I Kings 10:15, as do the same versions (with the exception of the Vulg. and the KJV, which follow the MT) in Ezek. 30:5, in both of which cases the MT has *'erebh,* "mingled people." In these two references the whole of Arabia is indicated by the context. Another designation for NW Arabia is ארץ קדם (*'ereṣ qedhem*), "EAST COUNTRY" (Gen. 25:6), E of Syria-Palestine.

***b. In the Apoc.*** In Jth. 2:25, Arabia is shown by the context to be near Damascus. In I Macc. 11:16, Arabia is the Nabatean kingdom, E and S of Palestine. The apocalyptic dragons in II Esd. 15:29 are said to be from Arabia.

***c. In the NT.*** "Arabia" in Gal. 1:17 has been taken to mean the Syrian Desert E of Damascus (so most moderns), or al-Balqā' in Transjordan (Arabic in Paris Polyglot), or Mount Sinai (but a more specific statement of this would be expected). Gal. 4:25 follows contemporary usage in including Mount Sinai in Arabia. In Matt. 12:42; Luke 11:31 "the South" is used for Sheba in S Arabia.

**2. Location, size, and boundaries.** Arabia is in Southwestern Asia. It is the largest peninsula in the world, covering almost 1,000,000 square miles—*ca.* one third the size of the continental U.S.A. The peninsula is roughly rectangular, the length of the W coast being 1,800 miles and the width from the Red Sea to the Persian Gulf *ca.* 600 miles. Arabia is bounded on the W by the Red Sea; on the S by the Gulf of 'Adan and the Indian Ocean; on the E by the Gulf of 'Uman and the Persian Gulf; and on the N, where there is no clear geographical boundary in the Syrian Desert, by modern Jordan, Syria, and Iraq. Since it is bounded on three sides by seas and on the N by the Euphrates, the Arabic name is Jazirat al-'arab, "Island of the Arabs."

**3. Divisions of Arabia. *a. Divisions of classical geographers.*** Classical geographers, following Ptolemy (second century A.D.), divided the country into three parts: Arabia Petrea, whose main city was Petra and which included Sinai, Edom, Moab, and E Transjordan; Arabia Deserta, the Syrian Desert; and Arabia Felix, "Fortunate Arabia," the S portion.

***b. Divisions of Arab geographers.*** Yāqūt in his *Mu'jam al-buldān* (under the heading *jazīrat al-'arab*) quotes a fivefold geographical division: Tihamah (the W coastal plain), al-Hijaz (the mountainous area E of Tihamah), Najd (the central plateau), al-'Arud (the lower areas to the E), and al-Yaman (the S region).

***c. Modern political divisions.*** These are Saudi Arabia, the majority of the peninsula, especially the N and the W; al-Yaman in the SW corner; 'Adan Protectorate along the S coast; 'Uman and Trucial 'Uman in the SE corner; and Kuwayt, adjacent to Iraq on the NE.

**4. Physical features.\*** ***a. Geology.*** The rocks of Arabia belong to three main types: the old, igneous and metamorphic rocks of the mountains along the W coast; the later, sedimentary rocks of the NE; and the recent lava beds. The sedimentary rocks of the

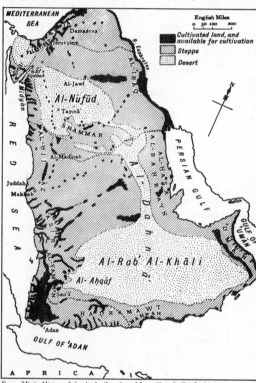

From Hitti, *History of the Arabs* (London: Macmillan & Co. Ltd.)

40. Arabia, showing land surface features

NE were laid down under ancient seas, whose organic matter produced the world's largest known accumulations of petroleum, exploited only since 1932. Arabia in general is often mentioned in the Bible as a source of gold (I Kings 10:2, 10, 15, 22; II Chr. 9:1, 9, 14, 21) and particularly OPHIR (I Kings 9:28; 10:11; 22:48; I Chr. 29:4; II Chr. 8:18; 9:10; Job 22:24; 28:16; Ps. 45:9; Isa. 13:12); HAVILAH (Gen. 2:11-12); SHEBA (Ps. 72:15; Isa. 60:6; with RAAMAH in Ezek. 27:22); and Parvaim, perhaps in Arabia (II Chr. 3:6). Other minerals from Arabia were silver (I Kings 10:22; II Chr. 9:14, 21) and

precious stones (Ezek. 27:22), including onyx from Havilah (Gen. 2:12). According to one interpretation of Ezek. 27:19, iron came from UZAL. The Letter of Pseudo Aristeas 119 refers to copper and iron mines in Arabia, probably those in Edom. *See* ARABAH. Fig. ARA 40.

***b. Coasts.*** The coasts of Arabia have been rising, and there are few good harbors, the best being 'Adan in the S. The most striking promontories are Ras Musandam in 'Uman and Qater projecting into the Persian Gulf. The W coast is fringed with coral reefs, and along the Persian Gulf are the Great Pearl Banks.

***c. Islands.*** The most important islands off Arabia are: Suqutrā to the S, and Bahrayn (perhaps the Sumerian Dilmun) in the Persian Gulf.

***d. Mountains.*** The rim of mountains along the W and much of the S coast intercepts moisture, leaving the interior dry. Most of al-Yaman is mountainous, the highest measured peak being 12,336 feet. The "hill country of the east" (Gen. 10:30) is somewhere in Arabia. Some of the mountains of NW Arabia are extinct volcanoes, and eruptions are recorded in medieval times. Some see in the smoke, fire, and earthquake of the theophany at Mount Sinai (Exod. 19:18) a description of an eruption, and wish to locate this mountain in NW Arabia.

***e. Lava fields.*** In central and N Arabia are many fields of broken lava (Arabic *ḥarrah*). Some think that חֲרֵרִים (*ḥarērîm*), "parched places" (Jer. 17:6), is the Hebrew for such lava fields.

***f. Valleys.*** The mountains of Arabia are cut by many valleys (Arabic *wādi*, plural *awdiyah*), along which are the caravan routes. Many of the wadies drain into deserts, and evaporation has produced "salt land" (Job 39:6; Ps. 107:34; Jer. 17:6).

***g. Plains and plateaus.*** Plains, usually narrow, are found along the coasts. The high central plateau is called Najd, and the stony N plateau is the Syrian Desert.

***h. Sandy deserts.*** In S Arabia is al-Rab' al-Khali, "the empty quarter," the largest continuous sandy area in the world. To the N is another great sandy desert, al-Nufud. As rocks are decomposed and the wind blows the sand, the sandy areas are spreading.

***i. Oases.*** There are oases, especially along the caravan routes in N Arabia, wherever a spring furnishes enough water to support vegetation.

***j. Meteorology.*** The climate of most of Arabia is dry and hot. Some places in al-Rab' al-Khali are rainless for ten years. Only in 'Asir, al-Yaman, and 'Uman is there enough rain for extensive regular cultivation. The average temperature in Tihamah is almost 90° F. Some identify שָׁרָב (*shārābh*) in Isa. 35:7; 49:10 with Arabic *sarāb*, "mirage," but the reference seems to be to the burning heat of the desert.

***k. Water.*** Because of the paucity and irregularity of rain, there are no large lakes and only one short perennial river, Wadi Hajar in 'Adan. After the occasional cloudbursts temporary freshets may rush down the valleys. These torrents soon disappear; and those who later seek water from them, like the Arab merchants of Job 6:15-20, will be misled. Water remains in the subsoil of some wadies, and Arabs dig to it with sticks, just as did the Israelites in the wilderness of Moab (Num. 21:16-17). The theory of the dessication of Arabia within historical times has been disproved by evidence for the same paucity of rain in antiquity; but in Arabia, as in Palestine and Iraq, the methods of conserving water (e.g., dams) have decreased in efficiency since ancient times.

**5. Plants connected with Arabia in the Bible.** The most important products of Arabia for ancient commerce were FRANKINCENSE and other perfumes. Arabia and the Arabians are often associated with SPICES in the Bible: Havilah (Gen. 2:12), Ishmaelites (Gen. 37:25), Sheba (I Kings 10:2, 10; II Chr. 9:1, 9; Isa. 60:6). The wandering Israelites found date palms, the most important Arabian fruit tree, in the oasis of Elim in Sinai (Exod. 15:27). The MANNA which the children of Israel ate in the wilderness (Exod. 16) may be derived from the tamarisk tree, which is common in Arabia. Mallow, bushes, broom, nettles, are typical desert plants (Job 30:4, 7). "Thickets" (Isa. 21:13) are thought by some to be inappropriate for Arabia, but travelers report thick underbrush in the oases. An emendation in Ezek. 27: 19 makes wine a product of Uzal, but the best wine in pre-Islamic Arabia was imported from Syria. ALMUG wood (I Kings 10:11-12) and EBONY (Ezek. 27:15) were imported by Arabian merchants from India or Africa.

**6. Fauna connected with Arabia in the Bible.** *a. Domestic animals.* The camel, the most important animal of Arabia, is often connected with Arabs in the Bible—e.g., Ishmaelites (Gen. 37:25; I Chr. 27: 30), Midianites (Judg. 6:5; 7:12; 8:22, 26), Amalekites (I Sam. 15:3; 30:17), the Queen of Sheba (I Kings 10:2; II Chr. 9:1); Hagrites (I Chr. 5:21), Kedar (Jer. 49:29), and Hazor in the desert (Jer. 49:32). Next in importance in the Arabian economy were sheep and goats, which Arabians and the princes of Kedar brought to Tyre (Ezek. 27:21). Solomon's ships brought pet monkeys from Ophir (I Kings 10:22), perhaps imported from Africa or India. Asses are associated with the Midianites (Num. 31: 28, 30, 34, 39) and with the Hagrites (I Chr. 5:21). Cattle were formerly more common in NW Arabia (Num. 31:33, 38). The horse is vividly pictured in Job 39:19-25, as in later Arabian poetry.

*b. Wild animals.* Some of the wild animals of NW Arabia are described in Job 38:39–39:12: the lion (38:39-40; found in Arabia in antiquity but not now), the mountain goat (39:1-4), the wild ass (39:5-8), and the wild ox (39:9-12; now extinct). Other Arabian desert animals are the jackal and the hyena (Isa. 34: 13-14; in Edom), the wolf (which the LXX connects with Arabia in Hab. 1:8; Zeph. 3:3), the gazelle (Isa. 13:14), poisonous serpents (Num. 21:6), and flying serpents (Isa. 14:29; 30:6; cf. the Arabian *aym*, which springs into the air). Ivory from Ophir (I Kings 10: 22; II Chr. 9:21) and from Dedan (Ezek. 27:15 MT) was imported from Africa or India.

*c. Birds.* Some birds of Arabia are listed in Job 38–39: the raven (38:41), the ostrich (39:13-18; extinct in Arabia since 1941), the hawk (39:26), and the eagle (39:27-30). Other birds associated with Arabia are: migratory quail (Num. 11:31; in Sinai), the owl, and the kite (Isa. 34:15; in Edom). The

"peacocks" brought from Ophir (I Kings 10:22) may have been imported from India, but the word may mean "baboons" (RSV mg.). *See* FAUNA § A2k.

*d. Insects.* Arabia may have been the breeding ground for locusts which attacked neighboring areas like Egypt (Exod. 10:13; brought by E wind) and Palestine (Joel 1-2). *See* LOCUST.

*e. Marine animals.* The oysters of the Persian Gulf were one of the main sources of pearls in the ancient world.

**7. Caravan routes.** The caravan routes for transporting Arabian incense and products of Africa and India began in Sheba (I Kings 10:1-13), al-Yaman. The main route went N via valleys and oases through Makkah, al-Madinah, al-'Ula (biblical Dedan), Mada'in Salih, Tabuk, and Ma'an, whence one route went W to Gaza and Egypt and another N to Damascus. From this main line other routes branched eastward—e.g., one from Mada'in Salih through Tayma' (biblical Tema) to Iraq. Another route led N from al-Jawf (biblical Dumah) through Wadi Sirhan to Transjordan.

**8. Biblical places in Arabia.** Biblical places which can be located with more or less certainty in Arabia include: Buz, Dedan, Dumah, Ephah, Havilah, Hazarmaveth, Hazor (Jer. 49:28), Massa, Midian, Ophir, Parvaim, Raamah, Sabtah, Seba, Sheba, Tema, and Uz. The detailed knowledge of Arabian geography in the OT is noteworthy.

*See also* TRANSJORDAN; MOAB; EDOM; SINAI. For tribes of Arabia, *see* ARABIANS.

*Bibliography.* Yāqūt, *Mu'jam al-buldān* (ed. F. Wüstenfeld; 1866-73); al-Hamdāni, *Sifat jazīrat al-'arab* (ed. D. H. Müller; 1891); D. H. Müller, "Arabia," in *Pauly's Real-Encyclopädie der klassischen Altertumswissenschaft*, N.B., vol. III (1895), cols. 244-59; F.-M. Abel, *Géographie de la Palestine*, I (1933), 288-98; J. A. Montgomery, *Arabia and the Bible* (1934); al-Hamdāni, *al-Iklīl*, book VIII, under the title *The Antiquities of South Arabia* (trans. N. A. Faris; 1938); R. H. Kiernan, *The Unveiling of Arabia* (1939), summarizes work and writings of explorers; G. Rentz, "Djazīrat al-'Arab," in *The Encyclopedia of Islam*, vol. I, fasiculus 9 (new ed., 1957), pp. 533-56; P. K. Hitti, *History of the Arabs* (6th ed., 1958).     J. A. THOMPSON

**ARABIANS** ə rā'bĭ ənz [ערב; ערבים; "Αραβες]. People from Arabia, more particularly N Arabia, with whose peoples dwellers in Palestine would have been very early in contact. In ancient times there seems to have been no one name for this area, nor any single ethnic name for its peoples, who are referred to by group names associated with various areas. Thus in the OT these Arabian peoples are referred to as Ishmaelites, Midianites, Dedanites, Sabeans, etc., rather than by the later terms Arabs, Arabians of Arabia.

1. The name
2. History
3. Beduin life
4. Religion
   Bibliography

**1. The name.** ערב properly means "nomad," and in II Macc. 12:10-12 the Arabians who attacked Judas are called νομάδες. It is doubtless connected with ערבה, the desert wilderness where the nomads wandered. It is the same word as the Egyptian *'emw*, which denotes nomads to the W of Egypt as well as those from Asia. Similarly in cuneiform inscriptions *Arubu* and *Aribi* are used for the nomads of Media as well as for those of Arabia. It has this meaning in both S and N Arabic, for the king whose titles are inscribed at Mārib is "ruler of Saba, Dhū Raidan, Ḥaḍramaut, Yemen with their *a'rab*" (*CIS*. IV, nos. 540-41), and the Koran uses *a'rab* (plural of *'arab*) for the Beduin, as contrasted with settled folk. Thus ערבי in Isa. 13:20; Jer. 3:2 means "nomad," and in I Kings 10:15; Isa. 21:13; Jer. 25:24; Ezek. 30:5, though translated "Arabia," probably means the same thing. The "ravens" of the Elijah story (I Kings 17:4, 6) were probably the Beduin, and the "mixed tribes" of Jer. 25:24 may also mean "nomads."

In Old Persian inscriptions, however, *Arabāya* has both a geographical and an ethnic meaning—i.e., Arabia as an Achaemenid province and the Arabs as inhabitants thereof. In Ezek. 27:21 ערב seems to have this ethnic sense, as it has in the earliest occurrences in Greek. This is the sense it bears in II Chr. 21:16; Neh. 4:7—H 4:1; in Syriac, where *Beth 'Arbāyē* is "the dwelling place of the Arabs"; in Nabatean, where ערביו is the common word for "Arabs"; and in Arabic, where even in the Nemāra Inscription the ruler is "king of all the Arabs."

**2. History.** Just when these Arabian peoples first appear in history is uncertain. Paleolithic sites exist in both N and S Arabia, but the remains tell little about these earliest inhabitants of Arabia, though they suggest a definite distinction between northerners and southerners even in the Stone Age. Representations of Asiatic *'emw* being smitten by Pharaohs interested in the Sinai mining appear on early Egyptian monuments, and doubtless represent the local Arabians of that date; necessities of intercourse with them would explain the "interpreters" mentioned among the officials at Sinai in inscriptions from the early dynasties. The Serabit el-Khadim inscriptions, so much discussed in connection with the origins of the Semitic alphabet, were the work of these local Sinai people. If R. P. Dougherty's theory that the "sealand" of early Akkadian inscriptions is the N Arabian sea of sand, the tribute therefrom to early Mesopotamian rulers would have been brought by nomads from this region.

Genealogical tables in the OT include Arabian peoples among the children of Cush (Gen. 10:7), of Aram (Gen. 10:23), of Eber (Gen. 10:25-30), of Abraham by Keturah (Gen. 25:1-4) and by Hagar (Gen. 25:13-16). These lists are not mutually consistent, doubtless representing variant ancient traditions concerning tribal relationships, but many of the names can be plausibly related to peoples and places in Arabia.

In the patriarchal narratives Abraham is represented as in contact with the BENē Ḥēth. From them Abraham purchased a burial ground for his family (Gen. 23), and among them Esau found wives (Gen. 26:34; 27:46; 36:2). Possibly these Hittites have no connection with the later Hittites from the Orontes region, but are the same people as the Ḥatti whom Tiglath-pileser III lists among the N Arabian peoples who sent him tribute, and with whom the Assyrians had trouble near Ashdod *ca.* 710 B.C. The

Ishmaelites appear in the Joseph story as camel people from Gilead engaged in caravan trade with Egypt. The description of Ishmael in Gen. 16:12 as a "wild ass of a man, [whose] hand [is] against every man and every man's hand against him," suits remarkably well the Beduin of N Arabia, whose raiding of settled folk has been a perennial factor in Near Eastern history. Gen. 21:20 speaks of him as dwelling in the desert country, while his "sons" belong to the desert area stretching from the land of Midian to the borders of Mesopotamia, which is precisely the area in which we find the Arab groups mentioned in the cuneiform inscriptions.

As early as 854 B.C. an inscription of Shalmaneser III mentions "Gindibu' the Arabian," who assembled a camel corps to oppose the Assyrians; and from Tiglath-pileser III (745-727) down to Nabonidus, the last Babylonian king, there is not infrequent reference to peoples of N Arabia and their rulers, among whom appear several "queens." These inscriptions mention the Masai (the Massa [משא] of Gen. 25:14 and the *Masei Arabes* of Pliny Nat. Hist. VI.30), the Temai (the Tema [תימא] of Gen. 25:15; Job 6:19; Jer. 25:23), the Sabai (the Sheba [שבא] of Gen. 25:3; Isa. 60:6; Jer. 6:20; Ezek. 27:22), the Ḥaiappa (the Ephah [עיפה] of Gen. 25:4; Isa. 60:6), the Ḥatti (the Benē Ḥēth of Gen. 25:10), the Idibaili (the Adbeel [אדבאל] of Gen. 25:13), the Qidri (the Kedar [קדר] of Gen. 25:13; Isa. 21:16; Jer. 2:10; Ezek. 27:21), the Nabaiti (the Nebaioth [נביות] of Gen. 25:13; 28:9; Isa. 60:7). Several Arabian place names mentioned in these inscriptions also have biblical correspondences—e.g., Taima is the Tema of Isa. 21:14; Adūma is the Dumah of Josh. 15:52; Isa. 21:11; Bāzu is the Buz of Jer. 25:23, the home of Job's friend Elihu (Job 32:2, 6) and the list of whose rulers given in Esarhaddon's Prism B inscription shows, for the most part, good Arabic names.

All these references are to N Arabia, for though the Sabai are by name connected with the Sabean kingdom in S Arabia, the references apparently are to S settlements in the N area. Throughout Arabian history there is a sense of a difference and even a certain antipathy between S and N Arabs which continued even under Islam. Perhaps as early as 1200 B.C. the S had developed a civilization the full greatness of which is only now beginning to be realized, and which survived till the advent of Islam. They were great builders of private and public works, great organizers of social and political life, great agriculturalists and traders. It was interest in the spice trade that led them to establish settlements on the trade routes in the N. They had learned an alphabet which they adapted and in which they have left numerous inscriptions, many of which have been found in their N settlements, where N Arabs in contact with them also learned to write a little in their N dialects. The Greeks knew four kingdoms in S Arabia—Minaean, Sabean, Qatabanian, and Hadramauti—but only recently has it become possible to understand more clearly their history. The Joctanid genealogical table in Gen. 10:26-30 contains several names with good S Arabian correspondences.

Possibly the distinction between Seba (סבא) and Sheba (שבא) in Gen. 10:7, preserved also in Ps. 72: 10, is meant to distinguish the Sabeans of S Arabia from those in the N settlements. All the references to Seba (cf. Isa. 43:3; 45:14) suit the S kingdoms, while those to Sheba suit better a N site. The Sabeans who attacked Job's herdsmen (Job 1:15, 19) were dwelling in the N, and though "It'amara the Sabean" of Sargon II's inscription has a good S Arabian name, it occurs also on a Lihyanite inscription from N Arabia. The question thus arises whether the Queen of Sheba who visited Solomon was really from the S and not rather from one of these N Arabian groups, for we know of no independent queens in the S.

The OT pictures these N Arabian groups as in contact with Palestine from the patriarchal age onward, in terms both of war and of peace. Ps. 83 lists the Ishmaelites and the Hagarenes as among the traditional enemies of Israel, and this, indeed, is part of the picture. In the Job story the Sabeans raid Job's lands; slay his herdsmen, and take his cattle as booty (Job 1:15). In the Gideon story (Judg. 6–7) the Midianites, Amalekites, and Bene Qedem (people of the East), raiding in from the E where they pitched their tents, plunder and retreat back into their deserts to escape pursuit. The tale of the capture of Ziklag by the Amalekites (I Sam. 30), and that of the raiders who carried away Jehoram's family and possessions (II Chr. 21:16-17; 22:1), are characteristic razzia stories. It was doubtless against such raiding that Uzziah needed the succor granted him (II Chr. 26:7). Raiding provokes retaliation, so that skill in eluding pursuit after a raid receives high praise among Arabs. It is such an escaping group to which the oracle in Isa. 21:13-17 is addressed. The Kedar (Qidri) are mentioned there, and Nebuchadrezzar's retaliation on these Qidri is the subject of Jer. 49:28-33. In the days of Hezekiah (I Chr. 4:43) a band of Simeonites exterminated the Amalekites whose roving bands had harassed the Israelites during their desert march (Exod. 17:8-16; Deut. 25:17-19), and had been troublesome raiders in the days of the judges (Judg. 6–7) and of Saul and David (I Sam. 15; 30). Though the historicity of some of these events may be open to doubt, it is evident that the writers are setting down accurately memories of what these nomadic N Arabian groups had meant in the history of Israel.

On the other hand, the writers picture these same peoples as contributing in peaceful ways to Israel's life. The Midianites, in one version of the Joseph story, are traders who lead caravans to Egypt (Gen. 37:28, 36). A gloss in Judg. 8:24 identifies Midianites with Ishmaelites, and many of their names have good Arabic correspondences. In Isa. 60:10 they are caravan people supplying Israel with luxury goods of S Arabian trade, but in the Moses story (Exod. 2–3) they are a pastoral people among whom Moses found a wife, to whose land he led the Israelites from Egypt (Exod. 17), and who supplied the guide to lead them through Moab to the Promised Land (Num. 10:29-32). The head of David's camel keepers was an Ishmaelite, the chief herdsman over his flocks a Hagarene (I Chr. 27:30); and Solomon is regarded as having profited from the trade of these Arabians (I Kings 10:15). Their wealth is mentioned in Ezek. 38:10-13, their supplying Israel with gold, precious stones, and spices in II Chr. 9:14; Isa. 60:6; Jer. 6:

20; Ezek. 27:22, their furnishing small cattle in II Chr. 17:11; Isa. 60:7; Ezek. 27:21, and the Dedanites' furnishing of textiles in Ezek. 27:20.

The exiles who returned and commenced, under Nehemiah, rebuilding Jerusalem found Arabs, under a leader Gashmu (RSV "Geshem"), among those seeking to hinder them (Neh. 2:19; 4:7; 6:1-6). This name is known from inscriptions as in use among Dedanite and Kedar groups, but in form it is a good Nabatean name. These Nabateans were the only N Arabians who established a civilization comparable with that of S Arabia. Some, indeed, think they were S Arabians who had migrated northward. When we first meet them, they are a nomadic group, though by the fourth century B.C. they had already wrested Petra, the ancient Sela', from the Edomites, making it a center from which they built up a kingdom stretching from the Red Sea to beyond Damascus and penetrating deeply into Arabia. Some remained nomads to the end, but groups settled at Petra and other "caravan cities" along the trade routes, where they developed their characteristic civilization. Their proper names reveal them as an Arab people, but they adopted Aramaic as their literary language, developing in their own way the Aramaic script so that it became the source of the later Arabic script.

Their first recorded king is Hārethath I (Aretas) *ca.* 169 B.C., contemporary with Antiochus Epiphanes and the Jewish high priest Jason (II Macc. 5:8). The Maccabees were in friendly relations with them (I Macc. 5:25; 9:35), but the Hasmoneans quarreled with them, and Alexander Janneus was beaten in battle with Obodas I, *ca.* 90 B.C. (Jos. Antiq. XIII. xiii.5). Under Aretas III (87-62 B.C.) their kingdom reached its greatest expansion, their culture becoming seriously Hellenized, and the king taking the title Philhellene. He intervened in Jewish affairs, supporting Hyrcanus against Aristobulus, and was attacked by Pompey's general Scaurus, who blockaded him in Petra, from which he freed himself only by buying off the Romans (Jos. Antiq. XIV.v.1). When war broke out between the Romans and the Parthians, the Nabateans had great difficulty in keeping friendly with both sides. From Pompey's day they had had their rulers recognized by Rome, but Aretas IV (9 B.C.–A.D. 40) seized the power without Roman acknowledgment, taking the title of Philodemos (*Rāḥem 'Ammeh*), though later he secured Roman recognition. He was the Aretas of the time of Paul (II Cor. 11:32). His son Malichos II lost Damascus and was compelled to aid Vespasian and Titus in the war against the Jews (Jos. War III.vii.9). After him there were but two rulers, and then in 106 Cornelius Palma put an end to their kingdom, which Trajan incorporated into the Roman province of Arabia (Dio Cassius LXVIII.14).

The Arabs Timotheus hired against Judas Maccabeus (I Macc. 5:39; II Macc. 12:10) may have been nondescript Beduin, as likewise that Arab chieftain Zabdiel who sent the head of Alexander Balas to Ptolemy (I Macc. 11:17), and the Imalkue who brought up Alexander's son Antiochus (I Macc. 11:39), though these may all have been Nabateans. Sylleus, who brought disaster on the Roman expedition in Arabia under Aelius Gallus in 25 B.C. (Strabo XVI.4.22-24), was certainly a Nabatean, and the

Arabians present at Jerusalem on the Day of Pentecost (Acts 2:11) were apparently Jews from some Nabatean settlement.

**3. Beduin life.** From the earliest times these peoples of Arabia, though dominantly nomadic, have included seminomadic and fully settled groups. Organization of settled life developed mostly in the S, the characteristic N Arabian life having always been the life of the nomad, and Arabic literature is full of references to the contempt the nomads have for settled folk and the scorn of the settled peoples for the nomad. The nomad is the *badu* (plural *badawin*), and the *bādiya* is the wilderness where he roams. The nomads' social unit is the tribe (*qabīla*), whose members are theoretically blood brothers, led by the sheik and his council of elders. Commonly tribes are named from an eponymous ancestor and known as Banu Murra (sons of Murra), Banu Taghlib, etc., just as the Benē Ḥeth and Benē Qedem in the OT. Necessities of water and pasturage dominate their economy, for without these their flocks cannot survive. There is consequently much seasonal migration. On their herds they live, and from them they derive the small wealth they need to purchase necessities not provided by their deserts. Their traditional beast of burden is the camel, but before its effective domestication they employed asses, which are still commonly used. The horse is rather a luxury animal. Their flocks are of sheep and goats. Of necessity their home is the mobile tent. The women do the domestic work around the tent, one half of which is "women's quarters," tend the small cattle, and engage in weaving. The men tend camels and horses, hunt, and raid. Raiding has ever been the traditional sport of the Beduin. It is preferable to raid some hostile group, but as their poets say: " 'Tis better to raid one's brothers than not to raid at all." Care is taken not to shed blood while raiding, yet blood does get shed, whence arises the dread duty of blood revenge which, through the ages, has dominated Beduin life.

This life the nomad lives has bred in him those qualities of hardiness, frugality, graspingness, stubbornness, and truculence for which he is famed, and makes him prize the virtues of manliness, fortitude, and hospitality. His individualism keeps him impatient of order and discipline, and unamenable to restraint or authority. In curious contradiction to Beduin love of freedom, slaves have had a definite place in the social system both in the N and in the S. In S Arabia their artistic sense found expression in architecture, decoration, and plastic art, though we know nothing of their literature. Petra and the delicate Nabatean pottery show what could be accomplished by N sedentary groups, but among the nomads the sole forms of artistic expression were poetry and pithy gnomic wisdom. It is curious that in I Kings 4:30; 5:10, Solomon's wisdom is said to have surpassed that of the Benē Qedem, and that Job's wise friends came from N Arabian groups.

This nomad life is reflected accurately in the OT. That they were tent dwellers appears in Judg. 5:6; 8:11; Pss. 83:6; 120:5; Jer. 49:29, 31; Ezek. 38:11. Representations of their tents on Assyrian monuments show them much the same as they are today. Assyrian representations of Arabs fighting from their

camels show them with that polling of the hair noted in Jer. 25:23; 49:32 and alsò by Herodotus (III.8). Their camels and flocks are often mentioned. Caravan routes are referred to in Judg. 8:11, while vss. 21-26 mention the amulets (RSV "collars") on the necks of camels and the men's earrings—customs which still survive. The nose ring and bracelets given to Rebekah (Gen. 24:22, 47) are still the ornaments given a Beduin girl. Joel 3:8 mentions their dealing in slaves.

**4. Religion.** From S Arabia we have material for a fair picture of the religious life in that civilization, but we are far from well informed about the religion of the N Arabian nomads, partly because Islam aroused an unfortunate enthusiasm for destroying all traces of the paganism of the "days of Ignorance." There were temples, some of them imposing structures, at the more important settlements in the N, but there were also numerous sanctuaries in the sparsely populated areas, forming centers to which the nomads went in pilgrimage, especially at festival times. At such centers there was generally a shrine with a sacred stone, and a sacred well with sacred trees near by. The stone represented deity, male or female. Sometimes they were but rough stones, sometimes rudely shaped, sometimes carved images. Sacred objects seem also to have been carried by the nomads during their wanderings. At shrines there were rites of circumambulation, animal and even human sacrifice, offerings, divinations, and festival rites. The territory for some distance around such shrines, being sacred to the divinity, seems to have offered sanctuary from the avenger of blood. Doubtless there were priesthoods, but they were of little significance. Theophorous names reveal the astral connections of many deities, as sun gods, moon gods, star gods. There were also deities with animal connections. Prominent among the goddesses was the ancient Mother Goddess, who would seem to have been the deity at the Meccan shrine. The old Arabian calendar had religious associations.

Lower in rank than deities were other angelic beings, and of still lower rank great numbers of spirits (*jinn*), sometimes benevolent, sometimes malevolent, whose influence on human affairs had to be guarded against by charms and conjurations. There was universal fear of the evil eye, and of soothsayers, and diviners flourished as mediators between this world and that of the spirits. There was a vague trend toward monotheism in both the S and the N.

**Bibliography.** C. Doughty, *Travels in Arabia Deserta* (2 vols.; 1884). G. Jacob, *Das Leben der vorislamischen Beduinen* (1895). J. Wellhausen, *Reste arabischen Heidenthums* (1897). R. Brünnow and A. Domaszewski, *Die Provincia Arabia* (3 vols.; 1905-9). T. Nöldeke, "Arabs (Ancient)," in J. Hastings, *Encyclopedia of Religion and Ethics*, I (1913), 659-73. H. Lammens, *Le berceau de l'Islam* (1914). A. Musil, *Arabia Petraea* (3 vols.; 1907-8); *The Northern Hijaz* (1926); *Arabia Deserta* (1927); *Northern Najd* (1928); *Manners and Customs of the Rwala Bedouin* (1930). J. A. Montgomery, *Arabia and the Bible* (1934). L. Dubertret and J. Weulersse, *La péninsule arabique* (1941). G. Ryckmans, *Les religions arabes préislamiques* (1951). M. von Oppenheim, *Die Beduinen* (3 vols.; 1939-52). D. Sourdel, *Les cultes du Hauran à l'époque romaine* (1952). R. Dussaud, *La pénétration des Arabes en Syrie avant l'Islam* (1955). J. Starcky, "The Nabataeans: a Historical Sketch," *BA*, XVIII (1955), 4.

A. JEFFERY

**ARABIC GOSPEL OF THE INFANCY** ăr'ə bǐk. A late compilation of wonder stories about the infant Jesus. Like all secondary infancy gospels (*see* APOCRYPHA, NT), it is heavily dependent upon the Protevangelium of James and the Gospel of Thomas (*see* JAMES, PROTEVANGELIUM OF; THOMAS, GOSPEL OF). These (together with highly imaginative expansions from hints in the canonical gospels) appear to have been respectively the chief sources for chs. 1-9; 36-55. The intervening chapters contain a long series of tasteless miracles wrought in Egypt through contact with the infant, his clothes, or his bath water (20-25), and in Nazareth (26-35). In all these tales Mary is the one who engineers the cures. The text, frequently reprinted, depends upon an Arabic MS first published by Henry Sike in 1697. That it was first published in Syriac has often been conjectured, but where and at what time it is impossible to determine, save that its highly oriental coloring suggests the East.

*Bibliography.* P. Peeters, *Évangiles apocryphes* (1914), vol. II. The text is summarized in M. R. James, *The Apocryphal NT* (1924), pp. 80-82, and given in full in *Ante-Nicene Christian Library*, XVI (Apocryphal Acts, Gospels, etc.), 100-124.

M. S. ENSLIN

**ARABIC VERSIONS.** *See* VERSIONS, ANCIENT, § 10.

**ARAD** âr'ăd [עֲרָד]. **1.** One of the sons of Beriah in the genealogy of Benjamin (I Chr. 8:15).

**2.** A Canaanite city of the Negeb in the time of Moses and the conquest of Canaan. It is mentioned in Egyptian texts as '*rd*. According to Num. 21:1-3, the king of Arad made a surprise attack on the Israelites at the end of the wilderness period as they were marching from Kadesh-barnea to Mount Hor by way of Atharim. The Israelites vowed vengeance on the Canaanites and destroyed the city, and its site was occupied by the nomadic Kenites (Judg. 1:16). Arad is included in the enumeration of the city kings conquered by Joshua (Josh. 12:14), probably because this is a summation of all the conquests W of the Jordan.

The site of the city is at Tell 'Arad, *ca.* sixteen miles S of Hebron.                              S. COHEN

**ARADUS** ăr'ə dəs ["Αραδος] (I Macc. 15:23). A place mentioned in a list of various places to which letters were sent about the conditions of the Jews. *See* ARVAD.

**ARAH** âr'ə [אָרַח, traveler, *or* ox(?), 'Αρές]; KJV Apoc. ARES âr'ēz. **1.** One of the sons of Ulla in the genealogy of Asher (I Chr. 7:39).

**2.** An ancestor of some of those who returned from Babylonian captivity (Ezra 2:5 = Neh. 7:10 = I Esd. 5:10). The number varies in the parallel passages and in the ancient versions. Shecaniah, an individual member of this family group, is mentioned in Neh. 6:18.                              F. T. SCHUMACHER

**ARAM** âr'əm [אֲרָם; Akkad. *Aramu, or a variant thereof*]. Alternately: SYRIA sĭr'ĭ ə [Συρία; English *versions often use the* Greek *name, especially in* 4 *below, although it is rather too late and specific to serve as a pre-*cise *equivalent*]. **1.** The fifth son of Shem; the father of Uz, Hul, Gether, and Mash in the conflate J and P genealogy of the sons of Noah (Gen. 10:22-23), which serves as a table of nations. The "sons of Aram" cannot with certainty be equated with known territories, though numerous suggestions have been made; in I Chr. 1:17 they are listed as his brothers. The sons of Shem indicate branches of the Semitic people, and thus the name is applied to a people, a language (*see* ARAMAIC LANGUAGE), and a land or area.

**2.** Son of Kemuel and grandson of Nahor, who was Abraham's brother (Gen. 22:21). The names mentioned here suggest the area of HARAN. This genealogical note suggests the close relationship between the people of Aram and the Israelite patriarchs.

**3.** The third son of Shemer in the genealogy of Asher (I Chr. 7:34).

**4.** Most frequently used as a singular collective for the ARAMEANS, an important Semitic people living throughout the Mesopotamian and Syrian areas in many scattered tribes and settlements (II Sam. 8:5-6; I Kings 20:20-21; I Chr. 2:23; 19:10, 12; plus sixty-four other times in Samuel, Kings, and Chronicles; Amos 1:5; 9:7; Isa. 7:2, 4-5, 8; 9:12; 17:3; Jer. 35:11; Ezek. 16:57; 27:16). Less frequently it is used in reference to the land of the Arameans (Num. 23:7; II Sam. 15:8; Hos. 12:12—H 12:13; probably Zech. 9:1) and often for land and people together, especially in phrases about kings or gods of Syria or Aram (Judg. 10:6; Isa. 7:1; and forty-three times in Kings and Chronicles).

The land of Aram is somewhat indefinite, since it is not a political or geographical unit but only indicates a concentration of Aramean population. Roughly for the OT, it covers the territory from beyond the Jordan and NE of Palestine around the Fertile Crescent into the upper Tigris-Euphrates Valley. Assyrian inscriptions, on the other hand, apparently limit it to areas E of the Euphrates, ascribing the W part to earlier powers such as HITTITES and AMORITES. The OT often uses the word as part of a compound to indicate particular subdivisions, thus indicating a more precise location (*see* ARAM-NAHARAIM; PADDAN-ARAM; ARAM MAACAH; ARAM-BETHREHOB; ZOBAH; DAMASCUS; *see also* GESHUR). In relation to patriarchal narratives the term usually refers to the Mesopotamian area. But simultaneous with the emergence of the monarchy in Israel, Damascus became the center of Aramean power and influence in the W. These two were neighbors and warring rivals through most of the period of the monarchy until Assyria destroyed first Damascus and then Israel and Judah. Consequently, in literature referring to the days of the monarchy, Aram means primarily Damascus and surrounding territory, even when no express indication is given.

**5.** KJV form (RSV mg.) of RAM 1 in Matt. 1:3 and of ARNI in Luke 3:33.                              F. T. SCHUMACHER

**ARAMAIC** ăr'ə mā'ĭk. A general term used to cover a group of Semitic dialects closely related to Hebrew, and even more closely related to one another, which have considerable interest for biblical studies. In the OT not only are Ezra 4:8–6:18; 7:12-26; Dan. 2:4*b*–7:28; and the gloss in Jer. 10:11 in Aramaic, but we find elsewhere a number of isolated Aramaic words, and in certain books the biblical Hebrew has been somewhat Aramaicized. In the NT such phrases as *talitha cumi, Marana tha, ephphatha, Eloi, eloi, lama sabachthani,* are in contemporary Aramaic, which also shows as substratum under much that is there written in Greek. The Targums to the OT books, the Syriac versions of the OT and the NT, and the originals of certain apocryphal and pseudepigraphical writings are in Aramaic.

Aram (*see* ARAM 5) is mentioned as a place name, designating an area NE of Syria, as early as 2500 B.C., but the name seems non-Semitic, the later Semitic-speaking peoples being named ARAMEANS by Tiglath-pileser I (*ca.* 1100 B.C.) because he found them in that area. He knew them as encroaching nomads, but much earlier—as early even as the beginning of the third millennium B.C.—we have evidence of similar nomads called Suti, coming from the deserts of N Arabia and raiding both Mesopotamia and Egypt. The relationship of these to the Arami, Kaldi, Akhlami, Pakudi, all similar nomadic invaders of whom we read in Assyrian inscriptions from Tiglath-pileser I onward, is uncertain, but it would seem that in these groups we are to see the speakers of proto-Aramaic. It is of interest that the OT associates the patriarchs with these Arameans (Gen. 24:3-10; 25:20; 28:2-5), and in Deut. 26:5 each Israelite is made to confess: "A wandering Aramean was my father." In the twelfth century such groups were establishing more or less settled communities all along the Tigris and Euphrates from the Persian Gulf to N Syria and southward into both Palestine and N Arabia. By the eleventh century they had succeeded in establishing little kingdoms, some of which in N Syria learned from the earlier-settled Canaanites the art of alphabetic writing. At first they attempted to use Canaanitish in their inscriptions, but they betrayed themselves by such Aramaisms as the use of *bar* instead of *ben* for "son." Before long they dropped this Canaanitish and began to use their own language in their inscriptions, so that from the tenth and ninth centuries we have our earliest texts in the Aramaic language.

It has been customary to divide the Aramaic languages (or dialects) into an eastern and a western group. A more accurate and significant division, however, is that into four groups: (*a*) Old Aramaic; (*b*) Official Aramaic; (*c*) Levantine Aramaic; (*d*) Eastern Aramaic.

1. Old Aramaic
2. Official Aramaic
3. Levantine Aramaic
   *a.* Palestinian Jewish Aramaic
   *b.* Samaritan
   *c.* Christian Palestinian Aramaic
   *d.* Modern Western Aramaic
4. Eastern Aramaic
   *a.* Babylonian Jewish Aramaic
   *b.* Mandaean
   *c.* Syriac
   *d.* Modern Syriac
Bibliography

**1. Old Aramaic.** This is the language of the inscriptions from N Syria, dating from the tenth to the eighth century B.C. When they ceased using Canaanitish, what these Arameans employed in their inscriptions was doubtless their local dialect, which they were gradually shaping into a literary form. Though all that has survived to us is what was written on durable stone, it is highly probable that they wrote also on less durable materials which have perished. For lack of contemporary texts written by Arameans in areas other than N Syria, it is not possible to say whether this dialect was used by other early Aramean groups.

**2. Official Aramaic.** Already in the inscriptions from N Syria, in the later inscriptions of the ruler Bar Rekub, whose earlier inscriptions had been in the Old Aramaic, a new dialect appears. It is the same dialect that later appears in official documents from Assyria, and then in texts from various parts of the Assyrian Empire, not only during the Assyrian period but more commonly in the succeeding Persian period. It seems fairly clear that it was a form of Aramaic developed as a lingua franca in the governmental offices—i.e., in the chancelleries—and so may be fitly designated "Official Aramaic." Even in the Assyrian period (*ca.* 1100-605 B.C.) Aramaic would seem to have been coming more and more into use throughout the Empire, and officials in the chancelleries, aware that Aramaic was far better known than Akkadian in the distant parts of the Empire, commenced using a simple, standard form of Aramaic for correspondence with such areas. In the heart of the Empire itself we find that there had grown up a practice of attaching Aramaic "dockets" to cuneiform tablets. Such "dockets," giving a brief indication of names and dates and a summary of the contents, were particularly useful to merchants, and it may well have been a kind of "merchant's Aramaic," based on the dialect of Aramaic spoken in Mesopotamia, that provided the basis for this Official Aramaic.

Once this type of Aramaic was recognized as having official sanction, the Aramaic-speaking people in various parts of the Empire would quite naturally begin to use it themselves, in preference to their own local dialect, for literary purposes. In Akkadian tablets we find that certain scribes are designated as "scribes for Aramaic"—i.e., for this Official Aramaic. On Bar Rekub's statue at Zinjirli a scribe stands before him with pen and ink and tablet prepared, doubtless, to write for him in this Official Aramaic, for Bar Rekub was a loyal subject of the Assyrian monarch. That such scribes wrote not only with a pen but with a stylus is evident from the existence of clay tablets from Assyria with the text incised in Aramaic. This Aramaic also appears incised on numerous metal weights, on seals and vessels, and is painted or written on pottery. Though the script in the Old Aramaic inscriptions was very close to the Canaanitish script, it early began to develop in its own way till presently it has so far evolved as to be a definite Aramaic script easily distinguishable from the Canaanitish script.

How widespread the use of this Official Aramaic was in Assyrian times is indicated by a number of bits of evidence. In II Kings 18:13-37 we read that in the year 701 B.C., when officials of Sennacherib appeared before the walls of Jerusalem, and the Rab-shakeh spoke in Hebrew to the officers of King Hezekiah, these latter begged him to speak rather in Aramaic, for they understood this official tongue and did not want the populace to hear the demand for submission made in Hebrew. Near Olympia in Greece a bronze bowl was found bearing a name incised in Aramaic characters, and it seems highly probable that the alphabetic signs the Greeks learned from the Semites in Asia Minor were of the Aramaic rather than the Phoenician type. From Egypt there are inscriptions in Aramaic from as early as the reign of Esarhaddon (681-669 B.C.), from Tarsus in Cilicia small inscriptions of perhaps an even earlier date, and it is clear that the use of the language had penetrated deeply into Arabia.

This Official Aramaic continued in use throughout the Neo-Babylonian period (605-538), and when the Persians succeeded as the dominant power, though the Persian monarchs used a system of cuneiform signs in which to carve royal inscriptions in their own Old Persian language, yet in their chancelleries Aramaic continued to be the official language. In fact, it is during this Persian period (538-330 B.C.) that we find the use of Aramaic at its widest spread. From Mesopotamia we have "dockets," ostraca, and seals with inscriptions in official Aramaic throughout this period. From Persia itself we have short inscriptions on stone and a number of clay documents. From Egypt have come funerary and dedicatory inscriptions on stone and graffiti scrawled on the rocks along the trade routes. From Palestine there are ostraca from Samaria and Ezion-geber, inscriptions on stone, jar handles from a variety of sites. From N Arabia come inscriptions from both Hegra and Taima, and from Anatolia inscriptions from Cilicia, Lydia, Lycia, together with a multitude of coins from various cities with legends in Aramaic. As far N as the Ural Mountains, as well as in the Caucasus and the Zagros Mountains, have been found metal objects inscribed with Aramaic words and names, from as far E as Afghanistan and Kurdistan, and even at Taxila in Pakistan, have come inscriptions, and to the W an inscribed bronze vessel from Greece and some short texts of Aramaic in Latin transcription show how widely this Aramaic was used as a lingua franca during this period.

Fortunately we have evidence that it was also used at this time for writing on less durable materials. The letters which the intercepted messenger Artaphernes was carrying from the Persian king to the Lacedaemonians, and which Thucydides (IV.50. 2) says had to be translated ἐκ τῶν Ἀσσυρίων γραμμάτων, may have been written in the cuneiform characters but are much more likely to have been written in Aramaic on parchment. The existence of writing on parchment seems clear also from the clay sealings in napkin-ring shape from Persepolis, but whether the perishable documents to which they were attached were written in Old Persian or in Aramaic we cannot be certain, though the number of Aramaic inscriptions from Persepolis favors the theory that they were Aramaic parchments. From Egypt, however, where documents on perishable material had a better chance to survive, we have the Borchardt collection, now published by G. R. Driver, containing thirteen letters, with fragments of several others,

addressed by high Persian officials to lesser officials in Egypt about administrative affairs. These are on leather, but numerous Aramaic papyri have been recovered from Edfu, Abydos, Abusir, Memphis, Hermopolis, and in particular the famous papyri from Elephantine and Assuan. Some mummy cases from the Persian-period necropolis near Alexandria bear names in Aramaic. The presence of the Ahiqar story and an Aramaic version of the Behistun inscription among these papyri from Egypt shows this Official Aramaic in use for literary as well as for practical purposes, so that it is not strange to find that the Aramaic portions of the OT, formerly set apart as biblical Aramaic or Chaldee, are really in this Official Aramaic. It is highly probable that the book of Daniel was originally written in Aramaic, for the Hebrew portions show in many places indications that they were translated from Aramaic. It has been suggested that the book of Ecclesiastes also was translated from an Aramaic original, but the arguments for this are far less cogent. It has long been held that several of the apocryphal and pseudepigraphical writings, which have survived to us only in versions in various languages, were originally composed in Aramaic, and now fragments from the Dead Sea Caves have actually presented portions of such texts copied from Aramaic originals.

This already brings us into the succeeding Hellenistic period. Official Aramaic continued in use throughout the Hellenistic period (330-30 B.C.). It is still found in use on "dockets" and on coins of this period, in papyri and ostraca from Egypt, in inscriptions from both Mesopotamia and Egypt, in a number of graffiti from Egypt, Herodian-age Palestine, and Nabatean Sinai, and particularly in several inscriptions, some of them bilingual, from Asia Minor, and the Parthian-period inscriptions from Hatra. One very curious phenomenon from this period is the existence of Aramaic texts in transliteration. From Egypt comes a papyrus written in the Demotic script, but Aramaic in language, dealing with some religious matter, and from Babylonia comes an Aramaic incantation text written in cuneiform syllabic signs. Greek was gradually ousting Aramaic during this period, but to compensate for losses in the more seriously Hellenized areas, Aramaic won an extension of influence in two areas—in Arabia where the Nabateans and Palmyrenes used Aramaic till well into the Christian era, and in Palestine, where the groups resistant to the penetration of Greek culture seem to have emphasized the use of Aramaic. To this we doubtless owe the Aramaic of Daniel and of *Meghillath Ta'anith,* as well as the Aramaic used in a number of inscriptions, and that of the Qumran documents from near the Dead Sea. It is known that Josephus wrote the first draft of his historical work in Aramaic. H. L. Ginsberg has noted that the Targum quotations and deed forms given in both the Babylonian and the Jerusalem Talmud are in Official Aramaic, as also certain rabbinic legal instruments of even later times. The Targums of Onkelos to the Pentateuch and of Jonathan to the Prophets, though redacted in Babylonia and somewhat influenced by the local Mesopotamian dialect, seem to have been composed with intent in a kind of general Aramaic, as perhaps the last efforts at literary composition in Official Aramaic.

Since this Official Aramaic continued in use for a long period of time over a widely extended area, it was inevitable that it should develop local peculiarities. Thus in Persia it was influenced both in structure and in vocabulary by the surrounding Iranian speech, in Egypt and Anatolia both by the local languages and later by Greek, in Palmyra and the Nabatean area by the native Arabic of the people who used it as their language of literary expression. For this reason it is possible to speak of Parthian Aramaic, Egyptian Aramaic, biblical Aramaic, Nabatean, and Palmyrene as dialects of Official Aramaic.

**3. Levantine Aramaic.** While early Aramean nomads were pentrating the Tigris and Euphrates area, other groups of them were penetrating Syria and Palestine, where they settled and where their language was spoken alongside Canaanitish in certain areas. After the fall of Samaria in 721, when the Assyrians replaced the inhabitants whom they carried off by colonists from various parts of the Empire, Aramaic seems to have come increasingly into everyday use in Syria and Palestine till by the time the exiles returned, it, and not Hebrew, was the commonly understood language. When the adversaries of the returned exiles wrote to the Persian king in Aramaic (Ezra 4:7) and received his reply in Aramaic, this was probably in the Official Aramaic of the chancelleries; but when Ezra read them the Book of the Law, his interpreters, who "gave the sense, so that the people understood the reading" (Neh. 8:8), doubtless used the local dialect. In spite of the widespread use of Greek, Levantine Aramaic was still the popularly spoken language in NT times and was only driven out of use by Arabic after the Muslim conquest. It has never become extinct, for it is still spoken, though in greatly changed form, in a few villages in the Anti-Lebanon.

The prestige of Official Aramaic as the language of official intercourse and culture retarded the use of this vernacular for literary purposes, much as the prestige of Latin retarded the literary use of the spoken dialects in Italy. Yet some groups did at length begin to use their local dialect for writing rather than the Official Aramaic, and these are sufficiently close to one another to be classed as representatives of Levantine Aramaic.

*a. Palestinian Jewish Aramaic.* Possibly some of the latest Palestinian inscriptions mentioned under Official Aramaic might have been included here. Its earliest appearance in literary documents, however, is in the Aramaic words and phrases embedded in the Greek of the NT. The dialect daily spoken by Jesus and the disciples was Galilean Aramaic, which, as is noted in Matt. 26:73, was recognizably different from the S dialect spoken in and around Jerusalem. It was in this same Galilean dialect that the Aramaic of the Palestinian Talmud and the older Midrashim was written. The Targum of Pseudo-Jonathan, the Fragment Targum, the Targum to the Hagiographa (i.e., the Yerushalmi Targums), and in particular the fragments of the old Palestinian Targum published by Paul Kahle in his *Masoreten des Westens* from the Geniza material, are all in this dialect. The vocalization is, however, uncertain, for that employed in the rabbinic texts is only a late, artificial system.

*b. Samaritan.* Much of the Samaritan religious literature is in Hebrew and Arabic, but the Samaritans have a Targum to the Pentateuch in their own dialect, which is very close to the Galilean dialect. They have also some liturgical works, hymns and poems, and devotional works in this dialect. After the Muslim conquest it died out of common use before Arabic. The curious alphabet in which the Samaritans write their Aramaic is a local development of the old Canaanitish script.

*c. Christian Palestinian Aramaic.* The earliest Palestinian Christians doubtless continued to use the local dialect among themselves, but the official language of the new religion was Greek, and its early literature was in Greek. When an Aramaic gospel began to circulate, it was in Syriac, the version made at the intellectual center in Edessa, a version which rapidly came into use in all the Aramaic-speaking areas both East and West. During the christological controversies of the fourth and fifth centuries the Syr. Peshitta version of the Scriptures seemed too closely associated with the Jacobites and Nestorians, who were condemned as heretics, and so those Christian groups in Syria and Palestine who sided with Byzantium and came to be called Melkites felt the need for religious texts in their own dialect, and produced translations, mostly from the Greek, both of the Scriptures and of various liturgical and devotional works. This is commonly called Christian Palestinian Syriac but was used also by Aramaic-speaking Christians in Egypt. Evidence that the dialect was also used for secular purposes has come from the Dead Sea Caves, where among the fragments from Khirbet Mird was a document in this dialect. By the ninth century it had died out before the advance of Arabic.

*d. Modern Western Aramaic.* In Christian villages in the Anti-Lebanon, more particularly in Ma'lula, Bakh', and Jubb 'Adin, a dialect of Levantine Aramaic is still the house language of people who in public use the Arabic of their neighbors. It has undergone considerable phonetic change and has been much influenced both in vocabulary and in syntax by the dominant speech of the area, but seems to be a survival of the vernacular Aramaic formerly spoken over a much wider area in the Levant.

**4. Eastern Aramaic.** The nomadic Arameans who invaded the Tigris-Euphrates region had their own local dialects which would have differed from the later, Official Aramaic much as did the Levantine dialects. Certain of these eastern dialects also, in spite of the prestige of the Official Aramaic, came to be written and used as literary languages. As spoken dialects they seem to have spread up into the mountains of Armenia and Kurdistan, and eastward as far as the Indus, but for the most part they died out after the Muslim conquest, though some are still spoken by Christian communities in N Mesopotamia and Kurdistan. Belonging to this Eastern Aramaic are:

*a. Babylonian Jewish Aramaic.* This appears in the Gemara of the Babylonian Talmud and in a number of documents ranging in date between the second and the seventh centuries A.D. It is not a uniform dialect even in the Talmud, and some of the texts available seem to have been written by non-Jews, but, as the Talmud is our chief witness to it, Babylonian Jewish Aramaic is a convenient name. As in the case of Palestinian Jewish Aramaic, the vocalization employed in the texts used by the rabbinic authorities follows an artificial system and is no sure guide to the pronunciation.

*b. Mandaean.* The religious literature of the Mandaeans of Iraq is written in a dialect of this Eastern Aramaic. Since these are original documents of an independent religion, written in a script indigenously developed from the Old Aramaic, they ought to show a pure form of Eastern Aramaic uninfluenced by Hebrew as the Jewish dialect is, or by Greek as is the case with Syriac. Unfortunately, however, all its documents come from a late period when the language has already undergone considerable phonetic change and been greatly influenced by the Arabic these people use in daily intercourse.

*c. Syriac.* This dialect, which became the Christian dialect of Eastern Aramaic, was perhaps already used as a literary language before the Christian era, but only a few scraps from the first century A.D. remain to illustrate its early form. As the language of the scholarly center at Edessa, particularly when a Christian school succeeded the pagan school there, it developed into a literary language of some importance. After the controversies over the decisions of the Council of Chalcedon in 451, it was accepted by most Aramaic-speaking Christians as their ecclesiastical and cultural language and one form of their defense against Byzantine influence. As such it was carried to Persia and Turkestan; to India and China in the E; to Asia Minor, Syria, and Palestine in the W; to Arabia and Egypt in the S. From Egypt we even have Greek texts in Syriac script. It greatly influenced the language of Armenia, the Middle Iranian dialects, and Arabic, and was used for religious purposes by pagans and Manicheans as well as by Christians. After the Muslim conquest it gradually gave way as a spoken language before Arabic, but was used for literary purposes till the fifteenth century, and is still in use as a liturgical language in the so-called Syrian churches.

*d. Modern Syriac.* Dialects of Eastern Aramaic still survive among Christian groups in the mountains of Kurdistan, on the E shores of Lake Urmia, in the hills of Tur 'Abdin and the Fellihi villages near Mosul in Mesopotamia. Like the still surviving dialects of Western Aramaic, they have suffered considerable phonetic change and have been much influenced both by the Arabic and Turkish spoken in daily intercourse and by the Syriac of their church. In the seventeenth century, under the influence of missionaries from the West, they began to use their dialect for literary purposes.

The Aramaic script already mentioned as a development from the Canaanitish script has had a quite extraordinary influence. One form of it, borrowed from some group in Asia Minor, was the source of the Greek alphabets and through them of the Latin, Gothic, and Cyrillic alphabets used in Europe and the Coptic scripts used in Egypt. Another form gave rise to the Pahlavi script of Middle Iranian, and through that to the Avestan, the Sogdian, and the Manichean alphabets, whence came the Uigur, Mongol, Manchu, Kalmuk, and Buriat scripts.

Another form gave rise to the Kharoshthi and Brahmi scripts, and through them the Tibetan and the various scripts in use throughout India, Southeast Asia, and Indonesia. Another form gave rise to the Armenian script, whence came the Georgian and Caucasian scripts. From yet another form came the "square" Hebrew, Palmyrene, and Nabatean scripts, from the latter of which came the Arabic alphabet with its modifications for Persian, Turkish, Urdu, and Malay. From another came the curious Mandaean script.

*Bibliography.* General: T. Nöldeke, "Beiträge zur Kenntniss der aramäischen Dialektes," *ZDMG,* XXI (1867), 183-200; XXII (1868), 443-527; XXIV (1870), 85-109; *Corpus Inscriptionum Semiticarum,* Pars secunda: Inscriptiones Aramaicae (1889—). M. Lidzbarski, *Ephemeris für semitische Epigraphik* (3 vols.; 1902-15). G. A. Cooke, *A Textbook of North Semitic Inscriptions* (1903). J. B. Chabot, *Les langues et les littératures araméennes* (1910). S. Schiffer, *Die Aramäer* (1911). E. G. Kraeling, *Aram and Israel* (1918). M. Jastrow, *A Dictionary of the Targumim, the Talmud Babli and Yerushalmi and the Midrashic Literature* (2 vols.; 2nd ed., 1926). W. R. Newbold, "Five Transliterated Aramaic Inscriptions," *AJA,* XXX (1926), 288-329. H. L. Ginsberg, "Aramaic Dialect Problems," *AJSL,* L (1933), 1-9; LII (1935), 95-103. F. Rosenthal, *Die aramäische Forschung* (1939). H. L. Ginsberg, "Aramaic Studies Today," *JAOS,* LXII (1942), 229-38. R. A. Bowman, "Arameans, Aramaic and the Bible," *JNES,* VII, 2 (1948), 65-90. J. Kutscher, "Ar.amith," in the Hebrew *Encyclopaedia Biblica,* I (1955), cols. 584-93.

Old Aramaic: D. H. Müller, *Die altsemitischen Inschriften von Sendschirli* (1893). S. A. Cook, *A Glossary of the Aramaic Inscriptions* (1898). M. Lidzbarski, *Handbuch der nordsemitischen Epigraphik* (1898); *Altaramäische Urkunden aus Assur* (1921). S. Ronzevalle, "Fragments d'inscriptions araméenes des environs d'Alep," *MFOB,* XV (1931), 235-60.

Dockets: J. H. Stevenson, *Assyrian and Babylonian Contracts with Aramaic Notes* (1902). A. T. Clay, "Aramaic Indorsements," *Harper Memorial Volume,* I (1908), 285-322; *Babylonian Business Transactions of the 1st Millennium B.C.* (1912). L. Delaporte, *Épigraphes araméens* (1912).

Biblical Aramaic: K. Marti, *Kurzgefasste Grammatik der biblisch-aramäischen Sprache* (2nd ed., 1911). H. L. Strack, *Grammatik des biblisch-Aramäischen* (6th ed., 1911). H. Bauer and P. Leander, *Grammatik des biblisch-Aramäischen* (1927). H. H. Rowley, *The Aramaic of the OT* (1929); "Early Aramaic Dialects and the Book of Daniel," *JRAS* (1933), 777-805. G. Messina, *L'Aramaico antico: indagine sull'aramaico del Vecchio Testamento* (1934).

Egyptian Aramaic: E. Sachau, *Aramäische Papyrus und Ostraka aus Elephantine* (1911). A. Cowley, *Aramaic Papyri of the Fifth Century B.C.* (1923). P. Leander, *Laut und Formenlehre des Ägyptisch-Aramäischen* (1928). N. A. Giron, *Textes araméens d'Égypte* (1931). L. Borchardt, *Allerhand Kleinigkeiten* (1933), pp. 47-49. E. G. Kraeling, *The Brooklyn Museum Aramaic Papyri* (1953). G. R. Driver, *Aramaic Documents of the Fifth Century B.C.* (1954).

Persian Aramaic: U. Melzer, "Die aramäischen Zeitwörter im Mittelpersischen," *WZKM,* XXXII (1925), 116-33; "Zur Aussprache der aramäischen Wörter im Mittelpersischen," *ZS,* V (1927), 312-38. H. H. Schaeder, *Iranische Beiträge,* I (1930), 225-54. O. G. von Wesendonk, "Ueber die Verwendung des Aramäischen im Achaemidenreich," *Litterae Orientales* (1932). E. Ebeling, "Das aramäisch-mittelpersische Glossar," *MAOG,* XIV (1941).

Palmyrene: J. B. Chabot, *Choix d'inscriptions de Palmyre* (1922). J. Cantineau, *Grammaire du Palmyrénien épigraphique* (1935). F. Rosenthal, *Die Sprache der palmyrenischen Inschriften* (1936). Du M. du Buisson, *Inventaire des inscriptions palmyréniennes* (1939). J. Schlumberger, *La Palmyrène du nord-ouest* (1951). J. Starcky, *Palmyre* (1952).

Nabatean: J. Euting, *Nabatäische Inschriften* (1885); *Sinai-*

*tische Inschriften* (1891). E. Littmann, *Nabataean Inscriptions from the Southern Hauran* (1914). J. Cantineau, *Le Nabatéen* (2 vols.; 1930-32). A. Grohmann, "Nabataioi," *Pauly-Wissowa,* XVI, 2 (1935), cols. 1,453-68. J. Starcky, "Un contrat nabatéen sur papyrus," *RB,* CXI (1954), 161-81.

Palestinian Jewish Aramaic: A. Meyer, *Jesu Muttersprache, das galiläische Aramäisch* (1896). M. Schultze, *Grammatik der aramäischen Muttersprache Jesu* (1899). G. Dalman, *Grammatik des jüdischpalästinischen Aramäisch* (2nd ed., 1905); *Aramäisch-neuhebräisches Wörterbuch* (3rd ed., 1938). W. B. Stevenson, *Palestinian Jewish Aramaic* (1924). G. Dalman, *Aramäische Dialektproben* (2nd ed., 1927). J. T. Marshall, *Manual of the Aramaic Language of the Palestinian Talmud* (1929). P. Kahle, "Fragmente des alten palästinischen Pentateuchtargums," *Masoreten des Westens,* II (1930), 1-13, 61-65. H. Odeberg, *The Aramaic Portions of Bereshit Rabba, with Grammar of Galilean Aramaic* (1939). P. Kahle, "Das zur Zeit Jesu in Palästina gesprochene Aramäisch," *Theol. Rundschau,* XVII (1949), 201-16.

Samaritan: S. Kohn, *Zur Sprache, Literatur und Dogmatik der Samaritaner* (1876). J. Rosenberg, *Lehrbuch der samaritanischen Sprache* (1901). P. Kahle, "Die zwölf Marka Hymnen," *Oriens Christianus,* III (1932), 77-103. D. Rettig, *Memar Marka, ein samaritanischer Midrasch zum Pentateuch* (1934).

Aramaic of the gospels: G. Dalman, *Die Worte Jesu* (2nd ed., 1905; English trans., 1902). F. Schulthess, *Das Problem der Sprache Jesu* (1917). C. F. Burney, *The Aramaic Origin of the Fourth Gospel* (1922). G. Dalman, *Jesus-Jeschua, die drei Sprachen Jesu* (1922). C. C. Torrey, *The Four Gospels, a New Translation* (1933); "The Aramaic of the Gospels," *JBL,* LXI (1942), 71-85. D. Daube, *Concerning the Reconstruction of the Aramaic Gospels* (1945). M. Black, *An Aramaic Approach to the Gospels and Acts* (1954). H. Birkeland, *The Language of Jesus* (1954).

Christian Palestinian Aramaic: T. Nöldeke, "Ueber das christlich-palästinische Aramäisch," *ZDMG,* XXII (1868), 443-527. F. Schwally, *Idioticon des christlich-palästinischen Aramäisch* (1893). F. Schulthess, *Lexicon Syropalaestinum* (1903). H. Duensing, *Christlich-palästinisch-aramäische Texte und Fragmente* (1906). F. Schulthess, *Grammatik des christlich-palästinischen Aramäisch* (1924). M. Black, *A Christian Palestinian Euchologion* (1938). H. Duensing, *Nachlese christlich-palästinisch-aramäischer Fragmente* (1955).

Ma'lula Aramaic: J. Parisot, "Le dialecte de Ma'lula," *JA* (mars-avril, 1898), pp. 239-312; (mai-juin, 1898), pp. 440-519; (juillet-août, 1898), pp. 124-76. G. Bergsträsser *Neuaramäische Märchen und andere Texte aus Ma'lula* (1915); "Neue Texte in aramäischem Dialekt von Ma'lula," *ZA,* XXXII (1918/19), 103-63; *Glossar des neuaramäischen Dialekts von Ma'lula* (1921). S. Reich, *Études sur les villages araméens de l'Anti-Liban* (1937). A. Spitaler, *Grammatik des neuaramäischen Dialekts von Ma'lula* (1938).

Babylonian Jewish Aramaic: S. D. Luzzato, *Grammatik der biblisch-chaldäischen Sprache und des Idioms des Thalmud Babli* (1873; English trans., 1877). C. Levias, *A Grammar of the Aramaic Idiom Contained in the Babylonian Talmud* (1900). M. Margolis, *Lehrbuch der aramäischen Sprache des babylonischen Talmud* (1910; English trans., 1910). J. A. Montgomery, *Aramaic Incantation Texts from Nippur* (1913). M. Schlesinger, *Satzlehre der aramäischen Sprache des babylonischen Talmuds* (1928).

Mandaean: T. Nöldeke, *Mandäische Grammatik* (1875). H. Pognon, *Inscriptions mandaïtes des coupes de Khouabir* (1898). M. Lidzbarski, *Das Johannesbuch der Mandäer* (1915); *Mandäische Liturgien* (1920).

Syriac: R. P. Smith, *Lexicon Syriacum* (2 vols.; 1868). E. Sachau, "Edessenische Inschriften," *ZDMG,* XXXVI (1882), 142-67, 345-52. R. Duval, *Traité de grammaire syriaque* (2nd ed., 1899). T. Nöldeke, *Compendious Syriac Grammar* (1904). A. Baumstark, *Geschichte der syrischen Literatur* (1922). C. Brockelmann, *Lexicon Syriacum* (2nd ed., 1928); *Syrische Grammatik* (5th ed., 1938). L. Costaz, *Grammaire syriaque* (1955).

Modern Syriac: T. Nöldeke, *Grammatik der neusyrischen*

*Sprache am Urmia-See und in Kurdistan* (1868). H. E. Prym and A. Socin, *Der neuaramäische Dialekt des Tur 'Abdin* (1881). A. Socin, *Die neuaramäischen Dialekte von Urmia bis Mosul* (1882). R. Duval, *Les dialectes néo-araméens de Salamas* (1883). E. Sachau, *Skizze des Fellichi-Dialekts vôn Mosul* (1895). A. J. Macleane, *A Grammar of the Dialects of Vernacular Syriac* (1895); *A Dictionary of the Dialects of Vernacular Syriac* (1901). J. Rhétoré, *Grammaire de la langue soureth ou chaldéen vulgaire* (1912). A. Siegel, *Laut und Formenlehre des neuaramäischen Dialekts des Tûr 'Abdîn* (1923).

A. JEFFERY

**ARAMAIC VERSIONS.** See VERSIONS, ANCIENT, §§ 1, 4.

**ARAMEANS** ăr'ǝ mē'ǝnz [ארמים; Akkad. *arumu, aramu, arimu*]. A people probably called after a country Arame. English translations follow the LXX in reading "Syrians" (Σύριοι).

1. Origins
2. Expansion
3. Migrations in patriarchal times
4. Aramean states
5. Arameans and Israelites
6. Assyrian invasions
7. Aramean culture
Bibliography

**1. Origins.** Arameans were a Semitic people, traditionally regarded as descendants of Shem (Gen. 10:22-23) or of the family of Nahor (22:20-21). The actual origin of the Arameans, like that of any other people, is obscure, but they seem to have formed part of the mass migration of nomads that moved northward through the W margins of the Syrian Desert toward Egypt, Canaan, and the lands along the Euphrates River. As early as the First Dynasty in Egypt (*ca.* 3100 B.C.) the nomads (*sttyw*) appeared in Egypt, and they are mentioned as the *Sutîu* or *Sutû* in Akkadian records as early as *ca.* 2700. When the term appears as an archaism in Late Assyrian times, it means simply "nomads." The same name was used for Amorites and for Arameans, since there was no great break in the continuity between such nomadic Amorites as settled at Mari on the Euphrates and the early Arameans that followed them into the same region.

References to the Arameans have been found in the Amorite texts from Mari and in the tablets recovered at Ugarit.

From the Amarna Age (*ca.* 1400 B.C.) onward, the appellation *Ahlame* ("confederates") is given to the nomads in the Akkadian records, and the use of the name *Sutîu* declines and finally ceases. Tiglath-pileser I (1114-1076) identifies the *Ahlame* as Arameans as he tells of his victories over the *Ahlame,* who by that time were flooding resistlessly into the W provinces of Assyria. Since there is no satisfactory Semitic etymology for the name Aram, it is doubtless a non-Semitic geographical term first applied by the Assyrians to a tribe or small group of the nomads found in the land of Arame, NE of Syria, in the foothills of Armenia; and then extended to the entire group of invaders.

**2. Expansion.** While still in the Syrian Desert, some of the nomads thrust toward Egypt; still others moved eastward, along routes still followed by

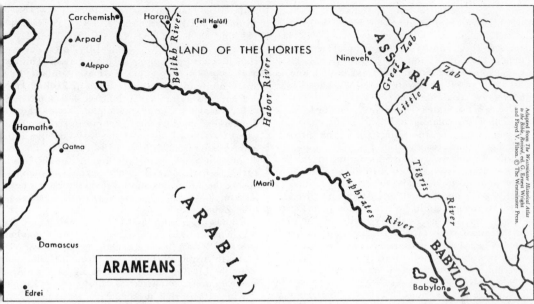

nomadic bedouins, toward Lower Babylonia. Among the latter were the Chesed, claimed as relatives by the Nahor Arameans (Gen. 22:22), who arrived in Babylonia, as the Chaldeans, *ca.* the time of David (*ca.* 1000 B.C.). These are the desert raiders mentioned in Job 1:17. In Babylonia they inhabited the swamps at the headwaters of the Persian Gulf, from whence they made incursions into Babylonia and in late Assyrian times became the allies of Elam against their Babylonian and Assyrian neighbors. Other E Arameans pushed up the Tigris River and settled in great numbers along its tributary, the Zab.

Most Arameans assaulted the Euphrates region from Rapiqu northwestward along the full course of the river, seeking entrance into Mesopotamia. From Rapiqu to Hindan they settled the land of Suḫu, the home of Bildad (Job 2:11; cf. Shuah in Gen. 25:2). Once across the Euphrates, they followed the great tributaries, the Ḫabur (Habor in II Kings 17:6) and, to the W, the Balih, to their sources and beyond. Many of their settlements were named in characteristic fashion, beginning with the word *Bît* ("House of") and followed by the name of the tribal dynast. N of the Euphrates and E of the Ḫabur, extending to Jebel Sinjar, lay Bit-Halupe. Small city-states lined the Ḫabur northward to Bît-Baḫianu in the vicinity of modern Tell Halaf and Ras-el-'Ain. In 808 B.C. the region became part of the Assyrian province of Guzâna, the Gozan to which some Israelites were exiled (II Kings 17:6; 18:11; cf. Isa. 37:12). Beyond, between the Kashiari Mountains and the E spurs of present Mount Karadja-Dagh, lay Shupria; and, to its NE, along the S bank of the upper reaches of the Tigris River, near Diyarbekir, was Bît-Zamâni, close to the land of Arame, which may have given the Arameans their name.

From Suḫu westward to Carchemish small Aramean groups settled along the Euphrates as early as the time of the Assyrian Ashurreshishi I (1132-1115), and Tiglath-pileser I (1114-1076) found great difficulty in expelling them and keeping them out of Mesopotamia. When Assyrian power broke in the early tenth century B.C., the Arameans seized their opportunity to invade, and by the time of the resurgence of Assyrian power in the ninth century B.C. their states were so firmly established that they could resist successfully and not be easily removed. The city Pitru (Pethor, the home of Balaam, in Aram-naharaim; Num. 22:5; Deut. 23:4), on the W bank of the Euphrates a few miles below Carchemish, at the confluence of the Sâjur River, fell to Assyria in the eleventh century B.C., after the decline of Hittite power in Syria; but it was taken by the Arameans in the time of Ashurrabi II (1012-972). It lay within the important Aramean state of Bît-Adini (Beth-eden in Amos 1:5; Eden in II Kings 19:12; Isa. 37:12; Ezek. 27:23). It lay within the great W bend of the Euphrates River and extended across it westward as far as the gates of Arpad. Through it ran the highway from Ḫarran to Syria. Bît-Adini formed the heart land of Aram-naharaim ("Aram of the Two Rivers"; Gen. 24:10; Deut. 23:5; Judg. 3:8; I Chr. 19:6), which originally extended from near Aleppo to almost as far E as the Ḫabur River. Its N border lay about in the line of present Edessa, Tell Halaf, and Nisibis. Most biblical references to it seem to refer particularly to its westward extension SW of the Euphrates. Bît-Adini blocked Assyria's rapid advance to the Mediterranean shore and very early became a leader of the W Arameans, uniting them to meet the Assyrian power.

**3. Migrations in patriarchal times.** Aramean nomads following the Baliḫ River to its source thickly populated the region around the great Assyrian commercial center Ḫarran, the Paddan-aram ("road of Aram," incorrectly rendered "field of Aram" in the MT of Hos. 12:12) of the Bible (Gen. 25:20; 28:2, 5-7; 31:18; etc. [all P]). Ḫarran, biblical Haran, was the ancestral home of Nahor and his descendants Abraham, Lot, Bethuel, and Laban (Gen. 22:20-24; 24:4, 7, 10; 25:20; 28:2 in the Hebrew text). From Ḫarran, Abraham migrated to

Syria (12:4-5) and the land of Canaan, but it was from his Aramean kinsmen that he drew the Aramean Rebekah as a wife for Isaac (Gen. 24), who later sent the "wandering Aramean" (Deut. 26:5) Jacob to the same vicinity for a wife (Gen. 28:2-5). Of the women that returned to Canaan with him, at least Leah and Rachel were Arameans, ancestors to the Hebrew people.

**4. Aramean states.** In moving westward, Abraham followed a common trend of Semitic migration. As the documents from Mari show, the Amorite settlements that preceded the Arameans along the Middle Euphrates were oriented toward the W. Later a strong Assyria (1326-1076) diverted the Aramean nomads to the NW, where they settled in isolated areas unoccupied by Hittites some decades before Arameans could be established in Mesopotamia nearer Assyria. At the W border of Bît-Adini the Aramean state of Yaḫan began. Its capital, Arpad (Tell Erfâd), was once ruled by Mati-ilu, whose treaty with Ashurnirari V (755-745) is preserved in both Akkadian and Aramaic forms. He rebelled against Tiglath-pileser IV (745-728 B.C.), with disastrous results (II Kings 18:34). Westward, Ḥattina developed in and about the plain of the Lake of Antioch, with its capital at Kunalua. Beyond, to the NW, at the foot of the Amanus Mountains, was the Aramean state of Ya'di or Sam'al, from which the oldest Aramaic inscriptions have come. Its capital, Zinjirli, commanded the Amanus pass to Que

Courtesy of Foto Marburg

41. Bar Rakab, king of Samal, on his throne before a scribe; Aramaic inscription above (from Zinjirli, last half of eighth century B.C.)

(Cilicia).* Judging from the names Gurgum and Marqasi (later Mar'ash), the Aramean population ranged still farther northward to Gurgum on one of the main highways from Mesopotamia to Cilicia. Ultimately Arameans pushed on into the Cilician Plain, which formed a natural extension of Syria. Fig. ARA 41.

S of Ḥattina, between Ḥalman (Aleppo) and Damascus, spread the important kingdom of Hamath, which once included nineteen districts. Hamath marked the boundary between Palestine and Syria (Num. 34:8; I Kings 8:65; II Kings 14:25; Ezek. 47:15; Amos 6:14). Its king, Toi, paid tribute to David (II Sam. 8:9-10; I Chr. 18:9-10). Later Zakir of Hamath called part of his kingdom La'ash. This district, between Aleppo and Hamath, contained the fortified city of Ḥazrak (Hadrach in Zech. 9:1). N of Damascus, in the metal-rich Anti-lebanon Mountains, was the powerful kingdom of Zobah, whose E frontier extended to the Euphrates (II Sam. 8:3), where Zobah probably took the Assyrian cities Pitru and Mutkinu from Ashurrabi II (1012-972). The tradition that Saul successfully fought Zobah (I Sam. 14:47) rather reflects David's spectacular successes among the Arameans and his invasion of their lands (II Sam. 8:5-8; 10:15-18). David's captain Igal came from Zobah (23:36).

Damascus, a fruitful oasis in the plain below the Anti-lebanon Mountains, was long an important "head of Syria" (Isa. 7:8). The terminus of caravan routes to Arabia, to Iraq, and, through Galilee and along the Mediterranean coast, to Egypt, Damascus was economically (Ezek. 27:18-19) and culturally (I Kings 16:10) rich and politically strategic. Tradition suggests that Abraham passed through it on his way to Hebron (Gen. 15:2). David conquered it and garrisoned it (II Sam. 8:5-6; I Chr. 18:5-6). When it was strong, it demanded commercial concessions from its neighbors (I Kings 20:34). Proximity to Israel often brought conflicts of interests, sometimes in competition for settlements E of the Jordan River (I Kings 20:34; II Kings 16:6), and sometimes actual warfare (I Kings 20:1-21, 23-33). Kings of Judah hired Damascus against the kingdom of Israel (I Kings 15:18-20), and kings of Israel made alliance with Damascus against Judah (II Kings 16:5). Assyrian records show that Israel was strongly represented as an ally of many Aramean states against Assyria at the Battle of Qarqar (854 B.C.). Afterward Elisha, while in Damascus, instigated the assassination of the Aramean king and the usurpation of the throne by a violent man (II Kings 8:7-15; cf. I Kings 19:15-18).

**5. Arameans and Israelites.** By the period of the judges (*ca.* 1225-1020) there was a strong concentration of Arameans about the sources of the Jordan River, and small Aramean states lined the N and NE borders of the land claimed by the Hebrews. E of the Sea of Galilee, contiguous to the regions claimed by Manasseh and Naphtali along the W border of the land of Bashan, were two small states, Geshur and Maacah, which the Hebrews could not conquer (Josh. 13:13). Geshur furnished for David's harem the daughter of its king Talmai, and she became the mother of Absalom (II Sam. 3:3; 13:37-38). Her daughter Maacah became the wife of King Rehoboam (I Kings 15:2; II Chr. 11:20-22) and a queen mother to the time of King Asa (II Chr. 15:16). It was to his grandfather in Geshur that Absalom fled when he had killed his brothers (II Sam. 13:37-38). The Arameans of neighboring Maacah, closely associated with Geshur, are traditionally related to the Nahor Arameans of Ḥarran (Gen. 22:24), as are those of Tubiḥi (Tebah of Gen. 22:24) of Zobah (I Chr. 18:8 LXX). The capital of Maacah,

Abel-beth-maacah (Abil el Qamh), S of Dan, overlooking the marshes of Lake Huleh, temporarily protected Sheba after his unsuccessful rebellion against David (II Sam. 20:15). The tiny state of Tob, which sent troops against David (II Sam. 10:8), was located near Edrei in Transjordan, at Et-Tayyibe on the road from Bosra to Der'a; it was in Tob that Jephthah sought asylum (Judg. 11:3-5).

Associated with Zobah and Maacah against David were the Arameans of Aram-beth-rehob (II Sam. 10:8). This state, among the Arameans hired by Ammon against David, was situated near the border of Hamath (Num. 13:21) with the city Laish-dan in its valley (Judg. 18:28-29), near the source of the Jordan River. Tradition explains that the Ammonites, who hired the Arameans, as well as their neighbors the Moabites, were also Arameans, related to Abraham and the Nahor Arameans of Ḥarran through Lot, son of Haran (Gen. 11:26-27; 19:30-38).

Most of the Aramean groups were small citystates relatively weak by themselves. The inscription of Zakir of Hamath, as well as II Sam. 8:10, indicates that they fought with one another and could readily be hired as mercenaries when it was to their own advantage (II Chr. 16:1-4). The strength of the Arameans lay in their readiness and ability to enter into more or less temporary alliances to meet an existing threat. At Qarqar, a "royal city" of Hamath, a coalition of about eleven such small states in 853 B.C. under the leadership of Damascus fought the Assyrians under Shalmaneser III to a stalemate and frustrated his plans to subjugate all of Syria and Palestine.

**6. Assyrian invasions.** So long as large Aramean states remained to organize and lead coalitions, such tactics were successful. But a series of strong Assyrian kings with constant assaults against plotters in the W destroyed Aramean resistance and ultimately converted their states into parts of Assyrian provinces. Bît-Adini fell to Shalmaneser III in 856 B.C. and became part of the Assyrian province of Kar Shulman-asharidu. Arpad of Yamḫad capitulated to Tiglath-pileser III in 740 B.C.; Zobah and Damascus in 732; and Hamath was taken by Sargon II in 720, shortly after the fall of Israel (722; II Kings 17:5-6). Men of Israel were exiled to the Aramean lands along the Ḥabûr River and to the region of Gozân (II Kings 17:6), as well as to Hamath (Isa. 11:11). Arameans of Hamath were among those placed in Samaria to replace those exiled (II Kings 17:24, 30). Tiglath-pileser III (745-727) reports that more than 40,000 N Syrians were exiled to remote regions of his kingdom. To repopulate those areas, men were exiled from trouble spots in the E. In 739 B.C., 12,000 Aḫlame Arameans from the Zab River region E of the Tigris were sent to Syria, along with 600 Arameans of the Damunu tribe which were taken from the city Amlate and 5,400 captives from the heavily Aramean center about Der in Babylonia. When the Assyrian officer in 701 before besieged Jerusalem boastfully recalled the humiliation of mighty Hamath and Arpad by the Assyrian armies (II Kings 18:34), Aramean political power in the W was gone, never to be restored. The states were but a memory. Individuals, however, still identified themselves as Ara-

means sometimes in the Jewish Aramaic papyri from Egypt of the Persian period. Far to the E, in Babylonia, the Chaldeans and Aramean settlers combined with their neighbors to humble mighty Assyria (612 B.C.), and a Chaldean kingdom persisted rather vigorously until the Persians took over Babylon and the world of the Semites (538).

**7. Aramean culture.** The great contributions of the Arameans, cultural rather than political, survived their national existence. Like the sticky "cake not turned" (Hos. 7:8), the Arameans caught and held cultural elements of their neighbors. They assimilated them and adapted them to their own use and, in their constant shifting about in the ancient world, spread them everywhere they went. They borrowed the alphabet from the Phoenicians, developed their own peculiar forms of it, and transmitted it to others everywhere they went—to the Persians, the Hebrews, the Arabs, and others even more remote. The simplicity and efficiency of the ARAMAIC LANGUAGE and ALPHABET vanquished the more difficult, cumbersome cuneiform scripts of the Akkadians and the Persians. By Late Assyrian times a Babylonian soldier wrote his report from Babylon in Aramaic, and an Assyrian officer was expected to be able to converse in the language (II Kings 18:13-37; Isa. 36). In the W provinces the language was widely used, and things written in it are found sporadically in the very heart of Assyria and Babylonia. When the Persians came to power, they recognized the value of the Aramaic script and language and not only used them themselves but also spread them to the widest reaches of their empire. Most preserved Aramaic was not written by Arameans but by those who borrowed their valuable tools. Aramaic maintained its importance until the conquest of the Near East by Alexander. Then it survived locally as special dialects and the script became highly diversified (Jewish Aramaic, Syriac, Nabatean, Palmyrene, Mandaic, etc.), continuing until it was finally displaced by Arabic.

**Bibliography.** S. Schiffer, *Die Aramäer* (1911). E. Kraeling, *Aram and Israel* (1918). R. A. Bowman, "Arameans, Aramaic, and the Bible," *JNES,* VII (1948), 65-90. R. T. O'Callaghan, *Aram Naharaim* (1948). A. Dupont-Sommer, *Les Araméens* (1949); "Les débuts de l'histoire araméenne," *Vetus Testamentum,* Supplement I (1953), pp. 40-49. R. A. BOWMAN

**ARAMITESS** ăr'ə mīt'əs [ארמיה, Aramean woman]. A designation of the concubine of Manasseh; mother of Machir.

**ARAM-MAACAH** âr'əm mā'ə kə [ארם מעכה]. Alternate name of MAACAH 1.

**ARAM-NAHARAIM** âr'əm nā'ə rā'əm [ארם נהרים, Aram of the rivers] (superscription of Ps. 60; elsewhere translated MESOPOTAMIA). A N Mesopotamian area, especially important as the home of the Hebrew patriarchs. The superscription of Ps. 60—H 60:2 alludes to David's warring against Aram-naharaim; perhaps this is a reference to the incident in I Chr. 19:6, when the Ammonites hired Mesopotamian chariots and horsemen against David.

**Bibliography.** R. T. O'Callaghan, *Aram Naharaim* (1948);

A. Malamat, *The Aramaeans in Aram Naharaim and the Rise of Their States* (1952).                                    C. H. GORDON

**ARAM-ZOBAH** âr'əm zō′bə [ארם צובה] (superscription of Ps. 60). An Aramean town and kingdom in the Biq'a. *See* ZOBAH.

**ARAN** âr′ăn [ארן]. The second son of the Horite clan chief DISHAN (Gen. 36:28; I Chr. 1:42). Cf. the Jerahmeelite OREN (I Chr. 2:25; also ארן).

**ARARAT** ăr′ə răt [אררט]. A country in the general district of Armenia. Its Assyrian name is *Urarṭu* and the country is best known from Assyrian historical references, although it has produced written records and archaeological data of its own. Its geographical center is Lake Van. Modern exploration of Urartu is conducted in three countries: Turkey, Russia, and Iran.

**1. History.** Urartu rose to importance as a political unit in the ninth century B.C. Ashurnasirpal II (884-859 B.C.) in his Nimrud Inscriptions refers to Urartu as the boundary of his conquests; but his successor Shalmaneser III (859-824) made several inroads in Urartian territory. Some of his campaigns are illustrated on the bronze gates of Balawat, where the capture of Urartian mountain fortresses is shown. Shalmaneser pursued an aggressive policy against Sarduri, an Urartian king also known from his own inscriptions, which are written in the Assyrian language.

During the period of Assyrian weakness after Shalmaneser, Urartian power expanded considerably. Under local kings by the names of Išpuini, Menua, Argišti, and Sarduri, new cities were built, citadels were ingeniously constructed out of a combination of masonry and rock cuttings, and aqueducts and irrigation systems were created. The sources for this period are partly local inscriptions in the Urartian language, an idiom probably related to Hurrian and written down in cuneiform. The geographical range of these inscriptions shows that Urartian influence began to expand to the W. It made itself felt as far as N Syria and seriously threatened Assyria, which lost several provinces to Urartu.

This situation changed radically under Tiglath-pileser III (745-727), who defeated the Urartian king Sarduri II or III when the latter wanted to come to the rescue of the city of Arpad in 743. The alliance of N Syria, SE Anatolia, and Urartu was broken up, and Assyria reconquered its ground on Urartu. Sarduri escaped to his capital Turushpa (Tushpa) on Lake Van, which Tiglath-pileser in 735 failed to capture, although much of the countryside was devastated by the Assyrian army.

The most famous campaign against Urartu was conducted by Sargon (722-705) in his eighth year. This expedition led to the capture of Musasir, a city which was ruled by a King Urzanu, a vassal of Rusa of Urartu. The inventory of this city as recorded in Sargon's inscriptions furnishes a literary description of Urartian material wealth.

The international situation in Asia Minor and Transcaucasia was complicated by the threat of Cimmerian (GOMER 1) invasions about this time.

There are references to Cimmerian warfare with Urartu. Rusa's natural allies against Assyria, the country of Tabal (TUBAL) and Mita of Mushki (MESHECH 1) were equally subject to Cimmerian aggression. Attention was diverted from the Assyrian front; and the later history of Urartu is marked by the further threat of invasions. The Scythians (*see* ASHKENAZ) arrived as successors to the Cimmerians, who had moved W; and the Medes came in pressing from the E. Although the seventh-century kings of Urartu still were active in building new citadels, the final destruction was brought about by Median (Madai) attacks of the early sixth century, after which Urartu ceased to exist as an independent ethnic and political unit. The Armenians, an Indo-European people perhaps related to the Phrygians (Herodotus VII.73), became the leading inhabitants of the country.

**2. Archaeology.** The knowledge of Urartian architecture used to be restricted to incompletely recorded excavations on the E shores of Lake Van, where two citadels exist: the rock of Van and Toprakkale. Russian excavations near Erivan have added much information.

It becomes increasingly clear that the architectural style of Urartu is related to that of Asia Minor, showing affinities to the earlier Hittite and contemporary Phrygian-Mushki tradition. The temple of the god Haldi at Musasir had a pitched roof of pedimental appearance like the contemporary *megara* at Gordion, capital of Phrygia.

Urartu had an outstanding metal industry, a branch also famous in Mushki and Tabal. The theoretical knowledge derived from Sargon's inventory of the temple of Haldi at Musasir is borne out by excavation. Urartian caldrons with siren handles, tripods, bowls, candelabra, and shields were exported to the W, where they have been found in Phrygia, Greece, and Etruria. The influence of Urartian art on the West was strong, because its *floruit* coincided with the opening of oriental trade to Greece and Italy.

**3. Biblical Ararat.** The fame of Ararat is now mostly based on Gen. 8:4. The mountains of the N were conceived as the likeliest candidates for an early emergence from the flood, and were labeled with the most readily available geographical name of Urartu. Modern Mount Ararat is in the ancient territory of Urartu, but it preserves the name in a restricted sense.

The references in II Kings 19:37; Isa. 37:38 are historical. Sennacherib was murdered by his son (Babylonian Chronicle III.34-38) in 681 B.C. The circumstances surrounding his death are not clear, and Ararat is not mentioned in preserved Assyrian texts as the land of refuge for the murderer(s).

The association of Ararat, Minni, Ashkenaz, and Medes (Jer. 51:27-28) recalls the military situation of the early sixth century B.C., when Urartu, Manneans, Scythians, and Medes were all active preceding the fall of Babylon.

*Bibliography.* F. Thureau-Dangin, *Huitième Campagne de Sargon* (1912). L. W. King, *Bronze Reliefs from the Gates of Shalmaneser* (1915), pp. 12 ff (first year, bands 1-2; third year, band 7). R. D. Barnett, "The Excavations of the British Museum at Toprak Kale Near Van," *Iraq,* XII (1950), 1-43: *Iraq,* XVI (1954), 3-22. B. B. Piotrovskiy, *Karmir Blur,* vols. I-III (1952-55). F. W. König, *Handbuch der Chaldischen Inschriften* (1955). K. L. Oganesian, *Karmir Blur,* vol. IV (1955). C. A. Burney, "Urartian Fortresses and Towns in the Van Region," *Anatolian Studies,* VII (1957), 37-53. A. Goetze, *Kleinasien,* Kulturgeschichte des alten Orients, III.1 (1957), pp. 187-200. M. J. MELLINK

**ARATUS** är'ə təs ["Αρετος]. A Stoic poet of Soli in Cilicia who flourished in the middle of the third century B.C. His astronomical poem "Phaenomena" (Φαινόμενα) is quoted in the Areopagus speech of Acts 17:28—"for we are indeed his offspring." *See* AREOPAGUS. B. H. THROCKMORTON, JR.

**ARAUNAH** ə rô'nə [ארונה] (II Sam. 24:20-24, 18, *Qere*); *Kethibh* [ארניה]. Alternately: ORNAN ôr'nən [ארנן] (Chronicles). The Jebusite whose threshing floor David purchased for the site of an altar to stay the ravaging plague by sacrifice (II Sam. 24:15-25; I Chr. 21:14 ff). When a severe epidemic broke out in Israel, with a mortality of some seventy thousand, it was considered to be a judgment of God because of the census of David (cf. I Chr. 21:12, 15, where the "destroying angel" or the "sword of the LORD" is equated with the "pestilence upon the land"; and the Plague Prayers of Mursilis in *ANET,* 394 ff). Although it appears that the disease reached the suburbs of Jerusalem, the capital itself was mercifully spared. Accordingly, the prophet Gad instructed the penitent king to purchase the threshing floor of Araunah, where the plague appeared to cease, as a fitting location for sacrifice. Although Araunah offered to give his property to the king as well as the provisions for the sacrifice, David insisted upon paying fifty shekels of silver for the purchase of the threshing floor. Here he offered sacrifices and supplications, and the plague was averted from Israel.

Araunah appears to have been the father of four sons, who isolated themselves during the epidemic (I Chr. 21:20). The threshing floor of Araunah was traditionally located on Mount Moriah, where the temple was subsequently erected (II Chr. 3:1).

The word הארונה (*Kethibh* [האורנה]) in II Sam. 24: 16 should be rendered, according to some authorities (cf. A. Speiser, *AASOR,* XX, 98-99), not "Araunah" but *iwirne,* a Hurrian word meaning "chief, ruler."

*Bibliography.* W. Feiler, "Hurritische Namen im AT," *ZA,* 45 (1939), 222 ff; C. H. Gordon, *Ugaritic Manual,* "Analecta Orientalia" 35 (1955), p. 77; H. B. Rosen, "Arawna—Nom Hittite?" *Vetus Testamentum,* V (1955), 318-20.

E. R. DALGLISH

**ARBA** är'bə [ארבע, four]. Presented as a prominent inhabitant of Hebron, or KIRIATH-ARBA, at the time of the Conquest, although improbably a personal name (Josh. 14:15; 15:13; 21:11). Arba is said to have been the ancestor of Anak and the greatest man among the Anakim, or "race of giants." It is unlikely that "Arba" is a personal name, although it is so construed in the three verses cited above. The LXX reading, "Kiriath-arba the metropolis of the Anakim," suggests that "Arba" is a corruption from "Kiriath-arba," the older name of Hebron, and that the Hebrew text originally referred to Kiriath-arba

as the metropolis (mother city) of the Anakim rather than to Arba as its "greatest man."

R. F. JOHNSON

**ARBATHITE** är'bə thīt [ערבתי]. A resident of BETH-ARABAH, the home of Abialbon, one of David's Mighty Men (II Sam. 23:31; I Chr. 11:32).

**ARBATTA** är bắt'ə [Αρβαττα] (I Macc. 5:23); KJV **ARBATTIS** —ĭs. According to some, the lowlands of the Jordan Valley; but more likely a toparchy W of Samaria, bordering upon Galilee. The district is called Ναρβατηνή by Josephus (War II. xiv.5; xviii.10), and this spelling is confirmed by the Syr. version of I Maccabees. In the Jewish War of A.D. 66-70 this area served as a refuge for Jews who fled from Caesarea.

In campaigns against Galilee and Arbatta, Simon defeated the Gentile forces and delivered the Jewish inhabitants, many of whom followed him back to Judea.

*Bibliography.* H. Bévenot, *Die beiden Makkabäerbücher* (1931), p. 82; F.-M. Abel, *Géographie de la Palestine,* II (1938), 250-51.

E. W. SAUNDERS

**ARBELA** är bē'lə ["Αρβηλα] (I Macc. 9:2). A site along Bacchides' line of invasion from Syria, which may be identified with BETH-ARBEL in Gilead, but it is more likely to be the Galilean Khirbet Irbid overlooking the Wadi el-Hamam to the W of the Sea of Galilee. Josephus has described this famous district of caves which were connected by stairs cut in the rock, a favorite refuge for rebels and brigands (Antiq. XII.xi.1; War I.xvi.2-4; Life 37, 60, 188).

*Bibliography.* F.-M. Abel, *Géographie de la Palestine,* II (1938), 249. E. W. SAUNDERS

**ARBITE** är'bīt [ארבי]. A resident of ARAB, the home of Paarai, one of David's Mighty Men (II Sam. 23: 35; in I Chr. 11:37, Naarai son of Ezbai).

V. R. GOLD

**ARBONAI.** KJV form of ABRON.

**ARCH.** KJV translation of אילמים and אלמות in Ezek. 40 (RSV VESTIBULE).

*****ARCHAEOLOGY** är'kĭ ŏl'ə jĭ. The study of the material remains of man's past. "Material remains" include all tangible things made by man, and can be divided into two groups: written documents, including texts of ancient languages on stone, metal, clay, parchment, and papyrus; and unwritten documents, comprising all other objects—e.g., fortifications, buildings of various kinds, sculpture, household vessels, tools, weapons, and personal ornaments. These remains are generally recovered by means of excavation; when carefully studied and evaluated, they supply important data for political, economic, social, and cultural history. "Man's past" limits the coverage of archaeology to the period of man's occupation of the earth, from at least 200,000 years ago—the Pleistocene period—to the present. With reference to time, archaeology is divided into two major branches, prehistoric and historic. The former is concerned with the Stone Age; the latter is devoted to the period between the end of the Stone Age—the date of which varies in different parts of the world—and the present; the interests of these two major divisions overlap in regions such as the Near East, where Neolithic deposits underlie historic remains in many sites.

Archaeology is world wide in scope, and there are special branches for every region from America to the Far East, and from South Africa to Scandinavia. This article deals with historic archaeology of the ancient Near East, with special emphasis on the archaeology of Palestine.

A. Types of remains
   1. Towns
   2. Tombs
B. Method of excavation
   1. Where to dig
   2. How to dig
      *a.* Mounds
      *b.* Tombs
   3. Recording
   4. Disposition of finds
   5. Excavation report
   6. Uses of objects
      *a.* Dating sites
      *b.* Describing and comparing cultures
C. Dating archaeological evidence
   1. Literary references
   2. Inscriptions and paleography
   3. Local objects
      *a.* Pottery
      *b.* Coins
      *c.* Other objects
   4. Imported objects
   5. Stylistic development in art and architecture
   6. Techniques of natural sciences

D. Contributions of archaeology to the Bible
E. Explorations and excavations in Palestine
   1. Exploration
   2. Excavation to World War I
   3. Excavation between World Wars I and II
   4. Excavation since World War II
F. Table of archaeological periods of Palestine
Bibliography

A. *TYPES OF REMAINS.* Some ancient remains have always been either partially or completely exposed, because of their location, size, or state of preservation—e.g., the Colosseum in Rome, the Parthenon in Athens, the pyramids and temples of Egypt, Baalbek in Lebanon, and Jerash in Jordan. At such sites archaeological work is largely devoted to the study of remains above ground level, but excavation is usually necessary to uncover floors, streets, architectural fragments, and evidence of occupation. Most ancient remains are buried beneath tons of debris or drifted sand, and are recovered by means of excavation. Near Eastern and particularly Palestinian sites are generally of this type. For the most part, these sites contain remains of ancient towns and tombs, although other kinds of remains—e.g., water distribution and conservation systems, isolated fortresses, temples, and palaces—are also found. Of these, towns and tombs will be considered here.

1. **Towns.** Ancient towns vary in size from a cluster of houses occupying as little as two to three acres, to planned cities covering as much as two hundred acres. Their locations were largely determined by natural features. Abundance of good water, and proximity to major trade routes, to a natural harbor, to economically important raw materials, and to tillable land were the principal factors which, singly or in combination, governed the selection. Barring nat-

Courtesy of the Arab Information Center, New York

42. Ruins at Gerasa (Jerash), with forum in the foreground

ural catastrophes, these advantages remained the same generation after generation, and towns continued to occupy the same sites for centuries and often millenniums, though occasionally with gaps.

When the initial settlement of a site was destroyed, the next occupation was built on top of the remains and accumulated debris of the first town, so that the level of the second town was higher than that of the first. This process, repeated time and time again, resulted in the formation of mounds (tells) which often reach a height of seventy-five feet or more above the natural surface. Generally these mounds are shaped like truncated cones. This characteristic shape, together with the thousands of fragments of broken pottery (sherds) that litter the top and sides of the mound and the remains of walls that are sometimes visible, makes archaeological sites of this type easy to recognize. Figs. ARC 42; BET 32; LAC 3.

Thus a mound contains the remains of many occupations; the earliest is at the base of the mound and the latest is at the top. Each occupation or stratum is represented by one or more layers of debris. These layers are distinguished by differences in color and texture. They are neither absolutely level nor uniformly deep, but tend to slope, thin out, or deepen, depending on the natural configuration of the site and the surface of the debris on which they lie. Various kinds of holes—e.g., storage and rubbish pits, cisterns, and foundation and robber trenches—were often sunk into earlier layers, and contribute to the unevenness.

In the layers of debris that make up a stratum are found the remains of buildings and structures of ancient towns. Houses, shops, warehouses, temples, palaces, streets, and fortifications form the bulk of the architectural remains, although special structures such as stables and governmental buildings are occasionally found. They are built of either sun-dried mud brick or stone and sometimes both. In stone construction, rubble (undressed stone) was commonly used, but examples of well-dressed ashlar appear in a number of sites—e.g., Solomonic Megiddo and Samaria during the time of Omri and Ahab. Floors are made of flagstones, plaster, or packed earth. Various kinds of objects (for a partial list, *see* § B6 *below*) are also found in these layers. The most common class of object is pottery, and tens of thousands of sherds (fragments of broken pottery) are brought to light in a season of excavation on a Palestinian mound. Most of the objects recovered were broken in antiquity, either through normal everyday use or as a result of a catastrophe in which walls fell and crushed them. Generally the occupation layer, which is immediately above the floor, has the greatest concentration of objects.

**2. Tombs.** Many kinds of tombs were used in antiquity: natural or artificial caves in the side of a hill or cliff; pits or chambers sunk in fields and entered through shafts; individual graves dug in houses or open areas; mausoleums, either stone-built or cut out of rock, and either exposed to view or covered with earth; massive monuments such as the pyramids of Egypt; and a number of others.

Generally, ancient tombs contain skeletons in various stages of preservation, and many objects including vessels, weapons, jewelry, and occasionally furni-

By permission of the Palestine Exploration Fund

43. Interior of shaft tomb, showing body on bier, with table, wooden bowl, and basket; from Jericho, Middle Bronze Age

ture, intended to care for the needs and desires of the deceased in the afterlife.* Tombs of prominent persons were almost always plundered in antiquity by enterprising robbers, and aside from pottery, little is found in them. Stratification is rarely found in tombs, because once the tombs were closed, little debris accumulated over the remains. Frequently tombs were reused by succeeding generations, with the result that they contain many burials and hundreds of objects. In such instances, burials and funerary equipment are usually found in hopeless disorder, because of the common practice of pushing old bones and objects to one side, or out of the chamber altogether, in order to accommodate new burials. This practice, of course, largely destroyed whatever stratification there once was. As a rule, tombs yield a much higher percentage of whole and only slightly broken objects than mounds (*see* § A1 *above*). Since whole and restorable objects illustrate the incomplete forms found in mounds, the discovery and excavation of tombs is very important in archaeology. Fig. ARC 43.

**B. METHOD OF EXCAVATION.** To evaluate and interpret the results of archaeological excavations, one must understand archaeological method, including both the technique of excavation and the study of objects. This brief survey includes only the chief features of archaeological method. (For further discussions, *see bibliography*.)

**1. Where to dig.** The choice of the site largely depends on the excavator's purpose in digging. He may want to excavate a particular mound because of its historical importance, or because previous excavations of the site have left many questions unanswered. Sometimes he has a definite cultural or chronological problem to solve, and from the hundreds of sites in the region, he selects a few that would be of value in solving it. Practical considerations such as accessibility to transportation and sources of supply, the availability of the mound for excavation, and the status of security usually make one site more attractive than the others.

After the site has been chosen, much preliminary work must be done before excavation can begin. A permit to excavate must be secured from the governmental department in charge of archaeological sites;

arrangements to purchase or rent the site must be made with the owner or owners; and the site and surrounding area must be surveyed. Using the plan of the site, the archaeologist selects the area he plans to excavate and determines the location of dumps. The choice of the area, like the selection of the site itself, depends largely on the particular problem or problems that the excavator is trying to solve. E.g., if he wishes to study the sequence of fortifications, he will dig one or more trenches at right angles to the line of the walls on the perimeter of the mound. Housing facilities and equipment for the staff must be arranged on or near the site. Sufficient tools, equipment, and supplies must be purchased for the staff and workmen. When everything is ready, laborers are hired and excavation begins.

**2. How to dig.** Good excavation technique is much the same the world over, but each region and, in fact, each site has its own stratigraphic problems, the solution of which demands special methods. The following is a description of basic technique for Palestine and much of the Near East, leaving aside all special procedures.

**a. Mounds.** Excavation of a mound begins with laying out and surveying the area selected by the archaeologist. If the area is large, it is divided into smaller units or sections; each section usually meas-

44. Pottery found in excavations at Tell Qasile

ures about five meters (*ca.* sixteen feet) square, a size which is small enough to control, yet large enough to provide ample work room and light as excavation progresses downward. The surface of the section is then cleared of plants and rubble, and all objects found are saved and recorded as surface finds. If the archaeologist is to gain a clear and true picture of each occupation in a site, it is imperative that he excavate stratigraphically; i.e., he must remove each layer of debris as a unit, being careful not to dig into the layer below; and he must also keep the objects of each layer separate from those of other layers. Fig. ARC 44.

These layers are distinguished by differences in color and texture. Since it is difficult to see and feel such subtle differences when digging downward, the excavator always digs one or more small test trenches to a depth of two to three feet in the area, and smooths the sides with a mason's trowel. When seen from the side, the various layers and their relationship to one another become clear, and provide a preview of the stratification of the area. Using this test trench as a key, he excavates the remainder of the area layer by layer to the lowest layer of the test trench. The objects found in each layer are placed in baskets which are identified by tags giving the name of the site, area, layer, and part of the layer—i.e., the room, street, cistern, pit, etc.—in which the objects were found. A careful description of each layer, sketches with exact measurements of all building remains, and a rough description of the objects discovered are entered in the field notebook. This process is repeated time and time again until the exacavation of the area is complete.

When walls appear, the archaeologist immediately begins to look for floors. Since objects on the floor usually belong to the final occupation of the structure and those below the floor belong to an earlier period, the objects from above the floor must be kept separate from those below. For this reason, he guards against inadvertently cutting through the floor and mixing the objects from the two periods. To discover the floor, and to study the relationship of the floor, the layers of debris, and the wall, the archaeologist digs one or more small test trenches *at right angles* to the wall, similar to those described above. In this manner, he usually discovers the floor, and sees in advance the construction of the wall and the relative position of the various layers of debris. Removing the layers revealed in the test trenches, he excavates the remainder of the area within the building. Floors and walls are cleaned, drawn to scale, photographed, and are studied in detail for evidence of repairs. They are then dismantled, and excavation proceeds downward. When the excavation of the area is complete or the season closes, scale drawings of the sides of the section are made; these enable the archaeologist to reconstruct the relative position of all layers, building remains, and objects; such reconstruction is absolutely essential for an accurate record of the excavation. Fig. ARC 45.

If this procedure seems time-consuming and unnecessary, it must be remembered that all excavation is destruction; once a section is dug, it is gone forever and cannot be restored except in the excavator's notebook and drawings. There is no opportunity to

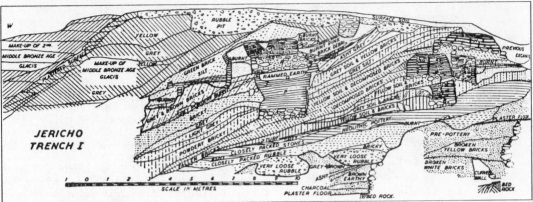

45. Section drawing showing relationship of walls and layers of debris, Jericho Trench I

duplicate the experiment exactly; in this respect archaeology is unlike all other branches of science. All excavation, therefore, must be done with the best possible technique, and all records must be kept fully and carefully.

*b. Tombs.* Except for monumental tomb structures and those that come to light in the course of excavation on mounds, tombs are generally difficult to find, owing to the fact that they are covered over and their location is unmarked. Frequently they are found by accident, as when a peasant's plow breaks through the roof; often excavators strip promising hillsides and fields in their search. Once a tomb has

46. Entrance to tomb 77 at Megiddo, Late Bronze I (*ca.* 1550-1400 B.C.)

been discovered, the excavation of it is a straightforward though difficult task. Most of the difficulty is inherent in the nature of tombs; space is small and cramped; the air is dust-filled, and ventilation is poor; some of the objects and bones are friable and tend to disintegrate when exposed to air. Figs. ARC 46-47.

Using small hand tools, the excavator clears the debris from the objects and bones without disturbing their position. Extremely delicate objects such as wooden utensils and furniture are treated with preservatives immediately. The debris is usually sifted to recover beads, tiny bits of jewelry, and seals. When all the objects and skeletons are exposed, they are then drawn and photographed in position. If several layers of undisturbed burials are found, each layer is cleaned, planned, and photographed as a unit before it is removed, so that the stratigraphic relationship of the burials can be established. When all objects have been removed, the entrance and chamber are drawn and photographed. *See* TOMBS, SEPULCHERS.

**3. Recording.** Accurate recording of all phases of excavation is absolutely essential for a correct interpretation of the site. The various layers of debris are described in the archaeologist's notebook as they are excavated.* At the end of the season, scale drawings and both black-and-white and color photographs are made of the sides of the sections, showing the exact position of each layer. Fig. SAM 13.

All features of the excavated area such as room deposits, walls, floors, and ovens are thoroughly cleaned, planned, and photographed. Since the play of light and shadow is important in photography, the archaeologist schedules his photography for the hour when the lighting of the area is optimum, and arranges the cleaning accordingly.

The objects recovered are brought from the mound daily in baskets which carry identifying tags (*see* § B2a *above*). These tags are the sole means of identifying the layer, room, or tomb where the objects were found, and are therefore kept with the contents of the baskets until the objects are finally recorded in the catalogue. All objects are then washed and dried, with the exception of delicate objects of metal, bone, and wood which usually require cleaning in an equipped laboratory. Since it is not feasible to keep the tens of thousands of sherds found in each campaign, they are sorted, and only characteristic types, new forms, and both whole and restorable vessels are saved; the remainder is described in the excavator's notebook and discarded.

The objects that are saved are recorded in the catalogue, which shows all relevant details, particularly the area, section, layer, room, or tomb, date found, and drawing and photograph numbers. In

Courtesy of the Oriental Institute, the University of Chicago

47. Interior of tomb 77 at Megiddo, Late Bronze I (*ca.* 1550-1400 B.C.)

addition to the catalogue, a pottery notebook is kept, in which the excavator enters the date, number of pieces, and his observations and impressions of the pottery of each layer or group as a whole before any is discarded. The over-all view obtained from the preliminary study often points up new problems in the section which can be solved during the season.

If the staff is sufficiently large, the restoration, drawing, and photography of objects are done in the field, since many or all of them may be kept by the department of antiquities of the country in which the excavation takes place.

**4. Disposition of finds.** Governments differ on regulations covering the disposition of finds. Some keep everything; others divide the finds on an agreed ratio; still others take only unique objects to round out collections in the national museum. The policy is known to the archaeologist before he excavates, and it affects the organization and operation of the expedition. If all objects must remain in the country, all drawing, photography, and much of the study must be done in the field; this requires more personnel, shorter digging seasons, or lengthy stays in the country after the close of the work. If the government divides the objects, representatives of the department of antiquities visit the site at the end of each campaign and divide the finds. Once this is completed, objects retained by the expedition are packed in bags and boxes, export licenses are obtained, and transportation is arranged.

**5. Excavation report.** At the end of each season, the excavator normally prepares several preliminary excavation reports which are published in various journals to give others a general view of the results of the dig. But he is not finished until a final, comprehensive report on the excavation is published. Having excavated and destroyed all or part of a site, he is morally responsible for making available to all a full and accurate record and interpretation of his excavation. In general, it is a task of reducing the excavated area to a printed text with illustrations. He carefully studies the stratification of the site as it is preserved in his notebook, drawings, and photographs, and determines the major strata or periods of occupation by correlating the layers of debris with building remains and with objects, particularly pottery. Representative pottery and other objects are

selected for publication, and lists are prepared which show all layers and loci in which each type was found. The selected objects are then described in detail, and finished drawings and photographs of all objects, together with final drawings of plans and stratification, are prepared. Since no archaeologist is an expert in all branches of science, he secures specialists in other fields to prepare technical reports on those objects which are outside his field of competence (*see* § C6 *below*). When these reports are in and he has completed his own research, he is able to see the results of his excavation as a whole. He then fits the site into the political, economic, and cultural history of the area and, if possible, into the larger framework of the ancient Near East as a whole. This is the ultimate goal of the archaeologist; the measure of his success largely depends on his skill in excavating and his competence in analyzing and interpreting the material recovered.

While the aim of every archaeologist is to make his final report as perfect as possible, mistakes are inevitably made, problems are left unsolved, and errors creep into his interpretation of the history, chronology, and culture of the site. Moreover, every new excavation adds to our knowledge of material cultures, with the result that some of the earlier analyses and interpretations become obsolete. For these reasons, the study of an excavation goes on for years after the publication of the final report. Other archaeologists, linguists, and historians correct, refine, and reinterpret the published raw material, and frequently make enormous contributions to our knowledge of the site.

**6. Uses of objects.** In every excavation tens of thousands, and often hundreds of thousands, of objects are found. Few if any of these are of intrinsic value; they consist, for the most part, of potsherds; broken bits of stone, metal, and glass vessels; flint and metal tools; implements and weapons; clay figurines; bits of sculpture in stone or metal; architectural fragments; bones; rings; stone and metal beads; scarabs; seals; etc. Of course, exceptional finds, such as objects made of gold, are occasionally recovered in some regions, but are very rare in a poor country like Palestine. The lack of intrinsic worth, however, does not lessen their value to archaeology; they are extremely important because they enable the archaeologist (*a*) to date the occupation levels or strata in the site, and (*b*) to describe and compare material cultures. *See* POTTERY § 2. Fig. POT 63.

*a. Dating sites.* The use of objects for dating strata presupposes a knowledge of the principle of change. Change takes place in all classes of man-made objects. New styles appear and remain popular for undetermined periods, during which they are modified to suit changing tastes and needs. Ultimately they lose favor altogether and disappear, being replaced by still newer styles. The length of time that a style is manufactured and used, and the number and rate of changes, are variable; there is no fixed rule governing the operation of change in man-made objects.

But the simple fact that change takes place is of the greatest importance, because it enables archaeologists to trace the history of each class of object.

To this end, excavators carefully keep the objects from each layer of debris separate; if they become mixed with earlier or later material, the direction and date of changes that have occurred in the different classes of objects cannot be determined.

The procedure used in tracing change in objects varies with different archaeologists, but is essentially this: Upon completion of the excavation, all the examples of a single class from each layer of debris are picked out and arranged according to their place in the sequence of layers from the lowest (earliest) to the highest (latest). They are then carefully studied; all changes in manufacturing technique, form, and finish are noted. The layer in which the class first appears, each layer in which it undergoes change, and the layer in which it is last found are recorded. This process is repeated with each class of objects. The histories of the various classes are then correlated, so that for any period the classes that were being made can be listed, and the exact stage of development of each class can be described. This correlation is called a typological sequence or a relative chronology.

The various types of objects are assigned dates when they occur in strata that can be dated by other means (see § C below). Since objects in a stratum are virtually identical with objects in contemporary strata of other sites in the same cultural area, an absolute date for a stratum in one site equally applies to strata with similar objects in all other sites in the area. Absolute dates, of course, are not found for all strata in a site; frequently one or two can be established, and sometimes none at all. But as the number of excavated sites in an area increases, the number of absolute dates also increases, and a precise chronological framework for the cultural area is gradually developed. When dates are assigned to the classes of objects in this sequence, we have what is known as an absolute chronology. Once this framework is established, objects can be used to date the occupational periods in other sites where other kinds of chronological evidence is lacking.

At this stage, archaeologists can omit some of the steps in this procedure. The objects of each layer are compared with those found in other sites, and dated accordingly. This enables excavators to trace the history of sites adequately, and has the advantage of being faster than the procedure described above. It is desirable, however, to trace the typological development of each class of objects, so that subtle changes, which may have been overlooked by previous excavators, but which may fill gaps in our typology and render our chronology still more precise, can be detected.

*b. Describing and comparing material cultures.* The various objects from contemporary strata in neighboring sites are very much alike; there may be minor differences, but they are far outweighed by similarities. When all the sites in a region share similar objects, they can be said to belong to a material culture. Each region has its own characteristic objects which differ from those of other regions in technique of manufacture and style. By means of the intensive study of objects, archaeologists have been able to isolate and describe the major material cultural centers of the ancient Near East—Egypt, Mesopotamia, Anatolia, and Syro-Palestine. Much progress has already been made in distinguishing local differences within each of these larger cultural areas, and this, too, is accomplished through the careful analysis of material remains. E.g., in antiquity Palestine and Transjordan belonged to the same material culture, as shown by many common features, one of which is ceramics. Yet in certain periods there are minor variations in shapes and styles of decoration that enable archaeologists to separate Palestinian and Transjordanian pottery, even though they belong to the same basic categories.

When the characteristic objects of the various cultures are known, many important facts bearing on our over-all knowledge of antiquity can also be deduced. The discovery of foreign objects suggests that the site figured in trade and commerce, or was subject to a foreign power. Here the type of object usually indicates which is the case—e.g., foreign pottery points to trade, but a victory stele establishes subjugation. Most foreign objects, of course, came through trade, and much has been learned from them about commercial relations in the ancient world. By noting the quantity of imports from one region that are found in different strata of sites in another region, archaeologists can throw light on the fluctuations of trade and commerce between these regions. By observing both the number and the kinds of the objects imported, the level of economic prosperity of the country can also be roughly estimated.

In certain cases, archaeologists can demonstrate both the existence and the date of foreign contacts even though no imported objects are found. Occasionally objects are recovered which were made locally—as shown by the material and sometimes the technique used—but which imitated the shape and finish of objects from another region. In such cases, it must be assumed that the local craftsman had models or prototypes which he copied. If the homeland of the prototype is known and if the date of the prototype is fixed, the existence of the local imitation proves that there was contact with the land where the prototype was made at that time, in spite of the fact that the genuine imported object which served as a model may never be found.

Objects also throw light on immigration and colonization. It sometimes happens that classes of objects which have been common at a site for several centuries are suddenly replaced by new objects which are completely different typologically. This indicates that the site has been occupied by people from another cultural region. Archaeologists then compare the new objects with contemporary objects of other regions, in order to ascertain their source, and, in turn, the homeland of the new people. Such is the case with the Philistines. In the second quarter of the twelfth century B.C., a new kind of pottery, featuring different shapes and decorative styles, suddenly appears at sites on the coastal plain and the Shephelah (foothills) of W Palestine. Even though no Philistine site has been extensively excavated to date, the geographical distribution and date of this pottery, which was fixed by the discovery of many examples in Israelite sites and in contexts with pottery of known date, indicated that it was Philistine. (Fig. POT 63.) Analyses of its shapes and motifs, and comparisons with other contemporary pottery of the ancient world, have shown that its ultimate source was Aegean pottery (specifically Mycenaean IIIC:1 pottery). The ancestral home of the Philistines was therefore in this general area, although it cannot be located more precisely as yet.

**C. DATING ARCHAEOLOGICAL EVIDENCE.** Dating the various strata in a site requires the careful sifting and study of many lines of evidence.

**1. Literary references.** References in ancient literature, including the Bible, texts in other Near Eastern languages, and Greco-Roman literary works, are the best sources for chronology. They sometimes supply information about cities, including names of founders and conquerors, with the result that dates of the establishment and destruction of various occupations can be fixed closely. E.g., we know from the Bible (I Kings 16:23-24) that the city of Samaria was founded by Omri in the seventh year of his reign (ca. 870 B.C.), and from both the Bible (II Kings 17:5-6) and the annals of the Assyrian king Sargon II that it was destroyed ca. 721 B.C. Unhappily, references of this type are not common for any period, and are especially rare for the second millennium B.C. and earlier.

**2. Inscriptions and paleography.** INSCRIPTIONS are occasionally found which contain names of persons or allude to events dated by other sources. These may be written on clay tablets, stone stele or seals, ostraca (sherds reused as writing material), parchment, or papyrus. At first sight it seems that this material should be extremely useful for purposes of dating. But these objects were often removed from their original contexts, and are found in strata dating hundreds of years later than the period in which they were made—e.g., stone inscriptions were frequently reused as building material in later periods, and seals were sometimes kept in families for generations. For these reasons, caution must be used in dating strata by the literary material found in them. On the other hand, if it is clear that the inscriptions are in situ—i.e., in the stratum to which they properly belong—they are useful for dating.

Paleography is also used for purposes of dating. Just as objects undergo change, the forms of signs or letters used in writing change in the course of time. Great progress has been made in dating these changes, and paleography now supplies approximate dates for strata in which written documents are found in situ. See ALPHABET, HEBREW AND GREEK; WRITING AND WRITING MATERIALS.

**3. Local objects.** Although virtually all objects are useful for dating, some are of greater value than others. They fall into two groups, those that were locally made, which includes the bulk of finds, and those that were manufactured in other countries. They can be further classified by kinds of objects.

**a. Pottery.** Because pottery is the most common and indestructible artifact made by man, and because it is an excellent medium for the expression of change, it is the most useful class of objects for determining dates. In Palestine, where many sites of all periods have been excavated and where there are a number of absolute dates, a pottery chronology has been perfected that is accurate within a maximum error of about two centuries, and for most periods

within a century or less. With more and better stratigraphic excavation, it will become even more precise, and may enable us to date strata of most periods within surprisingly narrow limits, perhaps twenty-five to fifty years. (See POTTERY. See also Fig. POT 63.) At present, an archaeologist who has mastered Palestinian pottery can collect and study sherds that have eroded to the surface on the top and sides of a mound, and predict accurately the various periods of occupation of the site without digging at all. This technique is known as surface exploration.

**b. Coins.** Coins are also valuable chronological evidence when found in quantities sufficient to prove that they were contemporary with the stratum in which they were discovered. In the absence of other clear-cut chronological evidence, the discovery of one or two coins in a stratum only supplies an approximate date for the occupation, since (a) they may have been kept in a family for some time, and are therefore found in a deposit somewhat later than their period, and (b) they may work downward or upward in the debris, because of their small size. Of course, coinage is a relatively late invention (seventh century B.C.), and for this reason coins are only useful in dating relatively late strata. See MONEY, COINS.

**c. Other objects.** Metal and stone objects also undergo typological change—toggle pins, tools, weapons, metal containers and utensils, stone containers of all types, incense burners, beads, etc. While they are not so common, and hence not so valuable for purposes of chronology, as pottery in Palestinian sites, they can sometimes be used to fix the dates of strata when found in situ. But more excavation and study will be necessary before certain classes of objects can be confidently used for dating.

**4. Imported objects.** Frequently examples of the above-mentioned objects were imported from abroad. If the imported object is securely dated in the place of its origin, and if it is found in situ, it is extremely valuable for dating the stratum in which it is found. A time lag, determined by the distance and the amount and frequency of trade between the respective countries, must be reckoned. The date of the stratum is then computed by adding the length of this time lag to the known date of the import. Generally a time lag of no more than twenty-five to fifty years —and usually much less—is sufficient in the ancient Near East. Of course, an imported object may have become a family heirloom and survived for several generations. In such cases it will be found in a stratum dating somewhat later than the period in which it was manufactured and imported. Here the archaeologist weighs the known date of the object against other lines of dating evidence.

**5. Stylistic development in art and architecture.** Stylistic development in art as represented by sculpture, seals, scarabs, etc., is becoming increasingly useful for purposes of chronology as more is learned about ancient art forms and motifs. Unfortunately objects of this type, and particularly sculpture, are not plentiful in Palestine, largely because of the poverty of the country and because of Israelite religious prohibitions.

Architecture also contributes important chronological evidence. Plans and elevations of all types of buildings and structures, methods of construction, styles of masonry, and architectural orders change in different periods, and the dates of many of these changes are now known. In the absence of other clear-cut chronological data, architectural material can be used to date strata approximately and, in some instances, exactly. Architectural styles are more difficult to recover in Palestine than in countries such as Egypt, Greece, and Italy, because of the widespread use of sun-dried mud-brick construction, which lacks permanence and was used for poorer, nondescript structures, and because of the practice of building over and over again on the same site, which tends to destroy structures below. But progress is being made in using architecture for purposes of chronology. *See* ARCHITECTURE.

**6. Techniques of natural sciences.** The natural sciences increasingly assist archaeology in the classification and analysis of artifacts. Every excavation brings to light many objects which require expert description, and archaeologists turn these over to specialists in other disciplines for study whenever possible. Botanists classify samples of wood and grain; zoologists and physical anthropologists classify animal and human bones. Their findings, together with information gleaned in the course of excavation, often reveal many details of the life of ancient man— e.g., the state of his health, his diet, aspects of his domestic economy. The classification of shells by conchologists is useful in determining sources of trade and probable trade routes. Geology is also making substantial contributions. If the region in which the site is located is geologically known, the quarries from which stone was taken to fashion building blocks, sculpture, beads, and other objects can often be found. Usually quarries are nearby, but occasionally they are located many miles away, and the discovery of objects made of stone from distant quarries points to ancient commerce.

A number of established scientific techniques of analysis are now being used on archaeological objects with excellent results. Among these are: (*a*) petrographic analysis, in which thin sections or slices of potsherds are studied under a petrographic microscope to determine the minerals present in the ware; (*b*) neutron activation, in which sherds are placed in a nuclear reactor and the chemical composition of the clay is determined from the induced radioactivity; (*c*) qualitative and quantitative chemical analyses, in which the identity and proportions of the constituents of clays and metals are determined; (*d*) spectrographic analysis, in which the compositions of metals and, to a lesser degree, clays are determined by measuring the spectrum of the material when burned in an arc. Each of these methods has its advantages and disadvantages; often two or more must be used on objects to obtain the desired information.

Taken as a group, they make two important contributions to archaeology: (*a*) They provide a means of describing objects exactly and objectively. In the case of pottery, the minerals native to the clay and those used as temper can be determined accurately; as for metal objects, the composition of ancient alloys can be described precisely. (*b*) They are also used to distinguish foreign from locally made objects and thus supply data on ancient trade. A good example of this is pottery. In the manufacture of ancient pottery, local clay and temper were almost always used. The composition of clays and the kinds of temper vary widely in different parts of the world, and even in the same region in different periods. Thus the discovery of pottery of similar shapes and finishes and made of similar clay and temper points to a common origin and date, regardless of where they were found. Until recently, however, pottery could be identified only by form and finish, both of which were successfully imitated by skilled ancient potters. For this reason it was often difficult to distinguish between an import and a good imitation. Now, with these analyses, it is usually possible to determine whether they were made locally or abroad.

The natural sciences also aid archaeology in fixing dates more precisely. A method of measuring time known as radiocarbon dating has recently been developed by nuclear physics. Since the intake of carbon[14] by living things stops with death and thereafter disintegrates at a fixed rate, reasonably accurate measurements can be made of the amount remaining in organic matter, with the result that the approximate age of the material can be determined. For the late periods and for regions where chronology is already fixed by other means, it is of little value; but for the early periods of every ancient culture and in regions which have only recently been opened to archaeology, it is of the greatest value for confirming and correcting dates.

In sites which have not been excavated stratigraphically—and this includes most of the older excavations as well as a number of recent ones—the layers of debris cannot be dated precisely, because they were not systematically removed one by one, and their objects were hopelessly mixed. In such instances, the objects of each building or locus are dated by comparing them with objects from strata and loci of known date in other sites. At best, this method is not so accurate as dating layers which have been carefully peeled off and objects which have been kept from contamination with earlier or later material. But it is the only technique that can be used with poorly excavated sites, and it does permit us to use the results of these excavations, though of course with caution.

**D. CONTRIBUTIONS OF ARCHAEOLOGY TO THE BIBLE.** No one can understand the Bible without a knowledge of biblical history and culture, and no one can claim a knowledge of biblical history and culture without an understanding of the contributions of archaeology. Biblical events have been illustrated, obscure words defined, ideas explained, and chronology refined, by archaeological finds. To say that our knowledge of the Bible has been revolutionized by these discoveries is almost to understate the facts. The following discussion is limited to the major areas in which archaeology has contributed to our understanding of the Bible (for detailed discussions, *see bibliography*).

One of the most important contributions of archaeology is the recovery of a number of ancient Near Eastern languages. Even though many of these were discovered by chance or by non-archaeological exploration, and were deciphered by linguists rather than archaeologists, they can be classed as archaeological finds because the quantity of texts necessary to make them intelligible was brought to light by means of excavation. Most of these languages are Semitic, including Akkadian (Assyrian and Babylonian), Ugaritic (Canaanite), and the pre-Islamic languages of South Arabia. Several non-Semitic languages, particularly Egyptian, Sumerian, and Hittite, have also been recovered by archaeology. A staggering volume of documents written in these and other previously known languages has been discovered. These documents range in time from man's earliest writings—in the Chalcolithic period—through the biblical and postbiblical periods, and include all literary genre: epics, historical narratives, annals of kings, law, poetry, wisdom literature, rituals, theological works, business documents, and correspondence.

The continuing study of ancient Near Eastern languages and literatures has made the Bible more intelligible. Many words and phrases in Hebrew which could not be accurately translated—because their meanings were unknown—can now be understood perfectly, because of the discovery of identical words and phrases in these texts. E.g., the word אֵד (Gen. 2:6), which is translated "mist" (RSV-KJV), actually means "river" in Sumerian and "river (god)" in Akkadian; the meaning "river" admirably fits this context.

In addition to rendering the biblical text more lucid, this literature illustrates and explains many laws, social customs, religious practices, and theological ideas of the Bible whose meanings are obscure. Many of the same ideas and customs are found in these documents, but in a fuller setting, which clarifies their significance in biblical times. E.g., the curious arrangement whereby a servant, Eliezer, was to become Abram's heir (Gen. 15:2-4) is explained in the NUZI tablets, where the same custom appears as a normal procedure among childless couples. The couple adopted a son and designated him heir to their estate; in return, the adopted son promised to provide both security and a fitting burial for them. Such agreements were nullified, or at least modified, if a son was born to the couple later. (For other examples, see also COVENANT; TERAPHIM; DEAD SEA SCROLLS.)

This literature, together with other archaeological discoveries, adds much to our knowledge of the history of Palestine. While the Bible is a veritable treasury of historical information, its whole approach to history is religiously rather than politically or economically oriented. Moreover, much of its historical material consists of summaries or sketches with references to more detailed sources which have not survived—e.g., the "book of Jashar," the "book of the chronicles of the Kings of Judah," and the "book of the chronicles of the Kings of Israel." For these reasons, important persons and periods are frequently given only brief notice. Here other literature and excavation fill in many details missing from the historical accounts of the Bible. E.g., I Kings 14:25-26; II Chr. 12:2-9 describe the Judean raid by the Egyptian king SHISHAK during the reign of Rehoboam in Judah. These brief accounts are supplemented by an inscription at Karnak, commemorating Shishak's victory, which preserves the names of captured towns in both Judah and Israel, showing that it was

a more far-reaching campaign than the brief biblical account suggests. Furthermore, excavations at a number of Palestinian sites, including Tell Beit Mirsim (Debir), Tell er-Rumeileh (Beth-shemesh), and Megiddo, have uncovered evidence of destruction at precisely this time. Similarly, the reign of Ahab in Israel receives a great deal of attention in the Bible (I Kings 16:29-22:40), but most of the biblical account is devoted to the Elijah narratives and to Ahab's wars with Ben-hadad of Syria. Yet Ahab's alliance with Ben-hadad of Syria and Irhuleni of Hamath, and their war against Shalmaneser III of Assyria, are not mentioned at all in the Bible; the account of this important struggle is found in an Assyrian text, the Monolith-Inscription from Kurkh (see AHAB). Excavations at Samaria (see SAMARIA [TOWN]) have also furnished much new information about Israelite material culture during Ahab's reign.

Archaeology has also confirmed many details of biblical history. Various biblical events have been considered unauthentic by scholars, not because they contradicted known facts, but because they seemed implausible or did not fit preconceived patterns of historical or literary development. E.g., the historicity of the Exile has been questioned in some circles, but these doubts have vanished in the face of evidence discovered through excavation. Every Judean site excavated to date, which was inhabited at the end of the seventh century B.C., has been found to have been destroyed in this period and either reoccupied only after a gap of at least several decades or never inhabited again. The dearth of occupied sites in Judah during most of the sixth century B.C. indicates a depopulation of the country, which agrees perfectly with the biblical account of the Exile. Similarly the description of the power, fame, and wealth of Solomon (I Kings 2:12-11:43; II Chr. 1-9) has been considered legendary and grossly exaggerated by some scholars. But excavations at Megiddo, Ezion-geber, and virtually every site occupied in this period have illustrated aspects of an elaborate state organization, a high material culture, and a thriving economy in Israel; it is now clear that during Solomon's reign, Israel comprised the greatest and the most prosperous land empire in the ancient Near East and indeed enjoyed a Golden Age. In this instance, archaeology has shown that the Bible actually understates the facts. These examples can be multiplied to cover every period of Israelite history. See specific sites, such as MEGIDDO; SAMARIA; LACHISH; DEBIR.

It would be misleading to conclude that archaeology confirms all details of biblical history, because it does not. Most discrepancies are small and can be readily explained in one of several ways, but some are more serious and cannot be accounted for easily. In these cases, scholars do not arbitrarily hold that the biblical authors are wrong, although they may be. In view of the increasing confirmation of the Bible in recent years, they now approach major discrepancies with more caution than was previously used, and usually reserve final judgment until more evidence is forthcoming.

One of the most valuable contributions of archaeology is the feeling of intimacy with the past that it brings to biblical studies. Almost every biblical student or scholar experiences a barrier of time and culture when he seeks to project himself into biblical times. Much of this barrier is broken by archaeology, and the student acquainted with the results of excavations finds that ancient man and ancient times become real to a degree that would be unattainable if he depended solely on the written word. All aspects of material culture brought to light by excavation contribute to this intimacy. While the field archaeologist is inevitably caught up in the life and times of ancient man during his excavation and his study of objects, the student can also share this intimacy—though to a lesser degree—if he studies excavation reports and becomes acquainted with objects through visits to museums.

These are the most important contributions made by archaeology to the Bible. Through excavation the world of the Bible is being resurrected, and as a result the Bible can be seen in its true background. Archaeology reveals both the similarities and the differences between the culture of Israel and the cultures of Israel's neighbors; it permits scholars to determine the common ground, which relates the Bible to other ancient literatures, and the areas of uniqueness, which set it apart from them. Archaeology does not and cannot prove the Bible. The Bible deals with man's relationship to God, and is, therefore, beyond the proof of archaeology or any other discipline. While archaeology confirms many details of history and lays bare the environment of the Bible, the history and environment with which it deals is human, not divine. It can neither confirm theology nor open the realm of faith.

**E. EXPLORATION AND EXCAVATION IN PALESTINE.** The history of exploration and excavation in Palestine is a long record of the labor of many individuals and organizations. A chronological summary of their work follows. In the section on excavation, only the more important sites dating between Chalcolithic and NT times are included. (For more detailed descriptions, *see* site entries and *bibliography*.) The modern place name of the site is given first, followed by the biblical name in parentheses, when known.

**1. Exploration.** Modern surface exploration of Palestine began in 1838 when Edward Robinson and Eli Smith traveled through the country studying topography and identifying many biblical places. From 1872 to 1878 a thorough survey of W Palestine was made by C. R. Conder and H. H. Kitchener under the auspices of the Palestine Exploration Fund. Beginning in 1884, G. Schumacher also undertook a systematic surface exploration of Hauran and N Transjordan. After a lapse of many years, exploration was resumed in 1933, when N. Glueck began his great archaeological survey of Transjordan from the Aqabah to Syria. This survey is especially significant because Glueck not only located hundreds of sites, but also determined their periods of occupation through the study of surface sherds. Since 1952, Glueck has been engaged in a similar systematic exploration of the Negeb. Important contributions to the identification of specific sites have also been made by a host of archaeologists, historians, and biblical scholars, including in particular C. Clermont-Ganneau, L. H. Vincent, W. F. Albright, G. Dalman, A. Alt, and F.-M. Abel.

**2. Excavation to World War I.** Scientific excavation in Palestine traces its origin to W. M. F. Petrie, who dug the mound of Tell el-Hesi (Eglon?) in 1890. There had been earlier excavations, notably F. de Saulcy's clearance of the "Tombs of the Kings" and C. Warren's work at Jerusalem, but results were meager and largely meaningless. Petrie's great contribution was the recognition of stratigraphy in Palestinian mounds and the discovery that common pottery undergoes typological changes which can be correlated with stratification. F. J. Bliss continued the work at Tell el-Hesi, and later collaborated with A. C. Dickie in excavating in Jerusalem (1894-97), and with R. A. S. Macalister (1898) in digging soundings at Tell ej-Judeideh (Moresheth-gath), Tell Sandahannah (Mareshah, Marisa), Tell es-Safi (Libnah), and Tell Zakariyeh (Azekah). Between 1902 and 1909 Macalister excavated Tell Jezer (Gezer). Meanwhile, a number of sites were excavated by German and Austrian scholars: Tell Ta'annak (Taanach) by E. Sellin from 1901 to 1904, Tell el-Mutesellim (Megiddo) by Schumacher from 1903 to 1905, and Tell es-Sultan (OT Jericho) by Sellin and C. Watzinger from 1907 to 1909. The first American excavations in Palestine were undertaken at Sebastiyeh (Samaria) by G. A. Reisner between 1908 and 1910. Reisner's great contribution was the development of good archaeological technique—i.e., careful analysis of stratigraphy, accurate surveying, thorough architectural study, and comprehensive recording. From 1911 to 1912, D. Mackenzie dug at Tell er-Rumeileh (Beth-shemesh); and in 1913 Sellin began the clearance of Balatah (Shechem), but was forced to postpone his work because of World War I.

This was the pioneering period in Palestinian archaeology. There were flashes of brilliance, notably Petrie's initial discoveries at Tell el-Hesi, and Reisner's introduction of new excavation methods at Samaria; unhappily the publication of the latter did not appear until 1924, and thus made no impression on pre–World War I archaeology. But as a whole, it was a disappointing and disillusioning period. Excavation technique was poor, and serious blunders were made in the interpretation of finds. By the outbreak of World War I, neither a systematic study of chronology nor a synthesis of finds could be made, so that chaos prevailed in the field.

**3. Excavation between World Wars I and II.** With the establishment of the British mandate in 1920, and the creation of a Department of Antiquities, excavation resumed in force. From 1920 to 1922 soundings were made at 'Asqalan (Ashkelon, Ascalon) by J. Garstang with W. J. Phythian-Adams. Beginning in 1921 and continuing until 1933, the great site Tell el-Husn (Beth-shan) was successively excavated by C. S. Fisher, A. Rowe, and G. M. FitzGerald. In 1922-23, Albright dug at Tell el-Ful (Gibeah of Saul). From 1923 to 1928 a series of campaigns at Ophel (City of David) in Jerusalem was directed by Macalister, J. G. Duncan, and J. W. Crowfoot. The largest excavation ever undertaken in Palestine was begun in 1925 and continued until 1939 at Tell el-Mutesellim (Megiddo), and was successively directed by Fisher, P. L. O. Guy, and G. Loud. From 1925 to 1934 G. Horsfield, Crowfoot, Fisher, and C. C. McCown undertook the clearance of Jerash (Gerasa). In 1926 H. Kjaer and

A. Schmidt began a series of limited excavations at Tell Seilun (Shiloh); and Sellin, followed by H. Welter and later by H. Steckeweh, resumed the excavation of Balatah (Shechem), which was carried on until 1934. Beginning also in 1926 and continuing until 1935, W. F. Badè excavated Tell en-Nasbeh, and Albright also undertook a series of campaigns at Tell Beit Mirsim (Kirjath-sepher, Debir) which lasted until 1932. In 1926-27 Petrie excavated at Tell Jemmeh (unidentified, but probably not Gerar as Petrie believed), and from 1928 to 1930 at Tell el-Far'ah (probably Sharuhen). E. Grant, assisted by Fisher, began a series of campaigns at Tell er-Rumeileh (Beth-shemesh) in 1928 which continued until 1933. From 1929 to 1936 Garstang excavated at Tell es-Sultan (OT Jericho), previously dug by the Germans before World War I. Father Mallon began clearance of the important Chalcolithic site Teleilat el-Ghassul in 1929; after his death, work was carried on by Fathers Koeppel, Mahan, and Murphey until 1938.* That year Horsfield, Agnes Conway, and Margaret Murray inaugurated a series of campaigns at the Nabatean capital, Petra. The Conway high place at this site was excavated by Albright in 1934. Fig. ART 62.

Upon completing his work at Tell el-Far'ah in 1930, Petrie conducted excavations at Tell el-'Ajjul (Beth-eglaim) until 1934. In 1931 O. R. Sellers and Albright dug at et-Tubeiqah (Beth-zur), and from 1931 to 1935 Crowfoot, Kathleen Kenyon, and E. L. Sukenik excavated Sebastiyeh (Samaria), and successfully solved many problems left by Reisner's earlier work. R. W. Hamilton excavated the small mound Tell Abu Hawam (Salmonah?) in 1932-33. Clearance was begun at the great site Tell ed-Duweir (Lachish) by J. L. Starkey in 1932 and was continued through a series of campaigns until his death in 1938. In 1933-34 Judith Marquet-Krause excavated at et-Tell (Ai), and in 1934 Albright and J. L. Kelso began work at the neighboring site, Beitin (Bethel). Minor excavations were also carried out by Petrie at Tell ez-Zuweyid (Anthedon) and at Petra in 1934-37. In 1937 Glueck cleared a Nabatean sanctuary at Khirbet et-Tannur, and from 1937 to 1940 he conducted several campaigns at Tell el-Kheleifeh (Ezion-geber), the site of a copper refinery going back to the time of Solomon.

The confusion that prevailed in Palestinian archaeology up to World War I was rapidly dispelled during these two decades. Although the technique of excavation left much to be desired in many instances, standards were generally much higher than those of pre–World War I excavations. Expeditions were better organized and more adequately staffed. Accurate surveying and careful recording of finds became the rule. The interpretation of the mass of material brought to light also proceeded rapidly. Pottery chronology was firmly established, especially by Albright's work at Tell el-Ful and Tell Beit Mirsim, and both architectural analysis and the study of other objects were immeasurably advanced. These developments vastly increased our knowledge of ancient Palestine, which in turn enlarged our understanding of the Bible. Great strides were also made in comparative archaeology, with the result that a clearer picture of the position and role of Palestine in the ancient Near East was formed.

**4. Excavation since World War II.** World War II and the Arab-Israeli conflict that followed two years later sharply curtailed excavation. But this period was not a total loss, since interpretation and synthesis of the material recovered between the world wars continued. Since 1944 work has been carried on at Khirbet Kerak (Beth-yerah) by a number of excavators, including B. Mazar (Maisler), M. Stekelis, M. Avi-Yonah, Guy, P. Bar-Adon, and Y. Yadin. In 1946 Père R. de Vaux began the excavation of Tell el-Far'ah (Tirzah) which continues, though with numerous interruptions.

With the end of Arab-Israeli hostilities and the partitioning of Palestine, excavation was resumed in both Israel and Jordan. Following the appearance of the first lot of Dead Sea Scrolls in 1948, clearance of numerous caves, and excavations at Khirbet Qumran and in Wadi Murabba'at have been carried on with few interruptions by De Vaux, G. L. Harding, Yusuf Sa'ad, Sellers, W. L. Reed, and a host of others. From 1948 to 1950 Mazar conducted important excavations at Tell Qasileh. In 1950 work was begun at Caesarea by Avi-Yonah, and at Jaffa by J. Bowman and B. S. J. Isserlin. During 1950-51 Tulul Abu el-'Alayiq (NT Jericho) was excavated by Kelso, A. H. Detweiler, F. V. Winnett, and J. B. Pritchard. A series of campaigns was also begun at Dhiban (Dibon) in 1951 under the successive direction of Winnett, Reed, A. D. Tushingham, and W. H. Morton. I. Ben-Dor and M. Dothan conducted small excavations at 'Affuleh (Epher) in 1951, and at Khirbet el-Bitar from 1952 to 1954. Work was resumed at Tell es-Sultan (OT Jericho) by Kathleen Kenyon, who inaugurated a series of campaigns in 1952 which have made numerous contributions to Palestinian prehistory and have revolutionized our knowledge of the history of the site. That same year J. Perrot undertook the excavation of Tell Abu Matar, and in 1953 J. P. Free began a series of campaigns at Tell Dotha (Dothan). During 1954 small excavations were started at Beitin (Bethel) by Kelso, at Ramath Rahel (Beth ha-Kerem?) by Y. Aharoni, at Nahariyeh by Dothan, and at Bir es-Safadi by J. Perrot and H. de Contenson. In 1955 Yadin undertook the excavation of the large and important site Tell el-Qedah (Hazor), and Avi-Yonah, N. Avigad, Aharoni, I. Dunayevsky, and S. Gutman began clearance of Herod's palace at Masada. During 1956 excavations at Balatah (Shechem) were resumed by G. E. Wright, and work was begun at el-Jib (Gibeon) by Pritchard, and at Tell Sheikh el-Areini (Gath) by S. Yeivin.

Since many of these excavations are still in progress, it would be premature to attempt a summary of developments and results at this time. Nevertheless, preliminary reports and the final publications which have already appeared clearly indicate that improvements are being made in excavation technique, recording, and interpretation. It is safe to predict that the rapidly accumulating mass of archaeological data will vastly enrich our knowledge of ancient Palestine and of biblical life and times.

**F. TABLE OF ARCHAEOLOGICAL PERIODS OF PALESTINE.**

| | |
|---|---|
| Mesolithic (Natufian) | *ca.* 8000-6000 B.C. |
| Pre-Pottery Neolithic | *ca.* 6000-5000 B.C. |
| Pottery Neolithic | *ca.* 5000-4000 B.C. |

| | |
|---|---|
| Chalcolithic | ca. 4000-3200 B.C. |
| Esdraelon | ca. 3200-3000 B.C. |
| Early Bronze (EB) | |
| EB I | ca. 3000-2800 B.C. |
| EB II | ca. 2800-2600 B.C. |
| EB III | ca. 2600-2300 B.C. |
| EB IV (or III B) | ca. 2300-2100 B.C. |
| Middle Bronze (MB) | |
| MB I (or EB-MB) | ca. 2100-1900 B.C. |
| MB IIa | ca. 1900-1700 B.C. |
| MB IIb | ca. 1700-1600 B.C. |
| MB IIc | ca. 1600-1550 B.C. |
| Late Bronze (LB) | |
| LB I | ca. 1550-1400 B.C. |
| LB IIa | ca. 1400-1300 B.C. |
| LB IIb | ca. 1300-1200 B.C. |
| Iron I or Early Iron (EI) | |
| Ia | ca. 1200-1150 B.C. |
| Ib | ca. 1150-1025 B.C. |
| Ic | ca. 1025- 950 B.C. |
| Id | ca. 950- 900 B.C. |
| Iron II or Middle Iron (MI) | |
| IIa | ca. 900- 800 B.C. |
| IIb | ca. 800- 700 B.C. |
| IIc | ca. 700- 600 B.C. |
| Iron III, Late Iron, or Persian | ca. 600- 300 B.C. |
| Hellenistic | ca. 300- 63 B.C. |
| Roman | ca. 63 B.C.-A.D. 323 |
| Byzantine | ca. A.D. 323-636 |
| Islamic | ca. A.D. 636-present |

**Bibliography.** N. Glueck, *The Other Side of the Jordan* (1940), a summary of archaeological discoveries in Transjordan, arranged geographically. M. Burrows, *What Mean These Stones?* (1941). C. C. McCown, *The Ladder of Progress in Palestine* (1943). J. Finegan, *Light from the Ancient Past* (1947), an excellent, easy-to-read summary of the history and archaeology of the ancient Near East. K. M. Kenyon, *Beginning in Archaeology* (1952), an excellent discussion of excavation technique. W. F. Libby, *Radiocarbon Dating* (1955). W. F. Albright, *The Archaeology of Palestine* (1956), the authoritative work on Palestinian archaeology, arranged chronologically; *Archaeology and the Religion of Israel* (1956); *From Stone Age to Christianity* (1957), a comprehensive study of the ancient Near East from literary and archaeological sources, with emphasis on the religion of Israel. L. H. Grollenberg, *Atlas of the Bible* (1956), contains the finest photographs of Palestine. A. O. Shepard, *Ceramics for the Archaeologist* (1956), pp. 138-47. M. Wheeler, *Archaeology from the Earth* (1956), an excellent discussion of principles and techniques of excavation. G. E. Wright and F. V. Filson, eds., *Westminster Historical Atlas to the Bible* (1956). E. V. Sayre and R. W. Dodson, "Neutron Activation Study of Mediterranean Potsherds," *AJA*, 61 (1957), 35-41. G. E. Wright, *Biblical Archaeology* (1957), a good discussion of biblical history, literature, and thought in the light of archaeological discoveries.                G. W. VAN BEEK

**ARCHANGEL** ärk ān′jəl. *See* ANGEL.

**ARCHELAUS** är′kə lā′əs ['Αρχέλαος]. Son of HEROD the Great and Malthace. On the death of Herod in 4 B.C., a codicil of his will which distributed his territory named Herod Antipas and Philip as tetrarchs, but Archelaus as the principal successor.

Archelaus did not try to ascend the throne immediately. Conscious of the hostility of the Jews to his family, he tried through kindliness and forbearance to win their approval; moreover, he wanted his right to the throne to be confirmed by Rome.

Despite his efforts to win over the Jews, they showed such unbroken animosity and rebellion that force of arms was needed to put down disorders, within the first months after his father's death. The revolts were addressed not so much against Archelaus as against his deceased father, Herod; and while Archelaus initially practiced some restraint, a notable bloodshed took place at the temple on Passover, when Archelaus felt it necessary to loose his army on the milling throngs.

As to the crown, Archelaus encountered rather quickly the intrigues which characterized the Herodian dynasty. His brother Herod Antipas was his rival for the throne, able to buttress his claim on the basis of Herod's will, which had named Antipas king; Archelaus' claim rested on a codicil added to the will (Jos. War I.xxxii.7; xxxiii.7). Both brothers sailed to Rome to lay their claims before Augustus. The mother, Malthace, accompanied Archelaus to Rome, but she was won over to the party of Antipas.

Before the case could be decided, Malthace died. Meanwhile, word came from Judea of rebellious disorders there which were put down by Roman might, so the issue was unsettled. Then a third deputation appeared, petitioning Augustus to abstain from appointing any of the Herodian family as king, and instead to allow the Jews to live by their own laws. (Antipas goes unmentioned at this stage in Josephus' account. Possibly the death of the mother ended his effort; or possibly the opposition to the family by the Jewish deputation made the brother close ranks, for the third brother, Philip, is mentioned as present in Rome to support Archelaus.)

When Augustus heard the case, his decision was to award half of Herod's land (principally Judea) to Archelaus, and the other half was divided between Philip and Antipas. The title accorded to Archelaus was TETRARCH, but it was promised to him that if he governed virtuously, he would be given the title of king (Antiq. XVII.viii.3–xi.4; War II.vi.3). *See* HEROD (FAMILY).

When Archelaus returned to Judea, he interfered in the high priesthood, replacing a certain Joezer with Joezer's brother Eleazar. He further affronted Judean sensibilities by the circumstances of his second marriage. Archelaus, meeting and loving a certain Glaphyra, divorced his wife Mariamne in order to marry her. He was her third husband. Her first husband had been Archelaus' half brother Alexander; on being widowed, she had then married a Libyan king, Juba. Widowed again, she had returned to her royal father's home in Cappadocia. Josephus states (Antiq. XVII.xiii.1) that in marrying his brother's widow, Archelaus "transgressed the law of our fathers" (probably on the basis of Lev. 18:16; 20:21).

Eleazar, whom he had appointed as high priest, he now removed. He appointed Jesus son of Sie.

Josephus abstains from supplying details of the oppression by Archelaus of Samaritans and Jews; he summarizes that the brutal treatment of them prompted them to send deputations to Caesar to denounce Archelaus. In A.D. 6, Archelaus was banished to Gaul, to a city now known as Vienne. His territory was added to Syria; a PROCURATOR, Coponius, was sent to administer Judea.

Archelaus is mentioned only once in the NT (Matt. 2:22).

*Bibliography.* Jos. Antiq. XVII.xi–xiii; War I.xxxiii.8–II. vii.4. E. Schürer, *A History of the Jewish People in the Time of Jesus Christ* (English trans., 1899), div. 1, vol. II, pp. 1-9, 38-42. Pauly-Wissowa, *Real-Encyclopädie der klassischen Altertumswissenschaft*, Supplement II (1913), pp. 191 ff.

S. SANDMEL

**ARCHER** [מוֹרֶה בַקֶּשֶׁת, מוֹרֶה, יוֹרֶה, דֹּרֵךְ קֶשֶׁת, בַּעַל חִצִּים, מַחֲצִים קֶשֶׁת(?), רֹמֵה קֶשֶׁת, רַב; KJV מַחֲצִים (*plural; RSV* MUSICIANS)]. A soldier equipped with bow and arrows for offensive warfare.

A noun of vocation for "archer" is not certainly attested in Hebrew, since the word קַשָּׁת (*qashshāth*), occurring only at Gen. 21:20, is uncertain in meaning (וַיְהִי רֹבֶה קַשָּׁת). Since רֹב is attested in Job 16:13; Jer. 50:29 in the technical sense of "archer," it may be necessary to divide the text differently: וַיְהִי רֹב הַקֶּשֶׁת, "and he became an archer among the bowmen"—i.e., an outstanding archer (RSV "and [he] became an expert with the bow").

מַחֲצִים is a *hapax legomenon* in Judg. 5:11. The KJV "archers" constitutes an interpretation of the word as derived from a denominative חָצַץ, from חֵץ, "arrow," which is unlikely. The LXX interprets the word (Codex B) as ἀνὰ κρουομένων, "those starting up," to which the Minuscule K adds ἐν ὀργάνοις; this is also reflected in the OL reading *percutientes organa*. Thus the RSV may be right in its rendering "musicians."

It is not certain whether the archer corps was a well-developed unit in the Hebrew ARMY, as it was among the Assyrians. Saul was wounded by Philistine archers on Mount Gilboa (I Sam. 31:3; I Chr. 10:3). Ammonite archers slew Uriah the Hittite (II Sam. 11:24). According to II Chr. 35:23, King Josiah

48. Assyrian soldiers attacking with siege-engine supported by archers, time of Tiglath-pileser III (745-727 B.C.)

was shot by the archers of the Egyptians. Jeremiah refers to the archers of Babylon and her enemies (50: 29; 51:3). The fewness of the archers of Kedar indicates the loss of Kedar's glory (Isa. 21:17). The tribe Joseph is represented as an invincible archer attacked by archers (Gen. 39:23). In a most difficult passage in Proverbs (26:10) an archer (רֹב; KJV "the great God") who wounds indiscriminately is an analogy for one who hires a passing fool or drunkard. Job pictures the Lord attacking him, surrounding him with his archers (Job 16:13).

For the archer's weapons, *see* BOW AND ARROW; WAR, METHODS OF; WEAPONS AND IMPLEMENTS OF WAR. Fig. ARC 48.

J. W. WEVERS

**ARCHEVITES** är′kə vīts [Aram. אַרְכְּוָיֵא, *Kethibh* אַרְכְּוָי; Akkad. *Uruk-a-a, A-ra-ka-a-a*]. Inhabitants of the city of ERECH (Uruk) in Babylonia (Ezra 4:9). With Persians, Babylonians, Elamites, and others, men from Erech were settled in the cities of Samaria and other parts of the province Beyond the River by Ashurbanipal, called OSNAPPAR in Ezra 4:10.

H. G. MAY

**ARCHI.** KJV form of ARCHITE in Josh. 16:2.

**ARCHIPPUS** är kĭp′əs [Ἀρχίππος]. One of the persons to whom Paul addressed the letter entitled in the NT "To Philemon." He is designated there as Paul's fellow soldier (vs. 2). He is also mentioned in the Letter to the Colossians, where the Colossian Christians are commanded to "say to Archippus, 'See that you fulfil the ministry which you have received in the Lord' " (4:17). On the interpretation of the word translated "ministry" hangs an important question in NT criticism.

It has often been held that Archippus was the son of PHILEMON and APPHIA. But there is no evidence for this assumption that a family was being addressed in the Letter to Philemon. A hypothesis advanced by John Knox suggests that the ministry (διακονία) which Archippus is being urged to fulfill is the freeing of the slave Onesimus, of whom he is the owner, not merely to be reinstated in his household, but to become an evangelist in the work of the Christian church.

This view has much to commend it. If Philemon lived at Laodicea, the largest and most important town in the Lycus Valley, he might well have been a sort of presiding elder for the churches in that region, and this fact would explain why the letter was addressed to him as well as to Archippus. The letter would have gone first to him and then to Colossae, where Archippus lived, and where Onesimus was "one of" the Christian group (Col. 4:9). Such a plan on Paul's part that the letter should go first to Laodicea would explain the otherwise strange wording of his request in Col. 4:16: "And when this letter has been read among you, have it read also in the church of the Laodiceans; and see that you read also the letter from Laodicea." This view is also helpful in accounting for the strange mixture of singular and plural pronouns which the letter uses toward the persons addressed (vss. 3, 5, 8, etc.).

If this ingenious reconstruction is accepted of the situation and relationships that the two letters of Colossians and Philemon presuppose, and we assume that Archippus is the chief recipient of the letter now entitled "To Philemon," then he is the owner of the slave. It is he who must fulfil the most urgent request made in the letter, that the slave be freed for evangelistic work, and it is he who needs the support of the group in Colossae in bringing this good result to pass. The letter entitled "To Philemon" was intended to go to him by way of Laodicea, and it may indeed be the letter referred to in Col. 4:16 as the "letter from Laodicea." The naming of the letter "To Philemon," when the collection of Paul's letters was made up, can be accounted for on the ground that he is named first among the recipients of the letter (Philem. 1:1). This order would be a natural one if Philemon were a sort of overseer of the churches in the region.

*Bibliography.* For J. Knox's views on Archippus, see *Philemon Among the Letters of Paul* (rev. ed., 1959).

M. E. LYMAN

**ARCHISYNAGOGOS** är′kĭ sĭn′ə gŏg′əs. *See* RULER OF THE SYNAGOGUE.

**ARCHITE** är′kīt [ארכי]; KJV ARCHI —kī in Josh. 16:2. A clan of Benjamin, established in the territory SW of Bethel. Its most noteworthy member was HUSHAI, the counselor of David and later of Absalom (II Sam. 15:32; 16:16; 17:5, 14; I Chr. 27: 33). According to the description of the boundary between Ephraim and Benjamin (Josh. 16:2, 5), with due correction of the corruption into which the Hebrew text has fallen, the border of the territory of the clan was at ATAROTH-ADDAR.      S. COHEN

**ARCHITECTURE.** The art of building; herein confined to ancient Palestine from the Neolithic Age until the first century A.D. Modern knowledge of the subject is restricted both by the inattention of ancient writers to matters of architectural interest and by the scanty survival of the buildings themselves, most of which time and succeeding generations of builders have utterly destroyed. Of those buildings which remain among the ruined cities of Canaan and early Israel, we are lucky if one or two courses of masonry survive above their foundations.

1. General characteristics
2. Materials
3. Construction and plans
4. Stylistic trends
Bibliography

**1. General characteristics.** Throughout most of the period men built their own houses; and the towns and villages in which they lived were the creation of their own unskilled communal labor. The vast majority of buildings that have survived, consequently, including town walls, gates, and temples, are "homemade" in character, dependent on the native, but unprofessional, skill in masonry of the common people. Only in periods of exceptional prosperity or political expansion do we find, in Israel and Judah, the traces of ambitious architecture, official, religious, or sepulchral in character, which display the hand of professional craftsmen and the sophistication of foreign styles or materials.

**2. Materials.** Native building in Palestine has always depended on the materials provided by the soil —limestone of varying qualities, and a few other rocks; wood; reeds; and mud. When rarely we can recognize the work of professionally skilled masons, it is in the fine shaping and carving of these materials, and in the use of exceptionally big structural members—large tree trunks for increased roof spans, and accurately dressed masonry, sometimes of great size, for aesthetic effect or special strength. Such marks of professional skill can hardly be found before the Late Bronze Age (1600-1200 B.C.), when true ashlar masonry is occasionally incorporated in late Canaanite buildings, like a city gate at Megiddo dated by its excavators between 1479 and 1350 B.C.

Until that time the finest masonry structures were composed of stones shaped, indeed, and fitting together, but without squared corners or true plane surfaces.

Throughout the period mud was used, either raw as mortar for solidifying or rendering rubble walls, or dried in the sun as bricks. The first bricks were modeled singly by hand. They were oval or rounded in form and varied in shape and size as the centuries passed. Examples showing the varying forms have been recorded in early houses from Jericho, Bethshan, Gezer, and Teleilat Ghassul. In the Early Bronze Age the manufacture of bricks was speeded up by the use of wooden molds, and this naturally brought in the square or rectangular forms that remained standard for all future ages. It also involved devising some way of preventing the glutinous clay from sticking to the molds; and for this the addition of chopped straw was found to be effective. It was the labor of having to fetch this straw, added to that of puddling the clay, which seemed so grievous to the Israelite laborers in Egypt (Exod. 5:7). *See* BRICK.

Archaeological technique cannot easily detect the use of reeds in building; but we can be sure that people living in the low-lying, marshy ground that occurs in the coastal plain, and round the upper reaches of the Jordan, built their houses, at least in part, of what was the easiest material at hand. And indeed, in the earliest Neolithic strata at Jericho there are traces of round or apsidal houses in which reeds were combined with ridge-backed bricks to produce, as we may infer, some kind of boothlike or possibly beehive dwelling (*see* JERICHO § 2). Further, there have been found, in Chalcolithic burials on the Plain of Sharon, clay ossuaries of rectangular form with ridged tops, which are most naturally interpreted as model houses copying a prototype of which the roof was formed by reeds drawn together at the top in a gable (*see* OSSUARIES; Fig. OSS 14). To this day, marsh reeds bound together and packed with mud form the most efficient and economical roofing material for houses in the Jordan Valley.

In the earliest town settlement of which we have knowledge, Neolithic Jericho, not only mud and reed, but also stone was used for building. Not only were the foundations of brick-built houses sometimes composed of stone, but as early as the seventh, or even the eighth, millennium, the town was enclosed in a protective rampart of boulders, some of them of enormous size, forming a compact revetment which confronted a rock-cut fosse and retained the higher ground within it. The stones were not dressed at all, but selected for shape and regularly arranged. The face of the wall showed the slight batter demanded for stability; and traces of mud or clay adhering to parts of the surface suggested that the whole structure had once been rendered in plaster.

Ancient as it is, the Neolithic wall of Jericho may truly be called the prototype of all succeeding native Palestinian stone building; for the essence of this has consisted at all times in the skilful selection and fitting together of large or small, but crude or only roughly shaped, boulders. Even the most monumental works of the Middle and Late Bronze Age, when megalithic construction reached its height, like the city rampart and a gate to be seen at Shechem, or a

Bronze Age rampart at Jericho, represent basically no more than that. Whether in civic or in common domestic building, the technique and the art are one; and from the earliest times until the end of the period the native house was a thing of rubble walls, reinforced on occasion by long stones used as coins or orthostats, and sealed on both faces with mud mortar.

The perpetuation of this style of masonry for so many centuries makes the more notable an exceptional building of the Early Bronze Age which was found at Ai (et Tell), composed of stones roughly dressed to a uniform size and laid in regular courses suggestive of brickwork (Fig. TEM 21). This building occupied a prominent position in the citadel of the town, and had all the appearance of an official residence. There is some reason to think that the upper parts of the walls were built of brick. But whether its peculiar style of masonry, which is not matched by any other building of the period, was due to foreign influence inspired by a brick tradition, or simply to a local mason of exceptional talent, is a matter for speculation. In any case we may regard the "residence" at Ai as the earliest example of the more ambitious planning and construction which periodically distinguished individual Palestinian buildings from the common run of village architecture. *See* AI; TEMPLES.

3. **Construction and plans.** For any builder the crucial problem is not how to raise his walls but how to roof the area between them. Until *ca.* the fifth century B.C. the Jewish or Canaanite builder had no other means of roofing an area than by laying wooden beams or long stones across it, resting their ends on walls at either side. He could increase the spans attainable by erecting pillars or posts as intermediate supports; or rarely, as in certain Bronze

Age tomb chambers found at Megiddo, by corbeling out the walls. But basically he remained limited, in the size of the rooms he could roof, by the length and strength of the timbers or stones at his disposal and his capacity to lift them. It is not until the Persian period that we meet, in the governor's residence at Lachish, the earliest extant vault (Fig. ARC 49), embodying in stone a device long known in Egypt and Mesopotamia, whereby small, manageable units by mere resistance to compression could be made to span a gap far greater than the longest of them. The stones in the vaults at Lachish were laid in diagonal lines, following a practice devised by builders in timberless countries for eliminating the necessity of wooden centering to support the vault in building.

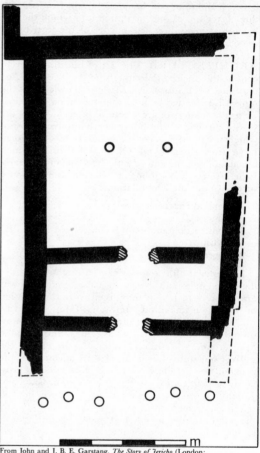

50. Plan of early Neolithic building at Jericho

Vault and arch remained rare in Palestine until the late first century B.C., when the grandiose foundations of Herod the Great, in Jerusalem, Caesarea, Sebaste, and other cities, gave general currency to Roman architectural forms. Until that time, we may say, the principle roofing material was timber, of which the mountains and foothills of Galilee, Samaria, and Judea would have afforded an ample supply. Such roofs would have been laid flat across the wall tops, with a gentle slope to run off rain water. The traces of them are rare; but some evidence

49. Plans of a fifth-century Persian residence at Lachish

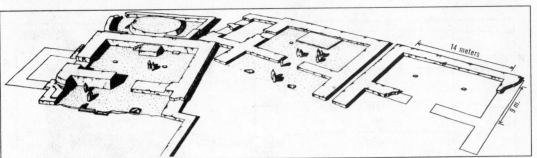

51. Isometric view of restored plan of three shrines and altar for burnt offerings (*ca.* 1900 B.C.), from Megiddo, Stratum XV

comes from the ruins of an early Bronze Age structure at Jericho, where the charred remains of parallel crossbeams were found fallen athwart a single longitudinal beam. These fairly heavy timbers may have been covered with a layer of flexible branches or reeds packed and surfaced with mud and chopped straw.

These simple materials, and the elementary methods of construction which they imply, gave rise, in the native architecture of Palestine, to no striking or complex building plans. The normal house throughout the Bronze and Iron Ages, as even today, was a loose agglomeration of small rectangular rooms, often grouped beside or around a little open-air yard, with a single door giving access from the outer world.

The only feature which survives to give an impression of architectural distinction to certain buildings in this long tradition of village masonry is the post or column. A building excavated in Neolithic Jericho consists of an inner and outer chamber, whose walls were composed of sun-dried bricks coated with a red-tinted and finely polished clay plaster; the roof, spanning a room seventeen feet wide, was supported by two wooden columns. Six more columns in front carried the roof forward to shelter an open porch (Fig. ARC 50). In the residence at Ai, again, four limestone plinths with neatly trimmed bearing surfaces had been aligned on the long axis of the main hall (*BA,* vol. VII, no. 4 [1944], fig. 3), to carry four wooden columns, of which the charred stump of one was still visible. The heavy columns implied by the size of these plinths, themselves resting on the rock, suggested the existence of an upper story; and the curious passage which surrounds the hall on three sides may perhaps be explained as the housing of a wooden staircase. Unfortunately all attempts to reconstruct this third-millennium two-storied house in elevation are doomed to remain pure guesswork.

The conjunction of wooden columns with rubble masonry is illustrated in three adjacent shrines discovered in Middle Bronze Age Megiddo (Fig. ARC 51). The columns stood on heavy limestone bases, and two of these on the long axis of each rectangular shrine betoken a roof supported by two transverse beams; while the remains of two similar supports between projecting side walls imply a colonnaded porch preceding each shrine. Columned porticoes similarly fronted some late Canaanite temples at Beth-shan.

"The cities are great and walled [RSV 'fortified'] up to heaven"—so the Hebrew spies are quoted as reporting; and nowhere did the native rough stone architecture of Palestine achieve a more monumental effect than in the gates and ramparts of the Bronze and Iron Age cities.

By the Middle Bronze Age most Palestinian cities were perched on considerable mounds of accumulation (*see* CITY § 2). Lines of defense would be chosen near the top of the slope, and the lower parts revetted with a compact glacis of rammed earth or marl, or of boulder masonry. This would be crowned with a vertical wall of smaller rubble set in mud mortar, or of bricks. In later centuries these great revetments were not maintained; but it was common to see the cities of the Iron Age defended by lines of vertical walling, which encircled the slopes at one or more levels, often strengthened by projecting towers or spaced offsets. A relief from Sennacherib's palace

52. Defenders of Lachish fighting from a tower; detail from the Lachish Relief

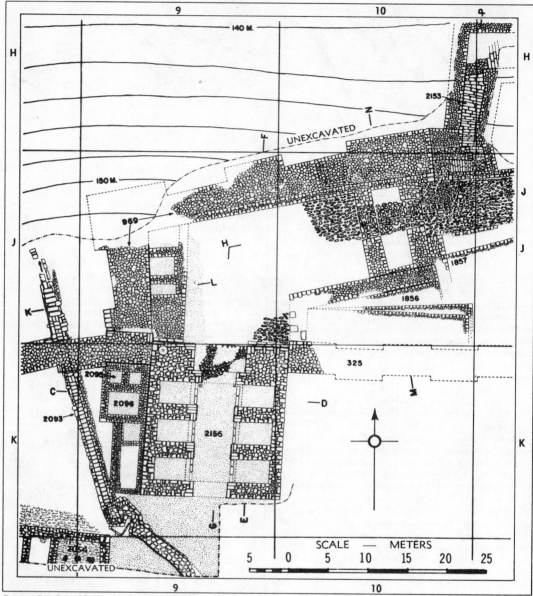

53. The Solomonic gate plans at Megiddo: 325 = city wall; 969 = wall of outer court; 1856 = wall; 1857 = wall; 2054 = row of rooms; 2093 = drain; 2095, 2096 = rooms, later added; 2153 = stairway; 2156 = city gate

at Nineveh (Fig. ARC 52) represents the city of Lachish so protected, and the general accuracy of the picture has been remarkably confirmed by excavation.

The approach to these high embanked cities was necessarily up a sloping road, dangerously flanked by the walls, toward a gate at the top. At Lachish the axis of the gate was parallel to the line of the wall, the gate itself being set in the side of a great salient or bastion. It gave access to a sloping piazza in which the visitor must needs turn to the right to reach a second gateway piercing an inner wall. The entrance to Lachish was thus dog-legged in plan. It represents, on a large scale, one of two main types of protected entrance employed in the fortified cities of the Near East. A closely analogous dog-legged gateway led into the Solomonic city of Megiddo. Figs. ARC 53; MEG 36.

A somewhat similar entrance, set sideways to the main wall, was discovered in good preservation at Mizpah, where the gate passed through a salient offset in the wall, protected by a massive external tower. Both the Megiddo and the Mizpah gates embodied a second defensive system: the former had three, the latter two, pairs of jambs, or projecting piers, within the length of the gate passage, which was thus in effect flanked by recesses or guard rooms on either side, from which intruders could be harassed, or where citizens could transact their peaceful affairs. This was an ancient protective device found not only in Canaan but also throughout the ancient East. An earlier example from Megiddo, of the Middle Bronze Age, is illustrated by Fig. ARC 54; and a Late Bronze example of the dog-legged type by Fig. ARC 55.

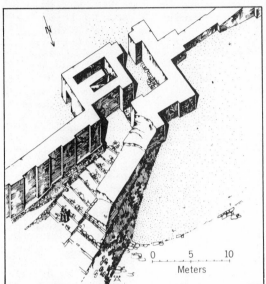

Courtesy of the Oriental Institute, the University of Chicago

54. Middle Bronze Age roadway and gate at Megiddo, Stratum XIII

The appearance of architecturally refined buildings in Palestinian cities coincides with that of finely dressed masonry; and it is a reasonable inference that the builders who perfected the art of squaring stones were the same people who planned the monumental structures of which we have some knowledge from ruins and literary sources of the Iron Age. Of these the most famous was the temple at Jerusalem, built for King Solomon, and the earliest known masterpiece of a tradition of dressed stone and timber construction of which the great rebuilding under Herod the Great was the culminating achievement.

The book of Kings makes it clear that Phoenician masons and joiners, lent by King Hiram of Tyre *ca.* 950 B.C., were the effective creators of the temple. From I Kings 6, and from extant remains of nearly contemporary buildings at Megiddo and Samaria, we can recover a general idea of what the building was like. The temple was a structure of squared stones, with a timber roof, raised on a podium above the enclosure in which it stood. The floor, internal walls, and ceiling were lined throughout with boards of fir and cedar decorated with carvings in relief and heavily overlaid with gold leaf. The internal doors and their frames were of similarly carved wood —olive or fir. The ornament throughout represented stylized palm trees, floral motifs, and winged sphinxes (cherubim). *See* TEMPLE, JERUSALEM.

The only explicit statement of structural method refers, not to the temple proper, but to the enclosure wall, which was composed of three courses of cut stone surmounted by a row of cedar beams (I Kings

6:36). This is explained by the remains of the contemporary city gate at Megiddo, of which the substructure was found to consist of five courses of closely jointed limestone ashlar with a bond timber *ca.* four inches thick between the second and third. It is possible that the description of this enclosure wall refers only to the substructure, and that the upper part was of some lighter material, perhaps of brick; for so it was probably in the gate, and in some other buildings in a similar style at Megiddo. These buildings, of the Solomonic city, had brick and timber superstructures resting on foundations composed of narrow piers of finely dressed and bonded limestone ashlar set between lengths of rubble walling, with well-jointed and bonded masonry corners. At Samaria, built in the following century, the acropolis wall was composed of a varying number of ashlar courses whose level top suggests that there, too, the upper walls may have been of some different construction, possibly incorporating timber tie beams, of which the traces in some sections of the lower city wall still remain.

The jointed masonry at Samaria and Megiddo was laid with fine precision; whether the surface was chiseled smooth, or left with a rustic boss, the masons were careful to smooth meticulously as much of the front margins of each stone as was needed to ensure its perfect alignment and impenetrable jointing. We can safely ascribe to the temple at Jerusalem the same perfection of finish.

The Jerusalem temple consisted of two chambers preceded by a porch or vestibule, and was enclosed on three sides by a series of abutting rooms in three tiers (Figs. TEM 17; 31). The dimensions of the whole structure embodied simple arithmetical proportions,

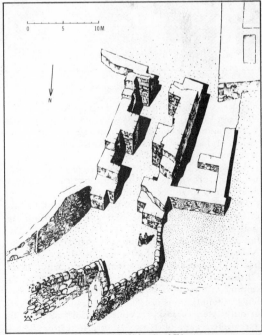

Courtesy of the Oriental Institute, the University of Chicago

55. Partial restoration of Middle Bronze Age gate at Megiddo, Stratum VIII

which demonstrate for the first time in Palestinian architecture the operation of a professional and probably hereditary craft. This we may confidently attribute to the masons of Phoenicia. For the more detailed architectural aspects of the Jerusalem temple, *see* TEMPLE, JERUSALEM. *See also* JACHIN AND BOAZ.

The temple was built to its full height in squared stone; and so also were the buildings of King Solomon's palace complex (I Kings 7:2-9; *see* HALL 2-4; PALACE). The account of these buildings, however, is far too brief to give any idea of their architecture beyond the facts that timber was freely used for roofs and columns, that windows and doors were aligned and opposed in calculated architectural relationships, and that columned porticoes were an important element in their design. Finally, we should probably be justified, by analogies to be observed throughout the Near East, in guessing that the plan of the palace incorporated a central courtyard, or a series of successive courtyards, giving access through columned porches to individual suites of rooms.

Of specifically architectural ornament at this period very little has survived; but both Samaria and Megiddo have yielded examples of a special form of pilaster capital decorated with volutes (Fig. ARC

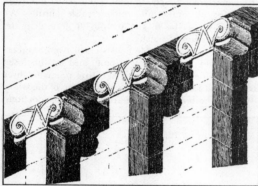

56.  Pilaster capital with volutes at Samaria

56),* of which the design is derived from a palm-tree motif used in earlier Canaanite decorative art. Such capitals seem generally to have topped the jambs of doorways, or to have surmounted pilasters attached to walls. Fig. CAP 8.

**4. Stylistic trends.** The finely dressed and squared masonry, of which we may suppose the temple of Solomon to have been built, is nowhere better seen than in Samaria, a city built *ca.* 875 B.C. by Omri of Israel, a king allied, as Solomon was, with Tyre. It is significant that the fine masonry there is confined to buildings attributed to Omri or his son Ahab; all those erected after the Phoenician alliance had been broken were consistently inferior in quality. Of the palace occupied by the kings of Israel on the summit of the hill of Samaria nothing has been seen but the foundations of a few rooms, some lengths of its outer wall enclosing a courtyard of beaten earth, and some scraps of its ivory-encrusted furniture. It is impossible to guess the plan (*see* SAMARIA). Whenever foreign influences are withdrawn from Palestine, its architecture reverts to the "village"

style described *above;* and so it was in Judah and Israel when Solomon, in the one, and Ahab, in the other, died. It is not until the destruction of both kingdoms, and the return of Judah from captivity under the Persians, that we meet the next actual building that displays the marks of deliberate architectural enterprise, beyond the limited capacity of village building. This is the fifth-century governor's residence at Lachish (Fig. ARC 49). The occurrence in this building of stone vaulting and arched doorways constructed by the characteristic method adopted by builders in brick, in timberless countries, points unmistakably to Persia or Mesopotamia as the source of its architecture. But the plan is a typical oriental house. It was enclosed by an outer wall pierced by one surviving external door. Its rooms were grouped round a central court, but not symmetrically. Beside single rooms the accommodation comprised two separate residential apartments, each approached up a few steps and through a colonnaded porch. In each apartment the main rooms were broader than deep, contrary to the temple at Jerusalem, but conforming to general practice elsewhere. The residence was built of rubble masonry, except for the columns supporting the porch of the W suite, which were made of cut-stone cylindrical drums and rested on cut-stone bases. These last consisted of a rounded pulvin superimposed on two diminishing square plinths. *See* LACHISH § 2.

Although the Lachish residence stands almost alone, among those recovered by excavation at this period, as a building of some distinction, we have some evidence in the rock-cut tombs of Jerusalem that foreign influences and architectural enterprise were never quite extinguished in the immediate vicinity of the Jewish royal court. When we read in Kings and Chronicles that this or that Jewish king was buried in his own sepulchre or in that of his fathers, we may reasonably imagine this to have been a rock-cut tomb distinguished by some sort of external monument. The appearance of such a monument may be inferred from one surviving example from the village of Silwan, of which Fig. ART 57 shows the present cross section and the restored elevation.

57.  The monolithic tomb at Silwan

The cemetery to which it belonged may be dated by inscriptions to the period of the Jewish Monarchy. The monument is entirely hewn in the rock; but it reflects a true architectural style, recognizably Egyptian. And we must infer that the Egyptian features, like the pyramidal form and heavy cavetto and torus moldings, were derived from an Egyptianizing style in building acceptable to Jewish taste under the Monarchy.

After Alexander's conquest of the East, Greek motifs mingled with those derived from Egypt and Persia to produce a Syrian-Hellenistic style of architecture. An example of this at Jerusalem is the tomb of the Hezir family (Fig. ART 80), a monument entirely cut in rock, in which the Egyptian features of the older Silwan pyramid are poised on a Hellenizing Ionic colonnade. On historical and stylistic grounds this has been attributed to the third century B.C. Another, and perhaps rather later, example of the same mixed style is the so-called "Absalom's Tomb" (Fig. KID 6), of which the cylindrical and conical upper parts are built of finely dressed and jointed masonry, but rest on a rock-cut base. That the style of architecture exhibited in these Jerusalem monuments was widely fashionable in the half-Hellenized East, is proved by its reappearance in the famous rock-cut tombs of Nabatean Petra, which embody in their elegant façades the same mixture of Greek and oriental motifs. Fig. SEL 38.

The Hellenizing tendencies in Jewish architecture of the first centuries B.C. coincided with a revival of the art of finely jointed and squared masonry; and both received a great stimulus from the boundless wealth, architectural enterprise, and Western sympathies of Herod the Great (30-4 B.C.), who both founded numerous cities within his kingdom and endowed them with public buildings, temples, theaters, hippodromes, and baths, which were customary in Greek and Roman cities of the time. The greatest of these foundations was the reconstructed temple of Jerusalem, of which Josephus has left a long but not very precise description (War V.v). The temple stood within a system of enclosed courts surrounded, like the precincts of other Eastern Hellenistic temples (Palmyra, Baalbek, Gerasa), by porticoes. Of the outer court the porticoes were two aisles deep on the N, E, and W sides, and three aisles deep on the S. The roofs were of timber, with carved cedar ceilings, and were carried by monolithic marble columns with Corinthian capitals. The three-aisled S portico was basilical in form, its broad central nave rising above two narrower side aisles. The upper walls of the nave were relieved by engaged columns; and engaged columns, corresponding with the free-standing colonnades, were set along the S wall of the portico.

The temple itself followed the plan of the old Solomonic building, except that its porch was extended sideways and in height to present a façade ca. 150 feet square toward the E. In the center of this stood an open doorway of giant proportions, over 100 feet high. The inner door of the shrine was lower; for, as Josephus tells us, the height of the cella was divided inside into two floors, the lower flanked by side chambers in three tiers, the upper story rising above their roofs. See TEMPLE, JERUSALEM, § C.

Nothing of all this can be seen today, except parts of the gigantic enclosure wall of the precinct, built, like another Herodian wall, which enclosed the tombs of the patriarchs at Hebron, of squared and paneled blocks of impeccable jointing and prodigious size. Besides this characteristic masonry, the Herodian age in Palestine was distinguished by the widespread introduction of cut-stone vaulting, which made possible such daring enterprises as the harbor at CAESAREA (Jos. Antiq. XV.ix.6), the vast substructures of the Jerusalem temple, and a great viaduct, of which the springing is still visible, that spanned the central valley of the city.

Much of the building under Herod was cosmopolitan in character, and could be matched in any province of the Roman Empire. But from rare surviving buildings of the period, like the ruins of Herod's palace lately discovered at MASADA, and from rock-cut tomb façades near Jerusalem, we can infer that the prevailing Hellenistic forms were strongly infused, in structure and ornament, with native oriental motifs. The temple itself, for all its Corinthian colonnades, followed the lines of its Phoenician predecessor. Of its architectural detail we know little or nothing; but it is safe to assume that it was kin to the façades of contemporary tombs, like that of Queen Helena of Adiabene, the tombs (so called) of the Judges and Jehoshaphat at Jerusalem, and the amazing cliff sculptures of Petra. The entrance to the "Tomb of the Judges" was a broad recess enclosed in a molded rectangular frame, which was surmounted by a pediment of classical aspect but filled with an acanthus-scroll relief carved in a distinctive local style (Pl. XXVIa). Similarly Queen Helena's monument, surmounted by three pyramidal structures, was entered through an Ionic portico beneath an entablature combining Greek structural features with wreaths, grapes, and foliage of a symbolical and distinctly Jewish or Levantine character. We are reminded by these floral elements of the golden vine that overhung, in Josephus' account, the inner door of the temple.

Architectural history in Palestine repeats itself. Solomon's temple reflected the cosmopolitan brilliance of his reign; and just as Herod the Great, his subjects, and his neighbors were Orientals aspiring momentarily to partnership in a Western civilization, so the public buildings of Jerusalem and other great cities of the Levant were an adaptation of Grecian forms, disciplined and intellectually defined, to the brooding purposes, obsessed with antique symbolism, of the Semitic East.

**Bibliography.** C. Watzinger, *Denkmäler Palästinas*, vols. I–II (1933-35); A. G. Barrois, *Manuel d'archéologie biblique*, vol. I (1939); H. Frankfort, *The Art and Architecture of the Ancient Orient* (1954). For pertinent bibliography on architectural data at excavated sites referred to *above, see* the bibliographies under JERICHO; AI; MEGIDDO; JERUSALEM; BETH-SHAN; LACHISH; SAMARIA; MASADA; TOMBS.        R. W. HAMILTON

**ARCHIVES, HOUSE OF THE** [בית ספריא]. A place in which public records and historic documents or decrees are stored. These may be in the temple area or in the royal treasury (*see* TREASURE). It is probable that the king placed Jeremiah's scroll in such an archive (Jer. 36:20 ff). Such a temple archive was the place for the finding of the scroll of the law under Josiah (II Kings 22:8 ff). Solomon undoubtedly kept annals in such a house of archives. Some of these annals of the kings are referred to in the historical books of the OT. In later days genealogical records may have been stored in the archives (Ezra 4:15). The Persian archives were searched for the royal decree pertaining to the end of the Exile (Ezra 5:17; 6:1). The Aramaic phrase literally means "house of books" (cf. KJV "house of the rolls" in Ezra 6:1). In still later times the Aramaic word GENIZA, used in Ezra 5:17, was applied to the storehouse for worn-out biblical scrolls. Archaeologists have certainly discovered archives or treasuries of tablets and scrolls at Persepolis, Nineveh, Ras Shamra, Elephantine, Cairo, etc. *See* WRITING AND WRITING MATERIALS.

C. U. WOLF

**ARCTURUS** ärk tōŏr′əs. The LXX-KJV rendering of עַשׁ, עָיִשׁ (RSV BEAR), the designation of a group of stars. The two variants of the form are likely of the same root, עָיִשׁ. Elsewhere עָשׁ is "moth," which is obscure in a stellar context. The term is astral, but closer identification is uncertain.

The versions yield a variety of evidence, indicating that the translators knew nothing of the original term with which they were dealing. The Job 9:9 LXX rendering is disordered, but probably translates ἀρκτοῦρος, perhaps from ἄρκτος, "bear," and οὖρος, "guardian" (cf., e.g., Rev. 13:2). The Vulg. follows the LXX reading *Arcturum;* Aben Ezra also reads "Great Bear." In Job 38:32 the LXX, followed by the Vulg., has ἕσπερος, "evening (star)," which is no help in identification. The Syr. in both cases has *Iyutha.*

The term עָיִשׁ has been related to the Arabic *na'š,* "bier," a portable litter. Supported by a myth, this has been applied to the constellation known as the "Great Bear" or "Wain." In popular form, this came to be simply *'aš.* The single clue from the OT is that the star has "children" (Job 38:32): The four central stars of the Great Bear have three lesser stars (children), which form the tail of the bear and the pole of the Wain.

Another conclusion is from the Syr. Possibly *Iyutha* is equivalent to αἴξ, or *Capella;* the small stars in this group are the children. More plausible is the proposal that *Iyutha* refers to the group Hyades, which in other Syriac literature is the case. On this basis, עָיִשׁ is the brightest star of the group, Aldebaran, of which the lesser stars of Hyades are the children. This is supported by early classical writers who grouped Pleiades, Hyades, and Orion, as in Job, to mark the change of seasons. Evidence from the Syr., however, is confused by the use of *Iyutha* as a translation of כְּסִיל (*see* ORION; Amos 5:8). This reflects the uncertainty of the translators. Nonetheless, Aldebaran is the most probable alternative to Arcturus, "Bear."

A third, less cogent proposal is that עָיִשׁ refers to PLEIADES. This proposal is based on the Targ. reading "hen with her chickens." This is understood as the cluster of Pleiades. The weakness of this proposal is intensified by the greater problem it creates, since the identity of כִּימָה in the same verses is generally held to be Pleiades.

The identification of Pleiades being rejected, the possible alternatives remain "Bear" (Arcturus) and Aldebaran. Though the latter is more probable, the identification is not certain.

*Bibliography.* E. W. Maunder, *The Astronomy of the Bible* (n.d.); G. Schiaparelli, *Astronomy in the OT* (1905); G. R. Driver, "Two Astronomical Passages in the OT," *JTS,* vol. 7 (1956).

W. BRUEGGEMANN

**ARD** ärd [אַרְדְּ, humpbacked; *cf. personal names* אַרְדּוֹן, אָרוּד, Jewish Aram. אַרְדָּא]; **ARDITES** är′dīts [הָאַרְדִּי]. Alternately: **ADDAR** ăd′är [אַדָּר] (I Chr. 8:3). A descendant of Benjamin, listed among the seventy "persons of the house of Jacob, that came into Egypt" (Gen. 46:27); ancestor of the "family of the Ardites" (Num. 26:40).

Both name and family relationship vary. The MT of Gen. 46:21; Num. 26:40 gives "Ard" (אַרְדְּ), which is a prior form of "Addar" in I Chr. 8:3 (LXX Αρεδ [A], Αδερ [S], Αδαρ [L]). His relationship to BENJAMIN (1) appears as son (Gen. 46:21 MT), grandson (Num. 26:40; I Chr. 8:3), and great-grandson (Gen. 46:21 LXX).

L. HICKS

**ARDAT** är′dăt [Lat. *Ardatte*] (II Esd. 9:26); KJV **ARDATH** —dăth. A field where Ezra received a vision. It may be related to ARAD 2.

**ARDITES.** Gentilic form of ARD.

**ARDON** är′dŏn [אַרְדּוֹן] (I Chr. 2:18). One of the sons of Caleb in the genealogy of Judah.

**ARELI** ə rē′lī [אַרְאֵלִי, *see* ARIEL]; **ARELITES** —līts. Son of Gad; ancestral head of the "family of the Arelites" (Gen. 46:16; Num. 26:17).

**AREOPAGITE** ăr′ĭ ŏp′ə jīt, —gīt [Ἀρεοπαγίτης]. A member of the "most reverend council" of the Areopagus, so called because it met on the hill of the AREOPAGUS (Acts 17:19, 22) at Athens. *See also* DIONYSIUS.

F. W. BEARE

*****AREOPAGUS** ăr′ĭ ŏp′ə gəs [ὁ Ἄρειος πάγος] (Acts 17:19, 22). A rocky hill at ATHENS; also, a council or court which originally met on it. Figs. ARE 58; ATH 112.

58. The Areopagus at Athens

The Areopagus hill, 370 feet high, is between the Acropolis and the Pnyx and somewhat N of them. The Agora lies still farther to the N, and of the roads coming S across the Agora the Panathenaic Way ran between the Areopagus and the Acropolis, and another between the Areopagus and the Pnyx. The name may mean the "hill of Ares" (*see* MARS' HILL); and it is supposed by some that the Temple of Ares, the ruins of which have been identified near the center of the Athenian Agora, once stood on the Areopagus. Another theory derives the name from the Arai ('Αραί), or "curses"—i.e., the goddesses of revenge and destruction whose shrine was in a cave at the NE foot of the hill.

The court which anciently met on this eminence was known as the "council in the Areopagus," or the "council of the Areopagites." The fact that in later times the usual expression for appearing before this tribunal was "to go up into the Areopagus" seems to reflect its early meeting place on an elevated point. A flight of some fifteen steps cut in the SE side of the rock, and the remains of rock-hewn benches on the top, may show where the assembly came together. Pausanias (I.xxviii.5) states that there were two stones on the Areopagus named the stone of Outrage and the stone of Ruthlessness, on which the accused and the accusers respectively stood. He also reports the tradition that Ares was the first to be tried on the Areopagus, for the slaying of Halirrhothius, and that Orestes was later tried there for the murder of his mother, Clytemnestra.

The functions of the court varied from time to time. At some periods its jurisdiction was limited chiefly to cases of capital crime; at others it had to do with wider areas of legal, political, educational, and religious affairs. The council also came to meet in other places than on the Areopagus hill. In 1952 a sculptured marble stele was found under the Stoa of Attalus with the text of a law against tyranny proposed by Eukrates in 337/336 B.C. and the statement that the law was to be inscribed on two steles of stone, one of which was to be set up "by the entrance into the Areopagus, the one as you enter the Bouleuterion." Whether the rather ambiguous language means that the entrance to the court of the Areopagus was near the entrance to the Bouleuterion, or that the same entrance gave access both to the court and to the Bouleuterion, it is evident that the council of the Areopagus was meeting at this time in a place in proximity to the Bouleuterion. In the late fifth century B.C. the New Bouleuterion was built to accommodate the Council of Five Hundred. If we look for a nearby building available in the fourth century for the Areopagus court, we think naturally of the Old Bouleuterion, which was close at hand and was not replaced by the Metroon until the late second century. At the same time, the following statement is found in a speech incorrectly attributed to Demosthenes (XXV.23) against Aristogeiton, a person who was tried and fined ca. 338-324 B.C.: "The council of the Areopagus, when it sits roped off in the Stoa Basileios, enjoys complete freedom from disturbance, and all men hold aloof." Pausanias (I. iii.1) describes the Stoa Basileios as the first building on the right upon entering the Agora when coming from the Dipylon gate, and it may be that it was identical with the Stoa of Zeus, a large colonnade with two projecting wings, which has been found in the NW corner of the area reached by the Athenian Agora excavations. It is also possible that the Stoa Basileius yet awaits discovery and identification in the still unexcavated region N of the Stoa of Zeus. Since the Old Bouleuterion gave way in the Hellenistic period to the Metroon and the latter was

used to house the state archives, it is not likely that the Areopagus could meet there any longer. As far as present information goes, therefore, the Stoa Basileios or Royal Stoa, remains one of the attested meeting places of the Areopagus, in which it is likely that this council might have been meeting at the time Paul came before it, although it is also possible that sessions were still held on the hill itself.

**Bibliography.** K. Wachsmuth and T. Thalheim, ""Αρειος πάγος," *Pauly-Wissowa*, vol. II (1896), cols. 627-33. *Pausanias's Description of Greece* (trans. with commentary by J. G. Frazer; 2nd ed., 1913), II, 362-64. B. D. Merritt, "Greek Inscriptions," *Hesperia*, XXI (1952), 355-59; "The Entrance to the Areopagus," *Hesperia*, XXII (1953), 129. H. A. Thompson, "Excavations in the Athenian Agora: 1952," *Hesperia*, XXII (1953), 51-53. H. J. Cadbury, *The Book of Acts in History* (1955), pp. 51-52, 57, n. 43. O. Broneer, "Athens, City of Idol Worship," *BA*, vol. XXI (1958), pp. 4, 27, n. 4.

J. FINEGAN

**ARES.** KJV Apoc. form of ARAH.

**ARETAS** ăr'ə təs ['Αρέτας; *cf.* ἀρετή, goodness, excellence]. The name borne by kings of Arabia at Petra and Damascus.

Gen. 25:13 (cf. I Chr. 1:29) lists Nebaioth as the "first-born of Ishmael." Nebaioth's sister, Mahalath, was one of Esau's wives (Gen. 28:9), although her name is elsewhere given as Basemath (36:3). Josephus identifies the Nabateans with the descendants of Nabaioth. The twelve sons of Ishmael, he says (Antiq. I.xii.4), "inhabited all the country from the Euphrates to the Red Sea, and called it Nabatene. They are an Arabian nation, and name their tribes from these, both because of their virtue—and because of the dignity of Abraham their father."

Their capital city and stronghold was Sela (סלע, "the cliff"; Judg. 1:36; II Kings 14:7; Isa. 16:1; 42: 11). This term is represented in Greek by Πέτρα, and from this circumstance is derived the name by which their country is known, 'Αραβία ἡ πρὸς τῇ Πέτρᾳ. Though the inhabitants were of the Arab race, Aramaic was the language of their writings and inscriptions. They first appear as a formidable power in connection with the wars of Antigonus (312 B.C.).

The Aretas of II Macc. 5:8 is their first known ruler. He appears as king of the Arabians during the days of the Maccabees. The high priest Jason, having heard a false report of the death of Antiochus, undertook by violent measures to gain control of the government. When the conspiracy failed, he became a refugee, and was "imprisoned (ἐγκλεισθείς; the RSV here adopts the conjecture ἐγκληθείς, accused] before Aretas the ruler of the Arabs." Some versions list Aretas among the sovereigns to whom the consul Lucius sent assurance of Roman friendship for the Jews, but the preferred reading here is "Ariarthes" (I Macc. 15:22).

Other references indicate that the Nabateans were friendly to the Maccabean party. "Judas Maccabeus and Jonathan his brother crossed the Jordan and went three days' journey into the wilderness. They encountered the Nabateans, who met them peaceably" and related how their own brethren had been "shut up in Bozrah," which city Judas promptly liberated (I Macc. 5:24-28). When Bacchides pursued Jonathan and Simon across the Jordan, "Jonathan sent his brother as leader of the multitude and begged the Nabateans, who were his friends, for permission to store with them the great amount of baggage which they had" (9:35).

At a somewhat later time Antipas father of Herod the Great was at enmity with Aristobulus because of good will shown by the latter to Hyrcanus. Through the machinations of Antipas, Hyrcanus became so frightened that he "fled to Aretas, of Arabia, who gave him refuge at Petra" (Jos. Antiq. XIV.i.3-4). Supported by Aretas, Antipas and Hyrcanus led an expedition against Aristobulus and gained a temporary victory. However, Scaurus, who had recently come from Pompey, sided with Aristobulus, and the army of Aretas and Hyrcanus was badly beaten at Papyron (Antiq. XIV.vii.3).

By 85 B.C., coins were made in Damascus, indicating that Aretas III had extended Nabatean control to that region. In NT times we find the Nabateans still exercising authority in Damascus. Paul tells how "at Damascus, the governor under King Aretas guarded the city of Damascus in order to seize me, but I was let down in a basket through a window in the wall, and escaped his hands" (II Cor. 11:32-33). Acts 9:24 relates that, before this escape, the gates were being watched day and night in order that Paul might be killed and his threat to the Jewish religion be brought to an end. The city of Damascus was at this time within the Roman province of Syria. That it should have been under the protection of an officer of King Aretas is difficult to explain. Rome displayed a large measure of tolerance in ruling her empire. If not actually a threat to Roman rule, political arrangements were often undisturbed, and considerable autonomy remained in the hands of local officials. However, in matters of final sovereignty Rome brooked no interference.

The Aretas who posed such a threat to Paul was Aretas IV (9 B.C.–A.D. 40), who before his accession was named Eneas (Jos. Antiq. XVI.ix.4). As already noted, Josephus described the Nabatean kingdom as extending from the Euphrates to the Red Sea (Antiq. I.xii.4). He attacked and defeated Herod Antipas, partly in revenge for the divorce of his daughter by the latter (Antiq. XVIII.v.1-2). The two of them also, says Josephus (Antiq. XVIII.v.2), had some quarrel "about their limits at the country of Gemalitis."

J. C. SWAIM

**AREUS.** KJV form of ARIUS.

**ARGOB** är'gŏb [עַרְגֹּב, mound]. **1.** A man mentioned with Arieh in II Kings 15:25 KJV, either as a victim, with Pekahiah, of Pekah's conspiracy, or as a fellow conspirator with the latter. This reference, omitted in the RSV, is generally taken as a textual gloss to vs. 29, perhaps referring to Argob and Havvoth-jair in Transjordan (cf. I Kings 4:13).

*Bibliography.* J. A. Montgomery, *Kings,* ICC (1951), p. 455.

J. M. WARD

**2.** A part of the kingdom of Og, situated in N Gilead. It was assigned by Moses to the tribe of Manasseh and was conquered by Jair the son of Manasseh (Deut. 3:4, 13-14; I Kings 4:13). It was said to contain sixty cities.

The location of the Argob district is extremely uncertain. The Targ. renders the word as *ṭarkônâ,* "stony region," which is equivalent to the Trachonitis of Hellenistic times and the modern el-Leja, a lava-covered region *ca.* twenty miles S of Damascus; but as this identification depends on a conjectural derivation of "Argob" from a root meaning "stony," most authorities are skeptical of it.

S. COHEN

**ARIARATHES** ăr'ĭ ə rā'thēz [Ἀριαράθης]; in RSV first ed. misspelled "Ariarthes." A Cappadocian king, fifth of the name; one of the sovereigns to whom the consul Lucius sent assurance of the friendship of the Romans for the Jews (I Macc. 15:15-24).

J. C. SWAIM

**ARIDAI** âr'ə dī [אֲרִידַי, *perhaps from* Pers. *haridayas,* delight of Hari] (Esth. 9:9). A son of Haman who was slain in the Jews' purge of their enemies.

**ARIDATHA** ăr'ə dā'thə [אֲרִידָתָא, *perhaps from* Pers. *haridata,* given by Hari] (Esth. 9:8). A son of Haman who was slain in the Jews' purge of their enemies.

**ARIEH** âr'ĭ ə [אַרְיֵה, lion]. *See* ARGOB 1.

**ARIEL** âr'ĭ əl [אֲרִיאֵל; LXX 'Αριήλ]. **1.** One of the "chief men" summoned by Ezra (Ezra 8:16). The meaning here may be "lion of El." Areli (אַרְאֵלִי; Gen. 46:16; Num. 26:17) is the name of a Gadite clan. In II Sam. 23:20=I Chr. 11:22 "the two *sons of* Ariel of Moab" follows the LXX. The MT has "the two ariel(s) of Moab" (cf. RSV). The meaning may be as in the Mesha Inscription (*cf.* 2 *below*), since the verb הכה can be used of striking an inanimate object (e.g., Exod. 8:12-13; 17:6).

**2.** A cryptic name for Jerusalem (Isa. 29:1-2, 7). For exegesis of Isa. 29 (in vss. 1-4 Yahweh is to bring distress on Ariel, and in vss. 5-8 he is to annihilate her enemies), see the Commentaries.

The name Ariel has been interpreted "the lion of God" or "the hearth of God." These meanings may go back to OT times. The word is used as a common noun in Ezek. 43:15-16 in the forms הַראֵל ("mountain of God"[?]; אֲרִיאֵל in versions and five MSS) and אֲראִיל ("hearth of God"[?]; אֲרִיאֵל in *Qere* and many MSS). The object described was a square altar hearth with "horns" at the four corners. It was superimposed upon the base of the altar and was presumably removable. This agrees with "the *'AR'L* [*'ar'ēl?*] of *DWDH'*" which Mesha of Moab "dragged" before Chemosh (Moabite Stone, line 12). Since the word there is in the construct state, it could hardly be a compound noun. The original meaning was probably "altar hearth" (cf. Arabic *'ira^{tun},* "hearth"), from the root אֲרִי, "burn," with afformative *lamedh,* similar to כַרְמֶל ("Carmel"), "garden land," from כֶרֶם, "vineyard" (cf. G-K § 85s). Targ. Isaiah has "altar." "Ariel" in Isa. 29:2*b* is probably to be taken as a common noun, and the meaning will be that Ariel/Jerusalem, where festal sacrifices are offered with such enthusiasm, will become an "altar hearth (indeed)," scene of fire and slaughter.

*Bibliography.* See Commentaries on Isaiah, especially those by Procksch and Duhm.

C. R. NORTH

**ARIMATHEA** ăr'ə mə thē'ə ['Αριμαθαία *or* (W-H) 'Αριμαθαία; *from* הרמתים]; KJV ARIMATHAEA. A town. Although the site is uncertain, a consensus today locates it *ca.* ten miles NE of Lydda (Ludd, Lod), and *ca.* ten miles SE of Antipatris. It would have been *ca.* twenty miles E of Tel-abib or Jaffa (Joppa), nestling in the hills of the Shephelah area. Other forms of the name are Harmathaim Ramathem, Ramatha, Ramah, Rama, and er-Ram.

Arimathea is named but once in each gospel and always in the same context—the story of Joseph of Arimathea, who obtained the body of Jesus and interred it in his own unused rock tomb (Matt. 27:57; Mark 15:43; Luke 23:50; John 19:38). Luke describes it as a Jewish town, and Joseph himself was a Jewish official of some standing.

This town is not to be confused with RAMAH (Ramleh or er-Ram) in Benjamin, six miles N of Jerusalem. But Arimathea may be the same as Ramathaim-Zophim ("the two Ramahs" or "twin heights") in the "land of Zuph" within Ephraim, where the prophet Samuel lived (I Sam. 1). It is also mentioned in I Macc. 11:34 and Jos. Antiq. XIII.iv. 9 (Ramatha), where it is reported that the Syrian king Demetrius II Nicator delivered to the Jewish leader Jonathan three Samaritan toparchies, including Arimathea (145 B.C.).

In the late fourth century Jerome reported that the Holy Paula visited Arimathea (which C. W. Wilson identifies with Rantieh). In the same century Eusebius called the town Remphthis (modern Rentis). In the Middle Ages, this town was celebrated as the home of the prophet Samuel and also possessed a monastery of Joseph of Arimathea. It is less likely that modern Beit Rima should be identified with Arimathea.

*Bibliography.* E. Robinson, *Biblical Researches in Palestine,* II (1867), 239-41; F.-M. Abel, *Géographie de la Palestine,* II (1938), 428-29. K. W. CLARK

**ARIOCH** âr'ĭ ŏk [אריוך]. An ally of Chedorlaomer who joined a punitive campaign against five kings in S Palestine, routing them in the Valley of Siddim (Gen. 14:1, 9). Chedorlaomer's league was then defeated by "Abram the Hebrew" and his associates (vss. 13-16). *See* ABRAHAM § C3*b.*

The district over which Arioch ruled remains uncertain. The OT calls it "Ellasar," a name often identified formerly with Larsa in Babylonia (*see* ASSYRIA AND BABYLONIA § C2). However, the ancient versions vary; the Dead Sea Genesis Apocryphon gives כפתור, which may have arisen from Caphtor (כפתור, pointing to Cappadocia?); and recent opinion favors Ilanzura, a city located between Carchemish and Haran, mentioned in the Mari texts. *See* ELLASAR.

The identification of the name Arioch is also uncertain. Earlier Arioch was compared with a king of Larsa whose name Warad-Sin might also be written Eri-aku. Recently, however, Arriwuk has turned up in the Mari correspondence (*ARM* II.63.3; 64.3) as the name of the fifth son of Zimri-Lim, king of Mari *ca.* 1750 B.C., and thus, regarding both form and date, offers a highly probable parallel to OT Arioch. Further, this obviously Hurrian name occurs in the form *Ar-ri-uk-ki* also in the Nuzi Documents from

the fifteenth century B.C. Nevertheless, since little is known about these two men, the question of the relation of either to Arioch remains open, even if the names are parallel in form.

*Bibliography.* R. de Vaux, "Les patriarches hébreux et les découvertes modernes, I," *RB,* LV (1948), 333; M. Noth, "Arioch—Arriwuk," *Vetus Testamentum,* I (1951), 136-40; F. M. T. Böhl, "Das Zeitalter Abrahams," *Opera Minora* (1953), pp. 45-46. L. HICKS

**ARISAI** âr'ə sī [ארסי] (Esth. 9:9). One of the ten sons of Haman put to death by the Jews.

**ARISTARCHUS** ăr'ĭs tär'kəs ['Αρίσταρχος, best ruler(?)] (Acts 19:29; 20:4; 27:2; Col. 4:10; Philem. 24). A Macedonian from Thessalonica (Acts 19:29; 20:4), a Gentile associate of Paul, who was arrested with Paul in Ephesus when the devotees of Diana threw the city into an uproar because of Paul's preaching of Christ. He was a traveling companion of Paul and seems to have accompanied him from the time of the work in Macedonia until the end (Acts 27:2). Tradition says that he was martyred in Rome under Nero.

An Aristarchus, evidently the same individual mentioned in Acts, is seen in Col. 4:10 as a fellow prisoner of Paul, probably in Rome. It is not necessary to suppose that this Aristarchus is a Jew, as are Mark and Jesus Justus, who are next named in this passage. But if he is understood to be a Jew, he cannot be identified with the Aristarchus mentioned in Acts. However, it is improbable that there were two men of this name intimately associated with Paul, for in that case there would have been some differentiation in references to them. Aristarchus, mentioned in Philem. 24, is to be identified with the individual named in Colossians. Both Acts and Paul's letters show Aristarchus as a valued and intimate associate of Paul. J. M. NORRIS

**ARISTEAS** ăr'ĭs tē'əs. The pretended author of a small Greek book (about the size of the Fourth Gospel) addressed to "his brother" Philocrates and hence widely, but wrongly, styled the "Letter of Aristeas." The author, presenting himself as a Greek courtier to Ptolemy II Philadelphus (283-247 B.C.), tells, as though an eyewitness and assistant, the series of events connected with the first Greek version of the Torah. Hence the "To Philocrates" has been studied, from antiquity to the present day, mainly and widely for its bearing upon the origin of the SEPTUAGINT.

1. Contents
2. Authenticity
3. Date
4. Analysis
5. Sources and literary connections
6. Value and afterlife
Bibliography

**1. Contents.**
I. Introductory address to Philocrates, vss. 1-8
II. The scheme, vss. 9-50: Demetrius of Phalerum proposes to Ptolemy to have the "Jewish laws" translated for incorporation in the Alexandrian library, of which he is the head

(9-11). Aristeas seizes the opportunity to obtain from the king the liberation of all Jewish slaves in his empire (12-27). Demetrius' detailed proposal (28-33) is accepted by Ptolemy, who requests the Jerusalem high priest Eleazar by letter to send seventy-two competent translators (34-40). Eleazar, in his reply, agrees cordially, subjoining the names of the translators (41-50).

III. The embassy, vss. 51-171; Aristeas, himself envoy to Jerusalem, describes the royal presents for Eleazar (51-82), Jerusalem and its vicinity (83-120), and Eleazar's high esteem for the translators (120-27), and reports his "philosophical" *apologia* for the Jewish law (128-71).

IV. The arrival of the translators, vss. 172-81: Carrying the Torah written with golden letters on parchment, they are received with profound respect and joy by Ptolemy.

V. The seven banquets, vss. 182-300: On seven successive nights the translators answer, to everyone's admiration, seventy-two questions put, one to each, by the king. He rewards them with presents (294); Aristeas stresses the truthfulness of his report (295-300).

VI. The translation, vss. 301-21: It is carried out on the island of Pharos in seventy-two days (301-7) and approved and hailed by the Alexandrian Jews (308-11) and the king (312-17), who dismisses the translators with thanks and further gifts (318-21).

VII. Epilogue, vs. 322

**2. Authenticity.** The book has for centuries been recognized to be a literary fiction. The writer's all-pervading concern to demonstrate Jewish superiority in every field and his use of the LXX (allegedly not yet existing), together with some Semitisms (vss. 81, 140) in his generally awkward Greek, prove the writer to have been a Jew (Alexandrian, as the whole story shows and his correctness in official Ptolemaic terminology confirms), and several factual slips refute his claim to have witnessed the events he describes. Aristeas looks back upon the age of Philadelphus as a romantic past (especially 28, 182); Demetrius of Phalerum, the philosopher and statesman, friend and adviser of the first Ptolemy, was dead at the time implied by the story (which is fixed to 276-270 by references to Queen Arsinoë II); and how could an eyewitness report that the Jordan flows around Jerusalem and, joined to another river, on into the Mediterranean (117)?

**3. Date.** Widely different datings (*ca.* 200 B.C.–*ca.* A.D. 50) have in the past been suggested on the basis of supposed historical implications. In view of the fantastic character of the whole book, this approach is today fairly generally abandoned. Arguments general and linguistic, and in particular the use of certain standard formulas, make a date near the end of the second century B.C. most probable. The prologue of ECCLESIASTICUS, often cited in this connection, may with as much reason be put before as after Aristeas. A definite *terminus ante quem*, at any rate, is given by Philo's use of the book. *See* § 5 *below*.

**4. Analysis.** From the summary of contents (§ 1 *above*) it will be evident that the story of the transla-

tion of the Law forms but a slender frame which serves to hold together a number of chapters by no means essential to it. This fact invites the suspicion that some sections may be later additions—a suspicion strengthened by the imperfect connection between some of them. Thus, e.g., Eleazar tells the king in his letter (46) that he has selected and dispatched the translators; in 121 he selects them again, and once more in 172 (when at last they actually travel to Alexandria); it would thus be easy to posit an original connection between, say, 50 and 172, and to describe all in between as interpolation. It would be similarly simple to jump from 186 to 301, omitting the "seven banquets" (Josephus does just about this in both these cases). In fact, the same procedure could be applied to every one of the sections in excess of the "frame" (see also, e.g., the duplication of 9-11 in 28-40)—and this is a counterindication against a surgery which, if applied consistently, would reduce Aristeas' book to about three pages. In fact, the features mentioned are merely indicative of Aristeas' clumsy literary technique; to substantiate a theory of interpolation, they would have to be reinforced by cogent literary or material considerations. Such have not so far been advanced (for the "biblical allegory" in 128-71, *see* § 5 *below*), and the identical style and method throughout the book are evidence of its unity.

**5. Sources and literary connections.** The translation story being used as a framework by the writer must have existed before it was thus used. Philo (*Life of Moses* 41) tells of an annual feast celebrated on Pharos in commemoration of the translation; this fact (and perhaps Aristeas 180) can be quoted in support of the inference that the frame story rests upon a popular tradition of Alexandrian Jewry. This inference is confirmed by some references in the Talmud and by the "Hellenist" ARISTOBULUS, writing *ca.* 170 B.C. (unless the theory be accepted which would make him a forger writing in the Roman age); for he gives (*apud* Euseb. *Praep. Ev.* XIII.12.2) in four lines the gist of the story, mentioning both Philadelphus and Demetrius. All the expansions are Aristeas' work, but not necessarily all of his invention. The turgid description of the royal gifts (51-82) —a rhetorical *ekphrasis*, utilizing Exod. 25:23 ff; 37: 10 ff—indeed is his own.

But the tale of the liberation of Jewish slaves (12-27) has a neat parallel in a papyrus document of 260 B.C., comparison with which will show how ruthlessly Aristeas could adapt historical data for his purpose. This purpose, the glorification of Jewish thought and tradition, is the one unifying bond of the diverse chapters; and the question of what written sources, if any, the author may have used in composing those not yet touched upon is far from settled. Suggestions, however, have not been wanting. In 31 he refers to Hecateus of Abdera in support of the "holy and solemn cogitations" contained in the Jewish law which prevented it—one wonders how—from becoming known among the Greeks. Following this cue, various sections (12-13, 22, 35-36, 83-120, 312-16; and at least part of the "Questions," 182-292) have been traced to various books ascribed to Hecateus (who wrote before 300 B.C.). This conjecture is open to devastating criticism. Eleazar's *apologia* (128-71) strikingly anticipates

Philo's allegorical expositions of the Torah and the questionable methods of later Jewish and Christian apologists; for this reason, to bracket it as a later insertion, dependent upon Philo, is to ignore the loss of almost all the literature on which Aristeas could draw.

**6. Value and afterlife.** Of this Hellenistic Jewish literature, Aristeas' book is, outside the Scriptures, the one extant complete representative (supplemented by the invaluable fragments preserved, mainly, by Eusebius). It illustrates the amalgamation of Greek and Jewish traditions in the Diaspora—on, it must be admitted, a distressingly low level of art and thought. The interest of posterity, however, has been focused, to this day, mainly on the framework of Aristeas' tale. The story of the seventy-two translators has been repeated, embroidered, and amplified by successive Jewish (Philo, Josephus) and Christian writers (Justin, Irenaeus, Tertullian, Clement, Epiphanius, etc.) and has helped to establish the canonical authority of the LXX. Eusebius, who included long excerpts in the *Praep. Ev.*, no doubt found the complete text in the Caesarean library; another user of the same library, Procopius of Gaza (in the sixth century A.D.) included it among the prolegomena of his huge variorum commentary on the Octateuch, and it is exclusively in MSS of this "catena" that the full text (though sadly corrupted) of Aristeas has survived.

Its legendary character, perceived by L. Vives (1522) and J. Scaliger (1606), was irrefutably demonstrated by H. Hody (1684; 1705). Therewith, though retaining its value as a document of its own age, it has lost the quality of a historical report. It is still permissible to inquire how much reality, if any, lies behind the legend which Aristeas elaborated. But the attempt, repeated at intervals, from his elaboration to extract particulars of the earliest history of the LXX rests precariously on an imperfect grasp of his general purpose and the misunderstanding of decisive passages.

*Bibliography.* Text: P. Wendland (1900): basic. H. St. J. Thackeray, in H. Swete, *Introduction to the OT in Greek* (2nd ed., 1905). R. Tramontano (1931): with full introduction and commentary.

English translations: H. T. Andrews, in R. H. Charles, *The Apoc. and Pseudep. of the OT* (1913), vol. II. H. St. J. Thackeray, *SPCK* (1917). M. Hadas (1951).

German translation: P. Wendland, in E. Kautzsch, *Die Apokryphen*, vol. II (1900). All the translations listed here, both English and German, contain valuable commentary.

General discussion: H. Hodius, *De Bibliorum text. origin.* (1705, resuming his thesis of 1684). H. G. Meecham, *The Oldest Version of the Bible* (1932); *The Letter of Aristeas* (1939; linguistic).

Special studies: E. J. Bickermann, *ZNW*, 29 (1930): 288: date; *JBL*, 63 (1944), 343; *A. Marx Jubilee*, I (1950), 156: on the LXX, against P. Kahle, *The Cairo Geniza* (1941), p. 132. G. Zuntz, "Zum Aristeas-text," *Philologus* (1958); "Aristeas Studies," *Journal of Semitic Studies* (1959).

The papyrus: *Aegyptus*, 17 (1936), 257.

H. G. Meecham and E. Schürer give full bibliographies.

                          G. ZUNTZ

**ARISTOBULUS** ăr'ĭs tŏb'yə ləs, ə rĭs'tə bū'ləs ['Αριστόβουλος]. **1.** A teacher of Ptolemy to whom Judas the Maccabee sent letters (II Macc. 1:10). He is often identified fancifully, even as early as the sec-

ond Christian century, with a Greco-Jewish philosopher (possibly 170-150 B.C.), of whom two fragments are preserved by Eusebius (*Praep. Ev.* VII.10; XIII.12).

*Bibliography.* E. Schürer, *A History of the Jewish People in the Time of Jesus Christ* (1899), div. 2, vol. III, pp. 237-43. The identification is strongly urged in Kahana, *Sefarim Hitzonim*, I, 176-77, but is not to be accepted. See P. Wendland, "Aristobulus of Paneas," *Jewish Encyclopedia* (1903), II, 97-98.

**2.** Aristobulus I (יהודה), the oldest son of John Hyrcanus, and the first of the HASMONEAN line to claim the title of king. He reigned only one year—104-103 B.C.—dying apparently from some painful disease. There is good reason to suppose that Josephus (Antiq. XIII.xi.1-3; War I.iii.1-6) has confused incidents in the career of Aristobulus' brother and successor, Alexander Janneus, with those in the time of Aristobulus. According to Josephus, Aristobulus imprisoned his (step?)mother and (step?)-brothers (except for his brother Antigonus) after the death of Hyrcanus in 104. His mother starved to death in prison; Antigonus he slew in a fit of unjustified suspicion and jealousy.

*Bibliography.* E. Schürer, *A History of the Jewish People in the Time of Jesus Christ* (English trans., 1899), div. 2, vol. II, pp. 291-94; R. H. Pfeiffer, *History of NT Times* (1949), p. 21.

**3.** Aristobulus II, the younger son of Alexander Janneus and Salome Alexandra. The latter survived her husband, who died in 76 B.C. On her death, in 67, the throne properly belonged to the older brother, Hyrcanus II. Aristobulus attempted to seize the throne by force; he defeated Hyrcanus in battle and supplanted him as king after only three months. Hyrcanus retired to private life.

A foe of Aristobulus, Antipater, emerged as a counselor and gadfly to Hyrcanus. The latter, after elaborate preparations, fled to the Nabatean king Aretas, who thereupon waged war on Aristobulus and defeated him. Aristobulus fled to the temple, there to be besieged by Hyrcanus and Aretas.

Meanwhile the Roman general Scaurus had been sent to Syria by Pompey. Both Aristobulus and Hyrcanus offered generous gifts in return for support. Scaurus elected to support Aristobulus; and Aristobulus then defeated Hyrcanus and Aretas in battle.

When Pompey arrived in Syria, new deputations came to him, both on behalf of the rival brothers and on behalf of Jews opposed to both of them. Pompey deferred his decision; after a series of gambits Pompey seized Aristobulus, besieged Jerusalem, and captured it, thus ending Jewish independence (63 B.C.). Aristobulus was taken to Rome. In 57 his son Alexander nearly succeeded in overthrowing the Roman governor Gabinius, but met defeat; a year later (56) Aristobulus escaped from Rome and, like his son, was almost successful, but was finally defeated and was returned a prisoner to Rome a second time. After civil war broke out in Rome between Caesar and Pompey, Caesar liberated Aristobulus so as to send him to Syria against Pompey's forces. Partisans of Pompey in Rome poisoned Aristobulus in 49.

*Bibliography.* Jos. Antiq. XIV.i; 1–lv.5; vii.4; War I.vi; l–ix.1. E. Schürer, *A History of the Jewish People in the Time of*

*Jesus Christ* (English trans., 1899), div. 2, vol. II, pp. 313-25, 376.

**4.** The last prominent male of the Hasmonean line; a grandson of Aristobulus II and a brother of Mariamne, wife of Herod the Great. Herod removed from the high priesthood a man named Ananelus and appointed Aristobulus in his place, although he was only seventeen or eighteen years old. Public acclaim of Aristobulus so displeased Herod that within a year Herod contrived to have the youth drowned (*ca.* 35 B.C.).

*Bibliography.* Jos. Antiq. XV.ii.5–iii.3.

**5.** The younger of two sons born to Herod by the Hasmonean Mariamne. With an older brother Alexander, Aristobulus was sent to Rome (23 B.C.) for education. Herod had executed Mariamne in 29. When the sons returned to Judea, Herod was torn between affection for them and fear that they would avenge their mother's death. Herod's sister and brother plotted against the youths, and Herod was moved to return to his court a son Antipater, whose mother, Doris, was Herod's first wife. Antipater contributed to the plot. In 12, Aristobulus and Alexander were charged with attempted panicide, but a reconciliation with their father saved them; five years later, however, the sons were condemned to death and strangled.

Aristobulus was married to Bernice, a granddaughter of Herod's sister Salome. They had four children, one a Herod, king of Chalcis; a second was Herod Agrippa I, king of Judea; a third was Aristobulus (*see* 6 *below*); and the fourth was Herodias, the wife of the tetrarch Herod Antipas. *See* HEROD (FAMILY).

*Bibliography.* Jos. Antiq. XVI.i; ii; iv.1-6; xi.1-7; War I.xxiii.1-5.

**6.** Son of 5 *above*. Little is known of him. He plotted against his brother Herod Agrippa (Jos. Antiq. XVIII.vi.3) and made a plea before the governor of Syria, Petronius, in A.D. 40, against the erection in the temple at Jerusalem of a statue of Caligula (Jos. Antiq. XVIII.viii.4).

**7.** A Christian whose family is mentioned in Rom. 16:10; he is otherwise unknown. It has been suggested that this was 6 *above*, and that the "family" were his slaves, but modern scholarship uniformly rejects this conjecture.                         S. SANDMEL

**ARIUS** âr′ĭ əs [″Αρειος]; KJV AREUS. King of the Spartans (I Macc. 12:20). Jonathan addressed a message to the Spartans, reminding them that their former king, Arius, had sent a letter "to Onias the high priest . . . stating that you are our brethren" (I Macc. 12:7; for the contents of the letter see vss. 20-23).                                      J. C. SWAIM

**ARK (OF MOSES).** KJV translation of תבה (RSV BASKET).

\***ARK OF NOAH** [תבה; Egyp. *ḏbȝ.t*]. A vessel described in Gen. 6:14-16, which Noah was ordered to build and in which he and his family floated about during the great Flood (Gen. 6:14–8:19). Commonly portrayed as a sailing vessel, the ark described in Genesis is nothing more than a floating house. Its function was simply to stay above water, not to sail or travel.

The biblical description is too meager to permit reconstruction. Built of GOPHER WOOD, the ark was a sizable vessel, measuring 300 cubits long (*ca.* 450 feet), 50 cubits wide (*ca.* 75 feet), and 30 cubits high (*ca.* 45 feet), and having three decks. Only one door is mentioned, and only one window (Gen. 8:6). The total deck space was approximately 100,000 square feet, and the cubic content *ca.* 1,500,000 cubic feet.

The Sumerian-Babylonian story of Utnapishtim bears marked resemblance to the Genesis account. The vessel built by the Babylonian hero for the same purpose as Noah's ark has a parallel description but with more detail concerning the inner structure. *See* FLOOD.

The purpose of the ark was to carry Noah's family of eight persons, and at least one pair of all living creatures. One source lists only one pair each of all creatures, but the other source indicates one pair each of unclean creatures and seven pairs each of clean animals and birds (7:2). This source omits all mention of "creeping things" (reptiles), and nothing is said about insects.                   W. G. WILLIAMS

**ARK OF THE COVENANT.**

1. Terminology and definition
2. Early traditions
3. The ark of the monarchy
4. Origin of the ark
5. Other references to the ark
Bibliography

**1. Terminology and definition.** "Ark" translates the Hebrew word ארון (Akkadian *arānu*) through the Vulg. *arca,* "chest"; Greek κιβωτός.

There are some two hundred references to the ark in the OT, and these references include not fewer than twenty-two designations. These designations include the frequent "the ark," and, no doubt an old title, "ark of Yahweh" (cf. "ark of God"—i.e., "divine ark"); the D group of titles—e.g., "ark of the covenant," but more frequently "ark of the covenant of Yahweh"; and P's special title, "ark of the testimony." Nearly a third of the references, including seven designations to the ark, occur in I–II Samuel, and there are also some oblique references to the ark which will be noted below. The varying designations reflect several schools of thought in ancient Israel. There are references to the earthly (Heb. 9:4) and heavenly arks (Rev. 11:19) in the NT.

The tabernacle and the ark have been compared with nomad tent shrines—e.g., the *utfah* (*markab mahmal* and *qubbah*). But since these are tent shrines —i.e., portable shrines—the parallel is more accurately to the tabernacle than to the ark.

The simple wooden chest of the earlier narratives and the elaborate golden shrine of the P document are viewed from various points of view. There is no doubt that the ark was interpreted (*a*) as the extension or embodiment of the presence of Yahweh, a counterpart to the divine soul (cf. e.g., Num. 10:35-36; I Sam. 6:3, 5, 8, 20); (*b*) as a war palladium of Israel's amphictyony in the days before the monarchy (I Sam. 4); (*c*) as a container, whether of a fetish stone from a sacred place like Sinai, as some of the older scholars thought, or of the two tables of the Decalogue (ברית, "covenant" = "law" [I Kings 8:21 = II Chr. 6:11]; עדות, "testimony" [Exod. 25:16, 21]); (d) as a portable throne for the invisible presence of Yahweh. It should, however, be remembered that something of each interpretation is to be found in each of the major representations, for the container idea does not exclude the throne idea, and neither excludes the extension idea. It is accordingly a mistake to think that the I–II Samuel idea of the extension is succeeded by the correcting and "container" idea of D, and that this in turn is replaced by the elaborate P conception. Rather are we in the presence of several parallel ancient ideas which largely overlap, even though different aspects may be emphasized in different parts of the literature.

**2. Early traditions.** A survey of the references to the ark in the narratives shows that it first appears in the wilderness wanderings in the so-called Song of the Ark (Num. 10:35-36). In this song the ark is not only seen as the leader of Israel's host, but it is directly addressed as Yahweh. There is virtually an identification of Yahweh and ark, and it is only because this passage must be interpreted in the light of other passages on the nature of Yahweh, that we do not infer an actual identification of Yahweh and ark. Hence the term "extension" or "pervasion" to describe the relation between Yahweh and ark. The ark is conceived in terms of an extension of Yahweh's personality. In Num. 14:44 again in a military context the ark and Moses are most closely related. This is important for the origin of the ark, but it should also be noted that the fact that the ark remained in the camp and did not go forth with the people into the hill country of the Promised Land, is controlled by the statement in vs. 42 that "Yahweh is not among you" (cf. vs. 43). The Song of the Ark is an ancient military poem of Yahweh and the ark which could well belong to the desert period itself. In any event, the origin of the ark lies behind it.

The ark is said to lead Israel over Jordan into Canaan. The account of the crossing in Josh. 3–4 is, no doubt, the liturgical adaptation of the original tradition of the crossing. In turn it has been suggested, and probably with justice, that this liturgical adaptation was, in fact, used annually at a celebration of the anniversary of the crossing. Thus Josh. 3–4 would contain the original tradition adapted to a form of service which was the founding legend of the sanctuary at Gilgal, where the crossing took place. The ark figures prominently in the present form of the story of the capture of Jericho, and the same combination of the military and cultic use of the ark is again evident (chs. 6–7). The religious use of the ark is seen again in the Gerizim-Ebal story (8:30-35), which may be a confused part of the Gilgal tradition (cf. 9:6; 10:43).

The story of the ark becomes obscure until its reappearance at the Shiloh sanctuary. In the meantime it may have been at Bethel (cf. Judg. 2:1 ff [MT "Bochim"]; 20:27-28). A reference to the settlement of the ark at Shiloh may be implied in the P passage at Josh. 18:1, but at the end of the Judges period it is found at Shiloh in the care of Eli and his family and Samuel.* The legends of the ark preserved in I Sam. 4–7 are important for the understanding of the ark.

The Israelites are defeated by the Philistines, but attribute their defeat to the absence of the ark. Whereupon they decide to fetch the ark from Shiloh and attempt a second battle with the ark in their midst. The Philistines greet the advent of the ark, with its attendant priests, with the words: "The gods have come into the camp. . . . Who can deliver us from the power of these mighty gods?" Nevertheless, the Philistines again defeat Israel, capture the ark, and remove it to Ashdod. Its departure from Israel is described as the exiling of glory from Israel (I Sam. 4:21). Fig. SHI 44.

Three conceptions are prominent in these stories. There is again the virtual association of Yahweh and ark; there is the military and cultic use of the ark; and, thirdly, the role of the ark as the rallying point of Israel suggests that it was an amphictyonic institution belonging to the amphictyonic cult at Shiloh.

The sojourn of the ark in the Philistine cities brought only disaster to them, though usually possession or care of the ark meant good fortune, even for non-Israelites (II Sam. 6:11). The bubonic plague (I Sam. 6:5), which ravaged Philistia at the time of the sojourn of the ark there, led the Philistines to arrange for the return of the ark to Israel. The newly calved cows which were to haul the new cart which carried the ark made no attempt to rejoin their calves, which had been removed from their mothers, but instead went directly to the village of Beth-shemesh. After some disaster there, possibly an outbreak of the plague, the ark was taken farther into the hill country, finally to rest in Abinadab's house. This man consecrated his son Eleazar to minister to the ark, and the ark remained in the care of Abinadab's household for twenty years—i.e., before, during, and after the reign of Saul—until, in fact, the eighth year of David's reign, when the latter removed the ark to his newly captured capital at Jerusalem (II Sam. 5–6).

It has been conjectured that the historical basis of these stories is as follows: The ark was taken to Philistia but remained there in Obed-edom's house at Gath until after the Battle of Gath (II Sam. 21:20), when David removed the ark first to Baal (cf. 6:2) and thence later to Jerusalem. This theory involves the neglect of the Beth-shemesh–Abinadab incidents and the view that most of II Sam. 6 is legendary, and it is a theory which is hardly possible in view of the new assessment of the value of Ps. 132 in this connection. Nevertheless, there may be a gleam of the truth in the theory which helps us to understand the present narratives. No doubt, the ark did journey to Kiriath-jearim via Beth-shemesh, but this may not mean that it passed beyond Philistine control. The fact that Israel lamented after the Lord after the deposit of the ark with Abinadab suggests that the ark, though nominally in Israel, was in effect still very much under the control of the Philistines. Whether this was so or not, it is clear that the ark was not present again in Israel, as it had been at Shiloh, for many a long day. From I Sam. 6 to II Sam. 6 we hear nothing of the ark. (In I Sam. 14:18, "ephod" should be read for "ark," as usage, language, and the LXX suggest.)

There seems no valid reason to doubt that for some time the ark remained in Philistia. It seems equally clear that the bare facts of the tradition have received by way of interpretation a religious overlay. The meaning of this part of the legends of the ark is that Yahweh let the ark be captured in order to punish Israel and its chief priestly house, and in order to show that Yahweh could alone overcome the Philistines and compel them to return the ark to Israel. Even if secluded from Israel and supervised by Philistines at a safe distance, Yahweh has regained his liberty; he has saved himself, even if Israel was not to recognize this until the days when David led the ark in honor to Jerusalem. The religious interpretation of the facts thus includes consideration of II Sam. 6; Ps. 132.

**3. The ark and the monarchy.** II Sam. 6 contains a story remarkable not only for its features of individual bravery, but also because it is virtually a cult legend of the Jerusalem sanctuary from the Yahwistic point of view. In spite of textual disturbances the story, which should also be read in its Chronicles form (I Chr. 13; 15–16), is reasonably clear. By means of a religious procession David begins to bring the ark to his new capital. Abinadab's sons accompany the new cart on which the ark is borne, Ahio leading the oxen and Uzzah walking beside the cart. A sudden accident causes Uzzah's death. He inadvertently shoots out his hand to steady the ark, and the shock of realizing that he had done so in sacred procession and before everybody's eyes kills him. Now David makes a mistake, attributing the death to the anger of Yahweh and concluding that Yahweh does not desire the removal of the ark. The story continues: "So David . . . took it aside to the house of Obed-edom the Gittite," where it remained three months, to the Gittite's very great advantage. The last man to touch the ark fell dead, so when the decision was taken not to go to Jerusalem, it was none other than David who ventured to carry the ark aside. No wonder that the soldiers loved David. He would not ask them to do what he was not prepared to do himself.

No doubt, it was the report of Obed-edom's good fortune that made David question whether he had not made a mistake and induced the king to try once more to remove the ark to Jerusalem. Probably volunteers were called for, and they were instructed to lift the ark and to try to walk six paces in the direction of Jerusalem. No doubt, too, that if Yahweh was against the removal, he would show his hand before the bearers had gone six paces. But the six paces were safely accomplished, and David realized that now, at least, he was free to transfer the ark to Jerusalem. Thus with sacrifices, with a royal dance in a priestly garment, with shouting and with trumpet, David and all the house of Israel brought the ark to the city of David. Thus David put Israel's most treasured religious emblem at the heart of Israel's life. The ark and all it stood for, and David, Yahweh's elect and anointed one, were united in Israel's new capital at Jerusalem.

It is possible to infer certain things from this account of the ark in the books of Samuel. It was the cult object of the amphictyonic shrine of Shiloh. Apparently Saul made no effort to recover it from the Philistines (unless II Sam. 21:2 is such an attempt), or to rescue it from oblivion at Kiriath-jearim. Saul's neglect of the ark may well have been the historical

reason for the estrangement between Samuel and Saul (besides the two reasons given in the text, cf. I Sam. 13:8-14; 15:10-35 for the rejection of Saul). In turn, David's resolve to seek the ark and remove it to Jerusalem reveals a religious spirit and an attitude toward Yahwism and the future of Yahwism in Israel, which are the foundation of the messianic idealization of David and his house. The different attitudes toward the ark shown by Saul and David appear to have been decisive features in the founding of the monarchy, and in the evaluation of these two kings.

Recent study, too, has shown the importance of considering the ark narratives in I–II Samuel in close connection with Ps. 132, which contains the only explicit reference to the ark in the Psalter, and with other psalms. The day is gone when, in particular, II Sam. 6 could be the history, and Ps. 132 a lyrical memorial of an ancient royal exploit. Indeed, there is a danger of going to the other extreme. The danger is that II Sam. 6 should be emptied of its history and considered merely as a cultic rubric subordinate to and supplementing such psalms as Ps. 132. II Sam. 6; Ps. 132 are very closely related; the former contains the historical tradition of the removal of the ark to Jerusalem, the psalm the rubric for the annual celebration of that removal, in the years that followed, in the royal festivals celebrated at the Jerusalem sanctuary. However much "myth" there is to be found in II Sam. 6, over against the ritual of Ps. 132, there is a solid historical basis to both. David did recover the ark, did thereby signalize the national liberation from the Philistine yoke; the sin of Israel in the days of Shiloh is atoned. Ark, Yahweh, royal house, and Israel exist in a new unity in Jerusalem, a unity virile enough to adopt and transform and be enriched by the existing El Elyon cult of old Jerusalem, a unity which was to break down through and after the reign of Solomon, but a unity which was to survive spiritually in the "messianic" prophecies of Isaiah, in the Servant Songs of Second Isaiah, etc.

At first in Jerusalem the ark remained in a tent (II Sam. 7:2). In II Sam. 11:11 we hear of the ark on a military expedition against the Ammonites. Later, during Absalom's revolt, David orders Abiathar and Zadok to carry the ark back to Jerusalem. David's decision is often interpreted as if it meant that David had now emancipated himself from any view that the ark was the guarantee of Yahweh's presence. Rather, David fatalistically concludes that if he is ever to enjoy his kingship again, it will be at Jerusalem. He therefore resigns himself completely to the will of God, and sends the ark back to Jerusalem. The story thus means: "Either Jerusalem or nowhere."

Lastly Solomon removes the ark from Zion to its place in the holy of holies, the inner sanctuary of the temple (I Kings 8). No further mention of the ark occurs in the historical books. Shishak may have removed it (14:26), Manasseh may have replaced it with his image of Astarte (II Chr. 33:7), and then Josiah restored it (35:3), though it is most likely that it was destroyed or stolen during Nebuchadnezzar's invasion. Jer. 3:16-17 may imply the existence of the ark, and the legend of II Macc. 2:4 is related to the passage in Jeremiah. The fate of the ark is a bigger mystery than its origin.

**4. Origin of the ark.** The question of the origin of the ark is difficult, though it is extremely likely that it goes back to Moses himself. The evidence suggests that it was not a Canaanite cult object adopted by Israel, or a cult object copied from the Canaanites after Israel's settlement in Palestine. Even if there were several arks, nevertheless there was only one of supreme importance, and this was the ark which was named with the name of Yahweh of hosts.

Deut. 10:1-5 tells how Moses made an ark and put the two stone tables of the Ten Commandments inside. It is therefore almost certain that the JE tradition in Exodus contained originally an account of the making of both the tent and the ark. Such an account, if it existed, would have occurred in Exod. 34: 1-4—i.e., immediately before Moses' (third) ascent of the mountain to receive the second tables of stone. According to P, Moses instructs Bezalel to make the ark in 25:10-21, and Bezalel actually makes the ark in 37:1-9, so according to P the ark is made after Moses' descent from the mount. Thus P confirms the (JE) D tradition that the ark goes back to Moses, and confirms too that it was actually constructed after the golden-calf incident, though planned in P before this incident. The time of construction is important.

P's name for the ark is the "ark of the testimony" —the testimony being, of course, in this context the Decalogue. In P this title is used thirteen times, and it is exclusive to P. P's account of the character, function, and location of the ark vis-à-vis the camp, is a problem discussed in Tabernacle, of which the ark is so much a part.

There are thus three facts which suggest the Mosaic origin of the ark: (a) the witness of the Pentateuchal traditions; (b) the close association of Moses and the ark in these traditions and in such a passage as Num. 14:44: (c) the testimony of the Philistine version of Israel's kerygma given in I Sam. 4:8 can only be described as garbled, but in the errors there is enough truth to suggest that it was common knowledge among the Philistines that the ark went back to the desert period. All in all, this is probably the wisest view, and the one that most nearly explains the traditions of the Pentateuch and those of the books of Samuel.

A comparison of the Pentateuchal traditions with those of the books of Samuel reveals no certain conclusions concerning the function of the ark. It is clear that D and P regard it as a container from the beginning, though there is little evidence of this in the Samuel stories. In these stories the ark is more an extension of or pervasion by Yahweh's personality than a container. Indeed, some have claimed that it stood for varying forms of the presence, except, of course, when it was temporarily eclipsed during the days when the Philistines captured it. But, as shown above, the sojourn in Philistia was one of the most triumphant periods of the ark. Others have seen in the Deuteronomic view of the ark a "demythologizing" of the ark, so that the ark ceases to be the throne of the invisibly present God and becomes a mere receptacle. Such a view involves setting aside the tradition that the ark, whatever else it was, was a container from the beginning. Again, it is likely that to oppose the container and the presence conceptions is to make a distinction not made by Israel itself.

**5. Other references to the ark.** Mention has already been made of the cultic significance and use of the ark, and big claims are current for the cultic interpretation of the Psalms and for the role of the ark in the royal New Year festivals celebrated in Israel. It is therefore strange that Ps. 132 is the only psalm which explicitly refers to the ark. Nevertheless, it is only necessary to read commentaries on the Psalms to find that the commentators point to passages where the ark is implied, even though the commentators often disagree on such passages. It is not possible to review all the evidence, but certain obvious clues may be mentioned.

*a*) Ps. 132:8 speaks of "thou and the ark of thy might," and thus affords a first clue. Following the Hebrew word for "might," here עֹז, it is impossible to avoid the conclusion that "power" in Ps. 78:61 means the ark, that "Seek Yahweh and his strength" means "Seek Yahweh and his ark" (Ps. 105:4=I Chr. 16:11). It does not follow that all references to עֹז in the Psalms mean the ark, but it is likely that such passages as Ps. 96:6=I Chr. 16:27; Pss. 21:2, 14; 63:3; 77:11-16; 81:1; etc., are best explained as either a reference to the ark or a description prompted by the thought of the ark.

*b*) In the Song of the Ark in Num. 10:35-36 the ark is addressed: "Arise, O Yahweh . . . . Return, O Yahweh." It is not unlikely then that some, at least, of the six repetitions of "Arise, O Yahweh," and of the three references to "Return, O Yahweh," in the Psalms also refer to the ark (3:7—H 3:8; 6:4—H 6:5: 7:6—H 7:7; 9:19—H 9:20; 10:12; 17:13; 90:13; 126: 4; 132:8). The following passages in the Psalms should also be consulted: 21:13—H 21:14; 35:1—H 35:2; 44:26—H 44:27; 74:22; 80:14—H 80:15; 82:8.

*c*) Another clue is provided by the phrase "before Yahweh" in II Sam. 6:5, which is explained by the words "before the ark" in the previous verse. It is evident, then, that the words "before Yahweh" may often conceal a reference to the ark. "Before Yahweh" comes some 225 times in the OT, and in some of these passages, especially in cultic contexts, the ark may be presupposed. Likely passages include Num. 10:33 ff; 14:44; Joshua, *passim;* I Sam. 4:1-7:1; II Sam. 6; 11; 15; I Kings 8; and in the laws, Exod. 25:10-22 = 37:1-9; and in the "Enthronement" Psalms, 95:6; 96:13; 98:9; cf. 116:9. The only other occurrence of the phrase in the Psalms—viz., 102:1— is too vague for a decision. The seventeen occurrences in the OT of "before (the) God" likewise conceal some references to the ark (cf. especially Pss. 56:13—H 56:14; 61:7—H 61:8; 68:3—H 68:4).

*d*) תִּפְאֶרֶת, "glory," in Ps. 78:61 refers to the ark; the "Mighty One of Jacob" in Ps. 132:2, 5, also refers to the ark; so that these terms provide further clues. Likewise כָּבוֹד, "glory," in I Sam. 4:21-22 can only refer to the ark. Many commentators conclude that the "King of glory" in Ps. 24:8, 10, refers to the ark. Thus the "place where thy glory dwells" (26:8) suggests the temple with the ark, and the shout of "Glory!" in 29:9 may have been the congregation's welcome to the ark as it came into sight.

*e*) Another clue is provided for us by the identification afforded in such verses as II Sam. 6:2, 18 (cf. 7:27; I Sam. 4:4). Even if in II Sam. 6:2 we omit, with the LXX, one of the words for "name," the sense is clear. The name of the ark was the name of Yahweh of hosts, who dwells between the cherubim. This could mean that the Hebrew words for "Yahweh of hosts" were actually inscribed upon the lid of the ark. Again, it is possible that other examples of the use of "Yahweh of hosts" really veils a reference to the ark, as is clearly the case in Ps. 24:10 (cf., e.g., Isa. 6:5).

It is clear, then, that the above titles and references pave the way for a new evaluation of the presence and the role of the ark in the Psalms. The question, of course, depends on whether the references are merely metaphorical or whether they contain precise cultic allusions. Cultic contexts of such references are therefore important. There is also the fact that II Sam. 6; Ps. 132 undoubtedly show the king and the ark in very close contact. Thus those references which appear in cultic contexts are further supported when these contexts are also royal contexts, as in the so-called Royal Psalms. It is a sufficient conclusion that the ark figures far more largely in the Psalms than has previously been supposed.

*Bibliography.* J. Meinhold, *Die Lade Jahwes* (1900). K. Budde, "War die Lade Jahwes ein leerer Thron?" *TSK*, LXXIX (1906), 489-507. M. Dibelius, *Die Lade Jahwes* (1906). W. Caspari, "Die Bundeslade unter David," *Theologische Studien: Th. Zahn dargebracht* (1908), pp. 23-46. G. Westphal, *Jahwes Wohnstätten* (1908), pp. 55-59, 85-91. W. R. Arnold, *Ephod and Ark* (1917). R. Hartmann, "Zelt und Lade," *ZAW*, XXXVII (1917-18), 209-44. H. Gressmann, *Die Lade Jahwes* (1920). H. Schmidt, "Cherubenthron und Lade," *Eucharisterion; Gunkelfestschrift* (1923), pp. 120-44. H. Torczyner, *Die Bundeslade und die Anfänge der Religion Israels* (2nd ed., 1930). G. von Rad, "Zelt und Lade," *NKZ*, XLII (1931), 476-98. H. G. May, "The Ark—A Miniature Temple," *AJSL*, LII (1936), 215-34. O. Eissfeldt, "Lade und Stierbild," *ZAW*, LVIII (1940/41), 248-51. W. J. Phythian-Adams, *The People and the Presence* (1942). J. Morgenstern, *The Ark, the Ephod, and the "Tent of Meeting"* (1945). A. Bentzen, "The Cultic Use of the Story of the Ark in Samuel," *JBL*, LXVII (1948), 37-53. T. Worden, "The Ark of the Covenant," *Scripture*, V (1952), 82-90. G. B. Caird, Introduction to I-II Samuel, *IB*, II (1953), 872-75. E. Klamroth. *Lade und Tempel* (1933), pp. 17-36. J. R. Porter, "The Interpretation of 2 Samuel VI and Psalm CXXXII," *JTS*, N.S. V (1954), 161-73. G. von Rad, "Zelt, Lade und Herrlichkeit Gottes," *Theologie des ATs*, I (1957), 233-40. W. Eichrodt, *Theologie des Alten Testaments*, I (1957), 59-63.

G. HENTON DAVIES

**ARKITE** är′kīt [עַרְקִי]. A person living in or coming from the town of Arqa (Akkadian *Arqâ;* Amarna *Irqata;* Greek ″Αρκη). The town was situated some miles NW of Tripolis in Syria. It was in Roman times called Caesarea Libani, today Tell ′Arqa. In Roman times the town was famous for its Ashtart (Astarte) cult. In the genealogy of Noah the Arkites are mentioned as sons of Canaan (Gen. 10:17; I Chr. 1:15). A. S. KAPELRUD

**ARM** [זְרוֹעַ; βραχίων]. A word ordinarily used in a metaphorical sense in the Bible; only in rare instances, such as Judg. 15:14, used in its common literal meaning. As man's chief member for putting into effect the dictates of his will—for fighting and building—the arm provides a natural metaphor for "strength." Thus, to "break the arms" of an enemy is to destroy his capacity to fight (Ps. 10:15; Jer. 48: 25; Ezek. 30:22). In Dan. 11:15, 22, 31, the KJV

"arms" is exactly equivalent to "armies" or "forces," and is so rendered in the RSV.

Although the word "arm" must have been commonly used in ancient colloquial Hebrew to designate the strength of men, it is used in the overwhelming majority of instances in the Bible for the strength of God. The most vividly anthropomorphic picture of God's arm in action is in Isa. 30:30, which depicts the lightning as the "descending blow of his arm." There are many references also to God's arm as "outstretched" in a militant gesture (e.g., Exod. 6:6; Ps. 136:12; Jer. 27:5), but in most of these cases it is probable that the phrase has lost its original pictorial vividness and is merely a conventional expression for God's irresistible power, as is obviously the case in Jer. 32:17, where "outstretched arm" is synonymous with "great power." It is only rarely that God's arm is connected with help for individuals (e.g., II Chr. 6:32). Its normal associations are with his work in creation (Isa. 51:9, referring to the destruction of RAHAB, the dragon of chaos); with his deliverance of Israel from Egypt (Deut. 4:34; Ps. 77:15; Isa. 63:12; this is the most common context); with the direction and preservation of the people in the present (Ps. 89: 13); and especially with his future, eschatological intervention on their behalf (Isa. 51:5). Although the "arms" of God are ordinarily pictured as engaged in militant action, two passages represent them as supporting or enfolding his people (Deut. 33:27; Isa. 40:11).

The word "arm" occurs only three times in the NT, each time with reference to God, but only in passages which are either a quotation from the OT (John 12:38) or deliberate imitations of OT style (Luke 1:51; Acts 13:17). R. C. DENTAN

**ARMAGEDDON** är′mə gĕd′ən ['Αρμαγεδών= הַרְמָגֵדוֹ, Mount Megiddo; *see also* מְגִדּוֹן (Zech. 12:11); LXX Μαγεδδω (A) or Μεγεδδω (B)] (Rev. 16:16). A word said by the Seer to be a "Hebrew" word, designating the scene of the last struggle of the forces of good and evil against each other. Unfortunately for our understanding of its meaning, the word (or phrase) does not occur anywhere in Hebrew, and some doubt even exists as to its proper spelling in Greek. The reading "Harmagedon" (alternately "Armagedon") is found in MSS א A, 1 al, in the Syr., Egyptian, Lat.Vulg., Ethiopic, and Armenian versions, with slight variations in the consonants ("k" for "g" and the like), and in the Greek commentary of Andreas (sixth century); whereas "Maged(d)on" (apparently following the LXX) occurs in MSS 046, 14, 92, in one Vulg. MS (Fuldensis) and one Syr. MS (Gwynn), and in Tyconius and Primasius. The latter reading may reflect the OT references to the city of Megiddo in Josh. 12:21; Judg. 1:27; 5:19; II Kings 9:27; etc.

Suggested interpretations include: (a) "city [Αρ, transliterating עַר or עִיר] of Megiddo"; (b) "land [Αρ for Aramaic אַרַע and Syriac *'ara*'] of Megiddo"; (c) "Mount Megiddo," as designating that portion of Mount Carmel upon or near which the city of Megiddo lay; (d) a corruption of Hebrew *har mo'edh* ("the mount of assembly"; Isa. 14:13, where the assembling of pagan gods is in question), or Hebrew *'ar himdah* ("the city of desire"—i.e., Jerusalem), or again Hebrew *har migdo* ("his fruitful mountain"—i.e., Mount Zion).

The last suggestion appears the most likely, in view particularly of the fact that in the book of Revelation 9:13-11:14; 14:14-20; 16:12-16 are all co-ordinate passages taking much of their imagery from Joel and that here it is from Mount Zion that the power of God in his warfare against the forces of evil is to proceed (Joel 2:32; 3:16-17, 21; *see* REVELATION, BOOK OF). As no Mount Megiddo is known to either ancient or modern geographers, it appears the more likely that in a book abounding in symbolical language this term also should be meant to carry a symbolical meaning such as that suggested. It is to be noted, moreover, that the battle said to take place on this spot is clearly one of ideologies (the gospel versus the "badspell," God's truth opposed to Satan's error)—cf., e.g., the "prophesying" of the two witnesses in Rev. 11:4 ff; the fact that Satan fights by means of "demonic spirits" which issue from the mouths of dragon, beast, and false prophet in Rev. 16:12-16; and that in the co-ordinate passage at 19:11-16 the "Word of God," who leads the forces of righteousness, wields as his weapon a "sharp sword" issuing from his mouth (vs. 15).

*Bibliography.* See the Commentaries listed in the bibliography under REVELATION, BOOK OF, particularly that of R. H. Charles, II, 50-51.      J. W. BOWMAN

**ARMENIA** är mē′nĭ ə. KJV translation of אררט (LXX Ἀρμενία) in II Kings 19:37; Isa. 37:38 (RSV ARARAT). This is a later name of Urartu-Ararat. The name Armenia (Armina) first occurs in the inscriptions of Darius at Behistun (section 6).     M. J. MELLINK

**ARMENIAN GOSPEL OF THE INFANCY.** A late and verbose infancy gospel, which, like all these secondary accounts (*see* APOCRYPHA, NT), is based largely upon the much more sober Protevangelium of James and the Gospel of Thomas (*see* JAMES, PROTEVANGELIUM OF; THOMAS, GOSPEL OF). The stories are very diffuse and contain interminable dialogues. There is little or nothing in this writing not found elsewhere in tradition in far earlier form. It is thought to have passed into Armenian from Syriac.

*Bibliography.* The complete text is available in P. Peeters, *Évangiles apocryphes* (1914), vol. II. It is briefly summarized in M. R. James, *The Apocryphal NT* (1924), pp. 83-84.      M. S. ENSLIN

**ARMENIAN VERSION.** *See* VERSIONS, ANCIENT, § 7.

**ARMLET** [אצעדה, צעדה (KJV ORNAMENT OF THE LEGS *in* Isa. 3:20; KJV BRACELET *in* Num. 31:50; II Sam. 1:10); כומז (Exod. 35:22; KJV TABLET)]. A ring or band worn on the upper arm, as distinct from a bracelet worn on the lower arm. Armlets were among the booty taken from the Midianites and offered to the Lord (Num. 31:50), and among the luxury articles of the daughters of Zion (Isa. 3:20). The armlet of Saul was brought as partial evidence to David after Saul's death (II Sam. 1:10).

Fig. ARM 59.      J. M. MYERS

From H. Gressmann, *Altorientalische Texte und Bilder zum AT* (Berlin: Walter de Gruyter & Co.)

59. Armlets on a clay figurine of a goddess, from Gezer

**ARMONI** är mō′nī [ארמני]. One of the two sons of Rizpah, a concubine of Saul and the occasion of Abner's defection. David delivered Armoni and his brother, Mephibosheth, to the Gibeonites to be hanged in order to satisfy their vengeance for the bloodguiltiness of the house of Saul (II Sam. 21:8-9).      E. R. DALGLISH

**ARMOR.** *See* WEAPONS AND IMPLEMENTS OF WAR § 4*b*.

**ARMOR OF GOD** [πανοπλία τοῦ θεοῦ]. The word for "armor" is a fusion of two Greek words, πᾶν ("all") and ὅπλα ("weapons"). The phrase "armor of God" refers to the full combat equipment of a soldier, and is used figuratively to indicate the total resources which God makes available to those who enlist under his command. OT and NT writers alike use weapons metaphorically, comparing contemporary types of arms with spiritual weapons received from God. For this symbolic use of the verb "to arm," ὁπλίζω, cf. I Pet. 4:1. For weapons in general, ὅπλα, cf. Rom. 6:13; 13:2; II Cor. 6:7; 10:4. Sometimes a single instrument of defense or offense is mentioned: breastplate, θώραξ (I Thess. 5:8; Rev. 9:9); helmet, περικεφαλαία (I Thess. 5:8; Isa. 49:17 LXX); sword, μάχαιρα (Heb. 4:12).

The whole armor, πανοπλία, is mentioned in two writings. In a parable of Jesus, Luke 11:22 has in mind the total equipment with which Beelzebul, the devil, fights to protect his property from seizure. But when a stronger power enters the battle, the devil's *full armor* is seized and his possessions are despoiled.

In the second writing (Eph. 6:11, 13), it is God's armor which is discussed allegorically. Here the symbolic scope of the warfare is depicted more fully and clearly than elsewhere. The warfare rages between God and the devil. Because man's enemy is not human but superhuman, man can win the battle only by relying on God's strength. The armor of God includes: truth, righteousness, the gospel of peace, faith, salvation, and the Spirit. Praying in the Spirit, relying wholly on the word of God, ceaselessly alert for every attack, being devoted wholly to the triumph of God's cause, the army of Christ can overcome every subtlety and every onslaught of the devil. But the spiritual battle against the "spiritual hosts of wickedness" can be won only if soldiers utilize fully these weapons. Although this armor is furnished by God, it must be put on by men if they are to conquer the immediate temptation and thereby the hidden source of every temptation, the "world rulers of this present darkness."

Paul relates this battle to the mystery of the gospel —i.e., through the prayer of total dependence, God's mighty power operates in human weakness, and his peace becomes a means of final conquest. The battle is not a matter of virtue's overcoming vice, nor is it a self-righteous crusade against human enemies, nor a way to gain mental and psychic poise, but a way of vindicating God's power over Satan in every situation (cf. 5:22–6:9) where the believer encounters (in his own heart) the craftiness of primal evil. The thought concerning what weapons are effective depends, not upon the part of the soldier's body to be protected, but upon the force of the enemy to be overcome. The devil's weapons, adequate though they are to defeat merely human opponents, fail to overcome God's power. God's weapons, when wielded by men (the Spirit, the Word, etc.), are sufficient to enable men to resist successfully the attacks of the devil.

*Bibliography.* A. Harnack, *Militia Christi* (1905), pp. 12-20; F. Boll, *Aus der Offenbarung Johannis* (1914), pp. 76-77; E. F. Scott, *Ephesians* (1930), pp. 247-56; R. Leivestad, *Christ the Conqueror* (1954), pp. 150-63. P. S. MINEAR

**ARMOR-BEARER** [נשא כלים]. A personal attendant of a warrior chieftain.

The armor-bearer is attested only in early times, being mentioned in the OT as a servant of Abimelech (Judg. 9:54), Jonathan (I Sam. 14), Saul (I Sam. 31), and Joab (II Sam. 18:15; 23:37; I Chr. 11: 39). Jonathan's armor-bearer is said to have killed those who had been felled by his chief (I Sam. 14: 13). Both Abimelech and Saul ordered their armorbearers to kill them in order to avoid capture by the enemy (Judg. 9:54; I Sam. 31:4; I Chr. 10:4-5). Such servants were often extremely devoted to their masters (I Sam. 31:5), and accompanied them on dangerous missions (14:6 ff). David is said to have been chosen by Saul as his armor-bearer for a period (16:21). Joab's armor-bearer, Naharai of Beeroth, was himself a mighty warrior, being one of the "Mighty Men" of David (II Sam. 23:37; I Chr. 11: 39). J. W. WEVERS

**ARMORY** [תלפיות, נשק, בית כלים, אוצר]. An official storehouse for military weapons.

Both אוצר and נשק are ellipses for phrases compounded with בית, "house of"; אוצר (Jer. 50:25), "treasure"; and נשק (Neh. 3:19), "arms." The meaning of תלפיות, a *hapax legomenon* in Song of S. 4: 4 ("arsenal"; KJV "armory"), is completely unknown, the renderings in the versions being based entirely on the context.

With the establishment of a standing ARMY came the necessity for storing arms. It is thought that the "House of the Forest of Lebanon" built by Solomon (I Kings 7:2; cf. 10:16-17) was such a storehouse (Isa. 22:8). The temple was also used as an armory during Athaliah's reign (II Kings 11:10). An armory existed in Jerusalem as late as the reign of Hezekiah (II Kings 20:13; Isa. 39:2), and the term "armory"

still served as a landmark at the time of the rebuilding of Jerusalem's walls (Neh. 3:19). J. W. WEVERS

**ARMS, ARMOR.** *See* WEAPONS AND IMPLEMENTS OF WAR (especially § 4*b* for armor).

*****ARMY.**

1. Linguistic usage
2. Before the Monarchy
  *a.* Patriarchal period
  *b.* The judges
3. Under the Monarchy
  *a.* Saul
  *b.* David
  *c.* Mercenary troops
  *d.* Cavalry and chariot corps
  *e.* Maintenance of the army
  *f.* Organization of the army
4. During the postexilic period
Bibliography

**1. Linguistic usage.** The common words for "army" in Hebrew are חיל and צבא, the former literally meaning "strength, force" (cf. "forces"), and the latter, "host, army." In Isa. 36:2 a number of MSS vocalize חיל as *ḥayil*, "army," rather than *ḥêl*, "fortress, rampart." The word גדוד refers to a "troop or band" (*cf. below*). For מחנה, *see* CAMP. The word מערכה means "arrangement, rank, battle line," and in the singular should be translated as "line of battle, battle." In the plural it means "ranks," hence "armies" (see I Sam. 17:26, 36; 23:3). מצבה (Zech. 9:8) may be an error for מצבא (מ + צבא; KJV "because of the army"; cf. Vulg.), but may also be taken as a noun meaning "guard" (so RSV). *See* GARRISON.

In the NT, παρεμβολή is rendered "army" (Heb. 11:34), "camp" (Heb. 13:11, 13; Rev. 20:9), and "barracks" (KJV "castle"; Acts 21:34, 37; 22:24; 23:10, 16, 32). Ὁτρατόπεδον is "army" (Luke 21:20). Ὁτράτευμα is "troops" (Matt. 22:7; KJV "armies"), "soldiers" (Luke 23:11 [KJV "men of war"]; Acts 23:10, 27).

**2. Before the Monarchy.** The establishment of the Monarchy marks the beginnings of an organized army in ancient Israel.

*a. Patriarchal period.* In patriarchal times a crisis would promote a levy on the male membership of a clan by its chieftain. When the Cities of the Plain had been raided by a coalition of kings, Abram led out his trained men and in typical Bedouin fashion pursued them by night, divided his 318 followers into three groups, and brought back his relatives and all the spoil (Gen. 14). Various clans would cooperate to meet a common danger (as in the battle with Amalek [Exod. 17:8-13]) or for common advantage (as in the raids of seminomads on settled areas [Judg. 1]).

*b. The judges.* The period of the judges saw irregular troops organized along tribal lines for defense and/or plunder. Such bands (גדודים) consisted of volunteers who served under some popular leader. These bands were usually small, allowing for pinpoint attacks and maneuverability in the hill country (Judg. 7:7-23). Many of these volunteers continued their allegiance in times of peace and formed bands of freebooters, who received provisions from the countryside in return for "protection." In times of peace such groups might pillage the countryside (e.g., Jephthah [Judg. 11:3]), or go into the service of some alien power (e.g., David [I Sam. 27]). Such razzia training often made these freebooters men of the hour in times of crisis; in fact, it was David who eventually translated the peasant kingdom of Saul into an empire with a fully organized army.

**3. Under the Monarchy.** With the establishment of the Monarchy the need for a permanent military force became apparent.

*a. Saul.* Saul began as a charismatic leader (I Sam. 11:6-11), but after his victorious return from the battle with the Ammonites he became king in earnest, choosing three thousand men for a standing army (I Sam. 13:2; cf. 24:2; 26:2). In the early part of his reign the army stood under the direct command of the king and his son Jonathan alone, whereas later on, reference is made to Abner as being the "commander of the army" (I Sam. 17:55). The exact duties of Abner are not at all clear, since Saul personally led his troops to the end of his life.

*b. David.* David's military genius was apparent long before he became king. Up to this time the Israelites were actually organized only for defensive warfare. David appointed as commander in chief (שר הצבא) Joab, whose tactical brilliance revolutionized Israelite warfare. He taught the Israelites the art of siege warfare (II Sam. 20:15), and captured the Jebusite stronghold of Jerusalem, which David thereupon chose as capital city of his kingdom.

*c. Mercenary troops.* Saul had been unable to establish a dynasty. David, profiting by Saul's mistakes, set about to consolidate his own position by the creation of a bodyguard of mercenary troops composed partly of old comrades from his outlaw days and partly of aliens. Since they were paid out of the royal purse, their allegiance was to David alone. These troops served not only as personal bodyguard but also to hold up the central authority of the Davidic house—an authority regularly disputed by the various tribes—as well as for purposes of defense against external enemies. These foreign mercenaries were mainly Philistines, the CHERETHITES AND PELETHITES under the command of Benaiah (II Sam. 8:18), and the Gittites under Ittai's command (15:19-22; *see* GITTITE). When David was forced to flee because of a palace revolution sponsored by his son Absalom, their loyalty remained unquestioned, and it was they who eventually put down the revolt and rewon the crown for David.

Apparently such hired troops became a fixed institution with the Davidic dynasty, in contrast to the Northern Kingdom, where army rule and military revolution only too often characterized palace government.

*d. Cavalry and chariot corps.* In spite of the great advance made by David, the army essentially remained an army on foot. Infantry always remained the basic corps of the Israelite army throughout its history. Furthermore, cavalry was cumbersome and impractical in the hilly terrain of Palestine. With the establishment of an empire and the consequent occupation of the Aramean plains, however, cavalry and chariot corps became necessary. These were in-troduced by Solomon, who was influenced by grandiose ideas of royalty. Since the Philistines were masters of chariot warfare (I Sam. 13:5; II Sam. 1:6; as were the Syrians [cf. II Sam. 10:18]), David must have been well acquainted with this type of army, but he wisely avoided it. His son's introduction of these expensive and impractical elements into his army (cf. I Kings 10:26) certainly contributed to the eventual disruption of the kingdom. Later Davidic kings had to abandon chariots and cavalry; in fact, Hezekiah apparently had no horsemen at all at his disposal (II Kings 18:23).

In the Northern Kingdom chariot and cavalry corps were part of the army at least under the Omrids. Ahab, according to the Annals of Shalmanezer III, contributed two thousand chariots to the Syrian coalition, as well as ten thousand infantry for its revolt against the Assyrians at Karkar.

*e. Maintenance of the army.* Little is known about the maintenance of the standing army. Before the time of David, soldiers had to provide their own weapons as well as their food (I Sam. 17:17-18). Once foreign soil was reached, the army lived off the land, pillaging as it went. The ordinary Israelite was by nature antimilitaristic and ill-disposed to the discipline required in army life. This was but natural over against the privileges and pay accorded the mercenaries, who were normally foreigners as well. Solomon wisely excused Israelites from the *corvée;* citizens were to serve only as officers.

*f. Organization of the army.* Even less is certain about the organization and officer ranks in the Israelite army. The OT makes frequent reference to corps of thousands, hundreds, and fifties, along with their respective officers, but the numbers were more ideal than accurate. For the difficulties of determining officer classes and duties, *see* CAPTAIN.

**4. During the postexilic period.** After the dissolution of the Palestinian kingdoms (in 722/21 and 586 B.C. respectively), separate national existence, and with it the army, came to an abrupt end. The return from exile in 538 B.C. simply meant incorporation into a Persian province. Not until the wars of liberation under the Maccabees was a Jewish army again a reality. Originally this was not an organized army at all, but rather scattered guerrilla bands of volunteers. Under the later Hasmoneans, however, paid soldiers, both Jewish and Gentile, constituted a standing army. Josephus states that John Hyrcanus began the custom of hiring mercenaries (Wars I.ii.5), and that under Alexander Janneus these paid troops consisted specifically of Pisidians and Cicilians (I.iv.3).

When the Hasmonean state came to an end in 63 B.C., Palestine came under Roman rule. Herod the Great as a loyal vassal to Rome not only put his forces at Rome's disposal but also modeled his own troops on that of his sovereign. The presence of Thracians, Germans, and Gauls (Jos. War I.xxxiii.9) as foreign mercenaries undoubtedly helped to fan the hatred which the Jews felt for Herod.

For further information on the functions of the army, *see* WAR, METHODS OF.

**Bibliography.** J. Kromayer and G. Veith, *Heerwesen und Kriegsführung der Griechen und Römer (Handbuch der Altertumswissenschaft* IV, 3:2); B. Meissner, "Das Heer und das

Kriegswesen," *Babylonien und Assyrien,* vol. I (1920), ch. 4; A. von Pawlikowski-Cholewa, *Die Heere des Morgenlandes; militärische Beiträge zur Geschichte des nahen und fernen Orients* (1940); A. G. Barrois, "La Guerre," *Manuel d'archéologie biblique,* vol. II (1953), ch. 16.      J. W. WEVERS

**ARNA** är′nə [Lat. *Arna*] (II Esd. 1:2). An ancestor of Ezra; apparently parallel to Zerahiah (Ezra 7:4).
                 J. C. SWAIM

**ARNAN** är′nən [אַרְנָן; Arab. quick] (I Chr. 3:21). A descendant of Zerubbabel in the extended genealogy of David; son of Rephaiah and father of Obadiah. The KJV speaks of the "sons of Arnan" (MT בְּנֵי אַרְנָן), but ancient versions are probably correct in reading "his son, Arnan" (בְּנוֹ אַרְנָן).
             F. T. SCHUMACHER

**ARNI** är′nī [᾿Αρνί; *variant* ᾿Αράμ] (Luke 3:33). An ancestor of Jesus. On the difficult problems concerning this and other names in the genealogy, *see* GENEALOGY (CHRIST).      F. W. GINGRICH

**ARNON** är′nən [אַרְנוֹן]. A perennial stream flowing from the plateau of Transjordan through a deep canyon into the Dead Sea, just N of the mid-point of its E shore. The Arnon divided the kingdom of SIHON from MOAB (Num. 21:13, 26), and later was the S boundary of the tribe of Reuben (Deut. 3:8, 16;

Courtesy of Denis Baly

60. Gorge of the Arnon River, cut in the Nubian sandstone

Josh. 13:16), although Moab frequently expanded N of it. Mesha claimed to have made a highway in the Arnon Valley (*see* MOABITE STONE).

The source of the Arnon is in the area of Lejjun, whence it flows N-NW for *ca.* fifteen miles and then W about an equal distance to the Dead Sea. The canyon through which the Arnon flows is tremendous, being, e.g., 2½ miles wide in the area S of Dibon, with the river bed 1,650 feet below the top of the cliffs.* The Seil Heidan, the Arnon's most important tributary, enters it from the NE, *ca.* two miles from the Dead Sea. The modern name for the Arnon is the Wadi Mojib. Fig. ARN 60.

*Bibliography.* F.-M. Abel, *Géographie de la Palestine,* I (1933), 177, 487-89.      E. D. GROHMAN

**AROD** är′ŏd [אֲרוֹד, hunchbacked; *cf.* אֲרַד, אַרְדּוֹן] (Num. 26:17); **ARODI** —ə dī [אֲרוֹדִי] (Gen. 46:16); **ARODITES** —dīts. Son of Gad; ancestral head of the "family of the Arodites."

*****AROER** ə rō′ər [עֲרוֹעֵר, juniper(?)]; **AROERITE** —īt [עֲרֹעֵרִי] (I Chr. 11:44). **1.** A well-known city situated on the N rim of the Arnon Gorge. It marked the S extremity of the Amorite kingdom of Sihon (Deut. 4:48; Josh. 12:2) and, consequently, of the territory captured by Israel E of the Jordan (Deut. 2:36; Josh. 13:9). It was fortified by the sons of Gad (Num. 32:34), though originally assigned to the tribe of Reuben, for whom it served as southernmost sentinel (Josh. 13:16). Because of its border position, it was the logical starting point for the taking of David's census (II Sam. 24:5). In the second half of the ninth century B.C., it is mentioned as marking the extent of Syrian occupation of Israel under Hazael (II Kings 10:33) and, on the MOABITE STONE as being fortified by Mesha after his defeat of Israel. When last mentioned in the OT, it was in Moabite possession (Jer. 48:19).

The ancient site is marked by the mound beside the modern village of ʿAraʿir *ca.* three miles SE of Dhiban and a short distance E of the N-S route which, from earliest biblical times to the present, has traversed the Arnon. From its magnificent vantage point on the lip of the canyon, it commanded all crossings of the forbidding gorge. Among the ruins occupying the mound are the heavy walls of two strong buildings—possibly fortresses from the Iron and Nabatean periods.

**2.** A town of Gilead on the border of the inheritance of Gad, located near the Ammonite capital of Rabbah (modern ʿAmman) and marking a part of Israel's frontier with Ammon (Josh. 13:25; *cf.* Judg. 11:33). The exact location is unknown, and its description as "opposite" or "before" Rabbah (Josh. 13:25) does not demand that it be sought to the E of that site. Geographically such a border would be difficult as long as Rabbah remained the capital and chief center of Ammonite strength. A site S of ʿAmman, in the vicinity of es-Sweiwina, would seem more appropriate.

**3.** A town in the S country of Judah, to the elders of which David sent a share of the spoil recovered from an Amalekite band which had raided the Negeb (I Sam. 30:28). The site is to be identified with modern ʿArʿarah, approximately twelve miles SE of Beer-sheba. "Adadah" of Josh. 15:22 is possibly a corruption of the same name. The Aroerite Hotham, father of two of David's Mighty Men (I Chr. 11:44), was probably a native of this town.

*Bibliography.* F.-M. Abel, *Géographie de la Palestine,* II (1938), 250; N. Glueck, *Explorations in Eastern Palestine,* I, *AASOR,* XIV (1934), 49-50; *Explorations in Eastern Palestine,* III, *AASOR,* XVIII-XIX (1939), 246-50.   W. H. MORTON

**AROM** ârʾɔm [ʾΑρόμ] (I Esd. 5:16). Ancestor of a family who returned from exile with Zerubbabel. The name is omitted in the parallel lists of Ezra and Nehemiah. It may represent HASHUM (Ezra 2:19; Neh. 7:22).   C. T. FRITSCH

**AROMA.** *See* ODOR.

**AROMATIC CANE** [קנה בשם; LXX κάλαμος] (Exod. 30:23; KJV CALAMUS). Alternately: SWEET CANE [קנה הטוב] (KJV CALAMUS); LXX θυμίαμα in Isa. 43:24; κιννάμωμον in Jer. 6:20; *cf.* Akkad. *qanû ṭâbu*]; CALAMUS [קנה; LXX κάλαμος in Song of S. 4:14; LXX *omits* in Ezek. 27:19]. A species of fragrant reed used by the Israelites as a perfume (Song of S. 4:14; Isa. 43:24; Jer. 6:20) and as an ingredient of the sacerdotal "anointing oil" (Exod. 20:23 P). It is commonly identified as the sweetflag (*Calmamus odoratus*), the scented rootstock of which (*Acorus calamus* Linn.) is still employed in confectionery, distilling, and brewing. Described by Ezekiel (27:19) as an import from Uzal—i.e., Sanʿa, the capital of Yemen—and by Jeremiah (6:20) as coming from a "distant land," sweetflag is said by Pliny (*Nat. Hist.* 12.248) to have been native to Arabia and India. (However, his subsequent statement that an even superior variety of it grows in Syria has not been confirmed.)   T. H. GASTER

**ARPACHSHAD** är păkʾshăd [ארפכשד; ʾΑρφαξάδ]; NT and KJV ARPHAXAD är făkʾsăd. The third son of Shem (Gen. 10:22); and the grandfather of Eber (vs. 24), the ancestor of the Hebrews (cf. Gen. 11:10-13; I Chr. 1:17-18, 24). Many attempts at etymologizing this name have been published, but none has gained general acceptance. The first three letters may correspond to Hurrian *arip-;* the last three may represent *Kasd-,* the eponymous ancestor of the Kasdim (i.e., Chaldeans). The Hurrian name Arip-hurra, occurring in the Nuzu (Nuzi) Tablets, would thus be an exact parallel, with the second element having ethnic affinities in both cases.

*Bibliography.* I. J. Gelb, P. M. Purves, and A. A. MacRae, *Nuzi Personal Names* (1943), p. 204.   C. H. GORDON

*****ARPAD** ärʾpăd [ארפד; Akkad. *Arpadda*]; KJV ARPHAD ärʾfăd in Isa. 36:19; 37:13. A city and a minor state in the N part of Syria. The ruin hill Tell Erfad, *ca.* twenty-five miles N of Aleppo, probably indicates the site. In the Bible the city is always mentioned with the city of Hamath (II Kings 18:34; 19: 13; Isa. 10:9; 36:19; 37:13; Jer. 49:23), both being proverbial examples of places destroyed by the Assyrians. The destruction is supposed to have taken place in 738 and 720 B.C.

*Bibliography.* A. Alt, "Die syrische Staatenwelt vor dem Einbruch der Assyrer," *ZDMG,* N.F. 13 (1934), pp. 233-58.   A. S. KAPELRUD

**ARPHAXAD** är făkʾsăd [ʾΑρφαξάδ]. **1.** A king of the Medes (Jth. 1:1-5, 13-15), otherwise unknown to history.
**2.** NT and KJV form of ARPACHSHAD.

**ARRAY, BATTLE** [ערך; מערכה, מערכה, חמשים; *cf.* חלוץ, *as* in Josh. 6:7]. The arrangement of forces on a field of battle in readiness to launch or withstand attack. The expression or similar terminology is used descriptively of a battle (cf. Josh. 1:14; I Sam. 17:10; II Sam. 10: 8-17), prophetically (e.g., Jer. 6:23), or figuratively (e.g., Job 6:4, where it is said that God's terrors are arrayed against Job). The quotation in Acts 4:26 of Ps. 2:2 follows the LXX. A figurative use (of ἑτοιμάζω) is found in Rev. 9:7, where it is said that locusts were arrayed like horses in battle.   J. A. SANDERS

**ARRAY, HOLY** [הדרת קדש] (I Chr. 16:29; II Chr. 20:21; Pss. 29:2; 96:9); KJV BEAUTY OF HOLINESS. An expression indicating "proper attire" (cf. Egyptian *hᵎdrt,* "neckband, necklace") or "proper form." All except one of the passages are poetic and are based on the very old Ps. 29. "Array" (הדרת) qualifying "king" in Prov. 14:28 obviously signifies royal splendor, majesty, or glory, one of whose aspects is a "multitude of people." The word occurs also in Ugaritic (I Krt. 155), where it is in parallelism with "dream."   J. M. MYERS

**ARROW.** *See* BOW AND ARROW.

**ARSACES** ärʾsɔ sēz [ʾΑρσάκης]. The name or title assumed by the Parthian kings in honor of the founder (*ca.* 250 B.C.) of the dynasty of the Arsacidae. Among the approximately thirty who bore it were Tiridates, Mithridates I and II, and Phraates IV. Those whom Josephus, in the Greek manner, calls Parthians, the E nations referred to as Persians and Medes. I Macc. 14:1-3 relates that Demetrius, having invaded the territories of "Arsaces the king of Persia and Media," was captured and taken before "Arsaces, who put him under guard." Appian says this Arsaces was Phraates, but he appears rather to have been Mithridates I (171-138 B.C.). Josephus (*Antiq.* XIII.viii.4) relates that Antiochus "lost a great part of his army to Arsaces, and was himself slain."   J. C. SWAIM

**ARSARETH.** KJV Apoc. form of ARZARETH.

**ARSENAL** [תלפיות] (Song of S. 4:4); KJV ARMORY. A store of battle weapons. The meaning of this Hebrew *hapax legomenon* is unknown; "arsenal" is a conjecture based on the context. "Weapons" and "courses of stone" are other conjectures, based on Arabic etymologies. The use is figurative and poetic. *See also* FORTRESS.   J. A. SANDERS

*****ART.** We are concerned here with the processes and realizations of painting, carving, engraving, etc., and with the origin and evolution of decorative themes and patterns, rather than with the nature of the monuments and objects thus decorated. Hence sigillography (i.e., the description and classification of seals; *see* SEALS AND SCARABS); ARCHITECTURE; and iconography (i.e., the study of images, especially divine images; *see* IDOL; IDOLATRY) do not fall within the scope of this discussion. Pls. XVII-XXIV.

1. Art in prehistoric Palestine
2. Canaanite art
   *a.* Ugaritic art
   *b.* Sculpture in Canaanite Palestine
   *c.* Ivory carving
   *d.* Decorative patterns of painted pottery
3. Hebrew art
   *a.* Decoration of the temple
   *b.* Ivory carving
4. Jewish art
   *a.* Decoration of funeral monuments
   *b.* Decoration of the early synagogues
Bibliography

**1. Art in prehistoric Palestine.** The earliest manifestations of artistic creativity thus far discovered in Palestine date from the Middle Stone Age (so-called Natufian culture; *ca.* 8000 B.C.), when the cave-dwellers of Mount Carmel and of the hilly country E of the Plain of Sharon carved and engraved their bone implements. Two objects may be singled out: the handle of a sickle haft representing a young fawn in full relief, and a slab of gray limestone with touches of red ocher, showing the profile of a gazelle (Fig. ART 61). There are attempts at representing the human figure, and the skulls of several individuals buried in a cave of the Carmel range were adorned with diadems of *Dentalium* shells. *See* PREHISTORY; MUGHARAH, WADI EL-.

The pre-pottery levels of Neolithic Jericho, tentatively dated *ca.* 6000 B.C., have yielded a number of human masks modeled of lime marl and touched with red paint, the eye globes being represented by means of sea shells. A framework of reeds had been used as a skeleton to mount each piece. These masks occurred apparently in groups of three—man, woman, and child. They were found together with animal figurines (bovines, sheep and goats, pigs) and plastic representations of the human male organs.

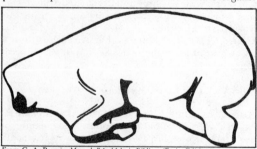

From G. A. Barrois, *Manuel d'Archéologie Biblique* (Paris: Editions A. & J. Picard & Cie.), vol. I

61. Mesolithic sculpture of a gazelle from Wadi el-Mugharah

All these objects had possibly a ritual or magic significance, as also the human skulls discovered in a nearby area and in a similar archaeological context.

They had been partly completed with fine clay in order to represent live human features. The eye sockets had been filled and inlaid with sea shells, and touches of paint had been applied to indicate eyebrows, eyelashes, etc. Figs. JER 14-15. *See also* JERICHO § 2.

The earliest, and outstanding, examples of wall paintings were found in the ruins of Teleilat Ghassul, a village of mud-brick houses of the Chalcolithic period (*ca.* 3500 B.C.), located in the lower tract of the Jordan Valley, on the E side. The artists, using a fresco technique, made use of mineral pigments, black, dark red, red and yellow ocher, and white. Geometrical patterns, as those used for the decoration of the unbaked earthenware of the same period, were combined with naturalistic motifs. One of the frescoes represents an eight-ray star around which geometrical designs, dragons(?), and masks somewhat similar to those worn by medicine men and sorcerers, were distributed irregularly (Fig. ART 62). On another panel, almost completely ruined, a bird, realistically painted, was seen together with masks like those of the star painting. There remained only the lower rim of a third painting, and the interpretation of what has been registered by archaeologists is rather hopeless. There was possibly a star in the left corner; a man, whose legs only are visible, turns his back to this emblem, and faces a series of figures, human or animal, whose feet are the only part still visible. It would be idle to attempt an interpretation of the scenes represented, because of the poor state of preservation of these frescoes.

**2. Canaanite art.** We use the ethnical term "Canaanite" for the populations of Palestine, predominantly Semitic but widely open to diversified cultural and artistic influences, prior to the definitive settlement of the Israelite tribes in the course of the thirteenth century B.C. Their artists drew their inspirations and techniques from Mesopotamian, Egyptian, Anatolian, and Aegean—i.e., pre-Hellenic —sources. Now the blending of these various elements was never a simple affair, but the result of complex interreactions. As a matter of fact, the art of ancient Asia Minor resulted from the modification of Mesopotamian themes in Hurrite, Mitannite, and Hittite workshops. The art of the eighteenth Egyptian dynasty is in itself a syncretism, and the cultural and artistic connections between the Aegean world and the E Mediterranean seaboard never ceased to work in either direction, from the Asiatic mainland to Cyprus and the isles, and from the isles to the Phoenician coast. For these reasons the process of fusion of the various strains was never completed, and did not result in anything organically unified or stable. The progress of Canaanite art, negligible during the Early Bronze Age (*ca.* 3000-2000 B.C.), when Anatolian influences were first felt along the Syro-Palestinian coast, flourished during the Late Bronze Age (*ca.* 1600-1200 B.C.), presumably because of an increased interchange with the fast-developing pre-Hellenic cultures.

**a. Ugaritic art.** Even though the classification of the people of Ras Shamra (Ugarit) on the Syrian coast as Canaanites may be challenged linguistically, yet their productions from the fifteenth to the fourteenth century B.C. are good illustrations of the com-

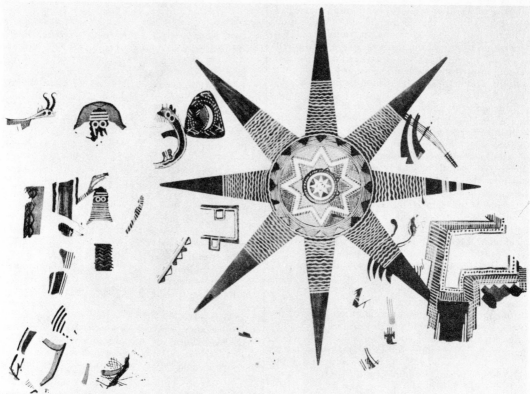

Courtesy of the Pontificio Instituto Biblico, Rome

62. Chalcolithic-period fresco from Teleilat Ghassul

posite art which flourished in Canaan until the Israelite conquest. Nothing is more revealing, from this particular standpoint, than the images of the gods of UGARIT. An outstanding example is a limestone stele representing the thunder-god. The god is standing. In his right hand he holds a mace; his left hand strikes downward with a spear, most likely the symbol of lightning, as the flamelike appendages of the butt end are meant to show. The Egyptian influence is obvious if one considers the tight loincloth, and the left shoulder seen full-face, while the head, body, and legs appear in right profile. However, the helmet, the pigtails, and the curved dagger are definitely borrowed from the art of Asia Minor, while the little figure shown in front of the god, probably the dedicator, is dressed in long, fringed Syrian robes (Fig. UGA 6). The same mixture of Egyptian and Asian features appears, in varying proportions, in other reliefs and statues. In contrast with these, an ivory plaque representing a female deity seated on a mountaintop and holding ears of corn, while two wild goats stand on their rear legs right and left of the goddess, shows an unadulterated Mycenaean influence. Still, the symmetrical disposition of the animals facing each other ultimately originates in the early phases of Mesopotamian art. Fig. UGA 5.

Decorative patterns using naturalistic or mythological motifs also reveal the composite nature of Ugaritic art, as can be seen from a golden paten representing a charioteer hunting a herd of wild oxen with bow and arrow, while an antelope gallops by the

side and a large mastiff follows the chariot. The well-balanced composition and the dynamic character of the animal representation are typically Aegean; the artificial combination of profile and full-face shoulder of the charioteer belongs to the Egyptian tradition, while the chariot, the harness, and the

From Schaeffer, *The Cuneiform Texts of Ras Shamra-Ugarit* (British Academy, Schweich Lectures, 1937)

63. Golden patera of king of Ugarit(?) hunting (fifteenth or first half of fourteenth century B.C.)

manner of hunting seem to originate in the art of Asia Minor rather than in Egyptian art.* The integration of disparate elements is complete in the decoration of a gold cup adorned with a frieze of sphinxes, winged figures, and stylized animals converging toward the emblem known as "tree of life." with its symmetrical volutes and palmated motifs. Fig. ART 63.

**b. Sculpture in Canaanite Palestine.** The few monuments which can be ascribed to the Canaanites, in contradistinction to foreign products such as Egyptian steles or reliefs found in Palestine, are generally uninspiring imitations of foreign models and patterns, the specific details of which were often misunderstood by the local artists. During the intermittent Egyptian occupation of Palestine under several Pharaohs of the eighteenth and nineteenth dynasties, stone carvers from Beth-shan had sculptured steles and votive plaques of limestone for the temple of the local god, Mekal, and his female consort, which were worshiped by the indigenous population as well as by the Egyptian commanders and the personnel of the garrison. One such stele dedicated to Mekal, as we learn from the crude hieroglyphic inscription, represents the god in right profile, seated on his throne, and receiving an offering of lotus flowers by two Egyptians. The sculptor did his best to give the "Egyptian look" to his god by conventionally representing the left shoulder full-face, and by placing in the left hand of the god the *was* scepter and in his right hand the *ankh* symbol of the Egyptian deities. But the full beard, the horns, the high pointed bonnet unwittingly substituted for the white crown of the Pharaohs, with a long streamer ending in a lotus flower, would never have been dreamed of on the banks of the Nile. (Fig. BET 36.) A small plaque representing the female deity of Beth-shan, with Egyptian emblems arbitrarily chosen and associated with fancy motifs, belongs in the same category as the stele of Mekal. Fig ASH 91.

The relief carved toward the twelfth century B.C. on a stele found at the Khirbet Balu'a in Transjordan shows a similar combination, by local craftsmen. of Canaanite and Egyptian elements: a male figure. dressed in flowing oriental garments, and wearing a headdress like that of the *Shasu*-Bedouins represented on Egyptian reliefs from Seti I to Rameses III, stands in left profile between two unidentified deities, male and female, whose emblems were borrowed at random from the current iconographic repertory of Egypt. Fig. MOA 61.

A bronze statuette from Megiddo, overlaid with gold foil, represents a Canaanite deity seated on a throne, dressed with a tight ankle-long garment, and wearing a conical tiara.* This statuette, dating from *ca.* the thirteenth century B.C., is reminiscent of similar figurines from Byblos and from Ras Shamra. The posture might suggest an Egyptian influence. except for the extended forearms; the features, however, recall Mesopotamian models. Figs. ART 64, UGA 7. *See also* MEGIDDO § 3c.

The legacy of the arts of Asia Minor and N Syria is undeniable in the case of a stone panel found in Beth-shan and tentatively dated from the fourteenth century. It consists of a heavy slab of basalt representing the fight of a lion and a mastiff (Fig. BET 37).

Courtesy of the Oriental Institute, the University of Chicago

64. Baal figurine of bronze, covered with gold; from the Megiddo Late Bronze temple

It is stylistically related to the massive statue of basalt and an orthostat of the same material, decorated with the figure of a roaring lion whose rear legs are disproportionately small, discovered in a thirteenth-century Canaanite temple at Hazor (Fig. ART 65). Affinities with the art of Asia Minor may be recognized also in the decoration of the so-called "altar" of Taanach, made of terra cotta, and which is in reality a stand for placing offerings and possibly for burning incense. Its side panels show the superposed profiles of winged four-footed animals, the heads of which were modeled in full relief. A floral ornament with multiple volutes, however, must be traced back to Aegean models. This object is not accurately dated. Fig. ART 66.

Courtesy of Yigael Yadin: The James A. de Rothschild Expedition at Hazor, The Hebrew University, Jerusalem, Israel

65. Basalt orthostat with lion carving, from a thirteenth-century-B.C. Canaanite temple at Hazor

From H. Gressmann, *Altorientalische Texte und Bilder zum AT* (Berlin: Walter de Gruyter & Co.)

66. Incense altar, from Taanach

As for the countless clay figurines, the nature, typology, and even the chronology of which are far from being well defined, they can scarcely be considered as works of art, if by this are meant those productions in which the imagination and inventive genius of the craftsman play the major role. There is scarcely any justification for discussing here either these objects or the earthenware vessels modeled in the shape of grotesque (intentionally or not) human figures by local potters, and appropriately nicknamed "toby-jugs" by some archaeologists. Exceptionally, two goblets of high-glazed ware from Tell Abu Hawam near Haifa, representing respectively a woman's head with ear and nose rings, and a ram's head, may be listed as local artifacts showing a strong affinity with similar objects, artistically somewhat poorer, of Ras Shamra and Cyprus. The human masks decorating the lid of pottery sarcophagi found in various sites of the coastal plain, in the necropolis of Beth-shan, and one of them even in Transjordan, may also be mentioned, on account of a possible link with the art of the golden masks of the royal tombs of Mycenae. The crude Palestinian substitutes for the latter date from the end of the Late Bronze and Early Iron Age, a period which coincides with the greater expansion of the Philistines. Fig. BET 38.

*c. Ivory carving.* Whereas the artistic level of Canaanite sculpture is distressingly low, the ivory carvings are abundant and unusually attractive.* They reveal not only an able technique, but also a great ingenuity on the part of the artists in combining patterns and motifs drawn from heterogeneous sources. An ivory plaque from Lachish (thirteenth century B.C.) shows in a continuous frieze bulls and lions fighting, while an eagle or vulture hovers over the scene. This theme is common in the glyptic of Mesopotamia, where it has mythological connotations. A box of ivory from Tell el-Far'ah in the Negeb is adorned with scenes which point to Egyptian prototypes, a banquet scene and the capture of wild ducks

By permission of C. F. A. Schaeffer, Director of the Ras Shamra Expedition and Professor of the Collège de France

67. The victorious king, on a plaque of ivory, from Ugarit

From G. A. Barrois, *Manuel d'Archéologie Biblique* (Paris: Editions A. & J. Picard & Cie.), vol. I

68. Ivory box from Tell el-Far'ah, depicting scene of a hunt in a swamp

From G. A. Barrois, *Manuel d'Archéologie Biblique* (Paris: Editions A. & J. Picard & Cie.), vol. I

69. Design on an ivory box from Tell el-Far'ah (*ca.* fourteenth century B.C.)

70. An ivory plaque from Megiddo, showing tribute-bearers and captives before the prince seated on a throne (*ca.* thirteenth century B.C.)

in the marshes.\* Miscellaneous details betray non-Egyptian influences—viz., Syrian (the costumes in the banquet scene), Mesopotamian (the palm trees), and Aegean (the bullocks standing at the edge of the thicket). This object cannot be dated with absolute precision; it may not be older than the twelfth century B.C. Figs. ART 67; 68; 69.

Most important is a collection of sculptured and engraved ivory inlays from Megiddo, dating from the early twelfth century B.C. They show forth an amazing variety of decorative themes, ranging from geometrical patterns to the palmated ornaments and the volutes so common in the art of Cyprus and of the Phoenician coast, to figures from the religious iconography of Egypt, and to naturalistic animal figures and scenes. These inlays once decorated the palace and the furniture of one of the Canaanite chieftains who held the fortress of Megiddo prior to the centralized rule of the Hebrew kings. Two pieces of the collection deserve a special mention. The first one is a long, thin plate of ivory, on which a scene was engraved, which might be entitled "the king's triumph." The right half represents the king, standing on his chariot, ahead of which march a musician and a warrior, while two naked prisoners have their hands tied to the harness of the horses. On the left half of the ivory, the queen is shown presenting flowers to her lord, who sits on his throne and sips from a bowl a brew which stewards actually prepare behind the throne. Egyptian conventions and techniques are combined here with local and foreign elements, such

as the long Syrian garments, and the winged solar disk, which is of the Asian, not Egyptian, variety. (Fig. ART 70.) The other outstanding piece of the treasure of Megiddo is an ivory casket decorated with sphinxes and lions carved in high relief. The sphinxes resemble more the prototypes from Asia Minor than Egyptian sphinxes, and the entire object reminds one of the massive bases on which stand the statues or emblems of Hittite deities. (Fig. ART 71.) Articles of daily use, such as combs, mirror and spoon handles, game boards, etc., were similarly enriched with engraved geometrical patterns and with animal figures, realistic and mythological. *See* IVORY.

*d. Decorative themes of painted pottery.* The purpose here is not to list the numerous varieties of painted pottery, for this task does not belong in art history, but rather in the history of the ceramic industry. The following is an attempt to analyze selected patterns used in the decoration of earthenware vessels, inasmuch as they cast some light on the sources, resources, and development of Canaanite art as a whole.

One class of painted pottery from the initial phase of the Late Bronze Age (*ca.* 1500 B.C.) is particularly instructive from this point of view. It consists in large vessels, pots, and craters found on various Palestinian sites such as Tell el-'Ajjul, Tell el-Far'ah, Lachish, and Megiddo. In contrast with the imitation of Aegean geometrical designs then fashionable in Palestine, they show forth a combination of stylized motifs with realistic animal representations, within panels separated by straight or wavy lines,

71. Ivory box with sphinxes and lions in relief, from Megiddo (*ca.* thirteenth century B.C.)

From G. A. Barrois, *Manuel d'Archéologie Biblique* (Paris: Editions A. & J. Picard & Cie.), vol. I

72. Painted pottery, Late Bronze Age III: (1) from Megiddo; (2) from Sharuhen; (3) from Beth-shemesh

From G. A. Barrois, *Manuel d'Archéologie Biblique* (Paris: Editions
A. & J. Picard & Cie.), vol. I

73. Painted pottery from Tell el-'Ajjul, Late Bronze I
(*ca.* 1500 B.C.)

From G. A. Barrois, *Manuel d'Archéologie Biblique* (Paris: Editions
A. & J. Picard & Cie.), vol. I

74. Painted pottery, Late Bronze I (*ca.* 1500 B.C.): (1)
from Gezer; (2) from Tell el-'Ajjul; (3) from Megiddo

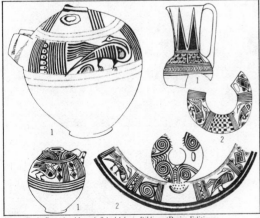

From G. A. Barrois, *Manuel d'Archéologie Biblique* (Paris: Editions
A. & J. Picard & Cie.), vol. I

75. "Philistine" painted pottery: (1) from Beth-shemesh;
(2) from Sharuhen (Tell el-Far'ah)

and rows of triangles, checkerboard designs, etc.
Two colors are used, red and black or sepia.* Vessels
similarly decorated have been found on the island of
Cyprus, and this style of ceramic painting may accordingly be described as Mediterranean. The motifs
inside the panels, which had obviously become the
common good of the pottery painters of Cyprus and
the Syro-Palestinian coast, go back partly to old

Mesopotamian prototypes; this is certainly the case
for the symmetrical group of the stylized tree, at
times identifiable as a palm tree, and of the antelopes or wild goats; also for the theme of the cranes
picking at each other or at a dead fish. These two
themes are attested since the beginning of the second
millennium in the art of lower Mesopotamia, a land
of palm groves, channels, and lagoons, where cranes
and gulls wade and catch fish on the shoals. Figs.
ART 72-74.

During the initial phase of the Early Iron Age, *ca.*
1200 B.C., another class of painted jugs and craters,
with spiral decorative patterns and overstylized large
birds turning their heads to smooth their feathers,
has been attributed to the Philistines, on the grounds
of their being found almost exclusively on sites of the
coastal plain of Palestine.* Their style suggests a
strong Mediterranean influence, as can be shown
from analogies from the pottery of Ras Shamra
(Ugarit), and from sub-Mycenaean wares found in
the isles and on the Greek mainland. Figs. ART 75;
PHI 50. *See also* PHILISTINES § 3*d.*

**3. Hebrew art.** When they established their rule
in Palestine, the Hebrews had no artistic tradition of
their own. This is quite natural on the part of tribes
which had been forced to keep on wandering because of political circumstances, but it is also true of
these clans or fractions of clans which had eventually
managed to settle prior to the days of Joshua. At any
rate, the troubled period which followed the Conquest, and which was brought to an end by the rise
of the Davidic dynasty, was not favorable to artistic
creativity. Not until the reign of Solomon did art
flourish again in Palestine, and still the Israelites had
to rely largely on foreign craftsmen, resources, and
techniques, as can be inferred from such texts as
I Kings 5:6, 18; 7:13-14; II Chr. 2:7, 14. The construction and the furnishing of the temple and of the
palaces of the kings of Judah and Israel seem to
have drained nearly all the artistic potential of the
Hebrews. Household utensils, earthenware vessels,
miscellaneous objects in the production of which the
Canaanite craftsmen had exercised their artistic gifts,
were now manufactured, not without a certain technical ability, but without much regard for aestheti-
cism. *See* POTTER.

*a. Decoration of the temple.* The art of Solomon's
temple is known to us through the descriptions given
in I Kings and II Chronicles. Now these texts are
not to be read as if they were the record of the architect's specifications, or a technical description of the
building and the furnishings. They were compiled by
scribes who were no art specialists, but whose chief
concern was to convey in their writings some idea of
the unique splendor of the "house of Yahweh." It is
even probable that at least those responsible for the
final redaction had not actually seen the monument.

In spite of the fact that nothing is left from the
temple, and despite the lack of precision and incompleteness of the texts, often corrupted in the process
of transmission, it is nevertheless possible to obtain
some idea of the general disposition of the buildings
and of their decoration. As the latter goes, the Bible
records suggest that the inner walls of the sanctuary,
doors, passages, etc., were covered with sculptured
panels of wood brightened with gold inlays (or gold

foil). The Hebrew terms that are used in the description of the ornamental patterns and motifs of these panels, as well as of the furnishings of the temple, are obscure, and their translation in the various versions is only tentative and often inconsistent. The passages relative to the temple itself mention ornaments from the plant world geometrically arranged, and live figures coming under the name of cherubim (*singular* "cherub"; *see* CHERUB 2). Among the former, the RSV names gourds, open flowers, and palm trees (I Kings 6:18, 29, 31, 35, and parallels). The cherubim of the temple may be understood as composite creatures, with human faces and wings, akin to the winged figures guarding the doorsteps of the gods in the temples of Mesopotamia and Asia Minor, while the cherubim of the ark as described in Exod. 25:18-20 may be closer to the winged figures painted on the panels of the processional shrines of Egyptian deities, from the Eighteenth Dynasty onward. Analogies to both types abound in the art of the ivory carvers (*see* § 3b *below*). The capitals of the pillars JACHIN AND BOAZ, and the other utensils of the cult, were also decorated with ornaments from the plant world in geometrical patterns, identified in the RSV as pomegranates, lilies, palm trees, flowers, and gourds (I Kings 7:18, 22, 24, 26, 36, 42, 49, and parallels). Figures of oxen adorned the square basis of the huge vat known as the Molten Sea (*see* SEA, MOLTEN), arranged three on each side (I Kings 7:25; II Chr. 4:4. Fig. SEA 34). The analogy of N Syrian and Hittite pedestals of divine emblems and statues comes here to mind. Cherubim and animal figures, lions and oxen, on the side panels of the bronze wagons for carrying water (I Kings 7:27-37 and parallels), point to similar analogies. As a whole, all this ornamentation runs parallel to what we know of the syncretistic art of Syria and Palestine, so well exemplified in the ivory carvings. What is distinctive in the sacred art of the Hebrews is that it involves a certain "demythologization" of foreign symbols, or at least an adaptation of the same in view of Yahweh worship.

It is about pointless to attempt to define, even tentatively, the art of the TABERNACLE, on the basis of Exod. 25-27. As the description reads now, its primitive elements, scarce and not explicit, were combined with anachronistic details drawn from the description of the Jerusalem sanctuary and artificially transposed to suit the portable nature of the tabernacle and its furnishings.

**b. Ivory carving.** The art of the Canaanite ivory carvers (*see* § 2c *above*) revived with the rise of the various W Semitic monarchies, following the artistic vacuum caused by the troubled period in the course of which the Israelites conquered Palestine. Occasional references to the decoration of houses and furniture by means of ivory inlays are found in the Bible (I Kings 10:18; 22:39; Amos 3:15; 6:4). These references are adequately illustrated by two important collections of ivory plaques. The first one, discovered in the ruins of the Assyrian palace at Hadatu (Arslan Tash), can be dated with precision, since a thin plate of ivory engraved with a dedicatory inscription in Aramaic mentions the name of Hazael, king of Damascus, who was defeated by Shalmanezer III in 841 B.C., and whose palace was

From G. A. Barrois, *Manuel d'Archéologie Biblique* (Paris: Editions A. & J. Picard & Cie.), vol. I

76. Ivory from Arslan Tash: sphinx with the head of a ram

From G. A. Barrois, *Manuel d'Archéologie Biblique* (Paris: Editions A. & J. Picard & Cie.), vol. I

77. Ivory from Arslan Tash, with stag in open relief

From G. A. Barrois, *Manuel d'Archéologie Biblique* (Paris: Editions A. & J. Picard & Cie.), vol. I

78. Ivory from Arslan Tash, showing cow and calf

From G. A. Barrois, *Manuel d'Archéologie Biblique* (Paris: Editions A. & J. Picard & Cie.), vol. I

79. Ivories from Arslan Tash

plundered, his treasures being carried away as booty and placed by the conquerors in the palace of Hadatu. The ivories of Arslan Tash, occasionally brightened with gold foil, show a great variety of motifs such as sphinxes, female winged figures facing one another on each side of the familiar tree pattern with its volutes and palmated ornaments, and a woman's face appearing in a threefold window frame. These motifs are treated in the manner of the Egyptian art of the New Empire, which itself is a syncretism drawing at least in part from oriental and Mediterranean sources. The craftsmen who carved the Arslan Tash ivories copied the Egyptian themes quite freely, transforming emblems and symbols having a theological significance into mere ornaments. Some pieces show an affinity with Assyrian prototypes, especially a plaque representing a bearded man standing full face, wrapped in a fringed shawl. Animal motifs such as the cow turning her head to lick her suckling calf, and the stag grazing, are borrowed from the Aegean repertory, while lion heads in full relief bring us back to oriental traditions. Figs. ART 76-79; ARC 43.

Another collection of ivories comes from the excavation of the royal palace of SAMARIA. Some plaques, enriched with gold foil and inlays of blue stone and glass paste, show genuine Egyptian motifs, such as Harpocrates in the lotus flower, Isis and Nephthys adoring the *djed* pillar. Others reproduce some of the most conventional types of the collection of Arslan Tash—the sphinxes, the woman in the window, etc. Figs. INL 8; IVO 22; WIN 22.

These examples, as well as the much-dilapidated ivories of Nimrud, the biblical Calah in Mesopotamia, obviously the booty of some expedition in Syria or Palestine, give evidence of a most active industry of ivory carving in the Semitic West, toward the ninth-eighth century B.C.

**4. Jewish art.** This section will not deal with the productions of foreign art, Hellenistic or Roman, on Palestinian soil, but rather with specifically Jewish artistic achievements. These are understandably rare and poor in the postexilic period, when home-coming exiles struggled for existence, as well as during the long fight of the Jews for independence from the Seleucid kings. They are more numerous, while still at a mediocre artistic level, when the Jews obtained a limited autonomy under their own rulers, or political freedom within the framework of the Roman imperial administration. Jewish art, however, was never entirely original, influenced as it was by the cultural and artistic expansion of Hellenism in West Asia, which resulted in an all-pervading, vigorous Greco-oriental syncretism. Examples of it abound in Palestine and the neighboring countries—the painted tombs of the Hellenized Sidonian colony of Marissa in Idumea, with their mythological motifs, and the mixture of animal figures, local and exotic, with a fantastic fauna of chimeras, griffins, and phoenixes; Nabatean and Palmyrenian tombs and temples with their sculptured or painted decoration; the pseudo-classic Herodian buildings. Jewish art in the Hellenistic and Roman periods is a particular variety of this widespread artistic koine. The decoration of Herod's temple may have been the paramount achievement of this art, but nothing of it is left, and

Josephus' descriptions are utterly insufficient, as far as style and technique go.

**a. Decoration of funeral monuments.** The richest Jewish rock-cut family sepulchres toward the end of the pre-Christian era were often adorned with columns imitated from the classical orders of architecture, Doric and Ionic, together with Egyptian and Asian elements, such as pyramidal structures, floral motifs, and deep concave moldings. The group of tombs located in the upper valley of the Kidron at

Courtesy of Herbert G. May

80. The tomb of the Hezir family in the Kidron Valley

the foot of the Mount of Olives offers good examples of this oriental syncretism; cf. the monuments commonly referred to as tombs of Absalom, Zechariah (Zacharias), and James (the lesser); also the tomb of Queen Helena (of Adiabene), erroneously labeled Sepulchre of the Kings, in the N suburb of Jerusalem (Pl. XXV*a*). The triangular gables of some monuments, such as the so-called tomb of Jehoshaphat in the Kidron Valley,* the tomb of Queen Helena, and the so-called tomb of the judges in the NW necropolis, are filled with intricate motifs from the plant world. Figs. ART 80-81.

From G. A. Barrois, *Manuel d'Archéologie Biblique* (Paris: Editions A. & J. Picard & Cie.), vol. II

81. Vestibule of the so-called "Tomb of the Judges," in the Sanhedrin area, Jerusalem (probably *ca.* 150 B.C.)

***b. Decoration of the early synagogues.*** The façades of some Galilean synagogues—e.g., at Kefr Bir'im and Tell Hum (Capernaum)—none of which is anterior to the third Christian century, were lavishly decorated with sculptured vegetable ornaments similar to those seen on the gables of Jewish rock-cut tombs, with the addition of a few typical emblems

The British Academy; from collection of the Hebrew University, Jerusalem, Israel

82. Keystone of arched window from Capernaum synagogue

The British Academy; from collection of the Hebrew University, Jerusalem, Israel

83. Frieze from the Roman-period synagogue at Capernaum

such as the seven-branch candlestick, the six-pointed "Star of David," the Torah-shrine, the wheeled chariot of I Chr. 28:18, and, quite unexpectedly, figures of Eros and sea horses. Figs. ART 82-83.

Human and animal figures are common on the mosaic pavements of Palestinian synagogues of the fourth-fifth century of our era. Originally pagan motifs from the mythology, such as the chariot of the sun-god, the figures of the zodiac and of the seasons, were borrowed without qualm by Jewish artists and combined with their own emblems, among which the candlestick and the Torah-shrine are favorites. An outstanding example is the pavement of the synagogue at Beth Alpha in the E portion of the Plain of Jezreel (Fig. SYN 100). Some iconoclasts, however, systematically destroyed the figures of the zo-

diac of the synagogue of 'Ain Duk near Jericho, and hammered the Eros and animal figures of Capernaum. The mosaic pavement of the synagogue of Djerash (Gerasa) featured the theme of animals seeking refuge in Noah's ark.

Wall frescoes, executed in a technique and style similar to those of Roman and Alexandrian paintings, decorated the synagogue of Dura-Europos on the Euphrates (third century). They represented miscellaneous episodes from the entire Bible—the child Moses rescued from the Nile, the well of Moses at Beer, the ark of the covenant causing havoc in the country of the Philistines, the anointing of David, Elijah's sacrifice on Mount Carmel, Mordecai honored by Ahasuerus, etc. Such an epitome of biblical history was, of course, best adapted to the very purpose of a Synagogue building, which is above all a place of instruction. Figs. ART 84; SYN 104-6.

Courtesy of Yale University

84. Mural painting of Moses and the burning bush, from the synagogue at Dura-Europos (*ca.* 250 B.C.)

***Bibliography.*** G. A. Barrois, *Manuel d'Archéologie Biblique* (1939), pp. 356, 425-28 (cf. p. 508), 488-507. Miscellaneous art productions directly related to the care for the dead and to religious cults are described in vol. II (1953), pp. 303-8; 372-74; 384-85; 389-98; 440-43; the art of the synagogue is discussed also in vol. II, pp. 466-68.

More detailed information on single techniques or groups of objects can be gathered from the following: H. Kohl and C. Watzinger, *Antike Synagogen in Galilaea* (1916). G. Orfali, *Capharnaum et ses ruines* (1922). A. Rowe, *The Topography and History of Beth Shan* (1930). F. Thureau-Dangin, G. A. Barrois, *et al., Arslan Tash* (1931). E. L. Sukenik, *The Ancient Synagogue of Beth Alfa* (1932). A. Mallon *et al., Teleilat Ghassûl*, I (1934).

D. A. E. Garrod and D. M. A. Bate, *The Stone Age of Mount Carmel*, I (1937). M. Rostovtzeff, *Dura Europos and Its Art* (1938). G. Loud, *The Megiddo Ivories* (1939). A. Rowe, *The Four Canaanite Temples of Beth Shan*, I (1940). J. W. Crowfoot, *Early Ivories from Samaria* (1942). Y. Yadin, "Excavations at Hazor," *BA*, XIX (1956), 2-12.       G. A. BARROIS

**ARTAXERXES** är′tə zûrk′sēz [Heb.-Aram. ארתחששתא, ארתחששפ (*Papyri*); Old Pers. *artaxšaça;* Elam. *ir-tak-ša-aš-ša;* Akkad. *ar-tak-šat-tu;* ᾿Αρτα-ξέρξης]. **1.** Artaxerxes I (465-425 B.C.), son of Xerxes I; known as Macrocheir (Μακρόχειρ) or Longimanus. He overcame revolts in Egypt, where, with Athenian support, unrest started in 460 and lasted until 454, and in other parts of the Persian Empire. During that time some of the E possessions were lost. By the peace treaty of Callias (449), signed at Susa, the relations between Athens and Persia were stabilized on a *status quo ante bellum* basis. Artaxerxes was buried at Naqš-i Rustam next to the tombs of his father and grandfather.

Courtesy of the University Museum of the University of Pennsylvania

85. Alabaster vase of Artaxerxes I with his name in Old Persian, Elamite, Babylonian, and Egyptian

Artaxerxes I authorized Ezra's mission to Jerusalem in 458 (Ezra 7:8, 11-26). He temporarily halted the reconstruction of Jerusalem (4:7-23). Nehemiah's two missions were under his reign and with his permission, the first in 445 (Neh. 2:1 ff; 13:6). *See* EZRA AND NEHEMIAH, BOOKS OF. Fig. ART 85.

**2.** Artaxerxes II (404-359 B.C.), son of Darius II and grandson of Artaxerxes I; known as Mnemon (Μνήμων). He crushed the rebellion of his brother Cyrus (Battle of Cunaxa, 401), as related by

Xenophon in his *Anabasis*. He lost Egypt probably in 402 or 401, repelled the meddling of Sparta in the affairs of Asia Minor (Peace of Antalcidas, 386), and suppressed other rebellious movements led by local satraps. Several of his inscriptions refer to his building activities. The palace he built at Susa is considered by some authorities to be identical with the palace described in Esth. 1:5-6. *See*, however, AHASUERUS.

Courtesy of the Oriental Institute, the University of Chicago

86. Artaxerxes III stairway, W of the palace of Darius at Persepolis

**3.** Artaxerxes III (359-338 B.C.), son of Artaxerxes II; known as Ochus. By the use of skilful diplomacy and military force he succeeded in maintaining a superficially strong empire, until the time when he was murdered as the result of a conspiracy led by Bagoas (338). *See* ARPACHSHAD. Fig. ART 86.

*See also* PERSIA, HISTORY AND RELIGION OF, § D3a.       M. J. DRESDEN

**ARTEMAS** är′tə məs [᾿Αρτεμᾶς, *short for* ᾿Αρτεμί δωρος (Artemidorus) given by ARTEMIS] (Tit. 3:12). An early Christian. Paul expected to send Artemas or Tychicus to Titus in Crete so that Titus could join Paul in Nicopolis.       B. H. THROCKMORTON, JR.

**ARTEMIS** är′tə məs [῎Αρτεμις]. A goddess of the most diverse characteristics, worshiped more widely than any other female deity in the communities of the Greek world and identified with the Latin Diana among the Romans. In classical mythology Artemis is the sister of Apollo, daughter of Leto and Zeus; the virgin huntress, protector of the chastity of her nymphs and devotees; a moon-goddess; the patroness of maidens of marriageable age, the helper of women in childbirth, and the giver of a gentle death to women. But in the popular religion, the traits of tenderness are not so marked; even in later times she retains striking aspects of savagery. Her cult shows numerous traces of totemism. Several animals are sacred to her—the stag, the wild boar, the hare, the wolf, the bear, and in some cases birds and fishes; but it is noteworthy that none of these is a domestic animal. She is pre-eminently a goddess of wild nature, of the hunter and the fisherman rather than of the cultivator of the soil.

The Artemis of the Ephesians (Acts 19:23-40; KJV "Diana of the Ephesians") has little but the name in common with this Hellenic goddess and nothing at all in common with the Latin Diana. She is really a form of the Asian mother-goddess, and was worshiped in a primitive sanctuary near the mouth of the Caÿster for centuries before the first Greek settlers arrived to found the city of Ephesus (ca. 1100 B.C.). For a long period, she was the focal point of indigenous resistance to the Greek city, but toward 800 B.C. she had been adopted by the Greeks and a new temple had been laid out for her close to the city. Lydians and Persians contributed to its magnificence and introduced new elements into the cult, which was sensuous and orgiastic but not impure.

The Ephesian Artemis was not a virgin huntress, but a fecund mother; not a moon-goddess, but a goddess of fertility in man and beast and vegetation. Her temple was a huge landholding corporation served by eunuch-priests called *Megabuzoi* (a Persian title); by other attendants called Essenes, who were subject to rigid rules of purity and abstinence; and by thousands of female slaves, hierodules. It appears that the latter were not prostitutes, as was the case in nearly all the other cults of the Great Mother in Anatolia. Her worship was not confined to Ephesus, but was practiced in nearly all the cities of Asia, in many places on the Greek mainland, in the S of Gaul, in Syria, and in Rome itself; so that there is no exaggeration in the description of her magnificence as one "whom all Asia and the world worship" (Acts 19:27). It is probable that her primary image, which was preserved in the sanctuary of the temple at Ephesus, was a meteorite (Acts 19:35: "the sacred stone that fell from the sky"[?]); but she was usually represented in sculpture as a female figure with multiple breasts, with lions, bulls, and rams worked in relief upon her shoulders and legs, with a bee just above her feet, and her head surmounted by a turret-

crown; the lower part of the body is not fully shaped to human form. The "silver shrines of Artemis" made by Demetrius (Acts 19:24) were not images, but were probably replicas of the primitive sanctuary which was replaced by the great temple of the later period. The title νεωκόρος ("temple keeper"—lit. "temple sweeper") was accorded officially by the Romans, usually in connection with the imperial cult, but there is evidence from coins and inscriptions that Ephesus was acknowledged as temple keeper both of the emperor and of Artemis. Figs. ART 87; SAR 26. *See also* GREEK RELIGION AND PHILOSOPHY § 4*b*.

*Bibliography.* W. M. Ramsay, *Cities and Bishoprics of Phrygia* (1895); L. R. Farnell, *Cults of the Greek States,* vol. II, c. XIII (1896); D. G. Hogarth, *British Museum Excavations in Ephesus: the Archaic Artemisia,* 2 vols. (1908). F. W. BEARE

**ARTIFICER.** KJV translation of חרש in Gen. 4:22 (RSV "forger"); I Chr. 29:5 (RSV "craftsman"); II Chr. 34:11 (RSV "carpenter"); Isa. 3:3 (RSV "magician"). *See* CARPENTER; MAGIC; METALLURGY.

**ARTILLERY.** KJV translation of כלי (RSV "weapons") in I Sam. 20:40. *See* WEAPONS AND IMPLEMENTS OF WAR.

**ARTISANS.** *See* CRAFTS.

**ARUBBOTH** ə rŭb'ŏth [ארבות] (I Kings 4:10); KJV ARUBOTH ə rōō'bŏth. A town in one of Solomon's twelve administrative districts, where Benhesed, an official of Solomon's court, was charged with the responsibility of collecting provisions. Recent studies favor a location in the territory of Manasseh, between Megiddo and Samaria. Though the administrative district may not have been identical with the territory of Manasseh, it is probable that Solomon did not ignore completely the old tribal lines when he set up his system of taxation. It has been proposed that modern 'Arrabeh, *ca.* nine miles N of Samaria, is the site of ancient Arubboth. ARBATTA (I Macc. 5:23) was perhaps the form of the name in the Maccabean period.

*Bibliography.* W. F. Albright, "The Administrative Divisions of Israel and Judah," *JPOS,* V (1925), 25-31. W. L. REED

**ARUMAH** ə rōō'mə [ארומה] (Judg. 9:41). The place of residence of Abimelech after he had been driven from Shechem. In vs. 31 the RSV emends to read "Arumah" (תרמה, *tormâ;* KJV "privily"). The name Arumah should be read in vs. 31 as well as in vs. 41; Abimelech could have launched his attack upon Shechem from the same place to which he later retreated.

The exact location of the city is unknown. An Arumah is mentioned in an Assyrian inscription of Adad-nirari III, but without a specific location. It is not likely that the city is to be identified with RAMAH near Lydda, or with ARIMATHEA. Some scholars identify Arumah with El 'Ormeh, located *ca.* halfway between Shechem and Shiloh. W. L. REED

**ARVAD** är'văd [ארוד; Akkad. *Armada, Aruda, Aruadi;* Amarna *Arvada*]; **ARVADITE** är'və dīt. A

87. Coin showing the temple of Diana (Artemis)

From *Atlas of the Bible* (Thomas Nelson & Sons Limited)

88. The island of Arvad (modern Erwad)

city and a minor state in N Syria, on an island of the same name, near the coast. The island is found between Tripolis and Ladhigiyeh and is now called Ruad. The people of Arvad, the Arvadites (ארודי), are mentioned in the genealogy of Noah as sons of Canaan (Gen. 10:18; I Chr. 1:16). They were famous as sailors and warriors and served in the navy and the army of the rich city-state Tyre (Ezek. 27:8, 11). The city existed also in Greek and Roman times, and appears in I Macc. 15:23 under the name Aradus.

Fig. ARV 88.         A. S. KAPELRUD

**ARZA** är′zə [ארצא, gracious(?)] (I Kings 16:9). Elah's chamberlain at Tirzah, in whose house the latter was assassinated, while drunk, by Zimri.

**ARZARETH** är′zə rĕth [ארץ אחרת, another land (*cf.* Deut. 29:28—H 29:27)] (II Esd. 13:45); KJV **ARSARETH** är′sə rĕth. A distant region beyond the Euphrates River where the ten tribes supposedly went after they were taken captive into Assyria, and from which they will return in the last days.

C. T. FRITSCH

**ASA** ā′sə [אסא, he has given, *with hypocoristic* א, *and root* ’wš, to give]. **1.** King of Judah *ca.* 913-873 B.C.; son and successor of Abijah.

The name is perhaps a contraction of אסאאל or אסאיה, "God (or Yahu) has given." The root, however, may be the Arabic *’asā*, "to heal," and the name may mean "healer" (*cf.* Aramaic אסיה, a "medical man"); thus perhaps the name means "God (or Yahu) has healed" and indicates a duty that was laid upon the king.

Asa reigned forty-one years. His mother's name is given as Maacah the daughter of Abishalom (I Kings 15:10). But this was also the name of his grandmother (vs. 2). The easiest correction is arbitrarily to change "his son" (I Kings 15:8; II Chr. 14:1—H 13:23) to "his brother," thus making Asa the younger brother of Abijah. The Chronicler actually gives King Abijah two mothers—Maacah the daughter of Absalom (II Chr. 11:20) and Micaiah (Greek Maacah) the daughter of Uriel of Gibeah (13:2). The probable explanation is that confusion arose in the traditions because of the similarity of the names. We may conjecture that Abijah's mother was Micaiah the daughter of Uriel of Gibeah and that Asa's mother was Maacah the daughter of Absalom. The whole section (II Chr. 11:18-23), which makes Rehoboam's favorite wife Maacah the daughter of Absalom, is an intrusion into the Chronicler's account from another source.

Asa was remembered by later tradition as a loyal supporter of Yahweh. In keeping with this character he instituted a series of reforms to rid the land of heathen deities and practices (I Kings 15:12). The Chronicler reports a more sweeping reformation in two stages, culminating in a great sacrifice in Jerusalem in the third month of the fifteenth year of Asa's reign (II Chr. 14:2-5—H 14:1-4; 15:8-15). These, however, are parallel passages. In addition, Asa removed Maacah from being queen mother because she had made an image for Asherah, the Canaanite goddess of fertility, and worshiped it. Because the climax of these reforms took place in the fifteenth year of Asa's reign, according to the Chronicler, it has been assumed that Maacah the queen mother acted as regent for the young king until this time. This assumption is unnecessary. The general picture is clear. Pagan worship and practices were to be found everywhere, even in court circles. Asa undertook to remove them and so restore the worship of Yahweh to its rightful place in Judah.

The border warfare with Israel continued. It seems clear (II Chr. 16:1) that Asa had been unable to hold the cities previously conquered by Abijah (II Chr. 13:19). According to Kings, war continued throughout the reigns of Asa and Baasha king of Israel (I Kings 15:16). Baasha moved against Judah and fortified Ramah in the territory of Benjamin. His purpose was twofold—to recover Benjamin, and to control the territory N of Jerusalem. It is clear that despite the Chronicler's statements about the fortified cities which Asa built, and the huge army at his command (II Chr. 14:6-8—H 14:5-7), he was unable to deal with the situation from his own resources. In this crisis he took what was left of the temple treasures and the royal treasures (*cf.* I Kings 14:26) and sent them to Ben-hadad king of Syria with the appeal that he should break his league with Baasha king of Israel, make an alliance with Judah, and attack Israel. To this appeal Ben-hadad responded. He invaded N Israel and captured several towns and some territory in Galilee, as well as all Naphtali (I Kings 15:17 ff; II Chr. 16:1 ff). This is the first report of Syria's contact with Israel. Ben-hadad was probably glad of the opportunity to open a trade route to the sea. On hearing of Syria's attack, Baasha withdrew from Ramah and returned to Tirzah. Thereupon Asa took the building material gathered by Baasha and fortified Geba (Gibeah with the Greek) of Benjamin and Mizpah (I Kings 15:22). If Mizpah is Tell en-Nasbeh, this story is confirmed from archaeological sources. The fortifications, which belong to this period, were very strong. Archaeology gives a similar date for the rebuilding of Saul's fortress at Gibeah, *ca.* 900. Asa's purpose was clearly to safeguard the approaches to Jerusalem from the N. Both towns are said to have been built by the conscripted labor of all Judah (I Kings 15:22).

The Chronicler records an undated invasion of Judah by Zerah the Ethiopian (II Chr. 14:9-14—H 14:8-13). The figures he gives are clearly unhistorical. The reference is probably to an attack made by Zerah, the Ethiopian commander of the Egyptian frontier city of Gerar. This attack may have been made on orders from Egypt. It was beaten back, and much booty was taken.

The Chronicler adds a further note in the form of a prophecy of Hanani the seer, condemning Asa for his reliance upon Syria. This enraged Asa so much that he put Hanani in prison and inflicted cruelties on others as well. Toward the end of his reign he contracted dropsy (II Chr. 16:12). The Chronicler saw in this the punishment of God. Asa was buried with royal honors in a tomb which he had built for himself in the city of David.

The unusual position in which the information about Asa's disease is placed, after the mention of the sources, may indicate that he was incapacitated and so was unable to perform his royal duties. In this event a regent may have ruled for him during the last years of his life.

A difficulty arises from the statement of the Chronicler that Asa "put away the abominable idols from all the land of Judah and Benjamin and from the cities which he had taken in the hill country of Ephraim" (II Chr. 15:8). No mention is made in our sources of these N cities captured by Asa. One of two explanations is possible: (a) The reference is to the cities captured by Abijah; (b) in the course of border warfare cities were likely to change hands several times.

The reference to Simeon (II Chr. 15:9) is puzzling. It is possible that since the death of Solomon, S Judah had been under the control of Edom.

**Bibliography.** E. G. Kraeling, *Aram and Israel* (1918), pp. 46 ff. W. F. Albright, "Excavations and Results at Tell el-Fûl (Gibeah of Saul)," *AASOR*, vol. IV (1924). M. Noth, *Die israelitischen Personennamen* (1928), p. 40. F.-M. Abel, *Géographie de la Palestine*, I (1933), 12 ff. A. Alt, "Die Syrische Staatenwelt vor dem Einbruch der Assyrer," *ZDMG* (1934), pp. 233 ff. W. F. Albright, Review of *Géographie de la Palestine*, *JBL*, LVIII (1939), 179 ff; "A Votive Stele Erected by Benhadad I of Damascus to the God Melcarth," *BASOR*, 87 (1942), 23 ff. J. Muilenburg, in C. C. McCown, ed., *Tell en-Nasbeh* (1947), pp. 13-49.

**2.** A Levite, son of Elkanah, ancestor of Obadiah, who lived in one of the villages of the Netophathites (I Chr. 9:16).                    H. B. MacLean

**ASADIAS.** KJV Apoc. form of Hasadiah.

**ASAEL.** KJV Apoc. form of Asiel.

**ASAHEL** ăs′ə hĕl [עשׂהאל, God has made; Ασαηλ]; KJV Apoc. AZAEL ā′zĭ əl. **1.** The brother of Joab and Abishai, sons of Zeruiah, the sister of David; named among the "Thirty" (II Sam. 23:24; I Chr. 2:16; 11:26). After the Battle of Gibeon, when Abner and his forces were routed by Joab, Asahel, "swift of foot as a wild gazelle," pursued relentlessly the fleeing Abner. Having warned Asahel twice to turn aside, but to no avail, Abner mortally transfixed the youth with his spear (II Sam. 2:18-23). This action precipitated a blood feud with the sons of Zeruiah and resulted in their treacherous murder of Abner at Hebron (3:27-30). Asahel was buried in the tomb of his father in Bethlehem (2:32).

The inclusion of Asahel in the list of officers of the monthly militia of David, serving as the commander of a division of 24,000 for the fourth month, is an insoluble difficulty (I Chr. 27:7). Some contend that his name was placed upon this division posthumously to honor him. Others view the list as a

production of the Chronicler and are skeptical of its historicity. However, it is possible that we may have here the prototype of the Davidic militia, organized early in the Judean rule of the king, and that this original list has been brought up to date by the inclusion of Zebadiah, son and successor of Asahel in this command (cf. I Chr. 12).

**2.** One of the Levites who, in company with the princes of Judah and priests, instructed the people in the law in an itinerant teaching mission in the cities of Judah in the third year of Jehoshaphat (II Chr. 17:8).

**3.** One of the subordinate overseers who assisted in the collection of contributions in the house of Yahweh in the time of Hezekiah (II Chr. 31:13).

**4.** The father of Jonathan, who opposed the formation of the Jerusalem commission to consider the cases of the Jews who had married foreign wives in the time of Ezra (Ezra 10:15; I Esd. 9:14).

E. R. Dalglish

**ASAIAH** ə zā′yə [עשׂיה, Y has made]; KJV ASAHIAH ăs′ə hī′ə in II Kings 22. **1.** An official ("king's servant") under Josiah; one of the delegation sent to Hulda the prophetess regarding the law book (II Kings 22:12, 14 = II Chr. 34:20).

**2.** One of the "heads of families," or chieftains, in the tribe of Simeon; among those who dispossessed the Meunim (I Chr. 4:36-41).

**3.** Son of Haggiah; chief of the Levitical group called the sons of Merari and thus among those who helped David bring the ark to Jerusalem (I Chr. 6: 30—H 6:15; 15:6, 11).

**4.** The first-born of the Shilonites, as listed among those who returned from the Babylonian captivity (I Chr. 9:5); but a similar list in Neh. 11:5 has the Shilonite named Maaseiah.

F. T. Schumacher

**ASAIAS** ə zā′yəs; KJV ASEAS ə sē′əs. *See* Isshijah.

**ASANA** ăs′ə nə. KJV Apoc. form of Asnah.

**ASAPH** ā′săf [אסף, *perhaps for* (Yahu) has gathered to himself; *in* 3 *below, possibly from some non-Hebrew root* (*see bibliography*)]. **1.** Apparently the father or ancestor of the Joah (4) who was King Hezekiah's recorder (II Kings 18:18, 37; cf. Isa. 36:3, 22). The precise signification of the phrase "son of" is, as often, uncertain; and this Asaph may relate to 2 *below*.

**2.** The eponymous ancestor or founder of one of the three chief families or guilds of Levite temple musicians, the "sons of Asaph" (e.g., I Chr. 25:1-2, 6, 9). Asaph himself, according to the Chronicler, was a Gershonite Levite, son of Berechiah, and, with Heman and Ethan (Jeduthun), was given by King David charge of the "service of song" in the tabernacle (I Chr. 6:39—H 6:24; cf. vss. 31-32—H 16:17). Whether or not Asaph himself was actually a Levite remains unknown, along with other details of his life; but his contemporaneity with David seems not improbable, even though mention of him is confined to the work of the Chronicler (cf. especially II Chr. 29: 30; 35:15; Neh. 12:46). Pss. 50; 73–83 contain ascriptions to Asaph in their titles, perhaps indicating a tradition of his authorship of them, or a style peculiar to them and originated by him, or again, perhaps referring simply to the Asaphite guild or to their hymnal.

In the Chronicler's history of Judah the sons of Asaph participated in nearly every major celebration relating to the temple, both before and after the Exile. Occasionally they are represented as striking the cymbals, but pre-eminently they were singers (I Chr. 15:17, 19; 16:5, 7, 37; II Chr. 5:12; 29:13; 35: 15; Ezra 3:10; Neh. 12:35). In I Esd. 1:15 they are called the "temple singers." Because of their evident importance in the view of the chronicler it has been suggested that he himself was a member of this guild (*see bibliography*), but this remains a conjecture.

Their musical function was referred to in some instances as prophesying (I Chr. 25:1-2), and according to II Chr. 20:14-23 it was one Jahaziel, a "Levite of the sons of Asaph," who, inspired by the divine Spirit, aroused Judah to victory over the Edomite coalition by means of song and praise to God. II Chr. 29:30 speaks, moreover, of "Asaph the seer" (cf. 35:15).

The guild is prominent in the postexilic name lists (I Chr. 9:15; cf. Ezra 2:41; Neh. 7:44; 11:17, 22; I Esd. 5:27, 59).

*See also* CHRONICLES, I AND II; HEMAN; JEDUTHUN; MUSIC; PRIESTS AND LEVITES; PSALMS, BOOK OF.

**Bibliography.** M. Noth, *Die israelitischen Personennamen* (1928), pp. 22, 181-82; R. H. Pfeiffer, *Introduction to the OT* (1948), pp. 621, 623-24, 797; R. A. Bowman, Exegesis of Nehemiah, *IB,* III (1954), 801. On the Asaphite psalms, see especially, besides other Commentaries, A. F. Kirkpatrick, *Psalms* (1902), pp. 427-30.

**3.** Someone mentioned in I Chr. 26:1; some have thought him to be the eponymous ancestor of the musical guild (*see 2 above*), but this is doubtful. Instead of "Asaph," "ABIASAPH" should probably be read, with the LXX (cf. "Ebiasaph" in the parallel in I Chr. 9:19; note Exod. 6:24).

**4.** The "keeper of the king's forest," probably in Lebanon, to whom the Persian king Artaxerxes sent a letter by Nehemiah, ordering in the latter's behalf timber for the construction work in Jerusalem (Neh. 2:8).

**Bibliography.** M. Noth, *Die israelitischen Personnenamen* (1928), pp. 22, 181-82; R. A. Bowman, Exegesis of Nehemiah, *IB,* III (1954), 674-75.                           B. T. DAHLBERG

**ASARAMEL** ə săr′ə mĕl [ἀσαραμέλ (א V La)] (I Macc. 14:28); KJV SARAMEL săr′ə mĕl. A place name according to the Vulg. and KJV-RSV; but it has long been thought to rest upon a corruption of a Hebrew phrase, arising perhaps out of the reluctance of I Maccabees to mention the name of God. Some consider it to represent Jerusalem, others בחבר ישראל, "in the congregation of Israel." The RSV note states: "This word resembles the Hebrew words for *the court of the people of God* or *the prince of the people of God.*" If the former, it would be חצר עם אל—i.e., the great court of the temple (lit., the "court of the people of God"). If the latter, it would be שר עם אל, "prince of the people of God." This would make it, not a place name, but an honorific title. Simon the high priest would thus be

referred to as "leader of the people of God" (cf. I Macc. 14:47; 15:1).                           J. C. SWAIM

**ASAREL** ăs′ə rĕl [אשראל] (I Chr. 4:16); KJV ASAREEL ə sâr′ĭ əl. One of four sons of Jehallelel in the genealogy of Judah. The LXX has ισεραηλ = Israel (אשראל).

**ASARELAH.** KJV form of ASHARELAH.

**ASCALON.** KJV Apoc. form of ASHKELON.

**ASCENSION** [עלה; ἀναβαίνειν, *also* ἀναλαμβάνεσθαι, ἐπαίρεσθαι, πορεύεσθαι (Acts 1); ὑπάγειν, ἀφιέναι (John); εἰσέρχεσθαι, διέρχεσθαι (Hebrews); ἁρπάξεσθαι (Rev. 12:5); χωρεῖν (Ign. Magn. 7:2)]. A voyage from the earth to heaven above; Christ's exaltation (following upon his humiliation), on which the transcendence of Christian existence is based.

**1. In the religious environment.** A divinity's ascension is a widespread mythological motif (e.g., Isa. 14:12-14). The ascension of an OT dignitary was an increasingly popular and detailed motif in Judaism: Enoch (Gen. 5:24; Jub. 4:23; Ecclus. 44:16; 49:14; Wisd. Sol. 4:10-11; I Enoch 39:3 ff; 70-71; II Enoch; Heb. 11:5; I Clem. 9:3); Elijah (II Kings 2:1-12; I Macc. 2:58; I Enoch 89:52; 93:8; Ecclus. 48:9; [Mark 9:2-8 and parallels; Rev. 11:3-12]); Levi (Test. Levi 2-5); Baruch (II Bar. 13:3; 25:1; 46:7; 76; III Baruch); Ezra (IV Ezra 14:9, 49); Moses (Jos. Antiq. IV.viii.49; Assumption of Moses [Mark 9:2-8 and parallels; Rev. 11:3-12; Jude 9]; Clement of Alexandria, Strom. VI.15); Zephaniah (Apocalypse of Zephaniah, in Clement of Alexandria, Strom. V.11); Abraham (Apocal. Abraham 15-29); Isaiah (Ascension of Isa. 6-11); Adam (Life of Adam and Eve 25-29); and even Raphael (Tob. 12:16-20). This tradition merged with that of the soul's ascent in ecstasy (see II Cor. 12:2-4) or at death, which developed in the Zoroastrian Avesta, Mithraism, Mandaeism, and Gnosticism into a detailed voyage (of Jesus: Ascension of Isa. 10-11) through the three or seven heavenly spheres with their gates, hostile spirits, and other obstacles (echoed in Eph. 2:14), to be passed by means of esoteric knowledge (e.g., Irenaeus I.xxi.5), passwords (e.g., Irenaeus I.xxiv.5-6), and the aid of friendly spirits (Jesus' aid: Acts of John 114; Acts of Thomas 148; Acts of Philip 144). Syncretistic theology developed the pattern of descent from heaven and ascent to heaven for describing the Gnostic "Redeemer," as well as the "divine men" of the Hellenistic age, such as Mani, Simon Magus, Apollonius of Tyana, and the Roman Caesar. Justin (Apol. I.54; Dial. 69) lists Dionysus, Bellerophon, Perseus, Heracles, all as mimicking Jesus.

**2. In the NT. *a. The meaning.*** When the earliest Christology identified Jesus with the Son of man, expected shortly from heaven, the theological necessity of the Ascension was apparent (see, e.g., Luke 22:69; Acts 7:56; Euseb. II.xxiii.13). This orientation can still be sensed when the ascension is for the purpose of installation in an office (Acts 2:36; 5:31; Phil. 2:9; etc.), or is associated with the title "Son of man" (John 3:13-14, etc.; cf. Mark 8:31, etc.), or with the Parousia (Luke 19:11 ff; Acts 1:11; 3:21; see also Phil. 3:20; Col. 3:1-4; I Thess. 1:10). Thus the Son of man's functions of dominion, glory, a

kingdom, the subservience of all (Dan. 7:14), amplified by Ps. 8 of the Son of man (Eph. 1:22; Heb.
2:6-9; etc.), Ps. 110 of the enthroned Lord (Mark
14:62; Acts 2:34-35; Eph. 1:20; Col. 3:1; Heb. 1:3,
13; etc.), and Ps. 2 of the adopted Son (Acts 13:33;
Heb. 1:5; 5:5; Rev. 2:26-27; 12:5; etc.), pointed the
direction in which the Ascension's significance (and
terminology) grew. For as these functions were
progressively transferred from the future (I Cor.
15:25-27; Heb. 10:13; cf. Matt. 19:28; etc.) to the
present, the Ascension became Jesus' decisive subjugation of and revelation to the spirit world controlling the cosmos, at the culminating climax of
confessional formulations (Eph. 1:21-23; Phil. 2:9-11;
Col. 1:18*b*-20; 2:15; I Tim. 3:16; I Pet. 3:22; Ign.
Eph. 19; *see* DESCENT INTO HADES § 2*b*). Hebrews
builds upon this form of the confession (1:3; cf. 5:7-
10), supported by the ascension psalms—2, 8, 110
(see Heb. 1–2; 5:5-6; 8:1)—and the cultic overtones
of "ascend," to present a theology centering in the
"great high priest who has passed through the
heavens" (4:14; see also Rom. 8:34; I John 2:1-2).

The Ascension becomes the key to all the spiritual
gifts—i.e., the religious experience—of the church,
by a shifting of the reference of the Pentecost psalm
(68:19) from Moses to Christ (Acts 2:33; Eph. 4:8 ff),
with the help of Ps. 110:1 (Acts 2:33-36). This
theme is further developed in John. Thus the Ascension tends to replace the Parousia as the beginning
of Christ's kingdom (Matt. 13:41; Luke 23:42-43;
Col. 1:13; Heb. 1:8), the doctrinal basis for the
church (Ephesians) and the Christian mission (Matt.
28:18-20), the focus of ethical aspiration (Col. 3:
1 ff), and the key to the believer's final destiny
(John 14:1 ff; Heb. 6:20; 12:2; the Good Shepherd).
When the Ascension is cast in the Hellenistic pattern
of descent and ascent, it becomes the form in which
Jesus finds a place within Gnostic systems, but also
a central doctrine of anti-Gnostic polemic from
Colossians on, and provides a central Johannine
category for the Christian message: In the humiliated Christ's transcendence over the world resides
man's hope of rising to true selfhood.

The perversion of the true Christian meaning of
the Ascension by the heretics in Paul's congregations
(especially Corinth and Philippi), as well as by subsequent Gnosticism, focuses attention upon the need
to clarify the meaning of the Ascension also for our
day. They took Christ's enthronement at his ascension for the finality of God's victory, and hence were
naïvely ignorant of, or presumptuously ignored, the
persisting ambiguities of human existence and the
all-embracing extent of God's ultimate claim upon
his creation, insights which had been kept alive by
the futuristic eschatology they rejected in favor of
the finality of Christ's work at the Ascension. Since
baptism meant union with Christ, they interpreted
their dying with Christ as the end of their finitude
—i.e., as becoming immortal (deification)—and
hence they identified their present status as that of
having risen and ascended with Christ; they assumed
they had moved beyond the historicity of human
existence and were above suffering and service. Over
against this false doctrine of the Ascension, Paul
worked out his theology: His retention of a futuristic
eschatology is not simply an inconsistent vestige of

mythology or of Jewish thinking, but rather a position which in his situation was necessary to preserve
a valid understanding of man's situation in the world
and of God's total claim on the cosmos. Within this
life, our union with Christ identifies us with his position in this life: on the way to the Cross. This is not
to deny our identification with the Christ who has
ascended, but rather to interpret correctly his ascension: His enthronement in heaven as Lord of the
cosmos means that human existence is ultimately
under the control of the Humiliated, the Crucified,
whose obedience is the key to meaningful existence.
Faith in Christ's ascension thus means not only that
his service and suffering were his freedom and his
victory, but that in his "obedience unto death" the
path of transcendence within service and suffering is
revealed as a reality for us and made accessible to
us as authentic existence. It is this which comes to
expression in Paul's position that our ascension has
not already happened so as to remove us from historical involvement, but rather that our future ascension does await us, thus giving transcendent meaning
to that involvement (Phil. 3).

***b. The story.*** The description of the Ascension is
for the NT of secondary importance to its theological
meaning. It is rarely narrated explicitly: only Acts
1:9-11 in the NT; in the Apocalypse of Peter the
transfiguration narrative becomes the Ascension; in
the Letter of James (Jung Codex) Jesus ascends in a
chariot of spirit, waving to his disciples. When opinions on such details as place (Luke 24:50: Bethany;
Acts 1:12: Mount Olivet) or time are suggested, they
often vary: at the time of the Crucifixion (perhaps in
kerygmatic usage of ὑψοῦν, the flesh-Spirit contrast,
and the suffering-glory combination; see also Luke
23:43, 46; Gospel of Peter V.19; Acts of John 102);
at the Resurrection (evident from the association or
interchangeability of resurrection and ascension terminology, and from presentations of appearances as
from the beyond; see also Col. 3:1; Eph. 1:20; Rom.
8:34; Gospel of Peter X); between appearances
(Matt. 28:18; John 20:22); at the end of the appearances on Easter Sunday (Luke 24:51; Epistola Apostolorum 62); on the eighth day—i.e., (Easter) Sunday
(Barn. 15.9); after many days (Acts 13:31); after 40
days (Acts 1:3; next Tert. Apol. 21); after 50 days
(in early Syrian liturgical observance); after 545 days
(Ascension of Isa. 9.16), or 550 days (Letter of
James, Jung Codex)—i.e., eighteen months (the Val-
entinians and Ophites: Irenaeus I.iii.2; I.xxx.14);
after 12 years (Pistis Sophia; II Book of Jeu 44).

The particular crystallization of the ascension
motif in Luke-Acts is primarily a reflection of theological considerations: The "ascent" is the climax of
the kerygma about Jesus (Luke 9:51; Acts 1:22; see
also Luke 19:12; 24:26), so that the gospel was
brought to an end here (Acts 1:2), for even the
shorter reading of Luke 24:51 alludes to the Ascension, and its conjectured elimination from Acts 1:2
multiplies, rather than reduces, difficulties. Acts opens
with the Ascension (1:9-11) as involved in the definition of the apostle (1:22) and prerequisite to Pentecost (2:33; 1:4-8). Since the resurrected Jesus was
available on earth for a period of time (Acts 1:3; 10:
40-41; 13:31), a specific terminal date was needed.
Since the period could not exceed fifty days, the

Ascension being prerequisite to the gift of the Spirit at "Pentecost"—i.e., the "fiftieth" (day after Passover)—the biblical number forty was chosen, just as in the cases of the ascensions of Ezra (IV Ezra 14:23, 49), Baruch (II Bar. 76), and Abraham (Apocalypse of Abraham 9, 12). The two white-robed men are familiar from resurrection narratives (Luke 24:4; John 20:12; Gospel of Peter IX–X; see also Luke 9:30), and the cloud of an epiphany is typical at ascensions (e.g., Luke 9:34; I Thess. 4:17; Rev. 11:12). Beholding Jesus ascend may reflect II Kings 2:9 ff, so as to point to Pentecost as the near goal of hope (Acts 1:4-5, 8) rather than to the Parousia (Acts 1:6-7; see also 3:21), whose final coming, however, is assured graphically by the form of the Ascension (1:11; e.g., on the Mount of Olives: Zech. 14:4; on a cloud: Luke 21:27; Rev. 1:7; etc.).

Bibliography. W. Bousset, "Die Himmelsreise der Seele," *ARW*, IV (1901), 136-69, 229-73. G. Wetter, "Der Gottessohn wird zum Himmel auffahren," *"Der Sohn Gottes"* (1916), pp. 101-13. R. Holland, "Zur Typik der Himmelfahrt," *ARW*, XXIII (1925), 207-20. G. Bertram, "Die Himmelfahrt Jesu vom Kreuz aus und der Glaube an seine Auferstehung," *Festgabe für Adolf Deissmann* (1927), pp. 187-217; see also *ZAW*, LXVIII (1956), 57-71. A. Fridrichsen, "Die Himmelfahrt bei Lukas," *ThBl*, VI (1927), 337-41. M. S. Enslin, "The Ascension Story," *JBL*, XLVII (1928), 60-73. H. Schlier, *Christus und die Kirche im Epheserbrief* (1930). K. Lake, "The Ascension," *The Beginnings of Christianity*, V (1933), 16-22. H. Jonas, "Der Aufstieg nach dem Tode," *Gnosis und spätantiker Geist*, I (1934), 205-10. P. Benoit, O. P., "L'ascension," *RB*, LVI (1949), 161-203. K. Galling, "Durch die Himmel hindurchgeschritten (Heb. 4:14)," *ZNW*, XXXIII (1950-51), 263-64. H. Bietenhard, "Der zum Throne Gottes erhöhte Christus," *Die himmlische Welt im Urchristentum und Spätjudentum* (1951), pp. 63-71. J. G. Davies, *He Ascended into Heaven* (1958).

Liturgical and iconographic: G. Kretschmar, "Himmelfahrt und Pfingsten," *ZKG*, LXVI (1954-55), 209-53.

Relation to the Copernican revolution: A. Oepke, "Unser Glaube an die Himmelfahrt Christi," *Luthertum*, XLIX (1938), 161-86.

Textual problems: J. H. Ropes, in *The Beginnings of Christianity*, III (1926), 256-61; K. Lake, in V (1933), 1-4. D. Plooij, "The Ascension in the 'Western' Textual Tradition," *Mededeelingen der Koninklijke Akademie van Wetenschappen, Afdeeling Letterkunde*, Deel 67, Serie A, no. 2 (1929), pp. 39-58. J. M. Creed, "The Text and Interpretation of Acts 1:1-2," *JTS*, XXXV (1934), 176-82. P. H. Menoud, "Remarques sur les textes de l'ascension dans Luc-Actes," *Neutestamentliche Studien für Rudolf Bultmann* (1954), pp. 148-56.

Complete résumé of scholarship: V. Larrañaga, S. J., *L'Ascension de Notre-Seigneur dans le NT* (1938).

J. M. ROBINSON

**ASCENSION OF ISAIAH.** See ISAIAH, ASCENSION OF.

**ASCENT, DESCENT** [מַעֲלָה, LXX ἀνάβασις, place of going up; מוֹרָד, LXX-NT κατάβασις, place of going down]. An ascending road or stairway; specifically, a mountain pass.

The terms "ascent" and "descent" apply in general to any roadway by which one goes up or down, the choice of words depending on the position of the observer or the direction in which he was going. Thus David left Jerusalem by the "ascent of the Mount of Olives" (II Sam. 15:30), and Jesus came toward the city by the "descent" of the same mountain (Luke 19:37). A stairway on the wall of Jerusalem (Neh. 12:37), the road to the armory within the city (Neh. 3:19), and the slope up to the royal tombs (II Chr. 32:33) are called "ascents." See STAIR.

The principal Israelite occupation of Palestine was in the rugged mountains W of the Jordan, and the passes by which the roads entered the mountains were of great economic, geographic, and military importance. They were usually called "ascents," since they were thought of as entrances to the mountain range. On the W side of the highlands two such passes are named: the Ascent of Beth-horon, near Upper Beth-horon, where Joshua pursued a coalition of Amorite kings (Josh. 10:10-11), and the Ascent of Gur in the mountains of Samaria, where Jehu killed Ahaziah (II Kings 9:27). The rift valley of the JORDAN, which bounds these highlands on the E, has steep cliffs on either side through which travel is possible only along secondary rifts that run into the valley roughly at right angles. Three of these rifts running into the Judean mountains are called "ascents." The Ascent of Akrabbim (Scorpions), beginning in the Wadi Arabah *ca.* sixteen miles S of the Dead Sea, slopes rather gradually upward in a northwesterly direction (Num. 34:4; Josh. 15:3; Judg. 1:36). From a point seven miles N of En-gedi the Ascent of Ziz leads westward through the high cliffs along the Dead Sea (II Chr. 20:16). Still farther N the Ascent of Adummim (Blood), so called because of the patches of red soil still to be seen near the Inn of the Good Samaritan, goes up from Jericho toward Jerusalem; it formed part of the N boundary of Judah (Josh. 15:7; 18:17). Named passes leading from the E side of the Jordan Valley are the Ascent of Luhith (Isa. 15:5; Jer. 48:5) and the Descent of Horonaim (Jer. 48:5), both in Moab, and the Ascent of Heres in Gilead (Judg. 8:13). A pass at Shebarim near Ai was the scene of one of Joshua's victories (Josh. 7:5), and in Josh. 8:14 the Hebrew text is usually emended to read "the descent toward the Arabah" (MT מוֹעֵד, "appointed time").

L. E. TOOMBS

**ASCENT OF THE CORNER.** See CORNER, ASCENT OF THE.

**ASCENTS, SONG OF** [שִׁיר הַמַּעֲלוֹת]; KJV DEGREES, SONG OF. The title of the psalms forming the group 120–34 incorporated in the canonical psalter (*see* PSALMS, BOOK OF). The meaning of this title has not yet been explained beyond doubt. Probably they are songs for the procession of the New Year's Festival "ascending" to the temple or for the pilgrims "ascending" to Jerusalem.

Bibliography. S. Mowinckel, *Psalmenstudien*, IV (1923), 3-4; G. Hylmö, *De s.k. Vallfartssångerna i Psaltaren* (1925); J. Liebreich, "The Songs of Ascents and the Priestly Blessing," *JBL*, 74 (1955), 33-36; H. D. Preuss, "Die Psalmenüberschriften in Targum und Midrasch," *ZAW*, 71 (1959), 44-53.

J. HEMPEL

**ASEAS** ə sē'əs. KJV Apoc. form of ISSHIJAH.

**ASEBEBIA.** KJV Apoc. form of SHEREBIAH.

**ASEBIA.** KJV Apoc. form of HASHABIAH.

**ASENATH** ăs'ə năth [אָסְנַת; Egyp. *ns-nt or 'ws-n-n(j)t*, belonging to *or* the servant of (the goddess)

Neith]. Daughter of POTIPHERA priest of On. The pharaoh gave her to JOSEPH SON OF JACOB as a wife, and she became the mother of Ephraim and Manasseh (Gen. 41:45, 50-52; 46:20). Later Jewish legends attempted to explain the apparent heathen origin of Joseph's wife. In one recension she is pictured as a Hebrew (daughter of Shechem and Dinah) who was adopted by Potiphera; elsewhere it is claimed that although she was Egyptian, she was converted to Yahwism by Joseph.

*Bibliography.* W. Spiegelberg, *Ägyptologische Randglossen zum AT* (1904), pp. 18-19; on the name; L. Ginzberg, *Legends of the Jews,* II (1910), 38, 170-78; on the legends. J. F. Ross

**ASER** ā'sər. KJV translation of 'Ασήρ in Tob. 1:2; Luke 2:36; Rev. 7:6. Whether the author of Tobit intended "HAZOR" (cf. II Kings 15:29) and misspelled the Greek word, or meant "Asher" in the mistaken opinion that the tribe of Asher was involved in the deportation, cannot be determined. G. W. VAN BEEK

**ASERER** ăs'ə rər. KJV Apoc. form of SISERA.

**ASH.** KJV translation of אֹרֶן (*'ōren*) in Isa. 44:14 (RSV CEDAR). In a few MSS the word "cedar" (אֶרֶז, *'erez*) appears in this passage. There is no evidence to support the translation "ash" (*Fraxinus* L.). *See* PINE. J. C. TREVER

**ASHAMED.** *See* SHAME.

**ASHAN** ā'shən [עָשָׁן, smoke]. Alternately: BOR-ASHAN bôr— [בּוֹר עָשָׁן, cistern *or* well of Ashan]; KJV CHORASHAN kôr—(*from a typographical error in a printed Hebrew text;* I Sam. 30:30). A city in the Shephelah originally assigned to Simeon (Josh. 19:7; I Chr. 4:32); designated a Levitical city of Judah in David's administrative reorganization (Josh. 21:16, where "Ain" should be read "Ashan" with the LXX B; cf. I Chr. 6:59—H 6:44); and later evidently a part of the administrative district of Hormah (Josh. 15:32, where, instead of vs. 42, comparison with the above lists indicates it must have appeared originally). It is mentioned as one of the places where David roamed with his men during his outlaw period (I Sam. 30:30). Ashan is identified with Khirbet 'Asan, *ca.* 1½ miles NW of Beer-sheba. V. R. GOLD

**ASHARELAH** ăsh'ə rē'lə [אֲשַׂרְאֵלָה *or* אֲשַׂרְאֵלָה]; KJV ASARELAH ăs'ə rē'lə. One of the sons of ASAPH who prophesied with musical instruments in the temple under the direction of the king (I Chr. 25:2). Another, and perhaps preferred, tradition of the MT reads "Asarelah." He is called Jesharelah in vs. 14, where the singers cast lots for their duties. F. T. SCHUMACHER

**ASHBEA** ăsh'bĭ ə [אַשְׁבֵּעַ]. KJV proper name applied to an otherwise unknown family of linen workers (I Chr. 4:21). The RSV is probably correct in translating the word as referring to their place of residence, BETH-ASHBEA, an otherwise unknown town, presumably in the Shephelah. F. T. SCHUMACHER

**ASHBEL** ăsh'bĕl [אַשְׁבֵּל, having a long upper lip]; ASHBELITES —bə līts [אַשְׁבֵּלִי]. Son of Benjamin, listed as either the second or the third son; ancestor of the family of the Ashbelites (Gen. 46:21; Num. 26:38; I Chr. 8:1). Ashbel would appear consistently as the third son of Benjamin if "BECHER," now misplaced in Num. 26:35 and apparently supplanted by בְּכֹרוֹ, "his first-born," in I Chr. 8:1, were inserted into the Benjaminite genealogies in Num. 26; I Chr. 8.

*Bibliography.* M. Noth, *Die israelitischen Personennamen* (1928), p. 227. R. F. JOHNSON

**ASHCHENAZ.** KJV form of ASHKENAZ in I Chr. 1:6; Jer. 51:27.

*****ASHDOD** ăsh'dŏd [אַשְׁדּוֹד, fortress(?); Akkad. *Asdudu*]; Apoc. and NT form AZOTUS ə zō'təs [Ἄζωτος]; ASHDODITES —īts; KJV once ASH-DOTHITES ăsh'dŏth īts (Josh. 13:3). One of the five principal cities (pentapolis) of the Philistines (Josh. 13:3), the northernmost of the three on or near the coast. It lay inland *ca.* three miles, halfway between Gaza and Joppa, *ca.* ten miles N of Ashkelon.

Like its sister cities, it was reputed to be very old, having once been inhabited by the primitive Anakim (Josh. 11:22; *see* ANAK). It was assigned, along with surrounding territory, to the tribe of Judah (Josh. 15:46-47), but remained in the hands of the Philistines (Josh. 13:1-3). When the Philistines, warring with Israel, captured the Ark (*see* ARK OF THE COVENANT), they took the sacred object to the temple of their god DAGON in Ashdod; but ill omens ensued, and the Ark was hurried on to Gath (I Sam. 5:1-8; 6:17).

At the height of Judah's power in the time of Uzziah (*ca.* 783-742), Ashdod and the surrounding territory under its control were conquered by the Judean king (II Chr. 26:6). However, the city and its territory were soon again independent, to the extent of revolting against Sargon II shortly before 711. Sargon ordered Azuri, the local king, deposed and a younger brother, Ahimiti, installed in his place. Still the "Hittites" (as Sargon called those opposed to him; cf. Gen. 27:46) in the city continued their revolt under Iamani (a Greek or Cypriote, judging by his name; there seems to have been a mixed population by this time). Sargon was enraged, made a special campaign, conquering Ashdod, Gath, and "Asdudimmu" (Ashdod-by-the-Sea, a separate place on the seacoast, which later became more important than the parent city). Iamani fled to Ethiopia, whence he was extradited to Assyria, and the territory that had revolted was made an Assyrian province (cf. Amos 1:8; 3:9 should read "Assyria" with RSV). Isaiah warned Judah against becoming involved in this rebellion, pointing out that the Ethiopian rulers of Egypt would instigate plots but offer no real help (Isa. 20:1-6; some also connect Zech. 9:6 with these events).

In 701 Ashdod was still loyal to Assyria; it paid its tribute to Sennacherib and in return received some of Judah's territory. At that time the king was named Mitinti (not to be confused with earlier and later kings of Ashkelon by the same name). Both

Esarhaddon (680-669) and Ashurbanipal (668-633) collected tribute from Ahimilki, king of Ashdod, presumably Mitinti's successor, as they advanced against Egypt (671 and 667). After this arose a new and stronger king in Egypt, Psamtik I (663-610), who, according to Herodotus (II.157), took Ashdod after a siege of twenty-nine years, said by some to be the longest siege in history. The Scythians also probably took their toll at this time (Zeph. 2:4; Jer. 25:20—note the word "remnant"; Herod. I.105). Later, perhaps because of lingering Egyptian influence, the city was involved in rebellion against the Chaldeans, probably at the time of the fall of Jerusalem (587); for an inscription from the later years of Nebuchadnezzar mentions the king of Ashdod, along with many similar rulers, as a prisoner at the Chaldean court.

In spite of these vicissitudes, Ashdod seems to have been the strongest of the Philistine cities in the Persian period, controlling a considerable amount of territory and presenting a real threat to the Jews through cultural contacts (Neh. 4:7; 13:23-24; Zech. 9:6[?]; Jth. 2:28). During Maccabean times it was devastated successively by Judas (I Macc. 4:15; 5:68), Jonathan (after a great battle nearby: I Macc. 10:77-85; 11:4), and John Hyrcanus (I Macc. 16:10). In I Macc. 14:34 Gazara (Gezer) is located on the borders of Azotus (Ashdod), but the places are more than fifteen air miles apart, and the reference may be to the larger Ashdod territory as in the Persian period (cf. Neh. 13:23-24). During the time of Alexander Jannaeus it was under Jewish control (Jos. Antiq. XIII.xv.4). Pompey freed it (63 B.C.), making it a part of the province of Syria (Jos. Antiq. XIV. iv.4; War I.vii.7).

Under Gabinius (governor 57-55 B.C.), Ashdod, now called Azotus, was rebuilt and repopulated as a Roman town (Jos. Antiq. XIV.v.3; War I.viii.4). Herod controlled it, bequeathing it to his sister Salome (Jos. Antiq. XVII.viii.1; War II.vi.3). Ca. A.D. 38 Philip the Evangelist, after baptizing the Ethiopian eunuch near Gaza, passed through Azotus on his way to Caesarea, preaching as he went. Thus many in the former Philistine cities heard the gospel for the first time (Acts 8:40). During the revolt against the Romans of 66-70, there was apparently enough Jewish influence in Azotus (perhaps from the time of Herod) to make it necessary for Vespasian to march against the city and leave a garrison there (Jos. War IV.iii.2). Eusebius mentions it as still being an important town at the beginning of the fourth century. It had Christian bishops from the fourth to the sixth centuries. During the Middle Ages it declined, and remains today only a small village.

No significant archaeological work has been undertaken at the site, now called Esdud. The site of the former seaport town, three miles away, is now called Minet el-Qal'a.

*Bibliography.* E. Klostermann, *Das Onomastikon der biblischen Ortsnamen,* Die gr. chr. Schriftsteller d. erst. drei Jahrhunderte, Eusebius Werke, III, 1 (1904), 20, 22, F.-M. Abel, *Géographie de la Palestine,* II (1938), 253-54; A. Malamat, "The Historical Setting of Two Biblical Prophecies on the Nations," *IEJ,* I (1950-51), 149-59; J. Kaplan, "Ashdod," *IEJ,* V (1955), 118; J. B. Pritchard, *ANET* (2nd ed., 1955), pp. 284, 286-88, 291, 294, 308.                 W. F. STINESPRING

**ASHDOTH-PISGAH** ăsh'dŏth pĭz'gə. KJV transliteration of אשדות הפסגה, אשדת הפסגה, in Deut. 3: 17; 4:49; Josh. 12:3; 13:20. In Deut. 4:19 the KJV translates "springs of Pisgah." The reference is to the slopes of Mount Pisgah. *See* PISGAH.

**ASHER** ăsh'ər [אשר, *from* to be a bearer of salvation; *an abbreviated form, actually the name of a god of fortune* (?); NT 'Ασήρ]; KJV NT ASER ā'sər. ASHERITE —ə rīt [אשרי]. The eighth son of Jacob and the eponymous ancestor of one of the twelve tribes. He was born of Leah's personal maid Zilpah (Gen. 30:12 ff) and was the younger full brother of Gad—therefore, always mentioned after him in the lists of descendants (Gen. 35:26; 46:17; Exod. 1:4; I Chr. 2:2).

The connection with the Leah group of tribes is clear; dwelling upon the W slopes of the Galilean highland (Josh. 19:24-31), the tribe of Asher had Zebulun and Naphtali as neighbors to the E. Because of its location it had close contact with the seacoast—i.e., with the maritime state of Tyre. This explains its half-caste nature. How little it was respected among the true Israelites is shown also by the references in the oldest literature. The passage in the Blessing of Moses (Deut. 33:24-25) starts with a special benediction:

> Blessed above sons be Asher;
> let him be the favorite of his brothers.

In reality, Asher was, apparently, just as little loved as its territory was safe from foreign influences, which is the reason the wish is also expressed:

> Your bars shall be iron and bronze.

The passage bears witness to the fertility of the territory of Asher:

> Let him dip [he dips] his foot in oil.

The short passage in the Blessing of Jacob alludes to the same thing:

> Asher's food shall [is] be rich,
> and he shall yield [yields] royal dainties
> (Gen. 49:20).

Since there is no reason to go into the period of the Israelite kings for the origin of the passage, the kings mentioned are certainly Canaanite-Phoenician city kings of the coastal plain, perhaps also of the Plain of Jezreel. It is not surprising that the Song of Deborah criticizes Asher for sitting still at the seacoast (Judg. 5:17) instead of taking part in the struggle for freedom against the coalition of the Canaanite kings. Asher was probably deterred by consideration for its customers, after the dream of possessing their cities had long since vanished in thin air (1:31 ff). In other cases, to be sure, Asher promptly fulfilled its obligation as a member of the Israelite amphictyony, as in the expulsion of the Midianites from the Plain of Jezreel by Gideon (6:35; 7:23). Later, too, as a result of its position apart, the tribe of Asher did not play a significant role. According to II Sam. 2:9 (read "Asherites"), Asher was the only one of the Galilean tribes to recognize the kingship of Ishbaal (Ish-bosheth) immediately. In I Kings 4:16 its territory is named as one of the districts of Solomon; to it belonged the district of Cabul—which in all probability was itself already strongly populated by Canaanites—with the twenty cities which Solomon relinquished to Hiram of Tyre as payment for timber deliveries (I Kings 9:10-14). In II Chr. 30:10, Asher probably serves merely as an example (cf. vs. 18) of the inhabitants of the former N kingdom who complied with Hezekiah's invitation to come to the celebration of the Passover in Jerusalem; aside from this the story is not historical.

The later literature mentions Asher otherwise only in lists and in listlike material. In the Priestly Code, as a rule, Asher appears separated from Gad, but between the other two half-caste tribes, Dan and Naphtali, at the close of the enumeration (Num. 1: 40 ff; 2:27; 7:72; 10:26; 13:13; 26:44-47); only in the list of the heads of tribes is Gad still included (Num. 1:14) in this group, but as the second. In the commission to divide the land, Asher is between Issachar and Naphtali (34:27). In Deut. 27:13, Asher, along with Gad (in the same order as in Gen. 30!), belongs to those who are to pronounce the curse on Mount Ebal. In the case of the Levite cities Asher is again classified, from a geographical point of view, in the N group, between Issachar and Naphtali (Josh. 21:6, 30-31=I Chr. 6:62, 74-75—H 6:47, 59-60). In Ezek. 48:34 the second W gate, directly next to Gad's (in the same order as in Gen. 30; Deut. 27:13), is named for Asher. One of the lists in Chronicles enumerates Asher last in the twelve-tribe series W of the Jordan (I Chr. 12:36); the other one (27:16 ff) strangely does not mention Asher (or Gad either). The genealogy in I Chr. 7:30-40, likewise at the end of the series of twelve, supplements Gen. 46:17 with material of unknown origin. The NT names Asher after Gad in the list of the sealed (Rev. 7:6) and ascribes the prophetess Anna to the tribe of Asher (Luke 2:36).

For the territory of Asher, *see* TRIBES, TERRITORIES OF, § 7.

*Bibliography.* In addition to the pertinent sections in general works on the history of Israel, see: M. Noth, *Die israelitischen Personennamen* (1928).

*See also* the bibliography under TRIBES, TERRITORIES OF.

K. ELLIGER

**ASHERAH** ə shĭr'ə [אשרה, אשירה]; ASHERIM —ĭm [*masculine plural;* אשרים (KJV GROVES)]; ASHEROTH —ŏth [*feminine plural;* אשרות (KJV GROVES)]. A Semitic goddess, and the cult object by which she was represented. *See also* CANAAN.

**1. The term.** The variety of words used in the versions to translate the Hebrew אשרה indicates an uncertainty concerning its meaning, except that it was associated in some way with pagan worship. In each of the forty occurrences of אשרה (including forms singular, plural, and with suffixes) the LXX translates "groves" (ἄλσος, ἄλση), except in two instances (Isa. 17:8; 27:9) where it has δενδρα, "tree," and two others (II Chr. 15:16; 24:18) where it has "Astarte" ('Αστάρτη, 'Αστάρταῖς, a confusion of אשרה with עשתרות, Ashtaroth). The Vulg. follows the LXX by using "wood" or "grove" (*lucus, nemus*) and the proper name Ashtaroth. The KJV is based on these readings and is in error, as can be observed from the context of passages which refer to the Asherah as having been worshiped with Baal (Judg.

3:7) and having been removed from the Jerusalem temple (II Kings 23:6). It is possible that the LXX has not been correctly interpreted and that ἄλσος was used, not to refer to a grove of trees, but merely to indicate a sacred area or object.

The Peshitta translates אשרה as the name of a goddess, but in most instances uses such words as *deḥlethâ* ("object of reverence, fearful thing"), *ḥešlâthâ* ("molten images"), *ṣalmê* ("image"), and *pethkᵉrê* ("idols"). In Deut. 16:21; Mic. 5:14—H 5:13, where the Peshitta has *štlt'* ("trees"), the translators may have been misled by the Hebrew verbs נטע ("to plant") and נתש ("to root out"), which could apply to an image as well as to a tree.

The Targ. follows the practice of merely transliterating the Hebrew word. The authors of the Mishna explained the Asherah as a tree that was worshiped, including grapevines and pomegranate, walnut, myrtle, and willow trees, and therefore, the wood and fruit must not be used ('Or. 1.7-8; Suk. 3.1-3; 'A.Z. 3.7, 9-10; Me'il. 3.8). By the time of the Mishna, the meaning of אשרה in the Hebrew scriptures had been forgotten, although the word could be used of forbidden trees because it had cultic associations and had to do with that which had been condemned in earlier periods.

The English translations vary in their methods of attempting to correct the "groves" of the KJV. Most, with the exception of the RSV, render the proper name as "Asherah" or "Astarte" (the latter would be more appropriate for עשתרות, "Ashtaroth"), and the cult object as "sacred pole." The RSV makes no attempt to distinguish the name of the goddess from the name of the cult object, using "Asherah" for both. In two passages (II Chr. 19:3; 33:3) it uses "Asherahs," an English plural; and elsewhere a Hebrew plural transliteration ("Asheroth," "Asherim") is used.

**2. The goddess.** Early studies either rejected the idea that the Asherah was a goddess or proposed that the word in the Hebrew text was a confusion with "Astarte" (עשתרות). However, with the discovery that the word was used as the name of a goddess, distinct from Astarte, in the Ras Shamra Texts where she figures prominently as the mother-goddess, Athirat ('ṯrt, 'ṯrt ym), it became evident that אשרה was the Hebrew name for an Amorite or Canaanite goddess who was worshiped in various parts of the ancient Near East.

In early Babylonian god lists Ashratum is mentioned as one of the deities, a temple was dedicated to her, and at various times she was named as the consort of Ramaanum or Amurru. In the Tell el-Amarna Tablets her name appears in the name of one of the Amorite princes, Abdi-Ashirta ("Servant of Asherah"). In S Arabia, Athirat was worshiped as the consort of the moon-god. In N Arabia at Tema the Nabateans worshiped a triad of deities which included Salm, Shingala, and Asherah. Although there is some uncertainty concerning translation, it is probable that Asherah also appears in an Aramaean magical text from Arslan Tash in Syria as a goddess who was appealed to by women at the time of childbirth, and in a fragmentary inscription found at Tell Ta'anach (*see* TAANACH), where an oracle of Asherah may have existed in early Canaanite times.

Many details concerning the place of Asherah in the pantheon have been supplied from the Ras Shamra Texts. At ancient Ugarit she was the mother-goddess, consort of El, mother of seventy gods including Baal, who is called *bn 'ṯrt* ("son of Athirat"). Animal sacrifices were offered to her, as to the other deities at Ugarit. The term "holiness" (*qdš*) was applied to her; she has been identified with the nude goddess of Egypt called Qudšu. The designation of the goddess as Athirat Yam suggests that she may also have had some connection with the sea. As mistress (*rbt*), creatress of the gods (*qnyt, 'ilm*), and counselor of the gods, Athirat always appears in a most favorable role in her relations with the other deities of Ugarit. As an important fertility deity of the Phoenicians and Canaanites, she would represent a formidable rival to Yahweh under the sponsorship of the Phoenician princess Jezebel (*see below*).

In the OT it is not always possible to distinguish between references to the Asherah as a goddess and as a cult object. This is true also for the word דגן; the image of Dagon is certainly intended in I Sam. 5:2-4, but in Judg. 16:23-24 it is the god Dagon who grants victory to the Philistines. It is apparent that the Hebrew writer did not always make a distinction between the deity and its image. In a similar way אשרה referred both to the goddess and to the cult object by which she was represented. It has been proposed that the goddess is appealed to in Gen. 30:13, where Leah cried: "With Asherah's help" (באשרי), at the birth of Asher (but see RSV).

According to Judg. 3:7, there was an association of worship between Baal and Asherah. The passage states that the Israelites were evil because they abandoned the Lord and served the Baals and the Asherahs (אשרות). The reference to these deities in the plural may indicate that each locality had its Baal and its Asherah, who were consorts worshiped at the same sanctuary. In the Gideon story (Judg. 6:26-30) the presence of the object called Asherah beside the altar of Baal may be explained by the fact that the people of Ophrah served Baal and Asherah as consorts at one shrine.

The goddess Asherah is intended by the statement that Maacah, mother of Asa, made an abominable image of her (מפלצת לאשרה; I Kings 15:13; II Chr. 15:16). In the time of Elijah there were four hundred prophets of Asherah who ate at Jezebel's table (I Kings 18:19). Manasseh is said to have put a graven image of Asherah (פסל האשרה) in the temple at Jerusalem (II Kings 21:7), and it is probable that in his day there were numerous shrines throughout the land where the goddess was worshiped. Josiah's reformation attempted, among other things, to stamp out the worship of this goddess for whom vessels (כלים; II Kings 23:4) and garments or shrines (בתים; vs. 7) had been made by the women in the Jerusalem temple. It will be noted that in every case where the OT mentions the goddess Asherah it was to speak in condemnation of her or in approval of men like Elijah, Asa, and Josiah, who attempted to destroy her cultus among the Israelites. The very fact that such reforms were required makes it likely that the worship of Asherah was popular in ancient Israel.

**3. The cult object.** The passages cited above contain the OT references to the Asherah as a goddess, but it is probable that in some instances where a cult object is mentioned the Hebrew writers did not distinguish between the numen and the representation of it. The following passages refer to the Asherah as a cult object, as can be judged by the association with images, altars, etc., and by the verbs used to indicate its construction and destruction: Deut. 16:21; Judg. 6:25-26, 28, 30; I Kings 16:33; II Kings 13:6; 17:16; 18:4; 21:3; 23:6, 15. The word appears in a plural form (אשרים, with and without suffixes) in Exod. 34:13; Deut. 7:5; 12:3; I Kings 14:15, 23; II Kings 17:10; 23:14; II Chr. 14:3—H 14:2; 17:6; 19:3; 24:18; 31:1; 33:3, 19; 34:3-4, 7; Isa. 17:8; 27:9; Jer. 17:2; Mic. 5:14.

The form of the cult object and its use in the worship of Asherah are not described in the OT. An investigation of claims that pieces of an Asherah had been found at Qatna and Megiddo reveals that only charred pieces of wood were discovered which as well might be identified as parts of wooden beams. No object has been found thus far in any excavation which could be called with certainty an Asherah. Since the OT shows it to have been constructed of wood, this is not surprising; only in rare instances have wooden objects in ancient Palestinian temples escaped decay.

The following symbols which are represented in Semitic art have been proposed by various scholars as illustrating the Asherah: a plain pole, a carved pole, a staff, a triangle on a staff, a cross, a double axe, a tree, a tree stump, a headdress for priests, and a wooden image. In each case the identification is made on an assumption concerning the meaning of אשרה in the Hebrew text. Several of the symbols might as well be identified the massebah (*see* PILLAR).

From a study of the verbs used in connection with the Asherah it is clear that it was an object which could be both constructed and destroyed by man; it was not a tree, but was made of wood or contained wood, and could be burned; it was an object that stood upright rather than lying flat, and it was employed in the worship of the goddess by the same name. As in the case of Dagon (*see* § 2 *above*), it is probable that the cult object, in this case a wooden one, was an image of the fertility goddess Asherah. This would explain the fact that there are only four references to the object in prophetic literature; by implication all prophetic condemnation of idolatry would include images of Asherah as well as images of other deities. The same conclusion would hold if the cult object were a staff or pole, but in such a case there would be the problem of explaining how the same word came to be applied both to the goddess and to the object with which she was represented.

With respect to the location of the Asherah, it can be observed that it existed in both the S and N kingdoms at such places as Samaria, Bethel, and Jerusalem. As evidence of widespread use of the cult object in ancient Palestine, attention may be called to the report that the people during Rehoboam's reign "built for themselves high places, and pillars, and Asherim on every high hill and under every green tree" (I Kings 14:23). Concerning the location of the Asherah within the sanctuary, it can be said only that it stood with other cult objects beside the altar.

The chronology cannot be described in detail, but it appears that the cult object was not known, as was the massebah, to the patriarchs or to the kings of the United Monarchy. Taking account of the date of the laws which refer to it, the object appears to have been known in Palestine from the tenth to the beginning of the sixth centuries B.C. The Asherah was not the invention of the Hebrew people but was adopted from neighboring peoples, perhaps under the influence of such persons as Jezebel.

Scholars do not agree as to the etymology of the word. Until the discovery of the name in the Ras Shamra Texts it was proposed that the name was derived from the Hebrew אשר ("happiness, good fortune"), ישר ("to be upright"), or Akkadian aširtu ("temple, sanctuary"). Evidence from Ras Shamra makes it probable that the Hebrew "Asherah" goes back to the Ugaritic proper name *'atirat,* a nominal form of the verb *'tr* meaning "to walk," or "to tread." Athirat Ym would be the goddess who treads upon the sea.

The antipathy toward the Asherah on the part of the Hebrew leaders was due to the fact that the goddess and the cult object of the same name were associated with the fertility religion of a foreign people and as such involved a mythology and a cultus which were obnoxious to the champions of Yahweh.

**Bibliography.** P. Torge, *Ashera und Astarte* (1902), pp. 1-107; W. H. Ward, "The Asherah," *AJSL,* 19 (1902), 33-44; J. B. Pritchard, *Palestinian Figurines in Relation to Certain Goddesses Known Through Literature* (1943), pp. 59-65, 89-90; W. F. Albright, *Archaeology and the Religion of Israel* (1946), Index; W. L. Reed, *The Asherah in the OT* (1949), pp. 1-116.

W. L. REED

**ASHEROTH.** See ASHERAH.

**ASHES.** The term frequently used in the Bible to designate the substances remaining after combustion has occurred, as after sacrifices. It is often mentioned in connection with DUST and SACKCLOTH as a sign of MOURNING, grief, and humiliation; its application to the body at times of FASTING was a sign of penitence; figuratively, it had reference to worthless things or persons.

Three different Hebrew words are rendered "ashes":

*a)* אפר is used most often (Gen. 18:27; Num. 19:9; II Sam. 13:19; etc.) in referring to ashes, as a sign of mourning (Esth. 4:1, 3; Job 2:8; etc.) and penitence (Job 42:6; Dan. 9:3). The same word appears in I Kings 20:38, 41, where the KJV used "ashes"; more correctly, most English translations, including the RSV, use "bandage," as required by the context, which calls for an article of disguise such as a mask. A word with the same consonants but different vowels was used in referring to the ashes of the burnt offering having a purifying effect (Num. 19:17) and in designating the ashes produced by the burning of vessels used in pagan worship (II Kings 23:4). The term often designated merely ashes from a home, or the refuse from a city (Isa. 58:5; Jer. 6:26), and as a metaphor implied destruction (Ezek. 28:18; Mal. 4:3), worthless maxims (Job 13:12), or unworthy people (Gen. 18:27; Ecclus. 10:9; 17:32).

*b)* דשן was used to refer to the type of ashes formed by a mixture of burned fuel and fat resulting from sacrifice at altars (Lev. 1:16; 4:12; 6:10-11; I Kings 13:3, 5) and from burned corpses (Jer. 31:40).

*c)* פיח designated the ashes or carbon formed in a kiln (Exod. 9:8, 10), said to have been used by Moses to produce boils among the Egyptians.

The LXX regularly renders the Hebrew by σποδός, except for פיח, which is αἰθάλης, "smoky substance" or "soot." Σποδός appears in Matt. 11:21; Luke 10:13 in referring to ashes for mourning, and in Heb. 9:13 to recall the OT rite of purification with ashes. The use of ashes for ritual purposes was not peculiar to the Hebrews; it has been observed among primitive Arab tribes, and it may be implied among the Phoenicians by the representations on the famous Ahiram Sarcophagus of two women with hands touching their heads.

W. L. REED

**ASHHUR** ăsh′ər [אשחור]; KJV ASHUR. According to the suspect MT, the posthumous son of Hezron (I Chr. 2:24 KJV); the reconstructed text (LXX, Vulg.) makes him the son of CALEB by Ephrathah (Ephrath in vs. 19). Perhaps vs. 19 and vs. 24 are duplicates, with "HUR" simply an abbreviation of "Ashhur." Ashhur's own children are listed in I Chr. 4:5-6. He was the settler or founder of the town of TEKOA.

F. T. SCHUMACHER

**ASHIMA** ə shī′mə [אשימא] (II Kings 17:30); ASHIMAH (Amos 8:14). A deity worshiped by the colonists from Hamath whom the Assyrians settled in Samaria after 722 B.C. (II Kings 17:30). This is possibly a deliberate Hebrew corruption (אשם, *āshām,* "guilt") of "Ashera," the name of the Canaanite mother-goddess. Of similar significance may be אשמת שמרון, *'ashmāth shôm*ᵉ*rôn,* by which the contemporaries of Amos swear (Amos 8:14). Greek sources from the Roman imperial period, however, attest a deity Σίμι, or Σειμίος, who may be named in the composite divine name Ashembethel in the Elephantine Papyri. Here, however, the first element may be a dialectic variation of the common Semitic word for "name."

**Bibliography.** A. Vincent, *La religion des Judéo-araméens d'Éléphantine* (1937), pp. 566, 654-56, 662-76; J. A. Montgomery, *Commentary on Kings,* ICC (ed. H. S. Gehman; 1951), p. 475.

J. GRAY

**ASHKELON** ăsh′kə lən [אשקלון; Egyp. *'Asqanu, 'Asqaruna;* Akkad. *Ašqaluna, Asqaluna, Isqiluna*]; in I Macc. 10:86 ASKALON ăs′— [Ἀσκαλών]; KJV variants ASKELON, ESHKALONITES ĕsh′kə lə nīts′, ASCALON. One of the five principal cities (pentapolis) of the PHILISTINES, the only one of the five located on the seacoast (Jer. 47:7). The site is *ca.* twelve miles N of Gaza and ten miles S of Ashdod. Fig. ASH 89.

Ashkelon has had a long and rich history. It is first mentioned in the Execration Texts of the Middle Kingdom in Egypt (*ca.* 1850 B.C.) as one of the rebellious elements in Egypt's empire (along with Jerusalem). In the Amarna Age (*see* TELL EL-AMARNA) the city, though affected by the rebellion, seems to have remained loyal to Egypt (Letters 287, 320; *ca.* 1375-1350 B.C.). However, it revolted against

From *Atlas of the Bible* (Thomas Nelson & Sons Limited)

89. Palestinian coast near ruins of ancient Ashkelon

Ramses II, who took it by storm and had inscribed on the temple wall at Karnak a dramatic representation of the battle.* The stele of Mer-ne-Ptah also speaks of Ashkelon's defeat (*ca.* 1220 B.C.). The Megiddo Ivories attest Egyptian religious influence in the city as late as *ca.* 1200 B.C. Fig. ASH 90. *See* IVORY.

Courtesy of the Pierpont Morgan Library

90. Ramses II's conquest of the fortress of Ashkelon (from Karnak)

At this point the Philistines came and the biblical record begins. Ashkelon and her sister cities were in territory not taken by Joshua (Josh. 13:3), though there is a tradition that Judah later took Gaza, Ashkelon, and Ekron (Judg. 1:18 MT; LXX says they were *not* taken). During the times of the Judges, Saul, and David, Ashkelon was definitely a Philistine city (Judg. 14:19; I Sam. 6:17; II Sam. 1:20).

Nothing more is heard of the city until the Assyrian period. Amos 1:8 predicts punishment on king and city (*ca.* 750 B.C. if from the prophet himself). This came to pass when "Mitinti of Ashkelon" revolted, after first paying tribute, against Tiglath-Pileser III. When Mitinti saw his desperate position, he became insane, and was succeeded by his son Rukibtu, who was more loyal to Assyria (733-732).

Later we find one Sidqia, apparently a usurper, in control of Ashkelon and several nearby places. Sidqia, after refusing to yield to Sennacherib during the latter's campaign against Jerusalem, was deported with his whole family to Assyria, and Sharruludari, son of Rukibtu, was restored to the kingship as an Assyrian vassal (701). Still later, another king, again named Mitinti, paid tribute to Esarhaddon (680-669), the conqueror of Memphis, and to Ashurbanipal, on his first Egyptian campaign (*ca.* 667).

Herodotus (I.105) mentions Ashkelon as the seat of a temple of "heavenly Aphrodite" (Astarte?) plundered by the Scythians *ca.* 626 B.C. (or shortly thereafter). From this time or later comes the oracle of doom in Zeph. 2:4, with the added prediction that Judah will eventually occupy the city (vs. 7).

After the defeat of the Egyptians at the battle of Carchemish in 605, the Chaldeans and Nebuchadnezzar (more correctly Nebuchadrezzar) wished to insure control of the West. Nebuchadrezzar immediately demanded submission and tribute of all the Palestinian states. Jeremiah warned that all should submit (Jer. 25:1, 17, 20). Apparently Ashkelon alone refused on this occasion. Punishment came quickly. An Aramaic letter found in Egypt from one Adon, probably king of Ashkelon, presumably to Pharaoh Neco, states that the "king of Babylon" has reached Aphek (forty miles to the N), and pleads for help. No help was forthcoming; Nebuchadrezzar "turned the city into a mound and heap of ruins" (Dec. 604; cf. Jer. 47:5-7). Later documents inform us that in 592 Ashkelonite captives (skilled laborers and members of the royal family) were living in Babylon.

According to the Greek geographer Scylax (*Periplus* 104), the city was under the control of Tyre in the Persian period. The Jews continued to view it with hostility (Zech. 9:5). After the coming of Alexander the Great, Ashkelon (or Ascalon, as it was now called) passionately embraced Hellenism, becoming a center of literature and scholarship. When Joseph son of Tobias, a Jewish tax collector under Ptolemy V Epiphanes (203-181 B.C.), came to Ascalon and demanded tribute, he was refused; the city paid with the loss of the lives and property of twenty principal men (Jos. Antiq. XII.iv.5). Nevertheless, it was conciliatory toward the Maccabees, suffering no damage from them (I Macc. 10:86; 11:60; 12:33). There was a considerable Jewish population at this time, though Jth. 2:28 lists the city as non-Jewish. Later, upon appeal to the Romans, Ascalon was made a "free town" (*oppidum liberum,* on coins of *ca.* 104 B.C.). The tradition that Herod the Great (*ca.* 73-4 B.C.) was the descendant of an Ascalonite temple slave, or even a native of the city (Just. Dial. 52.3; Euseb. Hist. I.vi.2; I.vii.11), is thought by some to be only Jewish slander. At any rate, Herod, though he did not control the city, built baths and other costly structures there (Jos. War I.xxi.11), including apparently a palace which his sister Salome inherited (Jos. War II.vi.3). When the war against Rome broke out (A.D. 66), the Jews attacked and partially destroyed Ascalon (Jos. War II.xviii.1); but the city recovered and repulsed with great slaughter a later Jewish attack (Jos. War III.ii.1-2).

By the fourth century, Ascalon's enthusiastic

paganism had given way to Christianity, and the city had become a bishopric. To the conquering Moslems it became the "bride of Syria" or "Syria's summit" (seventh century A.D.). It held out against the Crusaders until 1153. Saladin regained it in 1187, after the battle of the Horns of Hattin, breaking down its walls in 1191 lest it serve as a base for the Christians. An attempted restoration by Richard I succeeded only in part. What remained was finally dismantled by order of Sultan Baibars in 1270, since which time it has been a largely uninhabited ruin.

During early Christian times there was a separate seaport several miles to the S called Maioumas of Ascalon, which in the sixth century had its own bishop (*see* GAZA for a similar place bearing the same name).

In 1815, Lady Hester Stanhope, an Englishwoman living in Syria, conducted an excavation at Ascalon seeking treasure. She found instead a headless Greco-Roman statue of good quality, which she ordered destroyed, lest she be suspected of seeking works of art for the pleasure of Europeans instead of treasure to be turned over to the sultan! Two similar statues were found by a Turkish official in 1887.

During the years 1920-22, the Palestine Exploration Fund excavated at the site of Ashkelon-Ascalon. The history of the city was traced as far back as *ca.* 1800 B.C. (Middle Bronze Age), the time from which comes our earliest literary reference (*see above*). Evidence of the coming of the Philistines was found. The most extensive finds, however, came from the Hellenistic and Roman periods, during which the city flourished so greatly. Noteworthy are "Herod's Cloisters," the statues of "Peace and Victory," and the "Statuette of a Kneeling Venus."

The scallion, a kind of onion, derives its name from this city.

*Bibliography.* A. Neubauer, *Géographie du Talmud* (1868), pp. 69-71. H. Guthe, "Die Ruinen Ascalons," *ZDPV*, II (1879), 164-71. C. Schick, "Statues at Askalon," *PEQ* (1888), pp. 22-23. G. Le Strange, *Palestine Under the Moslems* (1890), pp. 400-403. J. Garstang and W. J. Phythian-Adams, "Excavations at Ascalon," etc., *PEQ* (1920-24). H. L. Ginsberg, "An Aramaic Contemporary of the Lachish Letters," *BASOR*, CXI (1948), 24-27. J. Bright, "A New Letter in Aramaic," *BA*, XII (1949), 46-52. J. B. Pritchard, ed., *ANEP* (1954), pp. 112, 288; *ANET* (2nd ed., 1955), Index, p. 526. A. Malamat, "A New Record of Nebuchadrezzar's Palestinian Campaigns," *IEJ*, VI (1956), 251-52. D. J. Wiseman, *Chronicles of Chaldaean Kings (626-556 B.C.) in the British Museum* (1956), pp. 66-75. W. F. STINESPRING

**ASHKENAZ** ăsh'kə năz [אשכנז]; KJV ASHCHENAZ. Son of Gomer (Gen. 10:3; I Chr. 1:6), and a kingdom associated with Ararat and Minni (Jer. 51:27). The identification with Assyrian *Aš-gu-za-a* for the SCYTHIANS seems certain. The Scythians were the pushing force behind the Cimmerian invasions (Herodotus IV.11), which accounts for their being the son of GOMER. They fought the Assyrians in conjunction with the Manneans (MINNI), and they were instrumental in the fall of the ancient kingdoms of Urartu (*see* ARARAT) and Assyria (Esarhaddon *Nineveh Prism* A.III.59-61). M. J. MELLINK

**ASHNAH** ăsh'nə [אשנה]. The name of two cities in Judah, both in the Shephelah below the mountains of Judah (Josh. 15:33, 43). Their location is uncertain. The first of these may possibly be 'Aslin, a village at the edge of the coastal plain of Judah. The second has sometimes been identified with Idhna, between Hebron and Lachish. S. COHEN

**ASHPENAZ** ăsh'pə năz [אשפנז] (Dan. 1:3-4). The chief eunuch of Nebuchadnezzar. He was commanded to bring handsome and intelligent Jewish youths to the king's palace.

**ASHRIEL.** KJV form of ASRIEL in I Chr. 7:14.

**ASHTAROTH** ăsh'tə rŏth [עשתרות]; ASHTERATHITE ăsh'te răth ĭt' [עשתרתי] (I Chr. 11:44).
**1.** The plural form of "ASHTORETH," the name of the Canaanite fertility-goddess. As such it probably denotes various local manifestations of Astarte, just as "Baalim" (RSV "Baals") denotes local varieties of the Canaanite BAAL. In the fertility cult of Ras Shamra, relative to the vicissitudes of Baal as a vegetation deity, the leading role during the eclipse of the god is played by the goddess Anat. This goddess is less conspicuous in Palestine than Astarte, who apparently assumed the role of Anat there, to judge from the close association of Ashtaroth and Baalim in the OT. *Cf.* ASHERAH.

In the Hebrew settlement it is said (Judg. 2:13; 10:6) that the Israelites practiced the cult of Baalim and Ashtaroth, though this might denote the observance of seasonal rituals of the fertility cult without the positive worship of Baal and Astarte. In any case, the references, being by nature of commentary in the Deuteronomic redaction of Judges, seem general references, which may not be emphasized in full detail. The same may be said of Samuel's injunction to Israel at the assembly of Mizpah at the election of Saul, to put away the Baalim and Ashtaroth (I Sam. 7:4) and of Israel's confession of apostasy to Baalim and Ashtaroth after the defeat at the hands of the Philistines (I Sam. 12:10).

In I Sam. 31:10 in the reference to the temple of the goddess, probably at Beth-shan, Ashtaroth of the MT should probably be emended to the singular Ashtoreth. Here there is no question of worship by the Hebrews, since Beth-shan was never occupied by the Hebrews, having been destroyed in the time of David. *See* ASHTORETH; BETH-SHAN § 4.
**2.** An abbreviated form of a place name compounded with the name of the goddess Ashtaroth. Ashtaroth is found as the name of a town in N Transjordan (Aštarti of the Amarna Tablets) associated with Edrei (modern Deraa) as the home of Og, king of Bashan (Deut. 1:4; 3:10; Josh. 12:4). Later settled by Machir (Josh. 13:12, 31), Ashtaroth was one of the Israelite cities of refuge (I Chr. 6:71; cf. Josh. 21:27). The same place is apparently denoted in Gen. 14:5 as a city of the Rephaim in the account of Chedorlaomer's raid. There it is termed ASHTEROTH-KARNAIM, "Ashtaroth of the Horns." This may refer either to the goddess Astarte, who is often represented with a horned headdress as the Egyptian cow-goddess Hathor, or to some topographical feature. The place was a notable cult center in Hasmonean times, when its sanctuary was destroyed by

Judas Maccabeus (I Macc. 5:44—"Carnaim"), which suggests that the former conjecture is the more probable.

**3.** A common noun meaning either "young" or "breeding stock," in passages referring to productivity of sheep (Deut. 7:13; 28:4, 18, 51)—עשתרות צאנך, 'ashᵉrôth ṣônᵉkâ, in parallelism with שגר אלפך, shᵉghar 'ᵃlāphᵉkâ. The possible connection with Ashteroth, the fertility-goddess, suggests that the first phrase might designate ewes, but the parallel "young of thy cattle" suggests that the first phrase means "young of thy flock." The etymology of the term is obscure, though a connection between the fertility-goddess and breeding ewes or their offspring is natural. W. R. Smith suggests that Ashtaroth, "Ashteroth," had the form of a sheep, but this is a pure conjecture unsupported by any known evidence.

For bibliography, *see* ASHTORETH. J. GRAY

**ASHTERATHITE** ăsh'tᵊ răth īt' [עשתרתי] (I Chr. 11:44). A native of ASHTAROTH.

**ASHTEROTH-KARNAIM** ăsh'tᵊ rŏth kär nā'ᵊm [עשתרות קרנים, twin peaks near Ashtaroth]. Alternately: KARNAIM [קרנים] (Amos 6:13); CARNAIM [Καρνάιν] (I Macc. 5:26, 43-44); CARNION kär'nĭ ᵊn [Κάρνιον] (II Macc. 12:21, 26 KJV). An important fortress city in Gilead. It has been located at Sheikh Sa'ad, *ca.* twenty miles E of the Sea of Galilee and three miles N of Tell 'Ashtarah, the site of ASHTAROTH. Archaeological investigations have shown that the two cities seldom flourished simultaneously but rather alternately; thus the great stele of Ramses II, originally set up at Ashtaroth, was found at Karnaim, whither it had been removed. This makes impossible the attractive supposition that the two towns were united under the name of Astarte of the two horns (i.e., the lunar crescent). As a matter of fact, the patron goddess of Karnaim was not Astarte, but ATARGATIS, the Canaanite 'Attar-'Ate (II Macc. 12: 26).

Ashteroth-karnaim was occupied by the Rephaim, or prehistoric inhabitants of Canaan, when it fell victim to the attack of Chedorlaomer and his confederate kings as they marched southward through the Transjordan (Gen. 14:5). It was so thoroughly destroyed that it was not occupied during the entire Late Bronze period (sixteenth–thirteenth centuries B.C.) and was rebuilt only after the Israelite conquest. Since it was a bone of contention between Syria (Aram) and Israel in the time of the kings, it may have been rebuilt by either of these nations. Jeroboam II of Israel (781-741 B.C.) captured it together with the nearby Lo-debar (Josh. 13:26). *See* DEBIR § 3. Amos later made a sarcastic pun on this exploit, in the sense of: "Have we not taken horns for ourselves?" (Amos 6:13; perhaps a reminiscence of the action of Zedekiah the son of Chenaanah as described in I Kings 22:11). Tiglath-pileser III of Assyria mentions the city under the name of Qarnen (Qarnini); he conquered the whole region in 732 and made the place the capital of the district.

In the postexilic period the city, known as Carnaim or Carnion, was settled both by Jews and by Greeks. At that time it was regarded as a very strong fortress, but it was captured and destroyed by Judas Maccabeus after the Jews there had appealed to him for rescue (I Macc. 5:26, 43-44; II Macc. 12:21, 26).

S. COHEN

**ASHTORETH** ăsh'tᵊ rĕth [עשתרת]. The deliberate Hebrew misvocalization of the name of the Canaanite fertility-goddess called עתתרת (Athtarath) in the Ras Shamra Texts and עשתרת (probably pronounced Ashtarath or Ashtereth) in later Phoenician inscriptions; the Greek approximation is Ασταρτη. The Hebrew scribes, as usual in reproducing the name of a pagan deity, retained the consonants and substituted the vowels of בשת (bôsheth), "shame," in the last two syllables. The name is so found in I Kings 11:5, 33; II Kings 23:13, the only instances in the OT of its use in the singular form. More commonly the plural ASHTAROTH is used in general statements about Canaanite paganism, the reference being to various local manifestations of the fertility-goddess. In I Sam. 31:10, where the reference is to a certain temple, probably at Beth-shan, where the Philistines deposited the armor of Saul after the Battle of Gilboa, the singular Ashtoreth should probably be read for Ashtaroth of the MT.

The passage in I Kings 11:5 refers to Solomon's patronage of the cult of Ashtoreth and II Kings 23: 13 to the abolition of her cult place on the "Mount of Corruption," probably the Mount of Olives, in Josiah's reformation. In both cases the cult of the goddess is related to the Phoenicians, specifically the Sidonians. It is perhaps significant that in both passages her worship is mentioned together with that of Milcom, the god of Ammon (*see* MOLECH), and in the latter passage with the cult of CHEMOSH, the god of Moab. Since there is good reason to believe that Milcom and Chemosh were local forms of the one astral deity, the Venus Star, Athtar, this may indicate that Ashtoreth had also been an astral deity, the female counterpart of Athtar. In this connection it is noteworthy that her Mesopotamian counterpart, Ishtar (*see* ASSYRIA AND BABYLONIA), retained her character as an astral deity, though at the same time the goddess of love and fertility. Apart from the known astral character of Ishtar and the association of the cult of Ashtoreth with that of Milcom and Chemosh in the passages we have cited, there is no evidence from Canaan that she was an astral deity except that Athtar, of which "Ashtoreth" is the female form, had certainly this character.

In Canaan the goddess is first encountered in the Ras Shamra Texts in offering lists and in mythology, where she is apparently the ally of BAAL in his conflict with the turbulent Sea-and-River. Unfortunately this text is fragmentary, and we cannot tell precisely the role played by the goddess. There is a later version, however, preserved in an Egyptian papyrus from the Nineteenth Dynasty, wherein Athtarath is the bride claimed by the tyrant Sea. Here also the text is fragmentary, precluding further particularization. From a certain passage in the saga of King Keret among the Ras Shamra Texts, where the king invokes a curse in the name of "Athtarath-the-Name-of-Baal," we see that the goddess, at least in the heroic past, was associated with Baal as the giver of life or death. From the Ras Shamra Texts generally, however, it would seem that the functions of Ashtoreth as the patroness of fertility were taken over by Anath, the sister of Baal, who is by far the most active deity in the pantheon of Ras Shamra. In Palestine and probably S Syria, however, on the evidence of Phoenician inscriptions of the first millennium and of the OT, Ashtoreth was much more prominent than Anath.

The goddess appears in Egyptian inscriptions and sculpture, particularly from the Nineteenth Dynasty, when a number of Semitic cults were introduced to Egypt. In an inscribed sculpture from the Ptolemaic period at Edfu, she is depicted with the head of a lion. The association with the lion suggests that Ashtoreth is the subject of the Nineteenth Dynasty sculptures where a naked goddess named Qodshu ("holiness"), holding a papyrus plant and a serpent, stands on a lion between Min, the virile Egyptian fertility-god, and RESHEPH, the Semitic god of destruction and death. Here the goddess wears her hair in the fashion of stylized horns characteristic of the Egyptian cow-goddess Hathor, and bronze figurines from Gezer actually depict a nude female with horns, which may well be representations of Ashtoreth. On

Courtesy of the University Museum of the University of Pennsylvania

91. Stele of "Ashtoreth," from Beth-shan

such evidence of the identity of the goddess, her cult seems to have flourished at Beth-shan from the fifteenth to the thirteenth centuries,* and a votive inscription of a man of Ascalon at Delos in the second century B.C. naming "Astarte of Palestine" may indicate Ascalon as another of her cult centers. Coins of the Roman imperial period from Sidon and Beirut also depict Astarte, who is known by her association with the lion. Fig. ASH 91.

Generally related to the fertility cult in Palestine are figurines usually molded of clay representing nude females with breasts and pudenda emphasized. These are frequently termed "Astarte plaques," though it has been suggested that they are models, not of the goddess, but of concubines to be placed

with the defunct in the tomb—a custom definitely attested in Egypt and Greece. The horned Hathor coiffure, however, suggests that these were figurines of the goddess, and the lotus flower and serpent which the figure occasionally holds certainly indicate Astarte, though the symbol of a dove clutched to the breasts indicates Ashera, the mother-goddess. The figurines, which from their great number appear to have been associated with the home rather than the sanctuary, may have been popularly used as symbols of prayers or vows to the goddess of fertility, or have been made and exposed on the principle of imitative magic, to influence the deity by autosuggestion and thus procure family.

The character of Ashtoreth as the giver of life is suggested further by her association with the Phoenician god of healing, Eshmun, in an undated inscription from Carthage (cf. the Assyrian name Ishtar-miti-uballiṭ—"Ishtar, make the dead to live").

*Bibliography.* S. A. Cook, *The Religion of Ancient Palestine in the Light of Archaeology* (1930), pp. 123-28, 173-74; A. H. Gardiner, "The Astarte Papyrus," *Studies Presented to F. L. Griffiths* (1932), pp. 74-85; R. Dussaud, *Les découvertes de Ras Shamra (Ugarit) et l'AT* (1941), pp. 106-11; J. B. Pritchard, *Palestinian Figurines in Relation to Certain Goddesses Known Through Literature* (1944); W. F. Albright, *Archaeology and the Religion of Israel* (1953), pp. 74-77. J. GRAY

**ASHUR.** KJV form of ASHHUR.

**ASHURBANIPAL** ăsh'ər băn'ə pəl [Akkad. *Aššur-bāni-apli,* Aššur is the creator of the heir]. King of Assyria (668–629[?] B.C.); son of ESARHADDON. Figs. ASH 92-93.

Ashurbanipal was the last of the great kings of Assyria. The main event of his reign was his long-drawn-out fight with the coalition which his brother Shamashshumukin king of Babylon had set afoot against him. In the first years of his reign, Ashurbanipal continued the policy of his father against Egypt. In 663 he even succeeded in penetrating beyond MEMPHIS and in destroying THEBES. The frontiers in Asia Minor, where Gyges of Lydia was threatened by the Cimmerians, and those toward the N, where the Manneans continued to exert pressure, remained rather stable in the first decade of Ashurbanipal's reign. In 652, Shamashshumukin apparently thought that the appropriate moment had come for a rebellion against his brother. It is difficult to see what caused the Babylonian king to rebel, surrounded as his capital was by strong Assyrian garrisons stationed under efficient commanders in all the major cities of Babylonia, which had always been genuinely loyal to Assyria. As an Assyrian he should also have known how unreliable Elamite assistance was and should not have been under any illusions as to the military value of the Chaldean tribes, his main allies, nor as to that of the Arabs, in a clash with the well-disciplined and efficiently led Assyrian troops. When the army of Shamashshumukin and his allies had failed to conquer such essential Assyrian-held cities as Ur and Uruk, and when the Elamite king was defeated by the Assyrians and internal unrest made Elam unable to participate further in the war, the Babylonian king was forced into a defensive fight, which, of course, sealed his doom. The year 650 saw Assyrian generals keeping Elam and

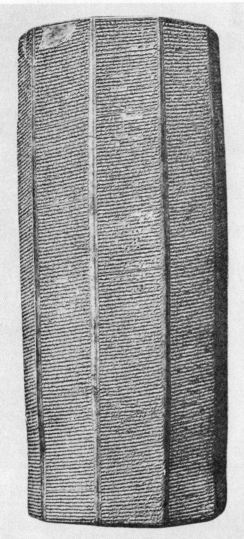

92. Baked clay prism with the annals of Ashurbanipal

the Chaldean tribes in check. An expeditionary force of Arabs was defeated and driven into Babylon, and eventually siege was laid to the city. This siege lasted for two years, and it was famine that eventually led to the downfall of Babylon, which had been defended with courage and tenacity (648). Ashurbanipal then undertook punitive campaigns against the Arabs and Elam, the latter ending with the destruction of Susa. With the year 639, the sources for Assyrian history cease, although we know that Ashurbanipal ruled till 629(?). No explanation can be given for this curious blackout. With appalling suddenness, the Empire disintegrated, under his son Sinsharishkun (627-612), who succeeded him. Babylonia fell to Nabopolassar; the N and the W threw off Assyrian domination nearly immediately; and in 612 the capital itself, Nineveh, was destroyed by the Medes.

As befits the only Assyrian king who ever prided himself on his literacy, Ashurbanipal's library in Nineveh, now partly excavated and kept in the British Museum, will be his perennial monument.

**Bibliography.** Translations of historical texts: M. Streck, *Assurbanipal und die letzten assyrischen Könige bis zum Untergang Niniveh's* (1916); A. C. Piepkorn, *Historical Prism Inscriptions of Ashurbanipal* (1933); T. Bauer, *Das Inschriftwerk Assurbanipals* (1933); R. Borger, "Mesopotamien in den Jahren 629-621 v. Chr.," *Wiener Zeitschrift für die Kunde des Morgenlandes*, 55 (1948), 62 ff.                    A. L. OPPENHEIM

**ASHURITES** ăsh'ə rīts [אשורי]. A people in N Israel mentioned between Gilead and Jezreel as part of the kingdom of Ish-bosheth (II Sam. 2:9). The Syr. and Vulg. read "GESHURITES" (cf. Josh. 12:5), whose situation would suit the context; but Geshur was an independent kingdom (II Sam. 3:3; 13:37). The Targ. has "ASHERITES," which is preferred by some commentators.                    R. F. SCHNELL

**ASHVATH** ăsh'văth [עשות] (I Chr. 7:33). One of the sons of Japhlet in the genealogy of Asher.

**ASIA** ā'zhə, ā'shə ['Ασία]. A portion of the continent of Asia; in the NT normally a province in Asia Minor.

**1. Extent.** Differences as to the extent of the area meant by "Asia" are due to the fact that the word

93. Ashurbanipal before an offering table and incense stand, pouring a libation over dead lions

Adapted from *The Westminster Historical Atlas to the Bible, Revised*, ed. G. Ernest Wright and Floyd V. Filson. © The Westminster Press.

meant different things at different times and that the borders were often not defined with precision. Among Greek geographers the word was used to denote the continent of Asia or some major portion of it. This usage is not unknown in the writers of the Roman Empire (Jos. Antiq. XI.viii.3; II Esd. 15:46; 16:1).

In the Apoc. the word is used of the kingdom of the Seleucids, for their ruler is referred to as "king of Asia" (I Macc. 8:6; II Macc. 3:3; cf. I Macc. 11: 13; 12:39; 13:32; Jos. Antiq. XII.iii.3). In the NT the word refers to the Roman province of Asia, with only a few possible exceptions (e.g., Acts 2:9; 19:10).

**2. The Roman province.** This portion of Asia Minor had been conquered by the Romans earlier in the second century B.C. in its war against Antiochus the Great, and had been given to their allies, the Attalids. When Attalus III died in 133 B.C., he willed his kingdom to Rome, but the province was not organized until after a revolt had been put down. The Romans knew the Attalids as "kings of Asia"; hence the new province was called Asia. The province included the W parts of Asia Minor, including Mysia, Lydia, and Caria, plus the coastal areas— i.e., Aeolia, Ionia, and the Troad—and many of the islands of the Aegean, including Rhodes and Patmos. The province was enlarged in 116 B.C. with the addition of Greater Phrygia. Asia could then be described as between Bithynia, Lycia, Galatia, and the Aegean Sea. It was not a solid territory, for within it were various free cities and temple states. *Ca.* A.D. 285 the province was greatly reduced in size and restricted to the coastal areas and the lower river valleys of the W.

The first capital of this Roman province was Pergamum, the capital of the former kingdom of the Attalids. By the time of Augustus the capital was changed to Ephesus, as that city grew in importance as a seaport and communications center for Rome.

It became a requirement that the governor should land and take office there.

Asia was a senatorial province and as such was ruled by a governor with the title of proconsul, who was appointed by the Senate from the senior ex-consuls. Although the appointment was usually for only one year, in exceptional cases it could be extended for a second or even a third year. Under the Republic the Roman provincial officials and the *publicani* had systematically exploited the wealth of Asia, and the short tenure of office encouraged their rapacity. Therefore Asia welcomed Augustus and the beginning of the Empire, for he brought relative peace and prosperity, a responsible and stable administration. Asia soon developed a strong sense of loyalty to the emperor.

Asia was regarded as the richest of the Roman provinces, as Cicero testifies: "In the richness of its soil, in the variety of its products, in the extent of its pastures, and in the number of its exports, it surpasses all other lands" (*De. Imp. Cn. Pomp.* 14). Other sources of wealth were minerals and timber.

This province possessed a high degree of culture and intellectual activity, which dated back to the early Greek cities along the coast. Long before Alexander the Great, such Greek cities as the two Magnesias, Miletus, and Tralles had become firmly established. After Alexander these Greek foundations multiplied, and the interior was rapidly Hellenized. Although Asia contained many diverse peoples, by the first century A.D. the culture and language had become predominantly Greek, as the province became the most thoroughly Hellenized portion of Asia Minor. The province was never dominated by a single city, like Alexandria or Antioch, but there were many medium-sized cities. Under the Empire the chief cities, which held the rank of metropolis, were Ephesus, Smyrna. Sardis, Pergamum, Lampsacus, and Cyzicus.

The religion of Asia included a great variety of cults and gods. There were native Anatolian rites, such as the worship of the Great Mother. There was the worship of Greek and Roman deities, such as Artemis or Diana at Ephesus (cf. Acts 19) and Asclepius at Pergamum. These Greco-Roman deities were often identified with the native gods. An important development for early Christianity was the rise of emperor-worship, which became both popular and powerful in Asia during the period of peace and prosperity inaugurated by Augustus. This province was one of the first to request permission to worship the living emperor. Augustus granted this request in 29 B.C. and then only to non-Romans. By the end of the first century A.D. emperor-worship in Asia had incited hostility toward the Christians, who refused to participate.

**3. In the NT.** With one or two possible exceptions, in the NT "Asia" refers to the Roman province (*see above*). At Pentecost there were Jews in Jerusalem who had come from Asia, although the inclusion of Phrygia in the list of places seems to indicate that only a portion of the province was meant, for Asia normally included Phrygia (Acts 2:9-10). The strength of the Jewish community in Asia is also indicated by the mention of Jews from there, who disputed with Stephen (6:9).

On Paul's second missionary journey he and Timothy were forbidden by the Spirit to preach in Asia, yet they apparently crossed the province to reach one of its cities, Troas (Acts 16:6-8). On Paul's return from Greece he stopped briefly at Ephesus (18:19-21). During his third journey Paul spent over two years in and around Ephesus, "so that all the residents of Asia heard the word of the Lord" (19:10; cf. vs. 22). This may be a reference to only that portion of Asia around Ephesus, and so possibly also in vss. 26-27. On Paul's final journey to Jerusalem he decided to pass by Asia and touched only at Miletus (20:16-17). Paul's extensive stay in Ephesus is reflected in references in his letters (Rom. 16:5; I Cor. 15:32; 16:8, 19; II Cor. 1:8).

Asia is the center of interest for the author of the book of Revelation. The seven churches which he addresses are all in the W portion of the province. His selection of only certain cities probably reflects his interest in the churches he knew best. It should be noticed that his list puts first the three chief cities of the province: Ephesus, Symrna, and Pergamum, and then adds Thyatira, Sardis, Philadelphia, and Laodicea (Rev. 1:11). Other cities of Asia mentioned in the NT are Colossae, Hierapolis, Adramyttium, and Assos.

*Bibliography.* T. Mommsen, *The Provinces of the Roman Empire* (1866), ch. 8: "Asia Minor"; W. M. Ramsay, *The Letters to the Seven Churches of Asia* (1904), ch. 10: "The Province of Asia and the Imperial Religion"; D. Magie, *Roman Rule in Asia Minor* (1950), chs. 1-7.　　　　D. C. Pellett

**ASIARCH** ā'zhĭ ärk ['Ασιάρχης] (Acts 19:31). As yet, the evidence is inadequate to permit a precise definition of the origin and meaning—perhaps a shifting one—of this term. Most of the notes in the commentaries on Acts 19:31 are more precise than the ambiguity of the evidence permits. The term occurs in Strabo 14.1.42; *Martyrdom of Polycarp* 12.2;

in some late juridical sources (cf. *Digesta* 27.1.6.14); and in numerous inscriptions on coins and stones of the cities of Asia.

It may be stated with assurance that the Asiarchs were men of wealth and public influence in the cities they represented or served, and that some of them may have been of provincial importance. For the very reason that they were not technically a part of the structure of Roman provincial government, but offered themselves in the cities of the Asian League or commune and were accepted, appointed, or elected as protectors and promoters of the expanding imperial cult and the worship of the goddess Roma, they would rate as Romans of the most loyal kind. Such religio-patriotic functions further involved defraying the expenses of the cult festivals, including the games associated with them. On occasion, an Asiarch might repair at his own expense a public bath, or pay for minting an issue of bronze coins which would bear his name, or finance gladiatorial combats and wild-beast hunts in the arena. In the interesting account of the *Martyrdom of Polycarp*, bishop of Smyrna (12.2) it was an Asiarch who in defiance of the mob refused to let loose a lion on Polycarp, on the ground that he had already closed the sports. At times the connection of the Asiarch with the emperor cult brought him the appointment of high priest of the local temple, or even carried the grandiose title of "high priest of Asia." Although the term of office was one year, re-election or reappointment was possible, and the title might survive the term of office. In this sense a city like Ephesus might have several Asiarchs at any one time.

If we may suppose that Luke and his first readers were aware of the varied functions of the Asiarchs, the importance of the mention of them in Acts is clear. Among Paul's "friends" and protectors, Luke will say, are the most noble and loyal Roman provincials, even the religious patriots and civic benefactors. Luke introduces the Asiarchs as an elite supporting Paul against the Ephesian rabble.

*Bibliography.* L. R. Taylor, "The Asiarchs," note XXII, pp. 256-62, in F. J. Foakes-Jackson and K. Lake, eds., *The Beginnings of Christianity*, pt. I, vol. V (1933), is the most influential of recent discussions. D. Magie, *Roman Rule in Asia Minor* (1950), pp. 449-50, 1298-1301, 1526, is the most searching discussion of the term since Taylor's, and one which questions some of Taylor's conclusions.　　　F. D. Gealy

**ASIBIAS.** Apoc. alternate form of Hashabiah 8.

**ASIEL** ăs'ĭ əl [עֲשִׂיאֵל; 'Ασιήλ]; KJV Apoc. Asael. **1.** Great-grandfather of Jehu in a list of Simeonite chieftains and their conquests in the time of Hezekiah (I Chr. 4:35).

**2.** A scribe who served Ezra (II Esd. 14:24).

**3.** Ancestor of Tobit (Tob. 1:1); a Naphtalite.

**ASIPHA.** KJV Apoc. form of Hasupha.

**ASKELON.** KJV alternate form of Ashkelon.

**ASMODEUS** ăz'mō dē'əs ['Ασμοδέυς, *probably from* שׁמד, *hence* the Destroyer (*cf.* ὁ ἀπολλύων Apollyon, *in* Rev. 9:11); *derived by some from the Zend Aesma Daēva*, demon of anger). An evil being described in later Jewish tradition as "king of the demons"; sometimes identified with Beelzebul (cf. Mark 3:22); in the Talmud he often appears in the events concerning Solomon.

Asmodeus plays a leading role in the book of Tobit. Himself in love with Sarah, he slays her seven successive husbands on the wedding night (is Mark 12:20-22 an allusion to this?). With the help of Raphael, Tobias brews a potion which drives Asmodeus away, and so he is able to possess his bride.

In literature, Asmodeus has come to symbolize marital discord. J. C. SWAIM

**ASNAH** ăs'nə [אסנה, *probably an Egyp. theophorous name, with* נה *referring to a god:* he who belongs to Nah]. The head of a family of temple servants who returned to Palestine after the Exile (Ezra 2:50; I Esd. 5:31).

**ASNAPPER.** KJV form of OSNAPPAR.

**ASOM.** KJV Apoc. form of HASHUM.

**ASP** [פתן (ADDER *in* Pss. 58:4—H 58:5; 91:13); Ugar. *btn;* Akkad. *bašmu;* ἀσπίς] (Deut. 32:33; Job 20:14, 16; Isa. 11:8; Rom. 3:13). English term refers to one of several poisonous snakes, with special reference to the cobra, or may indicate the common European type of viper or adder. Bodenheimer (*see* FAUNA § C) believes the identification of פתן is unknown; many have suggested the cobra is intended, but without adequate basis.

"Asp" is used in figures of speech in poetry. The wine of the enemy is the "cruel venom of asps" (Deut. 32:33), the food of the wicked becomes in his stomach the gall of asps (Job 20:14), and the venom of asps is under the tongue of the unrighteous (Rom. 3:13). The wicked will suck the poison of asps (Job 20:16), and in the new age of peace the child will play safely on the hole of the asp (Isa. 11:8).

H. G. MAY

**ASPALATHUS** ăs păl'ə thəs. KJV translation of ἀσπάλαθος (RSV CAMEL'S THORN).

**ASPATHA** ăs pā'thə [אספתא, *perhaps* Pers. *loan word*] (Esth. 9:7). One of the ten sons of HAMAN who were killed by the Jews in retaliation.

**ASPHAR** ăs'fär ['Ασφάρ] (I Macc. 9:33). A pool in the desert; the scene of a camp of Jonathan Maccabeus and Simon Maccabeus. N. TURNER

**ASPHARASUS.** KJV Apoc. form of MISPAR.

**ASRIEL** ăs'rĭ əl [אשריאל, God has filled with joy, *or* (the object of) joy is God(?)]; KJV ASHRIEL ăsh'rĭ əl in I Chr. 7:14; ASRIELITES ăs'rĭ ə līts. A descendant of Manasseh; a Gileadite enumerated in the list of the second census taken by Moses in the wilderness (Num. 26:31; Josh. 17:2; I Chr. 7:14, where "Asriel" should be deleted). He is the eponymous ancestor of the Asrielites, one of the families of Manasseh to whom land was allotted by Joshua.

*Bibliography.* M. Noth, *Die israelitischen Personennamen* (1928), pp. 167, 183. R. F. JOHNSON

**ASS** [אתון, she-ass, *cf.* Akkad. *atânu,* she-ass; חמור, *from* חמר, be red, *cf.* Akkad. *emêru,* ass; עיר, young, vigorous male ass (*alternately* FOAL; COLT; KJV ASS COLT; YOUNG ASS), *cf.* Arab. *'âra,* roam, rove, *and 'ayr,* ass, wild ass; ὄνος; ὀνάριον, *diminutive of* ὄνος; ὑποζύγιον, *lit.* under the yoke]. Centuries before Israel's patriarchal age, the ass had been domesticated and had become part of the civilized life of Western Asia. Tamed onagers appear in Mesopotamia in the third millennium B.C., and the domesticated Nubian wild ass is seen in Egypt in the same period. It is probable that the latter variety was the ass of ancient Palestine and the Bible. *See* WILD ASS; FAUNA § A1aii. Fig. ASS 94.

94. Hunt for wild asses, from an alabaster relief of Ashurbanipal at Nineveh

For a summary of Roman ideas about the ass and the utility of ass's milk, current in the first century A.D., see Pliny Nat. Hist. VIII.68; XXVIII.50.

1. As a work animal
2. As a riding animal
3. As food
4. As an economic asset
5. In Israel's religious tradition

**1. As a work animal.** The ass was used for carrying burdens (Gen. 42:26; I Sam. 16:20; 25:18; Neh. 13:15; etc.), and also for agricultural operations (Isa. 30:24). The proverbial strength of the ass furnished an apt figure for Issachar (Gen. 49:14). The prohibition against plowing with an ox and an ass together (Deut. 22:10) may have arisen in part out of solicitude for the ass, but it also appears to reflect the conviction that different species of things must not be confused in any way (cf. M. Kil. 8.2, 4). In ancient Egypt asses were used on threshing floors, but they are not mentioned in this capacity, as the ox is, in Deut. 25:4. For later Jewish views, recorded in the Mishna, about hiring an ass, see B.M. 6.3, 5; on ass-drivers, see Kid. 4.14.

**2. As a riding animal.** The ass, controlled by a bridle (Prov. 26:3), was the animal ordinarily used for riding by men (Num. 22:21; II Sam. 17:23; etc.) and by women and children (Exod. 4:20; Josh. 15: 18; II Kings 4:24; etc.). Even people of influence and position used the ass (Judg. 10:4; 12:14; I Sam. 25: 20). Zion's future king's coming riding on an ass (not on a horse or in a chariot) emphasizes his essential peaceableness (Zech. 9:9; cf. Matt. 21:1-7; John 12: 14).

**3. As food.** Both Xenophon (cf. *Anabasis* I.5) and Pliny (*see above*) speak of the flesh of the ass as food, and II Kings 6:25 implies that in the ninth century B.C. the Hebrews were familiar with the meat of the ass. But the dietary norms of Israel (Lev. 11:1-8; Deut. 14:3-8) treated animals like the ass, which neither part the hoof nor chew the cud, as unclean and therefore unacceptable as food, and these views eventually determined the established Jewish practice.

**4. As an economic asset.** Possession of an ass was almost the bare minimum for existence (Job 24:3); and wealth was indicated by the ownership of large numbers of animals, among which were commonly included asses (Gen. 12:16; 24:35; Job 1:3; etc.). Asses served as an acceptable gift (Gen. 32:13-15). In the summary of the resources of the early post-exilic Judean community the numbers of asses far exceed those of all the other animals (Ezra 2:66-67; Neh. 7:68-69). The death of an ass involved hasty disposal of the carcass, a circumstance which Jeremiah used to prefigure the burial of Jehoiakim (Jer. 22:19).

**5. In Israel's religious tradition.** The ass, like the ox, shared in the rest of the sabbath day (Deut. 5:14; on a later Jewish development of this principle, see M. Shab. 24.1). The ass on the sabbath received the care necessary for its survival (Luke 13:15; 14:5). It was subject to the law of firstlings (Exod. 13:13; cf. M. Hal. 4.9; Bek. 1.1-6). The Lord uses an ass to frustrate the purpose of the prophet Balaam (Num. 22-24; cf. II Pet. 2:16). On the later charge, voiced by the Egyptian Apion, that the Jews worshiped an ass's head, see Jos. Apion II.80-88, 114, 120.

W. S. McCULLOUGH

**ASSABIAS.** KJV Apoc. alternate form of HASHA-BIAH.

**ASSALIMOTH.** KJV Apoc. form of SHELOMITH.

**ASSANIAS.** KJV Apoc. alternate form of HASHA-BIAH.

**ASSASSINS** [σικάριοι; *loan word from* Lat. *sicarii*, dagger men, murderers, *from sica,* dagger]. In Palestine this term was used by the Romans with reference to those Jews who engaged in organized political killings in which the element of surprise was highly exploited (cf. Jos. War II.viii.3; xvii.6). From the point of view of the Roman authorities and their sympathizers (of whom Josephus was a paragon), such political killings were criminal.

Josephus uses the name to identify a particular revolutionary party in the war of 66-70. But it is doubtful whether this particular group was the only one which engaged in political killings, or that they were the only ones called *sicarii* by the Roman authorities in Palestine. Josephus calls them "brigands" (another depreciatory appellation) and declares that they were the first to set the example of lawless plundering (cf. Jos. War II.xiii.3; xvii.6; xxii.2; IV.ix.3; VII.viii.1). He traces their origins back as far as the national reaction against the Roman census under Quirinius: "In those days the Sicarii banded together against those who consented to submit to

Rome and in every way treated them as enemies, plundering their property, rounding up their cattle, and setting fire to their habitations; protesting that such persons differed not at all from Gentiles, by betraying in so cowardly a manner the hard won liberty of the Jews and admitting their preference for the Roman yoke" (War VII.viii.1).

The sicarii of Josephus held out until the last against the Romans, who did not successfully breach their defenses at Masada in the wilderness of Judea until A.D. 73. When the Romans broke through, they found that the sicarii had systematically carried through a mass act of self-destruction (Jos. War VII.viii.6–IX.1). Even Josephus represents this deed as motivated by patriotism and devotion to God and his Law (Jos. War II.viii.6; VII). The sicarii are probably best understood as patriotic Jews living in that main stream of the Phineas-Maccabean tradition of zeal for the law which ran strong throughout the period of the Roman occupation of Palestine. In that tradition there was adequate motivation, and there were ample precedents for their behavior as "assassins" and "robbers," as well as "martyrs." *See* ZEALOT.

In Acts 21:38 there is a reference to four thousand Assassins who went out into the wilderness under the leadership of a man whom the tribune believed might have been Paul. W. R. FARMER

**ASSAYER** [בָּחוֹן, *from* בָּחַן, examine, test] (Jer. 6:27); KJV TOWER (בַּחַן; cf. Isa. 32:14). One who tests ores for their gold or silver content. Jeremiah's prophetic task is to be an assayer of the people. He finds them entirely base metal.

**ASSEMBLY.** *See* CONGREGATION.

**ASSHUR** ăsh'ər [אַשּׁוּר]. Alternately: ASSYRIA ə sĭr'ĭ ə. KJV ASSUR ăs'ər. **1.** One of the sons of Shem; the eponymous ancestor of the Assyrians (Gen. 10:22; I Chr. 1:17).

**2.** The chief god of the Assyrian pantheon. In the Bible the name appears as a part of proper names, such as Esarhaddon ("Asshur has given brother[s]"). Fig. ASS 95.

**3.** A city in Assyria. The core of the land of Assyria (*see* ASSYRIA AND BABYLONIA) lies along the banks of the Tigris in N Iraq. Its capital cities were, at different periods, Asshur, Calah, Nineveh, and Dur-Sharrukin. The city of Asshur (modern Qal'at Sherqat) has been excavated by the Germans and has yielded important texts and monuments.

The city or the nation may be intended in Ezek. 27:23, although an alternative textual reading, "Aram" (Syria), may better fit the context. Asshur in Balaam's oracle (Num. 24:22, 24) is probably the nation Assyria, as the word is usually translated.

C. H. GORDON

**ASSHURIM** ăsh'ər ĭm [אַשּׁוּרִים] (Gen. 25:3). An obscure tribe, probably N Arabian, living in the S of Palestine, traced back through Dedan to Abraham and Keturah. They are not to be confused with the Assyrians.

**ASSIDEANS** ăs'ə dē'ənz. KJV form of HASIDEANS.

From H. Gressmann, *Altorientalische Texte und Bilder zum AT* (Berlin: Walter de Gruyter & Co.)

95. Asshur is asked to free the people from the locust plague.

**ASSIR** ăs'ər [אסיר, prisoner, captive]. **1.** One of the sons of Korah (Exod. 6:24; I Chr. 6:22—H 6:7). However, in the Chronicler's genealogy of the Levites, Assir is called the son of Ebiasaph and the father of Tahath (I Chr. 6:23, 37—H 6:8, 22). One must either assume two persons by the name of Assir among the early Korahites or attribute the mistake to the artificiality of these lists.

**2.** According to the KJV, a son of King Jeconiah (I Chr. 3:17); perhaps he was born in captivity. But he is nowhere else mentioned, and the right of succession passed from Jeconiah to Shealtiel. Jeconiah was carried into captivity, and "Assir" is probably not a name but an adjective: "Jeconiah, the captive," as in the RSV. The definite article (ה) could easily have dropped out, since the previous word ends with this letter.                F. T. SCHUMACHER

**ASSOS** ăs'ŏs ["Ασσος]. A seaport of MYSIA in the Roman province of ASIA (Acts 20:13-14). It was on the Gulf of Adramyttium on the site of the present village of Behramköy. Originally an Aeolic colony of Lesbos, the city was refounded by the kings of Pergamum as Apollonia (Pliny Nat. Hist. V.123).

The city was ideally located on the terraces of a steep volcanic cone and with a beautiful view. *Ca.* half a mile from the sea, it was protected by the steep ascent. Its natural defenses were strengthened by a city wall two miles long and sixty-five feet high (Strabo XIII.i.58). The harbor, formed by a large artificial mole, was adequate for coastal shipping.

Limited archaeological exploration has discovered extensive remains, including a Doric temple to Athena, which contained important sculptures, a market place, a gymnasium, baths, and a theater. Assos was famous as the home of the Stoic philosopher Cleanthes. In a predominantly agricultural area, it was famous for the quality of the wheat which it exported (cf. Acts 27:2).

At Troas, Paul sent his companions by sailing vessel around cape Lectum, while he went by land to Assos, a journey of *ca.* twenty miles, requiring less time than the voyage around the promontory.

*Bibliography.* W. Leaf, *Troy, a Study in Homeric Geography* (1912), pp. 260-61, 311-12; J. T. Clarke, *et al.*, *Investigations at Assos* (1902-21).                D. C. PELLETT

**ASSUMPTION OF MOSES.** *See* MOSES, ASSUMPTION OF.

**ASSUMPTION OF THE VIRGIN.** A legend widely circulated and variously elaborated, of the death and translation of the Virgin Mary; belonging to what is known as the Apoc. of the NT (*see* APOCRYPHA, NT). None of the many versions of the legend, which may have originated in Egypt, is earlier than the fourth century, although the nucleus of the story may go back to the third. Versions of it are extant in Coptic, Greek, Latin, and Syriac. There are two principal forms, one represented by the Coptic, the other by the Greek, Latin, and Syriac. In the Coptic versions Jesus himself appears to Mary, before the apostles depart on their missionary labors, and announces her coming death and translation —which events, both glowingly described, are separated by 206 days. In the other form an angel makes the announcement, Mary requests the presence of all the apostles, who are forthwith miraculously brought on the clouds from their several places of labor. Mary is transfigured; many healings result from contact with her dead body. She is transported to heaven by Jesus shortly after her death and burial.

The so-called Homily of Evodius and the Discourse of Theodosius are the chief sources for the Coptic version of the tale. The standard Greek form is the Discourse of St. John the Divine, and is found in five late (eleventh–fourteenth century) MSS. The standard Latin form is that wrongly attributed to Melito, with the Narrative by Joseph of Arimathaea a late Italian modification. This Narrative is totally distinct from the *Story of Joseph of Arimathaea,* which is a Greek appendix to the Acts of Pilate. The Syriac narratives are many and with distinct variations.

The legend itself took on a new interest and importance when in 1950 "the Assumption of the Blessed Virgin" was made a part of official Roman Catholic dogma.

*Bibliography.* M. R. James, *The Apocryphal NT* (1924), pp. 194-227, provides a convenient sampling of the various forms of this widely different and constantly elaborated theme. Additional bibliographical material is listed in J. Quasten *Patrology* (1950), I, 247-48.                M. S. ENSLIN

**ASSUR.** KJV form of ASSHUR; ASUR.

**ASSURBANIPAL.** *See* ASHURBANIPAL.

*ASSYRIA AND BABYLONIA ə sĭr'ĭ ə, băb'ə lō'-nĭ ə. Designation of the two civilizations which

flourished in Mesopotamia from the middle of the third millennium B.C. up to the last centuries before the Christian era. They take their names from their capital cities, Asshur and BABYLON. Assyrian and Babylonian civilization rivaled in antiquity that of roughly contemporaneous Egypt but excelled it in respect to influence exercised upon surrounding civilizations.

**A. THE COUNTRY.** Both Assyria and Babylonia lay within the borders of today's Iraq. Babylonia proper occupied the alluvial region between the rivers EUPHRATES and TIGRIS, from Baghdad S to the Persian Gulf, and reaching at times into the flatlands between the Tigris—along its tributaries—and the foothills of the Zagros Range and, upstream, on the Euphrates as far as Hit. The homeland of Assyria originally occupied only the region to the E of the middle course of the Tigris as far as the piedmont region. Its holdings extended upstream in the course of its history, as well as across the land "between the rivers," as far as the large bend of the Euphrates.

   **1. Geographic conditions.** Toward the S and the W, Mesopotamia is clearly separated from the deserts of Arabia and the Syrian Plateau by the course of the Euphrates. Toward the N and the NE, however, the political and cultural frontiers never became quite stabilized in the numerous parallel valleys of the piedmont or in the plains to the N and the E of the lower course of the Tigris. Two main types of landscape can be observed: First, there are the alluvial plains piled up by the two rivers, which push their accumulation of silt into the Persian Gulf and slowly raise the level of the land—a development that is, however, counteracted by a tectonic sinking movement. The higher-lying land is suitable for pasture, mainly in the spring, and also for agriculture (and date growing) when irrigated. The numerous swamps yield cane, which the first inhabitants used with great ingenuity, especially in combination with the abundant clay, for a semiaquatic way of living along the rivers and around the lakes and swamps. Second, there are the fertile valleys between the hills or along the tributaries of the Tigris, where rain is sufficient to grow barley and to raise sheep and goats. The region contains wood and stone for building purposes. The region around the sources of the Habur River, a tributary of the Euphrates in central Upper Mesopotamia, deserves special mention here because its volcanic soil makes it the most fertile of that between the two rivers.

As to the relationship of Mesopotamia with other geographical units, we have to the SE the Persian Gulf and its islands and coastal region, which were connected with S Babylonia by means of shipping lanes and which constituted a link between the "Fertile Crescent" and the East, through which plants, animals, and raw materials came intermittently into Mesopotamia from a very early period on, and were transmitted to the West, the countries around the Mediterranean Sea. To the S and the SW lies the Arabian Desert, from which occurred repeated infiltrations of Semite nomads, who, apart from their languages, brought few, if any, contributions to the culture of Mesopotamia. The most important line of cultural contact was in the Zagros Mountains and along the accesses to the Mediterranean via Upper Syria. Through the mountain passes came materials such as metals and precious stones, of the lack of which the early settlers had become increasingly conscious; also new techniques. However, relations with the mountain peoples were rarely peaceful; they exerted a continuous pressure that expressed itself in many ways, according to the resistance which the dwellers of the plain were able to mount. The mountain men entered as workmen or soldiers, or penetrated into the fertile regions to become bandits, mercenaries, or kings. Only Assyria attempted to colonize and thus pacify these tribes, and in the course of the history a series of hybrid civilizations arose here and there in the mountain valleys, to become ephemeral buffer states. The accesses to the "Upper Sea"—as Assyrian kings liked to call the Mediterranean—and to Anatolia permitted cultural contact by a process of continuous osmosis. This connection was, at times, intensified for commercial and political purposes.

The over-all settlement pattern of Mesopotamia shows a cluster of very old cities in S Babylonia, especially along the lower course of the Euphrates, and very few cities elsewhere. In the center of the urbanized region, the southernmost group contained the cities of Eridu, Ur, Larsa, and Uruk; then there was a central group around Nippur—i.e., Isin, Adab, Shuruppak (Fara)—and more to the E of it, Umma and Lagash, and finally the N group Borsippa, Babylon, Kutha, Kish, and the northernmost Sippar. To the E of the Tigris (Der, Eshnunna) and along the Euphrates (Mari, Terqa), more or less ephemeral cities grew up when accidental political conditions or trade routes favored a specific region. In Assyria proper, Asshur's unique position could well have been based on the sacredness of its locale, while the origins of another sacred city, Arbela, remain hidden under the modern town. All other large urban sites in this region were cities founded by kings for political or military purposes.

**2. Hydrographic conditions.** The two rivers Euphrates and Tigris are fed by a number of mountain streams in Armenia whose sources are, at one place, only *ca.* fifteen miles apart. Their courses are, however, very much different. The Tigris, upon breaking through the last ranges, flows E and then SE in a swift course; it is navigable in its lower reaches only by means of keleks (reed floats supported by inflated skins). It flows past NINEVEH, Calah, and Asshur—all capitals of Assyria—to enter the plain near Samarra, touching Opis (Upi, old Akshak) and SELEUCIA. In the historical period the lower course underwent many changes which did not favor the growth of permanent settlements. It now joins the Euphrates at Shatt-el-'Arab but formerly fell independently into the Persian Gulf. All the tributaries of the Tigris rise in the Zagros: the Khoser River, which flows past Nineveh; the Upper or Greater Zab, which joins the Tigris near CALAH; the Lower or Lesser Zab; the Adhem (Akkadian *Radānu*); the Diyala (Akkadian [*Mê*]-*Turna*[*t*]); and eventually the Duweirig (Akkadian *Tupliaš*).

The Euphrates, after leaving the mountains, runs first SW to reach a point where it is but ninety miles from the Mediterranean Sea, then turns S and eventually E. Its sole tributaries are the Belikh and the Habur, which come from the W side. The Euphrates reaches the plain only twenty miles from the Tigris. Its course is *ca.* five hundred miles longer than that of the Tigris; it carries less water, but its current is much slower, permitting navigation farther upstream.

A characteristic feature of the two rivers is their annual flooding. Their behavior is as follows: A general swelling of the water is caused by the autumn rains and continues through winter and spring till the snow melts in the Armenian mountains and the flood wave reaches the plains in April and especially May. It subsides in June, and the rivers reach their lowest level in September and October. It should be stressed that the time of the inundation in Mesopotamia is not nearly so favorable for cereal agriculture as it is in Egypt. The flooding of the Tigris and Euphrates is late and requires special work—preparation of dikes, etc.—to prevent the fields from getting too much water, apart from the problem of storing and distributing it. An equally important drawback is the tendency of the soil toward salination caused by the late flooding, which, together with the silting up of the distribution canals, cuts down the yield of fields and necessitated the relocation of agricultural territory after relatively short periods of prosperity. The digging of new canal systems and the resettlement of the population therefore formed an essential part of the economic and political program of a good sovereign as much as the maintenance of existing dikes and canals.

**3. Domesticated plants and animals.** In Assyria agriculture could reasonably rely on the rain which falls normally in October and November and which made it possible to prepare the fields for the next harvest. In Babylonia, irrigation, if properly managed, could be expected to secure a good harvest every year. The main cereal grown was barley, and only second to this were emmer—a primitive type of wheat—and wheat. The crushed seeds of the sesame plant were the only source of vegetable oil, and the main supplier of sugar was the date palm, grown in Babylonia proper. Of vegetables, onions, garlic, and leek are most frequently mentioned. Mustard was grown for its seeds, which were used as a spice. Millet, flax, and legumens were relatively rare, and so were fruit trees. Vineyards were cultivated only in Upper Mesopotamia. Not much change in these crops can be observed throughout the known period, except for the addition of rice, which the Persians are said to have introduced into Babylonia.

While herds of goats and sheep provided a ready supply of fresh meat, the wool of the latter was of major importance as raw material for the production of textiles, exported from Babylonia as far as Anatolia. Cattle were essential for plowing but seem to have been kept in larger herds only by palaces or temples. The donkey was used as the main beast of burden. Horses, Bactrian camels and dromedaries, and even elephants were well known. The horses acquired military importance when used with the chariot, and especially when the Assyrians introduced cavalry into their army after the ninth century B.C.

**B. THE PEOPLE.** The inhabitants of Mesopotamia, from the time when their linguistic affinities become clear, are referred to successively as Sumerians, Babylonians, Hurrians, Assyrians, and Chaldeans. Apart from them a series of invaders are known, such as the Guti, the Amorites (speaking a West Semitic tongue), and the Kassites, who succeeded at one time or another in ruling over parts of Mesopotamia. Others, like the Hittites or Elamites, came in on short raids until, with the conquest of Nineveh by the Medes (612 B.C.) and of Babylon by the Persians (538 B.C.), the political independence of Mesopotamia came to an end. Alexander the Great conquered Babylonia, then a satrapy of the Persian Empire, but the Seleucids succeeded for a short time in making Babylonia again politically important before the rising tide of Iranian rulers (the Sassanids and Arsacids) sealed the doom of Mesopotamian civilization.

**1. Ethnic background.** With the first intelligible written documents (from Ur and Djemdet Nasr), we meet the SUMERIANS, by any standards the most interesting people of the ancient Near East. There are indications that they only adapted an already existing system of writing to their own language; but the civilization the Sumerians created, and led in an astonishingly short period to a flowering, left its imprint on all subsequent civilizations which rose in, and also around, Mesopotamia. Their ethnic affiliations remain obscure, but it should be stressed that they represent only one of several ethnic groups which inhabited Mesopotamia in the formative centuries of the protohistoric period. Uruk (*see* ERECH) in the S seems to have been the place where Sumerian civilization reached its peak. This is shown by references to this city in religious texts, and especially in myths, as well as by the historical tradition, etc.

At the time when the Sumerian rulers created an empire from Ur, they seem to have already been fused to a large extent with Semites speaking the Old Akkadian dialect, as the names of the last kings of Ur and the number of Akkadian loan words in the Sumerian of that period suggest. The first bid of the Semites for political power in Mesopotamia was highlighted by the appearance of King Sargon of Agade (*ca.* 2350), whose influence on the political concepts of Mesopotamia was not only reflected in the subsequent Sumerian empire of Ur III (2125-2035) but also remembered in far-off Assyria. *See* SARGON 1.

Akkadian began to supplant Sumerian, first outside the well-established and formalized literary forms (such as legal and administrative documents), mainly in letters, then in texts of the growing Akkadian literary tradition, and in royal inscriptions, which were often edited in Sumerian as well as in Akkadian. The rise of the dynasties of Isin, Larsa, and Babylon (1894-1592) saw Sumerian as a spoken language clearly on the decline, but interest in Sumerian literary works remained very much alive. The first interlinear translations of Sumerian texts appeared, and in the training of the scribes much stress was placed on the teaching of Sumerian grammar and a specialized Sumerian vocabulary, as the school texts of that period (grammatical tablets and dictionaries) indicate.

It should be noted that there are no signs of any stress which this change in language might have produced, although it reflects an important ethnic shift. Apparently a deep-rooted, truly Mesopotamian (i.e., Sumero-Akkadian) civilization had already developed and become stabilized before the Old Akkadian period, so that the change-over was only one in political outlook and aspiration, which made the linguistic and even the ethnic transition of secondary importance. The scribal tradition succeeded in keeping Sumerian, as a scholarly and, in certain instances, even a sacred language, from oblivion until the disappearance of the entire Mesopotamian civilization. It was even able to achieve a somewhat artificial and short-lived renaissance of Sumerian in the Kassite period.

The role of the Semites in Mesopotamia was, of course, paramount. Semitic-speaking ethnic groups infiltrated in repeated waves throughout the entire history of the region, and it must be assumed that this situation was no different in the preceding protohistoric periods. It will never be known to what degree these migrants contributed to the rise of civilization in that region, especially to the unique phenomenon of urbanization which materialized there so early.

According to their attitude toward urbanization, two sets of Semitic migrants have to be differentiated in Mesopotamia. There were those who preferred to drift between the existing cities or to settle in small villages, reluctant to pay with taxes, military service, and *corvée* work for the security granted them by some central authority; and there were those who moved into cities—and perhaps even helped to found them. Only the latter spoke Akkadian up to the disappearance of this language in the second half of the first millennium B.C.; the former used a number of Semitic dialects: first, that which is termed Eastern Canaanite or Amorite, up to that period in the second millennium B.C. which is termed the Dark Age (*ca.* 1600-1350); after that, Aramaic (in various subdialects); and eventually Arabic. These non-Akkadian-speaking Semites succeeded at times—before the Dark Age—in conquering one or another city and in establishing dynasties in them, which contributed essentially to the political development of the region. Only from Mari on the middle course of the Euphrates do we have texts to show us the process of urbanization and "Akkadianization" of an ethnic group rather than of a small ruling class. The situation which arose after the Dark Age, under similar circumstances—i.e., during the invasion and immigration of the Aramaic-speaking Semites—led, however, to rather different results. Most of the new Aramaic states preserved their native language, while others assimilated foreign languages and cultures and created, to the W of Mesopotamia, various hybrid civilizations using as systems of writing the Phoenician and the hieroglyphic Hittite. The Arameans failed to exert any political influence upon the already well-established Assyria and Babylonia of the first millennium. The impact of their language and especially of their alphabetic system of writing, however, began to sap the strength of the Akkadian tradition, reducing it eventually to the lore of a narrow class of specialists. Obviously this linguistic change again reflects a decided shift in the ethnic composition of the population. The nomadic background and specific outlook of all these non-Akkadian population movements, before and after the Dark Age, were favorable to the growth of intercity and international political and commercial relations, as contrasted with the sedentary and autarchic outlook of the city-state tradition. *See* PATRIARCHS.

Most important among the several foreign (i.e., non-Sumerian and non-Akkadian) ethnic groups which passed through or penetrated into Mesopotamia were the Hurrians (*see* HORITES), who are in evidence as early as the beginning of the second millennium in Babylonia. They rose to primary importance in the W even before the Dark Age, at the end of which we see their vestiges in personal names, technical terms, institutions, and in the arts, everywhere from the Zagros Mountains, across Assyria, and up to the Mediterranean coast. The extent of their influence on Assyrian civilization is still difficult to evaluate, because it is not yet possible to gauge how much Assyria owes to other contacts with the mountain peoples. The latter had always been pressing down into the fertile plains and their rich settlements, and appear there under several names, such as Guti, Kassites, or Kurds—not to speak of similar movements which must have existed in the protohistoric period.

Contacts with the Arabs of the desert were always only slight and incidental to the continuous expansion policy of the Assyrian Empire. That there were commercial relations with them is likely, but they are not documented.

The existence of a number of completely undefined ethnic groups in Babylonia is revealed by such indications as the frequent occurrence up to the Old Babylonian period of personal names which cannot be assigned to any known language; by the oldest geographical names (for cities, rivers, and regions), which are, with very few exceptions, neither Sumerian nor Semitic; as well as by a body of words referring to essential materials, tools, plants, and animals, appearing as loan words in both Akkadian and Sumerian. Some of these ethnic groups have certainly to be considered among the first settlers.

**2. Languages.** The linguistic affinities of Sumerian have withstood so far any attempt of modern scholarship toward identification. The documentary evidence is very rich, ranging from the earliest economic texts (Uruk, Fara, Djemdet Nasr) to royal inscriptions (predominantly of the rulers of Lagash), poetic texts (such as hymns addressing gods and kings, and lamentations), myths of wide variety, proverbs, word lists, etc. There are interesting religious poetic texts and private letters, a unique type of legal document regarding procedures in court, and at least two law codes, all covering more than half a millennium. The language is now quite well understood, and many texts are translated.

For the Semitic language of Mesopotamia, the term "Akkadian" has come into use, replacing the earlier, clumsy designation "Assyrian and Babylonian," which refers to its main dialects. It should be noted, however, that the designation *akkadû*, "[language] of Agade," which has been adopted by modern Assyriologists, was in ancient times used when referring to the Semitic versus the Sumerian version of a text, while the Hittites referred to what we call Akkadian as "Babylonian," and the Assyrians themselves called their language "Assyrian" when contrasting it with Aramaic. Akkadian is the earliest recorded Semitic language and is commonly assigned to the E branch of this family of languages, of which it is the only representative. Probably because of its age and isolation, Akkadian shows a series of unique features in its phoneme inventory, its system of tenses, and its syntax. It shares certain morphological peculiarities with the old South Arabic dialects, but its vocabulary shows important links with the West. It is heavily influenced by foreign, mostly Sumerian, elements, but also contains words from roots which must have disappeared from the Semitic languages recorded at a later date.

As to the dialects of Akkadian, it is customary to set aside the oldest material coming from the Babylonia of the time of Sargon as Old Akkadian and then to posit a division into two main dialects, Babylonian and Assyrian, which in themselves fall easily into three stages according to periods.

The classical texts in Old Babylonian are the Code of Hammurabi and letters issued by the chancellery of this king, but an increasing number of literary and scholarly texts are becoming known, illustrating the wide range of written material in this dialect. Traces of local differences (N and S Babylonia, provincial peculiarities in the region beyond the Tigris and in the extreme S) as well as of period differences (early and late Old Babylonian) have been observed. Primary Middle Babylonian material is relatively rare. The letters of Middle Babylonian kings in the Amarna archive (*see* TELL EL-AMARNA) and the texts of Kassite NIPPUR, Ur, and Dur-Kurigalzu (1373-1160) are the most important representatives, apart from a few boundary stones, while secondary evidence is contained in a number of literary texts which seem to have been composed in that period but are preserved only in late copies. A much wider gap than that which separates the last Old Babylonian from the Middle Babylonian texts lies between the latter and those Neo-Babylonian texts that can be considered representative of the new dialect which came into evidence in the Babylonia of the seventh century B.C. While the Neo-Babylonian kings strove to imitate the paleography, the spelling, and even the wording of the Old Babylonian royal inscriptions, and the literary texts of the period maintain the standards of the Middle Babylonian period, the Neo-Babylonian legal documents, and especially the administrative letters, are written in a dialect which deviates in essential points such as spelling, morphology, and vocabulary from similar documents of the preceding period. The Akkadian of the royal inscriptions of the Persian period is usually called Late Babylonian.

In Assyria, the development of Assyrian—apart from Old Assyrian, which is almost exclusively attested in texts from Asia Minor (Cappadocia) and early royal inscriptions—took place under the shadow of Babylonian influence, in Middle Assyrian but especially in Neo-Assyrian times. The increasing and conscious Babylonization of Assyria expressed itself in the acceptance of a Babylonian dialect for the writing of royal inscriptions, royal letters, and other official documents. We call this dialect "Standard Babylonian." It is presumably a scholarly creation originating with the scribes of the Assyrian kings who had been trained by copying Babylonian literary texts. Whatever segment of Assyria's cultural life was not under the overpowering influence of Babylonian literary conventions and scribal customs expressed this fact by using Middle Assyrian or Neo-Assyrian dialect forms (and sometimes even paleographic features), doubtless as a demonstration of that nationalistic and anti-Babylonian attitude that was powerful enough to reach even to the throne and cause much bitter civil strife and wars.

The history of the Akkadian language, strangely enough, does not parallel the ups and downs of the political power of Mesopotamia. Before the Dark Age, Akkadian and the cuneiform system of writing spread into Anatolia, where it was adapted to write the Indo-European language of the newly rising Hittite Empire, and reached the Mediterranean

(Alalakh and Qatna). These writings show by certain peculiarities that they stem from the scribal tradition of the Ur III period via unknown intermediaries. A second period of expansion, derived from a later, Old Babylonian fountainhead, reached Mari, where, in a systematic process of the Babylonization of a non-Akkadian-speaking Semitic people, the scribal tradition of Babylonia was introduced. Earlier still, Sumerian and Akkadian had spread to Elam (where it is attested from the Old Akkadian to the Old Babylonian period), to Mari, and to some of the small hybrid states in the Zagros valleys (Lulubi, etc.).

After the Dark Age—an age which saw Babylonian political influence at a low ebb—Akkadian achieved its maximum extension, reaching Cyprus and Egypt to the W and the S, and Asia Minor to the N. The language was accepted as the diplomatic language in Palestine and Syria, and by the Hittites and the Hurrians. The system of writing was used to write texts in the Hurrian language and, some centuries later, royal inscriptions in Elamite (beginning with King Humban-ummena). Later still, the kings of Urartu wrote inscriptions in Assyrian as well as in their native tongue, using cuneiform. This last, however, constituted an exception, because with the increasing spread of the Assyrian Empire, at the beginning of the first millennium B.C., the influence of Akkadian (the language as well as the system of writing) was on the downgrade; Phoenician and Aramaic princes in Asia Minor and Upper Syria inscribed their stelae in their own languages, using an alphabetic script, or in Hieroglyphic Hittite. When Persian and Seleucid (Antiochus I, Soter; 280-262 B.C.) kings had inscriptions written in Akkadian, this is to be considered a political gesture rather than a means of communication, since at that time Aramaic had become the lingua franca in Babylonia.

The tracing of the internal development of Akkadian is greatly hampered by the traditionalism of the scribes, who painstakingly strove to preserve the wording and even the spelling of the originals which they copied. Secular documents only permit of observing changes in the vocabulary, the influx of foreign words, and traces of the everyday speech. Akkadian showed much resistance to the introduction of foreign words. Apart from the *Kulturwörter* of the earliest periods, we find foreign words nearly exclusively in texts written outside Mesopotamia (Nuzi, Qatna, Elam, Alalakh, Ras Shamra) and by foreign scribes (Mari). Even the influence of Aramaic and Persian in the Neo-Babylonian period did not produce more than a very small number of foreign words accepted by the well-trained scribes. On the other hand, quite a number of Akkadian words—mostly religious, legal, and technical terms—have penetrated the languages of the adjacent civilizations, either directly as loans or through a temporary adoption of the Akkadian language itself.

The eclipse of Akkadian by Aramaic toward the second half of the first millennium B.C. progresses from the fields marginal to literary and scholarly production. First the language of daily life must have changed, then that of records made for administrative and commercial purposes, and letters, and finally that of legal documents. The new language, Aramaic, was written in its own, alphabetical system; and, except for a few inscriptions on pottery and names scratched on clay tablets beside cuneiform writing, it was written on perishable materials. Special resistance to a change-over in language is shown in astronomical texts, written by specialists in very abbreviated and stereotyped forms, which could not be divorced from the cuneiform system of writing. These texts maintained the old language into the first century of our era. Whether any attempts were made to save the literary heritage of Akkadian by means of translation into Aramaic remains unknown, because, as already mentioned, the new material used for alphabetic writing did not withstand the ravages of time. It may, however, be noted that there exists an Aramaic text written down in the Seleucid period in the cuneiform system of writing, exactly as the demotic system of writing was used to write down an Aramaic text in Egypt.

As to the other languages written in non-Akkadian cuneiform characters, Hurrian and Elamite have already been mentioned. For Hurrian we have the so-called Mitanni letter written by King Tushratta (fourteenth century). Then there are, also in Hurrian, some glosses added to a Sumero-Akkadian vocabulary in Ras Shamra, a very early foundation inscription, and a small number of literary tablets found in Mari, together with a substantial number of Hurrian words occurring in Akkadian texts (mostly in Nuzi and Alalakh, but also in Mari and Ras Shamra and even in Asshur [Middle Assyrian]), in Hittite texts (from Boghazköy), and in personal names. The results of the investigation of Hurrian are, however, rather meager; and this is also the case with regard to Elamite, where we have texts from the Agade period to the Persian, without being able to cull much information from the type of material preserved. It is partly too repetitive and partly too much diversified and obscure in context for interpretation.

**C. HISTORICAL SURVEY.** It is the purpose of this survey to sketch an outline of the history, but not primarily the political history, with special consideration given to the limitations of our present knowledge. For the sake of convenience a median chronology has been accepted.

**1. Source material.** Mesopotamian historiography, in the stricter sense of the term, covers only the period from TIGLATH-PILESER III (745-727) and the contemporaneous Babylonian king, Nabû-nāṣir, to Antiochus I, Soter—to be exact, to the thirty-seventh year of the Seleucid era. Not very many years of this stretch of nearly half a millennium are represented in the Chronicles, which contain in annual records data concerning war and peace, the deaths of kings and of members of their families, etc. Their style is factual and terse, and they are of great importance, not only for the historian of Mesopotamia, but also for OT and even Greek history. Some of these texts record in similar style events before the Dark Age, thus attempting a *historia mundi*. Their content is necessarily more legendary but still an important source of information for the time from Sargon of Agade (and Ilushuma of Assyria) to Sumuabu of Babylonia and, overlapping partly, from Irra-Imitti of Isin to a Kassite king, Agum, son of Kashtiliash. For contemporary records of historical events, often on a rather local scale and from day to day, one has to mention the Astronomical Diary texts of the Seleucid period.

Another expression of consciousness of history is the king lists which reach from that mythical moment "when kingship descended from heaven" to the Diadochi. They cover in a nearly uninterrupted sequence all of Babylonian and Assyrian history, bridging even the gaps of the several Dark Ages. They give the names of the kings and the lengths of their reigns, divide them into "dynasties," and at times enter more or less cryptic remarks of a historical nature which show the influence of political concepts. For the last centuries of Assyro-Babylonian history, there is one list that co-ordinates the reigns of the kings of the two lands. All these lists constitute an important historical source, although their reliability decreases quite naturally for the older dynasties. Awareness of history expresses itself in royal inscriptions also in occasional references to kings of the past, who are dated by means of the number of years that had passed since they ruled. For this information the scribes clearly relied on their king lists.

Of great value for the historian, but not conceived by the Mesopotamians themselves as historiographic texts, are the so-called date lists of the Old Babylonian period and the Assyrian lists of eponyms. Since in Babylonia, up to the Middle Babylonian period, every year was named after an event that had occurred in the preceding year, it was necessary, for practical purposes, to draw up lists of such year names. Their value as a source of historical information is somewhat restricted by the tendency to record in these formalized names only victories, pious acts of the king, dedications of votive offerings to the temples, and similar events. However, references to the death of foreign rulers occur at times, and a change of the year name in the middle of that year can be taken to reflect an actual event, usually a calamity. The Assyrian system of identifying the years of the reign of a king by means of a consistent sequence of names of high officials used as eponyms, beginning with the king himself, likewise necessitated the drawing up of lists of the eponyms; some of these lists are provided with short remarks referring to campaigns, pestilences, etc.

The main body of historical information, however, is contained in the so-called royal inscriptions which come to us from such early kings as Mesannepadda of Uruk and continue on to Antiochus I, Soter. They range from a few signs on votive offerings to the rock inscriptions of Behistun, from small clay cones to prisms containing many hundreds of lines. Very few of them were written primarily to inform us of the deeds and achievements of the king whose name they bear; they were buried as foundation deposits or, written on relief-decorated stone slabs, were placed in dark corridors or on inaccessible rocks. They sing the praise of the king, list his heroic deeds, and have in most cases the purpose of dedicating a temple or palace. In fact, in terms of their stylistic development, they grew out of dedicational inscrip-

tions which listed the royal titles, embellished by numerous epithets recording specific victories, or which referred to such victories in connection with the dedication.

As essential as texts of this type are for the reconstruction of Mesopotamian history, it must be kept in mind that they are written in a highly stylized, sometimes poetic, language, in which only carefully selected happenings are recorded in a very conventional way. Events are arranged according to certain principles, sometimes geographical and sometimes chronological as annals. They are extended, embellished, reduced, or telescoped to fit the requirements of space or of the specific purpose of the inscription. Still, careful study is able to reveal in many instances something of the real nature of the recorded events. It is even possible to discover certain personal preferences and mannerisms of the kings, especially in the inscriptions of the Sargonides that form the largest body of material among these texts. While the Assyrian kings seem to have had a love of details and exact figures, and the text may even include episodic happenings, the Neo-Babylonian rulers preferred to avoid indications of a factual nature, and couched their reports in piously archaizing and vague terms.

Lastly, mention should be made of the fact that Hittite, OT, Egyptian, and Greek material can, at certain periods, be of great importance for the student of Mesopotamian history.

As to the much-discussed problems of chronology, one can state that absolute chronological certainty does not extend beyond the eighth century B.C. For anterior periods, the historian has to rely on an increasing amount of dead reckoning and more or less tenuous synchronisms, together with whatever accidental information archaeology or other sources can provide. All these have to be utilized and combined with the evidence offered by the texts to erect a chronological framework. It happens that the excavations in Alalakh have yielded reasons to believe that the reign of Hammurabi of Babylon must have fallen within a period of time that can be determined objectively. Then there is the fact that, quite by accident, astronomical observations concerning the passing of the planet Venus were recorded by the Babylonians at a time within the Hammurabi Dynasty which can be determined by modern astronomers. Since this astronomical event recurs in intervals of more than sixty years, three dates for the accession of Hammurabi can be proposed—1856, 1792, and 1728. Unfortunately, none of these dates can be selected as fitting all the requirements of the evidence known today. The chronology adopted here is based on the median date, 1792 B.C.

**2. History of Babylonia.** Babylonia experienced two climaxes of political power, one near the beginning of the two millenniums of its history and the other toward the end. The names of Sargon of Agade (*ca.* 2350) and NEBUCHADREZZAR II (605-562) characterize these two periods. Strangely enough, however, not much is known of these periods with regard to historical facts. The best-attested period of Babylonian history is that of Hammurabi (1792-1750) and his immediate predecessors and successors;

here only can one observe essential features of the economic and social life, details of relationships with foreign powers, etc.

With the downfall of Uruk, the very center of the classical stage of Sumerian civilization under Lugal-zaggisi, the Dynasty of Agade, founded by Sargon, achieved for the first time a type of unification of Mesopotamia which differed in kind from the hegemonic rule of one city-state over the others. It matters little whether Sargon was actually the first king of such stature, but legend and tradition made him the exponent of imperial aspirations. Sargon's military aggressiveness, reaching beyond the borders of Babylonia, was based upon the maintenance of a standing army supported by taxes which were levied and collected by a centralized bureaucracy. His and Narâm-Sin's extremely long reigns (fifty-five and fifty-six years respectively) might well have stabilized the organization of the country if an invasion of the Guti mountaineers had not brought about its ruin. Fig. ASS 96.

When the rule of the Guti was broken by Utuhegal of Uruk, the Neo-Sumerian empire of Ur (2125-2025; called Ur III, the first ruler being Ur-Nammu, and the most important, Shulgi) seems to have taken up the Agade tradition. We witness in the abundant documentation, especially of the last years of this dynasty, the workings of an elaborate administration, with provincial governors residing from as far E as Elam and as far N as Asshur, and taxes flowing into the capital, which was being embellished on a large scale by the kings of this, the third dynasty, of Ur. For reasons undetermined—possibly the social unrest provoked by the pressure of newly infiltrating peoples—the empire collapsed with long-remembered spectacularity under an invasion of the Elamites. The center of gravity of political power shifted slowly to the N—successively to Isin, Larsa, and eventually Babylon—in all instances under the leadership of a new class of rulers with Semitic but non-Akkadian personal names.

Babylon, the youngest of these cities, gained the upper hand under Hammurabi. He defeated Larsa to the S, Eshnunna to the E, and Mari to the N in a long-drawn-out series of wars, alliances, and political maneuvering. The political horizon of that era reached from Elam and Telmun in the Persian Gulf up to CARCHEMISH and Aleppo, and even to Hazor in Palestine. Kings, caravans in long-distance trade, and armies moved within this compass. Friends and foes among these newcomers bore the same non-Akkadian names. All were ready to change sides or to outmaneuver the enemy, bent on ensuring their hold over the city dwellers, who belonged to a different economic, cultural, and probably ethnic stratum. Only two of the rulers attempted a policy of integration, striving to organize a territorial state, Shamshi-Adad I (*ca.* 1812-1780) in Assyria and also Hammurabi in Babylonia on a different level.

We are fortunate enough to be able to observe Hammurabi's carefully and efficiently organized administration, and to see in some detail his social policies (Codex Hammurabi), which earned him fame within Mesopotamian civilization. The main political achievement of Hammurabi must be considered to be the successful change of his realm into a territorial state ruled from a capital, with all other cities on the provincial level, a political setup which was able to withstand the centuries of disorganization of the Dark Age. After Hammurabi there was hardly a question any more where political power was located in S Mesopotamia; it was from Babylon that Babylonia was to be ruled. Yet in spite of all the obvious prosperity and security of the middle period of Hammurabi's reign, we begin to encounter, from his thirtieth year on, an increasing number of year names that speak of victories won over the coalitions of the enemies of "Sumer and Akkad" reaching from Elam as far as Assyria, until the year names of his last years (forty-second and forty-third) show him clearly on the defensive, erecting fortifications where the Tigris and the Euphrates enter the Mesopotamian Plain.

The successors of Hammurabi seem to have been restricted to Babylonia proper, with the exception of the southernmost region, where the Sea Country arose protected by the inaccessibility of its marshes that enabled it to survive even the catastrophe which befell the entire Fertile Crescent and culminated in the conquest of Babylon (under

Courtesy of the Musée du Louvre, Paris

96. Stele of victory of Narâm-Sin

Samsuditana) by the Hittite king Murshili. Then the Dark Age set in, not only over Babylonia but also over nearly the entire Near East. We have no documents concerning the period of the last king of the Hammurabi Dynasty nor of any period up to Burnaburiash II (*ca.* 1370-1340), the nineteenth king of a new dynasty of foreign stock. This is the dynasty of the kings set up by the invading Kassites. Until Burnaburiash II we have neither royal inscriptions nor other documents, and even the following Kassite kings, whose dynasty ruled for nearly half a millennium, provide us with only meager and stereotyped inscriptions, mostly in Sumerian. We have, however, some of their letters sent to Egyptian kings and found in Amarna in Egypt. These and the letters and administrative texts excavated in Nippur (and others written three or four generations later in Ur) show a number of changes in language, writing, and, above all, scribal practices. The Nippur texts of the Kassite period (Burnaburiash II to Kashtiliash III, 1235-1228) indicate a royal palace well organized with regard to the administration of its estates, the handling of its personnel, etc.; but they have not been fully studied from this point of view, and they do not shed light on other cities of Babylonia. The letters of Kadashman-Harbe and Burnaburiash to Amenophis III and IV of Egypt show Babylonia as a minor political power exactly as does the letter of the contemporaneous Assyrian king Ashur-uballit. These rulers sent small presents to Egypt and expected gold and political favors in exchange. Still, one has the impression that the Babylonian kings did enjoy a certain prestige and were striving to maintain their dignity and their aspiration to make Babylonia an important state. Possibly, the preceding dark centuries hide certain political achievements of the rulers of Babylon. We may have also to deal here with trade relations on the royal level as they are attested elsewhere in the ancient Near East of that period.

During the rule of the last Kassite kings—who now shift from Kassite to Akkadian personal names —an increasing decline of royal authority is illustrated by the frequency of royal land grants to officials, inscribed on stone documents called *kudurru*, and carrying exemption from taxation and *corvée* duties. This fragmentation of the country, combined with the increasing infiltration of Arameans into the open country, which interrupted communication, further reduced the power of the kings of Babylon. A resurgence in the military potential of Elam led to the invasion of Shutruk-Nahhunte into Babylonia, in the course of which the Elamite king brought the stela with the laws of Hammurabi and other trophies back to Susa as booty. For Babylonia, already weakened by conflicts with Assyria, this event spelled the end of the Kassite Dynasty (*ca.* 1151).

The next centuries saw the slow comeback of Babylonia, heralded by the victory of Nebuchadrezzar I (1146-1123) over Elam and culminating, after many setbacks, in Nabopolassar (626-602), the first king of a new dynasty which was to become heir to Assyrian supremacy. This half millennium, from Nebuchadrezzar I to Nabopolassar, was in many important respects as dark for Babylonia as the Dark Age itself. Whatever light the Assyrian royal in-

scriptions reporting on the increasingly severe conflicts with Babylonia shed on this period, or whatever can be gleaned from occasional *kudurru* texts, royal inscriptions, and the extremely few administrative documents preserved, does not suffice to suggest any answer for the obvious query as to the nature of the cultural, social, and economic forces which kept Babylonia alive and even started it out on the road back to political power. Merodachbaladan's tenacious fight against Sargon II (721-705) of Assyria represents a strange but not unique phenomenon. The correspondence of the last Sargonides with their generals, political agents, spies, etc., shows that the stubbornness of Babylonian nationalism had its roots in the open country, mainly in the S, while the city dwellers, especially in the large cities, preferred Assyrian rule. This may be taken to indicate that large-scale commercial activities—i.e., long-distance trade—had, since Nebuchadrezzar I, been again moving through Babylonian cities and that this trade was protected and furthered by Assyria. This would also explain the emphasis placed by Esarhaddon of Assyria upon the fact that he again granted the inhabitants of Babylon the privilege of trading with all the regions of the world after his father, Sennacherib, had destroyed their city in one of those recurrent sudden shifts in Assyrian foreign policy toward Babylonia. *See* Hezekiah; Isaiah; Merodach-baladan; Sargon 3; Esarhaddon; Sennacherib.

Such trading—apart from booty taken—must have brought to Babylon the riches which become evident in the inscriptions of the rulers of the Chaldean Dynasty (such as Nebuchadrezzar II, 605-562), reporting on their rebuilding and sumptuously decorating the sanctuaries, and which are also amply illustrated in the thousands of administrative documents of the temples of Sippar, Babylon, and Uruk that are in our hands. As a matter of fact, Babylonia, when incorporated in the Persian Empire, was its richest satrapy. Only the kind of carrying trade on which the wealth of the caravan cities of Palmyra and Volegesia (in Babylonia) was later founded could have made such wealth come into Babylonia. Since this trade is not evidenced by any cuneiform document, one has to assume that it was in the hands of persons using another writing material, which indicates another language, necessarily Aramaic—and it is not without interest, in this context, to draw attention to the fact that Nebuchadrezzar had a "chief *tamkaru*" among his major court officials and that this man had the unmistakably Phoenician name of Hanno. *See* Jeremiah; Jehoiakim; Zedekiah.

The last ruler of Babylonia, Nabonidus (555-539), provides a somewhat queer finis for a development of nearly two thousand years. He rose to power as a middle-aged general in the confusion created by the conflicts between the short-lived successors of Nebuchadrezzar II, although he seems to have been a native of Harran in Assyria. After a stay in Tyre to install a pro-Babylonian king there, he seems to have dedicated all his efforts to the rebuilding of the temple of Sin in Harran in Upper Mesopotamia. He tried to stress the worship of Sin, his favorite god, in Babylon; this led possibly to conflicts with the priests. It seems, however, that these preferences and his archaeological pursuits reveal only one side of his character—though they gave him the worldwide reputation of being insane. From newly discovered inscriptions in Harran, it has become evident that he visited the large cities of Arabia during the years of his protracted absence from Babylon. From the Babylonian Chronicle we know already that he stayed away for years on end while his son and coregent, BELSHAZZAR, acted as king in Babylon. It is possible that these strange overland journeys of a Babylonian king are connected in some way with overland trade, the control of which might well have been in his hand. At any rate, when Cyrus suddenly invaded Babylonia and moved, without encountering resistance, into Babylon, Nabonidus returned and was treated by Cyrus with his characteristic leniency toward defeated kings. This was the end of Babylonian sovereignty, but that the spirit was not yet quite dead is shown by the fact that two subsequent pretenders to the Babylonian throne took the name Nebuchadrezzar. *See* ISAIAH § B2.

**3. History of Assyria.** In the history of Assyria an essential difference can be observed between the periods before and after the Dark Age. Although little evidence is available for the former, it definitely lacks that spirit of military aggressiveness which characterizes the latter, but shows an efficiency in organizing trade relations and commercial activities that is not conspicuous after the Dark Age. In the centuries after the Amarna Age, with Asshur-uballit (*ca.* 1365-1330) the Assyrian kings succeeded, by means of institutionalized annual campaigns, in building up a series of more or less ephemeral empires which often suddenly collapsed but were quickly reconquered and even extended. The frequency of these sudden changes in the political and military potential of Assyria constitutes a very important problem. As startling as the collapses, which drastically reduced the sphere of Assyrian influence, is the ever-undiminished vigor with which its political aspirations make Assyria rebound. It is obvious that both the ability to recuperate and regain strength and the curious instability of this strength have to be considered characteristic qualities of the new Assyria. They may perhaps be understood when one investigates the entire assemblage of Assyrian culture traits with respect to its native and to its Babylonian components.

On the surface, Assyrian civilization was patently dependent upon its sister civilization for the bulk of its religious concepts, its literary tradition, etc., although there exist some obvious deviations, mainly in point of political organization and in the preferred styles in the realm of the representational arts. But hidden under the surface of conscious and intensive Babylonization, Assyrian civilization remains alien. The position of the Assyrian king is quite different from that of the Babylonian. His relationship to the high officials and feudal lords, the social structure of the country, and the policy of the royal administration bespeak an utterly different attitude and different goals. Then there are the cultural and intellectual differences which come sharply to the fore in the political relationship between Assyria and Babylonia, and many other distinctive contrasts which future research will have to trace and to identify if an understanding of the singularity of Assyrian history is to be obtained. It is certainly far too naïve to look for an explanation—as has been done in the past—in terms of economic determinism or racial and climatic differences.

Assyrian history begins with a governor (*ensi*) of the Ur III Empire (up to 2025) residing in Asshur. After the collapse of this empire, the city, ruled by a series of kings who often called themselves only *waklum,* "overseer," rose to be a center of commercial activity which reached deep into Asia Minor and also into the mountains to the N and the E of Asshur. Of this development we know only what can be deduced from letters and commercial documents found in Kültepe (on the bend of the Halys River) and in a few other places in Asia Minor, among them Boghazköy—the Cappadocian Texts. They record the dealings of Assyrian merchants residing in Asia Minor and traveling through that general region, partly concerned with exportation of textiles manufactured in or distributed from Asshur, partly investing Assyrian money in inner Anatolian trade.

The Assyrians bought and sold copper and also provided the coppersmiths of that region with the tin essential for the production of bronze, tin which Asshur seems to have imported from far in the Iranian Plateau and distributed (as Mari did somewhat later) in the tin-hungry West. Dealing with the numerous native rulers by means of treaties, the Assyrian merchants enjoyed freedom of movement and communication, and a social status on which was based a specific code of ethics which has no parallels in the history of the ancient Near East. We are completely in the dark as to the development and the circumstances which led to this state of affairs but know only that some catastrophe put an end to communications with the capital and that the merchant settlements withered away quickly thereafter, terminating a period of commercial dealings of roughly three generations.

Most important for the history of Assyria is the person of Shamshi-Adad I (*ca.* 1812-1780). He was, according to many indications, a foreign conqueror who seized Asshur soon after the above-mentioned period and strove to create a territorial state in Upper Mesopotamia. His concept of organizing such a state is clearly that of a foreign king who relies on his nomadic and energetic followers to rule a population of different social and ethnic composition by founding new cities, bringing in new agricultural methods, reorganizing the subjects in order to improve their low standard of living, and, above all, attempting to settle the seminomadic strata in order to provide, through their taxes and services, the economic basis for the administration of his empire. With the death of Shamshi-Adad I, his empire disintegrated quickly—this sequence of events was to be repeated over and over in Assyrian history. His son, Ishme-Dagan, could hold only Asshur, and even this city soon disappeared from the historical scene. This is the era of Hammurabi, of the warring Amorite and Hurrian rulers of caravans moving from Telmun on the Persian Gulf to Cyprus, the era of the growth of the Old Hittite kingdom which was soon to engulf in one sweep the entire region and to usher in the Dark Age that brought the Hittite even to Babylonia and threw the entire Fertile Crescent into confusion.

During the Dark Age, Assyria proper was incorporated for quite some time into the Mitanni Empire of mottled and only partly known history. We have but a string of royal names with which the official king lists span this period—and it is worthy of note that the names of Shamshi-Adad and Ishme-Dagan each appear three times in the three centuries between the death of the first Shamshi-Adad and the ascendance of Ashur-uballit, the first king of stature after the Dark Age. This bespeaks a political tradition somehow kept alive in Asshur in spite of foreign domination and the loss of power. When the conflict between the rising New Hittite kingdom and the Mitanni Empire was eventually decided by the victory of the Hittite king Shuppiluliuma (*ca.* 1380-1340), Syria was brought under Hittite influence, and Assyria began the slow and difficult ascent toward becoming a major power among the nations of the post-Amarna age.

In these formative centuries Assyria developed a body of foreign-policy concepts which determined to a very large extent the history of the ancient Near East. There was first the vital front against the pressure of the mountain people—the trauma of the Hurrian experience made Assyria very much aware of this danger. Here, attack whenever possible and extermination, or forced urbanization combined with the building of strategic roads, were applied with varying success, to obtain not only security from invasion, but also soldiers and horses for the Assyrian army. Tragically enough, the battle on that front, which lasted for more than half a millennium, was eventually lost when the Sargonides succeeded in destroying the Urartean buffer state and thus broke the dike which perhaps could have held the Medes and other tribes in check.

A second front, that against Babylonia, proved equally difficult and eventually fatal. It is possible that the political situation which developed at the end of the Amarna period gave an especially bitter turn to the relations between Assyria and Babylonia. The Hittites at that time seem to have been well aware of the menace implied by the rise of an Assyrian kingdom and tried to find an ally in Babylonia, exactly as the Egyptians gave at least encouragement to Assyria to exercise pressure upon the Hittite enemy. Assyria's attitude toward Babylonia showed its characteristic aggressiveness and led to the first conquest of Babylon under Tukulti-Ninurta I (1244-1208), who triumphantly carried off the statue of Marduk. In the following centuries, however, Assyria experienced a cultural invasion from Babylonia which led to a slowly intensifying Babylonization of many essential aspects of her intellectual life, probably penetrating much deeper than we are able to see in documents. The effectiveness of this process is made clear by the violent reaction of Assyrian nationalism against it, and it created a dangerous ambivalence in the attitude of Assyria toward Babylonia. The sudden reversals in the Babylonian policy of the Sargonides (*see below*) show definitely that ideological conflicts dominated this relationship.

The third front, that toward the W and the "Upper Sea," influenced world history to a much greater extent than the other two. After the conquest of Carchemish (first by Asshur-uballit I and then by Tukulti-Ninurta I), and after Tiglath-pileser I (1115-1076) advanced as far W as Palmyra (Tadmor), Shalmaneser III (859-824) laid siege to Damascus and reached the Mediterranean Sea at Nahr-el-Kelb. From that moment on up to Sargon II (722-705), Assyria posed an immediate threat to the two small kingdoms of Judah and Israel (i.e., in the period from Omri [876-869] to Manasseh [687-642]) but, in fact, all the fluctuations of Assyrian military might, beginning with Tiglath-pileser II (966-935; a contemporary of Solomon), had their reflections in the political stability of Syria and Palestine. *See* SHALMANESER 3.

The first culmination point in Assyria's rise to power was attained when Ashur-uballit I and Tukulti-Ninurta I reached out to the W, toward the Euphrates, and toward the S, to Babylon. The so-called Synchronistic History reports the relations between Assyria and Babylonia from Ashur-uballit down to Adad-nirari III (810-783) in terms of treaties concluded by their kings. We read here of invasions and defeats, of marriages between the two dynasties, booty taken and boundaries determined, again and again. Tukulti-Ninurta's triumph was short-lived; the so-called Aramaic invasion again shattered the always precarious economic structure of Assyria and of its enemies alike, interrupting communications and scattering whatever the efforts of the Assyrian kings toward organization and urbanization may have achieved. Tiglath-pileser I, however, conquered Babylon and Babylonia and fought the Arameans along the Euphrates, and the Nairi coalition in the Armenian Mountains. He went as far as Palmyra and reached the Mediterranean. His successors again failed to maintain Assyrian power, and another eclipse engulfed the country until the time of Adad-nirari II (911-891).

With Tukulti-Ninurta II (890-884) and Ashurnasirpal II (884-860) a new spirit of aggressiveness and cruelty becomes evident in the royal inscriptions. Ashurnasirpal II* and his son Shalmaneser III (859-824) determinedly pushed into Syria and the entire Mediterranean coastal region, in spite of the fierce resistance of the Aramaic kings of that region (battle of Qarqar, 853), receiving tribute from Israel and the Phoenician cities. Both likewise battled the newly arisen and dangerous kingdom of Urartu to the N and repeatedly interfered in Babylonian rebellions; Shalmaneser fought there a new foe, the Chaldeans. Fig. ASS 97. *See* AHAB; ISRAEL, HISTORY OF, §§ 7-8.

Another outstanding conqueror among the Assyrian kings of this period was Tiglath-pileser III (745-727), the originator of large-scale deportations of conquered peoples, who made himself king of Babylon (under the name of Pulu) and received tribute from the kings of Asia Minor and Syria, and even from two queens of the Arabs. His son, Shalmaneser V (727-722), likewise king of Babylon (under the name of Ulūlaj), laid siege to Samaria for three years; but only his brother and successor, Sargon II, actually conquered the city. It took Sargon nearly his entire reign to reconquer the countries

Courtesy of the Mansell Collection, London
97. Statue of Ashurnasirpal II, from Nimrud

which Assyria had lost at the death of his father. Egypt stirred up Palestine and Syria, Elam Babylonia, and Urartu the kings of the Taurus region. Sargon turned first against Urartu, which he conquered and destroyed, reporting this achievement to his god Asshur in a letter which represents one of the finest creations of cuneiform historiography; then against Merodach-baladan of Babylon, where he made himself king; and he finally fell in battle in a campaign in the mountains before he could enjoy the new city, Dur-Sharruken (Khorsabad), which he had built as his residence E of Nineveh.* His death again brought general defection and rebellion, showing that the resistance against Assyria was growing in determination throughout the entire ancient Near East. Figs. SAR 27-29. *See* AMOS; HOSEA; JEROBOAM 2; SHALMANESER 5.

Sargon's son Sennacherib (704-681) had to fight

for his empire for a long time on all three fronts.* He attacked Elam with Phoenician ships brought down on the Tigris and destroyed Babylon after many battles; but, curiously enough, he made his son, Esarhaddon, who was patently pro-Babylonian, governor there. In the anti-Babylonian rebellion which this step caused, Sennacherib was killed, and Esarhaddon (680-669) had to take it upon himself to pacify Assyria.* He was the first Assyrian king to attack Egypt, which had kept stirring up revolts in Palestine, and above all had influenced the loyalty of Tyre and Sidon, apparently considered essential for Assyrian welfare. Sidon was destroyed, but the conquest of the Nile Delta was of no great consequence, since Esarhaddon was soon compelled to return to fight the Scythians and Cimmerians menacing his

Courtesy of Staatliche Museen, Berlin
98. Stele of Esarhaddon, from Zenjirli

99. The defeat of the Elamites, from Nineveh (Quyunjiq)

mountain front. He died on the march to Egypt on another campaign. As a result of an unprecedented arrangement of Esarhaddon, the change of ruler occurred without trouble; he had made the attempt to solve the eternal "Babylonian question" by making his son Ashurbanipal king of the realm and another son, Shamashshumukin, king of Babylon. This gave ASHURBANIPAL (668-626?) some sixteen years of respite, interrupted by the usual but minor campaigns, until Shamashshumukin succeeded in 652 in forming a formidable alliance of all the enemies of the Assyrians from Elam to Israel. It took six years of civil war to subdue the rebels and to destroy Babylon once again. Figs. SEN 41; ASS 98-99. *See* ISAIAH; MANASSEH.

Whether this fight taxed the strength of Assyria too much or whether it was for other, unknown reasons, a strange period of silence blacks out the last twenty years of the reign of Ashurbanipal. From the prosperity and the apogee of Assyrian power and prestige—two topics on which the scribes of Ashurbanipal do not tire of elaborating in glowing terms—the country seems to have fallen with appalling suddenness into obscurity. Two sons followed him in quick succession; we know only their names. Nabopolassar, representing an aggressive Babylonia under a new dynasty, attacked the old cities in Babylonia which still kept their loyalty to Assyria, and they fell, one after the other; while Cyaxares the Median descended upon Assyria from the Iranian Plateau. Both kings succeeded, in a series of campaigns, in destroying Asshur, the old capital (614), and eventually Nineveh (612). There is still a strange and heroic epilogue. Parts of the Assyrian army held out for a time in Harran, waiting for Egyptian help, which failed to reach them in time. They even set up a king, but the history of Assyria had come to an end. Babylonia, under Nebuchadrezzar, was to take up Assyrian policy and to rule the Near East as far as Cilicia and Egypt, and even to conquer Jerusalem (586), which had miraculously escaped up to then.

**D. *THE DISCOVERY OF THE PAST.*** The memory of Egypt's grandeur has been kept alive through impressive remains, through the tales of Herodotus and his successors, and through the biblical record. Mesopotamia was not so fortunate; but when the first travelers with antiquarian interest in 1576 began to pass through, their curiosity was quite naturally stimulated by the Bible stories about the Tower of Babel and the destruction of Nineveh. They saw the Tower of Babel in the impressive ruins of Aqar Quf (Dur-Kurigalzu) or of Birs Nimrud (Borsippa), in spite of the fact that the fame of Babylon kept on clinging to the ruins near Hilleh through a millennium of complete oblivion. The far more spectacular ruins of Persepolis—outside Mesopotamia—have to be credited with attracting most of the attention, especially through their inscriptions on stone, which led to the decipherment of the cuneiform script. The interest in the ruins of Babylon, as well as the quest for the site of Nineveh, was sharpened by accidental finds of inscribed objects such as the Caillou Michaux (a *kudurru* found near Ctesiphon), the East India House inscription (a basalt slab with 621 lines, inscription of Nebuchadrezzar II), and the Bellino Cylinder (Sennacherib), and it led to more or less systematic searches for remaining ruins and monuments throughout Babylonia and in the neighborhood of Mosul.

French and English diplomatic personnel and interested amateurs vied with one another to send to their respective governments Assyrian reliefs and colossi, cylinder seals, etc. P. E. Botta started digging in 1842 in the ruins of Nineveh and later in Khorsabad with spectacular results; A. H. Layard excavated in Nimrud (Calah) and discovered the rock reliefs of Maltai and Bavian; H. Rawlinson copied the Behistun Inscription; W. K. Loftus began work in 1851 in the desolate and dangerous Babylonian plain and discovered the tells at Nuffar (Nippur), Warka (Uruk), Muqayyir (Ur), and Senkereh (Larsa).

In the last quarter of the nineteenth century began the era of the great expeditions, French, British,

American, and German. The French started in 1842 in Nineveh, in 1877 in Telloh, and in 1897 in Susa; the British in 1847 in Khorsabad, in 1854 in Uruk (Erech) and Ur; the Americans in 1889 at Nippur; the Germans in 1897 at Babylon and in 1903 at Qal'at-Shergat (Asshur). The results have been truly staggering, measured not so much in museum pieces (with the exception of Telloh and Susa) or in discoveries of ruins of large architectural structures, but primarily in epigraphic evidence, of which a vast amount was uncovered. Telloh, Nippur, and Asshur have yielded many tens of thousands of tablets which shed light on nearly every phase and aspect of Mesopotamian civilization from the earliest to the Persian period and which supplement in a very fortunate way the treasures found previously by the English in Ashurbanipal's library and archives at Quyunjiq. If the publication of the immense body of material has not been able to keep up with the number of texts found (the dignified apathy, petty jealousy, and sheer incompetence of many large museums is to be blamed for this state of affairs), it nevertheless forms the basis of modern Assyriology and Sumerology.

Before the First World War, the spade of the archaeologist turned to the region along the Upper Tigris and the Euphrates (Tell Halaf, Carchemish, etc.), not to speak of Boghazköy, the Hittite capital in Anatolia, and of the sites in Upper Syria.

After the First World War came the period when the main tells bearing upon Mesopotamian prehistory (El Obeid, Uruk, Djemdet Nasr, etc.) were explored and the deep S (Ur and Eridu) and the region beyond the Tigris (Eshnunna, etc.) began to yield their information. Accidental discoveries by natives of the region lent a helping hand to the archaeologist; Tell-Hariri (Mari) in Mesopotamia, and Ras Shamra (Ugarit) outside it, are typical examples.

After the Second World War the difficulty of financing large-scale expeditions and the changed political situation forced archaeologists toward the older sites with follow-up operations, and toward smaller tells that promised results in short periods. More than before, they depended on accidental surface finds which might open new vistas for them. The rising water table reduces the chances of obtaining information from the oldest period and, for such older material, restricts the scholar to the investigation of tells that were abandoned very early and thus not covered by subsequent layers. Moreover, archaeological methods have been so successfully refined that old-style spectacular expeditions have become impractical. Such an immense amount of data has been amassed so far that a period dedicated solely to a systematic digesting and co-ordinating of this material would be a blessing for both the philologist and the archaeologist.

When Pietro della Valle (1621) and Carsten Niebuhr (1761—) brought copies and, later on, actual cuneiform inscriptions (from Persepolis and Ur, respectively) to Europe, the curiosity of scholars was aroused. The increasing number of objects with such writings arriving from the Near East kept this interest alive and eventually led to the decipherment of the cuneiform script. The task was much more

difficult than any of the participating scholars could possibly have imagined it to be, and it took more than fifty years.

These were years full of ingenious discoveries, of stubborn misunderstandings, errors, and bewildering confusion, because the pioneers were faced with three rather different systems of cuneiform writing: the Old Persian, the Elamite, and the Babylonian, in monolingual, bilingual, and trilingual texts. The German G. Grotefend tackled in 1802 the simplest system (Old Persian, on the first column of the trilingual Behistun Inscription) and made a decisive step forward by applying the vocabulary of the Zend Avesta, the newly discovered (Anquetil du Perron, 1771) Middle Persian religious book. He applied the correct words to the sign groups which he assumed to mean "king" and "king of kings" and came to identify in this way the names of the kings Darius and Xerxes. This resulted in the correct reading of ten signs. The Danish orientalist I. R. C. Rask (1823) added some readings, but definite progress was made only when the Englishman E. Burnouf discovered the value for decipherment of the list of geographical names in the trilingual Behistun Inscription (1836), and C. Lassen added new values in 1836 and 1844. A new impetus was given to this slow process when H. Rawlinson succeeded in reading seventeen signs, allegedly independently of Grotefend. He based his work on royal names and also on the Behistun Inscription (1836, 1838, 1846). His final publication was followed by J. Oppert's discovery (1847) that the Old Persian system of writing was syllabic in nature. This completed the decipherment of this type of cuneiform writing.

When N. L. Westergaard (1844) and E. Norris (1855) turned to the writing of the second column of the Behistun Inscription, the Elamite version, they were greatly hampered by the fact that it contained many more signs than the first and that the nature of the language could not be determined. It was the decipherment of the third, the Babylonian, column that shed decisive light on the second. In spite of the efforts of Westergaard and Oppert (1859), it was F. H. Weissbach who, as late as 1890, completed the decipherment of the column written in Elamite.

The decipherment of the third column proved to be the most difficult, because its system of writing was the most complicated, since it had signs for both syllables and words (logograms). Grotefend, however, discovered as early as 1814 the meaning of certain logograms and even the reading of the sign ša. An essential advance was made by I. Löwenstern, who established (1847) the principle of polyphony—i.e., that one and the same sign could represent different syllables. Botta's publication of texts in the same system of writing, found in Khorsabad, proved a great boon to Assyriology, because he carefully noted variant writings in parallel texts. E. Hincks's success (1847) in correctly identifying eighteen signs (and several logograms) out of the seventy-six readings he proposed was still based on an intensive analysis of the proper names in the Persepolis inscriptions and newly found texts from Armenia.

The third column of the Behistun Inscription furnished new material to Rawlinson (1850), who, as

Hincks had already done, identified the language of this column as Semitic and began to outline the structure of the verbal system. Oppert joined these efforts in 1855 and succeeded, in 1857, in giving the first translation of an Assyrian text without the help of an Old Persian version. In the same year a curious test was made by the Royal Asiatic Society, upon the suggestion of the Assyriologist Fox Talbot, who had just translated an inscription of Tiglath-pileser I. He sent it to the society in a sealed envelope to be compared with a translation of the same document by Rawlinson. The society thereupon invited Hincks and Oppert to participate in order to demonstrate the correctness of the decipherment. The successful outcome of the test, however, failed to stop such orientalists as J. A. de Gobineau, E. Renan, and H. Ewald from either declaring the readings impossible or remaining extremely skeptical. E. Schrader recognized the correctness of the results obtained, in spite of the peculiarities of the system of writing, defended opinions as to the Semitic nature of Assyrian (1869 and 1872), and did much to gain acceptance for Assyriology in Germany.

The so-called Sumerian problem created new complications and aroused much discussion. Hincks recognized as early as 1850 that the system of writing had been invented by a non-Semitic people, who Rawlinson had first thought were Egyptians, then Scythians (also Oppert), or Turanians; but to Oppert goes the credit of having called this civilization Sumerian (1869). F. Lenormant succeeded (1873) in giving the first outline of the language of this people, whose very existence J. Halévy stubbornly denied. This caused a complex and heated discussion which lasted until the end of the nineteenth century.

The Semitic character of "Assyrian"—as Akkadian was called, because the first well-understood texts were actually written in Assyrian—proved both a boon and a drawback. It offered vital help in the course of the decipherment, and stimulated interest in the newly discovered Semitic language on the part of those interested in comparative linguistics, and above all on the part of students of the OT, when the cuneiform texts started to reveal historical material bearing directly on the Bible and on concepts, customs, and literary patterns, which provoked comparison and evaluation. However, these attitudes thoroughly vitiated appreciation and investigation of Akkadian as a language with quite unique and distinct characteristics, and of Mesopotamian civilization as an integrated whole. Delitzsch's genius put order into the unsystematic ramblings of early Assyriology, and the school of B. Landsberger began to explore the morphology, vocabulary, and syntax of Akkadian in view of specific and individual features (*Eigenbegrifflichkeit*). This approach is still very much in its beginning, but it promises to lead to a better understanding of the language. The study of the numerous dialects is progressing slowly, because large bodies of material—such as the Old Assyrian texts from Kültepe, the Mari Texts, etc.—are difficult to handle for the few scholars interested in this type of research.

As important as the linguistic approach for Assyriology is that of cultural anthropology. Here very little understanding has been achieved so far, with the exception of a number of areas in family law (marriage and adoption). The vast field of social institutions has hardly been touched, the social structure remains obscure, and so do the economics of Mesopotamia, in spite of an overabundance of available data. Here lies a field of research that will reveal the links between Mesopotamia and the neighboring civilizations, not on the level of accidental similarities, but on that of institutional analysis. The main terra incognita, however, is the religion, which originally attracted much interest, especially on the part of OT scholars. Instead of dilettante oversimplification, the need here is for detailed studies of specific key words, of form patterns, and especially of diachronic and geographical differences.

**E. *LITERATURE*.** The written documents in cuneiform yield an unparalleled insight into nearly all the aspects of the complex civilization of Mesopotamia. The variety of the contents, and the coverage in time and space, as well as the ever-increasing number of tablets, creates a body of evidence which no other dead civilization can rival. The full exploitation of the information the cuneiform documents contain has only started, and new material is being unearthed and published every year.

**1. System of writing.** Better than in the writing system of any other civilization, we can see in the Sumerian the change from a logographic into a phonographic system of writing. The use of word signs (logograms) was essential for accounting and recording in a bureaucratic setup in which officials had periodically to render accounts on the movement of goods belonging to an authority. When the need arose to refer, for similar purposes, to proper names (geographical or personal) or to new objects and materials, the Sumerians made ingenious use of word signs (normally monosyllables stripped of their original meaning) to write the syllables of the names. It was, however, somewhat a drawback that their scribes still maintained the word signs and thus created a hybrid system which led to endless complications and in the long run caused the disappearance of the entire system of writing, when it had to compete with a far more efficient and easy alphabetic system.

The principle of logographic writing seems to have been invented by non-Sumerians; but it remains quite uncertain what relation, if any, exists between proto-Sumerian writing, the somewhat later and still undeciphered proto-Elamitic system of writing, and the script of the Indus Valley. Because the concept of writing spreads very easily at a certain level of social organization, it is tempting to link the mentioned systems in some way to that of Egypt, and it is customary to do so. More important than to inquire for the point of origin of the primary stimulus is to draw attention to the characteristic use made of it in the individual civilizations and to point out the achievement attained specifically by the Sumerians. The practice of using signs to express single syllables rather than entire words was well adapted to the polysynthetic character of Sumerian, and the use of class determinatives before nouns facilitated the transfer of homophonous word signs. The development was clearly toward simplification and standardization of sign forms, toward their reduction in number, and toward rendering more and more of the spoken relators in writing—in short, toward phonetization. When the Akkadians took over the Sumerian system of writing, this promising development was interrupted. Apart from applying the Sumerian syllabic signs to render the syllables of their own language, the Akkadian scribes used a large number of Sumerian word signs to render corresponding Akkadian words (mostly nouns but also verbs), sometimes adding syllabic signs to indicate more fully what Akkadian word was meant and in which grammatical form it was to be read. This somewhat cumbersome use of word signs was never completely discarded wherever Akkadian was written in cuneiform. However, the use of word signs was subsequently (especially in the Old Babylonian period) greatly reduced and restricted to certain often-occurring nouns (such as "god," "king," "city," etc.). Only the learned scribes of the first millennium returned to the earlier, more extensive use of word signs, for reasons of style rather than for practical purposes.

The shift from Sumerian to Akkadian resulted in a number of ambiguous writings caused by the widely differing phoneme inventories of the two languages. Slowly a small number of new signs came into use, and practices were evolved, which served to render phonetic differences that were immaterial in Sumerian but significant in Akkadian. However, quite a number of signs remained phonetically ambiguous, with regard both to differentiation between voiced and voiceless consonants and to the so-called emphatic pronunciation. This and the polyvalence of certain signs added more complications to the system of writing—all of which made a long period of study necessary for the scribes, required the use of many reference works (*see* § E6d *below*) and thus put writing into the hands of a class of trained specialists. These specialists were by nature conservative and allowed only scant development during the two millenniums of their authority. Although certain complicated signs did become obsolete, and—in very technical texts—the most frequently used logograms appear in abbreviated forms, no meaningful changes occurred any more. Still, it should be said that the system was elastic enough to be used for foreign languages such as Hittite (with a few rarely used diacritical signs), Elamite, Hurrian, and Urartean.

Paleographically, certain periods and regions became quite distinct. Further, there was a definite development toward a differentiation between cursive and monumental writings and between an Assyrian and a Babylonian style. There are certain confusions between signs, conflations of two or more signs, artificial fusion and differentiation of forms, etc., that occur here and there. Schools of scribes developed locally (with regard to use, form, and selection of signs), such as the Ur III tradition, which spread to Asia Minor (Hittite and Boghazköy Akkadian), or the Old Akkadian tradition, which survived in the Old Assyrian from Kültepe in Anatolia but was supplanted in Babylonia by the Old Babylonian.

**2. Writing material and technique.** Clay, as used in Mesopotamia, can safely be called the best writing material ever used from the standpoint of the permanency of the record. It is also extremely cheap and present everywhere. Pressed into all kinds of shapes, clay offers a smooth and plastic surface in which impressions can be easily made with appropriate tools, and when the clay dries or is fired, these impressions become permanent. The clay surface is very sensitive and not only retains the finest lines of the stylus but also renders all the fine details of a seal rolled over it or impressed upon it.

Clay was used in Mesopotamia for writing purposes in three main forms: tags protecting the knots of strings safeguarding the contents of bags, baskets, or containers; tablets of many sizes and shapes; and larger, prismatic—sometimes, but rarely, barrel-shaped—forms that could hold many more lines in less space, more compactly, and with less danger of damage than could a breakable tablet. The wedges were impressed with a stylus, usually of reed but sometimes of wood or even bone. Sometimes the clay tablet was covered with a slip of finer clay, on which the marks were made. The stylus was also used to make rulings, while vertical lines for texts to be written in columns, or with special care, were made by means of a snapped-on thread.

In the earliest period individual words were written, always from left to right, in boxes arranged in vertical columns. Later on they were arranged in rows (lines) across the width of the tablet, filling first one side (the obverse), then, turning the tablet along its lower and shorter edge, on the second side (the reverse). Often the tablet was inscribed in carefully laid-out columns of equal width, arranged on the obverse from left to right, and on the reverse in the opposite direction.

Literary texts show at the end of the last column of the reverse the title of the composition (usually the first line of the text), the owner of the tablet, the name of the scribe, and the date, in a stereotyped sequence that often refers to the original which was copied, its provenience, etc. Sometimes curses are added against those who remove the tablet from its place without authorization, or the text may be marked as secret, etc. If a composition is too long to be contained in one tablet, the colophon refers to this fact and indicates the first line of the next tablet of the "series," as the scribes called such an opus.

In libraries the tablets seem to have been stored on shelves or clay banks in bundles secured by strings and tags. A few of these tags have been preserved. Archives, private or administrative, were kept in large clay jars.

The clay tablets used by the administration of temples and palaces, as well as for recording legal transactions, for writing letters, etc., have very characteristic shapes. Some are small, thin squares down to the size of a postage stamp; others, cushion-shaped with narrow or thick rims, longish or squat, most of them inscribed parallel to the short side but some to the long. Each period or region is characterized by its preference for a specific shape, and, moreover, the content of the tablet is very often directly connected with its form.

Quite frequently, tablets are imitated in stone or metal, especially when used for foundation deposits. It should be noted that the custom of inscribing bricks for important buildings with the name of the building, the king, etc., led to the invention of brick stamps, some even with interchangeable sign units. Curiously enough, the scribes in Susa even resorted to the use of cylinders inscribed with curses, etc., and rolled them over the surface of legal documents instead of writing these formulas down.

In spite of the obvious advantages of their permanent writing material, the Mesopotamian scribes of the early first millennium sometimes wrote on wooden tablets with a thin layer of wax. A set of such tablets (made of ivory), to be hinged to one another so as to open up like a screen, has been found. This find was due only to a fortunate accident, which brings home the fact that we would have lost most of the literary texts in cuneiform if this practice had been adopted generally instead of only in luxury items for the king. Such "books" seem to have been used primarily for Aramaic texts, and they have perished in Mesopotamia, as have perished there all the Greek papyri of Hellenistic origin, while, on the other hand, the Egyptian soil preserved such documents very well.

**3. Nonliterary texts. *a. Administrative documents.*** Whenever a storage economy or a complex bureaucratic system is to be run by individually responsible officials of restricted office tenure, strict and written accounting is essential if one is not to resort to complex operational devices such as the quipus of Peru. Sumerian bureaucracy left an immense number of texts, from the modest beginnings in nearly pictographic writing from Uruk, to the archives of the Third Dynasty of Ur. These are records covering the movement of goods and animals into or out of the custody of an official, lists which sum up these dealings monthly or annually, records of rations given out, etc. All are extremely neatly written, often in several columns and with column headings, all dated, often sealed, indexed at their rims so as to be quickly found in the tablet boxes, of which we have a great number of identifying tags. In the Old Babylonian period, the style of these records changed somewhat; they refer mostly to the transactions of the palace administration, to tax collections, etc., as they likewise do in the Kassite period (Nippur). From the time of the Chaldean kings we have a large number of tablets dealing with the administration of the temple Eanna in Uruk, of the temple Ebabbar in Sippar, etc. Wherever Babylonian civilization and cuneiform writing penetrated outside Mesopotamia, we find the same bureaucratic techniques, invented by the Sumerians, as in, e.g., Elam, Mari, Chagar-Bazar, Nuzi, and Alalakh. These techniques were often adapted to special needs, and sometimes simplified.

***b. Letters.*** The formula of the Sumerian letter represents an order given to the messenger instructing him to recite the message to the addressee. The message itself was originally in the form of an imperative and was solely concerned with administrative matters. Akkadian letters which imitated this pattern were primarily vehicles for administrative dispositions and only secondarily contain reports to higher authorities regarding executed orders or requesting instructions. Commercial activities overland likewise had to rely on letters in matters of disposition and execution. These letters, however, contain quite a bit of extraneous matter and thus are often of historical or cultural interest. Genuine private letters are an exception and appear, as a rule, only in the Old Babylonian period.

Another domain in which letters were amply used is that of international relations, and these are, of course, of great interest to the historian. Of these we have, first, the exchange of letters between Ibbi-Sin, the last king of the Ur III Dynasty, and Ishbi-Irra, the first king of the Dynasty of Isin, and other rulers, preserved in a Sumerian collection of historical source material bearing upon that important period; then the correspondence of Hammurabi with Zimrilim of Mari, found in Mari; and all the letters from the lesser kings sent to Iasmah—Addu, king of Mari, son of Shamshi-Adad I.

The diplomatic letters of the Mari period are far overshadowed in importance and general interest by those found in the ruins of the new capital of Akh-en-Aton in Egypt, the so-called Amarna Letters. The royal archive there contained not only letters addressed to various pharaohs by kings and rulers of Babylonia, Assyria, the Hittite Empire, Mitanni, and Cyprus, and—the vast majority—by the kings and kinglets and Egyptian officials of Upper Syria and Palestine, but also some copies of letters sent from Egypt. Apart from the letters, there are lists of royal gifts sent to or by the pharaoh, and a small group of literary texts and vocabularies which show that the Akkadian scribes in Egypt had been trained there. Moreover, the archive contained one letter in Hurrian and two in Hittite. The importance of this fortunate find can hardly be overestimated. It sheds light on a period of Near Eastern history which otherwise would have remained completely dark, and it gave the impetus for the discovery of the remains of the Hittite capital at Boghazköy.

Similar texts were discovered in Palestine—in Sichem and Lachish. A new source of historically important letters from this region is Ugarit, from where we now have many letters written in Akkadian. Here, too, the presence of lexical texts shows that the scribes were locally trained and not imported. In the archives of the Hittite capital, Boghazköy, letters of Ramses and the Babylonian kings Kadashman-Enlil and Kadashman-Turgu were found, as well as copies of letters sent to foreign kings. Smaller bodies of letters come from Nuzi (with some royal letters) and Asshur of the Middle Assyrian period, and from Tell Halaf (Neo-Assyrian; among them some royal letters).

Another find which deserves the designation "archive" has been made in Quyunjiq, consisting of more than 1,200 letters, of which only *ca.* 200 could be called royal correspondence. These letters cover the period from Sargon II to Ashurbanipal. Most of them were written by or to Ashurbanipal, many to Sargon and Esarhaddon, but none by or to Sennacherib, except six addressed to him while he was crown prince.

Formally, the Assyrian kings introduced a change of style in some of their own letters, inasmuch as they begin with the words *abat* (or *amat*) *sharri,* "order of the king." Another innovation is the reports of scholars (*ca*. three hundred are known) concerned with the interpretation of ominous happenings to the king in answer to specific queries by the latter. As a rule, the scholar begins his letter by quoting a passage from an omen text dealing either with astrological omens or with those derived from other happenings (usually of the type contained in the series *šumma ālu* [*see* § E5 *below*]) which fit the circumstances or the event that had prompted the king to ask the scholar for information. At the end, he gives his name in an equally businesslike form, "from NN," but there are quite a number of cases where explanations—mainly to twist a bad omen into one of good portent—were added after the quotation, or personal requests of the scholar, and all sorts of accidentals.

The Neo-Babylonian letters show again a slightly different formula ("letter of NN to NN"). They are *ca*. one thousand in number. They are mostly concerned with administrative matters, with the exception of the political letters found in Kouyunjik, and represent the most valuable source material for the study of a new dialect of Babylonian.

Finally, mention should be made of a literary use made of the letter form. These are the letters addressed to various gods, of which we have examples from the Sumerian period on up to the Neo-Babylonian, with the inclusion of Mari and the library of Ashurbanipal. There are two types. First are those written by Assyrian kings to their god Asshur, to the other gods of the capital, and to its citizens to report on a victorious campaign. Of this type we have two examples, one of Sargon II and one of Esarhaddon, and it is remarkable how much more lively and realistic these reports are in comparison with the corresponding royal inscriptions. The second type of literary letter is written to gods by private persons as an expression of piety. There is only one example of a letter written by a god, and that is one in which Asshur apparently acknowledges the receipt of a report in letter form sent to him by Shamshi-Adad V.

The art of letter writing seems to have been greatly appreciated in the Sumerian scribal schools, as a number of practice letters, and even a letter writer, show. These letters are primarily congratulatory letters directed to kings, with all kinds of requests, and are couched in that language of learned and long-winded obscurity which court style has preferred at all times and everywhere.

*c. Public legal documents.* A number of law codes are extant—two Sumerian, one attributed to Ur-Nammu, king of Ur, and the other to Lipit-Ishtar, king of Isin; two Old Babylonian, one coming from Eshnunna, beyond the Tigris, mentioning king Dadusha, and the other the well-known stela of Hammurabi; then a Middle Assyrian law code of the eleventh century B.C.; and a small collection of Neo-Babylonian laws which could be taken to indicate the existence of a code at that period.

The code of Lipit-Ishtar may have contained *ca*. 1,200 lines and was discovered among the tablets excavated at Nippur (as was also the small code of Ur-Nammu) and is also preserved in a small group of excerpt tablets. Besides it we have a badly dam-

aged tablet from Uruk of *ca*. 190 lines with nine sections of a law code readable. It is the last tablet of a series containing Sumerian laws. The larger Sumerian code and the two Old Babylonian codes are provided with an introduction. Lipit-Ishtar's laws and the Codex Hammurabi also have lengthy epilogues. The prologues extol the king who has promulgated the laws, and Hammurabi's is most explicit in this respect, adding in the epilogue the usual curses and blessings intended to preserve the basalt stela upon which the code is engraved.

The individual laws are in all instances (Sumerian and Akkadian) styled in a casuistic and very condensed way, each section beginning with "if." The earlier codes add minimal prices to be paid for essential staples and services. The Codex Hammurabi happens to be the largest of the extant codes, but the numerous fragments of the Middle Assyrian collection of laws suggest that the original series may well have rivaled it in size. In spite of its size, the Codex Hammurabi fails to cover essential fields of the law, such as murder and sales, so that one has to conclude that the text is intended to reformulate only those sections in which changes had been made by the lawgiver. More important, however, for the appreciation of these codes, are the facts that, first, there are practically no allusions in legal texts or in letters—or even in royal inscriptions—to these collections of laws; and, secondly, those legal texts which happen to deal with topics regulated by these laws do not show that they were ever actually in force. Still, the Codex Hammurabi and the slightly younger Eshnunna Code present us with a unique insight into the social concerns and interests of the Babylonian kings, the efforts of their legal advisers to free themselves from a number of primitive notions concerning guilt and responsibility, and their striving for more concise, clearer formulations. Detailed comparison of both collections and their relationship to the Hittite laws and to those of the OT will help us discern more of the motifs and trends of thought which are reflected in the interpolations contained in the texts of the Babylonian laws.

Contractual arrangements between kings or cities to terminate a state of war are known from the Sumerian period but are quite rare in Babylonia. In fact, apart from the Sumerian Stela of the Vultures, which proclaims the new boundaries between the city Lagash, victorious under Entemena, and the "people of Umma," we have no text of this type from the S. There exists, however, a treaty of Naram-Sin (of Agade) in the Elamite language, which is, unfortunately, hardly understandable, but still bespeaks the existence of the legal and political concept underlying such arrangements.

Allusions to international treaties occur, at times, in the diplomatic correspondence from Mari, as is to be expected, since the political situation there had many parallels with that of the Amarna and the post-Amarna ages. From Assyria we have a treaty between Ashurnirari VI (754-746) and an Aramaic ruler of Upper Syria (Mati'ilu), and one between Esarhaddon and a king of Tyre (Ba'lu), while treaties of this Assyrian king with petty Median rulers have been discovered in Calah (Nimrud). From among the many treaties concluded between the warring kingdoms Assyria and Babylonia (a summary of such agreements is contained in the Synchronistic History) we happen to have only one, that between Shamshi-Adad V (824-810) and Mardukzakirshumi I (852-828), but in a rather fragmentary state.

Most of the treaties whose texts have been preserved were found in the Hittite capital and are written in Akkadian or Hittite. First should be mentioned the only international treaty in this archive, that between Hattushili III (*ca.* 1289) and Pharaoh Ramses II, of which we have the Egyptian version carved on the walls of one of the temples at Karnak and of the Ramesseum, as well as a badly preserved Akkadian copy. There were also found treaties between a number of Hittite kings and their vassals in Asia Minor and Upper Syria, some of which are in Akkadian, others in Hittite, and one attested in both languages. The treaties establishing vassalage very carefully circumscribe the duties and obligations of the vassal and what protection he could expect from the Hittite ruler. They end with an invocation to the gods of both parties to serve as witnesses to the treaty and provide the customary curses and blessings they are to inflict or bestow upon those who break or keep the agreement.

The Neo-Assyrian treaties of Ashurnirari VI and Esarhaddon are much more primitive with regard to appeals to supernatural sanctions relied on for the enforcement of the agreement. Both describe symbolic acts which illustrate in a very crude manner the fate of the offender, corresponding exactly to certain magic practices used for evil purposes and mentioned at length in certain religious texts in cuneiform. Obviously, the Assyrian kings had to accept the customs of the Western Semites (we also happen to have an Aramaic stela dealing with a treaty between Mati'ilu and his vassals couched in quite similar terms) as we know them from the OT and as they are alluded to in passages from Mari referring to the sacrificing of animals, etc., to sanctify the conclusion of such treaties.

In the general category of treaties also belong the so-called Charter of Asshur and the text of the oath of loyalty which the officials of the Neo-Assyrian Empire had to take. In the former, Sargon grants the inhabitants of Asshur, for political services rendered to him during his fight for the throne, those special tax exemptions which his predecessor had abolished. It may well be assumed that the free cities had to have their privileges renewed by every king who came to the throne, and such records, which happen not to be extant but for this one small tablet, should be interpreted as a treatylike arrangement between king and city. The oath of loyalty which the Assyrian high officials had to take is quite frequently mentioned in the letters of the Quyunjiq Collection, and there even exist some fragments which give us its wording. The main duty of a loyal official seems to have been to report everything to the king. It remains uncertain whether the text is legally to be interpreted as a contract between ruler and subject or as some sort of royal edict. No complete text of the oath is known.

Among the royal edicts, the official instructions addressed by the king to high officials are to be considered a text type which the Assyrians had in common with the Hittites, among whose documents they are, however, much more frequent. Up to a short time ago, only one text from Nuzi was known which determined the duties and responsibilities of the mayor of a city, but recently a collection of royal edicts has been published in which nine Assyrian kings of the post-Amarna period in great detail regulate the duties of the officials in charge of, or serving in, the royal harem. From the Old Babylonian period comes a unique royal edict—again an accidentally preserved representative of a category of texts that must not have been too rare. This is the decree of Ammizaduga, the last king but one of the Dynasty of Hammurabi, concerning the lifting of certain debts; this decree was issued during the first year of his reign. Although such social acts of the Old Babylonian kings are known from date formulas and other indications in texts, this decree shows for the first time the extent of the royal act, the details concerning exceptions granted, etc.

Royal grants found a specific documentary vehicle during the Middle and Neo-Babylonian periods in the boundary markers called *kudurru* stones. There exist over eighty monuments of this type, mostly oval or longish cylindrical stones, but also stone tablets, covering the period from Kadashman-Enlil (*ca.* 1380) to Shamashshumukin (668-648)—i.e., roughly one millennium—although only thirteen texts can be dated exactly. With very few exceptions, these stones record royal grants and privileges concerning fields or entire regions, and, sometimes, income grants to temples. Internal evidence shows that *kudurru* stones were set up on fields, while tablets were deposited in temples. In both instances, however, the purpose was to make the grant public.

An essential feature of these stones was the designs engraved upon them; they include or consist of divine symbols of all kinds corresponding to the major deities of the pantheon, and are sometimes even provided with identifying inscriptions. These symbols—the texts call them "gods," "standards," "weapons," "drawings," and "seats" because the symbols are placed on "seats" such as are often shown in representations of enthroned deities—obviously have the function of protecting the monuments. For the same purpose, we find reliefs carved upon them representing kings, either alone or with the grantee, or in worship before a deity. Another kind of protection is provided by the sometimes extremely elaborate curses and blessings inscribed on the *kudurru*. They invoke the gods represented there by means of symbols, etc., to prevent the removal of the document, the presence of which guarantees the validity of the grant. For a period as little documented as that in which these *kudurrus* originated, they represent a unique source of information as to language, legal practices, history, and onomasticon, not to speak of their value as monuments of Mesopotamian art.

The use of stone for legal documents does not, however, begin with the Middle Babylonian period. We have a number of quite early stone tablets which record the acquisition of land by kings and are dated to the early Old Akkadian period.

*d. Private legal documents.* All private legal documents written in cuneiform, be they Sumerian or

In the Harvard Semitic Museum; by permission of Harvard University Press

100. Old Babylonian contract impressed with seven seals of the contracting parties and witnesses

Akkadian, show the same pattern. They first mention and identify in various ways the object of the transaction—a house to be rented, a field to be sold, a girl to be married, or a child to be adopted. Then they give the names of the persons who are concluding the transaction, taking care to establish the relationship of the object to the person who is disposing of it. The core of the text is formed by the verbal form which specifies the nature of the transaction: "he has bought," "he has hired," ". . . rented," etc. The subject of the verb is normally the person who acquires the rights or objects. To these minimal requirements of form may be added a number of clauses referring to details of payment, to declarations of the participants concerning secondary points, etc. These clauses are equally uniform and condensed in style.

This consistent formalism may make it necessary to divide a more complex transaction into several simple ones for which there existed established formulas. In fact, we not only have collections of such formulas—in Sumerian and in Akkadian—from the Old Babylonian period (the series called *ana ittišu*) but also Neo-Babylonian practice texts used by apprentice scribes to familiarize themselves with the strict stylistic requirements of legal documents.

There exist, of course, special developments in certain regions and certain periods. Suffice it to mention here a group of texts from Nuzi, which are drawn up in subjective instead of the customary objective form, inasmuch as the person who acts makes his dispositions in the first person (after a short objective introduction); and a group of Neo-Babylonian

texts in which one party expresses his intention to buy or rent or marry in a formalized offer, to which the disposing party answers in an exactly corresponding wording and thus accepts the offer.

Every private legal text, whatever its formulation or content, lists the names of the witnesses present at the transaction. Sometimes these witnesses affixed their seals in order to demonstrate objectively that they had been present when the contract was drawn up.* Of the two parties to the contract, the one who assumed an obligation rolled his seal over the soft clay, or—at certain periods and in certain regions—made an impression with his fingernails or the edge of his garment, all this for the purpose of indicating his presence and not for identification. Nearly always the name of the scribe who wrote the tablet is given, but it should be stressed that he never had the function of a notary. The date and sometimes the place where the tablet was drawn up usually terminate the text of the document. Fig. ASS 100.

In the earlier periods—in Babylonia up to the Middle Babylonian period, in Assyria nearly throughout the entire development—the tablet was placed in a clay envelope (which we technically term a "case") on which the entire text was repeated to protect the original against fraudulent alterations.* In the Neo-Babylonian period this protection was achieved by making a copy of the original so that each of the two parties received a copy of the agreement. Fig. ASS 101.

The earliest known private legal documents deal with the sale of slaves (Ur III period). The sale of

In the Yale Babylonian Collection; by permission of the Yale University Library

101. Legal document and its envelope, from Cappadocia

houses and fields became common only beginning with the early Old Babylonian period. Texts recording the sale of children are extremely rare; such transactions occurred only in great emergencies. Sales of animals or boats were rarely written down, but sales of temple incomes which appear sporadically in the Old Babylonian period (mostly from Nippur) became quite frequent in Neo-Babylonian and Seleucid times.

Transactions styled as loans were often in reality of a different nature, being sales on credit, or obligations to deliver goods or services at a certain time, etc. The rigid formalism of the cuneiform legal document made these practices necessary. Loans of silver or barley are recorded from the Ur III period onward, with a variety of stipulations concerning interest and antichretic arrangements.

Rent of fields, houses, and boats, and the hire of persons are well attested throughout the entire period. This also holds true for marriage and adoption contracts, although they are rather rare in the Neo-Babylonian period. Here should also be mentioned divorce settlements, wills (i.e., division of property among survivors), and contracts dealing with the nursing and upbringing of small children (only Old Babylonian). Finally, apprenticeship contracts (only Neo-Babylonian), settlements in court, and warranty arrangements of all kinds are to be listed, not to speak of documents from peripheral regions (Susa, Nuzi, Ugarit, etc.) which recorded in Akkadian transactions that were an expression of alien social and economic situations.

Criminal proceedings were apparently not recorded on tablets; the strange Sumerian tablet dealing with the trial of a murderer and his execution, found in Nippur, seems to belong to a group of legal documents which were copied solely for their literary merit. Murder as such is extremely rarely mentioned —one Old Babylonian text refers to the strangling of a kidnaped slave—and even thefts and burglaries are recorded only in a very few documents up to the Neo-Babylonian period.

**4. Religious texts.** Under this subtitle should be passed in review some representative groups of the numerous cuneiform texts which deal more or less directly with the cult as enacted in sanctuaries of all kinds, or as utilized elsewhere for the benefit of a suffering individual with the assistance of priestly experts who relied upon established texts.

Paramount among the cultic texts in the strictest sense of the term is the Creation Epic (*Enūma eliš*). Its seven tablets, numbering each between 115 and 170 lines, were recited in Esagila, the temple of Marduk in Babylon, after the evening repast of the god on the fourth day of the New Year's Festival. Written in the solemn and hymnical style of the Old Babylonian period, the text tells the story of the theogony, the sequence of the generations of the primeval deities up to Ea, the first-born of Anu. Then the conflict of the *dei superi* with the powers of the abyss and the ensuing desperation of the gods are described in rather lively fashion. The text is replete with mythological allusions, prephilosophical concepts, and personifications, but the allusions were reduced to a minimum, so that we are offered only a tantalizing glance into the riches we have lost. The story, told with many cumbersome repetitions, follows the pattern, common in mythology, of the young god—in this case Marduk—who saves the elder gods from an emergency which even the wise elder god Ea could not handle. Marduk, after having secured from the assembly of the gods a promise of his full enjoyment of the fruits of his victory, defeats the evil powers; but for this battle it is obvious that the priestly poet could muster but little enthusiasm. With much more gusto and patent interest he describes the organization of the cosmos by its new ruler in tablets 5 and 6, which end with the assembled gods in their newly built heaven solemnly recognizing the superiority of Marduk. The last tablet enumerates the fifty honorific names bestowed by them upon their ruler, on which the author elaborates by means of playful though pious etymologies. *See* CREATION; GENESIS.

Directly concerned with the cult are the ritual texts, which prescribe in detail the activities of the priests in certain ceremonies. Not many of these texts are preserved. The earliest comes from Mari, and describes the ceremonial visit of the king to the temple of Ishtar and his presence during a complicated religious service. It belongs perhaps to the rituals which deal with religious acts performed by the king; this text type is so far known only as referring to Assyrian kings.

There is a group of rituals coming from Seleucid Uruk (with Assyrian parallels, however) and one from Babylon. The latter contains a description of the rituals for the second to the fifth day of the New Year's festival and belongs to a series encompassing at least twenty-three tablets. Hence, there may have existed in Esagila of Babylon a series of ritual texts that covered the entire cultic year. The description of the ritual is very elaborate; it gives the time and the place for every act of the priest, often quotes verbatim the prayers and benedictions to be said instead of giving them by title only. A quite important insight into the routine ritual activities of a Babylonian sanctuary is gained from a Seleucid tablet enumerating the repasts that were served to Anu and to the other deities of his temple in Uruk. The text is very explicit; it not only gives quantities and qualities but also refers to the preparing of the divine repast.

The main body of religious texts for cultic use are the prayers, mainly those of the *šu-illa* type—i.e., prayers to be recited with lifted-up hands. These texts follow a few well-established patterns and were assembled after the Old Babylonian period in very large series. Each prayer begins with an invocation and the praise of the deity addressed; has as middle section the complaint of the worshiper, to which is joined his request; and ends with formulas expressing anticipatory thanks and blessings. The prayer itself is considered only one part of the cultic act—in Akkadian terms it is viewed as a "conjuration"—while the accompanying ritual (consisting of the offering of food or incense) forms the equally essential second part. Stylistically, the individual elements of the pattern are subject to more or less elaborate embellishment and enlargement, and certain of the *šu-illa* prayers are not for cultic use but serve rather as a literary vehicle for the expression of religious feeling. They are also used to impart magical effectiveness to the objects and paraphernalia employed in conjurations, etc. Apart from the prayers of this type, there are those of a different tenor, such as the *šigû*, mainly containing lamentatory complaints; the *ikribu*, with its blessings and benedictions; and others, of minor importance. According to the functions of the deities addressed, and also according to other, not so obvious criteria, "conjurations" could be used for a multitude of purposes, such as to ward off the evil consequences of eclipses, against diseases and evil spirits, etc.

Finally, we have texts which deal expressly with the cultic activities of special priestly experts; these are the manuals of their craft. Foremost among them are the tablets which inform us about the activities of the *kalû*-priest, whose function it was to appease the gods with special songs, whenever certain happenings were considered likely to arouse their wrath.

The suffering individual who had recourse to priests and their crafts found guidance and assistance in two important series called by the Akkadians *Šurpu* and *Maqlû*. These textbooks are designed for the incantation priest, whom they address in their directives, and for the patient who does not know either what evil influence on the part of somebody else or what mistake of his own has caused his suffering. In the series *Šurpu* the prayers are addressed to several deities of the pantheon but mainly to Marduk, whose exorcistic power is most appreciated. In all their repetitiousness and propensity toward rank growths, the texts of the conjurations proceed basically in three steps, the first to establish the cause of the suffering, the second to transfer it magically to a carrier, the third to destroy the carrier by burning it. Long-winded enumerations of all kinds of sins, misdemeanors, etc.—formerly misinterpreted as a confession of sins—purport to meet every possibility in order to counteract the influence which had brought about the suffering, and much room is given to description of the symptoms. There are also conjurations that address the torch, the fire, and the sulphur to ensure their effect in annihilating the sin; and, of course, Marduk is praised and besought in countless variations.

The sister series, *Maqlû*, is somewhat larger and exclusively concerned with alleviation of the sufferings caused by evil magic. Its main weapon is the burning of figurines made of various combustible materials representing the sorcerer or sorceress, under the accompaniment of conjurations that either address the figurines with harsh words and threats or invoke the fire-god to destroy them. The conjurations vary greatly in style and literary value, from the justly famous poetic "Prayer to the Gods of the Night" to hackneyed repetitions of the customary phrases. More often than elsewhere, allusions are made to mythological incidents, and even phrases of the abracadabra type are used at times. If the patient happened to be the king—that is, in all instances known, the Assyrian king—additional and apparently more appropriate means had to be used to avert any evil influence affecting his health and even life.

There exist a number of series dealing with specific lustration ceremonies to which the king was subjected, either periodically or under certain circumstances. Such are the *bīt rimki*, "House for Lustration"; *bīt salā' mê*, "House of Water Sprinkling"; and *bīt mēsiri*, "House of (Magic) Protection." In case of mortal danger, even a substitute king might have been installed under appropriate ceremonies to carry the brunt of the attack and to be put to death in order to spare the real king. Such an instance actually occurred, and this (*šar pūḥi*) ritual was enacted for Esarhaddon. It should be noted that written ceremonials seem to have existed for all the cultic activities of the Assyrian king. They include a description of his annual coronation in the temple of Asshur, detailed instructions for a royal repast of special, and most likely cultic, importance, and a complex but badly preserved ritual connected with the cult of Ishtar. Of special interest is the strange ceremony (*tākultu*) during which the king poured libations for Asshur and all the greater and lesser gods and goddesses of his empire, for which they severally bestowed upon him and his city elaborate blessings.

In the realm of theology proper belong the so-called god lists, of which we have many copies from early Sumerian and Old Babylonian times on, all overshadowed by one tablet from the library of Ashurbanipal that is the largest cuneiform tablet found there and compresses into its twelve columns, by means of its minute writing, approximately 1,500 names of deities. Beginning with Anu, the gods are arranged in elaborate groups, according to rank, with family, entourage, and court personnel down to lady hairdressers, gardeners, and the hunting dogs of Marduk.

Some of the peculiarities of this list used to attract the interest of OT scholars, inasmuch as the compiler made repeated attempts to link minor gods together by explaining their functions as the "Bel [or Ishtar] of the heaven" or "of the warriors," etc. In another passage Adad, the storm-god, is explained in a similar context as the "Marduk of rain" and the moon-god Sin as the "Marduk who illuminates the night," while still others group the various names of a major deity together, explaining each of them as referring to a specific function of the god, so that, e.g., U is the Adad of Lightning, but Ri-ḫa-mun is the Adad of the Windstorm, etc., or Asaru-alim is the Marduk of Life, and Sha-zu the Marduk of Mercy.* All this was interpreted by modern scholars as an expression of henotheistic or even monotheistic speculations of Mesopotamian priests. Fig. MAR 9. *See* GOD, OT VIEW OF; ISAIAH § B2.

There exist a small number of texts dealing with theological speculations of similar nature, the implications of which are difficult to grasp. Suffice it to mention here tablets that describe in great detail the representation of a god in terms of plants, objects, and animals ("A kettledrum is his heart, a date palm his backbone"), or offer quite obscure symbolic and mythological interpretations for every phase and gesture of cultic actions, etc.

Cuneiform religious literature only exceptionally allows the subjective lyricism which Western tradition admits as an expression of personal piety. A few literary products are cast in the form of hymns which are distinguished by originality and style, such as the long hymn to the sun-god and some of the Old Babylonian hymns to Ishtar which—especially in comparison with the contrived stylization of their Sumerian prototypes—show a certain measure of forceful creativeness. Quite exceptional is the impressionistic subjectivity of the "Prayer to the Gods of the Night," which is attested in a number of copies from the Old Babylonian period onward and thus bears witness to the appreciation it met. Prayers written for the Assyrian kings—such as Ashurnasirpal I, Tiglath-pileser I, Esarhaddon, and Ashurbanipal—are somewhat above the level in literary quality, especially in respect to the "complaint" section. Here, the scribes could draw on a large vocabulary of terms and standardized imagery, upon which they loved to elaborate by means of variations and amplifications that allowed them to add a personal element to the compilation. This is especially true of the one literary opus which may deserve to be called an original work of Mesopotamian religious poetry, the text named after its *incipit:* "Let Me Praise the Lord of Wisdom" (*ludlul-bēl-nēmeqi*), sometimes misnomered the "Babylonian Job." Little more than half the text of the composition is preserved. It first describes (a princely sufferer is speaking in the first person) with considerable elaboration the affliction caused by divine wrath, then dwells upon the effects of the grace of the deity that was bestowed upon him after a series of three dreams, which are rendered with much interesting detail. The balance seems to have been dedicated to praise the savior Marduk in hymnical style. The composition is technically quite primitive; it is characterized by repetitions and paratactic sequences of situations without any attempt toward inner development or even transitional passages. The juxtaposition of contrasting descriptions of a state of suffering and misfortune on one hand and that of bliss and success on the other is a favorite topic in Mesopotamian literature. There are two other categories of texts which elaborate on this topic though on a public, rather than on a private, level. These are descriptions of calamities caused by war, famine, and pestilence, as well as of times of prosperity and abundance. Sometimes these topics are couched in the language of prophecy or cultic lamentation—a Sumerian

legacy—and sometimes they are quoted in erudite letters and even in the predictions of omen texts.

**5. Omen literature.** The belief that whatever happens within the orbit of human perception—be it unusual actions of men or animals, unusual happenings in the sky, or unusual features of stones or plants—occurs not only through specific, if unknown, causes but also, at the same time, for the benefit of the observer as manifestations of a supernatural agent, is shared in varying degrees by many civilizations, past and present. In Mesopotamia, moreover, the Akkadians of the Old Babylonian period began more or less systematically to record such ominous events in a specific form and to assemble these observations in collections. With the transfer to the sphere of writing, divination moved from folklore to the level of scientific activity. The experiences of past generations were collected and filed for future reference. Thus we have collections of omen texts from the Old Babylonian period up into the Seleucid. They represent an important section of the scholarly literature in cuneiform, and, above all, they have to be considered an original product of the intellectual effort of the Semitic Akkadians, since no Sumerian omen text has yet been found, although Sumerian year names refer to the use of extispicy to appoint a high priest. All omen texts have a specific literary form: the protasis, which states the "case" (its form is that of a section of a law code), and the apodosis, which offers the prognostication. The individual omen items are arranged in topical lists of all kinds. Two observations should be made at this point: (*a*) only in exceptional instances is there any logical relation between portent and prediction; at best there are paranomastic associations, secondary computations, etc.; (*b*) the prediction contained in the apodosis is considered only as a warning, no matter how specific and detailed its wording. The application of appropriate apotropaic rituals was an effective means of obviating all evil consequences of the ominous event. From the point of view of literary history, it should be stressed that the originally purely practical purpose of omen collections was soon superseded by theoretical aspirations. Instead of expressing a general principle in abstract terms, the scribes attempted to cover the entire range of possibilities by means of systematic permutations in pairs or in long rows of casuistically styled individual items, each in one point differing from the preceding.

Most of the fields covered by the omen texts already appear in Old Babylonian texts, with the exception of specifically astrological omens, which have not yet been found in Old Babylonian, while others, such as omens derived from the form of movement of smoke from a censer, disappeared after the Old Babylonian period. First should be mentioned the teratological omens—i.e., those derived from the birth of monstrosities among animals. While the lone Old Babylonian tablet of this type refers only to lambs, the series that developed from this meager beginning appears in the library of Ashurbanipal (and in later texts) in twenty-four tablets, of which only the middle section (tablets 6-17) belongs strictly to the series *šumma izbu* (as these omen texts have been called by Mesopotamian scholars). To this core were added tablets referring to the malformed offspring of gazelles, mares, sows, bitches, goats, and cows. On the first four tablets are collected omens dealing with women (even queens) giving birth to malformed children, strange beings, objects, and animals, and the occurrence of multiple births. Another example of how the series of omen texts grew by accretion and compilation is offered by the so-called physiognomic omens—i.e., those which derive predictions from certain characteristics of the human body, from the color of the hair, the length of the nails, the size of parts of the body, and the nature and location of moles and discolorations of the skin, to mention only a few of the many topics. The Old Babylonian texts of this type refer mainly to moles, but in the library of Ashurbanipal at least three series of this kind are represented, the most important with ten or more tablets. In them are listed not only bodily features but also personal peculiarities and mannerisms in speech and walk, and even moral qualities; and predictions are derived from them. Texts of this type do not seem to have been very popular, with the exception of those referring to the interpretation of moles; the others belong more in the realm of scholarly activity. *See* DIVINATION; PROPHETS.

Dream omens are not often represented. They must have existed in the Old Babylonian period, but most of the text material comes from Nineveh. In the series there are eleven tablets, of which the first and the last two contain conjurations and rituals for the purpose of warding off the consequences of bad dreams or, prophylactically, of protecting the sleeping person against them. Faced with the difficult task of writing a dream book which was to cover the unending and ever-changing variety of possible dream contents, the scribes resorted to organizing the individual tablets on the basis of certain definite activities of the dreaming person. Thus we have a tablet dealing with eating or drinking in one's dreams; covering normal eating habits, with the items systematically classified as meat, fish, fowl, vegetables, etc.; and mentioning cannibalism and coprophagy. Another tablet deals with traveling in one's dreams, and here again we meet this kind of pedantic systematizing. First are treated dreams of ascending to heaven and of descending into the nether world, and then the text enumerates temples, cities (beginning with Nippur), and countries the person may visit in his dreams, deriving very definite prognostics on the basis of associations which we are unable to understand. Dreams of flying are mentioned, dreams of losing one's teeth, incestuous dreams, etc.

The divination technique that made Mesopotamia famous up to the recent past is, of course, astrology. Strangely enough, there exists only one Old Babylonian tablet with omens that could be called astrological. Still, such omen collections must have existed at that period in Babylonia proper, because we have found quite a number of them in various sites outside Babylonia on tablets which are datable to the Middle Babylonian period and even somewhat earlier. These are texts from Elam, Mari, Qatna in Syria, Boghazköy, and Nuzi, and there is one from Middle Babylonian Nippur. The main mass of astrological omen tablets comes from the library in Nineveh; some from Asshur (many of them still unpublished) and Calah; others from the S, from late periods, especially from Uruk, Nippur, and Kish. We now know of at least seventy tablets of the main series, apart from shortened series, excerpt texts, tablets with commentary, etc. The Akkadians called the series *Enūma Anu Enlil* ("When Anu and Enlil") after the first words of its solemn (bilingual) introduction. There even exist a number of catalogs of this series—i.e., texts which list the beginnings of each tablet in their correct sequence. The series first treats the moon (twenty-three tablets), then the sun, then meteorological phenomena—also earthquakes—and eventually the planets (beginning with Ishtar, the planet Venus) and fixed stars. Omens are derived from the time and circumstances of the appearance of the new and the disappearance of the old moon, from the moon's relation to the sun, and especially from the dates of its eclipses; furthermore, from the circumstances (color, cloud formations) of the rising and setting of the sun and its eclipses, and from halos and similar phenomena; from the movements of the planets among the fixed stars, their color, luminosity, etc.; and the rising and setting of other stars and of constellations. Not astrological in our sense are the tablets concerned with such meteorological phenomena as the time and intensity of, and the circumstances surrounding, thunderclaps and lightning, the time of rainfalls and the color of the rain, cloud formations, and weather. Others refer to the time, the force, etc., of earthquakes.

There is a Seleucid text which contains astrological omens of an entirely different nature. One section of it predicts the future of a child born under certain astronomical conditions, such as the rising and movement of planets, eclipses, the rising of fixed stars, etc. With such lists have to be related the few extant horoscopes (all of the third and second centuries B.C.), which state the date on which the child was born (once, when it was conceived), the astronomical report, and the pertinent predictions. The dating of these horoscopes shows that we have to deal here with a late development of Mesopotamian astrology itself rather than with a phenomenon that developed in Mesopotamia under Greek influence, as has been assumed up to now.

Even for the physician there existed a collection of omen texts. This is the series called "If the exorcist goes to the house of a patient," which contains fifty tablets. The contents clearly show that the series presents a late compilation, although certain of its components have parallels in earlier texts, such as a Middle Babylonian tablet and a Hittite text that was translated from a lost Old Babylonian prototype. Only the first two tablets are strictly omen texts—i.e., they derive predictions as to the prospects of the sick person from ominous happenings occurring while the exorcist was on his way to him. The main section of the series (tablets 3-34) are instructions to the physician for diagnosis and general prognosis concerning the disease of his patient, presented in the form of omens based on the appearance of parts of the latter's body, which are mentioned beginning with the skull and ending with the ankles and toes. The diagnoses do not refer to specific diseases in our sense but rather give the name of the god or demon who inflicted the symptoms upon the patient, while the prognostic omens tell in terse formulas whether the patient will survive or die, how long he will be ill, or when he will die; all this is expressed in a variety of ways and sometimes in rather specific terms. Only in a few instances is a treatment prescribed, but then it is always magical and not medical. Tablets 35-36 refer to pregnant women and 39-40 to newborn children. The sex of the child, its fate in general, the nature of the birth, etc., are predicted from a variety of physical features of the expectant mother, such as discoloration of the skin, the formation of her nipples, and a variety of other symptoms. The last two tablets deal with sick infants much in the same way as the main section of the series.

The largest omen series known is called *šumma ālu ina mēlê šakin* ("If a city is situated on a hill"). The tablets are numbered, and the highest number on a preserved colophon is 107. Exactly as the astrological series, *šumma ālu* must have originated as a systematic collection later than the Old Babylonian period, because only a very few and somewhat different omens of this type can be assigned to that period. The majority of the extant tablets come from Nineveh and Asshur and, in Babylonia, from Uruk. Since only one fourth of the 107 tablets are preserved —very poorly in many instances—it is difficult to form an exact idea as to the content of the series. It is, however, possible to fill some of the large gaps by means of excerpt tablets that cover more than one tablet, by means of a partly preserved commentary series, and by means of some fragments of a catalog, but it has to be kept in mind that of more than thirty-five tablets only the first line is known, and that nearly as many are completely unaccounted for. This series seems to have been compiled as a compendium to incorporate all the numerous smaller and larger groups of omen texts which, in the Old Babylonian period, existed by themselves, grew by accretion, or were fused with similar collections. The motley content of *šumma ālu*, as it is now known, shows the following larger grouping of topics: omens referring to cities (tablets 1-2), to houses and incidents in houses, etc. (tablets 3-21); omens dealing with the behavior of insects and animals such as snakes, scorpions, lizards, ants, and various still unidentified small animals, also cattle, donkeys, horses, pigs, and dogs (tablets 21-49). Then follow three tablets dealing with fire, one with political omens ("If the king respects the law," nothing more preserved), and a section dealing with agriculture (tablets 53-60). The balance is badly preserved; encounters with wild animals (tablets 66-79) and human relations (tablets 94 ff) take up most of it. As a particular feature of the omens assembled in *šumma ālu*, the text contains here and there short conjurations to ward off the evil portended or even prophylactic rituals, such as one against the sting of scorpions.

Once a connection between an ominous event or feature and a subsequent happening is discerned and expected, man wants to change this one-way communication between the deity and himself into a two-way system and to elicit divine responses to situations created for this very purpose. From accidental omens he progresses to provoked omens. There are, therefore, two kinds of omens to be differentiated, and consequently two types of omen texts: those dealing with signs that happen by themselves (*omina oblativa* in Roman terminology) and those that have to be provoked by an act of the diviner (*omina impetrativa*). Of the latter, it can be said that they are, with one important exception to be discussed presently, rather rare and unimportant in Mesopotamia. There are indications that birds were released for the purpose of observing their behavior and that dreams were expected and movements of animals were induced and omens derived from them, etc.; yet all this is not only late (Neo-Assyrian period) but also below the level of scholarly interest—i.e., no omen texts refer to such practices. In the Old Babylonian period there are tablets dealing with the movements and color of oil poured into water for divination purposes and others that refer to the motion of smoke rising from a censer (although it is not certain whether the smoke was produced for this purpose). Both divinatory practices, however, fell into desuetude after the Old Babylonian period.

The only exception is divination by means of extispicy, which the Mesopotamian priests considered as *omina impetrativa;* i.e., they assumed that the deity, in this case always Shamash, "wrote"—as they put it—his answer to the prayer of the diviner then and there upon the intestines of the sacrificial lamb, on which it could be "read" in the formations, deviations, etc., that the collections of omens interpret. This divination technique is well attested in all periods in Mesopotamia; it was used exclusively for divination performed for the king and the army. In fact, the *bārû*-priest, who we know accompanied the army on campaigns, must have had the function of establishing the will of the gods on the spot. This is also illustrated in letters from Mari.

The corpus of texts dealing with extispicy—this term (derived from the Latin *exta*) is more appropriate than hepatoscopy, since the liver was by no means the sole carrier of the divine message—surpasses in size all other omen texts. No serious attempt has been made so far to organize the individual tablets according to a main series or shortened excerpt series, commentary series, excerpts, etc., or to trace the development from the Old Babylonian period to the Seleucid, or to distinguish local traditions. As far as one can see, the individual tablets are organized according to the part of the *exta* to be investigated. Thus we have texts dealing at length with the lungs, the liver, the gall bladder, the spleen, the kidneys, the diaphragm, etc., as well as with the formation of the coils of the intestines.

There existed a very complicated and elaborate technical terminology which referred to specific features of the individual parts, with terms such as "door of the palace," "gate," "path," etc., and also to certain characteristic markings, such as "weapon," "spot," etc. We also have a number of clay models of livers and lungs; some are very elaborate, others rather crude. They seem to have served two main purposes: for instruction, such as a highly detailed inscribed Old Babylonian model in the British Museum, or the models from Boghazköy, or models which illustrate the protasis of an omen written upon them; and for recording, such as those from Mari of the Old Akkadian period, which show how a liver looked when the historic event to which its inscription refers occurred. Such empirical cases must have been incorporated into the collections where we find, more frequently than in any other group of omen texts, references to historic rulers and their tragic fates. We also have, especially from the earlier periods, reports which list in a standardized arrangement all the ominous features observed at an extispicy; they are obviously intended for the expert who is to look up in the corresponding tablets the pertinent apodoses. If these apodoses show a majority of good predictions, the result is considered an affirmative answer of the god. If this is not the case, the extispicy can be repeated. At any rate, the predictions, whatever their specific content was, count solely as positive or negative items. Before the extispicy the diviner addressed a prayer to Shamash, asking for a reliable and positive answer, and even enumerated all the possible good features which he hoped to find in the *exta* he was to inspect. Moreover, there exists a small collection of omens which are derived from the movements and the behavior of the sacrificial lamb, from the moment it was brought in until its last convulsions; the god was assumed to communicate through everything that happened during the ceremony.

A special category of extispicy texts comes from the archives of the last Assyrian kings. They are queries addressed to the sun-god on matters of state, such as the appointment of officials, military decisions in a calamity, the reliability of generals, etc., accompanied by a prayer. At the end of the text are noted the results of the extispicy performed to obtain the answer of the god. This might have constituted material for scholars to check on the reliability of the collections of omens or a record made to protect the diviner. In fact, Nabonidus considered it necessary to add in an inscription an exact enumeration of all ominous features of an extispicy (with added apodoses) that was performed when he decided to change the tiara of the sun-god, as a proof of the god's consent.

**6. Secular literature.** Under this heading shall be united four groups of literary documents primarily characterized by the complete absence of any connection with cult and personal piety. These are: epical texts, royal inscriptions, the wide range of wisdom texts, and miscellaneous works.

*a. Epical texts.* The astonishing richness and variety of the Sumerian epical texts that are only now beginning to be known and investigated—with a prospect of still more to come—hampers any intensive literary study of the relatively few extant Akkadian texts of this type. They demonstrate that the Akkadian epic has its roots deep in Sumerian soil and that it will be a major problem to disentangle what is genuinely non-Sumerian, what is to be credited to that hybrid Sumero-Akkadian civilization which certainly flourished in what we call the Sumerian pe-

riod, and what is of Sumerian extraction. Apart from all this, there is the problem of the internal development of epical literature in Akkadian. The existence of such a development is clearly indicated when one compares what is left of the Old Babylonian epical texts with the appallingly poor products of the later period, such as the Epic of Era.

Foremost among the epics—and not only in size— is the Epic of Gilgamesh, which the Akkadians called, after its *incipit: ša naqba īmuru.* Its twelve tablets, containing more than three thousand lines, were found in the library of Ashurbanipal, but much outside material is available, which shows the complex development undergone by this literary work. Apart from Sumerian sources and parallels, four Old Babylonian tablets containing parts of the Gilgamesh story are known; two copies have been found in the W, one in Boghazköy, and one in Megiddo; translations into Hittite and Hurrian come also from Boghazköy. The epic in its latest form shows a composite character. The story itself is told on tablets 1-11. Tablet 12 gives, as a kind of appendix, a description of the nether world. There are two parallel scenes, one at the beginning and the other at the end of the story. After a short preamble in which the poet expresses the intention and scope of his opus, the listener is invited to admire the walls of Uruk, built by Gilgamesh; from this point on, the story of the latter is told. Quite intentionally, the story ends with Gilgamesh showing these same walls (referring to them in identical words) to one of his partners in his adventures. Within this frame, the story of Gilgamesh proceeds with stately grace, elaborate descriptions, and lively dialogues alternate with episodes that are well told and integrated into the flow of happenings. Few other, if any, cuneiform literary works are distinguished by such features. The basic topic is the all-powerful and famous king who rebels against the idea that he must die, exactly as every other human being. This topic already appears in the Sumerian Gilgamesh stories, especially in the often-copied Huwawa episode, which shows that the expedition to the Cedar Mountain in the Nineveh version originally represented the first attempt of Gilgamesh to obtain immortality. The Akkadian poet, however, seems to have changed it into one of the several famous deeds of his hero (such as the rejection of Ishtar's love, the oppression of Uruk, the fight against the Bull of Heaven) because he preferred to have the quest for life motivated by the death of a friend rather than by selfish considerations.

In his quest for immortality, once he has arrived in the "Fortunate Isle," where he finds the only man who had succeeded in becoming immortal, Gilgamesh is three times given the opportunity to realize his goal, but every time he fails or is cheated of it. He fails to pass the test of keeping awake for six full days; he does not realize that he washed himself and his garments in the "Fountain of Youth" and yet did not drink of it; and, finally, he loses the "Plant of Life" to a snake. Defeated, he returns to Uruk. Into this story of the quest for life has been skilfully woven the story of Enkidu, here the friend of Gilgamesh, while in the Sumerian stories he is his servant. The Enkidu story brings its hero as a subhuman being from the wilderness to civilization and lets him vie with Gilgamesh, become his friend, and accompany him to the Cedar Mountain. Here the text is very poorly preserved, but Enkidu may have been instrumental in bringing about the triumph of Gilgamesh over Huwawa, the guardian of the cedar, because here he commits an act for which he has to pay with his life later on, and it is precisely his death that starts Gilgamesh on his quest. All this, however, forms only the structural framework of the epic, which the poet has ornamented with a plethora of genre scenes, sophisticated fill work that reflects the main themes, and all the trappings of refined literary technique. There are two dreams which warn Gilgamesh of Enkidu's arrival, and presage with their symbolism the subsequent events; there is the description of how Enkidu was civilized—on both the mythic-symbolic and the social level; the warnings of the elders of Uruk of the dangers of the expedition against Huwawa; a description of a fairytale jewel garden, which may reflect some lost episode; the description of the nether world in Enkidu's dream, which brings up a topic that is connected with Gilgamesh' destiny—to become the judge of the nether world, etc. The poet uses dramatic developments as well as retarding digressions. Note the suddenness with which Enkidu has his death dream immediately after the celebration of the victory festival, and that the immortal Utnapishtim tells the story of how he achieved eternal life with deliberate ease. The wonders of the cedar forest are described with much love of nature and the apprehensions of the mother of Gilgamesh with interest in genrelike episodes. Of much appeal for the listener must have been the detailed descriptions of the marvels of the cosmos, such as the journey through the sunset mountains, the crossing of the waters of death, the diving for the "Plant of Life," etc. Yet, for all its sweep, from heaven to the nether world, and all its intense human appeal in the themes of friendship and the horror of death, the epic of Gilgamesh failed to appeal to the Akkadians. There are no copies extant from the scribal schools of Nippur and Uruk or other centers of learning in the S; none has been found in the large collections of Asshur; only two small fragments in Sultantepe attest that the text existed in that provincial collection. What is still more puzzling is that there are no allusions at all in cuneiform texts or in Mesopotamian iconography to the epic and its world of persons and scenes. Of course, there are quite a number of parallels with the OT and Greek mythology, and there is a reference in the Greek philosopher Aelian (second century A.D.) to Gilgamos, but within Mesopotamian literary tradition the epic had no place of importance. To speak of the work as a national epic is to use alien concepts. *See* EDEN, GARDEN OF.

The situation with regard to the other epical texts is likewise strange, inasmuch as there is only one Old Babylonian text of this nature—that which we call the Atrahasis story—coming from Babylonia proper. The Epic of Zû is preserved on two tablets from Susa, and the Adapa story, as well as that of Nergal and Ereshkigal, on tablets found at Amarna. Such an important text as the Descent of Ishtar has no

Old Babylonian version, although the Sumerian prototype is well known. This might be accidental— only recently a Standard Babylonian version of the Nergal and Ereshkigal story was discovered in the collection of tablets found in Harran—but this circumstance could also illustrate the relative unimportance of this type of text in contrast with, e.g., omen texts.

The Epic of Zû—to begin with the best preserved of these stories—is contained on a number of tablets from the library of Ashurbanipal from Asshur, Sultantepe, and on two tablets from Susa—not to speak of the much larger Sumerian epics dealing with Zû. It deals with the heroic exploits of a junior god, Ninurta, who succeeded where all the other gods failed. He recaptures from the mythical Zu-bird the all-powerful charm of Enlil (called *ṭup-šīmāte*), which ensures the correct functioning of the universe, by making certain that all gods, human beings, and objects will act according to their natures and purposes. The story seems to be well told, with the usual peripateia and references to the wisdom of Ea. Far more interesting is the famous short text (*ca.* 150 lines; only Asshur and Nineveh text) called the Descent of Ishtar to the Nether World. Obviously patterned after the well-preserved Sumerian version, it sets the story forth at the slow pace of its prototype and describes the entrance and the exit of the goddess through the seven gates of the nether world, as well as Ea's ruse to save her from imprisonment there. The last thirteen lines seem to have been appended for unknown reasons and taken from the contexts of several myths of the same cycle. To the same cosmic locale as the Descent of Ishtar the story known as "Nergal and Ereshkigal" brings us. It tells how Nergal became king of the nether world.

Quite substantial again are the extant fragments of the Etana story. There are some Old Babylonian texts, some from Susa, Asshur, from a Middle Babylonian tablet, and from fragments in the library of Ashurbanipal. Etana appears, like Gilgamesh, in the Sumerian king list. His miraculous flight to heaven, however, is represented on seals and mentioned in cuneiform texts, in contradistinction to the exploits of Gilgamesh. Etana is king of Kish but without offspring, and is sent by Shamash, upon his prayer, to the eagle who is to show him the wondrous plant that will give him a son. Into this "dynastic" story the poet did skilfully weave the conflict between the eagle and a snake, who lives together with him in a tree. This is only a reflection on the fairy-tale level of a Sumerian myth; the eagle corresponds to a "cloud bird" nesting in the "world tree." The eagle of the Etana story breaks his oath of friendship and eats the young of the snake, which in turn overpowers him and imprisons him in a pit, upon the advice of Shamash. Etana frees the eagle and, riding upon his back, reaches the heaven of Anu. The story breaks off here, but one can safely assume that Etana obtained the "plant of birth," and that the precociously clever son of the eagle, who is always presented as warning his rash father with pious speeches, had his share in the adventures.

Adapa is a hero in the Greek sense of the word. Like Gilgamesh, he is of divine extraction but mortal;

as in the case of Gilgamesh, immortality escapes him narrowly. His story is told on a tablet found in Egypt and on some fragments in the library of Ashurbanipal. As a son of Ea and caretaker of the city of Eridu, Adapa breaks the wings of the S wind, which has overturned his fishing boat, and is called before Anu to answer for his deed. Upon the advice of his father, Ea, Adapa refuses to eat or drink what Anu offers him and thus forgoes immortality, which partaking of the food of the gods would have bestowed upon him. The end is damaged, but Anu seems to have compensated Adapa for his loss and to have granted the exorcists of Eridu magic power to fight demons and diseases; thus, the story is etiological in purpose. It is to be noted, however, that the ending, contained on a fragment from Quyunjiq, is quite abrupt. In fact, the phrase "and so forth" shows that we have here an abridgment of the epic. The lines following this phrase clearly show that the text was copied for apotropaic purposes.

This practice of writing epical texts on tablets that were to serve as charms is well attested for the Epic of Era, a late (probably from the end of the second millennium B.C.), rather wooden poetical concoction. A number of copies of this text are written on amulet-shaped tablets obviously to be hung up to protect a house against the rage of the dangerous god Era (Irra). The five tablets of the text are extant on a number of copies, from Sultantepe, Asshur, Nineveh, etc., but they give us only about two thirds of the original text. As a *novum,* the author asserts in an epilogue that the entire content was revealed to him in a dream and that he did not change a single line when he wrote it down. Then, Era himself bestows blessings on those who praise it, from king to scribe, and assures the house where the text is kept freedom from pestilence. The content of the epic is still rather obscure; its main purpose seems to have been to explain to the pious how it was possible that Babylon, beloved by Marduk, was destroyed—this refers possibly to the sack of the city by Shutruk-Nahhunte of Elam. In the first tablet the poet attempts to motivate the fateful decision of Marduk to leave Esagila and to descend into the nether world, entrusting the city to Era and his vizier Ishum, the fire-god. The evil consequences of this decision seem to be elaborated in the poorly preserved second and third tablets, while the fourth contains a long lament over the destruction of Babylon in the traditional pattern for this type of literature. The fifth and last tablet ends with the prospect of recovery and Babylon's future prosperity.

In the Old Babylonian epical text, which originally contained 1,245 lines on three tablets and was entitled *enūma ilū awēlum* ("When the gods and man"), and of which we have but one tenth of the lines and some smaller fragments from Nippur(?) and Nineveh, we seem to have at hand a larger collection of stories. Among them is preserved that of Atrahasis, the wise hero of the flood, a favorite of Ea. The text is too incomplete to be discussed here, and this also holds true for the various creation stories that happen to be extant and a number of fragments of myths, as well as quotations and allusions in incantations, etc.

*b. Royal inscriptions.* The inscriptions of the Assyrian and Babylonian kings are primarily considered source material for the historian, and their literary merits have hardly been investigated. Although the origin of the Assyrian and the Babylonian inscriptions is patently the same (*see* § C1 *above* for details), they developed formal and topical differences which should be pointed out in a presentation of Mesopotamian literary activities. In Assyria, Arik-den-ili (1319-1308) and Shalmaneser I (1272-1242) are the first kings to arrange their records in the form of annals. Tiglath-pileser I (1115-1076) introduces his main inscription with a long, solemn invocation, and presents himself with strings of titles and panegyric attributes; he also has short paeans between the descriptions of the individual campaigns, and ends the text with a triumphal hymn. Adad-nirari II also introduces his annals with an overlong and rather hymnical introduction full of pompous self-praise, but the subsequent kings tend to return to more modest prologues. Characteristic of royal inscriptions of the Babylonian kings—and clearly in accordance with the Sumerian prototype—is the initial self-presentation of the king with titulary epithets describing his piety and achievements and—in Neo-Babylonian—the final prayer to the deity to which the object or building was dedicated. The kings of the Hammurabi Dynasty started the Akkadian practice of enumerating in inscriptions blessings which they expected in return for their pious deeds, especially in answer to the dedication. Outside the traditional pattern for such inscriptions—a pattern which is kept up in Babylonia, from the earliest time to Nabonidus—there are always topics preferred by certain kings, and there are a small number of quite irregular texts. Thus, the kings of the First Dynasty of Babylon like to name their adversaries and refer in some detail to their victories, which the kings of the Chaldean Dynasty avoid, with the exception of Nabopolassar's reference to his victory over Assyria. Nabonidus loves to enliven his inscriptions with dialogues in which gods, priests, and workmen appear, for which there is only one parallel in an inscription of Samsuiluna. He even quotes verbatim, in quite scholarly fashion, the texts of foundation tablets which his workmen had excavated, and thus gives us the text of an inscription of a Kassite king that would otherwise have been lost. His preference for reporting his own dreams is another piece of evidence for his untraditional attitude with regard to these inscriptions.

Topically, the inscriptions of the Sargonides, which surpass in bulk all other Assyrian royal inscriptions, are far less diversified. Reports on hunting expeditions that begin with Tiglath-pileser I and references to the care given to botanical gardens and to rare and foreign animals either bought or captured and kept in game parks or menageries (by the same king) should be mentioned here, as well as Ashurbanipal's detailed descriptions of his training as a scholar and a warrior.\* Sargon's preference for extremely poetical terms, Sennacherib's pride and interest in things technical, and Ashurbanipal's admittance of episodes and descriptions to the text show that these kings took personal interest in what the court scribes wrote under their names. Fig. ASS 102.

102. Killing of lions released from lair, from Nineveh (Quyunjiq)

Interest in royal inscriptions is further illustrated by the numerous copies of old inscriptions on statues, bricks, etc., made by later scribes who often even imitate the paleography. We owe to their interest in history much of what we know, e.g., of the Old Akkadian period. This interest began quite early. In the Old Babylonian period scribes from Nippur collected not only royal letters (*see* § E3*b above*) but also building inscriptions pertaining to a sanctuary (Tummal), and it can well be assumed that many of the references to special achievements or sins of the kings of old, as expressed in omen texts, in the Sumerian king list, and in proverbs, etc., were excerpted from such collections. Here belong the legends that attached themselves to famous rulers, either founders of a dynasty or the unfortunate kings whose empires were crushed by invasions. Sargon of Agade is the most famous representative of the former category, Ibbi-Sin of Ur of the latter. Among the legends concerning Sargon, that of his birth, his exposure in a basket floating down the river, his rescue and rise to power, is best known on account of its biblical associations, but the story of Sargon's adventure-filled campaigns to the W, as told in the epical text *šar tamhari*, was far more popular in the second millennium. Copies were found in Amarna and Boghazköy, where even Hittite and Hurrian translations were made of it. His son, Naram-Sin, rivaled him in military achievements, and the so-called Cuthean Legend tells about his desperate, but victorious, effort against an invasion of his empire, from Asia Minor to Telmun in the Persian Gulf, and even as far as Meluhha to the E of Telmun. Of this we have one Old Babylonian version, one from Boghazköy in Akkadian, and a number of fragments from Nineveh and Sultantepe. In the chronicles of the old period, as well as in omen texts, a number of episodes concerning famous rulers are mentioned. Among these rulers are Ku-Baba, a female innkeeper who founded the Third Dynasty of Kish; Utu-hegal, who drove out the Guti; Shulgi, the most famous king of the Third Dynasty of Ur; and Irra-imitti of the Dynasty of Isin, who died a strange death.

While such more or less historical personages belonged to the distant past when these texts were written, other literary documents refer to historical events and kings of the present or the still living past. Only extraordinary circumstances or extraordinary acts are reflected in this type of text. The destruction of Babylon by the Hittites (under Murshili), as well as by the Elamites (under Shutruk-Nahhunte), were such events, and the military triumphs of the Assyrian king Tukulti-Ninurta I, who conquered Babylon, and the spectacular (and very rare) successes of the Babylonians under Nebuchadrezzar I against Elam, likewise found literary expression. The scribes and poets take great pains to explain why Marduk abandoned his city to the enemy; in fact, one text has Marduk himself speaking like a king in a royal inscription, reporting on his journey westward (the Hittites obviously carried off his statue) and his return, while a more poetic version, preserved in the so-called Epic of Era, blames the calamity that befell Babylon on the fumblings of minor gods during an absence of Marduk (*see* § E6*a above*). It was much easier, of course, to extol the military achievements of the great king, Tukulti-Ninurta I, in a large epic that deals with his fight against Kashtiliash and is the only text in cuneiform which deserves the designation "historical epic." There are, however, a number of Babylonian fragments which may well come from similar literary productions written in the time of Nebuchadrezzar I. From the very end of the era of Babylonian political independence comes a strange text that should be mentioned, although it does not sing the praises of a king but, on the contrary, vilifies him. This is the poem directed against Nabonidus by the clergy of Babylon. It first describes the evil deeds of this last, but most interesting, Babylonian ruler and then turns to praise the arrival of the liberator and savior Cyrus, who delivered Babylon and returned its priests to importance and power. Among the sins of Nabonidus we find his building a temple which was to rival the venerable shrines Ekur and Esagila, and making a newfangled image of the moon-god; his departure for the W; and his taking up residence in the city of Tēma, which he rebuilt and turned into a fortress. The priestly author takes pains to point out that Nabonidus was not at all the scholar and inspired mantic he purported to be but, in fact, an ignoramus and a blasphemer. At the end of his diatribe he mentions by name some of the most hated officials of the king. Cyrus, however, is represented as loving Babylon, restoring the old cults, eradicating and abolishing whatever was instituted or changed by Nabonidus, and thus bringing happiness to all the inhabitants of the city. It is quite clear that the polemics against Nabonidus on the clay-barrel that purports to contain an inscription of Cyrus go back to the same source.

*c. Wisdom texts.* An important source for the study of the moral and social attitudes of Mesopotamian man is to be found in the texts customarily called wisdom texts. This category is taken here not only to embrace proverbs, fables, and other didactic tales, but also to include a number of specifically Mesopotamian literary products which shed light on these attitudes. Many of these texts have prototypes in Sumerian, and it must be stressed that the historian of literature competent to deal with this material should be at home in both fields, Assyriology and Sumerology. *See* ECCLESIASTES; JOB; PROVERBS; WISDOM.

Large quantities of systematically organized collections containing Sumerian "proverbs" have begun to be studied. By their very nature they represent one of the most difficult text categories to be investigated linguistically, not to speak of the difficulties presented by the subject matter and the pithy style of such sayings. In Akkadian we likewise have a variety of smaller collections of proverbs, often in bilingual texts, but no over-all arrangement is discernible. A small Old Babylonian fragment and two more from Boghazköy connect the library texts from Nineveh with the bulk of Sumerian proverbs. Quite a number of proverbial sayings and colorful phrases can be found in letters, such as those from Mari and Amarna, and in the archives of Nineveh, etc. Since Ashurbanipal and especially Esarhaddon were fond of quoting proverbs in their letters, reference has to be made to the Aramaic collection of proverbs that appears in the story of the wise Ahiqar, said to have been the adviser of Sennacherib and Esarhaddon alike, because some of the proverbs in which Ahiqar hands down the sum of his wisdom to his nephew are actually cited by these kings. The imagery of these proverbs is mainly rooted in the context of the daily life and the daily worries of Mesopotamian man, and this happens to be just the most obscure section of the Mesopotamian world. This imagery loves pointed contrasts, rhetorical questions, and riddlelike statements, all of which are imbued with a healthy cynicism and quite devoid of sentimentality or sadness. These proverbs represent a *summa* of practical wisdom, which is nowhere contrasted with a pattern of ideal behavior or normative aspirations. Good advice is also the topic of a lengthy collection of precepts conveniently dubbed "Counsels of Wisdom," where the arrangement is more coherent than in the collections of proverbs, and a definite moralizing tendency is in evidence, as references to Shamash illustrate. There are also repeated references in these precepts to court life, to religious duties, etc.; the social level of the reader to whom they seem addressed must have been high. There is no folk character in the topics of these precepts. They are comparable with that type of Egyptian literature called "instructions" (of Ptah-hotep, Amen-em-Opet, etc.).

Like the proverbs, the Akkadian fables have to be related to Sumerian texts. This is especially true for the type of fable which sets forth so-called disputations between animals, plants, and even materials, etc., considered personified and presented as arguing with each other about their respective good qualities, usefulness for man, etc. This genre is very well represented in Sumerian, where we have such dialogues as between Winter and Summer, Silver and Bronze,

the Pickax and the Plow, and others, while from Akkadian we have fragments of the Date Palm and the Tamarisk, the Bull and the Horse, etc. There also exist a number of short beast fables, or rather extended proverbs with animals as actors, that appear in a text type somewhat akin to the "Counsels of Wisdom" but more humorous in mood. These items are often arranged in groups according to the animals, and similar texts—especially one referring to the fox—are among the Sumerian proverb collections. Some fragments from the library of Ashurbanipal suggest the existence of a corresponding Akkadian version. Other fragments from Asshur and Nineveh seem to contain epical texts with animals (wolf and dog, mostly) as protagonists, but not enough is preserved to indicate the content of this type of text.

Four more texts should be discussed here, which, although quite different in tenor and style, could for one reason or another be termed didactic in purpose: the Theodicy, the *Speculum Principis* ("*Fürstenspiegel*"), the Dialogue Between Master and Servant, and the tale of the Poor Man of Nippur. While the first two reach, respectively, into the realms of philosophy and politics, the last two simply represent humorous folk tales, as is also shown by the fact that parallels to them are well known in other civilizations.

The Theodicy consists of a dialogue written as an acrostic poem (the acrostic gives the name of the poet) in stanzas of eleven lines each. The skeptic elaborates on the eternal topic of his misfortunes, which he contrasts with the success of the ungodly; on the worthlessness of all human endeavors; on the lack of social justice, etc.; while his pious adversary extols the virtues of devotion to the gods, whose wisdom in distributing success and failure remains beyond human understanding, and suggests that the skeptic resign himself to accepting good and evil as the gods have allotted them. The text is full of learned abstrusities and farfetched poetic expressions, so that the Akkadians themselves needed a commentary to understand it. Its tenor is ceremoniously polite, but the argumentation is completely devoid of vigor and cogency. There are Babylonian and Assyrian fragments (from Asshur and Nineveh) that show that this composition, which may date back to the turn of the first millennium, was widely appreciated.

Of the *Speculum Principis*, we have only one short (sixty lines) tablet, from the library of Ashurbanipal. It contains tersely styled political precepts for the king, each followed by a short phrase describing the punishment or reward which he is to expect. The pattern is that of the omen texts, and the intention is clearly to impress upon the ruler his obligation to act justly toward his subjects, by obeying the law of the country and heeding the advice of the chancellor. The main section of the text (fifty lines) is devoted to bringing it home to the king that the privileges of the free cities Sippar, Nippur, and Babylon are under divine protection and that the gods Shamash, Enlil, and Marduk will punish him direly for any infringement against the specifically enumerated rights of their cities. The text seems to be late, but it is possible that similar compositions were in circulation early in the first millennium, when the free cities of Mesopotamia became powerful enough to assert their independence.

On a Seleucid tablet from Babylon and an Assyrian one from Asshur we have preserved a unique text, again in dialogue form. Master and servant are engaged in an obviously comical dialogue, the master giving an order, to which his servant reacts by quoting proverbial sayings which demonstrate the wisdom of the master's decision, whereupon the latter changes his mind and revokes his order. For this the servant supplies equally good reasons from the same source, thus showing, to the amusement of the listener, that even the wisdom of the proverbs gives no unequivocal guidance. The servant is everywhere shown as much brighter than his master, and he proves it with his last retort.

Equally on the folk level is the story of the Poor Man of Nippur, which was found in Sultantepe, and of which a fragment shows that it was also kept in Nineveh. Again a unique topic: the roguish pranks of a poor man who, having been mistreated by an official, takes his revenge. The story is set in Nippur and is replete with wonderful information about everyday speech, the mores of the lower classes, and workaday life. The style of the poem is extremely lively, although in some passages somewhat compressed, as if a well-known story were being told.

**d. The education of the scribe.** While Sumerian and Egyptian literatures have texts that extol the scribal craft and its importance, there is no Akkadian reference to this topic. We know very little about the social position of the scribes. Their importance for the administration of city and state is illustrated by the fact that in Middle and Neo-Assyrian texts the city scribe appears among the highest officials, and that in the court of Nebuchadrezzar II the "scribes" of the palace are mentioned. The craft was handed down in families, as shown by the names appearing at the end of legal texts and in the colophons of scholarly tablets. The patron deities were the goddess Nisaba and, later, Nabû. There are traces of specialization—such as in medical or astronomical texts—but in general the education of the scribe prepared him, as we know from the Sumerian series "e d u b b a," to write every kind of text.

From countless "school tablets"—mostly lentil-shaped—we learn that the teaching method consisted in the teacher's writing a sign or word or short sentence on one side of the tablet while the pupil copied it as best he could on the other. Progressing to sign lists, the student began to copy, and probably learned by rote, first lists of the simpler signs and then those of the more complex signs. When the junior scribe advanced to the copying of literary works, he probably followed a definite curriculum, as the large number of extant copies of certain texts seems to indicate. Of certain important series copied by student scribes for practice, we have dozens of copies of the first tablets, but their number decreases for the subsequent tablets, so that the last tablets are very meagerly, if at all, attested.

Motivated by personal scholarly interest, individual scribes could accumulate, by having their pupils copy them as part of their training, a large number of literary texts to build up a personal collection of tablets. Since the scribes were attached to temples as well as to palaces, leisure induced by economic security and devotion to specific subject matters could easily contribute to what we might call a library, such as those found in Asshur, Sultantepe, etc. It should, however, be stressed that a library in the Western sense of this term existed only in Nineveh, where it was collected at the instance of Ashurbanipal. We know from his letters that this king was very eager to assemble such a collection, and that he sent emissaries to Babylonia to hunt for specific tablets and even showed so much interest in the project that he decided which tablets should be incorporated and which omitted. These texts were copied and bear the name of Ashurbanipal in a series of elaborate but standardized subscriptions that pointedly bear witness to the literary interests of the king. It has been estimated that far more than a thousand literary texts were stored in that library, apart from texts which were deposited there as a royal archive. There are, however, indications that substantial parts of the collection came from Calah, where Tiglath-pileser I may earlier have brought Babylonian originals after his conquest of Babylon, and also from private collections of certain priests.

Indispensable for the teaching of the complex system of cuneiform writing, for reference purposes, and for the study of the Sumerian texts, and also as a vehicle for scholarly activities, a staggering number of texts usually called syllabaries or vocabularies have been left to us by the Akkadian scribes. All this grew out of the practice of the Sumerian scribes of drawing up lists of signs (sign forms) as well as lists of objects, and of gods, stars, canals, rivers, personal names, etc. While the former type may well have had primarily practical purposes, the lists of the latter type are difficult to evaluate. To impute to these scribes scientific interests in our sense should be considered an attempt to romanticize what may well have been a purely mnemotechnical device. However, when Sumerian became an object of scholarly research for the Akkadians, both types of lists underwent an important development. The lists of objects, etc., were provided, in the Middle Babylonian period, with Akkadian translations and organized in two large series that were strictly standardized. Thus we have the famous series ḪAR . ra=*ḫubullu,* with twenty-two tablets (tablets 3-24), dealing, in this sequence, with: trees, wooden objects, reed objects, earthenware, leather objects, metal objects, domestic animals, wild animals, parts of the human or animal body, stones, fish and birds, plants, wool and garments, localities of all kinds, beer, honey, oils, barley, and other foodstuffs. When many of the Akkadian designations became obsolete, a commentary series (HAR.GUD=*imrû=ballu*) was used that added terms which were to explain the older expressions. Another Akkadian vocabulary of this type is l ú=*ša,* the four tablets of which list designations of human beings (officials, craftsmen, social classes, etc.), from king to brickmaker.

More complicated is the development of the sign lists. In the early Old Babylonian period there were three types of arrangement of sign lists, one in which the syllables followed each other according to the vowel sequence u-a-i, one which arranged the signs according to their form (called $S^a$ and provided in the left column with the reading of the sign and in the right with its Akkadian name), and one which is termed Ea by Assyriologists. The first two were used in primary education outside Nippur and the third in Nippur. While the first type disappeared soon and the use of the second remained limited, the Ea arrangement proved very fertile. Originally it was an elementary sign list (Proto-Ea) containing all the Sumerian signs and their polyphonic values, information needed to read and write Sumerian. This was soon enlarged into an exhaustive series called á—A = $nâqu$, which comprised forty tablets and added to the signs a column with Akkadian translations, giving several Akkadian words for each Sumerian sign. In some recensions of this series a column with the names of the signs was placed between the column with the signs and that with the translations. Excerpts were made of this forty-tablet series, such as: ea—A = $nâqu$, with eight tablets, further excerpted on two tablets which we call $S^b$, containing only the most common signs and values, for elementary training. For advanced training, the scribes of Nippur used an acrophonic list of signs and their compounds (Proto-Izi) that likewise was later provided with Akkadian translations and enlarged into the series i z i = $išâtu$, with at least sixteen tablets. They also had a bilingual series, diri-DIRI—siāku = $watru$, which gives in an acrographic arrangement only sign groups whose Sumerian reading differs from that of the individual components (seven tablets). In the Middle Babylonian period a new and different crop of bilingual lists appears: two that contain groups of synonyms (usually three), one called antagal = $šaqû$ (more than ten tablets), and the other, erimḫuš = $anantu$ (more than six tablets). Then we have one arranged according to topics, called alan = $lānu$, and one according to Akkadian meanings, sa₇.alan = $nabnītu$. The latter lists parts of the body and activities connected with them in a sequence running from the head to the feet, on more than thirty tablets. To this impressive body of material belong quite a number of less extensive syllabaries—besides a large number of still unassigned fragments presumably belonging to less widely used series—which attest to special traditions in different periods and localities.

Once the list as a form of scholarly presentation had become accepted, a number of works for the training of the scribe were cast in this mold. These are grammatical texts, used to teach Sumerian grammar to Akkadian scribes. They include the series dimmer = dingir = $ilu$ (which illustrates dialectal differences in Sumerian), the series $ana ittišu$, an Old Babylonian book of legal formulas from Nippur (of which tablets 1-2 of ḪAR . ra = ḫubullu represent an excerpt), and uru.an.na = $maštakal$, a kind of pharmacopoeia, to mention only the most important representatives of this type of literature. We also have synonym lists, which explain rare and obsolete Akkadian words by more common terms, and thus have columns of Akkadian words only.

There can be no doubt that the traditionally enforced bilingualism of the scribal tradition kept interest in grammar and lexicography alive in Mesopotamia. From the Old Babylonian period onward, Sumerian religious texts—and, infrequently, Sumerian learned poetry, such as the poems l u g a l e u m e l a m b i Nergal and Andimdima—were provided with Akkadian translations, first written as glosses below the line and in the free spaces left in the line, then interlinearly, and, very rarely only, on the reverse of the tablet. The translations are not always reliable, but they do quite often shed light on both the Sumerian and the Akkadian. The largest of these texts is the series $utukkī lemnūti,$ "the evil demons." In addition to scholarly bilingualism, there was another bilingualism caused by the accidents of history. In early times the kings of the Akkad Dynasty had Akkadian as well as Sumerian versions of their inscriptions made. Later on, Hammurabi had both versions written side by side in one inscription; interlinear royal inscriptions are rare and quite late. With the Persian conquest appeared trilingual inscriptions—in Old Persian, Late Babylonian, and Elamite—not to speak of the Aramaic version of the trilingual Behistun Inscription written on papyrus. Throughout its entire history, Mesopotamia was in contact with persons speaking foreign languages. We have the seal of a person (in Ur of the Third Dynasty) who was an interpreter for the language of Meluhha, and we have Greek transcriptions of Akkadian words written between the lines of Seleucid school tablets containing a text taken from the series ḪAR . ra = ḫubullu, and even an Akkadian text transcribed with Greek letters.

**F. *INSTITUTIONS.*** Since in every civilization social relations are articulated within established channels co-ordinated in a characteristic pattern, it is essential to deal, however cursorily, with these channels—institutions—in this survey of Assyro-Babylonian civilization. This framework is indispensable for the understanding of the innumerable data provided by the legal and administrative texts in cuneiform. Only three major institutions will be discussed here: kingship, city, and temple, after an introductory excursus on the social and economic background of the civilization.

**1. Social and economic background.** It is important for any understanding of Mesopotamian civilization to keep the Babylonian and the Assyrian social and economic backgrounds strictly apart and to realize that the Sumerian is to a large extent beyond our reach. Although Sumerian epical literature and mythological texts do reflect a society that flourished beyond the area illuminated by written documents, no co-ordination of the extant data from literary and nonliterary sources, in depth (time) and width (local range), is yet available.

The social structure of both Babylonia and Assyria is characterized first by the absence of any tribal organization of the free population, and second by the absence of status stratification above the level of slave. As a Sumerian heritage, there existed up to the Old Babylonian period a small number of groups whose freedom was restricted in various ways, but they disappeared in the course of time. The slave population—outside the large economic units of temple and palace—was at all times very small.

The basic cleavage within the population of Assyria and Babylonia was that between city dwellers and those who lived in villages of semipermanent habitations between the cities. The latter were often crowded out into near-nomadic conditions or else compelled by powerful city kings to live in abandoned or newly built settlements to till the soil, pay taxes, or do *corvée* work or military service. They also worked as laborers for the city dwellers or joined temples and palaces as mercenaries or serfs. Their number was easily added to by infiltrating foreign groups. In times of economic stress their ranks swelled until a king pressured them into projects of forced urbanization, internal colonization, etc. This rather fluid and at times quite substantial element of the population could, under certain conditions, engulf the cities and attain political power. Such conditions could have been brought about by an increase in foreign elements, by depression and internal strife in the cities. These factors, either singly or in combination, may have caused political, economic, and even linguistic changes which, though they appear to us to have occurred suddenly, may have been gradual. This situation contributed greatly to the curious lack of stability of the political structure of all the Mesopotamian states, where the power of the central authority depended to a large extent upon its ability to overcome the resistance of a large section of the population.

In respect to economics, the country primarily relied on agriculture, supplementing it with animal husbandry, mostly keeping sheep and goats, with some large cattle used for traction (plow and wagon). The maintenance of the latter required pasture and transhumance, which made the keeping of cattle a virtual monopoly of temples and palaces. Industrial activity—which in the ancient Near East means the weaving of textiles—and such enterprises as large-scale fishing, for the preparation of dry or salted fish, required man power which, in a nontribal society, could be levied only on a village organization level or by a redistribution system, such as that of the temple or the palace.

Because cereal agriculture by means of irrigation can operate on a larger scale only under authoritarian guidance, villages were quite rare in Babylonia; their place, it seems, was taken by manorial settlements, and all social and economic life was concentrated in cities. It happens (*see* § A2 *above*) that the annual flooding of the rivers in Babylonia was not so favorable for cereal agriculture as was the case in Egypt. Its timing was not advantageous. Much protective work was required, and the flooding caused an increasing salination of the soil, which had to be counteracted by the digging of new canals that dislocated the boundaries of the arable territory and affected the distribution of the population. The consequences for Babylonia were rather far-reaching, for they materialized, as a rule, in a centrifugal movement which could break the economic prosperity of a city, move political power to marginal regions, and leave large segments of the country agriculturally exhausted and culturally stunted. Only when a city had become the seat of a dynasty and could live off the spoils of war or on tribute—or when it was integrated in trade routes—could it survive such changes.

In Assyria, the economic situation presents itself quite differently. There was little, if any, genuine urbanization; and agriculture, dependent here on rainfall, was primarily a village affair, if not run from manors. This holds true for the entire region from the piedmont of the Zagros to the Mediterranean. The population consisted basically of poor farmers living in village communities and of a thin layer of a ruling class of feudal lords or foreign conquerors. The village units showed a definite and tenacious resistance to urbanization but adapted themselves easily to a feudal organization that knitted them together into more or less ephemeral states. They were willing to pay with products and work for the support of a feudal lord, who might be replaced overnight or be permanently absent at court. These feudal lords demanded a kingship quite different in concept from that of Babylonia; with their king they went to war annually and made raids upon the enemy after the harvest. The king obtained wealth and power by conquest and internal colonization centered in newly built royal cities populated with displaced conquered peoples, prisoners of war, and whatever natives could be forced into them, to pay taxes, build temples and palaces, and serve in the army. All this was kept together and functioning by sheer force, and any political change caused immediate disintegration and collapse. The people forced into urbanization then scattered, but the village communities continued undisturbed, and the few big cities usually managed to survive until a new ruler or a new conqueror came along.

Foreign trade was an important economic factor in both Babylonia and Assyria. But in this respect, too, essential differences can be observed in certain periods.

The export of textiles produced by slaves and serfs in the self-contained redistribution systems of temple and palace created in Babylonia, up to the end of the Ur III period, the means of importing metals for essential and prestige purposes and stone for decoration. These activities could be combined with a carrying trade between barbarian peoples, who lacked the prestige, political power, and interest necessary for organizing trade relations by means of treaties, diplomacy, etc., as was the case in Asia Minor and probably also around the Persian Gulf. Up to the time of Shamshi-Adad I (*ca.* 1812-1780), in Asia Minor the Assyrian traders were active; in the Persian Gulf region, the seafaring merchants of Ur.

Before the Dark Age the following situation in the domain of international trade can be observed: The texts of the *tamkaru* (traders) of the period of Ur III tell us of the import of spices, perfumes, and precious woods, apart from timber, stone, and metals; the Old Assyrian documents (letters, accounts, etc., often termed "Cappadocian Texts") from the merchant settlement at Kanish in Anatolia and other localities in this general region show in detail how Assyrian traders transacted business; the letters of the merchants of Ur (Old Babylonian period) show that they trafficked in copper imported by ship from across the Persian Gulf; and the evidence from Mari tells of trade relations joining the Mediterranean coast to the islands of the Gulf.

After the Dark Age we find a somewhat different situation. The traders who formerly traveled the route along the Euphrates, through Syria, and to the Hittite capital had now become royal emissaries, carrying precious gifts from court to court and enjoying royal protection, as we know from the letters found in Amarna and Boghazköy. In Ugarit and also in Nuzi, we again find indications of growing trade relations based on treaties but intensified by private initiative. From then on, strangely enough, our texts remain quite silent with regard to trade and traders—for which silence (after the twelfth century B.C.) one could perhaps blame the so-called Aramaic invasions, the wars accompanying the expansion of Assyrian power, etc. There exists, however, especially for the first half of the first millennium B.C., circumstantial evidence that speaks for the continuous existence, if not the growth, of foreign trade in and around Mesopotamia. Such evidence is the ease with which the kings of the Chaldean Dynasty took over the political and commercial role of Assyria after its collapse, when we find Nebuchadrezzar II, Neriglissar, and Nabonidus fighting in Asia Minor, dealing with Phoenician cities, traveling deep into Arabia, and filling their temples with unheard-of amounts of precious metals and stones. Further evidence is the fact that Nebuchadrezzar lists a Phoenician, Hanno, as his court *tamkaru*. It is also to be noted that Sargon II of Assyria forced the Egyptians to allow a trading station at the Palestinian border and that Esarhaddon granted the rebuilt city of Babylon again the privilege of unrestricted trade relations with the entire world. While the lack of any written evidence for this trade may be explained by suggesting that it was in the hands of Aramaic merchants using papyrus for records, the question as to what the merchandise was is more difficult to answer. It may have been that Mesopotamian trade had changed from an export-import activity to the more profitable carrying trade linking the East— i.e., the Iranian Plateau and the countries beyond the Persian Gulf—with the countries around the Mediterranean Sea. Some words should finally be said concerning the accumulation of wealth in private hands. It is clear that the trader in royal service profited personally and may well have grown rich (this seems to have been the case in Old Babylonian Larsa); but without the freedom of disposition and assumption of financial responsibility on the part of the trader, we cannot speak of private initiative in long-distance trade. It remains obscure whether such a situation actually ever evolved in the ancient Near East. Only participation in profits, and sharing of responsibility and pooling of funds, as is illustrated in the case of the *karum* of the Old Assyrian period and of Old Babylonian Ur, seems to have occurred. As to the late period, exemplified by the banking house of Murashu in fifth-century Nippur, we have apparently a fusion of feudal status and private commercial enterprise, still impossible to disentangle.

**2. King and palace.** From the point of view of Mesopotamian civilization, there existed only one institution in our sense, and that was kingship. It was of divine origin and therefore sacred in nature. This essential divine quality of kingship was expressed in two ways. In Babylonia up to the Hammurabi period, the name of the king could be written with the determinative used for gods and objects of worship, or (as is attested only for Ur III) statues of kings could receive shares of the offerings in the temple. To speak here of "deification" is a gross rationalization. In Assyria, the sanctity of the royal person was said to be expressed by its supernatural and awe-inspiring radiance (*melammū*), which was also a characteristic of deities and all things divine. This sheen or halo terrified his foes but was taken away from the king when he lost divine support. The royal apparel underlines this aspect of kingship; the horned miter of Naram-Sin, the *kusītu* garment of Neo-Assyrian kings, were also worn by the images. The special relationship existing between the king and his god, which materialized in the successes of the ruler in war and the prosperity of his country in peace, was often couched in terms of family relations, and the scribes and artists at court loved to elaborate upon this topic in their hectic and adulatory style. *See* KING.

There are deep-seated differences between the Babylonian and Assyrian concepts of kingship, which can only be touched upon here. The Assyrian king was the high priest of the god Asshur, while the Babylonian king was admitted into the cella of Marduk only once a year, and then without royal insignia. The Assyrian king had to be crowned as king anew every year, whereas this was not necessary in Babylonia. The stress put on the annual crowning in Assyria and the custom of having the king act as eponym on a par with the officials of the realm suggest the explanation that he was originally only the *primus inter pares* of an amphictyonic union of sheiks (as we know it of the kings of Hana) living around the sacred city of Asshur. The person of the Assyrian king had to be carefully protected from disease and evil magic influences. A host of physicians and diviners surrounded him, and he had to undergo elaborate lustration ceremonies. Adjoining the throne room of each Assyrian palace there is a room for ritual ablutions. Access to the king was carefully regulated; even the crown prince could not freely approach him. The personnel of the Assyrian and Babylonian courts differed widely. The Assyrian king was surrounded by officials whose task it was to execute his orders; the Babylonian king was surrounded by the administrators of his palace. The Babylonian king after the Middle Babylonian period had a vizier—a development rare and late in Assyria. Since obedience to the proper authorities was considered by the Mesopotamians the main characteristic of civilized living, service to the king was put on the same level as service to the gods. However, the kings were anything but oriental despots. The Assyrian kings—of whom we know much more than we do of their Babylonian counterparts—were always careful not to offend their high officials, whose loyalty to the dynasty they had to secure by oaths and agreements to assure the succession of the crown prince.

The king's palace represented an organization of major economic importance for the city. Into it poured tribute, the yield of the royal estates, and the products of the royal workshops. From its stores were fed and appareled according to status the royal family, the officials and personnel of the court, the administrators of the royal estates, the standing army, serfs, slaves, etc. A redistribution system of this magnitude quite naturally created conflicts when in contact with other systems of this type—such as, in Babylonia, that of the temple. Whether the palace organization developed from manorial roots or is to be considered an offshoot of the temple organization can hardly be determined now.

**3. City.** While the economic importance of the temple in Mesopotamia constantly declined, the conflict between the palace and the free city gained in importance. It resulted in royal attempts to restrict the freedoms and privileges of the old cities and also in the creation of new cities subject to the king's authority. A bevy of small cities—often actually in sight of one another—developed astonishingly early in S Mesopotamia. They were walled; divided into city quarters, each of which had a gate; and provided with a suburb, and with a harbor that had a specific political status connected with trade. Each contained a palace and at least one temple, that of the city god. Surrounded by fields and gardens which the river provided with the essential water, the cities housed a community of farmers, with a few craftsmen for immediate needs (potter, brickmaker, etc.). There was but little contact with other cities, and money was used for only a few purposes. The communal bond superseded all relations beyond that of the immediate family. The city acted as a legal person in our sense—e.g., when selling a vacant lot within its walls—and as a political body, through an assembly which could write or receive letters, etc. The growth or decay of such a city depended on the importance of the two institutions it harbored—temple and palace—and, of course, on its supply of irrigation water. The prestige and power of the king was paramount—the wealth of the palace attracted traders and mercenaries and enriched the city. However, the growth of a tradition of civil liberties—mostly exemptions from taxes, and other privileges—placed under divine sanction, created tension between the city and the king. This assumed increasing importance in the Neo-Assyrian period, where the Babylonian cities especially (apart from the capital) played a political role in the conflict between Babylonia and Assyria.

Each city had a definite individuality which is often reflected in its history. Nippur was a sacred town, particularly up to the Middle Babylonian period. Sippar occupied a unique position in the Old Babylonian period, with its commercial relations and as a link between N Babylonia and the seminomadic tribes of the Upper Euphrates region. Borsippa, a city without a king like Nippur and Sippar, has not yet been touched by the spade of the archaeologist. Uruk, of Sumerian fame, rose to new importance in the late period. The two millenniums of the history of Ur are best known, along with that of Nippur, while Eridu, Isin, and Larsa disappeared in and before the Old Babylonian period. Asshur in the N, deified as the god Asshur, has been well explored, but Arbela still lies under the modern city.

From the point of view of urbanism, the cities of the alluvial plains, in Babylonia, show a significant separation between the cultic focus and the palace, each being situated in a separate walled enclosure within the circumvallation, while the civic centers were in the city gates, where the inhabitants of the city quarters met in assembly. The urban pattern is definitely different in Assyria and the westward regions. There temple and palace moved together; one wall enclosed them and their essential dependencies, the treasury and the barracks of the royal guard. All this formed a city within the city. The compound containing the palace and the temple could be situated either in the center of the city—preferably upon an elevation, so that one could speak of citadel-cities—or at the periphery of the city. The latter arrangement is evident in all the new cities which the Assyrian kings built for themselves. There we find a high artificial terrace straddling the city wall and harboring the palace and the temples. Since these new cities represent royal city planning, another of their characteristic features should be mentioned, the rectangularity of the outlines of the walls though there is no over-all regularity in the distribution of the gates, so that no grid arrangement for the streets can be assumed. This is clearly a layout patterned after the military camps, which are often represented on Assyrian reliefs. The peripheral emplacement of the "inner city" and the fact that its buildings were placed on a terrace show the king as high priest separated in a sacred city by an enclosure.

At the turn of the second millennium the inhabitants of the oldest cities, such as Nippur, Babylon, and Sippar, in Babylonia, and Asshur and even Harran, in Assyria, began to acquire a special legal status with regard to the king. Apart from the exemptions from taxation, *corvée*, and military service, there were a number of privileges, some of which are mentioned in the text called *Speculum Principis,* while others are more or less accidentally brought to light by isolated references. E.g., Esarhaddon complained that his rebellious brothers "even drew the sword in the city of Nineveh, which is a godless thing to do"; the Babylonian king had to assure the high priest of Esagila at the New Year's Festival that he never had offended a citizen of Babylon by slapping his face; and there is a letter from the inhabitants of Babylon to Ashurbanipal that asserts, in the heat of an argument, that even a dog enjoys the privileges of a citizen of Babylon once it has entered that city.

**4. Temple.** The history of the Mesopotamian temple as an institution is very much in the dark, although there is an abundance of text material, especially for the Sumerian period (from Lagash) and the Neo-Babylonian period (from Sippar and Uruk). Economically, the temple was organized as a redistributive system, with its characteristic double aspect: incoming gifts and rents and outgoing rations and other payments. The numerous administrative documents illustrate this situation in detail. It seems that the *šangû*-priest headed the administrative side of the temple's activity, while the *en*-priest related the sanctuary to its deity in various ways. In relation to the community, the temple had specific functions, such as that of administering oaths (only Old Babylonian), establishing the standards of weights and measures (only Old Babylonian) and the interest rate for loans, and granting small loans in hardship cases (mostly Old Babylonian). The building of sanctuaries and providing them with funds was a royal privilege at all times, and in the Neo-Babylonian period we even find a royal commissary as a member of the ruling board of the temple to see to it that a tax on pious gifts (consisting of small silver payments collected in boxes at the entrance of the temple) was correctly paid to the king. Later on, the internal affairs of the temples were handled by an assembly of priests, together with the citizens of the city, sitting as a court. No conflicts are known in Babylonia between temple and king, except for the attempts of Nabonidus to introduce cultic innovations, apparently imitating the practices of Assyrian kings.

**G. RELIGION.** The interest of Assyriologists in Mesopotamian religion has been on the wane for more than twenty years, thus patently expressing an acute disappointment in the numerous books and articles which dealt with this topic in the first decades of the twentieth century. The main reason for the glaring fruitlessness of these efforts is the fact that scholars either have wanted to handle the vast amount of material in terms of OT religion or have applied preconceived romantic patterns to the amorphous mass of data, philological and archaeological alike. The following presentation intends solely to introduce the reader into the typology of the teeming pantheon and to trace some of the more obvious characteristics of the god-man relation in Mesopotamia.

The extant sources offer an extremely complex picture of the Mesopotamian pantheon, as is to be expected, not only on account of its long history but also because it represents a fusion of Sumerian and Akkadian deities. This fusion created a number of hybrid figures in whose names were preserved the names of the gods who had merged, and thus were kept alive in a plethora of local and minor deities who would otherwise have been forgotten. However, many of them survived only in learned and theological texts. The result is perhaps best illustrated by the god list (Series A n = Anum), which originally contained more than 1,500 names and still fails to mention names well known from other sources. More names could be added from the countless theophoric personal names. There the ever-changing preferences in time and region mirror the fluctuations in the popularity of individual deities, their rise and their fall into oblivion, in accordance with political trends or changes in popular religion. These personal names throw much light on the religious history of Mesopotamia proper and of some of the adjacent regions under Mesopotamian influence. Far more difficult is the utilization of religious texts dealing with the cult of certain gods.

The formalization and standardization of religious expressions and the narrow range of the hymnical terminology favor an extensive interchange of epithets, thus blurring the individuality of all but the most outstanding and characteristic divine figures. Even among these, a typological classification is evident. They easily fall into old gods and young ones, astral deities, and a few, very rare, unique figures. Anu and Enlil, and, later on, even Marduk, belong to the category of old gods. In the theogony of the Epic of Creation, Anu, the "Heaven," is the oldest god, and his realm the remote heaven. Originally, Enlil was by no means the misanthropic "Old Man" of the pantheon; but when he developed from god of the sacred city of Nippur to ruler of the gods, he assumed much of the characteristic remoteness of Anu. Enlil's temple, the "Mountain House" in Nippur, stood in a very specific relation to the nether world and to the evil demons who lived there, so that the conjurations performed against them often necessarily refer to Enlil. Marduk was at first one of the "young" gods, but the political development of his city, Babylon, moved him into the rank of the rulers of the cosmos. Ea, in Sumerian E n . k i, although in certain respects the local deity of Eridu, shared, in late theological speculations, the rule of heaven and earth with Anu and Enlil inasmuch as his realm was the waters surrounding the earth and those below it. He was the patron deity of the essential profession of exorcism, but he developed into the god of all the arts and crafts, and his wisdom and cunning is extolled in many myths and stories. Since the Marduk theologians made him the father of their god, Ea must at an early period have been more important than a local deity, probably some kind of "culture hero," comparable to the Oannes of Berossos.

Either the young gods had no city or their cities were new. A typical young god is Enlil's son, Ninurta. He had no city of his own and is the central figure in a cycle of myths that describe his prowess and achievements. Nabu, however, though called the son of Marduk, does not quite fit the pattern, since he became the city god of Borsippa, an old city. He was the patron deity of the scribes, and his popularity increased in the late period.

The foremost astral deities were, of course, Shamash, the sun-god, and Sin, the moon-god. Each of them was worshiped in two important cities, Shamash (Sumerian Utu) in Larsa and Sippar—both his temples are called the "White House"—and Sin (Sumerian Nanna) in Ur and in far-off Harran. As the god of light, Shamash was the judge of heaven and earth and was concerned with the protection of the poor and the unjustly treated. He and the moon-god, Sin, maintained their popularity throughout the entire duration of Mesopotamian civilization. Apart stands the figure of the storm-god, who was without a city in the alluvial plain but was worshiped under many names, from Assyria to the Mediterranean and in all the adjacent regions, by Semites, Hittites, and Hurrians alike. In Mesopotamia he appears in the role of the oracle-giver, together with Shamash. Unique in many respects among the parochial gods of Mesopotamia is Asshur, the city god of the capital of Assyria. Asshur was provided by his theologians with all the trappings of a lord of the universe, creator and organizer of the cosmos, father of the gods, etc., when Assyria rose to be the foremost power in the region. He represents a phenomenon quite unique in his relation to his city, with which he shared his name. As befitted a deity of that region,

Asshur was connected with a mountain sacred to him (Mount Ebih), where he had a sanctuary. Among the lesser gods, Nergal should be mentioned, because he was not only the city god of Cutha but, with his spouse, Ereshkigal, the ruler of the realm of the dead; and Dumuzi (TAMMUZ), more important to the Sumerians than to the Akkadians, whose death is the topic of an important body of hymns and lamentations.

Among the goddesses of the pantheon, Ishtar (Sumerian Innin) stands out against the various figures of the mother-goddess type such as Mama, Baba, etc., and against the goddess Gula, the patron of physicians and probably originally a goddess of death. Characteristic of Ishtar is the essential dichotomy of her functions. On the one hand she is the battle-loving warrior-goddess who gives victory to the king she loves, while on the other she is connected with sexual life. She is furthermore linked with the planet Venus, and her Sumerian prototype is connected with the Tammuz cycle, while she appears in Uruk first as daughter, later as spouse, of Anu.

There is remarkably little foreign influence in the Babylonian or Assyrian pantheon apart from occasional references to such gods as Amurru, Dagan, Shimaliya, etc., brought in by conquerors. In the regions outside Mesopotamia where cuneiform writing was used, the logograms for the names of the Sumerian and Akkadian gods referred to the local deity of the corresponding type, such as Teshup (Adad), Shaushka (Ishtar), etc.

While the gods were thought to reside in various cosmic localities—if they were not present in their images—a varying amount of sanctity was considered inherent in a number of localities on earth, in certain trees and animals, even in man-made objects. As sacred, these participated in the nature of the divine and deserve more than cursory mention. The sacredness of mountains is well attested, especially in Assyria, where kings erected stelae in the mountains, and a number of individual mountains were connected with specific deities, not to mention representations of gods walking over or growing out of mountains. The two rivers Tigris and Euphrates were likewise considered sacred, especially their sources (also those of the Habur River). Such numinosity also attached to the seashores, where the kings erected stelae, washed their weapons, and sacrificed, and to the bitumen wells of Hit, "where the stelae of the great gods are erected." Myths and iconography deal very often with sacred trees, such as the cedar guarded by Huwawa, the *kiškannu* tree in Eridu, the m e s tree of Nergal, and the *huluppu* tree of the Sumerian Gilgamesh story. Nothing, however, is known, from the historical point of view, of the sacredness of actual trees, and this also holds true for animals.

As to man-made objects, attention should be drawn to the role of the so-called sacred "symbols," as far as they are meant to indicate a divine presence.* These either represent cosmic phenomena— such as the sun disk, the crescent, the star of Ishtar —or are weapons of specific forms (lion-headed clubs, ram-headed staffs, etc.) and implements such

103. Boundary stone of Marduknadinahhe (note sacred symbols)

as the spade, lamp, and plow. Mythological animals are rare; the bull stands for Adad and the dog for Gula, while such composite monsters as the *mušhuššu* (lion-snake-eagle) or the *kusariqqu* (goat-fish) are linked respectively to Marduk and Ea. There are several still undetermined objects that served as symbols. The cultic function and importance of these objects remains largely unknown, but they seem to have represented the deity outside the sanctuary more often than the images did. Where, when, to what extent, and under what circumstances they replaced the images remains to be investigated. Fig. ASS 103.

Fundamentally, the deity was considered present in his image, living in the temple much in the same way as the king resided in his palace. Only a few images intended for cult purposes are preserved, but we know of them from iconography and from the pious custom of keeping cheap clay figurines representing images in private houses as objects of worship. Literary texts tell that most images were made of precious wood plated with gold (outside the areas decked out with garments), with staring eyes of precious stone, and were clad in sumptuous garments that were changed according to ritual requirements. It should be stressed that the image was always of human shape and proportion. Exceptions are rare and occur only with minor deities (bull-shaped son of Shamash) or for special reasons (snake-god). Asshur seems to have been fashioned, at times, in the likeness of the king, as can be seen from seals and reliefs which represent him and the king in identical dress and pose, and from the description of the bronze reliefs mounted on the gate of the New Year's Chapel, which reads: "The figure of Asshur going to battle against Tiamat is that of Sennacherib." In Babylonia the conservatism with regard to images was far-reaching—Nabonidus' attempt merely to change the tiara of the sun-god ran into strong opposition on the part of the priests and the assembly of the city. Assyrian kings, however, state repeatedly that they had images made of important deities according to their own ideas.

These images were constructed or repaired in special workshops of the temple and had to undergo a complex ritual of consecration, during which they were endowed with "life," their eyes "opened" so that they could see, and their mouths washed to purify them. Attired in gold-decorated garments, crowned with characteristic headgear (horned miters or feather crowns) and hung with golden pectorals, they were placed on pedestals in their cellas.

In the morning, the statues of the minor gods were brought before them—exactly as the courtiers had to be present at the king's levee—and the morning repast was enacted, to be followed by noon and evening meals, each consisting of two courses. Platters and jars were "passed" before the image, but sometimes the food was set on a table and curtains drawn around it and the image, so that the process of partaking remained hidden. The "leftovers" were at times sent to the king, sometimes even by express messenger, to have him partake of the food blessed by contact with the deity. The food itself was to be ritually clean and prepared in prescribed ways to the accompaniment of blessings at each stage. After the meal, the image was shown a finger bowl, with the water of which afterward the king and others present were sprinkled on certain occasions.

The images were often carried in procession through the spacious yards of the temples to visit other images in elaborate ceremonials or—especially at the New Year's Festival—to out-of-town sanctuaries amid the jubilation of the citizenry. From a Neo-Assyrian letter we even learn that Nabû went hunting in the game park, thus following also in this detail the behavior of the Assyrian king. There were the sacred ceremonial marriage festivals in which the god met his spouse. Only exceptionally do we hear of an image confined within its cella, as when Ashurnasirpal II warns his successor never to allow the sun to shine upon the image of Ishtar.

The functions of the personnel of such a sanctuary followed the pattern of the palace. The god, like the king, had to have a staff to prepare and serve food and drink, to manufacture and keep in good repair the utensils and paraphernalia of the cult, quite apart from the apparatus needed to keep up the temple as an economic unit. There were priests concerned with the performance of cultic obligations—not only those who officiated, but also the exorcists and the

singers and musicians, always according to the very diversified requirements of the cult of the god or goddess they served. It should not be forgotten that the importance and size of these temples differed greatly, from such world-famous temples as Esagila in Babylon, Eanna in Uruk, etc., down to dilapidated sanctuaries in decaying provincial cities. Fig. ASS 104.

Courtesy of the Musée du Louvre, Paris

104. Men bringing offerings, from Khorsabad

Thus the temple served to house the city's deity in a dignified way, so as to please him and keep him concerned with the city's well-being. It was the king's duty to keep the temple in good repair and provided with funds, preferably in a way that made the organization economically independent. Private piety may have contributed, but only in the Neo-Babylonian period do we know this was so. Since the image guaranteed the divine presence, victorious conquerors would want to carry it off in triumph, and we have many instances of such happenings, the last of which is mentioned in Herodotus' report that Xerxes brought the famous statue of Marduk from Babylon to Susa. With changing fortunes, many a Mesopotamian king succeeded in bringing back the image from its captivity. *See* TEMPLE, JERUSALEM.

It is extremely difficult to establish what the temple meant for the private citizen in the frame of his personal religious life. In Babylonia the sanctuary itself (antecella and cella) was accessible only to priests, while it seems to have been different in Assyria. It could therefore be that the participation of the private person was restricted to the cycle of those annual cultic events when the image was moved outside the temple, such as the New Year's Festival or the festive day on which the consecration of the sanctuary (*isinnu bīti,* "*natalis templi*") was celebrated by the city. There seem to have existed ritual mourning ceremonies, in which the city as a whole participated, and special occasions such as victories and great perils that may have compelled the priesthood to abandon its traditional isolation. The private person, however, was far removed from any intimate or personal contact with the cult of the gods. Within the eternal compass of health and sickness, success and failure, he was without expectation beyond death and devoid of the redeeming support of personal moral responsibility. *See* NEW YEAR.

Whatever comfort or help he can expect from charms, the efforts of exorcists, and the anxious observation of portents, man has to evolve in such a situation some kind of ideological structure in order to remain man. This seems to have been the case in Mesopotamia, as we know from sparse indications which are difficult to piece together. The concept of *šimtu* (commonly translated with the inadequate and misleading term "fate") was considered as applicable to the individual as it was, since Sumerian times and on a specific level of religious interpretation, to the cosmos. Each human being was considered endowed with a unique and personal "nature" (such a translation of *šimtu* helps us understand this alien concept), and this "nature" circumscribed his life in terms of luck or misfortune, survival or death, exactly as each stone or animal had its "nature," and parallel to the divinely ordained "nature" (here the term *parṣu*, Sumerian *m e*, is used) of cosmic phenomena and divine and human institutions and achievements. Although he was ever ready to turn to the unseen powers with prayers to change his "nature" for the better, a basic attitude of dignified resignation, which must have been part of the pre-Sumerian legacy, characterized the outlook of Mesopotamian man as individual.

**H. *THE ARTS.*** Mesopotamian art showed major achievements in only two mediums of artistic aspiration: monumental architecture (temple and palace) and small-scale engravings on precious stone (cylinder seals). In these widely differing fields it was able to express itself not only with great success but again and again with originality, in spite of the restricted functional and physical confines of these mediums.

The use of bricks and roof beams determined the range of technical possibilities in Mesopotamian architecture, and their application was further restricted by certain technological inhibitions. Thus bricks were joined with mud instead of mortar and hidden behind a mud facing, and the width of rooms was determined by the length of the beams, since columns, etc., were not used to remedy this restriction. The mud as mortar made the walls thick and continuous, whereas walls can be built much thinner and higher and can give the architect the freedom to curve them, open them up, etc., when the individual bricks are held in place with the adhesive power of real mortar.

Mesopotamian brick walls were, instead, articulated with rhythmically distributed stepped recesses and buttresses in strategic locations. Whatever the functional origin of this distinctive ornamentation was, it was restricted to nonsecular buildings and used skilfully to enliven the monotony of the endless blank walls.

A variety of techniques were invented to decorate the mud layer that hid the brickwork: white and colored plaster with painted designs was used, and such designs were often made more permanent by executing them in mosaics consisting of colored clay cones; while mural designs, at first painted on stucco, were transferred in Assyria to glazed brick panels and eventually to reliefed stone slabs. Only as a foreign import does the technique appear of imitating stone reliefs by means of premolded bricks, as in a temple in Uruk built by a Kassite king. Nebuchadrezzar improved upon this technique by providing the molded surface of the brick with polychromatic glazes, such as we see on the well-known Ishtar gate in Babylon.

Mesopotamian temple architecture not only used recesses in the walls to characterize a sanctuary but also differences in level. The entire building was often lifted above the plain by means of terraces, and at times the sanctuary (cella) itself was placed on a still higher level.

From the layouts of sanctuaries that were rather diversified at the beginning, we can observe an impressive development toward a well-organized setting up of a complex of rooms, corridors, and courtyards which made up the temple. The arrangement in smaller sanctuaries was often more harmonious and efficient than that of the far larger and more famous sanctuaries, which sometimes show a lack of "grand design." A major entrance provided with buttressed towers led more or less directly into a spacious paved yard surrounded on three sides by rows of auxiliary rooms, minor sanctuaries, etc., and containing, in eccentric position, an altar or well. In the fourth side was a buttressed or intricately recessed entrance that opened into the cella, which was often divided into one or more antecellas and the cella proper. The cella sheltered the god, whose image was placed on a slightly elevated podium before a recessed niche. There exist quite a number of variables in this general arrangement of Mesopotamian temples, among which two should be singled out here: (*a*) the appearance of a long and narrow, or a broad and shallow, cella; and (*b*) the position of the image in respect to the entrance into the cella —i.e., these two are sometimes coaxial, and at times they require the entering person to turn ninety degrees to face the god. In spite of a number of exceptions, the latter arrangement in both instances is the general rule in the S, the former in Assyria.

An essential feature of a Mesopotamian temple complex was, from the Ur III period on, the temple tower.* In fact, these garishly colored, staged, and crenelated towers rising high above the white-faced temples made Mesopotamia famous, as their mention in the Bible shows. With respect to the temple towers (Akkadian *ziqquratu*), there likewise existed a difference between Babylonia and Assyria. In the S these structures, made of an earthen core sheathed with bricks, were placed in separate enclosures apart from the temple and were accessible by monumental outside stairways in varying arrangements, while the Assyrian temple tower was within the temple, even so that the image's niche penetrated into the core of it, and it either had no means of access or held the stairways within its confines. Neither the purpose nor

105. Ziggurat at Ur

the function of these impressive structures is yet known. Fig. ASS 105.

There are a number of similarities between temple and palace architecture with regard to layout. The essential part of the palace was the throne room, where the king received ambassadors and tribute-bearing vassals. The placement of the throne in this room corresponded in Babylonia and Assyria respectively to the preferred position of the image in the cella. As important as the throne room was the large courtyard into which this room opened through a monumental gate, and a large hall, the purpose of which is not clear.

Assyrian palaces had a characteristic topic for their mural decoration—representations of the king as a protégé of the gods and as an ever-victorious warrior. Hence we see battle scenes, the bringing of tribute, and the slaughter of the defeated, all intended to impress and terrify the visitor. These representations, first on murals and later on shallow cut-stone orthostats, lined the courts, the throne rooms, and other important halls ever since Tukulti-Ninurta I (*ca*. 1244-1208). They show definite traces of artistic development, marked by the emergence of landscape and by the increasing attention given to anecdotal happenings, which endow the scenes with a convincing realism that often makes one forget the jarring pseudoperspective and the ingeniously hidden schematism of the numerous figures with which the battlefields are teeming.

Turning to the seal cylinders, we meet within the confines of their circumference a fairy-tale world of monsters and demons, with enthroned deities, numerous animals heraldically displayed, pious worshipers and battling heroes, and a host of ornaments to fill in any gaps. The iconographic inventory, as well as the styles of presentation—shifting from charming realism to geometrically accentuated abstractions—and also the engraving techniques employed, change from period to period, and from region to region. They act as a sensitive barometer of foreign influence and of the artistic creativity of an artist or a school of artists that otherwise could not have broken through the heavy crust of traditionalism in Mesopotamia that hampered artistic expression in other mediums. Without, e.g., a small body of Middle Assyrian seals and impressions, we would have missed the startling vitality and appealing immediacy of the art of that period, for they are not reflected in the

few preserved monuments. This *élan* and the superb technique which was its vehicle live on in the animals that appear fighting and dying on the Neo-Assyrian wall reliefs, and evoke a comparison with Old Akkadian art, whose impact on the Babylonian representation of human beings the following millenniums of delicate refining and tired but polished conventionality could not quite efface. Figs. ASS 106-8.

106. Cylinder seal depicting animals and heroes, from Second Early Dynasty period

107. The sun-god: Dynasty of Akkad

108. Cylinder seal showing Shamash enthroned, from First Babylonian Dynasty period

Of the few preserved art objects from Mesopotamia outside the two mentioned fields, only a small number happen to appeal to Western aesthetic conventions, such as the marble face of a Sumerian goddess from Uruk that may have looked much less fascinating with naturalistic set-in eyes; the head of a king of the Akkad period, made of bronze and endowed with a sweep of forceful elegance found in hardly any other work of Mesopotamian art; and, finally, the various statues of Gudea of Lagash (*ca*. 2200).* The latter show under their smooth dignity much of that well-contained inner pressure that seems to characterize Sumerian statuary (after its crude beginnings) and of which Babylonian art could only maintain the external formalism. In this again it is in contrast with Neo-Assyrian human representations, whose gesticulations are all too mechanically contrived and without meaning. Of course, countless art objects have been lost, and the few carved stone bowls, the remnants of metal work riveted into shape or chased over bitumen cores, etc., make us feel this loss only more. Stelae and reliefs carved on walls would emanate solely the boredom of extreme traditionalism, were it not for the array of monstrous beings which Mesopotamian artists knew how to endow with startling persuasiveness. Fig. SUM 87.

I. *SCIENCE AND TECHNOLOGY*. 1. **Astronomy**. In the domain of the exact sciences, Mesopotamia's achievements in mathematics and mathematical astronomy can well stand comparison with the accomplishments of other civilizations in these fields up to the time of Newton. As to mathematics, we have two types of texts: multiplication and division tables of all kinds, and problem texts. The latter are written either in Akkadian or in Sumerian and address the reader in the second person. Their presentation varies in explicitness. Some state only one problem and show in detail all the steps needed for its solution, while others list hundreds of problems in maximal condensation without giving their solutions. The sequence in which related problems are arranged takes the place of any abstract statement of a general nature. Babylonian mathematics never used such statements. Mathematically speaking, the problems are algebraic in nature, although normally formulated in geometric terms.

It is important to note that these mathematical problem texts appear in two bodies separated by a millennium of silence: the texts of the Hammurabi period and those of the Seleucid. There are no traces of any significant internal development between these groups, nor are texts known that would reveal any preliminary stage of development leading up to the Old Babylonian material. There exist lists specifically designed for the application of mathematical methods to practical problems, but there are no allusions to mathematics in the vast cuneiform text material, with the exception of a statement of King Ashurbanipal, who proudly reported that he knew how to make multiplications and divisions.

In contrast with the situation in the field of mathematics, we are able to establish the period in which the rise of Babylonian astronomy took place. Before the fifth century B.C. we have merely some observations of the appearance and disappearance of the planet Venus, dated from the end of the Old Babylonian period (for their relevance to chronology, *see* § C1 *above*); a short series of two tablets (called m u l . a p i n) that sum up the astronomical knowledge of the time, *ca.* 700 B.C. (the arrangement of the fixed stars in three "ways," their rising and setting, the planets, moon, seasons, etc.); and roughly contemporary reports to the Assyrian kings concerning eclipses, the movements of planets, etc., still on a par with reports of strange cloud formations, halos, the births of malformed animals, etc. Then, however, begins with amazing speed the development of mathematical astronomy in Mesopotamia—to be more exact in Babylonia—which started with the need of establishing a workable fixed lunar-solar calendar. For this purpose was created a zodiac to refer to the movements of the sun and the planets. Observations were made of the varying lengths of the days and nights during the year, and, above all, arithmetical progressions were used to express in mathematical terms the variations in the movements of heavenly bodies with regard to a fixed point. From description, the astronomers made the decisive step to prediction by ingeniously using these and more complex mathematical methods.

The astronomical texts, like the mathematical texts, fall into "procedure texts," which establish the rules for computing the positions of the moon and the planets from month to month or for other regular intervals, and the *"ephemerides,"* in which these computations are listed.

2. **Medicine**. It is customary to speak of Mesopotamian medicine under the heading of "science," but it should be stressed that, in comparison with Egyptian medicine, the Babylonian is as primitive and crude as are Egyptian mathematics and astronomy in comparison with Mesopotamian. The main characteristic of Mesopotamian medicine is that it is intrinsically connected and interwoven with exorcistic and other ritual practices. Its use of the pharmacopoeia seems rather confused, and the methods of applying medical treatment are quite unsophisticated.

There are relatively few medical texts extant, mostly organized according to the affected organs of the patient. Our understanding of them is greatly hampered by our inability to identify the numerous drugs, plants, and vegetable and mineral materials with sufficient certainty to establish a rationale between remedy and disease. The large "pharmaceutical" series (a r u a n n a = *maštakal*) is still too obscure, as to arrangement and purpose, to be of any help. The therapeutic texts follow the pattern of the omen texts, except that instead of the protasis they refer to the symptom or symptoms of the patient, while the apodosis is replaced by a prescription, in which the physician is addressed in the second person, or by a diagnosis of the disease, followed by advice to the physician to stay away. Apart from some obscure passages in these texts and an equally understandable section of the Codex Hammurabi, there is no evidence available that the Mesopotamian physicians practiced surgery.

3. **Technology**. In point of technology, Mesopotamian civilization fails to impress us with its achievements. In fact, it was not even able to keep up the Sumerian heritage in this respect. The Mesopotamians themselves seem to have been fully aware of this state of affairs. They imported from Egypt wonderful thin-walled alabaster vases; they took as booty from the mountain tribes copper containers and other large metal objects; and, above all, their kings expressed unrestrained admiration for all the technical achievements of the Egyptians and the Urarteans, whom they defeated in battle. In none of the various fields of technology, such as agriculture, metallurgy, weaving, the applied arts, etc., can one observe any marked advance beyond the level at which we meet them at the time of the flowering of Sumerian civilization.

There are definite indications of a technological impoverishment in Babylonia: the beautifully shaped and decorated pottery disappears with the Obeid period; the carved and polished stone vases, the containers, animal figures, etc., made of metal sheets go with the Akkad period; and the small metal objects made in cire-perdue technique vanish with the Old Babylonian period. After that, Babylonia resisted, nearly always with success, any outside stimulus.

Assyria was much more open to foreign influence: polychrome glazes came from Egypt via Syria, the stimulus to the advancement of metallurgic techniques from the mountains of Armenia, innovations in the building and decoration of palaces again from Syria, not to speak of the contributions of the steady influx of prisoners of war and foreign craftsmen, experts (dream interpreters and veterinarians from Egypt), and artists (singers from Syria).

In the basic techniques, the main achievements were handed down from the unknown civilizations of the past, achievements such as metallurgy, the domestication of the essential cereals and of the date palm, the use of the sheep as a wool-bearing animal, and the use of the plow—provided with a curious seeding apparatus that has a parallel only in China.

**J. CONTACTS WITH THE OUTSIDE WORLD.** From India in the E, in a wide arc to Egypt in the W, Mesopotamia maintained contacts with foreign civilizations in varying degrees of intensity over the three millenniums of its known history. Strangely enough, these contacts were far more effective in the earliest periods, up to the middle of the third millennium B.C., than they were later on. Only under Alexander the Great did they reach an intensity that can be compared with that of the earlier relations. As to the direction of the flow of outside contacts, it could be said that Mesopotamia, in respect to technology, received from the East and gave to the West. In respect to culture, Mesopotamia exercised influence upon its neighbors to the N, NW, and W by means of its language and system of writing. Only in its very last phase was a specific set of Mesopotamian achievements transmitted farther to the West.

As to the transmission of Mesopotamian civilization beyond the territory of the neighboring countries, we may mention the Bible as a vehicle for a number of religious and literary concepts of Mesopotamian origin; Hellenistic Egypt, which spread Babylonian (Chaldean) astrology and astronomy to the West; Assyrian art in certain of its late forms that reached the Greek world through Asia Minor; and finally, Assyrian court ceremonial that can be traced to Byzantium via Sassanian practices, and eventually to Europe.

From India, Mesopotamia received its various bovidae, the chicken, and eventually the peacock, and from Central Asia its equidae, to pass all these animals on to the West. From the islands and the coastal regions of the Persian Gulf came copper and precious stones, and eventually pearls, and from unknown regions came tin.

As to the immediate neighbors, Elam was the first of the civilizations that, although independent in origin, grew up under the shadow of Mesopotamia. Of Elam we still know very little. What has been unearthed in Susa, its capital, shows an independent and deeply alien civilization, where the Akkadian language was accepted for a time, but which turned later to the native idiom, using, however, the cuneiform system of writing. In its past (this should be stressed because it underlines the complexities of the development) the region had its own primitive and yet undeciphered system of writing. Although the Elamites for a long time had contacts with the Babylonians and the Assyrians, they left little if any vestige of their influence upon Mesopotamian civilization. In the valleys of the Zagros between Elam and Urartu may still be buried the remnants of cities in which, as in Nuzi, hybrid and short-lived civilizations flourished sometime during the second millennium B.C. and where Akkadian was used and—possibly but not likely—a native dialect was written with cuneiform signs.

In Armenia proper, around lakes Van and Urmia, at the beginning of the first millennium, grew the kingdom of Urartu, of which we have important archaeological evidence: its own inscriptions in Akkadian and in Urartean and, above all, a revealing description by Sargon II, who destroyed it.

On a much larger scale in time, space, and political and cultural importance, the same situation is repeated in Asia Minor, in the Hittite kingdom and its capital, Hattusha. Here, however, Mesopotamian civilization was accepted in a more than superficial way; large segments of Babylonian literature were copied and many texts translated into Hittite.

Much more complicated and far less well known are the relations between Mesopotamian civilization and that of the Hurrian kingdom of the Amarna period, whose capital was Wassukanni, near the sources of the Habur River. While the Hurrians accepted the Akkadian language and writing in much the same way as the Hittites, their influence on Assyria seems to have been rather important in the iconography of that region; it also expresses itself in certain religious practices peculiar to Assyria.

When we move to Upper Syria and the Levant, we meet the same traces of Mesopotamian influence but complicated, as it were, by the existence of, at least, one other center of diffusion, Ugarit.

Still farther to the S, we reach Palestine, where the same conflict is present but with a highly important additional factor: the development of a new civilization on which we happen to be exceedingly well informed by the Bible. Historical circumstances, especially the absolutely unique instance of the return of a deported nation to its homeland, make Mesopotamian-Hebrew cultural relations a most difficult and interesting problem.

As to Egypt, Mesopotamian influence reached it quite early and through still unknown intermediaries, to bring to that country the cylinder seal, the stimulus to develop a system of writing, and probably also certain features of monumental architecture.

*See also* CHALDEA; ETHIOPIA; EXILE; MEDIA; MENE, MENE, TEKEL, AND PARSIN; NEBO 1; NEBUZARADAN; NERGAL-SHAREZER; NISROCH; OSNAPPAR; PEKOD; RAB-MAG; RAB-SHAKEH; TEL-ABIB.

*Bibliography.* The following works, which are suited to familiarize the reader with Mesopotamian civilization, are in each case the best or latest or only available study on a specific topic: B. Meissner, *Babylonien und Assyrien* (2 vols.;

1920, 1925); A. Goetze, *Hethiter, Churriter und Assyrer* (1936); E. Chiera, *They Wrote on Clay* (1938; paper ed., 1952); A. Parrot, *Archéologie mésopotamienne,* I (Les Etapes; 1946); E. Dhorme, *Les religions de Babylonie et d'Assyrie* (1949); A. Moortgat in Scharff and Moortgat, *Ägypten und Vorderasien im Altertum* (1950); O. Neugebauer, *The Exact Sciences in Antiquity* (1952); J. B. Pritchard, ed., *ANET* (2nd ed., 1955).

A. L. OPPENHEIM

**ASTAROTH** ăs′ tə rŏth. KJV form of ASHTAROTH in Deut. 1:4.

**ASTARTE** ăs tär′tĭ. Greek form of ASHTORETH.

**ASTATH** ăs′tăth. KJV Apoc. form of AZGAD.

**ASTONISHMENT** [שׁמה; ἔκστασις, θάμβος]. Astonishment in the Bible is a reaction of man to an act of God within history. In the OT it is always awakened by the judgment of God upon Israel or one of her neighbors. In the NT it is most often brought about by an act or saying of Jesus Christ. Only once is it attributed to inanimate objects—in Job 26:11, where the pillars of heaven are said to tremble and be astounded at the rebuke of the Lord.

In the OT, שׁמה (II Chr. 29:8), from the verb שׁמם, "to be astonished" (II Chr. 7:21 = I Kings 9:8; Lev. 26:32), is the Hebrew equivalent of "astonishment." Unlike the KJV, the RSV frequently translates שׁמה "horror" (Deut. 28:37; Jer. 25:9, etc.), "dismay" (Jer. 8:21), or "waste" (Jer. 25:11, 18; 44:22).

In the NT the nominal Greek equivalent is ἔκστασις, translated "amazement" (Mark 5:42), or θάμβος (Luke 5:9). The verbs are ἐκπλήσσομαι, "to be astonished" (Matt. 7:28); ἐξίστημι, "to be amazed" (Luke 2:47); or θαμβέομαι, "to be amazed" (Mark 10:24).

Astonishment in the OT combines a sense of wonder, surprise, dread, and horror. It is occasioned by the unexpected, such as Yahweh's judgment upon his own temple and people (I Kings 9:8 = II Chr. 7:21). It has within it both the element of wonder at the power and sovereignty of God (Job 26:11) and the element of dismay that such a God is chastising the people Israel, with whom he has covenanted (Jer. 8:21; Ezek. 4:16; 12:19). It is awakened by the "otherworldly," by an act of God which man cannot understand, and by a turn of divine purpose seemingly dissonant with the past. Thus astonishment in the OT contains also dread—dread of the unknown and the holy (*see* HOLINESS; FEAR). Further, he who has been visited by Yahweh in judgment becomes an object of horror (Jer. 25:9; 42:18; 51:37; Ezek. 5:15, etc.), a person cast out from the realm of the light and the living, a person unclean and defiling to all around him (Deut. 28:37; II Chr. 29:8; Jer. 29:18; 44:12; 51:41). In the OT, astonishment comes when man is confronted by a jealous God (*see* JEALOUSY).

In the NT, it is aroused by Jesus Christ. Here, too, it contains the element of surprise, of being met by the unexpected (Matt. 13:54; Mark 10:24-27; Luke 2:47; 4:32). And there is wonder before the authority of the Lord (Matt. 7:28; 22:33; Mark 7:37). But dread is here, too, present. Thus Peter in his astonishment at the miraculous catch of fish cries out: "Depart from me, for I am a sinful man, O Lord" (Luke 5:8-9), and Jesus' own people are "of-

fended" by him (Matt. 13:53-58 = Mark 6:1-6). It is sinful man's dread before the holy.

Yet in the NT astonishment includes not only dread but also fascination and attraction. Jesus so astounds the multitude that the chief priest and the scribes seek his death, before he gains too much following (Mark 11:18). The Proconsul Sergius Paulus, astonished at the teaching of the Lord delivered by Paul, believes on Jesus Christ (Acts 13:12). The moment of dread before God is overcome in the love and submission of faith.

E. R. ACHTEMEIER

\*  **ASTROLOGER** [אשׁף, הברי שׁמים]. The longing to ascertain what the future has in store for the individual or society gave rise to the pseudo science of astrology. The heavenly bodies were minutely observed by the Babylonian and Egyptian astrologers in the belief that the variations and conjunctions occurring in the sky foretell future events that will take place on earth. Astrology, to judge from the evidence of the OT, was unknown in ancient Israel, and the few passages that mention astrologers refer exclusively to the Babylonian practice. Isaiah (47:13) scornfully points to the Babylonian astrologers when he says:

> You are wearied with your many counsels;
> let them stand forth and save you,
> those who divide the heavens
> 　[הברי שׁמים; LXX ἀστρόλογοι],
> who gaze at the stars
> 　[החזים בכוכבים],
> who at the new moons predict
> 　what shall befall you.

Jeremiah (10:2) admonishes the people not to be terrified by the "signs of the heavens" [אתות השׁמים] because the other nations are dismayed at them (see also Dan. 2:27; 4:7—H 4:4; 5:7, 11).

I. MENDELSOHN

**ASTRONOMY.** *See* SCIENCE §§ A2, B2, C2.

**ASTYAGES** ăs tī′ə jēz [′Αστυάγης]. The last ruler of the Median Empire (585?-550); son of Cyaxares.

As part of the peace arrangements between Alyattes king of Lydia and his father, Cyaxares, Astyages married Aryenis, daughter of Alyattes (Herodotus I.74). His daughter Mandane married Cambyses I, and their son Cyrus II, after being exposed, grew up with a shepherd and his wife (Herodotus I.108-16).

Later Cyrus turned against his grandfather, and the fate of the Median Empire was decided in two battles between the Medes and the Persians. In the first the major part of the Median army under Harpagus, general of Astyages, whose son had been murdered by Astyages (Herodotus I.117-20), deserted and joined forces with the enemy (I.127); in the second, Astyages was made prisoner (I.128). Ecbatana, the Median capital, was captured in 550, and Cyrus "became king of all of Asia" (I.130). *See* CYRUS; MEDIA; PERSIA, HISTORY AND RELIGION OF, § D3.

M. J. DRESDEN

**ASUERUS.** KJV Apoc. form of AHASUERUS 3.

**ASUPPIM** ə sŭp′ĭm. KJV translation of אספים ("gatherings," "storehouse") in I Chr. 26:15, 17. The word is correctly rendered, not as a proper name, but as the temple "storehouse" (so RSV; *see* TEMPLE, JERUSALEM; cf. אספי השערים, "storehouses of the gates," in Neh. 12:25).      W. L. REED

**ASUR** ā'sər ['Ασούρ]; KJV ASSUR ăs'ər. Eponym of a family of temple servants listed among the returned exiles in I Esd. 5:31. The name is not included in the parallels in Ezra 2:51; Neh. 7:53.

**ASYLUM.** *See* REFUGE.

**ASYNCRITUS** ə sĭng'krĭ təs ['Ασύγκριτος, incomparable]. A Christian greeted by Paul in Rom. 16: 14. The word appears in Ign. Smyr. 13:2, but not as a proper name. The name is found in papyri and inscriptions.      F. W. GINGRICH

**ATAD** ā'tăd [אטד, thorn]. A place in Canaan mentioned in the account of the burial of Jacob. The funeral cortège, on its way to Hebron, halted at the threshing floor of Atad, where the Egyptians observed a special seven-days' mourning for the patriarch; as a result of this the place received the additional name Abel-mizraim, interpreted to mean "mourning of the Egyptians" (Gen. 50:10-11). Apparently the latter detail is an attempt to explain a place name which more likely means "meadow of Egypt."

The statement that Atad was "beyond" (i.e., E of) the Jordan is puzzling in view of the fact that the direct route from Egypt to Hebron would be entirely W of the Jordan. One possible explanation is that the cortège followed an old trade route via the Sinai peninsula; another, that the viewpoint is from Transjordan, and "beyond" in this case means "west of." The sixth-century A.D. mosaic map at Medeba indicates an Alon Atad (terebinth of Atad) by the side of Beth Agla (the biblical Beth-hoglah) and between Jericho and the Dead Sea.      S. COHEN

**ATARAH** ăt'ə rə [עטרה, crown *or* wreath] (I Chr. 2:26). The second wife of Jerahmeel; the mother of Onam.

**ATARGATIS** ə tär'gə tĭs [Ατάργατις, *transliteration of* עתרעתה; *also found in shortened form* תרעתה, *whence* Δερκετώ, Derceto]. The great female deity of the Aramaeans, consort of HADAD; often called by the Greeks and Romans the "Syrian goddess," as in Lucian's *De Dea Syria*. Her name is compounded of two divine names—'Atar (philologically equivalent to Ishtar, Astarte, Ashtoreth), and 'Ate or 'Attah, the latter a male deity otherwise unknown, though sometimes the identification with Attis has been suggested. In origin, she is one of the mother-goddesses of Asia Minor; like Cybele, she had castrated priests, and her throne was mounted on lions; but after her adoption by the Syrians, she acquired many of the traits of the Babylonian Ishtar. Hierapolis (Bambyce) in Syria was the main center of her worship, but she had temples in many other places of the Near East, and in Hellenistic times her cult was carried into the Greek world and westward even as far as Britain. Her temple at Carnaim in Gilead is mentioned in II Macc. 12:26 (cf. I Macc. 5:43-44) as the scene of a

slaughter by Judas Maccabeus of the inhabitants who had fled to it for refuge.      F. W. BEARE

**ATAROTH** ăt'ə·rŏth [עטרות, *plural of* עטרה, crown, wreath, fold]. **1.** Ataroth of Gad (Num. 32:3, 34), one of the towns requested by the tribes of Reuben and Gad for their possession. It is to be identified with Khirbet 'Attarus, *ca.* eight miles NW of Dibon (modern Dhiban) and *ca.* ten miles to the E of the Dead Sea. It is mentioned in the Mesha Inscription: "Now the men of Gad had always dwelt in the land of Ataroth, and the king of Israel had built Ataroth for them" (*ANET* 320).

**2.** One of the boundary towns of the tribe of Ephraim (Josh. 16:7), located on its E border, identified by Glueck with the prominent mound of Tell el-Mazar, which dominates the highway leading to the hill country of Palestine alone the Wadi el-Far'ah, and of Transjordan along the Wadi Zerqa (the River Jabbok).

*Bibliography.* K. Elliger, *ZDPV*, 53 (1930), 265-309. M. Noth, *ZDPV*, 58 (1935), 201-15; *Josua*, HAT, 7 (1953). These have been superseded by the detailed treatment of N. Glueck, *Explorations in Eastern Palestine*, vol. IV, pt. I; Text in *AASOR*, vols. XXV-XXVIII (1925-28).

**3.** A town mentioned in Josh. 16:2; same as ATAROTH-ADDAR in vs. 5.

**4.** KJV translation ("Ataroth, the house of Joab") in I Chr. 2:54 (RSV ATROTH-BETH-JOAB).      J. MUILENBURG

**ATAROTH-ADDAR** ăt'ə rŏth ăd'ər [עטרות אדר, glorious crown] (Josh. 16:5; 18:13). A town on the boundary between Ephraim and Benjamin. As Noth has shown, the description of the S boundary of Ephraim in Josh. 16:1-3 has as its basis the same series of boundary points given in the description of the boundary of Benjamin in 18:12-13; we are dealing then with a single source here. That the text has suffered some corruption is shown by the accidental omission of *addar* in 16:2, but more particularly by the confused state of the versions. At the foot of Tell en-Nasbeh (*see* MIZPAH 5) there is a small modern village known as Khirbet 'Attara, but it contains no remains of pre-Roman times. Moreover, it is unlikely that two towns would have been so close together as Ataroth-addar in this location and another town on the top of the hill. Some scholars believe that the original site of Ataroth was on Tell en-Nasbeh, and others have proposed Ataroth-addar as the name of the town before it was changed to Mizpah at the time of Asa's fortifications (I Kings 15:16-22). This is possible, although it is strange that it has left so small a trace in the OT records, especially in view of the strategic location on the great road and the unusual prominence of the mound.

*Bibliography.* The articles in *PJB, BASOR, ZDPV*, and *ZAW* may be consulted. The following are among the most important discussions: L. Heidet, *Dictionnaire de la Bible*, Supplement (1928), vol. I, cols. 664-66. H. W. Hertzberg, "Mizpa," *ZAW*, 47 (1929), 161-96. A. Jirku, "Wo lag Gibe'on?" *JPOS*, 8 (1928), 187 ff. J. Hempel, "Atrot-'Addar," *ZDPV*, 53 (1930), 233-36. W. F. Albright, a review of G. Dalman's *Jerusalem und sein Gelaende, JQR*, 22 (1932), 412-16; a review of Abel's *Géographie de la Palestine, JBL*, 58

(1939), 179-88. M. Noth, *ZDPV*, 58 (1935), 201-15; *Josua*, HAT (1953), p. 101. J. Muilenburg, "Ataroth Addar," in C. C. McCown, *Tell en-Naṣbeh*, I (1947), 38-39.

J. MUILENBURG

**ATBASH** ăt′băsh. A variant spelling of ATHBASH.

**ATER** ā′tər [אָטֵר, crippled one, left-handed one, *or possibly the common name* Etir]; KJV Apoc. ATEREZIAS ə tĕr′ə zī′əs (I Esd. 5:15); JATAL jā′təl (I Esd. 5:28). The head of a family which returned to Palestine after the Exile (Ezra 2:16; Neh. 7:21; I Esd. 5:15). Some of the family were gatekeepers (Ezra 2:42; Neh. 7:45; I Esd. 5:28), and Ater alone is mentioned as one who sealed Ezra's covenant (Neh. 10:17—H 10:18).

M. NEWMAN

**ATEREZIAS.** KJV Apoc. alternate form of ATER.

**ATHACH** ā′thăk [עֲתָךְ]. A city in the S Shephelah to which David sent gifts from the booty taken from the defeated Amalekites (I Sam. 30:30); probably a scribal error for ETHER, כ (*k*) being read for ר (*r*). Cf. Josh. 15:42; 19:7.

V. R. GOLD

**ATHAIAH** ə thā′yə [עֲתָיָה]. A man of Judah; son of Uzziah; included in the list of postexilic inhabitants of Jerusalem (Neh. 11:4). Some identify him with Uthai in the parallel list (I Chr. 9:4); both are descendants of Perez, but the intervening generations diverge completely.

F. T. SCHUMACHER

**ATHALIAH** ăth′ə lī′ə [עֲתַלְיָה, עֲתַלְיָהוּ, Y is great, exalted, *based on* Akkad. *etellu*]. **1.** Wife of Jehoram, king of Judah; daughter of AHAB and JEZEBEL; granddaughter of Omri; mother of Ahaziah. She reigned over Judah for six years, *ca.* 842-837 B.C. (see II Kings 11; II Chr. 22-23). She represents a northern intrusion into the otherwise uninterrupted Davidic dynasty in Judah and the apogee of Baalistic influence in the Southern Kingdom.

Reared in Samaria, she became as zealous and capable a proponent of Baal-Melkart as her infamous mother and apparently exercised considerable influence, first as Jehoram's queen (II Kings 8:18= II Chr. 21:6; cf. II Chr. 21:11 ff), and then as queen mother "over" Ahaziah (II Kings 8:26-27; II Chr. 22:2-3). While visiting his uncle and wounded co-warrior against Aram—King Joram of Israel— Ahaziah was killed in the bloody usurpation by JEHU (1). If the Yahwistic-prophetic party seized the throne in the N, it was now the Baalists' turn in Judah. Athaliah determined to rule in her own right by destroying all surviving male heirs (II Kings 11: 1=II Chr. 22:10; but cf. II Kings 10:12 ff; II Chr. 22:17).

She managed to stay on the throne for six years— a tribute to her cold-blooded competence—though no information about her reign is preserved except that her partisans ("sons of Athaliah") vandalized the temple in favor of the house of Baal (II Kings 11:18; II Chr. 24:7). Her deposition, recorded in detail (II Kings 11; cf. II Chr. 23), was accomplished by Jehoiada the priest through mercenary soldiers and an infant son (Joash) of Ahaziah whom he and

his wife had hidden and secretly reared (II Kings 11:2-3=II Chr. 22:11-12). Apparently in some secrecy, they crowned and anointed him king. In a climax of magnificent personal bravery Athaliah tried to stem the tide, but the soldiers were too much, and she was taken out of the temple and slain (II Kings 11:13-16=II Chr. 23:12-15).

The priest presided over a covenant between Yahweh, king, and people. The fact that a mob destroyed the Baal cult and yet soldiers must be posted over the temple (II Kings 11:18=II Chr. 23:17-18) indicates that the populace was badly split between the two parties (perhaps with the Yahweh party being more rural than urban). The Chronicler emphasizes the role of Levites from outside Jerusalem and generally strives for greater sanctity, though he does not disguise his joy over the outcome.

**2.** One of the sons of Jeroham, a Jerusalem family listed in the genealogy of Benjamin (I Chr. 8:26).

**3.** The father of Jeshaiah, head of the sons of Elam who returned with Ezra (Ezra 8:7). He is called Gotholiah (KJV Gotholias) in the parallel passage, I Esd. 8:33.

F. T. SCHUMACHER

**ATHARIAS** ăth′ə rī′əs. KJV translation of ᾿Αθαρίας (BA), Αταρασθας (Luc.), an official title of the Persian GOVERNOR (so RSV mg.) of Judah (תִּרְשָׁתָא). See I Esd. 5:40.

C. T. FRITSCH

**ATHARIM** ăth′ər ĭm [הָאֲתָרִים]; KJV SPIES. The way along which the Israelites under Moses were marching at the time they were attacked by the king of Arad (Num. 21:1). The word is obscure; the LXX, followed by the KJV, translates it "spies"; however, it may be a place name, or it may mean "tracks." The location has not been identified.

S. COHEN

**ATHBASH** ăth′băsh. A Hebrew cryptographic scheme in which the letters of the alphabet in reverse were substituted. The term *athbash* (אתבש) is manufactured from the first two pairs of substitutes—i.e., the first, last, second, and next to last letters of the alphabet.

There are three demonstrable instances of *athbash* in Jeremiah, though how and when they entered the text is an enigma. In 51:1 are found the letters לֵב קָמָי. The Masoretes divided and pointed these to give *lēbh qāmāy* (lit., "the heart of those who rise against me"; cf. KJV), and are supported by Aq. and Symm. However, the LXX (28:1) had Χαλδαίους, revealing the hidden word. By *athbash* the letters become כַּשְׂדִּים, *kasdîm*, meaning "Chaldeans."

In 51:41 appears the word שֵׁשַׁךְ, rendered "Sheshach" in the KJV, which is *athbash* for בָּבֶל, "Babylon" (LXX 28:41 Βαβυλῶν). It is used also in 25:26 but may be a gloss (the LXX omits the clause). Since ch. 51 is full of references to Babylon, so that there would appear to be no value in concealing one, there have been various attempts to explain the word otherwise; but none seems successful.

The use of *athbash* is recognized in the Talmud, Midrashim, and Kabbala. An attempt has been made to employ it as an aid to elucidating the Dead Sea Scrolls. *See* TEXT, OT.

*Bibliography.* W. Gesenius, *Thesaurus Linguae Hebraeae* (1833-53); lexicons of Briggs, Browne and Driver, Gesenius-Buhl; S. A. Horodezky, "Gematria," *Encyclopedia Judaica,* VII, 170-72. H. J. Schonfield, *Secrets of the Dead Sea Scrolls* (1956).

B. J. ROBERTS

**ATHENOBIUS** ăth′ə nō′bĭ əs ['Αθηνόβιος] (I Macc. 15:32-36). Courtier of Antiochus VII Sidetes, from whom he had received the title ὁ φίλος τοῦ βασιλέως (cf. John 15:15; 19:12). Antiochus sent him as envoy to Simon the high priest.                    J. C. SWAIM

*****ATHENS** ăth′ĭnz [αἱ 'Αθῆναι] (Acts 17:15-16, 22; 18:1; I Thess. 3:1). The chief city of the ancient district of Attica, and the capital of modern Greece. The name of the city was probably derived from that of the goddess Athena (ἡ 'Αθήνη). Paul visited Athens and spoke in the synagogue and the market place, and in the Areopagus; but he established no church there (Acts 17:16-34). Fig. ATH 109.

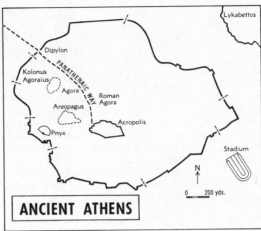

ANCIENT ATHENS

Jack Finegan

Discovery of Neolithic pottery on the slopes of the Acropolis shows that there was settlement at this place in the Late Stone Age (before 3000 B.C.). By the Late Helladic period in the Late Bronze Age (*ca.* 1600–*ca.* 1100) the Acropolis* was a strongly fortified citadel, as evidenced by the remains of walls of this date. In the Geometric period in the Early Iron Age (*ca.* 1100–*ca.* 750) the numerous cemeteries contain much pottery painted in formal designs sharply contrasting with the free and spacious style previously prevailing. Pl. XXVI*b*.

At the beginning of the sixth century Solon the Lawgiver is credited with doing much to establish the democratic organization of Athens. At this time the Agora, or main city square, which may previously have been just outside the entrance to the Acropolis, was located farther to the NW beside the hill Kolonus Agoraius. In this area have been discovered

Courtesy of the American School of Classical Studies, Athens

109. General air view of Athens; the Agora is in the foreground, and the Acropolis is in the background.

the foundations of the oldest known public buildings and sanctuaries, which include the predecessor of the Old Bouleuterion, and the archaic Temple of Apollo. *Ca.* the middle of the century the tyrant Pisistratus may have built the Heliaia, or law court, and the predecessor of the Tholos, both in the Agora; while some attribute to him also the Old Temple of Athena, the foundations of which have been found on the Acropolis between the Parthenon and the Erechtheion. At the end of the sixth century came the democratic reforms of Kleisthenes. The Boule (βουλή), or advisory council, which was probably as old as, or older than, the time of Solon, was increased to five hundred persons, fifty from each of the ten tribes into which Kleisthenes also divided the people of the state. In each of ten periods of the year, fifty councilors served as Prytanes, or presidents of the council, and met continuously as an executive committee. The Old Bouleuterion was probably built at this time as a meeting place for the enlarged Boule, and additions were made to the rooms, above which the Tholos was later built, where the Prytanes met.

At the beginning of the fifth century Athens was enclosed by a strong wall, which was constructed or repaired by Themistocles (*ca.* 525–*ca.* 460) in the

Courtesy of the American School of Classical Studies, Athens
112. The Acropolis at Athens, viewed from the W, with the Areopagus (Mars Hill) in the foreground

Courtesy of the American School of Classical Studies, Athens
·113. Temple of Hephaestus at Athens

Temple of Ares. In the same century the circular Tholos, the Stoa Poikile, the New Bouleuterion, the Stoa of Zeus, and other structures were built in the Agora. Meanwhile the work of Pheidias (died *ca.* 432 B.C.) and his pupils further beautified the city with a wealth of friezes and a forest of statues. Athens had reached its most glorious age, and was saluted by Aristophanes (*Knights* 1329) in the exclamation:

> Oh thou, our Athens, violet-wreathed, brilliant, most enviable city!

Figs. ATH·110-13; Pl. **XXX***b*.

Courtesy of the American School of Classical Studies, Athens
110. The Parthenon at Athens

Courtesy of the American School of Classical Studies, Athens
111. The Erechtheion on the Acropolis at Athens

face of the threat of Persian invasion. By the time the Persians actually destroyed Athens in 480/479, the Older Parthenon and the Old Propylea had already been founded on the Acropolis. When the Persians were driven away, an extensive program of rebuilding and of new building was instituted. Under the administration of Pericles (461-429) the famous Parthenon* and Propylea were erected, and the Erechtheion was built soon afterward.* In the time of Pericles probably belong also the Temple of Hephaestus* on Kolonus Agoraius and the original

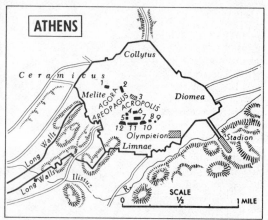
From E. G. Kraeling, *Bible Atlas*, copyright by Rand McNally & Co.

1) Hephaesteum; (2) Stoa of Attalus; (3) Market Place; (4) Propylea; (5) Temple of Wingless Victory; (6) Erechtheion; (7) Parthenon; (8) Odeum of Pericles; (9) Mon. of Lysicrates; (10) Theater of Dionysus; (11) Stoa of Eumenes; (12) Odeum of Herod Atticus

114. Athens from the SW, showing the ruins of the Agora, with the restored Stoa of Attalus

In the fourth century the financial minister of Athens, Lycurgus (338-326), interested himself in many public buildings and was probably responsible for the construction of what was afterward known as the Dipylon Gate, the building of the earliest known Stadium at Athens, the reconstruction of the Theater of Dionysus, and the enlargement of the auditorium on the Pnyx Hill.

In the Hellenistic period the Syrian king Antiochus IV Epiphanes (175-164) rebuilt on a magnificent scale the Temple of Olympian Zeus, which had been begun by Pisistratus; King Attalus II of Pergamum (159-138 B.C.) gave the large Stoa of Attalus which stands on the E side of the Agora and has been restored to serve as the modern Agora Museum;* and other large stoas were built on the S side of the Agora. In the second half of the same century the Old Bouleuterion and the nearby Temple of the Mother of the Gods were replaced by the Metroon, a building which took its name from a sanctuary of the Mother of the Gods (μήτηρ θεῶν) it contained, in protective proximity to which it housed the archives of state. Fig. ATH 114.

The sack of Athens by the Roman general Sulla in 86 B.C. did damage chiefly to private quarters, and in the reign of Augustus (27 B.C.–A.D. 14) new public buildings were added. On the Acropolis a small circular Temple of Rome and Augustus was erected by the people. In the center of the Agora the concert hall known as the Odeum or Agrippeum was built by M. Vipsanius Agrippa, minister and son-in-law of Augustus; and nearby was placed the Temple of Ares, which was moved from whatever its original location may have been.

By the time of Augustus the old Agora was well filled with buildings, and accordingly a new Roman Agora was laid out a short distance to the E. While further excavation is awaited in this region, the ruins of a large structure just N of the Augustan Market have long been known and are identified as the Stoa and Library of Hadrian (A.D. 117-38). The latter emperor also did further work on the Temple of Olympian Zeus. Ca. A.D. 143 a wealthy Roman resident, Herodes Atticus, rebuilt in splendid marble the Stadium of Lycurgus, and later built an Odeum at the SW base of the Acropolis.

Between A.D. 143 and 159 the geographer Pausanias visited Athens, and the detailed account of the city which he gives in the first thirty chapters of his *Description of Greece* has been of great value in the identification of the ancient monuments. Except for some later Roman buildings, such as those mentioned in the preceding paragraph, the appearance of Athens in the time of Pausanias must have been much the same as in that of the apostle Paul a century earlier.

*See also* AREOPAGUS; UNKNOWN GOD, ALTAR TO AN. Fig. ARE 58.

*Bibliography.* K. Wachsmuth, "Athenai," *Pauly-Wissowa*, Supplement I (1903), cols. 159-219; W. A. McDonald, "Archaeology and St. Paul's Journeys in Greek Lands: Part II, Athens," *BA*, IV (1941), 1-10; I. T. Hill, *The Ancient City of Athens* (1953); The American School of Classical Studies at Athens, *The Athenian Agora, A Guide to the Excavations* (1954); O. Broneer, "Athens, City of Idol Worship," *BA*, XXI (1958), 2-28.                          J. FINEGAN

**ATHLAI** ăth′lī [עַתְלָי, *shortened form of* (ו)עֲתַלְיָה, Yahweh is exalted; οθαλι (Ezra 10:28; I Esd. 9:28); KJV Apoc. AMATHEIS ăm′ə thē′əs. One of those compelled to put away their foreign wives in the time of Ezra.

**ATIPHA.** KJV Apoc. form of HATIPHA.

*\*ATONEMENT. The English word "atone" is derived from the phrase "at one." To be "at one" with someone is to be in harmonious personal relationship with him. Similarly, "atonement" originally meant "at onement," or "reconciliation." In modern usage, however, "atonement" has taken on the more restricted meaning of the process by which the hindrances to reconciliation are removed, rather than the end achieved by their removal. "To atone for" a wrong is to take some action which cancels out the ill effects it has had.

Here the wider, more positive meaning sometimes given the word "atonement" will be largely ignored, since it will be dealt with under such headings as RECONCILIATION; SALVATION. The concern here will be to notice what is said in the Bible about the means by which obstacles to reconciliation between man and God may be removed.

In the OT the word "atonement" occurs frequently, even in the RSV. But it is not so in the NT. Even in the KJV the word occurs only once, and then to translate καταλλαγή at Rom. 5:11, and in the RSV this is replaced by "reconciliation," so that in the more modern versions of the NT there is no use of the word "atonement." Indeed, in all other contexts in the KJV, καταλλαγή is translated "reconciliation." Though, however, the word itself is absent from the NT, the idea which the word seeks to express is constantly present.

The Bible as a whole assumes the need for some "atoning action," if man is to be right with God. It is accepted as a fact beyond dispute that man is estranged from God, and is himself wholly to blame for this estrangement. His disobedience to the will of God—i.e., his sin—has alienated him from God, and this alienation must first be remedied if right relationships are to be restored. The barrier raised by man's past sins must be removed.

A. In the OT
B. In the LXX
C. In the NT
  1. Man's need of atonement
  2. The cause of man's need
  3. The means of atonement
  4. The source of atonement
  5. The consequences of atonement
  6. The words and symbols used
    *a.* Sacrificial terms
    *b.* Lamb of God
    *c.* Ransom
    *d.* Redemption
    *e.* Propitiation or expiation
    *f.* "Bought"
D. Conclusion
Bibliography

**A. *IN THE OT.*** The usual Hebrew word for "atone" is כפר. Probably its original meaning was "cover," though some have suggested that it was "wipe off." In its developed use, however, it is doubtful whether there was any awareness of its original meaning, since the word could be used of the effect, not only of sacrifices, but also of the scapegoat. Whereas a sacrifice may be thought of as "covering" sin, this metaphor does not fit the scapegoat, who "bore it away." The word therefore came to be used in a general sense of removing the effects of sin.

One purpose of the elaborate sacrificial system of OT religion was to provide such an "atonement," and the word כפר is frequently used in relation to sacrifice. In the ritual for the consecration of priests, e.g., it is required: "Every day you shall offer a bull as a sin offering for atonement" (Exod. 29:36). Similarly, the priests must make sacrifice for the sins of all the people that they may be forgiven (Lev. 4:20). So also in the ritual of the Day of Atonement the first of the two goats is slain (Lev. 16:9), but the second "shall be presented alive before the LORD to make atonement" (vs. 10). This live goat is driven out into the wilderness, laden with the sins of the people.

Atonement is therefore commonly associated with the death of a victim. It is not, however, exclusively so, for not only can the live scapegoat make atonement, but also the offering of money for the temple may be an offering "to make atonement for yourselves" (Exod. 30:16). Incense can be effective in making atonement (Num. 16:47), and Moses seeks to make atonement through prayer (Exod. 32:30).

Usually it is man who must make atonement to God, by offering something which will be thought adequate to make amends for the bad effects of his sin. But sometimes it is God who is said "to make atonement." In the RSV this is translated as "pardon" in II Chr. 30:18, and as "forgive" in Ezek. 16:63; Deut. 21:8; Ps. 78:38.

It has often been discussed how far these means of atonement were thought of as "propitiating" God, or alternatively as "expiating" the offense. The word "propitiation" suggests that God, alienated by man's sin, requires something to appease his anger before he will again show favor to the sinner. "Expiation" recognizes that a hindrance to right relationships has been created by the sin, and that this is removed by the means of atonement, but it does not locate the hindrance in God.

The word "propitiation," however, is not used at all in our English versions of the OT; and "expiation" occurs only rarely.

The fact that in some contexts it is God who "makes atonement" should make us hesitate to affirm that the hindrance to reconciliation lies in his reluctance to forgive, and his demand for some appeasement. Almost certainly this idea would be present in the early stages of religion, but the claim that it is not to be found in postexilic writings probably should be accepted. In these it is customary to speak of making atonement, not "to Jehovah," but "for the people." Sacrifice, therefore, should probably be interpreted as an endeavor to expiate sin (i.e., remove the barrier it has raised against God) rather than to appease the anger of God toward man. Certainly in the context of Isa. 6:7, where the prophet hears the assurance: "Your sin [is] forgiven" (כפר), the word unmistakably indicates the cancellation of sin and its consequences. So too in Prov. 16:6: "By loyalty and faithfulness iniquity is atoned for" (כפר), it is expiation and not propitiation which is meant.

On the other hand, in Gen. 32:20 the word "atonement" (כפר) is used to describe Jacob's offer of a gift to Esau to appease the resentment which Jacob so understandably expected to find. This, however, appears to be an isolated instance. Other uses of the word do not point clearly to the meaning "propitiate," and many favor "expiate."

Even if it be insisted that in sacrifice man was, indeed, aiming to make an offering to God which would change God's attitude toward him from one of hostility to one of friendliness, it must nevertheless be acknowledged that the sacrificial system itself is a means which God himself ordained and established for this very purpose. It is never a merely human device for overcoming God's reluctance to forgive. God was thought of as one who himself had provided the means by which his forgiveness could be obtained.

**B. *IN THE LXX.*** Before proceeding to the NT it is well to note the Greek words which are used in the LXX to translate the Hebrew words (כפר and its derivatives) with which we have been dealing. The commonest are the verb ἐξιλάσκομαι (Exod. 30:15; Lev. 1:4; etc.) and the noun ἐξιλασμός (Lev. 23:27; Num. 5:8; etc.). The Hebrew word כפרת, which means the mercy seat, where God was believed to appear to declare forgiveness to his people, is translated by ἱλαστήριον (Lev. 16:2, etc.). Occasionally λύτρον is used (e.g., Exod. 21:30; 30:12).

In the NT, therefore, we must have before us such words as (ἐξ-)ἱλάσκομαι, (ἐξ-)ἱλασμός, ἱλαστήριον, and words derived from the same root. Also, attention must be given to λύτρον and words akin to it, such as λυτρόω, (ἀπο-)λύτρωσις, and ἀντίλυτρον.

Other words also, which have something of the same connotation, such as (ἐξ-)ἀγοράζω, must be borne in mind.

**C. IN THE NT.** Even though the word "atonement" does not occur in the NT, the meaning behind the word is constantly present. Here, however, it is no longer associated with the temple sacrifices, still less with payments of money, or incense, or even with prayers. It is related entirely to Jesus Christ and his coming to earth, and especially with his death upon the cross (see DEATH OF CHRIST). Words had to be found to declare that in Christ is that which overcomes the estrangement between man and God. It was inevitable that these words should largely be drawn from the familiar practice of sacrifice, partly because in this there was language all would understand, and partly because his death by crucifixion, with the actual shedding of blood, had so many unmistakable similarities to the actual practice of sacrifice.

The NT declares that in Christ and his death is all that man needs in order to find his sins forgiven and his life reconciled to God; in him is that which can cancel out the ill effects of sin, release man from the burden of its guilt, and grant him peace with God.

**1. Man's need of atonement.** The NT assumes man's need of being put right with God, and his own helplessness to put himself right. Man's life in its natural state is in a condition of estrangement from God. Men are "estranged and hostile in mind, doing evil deeds" (Col. 1:21), "without God in the world" (Eph. 2:12), and "alienated from the life of God" (Eph. 4:18). They are "enemies of God" (Rom. 5:10), and "hostile to God" (Rom. 8:7). This was obviously true of Gentiles, but it is affirmed that Jews, in spite of their great privileges, are in the same dire need (Rom. 3:23).

**2. The cause of man's need.** The cause of man's estrangement from God is the sin of man, his persistent disobedience to the will of God. God is a holy God. In spite of his great love and boundless mercy, he cannot treat sin as though it did not matter, for it corrupts and degrades human life, and thwarts all the purposes of God for man's good. God stands ready to forgive and to heal the penitent sinner, but where man continues deliberately and defiantly in his wrongdoing, God by his very nature cannot be complacent about it or indulgently indifferent to it. Dreadful penalties are ordained as a consequence of sin. "God is not mocked, for whatever a man sows, that he will also reap" (Gal. 6:7). This law of retribution is part of what is meant by the wrath of God which rests upon the unrepentant sinner (Rom. 1:18), and which finds expression in the solemn

warning: "The wages of sin is death" (Rom. 6:23). Indeed, the sinner is already "dead through . . . trespasses and sins" (Eph. 2:1).

**3. The means of atonement.** The NT declares frankly and uncompromisingly God's unremitting antagonism to sin, and the terrible consequences which he has determined shall follow it. He does not, however, hold aloof in cold contempt from the sinner, or turn from him with implacable resentment. Rather, he comes again and again seeking to deliver man from this evil thing which is destroying him, and holding him apart from God. Especially he has come in a final gesture of love and mercy in his Son, Jesus. The purpose of his coming was to seek and to save the lost. In fulfilment of this purpose he became known as the "friend of sinners." Not only did he come to earth, and live humbly among men, going about doing good and healing all that were oppressed by evil; he died at the hands of sinful men for man's sake. And all this was done for men who were still sinners. "While we were yet sinners Christ died for us" (Rom. 5:8).

The atoning work of Christ is particularly associated with his death on the cross. "He came to give his life as a ransom for many" (Mark 10:45). "We were reconciled to God by the death of his Son" (Rom. 5:10). "We have been brought near in the blood of Christ" (Eph. 2:13). "He himself bore our sins in his body on the tree" (I Pet. 2:24). Christ was "offered once to bear the sins of many" (Heb. 9:28). On this subject the writers of the NT speak with one voice. As he himself declared, the New Covenant, the possibility of a new relationship between man and God, is in his blood—i.e., inaugurated and made effective in his self-giving on the cross (I Cor. 11:25).

This utter self-giving of Christ, even in death, is the means of man's return to God. He is the new and living way to God (Heb. 10:20). Through him we have access to the Father (Eph. 2:18).

This access, however, is ours only "through our faith in him" (Eph. 3:12). What God has provided must be appropriated by faith. "God put [Christ] forward as an expiation by his blood, *to be received by faith*" (Rom. 3:25).

**4. Source of atonement.** Even the OT sacrificial system, by means of which it was claimed that man could find forgiveness from God, was thought of as an ordinance instituted by God, in order to provide for man's need. Still more in the NT we find that the new means of atonement is proclaimed, unanimously and insistently, as the gift of God to man. Christ's coming to earth and his self-giving on the cross for man's sin are all God's doing. Nor is it merely that God conceived and initiated the plan; God was in Christ actually carrying it forward to completion.

The NT does not lend support to theories of the Atonement which put Christ in contrast to the Father, as though the merciful Christ had to induce the severe Father to some grudging act of forgiveness which of himself he would not have committed. What Christ did for man, God himself was doing in Christ. "God was in Christ reconciling the world to himself" (II Cor. 5:19). ". . . Jesus Christ, whom God put forward as an expiation by his blood" (Rom. 3:25). "He . . . did not spare his own Son, but gave him up for us all" (Rom. 8:32).

**5. The consequences of atonement.** The immediate consequence of atonement is that man's relationship with God is restored; he has peace with God. This finds various ways of expression. Since it is sin that disrupts this relationship, and sin represents the victory of Satan, "the Son of God appeared . . . to destroy the works of the devil" (I John 3:8). "Christ . . . died . . . that he might bring us to God" (I Pet. 3:18). The way to God has been opened (Heb. 10:20). We are "justified by his blood" (Rom. 5:9), and reconciled by his death (vs. 10). Christ "died . . . that . . . we might live with him" (I Thess. 5:10).

From this restored relationship with God come all kinds of other good things. The sinner's conscience is cleansed, and he is equipped with new moral power (I Pet. 1:18). Man is delivered from the tyranny of self and enabled to live for Christ, with Christ reigning as Lord in his life (II Cor. 5:15; Rom. 14:9). All these good effects of the atoning work of Christ are gathered up in the word "salvation."

**6. The words and symbols used to interpret the Atonement.** The NT does not explain how Christ is able to cancel out the effects of man's sin and reconcile him to God. It is content to affirm the truth of it in an abundance of vigorous metaphors. It is the problem of theologians, basing their arguments on the data of the NT, to seek an explanation, and to determine how far the picture language of the NT should be interpreted literally or only metaphorically.

*a. Sacrificial terms.* Not surprisingly, the atoning power of the death of Christ is frequently expressed in terms taken from the sacrificial practices of Judaism, where atonement was associated with the shedding of the blood of an animal victim and its consequent death. Christ's death is called a "sacrifice for sins" in Heb. 10:12 and a "sacrifice to God" in Eph. 5:2. The "blood" of Christ is often mentioned as of special significance. This cannot mean the physical blood, but rather the life of Christ as it is yielded up to God in complete obedience to his will. This is in accord with the OT belief that "the life . . . is in the blood" (Lev. 17:11; cf. Gen. 9:4).

The Letter to the Hebrews links the power of Christ's death quite precisely with his unfaltering obedience to his Father's will (Heb. 10:7-9; cf. Mark 14:36). Paul too makes special mention of this element in the Cross: Christ became "obedient unto death, even death on a cross" (Phil. 2:8). This utter yielding of himself in full surrender to God's purposes is one element in the complete effectiveness of his work.

It is the task of theologians to decide whether these sacrificial metaphors imply that Christ's death is best understood as itself a sacrifice to God, or whether they are merely vivid ways of declaring that what the Jews sought to achieve by sacrifice has, in fact, been fully accomplished by Christ.

*b. Lamb of God.* Another metaphor which is usually understood as "sacrificial" is the title ascribed to Jesus: "Lamb of God." Paul speaks of "Christ, our paschal lamb," who has been sacrificed (I Cor. 5:7); and in John 1:29, 36, Jesus is referred to as the "Lamb of God, who takes away the sin of the world."

The difficulty in John 1:29 is that the paschal lamb is not a sin offering. John therefore seems to be combining in his affirmation two separate truths: (*a*) Jesus may be thought of as the paschal lamb, because his death heralds our great deliverance from bondage, and a share in his blood delivers us from destruction and secures our salvation. (*b*) Jesus takes away sin (as the goat on the Day of Atonement was believed to do). It may be, however, that the paschal lamb is not in John's mind, but rather the lamb mentioned in Isa. 53:7-8. Indeed, the so-called "Servant passages" in the later chapters of Isaiah have very greatly influenced the NT understanding of the significance of the death of Jesus.

Other references to Christ as the Lamb are in Revelation (5:6, 12; 13:8; etc.). In the older versions, but not in the RSV, 13:8 was translated to refer to the "Lamb slain from the foundation of the world." This translation is open to dispute, but it did serve to declare the truth that the Atonement is not a single act on Calvary, but an eternal fact in the character of God himself. Christ on the cross is the incarnation of the eternal, suffering love of God for man. I Pet. 1:20 suggests this same truth when it speaks of Christ's death as "destined before the foundation of the world, but . . . made manifest at the end of the times for your sake." The basic fact of the Cross is not something new, but an eternal truth about God.

*c. Ransom* (λύτρον). Mark 10:45: "The Son of man . . . came not to be served but to serve, and to give his life as a ransom for many," is the saying which, understood literally, has given its name to a well-known theory of the Atonement, as though the life of Christ were actually an agreed price paid to secure for man freedom from bondage to Satan, although it is far from clear to whom the ransom is to be paid.

Not only the word "ransom" but also the Greek phrase "for many" (ἀντὶ πολλῶν) is claimed as strong support for a substitutionary theory of the Atonement. The accurate meaning of ἀντὶ is, indeed, "instead of." In Hellenistic Greek the preposition is, however, not always used precisely, and there are cases where it is merely a synonym for ὑπέρ, meaning "on behalf of" (e.g., Matt. 17:27). Almost certainly Isa. 53 is once again influential in this saying.

It may be argued, however, that the word "ransom" is merely a vivid metaphor by which our Lord is declaring it to be his purpose to set men free from their present bondage, as Paul declares in Gal. 5:1: "For freedom Christ has set us free."

I Tim. 2:6, with its use of ἀντίλυτρον, seems clearly to echo the above passage. Cf. also the use of λυτρόω in Tit. 2:14.

*d. Redemption.* The word ἀπολύτρωσις is normally translated "redemption." By derivation it is clearly linked with λύτρον, and should mean "deliverance by the payment of a ransom." Certainly the idea of "freedom from bondage" is prominent in the meaning of the word, but it is doubtful whether the payment of a price has remained an integral part of the word's meaning. At any rate, the meaning of the word in Eph. 1:7; Col. 1:14 is further explained as simply the "forgiveness of sins."

In these contexts this forgiveness (redemption) has been already bestowed. Elsewhere (e.g., Rom. 8:23) the redemption referred to still lies in the future.

*e. Propitiation or expiation.* Ἱλάσκομαι (Luke 18:13; Heb. 2:17), ἱλαστήριον (Rom. 3:25), and ἱλασμός (I John 2:2; 4:10), all from the same verbal root, carry the meaning "propitiate," "appease," in classical Greek. Indeed, the last two are translated in the KJV by the word "propitiation," though the RSV in each case changes it to "expiation." Our guide to the real meaning of the word should be the LXX rather than pagan classical usage, and in the LXX these words can be used without any reference to "appeasement."

In Luke 18:13 the verb ἱλάσκομαι means "be merciful to," and is used of God's attitude toward a penitent sinner. In Heb. 2:17 the object of the verb is not "God," but the "sins of the people." So it must mean "expiation" rather than "propitiation."

The noun ἱλασμός may be used to mean "propitiation," but need not carry this significance. E.g., in the LXX version of Ps. 130:4: "There is forgiveness with thee," the word "forgiveness" (סליחה) is rendered by ἱλασμός. There is no implication of "propitiation" in the Hebrew original. Its normal Greek equivalent would be ἄφεσις. Ἱλαστήριον (Rom. 3:25) *may* be regarded as a noun formation meaning "propitiation," but modern commentators prefer other explanations. Some take it, not as a noun, but as an adjective, applied to Christ, and meaning "with reconciling power." Others, as the RSV, use "expiation." Still others point out that the normal use of the word in the LXX is to mean "mercy seat," the canopy in the Holy of Holies where God was thought to appear to declare forgiveness to his people. This is the meaning of the word also in Heb. 9:5. Therefore, it is claimed, the probable meaning in Rom. 3:25 is that Christ is the new mercy seat, his cross being the appointed place to which men may come to gain assurance that their sins are forgiven them.

There is therefore no clear case for insisting that any of these words in its NT context implies that God's anger needs to be placated by the sacrifice of Christ on the cross.

*f. "Bought."* (ἐξ-)ἀγοράζω means "buy," implying the payment of a price. It occurs in I Cor. 6:20; 7:23; Gal. 3:13; 4:5. It belongs to the same context of thought as the payment of a ransom. But the metaphor may seek to declare, not so much the means by which an end is achieved, as the end which is attained. In this case it is the truth that man now belongs utterly to God ("you are not your own") which is being emphasized.

The fact that ἐξαγοράζομαι in Eph. 5:16; Col. 4:5 is used metaphorically of "redeeming the time" (KJV), to mean "making the most of the time" (RSV), is a pointed reminder that the literal meaning should not necessarily be stressed.

**D. CONCLUSION.** It is sin which has created the need for atonement, because sin, besides corrupting the heart and deadening the conscience and making man increasingly prone to sin again, causes man to be estranged from God, separated from God by an unseen barrier, a "dividing wall of hostility" (Eph. 2:14). This barrier of separation God in Christ has broken down. Christ reconciles man to God and gives him peace with God. It is one task of theologians to attempt to explain how Christ in his self-giving on the cross has achieved this end. No precise explanation, however, is offered in the NT, nor has the church officially sponsored any one of the theories of the Atonement which have been propounded. But both church and NT agree in declaring with full assurance the *fact* of the Atonement—that God has himself prepared the way by which man may be reconciled to him, and the means by which the evil consequences of past sin can be annulled. This Way is Christ. This Means is Christ. "He is our peace, who . . . has broken down the dividing wall of hostility, . . . that he might . . . reconcile us . . . to God" (Eph. 2:14-16).

*Bibliography.* R. W. Dale, *The Atonement* (1875). J. S. Lidgett, *The Spiritual Principle of the Atonement* (1901). J. Denney, *The Death of Christ* (1902). G. Aulen, *Christus Victor* (1931). E. Brunner, *The Mediator* (1934). V. Taylor, *Jesus and His Sacrifice* (1937); *The Atonement in NT Teaching* (1940). C. R. Smith, *Bible Doctrine of Salvation* (1941). D. M. Baillie, *God was in Christ* (1948), pp. 157-201.      C. L. MITTON

\*ATONEMENT, DAY OF [יוֹם (ה)כִּפֻּרִים, (the) day of coverings *or* propitiations (Lev. 23:27-28; 25:9); LXX ἡμέρα ἐξιλασμοῦ (Lev. 23:27-28), τῇ ἡμέρα τοῦ ἱλασμοῦ (Lev. 25:9)]. Alternately: ATONEMENT [הכפרים], with DAY implied (Exod. 30:10 [LXX τοῦ ἐξιλασμοῦ]; Num. 29:11 [LXX τῆς ἐξιλάσεως]). The great annual fast day of Judaism, the tenth day of Tishri, described in Lev. 16, on which, when the temple stood, the high priest entered the holy of holies to atone for the sins of all Israel; now known as Yom Kippur. In the NT, ἡ νηστεία, "the fast," is the title (Acts 27:9). Other titles are "the feast of the fast" (Philo); "the Day," or "the Great Day" (Mishna).

The annual Day of Atonement is the only fast day prescribed in the Mosaic law. Its rites are set forth in Lev. 16, and supplementary stipulations about its observance are found in Lev. 23:26-32; Num. 29:7-11. Though apparently developing late, it played a formative and influential role in the whole of Judaism, especially in the two or three centuries just before the rise of Christianity. The spirited account of it in the Tractate Yoma in the Mishna shows this, as do the exalted references to it in many other Jewish sources. Further, in the NT the passion narratives, the Letter to the Hebrews, and the writings of Paul are all in various ways under its impact. This vitality helps also to explain the fact that the Day of Atonement survived the destruction of the temple, even though its rites epitomized the sacrificial system.

The words "you shall afflict yourselves" (Lev. 16:29; 23:27, 29; Num. 29:7) designate the Day as a fast. But it was also a "sabbath of solemn rest" (Lev. 16:31; 23:32)—literally, a sabbath of sabbatical observance, on which all work ceased (Num. 29:7). Its complex series of rites, of diverse origin, were unified by a single purpose: to ward off the wrath and make available the protection of the holy God who dwelt in the temple in the midst of his people (Ezek. 43:7-9; 48:35). The function of the sprinkling of blood and of the dismissal of the scapegoat was the same: to cleanse Israel, its priesthood, and its temple from the pollution of sin.

The whole exilic and postexilic period of Judaism was increasingly troubled by the sinfulness of man and the holy justice of God. On the one hand, among Ezra and his rabbinic successors, this produced an intense mood of moral and legal obligation. But on the other, in the priestly movement, it led to new developments in worship so that contrition, confession, and, especially, propitiation became increasingly prominent. The Day of Atonement embodies these motifs and brings this whole sacerdotal development to its climax. It has very appropriately been described as the "Good Friday of the OT."

1. Origin
2. The rites
   *a.* The sacrifice for the priests
   *b.* The sacrifice for the people
   *c.* The scapegoat
3. Significance
Bibliography

**1. Origin.** The canonical references to the Day of Atonement are confined to the priestly writings. As is true of the cultus as a whole, we are told Moses instituted it. But this may have the same meaning as the common statement of Christians today that a given practice or teaching is "biblical." The death of Nadab and Abihu (Lev. 10:1 ff) serves as a warrant for the Day; and it stresses the sovereign holiness of God, which they had ignored. Jub. 34:17 associates the origin of the Day with the mourning of Jacob for Joseph (Gen. 37:29 ff). But this is the only attempt to reinterpret this symbolic cultic institution as a historical memorial.

Ezek. 40–48 provided the climate in which the Day of Atonement could develop. The architectural plans and the expiatory character of the guilt and sin offerings honor the holiness of God who dwells in Israel's midst. But the Day as described in Lev. 16 does not seem to exist. In Ezek. 45:19-20 two days a year are designated for the cleansing of the temple. According to the more probable LXX reading, they fell on the first day of the first and seventh months respectively. This atonement of the temple corresponds most closely to the rite for the high priest in Lev. 16:11-14. It raises the important question of the relation of the Day of Atonement to the New Year. The observances in Ezekiel are very probably to be thought of as New Year ceremonies, assuming that an ancient autumnal New Year had not been fully supplanted by the spring observance of the priestly legislation (Exod. 12:2). It is to be noted also that the Year of Jubilee began on the Day of Atonement (Lev. 25:9). It is not easy to explain, however, why an interval of ten days should later separate the two observances. Some, drawing on analogies of Babylonian practice, suppose the Day of Lev. 16 was the culmination of a continuous complex of New Year observances. Others, troubled by the fact of the unusual ten-day interval, have tried to explain the problem as an attempt to synchronize a lunar year with a solar one. In any case, the atonement in Ezekiel is less complete than in Leviticus. A propitiation for the people as a whole does not occur, either by sprinkling of blood or by scapegoat. We must conclude that while a day of atonement was emerging, the Day of Lev. 16 did not yet exist. Special fast days were becoming increasingly frequent (Ezra 8–9; Zech. 7:3-5; 8:19). In Neh. 9:1, following an account about the teaching of the law on the first day of the seventh month and about the celebration of Tabernacles, we hear of a fast on the twenty-fourth day. No reference to the tenth day occurs, and the observances on the twenty-fourth bear little resemblance to those of the Day of Atonement. Apparently, even at this late date the Day was not yet generally recognized, but only by the temple priesthood. For it seems probable that the Day began as a priestly rite of propitiation which, through the assimilation or development of other rituals, gradually became a day of penitence and atonement for all. The spattering of the blood of the sacrifice seems to stand at the core of this development, rather than the scapegoat.

The question of the development of the Day in Israel involves the issue of the history of Lev. 16. In view of its repetitiveness, the occurrence of a doublet such as in vss. 6, 11, and the different ways of describing the scapegoat (vss. 8, 21), it has long been recognized that the writ is composite. Until recently, vss. 6-10, which contain rubrics for all three main rites, including the scapegoat, were considered all or a part of the original nucleus. Recently, under the influence of form criticism, this has changed. Vss. 11, 14-16, 20*b*-21, exhibit a characteristic ritual style. In vss. 14-16, in the rite of the goat of expiation, there is no reference to the scapegoat, though the two are treated together in vss. 5-10. This has increasingly led to the conclusion that vss. 5-10 are probably secondary to 11-16 though perhaps antecedent to 20*b*-21. The incorporation of the rite of the scapegoat into the Day of Atonement ritual may represent a concession to popular taste.

**2. The rites.** In later Judaism, the New Year again fell in autumn. Perhaps even before this transfer, preparation for the Day of Atonement began on the first day of the month with a "blast of trumpets" and a "holy convocation" (Lev. 23:23), to usher in a period of repentance. The Day itself, with its fast, began on the evening of the ninth day, at sunset, and lasted until the evening of the next day (Lev. 23:32). The strict abstinence included eating, drinking, washing, anointing, putting on sandals, and marital intercourse (Yom. 8.1; cf. Heb. 9:10). Only children and the sick were exempt.

Since he was the central figure in all the ceremonies, the preparation of the high priest was intense. Seven days before the Fast he left his home to take up residence in his apartment in the temple (Yom. 1.1). During these days he officiated at the daily burnt offering and rehearsed the solemn rites he was to perform on the Great Day. On the eve of the Day he ate very lightly, for he was to maintain an all-night vigil. The elders admonished him to be correct in the ritual and to weep at his vigil. During the night younger priests kept him awake by reading. On the morning, having bathed (Lev. 16:4), and in his finest array, he offered the burnt offering, which was elaborate on this day (Num. 29:8-11). Then he changed to the white linen garb of a penitent (Lev. 16:4) and was ready to officiate at the atonement ceremonies.

While overlapping at many points and forming a continuous liturgical action, it seems that there are three distinct rites: (*a*) the sacrifice for the priests, (*b*) the sacrifice for the people, and (*c*) the scapegoat.

***a. The sacrifice for the priests.*** The sacrifice for Aaron and his house (Lev. 16:6) was a young bull, the same as a priest's private sin offering (Lev. 4:3-11). The priest came to the animal at the usual place of slaughter in the area of the temple court (Yom. 3.8; cf. Ezek. 40:35-43). Before slaying it he placed his hands on its head and confessed his sins and the sins of his house. A similar confession prefaces each of the rites. All end with the pronunciation of the sacred name, the utterance of which survived on the Day long after it had otherwise ceased. According to the Mishna the casting of lots over the two goats (16.8) took place at this point and was followed by a repetition of the priest's confession (Yom. 4.2), but this is probably due to the composite character of Lev. 16:6-11.

With incense and the blood of the slain bull the high priest enters the holy of holies (Lev. 16:12-14). According to the Mishna this was done in two stages. First, with live coals on a censer in his right hand and a container of incense in his left, he entered to cense the shrine so that he might be safe from the divine mystery (Exod. 33:20). He set the smoking censer on the poles in the ark (Exod. 25:13-14) and, later, after the ark was lost, on the *Šetiyah*, or Foundation stone (Yom. 5.2). Then he retired to the nave of the temple to pray, but briefly, lest the people become terrified. He then took the blood from an attendant, who had been stirring it, to prevent its congealing, and entered the holy of holies for the second time. He sprinkled blood on the mercy seat (*kapporeth*) once, and seven times he spattered the ark with blood in front, to "cover" the pollution of the sins of the priests. He returned to the nave, and, setting the vessel with the bull's blood on a stand, he went out to perform the next rite, the atonement of the people.

*b. The sacrifice for the people.* The sacrifice for the people's atonement was a goat chosen by lot from two identical specimens presented in the area of the temple court N of the altar. There was a special urn for the two lots, one marked "For the Lord," the other "For Azazel." Standing between the two goats and facing them, the high priest thrust both hands into the urn and brought up a lot in each hand. Then he brought down the lots in his hand on the heads of the rams as he stood before them and uttered the dedication: "To the Lord," pronouncing the name. To this, as in the case of all the confessions, the attendants responded: "Blessed be the name of the glory of his kingdom forever and ever" (Yom. 4.1). A red ribbon was tied to the goat for Azazel.

The priest slaughtered the other goat, and with its blood he entered the sanctuary for the third time to sprinkle the ark seven times with the sacrifice of the people. Then, returning to the nave, he exchanged the vessel of goat's blood for the one with the blood of the bull and sprinkled the veil facing the ark seven times. Then, once more taking the goat's blood, he did the same. He then combined the remainder of the blood in the two vessels and proceeded with the anointing of the horns of the golden altar of incense (Exod. 30:1-10), which stood before the veil and was a symbol for the prayers of all Israel. With his fingers he sprinkled it with blood to rid it of Israel's uncleanness. Thus the instruments of the cultus on which the relation between

God and Israel depended were again "holy" and usable by God. We are told that the priest took the remainder of the blood and poured it out at the base of the altar of burnt offering and that an underground channel carried it thence to the Kidron (Yom. 5.6). There it was collected and sold to gardeners as manure—a startling statement which serves to remind us that the blood was sacred and effective, not by its intrinsic nature, but by the action of God through it in the divine priestly institution which was his gift to Israel.

*c. The scapegoat.* If the sacrifices of the bull and the goat effect the removal of Israel's pollution of its cult forms, the rite of the scapegoat serves to remove the guilt resting on the people themselves. Scholars have shown the wide prevalence of rites involving the transferral of contamination or guilt. Among the ancient Hittites we learn of a woman and a goat of multicolored wool driven through the camp toward the camp of the enemy as a sacrifice to their god, who had brought the plague. In Israel itself the rite for the cleansing of the leper (Lev. 14:6-7) employs the idea. It occurs also in Zechariah's vision of the expulsion of wickedness (5:5 ff) and has its most profound OT application in the Suffering Servant in the book of Isaiah (cf. 53:6, 11-12). In the NT it stands at the center of the atonement by Jesus Christ.

We have noted that in Israel the goat was dedicated to the Lord, rather than to an alien power. It was originally probably thought of as becoming a desert demon when sent into the wilderness (Lev. 16:22). Demons, sometimes of goatlike form, were thought to inhabit the desert (Isa. 13:21; 34:14; Tob. 8:3; Bar. 4:35; Matt. 12:43). The original etymology of "Azazel" is uncertain, and the term seems to have had a variety of meanings from time to time. In connection with the scapegoat it connoted a complete removal, beyond the inhabited world. In Enoch (6:7; 8:1; 13) "Azazel" was the term for the chief of the fallen angels, synonymous with "Satan."

After the confession of sins on behalf of the people, accompanied by the laying on of hands, the high priest turned the goat over to a man appointed to lead him away. Increasingly the people participated in the goat's departure, pulling out its wool, pricking it, spitting on it, and urging it to begone (Barn. 7.8; Yom. 6.4). The route led over Kidron into the Judean wilderness. Stations were set up along the way. At the end of the route, at the edge of a cliff, the attendant tied an end of the scarlet thread around the goat's neck to a rock and then pushed it over the cliff to its death. The announcement of this completion of the rite was relayed to the temple by the stations along the route. However, according to legend, a scarlet thread tied to the door of the sanctuary turned white at the very moment the goat was pushed over the precipice, as a sign that the people were cleansed of their sins (Yom. 6.8; cf. Isa. 1:18).

This ended the rites of the Day of Atonement. The high priest laid aside his penitent's garb and put on his magnificent cloth of gold costume to offer burnt offerings at the great altar, together with the fat of the bull of sacrifice and the goat (Lev. 16:24). A man was appointed to take the rest of the remains outside the camp to be burned. Both he and the attendant of the scapegoat became unclean and had to bathe and wash their garments before rejoining the community. Having completed the burnt offering, the high priest once more changed to the sacred white garments to enter the holy of holies for the fourth and final time, to bring back the censer which had stood there throughout the rites. Then, at sunset, he returned to his home and entertained his friends. The people danced and rejoiced. This was the moment when the words of Ps. 103:12:

As far as the east is from the west,
so far does he remove our transgressions from us,

were applicable; and about it Rabbi Akiba said: "How fortunate you are, O Israel! Before whom are you pure and who purifies you? Your father who is in heaven." Tabernacles began five days later, and "the joy of Tabernacles was the fruit of Kippur."

3. Significance. From what has just been said, it is evident that the Day of Atonement was a tremendous moment of renewal that permeated all Israel and united it in a solemn joy. Philo describes it as a fast that was a feast, "the greatest of the feasts" and "a seven of seven, a holier than the holy" (On the Special Laws II.xxxii). Ben Sirach was filled with awe at the splendor of the high priest through whose ministry God mediated forgiveness (Ecclus. 50:5 ff). On this day, it was said, for three hours Satan does not accuse Israel before God. It was a moment when the covenant relationship was pure and God's intervention was anticipated. In his brief prayer in the temple following the censing of the holy of holies, the high priest asked for a year of abundance and for the coming of Messiah (Gemara 53b).

On a Jewish cemetery in Delos two monuments to murdered Jews were discovered. They date from ca. 100 B.C., and on both, except for a change of name, there was inscribed the same prayer: "I invoke and beseech the most high God, the Lord of Spirits, and of all flesh, against those who by stealth have slain or poisoned the young unfortunate, Heraclius (Martin), spilling his innocent blood: may it happen even so to his murderers and their children. Master, whose all is, and you, angels of God, to you before whom all flesh humbles itself on this day in supplication: avenge the innocent blood, avenge it speedily." This prayer, with its obvious reference to the Day of Atonement, points to the established universal observance of the Day, in the Diaspora as well as in the Holy Land, at a relatively early date. What is more important, it shows that Israel believed that the cleansing from its sins accomplished by the rites and the forgiveness of God which this represented was the ground for faith in the redeeming action of God in behalf of his covenanted people.

The Day of Atonement was the most solemn expression of faith and worship developed by the priestly movement in postexilic Judaism. In its basic outlook it was profoundly theocentric, and its central function was to mediate the grace of God in forgiveness and redeeming action. While the symbol of the rabbinic movement, with its emphasis upon human obligation, was the two tables of the law placed in the ark (Deut. 10:5), the focal symbol of the priestly atonement rites was the mercy seat on it, where the

sins of Israel were "covered." According to the Mishna (Yom. 8.8-9) repentance was indispensable if one were to participate in the fruits of the Day of Atonement; on the other hand, not the repentance but the sacred Day and its ordinances effect atonement until the Day of Atonement; but only the action of God through and by the cultus he himself had instituted could wipe out man's sin. The interpreters of the Day guarded against "subjectivism."

Since the rites were elaborate and meticulously performed as part of an institutionalized cultus, there was a danger that they would be performed for their own sake and that the understanding of their effectiveness should become separated from the divine action. This danger was probably not fully avoided. The Letter to the Hebrews refers to the Day of Atonement mainly to stress the eschatological finality of the event of Christian faith: the high priest entered an earthly sanctuary, annually; Christ has entered the heavenly sanctuary, once for all. But beneath this dominant messianic theme one also detects a subsidiary polemic that hints that the rites of the Day were considered self-sufficient. Heb. 10:4 implies that the blood of the bull and the goat was held to be potent per se. If so, this was an aberration. No magical power was attributed to the blood as such; the disposal of the surplus and the account of what was done with it, noted above, makes this clear. Israel, indeed, shared the view of the nature mysticism all around her that "life is in the blood" (Lev. 17:11). This may even account for the use of blood in the ritual. But its effectiveness in mediating forgiveness did not depend on its natural vitality, but upon the faith that God had chosen to use it. Likewise, in the New Covenant, the blood of Christ avails, not because it is human blood, but because it is the blood of God's elect One (cf. Heb. 5:5).

Bibliography. For description of the rites, see A. Médebielle, L'expiation dans l'AT (1923). S. Landersdorfer, Studien zum biblischen Versöhnungstag (1924). G. B. Gray, Sacrifice in the OT (1925), pp. 306-22. A. Büchler, Studies in Sin and Atonement (1928), ch. 4. W. O. E. Oesterley, Sacrifices in Ancient Israel (1938), ch. 17. For form criticism of Lev. 16, see R. Rentdorf, Die Gesetze in der Priesterschrift (1955). On the etymology of "Azazel," see G. R. Driver, "Three Technical Terms in the Pentateuch," Journal of Semitic Studies, I (1956), 97-105.
J. C. RYLAARSDAM

**ATROTH** ăt′rŏth. KJV translation of עטרת in Num. 32:35. See ATROTH-SHOPHAN.

**ATROTH-BETH-JOAB** ăt′rŏth bĕth jō′ăb [עטרות בית יאב, crowns (or sheepfolds?) of the house of Joab] (I Chr. 2:54); KJV ATAROTH ăt′ə—, THE HOUSE OF JOAB. A village near Bethlehem, listed as one of the "descendants" in the genealogy of Judah. The location is unknown.    V. R. GOLD

**ATROTH-SHOPHAN** ăt′rŏth shō′făn [עטרת שופן] (Num. 32:35); KJV ATROTH, SHOPHAN. A city built by the Gadites in the territory conquered from Sihon. The name seems to be derived from that of the larger city of ATAROTH. It is probably Rujm ʿAtarus, situated on a lofty hill ca. 1½ miles NE of the site of Ataroth, so located as to protect the latter.

Bibliography. N. Glueck, AASOR, XVIII–XIX (1939), 135-36.
S. COHEN

**ATTAI** ăt′ī [עַתַּי, timely, *or perhaps an abbreviation of* Athaiah]. **1.** Son of Jarha, an Egyptian slave belonging to Sheshan; father of Nathan; mentioned in the genealogy of Jerahmeel (I Chr. 2:35-36).

**2.** Sixth in the list of warriors from Gad who went over to David at Ziklag (I Chr. 12:11).

**3.** One of the sons of Rehoboam by his favorite wife, Maacah (II Chr. 11:20).      F. T. SCHUMACHER

**ATTALIA** ăt′ə lī′ə ['Ατταλεία]. A harbor city on the SW coast of Asia Minor. Attalia was founded by and named after Attalus II of Pergamum (159-138 B.C.) to be the chief outlet on the coast of Asia Minor W of Pamphylia. The city and port are mentioned in Acts 14:25. Fig. ATT 115.

Courtesy of Machteld J. Mellink

115. The harbor of Attalia (modern Antalya)

Attalia (modern Antalya) still flourishes on a modest scale, and its port has preserved its picturesque ancient character. Fragments of the Hellenistic defenses can still be seen in the surviving medieval city walls. The most impressive ancient landmark is a triple gate built by Hadrian.

*Bibliography.* K. Lanckoronoski, *Städte Pamphyliens und Pisidiens* (1890), pp. 7-32, 153-63.      M. J. MELLINK

**ATTALUS** ăt′ə ləs [῎Ατταλος]. The name borne by three kings of Pergamum. Among those to whom the consul Lucius sent assurances of Roman friendship for the Jews (I Macc. 15:22) was Attalus II (*ċa.* 200-138 B.C.), founder of Philadelphia, the city named for him in deference to the "brother-loving" loyalty he had shown toward his predecessor, Eumenes II.

J. C. SWAIM

**ATTHARATES** ăth′ə rā′tēz ['Ατταρατή (B), Ατθαρατης (A), Αθαρασθας (Luc.)]. A corruption of the title TIRSHATHA (תִּרְשָׁתָא; Neh. 8:9=I Esd. 9:49—G 9:50).

**ATTHARIAS** ăth′ə rī′əs ['Αθθάριας] (I Esd. 5:40); KJV ATHARIAS. An official, named with Nehemiah, as giving orders to the priests among the returning exiles.      N. TURNER

**AUGIA.** KJV form of AGIA.

**AUGURY** [נַחַשׁ]. A form of DIVINATION. The term "augury" properly refers to the practice of the Greeks and Romans to foretell future events by the flight, chattering, or singing of birds. This method was practically unknown in ancient Mesopotamia and Palestine (but see Eccl. 10:20 for a possible allusion to it).      I. MENDELSOHN

**AUGUSTAN COHORT** ə gŭs′tən kō′hôrt [σπεῖρα Σεβαστή; Lat. *cohors Augusta*] (Acts 27:1). A term of disputed meaning. Inscriptions attest the presence of an Augustan cohort (*Cohors I Augusta*) in Syria after A.D. 6 and at Batanea in the time of Agrippa II (*ca.* 50-100). Acts 27:1 probably refers to this cohort. We may suppose (*a*) that Luke was aware of the fact that of five auxiliary cohorts stationed in Caesarea, one bore the honorary cognomen *Augusta;* (*b*) that Luke designates the name of the cohort less to define Julius than to promote the prestige of Paul by placing Paul in "Augustan" custody; and (*c*) that although, in general, auxiliary cohorts (*see* COHORT) in the Roman army were mustered from the localities in which they were stationed, and in particular, according to Jos. Antiq. XIX.ix.1-2; XX.viii.7 (see also War II.iii.4, with footnote, vol. II of Josephus, Loeb Classical Library, p. 343), the Roman troops stationed in Caesarea were for the most part local people from Caesarea and Samaria (Sebaste), nevertheless, it is quite gratuitous to suppose that Luke misunderstood *Sebastene* ( ="of Sebaste"=Samaria) for Sebaste ( =Augustan) or that "Augustan Cohort" is a (wilful?) mistranslation of "Cohort of the Sebastenes." Although the troops may have come in the main from Sebaste ( =Samaria), Luke is not the least concerned with their provenance; he is, rather, concerned with the prestige which falls upon Paul from the bright imperial name of Augustus.

Given Luke's intent, there appears to be no need to attempt to show that "Augustan cohort" was a popular name for the corps of officer-couriers (*frumentarii*) detailed for communication service between the emperor and his armies and responsible, among other things, for conducting prisoners to Rome. Nor is it necessary to question whether an important prisoner like Paul would be handed over to a centurion of a Syrian auxiliary troop. To Luke, Julius and Augustus were prestige-carrying Roman names. What rabble the cohort was composed of was not important; the weight falls wholly on the fact that Paul was put in charge of a (Roman) centurion, of the Augustan cohort, Julius by name.

*Bibliography.* T. R. S. Broughton, "The Roman Army," n. xxxiii, pp. 427-45, in F. J. Foakes-Jackson and K. Lake, eds. *The Beginnings of Christianity,* pt. I, vol. V (1933) (see especially pp. 443-44); G. H. C. Macgregor, Exegesis of the Acts of the Apostles, *IB,* IX (1954), 332; E. Haenchen, *Die Apostelgeschichte* (1956), p. 628, n. 4.      F. D. GEALY

**AUGUSTUS** ə gŭs′təs [Αὔγουστος, *from* Lat.]. The title given by the Roman Senate on Jan. 16, 27 B.C., to Gaius Julius Caesar Octavianus, founder of the Roman Empire and ruler of the Mediterranean world at the time of Jesus' birth (Luke 2:1). The title means "reverend," and when translated into Greek, it bore implications of divinity. It was borne by later Roman emperors and, with a feminine ending, by empresses; but when used as a name by itself, it refers to its most famous bearer. Figs. AUG 116-17.

Born on September 23, 63 B.C., into a family which had recently acquired senatorial rank, young Gaius met Julius Caesar (*see* CAESAR, JULIUS), his greatuncle by marriage, in 46. The next year the dictator adopted him in his will but did not make this fact

Courtesy of the American Numismatic Society

116. Coin with head of Augustus

public, and it was only after Caesar's murder and the reading of the will in 44 that the young man changed his name from Gaius Octavius to that given above. He first broke with Mark Antony, who had been Caesar's chief aide, and appealed to Caesar's troops for support. Supported halfheartedly by the Senate, he soon decided to break with it, and in 43 he occupied the city of Rome, where he was elected consul. His next move was to join Antony and the latter's ally Lepidus, forming a "triumvirate" with them and putting to death three hundred senators (including the famous orator Cicero) and two thousand knights. They next moved against the forces of Brutus, Caesar's murderer, and defeated them; then Antony and Octavian sent Lepidus off to Africa (he ultimately died as Pontifex Maximus in 13 or 12 B.C.). Antony married Octavian's sister Octavia, and the two active leaders of the Triumvirate proceeded to defeat the forces of an old-fashioned republican general in Sicily.

In the years after 41, Antony was chiefly engaged in the East, preparing and finally waging a war against the Parthians which Caesar had planned. In 36, however, he was beaten back by the Parthians and retired to Alexandria, where he fell under the spell of Cleopatra VII, queen of Egypt and former mistress of Caesar. He was so infatuated, and so politically inept, that he promised to give her and her children (both Caesar's and his) territories in the East which belonged not only to foreign kings but also to Rome itself. After 35 he abandoned Octavia; in 33 he married Cleopatra; in 32 he divorced Octavia. The following year Octavian was able to persuade the Senate to declare war on Cleopatra. Antony and Cleopatra advanced as far as the bay of Actium (Greece). Attacked by Octavian's troops by land, they attempted to withdraw their fleets to Asia Minor, but almost all of Antony's fleet was captured, and in 30 Octavian invaded Egypt. Both Antony and Cleopatra committed suicide, and Egypt became a Roman province.

Octavian had promised in 36 that he would restore the republic, and there is no reason to believe that he was not sincere. It was evident, however, that to turn the seventy legions now under arms over to the Senate could lead only to further troubles, and he therefore retained control over the army and foreign affairs, while restoring the operation of civil government to the Senate (sharply reduced in num-

bers) and the equestrians. In 27 he offered to resign his various offices; the Senate refused his offer and instead voted him the title "Augustus" as a person commended to gods and men. The Senate recovered control over Rome, Italy, and those provinces which did not need to be guarded by legions. Augustus had proconsular authority over the others and directed the work of their governors, men responsible only to him. Over a period of time he came to make more use of the perpetual tribunitian power which had been voted him in 30; this meant that he convened the meetings of the Senate and was the supreme criminal judge of the state. And he carefully observed the forms of republican rule, consulting the Senate and avoiding the trappings of royalty. This observance was obviously formal, for he actually controlled the imperial provinces with their legions and had been given the right to make binding treaties with foreign powers. The fact that he summed up his position in the title *princeps* ("first citizen") is irrelevant when compared with his actual powers, though he himself was no despot.

Toward the end of his long life he arranged for his stepson and son-in-law, TIBERIUS, to become co-regent; and when he died, Tiberius succeeded him. He also arranged for an inscription to be published in the provinces and at Rome; this has been recovered almost completely and describes the emperor's accomplishments (*res gestae divi Augusti*) in relation to honors given him, expenditures for public pur-

Courtesy of Editions des Musées Nationaux, Paris

117. Statue of Augustus, in the Louvre

poses, and achievements in war and peace. Among his construction projects were many temples, since he was anxious to restore Roman religion, at a fairly low ebb in the first century B.C., and to provide the state with the protection of the gods. "In my sixth consulship [28 B.C.] I repaired eighty-two temples of the gods in the city." In the provinces he accepted and encouraged the building of temples, not to himself alone, but to "Rome and Augustus." He was unenthusiastic about foreign cults except those of the Greeks which were "ancient and well established" (Suetonius *Augustus* XCIII).

Among Romans of every class there was strong admiration for him as the bringer of peace and prosperity to the inhabited world. An inscription celebrating his birthday in 7 B.C. states that "it is hard to say whether the birthday of the most divine Caesar is more joyful or more advantageous; we may rightly regard it as like the beginning of all things, if not in the world of nature, yet in advantage; everything was deteriorating and changing into misfortune, but he set it right and gave the whole world another appearance. . . . The birthday of the god was the beginning of the good news [cf. Mark 1:1] to the world on his account." And in the last year of his life, as Suetonius tells us (*Augustus* XCVIII), "as he sailed by the gulf of Puteoli it happened that from an Alexandrian ship which had just arrived there the passengers and crew, clad in white, crowned with garlands, and burning incense, lavished upon him good wishes and the highest praises, saying that it was through him they lived, through him they sailed the seas, and through him they enjoyed their liberty and their fortunes." There is no reason not to regard this offering of divine honors as spontaneous. He died on August 19, A.D. 14, and was deified by the Senate a month later. *See* EMPEROR-WORSHIP.

Popular, determined, fortunate, and long-lived, Augustus left a deep impress on the empire which he founded, and it followed the general lines he had established for the succeeding three centuries. No later emperor was remembered so favorably.

**Bibliography.** Articles and bibliography in *Cambridge Ancient History*, vol. X (1934); J. Buchan, *Augustus Caesar* (1937); R. Syme, *The Roman Revolution* (1939).    R. M. GRANT

**AURANUS** ô rā′nəs [’Αυράνος] (II Macc. 4:40). Leader of an insurrection in Jerusalem in the time of the Maccabees.    J. C. SWAIM

**AUTEAS.** KJV Apoc. form of HODIAH 2.

**AUTHOR OF LIFE** (Acts 3:15). An expression referring to Jesus. The word translated "author" (ἀρχηγός) is translated in Acts 5:31 as "leader"; and in Heb. 2:10; 12:2 as "pioneer." It refers in all cases to Jesus. The word is used by Plato (*Timaeus* 21.E) of an Egyptian goddess who is the "founder" of a city. In Acts 3:15 he who was crucified is recognized as the founder of a new life, which his followers now share with him.    B. H. THROCKMORTON, JR.

**AUTHORITY** [שׁלט, to be master of, have dominion over; ἐξουσία; Lat. *auctoritas*]. In the Bible, as in modern usage, authority is closely connected with power, though usually, but not always, distinguished from it. Its meaning covers the actual possession or use of power, the legal or moral right to exercise it, the domain (dominion) within which it is exercised, and the person or precedent appealed to in support of action or opinion. The focus of biblical usage is in the authority which belongs to God alone, all other authority being subordinate and derivative. This same divine authority was exercised by Jesus and claimed by him for the church.

**1. In the OT.** The concrete Hebrew language has no word for the abstract notion of authority. The KJV uses the word "authority" only twice in the whole OT. The LXX translates a number of Hebrew words, the chief being שׁלט, by ἐξουσία, though always in a late text. But there is sufficient to indicate, nevertheless, that the chief ingredients of the biblical notion are present. It is used of the seizure or exercise of political power (Neh. 5:15; Esth. 9:1; Eccl. 8:9); it can be distinguished as the legal right rather than the power to do a thing; it can be used to indicate the realm governed rather than the authority exercised (II Kings 20:13; Ps. 114:2); it can be used of the absolute authority wielded by the king (Eccl. 8:4), or of the life-and-death authority by king and judge (Ecclus. 9:13). When these ideas are applied to God, it is seen that his authority is absolute—everlasting, universal, and unquestionable (Dan. 4:34-35). But in his steadfast love he has imparted some authority to the natural order (the sun "rules" the day, and the moon and stars the night; Ps. 136:7-9). The relationship of human authorities to the absolute divine authority is articulated, instead of in words, in the mutual relationships of king, priest, and prophet. Surrounding peoples regarded their kings as divine beings, or descendants from gods, and so provided some sort of theological basis for the despotism they exercised. But in Israel and Judah the power of the monarch, though great, was always recognized as part, and not the supreme part, of a manifold delegation of authority by God. King, prophet, priest, judge—these together exercised the divine provision of ordered government. Kings must rule in righteousness, judges deal justly, priests make due expiation for sin; the watchman over all was the prophet, bound to no earthly master, servant only of God, speaking with divine authority the judgments of the Lord on church and state alike. The theology of this multiform authority was never stated explicitly in the OT; but it forms the fruitful basis for the insights of the NT.

**2. In the NT.** In Jesus Christ there has been a new disclosure of what divine authority is like. As incarnate Son of God he taught with authority (Mark 1:22), not as the scribes, appealing elsewhere; not even, we may add, as the prophets, declaring: "Thus saith the Lord," but with authority: "I say to you . . ." (Matt. 5:22, 28, 32, 34, 39, 44). He forgave sins, deliberately accepting the scribes' point that to do so was God's prerogative (Mark 2:10). He exorcized demons, agreeing with his opponents that to do so was either a divine or a demonic activity (Luke 11:14-20). Even before his ministry began, he defeated Satan, to whom God had given authority on the earth (Luke 4:1-13, especially vs. 6; I John

5:19). He claimed to have the authority of life and death over himself, which rightly belonged to God alone (John 10:18). He claimed that all authority was his (Matt. 28:18; John 17:2), and he gave his followers the right they did not otherwise possess to become sons of God (John 1:12). His kingdom was universal and eternal (II Pet. 1:11), and even his trial showed that his sentence by human authorities was within the authority of God (John 19:10-11).

**3. Subordinate authorities, human and superhuman.** With this new conception of the range and power of God's authority, the NT claims all other authority as subordinate to him. "There is no authority except from God" (Rom. 13:1) appears in a political context, but it asserts the final truth about all authority other than God's. Because Christians are sure of God's authority, they can use the word to describe a human magistrate, though they can also realize that obedience to God must always take precedence over mere political obedience (Acts 4: 19). But the greatest advance of NT thought was to claim that the whole world of supernatural beings and their authority were entirely subordinate to God. That Christ had been raised "far above all rule and authority and power and dominion" (Eph. 1:21) was their way of saying that no powers, human or superhuman, could undo what God had done in Christ. Most of all, Satan himself has authority in this world only within God's authority (Rev. 2:10, etc.), as has Antichrist (I John 4:1-6). So the Christian church can enunciate a conception of history where God's will is universally authoritative, and where the believer can gratefully accept all that God ordains. There is no possible basis for rebellion or complaint (Rom. 9:21). God can do as he will; his writ runs everywhere; his authority is absolute; and he has established his saving purpose in Christ.

Christ gave to his followers his own authority to forgive sins (Matt. 16:19; 18:18; John 20:23), to heal diseases (Luke 9:1), to expel demons (Mark 6:7), and to proclaim the coming of the kingdom (Matt. 10:7-8). J. MARSH

*AUTHORIZED VERSIONS. The term used to denote ecclesiastically endorsed translations of the English Bible. The Great Bible (1539), prepared by Miles Coverdale at the request of Cromwell, was the first Authorized Version. Printing was started in Paris, but, being interrupted by the Inquisition, was transferred to London. This Bible was set up in massive pages, hence the name of "Great Bible." The text was essentially from TYNDALE's VERSION and the Matthew Bible. The Bishops' Bible (1568), the second Authorized Version, was edited by Archbishop Parker, with the assistance of several bishops; hence the "Bishops' Bible." It was a revision of the Great Bible, but the Geneva Bible was also consulted. It was never endorsed by Queen Elizabeth, but was sanctioned by the bishops at the Convocation of 1571. The third Authorized Version, the King James Version (1611), was projected in 1604 by James I. Fifty-four able scholars and churchmen (only forty-seven actually worked) were appointed to the task. The Bishops' Bible provided the basis, but Tyndale, Coverdale, Matthew, and the Great Bible were used.

Latin versions, Luther's translation, and the Rheims NT were also consulted. Chapter divisions of Stephen Langton and verse divisions of Robert Estienne were introduced. No record of its official authorization exists, but it obviously was so regarded.

The Revised Version (1881-85) and the American Standard Version (1901) were official revisions of the King James. The Revised Standard Version (1946-52) is the latest revision. *See* VERSIONS, ENGLISH.

J. R. BRANTON

**AVA.** KJV form of AVVA.

**AVARAN** ăv′ə răn [Αὐαράν, beast-sticker(?); Vulg. *Saura*] (I Macc. 6:43-46); KJV SAVARAN săv′ə răn. Epithet or surname of Eleazar, fourth son of Mattathias. He died heroically at BETH-ZECHARIAH.

J. C. SWAIM

**AVE MARIA** ä′vĭ mə rē′ə, ä′vä mä rē′ä [Lat., Hail Mary]. An anthem in praise of Mary, the Lord's mother, composed of the salutations addressed to her by the archangel Gabriel and by Elizabeth, in Luke 1:28 and 42 respectively. Its earliest liturgical use occurs in the fifth-century Liturgies of Saint James (Jerusalem) and Saint Mark (Alexandria), where it is placed immediately before the commemoration of the saints in the Eucharistic Prayer of Consecration. The Roman mass first used the Ave Maria as an Offertory anthem for the Annunciation, a feast introduced at Rome in the latter half of the seventh century, whence it passed to other masses in honor of the Virgin and the mass for the fourth Sunday in Advent. As a popular devotion, it did not come into general use until the end of the twelfth century. With the addition of a nonscriptural, petitionary clause, the Ave Maria was officially admitted to the breviary of Pius V in 1568.

*Bibliography.* H. Thurston, "Hail Mary," *The Catholic Encyclopedia* (1907-53), VII, 110-12; R. J. Hesbert, *Antiphonale missarum sextuplex* (1935), pp. xxxviii-xxxix; H. Leclercq, "Marie (je vous salue)," *Dictionnaire d'archéologie chrétienne et de liturgie*, X, 2043-62. M. H. SHEPHERD, JR.

**AVEN** ā′vən [אָוֶן, 'āwen, wickedness]. **1.** A place mentioned in the phrase "high places of Aven" in Hos. 10:8. This phrase is probably a figure of speech referring to the pagan sanctuaries at Dan and Bethel, and perhaps others near Samaria. It has been taken as a specific reference to Bethel, called Beth-aven in Hos. 4:15; 5:8; 10:5. By his use of the term, Hosea was calling the high places wicked and implying a comparison with other well-known shrines where idolatry was practiced. W. L. REED

**2.** An element in certain compound names. In the circles opposing the Canaanizing cult, the Canaanite divine names—e.g., El and Baal—were replaced with "Aven." Accordingly, instead of "Bethel," "Beth-aven" was used (Josh. 7:2; 18:12; I Sam. 13:5; etc.). *Biq'ath 'āwen*, "the Valley of Aven" (Amos 1:5), is perhaps another instance; but a number of scholars try to emend the text. A. HALDAR

**3.** KJV translation of a place mentioned only in Ezek. 30:17 (RSV ON). Because the LXX has ἡλίου πόλεως, which is the usual rendering of the Hebrew 'ôn, HELIOPOLIS, the reading 'āwen is generally taken as a pun writing of 'ôn, effected by a change in vocalization only, on the basis of the homonymous noun 'āwen, "idolatry." It may, however, be a simple error in punctuation.            T. O. LAMBDIN

## AVENGER OF BLOOD [גאל הדם, redeemer of

blood]. The kinsman (brother, son; see below) of a slain man who, as his redeemer (see REDEEM), was duty bound to claim back his life from the slayer by killing him. Cf. the LXX rendering, ὁ ἀγχιστεύων τὸ αἷμα (Num. 35:19): "he who performs the kinsman's office with regard to blood."

In societies that lack a strong central authority the defense of private property and life is the task of the kinship group. The kinship group is both a defensive and an offensive unit: all are obliged to defend the right of any member, and all are accountable for the delict of any member. If a person is slain, his kin take vengeance for him upon the slayer, or on one or more of the slayer's kinship group. This in turn may give rise to countervengeance, and a blood feud, terminating at times only with the extinction of a family, is set in motion.

In biblical Israel the sovereignty of the kinship group over matters affecting its private interest was just beginning to be superseded by communal authority. Biblical law still recognizes the kinsman as responsible for prosecuting homicide (Num. 35:19). However, it sanctions retribution only within the bounds of talion ("a life for a life"; Exod. 21:23) and only on the person of the culprit (Deut. 24:16; cf. CRIMES AND PUNISHMENTS §§ A2, D2). Moreover, the law seeks to control the redeemer through the agency of the asylum, which, by giving refuge to the homicide from the hand of the redeemer, makes it possible for the juridical organs of the community to interpose between them. Once the case has come before the public court, the redeemer has no more say in the matter. If the court finds the slayer guilty of murder, the law requires that he be put to death. To be sure, execution is still the prerogative of the kinsman (Deut. 19:12), but he is not free to pardon or accept a monetary composition instead (Num. 35: 31; see CRIMES AND PUNISHMENTS § C2a; CITY OF REFUGE; BLOODGUILT). Though biblical law never replaced the private prosecutor for homicide with a public one, under the monarchy it appears that the king had the power to intervene and grant immunity to a slayer from the avenger (II Sam. 14: 8-11); to this extent, at least, even prosecution of the homicide had come under state control. However, the characterization of this procedure as guilty (vs. 9) shows that the right of blood redemption was yet regarded as so sacred that no abridgment of it could be held guiltless.

The following instances of blood redemption occur: (a) Gideon slays the Midianite killers of his brothers (Judg. 8:18-21). Since the culprits are non-Israelite, this may not reflect normal practice, for (b) Joab's slaying of Abner for killing his brother in combat (II Sam. 3:27, 30) is not considered legitimate (I Kings 2:5), whence it is to be inferred that slaying in combat does not normally privilege blood redemption. (This will account for David's failure to hold Joab guilty for killing Absalom.) (c) The Gibe-

onites secure the death of Saul's sons for his massacre of them (II Sam. 21)—extraordinary for its being a vicarious punishment (on which see CRIMES AND PUNISHMENTS § B2; BLOODGUILT). (d) A scrupulous refraining from vicarious punishment marks Amaziah's execution of his father's assassins (II Kings 14:5-6). (e) Finally, there is the fictitious, but instructive, case of the Tekoite woman (II Sam. 14:6-7), showing that redemption of blood was (paradoxically) carried out within a family as well— an internecine practice that sheds light on the fear of Rebekah in Gen. 27:45.

The kinsman's duty of redeeming blood is not to be confused with the actions of persons in authority undertaken to remove an imputed bloodguilt: e.g., David's execution of Ish-bosheth's assassins (II Sam. 4:11-12), and Solomon's execution of Joab (I Kings 2:31-33; cf. vs. 5 [RSV follows Luc. and OL reading the suffix "my" rather than the less pointed Hebrew "his"]). God's avenging of innocent blood is expressed by נקם, "avenge" (Deut. 32:43; II Kings 9: 7); דרש or בקש, "require, exact vengeance (for)" (Gen. 9:5; Ps. 9:12; Ezek. 33:6), with דם as the object. גאל דם, which refers to the kinsman's duty of redeeming family blood, is never used with God.

*Bibliography.* W. R. Smith, *Religion of the Semites* (1914), Index under "blood-revenge." E. Merz, *Die Blutrache bei den Israeliten* (1916): comprehensive and illuminating, but not always sufficiently discriminating. J. Pedersen, *Israel*, I–II (1926), 378-92. D. Daube, *Studies in Biblical Law* (1947), pp. 123-26. For blood feud in cuneiform law, see G. R. Driver and J. Miles, eds., *The Assyrian Laws* (1935); *The Babylonian Laws*, vol. I (1952), Index under "blood-feud."
           M. GREENBERG

## AVESTA ə věs'tə. The corpus of preachings of

ZARATHUSHTRA and teachings of the Zoroastrian religion, written in a language known as Avestan, which, along with Old Persian, the language of the Achaemenian inscriptions (see PERSIAN, OLD), represents the most ancient known stage of the Iranian language group. The name for the Avesta in Pahlavi (Middle Persian) is 'pst'k (Syriac 'bstg; Arabic 'bstq, 'bst', and other forms)—i.e., *Apastāk* or *Abastāg*—for which the meaning "injunction" (of Zarathushtra) has been suggested. See bibliography.

The Avesta became known to the Western world only at the end of the eighteenth century through the efforts of the Frenchman Anquetil Duperron. After having studied the sacred texts preserved by the Parsi communities in Bombay and other parts of NW India, where immigrant Zoroastrians from Persia settled from the eighth century onward after the collapse of the Sassanian Empire under the impact of the Arab invasion (see PERSIA, HISTORY AND RELIGION OF, § D6) and the conversion of most of the inhabitants of that country to Islam, he published his edition of the *Zend-Avesta* in 1771.

Within the Avesta several groups of writings are to be distinguished: (a) *Yasna*, formulas of prayer and liturgy, part of which is known under the name of *Gāthā* (lit., "chant"), traditionally attributed to Zarathushtra and written in a language slightly different from the rest of the Avesta; (b) *Vispered*, addition to *Yasna* and also containing prayers and formulas; (c) *Yasht*, sacrificial hymns addressed to individual deities; (d) Vidēvdāt (less correctly Vendī-dād), or "law [dāt] against [vi] the demons [dēv]"; (e) Nīrangistān, which deals with matters of ritual; (f) Hadōxt Nask, a fragmentary text on the fate of the soul after death.

There is reason to assume that none of the groups of texts is complete, as a result of the long lapse of time between the date of composition of, e.g., the Gāthā, which presumably contain Zarathushtra's own words (early sixth century B.C.), and the accession of Ardashīr, the founder of the Sassanian Dynasty, at whose initiative the first codification of the Avesta, in all probability, was made (first half of the third century A.D.). In addition, a considerable portion of it became lost in the troubled centuries following the conquest of Iran by the Arab armies. The codified text of the Avesta, written in an especially designed alphabet, was accompanied by the so-called zand, a translation and commentary in Pahlavi. This term was and is sometimes used, wrongly, for the Avestan text itself.

In addition to the pitfalls resulting from the incompleteness of the Avesta in its present form, the interpreter is faced with several other problems. As in some other, similar cases, the Avestan corpus of writings is not homogeneous. The commonly used linguistic distinction between Gāthic, the language of a presumably more ancient character in which the Gāthās are written, and "Younger Avestan," the language of all the rest of the Avesta, has come to be recognized as misleading, since the phonological, morphological, and other differences between the two types of language have to be viewed in local, rather than in chronological, terms. In other words, these two types are not two subsequent phases of one and the same language or dialect, but rather two different languages or dialects which, for that matter, may be even more or less contemporaneous. Whatever the result of further investigation of this question may be, the terms Gāthic and "Younger Avestan" do not apply to the contents of the texts.

If the lifetime of Zarathushtra falls in the second half of the seventh and the first half of the sixth century B.C., the Gāthās, his own preachings, were composed within that period. In the case of the other writings the situation is more complicated. The Yashts may be taken as an example. A considerable amount of the materials they contain clearly date from a time prior to Zarathushtra's lifetime. In both religious beliefs and social institutions these materials show affinity with the Rig-Veda, the collection of sacred texts of ancient India and the oldest known document in Sanskrit (twelfth-tenth centuries B.C.), to such an extent that the assumption of a common origin is clearly indicated. This kind of materials can be safely assigned to the period in which ancient Indians and ancient Iranians still formed one community. In some cases it is even likely that their origin goes back to the even more ancient period of Indo-European linguistic unity. In the hands of the Zoroastrian doctors these Indo-European and Indo-Iranian materials were, of course, covered with a layer of Zoroastrian orthodox theology. They were, in other words, adapted to the accepted beliefs and dogmas of the Zoroastrian priesthood. On another

line of approach, which has to be further pursued, analysis of the contents of the Yashts has resulted in the discovery of internal evidence leading to a tentative chronology of their composition. See bibliography.

The history of the Avesta text offers many obscurities. From both traditional Zoroastrian and non-Zoroastrian evidence it appears that the text went more than once through the process of collection, destruction, and recollection. Tradition holds, e.g., that one of the Arsacid kings (ca. 250 B.C.–A.D. 226; see PERSIA, HISTORY AND RELIGION OF, § D5) ordered the collection of the books surviving at the time. The existence of a written text in Arsacid times seems to receive confirmation from a statement made by Mani, the founder of Manicheism, in the third century A.D. that Zarathushtra "did not write any books, but his disciples after his death remembered [his words] and wrote the books which they read today." Another collection which in this and in the previous case is possibly to be taken as "collection of the oral tradition" took place in Sassanian times, this time in the newly invented, complex script of forty-eight characters of the Vulg. text known today.

*Bibliography.* Edition of most of the extant texts in the original script: K. F. Geldner, *Avesta* (3 vols.; 1886-95). A facsimile of *Yasna, Vispered,* and *Vidēvdāt* is to be found in *Codices Avestici et Pahlavici Universitatis Havniensis,* vols. VII-XII (1937-44), with introductions by K. Barr. For a survey of Avestan literature, see K. F. Geldner, "Awestaliteratur," in *Grundriss der iranischen Altertumskunde,* II (1896-1904), 1-39. A monumental and very complete dictionary of Old Iranian (Avestan and Old Persian) was written by C. Bartholomae; based on this dictionary are H. Reichelt's grammar, *Awestisches Elementarbuch* (1909); and F. Wolff's translation, *Avesta, Die heiligen Bücher der Parsen* (1910; reprinted 1924). For elementary teaching and learning purposes, A. V. W. Jackson, *An Avesta Grammar* (1892); H. Reichelt's *Avesta Reader* (1911), the latter with notes and glossary, are useful. The *Yashts* are translated in H. Lommel, *Die Yäshts des Awesta* (1927); the *Gāthās* in M. W. Smith, *Studies in the Syntax of the Gāthās* (1929); and in J. Duchesne-Guillemin, *Zoroastre, étude critique avec une traduction nouvelle des Gāthā* (1948; English trans. by Mrs. H. Henning, *The Hymns of Zarathustra,* 1952).

The literature on the Avesta is very extensive. In addition to the bibliography under ZARATHUSHTRA, the following recent studies on philological, linguistic, and religious problems connected with the study of the Avesta deserve to be mentioned: A. Christensen, *Études sur le zoroastrisme de la Perse antique* (1928). E. Benveniste and L. Renou, *Vŗtra et Vŗθragna* (1934). E. Benveniste, *Les infinitifs avestiques* (1935). J. Duchesne-Guillemin, *Les composés de l'Avesta* (1936). H. S. Nyberg, *Die Religionen des alten Iran* (1938). G. Morgenstierne, "Orthography and Sound System of the Avesta," *Norsk Tidsskrift for Sprogvidenskap,* XII (1940), 30-82. W. B. Henning, "The Disintegration of the Avestic Studies," *Transactions of the Philological Society* (1942), pp. 40-56. A. Christensen, *Essai sur la démonologie iranienne* (1941); *Le premier chapitre du Vendidad* (1943). H. W. Bailey, *Zoroastrian Problems in the Ninth-Century Books* (1943). P. Thieme, "Vorzarathustrisches bei den Zarathustriern und bei Zarathustra," *ZDMG,* 107 (1957), 67-104.

For further bibliographical references, see also W. B. Henning, *Bibliography of Important Studies on Old Iranian Subjects* (1950).                                    M. J. DRESDEN

**AVIM; AVIMS; AVITES.** KJV forms of AVVIM.

**AVITH** ā'vĭth [עֲוִית, ruin]. The home of Hadad son of Bedad, a king of Edom (Gen. 36:35; I Chr. 1:46).

Hadad apparently became king as a result of his father's defeat of the Midianites in Moab (cf. Abimelech son of Gideon in Judg. 9). A suggested site for Avith is Khirbet el-Jiththeh, between Ma'an and Khirbet el-Bastah.                          V. R. Gold

AVVA ăv'ə [עוה‎ or עוא‎, 'awwā] (II Kings 17:24); KJV AVA ā'və. One of the towns from which colonists were sent to Samaria to replace the Israelite natives deported after the capture of the town in 722 B.C. The other towns mentioned are Babylon, Cuthah, Hamath, and Sepharvaim.                          A. Haldar

AVVIM ăv'ĭm [העוים‎]; AVVITES —ĭts; KJV AVIM ā'vĭm (Josh. 18:23); AVIMS ā'vĭms (Deut. 2:23); AVITES ā'vĭts (Josh. 13:3; II Kings 17:31). 1. An aboriginal people of the Canaanites, who lived in villages near Gaza and were destroyed by the Caphtorim (Philistines; Deut. 2:23; Josh. 13:3).
2. A city of Benjamin, located near Bethel (Josh. 18:23).                          S. Cohen

AWE. See FEAR.

AWL [מרצע‎; ὀπήτιον, diminutive of ὅπεας]; KJV AUL. An instrument mentioned in connection with piercing the ear lobe to mark one who voluntarily

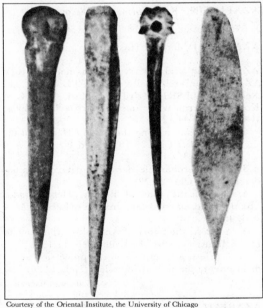

Courtesy of the Oriental Institute, the University of Chicago
118. Bone awls, from Megiddo

took a vow of perpetual slavery (Exod. 21:6; Deut. 15:17). It was an exceedingly common tool beginning with the Stone Age (Upper Paleolithic), and abundant specimens are known from excavations. It might be made of wood, bone, flint, or metal. Fig. AWL 118.
                                       R. W. Funk

AWNING [מכסה‎, from כסה‎, to cover, conceal, spread over] (Ezek. 27:7); KJV THAT WHICH COVERED. Literally, a covering (cf. Lev. 9:19; Isa. 14:11; "clothing" in Isa. 23:18); the parallel with מפרש‎

("that which is spread out," the sail) and נס‎ ("signal," perhaps "ensign") suggests that the reference is to the deck awning to cover the ship's passengers from the sun. The mention of "fine embroidered linen" and of "blue and purple from the coasts [or islands] of Elishah" indicates woven material.

A number of scholars suggest that in Ezek. 27:7, מכסה‎ (mᵉkhassê) should be repointed mikhsê, a word used of the covering of the ark in Gen. 8:13—perhaps a roof over the deck, if not a covering of cloth (see ARK OF NOAH), and of the skins or woven cloth which made up the tent of meeting (cf. Exod. 26:14; 35:11; 36:19; etc.). See TABERNACLE.       E. M. Good

AXE [חצב‎, גרזן‎, ברזל‎ (see below), כשיל‎, מגרה‎, מגזרה‎, קרדם‎, מעצד‎; ἀξίνη]; KJV AX. A hafted cutting tool, used (a) for work in both wood and stone (quarrying, tunneling, tomb preparation) and (b) as a weapon; characterized by the parallel arrangement of cutting

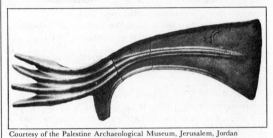

Courtesy of the Palestine Archaeological Museum, Jerusalem, Jordan
119. Bronze axe head, shaped like extended fingers of a hand, from Beth-shan, Stratum VII (thirteenth century B.C.)

edge and handle. Formally the axe is to be distinguished from the adze (cutting edge at right angles to the handle); MATTOCK (the head consists of a combination axe and adze); pick mattock (combination pick and mattock); pickaxe (combination pick and axe); hoe (see MATTOCK; an adze in form but used to work the ground); and HATCHET (the differentiation in this case is only in size and weight). The axe was one of the earliest tools invented by man, the head being made of bone, ivory, flint, or stone before the advent of metal. Figs. AXE 119-20.

The form and function of the axe and related implements cannot always be determined by reference to Hebrew and Greek terms found in the Bible and must, therefore, be conjectured from the context. The most common use of the axe was in cutting wood. The function of the מגזרה‎ of II Sam. 12:31 (=the מגרה‎ of I Chr. 20:3) is not clear.

חרב‎, "sword," is translated by "axe" in Ezek. 26:9, but neither the Hebrew word nor its Greek counterpart, μάχαιρα, ever means "axe."

The גרזן‎ of I Kings 6:7 was a tool used for working stone (the stone for the temple was prepared at the quarry to avoid the sound of hammer or axe or any tool of iron in the temple precinct). The same word is used three times in the Siloam Inscription (see SILOAM) of axes used to hew a tunnel out of rock from Gihon to the Pool of Siloam (cf. II Kings 20:20; II Chr. 32:30). It is probably safe to infer that the גרזן‎ in these instances was a mattock or pickaxe.

The מעצד‎ of Jer. 10:3 was a carpenter's hand tool,

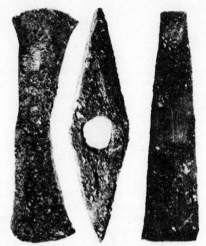

Courtesy of the Oriental Institute, the University of Chicago

120. Bronze axe heads from Megiddo, Late Middle Bronze I (*ca.* 1800-1750 B.C.); Stratum XIII

probably in the form of an adze, used to smooth and work wood; a number of good specimens were found at Gezer.

The use of the axe as a weapon in the Bible may be inferred from Judg. 9:48, where Abimelech and his men cut brushwood to burn the stronghold of Shechem. It is probable that these axes served the double purpose of tool and weapon, since it is unlikely that an extra set of axes was carried solely for the purpose of cutting brush. For the axe as an implement of destruction and hence a weapon of war, cf. Ps. 74:5; Jer. 46:22. Also cf. Jer. 51:20 (*see* HAMMER); Ezek. 9:1-2.

The difficulty of binding the head securely to the handle is illustrated by the law on manslaughter (Deut. 19:5) and the story of Elisha's recovery of the axe head from the water (II Kings 6:5).

**Bibliography.** W. M. F. Petrie, *Tools and Weapons* (1917), chs. 1-3, plates I-XVIII (copious illustrations of known types); K. Galling, "Axt," "Beilhacke," "Hacke," "Dächsel" (for a definition of types), *Biblisches Reallexikon* (1937); H. H. Cozhlan, "The Evolution of the Axe from Prehistoric to Roman Times," *Journal of the Royal Anthropological Institute,* LXXIII (1943), 27-56; C. Singer *et al.,* eds., *A History of Technology* (1954), ch. 22 *passim.*      R. W. FUNK

**AXLE.** *See* WHEEL.

**'AYELETH HASHAHAR.** *See* MUSIC.

**AYYAH** ä'yə [עַיָּה, 'ayyâ] (I Chr. 7:28); KJV GAZA gā'zə [עַזָּה]. One of the towns which were the possession of Ephraim. For the KJV "Gaza" there is evidence in a number of Hebrew MSS. In any case, however, this could not be the Philistine city of Gaza. The context and similarity of names suggest a connection with AI; several scholars have proposed as the location of Ayyah ancient Ai (et-Tell) or Khirbet Haiyan, less than one mile from Ai. Although archaeological evidence is lacking, it is probable that the reference in Neh. 11:31 to Aija (עַיָּה, 'ayyâ) is to be understood as "Ayyah" or "Ai" (cf. Ezra 2:28).

**Bibliography.** W. F. Albright, "Ai and Beth-Aven," *AASOR,* IV (1922-23), 141-49.      W. L. REED

**AZAEL** ā'zĭ əl ['Αζάηλος (B), Αζαηλ (A), Εσριηλ (Luc.)]; KJV AZAELUS ăz'ĭ ē'ləs in 1 *below.* **1.** An Israelite who put away his foreign wife and children (I Esd. 9:34). The name is omitted in the parallel Ezra 10:41.

**2.** KJV Apoc. form of ASAHEL 4.

C. T. FRITSCH

**AZAL** ā'żəl. KJV translation of אָצַל in Zech. 14:5. It was formerly considered an unidentified city. Now, after Symm., the word is generally read אֶצְלוֹ and translated "the side of it." Even then the verse is obscure.

**AZALIAH** ăz'ə lī'ə [אֲצַלְיָהוּ, Yahu has set apart; *perhaps related to* אֲצִילִי, chief men (Exod. 24:11), *and* Arab. *'asula,* to be distinguished]. The father of Shaphan, Josiah's secretary, who figured prominently in the publication of the celebrated Book of the Law (II Kings 22:3).      J. M. WARD

**AZANIAH** ăz'ə nī'ə [אֲזַנְיָה, Yahu has heard] (Neh. 10:9). A Levite; the father of Jeshua, a witness to the covenant.

**AZAPHION.** KJV form of Hassophereth. *See* SOPHERETH.

**AZARA.** KJV form of HASRAH 2.

**AZAREL** ăz'ə rĕl [עֲזַרְאֵל, God has helped]; KJV AZAREEL ăz'ə rēl usually; AZARAEL ăz'ə rā'əl in Neh. 12:36; ESRIL ĕz'rĭl in I Esd. 9:34. **1.** A Korahite warrior who came over to David at Ziklag (I Chr. 12:6—H 12:7).

**2.** A musician among the sons of Heman at the time of David (I Chr. 25:18); called Uzziel in vs. 4 (cf. Azariah = Uzziah).

**3.** Son of Jeroham; leader of the tribe of Dan under David (I Chr. 27:22).

**4.** One of the sons of Binnui (Hebrew adds "Bani") who married foreign wives (Ezra 10:41; I Esd. 9:34).

**5.** A priest; the father of Amashsai, who came to live in Jerusalem after the Exile (Neh. 11:13).

**6.** A priest; a trumpeter in the procession at the dedication of the wall of Jerusalem (Neh. 12:36).

F. T. SCHUMACHER

**AZARIAH** ăz'ə rī'ə [עֲזַרְיָה, עֲזַרְיָהוּ, Yahu has helped]. KJV Apoc. AZARIAS —əs; EZERIAS ĕz'—; AZIEI ə zī'yī. **1.** Alternate (probably personal) name of UZZIAH (3), king of Judah (II Kings 14:21; 15:1, 6-8, 17, 23, 27; I Chr. 3:12).

**2.** Son of Nathan; in charge of the officers over the twelve districts of the kingdom of Solomon (I Kings 4:5), probably responsible for ensuring their prompt delivery of provisions for the royal establishment; brother of Zabud. Scholars disagree as to whether he is the son of Nathan the prophet (II Sam. 12) or is Solomon's nephew (II Sam. 5:14).

**3.** The prophet who encouraged Asa, king of Judah, to undertake a religious reform (II Chr. 15:

1-8). He was the son of Oded, to whom the MT attributes the prophecy in vs. 8 (cf. II Chr. 28:9).

**4.** Son(s) of Jehoshaphat, king of Judah (II Chr. 21:2), who were slain when their elder brother, Jehoram, succeeded their father. The name appears twice in the list of six sons. This is probably an error resulting from the two alternative forms (*see* 1 *above*). It seems far-fetched to suppose that the name was used twice because the boys were only half brothers or because one had already died in infancy.

**5.** A high official under Solomon; son of Zadok and presumably brother of Ahimaaz (I Kings 4:2). The text is ambiguous: "the priest" could identify Zadok (KJV) or state the position of Azariah (RSV).

**6.** High priest under Uzziah (II Chr. 26:17, 20). He was the leader of the priests who opposed the king's exercise of the priestly office.

**7.** High priest under Hezekiah (II Chr. 31:10, 13) who, with the king, prepared storerooms in the temple for the contributions of the people. He was of the house of Zadok and was "chief officer of the house of God" (vs. 13; cf. I Chr. 9:11; Neh. 11:11; Jer. 20:1). It is conceivable, but not likely, that he is the same as 6 *above*.

**8.** A priest included in the list of those who lived in Jerusalem after the Exile; son of Hilkiah; probably also described as "chief officer of the house of God" (I Chr. 9:11). However, this list is parallel to one in Neh. 11:11, where this name is Seraiah, probably the more correct reading.

**9.** A name included three times in the Chronicler's list of high priests (I Chr. 6:4-15—H 5:30-41); they are probably to be identified with several of the priests above, but there is little general agreement as to the exact identifications. The references are to:

*a*) Son of Ahimaaz and grandson of Zadok (I Chr. 6:9—H 5:35). The parenthetical note of 6:10 is usually taken to be out of place and inapplicable here. Many therefore equate him with 5 *above*, despite the ambiguities.

*b*) Son of Johanan and grandson of *a* in I Chr. 6:10—H 5:36; Ezra 7:3; II Esd. 1:2. Posterior to Solomon, he can be related to 6 *above* or, by the parenthetical note, to 5 *above*.

*c*) Son of Hilkiah and father of Seraiah (I Chr. 6:13-14—H 5:39-40; Ezra 7:1; I Esd. 8:1; II Esd. 1:1), about two generations before the Exile. Some relate him to 7 *above*, who seems too early; others to 8 *above*, who seems a little late.

**10.** An ancestor of Heman the musician among the Kohathite Levites (I Chr. 6:36—H 6:21). His son was Joel. He is called Uzziah in I Chr. 6:24—H 6:9.

**11.** The father of a Kohathite Levite named Joel in the time of Hezekiah (II Chr. 29:12). Despite the duplication of names, he is probably not to be identified with 10 *above*.

**12.** A man of Judah; son of Ethan; listed in the genealogy of the sons of Zerah (I Chr. 2:8).

**13.** A man of Judah; son of Jehu and grandson of Obed; listed in the genealogy of the sons of Jerahmeel (I Chr. 2:38-39).

**14.** A Judahite army officer; son of Obed. He took an active part in the conspiracy to overthrow Athaliah and make Joash king (II Chr. 23:1). He is not to be identified with 13 *above*.

**15.** An officer who conspired to overthrow Athaliah; son of Jeroham (II Chr. 23:1). The name is probably not a mistaken repetition of 14 *above*, since they have different fathers.

**16.** A chieftain of Ephraim; son of Johanan; among those who persuaded the army of Pekah to release captives (II Chr. 28:12).

**17.** Son of Jehallelel; a Merarite Levite in the time of Hezekiah (II Chr. 29:12).

**18.** Son of Hoshaiah; one of the opponents of the prophet Jeremiah in Jer. 42:1 (according to the LXX); 43:2. The Hebrew in 42:1 has "Jezaniah."

**19.** A priest who put away his foreign wife in the time of Ezra (I Esd. 9:21; called Uzziah in the parallel list, Ezra 10:21).

**20.** A man who supported Ezra while reading the Law (I Esd. 9:43; missing in the parallel, Neh. 8:4).

**21.** A Levite (or an order) who instructed the people in their understanding of the Law in the time of Ezra (Neh. 8:7=I Esd. 9:48); the name is omitted in B, ℵ, A of the Greek.

**22.** A priest included among those who set their seal to the covenant in the time of Nehemiah (Neh. 10:2—H 10:3).

**23.** A man of Jerusalem who repaired the wall beside his house; son of Maaseiah (Neh. 3:23-24).

**24.** A leader or group in the postexilic period; listed among those who returned with Zerubbabel (Neh. 7:7). In the parallel list he is replaced by Seraiah (Ezra 2:2; cf. Neh. 12:1).

**25.** A prince or priest of Judah, included among those who marched at the dedication of the rebuilt wall of Jerusalem (Neh. 12:33).

**26.** The original name, in Hebrew, of Abednego (*see* SHADRACH), one of the companions of Daniel (Dan. 1:6-7, 11, 19; 2:17; I Macc. 2:59; Song Thr. Ch. 1:2, 66).

**27.** An officer in the army of Judas Maccabeus (I Macc. 5:18, 56, 60). He shared command during the absence of Judas and was badly defeated by Gorgias.

**28.** MT error for AHAZIAH 2 in II Chr. 22:6 KJV.

F. T. SCHUMACHER

**AZARIAS** ăz′ə rī′əs [’Αζαρίας]. **1.** The name used by the disguised angel Raphael (Tob. 5:12; 6:6, 13; 7:8; 9:2).

**2.** KJV Apoc. form of AZARIAH.

F. T. SCHUMACHER

**AZARU** ăz′ə roo [ἄζουρος (A), ἄζαρος (B); Vulg. *Azoroc*]; KJV AZURAN ăzh′ə răn. Ancestor of some who returned from the Exile (I Esd. 5:15; cf. Azzur in Neh. 10:17-18). J. C. SWAIM

**AZAZ** ā′zăz [עָזָז] (I Chr. 5:8). The father of Bela in the genealogy of Reuben.

**AZAZEL** ə zā′zəl, ăz′ə zəl [עֲזָאזֵל] (Lev. 16:8, 10, 26). The scapegoat dispatched on the Day of Atonement is described as being consigned "to/for Azazel." There are three principal interpretations of this term:

*a*) It characterizes the animal itself, and stands for עֵז אֹזֵל, "goat that departs"—i.e., (e)scape-goat. This is the view of the LXX (vss. 8, 10: τράγος ἀποπομπαῖος [cf. Pollux 5.26; Suidas]; vs. 26: τράγος διεστάλμενος εἰς ἄφεσιν), Symm. (τράγος ἀπερχόμενος), and the Vulg. (*hircus emissarius*). A variation of it connects the word rather with Arabic '*azāla,* "banish, remove," though the formation would then be unusual.

*b*) It denotes the place to which the animal was dispatched. This is the view of most of the rabbinic exegetes (cf. Saadya's rendering, *jubl 'azaz,* "a rugged cliff"). Some have sought to support it by connecting the name with Arabic '*azza* in the sense of "be rugged," and thus identifying it with the Beth Ḥiddudo, "sharp place," named in M. Yom. 6.8 and Targ. Ps. Jon. on Lev. 16:21 as the destination of the scapegoat. This, in turn, is the Dudael "in the desert" to which Azazel is consigned in Enoch 10:4.

*c*) It is the name of a demon inhabiting the desert. This view is adopted by most modern commentators, and is anticipated in Enoch, where Azazel appears as a ringleader of the rebel angels, who seduces mankind. Against it, however, stands the fact (strangely overlooked) that in no other culture are scapegoats offered to demons. Indeed, in view of the very fact that sin and impurity are unloaded upon them, they can be (and are) used only as vehicles of elimination, but not of propitiation.

*See also* SACRIFICE AND OFFERINGS; EXPIATION; ATONEMENT, DAY OF. T. H. GASTER

**AZAZIAH** ăz'ə zī'ə [עֲזַזְיָהוּ, Yahu is strong, *or* Yahu strengthens]. **1.** A Levitical musician in David's provision for the Jerusalem temple (I Chr. 15:21).

**2.** The father of Hoshea, the Ephraimite commander under David (I Chr. 27:20).

**3.** An officer of third rank in the temple during Hezekiah's time (II Chr. 31:13). J. M. WARD

**AZBAZARETH** ăz băz'ə rĕth. KJV translation of Ἀσβασαρέθ in I Esd. 5:69. The parallel passage, Ezra 4:2, indicates that ESARHADDON is meant (so RSV). J. C. SWAIM

**AZBUK** ăz'bŭk [עַזְבּוּק] (Neh. 3:16). The father of a certain Nehemiah who took part in rebuilding the wall of Jerusalem after the Exile.

**AZEKAH** ə zē'kə [עֲזֵקָה, hoed ground(?)]. A fortress city to the S of the Valley of Aijalon, dominating the passage into the Valley of Elah (*see* ELAH, VALLEY OF). It is identified with Tell ez-Zakariyeh, *ca.* nine miles N of Beit Jibrin (Eleutheropolis) and fifteen miles NW of Hebron.* Ruins of the wall and towers can be seen on the small plateau on the top of the

Courtesy of Herbert G. May

121. Azekah (Tell ez-Zakariyeh)

tell. To the E of the tell is Khirbet el-'Alami, which may be the site of Azekah during the Byzantine period. Fig. AZE 121.

Azekah was one of the points to which Joshua's forces chased remnants of the Canaanite coalition led by Adonizedek of Jerusalem after raising the Canaanite siege of Gibeon (Josh. 10:10-11). It was a city in the Shephelah district of Judah (15:35). It is noted as a location point in describing the battle lines of the Philistines in the engagement which was won by Israel after David's slaying of the Philistine champion, Goliath (I Sam. 17:1).

It was one of those cities whose fortifications were strengthened by Rehoboam (*ca.* 922-915) after the revolt of the N kingdom, and possibly after Shishak's invasion (*ca.* 918 B.C.; see II Chr. 11:9). The citadel was a heavily fortified enclosure on the highest point of the hill on which Azekah was built.

It was one of the last of Judah's fortified cities to fall to Nebuchadnezzar's forces before the attack on Jerusalem (*ca.* 588 B.C.; Jer. 34:7). In the fourth of the letters found at LACHISH, Hoshaiah, the commander of the garrison to the N of Lachish, tells his commanding officer, Yoash, whose headquarters are in Lachish, that he can no longer see the (fire or smoke) signals from Azekah, which lay to the N of his outpost, implying that Azekah had probably fallen to the invader and now only Lachish, and Jerusalem, remained to be captured by the Babylonians.

After the Exile, Azekah was reoccupied by Jewish returnees (Neh. 11:30). V. R. GOLD

**AZEL** ā'zəl [אָצֵל]. Son of Eleasah, and one of the descendants of Jonathan son of Saul. He was the father of six sons (I Chr. 8:37-38; 9:43-44).

**AZEM.** KJV form of EZEM.

**AZEPHURITH.** KJV Apoc. form of JORAH.

**AZETAS** ə zē'təs ['Αζητάς] (I Esd. 5:15). An ancestor of some who returned from the Exile with Zerubbabel. The name is omitted in the parallels Ezra 2:16; Neh. 7:21. C. T. FRITSCH

**AZGAD** ăz'găd [עַזְגָּד, *a theophorous name with* Gad, *the god of fortune:* Gad is strong]. The head of one of the families that returned to Palestine after the Exile (Ezra 2:12; Neh. 7:17; I Esd. 5:13). Johanan son of Hakkatan and 110 other male members of this family returned with Ezra (Ezra 8:12; I Esd. 8:38). Azgad appears as one of those who signed Ezra's covenant (Neh. 10:15—H 10:16). M. NEWMAN

**AZIAS.** KJV Apoc. form of UZZA.

**AZIEI.** KJV Apoc. form of AZARIAH.

**AZIEL** ā'zĭ əl [עֲזִיאֵל] (I Chr. 15:20). A minor Levite, among the harp players when the ark was brought to Jerusalem. His full name was JAAZIEL.

**AZIZA** ə zī'zə [עֲזִיזָא, the strong one] (Ezra 10:27). Alternately: ZERDAIAH zər dā'yə [Ζερδαιας] (I

Esd. 9:28); KJV SARDEUS sär dē'əs. One of those forced to put away their foreign wives in the time of Ezra.

**AZMAVETH** ăz'mə věth [עזמות]; BETH-AZMA-VETH běth—[בית עזמות] (Neh. 7:28). **1.** A member of the company of military heroes of David known as the "Thirty." He came from Bahurim (II Sam. 23:31; I Chr. 11:33).

**2.** The father of Jeziel and Pelet, two of the ambidextrous slingers and archers from the tribe of Benjamin who joined the outlaw band of David at Ziklag (I Chr. 12:3). He may plausibly be identified with 1 *above*.

**3.** Son of Jehoaddah; one of the descendants of the family of Saul (I Chr. 8:36; 9:42).

**4.** Son of Adiel. He was in charge of the royal treasuries under David in Jerusalem (I Chr. 27:25).

E. R. DALGLISH

**5.** A town identified with modern Hizmeh, five miles N-NE of Jerusalem, from the region of Geba. Forty-two men of Azmaveth came back from Babylon with Zerubbabel (Ezra 2:24). Singers from there participated in the dedication of the wall of Jerusalem (Neh. 12:29).      O. R. SELLERS

**AZMON** ăz'mən [עצמון]. A place on the S border of Judah, the last town to the W before the river of Egypt (Wadi el-'Arish; Num. 34:4-5; Josh. 15:4). It is possibly the same as EZEM. A location at 'Ain el-Qoseimeh near the ancient Kadesh-barnea, a place where prehistoric relics have been discovered, has been suggested.      S. COHEN

**AZNOTH-TABOR** ăz'nŏth tā'bər [אזנות תבור] (Josh. 19:34). A point on the S border of Naphtali. It is perhaps located at Umm Jebeil, near Mount Tabor.

**AZOR** ā'zôr ['Αζώρ]. An ancestor of Jesus (Matt. 1:13-14; also Luke 3:23 ff in MS D).

**AZOTUS.** Apoc. and NT form of ASHDOD.

**AZRIEL** ăz'rĭ əl [עזריאל, God is my help]. **1.** One of the chieftains or heads of families in the half-tribe of Manasseh (I Chr. 5:24).

**2.** The father of Jeremoth, who was head of Naphtali under David (I Chr. 27:19).

**3.** The father of Seraiah at the time of Jehoiakim (Jer. 36:26).      F. T. SCHUMACHER

**AZRIKAM** ăz'rə kăm [עזריקם, my help has arisen]. **1.** Son of Azel; a descendant of Saul and Jonathan in the genealogy of Benjamin (I Chr. 8:38; 9:44).

**2.** "Commander of the palace" under King Ahaz; slain in battle by Zichri, an Ephraimite warrior (II Chr. 28:7); possibly the same as 1 *above*.

**3.** Grandfather of Shemaiah, a Merarite Levite dwelling in Jerusalem (I Chr. 9:14; Neh. 11:15).

**4.** Son of Neariah; a postexilic descendant of David through Zerubbabel (I Chr. 3:23).

F. T. SCHUMACHER

**AZUBAH** ə zōō'bə [עזובה, forsaken, abandoned (*but later* bought, received?)]. **1.** The mother of Jehoshaphat; daughter of Shilhi (I Kings 22:42; II Chr. 20:31).

**2.** Wife of Caleb; mother of Jesher, Shobab, and Ardon (I Chr. 2:18-19).

**AZUR.** KJV form of AZZUR 1-2.

**AZURAN.** KJV form of AZARU.

**AZZAH.** KJV alternate form of GAZA.

**AZZAN** ăz'ən [עזן, (the deity) has shown strength] (Num. 34:26). The father of the Issacharite leader Paltiel, who was selected to help superintend the distribution of W Jordanian Canaan among the tribes to occupy that territory.

*Bibliography.* M. Noth, *Die israelitischen Personennamen* (1928), pp. 38, 190.      R. F. JOHNSON

**AZZUR** ăz'ər [עזור; עזר *in 2 below,* helped(?)]; KJV AZUR ā'zər in 1-2. **1.** The father of Hananiah, a false prophet from Gibeon (Jer. 28:1).

**2.** The father of Jaazaniah, an acquaintance of Ezekiel (Ezek. 11:1).

**3.** A "chief of the people"; one of those who set their seal to the covenant (Neh. 10:17—H 10:18).

F. T. SCHUMACHER

**B.** A symbol used to designate the biblical MS
Vaticanus.

**BAAL** bā′əl, bāl [בַּעַל, owner *or* lord]. **1.** The fourth
son of Jeiel, a Gibeonite ancestor of Saul (I Chr. 8:
30 = 9:36).
**2.** The father of Beerah, a Reubenite chieftain
who was exiled by the Assyrians (I Chr. 5:5).
**3.** A scribal error for Baalath-beer in I Chr. 4:33.

*__BAAL (DEITY)__ [בַּעַל, master]. The god Hadad, the
fertility-god par excellence of Canaan.

The term בַּעַל (*báʻal*), applied to men as well as to
gods, signifies ownership and may denote locality—
e.g., Baal-peor (Num. 25:3, 5; Deut. 4:3), Baal-
hermon (Judg. 3:3), etc., or sphere of interest—e.g.,
Baal-berith, the "god of the covenant" (Judg. 8:33;
9:4). Thus any local god might be so designated—
e.g., Dagon is termed the *báʻal* of a devotee who set
up a stele to him at Ras Shamra; this fact qualifies
the statement of one scholar that *báʻal* does not indicate sovereignty over a person, but simply implies
possession of a locality or attribute. Generally, however, a deity was entitled Baal only when he and his
worshipers had taken possession of and settled in a
given locality.

From the end of the third millennium probably,
and certainly by the middle of the second millennium, the title was applied specifically to the Amorite
god of winter rain and storm, whose name, known
from texts from Mesopotamian and Ras Shamra, was
Hadad (*see* Hadadrimmon). In support of the view
that a god was termed Baal only after his worshipers
had settled to sedentary life, it may be noted that in
Egyptian execration texts published by G. Posener
(date *ca.* 1800 B.C.) relating to Amorite chiefs, the
plurality of whom in certain localities in Syria and
Palestine probably indicates a tribal stage of social
and political development, the god Hadad, often
named in theophorics, is never termed Baal.

The Ras Shamra Texts, in redactions, certain—
and probably all—of which date from the Late
Bronze Age (*ca.* 1400 B.C.), contain a large complex
of myths pertaining to Baal, who was the most active
deity in the fertility cult of Canaan, though his activity was limited to nature; El, the senior god of the
Canaanite pantheon, was supreme in the social or
moral sphere.

Herein the contention is that in these Baal myths
there are really two separate complexes, the myth of
Baal and the Waters and that of Baal and Mot
("death, sterility"); this view is not generally held.
In his conflict with the Waters, Baal champions the
gods against the insults and tyranny of the unruly
waters, Sea-and-River, and after a grim struggle
overcomes him, disperses him (distributing the waters
so that they are a good servant rather than a bad
master), and is himself acclaimed "king"—his kingdom being an everlasting kingdom. This was apparently the Canaanite declaration of faith in Providence in nature, at once an assurance of faith and a
means of influencing the course of nature by an
articulate word and possibly an accompanying ritual
with the force of sympathetic magic.

The main motifs of this myth are reproduced in
the OT, notably in such psalms as assert or imply
the kingship of God—e.g., Pss. 9; 29; 46; 88; 93;
96–98—and in passages in the Prophets on the theme
of the kingship of God. The conception of the "day
of the Lord," implying as it does conflict and victory
over the powers of Chaos (e.g., Isa. 2), is also a development of the old Canaanite theme of Baal's conflict and victory over the waters and his assumption
of kingship. In addition to the correspondence between such Hebrew passages and the Canaanite
mythology in general features, there is occasionally
a striking correspondence in details and imagery—
e.g., Pss. 29; 93—Yahweh being depicted with the
attributes of Canaan. In this matter the influence of
Canaan on Israel seems to have been at its strongest, with Israel appropriating, though adapting,
Canaanite thought as well as external forms and
imagery. The theme continued to be developed
throughout the history of Hebrew literature in the
Prophets and in apocalyptic, both Jewish (e.g., Dan.
7:7 ff) and Christian (e.g., Rev. 12). Apparently
this Canaanite matter influenced Hebrew thought
through the Hebrew adoption of the myth together
with appropriate seasonal ritual, which was deemed
by the Hebrew settlers as necessary as the new techniques of local agriculture. Jewish tradition and the
passage Zech. 14:16-19 associate the kingship of
God with the autumnal New Year (Feast of Tabernacles) on the eve of the "early rains," and it was
probably this that was the occasion to which the
myth of Baal's victory over the Waters was proper.

Baal's character as the storm-god is expressed at
Ras Shamra in a sculptured stele of the god as a
helmeted warrior in a short kilt, striding into action
with a thunderbolt as spear and a mace uplifted. His
power of fertility is expressed by his association with
the bull as his cult animal, horns of which he wears
on his helmet.* His stock epithet is "he who mounteth
the clouds" (*rkb bʻrpt*); cf. Yahweh as him "who
maketh the clouds [his] chariot" (Deut. 33:26; Pss.
68:4—H 68:5; 104:3). The wavy line beneath the feet
of the god possibly represents the waters in the
clouds, or the mountaintops; cf. Yahweh,
"who treads on the heights of the earth" (Amos 4:
13; Mic. 1:3). These essential features of Baal are

reproduced in the round in bronze figurines from Ras Shamra and its vicinity and from Megiddo and Lachish (Tell ed-Duweir) in Palestine, indicating the distribution of the cult of the god. Fig. UGA 6.

Baal was one of the Semitic deities whose cult penetrated to Egypt, possibly with the great numbers of Semites deported from Syria and Palestine in the Eighteenth and Nineteenth Dynasties. The Pharaoh Ramses II seems himself to have affected Syrian cults. The most notable cult center of Baal in Egypt was Baal Saphon near Pelusium, E of the Delta; this name reflects the proper domain of the god—Mount Sapon, modern Jebel el-Aqra, Mount Kasios of the Greek geographers, on the N horizon of Ras Shamra, which was a kind of Canaanite Olympus and the seat of Baal.

The bulk of the remainder of the Baal mythology at Ras Shamra concerns Baal's conflict with Mot, the power of drought and sterility; and here Baal is a dying and rising god, the spirit of vegetation which wilts and dies in the heat of summer but revives again with the winter rains; local variations of Baal in this character were TAMMUZ and ADONIS. There are certain indications that the texts in question are related to the seasonal ritual of the Syrian peasant. One long text, e.g., concerns the building of a house for Baal, the completion of which coincides with the rain, thunder, and lightning, which is a feature of the "early rains" of autumn and winter inaugurated by the Hebrew Feast of Tabernacles, of which the "house" of Baal is believed to have been the prototype. Again, after Baal has succumbed to Mot, this sinister god suffers the vengeance of the goddess Anat, the sister of Baal; she cuts him with a blade, winnows him with a shovel, parches him with fire, and grinds him in a millstone and scatters him in a field. Here obviously rites of desacralization of the first or last sheaf of corn underlie the myth—such a rite, in fact, as is described in Lev. 2:14, which refers to the offering of the first sheaf, "crushed new grain from fresh ears, parched with fire." Baal eventually revives, and with his revival there is the prospect of the heavens raining oil and the wadis running with honey, and finally "after seven years" he engages Mot in a great struggle and overcomes him. Here seven years, as regularly in Semitic folklore, may indicate an indefinite lapse of time, but the reference may be to the seven-year cycle of agriculture terminated among the Hebrews by a sabbatical year. The belief seemed to be that in all the vicissitudes of local agriculture, with the menace of drought, locusts, and the like, if a few years of plenty were experienced, disaster was overdue. It was wise, therefore, to anticipate this by allowing the power of sterility full scope, either in a year of artificial famine when the land was allowed to lie fallow, or in combat with Baal, the power of fertility, in order that the sinister forces might thereby be exhausted.

Certain features of the myth suggest rites indicated in the OT. On the death of Baal, e.g., his sister "the virgin Anat" ranges the mountains searching for him and makes the hills resound with her mourning. This suggests the mourning for Hadadrimmon mentioned in Zech. 12:11, or the weeping for Tammuz by the women of Jerusalem (Ezek. 8:14), and prob-

ably the mourning of the virgins of Israel traditionally associated with Jephthah's daughter (Judg. 11: 37-40). The theme of the vicissitudes of Baal as a dying and rising god, however, was not assimilated to Hebrew thought as was that of Baal's victory over Chaos, but the imagery of the myth of Baal and Mot was freely drawn upon in Hebrew poetry.

From the references in the book of Judges to repeated lapses to the cult of Baalim and Ashtaroth, we may infer that in the early days of the settlement the Hebrews tended to assimilate the Baal cult without adapting it, and at various crises in Hebrew history—e.g., under Ahab and Jezebel (I Kings 16:32)—there was a recrudescence of Baal-worship in its native form in Israel. The prophets, especially Hosea (ch. 2), inveigh against this materialistic nature cult and the licentious rites by which it was practiced as rites of imitative magic; and, though Hezekiah and Josiah suppressed it (II Kings 18:4; 23), it is mentioned as the cult of Tammuz in the early days of the Exile (Ezek. 8:14) and in the Persian period (Zech. 12:11).

*Bibliography.* W. R. Smith, *The Religion of the Semites* (1927); E. Dhorme, "Le dieu parent et le dieu maître," *RHR*, CV (1932), 229-44; O. Eissfeldt, *Baal Zaphon, Zeus Kasios, und der Durchzug der Israeliten durchs Rote Meer* (1932); G. Posener, *Princes et pays d'Asie et de Nubie, Textes hiératiques sur des figurines d'envoûtement du Moyen Empire* (1940); R. Dussaud, *Les découvertes de Ras Shamra (Ugarit) et l'AT* (1941), pp. 97-103; C. H. Gordon, *Ugaritic Literature* (1949), pp. 9-56; A. S. Kapelrud, *Baal in the Ras Shamra Texts* (1952); G. R. Driver, *Canaanite Myths and Legends* (1956), pp. 10-21 (introduction to Baal mythology), 70-120 (text and translation of Baal myths); J. Gray, "The Hebrew Conception of the Kingship of God: Its Origin and Development," *Vetus Testamentum*, VI (1956), 268-85; *The Legacy of Canaan* (1957), pp. 120-23. E. O. James, *The Ancient Gods* (1960), pp. 87-90.     J. GRAY

**BAALAH** bā'ə lə [בַּעֲלָה, wife, lady]. **1.** An earlier name of Kiriath-jearim (Josh. 15:9; I Chr. 13:6).

**2.** A mountain on Judah's N border (Josh. 15:11); probably the hill of Mughar, just N of the Valley of Sorek (*see* SOREK, VALLEY OF), and *ca.* five miles NW of Khirbet el-Muqanna (EKRON).

**3.** A village in the Shephelah district of Judah; formerly a part of Simeon (Josh. 15:29; see 19:3, where "Balah" is to be read "Baalah"; I Chr. 4:29, where "Bilhah" is to be read "Baalah" [*cf.* LXX Βαλαά]). The village is to be identified with Tulul el-Medhbah, near Khirbet el-Meshash, probably.
    V. R. GOLD

**BAALATH** bā'ə lăth [בַּעֲלָת, mistress]. A town included in the original territorial allotment of Dan. It is listed between Gibbethon and Jehud (Josh. 19: 44-45) and in company with Gezer and Lower Bethhoron as one of the cities which Solomon fortified (I Kings 9:17-18; II Chr. 8:5-6). Though its exact site is unknown, Josephus (Antiq. VIII.vi.1) places it near Gezer.     W. H. MORTON

**BAALATH-BEER** bā'ə lăth bē'ər, bĭr [בַּעֲלַת בְּאֵר, lady of the well]. A city of Simeon, apparently the shrine of a Canaanite goddess. In Josh. 19:8 it is identified with Ramah of the Negeb (*see* RAMAH 5), and by some it has been identified with the BEALOTH of Josh. 15:24. The reading "Baal" (בעל) in the parallel passage in I Chr. 4:33 is a scribal error.

The site is unknown.     S. COHEN

**BAALBEK** bāl'bĕk. A Lebanese town in the Beqa'a near the source of Nahr el-'Aṣi (Orontes). Fig. LEB 21.

The Semitic name Baalbek probably contains an allusion to the deity worshiped there, Baal of the Beqa'a. The Greek name was Heliopolis, "city of the sun," which came to be used in the Seleucid period, since Baal was identified with the sun-god. In the fourth or fifth century the ancient name was introduced again. At that time the importance of the town had receded because of the wars between the Romans and the Sassanid princes. Therefore, the prospering which began during the reign of Augustus prevailed for two or three centuries.

Today Baalbek is famous because of its temple ruins. The most ancient temple was originally built for the cult of the West Semitic storm-god Hadad. Later it was dedicated to the cult of the sun-god and

afterward to Jupiter.* Macrobius, in his *Saturnalia,* explicitly says that the sun-god was identical with Jupiter. The ancient Phoenician sky-god Baalshamen also merged with Jupiter. Another important temple was that dedicated to Dionysus;* and finally there was a third important temple, the so-called round temple. The emperors Antoninus Pius (138-61) and Caracalla (211-17) were the most important builders, and in the reign of the latter the temples of Baalbek were generously completed, perhaps because his mother was a Syrian lady. Other deities worshiped at Baalbek were Venus and Mercurius. Together with Jupiter, these two formed a triad: the chief deity, the mother-goddess, and the young god. Figs. BAA 1; JUP 33; BAA 2.

In 637, Baalbek was captured by the Arabs, and it was devastated by the Mongols in 1401. Furthermore, the town has suffered from a number of earthquakes. In spite of this, there are valuable remains left, and in the years 1900-1904 Baalbek was excavated by German expeditions. Fig. BAA 3.

*Bibliography.* E. Weigand, "Baalbek und Rom," *Jahrbuch des Kais. Archäologischen Instituts,* vol. 29 (1914); E. Weigand, "Baalbek, Datierung und kunstgeschichtliche Stellung seiner Bauten," *Jahrbuch für Kunstwissenschaft* (1924-25); O. Eissfeldt, *Tempel und Kulte syrischer Städte in hellenistisch-römischer Zeit* (1941); R. Dussaud, "Temples et cultes de la triade héliopoli-

Courtesy of Pan American World Airways System

1. Six remaining columns of the temple of Jupiter at Baalbek, with the temple of Bacchus (Dionysus) beyond it

Courtesy of the Arab Information Center, New York

2. Temple of Dionysus (Bacchus) at Baalbek, with its many gigantic columns

From *Atlas of the Bible* (Thomas Nelson & Sons Limited)

3. View of the Great Court of the Altar or Parthenon of the acropolis at Baalbek

taine à Baalbek," *Syria*, vol. 23 (1942-43); P. Collart and P. Coupel, "L'autel monumental de Baalbek," *Bibliothèque Archéologique et Historique*, vol. 52 (1951); M. I. Aluf, *History of Baalbek* (21st ed., 1953).       A. HALDAR

**BAAL-BERITH** bāl bĭr'ĭth [בעל ברית, lord of covenant]. A god whose shrine, according to Judg. 9:4, was at Shechem, and whose cult, according to a comment in the narrative of Gideon and its sequel (8:33), became popular in Israel together with the worship of the local manifestations of the Canaanite fertility-god Baal after the death of Gideon.

In the case of the cult of Baal-berith this probably applied only to the Israelites in the vicinity of Shechem, rather than to all Israelite elements in Palestine. Shechem was one of the strong cities of Palestine, with which the Israelites reckoned rather by agreement than by force of arms, and the sanctuary of a covenant-god here probably reflects these conditions. Because of lack of evidence the actual identity of the god must be a matter of speculation. The term "Baal" in the name Baal-berith need not necessarily signify the Canaanite fertility-god Hadad, for it is a neutral term which may, in fact, be used of men as well as of gods, signifying locality, sphere of interest, or a particular feature or attribute. In Judg. 9:46 the temple at Shechem is referred to as that of El-berith, "covenant-god," though the substitution of "El" for "Baal" here may be due to scribal orthodoxy. The association of the cult of Baal-berith with that of local Baals in Judg. 8:33, on the other hand, and the location of an actual shrine in Shechem imply that the god was of long standing in the land, so that we have probably to visualize him as the local manifestation of the Canaanite Baal, in whose temple an agreement had been made and was regularly ratified between the Israelites and the people of Shechem, the god thus becoming secondarily for the Shechemites and primarily for the Israelites the "covenant-lord." W. F. Albright conjectures that the covenant here refers to an Amorite confederacy.

*Bibliography.* H. H. Rowley, *From Joseph to Joshua* (1950), pp. 125-28; W. F. Albright, *Archaeology and the Religion of Israel* (1953), p. 113.       J. GRAY

**BAALE** bā'ə lĭ [בעלי, Baals (*or* lords) of]. KJV translation in II Sam. 6:2; the RSV combines with "Judah": BAALE-JUDAH. *See* KIRIATH-JEARIM.

**BAALE-JUDAH** bā'ə lĭ joŏ'də [בעלי יהודה, Baals (*or* lords) of Judah] (II Sam. 6:2); KJV BAALE OF JUDAH. The same city as KIRIATH-JEARIM (I Chr. 13:6).

**BAAL-GAD** bāl găd' [בעל־גד, Baal of good fortune(?)]. A town near Mount Hermon marking the N limits of the conquest of Joshua (Josh. 11:17; 12:7; 13:5). It was situated in the valley between Mount Lebanon on the W and Mount Hermon on the E. The exact site is unknown, although modern Hasbeya has been suggested as a possible location.

*Bibliography.* F.-M. Abel, *Géographie de la Palestine*, II (1938), 258-59.       G. W. VAN BEEK

**BAAL-HAMON** bāl hā'mən [בעל המון, Lord of abundance *or* of wealth]. A place where there was an especially fruitful vineyard of Solomon (Song of S.

8:11). The site is unknown; emended readings and suggested locations have not proved to be well founded. It is possible that the name is a locale of poetic imagination, created to convey the position of the "possessor of wealth."

*Bibliography.* R. Gordis, *The Song of Songs* (1954), p. 98.       W. H. MORTON

**BAAL-HANAN** bāl hā'nən [בעל־חנן, Baal is gracious]. 1. A king in Edom before the Israelite monarchy; son of Achbor. He succeeded Shaul, who came from the Euphrates, and was succeeded by Hadad (Gen. 36:38-39 = I Chr. 1:49-50).

2. A Gederite official under David; he was in charge of olive and sycamore trees in the Shephelah (I Chr. 27:28).       F. T. SCHUMACHER

**BAAL-HAZOR** bāl hā'zôr [בעל חצור, Baal of Hazor]. Possibly the mountain home of Absalom, near the town of Ephraim, the scene of a festival to which Absalom invited the other sons of David and where Amnon was slain by the servants of Absalom at Absalom's instigation (II Sam. 13:23).

This place is not to be confused with the Hazor N of the Sea of Galilee. Hazor, listed in Neh. 11:33, is sometimes identified with Baal-hazor. The probable location is Jebel 'Asur, *ca.* six miles NE of Bethel. One of the Dead Sea Scrolls, the so-called Genesis Apocryphon, names Ramath-hazor as the place where the Lord appeared to Abram after his separation from Lot (Gen. 13:14). A late tradition, it suggests that another name for Baal-hazor was Ramath-hazor and that Absalom's mountain home may have been the site of an ancient Canaanite-Hebrew sanctuary.       W. L. REED

**BAAL-HERMON** bāl hûr'mən [בעל חרמון, lord of Hermon]. A city of the Hivites on the border of Manasseh, which was untouched by the Israelite conquest (Judg. 3:3; I Chr. 5:23). It must have lain on the N border of Israel close to Mount Hermon. Tristram and Wetzstein suggest a place on top of the mountain; others think it is another name for BAAL-GAD.       S. COHEN

**BAALI** bā'ə lĭ [בעלי, my lord, *or* my husband]. A title by which Hosea (2:16) depicts God as rejecting in favor of Ishi ("my husband"), thereby asserting the social, covenantal relationship between Israel and her God and rejecting all implications that God is for Israel what Baal was for the Canaanites, simply the power of Providence in nature.

*Bibliography.* W. R. Harper, *Commentary on Hosea*, ICC (1936), p. 234. For further bibliography, *see* BAAL (DEITY).       J. GRAY

**BAALIM** bā'ə lĭm [בעלים, Baals *or* lords]. Plural of Baal, possibly a plural of majesty, but probably various local manifestations of BAAL (DEITY).

**BAALIS** bā'ə lĭs [בעלים]. A king of the Ammonites. He sent Ishmael to murder Gedaliah soon after the destruction of Jerusalem (Jer. 40:14—G 47:14). He probably hoped by this means to take over some of the devastated territory of Judah.

      F. T. SCHUMACHER

**BAAL-MEON** bāl mē'ŏn [בעל מעון, *apparently* lord of habitation]. A town in N Moab, also called Beth-baal-meon, Beth-meon, and Beon (probably). It was assigned to the tribe of Reuben (Num. 32:3, 38; Josh. 13:17; I Chr. 5:8). *Ca.* 830 B.C. it was in Moabite possession, since Mesha "built Baal-meon, making a reservoir in it" (MOABITE STONE, line 9), and also built "Medeba, Beth-diblathen, and Beth-baal-meon" (line 30). Ostracon 27 from Samaria speaks of "Baala the Baalmeonite" (בעלא בעלמעני), showing Israelite possession *ca.* 772 B.C., if this is the same Baal-meon. Later it was once more in Moabite hands (Jer. 48:23; Ezek. 25:9).

The site has been identified with Ma'in, a large mound *ca.* four miles S of Medeba. No evidence of occupation from the OT period has been found, but the heavy subsequent occupation may well have destroyed it. E. D. GROHMAN

**BAAL-PEOR** bāl pē'ôr [בעל פעור, Baal of Peor]. Alternately: BAAL OF PEOR. The god of Mount Peor (*see* PEOR 1-2). While Israel was encamped at SHITTIM, the people entered into illicit relations with the Moabite women. Israel "yoked themselves to Baal of Peor" and indulged in licentious worship rites. In punishment, Israel was smitten with a plague. The Midianites were also involved in leading Israel astray. Cf. Num. 25:1-9; Deut. 4:3; Ps. 106:28; Hos. 9:10.

*See also* BETH-PEOR; BAAL (DEITY).

E. D. GROHMAN

**BAAL-PERAZIM** bāl pĭ rā'zĭm [בעל פרצים, Baal (lord) of breaking through (popular etymology)]; MOUNT PERAZIM [הת פרצים] (Isa. 28:21). A place near the Valley of Rephaim where David defeated the Philistines shortly after his being anointed king of Israel (II Sam. 5:20 ff; I Chr. 14:11 ff). In Isaiah's warning to Jerusalem, it is placed in parallelism with the Valley of Gibeon (Isa. 28:21). Probably it is modern Sheikh Bedr, on Ras en-Nadir, NW of Jerusalem, above Lifta (Nephtoah). V. R. GOLD

**BAALSAMUS** bāl sā'mэs [Βαάλσαμος]; KJV BALASAMUS bэ lăs'э mэs. Apoc. name of MAASEIAH 18.

**BAAL-SHALISHAH** bāl shăl'э shэ [בעל שלשה] (II Kings 4:42); KJV BAAL-SHALISHA. A city or region, the home of the man who came to Elisha at Gilgal bringing twenty loaves of barley and fresh ears of grain. This reference and the Talmudic statement (Sanh. 12*a*) that fruits ripened earlier there than elsewhere in Palestine may indicate that the place was in a fertile section of the country. Some scholars identify the site with SHALISHAH. The village of Kefr Thilth, SW of Shechem, preserves the name Shalishah and is a possible, though not certain, location.

W. L. REED

**BAAL-TAMAR** bāl tā'mэr [בעל תמר, lord of the palm] (Judg. 20:33). A place near Gibeah of Benjamin, where the Israelites assembled to fight in their last and successful assault upon the city. The site has not been identified; it may not have been a city at all, but a prominent landmark. S. COHEN

**BAAL-ZEBUB** bāl zē'bŭb [בעל זבוב]. A god of the Philistine city of Ekron, to whom King Ahaziah of Israel (*ca.* 845 B.C.) sent to inquire whether he would live after falling from an upper chamber (II Kings 1:2-18).

The Hebrew word זבוב (*zebūb*) means "fly," and the name is accordingly rendered "Baal of flies" by the LXX and Josephus (Antiq. IX.ii.1). Modern scholars have interpreted this as referring to a god who drove away infectious pests, and have compared the Greek Zeus Apomyios—i.e., "Averter-of-flies"—mentioned by Pausanias (V.14.2; cf. Clement of Alexandria *Protr.* II.38.4), and the demon Myagros, "Fly-driver," worshiped at Aliphera in Arcadia (Pausanias VIII.26.7). But (*a*) it is difficult to see why a god who averted pestilence should have been appealed to in the case of a fall; and (*b*) the Greek deities in question were not in fact averters of pests in general, but were simply propitiated before sacrifice, in accordance with a not uncommon practice (cf. Aelian *De natura animalium* II.8; V.17; Antiphanes III.134 Meineke) as a means of placating the flies who swarmed around the altar. If, therefore, the name is indeed to be associated with זבוב, it is more probable that Baal-zebub was a god who gave oracles by the flight or buzzing of a fly. A modern Scottish parallel, from the holy well at Kirkmichael, Banffshire, is adduced by R. A. S. Macalister (*see* bibliography), and others may be found in the *Handwörterbuch des deutschen Aberglaubens*. It is, however, equally possible that "Baal-zebub" is a deliberate, pejorative distortion of the god's true name. It has been suggested that this was the Zebul Baal ("Lord Baal") of the Ras Shamra Texts, but "Zebub" might more probably conceal a Philistine word. In short, the problem of identification must at present be left open.

*See also* BEELZEBUL.

*Bibliography.* R. A. S. Macalister, *The Philistines* (1914), pp. 91-93. T. H. GASTER

**BAAL-ZEPHON** bāl zē'fŏn [בעל צפן, בעל צפון; LXX Βεελσεπφων, Βεελσεφων]. A station of the Exodus in NE Egypt.

The exact location of Baal-zephon is unknown. Because neither Pihahiroth nor Migdol, with which Baal-zephon is mentioned (Exod. 14:2, 9), can be identified with certainty, only a general location in NE Egypt can be suggested. Eissfeldt identifies the site with that of Greco-Roman Casium ( = Kasion), which, following Clédat and Abel, should be placed at Ras Kasrun, *ca.* twenty-five miles E of Mohammediyeh. Albright argues, however, that because Kasion as a town does not appear before Hellenistic-Roman times and is furthermore in a location inappropriate to the nautical significance of the divinity Baal-zephon and to the best commercial interests, the site of Baal-zephon is more likely to be sought in N Egypt proper, on the Mediterranean or a reasonably deep body of water off it.

The divinity Baal-zephon, after whom the village was named, is becoming increasingly well known, as a result of modern research. The name is Northwest Semitic and means Lord of the North, although a more local association with Casius Mons, just N of Ugarit, called *Ṣpn* in North Canaanite, is suggested.

The earliest references to Baal-zephon occur in Ugaritic literature, where he is mentioned both in sacrificial lists and in the Keret Epic; it is in the latter that he is associated with a sacred bark and with the mythical *ḥol* bird (phoenix). An Egyptian source (Papyrus Sallier IV, *ca.* 1270-1250 B.C.) numbers him with the Semitic deities Qudshu and Baaltis, and in the curse formula of a treaty between Esarhaddon and Baal of Tyre (*ca.* 675 B.C.) he is listed with Baal-shamêm and Baal-malagê. The same formula affords us positive information on the god's role as a sea- and storm-god. A Phoenician papyrus letter from the sixth century tells us, further, that Baal-zephon was closely associated with the Egyptian port TAHPANHES. Eissfeldt has ably demonstrated the identity of Baal-zephon and Zeus Casius.

*Bibliography.* O. Eissfeldt, *Baal Zaphon, Zeus Kasios und der Durchzug der Israeliten durchs Meer* (1932); F.-M. Abel, "Les confins de la Palestine et de l'Egypte sous les Ptolémées," *RB,* 49 (1940), 232-33; W. F. Albright, "Baal-Zephon," *Festschrift Albert Bertholet* (1950). T. O. LAMBDIN

**BAANA** bā'ɔ nɔ [בַּעֲנָא]; KJV BAANAH in I Kings 4:16. **1.** Son of Ahilud; one of the twelve commissariat prefects of Solomon. His district was Taanach and Megiddo (probably his headquarters) as far as beyond Jokmeam, and all Beth-shean below Jezreel, from Beth-shean to Abel-meholah, which is near Zarethan (I Kings 4:12, corrected text of Albright). **2.** Son of Hushai; one of the twelve commissariat prefects of Solomon. His district was Asher and Bealoth (I Kings 4:16). **3.** The father of Zadok, who participated in the rebuilding of the walls of Jerusalem in the time of Nehemiah (Neh. 3:4); perhaps the same as BAANAH 4.

*Bibliography.* W. F. Albright, "The Administrative Divisions of Israel and Judah," *JPOS,* V (1925), 26 ff; F.-M. Abel, *Géographie de la Palestine,* II (1933), 80 ff; J. A. Montgomery and H. S. Gehman, *The Books of Kings,* ICC (1951), pp. 120 ff. E. R. DALGLISH

**BAANAH** bā'ɔ nɔ [בַּעֲנָה]. **1.** One of the sons of Rimmon, a Benjaminite from Beeroth. With his brother Rechab he shared in the regicide of Ish-bosheth (II Sam. 4:2-12). This violent deed appears to have been a frantic effort on the part of these two captains of Ish-bosheth to ensure the success of the plans of the deceased Abner for a united kingdom under David, by the elimination of its most dangerous opponent. Baanah and Rechab gained access to the royal chamber by eluding the dozing portress and slew Ish-bosheth as he was taking a siesta. Fleeing to the Judean court with the head of the monarch in their hands, they informed David of their accomplishment; but what seemed to them a most commendable political service was to David unmitigated murder. He ordered their summary execution and hanged their severed hands and feet beside the pool of Hebron as a public example. **2.** A Netophathite; the father of Heled (preferable to Heleb—II Sam. 23:29), who was a member of the "Thirty" (II Sam. 23:29; I Chr. 11:30). **3.** One of the Babylonian exiles who returned to Judah accompanying (KJV) or, more likely, sharing the leadership with (RSV) Zerubbabel (Ezra 2:2; Neh. 7:7; cf. I Esd. 5:8, where they are called "leaders").

**4.** One of those who set their seals to the covenant made in the time of Nehemiah (Neh. 10:27). He may perhaps be identified with BAANA 3.

**5.** KJV form of BAANA 2. E. R. DALGLISH

**BAANIAS.** KJV Apoc. form of BENAIAH.

**BAARA** bā'ɔ rɔ [בַּעֲרָא, *possibly hypocoristic for* Baal has seen] (I Chr. 8:8). Apparently a wife of Shaharaim, a Benjaminite. The text is corrupt.

*Bibliography.* E. L. Curtis, *Chronicles,* ICC (1910), pp. 159-60; M. Noth, *Die israelitischen Personennamen* (1928), pp. 40, 119. B. T. DAHLBERG

**BAASEIAH** bā'ɔ sē'yɔ [בַּעֲשֵׂיָה] (I Chr. 6:40—H 6:25). A Levite of the family of Kohathites; ancestor of Asaph the musician. The name is probably to be read with several MSS "MAASEIAH" (מַעֲשֵׂיָה).

**BAASHA** bā'ɔ shɔ [בַּעְשָׁא]. King of Israel *ca.* 900-877 B.C.; successor of Nadab whom he murdered.

The name is perhaps a contraction of בַּעַלְשִׁמַע, "Baal hears." The first part of the name is בַּעַל; the second has been shortened and now appears as a hypocoristicon. Or "Baasha" may be a contraction from בַּעַלְשֶׁמֶשׁ, "The sun is Baal."

Baasha was a son of Ahijah and came from the tribe of Issachar (I Kings 15:27). He reigned for twenty-four years at Tirzah (vs. 33). This is the first occasion on which Tirzah is actually mentioned as the new capital of the N. That a change had been made from Shechem has been hinted at previously (14:17; 15:21). Tirzah continued as the capital city until Omri became king. It has now been identified almost certainly with the modern Tell el-Far'ah, nearly seven miles NE of Nablus. It had previously been a Canaanite royal city (Josh. 12:24), and was renowned for its beauty (Song of S. 6:4).

Baasha came to the throne as the result of a military revolt against King Nadab, whom he murdered while the Israelites were besieging Gibbethon (I Kings 15:27-28). The revolt was a clear indication of the unsettled conditions prevailing in the N and showed that the concept of charismatic leadership was still strong.

In the summary of his reign (I Kings 16:5) mention is made of "his might." Apart, however, from the incident recorded in connection with the fortifying of Ramah (15:17), no other details are given (*see* ASA). When Baasha attempted to fortify Ramah (the modern er-Ram), some five miles N of Jerusalem, Asa king of Judah reacted by buying the support of Ben-hadad king of Syria. Syrian raids into N Israel forced Baasha to withdraw (vss. 17-21). That this border warfare continued against Asa king of Judah throughout Baasha's reign is certain (vs. 16).

In I Kings 16:1-7 appears a prophetic denunciation of Baasha and his house for their sin and disobedience by Jehu the son of Hanani. The concluding phrase: "and also because he destroyed it," is difficult. The later writer apparently saw the murder of Nadab, with the end of Jeroboam's house, as a mistake.

*Bibliography.* W. F. Albright, "The Site of Tirzah," *JPOS* (1931), pp. 241 ff; F.-M. Abel, *Géographie de la Palestine,* II (1938), 485. H. B. MACLEAN

**BABEL** bā'bəl [בָּבֶל]. The Hebrew form of the name BABYLON. In Gen. 11:1-9 it is told that mankind after the Flood came to the plain of SHINAR. There, to set themselves a lasting monument and to have a common purpose to unite them and prevent their scattering all over the earth, they decided to build a city and a tower that would reach to heaven. God, however, mixed up their language so that they no longer understood one another, and they had to disperse. The city and the tower were therefore—in a play on the Hebrew word *bālāl*, "to mix"—called Babel.

The story, as we have it, has such clear reference to Babylon that the tower which plays a central role in it can hardly be but the great ziggurat or stage tower of the Marduk temple in Babylon, Etemenanki, which consisted of six square stages one on top of the other, the last one crowned by a small chapel for the god. The ground plan of this tower was recovered by Koldewey in his excavations in Babylon, and an important cuneiform text which gives the measurements of the temple and its parts furnishes valuable evidence for a reconstruction. In addition we have a description of the tower as it looked in Hellenistic times, given by Herodotus. All questions about how the tower looked are, however, not solved. Various, in part quite different, reconstructions have been proposed (Fig. BAB 4), and

Courtesy of the Oriental Institute, the University of Chicago

4. Model of the ziggurat of Babylon (Tower of Babel), after Unger

discussion of the questions involved has given rise to a considerable literature (*see bibliography*). The story in Genesis would seem to have been inspired by the tower at a period when that great monument was in ruins between two rebuildings.

*Bibliography.* F. Wetzel and F. H. Weissbach, *Das Hauptheiligtum des Marduk,* Wissenschaftliche Veröffentlichungen der Deutschen Morgenländischen Gesellschaft, vol. 59 (1938).
T. JACOBSEN

**BABI** bā'bī. KJV form of BEBAI.

**BABOON** [תֻּכִּיִּים] (I Kings 10:22 RSV mg.). *See* PEACOCK.

**BABYLON (OT)** băb'ə lən [בָּבֶל; Assyrian-Babylonian *Bâb-il(im); Βαβυλών*]. An ancient capital city of Mesopotamia (modern Iraq). Its ruins are situated on a branch of the Euphrates near the modern town of Hilla, SW of Baghdad.

1. Excavations
2. History
3. Topography
4. Fortifications
5. Palaces and Ishtar Gate
6. Private houses
7. Marduk temple
8. The bridge
9. Reputation of Babylon
Bibliography

**1. Excavations.** The site of Babylon was visited by not a few early travelers and archaeological explorers, but no reliable and comprehensive picture of the city and its remains was obtained until systematic excavations at the site were undertaken by the Deutsche Orient Gesellschaft under the direction of Robert Koldewey from 1899 to 1918. Later work has been done on the site by Heinrich Lenzen. Because of the vast extent of the ruins, only selected areas could be investigated; and since the high water table makes penetration in depth difficult, the excavations have of a necessity concentrated on the later phases of the city, particularly on the remains of Neo-Babylonian and later times.

**2. History.** Since strata of the third millennium and earlier date could not be reached, the beginnings of Babylon as a city are not known. The earliest mention of it dates to the Akkad period (*ca.* 2500 B.C.) and occurs in a date formula of King Shar-kali-sharri which commemorates the construction of temples to the goddess Anunitum and the god Aba in KÁ-DINGIR[ki]. Because of the ambiguities of the older cuneiform writing, it is not possible to decide with certainty whether this writing renders the Sumerian name of the city (Ka-dingirak) or its Akkadian name (Bab-ilim). Both names mean "the gate of the god." The first certain occurrence of the name Bab-ilim is in texts of the period of the Third Dynasty of Ur—*ca.* twenty-second–twenty-first centuries—(e.g., YOS IV, no. 66: *ki ensik Bab-ilim-ma* [ki]*-ta,* "from the governor of Bab-ilim"). As shown by this and other references, Babylon served at the time of the Third Dynasty of Ur as provincial capital and seat of a governor. During the following Isin-Larsa period it became the capital of a small independent kingdom under a dynasty of Western (Amorite) descent, the founder of which was a certain Sumu-abum. Under Hammurabi, the best-known king of the dynasty, Babylon extended its sway over most of S Mesopotamia; but already under Hammurabi's son Samsu-iluna the S part of the kingdom was lost to the kings of the Sea-land. The end of the dynasty came shortly after 1600 B.C. with a Hittite raid on Babylon. In the following Cassite and Middle Babylonian periods Babylon maintained its position as capital of S Mesopotamia. It was captured and partially destroyed by the Assyrian ruler Tukulti-Ninurta I (1235-1198 B.C.), but was vigorous enough to recover from its misfortune. When the Assyrians under Tiglath-pileser III (746-727) and Sargon II (722-705) subdued S Mesopotamia, Babylon became a center of resistance, so that eventually Sennacherib (705-681) in 689 saw no other alternative than to completely destroy the city. Sennacherib's son Esarhaddon, however, rebuilt the city; and when after Esarhaddon's death Ashurbanipal became king of Assyria, his brother Shamashshumukin served as regent of Babylon. A rebellion by Shamashshumukin led to a severe siege of Babylon, and when in 648 the Assyrians took the city, Shamashshumukin burned himself to death in his palace. In 608 B.C. the Assyrian Empire fell, and Babylon, which had been a prime mover, entered upon its most glorious period as capital of the Neo-Babylonian Empire. Under Nabopolassar and Nebuchadrezzar II (605-562) a vast program of public building and fortification was carried out. When the Neo-Babylonian Empire fell to the Persians, Babylon opened its gates to Cyrus in 539 B.C. without opposition. The city maintained its dominant position under the Persian rulers; and when the Persian Empire in its turn fell to Alexander the Great, Babylon again offered no resistance, but received the conqueror with open arms. It was a logical choice for capital of Alexander's new empire; but when Alexander's successor Seleucus I (Nicator) founded Seleucia on the Tigris a short distance away, Babylon found the new city a dangerous rival. Little by little the inhabitants of Babylon moved to Seleucia and Babylon itself became deserted, so that at the beginning of the Christian era only a small group of astronomers and mathematicians still continued to live in the ancient city.

**3. Topography.** Neo-Babylonian Babylon formed a slightly squeezed rectangle, with the long side oriented NE-SW, and covered an area of approximately a thousand acres. The Euphrates River entered this rectangle at the middle of its N side and left it again at a point a little to the W of the middle of the S side. The area E of the river constituted the older part of the city, with the royal palace and the

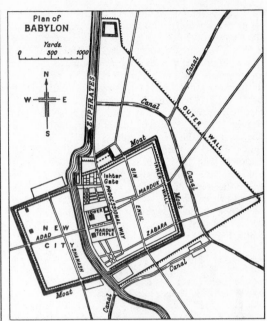

Courtesy of Edward Arnold (Publishers) Ltd., London

5. Plan of Babylon, *ca.* 600 B.C. (after Unger)

main temples; the area W of the river was younger and was known as the "new" city. Fig. BAB 5.

**4. Fortifications.** Two imposing walls enclosed the rectangle; the innermost of these, called Imgur-Enlil, measured *ca.* twenty-one feet in width, the

Courtesy of the Oriental Institute, the University of Chicago

6. Reproduction of the Ishtar Gate, from the time of Nebuchadnezzar

outermost, Nemetti-Enlil, *ca.* eleven feet. Outside the latter ran a water-filled defensive ditch. The walls were constructed of sun-baked bricks and had projected towers at *ca.* sixty–sixty-five–feet intervals. Access to the city was through ramps across the ditch and gates in the double walls. The best known of these gates, the Ishtar Gate,* was located in the E half of the N side of the rectangle. The system of fortification was further strengthened by Nebuchadnezzar II by the construction of a new double wall farther out in the terrain to the S and the E in order that "arrows of battle" should not be able to reach the inner wall. The outer wall of the new system was built of baked bricks and was *ca.* twenty-five feet wide; the width of the inner wall, which was of sun-baked bricks, was *ca.* twenty-three feet. For further security a system of artificial lakes and flooded areas was established to the N and the E outside these walls. Figs. BAB 6-7.

8. Babel, one of the mounds of the city of Babylon, probably the site of a palace of Nebuchadnezzar

7. City of Babylon, showing the Tower of Babel (from a painting by Maurice Bardin of the reconstruction by Unger)

9. The Ishtar Gate at Babylon (from a painting by Maurice Bardin, after the reconstruction by Unger)

**5. Palaces and Ishtar Gate.** A visitor to Babylon, arriving from the N, would, before approaching the Ishtar Gate, have passed Nebuchadnezzar's outer fortification line and a palace just inside them, called the "Summer Palace," on the bank of the Euphrates. The mound covering this palace still preserves the name of the city in the form "Babil." * Proceeding toward the city, the visitor would, just before he reached the Ishtar Gate and the inner fortifications, have passed a second large palace outside the walls to his right and a similar structure, interpreted as an "armed camp," to his left. The walls of these buildings facing the street were decorated with processions of lions in colored relief made of enameled bricks.* Approaching the Ishtar Gate, the visitor saw an arched entry *ca.* fifteen feet wide and perhaps thirty feet high, flanked on each side by a massive square tower.* The towers and the gate were faced with lapis-lazuli blue tiles and decorated with rows of bulls and dragons in colored relief.* Entering the Ishtar Gate, one crossed a broad gate room, in the W section of which was a dais for a divine statue or emblem; on leaving, one passed through the outer wall, Nemetti-Enlil, and faced a second larger gate leading through Imgur-Enlil. This gate was also flanked by lapis-lazuli blue towers, but these towers were higher, more massive, and without reliefs. Behind them stretched a long rectangular gate room, *ca.* one hundred feet deep, through which the visitor would finally emerge on the processional street Aibur-shabu, which led in a straight line S through the city. Standing at this point and looking toward the center of the city, the visitor would have immediately to his left a temple for the goddess Ninmakh, one of many such major temples within the city; immediately to his right he would see the largest of

Courtesy of the Oriental Institute, the University of Chicago

10. Eastern towers of Ishtar Gate, showing reliefs of animals

the palaces he had so far passed, the main palace of the city. This palace consisted of three major units, each with one or more central square courts surrounded by rooms. The first such unit, the one nearest the street, contained the official reception suite of the king, with the throne room, a broad hall on the S side of a large court and accessible from it through three doors. In the long wall of the room opposite the middle and main doorway was a niche before which the throne and dais of the king were located. A section of this part of the palace with unusually solid and heavy walls has been interpreted as the foundations for the famous "Hanging Gardens" of Babylon, said to have been constructed to please a queen who longed for the mountainous scenery of her homeland in the E mountains. Continuing westward, one entered a unit of the palace which has been interpreted as the living quarters of the king, and still farther W there was a last unit interpreted as the harem, the part of the palace which accommodated the royal family. W of this, on the bank of the Euphrates, lay a massive bastion protecting the palace against attack across the river. Figs. BAB 8; LIO 31; BAB 9-10.

**6. Private houses.** Moving on from the Ishtar Gate past the palace and continuing southward through the town along Aibur-shabu, the visitor would pass on his left a section of private houses which has been excavated. It shows relatively straight, somewhat narrow streets crossing one another at right angles. The houses varied in size from some 60 by 60 feet to as much as 130 by 130 feet and had from eight to twenty-six rooms grouped around one or more courts. These houses were generally one story high; and their walls toward the street, unbroken by windows, showed only a door opening. The roofs were flat. At street crossings large square daises with divine statues or emblems frequently stood.

**7. Marduk temple.** Continuing along Aibur-shabu, one reached on the right the pilastered walls of the complex Etemenanki with the ziggurat (temple tower) of Babylon (*see* BABEL, TOWER OF). The complex consisted essentially of a large, open square surrounded by building units interpreted as storehouses. Once along the E side, toward Aibur-shabu, and four times along the S side of the complex, the outer wall of the belt of storehouses formed a broad and deep recess, at the bottom of which stood a gate into the central open square. At the S side of this square the temple tower of Babylon was situated (Figs. BAB 4; 7). Turning right at the corner of Etemenanki on Aibur-shabu and following a street leading down to the river, the visitor would have on his right the S façade of the Etemenanki complex, while on his left, back from the street, stood the Marduk temple Esagila. The main gate to this temple was in its E wall. It led into a large, rectangular forecourt surrounded by rooms as yet unexcavated. To the left of this court was a smaller subsidiary court, also rectangular and surrounded by rooms and also unexcavated. A gate at the far, W end of the forecourt opened into the main unit of the temple. Through a gate room one entered a square court with double rows of rooms on the N and S sides. Opposite the entrance a monumental gate led into the antecella, and from there one passed into the cella proper, known as Ekua. The cella was rectangular in shape, entered through a door in the middle of the long side opposite which the dais with Marduk's image was placed. In the wall behind the dais was an ornamental niche. The decoration of the cella was lavish in the extreme. The roof beams were covered with gold and silver; the walls were covered with gold; and the colossal seated statue of Marduk on the dais was, according to Herodotus, fashioned of gold, as were also the throne on which it sat, the dais which carried the throne, and an offering table which stood before it. Altogether Herodotus estimates that some eight hundred talents of precious metal went into the furnishings.

**8. The bridge.** The street which ran from Aibur-shabu between Esagila and Etemenanki down to the river led to a bridge which connected the E and W parts of the city. The bridge was excavated by Koldewey and found to have rested on six boat-shaped pillars of baked bricks laid in bitumen. According to Herodotus, the covering of the bridge consisted of wooden planks which were taken up every evening so that the inhabitants of one part of the city could not cross over by night and steal from those of the other part.

**9. Reputation of Babylon.** Archaeological and contemporary written records fully confirm Babylon's reputation as a great and wealthy city of lavish splendor. They contain little which would allow a judgment of whether its reputation for moral laxity is equally well founded. All large cities tend to be vulnerable to moral judgment, as seen by the ease with which the epithet "Babylon" can be applied to them; and it may be remembered that the biblical tradition is of a necessity a hostile tradition, since neither religious conviction nor the harsh treatment of the Jews by the Babylonian rulers could endear the city to the biblical writers. The passage which has damaged the city's memory most severely: "Mystery, Babylon the great, the mother of harlots and abominations of the earth" (Rev. 17:5), refers undoubtedly, not to Babylon at all, but to Rome.

*Bibliography.* See the various final excavation reports published in *Wissenschaftliche Veröffentlichungen der Deutschen Orient Gesellschaft.* See also: R. Koldewey, *Das wieder erstehende Babylon* (1925); E. Unger, *Babylon, die heilige Stadt* (1931); O. E. Ravn, *Herodots Beskrivelse af Babylon* (1939).

T. JACOBSEN

**BABYLON (NT)** [Βαβυλών]. **1.** The E city and kingdom into which the people of Israel and Judah had been taken captive. The memory of this captivity among early Christians kept alive two themes common to the exilic prophets: (*a*) The captivity was God's punishment upon his people for their sins of idolatry and disobedience (e.g., Jer. 25:8-11; Acts 7:43, adapted from Amos 5:27); (*b*) Babylon the haughty empire would itself be destroyed by God (Jer. 25:12-14; Isa. 13; 14; 47; 48) and his people redeemed from their exile. Babylon, in retrospect, represented both the place and the time of this exile, a pivotal epoch in Israel's history, second in importance only to the captivity in Egypt. In the Matthaean genealogy, for example, the generations are divided: Abraham, David, Babylon, Christ. The movement from King David to slavery is reversed by the movement from slavery to the son of David (Matt. 1:1-17).

**2.** The contemporary realm which, as the realm of the devil, contains all blasphemies and idolatries. The ancient Babylon is here understood as the archetypal head of all entrenched worldly resistance to God. Babylon is an agelong reality including idolatrous kingdoms as diverse as Sodom, Gomorrah, Egypt, Tyre, Nineveh, and Rome. She is a harlot, riding the beast, ruling many kingdoms, corrupting kings, drunk with the blood of saints and martyrs (Rev. 17; 18). Babylon, the mother of all harlots, is the great source and reservoir of enmity to God, as well as the objectified product of the "one mind" which gives power and authority to false gods. As such, she is the antithesis of the virgin bride of Christ, the holy city, the new Jerusalem, the kingdom of God. Yet, although she was the fountainhead of all earthly rebellion against God, Babylon was also God's tool in punishing Israel (Jer. 25:8-11). Her power over God's people was granted by God himself (Rev. 17:17).

This demonic kingdom is, however, subject to great and final desolation. Drawing from OT pictures of the fate of the city, the prophet depicts the utter destruction of this "haunt of every foul spirit" (Rev. 18). All the plagues that had fallen on Egypt, Sodom, Tyre, Nineveh, are seen as embodied in one transcendent cataclysm. Ancient dooms are absorbed into this total doom, which falls on the rulers, sailors, merchants, and citizens—all who had drunk the wine of her fornication. Her judgment at the hands of God "in one hour" parallels in reverse the vindication of the saints and the descent from heaven of the holy city.

In the prophet's vision, the name Babylon is a mystery, and an aspect of the ultimate mystery of God's victory over evil (Rev. 17:5, 7). The truth concerning the sin and doom of Babylon is revealed

from heaven. It is due to prophetic disclosure that this apotheosis of evil can be detected in spite of its disguise in earthly prosperity, luxury, pride, and power. And only a disclosure like this can reveal the process of swift and final judgment.

If we must choose an empirical equivalent for Babylon, it would be Rome (city, empire, civilization), which to the prophet was a contemporary localization and embodiment of Babylon. In the events of his own day, through which the church was being tried and corrupted, he perceived both the idolatries and the sure doom of Babylon. In thinking of Rome in these terms, the prophet adopted an idiom which was current among Jewish seers (II Bar. 11:1; Sibylline Oracles 5:143, 158; IV Ezra 2) and Jewish rabbis. That it was current also among Christians is indicated by I Pet. 5:13. It is almost certain that the author of this letter was writing from Rome to churches in Asia Minor. Yet he speaks of writing from Babylon. He assumes that his readers will understand that the city which Romans call Rome is really a manifestation of the age-old domain of idolatry. As Tertullian wrote: "Babylon, in our own John, is a figure of the city Rome, as being equally great and proud of her sway, and triumphant over the saints" (*Against the Jews*). Yet it is not sufficient to identify Rome and Babylon. Babylon embraces more than one empire or culture. It is defined rather by dominant idolatries than by geographical or temporal boundaries. Babylon is coextensive with the kingdom of that beast which has corrupted and enslaved mankind, and whom the Lamb must conquer (Rev. 17:14) if mankind is to be freed. Babylon is an eschatological symbol of satanic deception and power; it is a heavenly mystery, which is to be comprehended prophetically, and which is never wholly reducible to empirical earthly institutions.

*Bibliography.* E. Lohmeyer, *Die Offenbarung des Johannes* (1926), pp. 135-44; P. Carrington, *The Meaning of Revelation* (1931), pp. 271-77; R. Schütz, *Die Offenbarung des Johannes und Kaiser Domitian* (1933); M. Kiddle, *The Book of Revelation* (1940), pp. 337-76; E. G. Selwyn, *First Peter* (1946), pp. 243, 303-5; O. Cullmann, *The State in the NT* (1956), pp. 71-85.

P. S. MINEAR

**BABYLONIA.** *See* ASSYRIA AND BABYLONIA.

**BACA, VALLEY OF** bā′kɔ [עמק הבכא, valley of the balsam trees(?)] (Ps. 84:6). A Palestinian valley the name of which was probably taken from a species of gum-exuding (weeping) tree—perhaps the BALSAM —which grew along its course. The word itself would seem to be a variant derivative from a root meaning "to weep." No valley of such a name has yet been identified, but a similar situation is perhaps suggested by the Valley of Rephaim, in which there were well-known balsam trees.

The valley was presumably a rather arid and inhospitable route along which ran a toilsome pathway to Zion (Jerusalem), which pathway was made to appear much less forbidding because of the joyous faith and mission of the pious pilgrim traveling it. In the same vein, it is quite possible that the valley was entirely symbolic.

*Bibliography.* A. F. Kirkpatrick, *The Book of Psalms* (1951), p. 507.

W. H. MORTON

**BACCHIDES** băk'ə dēz [Βακχίδης]. Friend of King Demetrius I (*see* DEMETRIUS 2), and governor of the area W of the Euphrates (I Macc. 7:8 ff). He was sent with an army to suppress the revolt of Judas Maccabeus and to install Alcimus as high priest. His mission was partly successful. He sought to deceive Judas and his brothers with peaceful words but was disregarded. When a company of scribes (or Hasidim) appeared before Bacchides and Alcimus for justice, both leaders took an oath not to harm them. These Hasidim trusted Alcimus as a priest and relied upon the assurance of religious freedom from the Syrian government. Sixty of the Hasidim were treacherously massacred, because the leaders became suspicious of their loyalty (Antiq. XII.vi.2). Bacchides also arrested deserters from the Hasmonean army because of his distrust.

After handing the country over to Alcimus with an army, he returned to the king. When Nicanor, a second general, had fallen in battle with Judah, King Demetrius again sent Bacchides to Judea. He was victorious in Arbela (I Macc. 9:2). Later at Elasa, Judah fell in battle against Bacchides.

As a result of a famine and Judah's death, Bacchides was able to dominate Judea and torment the loyal Jewish adherents. He fought Jonathan on the sabbath day (I Macc. 9:46) on the banks of the Jordan. Though a thousand of his men were slain, Bacchides gained the upper hand. Returning to Jerusalem, he took the sons of the leading men as hostages. He also fortified many places around Jerusalem, placing his men in the citadel. Fearing no more the Hasidim, Bacchides returned to Syria. This return is recorded as occurring after the death of Alcimus, and the land of Judea was quiet for two years till 158 B.C.

Bacchides was induced to return to Judea a third time. He fought against Jonathan at Bethbasi but met with stubborn resistance. To cover up his unsuccessful attempt to destroy Jonathan, Bacchides put the blame on the Hellenized Jews who had sent for him, accusing them of deception and consequently slaying many of them. As a result Jonathan now proposed peace and sought the release of prisoners. Bacchides agreed and swore never again to seek evil against Jonathan as long as he lived. Returning to his own land, he never again returned to Judea. As a result of the peace with Bacchides, Jonathan became the recognized leader, now having no rival, because of the death of the high priest Alcimus.

S. B. HOENIG

**BACCHURUS.** KJV form of ZACCUR 6.

**BACCHUS** băk'əs. *See* DIONYSUS.

**BACENOR** bə sē'nôr [Βακήνωρ]. A name in the phrase "Bacenor's men" (KJV "Bacenor's company") in II Macc. 12:35. These persons seem to be identical with those called Toubiani in vs. 17 (*see* TOB; DOSITHEUS). The meaning of the name is obscure. S. B. HOENIG

**BACHRITES.** KJV form of BECHERITES. *See* BECHER.

**BACKSLIDING** [שׁוֹבָב, מְשׁוּבָה]. A prophetic term, almost exclusive to Jeremiah and Hosea, describing Israel's infidelity to Yahweh, more properly "backturning," often translated "faithless" (Isa. 57:17; Jer. 8:5; cf. Jer. 3:14, 22; 31:22; 49:4; Hos. 11:7; 14:4). The word undoubtedly has covenantal associations. Israel, as the wife of Yahweh, has proved unfaithful and embraced paganism. But Israel's backsliding is not simply religious apostasy (a rejection of Yahweh for pagan deities, or the introduction of pagan rites into Yahweh-worship), but also moral apostasy—a forgetting, or rejection, of the ordinances of the Lord (Jer. 8:7); covetousness (Isa. 57:17); practicing deceit (Jer. 8:5); dealing falsely (Jer. 8:10). People, prophets, and priests together were guilty, refusing to respond to prophetic entreaty.

In the NT, Jesus predicts times of falling away (Matt. 24:10, 12), and Hebrews is replete with warnings against this tendency. *See also* APOSTASY.

*Bibliography.* S. R. Driver, *The Book of the Prophet Jeremiah* (1907), pp. 340-41; P. Volz, *Der Prophet Jeremia*, KAT (1922), pp. 33-47. V. H. KOOY

**BADGER.** The translation of שָׁפָן in Ps. 104:18; Prov. 30:26 (KJV CONEY). *See* ROCK BADGER.

**BAEAN** bē'ən [Βαιαν; Vulg. *Bean; cf.* Beon (Num. 32:3)] (I Macc. 5:14); KJV BEAN. An otherwise unknown tribe destroyed by Judas Maccabeus because they had been "a trap and a snare to the people and ambushed them on the highways" (cf. II Macc. 10:18-23; Jos. Antiq. II.viii.1). J. C. SWAIM

**BAG. 1.** חָרִיט (II Kings 5:23). Alternately: HANDBAG (Isa. 3:22); KJV CRISPING PIN (hair curler). In II Kings 5:23 the reference is to money bags, each holding a talent of silver. In Isa. 3:22 the translation "handbag" is obviously right, since the context points to an article of luxurious feminine apparel.

**2.** כִּיס (Deut. 25:13; Prov. 16:11; Mic. 6:11). Alternately: PURSE (Prov. 1:14; Isa. 46:6). A small bag or pouch used for weights, and in the Proverbs and Isaiah passages for money.

**3.** צְרוֹר (Gen. 42:25 [KJV SACK]; Job 14:17; Prov. 7:20; Song of S. 1:13 [KJV BUNDLE]; Hag. 1:6). Alternately: BUNDLE (I Sam. 25:29). Something tied together, usually a bag or cloth drawn together to hold money (Proverbs, Haggai) or something loose such as myrrh (Song of Songs). The word is sometimes used figuratively (Job, Samuel) for "bag of transgressions" or BUNDLE OF THE LIVING.

**4.** צוּר (II Kings 12:10—H 12:11). A verb meaning "to tie up in bags." The reference is to the contributions collected in the Jehoiada chest.

**5.** כְּלִי (Gen. 43:11 [KJV VESSEL]; Deut. 23:25; I Sam. 17:40, 49). Alternately: SACK (Gen. 42:25; I Sam. 9:7 [KJV VESSEL]). A grain bag, food sack, container for grapes, or bag for a shepherd's supplies. In I Sam. 17:40, יַלְקוּט ("wallet"; KJV "scrip") is obviously meant to explain the shepherd's bag and so is practically synonymous with it.

**6.** πήρα (Matt. 10:10; Mark 6:8; Luke 9:3; 10:4; 22:35-36); KJV SCRIP. A traveling bag, shepherd's bag, or beggar's bag. It was also part of the Cynic preacher's equipment.

**7.** Βαλλάντιον (Luke 10:4; 12:33; 22:35 ff). A purse.

**8.** KJV translation of γλωσσόκομον (RSV MONEY BOX). J. M. MYERS

**BAGO** bā′gō. KJV Apoc. form of BIGVAI.

**BAGOAS** bə gō′əs [Βαγώας (Pers. *for* εὐνοῦχος?); Vulg. *Vagao*]. A eunuch in "charge of all [the] personal affairs" of Holofernes (Jth. 12:11). He made the discovery that his master had been slain by Judith (14:14-18). J. C. SWAIM

**BAGOI** bā′goi. KJV Apoc. form of BIGVAI.

**BAGPIPE.** *See* MUSICAL INSTRUMENTS.

**BAHARUM; KJV BAHARUMITE.** Same as BAHURIM.

**BAHURIM** bə hyōōr′ĭm [בחורים]; KJV BARHUMITE bär hū′mīt [ברחמי] in II Sam. 23:31. Alternately: BAHARUM bə hâr′əm (I Chr. 11:33); KJV BAHARUMITE —ə mīt [בחרומי]. A village at modern Ras et-Tmim, E of Mount Scopus near Jerusalem, where Paltiel and Michal parted as she was being returned to David (II Sam. 3:16). There Shimei cursed David, who was fleeing from Absalom (II Sam. 16:5; 19:16; I Kings 2:8). Jonathan and Ahimaaz, when they were spying for David, hid in the well of a man of Bahurim (II Sam. 17:18). It seems that David in his flight took a shorter and harder route to the Jordan than the one around the S side of the Mount of Olives.

Azmaveth, one of David's Mighty Men, was probably from Bahurim, as appears from comparison of the variants noted above in II Sam. 23:31; I Chr. 11:33. O. R. SELLERS

**BAITERUS** bā′tə rəs [Βαιτηροὺς (BA), Γαβαων (Luc.)] (I Esd. 5:17); KJV METERUS mə tir′əs. Ancestor of some exiles, 3,005 strong, who returned with Zerubbabel. The name is omitted in the parallels Ezra 2:3 ff; Neh. 7:8 ff. C. T. FRITSCH

**BAJITH** bā′jĭth [הבית, the house]. A word treated as a Moabite place name in the KJV (Isa. 15:2). The RSV slightly emends the Hebrew, translating "the daughter."

**BAKBAKKAR** băk băk′ər [בקבקר] (I Chr. 9:15). A Levite, of the sons of Asaph, in Jerusalem. His name is missing in the parallel list in Neh. 11:16, unless it be Bakbukiah.

**BAKBUK** băk′bŭk [בקבוק, flask]; KJV Apoc. ACUB ā′kŭb. Head of a family of postexilic temple servants of lower rank (Ezra 2:51; Neh. 7:53). *See* NETHINIM.

**BAKBUKIAH** băk′bə kī′ə [בקבקיה, Yahu's pitcher(?)]. A singer (Neh. 11:17; 12:9) and guard of the temple storehouse (12:25). Since Neh. 11:17 mentions "sons" of Asaph and Jeduthun, Bakbukiah may be a "son" of Heman, thus completing the represen-

tation of three classical groups of singers (cf. I Chr. 25:1-5; *see* BUKKIAH). J. M. WARD

**BAKERS' STREET** [חוץ האפים] (Jer. 37:21). It is natural for a group of small industrial establishments to develop in specific areas. So in ancient Jerusalem, as in other cities, a certain street would attract members of a particular craft. Jeremiah in prison had a daily ration of a piece of bread from the bakers' street. Bakers may have been among those for whom streets (RSV "bazaars") were provided in Dasmascus and Samaria (I Kings 20:34). Baking was recognized as a specialized trade (Gen. 40:1–41:13; I Sam. 8: 13; Hos. 7:4). Today in Jerusalem there are numerous bakeries between the Damascus gate and the Church of the Holy Sepulchre. Probably the shop was part of the dwelling, so that the baker lived, worked, and sold on his premises.

*See also* ARCHITECTURE; BREAD; HOUSE; STREET.

O. R. SELLERS

**BAKING** [אפה, to bake]. The Hebrew word and its derivatives refer specifically to the baking of BREAD and of cakes prepared with flour and oil, which formed a substantial portion of the daily food of the Canaanites and the Hebrews (Gen. 19:3; Exod. 12: 39; Lev. 26:26; I Kings 17:12-13; Isa. 44:15); they refer also to the baking of the BREAD OF THE PRESENCE (Lev. 24:5) and of baked offerings (2:4 ff). The abstaining from leaven in the dough was prompted either by reasons of necessity, such as baking in a hurry (Exod. 12:39), or by rules of the ritual (Exod.

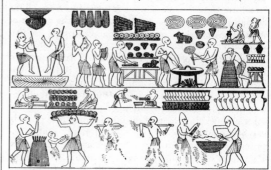

11. Royal bakery scenes, from the tomb of Ramses III (twelfth century B.C.)

Courtesy of the Metropolitan Museum of Art; Rogers Fund and contribution of Edward S. Harkness, 1920

12. Model of bakery and brewery, from Thebes

13:6-7; Lev. 2:5). The baking of bread was normally done in an OVEN. Travelers, however, baked flat cakes of coarse bread on pebbles upon which a fire had been built and the embers swept away (cf. I Kings 19:6). Modern Bedouins still use this method, unless they bake on a heated disk of iron (Arabic *sadj*). Pastries and baked offerings were baked either in special ovens or in pans or griddle irons (Lev. 2:4 ff). Figs. BAK 11-12; BRE 47.

Baking bread was normally a household chore performed by women. The feudal landlords in Canaanite Palestine used to draft maidens to serve as cooks and bakers, and the Israelites feared that their kings might do the same (I Sam. 8:13). In Egypt, the chief baker at the royal court seems to have been a personage of importance (Gen. 40:2). The development of city life under the Hebrew monarchies favored the creation of commercial bakeries in the larger towns. A street of Jerusalem was known as Bakers' Street (Jer. 37:21), presumably located toward what was at that time the NW angle of the city, which was protected by a fortress called the TOWER OF THE OVENS (Neh. 3:11; 12:38).

Hebrew אפה and its English equivalent, "to bake," are often synonymous with miscellaneous terms for "cooking," without reference to bread and cakes (cf. Exod. 16:23; see COOKING AND COOKING UTENSILS). Cooking, like breadmaking, was also a household affair, with the women in charge. Bible references to the art of cooking are few and not explicit. The specific Hebrew names for kitchen utensils, translated in the versions (which are not altogether consistent) by "cooking pot," "kettle," "caldron," "pan," and the like, cannot be applied with absolute certainty to the utensils of metal or the earthenware vessels discovered by the archaeologists (see VESSELS; POTTERY). The use of bronze or iron forks for the preparing and serving of meat is attested by I Sam. 2:13 and confirmed by archaeological discoveries.

The sacrificial meals, in the course of which the priests and certain categories of worshipers were partaking of the meats offered to Yahweh, made it necessary that kitchen facilities be provided for in the precincts of the temple. References to such kitchens appear in Ezek. 46:20, 23-24.

*Bibliography.* K. Galling, *Biblisches Reallexikon* (1937), cols. 75-78; G. A. Barrois, *Manuel d'Archéologie Biblique*, I (1939), 319-22. For modern parallels from Arabic villages in Palestine, especially with regard to breadmaking, see G. Dalman, *Arbeit und Sitte in Palästina*, IV (1935), 1-152.

G. A. BARROIS

**BALAAM** bāʹləm [בלעם; Βαλαάμ, the clan brings forth(?)]. A seer summoned by Balak king of Moab to curse Israel prior to its entrance into Canaan (Num. 22:5–24:25; 31:8, 16; Deut. 23:4-5—H 23:5-6; Josh. 13:22; 24:9-10; Neh. 13:2; Mic. 6:5; II Pet. 2: 15; Jude 11; Rev. 2:14).

The figure of Balaam is a singular one in the OT. He was a foreigner who was subject to the command of the God of Israel. Unlike Assyria, which is made to serve as the rod of Yahweh's anger (Isa. 10:5), Balaam is represented as consciously acknowledging the derivation of his powers from the Lord (Num. 24:13). Furthermore, the career of this seer, who was unable "to go beyond the word of the LORD, to do

either good or bad," is an extraordinary example of the potency attributed by the OT to the spoken word (cf. Gen. 12:3; 27:33; Exod. 21:17; Isa. 55:11; see BLESSINGS AND CURSINGS). A diviner of sufficient renown to be sought by the king of Moab, Balaam was summoned to pronounce a destructive curse upon Israel, but instead he uttered a series of blessings affirming present and promising future pre-eminence to Israel. In addition to these notable features in the career of Balaam, there is the well-known tale of Balaam's ass, with the folkloristic motif of the talking animal, paralleled elsewhere in the OT only by the serpent in the Garden of Eden (Gen. 3).

The general features of Balaam's career as presented in Num. 22–24 are clear, but detailed reconstruction of the Balaam tradition is confronted with numerous obscurities. The theory that the biblical account has resulted from conflation of different traditions, possibly continuous with the J and E Pentateuchal sources, has been widely adopted to clarify some of these obscurities.

Thus, the apparent divine inconsistency in first authorizing Balaam's trip to Moab (Num. 22:20) and then obstructing it by blockading the road before his ass (vss. 22-35a) is explained as the result of source conflation. In the E source God acceded to the request of a second embassy from the king of Moab, and Balaam was allowed to return with the princes of Moab to their land, although, of course, no permission was granted to comply with their request that Israel be cursed (22:15-16, 19-21). In the J source, on the other hand, Yahweh's opposition to Balaam's journey was made known after Balaam and his two servants had set out on their way. The angel of Yahweh, obstructing the narrow path between walled vineyards (vs. 24), would not permit the ass carrying Balaam to pass. The reason for Yahweh's opposition to Balaam's journey is no longer clear in the J source, although one may suppose that Balaam set out without having consulted Yahweh. It has been suggested that Balaam's journey was undertaken in response to a personal visit from the king of Moab, after the royal embassy had twice failed to secure it. A trace of such a visit from Balak may be preserved in Num. 22:37, 39a, but such an attempted reconstruction can remain only a hypothesis.

Once Balaam arrived in Moab, preparations were made to secure for him the powerful spoken curse which would significantly diminish the threat Moab considered Israel to be. The first attempt misfired, producing praise of Israel instead of a curse. Successive attempts, undertaken from different heights overlooking part or all of the Israelite encampment, were unable to alter the first result. In all, Balaam delivered four such solemn utterances or "discourses" (the word משל suggests a saying which implies more than its apparent or surface meaning). It is probable that the four Balaam sayings have resulted from inclusion of materials originally preserved in separate traditions. The movement of Balaam from height to height seems a contrived device to permit incorporation of all four poems into the saga. The two poems in Num. 23, usually attributed to E, are obviously acquainted with the story of Balaam in the employ of the king of Moab, while the J poems in ch. 24

could have originated apart from this particular tradition about Balaam.

The Balaam poems exhibit similarities to the deathbed blessings attributed to Jacob (Gen. 49) and Moses (Deut. 33), although without the developed tribal allusions of the latter. The pre-eminence of Israel among the nations is extolled in imagery that suggests, on the one hand, the return of the Paradise with its peace and bounty (Num. 24:5-7*a*); and, on the other, the martial triumph of Israel over its foes (vss. 7*b*-8). These are motifs which are not lost in subsequent biblical eschatology (cf. Isa. 40:10; 42:13; 49:22-26 with 49:8-11; 52:7; and Rev. 5:5; 12:7-8; 17:14 with 7:15-17; 22:1-5), and suggest already in ancient Israel a concern to affirm simultaneously both the goodness and the power of God.

Reflection of King David's subjugation of Moab and Edom (II Sam. 8:2, 13-14) is often detected in Num. 24:17*c*-18 ("Sheth" is best identified with Shutu, probably the ancient name of Moab). If this supposition is correct, the *terminus a quo* for at least the present form of the Balaam poems and narrative would be the tenth century B.C., with the emergence of the final form of the tradition considerably later. Conviction as to the Davidic influence behind the references to Moab and Edom would normally lead to the conclusion that it is David who is described in Num. 24:17*b:*

> A star shall come forth out of Jacob,
> and a scepter shall rise out of Israel.

However, these words have been interpreted messianically both in Judaism (in the name of the messianic claimant Bar Cocheba, "son of the star," in the time of Hadrian) and in Christianity (Rev. 22:16; and possibly in the manifestation of the star to the Magi in Matt. 2:2, 9-10). It is possible that this and other regal references in the poems (Num. 23:21; 24:7) are but slight modifications of ancient Semitic poetry which attracted Israel's attention during its own monarchy. A date in the thirteenth or twelfth century B.C. has, accordingly, been suggested for the composition of the Balaam oracles, but there has been vigorous dissent from this attempt to place the genesis of these poems prior to the Davidic monarchy.

The figure of Balaam, the renowned seer, may have had a history not always associated with the oracles now attached to his name. The close similarity between Bela (בלע) king of Edom (Gen. 36:32) and Balaam (בלעם) suggests the possible identity of the two, especially since both are named the "son of Beor." The present form of the tradition, however, locates Balaam's home in the Euphrates Valley at Pethor, evidently ancient Pitru in the vicinity of Carchemish (Num. 22:5; 23:7; Deut. 23:4—H 23:5). The "land of Amaw" (Num. 22:5) designates this same region, NE of Syria, as attested by its use in the Egyptian story of Sinuhe. The distant journey from Mesopotamia to Moab would normally be undertaken with more of a retinue and with better transportation than the two servants and ass which figure in the J account of Balaam's journey. This may imply that J located Balaam's homeland within a day's journey or two from Moab, perhaps in Edom or in Ammon (Num. 22:5 Samar., LXX) but it is

precarious to rest more than a supposition upon such an analysis.

With the exception of Mic. 6:5, subsequent biblical references to Balaam are unfavorable. His journey to Moab is considered motivated by base desire for gain (Deut. 23:4—H 23:5; II Pet. 2:15), and he is blamed as the instigator of Israel's defection to a Moabite Baal at Peor (Num. 25:1-3; 31:16 P; Rev. 2:14). Rabbinic sources generally make the same accusations of Balaam, although he is considered by some a prophet to the Gentiles.

The tradition of Israel's conquest of the Promised Land knows of no encounter between Israel and Moab such as is supposed in the Balaam narrative. Even if the latter reflects conditions of a later age, such as the Davidic or Omride monarchy (*see* OMRI), it is notable that a story set in the days of the Conquest could be so free of warfare and bloodshed.

**Bibliography.** S. Mowinckel, "Der Ursprung der Bil'āmsage," *ZAW*, XLVIII (1930), 233-71; O. Eissfeldt, "Die Komposition der Bileam-Erzählung," *ZAW*, LVII (1939), 212-41; W. F. Albright, "The Oracles of Balaam," *JBL*, LXIII (1944), 207-33; A. S. Yahuda, "The Name of Balaam's Homeland," *JBL*, LXIV (1945), 547-51.

R. F. JOHNSON

**BALAC.** KJV NT form of BALAK.

**BALADAN** băl'ə dən [בלאדן] (II Kings 20:12). The father of Merodach-baladan king of Babylon.

**BALAH** bā'lə [בלה, old, worn out] (Josh. 19:3). A city of Simeon in the Judean Negeb. The same site is probably indicated by Bilhah in the Chronicler's parallel passage (I Chr. 4:29) and by Baalah in the Judean list of Josh. 15:29. The precise location is unknown, but the context suggests the region S and E of Beer-sheba.                               W. H. MORTON

**BALAK** bā'lăk [בלק, the devastator; Βαλάκ (KJV BALAC)]. Son of ZIPPOR; king of Moab. After the Israelites defeated the Amorites, he became fearful for his kingdom and urged the seer BALAAM to curse the invaders (Num. 22–24). Balaam's refusal and Israel's subsequent victory were later remembered as examples of Yahweh's saving acts (Josh. 24:9-10; Mic. 6:5; cf. Judg. 11:25; Rev. 2:14).

J. F. ROSS

**BALAMON** băl'ə mən [Βαλαμών] (Jth. 8:3); KJV BALAMO —mō. A town near Dothan, probably the same as BELMAIN.

**BALANCES** [מאזנים]. Early in the development of civilization the balance was used to measure weights. It consisted of two pans suspended by cords from a beam which was suspended by a cord in its center or, probably later, with its center on a standard.* So far as we know, all balances in the Near East before the coming of the Romans were equal-armed, and the principle of leverage, giving the graduated scale, was not used. At a fairly early time there was added a plummet extending downward, rather than upward as in modern balances. Such balances are shown in Egyptian reliefs or papyri, and some of them indicate elaborate workmanship.* The metal pans were suspended by cords passing into the ends of a tubular beam.* The plummet was in front of the upright support, so that when the articles in the two pans were equal, the exact vertical position of the plummet would be evident. The Egyptians used balances in transactions, as is evidenced by many pictures showing the weighing of metals; and they also envisioned the use of balances by gods passing judgment on the deceased in the after life. There are scenes in which the heart of the one being judged before the gods is in the balance against the *ma'at* feather, the emblem of truth. In the Middle Kingdom story of the Eloquent Peasant the petitioner speaks repeatedly of balances in flattering or imploring the grand steward. "Thou art the balances. . . . Thy tongue is the plummet; thy heart is the weight, thy two lips the beam." In Mesopotamia balances were used, but apparently these were not so highly developed or esteemed as in Egypt. The simple hand balance there gave opportunity for fraudulent manipulation. Balances were well known in Canaan before

13. A pair of scales with a set of weights, from Ras Shamra (fifteenth to fourteenth century B.C.)

the coming of the Israelites. In the "Nikkal and Kathirat" text from UGARIT the family is described as operating the balances, with the father attending the beam, the mother the pans, the brothers the ingots, and the sisters the weights. Frequently in the Bible just balances are prescribed and false or deceitful balances denounced. Figs. BAL 13-14; WEI 12-13; GOL 34.

In the Apoc. balances are mentioned in II Esd. 3:34. In Ecclus. 28:25 the cross bar (ζυγός) and the upright (σταθμός) evidently are parts of a pair of scales, and their exactness is recommended in Ecclus. 42:4; the σταθμός is the weight in vs. 7. In Rev. 6:5 ζυγός means a balance.

*See also* WEIGHTS AND MEASURES § A.

*Bibliography.* J. H. Breasted, *The Dawn of Conscience* (1935), pp. 188-91, 251, 252, 260-63; C. H. Gordon, *Ugaritic Literature* (1949), p. 64. O. R. SELLERS

**BALASAMUS.** KJV form of BAALSAMUS.

**BALBAIM** băl bā'əm [Βελβάιμ] (Jth. 7:3); KJV BELMAIM bĕl mā'əm. A town near Dothan, probably the same as BELMAIN.

**BALDAD** băl'dăd. Douay Version form of BILDAD.

**BALD LOCUST** [סלעם, swallower, consumer] (Lev. 11:22). An orthopterous insect considered clean and therefore edible. Perhaps it is *Tryxalis nasuta* or *Tryxalis unguiculata*, with elongated head. *See* FAUNA § E2.

*Bibliography.* F. S. Bodenheimer, *Insects as Human Food* (1951). *See also* the bibliography under ANT.

W. W. FRERICHS

**BALDNESS.** Complete loss of hair from the head from natural causes was probably not common among biblical peoples, as can be judged from the

14. The god Anubis leads the deceased toward the balance, where his heart is weighed against the goddess Maat (1550-1090 B.C.).

fact that it is mentioned infrequently in the OT, not at all in the NT, and that representations of the human figure in ancient Near Eastern art usually picture Semites or Asiatics with long hair and beards. *See* HAIR; MOURNING; NAZIRITE; SHAVING.

The term for "baldness of the forehead" (גבח, גבחת) occurs only in Lev. 13:41-43, where the law states that such baldness is unclean only if the signs of leprosy appear. The same is said to be true for "baldness of the head" (קרחת, קרחה).

Artificial baldness as a sign of mourning (Amos 8:10) and possibly of enslavement (Isa. 3:24) was designated by קרחה, which is also the root of the proper name KORAH (Gen. 36:5; Exod. 6:21; Num. 16:1; etc.). "Baldhead" was a term of derision applied to Elisha (II Kings 2:23); the passage does not make clear whether natural baldness or the prophet's tonsure provoked the attack. The Hebrews were forbidden by law to make themselves bald by shaving (Deut. 14:1), doubtless because neighboring peoples did so (Jer. 9:26; 25:23). Tonsures were forbidden to the priests (Lev. 21:5; KJV "baldness"). Although it is not termed "baldness," the shaving of the head and the ceremonial burning of the hair at the termination of the Nazirite vow was a practice (Num. 6:19; cf. Acts 18:18; 21:24). Whereas priestly legislation forbids artificial baldness, the prophets mention it as a sign of mourning (Isa. 15:2; 22:12; Jer. 47:5; 48:37; Ezek. 7:18; Mic. 1:16). It is doubtful that the prophets approved the rite, or that it was common among the Hebrews; the prophets' allusions to it were merely a figurative way of designating impending doom and enslavement (cf. Ezek. 29:18, where baldness is said to have been produced by slave labor, probably from the carrying of burdens on the head).          W. L. REED

**BALL** [דור] (Isa. 22:18). The single biblical reference to a ball occurs in the story of the deposition of SHEBNA, the royal steward of Hezekiah (Isa. 22:15-25). Isaiah addressed Shebna, perhaps near the rock tomb which Shebna was constructing for himself, and predicted his downfall: "He [the LORD] will seize firm hold on you, and whirl you round and round, and throw you like a ball into a wide land"—i.e., the Lord would send Shebna into exile in Assyria. In the translation the words "and throw you" (KJV "and toss thee"), not found in the Hebrew, are supplied to give the sense. There is no necessary reference here to the ball used in games or sport.

In Isa. 29:3 the word דור means "circle," and the literal "like a circle" is translated "round about."          H. F. BECK

**BALLAD SINGERS** [משלים] (Num. 21:27); KJV **THEY THAT SPEAK IN PROVERBS.** A phrase which literally refers to the makers or repeaters of proverbs (*see* PROVERB). The context of several songs suggests that this "ballad" is somewhat similar to the modern "historical" ballad or folk song. *See* MUSIC.          C. U. WOLF

**BALM** [צרי; LXX ῥητίνη]. Despite its widespread therapeutic usage in antiquity, the true identity of this aromatic resin or gum is not easily established. It

is mentioned six times in the Bible, and from two references in Genesis (37:25; 43:11) it appears to have been a commodity of commercial value carried by Near Eastern trading caravans. Ezekiel (27:17) included balm among the early exports from Gilead to Tyre. Classical writers referred to it frequently under a variety of names, which renders proper identification difficult. Pliny regarded Jericho as the sole habitat of the shrub which yielded the balm resin, but Strabo maintained that it also flourished beside the Sea of Galilee. However, both writers were probably alluding to the species *Balsamodendron opobalsamum,* native to Arabia and Abyssinia.

Biblical references do not support the idea that balm trees grew in the rugged highland areas SE of the Sea of Galilee. Theophrastus recorded that spice caravans from the E passed through Gilead, which may account for the association of balm with that region. But there is no known tree in the area which would produce an aromatic resin with medicinal properties of the kind attributed to balm. The substance sent by Jacob to Joseph in Egypt (Gen. 43:11) was probably indigenous to Palestine, and therefore hardly *Balsamodendron opobalsamum* or "balm of Gilead" (*see* GILEAD, BALM OF). The balm mentioned in Jeremiah (46:11; 51:8) has been identified with *Balanites aegyptiaca* (L) Delile, a small shrub still found in North Africa, which produces an oil of reputed medicinal value. The ERV margin references in Genesis read "mastic," probably alluding to the resinous gum of the *Pistacia lentiscus* L. However, since healing virtues are not mentioned in this context, a different variety of balm may be meant. The ancients utilized the gum in cosmetic and EMBALMING techniques, as well as in medicine. It has dropped out of modern pharmacopoeias.

*Bibliography.* H. N. and A. L. Moldenke, *Plants of the Bible* (1952), pp. 84-85, 177 ff. *See also* bibliography under FLORA.          R. K. HARRISON

**BALNUUS.** KJV Apoc. form of BINNUI 3.

**BALSAM;** KJV **MULBERRY.** The translation of בכא, *bākhâ,* in II Sam. 5:23-24=I Chr. 14:14-15. The word apparently appears as a place name in Ps. 84:6 (*see* BACA, VALLEY OF). The true balsam (*Commiphora opobalsamum* [L.] Engl., also called *Balsamodendron opobalsamum* [L.] Engl.) trees, however, have never grown around Jerusalem, but are native to S Arabia.

The early rabbis translated the word "MULBERRY TREES," but these trees do not fit the context either. A type of aspen or POPLAR, such as the *Populus euphratica* Oliv. or *P. tremula* L., has been suggested on the basis of the context (but *cf.* FLORA § A2e). In North America the *Populus tacamahaca* is called the balsam poplar.

Others suggest the *Pistacia lentiscus* L. (*see* MASTIC), with no better support. It is possible that the Hebrew does not refer to a tree at all. *See also* BALM.

*Bibliography.* H. N. and A. L. Moldenke, *Plants of the Bible* (1952), pp. 183-84.          J. C. TREVER

**BALTHASAR** băl thăz'ǝr [Βαλτασάρ]. **1.** KJV form of BELSHAZZAR in Jth. 1:11.

**2.** In late tradition a king of Arabia, and one of the three Magi. *See* MELKON.

**BAMAH** bā'mə [במה (*plural* במות), *mainly rendered by* τὸ ὑψηλόν (*cf.* βωμός) *in the* LXX; ridge, of high rising ground (*cf.* going up *in* I Sam. 9:13, 19; Isa. 15:2; coming down *in* I Sam. 9:25; 10:5; *and parallel to* high hill *in* Ezek. 20:29)]. A word used:

*a*) Of Gilboa hill (II Sam. 1:19, 25) and of mountains above Arnon (Num. 21:28); also, in plural, of a town—high place—in Moab (Num. 21:19-20=22: 41; Josh. 13:17); twice on the Moabite Stone (lines 3, 27).

*b*) In figurative phrases for dominion: of Israel (Deut. 32:13 [cf. El Elyon motif]; 33:29; Ps. 18:33= II Sam. 22:34; Hab. 3:19; and eschatologically in Isa. 58:14); of God (Job 9:8; Amos 4:13; Mic. 1:3; often with "tread"); of divine aspirations of the king of Babylon (Isa. 14:14).

*c*) Figuratively of devastation (Jer. 26:18; Ezek. 36:2[?]; Mic. 3:12).

*d*) In Ezek. 20:29 of an artificially constructed word *Ba* ("come") + *Mah* ("what") for contemptuous but obscure purpose.

*e*) Of places of worship on natural heights, artificial mounds, and once (Ezek. 16:16) of portable colored sanctuary tents. *See* HIGH PLACE.

G. HENTON DAVIES

**BAMOTH** bā'mŏth [במות, high places]. A stopping place of the Israelites in Transjordan between Nahaliel and the "valley lying in the region of Moab by the top of Pisgah which looks down upon the desert" (Num. 21:19-20). The name is probably a short form of BAMOTH-BAAL.      E. D. GROHMAN

**BAMOTH-BAAL** bā'mŏth bāl' [במות בעל, high places of Baal]. A town of Moab. Balak took Balaam to the place, from which he saw the nearest of the Israelites (Num. 22:41; KJV: Balak took Balaam up "into the high places of Baal, that thence he might see the utmost part of the people"). The name of Bamoth-baal and the sacrifices of Balak and Balaam (Num. 23:1-12) would indicate that it was a sanctuary of Baal. Later, Bamoth was assigned to the tribe of Reuben, listed with the cities in the tableland of Heshbon: Dibon, Bamoth-baal, Beth-baal-meon, etc. (Josh. 13:17). Mesha says that he "built Beth-bamoth, for it had been destroyed" (MOABITE STONE, line 27). Beth-bamoth is probably Bamoth-baal. It is certainly on a height on the W edge of the Transjordan Plateau in the area of Mount Nebo, but its precise location is uncertain.      E. D. GROHMAN

**BAN.** KJV Apoc. form of TOBIAH 1.

**BAN (VERB).** In the RSV "ban" is used only in Ezra 10:8, to translate בדל. For the concept expressed in the OT by חרם *see* DEVOTED.

In the NT the idea of banning is present in references to (*a*) the proscription from the synagogues of those who confessed Christ and (*b*) the expelling of impenitent Christian sinners from the church.

Thrice the Fourth Gospel alludes to the fact that Christians were driven out from synagogues (John 9:22; 12:42; 16:2; cf, Luke 6:22). This practice, which was probably in use in John's days at the end of the first century, certainly does not go back to an earlier time (cf. Acts 28:16-22).

Deliberate offenders were banned from the church by virtue of the apostles' power of BINDING AND LOOSING. The NT offers two examples of the apostolic power of binding: First, a church member who committed some offense and refused to listen to two or three brethren and even to the community should be treated "as a Gentile and a tax collector" (Matt. 18:15-17)—i.e., as a man who was excluded from the fellowship of the church and to whom the gospel of salvation must be preached anew. Second, Paul writes to the Corinthians a summons to proscribe the incestuous man whose presence in the body of Christ had been too long tolerated, and the apostle expects that somehow this ban will bring about the final salvation of the guilty one (I Cor. 5: 1-5). Thus, "to ban" does not simply mean "to condemn"; it was a measure taken in view of the final welfare of the banned person.

*See also* BANISHMENT; EXCOMMUNICATION.

P. H. MENOUD

**BANAIAS.** KJV Apoc. form of BENAIAH 9.

**BAND. 1.** Anything with which a person is bound, as a shackle. The only RSV use of this translation is for עבת in Hos. 11:4. This same Hebrew is translated "rope" (Job 39:10) and "cords" (Ezek. 3:25; 4:8; *see* CORD, ROPE). More frequently מוסר is changed from KJV "band" to "bond" in the RSV (Job 39:5; Pss. 2:3; 107:14; Isa. 28:22; Jer. 2:20). Prisoners are shackled with "fetters" (אסור in Eccl. 7:26; δεσμός in Luke 8:29; Acts 16:26). Metaphorically the oppression of an enemy is a restraint (מוטה; Lev. 26:13; Ezek. 34:27; RSV "bars of their yoke"). In the NT, the KJV uses "band" for anything that joins together; so συνδεσμός is a "ligament" (Col. 2:19). Ζευκτηρία is for the fastener holding rudder to a ship (Acts 27:40; RSV "ropes").

**2.** Anything which encompasses another thing or person; a flat strip or border. The EPHOD is to be edged with a "binding around the opening" (שׂפה; Exod. 39:23; "band" in 28:8). The swaddling band is noted in Job 38:9 (*see* SWADDLE). The stands in the temple have bands (borders) around the top a cubit high (I Kings 7:35). In Dan. 4:15 a similar metal band is around the stump of a tree, but this could also imply the use of אסור, "fetter," of 1 *above*.

**3.** An organization of persons brought together by common purpose or character. The band of men does not fit into the usual tribal structure of Israel (*see* TRIBE). These may be raiders (I Chr. 12:21; Job 1: 17 KJV [RSV "company"]; Ezek. 38:6 KJV [RSV "horde"]), ruthless men (Pss. 59:3; 86:14), a group of drunkards (Hos. 4:18), a squad of soldiers (II Kings 6:23 KJV; Ezra 8:22; Prov. 30:27 KJV; Jer. 12:14 KJV [RSV "troop"]; John 18:12; *see* ARMY). A horde of locusts (Gen. 32:7 KJV; RSV "company") and the REMNANT are a band (II Kings 19:31).      C. U. WOLF

**BANDAGE. 1.** אפר (from Akkadian *apâru*, "head covering"; I Kings 20:38, 41*a;* KJV ASHES). A covering placed over the eyes to conceal one's identity.

**2.** חתול (from חתל, "to be swathed, wrapped up"; Ezek. 30:21; KJV ROLLER). A wrapping for a broken arm.

3. Κειρία (John 11:44; KJV GRAVECLOTHES).
A swathing band.                      J. M. MYERS

**BANDS, MAGIC** [כסתות, *cf.* Akkad. *kasū*, to bind
in a magic sense (*occurring frequently in the incantation
texts, Maqlu and Shurpu*)] (Ezek. 13:18, 20); KJV
PILLOWS. Objects connected with divination; just
how they were to operate is obscure. Late Aramaic
texts (fifth century A.D.) speak of persons' being
bound with magic charms to ward off evil.

J. M. MYERS

**BANI** bā'nī [בני, build, *or abbreviation of* Benaiah];
KJV Apoc. BANID bā'nĭd; MANI mā'nī; MAANI
mā'ə nī. A name similar to other names in postexilic
priestly writings (*see also* BUNNI; BINNUI). They are
easily confused, and it is difficult to distinguish individuals from family groups.
  **1.** A man of Gad; a warrior among David's
"Thirty" (II Sam. 23:36). He is missing in the
parallel list (I Chr. 11:38), unless "son of Hagri" is
a corruption of "Bani the Gadite."
  **2.** An ancestor or family line of Ethan, a
Merarite Levite at the time of David (I Chr. 6:46—
H 6:31).
  **3.** An ancestor or family line of Uthai, a Judahite
in postexilic Jerusalem (I Chr. 9:4). The LXX follows *Kethibh* and reads instead "Benjamin" (בנימן),
combining it with the next word.
  **4.** A family group—or founder thereof—included
in the great list of those who returned from the Exile
(Ezra 2:10; I Esd. 5:12). The parallel list, however,
reads "sons of Binnui" (Neh. 7:15). The Ezra list
numbers them at 642, the Nehemiah list at 648. If
Bani is to be omitted in Ezra 2:10, some scholars believe it should be restored later in the list (Ezra 2:
40 = Neh. 7:43), on the basis of I Esd. 5:26.
  **5.** Probably a family group, rather than an individual, in some passages:
  *a*) Several married foreigners (Ezra 10:29 = I Esd.
9:30 [KJV Mani]; Ezra 10:34 = I Esd. 9:34 [KJV
Maani]; Ezra 10:38, where the MT has both Bani
and Binnui; cf. I Esd. 9:34*b* [Binnui]).
  *b*) Representatives probably accompanied Ezra
from Babylonia (Ezra 8:10, where Bani should be
restored on the basis of I Esd. 8:36 [KJV Banid]).
  *c*) Representatives set their seal to the covenant:
Levitical in Neh. 10:13—H 10:14 and "chiefs of the
people" in Neh. 10:14—H 10:15.
  *d*) A representative is included among those who
assisted Ezra in instructing the people in the law
(Neh. 8:7 = I Esd. 9:48 Anniuth, KJV Anus).
  **6.** The father (or possibly the family line) of Uzzi,
who is described as overseer of the Levites in Jerusalem; of the order of Asaph (Neh. 11:22).
  **7.** The father (or possibly the family line) of
Rehum, a Levite who repaired an assigned section
of the Jerusalem wall (Neh. 3:17) and may have been
the representative in some of the cases listed under
5 *above*.
  **8.** A Levite (individual or group) who took part
in the celebration of the Feast of Tabernacles at the
time of Ezra (Neh. 9:4-5). The list has Bani twice
in vs. 4; one of these is probably an error.

F. T. SCHUMACHER

**BANISHMENT.** Condemnation to exile. Since, to
the Israelite, exile from his land meant being cut off
from Yahweh (Hos. 9:3-5; cf. Gen. 4:14; Ezek. 11:
15) and, in the worst case, being forced to worship
idols (Deut. 4:27-28; I Sam. 26:19; Jer. 16:13), biblical law never prescribes it as a legal penalty. In
Ezra 7:26, שרשי is usually rendered "banishment"
(cf. Vulg. *exilium*) or, better, "exclusion from the
community" (cf. 10:8). But LXX παιδεία, in combination with Aramaic סרושיתא G. R. Driver, *Aramaic Documents of the Fifth Century B.C.*, no. iii, line
6, p. 13), suggests "whipping" (cf. LXX παιδεύω at
Deut. 22:18 for Hebrew יסר, which tradition, as early
as Jos. Antiq. IV.viii.23, renders "whip").
  Voluntary exile was the last resort of hunted men:
Jacob flees to Haran (Gen. 27:43), Moses to Midian
(Exod. 2:15), David's parents to Moab (I Sam. 22:3-
4), David to Gath (I Sam. 27:1-4), Absalom to
Geshur (II Sam. 13:38), Jeroboam to Egypt (I Kings
11:40), Elijah to Phoenicia (I Kings 17:9), Uriah to
Egypt (Jer. 26:21-23). Taking asylum in another
country was commonly practiced by political refugees
in the ancient Near East (cf. II Sam. 15:19; I Kings
11:14-25; Si-nuhe of Egypt; Idrimi of Alalakh);
clauses dealing with the extradition of such fugitives
are frequently found in Hittite treaties.
  Since biblical law regards every homicide as guilty
in some measure, the enforced stay of the accidental
manslayer in the CITY OF REFUGE may be considered
a form of banishment (Num. 35:32; it is so regarded
by Philo *On the Special Laws* III.123; Jos. Antiq. IV
vii.4; M. Mak. 2).
  Roman law knew several forms of exile, from the
severe *deportatio,* which was perpetual and involved
confiscation of property and loss of citizenship, to the
milder *relegatio,* by which a person was excluded from
residence in a certain place, or confined to a particular place for a definite or indefinite period of time. A
very common form was *relegatio in insulam,* which, according to early church tradition, was inflicted upon
the author of Revelation (Rev. 1:9).

  *Bibliography.* On flight for asylum, see: M. Löhr, *Das
Asylwesen im AT* (1930), where the Hittite extradition texts are
adduced as well; S. Smith, *The Statue of Idri-mi* (1949), pp. 14-
15; J. Pritchard, ed., *ANET* (2nd ed., 1955), pp. 18 ff (Si-
nuhe), 199 ff (Egyptian and Hittite treaties).
  On the banishment of John to Patmos, see: E. Lohmeyer,
*Die Offenbarung des Johannes,* Handbuch zum NT, 16 (1926),
13.
  On שרשי, see F. Rundgren, "Zur Bedeutung von *šršw*, Ezra
vii 25," *Vetus Testamentum,* VII (1957), 400-404.

M. GREENBERG

**BANKING.** The development of international trade
in antiquity made it imperative that some methods of
banking be devised to facilitate the transfer of funds
and, after the invention of money, the circulation and
exchange of coins. During the historical period covered by the writings of the OT, all banking operations
were performed by landowners, merchants, and
traders. The profession of banker as such does not
seem to antedate the Hellenistic era. The Greek word
for "banker" is τραπεζείτης, from τράπεζα, "table,
counter," and, by extension, the "banking house," or
"bank," itself (Matt. 25:27; Luke 19:23). The exchange of currencies was part of a banker's opera-

tions. There were, however, specialized money-changers.

*See also* DEBT; MONEY-CHANGER; TRADE AND COMMERCE.      G. A. BARROIS

**BANNAIA.** KJV Apoc. form of ZABAD 5-7.

**BANNAS** băn'əs [Βάννος] (I Esd. 5:26); KJV BANUAS băn'yŏŏ əs. A Levite, ancestor of some who returned from the Exile with Zerubbabel. The name is omitted in the parallel Ezra 2:40.

C. T. FRITSCH

**BANNER** [אות, דגל, משאת, נס]. Alternately: EN-SIGN. Either a standard of a tribe or troops or a rallying or warning signal of some kind.

The word אות (LXX σημεῖον) simply means "sign," though in Num. 2:2 it is paralleled by דגל and specifically means a tribal standard. At Ps. 74:4 אתת occurs twice in the passage concerning the enemy: "They set up their own signs for signs"; the KJV interprets the first "signs" as "ensigns," probably on the basis of the Vulg.: *Posuerunt signa sua signa* (cf. the Roman *signa*).

The word דגל is principally employed to designate the various standards of the Israelite tribes in Num. 2; 10 (where it is incorrectly interpreted as τάγμα, "order, rank," in the LXX), whereas נס is broader

in meaning—"sign, ensign, banner, or signal." The word משאת (lit., "a raising up") is used in Jer. 6:1 as a "signal" (KJV "sign of fire"); this usage is now exactly paralleled in the Lachish Ostraca at 4.10: "We are watching for the signals of Lachish." *See* LACHISH § 5.

Nothing is known concerning the nature of the tribal standards. On the analogy of other nations (Babylonian, Assyrian, Persian, and Roman*), it is quite possible that these may have been animal standards raised on a pole or spear. (It might be noted that Joshua's javelin is represented as a palladium in the account of the conquest of Ai in Josh. 8:26.) Such an animal standard as a divine symbol was the fiery serpent of bronze set on a pole (Num. 21:8-9). A divine standard is implied in the name Moses gave to an altar in Exod. 17:15-16, but its significance is still obscure. Figs. BAN 15-17.

16. Assyrian standards

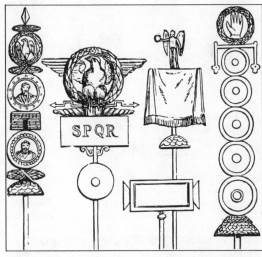

17. Roman standards

Banners were used as signals to rally an army (Isa. 5:26), and they would be set on a hill and accompanied (as in the Roman army) with the sounding of a trumpet (Isa. 13:2; 18:3; Jer. 4:21; 51:27). God's upraised hand is the raised "signal" for nations (Isa. 49:22; it might be added that the hand on a pole is thought to be the earliest form of the Roman *signum*).

Standards for army troops were common among the Egyptians, Babylonians, Assyrians, Hittites, Persians, and Romans. The eagle is attested as far

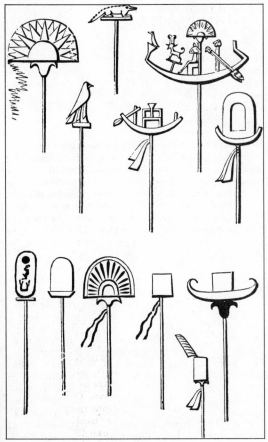

15. Standards used in ancient Egypt

back as the third millennium B.C. Army standards were commonly animal figures such as stags, steers, wolves, unicorns, serpents, lions, horses. Common among the Assyrians was the moon sickle mounted on a spear. The Assyrian royal chariot also carried the divine standards, the common form being that of the national god Ashur drawing a bow, or two running steers. A combination of the two is also attested. The eagle became for imperial Rome the official standard of the legion; but the wolf, unicorn, horse, and boar were all early standards. Under the emperors they became cultic symbols bearing the image of the emperor, and were therefore detested by the Jews. Sacrifices were made in the presence of the standards, but whether the *cultus signae* was earlier than Titus (cf. Jos. War VI.vi.1) is not known.

For standards in spiritual warfare, *see* DEAD SEA SCROLLS.

**Bibliography.** B. Meissner, *Babylonien und Assyrien*, I (1920), 82, 92-93; J. Kromayer and G. Veith, *Heerwesen und Kriegsführung der Griechen und Römer (Handbuch der Altertumswissenschaft* IV, 3.2; 1928), under appropriate entry; "Feldzeichen," in K. Galling, *Biblisches Reallexikon* (1937), pp. 160-63. J. W. WEVERS

**BANNUS.** KJV Apoc. form of BINNUI.

**BANQUET** [משתה, drinking]. The consumption of wine and rich foods was the chief feature of the banquet in biblical times. Amos provides a brilliant picture of the typical banquet: the guests lie on beds of ivory, eating lambs and calves; they drink wine and

Courtesy of the Oriental Institute, the University of Chicago

18. Preparing for the banquet, from the Megiddo Ivories (1350-1150 B.C.); a reconstruction

Courtesy of the Oriental Institute, the University of Chicago

19. Banquet scene, from the Megiddo Ivories (1350-1150 B.C.); a reconstruction

Courtesy of the Trustees of the British Museum

20. Banquet scene, from a basalt relief of Carchemish

sing songs; they anoint themselves with oil (Amos 6: 4-6; for more details on eating customs, *see* MEALS). Banquets were held on a variety of occasions: (*a*) at the arrival of a stranger (Gen. 19:3), (*b*) on a birthday (Gen. 40:20; Matt. 14:6), (*c*) when a child was weaned (Gen. 21:8), (*d*) after the sheepshearing (I Sam. 25:11; II Sam. 13:23), (*e*) at the grape harvest (Judg. 9:27), (*f*) after the completion of a public building (II Chr. 7:8), (*g*) when a treaty was ratified (Gen. 26:30; 31:54), and (*h*) at a wedding (Judg. 14: 10). No fewer than five separate banquets are described in Esther. *See* FEASTS AND FASTS; FOOD; WINE. Figs. BAN 18-20. J. F. Ross

**BANUAS.** KJV form of BANNAS.

*BAPTISM [βάπτισμα, *less commonly* βαπτισμός, *connected with* βαπτίζω, *an iterative form of* βάπτω, dip *or* immerse]. A rite using water as a symbol of religious purification. (In many NT passages the use of βαπτίζω and its cognates clearly implies immersion, but Luke 11:38 shows that this meaning is not demanded.) The term "baptism" is employed in the NT mainly of the rite practiced by JOHN THE BAPTIST, and of the Christian rite which, from the day of Pentecost onward, was the regular means of initiation into the Christian community.

1. Origin of baptism
    *a.* Proselyte baptism
    *b.* John the Baptist
    *c.* The baptism of Jesus
2. NT teaching about baptism
    *a.* The primitive church
    *b.* Pauline teaching
    *c.* Other NT references
3. Was baptism instituted by Jesus?
4. Possible traces of infant baptism within the NT period
Bibliography

**1. Origin of baptism.** The antecedents of Christian baptism are to be found within Judaism, and a careful study of this Jewish background renders improbable and unnecessary any hypothesis of the derivation of the Christian rite from the mystery cults.

*a. Proselyte baptism.* In common with other nations the Jews were accustomed to use water for the purpose of religious purification. A specialized use is to be found in the practice of proselyte baptism, one of the ceremonies by which new converts were admitted to Judaism. There is no reference to proselyte baptism in the OT or the Apoc., nor in Josephus or Philo. Some have therefore disputed whether this rite was practiced early enough to have influenced the origin of Christian baptism. It is now generally agreed, however, that the references in Epictetus, the Sibylline Oracles, and the Mishnah enable us, with some confidence, to date the beginnings of the practice not later than the first century A.D. Some have maintained that the significance of proselyte baptism was purely ceremonial, but in view of the fact that commandments of the Law were read during the administration of the rite, it is probable that we should, with H. H. Rowley, see proselyte baptism as "not an act of ritual purification alone but an act of self-dedication to the God of Israel, involving spiritual factors as well as physical with a fundamentally sacramental character."

**b. John the Baptist.** It was probably an extension of proselyte baptism when, "in the fifteenth year of the reign of Tiberius Caesar," John (who, in consequence, came to be known as the "baptizer" or the "baptist") went into all the region about the Jordan, preaching a baptism of repentance for the forgiveness of sins" (Luke 3:3). But there are striking differences between proselyte baptism and the baptism of John. John administered the rite to Jews as well as to Gentiles (Mark 1:5 and parallels). Further, for John the ethical significance of the rite became prominent. He bade the Pharisees and Sadducees "bear fruit that befits repentance." The most striking association of John's baptism is eschatological—he links the rite with his proclamation of the coming kingdom of God: "Repent, for the kingdom of heaven is at hand." John's baptism is thus a rite of moral purification designed to prepare those submitting to it for the approaching kingdom of God. In the gospel narratives John contrasts his own water baptism with a future baptism to be administered by the mightier one, "the thong of whose sandals I am not worthy to untie; he will baptize you with the Holy Spirit and with fire" (Luke 3:16).

Some scholars, arguing from an analysis of sources, have maintained that these references in the Baptist's teaching to the HOLY SPIRIT may not be authentic, and that John's original characterization of the future baptism spoke only of "fire"—i.e., "judgment" (cf. Matt. 3:10-12; Luke 3:9, 17). But, in view of the evidence furnished by the recently discovered DEAD SEA SCROLLS, there now seem less strong grounds than formerly appeared for denying the originality of these references by John to the Holy Spirit. The evidence of the Dead Sea Scrolls has (rather more questionably) been invoked to support the authenticity of such an utterance as John 1:29 on the lips of the Baptist. Further discussion would involve consideration of the alleged existence in NT times of a "Baptist" sect, the evidence for which shrinks on examination to very slender proportions. (The "disciples" at Ephesus [Acts 19:1] are probably to be understood, not as followers of John the Baptist, but as Christians whose instruction in the faith was incomplete.)

Fresh light has been thrown on the meaning of John's baptism by a comparison with the symbolic actions of the OT prophets. It has been suggested that these actions be understood not only as a vivid means of expressing the will of God, but also in some degree as helping to bring about its fulfilment. Seen in this light, John's baptism prepared those who submitted to it to face the coming Day of the Lord, confident that those who repented would be forgiven and granted a place in the future messianic community.

There is a brief account of John the Baptist in the Antiquities of Josephus (XVIII.v.2, § 117), the authenticity of which there seems no reason to doubt. Its representation, however, of John's mission as mainly ascetic seems historically less reliable than the Synoptic narrative, since the latter better accounts for the opposition John roused and the death he suffered at the hands of Herod.

**c. The baptism of Jesus.** The Synoptists record, and the Fourth Gospel implies, that Jesus accepted baptism at the hands of John (Mark 1:9-11 and parallels; John 1:32-34). The earliest account is told in such a way as to suggest that originally the record came from Jesus himself. Any attempt to regard the narrative as primarily invented by the early church founders on the evidence of Matt. 3:14-15, from which it is clear that the baptism of Jesus by John raised difficulties in the minds of the first Christians. That the ministry of Jesus was originally connected with the preaching and baptism of John is revealed by one of the most primitive passages in Acts (10:37-38). Recent study has stressed this connection. In the baptism of Jesus (historically speaking, a particular instance of John's baptism) a rite with water is intimately linked with a revelation of the Holy Spirit and a unique consciousness of divine sonship. It is noteworthy that these same two associations figure prominently in later NT teaching about the meaning of Christian baptism.

Further, the words of the voice heard by Jesus involve an allusion to Ps. 2 (vs. 7) and to one of the Servant Songs (Isa. 42:1). Admittedly the latter reference is not unmistakably to the *Suffering* Servant, but modern study of the OT in the NT has emphasized that sometimes the bare allusion to a word is meant to recall a far wider context. In view of this there is force in the theory that in the voice at the baptism of Jesus there is a foreshadowing of the Crucifixion. Greater point is thereby given to the passage in which, during his ministry, Jesus spoke of his death as a "baptism" (Luke 12:50). Though it has long been customary to treat this reference as purely metaphorical, there now seems good ground to make the reference to "baptism" more precise. Just as the baptism in Jordan inaugurated the ministry in Palestine, so the later "baptism" on Calvary inaugurated a wider ministry, unfettered by the limitations of the earthly mission. (*See also* § 3 *below* for the significance of the baptism of Jesus in a consideration of the authority behind Christian baptism.)

**2. NT teaching about baptism. a. The primitive church.** The rite of baptism with water as the symbol of entry into the Christian community was practiced from the day of Pentecost onward (Acts 2:38, 41). It was closely linked with repentance and with the reception of the Holy Spirit. From the frequency with which baptism follows upon "hearing" or "receiving the word" and "believing," the rite would seem, as it were, to embody the kerygma, and to represent the believer's response to, and acceptance of, the gospel message (Acts 2:37-38, 41; 8:12; 16:14-15, etc.). This continuance of water baptism is the more remarkable since both in the gospels and in the first chapter of Acts the contrast in the Baptist's teaching between his own baptism with water and the future baptism of the mightier one with Holy Spirit and with fire would suggest that in the new dispensation water baptism would have been superseded. (This has a bearing on the authority behind Christian baptism; *see* § 3 *below*.)

Sometimes the baptism is spoken of specifically as "in the name of Jesus Christ" (Acts 2:38; 10:48), or "in the name of the Lord Jesus" (8:16; 19:5). Ordinarily baptism preceded the reception of the Holy

Spirit, but in one instance—that of CORNELIUS—the gift of the Spirit was received before baptism; it is noteworthy that here, according to one account, Cornelius was subsequently baptized (10:48). In two passages the gift of the Holy Spirit is linked with another rite, the LAYING ON OF HANDS by an apostle (8:17; 19:6). It must be noticed, however, that there is no reference to the laying on of hands in the generally acknowledged Pauline letters.

The attempt has been made to dispute the view that baptism was practiced from the earliest days of the church, and instead to argue that the Christian rite originated in Hellenistic circles. Since, however, there are such close links between Christian baptism and the baptism of John, there is no need to discount the evidence of Acts, from which we infer that John's rite was continued and adapted by the apostles, some of whom we have reason to believe had themselves originally been followers of the Baptist. The precise nature of the impulse for this adaptation needs further elucidation (*see* § 3 *below*).

**b. The Pauline teaching.** The fullest NT exposition of the meaning of baptism is to be found in the Pauline letters. The most representative passages are:

I Cor. 12:12-13, where Paul teaches that baptism is the means of incorporation into the Christian community, which is the BODY OF CHRIST. Through baptism the Spirit is received, and the barriers that divide men, whether of race or of class, are thus overcome.

Gal. 3:26-29, where Paul draws out the connection of baptism with FAITH and sonship (*see* CHILDREN OF GOD). Baptism is described as a "putting on" of Christ. Again, it is stressed that this union with Christ overcomes all human divisions, whether of race, class, or sex.

Rom. 6:1-4. The vigorous exposition of the contrast between law and grace gives rise to the objection: "Are we to continue in sin that grace may abound?" Paul answers this objection by recalling his Roman readers to the significance of their baptism. When they underwent the rite (the imagery seems to imply baptism by immersion), they went down into the water, from which they subsequently emerged. This Paul sees as a symbolic representation of dying, being buried, and rising again with Christ. This "dying" is further explained as a death to sin, and this "rising again" as a resurrection to a new moral life. For those to whom these things have happened, the very thought of "continuing in sin" is patently absurd. This view of baptism as a moral death and resurrection has sometimes been unwittingly regarded as a form of personal teaching peculiar to Paul, but a careful reading of the context suggests that Paul must here rather be appealing to common Christian testimony (cf. "Do you not know . . . ?"); Paul himself had not visited Rome when he wrote this letter.

Col. 2:9-13. Paul is answering the false teaching at Colossae and asserting that Christ is all-sufficient for salvation. He strengthens his argument by an appeal to the significance of baptism, which he sees as the Christian counterpart of Jewish circumcision. Again he stresses that baptism means dying to sin and rising again to a new moral life. All things needful for salvation are given through our union with Christ in baptism; hence the Colossian insistence on ascetic rites is unnecessary.

Other references to baptism in the Pauline corpus elaborate these ideas further or guard against misunderstanding. Thus in Eph. 4:5 stress is laid on the relation of baptism to Christian unity; in I Cor. 10:2 Paul guards against a mechanical view of baptism which might suggest that salvation is thereby automatically assured. I Cor. 1:13-17 is not a belittlement of baptism but a protest against a misunderstanding at Corinth, whereby those baptized seem mistakenly to have thought that they had been baptized, not into the name of Christ, but into the name of the ministrant of the rite. In I Cor. 15:29 Paul alludes in passing to a local practice of baptism for the dead, according to which certain Corinthians would seem to have undergone the rite for the benefit of departed relatives. (Paul is not passing judgment on the practice but simply appealing to it as additional support for his argument about the resurrection of believers.)

The Pauline references to baptism all, in one way or another, bring out that close link between baptism and the preached message of the gospel which we have already observed in Acts. But by Paul the connection is far more fully explicated; and the whole Christian life is seen as the progressive laying hold on, and appropriation of, what was done once for all for a Christian at his baptism. It is in this that "faith" consists, and it is here that we see the full relevance of the Pauline teaching about baptism as a "dying and rising with Christ." It is improbable, as we have seen, that Paul himself was primarily responsible for this idea; indeed, it is far more likely that it stems from Jesus himself (*see* § 3 *below*). But Paul did much to set it in the forefront of normal Christian thinking. Just as the death of Christ and his resurrection from the dead took place once for all and yet had abiding consequences, so baptism, the application of that divine act to an individual, is administered once for all but has a continuing effect as it is increasingly appropriated and understood. Probably we come nearest to grasping the Pauline teaching when we view baptism as a sacrament of "realized eschatology." Divine sonship, the possession of the Spirit, the power to know God and to do his will, were all blessings connected, in the profoundest teaching of the OT, with the age to come. The Christian gospel consists in the fact that what in the OT was future expectation has now, because of what Christ was and did, become—at least in part —present realization. Baptism is the pledge to the Christian that here and now these blessings are his to be laid hold of; in a passage (Eph. 4:30) where the image of "sealing" involves an indirect reference to baptism, Paul reminds his readers that baptism also looks forward to a more complete redemption going beyond this present life.

**c. Other NT references.** The Fourth Gospel and the First Letter of John each contain a passage of considerable importance for the understanding of baptism. In the conversation with Nicodemus there is the saying attributed to Jesus (John 3:5): "Truly, truly, I say to you, unless one is born of water and the Spirit, he cannot enter the kingdom of God." Most scholars understand these words as containing a reference to baptism, but have some hesitation in regarding the saying, as it stands, as consisting of the *ipsissima verba* of Jesus. Some think, however, that the words may contain the nucleus of a genuine saying (*see bibliography*). The Johannine conception of "birth from above" is probably to be understood in the light of other Johannine teaching about divine sonship. It is noteworthy that here again the connection is to be observed between baptism, sonship, and the Spirit, which appears in the Synoptic narratives of the baptism of Jesus. The Fourth Evangelist clearly links sonship with baptism, but guards against any mechanical understanding of the rite by an equal stress on the activity of the Spirit. The indirect nature of the reference to baptism may be compared with the similar Johannine reticence about the Lord's Supper. Johannine theology is thoroughly sacramental, but this author expresses his teaching less directly than some other NT writers, in view of what seemed to him at the close of the first century A.D. unethical tendencies in current religious thought and practice.

The other striking Johannine passage about baptism is that in the First Letter (5:6): "This is he who came by water and blood, Jesus Christ, not with the water only but with the water and the blood." Like so much in I John, this teaching is to be understood as an answer to the Docetic heresy prevalent in Asia Minor at the end of the first century. In opposition to the teaching of CERINTHUS, who maintained that Christ was baptized but not crucified, John asserts the historical reality both of his baptism in Jordan and of his death upon the cross. This may be seen as the necessary answer to those who by their Docetic teaching were cutting loose the Christian faith from its foundation in historical fact. There may also be a secondary and derivative reference in the verse to the Christian sacraments of baptism and the Lord's Supper, though an allusion to the latter under the symbolism of "blood" seems without parallel. The truth may rather be that in this passage, as elsewhere in the NT, the close connection is again being emphasized between Christian baptism and the death of Christ.

Other references to baptism in the NT include two passages in the Letter to the Hebrews (6:2; 10: 22). The former suggests that teaching about baptism and its differentiation from other "ablutions," Jewish or pagan, formed part of the regular instruction of Christian catechumens; the latter passage brings out the moral significance of baptism and its connection with faith (cf. J. Denney's dictum, "Baptism and faith are but the outside and the inside of the same thing"). A similar purpose underlies the well-known passage in the First Letter of Peter (3: 21), where the importance of the new moral life is stressed, and this transformation is seen as an outworking of the same divine power by which Jesus was raised from the dead. Christ can communicate the new life because he has entered into it.

The only reference to REGENERATION in connection with baptism occurs in a passage in one of the Pastoral Letters: "He saved us, not because of deeds done by us in righteousness, but in virtue of his own mercy, by the washing of regeneration and renewal in the Holy Spirit" (Tit. 3:5). Some have traced here

the influence of ideas derived from contemporary mystery cults, but the evidence scarcely warrants such a conclusion. (The oft-quoted inscription, *taurobolio . . . renatus, Corp. Inscript. Lat.* 6.510, can be dated no earlier than A.D. 376.) It seems more probable that the language of this passage represents an extension of the concept of "birth from above," already linked in Johannine teaching with baptism and with the activity of the Holy Spirit.

**3. Was baptism instituted by Jesus?** Two Synoptic passages associate baptism with a command to preach the gospel throughout the world; of these, Mark 16:16 lacks original authority, since it occurs in the verses added in the second century A.D. to a gospel which (rightly or wrongly) was thought to be incomplete. The other passage, Matt. 28:19 ("Go . . . make disciples of all nations, baptizing them in the name of the Father and of the Son and of the Holy Spirit"), has also been disputed on textual grounds, but in the opinion of many scholars the words may still be regarded as part of the true text of Matthew. There is, however, grave doubt whether they may be regarded as *ipsissima verba* of Jesus. The evidence of Acts 2:38; 10:48 (cf. 8:16; 19:5), supported by Gal. 3:27; Rom. 6:3, suggests that baptism in early Christianity was administered, not in the threefold name, but "in the name of Jesus Christ" or "in the name of the Lord Jesus." This is difficult to reconcile with the specific instruction of the verse at the end of Matthew. At the same time, if it is part of the true text of Matthew, it provides evidence for a conviction in certain Christian circles toward the end of the first century that baptism rested upon the authority of Jesus. That such a conviction was well grounded is the more probable as we remember that the recorded teaching of John the Baptist would appear to suggest a supersession, rather than a continuance, of the practice of baptizing with water (cf. Mark 1:8 and parallels, and similar words attributed to Jesus in Acts 1:5). The fact that the basic rite of Christian initiation consisted of a baptism with water is more easily to be understood if the early Christians were justified in their conviction that the rite rested, in some sense, upon the authority of Jesus.

Such a dominical authority for baptism is to be found, not so much in the evidence of particular texts (which may be critically disputed), but rather in Jesus' life and ministry as a whole, with particular emphasis upon his baptism and death. Certain passages in Acts (cf. 1:21-22; 10:37; 13:24-25) make clear that in early Christian teaching the beginning of the mission of Jesus was traced back to the activity of John the Baptist. He was the forerunner of Jesus, and in his preaching and baptism the ministry of Jesus found its prelude. Further, the prominence given by the Synoptists to the narrative of Jesus' own baptism by John shows that the fact that Jesus submitted to John's baptism was regarded as highly significant. Recent study of the antecedents of Christian baptism has laid considerable stress on the importance in this connection of the baptism of Jesus. It is notable that both in the baptism of Jesus and in the Christian rite a baptism with water is linked with the descent of the Holy Spirit and with divine sonship. Further, in Acts baptism is frequently associated with, and regarded as expressive of, repentance. Some early Christians found it hard to understand how Jesus could submit to a "baptism of repentance for the forgiveness of sins." The difficulty is most satisfactorily resolved as we see Jesus corporately setting himself alongside those to whom he came to minister. He could not separate himself from the sinners whom he would save.

The other antecedent of Christian baptism in the ministry of Jesus is to be found in his death and resurrection. Notably in the Pauline letters, but also in the Johannine writings, Hebrews, and I Peter, baptism is connected with the death of Christ. To regard this association as a Pauline innovation breaks down on the evidence of Rom. 6:3 (*see* § 2*b above*). If Christian baptism is in some sense to be regarded as "the kerygma in action," the gospel of salvation dramatically brought to bear upon the life of a particular person, then it is scarcely surprising to find, when the full implication of the rite is being drawn out, that special stress is laid upon that divine act which is at the center of the gospel—the death and resurrection of Christ. The impulse for this linking of baptism with Christ's death and its sequel is to be sought in the utterances of Jesus which speak of his death under the figure of baptism—one of which suggests that it was only through his death that his wider ministry could be inaugurated: "I have a baptism to be baptized with; and how I am constrained until it is accomplished!" (Luke 12:50).

Thus the authority for Christian baptism in the ministry of Jesus is twofold, and corresponds with his own twofold baptism, that in Jordan and that on Calvary. Here the work of O. Cullmann is illuminating. He finds the link with the death of Jesus as far back as the baptism in Jordan, in virtue of the allusion in the voice from heaven to one of the Servant Songs in Deutero-Isaiah. Further, he sees the death of Jesus as what he terms a *Generaltaufe,* a universal baptism, which, lying as it does behind every individual act of Christian baptism, gives the rite its significance and potency. Such an understanding of the authority behind Christian baptism firmly grounds the origin of this gospel sacrament in the life and ministry of Jesus, and remains unaffected by critical reservations which may attach themselves to the interpretation of a particular text. *See* DEATH OF CHRIST.

**4. Possible traces of infant baptism within the NT period.** There is no direct evidence in the NT for the baptism of infants. Various lines of indirect evidence, however, converge—in the judgment of a number of scholars—to make the conclusion probable that in some quarters, at least, infant baptism was practiced in the early church during the NT period. Here a distinction should be drawn between the children of new converts and children born to parents already themselves baptized Christians. In regard to the former, the analogy of proselyte baptism would encourage the administration of Christian baptism to the children of new converts. But in regard to the latter, children of parents already Christian, the evidence from proselyte baptism would point the other way, since children born to a proselyte subsequent to his own reception were not baptized but only circumcised. It has been suggested that, as during the first century A.D. the early church increas-

ingly diverged from Judaism, the need was felt for some Christian counterpart to match the Jewish rite of circumcising infants, and this would encourage the practice of baptizing also the children of parents already Christian.

J. Jeremias has argued that Paul may have been instrumental in thus putting forward baptism as the Christian equivalent of Jewish circumcision (cf. Col. 2:11-12; Acts 21:21). Paul addresses children as "in the Lord" (Eph. 6:1). He would scarcely have used this distinctive phrase except of those actually included in the body of Christ, to which, according to Pauline teaching, baptism is the rite of entry.

Some have questioned whether the references in Acts to the baptism of "households" (16:15, 33; 18:8) may be held to include young children; here the evidence cited by Jeremias from Stauffer is important as showing that in the contemporary use of the term "household" young children were specifically included.

This indirect evidence within the NT agrees with certain indications in early Christian writers which appear to require a date for the beginnings of infant baptism within, rather than later than, the NT period. Thus the words of Polycarp at his martyrdom, "Eighty-and-six years have I been his slave" (Martyrdom of Polycarp 9), imply his reception into the church, and consequently his baptism as an infant, *ca.* A.D. 69 or 70. Again, Justin Martyr, writing *ca.* 155, refers to men and women of sixty or seventy years of age who in childhood "were made disciples" (Apol. 1.15; cf. the aorist tense of the verb μαθητεύω, used in Matt. 28:18). Toward the end of the second century Polycrates says that he has lived sixty-five years "in the Lord." The earlier examples, Polycarp and those referred to by Justin, may have been the children of new converts, but this is scarcely probable of Polycrates, since he refers to seven of his family who had been bishops before him, "he himself being the eighth" (Euseb. Hist. V.xxiv. 6-7). Tertullian in a well-known passage (*On Baptism* XVIII) deplores infant baptism, but fails to use what would have been his strongest argument—namely, that the practice was not primitive. The knowledge that, in some quarters, at least, infant baptism began to be practiced during the first century A.D. may lie behind the statement of Origen that infant baptism had been handed down "from the apostles."

Those who on grounds of faith and conscience oppose pedobaptism would set against this indirect evidence the silence of the NT about the baptism of infants. The strength of this argument should be balanced by the recognition that the NT is equally silent about any postponement of the baptism of the children of Christian parents to riper years. There is no recorded instance in the NT of the baptism on profession of faith of any but new converts. If the practice of the early church was to postpone baptism in such cases until years of discretion, it is remarkable that it has left no trace in documents written over a period of at least three generations. The direct historical evidence of the NT is insufficient to settle the question either for or against infant baptism; the case must be argued on other grounds.

*Bibliography.* D. Stone, *Holy Baptism* (1912). H. G. Marsh, *The Origin and Significance of the NT Baptism* (1941). K. Barth, *The Teaching of the Church Regarding Baptism* (English trans.

E. A. Payne, 1948). W. F. Flemington, *The NT Doctrine of Baptism* (1948). J. Jeremias, *Hat die Urkirche die Kindertaufe geübt?* (1949)—p. 43 contains a comparison of other sayings of Jesus with the one in John 3:5. O. Cullmann, *Baptism in the NT* (English trans. by J. K. S. Reid, 1950). M. Barth, *Die Taufe ein Sakrament?* (1951). G. W. H. Lampe, *The Seal of the Spirit* (1951). J. Murray, *Christian Baptism* (1952).

On infant baptism see especially an article by T. W. Manson, "Baptism in the Church," in *Scottish Journal of Theology*, vol. II, no. 4, pp. 391-403, with a reply by E. A. Payne in the following number, vol. III, no. 1, pp. 50-56.

W. F. FLEMINGTON

**BAPTIST.** *See* JOHN THE BAPTIST.

**BAR** [בד, בריח, מוט, מוטה, מטיל, מנעול; μοχλός]. Primarily, a piece of wood or metal used as a support, fastening, or barrier. Most of the biblical uses of the word are related to this general meaning—a bar of acacia wood used to join frames in the superstructure of the TABERNACLE; a bar of wood or metal used to secure a DOOR or GATE; an ingot of metal (*see* METALLURGY), particularly GOLD; the crosspiece of a YOKE; a verbal form meaning "to secure or lock" (Neh. 7:3); figurative uses (e.g., the "bars of Sheol" [Job 17:16]).

An interpretation of the bars (בריח) in the tabernacle (Exod. 26:26-29; 36:31-34; etc.) is difficult, but their function seems to have been to bond together the frames of the superstructure. The same Hebrew word often denotes bars used to secure gates or doors, to be distinguished from the bolt-and-LOCK combination, the latter being used on smaller buildings and houses. The second alone comes into consideration for the NT (e.g., Acts 5:23). The gate bar is used only with reference to city gates (Deut. 3:5; Judg. 16: 3; I Sam. 23:7; I Kings 4:13; Jer. 51:30; Amos 1:5; etc.) and citadels (Prov. 18:19; Bar. 6:18; I Macc. 9:50) in the OT and the Apoc. They were made of wood (implied in Nah. 3:13; cf. Jer. 51:30; Lam. 2: 9), bronze (I Kings 4:13), or iron (Ps. 107:16; Isa. 45:2). It is probable that gates which were barred as a defensive measure had more than one bar (cf. Neh. 3:3-15). At Tell en-Nasbeh the Iron Age city gate (*ca.* 900 B.C.) had a slot into which the bar could be thrust when the gate was open and a lock hole on the jamb opposite. Since the level was close to the ground, it is probable that other bars were placed higher up on the gate. The small, round lock hole indicates that the bar in this case was metal.

A city provided with high walls, gates, and bars was secure (Deut. 3:5; Ps. 147:13), but the breaking of the bars was the sign the city had fallen (Isa. 43: 14; Amos 1:5; Nah. 3:13). A quiet and secure people felt no need of gates and bars (Jer. 49:31; Ezek. 38: 11). Metaphorically, bars confine the sea (the abyss) in Job 38:10 and delimit Sheol (Job 17:16; cf. Jonah 2:6—H 2:7).

*Bibliography.* C. C. McCown, *Tell en-Nasbeh,* I (1947), 196-98 and pl. 71:5.

R. W. FUNK

**BARABBAS** bə răb'əs [Βαραββᾶς=בר־אבא, son of (the) father]. A man who, according to all the NT gospels, was held in prison by the Roman authorities at the time of Jesus' trial. Matthew calls him a "notable prisoner," but does not indicate what his crime was. The Fourth Gospel says that he was a robber, whereas Mark and Luke state that he had been arrested for insurrection and murder. The latter may indicate that he was of the party of ZEALOTS, who desired to throw off the Roman yoke by force. According to Jerome (*On Matthew*), the name in the apocryphal Gospel According to the Hebrews was *filius magistri eorum*—i.e., ברבן, "son of their teacher." Since "father" might be applied to a rabbi, both forms of the name may indicate that Barabbas' father held a position of leadership in the Jewish religious community.

According to three of the gospels (Matt. 27:15; Mark 15:6; John 18:39), Pilate the Roman governor used to placate the Jews at the time of a feast—John says specifically at the Passover—by releasing one prisoner of their choice. Luke, who may have been a more accurate historian, does not mention the custom (cf. Luke 23:18 ff), and nothing quite like it is referred to elsewhere in ancient literature. On the other hand, release of prisoners for various reasons was not unknown (cf. Jos. Antiq. XX.ix.3). The Roman historian Livy reported that prisoners were commonly relieved of their chains, though he does not actually say released from prison, at the Lectisternium.

All four gospels imply that the choice of a prisoner to be set free at this feast lay between Jesus and Barabbas. Urged on by the Jewish leaders, the populace clamored for Barabbas to be freed and for Jesus to be executed. Pilate gave in, and condemned Jesus to death (*see* TRIAL OF JESUS). Nothing is known of Barabbas' subsequent history. The Fourth Gospel does not actually say that he was let go.

Origen (*Commentary on Matthew*) said that the name appeared in some old MSS as "Jesus Barabbas" ('Ιησοῦς ὁ Βαραββᾶς), and this form appears also in the ninth-century Codex θ at Matt. 27:16. While the reading is not well attested, it is not impossible, from the historical standpoint. Jesus was a common enough name. Then Pilate's question would take the poignant form: "Whom do you want me to release for you, Jesus Barabbas or Jesus who is called Christ?"

P. PARKER

**BARACHEL** băr'ə kĕl [ברכאל, God blessed] (Job 32:2, 6). A Buzite; the father of Elihu, one of Job's three friends.

**BARACHIAH** băr'ə kī'ə [Βαραχίας] (Matt. 23:35); KJV BARACHIAS —əs. The father of Zechariah; same as OT BERECHIAH (5).

**BARAK** bâr'ak [ברק, lightning; Βαρακ]. Son of Abinoam. Barak shared with the prophetess DEBORAH in the leadership of a N Israelite militia in a victorious campaign against Sisera, the commander of the Canaanite forces of JABIN king of Hazor. The recital of the epic is preserved both in prose (Judg. 4) and in poetry (ch. 5), each of which contains its peculiarities. In the prose narrative Deborah summoned Barak from Kedesh in Naphtali to the seat of her juridical ministrations in Mount Ephraim and there divulged to him an oracle of Yahweh. It stipulated that Barak should bring about the overthrow of the Canaanite oppression by raising some ten thousand men from Naphtali and Zebulun, and await an engagement with the enemy at Mount Tabor. Apprised of the Israelite uprising, Sisera left his quarters at Harosheth-ha-goiim with his force of men and nine hundred iron chariots to crush the rebellion, but the Israelites swept down from Mount Tabor, completely routing the Canaanites. Retreating toward Harosheth-ha-goiim, Sisera fled northward toward Zaanannim and was granted asylum by Jael, the wife of Heber the Kenite. She perfidiously slew Sisera while he slept, and when Barak arrived on the scene in pursuit of Sisera, Jael informed him of her deed. This defeat of the N Canaanites under the command of Sisera forecast the ultimate doom of the power of Jabin.

An editor represents Barak as joining Deborah in singing the epinician ode (5:1).

Barak is included among the judges who liberated Israel from her oppressors in the valedictorian address of Samuel (I Sam. 12:11, where "Barak" [LXX; Syr.] should be read for "Bedan" [MT]). He is also mentioned in the NT catalogue of ancient worthies whose faith was exemplary (Heb. 11:32).

E. R. DALGLISH

**BARBARIAN.** The translation of βάρβαρος in Rom. 1:14; Col. 3:11; II Macc. 2:21. The word is elsewhere translated NATIVE (Acts 28:2, 4); FOREIGNER (I Cor. 14:11); SAVAGE WILD BEAST (II Macc. 4:25); BARBAROUS NATION (II Macc. 10:4); BARBAROUS FOE (III Macc. 3:24).

1. Origin
2. Derogatory connotation
3. Greeks and barbarians
4. NT usage

**1. Origin.** Βάρβαρος was originally an imitative word—like "dingdong," of bells; "twitter," of birds; "gibberish" or "yack-yack," of speech. In this sense a "barbarian" is a person who utters a sequence of sounds, but not sense. Or if the listener concedes that the barbarian speaks a real language, it remains nonsense if it is not understood. I Cor. 14:11 perfectly illustrates this meaning. Theoretically, at least, this use of the word need not carry pejorative meaning: a Greek might speak of a Hebrew as a "barbarian," a Hebrew might speak of a Greek as a "barbarian," and neither mean anything except that the other spoke a different language. In Herodotus, e.g., the word is not contemptuous but simply means "non-Greek." A barbarian is a "foreigner," and without further nuance of aversion or hostility. Thucydides could say: "I mean by the term Hellenes those who . . . had a common language" (I.3). Or Herodotus: "The Egyptians call by the name of barbarians all such as speak a language different from their own" (II.158). So the Jews may be barbarians to the Babylonians, Medes, and Romans; Egyptians or Greeks may be barbarians to the Jews (see II Macc. 2:21; 4:25; 15:2); and, of course, the term was applied by the Greeks to all non-Hellenic peoples. The Romans, too, followed suit, although they never called the Greeks barbarians. Indeed, one may generalize and say that all dominant peoples in antiquity called those who spoke a different language barbarians.

**2. Derogatory connotation.** In one stage of its de-

velopment, then, "barbarian" had simply linguistic-ethnographical-geographical meaning, without nuance of aversion or hostility. E.g., in Herodotus the term means simply "non-Greek," and is used without contempt. And we can say that the phrase "Greeks and barbarians" was a Greek way of classifying the totality of mankind, corresponding to the Jewish division of mankind into "Israel and the nations [Gentiles, heathen]." Since, however, (a) language is so powerful a means to consolidating a community and to exalting it in its self-esteem above other, alien linguistic groups; and (b) since the Greek language was so rich, massive, and masterly an instrument of speech and thought, and the civilization which it verbalized was so superb; and (c) since all in-groups tend to define themselves in terms of contrast, even hostility, to out-groups, it was inevitable that "barbarian," like "foreigner" among us, should quickly assume an air of contempt. This came more easily when, as in Greece, there were elements of genuine superiority. The Greek was a proud man.

**3. Greeks and barbarians.** "Barbarian," then, like "outlandish," comes naturally to mean "foreign in mentality or character." The barbarian is now, by definition and by nature, ignorant and untrained, crude and unpolished; as uncivilized he is wild, savage, cruel—in a word, "barbarous." By definition he is hostile and an object of enmity.

It was the Persian Wars (fifth century B.C.) which made clear to the Greeks the superiority of their culture to that of barbarians—set out in Aeschylus, Pindar, and Herodotus—and made the word imply boorishness and brutality and the contempt which free men have for slaves. Plato will say that barbarians are "by nature enemies" (*Republic* 470); that in war Greeks should be humane to Greeks but not to barbarians; and that Greeks should not have Greek slaves, only barbarian ones. And as Aristotle said: "Hellenes do not like to call themselves slaves but confine the term to barbarians" (*Politics* I.6.6), he consequently defended the enslavement of his two classes of barbarians, those of Western Asia and the Scythians (tribes around the Black Sea), as natural on the ground that the Orientals possessed intelligence without courage and the Northerners courage without intelligence. Yet not all Greeks held so hardened a position. Strabo (*ca.* 63 B.C.–A.D. 21) makes a point of saying that Eratosthenes (*ca.* 275–194 B.C.) "withholds praise" from those who divide mankind into two groups, Greeks and barbarians, and from those who advised Alexander to treat Greeks as friends and barbarians as enemies. "Eratosthenes goes on to say that it would be better to make such divisions according to good qualities and bad qualities; for not only are many of the Greeks bad, but many of the barbarians are refined—Indians and Arians, for example, and further, Romans and Carthaginians, who carry on their governments so admirably" (I.4, 9).

**4. NT usage.** In Acts 28:2, 4, βάρβαροι ("natives") means simply "foreigners"—i.e., here neither Greeks nor Jews. A difference in language is probably implied, although, if so, Acts 28:1-10 is not aware of a problem of understanding. Everybody seems to know Greek. That the natives' kindness is described as "unusual" may reflect the Greek assumption that all "barbarians" are inherently coarse, if not hostile. The context shows that the word carries no ill will.

In Rom. 1:14, Paul uses the two pairs: "Greeks"-"barbarians," "wise"-"foolish." Since the two pairs are probably to be taken as correlatives—i.e., the "Greeks" are the "wise" and the "barbarians" are the "foolish"—Paul will simply say that he is under obligation to preach the gospel to all mankind. The Greek stereotype "Greek"-"Barbarian" is here less geographical-ethnological than it is cultural in significance. In this sense, Romans, too, together with all who inhabit the important city-states of the Mediterranean, would be "Greeks." The "wise" would be the cultured peoples of the area, the well-Hellenized; the "foolish"—better, the uneducated (in the Greek sense)—would be those outside the Greco-Roman cultural orbit. The phrase on Paul's lips refers to the total non-Jewish humanity. J. B. Phillips' paraphrase: "from cultured Greek to ignorant savage," accurately reproduces the sense if one remembers that Paul would not have objected to the remark of Dionysius of Halicarnassus (born *ca.* 60 B.C.) *Roman Antiquities* I.89: "Let the reader . . . confidently affirm it [Rome] to be a Greek city."

In Col. 3:11, "barbarian" represents the non-Greek, non-Jewish population, but in close association with "Scythian" and "slave"—i.e., with human beings of the lowest and most degrading sort. Josephus describes the Scythians as those "who delight in murdering people and are little better than wild beasts" (Apion II.37; cf. II Macc. 4:47; III Macc. 7:5). Paul's use of "barbarian" is not different from that of Philo or Josephus; what is different is his insistence that in Christ "there cannot be Greek and Jew, circumcised and uncircumcised, barbarian, Scythian, slave, free man, but Christ is all, and in all."                                       F. D. GEALY

**BARBER** [גלב]. One who shaves or trims the BEARD and cuts and dresses the HAIR. Barbers are

Courtesy of the Metropolitan Museum of Art

21. An Egyptian barber at work dressing the hair of a soldier, from a wall painting from the tomb of User-Het, a royal scribe (fifteenth century B.C.)

busy in all periods of the biblical story (Num. 6:5; Ezek. 5:1) and into Talmudic regulations. They usually worked in the open air, and the RAZOR was their main tool. There is no evidence in the Bible that the modern Eastern custom of shaving the head was religiously significant. Fig. BAR 21.

C. U. WOLF

**BARHUMITE** bär hū'mīt [ברחמי, *apparently a copyist's error*]. KJV translation in II Sam. 23:31; RSV "of BAHURIM."

**BARIAH** bə rī'ə [בריח, fugitive] (I Chr. 3:22). Son of Shemaiah in the Zerubbabel line of Davidic descendants.

**BAR-JESUS** bär jē'zəs [Βαριησοῦς; Aram. בר ישוע, son of Jesus] (Acts 13:6-11). A Jewish magician and false prophet at Paphos on Cyprus, who became blind when Paul denounced him. *See* MAGIC; ELYMAS.

**BAR-JONA** bär jō'nə [Βαριωνᾶς]. The patronymic of Simon Peter. *See* PETER.

**BARKOS** bär'kŏs [ברקוס; Akkad. *and* Aram. *inscriptions suggest a theophorous name, perhaps* son (Aram. בר?) of Kos (a god)]. Head of a family of temple servants (Ezra 2:53; Neh. 7:55). *See* NETHINIM.

**BARLEY** [שערה, *śeʿōrâ*, usually plural, שערים; Ugar. *śʿr;* Arab. *šaʿîr;* κριθή]. An important grain in Bible times, barley is also mentioned frequently in the fourteenth-century-B.C. Ugaritic documents. The Semitic name was derived from the word for "hair," probably because of the long awns which project from the seeds to form the characteristic beardlike heads.

Barley ripened earlier than wheat (Exod. 9:31); the harvesting of wheat begins about two weeks later. Palestine was a "land of wheat and barley" (Deut. 8: 8). Barley was cheaper than wheat (II Kings 7:1, 16, 18; Rev. 6:6). It was used as food for animals (I Kings 4:28—H 5:8). Its grain was an important part of human diet, especially for the poor (Lev. 23:22; Ruth 3:15, 17; II Sam. 17:28; II Kings 4:42; 7:1, 16, 18; II Chr. 2:10, 15—H 2:9, 14; 27:5; Jer. 41:8), baked in the form of coarse loaves (Judg. 7:13; Ezek. 4:12; John 6:9, 13). It was used as a cereal offering (Num. 5:15; Ezek. 45:13; and probably Lev. 23:10-14, since barley was harvested first) and as a medium of exchange (Ezek. 13:19 [bribes!]; Hos. 3:2). Its harvest was a feature of the ancient CALENDAR (Ruth 1:22; II Sam. 17:28), as indicated by the tenth-century-B.C. Gezer Calendar, which says (line 4): "His month is barley-harvest" (i.e., April-May).

Several species of barley are found in Bible lands, but *Hordeum vulgare* L. (spring barley) is most common. *Hordeum hexastichon* L. (winter barley) is quite common in the Jordan Valley and the E plateau.

*See also* AGRICULTURE; FEASTS AND FASTS; FLORA § A1*c;* GRAIN; HARVEST; SACRIFICES AND OFFERINGS.

**Bibliography.** H. N. and A. L. Moldenke, *Plants of the Bible* (1952), pp. 112-13.                    J. C. TREVER

**BARLEY HARVEST.** The reaping of the cereal Hordeum. The barley harvest began as early as late April (especially in the lowlands; Josh. 3:15) or early May, preceding the wheat harvest by *ca.* two weeks (Ruth 2:23). The beginning of the barley harvest was marked by the bringing in of the FIRST FRUITS as a consecration of the harvest (Lev. 23:10).

H. N. RICHARDSON

**BARN** [מְגוּרָה; KJV גֹּרֶן (Job 39:12; RSV THRESH-ING FLOOR); ἀποθήκη]. A storage place for seed (Hag. 2:19) or grain (Matt. 13:30). The full barn is a sign of prosperity (Deut. 28:8; Prov. 3:10; Luke 12:18); an empty barn indicates dearth (Joel 1:17 KJV). *See also* STOREHOUSE; GRANARY; AGRICULTURE.

**BARNABAS** bär'nə bəs [Βαρνάβας; *understood by Luke to mean* בַּר נְבוּאָה, υἱός παρακλήσεως, son of encouragement (Acts 4:36)]. An apostle of the secondary group, companion of Paul on his mission to Cyprus and the Pisidian mainland. Originally named Joseph, he probably acquired the name Barnabas because of his ability as a preacher.

1. Jewish backgrounds
2. Mission work with Paul
3. Separation from Paul
4. Barnabas as a writer
Bibliography

**1. Jewish backgrounds.** Barnabas first appears in Luke's account of communal living in the Jerusalem church, as a man of some means who gave to the church the proceeds from the sale of a piece of land (Acts 4:36-37). He is also called a Levite and a native of the island of Cyprus (Acts 4:36). His priestly family had evidently separated from Jerusalem, and thus Barnabas had a career somewhat like that of John the Baptist. His birthplace makes him a Jew of the Diaspora, a fellow Hellenist of Saul of Tarsus in contrast to the Palestinian Jews like Peter, who are called "Hebrews" by Luke (Acts 6:1). Barnabas seems to be a part of the movement of Hellenists back to Jerusalem from Gentile lands, although Eusebius identified him with Luke's company of the Seventy (Luke 10:1). According to Acts, there was a large company of Hellenists in the city at the celebration of Pentecost just after the Crucifixion. The spiritual and cultural kinship of Barnabas and Saul is seen in the return of the latter to Jerusalem after conversion. The disciples in Jerusalem were suspicious of the convert, but Barnabas was there to introduce him favorably to them (Acts 9:27). Barnabas thus belongs to the company of first converts in Jerusalem who were won by the apostolic preaching, if not by Jesus himself.

**2. Mission work with Paul.** In the Christian Diaspora (Acts 8:1 ff), many Hellenists fled from Jerusalem and went to Antioch of Syria. That Barnabas did not flee is evidence of his good standing in Jerusalem, along with the "apostles." Though not a native, Barnabas had the confidence of the apostles. Later he was sent to join the company of workers at Antioch, to preach to Jews, Hellenists, and Greeks (Acts 11:19-22). As the work of the Antioch church expanded and more workers were needed, Barnabas went over to Tarsus and brought back with him Saul. It seems that Barnabas was the leader of the Antioch church, and the order which Luke gives, "Barnabas and Saul," indicates the pre-eminence. It was "Barnabas and Saul" who carried relief funds from Antioch to the famine-stricken Jerusalem (Acts 11:30).

Barnabas was commissioned by the Antioch church, along with Saul and John Mark, to undertake the missionary journey which led them to Cyprus and later to the provinces of the N mainland. It is not clear whether the church had Cyprus in mind in the selection of Barnabas and Mark, both natives, or whether it was the idea of Barnabas, who was the leader. But the Hellenistic character of all three workers is probably seen in their appointment to serve in Gentile lands. On the island of Cyprus, however, it seems that Saul, afterward called Paul, took over the leadership (Acts 13:9), and when they moved on to the mainland, they were known as "Paul and his company" (Acts 13:13). With exceptions to be noted, Paul is thenceforth named ahead of Barnabas. But in the city of Lystra there was a wave of enthusiasm on the part of the natives, and Barnabas was given the title "Zeus," while Paul was only "Hermes" the spokesman (Acts 14:12). The men of Lystra must have recognized a comparative dignity in Barnabas. Even Luke reverts to "Barnabas and Paul" (Acts 14:14). After the stoning in Lystra, Paul's leadership seems to have been temporarily suspended, and he "went on with Barnabas to Derbe" (Acts 14:20), since Barnabas does not seem to have been stoned.

Luke's account of the conference at Jerusalem (Acts 15) again places Barnabas at the front, indicating that Barnabas was in better standing than Paul in Jerusalem. "Barnabas and Paul" made the report in the conference relating to the work which had been done among the Gentiles (Acts 15:12). The document which was sent by the conference recommending "Barnabas and Paul" to the Syrian and Cilician churches again shows Luke's knowledge of the relative standing of the two men in Jerusalem.

**3. Separation from Paul.** The separation of Barnabas from Paul and their divergent missionary activity began in Antioch after the Jerusalem conference. The issue which Luke gives was the taking of John Mark on another journey (Acts 15:36 ff). Mark's defection at Cyprus (Acts 13:13) seemed to Paul to be sufficient grounds for dropping him from the party. But Barnabas was devoted to Mark as a cousin (Col. 4:10), and leaving Paul, Barnabas took Mark on a separate mission again to Cyprus. Luke's cryptic words "sailed away to Cyprus" (Acts 15:39) are his farewell to Barnabas.

The rift between Barnabas and Paul is further described by Paul himself in his Letter to the Galatians. At Antioch, Barnabas not only insisted on taking Mark on a second journey, but he had shown a wavering, along with Peter, on the issue of association with Gentiles, particularly eating with them at table (Gal. 2:11 ff). Peter was of Jerusalem, and the sympathies of Barnabas were there too. Neither Peter nor Barnabas measured up to the Pauline requirements for a mission to the Gentiles. The position of Barnabas seems to be fairly well defined. On the extreme left were Hellenists like Apollos, with Paul a little to the right of him. Barnabas was a Hellenist nearer center, or right of center, showing kinship with Peter and the Jerusalem group. On the extreme right were James and the Judaizers, sometimes referred to by Luke as "certain ones" who went out on tours of inspection in the country where the more liberal apostles were at work. Paul could later refer sympathetically to Barnabas as a "working" apostle, "working for a living" like himself (I Cor. 9:6). But beyond that, the rift was final, as far as the record goes.

**4. Barnabas as a writer.** The testimony of the later church gives Barnabas a role as writer. Tertullian assigned to him the authorship of the Letter to the Hebrews. Both Clement of Alexandria and Origen gave him credit for the epistle which bears his name, and they gave it canonical standing because they read its author as an apostle. However, the nature of both Hebrews and the Epistle of Barnabas is hard to reconcile with the conservative tendencies of Barnabas as indicated in Galatians, and the identification of Barnabas with Jerusalem in the book of Acts. Moreover, the Epistle of Barnabas seems to be dated *ca.* A.D. 130 on internal evidence, and too late for our Barnabas.

*Bibliography.* W. L. Knox, *St. Paul and the Church of Jerusalem* (1925), pp. 158 ff, 163-64; J. Weiss, *History of Primitive Christianity* (1937), I, 169-74; F. V. Filson, *Pioneers of the Primitive Church* (1940), pp. 83-113; E. J. Goodspeed, *A History of Early Christian Literature* (1942), pp. 30 ff (Letter of Barnabas).      M. J. SHROYER

**BARNABAS, ACTS OF.** A late and short apocryphon, heavily dependent upon the canonical book of Acts and purporting to describe the travels of Barnabas with Paul, their subsequent quarrel over Mark, their separation, and Barnabas' later travels and death by martyrdom in Cyprus. The book purports to be written by Mark, who tells of the vision which led him to join Paul and Barnabas, and of his departure, after the death of Barnabas, to Alexandria. The writing, extant only in Greek, was probably composed in Cyprus not earlier than the fifth century. This is an example of the soberer apocryphal Acts, with few garish wonder tales, but in essence simply an imaginative expansion of the cogent sections of the canonical Acts. *See* APOCRYPHA, NT.

*Bibliography.* The Greek text is printed as an appendix in Lipsius-Bonnet, *Acta Apostolorum Apocrypha* (1903), vol. II, pt. 2, pp. 292-302.      M. S. ENSLIN

\*BARNABAS, EPISTLE OF. A pseudepigraphal writing in the Greek language from the time of the later portions of the NT. It belongs to the so-called APOSTOLIC FATHERS and treats, first of all, the theme: Was the OT revelation concerned with the Jews or the Christians? and, secondly, adds a moral catechism in the pattern of "the way of light and way of darkness."

1. Form and general character
2. Contents
3. Sources
4. Theology
5. Date and authorship
6. Transmission of the text
Bibliography

**1. Form and general character.** This piece of writing purports to be a letter (1:5; 4:9; 17:2; 21:9), although it lacks the formalities of the LETTER of antiquity. It is, more correctly, a piece of didactic writing comparable to the Letter to the Hebrews (*see* HEBREWS, LETTER TO THE). Like the latter, it pursues a single, undivided subject, which is developed in the main part (chs. 1–17): namely, Judaism as the

great deception concerning the will and the way of God. More emphatically than anywhere else in early Christianity, the relationship of the OT with Judaism is severed. The letter stresses that the OT was intended for the Christians from the very beginning, with its entire contents to be interpreted as prophecy of Christianity. The author defends this view, not as a polemic directed abroad, but as a way to keep his Christian readers from taking seriously the historical origin of the covenant (4:6). These readers have just been baptized. In its designation for those who have been newly baptized the letter, particularly in its outline, suggests the baptismal catechisms of a later period. Hence we have before us in the Epistle of Barnabas the written result of baptismal instruction. *See* CHURCH, LIFE AND ORGANIZATION OF THE.

**2. Contents.**
   I. Introduction, with appreciation of baptismal grace, ch. 1
   II. The didactic main part, concerning the error of the Jews and the superiority of the Christians, chs. 2–17
     A. On sacrificing, ch. 2
     B. On fasting, ch. 3
     C. On the impending end of time and its demands on the believers, 4:1-6a, 9b-14
     D. On the inheritance of the covenant, 4:6b-9a; chs. 13–14
     E. On the work of redemption by Christ, whose incarnation, suffering, and dying are explained on the basis of the OT, chs. 5–8; 11–12
     F. On circumcision, ch. 9
     G. On dietary prohibitions, ch. 10
     H. On the sabbath, ch. 15
     I. On the temple, ch. 16
     J. Conclusion, ch. 17
   III. Practical moral instructions, chs. 18–20
     A. The doctrine of the two ways, ch. 18
     B. The way of the light, ch. 19
     C. The way of darkness, ch. 20
   IV. Conclusion of the letter, ch. 21

The author is not capable of tying the individual items together and achieving a tidy arrangement. This inability explains the incoherence and lack of orderliness of the letter; the text is complex, coming from the traditional subject matter of oral instruction (*see* FORM CRITICISM; TRADITION, ORAL). Then, too, the two main parts, which are apparently so dissimilar, do not indicate different origins, since the author attempts to bring about a transition from the theoretical to the practical portion (ch. 17) and prepares for the latter in the former (4:10; 16:9).

**3. Sources.** As has been pointed out, the author uses materials which are available to him. For the first part the OT is his main source. This serves him for his christological statements. Definitely one may say that the author has no need for a Christian source, such as a gospel, in addition to the OT. Naturally the tradition concerning Jesus is known to him, for it is on this basis that he directs his questions to the OT. But the use of a definite gospel, possibly Matthew, cannot be proved. It appears that the author still relies entirely upon oral tradition (*see*

FORM CRITICISM). His quotations from the OT follow only in part the LXX and are often attributed to a collection of testimonials, since they appear again in similar selection in later church writers. The doctrine of the two ways (chs. 18-20) is also found in Did. 1-6. The originality of the Didache version, which was formerly generally supported, has recently been given up in favor of the originality of Barnabas. The possibility that the author of the Epistle of Barnabas composed the two-ways doctrine independently is completely improbable. The textual content in chs. 18-20, as compared with that in chs. 1-17; 21, proves that an unfamiliar source begins here, and thus speaks against his independence. Hence, the third possibility may be the most probable: namely, that the two versions are independent of each other but dependent on a common source. This prototype, transmitted by means of connecting links, was probably a Jewish moral catechism. The pattern of the two ways is at home in the moral instruction of late Judaism; it has also turned up again just recently (1QS III.13-IV.26) in the Manual of Discipline of the Qumran discovery (*see* DEAD SEA SCROLLS). Compared with the Didache version, the two-ways doctrine of the Epistle of Barnabas turns out to be much less ordered and is especially lacking of Christian admixtures.

**4. Theology.** The discussion of the sources has proved that the author was at home in a heathen proselyte community which in its initial stages developed from the Judaism of the DISPERSION and thus represents a type similar to the Christianity of the First Epistle of Clement (*see* CLEMENT, EPISTLE OF). Like the latter, the Epistle of Barnabas shows itself somewhat influenced by Paulinism (*see* PAUL § B). To be sure, there are no indisputable signs of an acquaintance with the letters of Paul, but the Paulinian triad of faith, love, and hope is found in 1:4, 6 (cf. 11:8); the justification of Abraham by faith is exhibited in its significance for the conversion of the heathen (13:7); the Stoic Pan formula (*see* STOICS), doubly striking in a milieu of tradition so saturated by the Jewish, is applied to Christ (12:7) as it is by Paul in I Cor. 8:6; Col. 1:16. Above all, the Christology of pre-existence (*see* CHRIST § 9) is quite fully developed (chs. 5 ff). The preference for the word "gnosis" and the anti-Judaism of the author should not, however, mislead one to connect him with Gnosticism. The word means simply the deeper insight into Christianity with the help of the allegoric exegesis of the OT; and, in contrast to Gnosticism, the author never thinks of giving up the OT and its divine Creator. The allegorical method (*see* ALLEGORY), which he prefers along with the occasional use of typology, puts the author alongside Alexandrian Judaism (*see* PHILO JUDEUS; ALEXANDRIA), but he uses it in the service of his main theme as an awkward weapon against Judaism. That the allegorical exegesis is not slow to do violence to the meaning of the word, and resolves historical events into playful fantasy, can be clearly discerned in his letter (e.g., in chs. 9-10).

**5. Date and authorship.** The allusion in 16:3 to the fulfilment of an Isaiah prophecy concerning the destruction and the rebuilding of the temple at Jeru-salem by enemies was probably written in the time of Hadrian. The internal situation of the letter—the relative proximity to Deutero-Paulinism, the lack of reference to NT writings, the absence of the office of BISHOP (especially striking in 4:10*b*)—does not exclude an origin *ca.* A.D. 130, even though the letter suggests an earlier dating. In any case, composition by the apostle Barnabas is out of the question. The man (Gal. 2:13) who observed the Jewish regulations for cleanliness, and therefore separated himself from the heathen proselytes, cannot controvert the literally understood ritual law as being ungodly (Barn. 10:2, 12) and attribute the essence of the Jewish religion to the deceit of a bad angel (2:10; 3:6; 4:6; 9:4; *see* LAW IN FIRST-CENTURY JUDAISM). In addition to the title and the signature of the letter, which surely are secondary, ecclesiastical tradition after the time of Clement of Alexandria testifies to the name of Barnabas. In the letter itself, however, the author remains unnamed. He characterizes himself, with a modest defense against the title, as "teacher" (1:8; 4:6, 9; cf. 9:9; 21:1 ff). He might, according to the state of affairs in the letter, have been a representative of this early Christian office, who wanted by means of the letter to put into the hands of those whom he had just baptized a summary and continuation of his oral baptismal instruction.

**6. Transmission of the text.** Greek MSS are: (*a*) Codex Sinaiticus; (*b*) the Jerusalem MS (A.D. 1056) with the Didache; (*c*) Codex Vaticanus (Greek; 859), eleventh century (1-5:7*a* is missing). Another seven MSS with the same defective beginning are dependent on the Vaticanus or its prototype. An Old Latin translation is preserved in a Leningrad MS of the ninth-tenth century. There are quotations in Clement of Alexandria, who esteems the letter very highly; just as, after all, its inclusion in the Sinaiticus shows that in Egypt in ancient times it had almost canonical status.

*Bibliography.* German translation, with important commentary, by H. Windisch, in V. Lietzmann, ed., *Handbuch zum NT* (1920), Ergänzungsband Heft III. English translation by J. A. Kleist, in J. Quasten and J. C. Plumpe, eds., *Ancient Christian Writers* (1948), vol. VI.

Special studies: J. A. Robinson, *Barnabas, Hermas and the Didache* (1920). J. Muilenberg, *The Literary Relationship of . . . Barnabas and the Teaching of the Twelve Apostles* (1929). A. L. Williams, "The Date . . . of Barnabas," *JTS*, 34 (1933), 337-46. R. H. Connolly, *JTS*, 33 (1932), 237-53; 35 (1934), 113-46, 165-67, 225-48. (These three authors have established the homogeneity of the Epistle of Barnabas, possibly in opposition to H. Windisch.) See also: H. Lietzmann, *The Beginnings of the Christian Church* (1937), pp. 289-95. P. Meinhold, "Geschichte und Exegese im Barnabasbrief," Zeitschrift für Kirchengeschichte, 59 (1940), 255-305. J. Quasten, *Patrology*, I (1950), 85-92. J. Schmid, "Barnabas," Reallexikon für Antike und Christentum, I (1950), 1212-17. R. Bultmann, *Theology of the NT*, II (1955), 163-65. H. Köster, *Synoptische Uberlieferung bei den Apostolische Vätern* (1957), pp. 124-258. J. P. Audet, *La Didachè* (1958), pp. 122-63. G. Schille, "Zur urchristlichen Tauflehre," *ZNW*, 49 (1958), 31-52.          W. ELTESTER

**BARODIS** bə rō'dĭs [Βαρωδείς]. Head of a family of "sons of Solomon's servants" who returned with Zerubbabel (I Esd. 5:34). The name Barodis is omitted in the parallels Ezra 2:57; Neh. 7:59.

                                        C. T. FRITSCH

**BARREL.** The KJV translation of כד in I Kings 17:12-16; 18:33. The RSV correctly translates "jar." It was used for the storage of flour and the carrying of water. *See* POTTERY § 3*b*.     J. L. KELSO

**BARRENNESS** [עֶקֶר; στεῖρος, sterile]. Barrenness was believed to be a curse from God (Gen. 16:2; 20: 18; I Sam. 1:5; cf. II Sam. 6:23). When Elizabeth conceived, she exclaimed: "Thus the Lord has done to me . . . , to take away my reproach among men" (Luke 1:25). In the time of the end, so severe will be God's judgment that people will call the barren woman blessed (Luke 23:29). Barrenness is removed by the mercy of God, often through the use of prayer (Gen. 25:21; I Sam. 1:12 ff). As God blesses his people, the curse of barrenness is completely removed (Deut. 7:14). God in his mercy gives the barren woman a home and children (Ps. 113:9); and the nation is considered to be a barren woman, who will sing because of the promise of children (Isa. 54:1). Women who were barren prayed in the temple to the god of fertility, Tammuz (Ezek. 8:14).

*See also* FAMILY; MARRIAGE.     O. J. BAAB

**BARSABBAS** bär säb′əs, bär′sə bəs [Βαρσαββᾶς, son of the Sabbath, *or* son of Saba, *etc.*]. **1.** Joseph, surnamed Justus, one of the two candidates for the place left vacant by the defection of Judas Iscariot (Acts 1:23).

**2.** Judas (*see* JUDAS 5), sent by the Jerusalem church with Paul, Barnabas, and Silas to Antioch after the church council (Acts 15:22).

F. W. GINGRICH

**BARTACUS** bär′tə kəs [Βάρτακος (BA), Βαζακος (Luc.)] (I Esd. 4:29). The father of Apame, a concubine of Darius.     C. T. FRITSCH

**BARTHOLOMEW** bär thŏl′ə mū [Βαρθολομαῖος; Aram. בר תלמי, son of Talmai]. One of the twelve apostles, according to the four NT lists (Matt. 10:3; Mark 3:18; Luke 6:14; Acts 1:13).

Bartholomew may not have been this apostle's whole name. Names like Simon Bar-Jona (Matt. 16:17) indicate that a proper name along with a patronymic was common. Was it Nathanael Bartholomew, Jesus Bartholomew (as the thirteenth-century Syriac commentator Bar Hebraeus thought), or possibly Talmai Bar-Talmai? On the other hand, names like Barnabas or Barabbas, though they may technically have been patronymics, seem to have been used as independent proper names. This apostle may therefore have been known simply as Bartholomew.

The name appears in three of the lists (Matthew, Mark, Luke) immediately after Philip. The juxtaposition of the names has in part led to the view that the Nathanael of John 1:45-51; 21:2 and the Bartholomew of the lists are variant designations of the same person. According to the first Johannine passage, it was Philip who brought Nathanael to Jesus. In support of this identification it is also pointed out that Nathanael was called by Jesus to be a witness to the central role of the Son of Man in the salvation of men (John 1:50-51; *see* NATHANAEL)—surely an apostolic function; that Nathanael is named in connection with prominent apostles in John 1:35-51;

21:2; and that there is no mention of Nathanael in the Synoptics or of Bartholomew in the Fourth Gospel. It is argued that since Bartholomew is in form a patronymic, it is likely that its bearer would have another name as well.

Unfortunately these arguments fall short of proof of the identity of Nathanael and Bartholomew. The juxtaposition of Philip and Bartholomew in the lists may be quite fortuitous (in the Acts list they are not together). Jesus' comment concerning the greater things to be seen by Nathanael is not necessarily a formal call to apostleship. In view of the Fourth Evangelist's love of symbolism, Nathanael may be, not a historic personage, but a symbolic construction by which the writer depicts Judaism's incompleteness without Jesus Christ, even Judaism at its best. If Nathanael and Bartholomew are not the same, there is no problem in the mention of the former by the Fourth Evangelist and of the latter by the Synoptic writers. Many persons around Jesus appear in some but not all of the gospels. Bartholomew may quite well stand by itself in these lists as a proper name; it is not necessarily a patronymic. In fact, the patronymic is expressed in the lists by the Greek genitive, not by the Aramaic *bar*.

The uncertainties of the Nathanael-Bartholomew identification have led to other hypotheses: that Nathanael is Matthew, the apostle John, the unnamed companion of Cleopas on the road to Emmaus, James the son of Alphaeus, Matthias, or even Paul. If Nathanael and Bartholomew are not the same, we have no information about the latter in the NT beyond the meager amount to be gleaned from the four lists.

Church tradition makes Bartholomew a missionary to various countries and explains his death in divergent ways. Eusebius (Hist. V.x.3) reports that he preached the gospel in India and left behind the Gospel of Matthew "in the actual Hebrew characters." Armenia, Phrygia, Lycaonia, Mesopotamia, and Persia also have been claimed as the scenes of his labors. He is said to have evangelized with Philip and Thomas. Jerome, in the prologue to his Commentary on Matthew, mentions a number of apocryphal gospels, among them one by Bartholomew. Bartholomew figures in various apostolic romances of the Middle Ages.

*Bibliography.* M. R. James, *The Apocryphal NT* (1924), pp. 166-86, 467-68; D. Browne, "Who Was Nathanael?" *ET*, XXXVIII (1927), 286; J. R. Harris, *The Twelve Apostles* (1927), pp. 22-23, 78-80; R. B. Y. Scott, "Who Was Nathanael?" *ET*, XXXVIII (1927), 93-94; U. Holzmeister, "Nathanael fuitne idem ac S. Bartholomaeus apostolus?" *Biblica*, XXI (1940), 28-39.     E. P. BLAIR

**BARTHOLOMEW, GOSPEL [QUESTIONS] OF.** A work mentioned by Jerome, along with several other Gnostic gospels, in the prologue of his Commentary on Matthew, and in the list of apocryphal gospels condemned by the Gelasian Decree. There is no evidence, however, that Jerome himself knew the book, as it has been not unplausibly conjectured that his reference to it is due to a quite unwarranted conclusion drawn from the tradition preserved by Eusebius (Hist. V.x.3) that Pantaenus had discovered among the "Indians" a Gospel of Matthew written in Hebrew which had been earlier brought there by Bartholomew. The mention of the book in the Gelasian Decree may well be a simple repetition of the word of Jerome. Two sentences are quoted from "the divine Bartholomew" in one of the writings traditionally ascribed to Dionysius the Areopagite (de Myst. Theol. 1). None of these references gives any indication of the nature of the writing or any real proof of its actual existence.

There is, however, a writing now extant in Greek, Latin, and Slavonic under the title *Questions of Bartholomew*, which in its present, far-from-original form is not earlier than the fifth century but appears to be based upon much earlier, very possibly Gnostic, materials. It is now commonly conceded that this writing may well represent—at least contain relics of —the otherwise unknown apocryphal gospel. Composed in Greek, it is now extant in two Greek MSS, one in Vienna, the other in Jerusalem; in two Latin versions represented by two distinctly different types of text, one consisting of two leaves of abstracts perhaps of the ninth century, the other a greatly amplified and corrupt form in an eleventh-century MS; and in Slavonic.

It consists of a series of questions propounded to Jesus after his resurrection, to Mary, and to Satan (Beliar), by Bartholomew, who had followed Jesus from afar at the time of the Crucifixion and had seen many marvels at that time. Both in this apocryphon and in the Coptic Book of the Resurrection of Christ by Bartholomew the Apostle (*see following article*) this special ability of Bartholomew, to see visions not granted to others, is the consequence of the promise made to him (or to Nathanael, for the two were easily identified) by Jesus at the time of his call (John 1:50-51).

The contents of this curious writing, in essence the highly imaginative development and embroidery of such themes as the descent into hell, the annunciation to Mary and subsequent miraculous birth of her child, may for convenience be listed as five topics: (*a*) Christ's account of his descent into hell; the consequent terror of Hades and Beliar; the rescue of the patriarchs, with especial attention to "Adam the first-formed, for whose sake I came down from heaven upon earth." This section concludes with a most confusing account of the number of souls daily saved and lost. Either the texts are hopelessly corrupt or the arithmetic employed is distinctly esoteric. (*b*) The interrogation of the Virgin, at Bartholomew's instance, by Peter because he was "the chief"; her reluctant description of the advent of the angel; her supernatural levitation and besprinkling with celestial dew; the miraculous production of a loaf of bread and a great cup of wine from the garment of the angel; their solemn eucharist, and his promise that after three years she will conceive a son. At this point in her narrative fire proceeded from Mary's mouth and would have destroyed the whole world had not Jesus appeared and placed his hand upon her mouth. (*c*) A very brief account of the vision of the bottomless pit, which the apostles were granted upon the mountaintop, after Jesus had promised to reveal to them what they most wanted to know, now that in seven days he was to ascend to heaven. (*d*) A very long and turgid account of the questions put by Bartholomew to Satan, after the latter had been

brought heavily chained into the presence of the disciple and had been trampled upon by Bartholomew at Jesus' behest. This section is preluded by a discussion between Peter and Mary, in which the latter seeks to make clear in highly involved language how in her Jesus had been contained that she "might recover the strength of the female." (*e*) A brief colloquy regarding the deadly sins. Certainly in this section, at least in its present form, there is no hint of the ascetic disapproval of marriage. A single marriage "belongeth to sobriety" and is quite permissible, even though "virginity is best." The chief vices castigated are hypocrisy, backbiting, and speaking ill of a faithful Christian (which is actually "sin against the Holy Ghost").

*Bibliography.* A convenient English translation of this apocryphon is to be found in M. R. James, *The Apocryphal NT* (1924), pp. 166-81, together with references to critical studies. A more complete bibliography is given by J. Quasten, *Patrology* (1950), I, 127.      M. S. ENSLIN

**BARTHOLOMEW THE APOSTLE, BOOK OF THE RESURRECTION OF CHRIST BY.** A Coptic writing whose manifest purpose is the glorification of Bartholomew. It is scarcely one narrative but rather a very loosely constructed rhapsody. The writing purports to have been produced by Bartholomew and given to his son Thaddaeus with the injunction not to let it fall into the hands of unbelievers or heretics. As in the Gospel [Questions] of Bartholomew (*see preceding article*), among the chief themes are the resurrection of Christ, his descent into Hades and redemption of the souls there, and the restoration of Adam. As in most of the apocrypha (*see* APOCRYPHA, NT), stories from the canonical gospels are the sources for these tales, but they are expanded, altered, and combined with utter unconcern for either tradition or consistency. Jesus is twice buried —once by Joseph of Arimathea; once by Philogenes, the father of the boy whom Jesus had healed when he descended from the Mount of Olives with his disciples.

Among such episodes as the visit of Death to the tomb of Jesus and their colloquy there, of the ascent of the apostles to heaven, and of the women at the tomb (with an expansion of their number and detailed identification of them), is a highly imaginative expansion of the story of doubting Thomas. Thomas had been absent because of the death of his son Siophanes in a far-off land. He raises the son to life, listens to his account of how his soul had been taken in the hand of Michael to heaven to view the twelve thrones of the apostles, baptizes twelve thousand of the natives, sets his son over them as bishop, returns on a cloud to the Mount of Olives, doubts that Jesus has been raised from the dead (despite his own successful performance of such a miracle earlier on the same day), is confronted with Jesus, and touches Jesus' wounds.

Together with these very loosely articulated stories is a series of eight hymns which were sung in exultation in heaven to welcome the redeemed souls, chief among whom was Adam, whom Christ had brought back with him from his successful spoliation of Hades.

The work is extant only in Coptic. Several MSS,

all fragmentary, are known, the chief of which is one of the twelfth century, now in the British Museum (Or. 6804). The original work is commonly dated in the fifth or sixth century, the time during which these Coptic fantasies are supposed to have been produced.

*Bibliography.* An English translation is available in E. A. W. Budge, *Coptic Apocrypha* (1913); a convenient summary of its contents in M. R. James, *The Apocryphal NT* (1924), pp. 181-86.                          M. S. ENSLIN

**BARTIMAEUS** bär'tə mē'əs [Βαρτιμαῖος, *possibly from* Aram. בל טימי *or* בר טמאי, son of Timai *or* son of the unclean]. A blind beggar of Jericho healed by Jesus (Mark 10:46-52).

Matthew's and Luke's accounts (Matt. 20:29-34; Luke 18:35-43), while differing at significant points, agree in substance. Mark's circumstantial details— place, time, form of salutation of Jesus, attitude of crowd, discarding of mantle, etc.—seem derived from recollections of an eyewitness. Bartimaeus' perseverance, faith, and thankfulness, and Jesus' sympathetic response are noteworthy.

*Bibliography.* T. K. Cheyne and J. S. Black, eds., *Encyclopedia Biblica*, I (1899), 489-91; H. L. Strack and P. Billerbeck, *Kommentar zum NT aus Talmud und Midrasch*, II (1924), 25; V. Taylor, *The Gospel According to St. Mark* (1952), pp. 447-49.                          E. P. BLAIR

**BARUCH** bâr'ək [ברוך, blessed]. Jeremiah's amanuensis; a member of a prominent Judean family. His brother Seraiah was first chamberlain to King Zedekiah (Jer. 51:59). Baruch wrote for Jeremiah the oracles of destruction (36:4 ff) which were first read publicly (vs. 10) and then to King Jehoiakim (vss. 21 ff). In angry contempt the king burned the scroll piece by piece as it was read to him (vs. 23). It has been surmised from this event that the prophetic oracles were written on papyrus, since the odor of burning parchment would have been prohibitive (*see* WRITING AND WRITING MATERIALS). Baruch was then commanded by Jeremiah to re-record the oracles (36:27-32).

Innumerable hypothetical reconstructions of Baruch's roll have been proposed in modern times, and the subject is the starting point for most discussions of the composition of the book of Jeremiah (*see* JEREMIAH THE PROPHET). The materials most frequently assigned to Baruch's roll are Jer. 19:1–20:6; 21:1-10; and large portions of chs. 26; 28; 29; 34; 36-45. The prophet's oracles of restoration are in any case excluded by the description of the roll given in ch. 36.

Baruch also witnessed Jeremiah's purchase of a field in Anathoth and preserved the deed of purchase in an earthen vessel (32:12-15). He was accused by the leaders of the Judean remnant of the destruction of Jerusalem of prompting Jeremiah to oppose their flight after the death of GEDALIAH (2), and he was taken by them, along with the prophet, into Egypt (43:2-7).

Something of this noble man's agony in pronouncing for Jeremiah the nation's doom is disclosed in Jer. 45, where Jeremiah counsels his scribe and friend to stake his life on loyalty to the Lord rather than the lost cause of the dying kingdom.

Nothing else is known of Baruch. His name was attached to the pseudepigraphical book of Baruch and the Apocalypse of Baruch (*see following articles*). Furthermore, a variety of conflicting traditions arose concerning his ultimate destiny. One, reported by Jerome, held that he died in Egypt simultaneously with Jeremiah. Others would have had him go from Egypt to Babylon *ca.* 583 B.C., either with or without Jeremiah.

*Bibliography.* S. Mowinckel, *Zur Komposition des Buches Jeremia* (1914); T. H. Robinson, "Baruch's Roll," *ZAW*, XLII (1924).                          J. M. WARD

**BARUCH, APOCALYPSE OF.** A Jewish pseudepigraph, also called, somewhat confusingly, the "Syriac Apocalypse of Baruch" because the only complete text of eighty-seven chapters is in a sixth-century Syriac MS, and "Second Baruch," so as to distinguish it from other works attributed to Jeremiah's scribe. As the Syriac MS states, the Syriac was translated from the Greek, a statement borne out by numerous Grecisms and by comparison with a fragment of the Greek text preserved on a leaf of a fifth- or sixth-century papyrus MS. The Greek, in turn, according to competent linguists, is from a Hebrew original, a conclusion that is in keeping with the thoroughly Jewish contents.

**1. Contents.** As is indicated by certain discrepancies, inconsistencies, and apparently unnecessary repetitions, this apocryphon is probably based upon a number of sources. However, the ingenious source analyses of scholars like Kabisch and Charles may be too complicated to gain complete acceptance.

Baruch relates that prior to the event itself the capture of Jerusalem by the Chaldeans was revealed to him. After this had come to pass, he grieved over Zion, but was assured that the fall of Jerusalem was a necessary prelude to the divine judgment (chs. 9–20). God also told Baruch, who was impatient for this to occur, that he must wait until all who had been destined to live should be born. Then, and only then, the Messiah would appear, Behemoth and Leviathan would become a feast for the righteous, the earth would become marvelously productive, yielding ten thousandfold, and manna would descend from heaven. Then, for no apparent reason, the Messiah would return to heaven, and the righteous dead would be resurrected; however, the souls of the wicked would waste away and be tormented (chs. 21–34).

In an allegorical vision Baruch saw a mighty fountain (the dominion of the Messiah) uproot a forest (the kingdoms of the world) save for a cedar tree (Rome); it, however, would be burned, whereas a vine (the Messiah) would continue to grow (chs. 35–46). A prayer by Baruch, in which he praises the law, precedes an account of the resurrection of the righteous, who are justified because they kept the law, and of the fate of the wicked, who failed to do so (chs. 47–52).

In another symbolic vision appeared six black waters (evil periods of history, the last the Roman) alternating with six bright waters (the good periods, the last the destruction of the Romans), all to be consummated in a messianic kingdom. Accordingly, Baruch warns the people to keep the law, and prepares letters to send to the captive and dispersed Jews (chs. 53–77). In the letter to the 9½ tribes he exhorts them to be prepared by keeping the law, for the time of rewards for Israel and vengeance for the Gentiles is at hand (chs. 78–87).

**2. Special problems. a. Date.** The book was written sometime following the destruction of Jerusalem by the Romans (symbolically called Babylonians) in A.D. 70. Close similarities to II Esdras (ca. A.D. 100) are in keeping with this date. It may have been a source for the Last Words of Baruch (IV Baruch) of the second century.

**b. Author.** The work is quite Jewish, as the Talmudic parallels cited by Ginzberg show. The stress placed upon the law and the keeping of the law indicates that the author had much in common with the Pharisees.

**c. Messianic kingdom and resurrection.** Despite its title, there is no clear-cut apocalypticism in the work; instead, it is messianic in its expectations. First, there is no dualism between two opposing, supernatural world forces, Satan and God. Sin and corruption are evident, but they are due to Adam's fall, not to the activity of a Satan or Devil. Neither are there two distinct and different ages: the one evil and temporal, since it is under Satan's rule; the other good and eternal, since it is to be under God's rule. Instead, God is in direct control of this the present age, which will become better, culminating in a messianic kingdom (with or without a Messiah), to be accompanied by a resurrection. In an interesting passage (chs. 50–51) is described a physical resurrection in which the resurrected will be able to recognize one another. Then, following a judgment, the appearance of the resurrected will change. That of the wicked will become worse, and they will suffer torment; whereas the righteous will become exalted and glorified.

**d. Other features.** The law of God is to be observed. Adam's transgression introduced corruption and death into the world. His descendants are subject to sin and death; however, difficult though it is, each one has the freedom of will to live righteously and to have a blessed immortality, to be justified by his deeds, the works of the law, which are stored up in heavenly treasuries (whereas heavenly books record the sins of the breakers of the law). There is little angelology and no demonology. Considerable use is made of the OT, but there are few direct quotations. Much of the book, such as prayers, speeches, dirges, and a hymn, is in poetic form. The intermingling of prose and poetic passages is quite noticeable.

See also PSEUDEPIGRAPHA.

**Bibliography.** V. Ryssel, "Die syrische Baruchapokalypse," in E. Kautzsch, Die Apokryphen und Pseudepigraphen des Alten Testaments (1900), II, 406-46. L. Ginzberg, "Baruch, Apocalypse of (Syriac)," The Jewish Encyclopedia (1902), II, 551-56. R. H. Charles, The Apocalypse of Baruch (1896); "II Baruch," Apoc. and Pseudep. of the OT (1913), II, 470-526. F. C. Burkitt, "Baruch, Apocalypse of," in J. Hastings, Dictionary of the Apostolic Church (1915-18), I, 142-44. R. H. Charles and W. O. E. Oesterley, The Apocalypse of Baruch (1929).

M. RIST

**BARUCH, BOOK OF.** A little book of five chapters, reputed to have been written by the son of Neraiah, secretary or disciple of Jeremiah. Sometimes the Letter of Jeremiah (see JEREMIAH, LETTER OF) is included as the sixth chapter. It is divided into three parts, the first of which is written in prose and the others in poetry. Largely a mosaic of verses drawn from canonical works such as Jeremiah, Daniel, Deutero-Isaiah, and Job, it is addressed to the Jews who had been deported to Babylon. It was read aloud to them before it was sent to Jerusalem, where it was to serve as part of the liturgy. It is generally held among scholars that the book had three different authors and that a skilful redactor united their anonymous parts into a more or less consistent whole and ascribed the result to Baruch.

**1. Contents.** Most of the first third of the work consists of a prayer quoted freely from the ninth chapter of Daniel, expanded to about fifty-four verses. It starts with a confession of sins (1:15–2:10), followed by a petition for forgiveness and mercy (2:11–3:8). Isaiah, Leviticus, Deuteronomy, and Jer. 2:21-25 lend an effective mosaic of verses.

The second third (3:9–4:4) begins with a homily in poetry called "The Fountain of Wisdom," based on Job 28–29. Israel has forsaken this fountain; therefore she is in exile and has "waxed old in a strange country." True Wisdom—i.e., the Torah—is hidden from the world; not even the sages of the earth have been able to find her. God gave this hypostatized Wisdom to Israel alone.

The third division of the poem begins at 4:5 and is a prayer for comfort and encouragement. The meter changes from that of the second part.

**2. Original language.** Baruch was used in Jewish worship by the Diaspora in Upper Syria. In 1:14 the book itself directs that it shall be used in the liturgy of the synagogue. This liturgical use of Baruch would make inconceivable that it was written in any other language than Hebrew. This is universally acknowledged as regards the prose part of Baruch, but some scholars have proved that this is true also of the poetical portions. The Greek is manifestly a translation from the Hebrew. Some mistranslations from the Hebrew can be found. The characteristic parallelism of Hebrew poetry is also found in both poems.

The Greek work is clearly dependent on Greek versions of Jeremiah and Daniel. It has been argued that the Greek rendering of the book was the work of a single translator. It was this same translator who rendered the second half of Jeremiah into the Greek of our LXX. Indeed, the book of Baruch is often treated as though it were a part of Jeremiah.

The prologue of Sirach (see ECCLESIASTICUS) attests the existence of the Greek version of Jeremiah in Egypt in 132 B.C. Ben Sirach's grandson points to evidence afforded by Greek renderings of "The Prophets and the Rest of the Books." The Greek translation of Baruch was evidently in existence at that date.

**3. Date.** The verbal coincidences in the Greek of 4:36–5:9 and the 11th Psalm of Solomon are quite evident. The generally accepted date of the Psalms of Solomon is the middle of the first century B.C. It was formerly believed that the original language of this portion of Baruch was in Greek and that it was composed after A.D. 70. Now the view prevails, however, that the entire book of Baruch was written in Hebrew and then translated into Greek, no earlier than the middle of the second century B.C. This means that Baruch is older than the eleventh Psalm of Solomon, which must have borrowed from Baruch.

The date of the first third of the book (1:1–3:8; note especially 1:15-20; 2:1-2, 7-14, 16-19) must have been later than 164 B.C., because of its dependence upon the book of Daniel. This dependence is evident because of the fifty-four verses based on Daniel (9:7-11, 12-13, 13-17, 18) but also because the book repeats the error of Daniel (Dan. 5:2, 13, 18, 22) in making Belshazzar the son of Nebuchadnezzar (605-651 B.C.) when he was in fact the son of Nabonidus (555-538 B.C.).

The poetic section (3:9–5:9) must be later than Job and also later than Daniel. Some place it as late as A.D. 70, but so late a date is highly unlikely. The shock of the Roman attack would have left a clearer mark. A more probable time for this work is in the late Maccabean era—say the time of Salome Alexandra in 76-67 B.C.—a time of uneasy peace, following a period of stress and internecine strife, between Pharisees and Sadducees. Israel was still threatened and menaced by past mistakes. It was a time for contemplative prayer and literary endeavor in the manner of Baruch, whose age had been under a similar urgent necessity to return to God.

*Bibliography.* J. J. Kneucker, *Das Buch Baruch, Geschichte u. Kritik, Uebersetzung u. Erklärung* (1879); J. Knabenbauer, *Commentarius in Danielem prophetam, Lamentationes, et Baruch* (1905); R. H. Charles, *The Apoc. and Pseudep. of the OT* (1913); Harwell, *The Principal Versions of Baruch* (1915); St. J. Thackeray, *The LXX and Jewish Worship* (1921); W. J. Ferrar, *The Uncanonical Jewish Books* (1925); W. O. E. Oesterley, *An Introduction to the Books of the Apoc.* (1935); C. C. Torrey, *The Apocryphal Literature* (1945); R. H. Pfeiffer, *History of NT Times* (1949).                                    S. Tedesche

**BARZILLAI** bär zĭl′ī [בַּרְזִלַּי]; KJV Apoc. BERZELUS bər zē′ləs. **1.** A Meholathite whose son Adriel married Merab, daughter of Saul (I Sam. 18:19; II Sam. 21:8, where "Merab" must be read for "Michal").

**2.** An influential Gileadite of Rogelim who, with two other wealthy Transjordanian patricians—Shobi, the Ammonite prince of Rabbah, and Machir the son of Ammiel from Lo-debar—brought generous supplies of food and equipment for David and his men at Mahanaim during the perilous days of the rebellion of Absalom (II Sam. 17:27-29). After the defeat of Absalom, Barzillai provided a *cortège d'honneur* to escort the monarch beyond the ford of the Jordan, but, because of his advanced years, he declined the invitation of David to become a member of the royal court at Jerusalem; he proposed to the king that his son Chimham be accepted in his stead (II Sam. 19:31-39). In his last charge David commended to Solomon the sons of Barzillai as worthy members of the royal court because of the singular kindness of Barzillai (I Kings 2:7).

**3.** A priest who married one of the daughters of Barzillai the Gileadite (no doubt identical with 2 *above*) and assumed his name. His descendants were removed from the sacerdotal office in the postexilic period because they were unable to establish in the

genealogical register their priestly descent (Ezra 2:61; Neh. 7:63; cf. I Esd. 5:38, on which passage see Rudolph's Commentary).                    E. R. Dalglish

**BASALOTH.** KJV Apoc. form of Bazluth. *See* Bazlith.

**BASEMATH** băs′ə măth [בָּשְׂמַת, balsam, *or* fragrance]; KJV BASHEMATH băsh′— in 1-2, BASMATH băs′măth in 3. **1.** A daughter of Elon the Hittite, and a wife of Esau (Gen. 26:34 P).

**2.** A daughter of Ishmael; sister of Nebaioth; and a wife of Esau (Gen. 36:3-4, 10, 13, 17, P). She bore Esau one son, Reuel, who was the father of Nahath, Zerah, Shammah, and Mizzah (vss. 13, 17, P).

She is probably identical with 1 *above*, and the designation "daughter of Elon the Hittite" in 26:34 perhaps belonged originally only to Adah, another of Esau's wives (cf. 36:2). Basemath might also be identical with Mahalath, who is described in 28:9 (P) as a daughter of Ishmael, the sister of Nebaioth, and a wife of Esau. The Syr. consistently uses the name Mahalath for Basemath in Gen. 36.

Gen. 36:1 (P) indicates that Esau was the eponymous ancestor of the Edomites (*see* Edom), so it is probable that the genealogies of ch. 36 (all P) reflect Edomite tribal relations and history. Since the traditions in vss. 9-19 couple Basemath's four grandchildren (the eponymous ancestors of four tribes) with eight other legitimate descendants of Esau through two other wives, it is possible that the Basemath tribes belonged to a twelve-tribe amphictyony of Edom. That Basemath's father was Ishmael suggests the Ishmaelite origin of these tribes.

**3.** A daughter of Solomon; the wife of Ahimaaz, Solomon's administrative officer in Naphtali (I Kings 4:15).                    M. Newman

**BASHAN** bā′shən, bā′shăn [בָּשָׁן, הַבָּשָׁן, fruitful, stoneless plain]. The northernmost of the parts into which the region E of the Jordan was divided. Its exact dimensions are difficult to determine, since sometimes the Bible means by it only the wide, fertile plain, and in other cases includes all the territory that was in the kingdom of Og. In general, it may be said that Bashan was bounded by Mount Hermon on the N, Jebel Druze on the E, and the hills E of the Sea of Galilee on the W, and that it extended about six miles S of the Yarmuk. It included the districts of the Argob and Golan, and among its cities were Karnaim, Ashtaroth, Salcah, Kenath, and Edrei, and the later Greek cities of Hippos, Dion, and Abila.

The greater part of Bashan consisted of a tableland which ranges from 1,600 to 2,300 feet in height. It was well adapted for wheat growing and cattle raising, and was famous for its groves of oak trees. These natural features appear often in the poetry of the Bible. The strong bulls of Bashan typify the fierce enemies that beset the righteous man (Ps. 22:12); the luxurious, pleasure-seeking women of Samaria are "cows of Bashan" (Amos 4:1). The haughty and proud are described as tall cedars of Lebanon and spreading oaks of Bashan (Isa. 2:13); and a note is made in the description of the pride of Tyre that it made oars for its ships from Bashan oak timber (Ezek. 27:6). The description of the tribe of Dan as

> . . . a lion's whelp,
> that leaps forth from Bashan (Deut. 33:22),

may refer either to the situation of the tribe as being not far from Mount Hermon or to the fierce lions which lurked in the wooded part of the district.

Archaeological exploration indicates that Bashan was continually occupied from the Early Bronze period (thirty-second–twenty-first centuries B.C.). It was taken by the Israelites from the Amorite Og, and sixty walled cities fell to the former with but little resistance; it was assigned, for the most part, to the tribe of Manasseh. In the period after the division of the kingdom it was a constant battleground between the forces of Israel and Aram; later on, it became more or less identified with the district of HAURAN. The old name, however, survived in the Batanea of Hellenistic and Roman times and the modern Arabic el-Bathaniyeh. Batanea was given to Herod by Augustus and was later part of Philip's tetrarchy (Jos. Antiq. XV.x.1; XVIII.iv.6).

S. COHEN

**BASHAN-HAVOTH-JAIR.** KJV translation of חות יאיר (RSV HAVVOTH-JAIR) in Deut. 3:14.

**BASHEMATH.** KJV form of BASEMATH 1-2.

**BASHMURIC VERSION** băsh mŏŏr'ĭk. An obsolete designation of the Fayumic (Coptic) Version of the Bible. *See* VERSIONS, ANCIENT, § 5.

B. M. METZGER

**BASILIDES, GOSPEL OF** băs'ĭ lī'dēz [Βασιλείδης]. An apocryphal gospel mentioned by Origen ("Basilides dared to write a gospel 'According to Basilides' " —*Hom. in Luc.* 1) and subsequently by Jerome and Ambrose. Euseb. Hist. X.vii.6-7 refers to Agrippa Castor's refutation of Basilides, who "in expounding the mysteries compiled twenty-four books on the gospel." Clement of Alexandria (Misc. IV.7) cites a passage from the twenty-third book of the work, which he styled *Exegetica*. A fragment of this *Exegetica* (an exposition of the parable of Dives and Lazarus) is extant in the fourth-century *Acta disputationis Archelai et Manetis*. While the precise nature of this gospel is uncertain, the fact that Basilides wrote a commentary upon it would suggest that it was not an independent treatise of his own but an altered and revised form of one of the Christian gospels (not improbably, as in the case of Marcion, the Gospel of Luke), whereby he sought to establish his own views. *See* APOCRYPHA, NT.

M. S. ENSLIN

**BASIN;** KJV BASON. "Basin" and "bowl" are often interchangeable words in the Bible. For a detailed study of different basin forms *see* POTTERY § 3*a* for ceramicware, and VESSELS § 2 for metalware. Generally the largest basins were banquet bowls or mixing bowls for wine. The same size was used in the sacrificial system. These largest basins were beautiful works of art, whether ceramics or metalware. Smaller bowls were used at the table and also as wash basins. The water, however, was poured out of a pitcher over the hands, and a bowl collected the dirty water. The feet were washed the same way (John 13:5). The smallest bowls ultimately became cups. Among the ancients there were two cup shapes —one like ours and the other a shallow bowl which was used especially for wine. Each category of bowls ran in staggered sizes as today. Bowls were used for countless purposes, even to carrying coals and collecting ashes. They often served as lids for other vessels. The sacrificial service used a goodly variety of basins. *See* SACRIFICE AND OFFERINGS.

J. L. KELSO

**BASKAMA** băs'kə mə [Βασκαμα]; KJV BASCAMA. The scene of the murder and temporary burial of the Maccabean leader Jonathan by the Seleucid commander Trypho, who treacherously captured Jonathan when he accepted an invitation to accompany Trypho to Ptolemais in witness of their friendship (I Macc. 13:23; cf. 12:39-48). The place has not been identified definitely; it may be the modern Tell Bazuk in Gilead, NE of the Sea of Galilee. Josephus calls it simply Basca (Antiq. XIII.vi.5). The site has been identified with the nearby el-Gummeize, "the Sycamore," at the terminal point of the Wadi Djoummeizeh just above the NE edge of the lake, since the Syriac version of I Maccabees permits the reconstruction בית שקמא, "House of the Sycamore." Or it may refer to Tell es-Samak, the "Sycaminos" or "Sycaminon" of Strabo (*Geography* XIII.6.1) and Pliny (Nat. Hist. V.75).

*Bibliography.* F.-M. Abel, *RB* (1926), p. 513; *Géographie de la Palestine*, II (1938), 261.

E. W. SAUNDERS

**BASKET.** A vessel, usually plaited or woven, used to carry burdens. The precise distinctions among the various Hebrew and Greek words are not clear. Fig. BAS 22.

The most frequent term, סל, probably a cane basket (cf. LXX κανοῦν), occurs always as a container for foodstuffs: baked goods (Gen. 40:16-18), unleavened bread (Exod. 29:3, 23, 32; Lev. 8:2, 26, 31; Num. 6:15, 17, 19), or meat (Judg. 6:19). The טנא was used for bearing the first fruits of the ground to the priest (Deut. 26:2, 4; cf. 28:5, 17). The כלוב was likewise used for food (summer fruit in Amos 8:1-2), but may have been a net or net bag, such as a "cage" (KJV) for birds (Jer. 5:27; cf. Akkadian *kilubi*, "bird net"). The word דוד, properly referring to a cooking pot (*see* POTTERY § 3*a*), seems to mean also a similar large woven container, as used for figs (Jer. 24:1-2), for bricks or mortar or other heavy construction materials (parallel to "burden" in Ps. 81:6—H 81:7), and for the heads of seventy sons of Ahab delivered to Jehu (II Kings 10:7).

The תבה (perhaps from Egyptian *tb·t,* "chest") in which the infant Moses was placed (Exod. 2:3, 5) was probably a small chest made of bulrushes or papyrus (cf. LXX θίβις), with a cover (vs. 6), waterproofed with tar so that it would float. Papyrus boats are mentioned in Isa. 18:2. The same word is used of Noah's vessel. *See* ARK.

In the gospel accounts of the feedings of the crowds κόφινος is always the word for the twelve baskets in which the leftovers of the five thousand were

22. The plaited basket on the left dates from the New Kingdom in Egypt (1580-1085 B.C.); the open work basket dates from the Roman period (30 B.C.–A.D. 324).

gathered (Matt. 14:20; Mark 6:43; Luke 9:17; John 6:13), whereas σπυρίς (in some MSS σφυρίς) is used for the seven baskets of the four thousand (Matt. 15: 37; Mark 8:8). Since this distinction is observed even when the two stories are later mentioned together (Matt. 16:9-10; Mark 8:19-20), the two types of basket must have been noticeably different. Perhaps the σπυρίς was much larger, as indicated by its use to let Paul down over the wall of Damascus (Acts 9:25). However, Paul's own reminiscence of a σαργάνη, "rope hamper," as used on this occasion (II Cor. 11: 33) indicates that this word is doubtless to be preferred.                                       E. M. GOOD

**BASMATH.** KJV form of BASEMATH 3.

**BASON.** KJV form of BASIN.

**BASTAI.** KJV Apoc. form of BESAI.

**\*BASTARD** [מַמְזֵר (MONGREL PEOPLE *in* Zech. 9:6), *from* Aram. *loan word,* be foul, corrupt; KJV νόθος (Heb. 12:8; RSV ILLEGITIMATE CHILD)]. Bastards were not permitted to enter the Lord's assembly (Deut. 23:2). Ammon and Moab were hated as bastard peoples because of their incestuous origin (Gen. 19:30-38), according to the Talmud. "Bastards" (RSV "illegitimate children") in Heb. 12:8 are those who do not have the discipline of the Lord.
                                          O. J. BAAB

**BAT** [עֲטַלֵּף; νυκτερίς (Letter of Jeremiah 22—G 21), *from* νυκτερινός, by night, *from* νύξ, night]. Any of an order, Chiroptera, of nocturnal fruit-eating and insect-eating flying mammals, of which over four hundred species have been recognized. Eight varieties are specifically mentioned by Tristram, who also refers to others more generally, as being in Palestine in the nineteenth century.

In the OT bats are included in two lists of unclean birds (Lev. 11:19; Deut. 14:18), and in Isa. 2:20 as creatures to be found in dark caves. The Letter of Jeremiah 22—G 21 alludes to bats' lighting on the bodies and heads of idols, thus proving the latter's lifelessness.
                                   W. S. McCULLOUGH

**BATH** [בַּת; βάτος]. A liquid measure equal to the dry measure ephah (Ezek. 45:11, 14). From estimates of the contents of two eighth-century jars, fragments of which have been found with the letters בת, *bt,* in archaic Hebrew characters, it is thought that the bath contained 21-23 liters, or *ca.* 5½ American gallons. Fig. WEI 19.

*See also* WEIGHTS AND MEASURES § C4e.
                                        O. R. SELLERS

**BATHING** [רחץ, bathe, wash; *Pi'el of* כבס, wash (*of garments and poetically of persons*); שׁטף, wash off, rinse away; LXX *and* NT ἀπολούω, ἀπονίπτω, βαπτίζω, λούω, νίπτω = רחץ; πλύνω = *Pi'el of* כבס]. The biblical languages do not distinguish between bathing and washing, but between washing clothes and washing other objects, including the human body. The distinction is one of technique. Garments were pounded under water (כבס, "to trample"), and other objects were washed by pouring water or dipping them in water (root רחץ, "to overflow").

The dry climate of Palestine discouraged bathing except where a stream or pool was available (II Kings 5:10; John 9:7), but the ubiquitous dust made necessary frequent washing of the face, hands, and feet. Good grooming, especially for lovers, demanded washing of face, hands, or body, before anointing with oil (Gen. 43:31; II Sam. 12:20; Ruth 3:3; Ezek. 23:40; cf. Song of S. 5:3). During mourning or sorrow the face and garments were left unwashed (II Sam. 12:20; 19:24—H 19:25), a practice forbidden by Jesus during a fast (Matt. 6:17). A good host provided water for his guests' feet (Gen. 18:4; Judg. 19: 21); and to wash another's feet, the task of a servant, signified humility (I Sam. 25:41; I Tim. 5:10; especially John 13), a virtue ironically reversed in Ps. 58:10—H 58:11, where the righteous wash their feet in the blood of the wicked. Washing the hands, as Pilate did at the trial of Jesus, was symbolic of innocence (Deut. 21:6; Pss. 26:6; 73:13; Matt. 27:24), and semiritual washing of the hands before eating had become a requirement by NT times (Matt. 15: 2; Mark 7:3; Luke 11:38). Lambs were washed at shearing time (Song of S. 4:2), babies after birth (Ezek. 16:4), and bodies in preparation for burial

(Acts 9:37). Wine (Gen. 49:11) and milk (Song of S. 5:12) are mentioned as washing fluids in poetic passages.

References to ordinary washing are outnumbered by those to ritual cleansing with water (*see* CLEAN AND UNCLEAN). Priests and Levites washed clothes, hands, feet, or bodies before coming to the altar and on other ceremonial occasions (Exod. 30:20; Lev. 8:6; Num. 8:21; *see* LAVER), and cleansed the legs and entrails of burnt offerings (Lev. 8:21). Persons polluted with many kinds of uncleanness, and personnel involved in handling cleansing agents (*see* WATER FOR IMPURITY), had to wash the clothes (Num. 19:10), the body (Lev. 15:13), or both (Lev. 14:9; 15:5). Polluted garments were also washed (Lev. 6:27—H 6:20; 13:54).

Courtesy of James B. Pritchard

23. Pottery figurine of a woman bathing in a shallow bowl, from er-Ras cemetery, ez-Zib (*ca.* 800 B.C.)

Washing is an OT metaphor for cleansing from sin (Isa. 1:16; 4:4), a use continued in the NT (Acts 22:16; Heb. 10:22) with special reference to the water of baptism (Eph. 5:26; Tit. 3:5). Four times (Ps. 51:2, 7—H 51:4, 9; Jer. 2:22; 4:14) the word for "washing clothes" is used metaphorically of cleansing from sin—i.e., pounding it out of the sinner. Fig. BAT 23.                                L. E. TOOMBS

**BATH-RABBIM** băth răb'ĭm [בת רבים, daughter of a multitude]. A gate of Heshbon, near which there were fish pools (RSV "pools"; Song of S. 7:4—H 7:5). The picture evoked is that of the forehead and cheeks framing the eyes of the beloved, and this probably recalled a well-known aspect of one approach to the city.                                S. COHEN

**BATHSHEBA** băth shē'bə [בתשבע, daughter of abundance, *from* בש *plus* שבע; *cf. bibliography*]. Alter-

nately: BATH-SHUA—shōō'ə [בתשוע, *in error*(?)] (I Chr. 3:5). The wife of Uriah the Hittite, then of David. David saw her beauty, seduced her, and had Uriah killed in order to take her as his wife (II Sam. 11). Bathsheba later became the mother of Solomon (12:15-25). Still later, when Adonijah claimed succession to the throne, she and Nathan persuaded David to proclaim Solomon king (I Kings 1:5-40). She then carried Adonijah's request for Abishag to Solomon; this request resulted in the death of Adonijah (2:13-25).

*Bibliography.* E. Koehler, *ZAW*, LV (1937), 165-66.
D. HARVEY

**BATH-SHUA** băth shōō'ə [בת־שוע, daughter of Shua (*cf.* KJV *with* LXX Θυγάτηρ Σαύας *in* I Chr. 2:3); Ethio. *Betâsû'êl, Bêdsû'êl* (Jub. 34:20; 41:7; *see bibliography*)]. **1.** A Canaanitess; wife of Judah and mother of his sons Er, Onan, and Shelah (I Chr. 2:3; here probably, as in Gen. 38:2, 12, not a proper name). The marriage is treated with scorn by the writer of the TESTAMENTS OF THE TWELVE PATRIARCHS (Test. Judah 8:2; 10:6; 13:3; 16:4; 17:1; *cf.* Jub. 34:20; 41:7).

*See also* SHUA.

**2.** Alternate form of BATHSHEBA.

*Bibliography.* R. H. Charles, ed., *The Testaments of the Twelve Patriarchs* (1908), p. 78n; *Apoc. and Pseudep. of the OT* (1913). II. 65, 72, 318-21.                B. T. DAHLBERG

**BATHZACHARIAS.** KJV form of BETH-ZECHARIAH.

**BATTALION** [σπεῖρα]. The word used to translate the Latin *cohors*, a tenth part of a legion; hence usually *ca.* six hundred men, but the number varied.

Matt. 27:27; Mark 15:16 speak of the "whole battalion" as gathered together before Jesus, after Pilate had delivered him over to be crucified. These soldiers would probably have been the Second Italian Cohort, stationed in Palestine, or perhaps a detachment from them.                                B. H. THROCKMORTON, JR.

**BATTERING RAM** [כר]. An engine of warfare used by besiegers of a city to break down its walls.

Its earliest known form comes from the Assyrians. It consisted of a heavy pole suspended at the middle from a framework which also served to protect the wielders from the stones and arrows hurled from the walls by the defenders. The entire framework was usually propelled by four to six wheels. Figs. ARC 48; WAR 3.

The use of the battering ram may be referred to in II Sam. 20:15; Joab and his men are portrayed as battering (משחיתים; lit., "ruining") the walls of Abel of Beth-maacah. In Ezek. 4:2 the prophet is told to make a model of Jerusalem in siege with battering rams planted against its walls. In 21:22 they are mentioned as part of the siege weapons of Babylon in the anticipated siege of Jerusalem. A similar fate is promised for Tyre in 26:9 (*cf.* also Isa. 22:5).

*See also* WAR, METHODS OF, § 8.

J. W. WEVERS

**BATTLE.** See WAR, METHODS OF.

**BATTLE ARRAY.** See ARRAY, BATTLE.

**BATTLE-AX.** KJV translation of מפץ (RSV HAM-MER) in Jer. 15:20.

**BATTLEMENT** [טירה] (Song of S. 8:9; KJV PALACE), row or course of stones; פנה (Zeph. 1:16; 3:6; KJV HIGH TOWERS, TOWERS), corner, tower; KJV מעקה (Deut. 22:8; RSV "parapet"), נטישות (Jer. 5:10; RSV *correctly* "branches")]. A crenelated parapet. The phrase "battlement of silver" is used symbolically in Song of S. 8:9. The battlements of fortified cities are referred to in Zeph. 1:16; 3:6.      H. G. MAY

**BAVVAI** băv'ī [בוי] (Neh. 3:18). Son of Henadad; a Levite who helped rebuild the wall of Jerusalem. Several Hebrew MSS, the Syr., and certain Greek texts indicate that "Bavvai" is a corruption of "BIN-NUI" (cf. vs. 24).

**BAY.** The KJV translation of אמצים in Zech. 6:3, 7. The LXX omits reference to bay horses in these verses, and the RSV treats the term as a gloss in Zech. 6:3 and translates it as "steeds" in vs. 7. This word does not refer to color but signifies strength.      C. L. WICKWIRE

**BAY TREE.** The KJV translation of אזרח (lit., "a native") in Ps. 37:35. The text may not intend any particular tree; but if so, we need not choose the bay tree (*Laurus nobilis* L., noted for its aromatic

From *Plants of the Bible* (London: Crosby Lockwood & Son, Ltd.)
24. Bay tree

leaves), even though native to the area (*cf.* FLORA § A9*b*). In FLORA § A9*i* the ארן of Isa. 44:14 is identified with this tree (*see* PINE). Most scholars read with the LXX: "like a CEDAR of Lebanon" (so RSV), which suits the context (cf. Ezek. 31:1-14).
Fig. BAY 24.      J. C. TREVER

**BAZAAR** [חוץ, outside] (I Kings 20:34). A section of a street set apart for merchants. Ben-hadad of Damascus gave Ahab permission to establish bazaars in Damascus, as Ben-hadad's father had in Samaria.

**BAZLITH** băz'lĭth [בצלית]. Alternately: BAZLUTH băz'lǝth (Ezra 2:52; I Esd. 5:31); KJV BASALOTH băs'ǝ lŏth (I Esd. 5:31). The founder of a family group included among the NETHINIM in the great list of those who returned from the Exile (*Kethibh* of Neh. 7:54). The correct reading of the name is difficult to determine.      F. T. SCHUMACHER

**BDELLIUM** dĕl'ĭ ǝm [בדלח, *b*ᵉ*dhōlaḥ; cf.* Sanskrit *udukhala,* Akkad. *budulḫu,* Indian myrrh]. It is quite uncertain what this is. It has been defined as a gum or resin, a precious stone or a pearl. The cognates noted would seem to favor a gum. Its connection with gold and onyx as products of Havilah would point toward a stone (Gen. 2:12). In Num. 11:7 it is used to describe manna which was white like hoarfrost. This may give some basis for its being rendered "pearl" in the Syriac and Arabic versions. *See* JEWELS AND PRECIOUS STONES § 2.
     W. E. STAPLES

**BEADS** [כומז] (Num. 31:50); KJV TABLETS. Alternately: ARMLETS (Exod. 35:22). Articles of gold jewelry. The meaning of the Hebrew word is uncertain, and "breastplates" and "necklace" have been suggested. *See* JEWELS AND PRECIOUS STONES § 2.

**BEALIAH** bē'ǝ lī'ǝ [בעליה, Yahu is lord] (I Chr. 12:5). One of the ambidextrous slingers and archers of the tribe of Benjamin who joined the outlaw band of David at Ziklag.

**BEALOTH** bē'ǝ lŏth [בעלות]; KJV IN ALOTH ā'lŏth in 2 *below*. 1. A town in S Judah (Josh. 15:24); perhaps the same as BAALATH-BEER.
2. A town(?) in Solomon's eleventh administrative district (I Kings 4:16). Its location is unknown.

**BEAM.** The translation of a number of words.
The weaver's beam (מנור), the bar on which the warp was wound in the loom, evidently was large (I Sam. 17:7; II Sam. 21:19; I Chr. 11:23; 20:5). The word translated "beam" in Judg. 16:14 KJV (ארג; omitted in the RSV) is doubtful; it may mean "bobbin."
Words designating the beam used in building are: גב (I Kings 6:9); כפים (Hab. 2:11); כרתת (a plural; I Kings 6:36; 7:2, 12). The verb קרה means "lay beams" (Neh. 3:3, 6; Ps. 104:3). The corresponding noun, קורה, is translated "beam" in II Chr. 3:7; Song of S. 1:17 (where cedar beams are highly esteemed); but in the story of Elisha's making the iron axe float (II Kings 6:1-7) the RSV uses "log." צלע (I Kings 7:3), "beam" in the KJV, is "chamber" in the RSV; and עב (I Kings 7:6), "thick beam" in the KJV, is "canopy" in the RSV. The use of "beams" in I Kings 6:6 is conjectural, as indicated by the italics in the KJV. *See* ARCHITECTURE.
The KJV translates "mote" and "beam" (δοκός) in the parable in Matt. 7:3-5; Luke 6:41-42; but the RSV has "speck" and "log."      O. R. SELLERS

**BEAN.** KJV form of BAEAN.

**BEANS** [פּוֹל; Arab. *fûl;* Akkad. *pulilu*]. A leguminous plant, *Vicia faba* L., grown from very ancient times for its nutritious food. Beans were included with other foods and supplies brought to David in Mahanaim (II Sam. 17:28). They were combined with other grains to prepare a coarse bread symbolizing the siege of Jerusalem (Ezek. 4:9).

The dried bean is winnowed in a similar manner to wheat after the grain harvest. Also the green pod was cooked as a vegetable. *See also* AGRICULTURE; FLORA § A1*e;* FOOD.                    J. C. TREVER

**BEAR** [דֹּב, Aram. דֹּב (Dan. 7:5), *cf.* דבב, to move gently; Arab. *dabba,* to creep, *dubb,* bear; ἄρκος (Rev. 13:2), *variant of* ἄρκτος]. A large, heavily built carnivorous mammal, with coarse and generally long hair, a short tail, and five-toed plantigrade feet (family Ursidae). The bear of Palestine, which was known in the N regions as late as the early twentieth century, was the Syrian variety of the brown bear (*ursus arctos syriacus*). Like most bears, it subsisted on a diet of vegetables, fruit, and insects to a greater extent than on flesh.

The OT references indicate that bears were common in ancient Israel. Although these animals are generally inoffensive, when annoyed or extremely hungry they can be dangerous, which explains the allusion in Amos 5:19 and the simile for a wicked ruler in Prov. 28:15 (cf. Wisd. Sol. 11:17). A bear lying in wait for prey serves as a figure for God in Lam. 3:10; its attack on the flock points to David's prowess in I Sam. 17:34, 36-37. Such references throw light on the picture in Isa. 11:7 of the cow and the bear feeding together in the future age of peace. One of the commonest causes of the irritation of bears was (and still is) interference with their young (a possible explanation of II Kings 2:24), and a she-bear robbed of her cubs supplies a simile for human anger in II Sam. 17:8 (cf. Isa. 59:11; Ecclus. 25:17), and for the divine anger in Hos. 13:8, although Prov. 17:12 avers that confronting such an enraged animal is to be preferred to meeting a human fool.

Bears play a minor role in apocalyptic imagery. In Dan. 7:5 the second of the four beasts coming up out of the sea is a bear, doubtless chosen for its size, strength, and supposed voracity, and seemingly typifying the kingdom of Media. In Rev. 13:2 the composite beast, representing the Roman Empire, probably was inspired by Dan. 7, though the bear of the latter vision has contributed only the feet to the Johannine creation; bears' feet, being large, may signalize the trampling down of all opposition.

W. S. McCULLOUGH

**BEARD** [זָקָן, שָׂפָם]. Full beards were common among the Hebrews, who considered their removal a symbol of indignity (II Sam. 10:4-5), except in cases of leprosy (Lev. 14:9). Semites are often pictured wearing beards in ancient Near Eastern art. Egyptians and Romans preferred clean-shaven faces, although the rulers among the former wore artificial beards. Fig. BEA 25.

The regular Hebrew word for "beard" is זָקָן (Lev.

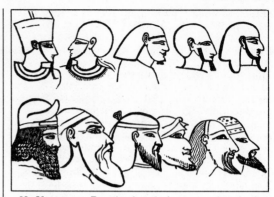

25. Upper row: Egyptian beards; lower row: beards of other nations

13:29-30, etc.), a cognate of the term for "old" which was applied variously to men (Judg. 19:16), slaves (Gen. 24:2), women (Zech. 8:4), and elders (Exod. 19:7). In II Sam. 19:24 only, the term שָׂפָם is usually rendered "beard," although it doubtless has reference to a "moustache" (so Moffatt, Amer. Trans.). The same word appears also in Lev. 13:45; Ezek. 24:17, 22; Mic. 3:7, where it is variously translated as "beard," "lip," and "moustache." Uncertainty as to the precise meaning of שָׂפָם in these passages is due to lack of information concerning the custom of covering lips or beard at times of distress or mourning.

The Hebrews were forbidden to mar the edges of their beards by cutting (Lev. 19:27); priests were enjoined against shaving off the edges of their beards (21:5), although Ezekiel was instructed to shave his head and beard to symbolize the coming destruction (Ezek. 5:1). David is said to have seized a lion or bear by its beard (I Sam. 17:35), and Joab took the beard of Amasa with his right hand to kiss him (II Sam. 20:9). Fearing Achish, and feigning madness, David let his spittle run down on his beard (I Sam. 21:13). The pulling of some of the hair from head and beard was a sign of mourning or anger (Ezra 9:3). The shaving of the beard was synonymous with impending doom (Isa. 7:20; 15:2; Jer. 41:5; 48:37). The practice of anointing the beard with precious oil is alluded to in a single reference to Aaron's beard (Ps. 133:2), but it is implied in Exod. 30:22-30; Lev. 8:30 as a priestly ritual associated with Aaron.

W. L. REED

**BEAST** [חַיָּה (Aram. חֵיוָא, חַיָוָה *in* Dan. 4:12; 7:5; etc.), living creature, *from* חָיָה (Aram. חֵיא), to live; טבח (Prov. 9:2; *cf.* Gen. 43:16), slaughtering; KJV זִיז (RSV ALL THAT MOVE[S]), *cf.* Akkad. *zâzu,* abundance, luxuriant growth; *for* מְרִיא, בְּעִיר, בְּהֵמָה (Isa. 1:11; Amos 5:22), *see* CATTLE; ζῶον, living being; θηρίον, wild animal, *diminutive of* θήρ, *and* LXX *translation of* חַיָּה *and* Aram. חֵיוָה; θηριομαχέω (I Cor. 15:32), to fight with wild beasts, *from* θηρίον *and* μάχομαι, to fight (*see* 2 *below*); κτῆνος, *see* CATTLE; KJV τετράπους (Acts 10:12; 11:6; Rom. 1:23; RSV ANIMALS), four-footed]; WILD BEASTS [צִיִּים (Isa. 34:14; *etc.*), *probably* desert-dweller]; SLAIN BEASTS [σφάγιον (Acts 7:42), *from* σφάζω, to slay, slaughter]. In some contexts the precise meaning of the word can only be surmised.

1. Any animal (Gen. 6:7; Lev. 11:2; Deut. 4:17; Job 12:7; 35:11; Ps. 36:6—H 36:7; Eccl. 3:18-21; etc.). Animals are divided into clean and unclean (Gen. 7:2; Lev. 11:1-8); the former may be used as food, provided the blood is removed (Lev. 7:26; cf. Prov. 9:2). Some serve as sacrifices (Acts 7:42; Heb. 13:11), and among these are those specially fattened for the purpose (Isa. 1:11; Amos 5:22). It is recognized that the mind of a beast is inferior to that of a man (Dan. 4:16; 5:21), and the beast's irrationality serves as a simile in II Pet. 2:12; Jude 10.

2. A wild and sometimes carnivorous animal (Gen. 1:24; 7:21; 37:20; Exod. 23:11; Deut. 28:26; I Sam. 17:44, 46; Mark 1:13; Acts 11:6; 28:5; Rev. 6:8; etc.). The lair of such an animal, which gets its food from God (Ps. 147:9), is referred to in Job 37:8; Zeph. 2:15. Israel's enemies are likened to wild beasts (Ps. 74:19; Jer. 12:9), as are the Cretans (Tit. 1:12). In I Cor. 15:32 the verb "to fight with wild beasts" is probably a metaphor for Paul's troubles with his enemies.

3. A domesticated animal (Gen. 1:24; 2:20; Exod. 19:13; 22:10—H 22:9; Num. 3:13; 31:47; Judg. 20:48; Prov. 12:10; Jer. 21:6; Jas. 3:7; Rev. 18:13; etc.). "Beast" means "ass" in Gen. 45:17, and an unspecified riding animal in Neh. 2:12, 14; Luke 10:34; Acts 23:24 (RSV "mount"). "Cattle," "property," and "beasts" (בהמה) occur together in Gen. 34:23, where it is probable that the third term refers to riding and pack animals and possibly also to oxen (cf. Num. 31:9; 35:3). In II Kings 3:9 the "beasts" following the army are presumably draft or pack animals. Domesticated animals are subject to the law of firstlings (Num. 3:13; 8:17), as well as to the sabbath regulation (Deut. 5:14); all sodomy with them is strictly forbidden (Lev. 20:15-16). In Exod. 22:10-15—H 22:9-14; Lev. 24:18 there is provision for restitution for an injury caused to the beast of another person. W. S. McCULLOUGH

4. The beasts of the Revelation to John. Two beasts are mentioned in the Revelation to John: (a) one described as the "beast that ascends from the bottomless pit" (11:7; cf. 17:8), as a "beast rising out of the sea" (13:1), as a "scarlet beast" (17:3), as the "beast with seven heads and ten horns" (17:7), as the "beast that was and is not" (17:11), and as the "first beast" (13:12) or simply "the beast" (13:2 ff, 14 ff, et passim); and (b) a second designated either as "another beast which rose out of the earth" (13:11), or as the "false prophet" (16:13; 19:20; 20:10).

The first of these beasts combines in itself the joint characteristics of the four beasts of Daniel's vision (Dan. 7:3-7; cf. the terms "lion," "bear," "leopard," a "fourth beast, terrible and dreadful and exceedingly strong," "ten horns," "out of the sea," and the like). Accordingly, this first beast represents the combined forces of all political rule opposed to God in the world and is the earthly, demonic messiah of the DRAGON, whose "power" is granted to it (Rev. 13:2). This false messiah imitates God's true Messiah at every possible point, notably in that it "was, and is not, and is to ascend from the bottomless pit and go to perdition" (17:8), even as Jesus, the Messiah of God, came in the Incarnation, died in the Atonement, rose in the Resurrection, and went into heaven by the Ascension.

The second beast represents every pagan cultus which exists for the express purpose of granting its religious sanction to further the political designs of the world power extant in any culture, insofar as that power is opposed to God's sovereignty over his world. This beast, therefore, combines in its activities the functions of priest (13:14), prophet (vs. 15), and grand inquisitor (vss. 16-17). In John's day the world power arrayed against God and his kingdom was the Roman Empire, and the cult established to further its aims was that of emperor worship and its priestcraft. Hence, the immediate reference of the two beasts arising respectively from sea and earth is, for John, to the Roman Empire and the imperial cultus. Together with the Dragon, these two beasts combine to form a sort of unholy trinity, the opposite to the true one!

*See* LEVIATHAN; BEHEMOTH.

**Bibliography.** *See* the Commentaries listed under REVELATION, BOOK OF. J. W. BOWMAN

**BEATEN GOLD** [זהב שחוט]. Thin sheet gold, produced by hammering (רקע) and used for overlaying objects of baser metals. The term is used only of the golden shields of Solomon (I Kings 10:16-17; II Chr. 9:15-16), which were not of solid gold but had gold overlay. The lampstands of the tabernacle were made of hammered work of gold (זהב מקשה; KJV "beaten work of gold"; Exod. 25:18, 31, 36; 37:7, 22; Num. 8:4; 10:2). Figurines of idols, made of bronze and covered with beaten gold, as described in Isa. 40:19, were found at Tell Abu Hawam and Megiddo.

**Bibliography.** R. W. Hamilton, "Excavations at Tell Abu Hawam," *Quarterly of the Department of Antiquities of Palestine*, vol. IV (1935), p. 60, nos. 370, 372, and pls. XV.2, XXXIX.1. I. BEN-DOR

**BEATEN OIL** [שמן כתית]. The highest quality of oil, used for the lamp in the sanctuary (Exod. 27:20; Lev. 24:2) or with the daily sacrifices (Exod. 29:40; Num. 28:5); also one of Solomon's barter products with Hiram (I Kings 5:11—H 5:25). Beaten oil was made by crushing fully ripe olives in a mortar. The oil which was produced without pressing was regarded as the purest and best. That produced by pressing was second grade, and that derived from further grinding and pressing third grade. *See also* OIL TREE; OLIVE TREE. J. M. MYERS

**BEATEN SILVER** [כסף מרקע] (Jer. 10:9); KJV SILVER SPREAD INTO PLATES. Thin plates or leaves of hammered silver, used along with gold leaf to overlay the wooden core of an image. Fine metalwork was imported from the Phoenician colonies of the W Mediterranean (here Tarshish). *See* METALLURGY. L. E. TOOMBS

**BEATING.** *See* SCOURGING.

**BEATITUDES.** The beatitude is a literary form, which commences with the word "blessed," and constitutes a declaration of praise for an individual regarded as an unusual example of moral rectitude and piety, who, as a consequence, might anticipate some appropriate reward from God. As expressions of joy and hope, and occasionally even of sorrow, beatitudes reflect varying, yet general, aspirations of human life.

1. Formal characteristics of the beatitude
2. Beatitudes of the OT
3. Beatitudes of the Apoc.
4. Beatitudes of the NT
Bibliography

**1. Formal characteristics of the beatitude.** Although the authors of OT documents did not limit their formulation of beatitudes to a single pattern, they generally began the declaration with אַשְׁרֵי ("happy" or "blessed"), after which they referred to a type of individual worthy of praise (Pss. 1:1; 2:12; Prov. 8:34; Isa. 56:2; Dan. 12:12). Similarly authors of NT documents usually constructed a beatitude by using the adjective μακάριος ("blessed" or "happy") with a substantive, a substantive adjective, or a relative clause, to designate the types of persons considered blessed, and frequently included a clause beginning with ὅτι ("because") to state the reasons for their fortunate state (cf. especially Matt. 5:3-11).

**2. Beatitudes of the OT.** Beatitudes appear almost exclusively in the writings of the psalmists and the sages, who used the form with varying religious overtones. These beatitudes are pronounced upon the man who is righteous, who keeps his hand from doing evil and does not profane the sabbath—such a one may look forward with confidence to such earthly rewards as peace, prosperity, the satisfactions of family life, the joys of temple worship, and renewal of strength (cf. Pss. 41:1; 65:4; 84:5; 106:3; 112:1; 128:1; Prov. 8:32; Isa. 32:20; 56:1-2). Generally God's deliverance was not eschatologically conceived but was regarded as a favor realizable during one's earthly existence. Even the chastened individual might be called blessed, for suffering was a means of learning God's law and might become the ground of hope for God's nonabandonment of the sufferer (Ps. 94:12). Rewards for obedience to God's commands appear to make the pleasures of a full and happy life the goal of human existence. In actual fact, however, the purpose of the beatitudes was not to emphasize these good fortunes as having value in themselves but as signs of God's nearness to the righteous. Blessed are those who trust God, who hope in him, who wait upon him, who fear and love him, and whose sins have been forgiven by him (Pss. 2:12; 32:1-2; 40:4; 84:12; 112:1; etc.).

**3. Beatitudes of the Apoc.** In the apocryphal writings of the OT the beatitude continued to be a gnomic saying used for purposes similar to those noted above. Fortunate are those individuals who live with wives of understanding, who are discreet in speech, who are not enslaved to inferiors, and who pursue wisdom and fear God (Ecclus. 25:7-10). Also fortunate are the Hebrew people, for to them has been given the privilege of knowing God and his will and consequently for feeling assured of deliverance from all the exigencies of human life—from toil and struggle, and from sorrow and anxiety. Significant for a clearer understanding of the beatitudes in the Sermon on the Mount (Matt. 5:3-12) is the first appearance of a collection of beatitudes in this apocryphal literature. Earlier authors had used single beatitudes rather sparingly, but the author of Ecclesiasticus lists nine types of men whom he conceives as blessed in some sense (Ecclus. 25:7-10).

**4. Beatitudes of the NT.** Beatitudes appear with greatest frequency in two of the Synoptic gospels (Matthew and Luke), seven times in the book of Revelation (1:3; 14:13; 16:15; 19:9; 20:6; 22:7, 14), three times in Paul's Letter to the Romans (4:7-8; 14:22), and once in the Fourth Gospel (John 20:29). They resemble the beatitudes of the OT in their formal structure and in their praise of individuals or the parts of the body associated with life—e.g., the eyes (Matt. 13:16) or the womb (Luke 23:29). In content, however, the NT beatitudes differ from those of the OT in one important respect: The NT beatitudes stress the eschatological joy of participation in the kingdom of God, rather than rewards for this earthly life. This typically NT outlook is implied even in those beatitudes which have closest affinities with certain OT beatitudes (Rom. 4:7-8 [cf. Ps. 32:1-2]; Jas. 1:25 [cf. Ps. 1:1]) and is clearly apparent in the beatitudes of the Sermon on the Mount (Matt. 5:3-12) and of the book of Revelation. Important for an interpretation of the collection of nine beatitudes at the beginning of the Sermon is a recognition of this eschatological rather than sociological orientation. Difficulties will be resolved, not by initiating a program of social and moral improvement, but by the coming of God's kingdom. Similarly the author of the book of Revelation has given the ancient gnomic form of the beatitude an eschatological significance and heightened its importance by enclosing his apocalyptic work within two beatitudes (Rev. 1:3; 22:14).

Consequently in the NT beatitudes the element of paradox becomes prominent. Men who in no way appear to be fortunate in the present (e.g., martyrs who have suffered death, the poor, the distressed, and the barren) are those declared blessed. These individuals will escape condemnation on the day of judgment, because they have prepared themselves by watching for its coming (Matt. 24:46; Luke 12:37-38; Rev. 16:15), by their ready willingness to hear the word of God without a feeling of offense (Matt. 11:6) and to see the signs of his coming with the eyes of faith (Luke 1:45; 10:23; 12:43; John 20:29), and by the expression of their newly found faith in concrete deeds (Matt. 24:46; Jas. 1:12, 25; Rev. 14:13; 22:7).

The beatitudes which appear in the Sermon on the Mount (Matt. 5:3-12; cf. Luke 6:20-23) are the most familiar. Luke includes four beatitudes in his report of the Sermon, in contrast to the First Evangelist's list of nine (cf. the collection of nine beatitudes in Ecclus. 25:7-10). The significance given to these beatitudes by these two evangelists is apparent from their formulation of the beatitudes and from their contexts. By having Jesus direct his words "Blessed are *you*" to the multitude and by matching each beatitude with a corresponding woe, Luke wishes to stress the specific situation and the factor of social change. The First Evangelist, on the other hand, stresses the general situation in which Jesus' followers of every age find themselves, by having him say: "Blessed are *the poor*," etc. Thus this evangelist makes the beatitudes an appropriate introduction to his code for Christian discipleship (Matt. 5–7). Since collections of beatitudes are a literary rather than an oral device for communicating laudatory comments about individuals, it hardly seems likely that Jesus spoke at one time as many as reported by the First Evangelist.

Analysis of the Matthean beatitudes suggests that three different types of beatitudes have been brought together to form the collection of nine. Reference is made in the first group to those individuals whose lot in life is evil. In this group are the poor, who have inherited the tradition of an elemental loyalty to God but have been disowned and oppressed by the observant Pharisees and the priestly Sadducees; the mourners, who bear the burden of grief for all men's sorrows; and the hungry, who yearn, according to the First Evangelist's interpretation, after righteousness. Release from the tensions of the present has a profound meaning for these individuals who in some way exhibit God's attitudes of mercifulness, of purity or singleness of heart, and of peacemaking. As God works to destroy evil and to create the good, so these individuals have learned from God's action what should be the character of their own activity. In the third group the ambassadors of Jesus, whose sufferings will be comparable to those of the prophets, are singled out as individuals who undertake the specific work of preaching the gospel. However difficult the present situation may be for men whom others would regard as most unfortunate, God will soon resolve the tensions of their present situation and grant them the gifts of his kingdom.

*Bibliography.* H. Windisch, *The Meaning of the Sermon on the Mount* (English trans. S. M. Gilmour; 1950), pp. 37-38, 87-88, 127, 175-80. L. Mowry

**BEAUTIFUL GATE** [ἡ θύρα ἡ ὡραία, ἡ ὡραία πύλη] (Acts 3:2, 10). The scene of the healing of a paralytic by Peter and John in the Temple. Jewish sources make no mention of such a gate, though Josephus describes the beauty of an Eastern gate fashioned of Corinthian bronze which opened upon the Court of the Women (War V.v.3), perhaps the Nicanor Gate of the Mishnaic tractate Middoth. This is more likely the gate of Acts 3 than the Susa or Golden Gate identified by Christian tradition.

*Bibliography.* F. J. Foakes-Jackson and K. Lake, *The Beginnings of Christianity*, V (1933), 479-86; S. Corbett, "Some Observations on the Gateways to the Herodian Temple in Jerusalem," *PEQ*, LXXXIV (1952), 7-15. E. W. Saunders

**BEAUTY.** The rich and diverse vocabulary for "beauty" in the Bible includes the root יפה, "be fair, beautiful," and derived words; צבי, "beauty, honor, gazelle"; the root פאר, "beautify, glorify," and especially the noun תפארה, "beauty, glory"; the roots אוה and חמד and derived forms suggesting "what is desirable to the eyes"; and the roots נוה "beautify"; נאה, "be comely, befitting"; נעם, "be pleasant, delightful, lovely," all with their derived forms. The adjective טוב, "good," also means "handsome, fair, beautiful, goodly." Other words are הדר, "beauty, splendor"; הוד, "splendor, beauty"; perhaps חסד, "faithful love, grace"; חן, "grace, beauty"; כבוד, "glory, splendor." There are also several infrequent terms such as the root שפר, "be beautiful, fair, comely," and the noun גזרה, "polishing" or "beauty." In the NT there are the terms καλός, "beautiful"; ὡραῖος, "charming, attractive"; ἀστεῖος, "handsome,

well-pleasing"; εὐπρέπεια, "fine appearance, beauty"; τιμή, "honor,"; etc. The study of all these terms in the concordances will reveal the range of reference.

Neither the OT nor the NT has any theory of the beautiful. Instead, there is the description of many things as beautiful. There are thus several descriptions of the beauty of women, as in Prov. 11:22; Jer. 4:30; Ezek. 16:9-14. Such passages as Isa. 3:18-24; Ezek. 23:40 show what aids to beauty were used. Naturally many women of much beauty are mentioned, including Sarai (Gen. 12:11, 14); Rebekah (Gen. 24:16; 26:7); though she was not so beautiful when she was older; and especially Rachel, who had a fine figure in addition to being beautiful. Abigail (I Sam. 25:3), Abishag (I Kings 1:3-4), Bathsheba, and both Tamars—Absalom's sister (II Sam. 13:1) and his daughter (14:27)—were beautiful. Delilah's younger sister (Judg. 15:2) and Esther were likewise (Esth. 1:11; 2:7), and especially the beautiful bride of the Song of Songs (4:1-6).

The fair sex does not have matters all its own way, for Absalom (II Sam. 14:25), Adonijah (I Kings 1:6), Benaiah's Egyptian (II Sam. 23:21), Daniel (Dan. 1:4, 15), David (I Sam. 16:12), Joseph (Gen. 39:6), Saul (I Sam. 9:2), and Jonathan (II Sam. 1:23) all were handsome in varying degrees. The baby Moses was goodly (Exod. 2:2), and the bridal pairs of Ps. 45 and the Song of Songs were alike distinguished. Other groups are mentioned as beautiful, such as the women of Gen. 6:2, fair virgins (Amos 8:13), and Job's daughters (Job 42:15); and cf. Prov. 6:25.

Parts of the body are singled out for special mention especially in the Song of Songs (*passim*); and cf. the voice (Ezek. 33:32), Ephraim's neck (Hos. 10:11), the feet of the herald (Isa. 52:7; Rom. 10:15) by synecdoche for the messenger himself. Particularly striking is: "Your lips are like a scarlet thread" (Song of S. 4:3). Inevitably women's hair and men's beards figure prominently (for the former, cf. Song of S. 4:1; Isa. 3:24; Luke 7:38; John 11:2; 12:3; and the latter, II Sam. 10:5; 14:25-27; Prov. 20:29). But reference in the NT to different parts of the body serves an entirely different purpose (Rom. 9:21). Aaron's garments were for glory and beauty (Exod. 28:2, 40; Rev. 1:14); also mentioned are a beautiful mantle from Shinar (Josh. 7:21); one of fine linen (Gen. 41: 42; Esth. 8:15; etc.); festal garments (Gen. 45:22; Judg. 14:12-13; II Kings 5:5; etc.); embroidered garments (Exod. 26:36; Judg. 5:30; Ezek. 16:18; 26:16; etc.); and white garments (Eccl. 9:8; Dan. 7:9; Matt. 17:2; Rev. 3:4-5; etc.). The phrases "fair garland" and "crown of beauty" or "beautiful crown" (Prov. 4:9; Isa. 62:3; Jer. 13:18; Ezek. 23:47) are used.

The natural scene in Palestine is described in terms of the beautiful. The land itself is a "heritage most beauteous" (Jer. 3:19; cf. Ps. 16:6). The beauty of Jerusalem, of Zion, of its temple, and of its houses is all described (cf., e.g., Ezra 7:27; Pss. 48:1 ff; 50:2; 93:5; Isa. 5:9; 64:11; Jer. 6:2; Lam. 2:15; Acts 3:2, 10). In Ps. 50:2; Lam. 2:15 the striking phrase "perfection of beauty" is used of Zion. "Beauty" in Pss. 27:4; 96:6, though represented by different Hebrew words, probably conceals references to the ark. Israel is the Lord's "beautiful flock" (Jer. 13:20; cf. Hos.

14:6). The beauty of the city of Samaria (Isa. 28:1-4), of Egypt and Pharaoh (Ezek. 31:1–32:21), and of Tyre and its princes (Ezek. 27–28) are all described. The beauty of Egypt is set forth under the figure of a cedar of Lebanon, and Tyre's beauty under precious stones (*see* DRESS AND ORNAMENTS; JEWELS AND PRECIOUS STONES; MANTLE). Jeremiah likens Egypt to a beautiful heifer (Jer. 46:20). Palestine's skies were bright and fair (Exod. 24:10; Job 26:13; Ps. 19:1; cf. Song of S. 6:10).

The OT in general shows a keen appreciation of the glory, and thus of the beauty, of God in nature. In God everything is beautiful in its time (Eccl. 3:11; such words as "clear, "bright," "shining," should be consulted in the concordance in this connection). Jesus himself crowns this attitude toward nature in his own famous words concerning "Solomon in all his glory" (Matt. 6:29 and parallels). The figure of beautiful or fair words is, of course, applied to flattering (Ps. 45:2) and false speech (Jer. 12:6; Rom. 16:18). But words of wisdom are beautiful (Prov. 1:9; 4:9). It is perhaps not amiss to mention here that while Israel's artistic genius expended itself in music, religious architecture and its decorations, and the dancing and processional activities connected with worship, the supreme expression of Israel's capacity for beauty is certainly in her gift of language, whether it be narrative description, the moving force of preaching, or the lyrical outpourings of psalmists and prophets in worship. At this point, too, Jesus' descriptive capacity in the parables reveals a sense of the beauty of diction never surpassed. The artistic principle is fully covered in Phil. 4:8.

Naturally, eschatological passages abound in references to what is beautiful. There is mention of the future beauty of Jerusalem (Isa. 52:1; 62:3; Zech. 9:17), and of the Messiah (Isa. 33:17; cf. 4:2), but the Servant of the Lord has no comeliness (Isa. 53:2). At the end God himself will become a beautiful diadem for his people (Isa. 28:5). Inevitably much beauty attaches to the persons, places, adornments, and general description of the book of Revelation.

The final word must be accorded to the beautiful deed of the woman who anointed Jesus in preparation for his burial (Matt. 26:6-13).

*Bibliography.* P. T. Forsyth, *Christ on Parnassus* (n.d.); J. A. Montgomery, "Aesthetic in Hebrew Religion," *JBL*, LVI (1937), 35-41; R. Wischnitzer, "Judaism and Art," in L. Finkelstein, ed., *The Jews*, II (1949), 985-91; H. A. Groenewegen and H. Frankfort, *Arrest and Movement* (1951); T. Boman, *Das hebräische Denken im Vergleich mit dem Griechischen* (1952), pp. 60-96, 133-40; H. Frankfort, *The Art and Architecture of the Ancient Orient* (1954); G. von Rad, *Theologie des ATs*, I (1957), 361-63. G. HENTON DAVIES

**BEBAI** bē′bī [Βηβαι] (Jth. 15:4). An unidentified Israelite city whose people joined in the destruction of the fleeing "Assyrian" forces after the death of Holofernes. It may be an early corruption of a name no longer recognizable. Some scholars identify it as BELMAIN.

*Bibliography.* F. Stummer, *Geographie des Buches Judith* (1947), p. 28. E. W. SAUNDERS

**BECHER** bē′kər [בכר, young camel]; BECHER-ITES—īts; KJV BACHRITES băk′rīts. **1.** The sec-

ond son of Benjamin (Gen. 46:21; I Chr. 7:6, 8). The genealogical list ascribed to Benjamin in I Chr. 7:6-12 must originally have belonged to Zebulun, now strangely missing from the Chronicler's genealogies. The Benjaminite list appears in its proper place beginning at I Chr. 8:1, and Zebulun, if restored to I Chr. 7:6, would follow Issachar, as it does in most other OT lists. The Benjaminite Becher must have been added to the list after it had been detached from Zebulun.

**2.** An Ephraimite, enumerated in the list of the second census taken by Moses in the wilderness (Num. 26:35). He is the eponymous ancestor of the "family of the Becherites" (KJV "Bachrites"). The names both of the ancestor and of the family are omitted in the LXX and in all probability do not belong in this verse. In the list of the sons of Ephraim in I Chr. 7:20, Bered is named in second place, the position occupied in Num. 26:35 by Becher. "Bered" may originally have been the reading of Num. 26:35.

*Bibliography.* M. Noth, *Die israelitischen Personennamen* (1928), p. 258. R. F. JOHNSON

**BECORATH** bĭ kôr′ăth [בכורת] (I Sam. 9:1); KJV BECHORATH. The father of Zeror; an ancestor of King Saul.

**BECTILETH** běk′tə lĕth [Βαικτειλαίθ, *from* Aram. house of the killing] (Jth. 2:21). An unidentified plain apparently situated in or near N Cilicia, reached by Holofernes and his army after a three-day march from Nineveh. Either this location or the time of the journey is impossible, for the distance between Nineveh and Cilicia is approximately three hundred miles. Some identify Bectileth with the *Bakataïlloi* of Ptolemy (*Geography* V.14) and locate it S of Antioch in Syria, or relate it to the Syrian *beqâ*. Others propose that it is a symbolic name referring to the slaughter of the peoples named in Jth. 2:22-23.

*Bibliography.* F. Stummer, *Geographie des Buches Judith* (1947), p. 27. E. W. SAUNDERS

**BED** [יצוע, מצע (Isa. 28:20), what is spread out; מטה, place of reclining; משכב, place of lying down; ערוגה (*see* 2 below); ערש, cf. Arab. 'rš, throne, arbor; κλινάριον (Acts 5:15), κλίνη, κλινίδιον (Luke 5:19, 24), all from κλίνω, incline, make recline; κοίτη (Luke 11:7; Heb. 13:4; cf. Rom. 9:10; 13:13), from κείμαι, lie outstretched; κράββατος]. Alternately: COUCH (Gen. 49:4; Job 7:13; Prov. 7:16; Ezek. 23:41; etc.); LITTER (Song of S. 3:7); MARRIAGE BED (Heb. 13:4). A place for reclining in sleep, sickness, or rest; often a movable article of furniture. Fig. BED 26.

**1. Types.** The various terms for bed cited above appear to be used loosely without any clear distinction in meaning. Most beds would be merely the place on the floor, sometimes a low ledge along a wall, where a person slept. The covering would commonly be one's garment (שמלה; Exod. 22:27—H 22:26). Such a sleeping place might be in an upper chamber (I Kings 17:19; *see* CHAMBER). Some beds, however, consisted of a wooden frame which could on occasion serve as a litter or stretcher (I Sam. 19:15; Matt. 9:2; Luke 5:18); this kind of bed might be of sufficient value to pay a debt (Prov. 22:27). The beds of the well-to-do were undoubtedly articles of furniture in keeping with their standard of living, and these might often be in bedchambers (II Kings 11:2). "Beds of ivory"—i.e., inlaid with IVORY—are referred to in Amos 6:4, and they are also included in the list of Hezekiah's tribute to Sennacherib (*ANET* 288). The perfumed coverings of the bed of an adulteress are mentioned in Prov. 7:16-17, but

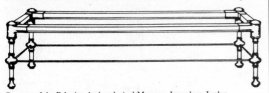

Courtesy of the Palestine Archaeological Museum, Jerusalem, Jordan

26. A bed with bronze fittings, from Tell el-Far'ah (Persian period; 550-330 B.C.)

the linen sheets and wooden headrests, so well known in connection with Egyptian beds, do not appear in the Bible (cf. "linen" in Prov. 7:16; Mark 15:46). Ten beds with silver feet are reported by Josephus to have been sent to Eleazar, high priest of Jerusalem, by Ptolemy (Antiq. XII.ii). The meaning of "BEDSTEAD of iron" (Deut. 3:11) is uncertain; the phrase may refer to a sarcophagus. Couches of gold and silver are said to have been in the palace of Xerxes at Susa (Esth. 1:6). The story of Judith (10:21) alludes to a canopied bed in the tent of Holofernes. *See also* COUCH; FURNITURE; HOUSE; LITTER.

**2. Uses.** Beds were used for sleeping at night (Job 7:13); for love-making (Gen. 49:4; Judg. 21:11; Song of S. 1:15-17; Ezek. 23:17); for a siesta (II Sam. 4:5-7; cf. the sluggard's bed of Prov. 26:14); for royal sulking (I Kings 21:4); for sitting on (I Sam. 28:23); for reclining on beside a table (Ezek. 23:41); for the sick (Gen. 48:1-2); for convalescence from a wound or injury (II Chr. 24:25; II Kings 1:4); for transporting the sick and the chronically ill (Mark 6:55; John 5:5-8); and for a bier (II Sam. 3:31; II Chr. 16:14; cf. Isa. 57:2).

**3. Religious use.** Beds were the scene of some acts of private devotion (Gen. 47:31; I Kings 1:47). The reference to beds in Isa. 57:7-8 is apparently to some non-Yahwistic sex cult. See also Hos. 7:14.

**4. Proverbial use.** Making one's bed in Sheol is a reference to the death of an individual (Job 17:13-14; cf. Ps. 139:8) or of a nation (Ezek. 32:24-25). A short bed appears in Isa. 28:20 as a figure for an intolerable situation. W. S. McCULLOUGH

**BED (GARDEN).** A level piece of ground in a garden. The word ערוגה (perhaps "what is ascended"), found only in Song of S. 5:13; 6:2; Ezek. 17:7, 10, is always used figuratively.

**BED CHAMBER.** *See* CHAMBER.

**BEDAD** bē'dăd [בדד; *cf. proper names* הדד, בן־הדד, בלדד, אלדד] (Gen. 36:35; I Chr. 1:46). The father of Edomite king Hadad.

**BEDAN** bē'dăn. **1.** The translation of בדן, the name of a Manassite, in I Chr. 7:17.

**2.** KJV-MT translation of בדן in I Sam. 12:11. "Abdon" (עבדן) has been suggested as the correct reading (cf. Judg. 12:13-15), but he is too unimportant a figure for the context. Better is "BARAK" (RSV-LXX). The rabbis, equating בדן with בךדן, "Danite," read "Samson." R. W. CORNEY

**BEDEIAH** bĭ dē'yə [בדיה, *possibly* branch of Yahu, *or perhaps a shortened form of* עבדיה, servant of Yahu] (Ezra 10:35). One of those compelled to give up their foreign wives in the time of Ezra.

**BEDSTEAD** [ערש, *'ereś,* bed; *cf.* Akkad. *eršu,* bed; Arab. *'arš,* throne, arbor, bier] (Deut. 3:11). The supporting framework of a bed.

ערש, usually translated "bed" (e.g., Job 7:13; Amos 6:4), is rendered "bedstead" only in Deut. 3:11, where it refers to the "bedstead of iron" of Og, king of Bashan, which is said to have been nine cubits in length. While it is conceivable that in the Early Iron Age iron may have been available for such a purpose in the Jordan area, the size of this particular bed suggests that it may have been some other object, such as a basalt sarcophagus. Basalt, which is both dark and hard, is common in Transjordan, and Pliny has been quoted to support the identification of basalt with iron. It is, however, a moot point whether Pliny's *"basanites* which in color and hardness resembles iron" is in fact basalt (Nat. Hist. XXXVI.7.11; cf. *basanites* in Isidorus Etymologiae XVI.5.6). Possibly the text refers to a DOLMEN, popularly thought to be the bed of a giant. *See also* BED § 1a.

*Bibliography.* On sarcophagi in the Transjordan region, see C. M. Doughty, *Travels in Arabia Deserta* (1888), I, 18.

W. S. McCULLOUGH

**BEE** [דבורה, *from* דבר; Arab. *dibr,* a swarm of bees; Syr. *debōrīthā',* wasp; μέλισσα]. The wild honeybee (*Apis mellifica*), a social insect, order Hymenoptera.

This bee was probably not domesticated until the Hellenistic period. Curiously, only one of the four occurrences of bees in the OT refers to the HONEY which they produced (Judg. 14:8). However, the fact that Canaan was so often referred to as the "land of milk and honey" suggests that bees were plentiful. The other occurrences (Deut. 1:44; Ps. 118:12; Isa. 7:18) all allude to their irritable, vindictive nature, and their painful sting, as symbols of Israel's enemies (see also IV Macc. 14:19). After praising the ant for her industriousness (Prov. 6:6-8), the LXX next extols the bee. Ben Sirach (Ecclus. 11:3), who appraises her appearance as nothing, considers her honey supreme. *See also* FAUNA § F4c.

*Bibliography.* See bibliography under BALD LOCUST.

W. W. FRERICHS

**BEELIADA** bē'ə lī'ə də [בעלידע, Baal knows]. One of the sons of David who were born in Jerusalem (I Chr. 14:7; cf. II Sam. 5:16 LXX). The name was altered to Eliada ("God knows") in accordance with the later disinclination to use the term "Baal" because of its associative ideas (II Sam. 5:16; I Chr. 3:8).

*Bibliography.* S. R. Driver, *Notes on the Hebrew Text of the Books of Samuel* (2nd ed., 1913), pp. 253 ff. E. R. DALGLISH

**BEELSARUS.** KJV Apoc. form of BILSHAN.

**BEELTETHMUS.** KJV form of BELTETHMUS.

**BEELZEBUL** bē ĕl'zĭ bŭl [Βεελζεβουλ; Coptic *Beel-zeboûî*]; KJV **BEELZEBUB** bē ĕl'zĭ bŭb. A designation applied by both Jesus and his opponents to the "chief of the devils"—i.e., SATAN (Matt. 10:25; 12:24, 27; Mark 3:22; Luke 11:15, 18-19). The Vulg. reads *Beelzebub*, evidently equating with the Philistine idol BAALZEBUB mentioned in II Kings 1:2. The connection is, however, far from clear, and this reading was probably no more than a *pis aller*, designed to explain a term the true etymology and meaning of which are alike obscure and which does not recur in any earlier or contemporary source.

The following are the principal interpretations:

*a*) In Ugaritic, *zbl* means "prince," and *zbl B'l* indeed occurs (I AB iv.4; III AB,A 8) as a designation of the god Baal. "Beelzebul" might thus represent a later application of this heathen style to the prime antagonist of God.

*b*) In postbiblical Hebrew, as also in Syriac and Arabic, a homonymous *z-b-l* means "dung," and in the Talmud, *zibbūl* denotes "stercorization." The name Beelzebul—i.e., *Baal zibbūl*—might therefore mean *Defoecator* (not simply *dominus stercoris*), as an opprobrious designation of the Evil One. An arresting analogy is afforded by the name Belchira (or Belachora) given in the pseudepigraphic Ascension of Isaiah (chs. 2–3) to a Samaritan who accused the prophet, for this is simply בעל חרא, "Lord of Dung." Similar characterizations of the Devil appear later in German folklore.

*c*) A third homonym, *zəbūl*, is said to exist in Hebrew with the meaning of "dwelling, abode." "Beelzebul" would thus have denoted primarily "Lord of the Abode [i.e., shrine]" and have come subsequently to be used as a designation of Satan, the rival of Yahweh. The existence of a root *z-b-l*, "dwell," is, however, somewhat doubtful. True, it has been assumed by several scholars to underlie the blessing on Zebulun in Gen. 49:13: "*Zebul*un shall *dwell* at the shore of the sea" (זבולן לחוף ימים ישכן); while in Gen. 30:20 the Vulg. and the Targums understand the phrase "Now my husband יזבלני" to mean: "Now my husband *dwells* with me"; and in Ps. 49:14, the words "Their form shall be for Sheol to wear away לו מזבל" are often rendered: "that there be no *habitation* for it" (RSV "Sheol shall be their *home*"). Such a meaning, however, does not exist in any of the cognate languages, and both in the passages cited and wherever else the noun זבל occurs in the OT (viz., Deut. 26:15; I Kings 8:13; II Chr. 30:27; Isa. 63:15; Jer. 25:30; Hab. 3:11), the meanings "exalt" and "height, zenith" (comporting with Akkadian *zabālu*, "lift up," and Ugaritic *zbl*, "exalted one, prince," and with LXX αἱρετιεῖ ;יזבלני Gen. 30:20), fit perfectly. Indeed, in Ps. 49:14, there may even be a pointed contrast between זבל, "eminence," and *Sheol*.

*d*) On the strength of OT usage, the Dead Sea Scrolls and early rabbinic literature employ the term זבל to denote one of the seven heavens. The name Beelzebul might therefore denote the Evil One (i.e.,

Satan, Belial, Samael) as lord of that region, in accordance with the express statement in Targ. Job 28:7 and with his designation as "prince of the power of the air" in Eph. 2:2.

A demon named Bizbath is mentioned in Mandean literature, and this name may conceivably be a corruption of "Beelzebul" (like "Bezebuth" in medieval *grimoires*), though an Iranian etymon has been claimed for it in an assumed *bazah-bat*, "lord of sin."

The Vulg. form, Beelzebub, becomes in later literature a not uncommon name for the Evil One. This tradition survives in Milton's *Paradise Lost;* while in the traditional English Mummers' Play, Beelzebub appears as a black-faced, clownish figure carrying a club.

*Bibliography.* W. E. M. Aitken, "Beelzebul," *JBL,* XXXI (1912), 34-53; W. F. Albright, *JPOS,* XII (1932), 7-8.

On Mandean Bizbath, cf. *Ginza,* trans. Lidzbarski, p. 20; *Johannisbuch,* trans. Lidzbarski, ii, 193; I. Scheftelowitz, *MGWJ,* LXXIII (1929), 231. T. H. GASTER

**BEER** bē'ər, bĭr [באר, a well]. **1.** A station of the Israelites where the princes and nobles of the people dug a well (Num. 21:16-18). The site is probably in the Wadi eth-Themed, since it would seem to be the only place N of the Arnon (vs. 13) offering an adequate water supply, easily obtainable by digging. Beer-elim (Isa. 15:8) may be the same location.

*Bibliography.* N. Glueck, *Explorations in Eastern Palestine,* I, *AASOR,* XIV (1933-34), 13.

**2.** A place to which Jotham fled (Judg. 9:21) after telling his fable; perhaps identical with BEEROTH. Some connect Beer with el-Bireh, N of Beisan and SE of Mount Tabor. Eusebius located it *ca.* 7½ miles N of Eleutheropolis. E. D. GROHMAN

**BEERA** bē'ə rə [בארא, a well] (I Chr. 7:37). The eleventh son of Zophah in the genealogy of Asher.

**BEERAH** bē'ə rə [בארה, a well] (I Chr. 5:6). A Reubenite deported by Tiglath-pileser III in the eighth century B.C.

**BEER-ELIM** bĭr ē'lĭm [באר אילים, well of chiefs *or* terebinths] (Isa. 15:8). A Moabite city; probably the same as BEER 1.

**BEERI** bē'ə rī [בארי, well]. **1.** A Hittite; the father of Judith, a wife of Esau (Gen. 26:34; LXX Βεηρ). Here, as elsewhere with P (cf. ch. 23), "Hittite" may be only a general designation of the Canaanite natives. *See* HITTITES § 3.

**2.** The father of Hosea the prophet (Hos. 1:1; LXX Βεηρι).

*Bibliography.* M. Noth, *Die israelitischen Personennamen* (1928), pp. 38, 224. L. HICKS

**BEER-LAHAI-ROI** bĭr'lə hī'roi [באר לחי ראי]. A well situated between Kadesh-barnea and Bered. Gen. 16:7-14 interprets the name as "well of the living one who appeared to me" (RSV mg. "well of one who sees and lives"), a name given to it by Hagar after she met the angel of the Lord there and received a reassuring promise. This is probably folk etymology of an older name meaning "well of the jawbone of a *rŏ'î* (perhaps some sort of antelope). The spot was a favorite encampment of Isaac (Gen. 24:62; 25:11, in which passages the KJV considers Lahai-roi the correct name—e.g., "the well Lahai-roi").

The location is uncertain; Arab tradition identifies it with 'Ain Muweileh, a caravan station *ca.* twelve miles W of Kadesh-barnea.                          S. COHEN

**\* BEEROTH** bē'ɔ rŏth [בארות, wells; Βηρωθ]; BEE-ROTHITE —ĭt; KJV BEROTH bĭr'ŏth (I Esd. 5: 19); BEROTHITE —ɔ thĭt (I Chr. 11:39). A city of Benjamin. It was one of the four cities of the HIV-VITES and followed the lead of Gibeon in coming to terms with the Israelites (Josh. 9:17).

The location of Beeroth on the border between Benjamin and Ephraim is plainly indicated in II Sam. 4:2, which finds it necessary to state that the town was reckoned to Benjamin. In the same passage there is a reference to a flight of Beerothites to GITTAIM farther S, which was probably due to a Philistine foray after their victory at Mount Gilboa. Naharai of Beeroth was the armor-bearer of Joab (II Sam. 23: 37; I Chr. 11:39). According to the story in II Sam. 4, two Beerothite brothers, Rechab and Baanah, were captains of Ishbosheth and assassinated the latter in the seventh year of his reign. The suggestion that this was an act of blood revenge for Saul's violation of the treaty with the Hivvites (cf. the case of Gibeon in 21:1-2) has no support in the text; it is far more probable that they perpetrated this act in the hope of currying favor with David—a hope in which they were grievously disappointed, as David had them killed for their deed (4:9-12).

The site of Beeroth has not been determined. Some authorities have favored el-Bireh, *ca.* a mile E of Ramallah, but the similarity of names is deceptive and the place hardly suitable. Albright has argued in favor of Tell en-Nasbeh, *ca.* a mile to the S, the site of an important city which was excavated by Badé and identified with MIZPAH. Another suggested location is Nebi Samwil, a mile S of el-Jib (ancient Gibeon).

*Bibliography.* W. F. Albright, *AASOR*, IV (1924), 102-11; J. Muilenburg in C. C. McCown, *Excavations at Tell en-Nasbeh* (1947), pp. 23-59.                          S. COHEN

**BEEROTH BENE-JAAKAN** bĭr'ŏth bĕn'ĭ jā'ɔ kɔn [בארת בני יעקן, wells of the sons of Jaakan]; KJV BEEROTH OF THE SONS OF JAAKAN. A place where Israel camped near the border of Edom and near which Aaron died (Deut. 10:6; called Bene-jaakan in Num. 33:31 ff). Possibly the site is el-Birein, *ca.* 6¼ miles S of el-'Auja. The place is found as Jaakan in the genealogical table in I Chr. 1:42.
                                          V. R. GOLD

**\* BEER-SHEBA** bĭr shē'bɔ [באר שבע]. The principal city of the Negeb and a noted sanctuary from very early times. It was the outstanding limit of Israelite population, so that the phrase "from Dan to Beer-sheba" (Judg. 20:1 and often) and its converse, "from Beer-sheba to Dan" (I Chr. 21:2), meant the entire nation, while "from Geba to Beer-sheba" (II Kings

23:8) is used to denote the territory of the kingdom of Judah.

The exact meaning of the name Beer-sheba is uncertain. According to the story in Gen. 21:25-31, it is the "well of the seven," \* from the seven lambs which Abraham gave to Abimelech, the king of Gerar, to seal their alliance; but in vs. 31 it is apparently the "well of the oath." According to Gen. 26: 32-33, the name was given to the city by Isaac, since after making an oath to seal a compact with the same or another Abimelech of Gerar, he learned that his servants had found a well the very same day; he named this well Shibah, "the oath," from which the name Beer-sheba was derived. However, it is possible that Beer-sheba is an old Canaanite name, and it has been suggested by one scholar that it means "well of the seven demons." There is also the possibility that the city named by Abraham was SHEBA, that the well about which Abraham spoke was not one nearby, and that Beer-sheba means merely the "well of (the city of) Sheba," and in course of time the two were counted as one city. In that case, Beer-sheba was a twin city, the modern Bir es-Saba', twenty-eight miles SW of Hebron, and Tell es-Saba', about two miles to the E. Fig. WAT 5.

Beer-sheba lies in a gap in the hills of Judah, at the junction of the water-parting route, southward from Hebron toward Egypt, and the route that ran northeastward from the Arabah to the coast. Hence it must have been a stopping place for most of the caravans that traversed the region in any direction. The patriarchs Abraham and Isaac, with their large flocks and herds, spent considerable time in the city before proceeding on their journeys. After the conquest of Canaan, Beer-sheba fell to Judah and was assigned to Simeon. An indication of its importance as a center of population is the fact that two sons of Samuel, Joel and Abijah, were judges there (I Sam. 8:2). Elijah, fleeing from the Valley of Jezreel because of the wrath of Jezebel, followed the route down to Beer-sheba (I Kings 19:3), after which he continued to Horeb, the mount of God. Zibiah, the mother of King Joash of Judah, who was dramatically crowned to overthrow the usurper Athaliah, also came from Beer-sheba (II Kings 12:1). Little is known as to the fate of Beer-sheba during the latter period of the kingdom, but it was one of the cities reoccupied by the Judeans returning from the Babylonian exile (Neh. 11:27).

Beer-sheba was a religious sanctuary as early as the time of the patriarchs. Its tutelary deity was originally El Olam, who was worshiped by Abraham there under a tamarisk tree (Gen. 21:33); but his worship was later assimilated to that of Yahweh and the name was reinterpreted as an epithet, the Everlasting God. Jacob consulted its oracle before journeying to Egypt (Gen. 46:1-5). In the time of Amos, the shrine in Beer-sheba was one of the most famous in the land; he mentions it as equal to Dan and Bethel (the sanctuaries with the golden calves), Gilgal (the ancient sanctuary founded by Joshua), and Samaria (the capital of Israel). Amos records a curious oath that is used: "As the way of Beer-sheba lives" (8:14); this may mean either that some especially sacred ritual was performed there, or that, as the prophet speaks in another place of "crossing over"—i.e., making a journey—to Beer-sheba (5:5), the city may have been a place to which pilgrimages were made.      S. COHEN

**BE-ESHTERAH** bē ĕsh'tə rə [בעשתרה]. A Levitical city in Manasseh E of the Jordan (Josh. 21:27). It is a contraction or scribal error for Beth-ashtoreth ("place of Astarte"), and the same as ASHTAROTH, the city found in the parallel passage, I Chr. 6:71— H 6:56.      S. COHEN

**BEETLE.** KJV translation of חרגל (RSV CRICKET).

**BEGGAR.** *See* ALMS.

**BEGINNING AND END.** *See* ALPHA AND OMEGA.

**BEGOTTEN.** *See* ONLY BEGOTTEN.

**BEHEADING.** *See* CRIMES AND PUNISHMENTS §§ D1, E3a.

**BEHEMOTH** bǐ hē'məth [בהמות, *intensive plural of* בהמה, dumb beast]. In the OT, a fanciful name for the hippopotamus, or some other mammoth living in marshes (Job 40:15-24). In the Apoc. and Pseudep., however, the name denotes a mythical beast, the male counterpart of Leviathan, which lives on land, while its mate lives in the sea (II Bar. 29:4; II Esd. 6:49, 52). In Enoch 60:7-8, Behemoth is located in the wilderness of Dendain, E of Eden; but in II Esdras he is said to dwell "where the thousand mountains are"—a fanciful interpretation of Ps. 50: 10 ("Behemoth [properly, 'beasts'!] on a thousand hills"). In rabbinic literature he is styled שור הבר, the "ox of the open field" (e.g., Targ. Ps. 50:10; Pir. R. El 11).

At the end of the present era, Behemoth, like Leviathan, will challenge God, but will suffer defeat. His carcass will then be served as food to the righteous (B.B. 74a; Palestinian Targ. Num. 9:26). This is probably a Jewish version of the Iranian myth concerning the ultimate defeat of the mythical ox Hudhayaos, for whom a similar fate is said to be reserved. But it was doubtless influenced also by a fanciful interpretation and extension of Ps. 74:14, taken to mean: "Thou it was that didst crush the heads of Leviathan; Thou wilt give it as food to the people, even to them that be parched."

Behemoth, like Leviathan, is said to have been one of the "great sea monsters" fashioned on the fifth day of creation (Gen. 1:21).      T. H. GASTER

**BEKA** bē'kə [בקע] (Exod. 38:26); KJV BEKAH. A weight, called "half a shekel, by the shekel of the sanctuary." By calculation from the shekel weight of 11.424 grams, the beka should be 5.712 grams; but stones inscribed בקע indicate a weight of over 6 grams. Fig. WEI 18.

*See also* WEIGHTS AND MEASURES § B4e.

     O. R. SELLERS

**BEL** bĕl [בל; Akkad. *belu,* he who possesses, subdues, rules]. The title of the state-god of Babylon, MARDUK,* upon whose discomfiture Jeremiah (50:2; 51:44) and Isaiah (46:1) animadvert in passages referring to the downfall of Babylon. Fig. MAR 9.

The title (Baal in Hebrew) denotes the supremacy

of the god in a certain locality, or refers generally to the specific attributes or sphere of interest of gods or men. Specifically, and in the passages above cited from the OT, Marduk, the god of Babylon, is denoted. He, assuming En-lil's role of conqueror of the chaotic waters (*see* SUMER), is the Mesopotamian counterpart of the Cannanite BAAL. Like Baal he is also acclaimed king as a result of his victory. In the extant Canaanite texts there is no evidence that Baal, like Marduk, was regarded as a creator-god, but his title "king" implies the establishment of Cosmos.

*Bibliography.* W. Muss-Arnolt, *A Concise Dictionary of the Assyrian Language* (1902), pp. 155-59. For further bibliography, *see* MARDUK.      J. GRAY

**BEL AND THE DRAGON** [Βήλ καὶ Δράκων]. An addition to the book of Daniel, illustrating his wisdom as "companion" to Cyrus. This accretion, generally following the Song of the Three Children and Susanna, contains two popular tales: that of Bel and that of the Dragon. Its primary purpose is to ridicule heathenism.

In the first story Bel is a great statue which nightly devours great amounts of food and drink and thus proves itself a living being. By means of a trick Daniel reveals that it is really the priests who are consuming the food and that Bel is inanimate. Thereupon Bel is destroyed by the king, and the priests are slain.

In the second story Daniel refuses to worship a monstrous dragon in Babylon. He offers to kill it and thus prove its falseness and impotence. He feeds it with a mixture of hair, pitch, and fat, and it bursts open. The people, angered by the death of this god, force the king to throw Daniel into the lions' den. Though they are starved, the lions do not devour Daniel. He is there for six days, and miraculously on the sixth day an angel transfers Habakkuk, the prophet, with food to Daniel. On the seventh day the king removes Daniel from the den and instead throws his enemies therein.

Many scholars believe that the original text of these tales was in Hebrew and composed in the first century B.C. This is because of the many Hebraisms in the text. Some scholars believe that it was written in Aramaic, as they find the story in the Chronicles of Jerahmeel, a fragment of the tenth century.

The text is generally assumed to have been written *ca.* 130 B.C., after the book of Daniel had been canonized. The value of the story is to stress the absurdity of idolatry and to uphold the notion of worshiping the one true God. No mention is made of Jewish practices or beliefs. The mention of angels may have been inserted later. The insertion of the Habakkuk element may be due to a gematria חבקוק = גור אריה, thus connecting the lion legends. This is found in a thirteenth-century record of R. Eleazar of Worms.

The association of Daniel with Habakkuk is indeed unique. The Codex Chisianus notes that the stories were taken from the prophecy of Habakkuk the son of Jeshua. Talmudically, Habakkuk is recognized as the Shunammite woman's son who was brought to life again by Elisha (II Kings 4:17-37).

The dragon perhaps may be a serpent, signifying snake-worship (although there is no other evidence that such worship was practiced in Babylon). On the other hand, some scholars believe that the story originated in Egypt, where serpent-worship definitely was prevalent.

Scholars also have noted in the story a symbol of conflict with Marduk or another Babylonian deity, but this has not been proved. *See* MARDUK.

*Bibliography.* R. H. Pfeiffer, *History of NT Times, with an Introduction to the Apoc.* (1949); B. M. Metzger, *An Introduction to the Apoc.* (1957).                                    S. B. HOENIG

**BELA** bē'lə [בֶּלַע, swallowing up]; KJV BELAH in Gen. 46:21. **1.** The first king of Edom; son of Beor (Gen. 36:32-33 = I Chr. 1:43-44). His city was Dinhabah. Nothing certain is known of his origin (probably Mesopotamian, not native Edomite) or exactly where he lived. His name is similar to that of the seer Balaam (בִּלְעָם), who was also a son of Beor. In fact, the Targ. calls him BALAAM, but the LXX has Balak—the seer's Moabite king.

**2.** The first son of Benjamin (Gen. 46:21); also founder of a family group, the Belaites (Num. 26:38). His sons are listed three times, but each time they differ completely in both name and number (Num. 26:38, 40; I Chr. 7:6-7; 8:1, 3).

**3.** Son of Azaz and descendant of Joel in the genealogy of Reuben (I Chr. 5:8).

F. T. SCHUMACHER

**4.** Apparently another name of ZOAR, one of the "cities of the valley." The names of the kings of the other four cities are given (Gen. 14:2), but not in the case of Zoar; instead, a seeming variant of the name of the town is given: "and the king of Bela (that is, Zoar)."

Since Bela appears also as a personal name, it may be that the "king of Bela (that is, Zoar)" came from the phrase "Bela king of Zoar."

For location and bibliography, *see* SODOM.

J. P. HARLAND

**BELEMUS.** KJV Apoc. form of BISHLAM.

**BELIAL** bē'lĭ əl [בְּלִיַּעַל]. A word which, usually in such compound expressions as "sons of Belial" (e.g., Deut. 13:13; Judg. 19:22; I Sam. 2:12), "daughter of Belial" (I Sam. 1:16), or "man of Belial" (II Sam. 20: 1; Prov. 16:27), but sometimes also by itself (II Sam. 23:6; Job 34:18), denotes reprobate, dissolute, or uncouth persons. Similarly, a "word of Belial" is a vicious canard (Deut. 15:9; Pss. 41:8; 101:3); a "witness of Belial," one who gives false testimony (Prov. 19:28); a "counselor of Belial," one who plots evil (Nah. 1:11); while "rivers of Belial" are currents of adversity, which bring neither benefit nor blessing and are likened to the streams of the nether world (II Sam. 22:5; Ps. 18:4).

In Nah. 1:15—H 2:1 the word is used absolutely to designate a malevolent power, either human or demonic.

The word means properly "worthless, useless," and is a compound of בְּלִי, "not," and יַעַל, "be of use" (cf. בְּלִימָה, "not-aught"—i.e., "nothingness"—in Job 26:7; Ugaritic *bl-mt,* "not-death"—i.e., "immortality" —in II AB, vi.26; *bl-mlk,* "not-king"—i.e., "commoner"—in II AB, vii.43; and the somewhat similar לוֹא־יוֹעִיל, "un-worth," in Jer. 2:11).

The LXX renders, according to context, by such terms as "lawless, lawlessness," "witless" (παράνομος, ἀνομία, ἄφρων); Aq. by "undisciplined, dissolute" (ἀνυπότακτος), and the Vulg., frequently, by "impious," "iniquitous," and "useless" (*impius, iniquus, inutilis*). There was, however, a clear tradition that the word was really a proper name, for in eight passages (viz., Deut. 13:13; Judg. 19:22; I Sam. 1:16; 2:12; 10:27; 25:17; II Sam. 16:7; Nah. 1:15—H 2: 1), the Vulg. simply transliterates it; and in a ninth (I Kings 21:13), it even ventures *diabolus.*

In the pseudepigraphic literature, Belial—often miswritten "Beliar"—is uniformly regarded as the proper name of that Prince of Evil (*alias* SATAN, "the Obstructor") who currently enslaves men by manipulating their instincts basely, but who will eventually be defeated by the Messiah, aided by God and his heavenly legions (cf. Test. Levi 3:3; 18:12; Test. Zeb. 9:8; Sibylline Oracles III.71-73; Ascension of Isaiah 4:2; cf. also Did. 16). This concept, in which Belial is the equivalent of the Iranian Druj, or Spirit of Deceit, and his human allies—the "men of Belial"— of the *dregvants,* is now well attested in the Dead Sea Scrolls (e.g., 1QS I.18; *Zadokite Document* IV.13 ff; 1QH III.27-39; VI.29-33), especially in the so-called War of the Sons of Light and the Sons of Darkness, which deals with the final conflict against him.

In the NT, the figure of Belial (Beliar) appears in II Cor. 6:15, where reference is made to the irreconcilability of the Messiah (Christ) with this opponent. A further allusion to him is recognized by some commentators in II Thess. 2:3, where the expression "man of lawlessness" is thought to represent the Hebraic "man of Belial."

*See also* ANTICHRIST.                                    T. H. GASTER

**BELIEF.** The translation of πίστις in II Thess. 2:13. *See* FAITH.

Courtesy of Staatliche Museen, Berlin

27. Bronze bell, probably rung to drive out evil spirits (*ca.* 700 B.C., Mesopotamia). The clapper is in the form of a serpent's head; and the bell is decorated with lizards, lion-headed demons, and a priest wearing a fishskin.

**BELL. 1.** פעמון (lit., "clapper," "striker"). An object attached to the vestment of the high priest (Exod. 28:33-34; 39:25-26; Ecclus. 45:9). Bells for this purpose were made of gold and were affixed to the vestment alternately with pomegranates—"a golden bell and a pomegranate, a golden bell and a pomegranate, round about on the skirts of the robe" (Exod. 28:34). The specified purpose of the bell varies: "Its sound shall be heard when he goes into the holy place before the LORD, and when he comes out, lest he die" (Exod. 28:35);

> to send forth a sound as he walked,
> to make their ringing heard in the temple
> as a reminder to the sons of his people
> (Ecclus. 45:9).

Josephus (War V.v) writes: "The bells signified thunder, and the pomegranates lightning." They may have been a survival of some magic purpose or for some kind of signal in connection with the rite involved. Fig. BEL 27.

**2.** מצלה ("that which tinkles"). A decorative ornament for horses in Zech. 14:20.                   J. M. MYERS
*See also* MUSICAL INSTRUMENTS § B1*a*.

**BELLOWS** [מפח, *from* נפח, to breathe, blow; Ugar. *mphm*]. Although the noun appears only in Jer. 6:29, the idea is found elsewhere in the OT.

The development of the bellows may be traced in stages: (*a*) the use of human lung power to blow fires; (*b*) the utilization of the blowtube (first reed, then metal) to concentrate the draft; (*c*) the addition of a mechanical device attached to the end of the pipe to replace the human lung. The last two stages are well known from antiquity. Down to the time of the New Kingdom (*ca.* 1550 B.C.), the blowtube exclusively seems to have been used in Egypt. On a nineteenth-century tomb painting from Beni-hasan, however, two objects on the backs of donkeys have been tentatively identified as portable hand bellows very much like the modern type. This painting depicts a party of Asiatic Bedouin who presumably engage in smithery (Fig. JOS 29). In the New Kingdom foot-operated bellows were used in metallurgy: bags mounted on bases were attached to iron or reed pipes (the latter were clay-tipped) which conveyed the draft to the hearth; two of these were arranged so that a man standing on them could pump air by alternately raising and lowering his feet; in each hand he held a cord which was used to open the bag after it had been depressed. The custom seems to have been to attach two such pairs to a single hearth, thus requiring two men for operation (*see* METALLURGY). At Beth-shemesh numerous clay tubes were found in connection with a metalworking establishment, indicating the type of draft employed. Under unusual conditions a natural draft could be employed, as at Ezion-geber by Solomon (in post-Solomonic times the natural-draft arrangement was replaced by bellows; *cf.* FURNACE).

"Bellows" in Jer. 6:29 may indicate a mechanical device, but elsewhere it is not clear that such a device is indicated (Job 20:26; 41:21—H 41:13; Isa. 54: 16; Ezek. 22:20-21; cf. Ecclus. 43:4 Amer. Trans.). The effect of a draft on a fire is also used metaphorically of the wrath of Yahweh (Ezek. 22:20-21; cf. Job 41:21—H 41:13).

*Bibliography.* L. Klebs, *Die Reliefs und Malereien des neuen Reichs* (1934), p. 109, Fig. 77; N. Glueck, "Ezion-geber; Elath—City of Bricks with Straw," *BA*, vol. III, no. 4 (1940), pp. 53-54; C. Singer *et al.*, eds., *A History of Technology* (1954), pp. 233, 577, 597, figs. 382-84.                    R. W. FUNK

**BELMAIM.** KJV form of BALBAIM.

**BELMAIN** bĕl′mān [Βελμαιν] (Jth. 4:4); KJV BELMEN bĕl′mən. An unidentified village in Samaria, apparently the same as Balbaim (7:3), Balamon (8:3), and possibly BEBAI (15:4). It has been conjectured that the place may be identified with BILEAM or IBLEAM; also that it may be the same as ABEL-BETH-MAACAH, which was near Dan, *ca.* twenty miles inland from Tyre.                     W. L. REED

**BELNUUS** bĕl′nōŏ əs [Βάλνουος (A), Βαλνοῦς (B)]; KJV BALNUUS băl′— (I Esd. 9:31). Apparently the same as BINNUI 3.

**BELOVED.** The translation of a number of words in the Bible. For discussion of various relationships underlying the use of "beloved" and "love," *see* LOVE IN THE OT; LOVE IN THE NT; CHRIST; SON OF GOD; CHURCH, IDEA OF; BROTHERHOOD; BROTHERLY LOVE.

**1. In the OT.** ידיד is applied to Benjamin (Deut. 33:12) and the chosen people (Pss. 60:5; 108:6; 127: 2; Jer. 11:15; cf. ידדות in Jer. 12:7). דוד is frequent in the Song of Solomon (sexual love) and appears in Isa. 5:1 (of God). Elsewhere a form of the verb אהב may be used (Deut. 21:15-16, of a wife; II Sam. 1: 23, of Saul and Jonathan slain; Neh. 13:26, of Solomon beloved by God; Hos. 3:1, of sexual love). מחמד occurs in Hos. 9:16, of children. Daniel was "greatly beloved" (חמדות; Dan. 9:23; 10:11, 19).

**2. In the NT.** Jesus, the Son and Servant of the Father, is ἀγαπητός, "beloved" (Mark 1:11; 9:7; and parallels; II Pet. 1:17; cf. Mark 12:6). At Eph. 1:6 "the Beloved" (ἠγαπημένος) seems to be a messianic title, combining the "elect servant" (Matt. 12:18, citing Isa. 42:1 with "beloved" substituted for "chosen") and the "only son" (cf. Gen. 22:2; Gal. 3:16; 4:4, 28-29, of Isaac, who is a type of Christ).

The church, successor to Israel and the body of Christ, is beloved (Rom. 1:7; 9:25 [cf. Hos. 2:1, 16 ff]; Col. 3:12; I Thess. 1:4 [cf. Deut. 33:12 LXX]; II Thess. 2:13). Congregations and their members are beloved, for Christ redeemed them and commanded them to love one another (John 13:34; Phil. 4:1, etc.; Heb. 6:9; I Pet. 2:11; II Pet. 3:1; I John 3:2, etc.; III John 1; Jude 1, 3, 17, 20). Christians form a spiritual brotherhood in love (I Cor. 15:58; Eph. 6:21; Col. 4:7-9; Jas. 1:16, 19; 2:5; of masters and slaves, note I Tim. 6:2; Philem. 16). The affectionate tone toward both women and men is remarkable, and not yet formal (Rom. 16:5-16; II Tim. 1:2; III John 1, 2, 5, 11; cf. Phil. 2:22 ff).

G. JOHNSTON

**\*BELOVED DISCIPLE.** A disciple of Jesus, referred to only in the closing chapters of the Gospel of John and never named. He cannot be identified with the rich man in Mark 10:21, for this man, the only one in the Synoptic gospels of whom it is said that Jesus loved him, did not become a disciple.

In John 13:23, at the Last Supper, "one of his disciples, whom Jesus loved, was lying close to the breast of Jesus"; and at a signaled request from Peter, he asked Jesus who would betray the Lord. At the Cross, Jesus committed his mother to the care of the "disciple whom he loved," who "from that hour . . . took her to his own home" (19:26-27). When Mary Magdalene found the tomb empty, she ran and told Peter and "the other disciple, the one whom Jesus loved." He outran Peter, but Peter first entered the tomb; then the "other disciple" entered and "saw and believed" (20:1-8). In John 21, the Appendix to the Gospel of John (*see* JOHN, GOSPEL OF), "that disciple whom Jesus loved" first recognized the risen Lord by the Sea of Tiberias (21:7). This chapter later reports a misunderstood saying of Jesus; he was supposed to have said that the "disciple whom Jesus loved" would not die. Apparently this disciple had died. It is explained that Jesus had only told Peter: "*If* it is my will that he remain until I come, what is that to you?" (21:20-23). Finally, 21: 24 gives the testimony of certain Christians ("we know") that "this is the disciple who is bearing witness to these things," and "his testimony is true."

Three other verses are sometimes understood to refer to the same disciple. John 1:41, however, implies no such reference, unless the inferior reading πρῶτος is accepted. Only then would it mean that, like Andrew, the unnamed companion also went and found his brother and brought him to Jesus; then this might be John the son of Zebedee bringing his brother James. In 18:15 "another disciple," "known to the high priest," *could* be the beloved disciple. In 19:35 also "he who saw" blood and water come from the pierced side of Jesus could be the beloved disciple, but this is not certain, since in vs. 27 the beloved disciple seems to have left the scene.

Attempts to identify the beloved disciple follow one of two methods:

One method argues that so favored a disciple must have been one of the Twelve, and a prominent one. He cannot have been Peter, with whom he appears; James the son of Zebedee was martyred early (Acts 12:2); James's brother John, then, the other one of the trio closest to Jesus, must be the beloved disciple. In both Luke (22:8) and Acts (3:1; 8:14), Peter and John appear together, as Peter and the beloved disciple do in John. This implies that John is the beloved disciple. The ancient church tradition supports this identification; it repeatedly names the apostle John as the beloved disciple. John 21:2 says that the sons of Zebedee were present at the Sea of Tiberias, and vs. 7 says that the beloved disciple was there. External evidence thus presents a strong case for identifying this disciple as JOHN THE APOSTLE.

The other approach is to examine the Gospel of John to see whether it indicates the identity of the beloved disciple. Since this gospel never mentions by name the apostle John, it alone cannot lead the reader to identify the beloved disciple as John. Three views based on the internal evidence of this gospel may be noted:

*a*) The beloved disciple is an idealized figure. He represents the true and worthy disciple of Christ. It is wrong to try to identify him with any particular disciple among Jesus' followers.

*b*) The beloved disciple is a Jerusalem disciple of priestly family or connections (this view assumes that 18:15 refers to the beloved disciple). He appears only in Jerusalem, except for the postresurrection appendix. The gospel centers in Jerusalem; this is unexpected and hard to explain if a Galilean fisherman is its writer or basic witness. The disciple has access to the high priest, and a curious tradition, found in a letter of Polycrates bishop of Ephesus, who, writing *ca*. 191, says that John "was a priest wearing the sacerdotal plate" (Euseb. Hist. III.31.3; V.24.3), may rest on John 18:15 and reflect the view that the beloved disciple was of priestly origin.

*c*) The beloved disciple was Lazarus. If the Gospel of John was written to be intelligible when read by itself, Lazarus would seem to be meant. He is the one man in the gospel whom Jesus is said to love. This love is emphasized in 11:3, 5, 11, 36. In 12:2 Lazarus shares a meal with Jesus. Then in 13:23 the beloved disciple is said to share a meal with Jesus. The alert reader can hardly avoid identifying him with Lazarus unless he knows another answer from some other source. Lazarus, moreover, lived near Jerusalem, at Bethany; he could easily have taken Jesus' mother home from the Cross "from that hour"; his resurrection is the climax of Jesus' public ministry, and for a gospel resting on this disciple's witness to have life through Christ as its theme is entirely fitting; for the resurrected Lazarus to be the first to recognize the risen Lord is likewise fitting; to identify Lazarus as the beloved disciple gives the gospel a unity it lacks when Lazarus is considered to be outside the circle of important disciples; and of the resurrected Lazarus a rumor could most easily have arisen that since he had already died and risen, "he was not to die."

Internal evidence thus points to Lazarus as the beloved disciple. External evidence points rather to John the son of Zebedee. It is difficult to reconcile the two lines of evidence. To regard Lazarus as unhistorical and created only to present in parable form the point of Luke 16:31, or the resurrection Christ effects in the believer from the death of sin, does not do justice to indications of the gospel that Lazarus is a real person. Perhaps the original draft of the gospel, which does not actually name the beloved disciple, became in time associated with a leader named John and so with the apostle John. John 21: 24 in the Appendix may reflect a stage in this process. A final decision is hardly possible.

*Bibliography.* F. V. Filson, "Who Was the Beloved Disciple?" *JBL*, 63 (1949), 83-88; W. F. Howard, *The Fourth Gospel in Recent Criticism and Interpretation* (4th ed., 1955), Index. *See also* bibliography under JOHN THE APOSTLE.

F. V. FILSON

**BELSHAZZAR** bĕl shăz'ər [בלשאצר; Akkad. *Bēl-šar-uṣur*, Bēl-protect-the king! Βαλτασάρ]. Son of, and coregent with, NABONIDUS. Belshazzar is, Assyriologically, of interest only as the unique example of a crown prince who was officially recognized as coregent. There exist two legal documents dated to the twelfth and thirteenth years of Nabonidus, which record oaths sworn by the life of Nabonidus, the king, and of Bēl-šar-uṣur, the crown prince, for which there is no parallel in cuneiform literature. Equally unique is the fact that the crown prince is mentioned in the prayer section of some of the inscriptions of Nabonidus, although the Akkadian inscription of Antiochus I, Soter (280-262 B.C.), asks for divine blessings even for the queen and the crown prince. From Assyriological sources nothing is known about Belshazzar's death.                A. L. OPPENHEIM

**BELT. 1.** אזור (Ezek. 23:15); KJV GIRDLE. Alternately: GIRDLE; WAISTCLOTH. A piece of the accouterment of Assyrian soldiers.

**2.** On חליצה, a belt worn by soldiers (Judg. 14:19; II Sam. 2:21), *see* SPOIL.

**3.** מזח (Ps. 109:19); KJV GIRDLE. A girdle worn next to bare skin.

**4.** מזיח (related to מזח; Job 12:21); KJV STRENGTH, mg. GIRDLE. A term used in the phrase "loosing the belt," which is figurative for rendering a soldier impotent.

**5.** On פתיל (Gen. 38:18, 25; "cord"; KJV BRACELETS), which has been interpreted as a wrestling belt, *see* WRESTLING.

**6.** Ζώνη (Matt. 10:9; Mark 6:8); KJV PURSE. Alternately: GIRDLE 5. A money belt, as the context indicates; confirmed by first-century A.D. papyri as an article used to carry money. This is a specialized use of ζώνη.                J. M. MYERS

**BELTESHAZZAR** bĕl'tĭ shăz'ər [בלטשאצר, *from* Akkad. *balaṭsu-uṣur*, May he protect his life]. The Babylonian name given to Daniel by the chief of Nebuchadnezzar's eunuchs (Dan. 1:7; 2:26; 4:8-9, 19—A 4:5-6, 16; 5:12; 10:1). Dan. 4:8 relates the first syllable to Bel, the title of Marduk, the chief Babylonian god. But this is popular etymology, unless the name is a shortened form of *Bel-balaṭsu-uṣur*, "May Bel protect his life."                M. NEWMAN

**BELTETHMUS** bĕl tĕth'məs [*corruption of* בעל-טעם; LXX Βααλταμ]; KJV BEELTETHMUS bē'əl—. A Persian officer in Palestine (I Esd. 2:16, etc.). It is not a proper name but seems to be the title for CHANCELLOR (cf. Ezra 4:8).

**BEN** bĕn [בן, son of]. Erroneously included among second-rank Levites in the MT of I Chr. 15:18 (KJV).

**BEN-ABINADAB** bĕn'ə bĭn'ə dăb [בן-אבינדב, father is noble]; KJV SON OF ABINADAB. A commissariat prefect (or his father) who was charged by Solomon with the district of Naphath-dor (on the coast between Phoenicia and Philistia) and who married the king's daughter Taphath (I Kings 4:11).

*Bibliography.* W. F. Albright, "The Administrative Divisions of Israel and Judah," *JPOS*, V (1925), 26 ff; J. A. Montgomery and H. S. Gehman, *The Books of Kings*, ICC (1951), pp. 120 ff.                E. R. DALGLISH

**BENAIAH** bĭ nā'yə [בניה, בניהו, Y has built]; KJV Apoc. BAANIAS bā'ə nī'əs (I Esd. 9:26); BANAIAS bə nā'yəs (I Esd. 9:35). **1.** The son of Jehoiada the priest; a native of the S Judean town of Kabzeel,

whose years of loyal military service ultimately gained for him the rank of commander of the army in the reign of Solomon. Although he never achieved the coveted rank of membership among the "Three," his valiant deeds distinguished him as more honorable than the company of the Davidic Mighty Men known as the "Thirty." His valor is illustrated by three heroic exploits: the liquidation of two warriors (אראל) of Moab, the slaying of a lion in a pit amid the winter snow, and a victory over an Egyptian giant won at considerable disadvantage (II Sam. 23:20-23; I Chr. 11:22-25).

Benaiah served as captain of the Cherethites (Cretans) and Pelethites (Philistines), foreign mercenaries who served as the royal guard under David (II Sam. 8:18; 20:23; 23:23; I Chr. 18:17). Although he was named as the commander of the Davidic militia of 24,000 men, who served annually during the third month, the command appears to have been honorary, since his son Ammizabad was in charge of the division (I Chr. 27:5-6).

In the final days of David, when Joab lent his support to the abortive plot of Adonijah to seize the throne, Benaiah supported Solomon, the Davidic nominee, and shared in his coronation at Gihon by responding to the act and proclamation of the coronation with an affirmation of loyalty, so it would seem, as spokesman for the people (I Kings 1:38). As captain of the royal guard Benaiah had the invidious task of destroying the enemies of Solomon—Adonijah, Joab, and Shimei (I Kings 2:25, 34, 46). As a reward for his faithful service Benaiah was made commander of the army by Solomon (I Kings 2:35). His son Jehoiada appears to have succeeded Ahithophel as the royal counselor to David (I Chr. 27:34).

**2.** A warrior from Pirathon of the hill country of Ephraim who is included among the company of the Mighty Men of David known as the "Thirty" (II Sam. 23:30; I Chr. 11:31). He was the commander of the Davidic militia which served each year during the eleventh month (I Chr. 27:14).

**3.** One of the Simeonite princes who enlarged by conquest their pastoral lands in the region of Gedor in the time of Hezekiah (I Chr. 4:36).

**4.** A Levitical musician, named among those who played harps set to ʿalāmôth (*see* MUSIC) in the sacred orchestra in the time of David. This group is first mentioned in connection with the transport of the ark to Jerusalem (I Chr. 15:18, 20; 16:5).

**5.** One of the priests who were charged with blowing trumpets before the ark of Yahweh and are named among musicians that accompanied the ark to Jerusalem (I Chr. 15:24; 16:6).

**6.** An Asaphite whose grandson Jahaziel delivered a favorable oracle to Jehoshaphat when he was threatened by a military coalition of Moabites, Ammonites, and Edomites (II Chr. 20:14).

**7.** A Levite, one of the subordinate overseers, who assisted in the collection of contributions in the house of Yahweh in the days of Hezekiah (II Chr. 31:13).

**8.** The father of Pelatiah, one of the princes of the people during the Exile. Pelatiah's counsel to Jerusalem was opposed by Ezekiel, and his death ominously occurred while the prophet spoke (Ezek. 11:1, 13).

**9.** The name of four Israelites who banished their foreign wives with their children in the purist movement of Ezra the scribe (Ezra 10:25, 30, 35, 43). While they share the same name in the book of Ezra, their names are given as Benaiah, Naidus, Mamdai, and Benaiah in I Esd. 9:26, 31, 34, 35.

E. R. DALGLISH

**BEN-AMMI** bĕn ăm'ī [בֶּן־עַמִּי, son of my kinsman (or people); LXX *inserts* Αμμαν, Vulg. *Ammon, before* בֶּן־עַמִּי] (Gen. 19:38). Lot's son by his younger daughter; eponymous ancestor of the Ammonites. *See* AMMON; LOT.

**BEN-DEKER** bĕn dē'kər [בֶּן־דֶּקֶר] (I Kings 4:9); KJV SON OF DEKAR. A commissariat prefect (or his father) who was over the second administrative district of Solomon, which corresponded generally to S Dan.

**BENE-BERAK** bĕn'ĭ bĭr'ăk [בְּנֵי בְרַק, sons of Barak (lightning)] (Josh. 19:45). A city of Dan, identified with modern Ibn Ibraq (Banai Baraq), one of the NW suburbs of Tel Aviv.

**BENEDICTION.** A prayer for God's blessing, or an affirmation that God's blessing is at hand. The Aaronic blessing (Num. 6:24-26) is the best known of the OT benedictions, while the blessings or prayers with which several of the NT letters conclude represent the most familiar benedictions of the NT (Rom. 15:13; II Cor. 13:14; Heb. 13:20-21; etc.). *See* BLESSINGS AND CURSINGS. W. HARRELSON

**BENEDICTUS** bĕn'ə dĭk'təs [Lat., blessed]. The Song of Zacharias, father of John the Baptist, in Luke 1:68-79; a psalm, like the MAGNIFICAT, emanating from the early Christian communities of Palestine, and constructed out of many reminiscences of OT poetry and prophecy. The Benedictus is more definitely messianic in character than the Magnificat, and celebrates the raising up of a leader ("horn"; vs. 69) out of the house of David. In line with early Christian tradition, John the Baptist is portrayed as the forerunner of Christ (the "prophet of the Most High" [vs. 76]; cf. Luke 1:32, of Jesus: "Son of the Most High"), who prepares the way for the time "when the day shall dawn upon us from on high" (vs. 78; cf. Mal. 4:2). In both the Eastern and the Western liturgies, the Benedictus is a canticle of the morning Office of Lauds.
*See also* HYMNS. M. H. SHEPHERD, JR.

**BENEFACTORS** [εὐεργέται, those who work well]. A title widely used of both gods and men from the fifth century B.C. on. Often assumed by kings, it was also bestowed upon them or upon outstanding men, generally to reward some conspicuous service or meritorious achievement (Add. Esth. 8:12c, 12n; Wisd. Sol. 19:14; II Macc. 4:2; III Macc. 3:19; 6:24). Εὐεργέτης occurs in the canonical books only in Luke 22:25, where Jesus forbids its use. Other forms of the same root usually refer the benefits they describe to God and not to men (Ps. 13:6—G 12:6; Acts 4:9; 10:38; I Tim. 6:2; Wisd. Sol. 16:2; II Macc. 6:13; 10:38).

*Bibliography.* A. D. Nock, "Soter and Euergetes," in S. E. Johnson, ed., *The Joy of Study* (1951), pp. 127-48.
I. W. BATDORF

**BENE-JAAKAN** bĕn'ĭ jā'ə kən [בְּנֵי יַעֲקָן] (Num. 33:31-32). A place where Israel camped near the border of Edom. *See* BEEROTH-BENE-JAAKAN.

**BEN-GEBER** bĕn gē'bər [בֶּן־גֶּבֶר]; KJV SON OF GEBER. A commissariat prefect (or his father) who was over the sixth administrative district of Solomon, with its seat at Ramoth-gilead (I Kings 4:13). However, some scholars consider him identical to Geber the son of Uri (vs. 19), since the geographical descriptions of their respective districts coincide. By conflating the two texts and removing the later glosses, Albright renders the presumable text of the original catalogue thus: "Geber son of Uri (or Uri son of Geber) in Ramoth Gilead; he had the *ḥawwôt Ya'îr* and the region of Argob."

*Bibliography.* W. F. Albright, "The Administrative Divisions of Israel and Judah," *JPOS*, V (1925), 17 ff; J. A. Montgomery and H. S. Gehman, *The Books of Kings*, ICC (1951), pp. 119 ff. For a different interpretation, see A. Šanda, *Die Bücher der Könige*, EHAT (1911), I, 72 ff.
E. R. DALGLISH

\***BEN-HADAD** bĕn hā'dăd [בֶּן־הֲדַד (*by faulty reading,* הֲדר *for* הֲדד *in three* Heb. MSS), Aram. בַּר הֲדד, son of (the god) Hadad; Akkad. ᵐᵈ*Adad-id-ri*, ᵐᵈ*Adad-'-id-ri*, ᵐ*BIR-ᵈda-ad-da*, ᵐ*a-pil* ᵈ*Adad*; LXX υἱὸν Αδερ]. **1.** Ben-hadad I (I Kings 15:18), son of Tabrimmon son of Hezion, whose throne name appears to have been Hadadezer (Akkadian Adad-'idri). He is first encountered as king of Damascus during the reign of King Baasha of Israel (909-885 B.C.), with whom he had an alliance which freed Baasha to attack King Asa of Judah (vs. 19). In 879 B.C., Asa bribed Ben-hadad I to break the treaty and invade Israel. By ravaging the N parts of Israel, Ben-hadad protected the caravan route through Galilee from Damascus to the Mediterranean coast, from whence Egyptian and Phoenician riches came to the bazaars of Damascus (I Kings 15:19-21; II Chr. 15:19–16:6). Later Omri of Israel (880-873) was forced to admit merchants of Damascus to the bazaars of Samaria (I Kings 20:34). At a critical moment, possibly shortly after the accession of Pygmalion in Tyre (*ca.* 860), Ben-hadad I seems to have made a treaty with Tyre, for he erected an Aramaic votive stele to his "lord," the Tyrian god Baal Melqart. Fig. BEN 28.

When newly enthroned King Shalmanezer III of Assyria (859-824) began to menace Syria with yearly campaigns (857-853), Ben-hadad I besieged Samaria and arrogantly demanded the utter submission of Israel (I Kings 20:1-22), evidently in an effort to compel King Ahab of Israel to join a Syrian alliance to resist Assyrian encroachment. Twice Damascus was defeated by Ahab and Ben-hadad I was captured (vss. 16-21, 26-33). Ahab spared his life and demanded only commercial advantages in Damascus bazaars (vs. 34) and the return of border cities that Damascus had taken from Omri. The treaty then made (856) instituted three years of peace between Israel and Damascus (I Kings 22:1).

In 853 B.C., Shalmaneser III faced a Syrian coalition led by Ben-hadad I, whom the Assyrians called

Courtesy of the National Museum in Aleppo

28. Stele of Ben-hadad, son of Tabrimmon, king of
Damascus, from Aleppo, bearing Aramaic dedicatory
inscription to the god Baal Melqart

Adad-'idri (Hadadezer), at Qarqar. The mighty conflict, in which Israel played an important part, resulted in a draw, as did later Assyrian assaults in
848 and 845. It was possibly in 853, after the Battle
of Qarqar, that Ahab of Israel and his ally,
Jehoshaphat of Judah, plotted to take Ramoth-gilead
from Ben-hadad I of Damascus (I Kings 22:29). In
the battle Damascus was victorious, and Ahab was
slain.

Ben-hadad I may be the anonymous "king of
Aram" mentioned in stories about Elisha's healing
powers. The king sent his leprous officer Naaman to
be healed by the prophet (II Kings 5:1-19), and later
the aged, ailing Ben-hadad I himself sent his servant
Hazael to consult with Elisha about his ailment (8:
7-10). When the prophet announced that Hazael
would be the next king of Damascus and presumably
anointed him (cf. I Kings 19:15-16), the servant returned to Ben-hadad I, murdered him, and seized
the throne of Damascus (II Kings 8:14-15). The annals of Shalmaneser III report the incident: "Adad-
'idri forsook the land; Hazael, the son of nobody,
seized the throne." Since "forsook the land" could
mean abdication, it is possible that the sudden death
of Ben-hadad I (ca. 842) was temporarily covered by
a rumor of his abdication.

Many scholars distinguish between a Ben-hadad
I of the time of King Asa of Judah and Baasha of
Israel and a Ben-hadad II, who was contemporary
with the dynasty of Omri of Israel. The son of
Hazael, listed below as Ben-hadad II, would then
become Ben-hadad III. Since it would at that time
be unusual for a son to bear his father's name, Kraeling suggests that another king, possibly the Rezon
of I Kings 11:23, intervened between the two kings
named Ben-hadad. Because Assyrians called the king
of Damascus contemporary with Ahab of Israel
Adad-'idri (Hadadezer), Luckenbill regarded Adad-
'idri as a usurper who succeeded Ben-hadad in 858,
after the Battle of Aphek. With him Kraeling identifies the anonymous "king of Aram" (I Kings 22:3,
31; II Kings 5:1, 5; 6:8, 11). Since the Assyrians call
the predecessor of Hazael Adad-'idri, Kraeling would
omit the name Ben-hadad in II Kings 8:7 as an error
or gloss. Albright, however, is perhaps right in insisting that the Ben-hadad of the Omride Dynasty
was identical with that of the time of Baasha. The
interval (ca. 880-842) is not too long for a single reign,
especially since the time of the death of Tabrimmon
is uncertain. The name Adad-'idri of the Assyrian
records may well have been the throne name of Ben-
hadad I, just as Pul was that of Tiglath-pileser III
(II Kings 15:19) and Zedekiah was that of Mattaniah (24:17).

**2.** Ben-hadad II, son of HAZAEL, who followed his
father (ca. 798 B.C.) on the throne of Damascus (II
Kings 13:3, 24). Some would identify him with the
king Mari' of Damascus, who paid tribute to Adad-
nirāri III in 804. This is possible if the phrase "all
the days of Jehoahaz" (813-798) is not to be taken
literally (II Kings 13:22). Ben-hadad II must have
been enthroned during the reign of Jehoash of Israel
(798-781). He inherited a kingdom weakened by Assyrian assaults and could not retain all the territory
that Hazael, his father, had taken. In three engagements with Jehoash (II Kings 13:14-19, 25), Ben-
hadad II lost the cities had taken from Israel (vss.
24-25). Jeroboam II of Israel (781-753) had additional successes against Damascus, expanding Israel
to its ideal limits (II Kings 14:25-28; Amos 6:14), but
the claim that Hamath and Damascus were taken by
Israel (II Kings 14:28) is absurd.

When the Aramean state of Hamath began to expand, Ben-hadad II organized a coalition of Syrian
kings to curb his neighbor Zakir king of Hamath.
Although they besieged Zakir in his stronghold
Hazrak (Hadrach in Zech. 9:1), Zakir withstood his
enemies. Kraeling conjectures that when Shalmaneser
IV besieged Damascus in 773, Ben-hadad II may
have died and been succeeded by the Tabeel of Isa.
7:6.

As noted under 1 *above*, some would regard this
Ben-hadad as Ben-hadad III.

**Bibliography.** D. D. Luckenbill, "Benhadad and Hadadezer,"
*AJSL*, XXVII (1910/11), 267-84; E. Kraeling, *Aram and
Israel* (1918); R. de Vaux, "La chronologie de Hazael et de
Benhadad III, rois de Damas," *RB*, XLIII (1934), 512-18;
W. F. Albright, "A Votive Stele Erected by Ben-Hadad I of
Damascus to the God Melcarth," *BASOR*, 89 (1942), 23-29;
J. B. Pritchard, ed., *ANET* (2nd ed., 1955), pp. 278-82
(L. Oppenheim), pp. 501-2 (F. Rosenthal).

R. A. BOWMAN

**BEN-HAIL** bĕn hāl' [בֶּן־חוּל, son of strength] (II Chr. 17:7). Prince and, in the commission to Judah, teacher, under Jehoshaphat.

**BEN-HANAN** bĕn hā'nən [בֶּן־חָנָן, son of gracious, favored one] (I Chr. 4:20). Son of Shimon in the genealogy of Judah.

**BEN-HESED** bĕn hē'sĕd [בֶּן־חֶסֶד] (I Kings 4:10); KJV SON OF HESED. A commissariat prefect (or his father) who was over the third administrative district of Solomon, which embraced generally W Manasseh—more specifically, Arubboth, Soco, and the land of Hepher.

> **Bibliography.** Albrecht Alt, *Israels Gaue unter Salomo*, BWAT 13: *Alttestamentliche Studien, Rudolf Kittel* (1913), pp. 1-19.
> E. R. DALGLISH

**BEN-HINNOM, VALLEY OF.** *See* HINNOM, VAL-LEY OF.

**BEN-HUR** bĕn hûr' [בֶּן־חוּר] (I Kings 4:8). KJV SON OF HUR. A commissariat prefect (or his father) who was over the first administrative district of Solomon, which was generally coincident with Ephraim.

**BENINU** bĭ nī'nōō [בְּנִינוּ, our son] (Neh. 10:13). A Levitical witness to the postexilic renewal of the covenant under Ezra. *See* NETHINIM.

**BENJAMIN** bĕn'jə mən [בִּנְיָמִין, *according to folk etymology,* child of fortune (Gen. 35:18); *in reality, originally the name of a tribe, with a geographical meaning; see below*]; **BENJAMINITE**—mə nīt' [בֶּן יְמִינִי]. **1.** A son of Jacob by Rachel (Gen. 35:18), and the eponymous ancestor of one of the twelve tribes. As the youngest son, especially beloved by his father and also favored by Joseph, his only full brother, Benjamin plays a special role in the Joseph story (Gen. 42:4, 36; 43:14-16, 29, 34; 44:12; 45:12, 14, 22). In lists he is always named along with Joseph (Gen. 35:24; 46:19, 21; I Chr. 2:2), save, necessarily, in Exod. 1:3.

The name of the tribe of Benjamin is to be correctly interpreted historically as "the southerner" (lit., "son of the south [right]"). To be sure, this designation hardly came into use for the first time in Canaan, as though it were for a unit which split off once more in the S from the large Joseph group which had divided in central Palestine into Manasseh and Ephraim. It is scarcely conceivable that this small fragment could have attained the same amphictyonic rights as the great tribes. Moreover, it has, indeed, its own tradition of conquest (preserved in Josh. 2-9), which indicates that the Benjaminites crossed the Jordan as outriders of the Rachel group. The blood toll paid in their so doing decimated the tribe, to be sure, but secured for it for the future the rights of an autonomous tribe in the circle of the Israelite amphictyony. That the name (and along with it the bearer) may very well have stemmed from the desert period is shown by its appearance in an entirely different nonbiblical connection. In the Old Babylonian texts of the archives of King Zimri-Lim, a contemporary of Hammurabi (*ca.* 1700), which

were brought to light in the excavation of MARI, there also appear Binu-Jamina, "southern people," a very rebellious Bedouin group, whose extensive pasture lands at that time began S of Haran and extended as far as the Terqa district. It is, indeed, not to be excluded that there is a historical connection between this group and the OT tribe.

The territory of the OT tribe is, according to the description of Josh. 18:11-21, a wedge, the small base of which lies in the mountains to the W and which stretches out lengthwise to the Jordan. The town list, which probably dates from the time of Josiah, names three ancient cities which by no means were settled by Benjaminites in the period before the kings: Jerusalem was conquered for the first time by David (II Sam. 5:6 ff); Bethel clearly lies to the N of the border, according to the description of the boundaries (Josh. 18:13); and Jericho was rebuilt first under Ahab (Josh. 6:26; I Kings 16:34). Moreover, in the W the territory of the towns of Gibeon, Beeroth, Chephirah, and Kiriath-jearim must be deducted; according to Josh. 9, this territory remained Canaanite—a situation which Saul first tried to change, with only partial success (II Sam. 4:2-3; 21:2). The Benjaminite settlement is thus rather scanty and is limited really to a few villages on the mountain ridge between Jerusalem and Bethel. For this very reason Benjamin is not to be regarded as having broken away from Joseph. On the contrary, because Benjamin found a place in the twelve-tribe scheme, it must be an old tribe; but in the course of taking possession of the land it was stunted like Simeon and others.

The smallness of Benjamin also shines through the rest of the tradition. Benjamin was the youngest son —i.e., the smallest tribe. This explains the fact that the Moabite king Eglon could make Benjamin pay tribute for almost two decades, until Ehud brought an end to the situation (Judg. 3:12-30). Also interesting in this connection is the very much touched-up account of the action which the federation took against Benjamin (chs. 19-21). At least the general conditions in it are historical. Also, Benjamin might have almost disappeared, had the men of the tribe not been permitted to kidnap wives. Six hundred men escaped (20:47); presumably this is the normal number of men in this tribe.

The oldest poetry adds some further features to the picture thus obtained. The Song of Deborah names Benjamin after Ephraim, evidently because of the geographical relationship, and as the second in the *Parallelismus membrorum*, since it is the smallest tribe; the Benjaminites remained true to their warlike tradition—their fame as slingers (Judg. 20:16) is probably also historical—and engaged in the fight for freedom (5:14). Something similar is evidenced in the short passage of Jacob's Blessing:

> Benjamin is a ravenous wolf,
>     in the morning devouring the prey,
>     and at even dividing the spoil
>             (Gen. 49:27).

The passage is probably to be explained by the geographical situation with respect to trade and refers, as in the case of Dan (Deut. 33:22), to attacks on caravans. The passage about Benjamin in the Blessing of Moses sounds considerably more peaceful and appears to be relatively late when it speaks of the beloved of Yahweh living in safety because Yahweh protects him always and dwells between his shoulders (vs. 12). A special holy place, having significance beyond Benjamin, must be meant, since it is the only topic of the passage: i.e., Gilgal (Josh. 4-5) or Gibeon (I Kings 3)?

Nothing in the preceding points to the fact that it was precisely Benjamin which would have been predestined to supply the first king. And yet, Saul, in whom, to be sure, the Ephraimite Samuel recognized the chosen man, evidently because of his personal capabilities, was Benjaminite (I Sam. 9:1, 4, 16, 21; 10:2, 20 ff; 22:7; II Sam. 21:14; Acts 13:21). The liberation of Israel from the Philistines had its beginning on Benjaminite ground when Jonathan killed the governor at Gibeah (Tell el-Ful) and when, following Jonathan's heroic deed at Geba (Jeba') and Michmash (Mukhmas), the first defeat was inflicted upon the Philistines (I Sam. 13:2, 15 ff; 14:16). After Saul's catastrophic end, Benjamin found itself among the few tribes which immediately recognized Ishbaal (Ish-bosheth) as his successor (II Sam. 2:9), even if participation of the Benjaminite levy in the historic battle of the mercenaries at the Pool of Gibeon belongs to legend (2:15, 25, 31). In any case, Abner soon succeeded in leading Benjamin over to David's side (3:19). However, the fact that David did not win the sympathy of all the Benjaminites is shown by the figure of Shimei (II Sam. 16:11; 19: 17 ff; I Kings 2:8) and is proved in a more dangerous fashion by the revolt of the Benjaminite Sheba (II Sam. 20:1). In Solomon's arrangement of districts Benjamin appears as a separate administrative district of the N kingdom (I Kings 4:18). After the breakdown of the personal union, the Judean kings succeeded in winning the territory of Benjamin as a glacis for their capital city; Asa was finally able to develop Mizpah (Tell en-Nasbeh) and Geba in Benjamin as frontier fortresses. Thus the historical basis was laid so that later writers could treat "Judah and Benjamin" as a unit (I Kings 12:21, 23; II Chr. 11:1, 3, 10, 12, 23; 14:7; 15:2, 8-9; 17:17 [cf. vs. 13]; 31: 1; 34:9; Ezra 1:5; 4:1; 10:9; Neh. 11:36). In Judg. 10:9 the Deuteronomic historian enlarges the same concept to include the "house of Ephraim." Ps. 68: 27—H 68:28 probably also fits in here, where "Benjamin, the least of them," is named with Judah in the parallel phrase, strangely enough, together with the Galilean tribes of Zebulun and Naphtali. In Ps. 80:2, Benjamin is probably an interpolation; but the psalm is native to the N kingdom, in any case. Perhaps it is a proof of the fact that the loss of the Benjaminite territory had not been forgotten there. This may perhaps also be true of Hos. 5:8 (cf. vs. 10); however, the prophet may recognize the status quo of that time and only refer to a repeated pushing out of the boundary toward the N by the Judeans.

In the later literature Benjamin usually appears in lists and similar material. The Deuteronomic historian places Benjamin after Joseph among the tribes who have to pronounce the blessing on Mount Gerizim (Deut. 27:12). In the Priestly Code, Benjamin's place is always immediately after Ephraim and Manasseh (Num. 1:11, 36 ff; 2:22; 7: 60; 10:24; 13:9; 26:38, 41), with the single exception of Num. 34:21, which is geographically conditioned. This combination is also popular in Chronicles, except that Benjamin usually stands first, in order to preserve, to some extent, the connection with Judah (I Chr. 12:29—H 12:30; also 6:60, 65—H 6:45, 50, as it was already in the source Josh. 21:17; cf. vs. 4); I Chr. 27:21 constitutes the only exception in both respects. Otherwise, the Chronicler adduces especially from Benjamin a lot of genealogical material (I Chr. 7:6-12, where Benjamin is in the eighth place in the whole series of tribes, between Issachar and Naphtali; 8; 9:3, 7-9), as well as several notes which cannot be checked (12:2-7, 16-18; 21:6). In Ezek. 48: 22-24, Benjamin receives the sector directly to the S of the central territory and thus the special relation to Judah, which receives the counterpart in the N, is once more preserved. On the other hand, the relationship to Joseph stands out in the case of the names of the gates. Benjamin is allotted the middle E gate next to Joseph, as Judah had already been allotted the middle gate on the N earlier. In Obad. 19, בנימן, Benjamin, is probably written erroneously for בני עמן, sons of Ammon. In the NT in the list of the sealed (Rev. 7:8) Benjamin ranks after Joseph at the end, in accordance with tradition.

Individuals who are expressly designated as Benjaminites include, in addition to those already mentioned, two of David's thirty heroes, Ittai from Gibeah (II Sam. 23:29=I Chr. 11:31) and Abiezer from Anathoth (I Chr. 27:12=II Sam. 23:27=I Chr. 11: 28). There is also Cush, who is named in the superscription of Ps. 7, and who is, perhaps, a combination of the unnamed messenger of I Sam. 4:14 and the other bearer of ill tidings in II Sam. 18:21 and is thus a literary figure like Mordecai, the hero of the book of Esther (Esth. 2:5). There are, in addition, two men of considerably more importance. One is the prophet Jeremiah from Anathoth (Jer. 1:1; 32:8, 44; 33:13; 37:12; cf. 17:26), who represents a conflict of the countryside with the capital city, as in the case of Micah (6:1; not, as many presume, the older N-S conflict!). The other one is the apostle Paul (Rom. 11:1; Phil. 3:5).

For the territory of Benjamin, *see* TRIBES, TERRITORIES OF, § 2.

*See* the bibliography under ASHER.

**2.** A great-grandson of Jacob, through Benjamin, Jediael, and Bilhan (I Chr. 7:10).

**3.** An Israelite of the time of Ezra, who pledged himself to dissolve his marriage with a foreign woman (Ezra 10:32).

**4.** A priest of the time of Nehemiah (Neh. 12:34); probably identical with the Benjamin who participated in the building of the wall (3:23).

K. ELLIGER

**BENJAMIN GATE** [שער בנימין]; KJV GATE OF BENJAMIN. A gate of Jerusalem, mentioned in Jer. 37:13; 38:7, perhaps to be identified with Nehemiah's SHEEP GATE or with the MUSTER GATE. *See* JERUSALEM § 6e.      G. A. BARROIS

**BENO** bē'nō [בנו, his son] (I Chr. 24:26-27). Son of Jaaziah, a Merarite Levite. Instead of a proper name some ancient versions translate "his son," meaning the son of Jaaziah.

**BEN-ONI** bĕn ō'nī [בֶּן־אוֹנִי, the son of my sorrow] (Gen. 35:18). The name given to her son by RACHEL as she died at his birth. He was renamed BENJAMIN (1) by his father, Jacob.

**BEN-ZOHETH** bĕn zō'hĕth [בֶּן־זוֹחֵת, son of Zoheth] (I Chr. 4:20). Son of Ishi in the genealogy of Judah; but the word could be a description rather than a personal name.

**BEON** bē'ŏn [בְּעֹן] (Num. 32:3). A town in N Moab requested by the tribes of Reuben and Gad; probably the same as BAAL-MEON.

**BEOR** bē'ôr [בְּעוֹר, בֵּעֹר, a burning(?); Βοσόρ]; KJV NT BOSOR bō'sôr. **1.** The father of Bela, who was an Edomite king prior to the introduction of the Israelite monarchy (Gen. 36:32; I Chr. 1:43).
**2.** The father of Balaam, the seer summoned to curse Israel (Num. 22:5; 24:3, 15; 31:8; Deut. 23:4—H 23:5; Josh. 13:22; 24:9; Mic. 6:5; II Pet. 2:15). It is possible that the names BALAAM and Bela, nearly alike in Hebrew, refer to the same person.
R. F. JOHNSON

**BERA** bĭr'ə [בֶּרַע; LXX Βαλλα]. King of Sodom, defeated after rebelling against Chedorlaomer (Gen. 14:2; cf. vss. 8, 10-11, 17, 22).

**BERACAH** bĕr'ə kə [בְּרָכָה, blessing] (I Chr. 12:3); KJV BERACHAH. One of the warriors from the brethren of Saul who joined the outlaw band of David at Ziklag.

**BERACAH, VALLEY OF** [עֵמֶק בְּרָכָה, valley of blessing]; KJV BERACHAH. A valley in the wilderness of Judah, S of Tekoa, identified with Wadi el-'Arrub, not far from Khirbet Bereikut (SW of Bethlehem), which seems to preserve the ancient name.
Jehoshaphat (*ca.* 873-849) reassembled his people in the Valley of Beracah after the defeat of the coalition of Edomites, Moabites, and Ammonites at the ascent of Ziz (II Chr. 20:26).
It is possible that the apocalyptic Valley of Jehoshaphat in Joel 3:2, 12 ff, is an allusion to this valley.
V. R. GOLD

**BERACHIAH.** KJV form of BERECHIAH 1 in I Chr. 6:39.

**BERAIAH** bĭ rā'yə [בְּרָאיָה, Yahweh has created]. A member of the tribe of Benjamin listed (I Chr. 8:21) as one of the sons of Shimei. It has been suggested that "BEDEIAH" in Ezra 10:35 ought also to be read "Beraiah," but this is not to imply that the two persons mentioned are one. Neither list can, with certainty, be dated before the Exile.

*Bibliography.* G. B. Gray, *Hebrew Proper Names* (1896), pp. 285, 287; M. Noth, *Die israelitischen Personennamen* (1928), p 171. H. H. GUTHRIE, JR.

**BEREA** bĭ rē'ə [ἡ Βερέα] (I Macc. 9:4). **1.** A place in Judea, not certainly identified. While Codices Alex-

andrinus, Sinaiticus, and Venetus (eighth century), and many minuscules read Βερέαν in this passage, it is possible that the original was Βέρεθ, since Latin MSS have *berethin* and similar forms, and the Syriac of the London Polyglot of 1657 (SyIII) has *byrt*. The place might then be the present el-Bireh, ten miles N of Jerusalem. The ninth- to thirteenth-century minuscules 19 93 542, supported by the Syriac published by Lagarde in 1861 (SyI), however, read Βερρζαθ, which is evidently the name found in Josephus (Antiq. XII.xi.1) in the form Βηρζηθώ and variants. This could be the present Bir ez-Zeit or Beerzeth, a village a little over four miles N-NW of el-Bireh.

*Bibliography.* F.-M. Abel, "Topographie des campagnes maccabéennes," *RB,* XXXIII (1924), 381-83. W. Kappler, ed., *Septuaginta* IX, 1: *Maccabaeorum liber* I (1936). F.-M. Abel, "Eclaircissement de quelques passages des Maccabées," *RB,* LV (1948), 187; *Les livres des Maccabées* (1949), p. 160. J. C. Dancy, *A Commentary on I Maccabees* (1954), p. 131.
J. FINEGAN

**2.** KJV form of BEROEA.

**BERECHIAH** bĕr'ə kī'ə [בְּרֶכְיָה, בֶּרֶכְיָהוּ, *contractions of* יְבֶרֶכְיָהוּ, Yahweh blesses; *see* JEBERECHIAH] KJV BERACHIAH in I Chr. 6:39. **1.** The father of Asaph in the genealogies of the Levites (I Chr. 6:39; 15:17).
**2.** A Levite, one of the "gatekeepers for the ark," mentioned in the Chronicler's account of the bringing up of the ark to Zion (I Chr. 15:23). The identification, sometimes made, of this Berechiah and 7 *below* may not be justified. Though both occur in confused and elaborated passages, I Chr. 9:16 is part of a list of singers, while 15:23 has to do with gatekeepers. An identification of the two may be justified by the supposition that a family which originally served as gatekeepers rose in status, in postexilic times, to singers.
**3.** A chief of the Ephraimites mentioned in the Chronicler's fanciful account of Ahaz' defeat by Pekah of Israel (II Chr. 28:12).
**4.** A son of Zerubbabel listed among the descendants of David in a genealogy which has as its point the fact that Zerubbabel was of the Davidic line (I Chr. 3:20).
**5.** Son of Iddo, and the father of the prophet Zechariah (Zech. 1:1, 7; cf. Matt. 23:35). Elsewhere (Ezra 5:1; 6:14) Iddo is said to have been the father of Zechariah. It may be that Berechiah came to be inserted between Iddo and Zechariah in Zech. 1:1, 7, under the influence of Isa. 8:2, where a Zechariah the son of Jeberechiah (a longer form of "Berechiah") is mentioned. *See also* BARACHIAH.
**6.** The father of Meshullam, one of those who led, under Nehemiah, in the rebuilding of the wall of Jerusalem (Neh. 3:4, 30; 6:18).
**7.** A Levite listed as one of the inhabitants of Jerusalem in postexilic times (I Chr. 9:16). The name, as well as the contents of the verse in which it occurs, is not found in the apparently parallel list in Neh. 11. *See also* 2 above.

*Bibliography.* M. Noth, *Die israelitischen Personennamen* (1928), pp. 21, 35, 183. H. H. GUTHRIE, JR.

**BERED** bĭr'ĕd [בֶּרֶד]. **1.** A son of Ephraim (I Chr. 7:20). The name is undoubtedly an eponym, and, on the basis of the parallel occurrence in Num. 26: 35, probably should be read "BECHER."

2. A place on the road from Canaan to Egypt, beyond Beer-lahai-roi (Gen. 16:14). The site is unknown, but the name may be preserved in the Wadi Umm el-Bared.

**BERI** bĭr´ĭ [ברי, *perhaps a shortened form of some kind* (*cf. Köhler*), *or possibly a corruption of* בני, sons of, *the first part of a name the latter part of which has fallen out* (*cf. Noth*)] (I Chr. 7:36). Mentioned in the genealogy of the tribe of Asher as a son of Zophah. The name, which is not mentioned in parallel genealogies in Gen. 46:17-18; Num. 26:44-47, is undoubtedly an eponym referring to a division of the Asherite clan of Zophah. It has no connection with the Beriites, since it does not come from the same Hebrew root. Neither is there any connection between this Beri and the Berites of II Sam. 20:14 KJV, since the RSV is undoubtedly correct in reading the latter as "Bichrites."

*Bibliography.* M. Noth, *Die israelitischen Personennamen* (1928), p. 240; L. Köhler and Walter Baumgartner, *Lexikon in Veteris Testamenti Libros* (1953), p. 149.

H. H. GUTHRIE, JR.

**BERIAH** bĭ rī´ə [בריעה, prominent, excellent; *cf.* Arab. *barā'atun*, Lat. *excellentia*]. **1.** The fourth son of Asher; the father of Heber and Malchiel (Gen. 46:17; Num. 26:44-45; I Chr. 7:30-31); ancestral head of the "family of the Beriites" (Num. 26:44).

2. The fourth son of Elpaal, one of the "heads of fathers' houses" (*see* FATHER'S HOUSE), "who put to flight the inhabitants of Gath" (I Chr. 8:13, 16).

3. The fourth son of Shimei the Gershomite, of the tribe of Levi, who with his brother Jeush "had not many sons, therefore they became a father's house in one reckoning" (I Chr. 23:10-11).

4. Son of Ephraim, so called "because evil [ברעה] had befallen his house" (I Chr. 7:23). The etymology is only approximate; the name here is uncertain.

L. HICKS

**BERIITES** bĭ rī´īts [הבריעי]. Descendants of BERIAH 1.

**BERITES** bĭr´īts. KJV translation of ברים (RSV Bichrites) in II Sam. 20:14, following the MT. *See* BICHRI.

**BERITH** bĭr´ĭth. KJV translation ("the god Berith") of EL-BERITH in Judg. 9:46.

**BERNICE** bər nēs´ [Βερνίκη]. A daughter of Agrippa I. She was probably born in A.D. 28. *See* HEROD (FAMILY) § H7.

Her first husband was a certain Marcus, whose father, Alexander, was a Jewish official ("alabarch") of Alexandria. On the death of Marcus, Agrippa betrothed her to his own brother Herod, for whom Agrippa obtained from the emperor Claudius the kingdom of Chalcis (Jos. Antiq. XIX.v.1). Two sons, Bernicianus and Hyrcanus, were born of this union (Antiq. XX.v.2; War II.xi.6); Herod died in 48.

In the ensuing years rumors of an incestuous relationship with her brother Agrippa II arose. Bernice

prevailed, through her wealth, on Polemo the king of Cilicia, to marry her; she hoped thereby to disprove the reports. Shortly after her marriage she left Polemo (Jos. Antiq. XX.vii.3; see Juvenal *Satires* 6).

She returned to Jerusalem and was present in 66 when the PROCURATOR Florus pillaged the temple and massacred a large part of the populace. She appealed to Florus to desist, but he ignored her. Indeed, she almost lost her life at the hands of the soldiers (Jos. War II.xv.1-2). Her presence at Jerusalem, according to Josephus, was to fulfil a Nazirite vow (cf. Mi. Naz. III.6; Acts 21:23-26). She wrote to the proconsul Cestius against Florus (Jos. War II.xvi.1). When later the populace assembled before Agrippa, and he addressed them, urging them against any action which would provoke war, she stood by his side (II.xvi.3). When the war broke out later that same year (66), the Jewish populace set fire to the palaces of Bernice and Agrippa (II.xvii.6).

Josephus gives no further information about Bernice, but Roman historians do. Tacitus (Hist. II.2) relates that she and Agrippa took an oath of allegiance to the Roman Vespasian, and that Bernice became the mistress of Vespasian's son Titus, even expecting to marry him (Suetonius *Titus* VII).

Perhaps Titus was willing, but Roman hatred of Jews compelled him to separate from her (Dio Cassius LXVI.15). Bernice is mentioned in Acts 25:13, 23; 26:30, in the narrative of Paul's appearance before Agrippa II.

*Bibliography.* É. Schürer, *A History of the Jewish People in the Time of Jesus Christ*, div. 1, vol. II (1891), 195-203; U. Wilcken, "Berenice," in Pauly-Wissowa, *Real-Encyclopädie der klassischen Wissenschaft*, III (1897), 287.    S. SANDMEL

**BERODACH-BALADAN.** KJV translation of ברדך בלדן (MT) in II Kings 20:12. *See* MERODACH-BALADAN.

**BEROEA** bĭ rē´ə [Βεροια] (II Macc. 13:4); KJV BEREA. **1.** The Hellenistic name of the Syrian city of Aleppo, where the renegade high priest Menelaus was put to death by being dropped into hot ashes at the order of the Seleucid king Antiochus Eupator at the instigation of Lysias. Josephus describes the execution in Antiq. XII.ix.7, but assigns it to the close of the war between Judas and Lysias.

*Bibliography.* F.-M. Abel, *Géographie de la Palestine*, II (1938), 264.    E. W. SAUNDERS

2. A city of Macedonia (Acts 17:10, 13; cf. 20:4), located *ca.* fifty miles SW of Thessalonica at the foot of Mount Bermios (Strabo VII.330, fragment 26).

*Bibliography.* Oberhummer, "Beroia, 1," *Pauly-Wissowa*, vol. III (1899), cols. 304-6.

**BEROTH.** KJV Apoc. form of BEEROTH.

**BEROTHAH** bĭ rō´thə [ברותה]. A town listed by Ezekiel (47:16) as part of the N boundary of the restored inheritance of the tribes of Israel; probably identical with BEROTHAI.

**BEROTHAI** bĭ rō´thī [ברתי]. A city in the Syrian (Aramean) kingdom of Zobah from which David took much booty of bronze in his campaign against Hadadezer (II Sam. 8:8). It is probably the same as

BEROTHAH, and is generally identified with modern Bereitan, *ca.* seven miles S of Baalbek in the W foothills of Anti-lebanon. Cun (Chun) in the parallel account in I Chr. 18:8 may be another name for the same place, but *see* CUN.                A. S. KAPELRUD

**BEROTHITE.** KJV alternate form of Beerothite. *See* BEEROTH.

**BERRIES.** The translation of גרגרים in Isa. 17:6 and of ἐλαία, "olive berries," in Jas. 3:12 KJV (RSV "olives"). In both instances the reference is to olives.

**BERYL** bĕr'əl. A silicate of beryllium and aluminum. The crystals are hexagonal prisms, usually green or bluish-green, but sometimes yellow, pink, or white. The emerald is a superior type of the same stone.

Three words are translated "beryl" in the Bible:

*a*) תרשיש, *taršiš*. The Hebrew gives us no clue to the qualities of the stone. The LXX χρυσόλιθος and the Vulg. *chrysolithus* suggest a yellowish stone, perhaps a yellow jasper. It is a stone in the breastpiece of judgment (Exod. 28:20; 39:13). In Dan. 10:6 the body of the man who appeared before the prophet near the Tigris River resembled beryl. The concept of brightness, rather than color, would seem to be implied here.

*b*) שהם, *šōham* (Ezek. 28:13; KJV ONYX). The Targ. agrees with the RSV in rendering this word as "beryl." In this passage תרשיש, which precedes שהם, is rendered "chrysolite." This agrees with the LXX and Vulg. renderings above. It is a stone in the covering of the king of Tyre.

*c*) Βήρυλλος (Rev. 21:20), the eighth jewel in the foundation of the walls of the New Jerusalem.

*See also* JEWELS AND PRECIOUS STONES § 2.
                W. E. STAPLES

**BERZELUS.** KJV Apoc. form of BARZILLAI.

**BESAI** bē'zī [בסי]; KJV Apoc. BASTAI băs'tī. Head of a family of postexilic temple servants (Ezra 2:49; Neh. 7:52; I Esd. 5:31). *See* NETHINIM.

**BESCASPASMYS** bĕs'kəs păz'məs [Βεσκασπασμύς] (I Esd. 9:31). Alternate name of MATTANIAH.

**BESODEIAH** bĕz'ə dē'yə [בסודיה, in the secret council of Yahu] (Neh. 3:6). The father of a certain Meshullam who helped rebuild the walls of Jerusalem in the time of Nehemiah.

**BESOM** bē'zəm. KJV translation of מטאטא in Isa. 14:23 (RSV "broom").

**BESOR, THE BROOK** bē'zôr [נחל הבשור]. A stream which David crossed on his expedition from Ziklag in pursuit of the Amalekites who had sacked the city (I Sam. 30:9-10, 21). It is probably Wadi Ghazzeh-Shellaleh, the largest of the wadis in the region SW of Ziklag (Tell el-Khuweilfeh).
                S. COHEN

*****BESTIALITY.** Sexual intercourse between a man or a woman and an animal, for which criminal act-

the various law codes of the OT provide the death penalty (Exod. 22:19; Lev. 20:15-16; cf. Lev. 18:23; Deut. 27:21). This practice may have been connected with the magical rituals of the pagan cultus. In a Babylonian myth Eabani (or Enkidu) had intercourse with a wild beast until enticed away by an agent of the goddess Ishtar.

*Bibliography.* For the text of the Gilgamesh Epic, see J. B. Pritchard, ed., *ANET* (2nd ed., 1955), pp. 73-99.
                O. J. BAAB

**BETAH** bē'tə [בטח]. A town (II Sam. 8:8; cf. טבח in Gen. 22:24); probably the same town as Tubihi, mentioned in a Tell-el Amarna letter. *See* TIBHATH.

**BETANE.** KJV Apoc. form of BETHANY.

**BETEN** bē'tən [בטן, abdomen] (Josh. 19:25). A border town in Asher. It is perhaps located at Abtun, approximately eleven miles S of Acco.

**BETH** bĕth (Heb. bāth) [ב, *b* (*Bêth*)]. The second letter of the Hebrew ALPHABET as placed in the KJV at the head of the second section of the acrostic psalm, Ps. 119, where each verse of this section of the psalm begins with this letter.

**BETHABARA** bĕth ăb'ə rə. KJV translation of Βηθαβαρά (=בית עברה, "ford, crossing"), a place of uncertain location beyond the Jordan where John was baptizing, in John 1:28. The word occurs in inferior Greek MSS. The great uncials indicate that the best reading is "BETHANY" (so RSV). Origen (*ca.* A.D. 250) found no evidence of a Bethany beyond the Jordan and so insisted on the reading "Bethabara," although he admitted that few MSS read it (*Commentary on John* VI.140). The site of this Bethany may have been forgotten and this common word for "ford" used to indicate either the true site or one thought to be suitable.

*Bibliography.* G. Dalman, *Orte und Wege Jesu* (1919), pp. 83-84, 88. E. G. H. Kraeling, *Rand McNally Bible Atlas* (1956), p. 370.                D. C. PELLETT

**BETH-ANATH** bĕth ā'năth [בית־ענת, house of Anath] (Josh. 19:38; Júdg. 1:33). A town in Naphtali. The earlier Canaanite town is mentioned in lists of several Egyptian rulers of the New Kingdom. It is perhaps located at el-Ba'neh, E of Acco.

**BETH-ANOTH** bĕth ā'nŏth [בית ענות, house (shrine) of the goddess Anath] (Josh. 15:59). A village of Judah in the district of Beth-zur; probably modern Khirbet Beit 'Ainun, 1½ miles SE of Halhul.

**BETHANY** bĕth'ə nī [Βηθανία; *Semitic derivation uncertain, but possibly* house of Ananiah *or* house of the poor, afflicted; *the Talmud has* בית היני, *which may refer to the late-season green figs of Bethany and Bethphage;* Βαιτάνη *or* Βατάνη *in* Jth. 1:9]; KJV BETANE bĕt'ə nī in Jth. 1:9. **1.** A small village *ca.* 1⅜ miles E of Jerusalem and lying on the E slope of the Mount of Olives. Fig. BET 29.

Jesus and his disciples lodged in suburban Bethany when attending temple ceremonies at Passover

Copyright: The Matson Photo Service
29. Bethany, with almond trees in spring blossom

time (Matt. 21:17; cf. Luke 21:37; Mark 11:19). One approach to Jerusalem from the E was through Bethany and over the ridge of the Mount of Olives; this was the course followed by Jesus when he arrived for this festival and made his "triumphal entry" (Mark 11:1-11 and parallels). Bethany is the setting for the story about Simon the Leper (Mark 14:3; Matt. 26: 6), and about Mary and Martha and Lazarus (John 11:1-44). It is also the site of Jesus' final "departure" from his disciples (Luke 24:50-51). Bethany and Bethphage are close to one another (note the joint reference in Mark 11:1; Luke 19:29).* Bethany is not named anywhere in the OT (unless one identifies it with ANANIAH in Neh. 11:32). Fig. JUD 32.

Today this village is called el-'Aziriyeh by its Muslim inhabitants, who hold Lazarus to be a saint and call the town after him. Both Muslims and Christians have marked many sacred sites in this little suburb. The traditional crypt of Lazarus was reported by the Bordeaux Pilgrim in A.D. 333. The "spot where Mary met the Lord" was enclosed in a church before 385. Another church was built over the crypt by that date (Jerome *Onomasticon*), and a monastery was added later (according to Arculf, *ca.* A.D. 670). In the eleventh century a basilica was erected to mark a site for the anointing of Jesus' feet by Mary, possibly the same structure later reported by the Abbot Daniel, E of the crypt. All these and other traditional sites reveal a confusing conflation of different gospel stories. Although an underground chamber is still honored as the crypt of Lazarus, all other ancient structures have suffered decay. Excavations of three successive churches on a site E of the crypt may possibly expose one of the churches reported by medieval pilgrims.

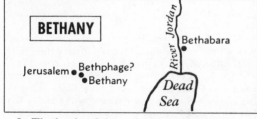

2. The locale of the activity of John the Baptist, according to John 1:28, where it is described as "beyond the Jordan" (i.e., E of the river). But such a

locale or such a town remains unknown and unidentified. Because of this passage alone, some maps show a Bethany on the E side of the Jordan, a little N of the Dead Sea (i.e., near the traditional site of the baptism). Origen, who lived in Palestine in the third century, suggested that the correct place in John 1:28 was really Bethabara, to be found on the W side of the Jordan, whereas Bethany was near Jerusalem. Many later MSS carry on this suggestion, which accounts for this name in the KJV. Others have proposed the term BETH-ARABAH, in the same region. However, the MS testimony is overwhelmingly in favor of "Bethany" as the original reading of John 1:28, although this cannot be the well-known Bethany near Jerusalem.

A few maps identify or relate this baptismal Bethany to "Aenon near Salim," where, "because there was much water," John baptized (John 3:23). As a result, another questionable Bethany is sometimes located W of the Jordan *ca.* thirty miles below the Sea of Galilee.

*Bibliography.* E. Robinson, *Biblical Researches in Palestine,* I (1867), 431-33; F.-M. Abel, *Géographie de la Palestine,* II (1938), 266-67; Babylonian Talmud (Soncino Ed.), Pes. 53*a;* S. J. Saller, *Excavations at Bethany* (1957).      K. W. CLARK

**BETH-ARABAH** bĕth ăr'ə bə [בית הערבה, house (shrine) of the Arabah]. A border point on Judah's N border (Josh. 15:6) and Benjamin's S boundary (18:18); perhaps to be identified with 'Ain el-Gharbah, SE of Jericho, on the N side of the Wadi el-Qelt. In the district list it appears as a town in the district of Jericho (Josh. 18:22) and the wilderness district (15:61).      V. R. GOLD

**BETH-ARAM.** KJV form of BETH-HARAM.

**BETH-ARBEL** bĕth är'bəl [בית ארבאל]. A town destroyed by SHALMAN, according to Hos. 10:14. Although various conjectures regarding its location have been advanced, it is now generally identified with the mound of Irbid in Gilead, which is situated at an important crossroads. Archaeological surface explorations have shown that the site was occupied in Iron I–II (*ca.* 1200-600)—as well as in other periods—which agrees with the historical requirements of this passage.

*Bibliography.* N. Glueck, *Explorations in Eastern Palestine,* IV, *AASOR,* XXV-XXVIII (1951), 153-54.
      G. W. VAN BEEK

**BETH-ASHBEA** bĕth ăsh'bĭ ə (I Chr. 4:21). *See* ASHBEA.

**BETHASMOTH** bə thăz'mŏth [Βαιτασμῶν]; KJV BETHSAMOS bĕth sā'məs (I Esd. 5:18). Alternate name of AZMAVETH 5 and Beth-azmaveth.

**BETH-AVEN** bĕth ā'vən [בית און, house of wickedness]. 1. A town near Ai and E of Bethel to which Joshua sent men from Jericho (Josh. 7:2). It was on the border of Benjamin in the wilderness (18:12). I Sam. 13:5; 14:23 do not indicate a relationship to Bethel but locate it W of Michmash, as the scene of a battle between Saul and the Philistines. The exact location is uncertain; some scholars take it as an older name for AI.

2. A condemnatory term for Bethel, place of idolatry (Hos. 10:5, where the "calf of Beth-aven" is mentioned; see also Hos. 4:15, 5:8). This would be comparable to the use of AVEN in 10:8.

W. L. REED

**BETH-AZMAVETH** bĕth ăz'mə vĕth [בית עזמות]. Alternate designation of AZMAVETH.

**BETH-BAAL-MEON** bĕth'bāl mē'ŏn [בית בעל מעון, *apparently* house of the lord of habitation] (Josh. 13:17). A town in N Moab assigned to the tribe of Reuben; more commonly called BAAL-MEON.

**BETH-BARAH** bĕth bâr'ə [בית ברה]. A town in or near the Jordan Valley. It was seized by the Ephraimites under the leadership of Gideon in the attack against the Midianites (Judg. 7:24). The context suggests a location W of the Jordan between the valley and the Plain of Esdraelon, perhaps in the Wadi Far'ah, NE of Shechem. Beth-barah is not to be confused with BETH-ARABAH, the Bethany E of the Jordan (John 1:28). W. L. REED

**BETHBASI** bĕth bā'sī [Βαιθβασι]. A village SE of Jerusalem fortified by Jonathan and Simon and besieged unsuccessfully by Bacchides (I Macc. 9:62, 64; cf. Jos. Antiq. XIII.i.5, which reads "Bethalaga"). It is probably the modern Khirbet Beit Bassa, in the wilderness of Judea, approximately three miles E of Tekoa.

*Bibliography.* F.-M. Abel, *Géographie de la Palestine,* II (1938), 269. E. W. SAUNDERS

**BETH-BIRI** bĕth bĭr'ī [בית תראי] (I Chr. 4:31); KJV BETH-BIREI —bĭr'ī ī. A city of Simeon in the S of Judah; the same as BETH-LEBAOTH, and apparently a postexilic form of this name.

**BETH-CAR** bĕth kär' [בית כר, house of a lamb, *or* house of pasture(?)] (I Sam. 7:11). An unknown site evidently between Mizpah and the Philistine country; possibly Beth-horon or 'Ain Karim. The Targ. has "Beth-sharon" and the Syr. "Beth-jashan."

**BETH-DAGON** bĕth dā'gən [בית דגון, בית דגון, house (shrine) of Dagon; Βηθδαγών, Βαγαδιήλ]. **1.** A village in the Shephelah district of Lachish in Judah (Josh. 15:41); possibly modern Khirbet Dajun.

2. A border point in Asher (Josh. 19:27). It is probably located near Mount Carmel, perhaps at Jelamet el-Atiqa.

*Bibliography.* F.-M. Abel, *Géographie de la Palestine*, II (1938), 67, 269.

3. A temple of the god Dagon in Azotus (Ashdod). Jonathan Maccabeus burned the temple and all who took refuge there (I Macc. 10:83-84).

**BETH-DIBLATHAIM** bĕth'dĭb lə thā'əm [בית דבלתים, house of two fig cakes(?)] (Jer. 48:22). A city of Moab. Preceding it in the list are Dibon and Nebo, and following are Kiriathaim and Beth-gamul. Beth-diblathaim may be the same as ALMON-DIBLATHAIM.

Mesha (*see* MOABITE STONE) speaks of building Medeba, Beth-diblathen, and Beth-baal-meon.

E. D. GROHMAN

**BETH-EDEN** bĕth ē'dən [בית עדן]. An Aramaic city-state, between the Euphrates and the Balikh River; identified with Bit-adini in the Assyrian records. Amos 1:5 predicts that its population is to be exiled to Kir. The "people of Eden" (KJV "children of Eden") were conquered by Assyria, according to II Kings 19:12 = Isa. 37:12. The place is called simply EDEN in Ezek. 27:23, where it is listed among the cities trading with Tyre.

*Bibliography.* A. Malamat, *The Aramaeans in Aram Naharaim and the Rise of Their States* (1952), pp. 39-47.

C. H. GORDON

**BETH-EGLAIM** bĕth ĕg'lĭ əm [בית עגלים, house (place) of the two calves; Βηθαγλαίμ]. The ancient name now applied by certain archaeologists to the site of modern Tell el-'Ajjul, four miles SW of GAZA, at the mouth of the Wadi Ghazzeh, near the seacoast. Excavation has shown the existence of an important town at the site from about the twenty-second to the tenth centuries B.C. This name does not occur in the Bible; the Hebrew has been inferred from the Greek form, Bethaglaim, found in the Onomasticon of Eusebius, and by analogy with EN-EGLAIM. It may refer to a temple of Baal (or Hadad) decorated with twin bullocks (cf. Jeroboam's "two calves of gold," in I Kings 12:28). The modern Arabic name means "mound of the little calf," preserving, as so often, a semblance of the ancient form and/or meaning.

The excavator, Sir Flinders Petrie, identified the site with ancient Gaza, alleging that the location of Gaza later shifted, as often happened (*see* JERICHO for an example of several such shifts). However, B. Maisler (now known as Mazar) and W. F. Albright have strongly denied the excavator's identification, and their claims for Beth-eglaim are now generally accepted, along with the view that the site of Gaza has *not* shifted. *See bibliography.*

The excavations, carried on in four campaigns from 1930 to 1934, were surprisingly fruitful. (A planned fifth campaign did not materialize.) The mound is not high or imposing, but it covers more than twenty-eight acres, being thus about six times the size of ancient Troy, three times the size of David's Jerusalem, twice the size of Megiddo. So abundant was the archaeological material in the small areas excavated that the excavator estimated fifty years would be required to investigate the whole site thoroughly.

From the excavation reports (as corrected by Albright) we see an important point on the trade route from Egypt to the N and the E, the last outpost on the way to Gaza, usually under control of Egypt. The earliest material came from a cemetery of what Petrie called the "Copper Age," but dated by Albright to the Tenth and Eleventh Dynasties (twenty-second to twenty-first centuries). This is the so-called First Intermediate period of Egyptian history, when Egypt was invaded by Asiatic peoples. The subsequently quickened pace of cultural interchange may have influenced the growth of the town.

The most important period began with the coming of the HYKSOS, as was also the case with Tell el-Far'ah, farther up the Wadi Ghazzeh (*see* SHARUHEN). The Hyksos built a great ditch or fosse about twenty feet deep, fifty feet wide, and nearly a mile long around the three unprotected sides of the town—the S was protected by a drop of fifty feet into the Wadi. The dirt from the fosse was thrown around the edge of the enclosed mound to a height of a hundred feet at an angle of thirty-five degrees. This glacis of so-called *terre pisée* is also characteristic of other Hyksos fortifications at various places in Palestine and Syria.

The chief architectural monument of the Hyksos was the so-called Palace I, made of sandstone quarried in the process of cutting the great fosse. The structure covered an area of more than six thousand square feet and had exterior walls more than six feet thick. This structure was destroyed, probably, by the Eighteenth Dynasty Egyptians, who invaded Palestine after expelling the Hyksos from Egypt. Its pottery and artifacts were of Middle Bronze II type (*see* BRONZE; POTTER).

Palace I was followed by Palace II, a very much smaller and more modest structure, built of yellow bricks according to Egyptian principles. Clearly Egypt was in control and Beth-eglaim had become less important, probably being now overshadowed by Gaza. Palace I and Palace II correspond to the two main levels of the town as a whole, which may be labeled, respectively, as Hyksos and post-Hyksos Egyptian. It has been suggested that Palace II was destroyed by Canaanite rebels just before the invasion of Thut-mose III. *See* EGYPT.

Palace III, so called, was not a residence at all, but rather a small Egyptian fortress surrounded by a cluster of houses, a station on the caravan route. This structure had two phases, A and B; it is to be dated in the latter part of the Eighteenth Dynasty (Late Bronze I).

Palace IV, a rebuilding of III B, was of Nineteenth Dynasty date (Late Bronze II). To this time belongs the horse burial interpreted by the excavator as evidence of the sacrificial use of horses. Since the Hyksos held horses in such high regard (and introduced them into Palestine and Egypt), Petrie dated this phase of the excavation to the time of the Hyksos. However, the pottery and stratigraphy are clearly against this dating. If this horse burial was due to Hyksos influence, it was left-over influence, for the Hyksos had disappeared long since. (There are also ass burials to complicate the problem!) Scholars have been too hasty in connecting every trace of horses with the Hyksos.

To this time also belongs the so-called Governor's Tomb, containing a gold ring of Tut-ankh-Amon and a scarab of Ramses II, along with much excellent pottery. Other interesting tombs of this period were found cut into the sides of the great fosse, which had gone out of use as the town became smaller and less important.

Palace V, also a fortress, represents the latest phase of the excavated area, marking the beginning of the Iron Age (*see* IRON [metal]) and the coming of the PHILISTINES. Egyptian influence waned. Gaza became more important, and apparently Beth-eglaim declined. However, in 1879 a large statue of Roman times was found at the site, and the name was known to Eusebius in the fourth century A.D., as noted above.

*Bibliography.* M. A. Meyer, *History of the City of Gaza* (1907), pp. 152-53, description of the Greco-Roman statue. F. Petrie, *Ancient Gaza*, vols. I-IV, Publications of the Egyptian Research Account and the British School of Archaeology in Egypt, LIII-LVI (1931-34), the original excavation reports. B. Maisler, "Der antike Name von *tel 'addschul*," *ZDVP*, LVI (1933), 186-88, suggested the identification with Beth-eglaim while the excavations were in progress. F. W. Freiherr von Bissing, "Das angebliche Weltreich der Hyksos," *Archiv für Orientforschung*, XI (1936-37), 333-34 and n. 61, warns against making a too easy connection between horses and the Hyksos. W. F. Albright, "The Chronology of a South Palestinian City, Tell el-'Ajjul," *AJSL*, LV (1938), 337-59, presents corrections and reinterpretations necessary for understanding the original excavation reports.      W. F. STINESPRING

**BETH-EKED** bĕth ē'kĭd [בֵּית עֵקֶד, house of shearing] (II Kings 10:12, 14); KJV SHEARING HOUSE. A place on the road from Jezreel to Samaria. At "Beth-eked of the Shepherds" Jehu met the kinsmen of Ahaziah king of Judah, and he slew them at the pit (rather, perhaps, "cistern") of Beth-eked. The place has been identified with Beit-Qad, three miles N of Jenin, where there are a number of cisterns.      W. L. REED

**BETHEL** bĕth'əl [בֵּיתאֵל, house of El (God)]. **1.** *See* BETHEL (SANCTUARY).

**2.** A city in the tribe of Simeon, called "Bethel" in I Sam. 30:27, "Bethul" in Josh. 19:4, and "Bethuel" in I Chr. 4:30. The site of this city is still unknown.

**BETHEL (DEITY).** A West Semitic deity, originally a deification of the temple of El. The earliest certain occurrence is in the seventh-century-B.C. treaty between Esarhaddon of Assyria and Ba'al of Tyre. It occurs as an element in personal names on Babylonian documents from Nebuchadnezzar to Darius II, such as *Bīt-ili-dalā*, *Bīt-ili-shēzib*, and *Bīt-ili-sharuṣur*. Some Jews of Elephantine (*see* ELEPHANTINE PAPYRI) bore names such as *Bethel-nāthan*, *Bethel-nûrî*, and *Bethel-'āqab*. Also found at Elephantine are the deities Eshem-Bethel, Ḥerem-Bethel, and 'Anat-Bethel. These are to be explained as deities having compound names, or—with W. F. Albright—as hypostatized aspects of Yahweh meaning respectively "Name of the House of God," "Sacredness of the House of God," and "Sign (of the Active Presence) of God" or "Will of God."

The deity possibly occurs twice at Ras Shamra: in a list of deities, and in the personal name *n'bt'il*. In the Phoenician theogony of Philo Byblius, *Baitylos* is a child of *Ouranos* ("Sky") and *Gē* ("Earth"). Thus the deity may have originated in Phoenicia in the second millennium B.C.; some scholars believe, however, that it is Aramean in origin.

In the OT, Bethel as a divine name occurs almost certainly in Jer. 48:13, possibly as a surrogate for Yahweh. Some scholars see the deity also in Gen. 31:13; Amos 5:5; and elsewhere. In Zech. 7:2 we should probably read a personal name, "Bethel-sar-ezer" (cf. Amer. Trans.).

*Bibliography.* J. P. Hyatt, "A Neo-Babylonian Parallel to *Bethel-sar-eṣer*, Zech. 7:2," *JBL*, LVI (1937), 387-94; "The

Deity Bethel and the OT," *JAOS*, 59 (1939), 81-98. W. F. Albright, *Archaeology and the Religion of Israel* (1942), pp. 168-74.                              J. P. HYATT

**BETHEL (SANCTUARY).** A city located on the main N-S ridge road where the boundaries of Benjamin and Ephraim meet. In Joshua's distribution of tribal allotments the city was credited to Benjamin (Josh. 18:21), but that tribe lost it to the Canaanites in the days of the judges. Ephraim reconquered it and retained possession of it thereafter. To the Canaanites, Bethel was a sanctuary city dedicated to the god El, one of the older major deities of that people. To the Israelites "el" became simply one of several generic terms for God, and the Hebrew identification of this place name has its setting in Jacob's vision at Bethel (Gen. 28:10-22). An earlier name of this city was לוז, LUZ (Gen. 28:19). Bethel is a site of major importance in the OT, being mentioned more often than any other city except Jerusalem.

*a. Identification of the site.* The identification of the city was made by Edward Robinson in his valuable geographical work early in the nineteenth century. He recognized Bethel in the Arabic place name Beitin—the last letters of the two words following a normal linguistic pattern. The site has been excavated in part, the work being done by joint expeditions of the American School of Oriental Research and the Pittsburgh-Xenia Theological Seminary with W. F. Albright and J. L. Kelso working in 1934 and Kelso alone in 1954 and again in 1957. The site afforded no military advantages, but the wealth of nearby springs on this high ridge made a city here inevitable. Indeed, cisterns were not needed here before NT times.

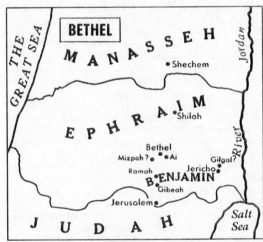

*b. History of the OT city.* The city first appears in the Abraham narratives. Abraham built an altar on the ridge E of Bethel (Gen. 12:8; 13:3-4). This was apparently already holy ground, as testified by tombs in the general neighborhood. The city itself was founded *ca.* 2000 B.C., at least a century before Abraham's time. A city wall on the N, about eleven feet thick and made of well-fitted stones, was faced with a wide clay revetment to keep battering rams away; it was built in the early Hyksos period (*ca.* 1750-1650). In the late Hyksos period (*ca.* 1650-

1550) a garrison complex was built just inside this wall near the gate. A city wall found on the W seems to have been even earlier, its gate being replaced by a tower with a Hyksos revetment. Archaeology throws no special light on any details of the Abraham and Jacob narratives at this point, although the narratives fit well into the general picture of the Middle Bronze Age. It is Jacob's experience there that lays special emphasis upon the term "Bethel" (Gen. 28:19; 35:1-7). God speaks of himself as the God of Bethel (Gen. 31:13) and also commands Jacob to return there. While en route, Jacob significantly orders his household to put away all their foreign gods, and at Bethel, Jacob's name is changed to Israel and the Abrahamic covenant is renewed (Gen. 35:10-15). "Israel" and "Bethel" are inseparable terms from that time on.

The story of Joshua's campaign against Ai and Bethel contains several puzzling features: (*a*) "Ai" itself is a puzzling term, as it simply means "the ruins." (*b*) Et-Tell, which is the common identification of Ai, shows no occupation here in the thirteenth century, which is the date of Joshua's conquest. (*c*) At the same time, the destruction of the city of Bethel is not specifically mentioned in the Joshua narrative, although the excavations there show the most terrific burning yet seen in Palestine. It may be that the two names, Bethel-Ai, are blended into a common episode. A second alternative is to locate a nearby ruin which can answer to Ai, but this has not yet been done. A third solution is to assume that the Bethel army moved to Ai and tried to make a preliminary defense there. For the relationship of the Bethel-Ai episode to the entire military campaign of Joshua, *see* JERICHO § 1.

The city which followed the burning of Bethel was of the crudest construction and in striking contrast to the city which preceded it, which represented some of the finest homes in pre-Greek times. The finds in the houses of the two periods are in equal cultural contrast. Indeed, the Israelite invasion brought so significant a cultural change that it marks the transition from Late Bronze Age to Iron I on the archaeologist's calendar. *See* ARCHAEOLOGY § F.

The excavators found that Bethel was destroyed several times in the period of the judges. It is hard, however, definitely to equate these phases with the scanty historical data furnished by the book of Judges. According to our present archaeological knowledge the picture seems about as follows: Bethel was apparently recaptured by the Canaanites early in the period of the judges, after which it was recaptured by the house of Joseph (Judg. 1:22-26). If the attempted extermination of the tribe of Benjamin (Judg. 20) was early in the period of the judges, then the Canaanite reconquest of the city can be easily understood. With Benjamin's power depleted, it was the strong tribe of Ephraim just to the N which reconquered the city; and from that time on, it remained Ephraimite territory (I Chr. 7:28). The road from Jericho to Bethel marked the boundary between these tribes (Josh. 16:1; 18:11-13). At Bethel the road branched, one unit going via Aijalon to the Philistine coast and the other via Gophna to the plain of Sharon.

In the early phase of the judges the ark was located at Bethel (Judg. 20:18-28), although the name Phinehas for the high priest does not of necessity imply that he was the same high priest identified with the Conquest. The Bethel-Shechem highway of Judg. 21:19 (cf. 20:31) locates Shiloh in terms of Bethel and not vice versa. The removal of the ark to Shiloh is later in the days of the judges. If one of the destructions of Bethel found by the excavators took place when the ark was at Bethel, then this would be a parallel military campaign to the later Philistine attack on Shiloh (at the time of the war in I Sam. 4-6?)—an attempt to destroy Israel's amphictyonic religious center.

Deborah's judgeship with its center "between Ramah and Bethel in the hill country of Ephraim" (Judg. 4:5) seems to come after Bethel's recapture by the Ephraimites. Her judgeship was somewhere ca. 1125. Although Bethel is not far from Saul's capital at Gibeah, and one of the Philistine campaigns took place all around Bethel (I Sam. 12-14), the excavators have not yet found any evidence of the capture of the city by the Philistines. Indeed, Bethel seems to have lived a charmed life, not only under the Philistines but for centuries thereafter, even up past the destruction of Jerusalem in 587.

After the fall of Shiloh, Samuel became the key figure of the judges; he worked a circuit of Bethel, Gilgal, and Mizpah (I Sam. 7:16). Bethel, however, soon lost power to Gibeah, Saul's new capital just to the S in Benjamin. Under David and Solomon the city saw still more fatal competition. Although the Bible is silent on the story of Bethel in the days of David and Solomon, archaeologists have found that the city grew and prospered as a result of new farming and commercial techniques introduced by the new dynasty.

It was Jeroboam I who lifted Bethel to new prominence, making it the Northern Kingdom's chief sanctuary and the rival of Judah's Jerusalem (I Kings 12:26-33; II Chr. 13:8-9). Jeroboam's revolt from the Jerusalem sanctuary was complete—new sites, new clergy, new calendar, new cult techniques (golden calves). Theoretically Jeroboam was still worshiping Yahweh, although the episode in I Kings 13:1-10 called down God's wrath on the king. The N sanctuary at Dan never seemed to be the equal of Bethel. Bethel was still the king's sanctuary as late as Amos. Three archaeological campaigns at Bethel have failed to locate the calf sanctuary, but much of the city has not yet been touched. An alternate location for the sanctuary is on a nearby hill to the SE. Here under Mamluk and Crusader remains at Burj Beitin there is a Byzantine church of about the sixth century, identifying Abraham's sanctuary. S of it there is a still earlier Byzantine ruin which is thought to commemorate the site of Jacob's vision.

The attitude of Elijah and Elisha toward this Bethel sanctuary is obscure, although there was a school of the prophets here (II Kings 2:2-3) when Elijah and Elisha were en route to Elijah's translation. On the return trip was the episode of Elisha and the boys who called him "you baldhead" (II Kings 2:23). Even as early as Jeroboam I an "old prophet" dwelt at Bethel (I Kings 13:11).

Upon Abijah's conquest of Bethel (II Chr. 13:19) he did not destroy the city but incorporated it into his own kingdom. We have no specific reference to

the king who reconquered it for Israel. Jehu left the city untouched. Apparently Jezebel's influence had been concentrated in the capital at Samaria and had not yet seriously influenced the Bethel sanctuary. Indeed, only a very few female figurines have been dug up from the city. Bethel was the center for the prophetic message of Amos, and he was ordered out of town by the sanctuary's priest Amaziah (Amos 7:12-13).

Although the Bible does not specify the Assyrian destruction of Bethel, commentators have usually assumed that the city suffered the same fate as Samaria. To date, excavators have not found any sign of an Assyrian destruction. Apparently the city was spared for some yet unknown reason. Its fame also seems to have lived on, for a Bethel priest was called in to put down the plague of lions in the province following the Assyrian conquest (II Kings 17:26-28). With the decline of Assyria, Josiah moved N to fill in the political and religious vacuum in the N tribes. His first action was against the Bethel sanctuary, which he annihilated. By his time, however, the sanctuary had increased its Canaanite features by adding an Asherah. He also tried to exterminate her clergy (II Kings 23:15-20). The city, however, was spared. Nebuchadnezzar, like the Assyrians, spared the city, probably because of the Babylonian colonists whom the Assyrians had planted here (II Kings 17:24, 30). The next major world conflict, however, finally brought a tragic destruction to the city, at the hands of either Nabonidus or the Persians. The city came back after the Exile. The excellent water supply made this inevitable. In the census list of Ezra the population is listed as 223 (Ezra 2:28), but that of Nehemiah (7:32) lists only 123.

*c. History of Bethel after OT times.* The Hellenistic period showed rapid and solid growth. Bacchides fortified the city (I Macc. 9:50), and a ruin on the ridge to the E shows shards of that date. The city continued to grow under the Maccabees, and there is no archaeological evidence of destruction in 63 B.C. when the Romans took over Palestine.

The NT makes no reference to Bethel, although the city was larger in extent at that time than in OT days. The S wall of this period enclosed within the city area the best spring on the site. It was the last city captured by Vespasian before he became emperor of Rome. He put a Roman garrison here. (Jos. War IV.ix.9). Vespasian was probably responsible for the destruction of the N gate as revealed by the excavations. This gate was then filled in. In the Second Jewish Revolt, Hadrian also placed a garrison here (Midrash *Ekha* II.3). The Roman city grew so extensively that cisterns had to be used.

The city reached its population climax in the Byzantine period. The best Byzantine street and gateway in Palestine still show plainly at the NE corner of the present village. The town's mosque is built over a Byzantine church, so excavations cannot be carried on there, but some digging to the E unearthed a large building which may be a monastery. Nearby Byzantine churches commemorating the experiences of Abraham and Jacob have already been referred to. No signs of destruction or other clues have yet been found which can account for the city's sudden death at just about the transition from the Byzantine period into the Arabic. The site lay in ruins until a little over a hundred years ago, when it was reoccupied by Arabs moving in from nearby Burka.

*Bibliography.* G. Sternberg, *ZDPV,* XXXVIII (1915), 1-40. W. F. Albright, *BASOR,* no. 55, pp. 24-25; no. 56, pp. 1-15. J. L. Kelso, *BASOR,* no. 137, pp. 5-9; no. 151, pp. 3-8.
         J. L. KELSO

**BETH-EMEK** bĕth ē'mĭk [בית העמק, house of the valley] (Josh. 19:27). A border town in Asher. It is probably at Tell Mimas, *ca.* six miles E-NE of Acco.

**BETHER** bē'thər [בתר, *a contraction of* בית הר, house (shrine) of the mountain(?); LXX(A) Βαιθής; Talmud ביתר]. A town in the Bethlehem district of Judah (Josh. 15:59 LXX; omitted by scribal error from the MT). The reference in Song of S. 2:17 KJV (RSV "rugged") may have some descriptive significance at present undetermined. The archaeological survey of Bether (Khirbet el-Yehud, just above modern Bittir, seven miles SW of Jerusalem) indicates almost continuous occupation from Early Iron I to the early Roman period.

Bether is best known as Bar Cocheba's capital after his designation by Akiba as a messiah in A.D. 132 (with attendant change of name from Simon bar-Kozeba to Bar Cocheba, "son of the star [of Jacob]"). Located atop an easily defended hill, Bether was the last Jewish stronghold to fall in 135. Its fall was accompanied by a massacre; according to Jerome, those not killed were sold as slaves by the victorious Romans. A Latin inscription on the site mentions the Roman Fifth (Macedonia) and Eleventh (Claudia) legions, known from other sources to have been in the region during the Second Revolt.

*Bibliography.* W. D. Carroll, "Bittîr and Its Archaeological Remains," *AASOR,* V (1924-25), 77-104.    V. R. GOLD

**BETHESDA** bə thĕz'də. KJV translation of Βηθεσδά in John 5:2 (from A C Π, etc.). A stronger MS testimony (א L 33, Euseb. Onom., etc.) favors Βηθζαθά as the original form (RSV BETH-ZATHA).

*Bibliography.* J. Jeremias, *Die Wiederentdeckung von Bethesda* (1949).        K. W. CLARK

**BETH-EZEL** bĕth ē'zəl [בית האצל, house, (shrine) of the noble(?)]. A place in S Judah mentioned among the wordplays of Micah (1:11); usually identified with modern Deir el-'Asal, two miles E of Debir (Tell Beit Mirsim).

**BETH-GADER** bĕth gā'dər [בית גדר, house (shrine) of the wall(?)] (I Chr. 2:51). A village in N(?) Judah; the location is unknown. It may be the same as GEDER.

**BETH-GAMUL** bĕth gā'məl [בית גמול, house of recompense] (Jer. 48:23). A town in the Moabite tableland; probably modern Khirbet el-Jemeil, the center of an area once intensively cultivated, *ca.* eight miles E of Dibon.

*Bibliography.* N. Glueck, *Explorations in Eastern Palestine,* I, *AASOR,* XIV (1933-34), 36-37.    E. D. GROHMAN

**BETH-GILGAL** bĕth gĭl'găl [בית הגלגל] (Neh. 12: 29); KJV HOUSE OF GILGAL. A place the exact site of which is unknown, though it is sometimes identified with Gilgal near Jericho, sometimes also with the Gilgal of Josh. 15:7. *See* GILGAL 1-2.

**\*BETH-HACCHEREM** bĕth'hă kĭr'əm, —hăk'ə rĕm [בית הכרם, house (shrine) of the vineyard]; KJV BETH-HACCEREM —hăk'sə rĕm. A village of Judah mentioned in Jer. 6:1 as a fire signal point and in Neh. 3:14 as chief city of a district; identified with modern Ramet Rahel, 2.1 miles S of Jerusalem; probably also identical with KAREM.

*Bibliography.* Y. Aharoni, "Excavations at Ramet Rahel, 1954," *IEJ,* 6 (1956), 102-11, 137-57.    V. R. GOLD

**BETH-HAGGAN** bĕth hăg'ən [בית הגן, the garden house] (II Kings 9:27); KJV GARDEN HOUSE. A town toward which Ahaziah fled in an attempt to escape Jehu. It is to be identified with EN-GANNIM 2 (Josh. 19:21; 21:29) and with the modern Jenin.
         W. L. REED

**BETH-HARAM** bĕth hâr'əm [בית הרם] (Josh. 13: 27); KJV BETH-ARAM —âr'əm. Alternately: BETH-HARAN —hâr'ən [בית הרן] (Num. 32:36). A fortified city of Gad, located S of Beth-nimrah in the Plains of Moab along the Jordan Valley. It was strengthened by the Gadites to serve as a place of security for their wives and children while they crossed the Jordan to aid in the conquest of W Canaan, so it must have been a place of unusual strength. Since Beth-nimrah is Tell el-Bleibil, Beth-haram is evidently Tell Iktanu, on the S side of the Wadi er-Rameh (Wadi Hesban), an imposing site which dominates the surrounding plain and contains sherds ranging from the Chalcolithic period to Iron Age II, before and during the Israelite settlement.

*Bibliography.* N. Glueck, *Explorations in Eastern Palestine,* IV, *AASOR,* vols. XXV-XXVIII (1951), pt. 1, pp. 389-95.
         S. COHEN

**BETH-HOGLAH** bĕth hŏg'lə [בית חגלה, house of the partridge]; KJV BETH-HOGLA in Josh. 15:6. A town of Benjamin, located on its S border a little W of Jericho. The site is either 'Ain Hajla or Qasr Hajla. A mistake on the part of the church fathers, followed by the Medeba Map, identified Beth-hoglah with the threshing floor of ATAD, the place of the mourning for Jacob (Gen. 50:10).    S. COHEN

**BETH-HORON** bĕth hôr'ən [בית חרון; Βαιθωρων]; KJV Apoc. BETH-ORON —ôr'ən. The name of two adjacent towns of strategic importance, Upper and Lower Beth-horon, located on the road from Gibeon to the Valley of Aijalon and the Shephelah.

The etymology of the name is uncertain; the most common one, "place of caves," has been proposed because of the presence of caves in the area and the similarity of "Horon" to the Hebrew word for "cave" (חר, *hor*). Another theory is that the place was an old Canaanite shrine where a god by the name of Hauron was worshiped; his name is known from Egyptian and Ugaritic texts.

Upper Beth-horon is *ca.* five miles NW of Gibeon

and *ca.* 1,750 feet above sea level; Lower Beth-horon is *ca.* two miles away, toward the Mediterranean, and *ca.* 700 feet lower. The ancient names are preserved in modern Beit 'Ur el-Foqa ("the upper") and Beit 'Ur et-Tahta ("the lower"). Visitors to the sites have reported various types of sherds whose dates would indicate a long history for Beth-horon. Traces of stone walls and rocky terraces at lower Beth-horon may go back to pre-Christian times.

Beth-horon was frequently the scene of military conflicts, beginning in the time of Joshua. It is included among the LEVITICAL CITIES in Josh. 21:22; I Chr. 6:68—H 6:53. An ancestress of Joshua was the builder of both Lower and Upper Beth-horon (I Chr. 7:24). In Joshua's battle with the five kings (Josh. 10:10-11) hailstones caused a great destruction of the enemy at the "ascent of Beth-horon." Lower Beth-horon is said to be on the border of the descendants of Joseph (16:3)—i.e., the S border of Ephraim, which adjoined the territory of Benjamin (18:13-14). Upper Beth-horon was also on the S border of the territory of the Ephraimites (16:5). In the time of Saul the place was raided by a company of Philistines (I Sam. 13:18). Solomon caused it to be rebuilt following an Egyptian raid (I Kings 9:17 mentions only Lower Beth-horon; II Chr. 8:5 refers to Upper and Lower Beth-horon). In the time of Amaziah king of Judah, Beth-horon was the scene of an attack by Ephraimites who were displeased by his treatment of them (II Chr. 25:13).

A king of Beth-horon in the time of Jacob is mentioned in Jub. 34:4. It was among the villages held by the Jews against Holofernes (Jth. 4:4). During the Maccabean Wars, Beth-horon was the scene of two victories under the leadership of Judas (I Macc. 3:16, 24; 7:39), and it was fortified by Bacchides after a battle with Jonathan (I Macc. 9:50; Jos. Antiq. XIII.i.3).                W. L. REED

**BETH-JESHIMOTH** běth jĕsh'ə mŏth [בית הישימות, בית הושימת, house of wastes]; KJV BETH-JESI-

MOTH—jĕs'ə mŏth in Num. 33:49. A town in the Plains of Moab, the S limit of Israel's encampment (Num. 33:49). It was assigned to the Reubenites (Josh. 13:20), but was later in Moabite possession (Ezek. 25:9). It is probably modern Tell el-'Azeimeh, *ca.* twelve miles SE of Jericho (Josh. 12:3).

*Bibliography.* N. Glueck, "Some Ancient Towns in the Plains of Moab," *BASOR*, no. 91 (1943), pp. 7-26, especially pp. 23-25.                E. D. GROHMAN

**BETH-LE-APHRAH** běth'lǐ ăf'rə [בית לעפרה, house of dust] (Mic. 1:10); KJV HOUSE OF APHRAH. An unidentified city. Parallelism with Gath suggests a Philistine city, although an allusion to Ophrah or Bethel may be intended. A play on words is evident in the phrase

In Beth-le-aphrah
roll yourselves in the dust
(עפר, *'āphār*).

W. L. REED

**BETH-LEBAOTH** běth'lǐ bā'ŏth [בית לבאות, place of lions] (Josh. 19:6). Alternately: LEBAOTH [לבאות] (Josh. 15:32). A city of Simeon in the S part of Judah; same as Beth-biri (I Chr. 4:31). The site is unknown, but it was evidently located near SHARUHEN.                S. COHEN

*BETHLEHEM běth'lǐ hěm [בית לחם, house (place) of bread *or* food(?), *or* house (place) of fighting(?), *or* house of (the god) Laḥamu(?); Βηθλέεμ]; BETHLE-HEMITE —ĭt; KJV Apoc. BETH-LOMON běth-lō'mən. **1.** A town in Judah; the home of David and the birthplace of Jesus; sometimes referred to in the KJV as Bethlehem-judah (Judg. 17:7-9; 19:1-2, 18; Ruth 1:1-2; I Sam. 17:12) to distinguish it from the town of the same name in Zebulun (*see 2 below*). It is located *ca.* six miles S-SW of Jerusalem near the chief N-S route linking Jerusalem with Hebron and the Negeb. Figs. BET 30-31.

The first historical mention of Bethlehem is found

From *Atlas of the Bible* (Thomas Nelson & Sons Limited)

30. Bethlehem. Between the bell towers in the center is the site of the basilica built by Constantine *ca.* A.D. 325 (but no longer there)

From *Atlas of the Bible* (Thomas Nelson & Sons Limited)

31. Bethlehem as viewed from the S

in one of the Amarna letters of the early fourteenth century B.C. in which 'Abdu-Heba, prince of Jerusalem, complains that *Bit-Lahmi* has gone over to the 'Apiru. In Gen. 35:19, the parenthetical phrase "(that is, Bethlehem)" following Ephrath is generally regarded as a gloss, since elsewhere (I Sam. 10:2) Rachel's tomb is located in Benjamin, not far from Ramah. Bethlehem was the home of the Levite who became the priest of Micah and later of the Danites (Judg. 17–18), and of the Ephraimite Levite's concubine whose death precipitated a war between Israel and Benjamin (ch. 19). Bethlehem was also the setting for most of the book of Ruth (Ruth 1:1-2, 19, 22; 2:4; 4:11). Its prominence in the OT, however, largely rests on its associations with David. It was his home (I Sam. 17:12, 15; 20:6, 28), the scene of his anointment by Samuel (16:1-13), the site of a Philistine garrison (II Sam. 23:14-16; I Chr. 11:16-18), and the home of Elhanan (II Sam. 23:24; I Chr. 11:26) and the burial place of Asahel (II Sam. 2:32). During the late tenth century the town was fortified by Rehoboam (II Chr. 11:6). Following the murder of Gedaliah, the fleeing Israelites stopped near Bethlehem en route to Egypt (Jer. 41:17). Its leading citizens participated in the Exile, and Ezra (2:21) and Nehemiah (7:26) record more than one hundred male Bethlehemite returnees (cf. I Esd. 5:17). It is also mentioned in Micah (5:2—H 5:1) as the home of the messianic ruler.

Bethlehem is best known as the birthplace of Jesus (Matt. 2:1-16; Luke 2:4-15; John 7:42). The site was venerated by early Christians, although no remains of the first three centuries A.D. have been found. The tradition that Jesus was born in a cave dates back to at least the middle of the second century, when it was mentioned by Justin Martyr. In 325, Constantine erected a basilica with an octagonal chapel over a series of caves. After this building was destroyed,

Justinian I (527-65) built a new and larger church, extensively altering the plan. Further modifications were made in the Middle Ages, but the present structure is basically the one built by Justinian.

**2.** A town in the territory of Zebulun (Josh. 19: 15); the home and burial place of Ibzan, one of the judges of Israel (Judg. 12:8, 10). It is generally identified with Beit Lahm, a town located approximately seven miles W-NW of Nazareth.

*Bibliography.* R. W. Hamilton, "Excavations in the Atrium of the Church of the Nativity, Bethlehem," *QDAP*, III (1933), 1-8. E. T. Richmond, "Basilica of the Nativity: Discovery of the Remains of an Earlier Church," *QDAP*, V (1936), 75-81. H. Vincent, "Le Sanctuaire de la Nativité d'après les fouilles récentes," *RB* (1936), pp. 545-74. F.-M. Abel, *Géographie de la Palestine*, II (1938), 276-77. J. W. Crowfoot, *Early Churches in Palestine* (1941), pp. 22-30, 77-85. J. B. Pritchard, ed., *ANET* (2nd ed., 1955), p. 489-*EA*, no. 290.    G. W. VAN BEEK

**BETH-MAACAH** bĕth mā'ə kə [בית מעכה, house of Maacah]. A clan, dynastic, or territorial name (II Sam. 20:14-15), which later became part of the town name Abel. *See* ABEL-BETH-MAACAH.

**BETH-MARCABOTH** bĕth mär'kə bŏth [בית המרכבות, בית מרכבות, place of chariots] (Josh. 19:5; I Chr. 4:31). A city of Simeon near Ziklag. As its name indicates, it was a place for the manufacture and storage of chariots, and, like the nearby HAZAR-SUSAH, was connected with Solomon's trade in munitions of war (I Kings 9:19; 10:29). Its older name may have been MADMANNAH. *See also* SOLOMON § 5.    S. COHEN

**BETH-MEON** bĕth mē'ŏn [בית מעון, *apparently* house of habitation] (Jer. 48:23). A town in the tableland of Moab; more commonly called BAAL-MEON.

**BETH-MILLO** bĕth mĭl'ō [בית מלוא] (Judg. 9:6, 20); KJV MILLO. A quarter in the city of Shechem. *See* MILLO 2.

**BETH-NIMRAH** bĕth nĭm'rə [בית נמרה, place of the leopard]; NIMRAH [נמרה] (Num. 32:3). A city in the Plains of Moab along the Jordan Valley, fortified by the Gadites (Num. 32:36; Josh. 13:27). The name is preserved in Tell Nimrin on the S side of the Wadi Nimrin (*see* NIMRIM, THE WATERS OF); but as this site was not settled before the Roman period, Beth-nimrah must be located at the nearby Tell Bleibil on the N side of the Wadi Sha'ib, which was occupied all through the Israelite period and then abandoned.

*Bibliography.* W. F. Albright, *AASOR*, VI (1924-25), 48; N. Glueck, *AASOR*, vols. XXV–XXVIII (1951), pt. 1, pp. 367-71. S. COHEN

**BETH-ORON.** KJV Apoc. form of BETH-HORON.

**BETH-PAZZEZ** bĕth păz'ĭz [בית פצץ] (Josh. 19:21). A border town in Issachar. It was located in the vicinity of En-haddah and Mount Tabor.

**BETH-PELET** bĕth pē'lĭt [בית פלט, place of refuge]; KJV BETH-PALET —pā'lĭt; BETH-PHELET —fē'lĭt. A city of S Judah near Beer-sheba (Josh. 15: 27). It was one of the cities rebuilt by the Judeans after their return from the Babylonian exile (Neh. 11:26). Flinders Petrie believed that he had found its site at Tell el-Far'ah, eighteen miles S of Gaza, which he excavated in 1928. However, the resemblance between the names is slight, and *far'ah* is an Arabic word meaning "ridge"; Tell el-Far'ah is rather to be identified with Sharuhen, and the site of Beth-pelet remains unknown. S. COHEN

**BETH-PEOR** bĕth pē'ôr [בית פעור, house of Peor]. A city of Moab, allotted to the tribe of Reuben (Josh. 13:20). The Israelites encamped "in the valley opposite Beth-peor" (Deut. 3:29; 4:46). This was probably their encampment while fighting against Sihon and Og (cf. Num. 21:20; 33:47-49), in the mountains of ABARIM. It was here "in the valley in the land of Moab opposite Beth-peor" (Deut. 34:6) that Moses was buried after he had seen all the land from Mount Nebo. Eusebius says that Beth-peor lay six miles from Livias (*see* BETH-HARAM) on the way to Heshbon. This would be three or four miles NW of Mount Nebo, but the identification is not certain.

*See also* BAAL-PEOR; PEOR. E. D. GROHMAN

**BETHPHAGE** bĕth'fə jĭ [Βηθφαγή; Aram. בית-פגי, house of unripe figs; *some MSS* Βηθσφαγή; Talmud בית-פאגי]. A village near Jerusalem and Bethany, and probably E of the latter. The name refers to a species of late-season figs which never appear ripe, even when they are edible; they are ascribed to both Bethphage and Bethany. Fig. JUD 32.

Bethphage is mentioned only in the story of the "triumphal entry" (Mark 11:1; Matt. 21:1; Luke 19:29). In Mark and Luke it is joined with BETHANY and is named first. This suggests that as Jesus approached from the E, he came first to Bethphage,

and that Bethany lies a little nearer Jerusalem. Today Bethphage is by many identified with the Moslem village of Abu Dis, which is situated SE of Bethany and lower on the SE slope of the Mount of Olives, separated from Bethany by a deep ravine. While this must be close to the true location, there is nothing about the modern village of Abu Dis to remind one of ancient Bethphage except the "Stone of Meeting" within the Greek church, believed to mark the spot where Martha met Jesus.

The gospels relate that in this vicinity Jesus sent ahead to the village two disciples to procure a young ass upon which to make the ascent of the Mount of Olives. Origen (third century) reflects these traditions when he calls Bethphage the house of triumph, of the meeting, of the mounting of the ass.

Medieval pilgrims (at least since the twelfth century) located Bethphage between Bethany and the summit of the Mount of Olives, although no evidence of an ancient village has been found in the area. The modern pilgrimages by monastic orders in Jerusalem recognize this westerly site.

Origen describes Bethphage also as the "house of the ravine" where priests dwell near the Mount of Olives (*see* NOB). This recalls the Talmudic idea (second-third century) of Bethphage as (literally or figuratively) a walled town which by a legal fiction was an extension of the holy city. It thus marked the farthest limit of Greater Jerusalem, for ritual purposes, and only from beyond it might one make a true pilgrimage to Jerusalem.

*Bibliography.* Migne, *Patrologia Latina*, XXIII (1883), cols. 1201, 1209, 1211-12, 1239-40, 1271. F.-M. Abel, *Géographie de la Palestine*, II (1937), 279. *Babylonian Talmud* (Soncino Ed.): Sanh. 14b; Men. 63a, 78b, 95b; *et al.* K. W. CLARK

**BETH-RAPHA** bĕth rā'fə [בית רפא, house of a giant(?) *or* of Rapha(?)] (I Chr. 4:12). A name listed in the genealogy of Judah as a son of Eshton. Either a clan or a place name in Judah is suggested, but neither can be identified at present.

W. H. MORTON

**BETH-REHOB** bĕth rē'hŏb [בית רחוב]; REHOB [רחוב] (Num. 13:21). A town marking the N limits of Canaan (Num. 13:21) in the vicinity of LAISH; DAN, according to Judg. 18:28. During the reign of David, it was one of the Aramean strongholds that sent forces to aid Ammon (II Sam. 10:6). It is probably to be identified with the Rehob (no. 87) of the Thut-mose III list. The exact location of the site is unknown; archaeological surface exploration does not support identification with Banyas.

*Bibliography.* W. F. Albright, "The Jordan Valley in the Bronze Age," *AASOR*, VI (1926), 16, 38-39; F.-M. Abel, *Géographie de la Palestine*, II (1938), 279.

G. W. VAN BEEK

**BETHSABEE** bĕth sā'bə ē. Douay Version form of BATHSHEBA.

**BETH-SAIDA** bĕth sā'ə də [Βηθσαϊδά; Aram. בית צידא, house of the fisher, *or* house of the hunter (*former preferable, because of its position; see below*)]. A city (πόλις; Luke 9:10; John 1:44; but cf. κώμη, "village," in D's version; so also Mark 8:26) mentioned several times in the NT in connection with the ministry of Jesus.

The position of Beth-saida on the shore of Lake Gennesaret can be inferred from Mark 6:45; Jesus and the disciples took ship from the (unidentified) location of the multiplication of loaves and fishes (according to Luke 9:10, this event occurred in Beth-saida or a deserted place belonging to it). The villages in the territory of CAESAREA PHILIPPI could be reached from it (Mark 8:22). These data seem to correspond to the village of the same name, placed near the lake, which the tetrarch Herod Philip raised to the status of a city, because of its numerous inhabitants, and named Julias in honor of Julia the daughter of Augustus (Jos. Antiq. XVIII.ii.2; as Julia was banished in 2 B.C., the foundation must have been made before that date). Philip died there and was buried in a sepulchre prepared in advance (Antiq. XVIII.iv.6). According to Josephus (War II.ix.1), this Julias was situated in Lower Gaulanitis (see GAULANITIS). Subsequently Julias marked the westernmost point of the kingdom of Agrippa II (Jos. War III. iii.5). The Jordan entered the lake below this town (War III.x.7); a furlong away (Jos. Life 72); it could be reached by ship from Tarichaeol (Life 73); the mountains beyond the Jordan began there (War IV. viii.2).

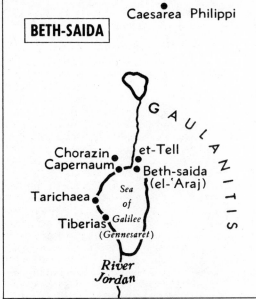

On these data Bethsaida-Julias has been identified with a double site, situated E of the Jordan, near its entry into the Sea of Galilee. The site called et-Tell, situated two miles from the sea and ca. 295 feet above its level, has been identified with the city of Julias, while the remains called el-'Araj on the shore of the lake are understood as marking the fisher's settlement of Beth-saida. Traces of an aqueduct and a Roman road leading uphill join the two sites. El-'Araj has a natural harbor, used till recent times by the fishermen of Tiberias. At et-Tell remains of a town wall, well-cut stones, and an ancient mosaic have been noticed; a strong spring rises in the vicinity.

Beth-saida is called (John 1:44; 12:21) the city of origin of the apostles Philip, Andrew, and his brother Peter (the latter, however, lived in Capernaum, where he had a house; cf. Matt. 8:14). Yet, although it furnished a quarter of the number of apostles, Jesus' ministry seems to have failed there, wherefore it is included in the imprecation: "Woe to you, Chorazin! woe to you, Beth-saida!" (Matt. 11:21; Luke 10:13).

Some confusion has been created by the passage in John 12:21, in which Philip is called "from Beth-saida of Galilee," as, according to Josephus and most other sources, the Jordan formed the boundary of Galilee on the E, and Beth-saida-Julias was beyond it. In order to explain this inconsistency, some scholars have sought to extend Galilee beyond the Jordan, while others have assumed the existence of another Beth-saida. We need not, however, assume a complete geographical exactitude for this verse; the same assumption concerning Julias occurs in Ptolemy's *Geography* (V.16.4).

Another source of confusion has been the calling of the pool of Bethesda (KJV) in Jerusalem (John 5:2) "Beth-saida" in some MSS (B Ψ W); but here the RSV carries the translation as "Beth-zatha."

On the other hand, the healing of the blind man, situated at Beth-saida (Mark 8:22, where the MSS D Λ read "Bethany"), belongs in its proper context to the city on the Sea of Galilee.

*Bibliography.* E. Schürer, *Geschichte des jüdischen Volkes,* II (1907), 208-9 and n. 487; G. Dalman, "Jahresbericht des Instituts," *PJ,* VIII (1912), 45-49; O. Proksch, "Jesu Wirkungskreis am Galiläischen See," *PJ,* XIV (1918), 18-19; A. Alt, "Das Institut in den Jahren 1929 und 1930," *PJ,* XXVIII (1931), 40, n. 32; G. Dalman, *Sacred Sites and Ways* (1935), pp. 161-68; G. A. Smith, *Historical Geography of the Holy Land* (1935), p. 457; F.-M. Abel, *Géographie de la Palestine,* II (1938), 279-80; C. Kopp, "Christian Sites Around the Sea of Galilee," *Dominican Studies,* III (1950), 10-40.

M. AVI-YONAH

**BETHSAMOS.** KJV form of BETHASMOTH. *See also* AZMAVETH 5.

*BETH-SHAN bĕth'shăn, bĕth shăn' [שָׁן בֵּית] (I Sam. 31:10, 12; II Sam. 21:12); BETH-SHEAN —shē'ən [שְׁאָן בֵּית] (Josh. 17:11, 16; Judg. 1:27; I Kings 4:12; etc.); BETHSHAN [Βαιθσάν] (I Macc. 5:52; cf. LXX, Josephus, etc.); KJV BETHSAN bĕth'săn, bĕth săn'. Apoc. alternately: SCYTHOPOLIS sĭth ŏp'ə lĭs [Σκυθῶν Πόλις; cf. Σκυθόπολις in Pliny, Josephus, Eusebius, etc.]. A city at the intersection of the valleys of Jezreel and the Jordan.

1. Name and identification
2. The site and its exploration
3. Prehistory
4. History
   Bibliography

**1. Name and identification.** The name of Beth-shan occurs, with slight linguistic variations, in ancient Egyptian, Akkadian, and Hebrew texts from the fifteenth century B.C. onward. In the OT both *Byt-šn* and *Byt-š'n* are written. Egyptian texts show numerous variations, the first element appearing as either *Bt* or *Bit,* and the second as *šl, sil,* or *šn,* the "l" sound being rendered either by *r* or by *nr*. Hieroglyphic renderings as a whole favor an "l" sound at the end of the name; some of them denote the final element as a "foreign deity" by including the "inverted legs" sign as a determinative. In Akkadian, *Bît-sâni* appears in one letter from TELL EL-AMARNA (no. 289). All the above variants are philologically interlinked and assuredly refer to the same place. We may call this by its shortest form, Beth-shan.

Where was Beth-shan? In Judg. 1:27 it is counted with Taanach, Dor, Ibleam, and Megiddo as one of the cities of Manasseh. In Josh. 17:16 it lies in the plain and is named in close sequence with the Valley of Jezreel. In I Sam. 31:10 it is a town of the Philistines near Mount Gilboa. And in the Egyptian didactic composition preserved in the Papyrus Anastasi I it occurs in a sentence which reads: "Tell me about Rehob; explain Beth-shan, Tirqa-el, and how the stream of Jordan is crossed." All these contexts point to a location at the E end of the Valley

Courtesy of the University Museum of the University of Pennsylvania

32. Tell el-Husn, with the valley of the River Jalud to the left

of Jezreel. Just there stands the imposing ancient mound of Tell el-Husn (Fig. BET 32); and in Tell el-Husn the name of Beth-shan has been found inscribed on no fewer than two Egyptian texts: the first a dedication to a god Mekal,* called Lord of Beth-shan; the other inscribed on a royal stela of Seti I commemorating a victorious reinforcement of the town of Beth-shan. On any natural interpretation this would have been set up in Beth-shan itself. Its identity with Tell el-Husn is thus doubly established. From the ancient city the neighboring Arab town of Beisan inherited its name (already so written in the Mishna). Fig. HIG 22.

**2. The site and its exploration.** Beth-shan lies well in the trough of the Jordan Valley, five hundred feet and more below sea level, on the S bank of the perennial River Jalud. Beside it passed the easiest route by which the traveler from Egypt turning inland might join the great valley or desert routes which linked Damascus and Arabia. Thus the city had strategic importance. But it possessed, too, the natural resources most prized by ancient man: cultivable soil, perennial water, and a subtropical climate. Excavations by the University of Pennsylvania, directed successively by Clarence S. Fisher, Alan Rowe, and G. W. FitzGerald, between the years 1921 and 1933, have thrown light on the history of the town, which supplements and extends what is known from ancient sources.

**3. Prehistory.** Although conditions must have favored settlement in the earliest times, the site does

not seem to have been occupied before the later Chalcolithic period, a few centuries before 3000 B.C. The inhabitants then lived in rough shelters partly dug in the ground and roofed over with light, perishable materials, probably reeds and mud. They used rough, handmade pottery, and flint tools. Before long they were improving their homes by making small, bun-shaped mud bricks to form solid bases to the low sides of their huts.

Of this society, during the first millennium and a half of its existence, little can be said; for the Early and Middle Bronze Age levels of the stratified mound were examined only in a restricted area. However, one significant fact emerged: the town was never defended with a wall. An unwarlike population must have accepted without resistance the waves of nomadic intruders from the E, who persistently invaded the lands of the Fertile Crescent. We may picture them through these centuries, with the slothful temperament induced by burning summers, quietly developing the arts of agriculture, cultivating their date palms and vines, and practicing without ambition the humble crafts of weaving, basketry, and pottery.

**4. History.** Beth-shan first emerges in history as one of the towns in Upper Retenu of which Thutmose III took possession after the battle at Megiddo (*ca.* 1468 B.C.).

This was the beginning of three centuries of close dependence on Egypt, entailing probably the posting of an Egyptian garrison or resident in the city. A letter to Amen-hotep from Abdu-Heba of Jerusalem (*EA* 289; *ANET* 489) reports that "men of Gath-carmel are as a garrison in Beth-shan" and

Courtesy of the University Museum of the University of Pennsylvania

33. Top part of stele of Seti I, dated the first year of his reign

makes them sound like intruders; but their leader
Tagi was friendly to Egypt, and scholars have pictured the men of Gath-carmel as a contingent of
mercenaries, perhaps Shardana or the like, posted
to defend the city, and historically the importers of
exotic burial furniture to be noted below.

So long as Egypt controlled the cities of Syria,
Beth-shan was a vital base for protecting her communications with the N. No fewer than thirteen inscribed hieroglyphic monuments or carved reliefs in
Egyptian style survive to show its importance. They
include two monumental inscribed stelae of Seti I
(1313-1292),* a stele of Ramses II (1292-1225), and
a seated statue of Ramses III (1198-1167). These
span the final period of Egyptian dominance in
Beth-shan. The statue of Ramses III may well have
been set up to commemorate the Pharaoh's second
defeat of the "Sea Peoples" in Galilee *ca.* 1187 B.C.
Of the two stelae of Seti I one, dated to the first year
(Fig. BET 33), relates that the princelings of Hamath
(on map, Hammat, Tell el-Hammeh) and Pahel
(Pella) had raised a force to attack Beth-shan and
Rehob (Tell es-Sarim), both loyal to Pharaoh. The
king sent the first army of Amon, "Powerful Bows,"
to Hamath; the first army of Re, "Many Braves,"
to Beth-shan; and the first army of Sutekh, "Strong
Bows," to Yano'am (Tell en-Na'am). "And in one
day they were overthrown." In the second stele, undated, it was the *'Apiru* (a word most scholars would
now identify with "Hebrews") of the mountain of
Yarmuth and the people of Tirqa-el who were attacking the people of Raham (both places unidentified). A force of chariots and infantry, detached from
the main army, defeated the enemy in two days and
rejoined the king at Yano'am. Beth-shan received
stelae to commemorate both victories. Fig. INS 9.

There is only vague evidence that the summit of
the city mound was protected, from about the time
of Amen-hotep III, with a brick wall, and that this
was pierced by a city gate partly of stone construction. Rowe also found the base of what he described
as a *migdôl,* or fortress tower, of the same period. In
the same level was discovered a bronze shaft-hole
axe with the "forked-lightning" points, behind the
socket, which are a feature of the weapon in the
hand of the famous warrior relief at Boghazköy.

As its name implies, Beth-shan was the seat of a
deity whose nature the word *sheʾ ān* should reveal.
Noth suggested an affinity with the Semitic root
*n-ḥ-sh,* meaning "serpent," or to the name of a Sumerian snake-deity *shakhan.* Albright compares with
*sheʾ ôl,* but reserves judgment. The discovery of clay
figurines of snakes with female breasts, and of pottery
shrines with plastic snakes attached to them,* is not
enough to recommend the philologically precarious
theory of a serpent-god; and most scholars have been
content to leave the eponymous god of Beth-shan
undefined. Fig. BET 34.

Digging in the S flank of the mound, the Pennsylvania expedition unearthed a succession of buildings
which appeared to have been temples. The earliest
and the latest, dated by Rowe respectively to Thut-
mose III * and Ramses III,* each comprised two adjacent shrines, apparently dedicated to a god and
his consort. The two best-preserved architecturally,

Courtesy of the University Museum of the University of Pennsylvania

34. A pottery model shrine from Beth-shan with a
rounded top which possibly was used as a support for
an incense bowl

attributed to Amen-hotep III and Seti I, had antechambers or forecourts roofed on pairs of wooden
columns with stone pedestals. Each temple contained
an inner sanctum reached from the antechamber by
a flight of steps. The antechambers were furnished

Courtesy of the Palestine Archaeological Museum, Jerusalem, Jordan

35. General view of the Mekal temple at Beth-shan;
sacred pillar or *massebah* encircled

with side benches and offering tables; and the inner sanctums had built tables against the back wall for their cult objects. The latest shrine remained in use until *ca.* 1000 B.C. It could have been the "temple of Ashtaroth" of I Sam. 31:10. Figs. BET 35; TEM 47-48.

Courtesy of the University Museum of the University of Pennsylvania

36. Stele of "Mekal the lord of Beth-shan," from the earliest Late Bronze Age temple at Beth-shan

Whatever their nature, the chief deities of Beth-shan were represented during the Egyptian period in human form. The first among them, on present evidence, was the baal named Mekal, whose effigy appears on a votive stele found lying on a platform in the earliest of the shrines (Fig. BET 36). The god is bearded, wears a high conical hat with a tasseled streamer, and with a pair of small horns tied on by a long ribbon knotted and hanging down behind. He holds an *ankh* in his right hand and a *was* scepter in his left, and receives two worshipers standing before him. In a lower register, which is damaged, are the remains of a female deity seated before an offering table; presumably she is the consort of the god. The words "Mekal, the great god, lord of Beth-shan," are written in hieroglyphics above the male figure in the upper register. Two other goddesses of Beth-shan are represented in human form. One of them, wearing a high plumed crown, is identified by an inscription as 'Antit ('Anat); she holds an *ankh* and a *was* scepter. The other, in a long, diaphanous robe, wears a similar composite crown with a long pendant ribbon above a pair of sheep's horns. She resembles 'Anat closely, but might be called a horned 'Ashtart or Ashtaroth, as Rowe suggests. She was found in the main sanctum of the Amenophis III temple. Fig. ASH 91.

Courtesy of the University Museum of the University of Pennsylvania

37. Battle between the temple-guardian, in the form of a dog, and Nergal, represented by a lion; from a basalt panel of the Mekal temple at Beth-shan

The finest of the religious monuments of Beth-shan was a basalt relief, three feet high, which was found in the Mekal temple (Fig. BET 37). In two registers it shows a rampant lion and a dog in conflict, and a lion assailed by a dog. Presumably apotropaic in purpose, it is one of few extant examples of native Canaanite sculpture.

The Israelite tribe of Manasseh failed to drive out the inhabitants of Beth-shan and its villages (Judg. 1:27); for the Canaanites had chariots of iron (Josh. 17). This probably explains why excavations have revealed no violent destruction at Beth-shan between the Bronze Age and the Iron Age. The Canaanites were those whom Ramses III had rewarded with a statue; perhaps the chariots were his. That they were not pure Canaanites is suggested by the presence, among tombs of this date explored by the Pennsylvania expedition, of burials using a peculiar kind of clay coffin not normally found in Canaanite cemeteries. They are slipper-shaped, having half-lids modeled in relief with a crude effigy of the corpse. Such coffins have been found in some few other Palestinian sites, dated *ca.* the twelfth or eleventh century (Fig. BET 38). They appear to imitate Egyptian anthropoid coffins. At Tell Fara', Petrie found two of them associated with "Philistine" pottery; and Rowe and others have attributed these from Beth-shan, on somewhat slender grounds, to mercenaries employed by the Egyptians, linking them in turn with the Philistines who possessed Beth-shan in the time of Saul (I Sam. 31:10, 12).

It is not related how soon the Israelites were able to avenge the death of Saul and Jonathan and the outrage to their bodies on the walls of Beth-shan. By the mid-tenth century Beth-shan was fully integrated into Solomon's fiscal system, and was counted

Courtesy of the University Museum of the University of Pennsylvania

38. Pottery anthropoid sarcophagus from Beth-shan (*ca.* twelfth to eleventh century B.C.)

with Megiddo and Taanach in the district, covering the whole Valley of Jezreel and reaching into Transjordan, which was controlled by Baana son of Ahilud. Soon after this, Sheshonk I plundered the city (*ca.* 926 B.C.); and his record of the event, engraved on the walls of Karnak, marks the end of a period in the history of Beth-shan.

The city is not heard of again until Hellenistic times, when it is called Scythopolis in addition to its old name (*see above* and Jos. Antiq. V.i.22: "Beth-shan which is now called Scythopolis"). Syncellus explains this as a relic of the Scythians, whose invasion of Palestine in the seventh century B.C. is recorded by Herodotus (I.105). According to Pliny (Nat. Hist. V.18.74), it had previously borne the name of Nysa in supposed honor of Dionysus or one of the nymphs who nursed him; and in imperial coinage the city is styled Nysa-Scythopolis. In II Macc. 12:29 it had a mixed population of Jews and Gentiles, who lived amicably together. John Hyrcanus captured but spared the city in 107 B.C. It was liberated by Pompey and remained a free city under the Roman Empire until the Arab conquest, being a member—and according to Josephus (War III.ix.7) one of the largest—of the Decapolis League.

To this period belong the foundations and fragments of a Hellenistic or Roman temple on the summit of the "tell," a marble head of Dionysus of the third century B.C., and other fragments of statuary. Scythopolis expanded beyond the limits of Tell el-Husn. There are remains of a colonnaded street, a hippodrome, and a theater in the low ground S of the

"tell," and of an extensive city wall which spans the River Jalud by a bridge. An inscription records the repair of this wall at the instance of a local magistrate, Pluvius Arsenius, under the emperors Anastasius and Leo (A.D. 508-10). The Pennsylvania expedition explored many Hellenistic and Roman tombs cut in the rock on the N side of the valley. One of these contained a stone sarcophagus inscribed with the name of Antiochus son of Phallion, possibly a cousin of Herod I.

In Christian times Scythopolis was the capital of Palestina Secunda and the see of a metropolitan bishop. It became the home, in the fourth century, of Count Joseph, one of the active promoters of early church-building, and was visited by Epiphanius and Eusebius. In the middle of the century, a notorious treason trial was held before Modestus, Count of the East; and numerous victims, accused of consulting oracles with disloyal intent, lost their lives.

Besides the restored city walls, the principal monuments of the period are the remains of an important circular church on the summit of Tell el-Husn, and the extensive mosaic floors, with many inscriptions, of a monastery founded in the sixth century A.D. by a pious Lady Mary on high ground N of the River Jalud.

Scythopolis-Beisan fell into the hands of the Arabs in 636, having witnessed in 635 the defeat of the Christian forces in the Battle of Pella.

**Bibliography.** Topography: G. A. Smith, *Survey of Western Palestine*, in *Memoirs*, vol. II (1881-83); *Historical Geography of the Holy Land* (1894), pp. 357-64. W. F. Albright, *AASOR*, VI (1926), 32-38.

History: F.-M. Abel, *RB* (1912), pp. 409-23.

Excavation: *Publications of the Palestine Section of the Museum of the University of Pennsylvania* (1930-40), I: A. Rowe, *The Topography and History of Beth-Shan* (1930; with bibliography to 1929). II: A. Rowe, *Beth-Shan, Four Canaanite Temples* (1940). III: G. M. FitzGerald, *Beth-Shan Excavations 1921-23; Arab and Byzantine Levels* (1931). IV: G. M. FitzGerald, *Beth-Shan, Sixth Century Monastery* (1939); *The Museum Journal* (1922-29), *passim*; *PEQ* (1923, 1927-31), *passim.*

R. W. HAMILTON

**BETH-SHEMESH** bĕth shĕm'ĭsh [בית שמש, house (shrine) of the sun (god)]. **1.** A city on the N border of Judah between Chesalon and Timnah (Josh. 15:

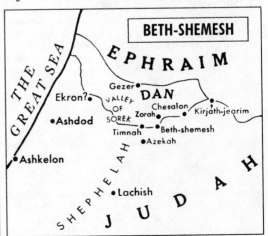

10); identified with Tell er-Rumeileh, in the Wadi es-Sarar (Valley of Sorek) below and just to the S of Sar'ah (ZORAH), fifteen miles N of Tell ed-Duweir (LACHISH), and *ca.* twenty-four miles W of Jerusalem on the main road to Ashdod and Ashkelon. Its name, "house of the sun (god)," suggests a possible ancient religious shrine. Fig. BET 39.

Copyright: The Matson Photo Service

39. Beth-shemesh (Tell er-Rumeileh)

Beth-shemesh was assigned to Dan (Josh. 19:41; Ir-shemesh), though the Danites did not immediately occupy it (Judg. 1:35; Har-heres). Its absence from the district list in Josh. 15 is possibly because it was unoccupied at the time of the list's preparation, though it would have been in the Zorah-Azekah district (vss. 33-36). It was designated a Levitical city (21:16, where it is now attributed to Judah; cf. vs. 9; cf. also I Chr. 6:59—H 6:44).

Located in the Shephelah, Beth-shemesh was the only fortified city in the Valley of Sorek and was an important frontier post between Judah and the Philistines. When the Philistines decided to return the ark of the covenant, captured from Israel after the Battle of Ebenezer, the cows pulling the cart were set on the highway between Ekron and KIRIATH-JEARIM in the direction of Beth-shemesh (I Sam. 6: 10—7:2; Jos. Antiq. VI.i.4).

Beth-shemesh belonged to Solomon's second administrative district (I Kings 4:9). It was the scene of a battle provoked by Amaziah of Judah (*ca.* 800-783) with Jehoash of Israel (*ca.* 801-786), in which Amaziah was defeated and taken prisoner (II Kings 14:11 ff; II Chr. 25:20 ff). During the unhappy reign of Ahaz (*ca.* 735-715) Beth-shemesh was captured by the Philistines (II Chr. 28:18). The biblical record contains no further references to Beth-shemesh.

The antiquity of Beth-shemesh was demonstrated by the excavations conducted by Duncan Mackenzie (1911-13) and C. S. Fisher and Elihu Grant (1928-31). It was first settled in Early Bronze IV (or IIIB, twenty-third to twenty-first centuries B.C.; Stratum VI).

Though it is not mentioned in any Egyptian texts, including the Amarna Letters, it seems to have been captured by the Hyksos in the mid–eighteenth century and was recaptured by the native Egyptian Eighteenth Dynasty, possibly by Amen-hotep I (Stratum V). The city was almost immediately reoccupied, the damage repaired, and it flourished from the fifteenth century on, to judge from the heavy fortifications and the S city gate, the well-

built houses, granaries, and cisterns. Trade with other areas is indicated by a smelting furnace which used imported copper ore and a fourteenth-century tablet written in Canaanite cuneiform (Ugaritic; Stratum IV).

It was effectively controlled by the invading Israelites (Danites; cf. Josh. 19:41 *and above*) for a short time until the establishment of the Philistines in the coastal plain. The general cultural level during the period of the judges was much inferior to the preceding one. The construction was of poorer quality. However, there was evidence of extensive metalworking, chiefly bronze but some iron, supporting the view that iron was introduced in this area by the Philistines and that they monopolized its production and distribution for some time. While the biblical record never suggests actual Philistine possession of the city, strong Philistine influence is indicated by the great quantities of their typical pottery. The city was almost certainly under Philistine economic, if not political, control during this period (cf. I Sam. 6). Stratum III was destroyed by a terrific conflagration in the middle of the eleventh-century for reasons still unknown.

Beth-shemesh was incorporated into the Judahite administrative system by David. Stratum II*a*, whose Davidic date has now been firmly established, contained a governor's residence and adjacent to it a large, thick-walled building with three long, narrow rooms which probably served as a district storehouse for goods and produce (one of the *miskenôth*, "storehouse cities" or "granaries," which later belonged to Solomon; cf. I Kings 9:17). The palace, or citadel, was built on an earth-filled platform, comparable to the Millo ("filling") which David built in Jerusalem (cf. II Sam. 5:9; also the storehouse at Lachish). The city itself was protected by a casemate wall similar to the one at Tell Beit Mirsim (DEBIR) and typical for this period—perhaps built by David as a protection against Philistine invasion. A bit later, near the government buildings, a huge stone-lined silo, twenty-three feet across at the top and nineteen feet deep, was dug.

Discovery of numerous grape and olive presses shows that the chief industry of Beth-shemesh at this period was oil and wine production. Metalworking was continued to some degree (especially in Stratum II*a*). The city expanded in the course of the century (Stratum II*b*) with growth in the wine and oil industries, rebuilding of houses, etc. Its occupation came to an end toward the close of the tenth century, probably as a result of Shishak's invasion *ca.* 918 B.C. Instead of rebuilding Beth-shemesh, Rehoboam strengthened the fortifications of Zorah on the hill above (II Chr. 11:10).

Though the city was never again fortified as it had been in the tenth century, it was reoccupied late in the ninth century. It was a poorer city, but life continued along the lines of II*a* and II*b*. Ca. 790 B.C. the battle between Amaziah and Jehoash was fought nearby (II Kings 14:11).

After its loss to the Philistines during Ahaz' reign, the city presumably remained in their hands until Josiah's effort to restore the Israelite empire. That it was again in Judahite hands and remained crown property until early in the sixth century is shown by the recovery of a stamped jar handle with the words "belonging to Eliakim, steward of Jaukin" (JEHOIACHIN; 598; now in exile), from 597.* It is possible that the reference to the Ashdodites in Neh. 4:7 implies a subsequent loss of the region of Beth-shemesh to Philistine control. Beth-shemesh itself was destroyed in the course of Nebuchadrezzar's campaign in 588-587. No further reference is made to the ancient city. In the fourth or fifth century A.D. a monastery was built on the site but was later destroyed. Fig. JEH 9.

The Roman-Byzantine city is located at the nearby site of 'Ain Shems. It belonged to the toparchy of Bethleptepha (modern Beit Nettif).

2. A city in Issachar, close to the Jordan River (Josh. 19:22). Though various sites have been suggested ('Ain esh-Shemsiyen, *ca.* seven miles S of Bethshan; Khirbet Shemsin, *ca.* two miles NW of el-'Abeidiyeh), present scholarship favors el-'Abeidiyeh, on the Jordan, just S of the Sea of Galilee and E of Khirbet Shamsawi, which may preserve the ancient name, even though Josh. 17:11 attributes Beth-shan to Manasseh.

3. A Canaanite city assigned to Naphtali (Josh. 19:38) but not occupied by the tribe (Judg. 1:33). The village of Haris, S of Tibnin (Taphnis), S-SE of Tyre, may preserve the name in the form of a synonym (שמש, *šemeš*=חלם, *ḥeres*). This Beth-shemesh may be the same as 2 *above;* it must then be sought farther S.

4. The famous religious city of On in Egypt (Jer. 43:13 KJV), also known as HELIOPOLIS (the RSV uses "Heliopolis" in this passage), *ca.* five miles NE of Cairo, where there was a temple of the sun-god Ra (cf. Isa. 19:18).

*Bibliography.* E. Grant and G. E. Wright, *Ain Shems Excavations,* pt. V (1939); G. E. Wright, review of *Lachish III, Vetus Testamentum,* 5 (1955), 97-105; G. E. Wright and F. M. Cross, Jr., "The Boundary and Province Lists of the Kingdom of Judah," *JBL,* 75 (1956), 215 ff; G. E. Wright, *Biblical Archaeology* (1957), *passim.*                           V. R. GOLD

**BETH-SHITTAH** bĕth shĭt'ə [בית השטה, house of the acacia] (Judg. 7:22). A place to which the Midianites fled after their defeat by Gideon and the Israelites. Its location is unknown—because of difficulties in the MT—but it must have been in the vicinity of Tell Sleihat, across the Jordan from ABEL-MEHOLAH.

*Bibliography.* W. F. Albright, "The Jordan Valley in the Bronze Age," *AASOR,* VI (1926), 47.      G. W. VAN BEEK

**BETHSURA.** KJV Apoc. form of BETH-ZUR.

**BETH-TAPPUAH** bĕth tăp'yōō ə [בית תפוח, house of apricots(?)]. A town of Judah in the hill-country district of Hebron (Josh. 15:53); identified with modern Taffuh, 4½ miles W of Hebron. This district was settled by the clan of Kenaz (vs. 13) and lay in the territory of the earlier "city-state" of Hebron and Debir. It is not the same as Tappuah.      V. R. GOLD

**BETH-TOGARMAH** bĕth'tō gär'mə [בית תוגרמה] (Ezek. 27:14; 38:6); KJV HOUSE OF TOGARMAH. Same as TOGARMAH.

**BETHUEL** bĭ thōō'əl [בתואל; *cf.* Canaanite *personal name Batti-ilu in the Tell el-Amarna Letters*]. Alternately: BETHUL bĕth'əl [בתול] (Josh. 19:4). **1.** The last son of Nahor and Milcah (Gen. 22:22); Abraham's nephew, and father of Laban and Rebekah (22:23; 24:15, 24, 47, 50 [J]). P calls him "the Aramean of Paddan-aram" (Gen. 25:20; cf. 28:2, 5).
                                                    L. HICKS

**2.** A town of Simeon near Hormah (I Chr. 4:30). The parallel passage in Josh. 15:30 gives it as Chesil, a scribal error. In I Sam. 30:27 David is recorded as having given some of the booty of the Amalekites to a city named Bethel; since this name never occurs in any of the lists of cities of Judah, it is undoubtedly a mistake for Bethuel. The site is unknown, but it was certainly not far from Beer-sheba.
                                                    S. COHEN

**BETHULIA** bĭ thōō'lĭ ə [Βαιτυλουα, Βετυλουα, Βαιτουλουα, Βαιτουλια]. A city in Samaria mentioned frequently in the book of Judith; the home of the heroine of the story. No place of this name is known; and despite the fulness of detail provided by the story, an exact identification has not been made. The fate of the nation is said to have fallen upon this hillcountry fortress (Jth. 8:21, 24); it is furthermore described as opposite Esdraelon near the Plain of Dothan (4:6); located on a hilltop above the valley (10:10); surrounded by mountains (6:10-12); and near springs (6:11).

It is conjectured that the original name was altered by copyists of the book, or that it was conceived as a pseudonym to disguise the true identity. The variant readings of the Greek name (*see above*) suggest a faulty transmission, but many scholars believe that it was contrived as a pseudonym, as may be true of most of the localities mentioned in the story. The name may represent בית אלוה or בית אל, "house of God," a fitting title for a fictitious city that persevered in its faith in the true God despite every danger. C. C. Torrey (*see bibliography*), who rejects this theory as improbable, strongly urges an identification with Shechem. This famous old Israelite city would satisfy most of the descriptive details furnished by the story. The need for a pseudonym would be easily explainable in terms of the violent hostility existing between the Samaritans and the Jews in the time that Judith was written; this would be expressed in an aversion to the actual name of this Samaritan city. Torrey proposes to derive the Greek name from the Hebrew *Beth'liya,* meaning "lofty abode." Others identify the city with the modern Meselieh, Sanur, or el-Barid. One scholar held that traditionally Bethulia was localized in the immediate area of the volcanic hill known as Hattin, *ca.* four miles W of the Sea of Galilee. Others argue that the actual site was on the summit of Jebel el-'assi, perhaps the OT Beth-eked of the Shepherds (II Kings 10:12), the modern village of Seih Sibel beyond Kefr Qud.

*Bibliography.* G. Dalman, *Sacred Sites and Ways* (1935), pp. 114-15; F.-M. Abel, *Géographie de la Palestine* (1938), II, 283; C. Steuernagel, "Bethulia," *ZDPV,* LXVI (1943), 232-45; C. C. Torrey, *The Apocryphal Literature* (1945), pp. 91-93; F. Stummer, *Geographie des Buches Judith* (1947).
                                                    E. W. SAUNDERS

**BETH-ZAITH** bĕth zā'ĭth [Βηθζαίθ; *transliteration of* בית זית, house of the olive] (I Macc. 7:19); KJV BEZETH bē'zĕth [Βηζέθ]. The place where Bacchides, one of Demetrius' generals, camped, after his act of perfidy in Jerusalem (161 B.C.; cf. Jos. Antiq. XII.x.2); identified with modern Beit Zeita, *ca.* three miles N of Beth-zur, near Khirbet Kufin, a large cistern.      V. R. GOLD

**BETH-ZATHA** bĕth zā'thə [Βηθζαθά, *indeclinable;* Aram.(?) בית זיתא, house of olives]; KJV BETHESDA bə thĕz'də. A pool in Jerusalem which had five porticoes.

The term appears only once in the Bible, in John 5:2, where the MSS offer variant forms, of which the best attested is Beth-zatha. There is also good support for "Bethsaida" (not to be confused with the town on the Sea of Galilee) and for "Bezetha" (*see below*). Poorly attested is the form "Bethesda."

The little that is known of the Pool of Beth-zatha is found in the episode of John 5:1-16. Tradition held that its waters were curative, and invalids lay about in its five porticoes. The story recounts that Jesus there spoke to a man who had been ill for thirty-eight years, and cured him through the spoken word rather than any use of the healing waters. The story implies that the power to cure lies in the waters only when they are "troubled." A second-century interpolation (vs. 4 in the KJV) explained that it was an angel's bathing in the pool that disturbed the water and imparted a healing power available to the first to follow.

The Pool of Beth-zatha has not been certainly identified, although several sites have been proposed. The story places it in Jerusalem, and near the Sheep Gate (although "gate" must be supplied). When postexilic Jerusalem was restored, the Sheep Gate was built by the priests; this indicates that it was an entrance to the temple area (Neh. 3:1). Mitchell (*JBL,* 1903) locates it in the N wall, then coinciding with the wall of the temple. Furthermore, such a gate would have faced the hill district of Bezetha (*see* BEZETH), which may have given its name to the pool. Most persuasive, therefore, are the excavations of Schick (1888), which have revealed twin pools with five porticoes, at the foot of Mount Bezetha. In the days of Jesus, this site lay N of the walled city, though today it lies inside and on the property of the "White Fathers," the Church of St. Anne. The two pools lie N and S, with a rock partition twenty feet thick; their total area may have been about 150 by 300 feet. Porticoes would have occupied the four sides and the partition.

The Madeba map (fifth century) located the Pool of Beth-zatha at Bezetha. Pilgrims in the fourth and fifth centuries attested to twin pools in this location, whose water turned ruddy upon periodic disturbance. The St. Anne excavations suit well the description by Origen, Eusebius, and Cyril of Jerusalem, except that there is now no spring of intermittent ruddy flow.

There are many rock cisterns about Jerusalem, and several have been proposed as the Pool of Beth-zatha. One such site is the double pool beneath the Convent of Our Lady of Zion. Others are the Fountain of the Virgin and the Pool of Siloam, whose intermittent waters are actually connected. But these and others have less claim today than the twin pools at St. Anne's.

*Bibliography.* K. Schick *et al.,* "Pool of Bethesda," *PEQ* (1888), pp. 115-34; E. W. G. Masterman, "The Pool of Bethesda," *PEQ* (1921), pp. 91-100; G. Dalman, *Sacred Sites and Ways* (1935), pp. 335-42.      K. W. CLARK

**BETH-ZECHARIAH** bĕth'zĕk ə rī'ə [Βαιθζαχαρια; Vulg. *Bethzacharam*]; KJV BATHZACHARIAS băth'zăk ə rī'əs. A place located by Josephus (Antiq. XIII.ix.4) seven stadia N of BETH-ZUR. Here "where the passage was narrow," the Maccabean army was defeated by the troops of Antiochus. In the battle, Eleazar was slain, having, as Josephus says, done no more than "attempted great things, and showed that he preferred glory before life" (Jos. War I.i.5; cf. I Macc. 6:32-33).      J. C. SWAIM

**BETH-ZUR** bĕth zûr' [בית צור, cliff house; Βαιθσούρα]; KJV Apoc. BETHSURA —sōōr'ə. A town of Judah, originally occupied by the Calebites (I Chr. 2:45); identified with Khirbet et-Tubeiqah, *ca.* 4½ miles N of Hebron, just off the N-S road along

Courtesy of the American Schools of Oriental Research

40. Beth-zur (Khirbet et-Tubeiqah)

the top of the watershed ridge.\* It is on a hill 3,325 feet above sea level, making Beth-zur the highest ruined town in Palestine. The modern town of Beit Sur is *ca.* ½ mile S of Khirbet et-Tubeiqah. Fig. BET 40.

Beth-zur became the capital of one of the hill-country provinces of Judah (Josh. 15:58). It was among the fifteen cities whose fortifications were strengthened by Rehoboam (II Chr. 11:7). During Nehemiah's administration, half its district was governed by a Nehemiah son of Azbuk, who was responsible for some of the repairs at Jerusalem (Neh. 3:16).

Beth-zur rose to its greatest importance during the Hellenistic period. It was a strategic frontier fortress between Judea and Idumea. In 165 B.C., Lysias, the Seleucid general, set up headquarters at Beth-zur in a campaign against the Jewish revolutionaries. In a spirited attack by Judas Maccabeus' smaller army, Lysias' forces suffered heavy casualties, so Lysias withdrew to Antioch to regroup and expand his army, while Judas (in 164 B.C.) occupied Beth-zur and fortified it (I Macc. 4:29, 61; 6:7, 26; II Macc. 11:5; Jos. Antiq. XII.vii.5).

In 162, Antiochus V, Eupator, and Lysias, his commander-in-chief, defeated Judas and his army. The Syrians recovered Beth-zur after a siege which the Jewish defenders could not sustain, since their food supply was low as a result of the sabbatical year.

Antiochus then stationed one of his own garrisons there (I Macc. 6:31, 49 ff; II Macc. 13:1-3, 18-26; Jos. War XII.ix.4-5). The Syrian general Bacchides, in behalf of Demetrius I, strengthened its fortifications (*ca.* 160; I Macc. 9:52). During Jonathan's administration it served as a refuge for Jewish collaborators with the Seleucids (10:12-14). While Jonathan engaged the army of Demetrius II in the Plain of Hazor, Simon Maccabeus finally recovered Beth-zur for the Jews and put a garrison in it (*ca.* 143; 11:65-66; 14:7). When Simon succeeded his brother Jonathan in 140 B.C., he ordered that the fortifications of Beth-zur be strengthened (14:33).

The partial excavation of Khirbet et-Tubeiqah has vividly illustrated the vicissitudes of the city. Apparently it was founded in the Middle Bronze II period (in the seventeenth century), though a few Early Bronze and Middle Bronze I sherds were found. Excavation has revealed massive fortifications similar in construction to those of the Hyksos period (*ca.* 1700-1550) at Bethel and Shechem. This prosperous city was destroyed in the fifteenth century, perhaps by Thut-mose III in one of his Syrian campaigns (after 1468). It remained unoccupied for the rest of the Late Bronze Age. In the late thirteenth or early twelfth century it was rebuilt by the Israelites, who reused the walls and buildings of the last MB city (cf. I Chr. 2:45). *Ca.* the mid-eleventh century the city was again burned, possibly by the Philistines. Thus far excavation has revealed nothing that one can definitely relate to Rehoboam's fortifying the city in the late tenth century (II Chr. 11:7). It may have been only a military post, for indications suggest an occupation gap during the tenth and ninth centuries. A great quantity of material from the eighth and seventh centuries has been recovered. This occupation also ended in a conflagration, this time perhaps in the course of the Babylonian invasion. Though it was a district capital in Nehemiah's day, little material from the Persian period was found. From this period may date the first phase of the central fortress.

The town prospered under the Ptolemies; coins from the first six Ptolemies (fourth to second centuries), as well as from most Seleucid rulers from Antiochus the Great until the coinage of John Hyrcanus (second century), were found. Repairing the old MB walls and adding a second outer wall (at least on the N and E sides) for added strength, Judas converted the city into a stronghold. He also rebuilt the central fortress. The third and strongest phase of this fortress was built by Bacchides (*ca.* 160), who used a Hellenistic plan in contrast to the earlier, oriental plan. This was destroyed by Simon (*ca.* 143). The period 140-100 seems to have been relatively peaceful. *Ca.* 100 B.C. the town was abandoned and not reoccupied, sometime between 120 and 100 B.C., perhaps as a result of the withdrawal of the military garrison after the annexation of Idumea by John Hyrcanus eliminating the need for a border fortress there.

*Bibliography.* O. R. Sellers and W. F. Albright, "The First Campaign of Excavation at Beth-zur," *BASOR*, 43 (1931), 2-13; O. R. Sellers, *The Citadel of Beth-zur* (1933); "The 1957 Campaign at Beth-zur," *BA*, vol. XXI, no. 3 (1958), pp. 71-76. V. R. GOLD

**BETOLIUS** bĭ tō'lĭ əs. KJV Apoc. form of BETHEL 1 (see Ezra 2:28) in I Esd. 5:21.

**BETOMASTHAIM** bĕt'ə məs thā'əm [Βαιτομασ-θαίμ]; KJV BETOMESTHAM —mĕs'thəm (Jth. 4:6); BETOMASTHEM —măs'thəm (Jth. 15:4). A locality mentioned in Jth. 4:6; 15:4; not known from the OT. The name is possibly derived from Beth-masthema ("house of the adversary," "house of Satan") and intended as an opprobrious term for SAMARIA. But the town's inhabitants appear to have joined the Jews in pursuing the fleeing pagan army.
P. WINTER

**BETONIM** bĕt'ə nĭm [בְּטֹנִים, pistachios] (Josh. 13:26). A city in the N part of Gad, marking its border. Its site is Khirbet Batneh, six miles SW of es-Salt.

**BETROTHAL.** The first stage of the marriage transaction. *See* MARRIAGE § 2a.

**BEULAH** bū'lə [בְּעוּלָה, married]. One of two symbolical names denoting the future prosperity of Jerusalem (Isa. 62:4; cf. 54:1-8). The other, Hephzi-bah, is a proper name in II Kings 21:1. In Isa. 62:4 the KJV places the names in the text and their meanings in the margin; the RSV transposes text and margin. (For Israel as the "bride" of Yahweh, see Jer. 2:2; Hos. 2:14-20—H 16-22.) This thought culminates in the NT in the conception of the church (Eph. 5:23-27) and the New Jerusalem (Rev. 21:2, 9 ff) as the bride of Christ.
C. R. NORTH

**BEVELED WORK** [מַעֲשֵׂה מוֹרָד, *lit.,* work of descent] (I Kings 7:29); KJV THIN WORK. Wreathlike scrollwork, probably in low relief, around the bronze panels of the stands for the lavers in Solomon's temple. *See* LAVER; TEMPLE; JERUSALEM.
L. E. TOOMBS

**BEWITCH** [βασκαίνω] (Gal. 3:1). Figuratively, "to charm" with arguments to a degree that the power of reasoning is lost.

**BEYOND THE JORDAN** [מֵעֵבֶר הַיַּרְדֵּן, עֵבֶר הַיַּרְדֵּן, מֵעֵבֶר לַיַּרְדֵּן, בְּעֵבֶר הַיַּרְדֵּן]. An expression indicating the territory either E or W of the Jordan, according to the viewpoint of the writer. Of the approximately thirty times it occurs, only five can be definitely thought of as meaning W of the Jordan: Gen. 50:10-11 (burial of Jacob); Deut. 3:20, 25; 11:30 (Moses speaking on the plains of Moab E of the Jordan). In all other passages the Transjordan region is indicated, and this became the standard usage in Talmudic sources and the NT (e.g., John 1:28).
S. COHEN

**BEYOND THE RIVER** [עֵבֶר הַנָּהָר; Aram. עֲבַר נַהֲרָה]. On the other side of the Euphrates. To one living in Palestine-Syria, "beyond the River" meant E of the Euphrates (II Sam. 10:16; I Kings 14:15; I Chr. 19:16; in these instances the RSV translates "beyond the Euphrates"). In Josh. 24:3, 14-15 (KJV "on the other side of the flood") the expression refers to the homeland of the patriarchs near Haran. To the Persians the same expression meant W of the Euphrates, and in the reorganization of the Persian Empire, Darius I named the fifth satrapy "Beyond the River" (Ebir-nari). Palestine-Syria was included in its bounds, and this official Persian usage is reflected in Ezra 4:10-20; 5:3, 6; 6:6, 8, 13; 7:21, 25; 8:36; Neh. 2:7, 9; 3:7 (KJV incorrectly "on this side the river").

                                  L. E. TOOMBS

**BEZAE, CODEX** bē′zē. A fifth- or sixth-century uncial codex MS of the gospels and Acts in Greek and Latin (symbols: Greek text, "D"; Latin text, "*d*"). The gospels are arranged in the Western order: Matthew, John, Luke, Mark. The codex apparently originally also contained the Catholic letters, as the end of III John is preserved before the beginning of Acts. It is one of the primary witnesses to the text of the NT. *See* TEXT, NT; VERSIONS, ANCIENT.

The codex contains 406 vellum leaves (plus 9 leaves that have been added by later hands) measuring 10 by 8 inches. Originally it probably contained 510 leaves or more. The Greek and Latin texts face each other on opposite pages—the Greek text on the left and the Latin text on the right. Each page contains one column of text with 33 lines of varying length (sense lines) per column.

The place of origin of the MS is unknown. The fact that it contains a Latin text, however, seems to indicate that it was copied in the West. Wherever it was copied, independent Greek and Latin MSS were used as exemplars, and they were corrected or assimilated to each other to produce this bilingual codex. It is the only known Greek MS of any extent that witnesses to the Western text of the gospels and Acts. Von Soden identified it as an Iᵃ MS which contained a large number of Old Syriac and African Latin readings. Westcott and Hort held that this codex gives a truer picture of the form in which the gospels and Acts were read in the third century and most of the second century than does any other extant Greek MS.

In the year 1546, Codex Bezae was taken to the Council of Trent by the bishop of Clermont, who probably had borrowed it from the Monastery of St. Irenaeus in Lyons. With this MS, the bishop tried to lay a biblical foundation for celibacy by using its reading in John 21:22: ἐὰν αὐτὸν θέλω μένειν οὕτως ἕως ἔρχομαι ("If I wish him to remain *thus* until I come"). It is the only known Greek MS which reads οὕτως ("thus") in this passage, although the reading is found in the Latin Vulg. After the council was over, the MS was returned to the monastery in Lyons. There it remained until the city was sacked by the Huguenots in 1562. In some way, it then came into the possession of Theodore Beza, who presented it to Cambridge University in 1581. Fig. BEZ 41.

*Bibliography.* For a photographic facsimile of the MS, see *Codex Bezae Cantabrigiensis. Quattuor Evangelia et Actus Apostolorum complectens Graece et Latine Sumptibus Academiae phototypice repraesentus* (1899). See also: F. H. A. Scrivener, *Plain Introduction to the Criticism of the NT* (4th ed., rev. E. Miller; 1894), I, 124-30; C. R. Gregory, *Canon and Text of the NT* (1907), pp. 350-53; W. H. P. Hatch, *Principal Uncial MSS of the NT* (1939), plate XXII; F. G. Kenyon, *Our Bible and the Ancient MSS* (5th ed., rev. A. W. Adams; 1958), pp. 207-12 and Appendix I (for some of the most interesting readings in Codex Bezae).

                                  M. M. PARVIS

41. Codex Bezae (fifth or sixth century A.D.)

**BEZAI** bē′zī [בֵּצָי, *shortened form of* בְּצַלְאֵל, *see* BEZALEL]. The head of a family that returned to Palestine after the Exile (Ezra 2:17; Neh. 7:23; I Esd. 5:16). According to Neh. 10:18—H 10:19, he set his seal to Ezra's covenant.      M. NEWMAN

**BEZALEL** bĕz′ə lĕl [בְּצַלְאֵל, in the shadow (protection) of God]; KJV **BEZALEEL** bĭ zăl′ĭ əl. **1.** A Judahite in charge of making the wilderness TABERNACLE and its equipment; he was descended from Caleb (Exod. 31:2; 35:30; 36:1-2; 37:1; 38:22; I Chr. 2:20; II Chr. 1:5). Bezalel's skill as a versatile craftsman is attributed to his being filled with the Spirit of God. Assisted by Oholiab and unnamed workers, Bezalel devised designs for the adornment of the ancient sanctuary, executed them in various media, and constructed the ark, altars, and other items.

**2.** One of the sons of Pahath-moab who divorced their foreign wives at Ezra's instigation (Ezra 10:30).

*Bibliography.* M. Noth, *Die israelitischen Personennamen* (1928), pp. 32, 152.      R. F. JOHNSON

**BEZEK** bē′zĕk [בֶּזֶק]. **1.** A city where the tribes of Judah and Simeon inflicted a defeat upon the Canaanites and the Perizzites (Judg. 1:4-5). Adoni-bezek fled from Bezek, only to be captured and mutilated. Because Adoni-bezek was taken to Jerusalem, where he died, it is thought that Bezek is to be located in the vicinity of Jerusalem. Modern Bezqa, *ca.* two miles SE of Lydda, has been proposed as a probable site.

**2.** The rallying point for the men of Israel and Judah by Saul for the purpose of repulsing the attacking Ammonites under the leadership of Nahash (I Sam. 11:8). The distance from Bezek to JABESH could be covered in the course of one night (cf. vs. 9). Modern Khirbet Ibziq, thirteen miles NE of Shechem on the edge of the hill country overlooking the Jordan Valley, is a probable location.

*Bibliography.* N. Glueck, *Explorations in Eastern Palestine,* IV, *AASOR,* vols. XXV-XXVIII (1951), pt. 1, pp. 269-72.      W. L. REED

**BEZER** bē′zər [בֶּצֶר, precious ore(?), *or* fortress(?)] (I Chr. 7:37). **1.** A division of the Zophah clan of the tribe of Asher.

*Bibliography.* M. Noth, *Die israelitischen Personennamen* (1928), p. 223.

**2.** A city of Reuben, appointed a CITY OF REFUGE (Deut. 4:43; Josh. 20:8), allotted to the Merarites (Josh. 21:36; I Chr. 6:78—H 6:63; *see* MERARI), rebuilt by Mesha of Moab (*see* MOABITE STONE). It is perhaps modern Umm el-'Amad, eight miles NE of Medeba.      E. D. GROHMAN

**BEZETH.** KJV form of BETH-ZAITH.

**BIATAS.** KJV Apoc. form of PELAIAH 2.

**BIBLE** [τὰ βιβλία, the books, *plural of* τὸ βιβλίον, *diminutive from* ἡ βίβλος (*specialized sense,* the sacred scriptures, *goes back to* ca. A.D. 400); Late Lat. *biblia, feminine singular for earlier neuter plural;* Old French *bible*]. The collection of writings to which the church attaches canonical authority. The limits of this collection have varied considerably at different periods, and there are profound differences within the church over the degree of authority which is to be attributed to the collection and to particular books within it. *See* CANON OF THE OT; CANON OF THE NT; INSPIRATION AND REVELATION.

**1. The English Bible.** The English Bible in its complete form contains eighty books—thirty-nine of the OT, twenty-seven of the NT, and fourteen of the Apoc. Since early in the nineteenth century, when the British and Foreign Bible Society decided against including the Apoc. in editions published under its sponsorship, it has become the general custom to publish Bibles of sixty-six books, containing only the "canonical" scriptures of OT and NT.

**2. The Greek Bible.** The Greek Bible includes the same twenty-seven books of the NT and a much more extensive OT—viz.: (*a*) Greek versions of all the books of the Hebrew OT, chiefly from the LXX but in part from the later translations of Theod. and Symm.; (*b*) additional works originally composed in Greek; (*c*) Greek versions of Hebrew works which are no longer extant in Hebrew; and (*d*) Greek supplements to the books of Esther and Daniel. *See* SEPTUAGINT.

**3. The Hebrew Bible.** The Hebrew Bible contains the thirty-nine books of the OT which the Christian churches, accepting in this the judgment of the rabbis of the age of the tannaim, have acknowledged as canonical. Jewish writers frequently refer to this collection alone as "the Bible."

**4. The Latin Bible.** The Latin Bible, according to the decision of the Council of Trent, contains seventy-two books—forty-five of the OT and twenty-seven of the NT. The forty-five OT books correspond with some difference of arrangement to the thirty-nine OT books in the English Bible with the Apoc. These are held to be "sacred and canonical," on the ground that "having been written by inspiration of the Holy Ghost, they have God for their author, and as such have been handed down by the church." *See* VULGATE.

The Bible has now been translated into more than a thousand languages, and the work of translation into other languages and dialects is still going on. No other literature has ever been rendered into any remotely comparable number of versions, and no book has ever approached the Bible in world-wide circulation.

In a more extended usage, the word "bible" is now sometimes applied to the sacred scriptures of other religions, and even to authoritative works on almost any subject.      F. W. BEARE

\***BIBLICAL CRITICISM.** All literature invites criticism; all important literature demands it, if the writing in question is to be used reliably (as for history or law) or worthily (as for artistic production) or in genuine reverence (as for religious or ethical guidance). For criticism in the widest sense is ἡ κριτικὴ τέχνη, the power of discernment, without which articulate thought is impossible. Everyday usage associates it too readily with mere disparagement. But art criticism, e.g., can be and often is the highest form of appreciation—not the gush of uninhibited first response, but a founded, comparing, contrasting, analyzing response—in other words, discriminating appreciation. But biblical criticism is not primarily aesthetic. Scripture is addressed to man, the whole man, heart, soul, and mind—and ultimately to hands and feet, too—but, since it is language, it is primarily addressed through his eye or ear to his mind, which alone can deal with language. Biblical criticism is one mode of the mind's response to this address, for sooner or later the mind must answer certain questions: As what is this addressed to me? In what circumstances? From what time? By or through whom? With what intent?

All these questions have been asked since the beginning, not merely of biblical scholarship but of the use of the Bible. And most of them received answers at one time or another, usually from tradition but also by deduction, either valid or invalid; and some of these answers in turn became written traditions that were repeated from copy to copy of the Scriptures themselves (see the inscriptions of the Psalms and the inscriptions and subscriptions of most of the letters).

1. Beginnings
2. Pioneers of modern criticism
   a. Grotius
   b. Hobbes
   c. Spinoza
   d. Jean Astruc
   e. Richard Simon
3. The eighteenth century
   a. Eichhorn
   b. Reimarus
   c. Semler
4. Later developments
5. Principles and processes
   a. Philological insight
   b. Textual criticism
   c. Literary criticism
   d. Historical criticism
   e. Form criticism
   f. Biblical theology
Bibliography

**1. Beginnings.** In the ancient church a science of biblical criticism first developed in connection with the text of the OT (*see* TEXT, OT), then of the NT (*see* TEXT, NT). The next area of this science to claim the attention of the ancient church was the history of the canon (*see* CANON OF THE NT; CANON OF THE OT). Here, however, we shall be limited to literary-historical criticism—the area somewhat misleadingly called "higher criticism" (to distinguish it from "lower" = textual criticism). The term is misleading because each area of criticism requires and uses the other. This kind of criticism lay beyond the horizon of the ancient and the medieval church, because it presupposes the possibility and right of free investigation, free both of a not-to-be-questioned tradition and of any institution that might claim to embody and guarantee such tradition. Only sporadically in this long period did questions arise which touched single details belonging to this discipline. Among these may be mentioned Julius Africanus' ingenious argument (*ca.* 325) that Susanna was originally written in Greek and hence cannot be a part

of the Hebrew-Aramaic Daniel (Africanus *Ep. ad Originem,* MSG, XI, 41); Theodore of Mopsuestia's conclusions (*ca.* 400) that the Song of Solomon is to be understood literally as an erotic poem (MSG, LXVI, 699) and that the author of Job was not a Jew (MSG, LXVI, 698); and Hugo of St. Victor's insight (twelfth century) that the Wisdom of Solomon was not written by Solomon and that Dan. 11 is to be understood with the help of I and II Maccabees (*Praenotatiunculae,* MSL, CLXXV, 9-28). But none even of these exceptional scholars was interested in systematically asking and answering similar questions for all the books in or near the canon.

The Reformation, as such, did not introduce this branch of criticism. Nevertheless, Luther on theological grounds did give his critical faculties free rein to the extent that he in principle excluded four books of the NT from his canon: Hebrews, James, Jude, and Revelation. In his original translation of the NT (September, 1522) he numbered the books Matthew to III John as 1 to 23, then after a significant space continued with the above-mentioned four books, leaving them unnumbered as if an appendix (just as the 1590 and 1592 editions of the Vulg. relegated the Prayer of Manasseh and III and IV Esdras to an appendix). His intention in doing this is still clearer in his Preface to Hebrews in that same edition—referring to the preceding twenty-three books, he says: "These are the true [and] certain *hewbt bucher* of the NT"; this phrase may reasonably be translated "the canonical books," inasmuch as in his Preface to Jude he clearly uses *hewptschrifft* to mean "canon." This was initially a theological judgment, but, having made it, he undergirded it with critical arguments: Hebrews is neither by Paul nor by any other apostle, but by some pupil to whom the apostolic doctrine had come, perhaps long after the apostles' time; James is not apostolic, because it contradicts Paul and neglects the passion, resurrection, and spirit of Christ; Jude is a copy of II Peter (the reverse of the modern critical view); Revelation is too confused, commends itself too much, and does not teach Christ. "Therefore," he concludes, "I will stay by the books that offer me Christ bright and clear"; and neither Revelation nor the other three did this.

Calvin likewise foreshadows biblical criticism in regard to these four books. It is an eloquent fact that Revelation is the one book of the NT on which he never wrote a commentary. As to Jude, he is uncertain about its canonicity—"yet as the reading of it is useful, and it contains nothing inconsistent with the purity of apostolic doctrine, and was received as authentic formerly by some of the best, I willingly add it to the others." (Was it Luther's curtailed canon to which Calvin was here mentally "adding"?) He sees "no just cause" for rejecting James, but evidently is aware that some were doing so. Hebrews he accepts as apostolic (i.e., canonical) but is clear that Paul was not its author; and by insight into its style he quickly recognizes it as not translation-Greek and hence dismisses the ancient explanation that its Greek style is that of a translator of Paul's alleged Hebrew. In the OT, at least in the case of Joshua and the books of Samuel, he suspends judgment on authorship; it is clear to him that their respective authors were not Joshua and Samuel. The germ of criticism is present in both reformers, but the conditions to cause it to bud and grow were not yet.

**2. Pioneers of modern criticism.** It was not until the eighteenth century that biblical criticism as a discipline within theological study first made its appearance. But from without it was anticipated by four nontheologians, the famous jurist Grotius (Huig de Groot, 1583-1645), the philosophers Hobbes (1588-1679) and Spinoza (1632-77), and the medical professor Jean Astruc (1684-1766). In the retrospect of four centuries it is easy enough to see that the ultra-orthodox church of the first post-Reformation century could not have given birth to biblical criticism, and also to understand why, by and large, the church of that and the succeeding century could regard these nonprofessional critics only as impertinent, derogatory, and blasphemous outsiders. But it was only outside the church professions that there was freedom to use one's eyes and powers of induction and deduction upon scripture without the necessity of arriving at foregone conclusions. Because these four men dared to seize this freedom, and by doing so ultimately paved the way for later professional theologians to do the same with better tools, their contributions must be described.

*a. Grotius.* During the busy decades of his diplomatic career Grotius was working on *Annotationes* to all the books of the Bible. Only those on the gospels (1641) and the OT (1644) were published during his life; two additional ones completing the NT were published posthumously (1646 and 1650). So far as he is a "critic," his criticism touches peripheral books of the canon. He expresses no doubt that Solomon is the author of the Song of Solomon and is one of the speakers in it; but it is simply a connubial dialogue between Solomon and a wife: "Here the secrets of marriage lie hidden under the modest wrappings of words." As a concession to tradition he goes on to pay noncommittal respect to the ancient Jewish and Christian allegories: "It is believed [he does not say "by me" or "by us"] that Solomon composed it with such art that without much distortion[!] allegories can be found in it which express God's love for the people of Israel. . . . Since this love was a type of Christ's love for the Church, Christians [not "I" or "we"] have exercised their wits toward applying the words of this song to that subject—with commendable zeal." To this ambiguous afterthought he prudently refrained from adding: "but questionable results." Nevertheless, his own annotations to the text are exclusively erotic, frequently more so than the Hebrew text, and never mention the Christ allegory. Koheleth, he thinks, should be called *Synathroistes* ("collector"), because he has here "collected" various opinions of wise men on *eudaimonia,* "happiness." And the collector was not Solomon—this judgment he backs up in a typical literary-critical manner: "As an argument for this view I have many words which are not to be found elsewhere except in Daniel, Ezra, and the Targums." Job, he decides, is not earlier than the Exile, and he has his doubts about the historicity of Esther. The Letter to the Hebrews, which he cannot attribute to Paul, he finally ascribes to Luke, not merely as its "translator" (Clement of Alexandria) but as its author. He recognizes the critical problem of the Thessalonian letters and proposes the ingenious solution of reversing their order.

But Grotius' true significance lies, not in occasional critical insights like the above, but in his quiet assumption of a right to study, analyze, and scrutinize the books of scripture exactly as one does any other book. In this he seems to be the pioneer among modern men. It is probably justified to assume that he deduced this right by generalizing the exceptional procedure of Arminius (Jacobus Harmans, 1560-1609), who on a single far-reaching point (predestination) had ventured to study scripture unhindered by any consideration for the reigning creed. After Arminius' death Grotius suffered prison and exile for the Arminian cause and became the chief literary light of the Remonstrant Church in its first decades.

*b. Hobbes.* Thomas Hobbes knew the legal writings of Grotius and presumably also the *Annotationes* —they had all been published before Hobbes's *Leviathan* appeared in 1651. Hobbes's real interest is neither in scripture nor in theology but in the theory of the state. Seeking a source of ultimate authority for the state, he turns his candid and rational eye to examine the Authority of authorities, the Christian scriptures. He does so with all the freedom of Grotius but with keener awareness of what he is doing, and now systematically inquiring after the authorship and date of each writing (of the OT, at any rate). Furthermore, the answers must be internal: "The light therefore that must guide us in this question [i.e., authorship of biblical books] must be that which is held out unto us from the books themselves: and this light, though it show us not the writer of every book, yet it is not unuseful to give us knowledge of the time wherein they were written." The second chapter of *Leviathan,* part III, reads like an embryonic introduction to the Bible such as our century knows. For Hobbes, titles of books are no reliable guide to their authorship, certainly not in the case of the Pentateuch. Moses, he notes, could not have written the last six verses of Deuteronomy or Gen. 12:6. In fact, the five books of Moses were written after Moses' time, though how long after is not manifest to him. From Josh. 4:9 he reasons that Joshua was written long after the time of the man Joshua, and from Judg. 18:30 that Judges was written after the Captivity. Samuel, Kings, Chronicles, are all later than the Exile, just as Ezra and Nehemiah obviously are. The Job of Ezek. 14:14; Jas. 5:11 is to him undoubtedly a historical person, but the book of Job, which he finds no way to date, is not a history but a moral tract on the paradoxical faring of the wicked and the upright. The Psalms are mostly by David, but Ps. 79, at least, is from the time of Antiochus Epiphanes. The Proverbs, though mostly by Solomon, include other authors, and the edited collection must be post-Solomonic. The titles or inscriptions (see KJV) of Ecclesiastes and the Song of Solomon are non-Solomonic, but he does not question the Solomonic origin of the body of either book. Hobbes recognizes that Jonah is not prophecy —all the "prophecy" it contains is: "Yet forty days, and Nineveh shall be overthrown!"—but is narrative, with Jonah's "frowardness" as its subject, so that there is small probability that he was also the author of it. The Latin version of the *Leviathan* (Amsterdam, 1668; translated by Hobbes) suggests that while Amos, Jeremiah, Obadiah, Nahum, and Habakkuk record prophecies really made by these prophets, it is unknowable whether the recorders and publishers of them were the respective prophets themselves or others.

The canon of the OT, Hobbes thinks, is not older than the end of the Captivity nor younger than Ptolemy Philadelphus (here he relies, apologetically, upon II Esd. 14). Significantly, he did not interrogate each book of the NT in this way—no one ventured to do this for another century. He carefully refrains from criticizing the NT and says summarily: "The writers of the NT lived all in less than an age [= generation] after Christ's ascension, and had all of them seen our Saviour, or been his Disciples, except St. Paul and St. Luke." But the ultimate authority which he was seeking Hobbes did not find in scripture, for *who* authorizes *it?* He would say: the church; only the church is not (any longer) a person. Therefore, he concludes that the authority of the canon, as law, rests upon the sovereign. Because he does not raise the issue of divine authority mediated through human authors, he might just as well have spared himself his criticism of the OT, but in not sparing he had started more than he could guess.

*c. Spinoza.* Fourteen years after he had been banned from the synagogue, Baruch Spinoza published anonymously his *Tractatus Theologico-Politicus* (1670). Its subtitle reads: ". . . in which it is set forth that freedom to philosophize not only can be granted without harming religion or the welfare of the state, but cannot be taken away without also taking away the welfare of the state and religion itself." Here the Enlightenment is clearly speaking, but a phase of the Enlightenment peculiar to this lonely man who was neither Jew nor Christian nor atheist. In the course of trying to prove that the light of nature and the light of revelation are ultimately identical, he comes in ch. VII, "Interpretation of Scripture," to describe what he calls *historia Scripturae,* by which he means, very nearly, biblical science. One portion of this discipline, he says, "must describe for all the prophetic books [=the whole Christian Bible] the circumstances of which we have record—viz., the life, character, and aims of each book's author, who he was, what occasioned his writing, when he wrote, to whom, and in what language." This is just what a modern Introduction seeks to do. In chs. VIII–X Spinoza proceeds to give for the OT books such answers as he has found. Taking his departure from the dark hints which Abraham Ibn Ezra (Spain; died 1167) had planted five centuries earlier in his commentaries on the Pentateuch (e.g., on Gen. 12:6: "The Canaanites were in the land," Ibn Ezra says: "It would seem that Canaan [Noah's grandson] had taken possession of the land of Canaan from someone else. But if this was not the case, there is a secret here. But let him who understands keep it quiet") and adding many observations of his own, Spinoza concludes that the Pentateuch was not written by Moses or Joshua by Joshua. He "suspects" that all twelve of the books from Genesis to II Kings were written by one man and that this man was Ezra, though he admits that he cannot prove it. But he

clearly sees that smaller works of earlier authors are here thrown together without harmonization (ch. IX). The books of Chronicles he thinks were written long after Ezra's time, perhaps even after Judas Maccabeus; he is surprised that they were admitted into the canon. He notices the chronological disorder in Jeremiah. Following Ibn Ezra, he thinks that Job was perhaps written by a Gentile in another language than Hebrew. Daniel, Ezra, Esther, and Nehemiah he supposes to have been written by one man, whose identity he refuses even to guess, at some time after the restoration of the temple service by Judas Maccabeus. He decides that there was no canon before the Maccabean period(!) and contends that the canon was established by the Pharisees.

Like Hobbes before him, whose work he certainly knew and used, Spinoza is much less free toward the NT. No more than Hobbes does he subject the books of the NT to the same detailed scrutiny as he did those of the OT, but contents himself with a brief chapter in which he arrives at the conclusion that the apostles, though they too were "prophets" in his sense, wrote mostly not as prophets but simply as teachers. But the OT was also a Christian book, and it was the Reformed Church of Holland which by 1674 succeeded in getting the high court of Holland to ban the *Tractatus* along with Hobbes's *Leviathan* and other books. It forbade "all and everyone the printing of these or similar writings, their distribution by auction, sale or other means, under pain of punishment." Spinoza had presumed too far upon Dutch freedom, but his critical insights, both right and wrong, had already become a sore and a stimulus that could not permanently be ignored.

*d. Jean Astruc.* Although Jean Astruc belongs to the eighteenth century, he is introduced here in order to keep together the four great nontheological pioneers. He was educated by his father, a Protestant clergyman of Jewish origin who shortly after his son's birth became Roman Catholic. Astruc became a professor of medicine, serving at various French universities, longest at Paris; in his own profession his fame rests mainly on his *De Morbis Veneriis libri sex* (1753). But when he was nearly seventy years old, he published, after long hesitation—and anonymously—*Conjectures on the Reminiscences Which Moses Appears to Have Used in Composing the Book of Genesis* (1753). It begins the epoch of modern source-criticism of the Pentateuch. Though others had noticed most of the phenomena, he was the first to put them together and offer the solution which for two centuries remained dominant. The phenomena which to him cry for explanation are chiefly three: (*a*) repeated narratives of the same event; (*b*) the strange distribution of Elohim and Jehovah (Astruc uses this mistaken medieval form of the Tetragrammaton); (*c*) chronological confusion. To demonstrate that all three of these perplexities are largely cleared up by his solution, he devotes half his book to a rearrangement of the text of Genesis (in the Genevan French translation of 1610) into four columns: A, C, D, and B (A and B occupy the outside places; C and D are printed between them). A is the Elohim source; B the Jehovah source; C only 7:20, 23-24, and perhaps ch. 34; D is non-Israelite matter and composite, falling into nine subsources, E-M. It does not greatly detract from his work that he offers some naïve conjectures about authors for portions of A and B; he is at least aware that they are mere conjectures. While he finds a few remarks of a compiler and a few marginal notes that have slipped into the text, basically it was Moses who formed the text. Here Astruc was more orthodox and less acute critically than Spinoza, whom he quotes in order to refute him. More naïvely, he assumes that Moses actually wrote Genesis in the same four columns which he has used himself and that the columns were abandoned and intertwined only by indolent or uncomprehending copyists. The future of Astruc's book lay not in France but in Germany.

*e. Richard Simon.* Returning now to the professional theologians and the seventeenth century, we come now the forerunner of modern "Introductions" to the Bible (or to its separate testaments): Richard Simon (1638-1712). The predominance of Protestant scholars in the biblical criticism of the eighteenth and nineteenth centuries would lead one to expect to find him a Protestant. Significantly, he was not: precisely the pre-eminence of scripture ("scripture only!") inhibited Protestant theologians from candid scrutiny of their highest authority, whereas the Roman scholar, with tradition as highest authority, could be relatively free toward scripture, particularly in times when there was polemic propriety in demonstrating the alleged need for an authority higher than scripture. Simon was a priest of the Oratory until the order expelled him in 1678 in consequence of his *Histoire Critique du Vieux Testament*, whereupon he became a parish priest.

Both Catholics and Protestants had produced "Introductions" before him, but they had been traditional, uncritical, medieval. Among them may be named Santes Pagninus (Roman Catholic), *Isagogae, etc.,* 1536; Petrus Palladius (Danish Protestant bishop), *Isagoge,* 1557; Sixtus of Siena (Roman Catholic convert from Judaism), *Bibliotheca sancta,* 1566; Andreas Rivetus (French Calvinist in Holland), *Isagoge,* 1627; Michael Walther (Lutheran), *Officina biblica, etc.,* 1636, based on Palladius. Simon goes over from textual criticism to literary criticism, "higher criticism." For the first time in a theologian's work, he dares to assert that "Moses cannot be the author of all the books attributed to him" (in later editions toned down to: ". . . of all that is in the books attributed to him"). The observations upon which he based this conclusion are already found in the nontheological pioneers, but in theology they were new. He proceeds to show that the other historical books of the OT cannot have been written in the times they describe but are the result of gradual compilation and a much later final redaction. His own theory of a guild of "public scribes" who kept the original records and handed them down is pure imagination, but his recognition of the long process of compiling and editing can never be completely lost. Although his work had been passed by the ecclesiastical censor, enemies within the church caused the edition to be confiscated and destroyed within a few months of its printing. On the NT a similar work from Simon's hand appeared in three parts (1689-93), but in matters of special introduction it is conventional except for a reservation that our Greek Matthew may not be identical with a hypothetical Hebrew Proto-Matthew and that Paul may not be directly responsible for Hebrews.

**3. The eighteenth century. *a. Eichhorn.*** Both at home and abroad, by both Roman Catholics and Protestants, Simon was forgotten until, nearly a century later, a Protestant theologian at Halle (Semler) revived his work by a translation into German at about the same time that the younger Astruc was also translated into German. It was the period when, late but virulently, the rationalism of the W countries of Europe penetrated German Protestantism. J. S. Semler (1725-91), of the more moderate wing of German rationalists, himself furnished footnotes to J. A. Cramer's translation which he had himself promoted (1776—). But the real innovator, Astruc, found his true successor in J. G. Eichhorn (1752-1827), professor of oriental languages at Jena since his twenty-fifth year. Before he was thirty, he began publishing his *Einleitung in das AT* (3 vols.; 1780-83), by which he began the long series of modern introductions to the OT. Of Astruc he says: "Finally Astruc, a famous physician, did that which no professional critic dared to attempt: dissected the whole of Genesis into separate fragments. . . . None of them all ever penetrated so far into this material with his gaze as did Astruc." Measured against many works of the nineteenth century, Eichhorn's critical results were decidedly conservative. He insisted, e.g., that Job is to be assigned to the time of Moses. But Eichhorn's enduring merit is that he, more than any other, naturalized within Protestant theological investigation the humanistic insight that the OT, like any other literature, may and must be freely scrutinized, free from tradition, dogma, and institutional authority. For the gradual spread of this view from the Pentateuch to all the books of the OT and for the varying fate of specific hypotheses, see the articles on each book of the OT.

*b. Reimarus.* Higher criticism of the NT, though far less prepared for by anticipatory works than that of the OT was, could not in the age of rationalism long be insulated from the work on its sister testament. But free investigation of the NT was still as dangerous as that of the OT had been in Spinoza's time. Spinoza and Astruc had been willing to publish anonymously, but we have now to mention a great and puzzling NT work of the eighteenth century which remained not merely anonymous but unpublished during the writer's lifetime; it circulated only as a secret MS among a select group of Hamburg intellectuals until, ten years after the writer's death, it was published by the famous dramatist Lessing (as the seventh in a series of fragments from the same writer) under the title *On the Purpose of Jesus and his Disciples—one more fragment by the anonymous writer of Wolfenbüttel* (1778). The violent reaction to this book, which really is offensive, proved the prudence of the author in withholding it. In its deistic polemic against all supranaturalism, all miracle, and its insistence upon casting down the halo worn by the conventional Jesus of that time, its conclusions may all be wrong, but the keenness of observation in it uncovered all the central problems of the life of Jesus: the eschatological message (political or transcendent?), the strange surprise of the

Resurrection if the passion predictions are historical, the possibility of creative additions in the oral tradition, the Messiah secret, the connection of both sacraments with the life of Jesus, the historical rivalry between the Synoptics and John. The author has long been known to have been Hermann Samuel Reimarus (1694-1768), not a theologian but a professor of oriental languages for forty years in the Hamburg Gymnasium. The "Fragments" were written over a period of twenty years, beginning *ca.* 1745, and this seventh one may well be contemporary with or even earlier than Astruc's published *Conjectures.*

*c. Semler.* The most important theological opponent of Reimarus' seventh Fragment was J. S. Semler (1725-91), theological professor at Halle. Though among the vanguard of biblical scholars of his time, he utterly failed to appreciate the greatness of the defiant little book. His criticism, with the weight of his name and position, devastated it; it had been written a century too soon. But Semler's books on the canon (*Abhandlung von der freien Untersuchung des Kanons,* 1771-75) and hermeneutics (*Apparatus ad liberalem Novi Testamenti interpretationem,* 1767) were a link in the development of the NT criticism, particularly as a stimulus upon J. D. Michaelis (1719-91), orientalist at Göttingen. Though Semler had recognized, e.g., that the Fourth Gospel and Revelation cannot have had the same author, he never wrote an Introduction to the NT; but under the influence of his ideas, Michaelis did. The first edition (1750) was very much in the wake of Richard Simon, but from the third edition (1777) on, Semler's influence increases. In the fourth edition (1788) he decides that the historical books and the books of non-apostles (including, apparently, Hebrews) are not inspired, and he finds the authenticity of Jude difficult to defend—as Luther also had.

**4. Later developments.** From then on, German Introductions to the NT came thick and fast, but the real advances were made in specific investigations of portions of the field. The long history of Pauline criticism was opened by Schleiermacher (1768-1834) with his demonstration that I Timothy was not written by Paul (1807); this denial was extended to all the Pastorals by Eichhorn in his Introduction (5 vols.; 1804-27). Still within the eighteenth century Lessing opened the modern discussion of the synoptic problem with his *New Hypothesis About the Evangelists as Merely Human Historians* (written 1778; published posthumously 1784): an Aramaic proto-gospel used independently by all three synoptists. The idea was taken up and expanded in Eichhorn's Introduction, but it was not the solution which many decades later was to win general support (*see* SYNOPTIC PROBLEM). The many problems surrounding the letters of Paul and the book of Acts were incisively opened up (and too radically solved, in the general opinion of later generations) by Ferdinand Christian Baur (1792-1860) in the middle of the century. (For the history of specific critical theories and present results, see the separate articles on each book of the NT.)

**5. Principles and processes.** There is no neat formula for the order in which the characteristic processes of biblical criticism have been, or ought to be, applied to a book under investigation. The nature and condition of the book itself set the order of the

problems to be faced. But the tools from which the scholar will choose the most appropriate for his task —now one, now another—are fairly constant.

*a. Philological insight.* Since biblical criticism concerns a literature, competence in the languages of this literature is the foundation for all serious work in it. Although there are living forms of these languages, natural or artificial, the languages are themselves "dead"; therefore, deeper penetration into them, both for the individual and for the scholarly community, is a never-ended, never-ending task.

*b. Textual criticism.* While the "higher critic" always strives to use the approximately "best" text available to him, and thus presupposes all the previous labors of specialists in the field, he is also constantly involved in text-critical decisions. Conversely, the textual critic also very frequently presupposes insights won by higher criticism; the two fields must work in constant interaction.

*c. Literary criticism.* As with any literature, the critic must ask himself whether the writing before him is integral or composite. He may be led to conclude the latter if he encounters: (*a*) striking and undistributed alternation of vocabulary (Elohim, Jahweh); (*b*) change of style (Pentateuch, Acts I and II, Pastorals, Ephesians); (*c*) change of point of view (Isaiah I and II); (*d*) repetitions (Pentateuch, Synoptics, I and II Thessalonians); (*e*) logical hiatus (John 14:31); (*f*) logical digression (II Cor. 6:14–7:1); etc. If he concludes for compositeness, he must then decide whether this phenomenon is due to the main author—who is then a compiler of earlier sources or is at least quoting already formed material—or whether it was subsequent to the main author. (In a complicated case both kinds of compositeness may be present; cf. Pentateuch criticism or Bultmann's theory of the Fourth Gospel.) In the case of subsequent compositeness the critic may discover: (*a*) an editor at work with systematic insertions, deletions, substitutions; (*b*) censorship of offensive expressions (*tiqqûnê sopherîm;* Matt. 1:18 in von Soden's view); (*c*) tacit copyist's "improvements," often by contamination with parallel passages (here textual criticism and higher criticism run together); (*d*) physical accident to the original MS (end of Mark? order of Fourth Gospel?).

*d. Historical criticism.* Involving both literary and historical criticism is the question of authorship: Is the writing actually the work of the ostensible author or an author named by ecclesiastical tradition? Is it pseudonymous? Or is it irretrievably anonymous? As with all literature, the answer to such questions is necessarily largely subjective; hence the wide diversity of opinion in this field. The answer can be found only from what is most certainly known about the writer, his opinions and style, and his historical situation. In general, historical criticism investigates the consistency of data within the book, within the total writing of the author, and within the whole canon. Further, it studies the agreements and disagreements between the book and secular writers, where such are available; this often brings in the wide fields of comparative religion and archaeology where they are relevant. While historical certainty is no more possible here than in history in general, relative probability is usually attainable. Where harmonization is impossible, a tentative theory to account for discrepancies is the best that can be hoped for.

*e. Form criticism.* Since Hermann Gunkel, attention has been increasingly directed to the various types of oral tradition and to the laws of modification in tradition. By it the investigator is often rescued from expecting of traditional material what it cannot yield and is given a new tool for estimating relative probabilities. *See* FORM CRITICISM.

*f. Biblical theology.* It is not always recognized that BIBLICAL THEOLOGY is itself a part of biblical criticism. The preceding methods can each be used as an end in itself, but they treat the Bible as what it incidentally is and not as what it essentially is. It is language but not a textbook on language. It is literature, and often superb, but it was not written for aesthetic ends. It is history but not history for history's sake. Essentially it is a book of faith. Biblical criticism within its sole proper framework—the totality of theological reflection—is all prolegomena to biblical theology. It clears the way to ask intelligently of each writer the questions which impelled him to write: What of God? What of man? What of the world? What of life and death and salvation? Biblical theology is the constructive and positive phase of biblical criticism, which, when it is responsible, justifies the description of it as "discriminating appreciation."

*Bibliography.* C. A. Briggs, *General Introduction to the Study of Holy Scripture* (1899). Standard Introductions to the OT and the NT, especially: L. Diestel, *Geschichte des ATs in der christlichen Kirche* (1869); E. König, *Einleitung in das AT* (1893); J. Moffatt, *Introduction to the Literature of the NT* (1911); R. Pfeiffer, *Introduction to the OT* (1941); H. Mosbech, *Nytestamentlig Isagogik* (1949).

Articles: "Bibelkritik" and "Bibelwissenschaft," in *RGG* (2nd ed.). K. GROBEL

# BIBLICAL CRITICISM, HISTORY OF.

Biblical criticism as the scientific study of the Hebrew and Christian scriptures is a comparative newcomer on the scene of history. Apart from isolated instances in earlier periods, it did not arise until a few centuries ago. Because of its usual connection with rationalistic and antisupernaturalistic philosophies, its development was long opposed by Christian orthodoxy, but it has come to be widely accepted, even by many who are theologically conservative.

1. The beginnings of modern criticism
   *a.* Interpretation in the post-Reformation age
   *b.* The groundwork of OT criticism
   *c.* The rise of radical NT criticism
2. A great century of progress, 1800-1900
   *a.* Liberalism's search for the historical Jesus
   *b.* The success of Wellhausen's school of OT criticism
   *c.* Forces preparing for change
3. Biblical criticism in the twentieth century
   *a.* New methods of interpretation
   *b.* Trends in OT study
   *c.* Trends in NT study
Bibliography

**1. The beginnings of modern criticism.** Medieval exegetes, with their love for mystical meanings, had done nothing to advance the historical understanding of the Scriptures. In their way the Reformers virtually rediscovered the Bible, insisting upon the simple grammatical meaning of its language, freeing it from the domination of hierarchical authority, and handing it back to the common people. Both Luther and Calvin were able exegetes and exhibited considerable freedom in some of their opinions, but neither they nor their co-workers concerned themselves with the literary and historical processes involved in the formation of this sacred book. *See* INTERPRETATION.

*a. Interpretation in the post-Reformation age.* If the originality and critical acumen of the great Reformers seemed to promise much for the unlocking of the Scriptures, this prospect was largely dissipated as both Protestantism and Catholicism hardened their lines of dogma. Post-Reformation divines became absorbed in dogmatic and ecclesiastical controversies, and for these they felt the urgent need of a Bible whose divine authority could settle all disputes. The Bible was God's book, infallibly and verbally inspired, and this was sufficient; they cared little that it had been mediated through man.

Nevertheless, potent forces were at work to reverse this trend. Intellectual and scientific interests awakened by the Renaissance were manifesting themselves widely. The observations of natural scientists and the explorations of geographers were challenging the traditional view of man's world based upon Bible cosmology. Philosophers like Bacon (1561-1626) and Descartes (1596-1650) were preparing the way for rationalism in their revolutionary epistemologies, upsetting the Thomistic synthesis long cherished by the church. The humanists were boldly investigating the composition and authorship of various ancient documents, making inevitable the application of a similar criticism to the Bible.

Unavoidably much of this new thought was condemned by ecclesiastical dogmatists, but there were some, especially in the Protestant churches, who were already cautiously welcoming it. In England, Hooker (1553-1600) was resisting the biblicism of Puritan rigorists. In Holland, Arminius (1560-1609) was challenging Calvinistic orthodoxy, while his supporter Grotius (1583-1645) was interpreting the Bible in an independent spirit, and Cocceius (1603-69) was emphasizing the progressive character of revelation in the Bible. In Germany, Calixtus (1586-1656) was protesting against Lutheran scholasticism, aided by Spener (1635-1705) and the Pietists.

Meanwhile, a significant beginning had been made in textual criticism. Elias Levita's discovery (1538) that the vowel points and accents in the Hebrew Bible were not original but dated from later than the sixth century A.D. aroused Christian scholars to a re-examination of their theory of inspiration. Johannes Piscator (1546-1625) and the elder Buxtorf (1564-1629) in vain attempted to maintain the high antiquity of the Masoretic points. Church opinion was strongly in their favor, but the arguments of Louis Cappel (1585-1658) proved the stronger. Cappel proved not only that the Masoretic apparatus was of late origin but that even the consonantal text was unreliable. His work became the basis for the literary criticism of subsequent generations.

Cherished views concerning the NT remained mainly undisturbed in this early period. New light came gently in the discovery of numerous variants to the accepted text. These were published in successive editions of the Greek NT, but scholarship settled generally upon a "Textus Receptus," which was taken as a norm. A new impulse was, however, provided by the publication of the great Alexandrian Codex (1628), and such textual scholars as John Mill (1645-1707) were working untiringly to recapture the wording of the original text.

*b. The groundwork of OT criticism.* Up until this time, church scholars had been unable to initiate the necessary work of literary and historical criticism. It was chiefly two independent political philosophers, Thomas Hobbes (1588-1679) and Baruch Spinoza (1632-77), who showed the way. In his *Leviathan* (1651) Hobbes denied that the Bible itself is God's revelation, and asserted that it merely contains the record of men who received this revelation. This implies that the Scriptures are subject to rationalistic interpretation. Hobbes outlined the method by which they should be studied, and through a penetrating exegesis of his own arrived at the conclusions that Moses did not write all of the Pentateuch and that much of the OT originated after the Exile. Spinoza in his *Tractatus Theologico-Politicus* (1670) likewise pleaded for the right of reason as judge of scripture, free from church tradition. Though not strictly a biblical scholar, some of his studies of the OT produced conclusions, among them the composite character of the Pentateuch and the postexilic date of the Psalter and Chronicles, which were prophetic of future trends.

These writings began to influence scholars in the church, such as the theologian Peyrerius, whose book *Praeadamitae* (1655) was burned by the Inquisition for teaching that the Pentateuch was by more than one author. Soon afterward a French priest named Richard Simon wrote a series of scholarly treatises on the Scriptures, applying the principles of Spinoza with a free scientific spirit, despite his own theological conservatism. In his first treatise, *Histoire critique du Vieux Testament* (1678), Simon laid the foundation for modern Pentateuchal criticism by bringing to light the archaeological remarks, diversities of style, contradictions, and repetitions which have ever since served as the staple of Pentateuchal analysis. Meanwhile, other scholars and exegetes were beginning to follow the techniques of literary criticism.

Another Frenchman, the court physician Jean Astruc, deserves the credit for providing the basis of the documentary theory of Pentateuchal composition. In an anonymous writing published in 1753, Astruc argued that the occurrence of the divine names Yahweh and Elohim is a distinctive mark of separate underlying documents. This is a theory which became an axiom in the later Wellhausen analysis.

In this same period there were some who were realizing the peculiar nature of Hebrew poetry. It was Bishop Robert Lowth in his *De Sacra Poesi Hebraeorum* (1753) who pioneered in this field by studying the parallelism and other technical features of Hebrew poetry. His book was followed by Von Herder's *Vom Geist der Ebräischen Poesie* (1782-83), which demonstrated not only that the OT is full of poetry, but also that the very genius of the Hebrew language is poetic. These scholars were influenced by the romantic movement of the time. Von Herder particularly was interested in the culture of the ancient Near East, and was a forerunner of the modern science of comparative religions.

As the eighteenth century drew to a close, OT scholarship was ripe for an attempt at a definitive statement of the results of criticism. Many scholars were active, especially in Germany, in preparing for such an attempt. Very prominent was a historian of great ability, Johann Semler (1725-91), but it was the task of Johann Eichhorn to write the first great "Introduction" to the OT. This was his three-volume *Einleitung*, published in 1780-83, in which he built upon all the research that had preceded his work, adopting what had been substantially Astruc's hypothesis of documents in the Pentateuch. Though many of Eichhorn's opinions did not differ radically from those held by tradition, the entire work was a demonstration of the results of independent historical investigation. Thus, as this century closed, it was already clear to scholarship that much could be expected from an open-minded criticism of the OT.

*c. The rise of radical NT criticism.* The eighteenth century similarly produced the beginnings of NT higher criticism. This was, however, very much under the dominance of rationalistic thought. Earlier, the English Deist Thomas Woolston (1670-1733) had expressed the antisupernaturalistic dictum that Jesus' miracles were mere superstitious wonder tales, and Deists generally were in agreement with this view. Gradually the center of rationalistic thought shifted to Germany, which thenceforth became renowned for its radical biblical criticism. The German universities became prominent seats of the Enlightenment because they were free from church control. At the same time Pietism was working within the church in Germany to effect a breakdown of orthodox dogmatism.

Rationalistic influence in German NT criticism showed its face very clearly when Hermann Samuel Reimarus wrote the notorious *Wolfenbüttel Fragments* (1774-78). These were published by the philosopher Lessing with the purpose of showing the full effect of rationalism on the biblical view of Jesus. Completely a child of the Enlightenment, Reimarus declared that faith is irreconcilable with reason and charged the disciples with deliberately falsifying the character and intent of Jesus.

During this period orthodox scholars were active in rebutting these extreme views, but the traditional pattern was slowly crumbling. Some conservatives were learning to respect the thinking habits, historical circumstances, and linguistic peculiarities of the writers of scripture, without accepting the antisupernaturalism of the rationalists. The devout Pietistic scholar J. A. Bengel employed in his *Gnomon Novi Testamenti* (1742) a painstaking philological skill, infused with fervent evangelical warmth. At this time NT textual criticism was making further progress, particularly in the work of Johann Wettstein (1693-1754).

**2. A great century of progress, 1800-1900.** The

nineteenth century was a period of rapid advances in the natural sciences. Traditional church dogma suffered severe shocks as it tried to adjust itself to such revolutionary views as Darwin's evolutionism. The dominant philosophy during the early decades of this century was the idealistic monism of Hegel (1770-1831). The most influential liberal theologian was undoubtedly Friedrich Schleiermacher (1768-1834), who subjected Christian doctrine and the Bible to a rationalistic interpretation. Schleiermacher did emphasize the centrality of Jesus Christ, but this Christ was little more than a symbol to him, since he interpreted the gospel narratives in much the same way as had Reimarus. Schleiermacher reflected the keen historical interest of this period in his *Leben Jesu* (published posthumously in 1865).

*a. Liberalism's search for the historical Jesus.* This attempt to produce a rationalistic reconstruction of the "historical" Jesus became very popular among NT scholars under Schleiermacher's and Hegel's influence. A biography of Jesus by Heinrich Paulus (1828) was one of them, but the most outstanding success was the *Leben Jesu* of David Friedrich Strauss (1835), which had tremendous influence while provoking storms of outraged opposition from conservatives. In Strauss's rationalistic oversimplification Jesus became nothing more than a Jewish wise man. This work failed to reconstruct the real Jesus, but it benefited subsequent Synoptic criticism in pointing out the principles by which the traditions appearing in our gospels had been preserved, paving the way for the formulation of the Markan hypothesis by Weisse in 1838, and subsequently of the long-dominant two-document theory by Holtzmann (1863) and Bernhard Weiss (1882).

The motifs of Hegelian philosophy were directly applied to NT criticism by Ferdinand Christian Baur (1792-1860). In his studies on the NT, Baur explained the rise of Christianity as a Catholic synthesis between a primitive Jewish thesis, in which Jesus was a purely human teacher, and the Pauline pagan antithesis, which had made of him the supernatural Christ. It was a consequence of this scheme that Baur denied most of the "Pauline" letters to that apostle.

Numerous "lives" of Jesus continued to appear during the course of the nineteenth century; most of them followed the lines of rationalistic interpretation previously laid down. Undoubtedly the most popular but perhaps the least serious of them was Ernest Renan's *La Vie de Jésus*, published in 1863. Even liberal critics agreed that Renan's sentimental reconstruction of the Man of Galilee was a caricature.

During this century rapid advances were made in various fields of NT study, particularly in textual criticism and in Synoptic analysis. It was the fashion among critics to reject the Johannine tradition as very late, and some, such as the radical Dutch school of Van Manen, tended to be overly skeptical toward the Pauline letters. Few, however, went so far as Bruno Bauer in his *Kritik der Evangelien* (1850-51), where he denied the very existence of a historical Jesus. In general, however, liberal critics continued to follow rationalistic principles in interpreting Jesus. Johannes Weiss's book *Die Predigt Jesu vom Reiche*

*Gottes* (1892) called attention to the eschatological, transcendental nature of the kingdom proclaimed by Jesus; but his view was, to an extent, counteracted by that of Wilhelm Bousset, who equated Jesus' kingdom with the fatherhood of God and the brotherhood of man in his *Jesu Predigt in ihrem Gegensatz zum Judentum* of the same year. This was also the view of *Das Wesen des Christentums* (1899-1900), wherein the prince of liberal critics, Adolf von Harnack, reduced the religion of Jesus to mere harmony between God and man. Shortly after the nineteenth century ended, Wilhelm Wrede stated the liberal view in an extreme form by denying that Jesus ever thought of himself as the Messiah (*Das Messiasgeheimnis in den Evangelien*, 1901).

Thus the "historical" Jesus whom the nineteenth century produced was little more than the ideal moral man of modern liberalism in the guise of a Galilean peasant. It will be seen that much of the contribution of the liberal school was in the negative form of supplying a radical antithesis to the traditional view of Jesus held by the church. Thus what this century produced was not enough. It was to be the task of twentieth-century scholarship to attempt the necessary synthesis between the Jesus of history and the Christ of Christian faith.

It must not be thought that liberalism was the only force to contribute to NT criticism during the nineteenth century. Always there were conservative scholars who were not simply polemic but who were contributing positively to the advance of this field of study by balancing the one-sided emphasis of the radicals. There was a distinguished *Heilsgeschichtliche* school in Germany, the most prominent of whom was a man of broad learning, E. W. Hengstenberg (1802-69). Equally influential were the great Cambridge trio of B. F. Westcott (1825-1901), J. B. Lightfoot (1828-89), and F. J. A. Hort (1828-92). These men did much to prepare scholarship for a return to a new appreciation of the biblical tradition.

*b. The success of Wellhausen's school of OT criticism.* During the first half of the nineteenth century OT scholarship was not so plainly under the dominance of rationalism as NT study was, and it was only gradually prepared to adopt the revolutionally different viewpoint of the Wellhausen school in the seventies and eighties.

By 1850 the theory of an exilic Second Isaiah had been widely accepted, and many scholars agreed on the late date of most of the Psalter and of the second part of Zechariah, as well as on the Maccabean date of Daniel. However, a real break-through had not yet come in the analysis of the Hexateuch, and with this OT scholars were the most intensely active. Three theories had been propounded: the simple documentary theory of Eichhorn; the fragment theory of A. Geddes (1792); and Heinrich Ewald's supplementary theory (1831), which was improved upon by Hermann Hupfeld in *Die Quellen der Genesis* (1853). The basic fault with all these was their failure to recognize the lateness of the great Elohistic source, which they called the *Grundschrift*. E. Reuss of Strasbourg recognized this fault as early as 1833 but failed to publish his opinions until later. Wilhelm Vatke's book, *Die biblische Theologie* (1835), plainly stated that this source was the latest and reconstructed Israel's history accordingly, but did not gain a sympathetic hearing because of the author's too obvious Hegelianism. The key to the solution had, however, already been provided early in the century by Wilhelm De Wette's *Dissertatio critica* (1805), in which he had forcefully argued that Deuteronomy dates from the time of Josiah.

With this clue a pupil of Reuss, Karl H. Graf, was able to demonstrate in *Die geschichtliche Bücher des Alten Testaments* (1866) that Vatke's theory had been substantially correct. The priestly laws contained in the *Grundschrift* he assigned to the post-exilic era, because they appear to be of later origin than those of Deuteronomy. The Dutch scholar Abraham Kuenen helped Graf see that this document's narratives, as well as its laws, belonged after the Exile, and the theory was independently confirmed by August Kayser in 1874. The most brilliant and prolific exponent of this hypothesis was undoubtedly Julius Wellhausen, whose works *Die Composition des Hexateuchs* (1876-77) and *Prolegomena zur Geschichte Israels* (1883) were tremendously influential in winning the majority of scholars for the new theory.

At issue were not only such cherished traditions as the Mosaic authorship of the Pentateuch but also the entire structure of Hebrew history and religion. Wellhausen and his school did not stop at literary analysis but went on to apply to the sources a historical criticism based upon Hegelian evolutionism. Believing that Hebrew religion originated in primitive forms like other religions, this school traced in ascending order its rise to the highest stage. The effect was revolutionary. Neither the patriarchs nor Moses were monotheists as depicted in the Pentateuch. Moses only introduced the worship of Yahweh as the chief among the gods. Until the eighth century B.C., Yahwism struggled hard to maintain a dominant position, and it was the combined influence of the great prophets, the Deuteronomistic reform, and the Exile which established absolute monotheism in Israel. The Levitical laws, far from being from Moses, resulted from the reforms of the post-exilic priesthood.

A great number of scholars labored in the closing decades of the nineteenth century and in the early decades of the twentieth to apply these principles to every part of the OT. There has been in recent years a reaction against their excessive analysis and against their too simple evolutionary scheme, but the major results of their studies are proving, even after much sifting, to have abiding value.

*c. Forces preparing for change.* As in NT studies, so here, the antithesis of Wellhausen's criticism to tradition was too extreme, and reaction was bound to come. Historical research in the nineteenth century was itself producing new knowledge about the world of the Bible. Archaeological exploration had not only revealed to scholars the great monuments and the geography of the Bible lands, but had also led to the decipherment of the Egyptian hieroglyphics and of the Mesopotamian cuneiform script. Thus a new flood of antique documents was becoming available, making possible a more scientific understanding of the history and religion of the Bible peoples while enriching Hebrew philology tremendously. The biblical text could now be established with greater exactitude, and its meaning could be better understood. Rabbinical studies, too, were beginning to lead to a clear picture of the relation between the Hebrew and Christian scriptures.

**3. Biblical criticism in the twentieth century.** Thus, as the twentieth century began, powerful forces were at work to correct the one-sidedness of a biblical criticism that had veered too far from the straight course of historical investigation, driven by the winds of rationalistic and evolutionistic thought. A new tack had to be taken if true progress was to continue.

*a. New methods of interpretation.* Realizing that literary criticism had passed its stage of greatest productivity, a group of German scholars associated with Hermann Gunkel (1862-1932) began to apply themselves to the study of comparative religions and of form criticism, with amazingly fruitful results for both OT and NT study. Gunkel laid stress on three methods of approach: (*a*) the determination of the oral tradition lying behind the written documents; (*b*) a comparison of the cultic and mythological motifs of the religions of Egypt and Mesopotamia with similar motifs in Hebrew religion, in order to show how Israel had both been attracted by and reacted against the cultures of her neighbors; (*c*) a sympathetic criticism of the literary forms in which the various tales, laws, and poems of the OT appeared. Gunkel employed all these techniques together, using the cultural situation (*Sitz im Leben*) to help understand literary forms, and vice versa. His most successful application of these methods was in his great commentary on the Psalms (1933).

Gunkel's methods have been widely applied by OT scholars everywhere, and they have also been used in NT criticism, though with less conspicuous success. Three pioneer works in which the literary forms of the gospel stories have been analyzed are M. Dibelius' *Die Formgeschichte des Evangeliums* (1919), K. L. Schmidt's *Die Rahmen der Geschichte Jesu* (1919), and R. Bultmann's *Die Erforschung der synoptischen Evangelien* (1925). These critics have, however, been unable to gain widespread assent to their results. Their work has been more successful in asking pertinent questions than in providing satisfying answers.

Some twentieth-century scholars have attempted to apply their knowledge of comparative religions to the NT. Under the leadership of Frazer and Reitzenstein, they have suggested that the mystery religions were dominant forces in producing Paul's version of Christianity, but their thesis has not gained wide acceptance.

Far more influential upon both OT and NT criticism during the past decades has been the revival of interest in a "theology of the Word of God," associated with Karl Barth and his school. That the Scriptures are the products of a living faith is now being taken seriously. Studies in the theology both of the OT and the NT are appearing in increasing numbers. This promises to be one of the most fruitful areas of future research.

**b. Trends in OT study.** As OT scholarship passed the mid-century mark, it could look back and observe a considerable distance between its present position and its position during the ascendancy of Wellhausen's school. It had rejected most of the too extreme views of that school, not because it had grown less critical but because it was proving itself capable of criticizing its own criticism in the light of advancing knowledge. Thus the relative conservatism of present scholarship is no retreat to traditionalism but a stirring vindication of the power of honest study to triumph over the subjective opinions of men. Without attempting to mention any but the most important names, the following summary of current trends may suffice to indicate where OT study stands:

In the study of almost all the OT books a growing sympathy for the writings and respect for their trustworthiness have been in evidence. Most present scholars still recognize the existence of the Pentateuchal documents outlined by the Wellhausen school, despite the attempt of some Scandinavian scholars to place oral tradition in the place of written documents. There is, however, an increasing interest in the individual narratives, stimulated by Gunkel's methods. It is now generally acknowledged that the Pentateuch and the Former Prophets contain many very old documents and record authentic traditions. The Alt-Noth school is skeptical about the oral traditions behind the stories of the settlement, but archaeological discoveries are often substantiating the biblical record in surprising ways.

Although the Priestly Code is still assigned in its completed form to Ezra's time, most present scholars agree that it, too, contains much old material. Moreover, it is now seen that the priests and the prophets worked in closer harmony than was formerly believed, and that the writings of a prophetic school may be as important as the original oracles of its leader.

Gunkel's form criticism on the Psalms has indicated their great liturgical importance, and it is being increasingly acknowledged that many of them are of pre-exilic origin. This has also been true with regard to the wisdom literature of Israel.

The development of Israel's religion and theology is being placed in a new light. It is no longer possible to arrange the OT writings according to a neat ascending scheme, because scholars realize that the age of a particular writing offers no indication of its underlying traditions and documents. Moreover, the study of the religions of the ancient Near East, particularly that of the Canaanites, the Hebrews' nearest neighbors, is making scholars less sure that Yahwism must be younger than the time of the patriarchs. At any rate, OT critics now generally acknowledge the uniqueness and grandeur of Yahwism, and they are ready to admit that the eighth-century prophets who so forcibly preached monotheism were heirs, and not simply originators, of a great religious tradition.

The Dead Sea Scrolls, which have been appearing since 1948, are illuminating a large blind spot in the later history of the Hebrews and promise to produce a rich harvest in various phases of OT research. To an extent, even NT study will be enriched by these finds.

**c. Trends in NT study.** Albert Schweitzer's book *The Quest of the Historical Jesus* (first published in German in 1906) signaled the end of the liberal Jesus. Far from being a mild Galilean teacher of morality and brotherhood, Jesus was a passionate eschatologist who died seeking to realize messiahhood, according to Schweitzer. This was an interpretation which NT scholarship has been long in accepting, but Schweitzer's book has had the effect of discouraging numerous attempts to write a history of Jesus. Some now despair altogether of finding the historical Jesus; others recognize that we must confess the Jesus of history to be the Jesus of the church which wrote the gospels.

Synoptic exegesis during the first half of the twentieth century avoided extremes of literary criticism on the one hand and of form criticism on the other. The four-document theory of B. H. Streeter (1924) has gained wide acceptance. The existence of an oral tradition preceding the documents appears more plainly than in previous periods. The Fourth Gospel is now often assigned a first-century date and is credited with a considerable historical trustworthiness. Similarly, much of the former skepticism concerning the authorship of Acts has disappeared, and this record is given wide credit as a historical source for the origin of Christianity. Paul's letters are no longer in doubt, except for Ephesians and the Pastorals, and this apostle himself is no longer looked upon as the archperverter of Jesus' religion but rather as a faithful follower and interpreter. A balanced conservatism similarly prevails in regard to the other NT writings.

While NT higher criticism's main effort since 1900 has been largely spent in reassessing the one-sided theories of the previous century, rapid forward progress has continued to be made in NT textual criticism and in linguistic studies. Discoveries such as that of the Chester Beatty Papyri and increasing understanding of the MS families have greatly aided the former, while new light from the papyri on the Koine of the NT, together with research into the Aramaic background of the gospels, has enriched the latter. A great monument of linguistic information, based upon the research of past generations, is Kittel's extensive *Theologisches Wörterbuch zum Neuen Testament.*

There has been increasing interest in the theology of the NT in recent years, paralleling a rising interest in OT theology. Present scholars are also being challenged to decide upon the merits of Bultmann's scheme of "demythologizing" the NT—i.e., of accepting its kerygma of a redeeming Christ without concern for the objective historicity of the gospel tradition. Thus biblical scholarship is once again facing the issue of judging the Scriptures on the basis of philosophical presuppositions. If some seem hesitant to be governed by an existentialist in the place of an idealistic philosophy, it may be because they are convinced that biblical criticism must remain primarily a theological discipline.

*Bibliography.* A classic definition of the meaning and method of historical criticism is A. Kuenen, "Critical Method," *The Modern Review*, I (1880), 461-88, 685-713.

On criticism of the Bible as a whole: A handy summary of modern criticism may be found in S. Terrien, "History of the Interpretation of the Bible, Modern Period," *IB*, I (1951), 127-41. More extensive are: C. W. Dugmore, ed., *The Interpretation of the Bible* (1944); R. M. Grant, *The Bible in the Church* (1948). Covering a restricted area or period are: J. E. Carpenter, *The Bible in the Nineteenth Century* (1903); W. B. Glover, *Evangelical Nonconformists and Higher Criticism in the Nineteenth Century* (1954). Valuable and detailed symposiums on recent trends are: H. W. Robinson, ed., *Record and Revelation* (1938); H. R. Willoughby, ed., *The Study of the Bible Today and Tomorrow* (1947); H. H. Rowley, ed., *The OT and Modern Study* (1951).

On OT criticism: E. M. Gray, *OT Criticism: Its Rise and Progress* (1923); J. Coppens, *The OT and the Critics* (1942)—from a Roman Catholic viewpoint; H. F. Hahn, *The OT in Modern Research* (1954); E. G. Kraeling, *The OT Since the Reformation* (1955); H. J. Kraus, *Geschichte der historisch-kritischen Erforschung des AT's von der Reformation bis zur Gegenwart* (1956)—by far the most detailed.

On NT criticism: A. Schweitzer, *The Quest of the Historical Jesus* (1st English ed., 1910), details research on the gospels to his time; while A. M. Hunter, *Interpreting the NT 1900-1950* (1951), summarizes more recent study.          S. J. De Vries

*BIBLICAL THEOLOGY, CONTEMPORARY.
A historical survey of major contributions to the field of biblical theology, such as in BIBLICAL THEOLOGY, HISTORY OF, makes it more than obvious that there is no one definition of this field on which biblical scholars can unanimously agree. It is true that a closer analysis of contemporary contributions to the field may well show that some of the older definitions are obsolete, as well as bring to light certain common tendencies in aim and method; but it will not eliminate the tensions between different conceptions of what a biblical theology is or should be. Such diversity was to be expected, since very different theological and philosophical presuppositions are necessarily involved.

And yet, in spite of these differences, recent biblical studies have gravitated with an unprecedented enthusiasm toward topics and problems which undoubtedly fall within the biblical theological field. This seems to be due to the fact that a new stage has been set for biblical theology, as a result of a new emphasis upon its descriptive task. Since consideration of this task has proved far more suggestive and creative than is often recognized, there is good reason to consider the nature of the new descriptive biblical theology and then to move toward its implications for other aspects of theology. This can be done only by way of hermeneutics. Thus we arrive at the following outline:

A. The descriptive task
   1. A new stage set for biblical theology
   2. What it meant and what it means
   3. Three approaches to NT theology
      *a.* Barth
      *b.* Bultmann
      *c.* Cullmann
      *d.* Conclusions
   4. Is a descriptive NT theology possible?
   5. The descriptive approach and the OT
   6. "Sacred history" and the unity of the Bible
B. The hermeneutic question
   1. As raised by a descriptive biblical theology
   2. Alternative answers to the hermeneutic question

   3. The significance of "canon" for biblical theology
   4. The preacher and biblical theology
Bibliography

A. *THE DESCRIPTIVE TASK.* 1. A new stage set for biblical theology. The alleged biblical basis for what has been called "liberal theology" in its classical form (the use of the term "liberal" in this sense, referring to the dominant theology *ca.* 1900, does not imply that many more recent types of theology are not just as "liberal" in their method and presuppositions)—i.e., the view that the OT is a witness to the evolution of a more and more ethical monotheism and that the gospels are biographies of Jesus as the even more refined teacher of the Golden Rule, the fatherhood of God, and the eternal value of the individual—the alleged biblical basis of this view was not shattered by the conservatives, but by the extreme radicals of the *religionsgeschichtliche Schule* ("history-of-religions school"; *see* BIBLICAL CRITICISM). They could show, on the basis of the comparative material, that such a picture of Jesus or of the OT prophets was totally impossible from a historical point of view and that it told more about the ideals of bourgeois Christianity in the late nineteenth century than about the carpenter from Nazareth or the little man from Tekoa. What emerged out of the studies of the *religionsgeschichtliche Schule* was a new picture of the men, the ideas, and the institutions of biblical history. Those elements and traits, which did strike modern man as crude, primitive, cultic, and even magical, were now given equal and often greater emphasis than those which happened to appeal to enlightened Western taste. The "peril of modernizing Jesus"—to use Henry J. Cadbury's phrase—was fully recognized. Johannes Weiss and Albert Schweitzer made a forceful plea for a most abstruse and appalling eschatology as the actual setting for Jesus and his followers; H. Gunkel, H. Gressmann, and S. Mowinckel placed the OT back in the matrix of Near Eastern myth and cult. Johannes Pedersen applied V. Groenbech's studies of human self-understanding in old Nordic religion to an extensive study of OT anthropology, where cherished distinctions between soul and body, magic and religion, cult and ethics, individual and collective, were thoroughly intermingled and lost much of their meaning. It became a scholarly ideal to creep out of one's Western and twentieth-century skin and identify oneself with the feelings and thought-patterns of the past. The distance between biblical times and modern times was stressed, and the difference between biblical thought and systematic theology became much more than that of diversification over against systematization or of concrete exemplification over against abstract propositions.

What emerged was a descriptive study of biblical thought—empathetic in the sense that it was beyond sympathy or antipathy. This was actually a new phenomenon in biblical studies, and yet it came as a mature outgrowth of the historical and critical study of the Scriptures. It differed in three ways from earlier contributions of historical criticism:

*a)* The strait jacket of doctrinaire evolutionism—in Darwinistic as well as in Hegelian terms—was considerably loosened. While development and stages were recognized and noticed, the later stages were not preconceived as progression (e.g., from priests to prophets) or regression (e.g., from Jesus to Paul). Each period and each ideology was given enough attention to be granted a careful description on its own terms.

*b*) The question of fact—i.e., whether, e.g., the march through the Red Sea or the resurrection of Jesus had actually taken place as described—was not any more the only one which absorbed the historian. Now there was more concern about what the function and the significance of such an item or of such a message as "He is risen" might have been to the writers and readers (or hearers) of the biblical records. Form criticism and *Sitz im Leben* became the catchwords for students of the documents of temple, synagogue, and church.

*c*) The question about relevance for present-day religion and faith was waived, or consciously kept out of sight. This statement will be, perhaps, the strongest reminder of how biblical theology was swallowed up or threatened by a history of biblical thought or a history of biblical religion. This historicism or antiquarianism, with its lack of interest in relevance, has been challenged on many scores by modern writers. And yet it remains a fact that modern biblical theology would be quite inexplicable were it not for the fact that the *religionsgeschichtliche Schule* had drastically widened the hiatus between our time and that of the Bible, between West and East, between the questions self-evidently raised in modern minds and those presupposed, raised, and answered in the Scriptures. Thereby a radically new stage was set for biblical interpretation. The question of meaning was split up in two tenses: "What *did* it mean?" and "What *does* it mean?" These questions were now kept apart long enough for the descriptive task to be considered in its own right.

**2. What it meant and what it means.** To liberals and conservatives alike, this distinction was not sharply in focus prior to the *religionsgeschichtliche Schule*. We may be justified in taking Harnack's *What Is Christianity?* as the most influential popular summary of liberal interpretation of the NT. It is not accidental that Harnack, as Bultmann points out in his Introduction to a reprint of the work (1950), "failed to realize the importance of the so-called *religionsgeschichtliche Schule* and never truly became sympathetic with it." Albert Schweitzer had brought this aspect of Harnack's interpretation to bear upon the problem now under consideration when he said in *The Quest of the Historical Jesus*: "Harnack, in his 'What Is Christianity?' almost entirely ignores the contemporary limitations of Jesus' teaching, and starts out with a Gospel which carries him down without difficulty to the year 1899."

The apologetic intentions of the "liberals" should not be forgotten. In the light of later development, "liberal" came to stand for the "leftists" in the theological assembly. By the turn of the century this was not so. The liberals understood themselves as the mediating party who, often with a deep concern for Christianity and its future role in our culture and with a genuine piety, refuted the radical assaults of

D. F. Strauss and others. But the way in which they carried on their apologetic task made them poor historians of religion. Their methods were basically the same as those used by the conservatives. Both were convinced that the Bible contained revelation which could be grasped in the clean form of eternal truth unconditioned and uncontaminated by historical limitations. The difference was only one of degree. While the orthodox interpreters found this revelation in the whole of scripture and systematized it by harmonization and by interpreting the less easily fitting by those passages which were hand in glove with their own systems, the liberals arrived at the pure revelation by way of more or less drastic reductions. This reductionist approach was often carried out by literary criticism, but once the *ipsissima verba* ("very words") of the prophets or of Jesus were established, these words happened to square well with the ideals of the modern age. Thus the tension between the past and the present meaning had been overcome before it could create any problems for interpretation. And this happened because the liberals were convinced that the teachings of the Bible were meaningful for modern man —just as the orthodox claimed the same for a vastly more challenging amount of biblical teaching. For the liberals the nucleus of revelation had to be that which could be hailed as relevant and acceptable to modern man.

The resistance to the *religionsgeschichtliche Schule* was openly or unconsciously aimed against its disregard for theological meaning and relevance. By and large, Gunkel's *Schöpfung und Chaos in Urzeit und Endzeit,* Mowinckel's *Psalmenstudien,* and Schweitzer's *Quest* appeared on the scene with no immediate relation to the ongoing theological discussion. Schweitzer's work did actually contain an Epilogue in which the author made a cautious attempt to draw out the ramifications of the thoroughgoing eschatology of Jesus for theology as well as for the life of the believer, but the return is rather small. When facing the shocking distance back to the Jesus of the gospels, Schweitzer finally takes refuge in an expectant mysticism where the Christ of faith comes to us as "One unknown," yet One who in an ineffable mystery lets man experience who He is. In the German edition this final sentence of the whole volume symbolically ends with ellipsis dots.

This ellipsis formed, however, a challenge, the response to which is the vigorous interest in biblical theology starting in the 1920's and showing no slackening tendencies toward the end of the 1950's. Once freed from the anachronistic interpretations of their predecessors, and forced to accept the hiatus between the ideas and ideals in the biblical material, the theologically minded student of the Scriptures slowly found a new and deeper relevance in what the *religionsgeschichtliche Schule* described for him as the pre-Westernized meaning of sayings and events. In the broader context of cultural climate this tendency had its obvious similarities in the taste for the primitive, with its crude vigor in art, music, and literature. It was akin to Rudolf Otto's reevaluation of religious phenomena in his study of holiness. It had striking parallels in the field of historical theology, where, e.g., Luther's own words and intentions were sharply contrasted with the teaching of seventeenth-century Lutheranism, the sympathies of the scholars always siding with the former. But it was primarily the experience of the distance and the strangeness of biblical thought as a creative asset, rather than as a destructive and burdensome liability.

Without this new and nonmodernizing look at the Bible, Karl Barth's programmatic commentary on Romans or Rudolf Bultmann's *Theology of the NT*—or his book written in 1926 on Jesus—would be inexplicable. O. Cullmann's *Christ and Time*, as well as his more recent *NT Christology*, are the typical examples of a somewhat different result of the same ideal of historical distance. In OT studies, W. F. Albright's *From the Stone Age to Christianity* and G. E. Wright's *God Who Acts*, as well as W. Eichrodt's and G. von Rad's OT theologies, are all inspired by the same tension between the mind of a Semitic past and the thought of modern man. Yet most of these writers launch strong attacks on the "historicism" of the "historian of religion." By these terms they do, however, usually refer to other elements in the *religionsgeschichtliche Schule* than the one to which attention has been drawn here—viz., the descriptive element, and its awareness of the distinction between what it meant and what it means.

**3. Three approaches to NT theology.** This distinction between past and present meaning has its specific problems for OT theology, and we may consequently be wise in first trying to clarify the issue in relation to NT theology. We may for this purpose go to three contemporaries who exemplify three different types of NT theology: Karl Barth, Rudolf Bultmann, and Oscar Cullmann. They are all aware of what we have called the distance between the centuries. Especially Bultmann's relation to the radical tradition—over against the liberal—in biblical studies is obvious—e.g., in his references to D. F. Strauss. The question raised by the distance should thus be faced in its most radical form: Do these old documents have any meaning for us—except as sources for our knowledge of a small segment of first-century life and thought, or as means for a nostalgic visit to the first era of Christian history? If they have a meaning in the present tense and sense, on what ground do they have this meaning?

**a. Barth.** In the Preface to the second edition of his commentary on Romans, Barth argues for the exegesis of Luther and Calvin over against that of men like Jülicher and Lietzmann. The former are the only ones who really have tried to "understand" Paul, since, e.g., Calvin, "having first established what stands in the text, sets himself to re-think the whole material and to wrestle with it, till the walls which separate the sixteenth century from the first become transparent, i.e., till Paul *speaks* there and the man of the sixteenth century *hears* here, till the conversation between the document and the reader is totally concentrated on the subject-matter, which *cannot* be a different one in the first and sixteenth century." The concentration on the subject matter (God, Jesus, grace, etc.) bridges the gap between the centuries, and it does so since they cannot but be the same. This identity in the subject matter guarantees the meaningfulness of the Pauline writings. They

must speak about what Calvin (or the modern interpreter) knows as the subject matter. This is apparently so since God, Christ, and all of revelation stand above history. Thereby the tension between the first century and ours is resolved, or rather transformed, into a theological category of "otherness."

It is also significant to note that Barth speaks as if it were a very simple thing to establish what Paul actually meant in his own terms. To say that the Reformers interpreted Paul by equating the problem of the Judaizers and the Torah in Paul with the problem of work-righteousness in late medieval piety and that this ingenious translation or application of Pauline theology may be 80 per cent correct but left 20 per cent of Paul inexplicable—and consequently distorted in a certain sense the true picture of Pauline thought—to say this is to call attention to a problem which could not be detected, let alone criticized, by Barth or any truly Barthian exegete. Thus biblical theology along this line is admittedly incapable of enough patience and enthusiasm for keeping alive the tension between what the text meant and what it means. There are no criteria by which they can be kept apart; what is intended as a commentary turns out to be a theological tractate, expanding in contemporary terms what Paul should have said about the subject matter as understood by the commentator.

When the term "biblical theology" is used of works where this method is applied, it does not designate anything basically different from systematic theology, except that its systematic task is so defined as to make the Bible central in its work. Thus it may be convenient for classification within the realm of systematic theology to speak of this theology as "biblical" rather than philosophical. But from the point of view of biblical studies such a theology is not automatically "more biblical" than other types of systematic theology.

**b. Bultmann.** On the last page of Bultmann's *Theology of the NT* we find a statement (in italics below), apparently made in passing, which is worth noting in relation to the question if or why the biblical documents have any meaning for the present. He places the reader before an alternative: "Either the writings of the NT can be interrogated as the 'sources' to reconstruct a picture of primitive Christianity as a phenomenon of the historical past, or the reconstruction stands in the service of the interpretation of the NT writings *under the presupposition that they have something to say for the present.*" Bultmann sides with the second alternative, and in so doing he takes for granted that the NT has such meaning. For Bultmann, as for Barth, the common denominator of meaning is the subject matter; but for Bultmann there is only one subject matter which is valid: the self-understanding as it expresses itself in the NT and as it is experienced through human history until the present time. This gives to his NT theology a strikingly uneven character. In dealing with the message of Jesus, the kerygma of the early church and its development into the second century, his method is by and large descriptive; but in the exposition of Pauline and Johannine material—and this is almost half the whole work—the tone and even the method are different, since these writings lend themselves so much more easily to anthropological interpretation.

Yet nobody could blame Bultmann for not having given reasons for what he is doing. Most of his later writings have centered around his plea for demythologizing, and it has become more and more obvious that this to Bultmann also implies a dehistoricizing of the NT. His attack on the historicism of NT interpretation (i.e., the use of the NT as a "source" for our knowledge of a historical past, be it the historical Jesus or the life and teaching of early Christianity) is centered in his emphasis on the NT as a message, a kerygma. The intent of NT theological utterances is not to state a doctrine (as for orthodoxy) and not to give the material for a concept (as treated by the historians). It is to challenge man in his own self-understanding, and consequently "the act of thinking must not be divorced from the act of living." When the NT kerygma witnesses to historical events (as in I Cor. 15:3-8), these "events" are of little significance as events; what counts is to recreate their effect on man's self-understanding. Thus —in Bultmann's own view—his NT theology becomes "theology" explicitly only where it clarifies the "believing self-understanding in its reference to the kerygma." As such—and only as such—has the NT "something to say to the present." Only on such terms does Bultmann find it possible to do justice to the intent of the NT.

*c. Cullmann.* In Cullmann, perhaps the most productive contemporary writer in the field of NT theology, we find a very different approach to biblical theology. If history is mute to Bultmann for reasons of hermeneutics and philosophy—a view which colors Bultmann's exegesis to the extent that he interprets NT eschatology as implying the end of history in Christ—Cullmann finds the key to NT theology in its understanding of time. Most discussions of Cullmann's *Christ and Time* have centered around a criticism of his distinction of linear time (biblical) versus circular time (Greek) and his idea of Christ as the center of time, but if these interpretations were refuted, the thrust of Cullmann's argument is still unchallenged when it urges us to recognize how the categories of time and history, rather than essence, nature, and eternal or existential truth, are the ones within which the NT moves (cf. Cullmann's "Le mythe dans les écrits du NT," *Numen,* I (1954), 120-35). Cullmann has thereby recaptured the mood of thought of the NT writers and stays within it long enough to work out its implication for different aspects of NT thought. On the other hand, it is not quite clear how Cullmann understands the relation between such a descriptive biblical theology in its first- and second-century terms and its translation into our present age; his hermeneutic discussions have nothing of the radical penetration of Bultmann's. His work is basically confined to the descriptive task, and when Bultmann could say about Cullmann—as he does about E. Stauffer's NT theology—that he "transforms theology into a religious philosophy of history," Cullmann's answer would be that NT theology *is,* whether we like it or not, a religious philosophy of history, and that he finds it difficult to see how this historical dimension can be translated away in any presentation of the gospel to the present age.

Such a discussion between Cullmann, Stauffer, and Bultmann would, however, be totally fruitless, for the following reasons: (*a*) All three take for granted that the NT has "meaning," but while Bultmann discusses from the vantage point of his own motivation for such a meaning, Cullmann (and Stauffer) have not clarified their answer to why or how they consider the NT as meaningful for the present age. Because of this lack of clarification, their works are read by many—perhaps most—readers as being on the same level of present meaning as Bultmann's or Barth's highly "translated" interpretations; and there are indications that they do not mind such a use of their works. A close study of Stauffer's NT theology makes it quite clear, however, that its method remains strictly descriptive; this is the more obvious in his extensive and impressive use of noncanonical intertestamental material as equally significant to picture the mood of NT thought. Cullmann's Christology follows suit in this respect. (*b*) Consequently, Bultmann's critique of such an approach should be the opposite to what it actually is. He could charge his opponents with not having seen the need for transforming or translating the NT religious philosophy of history into a contemporary theology, a need which he himself has epitomized in his quest for demythologizing. This would force his opponents to clarify why they consider such a dehistoricizing translation unnecessary or arbitrary. (*c*) Bultmann's case for the end of history in Christ and Cullmann's for ongoing history as the essence of NT eschatology have to be tested on the descriptive level. On this level a meaningful discussion can be carried on. If Cullmann seems to be much closer to the truth, Bultmann's interpretation may remain valid as a demythologized translation. But the "validity" of such an interpretation hinges then on the validity of the hermeneutic principles of the interpreter, and is of no direct consequence to the descriptive task of biblical theology.

In the present state of biblical studies, Cullmann's (and Stauffer's) contribution reminds us of Schweitzer, who felt himself compelled to present as forceful an eschatological picture of Jesus as he found in the sources, in spite of the fact that he did not see too clearly what its theological ramifications might be. This is the same as saying that these works carry the signs of hope which belong to every vigorous contribution to descriptive biblical theology, in spite of its hermeneutic unclarity. The pitfall for both the scholars and the common reader is the ambiguity by which the descriptive method is allowed to transcend its own limitations. (Stauffer later moved on to a quite different methodology, by which he claims to have established a new basis for the "historical Jesus.")

*d. Conclusions.* It thus appears that the tension between "what it meant" and "what it means" is of a competitive nature, and that when the biblical theologian becomes primarily concerned with the present meaning, he implicitly (Barth) or explicitly (Bultmann) loses his enthusiasm or his ultimate respect for the descriptive task. And yet the history of the discipline indicates that all types of biblical theology depend on the progress of this descriptive biblical theology, to which the contribution of the theologically irrelevant representatives of the *religionsgeschichtliche Schule* is strikingly great.

From the very beginning of the use of the term "biblical theology" in the seventeenth century, there has been the tension between the contemporary (be it scholasticism, conservatism, liberalism, or existentialism) and the biblical, but it is in the light of historical criticism that this tension has become clarified as one between two centuries with drastically different modes of thought. Once this difference became great enough to place the Bible further away from us—to the liberal theology the historical Jesus was closer to modern man than was the Christ confessed in the dogma of the church—the need for "translation" became a real one. Bultmann's plea for demythologizing—regardless of the way in which he carries it out—is certainly here to stay. But this makes it the more imperative to have the "original" spelled out with the highest degree of perception in its own terms. This is the nucleus of all biblical theology, and the way from this descriptive task to an answer about the meaning in the present cannot be given in the same breath on an *ad hoc* basis. It presupposes an extensive and intensive competence in the field of hermeneutics. With the original in hand, and after due clarification of the hermeneutic principles involved, we may proceed toward tentative answers to the question of the meaning here and now. But where these three stages become intermingled, there is little hope for the Bible to exert the maximum of influence on theology, church life, and culture. How much of the two last stages should belong to the discipline of biblical studies or to what extent they call for teamwork with the disciplines of theology and philosophy is a practical question, a question which in itself indicates the nature of the problem. If the three stages are carelessly intermingled, the theology as well as the preaching in our churches becomes a mixed or even an inarticulate language.

**4. Is a descriptive NT theology possible?** Many are those who express serious doubts about the possibility of the descriptive task as pictured above. Every historian is subjective in the selection of his material, and it is often said that he does more harm when he thinks himself to be objective—i.e., when he does not recognize, not to say openly state, what his presuppositions and preconceived ideas are. We can smile when we see how an earlier generation of biblical scholars peddled Kantian, Hegelian, or Ritschlian ideas, all the time subjectively convinced that they were objective scholars who only stated "facts." All this naturally calls for caution; but the relativity of human objectivity does not give us an excuse to excel in bias, not even when we state our bias in an introductory chapter. What is more important, however, is that once we confine ourselves to the task of descriptive biblical theology as a field in its own right, the material itself gives us means to check whether our interpretation is correct or not. To be sure, the sources are not extensive enough to allow us certainty in all areas; and the right to use some comparative material, while disregarding other such material as irrelevant for our texts, gives further reason for uncertainty; but from the point of view of method it is clear that our only concern is to find out what these words meant when uttered or written by the prophet, the priest, the evangelist, or the apostle—and regardless of their meaning in later stages of religious history, our own included. Such a program is by and large a new feature in biblical studies, a mature fruit of the historical method. It does not necessarily disregard the intent of the biblical texts, but captures the implication of their kerygmatic nature when it lifts them out of the framework of "theological concepts" and places them back into their *Sitz im Leben* (the "life situation") of Israel or the church.

This descriptive task can be carried out by believer and agnostic alike. The believer has the advantage of automatic empathy with the believers in the text—but his faith constantly threatens to have him modernize the material, if he does not exercise the canons of descriptive scholarship rigorously. The agnostic has the advantage of feeling no such temptations, but his power of empathy must be considerable if he is to identify himself sufficiently with the believer of the first century. Yet both can work side by side, since no other tools are called for than those of description in the terms indicated by the texts themselves. The meaning for the present—in which the two interpreters are different—is not involved, and thus total co-operation is possible, and part of their mutual criticism is to watch whether concern for meaning or distaste for meaning colors the descriptions where it should not.

**5. The descriptive approach and the OT.** The tension between the meanings becomes further complicated when we turn to the nature of OT theology, and this for two main reasons: (*a*) The OT contains material from many centuries of Israelite life. This makes it obvious that there are different layers of meaning within the same account. The account of the sacrifice of Isaac may well once have functioned as God's own command of substituting an animal for human sacrifices, but in its present setting in Gen. 22 the meaning is clearly seen as a witness to Abraham's ultimate obedience. Jacob's dream at Bethel seems to be a tradition by which the validity of the cult of the N kingdom was upheld by reference to how the patriarch had found Yahweh at that place, but once the rivalry between the two kingdoms was a dead issue, the story took on—or returned to—the meaning of a more general epiphany. This problem of interpretation and hermeneutics is certainly not confined to the OT; it forms the crucial problem of gospel research when we try to push beyond the evangelists to the actual words and deeds of Jesus. But in the OT it is a more flagrant and paramount problem. Thus already the descriptive task is faced with the constant question of "layers of meaning" through the history and transmission of OT traditions. The history of interpretation is woven into the very fabric of the biblical texts themselves, and the canonization of Torah, Prophets, and Writings did not disrupt the ongoing reinterpretation in sectarian or normative Judaism, as we learn from the intertestamental and the rabbinic material. Thus any statement of a descriptive sort about what an OT passage meant has to be accompanied by an address: for whom and at what stage of Israelite or Jewish history? The track along which the biblical theologian pursues the meaning of the OT is thus that of the ongoing religious life of Israel as the chosen people of God and as responding to the events in its history which they interpret as the acts of God.

*b)* Secondly, the church was born out of a dispute with Jewish interpreters of the OT regarding its meaning, and first-century Christian theology of the more verbalized sort, as that found in Paul, centers around the terms on which the church finds the OT meaningful—e.g., as promise now fulfilled or as law binding on the members of the church. The Christian claim to the OT rested on the conviction that Jesus as the risen Christ was the Messiah to whom the OT witnessed. The church thereby sided with those interpreters of the OT who, like, e.g., the Qumran community, saw the center of the OT in its prophecies and promises, including those found in the five books of the Law, while the Jewish exegesis which became normative more and more emphasized the law as the core of revelation and the precious token of Israel's chosen status (*see* LAW IN THE OT). Neither interpretation had any similarity with the one prevailing in the theologized form of the Wellhausen interpretation of Israelite history, where the significance of the OT was seen in the evolution of ethical monotheism. Here, again, it was the radicals of the *religionsgeschichtliche Schule* who caused the construction of this liberal interpretation to crumble, corrupted and weakened as it was by the apologetic interest in a meaning for the present.

Any writer in the field of OT theology must be aware of this double outcome of the ongoing interpretation of the OT material, each within the framework of a community of faith. For the descriptive task both outcomes appear as live options, and neither of them can claim to be the right one if judged by the potentialities of the OT material itself. The act of faith by which the interpretations parted ways does not add anything to the OT material as such. Thus a Christian and a Jewish OT theology differ only where the question of meaning is pursued beyond the material and the period of the OT texts themselves. Such a Christian OT theology may find its organizing principle in the NT understanding of the OT in first-century terms (another descriptive task being thus involved) or in any one principle of Christian hermeneutics from later centuries, our own included. Nobody could deny the validity or even the necessity for the church of such a task, especially since it is in the very tradition of the NT itself. Yet the same warning which emerged out of our study of the meanings in NT theology applies to such an enterprise. The distinction between the descriptive function as the core of all biblical theology on the one hand, and the hermeneutics and up-to-date translation on the other, must be upheld if there is to be any chance for the original to act creatively on the minds of theologians and believers of our time.

**6. "Sacred history" and the unity of the Bible.** In OT theology even more than in its NT counterpart, history presents itself as the loom of the theological fabric. In spite of its intentions to be historical, the liberal interpretation of the OT overlooked this fact, substituting its evolutionistic interest in the development of ethics and monotheism for the sacred history in which Israel experienced its existence. In more recent times an anthropological approach to OT theology—not much different from Bultmann's approach, but unaware of its implicit demythologizing and dehistoricizing—has been tried with some success. Its success is partly due to its superior descriptive power if compared with that of the liberals.

In sharp contrast to what is called—with a gross generalization—"the Greek," we find the Semitic or Hebrew or biblical anthropology spelled out, and sometimes this very anthropology is hailed as the essence of biblical theology. But in works like those of G. E. Wright and G. von Rad, OT theology seeks its center where the ongoing life of Israel—from a descriptive point of view—experienced it—i.e., in its own history as a peculiar people, chosen by God. Especially in Wright this approach is coupled with arguments for the uniqueness of Israel as compared with surrounding people and cultures, a claim which seems to be a carry-over from another methodology. Israel's uniqueness was hardly based on its ideas about God or man but in its ELECTION consciousness, which in turn has given its thinking distinctive features which we may well call unique. *See* COVENANT.

But the thrust of an OT theology which finds the center in the acts of God (Wright) or in Yahweh's revelation through words and deeds in history (von Rad), is ultimately to establish that HISTORY is not only a stage upon which God (*see* GOD, NT) displays his nature through his acts, but that the drama itself is one of history. The salvation which is promised is one within history, either in terms of return of the dispersed people from all the ends of the earth or as a New Jerusalem and a glorified Israel in a new age, which in spite of its otherworldly features comes in time and history at the end of this present age (*see* ESCHATOLOGY OF THE NT). This historical consciousness of Israel lives by the remembering of the past and the ever new interpretation of it as a promise for the future. The cultic festivals, with their roots in Near Eastern ritual and their manifestations in the sacred kingship of the Davidic dynasty, become projected toward the eschatological future of bliss, righteousness, and peace. In all this the common denominator—from a descriptive point of view—is neither certain concepts of God as One or as acting, nor an anthropology peculiar to the Bible, but the ongoing life of a people cultivating the traditions of its history in the light of its self-understanding. It is guided therein by its priests, prophets, and teachers of wisdom, and thus this people moves toward a sure but ever evasive *eschaton,* keeping the law, which is the token of their chosenness.

Such a framework for OT theology is the only one which takes the descriptive task seriously, since it does not borrow its categories from the NT or later Jewish or Christian interpretation but finds the organizing principle in the very life situations out of which the OT material emerges as meaningful to the life of the people. From such a layer of meaning we may move back into the meaning of the different elements which were placed in this framework of sacred history. This may lead us to patterns of thought and blocks of tradition originally quite unrelated to the historical consciousness of Israel; but only with a full recognition of this framework can we adequately go behind it and analyze what the original elements of the tradition may have been and how they were modified by their setting in the religion of Israel. Only so can we know to what extent they retained their character as remnants—whether weak or vigorous and creative—of an earlier period within the total tradition. As such remnants they deserve the fullest descriptive treatment and should not be swallowed up by a generalizing sweep of sacred history as though that sweep constituted the entire content of the OT.

When the OT is treated in this fashion as the living and growing tradition of a people, it yields a theology which brings us up to the parting of the ways by Jews and Christians. The description thereof places us where the NT stands, and we face the issues of NT theology as once Jews and Christians faced them in the first century. It brings into the NT the dimension of time and history which is essential to our understanding of the NT in its own terms. The announcement by Jesus that the new age is impending, and the faith of the early church that the Messiah is enthroned in heaven since he is risen and since the Holy Spirit has been poured out, comes as a vigorous claim for fulfilment of the OT promises, not accepted by the majority of the Jews. Yet Paul is convinced that before the kingdom is established on earth as it is now in heaven, the Jews will accept Jesus as the Messiah (Rom. 9–11). Thereby the drama of this age will come to its glorious end; the new age will be ushered in. Jewish exegesis in the Christian era went rather in another direction, and the eschatology which had reached its peak in Christianity as well as in parts of Judaism became more and more toned down. The emphasis shifted from the hopes for the future to the obedience in the present under the law. Rabbinic Judaism established itself as the normative interpretation of the OT, but the common denominator remained the same: the ELECTION consciousness which accepts the law as the gracious token of God's special favor to his people.

The only question which is beyond reach for such a descriptive approach is: Who was right—the Jews or the Christians? Its answer remains what it always was, an act of faith. If we approached OT theology in terms of developing ethical monotheism, we could, at least theoretically, arrive at an answer. This is, at any rate, what the liberal theologians implied when they hailed Jesus as a teacher superior both to the best of the prophets and to the wisest of the rabbis. But once we have accepted history as the fabric of biblical theology, we are thrown back to the same choice of faith which faced the first century. History does not answer such questions; it only poses them.

This highly simplified sketch of biblical theology in the encounter between the testaments suggests also in what sense there can be a biblical theology where the OT and the NT are held together as a unity. The significance of the OT for the NT is thus shown to be inescapable, just as it was in the early church before there was a NT in our sense. On the basis of the OT and its fulfilment in Christ rests the Christian claim to be the chosen ones of God, the true Israel in Christ, and—if Gentile by birth—"honorary Jews," heirs to the promises given to Israel. The crucial question arises when we ask what impact the NT should have on the presentation of

OT theology. When biblical theology allows for such impact, it goes beyond its descriptive task, unless what is being attempted is merely a description of how the early church understood the unity between the OT and its fulfilment in what came to be the NT. But if the biblical theologian should go on to say that this is consequently what the OT text meant, he would be making either a statement of his own faith or a statement about the faith of the NT. If he says that this is what the OT means for the present-day Christian, he has proceeded from description, via hermeneutics, to a contemporary interpretation.

Thus the treatment of the Bible as a unity in this sense is beyond the task of descriptive biblical theology. Indeed, such a biblical theology will tend to discourage and prevent too facile a unification. To cite one example: Paul's radical concentration on the OT promises and his view of the law as holy and yet obsolete, once Christ has come, led Marcion to do away with the OT. He was in a certain way faithful to Paul—far more so than some Jewish Christians—but since his conceptual framework did not allow for a God who dealt with mankind differently in different dispensations, he could not imagine God as the originator of a holy law which he later declared obsolete. In its defense against Marcion, the church by and large forgot Paul's dialectic of time, and leaned over backward placing the OT and the NT on an equal basis. A truly descriptive biblical theology would have prevented both extremes. Thus the historian, with his descriptive approach, may clarify the issue of the relation between the two testaments.

There is, however, one way in which descriptive biblical theology does consider the Bible as a unity. The "sacred history" continues into the NT. Israel's election consciousness is transferred and heightened by the Christians—Jews and Gentiles alike. History is still the matrix of theology. Jesus does not come with a new doctrine about forgiveness for sinners; when he comes, "it so happens" that sinners accept him and the righteous do not. The first shall be the last. He does not leave his disciples primarily as a group of pupils who have rehearsed the "teachings of Jesus" as a lesson to teach others, but he has promised them a place as princes in the new Israel and has urged them to watch for the signs of the times and the coming of the kingdom. They do so; and his RESURRECTION and the HOLY SPIRIT are indications to them that Jesus is now enthroned as the Christ on the right hand of God. The PAROUSIA must be close at hand, and the Spirit is the efficient and sufficient down payment of their share in the age to come. As Israel lives through its history as a chosen people, so are the Christians now gathered together as the chosen ones, the church enjoying a higher degree of anticipation of God's redeeming grace and power than did even the messianic sect at Qumran. God is still the God of a people with an ongoing history, however short it may be: the NT develops its ecclesiology.

It is in such a framework that NT theology can be properly described, and this framework is basically the same as that of OT theology. Here is the common denominator from a descriptive point of view. Within this framework, which gives us the *Sitz im*

*Leben* of NT thought as a message and a self-presentation, we may study different ideas and concepts. We may find out how they are related or how they conflict with one another. But none of these ideas exists as general and eternal truth apart from the self-understanding of the church as the chosen community.

Thus there is a unity of the Bible on a historical basis. And this is the basis on which the two testaments came together. If, on the other hand, we approach the unity of the Bible or one of the testaments from the point of view of concepts and ideas, we may still be able to discern a certain unity in its anthropology, in its concept of God, or in its attitude toward ethics. A descriptive study of, e.g., Paul's concept of justification would find the roots in the Song of Deborah, perhaps the oldest piece of tradition in the whole Bible (Judg. 5:11; צדקות = "saving acts of God"). The Gospel of Mark could be seen in relation to the kerygma in Acts 10; I Cor. 15, as we have learned from C. H. Dodd's *Apostolic Preaching and Its Developments*. But we would look for a *type* of unity which was different from the organic unity to which the testaments themselves witness. And we would be faced with a diversity of views without the means to understand how they fell into a meaningful pattern for the biblical writers themselves. Paul's dialectic attitude toward the law—mentioned above in comparison with Marcion—is a case in point. We would be inclined to see a great—or merely contradictory—paradox in his statement about the holiness and the obsoleteness of the law, if we did not recognize that Paul thought in the pattern of dispensations. The tension between the teaching of Jesus and the early theology of the church would remain a total enigma were it not for the fact that the disciples interpreted what followed after his death as a drastic step forward in the timetable of God, leading toward the Parousia. Our description has to detect and clarify such a development. It could, however, hardly answer the question whether the disciples were right or wrong in their interpretation. We can only describe what they did and why they thought they were right while others thought they were wrong.

What has now been presented as the first and crucial task of biblical theology—i.e., its descriptive function—thus yields the original in its own terms, limiting the interpretation to what it meant in its own setting. An attempt has been made to show that such a task does not necessarily imply the disintegration of the biblical material into unrelated bits of antiquated information. It is quite capable of presenting the different elements as an organic unity *if that unity is the one which actually holds the material together in the Bible itself.* It has been indicated that any question of meaning beyond the one suggested by the sources themselves tends to lessen the challenge of the original to the present-day theologian and makes him unaware of the hermeneutic problem as a *sine qua non* for any such interpretation.

**B. *THE HERMENEUTIC QUESTION.* 1. As raised by a descriptive biblical theology.** A more thorough familiarity with the net result of such a descriptive approach as the one outlined above raises the hermeneutic question in a somewhat new form.

No period of Christian theology has been as radically exposed to a consistent attempt to relive the theology of its first adherents. The ideal of an empathetic understanding of the first century without borrowing categories from later times has never been an ideal before, nor have the comparative sources for such an adventure been as close at hand and as well analyzed. There have always been bits and pieces of an appeal to the original meaning over against different later dogmas and practices of the church. The School of Antioch fought the School of Alexandria by such means; the Reformers argued with the papal theologians, and the Anabaptists with the Reformers, on such a basis; the pietists criticized the orthodox scholastics in the same fashion, and the liberal theologians claimed the same type of arguments against the evangelicals, etc. But never before was there a frontal nonpragmatic, nonapologetic attempt to describe OT or NT faith and practice from within its original presuppositions, and with due attention to its own organizing principles, regardless of its possible ramifications for those who live by the Bible as the Word of God.

The descriptive approach has led us far beyond a conglomeration of diverse ideas, the development of which we may be able to trace. We are now ushered right into a world of biblical thought which deserves the name "theology" just as much as do the thoughts of Augustine, Thomas, Calvin, and Schleiermacher. The translation of its content cannot any more be made piecemeal. The relation to the historical record is not any more one where systematic theology takes the raw material of nonsystematic data of revelation and gives to it systematic structure and theological stature. The relation is not one between a witness of a theologically innocent faith and a mature and sophisticated systematic theology. It is a relation between two highly developed types of theology. On the one hand, theologies of history, from which all statements about God, Christ, man, righteousness, and salvation derive their meaning and connotations, in terms of their function within the plan and on the plane of history; and on the other hand, theologies of an ontological sort, where Christianity is understood in terms of the nature of God, Christ, man, etc. *See* GOD, NT; CHRIST; MAN, NATURE OF (NT).

Within this pattern of nature or essence Christian theology has always tried to do justice to the historical element in the biblical material. But under the pressure of the thought-pattern inherent in the Western theological approach, biblical eschatology —i.e., the matrix of NT thought—was taken care of in a "last chapter" of systematic theology dealing with the "last things" (*see* ESCHATOLOGY OF THE NT). Thereby the very structure of biblical thought was transformed and its eschatology inactivated.

In more recent Protestant theology there have been serious attempts to do more justice to eschatology as the overarching category of systematic theology and the motif of the "two aeons," this age and the age to come, has been stressed—e.g., by the Lundensian theologians. But once again the outcome is a radical transformation, in that the aeons become internalized as levels of existence and experience in the mind and life of every Christian according to the formula "At the same time justified and sinner." The life on the border between the two dispensations as Paul knew them is lifted out of its historical context and becomes a timeless description of an inner dialectic of the Christian existence.

The focal point for a theological preservation of the historical dimension in the biblical material was found quite naturally in the stern insistence on the INCARNATION in Jesus Christ. But in this process the Incarnation was more and more intensively developed in terms of its ramifications for the nature of Jesus Christ, while its original connotations were far more centered in the chronological pattern of the Johannine Prologue: God had *now* come to men in Jesus Christ to tabernacle among them in a glory which outshone that of Moses and the law.

The situation could perhaps be best analyzed in the realm of NT Christology (*see* CHRIST), where significant strands of tradition display what later on came to be branded and banned as adoptionism—i.e., the concept of Jesus, who was made the Christ in his BAPTISM, or in his RESURRECTION, or by his ASCENSION. In the light of later doctrinal development it is easy to see why such a Christology was deemed heretical. But there is no indication that there was any conscious tension or argument, within the NT and in its time, between an adoptionist position and one which spoke of Jesus Christ in terms of pre-existence or virgin birth. This was apparently not a matter of conflict. It became so only when the biblical witness was forced to yield the answer to the question about the nature of Jesus Christ, and when this very question became the shibboleth of true doctrine. As long as the question remains within the theology of history, it does not ask what Jesus Christ is or how human and divine nature go together in him. It centers around the question: Who is he? Is he the Messiah or isn't he? In such a context an adoptionist answer coincides for all practical purposes with that of the pre-existence type. But once this framework is lost, the answers come miles apart from one another as contradictory, and the kerygmatic statements in Acts 2:32-37 are a sheer liability to the orthodox theologian when they hail Jesus as the one whom God has made both Lord and Christ after his crucifixion, placing him on his right side as the enthroned Messiah in heaven, whence he now could and did pour out the promised Holy Spirit as a sizable down payment of the age to come.

It is perhaps even more striking when Acts 3:18-21 urges repentance in order that times of refreshment might come from God and that he might send the aforetime-appointed Messiah, namely Jesus, who is now retained in heaven. Here the Parousia is really not the Second Coming of later theology. There is only one coming of the Messiah, the one at the end of time. We are used to considering the First Coming—i.e., the earthly ministry of Jesus, as a clear, uncomplicated "coming" of the Messiah, but recognize how many complications arose out of the interpretation of the Second Coming. To the theology manifested in Acts 3, the problem seems to have been the opposite one. The Parousia—what we call the Second Coming—was no "problem"; it was part of the Jewish expectations concerning the age to come. The problem was rather in the opposite

direction: To what extent was the First Coming, the earthly ministry of Jesus, a real coming? How much of an anticipation did it imply, and to what extent did Jesus exercise messianic power within it? Once he was hailed as the Messiah enthroned in heaven, it was clear to the gospel writers that Jesus was the Christ, but there are enough indications left in the Synoptic gospels to show that he was so by inference from what had happened after Calvary, and by references about what he was to become.

Thus the pattern of history in this type of NT theology sheds new light on the discussion about the messianic consciousness of Jesus. Those who deny such a consciousness and credit the church with having made Jesus their Messiah overlook the nature of this theology of history, for which there needed to be no distortion of facts in the belief that Jesus was made the Messiah in his ascension and enthronement. Those who claim a straight messianic consciousness in Jesus overlook the evidence that the messiahship in Jesus' earthly ministry has a strong futuristic note. But from the vantage point of post-Resurrection/Ascension the church confesses: Jesus is the Messiah now, and consequently he was the Messiah then—but he had not really become so by then, nor is he yet the Messiah here on earth as he is to be at the Parousia. Such an attempt to catch the theological meaning as found in Acts 2-3 gives no sense to one who inquires into the nature of Jesus Christ, and it sounds strange to a "yes-or-no" approach to the problem of the messianic consciousness of Jesus. But it was highly significant to those who were eager to understand where they were in the messianic timetable of Jewish and Christian eschatology. He who changes the question can only be misled or confused by using the biblical text as a direct answer to it.

Texts and problems have been chosen from some of the highly controversial areas of NT exegesis only as illustrations to clarify the problem before us. The exegesis involved may well require correction or refutation, but the thrust of the descriptive method would always be of the same nature. The hermeneutic problem of biblical theology therefore centers in the clash between two types of theology. Each type includes a wide variety of alternatives. On the biblical side there are the different types of OT theology, some contemporary with one another, some later developments of earlier strata. In the NT it is somewhat easier to discern a Matthean, Markan, Lukan, Johannine, or Pauline theology, etc. But they all live within the presupposition of their respective centuries, and they all answer questions which require a historical consciousness and an awareness of where in God's history they now stand.

On the systematic side there is perhaps an even greater diversity, but in our Western tradition we find the questions asked by the systematic theologian to be by their very nature above history and beyond change. Such a systematic approach has been considerably intensified by biblical criticism, with its conflicting answers to exegetical problems and its radical doubt or mild uncertainty about many events and data on which systematic theology would have to rest its case. Lessing's statement that eternal truth cannot be derived from historical data became the more pertinent to systematic theology once the biblical basis for orthodox Christianity was summoned to constant trial before the courts of historical criticism. But in a certain sense Christian theology had freed itself from its historical matrix already in the time of the apologists of the second century when the case for Christianity was spelled out in the terms of Hellenistic philosophy. It would be unwise to exclude some elements within the OT and the NT from a similar tendency; thus the need for and the possibility of a translation of biblical theology into new categories of thought is taken for granted from the very outset. Orthodoxy never had repristination as its program in the periods of its strength. The possibility of translation was given—as it is for Barth—in the reality of the subject matter, apart from its intellectual manifestation in the thought-patterns of the original documents. God and Christ were not Semites in such a sense that the biblical pattern of thought was identified with revelation itself.

Consequently, theology through the centuries acted in great freedom and with good conscience and considerable creativity. The fathers and the Reformers alike had no idea of a biblical theology apart from other theological endeavors. They were convinced that they were biblical theologians in the only sense one could be a theologian; in this respect Barth is certainly right in claiming the authority of Calvin and Luther for his biblical approach. But once the concern for a biblical theology as distinguished from other types of systematic theology has made itself manifest, a new problem arises. By way of a wide variety of hybrids where systematic and biblical categories were hopelessly intermingled, this concern has now brought us to the point where we can make reasonably clear statements about the meanings of the original in its own terms. This is why we have the right to say that the result of descriptive biblical theology has raised the hermeneutic problem in a somewhat new form.

**2. Alternative answers to the hermeneutic question.** In the light of descriptive biblical theology, it becomes possible to pass tentative and relative judgments on the alternative ways in which systematic theologians have stated the meaning for the present day—or for all times, if that is their conscious aim—of the biblical material. Such judgments can be made on the basis of the degree to which systematic theology succeeds in communicating the intention implied in the biblical texts, an intention which only a precise and uncompromised study of the original could detect. But such a judgment would always remain tentative, since the task of systematic theology is by its very nature one of translation from one pattern of thought into another, and every true and great translation is a creative effort, not just a painstaking and nearsighted exchange of the precise words of one language with its lexicographical equivalents in another language. Aquila's Greek text stands as the horrifying example of such a senseless approach. On the linguistic level we hold the view—at least Protestants do—that there is no language into which the Bible could not be translated well enough to communicate its message; and the student of the Greek gospels is already once removed from the Aramaic vernacular of Jesus' teaching. If this

analogy were one of considerable precision, it would imply that there could be few philosophies, epistemologies, anthropologies, etc., which could not furnish the framework for a systematic theology by which the meaning of the Christian scripture could be stated. The history of Christian theology gives us reason to accept the analogy to a considerable extent. And the fact that the original is available gives us the right and the audacity to encourage such translation activity.

The attempt of the so-called "liberal theology" to detect the meaning for today in the evolution of an ever more refined religious insight with a higher level of ethics could hardly be ruled out as one of the alternative answers to the quest for meaning. Its validity as a Christian theology would hinge upon its ability to live with a growing awareness that its categories of meaning are utterly alien to biblical thought. Such an awareness is harder for the liberals to take than for any other theologians, since they traditionally have rested their case on its historical truth, and claimed the historical Jesus as the first protagonist for their own views. In their attempt to grasp the intention of the biblical message, they were unusually handicapped.

In the wake of liberal theology in its academic form—in its popular form it is still very much with us—came the tendency to establish contact with the world of descriptive biblical theology by simply substituting its categories for those traditional to Western theology. Well aware of the peril of modernizing Jesus, one was less afraid of archaizing oneself. The achievements of the descriptive biblical theology were dumped right into the twentieth century. The fact that those results now displayed enough structure and religious intensity to give the impression of a real theology made it quite tempting to try such a return to the prelogical, the Semitic, the Hebraic, the first century. All these categories were now subsumed under the heading "biblical," and this in an evaluating fashion, so that the theological ideal became an ill-considered parallel to the well-considered descriptive ideal of divesting oneself of the twentieth century. The "biblical way of thinking" was spelled out over against "the Greek." Once more the descriptive and the contemporary became interwoven, this time on the terms of the result of the descriptive approach. From a theological point of view this meant that revelation was identified with patterns of thought and culture; the need or the possibility of creative translation—i.e., the very glory of systematic theology through the ages—was undercut. No serious attempts at a conscious translation were made.

Such a criticism could certainly not be directed against what we may call the thoroughgoing translations, where the tendency is ahistorical or even antihistorical. Paul Tillich and Rudolf Bultmann are two pronounced representatives of such answers to the hermeneutic problem. Neither of them finds anything normative in a theology of history as presented by the descriptive approach. To both of them history is utterly mute as far as theological meaning is concerned. Secondly, historical data are to them too shaky a foundation for the theological enterprise. Tillich thus approaches theology from an analysis of

Being, and he is consistent enough to claim no, or little, biblical support for such a category. Bultmann, on the other hand, finds his point of departure as well as arrival in human self-understanding, and for this he claims considerable biblical authority, since, according to him, the very intention of the kerygma (*see* PREACHING) is to challenge man's self-understanding. It appears, however, that Tillich, in spite of being perhaps the least "biblical"—in a conscious sense and by mode of language—of all contemporary theologians, is capable of communicating a wider range of biblical intention than does Bultmann with his highly anthropological concentration.

The most common response to the challenge of descriptive biblical theology is perhaps what may be called the semihistorical translation. Here the historical nature of revelation is taken seriously. The Bible is the record of the acts of God in history, and the kerygma is the powerful proclamation of these acts, a proclamation which shares in the creative power of the acts themselves. Thus the church is nurtured and renewed through the ages by this creative Word by which it rehearses the acts of God in sacred history. But somewhere along the line this sacred history has stopped, and there is only plain history left, with a more general PROVIDENCE at work. Thereby the God who acts becomes more and more the God who did act in biblical history. Consequently his acts appear as performed on the stage of history in order to demonstrate his nature. Theology reads his nature off the record of sacred history. The acts of God in history and the human response to them become calcified into a mold. This mold is then used by theology to make the true images or concepts of God as Him Who Acts. The difficulty with such a translation into nonpropositional and nonphilosophical concepts is that it accepts the historical framework of biblical thought for biblical times, since it yields the illustrations for our grasp of God's nature and will; but once the canon of the NT has drawn the line, there is a change of categories. Sacred history has come to an end, and what remains is a history where these deep-frozen images of God's acts are constantly brought to life in the remembrance of the church. The tension between a historical understanding of the Bible and a theologically void history of the church raises grave problems of inconsistency.

Such a problem would lead us to suggest that the only consistent alternatives would be either a radical, ahistorical translation as mentioned above, or—if the historical framework of biblical thought were to be retained—a systematic theology where the bridge between the centuries of biblical events and our own time was found in the actual history of the church as still ongoing sacred history of God's people. The blueprint for such a theology could be found in that self-understanding of Israel, both new and old, which descriptive biblical theology has laid bare as the common denominator of biblical thought. Such a theology would conceive of the Christian existence as a life by the fruits of God's acts in Jesus Christ, rather than as a faith according to concepts deduced from the teaching of the prophets, Jesus, and Paul regarding God's acts. It would exercise some of the same freedom which Paul's and the other NT letters do when they refrain from any nostalgic attempts to play Galilee into their theology by transforming the teaching of Jesus' earthly ministry into a system of theology and ethics. It would recognize that God is still the God who acts in history when he leads his church to new lands and new cultures and new areas of concern. A theology which retains history as a theologically charged category finds in its ecclesiology the overarching principles of interpretation and meaning. It does not permit its ecclesiology to be transferred to the second last chapter in its systematic works, followed by that on an equally inactivated eschatology. A theological awareness of sacred history seems to imply by inner necessity a growing recognition of the church as something far beyond an organization for the promotion of evangelism and theology. Through the ongoing sacred history, which is commonly labeled "church history," the fruits of God's acts in covenant and in the Christ are handed down to the present time. Within this history the task of preaching and theology under the guidance of the Holy Spirit is part of an ongoing sacred history. The chasm between the centuries is theologically as well as historically bridged by history itself, not only by a timeless kerygma which reaches the individual in an ever-repeated punctiliar action. The church lives, not only by the aorist of the Holy Spirit, but by the perfect tense as the Greeks understood it: an action which is completed and the effects of which are still with us.

**3. The significance of "canon" for biblical theology.** Such an approach would raise the question of the CANON (i.e., the limitation of the Bible to—usually—sixty-six books, thirty-nine in the OT and twenty-seven in the NT) in its sharpest form. As far as the descriptive approach goes, the canon can have no crucial significance. The church has a "Bible," but the descriptive approach knows it only as the "Bible of the church." In order to grasp the meaning of an OT or NT text in its own time, the comparative material—e.g., the intertestamental literature (Enoch, Testaments of the Twelve Patriarchs, Jubilees, etc.; *see* APOCRYPHA; PSEUDEPIGRAPHA) or the APOSTOLIC FATHERS, some of which clearly antedate some NT writings—is of equal or even greater significance than some canonical material. The revival of biblical theology in our own generation depends greatly on the way in which such material was brought to bear on the original meaning of biblical texts. But when the descriptive task is addressing itself to the interplay between different parts of the Bible, as, e.g., the NT understanding of the OT, it naturally takes cognizance of the limits of, as well as of the very idea of, canon. The descriptive approach also yields considerable insight into the nature and motivations for canonization itself and is capable of understanding the need as well as the rationalization connected with the long process of canonization. This in itself is one of the most puzzling and fascinating interplays of historical circumstances and theological concerns.

Once we go beyond the descriptive approach, the canon of scripture becomes crucial. To many of the modern types of biblical theology, the phenomenon of canonical scriptures seems to count little. To Barth it is INSPIRATION rather than canon that matters, and the process of canonization is an external feature which neither adds to nor substracts from the power of the inspired writings to allow the Word to authenticate itself ever anew to him who hears. This is actually consistent with an ahistorical theology, since canonization so obviously is a historical process. It strikes the historian, nevertheless, that the concept of inspiration was of little or no avail in the first centuries of church history, when the church moved toward a closed canon. Apostolic origin, a doctrine in agreement with the succession of teaching, and wide usage and recognition in the churches were the chief criteria when the early church dealt with a wide range of writings, many of which were recognized as equally inspired with those finally received among the twenty-seven. But once the canon was closed, the doctrine of inspiration served well as an answer to the question: Why are these books different from all other books? To Bultmann, canon seems to be of little significance. The Christian self-understanding, to which the Bible caters, is found within it, but there are also parts of it which do not display it. Furthermore, its meaning for the present rests on the same basis as that on which any historical document has "meaning" beyond its value as a source for historical information. Finally, the understanding of the intention of the Bible as kerygmatic is not deduced from its canonical nature; on the contrary, it is the kerygmatic nature which gives the Bible its claim to authority.

To the radically historical alternative, as outlined above, much depends on the understanding of canon as a crucial category of any theological enterprise. This is certainly what we would expect if the historical nature of revelation is retained in a theologically potent framework of the sacred history of God's people. It is quite significant that, e.g., a biblical theologian like Cullmann, who has given such a strong impetus to the historical alternative, has also addressed himself extensively to the problem of tradition and canonization (see the chapters "The Plurality of the Gospels as a Theological Problem in Antiquity" and "The Tradition," in *The Early Church* [1956]), and that his discussion takes the form of a new attempt to clarify how Protestant and Roman Catholic theology differ in their understanding of the interplay between the continuous tradition and the line drawn around the Bible by canonization.

To the historical approach the question raised by Harnack's studies in the NT canon becomes theologically significant: Why is there a NT, not only a fourth part added to the three units of the OT (Law, Prophets, Writings)? The descriptive approach suggests a theological answer: The NT—as well as the church itself—rests on the return of the Spirit. Judaism in the time of Jesus lived under the conviction that the Spirit had ceased, and when the question of valid scriptures was discussed, this cessation was related to the last of the prophets (i.e., Malachi). They recognized themselves as living in a period when Israel depended on the scriptural interpretations of scribes whose authority rested on faithful transmission, not on the Spirit in which one could say, as the prophets had done, "Thus saith the Lord." But they cherished the hope and the promise of the return of the Spirit. This would be one of the

crucial manifestations of the coming of the new age. Thus it is quite natural that the conviction of the church that this new age had arrived and manifested itself in the Holy Spirit also gave the basis and theological rationale for what came to be the NT.

It is worth noting, however, that the closing of the NT canon is not based on any argument similar to that of Judaism regarding the OT—viz., that the Spirit ceased again. Such a view would have undercut the very faith and life of the church and was never considered in the argumentation regarding the NT canon in the first centuries. The development from diversified oral and written traditions to the twenty-seven books of the NT was of a more historical nature, guided by the necessity to protect the original from more and more undependable elaborations and distortions, some "heretical" but quite a few properly orthodox in their intentions. The gift of prophetic and inspired teaching was still a recognized phenomenon, an ever-repeated "aorist" of God's dealing with his church. But the significance of Jesus Christ and his apostles as ἐφάπαξ ("once for all"), and as the very basis on which the church was built—i.e., the "perfect-tense" dimension of biblical thought, as referred to above—called for a distinction between this and what the church understood as original and as its magna charta. Thus Cullmann seems to be right when he suggests that early Christian tradition bore within it the element which served as a compelling cause for the process of canonization. This element may be defined as the "perfect-tense" element of Christian theology. As such it affirms the acts of God as unique in Christ and his apostles, but it also points toward an ongoing history of the theological existence of the church. God's acts are not punctiliar aorists, frozen and canned within the canon, nor do they belong to the timeless present tense of mysticism.

The question as to the meaning of the Bible in the present—as distinguished from the meaning in the past as stated by descriptive biblical theology—receives its theological answer from the canonical status of scripture. In its most radical form, the question was: Do these old writings have any meaning beyond their significance as sources for the past? On what basis could it be valid to translate them into new modes of thought? On what basis could such an original—and such a translation—have a normative function for the life of the church? Such questions can be answered only within the consciousness of the church. The answer rests on the act of faith by which Israel and its sister by adoption, the church, recognizes its history as sacred history, and finds in these writings the epitome of the acts of God. As such these writings are meaningful to the church in any age. It is as canon, and only as canon, that there is a Bible, an OT and a NT as well as the whole Bible of the church as a unity. The old question of whether the Bible rests on the church or the church on the Bible is a misleading question from the point of view of the historical alternative. To be sure, the church "chose" its canon. But it did so under the impact of the acts of God by which it itself came into existence. The process of canonization is one of recognition, not one of creation *ex nihilo* or *ex theologia*.

One could perhaps see the Protestant Reformation as a reaffirmation of the line drawn protectively around the canon. In a situation when the growth of tradition threatened to submerge the "original"—as had the traditions rejected as noncanonical in the second and third centuries—Luther and Calvin reinforce the distinctiveness of the original and its superior authority in the life of the church. There are many things which we would like to know, historically as well as theologically, beyond what the Scriptures tell us. In the Roman Catholic tradition such quite legitimate and pious curiosity has centered around Mary, the mother of Jesus. Against such and other elaborating traditions the Reformers take a firm stand on *sola scriptura* as sufficient, yea, more than sufficient, unto salvation. The canon is enforced, and such a return to the "original"—given the circumstances of the time—engenders one of the most spectacular renewals of theology and church life that history has seen.

This is in its own way a suggestive illustration of how an exposure to the "original" plays into the life of the church. It gives us theology in a new key and breaks through many cherished presuppositions. It is perhaps not too much to suggest that the highly developed descriptive biblical theology of our own period in the long run may have a slightly similar effect. This is not to hail our age as capable of a new Reformation. But it does suggest that all theological renewal and creativity has as one of its components a strong exposure to the "original" beyond the presuppositions and the inherited frame of thought of our immediate predecessors in the theological task. Otherwise the history of theology would be an uninterrupted chain reaction of a philosophical nature, with Augustine correcting the earlier fathers, Thomas Aquinas correcting Augustine, Luther refuting Thomas, Schleiermacher touching up Luther and Barth, and Tillich carrying the traditional discussion up to our own time. The exposure to the "original," as it is made accessible by descriptive biblical theology, could give an alternative to such a development. This alternative is not new in principle; it has been at work through the ages. What is new is the radical concern for the original *in its own terms.*

If we were to take an extreme example of what this could imply, we could return to the area of Christology. We saw how in the NT "adoptionism" stands as an equal, side by side with other types of Christology, and how the reasons for its downfall were found, not in the NT, but in the framework of later philosophical presuppositions. If the ontology which caused its downfall in the theology of the church were not any more a live option to the philosophical structure of a systematic theology of our time, it would be quite possible to speak meaningfully and in a most orthodox manner about Christ in "adoptionist" terms when witnessing to his function and his reality. There may be many and other reasons why this specific case should not be followed up; our only concern is to indicate in what way a descriptive biblical theology gives the systematic theologian a live option to attempt a direct translation of the biblical material, not a revision of a translation of a revision of a translation. . . . It is

easy to see the great need for such a possibility in the theology on the mission field and in the young churches, and there are signs that Western Christianity could be well served by a similar approach, with its sharp distinction between past and present meaning.

**4. The preacher and biblical theology.** A sharp distinction between what the texts meant in their original setting and what they mean in the present has considerable ramification for the work of the preacher, if he in any sense sees it as his task to communicate the message of the Bible to the congregation whose shepherd he is, and to the world which is his mission field. If we may use once more the analogy of the original and the translation—and this should not be considered more than an approximate analogy—the preacher is called upon to function as the bilingual translator. He should through his training and his ongoing studies attain the marks of a truly bilingual person—i.e., one who is capable of thinking in two languages. (By "languages" are meant, not the Greek and Hebrew of the Bible—although these would become more and more indispensable if the "bilingual" approach were taken seriously—but the modes and patterns of thought in the Bible.) His familiarity with the biblical world and patterns of thought should, through his work in descriptive biblical theology, have reached the point where he is capable of moving around in his Bible with idiomatic ease. His familiarity with the "language" of the contemporary world should reach a similar degree of perception and genuine understanding. Only so could he avoid the rhetorical truisms of much homiletic activity, where the message is expressed in a strange—sometimes even beautiful—mixed tongue, a homiletical Yiddish which cannot be really understood outside the walls of the Christian ghetto.

The demand for such a bilingual function of the preaching ministry may seem quite exacting, and indeed it is. It is also as it should be that the work of biblical as well as systematic theology finds its functional focus in the pulpit of the church. But it would be unreasonable to demand of the preacher—if now we may press our analogy once more—to become an academic grammarian of these two "languages" or a master of philosophical semantics. His task and his competence would remain by and large on the level of the vernacular, which he should have overheard long enough to be able to use it naturally and easily, as he would also use the Bible.

A mere repetition and affirmation of the biblical language, or even a translation which mechanically substitutes contemporary terms—often with a psychological slant—for those of the original, has little chance to communicate the true intention of the biblical text. To use an example from Bultmann's demand for demythologizing, the mere statement "Jesus is risen" directs the mind of most listeners toward a unique phenomenon, glorious or impossible as the case may be. On the basis of this phenomenon the believer is invited to base his hope for eternal life. A closer descriptive study of the resurrection passages suggests, however, that to the first listeners to the kerygma the phenomenon of the Resurrection was not surprising in the same sense. All Jews—

except the Sadducees—expected the Resurrection as the climax of God's history; the phenomenon was nothing strange and new to them. The only new thing was that it had happened. The claim of the church that Jesus was risen thus meant to those who accepted it that the general resurrection, to which they looked forward, had started to happen; Paul consequently says that Christ has been raised as the "first fruits of those who have fallen asleep" (I Cor. 15:20). In the same chapter the argument runs partly in the opposite direction to what we are used to think: "If there is no general resurrection, then Christ has not been raised" (vs. 13; cf. vs. 16). Those who first heard and believed the news about the Resurrection were not absorbed in a consideration of the phenomenon as such, but received it as a message that the new age had started to manifest itself here and now. This certainly affirmed their hopes in sharing in Christ's resurrection in God's good time, but the center of the message was that the power of the new age was at work in their own world and their own time.

Bultmann suggests that the task of the preacher is to free this message from its biblical nucleus, the proclaimed fact of the Resurrection as a historical event. But even for a preacher, who finds reason to object to such a demythologizing or dehistoricizing of the gospel, the problem which Bultmann points up remains a real one. Can the preacher say that he has communicated the message of Easter by stating and by underscoring the physical nature of the phenomenon of the Resurrection as a stumbling block for unbelievers, but a rock of salvation for those who believe? His familiarity with the results of a descriptive biblical theology would urge him to place the emphasis where the texts themselves put it and to meditate, e.g., along the lines of how the power of the new age manifested itself in Jesus Christ, not only as a token of our resurrection, but as the enthronement of Christ and as the possibility for man to live by the powers of the new age here and now. There would be many other lines like this which opened up from the gospel of Easter if the preacher did not become paralyzed—in faith or in doubts— by the phenomenon of the Resurrection, deducing from it theological propositions, but let his familiarity with the biblical world guide him through the concrete and diversified way in which the early church recognized and rejoiced in the resurrection of Jesus Christ. His homiletic imagination would become enriched, and the message would have a chance to find its live and relevant translation.

If the task of the pulpit is—as suggested here— the true *Sitz im Leben,* "life situation," where the meaning of the original meets with the meaning for today, then it is once more clear that we cannot pursue the study of biblical theology adequately if the two tenses are not kept apart. For the descriptive biblical theologian this is a necessity implied in his own discipline; and whether he is a believer or an agnostic, he demands respect for the descriptive task as an enterprise valid in its own right and for its own sake. For the life of the church such a consistent descriptive approach is a great and promising asset which enables the church, its teaching and preaching ministry, to be exposed to the Bible in its original

intention and intensity, as an ever new challenge to thought, faith, and response.

**Bibliography.** Biblical theologies (OT and NT): M. Burrows, *An Outline of Biblical Theology* (1946). G. Vos, *Biblical Theology* (1948).

OT theologies: L. Köhler, *Theologie des AT* (1936). O. J. Baab, *The Theology of the OT* (1949). A rich survey of major works in OT theology, with analysis and criticism, is given in R. C. Dentan, *Preface to OT Theology,* Yale Studies in Religion, vol. XIV (1950). G. E. Wright, *God Who Acts* (1952); cf. *IB,* I (1951), 349-89. G. von Rad, *Theologie des AT,* vol. I (1957). W. Eichrodt, *Theologie des AT,* vols. I-III (5th ed., 1957—). E. Jacob, *Theology of the OT* (English trans., 1958). Jewish OT theologies: K. Kohler, *Jewish Theology* (1918). E. Kaufmann, *Toledoth Ha-Emunah Ha-Yisraelith,* vols. I-VIII (1955-56). S. Blank, *Prophetic Faith in Isaiah* (1958).

NT theologies: A. Schlatter, *Die Geschichte des Christus* (1921); *Die Theologie des Apostel* (1921). E. W. Parsons, *The Religion of the NT* (1939). F. C. Grant, *An Introduction to NT Thought* (1950). R. Bultmann, *Theology of the NT,* vols. I-II (English trans., 1951-55); cf. especially N. A. Dahl's review article in *Theol. Rundschau,* XXII (1954), 21-49. E. Stauffer, *NT Theology* (English trans., 1955). Catholic works: M. Meinertz, *Theologie des NT,* vols. I-II (1950). J. Bonsirven, *Théologie du NT* (1951). By far the most significant contribution to NT theology—and, as background material, also to OT theology—is *TWNT;* a few of the articles have appeared in English translation—the articles "Love," "The Church," "Sin," "Righteousness," in one volume as *Bible Key Words* (1955); as separate monographs under respective main authors: K. H. Rengstorf, *Apostleship* (1952); R. Bultmann, *Gnosis* (1953); K. L. Schmidt, *et al., Basileia* (1957); W. Zimmerli and J. Jeremias, *The Servant of God* (1957); W. Foerster and G. Quell, *Lord* (1958). Cf. also A. Richardson, ed., *A Theological Word Book of the Bible* (1950). Indicative of and representative of the vigorous contemporary interest in biblical theology is the series *Studies in Biblical Theology.* Its monographs cover both the OT and the NT field.

The nature, method, and task of biblical theology: M. Kähler, *Der sogenannte historische Jesus und der geschichtliche, biblische Christus* (2nd ed., 1896). W. Wrede, *Über Aufgabe und Methode der sogenanntenntlichen Theologie* (1897). C. Steuernagel, "Atliche Theologie und atliche Religionsgeschichte," *ZAW,* IV (1925), 266-73. O. Eissfeldt, "Israelitisch-jüdische Religionsgeschichte und atliche Theologie," *ZAW,* XLIV (1926), 1-12. W. Eichrodt, "Hat die atliche Theologie noch selbständige Bedeutung innerhalb der atlichen Wissenschaft?" *ZAW,* XLVII (1929), 83-91. C. T. Craig, "Biblical Theology and the Rise of Historicism," *JBL,* LXII (1943), 281-94. P. Lestringant, *Essai sur l'Unité de la révélation biblique* (1943). J. D. Smart, "The Death and Rebirth of OT Theology," *JR,* XXIII (1943), 1-11, 125-36; cf. 186-87. W. A. Irwin, "The Reviving Theology of the OT," *JR,* XXIV (1945), 235-46. H. W. Robinson, *Inspiration and Revelation in the OT* (1946). A. N. Wilder, "NT Theology in Transition," in H. R. Willoughby, ed., *The Study of the Bible Today and Tomorrow* (1947), pp. 419-36; cf. A. N. Wilder, "Biblical Hermeneutic and American Scholarship," *ZNW, Beih.* XXI (1954), 24-32. C. H. Dodd, "A Problem of Interpretation," *Studiorum Novi Testamenti Societas,* Bulletin II (1951), pp. 7-18. H. Schlier, "Sinn und Aufgabe einer Theologie des NT," *BZ* (1951), 6-23. The presidential addresses of the S.B.L.E. by F. V. Filson, R. H. Pfeiffer, and E. R. Goodenough in *JBL,* vols. LXIX-LXXI (1950-52). J. Knox, *Criticism and Faith* (1952). B. Reicke, "Einheitlichkeit oder verschiedene 'Lehrbegriffe' in der neutestamentlichen Theologie?" *Theol. Zeitschrift,* IX (1953), 401-15. A. Vykopal, "Der Kampf um die Methode," *Jesus Christus Mittelpunkt der Weltanschauung,* vol. II (1954). R. Bultmann, "The Problem of Hermeneutics," *Essays* (English trans., 1955), pp. 234-61. G. Ebeling, "The Meaning of 'Biblical Theology,' " *JTS,* VI (1955), 210-25. A. Richardson, "Historical Theology and Biblical Theology,"

*Canadian Journal of Theology*, I (1955), 157-67. "Problems in Biblical Hermeneutics," a symposium with J. Muilenburg, J. C. Rylaarsdam, and K. Stendahl, *JBL*, LXXVII (1958), 18-38. J. L. McKenzie, "Problems of Hermeneutics in Roman Catholic Exegesis," *JBL*, 77 (1958), 197-201. E. Fuchs, *Zum hermeneutischen Problem* (1959).

Other works of general interest related to the task of biblical theology: J. Pedersen, *Israel: Its Life and Culture*, vols. I-II (1926); vols. III-IV (1940). C. H. Dodd, *The Apostolic Preaching and Its Developments* (1944). P. S. Minear, *Eyes of Faith* (1946). O. Cullmann, *Christ and Time* (English trans., 1950). E. Fuchs, *Hermeneutik* (1954). J. W. Bowman, *Prophetic Realism and the Gospel* (1955). P. Tillich, *Biblical Religion and the Search for Ultimate Reality* (1955). J. Hessen, *Griechische oder biblische Theologie?* (1956). W. F. Albright, *From Stone Age to Christianity* (1957). O. Cullmann, *The Christology of the NT* (1957). J. Knox, *Jesus Lord and Christ* (1958).

K. STENDAHL

**\*BIBLICAL THEOLOGY, HISTORY OF.** Biblical theology is a scholarly presentation of the witness to faith, and of the theological views, of the biblical writers, in the context of the covenanted people, Israel and the early church. It avails itself of the three theological disciplines: (*a*) the exegetical, which discloses the text; (*b*) the historical, which uncovers the circumstances in which the men of the Bible act and think; (*c*) the systematical, which embraces expressions of faith in an ordered and unified statement. Biblical theology is therefore the crown of biblical scholarship.

1. The beginnings of biblical theology in the eighteenth century
2. The dissolution of biblical theology in the religious history of Israel and of the early church in the nineteenth century
   *a.* OT
   *b.* NT
3. The theology of biblicism
4. Cult and kerygma: history of religion and biblical theology in the twentieth century
5. Conclusions
Bibliography

**1. The beginnings of biblical theology in the eighteenth century.** It is the Protestant view that dogmatics should present the teaching of Holy Scripture. The theological works of the reformers conformed to it far more than the subsequent scholastic systems of teaching in orthodoxy. The design and content of Melanchthon's *Loci* (1521) followed that of Romans to a large extent. Even the theological insight of Calvin's *Institutes* (1536) was grounded in biblical exegesis. By decisive appeal to Holy Scripture the Reformation laid the ground for biblical theology, the basic principle of which is that scripture should interpret itself. In the later, post-Reformation time scholars were deflected from the newly won recourse to scripture in their attempt to secure the Reformation heritage with dogma. There was in part a return to the teaching of the Bible with the "Collegia Biblica"—i.e., collections of biblical texts in support of dogmatic statements (S. Schmidt, *Collegium Biblicum* [1671]; J. Hülsemann, *Vindiciae* [1679]). But since these texts were selected to subserve dogmatic positions, neither the theology of the Bible nor that of its individual authors stood out. From pietism, which turned to the Bible because

dogmatic teaching did not edify, came the first biblical theology (C. Haymann; 1708).

However, scholarly exposition of the Bible presupposed that advance in the period of the Enlightenment which freed the mind from the authority of scholastic systems. For the Enlightenment, as in the Renaissance, which it resumed, man was the measure of all things — man whose horizon had been extended by far-reaching discoveries, whose conception of the universe had been radically altered, and who was now applying his reason to law and economics, science and art, history and philosophy. The Bible was also put to the test of reason. Two methods of inquiry evolved which have remained indispensable to biblical theology, with which it actually began: the literary-critical method, which seeks to distinguish the work of individual authors, the original form and setting of scripture; and closely related to it, the historical method, which looks into the factors out of which biblical events and views developed.

While the Englightenment in Germany engendered, above all, literary criticism (Reimarus, Lessing, Semler), English Deism concerned itself more with the historical development of Christianity (Toland, Tindal). At that time no one attempted to write biblical theology. Nonetheless, G. E. Lessing (1729-81), who stood at the threshold of a new era, went beyond purely critical reflection of the Bible to set forth a positive and constructive view. In his work *The Education of Mankind* (1780), he sketched a historical and systematic concept of biblical revelation. According to him, revelation served to educate mankind. God is the great Pedagogue, and the Bible his textbook. The OT, which contains the material for elementary teaching, shows how Israel, as a child, acquired the idea of one God and submitted itself to him. But its service lacked motive until the idea of resurrection, and the expectation of reward and punishment hereafter, emerged. Jesus not only taught this new idea, but also lived it out, and based his inner and outer action upon it. Man reaches the third stage when, on the basis of full insight, he does good for its own sake. This occurs in the time of the last gospel of reason.

Lessing's concept of biblical revelation is not theological, but philosophical. It revolves around mankind rather than God. For Lessing, revelation is simply the means to that end which mankind could have reached by natural progress. No trinity of divine persons is revealed, but instead the three central ideas of the Enlightenment: God, freedom, and immortality. At that, Lessing's view was pleasant.

In the second half of the eighteenth century biblical theology became increasingly independent of dogmatics. A. F. Büsching stated the *Advantage of Biblical Theology Over Scholasticism* (1758). Also J. S. Semler's critique aimed to make biblical theology a discipline of its own. The 1772 G. T. Zachariä wrote a biblical theology by which he examined the teaching of the church. But as he used biblical theology only as a criterion, it never acquired with him independent significance. Moreover, it left the teaching of the church intact, merely casting it in a new light.

J. P. Gabler took the step which was lacking. In his initial address as professor at Altdorf, "Oratio de justo discrimine theologiae biblicae et dogmaticae" (1787), he declared biblical theology to be a historical science. According to him, dogmatics should extract from the Bible that teaching with universal relevance, and leave to biblical theology those statements which were conditioned by time and place. While dogmatics needed philosophy, biblical theology must inquire into history. Gabler's distinction made a place at last for biblical theology, and gave rise to it, even though he himself did not pursue it further. G. L. Bauer took it up when he issued four volumes of biblical theology in 1800-1802, in which he set forth the religion of the Jews before Christ, the religion of Jesus, and that of the apostles. From the standpoint of the Enlightenment he criticized everything which conflicted with its concept of reason and morals, and explained it as a concession to the "erroneous ideas of common man."

The eras of romanticism and idealism which followed the Enlightenment contributed to the historical-philosophical basis of biblical theology. The Enlightenment had been unable to descend from its realm of pure reason to the plane of history. In contrast to it, romanticism brought in feeling, with which one could intelligently immerse himself in the spirit of other people. Then Hegel's philosophy imparted speculative imagination by which to order all the historical insights into one developing, spiritual process. J. G. Herder ("Vom Geist der hebräischen Poesie" [1782]) discovered literary beauty in the Bible, above all in the OT, regarding its stories and poems as expressions of the folk life in Israel. F. Schleiermacher (1768-1834) sought after the individual historical religions, in which alone religious consciousness becomes fruitful. As he did not grasp the significance of the OT, he was unable to write a biblical theology. W. M. L. de Wette succeeded with a *Biblische Dogmatik des AT und NT* (two volumes; 1813, 1816). He insisted on a purely historical approach; and using the available results of criticism, he undertook a thorough, exegetical investigation of the material. In the OT he distinguished two historically evident steps of revelation: the religion of Moses, and that of the Jews. Analogous to them he found two levels in the NT: the teaching of Jesus, and its interpretation in the message of the apostles. De Wette had a sharp eye for historical factors. He was the first who identified Deuteronomy with the law book which was found under Josiah. He evaluated historical facts in terms of religious-psychological conditions, and dogma was for him the expression of religious experience. The biblical theology of D. v. Coelln (1836) reflected the work of De Wette. B. Bauer (*Die Religion des AT* [1838-39]) cast aside criticism of sources and just followed the OT presentation. More significant was the historically oriented *Alttestamentliche Theologie* of H. Schultz (1869), which kept up with literary criticism in its several editions, offered many fine observations, and in its fourth edition comprised two parts, a historical and a dogmatic.

**2. The dissolution of biblical theology in the religious history of Israel and of the early church in the nineteenth century.** *a. OT.* A strong impulse emanated from the historical philosophy of Hegel. It was transmitted to OT study by W. Vatke and to the theology of the NT by F. C. Baur. W. Vatke's *Religion des AT* (1835) gave a brilliant treatment in the terminology of Hegel. He distinguished three periods of development in the OT: the preprophetic, the prophetic, and the postprophetic. He was the first to recognize that the Priestly Code was the latest source in the Pentateuch, and ascribed it to the postprophetic period. His hypothesis was rejected by the leading authority for OT study at that time, H. Ewald, so that not only his contemporaries disapproved, but even he himself finally lost confidence in it. It was later taken up by K. H. Graf and by A. Kuenen (*De Godsdienst van Israel* [1870]), and validated by J. Wellhausen (*Geschichte Israels* [1878; appeared in 1895 as Prolegomena]). By the end of the nineteenth century Wellhausen and his school, which had made tremendous strides in literary critical study of the OT scriptures, dominated the field of OT scholarship. Under their influence theological interest declined in favor of historical, and biblical theology of the OT was turned into the religious history of Israel. The *Alttestamentliche Religionsgeschichte* of R. Smend (1893) started a series of these treatments, which continued on in the twentieth century (A. Duff, 1892; F. Giesebrecht, 1904; M. Löhr, 1906; E. Kautzsch, 1911; K. Marti, 1907; K. Budde, 1910; E. König, 1915; R. Kittel, 1921; G. Hölscher, 1922; W. Oesterly-Robinson, second edition, 1937). The advantage of this type of analysis lay in the single line with which it moved toward its end in presenting the development of the Israelite religion. But it failed to evaluate the material theologically. The question of truth was overlooked; the claim of revelation by witnesses in the OT was disregarded. This deficiency was accentuated even more with discoveries which illuminated the religious world around Israel (Tell el-Amarna Tablets, 1887; Code of Hammurabi, 1910; *see* TELL EL-AMARNA; HAMMURABI). It was pointed out how much the faith of Israel had in common with the ideas of ancient, oriental religions. This seemed to put Israel on the same primitive, time-conditioned plane. Only a few scholars of the OT attempted to evaluate the theological significance. A. B. Davidson (*The Theology of the OT* [1904]) noted that the kingdom of God, which unfolds in the NT, did not announce itself alone in certain religious concepts of the OT, but was rooted in the life of the people, and made itself felt in their institutions. In the same year of G. Hölscher's *Geschichte der israelitischen und jüdischen Religion* (1922), which formed the apex of pure historical construction, there appeared E. König's *OT Theology*, in which he added a systematic part to his religious-historical treatment. He underscored the epoch-making character of Israel's faith, and as themes of "saving history" he discussed: God and his relation to the world and men, sin and the way to eliminate it.

*b. NT.* While the critical investigation of the gospels by D. F. Strauss implied the eclipse of NT theology, F. C. Baur (*Dogmengeschichte* [1847]; *Lectures on NT Theology* [posthumous]) broke fresh ground toward a constructive view of the NT. With a keen sense in evaluating historical sources, and with a comprehensive intellect, he saw in the NT the unfolding of the human spirit as it becomes conscious of itself. Consequently he applied Hegel's dialectical scheme of thesis, antithesis, and synthesis to primitive Christianity. It gave him a perspective on the contrasts among persons and their viewpoints, by which he also arranged the books of the NT in temporal sequence. In his view the teaching of Jesus formed the basis of the NT. It was not yet theology, but strictly religion—the immediate expression of religious consciousness. Theological reflection started over the place of the law. Paul was the first theologian. He proclaimed that type of gospel which was free from the law. This put him in opposition to the Jewish Christians, who, as his antithesis, adhered to the law. Out of his struggle came a compromise which issued in the Old Catholic church. As the scriptures of the NT were written in the course of this controversy, they may be ordered according to their stand in it.

Baur's work was carried to absurd extremes by his pupils E. Zeller and A. Schwegler. However, the picture which he projected of primitive Christianity remained alive in NT discussion throughout the nineteenth century. Much work was concentrated on individual persons in the NT: Jesus (K. Hase, D. Schenkel, H. Wendt, W. Baldensperger), Paul (A. Hausrath, K. Holsten, H. Lüdemann). In 1863 H. J. Holtzmann delineated the figure of the "historical" Jesus, and therewith started that line of liberal research. The classical work on primitive Christianity was C. F. Weizsäcker's *Apostolisches Zeitalter der christlichen Kirche* (1886). H. J. Holtzmann's *NT Theology* (two volumes; 1886-99) was a thorough and comprehensive work which concluded this period. Conservative were the biblical theologies of the NT by B. Weiss (1868; 1903) and T. Zahn (1928).

**3. The religion of biblicism.** Concurrent with the stream of theology which flowed from the Enlightenment and romanticism was another of pietistic biblical scholarship. In it one turned to the Bible to substantiate the orthodox position, as regards theological truth, and discerned in the Bible the providence of God in "saving history." J. A. Bengel (1687-1752) combined his linguistic and text-critical study with a keen and deep religious exposition of the NT (Gnomon = Fingerzeig [1742]). F. C. Oetinger (1702-82), who was influenced by the mystic J. Böhme, issued a biblical dictionary (1749) in which he sought to show the realism of biblical concepts. For him God and the world, spirit and body, belong together inseparably. Over against the rationalism of his time he insisted that the activity of God extended into corporeal nature. Both Bengel and Oetinger saw in the Bible a living whole, a glorious and complete system of truth, which required unified interpretation. This organic grasp of "saving history" in the Bible was pursued by J. T. Beck in the nineteenth century, the colleague of F. C. Baur in Tübingen (*Die christliche Lehrwissenschaft nach den biblischen Urkunden* [1841]). While the Hegelians saw reflected in the testimonies of the Bible the unfolding of the human spirit, Beck was convinced of the ordering power of God's Holy Spirit. Less original was E. W. Hengstenberg (*Christologie des AT* [1829-

35]), who from a reactionary standpoint contended for the identity of both testaments, laid the New back in the Old, and treated it on the same plane. J. C. K. von Hofmann (*Der Schriftbeweis* [1852-55]), on the contrary, the founder of the Erlangen School, held that the Bible documented the process of "saving history," which aims at the redemption of mankind. All revelation converges upon this end, and the Bible must be understood in this light, though the process will not be fully disclosed until the Eschaton arrives. History has a prophetic range, and all prophecy is embedded in history. Hofmann attempted to assign every book of the Bible its place in this scheme of redemption. Equally orthodox, and showing the revealing character of the Bible, were the treatments of OT theology by J. Steudel (1840), H. A. Hävernick (1848), G. F. Oehler (1873), W. L. Alexander (1888). H. Ewald, who defended the revelatory character of the Bible against oncoming liberalism (*Die Lehre der Bibel von Gott* [1871-76]), harmonized the OT and the NT in a peculiar and original way. Using his own religious experience with God, and life in the Christian church, as a norm to evaluate the Bible, he distinguished in it several levels of religious utterance. Other contributions to OT theology in line with this trend were those of F. Hitzig (1880), H. Schultz (fourth edition, 1889), E. Riehm (1889), A. Dillmann (1895), and A. C. Knudson (1918).

**4. Cult and kerygma: history of religion and biblical theology in the twentieth century. *a. OT.*** In the twentieth century the character of OT scholarship changed. Its one-sided historical approach was superseded by new methods of research and analysis. The religious picture was filled in by discoveries pertaining not only to the world around Israel but also to Palestine and its inhabitants. Systematic archaeological investigation penetrated far back into Palestine's past and provided a glimpse into the religious convictions of the people living then (W. G. Graham and H. G. May). Anthropology concerned itself with man's inner being (J. G. Frazer, R. Dussaud, W. Oesterly). M. Weber set sociological inquiry going. E. Guthe and G. Dalman applied themselves to geographical questions. All the data, together with the results of archaeology, presented a fully new picture of Israel's history and culture (A. Alt, W. F. Albright, M. Noth, K. Elliger).

H. Gunkel taught how from the form of biblical literature one can tell its setting in life (*Sitz im Leben*) among the people. Taking up the interest of Herder, he showed the attraction of OT stories, the beauty of Hebrew poetry, the impact of prophetic words. Along with the form criticism (*Formgeschichte*) of Gunkel, V. Grönbech's ideas about the soul of primitive man and his cult as creative drama were applied to the OT. J. Pedersen (*Israel*, I-IV [1934]; *ET* [1926-40]) considered Israel, apart from any theological norm, as a complete culture within itself. S. Mowinckel (*Psalmenstudien* [1922]) uncovered the strength and fullness of its religious life in the cult drama attending the ceremonies of ascension to the throne, which he found reflected in many psalms. These suggestions have been followed out by the cult-historical school among Scandinavian scholars (A. Bentzen, J. Engnell, H. Birkeland, S. Kapelrud).

Of especial importance for an understanding of the Hebrew religion were the cuneiform texts of Ras Shamra (1929; *see* UGARIT), which primarily described the Canaanite cult worship and threw into bold relief the previously shrouded being of the Canaanite religion. How great its influence upon the cult of Israel was, we learn from the OT itself. The Israelite prophets, who according to B. Duhm (*Die Theologie der Propheten* [1875]) stood upon a solitary ethical height and were opposed to Hebrew ceremonies, now appeared to be more closely connected with the cult.

At the same time, theological consideration of the OT recurred in the twentieth century. Ever since the eighteenth century OT scholarship had taken a line which increasingly detracted from the sublimity of the OT. From dialectical theology came a strong impulse to appraise anew the theological assertions of the OT. A front developed against liberalism in theology, wherein one rejected a descriptive, condescending attitude toward the Bible. Only a theocentric method, concentrating on the kerygma, and at the same time aware of its own inadequacy, was deemed appropriate for biblical statements. O. Eissfeldt (1926) urged both methods—historical investigation of the Hebrew religion and systematic presentation of the timeless truth of OT revelation. These methods are essentially different: the one resorts to reason to evaluate data, while the other relies on faith to perceive revelation. E. Sellin (1933) was the first to write a theology which corresponded to the conception of Eissfeldt. Its first part treats the Israelite religious history; the second, OT theology in its classical categories of God, man, eschatology, whereby the holiness of God is the central idea. On the other hand, O. Procksch and W. Eichrodt rejected this parallel approach and held that the presentation of OT theology is alone appropriate which proceeds from faith in Christ, to whom the OT points, rather than from historical philosophy. Likewise T. Lindblom (1936) and A. Weiser (1936) demanded theological treatment of the OT—the first in the form of a systematic presentation of the concepts of God contained therein, the latter on the basis of existential exegesis within the church. L. Köhler's *Theologie des AT* (1936) is constructed on a systematic framework, for which Köhler employs the same outline as Sellin. However, individual sections on historical development are inserted in the copious exegesis of concepts. W. Eichrodt's three-volume *Theologie des AT* (1933,1935, 1938; revised edition, 1957) takes its center—namely, the covenant of God—from the OT itself. The covenant idea implies a relationship in terms of which the theological assertions in the OT must be understood. According to Eichrodt the people as a unit, the world, and individual man are the three partners of God. The relation of the OT to the NT is also given in the covenant idea, for the New Covenant is based upon the Old, which it fulfils. Similarly O. Procksch sees in the OT the Bible of Christ, and therefore a book which is a source of revelation for Christianity. Procksch was influenced by von Hofmann so that his *Theologie des AT* (posthumous, 1956) is oriented to "saving history." The OT contains a history of prophetic witness which runs from the patriarchs to the prophets. In the first and larger part Procksch delineates this history, while a second part presents the thought-world of the OT in reference to those partnerships with God which Eichrodt distinguished. If for Procksch every theology is Christology, nonetheless by him the distinction between OT and NT was preserved, which W. Vischer (*Das Christuszeugnis des AT* [two volumes; 1934; English translation, 1949]) for the most part disregarded. By his exposition of the Pentateuch and the historical books Vischer sets OT statements in direct relation to those of the NT. On his view, taken from K. Barth, the OT shows what Christ is, the NT who Christ is. Vischer is fond of allegorical interpretation and adduces the exegesis of Luther, Augustine, and early Christian scholars. Thus he quite leaps over the channel of Enlightenment. The attempt to equate both testaments has not been pursued further, though T. C. Vriezen (*Theologie des AT in Grundzügen* [1956]) looks upon the OT as a book of revelation that converges on Jesus and finds its fulfilment in him. As with Procksch, God's guiding hand reveals itself to him in the history of Israel, in which the unique person of the prophet serves as his agent of communication.

The works of H. W. Robinson have contributed significantly to the development of OT theology: *Record and Revelation* (1938) and *Inspiration and Revelation in the OT* (1946), which contains the Prolegomena of an OT theology. Robinson sees the difficulties of OT theology lying in the fact that it does not appear systematically in the Bible, but is continually bound up with history. Eternal truth is embedded in time-conditioned state. Whoever will understand the truth must be gripped by it. Robinson's outline of theology provides for two systematic parts: the first makes clear the process of divine revelation in the categories of God-nature, God-man, and God-history; the second, in the figures of prophet and priest, in wisdom and psalms.

E. Jacob recognizes in *Théologie de l'AT* (1955) the historical character of OT theology over against the dogmatic approach. Of even later vintage is G. von Rad's *Alttestamentliche Theologie,* the first volume of which appeared in 1957. According to von Rad, theological thinking in the OT was not concerned with a *Weltanschauung,* but arose with the task of gathering, arranging, and interpreting different documents of traditions. Those documents gave details from the history of tribes, persons, and places, and had to be related to the whole of Israel, and its creed to Yahweh's mighty deeds and his will. The first period of Israel's history is told in the Hexateuch, whose theme is Yahweh's election of Israel and his gift of the Promised Land. The second period, covered by the Deuteronomist and the Chronicler, concentrates on God's covenant with David. Israel's response to God's revelation is given in the Psalms and in the wisdom literature.

The systematic approach prevails in the Roman Catholic treatments of recent times: P. Heinisch (1940); A. Gelin (1949); P. F. Ceuppens, J. Guillet, and P. von Imschoot (1954).

*b. NT.* By the end of the nineteenth century NT study was markedly enriched by religious-historical investigation, which has continued to occupy an important place in it. This material threw light on the Jewish (E. Schürer, G. Dalman, W. Bousset, J. Klausner, P. Billerbeck, J. Jeremias, W. D. Davies, D. Daube) and Hellenistic (W. Bousset, A. Deissmann, R. Reitzenstein, E. Norden) background of primitive Christianity, which was seen to assimilate in a unique way features from both patterns. It took its dominant ideas and eschatological urgency largely from apocalyptic Judaism, while Hellenism seemed to underlie the interpretation of the saving work of Christ and its representation in the cult.

When form criticism was applied to the NT scriptures, it set them in a new perspective, especially the gospels (M. Dibelius, *Formgeschichte* [1919; second edition, 1933]; R. Bultmann, *Die Geschichte der synoptischen Tradition* [1921; third edition, 1957]; V. Taylor; F. C. Grant; K. Grobel; K. Stendahl). Their content was seen to be shaped by the preaching and the cult of the primitive church, and in addition by the theological bent of the authors.

W. Wrede, in his pamphlet on the *Task and Method of So-called NT Theology* (1897), urged more concentration on the religious-historical method. He protested against the view that the writings of the Bible merely presented doctrinal teaching. For him primitive Christianity was a living religion whose essence could not be discerned from the canonical scriptures alone, but must be illuminated also from the material of the surrounding world. Wrede wanted to displace theology of the NT with the history of the religion of primitive Christianity. His thesis found expression in H. Weinel's *Biblische Theologie des NT* (1911) and J. Kaftan's *Neutestamentliche Theologie* (1927), both of which described the religion of Jesus as a moral redemptive religion. W. Bousset (*Kyrios Christos* [1927]) and W. Heitmüller regarded the cult as the center of primitive Christian piety. In contrast thereto, J. Weiss and A. Schweitzer pointed out that it was impelled by its expectation of the imminent end of the world.

It is understandable that the number of conservative scholars in the field of the NT was greater than in that of the OT. Of note was the *Theologie des NT* by P. Feine (1913; ninth edition, 1950), which followed the line of von Hofmann. E. Stauffer's vivid *NT Theologie* (1941) is likewise oriented to "saving history." This theme is less emphasized in the theologies of T. Zahn and F. Büchsel. A. Schlatter struck out on a line of his own (*Der Glaube im NT* [1885]; *Theologie des NT* [1909-18]), in which he objected to abstract contemplation. According to him the thinking of the NT witnesses is rooted concretely in their striving and acting. Schlatter was more receptive to Hebrew than to Greek thought, because he recognized that Judaism provided the background of primitive Christian religion.

R. Bultmann differs from Schlatter in that he stresses the Hellenistic influence in the formation of the Christian faith. Like Schlatter, he protests a rationalistic treatment of NT theology; his position, however, is derived from dialectical theology and existential philosophy (M. Heidegger). In the field of NT theology Bultmann (*Theologie des NT* [1948-53]) is the single, unqualified representative of this position. Since his work reflects the scholarly attainments of the twentieth century, and allows us to see

the problem of every NT theology, we must look at it closer.

The outline is historical. Bultmann gives only scant attention to the preaching of Jesus in itself (pp. 1-33). The reason is partly because radical form criticism leaves only a modest remainder of genuine Jesus sayings, but also because, in his view, the message of Jesus is source rather than object of NT theology. Likewise little space is given to the primitive church in Jerusalem (pp. 33-64). On the contrary, Bultmann devotes a large section to the gospel of the Hellenistic church, crystallizing it for the most part out of the traditional material in the letters (pp. 64-182). The central portion is given over to the treatment of Paul (pp. 183-348) and of John (pp. 349-439). Therein the theological concern of Bultmann becomes clear. For him, as for Luther, the teaching of justification is the heart of theology, and John the true evangelist. Bultmann is united with Luther, furthermore, in his emphasis on the gospel, on the power of the word of the Cross. The gospel awakens in man a new self-understanding which transforms the determining factors in his life so that he is freed from sin and becomes fully sensitive to God and his neighbor. Not until the post-Paulinian era did Christianity tend to turn the gospel into doctrine. For this reason Hebrews and James are not less sharply criticized by Bultmann than by Luther.

Yet Bultmann diverges essentially from Luther. His criticism of the NT goes much farther than that of Luther. Bultmann's is the attitude of the modern man who has attained a scientific picture of the world and lives by it. Not enlightened, the man of the NT spoke of heaven and hell, of angels and spiritual powers, as objective realities. Apart from the fact that this way of speaking alienates modern man from the gospel, it turns the living existential truth into an objective doctrine. The mythological and cosmological way of speaking must therefore be demythologized and made to concur with the self-understanding of man: that is to say, it must be interpreted anthropologically. Bultmann goes still further by saying that faith should not rely upon objectively tangible reality and self-evident historical facts. He runs into the danger of dissolving the facts set forth as historic events in the NT into purely meaningful symbols. Moreover, his conception of NT theology—to be sure, coherent—does not allow for the historical diversity of views in the NT, particularly as he quite underestimates the influence of the OT and Judaism.

**5. Conclusions.** The difficulty with biblical theology lies in the fact that the Christian church has continually made a system out of theology, when the Bible does not contain such a system. It comprises rather a diversity of witness interrelated with history. Biblical theology proper should take its principle of exposition from the Bible itself. It is not possible to grasp the Hebrew way of thought in the Bible with the systematic principle which came from the Greek mind and wove itself into Christian dogma.

Because the revelation of God occurred in history —in the history of the people of Israel and in the history of Jesus and his apostles—biblical theology is interwoven in this history. Any consideration of the theology of this history should follow the course of it. In this way one will get closer to the witness of the Bible, and be able to fit in better the knowledge which progressive research has gleaned from the surrounding religious world. The light which falls upon the thought and action of biblical persons from that source has made clearer the uniqueness of their witness as well as its historical conditions. Thus the task of OT scholarship today is to describe the covenant of Israel and the message of the prophets from the background of the Canaanite religion which has come to light through the Ras Shamra texts. For NT research the discovery of the Qumran writings (*see* DEAD SEA SCROLLS) has produced direct access to the features of a vital Jewish sect at the time of Jesus. The much-discussed questions in recent years of eschatology (as realized and awaited), and of Christology (the historical and the preached Christ) must therefore be re-examined. The hermeneutical question concerning the expression of biblical views in modern thought-forms is also affected.

But the historical approach is not without its pitfall. While the systematic method tends to dissect the thought of biblical authors and to subsume it under philosophical categories, a purely historical treatment may overly ascribe to biblical thought factors of the surrounding religious world, and assign it to a certain stage in the evolutionary development of religious consciousness. In either case the real thought is obscured. The question of truth does not fare better. In general, the systematic method overlooks the fact that the truth of the Bible is personal in character, resting upon the relation which God established between himself and men; while purely historical research seldom concerns itself with the existential truth of that which it describes. For this reason much of historical research is inadequate to biblical theology. The theology of the Bible cannot be understood as a type of view and teaching. It conveys a witness and an appeal. Whoever will present it cannot hold himself aloof from it, but must himself be gripped by it. If he wants to make it intelligible and believable to the people of today, he must put himself reverently back into the life and teaching of the Bible. He becomes truly scholarly and historical when he takes seriously what impelled the men of biblical times, when he looks at their attitude and activity from their own standpoint. He may avail himself of every method which modern scholarship offers insofar as it is applicable to the data of the Bible and to its presentation.

The ideal biblical theology in the Christian church must treat the witness and views of both OT and NT together. How much both testaments bear upon each other has become increasingly clear in the latest scholarship. We are now reaping the fruit of such unified research—e.g., in the articles in the *Theologisches Wörterbuch,* edited by G. Kittel and G. Friedrich.

**Bibliography.** O. Eissfeldt, "Israel.-Jüd. Religionsgeschichte und AT-Theologie," *ZAW,* XXXXIV (1926), 1-12; W. Eichrodt, "Hat die AT-Theologie noch selbständige Bedeutung innerhalb der Wissenschaft?" *ZAW,* XXXXVII (1929), 83-91; C. T. Craig, "Biblical Theology and the Rise of Historism," *JBL,* LXII (1943), 281-94; M. Burrows, *Outlines of Biblical Theology* (1946); J. Coppens, *Les harmonies des deux Testaments* (1949); G. W. Anderson and W. Porteous in H. H. Rowley, *The OT and Modern Study* (1952), pp. 283-345; G. Ebeling, "The Meaning of 'Biblical Theology,' " *JTS* NS, VI (1955), 210-25; E. G. Kraeling, *The OT Since the Reformation* (1955); H. J. Kraus, *Geschichte der hist.-krit. Erforschung des AT von der Reformation bis zur Gegenwart* (1956).

O. BETZ

**BICHRI** bĭk'rī [בכרי, *gentilic name from* [בכר]; BICHRITES —rīts (II Sam. 20:14); KJV BERITES bĭr'īts. Given as the father of Sheba the Benjaminite insurrectionist in II Sam. 20:1 ff; but since Bichri is a gentilic name, the phrase "the son of Bichri" may more correctly be understood to mean that Sheba was from the clan of Becher (Gen. 46:21; I Chr. 7: 6, 8).

E. R. DALGLISH

**BIDKAR** bĭd'kär [בדקר, son of piercing(?)] (II Kings 9:25). Jehu's charioteer at the slaying of Joram.

**BIER** [מטה; σορός]. A litter or bed on which a body was placed prior to burial (*see* BURIAL; MOURNING). It is mentioned only in II Sam. 3:31; II Chr. 16:14 (KJV BED); Luke 7:14. In these passages the information that David followed the bier of Abner, and that Jesus touched the bier of the young man of Nain, whose body was being carried out of the city, makes clear that a bier was portable, probably like the wooden boards used in Muslim funerals today. The description of the burial of Asa suggests that his bier was a more elaborate type of burial couch which was placed in the tomb.

The term מטה was a regular word for "BED," designating a bier only when used in referring to burials.

W. L. REED

**BIGAMY.** *See* MARRIAGE § 1c.

**BIGTHA** bĭg'thə [בגתא, *possibly from* Pers. *bagadata* and *bagadana,* gift of God] (Esth. 1:10). One of seven eunuchs who served Ahasuerus as chamberlains and whom he sent for Queen Vashti.

He is possibly identical with BIGTHAN of Esth. 2: 21; 6:2.

M. NEWMAN

**BIGTHAN** bĭg'thən [בגתן, *possibly from* Pers. *bagadana* and *bagadata,* gift of God] (Esth. 2:21); BIGTHANA —thə nə [בגתנא] (Esth. 6:2). One of two eunuchs of Ahasuerus who guarded his threshold. Their conspiracy against his life was discovered and revealed by Mordecai.

He is possibly identical with BIGTHA of Esth. 1:10.

M. NEWMAN

**BIGVAI** bĭg'vī [בגוי, *evidently a* Pers. *name with the initial syllable baga,* God; Elephantine Papyri בגוהי]. One of the Jewish leaders who returned to Palestine with Zerubbabel after the Exile (Ezra 2:14; Neh. 7: 19; cf. I Esd. 5:8). The "sons of Bigvai" also returned in the postexilic period (Ezra 2:2; Neh. 7:7; I Esd. 5:14). Certain members of this family are specifically said to have come with Ezra (Ezra 8:14; I Esd. 8: 40), and in Neh. 10:16—H 10:17 Bigvai appears as one who sealed Ezra's covenant.

M. NEWMAN

**BILDAD** bĭl'dăd [בלדד, beloved of the Lord(?), *or* the Lord has loved(?), *or* Dad (*proper name*) gives increase; LXX Βαλδαδ; *see bibliography*]. One of the three friends of Job (Job 2:11; 8:1; 18:1; 25:1; 42:9). The identification of Bildad as "the Shuhite" presumably makes him a member of a tribe of Aramean nomads who roamed an area somewhere to the SE of Palestine (Gen. 25:2, 6). *See* SHUAH.

*Bibliography.* T. Noldeke, *ZDMG*, XLII (1888), 479; K. Tallqvist, *Assyrian Personal Names* (1914), pp. 67 ff; W. F. Albright, "The Name of Bildad the Shuhite," *AJSL*, XLIV (1927-28), 31 ff. H. H. GUTHRIE, JR.

**BILEAM** bǐl'ĭ əm [בלעם]. A city listed in I Chr. 6: 70—H 6:55 as one of the LEVITICAL CITIES in the territory of Manasseh; identified by most scholars with IBLEAM.

**BILGAH** bǐl'gə [בלגה, brightness]. **1.** A descendant of Aaron, and head of one of the divisions of priests in the time of David (I Chr. 24:14; cf. vss. 1, 4).

*Bibliography.* E. L. Curtis, *Chronicles*, ICC (1910), p. 271.
**2.** One of the chiefs of the priests listed as having returned from Babylon with Zerubbabel (Neh. 12: 5, 18). B. T. DAHLBERG

**BILGAI** bǐl'gī [בלגי, cheerfulness] (Neh. 10:8). A postexilic priest who witnessed the covenant renewal under Ezra; probably identical with BILGAH 2.

**BILHAH** bǐl'hə [בלהה, simplicity(?), modesty(?), *or perhaps* unconcern, *from* Arab. *balaha,* to be without concern]. **1.** The handmaid of Rachel. She was given by Rachel to Jacob and bore him Dan and Naphtali.

When the barren Rachel became jealous because Leah was fruitful, she gave her handmaid Bilhah to Jacob as a concubine (Gen. 29:31-35; 30:1-8)—a custom paralleled in the Nuzi Texts (*see* NUZI). Bilhah gave birth to Dan and Naphtali, both of whom Rachel named, thus indicating her claim to them. The tribes, Dan and Naphtali, of which Bilhah's sons were the eponyms, resided in the far N of Palestine (after Dan's migration; Judg. 18) and belonged to the premonarchical twelve-tribe amphictyony reflected in the grouping of Jacob-Israel's family.
M. NEWMAN
**2.** A village somewhere in S Judah (I Chr. 4:29); probably the same as BALAH (Josh. 19:3) and BAALAH 3 (15:29).

**BILHAN** bǐl'hăn [בלהן; *cf.* Heb. *personal name* בלהה; *note ending -ān in other names in* Gen. 36:26-28]. **1.** The first son of clan chief Ezer (*see* EZER 1); ancestor of a native Horite subclan in Edom (Gen. 36: 27; I Chr. 1:42).
**2.** Son of JEDIAEL (1), a Benjaminite (I Chr. 7:10). However, vss. 6-11 may possibly be a lost genealogy of ZEBULUN. L. HICKS

**BILL** [ספר, writing, document; ἀποστασίον]. The document a man executed when he wished to divorce his wife. If he found her undesirable, he must write a bill of divorce and put it in her hands before he could send her away (Deut. 24:1, 3). This requirement is cited by Jesus also (Matt. 5:31; 19:7; Mark 10:4) as the recognized law of Moses.

The word ספר is used figuratively in the book of Isaiah, where God asks, relative to the children of Zion:

> Where is your mother's bill of divorce,
> with which I put her away?
> (50:1).

Harlotrous Israel was sent away by her God with a "DECREE of divorce" (Jer. 3:8).

*See also* DIVORCE. O. J. BAAB

**BILSHAN** bǐl'shăn [בלשן, *from* Babylonian, *probably an abbreviation of bel-shunu,* their Lord]; KJV BEELSARUS bē ěl'sə rəs. One of the leaders of the Jews who returned to Palestine with Zerubbabel after the Exile (Ezra 2:2; Neh. 7:7; I Esd. 5:8).
M. NEWMAN

**BIMHAL** bǐm'hăl [במהל, *probably a shortened form of* בן-מהל, son of circumcision, *or* circumcised one] (I Chr. 7:33). A division of the clan of Japhlet in the tribe of Asher in the Chronicler's postexilic genealogy.

*Bibliography.* M. Noth, *Die israelitischen Personennamen* (1928), p. 239; F. V. Winnett, *A Study of the Lihyanite and Thamudic Inscriptions* (1937), p. 21. H. H. GUTHRIE, JR.

**BINDING AND LOOSING.** The power of binding and loosing was entrusted to Peter by Jesus: "I will give you the keys of the kingdom of heaven, and whatever you bind on earth shall be bound in heaven, and whatever you loose on earth shall be loosed in heaven" (Matt. 16:19). Later on (18:18), Jesus gave to all disciples the same promise in the same terms, but without the first sentence on the keys. The POWER OF KEYS was entrusted to Peter alone. A parallel to the saying on binding and loosing is found in the words addressed by Jesus to the apostles on the eve of the Resurrection: "If you forgive the sins of any, they are forgiven; if you retain the sins of any, they are retained" (John 20:23).

The terms "to bind" and "to loose" translate the Greek δεῖν and λύειν, which doubtless represent the Aramaic אסר and שרא (Hebrew אסר and התיר). In the rabbinic literature these verbs have two distinct senses. First, they mean "forbid" and "permit" and express the verdict of a teacher of the law who declares some action "bound" (forbidden) or "loosed" (permitted). Second, they are used in reference to the imposition or the removal of the ban, meaning "condemn" or "absolve" respectively.

Both meanings have been applied to the texts of Matthew. In fact, the second should be preferred. For the disciples were not scribes, but the messengers of the gospel, which brings forgiveness of sins and peace with God to those who receive it with faith and which delivers up the unbelievers to the judgment of God (cf. Matt. 10:13-14). This is also the meaning contained in the Johannine form of the saying. In short, "to loose" is the divine power to forgive sins and thus to admit new converts in the church and to restore to the fellowship of the church repentant sinners. "To bind" is to announce God's judgment to unbelievers and impenitent sinners.

The power to bind and to loose was entrusted first to Peter as the leader of the disciples, and then to the other disciples (Matt. 18:11)—i.e., to the Twelve

(John 20:23), and not to the church. Similarly, at the end of the apostolic age this power was transmitted to the ministry and not to the community (II Tim. 2:24-26; Tit. 3:10).

Another interpretation holds that the opposite verbs "to loose" and "to bind" express together the totality of the power entrusted to the apostles. As sometimes in the OT "good and bad" means everything (Gen. 24:50), here both verbs should say that the apostles have the power to do "everything."

*Bibliography.* Books on Peter by F. J. Foakes-Jackson (1927); O. Cullmann (1953). H. L. Strack and P. Billerbeck, *Kommentar zum NT aus Talmud und Midrasch,* I (1922), 736-47. H. J. Cadbury, "The Meaning of John 20:23, Matt. 16:19 and Matt. 18:18," *JBL,* LVIII (1939), 231-34. J. R. Mantey, "The Mistranslation of the Perfect Tense in John 20:23, Matt. 16:19 and Matt. 18:18," *JBL,* LVIII (1939), 243-49; G. Lambert, "Lier-délier. L'expression de la totalité par l'opposition des deux contraires," *Vivre et penser,* III (1944), 91-103. O. Michel, "Binden und Lösen," *Reallexikon für Antike und Christentum,* II (1954), 374-80. C. H. Dodd, "Some Johannine 'Herrenworte' with Parallels in the Synoptic Gospels," *NTS,* II (1955-56), 75-86.
P. H. MENOUD

**BINEA** bĭn′ĭ ə [בנעא]. One of the descendants of the house of Saul; in the Benjaminite genealogies described as the son of Moza and the father of Rephaiah (I Chr. 8:37; 9:43).

**BINNUI** bĭn′yŏŏ ī [בנוי, *from* בנה, to build; *apparently confused with* BANI; BUNNI; BAVVAI, *all similar in Hebrew*]. Apoc. BELNUUS bĕl′nŏŏ əs; KJV BALNUUS băl′— (I Esd. 9:31); BANNUS băn′əs (I Esd. 9:34); SABBAN săb′ən (I Esd. 8:63). **1.** Head of a family returning with Zerubbabel and Nehemiah (Neh. 7:15); probably the same as the Bani of Ezra 2:10 and possibly the Bani of Ezra 10:34.

**2.** A Levite of postexilic times (Ezra 8:33; Neh. 10:9; 12:8). Since the Binnui of Neh. 10:9 is designated as a son of Henadad, Binnui the son of Henadad who aided Nehemiah in repairing the walls of Jerusalem (Neh. 3:24), though not called a Levite, is probably the same person, and Bavvai the son of Henadad must also be the same person (Neh. 3:18). Bani (Neh. 8:7; 9:4) may also be the same person, since the names are confused. Binnui the Levite may also have appeared in the original text of Neh. 7:43 (duplicated in Ezra 2:40), where, in unpointed Hebrew, there would be little difference between "the sons of" and "Binnui." *Cf.* BANNAS (I Esd. 5:26).

**3.** A postexilic Jew, son of Pahath-moab (Ezra 10:30; I Esd. 9:31).

**4.** Head of a postexilic family (Ezra 10:38; probably same as in I Esd. 9:34).

*Bibliography.* M. Noth, *Die israelitischen Personennamen* (1928), pp. 38, 172.
H. H. GUTHRIE, JR.

**BIRD** [כל בעל כנף, any owner of a wing; עוף, flier (Aram. עוף; Dan. 2:38; 7:6), FOWL *in* Lev. 7:26; פרח(ת), flying ones; צפור, chirper (Aram. צפר; Dan. 4:12—Aram. 4:9; etc.; *alternately* SPARROW); ὄρνεον, *variant of* ὄρνις; πετεινόν, flier (*mostly plural*); πτηνός, *from* πέτομαι, to fly]; KJV alternately FOWL. A class (Aves) of warm-blooded vertebrates, distinguished from other animals by the body's being more or less completely covered with feathers.

**1. Classification.** When Tristram was in Palestine in the nineteenth century, he identified 322 species of birds (to which, he thought, at least 30 others should be added), and of this number 260 appeared in European bird lists (*NHB* 167-68). It is likely that the same diversity of bird life existed in the Holy Land in the biblical period. Tristram also noted that what arrested his attention was the "number and variety of the larger birds of prey . . . which abound in every part of the . . . Land, and are at first sight its ornithological characteristic."

The OT distinguishes between clean and unclean birds. The unclean ones are specified in Lev. 11:13-19; Deut. 14:11-20: these, speaking generally, are birds of prey (*see* BIRD OF PREY). By implication the nonraptorial birds are clean, though the OT does not supply criteria for identifying them. They would appear to comprise passerines, pigeons, partridges, etc. The Mishna states: "Any bird that seizes food in its claws is unclean; and any that has an extra talon and a craw, and the skin of whose stomach can be stripped off, is clean" (Hullin 3.6).

The migratory habits of some birds are referred to (Song of S. 2:12; Jer. 8:7; Hos. 11:11); their nesting in trees (Ezek. 31:6) and in proximity to springs (Ps. 104:12); their singing (Ps. 104:12; Eccl. 12:4; Wisd. Sol. 17:18); their being tamed as pets (Job 41:5—H 40:29; Jas. 3:7). The survival of birds under the ordinary conditions of nature is cited by Jesus as illustrative of the Father's care for his creatures (Matt. 6:26; Luke 12:24).

We do not know how important edible birds (whose blood was not to be eaten; Lev. 7:26) were in the household economy of the biblical period. The numerous references to bird traps suggest that fowling was common (Lev. 17:13; Job 18:8-10; Ps. 124:7; Prov. 6:5; Jer. 5:27; Hos. 7:12; Amos 3:5; Ecclus. 11:30; 27:19; Bar. 3:17; etc.). Pigeons (*see* PIGEON), which served the poor as food and as religious offerings, were undoubtedly bred both in homes and in dovecots (Isa. 60:8; M. Shab. 24.3; Bez. 1.3). Small birds such as sparrows were also commonly eaten (Matt. 10:29). On domestic poultry, *see* FOWL.

**2. In the OT.** עוף (cf. כל עוף כנף, "every winged bird"; Gen. 1:21; cf. Ps. 78:27), which frequently appears in the phrase "birds of the air" (Gen. 1:26, etc.), is the most general term for all birds (Gen. 1:20, etc.), which are divided into species (Gen. 6:20) and into the categories of clean and unclean (Lev. 20:25). עוף is often associated with "beasts," "reptiles," and "fish," to make up the fauna known to ancient Israel (Gen. 1:26, etc.). It designates vultures and other carrion-eating birds (Gen. 40:19; Deut. 28:26; etc.), as well as game birds (Lev. 17:13; cf. Jer. 5:27) and the quail of the Exodus (Ps. 78:27). It is used of Noah's burnt offering (Gen. 8:20), and once of the burnt offering of doves and pigeons (Lev. 1:14). For the use of עוף in the phrase שרץ העוף ("winged insects"; Lev. 11:20-21; Deut. 14:19), *see* INSECTS.

צפור, while it may, like עוף, refer to birds of every sort (Gen. 7:14; Deut. 4:17; Ezek. 17:23; Dan. 4:12), including birds of prey (Ezek. 39:4, 17), usually designates the game birds (Ps. 124:7; Prov. 6:5; etc.) or the passerines (Ps. 102:7—H 102:8; Dan. 4:12). The allusion in Deut. 22:6-7 is to a nesting bird whose eggs are eaten, in Gen. 15:10 to doves and pigeons, in Lev. 14 to the birds used in the ritual for cleansing the leper and the leprous house. In Neh. 5:18 ("fowls") the reference is to edible birds suitable for a governor's table. See FOWL; SPARROW.

**3. In the NT.** Ὄρνεον is used in Rev. 18:2 to emphasize the utter ruin to descend on Babylon, which is to become the "haunt of every foul and hateful bird." In 19:17, 21, the reference is to vultures.

Πετεινόν is used (as πτηνός is in I Cor. 15:39) for birds in general (Matt. 6:26, etc.); in Acts 10:12-14 it includes unclean birds, and in Matt. 13:4, 32, it points to the passerines.

*See also* FAUNA § B.    W. S. McCULLOUGH

**BIRD OF PREY** [עִיט, screamer, *from* עִיט, to scream, shriek; *cf.* Arab. *'ayyaṭa,* to yell, scream]; KJV FOWL (Gen. 15:11; etc.); BIRD (Jer. 12:9); RAVENOUS BIRD (Isa. 46:11; cf. Ezek. 39:4). Any bird which seizes another animal for food.

Biblical Palestine was familiar with a large number of birds of prey—eagles, vultures, hawks, falcons, etc. All the members of this group were unclean to the Hebrews, and many of them are specifically mentioned among the forbidden birds in Lev. 11; Deut. 14. The fact that עִיט is not included in these lists supports the view that it is a general term to designate any bird of prey, as in Gen. 15:11. In Job 28:7 it appears in a parallel construction with אַיָּה, "falcon." It is used most commonly to emphasize a present or an anticipated desolation, as in Isa. 18:6; Jer. 12:9*b* (the text of vs. 9*a* may be corrupt; *see* SPECKLED BIRD); Ezek. 39:4. In Isa. 46:11 it apparently refers to Cyrus of Persia.

W. S. McCULLOUGH

**BIRSHA** bûr′shə [בִּרְשַׁע; LXX Βαρσα]. King of Gomorrah (Dead Sea Genesis Apocryphon XXI.24, 32: עוּמְרָם), defeated after rebelling against Chedorlaomer (Gen. 14:2; cf. also vss. 8, 10-11).

**BIRTH** [הוֹלֵד, *infinitive construct Niph'al or Hoph'al,* act of being born; מוֹלֶדֶת, birth, offspring; γένεσις, origin, source, manner of birth, nativity]. Many births were desired because of the importance of large families (*see* FAMILY). There was some understanding of the processes of conception and pregnancy, as well as birth, although there was a realization of the mystery of life as well (Eccl. 11:5). Although ovum was unknown to biblical writers, it was thought that only the seed of the male was determinative in conception and gestation, the woman providing in her womb a receptacle for its protection and growth (Wisd. Sol. 7:2-3). However, the famous Egyptian hymn to Aton refers to "seed" in woman and "fluid" in man. *See bibliography.*

The Bible reveals no evidence of attempts at birth control. Onan's deliberate wasting of his semen is condemned only because he refuses to raise an offspring to his brother's widow, thereby breaking the LEVIRATE LAW.

Two sources mention nine months' pregnancy (II Esd. 4:40; II Macc. 7:27; cf. ten months' pregnancy in Wisd. Sol. 7:2-3).

There are also allusions to the process of birth itself. The Hebrew women in Egypt were delivered quickly (Exod. 1:19), but usually birth was agonizing

and so unforgettably painful that various writers use this experience figuratively. We note the trembling of kings (Ps. 48:6), pangs, agony, anguish when the Lord's day is near (Isa. 13:8), cries, gasping, and panting (Isa. 42:14; cf. Jer. 6:24; 13:21; 22:23; 30:6; 48:41; 49:24; 50:43; John 16:21; Rev. 12:2). A son was born literally to the father, who received him on his knees (Gen. 21:3; 50:23). The words "Upon thee was I cast from my birth" may suggest the father's act of receiving his child when it came from the mother's womb (Ps. 22:10). Rachel, on the other hand, hoped to bear a child upon her knees through her maid Bilhah (Gen. 30:3). The use of MANDRAKE plants may have had the effect of relaxing the womb and facilitating the birth process. Women were assisted in childbirth by the use of the BIRTHSTOOL (*see* MIDWIFE). After birth the infant's navel cord was cut; then the infant was washed, rubbed with salt, and swathed in bands (Ezek. 16:4). The mother must undergo a cleansing process after the birth of her child (Lev. 12:2-8).

Sometimes birth was premature, because of the shock of bad news (I Sam. 4:19); or a woman might lack strength to bring a child to birth (II Kings 19:3). The UNTIMELY BIRTH enters the darkness and finds rest (Eccl. 6:4-5); one who is born thus can lie down and sleep, avoiding the agony of life (Job 3:11-13). A miscarriage could be caused by accident or violence (Exod. 21:22-25). It may have been regarded as a divine judgment (Ps. 58:8; Hos. 9:14). Miscarriage because of assault is covered by the Babylonian, Assyrian, and Hittite codes. *See bibliography.*

A birth was the occasion for rejoicing and ceremonial activities, especially the birth of a son (Ruth 4:14; Jer. 20:15; Luke 1:14, 57-58; 2:13, John 16:21). Children were named at birth (Gen. 29:32, 35; 30:6 ff). The birthday became an occasion for festivities (Gen. 40:20; Matt. 14:6). The day of birth may be cursed when life is miserable (Job 3:3; Jer. 20:14). In a spiritual sense, one may be born a second time, of the water and the Spirit (John 3:3-7)—figuratively, the new birth.

*See also* CHILD; FAMILY; MARRIAGE; SEX; WOMAN.

**Bibliography.** J. B. Pritchard, ed., *ANET* (2nd ed., 1955), p. 370.    O. J. BAAB

**BIRTH, VIRGIN.** See VIRGIN BIRTH.

**BIRTH OF MARY, GOSPEL OF.** See MARY, GOSPEL OF THE BIRTH OF.

**BIRTHRIGHT** [בְּכֹרָה, right of the first-born]. While all a man's sons had his protection and some benefits, the FIRST-BORN son had a special inheritance. His was the principal inheritance of property and name. Through him the FAMILY line was continued.

The stories of Jacob's appropriation of Esau's birthright as the first-born are important, for they show how Jacob, rather than his brother, continued the line of Abraham and Isaac (Gen. 25:29-34). Birthrights might be taken away from the eldest son. The birthright of Reuben was taken from him and given to the sons of Joseph (I Chr. 5:1; cf. Gen. 49:4). At a meal the sons were seated in order of their ages, "the first-born according to his birthright" (Gen. 43:33). The kingdom was given to the first-born as his right (II Chr. 21:3; cf. Ps. 89:27). Israel received the protection of her God, who made her his first-born (Exod. 4:22-23; Jer. 31:9). Paul had the privileges of Roman citizenship as a birthright (Acts 22:28).                                    O. J. BAAB

**BIRTHSTOOL** [אָבְן, *'óbhen*, wheel, disc; *variant reading*, *'ébhen*, stone, *in the plural*]. An object upon which a woman sat during labor. It was possibly of Egyptian origin.

*Bibliography.* For the custom of labor on a stool, see H. H. Ploss, *Das Weib* (3rd ed., 1891), pp. 35, 179 ff. For a view as to the Egyptian custom, see W. Spiegelberg, *Aegypten Randglossen* (1904), pp. 19-25.                                    O. J. BAAB

**BIRZAITH** bûr zā'əth [ברזית (*Qere*), well of the olive tree] (I Chr. 7:31); KJV **BIRZAVITH** —vĭth [ברזות (*Kethibh*)]. A name in a postexilic list of clans of the tribe of Asher. It does not appear in the parallel lists in Gen. 46:17; Num. 26:44-47, and seems, actually, to be the name of a place. It is probably to be identified with the modern village of Birzeit, which is located approximately 4.3 miles N of Ramallah, near ancient Tyre.

*Bibliography.* F.-M. Abel, "Une Mention Biblique du Birzeit," *RB*, XLVI (1937), 217 ff; *Géographie de la Palestine*, II (1938), 55.                                    H. H. GUTHRIE, JR.

**BISHLAM** bĭsh'ləm [בשלם, *possibly a shortened form of* בן־שלם, son of peace]; KJV Apoc. **BELEMUS** bĕl'ə məs. One of three men who took the lead in writing a letter of complaint against the Jews in post-exilic Palestine to the Persian king Artaxerxes (Ezra 4:7; I Esd. 2:16). The LXX, however, translates ἐν εἰρήνῃ, which would be a literal rendering of the Aramaic and comparable to the Hebrew בשלום. If this is correct, it would be part of the salutation of the letter. It has also been suggested that בשלם is perhaps a corruption of an original בירושלם, "against Jerusalem," which the letter in actuality was.
                                    M. NEWMAN

**BISHOP** [ἐπίσκοπος, overseer, guardian]. The title of the chief hierarchical order of ministry in the church, since post-apostolic times. In this sense the word occurs twice in the Pastoral letters (I Tim. 3:2; Tit. 1:7) in contexts describing the qualifications and duties of the office. It is used once (I Pet. 2:25 KJV) as a title of Christ. In the other two instances of the use of ἐπίσκοπος in the NT—in Phil. 1:1 by Paul, and in Acts 20:28 in a speech attributed to Paul—opinion has been divided as to whether the term has a technical sense. With these references should be associated Acts 1:20, where ἐπισκοπή is cited from Ps. 109:8 (LXX) with reference to the "overseership" forfeited by Judas' treachery and suicide. Also in I Pet. 5:2 some MSS insert the participial form of the verb ἐπισκοπεῖν to describe the pastoral oversight of elders (*see* ELDER IN NT).

The letters of Ignatius, martyr-bishop of Antioch (not later than A.D. 117), provide the earliest and most complete picture of the position and responsibilities of a bishop in the church. To the Christian community over which he was placed, he embodied the "authority of God the Father." No gathering of his church for baptism, Eucharist, or AGAPE was valid without his presence or authorization. He was the chief pastor of his flock, and the administrator and dispenser of its charity. The elders served him as a council of advice and acted as his deputies in his absence. The deacons were directly subordinate to him as assistants in worship and pastoral visitations. The bishop alone received the vows of virgins and enrolled widows (*see* WIDOW). He was the spokesman of his church in all correspondence with other churches and appointed ambassadors to other Christian communities as the need arose. He was responsible for all preaching and teaching, even though he himself might depute this function to others. He was also the guardian and representative of his people in its relations with the non-Christian community. In short, the bishop was chief priest, pastor, and ruler of his church.

In the light of these manifold responsibilities, the qualifications of character and ability for the episcopal office, as outlined in the Pastoral letters, is understandable. The DIDACHE (15:1-2) also enjoins that bishops (and deacons) should be ordained—men who are "humble, not avaricious, faithful, and well-tested," and who are to be honored in their ministry as the prophets and teachers.

The bishop was elected by the whole church that he was to serve, after being tested by the Spirit (or, as I Tim. 4:14 suggests, after being designated "by prophetic utterance"). He was ordained by prayer and the laying on of hands, but the ministers who acted in this ordination are not precisely noted in the earlier literature. I Tim. 4:14 has been taken by some critics to mean that the elders originally ordained the bishops. By the time of Hippolytus (*ca.* 200) it was considered an "apostolic tradition" that bishops of neighboring churches assembled for the ordination.

The major problem concerning the emergence in the church of the monarchical episcopate, as it is seen in Ignatius' letters, is not so much the cause of it, as the process by which it came about. With this problem is associated the question of "apostolic succession"—for from the middle of the second century, if not before, the bishops were viewed in the church as the direct heirs of the authority of the apostles, in an unbroken continuity of office, and the primary preservers for the church of the apostolic faith.

This viewpoint is presented for the first time *ca.* 95, in the Epistle of Clement (*see* CLEMENT, EPISTLE OF), written from Rome to the church in Corinth, in protest against the deposition by the Corinthians of their bishops and deacons. The apostles, said the writer, when they had preached in the villages and cities, "appointed their first converts, after testing them by the Spirit, as bishops and deacons of those who were to believe." This institution was foretold in scripture, according to Isa. 60:17. Knowing that there would be strife for the office, the apostles made arrangements that after their death other "tested men" should succeed to this office—namely, an office of "liturgy, . . . of offering the gifts" (chs. 42-44). *See* ELDER IN THE NT.

It is apparent from I Clement that the bishops' ministry was primarily a liturgical one of presidency at the Eucharist, in which they were assisted by the deacons. The same emphasis upon liturgical ministration is evident in the directives of the Didache, as already noted; and later works, such as Hippolytus' *Apostolic Tradition* and the references of Tertullian and Cyprian, make clear the primary function of the bishop as chief "priest" in the sacramental rites of the church. It is reasonable to suppose, therefore, that the bishops were originally those ministers of the Christian communities who were ordained as "overseers" of the Eucharistic banquet, by virtue of their evident "spiritual gift" (*charisma*) for this service. That they were selected and ordained for this office by the apostles, as I Clement says, is certainly possible; and that they were also members of the local presbyteries of "elders" is probable. Thus the apparent identification of bishops and elders in Acts 20:28; Tit. 1:5-7; I Clem. 44.5 may be explained.

It is also likely that Paul's greeting in Phil. 1:1 to the "bishops and deacons" was used in a technical sense. This letter was a note of thanks to the Philippians for the material assistance sent the apostle during his imprisonment. It would be only natural that Paul would single out for special mention those ministers of the church who had been particularly responsible for the overseeing of this charity. Such men would be the ministers in charge of the Eucharist, who received and dispensed the offerings of the people at the common meeting for the breaking of bread.

It is possible that in the early days there was a bishop-overseer for each house-church congregation. But the crises of the post-apostolic age brought about the concentration of authority in the hands of a single—i.e., monarchical—bishop. For the bishop's overseership of the Eucharist placed him in a favorable position for assuming such control. As presiding minister at the chief service of worship, he could decide which preachers, teachers, and prophets would be faithful to the doctrine of the apostles, and therefore he would allow them to speak or not, depending upon their orthodoxy. As the administrator of the offerings of the people, the bishop would assume primary pastoral responsibilities, with powers of excommunicating those who for one reason or another, doctrinal or ethical, would not be "in good standing," either for participating in the common worship or for receiving from its sacramental and charitable gifts. It would also be the responsibility of the bishop, in view of the increasing danger of persecution by the state, to safeguard the community, as far as possible, in its assemblies for worship, from detection and menace by the police. The evolution of the episcopal office in the church, therefore, was a response to pressing needs for authoritative guardianship in the period after the passing of the apostle-founders. But the office itself was of apostolic origin and appointment, and in this sense the bishops could legitimately claim to be the successors of the apostles.

Many attempts have been made to find prototypes of the bishop in the Jewish and Gentile background of Christianity. Some have seen in the headship of James over the Jerusalem community the first example of a monarchical bishop. Others have derived the office from that of the ruler of the Jewish synagogue, who presided over the worship of the synagogue and selected those who took part in its services

(*see* SYNAGOGUE). In the LXX (Job 20:29; Wisd. Sol. 1:6), the term ἐπίσκοπος is used of God (so also commonly in Philo), and in a number of instances of ordinary overseers; but it is never used of cultic ministers. Philo (*Who Is the Heir* 30) gives the title once to Moses. In I Macc. 1:51 (LXX) the word is used of the inspectors set over the Jews by Antiochus Epiphanes to carry out his religious policy.

The term is fairly common in Greek literature, papyri, and inscriptions, both in its general meaning of oversight and as a technical name for officials, civil and religious. From the time of Homer (*Iliad* XXII. 254) it is applied to the gods. The Cynic-Stoic philosophers were especially fond of the term to describe their own mission as messengers and heralds of the gods (though the form κατάσκοπος is more common than ἐπίσκοπος; cf. Epictetus *Discourses* III. 22, 38, 69, 72, 77, 97; Dio Chrysostom *Orat.* 9, 1). Many Syrian inscriptions note ἐπίσκοποι as overseers of buildings, provisions, coins, etc.; and cult associations of Greece and the Aegean isles record the term in reference to directors and cashiers. Until recently, it was a common view of scholars that the title of bishop was of Gentile origin in the church, first coming into usage in the mission churches founded outside Palestine, to denote those "elders" of the churches who were charged with the oversight of the common meals and the offerings of the faithful.

The recent discoveries of MSS of the Qumran community near the Dead Sea, however, have raised once more the question as to the possible Jewish origin of the title "overseer" (*see* DEAD SEA SCROLLS). The Damascus Document, published by Schechter in 1910, described an overseer or inspector of the camp (מבקר, *mebaqqer*), who taught the covenanters the "works of God," looked after them "as does a shepherd his flock," and, in particular, supervised the admission of new members, the disciplining of offenders, and all financial transactions. This same officer now appears in the Manual of Discipline from Qumran (VI.12-20; cf. CDC IX.18-22; XIII.7-19; XIV.11-13; XV.8, 14), and appears to be comparable to the "steward" of the Essenes (ἐπιμελητής) noted by Josephus (War II.viii.3; cf. Philo in Euseb. *Preparation* VIII.11). Whether or not there is any direct relationship between the overseer of these covenanters and the office of bishop in the church cannot be securely determined until research is more advanced in the larger question of the impact of the Qumran and similar communities upon the development of primitive Christianity. *See also* APOSTLE; MINISTRY, CHRISTIAN.

**Bibliography.** H. W. Beyer in Kittel, *TWNT*, II, 595-619, is fundamental; W. Lowrie, *The Church and Its Organization in Primitive and Catholic Times* (1904), especially pp. 331-71; H. Lietzmann, "Zur altchristlichen Verfassungsgeschichte," *Zeitschrift für wissenschaftliche Theologie*, LV (1913), 97-153; H. B. Swete, ed., *Essays on the Early History of the Church and the Ministry* (2nd ed., 1921), pp. 57-214; O. Linton, *Das Problem der Urkirche in der neueren Forschung* (1932); R. Dunkerley, ed., *The Ministry and the Sacraments* (1937), pp. 326-87; M. H. Shepherd, Jr., "Smyrna in the Ignatian Letters," *JR*, XX (1940), 141-59; K. E. Kirk, ed., *The Apostolic Ministry* (1946), pp. 113-303; H. F. von Campenhausen, *Kirchliches Amt und geistliche Vollmacht in den ersten drei Jahrhunderten* (1953); A. Ehrhardt, *The Apostolic Succession in the First Two Centuries of the Church* (1953); B. Reicke, "Die Verfassung der

Urgemeinde im Lichte jüdischer Dokumente," *Theologische Zeitschrift*, X (1954), 95-112; J. Daniélou, "La communauté de Qumrân et l'organization de l'Église ancienne," *RHPR*, XXXV (1955), 104-15. *See also bibliography* under CLEMENT, EPISTLE OF; IGNATIUS, EPISTLES OF.

M. H. SHEPHERD, JR.

**BISHOPS' BIBLE.** The Bible version published in 1568 under the editorship of Archbishop Parker as the second authorized version. At least nine of the revisers were bishops, hence the name "Bishops' Bible." *See* VERSIONS, ENGLISH, § 5.

**BIT** [מֶתֶג (KJV BRIDLE); χαλινός]; BRIDLE [מַחְסוֹם (*alternately* MUZZLE), רֶסֶן (*alternately* HALTER); KJV מֶתֶג (RSV BIT); χαλινός]. The bridle is the headgear of a horse's HARNESS, and the bit is the metal mouthpiece by which the bridle works to control or restrain the horse. This type of harness was not needed until the horse and chariot became popular. Fig. BIT 42.

Courtesy of the Palestine Archaeological Museum, Jerusalem, Jordan

42. A bronze horse's bit, from Tell el-'Ajjul (second millennium B.C.)

Early metal bits were a bar with a loop at each end for the reins. Just inside the loops were plates, or spiked wheels, which caused the animal pain and so made him tractable. A jointed bit is also known *ca.* the end of the second millennium B.C.

The words translated "bit" and "bridle" sometimes refer metaphorically to any form of control.

C. U. WOLF

**BITHIAH** bĭ thī'ə [בִּתְיָה, daughter (*i.e.,* worshiper) of Yahu] (I Chr. 4:17—H 4:18; cf. KJV). A daughter of Pharaoh and wife of Mered of Judah.

*Bibliography.* E. L. Curtis, *Chronicles*, ICC (1910), pp. 111-12.

B. T. DAHLBERG

**BITHRON** bĭth'rŏn [הַבִּתְרוֹן, the ravine]. KJV translation in II Sam. 2:29; the way by which Abner and his warriors returned to Mahanaim after their defeat near Gibeon. It was apparently not a wadi but a short cut through the mountains, well known at the time but now unknown. On the other hand, W. R. Arnold, pointing out the parallel between "all the night" and "all the Bithron," has suggested that the word means "forenoon," the translation adopted by the RSV (*AJSV*, XXVIII [1911-12], 274-83).

S. COHEN

**BITHYNIA** bĭ thĭn'ĭ ə [Βιθυνία]. A region in NW Asia Minor, named after a Thracian tribe. Its E neighbor was Paphlagonia; its S borders were formed by the Sangarius or Tembris valleys and Mysia. The Sangarius flows through Bithynia, and its lower valley forms the richest agricultural area of the country. The other fertile district is the plain near Mount Olympus. Large forests still exist in the inland areas.

Bithynia, like many other districts in Asia Minor, had some Greek cities along its coasts—e.g., Chalcedon and Heraclea Pontica—but the main body of its population consisted of Bithynians, Thracian (Indo-European) immigrants who moved into Asia Minor sometime in the dark ages after the fall of Troy (1200-800 B.C.). The region of Bithynia was only peripherally affected by Phrygian and Persian rule. In Hellenistic times a local dynasty increased the importance of the district (297-74 B.C.). Nicomedes I (279-250) was the founder of its capital Nicomedia, modern Izmit, on the Propontis. He invited the Gauls to come to his aid from Thrace, thereby fostering the dangerous movement of barbarians into Asia Minor. His grandson Prusias I (*ca.* 230-183) was an ally of Macedon against Pergamum, but his power was curtailed by Rome. Prusias was the founder of the city of Prusa ad Olympum, which as modern Bursa continues to be one of the leading cities of the district. Its prosperity is based on agriculture and the abundance of hot medicinal springs. The kingdom of Bithynia was bequeathed to Rome in 74 B.C.

Pompey organized Pontus and Bithynia into a single province in 65-63 B.C. Our best source of information about conditions in this district are the letters of Pliny the Younger, who was special commissioner of Bithynia and Pontus in A.D. 111-13. The number of Bithynian Christians was high in his days. Pliny wrote to Trajan that Christianity had spread even to the villages and rural districts (Letter 96), which implies that even the least Hellenized areas were reached by evangelization.

Paul apparently had planned to go into Bithynia from the S (Acts 16:7), approximately from the region of Dorylaeum in N Phrygia, from which Nicaea and Nicomedia could be reached. Dissuaded by the Spirit of Jesus from entering Bithynia, he traveled W to the Troad.

Of the two major cities of Bithynia, Nicomedia-Izmit has preserved some of the Hellenistic and Roman fortifications of its citadel. Nicaea-Iznik has a more impressive set of ancient walls, which, however, date from Roman to Seljuk times.

*Bibliography.* D. Magie, *Roman Rule in Asia Minor* (1950), pp. 302-20.

M. J. MELLINK

**BITTER, BITTERNESS.** Unpleasant experiences were described in the Scriptures in terms of the sense of taste, just as in English literature. In the Bible bitterness is symbolic of affliction, misery, slavery, and wickedness. All ten Hebrew words translated "bitter," "bitterness," are variants of the verb מָרַר, "to be bitter." Cf. the variants of Greek πικρός, "bitter" (Jas. 3:11, 14; cf. πικρία [Acts 8:23; Rom. 3:14; Eph. 4:31; Heb. 12:15]; πικρῶς [Matt. 26:75; Luke 22:62]; πικραίνω [Col. 3:19; Rev. 8:11; 10:9-10]). English expressions such as: "He made a bilious attack upon him," "It was a galling experience," and "She was tastefully dressed," have parallel derivation. Bitter taste was associated with the gall bladder and the acrid juices of upset digestion.

Experiences of bitterness may be classified for convenience under four headings:

*a*) Emotion. Subdivision may be made here of

active and passive emotion: cruel, biting words may be uttered (Gen. 27:34; Job 13:26; Ps. 106:33), or other manifestation of disposition (Rom. 3:14); or more subjective emotions may be experienced (Hos. 12:14; Jas. 3:14).

*b*) Living conditions, vividly described (Gen. 26: 35; Exod. 1:14; II Sam. 2:26; II Kings 14:26).

*c*) Food: bitter fruit (Deut. 29:18; 32:32); bitter herbs (Exod. 12:8; Num. 9:11); as opposed to food of pleasant taste (Isa. 5:20; Prov. 5:4 uses the contrast as a simile).

*d*) Water or other beverage (cf. Exod. 15:23; Isa. 24:9). Special reference is made to BITTER WATER, a concoction thought to reveal erring women of the community.

Figurative use was made of each of these types of experience. Particular attention was given to illustration of ethical values (Deut. 29:18; 32:32). The symbolism passed into major festivals. BITTER HERBS were used to make quick salads. Use of the bitter herb in the Passover meal took on increasing significance. The symbolism at first signified the haste with which the meal was prepared and eaten, but eventually it was used as a reminder of the bitterness of the experience of the Egyptian bondage.

W. G. WILLIAMS

**BITTER HERBS** [מררים]. Herbs eaten with the pascal lamb during the PASSOVER (Exod. 12:8; Num. 9:11), symbolically referring to the bitter experiences of the Hebrews in Egypt prior to the Exodus (M. Pes. 10.5). Many botanists have attempted to identify a specific herb intended by the injunction, including endives (*Cichorium endivia* L., native to India and unlikely in Bible times), common chicory (*Cichorium intybus* L., also called succory), lettuce (*Lactuca sativa* L.), water cress (*Nasturtium officinale* R. Br.), and several other bitter-tasting herbs. The selection of the *Centaurea* family of herbs ("star thistles"; *see* FLORA §§ A12*c*, 14*c*; THISTLES) is based on a desert (Exodus) setting for the origin of the custom, but the Pentateuch passages more likely suggest a postexilic Palestinian background (P source). The Hebrew word and its Greek equivalent, πικρίς, intend a general meaning which could include many different herbs, as shown by the Mishnaic reference to five kinds of herbs (Pes. 2.6), the exact identification of which is not entirely certain. Horse-radish (*Armoracia lapathifolia* Gilib.) is commonly used in Europe and America today as "bitter herbs" with the pascal lamb, but it was not known in Bible times.

מררים in Lam. 3:15 ("bitterness") might be translated "bitter herbs," in parallelism with לענה, WORMWOOD.

> He has filled me with bitterness [or bitter herbs],
> he has sated me with wormwood.

In Heb. 12:15 ρίζα πικρίας (cf. Deut. 29:18—H 29: 17), "root of bitterness," may have the symbolic meaning of "bitter herbs." *See* GALL.

*Bibliography.* A. L. and H. N. Moldenke, *Plants of the Bible* (1952), pp. 74-75. J. C. TREVER

**BITTER WATER.** KJV form of WATER OF BITTERNESS. *See also* MEDICINE.

**BITTERN.** KJV translation of קפד, קפוד. *See* HEDGEHOG.

**BITUMEN** bĭ tōō′mən, —tū′— [חמר]; KJV SLIME. Originally, mineral pitch or asphalt. Today the term includes numerous hydrocarbons.

The Hebrew word, from its derivation, may denote a "foaming up"; hence the word is used in regard to wells or pits in Gen. 14:10. It may also contain a concept of "covering"; hence it was used by Moses' mother to calk the ark of bulrushes (Exod. 2:3). Josephus (Antiq. I.ix) calls the Dead Sea "Lacus Asphaltitis" because of the presence of asphalt on its surface at the S end.

It has been suggested that bitumen was used by the Egyptians in their embalming, but this is doubtful. Bitumen was used as mortar in the Plain of Shinar (Gen. 11:3). Pits of bitumen were found near Kirkuk in Assyria, and at Hit on the Euphrates, whence it was shipped to Sumer. Bitumen was used as mortar in setting the burnt brick which formed the outer layers of the ziggurat of Ur. It was also used as calking for the rafts and basket boats on the Euphrates. It was used as a material for monuments. In some statuary it was used to simulate the pupils of eyes. *See also* PITCH. W. E. STAPLES

**BIZIOTHIAH** bĭz′ĭ ō thī′ə [בזיותיה] (Josh. 15:28); KJV **BIZJOTHJAH** bĭz jŏth′jə. A place in the Negeb district of Judah. The present text is probably corrupt, and one should read: ובנותיה, "and her daughters" (i.e., outlying villages; cf. LXX and the parallel list in Neh. 11:27). V. R. GOLD

**BIZTHA** bĭz′thə [בזתא, *perhaps* eunuch, *from* Pers. *besteh*, bound] (Esth. 1:10). One of seven eunuchs who served Ahasuerus as chamberlains and whom he sent for Queen Vashti.

**BLACK.** A word describing mainly natural objects and phenomena, calamity, gloom, and mourning. In the OT, שחר, חום, and קדר or their derivatives express varying degrees of darkness and are the Hebrew words most frequently translated "black." The word שחר, "to be black," is used of hair (Lev. 13:31, 37; Song of S. 5:11), skin (Job 30:30; Song of S. 1:5-6), the human face (Lam. 4:8), and horses (Zech. 6:2, 6). The black (KJV "brown") color of lambs (Gen. 30) is implied by חום, that which is "warm," "hot," or "burned."

Black in the heavens, as the sign of rain (I Kings 18:45), a symbol of cosmic mourning (Jer. 4:28), or desolation (Isa. 50:3), is expressed by קדר, This word, meaning "to be dirty, dark, or gloomy," also is employed to picture a visionless day (Mic. 3:6), treachery of Job's brethren (Job 6:16), and the mourning of individuals (Job 30:28; Jer. 8:21) and of Judah (Jer. 14:2).

The Greek word γέλας in the NT signifies "black" and is utilized in the description of hair (Matt. 5:36), apocalyptic horses (Rev. 6:5), and the darkened sun (Rev. 6:12). "Blackness" or "darkness" is intended by γνόφῳ (Heb. 12:18), and the "nether gloom or blackness of darkness" by ζόφος in Jude 13.

*See also* COLORS. C. L. WICKWIRE

**BLAINS.** KJV form of SORES.

**BLASPHEMY** [נאצה (Neh. 9:18, 26), βλασφημία (Matt. 12:31, etc.)]; **BLASPHEME** [נאץ (Lev. 24:11, 16), גדף (Ezek. 20:27), חרף (Isa. 65:7 KJV), קלל (I Sam. 3:13), βλασφημέω (Matt. 26:65; etc.)]. Slandering, reproaching, cursing, or showing contempt. In English the word "blasphemy" is specifically applied to dishonoring and reviling of the name, being, or work of God by word or action. This can occur through a deliberate and flagrant sin (Num. 15:30) and through speaking insultingly against (Isa. 37:6) or cursing (Lev. 24:11, 16; I Sam. 3:13 LXX-RSV; Rev. 16:9, 11, 21) God (cf. I Sam. 2:17; Neh. 9:18; Tob. 1:18 [LXX S]; II Macc. 10:34-36; 12:14; Acts 19:37).

Archetypal enemies of God are characteristically full of blasphemies (II Macc. 9:28; Rev. 13:1 ff; 17:3). The Jews accused Stephen (Acts 6:11) and Jesus of this crime, the latter because he presumed to forgive sins (Matt. 9:3; Mark 2:7; Luke 5:21) and claimed to be Christ the Son of God (Matt. 26:63-65; Mark 14:61-64; John 10:33, 36). On the other hand, the NT calls it blasphemy to revile Christ (Matt. 27:39; Mark 15:29; Luke 22:65; 23:39). Those who oppose the gospel (I Tim. 1:13; cf. Acts 26:11) and bring discredit to Christianity (Rom. 2:24; I Tim. 6:1; Tit. 2:5; Jas. 2:7; II Pet. 2:2) are blaspheming God by their actions.

As in classical Greek, βλασφημία in the NT also appears in a weaker sense as "mockery," "reviling," or "slander" directed against a human person (cf. Mark 7:22; I Cor. 4:13; Col. 3:8; I Pet. 4:4; Rev. 2:9; etc.). When directed against spiritual authorities (as against Christ; *see above*), it approximates blasphemy against God (Acts 13:45; 18:6; II Pet. 2:10-12; Jude 8-10).

The "unforgivable sin," blasphemy against the Holy Spirit (Matt. 12:31-32; Mark 3:28-30; Luke 12:10), must be understood as the deliberate and perverse repudiation of God's saving work, whereby one consciously hardens himself against repentance and the possibility of forgiveness (cf. I Tim. 1:20).

           S. J. DE VRIES

**BLASTING.** Translation of שדפון in the KJV and in Deut. 28:22 RSV. *See* BLIGHT.

**BLASTUS** blăs′təs [Βλάστος] (Acts 12:20). Chamberlain of Herod Agrippa I. This name, similar to the common noun meaning "bud" or "sprout," appears in both pagan and Christian writings. Nothing is known of Blastus beyond the information in Acts 12:20. The people of Tyre and Sidon, under sharp disfavor of Agrippa and fearful about their food supply, persuaded Blastus to aid them in making peace with Agrippa. Blastus, whose intimate position in charge of the royal bedchambers provided him with influence with Agrippa, was probably persuaded (cf. Matt. 28:14) with a royal bribe.    D. M. BECK

**BLEACH** [λευκαίνω] (Mark 9:3). To make white; used in describing the appearance of the garments of Jesus at the Transfiguration. The same Greek word occurs in the LXX in Lev. 13:19; Ps. 51:9—G 50:9; Isa. 1:18; Joel 1:7 (all from the root לבן, "to be white").       J. M. MYERS

**BLEMISH.** *See* SACRIFICE AND OFFERINGS § D.

**BLESSEDNESS.** KJV translation of μακαρισμός in Rom. 4:6, 9 (RSV "blessing"); Gal. 4:15 (RSV "satisfaction"). In the RSV the word "blessedness" does not occur at all. But the word "blessed" occurs frequently, in two different senses, as applied (*a*) to God and (*b*) to men.

In English the verb "bless" was taken into Christian usage originally to represent the Latin *benedicere*, which is used in the Latin (Vulg.) version of the Bible to translate, very literally, εὐλογεῖν, the usual (but far from literal) rendering in the Greek version of the OT (LXX) of the Hebrew verb ברך. The primary meaning of ברך is "to bend the knees" (cf. II Chr. 6:13), but it is most often used in the secondary sense, "to worship, adore, praise." So "blessed" came to be, through Latin *benedictus* and Greek εὐλογητός, the English rendering of the passive participle ברוך, which in its proper sense of "worshiped, adored," can be used only of God. But, rather surprisingly, the same verb, ברך, is also used in a very different sense, of God's "blessing" of men by manifesting his favor and goodness toward them (cf., e.g., Deut. 7:12-16). Then by a further development of meaning, men are said to "bless" other men, when they invoke upon them the blessing of God (cf., e.g., Gen. 14:19 —here the verb "bless" is used three times, once in each of the three meanings mentioned). But in English "blessed" (as an adjective) was used also for *beatus*, which in the Vulg. corresponds to אשרי and μακάριος. The Hebrew word is used only of men, never of God. In secular Greek μακάριος could be used equally well of the gods and of men, but in the NT there are only two instances in which it is used of God (I Tim. 1:11; 6:15).

When "blessed" is used of God (ברוך; εὐλογητός) in such an exclamation as: "Blessed be the LORD," the meaning is primarily: "Let God be worshiped, adored." Yet it is clearly implied that God is worthy of adoration; and when the reason God should be adored is stated, it is because of his goodness shown to the worshiper (cf., e.g., Ps. 28:6). There is no thought of any abstract blessedness which can be ascribed to God in himself.

When "blessed" is used of men (אשרי; μακάριος), the meaning is very different: men are "fortunate," "happy" (in the original sense of the latter word in English), because they are assured of the blessing of God. In the OT, whenever the nature of the blessing is clearly indicated, it consists in material prosperity (cf., e.g., Pss. 1; 128; 144, especially vss. 12-15; Prov. 3:13-35). It is the pious and good man who is blessed, but his blessedness does not consist in his piety and goodness, but in the material well-being with which God rewards his faithful servants. Usually this reward is regarded as still a thing of the future (cf., e.g., Pss. 128; 144:12-15).

In the NT, it is, of course, usually faithful Christians who are said to be blessed, and especially those who suffer because of their faithfulness (cf., e.g., Matt. 5:11; Luke 6:22-23). There is seldom any clear indication of the nature of the blessedness; but when it is in some sense a reward (μισθός) for faithfulness in suffering, it is, plainly, still in the future. The fact that this reward is "in heaven" does not necessarily mean that it is purely spiritual in quality. There seems, however, to be a progressive tendency toward a more spiritual conception of blessedness (cf., e.g., Jas. 1:12; and *see* BEATITUDES). In a few passages the blessedness is already present (e.g., Matt. 13:16; 16:17), and in these cases it is not clear that it is in any way a reward for anything which the "blessed" have done—it is a free, undeserved gift from God.

Both in the OT and in the NT, therefore, the only constant connotation of "blessed" is well-being, prosperity, which is the gift of God to men; the nature of this well-being is very variously conceived, and can be determined only from the context.

J. Y. CAMPBELL

**BLESSINGS AND CURSINGS.** Power-laden words, spoken on cultic or other occasions and often accompanied by gestures or symbolic actions, through which the wholeness of the religious community was understood to be safeguarded or strengthened, and evil forces controlled or destroyed. In the ancient Near Eastern world, as in most religious communities past and present, blessings and cursings were a fixed part of the cultus and had a prominent place in everyday life as well. It is very difficult to distinguish in many cases between blessings and cursings which belong to the realm of magic—in which the words and actions of the one who blesses or curses are entirely in his control and accomplish his purposes at his bidding—and those which are strictly religious in their understanding and use—where the blessings and cursings are conceived to have their origin and effect in the power and purpose of the deity (or of divine or demonic beings). In the OT there are clear traces of a magical understanding of blessings and cursings (Gen. 48:14-15; I Sam. 14:24; cf. I Cor. 12:1-3; Gal. 1:8), although most of the blessing and curse formulas, in their present form, attribute the power expressed through the formulas to the God of Israel.

1. Terminology
2. Forms of blessing and cursing
3. Blessings and cursings in the cultus
4. Blessings and cursings in Judaism and in the NT
Bibliography

**1. Terminology.** The most common Hebrew noun for "blessing" is ברכה. The term may refer at once to the power inherent in the spoken words, to the words themselves, and to their effect. The verb ברך in its active form designates the act by which a blessing is pronounced upon the community or an individual, either in the name of Yahweh or without reference to the deity. The passive form of the verb, ברוך, which occurs very frequently, has a somewhat ambiguous meaning in certain passages. The expression "Blessed be Yahweh" (ברוך יהוה) may mean, in its more primitive uses, that the power of Yahweh is itself increased through the pronouncement of words of blessing and the accompanying cultic acts. More frequently, however, the term is to be understood as an ascription of praise and gratitude for blessing received or as a prayer that Yahweh may show himself to be gracious in providing blessing.

In later Hebrew usage the term אשר, "happy,"

"blessed," appears as a synonym or a substitute for the term ברוך, particularly in reference to man as the object of divine blessing. In the NT the term μακάριος is the equivalent of the Hebrew אשרי (Matt. 5:3-11, etc.; cf. Ps. 1:1 and the LXX usage), while the verb εὐλογέω probably stands for the Hebrew and Aramaic verb ברך. The LXX generally renders the Hebrew noun ברכה by εὐλογία; the latter term is the common one for "blessing" in the NT (Rom. 15:29; I Cor. 10:16; Gal. 3:14; etc.).

The Hebrew nouns most widely used for "curse" in the OT are אלה and קללה. These may also refer to the power of the curse, to the words spoken, and to the effect of the words. The verb ארר is perhaps the earliest OT verb used to designate the act of cursing (Gen. 3:14, 17). It appears frequently in the passive form ארור, as the opposite of ברוך (Jer. 17:5-8). The verb קלל may originally have been a weaker term for the act of cursing ("to treat lightly, or with contempt"), but it appears to have become a synonym for ארר in early Israelite times (Exod. 22:28—H 22:27). Other terms for "curse" are considerably less common: מארה (Deut. 28:20); מגערת (Deut. 28:20); and תאלה (Lam. 3:65). In the NT the nouns used for "curse" are κατανάθεμα (Rev. 22:3), κατάρα (Gal. 3:10, 13; Heb. 6:8; Jas. 3:10; II Pet. 2:14), ἀνάθεμα (Acts 23:14; Rom. 9:3; I Cor. 12:3; Gal. 1:8-9), and ἀρά (Rom. 3:14). The chief verbal forms are ἀναθεματίζω (Mark 14:71; Acts 23:12, 14), καταναθεματίζω (Matt. 26:74), καταράομαι (Matt. 5:44; 25:41; Mark 11:21; Luke 6:28; Rom. 12:14; Jas. 3:9), and κακολογέω (Matt. 15:4; Mark 7:10).

**2. Forms of blessing and cursing.** Two major types of blessings appear in the OT: pronouncements of blessing and petitions for blessing. The first type is found in imperative (Gen. 1:28; 24:60) and in indicative (Gen. 27:29; I Sam. 25:33) forms, both of which reveal the Israelite conception of the power which is inherent in the spoken word of blessing. The second type has become more prominent in the later Israelite cultus and indicates how the power of blessing has become inseparably connected with the purpose of the deity.

An ancient blessing formula, probably used in connection with the ceremony of COVENANT renewal, is found in Deut. 28:3-6. Each of the blessings is introduced by the term ברוך. The objects of blessing are either the Israelite himself (אתה) or the basic sources upon which Israelite life was dependent: children, the soil, animals, and the produce of the soil ("basket and kneading-trough"; vs. 5). In other instances the name of the individual receiving the blessing is named: "Blessed be Abram by El Elyon . . . ; blessed be El Elyon" (Gen. 14:19-20). The expression "Blessed be Yahweh" (or "Blessed be God") is the most common form of Israelite blessing, often followed by an active participle indicating that action of the deity for which he is being praised. "Blessed is the man who . . ." is also a frequent form of blessing (Pss. 1:1; 84:12—H 84:13; Jer. 17:7). The term אשרי is probably more widely used by the laity, ברוך being reserved, in later Israelite times, for the priests.

The most complete curse formula of the OT appears in Deut. 27:15-26 (see also 28:16-19). Here the form is that of the passive participle ארור, followed by an active participle indicating the perpetrator of actions which fall under the curse: "he who dishonors his father or his mother," "he who removes his neighbor's landmark," etc. The expression "Cursed be the man who . . ." also appears (Deut. 27:15; Jer. 17:5).

Curses in the OT are often connected with oaths (I Sam. 14:24); with ordeals (Num. 5:16-28); or with the ḥérem, the devotion of a city or a people to the ban (Josh. 6:26). Such curses are seldom attributed directly to God. The curse upon the snake (Gen. 3: 14) and upon the ground because of man's sin (vs. 17) is attributed to God himself; on two occasions curses are uttered "before Yahweh" (Josh. 6:26; I Sam. 26:19). God does, however, threaten to send curses upon a faithless people, should they not keep the covenant (Deut. 28–29).

The cursing of the deity is strictly prohibited (Exod. 22:27; Lev. 24:23; Job 2:9). In fact, such a crime is so serious that the standard verbs for "cursing" are never found with "Yahweh" as their object (Exod. 22:27 [אלהים]; I Sam. 3:13, where the scribes have altered the original reading; Job 2:9 [ברך]). The prohibition against the use of the divine name in vain (Exod. 20:7; Deut. 5:11) probably indicates that the name of the deity must not be used in pronouncing maledictions upon one's enemies or otherwise wielding the power contained in the name.

**3. Blessings and cursings in the cultus.** Blessings and cursings had their primary place within the Israelite cultus. In the patriarchal period, the blessing of a dying father was transmitted to his heir (Gen. 27:1-45; 49; cf. Deut. 33), a rite by which all the powers which made for peace (שלום)—health, progeny, prosperity, victory in battle, wisdom—were continued, or even enhanced, after the death of the tribal leader. Such blessings, once pronounced, could not be revoked (Gen. 27:30-38). Within the confederacy of the twelve tribes of Israel prior to the establishment of the monarchy, blessings and cursings were probably a regular part of the festival of covenant renewal (Josh. 24; cf. Deut. 11:26-32; 27–29). After the establishment of the Jerusalem cultus (II Sam. 6), the powers of blessing and cursing were centered in the king, the priesthood of the royal cult, and the cult prophets. Baalam's assignment to curse Israel in behalf of Balak king of Moab (Num. 22–24) had its parallels in the royal cult of the kings of Israel (I Kings 22) and Judah (Jer. 23).

It was in the Israelite cult that the basic understanding of blessing was developed. Yahweh was understood to be the source of all blessing. He bestowed blessing as he saw fit, but his people were instructed to seek his blessing, to "pray for the peace of Jerusalem" (Ps. 122:6). In the Aaronic benediction (Num. 6:24-26) both the pronouncement of blessing and the petition for blessing were united in a single formula. The priest was enabled to declare blessing upon Israel, but only in the name of Yahweh. He was also the chief intercessor with the deity in behalf of blessing. The most distinctive aspect of blessing in the OT is the connection between blessing and historical experience. Yahweh's blessing found primary expression in his historical dealings with his people. Yahweh was blessed for all his gracious deeds in the past, and his continuing favor was sought (Pss. 34; 103).

Similarly, the cursings were drawn into the of-

ficial cultic practices. The old demonic powers continued to be threatening and had to be averted. It was not a matter any longer, however, of finding the right curse formulas to avert or destroy their power. Rather, Yahweh's intervention was sought to break the hold of such powers upon the individual or the community (Pss. 41; 58–59; 91; 141; etc.). The "workers of iniquity" (פעלי און) included those in whom evil powers were active to destroy the righteous. Such powers are occasionally spoken of as independent realities: קטב, "destruction," and דבר, "plague," along with death and Sheol (Hos. 13:14; cf. Ps. 91:6). None of these powers, however, could stand before the power of Yahweh's protection and blessing. Furthermore, the basic curse which befell Israel was the curse of sin and disobedience. Israel was set continually before two realities: life and death; blessing and curse. The call of Yahweh to his people was that they choose life (Deut. 30:19).

**4. Blessings and cursings in Judaism and in the NT.** In Judaism, the power to pronounce the Aaronic blessing (Num. 6:24-26) was reserved to the priest. Other blessings, however, such as the Eighteen Benedictions, were a regular part of the synagogue services. Blessings to God were pronounced both before and after meals; no food was to be eaten until it had been blessed. Curses were much less prominent and were forbidden (already in Job 31:30).

Blessing formulas are found in the NT as well. The BEATITUDES (Matt. 5:3-12) may have been intended as the new set of blessings accompanying the establishment of the New Covenant of the latter days (Jer. 31:31-34; note that Luke 6:20-26 contains both blessings and woes). The benedictions found in the introductory and concluding portions of the Pauline letters, plus the doxologies, benedictions, and woes of the book of Revelation (1:3; 4:8, 11; 5:9-10, 13-14; 8:13; 11:17-18; 14:13; 18:2-8; 19:9; 22:7, 14, 18-19), contain the major additional material bearing on blessings and cursing in the NT. Curses appear only seldom (Mark 11:12-14, 20-25); when pronounced upon Jesus' followers, they are to be met with blessings (Luke 6:28; Rom. 12:14; Jas. 3:8-10). In this manner Jesus is reported to have faced the curse of the Cross: "Father, forgive them; for they know not what they do" (Luke 23:34). The curse of sin and death is seen to have been abrogated, once for all, in the death and resurrection of Jesus (Rom. 5–8; Gal. 3:14), and the blessing of God is viewed as having come upon circumcised and uncircumcised alike (Rom. 4:6-9). For the NT, the definitive blessing has been bestowed upon mankind in Jesus Christ.

*See also* CURSE; OATHS; COVENANT; VENGEANCE; LAW IN THE OT.

**Bibliography.** S. Mowinckel, Psalmenstudien, V: *Segen und Fluch in Israels Kult und Psalmdichtung* (1924), pp. 1-57, 97-137; J. Hempel, "Die israelitischen Anschauungen von Segen und Fluch im Lichte altorientalischer Parallelen," *Zeitschrift der deutschen morgenländischen Gesellschaft*, N.F., 4 (1925), 20-110; J. Pedersen, *Israel, Its Life and Culture,* I-II (1926), 182-212; N. Nicolsky, *Spuren magischer Formeln in den Psalmen,* Beihefte zur *Zeitschrift für die alttestamentliche Wissenschaft,* vol. 46 (1927); B. Landsberger, "Das 'gute Wort,'" *B. Meissner Festschrift* (1929), pp. 294-321; H. Schmidt, "Grüsse und Glückwünsche im Psalter," *TSK,* 103 (1931), 141-50; H. Gunkel, *Einleitung in die Psalmen* (ed. J. Begrich; 1933), pp. 293-309; D. Daube, *Studies in Biblical Law* (1947); F. Horst,

"Segen und Segenhandlungen in der Bibel," *Evangelische Theologie*, 7 (1947), 23-37; S. A. Blank, "The Curse, Blasphemy, the Spell and the Oath," *HUCA*, 23 (1950-51), 73-95; J. M. Allegro, "A Possible Mesopotamian Background to the Joseph Blessing of Gen. XLIX," *ZAW*, LXIV (1952), 249-51; K. Koch, "Gibt es ein Vergeltungsdogma im AT?" *ZThK*, 52 (1955), 1-42; J.-P. Audet, "Esquisse historique du genre littéraire de la 'bénédiction' juive et de l'"eucharistie' chrétienne," *RB*, LXV (1958), 371-99; J. Scharbert, *Solidarität in Segen und Fluch im AT und in seiner Umwelt*, I. Vaterfluch und Vatersegen, *Bonner Biblische Beiträge*, vol. 14 (1958).

W. J. HARRELSON

**BLIGHT** [שְׁדֵּפוֹן, *from* שׁדף, scorch]; KJV and once RSV BLASTING (Deut. 28:22). The destruction of standing crops by the scorching EAST WIND.

The E wind, coming dry and hot from the Arabian Desert, is one of the most destructive natural forces in Palestine, withering grass and flowers in a day, and ruining fruit crops and standing grain. Its effect, blight, is listed along with mildew, hail, and pestilence among great natural catastrophes (I Kings 8:27 = II Chr. 6:28), and among the punishments visited by God on his people (Deut. 28:22; Amos 4:9; Hag. 2:17).

L. E. TOOMBS

**BLINDNESS.** OT writings use the word עִוֵּר predominantly to express loss of sight, whether of the purely physical variety or in allusion to metaphorical blindness. The NT most frequently employs the noun τυφλός and its corresponding verb in this connection. The prevalence of this affliction in Bible times is indicated by the frequency with which references to it occur in the Scriptures.

While it is not always either advisable or desirable to argue from the present state of specific diseases in oriental countries to their relative incidence in antiquity, there can be little question as to the widespread and serious nature of blindness in the ancient Near East. In Mesopotamia, the Sumerians and Akkadians employed a substance called kohl as an ointment for the eyes, partly as a cosmetic technique and partly out of hygienic considerations, since kohl was antiseptic and astringent in nature.

The Code of Hammurabi (*ca.* 1700 B.C.) included ophthalmic afflictions among the conditions which Babylonian medical men were permitted to treat. According to this legislation (*see* HAMMURABI), established fees appropriate to the social status of the patient could be charged for the treatment of ocular disorders. The mention of a bronze lancet as one of the instruments employed in the operation indicates the advanced nature of contemporary surgical procedures.

In ancient Egypt the predynastic Badarian culture (*ca.* 5000 B.C.) employed pulverized malachite and stibium in addition to kohl as an unguent preparation for the eyes; this usage still survives in parts of North Africa. The Ebers Papyrus (*ca.* 1550 B.C.) described the incidence of granular conjunctivitis, and recommended the use of forceps for extracting inverted eyelashes adjacent to the surface of the eye (trichiasis).

To the biblical writers blindness was the consequence either of frank ophthalmic disease or of physical degeneration. Of the former, the most widespread condition was ophthalmia, a severe form of conjunctivitis often involving the internal structures of the eye. This highly contagious disease was frequently transmitted by flies, aggravated by the glare of the sun, and irritated by dust-laden winds. Granular ophthalmia (trachoma), a chronic inflamed condition of the conjunctiva accompanied by enlargement and granulation of the eyelids, was particularly disabling. Blindness in infancy not infrequently resulted from *ophthalmia neonatorum,* an acute purulent conjunctivitis consequent upon gonorrheal or septic infection of the conjunctiva at birth by the mother. Ophthalmic diseases resulting from physical degeneration, such as glaucoma, cataract, and optic atrophy constituted other forms of blindness in Bible lands.

This dread affliction was frequently attributed to sin (Exod. 4:11; John 9:2), and as such could be cured by God alone. Particularly serious was a curse which invoked blindness as a punishment for misconduct (Gen. 19:11; II Kings 6:18; Acts 13:11). The nature of the Mosaic enactments on behalf of the blind (Lev. 19:14; Deut. 27:18) indicates that already blindness was a serious social problem which needed to be dealt with by means of appropriate legislation. While this humanitarian act doubtless did much to mitigate the sufferings of those afflicted by blindness, the nature of society in biblical times was such that under ordinary conditions, poverty and hardship formed the inevitable lot of the blind. In Lev. 21:20, impaired vision was included in the list of physical disabilities which disqualified a man from the priesthood, and presumably embraced both congenital and acquired blindness.

Several instances of blindness incident to senility are mentioned in the OT. The Genesis narrative indicates that the deception which Jacob perpetrated on his father (Gen. 27:1 ff) succeeded mainly because of the blindness of Isaac. In old age Eli the priest of Shiloh was blind, while Ahijah the prophet was similarly incapacitated (I Kings 14:4), though the latter was nevertheless able to penetrate the disguise adopted by the wife of Jeroboam. Isaac, Eli, and Ahijah were most probably afflicted with gray atrophy of the optic disc. This is a degenerative condition in which the optic disc, a whitish spot on the retina of the eye which marks the entrance of the optic nerve, becomes gray or blue-gray in color. A notable exception to the incidence of blindness in old age was Moses, who maintained vigorous eyesight until his death at an advanced age (Deut. 34:7). Leah (Gen. 29:17) was apparently afflicted with a mild form of ophthalmia, perhaps blepharitis, an inflamed condition of the eyelid.

One of the professed functions of Jesus' ministry was the "recovering of sight to the blind" (Luke 4:18). He used blindness and ocular deficiencies to illustrate spiritual truths (Luke 6:39 ff), and many of his healing miracles involved blind people. Of especial interest are the man who was blind from birth (John 9:1 ff), whose healing led Jesus to declare himself as the light of the world, and the man whose recovery of sight was gradual (Mark 8:22 ff). Jesus frequently employed different methods in his therapeutic acts (*see* HEALING), and in the above cases he anointed the eyes of the sufferers with saliva. While ancient folklore recommended applications of saliva,

(*a*) Latin MS, *Codex Amiatinus, ca.* A.D. 715

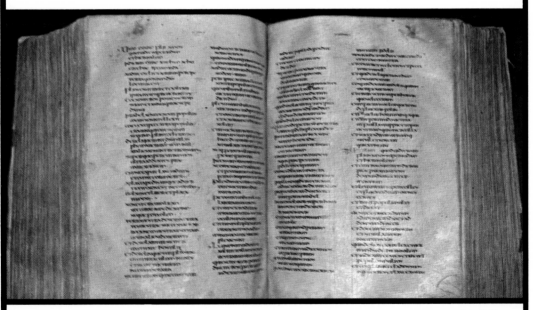

(*b*) Latin MS, *Codex Amiatinus, ca.* A.D. 715, showing leaves from Isa. 1–2

PLATE I

*(a)* *The John Wyclif Bible,* A.D. 1382

*(b)* *The Gutenberg Bible,* A.D. 1452-56

PLATE II

(*a*) Some of the *Greek minuscules used by Erasmus* in his Greek text of the NT, A.D. 1516

(*b*) *Samaritan Codex,* from the Samaritan synagogue, Nablus, Jordan

(*c*) *The Rule of the Congregation,* perhaps an appendix to the Manual of Discipline, from Cave I, Khirbet Qumran

PLATE III

(*a*) Facsimile from the *Duke of Sussex' Hebrew Pentateuch*, fifteenth century A.D.

(*b*) Facsimile of the *Hebrew Bible, in the Harleian Library;* fifteenth century A.D.

(*c*) Miniature of the beginning of the Gospel of Luke, from the eleventh century A.D.; from the *Harleian Gospels*, collated by Griesbach

(*d*) Portion of *Codex Genesos Cottonianus*, reputed to be an identical copy of one belonging to Origen in the third century A.D. This is considered to be one of the most ancient MSS of the Greek LXX.

(*e*) Miniature of the miracle at the Pool of Bethesda, from a seventh-century-A.D. *Syriac MS*

(*f*) Beginning of the Gospel of John in Coptic and Arabic, from *MS of the Gospels in the Bodleian Library*, written in the Year of the Martyrs, 890; A.D. 1173

PLATE IV

(*a*) Title page of Gospel of Luke, from *Codex Bombycinus,* an Arabic MS, now in British Museum

(*b*) *Evangelistarium of Charlemagne, ca.* A.D. 800, with miniature of Christ, and a group of birds and ornamental details

(*c*) *The Bible of Alcuin,* the top illumination showing the beginning of Paul's Letter to the Romans, and the bottom picture that of Adam and Eve and the first sin

(*d*) Miniature and beginning of the Gospel of John, from *a MS of the Duke of Sussex* (A.D. 1251)

(*e*) Picture of Mary Magdalene(?) from *King Henry VII's Prayer Book,* with a Latin script from the Psalter of King Henry VIII

(*f*) Anglo-Saxon Book of Moses, from a Cottonian MS of *Ælfric's Heptateuch.* Left: expulsion of Adam and Eve from the Garden of Eden; right: their instruction in agriculture

PLATE V

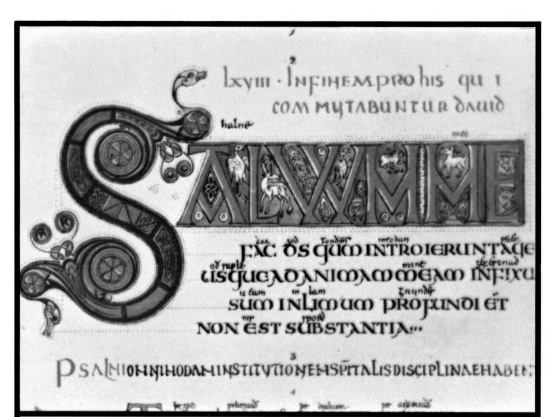

(*a*) Psalter of Augustine (*Codex Augustii*, from a Cottonian MS, fifth or six century A.D.): Script under "2" contains two verses of Ps. 68 [English 69]; the part headed "3" is the beginning of the second portion of the Preface to the Psalter.

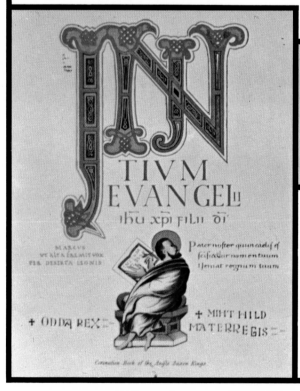

(*c*) Miniature of King David and his attendants, from a Latin and Anglo-Saxon Psalter, *Codex Augustii*, a Cottonian MS, the fifth or sixth century A.D.

(*b*) *Coronation Oath Book of the Anglo-Saxon kings,* from the fifteenth century A.D.

PLATE VI

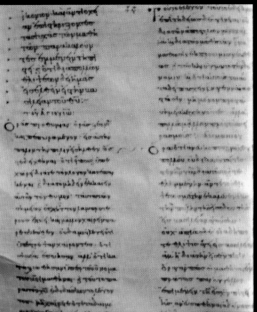

(*a*) Acts 14:22 with a related commentary, from a Commentary on the Book of Acts and the General Epistles, written *ca.* A.D. 900; *Greek MS 25,* Holy Cross College, Jerusalem

(*b*) A Byzantine portrait of Mark (left) and the beginning of the text of the Gospel of Mark under a head of Christ (right), from a complete NT of twenty-six books (minus Revelation), written by a scribe of the twelfth century; *Greek MS 47,* Holy Sepulchre, Jerusalem

(*d*) Thirteenth-century copy of Job with commentary, here the final verse doubly illustrated by (*a*) Job and four generations of offspring and (*b*) the death of Job; *Greek MS 5,* Holy Sepulchre College, Jerusalem

(*c*) A Lectionary of the Gospels (seventeenth century) open at the portrait of Mark, which stands before his text; *Treasury Collection MS 3,* Greek Orthodox Patriarchate, Jerusalem

(*e*) Psalter written in the ninth century, here open at Ps. 58; *Greek MS 96,* Holy Cross College, Jerusalem

PLATE VII

(*a*) The "Golden Gospels" lectionary, showing portrait of the evangelist John with his amanuensis Prochorus (left), and the text of John 1 (right); *Treasury Collection MS 2,* Greek Orthodox Patriarchate, Jerusalem

(*b*) Jeweled front cover of the "Golden Gospels": sixteenth-century depiction of the Resurrection; *Treasury Collection MS 1,* Greek Orthodox Patriarchate, Jerusalem

PLATE VIII

preferably the more alkaline variety from a fasting subject (cf. Pliny *Nat. Hist.* 28.7), Jesus related this symbolic act to the faith of the person concerned. In the second of these healings he exercised particular care in developing the visual accommodation of the patient to counteract the shock which might well have resulted from the sudden exposure of eyes totally unaccustomed to the strain of bright sunlight. The man who washed in Siloam (John 9:7) would have the advantage of the shade provided by adjacent buildings. Other recorded instances of Jesus' healing the blind, while not well documented clinically, indicate the use of a miraculous power which both restored the body and stimulated the soul (Matt. 20:34; Mark 10:52).

The blindness which overtook PAUL outside Damascus (Acts 9:3 ff) may be accounted for by reference to psychosomatic relationships. The fundamental reorientation of his spiritual values involved in his conversion produced a state of profound psychic conflict within his personality, and was expressed in somatic terms. Intense emotional strain of this sort can often produce amaurosis, in which blindness occurs without any concomitant lesion of the eye or optic nerve. Because this phenomenon is invariably emotional in nature, dramatic cures can result from suggestion and general psychotherapy; such was actually the case with Paul (Acts 8:17-18). Elymas (Acts 13:10-12) was similarly afflicted with temporary amaurosis. *See* DISEASE.

*Bibliography.* B. L. Gordon, "Ophthalmology in the Bible and in the Talmud," *Archives of Ophthalmology* (1933), IX, 751 ff; F. Dunbar, *Emotions and Bodily Changes* (4th ed., 1954), pp. 553-68.      R. K. HARRISON

\*BLOOD. *See* SACRIFICE AND OFFERINGS § A2*a,* 3.

**BLOOD, AVENGER OF.** *See* AVENGER OF BLOOD.

**BLOOD, FIELD OF.** A term which appears only in Acts 1:19 as the translation of χωρίον αἵματος, which in turn is the author's translation of the Semitic name for the place. The Semitic name, AKELDAMA, is, however, transcribed variously into Greek, and therefore the correct original is uncertain.

     K. W. CLARK

**BLOOD, FLOW OF** [ῥύσις αἵματος] (Luke 8:43); KJV ISSUE OF BLOOD. Hemorrhage, perhaps menorrhagia. The term used by Luke occurs frequently in the medical treatises of Hippocrates, Dioscorides, and Galen. *See* CLEAN AND UNCLEAN; HEMORRHAGE.

**BLOODGUILT** [דמים, דם] (Exod. 22:2-3—H 22:1-2; cf. Num. 35:27). Guilt—not always liable to a legal penalty—incurred through bloodshed.

The most ancient view would appear to be exemplified by the Greek concept of the miasma (stain, pollution) of homicide, an automatic, objective state. Every bloodshed—even that committed in self-defense—pollutes and requires a purification. When criminal and non-criminal homicide were distinguished, this miasma nonetheless persisted. Plato still recognizes the need for purification even from the miasma caught inadvertently from a murderer

(*Laws* 916). It was not the killer alone, however, who was affected; until the wrath of the slain man's ghost was appeased, his family as well lay under a pollution which could be cast off only by exacting vengeance.

In Israel, too, bloodguilt was defiling (Num. 35: 33-34), but it was incurred only through slaying a man who did not deserve to die (דם נקי, "innocent blood"; Deut. 19:10; Jer. 26:15; Jonah 1:14). Killing in self-defense and the judicial execution of criminals are explicitly exempted (Exod. 22:2—H 22:1; Lev. 20:9; etc.). On the other hand, where there is "innocent blood," there is always bloodguilt: for (*a*) intentional killing—including judicial murder (Judg. 9:24; I Sam. 25:26, 33; II Kings 9:26; Jer. 26:15)— as well as for (*b*) unintentional (*see below*); for (*c*) being an indirect cause of death (Gen. 42:22), even if only through negligence or dereliction of duty (Deut. 19:10*b;* 22:8; Josh. 2:19). Finally, (*d*) persons in authority incur bloodguilt for murder committed by those for whom they are responsible (I Kings 2:5, 31-33).

While the law does not privilege the AVENGER OF BLOOD to take action against persons bloodguilty under *c* and *d*, it does so in the case of murder and unintentional homicide. (Even a homicidal beast is considered bloodguilty: he must be stoned and his carcass treated as taboo [Gen. 9:5; Exod. 21:28-32].) The avenger may slay the accidental homicide outside the asylum without incurring bloodguilt (Num. 35:27), whence it may be inferred that the latter is not considered guiltless (this is borne out further by the character of the CITY OF REFUGE). Yet insofar as the accidental manslayer is not deserving of death, the community is held bloodguilty if it fails to provide him with an asylum (Deut. 19:10).

Since the bloodguilt of homicide lies on the entire community (Num. 35:33; Deut. 21:8-9), the communal interest and that of the avenger coincide insofar as both aim at eradicating the guilty party. When the criminal is known, his bloodguilt is expiable solely and entirely by his paying the legal penalty. No pecuniary composition or ritual expiation may be substituted for, or need be added to, this penalty: the murderer must die; the accidental homicide must serve out his term in the city of refuge (Num. 35:31-32; Deut. 19:13). However, if there occurs an untraceable murder in open country, the elders and priests of the town nearest to the corpse must perform a sacrificial purification—vicariously expiating life by life—accompanied by an avowal of innocence (Deut. 21:1-9).

Unexpiated bloodguilt is punished by God, the ultimate avenger (Gen. 9:5; II Sam. 4:11; II Kings 9:7; Ps. 9:12—H 9:13; Hos. 1:4). Unavenged blood cries to heaven for vindication—there is no trace of the idea that of itself it perils men (Gen. 4:10; Job 16:18; Isa. 26:21; Ezek. 24:7-9). As when God punishes idolatry (cf. Exod. 20:5; Deut. 5:9), here too he may exact retribution from the descendants of the bloodguilty person (II Sam. 3:28-29; 21:1; I Kings 21:29; cf. II Kings 9:25-26; Matt. 27:25). The writer of Kings reckons the bloodshed of Manasseh as a cause of Judah's fall three generations later (II Kings 24:4).

A peculiar extension of the idea is found in Lev.

17:4: bloodguilt is imputed to one who slaughters a sacrificial beast at an unauthorized altar—as if to say that not even a brute's life might be taken except for divinely sanctioned purposes. The penalty for such bloodshed is "excising" (a divine punishment; *see* CRIMES AND PUNISHMENTS § A2).

*Bibliography.* J. Pedersen, *Israel*, I-II (1926), 420-25. For the Greek idea, W. K. C. Guthrie, *The Greeks and Their Gods* (1954), pp. 189-93. *See also* bibliography under AVENGER OF BLOOD. M. GREENBERG

**BLUE** [תכלת; Sumer. *SIG-ZA-GIN;* Akkad. *takiltu;* LXX ὑάκινθος *or* ὑακίνθινος, *see* HYACINTH]. Alternately: VIOLET; PURPLE. A biblical color of uncertain hue, probably purple-blue, obtained from Mediterranean mollusks of the class Gastropoda and utilized for dyeing. Although "blue" has been associated with חלזון (cf. Targ. pseudo-Jonathan to Deut. 33:19), usually identified as the violet-producing *Helix-ianthina,* it is more likely that the desired color was obtained by varying the dyeing process and using different mollusks (*cf.* PURPLE). As a color of the clothing of idols it is rendered by "violet" in Jer. 10:9, and by "purple" in Ezek. 23:6, referring to the color of garments of young Assyrian nobles.

Tyre long enjoyed a monopoly in the "blue" and "purple" industry (II Chr. 2:7, 14), although both colors were available and obtained elsewhere (Ezek. 27:7, 24). While considered inferior to royal purple in antiquity, "blue" or "blue-purple" was a popular color. Materials dyed blue were widely employed alone and with scarlet and purple yarns and linen in the tabernacle (Exod. 25:4; 26:1, 4; Num. 4:6-7, 9; etc.), the clothing of the priests (Exod. 28:5-6, 8, 15; 39:1; etc.), and in Solomon's temple (II Chr. 2:7, 14; 3:14). Mention is also made of blue hangings in the palace of Ahasuerus (Esth. 1:6), and royal robes of blue and white (Esth. 8:15).

In Ecclesiasticus bonds of wisdom are compared to a cord of blue (6:30), and both blue and purple are identified in the clothing of Moses (45:10). Judas Maccabeus seized cloth dyed blue as plunder (I Macc. 4:23); and blue, with scarlet and purple, is prominent in the dress of the Qumran priests on the occasion of battle (1QM 7.10; cf. Exod. 39:28-29).

The word "blue" does not appear in the RSV or KJV of the NT; however, ὑακινθίνους as a breastplate color is rendered by "sapphire" (KJV "jacinth") in Rev. 9:17; and as a precious stone ὑάκινθος is translated "jacinth" in Rev. 21:20. *See also* VIOLET; COLORS.

*Bibliography.* Pliny Nat. Hist. V.19; IX.36; XIV.12; XXVI.10. A. Neuberger, *The Technical Arts and Sciences of the Ancients* (1930), pp. 186-89. J. R. Partington, *Origins and Development of Applied Chemistry* (1935), pp. 522-23. A. Schaeffer, "Neuere Ansichten über den antiken Purpur," *Chemiker-Zeitung,* 65 (1941), 273-75. A. Comfort, "The Pigmentation of Molluscan Shells," *Biology Review,* 26 (1951), 289. D. Barthélemy and J. T. Milik, *Discoveries in the Judean Desert, Qumran Cave I* (1955), pp. 18-20, 24-38.

C. L. WICKWIRE

**BOANERGES** bō'ə nûr'jēz [Βοανηργές, Βοανεργές, Βανηρεγές; *of* Aram. *origin, possibly related to* בני רגש *or* בני רגז] (Mark 3:17). A name of uncertain meaning given by Jesus to James and John, the sons of Zebedee.

Βοανη appears to be a corrupt Greek form of a word meaning "sons of" (בני). Ργες has been variously explained: from roots meaning "tumult" (רגש), "wrath" (רגז), "thunder" (רעם), "full brothers" (רחם).

Mark translates "sons of thunder," without indicating why the term was appropriate. Were the brothers stormy in temperament (Mark 9:38; Luke 9:54)? Were they once zealots or revolutionary agitators (Mark 10:37)? Were they perhaps twins, and this epithet a reflection of ancient mythology concerning the Dioscuri (Heavenly Twins)?

There is some textual evidence that the term originally may have characterized all the apostles, not just the sons of Zebedee.

*Bibliography.* G. Dalman, *The Words of Jesus* (1902), p. 49; J. R. Harris, *Boanerges* (1913), *passim;* W. Fischer, "Die Donnersöhne, Mc 3, 17," *ZNW*, XXIII (1924), 310-11; J. R. Harris, *The Twelve Apostles* (1927), pp. 101-3; G. Dalman, *Jesus-Jeshua* (1929), p. 12; J. A. Montgomery, "NT Notes," *JBL*, LVI (1937), 51-52; V. Taylor, *The Gospel According to St. Mark* (1952), pp. 231-32. E. P. BLAIR

**BOAR** [חזיר, *usually* SWINE]. A wild pig (*sus scrofa* in Europe and Western Asia), thought to be the ancestor of the domestic swine. חזיר, like the Greek word ὗς (or σῦς), can refer to both wild and domestic swine.

There is only one unambiguous reference to a boar in the Bible: the "boar from the forest" ravages the vine, Israel (Ps. 80:13—H 80:14). Such a danger to crops and orchards must have been ever present in the biblical period (cf. II Esd. 15:30; Enoch 89:72). The word חזיר, which appears as an unclean animal in Lev. 11:7; Deut. 14:8, and which is commonly translated "swine," probably designates both the wild and the domesticated pig, for the lists in which these references appear include both wild and tame animals.

*See also* FAUNA § A2eiii.

*Bibliography.* For a sculpture of a wild sow with young in Sennacherib's time, see A. H. Layard, *Discoveries in the Ruins of Nineveh and Babylon* (1853), p. 109; on a wild pig's skin, see M. Hullin 9.2; for Roman ideas about the wild boar, see Pliny Nat. Hist. VIII.78; for boars in Palestine in the nineteenth century, see Tristram, *NHB* (1867), pp. 54-56.

W. S. McCULLOUGH

**BOARD.** *See* PLANK.

**BOAT** [πλοιάριον (KJV SMALL SHIP *in* Mark 3:9; LITTLE SHIP *in* Mark 4:36; John 21:8), πλοῖον (KJV *and alternately* RSV SHIP), *from* πλέω, to sail; σκάφη, something scooped out, *from* σκάπτω, to dig, scoop out]; FERRY BOAT [עברה] (II Sam. 19:18—H 19:19 KJV; RSV *correctly* FORD). In the NT, πλοῖον sometimes means a vessel capable of sailing in the Mediterranean Sea (Acts 20:13, etc.), and in these cases the RSV uses "ship"; but oftener the word refers, like πλοιάριον (Mark 3:9, etc.), to a smaller craft used for fishing on the Sea of Galilee (Matt. 4:21, etc.). Σκάφη is a skiff, and in Acts 27:16, 30, 32, it refers to a ship's boat.

*See also* SHIPS AND SAILING. W. S. McCULLOUGH

**BOAZ** bō'ăz [בעז; Βόος, Βόοζ]; KJV BOOZ bō'ŏz (transliteration of LXX form) in Matt. 1:5; Luke

3:32. A wealthy and virtuous Bethlehemite, related to the family of Elimelech, whose inheritance he redeemed and whose daughter-in-law, Ruth the Moabitess, he married. It was in one of the fields of Boaz that the widowed Ruth chanced to glean when she had returned with Naomi, her mother-in-law, to Bethlehem. When Boaz met Ruth, he insisted that she glean exclusively in his fields and gave evidence of his deep appreciation for her noble character by showing her every consideration (Ruth 2).

These studied kindnesses, no doubt, prompted Naomi to suggest to her daughter-in-law that she ask Boaz to perform the duty of the next of kin (גאל). Accordingly, as Boaz guarded the grain at his threshing floor during the night, Ruth arrived there in festal garb and lay down at his feet while he slept. When Boaz awakened, he solemnly declared that if the one who was nearer of kin to Elimelech than he should refuse, he would gladly assume the right of redeeming the inheritance of the deceased (Ruth 3).

The next day Boaz had publicly transferred to him the right of redemption, which had been refused by the nearer kinsman because it involved a levirate marriage with Ruth. This marriage Boaz joyfully contracted, and in due time a son named Obed was born of the union (Ruth 4).

The genealogy of Boaz represents him to be of the family of Hezron of the tribe of Judah, and the great-grandfather of King David (Ruth 4:18-22; I Chr. 2:9-15; Matt. 1:3-6; Luke 3:31-33).

E. R. DALGLISH

**BOAZ AND JACHIN.** *See* JACHIN AND BOAZ.

**BOCCAS.** KJV Apoc. form of BUKKI 2.

**BOCHERU** bŏ′kə rōō [בכרו; LXX *and* Syr. *bə kō′rō* (*same consonants as* Heb.), his first-born] (I Chr. 8:38; 9:44). A Benjaminite, descendant of Saul and Jonathan.

*Bibliography.* M. Noth, *Die israelitischen Personennamen* (1928), p. 239.

**BOCHIM** bŏ′kĭm [בכים, weepers] (Judg. 2:1-5). A place between Gilgal and Bethel, where the angel of the Lord rebuked the people, and which received its name from their weeping. The site is unknown.

*BODY [בשר, flesh; σάρξ, flesh; σῶμα].* Usually an object with physical properties, such as extension, weight, solidity, and substance; but the word has also acquired social, spiritual, and metaphysical meanings.

A. Ordinary meanings in the OT and the NT
B. Religious meanings
  1. Primitive traditions of the Lord's Supper
  2. Paul's theology
    *a.* The body of sin
    *b.* The redeemed body
    *c.* The church as the body
    *d.* The immortal body
Bibliography

**A. *ORDINARY MEANINGS IN THE OT AND THE NT.*** Early Hebrew apparently had no term to designate the body as a whole in our sense of the word. It preferred to speak of various parts and organs individually. The nearest term to "body" is בשר, "flesh," which is used 127 times indicating the flesh of animals and men. But this word also has other meanings, such as kinship and as a metonym for man, or for all living beings, as over against God. The late Aramaic of Dan. 3:27; 4:30; 5:21 introduces the word גשם for "body"; and 7:15 uses נדנה. But none of these Semitic words acquired any important theological meanings.

In the NT the word σάρξ, "flesh," is closely parallel to בשר, but it acquired in addition profound psychological and theological meanings, especially in Paul. Σῶμα is the common word for "body" in the NT. It is applied to bodies of men or animals, living or dead. Σῶμα is also at times used as a synonym for σάρξ, and it came to have even more metaphorical meanings, as we shall see.

**B. *RELIGIOUS MEANINGS.* 1. Primitive traditions of the Lord's Supper.** Although Paul's letters are the oldest Christian documents that have survived, it is evident that some traditions are older. The first and most obvious of these is the tradition about the LAST SUPPER in I Cor. 11:23-29. The way in which Paul introduces this passage shows that it is something he has received from an earlier time. In vs. 24 it is reported that Jesus took bread and broke it and said, "This is my body which is for you" (τοῦτό μού ἐστιν τὸ σῶμα τὸ ὑπὲρ ὑμῶν). This saying introduces the idea that the loaf of bread which is broken in the communion ritual is the σῶμα or "body" of the Lord. In vs. 25 Jesus continues with reference to the wine: "This cup is the new covenant in my blood."

This tradition in almost the same form is preserved also in the Synoptic gospels (Mark 14:22; Matt. 26: 26; Luke 22:19). They all say: "This is my body" (τοῦτό ἐστιν τὸ σῶμά μου). In all three of these gospels there is also the drinking of wine, which in Mark 14:24; Matt. 26:28 Jesus calls "my blood of the covenant."

In both the above accounts of the Supper there is a possible ambiguity. Σῶμα may designate a body with all its elements, including blood. But the tradition continues and refers to drinking the blood separately. There is no ambiguity in fact. The rite is done in memory of the death of Jesus, and it is assumed that when he died, the blood flowed out of his body. Sacrificial rites of the OT need to be kept in mind as the background of this ritual. Both the sin offering and the covenant sacrifice (*see* SACRIFICE AND OFFERINGS) are involved.

A third form of the ancient tradition occurs in John 6:31-58. The exposition is based on the miracle of the loaves and fish, which precedes in 6:5-13. But the passage is nevertheless only a thinly veiled exposition of the Lord's Supper. Here instead of σῶμα we find σάρξ. Those who eat the flesh (σάρξ) of the Son of man and drink his blood achieve present union with him, life, eternal life, and will be raised up at the last day (vss. 52-58). Σάρξ evidently means the same thing in this passage that σῶμα does in the earlier ones.

**2. Paul's theology. *a. The body of sin.*** In Rom. 6:6 Paul refers to the "sinful body," and in 7:24, to "this body of death." It is more characteristic of him, notably in Rom. 7:4-25; Gal. 5:16-24, to regard the FLESH as the seat of sinful desires. But as the above passages indicate, he also uses σῶμα in the same way. Body and flesh are thus equated.

***b. The redeemed body.*** One of the paradoxes of Paul's theology is that the body of sin may be also at the same time the redeemed body. But he does not hold that it ever becomes a sinless body. As this idea involves the full range of Paul's doctrine of the Atonement, there is danger of oversimplification, yet the symbols are not too difficult. Paul makes much use of the spatial concept of being "in Christ" (Rom. 6:11; 8:2; Eph. 1:7; 2:13; 4:32; Col. 1:21; 2:11; etc.). It is baptism that brings one into the body of Christ (Gal. 3:27; Col. 2:12).

The union with Christ is expressed in I Cor. 6:13-20 by the figure of marriage. The individual Christian is the wife of Christ, the idea being that the husband and his wife are one body. So Paul argues in vs. 13 that the body is "not meant for immorality, but for the Lord, and the Lord for the body."

But vs. 19 changes to the figure of a temple in which a deity dwells: "Do you not know that your body is a temple of the Holy Spirit within you?" As the Lord is identified with the Spirit (II Cor. 3:18), this means that Christ resides in the body of the individual Christian; this reverses the imagery. I am no longer in Christ, but Christ is in me.

Paul's most startling image of identification with Christ is death. So he is able to say in Gal. 2:20: "I have been crucified with Christ; it is no longer I who live, but Christ who lives in me." With daring imagination, Paul grasps for one physical symbol after another in an effort to express his sense of the mystery of spiritual fellowship with Christ, which belongs to the redeemed.

***c. The church as the body.*** One of Paul's most sublime concepts is that the church is the body of Christ; this idea appears in many places. He explains in Rom. 12:5 that "we, though many, are one body in Christ, and individually members one of another." The imagery for the idea varies. With an allusion to the communion in which only one loaf is used, in I Cor. 10:17, he explains that "we who are many are one body." Also he comes back to the idea of the body of Christ as a building (I Cor. 14:12; Eph. 4:12). Col. 1:18 presents Christ as only the head of the body, which is the church. In Eph. 5:23-32 he is the husband of the church, which he loves as his own flesh. But regardless of his figures, Paul's basic idea is that there is only one body, that this body is the church, and that it is the body of Christ (Eph. 4:4; 5:23).

***d. The immortal body.*** Paul works out this view in I Cor. 15, which is his most sustained effort to present the Christian doctrine of immortality. The issue arose from the fact that Greek Christians believed in a spiritual life hereafter, but had an aversion to physical resurrection, regarding the body as a handicap of the soul. But Paul, with his Hebrew idea of man (*see* MAN, NATURE OF, IN THE NT), felt that as a human being is incomplete without a body, a resurrection is required for a future life. Some of his arguments, such as that based on the change of the planted seed into a living plant and the different

kinds of bodies, do not prove his point, but they are vivid allegories of his faith. He concludes that as there are heavenly (ἐπουράνια) and earthly (ἐπίγεια) bodies, so the human body which is buried is mortal (ψυχικόν), but that which is raised is immortal (πνευματικόν). The basis of his conviction, of course, is the personal testimony of those, including himself, who saw the Lord after his resurrection (vss. 1-8).

*Bibliography.* J. A. T. Robinson, *The Body, A Study of Pauline Theology* (1952). S. V. McCASLAND

**BODY OF CHRIST.** *See* CHRIST, BODY OF.

**BODYGUARD** [מִטָרָה; מַטָּרָה; מַשְׁמַעַת; מִשְׁמַעַת (Aram. טַבָּחַיָּא); שֹׁמֵר לְרֹאשׁ]. A person armed to protect another person, usually a sovereign, and responsible directly to him. David was captain of Saul's bodyguard, as well as personal bodyguard to Achish, king of Gath (I Sam. 22:14 [KJV "bidding"]; 28:2 [KJV "keeper of mine head"]). Benaiah ben Jehoiada was one of David's thirty veteran warriors and head of his bodyguard (II Sam. 23:23; I Chr. 11:25). Potiphar was captain of Pharaoh's bodyguard (Gen. 37:36; 39:1; etc.), and NEBUZARADAN and Arioch are called captains of Nebuchadnezzar's bodyguard (II Kings 25:8; Jer. 39:9 ff; 52:12 ff; Dan. 2:14). Zedekiah seems to have had a special body- or palace-guard, in whose quarters Jeremiah was imprisoned for a while (Jer. 32:2; cf. Neh. 3:25; 12:39). *See also* GUARD.

J. A. SANDERS

**BOHAIRIC VERSION** bō hī'rĭk. Among the several translations of the Bible into various Coptic dialects, the Bohairic Version gained the ascendancy throughout Egypt and is still today the authorized version used in the Coptic church. *See* VERSIONS, ANCIENT, § 5. B. M. METZGER

**BOHAN, STONE OF** bō'hăn [אֶבֶן בֹּהַן, stone of the thumb]. A boundary marker between Judah and Benjamin, known as the stone of Bohan the son of Reuben (Josh. 15:6; 18:17). The stone is located SE of Jericho on the edge of the hilly country in the NE corner of Judah. The descriptive name, "stone of the thumb [בֹּהַן]," was evidently misunderstood as containing a personal name, Bohan the son of Reuben. This development suggests that some elements of the Reubenite tribe were at one time settled in the NE corner of Judah.

*Bibliography.* M. Noth, *Die Welt des ATs* (3rd ed., 1957), p. 60. R. F. JOHNSON

**BOIL** [שְׁחִין; LXX ἕλκη]. A general term used to describe inflamed cutaneous swellings, whether of a staphylococcal nature or not. In Job 2:7 smallpox may be indicated, although the boils might be a secondary manifestation of *treponematosis*. The boils of the Egyptian plague (Exod. 9:9) were associated with BLAINS, and apparently described the small red papules encircled by white vesicles characteristic of cutaneous anthrax. The boil (furuncle) which afflicted Hezekiah (II Kings 20:7; Isa. 38:21) was probably a staphylococcal infection causing inflammation around a cutaneous follicle, with consequent suppuration and necrosis of the core. Isaiah prescribed a fig poultice, popular in contemporary therapeutics, which proved an adequate remedy for the infection.                    R. K. HARRISON

**BOLDNESS** [τολμάω; παρρησία; παρρησιάζομαι; θαρρέω]. The first of the Greek words that have been translated in terms of boldness and confidence, τολμάω, is used of action that rises above fear. The second and third by origin suggest free, unhindered speech, and carry the old Athenian tradition of free, democratic speech. In the LXX they are used in the sense of bold standing and action as well as boldness in speech (Wisd. Sol. 5:1; I Macc. 4:18).

"Boldness" in the NT becomes almost a stock term to describe the standing, the manner, and the spirit of those who proclaim the gospel. Jesus set the pattern, as in the straightforward preaching of his passion (Mark 8:32). Peter and John excite wonder by their courageous defense (Acts 4:13; cf. 4:31). Paul and Barnabas exhibit the same outspoken courage at Antioch in Pisidia (Acts 13:46). This spirit of confidence infects Paul's relations with the Corinthians: "I have great confidence [παρρησία] in you" (II Cor. 7:4).

The new Christian approach to God is marked by confidence and faith (II Cor. 3:4-5, 12, 18; Heb. 4:16; 10:19). There is a new assurance in prayer (I John 3:21-22; 5:14-15). Even before the dread Judge in the eschatological event the man of faith need not shrink back in shame, but he can stand confident and unafraid (I John 2:28; 4:17).

This bold, new spirit does not rest in self-confidence. Christian faith for living stands sure in the promises of God; the presence of the Spirit (or the Lord) brings inspiration and guidance; in Christ life has been undergirded with new insight and confident assurance both toward God and toward men. *See also* COURAGE.                    P. E. DAVIES

**BOLLED.** KJV translation of גִּבְעֹל in Exod. 9:31. The word is a KJV archaism meaning "having bolls"—i.e., pods—and so "in seed," as it is used of flax. The Hebrew may refer to the flower bud or the seed pod. The RSV translates "in bud."

**BOLSTER.** The KJV translation of רַאֲשֹׁת (I Sam. 26:12) and מְרַאֲשֹׁת (I Sam. 19:13, 16; 26:7, 11, 16). The Hebrew denotes simply the place where the head is while sleeping, and the RSV translates "at his head."

**BOLT.** *See* LOCK.

**BOND.** The translation of several Hebrew and Greek terms, used both literally and figuratively to mean "obligation," "dependence," or "restraint."

**1. In the OT.** The meaning is literal in such a phrase as "bond [עָצוּר] and free" (I Kings 14:10), and in speaking of Samson's bonds (אֲסוּרִים; Judg. 15:14) or those of prisoners (מוֹסֵר; Ps. 107:14) and slaves (Ps. 116:16; cf. Job 39:5).

The meaning is frequently figurative. The hands of an evil woman are like "fetters" or bonds (אֲסוּרִים; Eccl. 7:26). There are the bonds of wickedness (חַרְצֻבּוֹת; Isa. 58:6), of affliction and judgment (מוֹסֵר; Isa. 28:22; 52:2; Jer. 30:8; Nah. 1:13), the bonds or

authority of kings (Job 12:18; Ps. 2:3), and the bonds of covenant obligation (Jer. 2:20; 5:5; cf. Ezek. 20: 37) or of an oath (אִסָּר; Num. 30:3 *et passim*).

**2. In the NT.** The meaning of δεσμός and σύνδεσμος may also be literal (Luke 8:29; Philem. 13 KJV), meaning the bonds of imprisonment or the very sinews of the body (Col. 2:19); or figurative, meaning either the bonds of sin (Luke 13:16; Acts 8:23) or of peace and love (Eph. 4:3; Col. 3:14; cf. I Clem. 49:2). The "bond of legal demands" (χειρόγραφον; Col. 2:14) means a document or instrument of the law.                    J. A. SANDERS

**BONDAGE, BONDMAN.** *See* SLAVERY.

**BONES** [גֶּרֶם, עֶצֶם; LXX ὀστέον]. Despite the paucity of biblical anatomical references, the more familiar skeletal components are frequently mentioned. The most commonly found OT word for "bones," עֶצֶם, was derived from a Hebrew root "to be powerful," thus indicating the stability and firmness of bony tissue. The phrase "bone and flesh" signified the totality of an individual, which may account for the bones' being regarded as the seat of sensations (Job 4:14; 20:11; Jer. 20:9). גֶּרֶם was also used in a wider sense to denote character or personality (Prov. 17:22; 25:15).

In the creation narrative (Gen. 2:21) the word translated "rib" (צֵלָע) elsewhere means "boards" (I Kings 6:15-16), "leaves" of a door (I Kings 6:34), or "side" (II Sam. 16:13).

After death the bones were usually accorded careful burial (I Sam. 31:13). *See* DISEASE.                    R. K. HARRISON

**BONNET.** KJV translation of מִגְבָּעָה and פְּאֵר. *See* CAP; HEADDRESS.

**BOOK** [סֵפֶר, סִפְרָה; βίβλος, βιβλίον, βιβλαρίδιον, βιβλιδάριον]; often SCROLL. A document written on a strip of leather or papyrus and then rolled up (cf. Isa. 34:4) and often sealed (Rev. 5:1). The term may refer merely to a letter (I Kings 21:8) or to a longer literary work (Dan. 9:2; *see* WRITING AND WRITING MATERIALS). Certain books are referred to by name in the OT—e.g., the Book of the Covenant (Exod. 24:7), the Book of the Law (II Kings 22:8), the Book of the Wars of the Lord (Num. 21:4), and the Book of Jashar (Josh. 10:13). *See* BOOKS REFERRED TO.                    R. J. WILLIAMS

**BOOK OF LIFE.** *See* LIFE, BOOK OF.

**BOOKS REFERRED TO.** The various written documents to which reference is made in the Bible are of three types: source books used by authors or editors of our present OT and NT books; books mentioned as composed by Moses, the prophets, or other ancient worthies; and books presented as divinely authored.

The authentic written literary collections mentioned as used by OT writers as source materials include the following:

*a*) The "book of the Wars of the LORD" (Num. 21: 14), probably an anthology of old war poems on the fights of the invading Israelites with the original inhabitants of Canaan. *See* WARS OF THE LORD, BOOK OF THE.

*b*) The "Book of Jashar," a similar poetic anthology, containing both war poems (e.g., Josh. 10:12-13) and such authentic literary masterpieces as David's lament over Saul and Jonathan (II Sam. 1:17-27). *See* JASHAR, BOOK OF.

*c*) The "book of the acts of Solomon" (I Kings 11: 41), probably a primarily biographical document, perhaps compiled from royal annals and emphasizing King Solomon's wisdom. It may have included such examples of his justice and magnificence as the story of his judgment between the two harlots (3:16-28), the lists of his administrative arrangements (4:1-19), and the account of the Queen of Sheba's visit (10:1-10, 13). *See* KINGS, BOOK OF.

*d*) The "Book of the Chronicles of the Kings of Israel," which may have been a continuous journal compiled by scribes from royal records. It is mentioned eighteen times as containing further information about Jeroboam I, his wars and his reign (I Kings 14:19), Nadab (15:31), Baasha and his might (16:5), Elah (16:14), Zimri and his conspiracy (16: 20), Omri and his might (16:27), Ahab, his ivory house and the cities he built (22:39), Ahaziah (II Kings 1:18), Jehu and his might (10:34), Jehoahaz and his might (13:8), Joash and Jehoash and the might with which each fought against Amaziah of Judah (13:12; 14:15), Jeroboam II, his might and how he recovered Damascus and Hamath from the power of Judah (14:28), Zechariah (15:11), Shallum and his conspiracy (15:15), Menahem (15:21), Pekahiah (15:26), and Pekah (15:31). Jehoram and Hoshea are the only two Israelite kings for whom this source is not cited.

*e*) The "Book of the Chronicles of the Kings of Judah," containing the "rest of the acts of" Rehoboam (I Kings 14:29), Abijam (15:7), Asa, his might and the cities he built (15:23), Jehoshaphat, his might and how he warred (22:45), Joram (II Kings 8:23), Joash (12:19), Amaziah (14:18), Azariah (15: 6), Jotham (15:36), Ahaz (16:19), Hezekiah, his might and how he made the pool and the conduit and brought water into the city (20:20), Manasseh and his sin (21:17), Amon (21:25), Josiah (23:28), and Jehoiakim (24:5). This book, mentioned fifteen times, was for the S kingdom similar to *d above.* Before Josiah only Ahaziah and the usurper Athaliah are not mentioned as referred to in this source; after him only one of the four remaining kings—viz., Jehoiakim—is mentioned.

I and II Chronicles refer to several presumably authentic historians' source books: the "Book of the Kings of Israel" (I Chr. 9:1; II Chr. 20:34); the "Book of the Kings of Israel and Judah" (II Chr. 27: 7; 35:27; 36:8); the "Book of the Kings of Judah and Israel" (II Chr. 16:11; 25:26; 28:26; 32:32); and the "Commentary [or Midrash] on the Book of the Kings" (II Chr. 24:27). These were obviously not our canonical I and II Kings, but whether they were the same as or similar to *d* and *e above* used by the editors of I and II Kings, or whether they were authentic documents based on court record, is not known. *See* CHRONICLES.

The "Book of the Chronicles" mentioned in Nehe-

miah (12:23; cf. 7:5), not our canonical I and II Chronicles, may have been the official temple chronicle for the postexilic period containing historical data and lists of clerical personnel. Books of Persian kings' annals are mentioned (Ezra 4:15; cf. Esth. 2:23; 6:1; 10:2).

That the NT writers made frequent references to OT books as sources is, of course, well known, even though specific reference to the particular OT book is fairly infrequent (Mark 12:26; Luke 3:4; 4:17-20; 20: 42; Acts 1:20; 7:42; Gal. 3:10; Heb. 9:19).

Of all the biblical persons who are credited with the writing of books, the one who receives greatest acclaim is Moses. Earliest traditions refer to him as having written down Amalek's fate in a book (Exod. 17:14). At Yahweh's dictation he was said to have inscribed the words of the "book of the covenant" (24:3-7; *see* COVENANT, BOOK OF THE). Most frequent reference, of course, is to the "book of the law of Moses," which was carefully prepared (Deut. 17:18; 28:58, 61; 30:10; 31:24, 26) and contained explicit curses (29:20-21, 27). This book was cherished by Joshua (Josh. 1:8; 8:31, 34; 23:6), was neglected in the failures of King Amaziah of Judah (II Kings 14: 6; II Chr. 25:4), stimulated the reforms of King Josiah (II Kings 22:8-23:24; II Chr. 34:14-35:12) and King Jehoshaphat of Judah (II Chr. 17:9), and was central in the career of Ezra (Ezra 6:18; Neh. 8: 1-9:3; cf. 13:1).

Joshua is said to have written two books, one setting forth the allotment of Canaan to the Israelites (Josh. 18:9), the other containing the renewal of the covenant (24:26).

Various prophets are recorded as having been told to inscribe the words of Yahweh in a book (e.g., Isa. 30:8). Jeremiah's dictated book is particularly well known (Jer. 25:13; 30:2; 36; 45:1; 51:60, 63). The notation that "Samuel told the people the rights and duties of the kingship; and he wrote them in a book and laid it up before Yahweh" (I Sam. 10:25) probably inspired the Chronicler's frequent references to prophetic works as source materials, although these alleged sources are never termed "books" (I Chr. 29: 29; II Chr. 9:29; 12:15; 13:22; 26:22; 33:19).

The oldest book presented as divinely authored is probably the "book of remembrance" (Mal. 3:16), out of which Moses was willing to have his name removed (Exod. 32:32-33), and with which a number of psalmists were concerned (Pss. 40:7 [cf. Heb. 10:7]; 69:28; 87:6; 139:16). Identical with this book or related to it was the book of truth and of life of prophetic and apocalyptic writers (Isa. 4:3; 34:16; Dan. 10:2; 12:1, 4). It takes its most dramatic form in the NT "book of life" (Phil. 4:3; Rev. 3:5; 13:8; 17:8; 20:12, 15; 21:27). *See* LIFE, BOOK OF.

**Bibliography.** On historical source books used by OT writers, see, e.g.: J. A. Montgomery, *Kings,* ICC (1951), pp. 24-38; E. Nielsen, *Oral Tradition* (1954), ch. 3; N. H. Snaith, Introduction to I Kings, *IB,* III (1954), 4-6.        C. F. KRAFT

**BOOT** [סְאוֹן, *from* Akkad. *šēnu,* shoe; Egyp. Aram. שׁאן] (Isa. 9:5—H 9:4, in the phrase סְאוֹן סֹאֵן, "boot of the booted warrior"; RSV "boot of the tramping warrior"; KJV "BATTLE of the warrior"). The booted warrior is an Assyrian figure depicted in the Lachish reliefs from the period of Sennacherib (705-

681 B.C.). The boots appear as high leather boots laced up to the knees and thus in contrast to the sandals of the Israelite soldier. The Beni-hasan painting (nineteenth century B.C.) depicts Asiatic women wearing a low type of boot extending just above the ankle.      J. M. MYERS

**BOOTH** [סכה; שך (Lam. 2:6)]. A temporary shelter for cattle (Gen. 33:17), for men (Jonah 4:5), and especially on the battlefield (II Sam. 11:11; I Kings 20:12, 16). The booths used at the Feast of Booths

From *Atlas of the Bible* (Thomas Nelson & Sons Limited)

43. Booth in a Palestinian field

(*see* BOOTHS, FEAST OF) were to be made of branches, probably woven together (Lev. 23:40; Neh. 8:15). Fig. BOO 43.

"Booth" is also a figure of that which is flimsy (Job 27:18) and desolated (Isa. 1:8; KJV COTTAGE). *See also* PAVILION; TABERNACLE.      E. M. GOOD

**BOOTHS, FEAST OF** [חג הסכות, *from verb* to weave together, *referring to plaited branches with which booths were covered;* LXX ἑορτή (τῶν)σκηνῶν (σκηνω-πηγία)] (Lev. 23:34; Deut. 16:13, 16; Ezra 3:4; Zech. 14:16, 18-19; cf. II Macc. 10:6; Jos. Antiq. XIII.xiii.5). One of Israel's three great annual festivals, celebrated with great joy in autumn, at the completion of the agricultural year, to recall Israel's wilderness pilgrimage and, apparently, as a renewal of the covenant; commonly known as Tabernacles (cf. II Chr. 8:13). Other names for this festival in the Bible are: "the feast of ingathering" (חג האסף; Exod. 23:16 [LXX ἑορτή συντελείας]; 34:22 [LXX ἑορτή συναγωγῆς]); "the feast of the Lord" (חג יהוה; Lev. 23:39; Judg. 21:19); "the feast" (החג; I Kings 8:2, 65; II Chr. 7:8; Neh. 8:14; Isa. 30:29; Ezek. 45:23, 25).

Though Deut. 16:16 prescribes that all male Israelites must "appear before the LORD" three times a year, it seems that the Feast of Booths ranks as the original pilgrimage festival. Elkanah, father of Samuel, made an annual journey to Shiloh (I Sam. 1:3, 21) to make the "yearly sacrifice"; and the occasion of his pilgrimage probably was the "yearly feast of the LORD at Shiloh" (Judg. 21:19). This feast featured a vintage dance (Judg. 21:16 ff), indicating that it had close association with Canaanite agricultural celebrations. But it was an Israelite feast that is best understood as an early form of the Feast of Booths. The booths, later used to commemorate the wandering of Israel, are also derived from an agricultural practice: to protect the olive orchards in the month of harvest (September), their owners used to guard them by night, standing in shelters constructed of branches and vines. As will appear below, it is not clear when the booth was first reinterpreted as a symbol of Israel's wilderness experience. This is one aspect of the larger question whether, in pre-exilic times, the Feast of Booths was simply an agricultural festival borrowed from Canaan and celebrated in the name of Israel's God, or whether, from the beginning, it served as a vehicle for distinctive aspects of Israel's covenant faith. Until recently, under the influence of Wellhausen, preference was given to the former alternative; currently there is a strong shift toward the latter.

Booths became an extremely popular festival in postexilic Judaism. It was utilized especially as an occasion on which Jews from the Diaspora made pilgrimage to Jerusalem. Pilgrim parties came from Babylonia and from more distant places, bringing with them the accumulated offerings for the temple and the city. The plundering of such parties by highwaymen and the problem of their protection are sometimes alluded to (Jos. Antiq. XVII.ii.2; XVIII. ix.1). The eschatological visions which speak of the coming of all nations to worship at Jerusalem refer to the Feast of Booths as the occasion for their pilgrimage (Zech. 14:16 ff; cf. Isa. 2:2-4; 56:6-8). The season for the presentation of first fruits, which began with the Feast of Pentecost, concluded with the Feast of Booths (Bik. 1.10). The feast seems to have reached its most elaborate form shortly before the destruction of the temple.

1. Analysis of the feast
2. Early stages of its development
3. Antecedents
   Bibliography

**1. Analysis of the feast.** The feast began on the fifteenth day of the seventh month (Tishri). The first day of this month was a special holy day (Lev. 23:23-25), and the Day of Atonement (*see* ATONEMENT, DAY OF) fell on the tenth. The three events seem to signify a differentiation in what was originally a single observance. The sacred character of the first of the seventh month was probably a sign of the memory that Israel's year once began in autumn. But the original Feast of Booths was celebrated at the end of the year (Exod. 23:16; 34:22). All three festal calendars (Exod. 23:14-17; Lev. 23; Deut. 16) place Booths last in the series, intimating that it came at the end of the year, before the beginning of the new. Again, while we are told that the dedication of Solomon's temple took place at the feast in the seventh month (I Kings 8:2), it is also noted that he finished it in the eighth month (I Kings 6:38). And in the Mishna we learn that normally a booth was too old for use at the feast if it had been constructed thirty days before it; however, if it had been built intentionally for this ritual purpose, "even at the beginning of the year," it was acceptable (Suk. 1.1). Thus, originally, the feast seems to have come just before, rather than just after, the end of the year. The feast proper lasted seven days; to this two days of special observance were added.

Certain duties were incumbent upon every celebrant. He had to provide himself with a סכה or booth in which he slept and ate all his meals for seven days. This was a ritual requirement the proper fulfilment of which is specified in great detail in the Mishna. Further, every pilgrim had to collect twigs of myrtle, willow, and palm in the environs of Jerusalem. Originally these were used in the construction of the booths (Neh. 8:13-18); later some of them, at least, were bound together into a sort of festal plume, called the lulab, to which a citron was also attached. The lulab was a symbol of rejoicing and was carried ceremonially during the daily singing of the Hallel (Pss. 113-118), being waved aloft at the opening phrase of Ps. 118: "O give thanks to the LORD," and, especially, at the cry for salvation in vs. 25.

The water libation ceremony was the first common rite for each day of the feast. On the morning of the first day a procession of priests led down to the Pool of Siloam to bring up a container of water, which was to suffice for the seven days. The water was brought up in solemn fashion with the blowing of the שׁוֹפָר at the city gate (cf. Isa. 12:3). The pilgrims, singing the Hallel and carrying their lulabs, witnessed the circumambulation of the altar by the priestly procession and, waving their lulabs, joined in the great cry: "Save us, we beseech thee, O LORD." It was from this cry that the rite was given the title *"Hoshianah (Hoshono) Rabbah."* Having completed the circumambulation, the priest acting as celebrant ascended the ramp of the altar to perform the libation, using two silver bowls, one for water and one for wine. The people called out: "Lift up thy hand," so that they could verify the performance of the rite, for Sadducees denied the legitimacy of the rite, on the ground that there was no basis for it in the Pentateuch, and they had refused to perform it properly. On the seventh day the circumambulation of the altar was repeated seven times. As on the other days, the priests in the procession carried willows, but this time, instead of waving them aloft, they beat the earth with them at the conclusion of the ceremony.

The second great common rite occurred at night. It sought to give expression to the rejoicing of the feast. Four huge Menorahs fitted out with wicks made from the worn-out garments of the priests, illumined the entire temple area. Under them the celebrants danced a torch dance to the accompaniment of flute playing, and the Levites chanted the Psalms of Ascent (120-134), one each on the fifteen steps that led down from the court of Israelites to the Court of the Women. This, very probably, was the "holy feast" in the night mentioned in Isa. 30:29. It lasted most of the night for each of the seven days.

Each day at dawn there was a more solemn rite carried out by priests. At cockcrow they proceeded to the E gate of the temple area. Then, at the moment of sunrise, they turned W to face the temple and recited: "Our fathers when they were in this place turned with their faces toward the east, and they worshiped the sun toward the east; but as for us, our eyes are turned toward the LORD" (Suk. 5.4; cf. Ezek. 8:16).

The three common rites were performed on each of the seven days of the feast proper. The Hallel was also sung on the solemn assembly held on the eighth day. The ninth day is called *Simhath Torah*

("the Joy of the Law") and is a sign of the tendency to transfer the focus of the feast from nature to the law. It is an interesting fact, perhaps also bearing on the relationship of the feast to New Year, that the cycle of Torah readings began at this time. While in its postexilic development the feast is entirely Jewish in spirit, many of the forms in its three great rites seem to echo the nature mysticism of Canaan, from which they had been assimilated. The complex of observances had grown in bulk over the centuries, and the forms came from different sources; Israel's covenant with the Lord gave unity to the feast.

**2. Early stages of its development.** The Covenant Code, Deuteronomy, and the Priestly Law all contain provisions relating to Booths. In Exod. 23:16, representing the first of these, and in the related reference in Exod. 34:22, it is called חַג־הָאָסִיף, "the feast of ingathering." The observance is associated with the completion of agricultural work: "when you gather in from the field the fruit of your labor." There is no reference to booths; no memorial role is specified; nor is the manner or duration of the observance indicated. In the opinion of many, vs. 17, viewed as a pilgrimage requirement, represents a later addition to vss. 14-16; and, with the aid of I Sam. 1:21, the Feast of Ingathering in the Covenant Code is designated as the single pilgrimage festival in early Israel. The occasion at Shiloh at which Elkanah offered his sacrifice must have been the same as the "feast of the LORD" at Shiloh mentioned in Judg. 21:19 ff. The Feast of Ingathering appears, therefore, to have been an occasion of great rejoicing with features of carnival-like indulgence; it was supremely the time of sacrifices (in Num. 29 the quantity of sacrifices specified for Booths is greater than for any other feast); and this meant the eating of meat and the drinking of wine (cf. I Sam. 1:3-9); Eli's suspicion that Hannah was drunk (I Sam. 1:14) can be understood as reflecting the nature of the feast; and the dance of the maidens in the vineyards, apparently with seduction as an aim, hints strongly at traditional Canaanite vintage revelry. Yet it is a "feast of the LORD," and the rubric in Exod. 23:16 is the result of an early stage in the process by which Israel came to terms with Canaanite culture.

In Deut. 16:13-15 the Feast of Ingathering has become the Feast of Booths (to be celebrated at a place God "will choose"). No function or significance is specified for the booths, however. The feast is to last for seven days and is to celebrate the harvest of both threshing floor and wine press. There is a special admonition to rejoice in "your feast" (vs. 14), God's blessing of the agricultural enterprise being the warrant for joy. There is no overt connection between the feast and Israel's communal history. However, in Deut. 31:9-13 there is a supplement which introduces the reading of the law. Every seventh year, the year of release, at the Feast of Booths the law of the covenant is to be read out in the hearing of "all Israel." This not only gives us a relatively early basis for the development of the Joy-of-the-Law observance on the ninth day, but also hints at a connection between the Feast of Booths and a formal covenant ceremony at which the reading of the laws of the covenant was a standard feature (cf. Exod.

24:7 ff; Deut. 27; Josh. 24:22 ff). Alt, followed by Noth, holds that the year of release is an ancient institution in Israel that may date back to the era of Joshua. The seven-year interval, at which the land lay fallow, seems to owe something to the fertility theme of Canaanite religion; but in the release of slaves and the cancellation of debts this is combined with the communal character of Israel's faith.

In the priestly legislation (Lev. 23) the first day and the eighth, first mentioned here, are designated as days for a "holy convocation," a feature hinted in the LXX reading for Exod. 34:22. Sabbath rest is to be observed. However, the eighth day is not treated as one of the days of Booths proper (Lev. 23:36). In Lev. 23:39-43, in what appears to be a supplementary addition, we learn for the first time that the ritual residence in booths is to commemorate that God made Israel "dwell in booths" when he brought them "out of the land of Egypt" (vs. 43). The supplement is also first to mention the gathering of branches for the feast, implying (vs. 40) that they are to be used to make the lulab rather than for the construction of the booths (cf. Neh. 8:13-18), a fact which leads Auerbach to conclude that the supplement was added after the celebration described in the book of Nehemiah. As noted, the dedication of Solomon's temple took place on the occasion of "the feast" (I Kings 8:2). In the Hebrew text for I Kings 8:65 we read that he kept the feast "seven days and seven days, fourteen days" (RSV mg.). It is tempting to accept Auerbach's explanation that this error was due to the attempt of an editor of Kings who wanted to synchronize the account with Lev. 23, but who read the supplement as an additional prescription rather than as an amplification of Lev. 23:34-36.

**3. Antecedents.** The analysis just completed makes it clear that phenomenologically the associations of Booths with the agricultural life of Palestine were very close throughout. The nature mysticism implicit in the vintage dance recorded for the early period is more than matched by the fertility motifs exhibited by such late developments as the libation ceremony and the lulab. It is also difficult to escape the conclusion that Lev. 23:39-43 is supplementary even to the late Priestly Code; thus the only reference formally relating Booths to Israel's *Heilsgeschichte* is very late. This raises two different, though related, questions: namely, when did the Feast of Booths begin to function as a historical memorial for Israel, and what were the forces that operated to give it this role?

With respect to the former question it is well to remember that the rubrics governing a practice are always later, and often much later, than the observance they regulate. Consequently, it is not advisable in this connection to make the probable date of Lev. 23:39-43 determinative. But this only introduces the real problem. E.g., Auerbach suggests that the booths of the feast were first given a cultic-historical significance in Babylon, because in captivity there were no olive orchards to guard. I.e., following Wellhausen's thesis of *Denaturierung,* he assumed that "the feast" was fundamentally a nature feast of Canaanite origin and that the course of its develop-

ment in Israel was determined by historical factors in Israel's history extraneous to it.

There is the alternative view that there was from the first in Israel a tent festival, whose function served the purposes of a ceremony of "covenant renewal," and that the Feast of Booths is the outcome of the assimilation of the autumn agricultural observances of Canaan to this basically Israelite cultic institution. This view assumes that the "tribes" of Israel constituted a sacral amphictyony held together in covenant with Yahweh. The central cultic act of this community consists in the establishment and renewal of the covenant. The sealing of the covenant at Sinai (Exod. 24), the renewal of the covenant at Shechem (Josh. 24), and the reformation of Josiah (II Kings 22–23), as well as lesser instances of cult purification in the monarchic era, all seem to bear the marks of a covenant ceremony in which the reading of the law was a feature. In the opinion of Kraus, the covenant-renewal ceremony, in which the bases of communal life were purified and revitalized, played a role in Israel analogous to the role of the New Year's festival in Babylon. The action of God at the founding of the covenant is re-presented in a cultic action so that past meets present in a cultic "today" (Deut. 29:10 ff). The fact that in Deut. 31:9-13 the reading of the law is enjoined in connection with the seven-year cycle of the year of release may indicate that the times of Israel's covenant-renewal ceremonies were under the influence of the periodicity of the nature mysticism of Canaan. The underlying identity between the autumnal harvest feast of Canaan and Israel's observance of covenant renewal would consist in the revitalizing significance attached to both.

In the view of Kraus the Israelite covenant feast was at the same time a tent festival. In support of this he cites the frequency of tent feasts among nomads; but, even more, he appeals to the priestly reconstruction of the Israelite camp of the wilderness era with the "tent of meeting" at the center. And in Hos. 12:9—H 12:10, where the prophet announces Israel's return to the wilderness for judgment and regeneration (cf. Hos. 2:14), he notes that Israel's actual dwelling in tents is brought into relation with its days of appointment or meeting with God (RSV somewhat daringly renders the Hebrew "appointed feast"). It is to be noted in this connection that the "booths" of the feast are quite anachronistic as a "reminder" of the tents of the wilderness period. In contrast to the Wellhausen tradition, the booths did not suggest the idea of tents, Kraus holds, but the "booths" were an adaptation of an actual tent feast that preceded. He feels that this change began at Shiloh; it was there that the tent of the Lord was first displaced by a temple, and the tents of Israel's pilgrimage feast by agricultural booths. Many of the details in Kraus's reconstruction may have to be reconsidered. But a central thesis stands out: Israel had a cult-feast tradition rooted in its own history by means of which it could assimilate Canaan's vintage feast and develop the Feast of Booths. Though considerable tension exists between this thesis and an extreme emphasis placed upon universal cultic patterns by some scholars, it seems to merit general acceptance.

*Bibliography.* J. Morgenstern, "The Three Calendars of Ancient Israel," *HUCA*, vol. I (1924). G. von Rad, "Zelt und Lade," *NKZ* (1931), pp. 476 ff. L. Rost, "Sinaibund und Davidsbund," *TLZ*, 72 (1947), 129 ff. A. Alt, "Die Wallfahrt von Sichem nach Bethel," *Kleine Schriften I*, 70-80; "Zelte und Hütten," *Nötscher Festschrift* (1950), pp. 16-25. A. Kuscke, "Die Lagervorstellung der priesterlichen Erzählung," *ZAW*, 63 (1951), 74 ff. H. J. Kraus, *Gottesdienst in Israel: Studien zur Geschichte des Laubhüttenfestes* (1954). E. Auerbach, "Die Feste im alten Israel," *Vetus Testamentum*, 8 (1958), 1 ff.

J. C. RYLAARSDAM

**BOOTY** [בז, מלקוח, משסה]. Spoils taken in battle.

It was a general custom in antiquity for victorious raiders or troops to despoil the conquered territory of everything of value. A certain portion was often dedicated to the deity or to his sanctuary (cf. Num. 31:26 ff). Muḥammad decreed that one fifth of all booty was to be set aside for Allah (*Quran* VIII.41). For "spoil" as opposed to "booty" among the Hebrews, *see* SPOIL. J. W. WEVERS

**BOOZ.** KJV form of BOAZ in Matt. 1:5; Luke 3:32.

**BORASHAN** bôr ā'shən [בור עשׁן, cistern *or* well of Ashan]; KJV CHOR-ASHAN kôr— [כור עשׁן, *reading of the sixteenth-century printed Rabbinic Bible of Jacob ben Chayyim*, editio Bombergiana; כ is an error for ב]. Same as ASHAN.

**BORITH.** Apoc. alternate name of BUKKI 2.

**BORROW, LEND.** To take on security a thing given for its safe return, or to take on credit with the expectation of the return of it or its equivalent. The borrower obtains temporary use of the item from the lender. Sometimes a DEPOSIT was required of the borrower (Deut. 24:11, 13; cf. Exod. 22:7 ff). Money was frequently borrowed. Interest was not to be taken from fellow Israelites (Exod. 22:25; Lev. 25:35) but was allowed from Gentiles (Deut. 23:20). Usury was either exacting interest from an Israelite or taking exhorbitant interest from any creditor. Both lending and repayment were considered charitable actions (Ecclus. 29:1-14). Jesus also urges such a trust of one's neighbor (Matt. 5:42), even if repayment is questionable (Luke 6:34-35; 7:41 ff; cf. Prov. 19:17). Nevertheless, the debtor was not the happiest of persons (Prov. 22:7; Matt. 18:23 ff). *See also* DEBT.

C. U. WOLF

**BOSCATH.** KJV form of BOZKATH in II Kings 22:1.

**BOSOR** bō'sôr [Βοσορ]. **1.** One of the Gileadite cities where Gentile citizens persecuted the Jewish residents after the rededication of the temple in 165 B.C. (I Macc. 5:26, 36). It is identified with the modern Busr el-Hariri on the border of the Trachons, probably the BEZER of Deut. 4:43; Josh. 20:8.

**2.** KJV NT form of BEOR.

**BOSORA.** KJV form of BOZRAH 3.

**BOSSED, BOSSES** [גב, *gabh; cf.* Arab. *jabba,* cut, cut off; *jawb,* shield]. Bosses are knobs or protuberances, often ornamental, which stand out from a flat surface. Bosses on early shields strengthened the shield itself, which was often of leather stretched over a wooden frame. Later, on metal shields, bosses came to be largely decorative. *See* WEAPONS AND IMPLEMENTS OF WAR.

In Job 15:26 the wicked man is said to run against God "with a thick-bossed shield" (RSV; lit., "with the thickness of the bosses of his shields"); this is a figure for his insolent defiance of the Almighty.

W. S. McCULLOUGH

**BOTCH.** KJV translation of שׁחין (RSV BOIL) in Deut. 28:27, 35.

**BOTTLE** [נאד (Ps. 56:8—H 56:9); נד, *nōdh* (Ps. 33: 7; KJV HEAP, *with* MT *nēdh*); KJV אוב (RSV "wineskin"), בקבק (RSV "flask"), חמת (RSV "skin"; "cup"; "heat"), נבל (RSV "skin"; "jar"), ἀσκός (RSV "wineskin"; "skin")]. Translation is difficult, but the reference in Pss. 33:7; 56:8—H 56:9 seems to be to a waterskin (cf. Josh. 9:4, 13; Judg. 4:19; I Sam. 16:20, where the same word is used for "wineskin" and "milkskin"). Other words translated "bottle" by the KJV are designated more exactly by the RSV. J. L. KELSO

**BOTTOMLESS PIT.** The (literal) translation of ἄβυσσος in Rev. 9:1-2, 11; 11:7; 17:8; 20:1, 3. *See* ABYSS.

**BOUGAEAN** boo gē'ən [βουγαῖος] (Add. Esth. 12:6); KJV AGAGITE. A designation of HAMAN. It appears in the LXX for the original אגגי, "Agagite," in Esth. 3:1; 9:10. This epithet, however, the LXX elsewhere replaces with "Macedonian" (Esth. 9:24; cf. Add. Esth. 12:6) or omits entirely (Esth. 3:10; 8:3, 5). Some have identified "Bougaean" with the Homeric term of reproach "bully" or "braggart" (*Iliad* XIII.824; *Odyssey* XVIII.79). More probably it is the corruption of an original ἀγαγαῖος, "Agagite." M. NEWMAN

**BOUNDARIES, TRIBAL.** *See* TRIBES, TERRITORIES OF.

**BOUNDARY STONES.** *See* LANDMARK.

**BOW AND ARROW.** The words translated "bow" are קשׁת and τόξον. "Arrow" is used for חצי, חץ, and רשׁף. The phrase רשׁפי קשׁת (lit., "flashes of the bow") in Ps. 76:3—H 76:4 is translated "flashing arrows" (KJV "arrows of the bow").

The back of the Mesopotamian bow was made of wood, horn, or bones; decked with bark or leather; and then lacquered. In earlier times such costly weapons were carried only by princes and leaders. In the Assyrian assault bowmen, as well as lancers, were used effectively to protect those who scaled the walls of a besieged city. Fig. WAR 3.

In Thut-mose III's account of the spoils taken at the Battle of Megiddo, only 502 bows are listed, although almost 1,000 chariots and over 2,000 horses are included (*ANET* 237).

The arrow consisted of a shaft made of reed or light wood notched at one end, and a head or tip, either socketed or, as more commonly, equipped with

Courtesy of Editions des Musées Nationaux, Paris

44. Huntsmen shooting birds, from Khorsabad (eighth century B.C.)

a tang. Such tips were made of flint, bone, or bronze. Since metal was expensive, flint tips remained in common usage until the Late Bronze Age. Such tips were often equipped with barbs or dipped in poison (Job 6:4) in order to render them more effective.

The bow and arrow was the normal weapon in use by the nomad (Gen. 21:20) and the hunter (Gen. 27:3; Isa. 7:24); it was also used by the raider (Gen. 48:22; Josh. 24:12) and the warrior (Isa. 13:18; Ezek. 39:9; Hos. 1:7). Figs. BOW 44; ARC 48; HUN 34-35; WEA 11.

Arrows were sometimes used for divination (Ezek. 21:21—H 21:26), in accordance with Mesopotamian custom, and also for magical purposes (II Kings 13:15-19). "Arrow" is often used symbolically to represent violence (Pss. 11:2; 57:4—H 57:5) or divine judgment (especially in the Psalms; cf. 7:13—H 7:14; 38:2—H 38:3; 64:7—H 64:8).

See also WAR, METHODS OF; QUIVER; ARCHER.
J. W. WEVERS

**BOWELS** [מעים; σπλάγχνα]. The word "bowels" is used in the RSV only in the literal sense of "intestines," but the KJV uses it more loosely—e.g., in II Sam. 16:11 (for internal genitalia; cf. RSV); Ps. 71:6 (RSV "womb")—and metaphorically to refer to strong emotion (Job 30:27; RSV "heart"), especially love (Song of S. 5:4; RSV "heart") and compassion ("bowels of mercy" in Col. 3:12; RSV "compassion").     R. C. DENTAN

**BOWL.** In the Bible "bowl" and "basin" are often interchangeable terms, although usage has given certain priorities to each word. For the various uses of bowls and basins, see POTTERY § 3a; for metal bowls, see VESSELS § 2.

See Fig. POT 63 for pottery bowls of various periods.
J. L. KELSO

**BOX** [ארגז; KJV פך (RSV "flask"); KJV ἀλάβαστρον (RSV "jar"; "flask")]. A container. See also FLASK; MONEY BOX; PERFUME § 3; POTTERY; VESSELS.

**BOX TREE.** KJV translation of תאשור (Isa. 41:19; 60:13; RSV PINE) and πύξος (II Esd. 14:24; RSV "tablet"). The box tree is not found in the Holy Land (a box shrub, Buxus longifolia Boiss., has been found). Zohary (see FLORA § A9e) and others identify תאשור with the cypress.

The original Greek of II Esd. 14:24 was apparently πυξίον, "tablet"—probably a reference to boxwood, from which the tablets for writing were made in Greco-Roman times.     J. C. TREVER

**BOZEZ** bō'zĭz [בוצץ] (I Sam. 14:4). One of two rocks in the mountain pass between Michmash and Geba. It was apparently located on the N side of the Wadi Sweinit, but the exact spot has not been identified.

**BOZKATH** bŏz'kăth [בצקת, elevated ground]; KJV BOSCATH bŏs'— in II Kings 22:1. A village of Judah in the Shephelah district of Lachish (Josh. 15:39); its location remains unknown. Jedidah, the mother of Josiah (ca. 640-609 B.C.), was the daughter of Adaiah of Bozkath (II Kings 22:1).
V. R. GOLD

**\*BOZRAH** bŏz'rə [בצרה, fortified place; sheepfold; Βοσόρρα]; KJV Apoc. BOSORA bŏs'ə rə. 1. An important Edomite fortress city, home of King Jobab (Gen. 36:33; I Chr. 1:44); identified with modern Buseira ca. twenty miles S-SE of the Dead Sea and thirty-five miles N of Petra. Built on a flat spur, surrounded by deep wadis, and connected to the headland by a ridge protected by a fort, Bozrah was practically impregnable.\* Probably the strongest city in N Edom, it guarded the road along the W edge of the Jebel esh-Shera' and controlled the approaches to the copper mines in the Arabah. Fig. BOZ 45.

In the prophets' oracles against Edom, Bozrah is a symbol of Edom's strength, and its destruction signifies the destruction of all Edom (Isa. 34:6; 63:1; Jer. 49:13, 22; Amos 1:12). Bozrah in Mic. 2:12 KJV is better translated "(sheep)fold" (cf. RSV).

2. A city in Moab which will share in the impending destruction of the land (Jer. 48:24); probably the same as BEZER (cf. LXX B Βοσός, Bosor).

3. A city captured by Judas Maccabeus (165-160

Courtesy of Nelson Glueck

45. The spur on which Bozrah (Buseira) is situated

B.C.) in the course of his campaign in Gilead. Some Ammonite detachments, allies of the Seleucid Greeks, had taken refuge there (I Macc. 5:26, 28). It is identified with modern Busra eski Sham (Buṣruna of the Amarna Letters), ca. sixty-one miles S of Damascus and twenty-five miles E-SE of Dera'a. Located at the foot of the Jebel ed-Druz in SE Hauran, Bozrah was an important junction point during the Greco-Roman period for ancient roads leading to Mediterranean ports, Damascus, Aila (on the Gulf of Aqabah), and ports on the Persian Gulf.

After the invasion of Pompey (64 B.C.), Bozrah became the northernmost city of the Nabatean Empire, though from time to time the Nabateans' authority extended to Damascus (II Cor. 11:32-33). After Trajan's conquest of the Nabateans, Bostra (ἡ or τὰ Βόστρα; Bozrah) became the capital of the Roman province of Arabia, and general headquarters for the Legion III Cyrenaica. Alexander Severus (222-35) raised it to the status of a colony. Philip the Arab (Marcus Julius Philippus, 244-49), a native of Bostra, made it a metropolis.

Traditionally evangelized by one of the Seventy (Luke 10:1-20), Bostra was long the ecclesiastical center of the Hauran. In 244, Origen presided at an important church council convened to discipline the Monarchian, Beryllus. Later it became a Nestorian center. In the early seventh century, Muhammed, with his caravans from Mecca, visited Bostra. It is perhaps here that he learned much of what he knew about Christianity. In 634, Bostra fell to the Muslims in the course of their northward expansion. In 1113 and 1119 it was visited by invading Crusader forces.

*Bibliography.* N. Glueck, *Explorations in Eastern Palestine,* vol. I, *AASOR,* XIV (1933-34), 78-79; vol. II, *AASOR,* XV (1934-35), 83, 97-98. A. Alt, "Das Territorium von Bostra," *ZDPV,* 68 (1951), 235-45, and bibliography cited therein.

V. R. GOLD

**BRACELET** [צָמִיד; שֵׁירוֹת (Isa. 3:19; Aram. שֵׁירָא; *cf.* Akkad. *še'eru, šemēru*); KJV אֶצְעָדָה (RSV ARM-LET), חָח (RSV BROOCH), פָּתִיל (RSV CORD)]. An ornamental circlet worn on the lower arm, as may be seen from the reference to יָד ("hand") in each case except Num. 31:50, as against אֶצְעָדָה ("armlet"),

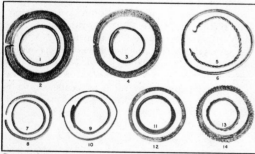

Courtesy of the American Schools of Oriental Research

46. Bracelets and anklets from Mizpeh (Tell el-Nasbeh): nos. 1-10, bronze; nos. 11-14, glass

used with זְרוֹעַ ("arm") in II Sam. 1:10. Bracelets were common all over Palestine, the archaeological remains show, and were worn by both men and women. Sometimes they were worn on one arm only,

sometimes on both arms. They were mostly of bronze, though there are examples of iron, silver, and glass bracelets, rarely of gold. Those mentioned in the biblical passages are, for the most part, said to have been of gold, notably those given to Rebekah. The שֵׁירוֹת were perhaps especially luxurious bracelets (Isa. 3:19). Fig. BRA 46.

J. M. MYERS

**BRAIDING** [ἐμπλοκή] (I Pet. 3:3; KJV PLAIT-ING); BRAIDED [πλέγμα] (I Tim. 2:9). An elaborate dressing of the hair in knots, or entwining a wreath in the hair. The term occurs also in Isa. 28:5 Aq. and Theod.

**BRAMBLE** [אָטָד, *'āṭādh* (Judg. 14:7-15; THORN *in* Ps. 50:9—H 50:10); βάτος (Luke 6:44; *elsewhere* BUSH)]. A shrub with sharp spines and runners, usually forming tangled masses of vegetation. "Bramble" is an apt translation for אָטָד in Jotham's fable (Judg. 9:8-15) and Jesus' parable (Luke 6:44).

About twenty biblical words seem to imply thorny flora (*see* THISTLES). The contexts give no hints for botanical identification, but often *Lycium europaeum* L. (European boxthorn), *Rubus sanctus* Schreb. (Palestine blackberry), and *Rhamnus palaestina* Boiss. (Palestine buckthorn) are mentioned as likely.

*See also* FLORA § A12; ATAD.

J. C. TREVER

**BRANCH.** The translation of a great variety of words in the Bible. General terms for "branch" in the OT are: עָנָף (Ezek. 17:6; 31:3); דָּלִיּוֹת (Jer. 11:16; Ezek. 17:6; 31:7); פֹּארָה (Ezek. 17:6; 31:5—here perhaps a pun on the title פַּרְעֹה, "Pharaoh"); קָצִיר (Job 14:9); נֵצֶר (Isa. 11:1) and יוֹנֶקֶת (Job 8:16 KJV) mean "shoot." צֶמַח (Jer. 23:5; cf. Akkadian *šamāḥu*) has the meaning "luxuriant sprout," referring to the royal descendant of David (*see below*). Other OT terms are: זְמוֹרָה (Num. 13:23), the "tendril" of a vine; כִּפָּה (Isa. 9:14; 19:15), the "frond" of a palm tree—figuratively used of nobles, contrasted with "reeds," the common people; and קָמָה (Exod. 25; 37), the "branch" of a lampstand (elsewhere REED). In the NT four words are translated "branch": βαΐον (John 12:13), a palm branch; κλάδος (Rom. 11:16-21), a figure for membership in Israel; κλῆμα (John 15:1-8), the branch of the "true VINE"; and στοιβάς (Mark 11:8), leafy branches.

The spreading branches of a tree or vine can symbolize the fruitfulness and prosperity of a man (Gen. 49:22; Job 8:16) or a nation (Ps. 80:11—H 80:12). Withered (Job 18:16), burnt (Jer. 11:16; Ezek. 15:2), or cut branches (Isa. 9:14) are used as figures for destruction.

"Branch" or "shoot" is employed as a designation of the present or future king of Israel. It has been suggested that this usage stems from an identification of the king with the TREE OF KNOWLEDGE; TREE OF LIFE, associated with the dying and rising god Tammuz (cf. Job 14:7, where the resurrection of a tree is contrasted with man, who "lies down and rises not again"; Isa. 17:10, where reference is made to "slips of an alien god").

The most important of the texts in question are: *a*) Isa. 11:1, though here we may have no more than a poetic metaphor; the offspring of Jesse can be considered a "shoot," even as the branch can be called the "daughter" of the tree (Gen. 49:22).

*b*) Jer. 23:5; 33:15, where the phrase "a righteous Branch" occurs. The same phrase is used in Phoenician to indicate the rightful heir to the throne. The second of these passages is generally thought to be a later addition to the book; the first may be from the hand of Jeremiah, in which case we have a contrast between a king righteous by name (Zedekiah) but not by nature, and a future ruler who will be in fact what his name implies. But possibly both passages are late, and depend on the third text (*below*).

*c*) Zech. 3:8; 6:12, where the reference is to Zerubbabel. In this instance the allusion to "branch" may have been suggested by the name of the king in question (*Zêr-Bâbili*, "shoot of Babylon"). Hence it is quite possible that in these texts we have poetic imagery rather than an actual identification of the king and the tree of life.

However, the vine branch put to the nose (Ezek. 8:17) probably does belong in the context of worship of the dying and rising god; it has also been suggested that the gesture is one of contempt, or that the phrase is a metaphor indicating the provocation of Yahweh (reading "my nose" for "their nose").

*Bibliography.* G. A. Cooke, *North Semitic Inscriptions* (1903), no. 29:11; R. Gordis, " 'The Branch to the Nose,' a Note on Ezek. VIII 17," *JTS*, XXXVII (1936), 284-88; A. E. Rüthy, *Die Pflanze und ihre Teile* (1942), pp. 52-62; G. Widengren, *The King and the Tree of Life in Ancient Near Eastern Religion* (1951), pp. 49-58; S. Mowinckel, *He That Cometh* (1955), pp. 160-61, 456-57; H. Ringgren, *The Messiah in the OT* (1956), pp. 35-36. R. W. CORNEY

**BRASS** [נחשת]. In Tudor English (i.e., KJV), "brass" was any copper alloy—e.g., copper-tin or copper-zinc. The RSV retains "brass" when נחשת is a metaphor for hardness or for obstinacy in sin (Lev. 26:19; Deut. 28:23; Isa. 48:4), but elsewhere the translation is "BRONZE." P. L. GARBER

**BRAZEN SEA.** *See* SEA, MOLTEN.

**BRAZEN SERPENT.** KJV form for BRONZE SERPENT. *See* SERPENT, BRONZE.

**BRAZIER** brā′zhər [אח, *perhaps loan word from* Egyp. '*ḥ*] (Jer. 36:22-23); KJV HEARTH. Probably a portable firepan for the heating of a room in cold weather.

**BREACH** [פרץ, שבר, בקיע, *see* 1 *below*; KJV בדק, מפרץ, *see* 1 *below*; פשע, *see* 2 *below*]. **1.** The act of breaking, or the state of being broken.

The common Hebrew word for "breach," פרץ, is used of a breach made in a city wall by the enemy (I Kings 11:27; Amos 9:11; etc.) and a breach among tribes (Judg. 21:15). In Gen. 38:29 it is used of a perineal rupture.

The word שבר literally means a "breaking in pieces" and is occasionally rendered "breach" in the KJV (Ps. 60:2—H 60:4 is the only RSV occurrence). It is often used as a colorful symbol for "wounds." At Lev. 24:20 it is better rendered as the RSV "FRACTURE."

The word בדק (cf. Akkadian *batâqu*, "cleave";

Ugaritic *bdqt*, "rift" [in the clouds]) occurs in connection with the state of disrepair of the temple during the reigns of Joash and Josiah. The RSV renders the Hebrew idiom "strengthen the breach of" as "repair" (II Kings 12:5, 8, 12—H 12:6, 9, 13; 22:5). The same Hebrew idiom appears in Ezek. 27:9, 27, alluding to "caulking the seam" of a ship.

The word מפרץ occurs only in Judg. 5:17; it is probably not derived from the root פרץ, "to break through," but is better rendered by the RSV "LANDINGS."

**2.** A betrayal of trust. Legislation for a breach of trust (KJV "transgression") is found in Exod. 22:9—H 22:8 and concerns failure in trusteeship and false claims. Legislation regarding "committing a breach of faith" (מעל מעל; KJV "commit a trespass") in matters of gifts due the sanctuary, deposits, robbery, and fraud occurs in Lev. 5:15; 6:2—H 5:21.

J. W. WEVERS

**BREAD** [לחם, *see* § 2a *below;* ἄρτος]. The baking and eating of bread are characteristic of the agricultural life. Bread is relatively scarce in the nomadic diet, since only a small quantity of grain can be transported. Thus Jesus' disciples protested: "Where are we to get bread enough in the desert to feed so great a crowd?" (Matt. 15:33; cf. Mark 8:4). Nevertheless bread was one of the staples of the diet. Ben Sirach points out:

> The essentials for life are water and bread
> and clothing and a house to cover one's nakedness
> (Ecclus. 29:21).

For more details on the importance of bread, *see* § 2a *below.*

47. Clay figure kneading bread, from the ez-Zib, excavation of 1941

1. Making of bread
   *a.* Ingredients
   *b.* Preparation of dough
   *c.* Baking
   *d.* Form of loaves
2. Use of bread
   *a.* Everyday life
   *b.* Offerings

3. Bread in biblical imagery
  *a.* In the OT
  *b.* In the NT
Bibliography

**1. Making of bread.** In the wealthier households bread was, of course, prepared by slaves; thus Samuel warns that the king demanded by the Israelites "will take your daughters to be perfumers and cooks and bakers" (I Sam. 8:13). And in the later history of Israel the making of bread became a profession; when he was in prison, Jeremiah was given a loaf each day "from the bakers' street" (Jer. 37:21; cf. the "Tower of the Ovens" in Neh. 3:11; cf. also Hos. 7:4, where the baker is probably a professional). In the average family, however, bread was prepared in the home. This was women's work, either that of the wife (Gen. 18:6), or of a daughter (II Sam. 13:8), or of some other female relative (Jer. 7:18; 44:19; cf. I Sam. 28:24). Usually the bread was made from three measures of meal at a time (Gen. 18:6; Judg. 6:19; Matt. 13:33; Luke 13:21), and only enough for the day was baked.

*a. Ingredients.* Usually bread was made from either wheat flour or barley meal in biblical times. But since FLOUR was more expensive than MEAL, wheat bread was preferred by the wealthier people, whereas the poorer classes had to be content with barley bread. The latter is specifically mentioned in Judg. 7:13; II Kings 4:42; John 6:9, 13 (the feeding of the multitude); cf. Ezek. 4:9. In times of need, however, other cereals and even leguminous seeds were mixed with the flour to increase the yield of bread. Thus as a symbol of the coming exile Ezekiel is ordered to bake a cake of bread made from "wheat and barley, beans and lentils, millet and spelt" (Ezek. 4:9).

*b. Preparation of dough.* The dough (בצק, from the root meaning "to swell") was prepared simply by mixing the flour or meal with water. In the nomadic period of Israel's history no leaven was added before kneading (cf. Gen. 18:6); the modern Beduin still eat UNLEAVENED BREAD generally. After the settlement in Canaan, however, it became customary to keep a small piece of the previous day's batch of dough and to crumble it into the water before mixing in the flour. Then the mixture was kneaded (*see* KNEAD) and allowed to stand "till it was all leavened" (Matt. 13:33; Luke 13:21; cf. Gal. 5:9). *See* LEAVEN. Figs. BRE 47-48.

*c. Baking.* In biblical times three main methods of baking were used. The simplest way was to build a fire over a large, flat stone, remove the ashes, place a flat piece of dough on the heated stone, and cover the whole with the ashes. Of course, the ashes had to be removed and replaced when the cake was turned. This method is probably referred to in the idol maker's remark that he "baked bread on [half of the idol's] coals" (Isa. 44:19); similarly Elijah is provided with a "cake baked on hot stones" (I Kings 19:6).

A more advanced method is to bake the cake on a griddle (מחבת; Lev. 2:5; 6:21—H 6:14; 7:9; I Chr. 23:29 KJV; cf. Ezek. 4:3) or in a pan (מרחשת; Lev. 2:7; 7:9). Throughout the Bronze and Iron I ages (*see* ARCHAEOLOGY § F) these were probably made

48. Disc platter used for forming cakes of bread, from Tell ed-Duweir shrine

out of clay (several were found at Gezer), but in Iron II they were iron (in Ezek. 4:3 מחבת is qualified by the adjective ברזל, "iron"). In either case a fire was laid in a pit, and the dough was baked directly on the griddle. Cakes made in this way were called חבתים (I Chr. 9:31: "flat cakes").

The most common method of baking, however, was in an oven. On the basis of modern Arabic parallels it may be assumed that the oven generally took the shape of a large inverted earthenware jar (Arabic *ṭabûn*). A fire was kindled the night before (cf. Hos. 7:6), and in the morning the ashes were raked out and the cakes were baked on the stones lining the bottom of the oven. Another type of oven presumably used in ancient times is the Arabic *tânnûr*. This consists of a tall earthenware cylinder in which a fire is again kindled; the dough is applied to the hot walls, either inside or outside. *See* BAKING; OVEN.

*d. Form of loaves.* Given these methods of baking, most bread was in the form of flat disks, probably with a diameter of approximately eighteen inches. Indeed, one of the Hebrew words rendered "cake" (עגה) comes from a root meaning "to be round." Furthermore, one of Gideon's soldiers has a dream in which a cake of barley bread rolls into the Midianite camp (Judg. 7:13); a circular form may be assumed. Another Hebrew term for "cake" is חלה, from the root meaning "to perforate"; such cakes were probably pricked either before or after baking.

Still others were apparently in the shape of a heart, since they are termed לבבות, related to the term for "heart." Not all cakes or loaves were flat, however. The arrangement of the BREAD OF THE PRESENCE in rows of cakes suggests the modern-day form. Indeed, long, thick loaves of (burnt) bread were discovered at Gezer. In addition special shapes may have been made by professional bakers; more than thirty different forms of bread are mentioned in an Egyptian papyrus document. See WAFER; CRACKNELS.

**2. Use of bread.** Since bread was one of the most important items in the diet, it was used not only at ordinary meals but also in cultic offerings.

*a. Everyday life.* Bread was of such importance that the expression "eat bread and drink water" could be used to signify eating and drinking as a whole (I Kings 13:8-9, 16-19; cf. Ecclus. 29:21, quoted above). Bread could thus be called a "staff" on which a man supported himself; when God comes in judgment, he breaks this "staff" (Lev. 26:26; Ps. 105:16; Ezek. 4:16; 5:16; 14:13; cf. Isa. 3:1; Ezek. 12:19). Indeed, the word לחם (lit., "bread") is often translated "food" in both the RSV and the KJV (sixty-four times in the former). Not to have bread is thus a mark of the most extreme poverty or distress; such was the situation during the final siege of Jerusalem (II Kings 25:3 KJV; cf. Job 15:23). Accordingly the psalmist praises Yahweh for providing

wine to gladden the heart of man,
oil to make his face shine,
and bread to strengthen man's heart (Ps. 104:15).

Specifically bread is mentioned as a gift to strangers. Melchizedek brings out bread and wine for Abram (Gen. 14:18), and the wandering Levite is careful to offer bread to his host's servants (Judg. 19:19). It was, of course, a common food of soldiers in the field (Jesse sends Saul a gift of bread and wine and a kid [I Sam. 16:20]) and harvesters (Ruth 2:14). Naturally it was taken along on a journey; Abraham provides Hagar with bread and a skin of water when he sends her away (Gen. 21:14), and Joseph presents his father and brothers with the "good things of Egypt," grain, and bread when they are on the point of returning to Canaan (Gen. 45:23).

Three loaves were sufficient for the average person at each meal (cf. Luke 11:5-6). But a prisoner was allowed only one loaf per day (Jer. 37:21), and a single loaf was all that was necessary as a gift (I Sam. 2:36). At the meal itself it was used as a spoon, its shape (*see* § 1*d above*) being appropriate for this function. It was thus natural for Jacob to give Esau bread with the pottage (Gen. 25:34) and for Rebekah to send along bread with the "savory food" which she had prepared for Isaac (Gen. 27:17). Bread therefore served as an eating utensil as well as a food in its own right.

*b. Offerings.* Bread was one of the most common elements of the cultic offerings of the ancient Near East. It is quite frequent in Babylonian and Mesopotamian ritual, and it may be assumed that bread offerings were made in Ras Shamra, since Keret sacrifices bread, wine, honey, a lamb, and a bird to El and Baal (*see bibliography*). Hebrew religion was no exception. The CEREAL OFFERING could consist of flour alone, but also of various kinds of cakes.

They could be "unleavened cakes of fine flour mixed with oil" or "unleavened wafers spread with oil" (Lev. 2:4); the bread could be baked on a griddle or in a pan (vss. 5, 7; *see* § 1*c above*). The only absolute requirements were that the bread be unleavened and seasoned with salt (vss. 11, 13). Part of the offering was to be burned on the altar, and the remainder was left for Aaron and his sons.

**3. Bread in biblical imagery.** Naturally a food as important as bread is often used in metaphorical expressions, both in the OT and in the NT.

*a. In the OT.* As something consumed, bread can be used as a metaphor for the enemy; Joshua and Caleb urge the Israelites not to fear the people of Canaan, "for they are bread for us"—i.e., they can be conquered easily (Num. 14:9). Various actions are also prefixed with "bread." The good wife does not eat the "bread of idleness" (Prov. 31:27); however, the ungodly

eat the bread of wickedness
and drink the wine of violence (Prov. 4:17).

Falsehood is called "bread of deceit"; its taste is sweet, but later the mouth is "full of gravel" (Prov. 20:17). And when Yahweh is angry with his people, he sends them the "bread of adversity and the water of affliction" (Isa. 30:20) or the "bread of tears" (Ps. 80:5—H 80:6). On the positive side, bread and wine represent the qualities of wisdom (Prov. 9:5) and the true word of God (cf. Isa. 55:2).

*b. In the NT.* Since the earliest form of the EUCHARIST (*see also* LORD'S SUPPER) involved the "breaking of bread," worship in general came to be called by the same phrase (Acts 2:42, 46; 20:7). Elsewhere in the NT, however, bread is used metaphorically only in reference to the coming kingdom of God or to Jesus himself. One of Jesus' dinner companions refers to the messianic banquet when he says: "Blessed is he who shall eat bread in the kingdom of God" (Luke 14:15; *see* MEALS § 4*b*). And the Christian proclaims the Lord's death until he comes, whenever he partakes of the bread and cup of the Eucharist (I Cor. 11:26). More significant than these, however, is Jesus' designation of himself as "true bread." The disciples had referred to manna as "bread from heaven" given by God (cf. Exod. 16:4; Neh. 9:15; etc.). Jesus then calls himself the "true bread from heaven" sent by his Father to give life to the world; the disciples ask that they be given this bread always (John 6:31-33). Thereupon Jesus strengthens his claim; he is the "bread of life," and those who follow him will never hunger or thirst (John 6:35). Finally, after a protest from the Jews, Jesus declares that those who "eat of this bread" will live forever, and that this bread is his own flesh (John 6:48-51; cf. 4:13-15). There are unmistakable references to the coming Last Supper in the narrative; the following verses (6:52-57) make this clear. But Jesus is also referring to his sacrificial death, particularly in 6:51. The mention of manna as an ordinary food is intended to show the superiority of Jesus to the law.

For the expression "daily bread," *see* LORD'S PRAYER § 3*e*.

**Bibliography.** J. Benzinger, *Hebräische Archäologie* (3rd ed. 1927), pp. 62-66; R. A. S. Macalister, *The Excavation of Gezer,*

II (1912), 42-44 (on griddles and loaves); C. H. Gordon, *Ugaritic Literature* (1949), p. 71 (on Keret's sacrifice).

J. F. ROSS

**BREAD OF THE PRESENCE** [לחם (ה)פנים, bread of the face (KJV SHEWBREAD); לחם התמיד, the continual bread; ἄρτοι τῆς προθέσεως, loaves to set before (God); πρόθεσις τῶν ἄρτων, a setting forth of the loaves]; SHOWBREAD [מערכת תמיד, the continual offering of (the bread of) the arrangement; לחם המערכת, the bread of the arrangement *or* row]. Twelve loaves, with two tenths of an ephah in each, baked of fine flour, like that used for the royal table and honored guests (Gen. 18:6; I Kings 4:22).

**1. Arrangement.** The loaves were arranged in two rows or piles on the table which stood before the Lord in the holy place—i.e., before the Holy of Holies (see Heb. 9:2 ff). This offering was required to be continually in the presence of the Lord (Exod. 25:30). Fresh loaves were brought into the sanctuary each sabbath, and the old loaves were then eaten by the priests in the holy place (Lev. 24:5-9). The Kohathites were responsible for baking and arranging the loaves (I Chr. 9:32).

Pure FRANKINCENSE was also placed on the table, probably in golden cups on top of the bread (Jos. Antiq. III.vi.6). This frankincense was regarded as a memorial and was later burned on the altar as an offering (Lev. 24:7). References are also made to an accompanying drink offering (Exod. 25:29; Num. 4:7).

Arrangements were made for the continual exhibition of the holy bread in the temple of Solomon, where there were probably ten tables for the bread of the Presence, though only one was in use at a time (I Kings 7:48; I Chr. 28:16; II Chr. 4:8, 19; 13:11; 29:18; for the dimensions, decoration, etc., of the table, see also Exod. 25:23-30; 40:22-23; Num. 4:7-8). Presumably the bread was unleavened (*see* UN-LEAVENED BREAD), though we have no explicit biblical regulation in this matter. Josephus states that it was unleavened and that the loaves, which were baked the day before the sabbath, were brought into the TEMPLE the morning of the sabbath and heaped in two rows of six, one loaf leaning against another. The supply of frankincense was changed as a part of this ceremony (Antiq. III.vi.6; x.17).

**2. Origins and early significance.** The earliest mention of the bread of the Presence is probably I Sam. 21. After David's entrance into Nob, he requested that the priest Ahimelech give him the holy bread which had been removed from the table in the holy place. David requested the bread in order to feed his hungry men (I Sam. 21:4-6; cf. Matt. 12:1-4; Mark 2:23-26; Luke 6:1-4). The passage suggests the antiquity of the practice in Israel. Ahimelech's concern lest David's men be in a state of impurity further suggests that the rite was regarded as an offering in the form of a meal partaken of by the deity and his devotees, who must be in a state of purity as they approach him (Exod. 19:10-15). The fact that all Pentateuchal passages referring to the bread of the Presence belong to the Priestly Code hardly supports the conclusion that the Hebrew rite was a late innovation reflecting Babylonian influences. It is possible that the Hebrew practice developed independently, though very similar practices in Babylon, Egypt, and elsewhere (Isa. 65:11; Jer. 7:18; 44:15-19) are expressions of the same root idea. Among the constituent parts of a Babylonian sacrifice was the laying of unleavened loaves before deity in sets of twelve or multiples of twelve. The Hebrew name לחם הפנים has its counterpart in the Assyrian *akal pānû*.

**3. The bread as a thank offering.** There is no evidence, however, that the bread of the Presence was ever understood technically as a sacrifice, even in early Israel. Originally thought of as an offering in the form of a meal for the deity, the bread would seem, in postexilic Israel, to have been offered as a thank offering. Whatever the original, possibly zodiacal, meaning of the twelve loaves, in later times the number suggested the twelve tribes of Israel (Exod. 24:4; 28:9-12; Lev. 24:5-9; etc.).

49. Table of the Bread of the Presence of Herod's temple, from the Arch of Titus

The table of the bread of the Presence which was in the second temple was taken away by Antiochus Epiphanes (I Macc. 1:22). A new one was brought to the temple and consecrated by Judas Maccabeus (I Macc. 4:49-51). Presumably it was this table which was carried to Rome by Titus (Jos. War VII. v.5). Fig. BRE 49.

*See also* SACRIFICE AND OFFERINGS; WORSHIP IN THE OT.

H. F. BECK

**BREAKFAST.** The noun used in John 21:12, 15 RSV to translate ἀριστάω. The KJV translates "dine" in these passages, though the context shows that it was an early morning meal. In later Greek the word could be used of the noon meal; so both KJV and RSV translate it "dine" in Luke 11:37. The noun ἄριστον is translated "dinner" by KJV and RSV in all its NT occurrences: Matt. 22:4; Luke 11:38; 14:12.

S. A. CARTLEDGE

**BREASTPIECE (OF THE HIGH PRIEST)** [חשן; LXX περιστήθιον in Exod. 28:4, *but mainly* λόγιον (λογεῖον) τῆς κρίσεως]; KJV BREASTPLATE. Literally, either a pouch or a beautiful thing such as an ornament, a garment. The breastpiece of the high priest was made of the best of fabrics, multicolored (Exod. 28:15). When folded, it made a double square *ca.* nine inches each way. By means of four golden rings it was attached to the EPHOD. On the outer squares were four rows of three jewels set in gold, each jewel bearing the name of one of Israel's tribes.

The breastpiece had a double purpose. It provided a receptacle for the sacred lot, the URIM AND THUMMIM (hence חשם המשפט, "breastpiece of judgment"; Exod. 28:15, 29-30). Thus God's judgments were conveyed to men. But, more important, it marked out the high priest as the representative, focus, and bearer of all Israel; and, in this capacity and by showing the breastpiece as a memorial before Yahweh, the high priest brought Israel into Yahweh's holy PRESENCE (Exod. 28:29).  G. HENTON DAVIES

**BREASTPLATE** [שריון, *cf.* Akkad. *siriam*, cuirass, armor; KJV חשן, *see* BREASTPIECE (OF THE HIGH PRIEST); θώραξ]. A piece of armor for the breast, often the front part of a corselet or cuirass. On the meaning of שריון *see* HABERGEON 1.

A breastplate (of scales, of chains, of solid metal) would be attached to, or worn over, a leather jerkin or tunic, and the latter would doubtless carry some additional armor for the back and other areas not protected by the central breastplate (cf. I Kings 22: 34; II Chr. 18:33). Iron breastplates, as well as multicolored ones, form part of the apocalyptic imagery of Rev. 9:9, 17.

The breastplate also serves as a figure of speech. In Isa. 59:17 the Lord, as a warrior, puts on righteousness as a breastplate. This symbolism is carried over into the NT: the Christian is to put on the "whole armor" (panoply) of God, which includes the breastplate of righteousness (Eph. 6:14) and of faith and love (I Thess. 5:8).

*See also* WEAPONS AND IMPLEMENTS OF WAR.

    W. S. McCULLOUGH

**BREATH.** The narrow, physical sense of this word is ordinarily conveyed by נשמה = πνοή. נפש is used of Leviathan's breath in Job 41:21—H 41:13. The word רוח is broadly translated as "breath," "wind," and, in the psychological and theological sense, "SPIRIT."

    R. C. DENTAN

**BREECHES** [מכנסים] (Exod. 28:42; 39:28; Lev. 6: 3; 16:4; Ezek. 44:18; Ecclus. 45:8). Part of the garb of priests. Linen breeches are specified (linen garments were customary for Egyptian, as well as Israelite, priests). The breeches served as a cover for the priest's body from the loins to the thighs, so that he would not be exposed when ministering at the altar. It was probably a kind of double-apron affair, rather than drawers, as frequently supposed, and could be put on or off easily when the ritual required change of garment. Sewn breeches come from the Persian and Scythian milieux.    J. M. MYERS

**BRETHREN.** *See* BROTHERHOOD.

**BRETHREN OF THE LORD.** *See* BROTHERS OF THE LORD.

**BRIBERY; BRIBE** [שלמנים, שלום, שחד, מתנה, כפר]. Bribery is the giving or receiving of a bribe—i.e., anything of value intended to influence one in the

discharge of a legal duty. The gist of the offense is the resultant tendency to pervert justice (cf. I Sam. 8:3; Prov. 17:23). Taking bribes is prohibited in the laws (Exod. 23:8; Deut. 16:19), though no fixed penalty is prescribed for the offense. Bribes were offered not merely to acquit the guilty and condemn (Ps. 15:5; Isa. 5:23), or even slay (Deut. 27: 25; Ezek. 22:12), the innocent; they were equally necessary at times to get justice done (Job 6:22). The practice of gift-giving to judges, denounced by the prophets (Isa. 1:23; Mic. 3:11; 7:3), meant that the poor, when they were not actively wronged in judgment, had difficulty in obtaining a hearing for their case (Isa. 1:23*b*). Against this, Deut. 1:17 exhorts: "You shall not be partial in judgment; you shall hear the small and the great alike."

Since giving gifts was viewed as a perfectly legitimate means of getting ahead (Prov. 18:16), and was even recommended to pacify antagonists (21:14), the distinction between gifts and bribes must sometimes have been extremely subtle. *See* GIFT.

*Bibliography.* E. A. Speiser, "Of Shoes and Shekels," *BASOR,* LXXVII (1940), 15-18; J. J. Finkelstein, "The Middle Assyrian *Šulmānu*-Texts," *JAOS,* LXXII (1952), 77-80.
    M. GREENBERG

**BRICK** [לבנה, *lebhēnâ, from* לבן, white; Akkad. *libittu;* Ugar. *lbnt;* Arab. *libn*]. In the ancient Middle East a most common building material was sun-dried brick; but, especially in Babylonia, kiln-burned brick was widely used. In the story of the Tower of Babel the people who migrated to the land of Shinar after the Flood said: "Come, let us make bricks, and burn them thoroughly." It is intimated that these bricks were hard, for "they had brick for stone" (Gen. 11:3).

50. Fallen brick walls at Shechem: above, Late Bronze Period; below: Middle Bronze Period

In the hills of Palestine, though stone was abundant and easily cut, brick was used extensively in some city walls, as in the Middle Bronze wall at Tell Beit Mirsim and in the Middle Bronze, Late Bronze, and Hellenistic walls at Shechem (Fig. BRI 50). In the lowlands, as at Jericho and Ezion-geber, sundried brick was used both for city walls and for houses. The Neolithic, pre-pottery houses in the lower levels at Jericho had first what Miss Kenyon calls "hog-back" bricks, hand shaped with thumb impressions in herringbone pattern,* followed by "bun" bricks, then in the Early Bronze Age rectangular bricks made in molds. Fig. JER 13.

In the Nile Valley, from prehistoric times to the present day, the making of bricks was an extensive occupation. From the Egyptian word for "brick," *db-t*, comes through Arabic and Spanish our word "adobe." The clay was thoroughly soaked, generally mixed with straw or other vegetable matter, and brought in baskets to the artisan, who shaped the bricks by hand or a wooden mold. Such ancient molds and the pictures of brickmaking have been found.* A few of the great monuments of ancient Egypt were made of sun-dried brick and still are standing. Some Egyptian bricks and many Babylonian bricks were stamped with the names of the kings for whose edifices they were intended. Near Babylon in peasants' houses today are bricks with Nebuchadnezzar's stamp. Fig. BRI 51.

From *Atlas of the Bible* (Thomas Nelson & Sons Limited)

51. Making of bricks in ancient Egypt (*ca.* 1460 B.C.), from the tomb of Thut-mose III

Mortar in Egypt and Palestine was of the same mud as the bricks; in Mesopotamia bitumen was used (Gen. 11:3). If the wall was to be plastered, it was allowed to stand for several months before the coating was applied.

Those who burn incense on bricks (instead of stone?) are denounced in Isa. 65:3. David made captives from Rabbah toil at the brickkilns (II Sam. 12:31). The best-known biblical story of bricks is in Exod. 5, in which the command of Pharaoh popularly is misunderstood as prescribing hardship on the Hebrews by compelling them to make bricks without straw. The hardship on the brickmakers was compelling them to find the straw, which previously had been furnished, and to keep up the quota of production. *See* ARCHITECTURE.

*Bibliography.* A. J. Neuburger, *Technical Arts of the Ancients* (1930), pp. 133-37; C. F. Nims, "Bricks Without Straw," *BA*, vol. XIII, no. 2 (1950), pp. 22-28; K. M. Kenyon, *Digging Up Jericho* (1957), pp. 70, 86, 175. O. R. SELLERS

**BRICKKILN** [מַלְבֵּן, *from* לבן, to make bricks; *Kethibh* מַלְבֵּן; Akkad. *nalbanu*] (II Sam. 12:31; Jer. 43:9 KJV;

Nah. 3:14 KJV). Alternately: PAVEMENT (Jer. 43:9); BRICK MOLD (Nah. 3:14). Probably a mold of rectangular shape; the word came to be used metaphorically of any rectangle (in Jer. 43:9 a terrace of bricks, or mastaba, has been suggested as the meaning). The interpretation "brick mold" is supported by the ancient versions (e.g., πλινθεῖον, "brick works") and the fact that bricks made in Palestine were seldom kiln fired (but contrast Gen. 11:3; *also see* BRICK). There was apparently no distinction between the kiln used to fire brick and other types of furnaces (*see* FURNACE). It is more probable that David set his captives to work at brick molds than at brickkilns.

*Bibliography.* N. Glueck, "Ezion-geber: Elath—City of Bricks with Straw," *BA,* vol. III, no. 4 (1940), pp. 51-55; C. Singer *et al.,* eds., *A History of Technology* (1954), pp. 464 ff, 473. R. W. FUNK

**BRIDE.** The translation of כלה (also "daughter-in-law"). The words אשה and γυνή, "woman," are also translated "bride" when they refer to a betrothed girl or a recently married wife. *See also* MARRIAGE; CHURCH.

**BRIDE (OF CHRIST)** [νύμφη, γυνή, παρθένος] (II Cor. 11:2; Rev. 19:7; 21:2, 9; 22:17; cf. Eph. 5:25-26); KJV alternately VIRGIN; WIFE. A metaphor for the church, with Christ as the bridegroom. The marriage of God to Israel is referred to in the OT (Ps. 45, often interpreted messianically; Isa. 54:6; Ezek. 16:8 ff; Hos. 2:19-20). See CHURCH, IDEA OF. B. H. THROCKMORTON, JR.

**BRIDLE.** See BIT.

**BRIER.** The translation of various Hebrew words denoting thorny plants. It is used figuratively of the enemies of Israel (Ezek. 28:24), and of that which is worthless (Mic. 7:4), especially land (Isa. 5:6; 7:23-25; 55:13).

**BRIGANDINE.** KJV translation of סריון (RSV COAT OF MAIL).

**BRIMSTONE** [גפרית, *cf.* Akkad. *kuprîtu,* brimstone, *and perhaps related to* כפר *or* גפר, pitch (*and other combustibles*); θεῖον, *cf.* θεῖος, divine]. Sulphur. It is said to be a means of divine retribution against Sodom and Gomorrah (Gen. 19:24; Luke 17:29), the apostate and the wicked (Deut. 29:23; Job 18:15; Ps. 11:6), the king of Assyria (Isa. 30:33), Edom (Isa. 34:9), Gog (Ezek. 38:22), idolators (Rev. 14:10), the beast and false prophet (19:20), the devil (20:10), and sinners in general (21:8). W. E. STAPLES

**BROAD PLACE. 1.** The translation of רחב (Job. 36:16) and מרחב (II Sam. 22:20; Pss. 18:19—H 18:20; 31:8—H 31:9), both used in figurative expressions. To set in a broad place may mean to deliver from danger, anxiety, want, or distress.

**2.** For רחוב, which the KJV translates "broad place" in Jer. 5:1, *see* SQUARE. See also CITY. O. R. SELLERS

**BROAD WALL, THE** [החומה הרחבה] (Neh. 3:8; 12:38). A section of the rampart of Jerusalem restored by Nehemiah. The context suggests a location on the NW side of the city. The Hebrew is perhaps to be emended into חומת הרחוב, the "Wall of the Square" (cf. LXX τεῖχος τοῦ πλατέως). *See* map under NEHEMIAH. *See also* JERUSALEM § 7*b*.

G. A. BARROIS

**BROIDERED.** *See* EMBROIDERY.

**BRONZE** [נחשת; נחוש, נחושה; חשמל]; KJV BRASS; STEEL; AMBER. An alloy of copper and tin. Copper ore sometimes contains a small amount of tin, but the presence of two per cent or more of tin is to be regarded as the result of a deliberate attempt to produce an alloy, and such an object is to be classed as a bronze. Chemical analyses of ancient bronzes show from two to sixteen per cent of tin.

**1. The terms.** After the invention of bronze the word נחשת was used to denote the new alloy, as well as COPPER. This may have been due to the fact that it is frequently difficult to tell from the appearance of an object whether it is made of copper or of bronze. Where, however, נחשת is said to have been used for casting, it is safe to assume that "bronze" is meant, for bronze makes a much cleaner cast than does copper. For objects which could be hammered cold into shape, doubtless copper was used. For the KJV rendering of נחשת by "steel" in four passages (II Sam. 22:35; Job 20:24; Ps. 18:34; Jer. 15:12), *see* STEEL. For חשמל in Ezek. 1:4; etc., *see* AMBER.

**2. The origin of bronze.** It is as yet uncertain where the discovery was made that the addition of a small amount of tin, up to four per cent, increases the strength and hardness of copper and at the same time lowers its melting point. The most probable location is one where copper and tin ores occur in close association. Such areas are to be found in Syria (the Kasrwan district behind Byblos), Armenia, the Caucasus, and NE Iran. Wainwright (*see bibliography*) favors Syria, but the earliest bronzes found in Syria, at Ras Shamra, date only from *ca.* 2050-1850 B.C., whereas bronzes have been found at Ur dating from *ca.* 2500 B.C. On the other hand, the absence of metal ores of any kind in Sumer makes it highly improbable that the art of making bronze was discovered there. Schaeffer (*see bibliography*) favors Armenia and Anatolia and believes that immigrant bronze-workers from this area, who had as the badge of their profession a bronze torque or neck ring, introduced bronze-working to Byblos, whence it spread to other areas, including Europe. A few bronze objects have been found in Egypt which seem to date from before 2000 B.C. Even if their dating be correct (which is by no means certain), they are probably to be regarded as the results of an accidental mixture of copper and tin, for there is no other evidence that the art of making bronze was understood in Egypt before the Middle Kingdom.

**3. Bronze in Palestine.** Because of the failure of the early archaeologists to subject their metal finds to chemical analysis, it is impossible to tell whether the "bronzes" mentioned in their reports are of bronze or of copper. However, the adoption of more scientific methods has shown that bronze made its first appearance in Palestine at the beginning of the Middle Bronze Age, or just before it. A few bronze studs found at Jericho are dated to the period 2300-1900 B.C. and associated with invaders from the N, probably Amorites from Syria. Many MB tombs at Jericho contained bronze rings set with scarabs of local manufacture. Lachish yielded a bronze toggle pin, a figurine, and a pin of Eighteenth Dynasty date (sixteenth-fourteenth centuries B.C.). A larger number of bronze objects was found at Megiddo. But, to judge from archaeological finds, bronze was by no means common in Palestine even during the Middle Bronze Age.

Metals were one of the chief spoils of war, as lists of booty taken by various conquerors show. When David defeated Hadadezer of Damascus, he is said to have carried off from two of the Syrian cities, Betah and Berothai, "very much bronze" (II Sam. 8:8). Similarly when the Chaldeans captured Jerusalem in 586 B.C., they carried away all the copper and bronze they could find (II Kings 25:13-17 = Jer. 52:17-23).

Solomon is said to have employed נחשת (copper and bronze) on a lavish scale in the adornment and furnishing of the temple (cf. I Kings 7:13 ff; II Chr. 3:15-4:1 ff). Since Israel had no long tradition of metalworking and, therefore, no highly skilled smiths, Solomon was obliged to import an expert from Tyre (*see* HIRAM) to supervise the work. The casting of the bronze objects was done in the Jordan Valley, between Succoth (probably to be identified with Tell Deir'allah) and Zarethan (site unknown; I Kings 7:46; II Chr. 4:17, where read צרתן [Zarethan] for צרדתה [Zeredah]). The reason for the choice of this location is not certain. Possibly smelters may already have existed here on the edge of Gilead. *See* IRON.

*Bibliography.* A. Lucas, "Notes on the Early History of Tin and Bronze," *JEA*, XIV (1928), 97-108; *Ancient Egyptian Materials and Industries* (2nd ed., 1934), pp. 174-81, 404-5. G. A. Wainwright, "The Occurrence of Tin and Copper near Byblos," *JEA*, XX (1934), 29-32. C. F. A. Schaeffer, "Porteurs de Torques," *Ugaritica*, II (1949), 49-120; "Corpus des armes et outils en bronze de Ras Shamra-Ugarit (1ʳᵉ partie)," *Ugaritica*, III (1956), 251-79.

F. V. WINNETT

**BRONZE SEA.** *See* SEA, MOLTEN.

**BRONZE SERPENT.** *See* SERPENT, BRONZE; NEHUSHTAN.

**BROOCH** [חח] (Exod. 35:22); KJV BRACELET. A fibula formed somewhat like a bent bow, with a pin. The brooches referred to in Exodus were gold; others were of bronze and iron. They came into common use in Palestine in the seventh century B.C., though earlier examples have been found. Fig. BRO 52.

J. M. MYERS

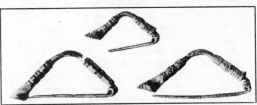

Courtesy of the American Schools of Oriental Research

52. Brooches, from Tell el-Nasbeh

**BROOD** [νοσσίον, *diminutive* of νεοσσός, nestling, *from* νέος, young; νοσσιά, *later form of* νεοσσιά, nest or brood of young birds; *cf.* νεοσσεύω, to hatch, build a nest]; KJV CHICKENS in Matt. 23:37. Young birds, especially of the domestic fowl. *See also* COCK.

W. S. McCULLOUGH

**BROOK.** A small stream and its bed, called in Arabic a *wadi*, which may be perennial when fed by springs, or completely dry and a raging torrent, depending on the amount of rainfall. *See* RIVER.

The Hebrew נחל is usually translated "brook" (Lev. 23:40; Deut. 9:21; I Sam. 17:40; I Kings 17:7; etc.). The same word may refer to a river or valley, depending on the context of the passage and the geography of the area involved—e.g., "river Jabbok" (נחל יבק; Deut. 2:37); "valley of the Arnon" (נחל ארנן; Deut. 2:36). The Hebrew text usually makes a distinction among "brook," "river" (נהר), and "valley" (עמק), although it was not always possible to do so, because of the tendency of the brooks to assume the proportions of rivers during the rainy seasons.

The brooks of ancient Palestine and the E Jordan area were numerous. They flowed into the coastal plain, the Sea of Galilee, the Jordan Valley, and the Dead Sea. Brooks were considered a pleasant feature of the land and important as sources of water for the villages often located near them (Deut. 8:7; II Chr. 32:4; Ps. 110:7; Jer. 31:9; etc.), although their treacherous nature in the rainy seasons was recognized (Job 6:15). They were often mentioned by name for the purpose of indicating important national or tribal boundaries, or other locations. *See* ARABAH, BROOK OF; BESOR; CHERITH, BROOK; EGYPT, BROOK OF; KANAH 2; KIDRON, BROOK; KISHON; WILLOWS, BROOK OF; ZERED, BROOK.

W. L. REED

**BROOK OF THE ARABAH.** *See* ARABAH, BROOK OF.

**BROOK OF EGYPT.** *See* EGYPT, BROOK OF.

**BROOM** [רתם, *rōthem;* Arab. *ratam*]. A desert shrub or bush which frequently grows quite large, offering a bit of shade. Elijah, on his way to Mount Horeb (I Kings 19:4-5), took refuge in its shade. Its roots and foliage were used for fuel (Job 30:4; Ps. 120:4). A place along the route of the Exodus, Rithmah, carried the name of this shrub (Num. 33:18-19). The figurative "broom" of Isa. 14:23 (KJV BESOM) could refer to a hand broom made from this shrub.

The KJV uses JUNIPER rather than "broom," but almost all scholars maintain now that it was the leguminous *Retama raetam* (Forsk.) Webb. (also called *Genista monosperma* L.), commonly known as the "broom tree," so abundant in the desert regions of S Palestine and Sinai. In Job 30:4 KJV לחמם is translated "their meat"; but the roots of the broom are nauseous, even poisonous, thus leading many botanists to assume that another plant is meant here (Moldenke: *Cynomorium coccineum* L., a parasitic plant). The RSV takes the word as an infinitive of the root חמם, "to become warm" (cf. Isa. 47:14),

leaving no need to change the identification. *See also* FLORA § A9*h*.

*Bibliography.* I. Löw, *Die Flora der Juden,* II (1924), 469-73; H. N. and A. L. Moldenke, *Plants of the Bible* (1952), pp. 91-92, 201-2.     J. C. TREVER

**BROTH** [מרק, פרק]. The water in which meat has been boiled. Since it retained many of the nutrients, it was not poured out, but eaten along with the meat. Gideon served the angel unleavened cakes, a kid, and broth (Judg. 6:19-20; cf. Isa. 65:4; Ezek. 24:10).

*See also* MEALS § 3*b;* FOOD.     J. F. ROSS

**BROTHERHOOD.** Scripture has no interest in brotherhood as such. Indeed, אחוה occurs only at Zech. 11:14 of union between Judah and Israel. The RSV "brotherhood" in Amos 1:9 translates an original "brethren." Similarly, the unusual Greek word ἀδελφότης is found only at I Pet. 2:17; 5:9, referring to the Christian community (cf. I Pet. 1:22: φιλαδελφία [*philadelphia*]; 3:8: φιλάδελφοι). To discover what the Bible has to say about brotherhood, it is essential to study its message about actual brothers.

**1. The OT teaching.** The OT teaches that God set mankind in families (Ps. 68:6; cf. Isa. 19:2, Egyptians; Deut. 2:4, Edomites and Israelites; Gen. 13:8, Abraham and Lot). Stories and genealogies exhibit interest in the history of some nations, chiefly Semitic (Gen. 1–11; I Chr. 1–9).

Quite apart from blood relationship, "brother" may be used of friends, allies, colleagues, and fellow citizens: II Sam. 1:26 (David and Jonathan); I Kings 9:13 (Hiram of Tyre and Solomon); Gen. 49:5 (within the sons of Jacob, Simeon and Levi were united in infamy; cf. Gen. 34:25-31); Lev. 21; Num. 8:23-26; II Chr. 29:34 (the brotherhood of priests and Levites); Amos 1:9 (Tyre broke an alliance by allowing slave raids); I Sam. 30:23 (David addressing his soldiers). Naturally, different degrees of affection were implied in such usage, but there was a proverb about a "friend who sticks closer than a brother" (Prov. 18:24). Brethren should be friends (Gen. 13:8; Ps. 133:1; Prov. 17:17), yet the OT candidly depicts disruption, war, and death caused by greed, cruelty, spoiled self-centeredness, injustice, and other forms of sin (cf. Ps. 50:20; Neh. 5:7; Jer. 9:4-6; Ezek. 18:10 ff; Zech. 7:9-10). We note especially Cain and Abel (Gen. 4:9), Esau and Jacob (Gen. 27:41), Joseph and his half brothers (Gen. 37:20), Moses and the quarreling Hebrews (Exod. 2:13), and Joab's vengeance on Abner for the death of Asahel (II Sam. 3:20 ff); and we contrast the love displayed in the intercession of Abraham for Lot (Gen. 18:23 ff), Judah for Benjamin (Gen. 44:18 ff), and Moses for the entire nation (Exod. 32:11-14, 31-32). *See* LOVE IN THE OT; BROTHERLY LOVE.

As the seed of Abraham and God's elect people (Exod. 19:5-6; Deut. 7:6 ff; Jer. 31:1; Amos 3:2), Israel was a family and her people brethren: "Have we not all one father? Has not one God created us?" (Mal. 2:10; cf. Lev. 25:46; Deut. 17:15; 18:18; Ps. 22:22; Hos. 11:1). It must be kept racially pure (Deut. 7:3-4; Ezra 9–10; Neh. 13:23-27), and a man might have to marry his deceased brother's widow to maintain a name and a line (Deut. 25:5 ff; Ruth 3:6 ff; cf. Matt. 22:23 ff). Hence too the rule: "You shall not hate your brother in your heart. . . . You shall love your neighbor as yourself" (Lev. 19:17-18; 19:34 extends this rule to the resident alien; cf. Deut. 15:2, and, for a practical application regarding usury, Deut. 23:19). Thus the OT teaches that, within the nation, a man is his brother's keeper—a truth that has bearing on matters of social welfare, trade, and religious customs. The OT also holds out hope that in Abraham "all the families of the earth will bless themselves" (Gen. 12:3; cf. Isa. 49:6).

**2. In the NT.** When we turn to the NT, we find genealogies of Jesus the Messiah in Matt. 1; Luke 3, and mention of his brothers and sisters in Mark 3: 31; 6:3; John 7:3; Acts 1:14; Gal. 1:19. There were brothers among the Twelve (Mark 1:16, 19; cf. Luke 6:16, variant reading). The NT writers were well aware of the different nations: Jews and Gentiles; Greeks, Romans, Scythians, Egyptians, Cypriotes (all represented in Jerusalem on the Day of Pentecost! Acts 2:9-11). But little is made positively of natural kinship; rather, such kinship may conflict with, and must yield to, the claims of God's kingdom (Matt. 10:37; Luke 9:61-62; 14:26). The ultimate goal is the city of God and the healing of the nations (Rev. 21: 24; 22:2).

Jesus probed the deepest meaning of the OT commandment to love one's neighbor (Mark 12:31; Luke 10:29 ff) and extended it to enemies (Matt. 5:44). Covetousness is excluded (Luke 12:13-15), and the censorious attitude (Matt. 5:22-24; 7:1-5). Invite the poor who cannot invite you back! (Luke 14:12-14). Kindness might be shown beyond Israel's borders (Mark 7:24 ff; cf. Matt. 5:41 of forced levies); and careless neglect of a fellow Jew might lead to the desolations of hell (the rich man and Lazarus [Luke 16:19 ff]; note the teaching on wealth [Mark 10: 23 ff], and Mammon [Luke 16:13]). The sons of God must abandon a narrow, selfish, harsh spirit (Matt. 5:43-48; 18:23 ff; Mark 11:25; Luke 15:25 ff [the elder "brother"!]; 17:3-4; cf. Col. 3:13). This ethic of Jesus derived from knowledge of God as Father, gracious and loving (Mark 14:36; Luke 11:2; Matt. 7: 11; John 14:2; 17:9 ff). For the apostolic church, too, God is Father, the Father of the Lord Jesus Christ (e.g., Acts 1:4; Gal. 4:6; Eph. 2:18; 3:15: "from whom every family in heaven and on earth is named"; I John 3:1). See GOD, NT; TEACHING OF JESUS.

The men and women who responded to Jesus with a measure of faith in his mission are his pupils or apprentices, but also his "brethren," for they seek to do God's will (Mark 3:34; Luke 11:27-28); he and they are the true Israel (John 15:1-17; Mark 8:29; cf. references to seed of Abraham: Luke 13:16, a woman; 19:9, a man; John 8:37 ff); the Twelve may anticipate the banquet of the messianic kingdom (Luke 12:32; 13:29; 22:29-30; cf. the Rule of the Congregation from Qumran, 1QSa), and their rewards will include "brothers and sisters and mothers and children and lands" (Mark 10:30). Christ's identification with his people and his disciples is notable (at baptism; in mission, Luke 10:16 and parallels; John 20:17; Matt. 25:40, the Judgment, where "brethren" need not be confined to disciples; Mark 9:41). Service and unity are keynotes of the brotherhood of disciples (especially Matt. 23:8-10; John 13: 12 ff).

Ideas of the church formulated after Pentecost gather up similar thoughts. In it the promise to Abraham is being fulfilled (Gen. 12:3; Gal. 3:8 ff; Acts 3:25; Heb. 2:16; 11:12, 18-19), so that it is a "first fruits" of a redeemed mankind (Gal. 3:28; Eph. 2:14; 3:9; 4:22-23; cf. Heb. 12:22-23; Rev. 14: 4, of the redeemed in heaven). It is the brotherhood of the new Israel (Gal. 6:16; Eph. 2:12; I Pet. 2:5, 9; Rev. 21:2, 7); the family of God through its joint-heirship with Christ, the true "Elder Brother" (I John 2:10; 3:1 ff; Gal. 4:6; Rom. 8:17-29; Heb. 1:6; 2:10-11; Eph. 1:5; 5:1; see ADOPTION). For Paul it is the "body of Christ," agent of the Holy Spirit, intended to be one, universal, and Christlike (I Cor. 12, etc.; cf. Eph. 1:22-23; see CHURCH, IDEA OF).

Brotherly love, therefore, should be typical of congregations as close-knit corporations of believers (I Pet. 3:8-9; Rom. 12:9 ff; 13:8-10). Such a love is redemptive (Jas. 5:20; I Pet. 4:8; cf. Luke 7:47); impartial (Jas. 2:1 ff); practical (Jas. 2:14-17; I John 3: 17-18), and so on (cf. Jas. 4:11-12; I John 3:12; III John 11; II Pet. 1:7). This love is commanded, and obedience to it alone attests love for God (John 13: 34; I John 4:20-21; see LOVE IN THE NT; BROTHERLY LOVE). Even in the first flush of the apostolic age, however, Ananias and Sapphira were defaulters (Acts 5), and "false brethren" bitterly opposed Paul (Gal. 2:4; II Cor. 11:26).

Nonetheless, "brethren" was the regular and perfectly genuine mode of address (Acts 1:16; Rom. 1: 13; I Tim. 4:6, etc.). Christians were "holy brethren" (Heb. 3:1; I Thess. 5:27 [variant reading], "beloved brethren" (I Cor. 15:58; Phil. 4:1; Jas. 1:16; cf. Acts 15:25; II Pet. 3:15). They constituted a spiritual brotherhood, distinct from the "world" as were the Qumran covenanters, and paradoxically exclusive because they made such high claims for themselves as the elect of God through Jesus Christ. Without sincere love like that of Christ himself, the brotherhood might easily degenerate into a self-righteous coterie; without wisdom its members might become lazy eschatologists or idealist revolutionaries (I Thess. 4:9-12; I Pet. 4:15-16). The wonder of the NT age was how slaves and masters became brothers beloved in the church of the living God, and how "from every tribe and tongue and people and nation" (Rev. 5:9) Christ was calling men and women into a redemptive society for which the word "brotherhood" was no unfitting title.

**Bibliography.** C. J. Cadoux, *The Early Church and the World* (1925); J. Pedersen, *Israel: Its Life and Culture*, vols. I–II (1926); J. H. Moulton and G. Milligan, *Vocabulary of the Greek Testament* (1929); W. A. Curtis, *Jesus Christ the Teacher* (1943); R. Niebuhr, *The Nature and Destiny of Man*, vol. II (1943).

G. JOHNSTON

**BROTHERLY LOVE** [φιλαδελφία]. A biblical concept given this name in the NT only.

The OT has the reality though not the word, for "neighbor" in Lev. 19:17-18 means "brother Israelite," and the rule of neighborly love is extended in Lev. 19:34 to the resident alien (cf. Deut. 10:19). The unity of a family is praised (Ps. 133:1; cf. Gen. 13:8, and the example of a clan rescue in Gen. 14:14-16). True friendship is a lasting and peculiarly close bond of love, often closer than that of blood brothers, as the immortal story of David and Jonathan shows

(I Sam. 18–II Sam. 1; Prov. 17:9, 17). Very moving is Joseph's affectionate reconciliation with his brothers (Gen. 43:30; 44:14 ff). Intercession expresses brotherly love: Abraham for Lot; Judah for Benjamin; and Moses for Israel (Gen. 18:23 ff; 19:29; 44:33; Exod. 32:11 ff). *See* LOVE IN THE OT; BROTHERHOOD.

In the NT φιλαδελφία occurs only at Rom. 12:10; I Thess. 4:9; Heb. 13:1; I Pet. 1:22 (cf. 2:17; 3:8 [φιλάδελφοι, "love of the brethren"]; 5:9); II Pet. 1:7. With these cf. 1QS 1.9; 2.24; 5.4; 10.26.

Christians are a family, a brotherhood in the service of Christ (Matt. 23:8), commanded to love one another in imitation of him (John 13:34; 15:12-13; Rom. 12:3; 13:8, 10; 16:5 ff; Gal. 5:13; 6:10; Eph. 4:2; Col. 1:4; 2:2-3; I Thess. 3:12; Tit. 1:8 [hospitality became distinctive]; Philem. 5, 16; I John *passim*). For them brotherly love is intense, because of their common covenant, faith, and hope; but it is comprised within that perfect love, *agape*, which is universal in its range. Since it is inspired by Jesus and his Spirit, it is gentle, kind, patient, pardoning, self-effacing, and sacrificial. *See* LOVE IN THE NT.

G. JOHNSTON

**BROTHERS OF THE LORD** [ἀδελφοὶ τοῦ κυρίου]. The men commonly thought of as brothers of Jesus. The phrase occurs in I Cor. 9:5, and Gal. 1:19 refers to "James the Lord's brother."

1. NT evidence
2. Three main views
   *a.* Helvidian
   *b.* Epiphanian
   *c.* Hieronymian
3. Critical evaluation of these views
4. Conclusion
Bibliography

**1. NT evidence.** Mark 6:3 lists them as James, Joses, Judas, and Simon; Matt. 13:55 names James, Joseph, Simon, and Judas; Joses and Joseph seem alternate forms of the same name.

The gospels of Matthew and Mark describe these four as children of Mary (Matthew mentions that his father was a carpenter) and as brothers of Jesus. They go on to mention that "his sisters" were living in Nazareth. Since Jesus is clearly said to be the first child of Mary (Matt. 1:18; Luke 2:7), any other children of Mary must have been younger than Jesus, and the two verses just noted would normally imply that Joseph and Mary had other children in the years following Jesus' birth. The people of Nazareth (Matt. 13:54-56; Mark 6:2-3) describe the four men as children of Mary and brothers of Jesus.

These brothers did not approve of Jesus' ministry. This is clear in the Synoptic gospels. Jesus himself, in the Nazareth incident mentioned above, said that a prophet is without honor "in his own house" (Matt. 13:57; Mark 6:4). This clearly implies opposition within his own family. On another occasion his family are so far from approving his zealous ministry that they think him to be "beside himself" (οἱ παρ᾽ αὐτοῦ in Mark 3:21 does not mean "his friends," but lit. "the ones from beside him," his family; and when they reach Jesus in Mark 3:31, they are identified as his mother and brothers). The Gospel of John agrees

that "even his brothers did not believe in him" (7:5). In view of these facts, none of the four brothers could have been numbered among the twelve apostles.

It is clear, however, that James saw the risen Lord (I Cor. 15:7). The brothers thus became members of the Jerusalem church from the earliest days —a fact attested by Acts 1:14, which explicitly distinguishes the brothers from the eleven apostles, who are named in the preceding verse. I Cor. 9:5 goes well with this distinction between the Twelve and the brothers of the Lord. James became the recognized leader of the church at Jerusalem (Acts 12:17; 15:13; 21:18). Paul reflects this leading role of James in Gal. 1:19. On Paul's first trip to Jerusalem after his conversion, he visited Cephas and also saw James. It is disputed whether Paul here ranks James as an apostle; the Greek words εἰ μή may mean that apart from Cephas, he saw no other apostle "except" James, which would class James as an apostle, or they may mean that he saw no other apostle, "but only" James. Either translation is possible, but it must be remembered that the word "APOSTLE" was not limited to the Twelve, since Paul, Barnabas, Andronicus, Junias, and others were included in the wider sense of the word as a designation of special pioneer missionary preachers. So even if, as seems likely, James was considered an apostle by Paul, this does not mean that Paul considered him one of the Twelve.

The NT thus regards the brothers of the Lord as sons of Joseph and Mary, younger than Jesus, unresponsive to his preaching during his earthly ministry, but active and leading members of the church from the beginning of the apostolic age.

**2. Three main views.** This NT view was challenged, however, by the middle of the second century. The debate became particularly fierce in the latter part of the fourth century, when each of three rival positions found a vigorous advocate whose name is now used to designate the view he championed. The three views are called (*a*) the Helvidian, after Helvidius, whose tract on the subject survives only in the citations and denunciation of it by Jerome; (*b*) the Epiphanian, after Epiphanius, whose discussion of his view survives in his tract *Against the Antidicomarianites*, included in his work *Against Heresies;* and (*c*) the Hieronymian, so named after Jerome (Latin *Hieronymus*), who wrote in opposition to Helvidius a work called *The Perpetual Virginity of the Blessed Mary*.

*a. Helvidian.* Unfortunately we do not possess the full argument of Helvidius, but from the quotations and hostile comments of Jerome, Helvidius clearly held the brothers of the Lord to be sons of Joseph and Mary and younger than Jesus. In this view he claimed to follow Tertullian and Victorinus of Pettau, but Jerome claims that Victorinus supported the Hieronymian view. The main argument of Helvidius evidently was that the NT, correctly interpreted, supports his position. Bonosus and, as it appears, Jovivianus held the same view.

*b. Epiphanian.* According to this view, Jesus' brothers were sons of Joseph but not of Mary. It claims secondary support in certain NT passages. E.g., it is argued that the attempt of the brothers to exercise control over Jesus, as in Mark 3:31; John

7:3-4, shows that they were older than Jesus and so not sons of Mary, whose first-born son was Jesus; and it is alleged that Jesus would not have committed his mother to the Beloved Disciple if the brothers had really been sons of Mary (John 19:26-27).

The main content of the Epiphanian view, however, is not found in the NT. The claim is that Joseph had been married previously, that the "brothers of the Lord" were Joseph's sons by this former marriage, that Joseph was over eighty years old when he took Mary as his wife and gave her the protection of his home, that he never had normal marital relations with Mary, and that Mary thus remained forever a virgin. The essential content of this view has no NT support, but it appears in apocryphal gospels from the middle of the second century, the earliest example being the Protevangelium of James. It found wide acceptance in the third and fourth centuries and in all later times. It is the view of the Greek Orthodox and other Eastern churches, and has been held by many Protestants.

*c. Hieronymian.* As far as can be learned, this view was first proposed by Jerome, but it at once won followers and is the Roman Catholic view. Jerome argues that James the brother of the Lord was an apostle (Gal. 1:19); he is to be identified with James the son of Alphaeus (Mark 3:18) and also with James "the younger" (Mark 15:40), the brother of Joses. Now James and Joses are called "brothers" of Jesus (Mark 6:3). Their mother, called Mary in Matt. 27:56; Mark 15:40, was "Mary of Clopas"; she was the sister of Mary the mother of Jesus (John 19:25). This makes James and Joses cousins of Jesus. Jerome points out that the word "brother" has a wide variety of meaning in the Bible. It can mean "kinsman," and is so used in this case. Thus, in effect, "brother" here means "cousin," and Mary never had marital relations with Joseph; Jesus was her only son.

Later writers identify two others of the Twelve, "Judas (not Iscariot)" (John 14:22) and Simon the Zealot (Luke 6:15; Acts 1:13), as brothers of the Lord (Mark 6:3); this view holds that three of the four brothers were among the Twelve. Another later addition to the theory is the assertion that the names Alphaeus and Clopas are identical, since both derive from the Aramaic *Ḥalphay* (חלפי). It has even been suggested that Matthew was one of the "brothers," since he seems to be named also Levi the son of Alphaeus (cf. Matt. 9:9 with Mark 2:14).

**3. Critical evaluation of these views.** The Helvidian view rests upon the natural meaning of the relevant NT passages. Against it one might urge that in John 2:12 the brothers seem favorable to Jesus' ministry; but their presence with Jesus, if conceded, is not definitely equivalent to approval of his work, and John 7:5 is unquestionable evidence that they were not then his disciples. It may also be urged that since the brothers were active in the church from the earliest days, they must have been favorable to Jesus during his ministry. To say this, however, would be to substitute an indecisive a priori assumption for the specific evidence of the gospels that the brothers were not his followers and apostles during his ministry. But even if both these criticisms

were accepted, they would leave untouched the basic fact that the NT thinks of the brothers as sons of Joseph and Mary, and younger than Jesus.

Jerome tried hard to establish his view by the NT evidence, but the boldness of his attempt is clear from the fact that before he wrote, toward the end of the fourth century, no one had proposed such a theory. His argument that James must have been one of the Twelve because he is called an apostle in Gal. 1:19 may interpret this verse correctly, but as seen above, there is in the NT a wider definition of the word "apostle," so that James (and Paul and others) could be an apostle without being one of the Twelve. The idea that "brother" (ἀδελφός) here means in effect "cousin" is rather startling. The second-century Hegesippus calls James and Jude "brothers" of the Lord but uses "cousin" when referring to another kinsman; this gives no support to Jerome's attempt to identify the "brothers" as cousins. Moreover, these brothers are always found in company with Mary the mother of Jesus, in a way that does not suggest that they are only cousins. Jerome's interpretation of John 19:25 is extremely unlikely, since it holds that two sisters both had the same given name, Mary. The linguistic equation of Alphaeus with Clopas is unconvincing, if not impossible. Jerome's argument that besides James the son of Zebedee there was only one other James among the early leaders, since "James the younger" implies there were only two Jameses to compare in rank, is a blunder; the Greek reads, not "James the younger," but "James the Little." No comparison is implied; the title may mean he was short of stature. In general, James, Joses, Judas, and Simon were four of the most common Jewish names at that time, and the appearance of such names among both the apostles and the brothers of the Lord is no proof that the two groups overlap. The real concern of Jerome, as the title of his tract shows, is not to define the relation of the brothers of the Lord to Jesus; it is rather to ward off the conclusion that Mary ever had normal marital relations with her husband or bore other children after the birth of Jesus. The argument he makes, that "knew her not until she had borne a son" (Matt. 1:25) and "gave birth to her first-born son" (Luke 2:7) do not necessarily imply that Mary later had other children, points to a possible but not natural interpretation of these passages; these passages, however, taken together with the later gospel passages concerning brothers of Jesus living in the home of Mary, point away from the interpretation that they are "cousins."

The Epiphanian view has one distinct advantage over the Hieronymian: it rests on a tradition that clearly runs back to the middle of the second century. But its crucial weakness is its lack of support in the NT. It, with Jerome's view, depends upon a doubtful interpretation of Matt. 1:25; Luke 2:7. Its assumption of a former marriage of Joseph is without NT basis. The idea sometimes proposed, that in Luke 1:34 Mary means that while about to establish the outward form of a marriage she intends to maintain permanently her virginity, reads too much into the words. The argument that the brothers of Jesus assume authority in a way which only older brothers would do, and so show that they must be sons of Joseph by a former marriage, is subjective and unconvincing; younger brothers could be critical and demanding if they agreed with a community conviction that Jesus was disgracing his family and home town by his zealous activity. The claim that Jesus would not have asked the Beloved Disciple to care for his mother if the brothers had been her children neglects the fact that his brothers did not yet believe in him; Jesus himself gives the answer to this objection, for he explicitly ranks spiritual kinship above family relationship (Mark 3:31-35).

The Protevangelium of James (*see* JAMES, PROTE-VANGELIUM OF), which J. B. Lightfoot (*see bibliography*) justifiably characterizes as "purely fictitious," is our earliest witness to the Epiphanian view. Of the later apocryphal gospels which tell the same story, Lightfoot rightly says: "Doubtless these accounts, so far as they step beyond the incidents narrated in the canonical Gospels, are pure fabrications." It may be added that the arguments of Epiphanius are neither substantial nor convincing, except when supported by the conscious or unconscious assumption that it would have been incongruous, or even unthinkable, for Mary to have given birth to other children. This widespread attitude includes two aspects: It finds it unbelievable that God would permit the mother of the sinless Christ, the Lord, to have at a later time other children who would share the sinful state of mankind. It also is convinced that Mary remained a virgin; she who experienced the miracle of being the mother of Jesus Christ never entered into normal marital relations with her husband.

**4. Conclusion.** Those who find these feelings justified may follow the Epiphanian view and accept its early church tradition, as Lightfoot did, in spite of the fact that its earliest traceable expression occurs in fictitious apocryphal narratives. Those who settle the question by NT evidence usually favor the Helvidian view, which seems to be the one view which is exegetically justified. The view of Jerome lacks clear support in the NT or in early church tradition.

**Bibliography.** Epiphanius *Against the Antidicomarianites,* in his *Against Heresies;* Jerome *Against Helvidius: The Perpetual Virginity of the Blessed Mary;* J. B. Lightfoot, "The Brethren of the Lord," *St. Paul's Epistle to the Galatians* (2nd ed., 1870), pp. 88-128; J. B. Mayor, *The Epistle of St. James* (1897), pp. vi-xlvii; T. Zahn, "Brüder und Vettern Jesu," *Forschungen zur Geschichte des Neutestamentlichen Kanons,* VI (1900), 227-364; J. H. Ropes, *The Epistle of St. James* (1916), pp. 53-62.

F. V. FILSON

**BROWN.** KJV form of BLACK in Gen. 30:32-33, 35, 40.

**BUCKET** [דְלִי]. A leather bucket was used for drawing water from a well or cistern (Isa. 40:15; Num. 24: 7). The mouth of the bucket was kept open by a stick made in the form of a Greek cross. A similar bucket is used in parts of Palestine today. Fig. BUC 53.

J. L. KELSO

**BUCKLE** [πόρπη]. A clasp for fastening an outer cloak or robe, the χλαμύς or *pallium,* worn over a tunic undergarment and pinned at the shoulder (*see* DRESS AND ORNAMENTS). In general use in the Med-

53. Man watering a garden with a bucket well, from a tomb painting of Thebes

iterranean world of the Greco-Roman period, brooches were sometimes given as rewards for valor and were emblems of rank. In the Eastern section of the Roman world the golden clasp and the wearing of purple, restricted to very distinguished persons or subject rulers, designated them as "friends and kinsmen" of the king (cf. I Macc. 10:89; 11:58; 14:44).

**Bibliography.** A. C. Bouquet, *Everyday Life in NT Times* (1954), pp. 56-69; G. E. Wright, *Biblical Archaeology* (1957), pp. 187-91, 241-42.                    E. W. SAUNDERS

**BUCKLER** [מָגֵן, *māghēn, from* גָנַן, defend, cover; סֹחֵרָה, *sōḥērâ* (Ps. 91:4), *cf.* Akkad. *seḥertu,* enclosure, circuit; צִנָּה, *ṣinnâ, cf.* Arab. *ṣāna,* preserve, keep]. Alternately: SHIELD (*see below*). A small, usually round, shield carried in the hand or worn on the arm.

Ancient shields fall into two main classes, a large one affording protection to the whole world of the body, and a small one carried usually on the left arm. This distinction is recognized in the OT in I Kings 10:16-17, where צִנָּה is a "large shield" and מָגֵן is a "shield." The latter term could therefore often better be translated "buckler," and this is sometimes the case (Song of S. 4:4; Jer. 46:3; etc.). In this respect the KJV is often to be preferred to the RSV (Job 15:26; Ps. 18:2, 30—H 18:3, 31; etc.). But more commonly מָגֵן is rendered "shield" by both KJV and RSV (e.g., Judg. 5:8), and in II Chr. 23:9 the RSV translates it "large shield." Conversely, צִנָּה is wrongly rendered "buckler" in Ps. 35:2; Ezek. 23:24; 38:4; etc. The KJV is also in error in I Chr. 12:8—H 12:9 when it renders רֹמַח, "spear," as "buckler." From all this it is evident that the English translators have not been too exact in their treatment of these terms. It is also probably true that the OT writers felt free to use these words rather loosely.

In the OT "buckler" is used both literally and figuratively. The literal usage calls for no comment here except to note that to it belongs I Kings 10:16-17, which describes Solomon's ceremonial bucklers and shields, decorated with gold. They were of no military value, although on occasion they may have been carried into battle (cf. II Sam. 8:7). Later, when these objects were looted, they were replaced by bronze ones (I Kings 14:25-28). The figurative use of "buckler" is illustrated by such passages as II Sam. 22:31 KJV; Ps. 18:2, 30—H 18:3, 31 KJV; Prov. 2:7 KJV; etc. In Job 15:26 KJV the resistance of the wicked man to God is described under the figure of a "buckler." *See* SHIELD; WEAPONS AND IMPLEMENTS OF WAR.                       W. S. McCULLOUGH

**BUGLE.** *See* MUSICAL INSTRUMENTS §§ B2*d-e*.

**BUKKI** bŭk'ī [בקי, *shortened form of* בקיהו, proved of Yahu; Apoc. Βοκκας]; KJV Apoc. BOCCAS bŏk'əs. Alternately: BORITH bôr'ĭth (II Esd. 1:2). **1.** A chief of the tribe of Dan; one of those who divided the land of Canaan among the Israelites (Num. 34:22).

**2.** An Aaronite priest, descendant of Eleazar and Phinehas (I Chr. 6:5, 51; Ezra 7:4; I Esd. 8:2; II Esd. 1:2; cf. the contradictory statements of Jos. Antiq. V.xi.5; VIII.i.3). *See* PRIESTS AND LEVITES § D1.

*Bibliography.* M. Noth, *Die israelitischen Personennamen* (1928), p. 226.                       H. H. GUTHRIE, JR.

**BUKKIAH** bə kī'ə [בקיהו, *possibly* vessel of Y (*see bibliography*)]. A Levite, son of Heman; one of those appointed by David to prophesy with musical instruments in the temple (I Chr. 25:4, 13; cf. vs. 1; on this passage *see also* GIDDALTI).

*Bibliography.* H. B. Gray, *Studies in Hebrew Proper Names* (1896), p. 205; M. Noth, *Die israelitischen Personennamen* (1928), p. 226; W. A. L. Elmslie, Exegesis of I Chronicles, *IB*, III (1954), 426-27.                       B. T. DAHLBERG

**BUL** bōōl [בול]. The old (Canaanite) name of the eighth Hebrew month (October-November), later called MARCHESHVAN. *See* CALENDAR.

**BULL, BULLOCK** [אביר (*alternately* STRONG BULL, MIGHTY BULL, STALLION; KJV *alternately* VALIANT MAN, STRONG ONE, STRONG HORSE), mighty one; *cf.* Akkad. *abâru*, be strong; Ugar. *ibr*, bull; *for the meaning* stallion, *see* Gordon 232; *for* בקר *and* שור (Aram. תור), *see* Ox; KJV עגל (RSV CALF)]; YOUNG BULL [פר בן בקר] (Lev. 4:3, etc.; KJV YOUNG BULLOCK). In English "bullock" meant originally "young bull"; it has been avoided in the RSV.

Bulls were part of a gift of cattle for Esau (Gen. 32:15—H 32:16). Successful breeding by a bull is referred to in Job 21:10.

"Bull" has various figurative meanings: the aggressive vigor of Joseph (Deut. 33:17); the pride and strength of Assyria (Isa. 10:13); the psalmist's enemies (Ps. 22:12—H 22:13); the kings of Gentile nations (Ps. 68:30—H 68:31); the leaders of Edom (Isa. 34:7) and of Babylon (Jer. 50:27). Probably the reference in Ezek. 39:18 is to be included in this category.

By far the commonest use of "bull" in the Bible is as a sacrificial animal. Such an animal would be uncastrated (Lev. 22:24); and since the English word "ox" has more specific reference to a castrated male

bovine, "bull" would be a better rendering in Lev. 4:10; 7:23 and similar contexts (*see* Ox). Its age is not usually specified, except that it must be at least eight days old (Lev. 22:27); the references are to a calf (Lev. 9:2), a three-year-old (I Sam. 1:24), and a seven-year-old (Judg. 6:25; cf. M. Par. 1.2).

The bull is mentioned as a sacrificial animal without reference to the particular occasion or purpose of the sacrifice in Lev. 22:23; Num. 23:1; Ezra 6:9; Pss. 50:13; 51:19—H 51:21; Isa. 1:11; Hos. 12:11. It is a sacrifice offering by individuals under certain special circumstances in Judg. 6:25 (Gideon); (I Sam. 1:24 (Hannah); I Kings 18:23 (Elijah); Ezra 8:35 (the returning exiles); Job 42:8 (Eliphaz, Bildad, and Zophar).

Most of the OT references to the bull are in the priestly narratives, and are connected either with the inauguration of the sacrificial system or with sacrifices on various sacred days. The more important of these occasions are: the consecration of priests (Exod. 29:1-37); the dedication of the altar of the tabernacle (Num. 7; cf. Ezek. 43:18-27); the purification of the Levites (Num. 8:5-22); various sin offerings Lev. 4; 16; cf. Heb. 9:13; 10:4); the New Moon Day (Num. 28:11-15); the Passover (Num. 28: 16-25; cf. Ezek. 45:21-25); the Feast of Weeks (Num. 28:26-31); the first of the seventh month (Num. 29: 1-6); the Feast of Booths (Num. 29:12-40). The latter has the distinction of exacting the largest number of bulls (seventy-one) for burnt offerings of all the annual feasts. We may compare the one hundred bulls of Ezra 6:17 and the one thousand bulls of I Chr. 29:21.

The use of bulls in Israel's cultus was a part of the religious tradition of Western Asia.* The sacrifice of bulls (and other animals) was an accepted way of satisfying the gods. Further, the bull was a widespread symbol of fecundity, and this may have made it a popular offering. The Canaanite recognition of El, head of the Ugaritic pantheon, as "father bull El" enhanced the cultic value of bulls along the Mediterranean littoral. Whether the Canaanite tradition of El as a bull or the association of the bull with BAAL

Courtesy of the University Museum of the University of Pennsylvania

54. Copper bull from a First Dynasty temple at al-'Ubaid, near Ur

had anything directly to do with the golden bulls ("calves") which Jeroboam set up at Bethel and Dan (I Kings 12:28) is speculative (*see* CALF, GOLDEN). There were twelve bronze bulls supporting the bronze sea at the Jerusalem temple ("oxen" in I Kings 7:25; II Kings 16:17, but more properly "bulls," as in Jer. 52:20). *See* SEA, MOLTEN. Fig. BUL 54.

See also FAUNA § A1*d*i.      W. S. McCULLOUGH

**BULRUSH** [גמא, *gōmê*] (Exod. 2:3). Alternately: PAPYRUS (Job 8:11; Isa. 18:2); RUSH (Isa. 35:7). A kind of REED which grew abundantly in swampy places and beside streams. In Exod. 2:3; Isa. 18:2 the reference is to some kind of basket or boat made from the papyrus plant (*Cyperus papyrus* L.). The KJV translates אגמן (Isa. 58:5) "bulrush," but *see* REED.

Fig. BUL 55. *See also* FLORA § A11*b*; MOSES; PAPYRUS.      J. C. TREVER

Courtesy of the Société Botanique de Genève

55. Bulrushes in the Lake Huleh swamp

**BULWARK** [אגם (Jer. 51:32; KJV REED); אשיה (Jer. 50:15), *from* Akkad. *asaittu, asîtu,* pillar, projection; חל, חיל, *cf.* Arab. *ḥawl,* strength, around, about; עז (Ps. 8:2; KJV STRENGTH), *from* עזז, be strong; KJV מצור (Eccl. 9:14; RSV SIEGEWORK), *from* צור, hunt (*but many emend to* מצור, *from* צור, besiege); KJV פנה (RSV CORNER *in* II Chr. 26:15; RAMPART *in* Ps. 48:13—H 48:14), *cf.* פנה, turn; ἑδραίωμα (KJV GROUND), *from* ἕδρα, seat, bench, base]. A barrier or wall constructed for defense.

**1. Literal usage.** In Ps. 48:13—H 48:14 (reading *ḥêlāh,* with the LXX and many Hebrew MSS, instead of *ḥêlâ*) the bulwarks (RSV "ramparts") of Zion are referred to, as also in II Chr. 26:15 (RSV "corners" of wall). In Jer. 50:15 the defenses of Babylon are meant. In 51:32 there is a curious reference to the "reedy pools" of Babylon: the word אגם, *'agam* (cf. Akkad. *agammu,* "swamp," "pond"), is translated "bulwarks" (KJV "reeds"). In Deut. 20:20; Eccl. 9:14, the allusions are to military works thrown up by besiegers, and in these passages the KJV "bulwarks" is therefore incorrect. *See* WEAPONS AND IMPLEMENTS OF WAR.

**2. Figurative usage.** In the difficult passage in Ps. 8:2 the RSV takes עז as "bulwark." In Isa. 26:1 God's salvation is described as "walls and bulwarks" (חל) for his people. In I Tim. 3:15 the church is said

to be the "pillar and bulwark of the truth," though ἑδραίωμα would be better translated "foundation" (cf. KJV GROUND).      W. S. McCULLOUGH

**BUNAH** bū'nə [בונה] (I Chr. 2:25). Head of a family of the clan of Jerahmeel of the tribe of Judah.

**BUNDLE OF THE LIVING** [צרור החיים] (I Sam. 25:29). A figure of speech expressing the state of being preserved among the living. The expression conveys the idea that, just as the owner of precious articles carries them in a bundle or pouch close to the body, so does the Lord keep in a bundle close to him those persons decreed to live. This figure of speech is apparently an ancient variant of the concept of the "book of the living" (Ps. 69:28; cf. Exod. 32:32-33; Dan. 12:1).      S. SZIKSZAI

**BUNNI** bŭn'ī [בוני]. **1.** A postexilic Levite who attended Ezra's public reading of the law (Neh. 9:4).

**2.** A Levite, the father of Hashabiah (Neh. 11:15), and perhaps identical with 1 *above.*

**3.** A chief of the people (Neh. 10:15).

**BURDEN** [משא, *from* נשא, to lift, carry; סבלה, *from* סבל, to bear a heavy load; βάρος, weight, burden; φορτίον, *from* φέρω, to bear, *hence* something borne]. Alternately: ORACLE. In addition to its literal usage, this term, as a translation of משא, is often used in a figurative sense—e.g., of the people of Israel (Num. 11:11, 17; Deut. 1:12) and of the individual (Job 7:20). The KJV uses "burden" in the prophetic writings for the "oracle" of guilt pronounced by the Lord upon a nation (e.g., Isa. 15:1; 17:1; 19:1) or the revelation of God to the prophet (e.g., Heb. 1:1), but the RSV always translates "oracle" in these instances.      B. D. NAPIER

**BURGLARY.** *See* CRIMES AND PUNISHMENTS § C2*d.*

**BURIAL.** The proper interment of the dead was a matter of great importance to the peoples of the ancient Near East. It is attested by frequent references to burial in the Bible and other ancient writings, and by the presence of thousands of tombs which modern archaeologists have excavated in Bible lands. For further discussion of places of burial, *see* DOLMENS; MACH-PELAH; OSSUARIES; TOMB; and on its rituals and significance, *see* BIER; EMBALMING; IMMORTALITY; MOURNING; RESURRECTION; SHEOL.

It is not easy to determine whether קבורה,

Courtesy of William L. Reed

56. Tomb entrance, Dibon (ninth century B.C.)

"burial," refers to the act or to the place. The custom of burying the dead may be implied in such passages as Eccl. 6:3; Isa. 14:20; Jer. 22:19, where no specific place of burial is mentioned. However, קבורה frequently denotes a tomb, and is variously rendered as "burying place" (Gen. 47:30), "sepulchre" (Deut. 34:6 KJV; RSV "place of burial"), "tomb" (II Kings 9:28; 21:26; 23:30; KJV "sepulchre"), and "grave" (Ezek. 32:23-24). The term מקברים designates the persons who bury the dead and is rendered "buriers" (Ezek. 39:15; Moffatt, Amer. Trans., "burial parties"). The Greek ἐνταφιάξω and ἐνταφιασμός designate the preparation of the body for burial (Matt. 26:12; Mark 14:8; John 12:7; 19:40), and θάπτω denotes the act of burying or entombment (Matt. 8:21-22; Acts 2:29; I Cor. 15:14). The latter, in the form συνθάπτω, is used figuratively in Rom. 6:4; Col. 2:12 in referring to being buried with Christ in baptism.

The antiquity of burial customs in Palestine is attested in the traditions concerning the cave of Machpelah, where Sarah was buried (Gen. 23:19) and also Abraham (25:9), Isaac, Rebekah, Leah (49:31), and Jacob (50:13). The position of skeletons found in the caves of Wadi el-Mugharah at Mount Carmel, and in tombs at ancient Jericho and Teleilat Ghassul near the N end of the Dead Sea, suggests that as early as the Stone, Chalcolithic, and Early Bronze ages care was taken in burying the dead. Figs. MUG 75-76.

Courtesy of Herbert G. May

57. Cemetery at Khirbet Qumran with burials in rows. Graves of about 1,200 members were found in this burial place.

Various places of burial, in addition to natural caves, are mentioned in the Scriptures. Frequently only the name of the city or region is mentioned; thus Aaron was buried at Moserah (Deut. 10:6; cf. Num. 33:38, where Mount Hor is named as his burial place); Moses in the valley in the land of Moab opposite Beth-peor (Deut. 34:6); Joshua in his own inheritance at Timnath-serah (Josh. 24:30; cf. Judg. 2:9); Jephthah in his city in Gilead (Judg. 12:7); Samson between Zorah and Eshtaol in the tomb of his father (Judg. 16:31); Saul and Jonathan, after

cremation by the Philistines, under the tamarisk tree in Jabesh (I Sam. 31:13), their bones later being buried in the land of Benjamin in Zela, in the tomb of Kish (II Sam. 21:14); David and Solomon in the city of David (I Kings 2:10; 11:43). The various kings of Israel and Judah are said to have been buried in the city of David (I Kings 15:8, 24; II Kings 8:24; 12:21; etc.), Tirzah (I Kings 16:6), Samaria (I Kings 16:28; 22:37), and Jerusalem (II Kings 14:20).

The precise location of the burial places is not described in these passages, but it is improbable that tombs were in the inhabited sections of the cities named. Although burials have been found beneath the floors of Neolithic homes at ancient Jericho and in the courtyards of Early Bronze Age homes at Gebal (Byblos), in later periods burials were usually made in natural or artificial caves outside the city walls in such places as Jericho, Lachish, Megiddo, Gezer, Tell en-Nasbeh (MIZPAH), Tell el-Far'ah (TIRZAH), Dibon,* Jerusalem, etc. Excavations reveal that tombs were often reused, and the bones from former burials were pushed to one side. Individual burials in single graves were not common, although a cemetery containing more than one thousand such graves has been discovered near the monastery of Qumran. *See* DEAD SEA SCROLLS. Figs. BUR 56-57.

Among the burial places for which a specific location is given may be mentioned: under an oak below Bethel (Gen. 35:8), in gardens (II Kings 21:18, 26; John 19:41—describing the burial place of Jesus as "in the garden a new tomb where no one had ever been laid"), and in a house (I Sam. 25:1; I Kings 2:34; II Chr. 33:20). The latter, named in connection with Samuel, Joab, and Manasseh, is unusual, and may indicate the revival of an ancient practice, or may merely be a euphemistic way of referring to a tomb (Ezek. 43:7 may mean that tombs were in the Jerusalem palace; the LXX of II Chr. 33:20 and the parallel in II Kings 21:18 locate Manasseh's burial in the garden of his house).

Coffins were not common among the Hebrews; the only reference to one is in connection with the body of Joseph in Egypt (Gen. 50:26; ארון, a portable box or chest). Elaborate wooden coffins, shaped in the likeness of human figures and ornately decorated, were often used in Egypt.* Terra-cotta coffins having on the lids designs of human features have been discovered in tombs at Beth-shean and Dibon.* Ossuaries containing the bones of the dead were used as early as the third century B.C. Figs. BUR 58-59; BET 38.

Ceremonies at the time of burial doubtless varied from generation to generation. The embalming of Joseph was unusual among Hebrews but was common among the Egyptians whose families could afford it. Likewise, cremation was not practiced by Jews or early Christians, as it was on occasion by Greeks and Romans. When bodies were burned, it was as a sign of vengeance (I Sam. 31:12), unrighteousness (Amos 6:10), or punishment of criminals (Lev. 20:14; 21:9; Josh. 7:25). The Mishna forbids cremation as idolatry ('A.Z. I.3).

Burial usually took place on the day of death (Deut. 21:23), as is still the case in the Near East, probably

58. An Egyptian painted wooden mummy case, used for burial

59. Terra cotta Moabite coffin, from Dibon (ninth century B.C.)

for reasons of sanitation and fear of defilement (Num. 19:11-14). Relatives prepared the body for burial and mourned the death (*see* MOURNING). Lack of burial was considered a great tragedy; to provide burial for another was a virtuous act (Tob. 1:17-18). Bodies

were carried to the tombs on litters or stretchers (*see* BIER), doubtless accompanied, as in modern times, by a procession of mourners. Possessions of the deceased were often buried with the body; Canaanite and Moabite tombs have been found to contain weapons, finger rings, earrings, bracelets, lamps, scarabs, food, and wooden furniture such as trays. The presence of the last item may account for the Hebrew law forbidding the offering of food to the dead (Deut. 26:14).

The full theological significance of biblical burial practices is not known, but it seems clear that they indicate an early belief in some type of survival after death, and the necessity of providing in a material way for such existence. W. L. REED

**BURNING** [שרף; בער (*see* HEIFER; SERAPHIM); יקד, מוקד; תוקד, KJV צרב (RSV SCORCHING); πύρωσις]. The act of consuming combustible materials by fire is mentioned frequently in the Bible, usually in describing an actual burning, but sometimes figuratively in referring to emotions of anger, lust, pain, etc. Among the materials described as burning are: BUSH, BURNING (Exod. 3:2); FIRE of the ALTAR (Lev. 6:9—H 6:2); LAMP (Lev. 24:2; Luke 12:35; John 5:35); MOUNTAIN (Deut. 5:23); INCENSE (I Kings 9:25; Jer. 11:17); RUSH (Job 41:20); COAL (Isa. 6:6; Rom. 12:20); PITCH (Isa. 34:9); sand (Isa. 35:7); wick (Isa. 42:3); TORCH (Isa. 62:1); fiery FURNACE (Dan. 3:6, 11, 15-26); CITY (Rev. 18:18). Figurative uses of "burning" include: ANGER of Yahweh (Josh. 7:26; Ps. 69:24—H 69:25); pain (Job 30:30; Ps. 38:7—H 38:8); LUST (Isa. 57:5).

*See also* BURIAL; CRIMES AND PUNISHMENTS; SACRIFICE AND OFFERINGS. W. L. REED

**BURNING BUSH.** *See* BUSH, BURNING.

**BURNT OFFERING.** *See* SACRIFICE AND OFFERINGS § C2; FIRE.

**BUSH, BURNING.** The flaming bush through which Moses became aware of the presence of Yahweh at Mount Horeb (Exod. 3:2-4). The Hebrew word for "bush" used here, סנה, is used only in this instance and in a parallel reference to it in Deut. 33:16.

Attempts have been made to identify the species of bush, but to no avail. It is assumed from early tradition that it was a thorn bush, and there is a possibility that the name of the bush is derived from a root meaning "thorny" or "sharp." Some have suggested thorn bushes of brilliant hue, or types of bushes that reflect the sunlight. The monks at Saint Catherine's monastery, Mount Sinai, have cultivated a species known as *rubus collinus*, assuming that this species (found only in Syria) was the bush seen by Moses. Objection has been made that no specimen of this species has ever been found growing wild in the Sinai region. It is better to assume an unidentified thorn bush.

It is to be noted that whereas Exod. 3:2 tells of the angel of the Lord appearing to Moses in the bush, Moses holds conversation directly with Yahweh in vs. 4. In this early period the term "angel," meaning "messenger," is thought perhaps to cover situations where there is manifestation of deity, rather than the appearance of a superhuman messenger of God.

The significance of the account is Moses' awareness of the presence of Yahweh. Modern attempts to rationalize or to find some natural explanation for such an account overlook two important aspects of early Semitic life: (a) the Semites used dramatic and picturesque language to portray spiritual and mental experiences; and (b) miracle and the supernatural were accepted facts of life, not subject to rational explanation. Modern rationale would have destroyed the spiritual value for the ancient Semite.

W. G. WILLIAMS

**BUSHEL.** The translation in Matt. 5:15; Mark 4:21; Luke 11:33 of μόδιος, a measure of 0.245 American bushel, here referring to a vessel which could cover a light; and in Bel 3, "bushels" (KJV "measures") in the translation of ἀρταβαι, a Persian measure of *ca.* 1 4/5 bushels, here used to designate amounts of flour presented as food to the idol Bel.

*See also* WEIGHTS AND MEASURES §§ C4*n-o.*

O. R. SELLERS

**BUTLER** [משקה, *from* שקה, to give drink, to irrigate]. An OFFICER who originally had charge of the wine for the royal table; hence one of high rank close to the person of the king and only nominally connected with the supply of wine. The term is used only of one of the fellow prisoners of JOSEPH (Gen. 40:1 ff). He is the chief butler, but his dream seems to indicate he is still the royal taster and keeper of the royal wine (vss. 11, 13, 21). The fact that the baker is also in prison suggests that the two were household servants and that only minor political influence belonged to them. However, because this butler speaks a good word to Pharaoh, Joseph is released to become an overseer in the land (Gen. 41:9, 40-41).

*See also* CUPBEARER.

C. U. WOLF

**BUTTER. 1.** The translation of מחמאת in Ps. 55: 21—H 55:22, as a figure for the smoothness of a traitor's speech.

**2.** KJV form of CURDS; KJV form of MILK in Job 29:6.

**BUZ** bŭz [בוז, contempt, *verb* to despise]. **1.** The second son of Milcah and Nahor, Abraham's brother (Gen. 22:21).

**2.** A man from the tribe of Gad (I Chr. 5:14).

**3.** A place (Jer. 25:23). *See* BUZITE.

**BUZI** bū′zī [בוזי, *a gentilic from* BUZ]. The father of Ezekiel (Ezek. 1:3).

**BUZITE** bū′zīt [בוזי]. An inhabitant or native of Buz (mentioned in Jer. 25:23 along with DEDAN and TEMA), probably an Arabian tribe or territory, the location of which is uncertain. Elihu's father (Job 32:2, 6) is called Barachel the Buzite.

**BUZZARD** [ראה (Deut. 14:13), *connection with* ראה, to see, *doubtful*]; KJV GLEDE. A medium-sized bird of prey of the family Accipitridae, of the genus Buteo, of which *ca.* twenty species are known. Tristram testifies that three varieties lived in Palestine in the nineteenth century.

The text of Deut. 14:13 is suspect, partly because ראה is not found in the parallel passage in Lev. 11: 14 (which has דאה), and partly because the Samar., LXX, and ten Hebrew MSS support the reading דאה (*see* KITE). Even if the MT is retained, the meaning of ראה remains unknown. W. S. McCULLOUGH

**BYBLOS** bĭb′lŏs [Βύβλος]. The Greek name of the ancient Phoenician town GEBAL.

**BYWORD** [משל, proverb; שנינה, sharp saying (*always in context with* משל)]. This word appears only in its negative sense in the Bible (e.g., "to become a byword, an object of derision among other people"), with minor exceptions always in the context of God's wrath against Israel or an Israelite. For the word in its wider usage, both negative and positive, *see* PROVERB. J. A. WHARTON

**C.** The symbol used to designate both the OT and the NT sections of Codex Ephraemi-syri. *See* EPHRAEMI-SYRI, CODEX. M. M. PARVIS

**CAB** căb. KJV form of KAB. *See* WEIGHTS AND MEASURES § C4*j*.

**CABBON** kăb'ən [כבון; *cf.* Aram. *kəban*, wrap around, surround]. A village of Judah in the Shephelah district of Lachish (Josh 15:40); perhaps to be identified with Hebra, E of Lachish; sometimes identified with Machbenah (I Chr. 2:49).

**CABIN.** A KJV archaism meaning "prison cell," used to translate חנות in Jer. 37:16. *See* DUNGEON.

**CABUL** kā'bəl [כבול]. 1. A border town in the territory of Asher (Josh. 19:27). It is generally identified with modern Kabul, a village *ca.* nine miles E-SE of Acre, overlooking one of the routes which descend from the Galilean hills to the maritime plain. The commonly held identification of Cabul with *kabura* in the Ramses III list (no. 23) is incorrect, since it and the towns mentioned with it are located farther N.
2. A district in Galilee. According to I Kings 9:13, Hiram of Tyre named a group of twenty towns, which Solomon had given him, Cabul. The parallel passage in II Chronicles (8:2) states that Solomon, rather than Hiram, was the recipient of the gift, but commentators generally agree that the fuller account in Kings is correct.
In all probability the administrative center of this district was the town of Cabul (*see* 1 *above*), but the location of the district cannot be determined, because of insufficient evidence. It has been plausibly suggested, however, that the towns were situated, not in the Plain of Acco, but in the hill country to the E, and that the comparative barrenness of the latter occasioned Hiram's displeasure.

*Bibliography.* A. Alt, *PJ*, 25 (1929), 43-44; F.-M. Abel, *Géographie de la Palestine*, II (1938), 14, 287.
G. W. VAN BEEK

**CADDIS.** KJV form of GADDI.

**CADES.** Douay Version and alternate KJV Apoc. form of KADESH; KEDESH.

**CADES-BARNE.** KJV Apoc. form of Kadeshbarnea. *See* KADESH, KADESH-BARNEA.

**CADMIEL.** KJV Apoc. form of KADMIEL.

**CAESAR** sē'zər [Καῖσαρ]. The family name of Julius Caesar (*see* CAESAR, JULIUS), taken by his adopted son AUGUSTUS, the first Roman emperor (27 B.C.–A.D. 14), and in turn by each of his successors so that it became a title (*cf.* EMPEROR). The name Caesar Augustus appears in Luke 2:1, and the title is found in some twenty-seven additional places in the NT. TIBERIUS CAESAR (A.D. 14-37) is specified in Luke 3:1 as reigning when Jesus began his ministry, and is the Caesar of the other references in the gospels (Mark 12:14-17 and parallels; Luke 23:2; John 19:12-15). In the book of Acts, CLAUDIUS (41-54), mentioned without the title in 11:28; 18:2, is the Caesar of 17:7; but the later references (25:8 ff; 26:32; 27:24; 28:19) probably mean NERO (54-68). Identification of the Caesar of Phil. 4:22, whether Claudius or Nero, depends on how the letter is dated (*see* PHILIPPIANS, LETTER TO THE). Other first-century Caesars, not mentioned in the NT, were: CALIGULA (37-41); Galba (68-69); Otho (69); Vitellius (69); VESPASIAN (69-79); TITUS (79-81); DOMITIAN (81-96); Nerva (96-98); Trajan (98-117). J. KNOX

**CAESAR, JULIUS** jōōl'yəs, —ĭ əs. Gaius Julius Caesar, father of the Roman Empire. He was born, sometime between 102 and 100 B.C., into a patrician but uninfluential family. In his youth he witnessed the Civil War and the dictatorship of Cornelius Sulla; he was surprised when Sulla restored the power of the Senate and resigned (79 B.C.). He was also aware of the interminable struggles for power among various generals, and like others took advantage of the chaotic situation to seek office with borrowed money. In 63 he was able to become pontifex maximus and praetor; in 61, after the conspiracy of Catiline had been put down, he became governor of Further Spain. Two years later he formed a coalition with Pompey and Crassus, both powerful generals, and was elected consul. He also obtained the governorship of those parts of Gaul which lay just to the N and the W of Italy, first for one period of five years, then for another. During his two terms of office he subjugated all the territory W of the Rhine.
Meanwhile Crassus had been killed in battle, and Pompey gradually became hostile toward Caesar. In spite of various efforts to reach compromises, the Senate finally (January, 49) voted to recall Caesar, who instead invaded Italy by crossing the River Rubicon. The result was a series of civil wars waged all around the Mediterranean—in Spain, Macedonia (Battle of Pharsalus, 48), Alexandria (where Caesar was helped by Antipater the Idumean, sent by HYRCANUS from Jerusalem), and Africa. In 46, Caesar was made dictator for ten years; he proceeded to the reform of the state, settling his veterans in Italy and elsewhere by founding colonies (*see*

COLONY). He reduced the number of persons on relief from 320,000 to 150,000; he expanded the Senate to 900 members; but, unlike Sulla, he followed a policy of clemency toward his former opponents. He also reformed the calendar and took time to write "commentaries" on the Gallic War from 58 to 52, and on the Civil War as well.

From experience and observation Caesar was well aware that the republican form of government was finished. It is said that he called it a "mere name without a substance." Indeed, since the end of the Carthaginian Wars (see ROMAN EMPIRE) the Republic had been going to pieces. This process has been explained in various ways, but at least three causes seem fundamental:

*a*) The most important was probably the rise of an urban debtor class, whose condition the Senate did almost nothing to improve. The gulf between rich and poor, instead of being narrowed by government policy, was actually widened when the new provinces were exploited. The equestrian class, ostensibly hostile toward the Senate, took advantage even of reform measures in order to acquire greater wealth. In Caesar's time class conflict produced near-anarchy.

*b*) The republican form of government possessed an inherent weakness because the Senate could only give advice to the consuls but could not compel them to follow it; the consuls could appeal to the popular assembly rather than to the Senate, if they so desired. This situation made for greater flexibility; it also meant that the power of the Senate was, or could be, severely limited. The foreign wars in which the late Republic was almost constantly engaged meant that the veterans were loyal, not to the Senate, but to their victorious generals, in whom they saw the power of Rome manifest.

*c*) The increasing contact between Rome and Hellenistic culture resulted in widespread acceptance, from the nobility downward, of Greek learning, including skeptical philosophy; and this acceptance resulted in the lessening of the authority of tradition. A world culture had come to overthrow the old Roman way of life, including Roman religion. These three forces (socio-economic, political, and cultural) were expressed in a series of crises which the machinery of government, designed for a small city-state, was unable to meet.

Caesar assumed absolute power. In his calendar the month of July now bore his name, and he issued coins with his own image on them. To be sure, he regularly informed the Senate of his decisions, but its function was purely consultative. On February 14, 44 B.C., he entered upon a perpetual dictatorship, issuing coins to celebrate the occasion; wearing a purple robe like that of the early kings, he sat on a throne. When hailed (not unnaturally) as king, he gave the ambiguous reply: "I am not a king but Caesar." A few senators, along with others determined to restore the Republic, therefore banded together to kill "the tyrant" (as Cicero described him), and at a Senate meeting on the Ides of March (March 15) they stabbed him to death with daggers (which appear on some coins of Marcus Brutus, nominal head of the conspiracy).

Power passed, however, not into their hands but into those of Caesar's former assistants, Marcus Antonius (Mark Antony) and Lepidus, and his heir Octavius (see AUGUSTUS). When a comet appeared in July, Octavius stated that it was an epiphany of Caesar, but Antonius refused to allow Caesar-worship. By 43, however, the three men had formed a "triumvirate," and in the following year a temple was erected to the "divine Julius" by vote of the subservient Senate. This event marked the beginning of Roman EMPEROR-WORSHIP, as well as the termination of the Republic.

Caesar himself can hardly be called a statesman but was a brilliant general who possessed remarkable political ability, used chiefly to advance himself. Believing in Fortune rather than in the gods, he took advantage of the weakness of the Republic to provide himself with supreme power. He had seen little but anarchy produced by senatorial rule, and it was not only his ambition but also the requirements of the situation which compelled him to take action. He intended to make the Danube a Roman frontier and to attack the Parthian Empire. The first project was achieved only by Augustus, the second by his successors.

**Bibliography.** T. R. Holmes, *The Roman Republic* (1923); R. Syme, *The Roman Revolution* (1939). For histories of Rome, *see* the bibliography under ROMAN EMPIRE.

                                     R. M. GRANT

**\*CAESAREA** sĕs'ə rē'ə [Καισάρεια, Καισαρία]. A city on the coast of Palestine *ca.* twenty-three miles S of Mount Carmel.

It first appears as a Phoenician city or fortification called Straton or Strato's Tower and apparently built by a king of Sidon of that name in the fourth century B.C. (Jos. Antiq. XIII.xv.4). In the Maccabean period it was captured from the tyrant Zoilus by Alexander Janneus (*ca.* 96 B.C.; Jos. Antiq. XIII.xii.4; xv.4). After the city was freed by Pompey in 63 B.C., it was given to Herod the Great by Augustus (Jos Antiq.

Copyright: The Matson Photo Service

1. Ruins of the ancient sea front at Caesarea

XV.vii.3). In honor of Caesar Augustus, Herod then named the city Caesarea and its seaport Sebastos (Augustus). His ambitious rebuilding of Caesarea required twelve years and was not finally completed until 10 B.C., when it was dedicated with magnificent games. Herod may have selected this site because he desired to have a seaport worthy of his kingdom and near Sebaste (Samaria). The location has excellent communications with the rest of Palestine. Figs. CAE 1; PAL 3.

Under the procurators Caesarea became their official seat and the capital of Palestine. Though predominantly pagan, the city contained a substantial Jewish minority. Riots between Jews and Gentiles in A.D. 66 marked the beginning of the Jewish war against Rome (Jos. Antiq. XX.viii.7-9; War II.xiii.7; xiv.4-5). In the later Roman Empire, Caesarea continued to be important, and especially as a seat of bishops and a center of learning under Origen (185-254), Pamphilius (240-309), and Eusebius (260-340).

Since there was no natural harbor, Herod constructed a mole 200 feet wide. The huge stones can still be seen extending 160 yards from the shore. The harbor included elaborate buildings and statues of Roma and Augustus at the entrance. The city included buildings typical of a Hellenistic city, such as a theater, amphitheater, hippodrome, aqueduct, colonnaded street, and an impressive temple dedicated to the divine Caesar (Jos. Antiq. XV.ix.6; War I.xxi.5-8). Only partial excavations have been attempted, but these have revealed a synagogue dating from the fourth or fifth century A.D.

In the NT, Caesarea first appears as a place where Philip preached (Acts 8:40). Peter converted the centurion who was stationed there (10:1, 24; 11:11). Herod (Agrippa I) had his residence at Caesarea, and there he died (12:19-23). Paul passed through the city on his way to Tarsus (9:30) and later when he returned from his missionary journeys (18:22; 21:8). After his arrest Paul was taken to Caesarea, where he was held prisoner and appeared before Felix and Festus (23:23; 25:12). After appearing before Agrippa II, Paul sailed from Caesarea for Rome (25:13-27:2).

*Bibliography.* G. A. Smith, *Historical Geography of the Holy Land* (1896), pp. 138-41; F.-M. Abel, *Géographie de la Palestine,* II (1938), 296-97.    D. C. PELLETT

**CAESAREA PHILIPPI** sĕs′ə rē′ə fĭl′ə pī [Καισάρεια ἡ Φιλίππου]. A city on the SW lower slope of Mount Hermon; mentioned in the Bible only in Matt. 16:13; Mark 8:27.

**1. Location and description.** The setting of this city is one of the most beautiful and luxuriant in Palestine, for it is on a terrace 1,150 feet above sea level overlooking the fertile N end of the Jordan Valley. To the NE towers Mount Hermon, 9,100 feet high. The terrace is well watered by one of the sources of the Jordan which springs from a cave nearby. The site was also selected for its strategic importance, because it guards the fertile plains to the W. The importance of the location was also assured by the presence of a shrine in the cave mentioned above. This shrine was, no doubt, already ancient when the Greeks arrived and dedicated it "to Pan and the Nymphs," as an inscription testifies.

This natural place of worship had probably been dedicated to various Semitic deities and was possibly the location of Baal-gad or Baal-hermon of the OT (Josh. 11:17 ff; Judg. 3:3; I Chr. 5:23). In NT times the name of the cave and its fountain was Paneion (τὸ Πανεῖον), and the city or district was called Paneas (ἡ Πανεάς; Jos Antiq. XV.x.3; XVII.viii.1; War I.xxi.3; III.x.7).

**2. History.** Paneas appears as the scene of an important battle (*ca.* 200 B.C.), in which Antiochus the Great defeated Egypt (Polybius XVI.18). In the first century B.C. it formed part of the territory of Zenodorus, but on his death in 20 B.C. it was given by Augustus to Herod the Great. He erected a temple of white marble and dedicated it to Augustus (Jos. Antiq. XV.x.3; War I.xxi.3). After Herod's death, in 4 B.C., it was included in the tetrarchy of his son Philip, who ruled until A.D. 34. Philip enlarged and beautified the city, giving it the name of Caesarea Philippi in honor of Tiberius Caesar and himself (Jos. Antiq. XVIII.ii.1; War II.ix.1). Later the city formed part of the kingdom of Agrippa II (*ca.* 50), who named it Neronias in honor of Nero (Jos. Antiq. XX.ix.4). It is mentioned as a stopping place for the Roman armies under Titus and Vespasian during the Jewish war of 66-70 (Jos. War III.ix.7; VII.ii.1). The city continued to be a place of importance in the later Roman and Byzantine periods and during the Crusades. The ancient name of Paneas survives in the name of the village Banyas on the same site. There are only a few remains of the ancient city.

In NT times Caesarea Philippi was an important city and a center of Greco-Roman civilization. The population was largely pagan (Jos. Life XIII). The city controlled a large area around it, which is indicated by "the district" (Matt. 16:13) or "the villages" (Mark 8:27) "of Caesarea Philippi." It was here that Jesus questioned his disciples about his messiahship and that Peter replied that Jesus was the Christ, the Son of God.

*Bibliography.* G. A. Smith, *Historical Geography of the Holy Land* (1896), pp. 473-81; F.-M. Abel, *Géographie de la Palestine,* II (1938), 297-98; D. Baly, *The Geography of the Bible* (1957), pp. 194-96.    D. C. PELLETT

**CAESAR'S HOUSEHOLD** [Καίσαρος οἰκία]. A collective term referring primarily to the imperial servants, including both slaves and freemen, usually at Rome but also in the rest of Italy and the provinces. It is used in reference to affairs at Alexandria by Philo (*Against Flaccus* 35): "If Agrippa had been not a king but one of Caesar's household, should he not have had some privilege and honor?" To "corrupt Caesar's household" (Jos. Antiq. XVII.v.8) means to seduce a slave belonging to Julia, wife of Tiberius Caesar. Paul mentions "Caesar's household" in Phil. 4:22 as that to which some Christians, sending greetings with him, belong (cf. Phil. 1:13: "throughout the whole praetorian guard"). The term also appears, presumably from Philippians, in the second-century(?) *Martyrdom of Paul* (pp. 104, 106; Lipsius), where on Paul's arrival at Rome he is greeted by a great crowd from "Caesar's household."

Scholars who claim that PHILIPPIANS was written from Ephesus or Caesarea have pointed out that the term can be used of persons outside Rome. It does not conclusively prove that Philippians was written from Rome itself.

**Bibliography.** J. B. Lightfoot, *Saint Paul's Epistle to the Philippians* (1903); G. S. Duncan, *St. Paul's Ephesian Ministry* (1929).            R. M. GRANT

**CAGE** [סוּגַר (Ezek. 19:9), *probably from* סָגַר, to shut, close; *cf.* Akkad. *šigâru, cage, and see below*]. Alternately: BASKET (Jer. 5:27; KJV "cage"); HAUNT (Rev. 18:2d; KJV "cage"). An enclosure, usually barred, for confining birds and other animals.

In the lament in Ezek. 19:2-9 a young lion (clearly Jehoiachin) is said to have been taken, put in a cage (vs. 9), and brought to the king of Babylon. While Ezekiel's language appears to be figurative (cf. II Kings 24:12-15; 25:27-30), the barbarous treatment of prisoners of war was common enough in the ancient world. We know, e.g., that Ashurbanipal, following an established practice, had earlier put a *šigâru* on the neck of a captured Arab prince Uate' (*ANET* 298). *See also* STOCKS.

**Bibliography.** On the probability that *šigâru* means a ladderlike wooden neck stock, in which as many as six men could be put at one time, see *Sumer,* X (1954), 116-19; XII (1956), 80-84.            W. S. McCULLOUGH

**CAIAPHAS** kā'ə fəs [Καιάφας, Καιαφᾶς, *probably from* קַיָּפָא]. The high priest in the TRIAL OF JESUS. *See also* ANNAS 1.

Caiaphas is mentioned twice in Josephus (Antiq. XVIII.ii.1; iv.3). The first reference contains little more than a mention of his appointment as high priest by Valerius Gratus; the second reference adds that the name was Joseph, but he was also called Caiaphas, and that he was removed from his office by the Procurator Vitellius (*ca.* A.D. 36 or 37) and replaced by Jonathan son of Ananus (probably the same name, and person, as Annas). The date of Caiaphas' appointment is uncertain; the first reference in Josephus would indicate that it took place *ca.* 18, so that Caiaphas served as high priest *ca.* eighteen years.

Apart from the NT, there is no additional information of substance about Annas and Caiaphas, though legends based on the NT arose (e.g., that Caiaphas became a Christian).

The gospels bring Annas and Caiaphas into relation with Jesus, but in a manner which creates problems for the interpreter. The problem, if at all solvable, needs to be seen clearly, prior to any attempt to solve it.

Mark 14:53 relates that Jesus, after his arrest, was led to the high priest; Mark abstains from naming him. The parallel, Matt. 26:57, names the high priest as Caiaphas. Earlier (vs. 3) Caiaphas is named as among those who gathered to plan "to arrest Jesus by stealth and kill him."

The parallel in Luke 22:54 omits the name of the high priest. But Acts 4:6, ensuing on the arrest of Peter and John, speaks of a gathering of Jewish leaders "with Annas the high priest and Caiaphas and John and Alexander." Since the account in Josephus clearly makes Annas precede Caiaphas, and Annas' tenure ended *ca.* 14 or 15, to speak of Annas as the high priest in the period of the 30's is surprising and

perplexing. Moreover, Luke 3:2, a sixfold chronological statement, provides the statement, whose puzzling character is clearer in Greek than in the usual English rendering, that the events took place in the priesthood (ἀρχερέως—singular, not plural) of Annas and Caiaphas.

· At this point the following questions may initially focus on the problem: (*a*) Did Annas precede Caiaphas? (*b*) If so, when did Annas cease to be high priest, and when did Caiaphas begin? (*c*) Does the suggestion in Luke 3:2 that both were priests at the same time conform to what is known of Jewish practice? (*d*) If Caiaphas was high priest simultaneously with Annas, or after Annas, why does Acts 4:6 list Annas as the high priest and Caiaphas as not a high priest?

In John the problems become more acute. John 11 relates that after the raising of Lazarus the SANHEDRIN gathered to discuss what to do about Jesus. Vss. 49-50 read: "But one of them, Caiaphas, who was high priest that year, said to them, '. . . It is expedient for you that one man should die for the people . . . .' " But 18:13 relates, after the arrest of Jesus, that "they led him to Annas; for he was the father-in-law of Caiaphas, who was high priest that year." 18:22 tells that "one of the officers standing by struck Jesus with his hand, saying, 'Is that how you answer the high priest?' " This verse makes it plain that Annas was regarded as the high priest. But vs. 24 tells that "Annas then sent him bound to Caiaphas the high priest."

Again, to resume, with questions which may focus on the problem: (*e*) Did the high priest ("that year") serve only one year? (*f*) Could there have been two, equal high priests at one and the same time? (*g*) Why do Luke and Matthew abstain from relating that Annas was the father-in-law of Caiaphas?

Considerable ingenuity has been expended in solving the problem, especially in conservative commentators (e.g., Godet, *Commentary on the Gospel of John*, II, 354-57), where the discordances are arbitrarily made to harmonize. Some commentators (e.g., Spitta, *Zur Geschichte und Literatur des Urchristentums*, I, 158 ff) tried to escape from the problems in John 18 by citing a different order of verses found in the Syrus Sinaiticus as proof of a disarrangement: Caiaphas was the high priest, but two examinations took place, one in the home of Annas and the second in the palace of Caiaphas; but see against this improbability Wendt, *The Gospel According to St. John*, p. 164, note 1, and the contention that the Syrus Sinaiticus is a harmonizing rearrangement.

Bultmann (*Das Evangelium des Johannes*, 12th ed., pp. 496-97) supposes that a non-Synoptic source has been utilized, which the evangelist has reworked but without thoroughness. In the source the high priest was listed as Annas; the evangelist blended with this source a quasi-Synoptic tradition naming the high priest as Caiaphas, and hence the confusion in John. Bultmann names (p. 497, note 4) the many commentators who want to omit "and Caiaphas" from both Luke 3:2 and Acts 4:6 as an interpolation, designed to correct the "error" in chronology. Moreover, a slight emendation of the Greek of Acts 5:17 would change the rendering from "But the high priest rose up," etc., into "But Annas the high priest," etc. (changing Ἀναστὰς into Ἅννας). This would bear out that Luke knew only Annas' name as the high priest, and that the careless blending of separate, discordant sources has produced the confusion.

A solution to the problem, especially in its various facets, is not available. Mark, we saw, did not name the high priest. It may be suggested that when the tradition after the time of Mark began to name the high priest, in some way the chronologically impossible Annas came to be the name, at least in one body of tradition. The tradition which names the priest Caiaphas is an effort to correct the chronological difficulties. But a by-product of the existence of the two names in a composite tradition was the association of Annas and Caiaphas, quite against Jewish practice, as dual high priests, as in Luke 3:2.

The interpretation found frequently that Annas remained influential in high-priestly matters long after his deposition is not supported by any evidence; it is a conclusion reached in any effort to escape the difficulties inherent in the problem.

Perhaps another by-product was the error of suggesting that the high priest served one single year; such appears to have been a pagan procedure (see Bultmann *Das Evangelium des Johannes*, p. 314, note 2), unknown to Jews.

Since the trial scenes in the gospels are scarcely accurate history, the details are scarcely apt to be accurate.

While in the usual growth of tradition a character nameless at an early stage acquires a name at a later stage, what we encounter in the present problem is that the initial naming of the man proved to be erroneous, so that a corrective name was added; and once there were the two names, they needed to be brought into an artificial chronological proximity—and even to be made father-in-law and son-in-law. It is to be doubted that the evangelists were concerned to be punctiliously accurate in a matter as minor as the name of the high priest; and surely they did not envisage that almost two thousand years later scholars would investigate such minor details with major scientific curiosity. S. SANDMEL

*CAIN kän [קַיִן, *see below;* Καιν; Vulg. *Cain*]. 1. Eldest son of ADAM and Eve (Gen. 4:1).

Gen. 4:1 connects קַיִן with קָנָה. But philologically *qáyin* points to the "hollow" root קין. If קנה, "to get, acquire, buy," is the true root, the relation of both its form and its meaning to the Genesis story remains unclear.

If the proper root is קין, the word may mean "spear" (II Sam. 21:16 [but corrupt; cf. I Sam. 17:38]); but it is best to consider it as an ancient personal name, from a word meaning "smith" or "worker in metal," cognate with Arabic *qayn* and Aramaic *qaináyâ*.

Both brothers brought to Yahweh an offering of their produce; but for Cain and his offering Yahweh had no regard. Therefore Cain became angry and, though exhorted to master sin, murdered his brother (Gen. 4:2-8).

Cain's punishment alienated him from his land,

his family, and his God. When Cain protested his banishment to the land of Wandering as being tantamount to death, Yahweh graciously mitigated it by placing his mark upon Cain (vss. 9-16).

Why Yahweh preferred Abel's sacrifice and by what means the preference was indicated, are not given in Genesis. The explanations found in the NT and postbiblical traditions, Jewish and Christian, are of necessity later retrojections (cf. Wisd. Sol. 10:3-4).

Form-critically, Gen. 4:17-24 must be separated from the Cain and Abel story. But *see* KENITES; TUBAL-CAIN.

Because he was "of the evil one" (ἐκ τοῦ πονηροῦ), Cain stands as a prototype of wicked men who "walk in the way of Cain" (Jude 11). Christians are exhorted not to be like him (I John 3:12) but rather to emulate the faithful Abel (Heb. 11:4).

L. HICKS

2. KJV form of KAIN.

CAINAN kā'nən [Καιναμ] (Luke 3:36; from LXX of Gen. 10:24; 11:12). Son of Arphaxad.

CAKE. See BREAD, particularly § 1d.

*CALAH kā'lə [כֶּלַח; Akkad. *Kalḫu*] (Gen. 10:11-12). One of the Assyrian capital cities. The site, now called Nimrud, is located at the NE angle of the confluence of the Tigris and Upper Zab rivers.

*Bibliography.* M. E. L. Mallowan, *Twenty-five Years of Mesopotamian Discovery* (1956). C. H. GORDON

CALAMOLALUS kăl'ə mŏl'ə ləs [Καλαμωλάλος (A); Καλαμωκάλος (B)]. Probably a corrupt combination of "LOD and HADID," names in the canonical parallel to I Esd. 5:22, where this is found. The RSV places this word in the mg. N. TURNER

CALAMUS kăl'ə məs [קָנֶה, *qānê;* κάλαμυς] (Exod. 30:23 KJV [RSV AROMATIC CANE]; Song of S. 4:14; Ezek. 27:19). A product of trade made from an aromatic REED (or grass) probably imported from India. *See* FLORA § A7e; SWEET CANE.

CALCOL kăl'kŏl [כַּלְכֹּל]; KJV CHALCOL in I Kings 4:31. One of the sons of Zerah, whom Tamar bore to her father-in-law, Judah (I Chr. 2:6). Calcol was celebrated for his wisdom, which was surpassed only by Solomon's, and is described as one of the "sons of Mahol"—i.e., "members of the orchestral guild" (I Kings 4:31—H 5:11).

*Bibliography.* W. F. Albright, *Archaeology and the Religion of Israel* (3rd ed., 1953), pp. 127-28, 210. E. R. DALGLISH

CALDRON. An English translation representing several varieties of Hebrew cooking pots, both ceramic and metalware. For exact terms, *see* POTTERY § 3a.

CALEB kā'ləb [כָּלֵב, dog (*i.e.,* slave) of, *or* snappish(?)]; CALEBITE —lə bīt; CHELUBAI kǐ lōō'bī [כְּלוּבַי], *probably a variant of* כָּלֵב] (I Chr. 2:9). One of the spies sent by Moses to reconnoiter the land of Canaan; subsequently conqueror of Hebron.

Within the band of spies sent from Israel's wilderness encampment Caleb represented the tribe of Judah. Caleb championed the view, upon the spies' return, that an immediate assault on Canaan should be made. This distinctly minority viewpoint was supported by Joshua but was rejected by the people, intimidated by the other spies' report of fortified cities and formidable opponents. This timidity was branded as rebellion against Yahweh and denial of his presence with his people (Num. 14:9); and because of it the adult wilderness generation, with the exception of Caleb and Joshua, was excluded from entering the Promised Land. Caleb particularly was lauded as Yahweh's servant, one who "has a different spirit and has followed [Yahweh] fully" (Num. 14:24; cf. Deut. 1:36).

Aside from his role as spy, Caleb is associated in the OT with the region around HEBRON. This territory was given to him as a divinely bestowed inheritance, but one from which Caleb himself must eject its former inhabitants, the Anakim, or "giants" (see ANAK). The conquest of nearby Debir, SW of Hebron, is also connected with the exploits of Caleb, although it was Othniel who actually took the town and so won Caleb's daughter Achsah as wife (Josh. 15:16-17; Judg. 1:12-13). The development of Hebron as a Levitical city of refuge is responsible for the explanation that Caleb controlled, not the city itself, but its outlying fields and villages (Josh. 21:12; I Chr. 6:56—H 6:41). Further indication of Caleb's association with territory in the S of Judah is afforded by the designation "Negeb of Caleb" (I Sam. 30:14), which applies to a section of the area in which David operated as an outlaw.

Behind the OT references to Caleb's career in the conquest of Judah lies fairly involved ethnological history. It is evident that the figure of Caleb represents the incorporation of a foreign strain into the tribe of Judah. While the priestly source (Num. 13:6; 34:19) and the Chronicler (I Chr. 2:18; cf. vss. 4-5) trace Caleb's ancestry back to Judah, older sources which know him as the son of Jephunneh the Kenizzite (Num. 32:12) or as the older brother of Kenaz, Othniel's father (Josh. 15:17; Judg. 1:13), point to the extra-Israelite origin of the Calebites. Kenaz was an Edomite clan or chief (Gen. 36:11; I Chr. 1:53), and the Kenizzites resided in (presumably S) Palestine in the patriarchal period (Gen. 15:19). It has been argued that both Caleb and Kenaz are Hurrian names (see HORITES), and Hur appears as a personal name in the Chronicler's Calebite genealogy (I Chr. 2:19, 50), although it is probable that Hur should be reckoned as the son of Hezron, not of Caleb (cf. I Chr. 2:24, 50aβ, with 2:19, which on stylistic grounds seems an intrusion into the Chronicler's genealogical tables).

The intricate Calebite genealogies in I Chr. 2; 4 apparently imply varying degrees of penetration by Calebite tribes into Judah and subsequent intermingling with that tribe. Caleb's several marriages and their respective progeny suggest such tribal history (cf. I Chr. 2:18-19, 24, 42-50; 4:15). Ephrathah as Caleb's wife symbolizes Calebite occupation of the Bethlehem countryside (I Chr. 2:24; cf. 2:50aβ-51; Mic. 5:2—H 5:1), as the names Ziph and Hebron (I Chr. 2:42) point to Calebite settlement farther S.

The troublesome reference to Caleb as the son of Hezron (I Chr. 2:18, 24; cf. vs. 9) can hardly suggest another person than Caleb son of Jephunneh, whom the Chronicler also knows (I Chr. 4:15), since Achsah is named as Caleb's daughter in both instances (cf. Josh. 15:16; I Chr. 2:49). The association of Caleb with Hezron, as also with Jerahmeel (I Chr. 2:42), is probably the Chronicler's strategy for affirming Caleb's lineal descent from Judah.

In the figure of Caleb the poignancy of OT particularism comes to expression. Possessing alien ties that were never quite completely concealed, Caleb nevertheless became the exponent of a fearless faith in the God who had promised Israel land.

*Bibliography.* H. Bauer, "Die hebräischen Eigennamen als sprachliche Erkenntnisquelle," *ZAW,* LXXXIV (1930), 73-80; M. Noth, "Eine siedlungsgeographische Liste in 1. Chr. 2 und 4," *ZDPV,* LV (1932), Heft 3, 97-124; H. L. Ginsberg and B. Maisler, "Semitised Hurrians in Syria and Palestine," *JPOS,* XIV (1934), 243-67; W. F. Albright, "Two Letters from Ugarit (Ras Shamrah)," *BASOR,* LXXXII (1941), 43-49. R. F. JOHNSON

**CALENDAR.** The Hebrews and early Christians did not possess a published and widely authoritative calendar similar to those in general use today. The present Jewish calendar is the crystallization of a long process of calculation and controversy carried on, not only in the centuries since the first published Jewish calendar (fourth century A.D.), but during the ages preceding it as well. Thus modern students of the Bible should realize that it is not possible to speak of *a* biblical calendar. A widely accepted pattern of time-reckoning there certainly was, but in the biblical period this was in process of continual change and experimentation.

Although we may assume that Gentile Christians in the NT era made a wide use of the Greco-Roman calendars, it may be understood that Jews and Jewish Christians, even when far from Palestine, continued to employ the official calendar of Jewish orthodoxy, particularly for observing the religious festivals (cf. Acts 20:6, 16). From extensive discussions of calendrical matters in the Mishna and the Talmud, we may be fairly certain of the main features of this calendar during NT times. However, the further we regress in Hebrew history, the greater our uncertainty becomes. Although it is obvious from numerous OT passages that the ancient Hebrews possessed at least a roughly calculated calendar (or calendars), they have nowhere given us a complete account of their system. The precise determination of this system remains one of the major problems of biblical research.

The need for a uniform schedule of time-reckoning, even for seminomadic people like the ancient Hebrews, is apparent. The complexities of their economic and political intercourse depended upon it more and more as they emerged from a tribal to a monarchical organization, and as they broadened their relations with other nations. It was also imperative for the orderly regulation of their religious festivals.

Sufficient as these motivations for calendar-making apparently were, the early Hebrews did not have the means for the accurate determination of a calendar. The criteria at hand either were unreliable or led to unavoidable conflicts in calculation. Thus the agricultural year fluctuated according to the weather and the region. It was difficult to determine the annual course of the sun and the stars—roughly 365¼ days —because methods of astronomical observation were inadequate; besides, the solar year failed to tally with the lunar year—one lunation lasted *ca.* 29½ days, and twelve lunations lasted roughly 354¼ days. It was the highly developed astronomical and calendrical science of the Babylonians which opened the way for a more accurate and refined calendar among the Hebrews. *See* SUN; MOON; ASTRONOMY.

1. The lunar-solar calendar
2. The year
3. The months
   *a.* The lunar month
   *b.* The Gezer Calendar
   *c.* The Canaanite names
   *d.* The numbering system
   *e.* The Babylonian names
   *f.* Intercalation
4. The religious festivals
5. Survey of historical development
6. Sectarian calendars
Bibliography

**1. The lunar-solar calendar.** In all likelihood the early Israelites followed a Canaanite calendar, which may at one time have been entirely solar like a later calendar used in Tyre (*see* YEAR). Calendars combining both solar and lunar reckoning were, however, widely used throughout the Near East even in very ancient times, and the Hebrews probably always had a lunar-solar calendar. The prestige of the Babylonian system certainly must have had effects even in pre-exilic Israel.

A lunar-solar calendar was adopted by the first Babylonian dynasty (*ca.* 1830-1550 B.C.), and became effective in Assyria during the first millennium B.C. The Babylonians gave Semitic names to the months, but in most other respects this calendar was substantially the Sumerian calendar of Nippur as observed in the third dynasty of Ur (*ca.* 2180-1960). This calendar reckoned the year from one vernal equinox to the next, while counting months from new moon to new moon, with an added month when this was needed to make up the discrepancy. These lunar months were of thirty days' length except when a new moon occurred on the thirtieth day, in which case this would become the first day of the new month. Until the Persian era astronomical observation was the primary means of determining calendrical periods, but thereafter mathematical calculation became a sufficiently dependable method of determination.

**2. The year.** It is fairly certain that in historical times the Israelites determined their year, not by the fluctuating agricultural and pastoral cycles, even though these natural phenomena must have influenced them deeply, but by observing the annual circuit of the stars and the sun. We have little evidence concerning the method they might have used for determining the completion of this circuit, but we do know that the new year began at one of the equinoxes, at the dividing point between winter and summer or between summer and winter. The Babylonians chose the vernal equinox as the beginning of their year, since spring is the time of new growth. The Hebrews, however, appear to have observed at different periods two new-year dates, one at the spring and another at the autumn equinox. The problem of the interrelation of these two systems, when each was employed and in which areas and for which particular purposes, is one that continues to vex OT scholars.

There is a hint of a primitive spring new year among the Hebrews in Exod. 12:2, 18, where the Passover month (Abib-Nisan) is solemnly established as the beginning of the year. Many scholars have considered this passage to be of postexilic origin and hence of little evidential value, but the importance of Abib as the "month to remember" persists in several passages of admittedly earlier date (Exod. 13:3-4; 23:15; 34:18; Deut. 16:1). It is striking that wherever the Hebrew months are mentioned by number—and this is the predominant method used in the OT (*see* § 3*d below*)—they are always counted from a first month in the spring. This is true even when the new year is observed in the fall, and certainly preceded the introduction of the Babylonian spring calendar at about the time of the Exile. Unless the month numbers have been corrected by a postexilic scribe, it is difficult to explain this persistent method of counting the months except on the supposition that far back, perhaps in patriarchal times, the Hebrews had observed a spring new year, and that this continued to affect the numbering of the months even when Israel adopted a fall new year.

There is, at any rate, abundant indication that a new year in the fall was standard during the monarchical period and probably for a long while before it. The Canaanites and the Northwest Semites in general seem to have had a fall new year, and probably the Hebrews took this as their own new year after their settlement in Palestine in the time of the Judges.

Thus both Exod. 23:16; 34:22 mention the end (or beginning) of the religious year after the fall Feast of Ingathering (cf. Lev. 23:24; Num. 29:1-6; Deut. 16:16). The SABBATICAL YEAR and the Year of Jubilee (*see* JUBILEE, YEAR OF) were agricultural years beginning in the fall and progressing through the cycle of sowing, pruning, reaping, and vintage (Exod. 23:10-11; Lev. 25:1-22). This agricultural year beginning in the fall is also the basis of the Gezer Calendar (*see* § 3*b below*), which probably dates from the last quarter of the tenth century B.C. Further evidence that a fall new year persisted at least until the time of Josiah and perhaps even after the Exile (though perhaps for restricted purposes) may be found in such passages as I Kings 6:1, 37-38; II Kings 22:3 (cf. 23:23); Neh. 1:1 (cf. 2:1). The fall new year may have been observed only in Judah after the time of Solomon, however. Recent chronological studies of the period of the Divided Kingdom indicate that Jeroboam's realm probably introduced (or reintroduced) a new year in the spring, at least for the purpose of counting reigns. *See* CHRONOLOGY OF THE OT.

Shortly before the Exile the Babylonian spring

new year began to come into vogue in the Judean kingdom, although it did not entirely supplant the fall new year. Jer. 36:22 speaks of the ninth month (called Chislev in Zech. 7:1) as falling in the winter; this may simply reflect ancient Hebrew practice, but likely it also resulted from increasing Akkadian influence. Chronological references in Jeremiah, as in 25:1-3; 46:2, depend upon a reckoning of the reigns of Judean as well as Babylonian kings from a new year in the spring, and Ezek. 33:21; 40:1 likewise presuppose a spring new year. (References in II Sam. 11:1; I Kings 20:22, 26; I Chr. 20:1; II Chr. 36:10 to the spring—lit., the "turning of the year"— as the "time when kings go forth to battle" may indicate a spring new year at an even earlier date.) The books of Kings generally maintain the fall reckoning, however, and long after the Exile we find Nehemiah reckoning the reign of his Persian monarch (who used a spring calendar) on the basis of a fall new year (1:1; 2:1). In the postexilic period the religious festivals were placed on a schedule beginning with Passover in the spring (Lev. 23). After the biblical period Judaism settled upon a religious new year in the month Tishri, while preserving reminiscences of other new-year days (M. R.H. I.1). *See* NEW YEAR.

3. **The months.** The primitive Hebrew word for "month" (*yérah*), like cognates in other Semitic languages, was related to the word for "moon" (*yārēᵃh*; *see* MOON). Significantly employed with the old Canaanite month names in I Kings 6:37-38; 8:2 (Abib is a consistent exception [Exod. 13:4, etc.]), this word continued to be used mainly in poetic (e.g., Job 3:6; 7:3) and archaizing (e.g., Zech. 11:8) texts. Perhaps because of polytheistic associations (cf. Ugaritic *yarih*, the moon-god), it was gradually supplanted by the word *hódhesh* (lit., "new"—i.e., "new moon"), particularly in texts where reference is made to the religious year, in which the new moon played so important a role.

*a. The lunar month.* There is no direct evidence that the ancient Hebrews ever observed any but a lunar month—i.e., a month of 29½ days, requiring alternation of 30-day months with 29-day months for practical purposes. Speculations concerning a purely solar reckoning, according to which the year was mathematically divided into twelve 30-day months without reference to the lunar phases, fail to explain why there should be months at all and do not take into sufficient account the widespread popularity of lunar calendars in very ancient times. It is true that 30 days are generally reckoned as a month's length (Gen. 7:11; 8:3-4; Num. 20:29; Deut. 21:13; 34:8; Esth. 4:11; Dan. 6:7, 12—A 6:8, 13) and that the year contained twelve months (I Kings 4:7; I Chr. 27:1-15) apart from intercalation. This formula is, however, only a practical way of reckoning and leaves undecided the precise calculation of the calendar. Arguments for a year of seven 50-day periods (the so-called pentecontad calendar) are even more precarious.

Very important in this connection is the fact that both the Hebrew words for "month" are associated with the moon (*see above*). The NEW MOON was an occasion requiring solemn religious observances even in early periods (cf. I Sam. 20:5, 18, 24; II Kings 4:23; Isa. 1:13-14; Ezek. 46:3; Hos. 2:11; Amos 8:5;

etc.). It marked the beginning of the new month, which continued for 29 or 30 days until another new moon was observed.

*b. The Gezer Calendar.* The months were, of course, closely associated with the seasons. This appears from such an old month name as Abib, which refers to the green heads of grain appearing in this month. The same agricultural interest is plainly the basis of the so-called Gezer Calendar, which was

Courtesy of Felice Le Monnier, Florence

2. The Gezer agricultural calendar; an inscription, possibly a school exercise tablet, on soft limestone

discovered by Macalister in 1908. Dating from the time of the early Divided Monarchy, this "calendar" appears to be a school exercise in which the months are mnemonically listed, not by the names current in that period, but by the chief agricultural activities of the year. Roughly inscribed on a limestone tablet are the words:

> His two months are (olive) harvest,
> His two months are planting (grain),
>   His two months are late planting;
> His month is hoeing up of flax,
> His month is harvest of barley,
>   His month is harvest and feasting;
> His two months are vine-tending,
>   His month is summer fruit
>   (trans. W. F. Albright, *BASOR,* 92
>       [Dec., 1943], 16-26).[1]

Fig. CAL 2.

*c. The Canaanite names.* During the biblical period three different systems were successively followed for naming the months. First, there was a series of Canaanite names used during part of the pre-exilic period. Four of these names are to be found

---

[1] From James B. Pritchard, *Ancient Near Eastern Texts* (Princeton University Press; rev. ed., 1955).

in the OT—the first of them, Abib, always in connection with the Passover (Exod. 13:4; 23:15; 34:18; Deut. 16:1), and the other three, Ziv, Ethanim, and Bul, in connection with the dedication of Solomon's temple (I Kings 6:1, 37-38; 8:2). In these passages these names are explained in terms of the later system of numbering the months. Abib is the first month (March-April), Ziv the second (April-May), Ethanim the seventh (September-October), and Bul the eighth (October-November). It should be noted that these four surviving names are associated with the two equinoxes.

That the agricultural year was still very influential in this period appears from the meaning of these names. Each refers to the most striking natural phenomenon of its season. Abib has already been mentioned. Ziv probably means "splendor" or "brightness," a reference to the brilliant colors of springtime. Ethanim refers to the perpetual streams which alone contained water in the fall. Bul may mean "produce" or "cattle"—another obvious agricultural reference. Two of these names, Ethanim and Bul, appear in Phoenician inscriptions. While not containing references to Abib and Ziv, these inscriptions do mention still other names which may have been originally employed by the Hebrews.

**d. The numbering system.** Probably already in the early monarchical period these Canaanite names fell into disuse. As commerce and the crafts grew more important, the Hebrews came to prefer a system of naming the months by number, and this system continued till late in the postexilic period. By far the largest number of biblical references to the various months are according to this method. As might be expected, there are almost as many references to the first and seventh months, when the great equinoctial feasts were held, as there are to all the others combined.

**e. The Babylonian names.** The third system of names did not arise until after the Exile, and did not find complete acceptance until rabbinical times. These names were those of the Babylonian months, which the Hebrews had certainly encountered long before the Exile through contact with the Assyrians.

There has been considerable uncertainty about the etymology of the Babylonian month names. It seems quite likely, however, that the Babylonians simply translated the general or explicit idea contained in the Sumerian names for the various months, which names had been closely associated with their mythology. The following list would, accordingly, indicate the order of the Babylonian months, beginning at the spring of the year, with their probable etymologies:

1. *Nisānu* (March-April), first month or month of sacrifice

2. *Ayāru* (April-May), procession month

3. *Sīmānu* (May-June), fixed season or time of brickmaking

4. *Du-uzu* (June-July), month of Tammuz the god of fertility

5. *Abu* (July-August), month of torches

6. *Elulu* or *Ululu* (August-September), month of purification

7. *Teshritu* (September-October), month of beginning

8. *Araḥ-samna* (October-November), eighth month

9. *Kislīmu* (November-December), of uncertain meaning

10. *Ṭebītu* (December-January), month of plunging (into water)

11. *Shabāṭu* (January-February), month of storms and rain

12. *Adaru* (February-March), month of the threshing floor

Taking these over by transliteration, and probably without a full understanding of their original mythological associations, the Hebrews gave this new series of names to their months. With the passages where they occur in the OT and the Apoc., and with their LXX equivalents for the latter, these Babylonian names appear in the following form in Hebrew:

1. Nisan (ניסן [Neh. 2:1; Esth. 3:7]; Νισα[ν] [I Esd. 5:6; Add. Esth. 1:1]; II Macc. 11:30, 33, 38, have the Macedonian equivalent, Xanthicus)

2. Iyyar (איר; not mentioned)

3. Sivan (סיון; Esth. 8:9)

4. Tammuz (תמוז; not mentioned)

5. Ab (אב; not mentioned)

6. Elul (אלול [Neh. 6:15]; Ελουλ [I Macc. 14:27])

7. Tishri (תשרי; not mentioned)

8. Marcheshvan (מרחשון; not mentioned)

9. Chislev (כסלו [Neh. 1:1; Zech. 7:1]; Χασελευ [I Macc. 1:54])

10. Tebeth (טבת; Esth. 2:16)

11. Shebat (שבט; [Zech. 1:7]; Σαβάτ [I Macc. 16:14])

12. Adar (אדר [Ezra 6:15; Esth. 3:7, 13; 8:12; 9:1, 15, 17, 19, 21]; Αδαρ [I Esd. 7:5; Add. Esth. 10:13; 13:6; 16:20; I Macc. 7:43, 49; II Macc. 15:36])

Thus seven of these Babylonian names are mentioned in the Bible, but all occur in late books. The five that do not appear are found in the Elephantine Papyri of the late fifth century B.C. All twelve of the names are listed in a tract probably dating from the pre-Christian era, *Megillath Ta'anith*. At first the use of these names was restricted to civil and historical records, but eventually they came to be employed in religious documents as well. Josephus makes frequent mention of them, as do also the Mishna and the Talmud.

**f. Intercalation.** As has been mentioned above, a cycle of twelve lunar months (354¼ days) falls short of the solar year (365¼ days). It is obvious, therefore, that in any lunar-solar calendar there has to be a system of intercalation by which the shortage of more than eleven days can be adjusted. The Babylonians inserted an extra month every two or three years, whenever observation showed it to be needed, and this also became the method used by the Hebrews.

Direct evidence of intercalation in the Bible is scarce, even though we may be quite positive that the Hebrews did employ it. Num. 9:11; II Chr. 30:2-3 seem to imply intercalation, and I Kings 12:32-33 can be best explained as referring to a unilateral act on the part of Jeroboam in decreeing an extra month after the first autumnal equinox of his reign. This is an indication that in early periods intercalation was generally made whenever the authorities thought it to be needed.

There is evidence that originally an extra month, when required, was inserted after Nisan (cf. II Chr.

30:2 ff), but eventually it was Adar, the twelfth month, that was duplicated. Because the spring Passover-Mazzoth festival, beginning the cycle of agricultural feasts, needed to be kept at a set time in the year, it can be understood why the intercalary month came to be inserted after Adar, the last month before the beginning of spring. M. Ned. VIII.5 gives the name of the intercalary month as *WeAdar* ("and-Adar").

In the rabbinical period precise calculation came to be employed to give seven out of every nineteen years an extra month, but this method was rejected by such a sectarian group as the Qaraites, and it long remained the source of numerous disputes.

**4. The religious festivals.** Briefly it must be noted that the entire Hebrew calendar was constructed upon the pattern of the religious feasts, which after the Exile came to assume a fairly rigid form. As observed in the postexilic cultus, the important feasts were: (*a*) the combined Passover and Mazzoth (Unleavened Bread) festivals on 14-21 Nisan; (*b*) the Feast of Weeks or First-fruits seven weeks later, on a Sunday in Sivan; (*c*) the Feast of Trumpets (the ancient New Year's Day) on the first of Tishri; (*d*) the Day of Atonement on the tenth of Tishri; and (*e*) the Feast of Booths (Ingathering) on 15-22 Tishri. (For further details about these and other festival days, *see* FEASTS AND FASTS.) One can hardly overemphasize the importance of the desire to maintain these festivals on a regular schedule throughout the successive years as a constant motive for calendrical study among the pious leaders of the Jews.

**5. Survey of historical development.** The majority of scholars are able to agree on the general characteristics of the calendar in successive periods of Hebrew history, even though data are lacking for a definitive description in all details, and the remote beginnings are especially obscure. Briefly summarized, the calendar's development can be stated as follows:

Although in patriarchal times the Hebrews may have observed a spring new year, it is clear that by the time the monarchy had become established they were beginning both their civil and their religious year at the fall equinox, probably as the result of Canaanite influence. It is likely, however, that a spring new year continued to be used in certain areas and for special purposes (apparently in the N kingdom for counting reigns). The old Canaanite names for the months began to disappear in favor of a system of naming the months by number. Intercalation was still experimental and erratic. We cannot be certain that any other than the Passover-Mazzoth Feast, the Feast of Weeks, and the Feast of Ingathering were in general observance (cf. Exod. 23:14-17).

After the return from Babylonian exile the Hebrews continued to use a solar-lunar calendar, but now the spring new year became more prominent. The months continued to be named by number, but gradually Babylonian names came into general use. The exact methods of astronomical observation developed by the Babylonians, together with their system of mathematical prognostication, enabled the Hebrews to define more exactly a schedule of intercalation, although this knowledge doubtless remained the professional secret of a select group of authorities.

The priesthood meanwhile elaborated in increasing detail prescriptions for observing the religious festivals, many of which came into being during the postexilic era. Postbiblical Judaism worked out many of these features to minute detail, but it also saw many of them fall into disuse and eventual oblivion.

**6. Sectarian calendars.** There is evidence that the authority of the normative calendar was never universally accepted, but that always there were individuals or groups who were promoting their own special calendars. Living in an age of uncertainty, the prophet Ezekiel envisaged a calendar which deviated from the official calendar of the priesthood in setting aside the first day of the first and the seventh months as days of cleansing and atonement (Ezek. 45:18-20 LXX). It seems likely, however, that Ezekiel's calendar, like his temple, was largely visionary and utopian.

A purely solar reckoning is employed in the calendar promoted by the sectarian book of Jubilees (*ca.* 105 B.C.). Throughout this remarkable book, but especially in 6:22-38, and also in I Enoch 72–82 ("The Book of Heavenly Luminaries," *ca.* 110 B.C.), a year of 364 days is prescribed, to be divided into four quarters, each of which contains thirteen weeks and three months of thirty or thirty-one days. It has been argued that this calendar was designed to begin each successive year on Wednesday, the day of the sun's creation, and to keep all the great religious festivals from falling on the sabbath. No provision for intercalating the necessary extra day at the year's end is mentioned in these books, and every arrangement is patently stylized and artificial. It is unlikely that this calendar was ever put into effect by any major segment of the Jewish populace. *See* ENOCH, BOOK OF; JUBILEES, BOOK OF.

There is evidence that the Qumran community who wrote the Dead Sea Scrolls followed the Jubilees calendar or one similar to it. As the study of these documents proceeds, the calendrical ideology of this sect as related to the normative calendar of orthodox Judaism and to other sectarian calendars will become increasingly clear.

**Bibliography.** A. Dillmann, "Ueber das Kalenderwesen der Israeliten vor dem babylonischen Exil," *Monatsberichte der Berliner Akademie* (1882), pp. 915 ff. M. P. Nilsson, *Primitive Time Reckoning* (1920). J. Morgenstern, "The Three Calendars of Ancient Israel," *HUCA*, I (1924), 13-78. S. Langdon, *Babylonian Menologies and the Semitic Calendars* (1933). J. Morgenstern, "Supplementary Studies in the Calendars of Ancient Israel," *HUCA*, X (1935), 1-148; "The Chanukkah Festival and the Calendars of Ancient Israel," *HUCA*, XX (1947), 1-36; XXI (1948), 365-496. E. R. Thiele, *The Mysterious Numbers of the Hebrew Kings* (1951), pp. 29-33. S. H. Horn and L. H. Wood, "Fifth Century Jewish Calendar at Elephantine," *Journal of Near Eastern Studies*, vol. XIII/1 (1954). J. B. Segal, "Intercalation and the Hebrew Calendar," *Vetus Testamentum*, VII (1957), 250-307. J. van Goudoever, *Biblical Calendars* (1959).

On the Gezer Calendar: R. A. S. Macalister, *The Excavation of Gezer* (1912), II, 24-28; III, pl. 127. D. Diringer, *Le iscrizioni antico-ebraiche palestinesi* (1934), pp. 18-20. W. F. Albright, "The Gezer Calendar," *BASOR*, 92 (Dec., 1943), 16-26.

On the pentecontad calendar: J. and H. Lewy, "The Origin of the Week and the Oldest West Asiatic Calendar," *HUCA*, XVII (1942-43), 1-152. J. Morgenstern, "The Calendar of the Book of Jubilees," *Vetus Testamentum*, V (1955), 37-61.

On the Jubilees calendar: The preceding title and A. Jaubert, "Le calendrier des Jubilés et de la secte de Qumran," *Vetus Testamentum,* III (1953), 250-64; "Le calendrier des Jubilés et les jours liturgiques de la semaine," *Vetus Testamentum,* VII (1957), 35-61; *La date de la Cène* (1957).

On the Qumran calendar: Jaubert (above); and J. Obermann, "Calendaric Elements in the Dead Sea Scrolls," *JBL,* LXXV (1956), 285-97. E. Vogt, "Kalenderfragmente aus Qumran," *Bibl.,* XXXIX (1958), 72-77.

On the Jewish calendar: S. Poznanski, "Calendar, Jewish," in J. Hastings, ed., *Encyclopedia of Religion and Ethics* (1913).

S. J. De Vries

**CALF** [בן בקר, *lit.,* a son of the herd, *see* BULL; בן (I Sam. 6:7, 10); עגל (עגול) *in* I Kings 10:19), עגלה; μόσχος, young shoot, *hence* calf; σιτιστός (Matt. 22:4), fattened; *see also* HEIFER]. The calf of a milch cow is referred to in I Sam. 6:7, 10 (cf. Job 21:10); its gamboling in Ps. 29:6 (cf. the "untrained calf" of Jer. 31:18); Mal. 4:2—H 3:20; its grazing in Isa. 27:10; its peaceful co-existence with other tame and wild animals in the future age in Isa. 11:6. Calves typify the Gentile peoples (as distinct from their leaders) in Ps. 68:30—H 68:31, and Egypt's mercenary soldiers in Jer. 46:21. A replica of a calf's head decorated the back of Solomon's throne (I Kings 10:19). In Ezek. 1:7 the feet of the cherubim are likened to those of a calf, and in Rev. 4:7 the second of the four living creatures who surround the heavenly throne is said to be like a calf (RSV "ox").

Calves, sometimes fattened in the stall, supplied veal for special occasions (Gen. 18:7-8; I Sam. 28:24; Luke 15:23, 27, 30). Amos suggests that it was usually the wealthy who enjoyed such a delicacy (Amos 6:4), though in I Sam. 14:32 calves were slaughtered for a large feast after Israel had defeated the Philistines. In Matt. 22:4 "fattened ones" (RSV "fat calves") can refer to calves, lambs, or kids.

The calf is much less frequently referred to as a sacrificial animal than the bull. A year-old calf serves as a burnt offering in Lev. 9:3 (cf. Mic. 6:6), and a calf of no specified age as a sin offering for Aaron in Lev. 9:2, 8 (cf. Heb. 9:12, 19). In a covenant-making rite the Israelites passed between the parts of a slaughtered calf (Jer. 34:18; cf. Gen. 15:9-10).

For the golden (or gold-plated) calves made by Aaron (Exod. 32) and Jeroboam (I Kings 12:28, 32), *see* CALF, GOLDEN.       W. S. McCullough

**\*CALF, GOLDEN** [עגל מסכה (Exod. 32:4), molten calf; עגלי זהב (I Kings 12:28), golden calves]. A representation of a young bull (the translation "calf" is misleading; see Ps. 106:19-20), perhaps made of wood and overlaid with gold, serving either as an image of Yahweh or as his pedestal or throne. Living bulls had a prominent place in the cultic practices of various regions of ancient Egypt. The bull appears in the art and the religious texts of Mesopotamia, Asia Minor, Phoenicia, and Syria. The gods of Syria in particular are frequently represented standing upon a bull.

In the OT, the golden calf appears primarily in connection with the calf made by Aaron in the wilderness period (Exod. 32) and the two calves made by Jeroboam I (*ca.* 922-901), one of which was placed in Bethel and the other in Dan. All references to golden calves in the OT (and in the NT [Acts

7:41]) have in view either the calf of the wilderness or those made by Jeroboam (Deut. 9:16, 21; II Kings 10:29; 17:16; II Chr. 11:15; 13:8; Neh. 9:18; Ps. 106:19). The denunciations of calf-worship by the prophet Hosea are directed against the worship of the bull of Bethel and (possibly) of the city of Samaria (Hos. 8:5-6; 10:5; 13:2).

The account of Aaron's making of the golden calf in Exod. 32 presents complex literary and historical problems. The earliest elements of the tradition are probably to be found in vss. 1-6, 15-16, 19-20, 35. The people, having waited for days for Moses to return from the holy mountain, summon Aaron to make a god who will go before them (the term אלהים sometimes takes a plural verb even when it refers to a god or to God). Aaron accedes to their wishes, but as soon as the bull has been fashioned, the people worship the god or gods represented by the bull in a way which this earliest tradition obviously condemns (vs. 6). Upon Moses' return from the mountain, he breaks the stone tablets, destroys the bull, and causes the people to submit to an ordeal (cf. Num. 5:11-28), and Yahweh then sends a plague upon the people for their sin.

Not even this early form of the tradition is free of difficulty. The connection of the bull with Yahweh

Courtesy of James B. Pritchard

3. Bearded storm-god with a three-pronged thunderbolt in his hand; from Aleppo

is unmistakable: "These are your gods, O Israel, who brought you up out of the land of Egypt!" (vs. 4; note also that Aaron proclaims a feast to Yahweh [vs. 5]). Yet how can one understand the reference to gods? (The demonstrative pronoun as well as the verb is in the plural in the Received Text.)

The difficulty is solved if Exod. 32 is brought into relationship with I Kings 12. In the latter chapter, Jeroboam I (*see* JEROBOAM 1) is reported to have made two golden calves, one of which was placed in BETHEL and the other in DAN. He did so for the specific purpose of preventing the people of Israel from continuing to worship Yahweh in Jerusalem (I Kings 12:26). The entire undertaking of Jeroboam appears to have been motivated by the desire to restore certain ancient and traditional features of Israelite life which had been suppressed under Solomon and Rehoboam: restoration of tribal integrity; concern for the poor and the oppressed; and perhaps the reform of Israelite worship—although this matter is obscured by the polemical attitude of the later tradition against Jeroboam (vss. 28-33; cf. II Kings 10:29, etc.). Jeroboam's effort could hardly have succeeded if the bulls erected at Bethel and Dan had been understood to be images of Yahweh; the effort would have been absurd if Jeroboam had introduced the worship of Hadad-Rimmon, the Syrian deity, in the form of a bull.

If, however, the bulls of Bethel and Dan represented pedestals or thrones upon which the invisible Yahweh was understood to be enthroned, then these bulls had virtually the same meaning as did the ARK OF THE COVENANT. On this hypothesis, the tradition of the golden calf made in the wilderness is illuminated. Just as the ark was most probably a portable throne-seat for the invisible Yahweh, representing his active presence and power particularly in time of battle (Num. 10:35-36), so also the young bull may have been. Exod. 32 would contain, on this view, a rival tradition of those of the ark and of the tent of meeting (*see* TABERNACLE), traditions which were originally associated with particular tribes or tribal groups, perhaps for centuries.

It is clear, however, that the bull was entirely too apt a symbol of fertility long to remain unrelated to Canaanite cult practices and religious understandings. The ark and the tent of meeting had no such associations. It was almost inevitable, therefore, that the bulls of Bethel and Dan should quickly have become marks of the apostasy of Israel to foreign gods (II Kings 10:29; 17:16; etc.; Hos. 8:5-6; 10:5; 13:2). Furthermore, the bull could not long remain as a representative merely of Yahweh's pedestal or throne; it would become identified with Yahweh himself in popular religious understanding.

The incident of the making of the golden calf in the wilderness has developed through tradition into one of the most magnificent depictions of Israelite faith contained in the OT. It relates, in two scenes enacted simultaneously, that Israel was bent upon breaking the covenant stipulations at the very time in which they were being promulgated by Yahweh upon the holy mountain (Exod. 32:1-14). The Levites appear as the zealous defenders of the faith even against son and brother (vss. 26-29). And Moses is portrayed as the intercessor before Yahweh

in behalf of a sinful people, ready to lay down his own life for them (vss. 31-32). Thus around a detested religious symbol, originally perhaps quite harmless, the community of Israel has gathered traditions of fundamental theological significance.* No one "makes" gods. Yahweh is the sovereign Lord, who tolerates no representations of himself or of other gods. No one establishes a priesthood, ordains sacred days and seasons, consecrates an altar (I Kings 12: 31-33). Yahweh himself is the ordainer and upholder of cult; he and he alone decrees where and how and why he is to be worshiped. Fig. CAL 3.

*Bibliography.* H. T. Obbink, "Jahwebilder," *ZAW*, 47 (1929), 264-74; O. Eissfeldt, "Lade und Stierbild," *ZAW*, 58 (1940-41), 190-215; J. B. Pritchard, *ANEP* (1954), pp. 163-64, 170.        W. J. HARRELSON

**CALIGULA** kə lĭg'yə lə. A nickname given the young Gaius Julius Caesar Germanicus, son of Germanicus and great-grandson of AUGUSTUS, who was Roman emperor A.D. 37-41. The name means "little boot" and refers to his upbringing in army camps. Enthusiastically hailed by the Roman people at his accession, when he was only twenty-four years old, he suffered first from a nearly fatal illness and, in mid-38, from the death of his favorite sister and

Courtesy of the American Numismatic Society

4. Emperor Caligula

heir Drusilla, who was deified by the Senate and given the title Panthea. During the next year he discovered the extent to which the Senate had intrigued against Tiberius, and began a series of investigations which led both to executions and ultimately to his own downfall. In September, 39, he went N to direct the field training of the legions in Germany and to prepare for an invasion of Britain, which was prevented either by a change of plans or by mutiny among the troops. By the summer of 40 he had become convinced of his own deity (some Alexandrians had earlier tried to set up statues of him in Jewish synagogues) and gave orders for a statue of himself as Zeus Epiphanios Neos Gaios to be prepared for erection in the temple at Jerusalem. At Rome he ordered a temple built for his own divinity, required oaths to be taken by his Genius, and had courtiers observe the practice of abasement (προσκύνησις). Delays by Roman officials in Syria, and the Emperor's own change of mind, prevented the desecration of the Jewish temple. During the winter of 40-41 a conspiracy was undertaken against him, and he was murdered on January 24. Only the influence of his uncle and successor, CLAUDIUS, prevented the Senate from condemning his memory.

It remains a question whether he was not quite

sane or whether he merely cultivated certain unpleasant traits in his character. Many of his contemporaries preferred to accept the former view. Fig. CAL 4.

*Bibliography.* J. P. V. D. Baldsdon, *The Emperor Gaius (Caligula)* (1931).      R. M. GRANT

**CALITAS.** KJV Apoc. form of KELITA.

**CALKERS.** KJV form of CAULKERS.

**CALL, CALLING** [קרא; καλέω, κλῆσις]. A summons issued by one in authority, especially God, to perform a particular function, or to occupy a particular status (*see* APOSTLE; PROPHET). Since Deutero-Isaiah, the religious concept has become almost synonymous with ELECTION.      G. E. MENDENHALL

**CALLISTHENES** kə lĭs'thə nēz [Καλλισθένης] (II Macc. 8:33). A Syrian who came with the Syrian general NICANOR against the Jewish leader JUDAS MACCABEUS. After the defeat of Nicanor, the Jews burned Callisthenes to death because he had helped set fire to the temple gates.      N. TURNER

\***CALNEH** kăl'nə [כלנה; Akkad. *kullanî, kulnia*]. Alternately: CALNO —nō [כלנו] (Isa. 10:9); CANNEH kăn'ə [כנה] (Ezek. 27:33). A Babylonian city, classed with Erech and Accad in Gen. 10:10 KJV (RSV "all of them," with a different vocalization of the consonantal text; *see bibliography*). So far, the site of Calneh has not been identified. In Amos 6:2, Calneh appears in the sequence Calneh, Hamath, Gath, suggesting that Calneh lies to the N. The discrepancy between the locations reflected in Genesis and Amos may be due to the N city's being a commercial colony named after the mother city in the S. This is substantiated by the mention of Canneh (usually regarded as assimilated from "Calneh," with -*ln*- becoming -*nn*-) between Haran and Eden in Ezek. 27:23. Similarly, Ur the birthplace of Abraham (which can only be located in the N) was a commercial colony named after the mother city of Ur in Babylonia.

The association of Calno (Isa. 10:9) with Carchemish points to the N location.

*Bibliography.* W. F. Albright, *JNES,* III (1944), 254-55.      C. H. GORDON

**CALPHI.** KJV Apoc. form of CHALPHI.

\***CALVARY** kăl'və rĭ [Vulg. *calvaria, translating* κρανίον, skull]. Given in Mark 15:22 as the translation of גלגלתא. *See* GOLGOTHA.

**CAMEL.** The camel has been a means of travel and carrying goods in the Near East for over three thousand years.
1. Terminology
2. Species
3. Date of domestication
4. OT possessors of camels
   *a.* Hebrew patriarchs
   *b.* Arabs and other nomads
   *c.* Israelites
   *d.* Other peoples

5. NT references
6. Uses
   *a.* Travel
   *b.* Bearing burdens
   *c.* Wool
   *d.* Food
7. Equipment and care
8. Characteristics
9. Figurative references
Bibliography

**1. Terminology.** The words translated simply "camel" are גמל (e.g., Gen. 12:16) and κάμηλος (Matt. 3:4; 19:24; 23:24; Mark 1:6; 10:25; Luke 18: 25). בכר (Isa. 60:6) is rendered "young camel" (KJV "dromedary"); the feminine, בכרה (Jer. 2:23), is also "young camel" (KJV "swift dromedary"). A related term is כרכרת (Isa. 66:20; "dromedary"; KJV "swift beast").

In addition, the KJV mistakenly finds "camel" or "dromedary" in the following words: אחשתרנים (Esth. 8:10, 14; RSV "in the king's service"; KJV "camels"); בני הרמכים (Esth. 8:10; RSV "bred from the royal stud"; lit., "offspring of swift mares"; KJV "young dromedaries").

**2. Species.** Most of the biblical references are to the one-humped *Camelus dromedarius,* or Arabian camel. This species has two main types: the slow, burden-bearing camel (e.g., Gen. 37:25), and the swift dromedary (e.g., I Sam. 30:17). The two-humped *Camelus bactrianus,* or Bactrian camel of Central Asia, is doubtless intended in Isa. 21:7 (from Media and Persia), in Tob. 9:2 (in Media), and perhaps in Jth. 2:17 (supposedly from Assyria).\* The Bactrian camel has the longer hair, and the Arabian dromedary is the faster of the two species. *See* FAUNA § A1*c.* Fig. OX 18.

5. A relief from Tiglath-pileser III (744-727 B.C.), showing a woman leading four camels; from Nimrud

**3. Date of domestication.** According to several references in Genesis, the Hebrew patriarchs in the early second millennium B.C. had camels (*see* § 4*a below*), but extrabiblical evidence for their domestication is mostly later. The camel is practically absent from Egyptian art and literature until Ptolemaic times. The first reference to domestic camels in Assyrian records is from the time of Tiglath-pileser I (*ca.* 1100 B.C.). The earliest known undisputed representation of a rider on a camel is from Tell el-Halaf in Mesopotamia in the tenth century B.C. On the other hand, bones of camels have been found in houses at Mari in the eighteenth century B.C. and possibly also in Palestine of the Bronze Age. The evidence seems to indicate that large-scale camel nomadism, as carried on by the Midianites (Judg. 6:5), did not appear before the late second millennium B.C. But for some time before such mass movements, individuals and families must have used camels as recorded in Gen. 24, which has seventeen circumstantial references to them. Some scholars have suggested that instances of camels in the patriarchal narratives are anachronisms. *See bibliography.*

**4. OT possessors of camels.** *a. Hebrew patriarchs.* Abraham is said to have had camels in Egypt (Gen. 12:16), and from Canaan he sent his servant to Paddan-aram with ten camels (24:10). Jacob had camels in Paddan-aram (30:43), and he traveled by camel back to Canaan (31:17) and sent camels as gifts to Esau (32:15—H 32:16).

*b. Arabs and other nomads.* The Ishmaelites who bought Joseph were carrying spices by camel caravan

Ezekiel predicts that Rabbah, the capital of Ammon, will become a pasture for camels (Ezek. 25:5). Job, whose chronology is difficult to fix, is pictured as an Arab sheik who had three thousand camels before his affliction (1:3) and six thousand after his restoration (42:12).

*c. Israelites.* Israelites from different parts of Palestine brought gifts by camel to David in Hebron (I Chr. 12:40). David had camels, but their chief caretaker was an Arab (I Chr. 27:30). The Judeans used camels to carry their gifts to Egypt to secure her support (Isa. 30:6). Sennacherib records that he took many camels from the cities of Judah, and a loaded camel is pictured among the spoils from Lachish in an Assyrian relief. According to the prediction in Isa. 66:20, the exiles employed camels in returning to Jerusalem (Ezra 2:67; Neh. 7:69). The writer of Tobit supposes that Israelite exiles in Media traveled by camel (9:2).

6. Camels and horses carrying soldiers, as Arabs flee from Assyrian forces of Ashurbanipal

to Egypt (Gen. 37:25). The Midianites used many camels in their raids of Israel (Judg. 6:5; cf. the Arab *ghazw*). A prophet (Isa. 60:6) foresees camels of Midian and Ephah bringing gifts to Zion in the messianic age. The Amalekites were associated with the Midianites in the raids of Judg. 6:3, and they used camels in the Negeb in the days of Saul (I Sam. 15:3) and of David (27:8; 30:17). During the reign of Saul the Reubenites captured thirty thousand camels of the Hagarites (Arabs) in Transjordan (I Chr. 5:21). Various other tribes in S Palestine also used camels: the Geshurites, the Girzites (I Sam. 27:8-9), and those near Gerar (II Chr. 14:15). The Queen of Sheba brought her gifts to Solomon by camel (I Kings 10:2). Many camels were included in the herds of the Transjordanian tribes of Kedar and Hazor (Jer. 49: 29, 32). The caravans of Tema (Job 6:19) and of the Dedanites (Isa. 21:13) were presumably of camels.

*d. Other peoples.* Ben-hadad, king of Syria, sent forty camels with gifts to Elisha (II Kings 8:9). In a vision a prophet (Isa. 21:7) sees camel-riding Elamites and Medes attacking Babylon. The writer of Judith imagines that the "Assyrian" army used camels (2:17).* Zech. 14:15 assumes that camels will be used by the enemies of Israel in the end times. Figs. CAM 5-6.

**5. NT references.** John the Baptist (Matt. 3:4; Mark 1:6) wore clothes of CAMEL'S HAIR.

Three gospels (Matt. 19:24; Mark 10:25; Luke 18:25) record Jesus' statement: "It is easier for a camel to go through the eye of a needle than for a rich man to enter the kingdom of God." The camel was the largest animal common in Palestine, and the eye of the NEEDLE was the smallest known opening. So the phrase is a hyperbolic, and therefore memorable, statement of the general truth stated immediately before: "It will be hard for a rich man to enter the kingdom" (Matt. 19:23; cf. Mark 10:23; Luke 18:24). A similar saying is found in the Babylonian Talmud: "Raba [died A.D. 352] said . . . 'A man is not shown (in a dream) a golden palmtree or an elephant passing through the eye of a needle' " (Ber. 55b; cf. B.M. 38b). Also Muhammad said of those who rejected his message: "And they shall not enter Paradise until a camel passes through the eye of a needle" (Koran VII.38, or 40). Such proverbs belie attempts to take the edge off Jesus' statement by substituting for κάμηλος the doubtful Greek word κάμιλος, "rope," in a few late MSS of Matt. 19:24; Luke 18:25.

In another vivid hyperbole Jesus condemns the Pharisees for "straining out a gnat and swallowing a camel" (Matt. 23:24). The reference to the camel and the lack of a sense of relative values here condemned are both illustrated by a saying of Rabbi Eliezer (ca. A.D. 90): "He who kills a louse on the Sabbath, it is as if he killed a camel" (T.B. Shab. 12a).

The NT does not mention what animals the wise men from the East rode (Matt. 2:1), but tradition is probably correct in making their mounts camels.

**6. Uses. a. Travel.** Some of the peaceful journeys by camel recorded in the Bible are: from Canaan to Paddan-aram by Eliezer and the return accompanied by Rebekah (Gen. 24); from Paddan-aram to Canaan by Jacob and his family (Gen. 31:17); from Ecbatana to Rages by Raphael (Tob. 9:2). The camel also was used as a mount in times of war: in the Midianites' attack from Transjordan into W Palestine and return (Judg. 6:5; 7:12; 8:21, 26), in the Amalekites' flight into the Negeb (I Sam. 30:17), and in the attack from Elam and Media against Babylon (Isa. 21:7). A riding camel can cover between sixty and seventy-five miles in a day.

**b. Bearing burdens.** In peacetime camels were used to carry merchandise, especially spices (Gen. 37:25). The desert caravans of Job 6:18-19; Isa. 21:13 probably consisted of camels carrying goods for trade. Gifts were also carried by camel: jewelry and clothes from Abraham to the family of Laban (Gen. 24:53); food from Israelites to David (I Chr. 12:40); spices, gold, and precious stones from the Queen of Sheba to Solomon (I Kings 10:2); products of Damascus from Ben-hadad to Elisha (II Kings 8:9); treasures from Judah to Egypt (Isa. 30:6); gold and frankincense from the Midianites to Zion (Isa. 60:6). In war camels are said to carry supplies for the "Assyrian" army (Jth. 2:17) and to accompany the armies attacking Israel in the end times (Zech. 14:15). A camel can carry from 450 to 550 pounds on good terrain.

**c. Wool.** See CAMEL'S HAIR.

**d. Food.** The Mosaic law forbade the eating of camel's meat (Lev. 11:4; Deut. 14:7), but it is eaten by the Arabs. Camel's milk is also drunk by the Arabs, and some see an indirect reference to this practice in the milch camels which Jacob gave to Esau (Gen. 32:15—H 32:16).

**7. Equipment and care.** The camel's saddle in which Rachel hid the teraphim probably had two bags or baskets, one on each side of the hump (Gen. 31:34). The saddle or pack was held on with a girth (Gen. 24:32). The Midianites decorated their camels with collars around their necks, from which hung crescent-shaped ornaments of gold (Judg. 8:21, 26). The Arabs today use similar decorations on their camels.

Several details about the care of camels are found in Gen. 24: making the camels kneel at the end of the day (vs. 11); watering them (vss. 14, 19-20); providing a place for them to spend the night, perhaps in an open court (vss. 25, 31); unloading them (vs. 32); provision of straw and provender (perhaps beans or barley, as today; vss. 25, 32). Since Arabs are the most experienced in the care of camels, it is natural that David chose an Ishmaelite, Obil, to be over his camels (I Chr. 27:30).

**8. Characteristics.** The large size of the camel gives point to Jesus' references to it (see § 5 above). The hump on which the load is placed is mentioned in Isa. 30:6. The Mosaic law notes that it chews the cud and that it has an undivided hoof (Lev. 11:4; Deut. 14:7). This flat foot of the camel fits it to walk on the sand without sinking. It will be noted that the camel is chiefly used in desert or semidesert areas (see §§ 4, 6a-b, above), for which it is admirably suited because of its ability to eat desert plants and to go for several days (as long as twenty in the winter) without water.

**9. Figurative references.** Israel in her following of foreign gods is compared to a restless she-camel in heat (Jer. 2:23). In Matt. 19:24 the camel is a metaphor for something important which the Pharisees overlook.

*Bibliography.* B. Meissner, *Babylonien und Assyrien*, I (1920), 100, 220, 326, 329, 353-54, 381. A. Erman and H. Ranke, *Aegypten und aegyptisches Leben im Altertum* (1923), p. 586. G. Cauvet, *Le chameau* (2 vols.; 1925-26). F. S. Bodenheimer, *Animal Life in Palestine* (1935), pp. 125-26. G. Dalman, *Arbeit und Sitte*, V (1937), 181-82; VI (1939), 147-60. E. D. Van Beuren, *The Fauna of Ancient Mesopotamia as Represented in Art*, *Analecta Orientalia*, XVIII (1939), 36-37.

W. F. Albright, *From the Stone Age to Christianity* (1940), suggests that the camels in the patriarchal narratives are probably anachronisms (see especially pp. 120, 196, 219; *cf.* § 3 above). It has aroused considerable discussion—e.g.: J. P. Free, "Abraham's Camels," *JNES*, III (1944), 187-93. R. de Vaux, "Les patriarchs hébreux et les découvertes modernes," *RB*, LVI (1949), 7-10. B. S. J. Isserlin, "On Some Possible Early Occurrences of the Camel in Palestine," *PEQ*, LXXXII (1950), 50-53. A. Pohl, "Das Kamel in Mesopotamien," *Orientalia*, XIX (1950), 251-53. R. Walz, "Zum Problem des Zeitpunkts der Domestikation der altweltlichen Cameliden," *ZDMG*, CI (1951), 29-51. A. Pohl, "Nochmals das Kamel in Mesopotamien," *Orientalia*, XXI (1952), 373-74. R. Walz, "Neue Untersuchungen zum Domestikationsproblem der altweltlichen Cameliden," *ZDMG*, CIV (1954), 45-85. R. J. Forbes, *Studies in Ancient Technology*, II (1955), 185-208. A. Parrot, *Syria*, XXXII (1955), 323 (camel bones at Mari).

J. A. THOMPSON

**CAMEL'S HAIR** [τρίχες καμήλου; D reads δέρριν καμήλου, skin of a camel] (Matt. 3:4; Mark 1:6). The material of the outer garment of John the Baptist. A rough cloak, in Arabic *'abâ'*, sometimes of camel's hair, is worn by the Bedouin of the desert today. Such a garment was suited to the austere life and message of John. Jesus contrasts John's dress with the "soft raiment" of courtiers (Matt. 11:8; cf. a similar contrast in Jos. War I.xxiv.3).

A "hairy mantle" (Zech. 13:4) was a sign of the prophetic office. Elijah, the prototype of John, wore a mantle of "haircloth" (II Kings 1:8), possibly of camel's hair, though some refer this description to Elijah's own hair.

**Bibliography.** G. Dalman, *Arbeit und Sitte,* V (1937), 5, 18, 163, 241.                                   J. A. THOMPSON

**CAMEL'S THORN** [ἀσπάλαθος]; KJV ASPALA-THUS ăs păl'ə thəs. A low, thorny shrub (*alhagi maurorum*) which yields a kind of manna; its root, according to Pliny (Nat. Hist. XII.24), was used for making a fragrant ointment. The word occurs in Ecclus. 24:15, and the Latin reading is *balsamum.* The passage says that Wisdom, like cassia and camel's thorn, has blessed Israel with the scent of perfumes.

B. H. THROCKMORTON, JR.

**CAMON.** KJV form of KAMON.

**CAMP** [מחנה ,מחנה ,תחנה; תרה; παρεμβολή]. A temporary protective enclosure for a tribe or army.

The common Hebrew word for "camp," מחנה ("encampment" in Josh. 8:13) derives from חנה, "to bend, curve"; hence it is thought that the Hebrew camp was originally circular in character. Such a circular camp—i.e., tents erected in a protective circle around the cattle—may derive from Israel's seminomadic days, since this form of tribal encampment is still common among Bedouin groups in the Near East. תחנה, found only in II Kings 6:8, is probably a scribal error (by metathesis) for תנחתו, "you shall go down" (instead of תחנתי, "my camp"). טירה is an encampment protected by stone walls. It is once rendered "camp" (Ps. 69:25—H 69:26; KJV "habitation"), once "settlement" (I Chr. 6:54—H 6:39; KJV "castle"), and elsewhere as "encampment" (Gen. 25:16 [KJV "castle"]; Num. 31:10 [KJV "castle"]; Ezek. 25:4 [KJV "palaces"]), with special reference to encampments of nomadic peoples, the Ishmaelites, Midianites, and people of the East. In Num. 24:5, משכנות, "dwellings," is properly rendered "encampments" (KJV "tabernacles"), as the context shows.

Israel is portrayed as a "camp" during its pre-Canaanite days, though a clear picture of its organization does not emerge. At Exod. 33:7, Moses pitched the tent of meeting far outside the camp, but according to the idealized account in Num. 2–4 (cf. especially 2:2) the tribes were to take their stations around the tent of meeting on every side. Furthermore, the Levites according to their families were to encamp in an inner circle about the tabernacle (1: 53). So dominant did this tradition become that the temple is called the "camp of the Levites" in I Chr. 9:18.

The word "camp" usually denotes a military camp outside the Pentateuch. A camp site would be chosen with two factors in mind: the availability of water (Josh. 11:5; Judg. 7:1; I Macc. 9:33), and lines of natural defense such as a hillside (I Sam. 14:4 ff; 17:3; 26:3). A camp pitched to await battle was fortified against attack, but it is doubtful whether anything as elaborate as the Assyrian camps, with their earthen walls, towers, and moats, ever obtained in Palestine. At best, the Palestinian camp may have been protected by a barricade of wagons. (The word מעגל ["encampment"; KJV "trench"] in I Sam. 17:

20; 26:5, 7, may well refer to this. The Hexaplaric recension of the LXX renders מעגל in 17:20 by στρογγύλωσιν, "a rounding," as does Aq. in 26:5, whereas the Lucianic recension has παρεμβολήν, from which the notion of a circular line of defense is taken.

The Greek word παρεμβολή is the regular rendering of מחנה in the LXX. It also occurs in the NT, where it refers to the stationary "barracks" of the Roman army in the Tower of Antonia (Acts 21:34, 37, *et passim*); in Rev. 20:9 the word is used figuratively of the militant Christian church.

J. W. WEVERS

**CAMPHIRE** kăm'fīr. KJV translation of כפר (RSV correctly HENNA). *See* FLORA § A7*d.*

**CANA** kā'nə [Κανά, *probably from* קנה, reed]. A village of Galilee of uncertain location; mentioned in the Bible only in the gospels. The full name was Cana of Galilee (e.g., John 2:1; 21:2), to distinguish it from other places of the same name (cf. Kanah in Josh. 16:8; 19:28; cf. also Jos. Antiq. XV.v.1).

**1. Location.** There is little basis for the identification of the site except etymology and tradition. Only two locations are likely for the Cana of the gospels. The less likely site is Kefr Kenna, even though it has the support of ancient and medieval tradition and both Greek and Roman churches. There is reason to believe that this identification was influenced by the accessibility of the site for pilgrims, for it is only *ca.* four miles from Nazareth and on the road to Capernaum and Bethsaida. The doubling of the middle "n" is difficult to explain if "Kenna" is derived from "Cana."

The more likely site and the one which has the support of most scholars is Khirbet Qana, the ruins of an ancient village *ca.* nine miles N of Nazareth. Various pilgrims, beginning with the twelfth century A.D., reported that they visited this site as the Cana of the gospels. The Arabic name Qana is much closer to the word "Cana" than is Kenna, and in the full form of Qana el-Jelil the Arabic has preserved the equivalent of the full expression "Cana of Galilee." The name, which means "place of reeds" (*see above*), is appropriate, for it overlooks a marshy plain where reeds are still plentiful. The site is at the N edge of the plain called el-Battuf, the ancient Plain of Asochis. This identification is supported by Josephus, who states: "My abode was in a village of Galilee, which is named Cana" (Life XVI). At this time he was apparently in the Plain of Asochis (Life XLI). Further support for this identification may be found in Eusebius as quoted by Jerome, for he places Cana in Asher near Sidon, which could be said of Khirbet Qana but not of Khirbet Kenna (*De Situ et Nom. Loc. Hebr.* 186). The ruins are on the top of a hill and have not been excavated, but there are cisterns and the remains of buildings. Nearby are tombs cut in the rock. It has been reported that sherds and coins of the first century A.D. have been found on the site.

**2. In the gospels.** Cana was the home of Nathanael, one of the Twelve (John 21:2). Although some have claimed that Simon was from Cana, this is not likely. In Matt. 10:4; Mark 3:18, in the KJV and in inferior Greek MSS, this Simon is called "the Canaanite" (ὁ Κανανίτης), but the preferred reading, as found in the RSV and in the better MSS, is "the Cananaean" (ὁ Κανανᾶιος), meaning "the Zealot" (cf. Luke 6:15).

Only two gospel incidents have their setting at Cana. One is the wedding feast at which Jesus turned the water to wine (John 2:1-11). The other is Jesus' being approached by an official from Capernaum who wished to have his son healed (4:46-54).

*Bibliography.* G. Dalman, *Orte und Wege Jesu* (1919), pp. 96-102. F.-M. Abel, *Géographie de la Palestine*, I (1933), 398; II (1938), 175, 412-13. E. G. Kraeling, *Bible Atlas* (1956), pp. 372-73.       D. C. PELLETT

*CANAAN kā'nən [כְּנַעַן; Χαναάν]; KJV NT CHANAAN. **1.** The ancestor of the CANAANITES (Gen. 10:15-19; I Chr. 1:13-16), said in Gen. 9:18; 10:6; I Chr. 1:8 to be the son of Ham and therefore grandson of Noah. However, in Gen. 9:24-27 Canaan himself appears to be the "youngest son" of Noah and the brother of Shem and Japheth. *See* NOAH § 2.

CANAAN

**2.** The country occupied by the CANAANITES in pre-Israelite times, consisting of PALESTINE W of the Jordan and part of Syria, or a limited portion of it, particularly the region along the coast, which was called PHOENICIA (Φοινίκη) by the Greeks.

      A. HALDAR

**CANAANITES** kā'nə nīts [כְּנַעֲנִים; *see* § 1 *below*]; **CANAANITESS** (I Chr. 2:3); **CANAANITISH** (Gen. 46:10). The people occupying Palestine W of the Jordan at the time of the Israelite invasion, and their descendants and successors. The word is also used as an appellative with the meaning of "merchants" (*see* § 1 *below*). For KJV "Canaanite" as a cognomen of one of Jesus' disciples, *see* CANANAEAN.

1. The name
2. The people and the country
3. The Canaanite language
4. History
5. Social structure
6. Literature and religion
Bibliography

**1. The name.** The actual form of the name of Canaan cannot be explained etymologically as a Semitic word. Since the final "n" has been taken to be a Hurrian grammatical element, the name has been considered to be a Hurrian word form (*see* HORITES), and this is perhaps the most plausible explanation.

The earliest document in which the Canaanites are mentioned is an inscription of Amenophis II (fifteenth century B.C.) reporting two campaigns in Asia. The inscription contains a list of war captives from Syria; 550 *maryana*, 640 *kyn'n.w*, are mentioned. The form *kyn'n.w* corresponds to Akkadian *kinaḫni/a, kinnaḫḫu,* which is found in the Amarna Letters. These equations make no difficulties, since the West-Semitic-Egyptian laryngeal ' often corresponds to ḫ in Cuneiform languages. The form *kinaḫḫu* consists of an element *\*kina-* and the Hurrian suffix *-(ḫ)ḫi,* "belonging to." The meaning of *\*kina-* cannot be decided with certainty—it may have the meaning "reed" or "red purple" or something else. Accordingly, "Canaan" may have the meaning "(Land) of Reeds [papyrus?]." Cf. Byblos, the place where the Greeks first were acquainted with papyrus; from the name of the place the Greek word for "book" derives. Red purple was another important product of the region, and in the Nuzi Texts we find *kinaḫḫu* with the meaning "red purple." With these semantic conditions we may compare the Greek name of the country, Φοινίκη, connected with *phoinix,* "red purple."

In the Amenophis II inscription *kyn'n.w* is in all probability a designation of a social or ethnic group, as it would seem closely connected with *maryana,* the Hurrian military aristocracy. If *kyn'n.w* is the designation of a social group, it would most likely be the class of merchants. For this opinion there is evidence in a number of OT passages as well (Isa. 23:8: according to this passage the Canaanites—i.e., the traders—were the aristocracy of Tyre in the days of Isaiah; Ezek. 17:4; Hos. 12:8; Zeph. 1:11; Zech. 11:7, 11, should perhaps be read כְּנַעֲנֵי הַצֹּאן, "sheep merchants"). If, in the fifteenth century and earlier, *kn'ni* was a term denoting the Hurrian merchants, it may have developed into an ethnic term denoting the inhabitants of the Phoenician coast, because the most important part of the population of that region was the class of merchants. If the basic meaning is "merchant," the use of Akkadian *kinaḫḫu* in the sense of "red purple" is easily understood, since the region of the Phoenician coast was particularly known for this commodity. Cf. the use of the name of Byblos as a designation of papyrus, referred to above.

**2. The people and the country.** The genealogies in which the name of Canaan appears are of a certain interest, in spite of the fact that they must not be taken too literally, since they are not based on ethnographical facts but contain allusions to cultural and geographical affinities. In Gen. 9:18; 10:6 Canaan is said to be a son of Ham. This would imply that the Canaanites were believed to be a branch of the Hamitic group. In Gen. 10:15 ff the sons of Canaan are mentioned: Sidon, his first-born, Heth, the Jebusite, the Amorite, the Girgasite, the Hivite, the Arkite, the Sinite, the Arvadite, the Zemarite, and the Hamathite. This list of various subdivisions of the Canaanites seems to reflect a certain geographical order from the S to the N. Of special interest is the association of the Amorites, one of the most important Semitic groups at the beginning of the second millennium, with the Canaanites (*see below; cf.* AMORITES). Another interesting detail is the fact that Ham is said to be the father of Canaan, and Heth a son of Canaan. This clearly indicates that the genealogy is not to be taken as a source for our knowledge of ethnographic relations, for it is not very likely that the Hittites were descendants of the Hamites, even if the Hittites of the OT tradition are not the same people as the Hittites of Asia Minor in the second millennium. When Ham is said to be the father of Canaan, it is a reminiscence of the Egyptian political domination of Canaan, which was exercised as early as during the Old Kingdom. In a similar way the relation maintained between Heth and Canaan may reflect traditions of migrations of the Hittites in the course of the second millennium and at the beginning of the first. The conditions at Ras Shamra at the middle of the second millennium give a good illustration of the mixed character of the population of Canaan during this period. According to Num. 13:29 (cf. Josh. 1:2-4), Hittites lived in the Judean hills. The fact that they came to live in such isolated places may find its explanation in the assumption that they had been pressed back by later migrations. According to the OT itself, the Hittites played an important role in the growth of the Israelitic people (cf., e.g., Ezek. 16:45). So did the Hurrians, from whom even the name of the Canaanites may derive (*see above*). At the time of Amenophis II they were in the country, and probably they had appeared there shortly after 2000 B.C. In any case, the Amarna Letters contain evidence for the opinion that non-Semitic ethnic elements settled in Palestine and Syria at a rather early date, for a number of these letters show a remarkable influence of non-Semitic tongues. As is evident particularly in one list from Ras Shamra, however, the Semites were the main part of the population at the middle of the second millennium, and gradually the Semitic element became still more dominating, and the Canaanites may be regarded as a Semitic people, even if they were never of pure Semitic blood.

In the OT, "Canaan" is used as a designation of the whole of the territory W of Jordan (Gen. 12:5; Num. 33:51), and the Canaanites are accordingly the inhabitants of this territory (cf., e.g., Gen. 12:6; 50:11; Josh. 7:9). But according to other passages (e.g., Num. 13:29; 14:25; Josh. 11:3) the Canaanites are the inhabitants of a limited area at the coast and in the plain. A few times the word is also used of the Phoenicians (Neh. 9:8; Isa. 23:11; Obad. 20; etc.). Accordingly, in the OT the country of Canaan may refer to a limited area, or to a wide area, which includes the whole of the district W of Jordan. In modern scholarly literature, "Canaan" is used as a designation of the whole area of Palestine W of Jordan and Syria, and the Canaanites are accordingly the inhabitants of this territory in pre-Israelitic times. It has been suggested that the Canaanites and the Amorites may be regarded as in reality identical (*cf.* AMORITES; *cf. also* § 3 *below*).

**3. The Canaanite language.** The Canaanite language belongs to the NW group of the Semitic languages. Since, however, Canaanitic was spoken in a vast area, local varieties and dialects must be assumed and can also be proved. Also the linguistic development of Canaanitic during the time from which the earliest Canaanite texts derive and up to the time when, e.g., the language of the OT obtained its final linguistic form, resulted in significant linguistic differences between various branches of the Canaanite language. In spite of this, the Canaanite language is rather homogeneous, and through a number of criteria it can be distinguished from other Semitic tongues. The question of the relation between Canaanitic and Amoritic has been of great importance, particularly after the Ugaritic language became known. Some scholars have contrasted these two languages, and as for Ugaritic put the question whether it is a Canaanite or an Amorite dialect. When dealing with such questions, it may be of importance to remember that "Amorite" is a term deriving from Akkadian. From the horizon of Mesopotamia all the territory W of its borders was called *Amurru,* "the western country." Hence Amoritic cannot be assumed to have been a homogeneous language, and because of this what we call Canaanite may be part of what the ancient Babylonians called Amorite. The theory has also been ousted that Canaanite and Amorite once were one and the same language.

Like all other Semitic tongues, Canaanite shows the distinguishing triconsonantism in the majority of the words, but a number of biconsonantal and quadriliteral roots exist. As is the case in other Semitic languages, the consonants are responsible for the basic meaning of the root, and through the vowels the meaning is modified. Because of this, the systems of writing in several Semitic languages are in the main consonantal; thus also in early Canaanite. The nouns were in the early periods inflected with case endings (cf. Akkadian and Arabic), and the case vowel was followed by the mimmation (cf. Akkadian). When the noun appeared before a genitive, the case elements were dropped. Later the case inflection was given up (cf. Akkadian). The tenses of the verb are the so-called perfect and the imperfect. The perfect shows conditions very similar to the corresponding form of the Akkadian verb, the so-called permansive, with regard to its formation, inflection, and syntax. The imperfect was used to describe actions in the present or future but was also used about actions in the past, in the sense of a preterit. Or, according to another opinion, there were two forms, corresponding to the Akkadian preterit and present-future respectively, of which the former was used to describe a completed action and the latter an action not completed.

A feature typical of Canaanite dialects was the occurrence of an initial "y" in all word stems which have an initial "w" in Akkadian and Arabic, an important criterion which distinguishes the Northwest Semitic from all other Semitic languages. Accordingly, Canaanite, Amorite, Hebrew, and Aramaic have this and other features in common. Other linguistic details, such as the definite article *ha-*, the mergence of certain sounds—e.g., the laryngeals *ḥ* and *ḫ*, etc.—appear relatively late. The fact that they do not appear in early dialects (Ugaritic) is, of course, no argument for separating them from dialects which show a number of later features (e.g., Hebrew).

Before 2000 B.C. a Canaanite script was in use containing about eighty characters. This early script was to some extent related to the Egyptian hieroglyphic system. A number of inscriptions on stone and copper have been found at Byblos. At Ras Shamra another Canaanite system of writing was used which derives from the Cuneiform writing. The alphabet which was used by the Phoenicians is a third Canaanite system of writing.

**4. History.** The countries of Syria and Palestine were inhabited since Paleolithic times. The Stone Age civilization discovered by A. Rust in caves in the vicinity of Negeb N of Damascus may be mentioned as one instance. Since several layers were found in the caves, that civilization was probably of a rather long duration. From the Mesolithic period, the Natufians of Mount Carmel discovered by Miss Garrod may be mentioned. Finally, the Chalcolithic men of Byblos found by Dunand are important evidence of early inhabitants in the region. The anthropological and linguistic types of these early men will, of course, never be known. But Semites undoubtedly settled in the region at an early date, and as early as 3000 B.C. a Semitic-speaking population most likely lived there. This may be concluded from the existence of towns with Semitic names, perhaps of a linguistic type related to Canaanite. One of the most ancient towns is Jericho; others are Beth-shean and Megiddo; at the coast in S Canaan, Byblos; and in the N, Ugarit. On the other hand, there are also place names of a non-Semitic type.

The period of Canaanite history which is best known is the Bronze Age. Through a number of excavations archaeological material has come to light through which the material culture of the Canaanites has become known. During the period of the Old Kingdom (2600-2200 B.C.), the Egyptians exercised political dominance in Palestine and Syria, and during the Fifth and Sixth Dynasties they undertook military invasions into the territory. During the Twelfth Dynasty (1990-1790 B.C.) the Egyptians dominated Palestine and part of Syria, as is evident from the finds at Byblos, Ras Shamra, and Qatna in Syria and a number of discoveries in Palestine, of which those at Megiddo may be the most important. Of Egyptian documents the so-called Execration Texts are important for this period. After the decline of the Egyptian power at the beginning of the eighteenth century, the Canaanites got free from the Egyptian domination. At the end of the nineteenth century, the Egyptian civilization was imitated, at least at Byblos, but this probably has regard only to the material culture.

A strong influence came also from the East, particularly during the centuries from *ca.* 2000 B.C. During these centuries there were intimate connections between the region in the W and Mesopotamia. The Amorites from the region of Mari invaded Mesopotamia and created local kingdoms, of which the first Babylonian dynasty was the most important. The Mari Letters make it possible for us to see how people came from the E to the region of Mari and continued down into Palestine (*see* HABIRU). Through these contacts an exchange of cultural elements took place, but, as, e.g., the texts from Ras Shamra show, the Canaanites tried to develop an independent culture. A homogeneous Canaanite civilization, however, could never be created, because the whole area of the Canaanites was divided in a number of local kingdoms with traditions of their own. Furthermore, new ethnic movements in the course of the second millennium gave new impulses.

The most important events are the Hyksos invasion into Egypt and the entering of the Hurrians and the Hittites into the domain of the Canaanites. The Hyksos were to some extent Semites, as appears from the Hyksos names which are known, such as 'Anat-har, Ya'qob-har, Abd Nahmān. These are Semitic like many others, whereas there are also non-Semitic names. Accordingly, there were several ethnic elements among the Hyksos. The cultural influence of the Hittites was strong, particularly in the N part of Syria. Because of all these complications Canaanite culture shows a rather heterogeneous character, and only in the region which is usually called Phoenicia—i.e., the region at the coast—did the civilization have a more unmixed structure. There was probably the real center of Canaanite civilization, whereas in the E part of Syria, Mesopotamian influence was stronger. As examples illustrating this, Mari and the region of Damascus may be mentioned, where the Amorites adopted many cultural elements from Babylonia. This holds true particularly with regard to the so-called Old Babylonian period, but as late as in the ninth century we know that Assyrian cults were practiced in Syria (e.g., Hama), and presumably this was the case also later. Even in the Damascene a strong Babylonian influence prevailed during the Old Babylonian period with regard to glyptic (e.g., cylinder seals), while the Amorites seem to have been more independent in the field of ceramics, as appears from finds of pottery in several places in that region, probably of an Amorite type (*see* AMORITES). But there are examples of art which might have developed into an independent Canaanite type if the development had not been broken by foreign influence—e.g., a picture of Jarimlim, king of Jamhad, contemporary of Hammurabi of Babylon; figurines of bronze; cylinder seals; etc.

After the expulsion of the Hyksos (sixteenth century), the Egyptians dominated politically. The text quoted above from the reign of Amenophis II (fifteenth century), listing war captives, is a witness of the military expansion of the Egyptians during this period. Later the power of the Egyptians declined, and the Amarna Letters inform us about the conditions prevailing during the first half of the fourteenth century. We see that the king of Byblos was almost the last ruler who co-operated with the Egyptians. He cries for help from the Pharaoh, but the latter is unable to support him. During this period a number of local kingdoms existed in Palestine and Syria fighting against one another. From that time on, the Israelite nation took its birth, and so the Canaanites merged with the Israelites, who became the political and cultural heirs of the Canaanites. Another branch were the Phoenicians, who for a short period played an important role as merchants and seafarers and extended their commerce in North Africa, where they founded a number of colonies, and as far westward as to S France.

**5. Social structure.** Canaanite social structure was, in the main, of the same type as that prevailing in the other Near Eastern countries. Three social groups existed: freemen, clients, and slaves. A great part of the slaves were war captives and foreign slaves, but most were natives—e.g., defaulting debtors and unemployed men and women, who sold themselves into slavery to obtain their livelihood; furthermore, children were often sold by their parents or exposed, and then they could sustain themselves only by slavery. The position of the slaves was of various character: there were state slaves, temple slaves, slaves working as farmers but without possessing their own land, and finally, a number of unfree men who worked in crafts. The clients were a class only half free.

Canaanite society and economy were based on agriculture. Part of the land was in the possession of the state and the temples, but there were also a number of private landlords. Also the tenant farmers, the *ḫupši*, possessed small pieces of land. King Rib-Addi of Byblos mentions that they, because of circumstances, were forced to sell the "wood of their houses, and their sons and daughters in order to procure food for themselves" (see the letters of Rib-Addi from Tell el-Amarna). The farmers were apparently a class of industrious people, and their work was the real basis of the economy and the prosperity of the nation. Generally the property of the farmer was not very large, and his household was, as a rule, the main help in his work. On the other hand, the tenants of land worked as dispossessed farmers under the owners of the large estates, to whom a great part of the land belonged. The top of the agricultural organization was the king, who possessed a large property. The royal lands were divided up among his subordinate supervisors, who in their turn leased pieces of land to free tenant farmers. Likewise the temples possessed large properties. This meant that an important part of the temple staff was responsible for their managing.

For long periods, ancient Near Eastern society was organized according to the principles of the feudal system. The king was the head of the society. He was the owner of the largest properties; he was the head of the military organization and of the religious organization; and he was likewise the most important industrialist and merchant. But under him there were guilds, the members of which took care of the special duties—guilds of priests, of warriors, of merchants, of craftsmen, etc.

The social conditions prevailing in the Canaanite feudal or semifeudal society are reflected in texts from Alalakh and from Ugarit, dating from the eighteenth to the thirteenth century B.C. To judge from certain texts, a great influence, deriving from Hurrian social conditions, can be observed in certain areas. The class of professional warriors was, e.g., called *maryannu*. The *maryannus* possessed a high position in society. Only the king could grant this rank, which was hereditary. The *maryannus* had superior military equipment, particularly their horse-drawn chariots. In texts from Alalakh and Ugarit cases of the king's granting this rank to citizens is mentioned. In return a *maryannu* had a special obligation to the king, and for the services he rendered the king he received areas of land. From these lands he derived the means of obtaining and maintaining his war equipment.

Akkadian documents from Ugarit throw light on the management of the royal lands and the revenues from them. Pieces of royal land were granted to members of the royal family, to state officials, and to other persons. For such grants of land, the receiver had to do services or pay taxes to the king, and he was often called the servant of the king. Such royal lands were fields, vineyards, orchards, and olive yards, including movable property, such as sheep, oxen, asses, and slaves.

For the expenses of the government, taxes were imposed on the citizens, and several kinds of taxes are mentioned in the texts from Ras Shamra. Also toll and fines are referred to in these texts. The king, furthermore, made people subject to labor for his constructions—e.g., of roads, of fortresses, of temples, and for work on royal lands. This semifeudal system prevailed in Palestine and Syria during the second millennium, as in other parts of the Near East. Also in the OT, where in so many ways we may observe reflections of the ancient Canaanite civilization, reference may be found to feudalism. As has been pointed out by an American scholar, this is undoubtedly the case in I Sam. 8:4-17.

**6. Literature and religion.** Until two or three decades ago, Canaanite literature and religion were almost unknown but for the scanty knowledge about them which may have been derived from late sources. But thanks to French excavations, directed by Claude Schaeffer, at Ras Shamra, ancient Ugarit, situated on the coast of N Syria, very important material has been discovered. The excavations at Byblos, directed by Maurice Dunand, are also of very great significance, but the finds of texts there have not been so rich. The excavations at Ras Shamra started in 1929 and were continued until the Second World War put a stop to them. Since that war they have been taken up again. Through the discoveries at Ras Shamra, a great part of the ancient Canaanite literature has been found, and through them we have for the first time obtained contemporary documents for our knowledge of Canaanite religion in the second millennium B.C. The texts, which date from the early fourteenth century, are written on clay tablets with a script invented by the Canaanites on the basis of the Cuneiform system of writing. The alphabet of Ras Shamra is an almost consistent consonantal system of writing. Only one letter, *alef,* appears in three forms, one for each of the three vowels "a," "i," and "u," the only survival of the syllabic system of Cuneiform. On these texts see UGARIT. Fig. UGA 3.

The question of the Ugaritic parallels to the Bible is a subject which has given rise to an enormous literature. Here only a few hints of some main points can be given. The chief deity of the Ugaritic pantheon is 'Il. He is a sky god. He is father of the other gods and is the supreme lord over the gods and ruler over the assembly of the gods on the mountain in the N—i.e., Mount Cassius. Baal is another important deity, previously well known from the OT. His wife was Anat. Roughly these two deities may be compared with the two Mesopotamian deities Tammuz and Ishtar. Like the latter, Baal and Anat are vegetation deities. The annual cycle of vegetation, its vanishing and its renaissance, is dramatically expounded in the cult of Baal and Anat, particularly in connection with the great New Year Festival. The texts for our knowledge of all this are included in the Baal and Anat cycle, which is found in an excellent English translation in C. H. Gordon, Ugaritic literature (1949), pp. 11 ff. Undoubtedly, Baal is a dying and reviving deity, and through the cult which is performed for him, life and prosperity are granted to his worshipers through the king, who represents Baal in the cult performances.

*Bibliography.* Since the literature on the Canaanites is very extensive, only a few of the most important works and special articles will be listed. There further references will easily be found. F. Böhl, *Die Sprache der Amarnabriefe mit besonderer Berücksichtigung der Kanaanismen,* LSS, V (1909), 2; "Kanaanäer und Hebräer," *BWAT,* vol. IX (1911). S. H. Hooke, *Myth and Ritual* (1933); *The Origins of Early Semitic Ritual* (1938). Z. S. Harris, *Development of the Canaanite Dialects* (1939). W. F. Albright, "New Light on the Early History of Phoenician Colonization," *BASOR,* no. 83 (1941); *The Rôle of the Canaanites in the History of Civilization,* Studies in the History of Culture (1942). M. Noth, "Die syrisch-palästinische Bevölkerung des zweiten Jahrtausends v. Chr. im Lichte neuer Quellen," *ZDPV,* vol. 65 (1942). B. Maisler, "Canaan and the Canaanites," *BASOR,* no. 102 (1946). I. Mendelsohn, *Slavery in the Ancient Near East* (1949). O. Eissfeldt, *El im ugaritischen Pantheon* (1951). W. von Soden, Bibliography on Mari, *Die Welt des Orients,* vol. I (1947-52). J. B. Pritchard, ed., *ANET* (2nd ed., 1955). I. Mendelsohn, "Samuel's Denunciation of Kingship in the Light of the Akkadian Documents from Ugarit," *BASOR,* no. 143 (1956).

A. HALDAR

**CANALS** [אֹרִים, *ye'ōrîm,* the Nile, *or* the Nile arms, Nile canals; *plural of* יאֹר, the Nile] (Exod. 7:19; 8: 5—H 8:1; Isa. 19:6); KJV RIVERS. A word referring to the Delta arms of the NILE and the network of connecting waterways in the Delta of Egypt.

T. O. LAMBDIN

**CANANAEAN** kā'nə nē'ən [κανανaîoς, *from* Aram. קַנְאָנָא, jealous one, zealot, *from* Heb. *root* קנא] (Matt. 10:4; Mark 3:18). A cognomen for a certain Simon, a disciple of Jesus, to distinguish him from Simon Peter. The ending -aîoς probably denotes a party (cf. Φαρισαîoς, "Pharisee"; Σαδδουκαîoς, "Sadducee"; Ἐσσαîoς, "Essene").

In Luke 6:15; Acts 1:13 the same disciple has the name Simon the Zealot, the Greek ζηλωτής being the equivalent of the Semitic original. See ZEALOT.

W. R. FARMER

**CANDACE** kăn'də sĭ [Κανδάκη] (Acts 8:27). A queen of ETHIOPIA. PHILIP (7) baptized her treasurer. "Candace" was a title (roughly, "queen"; exact meaning uncertain), not a personal name. It was used by a number of queens of the Ethiopian kingdom of Meroe, on the Nile in modern Sudan. The Candace of Acts 8:27 (not long after A.D. 30) cannot be certainly identified with any queen known elsewhere, though the title, apparently applied to the reigning queen-mother, was well known to ancient historians, and was used by queens at the times of Augustus (*ca.* 25 B.C.) and Nero (*ca.* A.D. 61).

*Bibliography.* Strabo *Geography* XVII.1.54; Cassius Dio *Roman History* LIV.5.4-5; Pliny Nat. Hist. VI.35.186; J. G. C. Anderson, in *Cambridge Ancient History,* X (1934), 242, n. 1; H. J. Cadbury, *The Book of Acts in History* (1955), pp. 15-18.

W. A. BEARDSLEE

**CANDLE.** KJV translation of נִיר; λύχνος. Candles were not used in biblical times. See LAMP; MENORAH.

**CANE** [קָנֶה, *qānê*]. An aromatic REED (apparently imported from India) from which a sweet-smelling substance or oil was extracted. See FLORA § A7e; SWEET CANE.

**CANKER.** KJV translation of γάγγραινα (RSV GANGRENE) in II Tim. 2:17 and of the verb κατιόω (RSV RUST) in Jas. 5:3.

**CANKERWORM.** KJV translation of ילק in Joel 1:4 (RSV HOPPING LOCUST); 2:25 (RSV HOPPER); Nah. 3:15-16 (RSV LOCUST). See FAUNA § E2.

*CANNEH. An alternate form of CALNEH.

*CANON OF THE OT. The great religions of the world have collections of writings which the faithful consider to be God's word and therefore to contain for all future time the ultimate standard of faith and practice. This is particularly true of Judaism, Christianity, and Islam; but Confucianism, Taoism, Buddhism, Hinduism, Zoroastrianism, have also bodies of sacred writings—whether or not inspired in the opinion of the believers—which carry the highest religious authority. Such a collection of books constitutes a "canon." But no book was ever regarded as God's Word before 621 B.C. (II Kings 22–23).

The Greek word "canon" (κανών) is derived from a Semitic root (Assyrian *qanû,* Ugaritic *qn,* Hebrew קנה, etc.) which is a loan word from Sumerian (GI, GI-NA) and originally meant "reed" (I Kings 14:15; Job 40:21; etc.). The word passed into Greek (κάννα) and Latin (*canna;* cf. English "cane") and gave rise in various languages to words literally meaning something made of reeds or straight like reeds ("cannon"), or figuratively something firm and direct like a reed (English "canon"). In Greek, e.g., "canon" means the stave of a shield, a weaver's rod, a ruler for drawing or measuring, a curtain rod, a bedpost (Jth. 13:6); and metaphorically a rule, a standard, a model, a paradigm, a chronological table, a boundary, a tax assessment, a tariff. The Greek and Latin church fathers used "canon" for the biblical law, an ideal man, articles of faith, doctrines of the church, contributions to the church, a catalogue, a table of contents, a list of clergymen or of saints ("canonized"). In the NT, "canon" means "rule," "standard" (Phil. 3:16—textus receptus; Gal. 6:16), "limit" (II Cor. 10:13, 15-16). Origen (died 254) may have used "canon" in the sense of the list of the divinely inspired books, although Athanasius (died 373) is the first of the church fathers known to have done so.

Before Origen the OT and its parts were called ἡ γραφή, "the scripture" (John 2:22; Acts 8:32; II Tim. 3:16; etc.); αἱ γραφαὶ, "the scriptures" (Mark 12:24; I Cor. 15:3-4; etc.); αἱ ἱεραὶ γραφαὶ, "the holy scriptures" (Philo *On Flight and Finding* 1.4 [546]; *On the Special Laws* 39, § 214 [243]; I Clem. 45.2; 53.1); ἅγιαι γραφαὶ, "holy scriptures" (Rom. 1:2); τὰ γράμματα, "writings" (John 5:47); τὰ ἱερὰ γράμματα, "the sacred scriptures" (II Tim. 3:15; Philo *Life of Moses* 2.51, §§ 290, 292 [179]; Jos. Antiq. I.iii.13; X.iv.210; etc.); τὸ βίβλιον, "the book" (Gal. 3:10; Luke 4:17; etc.); ἡ βίβλος, "the book" (Mark 12:26; Luke 3:4; 20:42; Acts 7:42; etc.); αἱ ἱεραὶ βίβλιοι, "the sacred books" (I Clem. 43.1); כתבי הקדש, "the holy scriptures" (M. Yadaim 3.2, 5; 4.6; Shab. 16.1; 'Er. 10.3; etc.). Later the Jews called their Bible מקרא, "what is read" (cf. Koran); הכתוב, "what is written"; הספר, "the book"; עשרים וערב ספרים, "twenty-four books."·

The OT was, and remained, the official collection of the holy scriptures of the Jews before becoming the first half of the Christian Bible. We must place ourselves several centuries before the rise of Christianity in order to understand how this collection began, grew, and was preserved; and we must deal with the Hebrew Bible rather than with the OT. This distinction is essential, although the contents are identical (except for the addition of the Apoc. in Roman Catholic Bibles), because the arrangement of the books in Jewish and Christian Bibles is quite different.

The Hebrew Bible counts twenty-four books and arranges them in three divisions: the Law, the Prophets, and the Writings (*see* § 8 *below*).

Christian Bibles, following the topical arrangement of the Greek and Latin Bibles, arrange the thirty-nine books (counting each of Samuel, Kings, Chronicles, and Ezra-Nehemiah as two books, and the minor prophets as twelve books) as follows:

a) The Pentateuch: Genesis, Exodus, Leviticus, Numbers, Deuteronomy

b) Historical books: Joshua, Judges, Ruth, I–II Samuel, I–II Kings, I–II Chronicles, Ezra, Nehemiah, Esther

c) Poetical books: Job, Psalms, Proverbs, Ecclesiastes, Song of Solomon

d) Prophetical books: Isaiah, Jeremiah, Lamentations, Ezekiel, Daniel, Hosea, Joel, Amos, Obadiah, Jonah, Micah, Nahum, Habakkuk, Zephaniah, Haggai, Zechariah, Malachi

The translators of the Hebrew Bible into Greek, working at Alexandria during the last two and a half centuries before Christ, did not know the reasons for the threefold division of the Hebrew Bible. Since they were trained in the Greek schools of rhetoric, they rearranged the books in a clear topical and chronological manner. They therefore ignored completely the boundary between the second and the

third divisions of the Hebrew canon. But this older arrangement, exhibiting clearly the three basic stages in the canonization of the Hebrew Bible, is basic for our study. It is first recorded in the Prologue to the Greek translation of Ecclesiasticus: "The law and the prophets and the other books of our fathers." When this was written in 132 B.C., the third division was not yet fixed for all time. There is here a true recollection of the gradual canonization of the OT. We must clearly distinguish the gradual process of canonization (which lasted almost five centuries) and the doctrine of canonicity which, regarding God as the real author of the books which he dictated to inspired writers, regards the chronological sequence as immaterial. Canonization, by stressing historical facts, does not exclude canonicity, which stresses divine written revelation.

The main part of this article will deal with the history of the canonization (§§ 1-8), and the final part with canonicity (§ 9).

1. Precanonical Hebrew literature
2. The canonization of the Law
3. The canonization of the Prophets
4. The canonization of the Writings
5. The Alexandrian Jewish canon
6. The Christian canon
7. The closing of the Jewish canon
8. The arrangement of the OT books
9. Canonicity
    *a.* Jewish doctrines
    *b.* The NT
    *c.* The Koran
    *d.* Roman Catholic doctrines
    *e.* Protestant doctrines
Bibliography

**1. Precanonical Hebrew literature.** Every sentence in the OT was profane literature before it became canonical sacred scripture. The only Hebrew author that expected his book to be canonized was Sirach (Ecclus. 24:32-33), and his writings failed to be canonized in the Hebrew Bible—although they were included in the Greek and Latin Bibles. Before the canonization of a book in 621 B.C., Israel possessed already a great national literature, including the early stories of Adam and the patriarchs, of Moses, of the judges; the early editions of the books of Amos, Hosea, Isaiah, Micah; the lives of Saul and David; some ancient poems and laws; accounts of kings of Judah and Israel; and other writings. Some of these ancient writings are literary masterpieces, but none of their authors expected to have his book canonized as scripture, any more than Homer, Vergil, Dante, and Milton expected to have their works either canonized for their religious teaching or declared "classic" for their literary greatness; on the contrary, Horace dreaded the thought that his books might become (as they did soon; see Juvenal *Satires* VII.226 ff) a textbook for the schools (Epistles I.20), although he regarded his verses as inspired by Apollo (*Odes* IV.vi.29 ff).

A sharp distinction was made between prophets' spoken words, which could be divinely inspired (Amos 3:8; Isa. 6:9-10; Jer. 1:7, 9), and their written words, which for centuries were not regarded as canonical even though they had been inspired (Deut.

18:18) when delivered orally—the words that God had spoken to Jeremiah (Jer. 36:2-4) were not considered canonical, when written in a book, for four centuries.

From time to time some parts of the existing literature were collected in bodies of canonical literature. It is only an accident in transmission that only this canonical literature (except for those apocrypha which had been written in Hebrew) has come down to us. This is only a small portion of the Hebrew literature which is mentioned in the Bible: the history of the kings of Israel, the history of the kings of Judah (I Kings 14:19, 29, etc.), and poetic anthologies (Josh. 10:13; II Sam. 1:18; Num. 21:14). Many other compositions have been lost without being mentioned, as happened in all ancient literatures. Some unknown Hebrew and Aramaic writings dating from the years about the beginning of our era have been discovered in caves near the Dead Sea.

We must therefore distinguish three stages in the process through which the writings contained in the OT have come down to us—the labors of the original authors (Jer. 36:4); the editing, arranging, and collecting of these writings; and their final canonization. The actual writing of parts of the OT took place from *ca.* 1150 (the Song of Deborah, Judg. 5) or a little earlier (some poems and laws), to *ca.* 125 (the book of Esther) or a little later (Ps. 2 seems to have been written on the accession and marriage of Alexander Jannaeus in 104 B.C.).

The span of a millennium, during which the OT was written, may be compared to the span from Beowulf to Tennyson in English literature, and from Homer to the NT in Greek literature. Even though the changes in culture and religion may not have been as radical in Israel as they were in England and in Greece, there is a world of difference between Deborah and Esther. In 1200 B.C. the Israelites were a group of tribes from the desert who were invading Canaan. After the wars of the judges, David established a short-lived empire, and eventually N Israel was absorbed by the Assyrian Empire and Judah by the Neo-Babylonian. The Judeans passed under the Persian and Hellenistic rule before attaining independence under the Hasmoneans from 141 to 63 B.C., when Roman rule began.

The literature and the religion of the OT reflect these political vicissitudes. The golden period corresponds to the years in which Israel conquered Canaan and was independent (1200-586). The silver age corresponds to the Judean subjection to the Babylonians (586-538), to the Persians (538-332), to Alexander and the Ptolemies (332-198), and to the Seleucids (198-142).

Out of a vast body of national Hebrew literature the books of the OT were selected because of their literary beauty or their nationalistic appeal, because they contributed to keep alive the nation and the worship of Jehovah. The men responsible for collecting and canonizing the Law, the Prophets, and the Writings were convinced that every word in them was divinely inspired by God. In reality, of course, only the prophets (including Moses, according to Deut. 18:18; cf. Hos. 12:13—H 12:14; Num. 11:24-30), in moments of ecstatic trance, experienced divine inspiration, feeling themselves filled by the divine spirit and uttering God's words; in normal condi-

tions, if they were sincere, they could not utter divine oracles (Jer. 28:10-14). The whole OT was regarded as scripture because it was supposed to have been written by prophets. We may therefore seriously question the assertion of Otto Eissfeldt that "in Israel there are . . . six kinds of words that are regarded as God's words"—namely, the judgment of a lawgiver or of a judge, the word of command or prohibition of a man announcing God's will, the instruction of a priest, the oracle of a prophet, the song of a singer, and the proverb of a wise man. Only the oracle of the prophet (and occasionally the response of a priest) were truly inspired when uttered. The other utterances were those of experts, and not of inspired men; they found their place in the Scriptures because their authors were regarded as inspired prophets.

The earliest literature of the Israelites, dating from the time of Moses or earlier, consists of poems (Gen. 4:23-24; Exod. 15:21; Num. 21:17-18) and of laws of the desert (Exod. 21:12, 15-17; 22:19; Lev. 20:10-13) or of Canaan (the Covenant Code: Exod. 21:2-11, 18-22; 21:26–22:17; and the ritual decalogue: Exod. 23:12, 15-17; 22:29-30, 18-19).

Between Moses and Solomon the Song of Deborah (Judg. 5) and other poems, such as David's two elegies (II Sam. 1:18-27; 3:33-34), were composed; and the stories of Adam, the patriarchs, and the judges were circulating orally. Prose writing at its best began in the time of Solomon (*ca.* 975-935 B.C.) and reached from fiction (the stories about Samson in Judg. 13-16) to brilliant historical writing (the biography of David, written probably by Ahimaaz son of Zadok). The best poems from this time are Gen. 49; Ps. 24:7-10. The best literature of the Northern Kingdom (935-722) is scantily preserved in some poems (Num. 23:7-10, 18-24; Deut. 33; Ps. 45), in remnants of the History of the Kings of Israel, in the stories of Elijah and Elisha, in the E Document of the Pentateuch, in the late source of Joshua and Judges, and in the prophetic oracles of Hosea. At the time, with the exception of the J Document and some superb prophetic oracles (Amos, Isaiah, Micah), the literature of the Southern Kingdom was not equally brilliant. The classical period came to an end in Judah with the fall of Jerusalem in 586 B.C., but it still includes a poetic masterpiece (Nah. 1: 10 ff) and the earliest and wittiest part of Proverbs (chs. 25-27).

After Jeremiah, prophecy began to decline (Zephaniah, Habakkuk), but inspired the Book of the Law (Deut. 5-26; 28), found in the temple in 621 B.C. The parts of the Pentateuch and of the historical books written at this time are likewise inferior to the earlier prose.

With the exception of Job and the Second Isaiah (Isa. 40-55), the sixth century lacks outstanding works: some psalms, proverbs, and the book of Lamentations illustrate the prolix and pretentious poetry of the times; Ezekiel, Haggai, and Zechariah illustrate the decline of prophecy; the Holiness Code (Lev. 17-26) illustrates the law of this period.

The two following centuries lack literary masterpieces—the best prose is found in Nehemiah, Ruth, and Jonah; the Priestly Code (*ca.* 450) and the final edition of the Pentateuch (*ca.* 400) were epoch-making, and proved fatal to prophecy (Isa. 56–66; Obadiah; Malachi; Joel; and additions to the prophetic books), which at the end of this period became apocalypse. The poetry (Deut. 32; Exod. 15:1-8; Nah. 1: 1-9; Hab. 3; I Sam. 2:1-10; many psalms and proverbs) is more and more elaborate and pompous.

In the third and second centuries the best poetry is in the Song of Solomon, Ecclesiasticus, Ecclesiastes, and late psalms; the best prose is in Chronicles and Esther; Daniel is the outstanding apocalypse (besides Isa. 24–27; Zech. 9–14); the final edition of the prophetic books (Isaiah, Jeremiah, Ezekiel, and the minor prophets) *ca.* 200 B.C. marks the death of prophecy.

**2. The canonization of the Law.** Since none of the literature preserved in the OT was written for the purpose of being included in a canon of inspired scriptures, we must ask ourselves how there arose in Judaism, and nowhere else, the notion that God wrote or dictated one or more books for the guidance of men. According to Jewish doctrine, God revealed himself to an unbroken series of inspired men going from Moses to Ezra. There may have been inspired prophets before Moses, but they wrote no inspired books; and no prophets arose in Israel after Ezra and Nehemiah (Jos. Apion I.viii; II Esd. 14:44-46; cf. Ps. 74:9; I Macc. 4:46; 9:27; 14:41), so that no Jewish apocalypse was attributed to an author later than Ezra.

No ancient religion doubted that the gods could reveal themselves and make known their will to human beings. They did so spontaneously, either appearing visibly, "face to face" (Exod. 33:11; *Iliad* I. 193-218, and often; *Gilgamesh Epic*, bk. VI; etc.) or in visions (I Kings 22:19-22; Isa. 6; Job 4:12-17; etc.) and dreams (Gen. 28:12-15; *Iliad* I.63; II.5-15; Gudea, Cylinder A, cols. I-VII). The deity could, on the other hand, speak to men through the mouth of prophets into whom its spirit had entered (Amos 3:8; 7:15-17; Vergil *Aeneid* VI.45-97; etc.). But the ancients had also the possibility of obtaining a divine oracle from the deity in answer to an inquiry; as Cicero said (*On Divination* II.26), there are two methods of divining the will of the gods—the artificial one, consisting in the interpretation of omens, and the natural, consisting of divine inspiration. Among the ancient Israelites both methods were used: according to I Sam. 28:6, God could answer human inquiries by dreams, by Urim (the priestly oracle), and by prophets. It may be safely asserted that in Israel priests and prophets were the only recognized recipients of divine oracles. For the stories of the visible appearances of Jehovah or of his angel to ancient heroes (from Adam to Samuel) are told only of men long dead, and never of contemporaries; and the same applies to a unique reference to "tables of stone, written with the finger of God" (Exod. 31:18). And the utterances of a seer·endowed with telepathy (identified with a prophet in the misleading gloss in I Sam. 9:9), of a gazer who interpreted omens, or of the magical practitioners denounced in Deut. 18:9-12, were never, as far as we know, regarded as oracles of Jehovah. We can therefore assert that canonical scripture had its origin either in the priestly or in the prophetic oracle, since dreams and visions belong mainly to prophecy.

The priestly oracle could not possibly have produced a canonical volume of sacred scripture and, of course, never did. When an inquirer asked a question of Jehovah, the priest bore a sacred box (the ark) containing lots, requested an answer from the deity, and after drawing the lots interpreted them and gave an answer, which of necessity could only be "yes" or "no," "A" or "B," and eventually "no answer" (I Sam. 14:37). Saul, David, and Solomon regularly inquired of Jehovah through a priest by this more or less mechanical method. It was in use since the early days of the settlement in Canaan, but it became obsolete at least in the reign of Ahab, a century after Solomon, when kings consulted prophets and not priests. It was still employed, apparently, in the more primitive regions of N Israel in the days of Jeremiah and had become a memory when Ezra 2: 63 = Neh. 7:65 was written; cf. Jos. Antiq. III.viii.9; M. Sot. 9.12 ("When the first prophets [living before Haggai, Zechariah, and Malachi] died, urim and thummim ceased"). Such oracular responses as could be obtained from the lots were limited to two alternatives, or to a simple "yes or no" answer to a special question asked on a definite occasion. They could therefore contain nothing having a permanent validity, worthy of preservation in a book.

The questions asked of Jehovah through a priest usually regarded military matters: Who committed a sin (I Sam. 14:40-42)? Will the men of Keilah deliver David into Saul's hand (I Sam. 23:12)? Should David pursue the Amalekite raiders (I Sam. 30:8)? Should David attack the Philistines (II Sam. 5:19)? The answers to these and other questions were vital to Saul, David, and other inquirers at a given moment, to help them choose between two alternatives, but had merely a historical interest to later generations, who could derive no guidance from these divine responses and who might consult the priestly oracle any time while it was still in use. There is nothing to indicate that the priestly law (Torah) and any of its articles were ever obtained through the manipulation and interpretation of the sacred lots.

The priestly oracle could not have given origin to the notion of canonical scripture; this notion could only have been derived from prophecy. The Hebrew prophets, like the Greek and Roman sibyls who face the prophets in Michelangelo's paintings in the Sistine Chapel, felt themselves to be physically invaded by the spirit of the deity at the moment of inspiration. The Hebrew word for "prophet," נָבִיא, possibly means "entered" (from בּוֹא, "to enter"). By entering into a man the deity could actually speak through the vocal organs of the prophet, even if he was reluctant to utter an unpopular message (Jer. 20:7-9); often when the prophet says "I," he means Jehovah (Amos 4:6-11; 5:21-24; etc.). But it was only in this overwhelming experience that the words of the prophet in the moment of their being uttered were regarded as divinely inspired; the inspiration of his book was an afterthought, and in the case of the earliest literary prophet (Amos, 750 B.C.), the idea of his having been inspired came more than five centuries after his time. In reality, of course, if one admits that the prophetic books contain actual oracles revealed to the prophets and uttered by them, one assumes that to this extent the books are inspired. Whether the individual books were written by the prophet or by a disciple does not matter in the least, provided the oracles are recorded faithfully.

It is probable that Jeremiah, who dictated the book of his oracles to Baruch during the seven years when he was in hiding and unable to preach, was the first prophet to write his book. In principle the first scripture was the written record of the inspired utterances of the eighth-century prophets, in spite of the fact that other writings attained canonical status much earlier. When Josiah came to the throne in 638, there were in circulation MSS containing prophetic utterances which their authors and their readers regarded as containing God's inspired words. Jeremiah (26:18) quoted Mic. 3:12, presumably from the book of Micah; and later Zechariah (1:4; 7:7, 12) must have read some of the prophetic books, for in 3:8; 6:12 he refers to Jer. 23:5; 33:15. Officially, the book found in the temple was the first writing to be canonized—through a solemn covenant in 621 (II Kings 22:8–23:3)—but for one century there were in circulation in Judah the books of the earlier prophets, and they were deemed by many readers to contain the word of God. In principle, therefore, the canon of the prophets was already in existence, although it was not closed until *ca.* 200 B.C.

It is generally admitted that the book found in the temple in 621 B.C. was the bulk of Deuteronomy (4: 44–8:20; 10:12–11:25; 12–26; 28:1-24, 43-46; 29:1). It is certain that the reforms of Josiah (II Kings 23: 4-24) were based on Deut. 5; 12; 16–18; 23 (the consternation of Josiah in II Kings 22:11 is explained by Deut. 28). No other part of the Pentateuch contains prescriptions for all the reforms; moreover, the one injunction of Deuteronomy which Josiah could not enforce (Deut. 18:6-8) is specifically mentioned in II Kings 23:9.

The Deuteronomic (D) Code was found in the collection box of the temple (II Chr. 34:14) in 621 and must have been written by a priest of Jerusalem a few years before. He had been deeply influenced by the teaching of the reforming prophets since Amos (750 B.C.), whose teaching had been extremely unpopular with nearly all Israelites (Amos 7:10-13) and Judeans. He made sure by two means that his book would not be consigned to the flames, as later Jeremiah's oracles (Jer. 36:22-23) were, but would reform the religion of the Judeans—first, by timing the finding of the book when Assyria, whose cults were introduced into the temple by Manasseh (692-639), was in a state of collapse after the death of Ashurbanipal in 625; and secondly, by combining the two religions contrasted in Mic. 6:7-8 by means of the doctrine of a divine covenant with Israel. Through this revelation to Moses, Jehovah made a covenant with Israel: if they obeyed God's commandments, he would bless them, as the current religion asserted; if they transgressed them, they would be wiped off the face of the earth (Deut. 28), as Amos (9:8*a*) had declared.

This divine covenant between Jehovah and Israel is first mentioned in Deut. 5:1-4; 29:1; etc. The author did not substantially modify the ancient religion of Israel, which had been denounced by the prophets as offensive to God (Amos 5:21-24, etc.), but he gave to it a prophetic interpretation. He stressed

with Amos the justice of God in punishing Israel for its sins (Deut. 28:15-24, 43-46), without going so far as Amos (9:8*a*) in announcing a total destruction of the nation. With Hosea (2:19; cf. 6:6) he regarded loyalty (Deut. 5:10) as the keynote of the relation between God and Israel, a relation which is one of great love (Hos. 3:1; 11:1-4; Jer. 2:2; 31:3; Deut. 5: 10; 6:5; 7:13). New, however, was the notion that love for God is expressed in keeping his commandments (Deut. 7:9; 10:12-13; 11:1, 13, 22; etc.); and that festivals and sacrifices, which the prophets had regarded as religiously indifferent or offensive to God if presented as gifts, tributes, or bribes, were to be regarded as expressions of gratitude to God and joy in his presence (Deut. 5:15; 12:11-12, 18; 14:26; 16:1-15; 26:10-11).

In form and contents the book found in the temple was inspired by the written prophetic oracles of Amos and his followers. Of course, this book (Deut. 5–26; 28, in part) was not written by Moses, as it purports to be, but by a priest of Jerusalem more than five centuries after the death of Moses. To say that the author was therefore a forger, a counterfeiter, means to show lack of historical sense (by accusing the author of violating literary conventions unknown at his time) and of understanding of human nature (by ascribing to the author disreputable motives rather than the highest ideals). The Deuteronomic author was absolutely honest—what he says about the history of the time of Moses he derived from the immensely popular national epics (J and E) reporting Israel's achievements under the guidance of Jehovah, from Abraham to the invasion of Canaan; the law contained in D is actual law (except for the closing of the provincial sanctuaries of Jehovah in ch. 12 and the celebration of the Passover at Jerusalem in connection with the Feast of Unleavened Bread [Deut. 16:1-8; cf. II Kings 23:21-23]); and as for religion, the forms are still those of the cult of Israel after the settlement in Canaan, and the spirit is that of the prophetic teaching. The author assumed, as did all his contemporaries, that truth is unchangeable—since Moses was divinely inspired, he knew and taught the true religion and the genuine law. Moses did not leave to future generations a book containing his inspired oracles, as Amos and his successors did; but if he had, it was generally believed in 621 B.C. that a book of his would have agreed with the teaching of the D Code.

Josiah and his contemporaries erred in attributing the book to Moses, in accordance with explicit statements of its author (Deut. 4:44-45; 5:1; 29:1). Only the authority of the great founder of the religion and nation of Israel could induce king and people to reform their faith and practice. As a result, Moses was regarded as the unique legislator of Israel, and no law which was not deemed to have been explicitly or implicitly revealed to him by God was thereafter considered to be valid.

No less epoch-making was a second error: the scroll found in the temple was regarded as the "book of the law" (II Kings 22:8, 11; cf. 23:24-25; Deut. 4:44; etc.), as a book of priestly torah, and not as a transcript of an oral prophetic oracle. In reality Deuteronomy is neither in form nor in substance a code of laws, but a sermon in three parts (4:44–11:°5;

12-26; 28). Moses in this book is a prophet (18:18), not a lawgiver (Exod. 15:25b) nor a priest of Levitical descent (Exod. 2:1 ff) who purified the people (Exod. 19:14) and gave oracular responses (Exod. 18:15). After Moses, Jehovah will raise up a prophet like Moses to transmit to the people the divine words (Deut. 18:18-22)—the author knows of no other method by which God communicates with man. But the misconception of Deuteronomy as the legal code of Moses has left a permanent impression on Judaism: the divine revelation consists primarily of law, not of prophetic exhortation; and faith, hope, and charity are less important than unquestioned obedience to every article of the law.

And yet the book is not a codification of the law (in spite of chs. 12-26), but a sermon, an appeal to the nation to do God's will as specifically set forth in it. Throughout the book the style is not that of a jurist, but discloses the eloquent diction of a pulpit orator (contrast, e.g., Exod. 21:2 and Deut. 15:12-15). The preacher pleads and warns, with the deep emotion and tender concern utterly lacking in an objective and serene legislator (see, e.g., Deut. 19). Philanthropic appeals are added to the civil-law articles, selected because they had some moral aspect; purely commercial law is omitted; and a pious and humane aura pervades the old civil laws as well as the philanthropic and religious exhortations. The influence of the prophets is pervasive: the doctrine of God (see, e.g., 10:12-18), the polemic against the worship of the Baals at the high places (see ch. 12), religion conceived as love for God expressed in doing his will (7:9; 11:1; etc.), and the stress on humane and moral obligations toward the weaker members of the community, all illustrate how deeply the noble religion of the prophets had modified the priestly point of view of the author.

In conclusion, it is clear that the writing of the D Code was inspired by the existing books of the prophets—the author provided a similar book for Moses, since the greatest of the prophets lacked a written record of his inspired speeches. Thus the book found in 621 was regarded as God's word (II Kings 22:19). However, it was not regarded by Josiah as a prophetic book, but as the "book of the law." In principle there was only one class of sacred scriptures—namely, the transcript of the inspired words of the prophets—and in principle the whole OT is in Judaism a collection of prophetic writings. But in reality, "the law" and "the prophets" were eventually distinguished. The initial basic revelation to Moses, growing gradually from Deuteronomy to the whole Pentateuch, was called torah (law) even though Deuteronomy was prophecy and the rest of the Pentateuch partly law and partly history. All subsequent revelations to prophets were secondary and in principle merely confirmed and explained the original, basic revelation. As often, the historical facts—prophecy precedes the law as inspired scripture—and the tenets of faith and dogma cannot be equated or even reconciled.

The publication of Deuteronomy in 621 B.C. marks substantially the end of the old religion of Israel and the beginning of Judaism, the death of a national religion and the birth of an ethical religion of salvation for all men. The immediate effect of the teaching of this book was the reformation of Josiah (II Kings 23:4-23)—Canaanite and Assyrian cult objects were removed from the temple; all shrines of Jehovah, with the sole exception of the temple in Jerusalem, were destroyed; all sanctuaries dedicated to foreign gods were annihilated. In spite of the obvious hardships which these measures imposed on the Judeans outside Jerusalem, the reforms of Josiah proved to be providential in their future effects. They preserved the nation after the state ceased to exist. Judah, when the monarchy ended and Jerusalem was destroyed in 586 B.C.—thirty-five years after the reforms—would have lost its national existence, as the Northern Kingdom had in 722 (the "ten lost tribes"). The reforms were the first step in the transformation of the state into a congregation, of the passage from monarchy to Sanhedrin, from temple to synagogue; thenceforth mankind was divided into Jews and Gentiles. The enactment of the proscriptions of Deuteronomy made it possible to abolish the most objectionable heathen practices in the worship, although many ancient harmless institutions of Canaan (like the three annual agricultural festivals) were preserved without recognition of their alien origin. Local shrines eventually disappeared, sacrifice was now distinguished from butchery (Deut. 12:15, 21-22), festivals became national events (even the family feast of the Passover, which was now combined with Unleavened Bread [Deut. 16:1-8]), the royal chapel and its worship in Jerusalem became unique and acquired a national character, while individual sacrifices eventually lost their importance; personal religion, eventually centered in the synagogue, suffered no loss with the destruction of the temple in A.D. 70. Another consequence of having a prophetic oracle of Moses as the constitution of the kingdom was that the state tended to become a theocracy, a religious institution that persisted after the monarchy came to an end thirty-five years later. The Jews became a divinely chosen people, a kingdom of God on earth, and they dreamed that eventually, when their condition became intolerable, God would intervene and place them at the head of his kingdom embracing all countries of the earth (Dan. 7:13-14, 27).

Aside from the reforms of Josiah, the book found in the temple in 621 had a lasting influence. It marked the beginning of the canonization of the Bible; nowhere before had a book been officially recognized as God's word. Judah now possessed a permanently valid revelation of God's will and mind, regulating religion and morals. This tended to make occasional and sporadic oral revelation through the prophets more and more superfluous. Since the priestly and prophetic instruction could not contradict any explicit statements of the book that God had revealed, and since there could only be one supreme authority, the priests henceforth became primarily interpreters and supplementers of the written law ("The law perishes from the priest" [Ezek. 7:26]), and the prophets either did the same (Ezek. 40-48; Haggai; Malachi) or disappeared as God's envoys to the people (Ps. 74:9; I Macc. 4:46; etc.). This result was not anticipated, much less desired, by the author (Deut. 18:15-19), although an addition to his book (13:1-5, in part; cf. Zech. 13:2-6) regards certain prophets as quacks who deserve to be put to death. Jeremiah, after preaching in favor of the reforms of Josiah (Jer. 11, in part), was sorely disappointed when the people refused to listen to the prophets because they had the "law of the LORD," and he declared the book to be the work of the false pen of the scribes (Jer. 8:8-10). In a sense, Jeremiah was the last of the prophets.

After 621 B.C. it was necessary to rewrite the history of Israel in the spirit and style of Deuteronomy. The existing stories from Abraham to the death of David were national epics, not religious tracts with historical illustrations in which the prophetic denunciation of sin was pervasive. The first edition of Kings, published ca. 600 B.C., denounces the pre-Deuteronomic years (with rare exceptions) as culpable defections of the law of Moses, particularly because the "high places" (village shrines of Jehovah) were not removed according to Deut. 12. Half a century later the books from Genesis to Kings were submitted to a Deuteronomistic retouching, which is pervasive in Joshua and supplies introductions and conclusions to the stories of Judges; the philosophy of history of these editors is plainly described in Judg. 2:6-3:6.

The book of the law revealed to Moses was canonized in 621 B.C., but it marks the beginning, rather than the end, of a process. Although the first edition of Deuteronomy was regarded as sacred scripture, it did not preclude future revelations of God in written form, nor did it diminish in the least the popularity of existing historical and prophetic writings, on which it was based: from the historical books it derived the national pride of the Judeans—a nationalism unknown before the Greeks and the Romans—and from the prophets, conversely, a sense of national shame in the presence of Jehovah. The finding of the book of the law seems to have stimulated literary activity—beginning with Jeremiah and Ezekiel, prophets began writing books, and were soon imitated by the author of Isa. 40-55, who was not a prophet; the homiletic edition of selected laws in Deut. 12-26 suggested within a century the publication of the Holiness Code (Lev. 17-26), which is likewise a "sermon of Moses."

Gradually Deuteronomy grew to the size of the whole Pentateuch. Ca. 550 the Deuteronomistic editor inserted the book found in the temple into the national epics (J and E) which had been amalgamated into one book a century before, placing it immediately before the account of the death of Moses (Deut. 34:1-6, in part). Deut. 11:26-30; 27 had been added shortly before 550, as had also the historical introduction and conclusion (9:1-10:11; 30:15-20; 31:1-13). This editor inserted into Exod. 34 his edition of the ancient ritual decalogue, extant in a much earlier text in Exod. 22:29b-30; 23:12, 15-19. The Holiness Code (Lev. 17-26) is an edition of the code of one of the sanctuaries closed by Josiah in 621; it was inserted into the Pentateuch as part of the Priestly Code, codified ca. 450 and included in the incomplete Pentateuch (JED) ca. twenty years later. The Priestly Code spans, with full genealogies, meager narrative, and exact artificial chronology, the period from the creation of the world to the occupation of Canaan under Joshua. It was not brought by

Ezra from Babylonia in 458 (Ezra 7:14, 25-25), but reflects in its legislation the ritual practices of the second temple (finished in 516 B.C.) during the first half of the fifth century. Its real significance was, however, its validity as the charter of the new Jewish congregation which arose between Haggai (520) and Nehemiah (444) and proved to be imperishable. After the Priestly Code was added, only small additions were made to the incipient Pentateuch—the Covenant Code (Exod. 20:22-23:19); a copy of those laws in an ancient civil code (1200 B.C.?) which had not been included in the book found in the temple in 621; an ancient document (Gen. 2:5-11:9; 14; 19; 34-36; 38, in part) depicting the mythical origin and early history of mankind and of nations around the Dead Sea; and miscellaneous poems (Gen. 49; Deut. 32; 33; etc.).

The Pentateuch embodies literary compositions dating from 1200 to 400 B.C., and is the edition of all the literature existing in 400 B.C. which could be regarded as composed by Moses ca. 1200 B.C. But it was only gradually that Moses was regarded as the author, not only of the laws, but also of the narratives which frame the legislation. The dates of the publication and canonization of the Pentateuch (which cannot be far apart) are unknown, but may be fixed a considerable time after the restoration of the temple (516 B.C.) and before the Samaritan schism (432, according to Neh. 13:28-29, but more probably a century later, according to Jos. Antiq. XI.viii.2, 4). The reading of the Law in 444 (Neh. 8) refers to the Pentateuch rather than to the Priestly Code—unfortunately the story is too unreliable to help us fix the date of the canonization of the Law. Nevertheless, a date ca. 400 B.C. cannot be seriously questioned; at that time the final editions of the five books ascribed to the inspired pen of Moses were issued substantially as we have them, and were adopted by the Jews as part of God's Word. Although the final editors of the Pentateuch aimed to include everything Mosaic or pre-Mosaic, they were not striving to embrace everything that was then holy scripture, such as the books of the prophets in circulation at the time. This edition was merely a stage in the process of codifying the law. In reality, this turned out to be, not a passing phase as the canonization of Deuteronomy, but the final edition of the canonical law of Moses. Why? Because it was widely circulated among the Jews all over the world. Synagogues were established wherever there were Jews, for the primary purpose of reading and interpreting the law of Moses; and the sect of the Samaritans, when it detached itself from Judaism, treasured the same text of the Torah, except for minor differences. The Pentateuch does not reflect the practice of the synagogue, but of the Jerusalem temple.

No single event in the religious history of the Judeans and of the early Jews, with the possible exception of the publication of Deuteronomy in 621 B.C., was as significant for the future as the publication of the Pentateuch, and its prompt canonization. An important factor was that manifestly measures were taken to circulate this book in a degree unknown for any other work. It was not kept in the temple, where the priests did not need it, but was taught assiduously to every Jew. It was compiled for this very purpose, and it enabled every Jew to know the details of his religion and what God expected from him. The need of acquainting every Jew with the contents of the Pentateuch brought into existence the synagogue, the most original and most vital institution of Judaism, before which the temple gradually lost significance until it ceased to exist in A.D. 70. Judaism is consciously based directly on the Pentateuch, and not on the teachings of the prophets. From the time of its publication, the Pentateuch was the supreme authority in Judaism, unequaled by any other part of the OT. The prophetic theology was received and accepted through Deuteronomy and other parts of the Pentateuch, rather than through the prophetic writings, which were considered confirmations of the teaching of Moses in times of ignorance. If Moses had actually written every word of his five books, the attitude toward them would not be more filled with veneration in the slightest degree. It makes no difference that historically Moses wrote practically nothing in his law, because its origin was regarded as a miracle without any relation to the mere facts of reality, and besides, nothing was known at the time about the development of religion. The attribution to Moses of later ideas and institutions raised accordingly no difficulties whatsoever. We know that the Pentateuch is the result of a development that continued for at least eight centuries after the death of Moses, but dogmatically it is the divine revelation to Moses.

In addition to the institution of the synagogue, other epoch-making effects of the codification of the Pentateuch were the stress on universal education among the Jews, so that each one might read the law; the emphasis in Judaism on conduct rather than faith; and the legal development, required to supplement the enactments of the Pentateuch or to interpret them for Jews living in later centuries, which was primarily accomplished in the Mishnah (ca. A.D. 200) and the Talmud (ca. A.D. 500). Judaism, to be followed by Christianity and Islam, became, through the canonization of the Pentateuch, a religion of the book, wholly and exclusively founded on a divine revelation fixed for all time in written documents: "You shall not add to the word which I command you, nor take from it" (Deut. 4:2). But the scripture was not sufficient in the field of ritual, civil, criminal, and moral law; many of its prescriptions, as the laws on divorce and on sabbath rest, require detailed elucidation. Thus around the Pentateuch there grew up the unwritten law, applying the revealed words to particular cases and to new circumstances. The rabbis believed that God had revealed the unwritten law to Moses at Sinai, but had forbidden him to put it into writing. But the law (written and unwritten) was transmitted faithfully, according to the *Sayings of the Fathers* (Pirke Aboth I.1). Jesus called the unwritten law the "tradition of the elders" (Mark 7:1-13; Matt. 15:1-6; cf. Gal. 1:14)—by observing it the Pharisees laid aside the written law. The oral law was finally committed to writing in the Mishnah and in the Talmud, and preserved the central and supreme position of the Pentateuch in inspired scripture.

The fact that the first book to be canonized (the bulk of Deuteronomy in 621 B.C.) was considered to be the "book of the Torah" (II Kings 22:8, 11), instead of the prophecy of Moses, tended to stress in religion the fulfilment of all the commandments of God, even the least ones. "Legalism" is often criticized for condemning violations of the divine law whether unconscious or deliberate, morally evil and harmful or indifferent, and for assuming that they could be atoned by ritual purifications and expiations. But this legalistic tendency in Judaism never silenced a more spiritual tendency, first stressed by Amos and the prophets who followed him.

Nevertheless the Torah became central in Judaism and has remained the supreme standard and norm of the Jewish religion. It was therefore natural that all revealed literature was identified with Torah, Law. Before the Pentateuch was canonized ca. 400 B.C., wisdom had been identified with Torah (Deut. 4:5-6; cf. Jer. 8:8; Ezra 7:14, 25-26). Earlier, wisdom had no connections with religion—in fact, was denounced by some prophets as objectionable to God (Isa. 5:21; 29:14; 33:6; 44:25; 47:10; Jer. 8:9; 9:23).

Since the Lord created wisdom before he made the world (Prov. 8:22-31), the Law, which is identified with wisdom, was said to have been made before heaven and earth. Lest there be any doubt about this eternal Law, which like wisdom is personified and could be something ideal, Ecclesiasticus emphatically states that it is

> the book of the covenant of the Most High God,
> the law which Moses commanded us
> as an inheritance for the congregations of Jacob
> (24:23; cf. 1:26; 6:37; 9:15; 19:20; 21:11;
> Bar. 4:1; IV Macc. 1:17).

The Law revealed to Moses not only existed before the creation of the world, but will last unchanged for all eternity (Ecclus. 24:9, 23; Bar. 4:1; Tob. 1:6; Enoch 99:2, 14; Matt. 5:18; Luke 16:17). After Ecclesiasticus (with the exception of Ecclesiastes if it is later) there is no wisdom literature which does not place the Law in a central position; see, e.g., Ecclus. 1:26; 6:37; etc.; Tob. 4:5; 14:9; Bar. 3:9; Aristeas 31, 168, 228, 279; Wisd. Sol. 2:12; 6:18; 16:6; 18:4; IV Macc. 1:17, 34; 2:6, 8-10; 5:16-36; 6:21, 27, 30; 8:25; 9:2; 11:5, 12; 13:9, 13; 15:9-10, 29; 16:16; 18:1, 4. As synonymous with wisdom, the law of Moses is said to teach the four cardinal virtues of Plato and the Stoics (IV Macc. 5:23-24; cf. 1:2-4, 18; Wisd. Sol. 8:7): temperance, courage, justice, and piety (prudence); and wisdom, according to the Stoic definition (Cicero *Tusculan Disputations* IV.26, 57; *On Duty* I.43, 153; II.2, 5), is a "knowledge of divine and human things, and of their causes" which is acquired through "education in the Law" (IV Macc. 1:16-17).

In addition to the supernatural origin and eternity of the Law, its identification with wisdom had other far-reaching and lasting effects. "The Law is a species of wisdom come down from wisdom on high" (Genesis Rabbah 17.5). It is a divine revelation, but, like wisdom (philosophy), it must be taught and learned (Deut. 4:1, 5, 9-10, 14, etc.; Prov. 4:1-11; Isa. 2:3; Ezra 7:25)—note that in Deut. 4; Ezra 7, where the Law is identified with wisdom, instruction is stressed. The immense prestige and authority of the Pentateuch gave rise to the synagogues by the side of the temple and of the scribes by the side of the priests. After the destruction of the temple in A.D. 70, synagogues, established originally for the reading of the Law, and scribes (biblical scholars and teachers; see Ecclus. 38:24–39:11; cf. Ezra 7:10-11), later called rabbis (masters, teachers), remained as the exclusive religious institutions of Judaism. The chronicler, who tends to date the institutions of Judaism too early, believes that general instruction in the Law (II Chr. 17:7-9) began in the third year of Jehoshaphat (872 B.C.), and he considers Ezra the first scribe (Ezra 7:10-11); he obviously reflects here conditions in his own time (300-250 B.C.). Synagogues and scribes, furthering the knowledge of the Law, presuppose the canonization of the Pentateuch (not before 400 B.C.), and are not mentioned in our sources before 300-250 B.C.; the sole possible mention of synagogues in the Bible and in the Apoc. is in Ps. 74:8, if "meeting places of God" actually means "synagogues." Philo and Josephus, of course, say that Moses established the synagogues. The first mention of a Jewish school is in Ecclus. 51:23, where the text reads "lodge in my school" (*beth midrashi* in the Hebrew; in the LXX, incorrectly, "in the house of learning"). "Rabbi Abdimi of Haifa said, From the day whereon the Temple was laid waste, prophecy was taken from the prophets and given to the scribes" (B.B. 12a). At the end of the second century of the Christian era, *The Sayings of the Fathers* (Pirke Aboth; ch. 6 is later) is full of references to the Torah and its study. Here Torah is both the written text of the Pentateuch and the inexhaustible divine teaching that may be derived from it through study and interpretation. R. Travers Herford compares the text of the Pentateuch to the mouth of a well, and the Torah to the water without limit, which may be drawn from it, exceeding in volume the capacity of the well. The study of the Torah was the contemplation of divine revelation, and through it such a hedge was made around the Torah (Ab. I.1) that it remained the peculiar treasure of Israel. Simeon the Just said that the world stood upon Torah, worship, and showing kindness (I.2). "Study of Torah [*talmud torah*] along with 'the way of the earth' [a worldly occupation or good behavior] is seemly" (II.2). "Be alert to learn Torah, and know what answer to an *Epicuros* [a freethinker, an atheist]" (II.19). "Whoever receives on himself the yoke [cf. Matt. 11:29-30] of Torah, they remove from him the yoke of the kingdom and the yoke of worldly occupation" (III.6). The study of the Law should be incessant, without distractions (III.9; cf. Deut. 6:7-9; Ps. 1:2), and without forgetting a single word (III.10). God's love was shown to Israel in his giving them the Torah, and even more in his making them aware of this supreme gift (Akiba, in III.18; cf. Prov. 4:2). The least important precepts of Torah are more essential than astronomy and geometry (III.23). Learning the Torah in order to practice it is better than learning it in order to teach it (IV.6).

It is not necessary to quote further passages in the rabbinical literature (Mishnah, Midrash, Talmud, etc.) to illustrate what the Torah meant to scribes, Pharisees, and rabbis. "Torah," which had originally meant the Sermon of Moses in Deuteronomy, found in 621, and then the whole Pentateuch *ca.* 400, came to mean the whole divine revelation, both written

(the Hebrew Bible) and unwritten—the "tradition of the elders," put into writing *ca.* A.D. 200, after the collections of juristic opinions made by Akiba (died A.D. 134) and his pupil Meir (died *ca.* 175), by Jehuda ha-Nasi (called "Rabbi"; 135-219), and expanded into the Talmud (*ca.* 500).

The Torah absorbed all forms of literature—not only wisdom, but also prophecy (Ezra 9:10-11), history, psalms, the Song of Solomon, etc. Religion thus became inextricably related to books, the Jews became the first people of the book, and prophetic inspiration became subservient to scripture and eventually disappeared. "The Bible became the primer, the congregation a school, religion a thing to be taught and learned. Piety and education belong together: the illiterate was not a perfect Jew" (J. Wellhausen).

The date of the canonization of the Pentateuch was probably close to 400 B.C. It was certainly later than 621 (Deuteronomy), than Ezekiel's visionary program of temple restoration in chs. 40-48 (dated in 573—40:1), later than the worship in the second temple (rebuilt in 520-516 B.C.; see Hag. 1:1, 15a; Ezra 6:15) reflected in the Priestly Code's description of the ritual ceremonies in the tabernacle of Moses written in the period 500-450. If Ezra's reading of the Law in Jerusalem (444; Neh. 8-10) is historical—and some scholars doubt that it is, or date it either before or after 444—the Pentateuch would have become canonical at that time or later. In any case, the Pentateuch cannot have been canonized long before 400. On the other hand, it cannot have become sacred scripture after the Samaritan schism, which seems to be dated by the chronicler in 432 (Neh. 13:28-29); but Josephus (Antiq. XI.viii.2, 4) dates it a century later, during the invasion of Alexander. The schism may have started politically in the days of Nehemiah and may have been made final religiously in the days of Alexander through the building of the Samaritan temple on Mount Gerizim (cf. John 4:20). At the time of the schism the Samaritans retained the Pentateuch, which had previously been canonized as their Bible. In conclusion, we may say that *ca.* 400 B.C. the Pentateuch was separated from Joshua–Kings and canonized for all time as the law of Moses.

Circulated among Jewish communities as no other book before or after, this edition could not be revised and enlarged, although minor textual changes and errors crept in through the accidents of MS transmission. This wide circulation and the regular reading in the synagogues erected for this purpose soon after 400—the LXX translation was made *ca.* 250 B.C. for the synagogues in Alexandria—precluded the addition of new legislation, which was confined to the "tradition of the elders" or oral law, said to have likewise been revealed to Moses on Sinai. Both the written and the unwritten law were transmitted by Moses to posterity through Joshua, the elders, the prophets, and the men of the Great Synagogue (in the time of Ezra [Ab. I.1]). After Simeon the Just, "one of the survivors of the Great Synagogue" (Ab. I.2), and Antigonos of Socho came the "Pairs" (*zugoth*) of learned scholars (last two centuries B.C.), ending with Shammai and Hillel during the reign of Herod (died 4 B.C.), followed by the tannaim (traditioners or teachers) in the first two centuries of the Christian era, and the amoraim (expositors), who expounded the Mishnah of the tannaim (ca. A.D. 200) in the Jerusalem (ca. 400) and the Babylonian (ca. 500) Talmuds.

**3. The canonization of the Prophets.** The fixation of the five books of the Pentateuch as the sacred canon of the Torah marks the second stage of the process which began in 621 B.C. with the recognition that the book of the law of Moses had been divinely inspired. In 400 the Jews had other ancient books which enjoyed considerable popularity but were not yet considered divinely revealed, notably four historical books (the Former Prophets: Joshua, Judges, Samuel, and Kings) and several volumes of prophetic oracles (eventually published, with additions, in the four volumes of the Latter Prophets: Isaiah, Jeremiah, Ezekiel, and the minor prophets). Growing public interest in these volumes and their value for enhancing the national pride and the hopes for a better future eventually resulted in their canonization as God's Word.

*a. The Former Prophets.* When the Pentateuch in 400 B.C. was separated from the four other volumes of the great corpus going from the creation of the world to the deliverance of Jehoiachin from Babylonian captivity in 561 B.C. (II Kings 25:27-29), the books of Joshua, Judges, Samuel, and Kings were left for almost two centuries in the realm of secular literature. In 550 B.C. this work had been edited by the Deuteronomists to inculcate the lesson that obedience to the Deuteronomic law was divinely blessed and violations of this divinely inspired law were punished by Jehovah. Eventually the history of the events following the death of Moses, where the cut was made, were supplemented with the Priestly Code account of the division of Canaan among the tribes of Israel (Josh. 13–21, in part), with ancient histories which had been omitted from the Deuteronomic edition (Judg. 1:1–2:5; 5; 9; 10:1-5; 12:8-15; 16–21; II Sam. 9–24; I Kings 1; 2:13-46a; 17–19; II Kings 1:2-17; 2–8; 13:14-21; 18:14-16; 19:9b-35; 20:1-19), and with numerous brief marginal annotations.

These marginal annotations (400-200 B.C.) are a valuable clue to the public interest in these books, which eventually led to their canonization and to the rewriting of Samuel and Kings in I–II Chronicles in 300-250 B.C. The correction of Esh-Baal and Merib-Baal (in Chronicles) to Ish-bosheth and Mephibosheth in Samuel was made later than the publication of Chronicles, to avoid the pronunciation of "Baal."

The glorification of David, entirely absent in the old source (see II Sam. 9–20, e.g.), inspired many additions both in Chronicles and in the glosses in Samuel. The chronicler calmly states that David set aside more than three billion gold dollars for the building of the temple (I Chr. 22:14; 29:3-4, 7-8). To bring the ark to Jerusalem, David called out, according to II Sam. 6:1, 30,000 picked soldiers (70,000 according to LXX [B]). David slew "the men of seven hundred chariots, and forty thousand horsemen" (II Sam. 10:18; 7,000 chariots according to I Chr. 19:18). David's army numbered 800,000 men of Israel and 500,000 men of Judah (II Sam. 24:9;

in I Chr. 21:5 the figures become 1,100,000 men of Israel and 470,000 men of Judah). In the plague which followed the census, 70,000 men are said to have died (II Sam. 24:15; I Chr. 21:14). The following statements are demonstrably unhistorical: (a) David took the head of Goliath to Jerusalem (I Sam. 17:54); (b) he had been crowned by Samuel in his childhood (I Sam. 16:1-13; his brothers were present, but knew nothing about it—17:28); (c) the hundred Philistines he killed (I Sam. 18:25; II Sam. 3:14) are doubled in I Sam. 18:27; (d) Joab's victory against the Arameans (II Sam. 10:13) is attributed to David (10:15-19).

This exaltation of David was due, first of all, to patriotic pride, and secondly to his genuine success in war and peace, which was interpreted (cf. Deut. 28) as evidence of divine favor for exemplary piety; similarly Samuel was raised from the humble position of an obscure village seer (I Sam. 9:6-8) to that of a judge over all Israel (I Sam. 7:3-17), a prophet (I Sam. 3:20-21; 9:9); he anointed Saul as king three times, according to the later legends (I Sam. 9:26–10:1; 10:17-24; 11:15); and he deposed him twice (13:14; 15:26-29; cf. 28:17-18), although no one seems to have known it. Hophni and Phinehas, who like Saul died heroically in battle, were regarded as scoundrels (I Sam. 2:22b). The theory that the pious prosper and the wicked suffer is pervasive in the books of Kings, in the verdicts of each reign, but is unknown in the sources earlier than 621 B.C.

These retouches helped to change historical accounts which were objective into lessons from history distorted according to the theory of divine retribution on earth. The publication of the Pentateuch in 400 B.C. involved other revisions. The allusions to the Pentateuch, wholly absent in the early sources, are numerous: the tent of meeting (I Sam. 2:22b); Aaron (2:27-28); the Egyptian plagues "in the wilderness" (4:8); the exodus from Egypt (6:6; 10:18; 12:8). Prophecy is extinct and is confused with clairvoyance (I Sam. 9:9), prognostication (II Sam. 24:11), and mere prediction (late prophetic oracles predict what has already happened—I Sam. 2:27-36; II Sam. 7; 12:7b-12). The Levites are mentioned three times in late texts (I Sam. 6:15; II Sam. 15:24; I Kings 8:4) as bearers of the ark in Samuel-Kings, but ninety-seven times in Chronicles and fifty-nine times in Ezra-Nehemiah, and in the vein of the chronicler the performance of orchestral music is added in II Sam. 6:5, 15.

In other ways, as well, the late annotations increased the popularity of the historical books by bringing (or by trying to bring) the ancient record "up to date" with the patriotic and religious feelings of the masses, proud of the past glories of David and Solomon, of the first temple, so much more imposing than the second (Hag. 2:3), and certain that the sole God (I Sam. 2:2; II Sam. 7:22; 22:32), the creator of heaven and earth (Gen. 1), is—or should be—the only ruler over Israel (I Sam. 8:7-8; 10:17-19; 12:12), instead of a king. After the publication of the Pentateuch the rituals described in Leviticus and elsewhere became standard for Israel, and the old texts were revised accordingly. It did not matter that these annotations, like Chronicles, utterly distorted the true picture of the past given in the old historical sources, and surrounded historical characters either by a glorious light or by a deceptive fog—the misunderstanding of the past by dating back the Law to a revelation to Moses on Sinai attained the dignity of a dogma, and the late annotations in this vein helped to give the four historical books the status of sacred scripture. Moreover, the connection of these books with prophecy, either by regarding their authors as prophets (I Chr. 29:29; II Chr. 9:29; 12:15; 13:22; 20:34; 26:22; 32:32), or because they contained stories about prophets (Samuel, Gad, Nathan, Ahijah, Jehu, Elijah, Elisha, Isaiah, etc.), strongly favored their canonization. Their growing popularity, their patriotic and religious significance, and their supposed prophetic authorship brought about their canonization *ca.* 200 B.C.—after Chronicles (300-250 B.C.) but before Ecclesiasticus (*ca.* 180 B.C.). The Chronicler quoted Samuel and Kings with great freedom—a proof that they were not at the time canonical—even making important corrections to the text: Satan (I Chr. 21:1), not God (II Sam. 24:1), tempted David to take the census; Elhanan did not kill Goliath (II Sam. 21:19), but Lahmi, the brother of Goliath (I Chr. 20:5). Ben Sirach, in Ecclus. 44–49, refers to the following books: the Pentateuch (44:16–45:26; 49:14-16); Joshua (46:1-10); Judges (46:11-12); Samuel (46:13–47:11); Kings (47:12–49:3); Isaiah (48:22-25); Jeremiah (49:4-7); Ezekiel (49:8-9); and the twelve minor prophets (49:10). We know from the preface of Ben Sirach's grandson to his Greek translation of Ecclesiasticus that the "Law and the Prophets" were not only canonical, but had already been translated into Greek (132 B.C.). A date *ca.* 200 B.C. for the canonization of the Former and Latter Prophets cannot be far wrong.

**b. The Latter Prophets.** Popular interest in the oracles of the eighth- and seventh-century prophets seems to have remained faint after the canonization of the D Code in 621. That book was ascribed to the pen of the greatest of the prophets, Moses, and contained so much of the noble religion of the prophets that they appeared to be mere plagiarists, repeating what had been said so eloquently by Moses. Moreover, the prophetic message had been a most unpopular threat of doom for the nation; and the ruin of Judah had been realized in 586 B.C. with Nebuchadnezzar's destruction of Jerusalem and the Exile. The career of Jeremiah illustrates vividly the violent hostility toward the prophets. After the prophetic warnings had been vindicated, their gloomy and menacing words were ill-suited to the prevailing pessimism and despair; and their aversion for the priestly rituals antagonized the growing importance of the temple services.

But already in the sixth century such prophets as Jeremiah and Ezekiel, who had been most bitter in their denunciation of Judah before 586, tried to comfort their people by picturing a better future. Ezekiel, by announcing the restoration of the temple and its services, and Second Isaiah (Isa. 40–55), by declaring to the exiles that Jehovah would bring them back to their country, lifted the eyes of the people from the pitiful present to a magnificent future. Then came Haggai and Zechariah with their prediction that a messianic king would restore peace and inde-

pendence to the Jews. Such alluring, Utopian visions proved immensely popular (until A.D. 200) and contributed to create an unprecedented interest in the prophetic volumes. It was believed that

> Surely the Lord GOD does nothing,
> Without revealing his secret
> to his servants the prophets
>     (Amos 3:7, an obvious interpolation);

and Ezekiel (38:17) and the Second Isaiah (Isa. 40:21; 41:26; 42:9; 44:7; 45:19; etc.) were certain that God had made known to the prophets his plans before carrying them out. Zechariah says that God had revealed through the "former" prophets his law and had punished his people for disregarding their inspired words (1:6; 7:12); at the time when Jerusalem and Judah were inhabited and prosperous, God spoke through the prophets (7:7), and the implication is obvious that if their words were obeyed, then prosperity might return.

The canonization of the Pentateuch (400 B.C.) tended to make the Jews a people of the book. Just as the historical books were revised and annotated to magnify past glories, so were the prophetic books to magnify future glories. The annotations in the prophetic books, especially the earliest (Isaiah and the minor prophets), by expressing the two conspicuous trends of the time—hostility toward foreign nations and assurance of a future triumph of Israel led by Jehovah or by his Messiah (anointed)—enhanced the popularity of the prophetic books. These dreams appeared in Ezekiel and Second Isaiah in the sixth century, but became dominant after Haggai and Zechariah in the fifth century, together with the glorification of the Law in the fourth century. Denunciations against foreign nations are found in Isa. 13–24; Jer. 46–51; Ezek. 25–32; 38–39; some of them are later additions, just as the first such series (Amos 1–2) has been supplemented with the oracles against Tyre, Edom, Judah, and possibly Gaza. In passages later than 400 B.C., Jehovah is said to pour down his wrath on the heathen (Isa. 34; Joel 3; Obad. 15 ff; Zeph. 2:4-15; Zech. 14; etc.).

The counterpart of the decimation of the heathen is the glorification of the Jews, although the two are not always contrasted as in Isa. 34–35. After Jeremiah (23:5; 33:15; cf. Isa. 4:2; Zech. 3:8; 6:12), a messianic king descended from David was expected to restore the independence and the prosperity of the Jews (Isa. 9:6-7; 11:10; Ezek. 34:23-24; 37:24-25; Hos. 3:5; Amos 9:11-15; Mic. 5:2-5; Zech. 9:5-6). According to other prophecies, however, the Jewish restoration would be accomplished by God without a Davidic Messiah, as in the Second Isaiah and much later in Daniel (Isa. 2:2-4 = Mic. 4:1-4; Hos. 1:7; Joel 3:13-21; Zech. 14:9).

When prophecy had become silent in the late fourth century, one or more scholars made a diligent search for prophetic books and prepared the present edition of the prophetic books in four volumes. The inclusion of such brief books as Obadiah, of a prophetic biography (Jonah), and of Nahum's triumphant ode, shows that the search was thorough, even though probably many valuable MSS failed to be found. The late-third-century annotations prove that, like the Former Prophets, the Latter Prophets were edited not long before 200 B.C. and not later than 180, when our edition was known to Ben Sirach, who read the poems of the Second Isaiah as part of the book of Isaiah (Ecclus. 48:24) and the twelve minor prophets as one volume (49:10)—a characteristic of this edition. Daniel, written in 164 B.C., could not be included; it quotes Jer. 25:11-12; 29:10 as scripture in 9:2. So in *ca.* 200 B.C. the Bible consisted of the "Law and the Prophets" (as known to Ben Sirach in 180; see Ecclus. 44-49), and is so called in IV Macc. 18:10; Tosef. B.M. 11, 23 (396); Midrash Ps. 90, § 4 (194*b*); Matt. 5:17; 7:12; 11:13; 22:40; Luke 16:16; John 1:45; Rom. 3:21.

The Law was read for instructions about the present, the Former Prophets with a sense of national pride for Israel's past glories, and the Latter Prophets for a glimpse of a better future. Sometime between 200 B.C. and A.D. 30 a reading from the prophetic canon (*haphṭārâ*) was part of the synagogue worship on certain days (Meg. 4.1-2); the earliest evidence is in Luke 4:16-19; Acts 13:15. The selection was fixed only on certain sabbaths, and we do not know whether Jesus selected Isa. 61:1-2 himself or whether it was prescribed; in early times the reading of Ezek. 1 was forbidden on account of its theosophical interpretation. The canonization of the Law and the Prophets allowed the future inclusion of other books in the sacred scriptures—Ben Sirach refers to Psalms, Proverbs, Ezra-Nehemiah, and perhaps to Job; and he even hopes that his own book will be regarded as inspired (Ecclus. 24:33).

**4. The canonization of the Writings.** The third division of the Hebrew Bible is simply called *Ketûbhîm* (כתובים), "Writings" (lit., "written [things]"), or in Greek, *Hagiographa* ("sacred writings"). No more precise title was possible, since it consists of a miscellaneous collection of widely different works. The Torah is a single work in five volumes; the Prophets includes two works of four volumes each; but the third canon consists of ten separate works (counting Chronicles-Ezra-Nehemiah as one work in two volumes), grouped as follows in the Hebrew Bible: (*a*) poetry (Psalms, Proverbs, Job); (*b*) the Five Scrolls (Song of Solomon, Ruth, Lamentations, Ecclesiastes, Esther), each one of which was read on an annual festival (Passover, Pentecost, the Ninth of Ab [when Jerusalem was destroyed in 586 B.C.], Tabernacles, and Purim); (*c*) prophecy (Daniel); (*d*) history (Ezra, Nehemiah, and Chronicles, in this order).

While the canonization of the Law and the Prophets consisted of the final, complete editions of certain types of literature, the Writings were a collection of separate works, each of which circulated independently until it was attracted like a satellite into the orbit of sacred scripture.

Two conditions had to be fulfilled before each book was canonized separately. The first was survival. When books had to be copied laboriously and expensively on papyrus or parchment, no work could survive for a few centuries unless it attracted readers. The Dead Sea Scrolls and the papyri found in Egyptian sands, without circulation among readers, disappeared in antiquity. Except for these documents, almost all Hebrew and Aramaic writings from the centuries before the Christian era have been lost; the

most important survival in Egyptian sands is a good portion of the Hebrew text of Ecclesiasticus and the Elephantine documents. As is well known, public taste is capricious—in Hebrew, Esther survived and Judith was lost; Ecclesiastes survived and Ecclesiasticus survived in part, by accident; Chronicles is extant, I Maccabees perished. Similarly some important Greek classics have come down to us in fragmentary copies found in Egypt, notably some fragments of Sappho and Menander; and *The Republic* of Cicero was discovered in part on a palimpsest in the Vatican, written below the commentary of Augustine on the Psalms, and published in 1822 by Cardinal Angelo Mai. Among the Jews, a book had to possess a strong appeal of some kind to survive; it must have attracted readers for its religious, nationalistic, or literary value.

The second condition for the canonization of a book after 200 B.C. was anonymous authorship. Only Nehemiah (and perhaps Ezra), who wrote his own memoirs, and the prophets whose public addresses were collected by them or by a disciple, have the genuine author's name attached to the book—it would be absurd to hide the name of the writer of an autobiography or of a public speaker well known to the audience. Other OT writers, not feeling the pride of authorship like Greek and modern writers, published their books as anonymously as telephone directories or railroad timetables. The first author who of necessity used a nom de plume to lend authority to his book was the author of the address of Moses in Deuteronomy; under his own name the book would not have transformed the religion of Judah after 621 B.C.

All the Writings are attributed to an imaginary author (David, Solomon, Daniel) or are anonymous (Job, Lamentations, Esther, Chronicles), except Nehemiah and perhap Ezra. We saw that prophecy ceased shortly before 200 B.C., and no inspired book could be written except by a prophet. It was, however, generally believed that prophecy came to an end soon after the death of Ezra when the men of the Great Synagogue collected the scriptures: no book known to have been written later than Ezra or Alexander the Great (in Jewish chronology this is practically equivalent; cf. Seder Olam Rabba 30) could be deemed inspired. The earliest statements of this doctrine date from *ca.* A.D. 90, and are found in II (IV) Esd. 14 (the twenty-four books of the OT were dictated, together with seventy esoteric apocalypses, to five scribes by Ezra in forty days) and in Jos. Apion I.viii.41, which says: "From the time of Artaxerxes [465-424 B.C.] to our own time, each event was recorded, but these writings are not deemed equally trustworthy with those written before them because the exact succession of prophets no longer existed." The Talmud (B.B. 14*b*-15*a*) likewise regards all canonical scriptures to have been written not later than Ezra (*ca.* 444 B.C.). The canonization of the Law is identified with that of the whole Hebrew Bible. We may fix the closing of the canon by the canonization of the Writings, *ca.* A.D. 90.

Ecclus. 39:1 (law, wisdom, and prophecies); II Macc. 2:13-14 (books about kings and prophets, books of David, and letters of kings about sacred gifts); and Luke 24:44 (Law, Prophets, and Psalms) allude to the gradual process leading to the final canonization of the Writings. Our earliest evidence is in the Prologue to the Greek translation of Ecclesiasticus, dated in 132: the Law, the Prophets, "and the others that followed them," or "and the other books of our fathers," or "and the rest of the books." What these "other books" which had been translated into Greek by 132 were, we have no way of knowing, but they probably included Psalms, Proverbs, and Job. As for Psalms, Ecclus. 47:8-10 in 180 B.C. knows a Davidic Psalter, and I Macc. 7:17 ca. 100 B.C. quotes Ps. 79:2-3 as scripture. Daniel may also have been regarded as inspired in 100 B.C. (I Macc. 2:59-60; and perhaps 1:54).

The interest in the rebuilding of the temple and the return of the exiles resulted in the separation of Ezra-Nehemiah from I–II Chronicles and their earlier canonization, for they incongruously precede Chronicles in the Hebrew Bible. The two earliest of the five scrolls (Ruth and Lamentations) reached canonical status before the other three (Song of Solomon, Ecclesiastes, Esther), the canonization of which was opposed by some rabbis, but (especially for Esther) was supported by popular demand. The discussions of the rabbis about Ezekiel were purely academic. We do not know whether the omission of references to Ezekiel, the five scrolls, Daniel, and Chronicles in Philo's writings, and the omission of Song of Solomon, Ecclesiastes, Esther, and Ezra in the NT are significant or merely accidental.

In any case, the destruction of Jerusalem and the temple in A.D. 70 and the propaganda of the Christians, quoting the gospel narratives (cf. I Cor. 11:23-26; 15:1-7, written before the gospels), forced the Jews to fix the canon of inspired scriptures for all time. Under the leadership of Johanan ben Zakkai, the Council of Jamnia (ca. A.D. 90) closed the third canon. The Hebrew Bible of twenty-four books is first mentioned at that time in II (IV) Esd. 14:44-46 —it included five books of the Law, eight in the Prophets, and eleven in the Writings (counting Ezra-Nehemiah and I–II Chronicles as only two books). Josephus (Apion I.viii), followed by Origen, Epiphanius, and Jerome, counted only twenty-two books, like the letters of the Hebrew alphabet; Josephus probably united Ruth with Judges, and Lamentations with Jeremiah. Jerome also knew of the total of twenty-four books, and also of twenty-seven books, adding to twenty-two the additional five "final letters" (דמנצפך). Josephus disregarded the three Hebrew canons (as the LXX did) and counted: five for the Law, thirteen for the Prophets (Joshua, Judges with Ruth, Samuel, Kings, Chronicles, Ezra-Nehemiah, Esther, Job, Isaiah, Jeremiah with Lamentations, Ezekiel, the twelve minor prophets, Daniel), and four for hymns to God and practical precepts to men (Psalms, Song of Solomon, Proverbs, Ecclesiastes). Possibly we should place Job in the third category and the Song of Solomon in the second. H. Graetz omits from this list Song of Solomon and Ecclesiastes; and S. Zeitlin likewise obtains the Bible of twenty-two books in Josephus by stating that the Song of Solomon and Ecclesiastes were added later to the canon of the Writings (which he dates from A.D. 65). But in view of the statements of II (IV) Esdras and in view of

the OT books quoted in Josephus and the NT, it is probable that the Hebrew Bible attained its present form, consisting of the Law, the Prophets, and the Writings, at the Council of Jamnia (Jabne) ca. A.D. 90.

The Pentateuch retained for the Jews its central position after the whole Hebrew Bible was canonized. It is natural to ignore religious progress through the centuries if the Law was revealed to Moses, together with the "tradition of the elders" or oral law (Mark 7:3-13; Jos. Antiq. XIII.x.6; cf. G. F. Moore, *Judaism*, I, 251-62), which was redacted in writing in the Mishnah (ca. 200) after having been transmitted orally. Revelation can hardly be improved or corrected, and consequently the Prophets and the Writings are considered *qabbalah* (tradition) which expounds the Law. Of course, as late as the Talmud the canon of twenty-four books was not always accepted blindly without suppressions or additions by the learned and by sectarians in Palestine, but eventually it was recognized as the sole revelation of God in written form.

The Dead Sea Covenanters at Qumran (usually identified with the Essenes) differed apparently from normative Judaism in 50 B.C.-A.D. 50 in recognizing some sacred books unknown or rejected by the rabbis. The Essenes, according to Josephus (War II.viii. 6; II.viii.7), studied ancient books, particularly medical or magical ones, and swore "to preserve carefully the books of the sect and the names of the angels." The so-called Zadokite Sect of Damascus (the Sect of the New Covenant) possessed the Book of the Hago (*sefer ha-hago*), containing regulations for the guidance of civil and religious leaders, and presumably also some noncanonical writings. The Apoc. and the Pseudep. preserved by the Christians illustrate the type of books that some Jews recognized as canonical.

**5. The Alexandrian Jewish canon.** Several circumstances contributed to make the Alexandrian canon (or the Hellenistic one in general) more hospitable to Jewish writings than the Palestinian official Bible. Since the discovery of the law of Moses in 621 (the D Code), Palestinian Jews made a sharp distinction between inspired scripture and human writings; canonization was a solemn recognition on the part of the leaders and the people that certain books were divinely revealed to prophets. Traditionally the final canonization of the whole Bible was accomplished by the men of the Great Synagogue (Assembly) in the time of Ezra and Nehemiah. Orthodox Judaism in Palestine after 400 B.C. always knew what was scripture and what was not.

In Alexandria, on the contrary, the Jews tended to accept as scripture any writing in Hebrew or Aramaic which came from Palestine. The Jews in the Dispersion spoke Greek, and their profane literature was in Greek, and after the translation of the Pentateuch into Greek (ca. 250 B.C.) they tended to regard all books translated into Greek from the Hebrew (as distinguished from those written in Greek) as divinely inspired. Moreover, they apparently did not believe, like the Palestinian Jews, that prophecy had ceased with Ezra and Nehemiah and the canon had been closed by the Great Synagogue. According to Philo of Alexandria (died ca. A.D. 50), inspiration has not ceased, but every wise and virtuous man is enabled, through the Spirit of God, to announce what is hidden to the human eye. Of course, for Philo and the Letter to Aristeas (*ca.* 100 B.C.), as in Palestine, the Pentateuch was unsurpassed in authority, but though subordinate to the law of Moses, other books were deemed inspired. There is evidence proving that the Bible of the Alexandrian Jews was not confined to the law of Moses (as some have claimed)—Philo quotes Psalms, Proverbs, Job, Ezra-Nehemiah, as scriptures; and in *On the Contemplative Life* § 25 (the authenticity of which has been questioned without decisive evidence) Philo says of the monastic Therapeutae that in their cells "they increase their knowledge and piety, and bring them to perfection, by studying the laws, and the sacred oracles revealed through the prophets, and hymns, and the other writings" (cf. Luke 24:44).

The Greek OT (incorrectly called the "Septuagint") is usually regarded as the Alexandrian Jewish Bible. In reality, except for a few papyrus fragments found in Egypt, all known copies of the LXX are Christian. Most MSS contain the books of the Hebrew Bible and the Apoc., but the Codex Alexandrinus (A) contains in addition III and IV Maccabees, the Odes (*cantica*) at the end of the Psalter (Exod. 15:1-19; Deut. 32:1-43; I Sam. 2:1-10; Jonah 2:3-10; Hab. 3; Isa. 38:10-20; Prayer of Manasseh; Dan. 3: 26-45 [Prayer of Azariah]; Dan. 3:52-90 [The Song of the Three Children]; Luke 1:46-55 [*Magnificat*]; Luke 2:29-32 [*Nunc dimittis*]; Luke 1:68-79 [*Benedictus*]; Luke 2:14 and selections [*Hymnus matutinus*]), and the Psalms of Solomon.

Strictly speaking, we therefore do not know what was the canon of the Alexandrian and Diaspora Jews before the time when the LXX was condemned in A.D. 130, under the leadership of Rabbi AKIBA, and Aquila's literal translation of the Hebrew Bible was substituted for it. But we may surmise that this earlier Greek Bible disregarded the arrangement of the Hebrew Bible and added the Apoc. (without II or IV Esdras).

In this Greek Bible the distinction between the Prophets and the Writings was completely disregarded, and after the Pentateuch the books were arranged according to literary types: (*a*) history: Joshua, Judges, Ruth, Samuel, Kings, Chronicles, I Esdras (Greek Ezra), II Esdras (Ezra-Nehemiah); (*b*) poetical and didactic books: Psalms, Proverbs, Ecclesiastes, Song of Solomon, Job, *Wisdom of Solomon, Ecclesiasticus;* (*c*) stories: Esther (with *additions*), *Judith, Tobit;* (*d*) Prophets: the twelve minor prophets, Isaiah, Jeremiah, Baruch, Lamentations, *Epistle of Jeremiah,* Ezekiel, Daniel (with *additions*); (*e*) *I and II Maccabees:* The apocryphal books are *italicized* in this list, which gives the contents of the great Vatican MS (Vaticanus Greek 1209, Codex B, *ca.* A.D. 350) with the addition of I and II Maccabees, which it lacks.

The earliest attestation for the threefold division of the Hebrew Bible (Law, Prophets, and Writings) is in the Prologue to the Greek translation of Ecclesiasticus (132 B.C.), and for the rearrangement of the books in the Greek Bible at Alexandria, Jos. Apion I.viii (*ca.* A.D. 95): five books of Moses, thirteen books of the prophets, four books containing hymns to God and precepts for men (Psalms, Proverbs,

Song of Solomon, Ecclesiastes). Although Josephus uses the books of the Apoc. as sources for his histories, in accordance with Palestinian usage he does not regard them as scripture, any more than Philo did. But in view of their inclusion in the LXX, it seems that most of the Jews in Alexandria regarded them as sacred writings. Both Philo and Josephus quoted the LXX in their writings, although Josephus was acquainted with the Hebrew Bible from childhood and claims (in most cases falsely) to have made his own translations from the Hebrew (Antiq. I. proem. 1-2). But Philo, who paraphrases in *The Life of Moses* II. 5-7, §§ 26-44 (cf. Jos. Antiq. I. proem. 1, 3; XII.ii.1-15) the story of the origin of the Greek translation of the Pentateuch given in the Letter of Aristeas, regarded the translation as literal and divinely inspired —it was his Bible just as the King James Version is the Bible for many English-speaking persons.

**6. The Christian canon.** The Bible of Jesus and of his disciples was the Hebrew Bible, but the Bible of Paul and his converts was the Greek LXX (including the Apoc., except II [IV] Esdras, which is found in the Vulg.). By far the great majority of Christians in the first century and later were Greek-speaking Gentile proselytes or pagans. The insignificant number of the Nazarenes and other Palestinian Jewish Christians who spoke Aramaic, first attested in Acts 15:5, the spiritual ancestors of the sect of the Ebionites, fled to Pella in Perea in A.D. 67 or shortly before. On Judeo-Christians, see H. J. Schoeps, *Theologie und Geschichte des Judenchristentums* (1949).

So the LXX became through Paul the official Christian Bible in the early centuries. The Christians followed Philo in claiming for the LXX the same inspiration as the original (Irenaeus III.ii.3-4; Cyril of Jerusalem *Catecheses* IV.33-34; Augustine *On Christian Doctrine* 22; *City of God* VIII.44). The differences between the LXX and the current Hebrew text were explained as textual errors in the transmission of the LXX, divine modifications for the use of the future church, or even Jewish corrections in the Hebrew text (Just. Dial. 71-73; Jerome on Gal. 3:13). The inspiration of the OT, presumably in the Greek version, is taken for granted in Heb. 1:1, and for the early church fathers the LXX was the only OT authorized by the church; even Origen, who was familiar with the Hebrew text and compared it with the LXX and other Greek versions in his Hexapla, preached on the LXX text and commented on it. Jerome was attacked for basing his Latin version on the Hebrew text; Augustine resented his change of "cucumber" to "ivy" in Jonah 4:6-10.

The citations and allusions to the OT in the NT are mostly (80 per cent) taken from the LXX, and every NT author is familiar with it; a detailed conspectus will be found in W. Dittmar, *Vetus Testamentum in Novo* (1903). The only quotations in Hebrew or Aramaic are the words on the cross (Matt. 27: 46=Mark 15:34 [Ps. 22:1—H 22:2]). Rarely do we find a new translation from the Hebrew, unless, as in other cases, the changes in the LXX are due to faulty memory: Matt. 12:18-21 (Isa. 42:1-4); Luke 1:17 (Mal. 4:5-6—H 3:23-24); 2:23 (Exod. 13:2); John 19:37 (Zech. 12:10); Rom. 9:17 (Exod. 9:16); 11:4 (I Kings 19:18); 12:19 (Deut. 32:35). At times the OT is quoted in a new version influenced by an

Aramaic interpretation: I Cor. 2:9 (Isa. 64:3-4); 15: 54 (Isa. 25:8). In very few other cases the LXX is improved through an examination of the Hebrew: Matt. 11:10 = Mark 1:2 = Luke 7:27 (Mal. 3:1); Matt. 26:31 = Mark 14:27 (Zech. 13:7); Matt. 22:24 corrects Mark 12:19 and Luke 20:28 according to Deut. 25:5. But in general the LXX is quoted with minor variants. Revelation, however, generally prefers Theod.'s Greek text of Daniel, which became standard in the Christian church; Heb. 11:33 alludes to Dan. 6:23 in Theod.'s recension although it is faithful to the LXX elsewhere; Mark 14:62 ("*with* the clouds") quotes Dan. 7:13 according to Theod., but Matt. 24:30; 26:64 according to the LXX ("*on* the clouds"). The most important use of the LXX instead of the Hebrew is, of course, in Matt. 1:23, which quotes Isa. 7:14 (LXX "virgin"; Hebrew and Greek Aq. "young woman"). Another striking case is Acts 15:17, which quotes Amos 9:12 according to the LXX ("the rest of men may seek" instead of the Hebrew "may possess the remnant of Edom," reading אדם as '*ādhām* instead of '*edhôm*, and the verb דרש, "seek," instead of ירש, "possess").

The following OT books are cited or formally quoted as scripture in the NT: Genesis, Exodus, Leviticus, Numbers (II Tim. 2:19), Deuteronomy, II Samuel (II Cor. 6:18; Heb. 1:5), I Kings (Rom. 11: 3-4), Psalms, Proverbs, Job (I Cor. 3:19), Hosea, Amos, Micah (Matt. 2:6), Joel, Jonah, Habakkuk, Zechariah, Malachi, Isaiah, Jeremiah, Daniel. There are some echoes from some other books of the OT but apparently no allusions to Song of Solomon, Ruth, Lamentations, Ecclesiastes, Esther, and Ezra. Conversely there are allusions to some of the Apoc. and Pseudep., notably: Ecclus. 5:11 (Jas. 1:9); II Macc. 6-7 (Heb. 11:35-36); Wisd. Sol. 2:13, 18 (Matt. 27:43); 5:17 (Eph. 6:11, 13); 7:26 (Heb. 1:3); 9:15 (II Cor. 5:4); 13:1-9; 14:22-31 (Rom. 1:20-32). Even more direct are references to some of the books of the Pseudep., some of which are quoted as scripture: the quotation in Matt. 27:9, according to Jerome, was taken from a Jeremiah apocryphon; an Apocalypse of Elijah is quoted in I Cor. 2:9, according to Origen, and in Eph. 5:9 according to Epiphanius; Jude 14-16 quotes Enoch 1:9, and in vs. 9, according to Origen, refers to the Assumption of Moses; Origen also says that II Timothy alludes to the lost book of Jannes and Jambres; "sawn in two" in Heb. 11:37 probably cites the Martyrdom of Isaiah; Luke 11:49-51*a* (cf. Matt. 23:34-35) quotes a lost work apparently called 'Η σοφία τοῦ θεοῦ (The Wisdom of God); the "scripture" quoted in John 7:38 is unknown (according to C. C. Torrey it is a mistranslated allusion to Ps. 46:4—H 46:3); the source of the quotation in Eph. 5:14 is unknown, unless it is a paraphrase of Isa. 26:19; 60:1; likewise unknown is the source of Jas. 4:5. For comprehensive lists of allusions to the Apoc. and Pseudep. in the NT, see F. Bleek in *TSK*, 26 (1853), 268-354; W. Dittmar, *Vetus Testamentum in Novo* (1903).

After Paul had said that the law of Moses was less important than the promises to Abraham (Gal. 3:16-20), was only an "old testament" to be supplemented by a "new testament" (II Cor. 3:6, 14), was merely a guide leading men to Christ (Gal. 3:24), the early Christians searched the Prophets and the Psalms for promises that had been fulfilled in the birth, life, and particularly the crucifixion and resurrection of Jesus Christ (Acts 2:22-36; 3:12:36; 4:8-12; and *passim* in the four gospels). Paul claimed that the divine promises to Abraham were made to the children of Abraham according to the spirit, whether Jews or Gentiles (Rom. 9-11), for Abraham was the "father of all who believe without being circumcised" (Rom. 4: 11). The church is the "Israel of God" (Gal. 6:16).

Paul thus claimed for the Christians the OT promises; the Letter to the Hebrews claimed for them the Levitical law. Moses was a servant, but Christ a "son over his own house" (Heb. 3:5-6), and the great ritual institutions of Judaism became mere images of spiritual, heavenly realities: the sabbath (4:1-11), the priesthood (5-8), the sanctuary (9:1-5), the sacrifices (9:6-14; 10:1-13), are but the "copy and shadow of the heavenly sanctuary" (8:5).

Conversely John sees no possible harmony between the law given by Moses and grace and truth, which came through Jesus Christ (John 1:17): the OT bears witness to Christ (5:39); but the Jews did not believe in Moses and the Scriptures, and how can they therefore believe in the words of Christ (5: 46-47)? Consequently they do not believe in God (7:28; 8:19); they hate him (15:23-25). The ritual institutions of the OT are futile and useless (5:16-17; 7:22-24), including the temple (4:20-21).

In conclusion, although the various writers of the NT differ in their attitude, they agree that the OT (without the Apoc.) is divinely inspired (cf. II Tim. 3:16) and predicts salvation through Jesus Christ; but some writers assume that the gospel has superseded the OT.

Although the total rejection of the OT by Marcion (second century) was declared heretical by most Christians, the Christian church never reached a complete agreement about the canonicity of the books called Apoc. ("hidden, spurious" books): I (III) and II (IV) Esdras, Tobit, Judith, Additions to Esther, Wisdom of Solomon, Ecclesiasticus, Baruch, Susanna, Song of the Three Children, Bel and the Dragon, Prayer of Manasseh, I and II Maccabees. All of them, with the exception of II (IV) Esdras, preserved in Latin in the Vulg., are extant in Greek in MSS of the LXX, but the canonicity of some was questioned.

After the NT, the Apostolic Fathers allude to the Apoc. or quote them as scripture: the Didache or Teaching of the Twelve Apostles (Ecclesiasticus), Barnabas (The Wisdom of Solomon, Ecclesiasticus, II Esdras), I Clement (The Wisdom of Solomon), etc. The popularity of the Apoc. increased in the church: Tertullian, Irenaeus, Hippolytus, Clement of Alexandria, Origen, Cyprian, regarded at least some specific books of the Apoc. as scripture.

But beginning with Origen, the church fathers who knew Hebrew realized that the books of the Apoc. were missing from the Hebrew Bible. As a scholar Origen limited the Bible to the twenty-two books, but as a churchman he defended their canonicity: in 238 Julius Africanus of Emmaus criticized Origen for quoting Susanna as scripture; Origen could merely appeal to the authority of the church and quoted Prov. 22:28 ("Remove not the ancient landmark"). For each book of the Apoc. and

Pseudep. E. Schürer (*Geschichte des jüdischen Volkes* [4th ed., 1909], III; *A History of the Jewish People* [1886-90]) gives the patristic quotations. Cyril of Jerusalem (died 386) in theory distinguished likewise books of unquestioned and of doubtful canonicity, but in practice followed the general usage. Jerome likewise made a distinction between the *libri canonici* (the *hebraica veritas* [Hebrew truth] confined to the Hebrew Bible) and the *libri ecclesiastici*—books outside the Hebrew Bible should be relegated among the apocryphal writings (*inter apocrypha*). Nevertheless, as a Christian believer he recognized the books of the Apoc. (including II [IV] Esdras) as scripture and included them in his Latin translation, the Vulg., which became the official Bible of the Roman Catholic Church. This divergent attitude toward the Apoc. has prevailed through the centuries in Christianity.

The authority of some or all of the Apoc. was recognized in the early councils. At Hippo in Africa (393), and at the third and sixteenth councils of Carthage (397, 419), all the books of the Apoc., as it seems, were regarded as scripture; and at the Council of Trent (1546), confirmed by the Vatican Council (1870), the anathema was pronounced against whosoever did not regard the whole Vulg. Bible "sacred and canonical." In the standard Clementine edition (1592) it contained I-II (III-IV) Esdras, omitted in the Sistine edition (1590); but these books were printed at the end of the OT in smaller type with a statement that they were not recognized as canonical at the Council of Trent.

In spite of some objections, the books of the Apoc. were regarded as scripture at the Trullan (692) and later councils; but the Council of Jerusalem limited the Bible to the Hebrew books and to Tobit, Judith, Ecclesiasticus, Wisdom of Solomon, and tacitly to I Esdras and the additions to Esther and Daniel.

At first the Syriac church read in the Peshitta version only the books in the Hebrew Bible, omitting Chronicles-Ezra-Nehemiah and Esther, but adding Ecclesiasticus. Eventually, except among the Nestorians, the influence of the LXX prevailed over the Hebrew Bible, and the Syro-Hexaplaric version of Paul of Tella (based on the LXX in Origen's Hexapla) contained also Wisdom of Solomon, Ecclesiasticus, Baruch, the Epistle of Jeremiah, and the Additions to Daniel. The most important MS of the Peshitta (Codex Ambrosianus, sixth century, A. M. Ceriani, ed., 1879-83) contains, in addition to the Apoc. (without I [III] Esdras, Prayer of Manasseh, Tobit, and Additions to Esther) III-IV Maccabees, II (IV) Esdras, and Jos. War VII.

In addition to the Syriac, other oriental churches used translations of books not included in the LXX. The Syriac versions of II (IV) Esdras and notably of II Baruch (the Syriac Apocalypse of Baruch) are important. G. Steindorff has published a Coptic (Fayumic or Middle Egyptian) version of the Apocalypse of Elias (1899). The Ethiopic versions of Jubilees, Enoch, and the Martyrdom of Isaiah are the most complete witnesses for these books. The Armenian versions of the Life of Adam and Eve and of the Testaments of the Twelve Patriarchs are valuable. The Greek versions of such books are mostly lost, and the Latin versions (except for II

[IV] Esdras, Apocalypse of Baruch, and Martyrdom of Isaiah) are not in existence.

It is clear that the Apoc. enjoyed a canonical status that was almost unchallenged, except by scholars, in the Roman and Greek churches during the Middle Ages. The situation changed with the Reformation. In their polemic against some Roman Catholic doctrines unknown to Jesus and Paul (justification by good works, the merits of the saints, etc.) the Reformers noticed that they were confirmed in some texts of the Apoc. Martin Luther said that II Maccabees and Esther Judaized too much and contained too much heathenism, so that he wished they did not exist; he denied that one could derive the doctrine of purgatory from II Macc. 12:43, "for the same book is not one of the books of Holy Writ." Another reason for rejecting the Apoc. was the revival of the study of Hebrew. Nicolaus of Lyra, a Christian of Jewish parentage, published in 1333 a pamphlet in Latin with the title "Treatise on the difference between our translation [the Vulg.] and the Hebrew truth." In 1520 A. R. B. Karlstadt (or Carlstadt) divided the scriptures into three classes: the Hebrew canon, the *libri hagiographi* or almost canonical (Wisdom of Solomon, Ecclesiasticus, Judith, Tobit, I-II Maccabees), and books worthless for Christians.

Since the Reformers, rejecting the authority of the Papacy, saw in the Scriptures their supreme guide, it was vital for them to fix the canon of Holy Writ, and to publish authentic translations from the inspired Hebrew, Aramaic, and Greek OT and NT. Accordingly Luther, in his epoch-making German translation of the Bible (1534), relegated the books of Wisdom of Solomon, Ecclesiasticus, Judith, Tobit, I-II Maccabees (the *hagiographi* of Karlstadt), together with Additions to Esther, Additions to Daniel, and Prayer of Manasseh (omitting I-II Esdras), to the end of the OT with this superscription: "Apocrypha, these are books which are not held equal to the sacred Scriptures, and yet are useful and good for reading." John Wycliffe's English translation of the Bible, made from the Vulg. (1380-82) and revised after his death (1384) by John Purvey (1388), included the Apoc.; it was printed in 1850. Miles Coverdale in his English Bible (1535) followed the example of Luther, placing the Apoc. at the end of the OT (adding, however, I-II Esdras and omitting the Prayer of Manasseh). The Prayer of Manasseh was added in the "Thomas Matthew" Bible (1537), which is an edition of the versions of William Tyndale (Genesis-II Chronicles) and Coverdale. The books of the Apoc. were included in later English Bibles—the Great Bible (1539), the Geneva Bible (1560, in which some of the Apoc. books were translated from the Greek), the Bishop's Bible (1568), and the KJV (made from the Hebrew and Greek, with the Apoc. scattered among the OT books; 1611). But beginning with 1629, some editions of the Bible appeared without the books of the Apoc. and, following some bitter controversies, since 1927 they have been omitted from most copies of the KJV and from most Protestant Bibles in other languages. So, while Roman Catholics regard the Apoc. as no less canonical than the books in the Hebrew Bible, the books of the Apoc. are placed outside holy writ by Calvinistic and other Protestant churches, but are read by the church "for example of life and instruction in manners; and yet doth it not apply them to establish doctrine" (*42 and 39 Articles of Religion* [1553, 1563]) according to the practice in the Lutheran, Anglican, and Zurich Reformed churches.

**7. The closing of the Jewish canon.** After the Writings were canonized in A.D. 90, the Jewish canon was closed for all time. The notion of sacred scripture was derived from that of prophecy—God himself speaking through an inspired man. At first, revelation was purely oral, but with Deuteronomy (621 B.C.) revelation became the written utterance of a prophet, and eventually a prophetic writing which had never been delivered orally. Oral prophecy declined after Ezekiel and gradually ceased after Malachi and Joel; Zechariah (13:1-6) has a very low opinion of the prophets of his day, and public opinion regards them as charlatans or agitators worthy of death. So genuine prophecy had ceased in the days of the Maccabees (164-142 B.C.; see I Macc. 4:46; 14:41; 9:27). According to Jos. Apion I.viii and the rabbis, the last prophets had been Haggai, Zechariah, and Malachi; accordingly no Jewish apocalypse was attributed to an author later than Ezra.

The conviction that prophetic inspiration, the source of inspired scripture, had ceased—and presumably had ceased forever—set aside the Law, the Prophets, and the Writings as a closed body of holy scripture, set apart from all other literature by its unique inspiration. The inclusion of the Apoc. in the LXX Bible of the Alexandrian Jews, which had been adopted by the Christians together with the gospel, made it imperative to close the sacred canon. This was not done without serious controversy, particularly about the Song of Solomon and Ecclesiastes, but also about Esther (see G. F. Moore, *Judaism* I, 242-47). Finally it was decided that these books were inspired and that the gospel, the books of the heretics, Ecclesiasticus, and the books written since "are not sacred scripture." So the Hebrew canon of scripture was closed forever shortly before or after A.D. 100.

**8. The arrangement of the OT books.** In the Hebrew Bible the books are divided into the successive canons as follows, in the printed editions:

a) The Law (*tôrâ*): Genesis, Exodus, Leviticus, Numbers, Deuteronomy

b) The Prophets (*nᵉbhî'îm*)
Former Prophets: Joshua, Judges, Samuel, Kings
Latter Prophets: Isaiah, Jeremiah, Ezekiel, the twelve minor prophets

c) The Writings (*kᵉthûbhîm*)
Poetry: Psalms, Proverbs, Job
The Five Scrolls: Song of Solomon, Ruth, Lamentations, Ecclesiastes, Esther
Prophecy: Daniel
History: Ezra-Nehemiah, I-II Chronicles

In the Talmud (Baraita B.B. 14*b*) the order is as follows: the Pentateuch, the Prophets (Joshua, Judges, Samuel, Kings, Jeremiah, Ezekiel, Isaiah, the minor prophets), the Writings (Ruth, Psalms, Job, Proverbs, Ecclesiastes, Song of Solomon, Lamentations, Daniel, Esther, Ezra [plus Nehemiah], Chronicles). For divergent orders in books and MSS, see S. Singer, ed., *The Jewish Encyclopedia*, III, 144. For the order in the LXX see H. B. Swete, *Introduction to the OT in Greek* (1914), pp. 201-14.

**9. Canonicity.** Up to this point we have been concerned with historical problems—how, why, and when certain Hebrew and Aramaic writings came to be regarded divinely inspired and included in a canon of sacred scriptures. Here we are concerned with theological problems—namely, the Jewish and Christian doctrines concerning the origin, sacredness, authority, and inspiration of the scriptures.

*a. Jewish doctrines.* The Jews believed firmly that the books of the OT had been inspired by God, and they called the OT the "oracles of God" (θεοῦ λόγια; Aristeas 177), "divinely revealed oracles" (θεόχρηστα λόγια; Philo *Legation to Caius* 31 [II, 577, Mangey]); the OT contains "decrees of God" (θεοῦ δόγματα; Jos. Apion I.viii); Moses wrote the Pentateuch under divine inspiration (Philo *Life of Moses* II.2 [II, 136, Mangey]; III.23 [II, 163, Mangey]). God revealed the books of the OT to prophets; the beginning of the Letter to the Hebrews expressed the Jewish doctrine: "In many and various ways God spoke of old to our fathers by the prophets." This is, of course, repeatedly stated in the OT: "The words of Jeremiah, . . . to whom the word of the LORD came" (Jer. 1:1-2); "The word of the LORD came to Ezekiel" (Ezek. 1: 3); etc. In the Pentateuch, God revealed his laws unto Moses (Exod. 20:1, 22; 21:1; 25:1; Lev. 1:1; 4:1; 6:1; 8:1; etc.).

The prophets also decided whether a book was divinely inspired or not (II Kings 22:14-16). But generally books were declared canonical by king and people (II Kings 23:2-3) or by clergy and people (Neh. 10:28-29); tradition attributed important roles in the canonization of the Scriptures to "Hezekiah and his college," who put into writing Isaiah, Proverbs (cf. Prov. 25:1), the Song of Solomon, and Ecclesiastes (B. B. 14*b*-15*a*); to the men of the Great Synagogue who put into writing Ezekiel, the Twelve (Minor Prophets), Daniel, and Esther; Nehemiah, who completed the OT (cf. II Macc. 2:13), a task also attributed to Judas Maccabeus (II Macc. 2:14) and to Ezra (II Esdr. 14). It is assumed in these passages that the whole OT was completed and canonized in the time of Ezra and Nehemiah, or of Artaxerxes I (465-424), according to Jos. Apion I.viii, or of Alexander the Great (Seder Olam Rabba 30). Consequently the last prophets were Haggai, Zechariah, Malachi, or, if we regard every biblical author as a prophet, Ezra and Nehemiah. After their death the Holy Spirit departed from Israel, and no inspired scriptures could be written. This doctrine, according to which the OT was completed and canonized in the time of Ezra or soon after, was accepted by the early church fathers (e.g., Tertullian, Irenaeus, and Clement of Alexandria) and by later Christian scholars until in 1877 A. Kuenen showed it to be historically incorrect.

On the other hand, the rabbis assert that the Law, together with repentance, paradise (Eden), Gehenna, the throne of glory, the (heavenly) temple, and the name of the Messiah were created before the world; the proof text is Prov. 8:22, on the assumption that Wisdom is identical with the Law (Baraita Pesakhim 54*a*). Some said the Law was created 2,000 years before the world, others said 974 generations. The pre-existence of the Torah implied that it was superior to the rest of the OT—for God alone was its creator and put it into writing, while human beings participated in the redaction of the other scriptures. The eleven psalms (90–100) which Moses wrote are not in the Torah because they are not words of the Torah (i.e., exclusively divine), but words of prophecy (Midrash Tehillin 90, § 4 [194*b*]). Those who deny the resurrection or the divine origin of the Torah, and the freethinkers ("Epicureans"), have no portion in the future world (Sanh. 10.1). The pre-existence of the Torah and its descent into the tabernacle and in Zion are already emphasized in Ecclus. 24:8-23. How did the Torah come to Israel? The Ten Commandments were proclaimed by the Lord with a loud voice to Israel at Sinai; they were engraved by him or by themselves on the two first tables of stone after angels (cf. Gal. 3:19) had passed around each one to every Israelite for acceptance. The rest of the Pentateuch, according to Rabbi Akiba, came to Moses through divine revelation, but it was generally certain that Moses did not contribute a single thought to the Torah; God revealed it either by word of mouth, as a teacher, or in writing, or by dictation, or through angels (Deut. 33:2 LXX; cf. Gal. 3:19; Acts 7:53; Heb. 2:2).

Ludwig Blau, in *The Jewish Encyclopedia*, writes: "The Torah is one of the seven things that existed before the Creation. According to Simeon ben Lakish, it is 2,000 years older. . . . Even Abraham obeyed all its laws [contrast Rom. 4; Gal. 3:8-12, 17-18]. . . . When Moses ascended to heaven, he found God with the Torah in His hand and reading the passage about the Red Heifer [Num. 19:1-10]. . . . It was given to Israel unconditionally . . . by Moses, who made one copy each for every tribe and corrected them all from the copy of Levi. . . . Before him who denies its divine origin the doors of hell shall never close, and he shall be condemned to stay therein eternally. . . . The Law will endure forever. . . . Any prophet who attempts to annul one of its laws will be punished by death. . . . Though all mankind should combine, they could not abolish one yod (the smallest letter) of it (compare Matt. 5: 18). When Solomon took unto himself many wives, the yod of ירב ('he shall multiply'; Deut. 17:17) cast himself down before God, and denounced the king. . . . Then spake God: 'Solomon and hundreds like him shall be destroyed, but not one of your letters shall ever be annihilated.' . . . The whole world is but a thirty-two-hundredth part of the Torah. . . . When a copy of the Law was burned, people rent their clothes as though one of their dearest relatives had died, and such rents were never to be sewed up. . . . But a copy written by a heretic (מין) might be burned, and one written by a non-Jew had to be buried. . . . Before the Torah the people had to stand up in the synagogue; and while it lay unrolled on the reader's desk, speaking . . . and leaving the synagogue were forbidden. . . . Before birth each one is taught the Torah; but when he sees the light of day an angel touches his mouth, and makes him forget it all." Many scholars were able to write the Torah from memory. Instruction in it was gratuitous.

The rest of the OT (the Prophets and the Hagiographa) is a supplement to the Torah. There is nothing in them which is not suggested in the Law. In other words, the Pentateuch is an inner zone, the Holy of Holies. The other scriptures are simply explanatory; they are Kabbala (tradition), and no legal decisions could be derived from them unless they were authenticated in the Torah. These books were given for instruction to the people in times of ignorance. Their divine origin was, of course, generally recognized, but three explanations of their origin were given: (*a*) God revealed the contents of these books to their human authors by inspiration; (*b*) God revealed these scriptures to Moses on Sinai, and the prophets received them by tradition; and finally (*c*) God revealed them to the pre-existent souls of their authors at Sinai.

The first theory is the most common. Divine inspiration of the Law and the Prophets is called by Josephus (Apion I.vii) ἐπίπνοια, "breathing upon," "inspiration." Esdras prays that God might send "the Holy Spirit into me"; God promises that he will light a candle of understanding in his heart; after he drank a cup of a liquid the color of fire, he dictated the twenty-four biblical books and seventy apocalyptic books to five secretaries in forty days (II Esd. 14:22, 25, 39-44). The rabbinical literature says the deity or the Holy Spirit (meaning the spirit of prophecy, or inspiration) rested over the authors of the canonical books so that they did not utter their own thoughts and wisdom, but spoke and wrote what God's mouth spoke.

The second theory, according to which the Prophets and the Hagiographa were revealed to Moses on Sinai and transmitted by him, was presented by Simeon ben Lakish (*ca.* A.D. 250). It assumed, as was generally thought, that these books added nothing new to the Torah—forty-eight prophets and seven prophetesses prophesied in Israel without adding or detracting what is written in the Torah, except the reading of the Esther scroll (on Purim; Baraita Meg. 14*a*). Others asserted that the book of Esther had also been revealed to Moses and had been transmitted orally until it was finally put in writing.

*b. The NT.* The OT is generally regarded as the inspired Word of God (Mark 7:13; Rom. 3:2; Heb. 1:1; II Tim. 3:16; II Pet. 1:19-21), which is given for life (Rom. 7:10; 10:5; Gal. 3:12), for guidance unto Christ (Gal. 3:24), for promising God's gospel (Rom. 1:2), for making one wise unto salvation (II Tim. 3:15).

Jesus did not come to abrogate the Law and the Prophets, but to fulfil them (Matt. 5:17-19); he saw in obedience to the summary of the Law (Deut. 6:5; Lev. 19:18) a condition for eternal life (Luke 10:25-28), and he declared that the Law is eternal (Matt. 5:18). But he considered the Law merely the first stage in progress, for it was given at times to correspond to human weakness (Mark 10:2-12) and was far below the requirements of the kingdom of God (Matt. 5:48).

Paul went a step further: although he recognized the divine origin of the Law, he regarded it merely as an "old testament" to be supplemented by a "new testament" (II Cor. 3:6, 13), incapable of producing life and righteousness (Gal. 3:21). Faith has delivered us from bondage under the Law (Gal. 3:23-26), as Paul tries to prove from the OT, which furnishes him and later Luther with the central motto of their religion: "The righteous shall live by his faith" (Hab. 2:4; Rom. 1:17; Gal. 3:11).

The prophetic books and the Psalms were more valuable than the Law for the early Christians, for they found in them promises fulfilled in the birth, life, death, and resurrection of Jesus Christ. The Jews had interpreted the whole OT as law, but the Christians found prophecies, if not predictions, on many pages (Luke 24:27, 44; John 5:39, 46; Acts 3:18).

*c. The Koran.* Through contacts with Jews and Christians, Mohammed became familiar with parts of the OT and retold, with legendary embellishments, some of its stories in the Koran. He recognized the divine origin of both the OT and the NT: "For he had sent down the Law and the Gospel aforetime; and now He has sent down the 'Illumination' " (Koran 3.2).

*d. Roman Catholic doctrines.* The NT contained echoes from the Apoc. and Pseudep. (Jas. 1:19; cf. Ecclus. 5:11; Heb. 11:35-36; cf. II Macc. 6-7; Jude 9; cf. Asmp. Moses), according to Origen (*De Principiis* 3.2.1) and the Book of Jannes and Jambres (II Tim. 3:8; cf. Origen on Matt. 23:37; 27:9; Heb. 11: 37; cf. the Martyrdom of Isaiah), and even quoted uncanonical writings as scripture (Matt. 27:9; cf. a lost apocryphon of Jeremiah, according to Jerome; cf. I Cor. 2:9; Eph. 5:14 with the Apocalypse of Elijah; cf. Jude 14-16 with Enoch 1:9). Since the LXX was the Bible of the early church, the Apoc. was known and quoted by the church fathers, who also referred to some books of the Pseudep., most of which were regarded as canonical in the oriental churches (Syriac, Coptic, Ethiopic, Georgian) and, in some cases, Greek (Psalms of Solomon, Enoch, III and IV Maccabees) and Latin (II Esdras). Clemens Romanus (I, chs. 8 and 17) quotes an Ezekiel apocryphon known to Josephus (*Antiq.* X.v.1) and the Assumption of Moses I.xvii, which is also quoted by Clement of Alexandria (*Stromata* VI.xv.132). The book of Enoch is regarded as canonical by Barnabas and Tertullian, and many fathers cited it until Jerome and Augustine declared it apocryphal. II Esdras is used by the Apocalypse of Baruch and by some Christian apocalypses; it is quoted by Clement of Alexandria, saying: "Esdras the prophet says"; it is utilized by Hermas and the Apostolic Constitutions, and it is cited as scripture by Ambrose of Milan, but Jerome spoke of its visions as "dreams." Its popularity surpassed greatly that of the Apocalypse of Baruch (cited by Papias in Irenaeus V.33.3). The Sibylline Oracles were highly regarded by Justin Martyr (Apol. I.44) and other fathers. IV Maccabees was included in a famous uncial MS of the LXX (Alexandrinus), but does not seem to have been generally regarded as canonical by the Christians. Slavic Enoch is cited by Origen (*De Principiis* I.iii.2).

The books of the Hebrew Bible were thus recognized as holy and canonical by all orthodox Christians from the beginning; for a while opinions varied about the books of the Apoc., but the Catholic church finally recognized their full canonicity. Only heretics rejected the twenty-two (or twenty-four) books of the Hebrew Bible—notably Marcion and the Gnostics in the second century, who were concerned only in developing Paul's teachings. They believed that the God of the OT, the creator of the material world and the revealer of the law of Levitical ceremonies, was distinct from the God of salvation and love. Marcion rejected the OT *in toto*, and adopted a canon consisting only of an expurgated edition of Luke and Paul's letters (without Timothy and Titus). In 144 he separated himself from the church and founded his own congregations, whose remnants continued as late as the seventh century (Paulicians) and lasted until the ninth century in the Byzantine church, and even later in Armenia; this tendency may have influenced the Albigenses.

The Catholic church fought these heresies with all its power, and defended the canonicity of the OT (including the Apoc.) with the utmost vigor.

There is a certain parallel in the Jewish canonization of the OT (*ca.* 400 B.C. to A.D. 100) and the Christian closing of its canon by *ca.* 200. Judaism was in danger of yielding to Hellenistic influence and Christianity to emperor-worship and other Roman practices, when they suffered cruel persecutions under Antiochus IV Epiphanes (168-165 B.C.) and under Domitian, who ruled from 81 to 96. The death of the faithful and the safety of the apostates, which seemed to question the power and the justice of God, moved noble dreamers to promise an imminent intervention of God to reward the martyrs and punish sinners after their death. Two brilliant authors wrote two superb apocalypses—the book of Daniel (164 B.C.) and the Revelation to John (*ca.* A.D. 90). Both were accepted as inspired scripture, but soon numerous apocalyptic writings appeared and threatened to change radically the nature of Judaism and Christianity, just as Hellenism had earlier (unorthodox Hellenistic Judaism and Christian Gnosticism). To counteract the insidious dangers of apocalyptic dreams (Jewish apocalypses, Shepherd of Hermas, Apocalypse of Peter, Apocalypse of Paul, Montanist writings, etc.), Jews and Christians used the same remedy: both groups drew up an official list of inspired books and excluded from this list writings declared uncanonical. The rabbis closed the canon at the first (A.D. 90) and second (A.D. 118) councils at Jamnia, in which it was decided that only the twenty-four books in the Hebrew Bible were canonical, and that "the gospel and the books of the heretics *are not sacred Scripture* [lit. "do not make the hands unclean"]. The books of Ben Sira [Ecclesiasticus], and whatever books have been written since his time, are not sacred Scripture" (Tosef. Yadaim 2.13). The Christian church did not deny that the Holy Spirit departed from Israel in the days of Ezra, but was certain that it had returned again and rested on the Christian apostles and prophets (Mark 1:10-12; Acts 2:1-4; 4:31; I Cor. 14:1-6, 29-32), and consequently God had now revealed a number of Christian scriptures. Just as the rabbis regarded only the writings of the prophets, from Moses to Ezra, to be inspired and therefore canonical, so the Christians after the second century refused to accept in their scriptures any book which was not apostolic. And just as the Hebrew scriptures had been transmitted by an unbroken succession of prophets (Jos. Apion I.viii), so the Christian scriptures had been transmitted by the apostles. "Moses received the Law from Sinai and delivered it to Joshua, and Joshua to the elders, and the elders to the prophets, and the prophets to the men of the Great Synagogue" (Sayings of the Fathers

I.1). "After they had proclaimed the Gospel, the apostles transmitted it to us by the will of God in the Scriptures that it might be the foundation and the pillar of our faith. In fact, clothed with the power of the Holy Ghost which had come down upon them, they received the gift of a perfect intelligence and went even to the ends of the earth, announcing to men the heavenly peace" (Irenaeus III.i.1).

Just as there were some doubts about the prophetic origin of some books of the OT among the Jews, so the church fathers took special pains to prove the apostolic origin of every book in the NT. Simeon ben Menasya (ca. A.D. 180) said: "The Song of Songs is sacred Scripture because it was spoken through the Holy Ghost; Ecclesiastes is not sacred Scripture because it originated from Solomon's own wisdom" (Tosef. Yadaim 2.14). Irenaeus (III.i.1) knew that only two of the gospels (Matthew and John) had been written by apostles, but says that Mark put in writing the preaching of Peter, and Luke the gospel preached by Paul; thus all four are "apostolic"; cf. Tertullian (Marcion IV.2), who speaks of the two testaments as "the Prophets and the Apostles" (Presc. Her. XLV), or "the ancient Law and the Apostles" (On Modesty XII). Some doubts were expressed on the apostolic origin of Hebrews and Revelation, but they were overcome. The prophetic and the apostolic origin of the sacred books excluded ipso facto books written after the disappearance of prophets and apostles, and also books the teaching of which contradicted the words of the prophets and apostles— late and heretical works were thus relegated outside the canon.

The spoken word of the prophets and of the apostles was recognized as the word of God as they uttered it (I Kings 22:19-23: "Hear the word of the LORD"; etc.; I Thess. 2:13: "When you received the word of God which you heard from us"), but many years elapsed before these inspired words attained canonical status when they were fixed in writing. The divine revelation was normally oral before becoming sacred scripture, although both testaments contain sacred books that were never delivered orally. Both the prophets and the apostles distinguished sharply between their own utterances and the inspired words that God spoke through their lips. On one occasion Jeremiah was silent until the divine revelation came to him (Jer. 28:10-14); and Paul distinguishes sharply between his own advice and an ordinance of the Lord (I Cor. 7:10-12); he gives an opinion, the Lord a commandment (7:25). Only the apocalypses (Daniel, Revelation, etc.) claimed to be divine revelation from the moment they were committed to writing; and only Jesus contrasted his own teaching to the Scriptures, and regarded it as superior (Matt. 5:21-22, 27-28, 33-34, 38-39, 43-44; cf. 19:8-9). The books of the OT were recognized as canonical through the authority of the prophets and, after them, of the men of the Great Synagogue; the books of the NT were recognized as apostolic through the authority of the apostles (II Pet. 3:15-16) and later through the authority of the church, guided by tradition (Serapion of Antioch, ca. 190, in Euseb. Hist. VI.12.3; Irenaeus III.1.1; IV.33.2; Augustine Contra adv. legis et proph. I.xx.39).

The Christians derived their understanding of the Scriptures, as well as their notions about canonicity, from the Jews. Like a man, the Bible has a body and a spirit, a literal meaning and a spiritual sense; it can be understood litteraliter vel carnaliter—according to the letter or the flesh—but also according to the spirit, allegorically—a distinction already familiar to Paul (Rom. 7:6; II Cor. 3:6). Beginning with Theagenes of Rhegium (ca. 525 B.C. ), by means of allegory a philosophical meaning had been discovered in Greece in the writings of Homer and Hesiod. This allegorical method was applied to the OT by Philo of Alexandria and passed from him to Paul (I Cor. 9:9; 10:1-4; II Cor. 3:13-16; Gal. 4:22-30) and to the author of the Letter to the Hebrews, according to whom the great religious institutions revealed in the OT are the "copy and shadow of the heavenly sanctuary" (Heb. 8:5). This allegorical method was used by Barnabas, Justin Martyr, and the School of Alexandria (Clement of Alexandria and Origen). Conversely the literal interpretation flourished in the School of Antioch (Lucian, Diodorus, Theodore of Mopsuestia, etc.). Like Philo, Clement of Alexandria and Origen believed that the whole OT, not merely certain passages, had a meaning deeper than the literal, to be explained through allegorical interpretation. In fact, Origen believed that the Scriptures had a body, soul, and spirit—a literal, moral, and allegorical sense (de Principiis IV.ii.18)—and, like Philo, he was so fascinated by the spirit that like Paul (I Cor. 9:9-10) he denied at times the validity of the literal sense (Homilia in Numeros XVI.9, where he interprets Num. 23:24 as eating the flesh and drinking the blood of the Son of man). The literal sense denies the hope of immortality, for two texts (Lev. 17:11; Deut. 12:23) imply that the soul (נפש) is in the blood—how then can it survive the death of the body? The blood mentioned in these texts must belong to spiritual man, as in Gen. 9:5 ("the blood of your souls"). But at the same time Origen founded the scientific study of the literal sense of the OT, and left us invaluable works on the geography of Palestine, sacred history, textual criticism, and exegesis. Through the Latin fathers and through the Latin translation by Rufinus of some of Origen's homilies, the allegorical exegesis became familiar to the medieval church. On the contrary, the literal exegesis of the school of Antioch (Theodore of Mopsuestia), except for Jerome and some learned Irish monks, was virtually forgotten, in spite of the works of Junilius Africanus (Instituta regularia divinae legis, based on the teaching of Paul the Persian, a learned teacher in the school of Nisibis), and of Cassiodorus (De institutione divinarum literarum), both dated shortly after 550.

Augustine's On Christian Doctrine places the spiritual (allegorical) sense of scripture above the literal; the spirit transcends the letter. But the narratives of the OT are regarded as historical truth, even more literally than by Jerome; before the spiritual meaning is sought, the facts are to be accepted.

Jerome (died 420) regards the spiritual sense as founded on the letter, but when the literal meaning is unedifying, he substitutes the allegorical for the literal. God did not dictate every word to the prophets, but, merely supplying the thought, left to the writer the choice of language, so that the style of the biblical authors varies.

Finally in the Middle Ages, Catholic scholars distinguished four senses in scripture: the letter teaches historical events; allegory, what you should believe; the moral sense, what you should do; and the mystical sense, what you should hope. One example will illustrate these four meanings: Jerusalem literally means the capital of Judea, allegorically it means the church, morally a well-ordered commonwealth, mystically the heavenly abode of the saved.

It is probable that this list of the four senses of scripture influenced Jewish exegesis. The Zohar (*ca.* 1300), possibly familiar with similar statements by Ibn Ezra (died 1167) and Bahya ben Asher (died 1291), distinguished *peshat* (פשט), the literal sense; *remez* (רמז), typological or allegorical sense; *derash* (דרש), expository or homiletical sense; and *sod* (סוד), secret or mystical sense. The initial letters of these words, forming the word *pardes* (פרדס), of Persian origin, meaning "park"; cf. "paradise"), designated these four meanings of scripture.

By these four manners of interpretation the church could force the OT to say whatever seemed desirable, and since the days of Paul its authority was imposed on it, in spite of Duns Scotus (died 1308) and Occam (or Ockam; died 1349).

*e. Protestant doctrines.* Soon after Martin Luther's disputation with Eck in 1519, Luther set aside the authority of the church and of the tradition, and regarded the Word of God as the supreme authority (Mark 7:13-14). This made the break between Protestants and Roman Catholics inevitable. Humanism shortly before had likewise reacted against the subordination of the Bible to the church—against the Catholic tendency to regard the Latin Vulg. as the Scriptures, it stressed the importance of the Hebrew and Greek original texts, and their literal (grammatical, stylistic, historical, and logical) interpretation. This exegesis was adopted in principle by the Protestant Reformation, in spite of the fact that it still retained the doctrine of the unity of scripture and the OT prediction of the coming of Jesus Christ. In place of the Catholic doctrine according to which the tradition of the church was the criterion by which the Scriptures were recognized to be the Word of God, the Reformation regarded the inner witness of the Holy Spirit as the final proof of scriptural inspiration. For Roman Catholics this is a purely subjective and individual test.

Luther does not ascribe equal authority to all parts of the Bible: the supreme message is not the "letter that killeth" but Paul's message of salvation through Jesus Christ (Rom. 3:21-26). The whole OT is to be interpreted in the light of the gospel: "All the stories of Holy Writ, if they are rightly regarded, refer to Christ." Unaware of the contradiction, which goes back to Paul, Luther could on the one hand regard the OT as a guide to Christ (Gal. 3:4), and on the other as the law of the Jews: "Leave Moses and his people together. . . . We have the Gospel." In the OT Luther valued Genesis for Paul's use of it, found little of value in the historical books, regarding Esther and Ezra-Nehemiah as Judaizing books, but prized the Prophets for their messianic prophecies (notably Isa. 53), the Psalms, and Job far above Proverbs, Ecclesiastes, and Song of Solomon. In conclusion, except for the quotations of the OT in the

NT and for its alleged witness to Christ, Luther would have tended to regard it as a purely human book.

Conversely, other Reformers, who did not stress like Luther merely individual salvation, but social righteousness and a community ruled by divine principles, esteemed highly the OT. For Zwingli at Zurich, Christ is not, as for Luther, the center of scripture, but one of the ancient men revealing God to man; Zwingli regarded some sayings of Plato and Seneca as the work of the Holy Spirit; of course, the difference is that the Scriptures are inspired throughout. Zwingli recognizes the validity of the literal meaning of each passage but questions its allegorical meaning, although he permits it; the Bible is consistent with itself. In his *Refutation of the Wiles of the Anabaptists* (1527), Zwingli denounced their rejection of the OT in favor of the Sermon on the Mount, but admitted the superiority of the NT over the OT. But Martin Bucer denied that the OT was inferior to the NT, for it contained the same Christology and doctrine of the Atonement—a view developed by John Calvin in his *Institutes* (1536).

Calvin, in controverting Augustine's words, "I would not believe the Gospel if the authority of the Catholic Church had not impressed me," cites the inner illumination by the Holy Spirit; elsewhere he quotes Eph. 2:20 to prove that the church is founded on the "apostles and prophets" (misinterpreting this to mean their inspired writings), and refers to the power of the Scriptures to prove their divine origin. He does not, like Luther, discriminate between biblical writings, but regards them equal in inspiration and authority. On the assumption of man's insignificance (Ps. 8:4) and God's primary concern with his glory, he developed an absolute determinism; Deuteronomy's idea of God's chosen people is transferred to God's elect, who belong to God's church. His exegesis is based on the letter and is remarkably historical. However, in successive editions of the *Institutes* he increasingly Christianized the OT and at times corrected the NT on the basis of the OT (the oath is commanded by Deut. 6:13; in Matt. 5:34 Jesus merely forbids the misuse of the oath). He maintained that God made only one covenant and that there is therefore only one people of God; he minimized Paul's contrast between the law and the gospel, and followed the Letter to the Hebrews in regarding the OT institutions as the shadow of NT reality.

Origen and Jerome, as well as Luther, Melanchthon, and Calvin, were devoted churchmen, eager to defend orthodox doctrine, and at the same time eminent biblical scholars searching for historical truth. Inevitably the contrast between faith and reason, between what Paul called the wisdom of God and the wisdom of the world (I Cor. 1:17–2:16), was bound to create a growing gap between doctrine and science. The great humanist Erasmus of Rotterdam, for instance, on the one hand reached critical conclusions still valid in denying the traditional authorship of Hebrews, James, II Peter, II and III John, and Revelation; but in 1527, when the theological faculty of Paris attacked his views, he admitted the supernatural character of the biblical books (without, however, repudiating his critical conclusions) and repeatedly submitted himself to the authority of the Roman Catholic Church.

In the sixteenth and seventeenth centuries the influence of the OT became pervasive in England—especially through the influence of Calvin—on the Free Churches, as is illustrated by the sabbath observance and the OT personal names among the Pilgrim fathers and Puritans in New England. The verbal inspiration of the Scriptures became a dogma: through the Holy Ghost, God had dictated to the individual authors every word, so that they were actually only scribes putting God's work into writing. Thus four characteristics were ascribed to the Bible: *auctoritas* (final authority in matters of faith), *perspicuitas* (transparent clearness, so that scripture explains itself), *perfectio* or *sufficientia* (scripture is so complete that it suffices to teach salvation), and *efficacia* (God, through scripture, accomplishes a man's conversion).

But historical and critical research on the OT began, after some rudimentary results achieved by pioneers through the centuries, in the seventeenth century with the textual criticism of Cappellus (1624 and 1650) and Morinus (1633); with the higher criticism of Hobbes (1651), Spinoza (1670), Simon (1678, 1685); with the discovery that the OT revelation is not instantaneous and uniform but progressive (Cocceius, 1648; Clericus, 1697); by the lay thinking emancipated from ecclesiastical control (Grotius, 1627; 1641-47) and reliance on reason (Descartes, died 1650; Bayle, 1645-47; Hobbes; Spinoza; the English Deists).

In the eighteenth century the critical analysis of the Pentateuch into separate sources began with Witter (1711), Astruc (1753), and Eichhorn (1780-83). Morgan (1737-40) influenced Reimarus (*ca.* 1747) and Lessing (died 1781) to submit the Scriptures to the test of "sense and reason" to see whether they are coherent with other knowledge; Kant (1781, 1793) denied divine revelation and identified true religion with the moral law written in the human heart; and Von Schelling (died 1854) began to use comparative mythology in explaining Gen. 3; Ernesti (1761) advocated the use of grammatical-historical exegesis; Semler (1771-75) regarded the sacred canon merely as a collection of books made by men for public reading, without normative authority unless they serve man's moral improvement (Song of Solomon, Ezra-Nehemiah, and Chronicles are thus rejected); Zachariae (1772-86), Eichhorn (1780-83), Gabler (1787), and Bauer (1796) pioneered in the historical study of biblical theology; and Bishop Lowth (1753) and Von Herder (1782) discovered in the OT the literature of an ancient nation rich in aesthetic values. In contrast with such secular attitudes toward the OT in the eighteenth century, we must not forget the deeply religious attitude of the Methodists (Wesley, died 1791) in England, of the Pietists in Germany (Spener, died 1705, and Francke, died 1727).

The nineteenth century witnessed incredible progress in the methods and results of the scholarly research on the OT, and a reaction against it on the part of orthodox Jews and Christians, whose "fundamentalist" views clung firmly to the traditional doctrines of the synagogue and various churches.

All attitudes mentioned were still present in the first half of the twentieth century, with or without some modifications. In whole or in part, the OT is regarded as God's Word, inspired literally or (following Jerome) merely in the thought; the OT is not divinely inspired and should be studied and read like the *Iliad,* or even (according to Marcion; Adolf von Harnack, died 1930; Friedrich Delitzsch, 1920-21) it is a liability to Christianity; besides the scholars that adopt one of these views, or at least keep them separate in their research (Otto Eissfeldt, 1926), others believe that the scholarly, objective study of the OT implies the recognition that it bears witness to Jesus Christ (Wilhelm Vischer, 1927, 1934, 1941), as the NT states, and as Augustine formulated when he said that Christ is latent in the OT and patent in the NT. In a less extreme form this latter tendency is obvious in the "biblical theologies," including both testaments, rather than in the histories of the religion of the OT and of the NT, in which the point of view of faith and the point of view of objective historical research are not kept distinct because they are regarded (in the investigation of divinely revealed scriptures) as inseparable: man's search for God and God's reaching out to man are two sides of a single process (H. H. Rowley, 1942).

**Bibliography.** J. Fürst, *Der Kanon des Alten Testaments nach den Überlieferungen in Talmud und Midrasch* (1868). L. Diestel, *Geschichte des Alten Testamentes in der christlichen Kirche* (1869). W. R. Smith, *The OT in the Jewish Church* (1881; 2nd ed., 1892; 3rd ed., 1926). F. Buhl, *Canon and Text of the OT* (1892). H. E. Ryle, *The Canon of the OT* (1892; 2nd ed., 1895); *Philo and Holy Scripture* (1895). G. Wildeboer, *The Origin of the Canon of the OT* (1895). K. Budde, *Der Kanon des Alten Testaments* (1900). I. Guidi, "Il canone biblico della chiesa Copta," *RB* (1901), pp. 161-64. M. Jugie, *Histoire du canon dans l'église grecque et l'église russe* (1904). R. H. Tyle, *The Canon of the OT* (1904). G. Hölscher, *Kanonisch und Apocryph* (1905). H. H. Howorth, "The Origin and Authority of the Biblical Canon in the Anglican Church," *JTS* (1906), pp. 1-40; "The Origin and Authority of the Biblical Canon According to the Continental Reformers," *JTS* (1906-7), pp. 321-65; (1907-8), pp. 186-230; "The Origin and Authority of the Biblical Canon Among the Later Reformers," *JTS* (1908-9), pp. 183-232. P. Heinisch, "Der Einfluss Philos auf die älteste christliche Exegese," *AA*, I (1908), 1-2. L. Dennefeld, "Der alttestamentliche Kanon der antiochenischen Schule," *BS*, XIV (1909), 4. W. Fell, "Der Bibelkanon des Josephus Flavius," *BZ*, VI (1909), 1-16, 113-22, 235-44. A. D. White, *A History of the Warfare of Science with Theology* (2 vols.; 1910). G. F. Moore, "The Definition of the Jewish Canon and the Repudiation of the Christian Scriptures," *Essays in Modern Theology and Related Subjects Assembled and Published as a Testimonial to E. A. Briggs* (1911), pp. 99-125; "The Theological School at Nisibis," *Studies in the History of Religion Presented to C. H. Toy* (1912). A. von Harnack, *Über den privaten Gebrauch der heiligen Schriften in der alten Kirche* (1912). M. Chaine, "Le canon des Livres Saints dans l'église éthiopienne," *Recherches de Science Religieuse* (1914), pp. 22-32. H. B. Swete, *An Introduction to the OT in Greek* (rev. ed. by R. R. Ottley; 1914). E. von Dobschütz, "The Abandonment of the Canonical Idea," *AJT*, XIX (1915), 416-29. W. F. Lofthouse, *The Making of the OT* (1915). J. Hänel, "Der Schriftbegriff Jesu," *Beiträge zur Förderung Christlicher Theologie*, XXIV (1919), 5-6. L. Ginzberg, "Some Observations on the Attitude of the Synagogue Toward the Apocalyptic-Eschatological Writings," *JBL*, XLI (1922), 115-36. M. L. Margolis, *The Hebrew Scriptures in the Making* (1922). W. R. Arnold, "Observations on the Origin of Holy Scripture," *JBL*, XLII (1923), 1-21; cf. *Ephod and Ark*, Harvard Theological Studies III (1917). A. von Harnack, *Marcion, das Evangelium vom fremden Gott,* Texte und Untersuchungen zur Geschichte der altchristlichen Literatur, XLX (1924). W. W. Christie, "The Jamnia Period in Jewish History," *JTS*, XXVI (1924-25), 347-64. G. F. Moore, *Judaism*, I (1927), 235-80. H. L. Strack and P. Billerbeck, *Kommentar zum NT aus Talmud und Midrasch*, IV/I (1928), 415-51. L. Pirot, ed., *Dictionnaire de la Bible*, Supplement, I (1928), 1022-45. A. Maichle, "Der Kanon der Biblischen Bücher und das Konzil von Trent," *Freiburger Theologische Studien*, XXXIII (1929). O. Michel, "Paulus und seine Bibel," *Beiträge zur Förderung Christlicher Theologie* (1929). W. Staerk, "Der Schrift- und Kanonbegriff der Jüdischen Bibel," *ZST*, VI (1929), 101-19. E. Stein, "Die allegorische Exegese des Philo von Alexandrien," *Beiheft ZAW*, LI (1929). B. H. Branscomb, *Jesus and the Law of Moses* (1930). S. Zeitlin, "An Historical Study of the Canonization of the Hebrew Scriptures," *Proceedings of the American Academy for Jewish Research*, III (1931-32), 121-58. K. Holl, *Gesammelte Aufsätze zur Kirchengeschichte: I. Luther* (6th ed., 1932). F. Horst, "Das AT als Heilige Schrift und als Kanon," *Theologische Blätter*, VI (1932), 161-73. B. Heiler, "La légende biblique dans l'Islam," *REJ*, XCVIII (1934), 1-18. O. Eissfeldt, *Einleitung in das AT* (1934; 2nd ed., 1956). J. Hempel, "Der synoptische Jesus und das AT," *ZAW*, N.F. XV (1938), 1-34. C. H. Dodd, *The Bible To-Day* (1946). H. A. Wolfson, *Philo*, I (1947), 115-38. H. Bornkamm, *Luther und das AT* (1948). A. Jepsen, "Der Kanon des AT," *TLZ*, LXXIV (1949), 65-74. J.-P. Audet, "A Hebrew-Aramaic List of Books of the OT in Greek Transcription," *JST*, N.S. I (1950), 135-54. R. C. Dentan, *Preface to OT Theology*, Yale Studies in Religion, XIV (1950). E. Dinkler, *Bibelautorität und Bibelkritik*, Sammlung Gemeinverständlicher Vorträge und Schriften aus dem Gebiet der Theologie und Religionsgeschichte, CXCIII (1950). H. H. Rowley, ed., *The OT and Modern Study* (1951). A. Richardson and W. Schweitzer, eds., *Biblical Authority for Today* (1951). A. Bentzen, *Introduction to the OT* (2nd ed., 1952), I, 20-41. A. Jeffery, "The Canon of the OT," *IB*, I (1952), 32-45. B. Smalley, *The Study of the Bible in the Middle Ages* (2nd ed., 1952). C. C. Torrey and O. Eissfeldt, "Ein griechisch transkribiertes und interpretiertes hebräisch-aramäisches Verzeichnis der Bücher des AT aus dem 1. Jahrhundert n. Chr.," *TLZ*, LXXVII (1952), 250-54. G. E. Wright, *The God Who Acts; Biblical Theology as a Recital* (1952). J.-S. Bloch, "Outside Books?" *Mordecai Kaplan Jubilee Volume*, English Section (1953). H. F. Hahn, *The OT in Modern Research* (1954). E. G. Kraeling, *The OT Since the Reformation* (1955). P. Katz, "The OT Canon in Palestine and Alexandria," *ZNW*, 47 (1956), 191-217. W. A. Irwin, "The Study of Israel's Religion," *Vetus Testamentum*, VII (1957), 113-26. P. W. Skehan, "The Qumran MSS and Textual Criticism," *Supplements to VT, Volume du Congress Strasbourg* (1957), pp. 155-60, for the Qumran LXX finds.

R. H. PFEIFFER

\*CANON OF THE NT. The collection of early Christian writings venerated as sacred scripture by the church, read in the liturgy, and recognized as the authoritative expression of the apostolic faith; or, the list of the books so recognized.

The history of the canon of the NT is a chapter of cardinal importance in the history of Christian literature. Its task is to investigate why and how the church came to attribute to a limited number of books written by Christian authors during the first century of her history an authority equal and ultimately superior to that of the venerable scriptures she inherited from Judaism. But this task belongs only in part to the history of the literature. It involves also the history of doctrine, the conflict with heresies and schisms, the development of Christian institutions, and, indeed, the entire scope of the manifold movement toward unity which issued in the ancient Catholic church. The importance of the creation of such a canon of Christian scriptures cannot

be too highly estimated, for in this one area the church achieved a unity which proved able to endure through the schisms which rent her in the fifth century, the division of the Greek from the Western church in the ninth century, and even the breakup of the Western church through the Reformation movements of the sixteenth century. In our own time, hopes of reunion could hardly be entertained, and the ecumenical movement would be all but inconceivable, were it not that all the churches concerned are in substantial agreement in recognizing the unique authority of the same twenty-seven books as constituting the canon of the NT, in employing them constantly in public and private devotions, and in appealing to them for guidance in faith and order.

This agreement was attained in substance by the end of the second century; for by that time the four gospels, the book of Acts, the Pauline letters (including the Pastorals but usually not Hebrews), and two or more of the Catholic letters (I John, I Peter, and sometimes others) were acknowledged as Holy Scripture in every part of the church. There remained on the margin a number of books whose canonicity was still in dispute. Hebrews, James, II and III John, II Peter, Jude, and Revelation were destined eventually to win general acceptance; and a somewhat larger number of other Christian writings enjoyed a temporary or regional canonicity but proved unable to maintain their high position. By the end of the fourth century, the limits of the collection were irrevocably fixed in the Greek and Latin churches of the Roman Empire.

The canon of the Syrian church still exhibited some major differences, but these were largely surmounted in the Peshitta (early fifth century), and entirely in the Philoxenian (508) and the Harklean (616) revisions of the Syriac NT (*see* VERSIONS, ANCIENT, § 4). It must be said that these revisions did not supplant the Peshitta in the major part of the Syrian church, which therefore still limits its canon of the NT to twenty-two books, rejecting Revelation and the four minor Catholic letters (II and III John, II Peter, and Jude). The Ethiopic canon, on the other hand, was enlarged to include eight additional books; and the Gothic NT never included Revelation. But these three churches were separated from the general body of Catholic Christendom by differences far more profound than marginal disagreements over the limits of the canon.

A. The apostolic age (to A.D. 70)
    1. The scriptures of the primitive church
    2. Modifying factors
        *a.* The presence of the Spirit
        *b.* The rejection of scribal tradition
        *c.* The authority of the words of Jesus

B. Preparations for the canon (A.D. 70-150)
    1. Collection of the Pauline letters
    2. The making of the gospels
        *a.* The one gospel and the many gospels
        *b.* Problems of early use
        *c.* Emergence of the great four
        *d.* Uncanonical gospels
    3. Other Christian writings of the period
        *a.* Writings which became canonical
        *b.* Marginal writings eventually rejected

C. The emergence of the canon of the NT (A.D. 150-200)
1. Growing veneration of the apostles
2. Earliest witnesses to the gospels
3. Marcion's canon
4. Effects of conflict with Gnosticism
5. Apologists and martyrs (A.D. 165-80)
6. The Old Catholic Canon
7. Effects of the introduction of the codex
D. The fixing of the canon (A.D. 200-400)
1. Origen
2. Dionysius of Alexandria
3. The persecution under Diocletian
4. Eusebius of Caesarea
5. Other Greek lists of the fourth century
6. Latin writers of the third and fourth centuries
E. The growth of the canon in the Syrian church (to A.D. 616)
Bibliography

**A. THE APOSTOLIC AGE (TO A.D. 70). 1. The sacred scriptures of the primitive church: the inheritance from Judaism.** Christianity from its very inception possessed an extensive and precious sacred literature inherited from Judaism—the books of the OT. From the mother faith Christianity also inherited the conception that these books were the very "oracles of God" (Rom. 3:2), and her teachers appealed to them constantly to validate their own message. Jesus himself had accepted the Jewish scriptures as the vehicle of a true, though not final, revelation of God, and explicitly disavowed any intention of repudiating them: "Think not that I have come to abolish the law and the prophets; I have come not to abolish them but to fulfil them" (Matt. 5:17). The apostle Paul likewise affirms that the gospel of God concerning his Son Jesus Christ was "promised beforehand through his prophets in the holy scriptures" (Rom. 1:2), and though it manifests God's righteousness apart from law, nevertheless the law and the prophets bear witness to it (Rom. 3:21). Other early Christian writers cite the ancient scriptures as the words of God himself, or of the Holy Spirit, or under such rubrics as "it is written," or "it stands in scripture."

The scriptures which the men of the early church held in such honor formed a much more extensive body of literature than that with which we are familiar in the OT and Apoc. of our own versions. They included an indeterminate number of other books, mainly apocalyptic writings, composed during the first two centuries before Christ or shortly afterward, and published under the names of ancient heroes of history and legend—Enoch, Ezra, Moses, Elijah, the Twelve Patriarchs. Several of these are actually cited as scripture in NT documents, but their influence is far more pervasive than the handful of citations would indicate. It is their understanding of history that determines the general world view of the early church and of the NT writers, and it is largely their reinterpretation of the ancient revelation that is inherited by the early church and is reflected in the apostolic writings. In them, far more than in the canonical books, we find the background of central themes of the NT such as the kingdom of God and the Son of man, the resurrection of the dead, and the doctrine of angels and demons. And once the mission moved into Greek territories, under the leadership of converts from the Diaspora (Paul, Barnabas, Philip the Evangelist, and others), it inevitably made use of the whole wide range of books available in the SEPTUAGINT, including a number which were originally composed in Greek. Almost all the OT quotations in the NT are taken directly from the LXX without concern for the meaning of the Hebrew text, which often enough would have no bearing upon the point at issue. Broadly speaking, the LXX is the Bible of the early church and of all the NT writers, though not of Jesus and the Twelve.

**2. Modifying factors in the Christian attitude toward the sacred books.** In a sense, then, Christianity was a book religion from its inception, heir to a revelation committed to writing in days gone by. Yet there were three factors in the new faith which made profound modifications in its attitude toward the ancient scriptures and in the role which they filled in its developing life, as compared with the dominance of the book in Judaism.

*a. The presence of the Spirit.* First of all, the Christians were persuaded that a new age of revelation had dawned: the Spirit of revelation was again active among them, the gift of God to every believer. Their ministers were "ministers of a new covenant, not in a written code but in the Spirit; for the written code kills, but the Spirit gives life" (II Cor. 3:6). The Spirit of Jesus, imparted through baptism, was identified with the Spirit who moved holy men of old to speak the oracles which were committed to writing and preserved in the books of the old covenant; and all Christians were inspired in different ways by one and the same Spirit, who apportioned his gifts to each one individually as he willed (I Cor. 12:4-11). Men so inspired, conscious of such inspiration, could not be in bondage to books, however highly revered.

*b. The rejection of scribal tradition.* Secondly, the oral tradition of the scribes was explicitly discarded, as "making void the word of God" (Mark 7:13). This left the field free for interpretations that owed nothing to the accumulated results of scribal labors. Still more broadly, the Christians no longer regarded the content of the OT as centering in the "law of commandments and ordinances" (Eph. 2:15), which occupied almost the entire attention of the scribes. They were not under law but under grace (Rom. 6:14), and they were not concerned with elaborate systems of casuistry. What they sought in the ancient scriptures was not a code of commandments to regulate daily living, but a testimony to Christ and his gospel; and their whole interpretation was governed by the conviction that in him the scriptures were fulfilled. To them, the burden of the scriptural message, given beforehand by the Spirit, was the "sufferings of Christ and the subsequent glory" (I Pet. 1:11; cf. Luke 24:25-27). They were convinced that a veil was over the minds of Jewish interpreters when they read the OT, and that only when a man turned to the Lord was the veil taken away (II Cor. 3:14-16).

*c. The authority of the words of Jesus.* Thirdly, alongside the ancient scriptures, the Christians had from the outset another authority, not as yet committed to writing, but transmitted by word of mouth

—the sayings of Jesus. "Remembering the words of the Lord Jesus, how he said . . ." (Acts 20:35)—this was the final court of appeal from the beginning. The words of Jesus were the words of eternal life. Treasured in the first instance by his disciples, in the same manner as the sayings of every rabbi were taken up and committed to memory by the students who followed him, they became in the developing church the words of the Master who still lived in their midst and governed all their life. Under the guidance of his Spirit, the words that he had spoken provided for his people instruction and comfort, challenge, appeal and counsel, answers to the criticisms of opponents, and above all that penetrating insight into the nature and will of God which still compels the confession: "No man ever spoke like this man!" (John 7:46). Before the gospels were written—and, indeed, for a good while longer—these words of Jesus, treasured in the memory of his followers and transmitted by word of mouth, carried final authority for the Christian believer and actually determined for him the sense in which he would understand the ancient scriptures. Here the church had in germ the essential canon of the new testament, long before she had any literature to canonize. And when the gospels came to be written and passed gradually into general use in the churches, the authority they acquired was accorded to them, not in the first instance as holy books, but as books containing the holy words of Jesus. The authority of the words was primary; that of the books was secondary and derivative.

**B. PREPARATIONS FOR THE CANON: THE PROVISION OF THE DOCUMENTS (70-150).**
**1. Collection and publication of the Pauline letters.** Jesus himself left nothing in writing, and the gospels which preserve for us the record of his teachings were not composed until the second Christian generation or later. The earliest Christian writings, the only documents of the apostolic age which have survived, are the letters of Paul. These were in the first instance occasional writings, addressed by the apostle to particular churches to deal with specific local problems and needs. With the possible exception of Romans, they were not intended for general circulation in the church, and it certainly never occurred to Paul himself that a letter which he wrote for the Christians of Thessalonica or of Philippi would ever be read in Antioch or in Jerusalem, let alone treasured by the whole church and given a place alongside the Law and the Prophets in worship and in study. There is no evidence to show that any of his letters were circulated in his lifetime beyond the region to which they were first directed. Only after they had been gathered into a collection did they obtain a wider circulation and become known throughout the church. The formation and publication of such a collection and even its general circulation could not forthwith raise these occasional writings to canonical status, but they established the conditions which alone made possible the later treatment of the letters as holy scripture.

Edgar J. Goodspeed has shown that there are good reasons for holding that the author of EPHESIANS was also the collector and publisher of the Pauline letters, and that he wrote Ephesians under Paul's name as a general introduction to the whole collection. He

was probably himself a man of Colossae; it has even been suggested that he was none other than Onesimus, once a fugitive slave, but won for Christ by Paul and sent home to his owner—perhaps the same Onesimus whom Ignatius knew as bishop of Antioch about fifty years afterward (*see* PHILEMON, LETTER TO). Whoever he may have been, he is the first Christian writer to make literary use of Paul's letters, and it is significant that he shows evidence of acquaintance with all of them, though he makes most use of Colossians, which provides him with the groundwork of his own distinctive thought. And from his time on, every single Christian writer known to us makes use of the letters in a manner which shows that he knows the whole collection. This appears sometimes in references to one letter or another in general terms (Clem. Rom. 47.1; Polyc. 3.2; 11.3), occasionally in direct citation (Polyc. 11.2), more often in the borrowing of characteristic words and phrases, and at least once in the composition of a letter collection to introduce a work of a totally different character. For the device of introducing an apocalypse by a sequence of letters addressed severally to seven churches but issued together under cover of a general letter (Rev. 1:4-3:22) is without parallel in apocalyptic, and can only be explained as indicating that the author had before him a corpus of Pauline letters similarly constructed. It is beyond dispute, then, that the collection of Paul's letters had been formed and published before the end of the first century, and that it quickly came into general use among Christians.

This earliest collection consisted of nine letters addressed to particular churches (Philemon, which seems to be an exception, is itself addressed to the "church [that meets] in your house"), with Ephesians as a covering letter addressed to all Christians everywhere. For, as the earliest MSS show, Ephesians was not addressed to any local church, but "to the saints who are also faithful in Christ Jesus." The Pastoral letters were added to the collection many years later; and Hebrews, under the influence of the Alexandrian church, won a peculiar place for itself later still. But even as a collection in general use, the letters were not yet regarded as holy scripture, despite the growing veneration of the apostles. Clement of Rome and the other apostolic fathers use them extensively, but never cite them in the terms they use to introduce passages from the OT scriptures. There is nothing to indicate that in the first half of the second century they were set upon a fundamentally different plane from the letters of the martyr-bishop Ignatius of Antioch, which were collected and published *ca.* 117. The earliest writer to mention them explicitly as included among the scriptures was the author of II Peter (3:15-16; *ca.* 150); and after that time, their canonical authority was taken for granted in all parts of the church.

**2. The making of the gospels. a. The one gospel and the many gospels.** The acknowledgment of the gospels was not in the least dependent upon the making of a gospel collection. On the contrary, each gospel must have first obtained a wide measure of acceptance, extending well beyond the community in which it was produced, before it was made part of a collection of such writings. All of them, indeed, with the partial exception of the Gospel According to John, were made not only in and for the community, but in a sense by the community as much as by the individual author. The materials they employed were, in the main, the common possession of the church, the store of traditions concerning Jesus as they had been accumulated and shaped through a generation or more of oral transmission in response to the needs and interests of the developing community. These traditional materials, especially insofar as they consisted of sayings of Jesus, carried his own authority from the outset, and contributed it in large measure to the books which contained them. The primary question here is how the church came to acknowledge four gospels instead of one; and secondary to that, how she came to acknowledge only four out of the many that were composed during the second and third generation of Christian believers. For not one of the gospels—not even John—was composed as a supplement to others, or with any thought that it would ever be read in conjunction with others. It is not too difficult to see why the church rejected most of those that came into existence at this time and were cherished in one circle or another; the extraordinary thing is that she did not settle upon a single authoritative account of the story of salvation and of the Lord's teaching. Each of the four—and the same is true of nearly all the uncanonical gospels as well—sought to provide such a unified manual for the church; and even after the four were established in a position of unassailable authority, there was at least one notable and partly successful attempt to weave out of them a single, harmonized account—the Diatessaron of Tatian (*see* VERSIONS, ANCIENT, § 4). But somehow by the end of the second century the fourfold gospel collection was accepted as a settled possession everywhere except in Syria (where the Diatessaron reigned supreme), though there is evidence for the occasional use of other gospels by Christian writers.

*b. Problems of early use of the gospels: the books and the oral tradition.* The history of the use of the gospels in the earliest period is very difficult to determine, because it is seldom possible to be sure that sayings or stories of Jesus which we find in writings of the post-apostolic age are taken from one of the great four, or from some uncanonical gospel, or even from oral tradition. As late as 135 or 140 the words of Papias, bishop of Hierapolis, make it quite clear that in some circles, perhaps even to the average Christian of the time, greater weight was still attached to an oral tradition resting on a living chain of testimony than to anything that was to be found in any book. Papias certainly had Mark, Matthew, and John at his disposal, if not also Luke, and quite possibly other gospels as well; yet he tells us: "If I met with a disciple of the elders, I questioned him about the words of the elders—what Andrew or Peter said, or what was said by Philip or by Thomas or by James . . . or by any other of the disciples of the Lord, and what things Aristion and the elder John, the disciples of the Lord, say. For I did not think that what was to be gotten from the books would profit me as much as what came from the living and abiding voice" (Euseb. Hist. III.xxxix.4). The maxim "Spoken

words vanish; written words abide" is here turned exactly in reverse! Yet only a few years later, the evidence of Justin Martyr shows that passages from the "memoirs of the apostles, which are called gospels," were being read liturgically in church, along with, or even in place of, readings from the Prophets; and this would certainly indicate that the gospels were being consciously or unconsciously regarded as holy scripture. But there were still wide varieties of attitude and practice with respect to them, nor is it certain which gospels or how many of them were in use at any given locality.

*c. Emergence of the great four.* The four canonical gospels are works of the second Christian generation (*ca.* 70-100). Mark, the earliest of them, appears to have been produced at Rome not many years after the outbreak of persecution under Nero (64), and may be taken to represent the deposit of the traditions concerning Jesus as they were known in the Roman church at the end of the apostolic age. Not many years later (*ca.* 80) it was incorporated almost *in toto* into a gospel composed in Palestine in a Jewish-Christian environment, being used as one of the principal sources of our Gospel According to Matthew. A like use of Mark, though less extensive, is found again in the Gospel According to Luke, which was published together with its sequel, the Acts of the Apostles, in some region of the E Mediterranean toward the close of the century or even somewhat later. In his Preface, Luke tells us explicitly that "many have undertaken to compile a narrative of the things which have been accomplished among us, just as they were delivered to us by those who from the beginning were eyewitnesses and ministers of the word" (1:1-2). His words make it evident that by the time he wrote, there were numerous gospels in circulation in the churches, and none of them enjoyed such an established position as to bar another writer from adding to the number. Neither for them nor for himself does he claim any special inspiration; he writes simply as one who has "followed all things closely for some time past" (1:3), to whom "it seemed good . . . to write an orderly account." Moreover, the way in which both he and Matthew treat the materials derived from Mark shows clearly that neither of them regarded the earliest gospel as inspired scripture. Both of them feel perfectly free, not only to add to Mark, but also to subtract, to abbreviate, to alter words and phrases, and even on occasion to alter the order of incidents. The author of the Fourth Gospel makes bold to treat the whole tradition with infinitely greater freedom, not holding himself bound to follow the general outline of events that underlies the Synoptic narrative, nor even to reproduce substantially the same teaching as the utterances of Jesus. And it cannot be doubted that the many other gospels which came into circulation during the same period and later, claimed for themselves at least an equal freedom. In short, the church of the early second century had at its disposal a large number of gospels, but accorded to none of them anything like canonical authority; and it still possessed a considerable mass of oral tradition, not committed to writing anywhere, which was by many valued more highly than any written record. The authority still rested in the words of the Lord, not in any of the books containing his words.

***d. Uncanonical gospels.*** It should be said that none of the uncanonical gospels, insofar as they have become known to us, adds anything significant to our knowledge of Jesus. The materials used in their construction are either quarried out of our four or are invented or distorted to support the religious views of some sect—usually a Gnostic school with Docetic conceptions of Jesus (regarding the human life of Jesus as phantasmal, or making a radical separation between the heavenly aeon Christ and the earthly body which he inhabited). Some are merely fictitious tales of the infancy and childhood of Jesus, attempts of the pious imagination to supply the information which was lacking about the years between the Nativity and the beginning of the public ministry. These are not by any means negligible to the historian, for they reflect aspects of the development of Christian thought, and some of them contributed themes to the Christian artist and so perpetuated themselves in painting, sculpture, and the minor arts, enduring in this way for centuries after their literary and theological influence had vanished. None of them ever attained the widespread circulation of any of the great quartet. *See* APOCRYPHA, NT.

**3. Other Christian writings of the period. *a. Writings which became canonical.*** The period that saw the publication of all these gospels and of the collected letters of Paul (say A.D. 70 to 140) witnessed also the production of a large number of other Christian writings—letters, apocalypses, apologies, homilies, manuals of teaching, "acts" of apostles. Several of these were destined to win a place in the canon along with the four gospels and the Pauline letters. The book of Acts, separated quite early from its companion volume, the Gospel According to Luke, seems always to have shared the fortunes of the latter in the esteem of the churches; and our earliest MS of the four gospels (P$^{45}$) also includes Acts. The three Pastoral letters (I and II Timothy, Titus), issued under the name of Paul to combat the heresies of the time, are generally dated around the beginning of the second century but may be as late as 150. Their acceptance as scripture depended upon their incorporation into the collection of Pauline letters, which cannot have taken place until late in the century; Marcion's canon did not contain them (*see* § C3 *below*), and they are not included in our earliest MS of the letters of Paul (P$^{46}$ —*ca.* 200).

The seven Catholic letters made their way individually, and were formed into a group relatively late. The Letter of James, a "diatribe" constructed after the model employed by Stoic teachers, is probably the work of a Jewish Christian steeped in Hellenistic literature and philosophy, and may be dated fairly early in the second century. Despite the apostolic name attached to it, it was slow to attain recognition or even to come into use; there is no trace of it in Christian literature until the third century. I Peter is a pseudonymous work published in Asia Minor, though perhaps emanating from Rome, early in the second century. It is used by Polycarp and other Eastern churchmen of the second century, but did not find recognition in Rome and the West

(except for Irenaeus and Tertullian) until much later. I John is closely related to the Fourth Gospel and may be by the same author; aided by this association, it won early and broad recognition. The four minor letters (Jude, II Peter, II and III John) were never widely used, and their canonicity remained in dispute in the Greek churches as late as the fourth century.

Hebrews is now held by some critics to be the work of a contemporary of Paul, but it seems to show such evidences of Pauline influence as to require us to place it in the generation after his death. In the Alexandrian schools it was given a place among the Pauline letters before the end of the second century, and in the Beatty papyrus P$^{46}$ it stands in the second place, immediately after Romans; but in the West, despite its extensive use in I Clement (*ca.* 95) and the strong advocacy of Tertullian, who attributed it to Barnabas, it did not attain general acknowledgment as canonical until late in the fourth century. Revelation, probably composed toward the end of the first century, quickly achieved a widespread popularity; but its authorship was disputed by Alexandrian critics, it was handicapped for a long time by the reaction against chiliasm, and its canonicity was still in dispute in the East in the fourth century.

***b. Marginal writings which were eventually rejected.*** Of other Christian writings which have survived, the group known as the APOSTOLIC FATHERS come from the same period as these later NT documents, and some of them enjoyed for a time a comparable prestige and popularity. I Clement, a letter written by the Roman church to the church of Corinth *ca.* 95, is never cited as scripture, but it was read in public worship at Corinth *ca.* 170, and is included in the Codex Alexandrinus (fifth century); and the extensive literature to which the name of Clement was later attached (II Clement, Clementine Recognitions, etc.) would indicate that it must have enjoyed something close to canonical authority in some circles at least. II Clement, really an anonymous homily of *ca.* 150, is also found in Codex A. The Epistle of Barnabas, a pseudonymous pamphlet of the early second century, probably of Alexandrian provenance, is found in the great Codex Sinaiticus (fourth century) and is treated as scripture by Clement of Alexandria and his renowned successor Origen, but it was never acknowledged in other parts of the church or by the later Alexandrians.

The little manual known as the Didache—"The Teaching of Jesus Christ Through the Twelve Apostles"—is of uncertain date, but is probably to be placed early in the second century. It was used by the early Alexandrians as holy scripture and continued to be so used in the Egyptian churches throughout the third century. There is evidence for its use in Syria as late as *ca.* 400 (in the Apostolic Constitutions), and it is included in some Greek lists of the fourth century. The fact that it was translated into Latin and into Georgian would indicate that it enjoyed for some centuries wide use and considerable prestige. The Shepherd of Hermas was highly regarded and immensely popular for two or three generations after its publication. Such great figures as Irenaeus and (for a time) Tertullian treated it as scripture, and even Origen regarded it as apostolic;

and it is included (incomplete) in the Codex Sinaiticus. According to the Muratorian Canon it was composed *ca.* 150 by Hermas, a brother of the Roman bishop of that time; but many investigators date it some decades earlier. The letters of Ignatius (*ca.* 115) and the Epistle to Diognetus (150 or later) were never cited as scripture.

At least five books attributed to Peter were composed during these years, but only the two letters were ultimately recognized. The Gospel of Peter, the Preaching of Peter, and the Apocalypse of Peter (*see* PETER, GOSPEL OF; PETER, PREACHING OF; PETER, APOCALYPSE OF) all enjoyed a period of use; the Apocalypse especially had distinguished sponsorship —Clement of Alexandria, the Muratorian Canon (which means the Roman church of the time), and Methodius (*ca.* 300). The Acts of Peter and the Acts of John (*see* PETER, ACTS OF; JOHN, ACTS OF) are works of a follower of the Gnostic Valentinus. The Acts of Paul (*see* PAUL, ACTS OF), composed by an Asian presbyter about the middle of the second century, was alone among the apocryphal Acts in obtaining some measure of ecclesiastical recognition. Its author was induced to confess his forgery and was deposed from office, despite his plea that he had written his book out of love for Paul. Nevertheless, it is cited by the great Alexandrians, and seems to have continued in wide use well into the third century.

## C. *THE EMERGENCE OF THE CANON OF THE NT: APOLOGISTS, HERETICS, AND OLD CATHOLIC FATHERS (A.D. 150-200).* 1. Growing veneration of the apostles. Toward the middle of the second century, then, the church was provided with a rich store of documents of her own creation —gospels, letters, "acts" of apostles, apocalypses, homilies, apologies, manuals of teaching. Some of these were coming into general use; others were more restricted in their circulation; none of them was yet being treated as holy scripture, on a level with the sacred scripture inherited from Judaism. Only the words of Jesus, whether recorded in books or transmitted by oral tradition, carried the fullest authority. At the same time, the apostles were gradually acquiring in the Christian mind a collateral, though subordinate, authority. Even before the end of the first century, a Christian writer could speak of the church as "built upon the foundation of the apostles and [Christian] prophets" (Eph. 2:20), and an inspired seer could picture the Bride of the Lamb as the "holy city Jerusalem coming down out of heaven from God," having under its walls "twelve foundations, and on them the twelve names of the twelve apostles of the Lamb" (Rev. 21:9-14).

The two-volume history of Luke is itself a striking manifestation of how the ministry of Jesus and the ministry of the apostles could be coupled in a single account of the origins of the Christian society; in the work of the apostles it is Jesus himself who is still acting through his Holy Spirit. Now this collective authority of the apostles was not exercised solely or even primarily through books—most of them, like their Lord, had left nothing in writing—but through the tradition of sound teaching which they had received from Christ and transmitted to their successors, the bishops. So in the Pastorals we have the repeated injunctions: "Guard the deposit [RSV 'what has been entrusted to you']" (I Tim. 6:20); "Follow the pattern of the sound words which you have heard from me" (II Tim. 1:13); "What you have *heard* from me . . . entrust to faithful men who will be able to teach others also" (II Tim. 2:2). There is no thought here of apostolic *writings*, although the author is well acquainted with the letters of Paul; the only "sacred writings" are those with which "Timothy" has been acquainted from childhood (II Tim. 3:15). The apostolic "deposit" is guarded by and transmitted through qualified teachers, by word of mouth. But just as the authority of Jesus was to be transferred from the words which he spoke to the books which contained them, so the authority of the apostolic deposit, still and always safeguarded by the bishops, was to be shared and verified by the books in which they themselves, or men closely connected with them, had committed it to writing.

The decisive development takes place during the second half of the century, and the evidence becomes increasingly abundant. First the gospels are treated as holy scripture in the citations of ecclesiastical writers and in the liturgy. Very soon afterward the letters of Paul are associated with them in similar usage; and before the end of the century a variable number of other writings gather around the nucleus of "the gospel" and "the apostle." The canon of the NT has emerged in essentials; it only remains to determine its limits by the exclusion of such writings as cannot secure and maintain a title of apostolicity. What is apostolic is canonical; whatever cannot be recognized as stemming from the apostles is not canonical.

2. Earliest witnesses to the canonical use of the gospels: II Clement and Justin Martyr. II Clement (*ca.* 150) is the earliest Christian document to cite passages from the gospels as holy scripture. After quoting some words from Isaiah, the writer proceeds: "And again another scripture says, 'I came not to call the righteous, but sinners' " (II Clem. IV.; Matt. 9:13). About the same time, Justin Martyr tells us that in the services of Christian worship which he is describing with some fullness, "the memoirs of the Apostles or the writings of the Prophets are read, as long as time permits" (Apol. I.67). He is using the word "memoirs" (ἀπομνημονεύατα) for the benefit of pagan readers; elsewhere, he speaks of the apostles as "those who have written memoirs of all things concerning our Saviour Jesus Christ"; and again, specifically identifying them, of the "memoirs made by (the apostles), which are called gospels" (Apol. I.33, 66). Thus he makes it clear, not only that books —the gospels—are the source of his knowledge of Jesus, but also that these same books are being read in the liturgy interchangeably with "the Prophets"— the ancient Hebrew scriptures. It is not clear which gospels he uses, or how many, or whether he restricts himself to those of our canon; but regardless of this, the decisive step has been taken. One group of Christian writings—the gospels—has been established in ecclesiastical usage in the place hitherto reserved to the inspired scriptures of Judaism.

3. Marcion's canon: the gospel and the apostle. The second step, of coupling letters with gospels as sacred scriptures of the new faith, was taken first by

the heretic Marcion, who came to Rome from Pontus sometime before 150. Reared in orthodox circles (his father was bishop of Sinope), this remarkable man came under Gnostic influence, and became persuaded that the God of the Hebrew scriptures, the Creator, the God of justice, was an inferior deity; and that Jesus had revealed the supreme God, the God of love, who had been previously unknown. He rejected the OT scriptures outright, and made a collection of Christian books the sole foundation of his teaching. He was persuaded that the Twelve had utterly corrupted the pure doctrine of Christ. For him, there was only one true apostle—Paul—who alone had stood faithful to the gospel of Jesus. He therefore took as his canon the ten letters of Paul known to him, those which, as we have seen, constituted the original collection; and he set beside them the one gospel of Luke, accepting it as the work of an associate of Paul. The text of the gospel suffered severe mutilation at his hands, as he sought to purge out anything which was incompatible with his basic doctrine; and his opponents charge that he altered the text of the Pauline letters also, though the evidence they offer points in most cases to nothing more than variant readings in the MSS which he had at his disposal; he did, however, excise some few paragraphs, chiefly in Galatians and Romans. Nevertheless, to him belongs the honor of making the first canon of the NT known to us. Limited as it is by his doctrinal predilections, it yet presents that combination of "the gospel" with "the apostle" which forms the heart of all subsequent canons.

It is probable, indeed, that the shape and scope of the canon as it finally emerged in Catholic usage was determined in large part by the reaction to Marcion. First, his coupling of "the apostle" with "the gospel" as a new corpus of sacred scripture, distinct from the Jewish scriptures, may well have had a direct effect in leading the church to think in terms of a canon of books of the NT, rather than of a series of additions to the one body of sacred writings. Next, his exaltation of Paul could hardly fail to stimulate the whole church to accord him equal honor, but as one wholly in accord with the other apostles, not as the lone bearer of truth amid the perversions of a horde of false apostles. It is significant that it is only after his time that we begin to have evidence for the ecclesiastical usage of the book of Acts, which represents Paul's ministry as flowing out of, validated by, and in a measure subordinate to, the ministry of the Twelve. It is even possible, as has been argued, that both Luke and Acts were edited in their present form in the course of the controversy with Marcion, and were only then associated to make a twofold work, again "gospel" and "apostle," to counteract Marcion's erroneous picture of conflict between Paul and the Twelve. The Pastorals, again, if not actually composed as anti-Marcionite tracts, at least found a ready acceptance into the Pauline collection when they were seen to range him solidly against Marcionite doctrine. Again, letters attributed to other apostles would be eagerly received and set alongside the Pauline collection, to give wider testimony to the apostolic faith which he shared; the way is opened for the canonizing of the Catholic letters. And finally, Marcion's rejection of all gospels except Luke would lead the church not only to maintain her own prior rights in that gospel but also to insist on according equal honor to other gospels for which she could claim an apostolic or quasi-apostolic origin. The publication of the fourfold gospel, the enlargement of the Pauline collection by the admission of the Pastorals, and the association with them of Acts and some of the Catholic letters, all appear to be significantly related to the struggle against Marcion.

**4. Effects of conflict with Gnosticism.** Though excommunicated by the church, repudiated by his father, and denounced by Polycarp as the "first-born of Satan," Marcion achieved an extraordinary success, in organization as in the propagation of his teachings. There were at one time some hundreds of churches in several provinces of the Empire, both in the East and in the West, which looked to him as their founder, and which were governed by bishops who traced their succession through him. Gnostic schools in general made no such efforts at organization and existed rather as groups on the margin of the great church or even within it; but in the aggregate, they represented a substantial influence, particularly as their doctrines, fantastic as they now seem, accorded with the mind of the age. Now all these sects required a sacred literature; and as they discarded the OT scriptures, they were obliged, like Marcion, to use Christian writings as their primary authorities. In part they made use of existing documents—gospels, acts, letters (they had little use for apocalyptic); and in part they created new documents, based on the existing models—gospels of Peter, of Thomas, of Philip, of "Truth" (recently discovered in a Coptic version; *see* APOCRYPHA, NT); acts of Peter, of Thomas, of John; etc. But they had no difficulty in applying the canonical gospels to the support of their doctrines, by the limitless freedom of allegorical interpretation; and the Pauline letters with their notorious difficulties offered them plenty of scope (cf. II Pet. 3:16).

Of necessity, this Gnostic use of Christian literature as sacred and authoritative had a twofold effect upon the conservative center of the church. On the one hand, it reinforced the existing tendency to glorify the legacy of the primitive church, the writings of the apostles; and on the other, it forced a process of discrimination between documents, of more and more exact delimitation of the writings that the church could recognize as canonical. The words of Serapion, bishop of Antioch, in a letter to the church of Rhossus, illustrate both aspects at once. On a visit to the town, he had been shown for the first time the Gospel of Peter, and as he had no reason to suspect heresy, he gave permission for it to be read. Since that time, it had been pointed out to him that the gospel in question was in fact heretical, and he now warned the church at Rhossus against it. "We receive both Peter and the other apostles as Christ," he writes, "but we reject the writings falsely attributed to them, for we know that such were not handed down to us" (Euseb. Hist. VI.12.3). It was, of course, a multitude of episcopal decisions such as this that gradually determined the usages of the churches; and it is amazing to see the degree of uniformity that was attained in this fashion.

**5. Apologists and martyrs, 165-80: Melito, Theophilus, Athenagoras, Tatian, the Scillitan Martyrs.** In orthodox circles the elevation of the Pauline letters occurred more slowly and less clearly. *Ca.* 180, Melito of Sardis made a list of the "old books," which he named the "books of the Old Testament"—a phrase which implies that there was something in the way of an aggregation of "new books" or "books of the New Testament"; but he did not himself coin the latter phrase, nor does he indicate at all clearly what books he would have included under such a description. Theophilus of Antioch, his contemporary, quotes from Matthew and John, and mentions the latter as one of the "Spirit-bearers" (πνευματοφόροι); but while he makes free use of the Pauline letters, the Pastorals, Hebrews, and I Peter, he does not appear to treat them quite as holy scripture. Athenagoras, an Athenian apologist of the time, appeals to the gospels under the same formula (φησίν) as to the Prophets, and cites sentences from Paul in such a way as to suggest that the words of the apostle carry the same divine authority as the Hebrew books. Tatian, in preparing his harmony of the gospels, the Diatessaron (*ca.* 170), appears to have employed our four gospels and no other—an indication that in the few years that had elapsed since the time of Justin, the four had acquired an undisputed pre-eminence. The influence of the Pauline letters upon him is quite marked, but it is not possible to determine exactly how highly he regarded them. Jerome (*ca.* 390) tells us that Tatian rejected some of them (possibly I and II Timothy?) but that he accepted Titus. The martyrs of Scilla in North Africa tell the examining magistrate that they keep in their cabinet "our books, and the epistles of the holy man Paul." These "books" would appear to include rolls of the OT scriptures and of the gospels, which are thus grouped together; the epistles are not counted among the "books," but are accorded a place in the same cabinet. There can be no great chasm to be bridged before they too will be reckoned among the "books."

**6. The Old Catholic Canon: the Muratorian Fragment, Clement of Alexandria, Irenaeus, Tertullian.** In the closing years of the century, evidence from a variety of sources shows clearly, a canon of Christian writings with only marginal variations was recognized and used in all quarters of the church. We now encounter the earliest Roman list—the Muratorian Canon. Irenaeus, a native of Asia, sat in his youth at the feet of Polycarp of Smyrna, came in middle life to Rome, and spent his last years as bishop of Lyons in Gaul; he may be said to represent in his single person almost half the Christian world. From Clement, the head of a great school of theological studies at Alexandria, we learn the doctrine of the church in Egypt; and Tertullian, a Carthaginian lawyer and presbyter, the first great representative of Latin Christianity, though in his later life a Montanist sectary, testifies to the views of the churches of North Africa and also of Rome. All four lines of testimony are in remarkable accord and take it for granted that the views they express are held by the catholic church everywhere.

The Muratorian Canon is a list of the books of the NT with brief remarks about their origin and au-

thenticity, found in a MS written at Bobbio in the eighth century but preserved in the Ambrosian library at Milan and published by Ludovico Antonio Muratori in 1740. It is a translation into barbarous Latin of a Greek original, which was drawn up at Rome some years before the end of the second century. The beginning is lost, but even the most perverse skepticism could hardly doubt that it dealt with the gospels of Matthew and Mark; Luke and John are listed as the third and fourth among the gospels. On the unity of the four it has this to say: "Although various fundamentals [*principia*] are taught in the several books of the gospels, nevertheless this makes no difference to the faith of believers; for in all of them all things are declared by the one guiding Spirit concerning the Nativity, the Passion, the Resurrection, the converse with his disciples, and his twofold coming." The divine inspiration and the essential unity of the four gospels could not be more explicitly affirmed. After this, the list mentions Acts; then thirteen letters of Paul, the three Pastorals being mentioned along with Philemon as written *pro affectu et dilectione*—"out of personal affection and love"—yet "held sacred in the esteem of the catholic church in the ordering of ecclesiastical discipline." Reference is then made to certain letters forged under the name of Paul by the Marcionites, and "several others which cannot be received into the catholic church, for gall ought not to be mixed with honey." It then affirms that "the epistle of Jude and two epistles bearing the name of John [probably I and II John; all three are actually anonymous] are received in the catholic [church], and Wisdom, written by friends of Solomon in his honor." Two apocalypses—that of John and that of Peter—complete the list of recognized books. The Shepherd of Hermas may be read privately, but cannot be read aloud in church to the people, either among the prophets or among the apostles; for Hermas wrote it "quite recently, in our own times, in the city of Rome, during the episcopate of his brother Pius."

This fragment, with its authoritative ring, is most revealing. Of the twenty-seven books included in our own canon, it recognizes no fewer than twenty-two—the four gospels, Acts, thirteen letters of Paul, three of the Catholic letters, and Revelation; and it includes only two which were ultimately judged apocryphal—the Wisdom of Solomon and the Apocalypse of Peter; and of the latter it admits that "some of our own [bishops?] will not allow it to be read in church." The remarks about Wisdom indicate that pseudonymity, even when recognized, is no bar to canonical recognition. The *age* of the writing is, however, decisive; it is implied that the Shepherd is not lacking in merit, but it is to be rejected for no other reason than that it was written too recently.

Clement of Alexandria lays down no such clearcut judgments, yet his writings show broad agreement with the Muratorian fragment in the general view of the Christian scriptures. He speaks of the documents generally as the "scriptures of the Lord," and employs the formula "the Gospel and the Apostle command." He distinguishes explicitly between the "four gospels that have been handed down to us" and the Gospel According to the Egyptians (Strom. III.93.1), but he does not hesitate to quote words of the Lord from other sources. His collection of Pauline letters has been enlarged to include fourteen, for he reckons Hebrews among them, following in this his revered master, Pantaenus. He never quotes Paul formally as "scripture," but he adduces the words of his letters in argument together with words of the Lord and citations from the OT, with no suggestion that they carry any lesser degree of authority. He makes use also of Acts; of at least four of the Catholic letters—I Peter, I and II John, and Jude—and according to Eusebius he commented on all of them; and of the book of Revelation. But he appears to show an equally high regard for a considerable number of other writings—the Apocalypse of Peter, the Shepherd, the Preaching of Peter, Barnabas, and I Clement. Clearly enough, the four gospels and the corpus of Pauline letters constitute for him also the substance of the canon; but he is still generous in his acceptance of other writings attributed to apostles and feels under no compulsion to make distinctions among them, except with regard to the gospels.

The Gnostic schools, as we have seen, discarded the OT entirely and as a consequence were obliged to use Christian writings as their holy scriptures and even to create new gospels, letters, and "acts" of apostles for the purpose. Their great Catholic opponent Irenaeus meets them by making a more extensive use of the NT documents than any earlier writer of orthodox views, and by discriminating more carefully between authentic and unauthorized books. He makes use of OT and NT writings without distinction: the gospels, acts, letters, and apocalypses (of John and of Hermas) are not in any sense secondary authorities with him. In fact, he shows greater precision in identifying the writers when he is dealing with the NT. He quotes freely from the four gospels, from Acts, from twelve Pauline letters (Philemon is omitted, no doubt from mere chance), from three Catholic letters (I Peter, I and II John—the omission of III John, again, is not significant), and from Revelation. He knows and values the Letter to the Hebrews, but does not seem to treat it quite as scripture. On the other hand, he fully accepts the Shepherd. His canon, accordingly, coincides with our own except for the addition of the Shepherd, the omission of James, Jude, and II Peter, and the lower place given to Hebrews. "The Scriptures are perfect," he tells us, "inasmuch as they were uttered by the word of God and his Spirit" (Iren. Her. II.28.2); and "the Scriptures" in this sense unquestionably include the NT books which he uses so freely. But the most striking feature of his evidence is the absolute and exclusive honor he accords to the four gospels as a God-given unity. "As there are four quarters of the world in which we are, and four universal winds, and as the Church is scattered over all the earth, and the Gospel is the pillar and bulwark of the church and the breath of life, it is seemly that it should have four pillars, breathing immortality from all sides and kindling men to new life. From this it is evident that the Word, the Fashioner of all things, . . . having been manifested to mankind, gave us the gospel in a fourfold shape held together by one Spirit" (III.11.8). And it is he who first suggests that the fourfold visages of the cherubim are "symbols of the economy of the Son of God"—the man symboliz-

ing Matthew, the calf Luke, the eagle Mark, and the lion John (later writers assign the symbols differently).

Tertullian, a lawyer of Carthage, converted to Christianity in middle life, is the first great exponent of Latin Christianity and the creator of its theological vocabulary. In later life he lapsed into Montanism and assailed with vigor what he regarded as the moral laxity of the church at large; but for twenty years or more he was the doughty champion of the faith against pagans, Jews, heretics, and the persecuting Empire. He is a little later than Irenaeus; his writings carry us into the early years of the third century.

Like Irenaeus, he confines himself rigidly to the four canonical gospels, and treats them as a unity. Together they form the "evangelic instrument" (a legal term which he employs alternately with *testamentum* to translate the Greek διαθήκη). They were written by apostles (John and Matthew) or by apostolic men (Luke and Mark); and the authority of the latter rests upon the authority of their masters, "which means that of Christ, for it was that which made the apostles their masters" (Tert. Marcion IV.2). A single gospel would not be authoritative in itself, certainly not that chosen by Marcion, for "Luke was not an apostle, but only an apostolic man; not a master, but a disciple and so inferior to a master. . . . Indeed, had Marcion published his gospel in the name of Paul himself, the single authority of the document, lacking all support from preceding authorities, would not be a sufficient basis for our faith." The authority of all the apostolic churches—those which can show an unbroken line of bishops descending by succession from the apostles—guarantees equally the authenticity of all four.

Tertullian is at one with Irenaeus in treating the four gospels as a unity; the "fourfold gospel" of the one is the "evangelic instrument" of the other. And he goes beyond Irenaeus or any previous writer in asserting the unity of all the apostolic writings. Together they form the "New Testament" (*Novum Testamentum*) alongside the Old. In bidding heretics to heed the apostolic churches, and especially that of Rome, "on which the apostles poured forth all their doctrine along with their blood," he affirms that Rome "mingles the law and the prophets in one volume with the writings of evangelists and apostles, from which she imbibes her faith" (Tert. Presc. Her. XXXVI). So he can write: "If I fail to settle this article of our faith by passages . . . out of the Old Testament, I will take out of the New Testament a confirmation of our view. . . . Behold, then, I find both in the gospels and in the apostles a visible and invisible God" (Adv. Prax. XV). With this he introduces testimonies from the Fourth Gospel, from Paul (including verses from the Pastorals), and from I John. He is the first writer to use the term "New Testament" in the sense of a collection of books, and he leaves no doubt that for him it possesses exactly the same authority as the ancient scriptures. In it he includes the four gospels, the thirteen letters of the Pauline collection, Acts, Revelation, and three of the Catholic letters—I John, I Peter, and Jude. Before he went over to the Montanists, he included the Shepherd in the list; but afterward he dismissed it with scorn as "that apocryphal Shepherd of the adulterers"; he indicates, however, that it was generally accepted and read in the churches. Hebrews is on the margin; ascribing it to Barnabas, whom he calls "a companion of apostles, . . . a person of sufficient authority," he still does not regard it as quite canonical. Thus for Tertullian the NT includes twenty-two books of our twenty-seven, and none that was rejected in the final establishment of the canon.

**7. Effects of the introduction of the codex.** The growing sense of the unity of the scriptures must have been fostered in some degree by a revolutionary change in the form of the book which took place during this period. In the second century, Christian scribes began to use the codex instead of the roll for new copies of their sacred books. To make the roll, sheets of papyrus were glued end to end to form a narrow strip which could then be rolled up from either end. For practical purposes, it was not convenient to make a roll much more than thirty feet long; and this was about sufficient to contain a single gospel, or one book like Acts or Revelation; the collected Pauline letters would require two such rolls. To make the codex, the sheets were folded, either one by one or in quires of two, three, or four sheets each, and were then sewed together quire upon quire, as in a modern book. It thus became possible to put the contents of any number of rolls into a single book of the codex form; and there is no reason to doubt that Irenaeus and Tertullian had before them the "fourfold gospel" in a single codex. All the Pauline letters could likewise be included in a single codex; and the day was to come when the entire NT and even the whole of the LXX would be brought within the covers of a single book. The oldest MSS of the NT known to us are all codices or fragments of codices; one of them contains the four gospels with Acts, and another originally contained the ten letters of the first Pauline collection. In such a form, it was obviously easier to think of the collection as a unity than when it lay before the reader in a number of rolls of different shapes and sizes. At the same time, it was always possible for a church to alter its collection of sacred books by adding or discarding one or two rolls; but the contents of the codex had to be decided in advance; and once made, it would remain fixed until the pages wore out. Thus the invention of the codex helped to hasten the fixing of the limits of the canon, as well as to promote the sense of its unity.

**D. *THE FIXING OF THE CANON IN THE GREEK AND LATIN CHURCHES (A.D. 200-400).***
**1. Origen.** At the beginning of the third century the canon of the NT had unquestionably come into being, and there is wide agreement about its constituent parts. Minor areas of disagreement, however, still remained. They did not affect the four gospels, the thirteen letters of the Pauline collection, or the book of Acts, which were all beyond dispute. Revelation appears to have been equally well established, but its authority was to be challenged in the course of the third century. Hebrews was still not secure, except in Alexandria; and of the Catholic letters, only I John was everywhere known and recognized, although I Peter had almost equally wide recognition. Several other letters and apocalyptic writings were able to claim a measure of ecclesiastical sanc-

tion. The fixing of precise limits was to be the work of the third and fourth centuries in the Greek and Latin churches; in the Syrian church it had to await the reforming bishops of the fifth and sixth centuries.

The situation in the early third century is analyzed by Origen, greatest of biblical scholars, who succeeded Clement as head of the school in Alexandria in 203 and for fifty years contributed his unrivaled learning and his great theological powers to the service of the church, at first in Alexandria, and in his later years, after a dispute with his bishop, at Caesarea in Palestine. He deals with OT and NT scriptures in exactly the same way, attributing to them the same authority and employing the same methods of interpretation. They are the "divine scriptures that have been entrusted to us"; and the same Spirit, the Spirit of the one God, has dealt in the same way with the gospels and the apostles as with the scriptures which were composed before the coming of Christ. In all of them there is a twofold or a threefold sense. Often enough, the literal sense of the narratives is neither true nor useful—he takes illustrations from the gospels as from the book of Genesis —and there are matters which cannot be admitted historically, which are meant to lead us on to inquire into a further sense, a spiritual significance, that we may "ascertain a meaning worthy of God in those scriptures which we believe to be inspired of him" (*On First Principles* IV.15-16).

Origen had traveled widely—to Rome, and in Greece and Asia Minor as well as in Egypt and Palestine—and had observed both the agreements and the differences among churches of different regions in their attitude toward the several NT writings; he was well aware that the views of his own church were not identical with those of other churches everywhere. Without attempting to lay down a judgment of his own, he makes note of the practice of the church, classifying the books as "acknowledged" or "disputed"; besides these, there are a number which are simply "false." Among the "acknowledged" he includes the four gospels, the Pauline letters (fourteen, including Hebrews, even though he knows that it is not by Paul and is not accepted everywhere), Acts, I John, I Peter, and Revelation. Among the "disputed" he includes James, Jude, II Peter, II and III John, and apparently also the Shepherd of Hermas, which he himself treats as apostolic and authoritative. He justifies the inclusion of Hebrews in the Pauline collection on the ground that the thoughts are the apostle's, though the style and diction show that the actual composition was done by one of his associates.

He is the first ecclesiastical writer to mention (and then it is done with some hesitation) "the epistle which is current [φερομένη] under the name of James." He has no doubt that Jude is the work of the Lord's brother, but he adduces its testimony with some hesitation, as if knowing that some will question its validity. He raises no objection of his own to II Peter and II and III John, but he does not cite them and remarks that they are in dispute. Revelation he accepts without question as the work of John the son of Zebedee, but he seems to suggest that it ought never to have been written; John "wrote the Apocalypse, though he had been commanded to be silent and not to write the utterances of the seven thunders." This appears to be the first faint note of disapproval of this book at Alexandria, where it was to come under heavy fire not long afterward. The Didache and the Epistle of Barnabas are not specifically classified, but are used by Origen as documents of high authority, even if not quite canonical. The books which he most rigorously excludes are the numerous uncanonical gospels, which he adjudges heretical; in this area he finds no disagreement among the churches. "The church has four gospels; the heretics have many [here he gives the titles of some of them]. . . . Four gospels only are approved, out of which we must bring forth points of teaching under the person of our Lord and Savior. . . . We approve nothing else but that which the Church approves, that is, four gospels only as proper to be received" (*Hom. in Luc.* 1). And again he speaks of "the four gospels which alone are uncontroverted in the church of God which is spread under heaven" (Euseb. Hist. VI.xxv.4).

**2. Dionysius of Alexandria and the questioning of Revelation.** Dionysius, who became head of the Alexandrian school *ca.* 231 and was afterward consecrated bishop, called in question the Johannine authorship of Revelation without denying its right to a place in the canon. He knew of others who rejected it outright and attributed it to the heretic Cerinthus, accusing him of portraying the glories of heaven in terms of sensual delights and material enjoyments. Dionysius would not deny that it was written by a man named John, or that he saw visions and received prophetic oracles; and though he admitted that he could make almost nothing of the meaning of the book, he laid the trouble to his own weakness of comprehension. He would not reject it, for it was held in esteem by many whose judgment he was bound to respect. But a comparison of its style and diction and of its central ideas with those of the gospel and letters of John showed that it had nothing in common with them and could not be by the same author.

Most of the other disciples of Origen, including many of the most influential bishops of the time, rejected the book entirely. In the later third century the great school founded by Lucian at Antioch, another nursery of bishops, joined the Origenists in rejecting it, while Methodius of Olympus upheld it strongly. In the Latin West, the book remained unchallenged, but in the East it never succeeded in regaining its former status. Even though the Greek churches were led to include it formally in their canon, they gave it no place in their liturgy, their scholars seldom commented on it, and their scribes did not often copy it—only a third of the extant Greek MSS of the whole NT contain it. In the Syrian churches it was never admitted to the canon at all, except among the Monophysites.

**3. The persecution under Diocletian.** In the year 303, after more than fifty years of religious toleration, the Emperor Diocletian launched against the church the most systematic, widespread, and determined persecution that she had yet faced. Besides the imprisonment, torture, and death of countless leaders and the wholesale destruction of church buildings, measures were taken to seek out the sacred scriptures and to consign them to the flames. Under these circumstances, Christians were compelled to decide which scriptures they might be justified in surrendering to the persecutors, and which they must guard from destruction at the risk of their own lives. A rigorous party in the church, indeed, regarded the surrender of any Christian books as an act of apostasy, and their hostility to those whom they stigmatized as *traditores* led to the long and bitter Donatist schism. But the church at large adopted the more sensible view that only the writings which were regarded as sacred in the highest sense need be safeguarded at the cost of life itself. The persecution thus provided the ultimate test of the esteem in which various books were held.

**4. Eusebius of Caesarea.** Nevertheless, even the pressure of persecution could not bring universal agreement in all particulars. The testimony of Eusebius, given in the great *Ecclesiastical History*, which he completed *ca.* 325, still reflects much the same differences as Origen had noted. For the first time we find mention of the "seven so-called Catholic epistles" as forming a distinct group, but Eusebius remarks that James and Jude are disputed (II.xxiii. 25), and in another passage he classes James, Jude, II Peter, and II and III John among the "disputed writings which are none the less known to most" (III.xxv.3). He is not always consistent in his statements, especially about Revelation. In his most nearly complete classification of the books, he lists it among the "acknowledged" with the qualifying phrase "if perchance it seem correct" (εἴ γε φανείη); yet a few lines later he includes it "among the spurious books" (ἐν τοῖς νόθοις), along with the Acts of Paul, the Shepherd, the Apocalypse of Peter, and the Didache, again with the qualifying phrase "if it seem correct," and the remark that some reject it while others include it in the list of accepted books. Those he lists without qualification of any kind are the "holy quaternion of the gospels," Acts, the letters of Paul (fourteen, with a note that some take objection to Hebrews on the ground that the church of Rome does not accept it as Paul's), I John, and I Peter. As Eusebius was charged by Constantine with the preparation of fifty copies of the Scriptures on vellum to be sent to him at Constantinople, his views on the canon had considerable practical importance, and it would be interesting to know what books he decided to include in the NT section; unfortunately, not one of these fifty copies has survived.

**5. Other Greek lists of the fourth century.** In the second half of the fourth century a number of bishops in different regions of the Greek church were moved to issue formal lists of the canonical books for the guidance of their people. Cyril of Jerusalem lists twenty-six of our twenty-seven, excluding Revelation; his contemporary Epiphanius of Constantia in Cyprus includes it with the others. Gregory of Nazianzus gives the same list as Cyril. In his thirty-ninth Festal Letter, written in 367, the great Athanasius of Alexandria gives a list of the "books that are canonized [κανονιζόμενα] and handed down to us and believed to be divine"; in this, after the books of the OT, he lists without hesitation the twenty-seven books of our own NT canon. All of these mention all seven of the Catholic letters, usually as a formally constituted group; they differ only over the acceptance of Revelation. There is no longer any mention of the doubts about the Pauline authorship of Hebrews, but the earlier hesitation is reflected in the fact that it is listed out of the order to which its length would otherwise entitle it, appearing sometimes in the tenth place and sometimes last of all. Bishops of the school of Antioch—John Chrysostom of Constantinople, Theodoret of Cyrrhus—make no use either of Revelation or of the four minor Catholic letters—i.e., II and III John, II Peter, and Jude. At the end of the fourth century, therefore, a considerable part of the Greek church acknowledged a canon of only twenty-two books. A section of the Apostolic Constitutions, however, published in Syria *ca.* 400, lists all our twenty-seven books except Revelation and adds to them I and II Clement. This canon was actually ratified by the Quinisextine Council, which met at Constantinople in 692.

**6. Latin writers of the third and fourth centuries.** In the Latin West, no writer between Tertullian and Jerome attempts to give a catalogue of the acknowledged books, but some idea of their general views on the canon may be gathered from their usage. The four gospels, Acts, the thirteen letters of the Pauline collection, I John and I Peter of the Catholic letters, and Revelation are consistently used by them (Cyprian, Lactantius, *et al.*) as holy scripture. The five other Catholic letters are not cited; and the Letter to the Hebrews, not being included among the Paulines, either is not mentioned at all or is explicitly rejected. No Latin writer of the period makes any use of the apocryphal gospels, acts, or apocalypses; they are seldom even mentioned, and then only to be condemned as heretical.

In the second half of the fourth century, however, the influence of Alexandria makes itself felt in the admission of Hebrews to the collection of Pauline letters and in the introduction of the minor Catholic letters. Hilary, bishop of Poitiers, sent into exile to the East (357-61) for his resolute opposition to Arianism, is the earliest Latin churchman to quote Hebrews as Paul's. Jerome, the great glory of Latin biblical scholarship, included in his famous translation of the Bible, which became the Vulg. of the Western church, the twenty-seven books of our canon; and his letter to Paulinus (Epistle 53; *ca.* 385) is the first Latin recognition of the corpus of seven Catholic letters. He remarks that the letters of James and Jude had been in dispute, but had acquired authority by the lapse of time and the usage of the church; that I and II Peter differ in style, character, and structure so much that we must believe the apostle to have made use of different "interpreters" in composing them; and that I John was approved by all "ecclesiastical and erudite men," while II and III John were said to be from the hand of the presbyter John. He is aware that the Pauline authorship of Hebrews has been disputed, and that the Greek churches do not fully accept Revelation; but he holds that the ancient and widespread testimony to these two books justifies their use as canonical and ecclesiastical.

The encouragement and support of Pope Damasus gave a quasi-official character to Jerome's work on the scriptures; but the effects of immediate recognition by authority were in the long run far outweighed by the silent influence of his version with its complete NT on the minds of men who were using it every day. There was, in any case, no conflicting opinion. Rufinus of Aquileia and Augustine of Hippo show, without dependence on Jerome, that they recognized precisely the same canon; Ambrose of Milan and Hilary of Poitiers are in essential agreement, except that they do not appear to have been acquainted with all the Catholic letters. This same list of twenty-seven books was given the sanction of conciliar authority in North Africa, first at a council held in Hippo in 393 and again at the Third Council of Carthage held in 397, with Augustine present at both of them. Canon 39 of the latter council decrees that "apart from the canonical scriptures, nothing may be read in the Church under the name of divine scriptures." After a list of the books of the OT, the canon goes on as follows: "Of the New Testament: of the gospels, four books; of the Acts of the Apostles, one book; epistles of Paul the apostle, thirteen; of the same, to the Hebrews, one; of Peter the apostle, two; of John, three; of James, one; of Jude, one; the Apocalypse of John, one book." These were the first conciliar pronouncements to be made anywhere on the limits of the NT canon; and it is to be noted that they did not come until the end of the fourth century, and were the decisions of provincial synods, not of an ecumenical council. The canon was determined by usage, by the common consent of the Christian community, testing the books in its daily life over centuries; not by formal authority.

**E. THE GROWTH OF THE CANON IN THE SYRIAN CHURCH (TO A.D. 616).** The history of the canon in the Syriac-speaking churches remains obscure until the beginning of the fifth century and the making of the Peshitta. Until that time, they used Tatian's Diatessaron almost exclusively in place of the four-gospel collection which had so early become dominant in the Greek and Latin churches; an Old Syriac version of the four gospels, made about the end of the second century, survives in two MSS, but there is no trace of its use by Syrian churchmen. It is not known when the book of Acts and the Pauline letters were first translated into Syriac, but it must have been before the end of the third century and may even have been done in the late second century, by Tatian. At all events, it is clear that in the fourth century the Syriac canon consisted of the Diatessaron, Acts, and the Pauline letters. A curious feature is that in Syria the Pauline collection was enlarged to fifteen letters by the inclusion of the spurious Third Epistle to the Corinthians, extant only in Armenian, Coptic, and Latin versions (*see also* PAUL, ACTS OF). This canon of seventeen books is used by Ephraem, the great scholar of the church of Edessa (*ca.* 320-73), and by his contemporary Afraates; and is given as authoritative in the Doctrine of Addai, a document composed *ca.* 370 at Edessa. However, a Syriac list of *ca.* 400 puts the four gospels in place of the Diatessaron and omits III Corinthians; this may be taken as an indication that the Syrian churches were now moving toward conformity with their Greek neighbors, probably under the influence of the school of Antioch.

The Peshitta, by far the most enduring and influential of oriental versions, was made under the direction of Bishop Rabbula of Edessa in the first quarter of the fifth century. It adopted the canon of Antioch: the four "separated" gospels, Acts, fourteen Pauline letters, and three Catholic letters—James, I Peter, and I John. The Syrian episcopate now made a determined and successful effort to end the use of the Diatessaron. Theodoret of Cyrrhus alone collected and destroyed more than two hundred copies of the Diatessaron in the churches under his government and replaced them with the four gospels of the Peshitta. The Diatessaron was so thoroughly suppressed that no copy of it has ever been discovered, apart from a single leaf of vellum containing a fragment of the Greek text of it.

The christological controversies of the fifth century destroyed the unity of the Syrian church and separated it from the catholic church of the West. From Edessa eastward through Mesopotamia and Persia it became Nestorian; in the W parts of Syria, it became Monophysite. The Nestorian churches continued to hold to the original canon of the Peshitta, which was the base also of the oldest Persian and Arabic versions. For the Monophysites, a revision of the Peshitta was prepared in 508 at the instance of a bishop called Philoxenus. This work was based on good Greek MSS and included the seven Catholic letters and Revelation. Thus the Syrian Monophysites, or Jacobites, as they are called, adopted the canon that had become established in the West. In 616, the Philoxenian edition was further revised by Thomas of Harkel, who retained the same canon. But these revisions never attained the authority of the Peshitta, and the Syrian churches generally have held fast to the shorter canon of twenty-two books, lacking the four minor Catholic letters and Revelation.

Except for occasional oddities, no further developments took place in the canon. The Ethiopic church added eight books to the established twenty-seven—a collection of decrees called the Synodus, and a series of "Clementines." In the Latin church of the Middle Ages, a number of important churchmen acknowledged fifteen Pauline letters, including in the collection a spurious Latin composition which first came to light in the sixth century under the title of the "Epistle to the Laodiceans." John of Damascus (ca. 730) reckoned the Apostolic Constitutions, which he attributed to Clement, among the books of the NT. In the sixteenth century some of the Reformers—Erasmus, Luther, Carlstadt, Zwingli, and Calvin—and even some Romanist divines raised again the problem of the "disputed" books, but without affecting the practice of any of the churches.

*Bibliography.* F. C. Burkitt, *Evangelion da-Mepharreshe* (1904) —the fundamental work on the history of the Diatessaron, the Old Syriac versions of the separate gospels, and the origins of the Peshitta. E. J. Goodspeed, *The Meaning of Ephesians* (1933), supplemented by J. Knox, *Philemon Among the Letters of Paul* (1935; 1959), deals with the origins of the Pauline letter collection. On Marcion's canon, see especially A. von Harnack, *Marcion* (2nd ed., 1924), and J. Knox, *Marcion and the NT* (1942). The standard Introductions to the literature of the NT generally give a sketch of the early history of the canon; among the best of these available in English are A. Jülicher (2nd ed., trans. J. P. Ward, 1904); A. H. McNeile

(2nd ed., rev. C. S. C. Williams. 1953). In German, see R. Knopf, *Einführung in das NT* (5th ed., rev. H. Lietzmann and H. Weinel, 1949).

General treatises: B. F. Westcott, *A General Survey of the History of the Canon of the NT* (7th ed., 1896); T. Zahn, *Grundriss der Geschichte des ntlichen Kanons* (2nd ed., 1904); C. R. Gregory, *The Canon and Text of the NT* (1907); J. Leipoldt, *Geschichte des ntlichen Kanons* (1907-8); E. J. Goodspeed, *The Formation of the NT* (1927); A. Souter, *The Text and Canon of the NT* (2nd ed., rev. C. S. C. Williams, 1953). Westcott's book, though marred to some extent by obsolete views of the Peshitta and the Old Latin versions, is still valuable for its weighty scholarship and sobriety of judgment, and is especially useful for its appendixes, which give the texts of the most important passages from early writers and from conciliar deliverances bearing upon the subject. Zahn brings his immense learning to the impossible task of proving that the canon of the NT was to all intents and purposes established before the end of the first century; he fails to distinguish between the circulation and use of writings and canonical recognition.                                    F. W. BEARE

**CANOPY** [סכה, booth, thicket (II Sam. 22:12=Ps. 18:11—H 18:12; KJV PAVILION), *from* סכך, to screen, weave together; חפה, chamber (Isa. 4:5; KJV DEFENSE), *from* חפף, to enclose, cover, surround; עב (I Kings 7:6; Ezek. 41:25, *perhaps in plural* 4:26 [*cf.* RSV *mg.*]; KJV THICK BEAM/PLANK)]; ROYAL CANOPY [*Kethibh* שפרור, *Qere* שפריר (Jer. 43:10; KJV ROYAL PAVILION), *from* Akkad. *šuparruru*, spread out; *cf. šipirri*, scepter]. A cover of some sort. There is a canopy over an outside vestibule on the Hall of Pillars of Solomon's House of the Forest of Lebanon (I Kings 7:6) and Ezekiel's temple (Ezek. 41:25). In Ezekiel it is specified as being of wood and may have been a cornice or roof (עב; *see* TEMPLE, JERUSALEM; HALL).

Figurative use of the idea of a canopy occurs in Isa. 4:5, where חפה signifies a protective canopy over the restored Jerusalem; and in II Sam. 22:12=Ps. 18: 11—H 18:12, where darkness is the concealing cover (סכה) for the theophanic presence of Yahweh. *See* BOOTH; PAVILION; THEOPHANY.

The "royal canopy" is the symbol of royal power which Nebuchadnezzar will establish over the court of the Egyptian Pharaoh, as a sign of Yahweh's sovereignty (Jer. 43:10). The Hebrew word for "royal canopy," שפרור, may mean a brightly colored pavilion or carpet, which is spread on the ground. "State-tent" and "scepter" have also been suggested as the translation of this word.                                    E. M. GOOD

**CANTICLES.** *See* SONG OF SONGS.

**CAP** [מגבעה] (Exod. 28:40; 29:9; 39:28; Lev. 8:13); KJV BONNET. A conical-shaped object of finely woven white linen tied on the head of the priest, as a sign of his investiture. The cap was a distinctive item of the priestly vestments. Fig. SYN 105.

*CAPERNAUM kə pûr′nĭ əm [Καφαρναούμ (great uncials), Καπερναούμ (TR)=כפר נחום, village of Nahum]. A city on the NW shore of the Sea of Galilee.

**1. Location.** Although Capernaum was named for some person called Nahum (*see above*), there is no proof of any relation to the prophet of that name in the OT. The evidence of the gospels and Josephus is not conclusive as to its location. There are also references to it in the rabbinic literature (e.g., Midrash Rabbah Koh. I.8; VII.26), but these do not indicate the location of the site.

Only two sites have been seriously considered. It was once thought to be the ruins now known as Khirbet (or Khan) Minyeh along the NW coast of the Sea of Galilee at the NE edge of the Plain of Gennesaret. This is perhaps supported by Josephus,

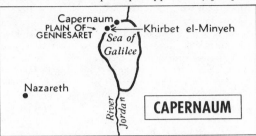

who refers to Capernaum as the name of a copious fountain in Gennesaret (War III.x.8; cf. Life LXXII). This spring may be the one now called 'Ain et-Tin or perhaps 'Ain et-Tabgha farther to the NE; both of these are near Minyeh. Although travelers as early as Arculf (A.D. 670) speak of this site as Capernaum, excavations in 1931 demonstrated that it is an Arab site, the ruins of an Umayyad palace.

It is now certain that Capernaum is Tell Hum, *ca.* 2½ miles farther NE than Khirbet Minyeh. The Arabic "Tell Hum" is probably a corruption of "Tanhum," a variant of the word "Nahum" (cf. Midrash Rabbah Shir. III.10; J.T. Ther. XI.7). There has been a strong Christian tradition since Theodosius (530) that this was Capernaum.

Tell Hum lies along the coast on a narrow plain. Its importance is indicated by the fact that it is regularly called a "city" (πόλις) in the gospels and that its ruins cover a strip a mile long. The prosperity of the city was promoted by its proximity to the major E-W highway and trade route which crossed the Jordan to the N of Capernaum. The neglect of the site and the pillaging of the ruins for building stones were ended when the site was acquired by the Franciscans in 1894. To preserve the ruins, they covered them with earth until they could be properly excavated.

**2. Antiquities.** Among the ruins of Tell Hum an octagonal-shaped building is shown as Peter's house, but it is more likely the remains of a church, perhaps the one mentioned by Etheria (385) as on the site of the home of the apostle Peter.

The most striking ruins are those of one of the best preserved synagogues in Palestine. The initial excavation was by Charles Wilson (1865-66), who thought it was the building mentioned in the gospels (e.g., Luke 7:5). Later excavations by Heinrich Kohl and Carl Watzinger in 1905 demonstrated that it could be no earlier than the third century A.D., although the site may well be that of the synagogue of Jesus' day. Further excavations and a partial restoration were made in 1922 under the direction of Gaudence Orfali.

The synagogue was an imposing building, sixty-five feet long and two stories high. It was built out

Courtesy of the Israel Office of Information, New York
7. Ruins of the Capernaum synagogue

of white limestone instead of the local black basalt. The building was a basilica with a gable roof. There were galleries on three sides for women; these galleries were supported on a single row of columns and were reached by two stairs in an annex on the NW corner. At the S end, toward Jerusalem, there was the ark of the law built of stone. Benches were built into the side walls. On the E there was an open court with a portico on three sides. Here there was a fountain for ceremonial washings. Figs. CAP 7; SYN 97-98.

The ornamentation of this synagogue was unusual in its use of figures not in accord with a strict interpretation of Jewish law. The remains reveal a surprising variety of animal, mythological, and geometric figures. Some of these, especially the geometric figures, may have been magical symbols. There is a unique likeness of what looks like a small temple on wheels, but it is probably the representation of a carriage and not of the ark. The unorthodox ornamentation may reflect the character of the Jewish community, for rabbinic literature speaks of Capernaum as a seat of the Minim (מנים) or sectaries (Midrash Rabbah Koh. I.8). On one of the pillars there was found an interesting Aramaic inscription which reads, "Alphaeus, son of Zebedee, son of John, made this column; on him be blessing."

**3. In the gospels.** Capernaum is one of the most important cities in the gospels, especially in Jesus' Galilean ministry. It is not explained why Jesus, early in his ministry, left his native Nazareth for the much larger city, "Capernaum by the sea" (Matt. 4: 13). This is the only place in the gospels of which it is said that Jesus was "at home" (Mark 2:1). In the Fourth Gospel it is following the cleansing of the temple that Jesus, his family, and his disciples go to Capernaum and stay "for a few days" (John 2:12). The home of Peter and Andrew was apparently there (Matt. 8:14; Mark 1:29; Luke 4:38).

Capernaum is named specifically as the setting of many incidents and is implied in others. In its synagogue Jesus healed a man with an unclean spirit (Mark 1:21-28; Luke 4:31-38). The synagogue is also referred to, in the story of the healing of the servant of the centurion, as the one built by this centurion (Matt. 8:5-13). The synagogue is also the setting of the incidents and the sermon which follow the feeding of the five thousand (John 6:16-59).

In Capernaum, Jesus healed the paralytic (Mark 2:1-12) and held the discussions on true greatness (9:33-37) and on paying the half-shekel tax (Matt. 17:24-27). Here he healed an official's son who was ill (John 4:46-54). The city was well known as the center of Jesus' ministry and where he had healed many people (Luke 4:23). Although it was his home, Capernaum shared in Jesus' condemnation of those cities which had seen his mighty works and yet had not repented (Matt. 11:23; Luke 10:15).

*Bibliography.* G. Dalman, *Orte und Wege Jesu* (1919), pp. 132-49; E. L. Sukenik, *Ancient Synagogues in Palestine and Greece* (1934), pp. 7-21; C. C. McCown, *Ladder of Progress in Palestine* (1943), pp. 257-60, 267-72; E. F. F. Bishop, "Jesus and Capernaum," *Catholic Biblical Quarterly*, XV (1953), 427-37.                                    D. C. PELLETT

**CAPH** käf [כ, *k* (*Kaph*)]. The eleventh letter of the Hebrew ALPHABET, as placed in the KJV at the head of the eleventh section of the acrostic psalm, Ps. 119, where each verse of this section of the psalm begins with this letter.

**CAPHARNAUM** kə fär'nĭ əm. Douay Version form of CAPERNAUM.

**CAPHARSALAMA** käf'ər säl'ə mə [χαφαρσαλαμα] (I Macc. 7:31). The scene of an engagement between Judas and Nicanor which resulted in a victory for the Jewish forces. This skirmish may be the one identified in II Macc. 14:16 with DESSAU. Others identify the name with the modern Khirbet Selma (el-'Id) near the Bethoron road *ca.* six miles NW of Jerusalem, perhaps the Salem of Euseb. Onom. 153-54.

*Bibliography.* F.-M. Abel, *Géographie de la Palestine*, II (1938), 293; J. J. Simons, *The Geographical and Topographical Texts of the OT* (1960), pp. 409-10.        E. W. SAUNDERS

**CAPHENATHA.** KJV form of CHAPHENATHA.

**CAPHIRA.** KJV Apoc. form of CHEPHIRAH.

**CAPHTOR** käf'tôr [כפתר]; CAPHTORIM —tə rĭm. According to biblical tradition, Caphtor was the place of origin of the Philistines.

The place name Caphtor first occurs in the form "Kaptara" in Akkadian texts. The oldest occurrence is in a geographic text available in a later copy, describing Kaptara as beyond the Upper Sea and within the sphere of influence of Sargon of Akkad. References to Kaptara are found in the economic archives of Mari (eighteenth century) and in texts in both Akkadian and Ugaritic (as *kptr*) from Ugarit.

In Egyptian sources a place name Keftiu (*kftyw* or *kftiw*) is found in texts from 2200 to 1200 B.C. It it commonly accepted among Egyptologists that *keftiu* is the Egyptian form of Kaptara/Caphtor. On the basis of geographical, historical, and literary considerations it is clear that the island of Crete, with which Egypt had commercial relations after *ca.* 2200, is meant by this term. Emissaries in Cretan dress bearing gifts of Cretan origin are depicted in Egyptian tombs.

In biblical tradition, the PHILISTINES came from Caphtor (Jer. 47:4; Amos 9:7). The archaizing his-

torical account in Deut. 2:23 uses the term "Caphtorim" rather than "Philistines" for those who displaced the AVVIM, the autochthonous inhabitants of the coastal area. Undoubtedly, the phrase "whence came the Philistines" in Gen. 10:14 is a misplaced learned gloss belonging after "Caphtorim" rather than after "Casluhim." The tradition itself is problematic, since there is no evidence for a Philistine occupation of Crete, nor do the facts about the Philistines, known from archaeological and literary sources, betray any relationship between them and Crete. Some scholars have favored equating Caphtor with a coastal area of Asia Minor (based on the LXX "Cappadocia" for "Caphtor") or with the island of Carpathos, but there is nothing in favor of this view. It is quite possible that the Philistines adopted the traditions of a colony of Cretan mercenaries—the biblical CHERETHITES, already resident in S Palestine. More likely is the possibility that by the thirteenth century the term "Caphtor" was used broadly for the Aegean area from which the Philistines as one of the "People of the Sea" emerged.

*Bibliography.* G. Dossin, "Les archives economiques de Mari," *Syria*, XX (1939), 97-113; H. J. Kantor, *The Aegean and the Orient in the Second Millennium B.C.* (1947); J. Vercoutter, *L'Egypte et le monde égeen préhellénique* (1956), contains a full bibliography and discusses in detail the various views on Caphtor.                                    J. C. GREENFIELD

**CAPITAL** [כתרת (CROWN *in* I Kings 7:31; KJV CHAPITER), צפת (KJV CHAPITER), ראש (KJV CHAPITER), כפתור (KJV KNOP *in* Exod. 25:31-36; 37:17-22; LINTEL *in* Amos 9:1; Zeph. 2:14)]. An ornament on top of a pillar. Figs. ARC 56; CAP 8.

Courtesy of the Oriental Institute, the University of Chicago

8. A "Proto-Ionic" capital found in Megiddo (tenth century B.C.)

The כתרת was a bronze sphere five cubits high on each of the bronze pillars Jachin and Boaz (I Kings 7:16-42; II Chr. 4:12; Jer. 52:22; in II Kings 25:17 the height is given as three cubits). In I Kings 7:31 the RSV interprets the word to mean "crown" (cf. כתר; Esth. 1:11, etc.). צפת appears only in II Chr. 3:15, where the reference clearly is to the same capitals. ראש (lit., "head") is used to designate capitals on pillars of the tabernacle (Exod. 36:38; 38:17, 19, 28).

See *also* ARCHITECTURE; LINTEL; TABERNACLE; TEMPLE, JERUSALEM.                                    O. R. SELLERS

**CAPPADOCIA** kăp'ə dō'shə [Καππαδοκία] (Acts 2:9; I Pet. 1:1). In NT times, a large Roman province in E Asia Minor.

The limits of Cappadocia varied greatly at different times, but in general it was the territory S of PONTUS and the mountains along the upper Halys

River, E of GALATIA and LYCAONIA, N of CILICIA and the Taurus Mountains, and W of Armenia and the EUPHRATES River (Pliny Nat. Hist. VI.3; Strabo XII.1).

Under the Persians, Asia Minor was divided into satrapies ruled by satraps. Later the Seleucids of Syria permitted these satraps to continue as client kings. After the Roman conquest this system continued, and Cappadocia was ruled by a king; but the last king, Archelaus, was accused of treason by Tiberius and summoned to Rome. When he died there in A.D. 17, Cappadocia was made an imperial province and placed under the direct rule of a procurator (Tac. Ann. II.42; Dio Cassius LVII.17). Its size at this time was ca. 33,000 square miles. Under the later emperors its size increased as it became more important as a frontier province.

Cappadocia was a wild, mountainous country with few large cities. The leading cities were Tyana and Mazaca (Caesareia). It had little timber, but was valued for its crops, especially wheat. It was noted for its cattle and famous for its horses. It exported some minerals, chiefly ocher, alabaster, mica, silver, and lead. Some sections produced excellent wine. Its position was strategic because of the roads which crossed it, such as the one from the Cilician Gates across to Pontus.

Cappadocia possessed a significant Jewish community as early as the second century B.C., indicated in a letter to Ariarthes, king of Cappadocia (I Macc. 15:22; cf. *Philo Legation to Caius* 36). Jews from Cappadocia were in Jerusalem at Pentecost (Acts 2:9). Christianity spread along the road N from Tarsus into Cappadocia and on to Pontus before the end of the first century A.D. (I Pet. 1:1). The new religion seems to have flourished, for by the fourth century Cappadocia was producing great leaders of the church.

*Bibliography.* T. Mommsen, *The Provinces of the Roman Empire* (1886), pp. 323-25, 332-33; D. Magie, *Roman Rule in Asia Minor* (1950), pp. 200-201, 491-96.      D. C. PELLETT

**CAPTAIN.** An officer of some kind. The word "captain" is used by English versions to render various Hebrew and Greek words mainly because little is known of army ranks in biblical times. "Captain" has been used to translate the following:

*a)* ראש (lit., "head"; by extension, the "one at the head" of a group).

*b)* רב (lit., "one who is great," thus "chief"), used mainly of Assyrian and Babylonian officers in such titles as רב טבחים, "captain of the guard" (II Kings 25:8-20; Jer. 39:9–52:30); רב שקה, RABSHAKEH (II Kings 18:17 ff; 19:4, 8; Isa. 36:2 ff; 37:4, 8); and רב סריס, RABSARIS (II Kings 18:17; Jer. 39:3, 13) and "chief eunuch" (Dan. 1:3; KJV "master of his eunuchs").

*c)* שר, the most common word to be rendered by "captain."

*d)* פחה (II Kings 18:24; Isa. 36:9; usually "governor"; "commander" in I Kings 20:24). This word is an Akkadian loan word, *pāḥatu*, an "administrative district"—hence, by extension, *bēl pāḥati*, the "ruler of a district."

*e)* שלט (Dan. 2:15), derived from שלט, "to rule."

*f)* שליש (alternately "officer"; "aide"), a word of

uncertain meaning. Since שלש means "to be three," it is thought that the word may refer to the third man in the CHARIOT.

*g)* Στρατηγός, in the phrase "captain of the temple" (Luke 22:4, 52; Acts 4:1; 5:24, 26; "general" [KJV "duke"] in I Macc. 10:65)—i.e., an officer of the temple police.

*h)* Χιλίαρχος (lit., "ruler of a thousand"), the regular NT designation for a military chieftain.

In addition, the KJV uses "captain" to translate the following:

*a)* אלוף (Jer. 13:21; RSV "friend"). There are two words identical in form: "tribal chieftain," possibly a denominative word from אלף, "thousand," hence originally a "leader of a thousand"; and a word from אלף, "to learn," hence "one who is well known, an intimate."

*b)* בעל, only in the phrase "captain of the ward" (Jer. 37:13; RSV "sentry"; lit., "one who has the oversight").

*c)* טפסר (RSV "marshal" in Jer. 51:27; "scribe" in Nah. 3:17). This is a Sumerian word borrowed through Akkadian. Sumerian *dub*, "tablet," and *sar*, "writer," were borrowed by Akkadian as *ṭupšarru*, and by Hebrew in turn as טפסר. Whether the Akkadian meaning of "tabletwriter" (hence "scribe") is germane for Hebrew is not clear.

*d)* כר (Ezek. 21:22; the RSV omits the phrase לשום כרים, lit. "to set battering rams"; LXX τοῦ βαλεῖν χάρακα; cf. BATTERING RAM). This KJV rendering is based on an invalid Jewish tradition (cf. Qimchi).

*e)* כרי (II Kings 11:4, 19; RSV "Carites"; *see* CHERETHITES). This KJV rendering derives from an early Jewish tradition (cf. Targ. Jonathan: גבריא).

*f)* נגיד (RSV "prince"; lit., "leader"), a charismatic ruler.

*g)* נשיא (Num. 2; RSV more literally "leader"), derived from נשא, "to lift up," hence "chieftain, leader."

*h)* קצין (RSV better "chief" in Josh. 10:24; "leader" in Judg. 11:6, 11).

*i)* Ἀρχηγός (Heb. 2:10; RSV "pioneer"). This word can mean either "leader" or "founder" and appears in both senses throughout the LXX.

                 J. W. WEVERS

**CAPTAIN OF THE TEMPLE** [ὁ στρατηγὸς τοῦ ἱεροῦ (Acts 4:1; 5:24, 26; *plural in* Luke 22:4, 52); ὁ πγοτάτης (one who stands over) τοῦ ἱεροῦ (II Macc. 3:4)]. The officer second in authority only to the high priest in the temple. He is mentioned in Jer. 20:1 LXX as ἡγούμενος (lit., "leader") and in Neh. 11:11 as ἀπεναντι τοῦ οἴκου τοῦ θεοῦ ("ruler of the house of God") = Vulg. *princeps domus Dei.* Josephus (Antiq. XX.vi.2; War VI.v.3) uses the simple στρατηγός. In the Mishna the chief officer is called סגן הכהנים ("captain of the priesthood") or simply סגן (*Sagan,* "captain").

The chief authority in the temple area was the high priest. The captain of the temple (translated "commander" by Moffatt, Goodspeed, Weymouth, Rieu; "officer in charge" by *The Twentieth Century NT*) was also a priest, having supervision over the cultus and the officiating priesthood, as the high priest's adjutant, as well as over the groups of Levites, themselves organized under "captains" into corps of guards functioning as police. The subordinate "captains" would be in direct charge of the watchmen who opened and closed the gates, of the sentries, and of the guards who protected the valuable treasures often stored in the temple, and would probably have more direct and frequent contacts with the people.

If the references in Acts suggest the chief "captain," the plural in Luke 22:4, 52, suggests the subordinate "captains." However, differentiation of function between the chief captain and the subordinate captains is not Luke's concern. Either he was uninformed as to the difference in status and function or he was indifferent to it. He may well have used the plurals in 22:4 ("chief priests and captains"), 52 ("chief priests and captains of the temple and elders"), to be impressive, and without entertaining the possibility of confusion between the captain and his subordinate captains. In Acts 4:1; 5:24, 26, since it was a question of arrest, it is the chief captain who is properly, even impressively, involved. Yet in neither case is it now possible to determine which sort of "captain" was actually involved. If the sober historian of the present day is inclined to decide for the officer with less prestige, Luke certainly was not.                                F. D. GEALY

**CAPTIVITY** [שְׁבִי; αἰχμαλωσία]. See EXILE; DISPERSION.

**CARABASION** kăr'ə bā'zhĭ ən [Καραβασειών (B), Καραβασιων (A)] (I Esd. 9:34). One of the Israelites who put away their foreign wives and children. His name is omitted in the parallel Ezra 10:34-37.
                                                C. T. FRITSCH

**CARAVAN** [ארחה, *from* ארח, to journey]; KJV **COMPANY** in Gen. 37:25, **TRAVELLING COMPANIES** in Isa. 21:13. A company of people, often merchants with pack animals, traveling together, especially through dangerous territory. The RSV repoints the MT ארחות ("paths") to obtain "caravans" in Judg 5:6a (KJV "highways"); Job 6:18 (KJV "paths"); Job 6:19 (KJV "troops"). In Job 6:19 הליכת (from הלך, "to walk"), which can mean "caravans," is translated "travelers" (KJV "companies").

Local caravans in Israel transported goods from one district to another, using mostly the ass; the camel, which came into use ca. 1100 B.C., was less common. Such trade might be interfered with by unsettled political conditions (Judg. 5:6). Most of the caravans mentioned in the OT are, however, related to Transjordan and Arabia. These Arab caravans of camels were engaged primarily in the lucrative spice and incense trade, whose products came largely from Hadhramaut in S Arabia. Such traders would come N via Timna and Marib through the Hijaz to Gaza or Damascus, or at a later date to Petra and Bostra. The rulers of Saba (Sheba) would be involved in this enterprise (I Kings 10:2), and Transjordanians might easily do business with Egypt (Gen. 37:25). Herodotus tells us that the Arabians rendered to Achaemenid Persia annually one thousand talents weight of frankincense (III.97). Pliny, who has much to say about the incense trade, notes that it takes sixty-five days to come by camel to Gaza from S Arabia (Nat. Hist. XII.32).

*Bibliography.* For a description of a caravan leaving Damascus in 1876 (the Haj or Meccan pilgrimage), traveling 2½

miles per hour, see C. M. Doughty, *Travels in Arabia Deserta* (1888), vol. I, ch. 1; for a caravan to Mecca with one hundred and seventy camels bearing thirty tons of butter (*samn*), see *op. cit.,* vol. II, ch. 16. For ancient and modern caravans in Hadhramaut, see W. Phillips, *Qataban and Sheba* (1955), pp. 4-6, 34, 76-78.
                                                W. S. McCULLOUGH

**CARBUNCLE.** A red stone such as ruby or garnet. In Exod. 28:17; 39:10 ברקת, a stone on the breastpiece of judgment, is incorrectly translated "carbuncle" (cf. Sanskrit *markata*, μάραδος = σμάραδος, "emerald"; Akkadian *barâqtu;* LXX and Vulg. "emerald"). Dark green beryl has also been suggested. In Ezek. 28:13, where it is one of the precious stones forming the covering of the king of Tyre, the RSV translates "emerald," but renders as "carbuncle" נפך ("turquoise"?), which in Exod. 28:18; 39: 11 appears as "emerald."

*See also* TURQUOISE; EMERALD; JEWELS AND PRECIOUS STONES § 2.                    W. E. STAPLES

**CARCAS.** KJV form of CARKAS.

**CARCHEMISH** kär'kə mĭsh [כרכמיש]; KJV once **CHARCHEMISH** (II Chr. 35:20); KJV Apoc. **CARCHAMIS** —mĭs. An important Syro-Hittite capital on the Upper Euphrates. The site, which has been excavated, is now called Jerablus. Fig. CAR 9.

9. Citadel mound of Carchemish, from the NW, the Euphrates River in the background

Isa. 10:9 alludes to the capture of Carchemish by the Assyrians. II Chr. 35:20 tells of Pharaoh Neco II's heading for Carchemish to wage war in the eighteenth year of Josiah; and it was there that Nebuchadrezzar defeated Pharaoh Neco II in the fourth year of Jehoiakim son of Josiah, according to Jer. 46:2 (see also I Esd. 1:25). The Battle of Carchemish is documented in the Nebuchadrezzar Chronicles, which describe Nebuchadrezzar's defeat of the Egyptian army and pursuit of them "so that not a single man escaped to his own country."

Carchemish is also well attested in Egyptian, and especially in cuneiform records. Fig. JEH 10.

The importance of Carchemish during and just after the Amarna Age is becoming clarified by the royal Hittite archives found at Ugarit. These texts show that for many administrational purposes, vassal kingdoms in Syria (such as Ugarit) were subject to Carchemish within the Hittite imperial system. Figs. CAR 10-11; BAN 20.

*Bibliography.* D. G. Hogarth and C. L. Woolley, *Carchemish* (1914, 1921); D. J. Wiseman, *Chronicles of the Chaldean Kings* (1956), pp. 23-27, 66-69.
                                                C. H. GORDON

10. King Araras of Carchemish and his son Prince Kamanas, from a basalt relief from Carchemish (second half of eighth century B.C.). Note Hittite hieroglyphs near top.

11. Basalt relief of a winged creature, from Carchemish

**CARE, CAREFULNESS.** The clear understanding of these terms in biblical usage is complicated by the number of words in Hebrew and Greek so rendered, by the history of "care" and "carefulness" in English usage, and by the range of meanings served by these words. In the Hebrew and Greek Bible the noun "care" translates at least ten words, and the verbs "care," "care for," "take care lest," translate at least thirteen words with some variety of meanings. In early English usage "care" meant "mental suffering," "anxiety"; and the word "careful" had a similar sense of overanxiety. The KJV illustrates the change of meaning in Phil. 4:6: "Be careful for nothing." Today the word "care" expresses concern, solicitude, responsible attention in one direction, and concern, regard, liking, even love, in another direction.

The OT terms frequently carry active and concrete connotations. In Gen. 39:22 the prisoners are committed to Joseph's hand (יד, ביד, "to Joseph's care"). In Deut. 11:12 God seeks out the land (דרש, "cares for"). In Jer. 23:2 the shepherds are to visit God's people (פקד, "care for, look after"). Note also Jer. 23:4, where other shepherds feed the flock (רעה, "care for, lead").

For the NT sense of care as anxiety, *see* ANXIETY. The word "careful" carries the meaning of being alive to obligation as in the commandments, or to risks in the sense of taking heed.

The whole Hebrew-Christian tradition opens up the channels of human awareness to the call of God and the claims of his law, to the risks of disobedience, to the presence and needs of other men. Over all are the care of God for his people and his attentiveness to their condition: "Cast all your anxieties [μέριμνα] on him, for he cares [μέλει] about you."

P. E. DAVIES

**CAREAH.** KJV form of KAREAH in II Kings 25:23.

**CARIA** kâr′ĭ ə [Καρία]. In early ancient times the name of the SW portion of Asia Minor. It was bounded on the N, in the Maeander River area, by Lydia, on the E by Phrygia, on the SE by LYCIA, and on the SW and the W by the Mediterranean and Aegean seas. The Ionian and Dorian Greeks established cities on the coast which maintained a rather independent status. Thus when *ca.* 139 B.C. the Romans sent a letter on behalf of the Jews to Caria (I Macc. 15:23), it probably went to the Carian confederacy which met at the temple of Zeus Chrysaoreus at Stratonicea, but the Romans sent separate letters to the cities of Myndos, Halicarnassus, and Cnidus. These letters imply a Jewish population in Caria and especially in these cities. *Ca.* 129 B.C., Caria was made part of the Roman province of Asia.

Bibliography. A. H. M. Jones, *The Cities of the Eastern Roman Provinces* (1937), ch. 2; D. Magie, *Roman Rule in Asia Minor* (1950), pp. 35-38, 50-52, 144-46, 155. F. V. FILSON

**CARITES.** *See* CHERETHITES.

**CARKAS** kär′kəs [כרכס, *perhaps* vulture, *from* Pers. *karkasa*] (Esth. 1:10); KJV CARCAS. One of seven eunuchs who served Ahasuerus as chamberlains and whom he sent for Queen Vashti.

**CARMANIANS.** KJV Apoc. form of CARMONIANS.

**CARME.** KJV Apoc. form of HARIM 1.

**CARMEL (CITY)** kär'məl [כרמל, vineyard]; **CAR-MELITE** —mə līt [כרמלי, of Carmel]; **CARME-LITESS** —līt'ĭs [כרמלית]. A village in the Maon dis-trict of Judah (Josh. 15:55); identified with modern el-Kirmil, seven miles S-SE of Hebron. Saul erected a monument at Carmel after defeating the Amalek-ites (I Sam. 15:12). Carmel was the scene of the in-cident between David and Nabal as a result of which David took Nabal's widow for a wife (I Sam. 25:2-40; 27:3; 30:5; II Sam. 2:2; 3:3; I Chr. 3:1). Hezro, one of David's Mighty Men, came from Carmel (II Sam. 23:35; I Chr. 11:37).           V. R. GOLD

\***CARMEL, MOUNT** [הכרמל, the garden *or* orchard; כרמל (Josh. 19:26; Jer. 46:18; Nah. 1:4)]. A promi-nent mountain on the coast of Palestine. It has sig-nificant associations with Elijah and Elisha.

Mount Carmel juts into the Mediterranean Sea at the head of a range of mountains to which it has given its name and of which it is geologically and geographically a part. The mountain itself, which is formed of hard, porous Cenomanian limestone, extends SE for a distance of *ca.* thirteen miles; it reaches a height of 470 feet at the promontory and a maximum elevation of 1,742 feet near 'Esfia. Its NE slopes are steep and precipitous, while those on the SW give way more gradually to the coast. A luxuriant growth of plants, for which it was famous in antiquity (*see below*), still covers its slopes.

Geographically, Mount Carmel is a wedge-shaped barrier, which splits the Palestinian coastal plain into two parts, the Plain of Acco to the N, and the plains of Sharon and Philistia to the S. Between the foot of the promontory and the sea is a narrow beach road which joins these plains, but throughout antiquity most commercial and military traffic crossed the Carmel Range inland by means of passes leading to IBLEAM; TAANACH; MEGIDDO; and perhaps JOKNEAM.

Courtesy of Herbert G. May

12. Mount Carmel from the Galilee foothills

As a result of its isolation, Mount Carmel has been sparsely occupied in historical times, though during the Stone Age, caves in its W slopes were inhabited by early man (*see* MUGHARAH, WADI EL). The first historical mentions of the mountain are found in lists of Thut-mose III, Ramses II, and Ramses III of Egypt, if the identification of *Rosh Qidshu* in these lists with Mount Carmel is correct, as seems prob-able. If *Rosh Qidshu*—which means "holy cape"—is an earlier name for Mount Carmel, it strongly sug-gests that the mountain was an early holy place or sanctuary. That special religious significance was attached to it during biblical times is indicated by I Kings 18:19-40, where it was the scene of the con-test between the prophets of Baal and Elijah; and by II Kings 2:25; 4:25, where it seems to have served as Elisha's spiritual retreat. The beauty (Song

of S. 7:5) and fertility of Mount Carmel greatly im-pressed biblical writers, who frequently mention it in parallelism with the Plain of Sharon, Lebanon, Bashan, and Gilead (Isa. 35:2; Jer. 50:19; Mic. 7: 14), or conversely employ the desiccation of Mount Carmel as a figure of great desolation (Isa. 33:9; Amos 1:2; Nah. 1:4).

Fig. CAR 12.

*Bibliography.* C. R. Conder and H. H. Kitchener, *SWP,* I (1889), 264-65; D. Baly, *The Geography of the Bible* (1957), *passim.*           G. W. VAN BEEK

**CARMI** kär'mī [כרמי, vineyard owner(?)]; **CAR-MITES** —mīts. 1. A son of Reuben, listed as the last of four sons of Reuben in the tribal genealogies (Gen. 46:9; Exod. 6:14; Num. 26:6; I Chr. 5:3). Carmi is the eponymous ancestor of the "family of the Car-mites."

2. A Judahite, the father of Achan (Achar in I Chr. 2:7), who violated the ban laid on Jericho (Josh. 7:1, 18; I Chr. 2:7; 4:1, where "Caleb" should probably be read instead of "Carmi").

R. F. JOHNSON

**CARMONIANS** kär mō'nĭ ənz [Lat. *Carmonii*]; KJV **CARMANIANS** —mā'—. A people from Carmania, a province of ancient Persia which was situated on the N shore of the Persian Gulf, to the W of Gedrosia. Its name survives in the modern Ker-man. In II Esd. 15:30 the Carmonians—more ac-curately, the Carmanians—are described as devastat-ing a "portion of the land of the Assyrians with their teeth." They joined battle with the "nations of the dragons of Arabia," who gained the upper hand, only to be defeated in their turn by an "enemy in ambush" from Assyria.

These events, described in veiled, apocalyptic lan-guage, probably refer to the time of the Sassanidae, especially Shapur or Sapor I (A.D. 240-73), who overran the Roman province of Syria—a "portion of the land of the Assyrians"—and destroyed Antioch. These Persian successes soon came to an end, how-ever, when Odenathus and his brave wife, Zenobia, Queen of Palmyra—the "dragons of Arabia"—drove Sapor and his forces back beyond the Euphrates. Zenobia's defeat later at the hands of Aurelian (A.D. 273) is probably referred to in vs. 33.

C. T. FRITSCH

**CARNAIM; KJV CARNION.** Apoc. form of Karnaim (II Macc. 12:21, 26). "Carnion" is either a Grecized form of "Carnaim" or the name of a sanctuary at Carnaim. *See* ASHTEROTH-KARNAIM.

**CARNAL** [σαρκικός (Rom. 7:14); KJV σάρξ, *see below*]; **CARNALLY** [זרע; KJV σάρξ (Rom. 8:6), *see below*]. "Carnal" is either equivalent to the Eng-lish word "material" (cf. II Cor. 10:4 KJV) or de-scribes human nature when under the domination of its lower, unregenerate impulses (cf. I Cor. 3:3 KJV). The adverb "carnally," meaning "sexually," is used in the OT to translate the modifying noun in the phrase שכבת זרע (Lev. 19:20) or לזרע (18:20), lit., "a lying of (or for) seed." Without sexual connota-tions, the adverb is used once in the KJV to translate (τὸ . . . φρόνημα) τῆς σαρκὸς (Rom. 8:6), a phrase more adequately rendered in the RSV "(to set the mind) on the flesh." *See also* FLESH IN THE OT; FLESH IN THE NT.      R. C. DENTAN

**CARNELIAN** [אדם (*cf. verbal cognate,* to be red); LXX *and* NT σάρδιον; Vulg. *sardius*]; KJV SAR-DIUS (mg. RUBY). A variety of chalcedony of a clear deep-red, flesh, or reddish-white color. Sardius is a darker variety of chalcedony. It is one of the few stones noted in the Bible which are found in any quantity in Palestine archaeological sites. אדם is a stone in the covering of the king of Tyre (Ezek. 28: 13). Σάρδιον occurs in the description of the one seated on the throne (Rev. 4:3), and it is the sixth jewel in the foundation wall of the New Jerusalem (21:20). *See* SARDIUS.

*See also* JEWELS AND PRECIOUS STONES § 2.
     W. E. STAPLES

**CARNION.** KJV Apoc. form of Karnaim. *See* ASHTEROTH-KARNAIM.

**CARPENTER** [חרש, *from* חרש, to scratch, engrave, *see below;* τέκτων, *see below*]. A craftsman who built yokes, plows, threshing boards, benches, beds, boxes, coffins, boats, and houses, and worked on temple and synagogue.

Frequently the Hebrew חרש is connected with wood, as in II Sam. 5:11; II Kings 12:11; I Chr. 14: 1; 22:15; II Chr. 34:11; Isa. 44:13; etc. The same word used with various metals is translated "smith."

The Greek τέκτων is used in the NT only for Joseph (Matt. 13:55) and Jesus (Mark 6:3). Justin Martyr suggests Jesus made plows and yokes (*Trypho* 88). Perhaps the Greek has the wider meaning of "builder."

Courtesy of Foto Marburg

13. A carpenter scene from the tomb of Ti at Saqqarah. The workman in the center is using a chisel and mallet; the other two are sawing boards.

The carpenter built the upper story on stone houses and made repairs on gates. Many a householder did the task of a carpenter in the days before there were specialists. Isa. 44:13 lists some of the carpenter's tools. His tools were the compass, pencil, plane, saw, hammer, axe, adz, chisel, plumb line, drill, file, square, etc. Many of these were made of stone and in the later periods bronze and iron. Both dowels and nails, as well as mortised, dovetail, and mitered joints, were used to join wood together.

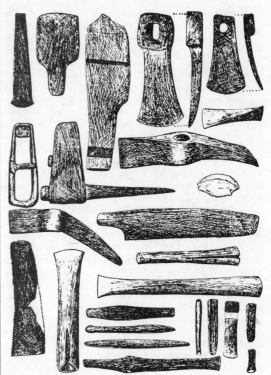

By permission of the Palestine Exploration Fund

14. Carpenter's tools, from Gezer

The early Israelites were probably backward in this skill because of their nomadic origin. David and Solomon both imported Tyrian carpenters to work on the palace and the temple (II Sam. 5:11; I Kings 5–7). Later, native carpenters were skilled enough to repair the temple (II Kings 12:11; 22:6). They were carried along with the wealthy into captivity (Jer. 24: 1; "craftsmen"). Phoenicians were again imported by Ezra (Ezra 3:7). In the latest OT times there were guilds of carpenters (I Chr. 4:14; "craftsmen"), and this is verified in the Oxyrhynthus Papyri. Less skilled workers in wood were the timber cutters. The most skilled carftsmen were engaged in carving and practiced inlay. Figs. CAR 13-14.

In Christian symbolism the carpenter's square is used for Jude and Thomas, and a saw is the symbol of James the Less.      C. U. WOLF

**CARPET** [גנז (Ezek. 27:24; KJV CHEST; *alternately* TREASURY)]; RICH CARPETS [מדין (Judg. 5:10; KJV JUDGMENT)]. The meaning of both these terms is in doubt.

The word used in Ezek. 27:24 is translated "treasury" in Esth. 3:9; 4:7. Its place in a list of types of merchandise imported by Tyre and the fact that it is described as being "of colored stuff" have given it the meaning "carpet." But that the objects are "bound with cords and made secure" may suggest that they are chests covered with beautifully woven material; this would fit the doubtfully presumed cognate, מדה, מד, "garment."

The word used in Judg. 5:10 refers to something on which people sit. Those who "ride on tawny asses," those who walk on the highways, and those who sit on מדין may be various types of professional storytellers or bards, who might well have had such informal soapboxes. E. M. Good

**CARPUS** kär′pəs [Κάρπος, *perhaps from* καρπός, fruit]. A resident of Troas with whom Paul had left a cloak, according to II Tim. 4:13. Paul asked Timothy to bring him this cloak from Troas.

According to one tradition, Carpus became bishop of Berytus in Thrace. He was also thought to have been martyred in Pergamum.

B. H. THROCKMORTON, JR.

**CARRIAGE.** The KJV translation of the following terms: כלי (I Sam. 17:22 [twice]; Isa. 10:28; RSV "baggage"); נשׂא (Isa. 46:1; RSV "burden"); כבודה (Judg. 18:21; RSV "goods"); ἐπισκευασά-μενοι (Acts 21:15; the RSV translates "made ready" instead of "took up our carriages"). In each instance the reference is to the object carried, not to a means of conveyance. The Greek term has to do with assembling the necessary baggage for a journey.

W. G. WILLIAMS

**CARSHENA** kär shē′nə [כרשׁנא, *possibly from* Pers. *keresna*, black] (Esth. 1:14). One of the seven princes and wise men of King Ahasuerus.

**CART** [גלגל, wheel; עגלה, *from* עגל, roll; צב, *from* Akkad. *ṣumbu*, wagon; ἄμαξα (Jth. 15:11), *from* ἅμα, with, *and* ἄγω, carry]. Alternately: WAGON. In English a "cart" is usually a light, two-wheeled vehicle and a wagon a heavier, four-wheeled one, but such distinctions for the biblical terms must be drawn principally from their context.

Courtesy of Foto Marburg

15. Assyrian soldiers leading away prisoners of war, the women being transported in a cart; from the palace of Ashurbanipal (629-626 B.C.) at Nineveh

In Num. 7:3-8; II Sam. 6:3 עגלה appears to be a wagon pulled by two oxen (in I Sam. 6:7 by two milch cows). This would be used for transporting both persons and things (Gen. 45:19, 21, 27; 46:5; Jth. 15:11). Such a four-wheeled vehicle is meant by ῥέδη in Rev. 18:13—not, with the RSV, "chariot" (cf. Amer. Trans. "carriage"). The meaning of עגלות צב (lit., "wagons of wagon"; Num. 7:3) is uncertain (KJV-RSV "covered wagons"; *see* LITTER). In Ezek. 23:24; 26:10 גלגל ("wagons") seems to refer to the transport wagons of an army. עגלות in Ps. 46:9—H 46:10 (lit., "wagons") may also mean military transport, though "chariots" (RSV) is not impossible. A wheeled vehicle, עגלה, was used in thresh-

ing operations (Isa. 28:27-28), possibly before the threshing sledge; but this is not to be confused with the "cart full of sheaves" in Amos 2:13.

Figs. CAR 15-17. W. S. McCULLOUGH

16. Upper: an ancient Egyptian cart; lower: a cart with captured women; from Lachish

Courtesy of the University Museum of the University of Pennsylvania

17. Clay model of wagon; from Tepe Gawra, in Mesopotamia (*ca.* 2500 B.C.)

**CARVING** [חרשׁת, *from* חרשׁ, cut in, engrave; מקלעת, *from* קלע, carve]; **CARVED FIGURES** [פתוחי מקלעות, engravings of carvings]; **CARVED WOOD** [פתוח, *from* פתח, engrave; *cf.* Akkad. *patāḫu*, bore a hole]; **CARVED WORK** [מחקה, *participle from* חקה, *variant of* חקק, cut in, inscribe]. Something cut, especially in an artistic manner. Cf. also משכית (probably "showpiece"), "figured stone" or "picture" (cf. Num. 33:52; Ezek. 8:12); אבן משכית, "figured stone" (Lev. 26:1; KJV "image of stone").

While the references in Exod. 31:5; 35:33 to the carving of stone and wood suggest that these skills were known to Israel in the Exodus days, the statement in II Sam. 5:11 that David was indebted to carpenters and masons from Tyre in his building operations supports the view that such craftsmen were developed in Israel only under the monarchy. This conclusion is strengthened by the account in I Kings 5:1-18—H 5:15-32 of Solomon's dependence upon the men of Phoenicia. As Israel's cultural life grew stronger, so, we may assume, did skill in carving, though the latter must have continued to be influenced by the older artistic traditions of Phoenicia and Egypt, and later of Mesopotamia.

Apart from the allusions, often satiric, to carved idols and their manufacture (Lev. 26:1; Num. 33:52; Deut. 4:28; Isa. 40:18-20; 44:9-20; Jer. 2:27; 10:1-10; Ezek. 8:10, 12; 23:14; Wisd. Sol. 13:13; 14:16), all the OT references to the carving of wood, stone, and metal pertain to the tent of meeting (Exod. 31:5; 35: 33), or to its successor the Jerusalem temple. In addition to the carving on the bronze stands of the temple lavers (I Kings 7:31, 36; *see* ENGRAVING), what is particularly recorded about the temple is the decoration of the olivewood and cypress doors and the cedar wainscoting with carvings (מקלעות) of "cherubim and palm trees and open flowers" (I Kings 6: 18, 29, 32, 35; cf. Ezek. 41:17-20; Ps. 74:6). Moreover, while the text does not use "carve" with respect to the cherubim of the inner sanctuary, it is obvious that these large creatures made from olivewood, each fifteen feet high, represent a good deal of joinery and carving (I Kings 6:23-28).

Carving skills were exercised on various materials other than wood. *See also* IVORY; GRAVEN IMAGE; SCULPTURED STONES.

*Bibliography.* For carving of ivory, see J. W. and G. M. Crowfoot, *Early Ivories from Samaria* (1938); many of the motifs of these objects are clearly Egyptian, doubtless mediated through a Phoenician tradition. For carved work in ivory, bone, and marble, found in biblical Hazor, see *BA,* XIX (1956), 1-11; XX (1957), 34-41.     W. S. McCULLOUGH

**CASEMENT.** KJV translation of אשנב (RSV LATTICE) in Prov. 7:6.

**CASIPHIA** kə sĭf′ĭ ə [כספא, place of silversmiths(?); LXX AB ἐν ἀργυρίῳ τοῦ τόπου, in silver of the place; ἐν τῷ τόπῳ τοῦ γαζοφυλακίου (I Esd. 8:44), in the place of the treasury; Vulg. *in chasphiae loco*]. A "place" from which Ezra obtained Levites for temple service in Jerusalem (Ezra 8:17). It could be a city or a district. Not certainly identified, it is assumed to have been in Babylonia, perhaps close to the route of Ezra's movement to Judah. Jewish tradition (Leviticus Rabbah 5; Rashi on Isa. 22:18) regards it as the "wide land" (Isa. 22:18) to which Hezekiah's officer Shebna was to be exiled. Winckler (*see bibliography*) proposed identification with Ctesiphon.

*Bibliography.* H. Winckler, "Kasiphja-Ktesiphon," *Altonentalische Forschungen,* Reihe 2, Band III, pp. 509-30.     R. A. BOWMAN

**CASLEU** kăz′loō. KJV Apoc. form of Chislev. *See* CALENDAR.

**CASLUHIM** kăs′lə hĭm [כסלחים; LXX Χασμωνιειμ]. A term of unknown origin which occurs in the ethnographic lists of Gen. 10:14; I Chr. 1:12 as the name of an offspring of Mizraim (Egypt) and as the source of the Philistines. It is preceded by the Lydians; the ANAMIM; the LEHABIM; the NAPHTUHIM; and the PATHRUSIM; and it is followed by the CAPHTORIM.     T. O. LAMBDIN

**CASPHOR.** KJV form of CHASPHO.

**CASPIN** kăs′pən [Κασπιν] (II Macc. 12:13). A strongly fortified town of mixed population taken by Judas, who massacred a great number of the people. It is probably the CHASPHO of I Macc. 5:26, 36, which has been identified with the modern Khisfin, nine miles E of the Sea of Galilee, and also with el-Muzeirib in the Hauran Plain.

*Bibliography.* G. Schumacher, *Across the Jordan* (1889), pp. 157-66; F.-M. Abel, *Les livres des Maccabées* (1949), pp. 435-36.     E. W. SAUNDERS

**CASSIA** kăsh′ə [קדה, *qiddâ;* קציעות, *qᵉṣî′ôth;* κασία; κιννάμωμον (Ecclus. 24:15; KJV CINNAMON)]. The aromatic bark of an oriental tree. Some scholars claim the two Hebrew words refer to different aromatic substances, but the evidence for identification is very meager and inconclusive.

In Exod. 30:24, *qiddâ* refers to an ingredient of the holy anointing oil, and in Ezek. 27:19 it is a product of trade with Tyre. In Ps. 45:8—H 45:9, *qᵉṣî′ôth* is mentioned along with MYRRH and ALOES in describing the fragrance of the royal robes. The latter word is used for one of Job's fair daughters, KEZIAH (Job 42:14). The copper scroll from Qumran Cave 3 by the Dead Sea mentions a "vessel of incense in cassia wood" (XI.1-4).

*See also* FLORA § A7*f;* SPICE.

*Bibliography.* H. N. and A. L. Moldenke, *Plants of the Bible* (1952), pp. 75-76, 218-19.     J. C. TREVER

**CASTANETS.** *See* MUSICAL INSTRUMENTS.

**CASTLE.** The translation of two words in the RSV and of several others in the KJV. In Neh. 7:2 the title "governor of the castle" (בירה; KJV PALACE) may be parallel to "ruler/governor of the city" in Judg. 9:30; I Kings 22:26; II Kings 23:8, although some have seen here a reference to the temple, since בירה is used of the temple complex in I Chr. 29:1, 19, and the Vulg. reads "house." Hananiah (=Hanani, brother of Nehemiah?) was "governor of the castle." In Prov. 18:19 quarreling is likened to the bars of a castle (ארמון; but "castle" is uncertain here, and the RSV elsewhere often translates the word "palace" but most often "stronghold" and twice "citadel"). "Castle" occurs in the KJV nine times in the OT, translating six different words, and six times in the NT for παρεμβολή (RSV "barracks").

Castles and strongholds of many kinds existed, "from watch tower to fortified city" (II Kings 17:9; 18:8). *See* CITY § B2*b.*

An archaeological example of a "castle" is the little fortress of Saul, rude but strong for its time and place, excavated at Gibeah (Tell el-Ful). The Herodian "castle of ANTONIA" (παρεμβολή; Acts 21: 34, etc.; RSV BARRACKS) is another. Dating from the beginning of the Hellenistic period, the ruins of the barbarous but picturesque Hyrcanium of 'Araq el-Emir in Transjordan, the *Bîrtâ* of the Tobiad family and the Zenon Papyri, still survives on its lonely mountain.      C. C. McCown

**CASTOR AND POLLUX** kăs'tər, pŏl'əks. *See* TWIN BROTHERS.

**CAT** [ἄιλουρος; *postbiblical* Heb. חתול, שונרא; *cf.* Arab. *sinnaur;* Syr. *šnartâ*]. A domesticated carnivorous mammal, *felis domesticus,* belonging to the family Felidae.

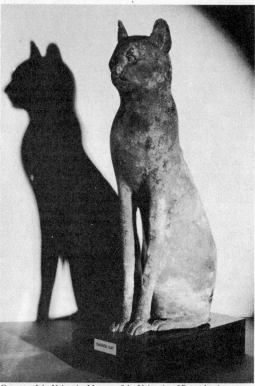

Courtesy of the University Museum of the University of Pennsylvania

18. Bronze statue of a cat, from the Twenty-second Dynasty or later

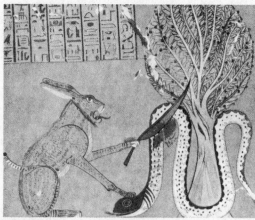

Relevé de Robichon. From *Histoire générale des Religions,* Quillet éd., Paris

19. A cat kills the serpent Apophis with a knife, from a Theban painting.

The absence of references to the cat in both the OT and the NT doubtless reflects the fact that the cat was not commonly known or kept as a pet in Western Asia in the biblical period. The Apoc. (Letter of Jeremiah 22—G 21) gives us the earliest Jewish reference to this animal. The cat, which was known to Greek zoologists (e.g., Aristotle *History of Animals* V.2; VI.35; IX.6), was probably first domesticated in Egypt, where, like certain other animals, it had a place in the religious practices of that country; e.g., Bastet, a cat-goddess, was the tutelary deity of Bubastis, and cats were sacred to her.* The cat was also closely associated with the sun-god Rē' (Fig. CAT 19). This Egyptian reverence for cats, which was recognized by Herodotus (II.66-67), Strabo (XVII.1.40), and Cicero (Tusc. Disp. V.27), may have been a factor in retarding the acceptance of these animals as pets by the non-Egyptian world. Fig. CAT 18.      W. S. McCULLOUGH

**CATARACT** [צנור] (Ps. 42:7—H 42:8); KJV WATERSPOUT. Alternately: WATER SHAFT (II Sam. 5:8); KJV GUTTER. Possibly an allusion to the waterfalls at et-Tannur on the most westerly source of the Jordan; or to Nahr Banias, the most easterly source of the Jordan, which bursts noisily forth from a cave at the foot of Mount Hermon. On the other hand, the context might also suggest an allusion to the waters of the underworld.

     H. G. MAY

**CATERPILLAR** [חסיל; *cf.* Jew. Aram. חסל, *Pael, Aphel,* to peel off, finish; KJV ילק, *see* CANKERWORM]; KJV CATERPILLER. Alternately: DESTROYING LOCUST (Joel 1:4); DESTROYER (Joel 2:25). The wormlike larva of a butterfly, moth, and sometimes of other insects.

Although the LXX generally takes חסיל, *ḥāsîl,* as ἐρυσίβη ("rust on grain"), Ps. 78:46; Joel 1:4; 2:25 favor a locust, probably in an immature state. Koehler (*Lexicon,* p. 319) suggests "cockroach," but there is no evidence that cockroaches were ever a destructive pest, as the biblical references demand. *See also* LOCUST; FAUNA § F2.     W. S. McCULLOUGH

**CATHOLIC LETTERS.** The traditional designation of the group of documents in the NT which is composed of JAMES; I and II PETER; I, II, and III JOHN; and JUDE (*see also* CANON, NT).

"Catholic" in English is derived from the Greek word *katholikos,* meaning "general." Church writers during the first four centuries used this term to designate the church throughout the world in distinction from churches in local communities. Cyril of Jerusalem (*ca.* A.D. 348) explicitly so defined it. Speaking of the church (Catechetical Lectures XVIII.23), he wrote: "It is called Catholic because it extends over all the world . . . and because it teaches universally and completely one and all the doctrines which ought to come to men's knowledge . . . and because it brings into subjection to godliness the whole race of mankind . . . and because it universally treats and heals the whole class of sins which are committed by soul or body." The church is, in other words, called "Catholic" by Cyril because it is world wide, because of the universality and completeness of its doctrinal teaching, because its evangelism encompasses the needs of all men, and because its remedies are effective for all the sins men commit.

Cyril's understanding of the term as meaning simply "universal" was generally accepted throughout the East during the first four centuries. Applied to certain non-Pauline letters, it described them as encyclical in character. Such letters were intended for the attention of Christendom in distinction from Paul's letters, each of which had a local address. So used, the term carried no suggestion of church-wide recognition of the letters.

In the West, especially in the usage of Augustine, "catholic" developed a theological meaning (*Letters of Petilian, the Donatist,* II.37.89; II.38.90; *City of God* XVIII.51). It distinguished the church in its unity from dissident, splinter groups, and the orthodoxy of the church's teaching from the heresy of dissenters. Applied to the letters under discussion, it designated them as worthy of inclusion in the canon of the NT because of their doctrinal soundness. Since the Middle Ages, "catholic" has generally been used in the sense of universal or general in distinction from local.

As early as the second century, "catholic" was used to describe individual letters. It was so used by Apollonius, Dionysius of Alexandria, and Origen. The earliest known instance of such use is by Apollonius (*ca.* 197), who says that the Montanist heretic Themiso, "aping the Apostle, dared to compose a 'Catholic epistle,' and therein to instruct those whose faith surpassed his" (Euseb. Hist. V.18.5). Similarly, Dionysius (*ca.* 200) is quoted as having described I John as "catholic" in distinguishing it from II and III John, apparently regarded as personal and local (Euseb. Hist. VII.25.7-10). Origen (*ca.* 250) also used "catholic" to designate I Peter (Commentary on John VI.18).

In the fourth century Eusebius applied "catholic" to the group of seven non-Pauline letters in the NT, noting that most of them were "disputed" (Euseb. Hist. II.23; III.25.1-3). He says, further, that Clement of Alexandria, in the *Hypotyposes,* gave "concise explanations of all the canonical scriptures, not passing over even the disputed writings," by which he meant "the Epistle of Jude and the remaining Catholic Epistles, and the Epistle of Barnabas and the Apocalypse known as Peter's" (VI.14.1; cf. II.23).

The gradual and relatively late acceptance of the seven letters in the church indicates rather clearly that they belonged to a time subsequent to Paul's career and to the publication of his letters as a corpus. Paul's letters, e.g., were approaching recognition as scripture when II Peter was written (cf. 3:15-16).

The Muratorian Canon, representing opinion at Rome *ca.* A.D. 200, includes, of the seven, only Jude and I and II John. Reflecting opinion in the East (*ca.* 250), Origen lists among the universally accepted writings I Peter and I John, noting that II Peter, II and III John, James, and Jude were strongly opposed by many, though he himself valued them highly and regarded them as canonical. The "Cheltenham List," believed to represent opinion in North Africa *ca.* 360, omits any mention of James and Jude, and indicates that only I John and I Peter of the remaining five enjoyed full recognition. The Teaching of Addai (*ca.* 350) and the Sinaitic Syriac list of *ca.* 400, reflecting opinion in Syria, make no mention of the seven Catholics. The Peshitta Version of *ca.* 425, however, lists James, I Peter, and I John.

The seven letters were included in the canon list of Codex Claromontanus, reflecting usage in Egypt *ca.* 300; in codices Sinaiticus and Vaticanus, representing the middle of the fourth century; in Athanasius' thirty-ninth Festal Letter (367), the list of Jerome (fifty-third Letter, *ca.* 394), the Codex Alexandrinus (fifth century), and the list of Augustine, who died in 430 (*On Christian Doctrine* II.8.13).

Location of the Catholic letters varies in the MSS and versions. Sometimes, with Acts, they follow Paul's letters, sometimes standing between Acts and Paul's letters. In the canon list of Codex Claromontanus they follow Paul's letters, with Acts coming after Revelation. In Eusebius' list, the order is Acts, letters of Paul, I John and I Peter, with the remaining Catholics listed after Revelation with the "disputed" books. They follow Paul's letters in the list of Gregory of Nazianzus, the PESHITTA, and the list of Augustine (Acts following the letters). They appear immediately after Acts in Codex Sinaiticus, the list of Jerome (where Acts and the Catholics follow Paul's letters), Athanasius, and Codex Alexandrinus.

A. E. BARNETT

**CATHUA** kə thōō′ə [Κουά (B), Καθουα (A)] (I Esd. 5:30). Head of a family of temple servants who returned with Zerubbabel. His name is omitted in the parallels Ezra 2:47; Neh. 7:49. C. T. FRITSCH

**CATTLE** [אלוּף (Ps. 144:14), *cf.* אלפים, oxen, *and see* Ox; בהמה, *cf.* Arab. *bahîmah,* beast, quadruped, *and bahmah,* young animal; בעיר, *cf.* Arab. *ba'r,* dung, *and ba'îr,* camel; בקר, *see* Ox; מלאכה (Gen. 33:14; *cf.* I Sam. 15:9), occupation, work, *cf.* Phoen. מלאכת, work; מקנה, *from* קנה, get, acquire, *cf.* Akkad. *qanû,* gain, obtain, *and* Phoen. מקנא, property in cattle; שוּר (Isa. 7:25), *see* Ox; KJV צאן (Gen. 30:39–31:43; Eccl. 2:7; RSV "flocks"), flock(s) of sheep and/or goats, *cf.* Akkad. *ṣēni,* small cattle, *and* Ugar. *ṣin,* sheep and goats; שׂה (Gen. 30:32, etc.; RSV "sheep"), sheep, *cf.* Akkad. *šu'u,* sheep, *and* Phoen. שׂ, sheep; θρέμμα (John 4:12), nursling, creature, *from* τρέφω, bring up, rear; κτῆνος (Rev. 18:13), a domestic animal, *mostly plural, from* κτάομαι, get, acquire]; FATLINGS [מריא (I Kings 1:9, 19, 25; KJV FAT CATTLE), fat one, *cf.* Akkad. *marā'u* III, 1, make fat, *and marû* (*adjective*), fat]. Domesticated bovine animals; in biblical usage often including sheep and goats and sometimes other animals.

"Cattle" may designate both wild and domesticated animals (Gen. 7:23 KJV; RSV "animals"); it seems sometimes to mean larger animals (oxen, asses), as distinct from flocks of sheep and goats (Num. 31:9), and it frequently means members of the ox family (Num. 31:9, 33, 44; I Kings 1:9, 19, 25; Ps. 144:14; Isa. 7:25; etc.). More commonly it refers to all the domesticated animals (Gen. 1:24; 2:20; 33:14; Num. 20:4, 8, 11; Ps. 50:10; John 4:12; etc.), specifically to oxen, sheep, and goats (Gen. 13:2-7; 46:32; Num. 7:87-88); to horses, sheep, goats, oxen, and asses (Gen.

47:16-17; to camels, as well, in Exod. 9:3; cf. I Chr. 5:21). On the other hand, it may mean only sheep and goats (Gen. 30:39–31:43; Eccl. 2:7 KJV). The KJV translates שה as "cattle" or "lesser [or 'small'] cattle" in Gen. 30:32; Isa. 7:25; 43:23; Ezek. 34:17, 20, 22, but the RSV uses "sheep."

Cattle, whose lowing is mentioned in Jer. 9:10, ordinarily eat the grass of the field (Deut. 11:15; Josh. 21:2; I Kings 4:23—H 5:3; Ps. 104:14; Isa. 30: 23), but some are kept in stalls (II Chr. 32:28). The temptation of bestiality is warned against in Exod. 22: 19—H 22:18. The view that all cattle are rather stupid is reflected in Bildad's question in Job 18:3. Different species of cattle must not interbreed (Lev. 19:19). All of them are subject to the law of firstlings (Exod. 13:12), and they are to enjoy the benefit of the sabbath rest (Exod. 20:10). Like all the other animals, cattle are divided into clean and unclean, and only the former can serve as food and as sacrificial victims (Lev. 5:2; 11:1-8). The possession of much livestock is the mark of position and wealth (Gen. 13:2; I Sam. 25:2; Job 1:3; etc.). Cattle are liable to taxation or even to confiscation by a foreign overlord (Neh. 9:37), and may become part of the booty of war (Josh. 8:2; Jer. 49:32).

*See also* FAUNA § A1*di*.                      W. S. McCULLOUGH

**CAUDA** kô′də [Καῦδα]; KJV **CLAUDA** klô′— (Acts 27:16). A small island S of Crete; the modern Gaudos or Gozzo. It was skirted by Paul's ship en route to Rome. Sailing along the S coast of Crete in search of a proper wintering place, perhaps after rounding Cape Matala, and being driven S below Cauda, Paul and his companions, struck by a NE wind, were forced to jettison their cargo (tackle?) and prepare the ship for the tempest.

The oldest MSS divide between two spellings of the island's name; א joins B and the Vulg. by altering Κλαῦδα to Καῦδα. Latin writers appear to prefer *Gaudus* (cf. Pliny *Nat. Hist.* IV.12), while Greek authors use the form Κλαῦδα.

*Bibliography.* R. Richard, "Navigations de S. Paul," *Études Religieuses*, LXIV (1927), 448-65; F. J. Foakes-Jackson and K. Lake, *The Beginnings of Christianity*, IV (1933), 322.

E. W. SAUNDERS

**CAUL.** KJV translation of יתרת (RSV "appendage") in Exod. 29:13, denoting the fatty mass which surrounds the liver; and סגור (*see* KIDNEY) in Hos. 13:8 (cf. RSV), referring to the pericardium.

**CAULKERS** [מחזיקי בדקך, RSV caulking your seams (Ezek. 27:9), your caulkers (Ezek. 27:27)]; KJV **CALKERS.** Those who drive some suitable substance (such as oakum) into the seams of a ship's planking to render them watertight.

The Hebrew phrase means "those who make strong (or repair) your (i.e., Tyre's) fissure (or rent)," and as the context is a nautical one, the reference could be to ships' carpenters or to shipwrights. It is usually assumed, however, that the allusion is specifically to caulkers.

Prior to the Hellenistic age the material generally used for caulking ships in the Near East appears to have been bitumen, which was usually mixed for this purpose with other substances to form a mastic (to

be distinguished from gum mastic). The bitumen would likely have come from Mesopotamia, where it was obtained from open seepages, the most important being near the town of Hit, NW of Babylon (cf. כפר, *kōpher,* "pitch," in Gen. 6:14, probably from Akkadian *kupru,* "asphalt"). *See also* SHIPS AND SAILING.

*Bibliography.* C. Singer, E. J. Holmyard, A. R. Hall, eds., *A History of Technology* (1954), I, 250-56.

W. S. McCULLOUGH

**CAVALRY** [ἱππικός]. A term occurring only in Rev. 9:16, where it refers to troops, "twice ten thousand times ten thousand" in number, which appeared when the four angels bound at the Euphrates River were released. They are part of the apocalyptic vision of destruction which the seer describes. The number rests ultimately on Ps. 68:17. Their number was "heard," frightening in its enormity; and a third of mankind was killed.

Demonic steeds occur prominently in chs. 6; 9 of Revelation as the bearers of destruction; and in ch. 19 white horses appear on which the armies of heaven ride, and especially the Messiah, who is called "Faithful and True."

B. H. THROCKMORTON, JR.

**CAVE.** Natural and artificial caves are numerous in the limestone and sandstone hills of Palestine and the E Jordan area and are frequently mentioned in the Bible as places of residence, refuge, and burial. *See* PALESTINE, GEOLOGY OF; ADULLAM; MACHPELAH; MAKKEDAH.

The Hebrew word most commonly translated "cave" is מערה (Gen. 19:30; 23:9; Josh. 10:16; Judg. 6:2; I Sam. 13:6; etc.). Less frequently the following words are used and have reference to various types or sizes of caves: חרים (KJV "caves"; RSV "holes"; Job 30:6), מחלות (KJV "caves"; RSV "holes"; Isa. 2:19), נקרות (KJV "clefts"; RSV "caverns"; Isa. 2: 21), חגוים ("clefts"; Song of S. 2:14; Jer. 49:16; Obad. 3), ארב (KJV "dens"; RSV "lairs"; Job 37:8), מעונות ("dens"; Job 38:40; Ps. 104:22; Song of S. 4:8; Nah. 2:12), סכה (KJV "den"; RSV "covert"; Ps. 10:9). Because robbers often used caves in the mountains as their headquarters, the figure of speech "den of robbers" (מערת פרצים, σπήλαιον λῃστῶν), when applied to the Jerusalem temple, is to be understood as implying a cave where evil deeds are planned (Jer. 7:11; cf. Matt. 21:13; Mark 11:17; Luke 19:46). The den of lions (גב אריותא) in the sixth chapter of Daniel may have been a type of artificial cave, although the Jewish writer seems to have thought of it as a cistern or pit. A cave was often used as a CISTERN or PIT and as a place of confinement and for the storage of water.

Three references in the NT to caves allude to them as a place of burial (σπήλαιον, the tomb of Lazarus [John 11:38]) and as places of refuge in times of persecution and distress (σπήλαιον, ὀπή [Heb. 11:38]; σπήλαιον [Rev. 6:15]).

Caves are mentioned most frequently in the OT in connection with the early settlement of the land of Canaan. According to Gen. 19:30, Lot dwelt in a cave with his two daughters because he was afraid to live in Zoar. The famous cave of Mach-pelah, which is usually identified with the grotto beneath the mosque at Hebron, was purchased by Abraham (Gen. 23:11-16) for use as a sepulchre for Sarah (vs. 19). Tradition identifies the same cave as his tomb (Gen. 25:9), as well as that of Isaac, Rebekah and Leah (Gen. 49:30-31), and Jacob (Gen. 50:13). The cave at Makkedah was used as a place of refuge by the five Canaanite kings following their defeat at the hands of Joshua, and it became their tomb when their bodies were placed inside and great stones were set against the entrance (Josh. 10:17-27).

The Israelites were forced to use caves as places of refuge during times of oppression by the Midianites (Judg. 6:2) and by the Philistines (I Sam. 13:6). David escaped from the wrath of Saul by fleeing to the cave of Adullam (I Sam. 22:1), and Elijah fled to a cave in Mount Horeb when his life was threatened by Jezebel (I Kings 19:9). Caves in the Mount Carmel region were used by Obadiah to conceal one hundred prophets who would otherwise have been put to death by Jezebel (I Kings 18:4, 13).

Thousands of caves have been discovered as a result of archaeological exploration, and the excavation of many that were occupied in ancient times has supplied much valuable information concerning their use as places of residence, worship, and burial. The excavation of large caves, such as those located between Bethlehem and the Dead Sea, and on Mount Carmel, has demonstrated that occupation in some cases extended from the Stone Age to the present, when they are used by shepherds and their flocks. Natural and artificial caves used as tombs have been found in the vicinity of many biblical cities such as Gezer, Beth-shemesh, Jerusalem, Beth-shean, Megiddo, and Dibon.* The culture of prehistoric man in Palestine has become increasingly clear as a result of the excavations of caves at Mugharet ez-Zuttiyeh, home of the "Galilee man," NW of the Sea of Galilee; at Wadi en-Natuf, NW of Jerusalem; at

By permission of the Palestine Exploration Fund

20. Two caves at Al Murabba'at

Wadi Khareitun, E of Bethlehem; at Wadi el-Mugharah (*see* MUGHARAH, WADI EL), S of Haifa on the Mount Carmel range; and at Tell Abu Matar, near Beer-sheba. Fig. BUR 56.

Among the caves which date from later periods are those at Wadi Murabba'at, W of the Dead Sea, occupied as early as the Chalcolithic period but also as a refuge for Jewish soldiers in the time of Bar Cocheba,* and those in the vicinity of Khirbet Qumran near the NW shore of the Dead Sea, where the famous DEAD SEA SCROLLS were stored. The Edomites (*see* EDOM) and the NABATEANS made use of the caves at Petra in Mount Seir, where the biblical Horites (Gen. 14:6) and the descendants of Esau (Deut. 2:12) once lived. Fig. CAV 20.

Muslim and Christian shrines have been erected over ancient caves in such places as Jerusalem, Bethlehem, Hebron, and Nazareth, although their identification with biblical sites remains uncertain because of the absence of archaeological data.

*Bibliography.* G. and A. Horsfield, "Sela-Petra, the Rock, of Edom and Nabatene," *QDAP,* VII (1938), 1-42; C. C. McCown, *The Ladder of Progress in Palestine* (1943), pp. 18-53; M. S. and J. L. Miller, *Encyclopedia of Bible Life* (1944), pp. 233-38; G. L. Harding, "Khirbet Qumran and Wady Muraba'at," *PEQ,* 84 (1952), 104-9; J. Perrot, "The Excavations at Tell Abu Matar, Near Beersheba," *IEJ,* 5 (1955), 17-40, 73-84, 167-89.    W. L. REED

**CEDAR** [אֶרֶז, *'erez;* Ugar. *arz;* κέδρος]. The mountains of Lebanon provided the major source of cedar in Bible times; thus David and Solomon imported huge quantities (II Sam. 5:11; 7:2, 7; I Kings 5-7; I Chr. 14:1; 17:1, 6; 22:4; II Chr. 2). The logs were floated down from the coast of Lebanon to Joppa as large rafts. One of Solomon's buildings was called the HOUSE OF THE FOREST OF LEBANON because of its three rows of fifteen cedar pillars (I Kings 7:2-5). In addition to pillars, cedar was used for roofing (vs. 7), supporting beams (vs. 2), ceilings (6:9), paneling 6:15), and even for carved work (vs. 18). Solomon "made cedar as plentiful as the sycamore of the Shephelah" (I Kings 10:27). Ship masts were made from it (Ezek. 27:5).

The cedar is frequently used as a symbol of strength (Ps. 29:5; 37:35; Isa. 2:13; 9:10; Zech. 11:2; etc.), of splendor (Song of S. 1:17; Jer. 22:14; etc.), and of glory (Ps. 80:10; Jer. 22:7; Zech. 11:1; etc.), often with a reference to Lebanon. The figure of the cedar in Ezek. 31 probably has mythological significance (cf. *IB,* VI, 233-38).

The reference in the oracle of Balaam (Num. 24:6) is difficult, since cedars do not grow by water. The poetic imagery here would not seem to demand ecological accuracy, but a transposition of this word with *'ₐhālîm* (ALOES?) in the previous stichos may account for the inconsistency. Cedar wood, together with HYSSOP and "SCARLET stuff," was used in the LEPROSY purification rite (Lev. 14:4-6, 49-52), and was associated with the RED HEIFER rite (Num. 19:6). Many botanists claim these references must be to a different cedar wood, such as *Sabina phoenicia* (L.) Antoine, since the context involves the Sinai Desert during the wilderness wanderings. More likely, it is a priestly anachronism representing post-Solomonic cultic practices in which Lebanon cedar was used as a symbol of longevity (cf. *IB,* II, 235).

Courtesy of Staatliche Museen, Berlin

21. Chiefs of Lebanon making obeisance to an Egyptian officer of Seti I (1318-1301 B.C.) as they fell cedars

Many scholars emend the obscure Hebrew *ke'ezrāḥ ra'ᵃnān* ("green BAY TREE"?) in Ps. 37:35 to "cedar of Lebanon" (RSV), following the LXX. *'Ôren* in Isa. 44:14 is emended to *'erez* by many scholars (but *see* PINE). *See also* FLORA § A9d; WOOD.

Fig. CED 21.

*Bibliography.* H. N. and A. L. Moldenke, *Plants of the Bible* (1952), pp. 66-70.                J. C. TREVER

**CEDARS OF LEBANON** lĕb'ə nən. *See* CEDAR.

**CEDRON.** KJV form of KEDRON; KIDRON.

**CEILAN.** KJV form of KILAN.

**CEILING** [ספן; *verbal form means* cover *or* panel]; KJV CIELING. Used only in the description of Solomon's temple (I Kings 6:9, 15). *See* HOUSE; PANEL; ARCHITECTURE.

**CELESTIAL BODIES** [σώματα ἐπουράνια] (I Cor. 15:40). Paul refers to "celestial," or "heavenly," bodies as different from "terrestrial," or "earthly," bodies. By "celestial bodies" he refers to the sun, moon, and stars, which, like his Hellenistic contemporaries, he understands as beings clothed in bodies of light—different from the matter, or substance, of which earthly bodies are made.

*See also* TERRESTRIAL BODIES; RESURRECTION IN THE NT.                B. H. THROCKMORTON, JR.

**CELIBACY.** Votive abstention from marriage—unknown in the Bible unless alluded to in Matt. 19:12; I Cor. 7:8. *See* MARRIAGE § 5; *also* ESSENES § 4b.

**CELLAR** [אוצר, *from* אצר, store up; Aram. אוצרא; κρυπτή, *from* κρυπτώ, conceal (Luke 11:33; KJV SECRET PLACE)]. The Hebrew word, generally translated TREASURE, TREASURY, is translated "cellar" in only one passage, where it refers to stores of wine or oil (I Chr. 27:27-28). The cellar, or room below the ground level, was not common in Palestine. *See* HOUSE.                O. R. SELLERS

**CELOSYRIA.** KJV Apoc. form of COELE-SYRIA.

*****CENCHREAE** sĕng'krə ē [αἱ Κεγχρεαί, αἱ Κεγχρεαί] (Acts 18:18; Rom. 16:1); KJV CENCHREA —krĭ ə. The seaport seven miles E of Corinth on the Saronic Gulf or Gulf of Aegina.

The place is first mentioned by Thucydides (IV. 42) in connection with the attack of the Athenians under Nicias upon CORINTH in 425 B.C. It is described by Strabo (VIII.369, 380) as a village and a harbor *ca.* seventy stadia from Corinth, the easterly naval station of the Corinthians, and the port used for trade from Asia. Pausanias (II.ii.3) says it was named from Cenchreas, son of Poseidon and Peirene. In the time of Pausanias (second century A.D.) there was a temple of Aphrodite at one side of the harbor, sanctuaries of Asklepios and Isis at the other, and a bronze image of Poseidon on a mole which ran out into the sea. Ancient ruins at the site include buildings and moles. The present village in the vicinity is called Kechriais.

*Bibliography.* Bölte, "Kenchreai," *Pauly-Wissowa*, vol. XI, pt. i (1921), cols. 167-70.                J. FINEGAN

**CENDEBEUS** sĕn'də bē'əs [Κενδεβαῖος]. Chief commander of the coastal country, appointed by King Antiochus to battle against Judea. The name may be derived from the city of Kanduba in Lycia. Cendebeus came to Jamnia and made incursions into Judea. He also built up Kedron (Gederoth in Josh. 15:41; Katra) to conduct raids against Judea. John Hyrcanus reported to Simon, his father, who sent him and his brother Judas to battle against Cendebeus.

John spent the night in Modin and then crossed into the plain where he saw Cendebeus' army. He crossed the mountain brook that separated them and with his army put Cendebeus to flight. He then pursued them to Kedron and burned the towers of Ashdod, whither some had fled. After this victory John Hyrcanus returned to Judea in peace (I Macc. 15:38; 16:1).

*Bibliography.* S. Tedesche and S. Zeitlin, *I Maccabees* (1950), p. 238.                S. B. HOENIG

**CENSER** [מחתה, *from* חתה, to carry (rake) fire; מקטרת, *from* קטר, to smoke (II Chr. 26:19; Ezek. 8: 11); מחלף (KJV KNIFE; Ezra 1:9); λιβανωτός (Rev. 8:3); KJV θυμιατήριον (RSV "incense altar"; Heb. 9:4)]. A portable ladle or shovel-like device for carrying live coals, etc., and for burning INCENSE. The word מחתה is variously translated "FIREPAN," "tray" (KJV "snuffdish"; *see* SNUFFERS), or "censer."

The implements of temple and tabernacle included shallow, open-topped pans of bronze (Exod. 27:3) or gold (I Kings 7:50) used for carrying live coals from the altar. They were somewhat similar to the dishes for incense (*see* INCENSE, DISHES FOR). When incense was placed on the sacred fire in these pans, they functioned as censers (Lev. 10:1; Num. 16:6). The double function appears also in Rev. 8:3, 5, where the angel uses his censer both to burn frankincense and to cast fire on the earth. The accounts of Korah's rebellion against Moses (Num. 16), Uzziah's affliction with leprosy (II Chr. 26:19), and Ezekiel's vision of abominations in the temple (Ezek. 8:11) show that the right to use the censer in the temple worship was a zealously guarded prerogative of the Aaronic priesthood. The censer appears as a necessary implement in the purification ritual of the Day of Atonement. *See* ATONEMENT. L. E. TOOMBS

**CENSUS.** The enumeration or enrollment of a people, among the Hebrews according to tribe, family, and lineage (Num. 1:18; Luke 2:4), for various purposes, including taxation (Exod. 30:13-16; Num. 3: 40-51; Luke 2:1-5; cf. Jos. Antiq. XVIII.i.1), determining man power for war (Num. 1:3; 26:2; II Sam. 24:9), and allotting the work of Levites in cultic service (Num. 3:4).

In Hebrew the nouns most frequently used to mean "census" are פקדים (Exod. 30:14; Num. 1:21; 26:9) and מספר (Num. 1:22; 26:53; II Sam. 24:2; I Chr. 21:2). מפקד also appears (II Sam. 24:9; I Chr. 21:5). The verbs used include פקד, ספר, and מנה (II Sam. 24:1; I Chr. 21:1). The use of the periphrastic idiom (שׂאו את ראשׁ, "lift up each head") seems to be limited to the initial divine command to take the census (Exod. 30:12; Num. 1:2, 49; 26:2).

In Greek the noun used is ἀπογραφή (Luke 2:1-5; Acts 5:37), meaning "enrollment" or "taxation."

An official census of all Israelites of military age was taken on three occasions, according to biblical tradition:

*a*) The first was effected at Mount Sinai in the second month during the second year after the exodus from Egypt. Of males twenty years old and over, able to bear arms, there were 603,550 (Num. 1:46; 11:21), not counting the Levites (Num. 1:47-54). The Levites one month old and over were counted separately and numbered 22,000 (Num. 3: 15, 39). The Levites were then to be the Lord's in the place of all the first-born males of all Israel, who at the time numbered 22,273 (Num. 3:43). A further numbering took place of all males from thirty years of age to fifty, of the sons of Korab, Gershom, and Merari, who "could enter the service, for work in the tent of meeting." These totaled 8,580 (Num. 4:34-49).

*b*) At Shittim in Moab, according to biblical tradition, another census was taken at the close of the forty years of wandering. Of men twenty years of age and over, able to bear arms, there were 601,730 (Num. 26:2, 51). The Levites were again counted separately. Of male Levites one month old and over, there were 23,000 (Num. 26:62).

*c*) Near the end of David's reign another census was taken. David commanded Joab and the military commanders to number all Israel from Dan to Beersheba. The report of Joab, according to II Sam. 24:9, was 800,000 men of military availability in Israel and 500,000 in Judah. According to I Chr. 21:5, the report was 1,100,000 in Israel and in Judah 470,000. In both accounts Joab vainly tries to dissuade David from his intention, and in both the Lord sends a pestilence upon Israel as punishment for the folly and sin of counting heads. Josephus indicates that David's mistake was in disregarding the method for census taking prescribed in Exod. 30:11-16, which was that of levying a half-shekel tax from each person of age (Antiq. VII.xiii.1). Such a method had the advantage of evading the ancient taboo of counting

heads. While the account in II Samuel does not specify, the Chronicler suggests that the Levites were again counted separately, those thirty years of age and over numbering 38,000 (I Chr. 23:3).

Interesting in a comparison of these two accounts are two major discrepancies. In II Sam. 24 it is said both that the Lord incited David to take the census and that he subsequently punished him for having done so. In I Chr. 21 it is said that Satan enticed David. (For the history of the name Satan and its meaning here, *see* SATAN.) The second discrepancy, that of the variance in Joab's report, is nothing short of intriguing.

The suggestion has been made that the figures used in Num. 1; 26 are basically the same as those appearing in conjunction with the Davidic census. That these figures, 603,550 (Num. 1) and 601,730 (Num. 26), reflect the Davidic census but were placed by the priestly editors back in the time of Moses, is not difficult to understand. II Sam. 24:9 gives a total of 1,300,000, and I Chr. 21:5 gives a total of 1,570,000 for both Israel and Judah. The same basic and original figures were used in each case, approximately what is given in Num. 1; 26, but through the confusion of whether Israel meant all the tribes or the N ones only, and through the normal tendency of later scribes to be victims of their own point of view, unwarranted mathematical additions and sums were compounded. Thus, the figures largely accurate for the Davidic census were relegated to the desert period (Num. 1; 26), and the larger figures, approximately double the original, were assumed for the time of David.

Another suggestion is that gematria was used to arrive at the figure in Num. 1:46, for the numerical value of the letters in בני ישׂראל ("sons of Israel") is 603, giving rise to the 603,550 recorded. Be this as it may, it may still be close to the original figure of the Davidic census as noted above.

A more recent suggestion (*see bibliography*) envisages the census report of Num. 1; 26 as reflecting the strength of the tribes of Israel early in the period of the judges.

An enumeration of the exiles who returned to Jerusalem with Zerubbabel is recorded in Ezra 2.

In the NT the enrollment under Augustus during the governorship of QUIRINIUS in Syria is noted in Luke 2:1-5 (cf. Acts 5:37). This census is related in Luke to the date and place of Jesus' birth.

**Bibliography.** W. F. Albright, "The Administrative Divisions of Israel and Judah," *JPOS* (1925), pp. 20-25; A. Alt, *Die Staatenbildung der Israeliten in Palästina* (1930); G. E. Mendenhall, "The Census Lists of Numbers 1 and 26," *JBL*, LXXVII (1958), 52-66. J. A. SANDERS

**CENTURION** sĕn tyo͝or′ĭ ən, —to͝or′— [κεντυρίων (Mark 15:39, 44-55), *also* κεντορίων, κεντουρίων; ἑκατόνταρχος; Lat. *centurio*]. The commanding officer of a "century," nominally a hundred foot soldiers, in the Roman army. There were ten centurions in a cohort and sixty in a legion. The number of centurions in the legion seems to have remained the same, even when the number of legionary soldiers increased or decreased beyond the usual six thousand. Fig. CEN 22.

Although theoretically the centurions were subordinate to the six legionary tribunes, and often deferred to them (Acts 22:26), yet the centurions were the actual working officers, the backbone of the army. The discipline and efficiency of the legion as a fighting unit depended on them. Polybius well describes the type: "Centurions are required not to be bold and adventurous so much as good leaders, of steady and prudent mind, not prone to take the offensive or start fighting wantonly, but able when overwhelmed and hard-pressed to stand fast and die at their post" (*History* VI.24).

22. A Roman centurion, from the Arch of Titus

Career men, the centurions were often the most experienced and best-informed men in the army. The office was the highest to which the ordinary soldier might aspire. Frequently chosen from the ranks, he may also have been a member of the equestrian order who, through insufficiency of means or failure to advance, was resigned to accept a centurion's commission, or from a class whose property qualification was below that of the equestrian order, or from town magistrates who in this way secured full Roman citizenship, or from veterans recalled to the service.

The centurion might be promoted, slowly or rapidly, as the case might be, in an ascending scale of responsibility, from cohort to cohort, even from legion to legion, until he might become the senior centurion, the *primus pilus*, of the first of the ten cohorts in the legion, thus occupying a position of very high importance. This system of promotion by transfer, in addition to facilitating the impress of the Roman stamp on the troops (even when the troops were recruited locally, the officers would most frequently be Romans) and preventing undue fraternization with their men, provided varied experience and wide acquaintance with the Empire, and must have made for an intelligent corps of officers.

The duties of the centurion were various. First, he was responsible for discipline; hence, his vine-staff (*vitis*) emblem, which he knew how to use on the backs of his men. This would include supervision of scourging and the execution of capital penalties (Tac. Ann. 1.6; 16.9; etc.; Matt. 27:54; Mark 15:39, 44-45; Luke 23:47). Then there was responsibility for drill, inspection of arms, quartermaster's duties, and command in camp and field. He assigned detail to his men, and might be bribed to the point of exacting tribute and thus greatly augmenting his already considerable pay.

He himself might be detailed for command of the auxiliaries, or for a variety of special tasks, such as those assigned to Cornelius and Julius in Acts—tasks which would seem to have separated them temporarily from their legions or from the main body of troops to which they were attached.

In addition to the prestige associated with the office, the high pay and generous bonus granted on discharge made the prospect of becoming *primus pilus* very attractive to the ambitious soldier. Often such officers remained in the army much longer than the required twenty years.

Usually after discharge, the centurion went back into private life; yet some became legionary tribunes, prefects of a cohort, or procurators, even the prefect of the praetorian guard.

The importance of centurions in the Roman army and in the life of the Empire is accurately reflected in the fact that they figure more frequently in the NT than does any other army officer. Likewise, the respect which accrues to their office is reflected in the fact that in Matthew (8:5 ff) and Luke (7:2 ff) the first Gentile to confront Jesus is a centurion. He is carefully described as a person of note: he has slaves; he is wealthy; he "loves" the Jewish "nation," and built the synagogue; and although he has soldiers under him who are abjectly obedient, yet he humbles himself before Jesus, declaring himself unworthy to have Jesus come "under his roof." Further, the centurion in charge of the Crucifixion is the first Gentile to make the Christian witness that Jesus is Son of God (Matt. 27:54; Mark 15:39). In Acts the conversion of the centurion CORNELIUS (second in importance only to Paul's conversion) is important enough in the plan of Acts to be called the Gentile Pentecost. And finally, Paul is "delivered . . . to a centurion" for safe conduct to Rome (Acts 27:1).

*Bibliography.* M. P. Nilsson, *Imperial Rome* (1926), pp. 302-4; H. M. D. Parker, *The Roman Legions* (1928), pp. 30-32, 196-205, 235-36; *Oxford Classical Dictionary* (1949), p. 180.

F. D. GEALY

**CEPHAS** sē′fəs [Κηφᾶς]. *See* PETER.

**CEREAL OFFERING.** *See* SACRIFICE AND OFFERINGS § A2b.

**CEREALS.** *See* SACRIFICE AND OFFERINGS § A2b; FLORA § A1; GRAIN.

**CEREMONIAL LAW.** Law concerned primarily with the festivals and cultic practices of Israel. *See* LAW IN THE OT; PRIESTS AND LEVITES; WORSHIP IN THE OT; SACRIFICE AND OFFERINGS; FEASTS AND FASTS.

**CERINTHUS** sə rĭn'thəs [Κήρινθος]. An early Gnostic active in W Asia Minor *ca.* A.D. 100. With Simon Magus he is listed in the Epistle of the Apostles (*see* APOSTLES, EPISTLE OF) as one of the two "false apostles, concerning whom it is written that no man shall cleave unto them." Irenaeus (Her. I.26) states that Cerinthus was educated in the wisdom of the Egyptians; that he taught that the world was not made by the primary God but by a certain power far separated from him; that Jesus was the natural son of Joseph and Mary, though more righteous, prudent, and wise than other men; that at his baptism there descended upon him the Christ in the likeness of a dove, endowing him with miraculous power; that at his death the Christ departed from him, and that then Jesus suffered and rose again, while the Christ remained impassible, since he was a spiritual being.

Epiphanius (Her. XXXVIII) turns him—Gnostic views and all—into a Jewish Christian heretic, at first the archopponent of Paul, later of John. This would appear his own irresponsible fabrication, due in no small part to the fact that in Irenaeus (his chief source of information) the brief account of Cerinthus is followed by that of "those who are called Ebionites . . . whose opinions with respect to the Lord are similar to those of Cerinthus and Carpocrates," and because in this account Cerinthus' reported views of Jesus' origin were definitely adoptionist.

Nothing from the pen of Cerinthus is known. Epiphanius' unsupported statements that he wrote a gospel (Her. LI.7) and that the Alogi considered him the author of all the Johannine writings (L.4) are not impressive. M. S. ENSLIN

**CERTIFICATE OF DIVORCE** [ספר כריתת; βιβλίον ἀποστασίου]. Alternately: BILL OF DIVORCE; DECREE OF DIVORCE; KJV BILL OF DIVORCEMENT. A document which a man under Jewish law was obligated to give his wife if he divorced her (Deut. 24:1; cf. Isa. 50:1). A woman was not permitted under any circumstances to divorce her husband. Divorce was possible if the husband found "some unseemly thing" (RSV "some indecency") in his wife. The rabbis differed in interpreting the meaning of "some unseemly thing": Rabbi Shammai took it to mean adultery; Rabbi Hillel, almost anything, even the act of scorching food. Jesus said (Matt. 5:31; 19:7; Mark 10:4) that Moses permitted divorce only as a concession to sin; and he (Jesus) appealed to Gen. 1:27; 2:24, stating that what God had joined in marriage the husband was not to put asunder. *See also* MARRIAGE.

B. H. THROCKMORTON, JR.

**CETAB.** KJV form of KETAB.

**CHABRIS** kăb'rĭs [Χαβρίς] (Jth. 6:15; 8:10; 10:6). Son of Gothoniel, and one of the elders of Bethulia to whom Judith sent her request for help.

**CHADIASANS** kā'dĭ ā'sənz [οἱ Χαδιάσαι (B); Χαδάσαι (A)] (I Esd. 5:20); KJV THEY OF CHADIAS kā'dĭ əs. A clan of exiles who returned with Zerubbabel. Their origin may be connected with the cities of Kedesh or Hadashah or Adasa.

N. TURNER

**CHAEREAS** kĭr'ĭ əs [Χαιρέας] (II Macc. 10:32-38). KJV CHEREAS. An Ammonite commander during the Maccabean period. When Gazara, which he held, fell to the Jews, he was slain by Judas Maccabeus. N. TURNER

**CHAFF** [מֹץ; *sometimes* חשׁשׁ (Isa. 5:24 KJV; 33:11); עוּר (Dan. 2:35); קַשׁ (Job 13:25; Ps. 83:13; Jer. 13:24), *see also* STUBBLE; KJV תבן (Jer. 23:28; RSV STRAW); NT ἄχυρον (Matt. 3:12; Luke 3:17)]. The fine dry material blown away by the wind in the process of WINNOWING. All the biblical references to chaff are figures of speech denoting the worthless or evil that is about to be destroyed (Job 21:18; Pss. 1:4; 35:5; Isa. 17:13; 29:5; 41:15; Hos. 13:3; Zeph. 2:2). H. N. RICHARDSON

**CHAIN(S).** The translation of several words in the Bible:

*a)* אזק (Jer. 40:1, 4), apparently a manacle.

*b)* זק (Isa. 45:14), properly a FETTER.

*c)* מעדנה (Job 38:31), chains which appear to hold together the six stars of the constellation Pleiades.

*d)* רתוקה, שׁרשׁרה, ornamental chains. They were employed in the decoration of the Jerusalem temple (I Kings 7:17; II Chr. 3:5, 16) and were also used on the priestly garment (Exod. 28:14; *see* EPHOD 2). Isa. 40:19 mentions silver chains which were attached to idols.

*e)* רביד (Aramaic המניך), a necklace. In Gen. 41:42; Dan. 5:29 the gift of such a necklace is a sign of royal favor (cf. Xenophon *Anabasis* I.2.27). In Ezek. 16:11 the word is used figuratively of Yahweh's care for Jerusalem.

*f)* Ἅλυσις (Mark 5:3-4; Acts 28:20; Rev. 20:1), chains of bondage. The Roman method of securing captives was to attach one end of a chain to the prisoner and the other to his guard (Acts 12:6-7).

*g)* Δεσμός (Acts 26:29; Heb. 11:36; Jude 6; KJV BONDS in the two former passages), a general term meaning anything used to tie or fasten.

R. W. CORNEY

**CHAIR** [כסא (II Kings 4:10)]; KJV STOOL. *See* SEAT 3.

**CHALCEDONY** kăl sĕd'ə nĭ, kăl'sə dō'nĭ. KJV translation of χαλκηδών (RSV AGATE) in Rev. 21:19. A translucent form of silica. *See* JEWELS AND PRECIOUS STONES § 2.

**CHALCOL.** KJV form of CALCOL in I Kings 4:31 —H 5:11.

**CHALDEA** kăl dē'ə; CHALDEANS —ənz. A region in S Babylonia. "Chaldeans," the designation of its inhabitants, is also a term referring to the last dynasty of Babylon (626-539 B.C.).

**1. The country.** From the ninth century B.C. onward, we read in the royal inscriptions of the Assyrian kings about a country called Kaldu, and its inhabitants, the Kaldai, situated along the Euphrates and the Tigris between the Persian Gulf and the southernmost cities of Babylonia. There were few, if any, urban settlements in this region of swamps, canebrakes, and lakes; and its inhabitants, of whom we know very little, seem to have relied on fishing, hunting, small-scale agriculture, and some cattle-breeding for their scant livelihood. The region was divided into tribal areas, called "houses," of more or less definable geographical distribution, under the leadership of tribal chieftains sometimes called kings. The largest among these tribes were the Bīt Dakkuri, S of Borsippa, with a subtribe called the Bīt Adini; and the Bīt Amukkāni, still farther to the S. Smaller tribes were the Bīt Sa'alli and the Bīt Šilāni. Along the Tigris were the Bīt Yakin, of great importance because of their proximity to the Elamite frontier. In their geographical isolation, these people did not seek contact with surrounding regions but kept to themselves. Thus a tradition of independence grew up and was maintained.

There is no indication that the Chaldeans spoke anything but the contemporary Akkadian dialects of the city people, although they certainly shifted to Aramaic earlier and more easily than those. The Chaldean tribes should, however, be clearly separated from the Aramean tribes of similar social and economic structure settled in the higher territory upstream along the two rivers.

Cuneiform and Greek sources speak without exception of Chaldea and the Chaldeans. while the Hebrew and the Aramaic of the books of Ezra and Daniel speak of כשדים and כשדיא, referring to the country, its inhabitants, and their crafts. No linguistically satisfactory explanation of this difference is known.

**2. History.** Apart from the historical texts, we have only a number of letters, found in the royal archive at Nineveh, referring to the dealings of the Assyrians with the Chaldeans at the time of the Neo-Assyrian kings. Although very little evidence is available for a study of Chaldean history in what may be called the first period, ending with the collapse of the Assyrian Empire, certain characteristics do become clear. What separates the Chaldeans from the city-dwellers is not a difference in cultural tradition —both worshiped the same gods, used cuneiform writing, etc.—but a difference in the social setup. The Chaldeans lived in loosely organized tribal groups, shifting allegiances according to the momentary distribution of wealth and power. They were unwilling to pay taxes or to render services, refused to recognize any loyalty beyond that of the clan, and were ready to plunder the riches of the city and to waylay its caravans. In short, they were the natural enemies of all urbanized society. The equilibrium between Babylonian city-dwellers and Chaldean tribes was upset when the Assyrian kings moved into their region. For obvious reasons they placed garrisons in the cities and attempted to police the tribal land. This made the Chaldeans, by necessity the leaders and carriers of any anti-Assyrian movement, the champions of national independence, while the city-

dwellers, as far as they lived on interurban trade under the security established by Assyrian armed might, became largely pro-Assyrian. The situation was further complicated by the fact that Babylon was not just a city among other cities, but a symbol of political aspiration and cultural power; the fight for supremacy in the land of Chaldea was therefore a three-cornered contest.

The Chaldean rulers were perfectly prepared for the type of warfare brought about by such a situation. Intertribal intrigues, guerrilla warfare, sudden attacks and flights, and complete disregard for treaties concluded with the enemy made these tenacious and crafty chieftains a dangerous enemy. After nearly two centuries of victories and defeats they came to be undisputed rulers of a Babylonian empire that stretched as far as Egypt and Cilicia.

The career of MERODACH-BALADAN, who fought with TIGLATH-PILESER III, Sargon II, and SENNACHERIB, but died in exile in Elam, can be taken as typical of those of Chaldean rulers. The political situation of the period had been mastered by him and other leaders of his type with great skill. There was Elam, more often than not, ready to send expeditionary forces in support of the Chaldeans against the cities and the Assyrian armies; there were diplomatic intrigues with far-off vassals of the Assyrians (such as, e.g., HEZEKIAH) to cause diversionary attacks; and there were always anti-Assyrian parties in the cities. Above all, when Assyrian military power and strategic know-how proved too menacing, Elam was always ready to grant asylum to the leaders of a rebellion. On other occasions, it was more advantageous to submit to the foreign invader, to take the oath of allegiance and to remain for a time a vassal of an Assyrian king, who was only too glad to concur with such an arrangement.

After the breakdown of the Assyrian Empire at the death of ASHURBANIPAL, the second phase of Chaldean history starts with NABOPOLASSAR, the founder of the so-called Chaldean Dynasty, and l is conquest of Babylonia. He made an alliance with the Medes, with whom he conquered Nineveh (614) and who apparently gave him a free hand within the limits of the Assyrian Empire to collect tribute, etc. Nabopolassar's great son, Nebuchadrezzar II, was powerful enough to throw the Egyptians out of Syria and Palestine and to keep up the territory ruled by Assyria to its maximum extent (with the exception of the mountain regions). In fact, "Chaldea" then began to replace the term "Babylonia." Nebuchadrezzar brought unheard-of booty into Babylon, whose splendor only then became proverbial in the ancient world. With him, however, the Chaldean Dynasty as such came to an end. His son (EVIL-MERODACH) and his son-in-law (Nergal-sharezer) ruled for only a short time. Nabonidus, usually assigned to this dynasty, represents an entirely different world.

The history of the Chaldeans went into its final phase when numerous Babylonians, then called Chaldeans, went into the outside world as magicians, astrologers, and diviners of all sorts. In these capacities they acquired great fame in Hellenistic Egypt, in Greece and Rome, and eventually in the Western world. In these places they gave their gentilic name to the arts they practiced.          A. L. OPPENHEIM

**CHALDEE VERSIONS** kăl dē'. An obsolete designation of the Aramaic Targums. *See* VERSIONS, ANCIENT, § 1.
B. M. METZGER

**CHALKSTONES** [אבני גר, *literally* stones of chalk, lime]. The Senonian chalk outcropping, a stratum of Palestinian rock, which predominates to the E and is found to a lesser extent W and N of the Judean hills, is soft, easily eroded, and nearly infertile. Its qualities are aptly utilized in Isa. 27:9 of the destruction of pagan altars:

> when he [Jacob] makes all the stones of the altars
> like chalkstones crushed to pieces.

*See also* PALESTINE, GEOLOGY OF. R. W. FUNK

**CHALPHI** kăl'fī [Χαλφεί, *cf.* Ἀλφαίος (Matt. 10:3); *from* חלף, *the designation given to a child thought of as a substitute for one lost*]; KJV CALPHI. The father of JUDAS 8; one of the commanders in Jonathan's army (I Macc. 11:70; Jos. Antiq. XIII.v.7).
J. C. SWAIM

**CHAM** kăm. Douay Version form of HAM.

**CHAMBER.** The translation of several words:
*a)* חדר, the regular word for a chamber or room.
*b)* לשכה, which is associated with the sanctuary in various ways—i.e., as a room where the sacrificial meal was eaten (I Sam. 9:22; "hall"), or as a room in the courts of the temple used for various purposes (II Kings 23:11; I Chr. 9:26, 33; Ezra 10:6; Neh. 10:38-39; 13:4-9; Jer. 35:4; 36:10 ff; Ezek. 40:17 ff; 42:1 ff; etc.).
*c)* נשכה, etymologically related to לשכה and also used of rooms of the temple courts (Neh. 3:30; 12:44; 13:7).
*d)* עליה ("upper chamber" in I Kings 17:19, 23; II Chr. 3:9; "roof chamber" in Judg. 3:23 ff; II Kings 4:10-11; "upper room" in I Chr. 28:11). In Ps. 104:3 this word is used of the Lord's heavenly abode (cf. vs. 13).
*e)* צלע, which has specific reference to the "side chambers" (so KJV-RSV) around the TEMPLE in Jerusalem (I Kings 6:5; Ezek. 41:5 ff).
*f)* KJV תא, "little chamber," "guard chamber" (Akkadian *ta'u*, "room"; RSV "guardroom," "side room"), used of the recessed chambers in the gateway, three on each side, such as are also illustrated in the excavations at Megiddo, Gezer, and Hazor (I Kings 14:28; II Chr. 12:11; Ezek. 40:7 ff).
*g)* KJV יציע (*Kethibh* יצוע; I Kings 6:5-6, 10; RSV "structure"), the side wings or storied side chambers of the temple.
*h)* Ὑπερῷον ("upper chamber" in Acts 20:8; "upper room " in 9:37, 39).
*i)* KJV ταμεῖον, "secret chamber" (Matt. 24:26; RSV "inner room"—i.e., a possible hiding place); alternately translated "room," "private room," "storehouse" (KJV "closet") in Matt. 6:6; Luke 12:3, 24.
H. G. MAY

**CHAMBERLAIN** [סריס (II Kings 23:11; Esth. 1:10; *alternately* EUNUCH ); κοιτῶν (Acts 12:20), *from* κοίτη, couch, bed; KJV οἰκονόμος (Rom. 16:23; RSV "city treasurer")]. One of the officers in charge of the private quarters of a king or noble. Like the cupbearer, he was able to be close to his sovereign by winning his confidence. NATHANMELECH was chamberlain at the time of Josiah (II Kings 23:11). Since these officials had access to the bedrooms of the women of the palace, they were frequently eunuchs.
C. U. WOLF

**CHAMBERS OF THE SOUTH** [חדרי תימן; LXX ταμιεῖα νότου; Vulg. *interiora Austri*]. A group of stars mentioned in Job 9:9 beside the Great Bear(?), Orion, and the Pleiades. It is identified by G. Schiaparelli (*see bibliography*) with certain stars distributed over the constellations of Argo, Centaurus, and the Southern Cross; whereas G. R. Driver (*see bibliography*), reading *ḥôdherê* and deriving the word from an alleged verb חדר, "encircle," would see in it the *circulus austrinus*. Another explanation is, however, that the expression refers, not to stars, but to the vacant stretches of the S sky, portrayed as the rear alcove of a tent (cf. Arabic *ḥidr;* and cf. Isa. 40:22); and that it is identical with the "chamber" (*ḥeder*) from which, in Job 37:9, the whirlwind is said to issue.

> *Bibliography.* G. Schiaparelli, *Die Astronomie im AT* (1904), pp. 58-59; G. R. Driver, *JTS,* VII (1956), 9-11.
T. H. GASTER

**CHAMELEON** kə mē'lĭ ən [כח (Lev. 11:30 KJV), *see* LAND CROCODILE; תנשמת (Lev. 11:30; KJV MOLE), *cf.* נשם, to breathe, pant (*see below*)]. A small, arboreal, lizardlike animal, of the suborder Rheptoglossa, notable for the way in which it changes the color of its skin as the occasion demands.

תנשמת (*tinshemeth*) cannot be identified, except that the context in Leviticus favors a reptile; possibly its appearance at the end of the list (11:29-30) points to some peculiarity that sets it apart from the preceding creatures (cf. the position of "bat" in vss. 13-19). The ancient versions indicate some uncertainty about this word (LXX "blind-rat"; Targ.-Vulg. "mole"; Syr. "hoopoe"); doubtless this confusion was furthered by another תנשמת among the unclean birds (Lev. 11:18; Deut. 14:16; *see* WATER HEN). In support of "chameleon" the possible derivation from נשם (*nāsham*) is cited. The chameleon makes a hissing or squeaking sound when disturbed, though it is doubtful if the verb "to pant" would describe this. It has also been supposed that the same derivation reflects the view, recorded in Pliny Nat. Hist. VIII. 51, that chameleons live on air; its breathing, therefore, may have been thought to be excessive.

*See also* FAUNA § C.

> *Bibliography.* On chameleons in Palestine, see Tristram, *NHB* (1867), pp. 262-63. W. S. McCULLOUGH

**CHAMOIS** shăm'ĭ. KJV translation of זמר (Deut. 14:5; RSV "mountain-sheep"). The chamois (*rupicapra*) is a small, goatlike antelope, strongly built and very surefooted, but inelegant in form, *ca.* two feet high at the withers. It is found mostly in mountainous regions and also in forests adjacent to mountains.
W. S. McCULLOUGH

**CHAMPAIGN** shăm păn'. KJV archaism which translates הבקע (RSV VALLEY) in Ezek. 37:2 mg.;

ערבה (RSV ARABAH) in Deut. 11:30. Πεδία in Jth. 5:1 (RSV "plains") is translated "champaign countries" by the KJV. The word is from Middle English *champayne*, "open, unenclosed land, plain."

G. M. LANDES

**CHAMPION** [איש הבנים (I Sam. 17:4, 23), man of the space between (*i.e.*, who fights the battle against a single opponent in the space between two armies), cf. μεταίχμιον; גבור (I Sam. 17:51), mighty one, warrior]. A term applied to Goliath. He stood for his army in the no man's land between the camps of the Israelites and the Philistines. *See* MIGHTY MEN.

J. A. SANDERS

**CHANAAN.** KJV translation of Χαναάν (RSV CANAAN).

**CHANCELLOR.** KJV translation of the Aramaic word בעל־טעם (for Persian "commander"), an officer in the Persian court, in Ezra 4:8-9, 17 (RSV "commander").

**CHANGE OF RAIMENT (GARMENTS).** KJV translation of חלפות שמלת in Gen. 45:22; חליפות בגדים in Judg. 14:12-13; II Kings 5:5, 22-23; and חליפות in Judg. 14:19. RSV FESTAL GARMENT.

**CHANNELS OF THE SEA** [אפקי ים, the stream beds of the sea; *cf.* Ugar. *apq thmtm*, the streams of the two deeps] (II Sam. 22:16; Ps. 18:15—H 18:16); KJV CHANNELS OF WATERS in Ps. 18:15—H 18:16. The channels, normally hidden, which control and direct the flow of the primeval sea that surrounds the earth and overlies the underworld.

*See also* SEA; SHEOL; WATER.     L. E. TOOMBS

**CHANNUNEUS.** KJV Apoc. form of HANANIAH.

**CHANT.** *See* MUSIC.

\***CHAOS** [אפל (Job 10:22; KJV DARKNESS), תהו (KJV CONFUSION *in* Isa. 24:10; 34:11; KJV IN VAIN *in* Isa. 45:18-19)]. Properly, a trackless waste (cf. Gen. 1:2; Deut. 32:10; Job 12:24; Ps. 107:40). The translation "chaos" must therefore be understood in the original Greek sense of "void, empty space" (χάος), rather than as a synonym of "confusion."

In Isa. 24:10 the meaning is that the city is reduced to a "ghost town"; in 34:11, that it will become a limbo which can be neither spanned nor plumbed. In the latter passage the term stands parallel to the assonantal בהו with which it is in turn conjoined for emphasis in Gen. 1:2; Jer. 4:23. The effect of the combination *tōhû wā-bhōhû* may perhaps best be conveyed by Ogden Nash's striking expression "limbo a-kimbo."     T. H. GASTER

**CHAPHENATHA** kə fĕn'ə thə [Χαφεναθά]; KJV CAPHENATHA (I Macc. 12:37). A place unknown today, just outside Jerusalem. Here the walls of the city had fallen down, and Judas Maccabeus built them up.     N. TURNER

**CHAPITER** chăp'ĭ tər. KJV translation of כתרת, צפת, ראש. RSV CAPITAL.

**CHAPMAN.** KJV archaism translating תור (RSV TRADER) in II Chr. 9:14.

**CHARAATHALAR** kăr'ĭ ăth'ə lär. KJV Apoc. form arising from the fusion of CHERUB and ADDAN.

**CHARACA.** KJV form of CHARAX.

**CHARACTERS, COMMON.** The translation of חרט in Isa. 8:1 (KJV MAN'S PEN). "Common character" is used for a symbol or letter used in writing that is recognized by the majority of literate persons as belonging to their system of notation; the letters of the alphabet written in the ordinary style of the period.

*See also* ALPHABET; WRITING AND WRITING MATERIALS.     C. U. WOLF

**CHARASHIM, VALLEY OF.** KJV translation of גיא חרשים (RSV GE-HARASHIM) in I Chr. 4:14.

**CHARAX** kâr'ăks [τὸν Χάρακα] (II Macc. 12:17); KJV CHARACA kăr'ə kə. A place unknown today, E of Jordan, with a colony of Jews. It existed during the period of Judas Maccabeus. *See* TOB.

N. TURNER

**CHARCHAMIS; CHARCHEMISH.** KJV forms of CARCHEMISH.

**CHARCOAL** [פחם (Prov. 26:21); ἀνθρακιά (John 18:18)] (KJV COAL). True mineral coal was not known in biblical times; charcoal, made from wood, was the common article of fuel. *See* COAL.

**CHARCUS** kär'kəs. KJV Apoc. form of BARKOS.

**CHAREA** kăr'ē ə. KJV Apoc. form of HARSHA.

**CHARGER.** The KJV translation of קערה (RSV PLATE) in Num. 7:13-85 and of πίναξ (RSV PLATTER) in Matt. 14:11. A large, flat metal serving dish.

**CHARGERS** [פרשים, *with emendation, for* ברשים] (Nah 2:3—H 2:4); KJV FIR TREES. Spirited horses used in battle to charge or attack enemy forces or positions. Cf. Isa. 31:1, 3; Jer. 8:6; Rev. 6:2, for horses used in battle.

*See* HORSE.     J. A. SANDERS

**CHARIOT** [רכוב, רכבה, רכב, עגלה, מרכבה, מרכב, הצן; ἅρμα, ῥέδα]. A wheeled vehicle drawn by onagers, oxen, or horses, and used for transport or war.

1. Terminology
2. Origin and development
3. History of its use in the Near East
4. OT usage
5. NT usage
Bibliography

**1. Terminology.** The common Hebrew words for "chariot" are רכב (collective) and מרכבה. The word מרכב (I Kings 4:26—H 5:1) literally means "place of riding," and may properly be used of "seat" or "saddle." At Ezek. 27:20 the KJV incorrectly translates רכבה by "chariot," whereas the RSV correctly uses "riding." The word עֲגָלָה is rendered at Ps. 46: 9—H 46:10 by "chariots." It normally means "carts used for transport" and in this passage probably refers to "supply wagons" used for military purposes (see CART). Ezek. 23:24 contains the only occurrence of the word הֹצֶן in the OT. The RSV adopts the common emendation מִצָּפוֹן ("from the north") on the basis of the LXX ἀπὸ βορρᾶ. A less complicated emendation is the transposed word צִנָּה, "shield."

**2. Origin and development.** Wheeled vehicles drawn by asses are attested in Mesopotamia as early as the end of the fourth millennium. A copper model of a chariot drawn by four asses found at Tell Aqrab (third millennium) has a single rider with two disk-wheels on which is mounted a body consisting of a simple board continuing the line of the heavy pole astride which stood the driver (Fig. CHA 23). The earliest spoked wheels are attested in the time of Hammurabi (cf. the Cappadocian cylinder seals). Wheels contained four or six spokes, the latter predominating,

23. Small copper war chariot drawn by four asses; from Shara temple, Tell Aqrab, Early Dynastic (first half of third millennium)

24. Upper part of bas relief on bronze band shows the war chariots of Shalmaneser III. Lower bas relief depicts the storming of the town of Hazor.

25. Assyrian relief of a royal chariot, with the king being shielded by an umbrella held by a servant

until the time of Shalmaneser III.* Under Ashurnasirpal II eight-spoked chariot wheels appear (also Syrian?), and were taken over by the Assyrians, where they remain characteristic until the Persian period.* Unusual was the twelve-spoked wheel, found only in Elamite chariots. Figs. CHA 24-25.

The body of the chariot was probably made of light wickerwork, open at the back, with a very high dashboard, to which was attached a case for spears, battle-ax, and whip. The earliest chariot box was four-cornered. In the Cassite period the chariot became lighter, with a rounded dashboard with two crossed quivers near it. After Tiglath-pileser III (746/5-728/7 B.C.) the four-cornered box type with a simple vertical quiver near the front became normal. The axle was usually under the rear of the box, though in its oldest known form it was directly under the middle. The chariot was normally low slung, but Sennacherib introduced the high chariot, of which the wheel was easily a man's height. Fig. CAR 15.

The chariot was manned by two men in the Egyptian and early Assyrian forms (coachman and warrior). The Hittite chariot was manned by a third (a shield bearer) as well, and this form was adopted in Assyria by the end of the second millennium. The three-man chariot was used by the Syrians and probably by the Hebrews, since the military official called שָׁלִישׁ is probably to be identified as this third man (Exod. 14:7; 15:4; I Kings 9:22; II Kings 9:25; etc.). After Ashurbanipal chariots sometimes carried four men.

"Charioteer" (רֹכֵב, rôkhēbh) is used once for the rider in a chariot (Jer. 51:21; cf. Hag. 2:22). For the driver (רַכָּב, rakkābh) of a royal chariot, see I Kings 22:34; II Chr. 18:33.

A chariot was normally drawn by two horses, though occasionally a third is shown on the monuments. The latter was, however, not yoked to the chariot, but was a spare.

**3. History of its use in the Near East.** It was the popularization of the use of the HORSE, instead of onagers and oxen, by the Hyksos that revolutionized ancient warfare (see WAR, METHODS OF). This speedier weapon for warfare enabled the Hyksos to conquer most of Syria and Egypt from ca. 1800 to 1600 B.C. Their influence in Egypt is attested by the adoption of such Semitic words as ssmj.t ("horses") and mrkb.t ("chariot") into their language. The use of the horse-drawn chariot permitted for the first time such large empires to be built as the New Kingdom, the Hittite Empire, and the later Assyrian Empire.

The chariot was not only used for warfare, but in ordinary life for the pomp and pleasure of kings and their principal officers as well. Such chariots were often preceded by runners (Gen. 41:43; Esth. 6:11) who heralded the approach of a dignitary. The use of chariots for processions and feasts became especially popular during the Hellenistic and Roman periods.

The importance of the chariot for warfare is demonstrated in numerous inscriptions. The inclusion of chariots in tribute lists may be seen in a number of inscriptions from the New Kingdom (Egypt). E.g., the Karnak Annals of Thut-mose III list 924 chariots as part of the booty from Megiddo, whereas the Memphis stele of Amen-hotep II lists 60 chariots of silver and gold and 1,032 painted wood chariots as part of the plunder from one of his Asiatic campaigns. The Annals of Shalmaneser III refer to the plunder of Hazael's army as including 1,121 chariots and 470 cavalry horses. In the Aramean coalition against Shalmaneser contributions from members are listed in the above-mentioned Annals as consisting in the main of chariots, cavalry, and infantry; that of Ahab the Israelite was 2,000 chariots and 10,000 infantry.

**4. OT usage.** The first mention of "chariot" in the OT is of Egyptian chariots. Joseph occupies a royal chariot (Gen. 41:43), uses it to meet his father (46: 29) and for Jacob's funeral (50:9). The destruction of Egyptian war chariots at the Red Sea (Exod. 14–15, *passim*) became a favored symbol for God's deliverance of his people (Josh. 24:6). Egyptian chariots are also mentioned as taking part in Shishak's invasion (II Chr. 12:3; cf. II Kings 18:24).

Chariots were introduced into Canaan by the Hyksos, as the number of horse skeletons found in the Tell el-'Ajjūl necropolis and the bronze (later iron) bridles in the Negeb attest. When the Israelite nomads invaded Canaan, they found the Canaanite iron chariotry too formidable to permit conquest of the plains (Judg. 1:19). Joshua defeated Jabin of Hazor and his coalition, which used chariotry, when they met at the "waters of Merom" (Josh. 11:4-9), burning their chariots and hamstringing their horses. Because chariotry was of no use in the hill country, the Israelites were gradually able to conquer it, but the plains remained for a long time held by the Canaanites. Judg. 4–5 relates the defeat of Sisera and his nine hundred chariots (4:3) by the N tribes of Naphtali and Zebulun.

The Philistines were able to dominate the Israelites because of their chariotry during the time of Samuel and Saul (cf. I Sam. 13:5, where, however, the number thirty thousand is almost certainly exaggerated). David's victories over the Philistines were doubtlessly due to his introduction of chariotry (II Sam. 8:4; I Chr. 18:4). Chariots were also used in the dynastic struggles of Absalom (II Sam. 15:1) and Adonijah (I Kings 1:5). It was Solomon, however, who developed an army of chariots in order to put his army on a par with, or on a higher level than, those of his neighbors. Chariot cities were established at Megiddo and Hazor to protect the NE frontier against the Syrians; at Lower Beth-Horon, Gezer, and Baalath, overlooking the districts of the plain, against the

Philistines; and at Tamar in the Arabah, against the Edomites (I Kings 9:15-19; *see* MEGIDDO § C4). Chariots were purchased from Egypt, the Hittites, and the Arameans (10:29), and after the division of the kingdom were prominent in the army of the N kingdom; in fact, under Elah there were two divisions of chariot forces (16:9), though later under Jehoahaz the chariot forces were almost completely destroyed by the Syrians (II Kings 13:7). In Judah chariotry was less developed, as the Assyrian invasions show, doubtlessly in large part because of the hilly terrain. As a result Judah was forced to depend on Egypt for help in chariot warfare (Isa. 31:1).

Chariots played a large part in Seleucid warfare (Dan. 11:40; I Macc. 1:17; 8:6). Seleucid war chariots were armed with scythes (II Macc. 13:2).

Chariots are often mentioned as symbolic of royal dignity (Gen. 41:43; I Sam. 8:11; II Sam. 15:1; I Kings 1:5; Jer. 17:25; 22:4). Elijah and Elisha are both called the "chariots of Israel and its horsemen" (II Kings 2:12; 13:14), as being equal in effectiveness, through their prophetic potency, to Israel's cavalry. Occasional mention is made of God's chariots as indicating divine power at the time of the Exodus (Hab. 3:8), or from Sinai (Ps. 68:17—H 68: 18, where the KJV "chariots of God" is idiomatically rendered "mighty chariotry" in the RSV), or as symbols of divine fury in judgment (Isa. 66:15).

In the last of Zechariah's night visions (Zech. 6: 1-8) four heavenly chariots are sent out in four directions as messengers of God to the Dispersion. The notion of chariots and charioteers of the deity was a widespread one in the Near East. Such sacred chariots were used in the cult of the sun in the time of Josiah (II Kings 23:11); in fact, the notion may well have originated in solar worship. The "chariot of fire and horses of fire" (II Kings 2:11) which transported Elijah toward heaven probably reflect an ancient solar legend (cf. also 6:17, where fiery chariots and horses are the invisible protectors of Elisha the man of God).

**5. NT usage.** The chariot of the Ethiopian eunuch (Acts 8:28-29, 38) was probably not a war chariot but a transport. Chariots and horses are mentioned among a merchant's cargo in Rev. 18:13, and the noise of a locust plague is compared to that made by horses and chariots rushing into battle in Rev. 9:9 (cf. Joel 2:4-5).

*Bibliography.* F. Studniczka, "Der Rennwagen im syrisch-phönizischen Gebiet," *Archaeology Jahrbuch,* 22 (1907), 147 ff; E. Unger, *Der Rennwagen in Vorderasiene* (1929); A. Salonen, *Die Landfahrzeuge der alten Mesopotamier* (1951); A. G. Barrois, *Manuel d'Archéologie Biblique,* II (1953), 98 ff; V. G. Childe, "Wheeled Vehicles," in Singer, Holmyard, and Hall, *History of Technology,* I (1954), 716 ff.　　　J. W. WEVERS

**CHARIOTEER** [רכב, *rakkābh*] (Jer. 51:21); KJV RIDER. The driver of a chariot. The same Hebrew word is used of King Ahab's driver (I Kings 22:34; II Chr. 18:33), and generally of a horseman (II Kings 9:17). Bidkar, Jehu's aide (II Kings 9:25), may have been his personal charioteer. *See also* CHARIOT; HORSEMAN.　　　J. A. SANDERS

**CHARISMATA** kə rĭz'mə tə [χαρίσματα, *plural of* χάρισμα, *free gift*]. Basically, favors, endowments, graces, offices, all bestowed by God's grace without claim of merit whatsoever on man's part. *See* SPIRITUAL GIFTS.                                   E. ANDREWS

**CHARITY.** A KJV translation of ἀγάπη (RSV more correctly LOVE).

**CHARM.** *See* AMULETS.

**CHARMER** חבר חבר (Deut. 18:11), מלחש (Ps. 58:5), בעל הלשון (Eccl. 10:11; KJV BABBLER); KJV אטים (Isa. 19:3; RSV SORCERER)]. A conjurer who uses spells or charms to achieve magic effects. *See* ENCHANTER; DIVINATION.

**CHARMER, SNAKE.** *See* SNAKE CHARMER.

**CHARMIS** kär′mĭs [Χαρμείς (B א), Χαλμείς (A)] (Jth. 6:15; 8:10; 10:6). Son of Melchiel; one of the three city magistrates of Bethulia to whom Judith made appeal for aid.                                   J. C. SWAIM

**CHARRAN.** KJV NT form of HARAN.

**CHASEBA.** KJV Apoc. form of CHEZIB 2.

**CHASM** [χάσμα]. A cleft or pit which separates two places. The word occurs in the NT only in Luke 16:26, where a valley separates the post-mortem abode of the rich man in Hades from that of Lazarus in Abraham's bosom. Used thus in a parable, the word does not encourage the effort to map the abode of the dead. The context makes clear, however, the emphasis on a final division, because the chasm cannot be crossed. Other uses in descriptions of final judgment may be found in I Enoch 18:11; Diogenes Laertius 8:31; Plato *Republic* X.614.                                   P. S. MINEAR

**CHASPHO** kăs′fō [Χασφω] (I Macc. 5:26, 36); KJV CASPHOR —fôr in I Macc. 5:26; CASPHON —fŏn in I Macc. 5:36. A city in Gilead stormed and taken by Judas, who released the Jews held captive there by the Syrians. It is probably the same place as CASPIN, and it has been identified with Khisfin, E of the Sea of Galilee, and with el-Muzeirib on the Yarmuk River.

*Bibliography.* H. Bévenot, *Die beiden Makkabäerbücher* (1931), pp. 228-29; F.-M. Abel, *Les livres des Maccabées* (1949), pp. 97, 99-100.                                   E. W. SAUNDERS

**CHASTENING.** *See* DISCIPLINE.

**CHASTITY.** *See* SEX; VIRGIN.

**CHEBAR** kē′bär [כבר; Akkad. *naru Kabari*] (Ezek. 1:3; 3:15, 23; 10:15, 20, 22; 43:3). A river. The exiles among whom Ezekiel the prophet lived were located at the village of Tel-abib on the River Chebar, and it was here that the prophetic vision came.                                   C. G. HOWIE

**CHECKER WORK. 1.** שבכה (I Kings 7:17), part of the ornamentation of the temple pillars. This word elsewhere denotes a LATTICE (II Kings 1:2) or NET (Job 18:8), and probably here indicates a crisscrossed design. For detailed discussion of the temple pillars, *see* JACHIN AND BOAZ. Fig. CHE 26.

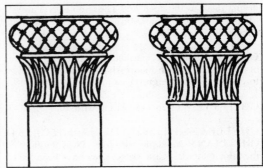

26. Checker work ornamenting the capital of the pillars of the porch in Solomon's temple

**2.** כתנת תשבץ ("coat of checker work"; KJV "broidered coat"; Exod. 28:4, 39), a kind of weaving employed in making the high priest's tunic. It was probably a checked design, with different colors in warp and woof, or a raised honeycomb design in one color. *See* CLOTH.                                   S. V. FAWCETT

**CHEDORLAOMER** kĕd′ər lā ō′mər [כדרלעמר, כדר־לעמר; LXX Χοδολλογομορ]. King of ELAM who led a punitive campaign against five kings in S Palestine and routed them in the Valley of Siddim (Gen. 14:1-12). His league was then defeated by "Abram the Hebrew" and associates (vss. 13-17). The Dead Sea Genesis Apocryphon agrees with Jubilees against the MT in naming Chedorlaomer at the head of the coalition (cf. vss. 5, 9, 17). The campaign may well have had economic motivation. *See* ABRAHAM.

The structure of the name Chedorlaomer is clear. *Kutir* (sometimes *Kudur*), meaning "servant," is a common Elamite word occurring regularly in Elamite proper names—e.g., *Kutir-Naḫḫunte*. *Lagamar* appears in several Elamite texts as a divine name. *Kutir-Lagamar* would therefore be a genuine Elamite construction meaning "servant of (the deity) Lagamar" and could quite properly be borne by a ruler. However, no one bearing this specific name has been found in any extrabiblical records, Elamite or otherwise. The name of a deity Lagamal—a Semitic form often identified with Elamite Lagamar—was used in Old Babylonian personal names during the age of Hammurabi; and this deity is called "king of Mari." The identification, if sound, could indicate the presence of Elamite officials on the political scene at MARI. But the name Lagamar is undeniably Elamite and must not be given a Semitic etymology.

*Bibliography.* G. G. Cameron, *History of Early Iran* (1936), p. 80. R. de Vaux, "Les patriarches hébreux et les découvertes modernes, I," *RB*, LV (1948), 334-36. F. M. T. Böhl, "Das Zeitalter Abrahams," *Opera Minora* (1953), pp. 46-47, 478; "King Ḥammurabi of Babylon," *Opera Minora* (1953), pp. 354, 514.                                   L. HICKS

**CHEESE** [גבנה (Job 10:10), חריצי החלב (I Sam. 17:18), שפה (II Sam. 17:29)]. On two occasions cheese appears in a list of provisions: (*a*) those brought by David to his brothers (I Sam. 17:18), and (*b*) those received by David at Mahanaim (II Sam. 17:29). In biblical times cheese was prepared by salting the strained curds, shaping them into small disks, and drying them in the open air. Thus Job asks Yahweh: "Didst thou not . . . curdle [lit., 'congeal'] me like cheese?" (Job 10:10). J. F. Ross

**CHELAL** kē'lăl [כְּלָל, perfection] (Ezra 10:30). One of the sons of Pahath-moab who were forced by Ezra to give up their foreign wives.

**CHELCIAS.** KJV form of HILKIAH 9-10.

**CHELLEANS** kĕl'ĭ ənz [Χελεοι] (Jth. 2:23); KJV CHELLIANS. A people who lived N of the home of the Ishmaelites (*see* CHELOUS). They have been identified with the ancient Cholle between Palmyra and the Euphrates River, the modern el-Khalle. Because of the broad, inclusive meaning of the term "Ishmaelite," other scholars are content to localize them somewhere to the N of these tribes, who lived in E Palestine beside the Arabian Desert.

*Bibliography.* F. Stummer, *Geographie des Buches Judith* (1947), pp. 24-25. E. W. SAUNDERS

**CHELLUH.** KJV form of CHELUHI.

**CHELOD** kē'lŏd. KJV translation of Χελεούδ (RSV "Chaldeans") in Jth. 1:6. Conjectures have been that Calneh is meant, or "sons of the weasel" (חלד). J. C. SWAIM

**CHELOUS** kĕl'əs [Χελους]; KJV CHELLUS. One of three cities in S Palestine named in Jth. 1:9; probably the modern Khalasa, identified with the ancient Alusa in Idumea and mentioned in the Palestinian Targums on Gen. 16:4, 7; Exod. 15:22 under the name חלוצה. It lay on one of the roads leading S from Jerusalem toward Egypt and on a caravan route between Gaza and Edom. Arab writers distinguish between an el-Khalus and an el-Khalasa, though it is not certain that Khalasa satisfies the description of the CHELLEANS in Jth. 2:23.

*Bibliography.* F.-M. Abel, *Géographie de la Palestine*, II (1938), 298, 313; F. Stummer, *Geographie des Buches Judith* (1947), pp. 12-13. E. W. SAUNDERS

**CHELUB** kē'lŭb [כְּלוּב, basket, *or* cage; *but in* I Chr. 4:11 (cf. LXX Χαλεβ) *perhaps variant of* CALEB].
1. A descendant of Judah (I Chr. 4:11). But it may be that "Caleb" should be read here and for "Carmi" in I Chr. 4:1.
2. The father of Ezri, one of David's officials (I Chr. 27:26).

*Bibliography.* M. Noth, *Die israelitischen Personennamen* (1928), p. 226. H. H. GUTHRIE, JR.

**CHELUBAI.** See CALEB.

**CHELUHI** kĕl'ə hī [*Kethibh* כְּלוּהִי, *Qere* כְּלוּהוּ, *probably corrupted, but* LXX χελια *suggests an original* כליה, Yahu is perfect] ; KJV CHELLUH kĕl'ə. One of those Ezra compelled to give up their foreign wives (Ezra 10:35; omitted in I Esd. 9:34).

**CHEMARIM** kĕm'ə rĭm. KJV transliteration of כמרים (RSV "idolatrous priests") in Zeph. 1:4. *See* PRIESTS AND LEVITES.

**CHEMOSH** kē'mŏsh [כְּמוֹשׁ]. The name or title of the god of the Moabites, who are called the "people of Chemosh" (Num. 21:29; Jer. 48:46); cf. theophoric names of Moabite kings, Chemosh —, the father of Mesha, and Kammusunadbi, contemporary with Hezekiah in Sennacherib's records. A sanctuary of Chemosh was built by Solomon "on the mountain east of Jerusalem" (I Kings 11:7) and was abolished by Josiah (II Kings 23:13). In Mesha's inscription, Chemosh is compounded with Athtar, the Venus Star; hence we suppose that Chemosh was the Moabite manifestation of this astral deity. The identity of Chemosh and Milcom (*see* MOLECH) of Ammon is indicated by Judg. 11:24.

*Bibliography.* G. A. Cooke, *A Textbook of North Semitic Inscriptions* (1903), pp. 1-14 (Mesha's Inscription); J. Gray, "The Desert God Attr in the Literature and Religion of Canaan," *JNES*, VIII (1949), 72-83; W. F. Albright, *Archaeology and the Religion of Israel* (1953), pp. 117-18.
J. GRAY

**CHENAANAH** kĭ nā'ə nə [כְּנַעֲנָה, *from* כְּנַעַן, CANAAN(?)]. 1. The father of Zedekiah the false prophet (I Kings 22:11, 24; II Chr. 18:10, 23).
2. Listed as part of the tribe of Benjamin (I Chr. 7:10)—probably incorrectly, since the list in I Chr. 7:6-12 is more likely one of the tribe of Zebulun.

*Bibliography.* M. Noth, *Die israelitischen Personennamen* (1928), p. 248. H. H. GUTHRIE, JR.

**CHENANI** kĭ nā'nī [כְּנָנִי] (Neh. 9:4). A postexilic Levite who was present at Ezra's public reading of the law.

**CHENANIAH** kĕn'ə nī'ə [כְּנַנְיָהוּ, כְּנַנְיָה, Y strengthens]. 1. A leader of the Levites in "lifting up" (משא) when David brought the ark to Jerusalem (I Chr. 15:22, 27). The understood object of משא may be the voice in song, as the context implies (LXX, KJV-RSV), or the ark. A third possibility is that משא means "prophetic oracle" (Vulg.), making Chenaniah a temple prophet.
2. An Izharite appointed for official duties outside the temple (I Chr. 26:29; cf. Neh. 11:16).

*Bibliography.* S. Mowinckel, *Psalmenstudien*, III (1923), 17-18. R. W. CORNEY

**CHEPHAR-AMMONI** kē'fər ăm'ə nī [כְּפַר הָעַמּוֹנִי, Ammonite village] (Josh. 18:24); KJV CHEPHAR-HAAMONAI —hā—. A town in Benjamin, apparently so called because it was settled by Ammonites. The site is unknown.

**CHEPHIRAH** kĭ fī'rə [הַכְּפִירָה, כְּפִירָה]; KJV Apoc. CAPHIRA kə—. A Hivvite city which followed the lead of Gibeon in making terms with the Israelites (Josh. 9:17). It was resettled after the Babylonian exile (Ezra 2:25; Neh. 7:29; I Esd. 5:19). Its site is Khirbet Kefireh, SW of el-Jib (Gibeon).
S. COHEN

**CHERAN** kĭr'ən [כְּרָן]. The fourth son of clan chief Dishon; ancestor of a native Horite subclan in Edom (Gen. 36:26; I Chr. 1:41).

**CHEREAS.** KJV Apoc. form of CHAEREAS.

**CHERETHITES AND PELETHITES** kĕr'ə thīts, pĕl'ə thīts [כְּרֵתִי; פְּלֵתִי]. Groups which constituted a section of David's personal army. They joined him after he defeated the Philistines and were part of his retinue after he was established in Jerusalem. Their leader, Benaiah son of Jehoiada, is listed as a member of David's administrative corps (II Sam. 8:18; 20:23). Their loyalty to David was absolute and was proved by their remaining steadfast with him by accompanying him on his flight from Jerusalem because of Absalom (15:18). They also participated in the punitive action against Sheba son of Bichri (20:7) and proved faithful once again in supporting the selection of Solomon as king (I Kings 1:38-44).

The name Cherethite most probably meant Cretans and alluded to the Aegean origin of part of the Sea Peoples who settled along the S coast of Palestine with the Philistines or to a band of Cretan mercenaries settled there by the Egyptians. They probably dwelt in the area to the SE of Philistia proper, which is once alluded to as the Negeb of the Cherethites (I Sam. 30:14). The Pelethites were, in all likelihood, recruited from the ranks of the Philistines with whom David had come in close contact during his sojourn in Ziklag. The form "Pelethite" (*pəlethi*) for "Philistine" (*pəlishti*) is explicable as an analogous formation modeled on "Cherethite" (*kərethi*), with which it always occurs. In the two passages in which the Cherethites are condemned by the prophets in parallelism with the Philistines, it is not clear from the context whether the terms are synonymous, or if separate peoples are meant (Ezek. 25:16; Zeph. 2:5).

The CARITES kâr'īts [כָּרִי], who were loyal to the royal house in the story of Joash (II Kings 11:4, 19), have been considered by many scholars as a later development of the Cherethites; others have seen in them the Carians, an Asianic people who often served as mercenaries in antiquity. The variant reading "Carites" preserved in the *Kethibh* of II Sam. 20:23 strengthens the former view.

*Bibliography.* W. F. Albright, "A Colony of Cretan Mercenaries on the Coast of the Negeb," *JPOS,* I (1920-21), pp. 187-94. J. C. GREENFIELD

**CHERITH, BROOK** kĕr'īth [נַחַל כְּרִית]. A stream where Elijah was told to hide; he remained there until the stream dried up because of the unprecedented drought (I Kings 17:2-7). Since the spot was E of the Jordan (vs. 3) and Elijah was a Gileadite, Cherith must have been one of the wadies in Gilead where there were many caves in the hills. The identification of the brook with Wadi Qelt, on the W side of the Jordan near Jericho, arose in the Middle Ages and is inconsistent with the text. S. COHEN

**CHERUB (ANGEL)** chĕr'əb [כְּרוּב; Akkad. *karubu*]. Plural CHERUBIM —ə bĭm; KJV CHERUBIMS —bĭmz. A winged bull, or similar mythological beast, adopted by the Israelites from earlier Mesopotamian and Canaanite mythology. On its functions and significance, *see* ANGEL § A4.

**CHERUB (TOWN)** kĕr'əb [כְּרוּב, cabbage (village?) *or* (place of the) cherub(?)]; KJV Apoc. CHARA-

**ATHALAR** kăr'ĭ ăth'ə lär [Χαρααθαλάν, *fusion of* Cherub *and* Addan]. Babylonian place, still unidentified, from which Jewish exiles, who could not prove their ancestry with genealogical records, returned to Palestine (Ezra 2:59; Neh. 7:61). The parallel in I Esd. 5:36 applies the name to a leader among the group.

**CHESALON** kĕs'ə lŏn [כְּסָלוֹן, back(?)] (Josh. 15:10). A city along the N section of Judah's boundary, bordering on Dan; usually identified with modern Kesla, *ca.* nine miles W of Jerusalem, in a region once noted for its oak forests.

**CHESED** kĕ'sĕd [כֶּשֶׂד] (Gen. 22:22). The fourth son of Nahor and Milcah; probably the assumed ancestor of an Aramean tribe from which came the Chaldeans.

**CHESIL** kĕ'səl [כְּסִיל] (Josh. 15:30). A city of Judah in the Negeb district of Hormah; present location unknown. Chesil seems to correspond with BETHUL (Josh. 19:4); BETHUEL (I Chr. 4:30); and BETHEL (I Sam. 30:27).

**CHESNUT.** KJV translation of עַרְמוֹן (RSV more correctly PLANE; *see* PLANE TREE) in Gen. 30:37; Ezek. 31:8. The common chestnut (*Castanea sativa* Mill.) is rare in Bible lands.

**CHEST** [אָרוֹן, chest, ark; KJV גִּנְזַךְ (Ezek. 27:24; RSV CARPET), treasure chest]. The box, probably of considerable size, which was placed beside the altar of the Jerusalem temple (II Kings 12:9—H 12:10) or outside the temple gate (II Chr. 24:8) to receive the offerings toward the repair of the temple under Joash. E. M. GOOD

**CHESULLOTH** kĭ sŭl'ŏth [כְּסֻלּוֹת] (Josh. 19:18). A border town in Issachar; same as CHISLOTH-TABOR. It is generally identified with modern Iksal, a town *ca.* three miles SE of Nazareth.

**CHETH** kĕth (Heb. ḤĀth) [ח, ḥ (Ḥêth)]. The eighth letter of the Hebrew ALPHABET as placed in the KJV at the head of the eighth section of the acrostic psalm, Ps. 119, where each verse of this section of the psalm begins with this letter.

**CHETTIIM.** KJV Apoc. form of KITTIM.

**CHEZIB** kĕ'zĭb [כְּזִיב; Χασεβά]; KJV Apoc. CHASEBA kăs'ə bə. **1.** Head of a family of temple servants at the return of the exiles, according to I Esd. 5:31. The name is not mentioned in the corresponding canonical list.

**2.** A place (Gen. 38:5). *See* ACHZIB.

**CHIDON** kī'dən [כִּידֹן]. According to I Chr. 13:9, the name of the threshing floor where Uzzah was struck dead for touching the ark. Whether Chidon was the place or the owner is not indicated. The parallel passage, II Sam. 6:6, has the "threshing floor of Nacon." O. R. SELLERS

**CHIEF** [אַלּוּף; נָסִיךְ]. A term preferred by the RSV to KJV "duke," which designates the leader of a

FAMILY; CLAN; or TRIBE, such as the Edomites (Gen. 36:15; Exod. 15:15; I Chr. 1:51) or the "clans of Judah" (Zech. 12:5). In I Macc. 10:65 the military chief (στρατηγός) is called a GENERAL (KJV "duke"). *See* also PRINCE; CAPTAIN.           C. U. WOLF

**CHIEF PRIEST** [הכהן הראש; ἀρχιερεύς (*alternately* HIGH PRIEST)]; HIGH PRIEST [הכהן הגדול]. In addition to the actual use of the term, certain references to Aaron (e.g., Exod. 27–31) veil a reference to the chief priest. *See* PRIESTS AND LEVITES.

G. HENTON DAVIES

**CHILD** [מַף, ילד; τέκνον]. The importance of children in the Bible is attested by the numerous allusions to them. The child in relation to the family was the recipient of love and care.

1. The child in relation to the family
2. The child as a descendant or posterity in the general sense
3. "Child" as a form of familiar address
4. Children of the covenant community and those hostile to it
5. "Child" as the designation of an inhabitant of a particular city
Bibliography

**1. The child in relation to the family.** Only by bearing children could a woman achieve her true purpose in life. She could properly look with disdain upon a barren woman (Gen. 16:4). A man was required to "raise up offspring" for his deceased brother by marrying the widow (38:8; *see* MARRIAGE § 1*g*). The children of the faithful are "like olive shoots" around a man's table and a sure sign of the favor of God (Ps. 128:3; cf. 127:5); and grandchildren are the "crown of the aged" (Prov. 17:6). It is impossible to suppose that a woman could "forget her sucking child" or "have no compassion on the son of her womb" (Isa. 49:15). The period of lactation is suggested in a late book (II Macc. 7:27) as being three years. The day of weaning was a time of celebration (Gen. 21:8); after weaning, children were taught bit by bit, line upon line (Isa. 28:10).

Children were named to express some aspect of God's relation to the father or to the entire family group at times (Gen. 4:1; 25:25-26; 29:32, 35; 30:6, 8, 11, 13, 18, 24; 41:51-52; etc.; note the naming of the prophet's children in Isa. 8:3; Hos. 1:2-9). They were dedicated to the God of their people at an early age. Prior to such a dedication, all male children were circumcised as the initial act of entrance into the community of the covenant (Luke 2:21; cf. Exod. 12:48). Children were the recipients of gifts; fathers know how to give good gifts to their children (Matt. 7:11). The child was expected to grow and become strong, full of wisdom and blessed by God's favor (Luke 2:40). It was the task of the parents to teach him diligently in the ways of the Lord and the traditions of his people through which these ways were made known (Deut. 4:9-10; 6:7, 21; 11:19; 31:12-13; Josh. 4:6-7; Ps. 78:4). *See* EDUCATION.

**2. The child as a descendant or posterity in the general sense.** The covenant community, represented by its founders, will have an abundance of children (descendants) as a sign of God's favor (Gen.

16:10; 17:2, 4-5, 20; Exod. 1:7). The children's children will know the wonder of God's steadfast love (Ps. 103:17) if they keep his covenant. In Pss. 11:4; 14:2 "children" signifies mankind (cf. 90:3). If the Israelites are truly penitent, God's words will never depart from the mouths of the children's children (Isa. 59:21; cf. 29:23).

**3. "Child" as a form of familiar address.** This word appears as a term of address by a teacher to his pupil or pupils in the wisdom writings of the Bible, or by a person with authority in the Christian community (II Tim. 1:2; Philem. 10). In a comparison of the usage of the books of Proverbs and Ecclesiasticus, we note that the former has "son" to symbolize his pupils and the latter makes considerable use of "child," τέκνον (Ecclus. 3:1, 17; 4:1; etc.). Jesus used the term in addressing individuals and crowds (Matt. 9:2; Mark 2:5; 10:24).

**4. Children of the covenant community and those hostile to it.** The term "children" (בנים; lit., "sons") occurs in a context that singles out Israel, the Christian people, individual members of either group, or nonbelievers. The "children of Israel" are members of the covenant community (Exod. 20:10; Isa. 17:3, 9; 29:22-23; 30:1; Ezek. 37:16; Hos. 4:6*e*). Similarly, the people who belong to the Christian community of faith are named as children of the "elect lady"—i.e., the church to which the letter is being written (II John 1, 4, 13; cf. Gal. 4:31). "Children of Abraham" are those who claim spiritual descent from him and thus membership in the covenant community (Matt. 3:9; Luke 3:8; John 8:39; Rom. 9:7; I Pet. 3:6). Negatively, Israel is called "rebellious children," "children of transgression" (Isa. 30:1; 57:4). Sinful Israel is denounced as being like "stupid children" (Jer. 4:22), and the scribes and Pharisees receive the appellative "child of hell" (Matt. 23:15). The "children of God" are set over against the "children of the devil" (I John 3:10). "Little children" (τεκνίον) is an intimate term for Christian people (John 13:33; Gal. 4:19; I John 2:12, 28; Test. Reuben 1:3).

**5. "Child" as the designation of an inhabitant of a particular city.** Jerusalem is personified as a mother and her inhabitants as children (Lam. 1:5). Jesus cried out over the plight of his beloved city and referred to her children (Matt. 23:37; Luke 13:34; 19:44; cf. Gal. 4:25). Translating the Hebrew word for "son" as "child," the LXX adds to the evidence of the usage here under discussion (Joel 2:23; Zech. 9:13; cf. Bar. 4:19, 21, etc.; I Macc. 1:38).

*See also* FAMILY; MARRIAGE; WOMAN; CHILDREN OF GOD.

*Bibliography.* H. L. Ginsberg, "The Legend of King Keret," *BASOR,* Supplementary Studies, nos. 2-3 (1946), p. 14; W. H. Brownlee, "The Dead Sea Manual of Discipline," *BASOR,* Supplementary Studies, nos. 10-12 (1951), p. 8.

*See also* the bibliographies under FAMILY; WOMAN; MARRIAGE.           O. J. BAAB

**CHILDREN, SONG OF THE THREE.** *See* SONG OF THE THREE YOUNG MEN.

**CHILDREN OF GOD.** For the (mainly OT) use of the phrase "sons of God" for supernatural beings, *see* SONS OF GOD. The singular, "SON OF GOD," is applied mainly to Christ or, in the OT, to the royal representative of the chosen people, or collectively to the people.

There is little to be gained by pressing a distinction between "children" and "sons" of God. In either case, the phrase, in both OT and NT, mostly connotes a moral or spiritual relationship to God. Even when it means "Israelites," it carries more than a quasi-physical idea of relationship. In the NT this becomes all the clearer, in that the believing Gentiles are expressly included and nonbelieving Israelites are excluded. The phrase is not, with only very few exceptions, applied to mankind as such, as though they were actually God's children, even if they are such potentially. Rather, it is in and through Christ that men are adopted or reborn into this relationship. And the glorious plan of God for mankind is to be achieved by his "bringing many sons to glory" through Christ—i.e., by the transmission of Christ's filial obedience to others. Thus, and not by any mere automatic evolution, will come the "glorious liberty of the children of God"; thus will be attained "mature manhood, . . . the measure of the stature of the fulness of Christ."

1. Terminology of children (sons) of God
2. OT usage
3. NT usage
    *a.* Moral content
    *b.* The sayings of Jesus
    *c.* Limited application of the term
    *d.* Children by God's favor
    *e.* Sonship and the future
Bibliography

**1. Terminology of children (sons) of God.** The difference (if any) between "children" and "sons" might represent a difference of emphasis as between nature or origin and status or relationship respectively. But if such a distinction may be faintly traced in the NT, as between τέκνα and υἱοί (*see* § 3*c below*), it does not seem possible in English to mark a distinction in the OT. It is worth noting, however, that in the Hebrew the regular word in our phrase is בֵּן (*ben*), not יֶלֶד (*yeled*); Jer. 31:20 (RSV "child"; LXX [38:20] παιδίον) is an exception. For the Greek of the OT, all that can be said is:

*a*) Τέκνον has, for whatever reason, a more limited range than υἱός. It is, in fact, seldom used in the LXX in our phrase. Among the few exceptions may be reckoned Deut. 32:5 (but in a negative form [contrast Phil. 2:15]: "They are no longer his children because of their blemish"; and in any case the text of the passage is uncertain); Jer. 3:19 (by implication: τάξω δε εἰς τέκνα, "I thought how I would set you among my sons"). In Hos. 11:1 the Greek has altered the sense of the original (τὰ τέκνα αὐτοῦ, "his children," for "my son").

*b*) Υἱός, by contrast, does duty not only in this connotation of relationship with God but also in a wide range of other meanings. (Strangely enough, in Deut. 32:43, υἱοὶ αὐτοῦ actually stands for עֲבָדָיו, "his servants.")

*c*) Παῖς, which can mean both "servant" and "child," occurs (in our phrase) in Wisd. Sol. 9:4; 12:7, 20 (RSV "servants," mg. "children"); 19:6 (RSV "children," mg. "servants"); and in II Macc.

7:34 οἱ οὐράνιοι παῖδες may mean the same ("the children of heaven"). In the NT this word is never found in the plural coupled with a genitive of the divine name.

**2. OT usage.** The OT makes it clear that Hebrew thought—at any rate, as represented by the final editings of the books of the Bible—had little or no use for the pagan idea of God as, in some physical sense, the father and begetter of his children, the tribe springing from him. If this is the meaning of Deut. 32:6:

> Do you thus requite the LORD,
>     you foolish and senseless people?
> Is not he your father, who created you,
>     who made you and established you?

and of Mal. 2:10: "Have we not all one father? Has not one God created us?" and, in the singular, of such phrases as Pss. 2:7: "You are my son, today I have begotten you"; 110:3:

> From the womb of the morning
>     like dew your youth will come to you (?),

then these are exceptions to the general rule that when God is thought of as "Father," the relationship is a moral, not a physical, one.

In Isa. 1:2 the reference is clearly to a father's care and education of his children:

> Sons have I reared and brought up,
>     but they have rebelled against me

(cf. Mal. 1:6); and it is probably in this sense, rather than in a quasi-physical one, that we are to understand Exod. 4:22: "Israel is my first-born son"; Deut. 14:1: "You are the sons of the LORD your God"; Hos. 11:1: "Out of Egypt I called my son." Indeed, it is in Hosea that the moral content of the term is made particularly clear. In Hos. 1:10 it is only in the future, when the punishment for apostasy and unfaithfulness is conceived of as over and done with, that Israel will be called "sons of the living God." This is the hoped-for future reversal of the doom contained in the phrase "not my people" (Hos. 1:9). So, in the vision of a future restoration, God is heard to say (Jer. 31:9):

> I am a father to Israel,
>     and Ephraim is my first-born;

and in Isa. 43:6 (perhaps alluded to in II Cor. 6:18) the exiles, chastened, purified, and at last returning, are designated God's sons and daughters (cf. Isa. 30: 1, 9; Jer. 3:4, 19, 22). Equally clearly it is a religious relationship in Isa. 63:16, in the moving address to God by persons who (perhaps) had been "unchurched" by orthodox Jews, but who claim that God is their Father, even if Abraham and Israel will not own them (cf. the words of John the Baptist in Matt. 3:8-9 [=Luke 3:8]: "Bear fruit that befits repentance, and do not presume to say to yourselves, 'We have Abraham as our father'; for I tell you, God is able from these stones to raise up children to Abraham").

In the writings of the Apoc. the following uses may be cited: In Wisd. Sol. 2:18 the upright, godly man is taunted by his enemies as they prepare to torture him. Let us see, they say, whether God will rescue him and vindicate his claim to be the son of God (*see* SON OF GOD; and cf. the taunts leveled at Jesus on the cross [Matt. 27:40 ff and parallels]). In 5:5 they utter a recantation (reminiscent of the change of mind in Isa. 53:4): We thought his life was madness; we mocked him; how comes it that, after all, he has been reckoned among the sons of God? In other passages God's sons are the Israelites as distinguished from the heathen nations (note that in Num. 21:29 the Moabites are sons and daughters of Chemosh; cf. Mal. 2:11)—e.g., Jth. 9:4, 13; Add. to Esth. 16:16; Wisd. Sol. 9:7; 12:19, 21; Ecclus. 36:12 (πρωτόγονος, "first-born son"); III Macc. 6:28; cf. Pss. Sol. 17:27.

**3. NT usage.** *a. Moral content.* In the NT the moral content of the term (whether with "children" or with "sons"—for any distinction there may be, *see* § *3c below*) becomes even more firmly established in proportion as its limitation to Israel in the narrower sense is abandoned and its application to the "Israel of God" (cf., perhaps, Isa. 63:16, cited above) is accepted. Very pointedly this occurs in Rom. 9:7-8, 25-26, where Hos. 1:10 is cited but applied to the acceptance of the Gentiles (cf. Gal. 3:7 ff: "It is men of faith who are the sons of Abraham"). Conversely, the merely nationalist claim (divorced from a deeply religious attitude) is sharply repudiated in John 8:41-42, 44: " 'We have one Father, even God.' Jesus said to them, 'If God were your Father, you would love me. . . . You are of your father the devil' " (for the latter phrase, cf. Matt. 13:38: "the sons of the evil one"; Acts 13:10: "You son of the devil"). With this may be compared the Baptist's words quoted above (Matt. 3:8-9 and parallel).

*b. The sayings of Jesus.* In certain passages to be adduced shortly from the Pauline letters, it is natural to see the reflection of the controversies, subsequent to the death and resurrection of Christ, over the admission of Gentiles into the Christian church; and it is possible that the passage already alluded to in John 8 bears a similar stamp. Its context contains words strikingly similar to the Pauline thought: "The slave does not continue in the house for ever; the son continues for ever. So if the Son makes you free, you will be free indeed" (John 8:35-36). But if in such passages the thinking and conflicts of the post-resurrection church may find an echo, there are sayings in the Synoptic gospels, simply carrying on and deepening the OT line of thought, which seem to fit quite naturally into the actual setting of the ministry of Jesus himself. Such are, e.g., Matt. 5:9: "Blessed are the peacemakers, for they shall be called sons [υἱοί] of God" (it is hardly plausible to interpret this as in Luke 20:36, as though it meant that they are destined to become angels); and again, Matt. 5:44-45: "I say to you, Love your enemies and pray for those who persecute you, so that you may be sons [υἱοί] of your Father who is in heaven; for he makes his sun rise on the evil and on the good." It is the impartially good, those who are deeply concerned for their fellow men, who are, by character, allied with God himself. Cf. Luke 6:35 ("sons of the Most High").

One might set side by side with this, as similarly "pre-christological" in outlook, the words in Heb. 12:5-8, where a measure of suffering is described as a sign that the Christians are truly sons (υἱοί) of God —not bastards about whom a father does not care, but under the careful discipline of the heavenly Fa-

ther. There is another saying of Jesus which, while in no way anachronous with his ministry on earth, anticipates in a striking manner the "christocentric" note of the idea of sonship in the letters—namely, Matt. 12:48-50 (cf. Mark 3:33-35; Luke 8:21): " 'Who is my mother, and who are my brothers?' And stretching out his hand toward his disciples, he said, 'Here are my mother and my brothers! For whoever does the will of my Father in heaven is my brother, and sister, and mother.' " Here are the Pauline ideas of filial obedience and of Jesus as the first-born among many brethren, but in a plausibly pre-resurrection form. Yet again the famous saying in Matt. 11:25 ff = Luke 10:21-22 (though this is primarily relevant under SON OF GOD), is reminiscent of the same thought; for here Christ as Son, in a unique sense, is able to make known the fatherhood of God to others, who are thus (it may be deduced) to become sons by adoption.

*c. Limited application of the term.* The NT does not seem to present a doctrine of all men as such being children of God, any more than the OT sees others than the chosen people (or those who, in some special sense, have become their counterpart, as possibly in Isa. 63:16, cited above) in this status. Adam, it is true, is the son of God in Luke's genealogy (3: 38), and all men are God's offspring in Acts 17:28. But these passages are far from typical. Even the strange application of Ps. 82:6 in John 10:35 ("You are gods," which in the psalm is continued by "sons of the Most High") is confined to those "to whom the word of God came" (*see* SONS OF GOD for the original meaning of the psalm). Thus, while all men are potentially the children of God, those alone are normally described as actually such who have been adopted (Paul) or begotten or born anew (John 3:3; I Pet. 1:3; 2:2) or given birth to by God (Jas. 1:18: "He brought us forth," which seems to be more easily interpretable of Christians than of the human race; strangely, the verb is appropriate to a mother's giving birth rather than to a father's begetting). *See* GOD, NT, § *5c*.

The variety of metaphors just alluded to—adoption, begetting, birth—lends some color to the possibility (*see* § *1 above*) that there is sometimes a just discernible distinction between "children" (τέκνα) and "sons" (υἱοί)—the former more appropriate to the metaphor of birth or begetting, the latter to that of adoption and the giving of status. But it is unprofitable to press the distinction, and the fact that υἱοί and τέκνα are both used by Paul in this connection, but only τέκνα in the Johannines (except in references to Christ, and once, by implication, in John 8:35), may be merely a matter of style.

*d. Children by God's favor.* Allusion to the limited application of the term calls for closer inspection of the most characteristic aspect of the NT conception of the sons of God—namely, that the status of son, belonging essentially and inherently to Christ, is mediated by him to men and only in Christ can belong to men. Thus, John 1:11-12: "He came to his own home, and his own people received him not. But to all who received him, who believed in his name, he gave power [better, 'the right'] to become children [τέκνα] of God"; or, in Pauline terms (Rom. 8:29): "Those whom he foreknew he also predestined to be conformed to the image of his Son, in order that he might be the first-born among many brethren" (cf. Heb. 2:10).

Putting the same thing in another way, Paul (though not very frequently) uses the analogy of ADOPTION, and, contrasting slave status with sonship, says that to be able to utter the same cry of filial obedience which Jesus himself uttered is a gift of the "spirit of sonship" (or, better, the Spirit who brings about adoption): "You have received the spirit of sonship [better, the 'Spirit who brings about adoption']. When we cry, 'Abba! Father!' it is the Spirit himself bearing witness with our spirit that we are children [τέκνα] of God" (Rom. 8:15-16). In Gal. 3: 23–4:7 the thought is worked out in fuller detail, showing that this filial attitude goes together with the conscious response of faith (see HOLY SPIRIT). So in Phil. 2:15 it is the Christians, in sharp contrast to the rest, who are described (evidently with an allusion to the "blemished" children of God, his unworthy representatives, in Deut. 32:5; see § 1a above) as "blameless and innocent, children [τέκνα] of God without blemish in the midst of a crooked and perverse generation."

"Baptismal regeneration" is the sacramental expression of this relationship; and the association of water and Spirit with the theme of rebirth in John 3:5 makes it natural to see there an allusion to it. But otherwise, the nearest that the NT comes to the phrase is in Tit. 3:5: "by the washing of regeneration and renewal in the Holy Spirit." Possibly I Pet. 3:21 ought to be added to this, if it contains an allusion to some aspect of ADOPTION in a baptismal context. See also BAPTISM; FAMILY; FATHER; GOD, NT.

It should be added that in I John 3:1 some commentators see a reference to some distinction between mere "adoption" and a more essential relationship: "See what love the Father has given us, that we should be called children of God; and so we are." Others, however, would treat "and so we are" as a contrast, less with our merely being "called" children than with the future condition to which reference is made in the next verse (see ADOPTION § 3).

*e. Sonship and the future.* Taking up I John 3:1 ff again, we find the affirmation that, while Christians are already sons (τέκνα) of God, there is yet to come some fuller manifestation of the meaning of this condition (or its confirmation is awaited in some fuller manifestation of Christ). This is to be when Christ "appears"; and the outlook thus expressed is in keeping with the NT doctrine that sonship to God is fraught with a high destiny which is ultimately to be revealed. This is described in Rom. 8:21 as the "glorious liberty of the children [τέκνα] of God." In its context this appears to mean the liberation of all creation (not only of humanity) from servitude to frustration and decay and mortality, a liberation which is to be divulged as soon as the glory of true sonship is achieved. Heb. 2:10 describes the same destiny as the "bringing of sons to glory." Christ, the absolutely obedient and perfect Son of God, having pioneered the way (cf. Heb. 2:10-18; 5:8-9), it remains for the rest, in him, to be brought to the full realization of God's plan for them. Expressing the hope individually, Rev. 21:7 promises to anyone who "conquers" that he shall be God's son (υἱός). This is the mes-

sianic promise (II Sam. 7:14) transferred to the Christian (see SON OF GOD). But in Eph. 4:13 the hope takes shape as the noble expectation of full-grown maturity: "until we all attain to the unity of the faith and of the knowledge of the Son of God, to mature manhood, to the measure of the stature of the fulness of Christ." This will be the coming of age of mankind. See PLEROMA.

*Bibliography.* M.-J. Lagrange, "La paternité divine dans l'AT," *RB* (1908), pp. 481 ff; *Le Judaisme avant Jésus-Christ* (1931), pp. 459 ff.      C. F. D. MOULE

**CHILDREN OF THE EAST.** KJV alternate translation of בני קדם (RSV EAST, PEOPLE OF THE).

**CHILEAB** kĭl′ĭ ăb [כלאב; LXX Δαλουιά] (II Sam. 3:3). The second son of David; born in Hebron, of Abigail the widow of Nabal. In I Chr. 3:1 he is called Daniel (דניאל; LXX Δαμνιήλ [B], Δαλουιά [A]).

**CHILIASM** kĭl′ĭ ăz′əm [χιλιάσμος, *from* χίλιοι, thousand]. A synonym of "millennialism." More specifically, "chiliasm" denotes an early Christian concept, which came into disrepute, of a MILLENNIUM characterized by materialistic and sensuous enjoyments.      M. RIST

**CHILION** kĭl′ĭ ən [כליון]. One of the two sons of Elimelech and Naomi, who migrated to Moab. Chilion married the Moabitess Orpah (Ruth 1:2 ff; 4:9).

**★CHILMAD** kĭl′măd [כלמד]. A place name listed in juxtaposition with Asshur (Ezek. 27:23); located near modern Baghdad.

**CHIMHAM** kĭm′hăm [כמהם (II Sam. 19:37-38—H 19:38-39); כמהן (II Sam. 19:40—H 19:41); כמוהם (Jer. 41:17 K)]. Son of Barzillai the Gileadite. He returned with David in lieu—and at the instance—of his father (II Sam. 19:37-40—H 19:38-41). In appreciation for the generous aid Barzillai had provided the king at Mahanaim, Chimham appears to have received a royal pension (I Kings 2:7) and a grant of land near Bethlehem, known in later times as Geruth Chimham (lit. "the lodging place of Chimham"), where Johanan ben Kareah and his band encamped as they prepared to go to Egypt (Jer. 41:17).      E. R. DALGLISH

**CHIMNEY.** 1. KJV translation of ארבה (RSV WINDOW) in Hos. 13:3.

2. KJV translation of Latin *caminus* (RSV, with Syr., FOOTSTOOL) in II Esd. 6:4.

**CHINNEROTH** kĭn′ə rŏth [כנרות] (Josh. 11:2; 12:3; I Kings 15:20); **CHINNERETH** kĭn′ə rĕth [כנרת] (Num. 34:11; Deut. 3:17; Josh. 13:27; 19:35); KJV **CINNEROTH** sĭn′ə rŏth in I Kings 15:20.
1. Early name of the Sea of Galilee. See GALILEE, SEA OF.
2. A district in Naphtali taken by Ben-hadad during the reign of Baasha in the early ninth century (I Kings 15:20).
3. A fortified city in Naphtali (Josh. 19:35), also mentioned in the list of towns conquered by Thut-

mose III. It is located at Tell el-'Oreimeh, situated on a hill dominating the fertile spring-fed plain along the NW side of the Sea of Galilee. Minor excavations have shown that the mound was occupied from MB to Iron I (i.e., *ca.* 2000-900 B.C.). On the hill itself, Paleolithic and Mesolithic artifacts have been found.

*Bibliography.* W. F. Albright, "The Jordan Valley in the Bronze Age," *AASOR,* VI (1926), 24-26; F.-M. Abel, *Géographie de la Palestine,* II (1938), 18-19, 299.

G. W. VAN BEEK

**CHIOS** kī'ŏs [ἡ Χίος] (Acts 20:15). A rocky and rather mountainous island in the E central region of the Aegean Sea. It measures thirty-two miles from N to S and eight to eighteen miles from E to W. A strait five or more miles wide and dotted with small islands separates it from the mainland of Asia Minor. Chios was famous for its wines, figs, and gum mastic, and was one of seven places which claimed to be the birthplace of Homer. Its chief city was Chios (now Scio).

Josephus (Antiq. XVI.ii.2) tells that King Herod, sailing N from Cos and trying to reach Lesbos, was driven back by a N wind to Chios, and gave the city funds to rebuild its colonnades.

In Paul's day Chios was a free city in the Roman province of Asia. Paul, on his final journey to Jerusalem, sailed S from Mitylene, anchored overnight "opposite Chios" under protection of the mainland, and the next day crossed more open sea to Samos.

F. V. FILSON

**CHISLEV** kĭz'lĕv [כסלו; Χασελευ]; KJV CHISLEU —lōō. The ninth month in the Hebrew CALENDAR; the Akkadian *kislīmu* (November-December).

**CHISLON** kĭs'lŏn [כסלון, slow] (Num. 34:21). The father of Elidad, who was selected from Benjamin to help superintend the distribution of W Jordanian Canaan among the ten tribes to occupy that territory.

*Bibliography.* M. Noth, *Die israelitischen Personennamen* (1928), p. 227.

R. F. JOHNSON

**CHISLOTH-TABOR** kĭs'lŏth tā'bər [כסלת תבר] (Josh. 19:12). A town in lower Galilee on the border between the territories of Zebulun and Issachar; the same as Chesulloth in Josh. 19:18. It is identified with Iksal, a village located *ca.* three miles SE of Nazareth and four miles W of Mount Tabor at the N edge of the Valley of Jezreel.

*Bibliography.* C. R. Conder and H. H. Kitchener, *SWP,* I (1881), 363, 366, 385-87; F.-M. Abel, *Géographie de la Palestine,* II (1938), 299.

G. W. VAN BEEK

**CHITLISH** kĭt'lĭsh [כתליש] (Josh. 15:40); KJV KITHLISH kĭth'—. A city of Judah in the Shephelah district of Lachish. It is possibly to be identified with Kentisha in the Palestinian list of Thut-mose III (*ca.* 1490-1436); the name (*k-n-ti-sa*) is also found on an ostracon from the reign of Mer-ne-ptah (*ca.* 1224-1216) found at Lachish.

V. R. GOLD

**CHITTIM.** KJV form of KITTIM.

**CHIUN.** KJV form of Kaiwan. *See* SAKKUTH.

**CHLOE** klō'ĭ [Χλόη, the Verdant] (I Cor. 1:11). A woman whose slaves or the members of whose household informed Paul—working in Ephesus—that there were partisan divisions among the Corinthian Christians. Whether she was herself a Christian, and whether she lived in Ephesus or Corinth, are matters impossible to determine with the evidence available. However, she was well enough known to Paul and to the Corinthian congregation to establish the standing of Paul's informants.

J. M. NORRIS

**CHOBA** kō'bə [Χωβα]. One of the N villages of Palestine which rallied to the fortification of the mountain passes against the invasion of the "Assyrian" forces under Holofernes (Jth. 4:4). In the rout of the enemy after the murder of their commander by Judith, the Jews of all Palestine pursued and slaughtered them to Choba (15:4-5) and beyond Damascus.

The exact location is unknown, but many identify it with el-Mekhubbi between Besan and Tubass on an important road leading from Besan into the Samaritan hill country. Abel (*see· bibliography*) thinks it is borrowed from the HOBAH of Gen. 14:15, N of Damascus.

*Bibliography.* F.-M. Abel, *Géographie de la Palestine,* II (1938) 299; F. Stummer, *Geographie des Buches Judith* (1947), p. 16.

E. W. SAUNDERS

**CHOIR.** *See* MUSIC.

**CHOR-ASHAN** kôr ā'shən. KJV form of Borashan. *See* ASHAN.

**CHORAZIN** kō rā'zĭn [Χοραζίν, Χοραζείν]. A city of Galilee reproached by Jesus (Matt. 11:21; Luke 10:13). Fig. CHO 27.

There is general agreement that the Chorazin of the NT should be identified with the ruins now known as Khirbet Kerazeh, which is two miles N of Capernaum, the modern Tell Hum. This agrees with Jerome (*ca.* A.D. 400), who places it two miles distant from Capernaum (*De Situ et Nom. Loc. Hebr.* 194).

Chorazin was built on the basalt hills above Capernaum. The extensive ruins indicate that it was a city of some importance. Typical of the buildings are the remains of a synagogue built out of the black

Courtesy of the Hebrew University, Jerusalem, Israel
27. Chorazin, the modern town of Khirbet Kerazeh

volcanic rock *ca.* the fourth century A.D. Among the ruins there was found a carved seat with an inscription, an example of "Moses' seat" (cf. Matt. 23:2). The city is mentioned in the Talmud in the Hebrew form "Chorazim" (כרזים) as a place famous for its wheat (T.B. Men. 85*a*).

Both Chorazin and Bethsaida were reproved by Jesus for their unbelief, and both were near the third city included in his censure, Capernaum, which was the center of his Galilean ministry.

**Bibliography.** G. Dalman, *Orte und Wege Jesu* (1919), pp. 149-51, 157; F.-M. Abel, *Géographie de la Palestine*, II (1938), 154, 299-300.        D. C. PELLETT

**CHORBE** kôr'bĭ [Χορβέ] (I Esd. 5:32); KJV CORBE. Alternate name of ZACCAI.

**CHOSAMAEUS** kŏs'ə mē'əs [Χοσάμαος (B), Χοσομαιος (A)]. A name attached to, or following, Simon in I Esd. 9:32, which is difficult to account for. While "Simon" represents "Shimeon" in Ezra 10:31, the following three names of Ezra 10:32 are wanting in I Esdras. The name Chosamaeus probably arose as the result of a scribal error in copying the three Greek proper names following Shimeon in the Ezra text.        C. T. FRITSCH

**CHOSEN ONE** [בחור, ἐκλεκτός]. In the OT, a name of honor, among others, of the SERVANT OF THE LORD (*see also* ELECTION); in the Ethiopian book of Enoch, the title of the SON OF MAN.

**CHOSEN PEOPLE.** *See* ELECTION.

**CHOZEBA.** KJV form of COZEBA.

*****CHRIST** krĭst [Χριστός, ὁ Χριστός; משׁח; Aram. משׁחא, anointed; the Anointed One, the Messiah]. A title applied to the coming king expected by the Jews (*see* MESSIAH, JEWISH), and in the NT the most common title of Jesus. Usually in the NT the word is translated into Greek, but twice (in John 1:41; 4:25) it is transliterated as Μεσσίας. In the gospels it usually retains its force as an adjectival epithet—e.g., "You are the Christ" (Mark 8:29); "the Lord's Christ" (Luke 2:26); "Jesus as the Christ" (Acts 5:42). But it soon became practically a name or surname for Jesus —e.g., "the gospel of Jesus Christ, the Son of God" (Mark 1:1); "While we were yet sinners Christ died for us" (Rom. 5:8); "baptized into Christ Jesus" (Rom. 6:3). "Christology" means properly the department of theology which deals with Jesus' messiahship; but since the word "Christ" in the NT is related to every aspect of Jesus' nature, it is the theology of his person, attributes, and mission.

1. The OT background
2. The Apoc. and Pseudep.
3. Rabbinic Judaism
4. Moses and the Logos in Philo
5. The Gospel of Mark
6. Q
7. Matthew
8. Luke-Acts
9. Paul
10. Later NT books
   *a.* Ephesians
   *b.* Hebrews
   *c.* Revelation
   *d.* I Peter
   *e.* The Pastoral letters
   *f.* Other documents
11. The Gospel of John
12. The Apostolic Fathers
13. The genesis of Christology
Bibliography

**1. The OT background.** Christology developed on the basis of the OT and Jewish hopes of the coming king and the future time of salvation. The Hebrew king (I Sam. 10:1; 16:13) and the high priest (Num. 35:25) were anointed on accession to office; hence the king was often called the "Lord's anointed" (I Sam. 16:6; cf. Luke 2:26). The later parts of the OT expect an ideal ruler, descended from David, in whose time God will establish a perfect and permanent reign on earth, characterized by peace and prosperity, righteousness, justice, and the knowledge and true worship of God. There are, however, books of the OT and noncanonical Jewish literature in which the future age is brought directly by God and no mention is made of any messianic figure. *See* ESCHATOLOGY OF THE OT.

It is not certain whether messianism first arises out of prophecies of the future destiny of Israel (e.g., Gen. 12:1-3; 49:10; Num. 24:17-19) or from the hope that David's dynasty will be permanent. Perhaps the earliest Davidic prophecy is Ps. 18 (= II Sam. 22:2-51). Hos. 1:11 prophesies that Judah and Israel will be united under a single head. Ezekiel, in the time of the Exile, includes in his picture of the future the permanent rule of a Davidic prince who will be a true shepherd of the people (37:24). The last clearly datable form of the Davidic hope in the OT is in Hag. 2:21-23; Zech. 4:6-10; both prophets apparently expect the restoration of the throne under Zerubbabel. This is not to occur by revolt against the Persian Empire: "Not by might, nor by power, but by my Spirit, says the LORD of hosts" (Zech. 4:6). Ps. 132 does not appear to go beyond the pre-exilic hope for a permanent monarchy (cf. Pss. 78: 65-72; 89:19-37). Amos 9:11-12 is probably a postexilic oracle:

> In that day I will raise up
>    the booth of David *that is fallen*
> . . . . . . . . . . . . . . . . . .
>    and rebuild it as in the days of old.

The oracles in Isa. 9–11 mark the highest point of the Davidic concept in the OT. There will be a "Prince of Peace," whose government on the throne of David will be established in justice and righteousness and will have no end (Isa. 9:6-7). A shoot will spring from the stump of Jesse; the spirit of the Lord will rest upon him, he will judge with justice and vindicate the poor of the land, and even brute nature will live at peace,

> for the earth shall be full of the knowledge of the LORD
>    as the waters cover the sea (Isa. 11:1-9).

In Second Isaiah, however, the Davidic king retires into the background. God's "steadfast, sure love for David" will not fail, and God will make an everlasting covenant (Isa. 55:3), but there is no explicit promise of the re-establishment of the monarchy. The people as a whole are the object of expectation. The servant of the Lord, who suffers, bears the sins of many, and makes intercession for the transgressors, is often described as an individual (Isa. 52:13–53:12), but he appears to be a symbol of Israel itself (Isa. 49:3). This idea was to be of great importance in the later development of messianism and Christology. *See* SERVANT OF THE LORD.

In Joel, Nahum, and Zephaniah, God himself will act directly, and no ideal king is mentioned. The same is true of Malachi, except that God will send Elijah the prophet before the coming of the day of the Lord (Mal. 4:5-6). In Daniel, God likewise will bring a new age, when "one like a son of man," representing the "saints of the most high," will take the place of the beast kingdoms and exercise an everlasting dominion (Dan. 7:13-14, 26-27; *see* SON OF MAN § 1).

**2. The Apoc. and Pseudep.** Thus the hope which was to become messianic appears only sporadically after the Exile. The small state of Judah was ruled by high priests in the Persian and Ptolemaic periods, and Davidic speculation retired into the background. Ecclesiasticus, or Ben Sirach, written just before the Maccabean Revolt, exalts the Davidic monarchy (Ecclus. 47:22) but says that all the kings except David, Hezekiah, and Josiah were sinners (Ecclus. 49:4); the high priest Simon son of Onias is Ben Sirach's great hero (Ecclus. 50:1-21). The Wisdom of Solomon has no concept of a Davidic Messiah.

The rise of a Maccabean dynasty of high priests turned the Jewish hope in a different direction. The Testaments of the Twelve Patriarchs celebrate the raising up of a new priest, whose star will rise in heaven like that of a king (Test. Levi 18:1-3). He will bring peace on earth, knowledge will come to the Gentiles, and sin will have an end (18:9); he will open the gates of paradise and give the saints to eat from the tree of life (18:11). The Lord has chosen Levi to be king over all the nation, and his reign will be eternal (Test. Reuben 6:10-12). The messianic reign has now become more miraculous and approaches the ideas of the book of Enoch, which perhaps was written about this time, and in which the messianic figure is the Elect One or Son of man. *See* SON OF MAN § 2; ENOCH, BOOK OF.

The cruelties of the later Maccabees and Pompey's capture of Jerusalem in 63 B.C. led to a revival of Davidic messianism. Not long after 63, the Psalms of Solomon denounce the Maccabees (1:8; 2:3) and pray that the Lord will raise up the true king, the son of David, who will destroy the godless nations with the word of his mouth, gather a holy people, and lead them in righteousness. Heathen nations will serve under his yoke. He will not trust in horse or rider or bow nor multiply gold and silver for war, for the Lord himself will be king (17:5-8, 23-28). This king is called the "Lord's anointed" (18:6-8).

The sectarians of Qumran, who wrote the Dead Sea Scrolls and were probably Essenes, rejected the Maccabean priests but not the priestly ideal. They expected a Messiah of Israel, presumably a civil ruler, and also a priest, who takes precedence over him in the sacred banquet (fragment of the Manual of Discipline, 1QSa 2.19-20). Yet it is not absolutely certain that both of these are messiahs in the strict sense of the word, for some of the writings speak of a "messiah from Aaron and Israel"—i.e., from the holy community—and others of "messiahs from Aaron and Israel" (1QS 9.11). One fragmentary collection of scriptural quotations combines Deut. 5:28-29; 18:18-19; Num. 24:15-17 (the prophecy of the star); and Deut. 33:8-11, and concludes with an excerpt from an apocryphal book. This is a close parallel to NT ideas and methods.

The first non-Christian book to use the phrase "the Messiah" in the absolute sense is the Syriac Apocalypse of Baruch, written perhaps at the time of the Jewish War (A.D. 66-70). When sin and misery have reached their climax, the Messiah will begin to be revealed; the monsters Behemoth and Leviathan will be given as food (29:3-4). Then follows a prophecy of miraculous plenty which Papias of Hierapolis attributed to Jesus (29:5). The treasury of manna will descend from on high (29:8). When the Messiah's time is finished, he will return in glory, and all who have fallen asleep in hope of him will rise again (30:1-2). The ideas of the messianic banquet and the manna are reminiscent of the gospels (e.g., Luke 14:15; 22:28-30; John 6:27-35).

The central portion of II Esdras is still later in date but related to the Apocalypse of Baruch. Here it is said that the Messiah will be revealed and will remain for four hundred years, after which he and all other living things will die, and the world will return to its primeval silence for seven days. Then follow the new world, the resurrection, and the judgment (II Esd. 7:28-35; the references in the present text to "my son" and "my son Jesus" are probably Christian interpolations).

Messianic expectation remained vivid until the end of the Second Jewish Revolt in A.D. 135. The numerous revolutionists mentioned by Josephus and by Acts (5:36-37; 21:38) may have been messianic pretenders like Simeon bar Cocheba, whom Rabbi Akiba hailed as Messiah. On the other hand, the Assumption of Moses, a document of the first century A.D., has no Messiah, and God brings in his kingdom directly. *See* ESCHATOLOGY OF APOC. AND PSEUDEP.

**3. Rabbinic Judaism.** The Messiah is not particularly prominent in the rabbinic writings, but enough traditions remain to show that in the first two centuries there were messianic speculations in Pharisaic circles. The rabbis taught that the Messiah would come at a time known only to God himself and would remain hidden until he revealed himself and proved his identity by messianic deeds and miracles (cf. Just. Dial. 8.4). Attempts to calculate the time of his coming were generally discouraged by the rabbis. It is occasionally said that the sins of Israel delay his advent. Several rabbinic ideas furnish interesting parallels to the NT, even though they may have arisen at a later time. E.g., the Messiah is the intermediary between God and the people; he intercedes for them and obtains their forgiveness. The Targums identify him with the Servant of Second Isaiah; however, the latter is turned into a conqueror, and his sufferings are minimized. The rabbis also emphasize the righteousness and wisdom of the

Messiah; he has God's holy spirit and will teach the right understanding of the law (cf. John 4:25). He is called "redeemer" and "comforter."

Along with the son of David, rabbinic literature mentions a Messiah known as the son of Joseph or son of Ephraim, who dies in battle. That Messiah should die and have a temporary kingdom was not unknown in first-century Judaism. The son-of-Joseph idea may have arisen from the defeat of Simeon bar Cocheba in the Second Revolt or from the failures of Hezekiah and Judas the Galilean. Deut. 33:17, which speaks of Joseph as a bull with horns like a wild ox, perhaps suggested the concept. Attempts have been made to find the dying Messiah in Zech. 12:10-14, where the tribes mourn for him whom they have pierced, but there is no clear evidence for the Joseph Messiah as early as the first century A.D. He does not suffer vicariously for the sins of the people, and he is primarily a warrior.

**4. Moses and the Logos in Philo.** It cannot be proved that the concept of the Logos or Word of God held by the Alexandrian Jewish philosopher Philo (first century A.D.) influenced NT Christology, but Philo illustrates a current trend of thought. He explains the relation between God and the world by means of the Logos doctrine. The Logos is called the ἀρχή (beginning) of the world, God's eldest son, his first-born son, and "second God." God created the Logos and the ideas, which in turn are the archetypes of all things modeled after them. Philo declares that the God who appeared to Jacob at Bethel (Gen. 31:13) was the Logos (*On Dreams* I. 229-30). The Logos is suppliant on behalf of the race of mankind and the ambassador of God to man (*Who Is the Heir of Divine Things* 205-6). He is once called the eldest of the angels.

Philo regards the high priest as symbolizing the Logos (e.g., *Life of Moses* II. 24, 117-26), but there is a particularly close relation between the Logos and Moses. Moses was not only a lawgiver, but also the prophet who saw with the soul's eye the immaterial forms of the material objects about to be made for the tabernacle so that the shape of the model was stamped on his mind. Philo also calls Moses a propitiatory priest and king, and quotes Deut. 5:5: "I stood between the LORD and you," as spoken by the Logos, thus nearly identifying Moses as the embodiment of the Logos. From such conceptions it is only a step to Christology, though it must be borne in mind that in Philo the Logos is not quite an independent person. *See* LOGOS; PHILO JUDEUS.

**5. The Gospel of Mark.** In the earliest of the gospels, Christology has already developed considerably. Mark's most characteristic title for Jesus is SON OF GOD. Jesus is at the same time the suffering, dying, rising, and returning SON OF MAN and is occasionally called the Messiah (8:29; 14:61-62), the Lord (11:3), and God's beloved (1:11; 9:7). The title Son of David is given him by others (10:47-49), but he rejects it as, not applicable to the one who is David's Lord (12:35-37). While the Jewish background is important for understanding the precise reference of these terms, their content is actually defined by Mark's picture of the earthly Jesus, for Jesus is greater than any of the titles applied to him. He is herald of the KINGDOM OF GOD and its good

news (1:14-15) and the inaugurator of a new age (2:19). He is a prophet (6:4) and an apocalyptic teacher with supernatural knowledge (ch. 13), but, more than this, he teaches with absolute authority (11:33), and calls his disciples with authority (1:16-20; 2:14), so that to receive him is to receive God (9:37) and to do the will of God is to be kin to him (3:35). He heals, forgives sins (2:10), and has power over nature (4:35-41; 6:34-44, 45-52). His disciples feel a sense of awe, for they are in the presence of the numinous (4:41; 6:51; 10:32). Once they see him transfigured (9:2-8), so that they share the experience Jesus himself had at his baptism (1:9-11). At the Cross even a Roman centurion can say: "Truly this man was a son of God!" (15:39).

Through most of Jesus' ministry his nature remains a mystery to his disciples, and they do not even understand the suffering of the Son of man (6:52; 8:17-21, 32-33). Even his teaching cannot be understood without special revelation (4:10-13, 33-34). He refuses to explain his authority to his enemies (11:27-33). But the demons, being spirits, recognize him immediately (1:34) and address him as the "Holy One of God" (1:24), "Son of God" (3:11), and "Son of the Most High God" (5:7; a title appropriate on pagan lips). Mark has to some extent imposed on his sources the "messianic secret" theory which helped early Christians explain why Jesus had been rejected. *See* SECRET, MESSIANIC.

In Mark, Jesus is human as well as divine. Behind the story of the baptism there may be the thought that on this occasion Jesus was adopted as Son of God, for the Spirit descends into him (1:10). Subsequently he is tested by Satan (1:13; *see* TEMPTATION OF JESUS). He asserts that no one is good but God alone (10:18); he cannot appoint disciples to sit at his right hand and left (10:40); the mark of his vocation is humble service (10:45); and he does not know all the details of the future (13:32). In Gethsemane he prays the Father that the cup may pass from him but leaves the decision to the will of God (14:35), and on the cross cries out: "My God, my God, why hast thou forsaken me?" (15:34). *See* PASSION, THE.

**6. Q.** The non-Markan passages of Matthew and Luke, usually known by the symbol Q, exhibit some variations in their interpretation of Jesus' mission and person.

In Q, Jesus appears as an authoritative ethical teacher, though his role as prophetic bringer of the kingdom is much more prominent. When addressed as κύριε ("Lord" or "Sir," perhaps "Rabbi"), he says that it is more important for his disciples to do his (or God's) will than to give him this title. The fact that they have eaten and drunk in his presence and he has taught in their streets will not save them when they confront him in the judgment (Luke 13:26-27).

In many passages which have christological importance there is no direct teaching about Jesus' person. The parable of the lost sheep (Matt. 18:12-14 = Luke 15:3-7) expresses Jesus' concern, as well as that of God, for the sinner, and implicitly justifies bringing the good news of the kingdom of God to outcasts. In the parable of the great supper (Matt. 22:1-10 = Luke 14:15-24) the defense of Jesus' mission becomes more explicit (cf. Matthew's parable of the laborers in the vineyard [20:1-15]). The parable of the talents or pounds (Matt. 25:14-30 = Luke 19: 11-27) may or may not have been specially applied to the disciples' responsibility to spread the gospel.

A whole group of passages contrasts the new age, inaugurated by Jesus' work, with the old. Jesus calls the attention of John the Baptist to his mighty deeds (Matt. 11:4-6 = Luke 7:22-23). He who is least in the kingdom of God is greater than John (Matt. 11:11 = Luke 7:28). The law and the prophets were until John, but the age of the kingdom of God is proclaimed, perhaps has dawned (Matt. 11:12 = Luke 16:16; cf. Matt. 12:28 = Luke 11:20; Matt. 13:16-17 = Luke 10:23-24).

The Q passage, in which Jesus sends his disciples to herald the kingdom of God (Luke 10:1-16 = Matt. 9:37-38; 10:7-16, 21-23, 40), teaches that he who receives the ones sent receives Jesus, and he who receives Jesus receives the one who sent him; Jesus is thus the emissary of God who is decisive for man's salvation. Connected with this in Q are numerous passages that reflect rejection of Jesus and his disciples, the conflict aroused by the new mission, and the sacrifices that must be borne by the faithful (e.g., Matt. 10:34-38 = Luke 12:51-53; 14:26-27; Matt. 12:30 = Luke 11:23).

Certain passages dealing with the new age (Luke 11:29-32 = Matt. 12:38-42), with the rejection of Jesus (Matt. 8:20 = Luke 9:58; Matt. 11:19 = Luke 7:34), and with discipleship (Matt. 10:26-33 = Luke 12:2-12; Matt. 24:43-51 = Luke 12:35-46) also identify Jesus as the Son of man. The collector of Q probably thought that Jesus would return as the celestial judge known by this title. *See* SON OF MAN § 3*a*.

All of the foregoing makes a reasonably consistent picture. But a new element is introduced in those passages where Jesus is identified as the Son of God and possibly also as the Wisdom of God. Jesus is addressed as Son of God in the temptation story, which is closely related to that of the baptism. Here the Son of God has superhuman powers. For him to possess the kingdoms of the world is a real possibility and temptation. "Son of God" in Q therefore describes a type of messiahship. In Matt. 11:25-30 = Luke 10:21-22, Jesus is the Son, but the emphasis is not now on his messianic office; it is on the hidden wisdom, revealed only to babes, delivered wholly to the Son, who alone knows the Father and alone is known by him. The idea that only the Son knows the Father is foreign to Judaism, and the whole passage introduces a new element into messiahship. Since it is based on Ecclus. 51:23-30, the discourse may identify Jesus with the heavenly WISDOM who figures so strongly in Proverbs, Wisdom of Solomon, and Ecclesiasticus. The oracle ascribed to the "Wisdom of God" in Luke 11:49-51 (= Matt. 23:34-36) may have been delivered by a prophet speaking in the name of the risen Christ. The lament over Jerusalem (Matt. 23:37-39 = Luke 13:34-35) likewise suggests Wisdom brooding like a dove over her children.

**7. Matthew.** The Christology of Q, like that of Mark, was highly developed. Matthew added little to the ideas of his sources. He gave increased emphasis to the interpretations of Jesus as Son of God, Messiah, and lawgiver. His principal contribution to the first is the story of the virgin birth (Matt. 1:18-25). As Messiah, however, Jesus inherited the royal dignity through his legal father, Joseph (1:1-17; *see* GENEALOGY OF CHRIST). The evangelist found it necessary to reconcile the known fact that Jesus' childhood home was Nazareth with the conviction that the Messiah must come from Bethlehem; hence both he and Luke emphasize Jesus' birth in that city. Matthew saw in the OT predictions of Jesus' messianic dignity and many incidents of his life (e.g., 1:23; 2:6, 15, 18; 4:15-16; 8:17; 12:18-21; 13:35). His special materials in the Sermon on the Mount are remarkable for the formula in which Jesus' teaching is contrasted with that of the ancients: "You have heard that it was said to the men of old . . . . But I say to you" (e.g., 5:21-22).

**8. Luke-Acts.** Though it is difficult to distinguish between the ideas of the evangelist and those of his special sources, Luke appears to have access to traditions dominated by the idea of the Messiah as son of David. Jesus was born in Bethlehem (Luke 2:4) and by a wondrous birth announced by the angel Gabriel (1:26-38). The virginity of Mary at the time of Jesus' birth is not specially emphasized, being suggested only in 1:34; 2:5. The language of 1:11, 32-33, 35; 2:26, 38, is the purest Jewish messianism, except that Jesus is also called Son of God. In 9:20, Peter hails Jesus as the "Christ of God," and in 23:35 Jesus is referred to as the "Christ of God, his Chosen One" (cf. 9:35: "my Son, my Chosen"). The hope that Jesus would restore the kingdom to Israel, or redeem it, is expressed in Luke 24:21; Acts 1:6 (cf. Luke 19: 11). Like Matthew, Luke emphasizes the fulfilment of scripture in the life of Jesus (e.g., Luke 24:25-27, 44-46, and frequently in Acts).

As Son of God, the boy Jesus thinks it only natural to be in his Father's house (Luke 2:49); on the other hand, he grew in wisdom and stature and in favor with God and man, and an important variant reading in 3:22, attested by the Western text, reads: "Thou art my Son, today I have begotten thee." The Spirit descends in *bodily form* at the time of his baptism, and afterward Jesus is filled with the Holy Spirit (4:1; cf. Acts 10:38, where Peter says that God anointed Jesus with the Holy Spirit and power). Luke's genealogy (3:23-38) traces Jesus' descent through Joseph to Adam, the son of God. Elsewhere in the special material Jesus speaks of God as his Father (22:28-30; 23:46; cf. 23:34, omitted by some MSS).

Luke's special material reflects an early interpretation of Jesus as prophet (7:16), and Jesus speaks of himself as a prophet (13:33). The same idea is expressed in 24:19: "a prophet mighty in deed and word before God and all the people"; and in Acts, Jesus is the prophet like Moses whom Moses promised (Acts 3:22-23). Several sayings of Jesus in the special material are prophetic in character (e.g., Luke 11:27-28; 12:14, 54-56; 13:1-9; cf. 16:19-31).

Other passages contain a larger miraculous element. Simon Peter, frightened by the wondrous catch of fish, asks Jesus to depart from him (Luke 5:8); Jesus sees Satan as fallen from heaven (10:17-20); on the cross he promises that the penitent thief that day will be with him in Paradise (23:43).

Luke differs from other synoptists in referring to Jesus as "the Lord," apparently in an absolute sense (e.g., 10:1; 11:39; 12:42; 17:5-6; 18:6; 19:8; 22:61; 24:34). The word κύριος (*see* LORD) has a wide range of reference in the NT, running all the way from "Sir" to a title or name of God. In his lifetime Jesus was frequently addressed as "Rabbi" or "Rabboni" (e.g., Mark 9:5; 11:21; 14:45), and the evangelists often render this as διδάσκαλος, "teacher" (e.g., Matt. 23:8; Mark 4:38; 13:1; Luke 7:40). Matthew twice in 23:10 uses the term καθηγητής, "instructor" or "teacher," and Luke several times ἐπιστάτης, "master" (e.g., 8:24; 9:33, 49). "Lord" is often used by the evangelists as a substitute for διδάσκαλος or "rabbi"—e.g., Matt. 7:21-22; 17:4, 15; Luke 7:6; 11:1; 18:41. But when Luke calls Jesus ὁ κύριος absolutely, he probably has in mind his heavenly dignity as Lord of all his people. Acts bears witness to the primitive idea that God raised Jesus up and made him both Lord and Messiah (2:36; cf. 3:13; 10:40-42; 13:32-35).

Other titles and predicates applied to Jesus in Acts are interesting as reflecting a rich tradition of preaching and teaching. He is called "savior" (5:31; 13:23), as in Luke 2:11, a term not very frequent in the NT (*see* SALVATION, SAVIOR); παῖς, "servant" or "child" (3:13, 26; 4:27, 30), a liturgical title that may refer to the Servant of Second Isaiah (*see* SERVANT OF THE LORD); ἀρχηγὸς τῆς ζωῆς, "prince," "pioneer or founder of life" (3:15; 5:31); the "Holy and Righteous One" (3:14; 7:52; 22:14); the "one who was to come" (19:4); etc. Some of these terms are nontechnical.

**9. Paul.** The letters of PAUL show that within a few years after the Crucifixion a very high Christology had developed. Paul has little interest in christological theory as such; what he has to say about the nature of Christ is incidental to his teaching about the work of Christ and the importance of faith in him as a saving person—and, coupled with faith, commitment and obedience. Yet his doctrine of Christ approaches that of the Fourth Gospel.

In all Paul's correspondence "Christ" is used as a name, either as a surname for "Jesus" or prefixed to it, or as a substitute for it. "Christ" also in a wider sense refers to the relationships of the risen Jesus. To be "in Christ" or "in Christ Jesus" means to be a Christian, with all that this implies (Paul does not use the word "Christian"). Furthermore, he uses a number of metaphors to express what has happened to the follower of Jesus. He has been justified or acquitted (Rom. 3:24); his defilement has been expiated (Rom. 3:25); he has been bought out of slavery to be Christ's slave and therefore free (Rom. 3:24; Gal. 3:13); by means of Christ's triumph over the forces of evil, the indenture which held him in slavery has now been canceled (Col. 2:14-15); though once an enemy, he is now reconciled to God (II Cor. 5:18-20); he has been adopted as God's son (Rom. 8:15-16) or has attained his majority (Gal. 4:1-5). All this depends on the life, death, and resurrection of Jesus and is made available by man's faith in Christ and identification with him. Thus, for Paul, Christ is the one who can do all this.

The Thessalonian letters, which are apparently the earliest, are concerned with the Parousia of

Christ (I Thess. 1:10; 3:13; 4:13-17; II Thess. 1:7-8; 2:8) and portray him in terms that suggest the "Son of man" figure of Enoch and the gospels. Over against him stands an antichrist, the "man of lawlessness," whom he will slay with the breath of his mouth (II Thess. 2:3-12). All these elements can be derived from Jewish apocalyptic (*see* ESCHATOLOGY OF NT; PAROUSIA). Jesus is, however, called Lord also (I Thess. 1:1).

Much is added to this in I Corinthians. As Christ or Messiah, he overturns the ordinary definition of messiahship; he is crucified, but nevertheless he is the power and wisdom of God (I Cor. 1:24). This wisdom is the foundation of all true knowledge and teaching (3:10) and is revealed through the Spirit (2:10); it is a mystery which the rulers of the world did not know (2:8). The Christian Messiah was active in the saving events of the OT; he was the rock, which according to Jewish midrash followed Moses and from whom the Israelites derived water; perhaps, too, he was the manna (10:1-4). Believers belong to his body, which is represented by the one loaf of the LORD'S SUPPER, and they share in his body and blood (10:16-17); the church, with its several members, is also his body (12:13-31). The Messiah is the heavenly man who is first to rise from the dead (15:20-23; *see* SON OF MAN; SECOND ADAM), and he will reign until he vanquishes all enemies, including death. But his rule ends when he hands the kingdom to God the Father, and God is all in all (15:24-27).

For Paul, Christ is in some sense subordinate to God; God is the head of Christ, as man is the head of woman (11:3). The term "Lord," used frequently in I Corinthians, suggests this also. There are many so-called gods and lords in the world, but in truth there is only one God, the Father, and one Lord, Jesus Christ (8:5-6). "Lord" suggests at one and the same time the Yahweh or Adonai of the OT; the term *Mar*, by which Aramaic-speaking Christians addressed Jesus (16:22); and the Gentile κύριοι, who were gods or heroes to their believers but demons to the Christians. One cannot share in the table of the (true) Lord and the tables of demons (10:21); on the other hand, the knowledge of Christ as Lord is, like the knowledge of his crucified messiahship, a gift of the Holy Spirit (12:3).

II Corinthians emphasizes the identification of the believer with Christ and adds three principal points: (*a*) The Lord Jesus Christ, who had been rich—i.e., possessed of divine wealth and power—became poor so that his followers might become rich (8:9; *see* INCARNATION). (*b*) His is the new covenant, as contrasted with the Mosaic covenant of condemnation, with its transient glory. Believers who gaze with unveiled face behold and reflect the glory of the Lord, who is the Spirit (3:4-18). But this is also the glory of Christ, who is the image (εἰκών) of God, and the glory of God in the face of Christ shines in the hearts (i.e., minds) of the apostles (4:4-6). Christ is therefore related as closely as possible to God and so closely related to the Spirit that the distinction is not clear (*see* HOLY SPIRIT); yet in 13:13 Paul speaks of the grace of the Lord Jesus Christ, the love of God, and the fellowship of (or sharing in) the Holy Spirit (*see* TRINITY). He emphasizes Jesus' humanity by saying that he was crucified in weakness (13:4).

Galatians and Romans express the creatureliness of Jesus and his subordination to God in another way. God sent his Son, made (γενόμενον) of a woman, made under the law (Gal. 4:4); Christ, in order to redeem man from the curse of the law, became a curse (Gal. 3:13; cf. II Cor. 5:21). God sent his Son in flesh like sinful flesh (lit., "in likeness [ὁμοίωμα] of flesh of sin"; Rom. 8:3) and planned that he should be the first-born of many brothers (Rom. 8:29). Jesus was an Israelite according to the flesh (Rom. 9:5). A careful distinction is drawn in Rom. 1:3-4: with respect to his flesh, Christ descended from David; with respect to the Spirit of holiness, he was declared Son of God in power by the resurrection from the dead.

Philippians and Colossians, like the other letters, still teach the future parousia (Phil. 1:6; 3:20; 4:5; Col. 3:4). The great christological passage, Phil. 2:5-11, does not add materially to what the other letters say except to fill out the picture of the condescension of the heavenly Christ. He was originally in the μορφή ("form") of God but willingly "emptied" himself and took the μορφή of a slave, which is also described as the ὁμοίωμα and σχῆμα ("form" or "fashion") of a man. As he had been obedient to death, God exalted him and gave him the highest of all names, Lord Jesus Christ. The terms are not clear. Probably Paul thought that Christ, in having the "form" of God in the Greek sense, also shared his nature. "Likeness" and "fashion" could mean that Christ only appeared to be human, but in view of what is said elsewhere, Paul must affirm the genuine humanity of Jesus. See HUMANITY OF CHRIST; INCARNATION, THE.

That Paul believed in Christ's divine nature seems clear from Col. 2:9, where he says that all the fulness (πλήρωμα) of divinity dwells in Christ bodily. The passage Col. 1:13-22 describes the Son of God in terms that suggest Philo's Logos and the heavenly man. Everything was created through him and for him; he is prior to all, and all holds together in him. Thus he is pre-eminent in creation, providence, and redemption.

It seems clear, then, that in Paul's thought the various approaches to the understanding of Jesus' nature—his human activity as teacher and loving friend of his disciples, and the categories of Messiah, heavenly man, Lord, inaugurator of the new covenant, and wisdom of God—are all combined in a harmonious and intelligible synthesis. A tremendous activity of thinking and teaching has gone into this, and all the materials used in later Christology are already present. In contrast to the gospel tradition, however, Paul says nothing of any miraculous activity in Jesus' ministry. He knows the earthly Jesus primarily as the crucified teacher, occasionally referring specifically to words of the Lord (I Cor. 7: 10, 25) but more often reflecting teachings existing in the gospel tradition without identifying the source (e.g., Rom. 12:14, 19; 13:8).

**10. Later NT books.** Toward the end of the first century the Pauline letters gained considerable popularity, probably because they were collected and circulated in the churches (see CANON OF THE NT), and other literature was modeled on them.

*a. Ephesians.* The first writing of this sort, Ephesians, adds very little to the Christology of Colossians except to suggest the descent of Christ into the lower parts of the earth (4:9-10), thus paving the way for the doctrine that he preached to the dead (I Pet. 3: 18-22). See DESCENT INTO HADES.

*b. Hebrews.* This homily, written when persecution was impending, seeks to strengthen Christian faith by pointing to the unique importance of Christ's person and work. Its idea of the Son of God as the agent of creation (1:1-12) may be a development of the doctrine in Colossians. It is God's purpose that the age to come shall be subjected to the Son; not everything is yet subject to him, but meanwhile he is crowned with glory and honor (2:5-9). More than most of the later NT books, Hebrews emphasizes the humanity of Jesus. As ἀρχηγός of salvation (cf. Acts 3:15) he leads many (other) sons to glory, and it is fitting that he should have been perfected by suffering (2:10). He tasted death for every man (2:9); thus Jesus is the representative of all humanity. In the days of his flesh he uttered cries and prayers to God and learned obedience through what he suffered (5:7-8). Having been tempted as other men, yet without sin, he has compassion on human weaknesses (4:15). Although he was God's unique apostle, or emissary, and high priest (3:1), he nevertheless did not glorify himself; it was God who glorified him (5:5). His high priesthood is perfect and permanent, as compared with the temporary and imperfect Aaronic system, and is typified by Melchizedek (5:6, 10; 6:13-7:17). It represents a new law and a new covenant (7:18-28). Jesus offers himself in the direct presence of God as a sacrifice that needs not to be repeated (9: 11-12); he lives eternally to make intercession for his people (7:25).

*c. Revelation.* This prophecy stands apart from the main christological development in that its view of Messiah is almost entirely that of late Jewish apocalyptic, combining as it does the thousand-year messianic age and the resurrection of the saints (Rev. 20:2-5) with the last onslaught of Satan (20:7-10), the general resurrection and judgment, and the age to come (20:11-22:5). Its picture of Messiah fits this pattern. He is the lion of the tribe of Judah, the root of David (5:5; 22:16), and the morning star (22:16), but he is also the Son of man, first-born from the dead, who comes with the clouds and is completely supernatural (1:5-7, 13-16; 14:14). Now is the first certain appearance in literature of the son-of-Joseph type of Messiah, for here Jesus is the warrior Messiah (6:16; 19:11) and the prophecy of Zech. 12:10-14 is applied to him (cf. Matt. 24:30; see §§ 2-3 *above*). But he does not die in battle, for he has already died and is alive again. The woman from whom he is born (12:1-15) is evidently the true and glorified Israel. The Messiah is not a bull, as in the Jewish tradition; he is the slain lamb (5:6) who has loved his people and loosed them from their sins by his blood (1:6).

In other respects the picture is Christianized. As the faithful witness (1:5) he is the pattern for Christian martyrs. He is the Son of God (14:1). His name is the Word of God (19:13), but here the reference is probably to the prophetic word which he gives (1:16) rather than the Logos idea. The new Jerusalem, described in Jewish apocalyptic terms, is his bride (21: 9-10), and the messianic banquet has become the marriage supper of the Lamb (19:9). Perhaps this supper is consciously connected with the eucharistic rite (3:20). *See* ESCHATOLOGY OF OT; ESCHATOLOGY OF APOC. AND PSEUDEP.; ESCHATOLOGY OF NT.

*d. I Peter.* By contrast, I Peter, written also in time of persecution, emphasizes the gentleness and lack of revenge on the part of the lamb without blemish or spot (1:19; 2:21-24). The new idea in this document is the descent of Christ into Hades to bring life to those who were there (3:18-22; 4:6). *See* DESCENT INTO HADES.

*e. The Pastoral letters.* The letters addressed to Timothy and Titus have a predilection for "Savior" as a title for Jesus (I Tim. 1:1; II Tim. 1:10; Tit. 1: 4; 2:13; 3:6); this word was originally secular and without very precise reference, though there are occasional earlier occurrences—e.g., Phil. 3:20. His humanity and his role in salvation are both emphasized; he is the "one mediator between God and men, the man Christ Jesus" (I Tim. 2:5; cf. 6:13-14; II Tim. 2:8; 4:1; Tit. 2:11-14). The little rhythmical formula in I Tim. 3:16 shows that something like a creed is beginning to develop.

*f. Other documents.* In II Peter the Transfiguration is regarded as a foreshadowing of the Parousia (1:16-18). This late document uses the term "Savior" several times (1:11; 2:20; 3:2, 18). James speaks of the parousia of the Lord (5:7) and of Jesus as the Lord of glory (2:1). For the Johannine letters, *see* SON OF GOD § 12.

**11. The Gospel of John.** Although the Fourth Gospel is not the latest book of the NT, it marks the highest point of its Christology. The evangelist develops earlier ideas found in the Synoptics, the Pauline letters, and Hebrews. Thus Jesus is Messiah (usually translated as Χριστός—e.g., 9:22; 11:27; 20: 31—but also transliterated Μεσσίας—e.g., 1:41; cf. 1:49) and Lord (13:13-14; 20:18, 28; 21:12). He is also SON OF GOD, but in the full sense that he has come out from God, returns to God (13:1-3), is not of human origin (1:12-14, 18; 8:58), does his Father's will and work in the world (2:16; 5:17, 19-29), and is restored to his original glory (11:4; 12:27; 14: 13, 28; 17:1; cf. Phil. 2:5-11). The doctrine of the hiddenness of Messiah is also worked out in connection with the Son of God (6:42; 8:19; 19:9). Passages in which Jesus is related to these concepts (1:51; 3:13-14; 6:27, 53; 8: 28; 12:34). Jesus is also called Savior (e.g., 4:42) without the term's being defined, and the prophet (7:40; cf. 6:14: the "prophet who is to come into the world"). The latter term is used by those who do not have full faith and knowledge. Jesus is the Lamb of God who "takes away" or "bears" the sins of the world (1:29), and it may be significant that in this gospel he suffers before Passover, at the time when the paschal lambs are slain, though the Passover sacrifice is more a sign of rescue from death than of removal of sin. Another possibility is that the "lamb" is the conquering ram of apocalyptic who represents the victorious Messiah. This Messiah does not "bear" sin or its consequences but puts a decisive end to it. He is supreme over the law of Moses (5:16-18; 7:22-24), but the only law which he gives is the new commandment of love (13:34). Nothing is said about the baptism of Jesus; instead, the function of

John the Baptist is to witness to one greater than himself (1:19-34; 3:22-30). The idea of the messianic secret is worked out elaborately in this gospel, where only a few disciples believe—and at that imperfectly —while Jesus' enemies are baffled and misunderstand him even when he speaks plainly. The discourse on the blinding of Israel concludes the public ministry.

In contrast to the other gospels, practically all of Jesus' teaching in John concerns faith and unbelief in himself. Not only is it true that to receive him is to receive God (13:20), but faith in Christ is absolutely essential to salvation (3:14-18, 36).

The gospel begins with a hymnic prologue (1:1-18) on Christ as the LOGOS. Since the word "Logos" in this technical sense does not appear again in the gospel, it is sometimes thought that the Prologue is an earlier hymn adapted by the evangelist. Its themes are used again, however, so that it has the character of an overture. E.g., Christ is always the life (1:4; 11:25; cf. 6:35, 51; 7:37-38) and the light (1:4, 9; 8:12; 9:5) of the world. The Prologue carries on the idea of Colossians and Hebrews that Christ was agent of creation (cf. Philo's idea of the Logos and the Jewish idea of Wisdom as creator). The emphasis is not, however, on Christ's role in creation but on redemption (1:11-13) and revelation (1:9, 14, 17-18). John goes beyond Paul in identifying the Logos as God, though he is "with" (πρός) God (1:2) and "only begotten God" in the bosom of the Father (1:18, MSS ℵ, B).

This last idea is also worked out in the body of the gospel. For the Son is equal with God (3:35; 5: 18; 10:18-30; 16:32; 17:10) and can appropriately be called God (10:34-36; 20:28). Christology thus reaches its climax in the full deity of Christ.

Some of the ideas and words used to describe Christ have striking parallels in Gnosticism, particularly the Mandaean literature (*see* GNOSTICISM). Thus Christ is the bread of life and the water of life (6:35; 7:37-38), life and truth (14:6), the way and the one who first treads out the way (13:36; 14:2-6), the true vine (15:1-10), the good shepherd (10:11) and the door or gate (10:7), and the helper or PARACLETE who sends another helper (14:16-17, 26; 16:13-15). Here and in the Logos prologue the difference between John and the Gnostics is that John does not separate the Creator from the revealer and the redeemer. They are one, and that one is God; thus creation was not a mistake or a tragic fall, and however sinful the world is, it is in a true sense the object of God's love (3:16).

Another and basic difference is connected with John's biblical-Christian idea of the world as God's creation. No Gnostic redeemer could ever assume full humanity, but only a semblance of it; nor could he redeem the whole personalities of his followers, but only the nonmaterial divine spark in them. But John believes that the Logos became flesh and tabernacled among his people (for the idea of the body as a tent, see II Cor. 5:1-5; II Pet. 1:13), for he was weary (John 4:6) and thirsted (4:7; 19:28) and died on the cross (19:30).

It cannot be denied, however, that the evangelist's story of Jesus' deeds and words is affected more by the doctrine of his divinity than by the record or the conviction of his humanity. As in Byzantine mosaics and paintings of Christ the Omnipotent (παντοκρά-τωρ), the humanity is only a vehicle of the divine, and the Fourth Gospel is a dramatic-theological representation of the meaning of Christ, a creed in gospel form. That which in Paul's view belongs to the risen and glorified Christ now shines out in the earthly ministry. The event which in the Synoptics is the baptism of Jesus now becomes the witness of John. There are no parables, but only allegories; no specific teachings about the law, but only the sovereignty of Christ over the law and the new law of love; no healings out of ordinary human compassion, but instead some great signs showing the divine compassion of the Omnipotent and Savior. The doctrines of eternal life, faith in Christ, and abiding in him reinterpret the idea of the kingdom of God. Jesus' mission is now explicitly to Samaritans and Greeks as well as to "his own" among the Jews.

His actions and style of speech are those which the evangelist deemed appropriate to divinity. Jesus' knowledge is supernatural (e.g., 1:47-51; 2:25; 4:17-19, 29; 13:21-27). He is sometimes enigmatic and rejects suggestions made to him, not because he is unresponsive but because the ways and thoughts of God are not those of man (e.g., 2:4-5). His prayers to the Father are those of complete communion and mutual understanding (11:41-42; 12:27-28; ch. 17). In the presence of Pilate he speaks as a witness to the truth, like a Christian martyr, and as a king whose realm is not of this world (18:19-21, 33-37; 19:10-11). It is of his own volition that he lays down his life and takes it again (10:17-18; 15:13), and therefore he cannot be arrested until he himself permits it (7:44-46; 18:5-8). His last word from the cross is: "It is finished"—i.e., complete—and he yields up his spirit (19:30). See DEATH OF CHRIST.

**12. The Apostolic Fathers.** A number of older christological ideas reappear in the Apostolic Fathers, a group of second-century Christian writings. E.g., God chose out Christ (I Clem. 64.1) and raised him from the dead (I Clem. 24.1). He is Lord, Savior, and high priest, and is typified by the Suffering Servant and the serpent in the wilderness. Certain ideas receive a fuller development. There is further evidence of the trinitarian formula (I Clem. 58.2; Did. 7.1, 3; see TRINITY), and of the beginnings of a creed, particularly the article "judge of the living and the dead" (II Clem. 1.1; Polyc. Phil. 2.1; Barn. 7.2). Ignatius affirms the VIRGIN BIRTH (Ign. Eph. 7.1; 18.2; 19.1); and against the Docetic error that Christ only seemed to be human, he insists that Christ came in the flesh (Ign. Trall. 9.1-2; 10.1; cf. Polyc. Phil. 7.1; Barn. 5.10). His nature is twofold: having originally been spirit, he became flesh (Ign. Eph. 7.1; 20.1; cf. II Clem. 9.5).

Occasionally the Apostolic Fathers emphasize the humility and condescension of Christ in becoming man (I Clem. 16.2; Diogn. 7.2-4). Ignatius develops the idea of Christ as the representative of all humanity. There has now appeared the dispensation of the new man (Ign. Eph. 20.1-2); Christians are the fruit of the tree on which Christ was crucified (Ign. Smyr. 1.1-2); Jesus received the ointment (μύρον) that he might breathe immortality on the church (Ign. Eph. 17.1) and was baptized that he might purify the water (Ign. Eph. 18.2).

It is not surprising then that one writer says the church was manifested in Jesus (II Clem. 14.3) and another that Jesus is shepherd of the catholic church (Mart. Polyc. 19.2). Ignatius teaches that the church is united with Christ as Christ is in union with the Father (Ign. Eph. 5.1; Magn. 1.2; 7.1). As the door of the Father, he is the way of entrance for the patriarchs and the prophets, the apostles and the church (Ign. Phila. 9.1). Some of these ideas are reminiscent of the Gospel of John. When Ignatius calls Jesus the Word of God, however, he thinks of him as God's (uttered) word "proceeding from silence" (Ign. Magn. 8.2), and the usage in Diogn. 11.2-3 appears to be similar.

The term παῖς, "servant" or "child," used in Acts, reappears in prayers and solemn passages (I Clem. 59.2; Did. 9.1-3; 10.2-3; Diogn. 8.9-10; 9.1); in the Martyrdom of Polycarp it almost certainly means "child" and is a synonym for "Son" (Mart. Polyc. 14.1, 3; 20.2).

Some other new ideas appear. Ignatius describes Jesus as the "will of the Father" (Ign. Eph. 3.2) and "born and yet not born . . . , first capable of suffering and then incapable of suffering" (Ign. Eph. 7.1), and he sees the star that announced his birth as destroying magic, wickedness, and ignorance (Ign. Eph. 19.3).

**13. The genesis of Christology.** One cannot trace with complete certainty the process by which Jewish messianism was transformed into Christology. Certainly Jesus' sense of his own mission and person must have been the largest single factor (see JESUS). The parables display him as a prophet announcing the kingdom of God, and to be a prophet was the highest category in which the Jews could place any human being. Even the rank of Messiah was partly based on the fact that he was a prophet. Jesus spoke with an absolute certainty of the truth of his message and his commission to proclaim it. Apparently he did not use the phrase "thus saith the Lord"; in fact, "the law and the prophets were until John," while Jesus stood on the threshold of a new age and saw in the events which accompanied his work the dawning of this age. Furthermore, the fate of Israel and the lives of individuals depended on their response to the message. Coupled with this authority is the absence from our sources of anything to suggest that Jesus had any consciousness of personal sin or alienation from God. On the contrary, he seems to have had a deep sense of filial relation to him. Other men were not excluded from this—indeed, Jesus sought to awake it in them—but with him it seems to have been so powerful and direct that the gospel tradition almost immediately described him as Son of God. He also very probably spoke of himself as Son of man.

He made his final trip to Jerusalem to arouse what can only be called a religious revolution, and he went fully conscious of the danger to himself and his disciples. His entry into Jerusalem had features that suggested to his followers that he had come as a peaceful messianic king, and an enthusiastic woman anointed him in Bethany. He cleansed the temple, perhaps as a sign that God would come with a more severe judgment unless men repented. At the Last Supper, certain that his body would be broken and his blood poured out, he gave the bread and wine to his disciples as signs that this death would be for their benefit, and he promised to meet them again in the banquet of the kingdom of God.

The Romans crucified him on the charge that he was or claimed to be the "king of the Jews." Within three days his disciples experienced him as risen. During his ministry he had received unusual allegiance from them, and now they no doubt concluded that God had made him both Lord and Messiah. It must have been almost immediately that they began to search the OT scriptures, which seemed clearly to prefigure the recent events. How natural and inevitable this was can be seen from the Qumran literature or Dead Sea Scrolls, which already employed an identical method. The growing faith was heightened and enriched by the experience of the Spirit which occurred at baptisms and on other occasions, and perhaps also by a sense of the presence of the risen Christ at the Lord's Supper. The word "Messiah" came now to mean for the disciples the prophet, the new lawgiver, the Son of God, and the Son of man, and in fact to denote everything that they knew and believed about Jesus. From this the rest of NT Christology developed without difficulty.

*Bibliography.* On the OT background: C. C. Torrey, "The Messiah Son of Ephraim," *JBL*, LXVI (1947), 253-77. C. R. North, *The Suffering Servant in Deutero-Isaiah* (1948). H. H. Rowley, *The Servant of the Lord* (1952). T. W. Manson, *The Servant-Messiah* (1953). A. Bentzen, *King and Messiah* (1955). J. Klausner, *The Messianic Idea in Israel* (1955). S. Mowinckel, *He That Cometh* (1956).

On the NT doctrine: K. Lake and F. J. Foakes-Jackson, *The Beginnings of Christianity,* I (1920), 345-68, 403-18; V (1933), 354-75. W. Bousset, *Kyrios Christos* (2nd ed., 1921). A. E. J. Rawlinson, *The NT Doctrine of the Christ* (1926). B. S. Easton, *Christ in the Gospels* (1930), pp. 175-99. J. Weiss, *History of Primitive Christianity* (1937), I, 1-44, 118-35; II, 446-95. W. Manson, *Jesus the Messiah* (1938). F. C. Grant, *An Introduction to NT Thought* (1950), ch. 9. R. H. Strachan, "The Gospel in the NT," *IB*, VII (1951), 14-20. C. H. Dodd, *The Interpretation of the Fourth Gospel* (1953), pp. 228-85. R. Bultmann, *Theology of the NT* (1955). E. Stauffer, *NT Theology* (1955), pp. 103-52.                S. E. JOHNSON

**CHRIST, BODY OF** [τὸ σῶμα τοῦ Χριστοῦ]. A phrase which connotes the many-faceted relations between JESUS CHRIST and those who belong to him, their relations to him as members (μέλη), and their relations to one another in him (*see* BODY). It expresses the bonds of mutuality and solidarity accomplished in his death (Rom. 7:4; II Cor. 4:10-12; Gal. 6:17; Col. 1:24), and the intimate and strong bonds created in his resurrection (Rom. 7:4-6; I Cor. 15:42-50; Eph. 1:20-23; *see* DEATH OF CHRIST; RESURRECTION IN THE NT). The corporate life of those who are in him is embodied in both this dying and this rising (Rom. 8:9-11; II Cor. 4:7-12; Phil. 3:10-11; Col. 2:9-15). Oneness with him is made real by the one baptism (Rom. 6:1-11; I Cor. 12:12-13; Eph. 4:4-5; Col. 2:9-19) and by the one Eucharist (Mark 14:22 and parallels; John 6:50-52; I Cor. 10:16-17; 11:23-32). Oneness in him is inseparable from the work of the one Spirit which supplies power, hope, peace, and love throughout the whole body (Rom. 8:9-11; I Cor. 6:17; 12:1-13; Eph. 2:14; 4:3-4, 16; Col. 3:19). As the body's head, Christ rules over it, loves and nourishes it, sanctifies and dies for it, and fills it with the fulness of God's glory (Eph. 1:23;

5:25-29; Col. 1:19; 2:9). The members of his body consider their own bodies as united to him (I Cor. 6:12-17; Phil. 1:20) and carry about in those bodies the death of Jesus (II Cor. 4:10-12; Gal. 6:17; Col. 1:24). As members of his "spiritual body," men share in the power of the resurrection and in the promised redemption of all things (I Cor. 15; Eph. 1:17–2:10; Phil. 3:10). Within the one body, the gifts of the Spirit are apportioned in such interdependence that each gift nourishes and is nourished by the whole, love being the "bond of perfection" (Rom. 12:4-8; I Cor. 12-14; Eph. 4:10-12; *see* SPIRITUAL GIFTS; HOLY SPIRIT). Within this body the division of mankind into Jews and Gentiles is overcome (I Cor. 12-13; Eph. 2:11-18; Col. 3:11). Participation in this body means freedom from the body of sin and death (Rom. 5-8). Through his body Christ struggles with the rulers of this age, overcomes them, and shares with his people the fruits of victory (Col. 1:16-20; 2:9-15). In the Pauline letters, where this pattern of thought is most highly developed, Christ's body is explicitly linked to the church (Eph. 1:22; 5:23; Col. 1:18, 24), to the one new man, the last Adam and those who bear his image (I Cor. 15:42-50; Eph. 4:12-13), to the household of God (Eph. 2:19), to the temple (Eph. 2:21), and to the commonwealth of Israel (Eph. 2:12). *See* CHURCH, IDEA OF.

*Bibliography.* E. Käsemann, *Leib und Leib Christi* (1933); S. Hanson, *The Unity of the Church in the NT* (1946); K. L. Schmidt, *The Church* (trans. J. R. Coates; 1950); J. A. T. Robinson, *The Body* (1952); E. Best, *One Body in Christ* (1955); A. Nygren, *Christ and the Church* (1956); H. Schlier, *Die Zeit der Kirche* (1956), pp. 159-85, 287-307.        P. S. MINEAR

**CHRISTIAN** [χριστιανός]. A name referring to the followers of the gospel of Christ; used only in Acts 11:26; 26:28; I Pet. 4:16.

Variant spellings of the word occur in the NT texts, and generally. In Acts 11:26, א 81 attest χρηστιανός; B D, χρειστανός. Tac. Ann. XV.44 (see also Suetonius *Claudius* 25; *Nero* 16) presupposes that in Rome in the sixties the people called the disciples *Chrestianoi*. Sometimes the fathers preferred *Chrestians,* even when knowing both spellings. The "e," indeed, is still retained in the French *Chrétien.* Leclerq affirms: "It is absolutely beyond doubt that *Christus* and *Chrestus, Christiani* and *Chrestiani* were used indifferently by the profane and Christian authors of the first two centuries of our era" (see Cabrol, *Dictionnaire d'archéologie chrétienne et de liturgie,* III [1948], 1464-78).

Since in Greek "e" and "i" were similarly pronounced and often confused, the original spelling of the word could be determined only if we could fix its provenance. If the name was coined by Christians themselves (so E. J. Bickerman), it could only have been spelled *Christianoi.* If the name was coined by pagans (Greeks or Romans), its original spelling could have been with an "e" or an "i." Pagans who were aware that the cult lord of the disciples was *Christos* could have formed the word as we now have it. Those to whom the word *Christos,* meaning "Messiah" or "Anointed One," was unintelligible might easily have confused it with the common Greek proper (slave) name *Chrestos,* meaning "good," "useful," "worthy." Having heard *Christos,* they might have thought *Chrestos,* and from the latter coined the name. In this latter case, the "e" would have been corrected to "i" when the Christians accepted the title.

The problem is further complicated by the fact that the word *Christianos* is a Latinism. The expected Greek ending would be ειος. Since there were only exceptional Greek formations in ιανος, a Syrian origin of the title, although possible, is brought into question.

Formed, then, like Herodiani or Caesariani, Christians were Christ's men or party members of a person named Christ.

Since χριστιανός is a Latinism and was contributed neither by Jews (who, not accepting Jesus as Messiah; would not have so entitled his followers) nor by the Christians themselves (they had other preferred designations like "disciples," "brothers," "saints," "believers," etc., nor did they make common use of the title until the second century), it has been maintained that the designation was coined by (*a*) the Roman police (in Antioch; so Leclerq), or by Roman officials (in Antioch) to designate the Christian movement as hostile to Herod Agrippa (*see* the work of Erik Peterson in the *bibliography*) for his collaboration with Rome (Harnack, H. Karpp); or (*b*) by the Roman populace (in Rome) in the sixties (F. C. Baur); or (*c*) that the term was of unspecified pagan provenance not earlier than 79 (Schmiedel) or from Asia Minor, *ca.* 90 (Lipsius).

It still remains possible that Luke's information is correct. The three occurrences of "Christian" in the NT suggest that the term was at this time primarily used as a pagan designation. Its infrequent use in the NT indicates not so much lateness of origin as pagan provenance. If current in Nero's time, its origin must have been fairly early. Also, if the term was first used in jest or scorn (this is not necessarily so), it is easily understood why the Christians should have avoided it. In any case it is clear that by the time of Ignatius (himself an Antiochene) the term was fully accepted in the church. As in I Peter, the name is one to suffer for.

It may well be, then, that the disciples were first called Christians in Antioch. I.e., the church which first accepted in its membership uncircumcised Gentiles was the locale where pagans first saw that this "synagogue" was organized on a new principle and center—which was "Christ," its cult lord. Mattingly (*see bibliography*) proposes that the *Christiani* were deliberately named after the *Augustiani,* Nero's claque of "handsome, tough youths," whose devotion to the rhythmic praise of Nero was really an act of worship. It was this group at Antioch which inspired the nickname *Christiani.* In disdain the populace heard the disciples sing hymns to Christ: "Were they not ludicrously like Nero's *Augustiani?* Christ had *his* claque at Antioch!"

**Bibliography.** A. Gercke, "Der Christusname ein Scheltname," *Festschrift zur Jahrhundertfeier der Universität Breslau* (1911), pp. 300-373. H. H. Wendt, *Die Apostelgeschichte* (9th ed., 1913). A. von Harnack, *Mission und Ausbreitung des Christentums* (1923), I, 424. H. J. Cadbury, "Names for Christians and Christianity in Acts," note XXX in F. J. Foakes-Jackson and K. Lake, *The Beginnings of Christianity,* pt. I, vol. V (1933), pp. 383-86. E. Schwyser, *Griechische Grammatik,* I (1939), 490. E. Peterson, "Christianos," *Miscellaneous Giovanni Mercati,* I (1946), 355-72. E. J. Bickerman, "The Name of Christians," *HTR,* XLII (1949), 108-24. H. Karpp, "Christianos," *Reallexikon für Antike und Christentum,* II (1954), 1131-38. F. V. Filson, "Christian," *The Twentieth Century Encyclopedia of Religious Knowledge* (1955), I, 239. E. Haenchen, *Die Apostelgeschichte* (1956), pp. 318-19, note 3; pp. 322-23. H. B. Mattingly, "The Origin of the Name Christian," *JTS,* N.S. vol. IX, pt. 1 (Apr., 1958), pp. 26-37.     F. D. GEALY

**CHRISTOLOGY.** *See* CHRIST.

**CHRONICLES (OF KINGS, ETC.).** *See* BOOKS REFERRED TO.

\*CHRONICLES, I AND II. A history from Adam (I Chr. 1:1) to Cyrus king of Persia (II Chr. 36:22-23), running parallel to Genesis–II Kings, concluded with Ezra-Nehemiah. I-II Chronicles and Ezra-Nehemiah (like I–II Samuel and I–II Kings) were single volumes in the MT, and were divided into two scrolls each in the LXX (and all later versions) because the Greek needed almost twice as much space as the Hebrew, which wrote no vowels. In the MT, Chronicles is the last book of the OT, incongruously following Ezra-Nehemiah, because it deals with events narrated elsewhere; in the LXX and in modern versions Chronicles-Ezra-Nehemiah follows II Kings, being grouped among the historical books, but in the MT it comes at the end of the Hagiographa (*Kᵉthûbhîm,* "Writings"). The Hebrew title of Chronicles is דברי הימים ("things of the days," meaning "events of [past] time," "history"); the Greek title is *Paraleipomena,* "omitted things," referring to the events added to Samuel and Kings; and it was adopted in the Vulg. Jerome suggested as a title "Chronicle of the Whole of Sacred History" and is thus responsible for the title in English and other modern languages.

1. Contents
2. Religious point of view
    *a.* Theological doctrines
    *b.* The clergy
3. Purpose
4. Sources
5. Date
6. Style
Bibliography

**1. Contents.** I Chronicles summarizes the period from Adam to David (chs. 1–9) and deals extensively with David's reign (chs. 10–29); II Chronicles deals with Solomon's reign (chs. 1–9) and with the kings of Judah, ending with Cyrus, king of Persia (chs. 10–36). The contents of the two books may be outlined as follows:

I Chr. 1–9 (from Adam to David). Genealogies: from Adam to Jacob (1:1-34); the sons of Esau (1:35-54); the sons of Jacob (2:1-2)—namely, Judah and his descendants (2:3–4:23), Simeon (4:24-43), Reuben (5:1-10), Gad and the war with the Hagrites (5:11-22), and E Manasseh (5:23-26); Levi (ch. 6—H 5:27–6:66), Issachar (7:1-5), Benjamin (to be read "Zebulon" [cf. Gen. 46:14]; 7:6-11), Dan (7:12, to be revised according to Gen. 46:23), Naphtali (7:13), W Manasseh (7:14-19), Ephraim (7:20-29), Asher (7:30-40), and Benjamin (8:1-5; Ehud, 8:6-28; Saul,

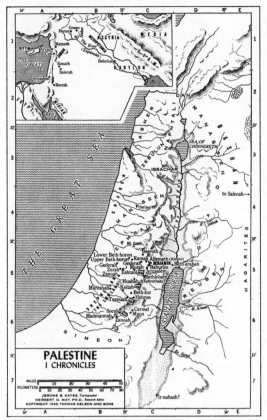

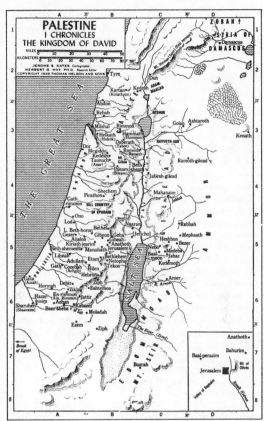

8:29-38, 39-40; the citizens of Jerusalem, 9:1-34; Saul, 9:35-44 = 8:29-38).

I Chr. 10–29 (David). (*a*) David's reign (10–20): Saul's death (10); David is appointed king of Israel (11:1-3) and conquers Jerusalem (11:4-9); the exploits of David's soldiers (11:10–12:40—H 11:10–12:41); the ark is brought to the house of Obed-edom (13); transaction of David's temporal affairs (14); solemn transportation of the ark to Jerusalem (15–16); Nathan's oracle (17); David's victories (18–20). (*b*) David's arrangements for the building of the temple (21–29): God reveals to David the site of the future temple, after Satan has induced David to take a census (21); David's provision of materials and workers for Solomon's building of the temple (22); David's organization of the clergy: Levites (23), priests, (24:1-19), Levites (24:20-31), temple singers (25), gatekeepers (26:1-19), treasurers (26:20-28), and administrators (26:29-32); organization of government officials: army generals (27:1-15), tribal chiefs (27:16-24), administrators of the king's property (27:25-31), and royal counselors (27:32-34); David's final instructions to the last assembly in his reign, concerning Solomon's succession and the building of the temple (28–29).

II Chr. 1–9 (Solomon). Revelation to Solomon at Gibeon (1:1-13); his riches (1:14-17); the building of the temple: negotiations with Hiram (ch. 2—H 1:18–2:17), description of the temple (3:1-13) and its furnishings (3:14–5:1), dedication of the temple (5:2–7:10), and God's answer to Solomon's prayer (7:11-22); various activities of Solomon: Hiram of Tyre

gives twenty cities to Solomon (8:1-2; contrast I Kings 9:10-11), Solomon rebuilds various cities (8:3-11), inaugurates the temple worship (8:12-13), and appoints the clergy (8:14-16); his commerce, wisdom, and wealth (8:17–9:28); concluding summary (9:29-31).

II Chr. 10–36 (the kings of Judah). Rehoboam and the division of the kingdom (10–12): secession of N Israel (10:1–11:4), Rehoboam's prosperity (11:5-23) and punishment through the invasion of Shishak (12:1-12), and concluding summary (12:13-16); Abijah defeats Jeroboam (13); Asa's victory over a million Ethiopians (14–16); Jehoshaphat's judicial reorganization and victory (17–20); Jehoram's crimes and punishment (21); Ahaziah (22:1-9); Athaliah (22:10–23:21); Joash (24); Amaziah (25); Uzziah's prosperity and pride (26); Jotham (27); Ahaz and his unsurpassed wickedness (28); Hezekiah's measures in behalf of the temple worship (29–32); Manasseh's captivity and repentance (33:1-20); Amon (33:21-25); Josiah's reforms (34–35); Jehoahaz (36:1-4); Jehoiakim (36:5-8); Jehoiachin (36:9-10); Zedekiah (36:11-21); Cyrus king of Persia (36:22-23 = Ezra 1:1-3*a*).

**2. Religious point of view.** *a. Theological doctrines.* The author of Chronicles, *ca.* two centuries later, wrote a sequel to the Priestly Code in the Pentateuch and Joshua, continuing the history from the death of Joshua to the edict of Cyrus (538 B.C.), adopting the juridical and ecclesiastical religion of that charter of Judaism—with some slight modifications due to later conditions. On a cosmic background, the priestly author had shown how the Creator of heaven and earth had become the sovereign of the Jews, and in his omnipotence had directed the course of events for the benefit of his people; for Israel yet unborn he had made a covenant with Abraham, revealed his law to Moses on Sinai, and distributed to the children of Israel the Holy Land through Moses, Eleazar, and Joshua. The apocalypses dreamed of a kingdom of God in the age to come, but the Priestly Code, with more practical sense, imagined that it had been established by God in the distant past, in the days of Moses and Joshua, and described it in such terms that it furnished the concrete pattern for the organization of the Jewish congregation.

On a more modest scale the Chronicler wrote a history of this kingdom of God after its establishment in the time of Moses and Joshua. The period from Adam to Joshua (treated by the Priestly Code) was briefly evoked by mere genealogies (as P had used generally from Adam to Abraham); the same applies to the time from Joshua to David (I Chr. 1–9), because Judah played then an insignificant role, and the period of the judges was (according to the Deuteronomists) a period of intermittent apostasy and war, irreconcilable with the establishment of God's kingdom in Canaan. The Chronicler followed P in regarding the tabernacle of Moses as the only sanctuary of the Israelites until Solomon built the temple. So the period before David is merely introductory, and only the period from David to Cyrus is treated in detail.

**PALESTINE**
2 CHRONICLES
KINGDOMS OF ISRAEL and JUDAH

MILES
0    10    20    30    40    50
KILOMETERS
0  10  20  30  40  50  60  70  80

JEROME S. KATES, Cartographer
HERBERT G. MAY, PH.D., *Research Editor*
COPYRIGHT 1949, THOMAS NELSON AND SONS

The general plan of the Chronicler is patterned after P: the four divisions of P (beginning with Adam, Noah, Abraham, and Moses), followed by an appendix dealing with the settlement in Canaan (Joshua), correspond to the periods beginning with Adam, David, Solomon, and Rehoboam, with an appendix dealing with renewed proclamation of the law and the settlement of the exiles in Canaan (Ezra and Nehemiah). In both the main events are the building of God's house (the tabernacle and the temple) and the organization of the clergy. In both histories God intervenes miraculously in the course of events and accomplishes his ends without needing human agencies.

Both authors lived in times of peace and had neither knowledge nor liking for battles, which they usually eliminated from their sources; when this was impossible for the Chronicler (in view of the accounts in Samuel and Kings), the outcome of battles was settled in advance by the Lord, who usually won the victory for the Jews in spite of all odds (II Chr. 13:8-15; 14:9-13; 15:14; 16:7-9; etc.), except when their wickedness was punished with defeat (II Chr. 12:1-5; 21:10, 16-17; 24:23-24; 25:20; 28:1-5; etc.). The enormous armies of Judah, reaching such fantastic totals as 400,000 (II Chr. 13:3),/ 580,000 (14:8), 1,160,000 (17:14-19), 307,500 (26:13), are considered useless in battle (20:12; cf. 17:14-19); but through divine help victory is won—not by fighting, but by singing a psalm (20:14-30) or by a priestly fanfare (13:14-15). The late accounts of the crossing of the Red Sea and of the capture of Jericho in P and elsewhere are familiar parallels to these supernatural events.

Such reports of miraculous interventions of God in the course of history were freely invented by P and the Chronicler in rewriting their sources, in order to illustrate God's omnipotence and his requirements —chiefly blind obedience to his orders or to his law, and complete trust in him. The pious Josiah, e.g., "did not listen to the words of Neco from the mouth of God" (II Chr. 35:22) and was killed in battle; Hanani said to Asa: "Because you relied on the king of Syria, and did not rely on the LORD your God, the army of the king of Syria has escaped you" (II Chr. 16:7; see also I Chr. 10:13-14; II Chr. 28:19; 33:10-11; etc.). Far from repentant, in an acute attack of gout, Asa "did not seek the LORD, but sought help from physicians" (II Chr. 16:12).

The Chronicler not only teaches the proper faith in God, after the manner of the Priestly Code, by such graphic fictitious stories, but also (with scarcely any previous model in P) uses sermons, oracles, and prayers after the manner of the Deuteronomists in Kings. The emphasis on faith (I Chr. 29:11-19; II Chr. 14:11; 16:8-9; 20:12) is derived from the prophets rather than from P, and so is the homiletic tone (influenced by Deuteronomy) which characterizes the numerous edifying utterances added to the sources (see, e.g., II Chr. 13:8-12; 15:1-7; 20:15-17; 29:5-11; 30:6-9; 32:7-8). It is not to be excluded that the Chronicler echoes here the homilies and the prayers which he heard in the synagogues; he is likewise familiar with the psalms sung in the temple.

The Chronicler was not a very original thinker, and made no contributions to the theology of the

Priestly Code. The notion that the sole universal Creator was the god of the Jews only—which the Priestly Code and the Second Isaiah explained in two opposite manners—did not trouble him in the least. His God was the "God of Israel our father, for ever and ever"; to him belonged the "greatness, and the power, and the glory, and the victory, and the majesty"; his is "all that is in the heavens and in the earth; thine is the kingdom, O Lord, and thou art exalted as head above all" (I Chr. 29:10-11). Although God rules over all kingdoms (II Chr. 20:6), over all (I Chr. 29:12), inconsistently he is king of and god of the Jews only (I Chr. 17:14; 28:4; 29:23), and "is not with Israel, with all these Ephraimites" (II Chr. 25:7). This universal God is so partial to the Jews, the "Lord's people" (II Chr. 23:16), that to fight against them is to fight against God himself (II Chr. 13:12). The N Israelites, who until Solomon (according to Chronicles) worshiped the Lord, are later "the wicked" and "those who hate the Lord" (II Chr. 19:2).

Thus the kingdom of God is, on the one hand, the kingdom of Judah (I Chr. 28:4-7; II Chr. 13:5); but on the other, as in the Priestly Code, it is not a state but a holy congregation, a church. Racial purity is neither necessary nor sufficient for citizenship in this sacred commonwealth: the subjects of the divine King are those—and only those—who worship the Lord exclusively and obey blindly the law which he revealed to Moses. Consequently, even the Ephraimites (i.e., the Samaritans) may join the Jewish congregation (II Chr. 10–22; cf. 11:16), and even heathen may pray in the temple (II Chr. 6:32-33, based on I Kings 8:41-43). Conversely, native Judeans may be excluded from God's kingdom: "The Lord is with you, while you are with him. If you seek him, he will be found by you, but if you forsake him, he will forsake you" (II Chr. 15:2). "For the eyes of the Lord run to and fro throughout the whole earth, to show his might in behalf of those whose heart is blameless toward him" (II Chr. 16:9).

In general, however, the kingdom of Judah was the holy congregation (II Chr. 30:12), eager to fulfil the law and particularly the temple rituals (I Chr. 29:6-9, 20-22; II Chr. 7:3-10; 13:8-12; 15:8-15; 24:8-11; 29:31-36; 31:2-8; 34:32-33; etc.). Even the worship on the high places was offered only to the Lord (II Chr. 33:17). In theory apostates were condemned to death (II Chr. 15:13), according to Deut. 12:29–13:18—H 12:29–13:19, but usually the Lord forgave repentant sinners (II Chr. 7:14): "For the Lord your God is gracious and merciful, and will not turn away his face from you, if you return to him" (II Chr. 30:9). Accordingly, Rehoboam (II Chr. 12:5-8) and Manasseh (33:10-13) were forgiven after their repentance.

After the apostasy of Jeroboam I (II Chr. 13:9), the holy congregation consists of Judah, some N Israelites, and the proselytes (II Chr. 30:25); its sovereign is the Lord, its law is the Pentateuch, the book revealed to Moses (II Chr. 23:18; 30:16; 35:12), found in the temple in the eighteenth year of Josiah; actually this book was part of Deuteronomy, and it was read at least twice in one day (II Kings 22:8, 10), but in II Chr. 34:14-15, 18, they read "in it" only once, for the Pentateuch could not be read

twice in a day. The Chronicler is thus the first author to attribute the whole Pentateuch to Moses; all the ritual practices which he attributes to Moses belong to the Priestly Code (I Chr. 6:48-49—H 6:33-34; 15:15; II Chr. 8:13; 24:6, 9; cf. I Chr. 16:40; II Chr. 2:4; 31:3).

*b. The clergy.* It is chiefly in matters concerning the status of the clergy that the Chronicler differs from the Pentateuch and discloses later developments.

Early in the Persian period (538-333) the high priest began to exert some civil authority, and the Priestly Code assigns to him some of the marks of royalty (Exod. 29:5-7), even mentioning Eleazar before Joshua (Josh. 14:1). This growth of temporal authority resembles that of the bishop of Rome. During the monarchy (before 586) it would have been inconceivable for a high priest to drive King Uzziah out of the temple for attempting to burn incense, violating the later prescriptions of the Priestly Code (Exod. 30:1-10; Num. 16:40; 18:1-7), as the Chronicler fancifully relates (II Chr. 26:16-21)—adding for good measure that the Lord made him a leper in punishment of his sin (contrast II Kings 15:5, where nothing is said of this ritual offense). Even greater is said to have been the authority of the high priest Jehoiada (II Chr. 23–24).

The high priest presides over a supreme court when it deals with sacred matters (II Chr. 19:8-11); this is presumably the earliest known allusion to the Sanhedrin.

Some rules practiced by the priests and Levites in the time of the Chronicler were still unknown in the Pentateuch, and could not be ascribed to Moses; the Chronicler attributes them to David or to a later king. The division of the priests into twenty-four courses, well known before the beginning of the Christian era (some of the courses are named in I Macc. 2:1; 14:29; Luke 1:5), is ascribed to David, "according to the procedure established for them by Aaron their father" (I Chr. 24:1-19).

The Chronicler was probably a Levite, and is far less concerned with the priests than with the Levites. The distinction of these two ranks in the priesthood began in 621, when the priests of the provincial sanctuaries ("high places") ceased to officiate (Deut. 18:6-8a; II Kings 23:9), and only the sons of Zadok at Jerusalem functioned as priests. This distinction was formulated by Ezekiel, for whom the Levites were temple servants (44:9-16), and was attributed to Aaron by the Priestly Code (Num. 18), with the difference that not only the sons of Zadok (descended from Eleazar, son of Aaron), but also the descendants of Ithamar, son of Aaron, or all the sons of Aaron, officiate as priests. This plan was approved by the Chronicler (I Chr. 24:1-3); but some protested that only the Zadokites should be priests (Num. 25:12-13, where God's covenant is made with the line of Phinehas, son of Eleazar; cf. also Ecclus. 45:23-24).

The Chronicler, after the manner of a modern labor leader, championed the improvement of the situation of the Levites against the "sons of Aaron," who wished to retain the Levites in their subordinate position (such anti-Levite tracts are found in Num. 3; 4; 8; 16; 17); conversely, supporters of the Levites wrote Num. 35:1-8; Deut. 33:8-11; Josh. 21 (cf. I Chr. 6:54-81—H 6:36-66); Mal. 2:4-8.

The Chronicler goes so far as to hint that the "hewers of wood and drawers of water" in the temple might go on strike when he reports that only 74 Levites, 128 singers, 139 porters, and 392 temple servants—in contrast with 4,289 priests—were willing to return from Babylonian exile with Zerubbabel in 538 (Ezra 2:36-58); and until Ezra persuaded 38 Levites and 220 temple servants to join his caravan of returning exiles, no Levite had appeared among the 1,500 men going back to Jerusalem (Ezra 8:15-20). Such figures imply the threat of a future strike, if we compare them with the Chronicler's large number of Levites in comparison with the priests (II Chr. 29:34); he would have us believe that David assigned tasks to 38,000 Levites (I Chr. 23:3-5).

The Chronicler's picture of the status of the Levites is far superior to that fixed in the Priestly Code. They are in charge of the holy objects (I Chr. 9:28; 23:28), which in the Priestly Code they could not even see lest they die (Num. 4:15-20; 18:3). The Levites left N Israel and came to Rehoboam (II Chr. 11:13-17; cf. 13:9-10); eventually they became teachers (II Chr. 17:7-9) and judges (19:8-11); they played a decisive role in the coronation of Joash and in the overthrow of Athaliah (II Chr. 23:2-20), but disobeyed Joash (24:4-7); they co-operated, however, with Hezekiah (29:4-19); 30:13-27; 31:11-19) and with Josiah (34:9-13; 35:3-18). Individual Levites are said to have been scribes (I Chr. 24:6; II Chr. 34:13) and prophets (II Chr. 20:14-17). The Chronicler's enthusiasm for the Levites was unlimited: "for the Levites were more upright in heart than the priests in sanctifying themselves" (II Chr. 29:34). He ascribes to them ritual functions belonging to the priests (I Chr. 9:32; 23:29-31; II Chr. 29:34 [contrast 29:22, 24]), and even the teaching of the law (II Chr. 17:8-9; 35:3) and the celebration of the Passover (II Chr. 30:13-22; 35:1-19); their ritual holiness is stressed twice (II Chr. 23:6; 35:3; cf. 29:34).

Singing in a temple choir was for the Chronicler (who probably sang with the guild of Asaph) the most important function of Levites (II Chr. 8:14). He is familiar with the choral parts of the temple services and is convinced that since David the Levites sang hymns on every important occasion, including war (I Chr. 15:16-24; 16:4-42; II Chr. 5:12-13; 20:19-22; 23:13, 18; 29:25-30; 35:15). The Chronicler occasionally gives the text of the hymns (I Chr. 16:8-36, a compilation from parts of Pss. 105; 96; 106) and of the doxologies which were sung (II Chr. 5:13; 20:21). He is more interested in choral than in orchestral temple music, but there is no compelling reason for attributing the allusions to the latter (I Chr. 15:19-24a, 28; II Chr. 5:11b-13a; etc.) to another author.

Music in the temple services is unknown in the Pentateuch and could not be attributed to Moses, so the Chronicler ascribed it to David (I Chr. 15:16-24; ch. 25; II Chr. 7:6; 8:14; 23:18; 29:25-30). David was advised by Samuel (I Chr. 9:22)—who was dead when David became king—Gad, and Nathan (II Chr. 29:25); both David and Solomon left written records about the organization of temple music (II Chr. 35:4).

Besides Levites and singers, the lower clergy included gatekeepers (I Chr. 26:12-18; cf. 9:17-27), the Nethinim ("given" [men]) or temple servants (I Chr. 9:2; often in Ezra-Nehemiah), and the descendants of Solomon's servants (Ezra 2:55, 58; Neh. 7:57, 60; 11:3), who seem to have been eventually united with the Nethinim (I Chr. 9:2; contrast Neh. 11:3). Even the humblest of these menials were exempted (or should have been exempted?), according to the Chronicler, from taxation (Ezra 7:24).

The Chronicler traces the ancestry of all priests to Aaron, and of all priests and Levites back to Levi son of Jacob (I Chr. 6:1-53—H 5:27-6:38). "Levi" has here no real genealogical reality, but is the supposed ancestor of all those concerned with the temple, with the exception of the Nethinim and the descendants of Solomon's servants. The doctrine that all clergymen are descended from Levi originated apparently with the Priestly Code, but has no historical basis. The Chronicler transforms the Ephraimite Samuel (I Sam. 1:1) and the Gittite Obed-edom (II Sam. 6:10-13) into Levites (I Chr. 6:22-28, 33-38—H 6:7-13, 18-23; 16:38; 26:4). An Ezrahite sage, Ethan (probably also called Jeduthum; I Kings 4:31—H 5:11), to whom Ps. 89 is attributed, became both a grandson of Judah (I Chr. 2:6) and a descendant of Levi through Gershom (I Chr. 6:42-43—H 6:27-28) and also through Merari (I Chr. 6:44—H 6:29; 15:17, 19)—unless there are two singers with the same name. No less bewildering are the genealogical transformations of Asaph and Korah.

The most probable explanation of this bewildering disregard for the facts in the genealogies and other data for the lower clergy is that the Chronicler is more eager to improve its status than to give us a true picture of the facts in his own day—and much less in the time of David or Jehoshaphat. It seems certain that the Levitical status of the singers and gatekeepers was not recognized in his day, and had never been recognized before, but he took it for granted and generally idealized their situation in order to improve their position as best he could. Some of the aspirations of the singers were eventually realized: shortly before A.D. 70, Agrippa II and the Sanhedrin granted them the right to wear linen garments like the priests (Jos. Antiq. XX.ix.6 [§ 216]).

**3. Purpose.** The main purpose of the Chronicler, variously pursued from several directions, is to glorify the Jews in Jerusalem and Judea in a period of utter political and economic insignificance, between the two vigorous revivals with Nehemiah and Judas Maccabeus. To raise the low morale at such times, the Chronicler exaggerated the splendor of the Jewish kingdom in the past, just as Daniel (2:44; 7:11) predicted the approaching world dominion of the Jews—when all seemed lost. Both authors contributed to the survival of the Jewish congregation and presumably had several imitators whose writings are not extant; both were greatly influenced by Ezekiel in stressing the cosmic importance of the Jews and of the temple worship, and the unique concern of the sole true God in their behalf. Both Chronicles and Daniel describe the past and the future, not according to realities or even possibilities, but on the assumption that the Creator of the world invariably intervened miraculously in behalf of the Jews. Both are dominated by this faith, and neither one ever allows facts to limit in the least the realm of faith.

Unless the Chronicler quotes reliable accounts from Samuel and Kings, it is useless to expect from him genuine historical information. Like the priestly author for the days from Adam to Joshua, the Chronicler is manifestly devoid of any desire to know any historical facts remote from the imaginary ideals and perfections of Utopia. Chronicles describes, not the epic struggles, ending in failure, of the Israelites to establish and maintain their independence in Canaan, but God's triumphant establishment of his imperishable kingdom on earth. Just as the Priestly Code had used the ceremonies of the second temple to describe those of the tabernacle of Moses, so the Chronicler transfers the institutions of his own day to the time of David.

To regard Chronicles as genuine history, as orthodox Jews and Christians have done, is to misunderstand the work, and fail to realize its nature and significance. The Chronicler set out to prove that the insignificant Judean community in the midst of the empires that arose after the death of Alexander was the glorious kingdom whose sovereign was the sole God in existence; his only earthly abode was the temple in Jerusalem. Mere historical facts could never prove the validity of this first apology for Judaism. Faith in such supreme claims could never be supported by actual occurrences—in fact, faith needs no proof and has no rational proof. The two arguments used by the Chronicler, as later by Josephus, are the antiquity of Judaism and the marvelous achievements of the Jews.

Like the Priestly Code, the Chronicler believed that the Jewish rites originated through divine revelation to Adam (the sabbath), Noah (Gen. 9:3-7), Abraham (circumcision), and Moses (the temple rituals and other sacred institutions). The temple music, unknown in the law of Moses, was ascribed to David, the Sanhedrin and general education to Jehoshaphat (II Chr. 17:7-9; 19:8-11), and missionary work among the Samaritans (a failure) and in Galilee (a partial success) to Hezekiah (II Chr. 30:1-12).

But the Chronicler did not regard the Jews as merely a holy congregation, as the Priestly Code had done following Ezekiel; he stressed at the same time the national achievements and royal glories of Judah. David not only reorganized the numerous clergy, and made extensive preparations for the building of Solomon's temple (I Chr. 22–29), but his fame "went out into all lands, and the LORD brought the fear of him upon all nations" (I Chr. 14:17; cf. II Chr. 17:10). This was inevitable if ca. 350,000 warriors came to crown David (I Chr. 12:23-40) and if later he commanded an army of more than 1,500,000, exclusive of Levi and Benjamin (I Chr. 21:5-6; 1,300,000 in II Sam. 24:9); for the construction of the temple, David set aside a sum about equal to three billion gold dollars (I Chr. 22:14; 29:3-4, 7-8)—a sum that at Solomon's incredible annual revenue of 666 gold talents (I Kings 10:14) David could have accumulated in ca: 150 years, if he had spent nothing.

In glorifying Judaism and the Jews through the centuries beyond all possibilities, the Chronicler necessarily rewrote the history from David to Cyrus: he freely omitted from his sources, added to them,

modified them, being blissfully unaware of anachronisms and impossibilities.

Whatever cast discredit on David and Solomon in the ancient sources is glibly forgotten: David's willingness to fight Saul at Gilboa in the ranks of the Philistines, his adultery with Bathsheba, the murder of her husband, Absalom's rebellion, and Solomon's sins (I Kings 11). Only David's taking of the census (I Chr. 21:1–22:1; cf. I Sam. 24) was necessarily recorded, for it resulted in the revelation of the site of the temple, but the Chronicler ascribed its suggestion to Satan, and not to the LORD. David and Solomon become saints.

Later, Levites from N Israel came to strengthen Judah (II Chr. 11:13-17). Judah in the fourth year of Rehoboam lapsed momentarily into paganism (II Chr. 12:1), but it immediately came to its senses through the invasion of Shishak (see II Chr. 12, which omits the apostasy of I Kings 14:22-24).

According to the Chronicler, all pious monarchs before Josiah removed the "high places," while all the wicked kings of Judah and Israel practiced paganism and persecuted the worshipers of Jehovah. Ahaz went so far as to close the temple (II Chr. 28: 23-24). Like the Deuteronomist in Judges, the Chronicler believed that the people alternated regularly between true and false worship: the true religion had been revealed to Moses on Sinai, but the people at times forgot it and worshiped the heathen gods. It was much later that scholars discovered that it was only slowly, through the teaching of the prophets, that the people eventually attained the noble level of the religion of the Pentateuch.

The utter exclusion from God's kingdom of N Israel would not be conceivable before the Samaritan schism, dated either in 432 (by Neh. 13:28-29) or about a century later (Jos. Antiq. XI.viii.2). If we accept the date of Josephus as the most probable (ca. 332) and of necessity date the Priestly Code before this (for the Samaritans had the complete Pentateuch), it seems incredible that, as some have argued, the books of Chronicles could have been written before the Priestly Code and the Samaritan schism, or in 450-350 B.C.—which, of course, would presuppose that the Chronicler had nothing to do with the edition of the books of Ezra and Nehemiah. The argument adduced is that after the publication of the Pentateuch the Chronicler would not have dared to attempt to elevate the Levites above their low status decreed by the Priestly Code. But this did actually happen (Jos. Antiq. XX.ix.6) when the Levitical singers were allowed to wear linen garments like the priests shortly before A.D. 70.

It seems highly improbable that the purpose of the Chronicler could have been to oppose the cruel, narrow-minded attitude of the priesthood in Jerusalem during the sixth and fifth centuries which was asserting its superiority over the "occasional" Levites, especially from Israelitish territory (but see IB, III, 344-46). As a matter of fact, the temple of Jerusalem was in ruins until 520-516, and for nearly a century after that was in a most depressing state, as shown by the books of Malachi and Nehemiah. Moreover, Levites from N Israel went to the temple only in the vivid imagination of the Chronicler (after the Samaritan schism); it would have been like Protestant pastors' begging to become priests in St. Peter's in Rome after 1517.

The rituals described in Chronicles are ordained in the Priestly Code or later, with the sole exception of II Chr. 35:6, 12, where the Levites (instead of the laymen, as in Exod. 12:3-8) slay the paschal lambs; this may have been done in the time of the Chronicler for pilgrims celebrating the Passover in Jerusalem or may have been done because of the large multitudes (II Chr. 29:34; 35:11), unless this is another instance in which the Chronicler enhances, as elsewhere, the position of the Levites for propaganda purposes. In any case, in two other instances of considerable importance, the Chronicler assumes the current practice of two basic religious institutions still unknown to the Priestly Code and the Pentateuch: temple choral and orchestral music, and the temporal authority of the high priest (II Chr. 24:15-24; 26:16-21). The Chronicler attributes to David the division of the priests in twenty-four courses (I Chr. 24:1-19); the organization of the Sanhedrin under the presidency of the high priest was begun by David (I Chr. 23:4; 26:29-32) and completed by Jehoshaphat (II Chr. 19:5-11). If the Chronicler wrote before the Pentateuch was canonized (*ca.* 400 B.C.), his books were abundantly interpolated by a later writer.

Every medal has two sides, and every apology needs a polemic as its counterpart. The Chronicler, in glorifying Judaism and the Jews, of necessity despised the heathen, and the Samaritans—most objectionable of all non-Jews. If Judaism is the only true religion, all others are false, and eventually all men must be converted to Judaism.

The Chronicler never doubted that the correct worship of the Lord, the only God in existence, as revealed in the Pentateuch, was the true religion, but he did not pour sarcasm on other religions and refrained from all polemic against them. In this respect he resembles Francis of Assisi, who, in the words of Paul Sabatier, "systematically avoided polemics, which are always more or less a form of spiritual pride; they merely dig the chasms which they claim to fill. Truth has no need to be proved: it prevails." The Chronicler never indulged in the viciously unfair caricature of Gentile religions beginning with the Second Isaiah (Isa. 44:9-17), according to which an imbecile hewed down a tree and with part of the wood warmed himself and cooked his meal, and with the rest carved a divine image and worshiped it. He probably felt that after the publication of the Pentateuch, heathen religions were no longer attractive to the Jewish congregation, and its occasional idolaters were immediately expelled or put to death. Moreover, the Chronicler hoped that the heathen would soon be converted to the true religion. Heathen had been converted before his time (Isa. 56:6-8), and allegedly there were proselytes in the time of Asa (II Chr. 15:9); missionary activity is said to have been begun by Hezekiah (II Chr. 30:1-12, 25), who failed dismally in his effort to convert the N Israelites (Samaritans), except for some Galileans (30:11); less than a century later the Jews were still a minority in Galilee (I Macc. 5:14-17, 20-23).

The obdurate Samaritans taxed the patience of the Chronicler beyond endurance: of course, he could usually ignore the Northern Kingdom as outside the pale of God's kingdom and regard the Samaritans as a half-heathen (II Chr. 13:4-12), godless (II Chr. 19:2; 25:7-10), and guilty mob (II Chr. 28:10-11). The heresies of the Samaritans are summarized in the sermon of Abijah (II Chr. 13:4-12); and, according to the Chronicler, are rejected by the Samaritans who repented and came to Jerusalem to worship (II Chr. 11:16; 15:9; cf. 28:12-15). On the whole, however, the Chronicler did not express in plain words his full contempt for the misguided heathen and for the apostate Samaritans, hoping for their future conversion.

**4. Sources.** Unquestionably the Chronicler drew his information on the history of Judah and Israel from the Pentateuch and the books of Joshua, Samuel, and Kings. From them he often quotes verbatim or draws information which he supplements or modifies according to his purpose. To show that the theocracy founded by Moses (according to the Priestly Code) continued without a break until Nehemiah, he did not hesitate to give both the text of his biblical sources and his own opinion, since the text of the Pentateuch was already canonical and that of the other books was soon to be canonized. In I Chr. 15:27, e.g., he says that David wore a robe of fine linen (according to his own view) and a linen ephod (according to II Sam. 6:14).

In general the Chronicler modified our canonical sources with complete freedom to suit his ideas. He simply omitted from Samuel and Kings what did not agree with his notions of the Jewish theocracy (the adultery of David with Bathsheba, the rebellion of Absalom, the accession of Solomon, etc.), and modified what did not agree with his religious views (contrast II Sam. 24:1 with I Chr. 21:1) or his notion of the facts of history (contrast II Sam. 21:19 with I Chr. 20:5). After reporting how the N tribes of Israel made David king (according to II Sam. 5:1-3), he adds: "according to the word of the LORD by Samuel" (I Chr. 11:3). To glorify Judah, the Chronicler does not hesitate to say without support in Samuel that David set aside for Solomon's building of the temple more than the equivalent of three billion gold dollars (I Chr. 22:14; 29:3-4, 7-8); 350,000 Israelites came to crown David at Hebron (I Chr. 12:23-40—H 12:24-41), and in Jerusalem he commanded an army of more than 1,500,000, exclusive of Levi and Benjamin (I Chr. 21:5-6; cf. II Sam. 24:9, where the much exaggerated total amounts to 1,300,000 men). Likewise he never hesitates to change his sources to cast aspersion on N Israel—in his day, the Samaritan community—as when he said that Abijah with 400,000 men defeated twice as many of Jeroboam's men, killing 500,000 (II Chr. 13:3-20; unknown in I Kings 15:1-5).

But in spite of his views that differed considerably from those of the authors of Samuel and Kings, the Chronicler preferred to reproduce his sources verbatim: I Sam. 31 and II Sam. 5:1-3, 6-10; 23:8-39 (in I Chr. 10-11, in part); II Sam. 7; 8; 10 (in I Chr. 17-20); etc. Any variations between the text of Chronicles and that of Samuel-Kings is due either to the better preservation of the text of Chronicles or to his own improvement of the diction (as in I Chr. 17:3-15; cf. II Sam. 7:4-17).

Elsewhere the Chronicler rewrote the narratives of

Samuel and Kings in order to express his own views, which often differed from those of his source: new details are added to the account of David's bringing the ark to Jerusalem (I Chr. 15:25-28; cf. II Sam. 6: 12b-15), to the taking of the census (I Chr. 21; cf. II Sam. 24), to the reign of Athaliah (II Chr. 22:10–23:21; cf. II Kings 11), to the repairs to the temple under Joash (II Chr. 24:4-14; cf. II Kings 12:4-16), etc. The Levites are mentioned only three times in the books of Samuel and Kings (I Sam. 6:15; II Sam. 15:24; I Kings 8:4, in late passages dealing with the transportation of the ark), but thirty-five times in I Chronicles and sixty-four in II Chronicles.

When detailed stories in II Kings could neither be omitted nor be reproduced in full, the Chronicler summarized them, stressing his own views (II Chr. 22:7-9 [cf. II Kings 9:1-28; 10:11-14]; II Chr. 32:1-23 [cf. II Kings 18:13-19:37]; II Chr. 34:4-7 [cf. II Kings 23:4-20]). Conversely the Chronicler expanded the brief account of the celebration of the Passover by Josiah (II Kings 23:21-23) and of his death (II Kings 23:29-30) into a detailed story (II Chr. 35:1-19, 20-25).

These examples suffice to illustrate the various methods by which the Chronicler rewrote, edited, shortened, expanded, and arbitrarily changed the passages in Samuel and Kings which suited his purposes, omitting the rest. The contrast between Chronicles and the earlier books brings out clearly the disregard of the Chronicler for historical accuracy or even likelihood, and his concern with the ritual worship, the importance of the Levites, and temple music. Only half of I-II Chronicles is even remotely inspired by biblical sources; in the other half the Chronicler, unless he had access to sources unknown to us, was able to display his vivid imagination by composing freely, without any guidance. Here we face the most difficult critical problem: did he use sources no longer accessible to us or write freely as he wished?

After the manner of Kings, the Chronicler refers the reader to other writings for further information on the subject. The historical works referred to—never our canonical Samuel and Kings, which are so frequently excerpted—are: the Book of the Kings of Israel and Judah (I Chr. 9:1; II Chr. 27:7; 35:27; 36:8); the Book of the Kings of Judah and Israel (II Chr. 25:26; 28:26; 32:32); the Royal Book of Judah and Israel (II Chr. 16:11); the Book of the Kings of Israel (II Chr. 20:34; in I Chr. 9:1, where this title appears, we should read the "Book of the Kings of Israel and Judah"); the Acts of the Kings of Israel (II Chr. 33:18); the Midrash (teaching) of the Book of Kings (II Chr. 24:27).

Another group of writings is attributed to various prophets and seers: the Acts of Samuel the Clairvoyant (I Chr. 29:29); the Acts of Nathan the Prophet (I Chr. 29:29; II Chr. 9:29); the Acts of Gad the Prognosticator (I Chr. 29:29); the Prophecy of Ahijah the Shilonite (II Chr. 9:29); the Visions of Iddo (sic) the Prognosticator Concerning Jeroboam Son of Nebat (II Chr. 9:29); the Acts of Shemaiah the Prophet and Iddo the Prognosticator (II Chr. 12: 15); the Midrash of the Prophet Iddo (II Chr. 13: 22); the Acts of Jehu Son of Hanani "which are recorded in the Book of the Kings of Israel" (II Chr. 20:34); a book by the prophet Isaiah the son of

Amoz, containing the history of Uzziah (II Chr. 26: 22); the Vision of Isaiah, the son of Amoz (cf. Isa. 1:1), the Prophet (II Chr. 32:32, and "in [sic] the Book of the Kings of Judah and Israel"); the Acts of the Prognosticators (II Chr. 33:19).

The following miscellaneous works are also mentioned in Chronicles: a genealogical register of Gad (I Chr. 5:17); the Chronicles of King David (I Chr. 27:24); the LORD's architectural plan of the temple (I Chr. 28:19); the plan for the organization of the Levites written by King David and the one written by Solomon (II Chr. 35:4); the Lamentations for Josiah written by Jeremiah and others (II Chr. 35: 25; the same as the book of Lamentations? cf. Jos. Antiq. X.v.1).

The first five books mentioned by the Chronicler, the histories of the kings of Judah and Israel, are manifestly a single work mentioned under different names. It is now often called the "Midrash of the Kings" (II Chr. 24:27), omitting "of the Book" with the LXX, and it is clearly not identical with our canonical books of Samuel and Kings, for it contained the Prayer of Manasseh (II Chr. 33:18). With the possible exception of the Acts of the Prognosticators (II Chr. 33:19), which is also said to have contained the Prayer of Manasseh, the prophetic books were part of the Midrash of the Kings. This historical work included also echoes from I-II Samuel (cf. I Chr. 29:29) and is said to have contained a parallel in the Vision of Isaiah (II Chr. 32:32; cf. II Kings 18:13–20:19; Isa. 36–39); moreover, the prophecy of Jehu son of Hanani (cf. I Kings 16:1-7, 12; II Chr. 19:1-3) was written in a book inserted into the Book of the Kings of Israel (II Chr. 20:34). It is significant that the information on a king is given either in a historical or in a prophetic book (except in II Chr. 20:34; 32:32; 33:18-19).

The Chronicler apparently quotes the same work under sixteen different titles, either as a Midrash of the Kings (five titles referring to historical books) or according to the ancient practice of referring to a passage by name, as Paul in Rom. 11:2-3 refers to I Kings 19:10, 14, as follows: "Do you not know what the scripture says 'in Elias'?"

If this Midrash actually existed—which is open to question—it was a work much more detailed than Chronicles, where it is referred to for information which was not reproduced from it. It began, to judge from the allusions to it, with David in I Chr. 11 and continued to Manasseh in II Chr. 33; we do not know if it contained a history of the kings of N Israel. The actual existence of the other writings listed by the Chronicler is extremely doubtful.

Two opposite conclusions as to the Chronicler's use of Samuel and Kings have been drawn: (a) that all the information parallel with the accounts in Samuel and Kings, as well as that not to be found there (e.g., II Chr. 24:27; 27:7; 33:18), was derived by the Chronicler from the Midrash of the Kings, without his ever using our canonical books of Samuel and Kings; and conversely, (b) that "the material of I and II Chronicles not derived from our canonical books . . . was all freely composed by the Chronicler himself, in pursuit of his apologetic aim"—in other words, that the Chronicler used exclusively our canonical books.

No objective final verdict on these two opposite opinions is possible, but the evidence slightly favors the second. What is not in the books of Samuel and Kings generally agrees closely with the contributions of the Chronicler in Ezra-Nehemiah. J. Wellhausen, who believed that the Chronicler used this Midrash, admitted that "whether one says Chronicles or Midrash . . . is more or less equivalent; they are children of the same womb, and can in no way be distinguished according to spirit and language, while conversely the sections preserved verbatim from the canonical Book of Kings are striking in both respects." In some cases Chronicles reproduces at the same time both the text of the canonical books and the later correction of it: Saul committed suicide (I Chr. 10:4; cf. I Sam. 31:4-5), and at the same time the Lord slew him because he consulted a ghost at Endor (I Chr. 10:13-14). Obed-edom was at the same time a Philistine from Gath (I Chr. 13:13-14; cf. II Sam. 6: 10-12), the ancestor of a Levitical guild of gatekeepers (I Chr. 15:18, 24; 16:38*b*, etc.), a Levitical temple musician (I Chr. 15:21; 16:5, 38*a*). Likewise Samuel was transformed from an Ephraimite (I Sam. 1:20) into a Levite (I Chr. 6:28) because he was also directly concerned with the ark of Shiloh (I Sam. 3:3), which was in the sole charge of the Levites according to the Priestly Code (Num. 3:31; cf. Deut. 10:8; etc.). Moreover, when the Chronicler did not reproduce his canonical sources without change, he often added his own contributions to the story such as references to the Levites, and freely invented personal names. In I Chr. 25:4, beginning with Hananiah, the names mean: "Have mercy, O Jehovah, have mercy on me!" "Thou art my God!" "I have magnified and extolled the help for the one sitting in hardship"; "I have made oracles overflow abundantly." At times he added many new details in place of some omissions (I Chr. 13:1-5; 15–16 [cf. II Sam. 6]; II Chr. 22:10–23:21 [cf. II Kings 11]; II Chr. 34 [cf. II Kings 22–23]). At times a brief notice in Kings is expanded, as the story of the death of Josiah (II Kings 23:29-30*a*) in II Chr. 35:20-25 (cf. II Chr. 18:28-34); the correspondence between Solomon and Hiram, of which there was no trace previously, is created by the Chronicler in II Chr. 2:2-16. In conclusion, "there is no internal evidence, anywhere, of an intermediate source between our Old Testament books and the Chronicler" (C. C. Torrey, *Ezra Studies*, p. 223).

**5. Date.** The date of the Chronicler cannot be fixed by definite clues between 400 and 200 B.C., for it is later than the Pentateuch (canonized *ca.* 400 B.C.) and earlier than Ecclesiasticus in 180 (I Chr. 23–29 is echoed in Ecclus. 47:8-10). A date *ca.* 250 B.C. or a little earlier is far more probable than 400-350 B.C., which W. F. Albright assigns to the work, by assuming that the Chronicler was Ezra and that Ezra came to Jerusalem after Nehemiah.

**6. Style.** Aramaic was for the Chronicler the spoken vernacular, and his Hebrew is somewhat artificial and postclassical, abounding in Aramaic expressions and late words; for details see E. L. Curtis and A. A. Madsen, *The Books of Chronicles,* ICC (1910), pp. 27-36. Nevertheless, when he writes freely without quoting a source, he delights in giving details taken from life (I Chr. 12:39; 28:2; II Chr.

16:14; 20:5, 16, etc.) and using vivid comparisons (I Chr. 11:23; 12:8, etc.). His imagination is picturesque and colorful, but in spite of its apparent realism it lacks connection with real facts and never reaches the level of truly great literature.

*Bibliography.* Commentaries: I. Benzinger, *KHC* (1901). R. Kittel, *HKAT* (1902). E. L. Curtis and A. A. Madsen, ICC (1910). J. W. Rothstein and J. Hänel, *KAT* (2 vols.; 1927). J. Göttsberger, *EH* (1939; Roman Catholic). M. Rehm, *Echter Bibel* (1949; Roman Catholic). W. A. L. Elmslie, *IB* (1954; cf. the Cambridge Bible [1916]).

Introductions to the OT: S. R. Driver (7th ed., 1898). C. H. Cornill (English trans. by G. H. Box, 1907; 7th ed. in German, 1913). C. Steuernagel (1912). L. Gautier (2nd ed., 1914; 3rd ed., 1939). J. Göttsberger (1928; Roman Catholic). W. O. E. Oesterley and T. H. Robinson (1934; 3rd ed., 1953). O. Eissfeldt (1934; 2nd ed., 1956). A. Weiser (1939; 2nd ed., 1949; 3rd ed., 1957). R. H. Pfeiffer (1941, 1948). J. E. Steinmueller (1942; Roman Catholic). A. Bentzen (1948-49; 2nd ed., 1952). E. J. Young (1949, 1953). C. Kuhl (1953).

Histories of the literature of the OT: K. Budde and A. Bertholet (1906; 2nd ed., 1909). J. Bewer (1922; 2nd ed., 1933; 3rd ed., 1949). J. Hempel (1930-34). A. Lods (1950).

Special studies: W. D. Crockett, *A Harmony of the Books of Samuel, Kings, and Chronicles* (1897). J. Wellhausen, *Prolegomena zur Geschichte Israels* (6th ed., 1905). C. C. Torrey, *Ezra Studies* (1910). G. von Rad, *Das Geschichtsbild des chronistischen Werkes,* *BWANT,* IV (1930), 3; "Die levitische Predigt in den Büchern der Chronik," *Festschrift für Otto Procksch* (1934), pp. 113-24. J. Hänel, "Das Recht des Opferschlachtens in der chronistischen Literatur," *ZAW,* LV (1937), 46-67. M. Rehm, *Textkritische Untersuchungen zu den Parallelstellen der Samuel-Königsbücher und der Chronik* (1937). A. C. Welch, *The Work of the Chronicler: Its Purpose and Its Date* (1939). A. Bea, "Neuere Arbeiten zum Problem der biblischen Chronikbücher," *Bibl.,* XXII (1941), 46-58 (Roman Catholic). M. Noth, *Überlieferungsgeschichtliche Studien,* I (1943). G. Gerleman, *Synoptic Studies in the OT* (1948). A. Bentzen, "Sirach, der Chronist und Nehemia," *Studia Theologica,* III (1949), 158-61. F. Zimmermann, "Chronicles as a Partially Translated Book," *JQR,* XLII (1951-52), 265-82, 387-412. W. Rudolph, "Problems of the Books of Chronicles," *VT,* IV (1954), 401-9. C. C. Torrey, *The Chronicler's History of Israel* (1954).

R. H. PFEIFFER

**\*CHRONOLOGY OF THE OT.**

1. From the Creation to the Exodus
   *a.* The early patriarchs
   *b.* From Abraham to the Exodus
2. From the Exodus to Solomon's temple
3. From Solomon's temple to the Exile
   *a.* Problems and methods
   *b.* From Solomon's temple to Jehu
   *c.* From Jehu to the fall of Samaria
   *d.* From the fall of Samaria to the Babylonian exile
4. After the return
Bibliography

**1. From the Creation to the Exodus.** *a.* **The early patriarchs.** Many generations of Bible readers have been led by the computations of Archbishop James Ussher, first published in his *Annales Veteris et Novi Testamenti* (1650-54) and printed in the margin of some editions of the KJV, to believe that the world was created *ca.* the year 4000 B.C. Ussher's chronology took at face value the years of the patriarchs as listed in the MT of Gen. 5; 7:11; 9:28-29; 11:10-32. However, the figures of the Hebrew Bible do not agree in many items with the Samar. and LXX versions, and these disagreements lead to differing totals. In Table 1 *below* a list is given of the age of each patriarch at the birth of his successor, of their remaining years, and of the total length of their lives, as these appear in the MT, Samar., and LXX respectively.

There have been three distinct ways of understanding this genealogy. The first interpretation is that of Ussher, which takes the list to indicate successive generations from father to son; the second interpretation is the same except that it assumes that many links have dropped out of the genealogy, as in the case of Kainan (retained by the LXX in Gen. 11:13); the third is to understand the names as dynasties or peoples instead of as individuals. With the latter two methods no estimate of the age of the world can be obtained.

The conventional and schematic structure of this list of patriarchs should be apparent. It contains two units of ten names each, the first extending from Adam to Noah and the second, counting Kainan, from Shem to Terah. This is analogous to the genealogy of Matt. 1, which artificially compresses all the generations from Abraham to Jesus into three equal units of fourteen. It will be observed that the MT places the death of Methuselah in the year of the Flood, as if to emphasize the radical break pro-

duced by that cataclysm in human life. The LXX overlooks this point, making Methuselah live fourteen years too long.

When the three lists of figures are compared, there can be little doubt that the Hebrew text is original. It will be seen that the LXX adds a century to the age of the early antediluvians at the time of their successor's birth, evidently through consideration of their extremely long lives. The Samar. does just the opposite with Jared, Methuselah, and Lamech in order to bring their deaths to the year of the Flood. While the LXX balances its additions to the first part of the patriarchs' lives by subtractions from the latter part, the Samar. simply shortens the whole life.

By adding a hundred years to most of the figures, the Samar. and the LXX avoid the abrupt drop in the ages of the postdiluvians at the birth of their successors, as compared with the corresponding ages of the antediluvians according to the MT. By making the year of each of Abraham's ancestors (except Terah [LXX]) to fall before Abraham's departure for Canaan at the age of seventy-five, the Samar. and the LXX emphasize this as a new beginning in human history. According to the MT, on the other hand, all these ancestors were still living at the time of Abraham's departure.

The great longevity of the Genesis antediluvians

**Table 1**

**Genealogy of the Early Patriarchs**

| Patriarch | Age at Successor's Birth | | | Remaining Years | | | Total Years | | |
|---|---|---|---|---|---|---|---|---|---|
| | MT | Samar. | LXX | MT | Samar. | LXX | MT | Samar. | LXX |
| Adam | 130 | 130 | 230 | 800 | 800 | 700 | 930 | 930 | 930 |
| Seth | 105 | 105 | 205 | 807 | 807 | 707 | 912 | 912 | 912 |
| Enosh | 90 | 90 | 190 | 815 | 815 | 715 | 905 | 905 | 905 |
| Kenan | 70 | 70 | 170 | 840 | 840 | 740 | 910 | 910 | 910 |
| Mahalalel | 65 | 65 | 165 | 830 | 830 | 730 | 895 | 895 | 895 |
| Jared | 162 | 62 | 162 | 800 | 785 | 800 | 962 | 847 | 962 |
| Enoch | 65 | 65 | 165 | 300 | 300 | 200 | 365 | 365 | 365 |
| Methuselah | 187 | 67 | 167 | 782 | 653 | 802 | 969 | 720 | 969 |
| Lamech | 182 | 53 | 188 | 595 | 600 | 565 | 777 | 653 | 753 |
| Noah | 500 | 500 | 500 | 450 | 450 | 450 | 950 | 950 | 950 |
| Shem | 100 | 100 | 100 | 500 | 500 | 500 | | 600 | |
| Total years at the Flood | 1656 | 1307 | 2242 | | | | | | |
| Arpachshad | 35 | 135 | 135 | 403 | 303 | 430 | | 438 | |
| Kainan | | | 130 | | | 330 | | | |
| Shelah | 30 | 130 | 130 | 403 | 303 | 330 | | 433 | |
| Eber | 34 | 134 | 134 | 430 | 270 | 370 | | 404 | |
| Peleg | 30 | 130 | 130 | 209 | 109 | 209 | | 239 | |
| Reu | 32 | 132 | 132 | 207 | 107 | 207 | | 239 | |
| Serug | 30 | 130 | 130 | 200 | 100 | 200 | | 230 | |
| Nahor | 29 | 79 | 79 | 119 | 69 | 129 | | 148 | |
| Terah | 70 | 70 | 70 | | | | 205 | 145 | 205 |
| Total years at Abraham's birth | 1946 | 2247 | 3312 | | | | | | |
| Plus the 2 years of Gen. 11:10 | 1948 | 2249 | 3314 | | | | | | |

finds a striking analogy in the fantastically long life spans of the antediluvian kings in the Sumerian King List. According to this list, one of the kings ruled as long as 43,200 years, and all eight ruled for a total of 241,000 years.

**b. From Abraham to the Exodus.** For the period before Abraham there is no event in secular history which may be used as a check point for establishing absolute dates. Many exegetes have believed, however, that Gen. 14 provides a basis for comparative chronology. This chapter records Abraham's contact with four invading kings, among them a certain

Canaan, as well as to the bondage in Egypt (cf. Gal. 3:17), thus reducing the latter by the 215 years elapsed between Abraham's entry into Canaan in his 75th year and the descent to Egypt in Jacob's 130th year. They make the sojourn in Canaan and the bondage in Egypt of equal length. It is to be doubted, however, that the additional words, "in the land of Canaan," can be considered as part of the original text, since in these two versions they occur in opposite order with relation to "in Egypt." Moreover, the term "people of Israel" would scarcely apply to the patriarchs before Jacob.

### Table 2
### Years from Abraham's Birth to the Exodus

| Period | Years |
|---|---|
| From Abraham's birth to his entry into Canaan (Gen. 12:4) | 75 |
| From Abraham's entry into Canaan to the birth of Isaac (Gen. 21:5) | 25 |
| From Isaac's birth to the birth of Jacob (Gen. 25:26) | 60 |
| From Jacob's birth to his descent into Egypt (Gen. 47:9) | 130 |
| From the descent into Egypt to the Exodus (Exod. 12:40-41) | |
| MT | 430 |
| LXX and Samar. | 215 |
| Total duration | |
| MT | 720 |
| LXX and Samar. | 505 |

Amraphel. Most attempts to identify these kings with personages in secular records have been highly hypothetical, but many scholars have confidently equated Amraphel with the famous HAMMURABI of the first Babylonian dynasty. A Babylonian chronology formerly accepted by most scholars dated this king 2123-2081 B.C. This agreed very well with a date for Abraham in the twenty-first century B.C., as required by a fifteenth-century exodus (*see below*). However, Hammurabi's dates have been radically revised by subsequent evidence that he was a contemporary of Shamshi-Adad I of Assyria and by new information from the Mari documents, from excavations at Alalakh in Syria, and from the Khorsabad King List. Many scholars now agree that Hammurabi reigned between 1728 and 1686 B.C.

Although the identification of Amraphel with Hammurabi remains problematical, there are some who feel that this identification should still be maintained, even on the basis of the low chronology, which would place Abraham in the seventeenth or eighteenth century. Nevertheless, it ought to be recognized that some of the figures in the OT definitely demand the early date for Abraham if their schematic character is not recognized (*see* Table 2). These are the 100 years of Abraham at Isaac's birth, Isaac's 60 years at the birth of Jacob, Jacob's 130 years at his descent to Egypt, the 430 years of Israel's bondage in Egypt (Exod. 12:40-41 MT), and the 480 years from the Exodus to the founding of the temple in Solomon's fourth year, *ca.* 967 (I Kings 6:1 MT). These figures add up to a total of 720 years from Abraham's birth to the Exodus and of 1,200 years to Solomon, placing Abraham's birth at 2167 and the Exodus at 1447.

It is true that both the LXX and the Samar. make the 430 years of Exod. 12:40 apply to the sojourn in

As a matter of fact, the genealogical lists of this period make a 430-year residence in Egypt impossible and even a 215-year residence very unlikely. There is record of no more than four generations from Jacob to Moses—viz., Levi, Kohath, Amram, Moses (Exod. 6:16-20; cf. Num. 3:17-19; 26:58-59; I Chr. 6:1-3). That this genealogy is intended to be complete is plainly implied in Gen. 15:16, where return from bondage is promised Abraham's descendants "in the fourth generation." Yet Kohath, who was one of those who went down to Egypt (Gen. 46:11), lived 133 years, his son Amram lived 137 years (Exod. 6:18, 20), and Moses was 80 years old at the time of the Exodus (7:7). Although we have no statement as to Jacob's age at the birth of Levi, or of Levi's age at the birth of Kohath, the likelihood is that the latter was a grown man at the descent to Egypt in Jacob's 130th year. Likewise it is probable that Amram was born within 40 or 50 years after his father's birth. But if we should go so far as to assume that Kohath was born the year before the descent; that his eldest son, Amram, was born 132 years afterward in the year before Kohath's death; and that Moses was born 137 years after this in the year of his father's death, the sojourn in Egypt would stretch to more than 349 years. A far more likely figure would be between 140 and 210 years, allowing 40 or 50 years for each generation. It has often been observed that most of the genealogical notices in the Pentateuch agree with this calculation. An early-seventeenth-century date for Abraham is made possible by this figure, depending on the date assigned for the Exodus.

**2. From the Exodus to Solomon's temple.** The statement in I Kings 6:1 that Solomon began to build his temple in his 4th year, which was the 480th year since the Exodus, has already been mentioned. Together with a statement ascribed to Jephthah in Judg. 11:26 that Israel had already occupied Heshbon and surrounding areas for 300 years, this calculation leads to a date for the Exodus in the middle of the fifteenth century, during the reign of Thutmose III (1490-1436) of the Eighteenth Dynasty. This Pharaoh, an ambitious builder, might fit very well the characteristics of the biblical king who set the Hebrews to building store cities (Exod. 1:11), were it not for the fact that the latter are said to have lived and worked in the Delta area, while the kings of the Eighteenth Dynasty had their residence far up the Nile at Thebes.

Further evidence for a fifteenth-century exodus has been found, however, in the Amarna Letters (see TELL EL-AMARNA). On the chronology under consideration, the Hebrews would have been conquering Palestine under Joshua in the years near and soon after 1400. According to the Amarna Letters, which

were sent from Palestine to Amen-hotep III (1413-1377) and Amen-hotep IV Akh-en-Aton (1377-1360), a group of marauders called HABIRU (probably to be associated with the Hebrews) were invading the central highlands at precisely this period. When J. Garstang, the excavator of Jericho, announced that that city had been destroyed before 1400 B.C., a fifteenth-century date for the Exodus seemed to many to be certain.

There are serious objections to this date, however. For one thing, archaeologists of competence have challenged Garstang's evidence as inconclusive and have pointed to the numerous contrary indications that various cities in the path of Joshua's conquest, such as Lachish, Debir, and Bethel, were destroyed in the second half of the thirteenth century. As a matter of fact, a date for the Exodus in this century fits the circumstances of contemporary history far better than does the earlier date. Counting 480 years

### Table 3
### Years from the Exodus to the Founding
### of Solomon's Temple, According to Biblical Data

| Intervals Associated With | Years |
|---|---|
| The wilderness wandering (Num. 32:13) | 40 |
| Period of Joshua and the elders (Judg. 2:7; duration not stated) | x |
| Oppression of Cushan-rishathaim (Judg. 3:8) | 8 |
| Othniel (Judg. 3:11) | |
|     MT | 40 |
|     LXX | 50 |
| Oppression of Eglon (Judg. 3:14) | 18 |
| Ehud (Judg. 3:30) | 80 |
| Oppression of Jabin (Judg. 4:3) | 20 |
| Deborah–Barak (Judg. 5:31) | 40 |
| Oppression of the Midianites (Judg. 6:1) | 7 |
| Gideon (Judg. 8:28) | 40 |
| Abimelech (Judg. 9:22) | 3 |
| Tola (Judg. 10:2) | 23 |
| Jair (Judg. 10:3) | 22 |
| Oppression of the Ammonites (Judg. 10:8) | 18 |
| Jephthah (Judg. 12:7) | 6 |
| Ibzan (Judg. 12:9) | 7 |
| Elon (Judg. 12:11) | 10 |
| Abdon (Judg. 12:14) | 8 |
| Oppression of the Philistines (Judg. 13:1) | 40 |
| Samson (Judg. 15:20; 16:31) | 20 |
| Eli (I Sam. 4:18) | |
|     MT | 40 |
|     LXX | 20 |
| Samuel; ark in Kirjath-jearim (I Sam. 7:2) | 20 |
| Saul (I Sam. 13:1; full number lacking) | y |
| David (I Kings 2:11; 7 years in Hebron, 33 years in Jerusalem) | 40 |
| Solomon (to building of temple; I Kings 6:1) | 4 |
| Total duration | |
|     MT | 554 plus x plus y |
|     LXX | 544 plus x plus y |
| Remaining years of Solomon (total reign, 40 years; I Kings 11:42) | 36 |

for the sojourn in Egypt, it makes possible an entry of the Hebrews into Egypt near the beginning of the semi-Semitic Hyksos Dynasty (*ca.* 1700-1565 B.C.). It also accounts for the fact that no mention is made of Egyptian inroads into Palestine in the books of Joshua and Judges, as very likely would have been the case had the Exodus occurred before the great Asiatic campaigns of Seti I (1319-1301) and Ramses II (1301-1234). Archaeological evidence from the Transjordan similarly favors a thirteenth-century exodus.

A date for the Exodus *ca.* 1290 or 1280, during the reign of Ramses II, has found wide favor (*see* RAMSES 2). In addition to the items of evidence just mentioned, a major argument for this date is based upon the statement of Exod. 1:11 that the Hebrews built Pithom and Ra-amses. The latter can hardly be any other than Per-Ramesese, almost certainly the same as Avaris-Zoan, the Delta capital of the Hyksos and the new capital of Ramses II, which he claims in his inscriptions to have built. That the name Ra-amses is not merely an anachronism, as some have claimed, is indicated by the fact that this city was apparently not occupied from the expulsion of the Hyksos (*ca.* 1565) until the accession of Ramses II.

As for the Habiru, there are several considerations which argue against their identification with Joshua's army. One is that further references to this people have been found in Babylonian and Hittite sources, in the NUZI texts, and in a text from Ras Shamra (*see* UGARIT), plainly indicating that the Habiru movement was far broader than the conquest of Canaan by the biblical Hebrews. Another major consideration is that when the Habiru raids in the Amarna Letters are compared with the report of Joshua's conquest, there are actually more differences than resemblances. A theory of a double entry into Canaan, appearing in several variations, attempts to reconcile an early fall of Jericho with this late date for the Exodus, and to account for an association of the Hebrew tribes with the fourteenth-century activities of the Habiru in Palestine. *See* ISRAEL, HISTORY OF, § 2.

In any case, most scholars agree that the Exodus must have occurred before 1229 B.C., the fifth year of MER-NE-PTAH, in which year this Pharaoh claims to have defeated "Israel" in the land of Palestine. There will continue to be uncertainty, however, concerning the exact time of the descent into Egypt and the duration of the Hebrews' sojourn there.

On the evidence for an exodus *ca.* 1290, it is apparent that the intervening period until Solomon is far shorter than the 480 years required by I Kings 6:1. Certain genealogies of this period demand a shorter interval, however. Thus Gen. 36:31-39 lists only eight Edomite kings reigning, according to the obvious intent of the passage, in the period culminating with the reign of Saul. Since a king was already ruling in Edom in Moses' time (Num. 20:14), these eight (or fewer) kings would have to fill a gap of approximately four hundred years if the Genesis passage is to agree with I Kings 6:1. Even worse, the six generations from Nahshon the contemporary of Moses (Exod. 6:23) to Solomon (Ruth 4:20-22) would have to stretch over this same period, unless long gaps in this genealogy are to be assumed.

It should be pointed out, moreover, that the chronology demanded by the books of Judges and Samuel actually far exceeds the figure of 480 years. As will be seen from Table 3, a total of 554 years plus two periods of unknown length occupy the interval from the Exodus to the founding of Solomon's temple. Josephus evidently based his estimate of 592 (Antiq. VIII.iii.1) or 612 (Apion II.ii) years for this period upon this observation (cf. Acts 13:18-21).

Unfortunately, there are no references to contemporary events in the records of this period sufficiently clear to be of use to us. The victory of Sisera (Judg. 4–5) is variously dated from 1200 to 1100 B.C., and references to the Philistines, who came to Palestine *ca.* 1175, offer little chronological help. Judg. 11:26, which might indicate a fifteenth-century exodus if this could be substantiated on other evidence, is perhaps the result of later calculation.

It is doubtless necessary to recognize that in many cases the judges were contemporaries of one another, exercising authority over limited tribal areas. This is certainly the case with Abimelech, who was regarded as an illegitimate ruler, and is very probable with regard to Samson and various others. *See* JUDGE; JUDGES, BOOK OF.

In any case, the figures of Table 3 indicate a tendency to schematization, with the employment of units, multiples, and fractions of 40 years. The schematic character of I Kings 6:1 itself has often been emphasized. Its 480 years, composed of 12 units of 40, was very likely obtained by subtracting all the years of oppression and the years of Abimelech, reducing the total of 554 years to 440, which would allow 20 years to Joshua and the Elders and 20 to Saul. Following a similar calculation, the LXX of I Kings 6:1 reduces its 544-year total to 430, the exact equivalent of the Hebrews' sojourn in Canaan and in Egypt according to its version of Exod. 12:40.

**3. From Solomon's temple to the Exile.** *a. Problems and methods.* When they come to the period of the Divided Monarchy, students of biblical chronology are at first sight delighted with the wealth of data available to them. First, there is a complete list of kings for both Judah and Israel, with the lengths of their respective reigns; second, synchronisms are provided for the accession of each king in terms of his contemporary's reign; third, the age of the kings of Judah at the time of their accession is stated; further, certain important events are dated either to a certain year or by the interval elapsed since another significant event; still further, certain biblical events are co-ordinated with contemporary occurrences in secular history. With so much information on hand, it would seem that the reconstruction of the chronology of this period should be a simple matter.

Nonetheless, various scholars who have worked with these data have found the chronology of this period almost beyond solution. They have discovered, to their dismay, that many of the above details seem to contradict one another. E.g., the total of years for Judah does not agree with the total for Israel; besides, the totals of either kingdom do not seem to fit the synchronisms. But worst of all is that the chronologies which many have attempted to construct from the biblical data fail to agree with historical information now available from a considerable variety of Assyrian and Babylonian documents.

Before discussing the problems connected with the biblical figures for this period, a statement of the high reliability of Assyrian chronology is in order. As contrasted, e.g., with the notorious ambiguity of many Egyptian historical records, the dependability of the Assyrian documents is outstanding. We know, for one thing, that the Assyrians (and Babylonians) kept their calendar year in precise accord with the solar year (*see* CALENDAR § 1). We also find in the Assyrian documents the employment of a method of dating which has proved to be of invaluable assistance for establishing absolute dates. Although the Assyrians did not date events by any given era, they did assign to each year the name of an eponym or limmu, as he was called, an official (sometimes the king himself) especially designated for this purpose. Assyriologists have been able to compile a complete list of these eponyms from 892 to 648 B.C.

Besides the name of the eponym for each year, this list mentions the years when the Assyrian kings began their reigns and gives the most notable political event of almost every year; but the most valuable of all its data is the mention of an eclipse of the sun in the month Simanu in the year of Bur-Sagale, which astronomers have calculated to have occurred on June 15, 763 B.C. Upon the basis of this calculation every other year in the eponym list can be fixed.

The dates of this list have been absolutely confirmed by other ancient chronological documents, the most important of which are the Khorsabad King List and the Canon of Ptolemy. The former was dated by the scribe who prepared it in the second eponymy of Adad-bel-ukin, the same as the eighth year of Tiglath-pileser III, 738 B.C. In the body of the Khorsabad List a complete succession of Assyrian kings is given from the beginning down to 745 B.C., in many cases with the length of reign, and the data of this list are in perfect agreement with the Eponym List. The Canon of Ptolemy, though coming from the second century A.D., records the reigns of Babylonian kings back to Nabonassar in 747 B.C., as well as the reigns of later Persian, Ptolemaic, and Roman rulers. Its accuracy has been established by Ptolemy's mention in another writing of numerous solar, lunar, and planetary positions, including eclipses, all dated in the reigns of the various kings mentioned in his canon. In every case astronomers have confirmed these data exactly.

With the aid of this fixed chronology for the Assyrian and Babylonian kings, some of their contacts with biblical kings mentioned in cuneiform records can be given an absolute date. The most important are the following:

*a*) The battle of Shalmaneser III (859-824) in his sixth year with Ahab and the Syrian allies at Qarqar, 853 B.C. (Monolith Inscription, *ANET* 278).

*b*) Shalmaneser III receives the tribute of Jehu in his eighteenth year, 841 (Annals and Black Obelisk, *ANET* 280, *ANEP* 122).

*c*) Tiglath-pileser III (745-727) receives tribute from Azariah and Menahem between 743 and 738, and is in contact with Jehoahaz (Ahaz), Pekah, and Hoshea in unstated years (Building Inscription, Annals, *ANET* 282-84).

*d*) Sargon II (722-705) captures Samaria in his accession year, 722/21 (Khorsabad Inscriptions,

*ANET* 284 f); but cf. the Eponym List and Babylonian Chronicle 1:28, which put this event in the last year of Shalmaneser V (727-722), 723/22.

*e*) Sennacherib (705-681) besieges Hezekiah in his fourth year, 701 (Oriental Institute and Taylor Prisms, *ANET* 287-88).

*f*) Neco at the siege of Harran, Tammuz to Elul in the seventeenth year of Nabopolassar (626-605), 609 (Gadd Chronicle, *ANET* 305).

*g*) The Battle of Carchemish in Nabopolassar's twenty-first year, 605 (B.M. 21946; cf. Jer. 25:1; 46:2).

*h*) Nebuchadrezzar II (605-562) captures Jerusalem on 2 Adar of his seventh year, March 16, 597 (D. J. Wiseman, *Chronicles of Chaldean Kings*, pp. 33, 73).

It is certain that most Assyrian and Babylonian chronological records deserve great confidence. Much of modern scholarship has denied this confidence to the biblical records, however, on the ground that these do not seem to agree with Assyrian chronology. There are still some, it is true, who prefer to ignore the demands of contemporary history for the sake of what they imagine to be a biblical chronology, explaining the discrepancies in the biblical figures as best they can, mainly by assuming several periods of interregnum in the lists of kings. This is a course, however, which enlightened scholarship refuses to follow. Convinced of the basic reliability of the cuneiform records, one is certain that something is wrong with the biblical data or with current methods of interpreting these data. Despite the fact that in recent decades more respect has been shown for the synchronisms and other figures than was usual during the ascendancy of the Wellhausen school, almost all chronologies of the Divided Monarchy are still forced to emend many of the biblical figures in order to bring them into a harmonious pattern and to make them agree with the Assyrian data.

Since scholarship in general has been passing through a period of profound doubt concerning the trustworthiness of the entire biblical tradition, it is small wonder that the Hebrew scribes have been easily accused of inaccuracy in recording chronological materials. Now, however, that the biblical tradition and the MT are being strikingly confirmed in countless ways, it is certainly in order that scholarship should again approach these chronological records with a mind open to the possibility, or even the likelihood, that they are, after all, substantially correct. A priori, the Hebrew scribes ought to deserve as much confidence, unless proved absolutely wrong, as the scribes of other peoples.

Happily, knowledge is at present available which makes it unnecessary to yield either the testimony of secular records or of the biblical text. It is possible to fit almost all the biblical data, unrevised, into a perfectly harmonious pattern while at the same time bringing this pattern into agreement with Assyrian and Babylonian records. One can do this by understanding thoroughly the methods and devices employed by the Hebrew scribes in recording their data.

It must be said that ancient attempts to improve the chronological statements of the MT, as in the LXX and in the writings of Josephus, have been demonstrated to be nothing more than that—attempts to emend what was not understood. They have no independent evidential value for the correct chronology of the Divided Monarchy, and modern systems based upon them are badly in error.

What then were the chronological methods of the Hebrew scribes? We must discover these through close study of the text and through careful experimentation. Several alternatives must be faced. First, it must be decided whether the scribes of Judah and Israel dated their kings by the accession-year or by the nonaccession-year method; then, which new-year day each kingdom employed, whether spring (Nisan) or fall (Tishri); further, how the scribes of each realm reckoned the reigns of their neighbors' kings, and whether each group of scribes was consistent in following a particular method throughout the whole period of the Divided Monarchy. Finally, the existence of any interregna or coregencies must be discovered. It will be apparent that possible combinations of these factors are numerous enough to lead to great complexity. Of the many combinations which have been tried by biblical chronologists, only the one here described, which is essentially that first proposed by Edwin R. Thiele (*see bibliography*), seems to give satisfactory results.

First of all, then, the method of counting reigns must be determined. The nonaccession-year system, in vogue in Egypt in ancient times, allowed a king to count the year of his accession as his first official year, while the same year also counted as the last official year of his predecessor. Also called the antedating system, this method resulted in counting one year too many in each reign. On the other hand, the accession-year or postdating system, which was the basis for reckoning in much of the Near East and in Mesopotamia, did not count a king's reign until the first new year after his predecessor's death. The portion of a year remaining between the predecessor's death and the new year was counted as the new king's accession year, and reigns which were too short to reach a new year were not counted. Under this system the true length of each reign was recorded.

A close examination of the early reigns of the Divided Monarchy reveals that Judah followed the postdating system, while Israel employed antedating, although later each kingdom changed its method. Thus the years of the kings of Judah till Omri's death (I Kings 14:21; 15:2; 16:29) total fifty-eight, while the years of the kings of Israel during the same period (14:20; 15:25, 33; 16:8, 23) total sixty-two, despite the fact that both kingdoms began in the same year. The only explanation of this phenomenon is that Israel's kings were antedated, resulting in excess years, while Judah's kings were postdated according to actual years of reign. The interesting fact that for this period Israel has only four excess years with five kings provides a vital clue to another of the chronological problems mentioned above—viz., the method of reckoning employed by Hebrew scribes for kings of the neighboring realm. Evidently the synchronism of I Kings 16:29, giving Asa thirty-eight years at Omri's death, is reckoned in terms of Israel's method of antedating. Omri actually died in Asa's thirty-seventh year, and the true length of the period in question was fifty-seven years. We have here then an illustration of the fact that the scribes

of each realm applied the methods of their own kingdom to the kings of the other realm, and this is a practice which proves to have been consistently followed.

A further problem concerns the beginning of the new year for each kingdom. For Judah we have direct evidence that the year was counted from the first of Tishri (September-October). I Kings 6:1, 37-38; II Kings 22:3; 23:23, together with the archaeological evidence of the Gezer Calendar, plainly demand such a reckoning. (For details, *see* CALENDAR § 2.) Moreover, a Tishri new year for Judah is demanded by the chronological data now under consideration.

The opposite is required for Israel. Although we have no direct statement that Israel reckoned the years of her kings from a new year in Nisan (March-April), a close scrutiny of certain synchronisms and lengths of reign makes it apparent that this was the case. Thus Rehoboam is said to have reigned seventeen years (I Kings 14:21), evidently from a new year in Tishri. During his seventeenth year he died, and his son Abijam reigned in his stead. This, Abijam's accession year, is said to have been Jeroboam's eighteenth year (15:1), even though it is a Judahite scribe who made the notation (*see above*). Since Rehoboam and Jeroboam began their reigns in the same year (ch. 12), it is evident that the latter reckoned his rule from a Nisan new year, and thus that Abijam must have begun his reign between the months of Nisan and Tishri. If it be supposed that, despite the fact that a Judahite scribe recorded this synchronism, the eighteenth year of Jeroboam was calculated by the antedating method (hence one year too high), then one must reckon with the synchronism given for Asa's accession after Abijam's three-year reign (I Kings 15:2, 8), which is the twentieth year of Jeroboam (vs. 9). If the scribe had been figuring Jeroboam's reign by Tishri years and by the antedating system, this would have had to be Jeroboam's twenty-first year. As it is, Asa began to reign between Tishri and Nisan—i.e., during the six months after the beginning of his father's third year and before the end of Jeroboam's twentieth.

Further examples could be given. Some will be noted in the discussion to follow, but at this point it must suffice to say that on the basis of Nisan years for Israel and Tishri years for Judah, many perplexing difficulties disappear and a pattern of harmony results. A Nisan new year was observed from ancient times in Babylonia and Assyria. The traveling new year of the calendar in Egypt, where Jeroboam found refuge from Rehoboam before the beginning of his reign (I Kings 11:40; 12:2), was celebrated in the springtime at this period. Since Jeroboam is known to have been an innovator with calendrical reckoning (cf. 12:32-33), it is easy to believe that he might have introduced the Nisan new year in his realm.

A further question which must be dealt with concerns the existence of interregna or coregencies. As has been mentioned, the totals of years for Judah and for Israel do not agree, and this discrepancy cannot be accounted for solely on an understanding of the modes of reckoning employed by the ancient scribes. From the disruption of the realm at Solomon's death to Jehu, Judah's years total 95, while

Israel's years total 98 plus 7 days. From Jehu to the fall of Samaria, Judah's years total 166, and Israel's total 143 plus 7 months. These discrepancies might be accounted for, at least in some instances, by the supposition of interregna (apart from the very unlikelihood of such a supposition), were it not for the fact that for the latter period Assyria's chronology allows no more than 120 years, indicating that both Judah's and Israel's totals must be shortened rather than lengthened. The only way in which a shorter total may be obtained is on the theory that coregencies existed at certain times in this period.

What is the evidence for the existence of coregencies in the Divided Kingdom? First of all, II Kings 8:16 (MT) plainly states that Jehoram of Judah began his reign while his father, Jehoshaphat, was still king. Another item of evidence for this coregency is found in 1:17; 3:1, where Joram of Israel is said to have begun his rule both in the second year of Jehoram and in the eighteenth year of Jehoshaphat. The only way to resolve these seeming inconsistencies is to posit a coregency for Jehoram beginning in his father's seventeenth year. The further statement of 8:16 that Jehoram began to reign in the fifth year of Joram of Israel must be understood to refer to the beginning of his independent reign.

There is good evidence, besides, for five additional coreigns during the period of the Divided Kingdom, plus one other in Judah after the fall of Samaria. Of these coreigns, the one for which there is the most direct statement is that of Jotham with Azariah (II Kings 15:5); others which may be legitimately deduced from chronological and similar indications are those of Jehoshaphat with Asa, Jeroboam II with Jehoash, Azariah with Amaziah, Ahaz with Jotham, and Manasseh with Hezekiah. Six of these coregencies pertained to the Judahite realm, while only one was in the N kingdom. Undoubtedly the wisdom of the kings of Judah in providing for the certain succession of their proper heirs through appointing them to coregencies before their own deaths, as was the case in most instances, accounts to a great extent for the remarkable stability of their dynasty.

On the basis of the above discussion we are now in a position to compare the biblical figures with known dates in contemporary secular records. If a pattern of harmony results, we have strong presumptive evidence that our interpretation is correct.

To recapitulate, then, one may say that the methods of the Hebrew scribes were the following: Judah's scribes dated their kings from a Tishri new year by the postdating method (changed, as we shall see, to the antedating method in Jehoram's reign and back again to postdating in the reign of Amaziah); Israel's scribes conversely dated from Nisan on the antedating basis (changed to postdating in the reign of Jehoash); both groups of scribes were consistent in figuring the reigns of the neighboring kingdom by their own methods; both took account of coregencies, sometimes expressing the length of a given reign from the beginning of a coregency and sometimes from the beginning of independent rule.

Since Ahab's son Ahaziah reigned two years (I Kings 22:51), and another son Joram (or Jehoram) reigned twelve years (II Kings 3:1), both figures being reckoned by antedating for a total of twelve

actual years; and since, as we have seen, this twelve-year period is the precise interval provided by the Assyrian records for the period between Shalmaneser III's contact with Ahab (853) and his contact with Jehu (841), we are forced to the conclusion that 853 was Ahab's last year, while 841 was the first year of Jehu. Thus we have two firm points for dating the various reigns of the Divided Monarchy. We also have a valuable confirmation that the antedating method was indeed in use in the N kingdom at this period.

Dating back from Ahab's death by the antedating method and subtracting a total of seventy-eight years and seven days, we arrive at 931 B.C. as the year of the beginning of Jeroboam's reign. This was also the year of Rehoboam's accession and of Solomon's death.

It will now be necessary to outline the chronology of the kingdoms of Israel and Judah from the Disruption to the Babylonian exile, using the dates already established as a firm basis for others and applying to the biblical figures the precise methods of the Hebrew scribes as described above. In Tables 4 and 5 all the reigns and coregencies of Israel and Judah are placed in graphic relationship with one another, along with the scripture references, lengths of reign and synchronisms, important events, dates, and contacts with foreign kings.

*b. From Solomon's temple to Jehu.* We have established the year 931 as the beginning of the reigns of both Rehoboam and Jeroboam. Thirty-six years previous to this, in Solomon's fourth year, the foundation of the temple had been laid. This was the year 967, the date furnished in our discussion above.

Although most scholars have favored a date for the Disruption close to 931, some recent chronologies have placed it as late as 922. Arguments for 922 have been based mainly on a Tyrian king list presumably cited by Josephus, and on the supposition that Shishak's raid in Rehoboam's fifth year (I Kings 14:25) must be dated too late to agree with 931 as the date of the Disruption. Such arguments are, however, too speculative in nature to weigh against the strong evidence for a 931 date.

The SHISHAK of I Kings 11:40; 14:25 was the vigorous Sheshonk or Shoshenq I, founder of the Twenty-Second Dynasty in Egypt. Recent dates assigned to him are 935-914, although the evidence for this is not altogether certain. This king has left in an undated inscription a record of the Palestinian cities captured by him on his campaign of 926/25.

After Jeroboam's reign of twenty-one actual years, his son Nadab came to the throne. In the statements that Nadab began to rule in Asa's second year (I Kings 15:25) and that Baasha slew Nadab in Asa's third year, after Nadab had reigned for two years (vss. 28, 33), we have another indication that in this period Israel reckoned by the antedating method, while Judah reckoned by postdating.

When we come to the reign of Baasha, an interesting chronological problem arises. I Kings 16:8 records that this king ruled for only twenty-four years (twenty-three by actual reckoning), after which he was succeeded by his son Elah. Confirmation for this figure is found in the further statement that Elah began to rule in Asa's twenty-sixth year. Yet we read

## Table 4
### Chronology of the Divided Kingdom

Legend: AR—accredited reign
CR—years of coregency
a/d—antedating or nonaccession-year system
p/d—postdating or accession-year system

| Scripture References | Rulers of Judah (Tishri Years) | Rulers of Israel (Nisan Years) | Dates B.C. | Dated Foreign Contacts |
|---|---|---|---|---|
| I Kings 14:20-21; II Chr. 12:13 | REHOBOAM<br>King 17 years p/d | JEROBOAM<br>King 22 years a/d | 931/30 | |
| I Kings 14:25; II Chr. 12:2 | 5 Rehoboam p/d | | 926/25 | Shishak's invasion |
| I Kings 15:1-2; II Chr. 13: 1-2 | ABIJAM<br>18 Jeroboam p/d<br>King 3 years p/d | | 913 | |
| I Kings 15:9-10; II Chr. 16:13 | ASA<br>20 Jeroboam p/d<br>King 41 years p/d | | 911/10 | |
| I Kings 15:25 | | NADAB<br>2 Asa a/d<br>King 2 years a/d | 910/09 | |
| I Kings 15:28, 33 | | BAASHA<br>3 Asa a/d<br>King 24 years a/d | 909/08 | |
| II Chr. 14:9, 15:10; cf. 15:19 | Victory celebration, 15 Asa p/d | | 896/95 | Zerah's invasion |
| II Chr. 16:1 | War with Baasha, 16 (MT 36) Asa p/d | Baasha builds Ramah | 895/94 | |
| I Kings 16:8 | | ELAH<br>26 Asa a/d<br>King 2 years a/d | 886/85 | |
| I Kings 16:10, 15 | | ZIMRI<br>27 Asa a/d<br>King 7 days | 885/84 | |
| I Kings 16:21-22 | | OMRI-------TIBNI | 885/84 | |
| I Kings 16:23 | | 6 years a/d<br>in Tirzah | | |
| I Kings 16:23 | | Sole rule, 31 Asa a/d; total rule 12 years a/d | 880 | |
| I Kings 16:29 | | AHAB<br>38 Asa a/d<br>King 22 years a/d | 874/73 | |
| I Kings 22:42; II Chr. 20:31; cf. 16:12 | *Jehoshaphat* coregent in 39 Asa a/d<br>Total reign 25 years | | 873/72 | |
| I Kings 22:41 | JEHOSHAPHAT, sole reign, 4 Ahab p/d | | 870/69 | |
| II Chr. 17:7 | Reform in 3rd year | | 867/66? | |
| cf. II Kings 1:17; 3:1; 8:16 MT | *Jehoram* coregent | | 854/53 | |
| | | | 853 | Battle of Qarqar |
| I Kings 22:51 | | AHAZIAH<br>17 Jehoshaphat a/d<br>King 2 years a/d | 853 | |

Based on the chronology of Edwin R. Thiele

**Table 4** (*continued*)

| Scripture References | Rulers of Judah (Tishri Years) | Rulers of Israel (Nisan Years) | Dates B.C. | Dated Foreign Contacts |
|---|---|---|---|---|
| II Kings 1:17<br>II Kings 3:1 | | J(EH)ORAM<br>2 Jehoram CR a/d<br>18 Jehoshaphat a/d<br>King 12 years a/d | 852 | |
| II Kings 8:16-17; II Chr. 21:5, 20 | JEHORAM, sole reign<br>5 Joram a/d<br>Sole reign 8 years a/d | | 848 | |
| II Chr. 21:19 | Sick 2 years | | | |
| II Kings 9:29<br>II Kings 8:25-26; II Chr. 22:2 | AHAZIAH<br>11 Joram p/d<br>12 Joram a/d<br>King (part of)<br>1 year | | 841 | |
| II Kings 10:36; 11:3-4; II Chr. 22:12 | ATHALIAH<br>(Queen 7 years a/d) | JEHU<br>King 28 years a/d | 841 | |
| | | | 841 | Jehu pays tribute to Shalmaneser III |
| II Kings 12:1; II Chr. 24:1 | J(EH)OASH<br>7 Jehu a/d<br>King 40 years a/d | | 835 | |
| II Kings 12:6 | Repairs on temple in 23rd year | | 814/13 | |
| II Kings 13:1 | | J(EH)OAHAZ<br>23 Joash a/d<br>King 17 years a/d | 814/13 | |
| ---------------------------------- (From this point all reigns are p/d) ---------------------------- ||||
| II Kings 13:10 | | J(EH)OASH<br>37 Joash<br>King 16 years | 798 | |
| II Kings 14:1-2; II Chr. 25:1 | AMAZIAH<br>2 Jehoash<br>King 29 years (counting years of retirement) | | 797/96 | |
| II Kings 14:23; cf. 15:1 | | *Jeroboam* coregent in 15 Amaziah<br>Total reign 41 years | 793/92 | |
| II Kings 14:21; II Chr. 26:1; cf. II Kings 15:2, 8, 13, 23, 27 | AZARIAH (UZZIAH)<br>King at his father's captivity | | 792/91 | |
| II Kings 15:2; II Chr. 26:3 | Total reign 52 years | | | |
| II Kings 14:23 | | JEROBOAM II, sole reign, 15 Amaziah | 782/81 | |
| II Kings 14:17; II Chr. 25:25 | Amaziah lives 15 years after Jehoash' death | | | |
| II Kings 15:1 | *Azariah's* sole reign, 27 Jeroboam CR | | 768/67 | |
| II Kings 15:8 | | ZECHARIAH<br>38 Azariah<br>King 6 months | 753/52 | |

**Table 4** (*continued*)

| Scripture References | Rulers of Judah (Tishri Years) | Rulers of Israel (Nisan Years) | Dates B.C. | Dated Foreign Contacts |
|---|---|---|---|---|
| II Kings 15:13 | | SHALLUM<br>39 Azariah<br>King 1 month | 752 | |
| II Kings 15:17 | | MENAHEM<br>39 Azariah<br>King 10 years<br>(Accredited reign<br>of Pekah) | 752/51 | |
| II Kings 15:32;<br>cf. 15:5, 30;<br>II Chr. 26:21 | *Jotham* coregent<br>2 Pekah AR | | 750 | |
| II Kings 15:33;<br>II Chr. 27:1, 8 | Jotham's reign from<br>coregency to core-<br>gency 16 years | | | |
| II Kings 15:19-<br>20 | | | 742/41 | Menahem and<br>Azariah pay<br>tribute to<br>Tiglath-<br>pileser III |
| II Kings 15:23 | | PEKAHIAH<br>50 Azariah<br>King 2 years | 742/41 | |
| II Kings 15:27 | | PEKAH<br>52 Azariah<br>Accredited reign<br>20 years (from<br>Shallum) | 740/39 | |
| | JOTHAM, sole reign | | 740/39 | |
| II Chr. 27:5 | At least 3 years<br>sole reign | | | |
| II Kings 16:1 | *Ahaz* coregent in<br>17 Pekah AR | | 735 | |
| II Kings 16:5-10;<br>II Chr. 28:5-<br>16, 20-21; cf.<br>Isa. 7:1 ff; 8:1-4 | Ahaz wars with<br>Israel and Syria,<br>appeals to Assyria | | 734-732 | Tiglath-<br>pileser III<br>in Palestine |
| II Kings 16:2;<br>II Chr. 28:1 | AHAZ, sole reign<br>Rule for 16 years | | 732/31 | Tiglath-<br>pileser deposes<br>Pekah |
| II Kings 15:30 | | HOSHEA<br>20 Jotham CR | 732/31 | |
| II Kings 17:1 | | King 9 years | | |
| II Kings 17:5;<br>18:9 | | 3-year siege of Sa-<br>maria begins in 7<br>Hoshea | 725/24 | |
| II Kings 17:6;<br>18:10 | | Samaria falls in<br>9 Hoshea | 723/22 | |
| | | | 722/21 | Accession year<br>of Sargon II |

in II Chr. 16:1 that Baasha built Ramah and began to wage war with Judah in Asa's thirty-sixth year. This is not the only point in which Kings and Chronicles seem to disagree about the details of Asa's and Baasha's reigns. I Kings 15:16, 32, states that there was war between these two kings all their days; yet II Chr. 14:1, 6, informs us that Judah enjoyed peace for the first ten years of Asa's reign, and in 15:19 we read the strange statement that "there was no more war until the thirty-fifth year of the reign of Asa."

Now if the thirty-sixth year of II Chr. 16:1 were correct, it is apparent that Rehoboam's reign would have to be substantially shortened, perhaps bringing his accession, with adjustments in the lengths of some of the other reigns, to the late date mentioned above, 922 B.C. This procedure would have the severe additional disadvantage, it should be realized, of reducing to meaninglessness a whole series of synchronisms (I Kings 15:1, 9, 25, 33; 16:8, 10, 15, 23, 29). Nevertheless, support for the superiority of II Chr. 16:1 has been sought in the references to Ben-hadad, king of Syria, as Asa's ally in I Kings 15:18-20; II Chr. 16:4. An inscription of Ben-hadad I has been dated by orthographic evidence between 875 and 825. However, the length of this king's reign is not known. There exists no argument which would make it impossible for him to have been Asa's ally shortly after the beginning of the ninth century B.C. See BEN-HADAD 1.

Actually, II Chr. 15:19 according to the Hebrew text does not contain the word "more." It simply states that there was no war in Asa's reign until his "thirty-fifth year." And then in the "thirty-sixth year" the conflict began with Baasha. I Kings 15:16, 32, can easily be understood to mean that continual enmity existed between these kings, although without open warfare until the hostilities under consideration. The clue to an understanding of the "thirty-sixth year of Asa" is doubtless to be found in the preceding reference to the "thirty-fifth year." What the conflict was that occurred in Asa's "thirty-fifth year" is not stated in II Chr. 15:19, but the context does contain reference to warfare—viz., the invasion of Zerah (see ZERAH 4) and Asa's triumph (14:9-14), culminated by a great victory celebration and covenant reratification in Asa's fifteenth year (15:10). Is it not altogether likely that II Chr. 15:19 is a misplaced reference to this conflict? And, since many people from Ephraim and Manasseh were defecting to Asa's apparently victorious cause (15:9), should we not seek here the motive for Baasha's building Ramah and closing the border (16:1)? Baasha certainly would not wait for twenty years to take such action.

There are two possible explanations for the "thirty-fifth" and "thirty-sixth" years of II Chr. 15:19; 16:1. If the figures are correct, they could originally have referred to the beginning of the Divided Monarchy; if the reference to Asa's reign is correct, they could represent a very understandable scribal error for "fifteenth" and "sixteenth." The latter alternative would seem the most likely, since there are no other examples of dating from the Disruption, while the books of Chronicles do contain instances of scribal slips in the recording of numbers. Besides, the first alternative would place the war with Zerah, thirty-five years after the Disruption, in Asa's fourteenth year, 897/96, while the victory celebration is dated in his fifteenth year, 896/95. The text does not seem to make very likely an interval of a year between these events. It is better, therefore, to date the war with Zerah and victory celebration in Asa's fifteenth year, 896/95, and the war with Baasha in Asa's sixteenth year, 895/94.

The figures provided in I Kings 16:23 for Omri's reign have caused considerable confusion. It is best to take this verse as a conflation of chronological data from various sources. According to the record Omri actually began to reign in Asa's twenty-seventh year, since Zimri reigned before him for only seven days (vss. 10, 15); but Omri's capital remained in Tirzah while he struggled against his rival Tibni (vss. 21-22), whom he killed in Asa's thirty-first year. With Tibni out of the way, Omri proceeded to build a new capital in Samaria (vs. 24). Omri's total reign was twelve years (by antedating), the first six of which had been spent in Tirzah.

We have good evidence that there were two coregencies in Judah in this period. The coregency of Jehoram with his father, Jehoshaphat, has been explained above. The other coregency was that of Jehoshaphat with his father, Asa. The evidence for this coreign is as follows: Ahab's reign began in Asa's thirty-eighth year (I Kings 16:29). Asa's forty-one-year reign (15:10) ended, therefore, in Ahab's fourth year, which is given as the beginning of Jehoshaphat's rule in 22:42. Yet this same verse states that Jehoshaphat ruled for twenty-five years, after which he was succeeded by Jehoram. Jehoshaphat's reign must count from the beginning of a coregency with Asa three years before the latter's death, because Joram of Israel became king in Jehoshaphat's eighteenth year (II Kings 3:1) and Jehoram began his sole reign in the fifth year of Joram (8:16). II Chr. 16:12 furnishes the valuable information that Asa became seriously ill in his thirty-ninth year, which would be sufficient reason for the establishment of a coregency at that time.

Ahab was included among the Syrian allies who fought against Shalmaneser III of Assyria at Qarqar on the Euphrates in the year 853. As has been indicated above, 853 was Ahab's last year. We know, however, that Ahab was not killed at Qarqar but lived long enough to turn against his erstwhile ally Ben-hadad (called Hadad-Ezer in the Assyrian record) with the help of Jehoshaphat. Since his army had suffered less severely at Qarqar than had the army of Ben-hadad, Ahab may have considered this an ideal time to throw off the Syrian hegemony. He was, of course, mistaken. As I Kings 22:29-38 informs us, Ahab died in battle at Ramoth-gilead, probably shortly before the month Tishri in his twenty-second year, in the seventeenth year of King Jehoshaphat (16:29; 22:51).

As has been mentioned, Jehoram of Judah began his sole reign in his brother-in-law Joram's fifth year (cf. II Kings 8:18). Since this is a synchronism for Judah, this ought to be the actual fifth year, calculated by postdating, and would fall in the year 847. However, if we assume postdating for Judah in this period, the one-year reign of Ahaziah (II Kings 8:26) plus the preceding eight-year reign of Jehoram (vs. 17), dating back from the beginning of Jehu's reign in 841, would demand 850 instead of 847 as the year of Jehoram's accession. It should be obvious that the Judean court, so much under the influence of the house of Ahab at this period, had changed to Israel's method of antedating. Thus Jehoram began his rule in Joram's actual fourth year, 848, and reigned only seven years, while his son Ahaziah reigned only part of one year. The double synchronism for Ahaziah's accession found in II Kings 8:25; 9:29 confirms this fact. A scribe who was obedient to the court's demands recorded this as occurring in Joram's twelfth year, while another scribe, perhaps in defiance of the court or else living in a later period, recorded it as Joram's eleventh year. Incidentally, these synchronisms are added confirmation that Judah was using a Tishri year, while Israel was observing a new year in Nisan, since only by this arrangement could Jehoram's eight-year reign, followed by the accredited year of Ahaziah, fall in Joram's twelfth and last year.

The house of Ahab came to a bloody end with the revolt of Jehu in 841, which was also the year that Jehu paid tribute to Shalmaneser III, according to the Black Obelisk. Not only did Joram of Israel die, but Jehu killed Ahaziah of Judah as well (II Kings 9:24, 27), taking the throne of Israel for himself and leaving the S kingdom to Athaliah (11:1). Thus the year 841 is of utmost importance for the chronology of the Divided Monarchy, marking as it does the end of two parallel reigns and the beginning of two others.

It must be stressed at this point that the figures in the MT for lengths of reign and synchronisms have so far proved to be in perfect harmony with one another and with the Assyrian dates, the only exception being II Chr. 15:19; 16:1. Difficulties arise, not so much from the figures as from erroneous ways of interpreting them. There is a strong presumption, therefore, that the figures for the following reigns can similarly lead to reliable results if they are properly interpreted.

c. *From Jehu to the fall of Samaria.* Although the length of Athaliah's rule is not stated in the Bible, we are informed that the boy Joash took her throne and that she was put to death in her seventh year (II Kings 11:4). Since it is also stated that Joash began to reign in Jehu's seventh year (12:1), it is apparent that both kingdoms were counting by the antedating method. Thus Athaliah actually reigned for only six years, and Joash' forty official years (12:1) actually amounted to only thirty-nine.

We may also be certain that antedating was in vogue in both kingdoms when Jehoahaz succeeded Jehu after the latter's twenty-eight-year reign (II Kings 10:36), since this is stated as taking place in the twenty-third year of Joash (13:1), and Athaliah's seven-year reign had preceded that of Joash. A change in method of reckoning was introduced in the next reign, however. After Jehoahaz had reigned seventeen official years, his son Jehoash came to the throne in Joash' thirty-seventh year (13:10). Since Israel was following a Nisan and Judah a Tishri year, this synchronism can fit the period between Nisan and Tishri of Joash' thirty-seventh year, but only if this year is counted by postdating. Thus we see that Jehoash of Israel changed to the method of postdating, the practice formerly in vogue in Judah and now apparently becoming increasingly prevalent throughout the Near East with the spread of Assyrian influence. That Amaziah the son of Joash soon followed suit is certain from the synchronism for his accession in the second year of Jehoash (14:2). Even though the latter had already adopted the postdating method, Amaziah would have counted his own accession year as the third year of Jehoash, had he not himself made the change to postdating. Until the end both kingdoms adhered to this method without further change.

Jehoash reigned sixteen years (II Kings 13:10),

after which he was succeeded by his son Jeroboam in the fifteenth year of Amaziah (14:23). Amaziah reigned twenty-nine years (14:2)—i.e., until Jeroboam's fifteenth year. However, we are informed that Azariah (or Uzziah) succeeded to the throne of Judah in Jeroboam's twenty-seventh year (15:1). We have here an excess of twelve years for Jeroboam. This excess of twelve years at Azariah's accession is plain indication of a coregency of Jeroboam with his father beginning in the latter's fifth year, 793/92, and it appears that we should count Jeroboam's forty-one-year reign (14:23) from this date. Since Jeroboam's coregency began in Amaziah's third year, 793/92, his above-mentioned accession in Amaziah's fifteenth year must be understood to refer to the beginning of his sole reign at the death of his father. As a matter of fact, II Kings 14:17 reports the unusual but significant item that Amaziah lived fifteen years after Jehoash' death (and the beginning of Jeroboam's sole reign), thus filling out his twenty-nine years.

There was, however, a second coreign involved in these reigns which further complicates our chronology, that of Azariah with Amaziah. II Kings 15:1 provides the synchronism for the beginning of Azariah's sole reign. This was in the twenty-seventh year of Jeroboam's coregency, as we have seen, yet the synchronism for Zechariah at the end of Jeroboam's forty-one years (fourteen years later) is the thirty-eighth year of Azariah (vs. 8). This indicates that Azariah shared his father's throne twenty-four years—i.e., from Amaziah's sixth year, 791/90.

There is doubtless great significance in the fact that Jeroboam II began his coregency in 793/92 and Azariah came to the throne so soon afterward, in 791/90. II Kings 14:7-14; II Chr. 25:6-25 tell of a war between Amaziah and Jehoash, provoked by the former after a successful campaign against Edom. In this war Jehoash defeated Amaziah at Beth-shemesh, destroyed part of the wall of Jerusalem, and took Amaziah captive, apparently at least until his own death in 782/81. In all likelihood Jehoash took the precaution of appointing Jeroboam as his coregent shortly before the beginning of this conflict, so that 792 is the probable date of Beth-shemesh and of Amaziah's capture. Although it is likely that Jeroboam released the latter after the death of his father, Jehoash (this being then the significance of II Kings 14:17), it is apparent that the people of Judah would place another king on the throne in Amaziah's absence. This would be Azariah, whose first (official) year was 791/90. But very likely Azariah was actually enthroned a year earlier, in 792/91, and counted this as his accession year, not expecting his father's release. It is doubtful, therefore, whether we should speak of a coregency in the usual sense. When Amaziah did return and attempted to reassert authority, a conspiracy arose to have him assassinated—the incident is recorded in the misplaced notice of II Kings 14:19-21.

The date of Azariah's accession is extremely important for the years to follow, because no fewer than five kings of Israel are dated by it. Zechariah took the throne at the end of Jeroboam's forty-one-year reign, in Azariah's thirty-eighth year, which would be between Nisan and Tishri, 753. Six months later, in Azariah's thirty-ninth year, 753/52, Shallum slew Zechariah, but reigned only one month (II Kings 15: 13), after which he was himself assassinated by Menahem, this being also in the thirty-ninth year of Azariah (vs. 17). Since we are not told exactly in which months the short reigns of Zechariah and Shallum fell, we must determine the beginning of Menahem's reign on the basis of Pekahiah's accession in Azariah's fiftieth year (vs. 23). This was the year 742/41. Sometime after Tishri, 742, and before Nisan, 741, Menahem's ten-year reign came to an end; hence his accession year was 752/51. This means that Shallum's one-month reign straddled the Nisan new year of 752, and that Zechariah's reign was from Elul, 753, to Adar, 752.

The reign of Menahem provides another contact with a king of Assyria, in this case Tiglath-pileser III, who came to the throne in 745 B.C. II Kings 15:19-20 speaks of Menahem's paying tribute to Pul of Assyria, whom we know from cuneiform sources to be the same as TIGLATH-PILESER (cf. I Chr. 5:26). In the "Annals" of this king both Menahem of Israel and Azariah of Judah are mentioned as among those who showed subjection to him in his first W campaign, which began in his third actual year of reign, 743. A problem arises because Menahem and Azariah are mentioned in the section appearing immediately before the record of Tiglath-pileser's ninth year. The assumption has therefore been that these kings were still alive in 738, too late for the chronology with which we are working. The "Annals" have revealed upon further careful study, however, that the entire six-year campaign of Tiglath-pileser III in the W is described in terms of a geographical unit and not by separate years. As a matter of fact, there is no mention of separate years between the third and the ninth. There are, on the other hand, indications which show that the events connected with Menahem and Azariah actually occurred toward the beginning of the campaign, perhaps in Menahem's last year, 742/41.

In an undated tablet of Tiglath-pileser, Ahaz of Judah is also mentioned as tributary to him; and in still another tablet of uncertain date this Assyrian king claims to have put Menahem under tribute, to have caused Pekah's overthrow, and to have placed Hoshea in Pekah's place. Since, as we shall see, Pekah died in 732/31, several years after Menahem's death by any reckoning, we have confirmation that Tiglath-pileser did not mention his contacts with the Hebrew kings in strict annalistic order.

After Pekahiah's two-year reign, Pekah seized the throne. This was in the fifty-second and last year of Azariah, 740/39 (II Kings 15:23-27). Pekah is said to have reigned twenty years, thus until 720/19; but in addition to creating complete confusion in the chronology of this period, this reckoning makes impossible the above synchronism with Tiglath-pileser III, who died in 727. The Assyrian Eponym List helps us at this point, listing the years 734-732 as "against Philistia" and "against the land of Damascus." Unfortunately we do not know in which year of this last W campaign of Tiglath-pileser Pekah was overthrown, but, as we shall see, the whole pattern of the period makes 732/31 the most probable. Now, if 732/31 was the year of Pekah's death, it

is apparent that II Kings 15:27 credits his reign with twelve years too many. A likely explanation for this is that Pekah usurped the reigns of Menahem and his son Pekahiah, reckoning his own reign from the death of Shallum in 752. Pekah is said to have been a high officer at the royal court (vs. 25). Having undertaken to wipe out the house of Menahem, which he may have secretly regarded as illegitimate even while working in its service, he sought to efface from the record the years that it had held the throne by claiming them as his own.

It has been noted that Pekah began to reign in Azariah's fifty-second year, 740/39. Presumably this would also be the year of Jotham's accession; however, II Kings 15:32 states that the latter began to reign in Pekah's second year, implying an interregnum. The truth is that, far from an interregnum existing between Azariah's and Jotham's reigns, we have a definite statement that Jotham ruled for a period as coregent when his father became a leper (vs. 5). Besides, Hoshea's accession in the year 732/31 is spoken of as occurring in Jotham's twentieth year (vs. 30), bringing the time when Jotham began to reign, evidently as coregent, to the year 751/50. The synchronism of Jotham's accession for Pekah's second year thus refers to the beginning of his coregency in terms of Pekah's accredited reign thrown back to 752/51. The conclusion is that Jotham became coregent between Nisan and Tishri, 750. Another synchronism in terms of Pekah's usurped reign is that of Ahaz, whose accession is dated in the latter's seventeenth year (II Kings 16:1), which was 735/34. There were evidently scribes in the Judean court who sympathized with Pekah's attitude toward the house of Menahem.

Jotham is credited with a sixteen-year reign (II Kings 15:33). That these years were counted from the beginning of his coregency in 750, and not from his father's death in 740/39, is certain for the reason that Ahaz began his sixteen-year reign in 732/31, reckoning back from the beginning of the reign of his son Hezekiah, whose fourteenth year (18:13) was the year of Sennacherib's invasion of Judah, 701. But if Jotham reigned sixteen years from 751/50, Ahaz must have ascended the throne in 736/35 (counting no accession year for Jotham, since he came to the throne as coregent). This points to the same date that we have obtained on the basis of II Kings 16:1. Ahaz began to reign with his father (or instead of his father) between Nisan and Tishri, 735. Vss. 5-10 and parallel references in Chronicles and Isaiah inform us of Ahaz' collaboration with Tiglath-pileser III in that king's campaign against Philistia and Damascus (dated by the Eponym List in 734-732, as we have seen), and it was doubtless a pro-Assyrian party that forced Jotham to yield the throne at this time and considered this to be the end of his reign. The total length of Ahaz' reign was, however, counted from the beginning of his sole rule, beginning in the year of Jotham's death, 732/31; this reckoning was doubtless the work of anti-Assyrian scribes in Hezekiah's reign.

Hoshea, the last king of Israel, seized the throne in 732/31 and reigned nine years (II Kings 17:1). The beginning of Shalmaneser V's three-year siege of Samaria is dated in Hoshea's seventh year (18:9), and Samaria's fall is dated in his ninth year (17:6; 18:10). According to this reckoning Samaria fell in 723/22, Shalmaneser's last year.

The biblical text asserts that Shalmaneser captured Samaria (II Kings 18:9-10). However, the Khorsabad texts of his successor, Sargon II, definitely claim the fall of Samaria for Sargon's accession year, 722/21, and this is the date that has been generally accepted for this momentous event. If Samaria fell in 722/21, it is obvious that there are errors in the biblical text. There are reasons, however, to doubt Sargon's claim. The first is that this king does not mention the capture of Samaria in his early annals; he boasts of this success only in the inscriptions in his palace at Khorsabad, which he completed shortly before his death. Moreover, the Babylonian Chronicle 1.28 (a more disinterested witness) claims the capture of Samaria for Shalmaneser. Even more important, the Eponym List mentions the repair of a temple as the memorable event of Sargon's accession year, 722/21, while listing a campaign against a city whose name is unfortunately lost for the last three years of Shalmaneser's reign, 725-723. There can be little doubt that the city in question was Samaria, and that therefore this city actually fell in 723/22. It is, of course, possible that Sargon took part in the Samaria campaign as a leading general, and this would be sufficient justification in his own mind for claiming it as an achievement of his own reign, which began so soon afterward.

All the biblical and Assyrian dates for the period of the Divided Monarchy have now been fitted into a harmonious pattern, with the exception of the following four: Hoshea's accession in the twelfth year of Ahaz (II Kings 17:1); Hezekiah's accession in the third year of Hoshea (18:1); Hezekiah's fourth year equivalent to Hoshea's seventh (18:9); Hezekiah's sixth year equivalent to Hoshea's ninth (18:10). It is obvious that these synchronisms threaten to upset the chronology which has here been worked out. As a matter of fact, they have caused endless trouble for generations of biblical chronologists. There is, however, a significant consistency about these four figures: they all pertain to Hoshea's reign; the figure for Hoshea is twelve years too low; the figures for Ahaz and Hezekiah are thirteen years too high. They are therefore best explained as a late and mistaken calculation by an editor who did not understand the correct method of figuring the twenty accredited years of Pekah (15:27). This editor failed to realize that Pekah had usurped the twelve years of Menahem and Pekahiah, and hence he placed the events of Hoshea's reign twelve years too late. He evidently did have reliable data indicating when Ahaz and Hezekiah began their reigns, but since these Judean kings followed a Tishri rather than a Nisan year, he placed their reigns thirteen years too high in relation to the reign of Hoshea.

*d. From the fall of Samaria to the Babylonian exile.* The campaign of SENNACHERIB against Hezekiah in the year 701 has already been mentioned. Since this took place in Hezekiah's fourteenth year (II Kings 18:13), we see that this king began to reign in 716/15. This accords with the description in II Chr. 29 of a Passover celebration in his first year, which implies that Samaria had already fallen. It is further attested by other figures concerning Hezekiah's reign. II Kings 18:2 states that he ruled twenty-nine years, thus for fifteen years after his contact with Sennacherib in 701. This is the exact length of time that was promised to him after he became sick during the siege of Jerusalem (20:6).

There has been considerable discussion of whether Sennacherib made one or two campaigns against Judah, because of the mention of the Ethiopian king TIRHAKAH in II Kings 19:9. Recent research has dated the beginning of Tirhakah's reign in 690/89, so that if Sennacherib came into conflict with him during Hezekiah's reign, this must have been *ca.* 688.

Between Hezekiah's accession in 716/15 and Jehoiachin's captivity in the 8th year of Nebuchadrezzar, 597 (II Kings 24:12), there are recorded seven reigns with a total of 128 years and 6 months. This is almost 11 years too long. Once again we face the alternative of errors in the record or of a coregency. In the face of the amazing accuracy of the chronological figures so far examined, it is not easy to assume an error. But if a coregency existed, who was it that shared his father's throne? Because there are no direct hints in the record, we must arrive at an answer by elimination. It was not Amon, Jehoahaz, or Jehoiachin, because their three reigns were too short, nor could it have been Josiah or Jehoiakim, whose reigns came between these three.

We have, as a matter of fact, definite dates for the accession of Josiah and of Jehoiakim. Both dates can be deduced from Jer. 25:1-3, which states that the fourth year of Jehoiakim was the first year of Nebuchadrezzar, and that Jehoiakim's fourth year came twenty-three years after Jeremiah's call in the thirteenth year of Josiah. These two synchronisms appear to have come from different hands, because they have been calculated by different methods. Since Nebuchadrezzar's first official year began in Nisan, 604, this would synchronize with part of Jehoiakim's fourth year, which began, however, in Tishri, 605, according to the established method for Judean kings. We may conclude from this that Jehoiakim's accession occurred in 609/08. Jeremiah's twenty-third year was apparently reckoned on a Nisan basis, beginning in 605. Thus his first year was in 627/26, Josiah's thirteenth year was in 628/27, and Josiah's accession was in 641/40. Amon's two-year reign began in 643/42.

We have now narrowed down the period of uncertainty to two reigns. Hezekiah came to the throne in 716/15, and Manasseh died in 643/42. In this period of seventy-three actual years the eighty-four accredited years must lie. Unless the figures are in error, there is no escape from the conclusion that Manasseh shared his father's throne eleven years, beginning in 697/96. A likely reason for this would be Hezekiah's probably chronic sickness and his knowledge of impending death. Even though his son was only twelve years old when Hezekiah placed him beside him (II Kings 21:1), we can readily understand this doomed man's taking such a precaution to ensure the continuation of his line.

For the chronology of Judah's last years there are three important Babylonian dates. The first is the siege of Harran from Tammuz to Elul, 609, Nabopolassar's seventeenth year. A cuneiform document

| | Table 5 | | |
| | Chronology of Judah, 716-561 B.C. | | |
| Scripture References | Rulers and Important Events (Tishri Years p/d) | Dates B.C. | Dated Foreign Contacts |
|---|---|---|---|
| cf. II Kings 18:13 | HEZEKIAH | 716/15 | |
| II Kings 18:2; II Chr. 29: 1 | King 29 years | | |
| II Chr. 29:3 ff | Passover in 1st year | 715/14 | |
| II Kings 18:13; Isa. 36:1 | Jerusalem besieged, 14 Hezekiah | 701 | Sennacherib's invasion |
| II Kings 20:6; Isa. 38:5 | Hezekiah sick; he lives 15 more years | | |
| II Kings 21:1; II Chr. 33:1 | *Manasseh* coregent; total reign 55 years | 697/96 | |
| II Kings 19:9; Isa. 37:9 | | 688? | Sennacherib against Tirhakah |
| | MANASSEH, sole reign | 687/86 | |
| II Kings 19:37 | | 681 | Esarhaddon king of Assyria |
| II Kings 21:19; II Chr. 33:21 | AMON<br>King 2 years | 643/42 | |
| II Kings 22:1; II Chr. 34:1 | JOSIAH<br>King 31 years | 641/40 | |
| II Chr. 34:3 | First reform in 12th year | 629/28 | |
| Jer. 25:1-3; 1:2 | Jeremiah's call in 13 Josiah; 23 years until 4 Jehoiakim (Nisan reckoning) | 627 | |
| II Kings 22:3; 23:23; II Chr. 34: 8; 35:19 | Finding of Law scroll; second reform in 18th year | 623/22 | |
| II Kings 23:29; II Chr. 35:20 ff | Death at Megiddo | 609 | Neco at Harran, Tammuz to Elul |
| II Kings 23:31; II Chr. 36:2 | JEHOAHAZ<br>King 3 months | Tammuz, 609 | |
| II Kings 23:36; II Chr. 36:5 | JEHOIAKIM<br>King 11 years | Tishri, 609 | |
| Jer. 46:2 | 4 Jehoiakim (Nisan reckoning) | 605 | Battle of Carchemish |
| | | Sept. 7, 605 | Nebuchadrezzar's accession, 1 Elul |
| Jer. 25:1 | Jeremiah's 23rd year, 4 Jehoiakim, 1 Nebuchadrezzar | 604/03 | Nebuchadrezzar's first official year |
| II Kings 24:1 | 3 years' subservience to Babylon | | |
| II Kings 24:8; II Chr. 36:9 | JEHOIACHIN<br>King 3 months (plus 10 days?) | Dec., 598 | |
| Jer. 52:28 | Jerusalem captured, 7 Nebuchadrezzar | Mar. 16 (2 Adar), 597 | |
| II Kings 24:12; cf. Ezek. 40:1 | Jehoiachin's deportation, 10 Nisan of 8 Nebuchadrezzar | Apr. 22, 597 | |
| II Kings 24:18; Jer. 52:1; II Chr. 36:11 | ZEDEKIAH<br>King 11 years | 597 | |

Based on the chronology of Edwin R. Thiele

**Table 5** (*continued*)

| Scripture References | Rulers and Important Events (Tishri Years p/d) | Dates B.C. | Dated Foreign Contacts |
|---|---|---|---|
| II Kings 25:1; Jer. 39:1; 52:4; Ezek. 24:1-2 | Jerusalem besieged on 10 Tebeth of 9 Zedekiah | Jan. 15, 588 | |
| Jer. 32:1 | Jerusalem under siege during 10 Zedekiah, 18 Nebuchadrezzar | 587 | |
| II Kings 25:3-4; Jer. 39:2; 52:6-7 | The wall is breached, 9 Tammuz of 11 Zedekiah | July 19, 586 | |
| II Kings 25:8; Jer. 52:12; cf. 52:29 | The city and temple are burned on 7 (10) Ab, 11 Zedekiah, 19 (18) Nebuchadrezzar Second deportation | Aug. 15, 586 | |
| Jer. 41:1 ff | Gedaliah's murder in 7th month | Sept.- Oct. 586 | |
| Ezek. 33:21 | News of the fall of Jerusalem reaches the exiles on 5 Tebeth of 12th year of Jehoiachin's captivity (Nisan reckoning) | Jan. 8, 585 | |
| Jer. 52:30 | Third deportation in 23 Nebuchadrezzar | 582/81 | |
| Ezek. 40:1 | Vision of new temple, 10 Nisan of 25th year of Jehoiachin's captivity, 14th of the destruction of the temple (Nisan reckoning) | Apr. 18, 573 | |
| II Kings 25:27; Jer. 52:31 | Jehoiachin released from prison on 27 Adar of the 37th year of his captivity, in accession year of Amel-Marduk (Evil-merodach) | Mar. 21, 561 | |

mentions that an Egyptian army joined with the Assyrians in this attack upon the Babylonian garrison. The king of the Egyptians was no other than the NECO who killed Josiah at Megiddo while marching to the Euphrates (II Kings 23:29), and who was back in Palestine three months later to set Jehoahaz off the throne of Judah (vss. 31-34). Since Tammuz to Elul is exactly three months, it is almost certain that Josiah's death occurred shortly before the siege of Harran in 609.

A second date is that of Nebuchadrezzar's victory over Neco at Carchemish. This is now definitely known to be 605, in Nabopolassar's twenty-first year, which was also the accession year of Nebuchadrezzar. Jer. 46:2, which speaks of this battle, evidently reckoned Jehoiakim's fourth year, with which it is synchronized, upon the Nisan basis used by Jeremiah in the passage mentioned above.

A third date is that of Nebuchadrezzar's first capture of Jerusalem and deportation of Jehoiachin. We now know definitely that this occurred on the second of Adar in Nebuchadrezzar's seventh year, March 16, 597. It is true that II Kings 24:12 speaks of Jehoiachin's captivity beginning in Nebuchadrezzar's eighth year; but since Adar is the last month of the year, the actual deportation, which probably did not take place for several weeks, may have occurred after the new year. Ezek. 40:1 indicates that Jehoiachin's captivity began on the tenth of Nisan, 597.

The important features of the period from Josiah's death to the Exile are accordingly as follows: Josiah died probably in Tammuz, 609, and was succeeded by Jehoahaz, who reigned until after Tishri of the same year. Thus the remaining months of 609 and 608 until the next Tishri counted as Jehoiakim's ac-

cession year. In 605 Nebuchadrezzar defeated Jehoiakim's ally Neco at Carchemish, and perhaps it was then that Nebuchadrezzar put Jehoiakim under tribute for three years (II Kings 24:1; cf. also Dan. 1:1). Shortly after the beginning of his eleventh year, in December, 598, Jehoiakim died and was succeeded by his son Jehoiachin (II Kings 24:6), who surrendered to Nebuchadrezzar, after ruling for only three months (vs. 8), on March 16, 597. Zedekiah then took the throne for eleven years (vs. 18). When he revolted, the Babylonian army again put Jerusalem under siege. This was on the tenth day of the tenth month in Zedekiah's ninth year, January 15, 588 (25:1). The wall was broken through on the ninth day of the fourth month of his eleventh year (vss. 3-4), and on the seventh day of the following month the temple was burned (vss. 8-9). A great deportation followed, as also the events recorded in chs. 39-42 of Jeremiah. After Jehoiachin had been a captive in Babylon thirty-seven years, during the latter part of which he was held in prison, he was released on the twenty-seventh of Adar in Amel-Marduk's accession year—i.e., shortly before the Nisan new year marking the official beginning of this new king's reign (II Kings 25:27).

There remains but one question more: in which year was Jerusalem destroyed? Formerly 586 was widely accepted as the year, because II Kings 25:8 places Jerusalem's fall in the nineteenth year of Nebuchadrezzar (cf. Jer. 32:1). But when 609 was shown to be the likely date of Josiah's death, Jehoiachin's captivity was most readily set in 598 and the fall of Jerusalem in 587. The three deportations mentioned in Jer. 52:28-30, synchronized for Nebuchadrezzar's seventh, eighteenth, and twenty-

| | Table 6 | | |
|---|---|---|---|
| | Chronology of Postexilic Judaism, 539-4 B.C. | | |
| Scripture References | Dated Events and Native Rulers | Dates B.C. | Foreign Rulers |
| Ezra 1:1; II Chr. 36:22 | Edict for return of exiles in 1st official year of Cyrus as ruler of Babylon | *ca.* 538 | Cyrus (ruler of Babylon) 539-530 |
| Ezra 3:6 | The altar set up on 1 Tishri of 1st year of return | Sept., 538 | |
| Ezra 3:8 | Work begun on temple, Nisan of 2nd year | Mar.-Apr., 537 | |
| | | 530-522 | Cambyses |
| | Elephantine colony of Jews established in Egypt before Cambyses' conquest in this year | 525 | |
| | | 522-486 | Darius I |
| Ezra 4:24; Hag. 1:1, 15 | Work on temple resumed in Elul of 2 Darius | Aug.-Sept., 520 | |
| Ezra 6:15 | Temple finished, 3 Adar of 6 Darius | Mar. 12, 515 | |
| | | 486-465 | Xerxes I (Ahasuerus) |
| Ezra 4:6 | Opposition to the Jews | | |
| | | 465-424 | Artaxerxes I Longimanus |
| Ezra 4:7-23 | Opposition to the Jews | | |
| Neh. 2:1; 5:14 | Nehemiah's first governorship, 20-32 Artaxerxes | 445-433 | |
| Neh. 13:6 | Nehemiah's return to Persia in 32 Artaxerxes and second governorship | 432 | |
| Ezra 7:7 | Ezra's return in 37 (MT 7) Artaxerxes | 428 | |
| | | 424-423 | Xerxes II |
| | | 423-404 | Darius II |
| | | 404-358 | Artaxerxes II Mnemon |
| | | 358-338 | Artaxerxes III |
| | | 338-336 | Arses |
| | | 336-331 | Darius III Codomannus |
| | | 336-323 | Alexander the Great |
| | Fall of Tyre, end of Persian rule | 332 | |
| | Palestine under the Ptolemies | 323-198 | |
| | Beginning of Seleucid era | Oct., 312 | |
| | | 223-187 | Antiochus III the Great |
| | | 187-175 | Seleucus IV |
| | | 175-163 | Antiochus IV Epiphanes |
| I Macc. 1:54 | Persecution of the Jews and pollution of the temple on 15 Chislev, 145th year of Seleucid era | Dec., 167 | |
| | **JUDAS MACCABEUS** | 166-160 | |
| I Macc. 4:52 | The temple purified on 25 Chislev, 148th year of Seleucid era | Dec., 164 | |

**Table 6** (*continued*)

| Scripture References | Dated Events and Native Rulers | Dates B.C. | Foreign Rulers |
|---|---|---|---|
| | | 163-162 | Antiochus V |
| | | 162-150 | Demetrius I |
| I Macc. 10:21 | JONATHAN<br>High priest in Tishri, 160th year of Seleucid era | 160-142<br>Sept.-Oct., 152 | |
| | | 150-145 | Alexander Balas |
| | | 145-142/1 | Antiochus VI |
| | | 145-139/8 | Demetrius II |
| I Macc. 13:41 | SIMON<br>Recognized as legitimate ruler in 170th year of Seleucid era | 142-134<br>142 | |
| | | 139/8-129 | Antiochus VII, Sidetes |
| | JOHN HYRCANUS | 134-104 | |
| | JUDAS ARISTOBULUS | 104-103 | |
| | ALEXANDER JANNEUS | 103-76 | |
| | ALEXANDRA | 76-67 | |
| | ARISTOBULUS II | 67-63 | |
| | Pompey takes Jerusalem | 63 | |
| | HYRCANUS II | 63-40 | |
| | ANTIGONUS MATTATHIAS | 40-37 | |
| | HEROD THE GREAT | 37-4 | |

third years, were taken as confirmation for these dates. Now, however, that Jehoiachin's surrender is definitely dated in Adar, 597, a 587 date for Jerusalem's destruction can be defended only on the unlikely supposition that II Kings (and parallel sources) dated Zedekiah's reign by Nisan years.

Actually there remains very little support for this supposition. It is true that we find Jeremiah reckoning by a Nisan new year (25:1; 46:2). This is also true of Ezekiel, but this fact cannot be adduced as support for 587, because if 587 were the year of Jerusalem's fall, Ezekiel's chronology would have to be based on Tishri years (this being the only likely explanation of Ezek. 33:21). The only data which still definitely favor the 587 date are the deportations mentioned in Jer. 52:28-30.

There is no sufficient reason to suppose that the writer or writers of the books of Kings, who had so long and consistently stuck to a Tishri reckoning for Judah, and who continued to reckon on this basis even for the date of Jehoiachin's release from prison long after the destruction of Jerusalem (II Kings 25: 27), would at this one point in the records change to Nisan reckoning. There is then no reasonable escape from a 586 date for Jerusalem's fall. This is demanded by Ezek. 33:21, which employs Nisan reckoning to date the arrival of a messenger in Babylon with the tragic news of Jerusalem's fall, presumably only a few months after this event, in the twelfth year of Jehoiachin's captivity. It is also demanded by Nisan reckoning in Ezek. 40:1, which

dates the fourteenth year of Jerusalem's fall in the twenty-fifth year of Jehoiachin's captivity.

It will be admitted that problems still remain in connection with the deportations of Jer. 52:28-30. It is very strange that this passage mentions so few captives, if these deportations are intended to represent those of Jehoiachin and of Zedekiah (cf. II Kings 24:14, 16; 25:11-12). Perhaps the captivity of the seventh year can be equated with that of 597, since we now know that Jehoiachin did surrender in Nebuchadrezzar's seventh year. But then we still have no adequate explanation for the deportation of Nebuchadrezzar's eighteenth year. Perhaps these three deportations have been reckoned by antedating, a method which had been earlier used in Israel and Judah and which continued to be used at various times in parts of the ancient Near East.

**4. After the return.** For the chronology of the postexilic period it is not necessary to go into any detailed explanations. Although much of the OT was put into final form during this period, historical records pertaining to it are exceedingly few. The period between 515 and 445 and the period between 428 and *ca.* 175 are almost completely blank. Nonetheless, the general chronology of the period is well established from many reliable historical sources. The beginning of the Seleucid era in 312 B.C. was particularly important. For the few chronological details concerning postexilic times that have come down to us in the OT and the Apoc., *see* Table 6.

A vexed problem has long been the date of Ezra's

return. If Ezra returned in the seventh year of Artaxerxes I (Ezra 7:7), the date would be 458, and he would have preceded Nehemiah. But there are indications that the latter came to Jerusalem before Ezra; hence the seventh year of Artaxerxes II (397) has been proposed. This, however, separates Ezra completely from Nehemiah. Perhaps the best solution is to adopt the suggested reading that Ezra's return was in the thirty-seventh year of Artaxerxes I, 428. *See* EZRA-NEHEMIAH.

*Bibliography.* H. H. Rowley, *From Joseph to Joshua* (1948), covers problems of early chronology and provides an extensive bibliography.

For the chronology of the Hebrew kings the most important studies are: A. Kamphausen, *Die Chronologie der hebräischen Könige* (1883). M. Thilo, *Die Chronologie des ATs* (1917). F. X. Kugler, *Von Moses bis Paulus* (1922). J. Lewy, *Die Chronologie der Könige von Israel und Juda* (1927). V. Coucke, "Chronologie biblique," in F. Vigouroux, ed., *Dictionnaire de la Bible*, vol. I (1928). J. Begrich, *Die Chronologie der Könige von Israel und Juda* (1929). S. Mowinckel, "Die Chronologie der israelitischen und jüdischen Könige," *Acta Orientalia*, IX (1931), 161-277. W. F. Albright, "The Chronology of the Divided Monarchy of Israel," *BASOR*, 100 (1945), 16-22. By far the most valuable is E. R. Thiele, *The Mysterious Numbers of the Hebrew Kings* (1951), which he has followed by "A Comparison of the Chronological Data of Israel and Judah," *Vetus Testamentum*, IV (1954), 185-95; "The Question of Coregencies Among the Hebrew Kings," *A Stubborn Faith* (1956), pp. 39-52; "New Evidence on the Chronology of the Last Kings of Judah," *BASOR*, 143 (1956), 22-27. Other important articles by Albright are: "A Votive Stele Erected by Ben-Hadad I," *BASOR*, 87 (1942), 23-29; "New Light From Egypt on the Chronology and History of Israel and Judah," *BASOR*, 130 (1953), 4-11; "Further Light on Synchronisms Between Egypt and Asia in the Period 935-685 B.C.," *BASOR*, 141 (1956), 23-27; "The Nebuchadnezzar and Neriglissar Chronicles," *BASOR*, 143 (1956), 28-33.

Important for Assyro-Babylonian chronology as related to the OT are: F. K. Ginzel, *Handbuch der mathematischen und technischen Chronologie* (1906). R. A. Parker and W. H. Dubberstein, *Babylonian Chronology 626 B.C.-A.D. 75* (1956). D. J. Wiseman, *Chronicles of Chaldean Kings* (1956).

S. J. DE VRIES

**CHRONOLOGY OF THE NT, THE.** The dating of the events narrated in the NT is a frustrating task, partly because of the paucity of available information and partly because of the complications of the ancient CALENDAR.

Early Christian history was beneath the notice of the secular historians, the only exception being when Tacitus, describing the fire of Rome and the persecution which followed, remarks that the Christians derived their name from Christ, who was executed in the reign of Tiberius by the procurator Pontius Pilate (Ann. XV.44). Among the NT writers only Luke had any interest in relating Christian history to world history, and even the facts which he supplies cannot always be successfully translated into dates. The other writers occasionally make statements from which chronological inferences can be drawn, but in almost every case there is room for doubt or divergence of opinion.

From the time of Julius Caesar the Romans used a solar calendar with the year beginning on January 1, but they had no single system of regularly numbered years. The Roman numerals made the use of the era *ab urbe condita* too cumbersome for general use, and years were commonly identified either by the names of the consuls or by the regnal years of the emperor, which were reckoned from the day of his accession and therefore did not coincide with the calendar year. The Jews used a lunar calendar, and a complicated series of calendar changes in the past had left them with two New Year's days, six months apart (R.H. I.1). The ecclesiastical year, which was used for reckoning festivals and the reigns of Jewish kings, began on Nisan 1 (which could fall anywhere from early March to early April). The civil year, which was used for other purposes including the reigns of foreign kings, began on Tishri 1. The lunar year of approximately 354 days was kept in line with the seasons of the solar year by the periodic intercalation of a thirteenth month (Veadar) between Adar and Nisan.

These two reasons together mean that it is rarely possible to date any NT event with precision and certainty; we must be content, for the most part, with probabilities and approximations.

A. The life of Jesus
  1. The Nativity
    *a.* The death of Herod
    *b.* The census
  2. The age of Jesus
  3. The beginning of the ministry
    *a.* John the Baptist
    *b.* The building of the temple
  4. The duration of the ministry
  5. The Crucifixion
    *a.* Patristic evidence
    *b.* The evidence of astronomy
B. The apostolic age
  1. Absolute dating
    *a.* The death of Herod Agrippa I
    *b.* The famine
    *c.* The edict of Claudius
    *d.* The proconsulship of Gallio
    *e.* The procuratorship of Festus
  2. Relative dating, A.D. 30-50
  3. Relative dating, A.D. 50-70
Bibliography

**A. *THE LIFE OF JESUS.*** The gospels provide a small amount of chronological data for the life, ministry, and crucifixion of Jesus. For each period or event the evidence can be variously interpreted, and all the possibilities must be set out in full in the hope that the combined results will indicate which way the balance of probability lies.

**1. The Nativity. *a. The death of Herod.*** According to Matt. 2:1, Jesus was born during the reign of Herod the Great, and the stories of the wise men and the flight into Egypt seem to imply that he was at least two years old at the time of Herod's death. Luke is less definite on this point, but he does say that John the Baptist was less than six months older than Jesus and that the annunciation of his birth to Zechariah came in Herod's reign (1:5).

Now Josephus tells us that Herod died in the thirty-seventh year after the decree of the Roman Senate which declared him king of Judea (40. B.C.), and in the thirty-fourth year after his actual assumption of power; that his last illness was immediately preceded by an eclipse of the moon; and that his death was closely followed by the Passover (Antiq.

XVII.viii.1; XVII.vi.4; XVII.ix.3). In an earlier passage (XIV.xvi.4) Josephus has explained that Herod became king *de facto* in the consulship of M. Agrippa and Canidius Gallus (37 B.C.) by capturing Jerusalem on the Day of Atonement—the same day on which, twenty-seven years earlier, Pompey had entered the city. This statement is important, not merely because it fixes the beginning of Herod's reign, but because it discloses Josephus' method of computation. Pompey came to Jerusalem on Tishri 10, 63 B.C.; and Tishri 10, 37 B.C., could be said to have fallen in the twenty-seventh year only if Josephus was using the inclusive system of dating whereby the first year was reckoned from the New Year immediately preceding. In that case the twenty-seventh year would begin either on Nisan 1 or on Tishri 1, 37 B.C. This conclusion is confirmed by Josephus' dating of the battle of Actium in the seventh year of Herod (Antiq. XV.v.2). The battle was fought on September 2, 31 B.C., less than six years after Herod's accession, and could be placed in his seventh year only if Josephus considered Herod's regnal years to have begun on Nisan 1, 37 B.C. This means that the thirty-fourth year of Herod's reign began on Nisan 1, 4 B.C. An eclipse of the moon which was visible in Palestine occurred on March 12 of that year. Herod's death, shortly before the Passover, must have happened during the first two weeks of the month of Nisan.

**b. The census.** According to Luke, Jesus was born at the time of a census when Quirinius was governor of Syria (2:2). Some scholars hold this to be an egregious blunder, on the grounds that no such census is recorded by Roman authorities; that P. Sulpicius Quirinius is known to have conducted a census and property assessment in A.D. 6-7, when he was governor of Syria; and that the governors of Syria during the last years of Herod's reign were C. Sentius Saturninus (9-6 B.C.) and P. Quintilius Varus (6-4 B.C.). Other scholars are more ready to believe that Luke knew what he was talking about and that, if he was wrong, he was at least not far wrong. They point out that the argument from silence, always notoriously weak, is particularly weak in connection with the ill-documented reign of Augustus; that Luke was well aware of the census of A.D. 6-7, which he mentions in Acts 5:37, and is not likely to have been guilty of the confusion so often ascribed to him; and that he was, in fact, at pains to distinguish the nativity census from others known to him. What Luke tells us is that Augustus issued a decree inaugurating a system of periodic enrollment throughout the Empire (this is the implication of the present tense, ἀπογράφεσθαι—if Luke had thought that the decree ordered only one particular world-wide census, he would have written ἀπογράψασθαι), and that the first census of the series was held in Palestine when Quirinius was holding office in Syria as imperial legate.

Our knowledge of the Roman census system is fragmentary, but such as it is, it gives a limited support to Luke's nativity story. Clement of Alexandria informs us (Strom. I.21) that Christ was born "when they first began to make enrollments," and, though he may have drawn his information from Luke, the form of his statement suggests that he was familiar

with a regular and long-standing system of census-taking which was not confined to Egypt. Tertullian (Marcion IV.19) places the nativity census in the governorship of Saturninus, and since Tertullian did not get this name from Luke, he must have had access to an independent, perhaps official, record. Census papers discovered in Egypt show that a census was held there at fourteen-year intervals from A.D. 90 to 258 and also in 62 and probably in 20. In each case, as with modern tax returns, the actual enrollment was carried out in the following year. The prefect issued an order requiring all persons absent from home to return for enrollment. There is every reason to suppose that this Egyptian system was initiated by Augustus. It was his organizing ability that laid the foundations of the whole imperial administration, and none of his successors before Vespasian had the statesmanship to originate such a scheme. If, then, we trace the fourteen-year cycle back to its point of origin, we shall conclude that the first census year was 23 B.C., 9 B.C., or A.D. 6, with the actual enrollment carried out in each case in the following year.

It is tempting to assume that the Egyptian system was followed in other parts of the Empire. The census which Quirinius is known to have conducted in 6-7 would fall into the same pattern. But as this enrollment was undertaken primarily for the purpose of tax assessment at the beginning of procuratorial rule in Judea, it is dubious how much weight can be allowed to this coincidence. A similar census and property assessment was carried out by Germanicus in Gaul in 14, which lies quite outside the series (Tac. Ann. I.31).

The only other evidence has to do with the census of Roman citizens. According to the *Monumentum Ancyranum* (ch. 8), Augustus held the censorship three times, once with Agrippa in 28 B.C., once alone in 8 B.C., and once with Tiberius in A.D. 14. Another census was held by Claudius in A.D. 48 (Tac. Ann. XI.25; Suetonius *Claudius* 16; Pliny Nat. Hist. VII. 48), and in this connection Pliny records a story of a man from Bologna who gave his age as 150, so that the officials felt it necessary to consult earlier census records to see whether his entries had been consistent.

It is too much to claim on the basis of this evidence that Augustus inaugurated a single, uniform system of census-taking for the whole Empire. But Luke, after all, does not claim this. All he says is that Augustus issued a decree that there should be regular enrollments of provincials, just as there had always been regular enrollments of Roman citizens. If we accept Luke's testimony, it would seem to be a reasonable hypothesis that this decree had some connection with the census of citizens held by Augustus as sole censor in 8 B.C. and also with the beginning of the Egyptian fourteen-year cycle in the same year. This would give us a *terminus a quo* for the Nativity, but we should have to allow for the possibility of delay on the first occasion of enrollment, particularly in a turbulent area under the jurisdiction of a native king.

There remains the problem of QUIRINIUS. The simplest solution is to say that Luke was right about the census but wrong about the name of the governor, and that his error was corrected by Tertullian.

But it is possible that even this would be an injustice to Luke. A damaged inscription in the Lateran Museum records the career of a nameless Roman who was twice governor of Syria, and since the time of Mommsen it has been generally agreed that the man in question was Quirinius. Sir William Ramsay, protesting hotly against the attitude which assumes Luke to be in error unless he can be proved to be right, has reconstructed the career of Quirinius so as to show that the probable time of his first term of office in Syria was in the latter years of Herod's reign, and has pointed out that there were other occasions when two men with the rank of *legatus Caesaris* were appointed to one province because one of them was expected to be fully occupied with the command of the army.

In view of all these difficulties, it cannot be said that the date of the birth of Jesus is securely established, but, taking the combined evidence of Matthew and Luke, we shall not be very far astray if we assign it to the year 7 B.C., with the understanding that it may be a year earlier or later.

**2. The age of Jesus.** Luke tells us that Jesus was about thirty years of age when he began his ministry (3:23). The sentence bristles with exegetical difficulties, and there is no agreement about its meaning. As Luke claims to know the exact date of the Nativity and the exact date of the public appearance of John the Baptist, it would seem that he was in a position to calculate the exact interval between them. But if we add thirty to the date we have proposed for the Nativity, we get the years 23-25 as the possible period for the beginning of the ministry, and this falls entirely outside the term of Pontius Pilate's rule as procurator of Judea (26-36). If, on the other hand, we take the expression "about thirty years of age" to be an elastic one, how far should we allow it to stretch? Could Jesus have been thirty-two or thirty-three or even thirty-four? Or did Luke simply mean to indicate that he had arrived at years of maturity? The last interpretation has a great deal to be said in its favor, for we know that members of the Qumran community had to be thirty years old before they were eligible for positions of religious leadership (CD XVII.5.6.)

**3. The beginning of the ministry. a. John the Baptist.** Luke begins his account of John the Baptist with an elaborate sixfold date (3:1-2), five parts of which serve only to fix the broadest of limits. Pilate was procurator from 26 to 36, Herod Antipas was deposed in 39, Philip died in 34, nothing is known of Lysanias, and Caiaphas was deposed at a Passover festival which cannot have been later than 36. The one precise date is the fifteenth year of Tiberius, and even this can be interpreted in three different ways. Augustus died on August 19, A.D. 14, and by the usual Roman reckoning the fifteenth year of Tiberius would run from August 19, A.D. 28, to August 18, A.D. 29. This normal system of dating puts the baptism of Jesus so late that many scholars have adopted the suggestion, originally made by Ussher, that Luke was counting from the decree by which Augustus took Tiberius into partnership as co-emperor. Mommsen, on the authority of Velleius Paterculus (II.121), assigned this decree to the year 11. This would make 25/26 the fifteenth year of

Tiberius, so that the ministry of Jesus could have begun late in 26 or early in 27. But there is no evidence, either from coinage or elsewhere, that the regnal years of Tiberius were ever reckoned in this fashion. There remains the possibility that Luke was using the Jewish system for dating the reigns of foreign kings, according to which the first year of Tiberius would begin on Tishri 1, A.D. 13, and his fifteenth year on Tishri 1, A.D. 27.

**b. The building of the temple.** John places the cleansing of the temple at the beginning of Jesus' ministry, associates it with a Passover, and records a discussion between Jesus and the Jews in the course of which the Jews say: "It has taken forty-six years to build this temple" (2:20). Mark places the same incident at the end of the ministry, and it might seem that John's contribution to chronology was invalidated by the discrepancy. This is part of a larger question —whether the arrangement of the Fourth Gospel is theological or chronological. But it is not necessary for our present purpose to settle this dispute. For the more independence we attribute to John in the handling of his sources, the more likely it becomes that he did not find the figure forty-six in the tradition but worked it out for himself from adequate evidence, independently of the story to which he attached it; and it is hard to see why he should have mentioned the figure at all unless he had good reason to believe that it was accurate.

Now according to Josephus (Antiq. XV.xi.1), Herod embarked in his eighteenth year (20/19 B.C.) on a plan for the complete rebuilding of the temple of Zerubbabel, and it must be this project to which John's figure refers. The earlier part of Herod's eighteenth year was occupied with a visit of Augustus to Syria, so that the rebuilding program probably did not begin until at least the autumn of 20 B.C. This means that the Passover, when it could be said that the temple had been forty-six years in process of building, is the Passover of 28, and this would synchronize with the third, or Jewish, interpretation of the fifteenth year of Tiberius. But the Passover of 27 would have fallen in the forty-sixth year, and this must remain as a second possibility.

**4. The duration of the ministry.** In early patristic times the belief sprang up that the ministry of Jesus occupied only one year. This theory seems to have originated in Gnostic circles, but was adopted by Clement of Alexandria (*Miscellanies* I.21) and Origen (*On First Principles* IV.5), among others. Clement makes it fairly plain that the belief was founded largely on the assumption that the "acceptable year of the Lord" (Luke 4:19) was to be taken literally as a description of the whole ministry. In favor of this theory was the paucity of biographical material provided by the gospels, since all four together do not supply enough incident to fill one year, let alone two or three. Mark's gospel, too, seemed to be susceptible of this interpretation. The grainfields episode of 2:23-28 belongs to early summer, the feeding of the five thousand when the grass was green to early spring, and the Crucifixion to the Passover season. It was found possible to compress even John's Gospel into the same small compass. The ministry here begins and ends with a Passover, and in between are a number of other feasts mentioned in their proper order—Pentecost in ch. 5, Tabernacles in ch. 7, and Dedication in ch. 10. It is true that 6:4 mentions another Passover, but Origen at least (*Commentary on St. John* 4.35) seems to have used a text from which the words τὸ πάσχα were missing, so that the feast mentioned in 6:4 could be identified with the Feast of Tabernacles described in the following chapter.

This one-year theory has had its modern supporters, but it is subject to the gravest disabilities. Every MS of John 6:4 contains the words τὸ πάσχα, and, even if the words were not in the text, the mention of "much grass" later in the story would compel us to assign the episode to the spring and not to the autumn. We could hardly claim, in any case, that Mark and John were agreed on a one-year ministry, if that agreement required that one of them should date the miraculous feeding in the spring and the other in the autumn. The natural interpretation of both gospels is that the miracle occurred in March or April and that at least another year elapsed before the final Passover.

But if the ministry of Jesus lasted for more than one year, how many years did it last? Matthew and Luke provide no evidence on this point, and Mark's three indications of season—the ripe grain (2:23), the green grass (6:39), and the final Passover—though they would fit admirably into a two-year ministry, cannot be said to exclude other possibilities. Almost all theories of a two- or three-year ministry have been based on the fuller chronological data of the Fourth Gospel.

There are seven passages which have been used to support one or another of these theories: "The Passover of the Jews was at hand" (2:13). "Do you not say, 'There are yet four months, then comes the harvest'? I tell you, lift up your eyes, and see how the fields are already white for harvest" (4:35). "After this there was a feast [A B D W Θ, etc.; "the feast": א C E L Δ λ 33, etc.] of the Jews" (5:1). "Now the Passover, the feast of the Jews, was at hand" (6:4). "Now the Jews' feast of Tabernacles was at hand" (7:2). "It was the feast of the Dedication at Jerusalem" (10:22). "Now the Passover of the Jews was at hand" (11:55). The last four passages clearly constitute a single ecclesiastical year; but do the other three passages imply one or two additional years? If the saying about the harvest is to be taken at its face value, it must have been spoken in midwinter; and if in 5:1 we accept the second reading—"the feast of the Jews",—we are bound to say that the only feast which could be so designated is Tabernacles. Granted these two suppositions, we should have to allot two years to the period between the cleansing of the temple and the feeding of the five thousand. On the other hand, it does not look as if the evangelist himself regarded the saying about the harvest in this light, for he tells us that when Jesus arrived in Galilee two or three days later, "the Galileans welcomed him, having seen all that he had done in Jerusalem at the feast [i.e., the Passover]." If there is any chronological inference to be drawn, it is that the events of ch. 4 follow fairly closely on those of ch. 2. This being so, the identity of the feast mentioned in 5:1 is of less consequence, and it should be added that in any case the reading without the article has the more impressive weight of MS authority behind it. We

may conclude then that according to the Fourth Gospel the ministry of Jesus lasted just over two years or just over three years, with the balance of probability heavily in favor of the former.

But is even this conclusion justifiable? Is there really any chronology in the Fourth Gospel? Are not the feasts mentioned for theological reasons? The first Passover is mentioned in connection with the cleansing of the temple, which John, probably for theological reasons, places at the outset of the ministry. The second Passover is mentioned in order to set the scene for the teaching that follows, on the bread of life. The Feast of Tabernacles is mentioned because its double ceremony of the water and the lights formed the background to the two great sayings of Jesus (7:37-38; 8:12). How then can we have any confidence that the events of the gospel story are given in chronological order? To all this we may reply that an interest in theology does not necessarily preclude an interest in history; indeed, John's whole thesis is that the earthly is the vehicle of the heavenly, that history reveals the divine. Because he had a theological reason for mentioning that the feeding of the five thousand was associated with a Passover, we have no right to assume that he invented the association. Yet, if even this one point is allowed, we shall return to our previous conclusion that the ministry of Jesus cannot be compressed into less than two years, and that there is no compelling reason for extending it to three years.

**5. The Crucifixion. a. Patristic evidence.** Almost all that the early fathers have to say on this subject can be shown to be deductions from the biblical data. The one possible exception is the tradition that the Crucifixion occurred in the consulship of the two Gemini (A.D. 29, when L. Rubellius Geminus and C. Fufius Geminus were consuls). This tradition is found in a work attributed to Tertullian (*Against the Jews* 8), in Hippolytus' Commentary on Daniel, in the prologue to the Acts of Pilate, in Lactantius (*Institutions* IV.10.18; *De Mortibus Persecutorium* 2), and in Augustine (*City of God* XVIII.54). But one of the earliest of these works, *Against the Jews,* gives as an alternative date the fifteenth year of Tiberius, which suggests that the whole Gemini tradition may have been based on a combination of Luke 3:1; 4:19.

**b. The evidence of astronomy.** The only other way of determining the date of the Crucifixion is by astronomical calculations based on the biblical data. All the gospels agree that Jesus died on a Friday during the Passover season. Mark and John disagree about the day of the month. The Jewish day began at 6 P.M., and the Passover was eaten in the early (evening) hours of Nisan 15. According to Mark 14:12, the Last Supper was the Passover meal, and this means that the arrest, the trial, the death, and the burial of Jesus also took place on Nisan 15. According to John 18:28; 19:14, the Passover was eaten that year on the Friday evening after the Crucifixion, which therefore occurred on Nisan 14 (*see* LAST SUPPER, THE). We have then to ask the astronomers in which years within the possible limits Nisan 14 or 15 could have fallen on a Friday.

In the time of Jesus the first day of the month was fixed not by calculation but by observation. A committee of priests met after the close of the twenty-ninth day and waited for two witnesses to testify that they had seen the sickle of the new moon. If the witnesses arrived before sunset, that day was declared to be the first of the new month; if not, that day became the thirtieth of the old month, and the new month began on the following day. It is possible to calculate for any given month the time at which the new moon first became visible, but there are two pieces of information which astronomy cannot give us. Even if the new moon was theoretically visible on a certain day, this does not necessarily mean that it was actually observed, since it may have been obscured by atmospheric conditions. And there are some years for which we cannot say with complete confidence which new moon was the new moon of Nisan.

It has usually been assumed, without adequate authority, that the paschal full moon was invariably that immediately following the spring equinox, and that the calendar committee inserted the intercalary month to prevent the Passover from coming before the equinox. This system may have been in force, in order to enable Jews of the Diaspora to attend the festivals. But if any such system had been adopted, intercalation would have been predictable and automatic, and the references to it in the Mishna strongly suggest that this was not so. The proclamation of the extra month might be made after the feast of Purim (Meg. 1.4; 'Eduy. 7.7), it had to be proclaimed by messengers (Yeb. 16.7), it could be proclaimed by a quorum of three (Sanh. 1.2), and legal provision is made for its unpredictable incidence (Ned. 8.5; B. M. 8.8). Moreover, on Nisan 16 the first sheaf of the barley harvest was waved in the temple, so that clearly the state of the harvest was more important than the equinox in determining intercalation, at least as long as the temple stood.

Taking these considerations into account, we can say that there are, astronomically, four possibilities: (a) In A.D. 27 Friday, April 11, was either Nisan 14 or Nisan 15. (b) In A.D. 29 Friday, March 18, may have been Nisan 14 (if there was no intercalation). (c) In A.D. 30 Friday, April 7, was either Nisan 14 or Nisan 15. (d) In A.D. 33 Friday, April 3, may have been Nisan 14. Of these four possible dates for the Crucifixion the third is by far the most probable. The first is by all accounts too early, and has never been seriously advocated by anyone. The second coincides with the Gemini dating, but involves an unusually early date for the Passover. The fourth would commit us to a three-year theory of the ministry and would also aggravate the already serious difficulty of dating the apostolic period. Nevertheless, none of the last three dates can be dismissed from our final reckoning.

When we come to survey the evidence which has been set forth under the last three headings, it is apparent that it can be combined in no fewer than six different ways. If the reign of Tiberius is reckoned, Roman fashion, from the death of Augustus, so that his fifteenth year is 28/29, we have to choose between a one-year ministry ending in 30 and a three- or four-year ministry ending in 33. If the reign of Tiberius is reckoned from his co-imperium, so that his fifteenth year is 25/26, we have to choose between

a two- or three-year ministry ending in 29 and a three- or four-year ministry ending in 30. If the reign of Tiberius is reckoned, Jewish fashion, from Tishri 1, A.D. 13, so that his fifteenth year is 27/28, we have to choose between a one-year ministry ending in 29 and a two-year ministry ending in 30. We have seen that the Jewish reckoning of the reign of Tiberius agrees best with the Johannine saying about the building of the temple, that two years is the most likely duration of the ministry, and that 30 is the most probable date for the Crucifixion. Thus, while none of the six combinations listed above can be entirely ruled out, there is a threefold probability in favor of the sixth.

The evidence we have at our disposal, then, points to the tentative conclusion that Jesus was born in 8-6 B.C., baptized late in A.D. 27 or early in A.D. 28, and crucified on April 7, A.D. 30.

**B. *THE APOSTOLIC AGE*. 1. Absolute dating.** The few indications of time which occur in the letters serve only to date events relatively to other events. For an absolute chronology we are totally dependent on Acts, and of the events mentioned in this book only five can be assigned even an approximate date from Jewish or Roman sources. There is as yet no evidence to provide a date for the proconsulship of Sergius Paulus in Cyprus.

*a. The death of Herod Agrippa I (Acts 12:23).* According to Josephus (Antiq. XVIII.vi.10; XVIII.vii. 2; XIX.v.1; XIX.viii.2), Agrippa succeeded to the tetrarchy of Philip shortly after the accession of Caligula (March 16, A.D. 37) and to that of Antipas in 39, became king also of Judea, Samaria, and Abilene on the accession of Claudius (January 24, A.D. 41), and died at a festival in Caesarea after completing three years as king of all Judea and in the seventh year of his total reign. On the basis of this evidence alone we should unhesitatingly place the death of Agrippa in the early months of 44. There have been listed among the coinage of Agrippa, however, two coins which purported to come from the eighth and ninth years of his reign. If these coins were accepted as genuine, Josephus' evidence would have to be set aside. The doubt raised by the coins is to some extent offset by the plausible theory that the festival which was in progress at the time of Agrippa's death was the quadrennial games instituted by Herod the Great at Caesarea in 9 B.C. in honor of the emperor and in commemoration of the founding of the city, since these games must have been held in A.D. 44.

On the whole, it seems safest to ignore the questionable numismatic evidence and to trust to Josephus, and this is the course adopted by the majority of scholars. This does not mean, however, as is often supposed, that the death of James and the imprisonment of Peter, which are described in Acts immediately before the death of Herod, are to be assigned to A.D. 44. At this point in Acts, Luke is compressing into a few paragraphs the events of many years, so that Agrippa's persecution of the apostles may have happened at any time during his reign over Judea; and since Agrippa's purpose was to win favor with the Jews, his action is more intelligible at the beginning of his reign than at the end of it, when his popularity was fully assured. Tentatively, then, we may say that the death of James took place just before the Passover of 41.

**b. The famine (Acts 11:28).** After the death of Agrippa, Claudius sent out Cuspius Fadus as procurator of Judea, and he was succeeded in turn by Tiberius Alexander and Ventidius Cumanus. Josephus gives us no information about the duration of their terms of office, except that Cumanus was procurator when Agrippa's brother Herod of Chalcis died in the eighth year of Claudius (48). It seems reasonable, however, to suppose that Alexander was procurator during 46 and probably for part, at least, of 47. It was during his administration that the great famine occurred which prompted the Christians of Antioch to send a relief fund to the church in Jerusalem.

**c. The edict of Claudius (Acts 18:2).** The edict by which Claudius expelled the Jews from Rome is mentioned by Suetonius (*Claudius* 25), though without any indication of date. Dio Cassius (LX.6.6) refers to it along with events which belong to A.D. 41, but it would be an exaggeration to say that he actually dates it in that year. The only writer to give a precise date is the fifth-century historian Orosius (VII.6.15), who places it in the ninth year of Claudius (49). As his authority he gives Josephus, though no mention of the decree appears in any of Josephus' extant works. Orosius' date fits perfectly with the next date we have to establish, and so is generally accepted. It has been argued, to be sure, that Orosius was usually a year off in his dates for the reign of Claudius, but it is dubious whether Orosius was so consistent, even in his errors.

**d. The proconsulship of Gallio (Acts 18:12).** The proconsular governors of senatorial provinces held office normally for one year only, and entered office on July 1. The year when Gallio was governor of Achaia has been determined by an inscription at Delphi. The inscription is badly mutilated, but enough of it remains to show that it was a copy of a letter from Claudius, called forth by a report from Gallio, and that at the time of writing Claudius had been acclaimed Imperator twenty-six times. These acclamations occurred at frequent but irregular intervals and by themselves do not establish a precise date. But other inscriptions have been preserved elsewhere which enable us to set fairly narrow limits for the Gallio inscription. There are two inscriptions (*C.I.L.* III.476, 1977) which show that the twenty-second and twenty-fourth acclamations belong to the eleventh year of Claudius' reign (January 25, A.D. 51, to January 24, A.D. 52). There is another inscription on a monumental arch of an aqueduct at Rome, dedicated on August 1, A.D. 52, which shows that by that date Claudius had celebrated his twenty-seventh acclamation. In the unlikely event that Claudius was acclaimed Imperator five times in one year, his twenty-sixth acclamation would have occurred at the end of his eleventh year, but it is much more likely that it belongs to the first half of his twelfth year.

It is theoretically possible that Gallio entered on his proconsulship on July 1, A.D. 52, and sent an immediate report to Claudius by courier about affairs at Delphi, which arrived in time for Claudius to write a reply and then to celebrate his twenty-seventh acclamation before August 1. But this possibility is so vastly improbable that it is better to disregard it altogether. There is an almost equally remote possibility that Gallio served for two years, beginning in July, 50. But the obvious interpretation of the Delphi inscription is that Gallio's term of office in Achaia extended from July, 51, to June, 52.

**e. The procuratorship of Festus (Acts 24:27).** Josephus and Tacitus agree that Cumanus was succeeded as procurator in A.D. 52 by Felix, who after a number of years was succeeded by Festus, but neither historian provides any satisfactory means of dating Felix' recall. Josephus tells us that when he was recalled by Nero, the Jews of Caesarea prosecuted him before the emperor, and that he would certainly have been convicted of maladministration had he not been the brother of Pallas, "whom Nero at that time held in special esteem" (Antiq. XX.viii.9). Some scholars have felt that Pallas could hardly have exercised such influence after his dismissal from office, and have therefore dated the recall of Felix very early in Nero's reign. Nero became emperor on October 14, A.D. 54. Pallas was dismissed before the poisoning of Britannicus, who at the time of his death had almost reached his fourteenth birthday (February 13, A.D. 55).

There are three serious objections to this early date for the recall of Felix. Josephus records a long list of events which occurred in Palestine while Felix was procurator and places them after his reference to the accession of Nero, which he would hardly have done if Felix' whole term of office had belonged to the reign of Claudius. Acts tells us that Paul had already been two full years in prison at Caesarea when Festus took up office, and even if Festus' arrival had been delayed until July, 55, there would be less than two years left between Paul's appearance before Gallio in the summer of 51 and his arrest in Jerusalem at Pentecost in 53. Moreover, it is plain that Nero had always disliked Pallas and intended to dismiss him from the moment he became emperor, so that it is hard to see why Pallas' influence with Nero should have been greater before his dismissal than after it. For Pallas was not disgraced; he was able to make his own terms with Nero, was exempt from the scrutiny normally undergone by retiring Roman officials, and was allowed to keep the vast fortune he had accumulated as secretary of the treasury under Claudius.

We are thrown back, therefore, on the evidence of Eusebius, which at first sight is unpromising. For in his Chronological Tables, Eusebius puts the arrival of Festus in the fourteenth year of Claudius and the tenth of Agrippa II. The first of these figures must be a mistake, since Eusebius was well aware that Felix was recalled by Nero; but it is a mistake which becomes intelligible if we assume that the second figure was the only one that stood in Eusebius' source. Knowing that Agrippa I had died in 44, Eusebius assumed that 45 was the first year of his son, Agrippa II, and therefore identified the tenth year of Agrippa II with 54, the fourteenth of Claudius. Actually, as we know from Josephus (War II.xiv.4), the beginning of Agrippa's reign was reckoned from Nisan 1, A.D. 50, so that his tenth year began on Nisan 1, A.D. 59. There is thus good reason for believing that, according to Eusebius' source, Festus became procurator in the summer of 59.

So we arrive at the dates in Table 1.

| Table 1 | |
|---|---|
| The death of Herod Agrippa I | 44 (early) |
| The famine | 46 |
| The edict of Claudius | 49 (or 50) |
| The arrival of Gallio in Corinth | 51 (summer) |
| The arrival of Festus in Caesarea | 59 (summer) |

**2. Relative dating, A.D. 30-50.** Of the dates listed above, the date of Gallio's proconsulship is the one which commands our most complete confidence. It may therefore be taken as the fixed point from which we can work both backward and forward.

We are told in Acts 18 that Paul spent eighteen months in Corinth, that he was prosecuted by the Jews soon after Gallio's arrival, and that he then remained in the city a good while. This means that Paul arrived in Corinth either in January, A.D. 50, or, if we take the eighteen months to be the total period of his residence there, sometime during the spring of that year. In either case his departure from Antioch with Silas cannot have been later than the previous spring. Immediately before this, Acts recounts the story of the apostolic conference and compels us to face the intricate problem of Paul's visits to Jerusalem. The evidence is found in Gal. 1–2 and Acts, and each source raises difficulties of its own which become doubly perplexing when we attempt to put the two accounts together.

In Galatians, Paul is defending himself against a charge of being a secondary authority, dependent for all his knowledge of the gospel on the older apostles, and under oath he gives a description of all the occasions between his conversion and his Galatian mission when he visited Jerusalem or had other contact with the apostles. Three years after his conversion he spent two weeks in Jerusalem, during which he met Peter and James. After fourteen years he went up again with Barnabas for a conference with James, Peter, and John about the admission of Gentiles to the church. Then finally he met Peter in Antioch and had a disagreement with him about table fellowship between Jewish and Gentile Christians. Since Paul is arguing that he had no opportunity to receive from the other apostles the gospel he preached in Galatia, we can assume that all these meetings occurred before the Galatian mission. But when did the Galatian mission take place? Was the letter addressed to N Galatians or to S Galatians? (*See* GALATIANS, LETTER TO THE.) Did Paul's second visit to Jerusalem come fourteen years after his conversion or fourteen years after his first visit? And at what point in his career did he write the letter?

In Acts, Paul visits Jerusalem five times in all, and the third occasion is the apostolic conference of ch. 15. The account of this conference appears straightforward enough, but it has some curious features. The reason for the conference was the rapid growth of Gentile Christianity through the successful missionary work of Paul and Barnabas, yet these successes are passed over in a single verse, and the main discussion has to do with the reception of Cornelius into the church by Peter. The chapter opens with a demand made by some former Pharisees that circumcision be made a condition of church membership and ends with the sending of a letter requesting the Gentile Christians to observe certain regulations, which cannot conceivably be regarded as conditions of church membership but are rather the terms on which Jewish Christians could eat with Gentile Christians without disloyalty to their national law. This letter is specifically addressed to the churches of Syria and Cilicia, but we are told that Paul delivered it also to the churches of S Galatia. These and similar anomalies have prompted some scholars to wonder whether the course of events was really as simple as Luke's account suggests.

The problem of combining the evidence of our two sources in a single, coherent chronology has produced a proliferation of theories, none of which can be said to command the support of a majority of scholars. The main varieties of theory can be quite simply classified if we tabulate the Jerusalem visits as in Table 2.

| Table 2 | | |
|---|---|---|
| A1 Acts 9:26-30 | | G1 Gal. 1:18-24 |
| A2 Acts 11:30; 12:25 | | G2 Gal. 2:1-10 |
| A3 Acts 15 | | |
| A4 Acts 18:22 | | |
| A5 Acts 21:17 ff | | |

G1 is, by common consent, the same as A1. But which visit in Acts corresponds to G2? This is the question which has produced such a bewildering assortment of answers.

The simplest, and perhaps the most widely accepted, view is that G2=A3. There is enough superficial resemblance to make this equation attractive. In each case Paul and Barnabas travel from Antioch to Jerusalem to discuss with James and Peter the status of Gentiles in the church. But over against these similarities there are formidable differences. In G2 Paul roundly asserts that he insisted on keeping the discussion a private one between himself and Barnabas on the one side and the three Jerusalem apostles on the other, whereas A3 describes a public meeting of the whole church. G2 is concerned with the admission of Gentiles to the church, but A3 leads to a resolution about intercommunion of Jewish and Gentile Christians. In G2 Paul assures his readers that the other apostles made no demands of him except that he remember the material needs of the Jerusalem church, whereas the letter of A3 requires of the Gentile Christians that they observe certain regulations from the Jewish food laws. Paul, writing on oath, omits all mention of A2, which on this theory must have given him a further contact with the Jerusalem church. Besides all this, it is very difficult to understand how the controversy at Antioch about table fellowship (Gal. 2:11 ff), which happened after G2, could have arisen after the matter had been settled to everybody's satisfaction at A3. There is also the further consideration that this view commits its exponents to the N Galatian theory, since no opponent of Paul's could have argued that A3 was the occasion when he received from the other apostles the gospel which he preached in S Galatia.

One of the objections to the first theory is eliminated if we add to it a further equation: $G2 = A2 = A3$. Paul and Barnabas, we must suppose, carried the famine-relief fund to Jerusalem and seized the opportunity of consulting the other apostles about the problems of the Gentile mission. Luke, deriving his information about this period from various sources, including an Antioch source which told him about the famine fund and a Jerusalem source which told him about the conference, failed to recognize that he was dealing with two accounts of the same visit, and he separated them by approximately three years. This theory explains why Paul swears he has been only twice in Jerusalem, but it is questionable whether this small gain justifies the elaborate hypothesis by which it is achieved. For all the other objections to the first theory still apply.

A theory which has been popular among British scholars is that $G2 = A2$. On this hypothesis the course of events runs something like this: Paul and Barnabas are sent by the church of Antioch to carry the famine fund and, while in Jerusalem, are able to have a private conference with the three Jerusalem apostles about the admission of Gentiles to the church. Full agreement is reached, but shortly afterward James realizes that the free social intercourse between Jewish and Gentile Christians at Antioch is going to be an embarrassment to him in his attempts to evangelize the Jews of Jerusalem. He therefore sends to Antioch a proposal that Jewish Christians celebrate the Lord's Supper separately from the Gentile Christians, and this precipitates the crisis of Gal. 2:11 ff. The matter is left without a permanent settlement while Paul and Barnabas embark on their missionary tour through Cyprus and Galatia, but is finally settled at the conference of A3.

This theory creates one serious problem. The famine visit cannot well be dated later than the autumn of 46. The first visit $(G1 = A1)$, fourteen years earlier—even if we use the ancient method of computation whereby each part of a year counts as a full year—cannot have been later than the spring of 33. Paul's conversion three years earlier would then come in the autumn of 31 at the very latest. This leaves only a year and a half between the Crucifixion of Jesus and the conversion of Paul. Some scholars, feeling that this is too small an interval, have suggested that Paul dated both his Jerusalem visits from his conversion, so that the fourteen years included the three. But it is safe to say that this interpretation of the dates in Galatians would not have occurred to anyone if the more natural interpretation had not created a chronological problem.

The critics have reasonably wanted to ask why Paul, writing to the Galatians about his visits to Jerusalem, failed to mention the conference of A3. The reply has commonly been that Paul did not mention the conference because it had not yet taken place, that Galatians was written in 48 or 49 shortly after Paul's return from the S Galatian mission. But this rider has done more to discredit than to commend the theory to which it has been attached. For there are very adequate reasons of language, style, and theology for assigning Galatians to the same period of Paul's life as II Corinthians and Romans. There is, however, a very simple alternative to this early dating of Galatians. Paul may have omitted mention

of the conference of A3 in writing to the Galatians because it had no bearing on his argument. For his sole reason for mentioning his visits to Jerusalem was to demonstrate that he had never sat at the feet of the "pillars" and could not have derived from them the gospel which he had preached in Galatia.

A critical analysis of Acts 15 led Johannes Weiss to the conclusion that the chapter was an amalgamation of two conferences. A3a (vss. 1-4, 12) dealt with the proposal to make circumcision a condition of church membership, and A3b (vss. 5-11, 13-33) dealt with the question of table fellowship between Jewish and Gentile Christians. It follows that $G2 = A3a$. Paul was not present at A3b, for in Acts 21:25 he has to be informed about the contents of the apostolic letter. Silas, on the other hand, must have been there, since he had a part in drafting the letter. A3b therefore must have taken place after Silas had parted from Paul.

The merit of this theory is that it explains Paul's silence about the apostolic letter. Its chief disadvantage is that the analysis of Acts 15 is purely speculative and, with the dubious exception of Acts 21:25, has not a jot of real evidence to support it.

In despair of ever untying this Pauline knot, John Knox has cut it by deciding to ignore Luke's chronological framework altogether, on the assumption that it was not drawn from his sources but was his own editorial contribution, and to construct a new framework entirely from the letters. He believes that the collection mentioned in I and II Corinthians and in Romans was Paul's response to the appeal of the Jerusalem apostles recorded in Gal. 2:10, and that therefore $G2 = A4$. A2 and A3 are unhistorical. Paul visited Jerusalem for the first time after spending three years in Arabia and Damascus, for the second time after eleven (or fourteen) years' missionary work with Barnabas in Asia Minor and Greece, and for the third and last time after a further period in the same territory. Into this framework selected episodes from Acts are fitted. The edict of Claudius, placed on the evidence of Dio Cassius in A.D. 41, marks Paul's first arrival in Corinth. The trial before Gallio, transferred to Paul's final stay in Corinth, marks the end of his missionary activity.

This theory naturally avoids all the difficulties which beset those who take Acts more seriously, but it raises some very awkward problems of its own. If Barnabas accompanied Paul to Greece, how are

| Table 3 | | | | | |
|---|---|---|---|---|---|
| | I | II | III | IV | V |
| Conversion of Paul | 33 | 33 | 31 or 33 | 33 | 34 or 37 |
| First visit to Jerusalem | 36 | 36 | 33 or 36 | 36 | 37 or 40 |
| Famine visit | 46 | — | 46 | 46 | — |
| First missionary journey | 47-48 | 47-48 | 47-48 | 47-48 | 37-51 or 40-51 |
| Apostolic conference | 49 | 49 | 49 | 49 | 51 |
| Paul's arrival in Corinth | 50 | 50 | 50 | 50 | 41 |

we to explain the presence of Silas-Silvanus there as his principal colleague, and how can we account for Barnabas' behavior at Antioch (Gal. 2:11 ff) after he had spent eleven years in the company of Paul? On what principle are the episodes from Acts to be selected and rearranged, and what justification is there for the assumption that the letters mention all the salient events of his career?

Each of these theories yields a different chronology for the initial period of Christian history, and the results may be tabulated as in Table 3.

**3. Relative dating, A.D. 50-70.** When we come to work forward from Gallio's proconsulship, we are dependent entirely on Acts. Paul was acquitted by Gallio sometime during the late summer or autumn of 51 and stayed on in Corinth many days before setting out for Jerusalem. He would not have sailed during the winter, so that his departure must be placed either in the autumn of 51 or in the spring of 52. There follows an undefined period during which he journeyed to Jerusalem, spent some time in Antioch, carried out an extensive tour of Asia Minor, and finally arrived in Ephesus. His stay in Ephesus lasted between two and three years and was followed by another tour of unspecified length through Macedonia to Corinth. He must have arrived in Corinth at the end of the year, for three months later he was celebrating the Passover in Philippi. From there he traveled quickly in order to reach Jerusalem in time for Pentecost, and very soon after his arrival he was arrested and taken to prison at Caesarea. He had been two years in prison when Festus arrived.

We have seen that the probable date for Festus' arrival is the summer of 59. From this we deduce that Paul was arrested in the summer of 57 and arrived in Corinth toward the end of 56. At this point in his life Paul was in a hurry to complete the collection he had organized for the Jerusalem church, and it is therefore unlikely that more than six months had elapsed since his departure from Ephesus. It had been his intention to leave Ephesus at Pentecost, and this must have been the Pentecost of 56 (I Cor. 16:8). His arrival in Ephesus then can be placed in the autumn of 53. Thus we arrive at the dates in Table 4.

| Table 4 | |
|---|---|
| Paul leaves Corinth | Autumn, 51, or Spring, 52 |
| Paul reaches Ephesus | Autumn, 53 |
| Paul leaves Ephesus | Summer, 56 |
| Paul reaches Corinth | End of 56 |
| Paul at Philippi | Passover, 57 |
| Paul reaches Jerusalem | Pentecost, 57 |
| Paul before Festus | Summer, 59 |
| Paul reaches Rome | Spring, 60 |

The only other event in this period which we can date with any confidence is the death of James, the Lord's brother, in 61. Festus died at some time during the year 60/61; and before the arrival of his successor, Albinus, James fell victim to mob violence. Not long after this the church in Jerusalem left the city, and was therefore not involved in the Jewish revolt of 66, which ended in the destruction of the city by Titus four years later.

*Bibliography.* C. H. Turner, "The Chronology of the NT," *HDB* (1908); W. M. Ramsay, *Pauline and Other Studies* (1908),

pp. 345-65; A. Deissmann, *Paul: A Study in Social and Religious History* (2nd ed., 1926), pp. 261-86; K. Lake, *The Beginnings of Christianity*, V (1933), 445-74; J. K. Fotheringham, "The Evidence of Astronomy and Technical Chronology for the Date of the Crucifixion," *JTS* (Apr., 1934), pp. 146-62; G. Ogg, *The Chronology of the Public Ministry of Jesus* (1940); J. Knox, *Chapters in a Life of Paul* (1950); J. Jeremias, *The Eucharistic Words of Jesus* (1955), pp. 1-13.     G. B. CAIRD

**CHRYSOLITE** krĭs′ə lĭt [תרשׁישׁ (*alternately* BERYL 1; "jewels"), *cf.* LXX *and* NT χρυσόλιθος, Vulg. *chrysolithus;* LXX λίθου ἄνθρακος, carbuncle, *in* Ezek. 10:9]. A magnesium iron silicate, usually olive-green. It is used in the description of wheels in the vision of Ezekiel (1:16; 10:9). It is a stone in the covering of the king of Tyre (Ezek. 28:13). It is used metaphorically in the description of the youth in Song of S. 5:14 and of Gabriel in Dan. 10:6. The use of χρυσόλιθος in Rev. 21:20, for the seventh jewel in the foundation of the walls of the New Jerusalem, would indicate a yellowish, rather than a green, stone.

*See also* JEWELS AND PRECIOUS STONES § 2.

W. E. STAPLES

**CHRYSOPRASE** krĭs′ə prāz [χρυσόπρασος] (Rev. 21:20); KJV **CHRYSOPRASUS** krĭs′ə prā′zəs. An apple-green variety of chalcedony, used as a gem in Egypt; the tenth jewel in the foundation of the wall of the New Jerusalem. *See* JEWELS AND PRECIOUS STONES § 2.     W. E. STAPLES

**CHUB.** KJV form of CUB (Ezek. 30:5).

**CHUN.** KJV form of CUN.

**CHURCH, IDEA OF.** For that reality which is designated in English most commonly by the word "church," there are in the NT many diverse terms, each with its own etymological and theological history. Each term conveys in varying contexts a large cluster of shifting connotations and associations. In contemporary English usage, "church" as a word dominates the ecclesiological vocabulary. It comes through German and Latin from the Greek κυριακόν, which means "that which belongs to the Lord." In NT Greek, εκκλησία (almost always translated in English by "church") is by no means so dominating or central a term. Of the 112 appearances of *ecclesia* in the NT, 90 per cent are found in Paul's letters, the book of Acts, and Revelation. From ten books (Mark, Luke, John, II Timothy, Titus, I-II Peter, I-II John, Jude) this word is absent. *Ecclesia* was used primarily to designate a particular communal reality, not to describe its qualitative aspects. Where the distinctive qualities and dimensions of community life were intended, other terms proved more flexible and evocative. In comparison with these other terms, *ecclesia* was relatively neutral and colorless, conveying by itself little theological meaning. It was open to use, without basic shift in meaning, by unbelievers as well as by believers. Even among those writers who made wide use of *ecclesia*, other terms were more expressive of the reality at hand. We turn first to the basic meanings of *ecclesia* as used in the NT and thereafter to the many cognate ways of expressing the idea of the church. Because the pictures and images are more frequent and forceful, and because they so effectively suggest the qualitative constituents of the church idea, the greater proportion of space here will be devoted to them. Throughout, "church" will be used as the more inclusive category (in line with modern English) and *ecclesia* in the more limited way in which NT writers employ the Greek word.

A. Basic meanings of *ecclesia*
  1. In the OT
  2. In the NT
    *a.* An assembly
    *b.* A community of believers
    *c.* A community gathered by God through Christ
    *d.* The eschatological people of God
B. Cognate ways of expressing the church idea
  1. The saints and sanctified
  2. Believers and faithful
  3. Slaves and servants
  4. The people of God
  5. Kingdom and temple
  6. Household and family
  7. The new exodus
  8. Vineyard and flock
  9. One body in Christ
  10. The new humanity
C. Essential traits in the church idea
Bibliography

A. *BASIC MEANINGS OF "ECCLESIA."* **1. In the OT.** The LXX uses *ecclesia* almost a hundred times as the translation for *qâhâl* (קהל). The basic meaning of both words is a meeting or gathering. People gather together or are summoned for any and every purpose. It is the people and the purpose which give significance to the *qâhâl*. *Qâhâl* may be a gathering of men called up for military duty (Gen. 49:6; Num. 22:4; Ezek. 16:40) or for civic action. Those who assemble may be prophets (I Sam. 19:20) or princes (Num. 16:3; I Chr. 28:8), or a disorderly mob (Ecclus. 26:6). *Qâhâl* is used as readily of those who gather to work evil (Ps. 26:5) as of those who worship God (II Chr. 30:13; Ecclus. 50:13, 20). Probably the most significant *qâhâl* in the OT is the assembling of Israel before God on Horeb (Deut. 4:10; 9:10; 10:4; 18:16), when God sealed his covenant with them. This served to define the significance of the ecclesia of Israel, but it did not give to the terms *qâhâl* or *ecclesia* a fixed, technical meaning.

*Qâhâl* was frequently rendered by other Greek words in the LXX. Of these the most noteworthy was συναγωγή, which also was a general term, applicable to meetings of all sorts. *Synagogue* was also used to translate the Hebrew *'ēdhâh* (עדה), which had one meaning not associated with *qâhâl*. It could be applied to a congregation apart from its act of meeting together. *Ecclesia*, however, never appears as a LXX rendering for *'ēdhâh*. And the Greek term συναγωγή is limited in NT usage to Jewish congregations, with rare exceptions (Jas. 2:2). The distinctive meanings of *ecclesia*, therefore, develop within Christian history and are due more to religious associations than to philological origins.

**2. In the NT.** *a. An assembly of persons which has been summoned for a particular purpose.* The purpose may be secular or religious. The meeting may be regularly constituted (Acts 19:39) or more spontaneous in origin (vss. 32, 40). In the NT *ecclesia* often refers to the occasion when a specific congregation gathers for prayer, instruction, and deliberation (Acts 11:26; 12:5; I Cor. 11:18; 14:4-5, 19, 28, 34-35; Col. 4:16).

*b. A community of believers which has been gathered from the inhabitants of a specific area.* The community meets in assembly, to be sure, but it is constituted as ecclesia prior to and apart from such assemblies. The area from which the community has been gathered may be a single household (Rom. 16:5; Col. 4:15; Philem. 2); a single city (Jerusalem [Acts 8:1; 11:22]; Cenchreae [Rom. 16:1]; Corinth [I Cor. 1:2; II Cor. 1:1]; Thessalonica [I Thess. 1:1; II Thess. 1:1]; Ephesus [Rev. 2:1, etc.]); or a province (Galatia [Gal. 1:2]; Judea [Gal. 1:22; I Thess. 2:14]); Macedonia [II Cor. 8:1]; Asia [I Cor. 16:19; Rev. 1:4, 11; etc.]). The multiple number of congregations in a province may be represented by the noun in the plural (I Cor. 16:1, 19; Gal. 1:2), but just as easily by the singular (Acts 9:31). The unity of many congregations is symbolized in Revelation by the number seven (Rev. 1–3). A group of congregations may be designated by reference to a common racial and cultural origin—e.g., the churches of the Gentiles (Rom. 16:4). In all these cases, the basic function of the word is to identify, without qualifying adjectives, a particular congregation or group of congregations (e.g., frequently in salutations: I Thess. 1:1; II Thess. 1:1). The idea of "having been gathered" persists in virtually all these contexts.

*c. A community gathered by God through Christ.* The nature of this community is therefore continually qualified by the One who summons or gathers it. This accent is made explicit in many cases: the ecclesia (or ecclesiai) of God (Acts 20:28; I Cor. 1:2; 10:32; 11:16, 22; 15:9; II Cor. 1:1; Gal. 1:13; I Thess. 2:14; II Thess. 1:4; I Tim. 3:5, 15). Often this qualification is implicit, but the contexts usually make clear the intention. The ecclesia belongs to God because he has called it into being, dwells within it, rules over it, and realizes his purpose through it. Whether referred to in the singular or the plural, the entire covenant community is considered a single unity because it has been gathered or summoned by the one God.

On occasion *ecclesia* is qualified by the phrase "the churches of Christ" (Rom. 16:16; Gal. 1:22), or by the double phrase "the church . . . in God the Father and the Lord Jesus Christ" (I Thess. 1:1; II Thess. 1:1). Even where the prepositional phrase is lacking, the context often assumes recognition that God in Christ is the power which has constituted this particular ecclesia. Because the ecclesiai belong to Christ, and to God, they constitute together a single reality—a world-wide covenant community, which is embodied in localized form wherever a congregation exists (Col. 4:15-16; I Thess. 1:1; etc.).

*d. The eschatological people of God.* The Christ who is the living foundation of the ecclesia is the Messiah promised to Israel. Because this Messiah is now gathering his people, *ecclesia* comes to include a strong sense of decisive finality. In later NT writings, *ecclesia* connotes the eschatological people of God, gathered from among the nations through the redeeming work of the Messiah, to participate in the new age which he inaugurates. Here the gathering of God's people spans all generations and all places, and fulfils all the covenants which have served as the ground of created community. As such it is a recipient and channel of God's glory, a participant in God's warfare with Satan, the heir of the promises, and the earnest of eternal life (Eph. 1:23-2:10; 3:8-12; Col. 1:21-27; Heb. 12:22-24; Rev. 1:20). Here we are farthest from the basic and initial reference of *ecclesia,* and it is only by absorption of meanings from other images that it develops this range of associations.

**B. COGNATE WAYS OF EXPRESSING THE CHURCH IDEA.** More than one hundred cognate expressions may be distinguished, but most of these can be grouped—somewhat arbitrarily, to be sure—under ten categories. In the case of each category it is recommended that the reader supplement the material in this article with that of related articles.

**1. The saints and sanctified.** *Ecclesia* may be viewed from the standpoint of God's action toward and upon men. In this case *ecclesia* becomes equivalent to those whom God has called, chosen, gathered, foreknown, justified, glorified, sanctified. Often these descriptions involve active verbs or participles, expressive of the dynamic character of divine action among men. To take as one example the designation of the church as "the saints" (*see* SAINT), even when the noun is used (οἱ ἅγιοι), the verbal action is to be assumed. Those who are "called saints" are men who have been "sanctified in Christ Jesus" (I Cor. 1:2). (For the virtual identification of saints and church, see John 17:17-19; Acts 9:31-32; Rom. 15: 16-31; I Cor. 14:33; II Cor. 1:1; Eph. 2:19; 5:26; Heb. 13:12; I Pet. 2:5-9; Rev. 20:9). The use of the term "saints" accents the work of the HOLY SPIRIT (πνεῦμα ἅγιον) in the integumentation of community, for saints are those who have received the Holy Spirit (ἡγιασμένοι) by rebirth in baptism. The Son who sanctifies is one with those who are sanctified (Heb. 2:11). Therefore, to be saints is to share in Christ, who is "our sanctification" (ἁγιασμός) from God (I Cor. 1:30). Thus the term "saints" illustrates clearly the dependence of the church on the activity of the Father (Luke 11:13; John 10:36; I Thess. 4:7), the Son (John 17:19; I Cor. 1:2; 6:11; Eph. 5:26; Heb. 10:10 ff), and the Spirit (Acts 10:44 ff; 11:15 ff; 15:8; Rom. 8). (For the rich significance of SANCTIFICATION in relation to community, *see* John 10:36; 17:15-20; Acts 10:44-47; 19:1-6; Rom. 8; I Cor. 3: 17; 6:1-19; 12:1-7; Eph. 1:13; 5:26; Col. 1:21-27; Heb. 6:4-10; 10:10-29). The use of the cognate expressions "saints," "the holy ones," "the sanctified," is as common as the use of *ecclesia* and also as widespread.

Less frequent and less widely scattered, but of genuine significance, is the use of the verb "to choose" (ἐκλέγεσθαι) and the noun "the chosen," "the elect" (οἱ ἐκλεκτοί), to designate the church. Jesus Christ is God's Elect, God's Chosen One; through him men are elect and chosen (Luke 9:35; John 15:6 ff; Acts 13:17; 15:7; I Cor. 1:27; Eph. 1:4; I Thess. 1:4; Jas. 2:5). To be described as "the elect" (*see* ELECTION) is to be designated as the covenant community which inherits the new age (Matt. 24:22, 24, 31; Luke 18:7; Rom. 8:33; Col. 3:12; II Tim. 2:10; I Pet. 2:9, Rev. 17:14). This category accents the priority of God's action in establishing the church, the continuity between Israel and the church, and the continuing dependence of the community on God's election (Rom. 9:11; 11:5, 7, 28; II Pet. 1:10).

A parallel expression is that which describes the ecclesia as those whom God justifies (οἱ δικαιούμενοι), and consequently as those who are justified or righteous (οἱ δίκαιοι). The interdependence of church and the justified is indicated in such sayings as this: "We are justified by faith" (Rom. 5:1; cf. Matt. 10:41; 25: 37, 46; Rom. 1:17; 5:9, 19; 8:30; I Cor. 6:11; Heb. 12:23). He who justifies, he who is the Just One, is God (John 17:25; Rom. 3:26; Rev. 16:5). But he justifies men through Christ (Matt. 27:19, 24; Acts 3:14; 7:52; 22:14; I Pet. 3:18; I John 1:9; 2:1, 29). And this JUSTIFICATION proceeds through the active power of the Holy Spirit (Rom. 8:4-30). In being justified, men are related to Jesus Christ, who is the true measure and ground of righteousness (Rom. 3: 26; Tit. 3:7; Heb. 12:23; I John 3:7). They are simultaneously related to all "just" men, from the beginning to the end (Matt. 13:17, 43, 49; 23:35; Rom. 4; Heb. 11:4; 12:23).

**2. Believers and faithful.** *Ecclesia* may be viewed from the standpoint of personal, communal response to God's action through Christ, a response which is empowered by the Holy Spirit. God calls men; in response they call upon the name of the Lord. Those who thus call constitute the ecclesia (I Cor. 1:2). Christ calls men to follow him, to be his disciples (*see* DISCIPLES), to be with him, and to be sent by him (Mark 3:14; 6:7); those who respond constitute the ecclesia. Consequently the terms "disciples" (μαθηταί) and "those who follow" (οἱ ἀκολούθεντες) become virtual equivalents to the term *ecclesia* (Matt. 28:19; John 10:4; Acts 11:26; 14:22, 28; 18:23; Rev. 14:4). In Christ, God justifies men, and pronounces them righteous before him; in response men commit themselves in confidence, in trust, in faith. Those who believe in God and in his Son constitute the ecclesia. The church is the company of believers (οἱ πιστεύοντες). Here again the same noun (ὁ πιστός) is applied to God (I Cor. 1:9; 10:13; II Cor. 1:18; I Thess. 5:24; II Thess. 3:3; Heb. 10:23; I Pet. 4: 19); to Christ (II Tim. 2:13; Heb. 2:17; 3:2; I John 1:9; Rev. 1:5; 3:14; 19:11); to the individual believers (Acts 16:1, 15; Rev. 2:13); and to the company of the faithful (John 1:12; 3:15; 5:24; 17:20-21; Acts 2:44; 4:4, 32; 5:14; 10:45; 14:23; Rom. 3:22; I Cor. 14:22; Eph. 1:1; Col. 1:2; Heb. 4:3; I Pet. 2:7). Constitutive of the church is this divinely imparted FAITH and faithfulness, justification and righteousness (*see* RIGHTEOUSNESS [IN THE NT]). In more than seventy-five passages, scattered through at least fifteen NT books, there are abundant data to support the thought of the church as the community of believers. Men who believe in the faithful God and his faithful Son are men in whom the faithfulness of God in Christ operates. By this faithfulness they are justified, sanctified, and glorified. In their confident commitment to the gospel, they are made alive and are united in the work of divine reconciliation (John 3; 17; Acts 4; 10; Rom. 4; Gal. 3; Eph. 1; Heb. 4; I John 5).

**3. Slaves and servants.** *Ecclesia* may be viewed

from the standpoint of the basic duties which this response of faith entails. The church is the company of those who through faith have accepted enlistment as slaves, servants, stewards, ministers, witnesses, confessors, ambassadors, soldiers, and friends. Of these terms as qualifying the nature of *ecclesia*, the two most frequently employed in the NT are at the same time the most menial in connotation ("slaves" and "servants") and therefore the most effective in stressing the paradoxical interdependence of humiliation and glory, of slavery and freedom. We should therefore review the basic reference of the term "slaves" (δοῦλοι). As in the case of faith and faithfulness, the ultimate lord to whom service is rendered is God revealed in Christ, who is in turn viewed as both lord and slave, both master and servant. Therefore, the status as a slave immediately involves a corresponding relationship to fellow slaves within the ecclesia. Because Christ became a slave (Phil. 2:7), those who belong to him become slaves of one another for his sake (II Cor. 4:5; Gal. 5:13). They are also bound in obligation to all the men to whom Christ came as a slave. The basic demand of obedience which Christ lays on the church thus becomes an inescapable obligation to the world (I Cor. 9:19).

The slave image, applied positively to the church, bears multiple connotations where it appears in the fifty passages in some eighteen writings. That every believer was considered a slave of God and of Christ is clearly indicated in such passages as I Thess. 1:9; Rom. 6:18, 22. That this description was grounded in the teaching of Jesus is made evident in all four gospels (Matt. 6:24; 10:24; 20:27; Mark 10:44; Luke 17:10; John 13:16). Furthermore, the parables of Jesus which center in a master's dealings with his servants were construed by early Christians to apply with special force to them (Matt. 13; 18; 22; 24; Mark 12; Luke 14; 15; 20).

It thus became the early custom of NT authors to introduce themselves as slaves of God (Tit. 1:1) and of Christ (Rom. 1:1; Phil. 1:1; Jas. 1:1; II Pet. 1:1; Jude 1:1; Rev. 1:1). They thus grounded their authority in this status (Acts 16:17; 20:19). Moreover, they often refer to the community as slaves of God (Acts 2:18; 4:29; Rom. 6:22; I Thess. 1:9; I Pet. 2:16; Rev. 7:3; 11:18) and of Christ (Rom. 14:18; I Cor. 7:22; Eph. 6:6-9). Fellowship in this company was a matter of motivation, a matter of obedience, a matter of the heart's allegiance.

They viewed this slavery as the opposite of slavery to FEAR, to the law, the flesh, the world, and Satan (Rom. 6:18; 8:12-15; Gal. 4:3, 24-25; 5:1; Heb. 2:15). In fact, SLAVERY to Christ was taken as ruling out the desire for the favor of men (Gal. 1:10; Eph. 6:6) or the security and prosperity of the self (Matt. 6:24; Rom. 16:18). Slaves now obey their earthly master because of their allegiance to their new Master. Slaves of Christ are free men in relation to their masters in the flesh (I Cor. 7:22; Eph. 6:6; Col. 3:24; I Pet. 2:16). Slaves of Christ are his friends and not like chattels who do not know what their Lord does (John 15:15-20). Thus to be slaves of Christ is not incompatible with being friends and brothers (Gal. 4:1-7). For to be slaves of Christ is to imitate his lowliness, humiliation, suffering (Matt. 10:24; Mark 10:44-45; John 13:16; 15:20). To be slaves of Christ is to be witnesses (*see* WITNESS), confessors to him (Rev. 19:2) as apostles and prophets. To be slaves of Christ is to proclaim his gospel and his kingdom (Acts 2:18; 4:29; 16:17; Rev. 1:1; 22:6), and to worship the one true God (Rev. 19:5; 22:30).

The connotations of *diakonia* as descriptive of the ecclesia form a similar pattern. All believers are *ipso facto* servants (διάκονοι), and the same Spirit energizes all forms of service (I Cor. 12:5). God supplies the strength and varied grace (I Pet. 4:10), with Jesus Christ serving as the great exemplar as well as the master whose commands all servants obey (Luke 22:26-28). There are many varieties of service—e.g., of the word and of tables (Acts 6:1, 4; II Cor. 8-9); but all forms of service in and to the church serve to strengthen it and to build it up. Although a special office of deacons appears (Phil. 1:1; I Tim. 3; *see* MINISTRY), their work does not diminish the truth that the whole church is a *diakonia* (II Cor. 3:1-11; 5:18; Eph. 4:12; Rev. 2:19). Christ serves his church, his church serves him—the mutuality constitutes the church as *diakonia* (Matt. 20:28; Luke 12:37; 22:26-27; Rom. 15:8; I Cor. 3:5-9).

**4. The people of God.** The Christian ecclesia is viewed throughout the NT as the people of God and therefore in many various ways as the continuation and consummation of his covenant community. The church understands itself in terms of the living scriptures, and interprets these scriptures, in turn, in the light of its own experience of community in Christ. Almost all the descriptions of ecclesia in the NT utilize concepts and images which in the LXX had been applied to God's people, and thus suggest a recognition of solidarity with Israel. But this kinship is often made entirely explicit. E.g., the church is identified as the Israel of God (Gal. 6:16), and God is known as the God of Israel (Matt. 2:6; Luke 1:54, 68; 2:32; Acts 13:17; Rom. 11:1). The Shema is accepted by the church as addressed to them: "Hear, O Israel" (Mark 12:29); the new COVENANT is sealed with the house of Israel (Heb. 8:8-10); Gentiles are incorporated within this commonwealth (Rom. 11:17; Eph. 2:12) and inherit the hope of Israel (Acts 28:20). Jesus is the shepherd-king sent to Israel for its glory and salvation, demonstrating God's faithfulness to the oath given to the patriarchs (Matt. 2:6; 15:24; Luke 1:68; 2:32; 24:21; John 1:49; 12:13; Acts 5:31; 13:23). Consequently the church may be appropriately addressed as the twelve tribes of Israel (Matt. 19:28; Luke 22:30; Jas. 1:1; Rev. 7:4; 21:12), as the true circumcision (Phil. 3:3; Col. 2:11-14), and as the sons of Abraham by repentance and faith (Matt. 3:9; John 8:39; Rom. 4:1-16; Gal. 3:7-29; Heb. 11). True circumcision is a matter of the heart (Rom. 2:29). Participation in circumcision is therefore inseparable from participation in Christ's death by baptism (Col. 2:11-14). Sonship to Abraham is dependent upon God's promises appropriated by faith (Rom. 4). "If you are Christ's, then you are Abraham's offspring" (Gal. 3:29). Those who rely on biological descent or on cultural and national heritage may be called Israel according to the flesh, but what constitutes men as the Israel of God is that qualitative communal relationship to God which is produced by God's promise and corporate hope, by God's election and man's faith, by

Christ's dying life and man's acceptance of that life as his own. The Israel of God is an eschatological community which relies on the coming salvation rather than on superiorities handed down from the past. Therefore, this community includes all those who from the beginning have lived by faith in God's covenant promises (Matt. 8:11; Luke 13:28-30; Heb. 11).

All these aspects are included, with others, in the NT description of the ecclesia as "the people of God" (ὁ λαὸς τοῦ θεοῦ). The use of this term in the NT is more frequent, more ubiquitous, more evocative of the sense of identity and mission, than the use of the term *ecclesia*. It is distinctive and yet dependent throughout upon the LXX perspectives. To avoid misunderstanding, the definite article should be preserved—"the people." Also the presence of the qualifying phrase "of God" should almost always be inferred. The nuances of this title are many-dimensioned and varied. In addition to those already specified (e.g., ISRAEL, HISTORY OF; CIRCUMCISION; etc.) the following are noteworthy: "the people of God" designates that society which God has chosen for his own possession (II Cor. 6:16; I Pet. 2:9; Rev. 21:3), and which he has created and brought into existence (Acts 13:17; 15:14; Rom. 9:25; I Pet. 2:10), by his grace in the forgiveness of sins (Heb. 2:17; 8:10; I Pet. 2:9). It is a community which is held together by its remembrance of deliverance (Tit. 2:14) and its hope of promised inheritance (Rom. 4:13-25). It is bound to God in a covenant written on hearts, a covenant which God will never repudiate (Acts 3:25; Gal. 4:24; Heb. 8:10-12). It is a realm pervaded by personal FAMILY relationships to God, for he lives in them and moves among them, acting toward them as a father toward his children (II Cor. 6:18). Corporate cohesion springs from the gift of the Holy Spirit and from the saving activity of Jesus Christ. The extension of the community comes through God's continued calling of men to be his people (Acts 18:9-10). The life of God's people involves essentially the praise and glorification of God among the nations, and the extension of the bounds of the covenant community to include men from every nation, tribe, tongue, and people (Rev. 5:9-10). Its distinctiveness, its separation from other peoples, is designed for the redemption of all peoples. Linked thus to the beginning and to the end of God's creative and fulfilling purpose, his people encompasses all generations. From beginning to end, Jesus Christ is the anointed king and shepherd of this people, his rule inseparable from his redemption of them through his death (Matt. 1:21; 2:6; 4:16; Luke 1:68, 77; 2:31-32; 7:16; Tit. 2:14).

All these positive qualifications of the true people of God are kept in constant tension with the actualities of a history filled with the treacheries of a people which rejects its God and repudiates its rightful King. The threat of the old covenant is repeated in various forms: "Every soul that does not listen to that prophet shall be destroyed from the people" (Acts 3:23; cf. Deut. 18:19; Rom. 10:21; Heb. 10:30). The Lord who owns the people is their sole judge. His judgment is the final criterion of their belongingness.

**5. Kingdom and temple.** The church, considered as the gathering of God's people, is viewed also in terms of those institutions which had long been central in the life of Israel—the kingdom and the temple. Believers are spoken of as kings and priests (Rev. 1:6; 5:10). Their society is called a holy nation and a royal priesthood (I Pet. 2:9). Usually each term—"kingdom" and "temple"—attracts a congeries of supporting images:

*a*) Although never completely identified with the KINGDOM OF GOD, the church includes those who have been transferred into the kingdom of his Son (Col. 1:13), who is King and Son of David. The church receives the keys of the kingdom (Matt. 16:18-19; 18:16 ff; *see* KEY). Believers are sons and heirs of the kingdom (Matt. 5:3, 10; 5:19; 8:12; 10: 11; 18:1, 4; Jas. 2:5). Through Christ they "reign in life" (Rom. 5:17), and are related to a kingdom which cannot be shaken (Heb. 12:28). Their strongest desire is to enter the kingdom (or to enter life—Matt. 19:13-30; Acts 14:22; Gal. 5:21), and they work together for the kingdom (Col. 4:11; I Thess. 2: 12). The way into the kingdom is narrow and steep, requiring total renunciation and humiliation. As servants of the King, they follow his road to power and glory. To those who conquer, crowns and thrones of GLORY are bestowed, emblem of royal grace and authority.

*b*) The center of Israel's kingdom was the City of David, the Holy City, JERUSALEM. This provided analogies for the idea of the church (Heb. 12; Rev. 2-3; 21-22). Here again the promises of God to Israel were fulfilled in the coming of Jesus as Messiah to Israel. The Messiah and the messianic people—always inseparable in biblical thought—were described as heirs and inhabitants of God's city, Jerusalem. This new city from above is a realm of freedom, in final conflict with the city from below, the realm of bondage. For the prophet John (Rev. 17-22), the Holy City which comes down from heaven is arrayed against its demonic counterpart BABYLON, Bride against Harlot, Christ against Satan. The two foes are both represented by the city of Jerusalem, which is both the scene of great apostasy—Sodom and Egypt, where the Lord was crucified—and also the scene of the redemption, where the Lord gathers his people in victory (Rev. 11:8). Each congregation is set at the juncture where the conflict between these two communities is maximal and where, therefore, the final victory of the messianic Jerusalem is to be revealed. Against this background, the gospels picture Jesus going up to Jerusalem to complete his work of salvation. It is there that simultaneously the Messiah's love for God's city and his rejection by his people are demonstrated.

*c*) Central to the mission and destiny of Jerusalem was the TEMPLE. In fact, it was the presence of the temple which made Jerusalem the Holy City. Early Christians, therefore, in thinking of their community as the new Jerusalem, also thought of it as the temple. In doing this, they rarely had in mind the visible structures on Mount Zion (ἱερόν). With them it was a fixed axiom that God does not dwell in a temple made by hands (Acts 17:24). Rather, God erects his people as a sanctuary (ναός) by choosing to dwell among men (II Cor. 6:16). Because his presence is the decisive element, Jesus' body is called a temple (John 2:19-21); so, too, is the whole church (Eph.

2:21; Rev. 21), the congregation (I Cor. 3:16-17), and each believer (I Cor. 6:19). The church is made a temple by the presence of God, the Holy Spirit, and Jesus Christ (John 1:14; I Cor. 3:16; 6:19; II Cor. 6:16; Rev. 7:15). And this temple is viewed as a single structure which is *growing into* a "dwelling place of God in the Spirit" (Eph. 2:20-22). The basic image suggests varying subimages of the cornerstone and the foundation and living stones (I Pet. 2:4-8). In every case, men are the substance of the temple—men who are "on earth"—but there is a close interdependence between this visible community and the temple in heaven in which God is glorified by all his creatures (Heb. 12:22-24; Rev. 3:12; 7:15; 12:12; 13:6; 21:3).

*d*) Because God's presence creates this temple, and because the fundamental function of the temple is to serve God day and night, there is no incongruity in thinking of Jesus as both CORNERSTONE and high priest, or of believers as both living stones and priests (*see* PRIESTS [IN THE NT]). In I Peter the whole church is described as both a royal and a holy priesthood (I Pet. 2:5, 9) whose corporate duty is the offering of spiritual sacrifices, or, in alternate expression, the proclamation of the gospel of mercy. In Revelation, likewise, the church is a community of priests (ἱερεῖς; 1:6; 5:10; 20:6) which appears as a fruit of the emancipating love, the atoning death, of God's Son and therefore as a witnessing and worshiping unit. By their participation in Christ's love they participate in his reign and life (5:10; 20:6). Here the conception is neither that of a separate order of priests within the church nor that of the individual priesthood of each believer, but that of the shared priesthood of a community which has received life and power through their dying Lord. In Hebrews, it is this Lord in whom the priesthood, or rather the eternal high priesthood, is vested. Through his perfect obedience and perfect sacrifice he became the "source of eternal salvation to all who obey him" (5:6-10; 7:16). He is the "surety of a better covenant" (7:22; ch. 8) by which the church lives; he is the access into the Holy of Holies, providing through his self-offering a way by which the community enters the sanctuary (9:11–10:25).

*e*) Because his priesthood is accomplished through his "sacrifice" of himself, so too the community of priests is created and sustained by self-sacrifice. Those who serve as priests present themselves, their bodies, as a living sacrifice (Rom. 12:1). Thus there is a close affinity among the images of temple, stones, priesthood, and sacrifices. Jesus Christ serves as "our altar" (Heb. 13:10-16); defined as worthy sacrifices, therefore, are such things as the praise of God, good deeds, and mutual sharing. The church continues as liturgical community, but the character of its λειτουργία is transformed. The self-sacrificing work of the apostle in his ministry of God's grace to the Gentiles is his priestly service (Rom. 15:16); likewise their contribution of financial aid to Jewish Christians is token of their priestly sacrifice (Rom. 15:27; II Cor. 9:12). Mutual sharing in suffering and in ministering to corporate needs is a genuine expression of both priesthood and sacrifice (Phil. 2:17, 25, 30). Faith itself is channeled through the sacrifice on the altar, the libation on the sacrifice, and the aroma of the sacrifice. All these images suggest the priestly character of the Christian community, which recognizes that mercy and love are greater than all burnt offerings (Matt. 9:13; 12:6-7; Mark 12:33; I Cor. 5:7-8). This priesthood is a royal priesthood because the source of its liturgical holiness is identical with the source of its kingly power, for its Lord revealed in his death and resurrection the meaning of both kingship and priesthood.

**6. Household and family.** The church is understood to be the eschatological gathering of God's people into his household, to become his "house" (οἶκος, οἰκία) and his FAMILY. A fluctuating configuration of images centering in the family suggests a wide complex of relationships as the structure of the church. Only a few of these relations can be suggested here.

Many of the OT concepts enter into new vitality in Christian thinking. As in the OT Israel is spoken of as a house, so too in the NT is the church described as the house of Israel or of Jacob, of Moses, of David, but also as the house of God (Matt. 10:6; Luke 1:33, 69; Acts 2:36; 7:42; Heb. 3:2-6; I Pet. 4:17). "House" and "household" are in some contexts virtually synonymous with "kingdom," "nation," "city," and "temple," with all their associations (Matt. 21: 13; John 2:16-17; Heb. 8:8-10; 10:21; I Pet. 2:5). The church is this house, and in slightly varied form this building (I Tim. 3:15). The work of construction (οἰκοδομεῖν) and the task of stewards and householders (οἰκονόμοι, οἰκονομία) are related concepts (Luke 12:42; Acts 7:47-49; 9:31; Rom. 15:20; I Cor. 3:9; 4:1-2; Eph. 2:21; I Pet. 4:10). God is related to his house in terms of owning, ruling, and dwelling within it. To him the household is related in terms of dependence, obedience, of stewardship, of watchful waiting, and of patient boldness (Heb. 5-6). In this family terminology as applied explicitly to the church, two related modes of thought receive major accent:

*a*) The church is thought of as the SONS (υἱοί) OF GOD (Rom. 9:26; II Cor. 6:16-18; Heb. 2:10). "You have one Father, who is in heaven" (Matt. 23:9). Existence as sons stems from God's act: "God sent forth his Son, . . . so that we might receive adoption as sons. . . . God has sent the Spirit of his Son into our hearts, crying, 'Abba! Father!' " (Gal. 4:4-6). The component elements of sonship vary in different writings, but there is assumed throughout a central, constant dependence on the Father's act. Among these elements may be detailed: peacemaking (Matt. 5:9); loving the brothers (I John 3:10-11); loving enemies (Matt. 5:41-45); acceptance of discipline (Heb. 12:5 ff); hope and purity (I John 3:3); conquering temptation (Rev. 21:7); freedom from fear of death (Heb. 2:15); freedom from the law (Gal. 4:5); direction by the Spirit (Rom. 8:14); redemption of the body (Rom. 8:23); humble obedience (Matt. 23:8-12); holiness and sanctification (Heb. 2:11). Sonship represents such fruits as these. All these are corporate, as well as personal, tokens of membership among God's people.

*b*) Corollary to the above is the conception of the church as a BROTHERHOOD (I Pet. 2:17; 5:9). Often the church is spoken ·of as a company of brothers (I Cor. 6:5; I John 3:10-17). In fact, the church is addressed as brothers (ἀδελφοί) no fewer than thirty times in the book of Acts alone (e.g., 15:22-23). "You have one teacher, and you are all brethren" (Matt. 23:8). Status as brethren is wholly dependent upon the work of God in Christ (Heb. 2:10-18). Jesus as the FIRSTBORN of many brethren provides the image to which they are predestined to be conformed (Rom. 8:29). This means that sonship and brotherhood are inseparably related to sharing in his sufferings (Rom. 8:17; Phil. 3:7-17), to counting everything else as loss for his sake, to becoming like him in his death. To be his brother in these terms is to be a fellow heir with him of God's life and kingdom. Thus the determining picture of sonship and brotherhood, and therefore of the being of the church, is provided by Jesus Christ himself. In him men see and imitate the personal embodiment of those constituents of sonship listed above. The character of the church thus depends upon the interdependence of the life of the elder son and his many brethren, and upon their common obedience to the Father's will.

*c*) This very interdependence is the core of another analogy from familial relationships—the church as the bride (νύμφη) of Christ. The incongruity of metaphors—the church as both the bride and the brothers —is due to reliance on separate idioms in OT thought, where similar incongruity appears. Israel had been visualized as the chosen bride of God in spite of her repeated adulteries (Jer. 2:1; Ezek. 16:23; Hos. 3:1-3). In the NT, Jesus is presented as the bridegroom; his disciples are his friends or sons (Matt. 9:15); his coming is symbolized as a wedding feast (Matt. 22:10; 25:1-13). To him the bride belongs (John 3:29). The faithful obedience of his church is viewed as preparation for the marriage (Rev. 19:7-9), which, in turn, signalizes the dwelling of God with men in the Holy City, Jerusalem (Rev. 21:2-27). Because of this conception, idolatry and adultery become vivid descriptions of sin, and the harlotry of the devil's bride, Babylon, becomes the final great antithesis to the faithfulness demanded of the church (Rev. 17-18). The worship of God's people is fittingly summarized by the prayer of the Bride: "Come" (Rev. 22:17). Paul speaks of having betrothed his Corinthian congregation to Christ as a pure bride, and of this bride as having been deceived by the serpent like Eve, when she preferred "a different gospel" (II Cor. 11:2-4). On Christ's side, the church becomes bride through his sacrificial love for it, his activity in nourishing, cherishing, and sanctifying it (Eph. 5:25-26, 29). On the church's side, life as his bride is expressed by reverence and obedience, by renouncing every other husband, and by seeking holiness (Eph. 5:21, 24, 27, 31). As various modes of expressing the existential relationship of the church to Christ, there is virtual equivalence in these images of the church as sons, brothers, bride; as citizens in the Holy City; and as members of Christ's body (*see* § 9 *below*).

7. **The new exodus.** The NT often thinks of the church in terms of typological comparison with key epochs in the scriptural history of Israel. Some of these typological references are incidental and indirect; some of them are central and decisive. Among the more incidental is the reference to baptism as comparable to salvation from the Flood at the time of Noah, suggesting the function of the church as the ark (I Pet. 3:18-22). More frequent and significant

is the conception of the church as exiles of the Dispersion, engaged in a continuing struggle with the tyrannical captivity of Babylon (Jas. 1:1; I Pet. 1:1; Rev. 16:12-18:24). Still more frequent and significant are the analogical references to the stories of creation with central interest in Adam (*cf. below*). Most pervasive and subtle are the associations of the church with Israel in Egypt: the sojourn; the conflict between Moses and Pharaoh; the plagues and the Exodus; the crossing of the Red Sea; the covenant of Mount Sinai; the wanderings in the wilderness, where the emigrants are guided by the pillars and nourished by the manna; the tabernacle, with the ark and the Aaronic priesthood; the succession from Moses to Joshua; and the Jordan crossing. Each of these items became a nucleus of living, corporate apperceptions in which memories, constantly fed from scripture, coalesced with contemporary experience, and gave shape to expectations. Different NT writers on different occasions focused their thought on different episodes in this saga. In Matthew, the relations between Jesus and the people of God are conceived to parallel in various ways the relations between Moses and Israel at Mount Sinai. In I Peter and Hebrews, the church is described as the community of strangers and pilgrims in sojourn in Egypt and as patient travelers toward the Land of Promise (Heb. 10:26 12:29; I Pet. 1:17; 2:11). Hebrews gives an elaborate comparison between Moses and Jesus, between the "day of testing" in the wilderness and the life of the church as it seeks the promised rest (chs. 3-4), and between the worship in the earthly sanctuary and the new and eternal Holy Place to which the people of God have access (chs. 9-10). For the prophet John, the plagues in Egypt have become analogies to God's final judgment in which Christians participate (Rev. 8; 15-16). The Supper of the church is a continuation and renewal of the feasts of PASSOVER and Unleavened Bread, a connection which is developed in various ways by Paul (I Cor. 10) and by the gospels (Mark 6:30-44; 8:1-21; Luke 22:1-30; John 6). It is by this long story of Israel as God's son that the thought of the church as God's sons is qualitatively conditioned throughout the NT. To recapture their sense of community, a thorough knowledge of the Pentateuch is required, in which is found the basic saga of God's dealings with his people. It is this knowledge which permeates the Psalms, the Prophets, and the intertestamental writings. Through them this saga conditioned the corporate sense of origins and destiny which the church claimed as its own. The story as a whole informs most of the agricultural images which had become in the OT customary descriptions of Israel and which were adopted as equally germane to the church.

8. **Vineyard and flock.** The church is described by a wide range of agricultural analogies, all evocative of the church's dependence on God, of the qualitative necessity of producing fruit, and of the imminent processes of judgment. E.g., the church is explicitly compared to God's plantation or field (I Cor. 3:5-9). The cycle from seedtime to harvest suggests many possible links to the life of the community: plowing, sowing, germination, growth, cultivation, harvest (Mark 4:14-29; Matt. 13:24-43; Jas. 5:7).

The image of FIRST FRUITS, with its association with the temple sacrifices and festivals, is freely employed and pictures the present moment in the life of the community as lying between the beginning of the harvest and its full reaping (Rom. 16:5; I Cor. 15:20; II Thess. 2:13; Jas. 1:18; Rev. 14:4).

The comparison of God's people to the vineyard (ἀμπελών) is also familiar. God rents his vineyard to tenants (Mark 12:1-12; Matt. 20:1-16; 21:33-43) and demands an accounting from them. The Gospel of John develops the symbol of Jesus as the vine, with his branches dependent upon him and with God treating various branches by pruning and purging in order to produce greater fruitfulness (John 15:1-6).

The OT conception of Israel as a FIG TREE informs the gospel parables concerning the fruitless tree (Luke 13:6-9; Matt. 21:18-22). Likewise the picture of Israel as the OLIVE TREE receives in the NT two notable supplements. To Paul the root of the tree is holy; therefore the branches also are holy. Fruitless and disobedient branches (unbelieving Jews) may be cut off, and branches of the wild olive (the believing Gentiles) are grafted into the trunk. The trunk remains the support of every branch, and God is able to save or to destroy branches as he wills (Rom. 11:16-24). To John the two witnesses and the two lampstands are two olive trees, which as prophets share in the mission of Jesus, a mission of prophesying, of dying, and of rising again in judgment on the world (Rev. 11:1-13). In Revelation, a related tree, the TREE OF LIFE, links the church as new Jerusalem to the Garden of Eden (Rev. 2:7; 22: 2; Gen. 3).

The most pervasive agricultural analogy, however, visualizes the church as God's flock (ποίμνιον), thereby appropriating a mode of thinking which had often been used of Israel (*see* SHEEP). "Take heed to yourselves and to all the flock [of God]," is a typical injunction to leaders of the church (Luke 12:32; John 10:1-16; Acts 20:28; I Pet. 5:2). At times this suggests a contrast between sheep and goats (Matt. 25:31-33), between sheep and wolves (Matt. 7:15; 10:16), between sheep lost and found (Matt. 18:10-14), between sheep without and with a shepherd (Mark 6:34). And there are different shepherds (ποιμένες)—strangers, hirelings, wolves, as well as good shepherds. A major accent falls upon those who serve as legitimate shepherds. God, of course, is owner of the flock who rejoices over each lost sheep which is recovered (Luke 15:3-7; Matt. 10:16; 15:24). Jesus Christ is the "great shepherd of the sheep" (Heb. 13:20) who gives his life for the sheep (John 10:1-16) and who commands his apostles and elders to feed his sheep (John 21:16; I Pet. 5:2). The ruling of Jesus over his people as well as over the nations is described in terms of shepherding (Matt. 2:6; I Pet. 2:25; Rev. 2:27; 7:17; 12:5; the Greek verb "to shepherd" [ποιμαίνειν] is sometimes rendered in the RSV as "to rule").

Jesus Christ, however, is often described as LAMB as well as Shepherd (John 1:29, 36; Acts 8:32; I Pet. 1:19; and twenty-seven times in Revelation). Here in the imagery of the flock is found the central paradox of the Cross, for it is in giving his life as a lamb (ἀρνίον, ἀμνός) that Jesus becomes qualified to shepherd the sheep (John 10:15; Acts 8:32; I Pet. 1: 19; Rev. 5:6-13; 7:17). His sacrificial death becomes the source and standard for the care which his representatives should give to his flock, the church (John 21; Acts 20:28 ff; I Pet. 5:2-4). More than this, it becomes the living example for all the sheep in his flock (Rom. 8:35-39; I Pet. 2:21-25; Rev. 7:14-17; 12:11). He is the Passover lamb, sacrificed for the church (I Cor. 5:7). He thereby both serves the church as host and feeds the church with his body (Mark 14; Matt. 26; Luke 22; I Cor. 10:14-21; 11: 23-32). "There shall be one flock, one shepherd" (John 10:16). In sharpest contrast to this Lamb-Shepherd is the deceitful dragon Satan, and the sharpest contrast among human societies falls between those who worship the dragon and those who follow the Lamb (Rev. 12–13).

**9. One body in Christ.** The ecclesia is described in the Pauline letters as "one body in Christ" (Rom. 12:5) and as the BODY OF CHRIST (Eph. 1:23). We should first note the antithetical expressions. Set over against the one body in Christ is the one body in sin (*see* SIN, SINNERS), both bodies being considered as solidarities in which all mankind participates. Over one realm, over one body, sin rules. The "old self" is representative of this body of sin; it is a member of a body which is in slavery to sin (Rom. 6:6). Consequently the whole man has become a weapon of wickedness (Rom. 6:12). This body of sin makes all men captives to the body of DEATH (Rom. 7:24; 8:10). From this captivity men can be freed only by divine help, help which will transform the whole creation, for the bondage to corruption has become universal (Rom. 8:23).

*a*) It is this tyranny of sin and death over mankind as a whole which Christ has destroyed in his body by his incarnation, death, and resurrection. The church refers to those who are united in him and through him. They become one body in him, and this oneness is described in many varying ways. E.g., they are baptized into his death (Rom. 6:1-5; I Cor. 12:13). Or they are crucified with him to the self, to the world, to the law of sin and death (Rom. 6:6-14; Gal. 2:19-21; 6:14-17). Or they participate in his body in the Eucharist. Having a partnership in the dying body of Christ (I Cor. 10:16-18), their bodies become members of him (I Cor. 6:15). They now glorify God in their bodies by carrying about the dying of Jesus, and by manifesting thus the life of Jesus in their mortal body (II Cor. 4:10-12; Phil. 1:20). Seeking to share his sufferings, they enter into the power of his resurrection. This power enables him "to subject all things to himself" by transforming humanity's body of humiliation into the form of the body of his glory (Phil. 3:10-21).

This body binds men together in a *koinonia* or COMMUNION of life and righteousness, over which Christ rules (Rom. 5:15-21), and through which a new creation emerges, a new humanity in Christ. This reality of communal life was often described prepositionally. Christ's members are "in him" and he is "in them" (Gal. 2:20); they are baptized "into him" (I Cor. 12:13); their deeds are done "to him" and "for him" (I Cor. 6:13); they belong "to him" because they have died "through his body" (Rom. 7:4). They suffer and are glorified "with him" (Rom. 8:17). The interaction represented by these prepositions can be described in terms of the presence in the church of the Holy Spirit (Rom. 8:9-11; I Cor. 6:19; 12:4-11) or in terms of being knit together and of being built into one another by the power of love. All these elements of interpenetration and interdependence are caught up in the description of the church as the body of Christ (τὸ σῶμα τοῦ χριστοῦ).

*b*) As used by Paul, the thought of the church as Christ's body conveys many nuances, not all of which can or should be systematically co-ordinated in a single pattern. We should not assume that all these nuances are present in every appearance of the concept, nor should we ignore the variations in the various letters. In particular we should recognize that the treatment is most highly developed in Colossians and EPHESIANS. In these letters we may be in touch with tradition which is only secondarily Pauline. But among the dominant accents are these:

Correlative to the idea of the body is the conception of believers as members (μέλη). In the church every person is a member of Christ's body and should so regard himself. He is no longer his own, but is bound in most intimate and significant ways to Another. His own body has become a member of Christ, and this must determine what he does with it (Rom. 12:4; I Cor. 6:13-19; II Cor. 5:10; Col. 2:16-23). In the new body all are members one of another, and this requires the recognition of mutual dependence, of a shared suffering, and of the power of love to knit together all parts of the body (Rom. 12:5; I Cor. 12:14-26; II Cor. 4:7-12; Eph. 4:16; Phil. 3:10-21; Col. 1:24). Each member, however unspectacular his role in the body, shares fully in the common glory and life; each, however prominent his gift, must know the humility of receiving this gift from Christ for the sake of the whole body (Rom. 12:3 ff; I Cor. 12:27-31; Eph. 4:11-16). All spiritual gifts are mediated through the body to its members, and through its members to the body. The same truth applies when the concept of members applies, not to individual believers, but to types of ministry and to the various races and classes which in Christ are reconciled (I Cor. 12:13; Eph. 2:14-22). There are many members, but there can be but one body (Rom. 12:4-5; I Cor. 10:17; 12:12; Eph. 4:4).

*c*) Also correlative to the idea of body is participation by all in the death and resurrection of Jesus. In participating in baptism and in the Eucharist, the community participates in the dying body of Jesus and in his risen body. By dying and rising Jesus establishes a lordship over both the dead and the living, and establishes a community among both (Rom. 14:7-9). Participation in his death conveys to those who constitute his body freedom from law, sin, and death (Rom. 6-8; Eph. 2:1-10; Col. 2:16-23). Through his death they receive the promise of cosmic redemption, for he overcame the rulers of this age, took captivity captive, defeated Satan, and subjugated all principalities and powers. His body is the realm where this redemptive power operates (I Cor. 10:18-22; Eph. 1:21-23; 4:12-16; Col. 1:20; 2:8-19). "In Christ shall all be made alive." His "spiritual body" is the image of mankind in the kingdom of God (I Cor. 15:20-28, 35-50).

*d*) Finally, related to the concept of body is the concept of Christ, not as the body, but as the head (only in Colossians and Ephesians). Herein is ex-

pressed the conviction that the head is the source and locus of authority, which the whole body must honor and obey (Col. 2:10). The head is the channel through which divine life and glory flow into the body (Eph. 1:22 ff). As its head, Christ loves, sanctifies, and saves the body (Eph. 5:25). "Bodily growth in love" springs from and moves toward the head (Eph. 4:15; Col. 2:19). The supremacy of Christ as head, however, is by no means limited to the church. Both Ephesians and Colossians present him as head over all things. We therefore must include in the thought of his body a reference to God's whole work of creation and redemption.

Although Paul alone of NT writers develops this theme explicitly, there are enough echoes in other writings to suggest that he was not alone among early Christians in employing this vocabulary. Like Paul, I Peter speaks of Christ's crucified body as the means of corporate death to sin and birth to righteousness (2:24). Hebrews speaks of Christ's body as the instrument of obedience and sanctification (10:5, 10; 13:11-12), and of the body as a realm of Christian solidarity in suffering (13:3). In John the body of Jesus is referred to as the temple, which is to be destroyed and built again (2:19-21). In all the Synoptics, the new covenant is sealed by the bread of the Passover, of which Jesus says: "This is *my body*" (Mark 14:22; Matt. 26:26; Luke 22:19).

Central and important as this description of the church is, it was seldom used alone, but rather in conjunction with associated images. In his thought about the body of Christ, Paul habitually fused many patterns and pictures—a fact which suggests the fruitfulness of synoptic flexibility in describing the church. His thoughts concerning the body constantly shift to the other pictures of the church which we have already surveyed: as the elect, the saints, the slaves and freemen, the commonwealth of Israel, circumcision, the temple and its sacrifices, the kingdom of Christ, the strangers who are made citizens, the city, the bride, the kingdom and household of God, the building and its stones. One other pattern of ideas is constantly fused into Paul's thought concerning the body—i.e., the community as a new humanity in Christ.

**10. The new humanity.** The church is viewed as the beginning of a new creation, a new humanity, in which Jesus Christ is the last Adam, whose image all are destined to bear. The foil for this concept is the existence of all men in the first Adam. In him all men are one through the fact of a shared creatureliness, a shared sin (Rom. 5:12), and a shared death (Rom. 5:14-15, 18-20). Jesus Christ entered into this bondage and died for the sake of all who in Adam are enslaved to sin and death (Rom. 5:6-11). As the last Adam he "became a life-giving spirit" (I Cor. 15:45), the first fruits of the dead (I Cor. 15:20). He is the "image of the man of heaven" (I Cor. 15:49), the image which all will bear. Those who belong to him are being transformed into this image, from one degree of glory to another (II Cor. 3:18). Born again as sons of God and as brothers of Christ, they receive as a free gift the grace of life and righteousness. This one man's "act of righteousness leads to acquittal and life for all men" (Rom. 5:18; I Cor. 15:22). Those who receive this gift are the first fruits of his creatures (Jas. 1:18; Rev. 14:4). They are each a new creation and should so consider themselves and one another. That which unites them to Christ unites them to one another in the ministry of reconciliation, a ministry which conveys the message that in Christ, God reconciles the whole world to himself (II Cor. 5:16-21). The individual is incorporated into the one new MAN, and this signalizes the transformation of his inward nature and his solidarity with all men. Whenever this transformation takes place, vicarious suffering produces life, and the wasting away of the "outer nature" produces daily renewal of the "inner nature" (II Cor. 4:7-15). The community participates in the fulness of God, a fulness of glory that is embodied in cosmic reconciliation (Col. 1:17-20). In this one new man it is impossible for hostilities to remain between Jew and Greek or between slave and master (Col. 3:5-15). The life of *this* man is characterized by peace, by love, by access "in one Spirit to the Father," and by growth toward the final purification and unification of all things (Eph. 2:11-22). As the body of Christ, as one body in Christ, the life of the church is the life of this Representative Man. Although this type of thought is most fully formulated by Paul, there are links to it elsewhere in the NT. E.g., the manhood of Jesus is viewed in Hebrews as inseparable from the manhood that is subjected to him and saved by him (ch. 2). The same kind of corporate singularity may be assumed wherever the person of Jesus is interpreted in the light of the Suffering Servant of Second Isaiah. And the gospel use of the term SON OF MAN, stemming as it does in part from Daniel, conveys the sense of one who represents the saints of the Most High (Dan. 7). And it probably conveys also the ancient oriental idea of the primal, archetypal man from whom true humanity is alone inherited.

**C. *ESSENTIAL TRAITS IN THE CHURCH IDEA.*** The foregoing summary of cognate ways of expressing the church idea is far from complete. An adequate survey would require not only more precise and thorough analysis of the above images but also a treatment of others, such as the pictures of the church as an army of soldiers and conquerors, as the realm of light, as sons of the Day, as salt, as leaven, as a fish net with its catch, as the "woman clothed with the sun," as a pillar of the truth, as a company coming from God and going to God, and finally as the Way. No list can exhaust the vivid imaginative power of the NT writers or do justice to the fluidity, vitality, and subtlety of their conceptions.

None of the separate titles or pictures can be taken as comprehending the total range of thought. None of them can be reduced to objective, qualifying definitions. These words and pictures are channels of thought rather than receptacles of ideas with fixed meanings. This is due, not alone to the character of the thinking, but also to the qualitative, relational character of the reality being described. Each thought-form was utilized with great freedom (and often with conceptual inconsistency) to point to the life-giving connections between the actual, visible people and its God.

Every pattern of thought described the church's dependence on the triune God in such a way as to accent the interdependence of all members of the community, past, present, and future. The cohesion was such as to encompass the whole existence of every person, and to indicate his relationship through Christ to the whole of mankind. Fellowship in the church was known to bridge those chasms which were viewed as impassable by the mind of this world —the chasm between heaven and earth, between the beginning and the end, between all races and nations, sexes and classes. Yet oneness in Christ also served to evoke new and radical lines of conflict, participation in which was requisite for understanding the character of the community ("We are not contending against flesh and blood, but against the principalities" [Eph. 6:12]). Participation in the life of the church was considered necessary for comprehending the implications of the pictures; e.g., participation in the shared allegiance to Christ was necessary for understanding how the community could be conceived simultaneously as a body, a city, and a bride. Moreover, whatever description be adopted as central (e.g., the people of God), the associations of this term need to be corrected and supplemented by the connotations of the other images. If we would fully understand the idea of the church in the NT, we should consider all the cognate expressions at once.

What are the motifs which appear in almost all these expressions? Multiple answers may be given, all of which may have substantial supporting evidence. But among these answers the following traits should not be overlooked:

The church is thought of as a profoundly theocentric reality, whose origins and destiny rest in the powerful initiative of God and whose life is comprised by God's call and man's response. It is a Christocentric community because Christ's work qualifies the existence of the community at every point. In history the church moves from the beginning in Christ of a new age toward the consummation in Christ of this age. Memory and hope are essential to its movement, and come to a focus in personal and corporate participation in the death and resurrection of Christ. The church is a charismatic reality, for the Holy Spirit knits together its life, and the gifts of the Spirit empower its work and determine its duties. The coherence of men in this community is characterized by the recognition of such gift-demands as love and mercy, obedience and freedom, humility and courage, holiness and sin-bearing, mutual suffering and mutual joy. There is participation, at a deep level, in common work, in daily tasks, and in an embassy to the world, wherein all members are summoned to share in worshiping and witnessing, in reconciling service and in vicarious suffering. The church is a new creation, a growing organism, a bearer of promise for the whole creation. It is localized and embodied in particular temporal events, in empirical social relationships, yet it points beyond these to a reality which is ontologically ultimate and eschatologically final. God's judgment begins with this household, but his presence in this household is the earnest and first fruit of final judgment and redemption for all things. The warfare between God and Satan cuts through the life of this community, whose every choice registers a divided loyalty, yet it remains God's chosen instrument of action in the world, his love for the church being the sign and the channel of his love for the world. Integral to its grounding in the fulness of God's glory is the oneness and the wholeness of the church. This oneness is enriched rather than destroyed by the diversities of his many gifts; the freedom of the many members; the scattered location of the many congregations; the gathering of men from many races, tongues, tribes, and peoples; and the inclusion at one table of men from all generations. The NT idea of the church is not so much a technical doctrine as a gallery of pictures. In this shifting panorama of thought we can detect recurrent themes which exhibit their vitality in the variety and flexibility with which they are voiced.

**Bibliography.** F. J. A. Hort, *Christian Ecclesia* (1897); E. Käsemann, *Leib und Leib Christi* (1933); A. M. Ramsey, *The Gospel and the Catholic Church* (1936); R. N. Flew, *Jesus and His Church* (1938); C. Chavasse, *The Bride of Christ* (1940); N. A. Dahl, *Das Volk Gottes* (1941); L. S. Thornton, *Common Life in the Body of Christ* (1942); G. Johnston, *The Doctrine of the Church in the NT* (1943); W. G. Kümmel, *Kirchenbegriffe und Geschichtsbewusstsein* (1943); S. Hanson, *The Unity of the Church in the NT* (1946); J. Y. Campbell, "Ecclesia," *JTS*, XLIX (1948), 130-42; K. L. Schmidt, *The Church* (trans. J. R. Coates; 1950); C. T. Craig, *The One Church* (1951); F. W. Dillistone, *The Structure of the Divine Society* (1951); E. Mersch, *Theology of the Mystical Body* (trans. C. Vollert; 1951); J. R. Nelson, *Realm of Redemption* (1952); A. Nygren, ed., *This Is the Church* (1952); A. Fridrichsen, ed., *Root of the Vine* (1953); J. E. L. Newbigin, *The Household of God* (1954); J. E. Best, *One Body in Christ* (1955); J. Knox, *The Early Church and the Coming Great Church* (1955); E. Stauffer, *NT Theology* (1955), pp. 153-204; H. de Lubac, *The Splendour of the Church* (1956); P. Minear, *Jesus and His People* (1956); L. S. Thornton, *Christ and the Church* (1956).

P. S. Minear

## CHURCH, LIFE AND ORGANIZATION OF.

During the time between his resurrection and his second coming, Jesus Christ continues his ministry in and through the church. The church makes known the living presence of its Lord by the diverse manifestations of its own life. When the first group of brethren gathered around the apostles had increased as a consequence of missionary activity, new ministries had appeared, and at the end of the apostolic age the first lines of church organization are visible.

**A. *THE LIFE OF THE CHURCH.*** From Jerusalem the church spread rapidly over the E Mediterranean area. The Spirit, without whom the church would not have existed, was also the director of its religious, moral, and material life, and its guide in its relations to the society of antiquity.

**1. Extent of the church.** Every living body must grow. Its harmonious development is the clearest outward evidence that it is alive. From the day of Pentecost the church manifested the vital force given by the HOLY SPIRIT, by beginning to expand. The plan of its extension had been given it in advance by its Lord: the apostles were to preach the gospel "in Jerusalem and in all Judea and Samaria and to the end of the earth" (Acts 1:8).

The point of departure was Jerusalem, the holy city of the Old Covenant which had now become the holy city of the new. Indeed, it was there that Christ died for the salvation of the world; there "he presented himself alive after his passion . . . and . . . was lifted up" (Acts 1:3, 9). It was there that the Spirit descended on the believers, that Christ preached for the first time, and that the church appeared as a great religious and social upheaval. It was from there that every Christian mission began, including that of the apostle Paul. It is striking to see that the Apostle to the Gentiles also counts as the factual starting point of his missionary journeys, neither Damascus nor Antioch, e.g., but Jerusalem (Rom. 15:19).

The three stages Judea, Samaria, the end of the world, are at the same time geographical and religious stages. The preaching must reach all men where they live; it must also reach all men, whatever may be their position as regards God, whether they are Jews, Samaritans, or Gentiles.

Peter preached first at Jerusalem, but very soon his activity was exercised in the towns around the holy city (Acts 5:16). Then the preaching of the apostles, of the evangelists Stephen and Philip, of Barnabas, and of Paul was heard in remote parts of Judea, in Samaria, Damascus, Phoenicia, Cyprus, Cilicia, Syrian Antioch, and in the regions situated in the S of what is now called Asia Minor (Acts 8–14). In short, thanks to this missionary work which extended from the year 30 to *ca.* the year 47, the church extended over almost all the E basin of the Mediterranean. Then, in the years 49-60 approximately, the apostle Paul, the Lord's "chosen instrument" (Acts 9:15), the new "witness" (Acts 22:15; 26:16) added to the Twelve, founded churches on all the shores of the Aegean Sea; he introduced the gospel into Europe and arrived at Rome, the capital of the empire and of the then civilized world (Acts 16–28).

The book of Acts, in its second half, speaks only of Paul's missionary journeys. But during this period the chief missionary was certainly not alone in this work. This is proved by two statements by Paul himself. First, he implies that the other apostles and brethren of the Lord are traveling, like himself, to announce the gospel (I Cor. 9:5). Further, when Paul has finished his activity in the East and in Greece, he writes to the Romans that, according to his "ambition to preach the gospel, not where Christ has already been named," he will go to Spain (Rom. 15:20-24). We conclude that at the time Paul was writing to the Romans, between the years 55 and 58, the gospel had been preached, or at least was being preached, in Egypt, on the coast of Africa, in Italy, and perhaps even in the S of France.

There is nothing surprising in this rapid extension of the church. The apostles were full of zeal, tireless in their desire to go farther afield, as we see from the example of Paul. On the other hand, the apostles and their immediate collaborators, such as Silas, Timothy, Titus, Apollos, were not alone in their work. Beside them were a great number of unnamed missionaries. Among the merchants, imperial officials, soldiers, and, last but not least, tourists—there was a lot of traveling in the Roman Empire—many were doubtless won over to the gospel and became active propagandists for the salvation they had found. Everything leads us to suppose that it was these unknown evangelists, nameless in church history, who were the first to carry Christianity to Italy and to Rome.

It must also be recalled that the apostolic mission was essentially a mission in towns. The apostles, and Paul in particular, made contact first with towns and preferably the provincial capitals, feeling that it was these vital centers which must first be gained for the faith. From these the gospel radiated into the villages and the country districts.

Along with this geographical expansion went extension on the religious or theological plane. The gospel, preached in the first place to the Jews alone, was soon preached also to the Samaritans, that despised race separated from the people of Jerusalem. In this way the preaching of Christ began re-establishing the unity of the people of God of the Old Covenant. Afterward the same gospel was preached to the proselytes and Gentiles—i.e., to men whom the Jews considered to be excluded even more than the Samaritans from the grace of God reserved for the chosen people of Israel. Thus by the gospel God "has broken down the dividing wall of hostility," as Paul says (Eph. 2:14). The book of Acts, moreover, points out on two occasions that to the Gentiles also God has opened a door of the faith (11:18; 14:27). Toward the middle of the first century at the COUNCIL OF JERUSALEM the Spirit bore witness, once again, to the fact that the gospel was also destined to the Gentiles, and the apostles, guided by the Spirit, established the few rules which were to allow the converts from Judaism and the converts from paganism to live in peace and harmony in the one church which gathers them all together (Acts 15). At this time, scarcely twenty years after the passion of Jesus, the church had already attained its full greatness on the religious plane. In fact, the human race does not consist of any men other than Jews and non-Jews, and both groups were admitted on an equal footing into the one and only church of Christ. Certainly the church was to increase further on geographical lines, but this extension of the church over the whole surface of the globe did not modify its structure; it was now and forevermore the church of the Jews and the Gentiles, united in the faith in one Savior.

There was not constituted, from the middle of the first century, one church for the Jews and a separate one for the Gentiles. The church remained one, and one only. This is accounted for by the living faith of the apostles and the believers and by their faithful attachment to the teaching of the Lord.

**2. The age of the Spirit.** It has been said, with reason, that the chief personage in Acts is neither Peter nor Paul, but the Spirit. The Spirit is the exalted Christ, present and active in and through his own, from the Ascension until the Parousia. This action of the Spirit in the church has three aspects:

First, the Spirit given at Pentecost (Acts 2:1-11) intervenes constantly to guide the missionaries in their journeys by which the church grows (Acts 8:26, 39; 9:10; 13:2; 16:6-7; 20:22). The Spirit makes it known to the church that it is part of the divine plan that the Gentiles too should share in the salvation in Christ (Acts 10:3, 13, 47; 15:8, 17, 28). The Spirit also intervenes in order to strengthen the apostles and to enable them to face the hostility which their preaching provokes (Acts 4:31; 18:9-10).

Second, the Spirit is the instigator of the unity of the church. The church is a body where racial and social differences are abolished (Gal. 3:28). The believers are "all one in Christ Jesus," because they all "were baptized into Christ" (vs. 27). "There is one body and one Spirit," just as there is one hope, one Lord, one faith, one baptism, one God (Eph. 4:4). This unity created by the Spirit is manifested in the communion which unites the Twelve to Paul and Barnabas (Gal. 2:9). At Jerusalem the first believers are "of one heart and soul" (Acts 4:32). Paul reminds the Philippians that by "participation in the Spirit" they are "of the same mind, having the same love, being in full accord and of one mind" (Phil. 2:1-2). Always and everywhere the Spirit makes the believers live with a new life, of which the sign is unity and brotherly communion.

Third, the Spirit teaches all things to the disciples and brings to their remembrance all that Jesus has said to them (John 14:26; cf. 15:26; 16:13-14). In other words, the Spirit gives to the believers the true meaning and understanding of Jesus' person and message and, accordingly, the true interpretation of OT scriptures in which the coming of Christ has been prophesied (cf. John 2:22). This explains two most decisive facts in the life of the primitive church: the formation of the gospel tradition and the adoption by the church of the OT as Christian scriptures.

The four canonical GOSPELS were written in the years 65-100 approximately. But before their publication the elements which compose them were transmitted orally, from the time of the first apostolic preaching. In the discourses by Peter we already find a sketch of gospel narrative (Acts 2:22-24; 3:13-21; 10:36-43). The apostle Paul himself also recalls the teaching of Jesus (Acts 20:35; I Cor. 7:10-11). Since the first days the believers knew that they were saved by the holy life, death, and resurrection of Christ; since the first days also, these facts were told them. The gospels were preached and thought long before they were written. Right from the start the church found in the tradition concerning Jesus its spiritual nourishment.

It is worthy of note that there exists, as compared with the four gospels, only one book of the Acts of the Apostles. We further observe that the richness of the gospel tradition in memories of Jesus is in striking contrast with the poverty of the book of Acts regarding details of the life of the church before the time of the apostle Paul. Only a few factual happenings illustrate the concrete life of the Palestinian communities. The reason for this is that the church lives neither by its own memories nor by the memories of the apostles, but by the person of Christ who always occupied the first place in the apostolic preaching and teaching and in the devotion of the believers.

On the other hand, it was the deepest conviction of the church since the beginning that in Jesus the OT promises had been fulfilled. In almost every NT book such terms as "according to the scriptures" are to be found (cf. Acts 8:35; Luke 24:44-46; I Cor. 15: 3-4). These terms mean that the Christ of the church's faith is the Messiah of Israel and fulfils the prophecies. The redeeming power of God, which has been at work since the beginning of Israel's history, when God brought his people out of the land of Egypt, was at work again in the resurrection of Christ to bring to the believers the forgiveness of sins and a new life by the Spirit. The same redeeming power will work again at the end of this world, when Christ shall return with glory and the kingdom of God shall be established. Thus the gospel is a fulfilment rather than a novelty. The gospel reveals the continuity of God's design of salvation in and through history.

Thence, we have two consequences. On one side, the OT scriptures, where Christ was announced, are, just as much as the writings which speak of the Christ who has come, the books where the church finds its edification. On the other hand, as the hope of the past has actually been fulfilled by the life, death, and resurrection of Christ, so the Christian hope in the consummation must also find its realization. The church's essential assurance that God's design is carried out according to the Scriptures explains this fact: the expectation of the first believers of the sudden end of history at a time when they themselves would still be alive (Mark 9:1; I Thess. 4:17) did not come true. The time between Christ's first and second coming soon appeared to be much longer. Yet the delay in the date of the final events destroyed neither the faith nor the hope of the church. The church lives in the age of the Spirit, and this age has its proper place in God's design. Whatever may be the duration of this age, the church always has the same task before her: to preach the gospel to the world and to maintain the spiritual life of the believers. *See* Preaching.

**3. Religious life.** The life of the church is a life of communion with Christ. For all believers this life is a new life. All men, former Jews and former Gentiles, have access to it through repentance (Acts 20: 21; 26:20), for all have to detach themselves from their past in order to become Christians. But the two groups which are united in the church have a different religious past. Before Christ the Jews lived under the law, and the Gentiles in idolatry. This is why the repentance by which all must pass has not the same significance for the Jews as for the Gentiles.

In the missionary discourses of Peter, the Jews are called upon to repent from their sins (Acts 2:38; 3: 19; 5:31). As is indicated by the context, their sin does not consist of moral faults. It is, on the contrary, a religious and theological error. Their sin is their unbelief in Jesus of Nazareth, in whom they see a man rightly condemned by the leaders of Israel, whereas he is the Christ and the Lord (Acts 2:23; 3:

13, 17; 5:30). Paul's experience is the typical example of the Jewish conversion to the gospel. Paul was not converted in order to turn from a worldly man into a religious one, or from a troubled spirit into a soul in peace with God and his own self. He was "as to righteousness under the law blameless" (Phil. 3:6), "extremely zealous" in his Jewish life (Gal. 1:14). God himself stopped him on the Damascus Road in order to reveal to him that Jesus, whom he was persecuting in the form of his believers, was in reality the Lord of glory, just as his worshipers said he was. Now as a believer in Christ, Paul lives in the same passionate zeal for the glory of God as he did in his recent past. Only he knows now that salvation is not to be gained by man's efforts but is given to him in the fellowship of the living Christ. Likewise for the Jews who passed over to the gospel, conversion did not mean a total change of life. As Christians they adore the same God they were worshiping as Jews; they continue to live in obedience to the will of God. Yet it is now expressed no longer in the law but in Christ. Consequently Christ is now the norm of their religious life and ethical practice. Fellowship with Christ takes the place of observance of the law. Nothing is more significant in this connection than the description of the life of the early Christians at Jerusalem. "They devoted themselves to the apostles' teaching and fellowship, to the breaking of bread and the prayers" (Acts 2:42). In other words, what inspires the religious and moral life of the believers is no longer the law recited at the service in the synagogue, but the living person of Christ, with whom they enter into communion through the gospel tradition transmitted in the apostolic teaching, through the Eucharistic meal or "breaking of bread," and through prayer. *See* Gospel; Preaching.

For the Gentiles, on the other hand, conversion to the gospel meant a radical change of the religious and ethical life. They had to turn away from idols and "to serve a living and true God" (I Thess. 1:9; cf. Acts 17:23, 30). Like the former Jews, they must believe in Jesus as the Son of God. But, in addition, they must give up the idolatrous polytheism and specifically pagan customs, which were incompatible with life in Christ. The passage from paganism to Christianity required a greater step than the passage from Judaism to Christianity. It is for this reason that the Apostle to the Gentiles writes to his readers: "Do not be conformed to this world but be transformed by the renewal of your mind" (Rom. 12:2). He exhorts them to "live in Christ" (cf. Rom. 6:11), in "obedience to the faith" (Rom. 1:5), to "walk by the Spirit" and not by the flesh (Gal. 5:16), to renounce the "works of the flesh," and to bear the "fruit of the Spirit" (Gal. 5:19-23).

Among the works of the flesh Paul names first, and with some insistence, the sexual faults. These were typical pagan vices. The Gentiles were much more free than the Jews as regards sexual life. The monogamous marriage was not held, in the pagan world, in the same respect as in Judaism, where it was considered a divine institution. Moreover, the Gentiles looked with indulgence on unnatural vices, which were an abomination in Israel. This is why the Apostle to the Gentiles gives in his letters so many exhortations to lead a pure life and to respect marriage (I Cor. 6–7; I Thess. 4:3-7). He recalls in particular that the body of the believers belongs to the Lord, that it is the temple of the Holy Spirit, and that it must not be polluted (I Cor. 6:13-20). Every sexual misconduct of the believer is much more than an ethical defect; it is an offense against Christ. For the believers "are the body of Christ and individually members of it" (I Cor. 12:27). It is therefore for a religious reason, even more than for a moral one, that the believer must turn away from the works of the flesh to bear the fruit of the Spirit.

To the "works of the flesh" in the plural, Paul opposes the "fruit of the Spirit" in the singular. This is a precious indication that Christ's spirit does create a unity of mind in the believer. This fruit is love and its connected consequences. In fact, all behavior and all sentiment on the part of the believer are grounded in his love for Christ and for his fellows. "For the love of Christ controls us" (II Cor. 5:14), so that the believers, loved by Christ, must "live no longer for themselves but for him who for their sake died and was raised" (II Cor. 5:15), and consequently must "love one another with brotherly affection" (Rom. 12:10). Thus, in the church, religious life is the foundation of moral life.

In a word, Christ takes possession of the entire man. The whole life of the Christian is under Christ's rule and guidance. This is true, not only of the religious, but just as much of the material and social, life of the believer.

**4. Material life.** There is no sphere of Christian life which is not governed by the spirit of Christ. The proof thereof is given by the fact that in the NT the term "fellowship" may designate so high a reality as the communion of the believer with his Lord, when the Eucharistic meal is celebrated (I Cor. 10:16), as well as such a trivial thing, at first sight, as the sharing of material goods (*see* COMMUNION; COMMUNITY OF GOODS). This sharing is recommended as a sacrifice which is pleasing to God (Heb. 13:16). Its factual examples in the NT are the corporate life of the first Christians and the collection undertaken by Paul for the Jerusalem church.

Among the first Christians at Jerusalem no one said that any of the things he possessed was his own, but they had everything in common (Acts 2:44; 4:32). It is further explained that the possessors of lands or houses sold them, and brought the proceeds to the apostles, who made distribution to each as any had need (Acts 2:45; 4:34-35). These were quite voluntary acts, inspired by the love which reigned in the church, and also, no doubt, by the feverish expectation of the imminent return of Christ. The same expectation of the end was to incite the Thessalonians to stop working (II Thess. 3:6-12). Since, however, the present world continued as before, the communism of the early church proved to be a wrong solution of the problem of community life. But this economic failure was not a spiritual one. On the contrary, the experience of the first believers teaches us that the Christian life is not compatible with a selfish attachment to earthly possessions, and that Christian communion affects all planes of life. Further, the experience at Jerusalem established the principle of sharing which rendered the collection organized by Paul necessary; and this is the most striking example

of financial, as well as religious fellowship in the primitive church.

In the eyes of Paul the *collection* (*see* OFFERING FOR THE SAINTS) was not a mere gesture of liberality. It expressed the communion which united all believers and which had its source in the fact that they all belonged to the same Savior and were all one in him. The collection was a religious act in the etymological sense of the word: it bound to one another those who, in Palestine on the one hand, in Asia and in Europe on the other, were bound to Christ. Paul bases his argument not on philanthropic and sentimental motives but on these spiritual ones, when he recommends the collection to the Corinthians (II Cor. 8). He states, in fact, that the Christians of Jerusalem, who are of Jewish origin, will be convinced, in receiving the sum from the collection, that the members of the Pauline churches, who were formerly Gentiles, believe in the same gospel as they do. The collection is an act of Christian communion, a sign of the unity of the church and of the material and spiritual solidarity of the Jews and Gentiles bound together in one body (cf. II Cor. 9:12-13). More than that, the collection is a debt which the Gentile Christians must settle with the Jewish Christians. They, children of Israel, are at the origin of the salvation; it is they who received through their father Abraham the divine promises and covenants; it is from them that Christ received his human nature; it is from them also that the apostles came, not excepting even the Apostle to the Gentiles. Now, all these spiritual riches have been transmitted by the Jews to the Gentiles, who now form with them the Israel of the Spirit, the church of Christ. Consequently the Gentiles must, on their side, share with them the material riches which they possess and which the Jews lack (cf. Rom. 15:26-27).

Paul is able to quote a similar example of this sharing of spiritual and material goods: the preacher who brings the gospel to men has the right to live in the temporal wealth of the believers (I Cor. 9:11; Gal. 6:6).

Thus the gospel places man in his entirety, with his soul and his worldly possessions, in a new relation to those who share with him the supreme riches —i.e., the salvation in Christ. The exchange of spiritual and material goods is the expression of the communion between one person and another among all those who believe in Christ.

**5. Church and society.** It remains to describe the social life of the church and the relations of this new society, which was the Christian community, with the society of antiquity in which it moved.

The church united people of every social status, from the rich who had slaves to serve them to the very slaves themselves. The current idea that the early church was recruited essentially from the lower classes of society does not appear to be founded on scripture. Paul says that in the Corinthian church there are not many "wise according to worldly standards, not many . . . powerful, not many . . . of noble birth" (I Cor. 1:26). This is a somewhat rhetorical way of saying that there are at least some such people, and above all that God appeals to all men without any consideration of social distinction. There were at Corinth rich Christians (I Cor. 1:11; 11:21-

22). Almost everywhere some men and women of good position entered the church (Luke 8:3; Acts 16: 16; 17:4, 12, 34), and well-to-do members placed their houses at the disposal of the church (Acts 12: 12; 16:14-15; Rom. 16:23; I Cor. 16:19; Col. 4:1; Philem. 2). Paul himself was, no doubt, of high social standing, as is more than suggested by his Roman citizenship inherited from his father (Acts 22:28); his wide culture, both Judaic and Hellenistic (Acts 21: 29; 26:24); and the funds he had at his disposal, at least at some periods of his life (Phil. 4:12; Philem. 19).

What is the attitude of the church toward the different social groups of which it is composed? Here we have two questions of particular interest: the attitude of the church toward women and toward slaves, for both of these groups were stirred, in the first century, by aspirations for emancipation from marital authority in the one case and for freedom from slavery in the other.

Not only did women enter the church, but they exercised therein a ministry of assistance which the apostle Paul approves (Rom. 16:1; Phil. 4:3). If the apostle forbids women to interrupt the worship by their chattering (I Cor. 14:34-35), he allows them to prophesy on condition that they do so wearing dress considered suitable at that time (I Cor. 11:3-15). In the question of mutual relations and reciprocal duties of husband and wife (Eph. 5:21-33; Col. 3:18-19; cf. I Pet. 3:1-7) Paul does not defend, as is ordinarily supposed, the old oriental conception according to which the first religious duty of a woman was absolute submission to a husband who, as far as he was concerned, had all the rights. In the first place, the Christian MARRIAGE, of which the apostle speaks, is strictly monogamous for the husband as well as for the wife, and this is a singular novelty as compared with pagan customs. Further, according to Paul, there should be complete harmony between husband and wife in love and mutual service, which corresponds to that which exists between Christ and the church. The submission of the wife is not the obedience of a slave to his master; it is the attitude with which the wife accepts the place God gives to her as a married woman. When the apostle bids the husband love his wife as Christ loved the church and gave himself up for her, he claims for the husband an authority which rests only on love and self-forgetfulness. He ordains for the husband an attitude of tenderness and faithfulness that no husband can adopt and keep unless he is animated by the spirit of Christ.

As regards SLAVERY, the apostle Paul, in a general way, advises slaves to submit themselves to their masters (Eph. 6:5-8; Col. 3:22-25; cf. I Pet. 2:18-21), but he reminds the masters that they themselves have in heaven one who is the Master of both slaves and masters (Eph. 6:9; Col. 4:1). Paul deals with the question in the same spirit in the letter to Philemon with reference to the slave ONESIMUS. The apostle sends back to his master, Philemon, in accordance with the law at that time, the fugitive slave, who, under his influence, has become a Christian. Paul does not ask for his liberation in so many words, but he reminds Philemon that this slave is now a brother, which means that the master and the slave are now, in their relations to each other, in a new situation created by the communion which they both have with Christ.

This cautious attitude of the early Christians in the social sphere can be explained by two facts. First, the end of history was believed to be at hand; "the form of this world is passing away" (I Cor. 7:31). Consequently, "every one should remain in the state in which he was called" (I Cor. 7:20). The church did not care, in the first place, to change the social order of the time. On the contrary, it accepted the political and sociological setting in which it lived, so long as God maintained that setting. Thus the apostle Paul advises the faithful not to break off personal relations with the heathen (I Cor. 5:9-10); to remain amenable to the state (Rom. 13:1-7; cf. I Tim. 2:1-2; I Pet. 2:13-17); to work like all men, not only in order to live honorably, but also to be in a position to help others (Acts 20:35; Eph. 4:28; I Thess. 4:11-12; II Thess. 3:7-12). In a word, the church did not think of making the gospel a ferment of social revolution any more than Jesus thought of confusing the preaching of the kingdom of God with the anti-Roman agitation of the Zealots.

Second, the church appealed primarily to the individual. It taught the believer to consider every man, whoever he may be, as a "brother for whom Christ died" (I Cor. 8:11; cf. Matt. 25:40, 45). If the church did not preach a revolution which would lead to disorder, neither did it sanction a social state inspired by the hardness and selfishness of the human heart. It wished to bring man first into communion with Christ, for the man who himself is changed by Christ will in his turn change the framework of society in which he lives.

The church, however, had also worked positively in the social sphere. It had created a new sociological form, the Christian community itself. In fact, the church as such ignored racial and social differences (Gal. 3:28); it exercised its own discipline (Matt. 18:18) without having recourse to pagan tribunals (I Cor. 6:1-6). Finally, it bestowed in itself a specific form of organization.

**B. *THE ORGANIZATION OF THE CHURCH.***
The church is the body of Christ, and each member of the body has to serve according to his calling and ability. There is no dead member in the living body of the church. "As each has received a gift, employ it for one another, as good stewards of God's varied grace" (I Pet. 4:10). While, however, all the faithful must serve in the church, the ministry of certain members is indispensable to the life of the church.

The work of salvation had been accomplished by Jesus Christ at a given moment in history. This work had been done once for all; it was not repeated. Besides, no repetition was necessary; for Christ had chosen certain men to be his witnesses, his apostles, to proclaim to the world what he had said and done. The witness of the apostles, who made the person and the work of Christ known to men, was therefore as important and as necessary as that work itself. The church was thus founded by the work of Christ and by the testimony of the apostles. But the construction or the edification of the church must be pursued until the second coming of Christ, well beyond the time of the apostles. This work of edification required other ministries than the apostolate.

These other ministries were quite as indispensable as the apostleship to the life of the church. This is why Paul considers the ministry as a divine institution. It is God (I Cor. 12:28) or Christ (Eph. 4:11) who gives to the church "apostles," "prophets," and "teachers."

The church draws its life from the gospel; it needs men to preach it and to explain it. On the other hand, the church is called on to be a structure and not a heap of materials; it must be a body and not an unorganized mass of believers. These two images of the edifice and the body, which in the NT are current similes for the church, show that it cannot exist without services of order and government.

Lastly, the church has had, from earliest times, the care of the poor and the unfortunate; it cannot dispense with ministries of assistance and benevolence either. This is why the different forms of the ministry appear very early in the church, during the lifetime even of the apostles. Their appearance is normal. It is the necessary expression of the life of the church. *See* MINISTRY.

**1. The apostleship.** It is generally admitted that the NT uses the term "apostle" in both a looser and a stricter sense. In the first case it is applied either to missionaries like Barnabas or to messengers of a particular community. In the second, it designates a limited group of men who have been recognized by both the NT and the Christian tradition as the authorized representatives of Jesus Christ. The Twelve and Paul are undisputed holders of the apostle's title in this second sense. For discussion of the most debated questions of the origin and meaning of the word "apostle" and of the number of early Christian missionaries who were apostles in the strict sense of the word, *see* APOSTLE.

*a. The meaning of apostleship.* The TWELVE were chosen by Jesus in his earthly life to join him (Mark 3:13-19). They saw the risen Lord and received from him the commission to be his witnesses in Jerusalem, in Palestine, and to the end of the earth (Acts 1:8). Thus the Twelve stood in a unique position. They were witnesses of the ministry and the resurrection of Christ, and they had been commissioned by him. The promise had been given them that in the world to come they would judge or rule the people of God (cf. Matt. 19:28; Luke 22:28-30). In other words, they were entrusted with a historical and eschatological mission. They were apostles forever.

In this respect two facts in the early church are significant. Between the Ascension and the day of Pentecost, Matthias was appointed to fill the vacancy in the Twelve left by Judas (Acts 1:15-26). But when James the son of Zebedee was put to death by Herod Agrippa I (Acts 12:2), no attempt was made to fill his place. The implication is that only apostasy such as that of Judas could create a vacancy. The death of one of the Twelve did not do so, because these men were chosen for this world and the world to come (cf. Rev. 21:14).

Now Paul stands in a position similar to that of the Twelve. Although he had not been a witness of the earthly life of Jesus, he claimed—and the Twelve acknowledged his right—to be recognized as an "apostle of Jesus Christ" in the same strict sense as those who were apostles before him (Gal. 1:1, 17).

First, Paul sets his experience on the Damascus Road alongside the experience of the Twelve on Easter Day (I Cor. 15:3-8). He too has seen Jesus our Lord (I Cor. 9:1). Second, Paul has been entrusted by Christ with the gospel to the Gentiles, just as Peter has been, in the name of the Twelve, with the gospel to the Jews (Gal. 2:7).

Moreover, Paul is highly conscious of the exceptional vocation of an apostle. He is also well aware that the circle of the apostles is one which has been formed once and for all and which is now closed. Paul reminds us that there were apostles before him. He never says that there will be any after him. On the contrary, he is persuaded that he is the last of the apostles. In fact, in order to be an apostle, one must be a direct witness of the glorified Christ. Now the appearances of the risen Lord are at an end.

Thus, according to the NT, the apostle occupies a unique position in the history of salvation. He has seen the risen Lord and has been commissioned by him to preach the gospel. To this specific status of the apostle a specific function in the church corresponds.

*b. The mission of the apostle.* It is not enough, if the world is to be saved, that Christ should have died and risen again. What is further necessary is that the death and the resurrection of Christ should be announced to the world. If there had been no eyewitnesses to the resurrection of Jesus Christ, or if the witnesses had remained silent, there would be, practically speaking, neither gospel nor salvation. God has elected to save the world by a work of redemption accomplished at a given moment and at a given place. The mission of the witnesses is to announce this work, which has been accomplished once and for all. By their testimony the apostles are the hinge between Jesus Christ, who has brought about salvation, and the church, which lives by it. Thus there is nothing contradictory between these two assertions of Paul: The foundation of the church is Christ (I Cor. 3:11), and the church is built upon the foundation of the apostles (Eph. 2:20).

Witnesses for Christ, the apostles are clothed with his power. They speak the word of God with all boldness (Acts 4:29; cf. 28:31) and perform signs, wonders, and mighty works as Christ did (Acts 4:30; II Cor. 12:12). The apostles exercise their authority over the whole church and not only over a local community. They hold ecumenical power, and they effect the unity of the one church of Jews and Gentiles. In the beginning the apostles exercise the whole ministry by themselves. The apostle Paul, e.g., acts as a prophet when he announces the conversion of Israel (Rom. 11), or as a teacher when he proves that Christ is the fulfilment of the law (Gal. 3), and as a pastor when he exhorts the elders at Ephesus (Acts 20). But as the church grows, the apostles leave certain of their functions in the hands of new ministers. Only their charge as witnesses of the risen Lord is not transmissible.

*c. Apostolic succession.* The church can have no other apostles than those chosen by Jesus himself, because the apostle is the witness of the risen Lord, of whom there have been no new appearances. In the history of salvation the apostleship is a unique fact, as the resurrection of Christ, of which it bears witness, is a unique fact. Until the end the church draws its life from the redemption effected by Christ and testified to by his apostles. This is why new apostles are not appointed to succeed those who die. The case of Matthias (*see* § B1*a above*) is unique. In taking the place of Judas, Matthias did not succeed an apostle who had died; he replaced one who had forfeited his position by his betrayal. His choice, made by the Lord, did not lay down the principle of apostolic succession. On the contrary, the conditions of apostleship which had been definitely recalled—to be a witness of the ministry and resurrection of Jesus (Acts 1:21-22)—emphasize in the clearest possible fashion the fact that the apostolate is, by definition, an institution bound up with the origin of the church. In short, considering what an apostle is, it is quite impossible that there should ever be a successor of the same kind. We might add that the apostles, in their capacity as witnesses, have no need of successors, for their testimony is always there; written down in the NT. But, at the same time as he founds the church by his testimony, the apostle begins to construct it, to build it up by his preaching and his teaching. This second function of the apostle, and only this, is transmissible. The ministry of Timothy and of Titus (*see* § 4 *below*) clarifies this point.

**2. The church of Jerusalem.** At first the apostles were the sole leaders of the church (Acts 1–5). But soon, as the church grew, the apostles were seconded by the Seven and then by the elders.

The growth of the church necessitated the appointment of the SEVEN "to serve tables," in order that the apostles might devote themselves "to prayer and to the ministry of the word." The Seven were chosen by the community, and the apostles installed them in their charge by prayer and the laying on of hands (Acts 6:1-6). Among the Seven, two played a great part as real preachers and missionaries: Stephen (Acts 6–7) and Philip (Acts 8; cf. 21:8). They were the forerunners of the apostles in the mission beyond Jerusalem and with the non-Jews. The Seven had no successors, and their missionary work in Palestine and in Antioch (Acts 11:19) was taken over by the apostles and fellow workers. The author of Acts does not seem to make of the Seven the precursors of the deacons. He never gives this name to the Seven. In any case, he never mentions deacons.

The ELDERS appear a little later in the church of Jerusalem. It was in their hands that Barnabas and Paul placed the collection made at Antioch for the brothers of Judea (Acts 11:30). At this point the apostles are not mentioned; they were doubtless detained at some distance by their missionary journeys (cf. I Cor. 9:5). The book of Acts says nothing of the nomination or of the duties of the elders. No doubt, they were the chief residents belonging to the church. They collaborated with the apostles when the latter were present and assumed the direction in their absence. Such is the position at the moment of the Council of Jerusalem (Acts 15). Later, when Paul arrives for the last time in the holy city, he finds at the head of the church James, the Lord's brother, seconded by the elders (Acts 21:18).

According to the book of Acts, elders existed in the churches founded by Paul (14:23) and notably at Ephesus (20:17-38). Paul himself never uses the term "elders" in his letters; at times they are mentioned in the Pastoral letters, which are ascribed to him but are generally considered as belonging to a later time. But Paul speaks of ministry equivalent to that of the elders. There is, moreover, an echo of this equivalence of terms in Acts. The Ephesian elders are also called guardians or bishops (Acts 20:28), and the passage underlines the point that their mission consisted in feeding the flock as good pastors of the church. Now, the church at Philippi, founded by Paul, was directed by bishops and deacons (Phil. 1:1), and in the Letter to the Ephesians both "pastors" and "teachers" apparently designate the same ministers. Thus we can establish an almost certain identity between the terms and the offices of elders, bishops, and teachers. In fact, "to feed the church of the Lord" (Acts 20:28) is to nourish spiritually the believers with the true apostolic teaching and to defend them against the peril of false doctrines (cf. vss. 29-30). Therefore, it should be admitted that the same pre-eminent ministry of the word was entrusted to elders, according to the book of Acts, and to teachers and bishops, according to the Pauline letters.

The elders are mentioned again in the letters traditionally attributed to the apostles of Jerusalem. According to I Peter, it is the duty of the elders to "tend the flock of God" (5:1-4). They have thus the same mission as the elders in Ephesus. According to James, the elders must also pray over the sick and anoint them with oil in the name of the Lord (5:14).

**3. The Pauline churches.** The apostle Paul had the care of organizing the churches which he founded. God is a God of order, and order must reign in the house of God (I Cor. 14:40). But the apostle never dealt with the question of the ministry as such. He confined himself to giving in each church directions in connection with local circumstances.

In the Letter to the Philippians he salutes the "bishops and deacons" (1:1). But he does not state what their duties consist of. The bishops are, without any doubt, those who watch over the church in order to make sure that the members are persevering in the teaching received from the apostle; their ministry seems to be the same as that of the teachers of Corinth and of the elders or bishops in Ephesus. The deacons are most certainly subordinate to the bishops, since they are named subsequently. The bishops and deacons make their appearance also later in the Pastoral letters. It is striking to meet them at Philippi, and at Philippi only, at the most active period of Paul's missionary life. On the other hand, Philippi is the only church which never caused the apostle any worry, either in theological or in practical matters. Philippi was the model church. Consequently, the simple organization which existed in this church —bishops to carry out the ministry of the word and deacons to take charge of all matters of assistance— might have been the organization answering most nearly the desires of Paul, and which he established there where he was able to act freely, without—as was the case at Corinth—being hampered by local difficulties.

The situation was, indeed, very different in the church of Corinth. Fanatical and lawless tendencies were at work there, and the difficulties Paul had in bringing the Corinthians back to the divine order in all fields are well known. The apostle reminds them that it is the will of God himself that there should be ministries to secure the normal life of the church. He writes: "God has appointed in the church first apostles, second prophets, third teachers, then workers of miracles, then healers, helpers, administrators, speakers in various kinds of tongues" (I Cor. 12:28; cf. vss. 29-30). In this sentence the apostle makes a distinction between two series of ecclesiastical functions, which he by no means puts on the same level. He first mentions the three ministries of the word, and he numbers them in order to mark their hierarchy and their importance. These ministries, indeed, are to be found in all churches, under somewhat different names, for they are indispensable to the life of the church. The apostle comes in at the head of the list, because it is he who founds the church by his testimony rendered to the risen Lord. The prophets are, no doubt, inspired preachers, who express themselves in clear and comprehensible language, unlike those who speak with tongues (*see* PROPHET IN THE NT). The particular task of the teachers here seems to be to interpret the Christian message, to show its relation to the OT, and to bring to light all its riches. In other words, the prophets and teachers explain to the believers, and apply to their lives and circumstances, the message of salvation that has been brought them by the apostle.

In the second part of his enumeration, Paul gives a list of SPIRITUAL GIFTS. He designates them by abstract, and not personal, terms, like the three first ministries, for these gifts are doubtless spontaneous and sporadic manifestations of the Spirit, which have not the permanent character of a ministry. Nor does Paul enumerate these spiritual gifts, for they are too free to form a complete, invariable set; by their very nature they elude all classification. When Paul resumes the same subject (I Cor. 12:29-30), he again places at the head of his list, and in the same order, the three ministries of apostle, prophet, and teacher, but he gives a rather different series of spiritual gifts. In a word, Paul recalls the fact that the Spirit pours out its gifts on certain believers in order to enrich the life of the church. But the church may, in certain cases, withhold these gifts. A church where no one spoke in different tongues would nevertheless be a real church. But on the other hand, a church cannot be formed without the testimony of the apostle, and it cannot continue to live without the ministry of the word, which is its spiritual nourishment. The three ministries of the apostle, the prophet, and the teacher are themselves indispensable to the life of the church.

In the Letter to the Ephesians, Paul gives an almost identical list of the essential ministries. He writes: "[God gave some to] be apostles, some prophets, some evangelists, some pastors and teachers" (Eph. 4:11). The last two terms, "pastors" and "teachers," refer to the same men: by their teaching the teachers feed the flock of God; the term "shepherd" is only an image taken from that of the flock, frequently found in the NT, to signify the church. The only new term in this list, as compared with the one in I Corinthians, is EVANGELIST. The evangelist has the same function as the apostle: to spread the gospel where as yet it has not been preached. If the evangelist is not quite the equal of the apostle, it is

because, unlike the latter, he is not an eyewitness of the risen Lord. The evangelists are seldom mentioned in the NT. Only two are known personally: Philip, one of the Seven (Acts 21:8), and Timothy, the faithful fellow worker with Paul (II Tim. 4:5).

In the Letter to the Romans (12:6-8) Paul names the following spiritual gifts, in speaking at one time of duties, at another time of the men who fulfil them: "prophecy, . . . service, . . . he who teaches, . . . he who exhorts, . . . he who contributes, . . . he who gives aid, . . . he who does acts of mercy." The list is vague, no doubt intentionally so. In writing to the Romans, Paul addresses himself to a church which he did not found and which he has not yet visited, and he has no direct knowledge of the particular circumstances of its inward life. But this list too gives an important position to prophets and teachers. We know besides, from the book of Acts (13:1), that prophets and teachers did exist in the church of Antioch, starting point of the apostle's first great missionary journey.

**4. The later church.** The letters to Timothy and Titus (the so-called PASTORAL LETTERS) are here our source of information. They were probably drawn up by a disciple who was perhaps prompted by oral indications given by Paul or who perhaps utilized written notes left by the apostle. At all events, these three letters bring to our knowledge a situation which was definitely more advanced than that which appears in the Pauline letters and in Acts. The apostle Paul has vanished from the scene. He is no longer the living, active link between the churches, busy directing and advising the ministers of the local churches. His disciples Timothy and Titus appear in these letters as the apostle's agents, whose task is to supervise the good organization of the church, and to specify the duties of the different ministers. These ministers are four in number:

The deacons (*see* DEACON) must be invested with strong moral and practical qualities (I Tim. 3:8-13). Their duties are not indicated in precise terms. Since practical qualities are required of the deacons, we may conclude that they have to devote themselves to works of assistance and administration. It is possible that the widows, who seem to form an order, may be deaconesses (*see* DEACONESS).

The elders (*see* ELDER IN THE NT) must be men of irreproachable character. They occupy a governing office, but some among them take up the work of preaching and teaching, and thus deserve a "double honor," which means most probably an additional material recompense rather than particular esteem on the part of the congregation (I Tim. 5:17-22; Tit. 1:5-6). It is evident from this that the functions of the elders vary, since not all are preachers and teachers, but here, as already in the time of Paul, the ministry of the word holds the pre-eminent place. We see, moreover, that the elders are remunerated, which implies that they devote at least part of their time, if not the whole, to their ministry.

The BISHOP is always spoken of in the singular, whereas deacons and elders are invariably mentioned in the plural (I Tim. 3:1-7; Tit. 1:7-9). It therefore seems likely that at the time of the Pastoral letters there was only one bishop to a community. The bishop fulfils the same ministry of the word as the elders, but he also undertakes duties which are distinct from those of the elders. The bishop must be hospitable—i.e., he must entertain traveling Christians, who were reluctant to use public inns, for moral as well as ceremonial reasons—and he must also have the respect of outsiders. In other words, it is the bishop who represents the church in the eyes of other churches and also in the eyes of the Gentiles among whom his community is established. What is more, the bishop does not confine himself to teaching like the elders; he must also be able to urge men to follow the sound teaching and to correct those who disagree with it; in other words, he must defend the traditional apostolic teaching against all deviation. The bishop is presumed to have had wider knowledge than the elders and a clearer understanding of the difficult situation in which the church was placed at the moment when the apostles, who were its mainstays during the first decades, disappeared from the scene of history. In a word, the bishop appears, at the head of the elders, as the leader of the local church.

TIMOTHY and TITUS acted, in Ephesus and Crete respectively, as the heirs of the apostle Paul and his authorized delegates. As was the case with the apostleship, their ministry overlapped the local church and extended over a whole province, to secure the link and the unity between the various churches of one district. Thus the functions of these apostolic delegates were quite distinct from those of the bishop, the elders, and the deacons. This ministry must also be continued in the church, since Timothy receives the command to entrust the teaching he has received to faithful men, who will be competent to teach others also (II Tim. 2:2).

5. **Church order in the NT.** The description just given (see § B4 *above*) of the ministries within the church during the first century brings to light the three following facts: First, all the believers were active members of the community and in this sense fulfilled a service; the ministry of men set apart to preside over the essential working of the church was, however, indispensable. Second, God himself gave ministers to the church, primarily the apostleship, which, through the testimony rendered to the person and work of Christ, founded the church and began its edification or construction. This construction was carried on by the work of other ministries. Third, the ministry which is of first necessity is always that of the word, whereby the gospel and the apostolic tradition continue faithfully to nourish the church.

The question of the organization of the church remains to be examined. On this point the NT contains very few precise indications, and they are always in reference to a local or regional church. It must not be forgotten that, in the first century, there was really no general, uniform organization of the church.

a. *The appointment of the ministers.* The twelve apostles were chosen by Jesus during his earthly days. Similarly, the new apostles Matthias and Paul are called by the Lord and not elected by the church. In the case of Matthias (Acts 1:21-26) it should not be lost sight of that the first congregation presents only two possible candidates who satisfy the conditions put forward by Peter—namely, to have been witnesses of the ministry and of the resurrection of Christ. These conditions, in fact, limit the choice of the community to men already designated by the Lord, for he did not appear to all people but only to those who were chosen by God (Acts 10:41). The will of the Lord expresses itself by the casting of lots. Now, as far as Paul is concerned, it is sufficient to quote his own words: he is apostle "not from men nor through man, but through Jesus Christ and God the Father" (Gal. 1:1).

In the appointment of the Seven (Acts 6:1-6) the first step is made by the apostles, who recommend that "men of good repute, full of the Spirit and of wisdom," be elected. Thus the Seven are picked out by the "brethren," but among men already set apart by their spiritual gifts.

Barnabas and Paul are sent out as missionaries by the Spirit, who has set them apart for this work (Acts 13:1-3). Similarly the elders in Ephesus were made leaders of the community by the Spirit (Acts 20:28). It is not told how this designation by the Spirit was practically carried out. Most probably the apostle was also the agent of the Spirit here, according to the practice followed elsewhere in Acts: during their first great journey Paul and Barnabas appointed elders for the disciples "in every church, with prayer and fasting" (Acts 14:23). This text is important. It shows us that the power that the apostle possessed, by virtue of his vocation, bestowed on him the capacity of discerning, by prayer, the will of the Lord and of being, in fact, the intermediary by which Christ gave to the church the necessary ministers.

It is by virtue of this same capacity, without the slightest doubt, that Paul chose Timothy and Titus as his successors, in the restricted sense mentioned *above* (see § B4), and transmitted to them, with the charge of directing the church at Ephesus and in Crete, the precise duty to see that the ministry was carried on. When the apostle commanded Timothy to entrust what he had received to faithful men who would be able to teach others also (II Tim. 2:2), he no doubt meant that it was his disciple's business to discriminate between such men. This is also what we may gather from the passages in which Timothy and Titus are given the order to establish elders in the church (Tit. 1:5; cf. I Tim. 5:22), as, according to the book of Acts, the apostle has done. So, at the moment when the apostle disappears from the pages of history, his power is not handed on to the church as a whole, but to men who have assumed a certain ministry.

b. *The ordination of the ministers.* In passing on the ministry the apostle was only acting as the agent of Christ or of the Spirit. For this reason ordination in the early church was always accompanied by prayer. Prayer is the genuine Christian rite of ordination. In the Jewish ordination of elders there is no prayer and no explicit statement of a gift of the Spirit, but only an imposition of hands. In the church, on the contrary, the laying on of hands is seldom used (see HANDS, LAYING ON OF). Only the Seven (Acts 6:6) and later Timothy (I Tim. 4:14; II Tim. 1:6) explicitly receive the imposition of the apostolic hands. In his turn Timothy must impose hands on the elders whom he creates (I Tim. 5:22). Prayer, more than the gesture of ordination inherited from Judaism, proves that there is nothing mechanical in the transmission of the ministry in the church, and that the new minister receives in truth his charge from the Spirit. In the NT, however, the imposition of hands is always done ·by the apostle or by the minister of the word who has himself received the imposition.

*c. The beginning of church order.* Jesus chose his own apostles. Subsequently the apostles presided with prayer over the choice and ordination of the new ministers required by the church, and these ministers were to act in the same manner toward their successors. The believers were consulted and called upon to express their approbation. But the ministry was not transmitted by the church. It was given from on high, and it was transmitted by those who had already received it. Yet the Spirit himself was at work in this transmission. The ministers were called from on high by the Lord of the church to accomplish their service in the church.

This is an absolutely original system. The church in the NT is not a democracy, in the sense that the power is in the hands of the people, who would then delegate it to ministers freely elected. Neither is the church in the NT an oligarchy, in the sense that the apostles, and after them ministers freely appointed by the apostles, are capable themselves of designating their successors with authority.

The original church order has its source in the idea of the church. Christ is the head of the church, which he rules through his Spirit. Power in the church belongs neither to the ministers nor to the community itself, but to Christ.

**Bibliography.** H. Lietzmann, *The Beginnings of the Christian Church* (1936). J. Weiss, *The History of Primitive Christianity* (1937). E. F. Scott, *The Nature of the Early Church* (1941). J. V. Bartlett, *Church Life and Church Order During the First Four Centuries* (1943). C. T. Craig, *The Beginning of Christianity* (1943). M. Goguel, *La naissance du christianisme* (1946); *L'Eglise primitive* (1947). K. E. Kirk, *The Apostolic Ministry* (1946). T. W. Manson, *The Church's Ministry* (1948). P. H. Menoud, *L'Eglise et les ministères selon le NT* (1949); *La vie de l'Eglise naissante* (1952); "Revelation and Tradition," *Interpretation*, VII (1953), 131-41. G. Dix, *Jew and Greek. A Study in the Primitive Church* (1953). J. L. Leuba, *NT Pattern* (1953). G. B. Caird, *The Apostolic Age* (1955). P. H. MENOUD

**CHURCH, WORSHIP OF.** See WORSHIP IN THE NT, CHRISTIAN.

**CHUSHAN-RISHATHAIM.** KJV form of CUSHAN-RISHATHAIM.

**CHUSI** kū'sī [Χουσεί, *also* Χούς *or* Οὔξ]. A locality mentioned in Jth. 7:18. The name is omitted from the Vulg. but occurs in OL. It is located to the W of Aqrabeh (*see* ACRABA), S of modern Nablus.
P. WINTER

**CHUZA** kū'zə [Χουδᾶ(ς); Aram. כוזא, little jug]. Steward of Herod Antipas (*see* HEROD [FAMILY]); husband of JOANNA, a Galilean woman, who followed and supported Jesus (Luke 8:3). Chuza, a man of position and of means, may have been a manager of Herod's property or a political appointee.
D. M. BECK

**CIEL, CIELD, CIELING.** KJV archaic verb forms used to translate the following Hebrew words:

*a*) חפה (II Chr. 3:5; RSV "cover").

*b*) ספן (Jer. 22:14; Hag. 1:4; RSV "panel"), "cover."

*c*) שחיף (Ezek. 41:16; RSV "paneled").
See PANEL; HOUSE; ARCHITECTURE.
O. R. SELLERS

**CILICIA** sĭ lĭsh'ə [Κιλικία] (Acts 6:9; 15:23, 41; 21: 39; 22:3; 23:34; 27:5; Gal. 1:21). A large and important district situated in the SE coastal zone of Asia Minor. It had various names in the earlier periods of its history. The Greek and Roman designation of Κιλικία is derived from a population first attested in Assyrian records of the ninth century B.C. as Hilakku (OT HELECH).

1. Geography
2. Prehistory
3. History
   *a.* Hittite period
   *b.* Dark Ages to Persian period
   *c.* Hellenistic period to 67 B.C.
   *d.* Roman period
4. Biblical references
5. Archaeology
Bibliography

**1. Geography.** The classical name of Cilicia is applied to an area which geographically is bipartite. The W part of Cilicia extends from Pamphylia to the Lamus River. This is Cilicia Tracheia (Aspera), true to its name in its forbidding mountainous appearance. Between Coracesium (modern Alanya) and Soli-Pompeiopolis the coast is steep and rocky. Promontories form small harbors. The hinterland is agriculturally unprofitable, although picturesque for its rocky plateaus and natural chasms and caves. The chief river descending from the Taurus Mountains

Courtesy of Machteld J. Mellink

28. The Cilician Gates: a view of a modern road through the narrowest part of the gorge

here is the Calycadnus (Göksu), which flows in deep gorges. Communications were difficult in the broken-up interior of this part of Cilicia, and traffic naturally followed the coast as well as it could. Of the resources, the forests covering the mountain slopes provided excellent timber.

The second part of Cilicia, the region E of the Lamus River, forms a vast contrast to the W. The coastal plain widens eastward and forms one of the most fertile regions of Asia Minor, extending to the Gulf of Issus. This is Cilicia Pedias (Campestris), modern Çukurova, a subtropical district well watered by several rivers, the Cydnus (Tarsus çay), the Sarus (Seyhan), and the Pyramus (Ceyhan). The plain is a vast expanse of rich land, intensively exploited for agriculture in ancient and modern times (grain, rice, flax, vines, fruit trees, nowadays citrus groves and cotton). Communications are rapid and easy within Cilicia Pedias, whereas ancient roads connected it with the country N of the Taurus Mountains via controlled passes, the most famous of which are the Cilician Gates (Gülek Bogaz).* In time of peace the Cilician Gates are adequate to maintain contact between Cilicia and the N, but they can be blocked if isolation is desired. The same applies to the connections with the E: the road to Syria and Antioch (Antakya) has to cross the Amanus Mountains, a S extension of the Taurus. Coastal defiles and a high pass (Beilan) make these "Syro-Cilician Gates" equally ambivalent as a thoroughfare or a closed border. Fig. CIL 28.

**2. Prehistory.** The earliest inhabitants of Cilicia Pedias lived in villages and towns all over the plain, which is dotted with ancient tells. Prehistory in Cilicia begins in the Neolithic period and shows strong affinities in material culture to N Syria and Mesopotamia. In this phase the Taurus was more of a border than the Amanus, but in the third millennium B.C. the situation was reversed. Contact with inner Anatolia was increased, and coastal navigation was also rapidly developing. New intrusions from Syria appear after 2000 B.C.

**3. History. a. Hittite period.** In the course of the second millennium B.C., Cilicia entered history under the name of Kizzuwatna, an independent country which negotiated treaties with the Hittites. The first treaty was concluded between Išputahšu and Telepinu (the fifth Hittite king after the fall of Babylon); the last one was made by Šunaššura with the famous Hittite king Šuppiluliuma in the early fourteenth century B.C. Sometime during Šuppiluliuma's rule Kizzuwatna was made part of the Hittite Empire, and it remained so until the downfall of the Hittites ca. 1200 B.C. The population of Kizzuwatna at that time was mixed, Luvian and Hurrian elements being attested. The country was literate, and part of its population lived in important towns such as Tarša (TARSUS) and Atania-Adana.

**b. Dark Ages to Persian period.** During the invasions by the Sea Peoples, Cilicia was also overrun and sacked. The Hilakku-Cilicians and some groups of Mycenean Greeks settled in the country in this period of disturbances. With the Assyrian expansion to the E, Cilicia re-entered history. In the late eighth century B.C. its people made a conspiracy with the invading Phrygians (see MESHECH) but were defeated by Sargon of Assyria (ca. 712 B.C.). The later Assyrian kings maintained some control in Cilicia, which in the meantime became an aim of renewed Greek interest and colonization.

In the course of the seventh century B.C., Cilicia emerged as an independent kingdom, a minor rival of Lydia, Babylon, and the Medes. The Cilician king Syennesis mediated between Alyattes of Lydia and Cyaxares the Mede in 585 B.C. (Herodotus I.74). It is not clear what the leading language of Cilicia was by this time, but several coastal cities had absorbed enough Greek colonists to be predominantly Greek. The use of Greek remained common in the Persian period, as is apparent from the coinage of the cities.

CILICIA

Cilicia was allowed some autonomy under its own kings until the fourth century B.C., when it was made into a Persian satrapy. The most important cities of this period were Nagidus, Celenderis, Soli, Tarsus, Mallus, and perhaps Mopsuestia.

*c. Hellenistic period to 67 B.C.* In the Hellenistic period Cilicia came under Seleucid rule. Seleucus Nicator founded several new cities in the coastal area—e.g., Seleucia ad Calycadnum—a practice followed by his successors. Many cities were renamed Antiocheia or Seleucia in the third century B.C. The coast of Cilicia Tracheia was encroached upon by the Ptolemies, who seized several cities after 246 B.C.—e.g., Soli. Under Antiochus III (223-187) these cities were reconquered, but this monarch had his territory reduced by the Romans in 188 B.C. E Cilicia remained firmly Seleucid and was actively Hellenized by Antiochus IV, Epiphanes (175-163). Local coinage of the cities was resumed or began under his rule. After his death Seleucid control broke down and dissension prevailed. Many cities dropped their Seleucid names after 150 B.C.

In Cilicia Tracheia, a local dynasty of priest kings, the Teucrids, maintained itself in the mountains at Olba, N of Seleucia. These rulers, supposedly descendants of Ajax, son of Teucer, based their prestige on the cult of Zeus Olbios. The coastal zone of Cilicia Tracheia became a paradise for robbers and pirates, who used the small harbors to escape detection and terrorize coastal shipping. Rhodes by this time had lost control of the seas, and it was Rome which had to combat the Cilician pirates. A first campaign was conducted in 102 B.C., without lasting results. In Cilicia Pedias, the Armenian king Tigranes established himself in 83 B.C. and deported many citizens to Tigranocerta. The Romans forced him to give up Cilicia in 69 B.C.

The major blow against the pirates was struck by Pompey in 67 B.C. He defeated them effectively, resettled the better elements in cities of Cilicia, and refounded Soli as Pompeiopolis. Cilicia, both the E and the W parts, was annexed as a Roman province, with Tarsus as its capital.

*d. Roman period.* The province of Cilicia was not ruled as a unified district. Some of the local princes were allowed to continue their rule as vassals of Rome—e.g., the Teucrid Dynasty of Olba and that of Tarcondimotus in the Amanus region. Shortly after Cicero's governorship (51-50) changes were made in the size of Cilicia, and *ca.* 38 B.C., Cilicia Pedias was attached to the province of Syria. It probably stayed under the governor of Syria until A.D. 72. The W part, Cilicia Tracheia, had a much more checkered career. It was given by Antony to Cleopatra (36 B.C.), later by Octavian to King Amyntas of Galatia. After his death it went to Archelaus of Cappadocia, who made his residence and built a palace at Elaeussa, a town he renamed Sebaste. His son succeeded him in A.D. 17.

The last Hellenistic monarch to rule over Tracheia was Antiochus IV of Commagene (A.D. 38-72). He again made an energetic effort to Hellenize the province, to found cities, and to defeat the insurgent mountaineers. His abdication in 72 led to the final unification of Cilicia Tracheia and Pedias as a Roman province known as Cilicia under Vespasian.

Probably under Theodosius the Younger (408-50), Cilicia was again divided into two parts, Cilicia Prima with Tarsus as its capital in the W, and Cilicia Secunda with its capital at Anazarbus in the E.

**4. Biblical references.** The joint references to Syria and Cilicia in Acts 15:23, 41; Gal. 1:21 indicate that Cilicia Pedias is meant, which administratively was part of Syria *ca.* 38 B.C.–A.D. 72. In the wider sense Cilicia is mentioned as the entire coastal strip E of Pamphylia (Acts 27:5).

The travels of Paul in his native country are not specified as to the cities visited, but he clearly followed the ancient road from Antioch to Tarsus and N through the Cilician Gates to Derbe on his second journey, a route which would have taken him to many of the old cities of Cilicia in addition to Tarsus.

**5. Archaeology.** The exploration of Cilicia is still far from complete, but the recording of inscriptions and monuments has covered a wide field. Extensive excavation has taken place at Mersin (a prehistoric mound near ancient Zephyrium) and Tarsus. Some work has also been done in Mopsuestia, and a spectacular discovery was made at Karatepe on the River Ceyhan in the Taurus Mountains, where a fortress with sculptures of *ca.* 700 B.C. also produced the first long bilingual text in Hittite hieroglyphs and Phoenician.

Of the aspect of Cilicia Tracheia in the first century A.D., the remains of Roman towns and cemeteries along the coast give a remote impression. Elaborate ruins line the road from Pompeiopolis to Elaeussa, Corycus, Seleucia; dilapidated aqueducts are left as marks of engineering which enabled the towns to exist under adverse circumstances. Most of the ancient towns of Cilicia Pedias are covered by new settlements, as its fertility is undiminished. In the mountains, grandiose ruins are left of such abandoned towns as Anazarbus—Anavarsa in the E and Olba in the W.

*Bibliography.* Monumenta Asiae Minoris Antiqua, vol. II (1930); vol. III (1931). A. H. M. Jones, *The Cities of the Eastern Roman Provinces* (1937), pp. 192-215. A. Goetze, *Kizzuwatna and the Problem of Hittite Geography* (1940). D. Magie, *Roman Rule in Asia Minor* (1950), pp. 266-77. M. Gough, "Anazarbus," *Anatolian Studies*, II (1952), 85-150; "A Temple and Church at Ayas," *Anatolian Studies*, IV (1954), 49-64; "Augusta Ciliciae," *Anatolian Studies*, VI (1956), 165-77.

M. J. MELLINK

**CIMMERIANS** sĭ mĭr′ĭ ənz. The Greek name of a people represented in the Bible by the name GOMER.

**CINNAMON** [קִנָּמוֹן, *qinnᵉmôn;* Ugar. *qnm?;* κιννάμωμον]. The fragrant bark of an oriental tree, highly valued as a spice. It was used for the holy oil (Exod. 30:23), in perfume (Prov. 7:17), in praise of the bride (Song of S. 4:14), and as a trade item of Babylon (actually Rome; Rev. 18:13).

*See also* FLORA § 7g; SPICES.

*Bibliography.* H. N. and A. L. Moldenke, *Plants of the Bible* (1952), pp. 76-77.      J. C. TREVER

**CINNEROTH.** KJV form of CHINNEROTH in I Kings 15:20.

**CIRAMA.** KJV Apoc. form of RAMAH.

**CIRCUMCISION** [מוּלָה; περιτομή]. The act of cutting off the foreskin (prepuce) of the male genital. Among the Hebrews circumcision was a religious ceremony performed on the eighth day after birth, as a sign of the covenant between Yahweh and Israel (Gen. 17:10-14). Not only Israelite children were circumcised, but also slaves owned by Israelites, whether they were bought or were born in slavery; furthermore, any resident alien who wished to keep the Passover had to undergo circumcision (Exod. 12:48-49).

Circumcision was widely practiced in antiquity, and was by no means unique with the Hebrews. It was practiced by the Egyptians* and by most of the ancient Semites, except the Babylonians and the Assyrians. Of the peoples living adjacent to the ancient Hebrews only the Philistines did not practice it; they were contemptuously referred to by Hebrews as "the uncircumcised" (עֲרֵלִים; Judg. 14:3; 15:18; I Sam. 14:6; 17:26, 36; 31:4; II Sam. 1:20; I Chr. 10:4). It was

29. Relief from a Sixth Dynasty tomb at Saqqarah (2350-2000 B.C.), showing the operation of circumcision

observed by pre-Mohammedan Arabs, and is now generally practiced by Muslims, although it is not even mentioned in the Koran. The custom has been found among many tribes of Africa, Australia, and America, some of whom have an analogous rite for females. It was apparently not known among the Indo-Germanic and Mongolian peoples. Fig. CIR 29.

**1. History of the rite.** The origin of circumcision is lost in the mists of antiquity. Gen. 17:9-27 ascribes its origin to the time of Abraham, but the account is a part of the late Priestly Code (fifth century B.C.). Exod. 4:24-26 is interpreted by some scholars as indicating an origin in the time of Moses, under Midianite influence. Others attribute the origin to the time of Joshua, on the basis of Josh. 5:2-7, noting that the LXX has a different text, which omits "again the second time." Herodotus says that the Jews and other peoples borrowed the rite from the Egyptians (II.104). None of these theories is satisfactory, in view of the widespread practice of circumcision in antiquity. The early use of flint knives

(Exod. 4:25; Josh. 5:2) points to an origin before the beginning of the use of iron for tools (eleventh century B.C.). Mention of the practice in Gen. 34:14-24 speaks for a pre-Mosaic origin. It is worthy of note that the earliest law codes of Israel do not enjoin the rite.

It is probable that in the early period of Hebrew history circumcision was performed at the onset of puberty or at marriage. Ishmael is said to have been circumcised at the age of thirteen (Gen. 17:25). The Hebrew word for "father-in-law," חֹתֵן, means literally "the circumciser." Among the other peoples who have practiced circumcision, childhood or puberty, rather than infancy, is the general rule.

It is not known when the rite was transferred by the Hebrews to infancy; at any rate, it was by the time of the writing of Gen. 17:12; Lev. 12:3, both in the Priestly Code. By the time of the NT, naming of the child on the eighth day accompanied the rite (Luke 1:59; 2:21).

Circumcision must have been widely practiced in the pre-exilic period, but there were prophetic circles in which the rite was not highly valued. Deuteronomy nowhere enjoins physical circumcision, but twice speaks of circumcision of the heart (10:16; 30:6). Jeremiah once pronounced God's judgment upon the various nations—Egypt, Judah, Edom, the Ammonites, Moab, and the desert Arabs—that were "circumcised [in the flesh] but yet uncircumcised [in heart]" (9:25-26).

It was apparently in the period following the Babylonian exile that circumcision assumed great importance for the Jews, being one of their most distinctive religious rites, along with sabbath observance.

When Hellenistic influence grew strong in Palestine, the Jews came into contact with Greeks who did not practice circumcision. Some Jews sought to overcome the effect of circumcision by epispasm, making foreskins for themselves (I Macc. 1:15; Jos. Antiq. XII.v.1; cf. I Cor. 7:18). Antiochus Epiphanes forbade circumcision, and his agents put to death women who had circumcised their children (I Macc. 1:48, 60). Yet followers of Mattathias forcibly circumcised many Jews. After the Hasmonean successes, the rite became most important as a mark of Jewish fidelity. In the book of Jubilees (second century B.C.) it is said that every child that is not circumcised "belongs not to the children of the covenant which the Lord made with Abraham, but to the children of destruction; nor is there, moreover, any sign on him that he is the Lord's, but (he is destined) to be destroyed and slain from the earth" (15:26). The view was developed that the higher angels and many of the early patriarchs were born circumcised. Circumcision became a requirement of proselytes, along with baptism; some rabbis of the Tannaitic period taught, however, that baptism alone was sufficient. The Roman emperor Hadrian issued an edict making circumcision a capital crime, along with castration. Reaction to this decree was one of the causes of the Jewish revolt led by Bar Cocheba (132-35).

Circumcision was a bitter source of contention in Christianity of the NT period. Both John the Baptist and Jesus were circumcised (Luke 1:59; 2:21). Those early Christians who were Jews had doubtless been circumcised, but when Christianity spread among the Gentiles, particularly away from Palestine, the question arose whether it was necessary for Gentiles to be circumcised in order to be Christian. Some Judean Christians taught that circumcision was necessary. The Jerusalem council which is reported in Acts 15 was summoned to deal with the question; the decision reached was that circumcision was not obligatory for Christians.

Paul was himself circumcised on the eighth day (Phil. 3:5) and insisted upon the circumcision of Timothy, who had a Jewish mother and a Greek father (Acts 16:3), but not of Titus (Gal. 2:3). Nevertheless, he was a leader among those who denied the necessity of physical circumcision and gave the word a spiritual meaning. He insisted that for the Christian neither circumcision nor uncircumcision was of any avail, but only "faith working through love" (Gal. 5:6), or "a new creation" (Gal. 6:15), or "keeping the commandments of God" (I Cor. 7:19). He taught that "circumcision is a matter of the heart, spiritual and not literal" (Rom. 2:29), and that "in him [Christ] also you were circumcised with a circumcision made without hands, by putting off the body of flesh in the circumcision of Christ" (Col. 2:11).

In Christianity circumcision has not usually been observed as a religious rite, except in the Abyssinian and Coptic churches, which probably were influenced by the Egyptian practice.

**2. The significance of circumcision.** In discussing the significance or meaning of this custom, we must distinguish between the meaning or purpose which it had in its beginnings, and the interpretation given to the developed form of the rite.

The purpose for which circumcision was originally practiced can only be conjectured. We cannot hope to fathom accurately the primitive or early mind. Many theories have been advanced to explain the origin of circumcision. Of these, three deserve mention here:

*a*) It was performed for physical reasons—such as to prevent disease, to prepare for marriage by facilitating intercourse, or for reasons of general cleanliness and hygiene. Philo, e.g., in writing in defense of circumcision says that it prevents a severe and almost incurable malady of the foreskin, that it promotes the cleanliness of the whole body as befits a consecrated order, and that it promotes fertility of offspring (*On the Special Laws* I.4-7). Philo's explanation is in part too sophisticated, but it seems probable, in view of the widespread occurrence of the custom and its frequent association with puberty or marriage (perhaps among the Hebrews in the earliest stage), that preparation for marriage was an important element in the early custom.

*b*) It was a form of sacrifice—perhaps a sacrifice of the reproductive powers to a fertility deity, or even a substitute for human sacrifice, a part being offered up in lieu of the whole. While this view is not impossible, the rite does not appear to have been considered a sacrifice among the Hebrews. The rite was not performed by priests, and no altar or sanctuary was involved. The rite presumably was performed in the home before being transferred to the synagogue *ca.* the ninth century A.D. This re-

mained the practice until the early nineteenth century, when it reverted to the home (or the hospital).

However, Targumic interpretations of Exod. 4:24-26 viewed the blood of Moses' son's circumcision as having expiatory value to avert the wrath of Yahweh from Moses (*see bibliography*). Also Judaism laid stress on the shedding of blood in circumcision, from the Tannaitic period on (M. Shab. 19.6). The notion of sacrifice, nevertheless, was not emphasized.

*c*) Circumcision was an act of initiation, either into membership in the tribe or nation, or into the duties of manhood. Thus circumcision may have been a kind of tribal mark.

For the later Hebrews circumcision was indeed an act of initiation into the covenant people. Whether this was the original purpose we cannot say. It does not seem likely that it was considered primarily as a "tribal mark," for its effect would usually be hidden from view, unless we assume that nudity was practiced at the time it originated.

It is probable that a combination of the above views, especially the first and third, is necessary to explain the original purpose of circumcision. For early man so much of life was penetrated by religion that we should not think that a simple, secular motive was dominant.

Our discussion thus far has suggested some aspects of the meaning of circumcision in its developed form, as we see it in the Priestly Code.

Above all, it was an act of initiation into the covenant community. The command to Abraham and his descendants was: "You shall be circumcised in the flesh of your foreskins, and it shall be a sign [אות] of the covenant between me and you" (Gen. 17:11). Paul spoke of Abraham's circumcision as a "sign or seal" of his righteousness (Rom. 4:11). The rite served to indicate that a Hebrew was a son of the covenant. Today a common name in Judaism for the circumcision ceremony is ברית (lit., "covenant").

Circumcision represented the removal of impurity, and thus was an act of purification. The word for "uncircumcised" is closely associated with "unclean" in Isa. 52:1, and is actually used of the fruit of a tree in its first three years as the equivalent of "unclean" or "prohibited" (Lev. 19:23). One of the words used by Arabs for circumcision is *ṭuhr,* "cleansing."

Circumcision was observed as an ordinance of divine origin, and was considered to be an occasion for joy and rejoicing. A passage in the Babylonian Talmud says: "R. Simeon b. Gamaliel said: Every precept which they accepted with joy, e.g., circumcision . . . they still observe with joy" (Shab. 130*a*). The ceremonies accompanying the rite include many expressions of joyfulness.

**3. Figurative circumcision.** In three different ways circumcision was given a figurative or spiritual meaning in the Bible.

*a*) Deut. 10:16 has the injunction: "Circumcise therefore the foreskin of your heart, and be no longer stubborn." In Deut. 30:6, it is said: "The LORD your God will circumcise your heart and the heart of your offspring, so that you will love the LORD your God with all your heart and with all your soul, that you may live." Jeremiah uses the figure in 4:4, and the "uncircumcised heart" is mentioned in Lev. 26:41. Paul uses the figure in Rom. 2:28-29 (cf. Col.

2:11). The circumcised heart is a heart open to God's command and obedient to him, not closed and stubborn.

*b)* Moses is described as one "of uncircumcised lips" in Exod. 6:12, 30. The context indicates that he did not consider himself to be eloquent and persuasive, but needed Aaron to serve as his spokesman.

*c)* In one passage Jeremiah speaks of the ears of the Israelites as being uncircumcised (6:10). Here the RSV renders: "Behold, their ears are closed." This gives the meaning, which is similar to that of the uncircumcised heart.

*Bibliography.* K. Kohler *et al.,* "Circumcision," *The Jewish Encyclopedia* (1907), IV, 92-102; D. Jacobson, *The Social Background of the OT* (1942), pp. 300-310. On Moses' son's circumcision, see G. Vermès, "Baptism and Jewish Exegesis: New Light from Ancient Sources," *NTS,* 4 (1958), 308-19.

J. P. HYATT

**CIS.** KJV form of KISH in Acts 13:21.

**CISAI.** KJV Apoc. form of KISH.

**CISTERN** [באר, בור]. A pit, hole; more often WELL, never "fountain" or "spring." The difference between "well" and "cistern" often is not apparent (cf. Prov. 5:15; Isa. 30:14; Jer. 14:3). Pits dug in Palestine's porous limestone were not satisfactory for water storage until lime plaster became common, apparently about the time of the Conquest.

The cistern brought a measure of comfort and security, especially in dry summers and times of siege (cf. Isa. 36:16), and it eased the labors of women. It contributed to the individual's prosperity and status (II Kings 18:31 = Isa. 36:16). The cisterns in the cities were fed by water from the roofs. Such may have been the cistern of Malchiah in the court of the guard, in which Jeremiah was cast (Jer. 38:6-13). The Israelites were to take over cities in which were cisterns they had not hewn out themselves (Deut. 6: 11). Uzziah hewed out cisterns to assure water supply for his herds and agricultural activities (II Chr. 26: 10). In Jer. 14 the pagan gods are symbolized as broken cisterns that can hold no water. In Eccl. 12:6 the wheel broken at the "cistern" is one of several symbols of cessation of life.

Cisterns were often roughly bottle-shaped, but most irregular. The mouth was sometimes finished with a prepared rim and was covered with a stone. Drains gathered water from flat roofs, courtyards, and even streets. Sometimes a small settling basin was placed beside the rim, and cisterns were occasionally cleaned, but in nearly every one under the mouth lay a heavy cone of debris containing earth, broken vessels, jewelry, coins, and rarely a skeleton of a beast or a man. They could be used for storage of grain.

Figs. CIS 30; GIB 29; SAL 7; WAT 6.

*See also* WATER WORKS § 2*a.*     C. C. McCOWN

**CITADEL** [ארמון; ἄκρα; *see* FORTRESS]. A stronghold of a city (Ps. 48:3, 13—H 48:4, 14) or palace (I Kings 16:18; II Kings 15:25) for purposes of defense or domination. David conquered Jerusalem by first taking the stronghold or citadel of the city (II Sam. 5:7, 9; I Chr. 11:5, 7). The Hebrew word may refer to a fortified tower or building, and, in addition to "citadel," is rendered variously TOWER (Ps. 122:7), STRONGHOLD, (e.g., Isa. 34:13; Amos 1:12; 2:2), PALACE (e.g., Jer. 6:5; Lam. 2:7), and CASTLE (Prov. 18:19).

The citadel or *akra* of Jerusalem in Maccabean times remained a Seleucid stronghold until Simon conquered it (*ca.* 142 B.C.; I Macc. 13:49-52; Jos. Antiq. XIII.vi.6-7). The last citadel of Jewish Jerusalem, the Antonia of the Herodian temple, fell under the Roman attack led by Titus in A.D. 70 (Jos. War VI-VII).

J. A. SANDERS

**CITHERN** sĭth'ərn. KJV translation of κιθάρα (RSV HARP).

**CITIES OF THE VALLEY** [עָרֵי כִכָּר]; KJV CITIES OF THE PLAIN. The five cities, SODOM, GOMORRAH, ADMAH, ZEBOIIM, and ZOAR, situated in the Valley of the Jordan and the Dead Sea. With the exception of Zoar, they were destroyed by the Lord because of their wickedness (Gen. 19:24-29). They are referred to as the "Five Cities" (Pentapolis) in Wisd. Sol. 10:6. In Gen. 14:3, 8, 10, the cities are located in the Valley of Siddim, thought to be in the area now under the waters of the S part of the Dead Sea.

For location and bibliography, *see* SODOM.

J. P. HARLAND

**CITIMS** sĭt'ĭmz. KJV Apoc. form of KITTIM, meaning "Macedonians." *See* MACEDONIA.

**CITIZENSHIP.** The state of being a citizen, whether of a Greek city-state or of the ROMAN EMPIRE. According to Acts 22:28 the apostle PAUL was a Roman citizen because he was born with this status. This suggests that his father was among the pro-Roman provincials who were given citizenship in the last years of the republic. Cicero tells us (*Philippic* II.92) that Mark Antony gave it, not to individuals, but to whole peoples, while Suetonius (*Julius* XLII.1) says that Caesar gave it to all the physicians and teachers of liberal arts at Rome, though not elsewhere. These examples show how widely citizenship was being extended. Under CLAUDIUS further extensions occurred: native auxil-

From *The People of the Dead Sea Scrolls,* by John Marco Allegro. Copyright © 1958, by John Marco Allegro and David Noel Freedman. Reprinted by permission of Doubleday and Company, Inc.

30. A cistern at Khirbet Qumran

iary soldiers became citizens upon their discharge from the army; and the emperor's wife, Messalina, together with the imperial secretaries, sold the privilege, at first for large sums, later for "broken bits of glass" (Dio Cassius LX.17; the statement reflects senatorial lack of enthusiasm for the new citizens). It was perhaps under such circumstances that the tribune Claudius Lysias paid a large sum to become a citizen (Acts 22:28).

We do not know how citizens provided proof of their citizenship at this time, though presumably they carried with them the equivalent of the modern passport. During Claudius' reign there were executions of some who falsely claimed to be citizens (Suetonius *Claudius* XXV.9).

The right of citizenship meant that a citizen could not be punished without trial; according to Acts 16: 39 either the lictors or the magistrates at Philippi apologized to Paul (and Silas, a citizen?) for a beating and an imprisonment. A citizen could not be examined by scourging, or even bound (Acts 22:24-29; so also Cicero *Against Verres* II.5.170), though Paul tells us that he was beaten three times (illegally?) by lictors (II Cor. 11:25). Most important of all was the right to "appeal to Caesar" and be tried at Rome (Acts 25:10-12); naturally, once the right was exercised, it could not be revoked by the appellant (Acts 26:32). During Claudius' reign the free state of Rhodes was deprived of its independence because some Roman citizens had been executed there (Dio Cassius LX.24). At a later date the question of citizenship continued to be important in dealing with Christians; Pliny (Epistle X.96) says that he segregated citizens from others in order to send them to Rome. The emperors gradually extended the citizenship until in A.D. 212 it was given to all free inhabitants of the Empire.

Paul was also, according to Acts 21:39, a citizen of TARSUS, capital of Cilicia, and according to Acts 22:3 was born there. At the end of the first century Tarsian citizenship was restricted to those who possessed at least five hundred drachmas (Dio Chrysostom *Oration* XXXIV.23), though it is not certain that such was the case earlier. A citizen of a provincial city had to be a member of a particular phyle (tribe); because of the religious character of such tribes, there must have been one at Tarsus consisting only of Jews.

Thus Paul's ethnos (nation) was Jewish (Acts 26: 4), as his tribe at Tarsus probably was; his citizenship was dual, since he was a citizen both of Tarsus and of Rome. Such dual citizenship had already been developed in the Greek world, when city-states banded together in leagues and "isopolity" was given the citizens of individual cities. Paul's status as citizen was one of the factors which fitted him to become an apostle to the Gentiles.

**Bibliography.** H. J. Cadbury in *The Beginnings of Christianity*, V (1933), 297-338; A. N. Sherwin-White, *The Roman Citizenship* (1939).

R. M. GRANT

**\*CITY** [עִיר, *less often* קִרְיָה; Aram. קִרְיָה, קִרְיָא, *also, rare and poetic*, קֶרֶת, *perhaps from* קרה, meet *or* gather; πόλις]. Since the Bible is by no means a parochial book, the biblical writers are concerned with Near Eastern, Greek, Hellenistic, and Roman cities, all

of which must be considered in their proper contexts and perspectives. It is hardly necessary to refer to such now well-known cities as Babylon, Ur, Carchemish, Byblos, and Alalakh, the cities of ancient Palestine, and the Hellenistic and Roman cities mentioned in the NT, to arouse mental pictures of opulence and magnificence. However, excavators have, quite naturally, been so much concerned with the artistic and magnificent, with palaces and temples, with baths and theaters, that they have neglected the actual living conditions of the people, the VILLAGE and the slum.

A. The general characteristics of the city
B. Hebrew cities
  1. Biblical usage
    *a.* Walls
    *b.* The city's villages
    *c.* Legal distinction between city and village
    *d.* Legal obligations and responsibilities
    *e.* Various types of cities
  2. Archaeological evidence
    *a.* City sites
    *b.* Sources of evidence concerning fortifications
    *c.* Walls and towers of a primitive village
    *d.* Walls of a border fortress city
    *e.* The gate
    *f.* Citadel with palace and temple
    *g.* The storage city
    *h.* Industrial, caravan, and seaport cities
    *i.* City plans
C. Greco-Roman cities
  1. Language usage
  2. General character
    *a.* Their effect on the Orient
    *b.* The Hippodamian city
    *c.* The agora
    *d.* The Roman city
Bibliography

**A. THE GENERAL CHARACTERISTICS OF THE CITY.** The definition and application of the three commonly used English terms "city," "town," and "village" vary with local custom and authors' individual experience. The word "suburbs" adds a fourth modern category. So it is in any language. None of our modern terms, such as those just used, covers exactly the same area of meaning or suggests the same mental picture as do the words of any ancient language, and the ancients were as capricious as moderns in their use of terms. Outstanding cases are easy, but in every class there are many borderline cases.

Cities varied among themselves in ancient as in modern times, probably much more in ancient times than today. Because intercommunication was greatly restricted, each city and its small region were, as far as possible, self-sufficient, and any society was much more at the mercy of local conditions than now. Defensibility, water, food, and therefore a hilltop site, springs, arable land, and building materials were prime necessities that tended to produce uniformity. Proximity to the sea, to the steppe, and to caravan routes, and a site on mountain or plain were modifying factors that produced diversity; but all cities needed to provide for shelter, food, drink, and security, for civic and cultic functions, for business and economic life, trade, commerce, industry, and social life.

**B. HEBREW CITIES.** The cities of Palestine bore little resemblance to Nineveh and Babylon, to Ephesus and Corinth, to Alexandria and Rome. Two sources of information regarding biblical cities are available—the Bible itself and the cities that have been excavated.

**1. Biblical usage. a. Walls.** The primary distinction between the city and the village was that the former was walled. This is equally true whether the term עִיר, קִרְיָה, or קֶרֶת is used; the difference in terms seems to have been purely rhetorical. The expressions "walled cities" (RSV "fortified cities"; KJV "fenced cities") and "country cities" (RSV "unwalled villages," "open towns") are contrasted (cf. I Sam. 6:18; Esth. 9:19; Ezek. 38:11), but such language is exceptional. The repetition of the phrase "walled cities" does not imply that there were any unwalled cities. The frequent enumeration of the doors, bolts, and bars of the city gate is a similar literary convention, a picturesque repetition for emphasis (Deut. 3:5; Judg. 16:3; I Sam. 23:7; II Chr. 8:5). Were there walled cities without gates? Hardly. The GATE was extremely important, not only in the defense of a city, but also in its social functions. *See* §§ B2*e, i, below.*

**b. The city's villages.** Its defenses were demanded by another basic characteristic of the ancient city to which there is no parallel in modern Western culture. The city was a place of refuge. In Palestine, as elsewhere in the Mediterranean world, one mark of a city was its villages—i.e., its surrounding agricultural area—which looked to it for protection. In the OT two expressions are used: the city had its "villages" (חֲצֵרִים) or its "daughters" (בָּנוֹת). The use of בָּנוֹת seems to be preferred for non-Israelite cities in Judges (1:17). There seems to be no difference between the two phrases, except that, in a series of statements in Joshua (15:45-47), the Philistine cities Ekron, Ashdod, and Gaza are credited with both "daughters" and "villages." In this case בָּנוֹת is legitimately translated "towns," as intermediate between cities and villages. Elsewhere, if "town" is used, it is because the translator introduces his belief that the known importance or size of the place does not call for the title "city."

One exception is to be noted. The cities given to the Levites had no villages, but מִגְרָשׁ, "pasture lands," (incorrectly translated "suburbs" in the KJV). Since these pasture lands included only an area within a radius of two thousand cubits from the cities' walls, there could hardly be any villages included (Num. 35:1-8; Josh. 20:7-8; 21:1-42; I Chr. 5:16; 6:40-66; etc.).

**c. Legal distinction between city and village.** In one passage (Lev. 25:31), the village (חָצֵר) is distinguished from the city by its having no walls, and as to redemption its houses are under the same law as the "fields of the country." A house in a village could not be permanently alienated, but must be returned in the year of jubilee. A house in a walled city, on the contrary, if sold, was open to redemption during one year only. After a year, if not meantime redeemed, it became the property of the buyer in perpetuity (Lev. 25:13-17, 25-31).

**d. Legal obligations and responsibilities.** The laws regarding relationships between city and village are nowhere set forth. The main value of such a relationship to the villagers was doubtless that the city could be a place of refuge in time of war. It would also be the natural center for selling produce and buying whatever the farmer could not produce.

**e. Various types of cities.** The usual Palestinian city served an agricultural population, both in the city itself and in its villages. It would have been essentially a market town. Various specialized types are mentioned in the OT: the store city, the chariot city, the city for horsemen (Exod. 1:11; I Kings 9:19; II Chr. 1:14; 8:4-6; 9:25; 17:12). There are also royal cities (Josh. 10:2; I Sam. 27:5), with which "country towns" are contrasted (I Sam. 27:5). Cities built especially for defense, fortress cities, are also mentioned, and, indeed, any fortified place, no matter how small, might be called a city (Num. 13:19; II Kings 17:9; 18:8).

**2. Archaeological evidence. a. City sites.** In ancient Palestine, since there was a great dearth of trees, there were, aside from caves, two completely diverse solutions of the problem of housing: the tent and the building of stone or mud brick; the latter was largely confined to plains like the coast and the Jordan Valley at Jericho. In the mountains chiefly limestone and, in the Hauran and about the Sea of Galilee, basalt were used. In all periods the tent must be reckoned as an important domicile. A "tent city" of great size might easily spring up overnight on the edge of the steppe in Transjordan or the Negeb when different sections of a tribe came together for a festival or for consultation. Cave dwellings were used by nomads for shelter and warmth in winter, and for storage in summer in addition to their tents. Otherwise they were used by the poor. Petra is a unique example of cave dwellings de luxe, in connection with free-standing buildings, used by an originally nomad people.

In selecting a site for a village or city, as actual practice shows, proximity to cultivable land was naturally a first consideration, but it was not infrequently overridden by the desire to be on a hilltop and near a spring. This consideration became less persuasive after cisterns came into use (*see* CISTERN) but was by no means forgotten. The hilltop allowed measures to be taken against approaching raiders. It also provided unintended sanitation, since the winter downpours washed the streets clear and put mosquitoes—if they had them—at a greater distance.

**b. Sources of evidence concerning fortifications.** Jericho stands apart. Under Tell es-Sultan, the mound of OT Jericho is a unique example of a walled city, the oldest yet discovered. Already before 7000 or 8000 B.C. (according to a Carbon[14] dating), in a Neolithic period when pottery was not yet known, it had a strong wall connected with a massive round tower. The walls belonging to the successive city levels make a most enlightening study. Unfortunately those connected with biblical history from Joshua's time on were excavated in the early days of archaeology in Palestine, and their history cannot at present be successfully unraveled.

Other excavations, especially at Kiriath-sepher, or Debir, Gibeah or Saul, Beth-shemesh, Samaria, Megiddo, Mizpah, and Lachish, throw light on many features of city life. Here use will first be made of the results of excavation at Tell en-Nasbeh (probably Mizpah of Benjamin), as yet the most completely excavated site in Palestine. It was first a little border city (*ca.* 1200-900) and was then turned (by Asa) into a strong border fortress (*ca.* 900-850), while it served also as a market town for a considerable area. According to stamped jar handles found there, it served as a local administrative center during a considerable portion of the postexilic period down to *ca.* 400 or 350. With it must be compared the excavated strata VI-I of Megiddo, which cover the same period.

*c. Walls and towers of a primitive village.* The city (really only a small village) had a crude rubble wall usually two stones in thickness and reaching a width of about a yard, rarely as much as two yards. Two heavily built towers, each having two rooms, may have belonged to this period or to the earlier, unwalled village. The towers are not unlike that at the corner of the fortress of Gibeah, Saul's capital, and the wall resembles those of Debir, but is much weaker. The size of this "city" was probably not half that of the later fortress.

*d. Walls of a border fortress city.* The great wall of the main period was still standing to a height of twenty feet or more. It had a foundation of large flat stones piled up on projecting limestone strata to a height of a yard or more, and projecting a foot or so beyond the face of the wall. Spaces between the rocks allowed for drainage. On the outside, from the surface of the ground, the wall was often overlaid

Courtesy of Chester C. McCown

31. Typical section of a city wall, from Mizpah (Tell en-Nasbeh)

with a thick coating of hard yellow plaster up to fifteen or eighteen feet, evidently intended to discourage scaling. Elsewhere there was a sloping glacis as a protection against battering rams. In some areas there was a dry moat at the foot of the wall. The average height of the wall was estimated to have been from forty to forty-six feet above the limestone strata on which the wall was based. Fig. CIT 31.

The construction of the wall was quite unmethodical; apparently it was done by gangs that worked separately, for in one place, at least, one section was not bonded into the next. The stones were only hammer-trimmed and were laid in irregular, ill-fitting courses in clay mortar, with small stones used to fill up the chinks. Many of the stones were large enough to require three men to lift them. The two faces of the wall were ashlar with a rubble filling. Rectangular towers were placed at irregular intervals, some of them as expansions of the wall itself, some as additions, as apparent afterthoughts. The thickness of the wall, like that at Megiddo IV, varied from *ca.* 11.5 to 13 feet; with the towers it ran to from 20 to 30 feet.

As elsewhere, the limestone strata of the hill were in horizontal layers, receding upward. The walls were built on the projecting strata and followed contours that ranged between 2,540 and 2,560 feet above sea level. The circuit of the walls amounted to 2,165 feet, or half a mile less about 150 yards. Megiddo IV and III measured *ca.* 2,600 feet in circumference. The coffin-shaped area at Mizpah measured a little less than eight acres, making it larger than the early "City of David" at Jerusalem.

The casemate, or casement, type of wall was formed by connecting two adjoining, parallel encircling walls by cross walls at right angles to them. It appears in the Late Bronze Age in Asia Minor and Syria, and reaches Palestine perhaps in the Early Iron period, at Jericho, Gibeah of Saul, Beth-shemesh (*see* § B1 *above*), Debir, and Shechem, and later at Samaria, but not at Tell en-Nasbeh.

The use of the stone glacis, as seen at Tell en-Nasbeh, is common in the Iron Age. As an alternative, the *terre pisée* (beaten-earth) rampart of the Hyksos period has been found all the way from Tell el-Yehudiyeh in Egypt far into Asia. Traces of it appear on at least a dozen mounds in Palestine. Hazor (Tell el-Qedah), where one of the largest Hyksos encampments lay, is reported to have housed later an immense population in stone houses on the encampment site.

*e. The gate.* For the ancient Hebrew, the city gate was much more than a means of ingress and egress, much more than an important part of the city's defenses. It was also the "center" (even though at one side) of the city's social, economic, and judicial affairs. A brief description of the excellently preserved gate at Tell en-Nasbeh will, therefore, eventually involve much more than details of stonework. *See* § B2*i below.*

Usually city gates were placed in the opening between the two ends of the wall.* The placement of the Tell en-Nasbeh gate was unusual; otherwise it had features in common with other gates of the period. It was built on the NE side of the city. The wall from the N came down on a slightly higher (inner) stratum than the one coming up from the S. They were continued until they overlapped one another *ca.* 40 feet, and there was a space of *ca.* 40 feet between the two walls, giving a square of nearly 40 by 40 feet. The gate proper absorbed *ca.* 17 feet. There were two sets of gate piers with an opening (a gateway) of 14 feet between them. The two "guard rooms" were *ca.* 6 by 8 feet. Figs. MEG 36-37.

Pivots fitted into stone sockets carried the two (doubtless solid, wooden) gate leaves, which were placed between the outer piers. (There was none between the inner piers.) The two gates, when closed, were made fast by a bar, the end of which was thrust into a lock hole in one pier, but which was run back into a long slot in the other pier when the gate was opened. The sizes of the slot and the lock hole indicate a metal bar. There was a very slightly raised stone door sill and, at the center, an embedded stone to serve as a gate stop, against which the two leaves of the gate pressed when closed.

The overlapping walls provided an unusually strong defense for the gate. A parallel has not yet been discovered elsewhere. The extended end of the outer, E wall was built into a tower measuring 30.8 by 32.8 feet, protected by a glacis that at its bottom was 43.3 by 43.8 feet. Defenders could thus be concentrated on the inner wall, on the wall over the gate itself, and on the great tower on the outside. If the gate were broken down or burned, there would be defenders who could take refuge in the rooms within the gate structure and attack entering enemies from the side.

How Hebrew gates and walls were completed above cannot be positively determined. In some cases (Megiddo), the upper courses may have been of mud brick. At Tell en-Nasbeh no evidence of mud brick and no voussoirs were found to indicate an arched gateway, and the mass of rubble at the foot of the wall seemed to point to the use of stone throughout. Fires, frequently mentioned and even depicted in the destruction of ancient cities, indicate a large use of wood. Heavy wooden lintels over the gateway may have carried the wall, but the arch is probable. Judged by the few Assyrian representations of Syrian towns, the walls would have been finished with parapets having stepped, triangular, or conical crenelations. *See* ARCHITECTURE.

At Tell en-Nasbeh, a three-pier, indirect-access gate at a point farther S in the E wall was belatedly discovered. This type of gate with three pairs of piers was long maintained in many cities—e.g., Megiddo—and has been found at Gezer, Beth-shemesh, Shechem, Tell Beit Mirsim, and in Syrian cities such as Alalakh and Carchemish, all of them from the middle second down to the early first millennium. Various forms of the indirect-access gate appear later at Megiddo, Samaria, and Tell Beit Mirsim. It has persisted down to modern times, as the Damascus and Bethlehem (or Jaffa) gates at Jerusalem illustrate.

*f. The citadel with palace and temple.* A small fortress city, such as Tell en-Nasbeh, may or may not have had a further interior defense. Evidence for or against at Tell en-Nasbeh is lacking, since there the central hilltop is bare. Larger cities usually had one. Hazor is an excellent example, where Khirbet Waqqas, with its great expanse (600 by 1,200 yards), is presided over by Tell el-Qedah at its SW corner, which rises to a much greater height. Cf. the situation at Tell el-Meqbereh—Tell Abu Kharaz (JABESH-GILEAD?), where the latter tell was a fortress towering over the former, which was probably the residential section of the city.

The citadel, or acropolis, was usually combined with the palace (*see* CASTLE), sometimes with a temple, also as at Jerusalem. Aside from the highest point, two positions seem to have been preferred—either the NW corner (or the W side), for the sake of the cool winds from that quarter, or a place by the city gate. At MEGIDDO in Strata VA-IVB and IVA, there was a governor's headquarters (?) by the gate, which was low on the NW side, while there was another complex of buildings on the highest part of the mound on the E shoulder of the mound, at first regarded as a temple, later as the palace of the commander of the chariot corps. This last has also been suggested as the governor's residence, as has a large residence with a walled paved courtyard on the S. In the Samaria of Omri and Ahab, the palace, which was strongly fortified, and eventually the Temple of Augustus were on the NW.

At Tell en-Nasbeh a well-constructed long-room building with a distinctive plan (sometimes called *hilani*) appears in three places: just inside the great

Courtesy of Chester C. McCown

32. A "governor's residence," just back of an abandoned triple gate. The central entrance and open court are right of the center; one long room is at the left; another room is across the back; a fourth room is beyond the wall at the extreme right.

gate, inside the position of the early gate, and at the extreme S end of the city (but near no present signs of a gate). The one by the later gate, with its upper story, its four long rooms and a fifth added later, could have served as the official residences of the city's "governor."* But it was not fortified. The long, narrow rooms were probably for the storage of taxes in kind. The room nearest the gate at Tell en-Nasbeh had many wine jars. Fig. CIT 32.

*g. The storage city.* In Hebrew Palestine no storage cities that can be distinguished as such have been excavated, although small storage pits for grain are frequent. At Tell Jemmeh on the S border of Philistia, Sir Flinders Petrie did discover great grain pits under a citadel or fortress of the Persian period (fifth century). Presumably they were of imperial design and construction and connected with provision for the Persian armies that invaded Egypt. The dry climate was especially favorable to storage, and the area produced abundant grain.

*h. Industrial, caravan, and seaport cities.* There were cities of still other types besides those mentioned in either the OT or the NT: industrial, seaport, and caravan cities played little part in Hebrew economy, and no caravan or industrial cities are mentioned as such. Tyre, Sidon, Joppa, and Ezion-geber are referred to, but none of them affected Hebrew life except indirectly. EZION-GEZER is the only industrial city.

As to caravan cities, the well-known international routes through Syria determined their sites and their character, even though they were not mentioned in the Bible as such. Gaza, Tyre, Damascus, and Petra are known as caravan cities, both from their locations and from written and archaeological records. Gaza and Tyre are ports for both ships and camels. Sela, later Petra, and possibly Teman were essentially caravan cities, as were Philadelphia, Gerasa, Pella, and Beth-shan. Principal seaports in NT times were Joppa, Caesarea, Stratonis, and Ptolemais.

***i. City plans.*** In general, Palestinian cities were not planned but merely grew. The nature of the terrain modified their growth. Plans at Megiddo and Samaria were not greatly affected by their gentle terrain and their walls. But there was some evidence of planning. At Tell en-Nasbeh and Tell Beit Mirsim the centers of the hills were decidedly higher than the base of the walls, and the houses followed the curve of the walls, allowing no really straight streets.

At Samaria and Tell Beit Mirsim the houses often used the inner wall of the casements as their back wall. Not so at Tell en-Nasbeh. There in almost its entire circuit there was a space of from *ca.* 13 to 33 feet between the houses and the wall. In some areas it is impossible now to discover how a house was approached. The unbuilt area along the wall is in one section practically filled with stone-lined pits for the storage of grains. Similarly cisterns were excavated throughout the city. The difference is that the storage pits were usually dug in the earth and built of small stones, which were probably plastered with mud mortar and were not watertight, whereas cisterns were dug in the rock under houses or courtyards and plastered.

Few Palestinian cities of Hebrew date have been sufficiently excavated to provide detailed data on their interior plans and on provisions for communal life. In both Tell en-Nasbeh and Tell Beit Mirsim what appears to be a street seems to be cut off by a projecting house corner or a wall. Appearances may deceive. However, cities on Palestinian hills were usually crowded in order to bring as many families as possible within the walls. Often today entrance to one house may be from the roof of one built below it on the hillside. Doubtless such practices have always been known.

The Hebrew words for "street" are significant in that none arrives at the clear-cut definition of a narrow, clearly bounded strip of land set aside for the wayfarer in a city or village. The Hebrew word most often translated "street" (חוץ) actually means merely "outside" the house or the city or any enclosure. The LXX often renders it ἔξω ("outside"), or ἔξοδος ("exodus"). The word שׁוּק appears only four times in the OT, and is rendered in the LXX by δίοδος, ὁδός, and ἀγορά (twice). Apparently the little lanes in the oriental city were thought hardly worthy of a name. Only the "broad way" (רחוב; πλατεῖα) has a designation.

The ordinary streets in Hebrew times received no paving. No attempt was made to clear them. They accumulated potsherds and small stones, and, trodden down, these gradually came to constitute a very unsatisfactory kind of macadam. Areas that called for pavement—e.g., floors and courtyards—might be paved with stone (slabs or cobblestones), or with limestone chips and powder. An earthen floor sufficed for ordinary houses and courts.

In larger cities, especially where there was a much-visited temple or a king's palace to be reached, room was taken for a "broad way" (רחוב; πλατεῖα), often with an enclosed courtyard before the temple or palace, and these were often paved. In large cities there were "streets" (special sections of streets) for craftsmen—copper and iron workers in one place, jewelers in another; the modern *sûq* (שׁוּק, *shûq*) had its parallels in ancient times. "Streets" (in the bazaar) for these commercial purposes were sometimes set aside for foreign merchants (I Kings 20:34; cf. RSV "bazaars").

No temples or provisions for worship are found in Hebrew cities outside of Jerusalem. At Megiddo one area was occupied by altars or sanctuaries, or was left vacant as if taboo, from the beginning down to Stratum IV, when a Solomonic stable and veterinary headquarters appear on it (*ca.* 1000). Since the top of the mound at Tell en-Nasbeh was denuded, no "high place" (במה) could be expected. Not so at Megiddo. The whole area of Stratum III was cleared. Yet, since high places would probably have no permanent structures or furniture, this negative evidence does not absolutely prove their absence.

A striking feature of cities all over the Near East is the immense labor spent on provisions for water (*see* WATER WORKS). Long shafts and tunnels became common in the Late Bronze Age. "Hezekiah's tunnel" at Jerusalem is a late imitation. Cisterns came into use at about the beginning of the Iron Age (*ca.* 1200), when the use of lime plaster became known.

In the larger cities, especially royal cities, there were streets of some width and directness that ran from the gates to a plaza, the "square" or "broad place," before the royal palace (Esth. 4:6; 6:9, 11; Dan. 9:25). Near the gate of the city (Neh. 8:1, 3, 16; Job 29:7, *et passim*) also, such a provision might be made. Tell en-Nasbeh illustrates the latter. Both inside the city by the "long-room house" that was by the gate, and outside between the walls, a "broad place" was left. Inside, the place was empty. Outside, stone seats were placed against the wall on both sides. At Megiddo along the approach to the gate of Stratum VA a platform and benches were installed. In the gate wares of all kinds were exchanged, justice was dispensed, business was carried on, assemblies met, proclamations and speeches were made, and social life was at its height. *See* BROAD PLACE.

To the Hebrew the gate was socially all-important. His concrete, visualizing way of thinking, therefore, coined various idioms in which "gate" (שַׁעַר) had pregnant meanings. Since the "judges sat in the gate," the one place where there was room and everybody congregated, "gate" stood for "justice." "They are crushed in the gate" (Job 5:4) has no reference to physical crushing, of course, but to injustice done them. In Genesis (23:18; 34:24) the expression "to go out of" and "to come in by" the city gate is used to mean the total (male) community. "Within thy gates" appears again and again in Deuteronomy, by synecdoche for "within thy city."

Occasionally a whole city moved to a new site, for reasons not now apparent. Cities were "built" (i.e., rebuilt) or "founded" (given local autonomy) usually for defense and often were border fortresses. The rebuilding and refounding of cities was a cultural, as well as military, policy among the Hellenistic-Roman rulers.

## C. GRECO-ROMAN CITIES. 1. Language usage.
In Greek there is the same ambiguity as elsewhere in such words as πόλις, "city," and κώμη, "village." There is no word for "town," except the rare Hellenistic compound κωμόπολις (Mark 1:38; Strabo XII.2.6, etc.). In one passage in Mark (6:56) there is an interesting illustration of the use of some of the significant words. It says that wherever Jesus went into villages or cities or fields (ἀγρούς), they placed the sick in the market places (ἀγοραῖς) for him to cure. Important MSS and versions replace the word for "market" (ἀγορά) with that for "broad ways" (πλατεῖα), the word that serves for "bazaar" (Arabic *sûq*), "street," and "plaza." In Greco-Roman cities, the agora supersedes the city gate as a place of general concourse. The word ῥύμη appears four times in the NT, as a lane, or street. For ῥύμη (Luke 14: 21), Matthew (22:9) has διεξόδους τῶν ὁδῶν, "the ends of the streets" (hardly the RSV "thoroughfares," which is an etymological translation not sanctioned by usage). But Acts 9:11 has ῥύμη for the "street called Straight" in Damascus.

**2. General character of Greco-Roman cities. a. Their effect on the Orient.** The Greco-Roman city is much better known than that of the Orient because of the closer connection of the Western world with Greek and Latin material culture than with that of the Near East. It is a notable fact also that whereas Judaism and the gospels had a distinctly agricultural background, Christianity almost immediately gravitated toward the city. Jesus was a man of the country; Paul, of the city. No book in the Bible is more thoroughly bound to the city than the book of Revelation. Judaism also moved to the city when it left Palestine.

Before this happened, Alexander and his successors took the Greek city to the Orient. Necessarily it was the external form, not the Greek spirit, that migrated to the East. (Indeed, the "Greek spirit" was already largely lost to Greece.) Not enough Greeks migrated to Syria and Palestine, to Mesopotamia and Egypt, to leaven the population. The people still lived in their country villages and spoke Aramaic, while the cities put on an alien veneer.

All around the Mediterranean, Alexander and the Seleucids were vigorous city builders. They intended the cities they founded to be citadels of Greek culture that would preserve their conquered lands for their successors. But their "foundations" were imposed, often far from successfully either as to form or culture, upon a tough oriental tradition. The Qaṣr el-ʿAbd at ʿAraq el-Emir, the Nabatean temple at Khirbet et-Tannur, and Petra itself are exhibitions of the mixtures that resulted.

**b. The Hippodamian city.** This type of city, which became the fashion in the fifth century, was marked by (*a*) its (fairly) rectangular form; (*b*) its agora, or market place; (*c*) its open-air theater; a smaller, roofed odeum; a gymnasium, or palestra; and an amphitheater or a stadium—i.e., various places of amusement; and (*d*) various temples. It usually had an acropolis. It also had its villas and its tenements. Fig. CIT 33.

The ideal city plan was oriented to the four points of the compass, but in practice the terrain and other factors decidedly affect both the direction and the regularity of the city plans. Orientation might take any direction, with preference for the main street running W, W-NW, and N.

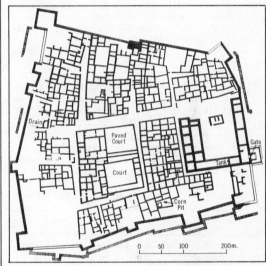

33. Plan of Idumean city of Marisa (OT Mareshah), a Hippodamian plan which, for some reason, is not exactly rectangular

**c. The agora.** The agora was a market place, but much more than this; it was actually a civic center. It took the place of the "gate."* Its shape varied in older Greek cities. Sometimes it had a horseshoe form. But in the Hellenistic (Hippodamian) scheme it was an open rectangular area of some size. No street passed through it, but a main city street along one side, while the other three sides were occupied with city office buildings, halls for the meetings of the citizens and official city bodies, and temples. Various monuments were set up there to be seen by all men, and, as time went on, the agora became filled with statues of men and gods. Figs. ATH 109; 114.

**d. The Roman city.** Superficially following the Hellenistic city plan came the Roman model, rectangular like its predecessor, but marked by its cardo and decumanus (the N-S and E-W lines respectively). They crossed at right angles, usually near the center of the city, and ran from a gate on one side through the city to a gate on the other side. The decumanus was supposed to end in a temple. Shops lined the main streets, which were bordered by stoas, and decorated with fountains and monuments of various kinds. The forum, or forums, took the place of the agora as sites for display of the statues of famous citizens and other supposedly decorative pieces. Streets passed through them. The bath was a necessary feature of the Roman city.

Usually Greek and Roman cities exhibited great care in providing for water by aqueducts and underground tunnels and pipes, and likewise in provisions for drainage and sanitation. Less attention in proportion was paid to city walls, although they were always built. The gates were largely ornamental, and often a triumphal arch preserved the name of some donor who had dedicated it to the emperor. Place was found also for many inscriptions in honor of governors, the imperial family, and benefactors of the city. A street of tombs outside the city along a prominent road was a standing feature.

**Bibliography.** A. von Gerkan, *Griechische Städteanlagen* (1924); A. H. M. Jones, *Cities of the Eastern Roman Provinces* (1937); W. F. Albright, *Excavation of Tell Beit Mirsim*, III (*AASOR*, XXI-XXII; 1943), pl. 3 (fig. 4); C. C. McCown *et al.*, *Tell en-Nasbeh*, I (1947), "Survey Map" and fig. 51 (figs. 1, 2, 4).                    C. C. McCOWN

**CITY AUTHORITIES** [πολιτάρχαι, politarchs]. A term occurring in Acts 17:6, 8, and nowhere else in extant Greek literature, but in inscriptions. Cf. πολίταρχος in Aeneas Tacitus 26.12.

The title politarch was mainly, although not exclusively, the Macedonian title for the non-Roman city magistrate. Most of its occurrences in inscriptions are from Macedonia; five of them are from Thessalonica.

The number of politarchs in a town varied with its importance. Amphipolis had five, Pella two; Thessalonica had five in the time of Augustus, and six later. The politarchs of Thessalonica would carry heavy responsibilities, since Thessalonica was both a free city and capital of the province of Macedonia. When Macedonia was conquered by the Romans in 168 B.C., it was divided into four districts, with Thessalonica the capital of the second district; in 146, however, the whole of Macedonia was reduced to a single province with Thessalonica as its chief city. In turn Thessalonica was made a "free city" by Octavius and Antonius and was ruled by its own assembly and magistrates. Although after A.D. 44 the head of the Roman administration in Macedonia was a proconsul of praetorian rank, supported by a legate and a quaestor, whose seat was in Thessalonica, yet it was not the intent of Rome to displace or supersede local governmental institutions in Macedonia any more than elsewhere. If the presence of the Roman government in Thessalonica is obvious from the form of the charge against Paul and Silas ("They are all acting against the decrees of Caesar, saying that there is another king, Jesus" [vs. 7]), nevertheless, in the story in Acts, it is the "city authorities" (politarchs) who are in full charge, and who are responsible both to the city and to Rome. They would hold executive power by the joint authority of senate and people. Although the freedoms granted a "free city" were real, they did not include freedom to recognize "another king."

**Bibliography.** E. D. Burton, "The Politarchs," *AJT*, II (1898), 598 ff.                    F. D. GEALY

**CITY OF DAVID.** *See* DAVID, CITY OF.

**CITY OF DESTRUCTION.** *See* HELIOPOLIS.

**CITY OF MOAB** [עיר מואב] (Num. 22:36). The place where Balak went to meet Balaam; probably the same as AR.

**CITY OF PALM TREES** [עיר התמרים]. A place mentioned as a part of Jericho (Deut. 34:3; II Chr. 28:15) and the residence of the Kenites (Judg. 1:16) and Eglon (Judg. 3:13). Since JERICHO lay in ruins from the time of the Conquest until that of Ahab, and the Kenites were tent-dwellers, the term probably does not refer to the city as such but to the groves of palm trees that flourished nearby.                    S. COHEN

**CITY OF REFUGE** [עיר מקלט] (Num. 35:11-12), intaking cities, *cf.* קלט, Mishnaic Heb. take in, receive=אסף in Josh. 20:4; עיר מועדה (Josh. 20:9), appointed cities]. One of six Levitical cities appointed to receive and give asylum to accidental manslayers.

Among many peoples of antiquity (e.g., Phoenicians, Syrians, Greeks, Romans) certain shrines or sacred precincts were regarded as providing absolute security to fugitives. Innocent and guilty, criminals, runaway slaves, debtors, and political fugitives passed beyond the reach of revenge and justice alike upon attaining sacred ground and claiming the protection of the deity (cf. Tac. Ann. III.60-63). In Israel as well, the altar of Yahweh afforded asylum to fugitives (I Kings 1:50-53; 2:28-34). But biblical law restricted the right of asylum to the accidental homicide alone (Exod. 21:12-14; Num. 35:9-34; Deut. 19:1-13; Josh. 20; *see* CRIMES AND PUNISHMENTS § 2*b*). Its aim was to control blood revenge by making it possible for public justice to intervene between the slayer and the AVENGER OF BLOOD, "that the manslayer may not die until he stands before the congregation for judgment" (Num. 35:12). Ensuring the safety of the accidental homicide was in the vital interest of the whole community: "lest innocent blood be shed in your land . . . and so the guilt of innocent bloodshed be upon you" (Deut. 19:10).

As to the nature of the asylum, Exodus speaks vaguely of a "place" to which the accidental manslayer might flee, going on to say that the murderer must be taken even from the altar to execution (cf. I Kings 2:31-33). Numbers says nothing of the altar, but prescribes that six LEVITICAL CITIES, three on each side of the Jordan, are to be appointed as asylums (Num. 35:6, 13-14). Deut. 4:41-43 records that Moses designated the Transjordanian cities of refuge. Moses further ordered that three more be appointed in Canaan, with the eventual addition of yet another three contemplated when "all the land which [God] promised to give to your fathers" was conquered (19:1-10). That these are Levitical cities is not said in Deuteronomy. Josh. 20:7-8 lists the six cities of refuge as follows: Kedesh, Shechem, and Hebron in Canaan; Bezer, Ramoth-Gilead, and Golan in Transjordan—all priestly or Levitical cities (cf. Josh. 21:13, 21, 27, 32, 36; I Chr. 6:63).

Both the viewpoint and the procedure for dealing with the manslayer vary from source to source. In Numbers the "congregation"—a tribunal outside the asylum—tries the fugitive manslayer. If it finds him innocent of murder, it "rescues" him from the avenger and "returns" him to the city of refuge, where he must remain until the death of the (local?) high priest. If he leaves before, he may be slain with impunity by the avenger. No ransom may be accepted from the manslayer in lieu of his remaining in the asylum (Num. 35:32)—his stay has, then, something of the nature of a punitive detention. Its termination at the death of the high priest was later interpreted—doubtless correctly—as a vicarious expiation of life by life (cf. T.B. Mak. 11a). The old idea of objective BLOODGUILT dominates these laws.

Deuteronomy stresses the responsibility of the community to establish easily accessible asylums for manslayers, and to keep murderers from enjoying immunity in them. Should a murderer flee to a city of refuge, the elders of his home town must send for him and surrender him into the hand of the avenger. Nothing is said of an enforced detention or of a release at the death of the high priest.

Josh. 20 reflects both Numbers and Deuteronomy: the elders—here those of the city of refuge—pass upon the fugitive's right of asylum at his arrival; later the congregation tries him; if innocent, he must remain in the city until the high priest's death.

It is commonly held that the cities of refuge were conceived of by Deuteronomy (which is followed by Numbers) as a replacement of the local altars—abolished by the Deuteronomic reform—that had heretofore served as asylums. Yet even during the period of local sanctuaries provision must have been made for the prolonged protection of the manslayer, for whom the local altar afforded only a temporary refuge. Furthermore, the ancient notion that bloodguilt is objective and defiles the land makes it necessary even for the accidental homicide to expiate his act. In Greece, where a similar notion of bloodguilt prevailed, the unintentional homicide was punished with banishment until the kinsman of the slain person forgave him. Since BANISHMENT is not a biblical penalty, the Israelite analogue to this could only have been an enforced exile of the manslayer from his home town. Moreover, since the law does not permit the kinsman to compose the homicide in any way, another means of expiating the guilt had to be found. The city of refuge, especially as conceived of in Numbers, at once takes account of all these considerations: It secures the life of the manslayer for an indefinite period while at the same time providing for the expiation of his guilt, first by an enforced detention—tantamount to banishment from his home town—and then by the death of the high priest. Viewed in this light, the cities of refuge are necessary adjuncts, rather than later replacements, of the local altars.

The asylums were presumably priestly towns containing important shrines (this is certain for Hebron and Shechem) that had become popular refuges. The six cities were all part of Israelite territory only during the heyday of the United Monarchy, shortly before and after the death of David. The United Monarchy may also be considered the most likely time for such a national program for regulating blood revenge to have been conceived. Deuteronomy transformed the ancient conception by effacing its sacerdotal side: the Levitical character of the cities of refuge—i.e., their being temple cities—as well as the role of the high priest's death, is ignored by Deuter-

onomy, whose doctrine of centralized worship entailed the virtual secularization of the asylums. The law of Numbers alone, whatever be the date of its formulation, preserves the cultic and expiatory features that are the earmarks of antiquity. Thus, although there is no mention of the cities of refuge outside the laws, it appears likely that the laws take their departure from a living custom of the early age.

*Bibliography.* W. R. Smith, *Religion of the Semites* (2nd ed., 1914), pp. 148-49; E. R. Merz, *Die Blutrache bei den Israeliten* (1916), pp. 125-36; M. Löhr, *Das Asylwesen im AT, Schriften der Königsberger Gelehrten Gesellschaft* 7/3 (1930); N. M. Nicolsky, "Das Asylrecht in Israel," *ZAW,* 7 (1930), 146-75; W. F. Albright, "The List of Levitic Cities," *Louis Ginzberg Jubilee Volume,* English Section (1945), pp. 49-73; M. David, "Die Bestimmungen über die Asylstädte in Josua XX," *Oudtestamentische Studiën,* IX (1951), 30-48. For the Greek custom, cf. Demosthenes *Against Aristocrates* [XXIII] 72; B. Dinur, "The Religious Character of the Cities of Refuge . . . ," *Eretz Israel,* III (1954), viii-ix, 135-46; M. Greenberg, "The Biblical Conception of Asylum," *JBL,* LXXVIII (1959), 125-32; Y. Kaufmann, *Sefer Yehoshua'* (1959), pp. 259-70.   M. GREENBERG

**CITY OF SALT.** *See* SALT, CITY OF.

**CITY OF THE SUN** (Isa. 19:18); KJV CITY OF DESTRUCTION. A translation of עיר ההרס (*'îr haheres*), to be emended, on the basis of several MSS, Symm., and Vulg., to עיר החרס (*'îr haḥeres*); generally taken as a reference to HELIOPOLIS.

T. O. LAMBDIN

**CLAMP** [מחברה, *from* חבר, to join] (I Chr. 22:3); KJV JOINING. An iron instrument among the materials prepared by David for use in the construction of the Jerusalem temple.

**CLAN** [משפחה]; KJV FAMILY; DUKE; THOUSAND; TRIBE; DIVISION; GOVERNOR. Alternately: FAMILY (generally); KINDRED (Gen. 24: 38). The word "clan" is used to distinguish a kin group more extensive than the FAMILY, although the Hebrew does not always make such a distinction.

The father's house and kindred, the "whole family" of a widow's husband, a clan united in the Passover sacrifice, and a man's clan which will be cut off for sacrificing a child to the god Molech are examples of biblical usage (Gen. 24:38; Exod. 12:21; Lev. 25:10; II Sam. 14:7). Further, "clan" indicates a technical division of the tribes of Israel (Exod. 6: 14 ff; Num. 3:15 ff; Neh. 4:14—H 4:7).   O. J. BAAB

**CLAROMONTANUS, CODEX** klăr'ə mŏn tăn'əs, —tā'nəs. A sixth-century uncial codex MS of the Pauline letters in Greek and Latin (symbols: Greek, "D^P"; Latin, "*d*"). It is an important witness to the early text of the NT. *See* TEXT, NT; VERSIONS, ANCIENT.

The codex contains 533 vellum leaves measuring 9⅜ by 7⅜ inches. Leaves 162-63 are palimpsest. Their under writing contains fragments of the *Phaethon* of Euripedes. The Greek and Latin texts face each other on opposite pages—the Greek text on the left and the Latin text on the right. Each page contains one column of text with 21 lines of varying length (sense lines) per column. The MS contains all the letters traditionally assigned to Paul (Hebrews follows Philemon). It has suffered some slight mutilation.

The place of origin of the MS is unknown, although it undoubtedly was written in the West. The Greek and Latin texts have not been harmonized to the extent that they have in Codex Bezae. The text is Western.

According to Theodore Beza, the MS was found in a convent at Clermont-en-Beauvais. He acquired it sometime between 1565 and 1582. The codex later (probably at Beza's death in 1605) came into the possession of Claude Dupuy, counselor to the Parlement of Paris. Upon his death, it passed to his sons, Jacques and Pierre. Jacques Dupuy was the king's librarian; and sometime before 1656 the MS was sold to Louis XIV and became a part of the Royal Library. Thirty-five leaves of the codex were stolen in 1707 by an apostate priest, John Aymont. One of these stolen leaves was sold by Aymont in Holland, but it was recovered and returned to Paris in 1720. The other thirty-four leaves were sold to Harley, Earl of Oxford. When his son learned the true identity of the leaves, they, too, were returned to Paris. The MS is now in the Bibliothèque Nationale.

*Bibliography.* F. H. A. Scrivener, *Plain Introduction to the Criticism of the NT* (4th ed., rev. E. Miller; (1894), I, 173-76; C. R. Gregory, *Canon and Text of the NT* (1907), pp. 350-53; W. H. P. Hatch, *Principal Uncial MSS of the NT* (1939), plate XXX; F. G. Kenyon, *Our Bible and the Ancient MSS* (5th ed., rev. A. W. Adams; 1958), p. 212.                M. M. Parvis

**CLASPS** [קרס, *from* קרס, to bend down, crouch down]; KJV TACHES. Alternately: HOOKS (Exod. 35:11; 39:33); KJV TACHES. Gold (Exod. 26:6; 36:13) or bronze (Exod. 26:11; 36:18) fastenings by which the linen curtains and the goatskin hangings of the tabernacle were held together. The veil which separated the Most Holy Place from the rest of the tabernacle was also hung from clasps (Exod. 26:33).
                                        E. M. Good

**CLAUDA.** KJV form of Cauda.

**CLAUDIA** klô′dǐ ə [Κλαυδία, *feminine of* Κλαύδιος, *for* Lat. *Claudius,* from *claudus*(?), lame]. A Christian woman, probably a Roman, mentioned in II Tim. 4:21 as sending greetings to Timothy. In the Apostolic Constitutions VII.46 she is mentioned as the mother (or wife) of Linus, the first "bishop" of Rome. There is also a tradition that she became the wife of Pudens.

*Bibliography.* Conybeare and Howson, *Life and Epistles of St. Paul* (1897), pp. 835, 844.
                                B. H. Throckmorton, Jr.

**CLAUDIUS** klô′dǐ əs. Tiberius Claudius Nero Germanicus, successor of Caligula as Roman emperor (A.D. 41-54). He is named in Acts 11:28; 18:2, and is evidently the Caesar intended in Acts 17:7. Fig. CLA 34.

Claudius was born in 10 B.C.; his father was Drusus, son of Livia and brother of Tiberius. Partly paralyzed, and regarded as stupid by Augustus, Tiberius, and Caligula, he came to the throne only because he was acclaimed by the praetorian guard during the chaos after the murder of Caligula. He

Courtesy of the American Numismatic Society

34. Claudius

repaid their favor with a series of military campaigns, including an invasion of Britain, which became an imperial province.

During his early years of retirement he had developed an intense interest in Roman history and religion, and in 47 he led a revival of Roman religious practices. Like Augustus and Tiberius, he suppressed the religion of the Druids, though there is no evidence that he attacked the popular worship of Isis.

At the beginning of his reign he endeavored to suppress the anti-Jewish activities which Caligula had favored, and Josephus cites some pro-Jewish decrees which come from this period. Probably, though not certainly, his action against Jews at Rome comes from a later period. Speaking of Claudius' treatment of foreign nations, Suetonius (Claudius XXV.3) says that "he expelled from Rome the Jews, who were constantly rioting under the leadership of Chrestus." Since we know that "Chrestus" and "Christus" were pronounced alike, we may assume that Suetonius has at least the name, if not the person, Christus in mind. It is very doubtful that he knew, or even thought he knew, that Christus, the founder of the Christian "superstition," was at Rome under Claudius, even though the Christian father Irenaeus places Jesus' death under this emperor. There were Christian Jews at Rome during Claudius' reign, and from Acts 18:3 we know that Paul's friends Aquila and Prisca were expelled from the city because of Claudius' edict. Presumably what Suetonius knows is that there were Jewish riots in Rome and that these had been related to the claims of someone named Christus. The actual edict of Claudius, discussed more fully by Dio Cassius (LX.6), seems to agree with this analysis. The edict did not actually expel the Jews from the city but forbade their assemblies because of Jewish turbulence. For a devout Jew such a decree could mean only that he would have to leave the city in order to continue his religious observances.

While Claudius rejected divine honors for himself, they were provided for him in the provinces, and in Britain a temple to him was erected at Colchester, the principal Roman base.

Two freedmen, Narcissus and Pallas, were extremely influential during his reign. Narcissus, his private secretary, exposed the plot of the emperor's third wife, Messalina, and confirmed reports of her promiscuity. Pallas, his financial secretary, persuaded him to marry Agrippina, the emperor's own niece, and ultimately to adopt her son Nero. Both freedmen were voted honors by the Senate in recognition of their power.

In the year 54 the emperor was reviewing the problem of the succession and reached the conclusion that his own son (by Messalina) Brittanicus should succeed him, rather than Nero. Before he could make his decision public, Agrippina gave him poison in mushrooms, which Nero called "divine food, since by eating them Claudius became a god" (Dio Cassius LXI.35). Publicly Agrippina and Nero arranged for a magnificent funeral and the deification of Claudius, though Nero's tutor, Seneca, soon derided the ceremony in his *Pumpkinification of Claudius*.

In spite of fiscal reforms and some military successes, the reign of Claudius was marred by domestic infelicity, a good deal of conspiracy and informing, and the emperor's own ineptness. The succession of NERO made a bad situation worse.

*Bibliography.* R. Graves, *I, Claudius* (1934); *Claudius the God* (1935): both of these are novels, but well grounded historically. M. P. Charlesworth, *Documents Illustrating the Reigns of Claudius and Nero* (1939). V. M. Scramuzza, *The Emperor Claudius* (1940).      R. M. GRANT

**CLAUDIUS LYSIAS.** *See* LYSIAS, CLAUDIUS.

**CLAY.** The OT is very skilful in its use of the various Hebrew terms for "clay," although the English translations do not always bring this out. Three different terms were used for a dry native clay and two for a wet native clay. Another designated a worked clay for use by either the potter or the brickmaker, although the clays were prepared differently. Five terms were used for fired clay. POTTERY § 3 discusses some of these technical terms.

Clay was used for the making of both sun-dried and kiln-fired brick. Marly clay was used as a cheap plaster and a floor surface. It also served as a roof covering, for a good marly clay sheds water. Jesus used clay when healing the blind man (John 9:1 ff).

The most skilled craftsman in clay was the potter. He made not only dishes of all kinds, but also toys, idols, cult objects, etc. Cuneiform writing was upon clay tablets. Potsherds were a common writing material when ink was used. Ownership seals were stamped on wet clay. Clay was not only used as a mold in metallurgy but also, when fired, served as a crucible. The clay referred to in Dan. 2:33 was a special type—terra cotta—used in this instance much as cloisonné. *See* POTTERY.      J. L. KELSO

**CLAY TABLETS.** The normal material for writing in Mesopotamia. Clay was ideally suited for this purpose, being always available in large quantities and, unlike papyrus in Egypt, inexpensive. Shaped into tablets when soft, the clay surface was smoothed, and the CUNEIFORM signs were impressed in it with a stylus. When dried or baked, the tablets became hard and almost indestructible. Initiated by the Sumerians, and then adopted by the Semitic Akkadians, the use of clay tablets soon passed to other Western Asiatic peoples such as the Hurrians, Hittites, Elamites, and Canaanites of Ugarit. *See* WRITING AND WRITING MATERIALS. Figs. ASS 101; CLA 35; TEL 10.      R. J. WILLIAMS

35. Clay tablet from Tell el-Amarna (*ca.* 1380 B.C.)

**CLEAN AND UNCLEAN.** To be unclean means to be contaminated by a physical, ritual, or moral impurity; the absence of such impurities constitutes cleanness. These concepts have very ancient rootage in tribal life, and in advanced religions evolve into a system of ritual laws, administered by the priests. At this stage uncleanness is thought of as what is displeasing to the deities or as what belongs to the sphere of the demonic.

OT laws of clean and unclean are applied to persons, foods, places, and objects. Human beings become unclean principally by contact with the dead or with the discharge of one of the body fluids, by the eating of tabooed foods, and by the disease of leprosy. Places and objects are usually clean in themselves and become unclean by contact with something impure. Procedures for purification involve a waiting period of one, seven, or more days; a ritual employing water, fire, or some other cleansing agent; and often a sacrifice of the nature of a sin offering.

Hebrew priestly tradition regarded the laws of cleanness as part of the Mosaic covenant, and essential to the survival of the nation, since violation of them was offensive to the holiness of God and estranged him from his people. In the Prophets, the wisdom literature, and the Psalms there is a tendency to emphasize moral cleanness, but the ceremonial aspects are not set aside, and actually increase in importance during the intertestamental period.

Impurity due to leprosy and to demon-possession are NT themes, but the main direction of NT thought is an almost exclusive emphasis on moral purity, and an abrogation of the dietary laws, necessary in order that the Gentiles might become part of the church.

1. Terminology
   a. Biblical Hebrew
   b. LXX and NT
2. General considerations
   a. Primitive concepts
   b. Evolution of ideas of cleanness
3. Laws of uncleanness
   a. Of persons
   b. Of animals and foods
   c. Of places
   d. Of objects
4. Purification rituals
5. Theology of cleanness
   a. Cleanness and holiness
   b. Uncleanness and sin
   c. Relation to the covenant
   d. Relation to the work of Christ
   Bibliography

**1. Terminology.** The words "clean" and "unclean" and such kindred words as "cleanness," "uncleanness," "cleanse(s)," and "cleansing" appear over five hundred times in English translations of the Bible, chiefly in the priestly laws of Leviticus and Numbers and in the legal parts of Ezekiel. Concepts related to cleanness are purity and impurity; HOLINESS; PROFANE; COMMON; DEFILEMENT; ABOMINATION; and pollution. Altogether the linguistic picture shows that questions of cleanness and uncleanness were major concerns of the biblical writers, and particularly of those who held most closely to the priestly tradition. This is to be expected, because an important part of the priestly function was "to distinguish between the holy and the common, and between the unclean and the clean" (Lev. 10:10; 11:47; 20:25; Ezek. 22:26).

The KJV uses "clean" in the now obsolete sense of "entirely" in such expressions as "clean escaped" (II Pet. 2:18), "clean gone" (Ps. 77:8), and "clean passed over" (Josh. 4:1, 11); the RSV has "clean cut off" in Ezek. 37:11. Also, the process of cleaning grain is mentioned in II Sam. 4:6; Jer. 4:11. Neither of these latter uses will be considered further herein.

**a. Biblical Hebrew.** The basic root for conveying the idea of "cleanness" is טהר (active, "to be clean" [Lev. 15:13; 22:4]; intensive, "to cleanse" [Lev. 16:30; Num. 8:6]; causative reflexive, "to cleanse oneself" [Num. 8:7; Josh. 22:17]; derived nouns טהר, "clearness" [Exod. 24:10] or "purifying" [Lev. 12:4], and טהרה, "cleansing" [Lev. 13:7; Num. 6:9]; adjective, טהור, "clean" [Gen. 7:2; Lev. 11:47]). In the priestly law and in Ezekiel (see also Ps. 51:7—H 51:9) the intensive and causative forms of the verb "to sin" (חטא) are used of purification rituals, and are normally translated "to cleanse" (Lev. 14:52; Num. 19:19; Ezek. 43:20) and "to cleanse oneself" (Num. 19:12-13, 20). The fact that the verb forms in question should mean "offer a sin offering for" indicates the close relationship in OT thought between SIN and uncleanness; both represent a contamination of the true nature by an alient element.

Three words for "cleanness" not found in the technical sense in the priestly literature are: בר (root ברר); the adjective זך and related verbs זכה and זכך; and the adjective נקי (from נקה). The first of these (בר),

judging by its Akkadian cognate, means "to make bright by polishing," and two similar Hebrew words (בר and ברית) are used of the alkali employed in refining metals (Job 9:30; Isa. 1:25) and in making soap (Jer. 2:22; Mal. 3:2). בר is used chiefly in the phrase "the cleanness of one's hands" (II Sam. 22:21, 25; Job 22:30; Ps. 18:20, 24—H 18:21, 25; but cf. Job 11:4), and it refers to moral purity. The second word (זך) is used in the priestly writings of pure frankincense (Exod. 30:34; Lev. 24:7) or olive oil (Exod. 27:20; Lev. 24:2). Outside the priestly writings it appears occasionally with the meaning "morally clean" (Job 15:14; 25:4; 33:9; Ps. 73:13; Isa. 1:16). נקי, basically "to be empty of," is normally rendered "innocent," but refers to "cleanness of teeth" in Amos 4:6, and of hands in Ps. 24:4—the latter indicating moral purity.

The idea of "uncleanness" is expressed by derivatives of the root טמא, the direct opposite of טהר. The verb (טמא) means "to be unclean" (Lev. 15:32; 22:6), the passive form "to defile oneself" (Lev. 11:43; Num. 5:13), the intensive form "to make or declare unclean" (Lev. 13:3, 8, 11, 15; Num. 35:34), the causative reflexive form "to defile oneself" (Lev. 11:43; Ezek. 14:11). The noun (טמאה) means "uncleanness" or "filthiness" (Lev. 5:3; 7:20; Num. 19:13; Ezek. 22:15), and the adjective (טמא) means "unclean" (Lev. 11:35; Isa. 64:6; Ezek. 4:13). The RSV twice translates a noun normally rendered "impurity" (נדה) as "unclean thing" (Ezek. 7:19-20), and gives the intensive passive form of the verb "to defile" (גאל) the meaning "exclude as unclean" (Ezra 2:62; Neh. 7:64).

Fundamentally, to be unclean means to be contaminated by some impurity, as a cloth is contaminated by dirt (Zech. 3:5), or a metal by dross (Dan. 11:35). A clean object or person has no such impurity and possesses its true nature in unadulterated form. Cleanness thus appears as a negative condition; the active, malignant state, calling for protection by taboos and purification rituals, is uncleanness. In keeping with this principle, uncleanness is contagious and transferable from one object to another, while cleanness, the passive state, cannot be transmitted (Hag. 2:10-19).

**b. LXX and NT.** The common LXX word for "clean" is καθαρός (noun καθαρότης, verbs καθαρίζω and καθαίρω). For "uncleanness" negative forms derived from the same root are used (ἀκάθαρτος, ἀκαθαρσία). The general sense is again to be free from, or contaminated with, any form of impurity, whether physical, ritual, or moral. This group of words is used to render all the Hebrew roots discussed above (e.g., טהר in Lev. 7:19; ברר in Hab. 1:13; זכך in Job. 15:15; and נקה in Job. 4:7). A LXX synonym for καθαρίζω is ἐξιλάσκεσθαί (Lev. 12:8; 16:30).

The NT employs concepts of cleanness and uncleanness in ways closely parallel to the OT, and its vocabulary is like that of the LXX, but concepts of cleanness and uncleanness occur relatively infrequently in the NT. The derivatives of καθαρίζω and their negatives are exclusively employed, except that the KJV has "lust of uncleanness" where the RSV reads "lust of defiling passion" (ἐπιθυμία μιασμοῦ) in II Pet. 2:10.

**2. General considerations.** The clean and the unclean take an important place in the religions of tribal societies, and the emphasis continues in modified and developed form in all the religions of mankind. The origins of this type of thought are complex and obscure, and, since cleanness is an inclusive idea incorporating many conflicting and contradictory elements, no logically satisfying account of the practices and beliefs associated with it is possible.

*a. Primitive concepts.* Primitive man makes no real distinction between animate and inanimate nature, but regards the whole universe as infused with a personality or personalities akin to his own. The vital force in the world may be conceived as a diffuse and mysterious presence (e.g., the "mana" of the Melanesians), or it may be made concrete and individual in a hierarchy of gods and demons (e.g., the pantheons of Canaanite, Babylonian, and Egyptian religions). The peoples of ancient Mesopotamia felt the presence of personal powers in everything from the majestic dome of the sky (the god Anu) to the worm which caused toothache.

Since the nonhuman powers may be hostile to man, any object—a rock, a stream, a tree, or an animal—may be dangerous to human life, and the survival of the group demands exclusion from it of the potentially destructive elements in the world about it. This is done by a system of taboos. Certain seasons, kinds of food, types of marriage, etc., introduce alien elements into the life of the group. Such things are unclean, and contact with them renders a person unclean.

Although self-preservation is the fundamental reason for laws of cleanness, a wide variety of secondary reasons may account for any particular object's being regarded as unclean. In sexual intercourse (II Sam. 11:11), birth (Lev. 12), and death (Num. 6:6) potent and mysterious forces are at work, and purification rituals are almost universally associated with these phenomena. Anything repulsive, abnormal, or distorted was likely to be regarded as unclean. Thus, the Israelite priests, whose holy office demanded scrupulous care in matters of purity, could not officiate if any blemish were found on them (Lev. 21:16-24). The pig was unclean for the Hebrews probably because of its extensive use by the Canaanites as a sacrificial animal. Pig bones were found in several Canaanite shrines excavated in Palestine, and the pig was considered sacred in Babylonia, Cyprus, and Syria. Altars with steps, a common pagan type, were prohibited by Israelite law (Exod. 20:26), and the regulation against boiling a kid in its mother's milk (Exod. 23:19; 34:26; Deut. 14:21) is a protest against a well-documented Canaanite practice. Tribal conservatism played a large part in establishing rules of cleanness and uncleanness. The traditional customs were venerated, and any innovation was easily regarded as a source of contamination. The camel, introduced relatively late into the Palestine area, was included with the unclean beasts (Lev. 11:4) probably because it was not one of the foods traditionally accepted among the tribes.

*b. Evolution of ideas of cleanness.* When a religion has developed to the point of possessing a pantheon of deities, uncleanness is defined in relation to the will of these supreme beings. The unclean is repulsive to or prohibited by the gods (Isa. 35:8; 52:1; Ezek. 39:24; Rev. 21:27), or belongs to the sphere of the demonic powers opposed to the gods (Zech. 13: 2; Mark 1:23; Luke 4:33; Acts 5:16). Uncleanness is often described in the OT as an ABOMINATION to Yahweh (Lev. 7:21; 11:10; Deut. 17:1).

The priesthoods of developed religions tend to systematize the laws and practices of clean and unclean, and to bring them into harmony with the theology of the priesthood. In Babylon rituals of purification were concentrated in the most meaningful of the festivals, the New Year celebrations, where they formed part of a developed theological understanding of the relationship of the state to the cosmic order. Similar tendencies are evident in the OT. While many of the laws of cleanness obviously have ancient origins and a long history, they were codified by the priesthood during the monarchy and after the Exile, and appear in systematized form in Leviticus and Numbers. The priests related them to the covenant theology by placing their origin in the Mosaic period and making them an integral part of the formative events which called Israel into existence and defined her nature (*see* COVENANT). The most important of the purification rituals were concentrated in the Day of Atonement. *See* ATONEMENT, DAY OF.

A third line of development runs in the direction of ethical cleanness. When the gods of a nation become concerned for the moral conduct of their worshipers, the concept of "cleanness" inevitably broadens to include ethical purity, "clean hands and a pure heart" (Ps. 24:4). It is possible to distinguish between ritual and moral cleanness, the former being the result of a contaminating element which comes into the life of the individual or nation from outside, and the latter of an act of rebellion arising from an inner defect of the HEART. Jesus makes this distinction very sharply: "There is nothing outside a man which by going into him can defile him; but the things which come out of a man are what defile him" (Mark 7:15). No such clear distinction is made in the OT. Both prophets and priests recognized that, since Yahweh is a moral God, he demands ethical purity, and that sinfulness is a form of uncleanness. The prophets occasionally seem to discount ritual practices and to emphasize ethical conduct as the only binding demand of Yahweh, but, by and large, immorality and ritual uncleanness stand side by side in the OT as equally displeasing to the God of Israel, and the priests consistently treated uncleanness as a form of sin. *See 5b below.*

The close connection between the holy and the clean remains to be noted (*see* HOLINESS). Since a holy person, place, or thing is specially set apart for the service of, or as the property of, the deity, it is removed from common use, filled with divine powers, and potentially dangerous to unauthorized persons who have not taken the proper ritual precautions in approaching it (II Sam. 6:1-8). The holy thing is removed from ordinary life and hedged around by ritual protections similar to those governing an unclean object. It is isolated because it is so close to the deity, while the unclean is isolated because it is so remote from him (*see* § *5a below*). The

COMMON may be put to ordinary uses because it is neither holy nor unclean, but ritually neutral.

**3. Laws of uncleanness. *a. Of persons.*** Since in priestly thought uncleanness was infectious, a human being might incur it by contact with any unclean person or thing (Lev. 5:3); but the law regarded three forms of uncleanness as serious enough to exclude the infected person from society. These were leprosy, uncleanness caused by bodily discharges, and impurity resulting from contact with the dead (Num. 5:2-4).

The appearance of swellings, eruptions, and raw sores on a formerly clear skin has an uncanny quality, which to the ancient mind indicated the work of evil powers or divine judgment on sin. The horrible effects of leprosy and the disfiguring nature of many skin diseases heightened the impression of mysterious forces at work in producing them, and brought them into the realm of the unclean. The Hebrew described such diseases as "leprosy" (צָרַעַת; λέπρα; *see* LEPROSY), and thought of them as producing an uncleanness which lasted until a cure was obtained, or the sufferer died. The uncleanness due to leprosy is mentioned in the story of NAAMAN (II Kings 5), and the full law of leprosy is given in Lev. 13-14. Frequent NT references to the healing of lepers show that OT ideas of the disease continued virtually unchanged into NT times (Matt. 8:1-4; 10:8; 11:5; Mark 1:40-45; Luke 4:27; 5:12-14; 7:22; 17:11-19).

The discharges issuing from the body—blood, semen, menstrual flow, and excretions accompanying childbirth—caused in ancient man irrational revulsion. The semen, ejaculated from the sacred genital organs (Gen. 24:2-3) at the climax of the sexual act and associated with the powerful forces of reproduction, was unclean, and its emission during sexual intercourse produced uncleanness in both the man and the woman (Lev. 15:16-18), or in the man, if discharged by accident (Deut. 23:10). In both cases the period of uncleanness was until evening, but an unnatural discharge from the male organs made the man unclean for seven days after the discharge had ceased (Lev. 15:1-15). A woman's menstrual flow, because of its cyclic occurrence analogous to such important cosmic rhythms as the phases of the moon, its connection with fertility, and its relationship to the life forces contained in the blood, was a potent source of uncleanness (Lev. 15: 19-24; II Sam. 11:4). It produced an impurity of seven days' duration in the woman and in any man who had sexual intercourse with her (Lev. 15:19, 24). Such intercourse was sternly forbidden (Lev. 18: 19; Ezek. 22:10). Analogous to, but more serious than, menstrual impurity was a persistent discharge of blood from a woman (Lev. 15:25-30). Childbirth produced a similar uncleanness, continuing seven days for a male child and fourteen for a girl, with an additional thirty-three- and sixty-six-day period during which the woman was excluded from touching holy things. All discharges produced uncleanness which could be transferred to objects and people by contact. Even the spittle of a man with a discharge made the one on whom it fell unclean (Lev. 15:8).

The dead body of a human being is an object of horror, and, to the primitive mind, of danger as well, for the spirit of the dead might be lurking nearby to do harm to anyone who approached. In the OT priestly laws (Num. 19) contact with a corpse (vs. 11), with a human bone (vs. 16; cf. Matt. 23: 27), or with a grave (Num. 19:16) caused uncleanness and made necessary elaborate purification rituals (vss. 13, 17-19). The need to bury the dead meant that this source of impurity could not be entirely avoided. Priests could bury only members of their immediate family (Ezek. 44:25); the high priest and the Nazirites could not contaminate themselves even for their parents (Lev. 21:11; Num. 6:7). No one unclean by a dead body could celebrate the Passover, but he was allowed to do so a month later (Num. 9:6-11).

A demon, one of the cosmic powers opposed to God, is an "unclean spirit" (ἀκάθαρτον πνεῦμα). When in intertestamental times Judaism developed a demonology under Persian influence (*see* DEMON), insanity was attributed to the presence of an unclean spirit (Matt. 10:1; Mark 1:23-27; Luke 4:36) or an unclean demon (Luke 4:33). The only use of "unclean" in the gospels is in reference to demon-possession (Matt. 12:43; Mark 3:11, 30; 5:2, 8, 13; 6:7; 7:25; 9:25; Luke 6:18; 8:29; 9:42; 11:24; Acts 5:16). In the OT the expression "unclean spirit" (רוּחַ הַטֻּמְאָה) appears once in a late passage (Zech. 13:2) in reference to the spirit of false prophecy, possibly demon-inspired.

Pagan idols and the cult practices associated with them belonged, like the demons, to the sphere of antigod, and rendered Israel unclean, when imported into her worship (Ps. 106:38; Isa. 30:22; Ezek. 24: 13; 36:25; 37:23). The presence of idols, pagan worship, and disregard for Israel's purity laws rendered all foreign lands and peoples unclean (Ezra 9:11; Jer. 43:12; Amos 7:17). In the postexilic period the nationalistic exclusiveness of Judaism became so rigid that anyone who could not prove pure Israelite descent was automatically excluded from the priesthood as unclean (Ezra 2:62; Neh. 7:64). The early church saw the purification of the Gentiles as part of the atoning work of Christ (Acts 15:9; Eph. 2:11-13), and Peter's vision taught him not to call any man common or unclean (Acts 10:28).

It is untrue to say that the concept of ritual uncleanness gradually gave way to a higher, moral conception of purity. In fact, both grew together and in close relationship to each other (*see* § 5*b* below), so that both moral and ritual laws reached their most stringent form in the postexilic Jewish community. Clean hands (II Sam. 22:21, 25; Job 17:9; 22:30; Pss. 18:20, 24—H 18:21, 25; 24:4), a clean heart (Pss. 51:7, 10—H 51:9, 12; 73:13; Prov. 20:9), clean lips (Isa. 6:5), and clean "innermost parts" (Prov. 20: 30) are symbolic of righteousness (II Sam. 22:21, 25; Pss. 18:20, 24—H 18:21, 25) and innocence (Job 11: 4; 33:9; Ps. 51:7, 10—H 51:9, 12; Prov. 20:9). Uncleanness comes from sin (Ps. 51:2—H 51:4; Isa. 64:6), and cleansing from forgiveness and from ceasing to do evil (Isa. 1:16). It will be noted that all these references come from outside the priestly cycle of writings. The NT repudiated the whole corpus of purity laws, food laws most vigorously of all (*see* § 3*b* below), and concentrated almost exclusively on uncleanness caused by lying speech (I Thess. 2:3), licentiousness (Eph. 4:19), and sin (Jas. 4:8). Cleanness is virtually equated with holiness (II Cor. 7:1; I Thess. 4:7).

*b. Of animals and foods.* Since food is taken into the human body, it represents a potential source of uncleanness, and food taboos are an early and important part of purity legislation. Samson's mother was warned against eating any unclean thing before the birth of her son (Judg. 13:4, 7). In the priestly view of human prehistory man was permitted from the Creation to eat green plants (Gen. 1:29-30), and this was not modified in the Mosaic law. If, however, unclean food was used in baking, the bread was unclean (Ezek. 4:12-13). Permission to eat meat came immediately after the Flood, the only restriction being that meat with the blood in it was not to be eaten (Gen. 9:3-4; cf. Lev. 17:14-15; Deut. 12:16, 23). According to priestly tradition the main body of food laws was given by divine revelation during the Mosaic period (Lev. 11; Deut. 14:3-21). In contrast to the priestly theory, the Yahwist represented the distinction between clean and unclean animals as existing in the time of Noah (Gen. 7:2, 8; 8:20).

OT food laws declared unclean any animal which died of itself (Deut. 14:21) or was torn by wild beasts (Lev. 17:15), and any meat which still had blood in it (Gen. 9:4; Lev. 17:14-15; Deut. 12:16, 23) or had touched an unclean thing (Lev. 11:34). In addition the law described those animals which were unclean in themselves, and were therefore called "abominable things" (Lev. 11; Deut. 14:3-21). The Deuteronomic legislation, the older of the two, divided the animal kingdom into four categories: animals (בהמה; Lev. 11:2; Deut. 14:4), water creatures (כל אשר במים; Lev. 11:9; Deut. 14:9), birds (עוף [Lev. 11:13]; צפור [Deut. 14:11]), and winged insects (כל שרץ השרץ; Lev. 11: 20; Deut. 14:19). To this classification Lev. 11:29 added swarming things (שרץ העוף). *See* FAUNA.

Beasts which did not both divide the hoof and chew the cud were unclean. Lev. 11:3-7; Deut. 14: 6-8 specify the camel, the rock badger, the hare, and the swine as unclean, and Deut. 14:4 lists ox, sheep, goat, hart, gazelle, roebuck, wild goat, ibex, antelope, and mountain sheep as clean. Among the water creatures only those with fins and scales were fit for food (Lev. 11:9-12; Deut. 14:9-10). In both books only the birds that are considered unclean are listed: eagle, vulture, osprey, buzzard, kite, raven, ostrich, nighthawk, sea gull, hawk, little and great owl, water hen, pelican, carrion vulture, cormorant, stork, heron, hoopoe, and bat! These birds are unclean probably because they are flesh eaters or scavengers. While Deut. 14:19 makes all winged insects unclean, Lev. 11:20-23 permits the eating of jumping insects, such as locusts, crickets, and grasshoppers. Swarming creatures form a miscellaneous class, including rodents and reptiles (Lev. 11:29-38). Those which crawl on their bellies, go on all fours, or have many feet are unclean, and the weasel, mouse, and several kinds of lizard are specified. All unclean animals produce uncleanness when they are eaten, or when their carcasses are touched or carried (Lev. 11:8, 11, 27-28, 31). The dead bodies of clean animals also produce impurity (Lev. 11:39-40). Animals suitable for food do not have to

be slaughtered at a sacred place (Deut. 12:15, 21).

The fact that the food of all Gentile nations was unclean (Hos. 9:3) posed a difficult problem for Jewish communities living in a foreign environment, and for the early church when it moved out into the Gentile world. There was a clear lead in the teaching of Jesus, who had declared that defilement could not be caused by any external agent (Mark 7:14-23; Luke 11:41), and who ate with tax collectors and sinners (Matt. 9:11; Mark 2:16; Luke 5:30; 7:34). Peter's vision of the sheet lowered from heaven and containing all types of animal, all of which the divine voice pronounced clean and fit for food, provided the church with a mandate to abandon the food laws, and by implication the other purity laws as well (Acts 10:9-16; 11:1-10). Nevertheless, whether or not to observe the Jewish food laws was a subject of controversy between the Judaizing and the Hellenizing branches of the church (Gal. 2:11-13; Col. 2:16). The Council of Jerusalem settled on the formula: Abstain from meat offered to idols, from blood, from things strangled, and from fornication (Acts 15:20, 29), freeing the Gentiles in other respects from the law. Paul's position was that "nothing is unclean in itself" but that Christian love demands a sympathetic understanding of those who are troubled by such matters (Rom. 14:14, 20-21).

*c. Of places.* In the matter of clean and unclean places the OT writers are chiefly concerned to prevent intrusion of the unclean into localities made holy by the presence of Yahweh. The holy soil of Israel could be defiled by oppression (Ezek. 22:24), by idolatrous or prohibited religious practices (Josh. 22:17, 19; Ezek. 36:17), or in Ezekiel's eschatology by the dead bodies of the slaughtered armies of Gog (Ezek. 39:12). The holy city, Jerusalem, might be polluted by sin (Lam. 1:8); by idolatry (Jer. 13:27); by the blood of those killed in its streets (Lam. 4:15); and by the ruin of the temple, which, like an unburied corpse, spread contagion through the city and the surrounding land (Hag. 2:10-19). The entrance of the unclean into the temple, where it would come directly into the presence of the holy God, was the most serious invasion of the holy. Hezekiah, therefore, cleansed the temple from the defilement caused by the apostate religion of Ahaz (II Chr. 29:12-19). Ezekiel prescribed cleansing rituals for altar and sanctuary when they would be re-established after the Exile (Ezek. 43:20-22; 45:18-20). Nehemiah purified the chambers of the temple which had been contaminated by an unclean person, Tobiah (Neh. 13:9). The impressive annual ritual of the Day of Atonement removed the pollution of the sacred place which the sins and impurities of Israel during the year past had caused (Lev. 16, especially vss. 19, 33). During the Maccabean Revolt one of the first acts of the victorious Jewish army was to cleanse the altar and the temple from the profanation to which they had been exposed (I Macc. 4:36-58).

The same concern to protect the holy from the unclean appears in the requirement that remnants of sacrifices be disposed of in a clean place (Lev. 4:12; 6:11), and that human excrement be buried outside the military camp, which in the theology of the holy war was a sacred place (Deut. 23:12-14; *see* WAR,

IDEAS OF). Unclean objects, such as the debris of a leprous house, had to be disposed of in an unclean place (Lev. 14:45).

**d. Of objects.** Objects are not unclean in themselves, but become unclean by contact with impure persons or animals. Exceptions are houses, garments of wool or linen, and leather objects which have contracted leprosy—greenish or reddish spots with a tendency to spread. An infected house was shut up fourteen days, the infected parts were removed, and the building was replastered. If this did not effect a cure, the building was destroyed. Garments and skins, uncured after a fortnight, were burned (Lev. 13:47-59; 14:33-52).

The carcasses of unclean swarming creatures defiled any object they touched, except water in a cistern or spring and dry seed (Lev. 11:29-38). Any type of discharge or the touch of a person with such a discharge contaminated any object, but especially the bed, seat, or saddle occupied by an infected person (Lev. 15:4-12, 17, 20, 26). Pottery vessels and clay ovens contaminated in this way were broken; other objects were washed and returned to use. Uncovered vessels in a dwelling where a dead body lay were unclean (Num. 19:15). Booty captured in war, coming from a foreign environment, was considered impure. Noninflammable material was cleansed by FIRE, other objects by the WATER FOR IMPURITY (Num. 31:21-34).

The Bible also describes objects as clean or unclean in a nonritualistic sense. The human teeth (Amos 4:6), a turban (Zech. 3:5), and the linen shroud which covered Jesus' body (Matt. 27:59) are called "clean," and the verb "cleanse" is applied to the washing of dishes (Matt. 23:25-26) and to shaking lice from a garment (Jer. 43:12). Metaphorically, Ezekiel declares that God has made the wealth in which Jerusalem trusts unclean, and Job insists that not even the heavenly bodies are clean in the sight of God (Job 15:14-15; Ezek. 7:19-20).

**4. Purification rituals.** A complete purification ritual consists of three elements: (*a*) a waiting period, beginning when the source of pollution ceases, as when a discharge stops running (Lev. 15:28), and lasting for one of the sacred units of time or a multiple thereof—one, seven, fourteen, forty, or eighty days; (*b*) a cleansing agent: fire (Num. 31:23), water (Lev. 15:5), blood (Lev. 14:25), or a complex mixture prepared by the priests, such as the "water for impurity" (Num. 19:9); and (*c*) a sacrifice of the type of the sin or guilt offering (*see* SACRIFICES AND OFFERINGS). The seriousness with which the priests viewed any case of uncleanness may be inferred from the duration of the waiting period, the complexity of the cleansing agent, and the elaborateness of the sacrifice.

Secondary infections—i.e., those which did not originate in the person himself but were acquired by contact with uncleanness—were usually "until the evening" (Lev. 11:24-25)—i.e., "when the sun is down" (Lev. 22:7). Exceptions to this general rule were semen, which produced only a one-day uncleanness (Lev. 15:16), and contact with the dead, which rendered unclean for seven days (Num. 19:11). Touching the dead bodies of animals (Lev. 11:24-25, 27-28, 32, 39), eating what dies of itself or is torn

by wild beasts (vs. 40), being in a house sealed up after a death (14:46), being contaminated by the discharge of another person (15:5-8, 10-11, 16-19, 21-23, 27), and preparing or using the "water for impurity" (Num. 19:7-8, 10, 21-22) produced one-day uncleanness. A waiting period of seven days followed contact with a corpse (Num. 19:11, 14; Ezek. 44:26), the birth of a male child (Lev. 12:2), the cure of a leper (14:9), or a discharge of any kind, except semen (15:13, 19, 28). Fourteen-day periods applied to the quarantine of a suspected leper (13:5-6), and to the birth of a female child (12:5). The forty- and eighty-day periods are the length of time during which the mother of a newborn child must stay away from holy things (12:4-5).

Water, the most common agent of purification, is symbolic of cleansing throughout the Bible (Ezek. 36:25; Zech. 13:1; John 13:10; Eph. 5:25-26; Heb. 10:22), and blood has the same symbolic value in more intense form (I John 1:7). In the actual rituals water alone was the normal cleansing agent for one-day uncleanness, the full formula being: Wash the clothes, bathe the body, and be unclean until evening (Lev. 15:5-8, 10-11, etc.). Sometimes only the washing of the clothes (11:25, 28; 14:47), sometimes only the bathing of the body (15:16, 18), is mentioned. Where no washing is specified (11:24, 27, 31, 39), it is probably implied. Washing the hands prevents a man with a discharge from spreading infection by his touch (15:11). Blood alone was used to cleanse the altar (Lev. 16:18-19; Ezek. 43:20) and the holy place (Lev. 16:15-16; Ezek. 45:18-20). Cedarwood, scarlet thread, and hyssop dipped in blood were used for cleansing lepers (Lev. 14:2-9) and leprosy in houses (vss. 49-51). The same ingredients mingled with the ashes of a red heifer and mixed with spring water constituted the "water for impurity," and cleansed from contact with the dead (Num. 19:1-11). *See* BLOOD; CEDAR; HYSSOP; RED HEIFER; SCARLET; WATER FOR IMPURITY.

Sacrifices, often combined with or preceded by ritual washing, were part of the purification following discharges, childbirth, and leprosy. Purification from discharges (except semen and menstrual fluid) required two turtledoves or two young pigeons, one for a sin offering and one for a burnt offering (Lev. 15:14-15, 29-30). After childbirth a lamb and a pigeon or a turtledove were offered (12:6); and a leper who had been healed presented two male lambs, a yearling ewe, three tenths of an ephah of fine flour mixed with oil, and a log of oil (14:10). The poor were allowed to substitute animals of lesser value (Lev. 12:8; 14:21-32; Luke 2:24). The elaborate nature of the leprosy sacrifices—a combination of guilt offering, cereal offering, sin offering, and burnt offering—witnesses to the seriousness attached to leprous uncleanness. *See* LEPROSY; SACRIFICES AND OFFERINGS.

An interesting feature of some purification rituals, showing that the priests regarded uncleanness as an almost physical thing, is the transference of human uncleanness to an animal, which is then sent away and carries the uncleanness with it. This occurs in purification after leprosy. Two birds are provided. The blood of one is used to make the cleansing agent; the other is released alive "into the open field" (Lev. 14:7). This rite recalls the release of the scapegoat on the Day of Atonement. *See* AZAZEL.

**5. Theology of cleanness.** The foregoing sections indicate that questions of cleanness and uncleanness, far from being peripheral matters, were of pressing theological concern to those OT writers most closely associated with the priesthood, and that their importance increased in postexilic times.

*a. Cleanness and holiness.* A pervasive principle of OT theological thought is that Israel should reflect in her community life the character and activity which she ascribes to God. If Yahweh acts in justice, the national conduct should be marked by justice (Amos 5:21-24). If the key to Yahweh's nature is steadfast love, this becomes Yahweh's chief demand on his people (Hos. 4:1-2; 11:1-4). If Yahweh is pre-eminently a holy God, then his people must be peculiarly a holy nation (Exod. 19:6; Num. 15:40; 16:3; Deut. 14:21). Holiness and uncleanness are as incompatible as light and darkness. Therefore, in fulfilling her destiny as a holy nation, Israel must rigidly exclude every form of uncleanness and must protect with special zeal those institutions, such as the priesthood (Lev. 16; Num. 8), the sacrifices (Lev. 7:19-21; 10:14; Num. 9:13; 18:11, 13; Deut. 26:14; II Chr. 30:17-18; Ezra 6:20), and the sacred buildings and vessels (II Chr. 23:19; Isa. 52:11), which were devoted in a unique way to the service of Yahweh. The concern for cleanness is, thus, not merely a set of conventions, inherited from paganism and blindly carried on in Yahwism, but an essential part of Israel's response to the holiness of Yahweh: "You shall be holy; for I the LORD your God am holy" (Lev. 19:2; cf. 11:45; 20:7). *See* HOLINESS.

There is nothing casual or optional in the demand for cleanness. It is a matter of national life and death. Uncleanness in Israel causes Yahweh to turn away his face, and without his saving presence the nation is doomed to exile and destruction (Ezek. 39:24). The same sense of the vital necessity of preserving the cleanness of the nation is seen in Lev. 15:31: "Thus you shall keep the people of Israel separate from their uncleanness, lest they die in their uncleanness by defiling my tabernacle that is in their midst." To profane Yahweh (Ezek. 22:26) by bringing uncleanness into his presence is to negate the holiness of Israel, and to forfeit Yahweh's protecting presence. At the end of the present age, when Israel is finally redeemed, all uncleanness will be excluded (Isa. 35:8; 52:1; Rev. 21:27).

It appears, then, that the distinction between holy and unclean is not simply a religious but a cosmic division, running through the whole universe and dividing animals, objects, and places into two categories which could be mingled only at the gravest peril. The priests were repeatedly charged to maintain the distinction between these incompatible aspects of reality (Lev. 10:10-11; 11:47; 20:25-27; Ezek. 22:26; 44:23). The incipient dualism which existed in the distinction between clean and unclean became more explicit when Jewish thought was exposed to Persian influences. The unclean was then identified with the demonic powers of darkness, which war against the forces of light. In the Manual of Discipline of the Qumran Community (*see* DEAD

SEA SCROLLS) "ways of defilement in the service of uncleanness" are included among the works of the spirit of darkness. The demons that cause insanity are regularly called "unclean spirits" in the NT.

*b. Uncleanness and sin.* The priestly literature does not distinguish moral wickedness from impurity. The law of jealousy in Num. 5 deals with cases of suspected adultery by means of the ordeal of the WATER OF BITTERNESS. Here a case of moral delinquency is named and treated as a problem of uncleanness (vs. 28). In like manner sin and guilt offerings are extensively used in purification rites (*see* § 4 *above*), and the ritual of the Day of Atonement removes simultaneously the accumulation of guilt for both sin and uncleanness (Lev. 16:16, 30). The Levitical law frequently uses "sin" and "uncleanness" as synonyms (5:3-4).

The Israelite cultus did not claim the power to remove the source either of sin or of uncleanness by ritual means. Only God could "bring a clean thing out of an unclean" (Job 14:4). The creation of a clean heart is the exclusive work of God (Ps. 51:10—H 51:12), and he may forgive apart from the "sanctuary's rules of cleanness" (II Chr. 30:19; cf. Isa. 4:4; Ezek. 36:25, 29; Zech. 3:4). Therefore, OT purification rituals could begin only after the source of infection had been removed, as when a leper was healed (*see* §4 *above*). Moral iniquity is a form of uncleanness of which the source is the inner life of the sinner, and unless God forgives the sin, the source of defilement remains. Deliberate and unrepented sin is, consequently, a continuing source of pollution which renders purification rituals useless.

When, however, the originating cause of uncleanness has been removed, a stain is left which continues unless and until taken away by the prescribed ritual. Involuntary transgressions and those for which forgiveness is sought likewise leave a stain on the individual and the nation. It is this "uncleanness of sin" with which the cult is competent to deal, by removing the continuing impurity left by forgiven sin or removed infection. Because the Jewish priests could not deal with the source of impurity, whether external or internal, without encroaching on the prerogative of God, they had no need to draw a sharp line between sin and ritual impurity. Although their theology conceived uncleanness in quasi-physical terms, there can be no doubt that the cultic purifications which they performed for the people fulfilled an important psychological function by relieving the worshipers of the debilitating sense of guilt and by mediating to them assurance of forgiveness and cleanness.

*c. Relation to the covenant.* The mighty act of God, which above all others revealed his holiness, was the deliverance of Israel from Egypt and the making of the covenant at Sinai. A priori, therefore, it appears likely that priestly theology would connect its laws of cleanness with these crucial events. This is done by the device of projecting back the Holiness Code, the Priestly Code, and Deuteronomy to the Mosaic period and representing them as secondary to and explanatory of the covenant itself. The connection is explicitly stated in Lev. 11:45: "I am the LORD who brought you up out of the land of Egypt, to be your God; you shall therefore be holy, for I am holy," a formula reminiscent of the beginning of the Ten Commandments (Exod. 20:2; Deut. 5:6; cf. Lev. 19:36; Num. 15:41). *See* COVENANT.

The structuring of the cleanness laws into the covenant theology not only gave them Mosaic sanction, but also made them unequivocally binding on Israel. The God who had delivered the nation, and who as its king gave the nation his law, had included the purity laws as part of his will. There was, therefore, no possibility of evading them as trivial or of regarding them as of lesser importance than the moral laws. They were part of the constitution of Israel's national life, and their observance was an inescapable necessity if the obligations of the covenant were to be met. The Zadokite Document, dating probably from the first century B.C., repeats and expands OT purity laws as part of the legislation for the community of the new covenant. *See* DEAD SEA SCROLLS.

*d. Relation to the work of Christ.* In the NT, concepts of cleanness and uncleanness are peripheral and metaphorical. Paul reversed the OT view that uncleanness was contagious while holiness was not (*see* §1*b above*). In a marriage between a Christian and an unbeliever, the Christian consecrates the other partner, and the children are "holy" (I Cor. 7:14). This usage is plainly *argumentum ad hominem*, and is in no way central to the apostle's thought.

Since the NT eliminates the concept of ritual uncleanness coming from external sources and concentrates on moral impurity arising from within (*see* § 3*a above*), its theology of uncleanness is reduced to a minor aspect of the doctrine of atonement (Heb. 10:22; Jas. 4:8; I John 1:9; *see* ATONEMENT). Cleansing is part of the redeeming work of Christ in his office as High Priest. He cleanses the disciples by his word (John 15:3), and, symbolically, by washing their feet (13:10). The NT applies the metaphor of the sin offering to the work of Christ, whose blood cleanses from all sin (I John 1:7) and who gives himself for the church and cleanses her by water and the word (Eph. 5:25-26). OT cleansing agents typologically foreshadow the water of Christian baptism (Eph. 5:25-26). The Letter to the Hebrews, the most priestly of NT writings, condemns OT rituals as inadequate because they had to be continuously repeated (Heb. 10:2), and declares that Christ, the perfect High Priest, sprinkles the heart clean from an evil conscience and washes the body with pure water (vss. 21-22).

*Bibliography.* R. Smith, *The Religion of the Semites* (1889), pp. 140-388. B. Stade, "Die Eiferopfertorah," *ZAW*, 15 (1895), 166-75. A. Menes, "Tempel und Synagoge," *ZAW*, 50 (1930), 268-81. D. J. Hänel, *Religion der Heiligkeit* (1931). I. Benzinger, *Hebräische Archäologie* (1937), pp. 401-402. J. Pedersen, *Israel*, I-II (1926), 474-96; III-IV (1940), 264-95, 447-65. R. Otto, *The Idea of the Holy* (trans. J. W. Harvey; 10th ed., 1946), pp. 117-35. W. Eichrodt, *Theologie des ATs*, I (1948), 57-81. H. Frankfort *et al.*, *Before Philosophy* (1949), pp. 11-38.

L. E. TOOMBS

**CLEMENT** klĕm'ənt [Κλήμης] (Phil. 4:3). An individual living in Philippi; one of Paul's fellow workers (συνεργοί) in the establishment of this first Pauline church in Europe. Clement is here distinguished as one whose name is written "in the book of life," while the others whose names are so written

are referred to as "the rest"; so Clement occupied a place of special esteem in Paul's memory of his days in Philippi. Perhaps this mode of mentioning Clement indicates that he was no longer living. The context in which Clement is mentioned shows that he—living or not—would be a favorable factor in the efforts to which Paul was exhorting his "true yokefellow" to bring about a Christian reconciliation between Euodia and Syntyche, two women of Philippi, who had worked with Paul and Clement and the rest in the establishment of the Philippian church.

Attempts to identify this individual with Clement of Rome (*see* CLEMENT, EPISTLE OF) fail for lack of evidence that this Clement ever went to Rome, and because of the chronological difficulty in thinking that this Clement—already quite mature, or possibly dead—could have lived until the end of the first century, when Clement of Rome was active. Also, the name is so common that identifications are precarious unless supported by evidence other than the name.

J. M. NORRIS

*CLEMENT, EPISTLES OF.** Two documents, the first a letter, the second a homily, attributed since the second century to Clement, reputed disciple of Peter and third Bishop of Rome; appended to the NT in Codex A; included in all modern editions of the APOSTOLIC FATHERS. I Clement has a good claim to authenticity. An extant Latin translation of it, made in the second century, is probably the oldest surviving piece of Latin Christian literature. There is also a Syriac version. The reason for the attachment of Clement's name to the homily known as II Clement, however, is, to date, an unsolved problem. The two documents have no inherent connection and will therefore be treated separately.

**1. I Clement.** This is an official communication of the church in Rome, dispatched with an embassy of three of its senior members, to the church in Corinth. The occasion of this missive was the deep concern at Rome over a factional dispute in Corinth created when certain younger members of the church there succeeded in deposing from the ministry elder men of the hierarchy, for reasons—whether theological or personal, but in any case not moral—that are not clearly indicated. The Roman church took strong exception to this deposition as an affront to the revealed will of God for the orders of ministry in the church, and to the arrangements made by the apostles before their death for a due succession of ordained men as bearers of their authority. The letter is thus of great importance for the development in the church of the threefold orders of bishops, elders, and deacons, and for the emergence of a theory of apostolic succession in the ministry. *See* MINISTRY, CHRISTIAN.

The situation at Corinth is utilized by the author as an opportunity to impart, with utmost gravity and dignity, a considerable amount of exhortation to the Christian virtues of faith, compassion, humility, self-control, and hospitality; and warnings against the unseemly vices of factiousness, jealousy, envy, doublemindedness, and pride. Christian ethic and piety are grounded in the beneficent creation and providential activity of God, and in the distinguished examples of humble and steadfast endurance of holy men and women in all ages. Among the noted witnesses of "recent" times, the author refers (ch. 5) to the patient endurance of martyrdom, because of jealousy and envy and strife, of the "good apostles" Peter and Paul.

The writer of I Clement has an excellent command of the LXX Version of the OT, and cites from all parts of it, copiously and, when it suits him, with considerable textual liberties. Three apocryphal passages (17:6; 23:3; 46:2) are cited as scripture, but remain otherwise unknown. He also uses Christian sources, though they are never advanced with the scriptural authority of the OT. He recalls sayings of Jesus (13:2; 46:8—similar to but not textually identical with any canonical gospel). He knows and quotes Paul's letters, especially Romans, I Corinthians, and Ephesians (ch. 49 is a hymn to "love" modeled upon I Cor. 13). He is also quite conversant with the Letter to the Hebrews. Chs. 59-61 contain a remarkably fine example of early Christian liturgical prayer of supplication, easily identifiable as a form that ultimately stems from the Jewish synagogue of the Dispersion. Many critics believe that chs. 33–34 also reflect a liturgical preface and *Sanctus* adapted from the synagogue.

Clement's style betrays marked influence from the rhetoric of the Hellenistic diatribe, and his vocabulary shows acquaintance with Stoic, and to a lesser degree Platonic, terms. Church tradition has identified the author with the Clement mentioned in Phil. 4:3, as also with the Clement spoken of by Hermas (*Visions* II.4.3). His name strongly suggests that he was related in some way with the household of the imperial Flavian Dynasty. The ancient basilica of San Clemente, one of the oldest parish churches of Rome, is thought by many archaeologists to stand on the site of his home.

The chronological limits for the writing of I Clement are set by its use of NT documents such as Hebrews and Ephesians, on the one hand, and by the extensive influence of the letter manifest in the Epistle of Polycarp (*see* POLYCARP, EPISTLE OF). But a reference to recent persecution at Rome in 1:1 has persuaded almost all critics that I Clement was composed in A.D. 95 or 96, shortly following the persecution associated with DOMITIAN.

**2. II Clement.** This homily was preached to Gentile converts following a lesson read from Isa. 54:1 ff (cf. 2:1; 17:3; 19:1). It deals principally with ethical themes—repentance, self-control, and watchfulness in view of the coming judgment. The principal theological interest of the homily is the speculation in ch. 14 concerning the spiritual church, pre-existent before creation.

In 2:4, the preacher cites Matt. 9:13 as scripture; and he also shows acquaintance with Luke, the Pauline letters, Hebrews, and possibly I Peter. Several noncanonical gospel sayings are employed, one of them derived from the apocryphal Gospel According to the Egyptians. There is likewise an unknown "prophetic word" quoted in 11:2 ff, which was also used in I Clem. 23:3, and which bears some relation to the apocryphon cited by Paul in I Cor. 2:9.

These indications suggest a date for the homily sometime toward the middle of the second century.

As a place of origin, Rome, Corinth, and Alexandria have all had their advocates. It is possible that Irenaeus (Her. IV.3.2) shows acquaintance with II Clement, alongside his summary of I Clement.

*Bibliography.* See the texts, translations, commentaries, and bibliographies under APOSTOLIC FATHERS.

For I Clement: J. B. Lightfoot, *The Apostolic Fathers,* pt. 1: *S. Clement of Rome* (2 vols.; rev., 1890); G. Bardy, "Expressions stoiciennes dans la Ia Clementis," *Recherches de science religieuse,* XII (1922), 73-85; A. von Harnack, *Einführung in die alte Kirchengeschichte . . . I. Clemensbrief* (1929); F. Gerke, *Die Stellung der ersten Clemensbriefes innerhalb der Entwicklung der altchristlichen Gemeindeverfassung und des Kirchenrechts, Texte und Untersuchungen zur Geschichte der altchristlichen Literatur,* vol. XLVII, no. 4 (1931); W. K. L. Clarke, *The First Epistle of Clement to the Corinthians* (1937); P. Meinhold, "Geschehen und Deutung im ersten Clemensbrief," *Zeitschrift für Kirchengeschichte,* LVIII (1939), 82-129; L. Sanders, *L'Hellénisme de saint Clément de Rome et le Paulinisme* (1943); A. W. Ziegler, *Neue Studien zum ersten Clemensbrief* (1958).

For II Clement: J. B. Lightfoot (*see above*); R. Harris, "The Authorship of the so-called Second Epistle of Clement," *ZNW,* XXIII (1924), 193-200; G. Krüger, "Bemerkungen zum zweiten Clemensbrief," in S. J. Case, ed., *Studies in Early Christianity* (1928), pp. 419-39; B. H. Streeter, *The Primitive Church* (1929), pp. 244-53.

*See also the bibliographies under* MINISTRY, CHRISTIAN; ROME (CHURCH).                                M. H. SHEPHERD, JR.

**CLEOPAS** klē′ə pəs [Κλεοπᾶς, *probably a shortened form of* Κλεόπατρος]. One of the two disciples who were confronted by the risen Jesus on the road to Emmaus (Luke 24:18). The other is not named. Tradition gives the name Simon to the companion and includes both among the Seventy of Luke 10:1-24. Cleopas is sometimes identified with CLOPAS. The connection is not impossible, but in the absence of clear supporting evidence it must remain uncertain.                                H. H. PLATZ

**CLEOPATRA** klē′ə pā′trə, —pā′trə [Κλεοπάτρα]. The name given to the queens of Egypt in the Ptolemaic Dynasty, four Ptolemies having had wives by that name. The Cleopatra of Add. Esth. 11:1 is thought to have been the wife of Philometor (181-146 B.C.). To them was brought the translated letter concerning Purim. Onias, son of the high priest of that name, when he saw the wicked Alcimus installed in the high priesthood, fled to Ptolemy Philometor, "king of Egypt; and when he found he was in great esteem with him, and with his wife Cleopatra, he desired and obtained a place in the Nomus of Heliopolis, wherein he built a temple like to that in Jerusalem" (Jos. Antiq. XII.x.7). It was the citation by Onias of the prophecy in Isa. 29:19 which won over Cleopatra and her husband (Jos. Antiq. XIII.iii.1).

The Cleopatra of I Macc. 10:57-58 is thought to have been the daughter of the above. The younger Cleopatra was given in marriage to Alexander Balas after he had taken the kingdom of Syria, following the slaying of Demetrius. Her father "celebrated her wedding at Ptolemais with great pomp, as kings do" (I Macc. 10:58; Jos. Antiq. XIII.iv.1). Some consider that Ps. 45 was either written or edited as an epithalamium on this occasion. Hearing later that Alexander was involved in a plot on his life, "Ptolemy blamed himself for having given his daughter in marriage to Alexander, and for the league he had made with him to assist him against Demetrius; so he dissolved his relationship to him, and took his daughter away from him" (Jos. Antiq. XIII.iv.7), and gave her to Demetrius.　　　　　J. C. SWAIM

**CLEOPHAS.** KJV form of CLOPAS.

**CLERK, TOWN.** See TOWN CLERK.

**CLOAK;** KJV CLOKE. The translation of several words referring to outer garments. See DRESS AND ORNAMENTS § A1.

**CLOPAS** klō′pəs [Κλωπᾶς; cf. Palmyrian קלופא] (John 19:25); KJV CLEOPHAS klē′ə fəs. The husband (or son or father) of one of the women who stood at the foot of the cross. No certain reference to him appears elsewhere in the NT, though he is sometimes identified with CLEOPAS and/or ALPHAEUS. There is no linguistic relationship between "Cleopas," a genuine Greek name, and "Clopas," which seems to be of Semitic origin. Grammarians recognize that the names may commonly have been interchanged, but this is hardly sufficient grounds for assuming personal identity. There is no indication that the Clopas named in John 19:25 was also known as Cleopas or that the names have been interchanged in the transmission of the text. The connection with Alphaeus can be established only if MARY the wife of Clopas is the same person as Mary the mother of James and Joses (Mark 15:40 = Matt. 27:56; cf. Luke 23:49; 24:10), and if the James mentioned here is the same as JAMES (2) son of Alphaeus (Mark 3:18 = Matt. 10:3 = Luke 6:15; Acts 1:13). Mary the wife of Clopas may thus be recognized as the wife of Alphaeus, and it is possible to suppose that Alphaeus and Clopas are the same person. Since other alternatives are present in each of the preliminary suppositions, as well as in the final identification, the question must remain undecided. "Clopas" can hardly be explained as a variant transliteration of חלפי, the Aramaic or Hebrew form from which "Alphaeus" is derived.

Efforts to connect Clopas, and therefore Alphaeus and his sons, with the family of Jesus, are based on the inference that only three women are named in John 19:25 (cf. Mark 15:40 = Matt. 27:56). Mary the wife of Clopas must then be identified as the sister of Jesus' mother. The text permits such an identification, but it certainly does not require it. In this connection it is interesting to note that Hegessipus mentions a brother of Joseph whose name was Clopas (Euseb. Hist. III.11; 32.1-4, 6; IV.22.4).

　　　　　H. H. PLATZ

**CLOSET** [חדר (Judg. 3:24; KJV CHAMBER); KJV חפה (Joel 2:16; RSV "chamber"); KJV ταμεῖον (RSV "room" in Matt. 6:6; "private room" in Luke 12:3)]. See CHAMBER; ROOM.

**CLOTH.** Because fabrics disintegrate in wet climates, not many of those made in Bible times have survived in Palestine, and the Bible references to fabrics give us a very hazy notion of what was made and almost no idea of how it was made. E.g., in Gen. 37:3 we find the vague phrase "long robe with sleeves" (KJV "coat of many colors"; cf. II Sam. 13:18-19).

John 19:23, speaking of Jesus' robe, reads: "His tunic was without seam, woven from top to bottom." Exod. 28:32, referring to a priest's robe, is not much more definite, but it does suggest that there was a customary way of making an opening for the head: "It shall have in it an opening for the head, with a woven binding around the opening, like the opening in a garment, that it may not be torn."

Exod. 26:2 gives us some exact dimensions of the curtains for the tabernacle: "The length of each curtain shall be twenty-eight cubits, and the breadth of each curtain four cubits" (ca. six feet). Vs. 8 mentions a length of thirty cubits but the same four cubits' width. This suggests that four cubits or ca. six feet was a standard width for curtains, though apparently they could be any length. The materials to be used in the fabrics for the tabernacle were fine twined linen, blue and purple and scarlet stuff, and goats' hair. The directions call for cherubim to be skilfully worked on the inner curtains and the veil, and for the screens for the door of the tent and for the gate of the court to be embroidered with needlework.

For the holy garments (Exod. 28:5) gold was added to the other materials. The coat was to be woven of checker work. There are no specific directions as to how to spin, how to weave, what type of loom to use, or the shape of the garments.

1. Archaeological specimens
2. Vegetable fibers
   *a.* Spinning
   *b.* Location and preparation
   *c.* Colors
3. Animal fibers
   *a.* Effect of climate and fodder on wool
   *b.* Colors and dyeing centers
4. Looms
   *a.* Egyptian vertical
   *b.* Greek vertical
   *c.* Horizontal
5. Weaving customs
   *a.* Long warp
   *b.* Shaping of garments
   *c.* Pairing yarns for strength
6. Interpretation of Bible texts
Bibliography

**1. Archaeological specimens.** Although few textiles have been preserved in Palestine, many are found in the dry climate of Egypt; and, as textiles are easy to carry either by boat or by camel, some may have come from Palestine. There are specimens six feet wide, as well as narrow tapes. There are textiles made of linen and textiles made of wool. Plain and patterned specimens have been found of both. The method of WEAVING was uniformly simple and therefore did not require mention, but the workmanship was in many cases extraordinary. However, we see at a glance that these specimens by themselves will not answer all our questions, for the colors do not confine themselves to the "blue and purple and scarlet" of the Bible, but cover the whole spectrum (cf. the "many-colored robes" in Ps. 45:14). There is little that seems to us like embroidery at first sight. But by studying the fabrics and ancient texts together we may be able to reconstruct much of the technology of the period and bring to light once more many points which were common knowledge in a nomadic society and so were referred to by formula instead of being described in detail. As natural phenomena and weaving habits are almost entirely unknown or forgotten in our modern urban economy, we do not understand the Bible texts. To rediscover the fascinating set of circumstances contributing to the evolution of man-made fabrics, let us start with the four fibers most used in making cloth.

**2. Vegetable fibers.** Flax and cotton are vegetable fibers. The people who cultivated them had to stay in one place long enough to sow and reap. They were luxuries in lands where the economy was based on flocks and herds. Conversely, sedentary people who grew crops were not so well supplied as shepherd folk with hides and leather from which to make clothing and shelter. Consequently, in all parts of the world it seems to have been the vegetable fibers which were first spun in order to make continuous yarns for weaving.

**a. Spinning.** In fact, it was probably the vegetable fibers themselves which suggested the idea of spinning to man, for when vegetable fibers are wet, they turn as they dry. Flax turns in the direction of the center part of the letter "S"; cotton turns quite actively in all directions but apparently rather more in the "Z" direction than in the "S." Flax was a medium-length fiber—12 to 20 inches—but the cotton in Bible lands was very short, 1¼ inches at most. Flax, therefore, was the easier fiber to spin, and the spinning in Egypt, where it was the principal fiber, followed the lead of the flax itself and turned in the "S" direction. This method of spinning reached the boundaries of Egypt's influence. Cotton from India, where it seems to have originated, was Z-spun, and this method traveled W over the trade routes. Vegetable fibers have been spun since the Stone Age, when sheepskins were being used whole and felt was made with the wool shed by sheep and goats. Wool began to be spun in the Bronze Age, but the practice became much more common in the Iron Age, when the invention of shears made it possible to shear sheep instead of plucking the wool. By this time both vegetable spinning crafts were well established, and either or both were adopted by people with wool to spin, since animal fibers have no innate preference as to direction of spin. By Bible times spinning was traditional and did not warrant description. (It may be said here parenthetically that when linen yarns are found Z-spun, they are mostly of superior quality, and we know that we have to do with a spinner trained on cotton, who could hardly fail to make good thread with a fiber ten times as long and much less active, even when he spun it the way it did not want to go. There is no evidence to show that linen spinners spun cotton, though wool spinners did so on occasion.)

**b. Location and preparation.** Flax grew abundantly in Egypt. The Pharaohs gave garments of fine linen* as presents, together with gold and jewels (Gen. 41:42). The chief characteristic of Egyptian linen was its softness and pliability. Clothes made of it were comfortable to wear, and sails did not cut themselves in a gale (cf. the fine embroidered linen from Egypt

used in the ship's sails in Ezek. 27:7). This pliability seems to have been produced by steeping or retting the flax in running water to decompose the woody parts of the stem and liberate the linen fibers; flax laid out on the roofs to be retted by the dew (Josh. 2:6)—Rahab's method in Jericho—produced fibers which were stiff and brittle. Some flax grew in Palestine, the linen of Galilee being likened to Egyptian linen, but most of the export linens other than the Egyptian came from Syrian towns. Solomon sent to Tyre for a man trained to work in fine linen (II Chr. 2:13-14). Greek historians tell us that the flax industry was very old in ancient Mesopotamia, and the Bible mentions cotton fabrics in Assyria. The cotton tree was introduced into Assyria *ca.* 700 B.C. by King Sennacherib, and over two centuries later we find "cotton curtains," both white and blue (Esth. 1:6), at the king's palace in Susa, with linen and

From *Workshop Notes*, no. 18 (The Textile Museum, Washington, D.C.); by permission of Louisa Bellinger

36. 1*a-b*) Tunic "without seam, woven from top to bottom" (John 19:23), with neck opening and sleeves; (2*a-b*) Egyptian gown of Dynastic times, of plain linen with a hole for the head in the middle of the weave; (3) Asiatic garment with arms bare and scallop at the bottom; (4) Egyptian plain white kilts, uniform in width

wool being used for the cords. Cotton grew in many lands, but it seems to have been spun only in countries with a damp or humid climate, which helped keep the short fibers together during the process. Isa. 19:9 probably refers to Upper Egypt or the Sudan, where cotton was indigenous. The climate of Lower Egypt seems to have been too dry to allow cotton to be spun there. Fig. CLO 36, nos. 2*a-b*.

**c. Colors.** In earlier Bible times, as in the Roman period, linen and cotton were used undyed, with certain exceptions. Cotton could be dyed or printed with indigo (Esth. 1:6); linen was harder to dye, but occasional blue threads either in warp or in weft do decorate some otherwise plain linen fabrics such as were found in the Scroll Caves and at Dura-Europos on the Euphrates. That the robe of the ephod (Exod. 28:31) was to be made all of blue shows how very special it was.

**3. Animal fibers.** Silk and wool are the two animal fibers most used for fabrics. Silk at our period was still largely confined to the Far East. The economy of Bible lands, except for Egypt, was based on wool. Sheep and goats were raised in many places, but few people nowadays stop to think what fodder and climate do to wool.

*a. Effect of climate and fodder on wool.* Sheep raised at high altitudes grow a special undercoat of fine wool to keep them warm. Those raised at sea level may not grow this undercoat, because they do not need it. According to Matthews (*Textile Fibers*) the wool in Egypt today is coarse and medium long, in Syria long and very resilient, in Asia Minor long and medium fine. This agrees with the archaeological specimens. Wool in Asia Minor is clear white; in the Caucasus and Upper Mesopotamia it contains a series of colors from clear white through yellow, tan, and chocolate brown, to dark brown. Thus we see that even today food and climate seem to produce the same basic results as they did in the time of the patriarchs, for though Laban removed "every speckled and spotted sheep and every black lamb, and the spotted and speckled among the goats" (Gen. 30:32-34), Jacob seems to have had little difficulty breeding speckled and spotted sheep and black lambs at Paddan-aram. In Anatolia he might not have managed it.

*b. Colors and dyeing centers.* This story points up the fact that there were many natural colors in wool which could be separated or used together. It seems also to have been customary to dye animal fibers. Therefore, any color mentioned in the Bible except blue, which was used sparingly on cotton or linen also, connoted wool. The reiteration of "blue and purple and scarlet stuff" in such places as Exod. 26:1 sounds as if these were the only three colors available. However, indigo dyed on white wool could give a light or medium dark blue; if dyed on gray wool, it would be darker still; on yellow wool it produced green. Madder or kermes on white would give red or pink; on yellow, orange; on gray, garnet. In fact, with a blue dye and a red dye and the natural colors in wool itself, the weaver had at his disposal a complete palette. By dyeing first with blue and then with red he could even approximate the Tyrian purple, which was such an expensive color. The habit of dyeing wool before spinning gave yet another method of achieving gradation of color, for wools of various natural shades or dye lots were often spun together to make a desired effect. In Palestine dyers were concentrated in certain towns. There was the "Magdala of the dyers" on the River Jarmuk. At Tell Beit Mirsim, Albright identified a house containing stone vats and weights as a dyers' workshop. Similar vats were found at Gezer, which in Hellenistic times and probably earlier too was an important dyeing center, as were also the "town of byssus" Beth-Asbea and Luz, a center for blue stuffs.

**4. Looms.** Three kinds of looms were in common use in Bible times. Of the two types of vertical looms Herodotus tells us that the Egyptians were the only people to use their loom, while all other peoples used the Greek type. Palestine, therefore, probably used the types discussed in §§ *4b-c below.*

*a. Egyptian vertical.* The Egyptian loom had two beams, a warp beam at the top and the cloth beam at the bottom. Two weavers stood, one on each side of the loom, and passed the shuttle back and forth through alternating sheds, beating the weft down. The fabrics made on this loom were sturdy, for

Courtesy of the Metropolitan Museum of Art

37. Egyptian wall painting of the Twelfth Dynasty, showing women weaving and spinning

gravity helped pack the wefts in tightly. As linen was a strong, sleek fiber, the Egyptians set their warps close together and put in a lesser number of wefts. Fig. CLO 37.

*b. Greek vertical.* The Greek loom used extensively for weaving wool had the cloth beam at the top and loom weights on the bottom of the warps. The weaver stood in front of this loom and beat the weft upward. Wide fabrics could be made, since the weaver was mobile. A whole shed was not opened at once on this loom. The wefts were darned or embroidered past five or six warps at a time, and this section was beaten up before the next section was put in. Near Eastern wool was springy and had many scales which caught at and clung to anything they touched. Consequently, wool warps were spaced and were usually entirely covered by the wefts, which were beaten up close to make compact fabrics. The weaving process was slow, but the fact that the weft traveled short distances at a time led to the weaving of color patterns, for it was as easy to substitute a new color for a space as to continue the old one.

*c. Horizontal.** This loom was an easy type for nomadic peoples to carry with them. It consisted of two beams held in place by four pegs driven into the ground. The weaver sat in front of the loom, which was generally narrower than those in §§ *4a-b above.* Since a whole shed was opened at once for the weft, the width had to be confined to the reach of the weaver's arms, or in some cases, to the reach of two weavers sitting side by side. This was obviously the loom mentioned in Judg. 16:13-14, which Delilah used when weaving the seven locks of Samson's head into her web; otherwise Samson would have had to sit up while sleeping. Both wool and linen were woven on this loom, and it was probably the loom on which linen weavers first tried weaving wool patterns into linen webs. Because linen yarns were so much finer than most wool, several linen warps had to be grouped together to approximate

38. Egyptian model of a weaving shop with horizontal loom, found near Girgeh, Upper Egypt, Twelfth Dynasty (1990-1780 B.C.)

the size and spacing of wool warps, or the pattern would not lie flat. Unless a linen weaver wove a pattern band across the whole web, he was plagued with the question of how to connect the pattern and background areas, for he threw his linen weft across the web in an open shed, but the pattern weft inched its way along, being embroidered on the grouped warps. Narrow tapes were woven on this loom, as well as wider fabrics. Fig. CLO 38.

5. **Weaving customs.** The specifications for the curtains for the tabernacle (Exod. 26:1-2, 7-8) show us that four cubits or six feet was a standard width for both linen and wool materials; the length was limited only by the amount of warp the weaver put on the loom.

a. *Long warp.* It is much easier to put a long warp on a loom than to thread the loom several times. This seems to have been the custom in Palestine, for the hangings for the court (Exod. 27:9) were to be 50 yards long. Their width was not given in the text, but as the height of the court was 7½ feet, 6-foot hangings were probably implied. It is customary to mention the warp material first, since the warp must be strung on the loom before weaving begins. Therefore, we assume that the inner curtains were to be linen, with inwoven wool patterns. This difficult technique seems to have been reserved for the most important place. The hangings for the court were to be plain linen, and the goats'-hair curtains for the tent were to be plain also. The veil (Exod. 26:31) and the screens for the door of the tent (vs. 36) and for the gate of the court (27:16) were to be wool, with linen probably used just to highlight the design. The veil was to be of "skilful work," and the screens were to be "embroidered."

b. *Shaping of garments.* Garments were woven on the same types of looms as the curtains, and a long warp would suffice for many garments. To weave a long robe with sleeves on a wide loom, the weaver would have made sure that his warp was twice as wide as the length of the gown he wished to weave. However, material was expensive and not to be wasted, so he wove the shape he wanted, as we knit a sweater. By weaving his tunic from cuff to cuff, the selvages, the strongest part of a fabric, came at the hems and at the neck opening, the two places that needed most strength. In the case of a wool robe, stripes could easily be made by changing the color of the weft, which ran up and down the tunic.

The weaver began his work on enough of the center warps to make a sleeve, leaving the warps at each side bare. These would be added when the sleeve had been woven from cuff to shoulder line, to form the length of the tunic. Across the shoulder he wove the whole width of the warp. When it was time to make the opening for the head, he would weave half the web at a time to separate back and front of the tunic, either leaving several inches of bare warp in the center to be cut away later and bound "with a woven binding around the opening" (Exod. 28:32) or weaving to adjacent warps so that no cutting was necessary. When the head opening was large enough, he wove the second shoulder across the whole warp and finished up with a sleeve to match the first one. The tunic was then cut from the loom and the raw ends finished.* The cut ends at the cuffs were either turned in and hemmed or the warp was left long enough to roll or braid into a warp cord. The free warps on the sides of the front and back panels were made into warp cords, which strengthened the sides of the tunic. In many cases these warp cords were begun at the hem, the ends being buried in the selvage of the sleeve. However, Num. 15:38 exhorts the people of Israel to make tassels on the corners of their gowns. This was done by beginning the cord at the top and leaving the ends at the bottom.* This is the way Jesus' tunic without seam was woven (John 19: 23). When a tunic was woven on a narrow loom, it was made in three pieces. The center section was woven as on a wide loom, from cuff to cuff with a head slit in the middle. Two other pieces were woven wide enough for the front and back skirts. These were seamed to the top section, selvage to selvage. When a circular garment was to be woven, the weaver broadened his web a warp or two at a time instead of all at once. Fig. CLO 36, nos. 1a-b.

c. *Pairing yarns for strength.* When narrow tapes were woven which had to be strong and still should be flexible, two yarns were quite often used together instead of a single yarn of larger size. Two yarns might be used together in both warp and weft or in either. The process of weaving was the same. Wide fabrics occasionally had two warps used together at the selvage, and it was quite usual to run an extra weft up each edge of a fabric, weaving it a little way in from the edge with the regular weft. Possibly such an extra weft would have been used to make the fifty loops on the edge of the curtains (Exod. 26:10).

As with the hangings, expensive materials and methods were used for important garments. Of the holy garments, the turban and breeches were to be made of plain linen, the coat was to be blue-and-white checked linen, and the girdle was plain linen with wool patterns. The breastpiece and the ephod were to be wool with gold and linen detail.

6. **Interpretation of Bible texts.** Now let us see how this data will help us interpret the Bible texts. The materials available in Palestine were linen, wool, goats' hair, and gold. Linen was referred to as "fine twined linen." As there is little difference in diameter of linen fibers from various places in the Near East, the "fine" must refer to the quality and method of preparation in running water, explained in § 2b *above.* As linen was used undyed, spun yarn was called for; and the spin, being traditional, did not

have to be mentioned. Wool was mentioned as "blue and purple and scarlet (stuff)." The formula of naming the three principal dyes apparently covered colors in general. The only mention of spinning wool in connection with the tabernacle is in Exod. 35:25-26, and it is probable that those "women who had ability spun with their hands" to the specifications of the master craftsman. The mention of goats' hair raises no question. The preparation of the gold thread, explained in Exod. 39:3 because it was a rare technique, is not translated in either the KJV or the RSV quite according to what we find archaeologically. "Gold leaf was hammered out and cut into threads" (RSV); "they did beat the gold into thin plates, and cut it into wires" (KJV). Apparently, drawn wire such as that used for the filigree (vs. 16) was beaten thin and cut in strips. A hank of such gold thread, spun but without a core, was found at Dura on the Euphrates. Textiles from Palestine or Syria used the metal thread flat. Gold leaf, beaten into parchment, was used in the Far East, but has not been found in Near Eastern fabrics. The method of weaving—over one warp and under the next—was not mentioned, for it was universal. However, the type of loom on which fabrics were to be made seems to have been implied by formula. Fabrics to be made on a Greek vertical loom were to be "embroidered"; those to be made on a horizontal loom were to be "skilfully worked," the exact manner being left, apparently, to the ingenuity of the craftsman.

One question we cannot answer conclusively concerns Lev. 19:19: "Nor shall there come upon you a garment of cloth made of two kinds of stuff" (KJV adds "mingled"). The ban may have been against spinning two fibers together. At least, this was never done. If it means that two fibers may not be used in a single garment, it goes counter to the specifications for the holy garments, since the girdle calls for wool and linen, and the robe, breastpiece, and ephod call for wool, linen, and gold. Only the turban, breeches, and coat are to be made all of linen.

The most interesting question still to be answered concerns the type of garment made by Jacob for Joseph (Gen. 37:3). Unlike Ps. 45:13-14:

> The princess is decked in her chamber with
> gold-woven robes;
> in many-colored robes she is led to the king,

neither version mentions weaving. The KJV, following the LXX, reads "coat of many colors." The meaning of the last word is obscure, and another proposed rendering of the expression is "robe of pieces." In looking for the best rendering we must begin by remembering that Jacob lived in the Bronze Age, when wool still had to be plucked from the sheep. A great proportion of plucked wool was sorted, dyed, and made into felt, and the yield per sheep was small, compared with that when shears had been invented in the Iron Age. Though tablets from Ur III (*ca.* 2200-2000 B.C.) do attest to spinning and weaving of wool as a female occupation, they do not mention male weavers. Apparently wool as a fiber to be spun and woven had not come into its own, and it is now realized that the *kaunakes* which figures so prominently in Sumerian and later art,

formerly thought to be tapestry weave with long pile, was originally a sheep's fleece and later often a fleece or fur mantle. Farther W the University Museum Excavations at Gordium disclose as late as the seventh century B.C. specimens of spun and woven linen of various qualities, but also felted wool, a few pieces with inlaid felt pattern and a piece or two with flocks of wool sewed to the felt. There is also fine tanned leather set with designs of large and small metal studs. At Naqada in Egypt, Petrie has found specimens with Old Kingdom dates, of painted leather with zigzag and herringbone patterns similar to the patterns on the garments of an Asiatic family—roughly contemporary with Abraham—shown in a wall painting in the tomb of a noble at Beni-hasan, together with scribes dressed in Egyptian kilts (Fig. JOS 29). A study of this mural shows that the Egyptian kilts are evidently made of oblong pieces of plain linen cloth draped around the wearer.* When the upper corner of the kilt falls below the belt line, the lower corner also falls below the straight line of the hem. The fabric is obviously uniform in width. The Asiatic garments, on the other hand, are scalloped at the hem and bias at the top, so that one shoulder and both arms are left bare.* In a part of the world where the pattern was made by the weft, there was no way to weave such garments, for if the color changes are to lie weft-ways, the weaver would have had to scallop one selvage while making the other bias. A bias edge can be made on a two-beam loom, but a scalloped one cannot. These garments all show a binding at the neck opening and also at the hem, like that mentioned in Exod. 28:32. However, because of their shape (which applies also to the Syrians depicted in the tile decoration from the palace of Ramses III, who have long robes with sleeves), it seems more likely that these garments were made of leather or wool felt than that they were woven. This supposition is strengthened by the costumes shown on the Megiddo ivories dating *ca.* 1200 B.C., after the Exodus, which have straight bands of decoration and are made in shapes easy to weave—shapes which are found in many places. Therefore, unless further archaeological evidence changes the picture, it seems logical to assume that Jacob made Joseph a garment of leathers or wool felt, with a woven binding to keep it from tearing (Exod. 28:32). For the painted garments in the Egyptian murals, whether long robes with sleeves or short robes without sleeves, do agree both with the KJV (LXX) interpretation, "coat of many colors," and with the alternate suggested translation of the Hebrew, "robe made of pieces." The same kind of garment (*kᵉthoneth happassim;* RSV "long robe with sleeves"; KJV "garment of divers colors") was worn by Tamar, David's daughter, and we are told that "thus were the virgin daughters of the king clad of old" (II Sam. 13:18). *See* JOSEPH § 2*b.* Fig. CLO 36, nos. 4, 3.

The questions we have been able to answer make it clear that Bible references to textiles and garments alike were meant for a civilization well acquainted with all weaving and tailoring processes and therefore, habitually, point to a technique or custom without explaining it.

**Bibliography.** E. Riefstahl, *Patterned Textiles in Pharaonic Egypt* (1944): a well-illustrated study gathering together much information. R. Pfister and L. Bellinger, *The Excavations at Dura-Europos, Final Report IV, Part II, the Textiles* (1945): five color plates which give an idea of the colors available in wool before A.D. 256; the gold thread and blue bands in a linen fabric are also illustrated. L. Bellinger, "Textile Analysis: Early Techniques in Egypt and the Near East," *Workshop Notes*, no. 2 (1950): detailed discussion of the characteristics of fibers. G. M. Crowfoot, "Linen Textiles from the Cave of Ain Feshkha in the Jordan Valley," *PEQ* (Jan.-Apr., 1951): illustrated article on fabrics from the Scroll Caves by an expert. R. J. Forbes, *Studies in Ancient Technology*, vol. IV (1956): the most comprehensive modern work written in English on fibers, fabrics, and dyeing in antiquity; however, it contains much information not applicable to the Near East.

L. BELLINGER

**\*CLOUD** [עָנָן, cloud, cloudiness, mist; עָב, a particular cloud, rain cloud; נָשִׂיא, towering cloud; עֲרָפֶל, murky cloud; νέφος, νεφέλη, cloud, cloudiness, mist]. The "pillar of cloud" (Exod. 13:21) is composed of עָנָן, as is the rain cloud (Exod. 19:9; Job 26:8). The עָנָן covering the tabernacle (Exod. 40:36-37) was not a defined, individual cloud, but morning mist or a cloudy sky. The עָנָן and darkness (חֹשֶׁךְ) between the Egyptians and the Israelites at the Red Sea (Exod. 14:20) was probably the dust storm of a sirocco or EAST WIND. For "cloud" as a visible token of Yahweh's presence, cf. Exod. 16:10; 20:21; Lev. 16:2; I Kings 8:10; Ezek. 10:4; Matt. 17:5. "To come with clouds" (Rev. 1:7) is to come as the instrument of divine judgment, since Mark 13:26 is dependent on Dan. 7:13, which in turn is derived from Jer. 4:13, with its unique plural of עָנָן.

*See also* PALESTINE, CLIMATE OF; GLORY; TABERNACLE; SON OF MAN. R. B. Y. SCOTT

**CLOUD, PILLAR OF.** *See* PILLAR OF CLOUD AND FIRE.

**CLUB.** A weapon. The following words are translated "club":

*a)* תּוֹתָח (Job 41:29—H 41:21; LXX σφυρά, "hammer, mallet"; KJV "dart"). Since this word is parallel to כִּידוֹן, "javelin," it must be a weapon of some sort. Since the Arabic cognate *wataḥa* means "to beat with a stick," "club" is probably a better rendering than "dart."

*b)* מֵפִיץ (Prov. 25:18). The Hebrew text has מֵפִיץ, "scatterer," but "war club" (KJV "maul"), following the LXX ρόπαλον, fits the context. See also Jer. 51:20, where מֵפִיץ, "hammer" (KJV "battle-axe"), along with "weapon of war," describes the Medes as the Lord's instrument.

*c)* Ξύλον. The kind of instrument which, along with swords, was carried by the crowd that came with Judas to Gethsemane to seize Jesus (Matt. 26:47, 55; Mark 14:43, 48; Luke 22:52).

J. W. WEVERS

**\*CNIDUS** nī′dəs [ἡ Κνίδος] (Acts 27:7). A Greek city on the coast of SW Asia Minor.

Cnidus was a city of some renown in antiquity. Colonized by Dorian Greeks, it lay in territory which had even attracted prehistoric settlers from the Aegean area. The promontory of Cnidus is the southernmost on the coast of Caria. Its length is *ca.* forty miles from W to E, consisting of rugged mountains to the E, and separated by an isthmus, some

fertile territory in coastal plains to the W. Ancient Cnidus probably lay at the central isthmus near Burgaz-Datça (the modern port of call) originally, and was moved to the site near Tekir on the W tip of the peninsula in the fourth century B.C. This Hellenistic Cnidus had two harbors (Strabo XIV. 656), a regularly planned town, many sanctuaries, and famous fourth-century Greek sculpture (e.g., the Aphrodite of Praxiteles). The site was explored in the nineteenth century.

The sailing beyond the S coast of the Cnidian Peninsula is often endangered by northerly winds, as Paul experienced on his voyage from Lycia westward.

*Bibliography.* G. E. Bean and J. M. Cook, "The Cnidia," *Annual of the British School at Athens*, XLVII (1952), 171-212.

M. J. MELLINK

**COAL, COALS** [גֶּחָל, *gaḥal, geḥāl*, used only in plural; גֶּחָלֶת (II Sam. 14:7; Isa. 44:19); פֶּחָם (Ps. 11:6; Isa. 44:12; 54:16; Prov. 26:21 KJV [RSV "charcoal"]); רִצְפָּה, a hot stone or coal (I Kings 19:6; Isa. 6:6); KJV שָׁחוֹר (RSV "soot"); ἄνθραξ (Rom. 12:20), ἀνθρακία (John 18:18; 21:9; RSV "charcoal")]. True mineral coal has not been found in Palestine, whose geological formation is too recent. Biblical references are not to mineral coal, but to charcoal. Charcoal was used for heating (Isa. 47:14; John 18:18) and cooking (Isa. 44:19; John 21:9), and by the blacksmith (Isa. 44:12).

Ps. 120:4 refers to coals of the broom tree (KJV "juniper"). W. G. WILLIAMS

**COAST.** A KJV archaism for "border" or "boundary." The RSV uses variously "country"; "territory"; "region"; "boundary"; "border," and, when the context fits, "coast" (i.e., Num. 34:6; Josh. 9:1; Judg. 5:17; Acts 27:2; cf. also Isa. 23:2, 6: אִי, usually "coastlands").

**COAT. 1.** כְּתֹנֶת. Alternately: ROBE; GARMENT. A long, shirtlike inner garment, usually of linen, sleeveless or sleeved, worn under the outer garment (מְעִיל). The RSV restricts the term to the undergarment of priests, except in II Sam. 15:32, but the KJV uses it more frequently. *See* DRESS AND ORNAMENTS § A2. On כְּתֹנֶת פַּסִּים ("long robe with sleeves"; KJV "coat of many colors"), *see* CLOTH § 6.

**2.** KJV translation of מְעִיל. *See* DRESS AND ORNAMENTS § A2.

**3.** שִׁרְיוֹן. *See* COAT OF MAIL.

**4.** סִרְיוֹן. *See* COAT OF MAIL.

**5.** מַד (Ps. 109:18). A garment.

**6.** KJV translation of סַרְבָּל. *See* MANTLE 10.

**7.** Χιτών. The inner garment worn next to the skin; distinct from the ἱμάτιον, which is the outer garment. *See* DRESS AND ORNAMENTS § A2.

**8.** KJV translation of ἐπενδύτης (John 21:7; RSV "clothes"), a general term for wearing apparel.

J. M. MYERS

**COAT OF MAIL** [שִׁרְיוֹן קַשְׂקַשִּׂים, שִׁרְיוֹן]. A protective cuirass worn from the neck to the girdle, probably formed of two pieces of leather joined below the arms.

Goliath wore such a coat covered with bronze scales (קַשְׂקַשִּׂים; I Sam. 17:5), the weight of which is reported to have been five thousand shekels (*see* SHEKEL). David refused to wear Saul's coat of mail (שׁרִיוֹן; vs. 38), because of its weight. The armored skin of the Leviathan is described as a double coat of mail (Job 41:13—H 41:5, with emendation after the LXX). For "coat of mail" as part of armament, see also II Chr. 26:14; Neh. 4:16; Jer. 46:4; 51:3.

*Bibliography.* A. L. Oppenheim, *JCS*, 4 (1950), 192 ff; E. A. Speiser, *JAOS*, 70 (1950), 47 ff.   J. W. WEVERS

**COCK** [זַרְזִיר] (KJV *translates* זַרְזִיר מָתְנַיִם GREY-HOUND); *cf.* Jewish Aram. זַרְזִיר, wrestler, antagonist, starling; Syr. *zarzīrā*, starling (*so also* Arab.); ἀλέκτωρ, *a poetic form of* ἀλεκτρυών, cock; *cf.* ἀλεξητήρ, protector, *from* ἀλέξω, to ward off, defend]; **COCKCROW** [ἀλεκτοροφωνία]. The male of the common domestic FOWL, as of various other birds. Figs. COC 39; JAA 1.

Courtesy of James B. Pritchard

39. Cock on a sherd of a cooking pot, found in the excavations at Gibeon

On the Jewish prohibition against the rearing of fowl (cocks) in Jerusalem, see B.K. 7.7. The Hebrew phrase in Prov. 30:31: "זַרְזִיר of loins," is obscure (RSV "the strutting cock"; KJV "greyhound"); Jewish Aramaic suggests "the powerful wrestler."

In Mark 13:35 the third watch of the night (approximately 12:00-3:00 A.M.) is "cockcrow"; this reflects the Roman custom of dividing the night into four watches (for three watches, which was the Jewish practice, see Jos. War V.ii.510). All the other NT references to "cock" are associated with its crowing at Peter's denial of Jesus (Matt. 26:34, etc.).
W. S. McCULLOUGH

**COCKATRICE.** KJV translation of צֶפַע (Isa. 14:29; RSV "adder") and צִפְעוֹנִי (Isa. 11:8; 59:5; Jer. 8:15; RSV "adder"). A fabulous reptile alleged to be hatched by a serpent from a cock's egg, and having the power to kill by its glance (cf. Pliny's reference to the "basilisks" found in Cyrene, in Nat. Hist. VIII.33). In KJV usage the cockatrice is merely a venomous serpent.   W. S. McCULLOUGH

**COCKLE.** KJV translation of בָּאְשָׁה (RSV "foul weed") in Job 31:40. *See* WEEDS 1.

**CODE.** A term used for various collections of OT legal materials. *See* LAW IN THE OT; COVENANT, BOOK OF THE; PENTATEUCH.

**CODEX.** The earliest book form. Derived from Latin *codex* or *caudex*, "tree trunk," the term came to be used for wooden leaves or tablets (*see* TABLET), and eventually for books consisting of leaves laid on one another. Finally, sheets of papyrus or vellum were folded and bound together. *See* WRITING AND WRITING MATERIALS.   R. J. WILLIAMS

**COELE-SYRIA** sē'lĭ sĭr'ĭ ə [Κοίλη Συρία, hollow Syria]; KJV **CELOSYRIA** sē'lō sĭr'ĭ ə. The Greek name of the region between the Lebanon and the Anti-lebanon mountains; modern Beqa'. During the Hellenistic period the name was also used more broadly of all Palestine and Phoenicia, which under the successive rule of the Ptolemies and the Seleucids was considered a single province under a single governor (Polybius V.87.6), perhaps corresponding to the former Persian province W of the Euphrates. Polybius (V.80) includes the Philistine coast, and Jerusalem seems to be considered one of its cities in II Macc. 3:5-8 (cf. Jos. Antiq. XIV.iv.5: "Coele-Syria as far as the river Euphrates and Egypt"). The name is also used of S Syria apart from Phoenicia (I Esd. 2:17, 24, 27; 4:48; etc.; I Macc. 10:69; II Macc. 4:4). When Herod in 47 B.C. was given military supervision over it by the Romans, it designated all the land E of the Jordan, as distinguished from Judea, Samaria, and Galilee (Jos. Antiq. XIV.ix.5; War I.x.8; cf. Pliny Nat. Hist. V.9). In Jesus' day, Coele-Syria thus included the tetrarchy of PHILIP (5), together with the land S of the Yarmuk to the Jabbok (Jos. Antiq. XIII.xiii.3).

*Bibliography.* E. Bevan, *The House of Seleucus*, I (1902), 207-8 *et passim*; G. A. Smith, *Historical Geography of the Holy Land* (9th ed., 1902), pp. 538, 553.   E. W. SAUNDERS

**COFFER.** KJV form of BOX in I Sam. 6:8, 11, 15.

**COFFIN.** *See* BURIAL.

**COHORT** [σπεῖρα] (Acts 10:1; 21:31; 27:1); KJV BAND. Alternately: BATTALION (Matt. 27:27 = Mark 15:16); BAND (John 18:3, 12); KJV BAND. One tenth of a LEGION. The paper strength of a cohort was six hundred men. However, the troops stationed in Palestine were not legionaries but auxiliaries; auxiliary cohorts had a paper strength of 760 infantry and 240 cavalry. Such cohorts, composed chiefly of local units, were usually posted on the frontiers in small forts, four to eight acres in area, each holding one cohort. Agrippa I, at his death in A.D. 44, left five cohorts and one *ala* ("wing"= "squadron") in Caesarea; the *ala* consisted mainly of cavalry (Jos. Antiq. XIX.ix.2; War III.iv.2). The cohort in Jerusalem was stationed in the fortress of Antonia, N of the temple (Jos. War V.v.8).
F. D. GEALY

**COIN.** *See* MONEY.

**COLA.** KJV form of KOLA.

**COL-HOZEH** kŏl hō′zə [כל־חזה, every seer] (Neh. 3:15; 11:5). Apparently the eponym of a clan of Judah; mentioned in postexilic lists of names.

*Bibliography.* M. Noth, *Die israelitischen Personennamen* (1928), p. 248.

**COLIUS.** KJV Apoc. form of KELAIAH.

**COLLAR.** 1. פה (Job 30:18; Ps. 133:2 [KJV SKIRTS]). On the basis of Exod. 28:32, obviously the opening for the head, and in no sense an ornament, of a garment.

2. ענק (Judg. 8:26); KJV CHAIN. A decorative ornament, with pendants, which hung around the necks of the camels of the Midianites. The word also occurs in Prov. 1:9; Song of S. 4:9 ("pendant"; "necklace"; KJV "chain").

3. ציִנק (Jer. 29:26); KJV STOCKS. A pillory into which a person's head was placed.

4. In Ps. 105:18 "in iron" is interpreted "in a collar of iron," in the context referring to "neck" (נפש).
J. M. MYERS

**COLLECTION (NT).** *See* OFFERING FOR THE SAINTS.

**COLLEGE, THE.** KJV translation of משנה (RSV SECOND QUARTER) in II Kings 22:14; II Chr. 34:22.

**COLONY.** Roman colonization really began as a measure taken by Julius Caesar (*see* CAESAR) to provide land and employment at low cost to the state for two kinds of persons: (*a*) able-bodied members of the Roman proletariat whom he had removed from the relief rolls, and (*b*) veterans of his legions. Most of the colonies he established were therefore in the provinces, and he thus relieved the overcrowded city of Rome while strengthening the Roman element outside Italy. Most of his colonies—more than twenty in number—were in the West, but in the East his foundations included CORINTH and PHILIPPI.

AUGUSTUS continued Caesar's policy. In his *Res gestae* (V.28) he expressed his pride in his work: "I settled colonies of soldiers in Africa, Sicily, Macedonia, both Spains, Achaea, Asia, Syria, Gallia Narbonesis, Pisidia. Moreover, Italy has twenty-eight colonies founded under my auspices which have grown to be famous and populous during my lifetime." Among his foundations were ANTIOCH (PISIDIAN); LYSTRA; TROAS; and SYRACUSE, all mentioned in the book of Acts. Also mentioned in Acts is Ptolemaïs (*see* ACCO), colonized by Claudius. It is not certain whether ICONIUM was colonized by Claudius or by Hadrian.

In addition to such colonies, other communities were given the status of Roman colonies simply in order to honor their inhabitants and strengthen their ties with Rome; but this practice was much more common in the West than in the East.

The colonies possessed autonomous government, in some cases immunity from taxation, and—by a legal fiction—use of Italian legal procedure and precedents. In Acts 16:12-40 a clear picture of such procedure is given us. The magistrates (vs. 19) included praetors (vss. 20 ff), who in colonies could deal with civil or criminal cases. (They are appar-

ently the "unrighteous" judges of I Cor. 6:1 ff.) They could impose floggings by the agency of lictors (Acts 16:22), though not legally in the case of uncondemned Roman citizens (16:37-38).

*Bibliography.* A. N. Sherwin-White, *The Roman Citizenship* (1939); G. H. Stevenson, *Roman Provincial Administration* (1939).
R. M. GRANT

**COLORS.** The OT has no word for the abstract concept "color." Words so translated have another basic meaning:

*a*) עין (Lev. 13:55), literally, "appearance" (as in Num. 11:7).

*b*) פסים (Gen. 37:3, 23, 32; II Sam. 13:18-19) describes the type of garment worn by Joseph and by Tamar. But the correct translation is doubtless "long, with sleeves" (RSV), rather than "many-colored" (KJV).

*c*) טלא (Ezek. 16:16 KJV), רקמה (I Chr. 29:2; Ezek. 17:3), חטבות (Prov. 7:16), ברמים (Ezek. 27:24), "variegated," "many-colored."

*d*) Aramaic זיו (Dan. 5:6, 9-10; 7:28), "complexion" (cf. Akkadian *zîmu*).

In the NT the word "color" does not occur; the phrase "color of fire" (Rev. 9:17) translates the single Greek word πυρίνος.

When one turns to the names for the individual colors, one is struck both by the relative poverty of terms and by the lack of precision in their definition. The most frequent, and apparently the most carefully differentiated, are the names of manufactured colors, especially of those used in the dyeing of fabrics (*see* BLUE; PURPLE; SCARLET; VERMILION; VIOLET). Natural colors rarely are used in descriptions, and then, as a rule, only when the writer desires to make a special point, as in the case of RED and Edom, or wishes to bring out the unusual character of that which is being described.

It has also been noted that colors in the OT can be classified as either somber or brilliant; indeed, the Hebrew appears often to have been concerned more with the lightness or "value" of a color—the amount of light which was reflected—than with its hue. A similar phenomenon has been noted both in Homer and in Old English poetry.

Colors are often used symbolically by various writers in the OT (*see* BAY; BLUE; BROWN; CRIMSON; DAPPLED; GRAY; GREEN; GRISLED; PURPLE; RED; SCARLET; VERMILION; VIOLET; YELLOW; *see also* BLACK; WHITE). But there is no evidence that colors were so employed in the decoration of such buildings as the tabernacle or the temple, or in the manufacture of the priestly garments. In later ages, however, the colors were given an allegorical meaning: the fine white linen was said to represent the earth from which the flax had sprung; purple stood for the sea, since "it is reddened with the blood of fish"; blue was the color of the air, and scarlet of fire. Thus the four elements from which the world had been formed were represented (Philo *Life of Moses* II.17; Jos. Antiq. III.vii.7).

*Bibliography.* W. E. Mead, "Color in Old English Poetry," *PMLA*, N.S. VII (1899), 169-206; F. E. Wallace, "Color in Homer and in Ancient Art," *Smith College Classical Studies*, no. 9 (1927); A. Guillaumont, "La désignation des couleurs en hébreu et en araméen," in I. Meyerson, ed., *Problèmes de la couleur* (1957), pp. 339-48; H. Janssen, "Les couleurs dans la Bible hébraïque," *Annuaire de l'Institut de Philologie et d'Histoire Orientales et Slaves,* XIV (1954-57), 145-71.

R. W. CORNEY

**COLOSSAE** kə lŏs'ĭ [Κολοσσαί]. A city in SW Asia Minor.

Colossae is a city with a Hellenized but originally non-Greek (Phrygian?) name. It lies in the valley of the River Lycus (modern Çürüksuçay), a tributary of the Maeander, in the SW confines of ancient Phrygia. The valley of the Lycus is the ancient thoroughfare from W to E. The modern railroad and highway still follow its course from Sarayköy to the E.

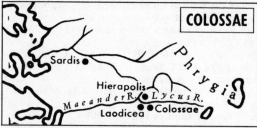

Of the three major Christian cities in the Lycus district, Colossae is the earliest to have achieved city status. Herodotus (VII.30) lists it as a "large city of Phrygia," a station on the expedition of Xerxes to Sardis in 481 B.C. At that time the population must have consisted primarily of Phrygians speaking their native language and worshiping their great goddess and associate deities. Colossae is mentioned again as a prosperous and large city by Xenophon in his account of the march of Cyrus the Younger in 401 B.C. (Anabasis I.2.6). This marks Colossae as the most prominent pre-Hellenistic city in the Lycus Valley.

Competition arose from LAODICEA and HIERAPOLIS in Hellenistic times, although Colossae maintained its status as a city under the Romans and was one of the active centers of the textile industry in the district. Its inscriptions and coins reflect its importance in the imperial period. The city must have been Hellenized and partly Romanized in a gradual process of assimilation to its neighbors, rather than by a new foundation.

The location of Colossae has been known since the travels of William J. Hamilton in 1835. He identified the ruins of the city and its acropolis on the left (S) bank of the river, where he still saw many architectural fragments in marble (columns, architraves, cornices) and the cavea of the theater with several of the stone seats preserved. On the N bank lies the necropolis, with rock-cut and partly built graves.

Also on the N bank, E of Colossae, a Byzantine church was built for Saint Michael, who had performed a miracle in opening the rock for the river to flow through at the time of an inundation. This late story about the spectacular gorge of the Lycus at Colossae recalls the fantastic tale Herodotus records from hearsay about the underground course of the river. The ruins remain of the Church of Saint Michael, which was destroyed in a raid by the Turks at the end of the twelfth century.

The site of the city of Colossae was abandoned in the eighth century and became a quarry for the inhabitants of the neighboring city of Chonai (modern Honaz), three miles to the S.

No excavations have taken place at Colossae. The epigraphic evidence is the only local material which has been examined by modern scholarship. The available archaeological and historical references do not yet match the importance of the city as based on the Letter to the Colossians.

**Bibliography.** W. M. Ramsay, *The Cities and Bishoprics of Phrygia* (1895), pp. 208-13; D. Magie, *Roman Rule in Asia Minor* (1950), pp. 126-27, 985-86.     M. J. MELLINK

\*COLOSSIANS, LETTER TO THE kə lŏsh'ənz [Κολοσσαεῖς or Κολασσαεῖς, see COLOSSAE]. A letter from Paul and Timothy to the Christians of Colossae, carried by Tychicus and Onesimus (the slave of Philemon); now the twelfth book in the NT canon. Notable are its advanced Christology in the impressive hymn, 1:15-20, and its refutation of a dangerous syncretistic heresy (2:6-23). Colossians is also the primary source of EPHESIANS.

1. Authorship
2. Date and place of writing
3. Purpose
4. Contents
   *a.* Doctrine
   *b.* Ethics
   *c.* Personalia
5. Text
Bibliography

**1. Authorship.** Colossians was canonical and accepted as Pauline by A.D. 200 (Iren. Her. III.14.1; Muratorian Canon), though traces of its use before then are remarkably few. Marcion included it in his NT, and the Alexandrian Gnostics naturally found it valuable. Mayerhoff in 1838 first questioned its authenticity, regarding it as based on Ephesians. On similar grounds of interrelationship and style De Wette reached opposite conclusions. Baur and his school rejected both letters because of alleged Gnostic and Montanist elements.

Hitzig and especially Holtzmann, however, suggested that the author of Ephesians used a much shorter, genuinely Pauline, Colossians which he later reworked into our present letter. This theory received almost no support during the first half of the twentieth century, but in 1950 Masson independently made a similar proposal. The short original lacked, he thought, 1:5-6, 9-29; 2:1-5, 7, 10, 11*b*, 12*b*, 13-15, 17-19, 22-23; 3:1-2, 5-11, 13*b*-17, 22*b*-24; 4:3*c*, 4, 8*b*, 12*b*, 13, 16. In these verses are found the closest parallels to Ephesians in style and vocabulary, as well as such un-Pauline features as the negative tone of the ethical instruction; the pre-Pauline hymn of 1:15-20, to which was added 1:18*a;* the feeble opposition of "barbarian" and "Scythian" in place of "Greek" and "barbarian" (3:11; cf. Rom. 1:14); and the "mystery of Christ" (1:26-27; 2:2; 4:3). The author of Ephesians has altered the "brethren from Laodicea" (i.e., a group of Laodiceans resident at Colossae) to the "brethren at Laodicea" and inserted 4:16 in order to designate his own composition as a letter to the Laodiceans. This solution of the close relationship of Colossians to Ephesians must not be dismissed too easily, because there probably was interpolation into the genuine letters when the Pauline collection was made (e.g., Rom. 16:25-27, which is in the style of Ephesians), and disciples did not hesitate to edit Pauline materials (as possibly II Timothy).

Persuasive as it is, nevertheless, Masson's theory, like Holtzmann's, should be rejected. The principal objections are: (a) minute differences are exaggerated; (b) the variety of expression in Col. 1:9-14 is unaccounted for on the view that it echoes Eph. 1:15-23; 2:2; 1:7; (c) the texts were assimilated during transmission (e.g., Col. 3:6; Eph. 5:6: "upon the sons of disobedience"); (d) various Colossian passages were conflated in one Ephesians passage, and this phenomenon demands that the Colossians used was our present letter; (e) the theory rests on too subjective criteria (e.g., that Paul could not have composed hymns like Col. 1:15-20; Phil. 2:6-11; in fact, however, poems from prison are not unusual, and Paul had poetic gifts, as I Cor. 13 shows).

Colossians has thirty-four words not found elsewhere in the NT; fifteen common with Ephesians but otherwise used in non-Pauline material; and ten common only with Ephesians (e.g., "men-pleasers" and "eyeservice"). All agree that vocabulary alone contributes little to the argument (Philippians has thirty-six *hapax legomena*), and the absence from Colossians of the Pauline words "righteousness" (justification), "fellowship," and "law" is not serious. Style is a more important concern, and, like Ephesians, Colossians has long sentences, many participles, synonyms, parallel clauses, heaped-up genitives, and epexegetic infinitives. It is true that each of these appears also in accepted letters (Phil. 1:3-8 is one sentence; Rom. 1–2 contains a number of examples of the use of synonyms; parallel clauses are used in II Cor. 10:4-6; genitives abound in I Corinthians, Romans, and Philippians). Yet arguments from vocabulary and style have a cumulative effect along with evidence of ideas. A similar style in Ephesians produces a ponderous tone marked by liturgical tautology, and the non-Pauline character is masked. It is otherwise in Colossians. Whereas Ephesians is dull and impersonal, Col. 2:6-4:6 is lively with personal feeling; definite people and places appear (1:2, 5-8, 27; 2:1; 4:7 ff, 13). We have to do with a real letter. No doubt, the crisis of the Colossian heresy is responsible for the introduction of unusual words like "beguiling speech," "philosophy," "deity," "disqualify," and "rigor of devotion" (2:4-23). In respect to ideas, the Christology is developed, but on lines compatible with Rom. 5; I Cor. 1:24; 2; 4:1; 15:45-49; II Cor. 4:4; 5:18-19; etc.; the doctrine of angelic spirits is quite Pauline (cf. Gal. 3:19; 4:8-11; Rom. 8:38-39); so is the doctrine of the church as the body of Christ (Rom. 12; I Cor. 10:18, 32; 12; and probably 11:29).

Despite Timothy's appearance, the letter is really Paul's (1:23; 4:18; cf. similar shifts in II Thess. 3:17; I Cor. 16:21), though 4:18 may mean that the letter was dictated.

The links between Colossians and PHILEMON support authenticity. Paul (a prisoner), Timothy, Onesimus, Archippus, Epaphras, Mark, Aristarchus, Demas, and Luke belong to both. The words "fellow

worker," "fellow prisoner," "knowledge" (ἐπίγνωσις —once in Philemon and four times in Colossians, which is four times as long), "church in a house," are common. The genuineness of Philemon carries with it that of Colossians, and Philemon is incontestably Pauline.

PHILIPPIANS shares with Colossians ἀξίως ("worthily"; of behavior); πλοῦτος ("riches") and δόξα ("glory"); ὑστέρημα ("what is lacking"); ἀγών ("conflict"); εὐχαριστία ("thanksgiving"). Γνῶσις ("knowledge") is used once in each; ἐπίγνωσις ("discernment") once in Philippians as in Philemon; σοφία ("wisdom"), used six times in Colossians, is absent from Philippians. This variation in emphasis on wisdom and knowledge marks the difference in situation and purpose. But notice too the "death and resurrection" theme in both (Col. 2:12; 3:1; Phil. 3:10-11; cf. Rom. 6:3-4); the spiritual "circumcision" (Col. 2:11-13; Phil. 3:3); Christ's enabling power (Col. 1:29; Phil. 4:13). Completing Christ's tribulations (Col. 1:24), an unusual idea, has a parallel at Phil. 3:10; and both letters contain great christological poems. The different tone in Philippians is also due to the intimate connections of Philippi with Paul, its founder. In Colossians, Paul is following up the work of Epaphras, who had done well but was not sent back (4:12). The RSV "on our behalf" (1:7) makes Epaphras the delegate of the apostle; but the reading is uncertain. Allowing for these changes in occasion, relationship, and destination, one finds little to suggest a different authorship. Whereas Philemon must belong to the same imprisonment as Colossians, Philippians need not, and it may be earlier (cf. Phil. 2:6-11 with Col. 1:15-20; Phil. 3:10-11 with Col. 2:12).

Angelology combined with legalism and Encratite practices is found in pre-Christian Jewish groups (e.g., at Qumran), and the type of heresy met at Colossae could certainly belong to Paul's day.

For all these reasons, then, the authenticity of Colossians should be accepted.

**2. Date and place of writing.** These belong together because one prison must fit Philemon and Colossians. On the evidence of Acts, Paul could have met Onesimus the runaway at Caesarea or at Rome. Scholars have presented strong claims for both places. EPHESUS has been proposed as the place of meeting, because Onesimus and Epaphras would have gone to a nearby city; Paul suffered there (I Cor. 15:32; II Cor. 1:8-10; 11:23) and encountered Jewish or Judaizing opposition when he was writing Galatians, Colossians, and Phil. 3; Paul's travel plans in Philippians and Philemon contradict Rom. 15:24, 28; there was a *praetorium* at Ephesus, where later tradition located a prison also. Acts, however, is silent, and Acts must not be dismissed as a poor source; I and II Corinthians need not imply imprisonment, and it is very doubtful that Paul could, legally, have been thrown to the lions. Judaizing or Jewish opponents troubled Paul and his congregations at many places and times. As for travel, the apostle could have changed his mind under new circumstances. Hence the Ephesian hypothesis must be rejected.

Paul was indubitably a prisoner at Rome and martyred there (I Clem. 5 and early tradition). Onesimus would run as far from Colossae as possible, and the ease of communication between Rome and Asia Minor makes the travel arrangements plausible. But the high Christology of Colossians contributes little to the case for Rome (II Cor. 4:4; 5:18-19 come from the end of Paul's Ephesian mission). If Colossians was written at Ephesus, the date would be *ca.* A.D. 56-57; if at Rome, *ca.* 61-62. *See* CHRONOLOGY, NT.

**3. Purpose.** The apostle wrote (*a*) to establish the Colossians in the true faith by exposing the deadly nature of the heretical teaching (1:23; 2:4, 7-8, 16); "Why do you submit to . . . ?" (2:20) may mean that the menace was making serious inroads; possibly he has one particular teacher in mind (2:4, 8, 16, 18), but this cannot be proved; (*b*) to instruct them in the Christian way of life (2:20; 3:1, 5, 12, 18 ff); (*c*) to encourage them to promote mutual love and harmony (2:2; 3:12-15; 4:8); and (*d*) to give news of the company at Rome and send greetings to his friends (4:7 ff).

What was the Colossian heresy? Apparently a mystery cult in which visions played a part (1:26-27; 2:2, the Christian use of "mystery" as a revealed secret; cf. the esoteric teaching of Qumran, 1QS 4.18; 5.11; 9.16-20; *see* DEAD SEA SCROLLS). More specifically: (*a*) the heretics assailed Christianity as an immature faith and denied the sufficiency of Jesus Christ as divine revealer and redeemer from sin. Paul dubbed it an empty deceit, based on mere human tradition (cf. Mark 7:8). Christ is the beloved Son of God, the Savior of the universe, victor over the angelic powers, mediator of the whole creative process (1:13-20; 2:15—at the Cross, according to RSV mg.). (*b*) The angelic powers were to be worshiped as well as Christ—or above Christ? (1:16; 2: 8-20). These *stoicheia* are the planetary and starry spirits that affected man's birth and destiny; probably also the angels standing behind the Mosaic law. It is believed that the heretics regarded the angels as intermediaries between holy, transcendent deity and the material world where man lives. The names of the angels played an important role among the ESSENES, and we find the same element in the Qumran literature. (*c*) Certain ascetic and liturgical practices were regarded as essential to the maturity or perfection of salvation. Paul mentions "food and drink" rules, possibly abstinence from meat and wine, and Jewish observances like New Moon, sabbath, and circumcision (2:11 ff). Should baptism be added? (Cf. 2:11-12, 20; 3:1-3, 10; and the lustrations so common at Qumran.) There is hardly enough evidence for a heretical practice of baptism. Paul vigorously objects that the Colossian usages constitute a new and negative legalism and deny the reality of faith union with the living Christ, "in whom are hid all the treasures of wisdom and knowledge" (2:3).

Thus the heresy seems to have been a syncretistic cult drawn from pagan and Jewish sources, perhaps by Gentile converts (2:13) who had enjoyed previous contacts with the synagogue. The Judaism in question may have been Essene or Zadokite (cf. 1QS 2.24 for "humility" and "charity"; CD 2.3, 13, for "wisdom"; 1QS 4.22 for "knowledge"; 1QH 3.21-22 and 11.11-12 for an "inheritance among the holy ones"; angels have been noticed above; Col. 1:12-13, "light . . . darkness," reminds one of Qumran dualism). We may have to do with a pre-Christian Jewish "gnosticism," though not necessarily with a fully developed speculative system like that of Basilides or Valentinus. *See* GNOSTICISM.

**4. Contents.** Analysis is, on the whole, a simple matter:

I. The greeting, 1:1-2
II. The true, apostolic gospel, 1:3-2:5
   A. A prayer for the church, 1:3-12
   B. The absolute pre-eminence of Christ, 1:13-23
   C. Paul's apostolic ministry and authority, 1:24-2:5
III. Christian liberty defended against the challenge of the Colossian heresy, 2:6-3:4
IV. Christian behavior, 3:5-4:6
   A. General ethical injunctions, 3:5-17
   B. Household duties, 3:18-4:1
   C. Exhortation to prayer, 4:2-6
V. Personal messages, 4:7-17
VI. Closing greeting and autograph, 4:18

Colossians is brilliantly conceived and written, an "example of great prose being addressed to a very little clan" (Moffatt). Paul is at his diplomatic best, graciously recognizing Epaphras' work and perhaps Timothy's (1:7-8; 2:7; 4:3, 12-13; cf. 1:24; 2:1-2, 5); yet he fights almost fiercely (2:8: "See to it that no one makes a prey of you") for the true faith of the crucified and risen Lord (1:23, 28; 2:3-4, 7; for Pauline "orthodoxy" cf. esp. Gal. 1:6-9). Nothing suggests an old man at the end of his course (cf. Philem. 9 RSV mg.); rather, we see the missionary to the Gentiles arrayed for battle and the defense of the church.

*a. Doctrine.* God is the Father (1:2, 12; 3:17), or the Father of our Lord Jesus Christ (1:3). He is at once the invisible and the knowable, revealed in his Son, the perfect Image, whom he raised from the dead (1:9, 15; 2:12). God the supreme Sovereign is righteous and gracious, Lord of history, and Judge of the immoral, on whom his "wrath" will fall at the End (1:6, 13; 2:12-15; 3:1, 6; 4:11; for "wrath" cf. John 3:36; Rom. 1:18; 2:5; Eph. 5:6). His plan to redeem the sinful and the fallen world is a mystery that was hidden from all eternity (or, "hidden from angels and men"), but has been revealed to his holy ones—i.e., the church (1:26). God "elects" or chooses a people and through missionaries like Paul proclaims his Word (1:12; 2:19; 3:10, 12, 15; 4:3).

Like Philemon but unlike Philippians, Colossians lacks teaching about the Spirit of God (unless at 1:8-9; love and wisdom are fruits of the Spirit; if so, cf. other references to wisdom). Paul may have been led to this strange position by his christological polemic or by heretical claims to a false spirituality.

Jesus is the Messiah and the Lord (2:6; RSV is not adequate; the historical manhood is stressed in 1:22; 2:6). He was put to death, but raised by God to reign at his right hand; he is the beloved Son, the Savior of the universe (1:20) and of men (1:14; 2:13-14). Moreover, he was the divine agent at Creation and is the principle of coherence for every creature (1:15-17). Paul may be thinking of the divine Wisdom (Prov. 8:12 ff) or of the immanent Logos of which Philo and the Stoics spoke. Christ is the eternal head (the "first-born") who directs every process of life and energy—there is no explicit reference here to an eternal generation of the Son; but cf. the "Adam" typology of Rom. 5:14; I Cor. 15:45; and the condescension theme of II Cor. 8:9; Phil. 2:7-8. Three propositions sum up the high Christology of Colossians: (*a*) Deity in its fulness chose to dwell in Christ "bodily"—i.e., in the concrete reality of a body (1:19; 2:9; cf. 1:22; 2:11; and the "substance" [Greek "body"] of 2:17. It is farfetched to refer 2:9, 17, to the church as the body of Christ). (*b*) Christ is Lord over all angels (1:16; 2:10, 15; cf. Heb. 1:4-14). Paul accepted the existence of good and bad angels, although he denied the reality of pagan idols (I Cor. 8:4). (*c*) Christ is the head of the church, his body, both as mediator of Creation and as Savior (1:18; cf. John 2:21; I Cor. 11:3). In this sense also he is "first-born," the first-born from the dead, the commencement of the new family of God, the new Adam (cf. Rom. 8:10-11; I Cor. 15:20 ff). The phrase "to present you" (1:22) may have in view Christ's high-priestly office; if so, cf. Heb. 3:1; I Pet. 3:18; and the priestly messianism of Qumran.

The salvation offered by such a Christ cannot therefore be a mere preparation, in need of the secret teaching and regulations of another discipline. Legalism of the Jewish type is repudiated; the faithful are liberated from the power of angels (2:15); and sins (conceived as debts listed on a bond, 2:14) are remitted (this phrase is used instead of "justification"). Paul thinks of salvation both as a future inheritance (1:5, 22, 28; 3:4, 24; 1:12 is ambiguous, but may be eschatological) and as a present possession (1:13-14, 22; 2:11-15, 20; 3:1, 3, 10). Christ is the "hope of glory" and yet "in you" or "among you" (1:27). Christian life "is hid with Christ in God" (3:3). This "mysticism" is related to the new-Adam idea (3:10, "manhood," not "nature" as RSV) and to baptism (2:12; but too much should not be deduced from the analogy of baptism with circumcision—e.g., to justify infant baptism). Because the "substance" is in Christ, he is not only the clue to ultimate reality, he is also the judge of every religion and the touchstone of morals (3:5, 11, 15-16, 24). He is God's own "secret" by whom all mankind can be redeemed (1:6, 23-29; 3:11). Hence Paul's powerful missionary impulse and adoring gratitude (1:29; 3:17).

Christ's redemptive work, man's response in faith and baptism, bring the church into being as the body of Christ (1:4, 22, 24; 2:12) and the temple of God (1:23, "stable and steadfast," and 2:7, "built up," imply this concept). Its range is universal (1:6, 28, where one notes the triple "every man"; 3:10, Adam; 3:11, race or culture or economic status count for nothing). This church is to become united, in love, and ought to grow, in wisdom, as each member becomes mature (1:8, 28; 3:14). Worship, with prayers and songs of thanksgiving at its heart, is central to the church's life (3:15-17). The eucharistic context of the hymn about Christ (1:12, 15 ff) has been emphasized by N. A. Dahl; cf. the same thought in 3:17. Paul may be indebted to the Jewish hymns and benedictions known to us in the Psalms of Solomon and the Qumran *Hodayôth;* and through him the line to the ancient prayers of the third century A.D. can be traced. The apostle is both teacher and ruler in the church (1:28), and in its service he completes the Messiah's sufferings (a daring idea, but no reflection on Christ's all-sufficiency can possibly be intended; 1:24). The phrase "that we may present" (1:28) answers Christ's work in 1:22 and so may indicate the priestly function of the apostle, in the setting of the eschatological hope (cf. Rom. 12:1; 15:16; Phil. 2:17, for priestly and sacrificial language). No local minister is addressed, except probably the Laodicean ARCHIPPUS (4:17). Christ is the Head who operates through his servants (2:19; implying the teaching of Rom. 12:4 ff). Clearly this doctrine is what the second century meant by catholicity.

Impartial judgment awaits the world (1:22-23; 3:6, 25), but little stress is laid on this idea (cf. 3:4).

*b. Ethics.* Paul's ethical teaching flows from his theology of salvation (1:10; 3:5—RSV "in you" represents Greek "the members." This difficult phrase may be a gloss. Masson ingeniously solves the problem by translating it as a vocative, "you, the members [of Christ's body, the church]," and ascribing it to the author of Ephesians). Christ's example is held up for imitation (1:11-12; 3:14-17; 4:2-6); hence love is the greatest virtue, the bond of unity (or of maturity), the motive for mutual forgiveness. This love is Christian charity, compassionate, tender, gracious, Christlike (*see* LOVE IN THE NT). Paul's converts and friends are his beloved, his brothers (1:7; 4:7, 9, 14; cf. 1QS 5.24–6.1; 8.1-6; and note the differences).

The teaching on household duties is summary, apart from the section on slaves (because of ONESIMUS). The inferior groups are told to be submissive, as befits the Christian community; but Paul fails to advise them to love their superiors, the husbands, fathers, and masters (3:18–4:1). Slavery is not condemned, presumably because the adventist hope is strong. An ethic for today would require fuller discussion of the duties and rights of other "superiors" —e.g., governments, industrial corporations, mortgage companies, schools, trade unions, etc. Yet the Pauline principle is always relevant: "as serving the Lord . . . , knowing that you also have a Master in heaven" (the Greek word "master" or "lord," κύριος, occurs nine times in the brief paragraph 3:18-4:1).

*c. Personalia.* Note the range and depth of Paul's friendships. MARK is probably the author of the Second Gospel (cf. Acts 12:25; 13:5, 13; 15:37).

House churches were usual in the primitive days (4:15—the text here is uncertain; Nympha or Nymphas is equally possible; cf. Philem. 2; Acts 16:15). The "letter from Laodicea," if not lost, may be Philemon; Marcion called canonical Ephesians "Laodiceans"; for a spurious letter with this title, see Lightfoot on 4:16 and LAODICEANS, EPISTLE TO THE.

LUKE is usually identified with the author of Luke-Acts or the "we sections" in Acts. Paul's thorn in the flesh (II Cor. 12:7) has been identified, dubiously, as epilepsy; hence his need of a doctor to accompany him (cf. Gal. 4:13). Other lists of friends and colleagues will be found in Rom. 16; I Cor. 16:12-17; II Tim. 4:9-12.

**5. Text.** There are major difficulties in 2:18, 23, and minor problems at 1:7, 12, 16; 2:2, 10, 22; 3:22. Even Lightfoot and Hort resort to conjecture at 2:18 ("taking his stand on visions"), by ingenious division of the letters. But Hort's "riding on the clouds" is not much better than the RSV, which may be a *terminus technicus* from the mystery cults. In the same verse, the RSV "insisting on" would be more accurately translated as "taking pleasure in" (θέλων ἐν; cf. I Sam. 18:22; Pss. 111:1; 146:10 LXX). Or θέλων alone may mean "willingly" or "deliberately." Again, on the plausible analogy of the Greek noun behind the RSV "rigor of devotion" in 2:23, Hort would emend so as to have: "Let no one disqualify you in a voluntary humility." The reference would then be to a false meekness in the presence of the angels or to ascetic mortification. Resort to conjecture is not really necessary, but "priding himself on" would be better than the RSV. Vs. 23 is a famous crux also. Some MSS omit "and" after "self-abasement," thus leaving the next phrase without connection. "Severity to the body" may be an intrusive gloss explaining "self-abasement"; similarly, "they are of no value" may be a gloss on "an appearance of"; while the last phrase is ambiguous—either "looking to indulgence of the flesh" or "to check indulgence of the flesh." Paul's point is that mortification does not promote spiritual health, that it leads rather to self-indulgence; this point can be verified in the history of monasticism.

*Bibliography.* NT Introductions by Goguel (1926); Behm (1950); McNeile-Williams (1953); Commentaries by J. B. Lightfoot (1875); H. von Soden (1893); T. K. Abbott (1897); E. Haupt (1902); M. Dibelius (1927); E. Lohmeyer (1930); E. F. Scott (1930); Ch. Masson (1950); F. W. Beare (1955); C. F. D. Moule (1957).

Special studies: H. J. Holtzmann, *Kritik der Epheser-und Kolosserbriefe* (1872); A. E. J. Rawlinson, *The NT Doctrine of the Christ* (1926); A. Schweitzer, *The Mysticism of Paul the Apostle* (1931); O. Roller, *Das Formular der paulinischen Briefe* (1933); S. Hanson, *The Unity of the Church in the NT: Colossians and Ephesians* (1946); E. Percy, *Die Probleme der Kolosser-und Epheserbriefe* (1946); F. Prat, *La Théologie de S. Paul* (1949); O. Cullmann, *Christ and Time* (1950); A. Galloway, *The Cosmic Christ* (1951); G. H. C. Macgregor, "Principalities and Powers: The Cosmic Background of St. Paul's Thought," *NTS*, vol. I, no. 1 (Sept., 1954), pp. 17-28; W. D. Davies, *Paul and Rabbinic Judaism* (2nd ed., 1955); G. B. Caird, *Principalities and Powers* (1956).                    G. JOHNSTON

**COLT** [בֶּן, son; עַיִר, see Ass; πῶλος, the young of various animals, *sometimes* horse; *cf.* Lat. *pullus*, young animal]. The young of the horse or of animals of the horse kind.

In the OT "colt" is used of the young of camels (Gen. 32:15), of the domesticated ass (Gen. 49:11; Zech. 9:9), and of the wild ass (Job 11:12).

In the NT πῶλος is used of the animal which was obtained by Jesus' disciples for their Master's entry into Jerusalem (Mark 11:2, etc.), in connection with which two of the evangelists quote Zech. 9:9 (Matt. 21:5; John 12:15). Matt. 21:2; John 12:14 indicate that the animal was a young ass, but Mark and Luke use πῶλος without qualification.

*Bibliography.* W. Bauer, *JBL*, LXXII (1953), 220-29, maintains that when πῶλος is used with no restriction, it means "horse," and he implies that this was the earliest Christian tradition about the animal on which Jesus rode. His discussion, which avoids the question of the original Aramaic term, does not give full weight to the fact that in Jewish Palestine it was the ass which was ordinarily used for riding.
W. S. McCULLOUGH

**COMFORT** [נחם (Pi'el); παρακαλέω, παράκλησις; *also* παραμυθέομαι, παραμυθία, παραμύθιον; *and*

παρηγορία]. While παρακαλέω may mean "to call (somebody) to one's side" for help (*see* PARACLETE; COMFORTER), it is also used of calling or speaking to someone else by way of comfort, encouragement, entreaty, or exhortation. With the noun παράκλησις it appears in the NT as a gospel key word, going back, perhaps, like other gospel key words, to the exordium of the good news of Isa. 40:1 ff:

> Comfort, comfort [נחמו נחמו] my people,
> says your God;

(cf. Isa. 51:12: "I am he that comforts you" [lit. "your comforter"—מנחמכם]; also 49:13; 51:3, 19; 61:2; 66:13). So in the NT, God is the "God of all comfort" (II Cor. 1:3). II Corinthians might, indeed, be called the letter of comfort, so repeatedly does Paul strike this note in it, especially in the opening paragraph (1:3-7) and in 7:4-13. Those who enjoy the comfort of God are best able to comfort others; and Paul, who had received such comfort by the reassuring news which Titus brought him from Corinth, is now eager to impart a full measure of that comfort to his readers as compensation for the distress which his "severe letter" had caused them.

In the teaching of Jesus those who mourn are congratulated because they are to be comforted (Matt. 5:4); Lazarus in Abraham's bosom is comforted after his wretched life on earth (Luke 16:25).

"Comfort" is a commoner word in the KJV than in the RSV, because its range of meaning was wider in older English than it is today. In accordance with the Latin *confortare* (from which the English word is derived), it meant "to strengthen," as well as "to aid, console, encourage, refresh, relieve, soothe." The RSV retains "comfort" only where it means "to console or relieve from distress"; elsewhere it replaces it by such words as "encourage" (cf. Rom. 1:12; 15: 4; I Cor. 14:31; Col. 2:2; I Thess. 5:14); "incentive" (Phil. 2:1); "cheer" (Phil. 2:19). In II Cor. 13:11 the RSV has "heed my appeal" for the KJV "be of good comfort" (παρακαλεῖσθε).

A "word of exhortation" (λόγος παρακλήσεως) apparently denotes a synagogue homily (Acts 13:15; Heb. 13:22). The "comfortable words" of Zech. 1:13 KJV are "comforting words" in the RSV; the "comfortable" word of II Sam. 14:17 KJV is literally a word "for rest" (RSV "The word . . . will set me at rest"). To "speak comfortably" (KJV) is literally to speak "upon the heart"; the RSV renders to speak "kindly" (II Sam. 19:7); "encouragingly" (II Chr. 30:22; 32:6); "tenderly" (Isa. 40:2; Hos. 2:14). *See* CONSOLATION.

*Bibliography.* L. A. Weigle, *Bible Words in Living Language* (1957), pp. 92-93.                    F. F. BRUCE

**COMFORTER.** KJV translation of παράκλητος in John 14:16 ff. *See* PARACLETE.

**COMMANDMENT.** An authoritative word or precept; most frequently found in reference to the divine commands. The OT expression "according to the mouth of Yahweh" is generally translated: "according to the commandment of Yahweh" (Exod. 17:1). The term דבר, "word," is frequently to be translated "commandment"; so also the term אמרה, "that which is said."

The two most common Hebrew and Greek terms

for "commandment" are, respectively, מצוה and ἐντολή. Both are derived from roots which have the basic meaning "to give an order," "to appoint," "to commission" (for a specific task).

In the OT, and often in the NT as well, the commandments of God generally refer to those found in the Pentateuch, the TORAH. In the NT, the commandments are summarized by Jesus in the command to love God and neighbor (Matt. 22:35-40; Mark 12:28-34; Luke 10:25-28). This combination of Deut. 6:5; Lev. 19:18 is already reflected, however, in certain intertestamental writings (Test. Iss. 5:2; 7:6; Test. Dan 5:3).                W. J. HARRELSON

**COMMANDMENTS, TEN.** See TEN COMMANDMENTS; LAW IN THE OT.

**COMMENTARY.** Anglicized form of Latin *commentarius*, which, usually used in the plural, first meant sketchy notes as in a pupil's notebook or a speaker's outline, then a book of unpolished history (cf. Caesar's *Commentarii*), and finally a book of notes explaining some earlier work (cf. Julius Hyginus' commentaries, late first century B.C., on Vergil). Jerome, the first great Latin biblical commentator, mentions many commentators (on secular texts) before his time.

A biblical commentary takes a section of scripture and seeks to make its meaning clear, or at least clearer, to the man of the author's own day. Typically it begins with the commentator's conclusions on the questions of introduction—who wrote it, why, etc. But some commentaries proceed inductively, leaving the reader to gather these matters in the course of the comment. Many reproduce the text in the original or in translation. The comment must deal to some extent with textual, grammatical, and lexical problems of the original; some do little more. More satisfactory commentaries strive to outline the author's thought, to relate each part to the aim of the whole, and to see it against the background of its religious and its sociopolitical matrix. Others place greater emphasis on exegetical history and the writing's bearing upon present religious needs.
                                K. GROBEL

**COMMERCE.** See TRADE AND COMMERCE.

**COMMISSION, THE GREAT.** A way of referring to Jesus' command in Matt. 28:18-20 that his disciples should go into all the world and "make disciples of all nations, baptizing them in the name of the Father, and of the Son, and of the Holy Spirit." The story presents a typically Matthean picture of the risen, exalted, yet abiding, Lord. From a new mountain of authority (cf. Matt. 5:1; 7:21-29), he sends his disciples on the final, universal mission (Matt. 24:14; John 20:19-23; Acts 1:8) of the newly begun messianic age.

Did the early church receive its universal commission through some such christophany, or was it learned gradually by experience (Acts 10:1-11:18; Gal. 2:9)? Is such an appearance of the risen Christ sufficient explanation for its baptismal practice, or had the latter (Acts 2:38; 8:16; I Cor. 1:14-16) some other origin? Since the threefold baptismal formula occurs only here in the NT, was it an original part of this Gospel (*see* BAPTISM)? The strophic form

gained by retranslating this passage into Aramaic supports the reading "in my name," found in Eusebius. The present text, however, is attested by all other evidence, and its joining of Father, Son, and Spirit appears in other primitive confessions (I Cor. 12:3-6; II Cor. 13:14; I Pet. 1:2).

*Bibliography.* F. J. Foakes-Jackson and K. Lake, *The Beginnings of Christianity,* I (1920), 300-344; K. H. Rengsdorf, "Apostleship" (trans. J. R. Coates), *Bible Key Words,* VI (1952), 32-53; E. Lohmeyer, *Das Evangelium des Matthäus* (1956), pp. 412-26; E. Stauffer, *NT Theology* (1956), pt. 3.
                                I. W. BATDORF

**COMMON** [חל (KJV *alternately* PROFANE); κοινός, δημόσιος]; **COMMON LAND(S)** [מגרש] (Lev. 25: 34; II Chr. 11:14; KJV SUBURBS). In OT priestly literature "common" is the opposite of "holy" (קדש; Lev. 10:10; *see* HOLINESS), the unconsecrated rather than the consecrated—e.g., "common bread" (I Sam. 21:4—H 21:5), a "common journey" (I Sam. 21:5—H 21:6).

Although in the OT the common is ritually neutral, and may be either clean or unclean, in the NT κοινός is synonymous with "unclean" (*see* CLEAN AND UNCLEAN; Acts 10:14-15, 28). The same Greek word means "shared"—e.g., "common faith" (Tit. 1:4), "common salvation" (Jude 3), "all things in common" (Acts 2:44). "Common" in the meanings "shared" and "ordinary" (δημόσιος; Acts 5:18) is omitted in Hebrew (Num. 16:29; I Kings 10:27; Jer. 23:28), or expressed by circumlocution—e.g., "a man's stylus," "a man's cubit," "people of the land," "sons of the people" for "common script" (Isa. 8:1), "the common cubit" (Deut. 3:11), and "the common people" (Lev. 4:27; Jer. 26:23).
                                L. E. TOOMBS

**COMMON LIFE.** The distinguishing characteristic of the Spirit-possessed community of the Christian body, expressing that fellowship between men which results from corporate communion with God and transcends secular divisions (Rom. 15:27; Gal. 3:27-29). It finds practical expression in mutual assistance (Rom. 12:13; 15:26; II Cor. 8-9); in the COMMUNITY OF GOODS, especially emphasized by Luke, for whom offenses against the common life are directed against the Holy Spirit (Acts 5:3, 9); and in the common table (cf. Acts 6:1; Gal. 2:12). Its source and focus lie in sacramental COMMUNION.

*Bibliography.* L. S. Thornton, *The Common Life in the Body of Christ* (1941).                G. W. H. LAMPE

**COMMONWEALTH.** The translation of πολίτευμα in Phil. 3:20 (KJV CONVERSATION) and of πολιτεία in Eph. 2:12.

Paul wrote to the Philippians: "Our commonwealth is in heaven" (Phil. 3:20). Implicit here are the following considerations: (*a*) "Our commonwealth"—i.e., the commonwealth of Christians—is distinct from all others. Christians are already citizens of the heavenly state, as contrasted with earthly states. (*b*) "Commonwealth" implies "community." The Christian lives out of, and shares in, Christian community. (*c*) The conduct of Christians is to be appropriate to their citizenship. (*d*) Only a miracle—the coming of the Savior from the commonwealth in heaven—will establish the fulfilment of the community's life.

Πολιτεία, translated "commonwealth" in Eph. 2:12, is translated "CITIZENSHIP" in Acts 22:28.

B. H. THROCKMORTON, JR.

**COMMUNICATION.** *See* MESSENGER; TRAVEL AND COMMUNICATION.

**COMMUNION** [κοινωνία]. A term literally meaning "sharing" and particularly important in connection with the covenant relation between God and his people. *See* COVENANT.

1. In the OT
   *a*. Between God and his people
   *b*. Between God and individuals
   *c*. In relation to Israel's hope
2. In the NT
   *a*. As participation in Christ
   *b*. Church and sacraments
Bibliography

**1. In the OT.** *a. Between God and his people.* The entire notion of the covenant involves the idea of communion between God and man, although this is generally implicit and not actually expressed in terms of "communion." The latter conception might suggest a participation in the divinity such as is foreign to the thought of the OT, although Philo (*Life of Moses* 1.158) is able to speak of the relation between God and Moses as a κοινωνία.

The covenant involves the closest fellowship between God and his people, but without compromising the completeness of the divine lordship or modifying the fundamental truth that the whole relationship is based upon the sovereign grace of God, who remains transcendent, calling his people into existence and resting his covenant with them upon his promises, which are the expression of his omnipotent will. There can be no tendency in the covenant theology of the Bible to suggest the possibility of an absorption of the human by the divine, or of any union which would obscure the basic distinction between the Creator and his creation or between the all-holy God and those who are made holy only by virtue of their vocation from him. Nevertheless, within the terms of the relationship of grace and obedience presupposed in the call of Israel, communion of a close and intimate kind is established between man and God. The foundation of the covenant is the divine promise: "I will be with you" (cf. Exod. 3:12), and it is expressed in the presence of God among his people, and the access to him which this implies (*see* COVENANT). The divine presence is symbolized in the ark, which represents and mediates it (cf. Num. 10:35-36), and in the ideas associated with the cloud of the presence (Exod. 33:7-11), and the angel of the Lord leading and directing the covenant people (Exod. 23:20-21; 32:34). Later, the presence of God among his people is represented chiefly by the temple at Jerusalem, and by Israel's possession of the revealed will of God as set out in the Law.

*b. Between God and individuals.* Certain individuals are granted a special and peculiarly close relationship to God. Moses is marked out from all other men as one with whom God communed directly, without an intermediary: "When Moses entered the tent, the pillar of cloud would descend and stand at the door of the tent, and the LORD would speak with Moses. . . . Thus the LORD used to speak to Moses face to face, as a man speaks to his friend" (Exod. 33:9-11). His communion with God was thus different from that of the prophets: "And there has not arisen a prophet since in Israel like Moses, whom the LORD knew face to face" (Deut. 34:10). The prophets themselves, however, are specially favored in their relationship to God. They are

> filled with power,
> with the Spirit of the LORD,
> and with justice and might,
> to declare to Jacob his transgression
> and to Israel his sin (Mic. 3:8).

> The Spirit of the Lord GOD is upon me,
> because the LORD has anointed me
> to bring good tidings to the afflicted
> (Isa. 61:1).

They are men to whom the word of the Lord comes (Jer. 1:2), to whom God reveals the meaning of his acts in history:

> Surely the Lord GOD does nothing,
> without revealing his secret
> to his servants the prophets
> (Amos 3:7).

*c. In relation to Israel's hope.* The hope of Israel, however, included the expectation that in the age of fulfilment all God's people, and not merely a selected few, would be admitted to a similar intimate, personal knowledge of God. This might be conceived in terms of a general effusion of the prophetic Spirit upon the whole people (cf. Num. 11:29; Joel 2:28-29). In a deeper sense it might be seen as the essence of a new relationship to God, which might properly be described as one of personal communion rather than external observances: "This is the covenant which I will make with the house of Israel after those days, says the LORD: I will put my law within them, and I will write it upon their hearts; and I will be their God, and they shall be my people. And no longer shall each man teach his neighbor and each his brother, saying, 'Know the LORD,' for they shall all know me, from the least of them to the greatest, says the LORD; for I will forgive their iniquity, and I will remember their sin no more" (Jer. 31:33-34). This is the hope of a deeper communion between God and man, which was seen by the NT writers as having been fulfilled in Christ. Under the system of the old covenant it could not be fully realized, although at its best devotion to the law as the principle of fellowship with God, seen, e.g., in Ps. 119, and also the liturgical system of the temple and its sacrifices, provided some measure of personal, and far from merely formal, communion with God. The sacrifices themselves were intended to supply a means toward this end. Whereas the sin offering and its associated sacrifices were meant to serve as a way of removing the barriers to fellowship with God set up by sins (at least unwitting and ritual offenses), the peace offering was evidently thought of as constituting a communion meal in which God and the worshiper were brought together in a mutual participation in the dedicated offering (*see* SACRIFICE AND OFFERINGS). The clearest indication that the sacrifice could be regarded as a real bond of close personal union is to be found in the illustrations and analogies adduced by Paul. "Consider the practice of Israel," he says; "are not those who eat the sacrifices partners [i.e., communicants] in the altar?" (I Cor. 10:18). The worshipers in the sacrificial system participate in the altar—i.e., in the divine presence as thereby symbolized. Paul believes that there is a similar participation on the part of heathen worshipers, but that in their case the communion is with demons: "I imply that what pagans sacrifice they offer to demons and not to God. I do not want you to be partners with [i.e., communicants with] demons. You cannot drink the cup of the Lord and the cup of demons. You cannot partake of the table of the Lord and the table of demons" (I Cor. 10:20-21). To partake of the sacrifice makes the worshiper a participant, either in fellowship with God in the case of the sacrifices of Judaism, or in fellowship with demons if he eats and drinks the offerings consecrated to pagan deities.

**2. In the NT. *a. As participation in Christ.*** In the Christian dispensation, communion between God and man has been established in a new and deeper sense through Christ. Through his life, death, resurrection, and glorification the new covenant has been brought into being (cf. Mark 14:22-25; I Cor. 11:23-26). Man's communion with God is now in and through Christ, and the Christian life is life "in Christ." This frequently repeated phrase of Paul indicates the heart and essence of the Christian experience of communion. The gospel proclaimed by Paul and the other apostolic missionaries is summed up in the words: "We beseech you on behalf of Christ, be reconciled to God. For our sake he made him to be sin who knew no sin, so that in him we might become the righteousness of God" (II Cor. 5:20-21). The vocation of those who are converted by the apostolic preaching is a calling "into the fellowship of his Son, Jesus Christ our Lord" (I Cor. 1:9).

This calling involves union with Christ in his death, burial, and resurrection. It is a sharing in the life of the new age, to be partially realized in the present time and to be consummated after death; the state of being "always with the Lord," in a complete and final sense, belongs to the future hope (I Thess. 4:17). It is, however, experienced now in the most profound personal communion with Christ, which is mediated by the Spirit and is identical with life in the Spirit of God, which is the Spirit of Christ (cf. Rom. 8:9-17). Its character is best expressed in Paul's acknowledgment of his death with Christ to the life of the "flesh" and his entry upon a life whose inner principle and motive is Christ, apprehended by faith: "I have been crucified with Christ; it is no longer I who live, but Christ who lives in me; and the life I now live in the flesh I live by faith in the Son of God, who loved me and gave himself for me" (Gal. 2:20). The Christian has died with Christ, believing that he will also live with him (Rom. 6:8). We suffer with Christ in the assurance of glorification with him (Rom. 8:17; cf. II Cor. 7:3). By anticipation the Christian can be said to be exalted with·Christ and enthroned with him, even while he still lives in the present age: "God, . . . even when we were dead through our trespasses, made us alive

together with Christ . . . , and raised us up with him, and made us sit with him in the heavenly places in Christ Jesus" (Eph. 2:4-6). The personal experience of Paul himself was of rejecting all that had seemed valuable to him in his unconverted days and accepting a righteousness given by God, the essential content of which is a new relationship to God through communion with Christ in death and resurrection: "that I may gain Christ and be found in him, not having a righteousness of my own, based on law, but that which is through faith in Christ, the righteousness from God that depends on faith; that I may know him and the power of his resurrection, and may share his sufferings, becoming like him in his death, that if possible I may attain the resurrection from the dead" (Phil. 3:8-10). The thought, however, though more profoundly expressed by Paul, is not peculiar to him. With a somewhat different emphasis, the idea of the Christian life as a sharing in the sufferings of Christ is found also in such passages as I Pet. 4:13; 5:1.

***b. Church and sacraments.*** This communion with Christ is not merely an individual experience. It is constitutive of the church as the body of Christ (cf. especially I Cor. 12:12-13). The community is a body indwelt by the Spirit, so that it can, in one aspect, be virtually equated with Christ. The effective sign of incorporation into Christ is baptism, in which the converts are buried with Christ to rise as participants in the resurrection life (Rom. 6:3; Col. 2:12). This new life is a participation or communion in the Holy Spirit (II Cor. 13:14), and results in communion between the human members of the one body which is Christ (the phrase "participation in the Holy Spirit" in the last-mentioned passage may also, or perhaps alternatively, convey the meaning of "fellowship brought about by the Holy Spirit"; cf. RSV text and mg.). In Christ the various earthly divisions and distinctions are transcended (Rom. 10:12; Gal. 3:28). *See* CHURCH, IDEA OF.

The communion of the church with Christ (which is a union through him with the Father; cf. John 14:20-23; I John 1:3-6; 3:24; 4:13), and culminates in the hope of the vision of God as he is (I John 3:2), is effectively signified and expressed in the Eucharist. Participation in the one loaf and the cup is the means and the bond of union with Christ, and continually constitutes the church as his body. It brings the community into present union with the ascended Christ, and both symbolizes and effects the unity of all Christians. It is the communion in and of the body and blood of Christ (I Cor. 10:16-17; 11:23-29). In this Eucharistic communion, there are gathered up the ideas underlying the commemoration of Christ's death, the re-enacting of the Last Supper, the meals of fellowship between the risen Christ and his followers (cf. Luke 24:30; John 21:13), and the "breaking of bread" in fellowship, practiced by the early Jerusalem church (Acts 2:42, 46).

Present communion with God in Christ is to be perfected when the future hope of total redemption is fulfilled. The proclamation of Christ's death in sacramental communion is "until he comes" (I Cor. 11:26). The promises of God thus imply a release from the "corruption that is in the world because of evil desire [RSV 'passion']," and participation, or communion, in the divine nature (II Pet. 1:4). This "deification" of the believer signifies chiefly participation in the future life, which is the life of God.

*Bibliography.* A. J. F. Higgins, *The Lord's Supper in the NT* (1952); J. A. T. Robinson, *The Body* (1952); A. R. George, *Communion with God in the NT* (1955); E. Best, *One Body in Christ* (1956); O. Cullmann and J. Leenhardt, *Essays on the Lord's Supper* (1958).     G. W. H. LAMPE

**COMMUNITY OF GOODS** (Acts 2:44-45; 4:32-5:10). In the first days of the church in Jerusalem, the believers, taught by the apostles, united in a communal life in which they joyfully and generously shared both spiritual and material possessions. Luke reports twice that they had all things in common. In 2:44-45 they sold their goods and divided to all as needed. In 4:32-35 no one selfishly claimed his own property. No one was in want, because owners of lands and houses sold these and gave the proceeds to the apostles to distribute to the needy. Luke graphically reports the gift of BARNABAS to the common fund, the lies and deaths of ANANIAS and SAPPHIRA.

The origins of this community of goods may be found in the example of Jesus and his disciples (Luke 8:3; Mark 10:21), and in the contagious new joy of a common life in the Spirit which overflowed into a sharing of wealth. The communal life of the Essenes was well known (Jos. War II.viii.3-4). The Dead Sea Scrolls show some parallels, or possible antecedents, in community of goods at Qumran (1QS 1.12; 5.2; 6.3, 19, 22; 7.25), where communism was required.

Because of Marxism today, "communism" is not a suitable term for the communal life of the first Christians. Their community of goods was voluntary, set up by sales, and shared by apostles with the poor. Its motivation was God's grace. It was not an equality of property or of production. It resulted in the first dissension in the church (Acts 6:1-6). It soon faded out, and the poor were aided by other plans (Gal. 2:10; I Cor. 16:1; II Cor. 8:1-15). But its influence continued long (Did. 4.8; Barn. 19.8), especially in the communal monastic orders of the church.

*Bibliography.* K. Lake, *Beginnings of Christianity,* V (1933), 140-51; H. Seesemann, *Der Begriff* κοινωνία *im neuen Testament* (1933).     D. M. BECK

**COMPASS POINTS.** *See* ORIENTATION.

**COMPASSION, PITY.** The words for "compassion" and "pity" in the original languages of the Bible are also frequently translated "mercy," and the meanings of these terms are interchangeable. *See* MERCY.

**CONANIAH** kŏn'ə nī'ə *Kethibh* כונניהו, *Qere* כנניהו, Yahu has established]; KJV CONONIAH in II Chr. 31:12-13. Alternately: JECONIAH jĕk'ə nī'ə ['Ιεχονίας] (I Esd. 1:9); KJV JECONIAS —əs. **1.** A Levite and chief officer over the collection of contributions and tithes in the reign of King Hezekiah (II Chr. 31:12-13).

**2.** A chief of the Levites in the reign of King Josiah (II Chr. 35:9).     B. T. DAHLBERG

**CONCISION.** *See* MUTILATION.

**CONCUBINE** [פילגש; πάλλαξ]. A slave girl who belonged to a Hebrew family and bore children. Concubines were acquired by purchase from poor Hebrew families, captured in war, or taken in payment of debt. A girl in this classification achieved a certain status if she had sons (Gen. 21:10; 22:24; 30:3; 31:33; Exod. 23:12; 21:7, 10). Her son might become a co-heir; her name was remembered because of her offspring; a barren wife might have a son through her; she might have her own quarters; she was to benefit by the seventh day of rest; and she had the right to food, clothing, and sexual intercourse. She had the affection of her "husband" (Judg. 19:1-3). Eunuchs were put in charge of concubines (Esth. 2:15); they are called "man's delight" (Eccl. 2:8), along with singers. A king might have many concubines (I Kings 11:3). The faithfulness of the daughter of a concubine induced David to give decent burial to the bones of Saul and Jonathan (II Sam. 21:10-14).

*See also* FAMILY; MARRIAGE.     O. J. BAAB

**CONCUPISCENCE.** A word occurring in the KJV and some other older versions in several NT passages with the meaning of "covetousness" (Rom. 7:8; Col. 3:5) and "sexual lust" (I Thess. 4:5), translating ἐπιθυμία. The term is not used in the RSV or other modern translations, because of technical theological connotations acquired by the concept in Roman Catholic theology. *See* COVETOUSNESS; DESIRE; LUST.     F. W. YOUNG

**CONDEMNATION.** Primarily, the act of judging guilty.

**1. In the OT.** In the OT the term "condemn" is used to translate רשע, except in four passages. It renders שפט in Pss. 109:31; 141:6; Prov. 19:29; and אשם in Ps. 34:21-22.

The concept of condemnation appears primarily in Job, Psalms, and Proverbs, but also in Exod. 22:9; Deut. 25:1; I Kings 8:32; and it is usually, but not always, used in connection with God. God will condemn one who breaks a trust (Exod. 22:9), the man of evil devices (Prov. 12:2), the unrighteous (Ps. 34:21); and Solomon prays that God will condemn the guilty (I Kings 8:32). But God will not condemn those who take refuge in him (Ps. 34:22), and he saves the needy man from those who condemn him to death (Ps. 109:31; cf. Ps. 37:33). The wicked are said to condemn the innocent (Ps. 94:21; Prov. 17:15), and the righteous condemn the wicked (Deut. 25:1; Ps. 141:6; cf. Prov. 19:29). Job condemns himself (Job 9:20; cf. 15:6); he fears that God will condemn him (9:29) and pleads with God not to (10:2). Job is asked both by Elihu (34:17) and by God himself (40:8) whether he will condemn God.

**2. In the NT.** "Condemn" and "condemnation" translate eight different Greek words, six of which have the same root. Of these six, two are verbs (κρίνω, κατακρίνω) and four are nouns (κρίμα, κατάκριμα, κρίσις, κατάκρισις). The other two Greek words are καταγινώσκω (Gal. 2:11; I John 3:20-21) and καταδικάζω (Matt. 12:7, 37; Luke 6:37; Jas. 5:6). The root of the first six words meant originally "to separate or distinguish"; then "to pass a judgment on"; and finally "to pass an unfavorable judgment on," or "to condemn." This root combined with the preposition κατά always means "to pass a sentence against," or "to condemn." The word "condemn," therefore, is to be understood primarily as referring to a verdict of guilty, and usually only by implication to a punishment.

In the NT, God is sometimes the source of condemnation, either explicitly—as, e.g., of "sin in the flesh" (Rom. 8:3) or of Sodom and Gomorrah (II Pet. 2:6)—or implicitly (cf. Matt. 12:37; Mark 12: 40=Luke 20:47; John 3:18*b;* Rom. 3:7; 13:23; I Cor. 11:32, 34; II Cor. 3:9; II Thess. 2:12; Jas. 5:12; II Pet. 2:3; Jude 4). But God sent his Son, not to condemn the world (John 3:17; cf. 3:18*a;* 8:11).

Men also condemn one another (cf. Matt. 12:7; John 8:10; Rom. 2:27; Heb. 11:7; Jas. 5:6); but they are forbidden to do so (Luke 6:37). Jesus warns that the men of Nineveh and the queen of the South will condemn his "generation" (Matt. 12:41-42=Luke 11:31-32); and Paul rejoices that no one whom God acquits can be condemned by any other (Rom. 8:34).

Jesus was condemned to death (Matt. 20:18= Mark 10:33; Matt. 27:3; Mark 14:64; Luke 24:20); and one may condemn oneself (Rom. 2:1; Gal. 2: 11; I John 3:20-21). The devil also condemns (I Tim. 3:6).

The word used only in Rom. 5:16, 18; 8:1 (κατάκριμα) probably means the punishment following sentence, and not the sentence itself. It refers in Rom. 5 to the punishment of servitude in which all men live following Adam's sin; and in Rom. 8 the servitude is said to be past for those who are in Christt. B. H. THROCKMORTON, JR.

**CONDUIT** [תעלה] (II Kings 18:17; 20:20; Isa. 7:3; 36:2). A water channel or tunnel. *See* WATER WORKS; JERUSALEM § 6*c.*

**CONEY.** KJV translation of שפן. *See* ROCK BADGER.

\*CONFESSION. An aspect of the worship of God. It involves acknowledgment of sin and helplessness, the declaration of the acts of God by which man is rescued from his troubles, and praise and thanksgiving to the mighty God who shows mercy to his people. In the NT the second aspect relates to Jesus as God's anointed one and develops into a liturgical and theological proclamation of the lordship of Jesus. As the Christian mission moved into the Hellenistic world, a variety of misinterpretations of the gospel arose. To combat them, the liturgical confession became more complex, moving toward the theological formulation found in second-century baptismal creeds.

1. Terminology
2. In the OT
3. In the NT
   *a.* Confession of sin
   *b.* Confession of Jesus
   *c.* Praise and thanksgiving
Bibliography

**1. Terminology.** Confession as proclamation, acknowledgment of sin, and praise of God is expressed by many terms in the OT. The commonest among them are the verb ידה, "to confess or declare"

(Pss. 7:17; 9:1; 28:7; etc.); the noun תודה, "confession, thanksgiving" (Pss. 26:7; 50:14; 100:4; Ezra 10:11); the verb נדר, "to vow" (Ps. 76:11; Isa. 19:21); the noun נדר, "vow" (Ps. 22:26; Jonah 1:16); the verb שבח, "praise, glorify" (Pss. 63:3; 117:1; 145:4); and the verb קרא, "call upon, proclaim" (Exod. 33: 19; 34:6; Isa. 61:2).

The LXX also has a great variety of expressions. The verbs ὁμολογέω, "to confess"; ἐξομολογέομαι, "to praise, thank"; ἀνθομολογέομαι, "to give thanks"; and the noun ὁμολογία, "confession," are used to render נדר ידה, שבח, and נדר. 'Επικαλέω and καλέω, "to call upon," render קרא; αἰνέω and ἐπαινέω, "to praise," translate שבח; αἴνεσις, "praise," is used for תודה. ידה is also translated by κράζω and ἐξαγορεύω.

In the NT the chief terms are the verb ὁμολογέω, "to confess, declare" (Matt. 10:32; John 1:20; Rom. 10:9); the noun ὁμολογία, "confession" (II Cor. 9:13; I Tim. 6:12; Heb. 3:1; 4:14); the verb ἐξομολογέομαι, "to confess, acknowledge, praise" (Matt. 3:6; 11:25; Mark 1:5; Luke 10:21); and ἀνθομολογέομαι, "to give thanks" (Luke 2:38).

**2. In the OT.** Confession roots in the liturgical tradition of the cultus. It is first the proclamation of the deliverance wrought by God: Israel's redemption (*see* REDEEM) from bondage in Egypt, or the deliverance of an individual oppressed by his enemies, crushed by disaster, or burdened by guilt:

> I waited patiently for the LORD;
> he inclined to me and heard my cry.
> He drew me up from the desolate pit,
> out of the miry bog,
> and set my feet upon a rock,
> making my steps secure
> (Ps. 40:1-2).

Secondly, it is the acknowledgment of SIN and helplessness. Under the chastening hand of God, Israel recognizes its sin. The worshiper ponders the desperation of his plight and his helplessness to escape. Confession of sin glorifies God by recognizing that he is in the right over against man:

> So that thou art justified in thy sentence
> and blameless in thy judgment
> (Ps. 51:4).

In the postexilic period individual confession of sin becomes an increasingly prominent part of religious life.

Thirdly, it is the praise of God, who rescues his people. The Psalter is the chief repository of Israel's eloquence in such confessional praise of God, particularly Pss. 22; 30; 34; 40; 51; 116. Similar hymns are to be found in I Sam. 2:1-10; Isa. 38:10-20; Jonah 2:2-9. *See* WORSHIP IN THE OT.

**3. In the NT.** The OT pattern of liturgical confession provides the framework of NT usage. The three basic elements recur: confession of sin, proclamation of the divine deliverance, and thankful praise. The centrality of the person of Jesus and developments in the early church, however, cause significant modifications.

*a. Confession of sin.* John the Baptist emphasizes strongly the importance of confession of sins. It is a sign of REPENTANCE and a part of the baptismal rite by which Israel is to be purified for the coming of the Messiah (Matt. 3:6; Mark 1:5). Jesus also stresses confession of sins, making it central in the parables of the prodigal son (Luke 15:18) and of the Pharisee and the tax collector (Luke 18:10), as well as in the Lord's Prayer (Matt. 6:12; Luke 11:4).

*b. Confession of Jesus.* Where the OT confession proclaims God's redeeming acts for Israel, the NT confession focuses on Jesus as God's redemptive deed. Jesus is himself the great example of confession, "who in his testimony before Pontius Pilate made the good confession" (I Tim. 6:13). Similar language is used in Rev. 1:5; 3:14. When false witnesses testified against him (Mark 14:56) and the disciples denied him (vs. 68), Jesus bore witness to his messianic vocation before the high priest (vs. 62) and Pilate (15:2).

The disciple is also required to make confession. It is a public event taking place "in the presence of many witnesses" (I Tim. 6:12), quite possibly in connection with the rite of BAPTISM. At the beginning of the ministry John the Baptist made confession (John 1:20, 29-34; 3:25-30). At Caesarea Philippi, Simon Peter confessed Jesus as Messiah (Matt. 16:13-20; Mark 8:27-30; Luke 9:18-21). Mary did so after the death of Lazarus (John 11:27), and Paul in his speech before Felix (Acts 24:14 ff).

The disciple commits himself in loyalty to Jesus as God's anointed one (Matt. 10:32; Luke 12:8; Acts 23:6), an identification which is by no means obvious, and which may involve risks, such as religious and social ostracism (John 9:22; 12:42). Jesus confronts his disciples with the necessity of choice: they cannot serve both God and mammon (Matt. 6:24; 19:23; Luke 16:13). The Fourth Evangelist puts the issue as the glory of God opposed to the glory of men. Those who crave glory among men are unable to confess Jesus (John 5:44; 12:43).

The apostolic church knows the necessity of confessing Jesus: "If you confess with your lips that Jesus is Lord and believe in your heart that God raised him from the dead, you will be saved. For man believes with his heart and so is justified, and he confesses with his lips and so is saved" (Rom. 10:9-10; cf. II Cor. 4:13). In the life of the early church a number of factors influenced the development of confessional formulas. There was the need for catechetical instruction as preparation for baptism. The Western text of Acts 8:37 relates that the Ethiopian eunuch confessed: "I believe that Jesus Christ is the Son of God." While the quotation may not be a part of the original text, it shows that the custom of confession at baptism is very early.

The worship of the early church also influenced the forms of confession. I Tim. 3:16 is believed to be an early christological hymn:

> He was manifested in the flesh,
> vindicated in the Spirit,
>      seen by angels,
> preached among the nations,
> believed on in the world,
>      taken up in glory.

Other liturgical formulations are to be seen in Phil. 2:6-11 and in I Cor. 15:3-7, where Paul's reference to "delivering" what he had "received" points to a liturgical and confessional tradition. The Jewish liturgical tradition of the Shema has probably influenced the confession: "There is one God, the Father,

from whom are all things and for whom we exist, and one Lord, Jesus Christ, through whom are all things and through whom we exist" (I Cor. 8:6); "There is one body and one Spirit, . . . one Lord, one faith, one baptism, one God and Father of us all" (Eph. 4:4-6).

Persecution also played a role. The Roman imperial cult required sacrifice to the emperor and the acknowledgment that Caesar was Lord, κύριος καῖσαρ. Early Christians were convinced that the one κύριος was revealed to them in Jesus the Messiah, and they therefore regarded EMPEROR-WORSHIP as idolatry. Jesus himself made the good confession before Pontius Pilate, and the Christian was obliged to confess his name before Roman authorities also. Out of this experience a close connection developed between confession of Jesus and the concept of witness of martyrdom (μαρτυρία). *See* MARTYR.

Growth of HERESY was a fourth conditioning factor. Some of the NT confessional formulations show sharp reaction to false teaching: "Who is the liar but he who denies that Jesus is the Christ?" (I John 2:22); "Every spirit which confesses that Jesus Christ has come in the flesh is of God, and every spirit which does not confess Jesus is not of God" (I John 4:2-3; cf. I John 4:15; II John 7). Confession is an affirmation of the historical character of God's redeeming deed in Jesus Christ; commitment to the lordship of Jesus, with all its risks; and rejection of all intellectualistic, moralistic, and mythological misinterpretations of the Christ event.

*c. Praise and thanksgiving.* While confession of Christ in its controversial setting is most prominent in the NT, confession as praise is not absent. The prophetess Anna praises God after seeing the child Jesus (Luke 2:38). Jesus makes a confession of praise to the Father for his gracious revelation (Matt. 11:25; Luke 10:21). The author of the Letter to the Hebrews sees the life of the Christian as confessional praise: "Let us continually offer up a sacrifice of praise to God, that is, the fruit of lips that acknowledge his name" (Heb. 13:15). Rom. 15:9 asserts that Christ became a servant of the circumcised in order that Gentiles might glorify God, and Phil. 2:9-11 envisages the triumph of the exalted Christ when "at the name of Jesus every knee should bow . . . and every tongue confess that Jesus Christ is Lord, to the glory of God the Father."

*Bibliography.* P. Carrington, *The Primitive Christian Catechism* (1940); A. M. Hunter, *Paul and His Predecessors* (1940); O. Cullmann, *Les premières confessions de foi chretiennes* (1943); E. Stauffer, *Theology of the NT* (1955), pp. 235-53.

W. A. QUANBECK

**CONFIRMATION.** The beginning of the church's rite of confirmation is found by some scholars in a narrative of Acts (cf. 8:14-17): The Samaritans have been baptized by Philip, one of the Seven, and they received the HOLY SPIRIT by the laying on of the hands of the apostles Peter and John. A somewhat similar case appears in Ephesus (Acts 19:1-7): Some "disciples" who have only received "John's baptism" are baptized in the name of the Lord Jesus and receive the Spirit on the imposition of Paul's hands. Elsewhere in the NT the Spirit is given at the moment of baptism (cf. Acts 2:38). The laying on of hands does not appear as an element of Christian BAPTISM or a rite of admission to the church. *See* HANDS, LAYING ON OF.

Different explanations of the origin of confirmation have been proposed by scholars. The most probable seems to be the following: With the mission in Samaria the gospel passed over to non-Jews for the first time. The solemn intervention of the apostles must then underline the fact that a great step had been made toward the fulfilment of the Lord's command (Acts 1:8), and that the new converts now fully shared in the communion of the one apostolic church. Similarly the Ephesian story emphasizes that the "disciples" were now real Christians incorporated in the church. In this sense both narratives may be considered as precedents of confirmation.

P. H. MENOUD

**CONFISCATION.** Appropriation of private property to the public use or treasury. Confiscation, not mentioned in biblical law, came into vogue in Israel with the rise of the monarchy. It was a prerogative of the king to seize private property for his personal use and for his officers (I Sam. 8:14; cf. 22:7); the abuse of this prerogative led to the reaction visible in Ezek. 45:7-8; 46:16-18. As a judicial punishment, Ahab's appropriation of Naboth's property was early interpreted—correctly, it would seem—as an exercise of the royal right to confiscate the estate of state offenders: "The property of persons executed by the king devolves upon the king" (Tosef. Sanh. 4.6, citing I Kings 21:15-16). Jewish authorities under Persian rule were granted the power to inflict property penalties (עֹנֶשׁ נִכְסִין; Ezra 7:26), illustrated by Ezra 10:8, where יָחֳרַם, "forfeited," means "confiscated to the public treasury." M. GREENBERG

**CONGREGATION, ASSEMBLY.** The translation of several words denoting a gathering. Most frequent and most important are the terms עֵדָה and קָהָל.

*a*) עֵדָה, from the root יָעַד, "to appoint," designates a company assembled by appointment. The idea of appointment, however, is not always apparent in the uses of the word; it is used, e.g., of a swarm of bees (Judg. 14:8) or a herd of bulls (Ps. 68:30). The word may be applied to any gathering, group, or class viewed collectively, especially the wicked—e.g., in Job 15:34 KJV ("congregation of hypocrites"; RSV "company of the godless"); Ps. 22:16 KJV ("assembly of the wicked"; RSV "company of evildoers"); Ps. 86:14 KJV ("assemblies of violent men"; RSV "band of ruthless men"); Ecclus. 16:6 ("assembly of sinners"). In Ecclus. 7:7; 42:11, עֲדַת שַׁעַר designates the town gossips who meet at the city gate. The partisans of Korah are referred to as "his company" (עֲדָתוֹ; Num. 16:5); and the same term is applied to Job's household (Job 16:7), if the text is not corrupt. The "congregation of the righteous" (Ps. 1:5) refers, perhaps, to a legal or judicial assembly rather than to the righteous in general. In Ps. 7:7—H 7:8 the "assembly of the peoples" (עֲדַת לְאֻמִּים; KJV wrongly "congregation of the people") applies to all the peoples of the earth, who are summoned for judgment before the Lord. In Ps. 82:1 the expression עֲדַת אֵל ("divine council"; KJV "congregation of the mighty") is nearly identical with Ugaritic 'dt ilm,

which is one of several designations of the pantheon in the Ugaritic texts.

The term עֵדָה is frequently used as a designation of the body politic of Israel, especially Mosaic Israel encamped in the wilderness. The name Israel may be added to make explicit the identification of the community as the "congregation of Israel" (עֲדַת יִשְׂרָאֵל; Exod. 12:3, 6, 19, 47; Lev. 4:13; Num. 32:4; Josh. 22:18, 20; I Kings 8:5) or "all the congregation of the people of Israel" (כָּל עֲדַת בְּנֵי יִשְׂרָאֵל; Exod. 16: 1-2, 9-10). Or the community may be identified by the addition of the divine name (the "assembly of Yahweh," עֲדַת יהוה), the "congregation of the LORD" (Num. 27:17; 31:16; Josh. 22:16); or by a possessive suffix referring to the Lord (Ps. 74:2). Frequently the word is simply determined by the article, "the congregation" (הָעֵדָה; Lev. 4:15; 8:4-5; 10:17; Judg. 20:1; 21:10, 13, 16; "the assembly" in I Kings 12:20) or amplified by the adjective "all" (Lev. 8:3, and some thirty times in the rest of the Hexateuch).

The word עֵדָה as a technical term applied to the nation Israel is characteristic of the P Document; it is not used in D or JE and is rare in other historical books; Judg. 20:1; 21:10, 13, 16; I Kings 8:5 (=II Chr. 5:6); 12:12 are the only other instances of such usage. As used in P, the term appears to designate the responsible element of the nation, the full citizens who have the rights and duties of looking after the affairs of the nation. At the head of the עֵדָה is Moses, and the tribes are represented by leaders or chiefs (נְשִׂיאֵי הָעֵדָה; Exod. 16:22; Num. 4:34; 31:13; 32:2; Josh. 9:15, 18; 22:30), or elders (זִקְנֵי הָעֵדָה). Another term for these "leaders of their ancestral tribes, the heads of the clans of Israel," is קְרוּאֵי הָעֵדָה (Num. 1: 16; 26:9; "[ones] chosen from the congregation"; KJV "renowned of the congregation," "famous in the congregation"). Males of the community twenty years of age and over who were fit for military service (Num. 1:20) are called פְּקוּדֵי הָעֵדָה (Exod. 38:25), "those of the congregation who were numbered." The signal for the summoning of the whole community was the blowing of two silver trumpets; and for the leaders only to meet with Moses, a single trumpet (Num. 10:2-4).

*b*) The term קָהָל, possibly derived from קוֹל, "speak," hence "convocation," is used to designate various sorts of human gatherings. It is not applied to animals, as is עֵדָה. Perhaps the oldest use of the word is in Num. 22:4, where it is applied to the numerous camp of Israel and is appropriately rendered "horde" by the RSV. In the Blessing of Jacob (Gen. 49:6) the word, in parallelism with סוֹד, "council" (*see below*), refers to the collusion of the tribes of Simeon and Levi in the treacherous attack on the Shechemites (34:25 ff) and is rendered as "company." In Ezekiel the term is applied to foreign military and naval forces and is variously rendered "host(s)," "company," "crew" (Ezek. 17:17; 23:46; 27:27, 34; 32:22; 38:4, 7, 13, 15). Apart from its use in the general sense of "multitude," the term, like עֵדָה, is rare in pre-Deuteronomic literature. While in P עֵדָה predominates (*ca.* one hundred occurrences) and קָהָל is used relatively infrequently (*ca.* twenty-five times), in Deuteronomistic literature the latter term is the regular designation of the theocratic convocation of Israel, the gathering of the nation for religious purposes, and עדה is not used. The term קהל is especially frequent in Deuteronomy, Chronicles, Ezra, Nehemiah, and Psalms. The use of the term is virtually identical with that of עדה: the name Israel may be added (קהל ישראל, the "assembly of Israel"; Deut. 31:30), or the divine name (קהל יהוה, the "assembly of the LORD" [Num. 16:3; 20:4]; or קהל אלהים, the "assembly of God" [Neh. 13:1]); or the word may be determined by the definite article and/or the demonstrative pronoun (Exod. 16:3; Lev. 4:13). A derived form, קהלה, occurs in Deut. 33:4; Neh. 5:7.

The distinction, if any, between עדה and קהל is difficult to determine. In Lev. 4:13 there appears to be a differentiation between עדה as the entire body politic, the community at large, and קהל as a select group, a judicial body, composed of elders. In Deut. 23:1-2 certain classes of people are excluded from the assembly קהל of the Lord; but since the term עדה is not used, there is no evidence here for the relation of the two terms. In general, the terms are used synonymously, without perceptible difference, to designate the cult community of Israel. In Num. 20 the terms are used interchangeably. The LXX generally translates עדה as συναγωγή and קהל as ἐκκλησία, uniformly so in Deuteronomy (except 5:22, where קהל is rendered συναγωγή), Joshua, Judges, Samuel, Kings, Ezra, and Nehemiah. In Exodus, Leviticus, and Numbers both terms are rendered συναγωγή, apparently for the sake of uniformity. In Psalms קהל is once rendered συναγωγή (40:10) and once συνέδριον (26:5), but otherwise ἐκκλησία. It appears that the words συναγωγή and ἐκκλησία are virtually synonymous and that the difference in usage is due to differences in time, place, and person of the various translators. In the OT Apoc. ἐκκλησία is used in the sense of a popular assembly (Jth. 6:16; 14:6; Ecclus. 15:5), but only rarely for a people as a whole (I Macc. 4:59). In the NT, ἐκκλησία is applied to the community of Israel in Stephen's speech (Acts 7:38), but συναγωγή became the normal term to distinguish Israel from other nations. An assembly of Jewish Christians is designated as συναγωγή in Jas. 2:2 and similarly ἐπισυναγωγή in Heb. 10:25 (though in II Thess. 2:1 the term has a different meaning). It was only natural that the Christian movement dispensed with the term συναγωγή, because of its Jewish associations, in favor of the term ἐκκλησία, although occasionally the early fathers used συναγωγή of the church. The developing opposition between church and synagogue is reflected in the reference to the Jewish community as the "synagogue of Satan" (Rev. 3:9). Augustine sought to establish a distinction between the Latin equivalents of συναγωγή and ἐκκλησία, *congregatio* and *convocatio*, the latter being, as he thought, the nobler term, since it is used only of men, while the former might also designate a herd of cattle. This distinction is certainly not true of the Hebrew word which the LXX usually translates συναγωγή, since עדה, while used of insects and cattle, also is applied to the assembly of the gods!

*c*) Other terms denoting a gathering are sometimes rendered "assembly." The term מועד, from the same root as עדה, means "appointed time" (καιρός), or "appointed place" (ἑορτή), and hence is used of sacred seasons and appointed feasts, probably set by the moon—the times at which all males had to present themselves at Yahweh's sanctuary (Lev. 23:2, 4, 37, 44; Hos. 9:5; 12:9). By extension, the term may also designate the assembly that celebrates the festival, the place of assembly, or any assembly. In Job 30:23 the nether world is called the "house appointed [בית מועד] for all living." Zion is called the "city of our appointed feasts" (Isa. 33:20), and the synagogues are termed מועדי אל, the "meeting places of God" (Ps. 74:8). The temple is designated by the term מועד (Ps. 74:4; Lam. 2:6). In Isa. 14:13 the "mount of assembly" (הר מועד) is an allusion to the holy mountain Zaphon of the Ugaritic myths. The use of מועד for the assembly of the gods, as with its cognate עדה, is attested also in the Ugaritic myths, where a plenary session of the pantheon is termed *phr mʻd*. On the "tent of meeting" (אהל מועד), *see* TABERNACLE.

*d*) The term עצרה or עצרת, apart from Jer. 9:2, is a technical term for certain cultic assemblies. It is applied to an assembly for the worship of Baal (II Kings 10:20). In Joel 1:14; 2:15, it is parallel to צום, "fast" (perhaps Isa. 1:13 should be emended to read "fast and solemn assembly"), but whether the parallelism is synonymous or antithetical is not clear. In Amos 5:21 the word is parallel to חג (*see* FEASTS AND FASTS), and the LXX renders πανήγυρις, which is used once in the NT (Heb. 12:23). In Isa. 1:13 the parallel is מקרא, "convocation" (RSV "assembly"). The term is applied specifically to the assembly of the seventh day of the Feast of Unleavened Bread (Deut. 16:8) and the eighth or supernumerary day of the Feast of Booths (Lev. 23:36; Num. 29:35; Neh. 8:18) and of Solomon's dedication of the temple (II Chr. 7:9).

*e*) The term מקרא, "convocation" (RSV "assembly"), is also used of a cultic assembly (Isa. 1:13) or the place(s) of assembly (Isa. 4:5). In P the term is מקרא קדש (LXX κλητή or ἐπίκλητος), "holy assembly" (Exod. 12:16) or "holy convocation" (Lev. 23; Num. 28:18, 25; 29:7).

*f*) The word סוד, "intimate, friendly conversation" (cf. Arabic *sāwada*, "speak in secret"), is applied to friendly or intimate gatherings of various sorts—a "gathering of young men" (Jer. 6:11), a "company of merrymakers" (Jer. 15:17), a "band of drunkards" (Hos. 4:18, as emended), a secret meeting of evil plotters (Ps. 64:2), the assembly of the upright (Ps. 111:1), and the privy council of God (Job 15:8; Ps. 89:7; Jer. 23:18).

*g*) The word מושב, "seat" (Ps. 1:1), is translated "assembly" in Ps. 107:32, where it is parallel to קהל, "congregation."

*See also* CHURCH, IDEA OF; SANHEDRIN; SYNAGOGUE.

**Bibliography.** L. Rost, "Die Bezeichnungen für Land und Volk im AT," *Festschrift für O. Procksch* (1934), pp. 125-48; *Die Vorstufen von Kirche und Synagoge im AT,* BWANT (1938). B. Luther, "Kāhāl und ʻedāh als Hilfsmittel der Quellenscheidung im Priesterkodex und in der Chronik," *ZAW,* 56 (1938), 44-63. J. D. W. Kritzinger, *Q<sup>e</sup>hal Jahwe, wat dit is en wie daaran mag behoort* (1957).     M. H. POPE

**CONGREGATION, MOUNT OF.** *See* MOUNT OF ASSEMBLY.

**CONIAH** kō nī′ə [כניהו] (Jer. 22:24, 28; 37:1). Same as JEHOIACHIN.

**CONONIAH.** KJV alternate form of CONANIAH.

**CONQUEST OF CANAAN.** *See* ISRAEL, HISTORY OF.

*CONSCIENCE [ἡ συνείδησις, τὸ συνειδότος, ἡ συνέσις, τὸ συνειδός]. Roughly, and mainly, a witness within man which condemns his sin. Other nuances in its meaning, such as "consciousness," will appear below.

1. Background of the term
    *a.* Not derived from the OT
    *b.* Hellenistic origin
    *c.* In Latin writers
2. Meaning in general use
3. In the NT
    *a.* Pauline usage
    *b.* In non-Pauline letters
Bibliography

**1. Background of the term. *a. Not derived from the OT.*** In the LXX, συνείδησις, "conscience," occurs only (Eccl. 10:20). The underlying Hebrew term is מַדָּע, rendered in the RSV by "thought" (elsewhere the Hebrew word occurs in II Chr. 1:10-12; Dan. 1:17, is translated by συνέσις, and simply means "knowledge"). Conscience, as the whole context shows, here merely means "the mind" or "the inner, secret place of thought." Codex Sinaiticus reads συνείδησιν instead of εἴδησιν at Ecclus. 42:18. But since we do not know the underlying Hebrew, the reading of Sinaiticus cannot safely be regarded as pertinent. Most significant is Wisd. Sol. 17:10. Here conscience emerges with a moral connotation, as a witness within man, which condemns his sin. This approximates to what we find later in the NT. At this point, it should be emphasized that the Wisdom of Solomon shows marked Hellenistic influences, and that the emergence of the term "conscience," with a moral significance, points to the Hellenistic world as its source. This is not surprising. Hebrew thinking is theocentric, not introspective. It emphasizes God as King, and man as his obedient servant. The obedience demanded by God has been revealed to man from a source outside him in the Law and the Prophets. Not knowledge of the self (including the conscience), but the fear of the Lord, was the beginning of wisdom (Prov. 1:7; 9:10). Hence, there was no urge to examine the inner motives of man's behavior, or to concentrate on what might be called subjective psychological phenomena. In such a soil, the development of an examined theory of conscience was not to be expected. Similarly in rabbinic Judaism, where again the law given on Sinai was the light of men, the absence of any term corresponding to "conscience" is natural. The concept of the "good impulse" (יֵצֶר טוֹב) affords no real parallel to conscience; in any case, this was far less developed than that of the "evil impulse" (יֵצֶר רַע). This is not to assert that the OT and Judaism were unaware of the phenomena which gave rise to the idea of "conscience," but that they lacked the theoretical interest to interpret them psychologically or anthropologically.

***b. Hellenistic origin.*** The Hellenistic world, then, seems to be suggested as the background of the term "conscience" (συνείδησις); and it has been customary to connect it specifically with Stoicism (*see* STOICS). Does the evidence support the Stoic derivation of "conscience," which most NT exegetes seem to assume without question? Stobaeus, who noted down, in the sixth century A.D., the most interesting passages that he had ever read, including those dealing with conscience (though the term he used was τὸ συνειδότος), refers to Periander (625-585 B.C.) and Bias (550 B.C.) as having used the term "conscience." But there is little doubt that he was mistaken in this. The term first occurs in a passage in Democritus (460-361 B.C.), whose philosophy was akin to that of Epicurus (342-270 B.C.) and whose works were praised by Cicero. The passage reads: "Some men, not knowing the dissolution of mortal nature, suffer wretchedly throughout their lifetime from distress and fear because of their consciousness of the evil-doing in their lives, making false speculations about the time after death" (Democritus 297, in Diels, *Fragmente der Vorsokratiker*, II [1952], 206-7). Here "conscience" (συνείδησις) has a moral connotation: it consists of the consciousness of wrongdoing, which causes man to spend his days in fears and anxieties, and leads him to form false ideas of the time after death, since man does not know that dissolution awaits him. The usage, however, is not precisely defined. The term next appears in Chrysippus, a celebrated Stoic philosopher born *ca.* 280 B.C. Words of his are cited by Diogenes Laërtius (240 B.C.) VII.85: "It is suitable [or fitting] for every living thing to be *aware of* its own structure and of itself." "Conscience" is here predicated of all living creatures and not only of man: it seems merely to designate a creature's self-awareness, and is without moral connotation. After Chrysippus we again note the appearance of "conscience" (συνείδησις) with moral significance in Wisd. Sol. 17:10 (*see above*), and in Philodemus (50 B.C.) *Rhetoric* II.40, and in Dionysius of Halicarnassus (died 7 B.C.) *Antiquities* VIII.1.3, where conscience disturbs Coriolanus in his approach to the Volsci, whom he had often treated brutally in battle. In Diodorus Siculus (a contemporary of Julius Caesar and Augustus) we find the term at IV.65.7, but here also it may mean "consciousness." In all these passages, with the exception of that by Chrysippus, the Stoic, συνείδησις has a moral reference.

Another Stoic, Epictetus (first century A.D.), is supposed to have employed the term in a famous passage which reads: "When we were children our parents handed us over to a nursery slave who should watch over us everywhere lest harm befall us. But when we were grown up, God hands us over to the conscience [συνειδήσει] implanted in us, to protect us. Let us not in any way despise its protection for should we do so we shall be both ill-pleasing to God and have our own conscience [συνείδοτι] as an enemy" (cited by Pierce [*see bibliography*]). This is the only passage in Epictetus, as far as is known, where συνείδησις occurs, and its ascription to him rests on the slenderest grounds, so that most scholars do not now regard the passage as authentic (*see bibliography*). But the ascription to Stoics of the term "conscience" has become very fashionable, as we saw. Stoics are said to have coined the term. Nevertheless, apart from its use by Chrysippus (and he used it without a moral connotation), there is no reason at all, to judge from the Greek sources, for regarding the term as peculiarly Stoic. Must we conclude that the Stoic origin of the term must be rejected? Not only do the Greek lexicographical data lead to this, but it is what we should expect. The term "conscience" (συνείδησις), as the passages cited already reveal, and as subsequent treatment will confirm, has undertones of emotion, anxiety, or concern, which little comport with the Stoic ideal of self-sufficiency (ἀπάθεια). Moreover, not only is "conscience" not a Stoic term, but some claim that there is no evidence that it was significant in Greek philosophy outside Stoicism. Thus it does not occur in Aristotle's *Ethics*. Consequently, they turn to popular Hellenistic thought for the origin of the term (e.g., E. Schwartz [*see bibliography*]).

c. *Usage in Latin writers.* The term is found in writers of Greek, such as Philo and Josephus, with a developed moral connotation, as in Paul, so that in Hellenistic circles, strictly so-called, it was in literary circulation in the time of the apostle. Latin authors, however, use it far more frequently than do the Greek. Cicero (106 B.C.), who used the term *conscientia* seventy-five times, and Seneca (born a few years before Christ) connect "conscience" with Epicureanism, which counseled the avoidance of wrongdoing for fear of the reproaches of conscience (Cicero *De Finibus* I.45; I.51; II.53-54; Seneca *Epistles* XLIII.5; CV.7-9), which had the role of accuser (Seneca *Epistles* XLIII.5; XXVIII.9-10), and the cultivation of a "good conscience" (Seneca *On a Happy Life* XIX.1; XX.5). Moreover, a connection has been traced between the idea of conscience in Epicurus and Euripides, on the one hand, and in Philo, on the other (*see bibliography*). As in Epicureanism, so in Cynicism, the Latin authors find conscience emphasized. It, rather than fear of men or of gods, is the rule and motive for conduct (Cicero *On the Nature of the Gods* III.85): it is not only punitive but also directive (Horace [65 B.C.] *Epodes* V.29; *Epistle* 1.61). It is his conscience that also gives to the Cynic his authority: he aims so to live that his conscience itself has become his public: he lives under his conscience always as in the public eye (Seneca *Epistle* XLIII.5; *On a Happy Life* XX.3-5; Epictetus III.22.94 [τὸ συνειδός]).

When we ask whether the Latin writers reveal in Stoicism an emphasis on conscience, the answer is in the negative. Seneca shows that Athenodorus, a Stoic teacher of Augustus, used the term "a good conscience" (*On Tranquility of Mind* III.4); he also ascribes the use of "conscience" to Musonius, the teacher of Epictetus, the Stoic (*Epistle* LII.9). Seneca himself uses the term in *On Benefits* IV.34.3, where the necessity of arriving at a strong conscience is urged. This enables a person to overcome all timidity, so that he is no longer at the mercy of the opinions of others. But the use of "conscience" in Stoicism cannot have been central, and whenever the term does occur in Stoic connections, it undergoes modification. Thus the strong conscience, desiderated by Seneca, really signifies strong character. The Latin writers, therefore, lend no support to the view that conscience was a peculiarly Stoic doctrine, while

they suggest that, in its Latin form at least, conscience was a concept much employed in literary circles. Two explanations of this are possible: (*a*) that Latin writers were closer to popular usage than the Greek, and had borrowed a popular term; (*b*) that many Greek documents from the Hellenistic period have been lost to us, so that we should be prepared to find in Latin writers much that had already appeared in Greek sources that are no longer extant. These Latin writers reveal that the term "conscience" was known to Epicureanism, Cynicism, and—although not native or even congenial to it—to Stoicism. The use of "conscience" by Stoic writers suggests that the needs of moral guidance overrode the niceties of philosophy. Thus Seneca, who deplored making the fear of conscience the motive for conduct, yet, inconsistently, in his instruction of Nero himself appealed to it (*De Clementiae* I.1.1). Probably in the teaching of popular moralists the term "conscience" was familiar. While it was not in use in the technical language of the "schools" of philosophy, it was well established perhaps in more popular, philosophic-moralistic teaching among Epicureans, Cynics, and even, at times, Stoics. This view, while it rests mainly on the assumption that Latin authors do reflect Greek usage, finds some support, at least, in the first century from Philo and Josephus, who can hardly be claimed to have been influenced by Paul (this although Philo prefers the term τὸ συνειδός to ἡ συνείδησις).

2. **Meaning in general use.** The term "conscience" (συνείδησις) is to be understood in conjunction with a number of similar words and phrases, which are sometimes used interchangeably. These are τὸ συνειδότος, τὸ συνειδός, συνέσις, αὐτῷ συνιστορεῖν τι, αὐτῷ συνειδέναι τι. All these stem from the verb σύνοιδα, which means "I know in common with." It usually implies knowledge about another person, which can be used in witness for or against him. Hence σύνοιδα came to mean "I bear witness." Of particular importance is the phrase αὐτῷ συνειδέναι τι, which means "to share knowledge with oneself," "to know with oneself," "to be a witness for or against oneself," because συνείδησις (like τὸ συνειδός and συνέσις) is its substantival equivalent. The necessity for finding a single substantive to convey the meaning of a phrase would be natural. It is also easy to see why συνείδησις and συνειδός, because of their greater similarity in form and sound to αὐτῷ συνειδέναι τι, would be more likely to be chosen for this than συνέσις. It is more difficult to understand why συνείδησις should have been preferred to συνειδός. Possibly συνείδησις is the wider term, including all senses of the verb σύνοιδα, while συνειδός was restricted to ἐμαυτῷ σύνοιδα. But this is uncertain. By the time of the NT, in any case, συνείδησις was the most popular term to express what was conveyed by the phrase αὐτῷ συνειδέναι τι.

An examination of the pertinent passages suggests the following connotations for the term:

a) Conscience is a faculty implanted in man, as part of his very nature, so that it functions by necessity, as an expression of his very constitution. Thus in Xenophon's account of the trial of Socrates, the latter believes that those induced to bear false witness against him will, *of necessity,* suffer the pangs of conscience ("It is necessary that they should be conscience stricken about much impiety and wickedness" [*Apology* 24]).

*b*) This faculty is a necessary characteristic of every man. Thus Polybius (204 B.C.—), using the term συνέσις, which is the equivalent of συνείδησις, claims that there is "no witness so fearful nor accuser so terrible as that conscience which dwells in the soul of every man" (XVIII.xliii.13).

*c*) Often the implanting of conscience is, by implication, if not explicitly, traced to God. Thus Xenophon *Cyropaedia* I.vi.4 connects it with prayer: "Owing to that very regard do you not come to the gods with a better heart to pray, and do you not expect more confidently to obtain what you pray for, because you feel conscious of never having neglected them?" Democritus asserts that, in the popular mind, conscience is connected with punishment, presumably at the hands of the gods after death. Euripides (480 B.C.—), using the term συνέσις, gives to conscience the function of the Eumenides or Erinyes, the avenging deities of Greek mythology. (These were concerned to punish the wicked both in this world and after death, those who had been disobedient to parents, disrespectful toward the aged, guilty of perjury, murder, etc. The Eumenides were consequently dreaded by gods and men.) Menelaus: "What aileth thee? What sickness ruineth thee?" Orestes: "Conscience [ἡ συνέσις]—to know I have wrought a fearful deed." (*Orestes* 395-96.) The equation of conscience with these figures is, therefore, highly significant. The same equation probably occurs in Diodorus Siculus (IV.65.7), who uses the phrase "on account of conscience" (διὰ τὴν συνείδησιν). Menander (342-291 B.C.) called "conscience" a god, but we cannot gather from his words what he meant by the term: "To all mortals conscience is a god" (*Gnomai Monostichoi* 654). Philo does not make explicit the divine origin of conscience but probably assumes it (*On the Decalogue* 87; *see below*).

*d*) As the above references reveal, conscience comes into activity in connection with a person's deeds, and particularly his bad deeds (as in Xenophon *Apology* 24).

*e*) Primarily, if not exclusively, it is a person's own acts that concern the conscience. In agreement with the verbal form αὐτῷ συνειδέναι τι, which it represents, conscience, comes to know something, if we may so express it, with the person himself, and bears witness against him. The operation of conscience is, so to speak, "automatic."

*f*) While it is conceivable that conscience could denote a constant state of criticism of a person's character (this is especially suggested perhaps by the identification of conscience with the Eumenides, although they too become avengers of particular acts of wrong), nevertheless, it is specific acts of wrongdoing, not so much a continued or habitual condition of character, that call forth conscience. And, usually, since conscience has been "called forth," it follows naturally that it has reference most frequently to past acts.

*g*) Stirred into activity, of necessity, by wrongdoing, conscience emerges as a pain. Philo reveals this: "For every soul has for its birth-fellow and house-mate a

monitor [ἔλεγχος] whose way is to admit nothing that calls for censure, whose nature is ever to hate evil and love virtue, who is its accuser [κατήγορος] and its judge in one. If he be once roused as accuser he censures, accuses and puts the soul to shame, and again as judge, he instructs, admonishes and exhorts it to change its ways. And if he has the strength to persuade, he rejoices and makes peace. But if he cannot, he makes war to the bitter end, never leaving it alone by day or night, but plying it with stabs and deadly wounds until he breaks the thread of its miserable and ill-starved life" (*On the Decalogue* 87; Loeb translation).[1] The term used is ἔλεγχος, but it is to be identified here with συνείδησις. Here conscience (the convictor) appears as a pain. Similarly, Plutarch describes conscience (τὸ συνειδός = συνείδησις). He quotes first Euripides *Orestes* 396: "My conscience [συνέσις], since I know I've done a dreadful deed, like an ulcer in the flesh, leaves behind it in the soul regret which ever continues to wound and prick it. For the other pangs reason does away with, but regret is caused by reason itself, since the soul, together with its feeling of shame, is stung and chastised by itself. For as those who shiver with ague or burn with fevers are more distressed and pained than those who suffer the same discomforts through heat or cold from a source outside the body, so the pangs which Fortune brings, coming as it were, from a source without, are lighter to bear; but that lament, None is to blame for this but me myself, which is chanted over one's errors, coming as it does from within, makes the pain even heavier by reason of the disgrace one feels" (*On Tranquility of Mind* 476F-477A; Loeb translation).[2] Xenophon asserted that no one who suffered the pangs of conscience could again be accounted happy (*Anabasis* II.v.7).

*h*) The passage from Philo depicts conscience also as an agent of pain—i.e., to inflict pain—as, by implication, do other sections by the same author (e.g., *Frag.* ed. Mang. 11. p. 652; *QDSI* I.128 (τὸ συνειδός); and possibly *QDPIS*.27). Plutarch refers to the chastising and gnawing of conscience in *Poblicola* IV.99B. That it could be equated with the dread Eumenides, speaks for itself.

*i*) Conscience is said to suffer pain (*The Orphic Hymn* LXIII.3-5 [τὸ συνειδός]; Dionysius of Halicarnassus in *On Thucydides* VIII.4; μηδὲ μιαίνειν τὴν αὑτου συνείδησιν—of Thucydides' care and conscientiousness as a historian; he refused to pollute his conscience). Perhaps the most widespread concept of conscience in the Hellenistic period can best be gleaned from the fragment wrongly attributed to Epictetus already cited above. There συνείδησις, "conscience," implanted by God, is by implication compared to the nursery slave (παιδαγωγός): its function was, not so much to teach morals, as to protest against immorality by inflicting pain designed to safeguard good conduct. With this concept, we must assume that the writers of the NT, who had connections with the Hellenistic world, at least would be familiar. But, before we turn to the NT, we must notice certain issues not yet faced—namely, whether

[1] Reprinted by permission of the publishers and of The Loeb Classical Library from Loeb Classical Library volume Philo, *Decalogue*.
[2] Reprinted by permission of the publishers and of The Loeb Classical Library from Loeb Classical Library volume Philo, *On Tranquility of Mind*.

the activity of conscience is concerned with the acts of others, as well as of its subject; whether it is a guide for the future, as well as a judge of the past; and, finally, whether any positive connotation can be given to the concept of a "good conscience"—in fact, whether such a thing exists at all, or whether the phrase merely signifies the absence of "conscience." Since we are dealing with a concept noted in popular, Greco-Roman philosophy, not with that of the schools, no "scientific" or philosophical accuracy and refinement in the use of the term should be expected.

**3. In the NT.** The NT usage further attests the Hellenistic derivation and affinities of συνείδηις. On the one hand, in the four gospels, which are concerned with a tradition which, however much under Hellenistic influences, was primarily Hebraic or Palestinian, the term does not occur. But perhaps we are to see synonyms of it in the term "heart" in Mark 3:5, and, more doubtfully, in Mark 6:52; Matt. 15:10-20 (here "heart" seems, in accordance with much Semitic usage, to be the equivalent of "mind," because it is the source of "thoughts," although in I John 3:20-21 "heart" seems to be identical with "conscience"). Again, we may have circumlocutions for συνείδησις: in Matt. 6:23: the "light within"; and in Luke 12:57 the reference may be to "conscience," although the appeal here too may be to the rational faculty in man. On the other hand, συνείδησις appears thirty times in the rest of the NT, always in documents which were wide open to the influences of the Hellenistic world. There are fourteen occurrences in Paul, six in the Pastorals, five in Hebrews, three in I Peter, two in Acts. Thus, among NT writers, Paul first used the term, and most frequently; and perhaps it was he who gave it prominence in Christian usage.

*a. Pauline usage.* The term occurs first in I Cor. 8, a chapter dealing with the eating of food offered to idols. On the ground of their superior knowledge that idols, to which the food had been dedicated, were literally nonentities, so that the dedication of food to them was without significance, "strong" Christians were tempted to ignore the scruples of their weaker brethren, and override their objections. But Paul insists that for them to do so would submit the weak to pains of conscience, and actually injure or wound that faculty in them. To avoid this pain and injury to the weak, the strong should forever avoid eating meat sacrificed to idols. But in I Cor. 10, more cautious than in I Cor. 8, Paul recognizes that the strong are not to be fettered in their freedom by the weak. As a general rule, a man should be guided by freedom; but he should pay respect, however, not to the weak brother's opinions, but to his pains of conscience. This means that, while the bludgeoning of the strong by the weak is not to be countenanced, because this would be tyranny, nevertheless, consideration for the pain of the weak becomes a principle of conduct.

I Cor. 8; 10 reveal, first, that Paul recognizes a variety in conscience. The weak conscience may be due to lack of knowledge (I Cor. 8:7), force of habit (I Cor. 8:7), or lack of ability to withstand the example of others (I Cor. 8:10); it is not merely feeble and vulnerable, but has a stronger connotation: the weak conscience does not have the force necessary to act according to knowledge. (The concept has been claimed to be original with Paul, but we meet the contrast between the strong and the weak in Latin authors. The sage is strong; in his strength, he is tempted to become presumptuous, puffed up. And the origin of the Pauline contrast between the strong and the weak in Corinth has been found in Stoicism. Others prefer to find a parallel to the Pauline contrast in such passages as Matt. 18:1 ff.)

The discussion raises the question whether conscience, in these passages, has a future reference. At least at first glance, in I Cor. 8:10; 10:25 ff, "conscience" seems to be a regulative principle. The weak brother, contemplating the strong brother in I Cor. 8:10, must have been cogitating over the problem of eating food offered to idols and is dissuaded from this by his "conscience"; so too in I Cor. 10:28. The translation of 10:25 is difficult: how are we to understand the phrase διὰ τὴν συνείδησιν, "on the ground of conscience"? It is possible to take this verse to mean: Eat any food that is sold in the meat market without letting scruples of conscience induce you to ask questions about it—i.e., avoid deliberating over the act beforehand in terms of your conscience. This implies that conscience has a future reference. But I Cor. 10:25 may merely mean: Because of conscience avoid asking questions; because, as long as you do not know the source of the meat, you can eat without suffering pangs of conscience afterward. Nevertheless, unless we are to draw a very rigid distinction between the scruples, at least discomforting, if not painful, which a man has before doing wrong, and the pain which follows his act, it is exceedingly difficult to exclude all future reference from conscience in both these sections. Rom. 13:5 may be adduced in support of this: "Therefore one must be subject [to the state], not only to avoid God's wrath but also for the sake of conscience." Submission to the state, Paul has argued, is a necessity, not merely because the state has power to enforce its demands. This power is derived from God (Paul is not here dealing with evil governments as such), and, therefore, commands a rightful obedience. To obey the state, therefore, will not bring on the pangs of conscience. For the sake of conscience, therefore, it should be obeyed. But it is difficult not to understand that the conscience has been informed about the nature of the state before obedience to it can be "according to conscience" or "on the ground of conscience"; the future reference can hardly be ruled out completely. Conscience in Paul, therefore, is at least on the way to becoming a regulative principle.

This raises the question of the relation between "the conscience" and "the mind" or "reason." Perhaps the difficulty of deciding whether conscience in Paul has a future reference arises from his failure to clarify the distinction between these. That he does distinguish them appears from Rom 2:14-15. Here three things are distinguished: all men are presumed to have (*a*) a law written on the heart, a moral awareness (here Paul may be influenced by Stoic concepts, although he would not subscribe to the Stoic view that for those who recognized the "natural law" it was possible to fulfil it); (*b*) the conscience; (*c*) reason or thought. But in Rom. 14:5 the "mind" (νοῦς) seems to have taken the place of what in I Cor. 8:10 is the "conscience." And in I Corinthians, Paul has not been careful at all to distinguish between reason and conscience; hence the problems of exegesis. It cannot be sufficiently emphasized that "conscience" was not a fully examined concept in Paul's day, and that he did not introduce scientific consistency into his use of it, although he did refine it.

I Cor. 8; 10 show the seriousness of ignoring the claims of conscience, be they regarded as prevenient scruples or as posterior pain. The effect of the inconsiderate conduct of the strong is to defile the conscience of the weak (I Cor. 8:7), so that he is destroyed; i.e., led to emulate the strong, and to ignore his own awareness of what is right, the weak Christian is likely, later, to lose his faith and relapse into pagan ways. To ignore conscience—i.e., to lay oneself open deliberately to its pains, and not to escape from them as frequently as possible—is to develop a resistance to them; to wound the conscience so as to blunt its attacks, to become "acclimatized" to conscience, so that its impact becomes dulled—this is to be destroyed. This raises the question as to the exact meaning of the phrase "a good conscience." Is its significance merely negative—i.e., does it simply denote absence of pain—or has it a positive sense?

In I Cor. 10:28-29, the implication is that conscience passes judgment, not on the subject's own acts only, but on those of others also. This is a meaning not to be ruled out in II Cor. 4:2; 5:11, although here the term συνείδησις may merely signify "consciousness" or "awareness." In II Cor. 4:2 every man, Jew and Gentile, is credited with a moral discernment, which assesses the conduct of others "in the sight of God"—i.e., the assessment is analogous to that of God himself. Thus there should be no criticism of Paul's exercise of his ministry. That the gospel does not find acceptance with some is due to the fact that their minds (τὰ νοήματα) have been blinded by the god of this world; these are the perishing (οἵ ἀπολλυμένοι). The same verb is used of what happens to the weak Christians in I Cor. 8:11. The blinded minds of unbelievers (νοήματα τῶν ἀπίστων) might be a synonym for the "perished consciences," as if νοήματα and συνείδησις were equivalent: in this case συνείδησις in II Cor. 4:2 should be rendered by something like "thoughts" (see above on the lack of precision in Paul's usage). The same applies to II Cor. 5:11: here "conscience" is the subject of "knowledge" or "awareness." Nevertheless, it is possible that in II Cor. 4:2 the reference is to conscience in all its forms, and that in II Cor. 5:11 the reference is specifically to the individual consciences of men, not to their intellects (the plural "consciences" occurs only here).

The other places where Paul uses συνείδησις may be claimed to fall well within the Hellenistic usage traced in § 1b above. But certain associations are noteworthy: (a) In Rom. 2:14-15; 13:5, conscience is associated both with necessity (ἀνάγκη) and with "the wrath" (ἡ ὀργή). In Rom. 2:14-15 "conscience" is a property of man by nature or necessity, and its operation, in part at least, insofar as it is a pain following upon acts of wrongdoing, may be regarded as the inner counterpart of the process of "wrath" which Paul found at work in the natural order and

in society (Rom. 1:18). (In II Cor. 1:12 "conscience" is used somewhat absolutely and calls for no comment.) (b) In Rom. 9:1 the witness of conscience is conjoined with that of the Holy Spirit and Christ. This is of the utmost importance for Paul's estimate of "conscience." There can be little doubt that Paul derived the term "conscience" from his opponents at Corinth. It was no favorite of his, and in Rom. 14:15, when he is dealing with precisely the same problem as in I Cor. 8:10, he avoids the term. In I Corinthians, following his policy of being all things to all men, he had used his opponents' term. But that he did not give to "conscience" the overriding significance in ethics that they did, appears in I Cor. 4:4. There, although he uses the verbal form (ἐμαυτῷ σύνοιδα), not the substantival (συνείδησις), he makes it clear that conscience is not his ultimate court of appeal. This is Christ himself. Open to corrupting influences, as it is, conscience is to be quickened by the Spirit and itself enlightened by Christ.

b. In non-Pauline letters. Outside the Pauline letters, "conscience" emerges in I Peter, the Pastorals, Hebrews, all of which probably reflect late Hellenistic literary usage. In I Pet. 2:19, συνείδησις probably simply means "consciousness"; the RSV is right (over against Selwyn) in rendering "mindful of God." So in 3:16, "conscience" refers to a consciousness of innocence of any misconduct which might justify the criticism of outsiders. The occurrence in 3:21 is difficult. The RSV (so also Moffatt), which takes baptism to signify, on its manward side, the prayer for a clean conscience, is probably to be rejected, the correct translation being that "baptism is the appeal made to God by a good conscience." The context does not allow us to define precisely what this means. Significant is the emergence here of the phrase "a good conscience." This is a mark of the Pastorals, and of the literature of the end of the first century and the beginning of the second (I Tim. 1:5, 19 ["good conscience"]; 3:9; II Tim. 1:3 ["clear conscience"]; I Tim. 4:2 and Tit. 1:15 refer to the corruption or searing of conscience). See also, e.g., Acts 23:1; I Clem. 41.1; Polyc. 5.3; II Clem. 16.4.

Noteworthy in the Pastorals are: (a) The close relation between conscience and loyalty to the faith (I Tim. 1:5, 19; 3:9; 4:2; less clearly, II Tim. 1:13). This association of conscience and loyalty to the gospel had already been prepared for by Paul (II Cor. 4:2). But here it is carried further. In I Tim. 1:19-20, in particular, the conduct of the Christian life is dependent upon having faith and a good conscience. To cast away the latter is to make shipwreck of the faith, which, a quasi-technical term in the Pastorals, here means right belief. (b) The concept of conscience emerges over questions concerning foods (I Tim. 4:1 ff; Tit. 1:13 ff). Those who make distinctions in this matter are "unbelieving" (Tit. 1:15), their mind and conscience corrupted, whereas a sound faith demands a conscience undefiled. While in Paul a tolerant attitude toward "the weak" is advised on the ground of their conscience (Rom. 14:14; I Cor. 8:10; Col. 2:20-23), in the Pastorals the attitude of "the weak" is condemned outright. It has become more of a menace and has to be openly opposed: under the influence of developing Gnosticism "the weak" have become diabolic and anti-

Christian (I Tim. 4:1-5). As there are degrees of enlightenment in conscience, so in the Pastorals there are degrees in the toleration of the dictates of the same. In both I Tim. 1:19-20; Tit. 1:13 ff, a "good conscience" implies a positive loyalty to the truth. The verb tenses are here significant. In I Tim. 1:19-20 the act by which the "good conscience"—which is not merely the absence of pain following evil deeds, but a determination to "wage the good warfare" (I Tim. 1:18)—is rejected, is in the aorist tense (i.e., it consists of a single, decisive event [ἀπωσάμενοι; I Tim. 1:19]), but the process whereby the conscience has been deadened is in other passages in the perfect tense (I Tim. 4:12; Tit. 1:15). This last regards the corruption of the mind (νοῦς) and conscience (συνείδησις) as a process, and sharply distinguishes the two concepts. The Greek perhaps suggests that the corruption of the faculty of remorse for sin (συνείδησις) is a worse calamity than the corruption of the rational faculty which enables us to distinguish sin. This should not be pressed. But the clear distinction between mind and conscience at this point should warn us against overemphasizing what directive function conscience may have had.

c) It has been urged that in the Pastorals the "conscience" has become domesticated in this world. Unlike Paul, who urged that our citizenship is in heaven, the Pastorals are concerned to develop an ethic for citizenship on earth. For them the "good conscience" signifies the soft pillow of the man who has not disturbed his society: it is a mark of the static conception of Christianity found in the Pastorals. But caution is necessary here. In the Pastorals also the Christian life is a battle and conscience is tied to the faith. But even more important is the usage of the phrase "a good conscience," and of conscience itself, in the Letter to the Hebrews, associated here with the literature to which the Pastorals belong. In Heb. 10:2 "conscience" again merely means "consciousness" (so RSV); in Heb. 9:14 it has an accusing function, where the dead works are not the works of the law, but works of sin, which are to be forgiven by God through the sacrifice of his Son. So in Heb. 10:22 we have a wicked conscience—i.e., an accusing conscience. From Heb. 9:9 we gather that the old sacrificial system cannot deal with that where man confronts God's holiness—i.e., his conscience. Throughout Hebrews, conscience is directed toward God—it is not primarily a moralistic, but a theological, concept. Here Hebrews differs from Paul, where conscience is not primarily oriented to God but to man; and if in the Pastorals conscience is domesticated, Hebrews differs from them also. In Hebrews the "clear conscience" occurs only once, in 13:18, and has reference to a concrete situation in a dynamic context. The author is sure that, in the particular situation confronting him, he is not at fault. But he is faced with the necessity to act honorably in all things, as befits a Christian—i.e., in response to God's truth. There is no suggestion of a "soft pillow" in this world, no bourgeois complacency, but the desire for that purity which comes from doing God's will, which is possible only through the blood of the eternal covenant.

*Bibliography.* Meineke, *Fragmenta Poetarum Comoediae Novae* (1891). On συνείδησις in Epictetus, see J. H. Moulton and G. Milligan, *The Vocabulary of the Greek NT* (1914-29). C. H. Dodd, "Conscience in the NT," *Mansfield College Magazine,* no. 66 (1916). On the connection between the idea of conscience in Epicurus and Euripides and in Philo, see E. Bréhier, *Les idées philosophiques et religieuses de Philon d'Alexandrie* (1925), pp. 259-300, which suggests perhaps a continuous literary and philosophical tradition. M. Dibelius, *Die Pastoral-briefe* (2nd ed., 1931), pp. 11-12. C. Spicq, "La conscience dans le NT," *RB,* 47 (1938), pp. 50-80; *Les Epitres Pastorales* (1947), Excursus pp. 29-38 with bibliography. J. Dupont, "Syneidesis aux origines de la notion chrétienne de conscience morale," *Studia Hellenistica,* 5 (1948), pp. 119-53. E. Schwarz, *Ethik der Griechen* (1951), pp. 90-91, 237 (n. 31). C. A. Pierce, *Conscience in the NT* (1955)—difficult but rewarding.

W. D. DAVIES

**CONSECRATE, CONSECRATION.** To set apart, dedicate, or sanctify a person or thing to some sacred purpose related to the service and worship of God, and so, often, to give the person or object itself a character of holiness. "Consecration" is therefore used as the proper word for the ordination and hallowing of persons to sacred offices or to sacred service (Exod. 29:9; Lev. 8:33; I Chr. 29:5; II Chr. 29:31), and the setting apart and dedication through religious rites of things from common to sacred uses (Josh. 6:19; II Chr. 31:6).

"Consecrate" and derived words are the usual, though not always exclusive, rendering of the following words:

a) קדש, "to separate or set apart," the most prominent of the Hebrew words which convey the idea of "cleanliness" or "holiness" (Exod. 13:2; 19:10, 14, 22-23; 22:31—H 22:30; 28:3, 41; 29:1, 27, 33, 36-37, 44; 30:29-30; 40:9-11, 13; Lev. 8:10-12, 15, 30; 11:44; 16:32; 20:7; 21:8, 10; Num. 3:13; 6:11; 7:1; 8:17; 11:18; 18:8; Deut. 15:19; 33:3; Judg. 17:3; I Sam. 7:1; 16:5; I Kings 8:64; 9:3, 7; I Chr. 23:13; II Chr. 7:7, 16, 20; 26:18; 29:33; 31:6; Neh. 3:1; Isa. 13:3; Jer. 1:5; Ezek. 48:11; Zeph. 1:7). The original meaning of the word is not clear, though Baudissin's view that the fundamental idea is one of "separation" is still widely held. In usage the term "holy" came to express the general notion of the godhead and in an early, though perhaps secondary sense, was applied to that which belonged to the sphere of deity, which lay near or had come into his presence (Exod. 3:5; Num. 16:37-38), or which belonged to him. "Consecrate" is therefore the correct rendering of this Hebrew word denoting "to be holy"—i.e., "to be separate from the common and the profane."

b) מלא יד, literally "to fill the hand" (Exod. 28:41; Lev. 16:32; 21:10; I Kings 13:33; I Chr. 29:5; II Chr. 13:9; 29:31; Ezek. 43:26). The same term is sometimes rendered "ordain" or "install" (Exod. 29:9, 29, 33, 35; 32:29; Lev. 8:33; Judg. 17:5, 12). Note such passages as Exod. 29:34; Lev. 7:37, where "hand" is simply understood. In these and other passages (Lev. 8:28, 31) the plural form מלאים is rendered "consecrations" in the KJV (but singular, "ordination," in the RSV). In the majority of instances where "consecrate" and "consecration" occur, they are the rendering of this idiomatic expression, and it is the only characteristic expression for "consecrate" in the OT.

The origins of this phrase are somewhat obscure. It is generally used of the consecration of priests (except in Ezek. 43:26, where the altar is consecrated).

In the most ancient practice the offerings were placed in the hands of the priest; by this symbolic act, involving contact with the holy offering, the priest was consecrated. Evidently the person who wished to make a sacrifice or offering could install a priest simply by "filling his hand" (Judg. 17:5; I Kings 13: 33; II Chr. 13:9; cf. Exod. 32:29). A suggestion of an early instance, if not the origin, of this practice in Israel is contained in the account of the ordination of the priests by Moses in Exod. 29. Deut. 26:13 ("I have removed the sacred portion out of my house") would seem to suggest that that part of one's produce or revenue which belonged to the deity and was therefore to be offered to him was infused with a quality of holiness which made it undesirable, perhaps dangerous, for the householder to retain such a portion in his possession. These goods were therefore passed into the hands of the priest, who had not only the right but also the risk of approaching the altar of the deity. The priest's hands were filled with the offerings, and by this very rite he was consecrated; from these offerings, once they had been presented to the deity and had proved acceptable, the priest derived his income.

*c)* נזר, "to separate, dedicate" (whence "separation," "dedication," or "consecration," and one "consecrated" or "devoted"), occasionally translated "consecrate" (Lev. 21:12; Num. 6:9, 18-19; Hos. 9: 10) but more commonly "separate" and its derivatives (see, e.g., Num. 6:2-21). *See* NAZIRITE.

*d)* Ἁγιάζω, "to separate, set apart, sanctify, be sanctified," in a few instances translated "consecrate" (John 10:36; 17:19; I Cor. 7:14; I Tim. 4:5; II Tim. 2:21) but generally "sanctify" (John 17:17; Acts 20:32; 26:18; Rom. 15:16; I Cor. 1:2; 6:11; Eph. 5: 26; I Thess. 5:23; Heb. 2:11; 9:13; 10:10, 14, 29; 13: 12; note also the differences in the translations of Matt. 23:17, 19; I Pet. 3:15; Jude 1).

*See also* PRIESTS AND LEVITES; SACRIFICES AND OFFERINGS.

*Bibliography.* T. F. Torrance, "Consecration and Ordination," *Scottish Journal of Theology,* XI (1958), 225-52.

H. F. BECK

## CONSOLATION [παράκλησις]. A synonym of

COMFORT. In Luke 2:25 the "consolation of Israel" coincides with the advent of the "Lord's Christ." When Acts 4:36 KJV explains BARNABAS as the "son of consolation" (RSV "encouragement"; ERV-ASV "exhortation"), the underlying Hebrew-Aramaic term may be נוח ("refreshment") or נביא ("prophet"; cf. Palmyrene *Bar-Nebo*). F. F. BRUCE

## CONSTELLATIONS. *See* SCIENCE § C2*d.*

## CONSUL [ὕπατος]. The title of the two chief mil-

itary and political magistrates in the Roman Republic. They were of senatorial rank and served a year's term of office. According to I Macc. 15:16 a certain consul named Lucius (probably Lucius Calpurnius Piso, 140-139 B.C.) was the author of a circular letter addressed to the Egyptian king Ptolemy (Euergetes II, 146-116 B.C.) and sent to neighboring states, declaring the friendship between the Roman Senate and the Jews. The identification of Lucius and the authenticity of the letter are disputed.

Josephus mentions a similar letter sent by the praetor (*strategos*) Lucius Valerius in 54 B.C. (Antiq. XIV. viii.5).

*Bibliography.* F.-M. Abel, *Les livres des Maccabées* (1949), pp. 275-76; S. Tedesche and S. Zeitlin, *The First Book of Maccabees* (1950), pp. 40-43. E. W. SAUNDERS

## CONSUMPTION. 1. The translation of שחפת (Lev.

26:16; Deut. 28:22; LXX ἀπορία), which originated from a root meaning "thinness" or "attenuation." From the context febrile disease, probably undulant fever, seems to be implied, although phthisis or even cancer may be indicated.

**2.** KJV translation in Isa. 10:22 (כליון); 28:22 (כלה). In both passages widespread "destruction," rather than specific pathology, is envisaged.

R. K. HARRISON

## CONTENTMENT [αὐτάρκεια]. The acceptance of

"things as they are" as the wise and loving providence of a God who knows what is good for us, who so loves us as always to seek our good, and whose power is adequate to his love.

In the OT contentment is of this godly sort. Moses was "content" (יאל) to dwell with Reuel (Exod. 2:21) because he knew his stay was divinely ordained. Even his disappointing inability to enter Canaan became, in God's overruling, something that "sufficed" him (Deut. 3:26). The spirit of contentment finds expression even in the absence of the word—e.g., in Ps. 23, where the devout soul is content even in the "valley of the shadow of death," provided God is present.

Occasionally such contentment may appear reactionary to modern social reformers, as when John the Baptist told some Roman soldiers: "Be content with your wages" (Luke 3:14). Yet neither in the OT nor in the NT does the proper contentment of godly men preclude the divine discontent with injustice and wrong which is the true source of social reform. The social teaching of the OT prophets, and the transcendence of the barriers of class, race, and sex in the NT church (Gal. 3:28) testify eloquently to this.

Jesus himself enjoins contentment in the Sermon on the Mount (Matt. 5–7, especially 6:19-34). In the Letter to the Hebrews (13:5), Christians are exhorted to "keep your life free from love of money, and be content with what you have." A Stoic could have said this much, but the NT writer gives a more-than-Stoic reason for Christian contentment, for he continues: "He has said, 'I will never fail you nor forsake you.'" The Sermon on the Mount also sees the love of money as a great enemy of true contentment, as does I Tim. 6:6-8: "There is great gain in godliness with contentment; for we brought nothing into the world, and we cannot take anything out of the world; but if we have food and clothing, with these we shall be content. But those who desire to be rich fall into temptation."

For the Christian, however, contentment is not self-regarding. Paul asked alms for the saints in Jerusalem from the church in Corinth. He told the Corinthians that "he who sows sparingly will also reap sparingly." And lest self-regard should make the Corinthians chary of generous giving, he assured them that "God is able to provide you with every blessing in abundance, so that you may always have enough of everything and may provide in abundance for every good work. . . . He . . . will supply and multiply your resources." (II Cor. 9:6-10.)

The innermost secret of this carefree, generous contentment lies in the Christian's life with God. This is the all-satisfying good. Paul writes (Phil. 4:11-13: "I have learned, in whatever state I am, to be content. I know how to be abased, and I know how to abound; in any and all circumstances I have learned the secret of facing plenty and hunger, abundance and want. I can do all things in him who strengthens me." The Christian's all-conquering contentment comes from his knowledge of Christ and his communion with him. Paul once more states it clearly: "I count everything as loss because of the surpassing worth of knowing Christ Jesus my Lord. For his sake I have suffered the loss of all things, and count them as refuse, in order that I may gain Christ and be found in him" (Phil. 3:8-9).          J. MARSH

**CONTRIBUTION FOR THE SAINTS.** *See* OFFERING FOR THE SAINTS.

**CONTRITE.** The translation of a form of the root דכא or דכה, "to crush" (Pss. 34:18 KJV [RSV "crushed"]); 51:17; Isa. 57:15), and of a form of נכה, "to smite" (Isa. 66:2). The religious sense of the word is indicated by the words or phrases with which it appears in parallel: "broken heart" (Ps. 34:18 KJV); a "broken spirit" (Ps. 51:17); "humble" (שפל; Isa. 57:15); "humble" (עני; Isa. 66:2). It belongs to the vocabulary of later, postexilic Israel, for which, as a result of the humiliating experiences of the Babylonian Exile, such qualities as humility, lowliness, meekness, had come to seem essential marks of the truly religious man—a point of view notably represented in the NT by the Beatitudes and the Magnificat (Luke 1:46-55).          R. C. DENTAN

**CONVERSATION** [דרך; ἀναστροφή, πολίτευμα, τρόπος]. Used in the KJV in its older sense of "way of life," "behavior" (cf. Latin *conversari*). In ethical injunctions ἀναστροφή is used at times in a context which contrasts the old, Jewish or pagan manner of life with the new, Christian one (cf., e.g., I Pet. 1:15, 18). In Phil. 3:20 KJV "conversation" represents πολίτευμα—i.e., civic life, constitution (cf. RSV "commonwealth"; ERV-ASV "citizenship")—a specially apt term in an admonition to inhabitants of a Roman colony.

In its modern sense of "speech," "talking," this word is not used in standard versions of the English Bible.

*Bibliography.* L. A. Weigle, *Bible Words in Living Language* (1957), pp. 8-10.          F. F. BRUCE

**CONVERSION** [שוב; ἐπιστρέφειν, ἐπιστροφή]. In biblical usage, a turning or a returning. The OT uses the term frequently; but the noun is found only once in the NT (Acts 15:3), to refer to the "conversion of the Gentiles." The verbal forms are used both transitively and intransitively in both the OT and the NT.

In the OT nouns and verbs are found with the physical meaning of "turn" or "return" (Judg. 8:13), though the action can be given added significance by association with some person (Jephthah [Judg. 11: 8]; Rehoboam [I Kings 12:27]) or purpose (Josh. 8:

21). The most characteristic use is to describe God's "turning" in respect of man, whether favorably (Deut. 13:17) or unfavorably (Josh. 24:20); and man's turning in respect of God, either to him (Jer. 3:14) or from him (Jer. 8:4-6; Ezek. 33:18). God's turning is not fickleness, but part of his unchanging pursuit of man's salvation. Man's turning from God is rebellion (Josh. 22:16); and his turning to God, though his own submission, is the work of God's grace (Ps. 85: 3—H 85:4; Lam. 5:21). Turning to God, or "conversion," is thus more than a change of mind, more than undergoing some experience; it is a concrete change to a new way of life, as the word "turn" suggests—a turning in one's tracks and going in a new direction. Such views found heightened expression in the prophets of the Exile, who spoke of "returning" to God at the same time as they foretold a "return" to Jerusalem (Isa. 44:22; 51:11; 55:7), an act of man which was possible only by the previous act of God.

In the NT the literal meaning of "turning" is found (Luke 2:39), and as in the OT the physical act sometimes gains significance by association with a person or action (Mark 5:30) or purpose (Acts 15: 36). The NT does not speak of God's "turning" to man; the Incarnation is the fulfilment of all such "turning." Though the word can be used of turning away from God (Gal. 4:9), its most characteristic use is of man's turning to him (Acts 9:35; 15:19). It is often associated with "repent" (Acts 3:19; 26:20), "believe" (11:21), or with some expression indicating the nature of the "turning"—from darkness to light (26:18), from idols to God (I Thess. 1:9), from vain things to a living God (Acts 14:15)—and Paul can say that "when a man turns to the Lord the veil is removed" (II Cor. 3:16).

The biblical emphasis is thus not upon a subjective psychological experience, but upon an objective change in man. But the change is not simply to be achieved by outward deed, for it was this conception which Jesus repudiated in Pharisaic teaching (Mark 7:6-23). True turning to God follows upon repentance and belief, and it leads not only to an observable new way of life, but to a spiritual transformation as well: "And we all, with unveiled face, beholding the glory of the Lord, are being changed into his likeness from one degree of glory to another; for this comes from the Lord who is the Spirit" (II Cor. 3: 18).          J. MARSH

**CONVICTION** [πληροφορία (I Thess. 1:5), full assurance, certainty, *from verb* to bring to full measure or certainty; ἔλεγχος (Heb. 11:1), proof, evidence]. Strong persuasion, certainty, or proof.

**CONVOCATION, HOLY** [מקרא קדוש, holy summons; LXX κλητή ἀγιά] (Lev. 23:2-4, 7-8, 21, 24, 27, 35-37; Num. 28:18). A term which refers to the SOLEMN ASSEMBLY and is virtually interchangeable with it (cf. Exod. 12:16; Isa. 1:13; 4:5). It stresses the summons to an assembly where Israel, in a state of special holiness, is called to fulfil its sacred functions. Holy convocations were central aspects of each of the three great FEASTS and of the Day of Atonement (*see* ATONEMENT, DAY OF). They were days of rest, like the sabbath, and in later times were known as sabbaths (cf. PENTECOST and Lev. 23:11). In Isa. 4:5 the eschatological hope of Israel is portrayed in a vision of great convocations. In Neh. 8:8 the Hebrew term is used of "the reading" of the Law; and thus it became the technical term for "holy scripture" in Judaism.                                    J. C. RYLAARSDAM

**COOK** [מבח]. One who prepares and serves food. Usually the women in the family were the cooks (Gen. 18:6; 27:9; II Sam. 13:8). Men could also cook (Judg. 6:19). Male or female servants could also be ordered to cook (Luke 17:8). The cook often had to butcher and boil (the Hebrew root meaning is "to boil") the meat (Gen. 18:7). Professional cooks were not unknown (I Sam. 9:23-24; cf. I Sam. 8:13).

*See also* COOKING AND COOKING UTENSILS; FOOD; SERVANT.                                    C. U. WOLF

**COOKING AND COOKING UTENSILS.** The women of the house did the cooking except in the palace (I Sam. 8:13) or in wealthy homes, where servants were employed. Baking of bread was often done during the day, but most of the cooking was done for the evening meal. This was the important meal, and for the poor it was often the only one. This last point is the key to the interpretation of the laborers in the vineyard (Matt. 20:1-16). A common laborer needed a whole day's wages in order to feed his family that evening.

1. **Cooking.** In the average home the courtyard served as the kitchen except in inclement weather, when the inhabitants had to stay indoors.

a. *Grains.* In Bible times bread was the most important food. The major grains used were wheat and barley, but their flour could be mixed with less desirable grains such as millet and spelt (Ezek. 4:9). The rich used wheat, the poor used barley. Bread. was often dipped in olive oil and then in some ground spice or herb, thus giving various flavors to the bread and counteracting the monotony of the diet. Cakes were often coated with honey and sprinkled with a variety of seeds and nuts. Cakes were not only baked in the oven but were also made by frying in deep fat. The fats most commonly used were olive oil and sesame. The nomads, however, used boiled butter. *See* BREAD.

A second common method of eating grain was to make it into porridge. For the best results the wheat was first steeped in water and then dried, and before cooking the grain was ground to about the consistency of our cracked wheat. There were a variety of ways to season it—with salt, honey, olive oil, condiments, etc. Prov. 27:22 alludes to another method of cooking grain, a sort of hash; cracked wheat and meat were pounded together in a mortar and then spread out in a shallow pan for baking.* In the Proverbs passage the meat is the fool, and nothing else can ever be made of him, no matter how long he is worked over. Fig. VES 14.

The first opportunity for cooking grain came in the harvest field itself, where the grain was being reaped. It was bound into small sheaves and then roasted or parched over an open fire (Ruth 2:14). Indeed, grain was an item of food so appreciated that it appears in the Levitical law of first fruits (Lev. 2:14-16). Only one who has lived on a bread diet all winter can appreciate this first taste of the new grain.

b. *Vegetables and fruits.* The poor man's variant for bread and porridge had to be vegetables and fruits, since he could seldom afford meat. Various kinds of lentils and beans were especially valuable, as they could be used the year around. The Esau story (Gen. 25:29-34) shows that even the most influential members of society appreciated these lentils and beans. These dishes were often flavored with onions and garlic.

c. *Meats.* The Hebrews were not great meat eaters. Indeed, the use of meat was a sign of wealth. This shows up well in the food budget of Solomon (I Kings 4:23), where we have both stall-fed and pasture-fed animals, as well as wild game and fatted fowl. For the poor man, meat was a rare item of diet reserved for religious occasions, family gatherings, and meals for special guests. The favorite meats were lamb and goat, with the rich adding veal. There was no easy way to preserve meat, so the whole animal had to be consumed the same day it was killed.

Meat had a wide variety of cooking possibilities. It was roasted in an oven, boiled in water, cooked in oil, or used on spit or griddle. When the meat was roasted in an oven, it was often the whole animal. It was always well cooked so that it could easily be pulled off the bone. Boiling was the most common method of cooking. Mic. 3:2-3 shows how stew was prepared: the meat was cut off the bones and then the bones crushed for the marrow. In this passage we have strong figurative language in which the rich are spoken of as cannibals making stew out of the poor. Broth from the meat was boiled down and served in a separate dish from the meat (Judg. 6:19). Fowl was cooked the same way as meat; fish was probably most commonly broiled over coals (John 21:9). An item of diet unusual to us but common to the Near East was cooked locusts (Lev. 11:22; Matt. 3:4; Mark 1:6). For cooking of sacrifices, *see* SACRIFICE AND OFFERINGS.

d. *Seasonings.* Food was made more palatable by the addition of salt; and with the heavy vegetarian diet of the common man, salt was an absolute necessity (see Job 6:6; Matt. 5:13; Col. 4:6). Common flavoring agents were onions, leeks, and garlic; and the Israelites in the wilderness missed these greatly (Num. 11:5). Condiments were whole or ground seeds such as anise, coriander, cummin, dill. Herbs such as thyme and mint were also used. Nuts of all kinds also added their flavor as well as their nutrient oils. The place of these flavoring agents in the ancient diet cannot be overemphasized, for these gave the common man the variety in his menu. Honey was the sugar of antiquity.

2. *Cooking utensils.* The Hebrews used several varieties of cooking pots (*see* POTTERY).* The most common form was wide and shallow. In early Israelite times it was without handles, but later it had two handles. There was also a two-handled small-mouth cooking pot almost spherical in shape and probably used for heating water. There was also a one-handled cooking pot. Two special vessels were used for deep-fat frying, and there was also a griddle. In the days of Isaiah and Jeremiah, potters were so proud of their cooking pots that they used trade-marks just as we do today. Furthermore, their vessels were made in standard sizes as ours are. Copper kettles and pans were much more efficient, but they were

also very expensive. Both the tabernacle and Solomon's temple list a goodly number of cooking vessels. Fig. COO 40.

Courtesy of the Royal Ontario Museum, Toronto

40. Cooking and other utensils from Palestine. From left to right: Basalt mortar and pestle (Middle Bronze Age II); two-handled mixing bowl (Iron Age); small bowl (Iron Age); pitcher (Iron Age); one-handled cooking pot (Iron Age); two-handled cooking pot (Iron Age)

The oven for baking bread looked like a large inverted bowl with the bottom missing. It was often a yard in width. At times it was built over a small hole in the ground, thus giving extra volume to the oven. The fire was built inside the oven; then, when only the embers were left, the thin bread was placed inside on the walls of the oven. If the oven had a plain exterior and was heavily heated, bread could also be placed on the outside. In the large cities there were public bakeries (Jer. 37:21) to which the housewives brought their bread for baking.   J. L. KELSO

**COOS.** KJV form of Cos.

**COPING** [מפה, handbreadth] (I Kings 7:9). The meaning of this architectural term is obscure.

**COPPER** [נחשת, החוש, נחשה; Aram. נחש (Dan. 2: 32, etc.); χαλκός; χαλκίον; χάλκεος; λεπτόν, a small coin (KJV MITE)]; COPPERSMITH [χαλκεύς] (II Tim. 4:14). The usual RSV translation of these words is "bronze," although the same Hebrew word may mean either "copper" or "bronze." The KJV uses "copper" only in Ezra 8:27 (RSV "bronze"), "steel" in four passages, but otherwise "brass," a term which in Tudor English could include any alloy of copper, such as copper and tin (bronze) or copper and zinc (brass). Brass was unknown in biblical days.

With the exception of gold and meteoric iron, copper was the first metal used by man (see METALLURGY). At first it was made into simple ornaments and then into tools; this development altered the whole course of human history, since it vastly increased man's power over his environment and made possible, among other things, the development of an architecture in cut stone.

In Palestine copper adzes dating from the thirty-fourth or thirty-third century B.C. (Late Chalcolithic) have been found at Meser. Similar adzes of about the same date have been found at Teleilat el-Ghassul and in Level XVI at Beth-shean. From Tell Abu Matar near Beer-sheba come four pear-shaped maceheads, some rings, and other copper objects. On the archaeological finds mentioned above, see bibliography.

From the Early Bronze Age (3000-2000 B.C.) come a few daggers and one axhead found at Jericho, but the impression gained from archaeological reports is that copper remained very scarce all through the Early Bronze period.

With the dawn of the Middle Bronze Age ca. 2000 B.C. copper became much more abundant; BRONZE also made its appearance. This greater abundance of metal seems connected with the arrival of invaders from the N, probably Amorites. The pottery which these newcomers have left at Jericho is frequently modeled on metal forms found in Syria. Tell el-'Ajjul has been rich in metal remains. See bibliography.

Copper continued to be used extensively even after the introduction of bronze, especially for objects which did not require to be cast (see BRONZE). During the second millennium B.C. the copper mines of Cyprus were an important source of supply for the countries of the Near East, although Egypt during the Eighteenth Dynasty drew her supply from a variety of sources, as Egyptian inscriptions attest. Much later, at the time of Ezekiel (sixth century B.C.), Tyre was importing copper from Tarshish, Javan, Tubal, and Meshech (Ezek. 27:12-13).

The idea that the ancients possessed the secret (later lost) of tempering copper has been shown by modern investigation to be completely without foundation. What they did discover was that copper can be given a reasonably hard cutting edge by cold hammering.

*Bibliography.* A. Lucas, "Copper in Ancient Egypt," *JEA*, XIII (1927), 162-70; *Ancient Egyptian Materials and Industries* (2nd ed., 1934), pp. 153-74, 401-4. A. G. Barrois, *Manuel d'archéologie biblique*, I (1939), ch. 9.

On the discovery of copper adzes, at Meser: M. Dothan, "Excavations at Meṣer," *IEJ*, VII (1957), 220, 226, plate 37C, D; at Teleilat el-Ghassul: A. Mallon, *Teleilat Ghassul*, I (1934), plate 34:2; at Beth-shean: *PEQ* (1934), p. 127, plate II:2; at Tell Abu Matar: *IEJ*, V (1955), 79, 84, plate 15A.

On the metal remains at Tell el-'Ajjul: W. M. F. Petrie, *Ancient Gaza: Tell el-'Ajjul* (4 vols.; 1931-34). For the assignment of the earliest remains at Tell el-'Ajjul to the MB period, see W. F. Albright, *Archaeology of Palestine* (1949), p. 39.

        F. V. WINNETT

**COPPERSMITH** [χαλκεύς]. A worker in bronze, then generally a (black)smith, a brazier.

The only NT use of χαλκεύς (II Tim. 4:14) indicates the occupation of a certain Alexander, from whom the author claims to have received great harm. Metalworkers or smiths (see CAIN) were the earliest full-time industrial specialists (cf. Gen. 4:22, with mention of TUBAL-CAIN). Etymologically the tribal name KENITES means "smiths." An Egyptian impression of such a traveling band of tinkers is given in a wall painting at Beni-hasan (ca. 1890 B.C.; Fig. OCC 3). The name Bezalel (Exod. 31:2; 35:30; etc.) has now good parallels from old Amorite usage. Alexander, like Solomon's χαλκεύς, Hiram of Tyre, before him, was one of an ancient and useful union of workmen; he apparently failed to uphold the honor of his craft in his Christian profession.   P. L. GARBER

**COPTIC VERSIONS.** The translations of the Bible into the several dialects of Egypt during the early Christian centuries. *See* VERSIONS, ANCIENT, § 5.

        B. M. METZGER

**COR** kōr [כֹּר; Sumer. *GUR*]. A large measure of uncertain quantity. *See* WEIGHTS AND MEASURES § C4*b*.

**CORAL.** The red coral of the Mediterranean area, used for jewelry. It is the calcareous skeleton of one of the Actinozoa. "Coral" is the translation of two Hebrew words:

*a*) ראמות, *râmoth* (cf. Arabic *ra'mat*, "sea shell"). The LXX and the Vulg. read the word as a plural feminine participle in Job 28:18 (cf. Prov. 24:7). The LXX transliterates λαμώθ in Ezek. 27:16, and the Vulg. reads *sericum*. This is evidence that the ancient versions were uncertain of the meaning of the word. In Job 28:18 the word is used with "crystal" and "pearls"(?) in the evaluation of wisdom. In Ezek. 27: 16 coral is an article of trade between Edom and Tyre.

*b*) פנינים, *penînîm* (alternately JEWELS; COSTLY STONES; PEARLS; cf. Arabic *fananun*, a branch of a tree, and so an indication of the character of coral). In describing the princes of Zion, Lam. 4:7 notes that "their bodies were more ruddy than coral" (KJV "rubies"; LXX λίθος, "stone"; Vulg. *ebur*, "ivory").

*See also* JEWELS AND PRECIOUS STONES IN THE OT § 2; PEARL.         W. E. STAPLES

**CORBAN** [קרבן, offering *or* oblation; κορβᾶν] (Mark 7:11). The term, in postexilic Judaism, for a gift consecrated to God for religious purposes. The Hebrew term is used in Ezekiel, the HOLINESS CODE, and the PRIESTLY CODE to designate any kind or class of "offering" (Lev. 1:2; 22:27; 23:14; Num. 7:25; Ezek. 20:28; 40:43). The absence of the word in any earlier writings indicates that it was not widely used until later times, and, probably, that its use originated in circles having to do with the Jerusalem cultus. The Mishna (*see* TALMUD) shows how, in later Judaism, anything set apart by the use of the term, even rashly, could not thereafter be used for any other purpose (Ned. III.6; IX). It is to this strict use of the word that the saying of Jesus in Mark refers.

*Bibliography.* J. H. A. Hart, "Corban," *JQR*, XIX (1907), 615-50; H. Strack and P. Billerbeck, *Kommentar zum NT aus Talmud und Midrasch,* I (1922), 711; M. Black, *An Aramaic Approach to the Gospels and Acts* (2nd ed., 1953), p. 101.
         H. H. GUTHRIE, JR.

**CORBE.** KJV Apoc. form of CHORBE; same as ZACCAI.

**CORD, ROPE.** In antiquity a great many fibers were used in the manufacture of rope. The Bible mentions flax (Esth. 1:6), silver (Eccl. 12:6), and gold (Exod. 28:24-25); Pliny speaks of hemp, esparto grass, papyrus, and palm leaves (Nat. Hist. XIII.72; XIX.29-31, 173). Goat's hair, wool, and later camel's hair were doubtless also employed for this purpose.

Some of the more common words translated "cord" or "rope" are:

*a*) חבל, a general term, used on the one hand of a rope strong enough to support a man's weight (Josh. 2:15; Jer. 38:6) or to drag stones (II Sam. 17:13), and on the other of cords which tie back curtains (Esth. 1:6) or suspend a lamp (Eccl. 12:6). It is employed figuratively of a trap by (Ps. 119:61) or for (Job 18:10) the wicked, and of a snare set by Sheol

or death (Ps. 18:4-5—H 18:5-6). The word is also used of a measuring line (Mic. 2:5; Zech. 2:1—H 2:5).

*b*) מיתר, the cords of a tent (Isa. 54:2; Jer. 10:20), of the court of the tabernacle (Exod. 35:18; Num. 3: 37); and the strings of a bow (Ps. 21:12 KJV—H 21:13; cf. יתר in Job 30:11).

*c*) עבת, from a root meaning "to wind, weave," hence probably "braided rope." In the majority of cases the word refers to bonds (Judg. 15:13; Ps. 2:3; Ezek. 4:8). Captives would be secured by binding the elbows or hands behind the back or over the head, and they could be led by ropes around the waist (cf. נקפה in Isa. 3:24) or neck. This word is also used of the gold braid on the high priest's garment. *See* EPHOD 2.

*d*) Σχοινίον, a rope made of rushes; possibly of esparto grass (John 2:15; Acts 27:32).

*e*) Ζευκτηρίας, the crossbar of a double rudder (Acts 27:40; cf. Euripides *Helena* 1556).

*Bibliography.* J. B. Pritchard, ed., *ANEP* (1954), figs. 1, 7, 10, 298, 332; R. J. Forbes, *Studies in Ancient Technology,* IV (1956), 2-80, *passim.*        R. W. CORNEY

**CORE.** KJV alternate form of KORAH.

**CORIANDER SEED** kôr'ĭ ăn'dər [גד, *gadh;* κόριον]. The fruit of an umbelliferous annual plant (*Coriandrum sativum* L.) which was used much as poppy,

41. Coriander

caraway, and sesame seeds are used today. The small, globular, grayish, aromatic seed with ridges is mentioned only twice in the Bible (Exod. 16:31; Num. 11:7) to describe MANNA.

*See also* FLORA § A6*b;* SPICE.

Fig. COR 41.

**Bibliography.** I. Löw, *Die Flora der Juden,* III (1924), 441-47; H. N. and A. L. Moldenke, *Plants of the Bible* (1952), p. 86.
J. C. TREVER

**\*CORINTH** kôr'ĭnth, kŏr'— [ἡ Κόρινθος] (Acts 18:1; 19:1; I Cor. 1:2; II Cor. 1:1, 23; II Tim. 4:20). The chief commercial city on the Isthmus of Corinth and the capital of the Roman province of ACHAIA.

Descriptions of Corinth are given by Strabo (VII. 378-82), who visited the city soon after its restoration by the Romans in 44 B.C., and by Pausanias, who wrote his *Description of Greece* (see book II) *ca.* A.D. 174. The excavation of the ancient city was begun by the American School of Classical Studies in Athens in 1896, and the work and the publication of the results have continued.

The site of the city was *ca.* two miles inland from the Gulf of Corinth on an elevated terrace at the foot of Acrocorinth, a rocky hill rising to 1,886 feet above sea level. Stone implements and pottery vessels attest the life of man here in the Neolithic period, while tools of metal show the transition to the Early Bronze Age *ca.* 3000 B.C. *Ca.* 2000 B.C. the settlement seems to have been devastated, and then at the beginning of the first millennium B.C. was occupied by the Dorian Greeks. By the eighth century B.C., Corinth had founded colonies at Corfu and Syracuse. In the seventh century Cypselus made himself tyrant of the city, and was followed by his famed son, Periander (*ca.* 625–*ca.* 583 B.C.), under whom Corinth reached great power and prosperity. The city was famed for pottery and bronze work, and its products were carried far and wide by extensive shipping.

Corinth survived the vicissitudes of the Peloponnesian War (431-404 B.C.) and the Corinthian War (395-387 B.C.), but in the third century B.C. as the leader of the Achaian League it came into conflict with Rome. In 146 B.C. the Roman consul L. Mummius captured, burned, and razed the city, slaying its men and selling into slavery its women and children. Corinth lay desolate for a century, then was refounded as a Roman colony in accordance with a decree which Julius Caesar issued in 44 B.C., not long before his death. The city was known earlier as Ephyra (Ἐφύρα), meaning "lookout" or "guard," but now in honor of its new founder was called Colonia Laus Julia Corinthiensis, a name which has been found in an inscription at Corinth (*see bibliography*). The colonists seem to have been freedmen from Italy, with whom soon Greeks and Orientals, including many Jews, were mingled.

Prosperity returned to the revived city. Corinth was strategically located on its isthmus and controlled the ports of Lechaion on the Gulf of Corinth and Cenchreae on the Saronic Gulf. The goods of East and West were shipped across the isthmus, and at its narrowest point the smaller vessels were themselves dragged over bodily on a sort of shipway of which some vestiges have probably been identified and which Strabo (VIII.335, 369, 380) called a δίολκος, or "haul-across." The isthmus was only 3½

miles across, and it occurred to Periander and others to cut a canal through it. This project was seriously undertaken by Nero upon his visit to Greece in A.D. 66 or 67, but abandoned when exigencies elsewhere proved more pressing. The same emperor was generous in restorations in Corinth when the city was shaken by an earthquake, and Vespasian and Hadrian also built there. By the second century A.D., Corinth was probably the finest city in Greece.

Strabo (VIII.379) states that Corinth was surrounded by a wall except where it was protected by Acrocorinth, and that this wall extended for as much as forty stadia. Modern exploration has found and traced the ancient wall in a circuit of more than six miles, which is actually in excess of Strabo's figure, since it amounts to some fifty-five Greek stadia. It would appear that the city did not need all this space, and the excavations which have laid bare many of the chief buildings have touched less than the hundredth part of the entire area.

Since Mummius conducted so thorough a destruction, relatively few remains of the ancient Greek city

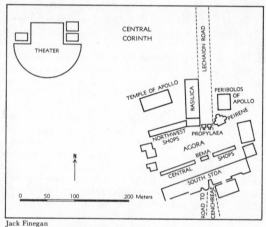

Jack Finegan

42. City plan of Corinth

have been found, and it is for the most part the ruins of Roman Corinth which have been brought to light. In the identification of the different structures the detailed itinerary and descriptions of Pausanias have been of the utmost value. In what follows, some of the chief features of Corinth will be noted which existed in the middle of the first century A.D.—i.e., at the time of Paul. Fig. COR 42.

Coming from the port of Lechaion to the N, a road led directly to the central area of Corinth. Where this road approached the agora, it was twenty to twenty-five feet in width and flanked by raised sidewalks on either side, both road and sidewalks being paved with hard limestone. Steps built into the road make it evident that it was not intended for wheeled traffic, and it was lined with colonnades and shops on each side.\* Above these shops on the W side of the road was a large basilica, a great rectangular hall divided by two rows of columns, with rooms at each end. Beyond the basilica to the W on a separate eminence stood the great Temple of Apollo.\* Built in the sixth century B.C., seven of its original thirty-eight columns still stand, nearly twenty-four feet tall and

Courtesy of the American School of Classical Studies, Athens

43. The Lechaion Road at Corinth

Courtesy of the American School of Classical Studies, Athens

44. Temple of Apollo at Corinth

six feet in diameter. Behind the shops on the E side of the Lechaion Road was a large open court, probably the peribolos or sacred enclosure mentioned by Pausanias (II.iii.3) as also dedicated to Apollo. S of the peribolos was an enclosure around a copious natural spring, the famous Fountain of Peirene. Figs. COR 43-44.

At the head of the Lechaion Road, splendid

propylaea gave access to the agora.* This large, generally rectangular area was divided into two parts, the N or lower, and the S or upper part. Colonnades, shops, basilicas, and other monuments surrounded the agora. The dividing line between the lower and upper areas was marked by a long row of central shops, in the midst of which was found the bema (*see below*). The S edge of the agora was adorned by the colonnades of the S stoa, which gave access to another row of shops and buildings. Many of these shops were provided with deep wells connected with the Peirene water system. The pottery found here included many drinking vessels inscribed with such names and words as Dionysus, Zeus, Health, Security, and Love, which suggest that these shops served chiefly as taverns. Fig. COR 45.

From the S edge of the agora, the road departed which led to Cenchreae. On a sloping hill NW of the agora was the theater. Consisting fundamentally of a semicircle of seats facing a large stage building, the theater originated in the fifth century B.C. and was rebuilt several times in the Greek and Roman periods. Farther N, adjacent to the city wall and beside the spring Lerna, was the sanctuary of Asclepius, the god of healing. The patients who came here often expressed their gratitude for healings received by leaving votive offerings in the form of representations of their afflicted parts; a vast number of terra-cotta replicas of hands, feet, and other members of the body were found in the ruins. *Ca.* a mile W of the agora was the potters' quarter, where the ancient craftsmen produced the wares which added to the fame of their city. On the summit of Acrocorinth was a temple of Aphrodite, the goddess whose worship Strabo (VIII.378) said brought so many people and so much wealth to Corinth; and this temple too has been identified with probability in the excavations.

In connection with the work of Paul at Corinth the bema is of special interest.* As indicated above, this structure was found near the center of the agora. It consisted of a high, broad platform raised on two

Courtesy of the American School of Classical Studies, Athens

45. The Agora at Corinth

steps and carrying a superstructure, with benches, on the back and part way along the sides. Below, on either side, were rectangular enclosures with benches, and beside these, passageways gave access from the lower to the upper areas of the agora. Built of white and blue marble, the bema must have presented an

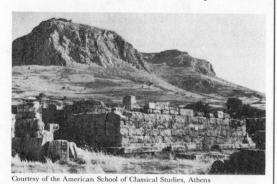

Courtesy of the American School of Classical Studies, Athens

46. The bema at Corinth, with Acrocorinth in the background

impressive appearance, and it served very well for the function of a public-speaking platform with the possibility of a large crowd assembled in front of it. The date of the construction is believed to be in the first half of the first century A.D., perhaps *ca.* A.D. 44. A Corinth inscription which states that a certain text had been read "from the rostra" probably refers to this structure and accords perfectly with the idea of a speaking platform in a public place. The Greek word *bema* (βῆμα), translated "tribunal" in the NT, corresponds to the Latin *rostrum*, and there can be little doubt that this is the very place where Paul was brought "before the tribunal" (ἐπὶ τὸ βῆμα), as recorded in Acts 18:12-17. Fig. COR 46.

In the vicinity of the theater at Corinth was a plaza, some sixty feet square, paved with limestone blocks, dating probably in the middle of the first century A.D. On one of the blocks was the inscription ERASTVS·PRO·AED / S·P·STRAVIT. This is probably to be read, *Erastus pro aedilitate sua pecunia stravit*, and means that in return for his aedileship, Erastus had laid the pavement at his own expense. "Aedile" (Latin *aedilis*) was the title of a Roman city official who was in charge of various public works. In Rom. 16:23, written doubtless in Corinth, Paul mentions an Erastus, whom he calls the "city treasurer" (ὁ οἰκονόμος τῆς πόλεως). It has been held that the Erastus of the paving inscription and the Erastus of Rom. 16:23 could not be the same, because "aedile" is usually ἀγορανόμος in Greek. However, since οἰκονόμος means, not only "treasurer" (Latin *arcarius*), but also more broadly "steward, manager, administrator," it seems that this word might easily be used as the equivalent of *aedilis*, and so it may well be held that we have here an inscription of the very man who later became a Christian and a friend of Paul.

Another inscription found in fragments in the vicinity of the Lechaion Road near the agora, dating probably in the last years of Augustus or the reign of Tiberius, mentions a shop or market with the same word in Latin, *macellum*, which Paul uses in Greek, μάκελλον (RSV "meat market"), in I Cor. 10:25. A similar fragmentary inscription contains a word restored as *piscario*, which suggests that in this case a fish market, or fish and meat market, is involved.

Yet another inscription was found on a block of white marble on the Lechaion Road near the propylaea. Rather roughly cut and now partially destroyed, it reads ΓΩΓΗΕΒΡ—i.e., [Συνα]γωγὴ Ἑβρ[αίων], "Synagogue of the Hebrews." The block probably formed the lintel over a doorway of a Jewish synagogue, which must have stood in that vicinity. While the style of lettering indicates a date later than the time of Paul, this synagogue may have been the successor to the very one in which, according to Acts 18:4, the apostle preached.

*Bibliography.* T. Lenschau, "Korinthos," *Pauly-Wissowa*, Supplement IV (1924), cols. 991-1036. T. H. Shear, "Excavations in the Theatre District and Tombs of Corinth in 1929," *AJA*, XXXIII (1929), 525-26. American School of Classical Studies at Athens, *Corinth, Results of Excavations* (1929—). H. J. Cadbury, "Erastus of Corinth," *JBL*, L (1931), 42-58; "The Macellum of Corinth," *JBL*, LIII (1934), 1934-41. O. Broneer, "Studies in the Topography of Corinth at the Time of St. Paul," Ἀρχαιολογικὴ Ἐφημερίς, περιοδικὸν τῆς ἐν Ἀθήναις ἀρχαιολογικῆς Ἑταιρείας (1937), 125-33; "Colonia Laus Iulia Corinthiensis, an Official Report from Corinth," *Hesperia*, VIII (1939), 181-90; X (1941), 388-90. C. C. McCown, "Book Review: Light from the Ancient Past," *AJA*, L (1946), 426—on Erastus. O. Broneer, "Corinth: Center of St. Paul's Missionary Work in Greece," *BA*, XIV (1951), 77-96. American School of Classical Studies at Athens, *Ancient Corinth, A Guide to the Excavations* (6th ed., 1954). H. J. Cadbury, *The Book of Acts in History* (1955), pp. 44, 55, n. 26-27. J. FINEGAN

\***CORINTHIANS, FIRST LETTER TO THE** kə rĭn′thĭ ənz [Κορίνθιους, *see* CORINTH]. A letter written by the apostle Paul to the church at Corinth; now found as the seventh book of the NT canon. Because of the variety of matters with which it is concerned, it is one of the most illuminating documents in all Christian literature. It casts a flood of light, not only on many aspects of Paul's thought, but also on typical problems that arose in early Gentile churches. 11:23-26 preserves the earliest account of the church's celebration of the Lord's Supper and of the words that Jesus used at the Last Supper. 15:3-11 has the earliest account of the origin of the faith in the Resurrection. The hymn about love in ch. 13 is perhaps the most familiar and most beloved chapter in all Paul's writings, but the entire letter is replete with spiritual depth and lyrical cadence.

**1. Destination.** The letter that was entitled I Corinthians when it was included in the collected letters of Paul was written by the apostle from Ephesus (I Cor. 16:8) to the church at Corinth, a city situated at the S end of the narrow isthmus that connects Greece with the Peloponnesus. Although the site had been inhabited as early as Neolithic times and ancient Corinth had played an important role in early city-state politics, the city in Paul's day was a new and burgeoning metropolis, more nearly comparable to Houston, Texas, than to Boston, Massachusetts. In 146 B.C. the old city had joined in an Achaean revolt against Rome and had been destroyed by the Roman general Mummius, about the same time and almost as thoroughly as Scipio had laid waste the city of Carthage. Then, in 46 B.C., it was refounded as a Roman colony by Julius Caesar and repopulated with Italian freedmen and dispossessed Greeks as *Laus Julia Corinthiensis*. It rapidly recovered its former commercial prosperity as a center of import and transit trade and grew in size and influence to become in Paul's day, after Rome, Alexandria, and Ephesus, the largest and most important city in the Empire. In 27 B.C., Augustus made it the capital of the province of Achaia and the residence of the Roman proconsul. The holder of that office in A.D. 51-52 was Gallio (Acts 18:12-17), an elder brother of the Stoic philosopher Seneca.

In the first century of the Christian era Corinth was a city to which immigrants had been attracted from all parts of the Mediterranean world. Egyptians, Syrians, Jews, and Orientals of other races had settled among the earlier Italian and Greek colonists and had brought with them their diverse cultural heritage, their distinctive social customs, and their differing religious beliefs and practices. Modern archaeological research at Corinth, carried out by the American School for Classical Studies at Athens, has identified the remains of temples to the Egyptian divinities Isis and Serapis, to the Phrygian goddess Magna Mater, to the Syrian deity Astarte and the Ephesian Artemis, as well as to Helios, Aphrodite, and others.

Even at a time when public morality everywhere in the Empire was at a low ebb, Corinth in Paul's day was notorious for its lax morals. From the time of the poet Aristophanes (*ca.* 400 B.C.), "to live like a Corinthian" or "to Corinthianize" was a proverbial expression for dissolute living. To some extent this immorality was a consequence of pagan religious rites. Many of the religions that flourished in the Near East and that had been introduced into Corinth were fertility cults, and their ritual of worship often included gross forms of imitative magic. According to Strabo (a Greek historian and geographer who died *ca.* A.D. 24), the cult of Aphrodite early in the first century of our era had a thousand priestess-prostitutes attached to its Corinthian temple.

**2. Paul's first contact with Corinth.** Jews in some numbers had settled at Corinth, as at every other center in the Mediterranean world. In 1898 a stone inscription was discovered that had stood in the first century over the doorway of a building not far from the agora, or market place, on the fringe of the residential area to the W of the city and near the road that leads to the nearby port of Lechaem. The inscription bears the legend "synagogue of the Jews." In this synagogue Jews who had been born at Corinth, Jews who had immigrated from Rome or Naples or Alexandria or Antioch, Jews of wealth and Jews of abject poverty, gathered each sabbath to express their group solidarity, to be reminded of the traditions, beliefs, and practices of their religion, and to be encouraged with the assurance of the glorious future in store for the people of God. There were some proselytes among them, men and women of non-Jewish birth who had identified themselves ritually and by formal initiation with the Jewish community; but there were not many of these, for to become a Jew involved a radical break with the Gentile environment of that day, as of ours. Far more numerous than the proselytes were the so-called "God-fearers," Gentiles who had informed themselves about the history and tradition of the Jewish people, who had undertaken to govern their lives by the regulations of the Mosaic law, and who had accepted the monotheism of Jewish theology, but who had not taken the final step of ceremonial identification with the Jewish group. In Corinth, as elsewhere in the Empire, this fringe of interested people, the majority of whom were women, was very large. In every respect save that of ceremonial and ritual adherence to the Jewish faith, they thought and acted as Jews, but hesitated to pass over as recognized converts for two reasons: the anti-Semitic prejudice of the day that made formal identification with the Jewish community a matter of some social consequence in Gentile circles; and—almost as important a barrier—the fact that even within the Jewish community a proselyte remained for his lifetime a second-class Jew. Only his children were admitted to the full rights and privileges of the religious group.

The first acquaintance of the Corinthian Jewish community with the troublesome Christian sect dated from A.D. 49, according to the usual reckoning (*see* CHRONOLOGY OF THE NT). Late that year a man and wife, Aquila and Prisca ("Priscilla" in Acts), had come to the city after an edict of the Emperor Claudius had expelled them from Rome (Acts 18:2), where, together with other Jews, they had been charged (according to Suetonius) with stirring up riots over a certain "Chrestos." In Corinth, Aquila and Prisca associated themselves with the synagogue, but, busy with their trade as leather-workers, they apparently made little attempt to debate their Christian faith or to make converts.

Early in A.D. 50 Aquila and Prisca opened their home to an itinerant Christian evangelist of the same trade, a Tarsian Jew by the name of Paul. On the sabbath their guest accompanied them to the synagogue and was invited as a distinguished visitor to address the congregation. Paul took aggressive advantage of the opportunity. On this and later occasions he attempted with enthusiasm and persistence to convince his hearers that a certain Jesus was the Messiah of Jewish expectation and the Lord of life. This "Christ" had been crucified in Palestine under Pontius Pilate but had been raised by God from the dead and waited now at God's right hand in heaven, from whence he would shortly return to inaugurate a new and eternal kingdom for all who by their faith would be qualified to enter it.

Although tolerant to the extreme, the rulers of the

synagogue found Paul an exasperating and contentious exponent of what seemed to them a dangerous heresy. After two assistants arrived from Macedonia to join him, Silvanus ("Silas" in Acts) and Timothy (Acts 18:5), the Jewish leaders feared a serious rift in their community and ordered Paul to withdraw. This the apostle did, but not without taking with him a number of Jewish converts, including Crispus, the president of the synagogue (Acts 18:8), and a following of non-Jews who had been frequenting the Jewish place of worship. These "God-fearers" found Paul's presentation of the new faith of Christianity an attractive substitute for the Judaism in which they had been interested. It seemed to offer all the values of the Jewish religion—a high monotheism, a high morality, and a claim as the true Israel to the sacred literature and divine prerogatives of the Jews—without requiring circumcision or obedience to Jewish dietary regulations as conditions of admittance and membership.

Paul chose to carry on his mission from the home of one such "God-fearer," a man named Titius Justus (Acts 18:7). The location was a strategic one, for it adjoined the synagogue, but its choice was scarcely calculated to make for good relations with the Corinthian community of Jews.

Converts to Christianity, both from Judaism and from paganism, submitted to the rite of baptism. Jews were familiar with the practice of ritual washing by which proselytes were admitted to the community of Israel. No doubt some had heard of John the Baptizer, the desert prophet who had baptized fellow Jews in the Jordan as a sign that they were ready for the advent of the Messiah and the new age, and whose followers still practiced the rite. Some may even have had knowledge of the repeated lustral washings of the monastic sect at Qumran. Non-Jews would think of the blood bath of Mithraism, by which the initiate shared in the life-giving power of the animal sacred to the solar deity, as its blood poured down upon him from the jugular vein of the slaughtered bull. Paul personally baptized only a few of the Corinthian converts—Crispus, Gaius, and the household of Stephanas (I Cor. 1:14-16). In the main he left this function of the missionary to his associates. Nevertheless, he thought of the rite as more than a symbol—as a sacrament. Writing to Roman Christians at a later time from Corinth, he implies that the convert when immersed shares Christ's experience of death, and when raised from the water enters in some fashion into the experience of his resurrection (Rom. 6:1-5). No doubt many Corinthian converts, familiar with analogous initiation ceremonies in pagan mystery cults, accepted an even more realistically sacramental interpretation of the rite by which they were admitted to the Christian fellowship.

Paul's Corinthian converts were drawn generally from the city's lower economic and social groups. In I Cor. 1:26-29 the apostle reminds his readers of their status when they had received their call: "Not many of you were wise according to worldly standards, not many were powerful, not many were of noble birth; but God chose what is foolish in the world to shame the wise, God chose what is weak in the world to shame the strong, God chose what is

low and despised in the world, even things that are not, to bring to nothing things that are, so that no human being might boast in the presence of God." Some converts were slaves. Others were poverty-stricken wage earners. Yet there were also some people of leisure, wealth, and social influence in the new church. In a later letter the apostle mentions a certain Erastus, whom he describes as the "city treasurer" (Rom. 16:23) and who presumably was a civic official of some importance. (A tablet with his name inscribed on it is among the interesting finds of a recent archaeological excavation at Corinth.) Gaius, who could serve as host to Paul and "to the whole church" (Rom. 16:23); Chloe, who appears to have been a woman of means who maintained establishments both in Corinth and Ephesus (I Cor. 1:11); Crispus, who had been president of the synagogue (cf. I Cor. 1:14 and Acts 18:8); Sosthenes, who may also have been synagogue president before he became a Christian (cf. I Cor. 1:1 and Acts 18:17); and possibly others whom we can no longer identify belonged to the so-called higher social and economic strata of the times.

Paul as a Christian missionary followed the rabbinical practice of supporting himself by his own labor. He worked at Corinth at his trade as a leatherworker and later boasted of his financial independence of the Corinthian congregation. He had "preached God's gospel without cost" to them (II Cor. 11:7). He had "robbed other churches" (to use his own phrase [II Cor. 11:8]) by accepting financial support from them in order to serve his converts at Corinth without becoming in any way a burden to them. Macedonian Christians (II Cor. 11:9)—more specifically, Philippian Christians (Phil. 4:15)—had supplied his most pressing needs. In one rather involved argument (I Cor. 9:6-18), he defends the right of a Christian missionary to receive support from those to whom he ministers, and at the same time his own refusal to make use of this right. He wished to make the gospel "free of charge" (I Cor. 9:18), to put no hindrance in the way of its acceptance.

The earliest historian of Christianity estimates that Paul spent eighteen months in Corinth during the course of his first visit (Acts 18:11). Toward the end of his stay, probably late in the summer of A.D. 51, GALLIO assumed office as Roman proconsul of Achaia. Corinthian Jews, who had been growing more and more indignant at the inroads that Christians had made on their following, charged Paul before the proconsul with "persuading men to worship God contrary to the law" (Acts 18:13)—presumably the Jewish rather than the Roman law. Gallio refused to intervene, contemptuously dismissed the case, and took no notice when the mob turned on Sosthenes, the president of the synagogue, and manhandled him (Acts 18:14-17).

Shortly after this incident, probably early in the autumn of 51, Paul took his leave of the congregation he had established in Corinth and sailed from Cenchreae on a ship bound for Syria (Acts 18:18).

**3. Developments subsequent to Paul's departure.** Paul took Prisca and Aquila with him as far as Ephesus (Acts 18:18), and this much-traveled married couple now became residents of the sprawling capital of the province of Asia. According to the account in Acts, the apostle himself stayed only briefly in Ephesus after leaving Corinth. However, impressed by the reception given him, he promised his new-found friends to return (Acts 18:19-21).

During Paul's absence a Jew by the name of Apollos arrived in Ephesus. He is described in Acts 18:24 as a native of Alexandria and an "eloquent" man; the adjective could also be translated "learned." It is a plausible inference from the closing verses of Acts 18 that the Alexandrian newcomer had heretofore been a follower of John the Baptist. (The alternative is to regard him as one whom Prisca and Aquila, as disciples of Paul, regarded as an inadequately instructed Christian, one familiar with "water" but not with "spirit" baptism.) Prisca and Aquila heard him speak in the Jewish synagogue, took him aside, and "expounded to him the way of God more accurately" (18:26)—i.e., converted him to the Christian faith (or to a Pauline interpretation of Christianity).

Armed with a letter of introduction and commendation from Ephesian Christians, Apollos journeyed to Corinth and proved of great service to the congregation of brethren at the Achaean crossroads (Acts 18:27-28). Paul later recognized this service when, in I Cor. 3:5, he ranked Apollos with himself as "servants through whom you believed, as the Lord assigned to each." Paul had sown the seed and Apollos had watered it (I Cor. 3:6).

Apollos had come back to Ephesus after Paul's return there from his journey to Syria (Acts 19:1) and before the writing of I Corinthians. (In I Cor. 16:12 Paul refers to Apollos' inability to pay a return visit to Corinth.) At Corinth, Apollos had impressed many of the new converts with his "wisdom." On his departure many of them claimed a position of preeminence in the Christian community as his personal followers, and "I belong to Apollos" became their watchword (I Cor. 1:12; 3:4).

It is possible that Cephas had also paid a visit to Corinth after Paul's departure and before the composition of I Corinthians. At any rate, a group of Corinthian Christians came to refer proudly to him as their personal apostle, rivaling the followers of Apollos with the party slogan "I belong to Cephas" (I Cor. 1:12).

The emergence in the Corinthian church of Apollos' and Cephas' cliques led to the formation of still others. Converts who remembered Paul affectionately as the "father," "planter," and "architect" of their faith, prided themselves on their superiority to the rest with the words: "I belong to Paul" (I Cor. 1:12; 3:4). Still others cried in effect: "A plague on all your houses! I belong to Christ!" (I Cor. 1:12; it used occasionally to be urged that the words were not originally a part of the text; that they were a marginal gloss by some pious reader. It is now widely believed that the "Christ party" were Christians at Corinth influenced by current Gnostic beliefs, and that ideas they held are frequently the subject of Paul's criticism in I Corinthians).

After developments such as these at Corinth, Paul came back to Ephesus in the course of what traditionally is called his "third missionary journey." Despite a busy and successful mission in Ephesus and contiguous areas, a mission that the author of

Acts tells us extended over the greater part of three years, the apostle contrived to keep in touch by correspondence and by direct inquiry with the turbulent little Christian community which he addresses in the letter we have under discussion. In his own words, his "anxiety for all the churches" was a concern that burdened him every day (II Cor. 11:28).

In I Cor. 5:9-11 Paul refers to a letter he had written shortly before the letter that is called I Corinthians in the NT canon. In it he had warned the Corinthian Christians against association with people guilty of sex immorality or greed, or who were idolaters, revilers, drunkards, or robbers. This advice had been regarded by its recipients as impossible in view of the conditions that prevailed at Corinth. In his later letter Paul himself admits that if they had taken his warning strictly, they would have had to "go out of the world." He had not meant to prohibit association with immoral people in general. He had meant only that Christians should have nothing to do with so-called "brothers" who were guilty of immorality. With such a one, he adds sternly, they "were not even to eat."

This "first" letter has not been preserved, but there is a possibility that a fragment of it is now embedded in II Cor. 6:14–7:1. Although there is no MS evidence to support the hypothesis, there are certain observations that lend the supposition a measure of plausibility. The passage breaks the continuity between II Cor. 6:13 and 7:2, which certainly would read more smoothly without this interruption (or digression). It differs in style and content from what precedes and follows it. And its categorical imperatives, its rhetorical questions, and its angry tenor are such as might have been characteristic of Paul's first, lost letter. *See* § 5 *below.*

**4. Occasion.** Our canonical I Corinthians is in part an answer to a letter that Paul had received at Ephesus from the church at Corinth (I Cor. 7:1). It is possible that this letter had been personally delivered by the Corinthian delegation of Stephanas, Fortunatus, and Achaicus. At any rate, they had arrived at Ephesus before Paul undertook to answer it, and their presence had greatly cheered him (I Cor. 16:17-18). The Corinthian letter had assured the apostle that he was always remembered and that the traditions were maintained as he had delivered them (I Cor. 11:2). It had expressed complacent satisfaction with conditions at Corinth (I Cor. 4:7-8) and the hope that Apollos might shortly return to resume his ministry (I Cor. 16:12). But in the main it appears to have consisted of a series of questions concerning which the Corinthian congregation desired the apostle's judgment: questions about sexual intercourse, about marriage, and, in particular, about a sort of "spiritual" marriage that had become a vogue in Corinth (ch. 7); questions about the propriety of eating the flesh of animals that had been sacrificed to pagan gods and then sold in the market place (ch. 8); and questions about the authentication of spirit possession, the relative worth of "spiritual gifts," and the proper ordering of public worship (chs. 12–14).

Paul might have contented himself with a series of verbal instructions to be delivered by the members of the deputation that had waited on him, but, fortunately for the later church, he felt the occasion important enough to warrant a lengthy letter. In our canonical I Corinthians he not only answered the questions that had been asked, but also made observations and issued instructions on a variety of other matters that needed correction: the existence of cliques in the church at Corinth (1:10–4:21); a case of flagrant immorality on the part of a member of the Corinthian congregation (5:1-8); litigation by Christians in pagan courts (6:1-11); loose sex mores (6:12-20); modernistic tendencies among women (11:2-16); the proper observance of the Lord's Supper (11:17-34); the meaning of the resurrection faith (ch. 15); and the proposed collection for the needy saints in Jerusalem (16:1-4).

**5. Unity.** The many different matters mentioned or discussed by Paul in what we call I Corinthians have encouraged some interpreters to regard the canonical document as a composite of several originally separate writings, and it is suggested that the abrupt transitions in our present letter from one issue to another help to support this hypothesis. In addition to II Cor. 6:14–7:1 (*see* § 3 *above*), it is held that the following passages in I Corinthians can be ascribed to the first or precanonical letter which Paul mentions in I Cor. 5:9-11: I Cor. 10:1-23 (attack on idolatry); 6:12-20 (attack on fornication); and (possibly) 11:2-34 (criticism of improper behavior at the Lord's Supper). The remainder is distributed between two hypothetical letters: (*a*) an answer to questions the Corinthians themselves had asked (in the letter to which Paul refers in I Cor. 7:1): I Cor. 7–9; 10:24–11:1; 12:1–16:6; and (possibly) 16:7, 15-19; (*b*) a letter written after Paul had heard from members of the household of Chloe (1:11) of the growth of factions in the church at Corinth: I Cor. 1:1–6:11; 16:10-14; and (possibly) 16:22-24.

There is nothing inherently improbable about such a partition hypothesis. The earliest recoverable text of I Corinthians is its text in the collected letters of Paul. It may be taken for granted that some editorial recasting of Pauline material available at Corinth was involved in publishing it as part of a message to be read by the whole church. Certain catholicizing phrases, as in 1:2; 4:17; 7:17; 11:16; 14:33, may have been added at that time. It is quite conceivable that much of Paul's first "lost" letter has actually been incorporated in our I and II Corinthians. However, it is a different matter to assume that passages from this "lost" letter can now be recognized with any confidence in their present context. And the theory of two later letters combined with these fragments to constitute our present letter is not demanded by any real difference in the situation that the material presupposes. I Corinthians can be readily understood as a letter composed at one time, and it may even be argued that Paul's admonitions in 13:4-7 are best understood in the light of the situation at Corinth as described in 1:10–4:21.

**6. Authenticity.** The authenticity of I Corinthians was never questioned in ancient times, was challenged in the late nineteenth century only by a few Dutch and German scholars, and is assumed in our day by every responsible interpreter. Its style, vocabulary, and ideas are indubitably Paul's. I Clement, a letter of the church at Rome to the church at Corinth *ca.* A.D. 96, contains a number of quotations from it and allusions to it, and in one passage (I Clem. 47.1) exhorts its readers to "take up the epistle of the blessed Paul the apostle." Ignatius' letters, from the early second century, often echo the language of I Corinthians and support the hypothesis that their author was familiar with it (as with other parts of the Pauline collection). The possibility that a few comments by early readers of the letter have been transferred by later copyists from the margin of their exemplar to the text (e.g., 1:12*d;* 4:6*b;* 14:34-35; 15:56) is still occasionally entertained.

**7. Outline.** The letter may be outlined as follows:

I. Introduction, 1:1-9
II. The problem of factions, 1:10–4:21
III. Problems of immorality, chs. 5–6
   A. A case of incest, 5:1-8
   B. Correction of a misunderstanding, 5:9-13
   C. Litigation in pagan courts, 6:1-11
   D. Sex immorality, 6:12-20
IV. Answers to questions, 7–14
   A. Marriage and celibacy, 7:1-40
   B. Food sacrificed to idols, 8:1–11:1
   C. The veiling of women in public worship, 11:2-16
   D. The celebration of the Lord's Supper, 11: 17-34
   E. Spiritual gifts and the conduct of worship, chs. 12–14
V. The resurrection, ch. 15
VI. Conclusion, ch. 16

**8. Contents. *a. Introduction.*** Paul's introduction follows the pattern evident in his other letters: the address, a greeting, and a paragraph of praise and thanksgiving. The "Sosthenes" whom he associates with himself in the address is probably to be identified with the "ruler of the synagogue" mentioned in Acts 18:17, who must then have been converted to Christianity at some point after the incident narrated by Luke. It is unlikely that he was in any sense a co-author of the letter. Since Paul customarily made use of an amanuensis (Rom. 16:22), it is possible that Sosthenes served as his scribe. More probably Paul mentions him only as a matter of courtesy, as one of his companions at Ephesus well known to the congregation at Corinth. It is interesting to note that Paul refers to the Corinthian congregation as the "church of God which is at Corinth." The whole church was mirrored in the local church—one church with local manifestations rather than an agglomeration of separate churches. Some of the phrases Paul uses in his prayer of thanksgiving seem rather extravagant in view of the evils he is shortly to denounce.

***b. The problem of factions.*** From members of the household of Chloe (*see* § 2 *above*), probably slaves, Paul had learned of the growth of cliques in the congregation at Corinth. The apostle knew of at least four that were competing for primacy—people who claimed to have an advantage over others because of a bond—in some instances that of baptism—that attached them to Paul, to Apollos, to Cephas, or to Christ. Some interpreters believe that the phrase "I belong to Christ" was not in the original text. They hold that it was a comment by some pious reader on the various party slogans, a gloss that some later scribe transferred to his copy from the margin of his exemplar. Others interpret the reference as one to people who prided themselves on being superior to others at Corinth on the grounds that they had received their call, not by any human mediation, but directly from the risen Christ. Still others regard the "Christ party" as Corinthian Christians influenced by current Gnostic ideas, folk who distinguished between the man Jesus and the divine Christ, and they believe that the apostle had this group in mind in such passages as I Cor. 12:3 (*see § 3 above*).

Paul protested that these various factions gave to individual apostles a place that belonged only to Christ. In particular he addressed himself to those who took pleasure and found confidence in a gospel phrased as a system of "eloquent wisdom." (It is possible that Paul had the "Apollos party" in mind.) Instead of the wisdom of the world, God had offered men the "foolishness" of the message of the Cross as a means of salvation. His very choice of members of the church at Corinth shows how little he values the wisdom of the world. Not many were powerful or of noble birth. God had chosen those who were regarded by the standards of the world outside the church as foolish and socially unimportant, as low and despised, those whom Platonic philosophers described as "things that are not," to bring to nothing "things that are." As a consequence no member of the church had any right to pride himself on any natural endowment, intellectual or other, for the wisdom and righteousness and sanctification and redemption that were his in his new life as a Christian were gifts of God "in Christ."

As a further demonstration that the gospel is not a philosophy related to other human systems, Paul reminds his readers that, when he had first come to Corinth, he had deliberately chosen to avoid lofty rhetoric and persuasive words of wisdom in his proclamation. "For I decided to know nothing among you except Jesus Christ and him crucified." Paul at Corinth had been no peripatetic philosopher or rhetorician. The Corinthians did not accept his message because of its impressive phrasing or logical demonstration, but because they saw in it a manifestation of the supernatural power of God.

This contrast between the "wisdom" of the world and the "foolishness" of the message of the Cross prompts Paul to a new train of thought. The proclamation of the gospel at times, and among people prepared to receive it, did include a "wisdom"—an esoteric system of thought which, like various forms of Gnosticism, sought to explain the riddle of existence and the inner meaning of history. But this divine wisdom could be presented only among the "mature," by whom Paul apparently means the "fully initiate," those who had been spiritually endowed to receive and understand what was spiritually imparted. It could not be understood by the "unspiritual" or "natural" man, the non-Christian, nor could Paul have preached it among his Corinthian converts. They were "babes in Christ," not yet ready for "solid food." And the emergence of factions among them was evidence that they had still not achieved the status of "spiritual men."

After this digression, Paul returns to the main theme, his criticism of the factions at Corinth. He and Apollos had been nothing but fellow workmen in the service of God, laboring in the field that God was cultivating and on the building God was erect-

ing, completely subordinate to and dependent on God. How foolish, then, were the party slogans!

But now Paul's words undergo a sharp change of tone. Like a "skilled master builder," he himself had laid the foundation well and true—the gospel about Jesus Christ—but the structure that had been erected on this foundation might not be above criticism. The events of the "last days" (Paul here uses conventional ideas of current eschatology) would reveal what sort of work had been done and would destroy the shoddy. The poor workman himself would share in the blessedness of the new age, but only as one had passed "through fire." With a final stern warning to those who would defile the temple of God (the church), Paul reiterates that the wisdom of this world is folly with God and that no one should boast of men, and ends with a psalm of praise about the glorious inheritance of the Christian.

In the final chapter of this section Paul enters a brief in his own defense. He had been a steward of the gospel, and whether or not he had been faithful was for God alone to judge. (It would almost appear from this passage that Paul's opponents at Corinth had summoned him to give an acount of his apostleship before some church court.) In words of wounded love, touched on occasion with bitterness, Paul rebukes the troublemakers at Corinth and pleads with his readers as his "beloved children" to mend their ways, that he may come to them in a "spirit of gentleness" rather than "with a rod."

*c. Problems of immorality.* The apostle now proceeds to abrupt and angry comment on the tolerance shown by the Corinthian congregation to a member guilty of incest. Apparently the case was one of marital cohabitation of a man with his stepmother, a relationship condemned both by Jewish and by Roman law. (There was no necessary association in Greco-Roman paganism between religion and morality, and Gentile converts to Christianity, as Paul frequently intimates, sometimes offended in this respect also as Christians.) Paul would have the church meet in solemn assembly, at which he himself, he says, would be present in spirit, and issue an edict of excommunication. He expects such action to be followed by the offender's death, but hopes that his spirit, because of its previous association with the spirit of Christ, may be saved in the "day of the Lord." Allegorizing the Jewish Passover festival, Paul finds in it a type of Christianity in which the "yeast" of pagan vice has no more place. "Let us, therefore, celebrate the festival," he exhorts his readers, "with the unleavened bread of sincerity and truth."

This brings to the apostle's mind an earlier letter that he had written on such matters (*see §§ 3, 5 above*) and that the Corinthian Christians had misunderstood. In warning them against association with immoral men, he had not meant those outside the church—it was God's task to judge such people—but those inside. The Corinthians were not only to avoid associating or even eating with such a one; they were also to excommunicate him.

Paul now turns to the problem raised by litigation in pagan courts. He regards the fact that Christians have differences at all as in itself a moral defeat. But how much worse, having differences, to drag them for settlement before pagans? Why not settle these matters among themselves? (Dispersion Jews often had their own civil courts.) All of which leads him, as in Gal. 5:19-21, to give a list of moral evils that shut a man out of the kingdom of God. (The list is modeled on similar ones in the Stoic literature of the time.) All such sins of the flesh ought to have ended among Christians at baptism, but continued to manifest themselves within the Corinthian congregation, and Paul calls upon his readers to become in fact what they already are in principle: people who are sanctified and justified "in the name of the Lord Jesus Christ and in the Spirit of our God."

Sexual immorality to Paul the Jew and Paul the Christian was a particularly offensive manifestation of moral evil, and he pleads with his Corinthian converts to shun it. In an argument that is not always easy to follow, he disputes the claim that evidently had been made by some at Corinth that sexual intercourse outside the marriage bond was no more a matter of consequence than partaking of food. Two factors are involved in the act of eating—food and the stomach—and both will pass away. Two factors are also involved in immoral sex intercourse—the harlot and one's own body. The latter is part of the body of Christ and is destined for resurrection. Since God has declared (Gen. 2:24) that sexual intercourse makes man and woman one body, he who makes Christ's body one with that of a harlot is guilty of an intolerable act of desecration. The Christian is no longer his own property. He has been bought and paid for. As the temple of the Holy Spirit, he should now glorify God in his body.

*d. Answers to questions.* The Corinthian church had sent Paul a letter in which they had requested his opinion on a number of matters (*see* § 4 *above*). Ch. 7 is a reply to some such question as, "Should believers marry, in view of the imminence of the end of this age?" Paul's answer is a classical example of what has been termed an "interim" ethic—an ethic for the interim between the end of one age and the advent of another and conditioned by such historical presuppositions. Marriage is a desirable state only for those who cannot sublimate the sex instinct. It has no value in itself, and, since the end of this age is at hand, it is not even necessary as a means of procreation. In principle marriage is religiously and ethically indifferent, but in practice it can easily interfere with an individual's dedication of himself to God.

Although Paul believed in celibacy as the ethical ideal, he disagreed with some in Corinth who apparently held that married people ought to practice rigorous continence. Continence in the married relationship was impossible except by mutual consent and for limited periods, and then only for cultic ends.

By appealing to a command of the Lord (possibly the tradition preserved in Mark 10:2-9), the apostle repudiated divorce but acknowledged that, in extending the prohibition to include the divorce of an unbelieving partner, he spoke on his own authority. His advice to unmarried persons to remain as they were was given likewise on his own initiative and "in view of the impending distress."

Toward the end of the chapter Paul discusses an experiment at Corinth in what later came to be called "spiritual" marriage. Convinced that celibacy was the religious and moral ideal, some men and women had undertaken to live together in spiritual

fellowship but without sex intercourse. Paul indicates a measure of sympathy with this procedure, but counsels that it should not be continued if it subjects the natural passions to too great a strain.

In the Greco-Roman world, meat sold on the market had been obtained by the vendors in most instances from a pagan temple. Ch. 8 is in answer to a question from Paul's correspondents that may have run something like this: "What is wrong with eating food that has been sacrificed to idols? It can do us no harm. We have 'knowledge.' We know that there is but one God and that there is no such thing as an idol!"

Paul agrees that for Christians there is but one God and one Lord. Nevertheless, out of consideration for those brethren who, by long habituation to the idea of the reality of idols, have not been emancipated from such belief, he urges his readers to refrain from sitting at table in an idol's temple. An act that involved no problem of conscience for the individual concerned might encourage others to act similarly, but in defiance of conscientious scruples. Unless one is governed in all his doings by the principle of consideration for others, declares the apostle, he may be led by his thoughtlessness to sin against Christ.

In ch. 9 Paul cites his own example in support of this principle of the renunciation of rights. The rhetorical questions with which the apostle begins may have been induced by some disparagement at Corinth of his apostolic credentials. He had waived two rights, that of support at the expense of the community and that of marriage, but in what follows he defends only his practice in the former instance. The right of the apostle to be supported by the community is established by four arguments: (*a*) a comparable principle is taken for granted in secular occupations; (*b*) there is scriptural authority for it (Paul discovers this authority by allegory); (*c*) temple procedure sets a precedent; and (*d*) a word of the Lord enjoins it (Paul's reference here may be to the saying of Jesus preserved in Luke 10:7). In a sentence that is grammatically almost incoherent in the Greek text, Paul protests that he had not written as he had in order to lay claim to such privileges in the future. He had deliberately waived his rights in order that his reward in preaching the gospel might be his pride in preaching it without reward.

As a final illustration from his own example in support of the principle of accommodation as set forth in ch. 8, Paul refers to his practice of becoming "all things to all men" for the sake of the gospel. This willingness was open to misunderstanding then and now, and Paul (according to both the account in Acts and references in his own letters) had often to defend himself against charges of inconsistency.

In the concluding paragraph of the chapter, which leads into his discussion in the next section of the need for self-discipline on the part of the community, Paul uses metaphors drawn from the language of athletic contests to describe his own practice of self-denial in view of a heavenly reward.

In ch. 10 Paul returns to a discussion of the matter of eating meat that had been sacrificed to idols. He deals in the first instance with the question of whether one who participates in the LORD'S SUPPER could also take part in a sacrificial meal celebrated in a pagan temple, and to this query he gives an emphatic and categorical "No!" The one rules out the other. Whether Paul in this passage is thinking in realistically sacramental terms, or whether he holds only that the risen Christ presides as host at the sacred meal, is still a matter of exegesis about which honest interpreters have differences of opinion. But there can be no doubt about the seriousness with which the apostle views the issue. "You cannot partake of the table of the Lord and the table of demons." And to drive home his warning, he cites illustrations from traditional embellishments of the OT story about the wanderings of Israel. Though the fathers had prototypes of the Christian sacraments of baptism and the Eucharist, they were overthrown in the wilderness. The Corinthians are in similar deadly peril if they "put the Lord to the test."

Toward the end of the chapter, Paul deals with the other aspect of the issue that had already been raised in ch. 8, the propriety at a private meal of eating food that originally had been offered as a pagan sacrifice. Anxious questions about where the host had obtained the meat need not be asked. However, if some scrupulous companion at the meal should point out that it is sacrificial meat, the apostle's advice again is to refrain from eating it, on the principle of consideration for the conscience of him who is troubled.

In the first paragraph of ch. 11 Paul criticizes the participation of some women at Corinth in public worship without wearing veils. In the first place, he declares, it is a breach of accepted social custom. Only prostitutes go about with shorn or shaven heads! Secondly, the veil is a symbol of woman's subordination to man, a status implied in the creation story. (The argument in 11:7-10 raises problems of exegesis about which competent interpreters have not been able to reach agreement.) Finally, the appearance of women at public worship without veils is an improper innovation that the apostle declares he is not prepared to tolerate.

In 11:17-34 the apostle condemns developments at Corinth in the celebration of the Lord's Supper that he regards as perversions of its true character and origin. In Paul's day, as we learn from this passage, it was the custom of Christians to gather as a congregation for a common meal with which the Eucharist was then associated. At Corinth the well-to-do often arrived early and ate and drank without waiting for the wage earners and slaves, who had little to contribute to the common pool and who found most of the food consumed before they could partake. As a consequence, Paul declares with emphasis: "When you meet together, it is not the Lord's supper that you eat." He then proceeds to recall the words with which the Lord Jesus had instituted the rite.

Paul's account of the Last Supper has marked variations in order, phraseology, and emphasis from the so-called "short text" of Luke; and the relative value of the one or the other for a reconstruction of the original words of Jesus is not to be settled on the basis of chronological priority alone. Nevertheless, Paul's account is much the earliest we possess, and the close agreement of Paul's account with Mark's cannot be ignored. The only really significant variation is in Paul's addition (or Mark's omission) of the command: "Do this in remembrance of me." In the parts of the church that Paul and Mark knew, the Last Supper was believed to have been much more than a feast anticipating God's triumph in the new age. It was already an interpretation by Jesus of his anticipated death as a sacrifice inaugurating a new covenant. And the rite in which the Last Supper was recalled had become a sacrament by which those who participated shared in some realistic way in the triumph of the Cross and the Resurrection. "Whoever, therefore, eats the bread or drinks the cup of the Lord in an unworthy manner," the apostle warns, "will be guilty of profaning the body and blood of the Lord."

Chs. 12-14 are in answer to some such question as: "Which spiritual gift is the more important, 'prophecy' or 'speaking with tongues'?" To begin with, the apostle offers a rough test by which inspiration "by the Spirit of God" might be distinguished from demonic inspiration. (It is possible that Docetists, who denied that the man Jesus was the divine Christ, are meant by the somewhat astonishing reference in 12:3 to those who could say, "Jesus be cursed!") He then goes on to insist that the varieties of gifts manifest in the life of the church are all from the same Spirit, as the varieties of service they make possible are from the same Lord and the varieties of forms they take are from the same God. Each is indispensable to the welfare of the whole, as each organ contributes to the proper functioning of the entire body. The church constitutes the body of Christ, and its individual members, whether apostles, prophets, teachers, social workers, administrators, or "speakers with tongues," are all endowed by the same Spirit for the good of all.

In what we call the "thirteenth chapter of I Corinthians," Paul interrupts his argument to assert, in rhythmic prose of a beauty and a cadence rarely approached in any literature, that no gift of the Spirit has any value except as it is exercised in love. The love of which he speaks is not the erotic attraction of an individual to a member of the other sex or the affection that characterizes family or group relationships at their best, but the discovery that believers have made of God's grace in Jesus Christ. It can be recognized both by what it is and by what it is not. And, unlike other gifts that are restricted to this age and are imperfect and incomplete, it will never come to an end. In what may be a quotation from some primitive Christian oracle, Paul concludes with the declaration that "faith, hope, love abide, these three." To which he adds: "but the greatest of these is love." (For the same triad of gifts in the order "faith, love, hope," see I Thess. 1:3; 5:8.)

Finally, in ch. 14, Paul comes to the relative value of "prophecy" and "speaking with tongues." By the former he means the intelligible proclamation of the purposes of God; by the latter, the unintelligible utterance of meaningless sounds under the stress of unrestrained emotion. Both are gifts of the Spirit, but the one edifies and encourages and consoles the church, while the other (unless its significance can be interpreted) has value only to the speaker himself. In public worship there is to be freedom of inspired utterance, but it is important that "all things be done for edification." No one should "speak in a tongue" unless there is someone present to interpret; and prophets, too, should be governed by considerations of moderation and of courtesy.

Vss. 33-34, which forbid women to participate in public worship, are in contradiction to the practice assumed in I Cor. 11:5, 13, are textually insecure (they appear at the end of the chapter in one important group of MSS), seem to be dependent on I Tim. 2:11-12 (the work of a later Paulinist), and should probably be regarded as an interpolation.

*e. The resurrection.* Ch. 15 is frequently but improperly called "Paul's great argument for immortality." It is, rather, Paul's argument for the Jewish (originally Iranian) doctrine of the resurrection, with modifications that he (or the church of his day) had introduced. The problem is stated in 15:12: "Now if Christ is preached as raised from the dead, how can some of you say that there is no resurrection of the dead?" It is improbable that there were any in the apostle's congregation at Corinth who were denying the hope of immortality. Both Jewish and Gentile converts would take this hope for granted. But, whereas Christian Jews would associate the life after death with the expectation of the resurrection of the body at the Last Judgment, former Gentiles would think in terms of their inheritance in this respect from Greek thought, which conceived of immortality in terms of the release of the spirit from the prison of this flesh and its return to the divine world from whence originally it had come. For the Jew there could be no real life in the coming age without a body; for the Greek there could be no true immortality with a body! In his discussion, Paul reveals both the Jewish and the Greek influences on his thinking.

In vss. 1-19 Paul begins by establishing the historical fact of Christ's resurrection. He reminds his readers that the proclamation of this was the heart of the gospel he had preached to them at the first, and that it was also the message he himself had received from the church before him. In what is the earliest account of the resurrection faith in Christian literature, and one of the greatest importance to our understanding of Christian beginnings, the apostle declares that faith in the resurrection of Christ rests on visions of the risen Lord, beginning with one to Cephas and including that to himself "as to one untimely born."

Having established the fact of Christ's resurrection and having asserted (in vss. 20-34) that it is the promise of the resurrection of believers, Paul in vss. 35-50 discusses the nature of the body that the Christian will possess when he is raised from the dead (cf. II Cor. 5:1-10). It will not be the body that clothed his spirit while in this life. It will be an ethereal, spiritual body, as different from the one that we now have as the plant is from the seed that was sown in the earth. "Just as we have borne the image of the man of dust [Adam], we shall also bear the image of the man of heaven [Jesus Christ]."

Paul brings the chapter to an end (vss. 51-58) with a forecast of the manner in which the resurrection will take place. It will be the first event in the new age. It will take place suddenly and dramatically. And it will involve the overthrow of death.

*f. Conclusion.* In the final chapter Paul first gives instructions for assembling the contribution at Corinth toward the collection being made in various Pauline churches for "the saints"—i.e., the congregation at Jerusalem (cf. Gal. 2:10; Rom. 15:25-28; II Cor. 8:9). He then discusses his own travel plans (*see* CORINTHIANS, SECOND LETTER TO THE, § 1) and adds some brief notices. Presumably Timothy (cf. 4: 17) and his unnamed companions had left by the longer land route and would not arrive at Corinth until after the receipt of the letter. Paul regrets that Apollos could not accompany them. After a few brief exhortations, the apostle urges his readers to show due obedience to the household of Stephanas (the first converts in Achaia) and others who had assumed administrative responsibilities, and refers to his pleasure at the coming to him of Stephanas, Fortunatus, and Achaicus. Greetings from the churches of Asia and from Prisca and Aquila (cf. Acts 18:1-3, 26; Rom. 16:3) and others are appended, and the letter ends with Paul's personal signature (cf. Gal. 6:11; II Thess. 3:17), a malediction, a traditional Aramaic prayer, a benediction, and an expression of love.

**9. Date.** In I Cor. 16:8 Paul declares that his intention is to "stay in Ephesus until Pentecost." Those who accept the estimate in Acts of an Ephesian ministry covering a period of from two to three years (Acts 19:8, 10) believe Paul's reference here to be to the late spring of A.D. 55. (For other calculations *see* CHRONOLOGY OF THE NT.) Paul's allegory of the Passover festival in 5:7-8 may have been suggested by the fact that the apostle was observing the Jewish feast at the time of writing. However that may be, it is reasonable to assume that I Corinthians is to be dated not long before the time of Paul's announced departure. On the basis of the chronology most commonly assumed, this would locate the composition of the letter in the late winter or the early spring of A.D. 55.

**10. Text.** Ordinarily I Corinthians was copied by early scribes as part of the Pauline collection, but occasionally also on papyrus rolls or in codices that included Acts as well as the letters (so-called *Praxapostoloi*). Therefore, problems of recovering the original text of the letter are problems related to those of the *corpus Paulinum* as a whole (*see* TEXT, NT). Except in a few instances, these affect matters of relatively unimportant detail rather than of substance.

*Bibliography.* Commentaries: W. Bousset (1907); J. Weiss (1910); A. Robertson and A. Plummer (1911); H. Lietzmann (1931); J. Moffatt (1938); C. T. Craig, *IB*, vol. X (1953).

Important special studies: J. Weiss, *The History of Primitive Christianity,* bk. II (English trans., 1937), ch. 12; W. Schmithals, *Die Gnosis in Korinth* (1956).

S. M. GILMOUR

\*CORINTHIANS, SECOND LETTER TO THE. A letter written by the apostle Paul to the church at Corinth; now found as the eighth book of the NT canon. One of the more personal (as contrasted with doctrinal), of the apostle's letters, II Corinthians gives us a wealth of information about Paul's movements, experiences, and states of mind during a period that the author of Acts passes over almost without comment (Acts 20:1-3). Together with I Corinthians, Acts 18, and I Clement (*see* CLEMENT, EPISTLE OF), it provides incomparable source material for a study of a first-century church and first-century Christianity.

**1. Background of the letter.** For any reconstruction of events in the life of Paul during the six months or more that followed the dispatch of I Corinthians, we are dependent wholly on hints in the apostle's own writings. At this point in its narrative the book of Acts leaves us entirely in the lurch.

Timothy's departure from Ephesus to Corinth to remind Paul's converts of his "ways in Christ" had been announced in I Cor. 4:17. From I Cor. 16:10 we may assume that he was to travel by the land route through Macedonia and would not arrive until after the receipt of the letter that we know as I Corinthians. From I Cor. 16:10-11 it would appear that Paul feared an unfriendly reception for him. Presumably Timothy paid the projected visit and, with the otherwise unidentified "brethren," rejoined the apostle at Ephesus, for Paul associates him with himself in the salutation with which II Corinthians opens. From the fact that he was replaced as an envoy in Paul's later dealings with the Corinthian church, it has been inferred that the apostle's fears were well grounded and that Timothy's mission proved unsuccessful.

Paul's next emissaries were his young friend Titus and an unnamed "brother" whose visit to Corinth is mentioned without elaboration in II Cor. 12:17-18. In all likelihood their mission was to further the collection of the offering for the church at Jerusalem (I Cor. 16:1-4)—the "gracious work" in which, according to II Cor. 8:6, Titus had "made a beginning" at Corinth. The mission (which may have included the delivery of I Corinthians) was a brief one, and Titus and his companion soon rejoined Paul at his Ephesian headquarters.

In the late winter or early spring of the year 55, Paul had informed his Corinthian readers of his travel plans (*see* CORINTHIANS, FIRST LETTER TO THE, § 9). He proposed to stay in Ephesus until Pentecost and then to journey to Corinth by land through Macedonia, with the intention of remaining at the Achaean capital for a considerable period—perhaps the whole winter. "For," said he, "I do not want to see you now just in passing; I hope to spend more time with you, if the Lord permits" (I Cor. 16:5-9; there are other references to this projected visit in I Cor. 4:18-21; 11:34).

There is reason to believe that these travel plans were abandoned and that Paul made a hasty trip to Corinth during the late spring or early summer of 55, traveling probably by the direct sea route. Two passages in II Corinthians (12:14; 13:1) refer to the visit he proposed to pay at the time these chapters were written as "the third," and in 13:2 reference is made to an earlier "second visit." No doubt this latter is to be identified with the "painful visit" mentioned in II Cor. 2:1, where the adjective was suggested to the apostle by the recollection of unhappy experiences during that second stay.

It was probably word of new developments in the turbulent little Christian community at Corinth that compelled Paul to revise his earlier plans and to pay it this second, precipitous visit. Certain Jewish Christians (II Cor. 11:22-23) to whom Paul later gave the sarcastic title of "superlative apostles" (II Cor. 11:5; 12:11) had arrived at the Achaean capital and by accusation and insinuation had attempted to undermine the apostle's influence with his converts. One influential member of the Corinthian congregation had lent himself to their program of disparagement and insult and had inflicted on Paul what the apostle considered a grievous wrong (2:5; 7:12).

On his return to Ephesus, Paul wrote a letter to the church at Corinth in the hope of correcting the situation there and of avoiding a repetition of his "painful" visit. "And I wrote as I did," he told his readers later, "so that when I came I might not be pained by those who should have made me rejoice, for I felt sure of all of you, that my joy would be the joy of you all" (II Cor. 2:3). Reflecting on the burden of the letter, he recalled his state of mind at the time of writing. "For I wrote you out of much affliction and anguish of heart and with many tears, not to cause you pain but to let you know the abundant love that I have for you" (2:4). From various references in chs. 2 and 7 it is apparent that Paul commissioned Titus to deliver the letter and to report back to him on its reception.

The author of the book of Acts refers to Paul's departure from Ephesus (Acts 20:1) as though it were a normal and uneventful episode in his ministry. (He makes it clear that the riot he describes in Acts 19 presented no threat to Paul's personal safety.) But there are indications in the opening chapter of II Corinthians that the apostle underwent some nerve-racking experience late in his stay at Ephesus which seemed at one time to threaten his very life and from which he felt he had been delivered only by the direct intervention of God. "For we do not want you to be ignorant, brethren, of the affliction we experienced in Asia [the Roman province of which Ephesus was the capital]; for we were so utterly, unbearably crushed that we despaired of life itself. Why, we felt that we had received the sentence of death; but that was to make us rely not on ourselves but on God who raises the dead; he delivered us from so deadly a peril, and he will deliver us; on him we have set our hope that he will deliver us again" (II Cor. 1:8-10).

Some have found support in the paragraph quoted above for a hypothesis of an Ephesian imprisonment, during which the so-called "Imprisonment letters" were written, and have seen in Paul's remarks in I Cor. 15:32 that he had "fought with beasts at Ephesus" an oblique reference to an actual ordeal as a prisoner. The latter observation is more plausibly understood as metaphorical, and the Ephesian imprisonment hypothesis, while attractive at many points, is frequently buttressed by a type of circular reasoning: The Corinthian "evidence" of an Ephesian imprisonment is supported by deductions from the Imprisonment letters, and the Ephesian origin of the letters is "established" by the Corinthian "evidence." (The argument that Rom. 16 is a letter by Paul from Corinth to the church at Ephesus and that vss. 3-4 remind Ephesian readers of the danger that threatened the apostle's life while he was with them is also an instance of supporting one hypothesis by another.)

Paul's original plan while at Ephesus had been to visit Corinth after passing through Macedonia (I Cor. 16:5). While at Corinth on his second, "painful" visit, he had apparently told the Corinthian Christians that he would come to them again before going on to Macedonia and returning en route to Judea (II Cor. 1:16). Back at Ephesus he once more changed his mind, wishing to spare the Corinthians a further personal reprimand and hesitating to repeat his previous "painful" visit (II Cor. 1:23–2:1). Reverting to his original plan, he left Ephesus and proceeded to Troas, a seaport on the NW tip of Asia Minor, intending to preach the gospel there and hoping to find Titus and get word of the success of the Corinthian mission. (Titus had apparently prearranged his return route.) Worried about affairs at Corinth and fearful of the reaction to his letter, the apostle was unable to make full use of his opportunities as an evangelist, and, when Titus failed to arrive, he left Troas for Macedonia (II Cor. 2:12-13).

In Macedonia, as at Troas, Paul was torn with anxiety, "afflicted at every turn—fighting without and fear within" (II Cor. 7:5). Then Titus rejoined him, and his whole mental attitude was transformed. "But God, who comforts the downcast, comforted us by the coming of Titus, and not only by his coming but also by the comfort with which he was comforted in you, as he told us of your longing, your mourning, your zeal for me, so that I rejoiced still more" (vss. 6-7). Titus' appeal and the apostle's letter had brought about a radical change of heart in Paul's beloved Corinthians. They had received the emissary with deference, heeded the spoken and written word, and acted to punish the offender and to demonstrate their zealous obedience (II Cor. 7:11, 15). They had been "grieved into repenting" and had now proved themselves "at every point . . . guiltless in the matter" (II Cor. 7:8-11).

Now that the crisis was over, Paul wrote again to the Corinthian church, partly to express his relief and reassurance at recent developments, partly to plead for lenient treatment of the offender, and partly to further the collection at Corinth of the "offering for the saints."

The apostle had written the "severe" letter, he told his readers, not to cause them pain but to let them know the abundant love he had for them (II Cor. 2:4). "For even if I made you sorry with my letter," he declares, "I do not regret it (though I did regret it), for I see that that letter grieved you, though only for a while. As it is, I rejoice, not because you were grieved, but because you were grieved into repenting" (7:8-9).

The "majority" had inflicted some form of punishment on the ringleader of the revolt against Paul, and the apostle now set himself against a minority that apparently favored imposing an even heavier penalty. With the resolution of the crisis, the duty of the Christian community was to turn to forgive and comfort him who had been punished (2:7).

While in Macedonia, Paul had assembled the collection from Christians in that area, to which he makes grateful reference in II Cor. 8:1-5. Since the situation at Corinth had changed so much for the better, he now pleads with the Corinthians (in chs. 8-9) to exhibit a similar generosity. He announces plans to come to Corinth soon, probably accompanied by "some Macedonians," and asserts his confidence that the collection will be ready on his arrival. To make sure that this will be the case, he once more introduces Titus, whom he had charged with completing the arrangements for the collection that had been begun a year before, and commends him to the respect and affection of the congregation. (No doubt Titus was also the bearer of the letter.) "Titus . . . is my partner and fellow worker in your service" (8:23). Accompanying Titus were two unnamed brothers: one "who is famous among all the churches for his preaching of the gospel" and who had been "appointed by the churches [probably Macedonian, but possibly Galatian (I Cor. 16:1)] to travel with us in this gracious work" (II Cor. 8:18-19); and one who had been "often tested and found earnest in many matters" (8:22). They are recommended to the Corinthians as "messengers of the churches, the glory of Christ" (vs. 23). By associating them with himself in this ministry, Paul was protecting himself against the possibility of being charged with misappropriation of funds. "We intend that no one should blame us about this liberal gift which we are administering" (8:20). For another instance of Paul's sensitiveness in money matters, see I Cor. 9:1-18.

Paul was confident that the Corinthians would respond to his appeal, but this advance party was to ensure that there would be no failure. "I know your readiness, of which I boast about you to the people of Macedonia, saying that Achaia has been ready since last year; and your zeal has stirred up most of them. But I am sending the brethren so that our boasting about you may not prove vain in this case, so that you may be ready, as I said you would be; lest if some Macedonians come with me and find that you are not ready, we be humiliated—to say nothing of you—for being so confident. So I thought it necessary to urge the brethren to go on to you before me, and arrange in advance for this gift you have promised, so that it may be ready not as an exaction but as a willing gift" (II Cor. 9:2-5). Rom. 15:26-27, written after Paul's arrival at Corinth, is evidence that his confidence on this occasion was well founded.

**2. Unity.** II Cor. 6:14–7:1 interrupts the connection between 6:13 and 7:2, differs in theme and temper from what precedes and follows, and is probably out of place in its present context. The suggestion that it is a fragment of the letter Paul wrote to the church at Corinth prior to our I Corinthians (I

Cor. 5:9-11)—the letter that warned its readers "not to associate with immoral men"—is attractive (*see* CORINTHIANS, FIRST LETTER TO THE, § 3). Some interpreters believe that certain passages in our canonical I Corinthians were also taken by the editor of the Pauline corpus from this "first" letter (*see* CORINTHIANS, FIRST LETTER TO THE, § 5). Pauline authorship of the material has not been called into question.

The hypothesis that II Cor. 10-13 is part of the "severe" letter Paul mentions in II Cor. 2:3-4; 7:12, was advanced as early as 1870 and has commended itself to many. On this assumption the last four chapters of our canonical letter were written some weeks earlier than the first nine and were addressed to a radically different situation.

The strongest argument for this hypothesis is the remarkable difference in tone between chs. 10-13 and the preceding section. Chs. 1-9 breathe a spirit of relief and gratitude as a result of the good news brought by Titus from Corinth. The storm had passed and the sky had cleared. Then, with the beginning of ch. 10, there is an abrupt change. Ch. 9 ends with the doxology: "Thanks be to God for his inexpressible gift!" In what follows, Paul's attitude is one of sharp defense, his words are charged with reproach and a sense of injustice, and there is a cascade of protest, threat, and appeal. To say that such a sudden change in tone could have been caused by a pause in dictation followed by a sleepless night, an attack of indigestion, or the receipt of fresh and disturbing information from Corinth, is not enough to account for the phenomenon and would leave us puzzled as to why Paul did not redraft the first section or omit it altogether.

If II Cor. 10-13 is earlier than II Cor. 1-9, passages in the former may account for and illuminate references in the latter. Most of chs. 10-13 is Paul's reluctant but vigorous defense of his apostolic authority, while in 5:12 the apostle protests that "we are not commending ourselves to you again," and in 3:1 he asks: "Are we beginning to commend ourselves again?" In 13:1 Paul refers to his forthcoming visit as his "third" (cf. 12:14) and warns his readers in what follows that, if he should come, he would not spare them. In 2:1 he says that he had made up his mind not to pay the Corinthians "another painful visit" (apparently a reference to the postponement of the visit he had had in mind when he wrote 13:1; 12:14). In 1:23 he calls upon God to witness that it was to spare them that he had refrained from coming to Corinth, and in this way defends himself against any charge of irresponsible vacillation (1:15-17). In 10:6 Paul declares that he is "ready to punish every disobedience," while in 2:9 he says that the purpose of the "severe" letter was to discover whether his Corinthian readers would be "obedient in everything."

The case for regarding II Cor. 10-13 as originally part of the "severe" letter is, therefore, a strong one, but the letter undoubtedly contained more than we now have in these four chapters. In 7:12 Paul declares that he had not written on account of the one who had done the wrong or on account of him who had suffered the wrong, but in order to bring his Corinthian readers to realize their devotion to him, and in 2:5-7 he makes further reference to one who

"has caused pain." From this it would appear that the case of some offender who had wronged Paul and, in some measure, the whole congregation at Corinth occupied part of the "severe" letter. No specific "offender" is the subject of discussion in chs. 10-13. Furthermore, while the "severe" letter could have ended with 13:11-13, 13:14 (the famous benediction) would be more appropriate at the end of chs. 1-9, and 10:1 ff must have been preceded by an address and other customary preamble.

A certain parallelism in the appeals in chs. 8-9 for a generous offering to the fund for the saints has persuaded some interpreters that the latter chapter is a note to the Corinthian church from a somewhat earlier period than the former. Others also claim to discover in II Cor. 1-8 evidence of a mildly polemical letter (II Cor. 2:14-6:13; 7:2-4), written by Paul after his second, painful visit but before the events that gave rise to the "severe" letter, embodied in another that expressed his thankfulness that happy relationships with the Corinthian community had been restored, repeated his urgent appeal for generosity in the matter of the collection, and commended Titus and his associates to the affection and obedience of the church (II Cor. 1:1-2:13; 7:5-8:24). There are some fine distinctions in emphasis between chs. 9 and 8, and one might have expected 7:5 ff to have followed immediately on 2:13. (As it stands, the intervening material has the appearance of an extended digression.) Nevertheless, all this, while lending impressive support to these more elaborate partition hypotheses, falls far short of demonstrating them. Chs. 1-9 can be readily understood in their entirety as the thankful letter Paul wrote and dispatched from Macedonia shortly before his own departure for Corinth on what was to prove his final visit.

**3. Authenticity.** Every test of style, vocabulary, and doctrine combines with the tradition of the church and the evidence of textual history to vouch for the authenticity of II Corinthians. While the author of I Clement (*ca.* A.D. 96) appears to have been unacquainted with this letter (although using and referring to I Corinthians), the author of the Letter to the Ephesians (assuming that he was someone other than Paul himself) shows unmistakable indications of familiarity with it. The letter was probably known to Polycarp early in the second century, and Marcion (*see* MARCION, GOSPEL OF) included it in his canon *ca.* 140. If our present II Corinthians is a patchwork of material from several originally separate letters (*see* § 2 above), the work of redaction was completed—probably by the original editor of the Pauline collection—before any portion of it was put into independent circulation.

**4. Date.** The dating of any letter written by Paul depends on conclusions that the interpreter has reached with respect to the absolute and relative chronology of the apostle's life and work; and for a discussion of the various problems and possibilities involved, *see* CHRONOLOGY OF THE NT. If our canonical I Corinthians was composed at Ephesus early in 55, as is often maintained (*see* CORINTHIANS, FIRST LETTER TO THE, § 9), the earlier letter referred to in I Cor. 5:9-11, of which II Cor. 6:14-7:1 may be a fragment, must have been written, likewise at Ephesus, late in 54. The "severe" letter, of which II Cor.

10-13 may be a part, is also a letter of Ephesian origin and, in light of the events discussed in § 1 *above,* probably dates from the summer of 55. The "thankful" letter, now found in whole or in part in II Cor. 1: 1-6:13; 7:2-9:15; 13:14, would then have been dictated and dispatched shortly after Paul's reunion with Titus in Macedonia, probably late in the autumn or early in the winter of 55.

**5. Paul's opponents in Corinth.** Sometime between the writing of I Corinthians and the time of the "severe" letter, a band of teachers came to Corinth, boasting of their pure Jewish descent, stressing that they were Palestinian rather than Hellenistic Jews, claiming to be Christians (II Cor. 11:22-23), and flourishing letters of commendation from Christian communities they had already visited (II Cor. 3:1). Representing themselves as true apostles and as "servants of righteousness" (II Cor. 12:15), they made a bitter attack on Paul's person, reputation, and apostolic credentials. He could write threatening letters, they said, but he was unprepossessing in appearance and an ineffective speaker (10:10; 11:6). He was a rank coward (10:1). He was unreliable and could say "Yes" and "No" in the same breath (1:17-18). He refused to accept any money from the Corinthian church for his support, either because he was not sure of his apostolate (11:7-9), or because he was a crafty and dishonest embezzler of the funds being collected for the poor Christians in Jerusalem (12:16-17; 8:20-21). He had an exaggerated opinion of himself (10:8) and liked to parade it (3:1), but he was really not an apostle at all, for his ministry had not been marked by "signs and wonders and mighty works" (12:1-12). His behavior indicated that he was mentally unbalanced (5:13).

Paul counterattacked vigorously and in kind. These "superlative apostles," as he caustically described them (11:5; 12:11), were actually spurious—false workmen who were only masquerading as apostles of Christ (11:13); ministers of Satan who had disguised themselves as "servants of righteousness," as their master on occasion could disguise himself as an angel of light (11:14-15). Their gospel was not his gospel, for they preached another Jesus and tendered the Corinthians another spirit (11:4). They loved to praise themselves rather than to await God's commendation (10:12, 18). Instead of pioneering as missionaries in new fields, they invaded communities other men had evangelized and took credit as parasites for work others had accomplished (10:15-16). Contrary to his own practice, they not only claimed and accepted remuneration (11:12), but actually tyrannized and exploited the congregation (11:20).

It has often been assumed that these "false apostles," as Paul terms them, were "Judaizers" such as he attacks in the Letter to the Galatians (*see* GALATIANS, LETTER TO THE)—Christian Jews who wished to impose the rite of circumcision and obedience to the Jewish law on Gentile converts to Christianity. But this assumption is surely incorrect. Such issues did not arise at Corinth. Nor is there any suggestion in our sources that Paul's opponents in this instance were emissaries of James and his associates in Jerusalem.

While Paul's references are often tantalizingly obscure to us, there is reason to believe that the heresy he had to combat at Corinth was related to the one

that occasioned his concern (perhaps about the same time) at Colossae—a type of Christian GNOSTICISM that adapted the Christian gospel of the risen Christ to the Gnostic myth of the "Redeemed-Redeemer" and took over the Gnostic views of the world and of man. The fact that his opponents were Palestinian, rather than Hellenistic, Jews does not rule out such a possibility, for it is now evident from much of the literature discovered since 1949 at Qumran (the DEAD SEA SCROLLS) that a form of Jewish Gnosticism flourished in Judea in pre-Christian times. It is probable that Jewish Christian Gnostics were a third force very early in Christian history along with "Judaizers" (e.g., James of Jerusalem) and HELLENISTS (e.g., Stephen and Paul). If the "Christ party" at Corinth that had troubled Paul when he wrote our canonical I Corinthians was composed of Christians with Gnostic tendencies (*see* CORINTHIANS, FIRST LETTER TO THE, §§ 3, 8*b*), then the visiting missionaries who caused him such acute concern at a later date were able to cultivate a fertile field.

**6. A warning against fellowship with unbelievers.** It has been suggested above (*see* § 2) that II Cor. 6:14-7:1 is a fragment of the first letter Paul wrote to the church at Corinth (I Cor. 5:9). Not only does the passage appear as an awkward digression in its present context, but its categorical imperatives, rhetorical questions, and appeals to OT scripture could have supported the apostle's warning "not to associate with immoral men" and caused the misunderstanding he later sought to correct.

**7. Paul's vindication of his apostleship.** The reasons for assuming that II Cor. 10:1-13:13 is part of the "severe" letter to which Paul refers in II Cor. 2:3-4; 7:12, have been given above (*see* § 2). This section of our canonical letter may be outlined as follows:

    I. Introduction, 10:1-6
    II. Refutation of malicious slander, 10:7-11:15
    III. Reluctant self-defense, 11:16-12:13
    IV. Projected third visit, 12:14-13:10
    V. Conclusion, 13:11-13

**8. Contents of chs. 10-13.** The chapters in which Paul vindicates his apostolic authority are comparable in the intensity of their passion only to parts of his Letter to the Galatians. Their content may be summarized as follows:

*a. Introduction.* In words that alternately plead and threaten, words of a hurt, indignant, and an angry man, Paul seeks to re-establish his authority in the church at Corinth as the first and necessary step in dealing with the troublemakers.

*b. Refutation of malicious slander.* The agitators had implied that Paul did not belong to Christ, had charged him with being a weakling who could only frighten men by his letters, had attacked his infelicity as a speaker, and had hinted at unworthy motives in his refusal to accept support. Paul lays emphatic claim to be Christ's, denies the charges of cowardice, reminds his readers that his knowledge makes up for any inadequacies in rhetoric, and explains once again that he had refused to accept remuneration out of motives of love and consideration and so that he might be able to preach "God's gospel without cost" to the congregation (cf. I Cor. 9:15-18). Interwoven with this is a vigorous counterattack. The troublemakers are conceited, invade areas God had assigned to others, pervert a pure and sincere devotion to Christ by another gospel, and, themselves a burden on the church, wish to deprive him of his singular independence. In short, they are false apostles doomed to certain destruction.

***c. Reluctant self-defense.*** Paul compares the achievements of these "false apostles" with his own. Despite an intense dislike of self-commendation, he cannot allow false modesty to prejudice his interests. His Jewish descent was as pure as theirs. His sufferings in Christ's service far exceed any that they can boast. (II Cor. 11:24-27 reminds us of how little we know of Paul from the account in Acts. Cf. also 6:4-10; I Cor. 4:9-13.) Although the signs of a true apostle were repeatedly exhibited in his ministry, his experience at Damascus (with the danger to himself from the Nabatean governor rather than from Jews as in Acts 9:23-25), an early ecstatic experience (occasionally regarded as that of his conversion), and some recurring physical ailment were evidence that even his weaknesses could make manifest the power of Christ.

***d. Projected third visit.*** With greater restraint Paul now seeks to correct some serious moral defects of the Corinthian Christians in advance of his forthcoming visit. (The "third" visit of II Cor. 12:14; 13:1-2 implies a second not mentioned in Acts—presumably the "painful" one referred to in 2:1. *See* § 1 *above*.) They themselves could witness that neither he nor Titus had taken any advantage of them, despite ugly insinuations to the contrary. His earlier defense of himself had been made in the hope that a renewed respect for his authority might lead his readers to repent of individual and social sins and make it unnecessary for him to take disciplinary action on his arrival. But if that should not be the case, he warns them that he would not hesitate to resort to the extreme measures he had threatened when he had last been with them. Pleading with them to "test themselves," he expresses the hope that such self-examination will lead to repentance and reformation, for the Lord had given him his authority for purposes of building up rather than of tearing down.

***e. Conclusion.*** A farewell and a final series of brief exhortations precede final greetings.

**9. A letter of reconciliation.** The last of Paul's letters to the church at Corinth of which we have any record appears to have been preserved, probably in its entirety, in II Cor. 1:1–6:13; 7:2–9:15; 13:14. It may be outlined as follows:

I. Introduction, 1:1-11
II. Explanation of a change in travel plans, 1:12–2:13
III. Paul's message and mission, 2:14–6:13; 7:2-4
IV. Restoration of confidence, 7:5-16
V. The offering for the saints in Jerusalem, 8:1–9:15
VI. Benediction, 13:14

**10. Contents of chs. 1-9. *a. Introduction.*** After the normal preamble of a letter, the apostle gives thanks to God for deliverance from deadly peril in Asia (*see* § 1 *above*) and asks for the supplications of the Corinthians on his behalf.

***b. Explanation of a change in travel plans.*** Paul defends himself against reproaches of fickleness and insincerity (*see* § 5 *above*). Just as the promises of God in Jesus Christ were trustworthy, so he whom God had commissioned to preach to them was trustworthy. He had refrained from coming again to Corinth, not as a wanton breach of promise, but to spare the congregation a repetition of his earlier, painful visit. Instead, he had written them a letter out of "anguish of heart and many tears." This had had the desired result, for the ringleader of the revolt had been punished. Now that the crisis had been surmounted, it was the duty of all to forgive and comfort the offender. Awaiting the return of Titus with a report on the response of the congregation to his letter, Paul had gone to Troas and then, plagued with anxiety when he still did not meet his emissary and unable to take advantage of his missionary opportunities, to Macedonia. For this section, *see* § 1 *above*.

***c. Paul's message and mission.*** The apostle postpones his account of his reunion with Titus and of his relief at the good news from Corinth until later (7:5-7), for reflection on the happy ending prompts a cry of thankfulness to God and leads him to undertake a general vindication of his ministry. For reference to another point of view on this apparent digression, *see* § 2 *above*.

As one divinely commissioned, Paul declares, his task has been to spread the fragrance of the knowledge of God in Christ. For this he needs no letters of commendation, as do his opponents, for the Corinthian Christians themselves are a letter of Christ that he has delivered. He is a minister of a new covenant —not of a written code that brings only condemnation and death, but of a life-giving Spirit. The glory that shone from Moses' face when he delivered the tablets of stone (Exod. 34:29-35) soon disappeared, but the surpassing splendor of the new covenant will never fade. The veil with which Moses hid the fading brightness of his face has been a veil that has hidden the truth of scripture from the Israelites to this day, and one that is lifted only by Christ. God shone in his apostle's heart at the time of his conversion to give him the light of the knowledge of his glory, and throughout his ministry he has never veiled that divine light.

Like treasure in an earthen vessel, this glorious gospel is entrusted to a frail and suffering minister to show that God is the only source of its transcendent power. Afflicted, perplexed, persecuted, and laid low by men, the apostle is always sustained by the knowledge that at the resurrection he who raised the Lord Jesus will also bring him and his beloved Corinthians with Jesus into his presence. Therefore, in his earthly body of flesh he waits longingly and confidently for the body God has prepared for him in heaven.

Once again Paul asserts his sincerity, not (he protests) to commend himself, but to enable his readers to answer those who had questioned it. He is controlled wholly by the love of Christ, who died that men might no longer live for themselves but for him. In Christ, God was restoring men who had been estranged by sin to fellowship with himself. As he does for all believers, he had made the apostle a new creature in Christ. Having been entrusted with the ministry of reconciliation, Paul's one aim had been to be an ambassador on Christ's behalf, one whom God could use as a spokesman. Reconciliation had been made possible by Christ's vicarious suffering and death. Entreating his readers to appropriate this gift of God's grace, Paul reminds them of the hardships he had endured, the ill-treatment he had suffered, the labors he had performed, and the evidences of possession by the Holy Spirit he had made manifest as God's minister. The section ends with the apostle's reiterated appeal to the Corinthian Christians to open their hearts to him. Any barrier that still separates them from him is not of his making, for he has wronged none of them, corrupted none of them, and taken advantage of none of them.

**d. Restoration of confidence.** Paul now resumes the thread of thought that he had interrupted at 2:14 with his reflections on his apostolic ministry. While in Macedonia he had been harassed without and distraught within, but all this had changed with the coming of Titus and the good news that his "severe" letter had effected a radical transformation in the situation at Corinth. Grief on the part of the Corinthians had led to repentance and reformation, and this, with the joy of Titus at being able to bring such good news, had gladdened him and renewed his perfect confidence in the congregation. See also § 1 above.

**e. The offering for the saints in Jerusalem.** Now that relationships of mutual confidence had been re-established, Paul feels free to urge his readers to complete the offering for the saints in Jerusalem that they had begun to collect more than a year before. (For other references to this first Christian benevolence fund, see I Cor. 16:1-3; Rom. 15:25-28; and [possibly] Acts 24:17.) As they excel in all other spiritual gifts, so the Corinthian Christians ought also to excel in the grace of sacrificial generosity, the grace that has already been so abundantly exhibited by the churches of Macedonia. In this they will demonstrate the sincerity of their love and will be acting under the constraint of Christ's own example. (With II Cor. 8:9, cf. Phil. 2:5-8.) To carry the matter through to a successful conclusion and to guard against any charge that he is diverting church funds to his own use, he is sending Titus and two other trusted brothers to Corinth. He hopes the offering will all be in hand in advance of his own arrival. He has already boasted to people in Macedonia that "Achaia has been ready since last year," and he is confident that the Corinthian church would not wish him to be humiliated by their failure. Furthermore, he assures his readers, God rewards generosity by providing the wherewithal to display it, and in practicing it the donors not only will help to supply the needs of the saints in Jerusalem, but also will fill those whom they aid with gratitude to God.

**f. Benediction.** This benediction is in a more elaborate form than Paul uses at the end of any other letter. May the saving grace that is mediated by the Lord Jesus Christ, the love that God has shown to his children, and the fellowship that is the work of the Holy Spirit in the church be the rich possession of all in the congregation at Corinth!

**10. Text.** The entire text of II Corinthians is found in the great uncials Vaticanus and Sinaiticus, but large portions are now missing from Alexandrinus and Ephraemi Rescriptus. Many fragments, some of considerable extent, have been preserved in the third century papyri known as P[46]. In its rendering of II Corinthians the RSV is based (as elsewhere) on an eclectic Greek text, but it is unlikely that any future research will require much serious departure from the readings its translators adopted.

**Bibliography.** Commentaries: W. Bousset (1907); A. Menzies (1912); A. Robertson and A. Plummer (1915); H. Windisch (1924); H. Lietzmann (1931); R. H. Strachan (1935); F. V. Filson, IB, X (1953), 265-425.
Important special studies: J. Weiss, The History of Primitive Christianity (English trans., 1937), bk. II, ch. 12; W. Schmithals, Die Gnosis in Korinth (1956).          S. M. GILMOUR

*CORINTHIANS, THIRD EPISTLE TO THE. A part of the apocryphal Acts of Paul (see PAUL, ACTS OF), long regarded as authentic in the Syriac and Armenian churches.          M. S. ENSLIN

**CORMORANT** kôr'mə rənt [שָׁלָךְ (Lev. 11:17; Deut. 14:17), cf. LXX καταρράκτης, swooper (a sea bird), and Vulg. mergulus, diver (a kind of bird), in Lev. 11:17; LXX νυκτικόραξ and Vulg. nycticorax, long-eared owl, in Deut. 14:17; Targ. (Onq.) שְׁלֵינוּנָא, a puller out of fish; KJV קָאַת (Isa. 34:11; Zeph. 2:14), see PELICAN]. Any one of a family of large sea birds (Phalacrocoracidae) which includes cormorants (of which there are ca. thirty species), darters, and gannets. The common cormorant (Phalacrocorax carbo carbo), which feeds almost exclusively on fish, was reported by Tristram to be found on Palestine's coast and also on the Sea of Galilee and the Jordan River. It would be natural for such a bird to be included in a biblical bird list, but whether שָׁלָךְ was the term used to designate it we do not know. G. R. Driver (see bibliography) proposes the identification "fisherowl." The Indian Fish-owl (Ketupa zeylonensis semenowi), a large bird twenty-five inches in length, feeds on fish, crabs, and small mammals. It was found in Palestine by Tristram, who, however, noted that it was not at all abundant.

**Bibliography.** G. R. Driver, PEQ (1955), pp. 14-15.
                                        W. S. McCULLOUGH

**CORN.** A general term used in the KJV for many different food-producing grasses. See GRAIN.

**CORNELIUS** kôr nēl'yəs [Κορνήλιος] (Acts 10:1, 3, 17, 22, 24-25, 30-31). A CENTURION of the Italian Cohort (see COHORT; ITALIAN COHORT), stationed in Caesarea. Acts describes him as a "devout man," who, with "all his household," "feared God" (φοβούμενος τὸν Θεόν, probably a technical term indicating a Gentile who worshiped the God of the Hebrews, but who was not a proselyte—i.e., who remained uncircumcised, and who did not observe the food laws or other separatist cult ordinances). Like the centurion at Capernaum who "loved" the Jewish people and "built us our synagogue" (Luke 7:5), Cornelius, too, "gave alms liberally to the [Jewish] people." In addition he "prayed constantly to God."

Obviously, Cornelius is here described as the type of Gentile ideally suited to bridge the gap between Judaism and Christianity: to show that Judaism is the proper preparation for the gospel; that the logic of belief in the God of Abraham, Isaac, and Jacob leads to belief in the God and Father of our Lord Jesus Christ; and that God has appointed that Gentiles shall receive "repentance unto life" (11:18) on the same terms as the Jews—namely, through faith in the Lord Jesus Christ and not by works of the law.

I.e., Gentiles are under no necessity of becoming Jews first.

Fully acceptable to Jews ("well spoken of by the whole Jewish nation"; 10:22), Cornelius was ripe for the church. As one who feared God, gave alms to God's people, and prayed constantly, Cornelius was ready for revelation. And that God should choose such a Gentile—a Roman, a soldier, an officer of centurion rank—is regarded as in itself sufficient to convince Peter and the church at Jerusalem—indeed, Judaism and the whole church of Luke's time—that "every one who believes in him [Jesus] receives forgiveness of sins through his name." When Peter and the "believers from among the circumcised" saw that "the gift of the Holy Spirit had been poured out" (10:45) on Cornelius, "his kinsmen and close friends" (vs. 24)—all uncircumcised men—they were amazed, and could not forbid baptism. I.e., since God publicly validated his call to Cornelius by the outpouring of the Holy Spirit, for Peter to reject Cornelius meant to "withstand God" (11:17).

Although Acts is not concerned to tell us what happened to Cornelius after his conversion—whether, e.g., he established a church in Caesarea, or what his career as a Christian may have been—it is obvious that the incident is set forth as the high point in the first half of Acts. Not only is the narrative made up of a double vision, a double miracle, but both are twice repeated and with great circumstantiality. Such a repetition of a conversion story in Acts is matched only by that of Paul's conversion, which Luke honors with a threefold repetition.

The importance of the conversion of Cornelius in the plan of Acts is: (a) it provides the occasion whereby Luke can put into Peter's mouth one of the most succinct and epigrammatic summaries of the primitive Christian proclamation; (b) it provides the event-datum by which in ch. 15 Peter is made to defend (in Pauline language) the Pauline mission to the Gentiles when Paul and Barnabas are under investigation before "the apostles and the elders" in Jerusalem; and (c) perhaps most important of all, Luke will show that Paul's mission to the Gentiles was preceded by Peter's mission to the Gentiles, and that in both cases it was not man's choice but God's call in which the mission was grounded. The two chief apostles here fully agreed (Acts contains no hint that Peter was "entrusted with the gospel to the circumcised"; cf. Gal. 2:7). And it was Peter who first stood trial before the circumcision party in Jerusalem (11:2), who silenced them (vs. 18) and won from the authentic apostolic church, the mother church, the definitive recognition: "They glorified God, saying, 'Then to the Gentiles also God has granted repentance unto life.' " In this way Peter definitively established the universal church before Paul began his Gentile work.

If the *intent* of Luke in chs. 10–11 is clear, nothing else is. It is generally conceded that Luke's narrative rests on some sort of event- and source-data, but beyond this there is no agreement. Although we have no information about Cornelius except what Acts gives us, the existence of such a person need not be contested. He may or may not have been the first Gentile convert; his importance for Luke is that he was the first Gentile convert of sufficient eminence

for use in challenging and overcoming Jewish particularism in the church. He may or may not have been the first Gentile to whom Peter preached; nor need we suppose that Peter refused to preach to Gentiles until Paul had radically settled the issue; in any case, Cornelius is made by Luke the decisive figure for Peter and the Jerusalem church in the pre-Pauline period. This may in some sense have been the case, although in what sense it now seems impossible to say. The historian's problem is set for him by the fact that as a sheer act of God both on Cornelius and on Peter, chs. 10–11 are a surd (a) in the book of Acts itself (although decisively settled here, the problem comes up again in ch. 15 for decisive settlement); (b) in the life of Peter as reflected in Galatians; (c) in Paul's struggles with the church in Jerusalem over his Gentile mission, as reflected in Acts and in Galatians; and (d) in the early church itself as it worked with the two problems: Should Gentiles be circumcised before becoming Christians? And, conceding that uncircumcised Gentiles might become Christians, should Jewish Christians, who had never eaten anything but kosher, join them in table fellowship?

One widespread attempt to save the narrative for history is to suggest chronological misplacement. It belongs, it is urged, after 12:1-18—i.e., after Peter's release from prison. It was then that Peter went to Caesarea (12:19), Lydda (9:32), Joppa (9:36), and Caesarea (again? 10:24). This has the advantage of placing Peter's preaching mission at the time of the earlier mission of Paul and Barnabas (11:19-26; 12:25), and subsequent to the "preaching [of] the Lord Jesus" to "the Greeks" in Antioch (11:20). Also, putting the incident after the death of Herod Agrippa (12:20-23; A.D. 44) makes the presence of a Roman garrison in Caesarea more credible, since Roman troops seem not to have been stationed in Caesarea while it was under the rule of Agrippa.

Perhaps the chief merit of such attempts at reconstruction of the order of events is that they call attention to the difficulty of the accounts as they stand. Rather than to place confidence in a sequence of events arrived at by juggling Luke's data, scant as they are and unverifiable in detail, and obviously tendentious, it seems better to recognize that here the establishment of the historic facts—i.e., of events in their initial context, sequence, and meaning—is beyond any certain recovery. The sources are too few and fragmentary, corroborative evidence is lacking, and Acts and the Pauline letters offer varying and not easily reconcilable accounts.

Success in analyzing and identifying the sources of Acts 10–11 has not been achieved. It is hard to escape the conclusion that Luke has here jumbled confusedly the two questions about admitting uncircumcised Gentiles into the church, and the propriety of table fellowship with such, although in the end the two were to find the identical solution.

Out of chs. 10–11, we cannot clearly determine the significance of the conversion of Cornelius in the establishment of the universal church, nor the contribution which Peter and the Jerusalem church made toward the work mainly accomplished by Paul in establishing a church in which the principle of salvation of all men by faith was fully accepted, and

Gentiles admitted to the fellowship apart from the "works of the law." Luke has here used history, but he has not written history; he has turned a faith-principle into historical form, in which faith both creates history and is created by it.

*Bibliography.* P. W. Schmiedel, "Cornelius," *Encyclopedia Biblica,* vol. I (1899), cols. 908-13. H. H. Wendt, *Die Apostelgeschichte* (1913), pp. 187-89. E. Meyer, *Ursprung und Anfänge des Christentums,* III (1923), 148-53. H. W. Beyer, *Die Apostelgeschichte* (1932), pp. 67-70. F. J. Foakes-Jackson and K. Lake, *The Beginnings of Christianity,* IV (1933), 112. F. W. Beare, "The Sequence of Events in Acts 9–15 and the Career of Peter," *JBL,* LXII (1943), 295-306. R. Liechtenhan, *Die urchristliche Mission* (1946), pp. 53-54. O. Cullmann, *Peter* (1953), pp. 36-37. G. H. C. MacGregor, "Exegesis of Acts, *IB,* IX (1954), 131-33. J. N. Sanders, "Peter and Paul in Acts," *NTS,* II (1955), 133-43. M. Dibelius, "The Conversion of Cornelius," *Studies in the Acts of the Apostles* (English trans., 1956), pp. 109-22; "The Apostolic Council," *Studies in the Acts of the Apostles,* p. 101. E. Haenchen, *Die Apostelgeschichte* (1956), pp. 298-513.       F. D. GEALY

**CORNER, UPPER CHAMBER OF** [עֲלִית הַפִּנָּה]; KJV GOING UP OF THE CORNER; ERV-ASV ASCENT OF THE CORNER. The last item of Nehemiah's description of the restoration of the walls of Jerusalem (Neh. 3:31). The "corner" is the NE corner of the city. The translations "going up," "ascent," presuppose a reading עֲלוֹת, easily confused with עֲלִית, the actual Hebrew spelling, correctly interpreted in the RSV. *See* map under NEHEMIAH. *See also* JERUSALEM § 7b.       G. A. BARROIS

**CORNER GATE** [שַׁעַר הַפִּנָּה; *also* שַׁעַר הַפּוֹנֶה (II Chr. 25:23)]; KJV GATE OF THE CORNER in Jer. 31:38. A gate of Jerusalem, close to the NW angle of the city, four hundred cubits E from the (old) EPHRAIM GATE (II Kings 14:13; II Chr. 25:23). Its towers had been built by Uzziah (II Chr. 26:9). It is not mentioned in the restoration of Jerusalem by Nehemiah. *See* map under NEHEMIAH. *See also* JERUSALEM § 6b.       G. A. BARROIS

**CORNERSTONE** [פִּנָּה, corner; זָוִית (Ps. 144:12 KJV; RSV "corner pillar"), corners, *perhaps from* Aram. זָוִיתָא; אֶבֶן פִּנָּה, stone of a corner; ἀκρογωνιαῖος, cornerstone, *from* ἄκρος, top, *and* γωνία, corner; κεφαλὴ γωνίας, head of a corner]. Normally the large stone placed at the foundation of a wall angle to bind two walls together (*see* ARCHITECTURE). In some passages it may refer to a topstone in a defense tower. "Cornerstone" is used in the OT as a symbol of stability and faith, interpreted in the NT almost entirely of CHRIST.

**1. In the OT.** In the OT "cornerstone" usually means the foundation stone (Job 38:6, the cornerstone of the world). Its most striking use is in Isa. 28:16. Though the MT clearly contains some doublets (e.g., doubled אֶבֶן, doubled מוּסָד), the passage contrasts the "shelter" of falsehood, which the wicked have built, and Yahweh's true building of the community of faith. The meaning of "cornerstone" in this passage has been variously explained as Yahweh, as the Solomonic temple, as the renewed community, as a messianic figure, and as the faith of a renewed Israel (*see bibliography*). The inscription on the stone: "He who believes will not be in haste," suggests that

Isaiah is comparing the life of the covenant people to the steadfast strength of the well-built temple.

In Isa. 19:13 פִּנּוֹת denotes chieftains who keep tribes firm (cf. Judg. 20:2). The "chief cornerstone" in Ps. 118:22 is properly the "head of the corner" (רֹאשׁ פִּנָּה; LXX κεφαλὴ γωνίας), perhaps the "top of the battlement" (cf. Zeph. 3:6; Zech. 4:7). The reference is probably to vindication of a king against internal dissension. Yahweh has made him the chief defense for whom malcontents (the "builders") had contempt.

The word in Ps. 144:12 may be best translated "corner pillars" (RSV), because of the parallel to זָוִיּוֹת of "plants full grown," suggesting vertical pillars. "Cornerstone" (פִּנָּה) in Zech. 10:4 is extremely enigmatic, and most commentators consider the whole verse a gloss. It may be a piling up of similes for a vaguely messianic implication of vs. 3, perhaps garnered from Isa. 19:13; 22:2; 41:2.

**2. In the NT.** All NT references to "cornerstone" are either quotations or echoes from the OT. Ps. 118:22 is quoted from the LXX in Matt. 21:42; Mark 12:10; Luke 20:17; I Pet. 2:7; and in a non-LXX form in Acts 4:11. The Synoptic quotations follow the parable of the wicked husbandmen and show the rejection and triumph of Christ as the "head of the corner" (κεφαλὴ γωνίας). I Pet. 2:7 implies that the faithful, like Christ, are "living stones" (vss. 4-5). Isa. 28:16 is quoted in a form similar to but not identical with the LXX in I Pet. 2:6, where the "cornerstone" (ἀκρογωνιαῖος) is Christ.

Eph. 2:20 echoes Isa. 28:16, though here the "foundation" (θεμέλιος) is the apostles and prophets and the "cornerstone" (ἀκρογωνιαῖος, "capstone"[?]) is Christ. A similarity to the metaphor of Christ as head of the body may exist in this passage.

Like Jewish tradition, the NT writers interpret these OT verses messianically (cf. Targ. Ps. 118:22; Isa. 28:16). The symbol shows Christ as the foundation on which the faith of the church rests, a foundation rejected by Judaism but the only stable basis.

On Rom. 9:33, partially quoting Isa. 28:16, *see* STONE.

*Bibliography.* J. Jeremias, "κεφαλὴ γωνίας—ἀκρογωνιαῖος," *ZNW,* 29 (1930), 264-80; E. E. LeBas, "Was the Cornerstone of Scripture a Pyramidion?" *PEQ,* 78 (1946), 103-15; J. Lindblom, "Der Eckstein in Jes. 28, 16," *Interpretationes ad VT pertinentes Sigmundo Mowinckel Septuagenario Missae* (1955), pp. 123-32, gives a survey of interpretations of Isa. 28:16; S. H. Hooke, "The Corner-Stone of Scripture," *The Siege Perilous* (1956), pp. 235-49.       E. M. GOOD

**CORNET.** See MUSICAL INSTRUMENTS § B5b.

**CORRECTIONS OF THE SCRIBES** [נְקֻדוֹת; *puncta extraordinaria*]. Dots placed over letters, or even words, in fifteen places to indicate the doubts of the scribes about the text. They are probably the earliest instances of scribal influence upon the text. Cf. Siphre on Num. 9:10. *See* TEXT, OT; MASORETIC ACCENTS.

*Bibliography.* C. D. Ginsburg, *Introduction to the Massoretico-Critical Edition of the Hebrew Bible* (1897), pp. 318-34; P. Kahle in H. Bauer and P. Leander, *Historische Grammatik der Hebräische Sprache* (1922), pp. 79-80.       B. J. ROBERTS

**CORRUPTION** [φθορά, διαφθορά, *from* φθείρω, destroy]. While this term is used in modern English with special reference to the decomposition of organic matter or to moral depravity, its chief biblical connotation (particularly in the KJV) is the transience of the present world order with all that belongs to it.

In Rom. 8:21, φθορά ("decay") refers to the liability of the material universe to change and decay; contrast the "incorruptible" (ἄφθαρτος) inheritance reserved for believers (I Pet. 1:4 KJV; RSV "imperishable"). In I Cor. 15:42 ff it denotes the liability of the "natural" body to death and dissolution; "corruptible" (φθαρτός; RSV "perishable") is practically equivalent to "mortal" (θνητός), as "incorruption" (ἀφθαρσία; RSV "the imperishable"), predicated of the "spiritual" body, is a synonym for "immortality" (ἀθανασία). In Acts 2:27 ff; 13:35 ff, "corruption" (in the sense of "decomposition") represents διαφθορά, from Ps. 16:10 LXX, where the MT has שחת (RSV "the Pit," in parallelism with "Sheol"). As a messianic "testimony," the LXX form of Ps. 16:10 lends itself even better than the MT form to the case of Jesus, whose body, being raised from death, "saw no corruption" (Acts 13:37). *See* DEATH; IMMORTALITY; PIT; SHEOL.

**Bibliography.** E. F. Sutcliffe, *The OT and the Future Life* (1946), pp. 76-81.       F. F. BRUCE

**CORRUPTION, MOUNT OF** [הר המשחית, *har ham mashḥîth*]. A hilltop E of Jerusalem, presumably the S end of the Mount of Olives, where Solomon had built a high place to the gods of his foreign wives (I Kings 11:7). The high place, together with other illicit centers of worship, was destroyed by Josiah. Its name (II Kings 23:13) may well be a derisive corruption of הר־המשחה, *har hammishḥâ*, "Mount of the Ointment," an extrabiblical synonym for "Mount of Olives." *See* map in MOUNT OF OLIVES. *See also* JERUSALEM.       G. A. BARROIS

**COS** kôs, kŏs [Κῶς]; KJV COOS kō′ŏs. An island with a city of the same name, in the Aegean Sea, off the coast of Caria. It was wealthy because it lay on an important shipping route. It was famous for wines and silk. It was known as one of the Isles of the Blessed. It became a great Jewish center in the Aegean. According to I Macc. 15:23, Lucius the Roman consul required the local authorities not to fight against the Jews (138 B.C.). One of the pursuits of the Jews here was banking. Herod the Great favored the island, and a statue to his son has been found there. Paul called here on his voyage from Miletus at the close of his third missionary journey.

**Bibliography.** W. R. Paton and E. L. Hicks, *Inscriptions of Cos* (1891).       N. TURNER

**COSAM** kō′səm [Κωσάμ = קסם, diviner] (Luke 3: 28). An ancestor of Jesus.

**COSMETICS.** The cosmetics mentioned in the Bible include ointment, perfume, eye paint, and possibly henna.

1. Ointment and perfume
2. Eye paint
3. Henna
4. Cosmetic palettes
5. Cosmetics in Egypt and Babylonia
6. Cosmetics among the Jews
Bibliography

Courtesy of the University Museum of the University of Pennsylvania

47. A variety of Egyptian toilet articles: The ivory duck is of the First Dynasty from Abydos; the bronze mirror and the ointment containers are from the New Kingdom; the small monkey is from the Middle Kingdom.

**1. Ointment and perfume.** Perhaps the most common cosmetic of the Bible is OINTMENT (*see* § 6a), which was often perfumed (*see* PERFUME § 5a). In the dry, hot climate of the Middle East ointment is necessary to keep the skin and hair from desiccation, and perfume counteracts body odors. Fig. COS 47.

**2. Eye paint.** A paste, usually black, was sometimes painted around the eyes for beautification; its recorded use in Israel was chiefly by women of evil reputation. *See* EYE PAINT.

**3. Henna.** HENNA is a cosmetic applied to hands, feet, nails, and hair, as an orange stain and perfume, in the modern Middle East. It is not clearly referred to as a cosmetic in the Bible. Song of S. 1:14; 4:13 mention the fragrant flowers of henna, and it may be significant that here it is associated with plants from which perfumes were derived. Some have found a reference to dyeing the hair with henna in Song of S. 7:5, but this is doubtful. Fig. HEN 14.

**4. Cosmetic palettes.** From the Iron II period in Palestine (*ca.* 800-600 B.C.) come cosmetic palettes of limestone in the form of small bowls about four inches in diameter with a flat base and a small round hole

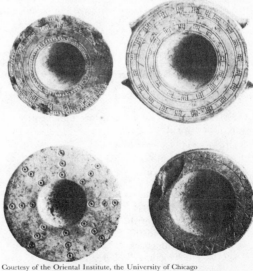
Courtesy of the Oriental Institute, the University of Chicago

48. Palettes from Megiddo

surrounded by a broad, flat rim often decorated in geometric design. They were used in preparing colors for the face, probably by means of a type of bone spatula also frequently found (Fig. COS 48). Ivory and metal kohl sticks and unguent spoons are also found.

**5. Cosmetics in Egypt and Babylonia.** Rouge for the face was used in Babylonia and in Egypt. An Egyptian sketch of the New Kingdom shows a woman holding a mirror as her hair is dressed (Fig. COS 49).

Courtesy of the Metropolitan Museum of Art

49. Hairdressing scene from the sarcophagus of Princess Kawit; as she holds a mirror in her hand, she is given milk by an attendant; from Deir el-Bahri (*ca.* 2000 B.C.)

The tombs of Egypt have yielded many cosmetic receptacles, ointment spoons, rods for eye paint, and metal hand mirrors. In Ur of the twenty-fifth century B.C. sets of toilet instruments were discovered, including tweezers, ear picks, stilettos, and paint sticks.

**6. Cosmetics among the Jews.** Some cosmetics used by the Jews in antiquity but not mentioned in the Bible are rouge, powder, and hair dye. The Mishna forbids the use of rouge on the sabbath (Shab. 10.6; also interpreted as parting the hair). Women's powder made of flour is to be removed from the house before the Passover (M. Pes. 3.1). Hair dyeing is said to have been practiced by Herod the Great (Jos. War I.xxiv.7).

*Bibliography.* S. Krauss, *Talmudische Archäologie,* I (1910), 233-44; B. Meissner, *Babylonien und Assyrien,* I (1920), 244, 412; E. Erman and H. Ranke, *Aegypten und aegyptisches Leben im Altertum* (1923), pp. 257-58; A. Schmidt, *Drogen und Drogenhandel im Altertum* (1924); C. L. Woolley, *Ur Excavations,* II: *The Royal Cemetery* (1934), 245; G. Dalman, *Arbeit und Sitte,* V (1937), 276, 286-87, 334, 346, 352-53; R. S. Lamon and G. M. Shipton, *Megiddo I* (1939), pls. 96, 108-11; W. F. Albright, *The Excavation of Tell Beit Mirsim,* vol. III, *AASOR,* XXI-XXII (1943), 80-81.            J. A. THOMPSON

**COSMOGONY.** Theory and lore concerning the origin of the world.

**A. *IN THE OT.* 1. Cosmos and creation.** To the ancient Hebrews, the world was not an organic unity, but a collection of disparate phenomena individually controlled and collectively disposed at the will and pleasure of their common Creator. This is shown most clearly by the fact that there is no word in biblical Hebrew corresponding to the notion of "universe" or "cosmos." The word עוֹלָם, which came later to be employed in that sense, bears in the OT the exclusive meaning of "eternity" or "indefinite time"; while תֵּבֵל, which is often rendered "world," really means no more than "terra firma" (cf. Akkadian *tābalu, nābalu*). The nearest approach to the idea of universality which the Hebrews could achieve was to speak of "the all" (הַכֹּל; I Chr. 29:12, 24; Ps. 103:19; Jer. 10:16; 51:19), but this referred, of course, to the totality or aggregation, rather than to any overarching unity, of existent things.

To the Hebrews, therefore, cosmogony was not—as it was to the Greeks—the search for the physical origin or central organic principle of the universe, but simply the account of how the various natural phenomena within it had come to acquire their respective roles and been assigned their functions vis-à-vis the life of man on earth. This, too, is clearly demonstrated by the evidence of language. The Hebrew words conventionally rendered "create" (viz., בּרא, connected with Arabic *b-r-y,* "cut out, pare, leather"; יצר, properly "mold"; and קנה [Gen. 4:1; 14:19, 22; Deut. 32:6; Ps. 139:13], related to Arabic *q-n-w/y,* "fabricate"), though they came eventually to be used in an extended, metaphorical sense, are derived from handicrafts and plastic arts, and refer primarily to the mechanical fashioning of shapes, not to biological processes or metaphysical bringing into existence. *See bibliography* § 1.

Furthermore, Hebrew thinking on the subject was mythopoeic rather than intellectual, issuing more out of imaginative fancy than out of logical inference or disciplined inquiry. Accordingly, all efforts to reconcile biblical cosmogony with modern science rest, in the last analysis, on a fundamental misunderstanding of its purport and intent and on a naïve confusion between two distinct forms of mental activity. Fig. COS 50.

**2. Creation stories.** There are in the OT four principal accounts of creation: two in the book of Genesis (chs. 1-2); a third in Prov. 8:22-31; and a fourth, which has to be pieced together from stray allusions in the prophetic and poetic books. However late be their literary redaction, all these accounts are

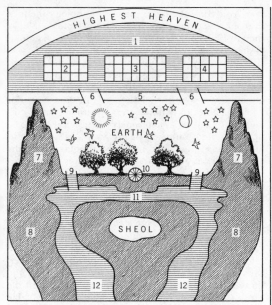

50. OT conception of the world: (1) waters above the firmament; (2) storehouses of snows; (3) storehouses for hail; (4) chambers of winds; (5) firmament; (6) sluice; (7) pillars of the sky; (8) pillars of the earth; (9) fountain of the deep; (10) navel of the earth; (11) waters under the earth; (12) rivers of the nether world

based upon traditional ancient Near Eastern lore. Each of them, however, accommodates and adapts the ancient material to a distinctive Hebrew viewpoint, breathing the Spirit of God into the rude clay. *See* CREATION; DEEP; WATER.

*a. Gen. 1:1–2:4.* This passage (commonly assigned to the P document, redacted in the sixth century B.C.) offers an account of creation in terms of a six-day process. The scheme is given in Table 1.

**Table 1**

| Day | Phenomenon | Function |
|---|---|---|
| 1 | Light | to distinguish day from night |
| 2 | Firmament | to divide the primordial waters into an upper and lower register |
| 3 | Earth and seas; vegetation | |
| 4 | Luminaries | to give light and regulate seasons |
| 5 | Animal life in sea and sky; sea monsters | |
| 6 | Animal life on earth; man, created in the image of God | to "subdue" the earth and rule the animal kingdom |
| 7 | Sabbath: Day of Rest | |

All things are represented as coming into being solely by the fiat of God. It is nowhere stated out of what substances they were composed, for the central theme is not the physical origin of phenomena but their role in human existence and the orchestration

of their several functions, what John Donne called the "concinnity of parts."

There are several features of this account:

*a*) Monotheistic orientation. In the earlier Mesopotamian cosmogonies, the phenomena of nature are represented as being directed by the distribution of their controlling "norms" (Sumerian *me;* Akkadian *parṣê*) among a host of gods, who severally assume government over them (cf. Enuma Êliš 6.39-46). Here, however, such powers are assigned to the phenomena themselves, which thus become the direct, unmediated exponents of their creator's will and pleasure. The firmament is ordered of itself to serve as the divider between the upper and lower waters of the primordial ocean; the earth is commanded of itself to produce self-germinating vegetation; etc. From the standpoint of the history of religion, this represents a significant transition from daemonism to dynamism. Phenomena, though primarily disposed by a supreme creator, are essentially self-determinant, and their functions and operations are no longer conceived as being due to the manipulations of external agents—i.e., spirits or daemons.

*b*) Light. The prescientific distinction between daylight and the sun is made also in the Mesopotamian Epic of Creation (Enuma Êliš 1.38), where, even before the creation of the luminaries, Apsu complains to Tiamat that he cannot rest by day nor sleep by night. *See bibliography* § 2.

*c*) The priority of water. The account is premised on the assumption that originally there was nothing but water pervaded by wind (vs. 2). This concept of the priority of WATER obtains also in the Mesopotamian Epic (Enuma Êliš 1.1-3), and it has been suggested by some scholars that it originated in the fact that the earliest cities of Babylonia (e.g., Eridu on the Persian Gulf) were built on lagoons; or that it was inspired by the seeming emergence of the earth, each spring, out of the waters of the winter floods. The truth is, however, that this concept figures equally in the cosmogonies of many peoples who do not happen to live under such geographical and climatic conditions. It appears, e.g., in ancient Indic lore (Rig Veda I.xiii.19; X.xix.1; Taithriya Samhita V.vi.4); in Homer (*Iliad* XIV.201, 246); in the Finnish Kalevala (Rune 1); among the Mexicans, the pygmies of Gabon, the Yoruba of the Sudan, and the Crow Indians, Iroquois, and Creeks of North America, not to speak of innumerable other primitive societies. It may therefore be explained far more naturally from the fact that water, having no fixed shape and appearing to be ungenerated, comes perforce to be regarded by the primitive mind as something that must have existed before all other things were created—i.e., given their specific and distinctive forms. It is to be observed especially in this connection that the scriptural account nowhere implies, in the manner of Thales, that all things actually issued out of water; it says only that water preceded them in point of time, but insists that they themselves were each created independently by successive fiats of God.

*d*) The priority of wind. Because it is likewise unrestricted by form and likewise seemingly ungenerated, the primordial quality of water is shared by wind. The latter is described poetically as the "breath of God" (רוח אלהים), just as thunder is regarded as his voice. This characterization recurs elsewhere in the OT (e.g., Exod. 15:8, 10) and possesses abundant parallels in the mythopoeic fancies of other cultures. Thus, in an Egyptian hymn from Hibeh, the four winds are said to issue from the mouth of the god Amon, while in Chinese mythology wind is likewise regarded as divine breath. It is therefore somewhat idle to speculate whether the Hebrew expression used in Gen. 1:2 means the "spirit of God" or the "breath of God" or "a mighty (divine) wind"; for the probability is that these notions were not differentiated. (For varying viewpoints, *see bibliography* § 3.) Moreover, in the Phoenician cosmogony recorded by Sanchuniathon (in Eusebius *Praeparatio evangelica* I.10), the divine wind is a primal force, and so it is also in a cosmogonic hymn of the Rig Veda.

The wind is said to have hovered, or fluttered, over the surface of the waters. The Hebrew word (רחף; LXX ἐπεφέρετο; Vulg. *ferebatur*) recurs in Deut. 32:11—its only other appearance in the OT—to describe the action of an eagle which hovers solicitously over its young, and it came to be used in Aramaic and Syriac in the sense of "brood." This has suggested that the scriptural expression may contain a faded reminiscence of the ancient conception that the world was hatched out of an egg—a notion which obtains alike in Egyptian, Greek, Phoenician, Indic, Iranian, and Polynesian mythology. The fact is, however, that the word in question has now turned up in the Ugaritic Poem of Aqhat (III.i.20, 31), where it is applied to the coasting of eagles in flight. Hence, all that the scriptural passage really implies is that the wind swept the waters as a coasting bird sweeps the air; and this metaphor is adequately explained by the fact that the wind was commonly regarded in the ancient Near East as possessing wings (cf. II Sam. 22:11; the Mesopotamian Story of Adapa in *ANET* 101).

*e*) The sky. The Hebrews distinguished clearly between the "great blue yonder" in general and the immediate ceiling or canopy of the earth, though the distinction is often obscured in the OT by the fact that the same word (שמים) tends to be used for both. The former was simply the upper part of the great cosmic ocean; the latter was conceived as a layer stretched across it to prevent its waters from overflowing. This finds an arresting parallel in ancient Mesopotamian lore, where the nethermost register of heaven is often styled the "celestial bulwark" (*šupuk šamê*). The author of our scriptural account pictures it as a strip of metal, for the word by which he designates it (viz., רקיע)—usually rendered "firmament" (after LXX στερέωμα; Vulg. *firmamentum*)—really has that meaning (cf. רקע [Exod. 39:3; Num. 17:3-4; Jer. 10:9]; Phoenician מרקע). In the Babylonian Epic of Creation (Enuma Êliš 4.137-45), on the other hand, the firmament is made out of the upper part of the body of Tiamat, which is slit lengthwise by the victorious Marduk, the lower half making the earth. In the Hittite myth of Ullikummi (*ANET* 124), heaven is said to have been sundered from earth by a cleaver or (magic?) knife.

*f*) Man. The scriptural writer is quite prepared to take over from the older, pagan mythology the idea that man was created in the divine image. Nor—though he incongruously suppresses the background—does he object to including in his "purified" version so blatantly polytheistic a trait of the original myth as the phrase: "Let us make man in our image" (vs. 26), with its implication that this had been effected at a meeting of the gods in common. But when it comes to defining the purpose of man's creation, he makes a supremely significant advance upon the time-honored pagan view. In contrast to the doctrine enunciated in the Mesopotamian myths and retained in Gen. 2 (*see below*), man is here represented, not as the menial of the gods, but as the ruler of the animal and vegetable kingdoms (1:28)—an idea which was eventually to be developed into the notion that he was, in fact, God's viceroy on earth (cf. Koran, Sura 2.28). See bibliography § 4.

No sooner is man fashioned than he is bidden "subdue the earth" (vs. 28). This is usually taken to refer to agriculture. It is equally possible, however, that the words are intended simply as a parallel to "having dominion" over the animal world, in the sense that man is enjoined to exploit the vegetable world for his sustenance and enjoyment. In that case, the writer's view would mark another break with the older tradition, for, as we shall see presently, in the Mesopotamian myths and in Gen. 2, the function of man is to till the soil *for the benefit of the gods*. Our author's view would also find a striking parallel in the concept of the Roman poets that in the primeval Golden Age man enjoyed the fruits of the earth without having to toil for them (cf. Tibullus I.3.41; 9.7; II.1.4; Ovid *Metamorphoses* I.104; *Amores* III.8.41). It is significant also in this connection that it is the fruits of earth and trees, not animal flesh, that is said to have been given to man for food (vs. 29), for this chimes with a widespread ancient notion that primeval man subsisted on an exclusively vegetarian diet (cf. Porphyry *De Abstinentia* II.5-7, 20-22, 27-31; Ovid *Fasti* I.347 ff)—sometimes, indeed, represented as consisting of acorns!

*g*) The six-day scheme. This is, in all probability, simply a device on the part of the priestly compilers whereby the ancient myth might be accommodated to the Israelitic institution of the seven-day week and at the same time provide validation for the seventh-day sabbath. Indeed, it has been suggested that since, according to one method of reckoning, ten separate acts of creation may be recognized, the story may have originated in an area and at a time when a ten-day week obtained. Such a system seems, in fact, to have left traces in the OT itself (Gen. 24:35; Exod. 12:3), and it is paralleled in ancient Egypt, among the pre-Islamic Arabs, in Greece (Hesiod *Theogony* 765-77) and among many primitive peoples of the present day. See bibliography § 5.

*b. Gen. 2:5-25.* Although, for logical reasons, it was placed second in the final edition of the Pentateuch (or Hexateuch), this account is, in fact, earlier in point of redaction and more archaic in point of view than Gen. 1. In its present form, it is assigned by modern critics to the J document, compiled in the tenth century B.C. The features of this account are:

*a*) The watering of the earth. This account is really an anthropogony rather than a cosmogony.

The only cosmogonic detail in it is the statement that the earth was at first watered, not by rains, but by a subterranean flood (אד = Akkadian *edu*), and this is introduced only by way of background and setting for the creation of man. The most natural explanation of this detail is that the story pictures primordial conditions after the pattern of what actually takes place annually prior to the "regeneration" of the earth in autumn. Just before the agricultural cycle begins—i.e., in the early days of October—the soil of Palestine depends for its moisture more on subterranean springs than on rain, which only commences to fall to any appreciable degree about a month later. An excellent illustration of this concept is afforded by the Ugaritic Poem of Baal, where dominion over the earth is first awarded to Yammu (alias Naharu), god of the sea and subterranean waters, and is subsequently wrested from him by Baal, lord of the rains. (Moreover, as soon as Baal has vanquished his rival, arrangements are made to secure the precipitation of his rains in due season: II AB,6-7: *'dn mṭrh B'l y'dn.*) See bibliography § 6.

*b*) The function of man. In contrast to the more exalted outlook of Gen. 1-2:4, this account retains the primitive view that the function of man is to tend and till the garden of God (2:15). The Mesopotamians likewise held that man was created to perform chores for the gods. In KARI I, no. 4, the divine Anunnaki recommend the creation of man so that he might "do the chores of the gods, fix bounds, carry basket and seed-bag, direct the course of canals, water the soil, cause plants and shrubs to grow." So, too, in Enuma Êliš 6.7-9, Marduk orders the creation of man that he might perform chores (*dullu*) for the gods and thus give them a chance to relax; while in another account (CT XIII.35-37) he creates man out of dirt to maintain earthly abodes for the gods. In yet a further version (*ANET* 99-100), man is formed out of clay, animated with blood, in order to "bear the yoke."

Since the function of man is thus to serve the gods rather than to rule the animal kingdom (as in Gen. 1), the latter has no organic place in the story. The creation of animals has therefore to be introduced solely as an afterthought, something done only for man's diversion (vss. 18-19). The same sequence obtains, for the same reason, in the Mesopotamian myth about the creation of man as the caretaker of shrines.

*c*) Man from dust. Nothing is said in Gen. 1 concerning the substance out of which man was made, nor is any reference made to a single primal pair. In Gen. 2, however, it is stated expressly that man was molded out of dust and animated by the divine breath (vs. 7).

The former idea recurs in Job 33:6 (lit., "I too was pinched out of clay") and is commonplace on Mesopotamian mythology (e.g., Epic of Gilgamesh I.2.34-38; Ea and Atraḫasis, IV.4-10). It was likewise familiar to the Egyptians, among whom the god Khnum was said to have molded man on a potter's wheel. Nor is it unattested in classical sources. Similar stories are told also among several primitive peoples. See bibliography § 7.

As for the notion that man was animated by the divine breath, it should be observed that, in accordance with the belief that blood, as well as breath, is the seat of life (cf. Lev. 17:10), it is often the divine blood, rather than the divine breath, that is said in ancient anthropogonic myths to have been intermingled with the primal clay (cf. Enuma Êliš VI.5-6, 32-33; KARI I, no. 4).

*d*) Woman. Woman is said, in Gen. 2, to have been created out of man's rib (vs. 21). It has been suggested that this legend derives from a Sumerian source and was inspired by the fact that in Sumerian script the sign "TI" stands both for "rib" and for "life," so that "NIN.TI" (a goddess), the primal mother of man, could be explained both as "Rib-lady" and as "Lady of Life." The latter explanation, it is added, is reflected in the Hebrew name Ḥawwah (Eve), which is, indeed, fancifully connected by the scriptural writer (Gen. 3:20) with the verb חיה (חוה), "to live"! The fact is, however, that the story of woman's origin from the flesh of man is common to many primitive peoples—e.g., the Tahitians, the Maoris, the Karens of Burma, and the Bedil Tartars of Siberia—where no such philological basis for it exists and where biblical influence (through missionaries) can be reasonably discounted. It is therefore far more natural to assume that the story has a social and biological, rather than a linguistic, basis! See bibliography § 8.

*c. Prov. 8:22-31.* Unacquainted as they were with physical laws and organic processes, the Hebrews were all the more impelled to find some mythopoeic explanation for that logic and reason of the natural order upon which they ever insisted (cf. Ps. 104:24; Prov. 3:19; Jer. 10:21; 51:15; Ecclus. 42:21; Wisd. Sol. 7:22; 9:9). This is the theme of Prov. 8:22-31, where Wisdom (חכמה) is introduced as an expert technician (אומן [so LXX, Vulg., Syr., for MT אמון, "nursling"; cf. Akkadian *ummanu*]) who attended upon Yahweh during the process of creation (vs. 30). The successive stages of this process are enumerated in six couplets, each relating two complementary acts, viz.:

*a*) The creation of the oceans (תהמות)—i.e., the partition of the primordial waters into an upper and lower register; matched by the filling of the subterranean springs (מעינות) with water (vs. 24).

*b*) The sinking of the mountains (הרים הטבעו)—i.e., the lowering of their roots over the nether ocean, to prevent its waters from rising and flooding the earth; matched by the raising of their summits (גבעות) above the level of the earth (vs. 25).

*c*) The exposure of the earth and open tracts (חוצות); matched by the production of vegetation (reading ודשא עפרות תבל for the obscure וראש עפרות תבל of the MT and versions; cf. Akkadian *duššu*; vs. 26).

*d*) The stabilization of the sky (שמים)—i.e., the firmament—designed to keep the upper waters from flooding the earth; matched by the prescription of an encircling bound (חוג)—evidently a range of mountains, like the Qaf of Arabic folklore—to prevent the flooding of the earth from the sides (vs. 27).

*e*) The condensation of the thin vapors into clouds (באמצו שחקים), to provide moisture from above: matched by the release of the subterranean waters through gushing springs (בְּעַזּוֹ עִינוֹת [so versions] תְהוֹם; cf. מַיִם עָזִים and Arabic *'azza,* in the specific sense of "produce a gush"; vs. 28).

*f)* The bounding of the main (בְּשׂוּמוֹ לַיָּם חֻקּוֹ); matched by the steadying of the bases of the earth (so versions; בַּחֲזָקוֹ מוֹסְדֵי אָרֶץ; vs. 29).

Although Wisdom is here regarded as older than all *created* things, it is not to be inferred that it was deemed older than the cosmic ocean. This would run counter to a well-established tradition of Semitic mythology, which insisted that Wisdom in fact dwelt (i.e., was inherent) in that primordial substance. In Mesopotamia, e.g., the word *abzu,* which denotes that ocean, was popularly interpreted as *ab-zu,* "abode of wisdom," and regarded as the seat of Ea, god of arts and crafts and of intellectual creativity. It was, indeed, largely by virtue of the "wisdom" latent in that ocean that magicians were able to operate; and it was from that ocean that the seven primeval masters *(apkallê)* of arts and sciences—or, according to Berosus, the culture hero, Oannes—were believed to have sprung. Moreover, in Ecclus. 24:5-6, it is stated explicitly that the deep was one of the original abodes of Wisdom. All that the scriptural writer really says is that Wisdom preceded the oceans (תְהֹמוֹת; the plural is significant)—i.e., the division of the primordial stream into the ocean above the earth and the ocean beneath it. *See* Deep.

*d. The myth of the primordial combat.* Of quite a different order is a cosmogonic myth to which allusion is made in several poetic passages of the OT (viz., Job 3:8; Pss. 74:13-14; 89:10-11; 93; Isa. 27:1; 30:7; 51:9-10; Hab. 3:8). The essence of this myth is that at the beginning of the present world era, the supreme God (Yahweh) did battle with a draconic monster, whom he subdued either by slaying him or by keeping him in bonds. The monster is variously named: Leviathan (לִוְיָתָן, "Coiled One"); Yam ("Sir Sea"); Nahar ("Sir Stream, River"); Tannin ("Dragon"); and Rahab ("Rager"; cf. Akkadian *ra'ābu*). Less frequent designations are: "Evasive[?] Serpent" (נָחָשׁ בָּרִחַ; Isa. 27:1); "Tortuous Serpent" (נָחָשׁ עֲקַלָּתוֹן; Isa. 27:1); and "Dragon-monster" (בְּשָׁן; Ps. 68:22; cf. Ugaritic *btn;* Akkadian *bašmu* [ancient and English versions wrongly "Bashan"]).

This myth represents a Syro-Palestinian version of one found throughout the literature of the ancient Near East. *See bibliography* § 9.

The closest parallel is afforded by the Ugaritic Poem of Baal (fourteenth century B.C.), which relates how that god of rainfall engaged the draconic monster Yammu ("Sir Sea"), *alias* Naharu ("Sir Stream"), Tannin, or Baṭhan, and subdued him as a necessary preliminary to securing his own dominion over gods, men, and earth. In one passage the antagonist is actually styled "Evasive[?] Serpent" (*btn brḥ*) and "Tortuous Serpent" (*btn 'qltn*), as in Isa. 27:1, showing the direct indebtedness of the biblical version to this Canaanite source.

The same story occurs also on Mesopotamian soil in the Babylonian "Epic of Creation" (Enuma Êliš), which relates the successful combat of Marduk (or, in the Assyrian version, Aššur) against the monstrous Tiamat and her confederates; and there is also a second version, in which the antagonists are respec-

tively the god Tišpak and the dragon Labbu, although there it is not said explicitly that the combat was primordial.

In Hittite, the battle royal between a mortal hero Hupasiyas, acting in behalf of the gods, and the serpent Illuyankas forms the cult myth recited annually at the festival of Puruli, in late summer.

Lastly, there is an older Sumerian version narrating how the god Ninurta subjugated the demonic Asag (cf. Akkadian *ašakku,* "demon") and kept him confined between the banks of the Euphrates.

The myth is frequently represented on Mesopotamian cylinder seals, and it is likewise portrayed on reliefs from Malatya and Karatepe. In both the latter cases, the dragon is shown with many heads, consonant with the description in Ps. 74:13. Fig. LEV 27.

More remote affinities may be recognized in the Greek myth of the fight between Zeus and Typhon, in the Indic story of the conflict between Indra and Vṛtra, and even in the much later legend of Saint George and the dragon (actually located in N Syria!).

All these stories are mere retrojections into cosmogony of the annual subjugation of the waters (personified as a draconic marplot), which, when the snow melts on the mountains, indeed rush down in fury, and which also well up, toward the end of summer, from subterranean springs. (It is significant in this connection that, in Chinese folklore, when an overflowing river is confined, it is said that "the dragon has been caged"). What has to be done at the beginning of each year is conceived as having been done at the beginning of the present era, when the earth was first called into being.

**B. *IN THE APOC. AND THE PSEUDEP.***
**1. Foreign influences.** During the intertestamental period the Jews were increasingly exposed to foreign philosophies and religious doctrines, and an important element of these was speculation about the origins of the world. Normative Judaism tended, on the whole, to deprecate such mental flights, on the grounds that they might lead to apostasy. Man, it was asserted, should not explore what was beyond his powers, but should occupy himself only with performance of what God had enjoined upon him (cf. Ecclus. 3:21-22; M. Ḥag. 2.1). Accordingly, formal accounts of creation (e.g., Ecclus. 43-44; II Esd. 6:1-6, 38-54) hew close to the descriptions contained in the OT, though there seems to have been a certain amount of ambivalence regarding the doctrine of *creatio ex nihilo,* this being emphatically affirmed in some places (e.g., II Macc. 7:28) but denied in others (Wisd. Sol. 11:17). *See bibliography* § 10.

Yet, with all this fidelity to tradition, in an increasingly cosmopolitan atmosphere intellectual isolation was obviously impossible, and in the interpretation of the sacred texts bearing on cosmogony the subtle influence of Greek ideas may indeed be detected, especially in such more philosophical works as the Wisdom of Solomon and II Esdras. The following are the more arresting instances of this development:

*a. The "goodness" of creation.* The scriptural statement that "God saw everything that he had made, and behold, it was very good" (Gen. 1:31), is developed into the notion that, since God is himself intrinsically good, nothing that comes from him can be other than "healthsome" (σωτήριος) and free from the "poison of destruction" (Wisd. Sol. 1:14; cf. Shab. 77a). This reproduces a familiar teaching of Plato (*Timaeus* 30).

Closely related is the concept that the scheme of things is necessarily beneficial to man, because it is the product of God's inherent love (Wisd. Sol. 11: 24). This in turn is subjected to an interesting development. Offsetting the popular Greek doctrine that the primal creative force was "sexual passion" (ἔρως) or "desire" (πόθος), which swept the chaotic abyss, the Palestinian Targum to Gen. 1:2 identifies the hovering "spirit of God" as the "spirit of love that proceeded from God" (רוח רחמין מן קדם אלקים).

*b. The creative Word.* The word wherewith God called phenomena into being (Gen. 1: Ps. 33:6) tends to become hypostatized as an ergative force (Ecclus. 42:15; Wisd. Sol. 18:15 [ὁ παντοδύναμος λόγος]; II Esd. 6:38; Targ. Isa. 45:12; 48:13). Indeed, in the Targums, "Word" (מימרא) is frequently employed as a pious circumlocution for "God." It is true that this concept may be traced ultimately to ancient oriental prototypes (*see bibliography*). Its increased articulation at this period, however, may well have been influenced by Greek philosophical ideas about the λόγοι as intermediate agents of God's creativity and about the Logos itself as the ergative force of deity (*see bibliography* § 11). *See* LOGOS.

*c. Wisdom as creative agent.* On the basis of Prov. 8:30, Wisdom was hypostatized as the "craftsman" (τεχνῖτις) who attended upon God during the process of creation (Wisd. Sol. 7:22; 9:4, 9-10; Enoch 42:1). Here again, an oriental background has been claimed on the strength of a passage in the Aramaic text of the Romance of Aḥiqar (lines 94-95; *see bibliography* § 12); but here, too, the rearticulation of the ancient concept—if such, indeed, it is—may well have been influenced by contemporary Greek notions about the creative role of Sophia, or "Wisdom"—ideas subsequently elaborated in Gnosticism. That this concept was, indeed, very much in the air and that it was even thought necessary by the more "orthodox" to combat it, is perhaps to be deduced from the pointed statement in Ecclus. 42:21 (text corrected after the Hebrew version) that God, "unique [read εἷς; *vulgo* ἕως] from everlasting unto everlasting, (himself) disposed the powers of his own wisdom . . . and needed no counselor." In the same vein, too, Philo makes a point of affirming (*Exposition of the Law* I.8) that God was the only "craftsman" (τεχνίτης).

*d. The doctrine of spirits.* Another favorite notion at this period was that God had activated phenomena by informing them with inherent spirits that controlled them. The most explicit statement of this view is to be found in the first of the Dead Sea Hymns of Thanksgiving (I.5-39), where it is said that all natural phenomena were at first parceled out among spirits, each assigned to a respective domain of authority (ממשלה), and that these spirits were subsequently turned into angels. Further expression of the same idea occurs in Ecclus. 16:27, which should be rendered: "He disposed [ἐκόσμησεν; RSV 'arranged'] his works for ever [RSV 'in an eternal or-

der'], and their spheres of authority [ἀρχάς; RSV 'dominion'] for their generations"; while, according to II Esd. 6:41, what God created on the second day was not the firmament *tout court*, but rather the "spirit" of it.

This, too, may betray the influence of Greek cosmogonic ideas, for Plato likewise speaks of intermediate "gods" (θεοί) as instruments of the creative process (cf. *Timaeus* 41); while Philo identifies the ἰδέαι or λόγοι of the Stoic cosmogony with angels or demons. On the other hand, it must be conceded that the idea may just as well have come from Iran and reflect the Mazdean notion of the *yazatas*. *See* ANGEL.

*e. Motion as a primal force.* Yet a further trace of Greek influence may be recognized in the statement of II Esd. 6:3 that God conceived the course of existence before the phenomena of nature were made and *antequam . . . confirmarentur motu virtutes* (so also Syr.). This is often rendered "or ever the powers *of the earthquake* were established"; but it may be suggested that the reference is really to the Greek idea, enunciated alike by Anaximander (cf. Simplicius *In Aristotelis Physica* f. 6a Aldine) and Plato (*Timaeus* 36D; *Phaedrus* 246C), that motion was a primal force. The correct translation would then be: "or ever the inherent qualities of things were reinforced by movement."

*f. The doctrine of opposites.* In Ecclus. 33:15; 42: 24, it is stated that all things were created "twofold [δισσά], one opposite the other." It is not difficult to recognize in these words an allusion to the doctrine of "opposites" taught by Anaximander (cf. Simplicius), Pythagoras (quoted by Alexander Polyhistor, in Diogenes Laertius, VIII.24), and Aristotle (*Physica* I.4), as part of their cosmogonic systems.

**2. The purpose of creation.** Quite apart from these foreign influences, there was in this period a certain amount of speculation concerning the purpose of creation. Two main theories appear to have been prevalent. According to the one—developed from the Scriptures themselves (e.g., Gen. 1:26, 28; Ps. 8:5-9) —the world had been brought into being for the sake of man (cf. II Esd. 6:46; II Bar. 15:7). According to the other, all things had been created solely for God's glory (cf. 1QH I; VI; VII.6-7; X.12; XIII.4; XVIII; M. Ab. 6.11). This did not mean, however, that the world was simply God's plaything—a view seemingly entertained by the cynical glossator who wrote Prov. 8:31—but that it was the inevitable self-expression of God's inherent nature, the realization of his being in a concrete medium.

**C. *IN THE NT.*** The NT offers no original view of cosmogony. The doctrine of *creatio ex nihilo* is reiterated in Rom. 4:17; Heb. 11:3; and the concept of the ergative Word in Heb. 11:3; I Pet. 3:5. The latter, however, is identified in John 1:14; Heb. 1:3 with the incarnate godhead of Jesus Christ.

The cyclic character of creation influenced the author of II Pet. 3:5-13, where it is pointed out that just as in the past the world was destroyed by the Flood and then renewed, so in the future the dissolution of all things in a cosmic conflagration (ἐκπύρωσις) will be succeeded by "new heavens and a new earth, in which righteousness dwells." In somewhat similar vein, the new dispensation ushered in by the triumph of Christ is regarded, in II Cor. 5:17; Gal. 6:15, as itself the "new creation."

Again, in Rev. 12:7-10; 20:2-3, the primordial battle against the dragon and his confederates (*see* § A2*d above*) is conceived as an event which must necessarily be repeated as a prelude to the new era.

Finally, attention may be drawn to the fact that the familiar portrayal of the Holy Spirit as a dove (Matt. 3:16) represents, in the last analysis, an interpretation of the cosmogonic "spirit of God hovering on the face of the waters" (*see* § A2*a above*). This interpretation, it may be added, is to be found also in early rabbinic sources (e.g., J.T. Ḥag. II.77*a;* B.T. Ḥag. 15*a;* Toseft. Ḥag. II.5).

**D. COSMOGONY AND ESCHATOLOGY. 1. Cosmogony as a cyclic process.** It was a widespread notion in antiquity that time was a cycle rather than a linear progression; and, in accordance with this idea, creation was necessarily envisaged as a recurrent, rather than a unique and punctual event. The cycle could be conceived as one that revolved over centuries or even millenniums, or as one that revolved annually. In the former case, a repetition of the primordial, archetypal process was to be expected at the end of the present era. Eschatology, or the lore of the last things, thus became, in effect, cosmogony in the future tense. In the latter case, on the other hand, every New Year was in fact a new creation; and this was expressed by a formal re-enactment of the cosmogonic process in the New Year ritual, albeit only in the attenuated form of a liturgical recitation. The latter form of articulation, moreover, worked both ways, for it led also (in reverse) to the projection of cosmogonic myths out of conditions which actually obtained at the beginning of the year. *See bibliography* § 13.

In Judaism, a radical transformation of this concept of cyclic creation found its most articulate and vivid expression during the postexilic and intertestamental periods, when it provided a ray of consolation and hope to a people whose light seemed to have passed into eclipse. The development and elaboration of it probably owed much to the infiltration of Iranian ideas, for the future "re-establishment" (*vidāiti*) and "wondrous re-ordering" (*frašo-kereti*) of the world is a cardinal tenet of Mazdean and Zoroastrian teaching, and all the concomitants of this doctrine—the final conflagration, the war against the Evil One, the trial in molten metal, the reward of the righteous, and the requital of the wicked—likewise find place in the Jewish presentations.

**2. The first and the last.** In accordance with this basic concept, almost every element of the traditional creation myths is duly reproduced in the apocalyptic visions of the last things.

*a. The new creation.* The world will be renewed (חדוש העולם; παλινγενεσία; Enoch 72:1; 91:16; Jub. 1:29; II Esd. 5:45; 7:75; II Bar. 32:6; 44:12; 57:2; 1QS IV.25; 1QH XI.13-14; XIII.11-14; Matt. 19:28).

The doctrine is well attested also in early rabbinic literature. In the Mekilta on Exod. 16:25, e.g., Eleazar of Modim (*ca.* A.D. 100) speaks of the "new world" (עוֹלָם חדשׁ); while reference to the "world which will be renewed" (עלמא דהוא עתיד לאתהדתא) is

likewise made in Targ. Mic. 7:14; Hab. 3:2; and in Palestinian Targ. Deut. 32:1, as well as in the form of the Ḳaddish prayer recited at funerals.

Nor will this renewal be solely a matter of moral regeneration. A new heaven and a new earth will be brought into being (cf. Isa. 65:17; 66:2; II Pet. 3:13; Rev. 22:1).

*b. The renewed combat.* The dragon which God defeated and chained at the beginning of the present era will burst his bonds and offer a new challenge, and again be vanquished in combat.

This idea appears already in Isa. 27:1, where the future discomfiture of the monster is portrayed in terms borrowed from the account of his primordial defeat by Baal in the mythological poem from Ras Shamra (Ugarit; I* AB, i.1-2). Similarly, in Job 3:8 —a passage commonly misunderstood—one of the curses which Job invokes upon his birthday is that the future rousing of Leviathan may take place on that date—i.e., that "all hell may break loose" upon it. The notion of the future battle with the dragon is further elaborated in II Esd. 6:52; II Bar. 29:3-8; B.B. 74*a*-75*a;* Shab. 30*b;* Keth. 11*b;* Palestinian Targ. Num. 9:26-27. The Iranian counterpart is the myth of Aži Dahak, the primordial serpent confined beneath a mountain, who will burst forth in the last days, eventually to suffer defeat at the hands of the hero, Keresaspa (cf. Yasht 13.62).

Moreover, just as in the ancient myths (e.g., the Mesopotamian Enuma Êliš and the Greek Titanomachia) the gods had to defeat a cabal of rebellious powers before the several phenomena of the world could be set in order, so will God again march forth with his hosts to do battle against the forces of evil (Zech. 14:2-5; Test. Levi 5:27; Test. Dan 2:10-11; Sibylline Oracles III.319, 519, 632, 663; II Bar. 70: 7-10; Enoch 56; II Esd. 5:6; 14:33; Asmp. Moses 8:1-2; 1QH III.35; VI.29; X.34-35; 1QM, *passim;* Palestinian Targ. Gen. 49:11; Num. 9:6; 24:17-20, 24; M. 'Eduyôth 2.10; Rev. 20:8). Here again, Iranian influence may be suspected; for much the same description of this conflict is given in the Zend Avesta—e.g., in Yasna 30.3; Yasht 19.11; 44.15; etc. Moreover, the specification, in the Jewish accounts, of the "outlandish" nations, Gog and Magog, as earthly representatives of the evil powers finds its exact counterpart in that of the wild tribes of Gilan and Mazanderan in Iranian sources (cf. Yasna 57.17; 77.1; Yasht 5.22; 9.4; 10.17; Vendidad 10.14, 16).

Finally, just as in the traditional cosmogonic myths (e.g., Enuma Êliš IV.14; the Ugaritic Poem of Baal III AB, A 9-10; Ps. 93:1-4) the issue of the combat is the assumption of sovereignty by the victorious god, so, in the apocalyptic vision, the result of God's combat against the heathen will be that "on that day . . . Yahweh will become king over all the earth" (Zech. 14:1-3, 9).

*c. The renewal of fertility.* Just as in the traditional myth God sent his special waters to moisten the earth (Gen. 2:6), so, at the future "re-creation" of the world a special stream of living waters will be released (Zech. 14:8). And just as in the Canaanite myth the reappearance of Baal is presaged by the fact that "the skies rain oil, the wadies run with honey" (I AB, ii.6), so, at the renewal of the world, precisely the same phenomenon will occur (cf. Joel

3:18; Amos 9:13; Sibylline Oracles III.774-77; II Enoch 8:5).

***d. The new light.*** Just as in the traditional myth God sent light to inaugurate the process of creation, so light will again burst forth upon a world shrouded in darkness (cf. Enoch 5:6; 38:4; 45:4; 48:3, 6; 92:4; 1QH VII 24-25; the nucleus of this idea may be found already in Isa. 30:26).

***e. The new man.*** The crowning point of the new creation will be the emergence of the new man (the "Son of man"; cf. בן אדם; Aramaic בר אנש), to whom —as at the former creation (Gen. 1:26-28)—all things will be subject (cf. Dan. 7:13; Enoch 46:1-4; 48:2-10; II Esd. 13:3-13). In the Christian development of this doctrine, the new man is identified, of course, with the divine man, Jesus Christ.

Moreover, the righteous, who will be spared for this consummation, will enjoy once more the bliss of the primeval age. They will again dwell—and not necessarily after death!—in the garden of God (Enoch 61:12) and eat freely of the fruit of the paradisal tree (24:4-5), and they will live as long as did the antediluvians (25:6). *Magnus ab integro saeclorum nascitur ordo.* The cosmogonic cycle completes its revolution. Once again, the creative breath of God moves in the darkness over the troubled waters of the world, and once again the sudden burst of his light heralds a new day.

The Bible opens with the story of creation, not because this is the beginning of all things, but because it wishes to proclaim at the outset that the world is under God. It is the breath of the eternal God that stirs the primordial waters, and it is the same breath that turns the dull clod into a living soul. All the subsequent narratives and chronicles of the OT are but a reaffirmation of this truth in terms of history, and therefore, in the last analysis, an epic of continuous creation: the divine breath is still hovering over the turbulent deep, still being breathed into rude clay. And it is in line with this tremendous concept that the NT ends with the vision of a new creation, or rather a completion of the continuous process, when God who at the first was all in nothing shall at the last be all in all.

*Bibliography.* 1. On Hebrew words translated "create":

*a*) ברא. F. Buhl, *Kittel Festschrift* (1913), pp. 42-60: J Van der Ploeg, *Mélanges Lefort (Le Muséon)*, vol. LIX; 1946), pp. 1-4; R. J. Wilson, *ET*, LXV (1953), 94-95.

*b*) קנה. P. Humbert, *Bertholet Festschrift* (1954), 259-66; G. Rinaldi, *Aegyptus,* XXXIV (1954), 61-65; W. F. Albright, *VTS*, III (1955), 7, note 5; M. Pope, *El in the Ugaritic Texts* (1955), pp. 51-52; F. Vattioni, *Review of Biblical Theology*, III (1955), 218-20. The meaning "create" is denied to this word by: G. della Vida, *JBL*, LXIII (1944), 1, note 1; J. A. Montgomery, *JAOS*, LIII (1953), 107, 116; P. Katz, *Journal of Jewish Studies*, V (1954), 126-31.

2. On the distinction between daylight and the sun, see: S. Aalen, *Die Begriffe "Licht" und "Finsterniss" im AT, im Spätjudentum und im Rabbinismus*, vol. I (1951).

3. For varying viewpoints on Gen. 1:2, see: W. H. McClellan, *Bibl.*, XV (1934), 512-27; K. Smorónski, *Bibl.*, VI (1935), 140-46, 275-93, 361-95; S. Moscati, *JBL*, LXVI (1945), 305-10.

4. For Mesopotamian parallels to the idea that man is created in the divine image, see: B. Meissner, *Babylonien und Assyrien* (1920—), i, p. 371. The idea was enunciated also by C. Masonius Rufus, a Stoic teacher of the first century A.D. (Stobaeus CXVII.8).

5. On the six-day scheme, see: J. Wellhausen, *Reste des arabischen Heidetums* (2nd ed., 1897), p. 142; J. Skinner, *Genesis* (1910), pp. 7-12; H. Webster, *Rest Days* (1916), pp. 188-90.

6. On seasonal conditions in Palestine at the beginning of the agricultural year, see: G. A. Smith, *The Historical Geography of the Holy Land*, p. 77; G. Dalman, *Arbeit und Sitte in Palästina*, I, i (1918), 119.

7. For primitive parallels to the idea that man was made from clay or dust, see: O. Dähnhardt, *Natursagen*, I (1907), 89-111; J. G. Frazer, *Folklore in the OT* (1919), I, 3-29. For Classical parallels, see: J. E. B. Mayor, Commentary on Juvenal iv.133, xiv.35; E. S. McCartney, *Classical Journal*, XX (1935), 367-78.

8. On the assumed Sumerian origin of the idea that woman was formed from the rib of man, see: V. Scheil, *Comptes rendus* (1915), pp. 534-36; S. N. Kramer, *Enki and Ninḥursag*, BASOR, Supplement I (1934), p. 9; E. Villa, *Studi e Materiali di Storia delle Religioni*, XV (1939), 126-29; H. Holma, *Orientalia*, XIII (1944), 225. But for primitive parallels, see O. Dähnhardt, *Natursagen*, I (1907), 115-20.

9. English translations of the ancient Near Eastern myths of the primordial combat:

*a*) Ugaritic. T. H. Gaster, *Thespis* (1950), pp. 133-224; H. L. Ginsberg in J. B. Pritchard, ed., *ANET* (2nd ed., 1955), pp. 129-42.

*b*) Babylonian (Enuma Êliš). A. Heidel, *The Babylonian Genesis* (1942), pp. 7-47, pp. 119-22 (Tišpak and Labbu); E. A. Speiser in J. B. Pritchard, ed., *ANET* (2nd ed., 1955), pp. 60-72.

*c*) Hittite. T. H. Gaster, *Thespis* (1950), pp. 316-36; A. Goetze in J. B. Pritchard, ed., *ANET* (2nd ed., 1955), pp. 125-26.

*d*) Sumerian. S. N. Kramer, *Sumerian Mythology* (1944), pp. 80-82; T. Jacobsen, *JNES*, V (1946), 146-47.

10. On cosmogony in the Apoc. and the Pseudep., see: W. M. Patton, *International Journal of Apocrypha*, no. 17 (April, 1909), pp. 33-37.

11. For oriental and Greek influences on the concept of the creative Word, see in particular: L. Dürr, *Die Wertung des göttlichen Wortes im AT und im Antiken Orient* (1938); W. F. Albright, *From the Stone Age to Christianity* (1940), pp. 145-46, 285; *JBL*, LX (1941), 206-9; E. Hatch, *The Influence of Greek Ideas on Christianity* (1957), pp. 246-50.

12. On the oriental background of Wisdom as "craftsman," see: W. F. Albright, *AJSL*, XXXVI (1920), 282-85; C. Story, *JBL*, LXIV (1945), 334.

13. On cosmogony and eschatology, see: H. Gunkel, *Schöpfung und Chaos in Urzeit und Endzeit* (1895). This classic discussion can now be augmented from more recent discoveries of ancient Near Eastern literature (*see above*), but these discoveries also require modification of Gunkel's conclusions at several points. On the idea of creation as a recurrent event, see: M. Eliade, *The Myth of the Eternal Return* (1954).

For translations of the Dead Sea Scrolls as indicated, see: T. H. Gaster, *The Dead Sea Scriptures* (1956).

T. H. GASTER

***COTTON*** [כרפס, *karpas;* κάρπασος; Heb. *and* Gr. *borrowed from* Sanskrit *karpasa, perhaps through* Pers.; חורי, *ḥôrāi*(?)]. The fibers from the fruit of a plant, *Gossypium herbaceum* L., which have been woven into thread and cloth from very early times. כרפס in Esth. 1:6 refers to hangings of cotton in the palace of Susa, while Isa. 19:9 mentions weavers of cotton in Egypt. In the latter passage the context and parallelism seem to favor the translation "cotton" for חורי (RSV "white cotton"; KJV "networks"), even though the word may mean just "white" (cf. Esth. 8:15, where חור may refer to cloth).

*See also* FLORA § A5; CLOTH; WHITE.

*Bibliography.* I. Löw, *Die Flora der Juden,* II (1924), 235-42, 244; H. N. and A. L. Moldenke, *Plants of the Bible* (1952), pp. 109-10.

J. C. TREVER

**COUCH** [מִסַּב (Song of S. 1:12), *from* סָבַב, go around; *also* יָצוּעַ, מִטָּה, מִשְׁכָּב, עֶרֶשׂ, *see* BED]. Something upon which to recline or sleep, but there is no clear distinction between the five Hebrew words cited above. The RSV uses "couch" thirteen times, either when the context favors a more elegant term than "bed," or to avoid the repetition of "bed" in successive clauses or verses. *See* BED; FURNITURE; HOUSE.

W. S. McCULLOUGH

**COULTER.** KJV alternate form of MATTOCK; PLOWSHARE.

**COUNCIL, THE COUNCIL, COUNCIL HOUSE, COUNSEL.** Words used to translate numerous Hebrew, Aramaic, and Greek terms. A council is a deliberative body charged with civic, legal, and religious responsibilities.

In the OT the term סוֹד refers to confidential discourse or secrets (Prov. 3:32; 11:13); frequently, however, it designates the council of Yahweh, his deliberation in the heavenly assembly with the host of heaven gathered about him (Ps. 89:7—H 89:8; Job 15:8; Jer. 23:18, 22; Amos 3:7; note also Ps. 82:1, where the Hebrew word translated "council" in the RSV is עֵדָה, usually rendered "congregation"). The king's council is represented by those who "see the face of the king" (רֹאֵי פְּנֵי הַמֶּלֶךְ; II Kings 25:19; Jer. 52:25). The commanders of armies also "sit" in council (II Kings 9:5: יָשַׁב).

The NT refers only to human councils. The term συνέδριον may refer to local councils of particular cities (Matt. 10:17; Mark 13:9) or to the high council, the SANHEDRIN (Matt. 5:22; 26:59; etc.). *The* council generally means the Sanhedrin (τὸ συνέδριον).

The most common term for "counsel" is עֵצָה, in reference both to counsel given by God and to that given by men. The wise men (חֲכָמִים) and elders (זְקֵנִים) of Israel have particular responsibility for counsel (Jer. 18:18; II Sam. 15:31, 34; Prov. 1:25, 30; 8:14). Yahweh's counsel is also provided through kings and prophets, and through participation in the worship of the community (I Kings 1:12; Jer. 19:7 [RSV "plans"]; Ps. 73:24). The verb יָעַץ is used with the meaning "to give or receive counsel," in reference to human and divine counsel. In postexilic times, under Persian influence, a number of terms for "counsel" and "counselor" appear (מְלַךְ [Dan. 4:24— A 4:27]; יָעַט, variant of יָעַץ [Dan. 6:7—H 6:8]; דְּתָבַר [Dan. 3:2-3]; עֵטָא or עֵטָה [Dan. 2:14]; הַדָּבַר [Dan. 3: 24, 27, etc.]). These terms refer primarily to the giving of advice on state matters, rather than to the counsel of God.

Although the OT does not directly connect the possession of sound counsel with the entrance of prophet, king, or worshiper into the council of Yahweh, it is clear that true counsel has its source in Yahweh and in him alone. One of the endowments of the eschatological king-savior of Isa. 11:1-9 is that of a "spirit of counsel and might" (רוּחַ עֵצָה וּגְבוּרָה [vs. 2]).

To take or give counsel in the NT is expressed by the verbs συμβουλεύω and βουλεύομαι, or by a verb plus the noun συμβούλιον. The majority of occurrences have reference to the enemies of Jesus who take counsel on how to destroy him (Matt. 12:14; 22:15; 26:4; etc.). It is remarkable that the NT as-

signs little specific place to the wisdom tradition of Israel or to wise counselors. The role of the elders (πρεσβύτεροι) in the early church may, however, have continued this tradition in part. The "secret and hidden wisdom of God" referred to by Paul (σοφίαν ἐν μυστηρίῳ, τὴν ἀποκεκρυμμένην [I Cor. 2:7]) has its closest connection in the OT with the heavenly council (סוֹד), where the determinations and decrees of God are first promulgated. The NT use of the term μυστήριον, "mystery," may also have behind it this Hebrew term סוֹד (note that the LXX translates the comparable Aramaic word רָז by μυστήριον [Dan. 2:18, etc.]; παιδεία is apparently intended by the LXX to render סוֹד in Amos 3:7). Thus the sacraments of the church (*sacramentum* becomes the standard term for the translation of the NT word μυστήριον) may be understood in part as dramatic enactments or representations of the secret counsel of God which has been revealed in Jesus Christ.

W. J. HARRELSON

**COUNCIL, HEAVENLY.** *See* GOD, OT; HOST OF HEAVEN.

**COUNCIL OF JERUSALEM** jĭ ro͞o′sə ləm. The name given to a conference at Jerusalem to determine the terms on which Gentiles would be received into the church. According to Acts, the issue became acute, not when one God-fearing household previously sympathetic with Judaism became Christians (ch. 10), nor when some Gentiles at Antioch believed the gospel (11:19-26), but only when a widespread mission in Cyprus and central Asia Minor won numerous Gentiles and showed that the church could easily become largely Gentile (chs. 13-14).

Both Acts 15:1-29; Gal. 2:1-10 report such a council. But the two accounts differ in important respects. In Galatians the council occurs during Paul's second visit to Jerusalem after his conversion; in Acts, during his third visit. In Galatians, Paul says he went to Jerusalem by divine direction; in Acts the Antioch church sends Paul and others to Jerusalem. In Galatians, Paul pictures his negotiations with Jerusalem leaders as a conference between equals, and states that his independent leadership of the mission to Gentiles was fully recognized; in Acts the Jerusalem leaders and church appear to hold superior authority over the entire church. In Galatians, Paul says he agreed to a request that he provide relief funds for the needy Jerusalem Christians; Acts says nothing of this. In Galatians, Paul asserts that the Jerusalem leaders "added nothing" to the gospel he had been preaching; in Acts the Jerusalem leaders, supported by the Jerusalem church, formulate a letter which requires Gentile Christians to abstain from meat sacrificed to idols, from blood, from meat of strangled animals, and from unchastity (15:29).

Of proposals made to provide a solution to this problem, five must be mentioned: (*a*) The visit of Gal. 2:1-10 is the one reported in Acts 11:27-30. This is Paul's second visit to Jerusalem in each writing; both passages refer to a collection; both say Paul and Barnabas came together to Jerusalem. But Acts 11:27-30 says nothing of a conference of any kind; Paul and Barnabas do not see the apostles; and the council of Acts 15 implies that no previous conference on Gentile Christians had been held.

*b*) Acts 11:27-30; 15:1-29 are two accounts of the same conference, wrongly described as two separate meetings. On this view, the date is usually thought to be that of Acts 11:27-30. But neither account resembles the other. If Acts is so confused on this crucial point, we can hardly hope to reconstruct a convincing history of the apostolic age.

*c*) Acts 15:1-29 combines two sources, one dealing with circumcision of Gentiles and the other with rules governing fellowship, especially at meals, between Jewish and Gentile Christians. There is no linguistic basis for distinguishing two sources, and the hypothesis wrongly assumes that a conference which rejected circumcision for Gentiles would not discuss the basis of Jewish-Gentile table fellowship.

*d*) Acts 15:1-29 is not historical material; the author, having expanded the Cornelius story to serve his favorite ideas, freely composes the council narrative for the same reason, using in the decree (vs. 29) a decision derived from another occasion. This radical denial of historical basis fits poorly the general historical value of Luke and the latter half of Acts.

*e*) The "apostolic decree" (Acts 15:28-29) is wrongly placed here; it was really issued at another time, probably later than the Council, and when Paul was not present. Acts 21:25 is thought to imply that James is here telling Paul about a decision previously unknown to him. This view is possible, to say the least, but not necessary.

Of these varied views, none has won general support, and none is so convincing as the view that Gal. 2:1-10; Acts 15:1-29 describe the same conference. Both deal with the place of the Gentiles in the church and face the question of circumcision. In both, this question had come up at Antioch and at Jerusalem. In both, Paul, Barnabas, and another or others went to Jerusalem to confer. In both, Paul won a sweeping victory: the Jerusalem apostles rejected circumcision for Gentiles. The two accounts are independent—Paul writes with the aim of vindicating his independent apostleship—but there is broad agreement.

The two most serious differences are: (*a*) Acts appears to assume that the Jerusalem leaders had supreme authority; Paul claims equal, independent authority. Certainly the decision of the Jerusalem leaders was crucial for Paul's work; he recognized this by going to seek their agreement with his gospel. Both sides had a sense of the unity of the church; but Paul is never given one-sided directives in Acts or treated as an inferior.

*b*) The "decree" in Acts seems to contradict Paul's claim that the Jerusalem leaders "added nothing" to his message and practice. If the decree was a later action of the Jerusalem leaders, Paul's statement clearly holds true. But as Acts stands, the "decree" is not impossible. By it Gentiles were excused from circumcision and from the great mass of Levitical ceremonial regulations; keeping the law was not necessary to salvation. If Paul accepted the decree, not as giving items essential to salvation, but as facilitating mutual friendship and social fellowship between Jewish and Gentile Christians, he won as great a victory as church history can show, with a minimum of pacifying concession to the opposing side. (The Western text of the decree, which omits "strangled things" and sometimes adds the Golden Rule, leaves a moral code, opposing idolatry, murder, and immorality. This is a later moralizing of an earlier concern for ceremonial rules.) Paul would oppose idolatry and fornication in any case; respect for Jewish aversion to meat containing blood and taken from strangled animals is as intelligible as not serving pork at a modern conference of Jews and Christians. If Paul did accept the decree, however, he later saw it used to support the binding character of the Mosaic ceremonial law for all Christians, and refused to continue his support of the decree. This could explain why he makes no reference to it in I Cor. 8-10.

Uncertainty over details should not obscure the broad-minded courage of the Jerusalem leaders in supporting Paul, and the magnitude of the victory which Paul won in this council.

*Bibliography.* K. Lake, "The Apostolic Council of Jerusalem," *Beginnings of Christianity,* V (1933), 195-212; H. Schlier, *Der Brief an die Galater* (1949), pp. 66-78; J. Dupont, *Les Problèmes du Livre des Actes d'après les Travaux Récents* (1950), pp. 51-70; F. F. Bruce, *The Acts of the Apostles* (1951), pp. 287-304; E. Haenchen, *Die Apostelgeschichte* (1956), pp. 387-419.

F. V. FILSON

**COUNSELOR** [יוֹעֵץ; *alternately* עֲצָתוֹ (Ps. 119:24; Isa. 40:13); דְּתָבַר (Dan. 3:2-3); הַדָּבַר (Dan. 3:24, 27; 4:36; 6:7); σύμβουλος (Rom. 11:34); παράκλητος (John 14:16, 26; 15:26; 16:7)]. One who counsels or advises.

Counselors seem to have been customary court officials of the Israelite kings (II Chr. 25:16; Isa. 1:26; 3:3; *see also* GOVERNMENT § C2*a*). In fact, it may be that the counselor was next in power to the ruler himself (Mic. 4:9; cf. Job 3:14; 12:17; *but see* CHANCELLOR; CUPBEARER). David's counselor Ahithophel had an outstanding reputation (II Sam. 16:23). After his defection and suicide he was succeeded by Jehoiada and Abiathar (I Chr. 27:34). Zechariah son of Shelemiah, and Jonathan, a relative of David, are also named as counselors of this period (I Chr. 26:14; 27:32). The schism between Israel and Judah is attributed to Rehoboam's heeding the wrong counselors (I Kings 12:6-14). Counselors are mentioned as serving the rulers of surrounding nations: the pharaoh of Egypt (Isa. 19:11), Nebuchadnezzar in Babylon (Dan. 3:2, etc.), and the Persian Artaxerxes, whose seven counselors (Ezra 7:14) no doubt correspond to the "seven princes of Persia and Media" consulted by Ahasuerus (Esth. 1:14).

In a general sense, parents (Prov. 1:8, etc.), elders (Ezek. 7:26), prophets (II Chr. 25:16; Jer. 38:15), and wise men (Jer. 18:18; 49:7; *see also* WISDOM) characteristically act as counselors. A prudent person consults an abundance of counselors before taking an important step (Prov. 11:14; 15:22; 20:18; 24:6), whereas the fool ignores counsel (Prov. 1:25, 30). Job recalls that in his happier days he was the sort of upright and substantial citizen whose counsel was respected (Job 29:21). On the other hand, some are misled by evil counselors (II Chr. 22:3; Ps. 1:1; Prov. 12:5; Nah. 1:11).

God himself is a counselor (Pss. 16:7; 32:8; 33:11;

73:24), and no one can counsel him (Isa. 40:13; Rom. 11:34). His law and his testimony are the people's counselor (Ps. 119:24). His Messiah is an ideal king, who can bring to pass the wondrous deeds he counsels (Isa. 9:6; 11:2). He is not an advice-giver, but his power is the strength of the community. So also the Holy Spirit is the Counselor (John 14:16, etc.; *see* PARACLETE). C. U. WOLF

\*COURAGE. Across the races and generations of men courage has been a widely celebrated virtue. The Greeks had a word for it (ἀνδρεία), and they ranked it among the four cardinal virtues. The Bible has its roll call of heroes who were courageous in battle and in martyrdom. But courage in the Bible does not usually stand as an independent virtue; it is generally found in a religious context, it is inspired by God, and it is exhibited in the service of God. The words "courage" and "courageous" were used infrequently in the KJV (fourteen times), but there are some fifty occurrences in the RSV. *See also* BOLDNESS.

1. Terminology of courage in the Bible
   *a.* In biblical Hebrew
   *b.* In LXX Greek
   *c.* In NT Greek
2. Courage in the OT
3. Courage in the Apoc. and the Pseudep.
4. Courage in the NT
Bibliography

1. Terminology of courage in the Bible. The spirit of courage and bravery pervades the Bible and should be recognized far beyond the actual vocabulary. The action of inspired men and groups of men assumes that strength of mind and determination which are the essence of courage.

*a. In biblical Hebrew.* Strength and courage are intimately related in OT usage, as in the expression so often used: "Be strong and of good courage." חזק means "to bind fast, to make firm," and so it is used in the sense "to show oneself strong, courageous" (II Sam. 10:12). So also אמץ means "to be alert, to strengthen," and so "to be of good courage." Deut. 31:7 combines both terms: חזק ואמץ, "Be strong and of good courage." By common transference the seat of feeling and emotion was used to connote the feeling or emotion; so "the heart," לבב, comes to stand for courage (Dan. 11:25; I Sam. 17:32). The word "spirit," רוח, is used in a similar sense in Josh. 2:11.

The expression "mighty men of valor" is used frequently in the battle chapters of the OT. Once again, the term used, גבור, has as its first meaning "strong, mighty, valiant," and it becomes the common term for a warrior or war chief (Josh. 1:14; II Kings 5:1).

*b. In LXX Greek.* The usual Greek words, ἀνδρεία (noun), ἀνδρεῖος (adjective), ἀνδρίζομαι (verb), carry an original force of the masculine quality of aggressive courage, but this significance is so far lost that in Prov. 12:4 we read: "A good [ἀνδρεία, "courageous"] wife is the crown of her husband," and in Prov. 31:10: "A good [ἀνδρείαν, KJV "virtuous"] wife who can find?"

The Wisdom of Solomon lists courage (ἀνδρεία) among the four cardinal virtues. The adverb, ἀνδρείως, is used in the incident of Eleazar (II Macc. 6:27).

The verb, ἀνδρίζομαι, is often coupled with words for strength, as in Josh. 10:25: "Play the man and be strong" (ἀνδρίζεσθε καὶ ἰσχύετε; cf. II Kings 10: 12). Mattathias on his deathbed challenges his sons: "Be courageous and grow strong in the law" (I Macc. 2:64 orig. tr.: ἀνδρίζεσθε καὶ ἰσχύσατε ἐν τῷ νόμῳ).

The noun, θάρσος, and the verb, θαρσέω (Attic θαρρέω), convey the sense of confidence, fearlessness, courage of spirit. Most often the imperative of the verb is employed to rally men: "Take heart, be of good courage" (orig. tr.).

*c. In NT Greek.* As noted *above*, the usual word for "courage," ἀνδρεία, is not found in the NT, but the verb, ἀνδρίζομαι, appears in I Cor. 16:13: "Be watchful, stand firm in your faith, be courageous [KJV "quit you like men"], be strong."

The noun, θάρσος, "confidence, courage," is found only in Acts 28:15, but the verb, θαρρέω, is used of the stout heart (II Cor. 5:6, 8), confidence in men (II Cor. 7:16), and boldness in human relations (II Cor. 10:1-2). The verb, θαρσέω, in the imperative is placed on the lips of Jesus: "Be of good courage" (θάρσει, θαρσεῖτε: Matt. 9:2; 14:27; John 16:33).

The sense of courage in free utterance is conveyed by παρρησία, παρρησιάζομαι, but these words are also used for confident assurance in the religious context.

A more reckless spirit of daring is suggested by the word τολμάω (Mark 12:34; Rom. 5:7).

2. Courage in the OT. Implicit in the action and movement of the patriarchs is a strong, even an adventurous, spirit, as when Terah left Ur of the Chaldees. But the accounts leave it to God to supply the initiative and provide the way. Similarly it is God who leads the Israelites out of Egypt, and their safety rests, not in their own military prowess, but in the pillar of cloud and the pillar of fire. When Israel goes in to possess the land, the Lord gives their enemies into their hand, and their confidence rests in God: "One man of you puts to flight a thousand, since it is the LORD your God who fights for you" (Josh. 23:10; cf. I Sam. 14:6).

There are cases of individual courage, but even David's victory over Goliath is credited to God (I Sam. 17:37). The strength of Israel's armies rests in the "mighty men of valor." No one would doubt the courage of the prophets in proclaiming God's message. In the OT in general, the loss of courage and faintness of heart come from sin and evil (Ps. 107:26; Jer. 4:9), but God supplies the stout heart and the courageous spirit (Pss. 27:14; 31:24).

3. Courage in the Apoc. and the Pseudep. The success of the Maccabean struggle is due, among other things, to the strong courage of leaders and men in the cause of the nation. From his deathbed Mattathias commits the struggle to his sons: "Be courageous and grow strong in the law" (I Macc. 2: 64). Judas calls for courage in the face of impossible odds: "If our time has come, let us die bravely [ἐν ἀνδρείᾳ] for our brethren" (I Macc. 9:10). Eleazar is broken on the wheel, giving a courageous example of patient endurance (II Macc. 6:27).

Courage sometimes shows up as a more individual virtue, but it is still called forth in the cause of religion (the law and the nation). In the Wisdom of Solomon the Greek spirit is apparent, and courage stands on its own feet as one of the cardinal virtues (8:7), a gift of God's WISDOM. In the Letter of Aristeas the question is asked: "What is the true aim of courage [ἀνδρεία]?" The answer follows: "To execute in the hour of danger, in accordance with one's plans, resolutions that have been rightly formed."

**4. Courage in the NT.** The Greek word for "courage" (ἀνδρεία) does not occur in the NT, and the verb, ἀνδρίζομαι, appears once (I Cor. 16:13). But the NT breathes the spirit of courage in its fullest strength—no longer the fighting spirit of the warrior in the emergency, but now the strong moral temper that rises above unpopularity, abuse, and hostility to take its stand on the unseen, spiritual realities. This spirit is shown in steadfast endurance (ὑπομονή), boldness of speech (παρρησία), undaunted faith (πίστις). Jesus' own example of courage in his ministry and passion is the inspiration of his followers (Heb. 12:2). Peter and John bravely face their accusers. Stephen goes to his death with words of forgiveness on his lips. Paul carries the gospel confidently to the great metropolitan centers; presents his gospel to the Areopagus; stands bravely before his judges. Heb. 11 is a tribute to faith and courage. The martyrs of the church demonstrate a brave endurance unto death (Rev. 7:14; 14:1).

*Bibliography.* J. B. Lightfoot, *The Apostolic Fathers* (1891), in which important references are I Clem. 55.3; Shepherd of Hermas, Vis. I.4.3. R. H. Charles, *The Apoc. and Pseudep. of the OT* (1913). J. H. Moulton and G. Milligan, *The Vocabulary of the Greek Testament Illustrated from the Papyri and Other Non-literary Sources* (1914-29). W. F. Arndt and F. W. Gingrich, *A Greek-English Lexicon of the NT and Other Early Christian Literature* (trans. from W. Bauer, *Griechisch-Deutsches Wörterbuch zu den Schriften des Neuen Testaments und der übrigen urchristlichen Literatur;* 1957). P. E. DAVIES

**COURIER** [רָץ] (II Chr. 30:6, 10; Esth. 3:13); KJV POST. A royal MESSENGER who traveled overland and by sea. Ancient Persians and Romans, as well as other civilized peoples, had well-organized carrier service to take swiftly messages from the king or emperor to all parts of the land. C. U. WOLF

**COURT OF BUILDING** [חָצֵר, enclosure, court]. An area enclosed by walls before a building, but without roof. See TEMPLE, JERUSALEM.

**COURT OF LAW.** Legal proceedings in the Bible are marked by considerable development throughout the centuries. During the period of the patriarchs, legal questions were decided between families and tribes (Gen. 31:37; 34:4-24), on the basis of legal precedents and tribal traditions. With the organization of the tribal system under Joshua (or perhaps under Moses), more difficult cases were settled "before God"—i.e., at the central sanctuary of the tribes (Exod. 21:6; 22:8—H 22:7; *see* LAW [IN THE OT]). The earliest court of law attested in the OT is the palm tree of Deborah, to which all Israel is reported to have come for judgment (Judg. 4:5). Generally, the city gate served as the place of judgment for local cases (Amos 5:10; Ruth 4:1).

With the establishment of the kingship, the king assumed the function formerly exercised by the judges (שֹׁפְטִים; *see* JUDGE) of Israel at the central sanctuary or in their circuits throughout the land (I Sam. 7:16-

17). The king served as a kind of supreme court, settling the more difficult cases or those in which one of the parties sought appeal to higher authority (I Kings 3:16-28; II Sam. 15:2-6). The city gate continued to be the gathering place for judgment. The king, or his representative (II Sam. 15:3), heard the case, including the testimony of witnesses, and rendered judgment.

In the case of acts of apostasy, the elders and leading citizens of the city placed the accused "on high" before all the people and heard the testimony of his accusers. If the accused were found guilty, all the people executed the punishment of death (I Kings 21:9-13).

The OT has no specific term for "court of law." The nearest equivalent is provided by the term שַׁעַר, the "gate of the city" (cf. תְּרַע, the gate or courtyard of the king [Dan. 2:49]). In later Hebrew and Aramaic usage the expression בֵּית דִּין, "house of judgment," sometimes refers to the judgment seat, the court of judgment (cf. Dan. 7:10, 26 [דִּינָא]). Where the term "court" is found in the English versions, the translation is generally not a literal one. Deut. 25:1 reads literally: "They draw near for judgment"; Prov. 25:8 would be translated literally: "Do not go forth quickly for contention." The same is true of NT passages in which "court" appears (Matt. 5:25: "on the way"; Acts 13:1: "an intimate friend of Herod"; etc.). Only in I Cor. 4:3 (ἡμέρα) and Acts 19:38 (ἀγοραῖοι) do we have precise terms for courts of law. W. J. HARRELSON

**COURT OF THE GUARD.** *See* GUARD, COURT OF THE.

**COUSIN.** There is no word for "cousin" in the Bible. The OT has such expressions as "son of your uncle" or "son of your father's brother." The cousin has certain obligations and rights pertaining to economic transactions and especially to marriage. Hanamel the cousin of Jeremiah requested him to exercise his right to purchase a parcel of land at Anathoth. So he bought the field from his cousin (Jer. 32:7-9, 12). The marriage of cousins was common, particularly of first cousins (Gen. 24:15; 28:2; 29:10, 19; 36:3). We may observe in this practice the effect of both exogamous and endogamous forces. The daughters of Zelophehad married the sons of their father's brothers in order to keep the inheritance in the tribe of their father (Num. 36:11). The daughters of Eleazar, who had no sons, married their kinsmen (cousins), the sons of Kish (I Chr. 23:21-22). Significantly, the laws governing incest, although listing women to whom a man is closely related, omit the category of cousin (Lev. 18:6-18).

The KJV translates συγγενίς as "cousin" when used of Mary's relation to Elizabeth (Luke 1:36), but the Greek term requires the translation "kinswoman" (so RSV). The συγγενίς of Luke 1:36 is held to be a peculiar form of the word that is more generally used, συγγενής, variously translated "kin," "kinsfolk," "kinsmen" (cf. Mark 6:4; Luke 1:58; 2:44; 14:12).

*See also* FAMILY; MARRIAGE. O. J. BAAB

**COUTHA.** KJV form of CUTHA.

*COVENANT. A solemn promise made binding by an oath, which may be either a verbal formula or a symbolic action. Such an action or formula is recognized by both parties as the formal act which binds the actor to fulfil his promise. Covenants may be between parties of different socio-political groups, in which case the covenant creates a relationship between them regulated by the terms of the covenant; or a covenant may take place within a legal community, in which case obligations are assumed which the law does not provide for—i.e., it makes new obligations binding.

Since the covenant usually had sanctions of a religious nature (an appeal to the gods to punish any breach of covenant), it was closely connected with religion. It also had close connections with law, since the obligations assumed by covenant tended to become legal obligations enforced by political means, and there is some reason to believe that, in late times at least, the covenant was simply a form of legislation.

## A. *COVENANTS IN THE ANCIENT WORLD.*

In the long time span covered by ancient history there is a great variety of forms and situations in which covenants appear, and much is yet to be learned of the history of covenants. It may be an exaggeration to speak of every relationship other than kinship as a covenant relationship, but it is nevertheless true that covenants were an exceedingly important means for the regulation of behavior, so that some measure of trust and predictability could be introduced into social and political life. The oath (verbal or symbolic) seems to have been the constitutive element which made covenants binding, though it is possible that other formal actions, such as a common meal, did not involve an appeal to the divine world to punish violation of the promise. Not every oath, however, was a covenant, for not all oaths in ancient law involved promises concerning future action. Ancient terminology clearly designated covenants as "oaths and stipulations" in international relationships, and this gives a working definition of ancient covenants. *See* OATH.

The covenants which are of greatest importance for OT history are those which regulate relationships between two distinct social or political units,
international treaties. Evidence for the existence of such treaties goes back to the mid–third millennium B.C. in Sumerian sources, and to Old Akkadian texts two centuries later. Though too fragmentary for a satisfactory juristic analysis, they nevertheless prove that there were already at that time well-formed patterns for the regulation of international affairs, usually associated with the subjection of the party which was defeated in war. Though the Mari archives (*ca.* 1700 B.C.) contain very frequent references to covenants, they do not describe the content and procedure in sufficient detail to be entirely satisfactory. By far the most useful and extensive body of material comes from the Hittite Empire of the Late Bronze Age (*ca.* 1400-1200 B.C.), which had far-flung relations from Mesopotamia to Egypt, as well as suzerainty over various city-states of N Syria.

The Hittite suzerainty treaties have been preserved in abundance, and can be taken as an illustration of a highly developed form known throughout the ancient Near East. These covenants were the formal basis of the Empire; it was on them that depended the relationship between the Hittite state and the vassals which owed it allegiance. They placed the vassal state under the protection of the Hittites, and at the same time placed the military resources of the vassal state at the disposal of the suzerain. There can be little doubt that the military alliance so formed was a primary intent of the treaties, but in addition, they were a means of preserving the peace within the Empire by regulating in advance the obligations of the vassal. Since it was the suzerain who stipulated the obligations of the vassal, the latter was, in effect, protected from arbitrary action on the part of the vastly more powerful overlord. The form of these treaties has been carefully analyzed, and the following characteristic elements of a treaty in this period may be isolated.

*a*) The preamble. The treaty text frequently opens with the statement: "These are the words of . . .," followed by the identification of the king who gives the treaty, his titles, appellatives, and genealogy. The treaty is thus a message from the suzerain to the vassal.

*b*) The historical prologue. This consists of a description of the previous relationships between the two parties, frequently in the "I-Thou" form of address, emphasizing particularly the acts of benevolence which the suzerain has performed for the good of the vassal. Often it is actually the Hittite power which placed the vassal on his throne. These preceding acts of the suzerain are evidently regarded as the foundation of the vassal's obligation, and therefore the historical prologue seems to be carefully composed; these prologues are actually most important sources for the history of the Hittite Empire.

*c*) The stipulations. This section contains the obligations to which the vassal binds himself in accepting the covenant, defined by the suzerain. The content varies widely, but military obligations are, as expected, treated in detail. First, the vassal must not enter into alliances with other independent kings, and he must be a friend to the suzerain's friends and an enemy to his enemies. The vassal must answer any summons for military forces, and engage wholeheartedly in any military campaign commanded by the suzerain. Second, regulations for the treatment of refugees are so frequent that it is necessary to conclude that this was an important issue during this period. Third, war booty is often regulated in advance; this also was evidently a fertile source of discord. In addition to these most common stipulations, many other types of actions are prescribed or prohibited. Most interesting is the frequent prohibition of "murmuring," the utterance of "unfriendly words," against the suzerain, and the obligation to report such words uttered by others. With this is often combined an exhortation to trust the suzerain, even in spite of appearances to the contrary. Finally, a stipulated tribute is imposed.

*d)* The deposit and public reading. Typically there is a provision for the deposit of the treaty document in the sanctuary of the vassal, and a requirement that it be read in public at stipulated intervals, from one to four times a year.

*e)* The list of witnesses. Ancient legal documents normally ended with a list of witnesses, and the international treaties are no exception. Here however, the gods of both states are named—in fact, some of the lists seem to attempt exhaustiveness in making all known gods of the cultural area witnesses to the covenant. In addition, however, important features of the natural world are included, such as mountains, rivers, springs, the great sea, heaven and earth, winds and clouds. It seems reasonably certain that the gods as witnesses were expected to punish breach of contract, and thus religious awe was appealed to as a ground for future obedience. Though the Hittite king certainly did act against a rebellious vassal with military force, the treaties mention only religious sanctions.

*f)* The blessings and curses. This consists of a list of goods and calamities which the divine witnesses were called upon to bring upon the vassal for obedience and disobedience respectively. The curses usually precede, and consist of the misfortunes usually attributed to the wrath of the gods in antiquity: destruction, sterility, misery, poverty, plague, famine. The blessings, conversely, are divine protection, continuity of the vassal's line, health, prosperity, and peace.

The foregoing analysis of the treaty form is schematic, more so perhaps than the treaties themselves, but is useful as a description of that which was evidently felt to be important in a valid treaty. This written document is, however, not all that is involved in a covenant. The text of the treaty frequently refers to the oath of the vassal, but the description of the words or forms by which the oath was sworn seems to be completely lacking and unknown. It is conceivable, but unlikely, that the mere existence of a written document was sufficient to put the covenant into effect. The description of the "soldiers' oath" in Hittite texts points to the probability of some formal ceremony for the ratification of the covenants as well.

So far as the validity of the covenant is concerned, it seems clear that the oath was binding only upon the one who swore, and therefore the death of the vassal and accession of his heir required the drawing up of a new covenant. The same was true evidently in the case of the death of the suzerain. It is true, of course, that the terms of a previous treaty were generally respected by a new king of a vassal state, but it is difficult to say whether or not changes of ruler tended to result in rebellion because the old covenant was no longer regarded as valid. There seems to be no evidence of any concept of a covenant binding in perpetuity.

The normal form of covenants was thus a treaty in which only the vassal is bound by oath. Parity treaties existed at this time, but are best regarded as the same form in which both parties are bound to identical obligations.

In comparison with the material from the Hittite Empire, relatively little is known of covenants from the Assyro-Babylonian periods. Enough treaties have been recovered to indicate that considerable change had taken place in the intervening dark ages. In contrast to the Hittite covenants which gave in the historical prologue the grounds upon which the vassal should willingly give up his freedom to become an ally of the Hittite king, so far nothing analogous has been found in these later treaties, but the fragmentary state of the later treaties warns against much confidence in this argument. So far it would be rather difficult to describe any consistent pattern to which all these later treaties conform, and there are very numerous differences (as well as similarities) between the two groups.

It is not only empires which produced treaties in the ancient world. Perhaps equally important were covenant alliances for the purpose of obtaining a concerted action against empires. There is unfortunately very little direct evidence of the form and content of such alliances, but a respectable body of material to prove that they existed. Already in the Mari period, there were several kings each of whom had ten to fifteen kings in his following, but in addition there were smaller social, tribal, or political groups which joined forces to resist their more powerful neighbors. The Egyptian kings of the New Empire had to fight coalitions of Syro-Palestinian kings, and one of the Amarna Letters (Knudtzon, No. 74) quotes what purports to be the message of an alleged rebel to other dissident groups, exhorting them to gather in a temple (or city containing a temple) to form a defensive coalition by covenant, so that they might drive out the (Egyptian) regents and establish peace in perpetuity. In the Iron Age as well, such coalitions were standard forms of organizing resistance to the Assyrian Empire, the most famous being that which fought Shalmaneser III at Qarqar in 853 B.C. We have no direct evidence that the coalitions condemned by the Hebrew prophets were bound together by a covenant, but it is difficult to see any other basis for them.

**B. COVENANT TERMINOLOGY IN THE BIBLE. 1. In the OT.** The most frequent word for "covenant" (286 occurrences) is ברית, but there are numerous references to covenants and covenant relationships where this term does not occur. The etymology of the term is uncertain. Most generally accepted is the derivation from Akkadian *birîtu,* "fetter," or a cognate root. The word is used as a direct object of a number of verbs to designate the establishment or breach of covenant. The phrase

כרת ברית ל (lit., "cut a covenant with [or for]") is by far the most frequent. Though the origin of this phrase has been the object of much speculation, it seems most likely that the original meaning was lost in antiquity before the time of Moses, and had simply become a technical term. Other verbs include הקים, "establish"; בוא ב, "enter a covenant"; and נתן, צוה, העבר, and שים: "give," "command," "cause to enter," "issue," respectively.

In view of the fact that the term for "covenant" is quite rare in the earliest sections of the OT, the tradition of the covenant with Yahweh must have been designated by other words than ברית. It seems quite likely that the oldest designation of the Decalogue as the עשרת דברים, "the ten words," rests on this early tradition, since covenants were regarded and called the "words" of the suzerain. The theological usage of the "word" of God may therefore be very closely bound up in its very origin with the covenant, though, of course, much expanded in scope with the passage of time.

In addition, the term עדות, "testimony" (in the usual Bible translations), almost certainly was an alternate designation for the covenant (Exod. 31:18), since the cognate Akkadian and Aramaic words were in common usage as terms for "covenant." The original meaning of this word would consequently have been "obligations sworn to" by the religious community.

Occasionally, the word אלה, "oath," may for all practical purposes be a synonym of "covenant," for it was the act which formally constituted a binding contract. It is difficult to say whether in Gen. 26:28 there is any real distinction between the oath and the covenant. "Oath" (שבועה) is occasionally used in similar fashion (Gen. 26:3; Josh. 9:20; II Chr. 15:15; Neh. 6:18).

**2. In the LXX.** In the vast majority of occurrences of ברית (270 out of 286), the LXX renders it with διαθήκη, which in Greek ordinarily (and very frequently) meant "last will and testament" (*see* TESTAMENT). One passage in Aristophanes (*Birds* 440 ff) shows, however, that the Greek language could use the word in other contexts. Here Peisthetairos demands that the birds enter into an oath to do him no harm, and that the covenant be written upon tablets before he will lay down his arms.

The same Greek word is used also to translate Hebrew אחוה, "brotherhood"; דבר, "word"; חוק, "statute"; and תורה, "law." Very rarely is the usual Greek word for "contract" used, but never (except in Aq.) as a translation of ברית (cf. Isa. 28:15; 30:1).

**3. In the NT.** The only word which has demonstrable connections with covenant concepts is the same one, διαθήκη, so frequently used by the LXX. It is entirely possible that μαρτυρεῖν, "to witness," may have grown out of covenant patterns, since it is known that elsewhere "witnesses" to a covenant were essential, and even more important after the oath as the binding element fell out of use. This, however, needs further investigation.

**C. OT COVENANT TRADITIONS.** In antiquity, covenants were a most frequent basis for human relationships which were not kinship ties. It is not surprising, therefore, that covenants are of great importance in OT history and religion. The classification here followed is based on an analysis of their content, so far as it is possible to draw conclusions from the narratives which describe them. It is not possible to classify them merely by appealing to the terminology (כרת ברית, עם, את, or ל) used in the narrative to indicate that a covenant was made.

**1. Secular covenants.** This term designates those covenants to which Yahweh is not one of the parties involved, even though all covenants were normally sworn by appeal to deity as witness. Such covenants may be conveniently grouped into four classes as follows:

*a. Suzerainty.* In suzerainty covenants a superior binds an inferior to obligations defined by the superior. Typical illustrations are I Sam. 11:1, in which Jabesh-gilead offers to "serve" Nahash in a covenant relationship. In this case, as elsewhere, some prior inducement is necessary before the one in superior power is willing to give up his freedom of action in a covenant relationship. Ezek. 17:13 refers to a standard type of suzerainty treaty between Babylon and Zedekiah. Probably Hos. 12:1—H 12:2 (the "bargain with Assyria") belongs here, though the terminology used does not point in this direction. The question of Yahweh to Job (Job 41:4—H 40:28) ironically inquires whether Leviathan will bind himself to serve Job as a vassal. Similarly, Job 5:23 implies such a relationship to the stones and beasts of the fields. Though suzerainty treaties bound only the one inferior in power, the superior nevertheless gave up some degree of freedom of action. His relationship to the vassal was not based on force alone, once a covenant had been established; he had stipulated what he required of the vassal, and further arbitrary exercise of his superior power was not expected of him.

*b. Parity.* In parity covenants both parties are bound by oath. These may be further subdivided, as it was done by Thucydides long ago, into two classes: those in which specific obligations are imposed, and those which impose no obligation but to preserve the peace between the two parties. The treaty between Jacob and Laban (Gen. 31:44-50) is most likely of the latter type, though somewhat more complex, since Jacob can be guilty of a breach of the peace by ill-treatment of Laban's daughters. The covenant of Abraham with Abimelech (21:25-32) seems to be a peace covenant. The parallel account of Isaac's covenant with Abimelech (26:27-31) seems certainly to be of this type, since no further obligations are stated. On the other hand, the description in Gen. 14:13 ff implies military obligations of Abraham's allies, but it is not possible to say definitely that this is a parity covenant. The covenant with the Gibeonites (Josh. 9:3-27) is certainly a parity peace treaty, which was subsequently changed by the consent of the Gibeonites to a suzerainty treaty, since the oath of the Israelites was obtained by misrepresentation. The frequent warnings against treaties with the Canaanites (Exod. 23:32; 34:12; Deut. 7:2; Judg. 2:2) presumably refer to both kinds of treaties, parity peace treaties, alliances, as well as suzerainty treaties. Any relationship regulated by covenant would ordinarily have been sworn to by Canaanite deities as well as by Yahweh; such recognition of Canaanite gods, many of whom must have had considerable local prestige, would have opened the way (as subsequently was the case) to reception of their cult and religious values by Israelite towns and villages.

It is difficult to interpret the covenant between David and Jonathan (I Sam. 18:3), since no stipulations and no oaths are mentioned in detail. No conclusions at all can be drawn from the mere fact of difference in social status between the two, nor from the fact that Jonathan is said to have made a covenant with David (this may indicate simply that the initiative appropriately came from Jonathan). Presumably this was simply an oath of undying friendship and loyalty, the establishment of a permanent relationship with no stipulated obligations. It is hard to imagine that only one party was bound by this covenant, and therefore this would seem to be a parity covenant, in which the difference in social status became irrelevant.

It is likewise impossible to analyze satisfactorily the narratives concerning the covenant(s) by which David became king. We are not told whether it was David or the elders of Israel (or both) who swore the oath (II Sam. 5:3). Since the kingship meant the conferring of sovereignty, it seems most probable that the elders must have sworn allegiance to the king "before the Lord," but there is no hint that David was bound by oath to any specific obligations.

The same difficulties are inherent in the narrative about David's covenant with Abner (II Sam. 3:12). David's statement of the conditions under which he would enter a covenant with Abner, as well as Abner's promise to "bring over all Israel," seem to imply obligation only on the part of Abner, but this may well have been a two-sided bargain in which David was bound to some promise as well.

At least from Solomon on, the kings had little hesitation in entering into treaties with foreign lands (I Kings 5:12). Asa bribed Ben-hadad to break a treaty with Baasha in order to form an alliance with Judah like that which had existed in the preceding generation (15:19). There is no indication that this was a suzerainty treaty which subjected Judah to Damascus. In I Kings 20:34, Ben-hadad offered concessions of territory and commercial rights as inducement to Ahab's entering into a treaty with him, but the specific terms are not given.

The prophetic indictments of foreign alliances indicate how frequent and commonly accepted such policies were in the later monarchy. It can be assumed that the foundation of such alliances was a covenant, but in the absence of further details, no further discussion is necessary here.

*c. Patron.* This is a type in which the party in superior position binds himself to some obligation for the benefit of an inferior. Surprisingly little evidence exists for this type other than the covenant traditions which bound Yahweh (*see* § C2 *below*). The curious and difficult passage of Isa. 28:15 (the covenant with death) seems to fall into this category, for only "death" seems to be bound not to touch those in the covenant; one suspects that this is a prophetic satire of some sort, ridiculing religious covenant concepts derived from the Abraham-David tradition.

*d. Promissory.* This type, which is extremely important in secular as well as religious tradition,

shows a considerable change from older patterns of behavior and thought, and may well have derived from age-old legal practices. A promissory oath is not primarily intended to establish a new relationship between two parties, but simply guarantees future performance of stipulated obligations. There is thus really one party to this type of covenant, which differs from a vow only in that the vow conditions future stipulated action upon action of deity, whereas the type here termed "promissory oath" is unconditioned. The narrative of II Kings 11:4-12, 17, involves several covenants; first, the "conspiracy" of Jehoiada bound the military leaders to a course of action which would re-establish the Davidic dynasty upon the throne. When this was successfully accomplished, the tokens of kingship (including the עדות, which may have had something to do with the older religious covenant; it is included here simply as one of several acts which established Joash as legitimate king) were given to the king's son. Next, Jehoiada acted as intermediary in establishing a covenant between Yahweh, king, and people, the only stipulation of which is that they "should be the Lord's people." Finally, a covenant between king and people is mentioned with no further detail. The complexity of this procedure is a good indication of the deep crisis which had preceded in the reign of Athaliah. It is an open question whether this covenant established a new relation between the Judeans and Yahweh. Certainly the main import of the covenant was to establish Yahwism as the religion of the state, but the older pattern in which Yahweh was regarded as the initiator, speaking in the first person, cannot be either affirmed or denied from this narrative.

Promissory oaths are more frequent in later narratives. Jer. 34:8 gives an excellent example, in which slaveowners covenant to free their slaves in time of siege—an oath conveniently forgotten when the siege was later, temporarily, lifted. In very similar fashion, Josiah made a covenant, joined in by the people, to obey the commands found in the Book of the Law found in the temple (II Kings 23:3); and in the same way the postexilic community bound itself by a curse and an oath to obey the laws of the Pentateuch (Neh. 10:28-29), to put away foreign wives (Ezra 10:3), and to refrain from foreclosing on real property taken as security for loans, and from taking interest on loans (Neh. 5:11-13). These are all essentially one-party covenants. No new relationship between parties is created by them; they are essentially legislation established by contract between political authority and people, the content of which is derived from religious tradition and regarded as religious obligation, the purpose being to avoid future calamities (Neh. 9:38).

**2. Covenants in which God is bound.** The classical and probably original covenant of this type is the Abrahamic covenant preserved in two forms coming from J (Gen. 15) and P (17:1-14). In the earlier version, Yahweh's covenant is specifically stated to be in response to Abraham's request for certainty of the promise which Yahweh had made. This covenant tradition is of considerable historical importance if, as is here proposed, it became the model for later covenant traditions (Davidic and Noachite). This covenant is attributed by J to pre-

Mosaic times, and is to be accepted as such for the following reasons:

*a*) The narrative of the means by which the covenant is formally established gives every indication of being a very archaic form. The cutting of sacrificial animals into two parts, followed by the promisor's passing between the parts, is paralleled only by Jer. 34 (much later than J, and probably a deliberate archaism there), and a possible parallel in Herodotus coming from Asia Minor. The "smoking fire pot and flaming torch" certainly are a symbolic (and unique) representation of the deity who thus binds himself. It still seems most likely that the passing between the parts is a symbolic identification of the promisor with the animal which was slaughtered —a graphic way of proclaiming the fate of the promisor if he violates the covenant.

*b*) It is known from extrabiblical sources that covenants between the head of a family and a particular deity were customary in pre-Mosaic times.

*c*) It is difficult, if not impossible, to account for the invention of this narrative in post-Mosaic times, or for the peculiar type of covenant involved, for which we have no really good parallel except in those covenant traditions which are here held to be dependent upon the Abrahamic tradition. It may be freely granted that the narrative of Gen. 15 has been colored somewhat by post-Mosaic Israelite tradition, but it can hardly be denied now that some kind of tradition of a covenant between a deity and the patriarchs was an important element in the pre-Mosaic heritage of ancient Israel. The important fact of this covenant in both versions, J and P, is that no obligations are sworn to by Abraham by oath or other formal act, and other later traditions are equally insistent that it is Yahweh who swore the oath to create of Abraham a nation and give to his seed the land. The connection of the covenant with circumcision in P is by no means to be taken as an obligation made binding by the covenant. Rather, it is the "sign" of the covenant, a guarantee through time of the validity of Yahweh's oath, and no more an obligation than it was Noah's obligation to put a rainbow in the sky as a sign of Yahweh's covenant with him. It tied deity and people together by serving simultaneously as a guarantee and as an identifying marker of those in later generations who should become the beneficiaries of Yahweh's promise. The connection of covenant with a "sign" in such fashion seems to be very late in OT history.

Of subsequent covenants in which Yahweh bound himself, the Davidic covenant is by far the most important. This is attested in several sources, from the "last words" of David (II Sam. 23:5) to the words of Abner (3:9) in a somewhat different context, and in various psalms (Pss. 89:3, 28-29; 110:4). In every form of this tradition it is Yahweh alone who is bound to a promise, and it is impossible to make out of this a bilateral covenant by appealing to the traditions (mostly, if not entirely, Deuteronomic) which emphasize the king's obligation to obey the Mosaic law, for there is never any reference to a king's oath until possibly Josiah. It is true that we have no narrative which states how this oath of Yahweh was formally established, that the Davidic dynasty should remain on the throne in perpetuity; and it is com-

pletely unclear how this covenant was promulgated so that it became evidently unquestioned religious conviction on the part of Judah (in sharp contrast to the situation in the N tribes). There can be little doubt that the effect of this covenant tradition, and probably the intention behind it, was to establish a stable state and dynasty to obviate the danger of constant revolution and struggle for power at the death of each king. It is generally accepted that this covenant was promulgated through a "court prophet"; II Sam. 7 (the oracle of Nathan) says nothing about an oath or other symbolic action, and is usually regarded by scholars as a late addition to the narrative of David. The similarity to the covenant with Abraham is formally most impressive, and it seems most likely that the two traditions have influenced each other, so that the promise to Abraham of the land is described in terms reflecting the Davidic empire (Gen. 15:18), as the kingship of the Davidic dynasty is described in terms of the Abrahamic tradition (Ps. 110:4), where, curiously enough, it is Melchizedek (to whom Abraham paid tribute) who is the predecessor of the Davidides (who collected taxes from the descendants of Abraham). In David, the promise to the patriarchs is fulfilled, and renewed.

Finally, in Num. 25:10-13, the same type of covenant is applied to the priestly line of Phinehas, in a passage which seems to be very late in its present form. It shows a complete reversal of the Mosaic covenant tradition, in that Yahweh binds himself in response to something done for his benefit by Phinehas. It establishes a legitimate priestly line, just as the Davidic covenant established the royal line. *See also* ELECTION.

The covenant with Noah is the third of this type, and certainly inspired by the Abraham-David covenant tradition. Again, only Yahweh is bound in a covenant in perpetuity, exactly as in P's account in Gen. 17; Num. 25:12, the benefits of which extend to the lineal descendants, and are guaranteed by a sign (cf. Num. 17:10).

**3. Covenants in which Israel is bound.** In contrast to the Abraham-David-Phinehas-Noah covenant traditions, there is another persistent complex of narratives which is almost directly opposite, and which is in origin almost completely unrelated to them. There can be little doubt that this covenant pattern derives ultimately from Moses and is to be identified with the original, short form of the Decalogue.

*a. The Mosaic covenant.* The OT criticism stemming from Wellhausen maintained that the relation between Yahweh and Israel was a "natural" one; it was a "tribal" religion in which Yahweh was little more than a symbol of the tribe, whose interests were identical to those of the deity, and consequently there could be no conditions attached to this relationship. According to this view, the prophets from Amos on were the first to maintain that the relationship had conditions of an ethical nature attached, and eventually the relationship was conceived of as a covenant in late pre-exilic times. Thus the covenant, from this point of view, was simply a theological idea, a concept for conveying religious truth.

It now seems much more likely that the covenant tradition stemmed rather from events in the time of Moses—the formation of a religious community by covenant, which took place by utilizing forms of action and organization as well as thought, which were widespread in the Late Bronze Age. Thus the covenant is not merely a theological concept, but is rather the original form of social and religious organization which tied together religious experience and conviction, the religious awe and gratitude of the Hebrews of Moses' time with religious obligations which preserved the peace (*see* PEACE IN THE OT) within the group. Thus the covenant, though a religious rather than a political structure, was no more a mere theological concept than politics is a purely philosophical concept today. It seems probable, on the other hand, that the covenant, which originally gave form and structure to the social life of the community, eventually became more of a symbol than a real foundation of the community, in that law in a political structure took the place of the older covenant community. Though religious convictions were held with no less fervor, the concepts and forms of action associated with covenant changed radically in the course of the centuries from Moses to Ezra. Stagnation is not necessarily a religious virtue.

Any comparison of the traditions associated with Moses and the international treaty forms of that time will reveal such striking similarities that the coincidence can hardly be held to be accidental. To a large extent this is true regardless of the particular source of the Pentateuch in which the traditions are preserved, though it is only to be expected that later sources refract and reinterpret older traditions in the light of experience and of other concerns. It is most striking that nearly all the characteristics of the old covenant form described above (§ A) are to be found in the narratives of the formative period of early Israel. Furthermore, it is possible to identify the Decalogue (the "ten words"; *see* TEN COMMANDMENTS) as the original text of the covenant between Yahweh and Israel, though in its present form it has undergone some expansion and interpretation. Early Israel emerged as a religious community on the foundation of this covenant, in which the relation to Yahweh was established in a fashion analogous to that between a suzerain of the Late Bronze Age empires and his vassals. Yahweh was not conceived of as a king, but as a king of kings, who had numerous semi-independent peoples under his control, but who entered into a covenant only with Israel. Since such relationships were inevitably involved with military alliances, it is not surprising that the military obligations of Israel, and reciprocally the features of Yahweh as a "god of war," are strongly emphasized in the narratives of the period from Moses to David. This transference of suzerainty from a flesh-and-blood emperor to a supreme and unique deity was not only a religious revolution; it was simultaneously a protest against the feudalistic imperialisms of that time, a religious expression of the human striving for freedom from an oppressive external political control and exploitation. It was also a development of utmost importance for the history of religion, for it placed moral obligations above political and economic interests in the scale of religious values. The continued existence of any political and economic

institutions was thus conditional upon obedience to the ethical norms stipulated in advance by deity. At the same time, it placed the religious-ethical obligations above institutions and political structures in the scale of human values. The history of the OT is the history of the attempt to harmonize or identify these two.

If the Hittite treaty form is used as the model by which the OT covenant is analyzed, the following features of the narratives about the period of Moses fall into place:

*a*) The preamble is in the Decalogue reduced simply to the words: "I am the LORD your God." No further identification of this suzerain is necessary or possible, except in terms which have to do with his action in history—the historical prologue. The biblical sources are insistent upon the fact that it is Yahweh who gave, commanded, or established the covenant. The exception in Deut. 29:1—H 28:69 is explicitly aware of the fact that what follows is a different covenant tradition.

*b*) The historical prologue is, like all other parts of the Decalogue, extremely brief in comparison with the Hittite treaties, but it has the essentials. The phrase "who brought you out of the land of Egypt" is inseparable grammatically from the identification of the covenant-giver, so that the revelation of the deity is inseparable from the historical events which are the foundation of the covenant itself, and the obligations which it stipulates. In view of the great importance of the historical prologue in covenant forms of this period, it is almost impossible to separate this from the fact that ancient Israel had unique and (from the point of view of ancient times) peculiar historical sense, from which Israelite history-writing ultimately sprang; though certainly the first elaboration of historical narrative, appropriately enough, took the form of poetry (Exod. 15; Judg. 5). Since the covenant itself combined HISTORY and LAW, there can be little doubt that it is this which explains the fact that narrative and law codes are so curiously interwoven in the present form of the PENTATEUCH, at least better than any alternative explanation.

*c*) The stipulations begin with the very same obligation so frequent in the Hittite treaties—the exclusion of relationships to other sovereign powers. Since a deity with whom one has no relationship is unreal and irrelevant (in contrast to a mighty ruler of an empire on one's borders), the beginning of monotheism is to be found here. This exclusive relation to a single god carried with it the obligation to engage in and refrain from war at his command. Little is known for certain of the means by which those commands were communicated, but human "charismatic" leadership certainly had much to do with it. Failure to wage war was breach of covenant among the Hittite vassals, and the same is repeatedly stated or implied in the early narratives (Num. 14; Judg. 5; 21:5). Unwavering trust in the suzerain was also mandatory, and murmuring against him was always regarded as violation of obligation. The narratives of the murmurings in the wilderness (e.g., Num. 11) also treat these actions as punishable. It may be coincidence, but the murmurings which precede the Sinai covenant in the narratives are not punished (cf. Exod. 17:2-7 J). Evil talk has so continuously been regarded as semicriminal that it is hardly safe to draw conclusions from this alone, but the contrast in the treatment of pre- and post-Sinai murmurings can hardly be dismissed with no further consideration.

The so-called "apodictic" form of the Decalogue stipulations ("You shall not . . .") cannot any longer be taken to be proof of a specific *Sitz im Leben* distinct from the "case law" form ("if . . . , then . . ."; Exod. 21:1–22:25 *passim*), for both the Hittite treaties and laws, and the "Covenant Code" of Exod. 21–23 include laws of both types.

The stipulations define the interests of the suzerain which the vassal is bound to protect, and to considerable extent have to do with regulations which preserve the peace within the domain of the suzerain. There can be little doubt that the content of the Decalogue, as well as its predominantly negative stipulations, points in the same direction. By placing the people under oath to refrain from the acts prescribed by these stipulations, there is a horror in the community of the sort of acts which are precisely those most likely to disrupt the peace. Murder, theft, adultery, false oaths, false accusation, insubordination of children, and religious schism are certainly among the most common sources of internal conflict, and all were actionable in ancient law outside Israel. Except for the SABBATH observance (even the prohibition of coveting has a partial parallel in Hittite sources), the content of the Decalogue was not so different from the customary law of the pagan nations of antiquity. It was the religious conception of God and the relation of man to God in the covenant that sharply distinguished Israel from ancient pagan peoples; above all it was the fact that obedience to the commands of God took precedence over other concerns, by making temporal blessing and calamity dependent upon ethical or moral norms, which law had to serve, not create.

*d*) The traditional text of the Decalogue ends with the stipulations, but in the narratives of the Pentateuch the other elements of the Hittite treaty form appear, and survive into the books of JOSHUA; JUDGES. The provision for deposit of the written covenant and its periodic public reading is found repeatedly, though in the later sources. Deut. 10:5 (and elsewhere in the Deuteronomic history) states that the tables of stone were placed in the ARK OF THE COVENANT, as does the Priestly source (here called the עֵדוּת as in Exod. 31:18) in Exod. 40:20. Since the ark was almost certainly a portable sanctuary, this tradition is exactly in keeping with customary procedure in pre-Mosaic times, and the fact that it is attested only in later sources proves nothing unless it can be shown that the later tradition contrasts with some more likely earlier narrative with regard to the disposition of the stone tables, unless a flat denial of the historical possibility of the existence of the stone tablets be regarded as the better solution of the problem. The provision for public reading of the stipulations is preserved in one form in Deut. 31: 10-11, but there are frequent references to the public recitation both of historical traditions and of the "laws" (Deut. 26:1-11; 27; 31:9-13, 22; Josh. 4:6-7; 8:30-35; private, family recitation is especially emphasized also in Deut. 6:20-25 and elsewhere). The 2½ centuries of history from Moses to David must have seen a variety of customs, covenant formulations, and the like which make it impossible for us to distinguish sharply between the Mosaic or postconquest patterns of covenant and cultic celebrations (which certainly were closely connected). If the covenant patterns of the Late Bronze Age were followed, a new covenant should have been established with (perhaps) new stipulations every generation for some ten generations before the time of David. The personal appearance of every male Israelite before the Lord (Exod. 34:23; Deut. 16:16) three times a year corresponds to a similar requirement of the Hittite vassals that they appear before the Hittite king at stipulated intervals.

*e*) The list of witnesses (*see* WITNESS), so characteristic of Hittite treaties and necessary for binding legal documents in ancient law, could not have a parallel in the exclusive covenant between Yahweh and Israel. Yet there exists a persistent search for adequate witnesses until the NT martyrs. It has been pointed out above that witnesses to the Hittite treaties, in addition to the gods, included features of the natural world. These appear also with regularity in biblical sources in a similar role, from Deut. 32 to the Prophets (Isa. 1:2; Mic. 6:1-2). Beyond this, other narratives appeal as witnesses to the people (Josh. 24:22), a stone (vs. 27; and cf. Gen. 31:47).

*f*) The BLESSINGS AND CURSINGS appear in such variety that little need be said of this as a part of the Israelite covenant traditions. The list of Deut. 27–28 is most detailed, but it is not only in the Pentateuch that the blessings and cursings appear. The entire prophetic tradition of pre-exilic times is tied to this aspect of the covenant. Both are predominantly natural phenomena (in extrabiblical covenants as well): fertility and famine, health and disease, victory and defeat in war, peace and utter destruction.

*g*) The OATH itself is lacking in both the Israelite and the Hittite covenants, though there is no doubt that this was the formality which made the covenant valid. There seems little reason to doubt that the oath was frequently a symbolic action, which took many forms in antiquity: it was that act or verbal statement which distinguished a most solemn, binding promise from any casual or even rash promise made on the spur of the moment. Frequently in antiquity this involved the slaughter of an animal. Almost any action recognized by both parties to a covenant as such might serve to make a promise one which could not, on pain of catastrophe, be violated. The OT alone gives a surprising number of such forms, from the purely verbal oaths of I Sam. 3:17; 25:34 to the symbolic actions of Gen. 15; Jer. 34; the covenant meals of Gen. 26:30 (where the oath-taking is distinguished from the feast, however); 31:54; the "covenant of salt" (Num. 18:19); and the ritual of Exod. 24:5-8, which is preceded by the words: "All the words which the LORD has spoken we will do." For this action of sprinkling blood upon altar and people there is no extrabiblical source which aids in interpretation; it is simply that which formally placed the covenant in effect, like the signing of a legal contract.

**b. The covenant of Joshua.** The narrative in Josh. 24 preserves almost all the features of the covenant as just described, but differs so radically in detail that it must be regarded as an independent narrative. In addition to the characteristic address in which Yahweh speaks in the first person, the historical content of the prologue contains unique features. Where the stipulations are expected, the narrative breaks off, and Joshua begins to speak. The break has already been noticed on other grounds by scholars; it is possible that the missing stipulations are to be sought somewhere in the Pentateuch (Deut. 27 has been suggested), but there is little use in speculating about this. Only the blessings and cursings are absent, and this would tend to reinforce the connection of Deut. 27 with Josh. 24. Whether this narrative preserves some historical connection with the formation of the federation of twelve tribes is uncertain, but it is still impossible to find any basis for the unity and yet diversity of these groups other than a covenant, which bound them to religious, ethical, and military obligations and yet left a very considerable degree of local self-determination and independence.

*c. The reform of Josiah.* After the long period of the monarchy, in which the old covenant traditions gave way to new social, legal, and religious patterns of thought and organization, there was a resurgence of the older traditions, initiated by the discovery of a lawbook in the Jerusalem temple. According to the narrative of II Kings 23, King Josiah made a covenant, joined in by all the people, to follow the "words of this covenant that were written in this book" (vs. 3). This event furnished in many important respects the foundations of the Judaism which arose after the Exile, for the action of Josiah was essentially a legislation by covenant, in which the accumulated body of legal customs and norms derived from the past (reflected fairly adequately in the present book of Deuteronomy) was identified with the covenant obligations to Yahweh. The prestige and coercive power of the state were put at the disposal of this tradition of religious law. Though this reform did not succeed, it established a pattern which held until the destruction of Jerusalem in A.D. 70, and after, in that it completely identified covenant obligations with a law code (or rather, collection of laws), and attempted to enforce them by political means. This covenant, however, was not one which established a relationship; it established a pattern of legal norms, and was more like a promissory oath than a covenant between two parties. If there were two parties in this covenant, it was king and people, not Yahweh and people. Though the broader aspects of religion as a personal relationship between deity and the individual were by no means lost, still this relationship could henceforth find legitimate expression only within the framework of the accumulated ethnic, cultural, and legal traditions of the Jews.

*d. The covenant of Ezra.* A century and more after the return of some exiles to Jerusalem and environs, initiative from the community still in exile resulted in action dedicated to bring the life of the Jerusalem community more into harmony with the demands of the religious legal traditions. A solemn convocation took place in which the law of God was formally enacted as binding upon the community with "a curse and an oath" (Neh. 10:29). Neh. 9-10 still preserves a historical narrative, but in the form of a prayer of Ezra, with emphasis upon the sins of Israel and the consequent punishment. In sharp contrast to the book of Job, the poverty, distress, and political subjection of the postexilic community are attributed to the failure of the Jews to obey the law, and "because of this" the princes, Levites, and priests make a firm covenant and set a seal to it (Neh. 9:38). From this time on, there is an official orthodoxy, in which the covenant is primarily the oath to obey the accumulated traditions as collected, interpreted, and preserved in the canonized Torah. Two traditions have fallen together. Yahweh is bound by the covenant with Abraham; and Israel is bound by the Sinai covenant as expanded in the collected law codes, now enforced by the political authority of the Jewish state. Henceforth, the primary problem is that of hermeneutics, of interpreting the Scriptures, which are final authority. History itself comes to an end with the Chronicler; no further historical work became canonical. The law was final; all that remained was securing obedience to it, and its adaptation to changes in outward circumstances.

**D. COVENANT IN POSTBIBLICAL JUDAISM.** The reform of Ezra was eminently successful, for covenant and law were entirely identified with each other during this period. Every Jew was presumed to be bound by the covenant at Sinai, but the problem of interpretation, of applying old legal norms to the contemporary world, remained. CIRCUMCISION (the covenant with Abraham) was the basis of obligation to Torah (cf. Gal. 5:3).

In the Qumran community, however, the covenant plays a more functional role in religious life, as a means for the accession of new members. The community regarded itself as that of the "new covenant" (Jer. 31:31), and in the description of the provisions for reception of new members there is a surprisingly close adherence to the old biblical traditions. The Manual of Discipline provides for a recitation of all the gracious acts of God, followed by a recitation of the sins of Israel and a confession of sin by those who are about to enter the community. There follows the priestly blessing, and the Levitical curse on those who "have cast their lot with Belial"; those who are entering the covenant respond: "Amen, amen." There is little room for doubt that the rules of discipline of the community are regarded as the authoritative, normative interpretation of Mosaic law, and the purpose of the initiatory rite is to bind every member to obedience to that discipline: "Everyone who is admitted to the council of the community shall enter into a covenant . . . and bind himself by an oath to abide with all his heart and soul by the commandments of the Law of Moses, as that Law is revealed to the sons of Zadok—that is, to the priests who still keep the covenant and seek God's will." As elsewhere in Judaism, the covenant is completely identified with the biblical law, but the community interpretation thereof is the only true one. In this respect, the most important fact about the Qumran community is that it is based, not on nationhood or statehood, but upon a solemn oath. It was a secret-covenant community whose members had a relationship to God and to one another based upon this solemn oath to obey the community interpretation of divine law. It is not surprising that the covenant is that symbol which sums up in one word the whole content of Qumran religious life and faith. The covenant is truth, everlasting, the source of joy, strength, and enlightenment; it is also Torah, the statutes of God, the law of Moses. Particularly interesting is the fact that even this solemn oath is not to be sworn by a divine name, for subsequent violation of the oath would require a penalty of death. Rather, the oath is sworn by the curses (a distinction impossible in earlier times), so that disobedience is punishable by "guilt-offering, confession, and restitution."

**E. COVENANT IN THE NT.** The surprising infrequency of references to covenant in the NT raises great difficulties, even though it is understandable. The covenant for Judaism meant the Mosaic law, and for the Roman Empire a covenant meant an illegal secret society. This two-sided conflict made it nearly impossible for early Christianity to use the term meaningfully. Of the thirty-three occurrences of διαθήκη, nearly half are either quotations from the OT or references to the OT covenants; hence it is very difficult to decide whether the covenant in the NT is a theological concept inherited from Judaism, or was taken seriously as the formal basis of the relation of the early Christians to one another and to Christ. On the basis of the little evidence available, one may conclude that, for a time at least, the early Christians did regard themselves as a community bound together by covenant, but that this covenant is a most free, creative reinterpretation of the older traditions.

The primary source for this conclusion is, of course, to be found in the narratives of the LAST SUPPER (Matt. 26:28; Mark 14:24; Luke 22:20; I Cor. 11:25). In every source the blood is very specifically stated to be related to the (new) covenant, with obvious reference to the blood of the old covenant in Exod. 24:8. In the light of covenant forms, there seems to be no reason to doubt that this act was intended as the formal rite which established a covenant relationship. Since Homer, libations involving a cup of wine were so normal a form of sealing treaties that σπονδαί ("libations") became the term for "treaty." Libations are frequently referred to (and condemned by the prophets; e.g., Jer. 7:18) in the OT, but never demonstrably as a form connected with the establishment of a covenant.

Is it possible to connect the Last Supper with OT covenant traditions, beyond the reference to the "blood of the covenant"? The very brief account yields little, but conjecture points to numerous possibilities. The tie between historical events and covenant relationship, so characteristic of the OT Mosaic tradition, may have its parallel in the generally accepted view that Jesus' reference to his blood was a deliberate reference to his anticipated death, and there can be no doubt that the church connected the two. The establishment of the covenant thus anticipated the historical event upon which the covenant was based. Furthermore, the absence of any obligations stipulated in the covenant can be treated in two ways. First, there can be no doubt that the covenant was one which, above all, created a personal relationship—a community of interest, so to speak— in which the stipulation of obligations of one party to the other was superfluous. Second, the Gospel of John, which preserves no historical narrative of the Last Supper, but which contains much interpretation of it, has a reference to a "new commandment" appropriate to a "new covenant" (John 13:34). The commandment of love (see LOVE IN THE NT) thus corresponds to the very nature of the covenant itself. There is nothing new about this command except its place in the covenant relationship, as the stipulated obligation assumed by those who enter the covenant community, if this interpretation is correct. The other usual elements in a binding covenant are not present in this narrative, but there are hints here and there in Paul and Hebrews (see below) that certain patterns of thought derived from them may be present in NT sources. As pointed out above, the very purpose of a covenant was to bind together the two parties in a firm relationship; this becomes the whole of the covenant in the NT, centering on Christ, for nothing is more strongly emphasized in the NT than this relationship between Christ and the NT church. It is not accidental, moreover, that the relationship finds its deepest expression in the Eucharist. Unfortunately, the clearest description of the NT church as a covenant-bound community comes from Pliny the Younger (ca. 112). In his famous Letter to Trajan he describes how the Christians "come together to bind themselves by an oath." It is easy to see why he would, in the light of Greek σπονδαί, interpret the Eucharist as an oath, but it is by no means clear that he can be trusted as an early witness to what the early Christians believed concerning the Eucharist. All that can be concluded here is the fact that both the words of institution at the Last Supper and the letter of Pliny point in the same direction: namely, that the Eucharist was regarded as the formal act which established a lasting relationship between the community and Christ, in analogy to the Mosaic covenant, but combining with it a number of motifs from OT sources, including the sacrificial animal, the Suffering Servant (Isa. 53:11-12; Matt. 26:28), and the new covenant of Jer. 31:31-34.

With this thesis several facts harmonize. The stern warning of Paul in I Cor. 11:27 that those who eat the bread or drink the cup of the Lord in an unworthy manner are guilty of "profaning" the body and blood of the Lord and bring condemnation upon themselves, can well be brought into the general context of patterns of thought involving breach of covenant; but, characteristically enough, it is not breach of a legal form, but an offense against the body of the living Lord which brings illness and death—and this is evidently regarded as the judgment of the Lord, as vss. 31-32 indicate. We find a very similar point of view in Heb. 10:26-31. In contrast to the Qumran oath, "there no longer remains a sacrifice for sins," and an even greater punishment than that provided for by the Mosaic covenant awaits him who has "spurned the Son of God, and profaned the blood of the covenant by which he was sanctified, and outraged the Spirit of grace." This is followed again by the reference to the judgment of God (vs. 30), but even more significant is the fact that in vs. 19 it is explicitly stated that entrance to the sanctuary is "by the blood of Jesus." All this again points to a pattern of thought inherited from the older covenant tradition, in which the cup takes the place of an oath by which a relationship is permanently established and cannot be broken without incurring a fearful judgment at the hands of God himself.

Since the relationship to Christ is both the content and the obligation (as well as the form, in the body and blood of Christ) of the covenant, all the detailed prescriptions of Jewish law are both unnecessary and (for Paul) inimical to Christianity. In Eph. 2:12-13 the Gentiles, once "strangers to the covenants of promise," and "far off," have been "brought near in the blood of Christ." Whether this refers to the Crucifixion or to the Eucharist is probably immaterial, for they are inseparable, and the latter is historically an anticipation of the former.

In Gal. 4:21-28 the old and new covenants are contrasted as the children of slavery and those born free. In II Cor. 3:6 also, the new covenant, of which Paul is a "minister," is a covenant in the Spirit, in contrast to the written code. There can be no doubt that Paul continues and expresses in detail that which is present in the Synoptic tradition—namely, that the new covenant rejected the detailed stipulation of religious obligation characteristic of the Jewish identification of covenant with law. This must go back to Jesus himself, for only John (and by implication only) connects any obligation of the Christian community with covenant—the obligation of love.

In Gal. 3:16, Paul applies the covenant of Abraham to Christ. It is ironical that the blessing of the nations takes the form of delivering them from the curse of the law which came after Abraham, in addition to the "promise of the Spirit through faith."

The Letter to the Hebrews utilizes much more frequently the covenant tradition, but in almost exactly the same way as Paul. Every possible argument is drawn on to show that the new covenant both fulfils and abrogates the old. In 7:1-22 the passage of Ps. 110:4 is applied to Jesus, with the conclusion that Jesus is the "surety" (or "mediator") of a better covenant. Ch. 8 strongly argues that the old covenant is obsolete, drawing on Jer. 31:31-34; and in the subsequent chapter (9), the concern for Levitical purity is contrasted with the purifying of the conscience by the blood of Christ. The regular, repeated sacrifices of OT law are contrasted sharply with the once-for-all sacrifice in which Christ gave his own blood to put away sin. There is an incidental argument drawn from the Greek usage of διαθήκη to refer to a "last will and testament." There can be no doubt, however, that this is simply an apologetical argument, and cannot be taken seriously as the framework of the author's conception of the covenant, which is entirely within the OT pattern of thought. This great emphasis on covenant in the Letter to the Hebrews, which argues for the substitution of the new covenant for the old, is itself a strong indication that the early church did take the covenant seriously. The old religious security of the Jewish covenant traditions would not likely have been used as the point of attack were it not for the fact that Christianity also had a covenant regarded as just as real as those of the OT.

In spite of all that has been proposed above, it is difficult to avoid the conclusion that for Western Christianity at least, both the astounding creativity of the early church and the radical break with Jewish forms and associated patterns of thought very soon produced a structure of religious thought and life in which the old covenant patterns were not really useful as a means of communication, and may have been dangerous in view of the Roman prohibition of secret societies.

All we can conclude is that the Last Supper is certainly the central feature of early Christian life, in which the community was bound together with Christ; but the important features of the Mosaic covenant, the stipulations, are absent. On the other hand, the history of God's act in Christ, the exclusive relationship to God through Christ, the curse done away with by the Cross, the blessings of freedom in Christ and life here and hereafter, and even the judgment of God for rejection of the covenant relationship—all so important and constant features bound up with covenant traditions in the OT—are taken up in the NT and are inseparable both from the person of Jesus and from the sacrament of the Eucharist.

The NT experience of Christ was one which could not be contained within the framework of a quasi-legal terminology or pattern of thought and action. Neither the act of God in Christ nor the religious obligation of man to God could be adequately expressed in language. Therefore the Word became flesh. The letters of man's poor alphabet had to take second rank behind the person of a living being, the Christ, as the means of communicating the message of God. And yet the Sinai covenant of the OT and the NT covenant in Christ's blood are one: each created a people of God out of those who were no people, demanded the complete self-surrender to God as a joyful response to the love of God which preceded. The simple stipulations of the Decalogue were summed up in the yet simpler obligation of love at Jesus' command—but this is no command; it is rather the very nature of the relationship between God and the community.

*Bibliography.* V. Korosec, *Hethitische Staatsverträge* (1931); J. Jeremias, *Die Abendmahlsworte Jesu* (1949); G. E. Mendenhall, *Law and Covenant in Israel and the Ancient Near East* (1955); N. Clark, *An Approach to the Theology of the Sacraments* (1956); M. Noth, *Gesammelte Studien zum AT* (1957), pp. 142-54.

See also the various theologies of the OT, especially Eichrodt (1955), vol. I. G. E. MENDENHALL

**COVENANT, BOOK OF THE** [ספר ברית]. In Exod. 24:7, Moses is reported to have read from the "book of the covenant" in connection with the ceremony of covenant-making at Mount Sinai. The expression is frequently taken to refer to the collection of laws found in Exod. 20:23-23:33. More probably, however, it refers to the written stipulations of the covenant between Yahweh and Israel which developed throughout the course of Israelite history. See II Kings 23:2-3, 21; II Chr. 34:30-31.

*See also* LAW IN THE OT; TEN COMMANDMENTS; COVENANT; JOSIAH; MOSES.

*Bibliography.* A. Jepsen, *Untersuchungen zum Bundesbuch* (1927). J. Morgenstern, "The Book of the Covenant," *HUCA,* V (1927), 1-151; VII (1930), 19-258; VIII-IX (1931-32), 1-150, 741-46. R. H. Pfeiffer, "The Transmission of the Book of the Covenant," *HTR,* 24 (1931), 99-109. A. Alt, *Die Ursprünge des israelitischen Rechts* (1934). H. Cazelles, *Étude sur le code de l'alliance* (1946). W. J. HARRELSON

**COVERINGS** [מרבדים, *from* רבד, to bespread, deck]; KJV COVERINGS OF TAPESTRY. Fabric goods, used as bedspreads (Prov. 7:16, where the cognate verb occurs) or, apparently, as clothing (31:22).

**COVERLET** [מכבר] (II Kings 8:15); KJV THICK CLOTH. Apparently a cloth of some sort which Hazael dipped in water and spread upon the face of Ben-hadad until he smothered. From the cognates כברה, "sieve" (Amos 9:9), and מכבר, "grating" (Exod. 27:4, etc.), the suggestion is sometimes made that this is a netted cloth.                                    E. M. GOOD

**COVETOUSNESS** [אוה, חמד, בצע (Isa. 57:17), *more often* UNJUST GAIN; πλεονεξία]. Throughout the Bible, the desire to have something for oneself or to have more than one already possesses. The object of such desire is always material, even in Deut. 5:21; Exod. 20:17, where the neighbor's wife and servants are regarded as material possessions.

Covetousness is always considered in the Bible as sinful, for a variety of reasons. Its prohibition in the two forms of the Decalogue is based upon the promise of land and servants to Israel, a promise in which every Israelite is entitled to share. To deprive a man of his property is thus to deprive him of his God-given inheritance (cf. Mic. 2:2; Rom. 7:7; 13:9). The sin of Achan, however (Josh. 7:21), is his failure to obey the ancient law of ḥērem, to devote to the Lord that which is his. In Prov. 21:26, the whole background of the wisdom teaching is present: the care of the righteous for the needy, the faith that God's gifts will suffice for the good man, the divine reward for liberality. (In later Jewish literature almsgiving becomes synonymous with righteousness.) However, usually and especially in the NT covetousness is considered a hindrance to true worship and faith in God. Where a man's treasure is, there is his heart; he who loves material possessions cannot truly love God (Mark 7:22; Luke 12:15; cf. Rom. 1:29). Thus in some passages covetousness is identified with idolatry (Eph. 5:3, 5; Col. 3:5); recognition of this fact helps in interpreting the difficult text of Isa. 57:17.

                                    E. R. ACHTEMEIER

Courtesy of Foto Marburg

51. Cow with calf tied to her leg, from sarcophagus of Princess Kawit at Deir el-Bahri

**COW** [עגלה (Isa. 7:21), *see* CALF; *for* פרה, בקר, ארף (*feminine of* פר), שור, *see* Ox]; KJV KINE as the plural. The basic function of the cow, the reproduc-

tion of its kind, is referred to in Lev. 22:27-28; Deut. 7:13; 28:4, 18, 51; Job 21:10; and its suckling of calves in I Sam. 6:7. In one instance a milch cow is put to work drawing a wagon (I Sam. 6:7-8). Forty cows constituted part of the cattle gift to Esau (Gen. 32:15—H 32:16). CURDS were produced from cows' milk (Deut. 32:14; Isa. 7:21-22; the meaning of שפות [RSV "cheese"] in II Sam. 17:29 is uncertain), but such a product was incidental to breeding calves, and there is no evidence that cows were exploited for dairy purposes; moreover, the pasturage for milch cows in Palestine was much scarcer than that for goats. The MILK in Ezek. 25:4 would include that from cows, camels, and goats; the ten cheeses (lit., "cuts of milk") sent by Jesse in I Sam. 17:18 may have been made of goats' milk.

The only figurative uses of "cow" occur in the imagery of Joseph's dream (Gen. 41) and in Amos. In Amos 4:1 the luxury-loving women of Samaria, who condone the rampant injustice, are likened to the cattle for which Bashan was well known (cf. Deut. 32:14; Ps. 22:12—H 22:13; Ezek. 39:18).

Figs. COW 51; MIL 49.                    W. S. McCULLOUGH

**COZ.** KJV form of KOZ.

**COZBI** kŏz′bĭ [כזבי; Akkad. *kuzbu,* voluptuousness]. Daughter of ZUR, one of the chiefs of MIDIAN. Zimri took her to his family's house, and as a result both were slain by Phinehas, thus averting a plague (Num. 25:6-15). The Talmud (Sanh. 82*a*) also implies that Cozbi succeeded in seducing Moses himself.

                                    J. F. ROSS

**COZEBA** kō zē′bə [כזבה, falsehood] (I Chr. 4:22); KJV CHOZEBA. A village in the Judean highlands, possibly to be identified with Khirbet ed-Dilb (where there is Early Iron pottery) near el-'Arrub, W of Tekoa. Many writers identify Cozeba with ACHZIB (Josh. 15:44) and CHEZIB (Gen. 38:5).

                                    V. R. GOLD

**CRACKNELS.** The KJV translation of קדים (from נקד, to prick; RSV "some cakes") in I Kings 14:3. *See* BAKING; BREAD § 1*d*.

**CRAFTS.** The manual arts requiring special skill. Those engaged in the crafts are called artisans, skilled workers, craftsmen, etc. In the Bible translations, "craftsmen" is usually reserved for those who work in wood. *See* CARPENTER; CARVING; WOOD.

Many of the crafts were performed in the home by both men and women. There were probably no smiths in Israel until the time of David (*see* METALLURGY; I Sam. 13:19 ff). Contact with developed Canaanite civilization after the Conquest, and later with the Babylonians during the Exile, increased the number of craftsmen in Israel. Until after the Exile, it is thought, skilled workers were illiterate. After the Exile and in NT times the rabbis were often independent by virtue of their skill in some craft (*see* PAUL). In Talmudic times rabbis would not take money for their teaching but would take the exchange of skilled services from their students. Labor was honorable.

The craftsman was usually a free artisan. In the

ancient Near East only a small number of slaves were trained in these skills. There were guilds of craftsmen in Palestine after the Exile (Neh. 3:8). Goldsmiths helped rebuild the walls of Jerusalem. Synagogue reports from Alexandria refer to smiths in gold and silver and to weavers. A second-century-A.D. inscription in Asia Minor refers to a Jewish guild of dyers and weavers.

Shops were kept by craftsmen (Jer. 18:2), but business and much of the work was conducted out of doors (I Kings 20:34). The people of a single craft often occupied a special quarter in an Israelite town (Neh. 11:35; Isa. 7:3; Jer. 37:21). The list of craftsmen is great, including: carpenters; furniture makers; boatbuilders; wood carvers; carvers in ivory, ebony, and alabaster; smiths in gold, silver, and bronze; weavers; tanners; leatherworkers; tentmakers; carpetmakers; ropemakers; basket weavers; fullers; dyers; sculptors; jewelers; glassworkers; potters; lampmakers etc. *See* OCCUPATIONS.

God is described as the greatest artisan of all (Heb. 11:10).

**Bibliography.** I. Mendelsohn, "Free Artisans and Slaves in Mesopotamia," *BASOR*, LXXXIX (1943), 25 ff; A. Lucas, *Ancient Egyptian Materials and Industries* (1948).

C. U. WOLF

**CRAFTSMEN, VALLEY OF.** *See* GE-HARASHIM.

**CRANE** [עגור (KJV SWALLOW), *cf.* Akkad. *egerū;* KJV סוס, סיס (RSV "swallow")]. Any of a class of tall wading birds with long bills, necks, and legs, of the order *Gruiformes,* of the family *Gruidae.* Tristram noted the large number of these rather noisy birds which passed over Palestine in their spring migration to more northerly lands (*NHB* 239-41).

The meaning of עגור is uncertain. The LXX omits it in Isa. 38:14, and in Jer. 8:7 renders it as "small birds of the field." It is generally agreed that the verb צפף, "to chirp, peep," used in Isa. 38:14 (RSV "clamor"), can hardly describe the trumpeting or bellowing of the crane. G. R. Driver (*see bibliography*) notes various alternative identifications; his own preference is for the wryneck (of the genus *Jynx*). R. B. Y. Scott (*see bibliography*), on Isa. 38:14, favors an emendation to read עוגר (cf. Dead Sea Scroll 1QIs^a: עוגר), and obtains the phrase "like an unhappy swallow."

**Bibliography.** G. R. Driver, *PEQ* (May-Oct., 1955), p. 132; R. B. Y. Scott, Exegesis of Isaiah, *IB*, V (1956), 376.

W. S. McCULLOUGH

**CRATES** krā'tēz [Κράτης] (II Macc. 4:29). Viceroy of Cyprus during the brief occupation of the island by Antiochus Epiphanes. Crates was general of the mercenaries who came from Cyprus to support Sostratus, the governor of the citadel in Jerusalem; he served as the latter's deputy atnd successor after Sostratus demanded payment from Menelaus of the money he had promised to pay the king for the priesthood he obtained.

**Bibliography.** S. Tedesche and S. Zeitlin, *II Maccabees,* II (1954), 137.

S. B. HOENIG

**CRAWLING THINGS** [זחלי (Deut. 32:24; Mic. 7: 17), crawlers, *from* זחל, to crawl away; רמש (Hab. 1:

14), creeper, *from* רמש, to creep]; KJV SERPENTS (Deut. 32:24), WORMS (Mic. 7:17), CREEPING THINGS (Hab. 1:14). In Deut. 32:24 the reference is to poisonous snakes (cf. the same threat in Jer. 8:17); in Mic. 7:17 to reptiles generally, whose lowly life serves to symbolize the abasement of the Gentiles; in Hab. 1:14 to water creatures, seemingly other than fish, taken in a net.

W. S. McCULLOUGH

**CREATION.** In the Bible (with the possible exception of wisdom literature) the doctrine of creation does not stand by itself but depends upon and elaborates the redemptive activity of God in history. In the OT, creation is viewed in the light of Israel's covenant faith, of which it is both the presupposition and the fulfilment; and in the NT creation is viewed christologically—i.e., in the light of God's revelation in Jesus Christ and the "new creation" which through him has already become a historical reality. In both Testaments, the doctrine stresses the complete dependence of the whole creation upon the Creator, the supreme position of honor and responsibility which God has given man, and the divine purpose which undergirds and controls the historical drama from its beginning to its consummation.

1. History and creation
   *a.* Ancient cosmology and mythology
   *b.* The origin of Israel's creation faith
   *c.* Creation as the beginning of history
2. The sovereignty of the Creator
   *a.* Creation by the Word
   *b.* Creation *ex nihilo*
   *c.* The harmony and goodness of the creation
   *d.* Man's position of honor
3. Beginning and end
   *a.* Threats to God's creation
   *b.* The new creation
4. Creation viewed christologically
   *a.* Christ and creation
   *b.* The new creation in Christ
Bibliography

1. **History and creation.** The NT inherits and transforms the OT faith that God created all things (Acts 4:24; 14:15; 17:24; Eph. 3:9; Rev. 4:11; 10:6); and likewise the OT creation faith, as expressed consummately in the creation stories of Genesis, the message of Second Isaiah, and various psalms (e.g., Pss. 8; 19; 104), both presupposes and radically transforms the cosmological views of antiquity (*see* COSMOGONY; WORLD, NATURE OF THE). The OT affirms that Yahweh, the God of Israel, is the creator of heaven and earth. And since the meaning of the special divine name was given to Israel in her historical experiences, as interpreted by a series of prophetic figures beginning with Moses (*see* GOD, NAMES OF, § B), Yahweh's creative work was understood in a completely different sense from the prevalent creation beliefs among Babylonians, Egyptians, or Canaanites.

*a. Ancient cosmology and mythology.* In a formal sense there are numerous points of contact between Israel's creation faith and the cosmological views of antiquity. The Bible takes for granted a three-storied structure of the universe: heaven, earth, and underworld (Exod. 20:4). According to this *Weltbild,* the earth is a flat surface, corrugated by mountains and divided by rivers and lakes. Above the earth—like a huge dome—is spread the firmament, which holds back the heavenly ocean and supports the dwelling place of the gods (Gen. 1:8; Ps. 148:4). The earth itself is founded upon pillars which are sunk into the subterranean waters (Pss. 24:2; 104:5), in the depths of which is located Sheol. In this view, the habitable world is surrounded by the waters of chaos, which, unless held back, would engulf the world in chaos (Gen. 7:11; cf. 1:6).

In various ways ancient peoples affirmed that the world emerged out of primordial chaos. In Babylonian mythology the origin of the three-storied universe was traced to a fierce struggle between divine powers that emerged from uncreated chaos—Marduk the god of order and Tiamat the goddess of chaos. Victorious in the struggle, Marduk split the fishlike body of the monster down the middle, thus making a separation between the upper and lower parts of her body (cf. Gen. 1:6). The OT contains reminiscences of this creation myth, for we hear of Yahweh's primordial battle with sea monsters named Rahab or Leviathan (Job 9:13; Pss. 74:13-14; 89:10; Isa. 27:1; 51:9), and of his action in setting bounds for the sea (Ps. 104:7-9; Prov. 8:27-29; see WATER). Moreover, the Hebrew word for "Deep, Abyss" (תהום), is linguistically related to the Tiamat of the Babylonian myth (see DEEP, THE). But these are very distant echoes. Although the Bible takes for granted the contours of ancient cosmology, it has demythologized the ancient understanding of existence. The OT contains no theogony, no myth which traces the creation to a primordial battle between divine powers, no ritual which enabled men to repeat the mythological drama and thereby ensure the supremacy of the national god. Mythological allusions have been torn out of their ancient context of polytheism and nature religion, and have acquired a completely new meaning within the historical syntax of Israel's faith. The pagan language survives only as poetic speech for the adoration of Yahweh, the Lord of history.

***b. The origin of Israel's creation faith.*** The earliest cultic summaries of Israel's faith did not refer to Yahweh as creator but concentrated, rather, on his mighty deeds of history by which he made himself known and constituted Israel as his people. To be sure, the Israelite knew and confessed that the God who was mighty in history could also make the forces of nature serve his purpose. He prepared a path for his people through the Red Sea (Exod. 15:21), preserved them in the wilderness by performing SIGNS AND WONDERS, and rescued their army at the Battle of Megiddo by causing the stars to fight on their side and the River Kishon to overflow its banks (Judg. 5:20-21). Nevertheless, reference to the Creation is conspicuously absent in the early summary of *Heilsgeschichte* in Deut. 26:5-10, and this is the more striking when one compares the late summary found in Neh. 9:6-31, which begins with the Creation.

It is doubtful whether this silence necessarily argues that the creation faith was either unknown or unimportant in the early period of Israel. It would be strange indeed if Israel had taken no account of a belief which figured prominently in the religions of the cultural environment. Although the date of

Gen. 14 is uncertain, it is noteworthy that in this passage the title of El Elyon (*see* GOD, NAMES OF, § C2*b*), "Maker [קנה] of heaven and earth," is applied to Yahweh (vss. 19, 22). The title has been appropriated from Canaanite religion, as evidenced by the occurrence of the verb in the Ras Shamra mythological texts and the expression *El qn 'rṣ* in the Phoenician inscription of Karatepe. Furthermore, an old poetic fragment found in Solomon's temple address affirms that "Yahweh has set the sun in the heavens" (I Kings 8:12; text reconstructed on the basis of the LXX). Also, a number of scholars hold that in the pre-exilic period Yahweh's creative work was celebrated at the fall New Year's Festival, just as Marduk's victory over Tiamat was celebrated in the liturgy of the Babylonian New Year's Festival, and that several psalms have come out of that cultic situation (Pss. 24; 47; 93-100). Finally, the creation stories of Gen. 1-2 must be considered, not only in terms of their date of literary composition, but also in terms of the age of the tradition they preserve. The Yahwist's story (Gen. 2:4*b*-25; cf. 6:6-7; 7:4; *see* J), although it actually does not deal with creation in its broadest sense, dates back to the time of the early monarchy, probably Solomon's reign; and it is not impossible that its terse reference to the "day that Yahweh God made the earth and the heavens" implies a longer account of the creation of the earth which has been superseded by the priestly account (*see* P). Creation is dealt with most comprehensively and intensively in the latter (Gen. 1:1–2:4*a*). The P account is usually dated in the time of the Exile or later, but careful study of its form and content indicates that the present version is the end result of tradition, whose development extended over a considerable period of time.

Nevertheless, it is a striking fact that in the early period of Israel's history the creation faith did not have the prominence that was given it in later times. The first prophet to reckon seriously with the doctrine was Jeremiah, who declared that Yahweh's sovereignty over history is underscored by the fact that he is Creator (Jer. 27:5; cf. 32:17), and who perceived in the constancy of nature a pledge of Yahweh's covenant faithfulness (5:22-24; 31:35-36). Aside from the P account, the doctrine of creation comes to its deepest expression in the message of Second Isaiah during the Exile (*see below*). And, as is evident from the devotional, apocalyptic, and wisdom literature of the postexilic period, the doctrine came to be a cardinal tenet of Judaism.

The reason for the slow movement of this doctrine from the periphery to the center of Israel's faith is to be found in the nature of the Israelite faith itself. In contrast to other religions, which viewed man as living in a state of nature, Israel's faith insisted upon the radically historical character of human existence. The meaning of life was not to be found in the rhythms and cycles of nature, as, e.g., in the Canaanite mythology of Ras Shamra, but in decisive historical events in which men of faith perceived the revelation of God and heard his call to take part in his historical plan (*see* GOD, OT VIEW OF, § 1). The primary testimony of Israel's faith is that Yahweh is the Lord of history. He is the God of Abraham, Isaac, and Jacob; the God who brought his people up out of the land of Egypt; the God who disclosed his power and purpose historically, as at the crossing of the Red Sea, the Battle of Megiddo, or subsequent critical moments in Israel's historical pilgrimage. Thus Israel's faith was first confessed in the form of *Heilsgeschichte*—the story of Yahweh's mighty acts of salvation (Deut. 26:5-10). The conflict between Israel's historical faith and the nature religions of the Fertile Crescent continued right to the fall of the nation and the exile of the people, events which disclosed the futility of Baalism and confirmed the truth of the prophetic message.

During these years of conflict, creation was associated with the world view of the nature religions. Creation belonged to the mythology of Babylonia, Egypt, and Canaan—not primarily to the realm of history, which prophets interpreted as the sphere of Yahweh's saving activity. The nature gods had a mythology but not a history, and therefore they could not declare the divine purpose "from days of old" (cf. Isa. 37:26) and bring it to pass. Within this framework of understanding, creation is a timeless event—timeless in the sense that it belongs within a cyclical pattern of mythology, which must be repeated and re-enacted each year, as was the case with the Ras Shamra mythology or the Babylonian New Year ritual. So pervasive and appealing was this nature mythology that it was no simple task for Israel's interpreters to demythologize the doctrine of creation and to bring it into theological relationship with the sacred history of Yahweh's mighty deeds. When this was accomplished, however, the foundations of the ancient mythological world view were shaken. No longer was creation a myth to be repeated; but, incorporated into Israel's *Heilsgeschichte,* it was a history to be remembered and retold.

*c. Creation as the beginning of history.* In the Bible the story of creation does not stand by itself as though it were a prescientific attempt to explain the origin or evolution of nature. Rather, as indicated by the position of the creation stories at the very beginning of the Bible, creation is the starting point of history. It sets the stage for the unfolding of the divine purpose and inaugurates a historical drama within which first Israel and, in the fulness of time, the church were destined to play a key role. Thus the Creation stands in an inseparable historical relation to the narratives that follow, particularly those that span the generations from Abraham to Joshua. In the Yahwist's epic the story of man's creation, together with other stories of primeval time (*Urgeschichte*), is the prologue to the sacred history that unfolds with the call of Abraham, the deliverance from Egypt, the guidance through the wilderness, and the inheritance of the Promised Land. The priestly creation story, too, does not stand in isolation but prepares the way for a series of historical covenants and the climactic revelation of Yahweh to Israel in the Mosaic period. Moreover, it is significant that the Creation is embraced within the time scheme (תולדות) which P traces through succeeding "generations" (Gen. 2:4*a*). In this view, creation is a temporal event, the beginning of a movement of history.

Just as the Creation points forward to the Exodus and the making of the covenant, so the covenant

faith reaches backward and includes the Creation. The theological movement of Israel's thought is not from the confession "God is the Creator" to "Yahweh, the God of Israel, is the Redeemer," but in just the opposite direction. In the formulation of the traditions now included in the Hexateuch, the Exodus, together with historical events immediately associated with it, had decisive significance for the historical interpreter. This is evident, above all, in the epic of the Yahwist (*see* J). From the standpoint of faith provided by Israel's ancient confession (Deut. 26:5-10), he essayed the task of interpreting the whole human drama, right from the beginning. His unique contribution was the manner in which he prefaced a series of stories dealing with primeval time (Gen. 2-11) to the sacred history which begins with the call of Abraham. Thus a historical line was traced from the faith situation of Israel to the remotest historical beginnings imaginable, with the result that all human history was seen in the light of the revelation given to Israel and was embraced within the saving activity of Yahweh. In a similar manner the NT church, convinced of the decisive character of God's revelation in Jesus Christ, understood the whole sweep of historical time and the whole creation in a christological perspective (Eph. 1:9-10; *see* § 4 *below*).

In Israel's understanding, then, creation and history are inseparably related. Creation is the foundation of the covenant; it provides the setting within which Yahweh's saving work takes place. But it is equally true that creation is embraced within the theological meaning of the covenant and therefore is the first of his saving deeds (Ps. 74:12-17). In view of the inseparable connection between creation and history, it is not surprising to find that Yahweh's subsequent historical deeds are regarded as creative acts and, indeed, may be described by the same verbs as are applied to the original creation (יצר, עשה, ברא); and this is true, above all, of Yahweh's creation of Israel (Isa. 43:1, 7, 15, 21; 44:2, 21, 24; 45:11) or the Servant (49:5). No prophet grasps as profoundly as Second Isaiah the soteriological meaning of creation and the creative significance of redemption. He appeals to faith in Yahweh's wisdom and power as Creator in order to demonstrate to despairing exiles that Israel's God is sovereign over the whole course of history and that he therefore can and will redeem his people (Isa. 40:12-31; 43:1-7; 45:9-13; 48:12-13). Furthermore, he declares that Yahweh's imminent coming to redeem his people will result in nothing less than a new act of creation. *See* § 3*b below.*

**2. The sovereignty of the Creator.** The Bible does not have the equivalent of the Greek term κόσμος, which suggests the view of the universe as a rationally constituted and self-sustaining structure of reality. Instead, it speaks of the relationship between the Creator and his creation, a relationship which is essentially that of the covenant. For the belief that "heaven and earth" or "everything" (כל; Ps. 8:6—H 8:7; Isa. 44:24) is dependent upon Yahweh the Creator is a derivative from Israel's covenant understanding that her whole life is dependent upon the God who delivered his people and bound them to himself. The covenant, rather than a rational principle, is the ground of the unity of creation.

The doctrine of creation, then, is pre-eminently a religious affirmation about the sovereignty of God and the absolute dependence of the creature. To say that Yahweh made the earth is to confess that it belongs to him; he is its Lord (Pss. 24:1-2; 89:11—H 89:12; 95:5). Nothing in the realm of creation should be glorified, for the meaning of the Creation is that it points beyond itself to Him who is high and lifted up and therefore is worthy of the praise of man and all other creatures. Thus the proclamation that Yahweh is creator is a summons to worship, for the Creation testifies to his wisdom and power (Ps. 104:24; Prov. 3:19-20; Jer. 10:12-13), his steadfast love (Ps. 136:4-9), and his incomparable majesty, which he shares with no other (II Kings 19:15; Neh. 9:6; Isa. 40:25-26). To be sure, the Creation does not witness to the Creator so clearly that faith is unnecessary. In the wisdom books Ecclesiastes and Job, the rational mysteries of the Creation witness to a divine sovereignty which is beyond man's understanding; and even in other contexts, where Yahweh's historical revelation provides the standpoint of faith, the Israelite is aware of the hiddenness of God (*see* GOD, OT VIEW OF, § 2*a*). Although the language of creation was often mysterious, it was nevertheless sufficiently intelligible to the man who stood within the covenant so that he could exclaim that the heavens declare the glory of God (Ps. 19:1-4—H 19:2-5). Thus the sovereignty of God, manifest in his works of creation, is the basis for adoring, trusting, fearing, and obeying him (Ps. 95; Isa. 40:27-31).

*a. Creation by the Word.* Despite differences between the creation stories of Gen. 1-2, they agree in ascribing creation to the free and spontaneous initiative of God. The personal relation between Yahweh and his creation is vividly portrayed in the J account, according to which Yahweh "forms" man (יצר suggests the image of the potter molding clay) from the ground and provides him with an environment suitable for his welfare. The strong anthropomorphism of the story, however, does not reduce the Creator to the level of man or exalt the creature to a plane of equality with God (cf. Gen. 3:22). Elsewhere the image of the divine Potter expresses the sovereignty of God over his creatures (Isa. 29:15-16; 45:9-13; Jer. 18:1-6; Rom. 9:20-21).

The sovereignty of God is expressed more forcefully in the P account, which bears the marks of greater theological reflection about the creation in its widest sense. In this account, God is exalted and transcendent. His only point of contact with the Creation is his uttered command, which punctuates the creative drama with the refrain: "And God said. . . . And it was so." The same thought is echoed by a psalmist:

> He spoke, and it came to be;
>   he commanded, and it stood forth
>     (Ps. 33:9; cf. vs. 6).

and in other OT passages (Ps. 148:5; cf. Isa. 45:12). Creation by the Word came to be the normative expression of the mode of God's creative work (Ecclus. 42:15; Syr. Apocalypse of Bar. 21:4 ff; John 1:1-3; Heb. 11:3; II Pet. 3:5-6).

As Israel learned in her historical experience, the WORD of God is the sovereign power which shapes men's lives and controls the course of history. His word is active and dynamic; it is the means by which he accomplishes his will. The "word of the LORD," when put in the mouth of the prophet, makes the prophetic spokesman sovereign over nations and releases a divine power which both overthrows and builds (Jer. 1:9-10). As the rain and the snow descend from heaven and do not return thither until they have made the earth fertile, so the word that goes forth from Yahweh's mouth does not return empty, but accomplishes his purpose and effects his will (Isa. 55:10-11). His word is "living and active, sharper than any two-edged sword" (Heb. 4:12; cf. Rev. 19:13-15). In these instances, it is clear that the Word is not a sound or even an idea. God's word is an act, an event, a sovereign command, which accomplishes a result. The creation story affirms that God's word, mighty in history, is also the very power which brought the creation into being. Since the creative Word establishes a personal relationship between the Creator and his creation, the Christian faith affirms with theological consistency that the Logos became flesh in a person (John 1:1-18).

*b. Creation ex nihilo.* In later theological reflection upon the meaning of creation, the sovereignty of the Creator was further emphasized by the doctrine that the world was created out of nothing (II Macc. 7:28; cf. Rom. 4:17; Heb. 11:3). It is doubtful, however, whether this teaching is found explicitly in Gen. 1 or anywhere else in the OT. As suggested in the footnote of the RSV, it is grammatically possible to treat Gen. 1:1 as a temporal clause which introduces a main sentence beginning with vs. 2 or even vs. 3. It is probable, however, that vs. 1 should be construed as an independent sentence which serves as a preface to the entire creation account. On this view, the story actually begins in vs. 2 with a portrayal of uncreated chaos as the presupposition and background of God's creative work. The notion of creation out of nothing was undoubtedly too abstract for the Hebraic mind, and, in any case, the idea of a created chaos would have been strange to a narrative which is governed by the view that creation is the antithesis of chaos.

The main intention of the writer is to emphasize the absolute sovereignty of God. There is not the slightest hint that God is bound or conditioned by chaos, as in the Babylonian Enuma Êliš, which portrays the birth of the gods out of the waters of chaos. Nor does God have the character of a demiurge who works with material which offers some resistance or places limitations upon his will (*see* § 4 *below*). On the contrary, he creates with perfect freedom by his word—a view which is underscored by the use of the verb ברא. In the OT this verb is used exclusively of God's action and expresses the effortless divine creation which surpasses any human analogy such as the potter or the architect (cf. Pss. 51:10—H 51:12; 104:30; Isa. 43:1, 7, 15; 48:7). Since, however, this verb is used in connection with the verb עשה in Gen. 1:26-27 and elsewhere is linked with יצר, "mold" (Isa. 43:1; 45:18), it was undoubtedly employed to support the view of creation by the Word, rather than creation *ex nihilo.*

*c. The harmony and goodness of the creation.* God's creation is characterized by order. This order, however, is not that of Greek κόσμος, harmonized by reason, but rather a divinely decreed order within which each creature fulfils the Creator's will. The Creator commands, and thereby not only brings a creature into being but also designates its peculiar nature and assigns to it a specific task. The heavenly bodies, e.g., are not independent deities who control man's life, as was supposed in antiquity, but are servants of God whose appointed function is to designate the seasons and to separate the day and the night (Gen. 1:14-19). Earth is not just the fertile "mother," from whose womb all life proceeds and to which it returns (Job 1:21; Ecclus. 40:1), but is God's creature who produces vegetation and animals at his command (Gen. 1:11-12, 24-25). The idea of "nature" as an autonomous sphere governed by natural law or set in motion by a First Cause is not found in the OT. The Creator stands in personal relationship to his creation. It is the divine decree (חק) that determines order (Job. 38:33; Pss. 104:9; 148:6; Jer. 5:24; 31:35-36), and it can even be said that Yahweh has made a covenant with the day and the night (Jer. 33:20). At any moment the Creator could allow the creation to fall back into chaos, for his continuing power is necessary to uphold and renew the creatures (Ps. 104:29-30). The regularities of nature, as expressed in the promise to Noah (Gen. 8:22; cf. 9:13-17), are based upon Yahweh's covenant faithfulness.

When God looks upon his works, seeing that each creature corresponds to his intention and fulfils its assigned function, he pronounces the verdict: "Very good" (Gen. 1:31). Yahweh's name is majestic throughout all the earth (Ps. 8:1—H 8:2), for those who have eyes to see may behold his glory in all his works, and those who have ears to hear may listen to an anthem of praise sung by all creatures (Ps. 19:1-4—H 19:2-5; Rom. 1:20). The creation faith represents a repudiation of all metaphysical dualism which leads men to suppose that the created world is evil and to seek a pathway of escape into the higher realm of pure Being. Likewise it means the surrender of ascetic practices, "for everything created by God is good, and nothing is to be rejected if it is received with thanksgiving" (I Tim. 4:4). The positive view of man's life on earth, including bodily pleasures, is expressed admirably in Ps. 104, which climaxes with the prayer that God may "rejoice" in all his works even as the psalmist, contemplating the wonderful character of the creation, rejoices in the Lord.

Most striking, however, is the anthropocentric meaning of creation. Yahweh did not create the earth as a chaos, but he formed it to be man's dwelling place (Isa. 45:18); this idea is expressed in both creation stories, particularly that of P. In the deepest sense, God's creation was for the covenant—i.e., it provided both the setting and the foundation for the relationship between God and man which alone gives meaning to man's life (cf. Ps. 73:23-26). The works of God's creation are chiefly for the benefit of man (Syr. Apocalypse of Bar. 14:18), although they are intended to remind him constantly of the goodness of God and to awaken within him the impulse to praise his Creator. The natural world is man's God-given habitat, wherein he is to find joy in the service

of God. Thus the doctrine of creation frees man from the alternatives between which human thought often moves: either the materialistic enjoyment of the natural world for its own sake, or the verdict that the world of change and death is essentially meaningless.

***d. Man's position of honor.*** Both creation stories affirm, in different ways, that man is assigned the highest place of all God's creatures (*see* MAN, NATURE OF, OT). In the J story the man (האדם) is formed from the ground (האדמה), to which he must return at death. But his special status is symbolized by saying that he is created first (contrary to the P account), that a portion of the earth-wilderness is converted into a garden for his sake, and that the animals are created with the thought of finding a companion for him. His special relationship to God is symbolized by the animation of his body by the divine breath (Gen. 2:7), and his dominion over the animals is indicated by his authority to give them names (2:20; *see* CREATURES, LIVING). Above all, he is the creature who lives vis-à-vis God, and whose life is incomplete apart from the woman, the person who "corresponds to him" (2:18, 21-24; cf. the "male and female" of Gen. 1:27; 5:2).

In the P account the creation of man occurs at the climax of the creative drama. The plants and the animals stand in only an intermediate relation to God, for they are brought forth by the earth in response to his command (Gen. 1:11, 24). But the immediate relation of man to God is symbolized by a solemn decision, announced in the heavenly council: "Let us make man in our image, after our likeness" (1:26-27; cf. 5:1; 9:6). The anthropomorphism (*see* GOD, OT VIEW OF, § 3*a*) of this statement should not be toned down by attempting to define the IMAGE OF GOD as man's "spiritual nature," "soul," "freedom," "self-transcendence," etc. The application of the same language to Seth, a son in Adam's image (5:3; cf. vs. 1), indicates that man, in his total bodily existence, was made in the image of God, although the immediate reference is probably to the divine beings who surround God (cf. Ps. 8:5—H 8:6).

In Gen. 1, however, the intention is not to define man's essence or God's nature, but rather to indicate man's task and his relationship to God. As God's living image on earth, man is to act as his representative. He is the administrator of God's works. Hence the thought quickly moves from the "image" to the announcement that God has given man a special blessing and has commanded him to exercise dominion over the earth (1:28). Likewise in Ps. 8 the thought that man has been made but a little less than God (or the angels) is quickly followed by the thought that Yahweh has put all things under his feet (Ps. 8:6-8—H 8:7-9). Man is to exercise sovereignty within God's sovereignty, so that all earthly creatures may be related to God through him.

God crowns man with glory and honor, not only by making him a king within his empire, but also by singling him out for his special concern. To the psalmist, the greatness of God's creation prompts the wondering query as to why God chooses to notice and care for man (Ps. 8:3-4—H 8:4-5). Man is made to have fellowship with God. He is the only creature who can answer God, either in defiance or in trust. Although all God's creatures are summoned to praise him, man is the only creature in whom praise can become articulate. His life is made for conversation with God, for a dialogue in an I-and-thou relation. Thus it is said of Israel that Yahweh has formed a people for himself that they may declare his praise (Isa. 43:21) and thus fulfil the vocation of every man.

**3. Beginning and end.** Just as Israel traced a historical line back to the Creation, so it looked forward in hope toward the end when the Creator's purpose would be finally realized. The purpose of history is grounded in the will of the Creator, who, in the language of Second Isaiah, is "the First and . . . the Last" (Isa. 44:6; 48:12; *see* GOD, NAMES OF, § D4*b*). Creation is fundamentally an eschatological doctrine. The opening words of Genesis: "In the beginning God," correspond to the prophetic expectation: "In the end God."

**a. Threats to God's creation.** Although the Creator's work was finished in the beginning (Gen. 2:1), the Bible also speaks of threats to God's creation which he must overcome before his purpose is finally realized. The first threat is that of chaos. The priestly creation story, which is influenced by the mythopoeic thought of ancient man (*see* §1*a above*), portrays a creation out of chaos—the primeval waste and void (תהו ובהו) and the darkness of the Deep (תהום; Gen. 1:2). God's work of creation did not destroy the chaos and darkness but pushed them back, so to speak. Light was separated from the primeval darkness (vss. 3-5), a firmament separated the upper and lower waters (vss. 6-8), and the waters under the heaven were gathered together in one place so that dry land might appear (vss. 9-10). According to this view, chaos surrounds the habitable world on every hand. We can best understand this portrayal as one which comes out of experience, rather than objective, rationalistic inquiry. Ancient man knew existentially that his life was suspended above the formless Abyss and hemmed in by the waters of chaos (*see* WATERS, MANY), which threatened to engulf his world.

Chaos imagery recurs throughout the OT, especially in poetic contexts. A psalmist affirms that the earth belongs to Yahweh,

> for he has founded it upon the seas,
> and established it upon the rivers
> (Ps. 24:2; cf. 136:6).

God has made the firmament strong and assigned boundaries to the primeval sea (Job 38:8-11; Pss. 33: 7; 104:7-9; Prov. 8:27-31; Jer. 5:22). Indeed, God watches over chaos (Job 7:12), and if the rebellious waters lift up, he rebukes them and they flee (Pss. 18:15—H 18:16; 77:16).

He was victorious over the chaos monster, Rahab or Leviathan (Job 9:13; Pss. 74:13-14; 89:9-10—H 89:10-11), and he commands the serpent that still lurks at the subterranean basis of the earth (Amos 9:3). In the NT a seer declares that in the end time, when God's redemptive work is complete, the sea will be no more (Rev. 21:1), and there will be no more night (22:5). In the meantime, the Creator's work must continue. For unless he upholds the creation by his power, the waters of chaos would sweep in and the earth would return to the pre-creation void, as at the time of the Flood (Gen. 7:11; 8:2). In

a time when the foundations of the earth shake and the waters roar and foam, the man of faith confesses that God alone is his refuge and strength (Ps. 46:1-3—H 46:2-4).

To the prophets, the work of God was threatened even more by man's sin. Admittedly, the idea of a fallen creation seems not to have been expressed in the OT. In the J epic, the story of man's banishment from the Garden of Eden (Gen. 3) is intended as a background and preparation for the call of Israel, as personified in Abraham (Gen. 12:1-3), and otherwise had little influence upon OT tradition. Neither the priestly account of the Creation nor the creation psalms (Pss. 8; 104) contain the somber note that "every imagination of the thoughts of [man's] heart was only evil continually" (Gen. 6:5). Although the priestly account of the Flood portrays almost complete divine judgment upon the creation, the creation still bears the signature of God, and the divine image is not effaced (cf. Gen. 9:6). But if the OT does not speak of a fallen creation, some of its prophets speak of Israel's fallen or perverted history, whether the tragedy is traced to the entrance into Canaan (Hosea) or to the time of the people's beginning in Egypt (Ezekiel). Their diagnosis of Israel's sickness is not based upon a general teaching about man's sinfulness, but upon the empirical reality of Israel's persistent blindness and rebellion. Sin, it was said, is "unnatural," a mysterious fault which characterizes man alone (cf. Jer. 17:9). The animal knows his master, but Israel does not acknowledge her Lord (Isa. 1:3)! The birds follow their homing instincts, but Israel does not know Yahweh's ordinance (Jer. 8:7)! With something other than poetic exaggeration, Hosea declares that even nature has been affected by the corruption of Israel's sin (Hos. 4:3), and Jeremiah envisions Yahweh's judgment falling so heavily upon his people that the earth returned to pre-creation chaos (Jer. 4:23-26; the language in vs. 23 echoes Gen. 1:2).

From Jewish scripture the rabbis derived the view that man's heart is the arena of conflict and decision between two tendencies, the "evil impulse" and the "good impulse" (cf. Ecclus. 15:14-15; *see* FALL). It remained for Christian interpreters to view historical tragedy in the dimension of a fallen creation. The way was prepared, however, especially in the apocalyptic circles of Judaism, by the story of Satan's rebellion against the Creator and his fall from status within the heavenly council (*see* SATAN). According to this view, history is the scene of God's struggle with Satan, the ruler of the present age, who seeks to establish a rival kingdom and to seduce men into his service. But even this view presupposes a historical, rather than a metaphysical dualism. Satan is not coeternal with God, but is a parasite on God's creation. His rule lasts only as long as men are deceived by him; and in the last day, when God's victory is complete, he will be destroyed.

**b. The new creation.** According to Israel's prophets, when once the judgment of God has been accomplished, he will make a new beginning, giving man a new heart (Ezek. 36:26-28) and bringing him into a new covenant relationship (Jer. 31:31-34; cf. Hos. 2:18-23—H 2:20-25). Not only will man enter a new history, but the nonhuman creatures will be quickened and transformed (Isa. 11:6-9; Hos. 2:18—H 2: 20). Thus prophetic eschatology moves toward the vision of the new creation—"the new heaven and the new earth" (Isa. 66:22)—which figured prominently in exilic and postexilic prophecy.

The theme of the new creation dominates the message of Second Isaiah, who grasps profoundly the interrelation of creation and history (see § 1c above). At one level of thought, Yahweh's power and wisdom in creating heaven and earth is the ground of assurance that he will redeem his people (Isa. 40:12-31; 42:5-9); but at a deeper level the prophet perceives that the new beginning in history will be God's new act of creation. In a striking passage, he interprets the old myth about the chaos monster in historical terms (51:9-11). Yahweh's victory over Rahab occurred at the beginning of Israel's history, when he created (ברא) Israel to be his people (cf. 43:1). At that time Yahweh dried up the waters of the "great deep" (תהום רבה)—i.e., the Red Sea—so that his redeemed people could pass over (cf. Ps. 77:16-20—H 77:17-21). To the prophet, this creative event guarantees that the Creator-Redeemer is about to make all things new. The God who is Lord over the Deep (Isa. 44:27) summons Cyrus to be his agent of deliverance and the herald of a new day, not only for Israel but for the benefit of all mankind. Moreover, nature will be marvelously transformed (41:17-20; 43:18-21) as it is taken up into the new history (cf. Rom. 8:19-23).

It is characteristic of eschatology that the visions of the end time are drawn in terms of the pictures of the first things. Creation anticipates the consummation; and the consummation is the fulfilment of the beginning. The goal of history will be a return to the beginning, not in the sense of a historical cycle which repeats itself, but in the sense that the original intention of the Creator, frustrated by creaturely rebellion and threatened by the surging powers of chaos, will be fulfilled.

**4. Creation viewed christologically.** During the Hellenistic period the doctrine of creation was a cardinal tenet of faith which distinguished Judaism from other religions or philosophies. The LXX translators avoided using the Greek verb δημιουργέω with respect to God's creative action, owing to its association with the idea of a worker who manufactures or produces things out of previously existing material. The Creator is not the demiurge of Gnostic thought. They chose instead other verbs, especially κτίζω, which express the absolute sovereignty of God. The NT likewise avoids using δημιουργέω (although the substantive form occurs in Heb. 11:10) and prefers κτίζω and its derivatives. The Christian faith is at one with Judaism in affirming that God alone and by his word created the world and determines its purpose from beginning to end. Frequent reference is made to the original creation (Mark 10:6 = Matt. 19:4; Mark 13:19 = Matt. 24:21; Rom. 1:20; II Pet. 3:4) or to that which happened "from the foundation of the world" (Matt. 25:34; Luke 11:50; John 17:24; Eph. 1:4; Heb. 4:3; I Pet. 1:20; etc.). The apocalyptic vision of the Creator enthroned in glory, while his many creatures praise him (Rev. 4-5), vividly expresses God's sovereignty over the whole course of history.

*a. Christ and creation.* Just as in the OT creation is viewed in the perspective of the Yahweh's mighty acts of history, so in the NT the church understands creation christologically—i.e., in the light of God's action in Jesus Christ, who is the fulfilment of Israel's sacred history and the inaugurator of the New Covenant. Since Christ is the center of history, he is also the revelation of God's purpose, which undergirds the whole creation. The unity of creation is not disclosed in a rational principle but in God's purpose "which he set forth in Christ as a plan for the fulness of time, to unite all things in him, things in heaven and things on earth" (Eph. 1:9-10). In him all things cohere or "hold together" (Col. 1:17), and, indeed, he "upholds" the universe by his word of power (Heb. 1:3). He is the bearer of the meaning of history and creation. Therefore, men of faith, confessing the decisive character of God's action in Jesus Christ, could say that man's salvation was predestined in Christ before the foundation of the world (Matt. 25: 34; Eph. 1:4; I Pet. 1:20; Rev. 13:8; 17:8). *See* PREDESTINATION; ELECTION.

By making use of the conception of pre-existence, an important further step was taken in Pauline and Johannine circles: God created the world through Christ. The OT background for this view is the conception of WISDOM as the first product of God's creative work. Israel's sages not only declared that wisdom is the supreme trait of God, but they also regarded "her" as the form of God's creative activity and, indeed, the personal agent of his creation (Job 28:12-27; Prov. 8:12-36). Thus their thought moved in the direction of hypostatizing Wisdom (Wisd. Sol. 7:22–8:1). Furthermore, the doctrine of creation by the Word (*see* § 2a above) was the decisive line of theological thought in the OT. These two views— pre-existent and creative Wisdom and creation by the Word—converge in the Prologue to the Fourth Gospel, which declares that the redeeming Christ is none other than the Logos of creation (John 1:1-18; cf. I John 1:1-3; 2:13-14).

By his juxtaposition of the prepositions "from" and "through," Paul makes a similar affirmation. There is one God *"from* whom are all things and for whom we exist," even as there is one Lord, Jesus Christ, *"through* whom are all things and *through* whom we exist" (I Cor. 8:6). A deutero-Pauline writer says of Christ that "in him all things were created, in heaven and on earth," for he is "the image of the invisible God, the first-born of all creation" (Col. 1:15-17; and similar language is found in Heb. 1:2-3). Everything has its center in Christ, through whom God creates, upholds, and redeems the world.

The doctrine of creation, then, underlines and validates the truth that history, from beginning to end, is under the sovereign purpose of God as revealed in Jesus Christ. The Fourth Gospel begins by echoing the opening words of Genesis: "In the beginning" and speaks about the light shining in the darkness (cf. II Cor. 4:6). And even as Christ was in the beginning, so he will triumph at the end (I Cor. 15:24-28; Revelation). Indeed, the very title which Second Isaiah had applied to God is applied in the book of Revelation to Christ: he is "the Alpha and the Omega," "the first and the last," "the beginning and the end" (Rev. 1:17; 22:13; cf. 3:14). The whole sweep of history, from creation to the new heaven and the new earth, has its fulcrum in him.

*b. The new creation in Christ.* The heart of the NT gospel is the proclamation that in Christ, God has already inaugurated his kingdom, has already introduced the new history for which prophets of the OT hoped. Echoing the message of Second Isaiah, the NT declares that the new creation has already come. At the same time, however, the new creation is a promise and foretaste of the end time, when there will be a new heaven and a new earth, free from the corruption of evil and death (Rev. 21:1-4), and when all creatures in heaven and earth will join in an anthem of praise to the Creator (Rev. 4:8-11; 5:13). Wherever God's action in Christ is effective for man's salvation, he is creatively at work, after the manner of the original creation. Thus Paul, commenting on the transformed life of the man of faith, exclaims that God's redemptive deed is nothing less than a new act of creation: "For it is the God who said [at the dawn of history], 'Let light shine out of darkness,' who has shone in our hearts to give the light of the knowledge of the glory of God in the face of Christ" (II Cor. 4:6). In another context he declares that the new life of faith has its source in the sovereignty of God, who creates *ex nihilo* by calling into existence the things that do not exist (Rom. 4: 17).

The light of God's new creation, however, breaks forth in the darkness, which is the essence of the "world" (John 1:5, 10; 3:19; 8:12; 12:35-36, 46; I John 1:5-6; 2:8-9, 11). In both Pauline and Johannine writings κόσμος (*see* WORLD, NATURE OF THE) occasionally designates the world as God's creation (e.g., John 17:4; Rom. 1:20; Phil. 2:15), but usually it means man's historical sphere—not only the earthly stage of history, but the context of social relationships in which he lives. In the latter sense, the κόσμος is a fallen world, for it is characterized by enmity to God and lies under the dominion of evil powers (John 12:31; 16:11; I Cor. 1:21; Gal. 4:9; I John 5:19; etc.). Moreover, Paul goes so far as to say that the whole created order, affected by the sin of man, groans under the bondage of corruption, waiting eagerly for the creative and redemptive act that will reveal the sons of God (Rom. 8:19-25). But the promise of the coming redemption, not only of man in the fullest sense but of the whole creation as well, has already been given to those who receive the "first fruits of the Spirit." Through Christ, God has already won the decisive victory over the world, and thereby has initiated a new history, a new humanity. "Therefore," says Paul, "if any one is in Christ, he is a new creation; the old has passed away, behold, the new has come" (II Cor. 5:17; cf. Gal. 6:15).

In Jesus Christ, God has restored the human pattern intended at the original creation. He is the New Man, of whom Adam was a foreshadowing type (Rom. 5:12-14; cf. I Cor. 15:21-22). He is the "likeness of God" (II Cor. 4:4) and the "image of the invisible God, the first-born of all creation" (Col. 1: 15)—this language recalls the "image of God" of Gen. 1:26, just as Heb. 2:5-9 interprets the man "crowned with glory and honor" (Ps. 8:4-6) christologically. He is the beginning of the new humanity

into which any man may be born, not through biological parentage, but by his decision in response to divine grace. To be sure, the old Adam lives on, the flesh wars against the Spirit, the world presents its temptations and frustrations; but the new has come and the old is passing away, for "we all, with unveiled face, beholding the glory of the Lord, are being changed into his likeness from one degree of glory to another" (II Cor. 3:18). Through Christ, says a deutero-Pauline writer, men may put on the "new nature, which is being renewed in knowledge after the image of its creator" (Col. 3:10; cf. Eph. 4:24). The new man, "created in Christ" (Eph. 2:10, 15), lives in a new relation to God and therefore in a new relation to his fellow man. Mankind, separated by a dividing wall of hostility, is reunited by God's reconciling action in Christ (Eph. 2:11-22), and men begin to walk in "newness of life" (Rom. 6:4).

Thus the Christian community, from the standpoint of faith given by God's revelation in Christ, looks both backward and forward. It traces God's purpose to the first creation, saying: "In Christ all things were created"; and it lives toward the future, saying: "God will sum up all things in Christ." The full disclosure of the new creation lies in God's future, when his kingdom will fully come and the new heaven and the new earth will appear. Even as the dramatic story of Gen. 1 is not a scientific account of the origin of the universe, so the poetic visions of Revelation are not a speculative projection into the future. The truth of both is perceived by the person who participates in the new creation in Christ and who knows in faith that the whole span of history, from beginning to end, is embraced within the sovereign purpose of the Creator and Redeemer.

**Bibliography.** H. Gunkel, *Schöpfung und Chaos in Urzeit und Endzeit* (1895). W. Eichrodt, *Theologie des ATs*, II (1935), 45-97. H. W. Robinson, *Inspiration and Revelation in the OT* (1946), pp. 1-33. R. Bultmann, *Theology of the NT*, I (1951), 254-59; II (1955), 15-32. B. W. Anderson, "The Earth Is the Lord's: An Essay on the Biblical Doctrine of Creation," *Interpretation*, IX (1955), 3-20. E. Stauffer, *NT Theology* (1955), pp. 51-79. C. Tresmontant, *Essai sur la pensée hébraique* (1956). G. von Rad, *Theologie des ATs*, I (1957), 140-57; "Das theologische Problem des alttestamentlichen Schöpfungsglaubens," *Werden und Wesen des Alten Testaments*, Beiheft 66 zur ZAW (1936), pp. 138-47, found also in *Gesammelte Studien zum AT*, Theologische Bucherei, no. 8 (1958), pp. 136-47. E. Jacob, *OT Theology* (1958), pp. 136-50. G. A. F. Knight, *A Christian Theology of the OT* (1959), pp. 107-18.

B. W. ANDERSON

**CREATURE(S), LIVING** [נפש (ה)חיה, ψυχή ζῶσα, a living being]; **LIVING BEING** (Gen. 2:7). In the Yahwist creation story it is said that Yahweh breathed the "breath of life" into man he had formed from the ground, and that he became a נפש חיה (Gen. 2:7); and it is implied that the animals became "living creatures" in a similar manner (2:19-20; cf. Ps. 104:29-30). Elsewhere, however, the expression is always applied to animals or water creatures (Gen. 1: 20-21, 24, 30; 9:10, 12, 15-16 [all P]; Lev. 11:10, 46; Ezek. 47:9).

*See also* CREATION § 2d; LIFE; SOUL.

B. W. ANDERSON

**CREDIT, CREDITOR.** *See* DEBT.

**CREEPING THING(S)** [רמש, *from* רמש, to creep; שרץ (*usually* SWARMING CREATURES *or* SWARMING THINGS), *from* שרץ, to swarm, teem; KJV ἑρπετόν (*alternately* SERPENT; RSV REPTILE), *from* ἕρπω, to move slowly]. A term referring to reptiles, insects, or some other animals.

While רמש, *remeś*, designates all animals in Gen. 9:3 ("moving thing") and water animals in Ps. 104:25 ("living thing"), its usual sense is "reptiles," which are distinguished from the wild beasts, the domesticated beasts, the birds, and the fish (Gen. 1:24, 26; 7:14; I Kings 4:33; Ps. 148:10; etc.).

שרץ, *shereṣ*, refers to water creatures in Gen. 1:20 ("living creatures"); Lev. 11:10, and to certain flying "insects" in Lev. 11:21; Deut. 14:19; it more commonly serves as a general term for various creatures that appear in large numbers, small quadrupeds, reptiles, and insects (Gen. 7:21; Lev. 5:2; 11:29, 41, 44; 22:5; etc.). W. S. McCullough

**CREMATION.** *See* BURIAL.

**CRESCENS** krĕs'ənz [Κρήσκης] (II Tim. 4:10). A companion of Paul. If this passage may be taken as a genuine Pauline fragment, it indicates that Crescens had been with Paul at the place of one of the imprisonments but had left for Galatia. The reason for his going is not indicated, and the time cannot be determined. Some MSS read "Gaul" instead of "Galatia," but the latter is better attested.

J. M. NORRIS

**CRESCENT** [שהרנים] (Judg. 8:21, 26 [KJV ORNAMENT]; Isa. 3:18 [KJV ROUND TIRE

From *Zeitschrift des Deutschen Palästina-Vereins*, no. 49 (1926), Tafel 30; by permission of Otto Harrassowitz

52. Gold crescents, from Shechem

LIKE THE MOON]). A new-moon-shaped decorative pendant or AMULET worn around the neck or sometimes sewed on garments. Crescents were of gold, silver, or bronze. Fig. CRE 52. J. M. MYERS

**CRETE** krēt [Κρήτη]; **CRETANS** krē'tənz. A large island in the Mediterranean SE of Greece. The highly advanced Minoan civilization flourished there during the first half of the second millennium B.C. Crete was known as Kaptara to the Akkadians, Keftiu to the Egyptians, and CAPHTOR to the Hebrews. Jews were settled on the island by the second century B.C., if not earlier. Gortyna, on Crete, is one of the cities to which the Roman consul Lucius addressed a letter urging that the Jewish inhabitants be well treated (I Macc. 15:23). Crete is listed in Acts 2:11 as one of the places whence Jews came to Jerusalem. Paul sailed along the coast of Crete on his voyage to Rome (Acts 27:7-21). Christianity was introduced early into the island, despite the low moral conditions there. Titus was appointed to supervise the work of the churches and to counteract Judaizing tendencies (Tit. 1:5-14).

J. C. GREENFIELD

**CRIB** [אבוס, feeding trough, *from* אבס, to feed]. The receptacle for fodder; at times the stall or MANGER for the ox (Prov. 14:4 KJV) or the ass (Isa. 1:3). The wild ass will hardly use a crib (Job 39:9).

**CRICKET** [חרגל] (Lev. 11:22); KJV BEETLE. Any of several dark-colored insects of the family *Gryllidae*.

The identification of the edible creature designated by חרגל (*ḥargōl*) is uncertain, though it may be doubted if it is a cricket. The LXX takes it as ἀκρίς, "grasshopper, locust" (cf. Aristotle *History of Animals* V.28 [555b, 18]), and this is also the Jewish interpretation. Whether it is a long-horned grasshopper (*Tettigoniidae*), as in modern Jewish usage, or one with short antennae (*Acrididae*), cannot be determined. *See* FAUNA § F2. W. S. McCullough

**CRIMES AND PUNISHMENTS.** A crime is an act in violation of a penal law prohibiting such an act and imposing a penalty for the commission of it. The term "crime" refers properly to offenses of a public nature, to wrongs committed against society and punished by society in its own name. Biblical Law, however, does not, save for a few cases, place the responsibility of prosecuting offenses upon a public body. As in ancient law generally, it is the person injured who initiates action in biblical law, though there is the recognition—particularly in the case of capital crimes—that the private prosecutor acts in the general interest as well as his own. This expresses itself in the execution of judgments, where often the entire community participates in punishing the offender.

The fundamental biblical conceptions of crime and punishment are set forth in the law corpora of the OT. Their development and modification during the period of the second temple can be seen in the NT, in which Roman penal law is also reflected.

A. The OT concept of crime and punishment
  1. The nature of crime
  2. The nature of punishment
  3. Terminology
B. The sources
  1. Law corpora
  2. Nonlegal literature
  3. Extrabiblical Jewish writings
  4. Ancient Near Eastern law
C. The criminal law of the OT
  1. Crimes against God and religion
    *a.* Foreign cults and usages
    *b.* Blasphemy
    *c.* Violations of religious institutions
  2. Homicide
    *a.* Murder
    *b.* Accidental homicide
    *c.* The goring ox
    *d.* Justifiable homicide
  3. Sexual crimes
    *a.* Violations of marriage
    *b.* Violations of chastity

## A. THE OT CONCEPT OF CRIME AND PUNISHMENT.

**1. The nature of crime.** The criminal law of the Bible differs from that of the other legal traditions of the ancient Near East in being pervaded by religious conceptions. In the biblical view, the law is the command of God; hence violation of it is rebellion against God's will—i.e., crime is sin. Moreover, biblical tradition holds that the law was communicated to the Israelite people as a whole, and that responsibility for fulfilling it rests on the entire community. If the community does not punish offenders, God will punish the community. This idea dominates the epilogues of several law corpora, which condition the welfare of Israel upon observance of the laws (cf. Lev. 18:26-28; 26:3-45; Deut. 28). Worship of other gods, sexual offenses, and homicide are singled out as involving the entire community in guilt (cf. the above passages and Deut. 19:10; 21:1-9). Hence the tendency of the laws to punish these offenses by public actions.

The notion of objective guilt, which still operates in the realm of cult and taboo, has but faint echoes in the penal laws of the Bible. As a rule it is the subjective factor, the mind of the doer, which is determinant in evaluating the nature of the offense. The laws distinguish clearly between murder, on the one hand, and homicide through negligence or accident, on the other. Bodily injuries inflicted deliberately and with premeditation are treated differently from those inflicted in sudden heat of passion. However, in the case of homicide, bloodguilt—a religiously grounded concept—is so far considered an objective condition that (*a*) the slaying of the accidental homicide by the "redeemer of blood," while wrong, is not actionable; and (*b*) a homicidal beast must be put to death. In the cultic sphere, penal law recognizes the objectivity of the *ḥērem* status: whoever has incurred it, whether wittingly or not, must be punished. The religion of Israel heightened both the awesome sanctity of all that touched upon God—an objective datum—and the importance of the individual's moral

choice—a subjective datum; these laws illustrate the dilemma that may arise out of the clash of the two.

**2. The nature of punishment.** Punishment of wrongdoers is an attribute of divine justice. "Condemning the guilty by bringing his conduct upon his own head" (I Kings 8:32) is the way of God; in the penal laws, man is commanded to follow it, for "when the wicked perish there are shouts of gladness" (Prov. 11:10).

Capital crimes are a blot upon the whole community. When the law decrees that the capital offender must die, it is not merely to punish him but to "purge the evil from Israel" (Deut. 17:12; cf. 13:5—H 13:6; 17:7; 19:19; 21:21; 22:21-22, 24; 24:7; Judg. 20:13; II Sam. 4:11). Murder lays the "guilt of innocent blood" on the whole community; the murderer must be executed "so that it may be well with you" (Deut. 19:13). Sexual crimes "defile" the land and the people; such crimes too must be purged lest "the land vomit you out, when you defile it" (Lev. 18:24-28).

The deterrent value of the public execution of criminals is also recognized: "And the rest shall hear, and fear, and shall never again commit any such evil among you" (Deut. 19:20; cf. 17:13; 21:21).

Noncapital punishments aim at a correspondence with the offense. Crimes against property are punished in the property of the offender, with multiple damages in cases of theft and fraud. Wilful injuries to the person are governed by the rule of talion: "You shall give life for life, eye for eye, tooth for tooth, hand for hand, foot for foot, burn for burn, wound for wound, stripe for stripe" (Exod. 21:23-25; cf. Lev. 24:19-20; Deut. 19:21), whose object is to limit retaliation to the exact measure of the injury. Biblical law diverges from other law systems of the ancient Near East in not regarding any offense against property as a capital crime, and in restricting talion to the person of the offender. See §§ C7*b*, D2, *below*.

Despite the religious cast of biblical law, ritual expiation plays a negligible part in punishment. Intentional violations of the law do not, as a rule, entail expiatory offerings (for the exceptions, *see* §§ C3*a*, 7*c*, *below*). Except insofar as capital punishment itself is colored by the idea of expiation (*see* § D1 *below*), the penalties of all deliberate offenses are purely civil. The elaborate system of sin and guilt offerings in Lev. 4-5 is designed exclusively for unwitting violations of the law.

The priestly laws punish some three dozen religious and sexual offenses by the offender's being "cut off from [the midst of] his people" (e.g., Gen. 17:14; Exod. 31:14; Lev. 18:7-29; the complete list is in M. Ker. 1.1). The nature of this punishment, called *kareth*, "excising," by later jurists, is not clear. Many offenses punished by *kareth* are elsewhere in the priestly law punished by death (cf. Lev. 18:8, 29, with 20:11; 18:17 with 20:14; 18:23 with 20:15). In Exod. 31:14-15 *kareth* and death are found together as the penalty for violating the sabbath. It thus appears that a death penalty, rather than banishment or excommunication as has been supposed, is involved. Lev. 20:4-5, in which God threatens to "cut off" the Molech-worshiper himself if the people fail to do so, suggests that it is a divine rather than a human punishment. Specifically, it is punishment by God of an offender whom men have failed to punish, whether through dereliction or inability (cf. Mekilta at Exod. 31:14). This will answer for the cases which are punished both by *kareth* and by death. For the rest, in which *kareth* alone appears, a kind of penalty *in terrorem* seems to be intended (later law punished these by scourging; cf. M. Mak. 3.1-2). According to Num. 15:30 all violations of the law committed wilfully ("with a high hand") incur the penalty of *kareth*.

**3. Terminology.** The commonest expressions for criminal offenses are derivatives of חטא, "act amiss," and עוה, "do wrong" (Deut. 19:15; I Sam. 20:1). פשע, "transgression," also serves as "crime," "offense" (Gen. 31:36; 50:17; Exod. 22:8; I Sam. 24:11). Since these terms may also be rendered by "sin," it is not always clear whether a wrong is being considered as an offense against God or against man. The priestly writers call various dishonest acts מעל ביהוה, "trespass against the LORD" (Lev. 6:2—H 5:21; RSV "breach of faith against the LORD"). Particularly scandalous crimes are called נבלה, "base deed," "shameless act" (Deut. 22:21; Josh. 7:15).

The offender is a רשע, "criminal," "guilty man" (Exod. 23:1; Deut. 25:2), or a חטא, "offender" (I Kings 1:21). A capital sentence is משפט מות (Deut. 19:6), a capital crime, חטא משפט מות (Deut. 21:22). One guilty of a capital offense is רשע למות, "guilty of [i.e., justly liable to] death" (Num. 35:31), or בן־מות, "liable to death" (I Sam. 26:16; II Sam. 12:5). If the offense is punished by scourging, he is בן־הכות, "liable to be beaten" (Deut. 25:2). עון, "wrongdoing," may also serve as "punishment" (Gen. 4:13; I Sam. 28:10). "To fine" is ענש (Exod. 21:22; Deut. 22:19), which later comes to mean "punish" in general (so in Mishnaic Hebrew, and perhaps in Prov. 17:26). The penalty later called *kareth* is expressed by the sentence: "That person shall be cut off from his people" (e.g., Lev. 7:20), with slight variations.

The terminology of particular crimes is given in § C *below*.

**B. THE SOURCES.** The law corpora and narratives of the Bible are our chief sources of information. Later Jewish literature, particularly the juristic writings of the Tannaim, contains valuable supplemental and interpretative material. Other law collections of the ancient Near East provide instructive parallels and contrasts.

**1. Law corpora.** Because the three major law corpora—the laws of JE (in Exodus), P (including H; chiefly in Leviticus and Numbers), and D(euteronomy)—have each a history and style of their own (*see* PENTATEUCH), it is the more notable that, so far as rules of crime and punishment are concerned, there is agreement between them on matters of principle. One may discern degrees of development in the details of a law (e.g., the increasing detail in the law of accidental homicide from JE, to D, to P; *see* §§ C2a-b *below*). A given principle may stand out more clearly in one corpus than in another (e.g., the ban on vicarious punishment: explicit in D, implicit in JE; *see* § C2c *below*). Furthermore, the disparate origins and interests of the corpora are reflected in the selection of offenses with which they deal. The law corpus of JE, the biblical casebook par excellence, contains nearly all the rules concerning corporal and property injuries—rules for which the

casuistic formulation is most suitable. P deals most fully with incest, because of its bearing on impurity. In matters of principle, however, no change is evident.

The following characteristics are common to the criminal law of all the law corpora, and distinguish it as a whole from that of the other law collections of the ancient Near East:

*a*) All the law corpora regard God as lawgiver and as the ultimate sanction of the law.

*b*) All treat of religious as well as secular crimes.

*c*) All explicitly and consistently distinguish accidental homicide from murder.

*d*) None imposes a death penalty for violating a property right.

*e*) All iterate the principle of talion in such a way as to exclude vicarious punishment.

*f*) None recognizes class differences among Israelites in fixing penalties.

It must also be noted that the societal framework of all the law corpora is a nonmonarchic, tribal polity. Laws punishing offenses between man and man address themselves in the first instance to the injured man or his kin, rather than to a court; the right of self-help is recognized. Neither the judicial system of the monarchy nor the new categories of crime that came into being with the rise of a monarchic state are reflected in the laws.

This is not to say that the criminal law of the Hebrews had no history. Stages in the development of certain concepts are visible in the conflicts between law and practice as reflected in the narratives, and these will be discussed below. Our present data, however, are hardly adequate to speak of an evolution of criminal law during the biblical period. The inadequacy is twofold:

*a*) Even assuming the conventional critical dating of the law corpora, it is still not permissible mechanically to date a given law by the assumed date of the corpus as a whole. This is especially true of the criminal law, for rarely are the rules of one corpus taken up and revised by its supposed successor. The fact is rather that each corpus has some rules in common with the others, and some that are either ignored or only slightly touched upon by the others. More disturbing to the historian is the fact that the rules under one heading are commonly scattered through two or more of the corpora. Thus JE, which deals extensively with injuries to person and property, includes only one offense against chastity: seduction. D treats at length of crimes upon women, married and unmarried, but omits the case of seduction; at the same time, its one law concerning bodily injury fits best with the cases of JE. P, though frequently admonishing against idol-worship, contains but one penal law on the subject: the case of Molech-worship; the detailed laws of Deuteronomy are entirely missing. On the other hand, P's one law is not found in D (cf. Deut. 18:10—an admonition, not a penal law). Whatever be the cause of these omissions, it can hardly be the date of the law in question. Offenses against chastity other than seduction were surely known in JE's time, and they cannot have differed much from those enumerated in D. D's one law of bodily injury has its closest analogue in the Middle Assyrian Laws, and can scarcely be considered a Deuteronomic innovation. Nor is the punishment of Molech-worship likely to have been a fresh creation of P (or H), inasmuch as the offense is noted as early as the time of Ahaz (mid-eighth century).

In these, as in many other matters, it is necessary to combine the data of the various corpora in order to gain a view of Hebrew criminal law of the preexilic period. This doubtless involves the risk of obscuring a possible evolution of the law. But, when evidence of such an evolution is lacking, the agreement of the corpora when they do overlap gives grounds for this procedure forced upon us by the meagerness of the data. In these circumstances it is, of course, impossible to treat the laws historically save for a few exceptional cases.

*b*) The second obstacle in the way of writing a history of Hebrew criminal law is our ignorance of the extent to which biblical law was considered binding in the pre-exilic period. The laws of all societies contain ideal norms that are not actually enforced in life. This appears to be the case of a considerable number of biblical laws, whose ideal and reforming character is patent. The potential value of the historical narrative for dating laws is thus gravely impaired. Had only the account of Jer. 34:8-22 been preserved, it would hardly have been believed that the slave law in question was in fact part of Israel's earliest legislation (Exod. 21:2). But the amount of information available outside the laws concerning the criminal law of Israel is, at best, quite small. Records of criminal cases, court documents, and memoranda such as are found in profusion in Mesopotamia are altogether lacking. The occasional references to crimes in the nonlegal literature of the Bible either involve some unusual circumstance or are too brief to make up this lack. The ideal character of much of biblical legislation, together with our ignorance of the actual disposition of criminal cases in biblical times, makes highly problematic the attempt to date laws by reference to the nonlegal literature.

**2. Nonlegal literature.** Allusions to points of criminal law outside the legal corpora sometimes agree with the pertinent rule of law, sometimes do not. In the latter case it must be determined whether an evolution in law, or a gap between the ideal rule and actual practice, is involved. This cannot always be done.

Some allusions are of questionable relevance: Jacob's condemnation to death of whoever stole Laban's gods tells more of the power of the family head in a patriarchal society than of the legal penalty for theft at that time. David's impassioned declaration that the rich man of Nathan's parable deserved to die for robbing the poor man of his lamb (II Sam. 12:5) gives no firm basis for assuming that robbery was then a capital crime (note the soberer verdict of vs. 6, which coincides with the penalty—for theft—of Exod. 22:1—H 21:37). Nor does the warning of Prov. 6:31 that the thief "will pay sevenfold; he will give all the goods of his house," sound like more than a hyperbolic expression of multiple penalties.

A significant divergence between law and narrative appears in the attitude taken toward marriage of a paternal sister. Accepted in the patriarchal narratives (Gen. 20:12), condoned as late as the time of

David (II Sam. 13:13), it is banned in Lev. 18:9; 20:17 (on pain of *kareth*); Deut. 27:22. Marriage to two sisters, accepted in the Jacob narrative (Gen. 29:21 ff), is banned in Lev. 18:18. The laws reflect the later tendency to broaden the concept of incest. (The prohibited relations continued to increase as time went on; cf. Tosef. Yeb. 3.1.)

Vicarious punishment is prohibited in Deut. 24:16: "The fathers shall not be put to death for the children, nor shall the children be put to death for the fathers; every man shall be put to death for his own crime" (חטא; RSV "sin"). The observance of this prohibition is noted for the first and only time in the narrative of Amaziah's reign (beginning of eighth century; II Kings 14:6). Prior to this several instances of vicarious or collective punishment occur: the household of Achan (Josh. 7:24-26), the population of Jabesh-gilead (Judg. 21:10-11), the priestly clan at Nob (I Sam. 22:19), the sons of Saul (II Sam. 21), and the sons of Naboth (II Kings 9:26). Accordingly the Deuteronomic law has been assumed to be a later development. It is a question, however, whether the evidence warrants the assumption. The instances of Achan and the people of Jabesh come under the special law of the *ḥērem,* which, belonging to the realm of sacred and taboo, operates in accord with divine rather than legal principles (*see below; see also* § C1*a below;* BLOODGUILT; CURSES). The executions of the priestly clan at Nob and the sons of Naboth are nowhere represented as legally justified (the formally correct trial of Naboth in I Kings 21:8-19 results only in his execution). Both cases involve treason, for which it appears to have been customary to execute the whole household of the offender. This custom, by no means confined to ancient Israel, is not to be assumed to have had legal sanction, though it was so common that Amaziah's restraint deserved to be singled out for praise. Saul's sons were executed in extraordinary circumstances: their father had violated a sacred national oath, for which divine wrath had later struck at Israel; Saul was already dead, and the Gibeonites expressly rejected composition. The case is altogether too unusual to serve as a basis for generalization as to the procedure in ordinary crimes. Outside the realm of sacred and taboo, then, there is no evidence whatever of the legal infliction of vicarious or collective punishment. So far as the principle of Deut. 24:16 is concerned, it is already reflected in the early laws of JE: Exod. 21:31 forbids the vicarious punishment of children (*see* § C2*c below*). It can only be said, then, that before—and, one may add, after (cf. Jos. Antiq. XIII.xiv.2)—Amaziah there is evidence that Israelite extralegal practice fell behind a demand of Israelite law that is as old as the earliest law corpus. This is hardly decisive for the dating of that law.

To be sure, Exod. 20:5 represents God as holding children to account for the sins of their fathers "to the third and the fourth generation of those who hate me." This divine prerogative, however, has nothing to do with the legal penalty prohibited in Deut. 24:16, which is imposed and executed by men. (When later prophets transposed the legal formula of Deuteronomy into a theological one, they replaced יומת, "shall be put to death"—i.e., legally—with ימות, "shall die"—i.e., by divine decree [Jer. 31:30;

Ezek. 18:4 and *passim*].) Far from demonstrating a progression in the conception of punishment, the two passages refer to entirely separate domains, and it is the biblical view that both are concurrently valid. Deuteronomy is so unaware of a clash between the two principles that in 5:9 it reproduces the old formula of Exodus without demurrer. Their simultaneous application in a single law actually appears in Lev. 20:2-5: the people of the land must stone the Molech-worshiper—him alone; if they fail to do so, however, God "will set [his] face against that man and against his family, and will cut them off from among their people." As well consider the first clause of this law a repeal of the second as consider Deut. 24:16 a repeal of Exod. 20:5; Deut. 5:9. God's ways are not man's; a divine prerogative cannot be utilized as a source for penal law.

The nonlegal literature does furnish several examples of the operation of the laws: the redeemer of blood (II Sam. 3:27, 30; 14:6-11); the altar asylum (I Kings 1:51; 2:28 ff); the crime of "cursing" God (and king) and its punishment (I Kings 21:10—the fullest account we possess of a criminal process); the burning of a harlot (Gen. 38:24); the suppression of mediums (I Sam. 28:9); the false prophet (Jer. 26:7-24); and various instances of actions against the worship of other gods.

As a source for the law of the monarchy—virtually ignored by the law corpora—the nonlegal literature is particularly valuable. Whatever we know of crimes against the king and state is derived from it.

**3. Extrabiblical Jewish writings.** Philo (*On the Special Laws*) and Josephus (Antiq. IV.viii), and, to a lesser extent, the Apoc. and the Pseudep. (e.g., JUBILEES, BOOK OF), are valuable witnesses for the views on biblical law held in various quarters during the last half of the second-temple period. The earliest sources for normative Jewish jurisprudence, the legal writings of the Tannaim (rabbinic jurists of the first century B.C. to the third Christian century), contain much that illuminates biblical law. Of primary interest are the Tannaitic commentaries on the laws: the Mekilta on Exodus; Sifra on Leviticus; Sifre on Numbers and Deuteronomy; and the great codification of Tannaitic law, the Mishna. All were compiled in the third Christian century.

The Jews regarded biblical law as a harmonious whole, and in their disregard of historical considerations, employed exegetical methods that the modern critic must abandon. Yet to the extent that biblical law does share common principles, a synoptic view is an advantage rather than a hindrance. Judiciously utilized, these writings are richly suggestive for the exegesis of the laws.

**4. Ancient Near Eastern law.** Indispensable for the understanding of biblical law are the other law collections of the ancient Near East. In contrast to the laws of the Bible, the latter are the product of a secular jurisprudence which recognized the state and the king as the promulgators and ultimate sanction of law. To make just laws was considered by the king a divinely imposed duty, but the religious motive rarely enters the laws themselves. The primary concern of the penal law is economic: to safeguard property and make losses good. In the case of murder this may involve a monetary composition, or the replace-ment of the slain by another person. Life may be sacrificed to protect property. Social status is decisive in evaluating harms and assessing penalties. Sexual crimes, not having the nature of sins against God, are less severely punished. Inasmuch as biblical law is evidently an adaptation of a common law of the ancient Near East, the divergences between it and other representatives of that law are instructive even in details. The following law collections are pertinent to the discussion of the criminal law of the OT: the Laws of Eshnunna (LE), from the first half of the nineteenth century B.C.; the Code of Hammurabi (CH), from the beginning of the eighteenth century; the Middle Assyrian Laws (MAL), from between the fifteenth and thirteenth centuries; and the Hittite Laws (HL), from the fourteenth century(?).

**C. *THE CRIMINAL LAW OF THE OT.*** The following classification of crimes is based chiefly on the nature of the penalty—on whether the crimes involve capital, corporal, or property punishments.

**1. Crimes against God and religion.** While all violations of the law offend God as lawgiver (cf. the priestly formulation: the wilful offender "reviles the LORD . . . , has despised the word of the LORD" [Num. 15:30-31]), the following are direct affronts to the majesty and sovereignty of God, and subject the offender to the death penalty.

*a. Foreign cults and usages.* Having and serving other gods is forbidden in the Decalogue (Exod. 20:3-5). The offense, and incitement to it as well—a form of treason against the theocracy—is punished by stoning (Deut. 13:6-10—H 13:7-11; 17:2-7). The worship of Molech by child-sacrifice is singled out by P and punished in the same way (Lev. 20:2-5). One who prophesies in the name of another god is to be put to death (Deut. 13:1-5—H 13:2-6). A foreign cult pollutes the community; until it is extirpated, all will suffer God's wrath. Hence Num. 25:1-9 recommends the summary slaying of the offender caught in the act (cf. I Macc. 2:24-26; Philo *On the Special Laws* I.54-57).

All that relates to foreign cults is *ḥērem,* "object devoted to destruction": the idols and their decorations (Deut. 7:25), a person who sacrifices to them (Exod. 22:20—H 22:19), even a city that has apostatized (Deut. 13:12-18—H 13:13-19). Persons in *ḥērem* status are to be slain, and things are to be burned (cf. Deut. 7:25), with no possibility of ransom (Lev. 27:29). The *ḥērem* status is contagious: one who appropriates a *ḥērem* object himself becomes *ḥērem;* if he brings it into his house, all in his household become contaminated and must be destroyed (Deut. 7:26; cf. Josh. 6:18; 7:20-26). The effect is thus analogous to the contagious impurity of a corpse (cf. Num. 19:14). The slaying of Achan's household is not, then, an example of "putting sons to death for the sins of their father"; the contagiousness of a taboo status is not subject to limitations by a court.

MAGIC and DIVINATION of every kind—not merely antisocial sorcery (as in CH 2; MAL A 47; H L 9-10, 170)—are banned (Lev. 19:26*b*, 31; Deut. 18:10). One who consults a practitioner of these forbidden arts is subject to *kareth* (Lev. 20:6). A sorceress must not be permitted to live (Exod. 22:18—H 22:17); mediums must be stoned (Lev. 20:27).

Since these offenses are regarded as endangering

the public good, the obligation to prosecute them falls on the witnesses and the community (Lev. 20:2; Deut. 13:6-18—H 13:7-19). Execution usually takes the public form of stoning. The nonlegal literature affords abundant examples of these crimes and their punishment. Here it may be noted that in the monarchy it fell to the king to prosecute them (I Sam. 28:3, 9; I Kings 15:11-13; II Kings 10:18-28; 23).

*b. Blasphemy.* "Cursing" God is banned in Exod. 22:28—H 22:27, and punished by stoning in Lev. 24:15-16. The verb in question, קלל, means "to contemn," whether by words (cf. II Sam. 16:5-12) or by deeds (I Sam. 3:13; cf. 2:17, 29-30; the RSV "blaspheming" is inept). Later law uses the term גדף, which has the same range of meaning (cf. II Kings 19:22, referring to the speech of 18:33-35; 19:12; and Num. 15:30, where, since a deed is involved, the RSV "reviles" is inept). The euphemism ברך of I Kings 21:10 indicates that קלל of the Exodus law, which appears to have been the basis of the indictment of Naboth, was referred to verbal contempt. This is clearly the meaning of the law of Leviticus, which further restricts the death penalty to the case in which the Tetragrammaton has been uttered (נקב, "pronounce," "designate," as in Num. 1:17; Isa. 62: 2; so M. Sanh. 7.5: "The blasphemer is not culpable unless he expressly utters the Name"). This restrictive tendency reaches its culmination in the gloss "unless he abuses the Name by the Name" (Gemara). The narratives of Lev. 24:10-23; I Kings 21:8-14 illustrate the operation of the law, and show that it fell upon the witnesses to prosecute the offender.

*c. Violations of religious institutions.* The prohibition of labor on the sabbath (Exod. 20:8-11; 23:12; 34:21; Lev. 23:3; Deut. 5:12-15) is enforced in the priestly writings by the death penalty (Exod. 31:14-15; 35:2), specified as stoning in the exemplary story of Num. 15:32-36. From this story it appears that prosecution of sabbath-breakers was regarded as a duty of the witnesses. There is no other evidence for the enforcement of the death penalty. In Israel of the eighth century it was the custom to suspend all commerce on the sabbath (Amos 8:5); later, however, the ban was not observed (Jer. 17:19-27), and had to be harshly enforced by Nehemiah (Neh. 13:15-22).

The false prophet, who "presumes to speak a word in my name which I have not commanded him to speak, or who speaks in the name of other gods," must die (Deut. 18:20-22). The law is alluded to in several passages of Jeremiah (26:9, 15-16; 28:5-9); the issue is as old as the reign of Ahab (I Kings 22:19-28).

**2. Homicide.** In the biblical view human life is invaluable. Criminal homicide imposes a culpability that can be expunged only by the killer's life: "Whoever sheds the blood of man, by man shall his blood be shed; for God made man in his own image" (Gen. 9:6). The guilt of bloodshed is so far objective that it extends even to beasts: "For your lifeblood I will surely require a reckoning; of every beast will I require it" (vs. 5). Prosecuting the homicide is the duty of the Avenger of Blood, but the law holds the community responsible for keeping the redeemer's activity within legal bounds.

Biblical law distinguishes the following types of homicide: murder, accidental homicide, the goring ox, and justifiable homicide.

*a. Murder.* When a homicide was committed personally and with intent to harm, the killer was a murderer (רוצח) and must be put to death. Intent was presumed if (*a*) the killer lay in wait (Exod. 21:13; Num. 35:20, 22; Deut. 19:11); (*b*) there was enmity between the parties (Num. 35:20-21; Deut. 19:11); (*c*) a murderous implement was used (Num. 35:16-18; note the increase in the detail of the law from JE to D to P). The presumption established by *c*—and surely that of *b* as well—could be defeated by proof of accident.

The murderer was not permitted to ransom his life: "You shall accept no ransom for the life of a murderer who is guilty of death; but he shall be put to death . . . ; for blood pollutes the land, and no expiation can be made for the land, for the blood that is shed in it, except by the blood of him who shed it" (Num. 35:31-33). This prohibition of composition for murder is unparalleled among the laws of the ancient Near East (contrast, e.g., MAL A 10; HL 1-5; CH knows of talion but not of a ban on composition); it is the legal expression of the sanctity of human life expressed in Gen. 9:6*b*. That capital punishment is a paradoxical consequence of this view was recognized by later jurists, and believed by them to have been sensed already by Deut. 19:13*a:* "Lest you think, 'Since one man has already died why should we be guilty of another's death?' Scripture says, 'Your eye shall not pity him' " (Sifre).

It was the privilege of the redeemer of blood to slay the murderer (Num. 35:19; Deut. 19:12), but if he did not, others appear to have had the right to do so, to cleanse the land of evil (II Sam. 4:11).

Homicide resulting from an act committed with a purpose to harm is not distinguished from murder: death caused by a blow struck in a sudden heat of passion (by inference from Exod. 21:18-19; this case is excluded from talion by CH 206-7); death of a pregnant woman who miscarried after having been struck by fighting men (Exod. 21:22-23; cf. CH 210, where also talion is applied, but to the daughter of the killer); death of a slave under the rod (Exod. 21: 20). The last law is unparalleled for its interest in the slave as human being rather than chattel: because he has no kin to avenge him—a foreign slave is intended—the law demands that he "be avenged" (ינקם) by Israelite justice. To this extent only does the law take the slave's status into account: since the owner of the slave is privileged to beat him (he is "his money"), death ensuing a day or two after the beating is not punishable. Contrast vss. 18-19, where one who strikes a freeman so that he is confined to bed is not cleared until his victim recovers sufficiently to walk about.

*b. Accidental homicide.* When the homicide was unintentional, the laws provide an asylum for the killer (Exod. 21:13; Num. 35:9-15, 22-28; Deut. 19:1-10; note that in Numbers and Deuteronomy the killer is still called רוצח, "manslayer"). The examples given are of accidental homicide: while a man is chopping wood, the head of his ax flies off and kills his companion (Deuteronomy); a man involuntarily (בפתע, "of a sudden") pushes another to his death, or, without seeing him, throws a stone or an implement that kills him (Numbers). Exodus characterizes the slaying as occasioned by God. Establishment of the asylums is a communal responsibility: if the manslayer is slain by the redeemer of blood before he can reach the asylum, there is bloodguilt on the community—though the redeemer is not accountable (Deut. 19: 10). *See also* CITY OF REFUGE.

*c. The goring ox.* When a man's beast—the law speaks of an ox—commits homicide, two legal personalities are involved: the beast, upon which an objective bloodguilt lies, and the owner, whose degree of responsibility is the subject of the law of Exod. 21:28-32. If the ox was not known for goring, it is stoned, and its carcass is taboo and may not be eaten; the owner is innocent. But if the ox was known to gore, and its owner, despite notice thereof, neglected to keep his ox in, and it gored someone to death, both ox and owner must die. However, since the owner neither purposed harm nor committed it personally, the law permits him to ransom himself, with the consent of, and by the sum fixed by, the victim's kin. The law is the same if the victim was another's son or daughter: then too it is the owner—not his son or daughter—who must suffer punishment. Should the habitual gorer kill a slave, it must be stoned, and, kin being absent, the slave's owner receives his value.

These laws are illuminated by comparison with the corresponding Babylonian laws (LE 54-55; CH 250-1). While in language and style there is a striking resemblance, the latter know nothing of the one constant factor in all the clauses of the biblical law: the stoning of the ox and its taboo status. The religiously grounded notion of bloodguilt has no echo in these laws, whose sole interest is to compensate the victim's party for their loss. The Babylonian laws are silent concerning the goring of a son or daughter, but in other cases of criminal negligence (CH 116; 229-30) it is laid down that if the victims are children, the child of the offender is put to death. Such a conception appears to underlie, and to be repudiated by, Exod. 21:31, which thus anticipates the principle expressed in Deut. 24:16. The Babylonian laws make it possible to appreciate the distinctively Israelite cast of the biblical laws on the goring ox.

*d. Justifiable homicide.* Slaying in self-defense entails no bloodguilt. A householder is privileged to slay a burglar breaking into his house, the presumption being that the night housebreaker would not shrink from murder. (Presumption of thievery alone does not justify killing in Hebrew law, since even the convicted thief is punished only in his property, not his life; cf. Mekilta at Exod. 22:1.) The daytime housebreaker, against whom there is no such presumption, may not be slain, but is subject to multiple damages (H Exod. 22:1-2; the RSV has transposed the verses). Comparison with Babylonian law is instructive: LE 12-13 subjects daytime trespass to fine, nighttime trespass to death. However, since CH 21 makes every housebreaking, regardless of whether by day or by night, liable to summary slaying, it is clear that presumption of theft is sufficient to warrant killing the culprit in Babylonian law. LE's distinction between day and night is to be understood in this light: the night trespasser is presumed a thief and may therefore be put to death.

The narratives furnish one other type of justifiable homicide: slaying in battle, which does not privilege the redemption of blood (II Sam. 2:18-23; cf. 3:26-30; I Kings 2:5).

**3. Sexual crimes.** Sexual offenses cause "impurity" (טמאה) and "defile" (חלל, טמא) the victim (Gen. 34:5, 13, 27; 49:4; Lev. 19:29; 21:9; Num. 5:29; Deut. 24:4; Hos. 5:3; 6:10). Except for cases in which amends can be made (viz., the rape or seduction of an unmarried woman), the legal penalty for such offenses is death. The guilt and pollution they bring on lies upon the whole community (Gen. 20:9; 26:10; Deut. 24:4).

*a. Violations of marriage.* While the Israelite conception of marriage had, in common with the rest of antiquity, a secular, economic aspect, it went its own way in considering the marriage bond as divinely sanctioned. Later texts speak of a sacred covenant (Prov. 2:17; Mal. 2:14), but the idea is as old as the parable of Hos. 1-3, which presupposes it (cf. also Ezek. 16, especially vs. 8). Hence ADULTERY is conceived of, not merely as a violation of the husband's rights, but as a sin against God (Gen. 20:6; 39:9; Ps. 51:1, 4). This accounts for the salient difference between biblical and Near Eastern law on this head: the latter, regarding adultery as a wrong against the husband alone, gives him the right to pardon his wife (and her paramour) if he wishes (CH 129; MAL A 14-16; HL 198).

The laws define as adultery the voluntary cohabitation of a married woman—biblical, like Babylonian law (CH 130), does not distinguish the betrothed from the married woman in this respect—with a man other than her husband. Both the woman and the man are put to death (Lev. 20:10; Deut. 22:22-24, where stoning is specified; cf. John 8:3-7). The presumption of consent is the subject of Deut. 22:23-27: when the offense was committed in open country, where no help was available to the woman, she is presumed to have been forced, and the man alone is executed; when it occurred in the city, she is presumed to have been willing, and is stoned too (cf. HL 197). What constitutes a marriage tie requisite for adultery is treated in Lev. 19:20-22: the violation of a slave woman who has been designated (יעד=חרף of Exod. 21:8) to marry a man, but has not yet been freed or redeemed, is not considered adultery. "Designation" of a slave woman, unlike betrothal (which is possible only with a freewoman), does not create a tie constitutive of adultery. The violator must indemnify the injured man (cf. LE 31; בקרת is best taken as related to Akkadian *baqāru*, "have a claim"), and bring a guilt offering.

Prosecution of the adulteress (and her paramour) was the duty of the husband (cf. Num. 5:11-31; *see* JEALOUSY, ORDEAL OF; Prov. 6:32-35). The law does not recognize the wife's right to proceed against her husband in case of infidelity.

*b. Violations of chastity.* From the law of the seducer (*see below*) it appears that ordinary fornication —in polygamous Israel the nonmarital union of any man with an unmarried woman—was not punishable. Hence it is that harlotry (זנות) is prohibited (Lev. 19:29; Deut. 23:17—H 23:18) but not penalized. From Lev. 21:7 it is clear that a nonpriest could marry a harlot, and this is borne out by the narrative of Judg. 11:1. An exception is the case of the priest's daughter, whose harlotry profanes her father; she must be burned (Lev. 21:9; cf. CH 110). The law of the newlywed wife who is discovered to be non-virgin and is stoned (Deut. 22:20-21) leaves it uncertain when defloration occurred. That she was still "in her father's house" is consistent with an interpretation that she was violated after betrothal (cf. CH 130), making her an adulteress (so Sifre). But it is equally possible to take it as having occurred before, in which case the law of Deuteronomy will be more severe than the others (Philo *On the Special Laws* III. 81 so interprets, in accord with his view that fornication is a capital crime [51]; so too Jos. Antiq. IV.viii. 23). Judah condemns Tamar to burning (Gen. 38:24) because she was considered inchoately married to her levir, Shelah (she is still Judah's "daughter-in-law"); her harlotry was therefore adulterous. *See* MARRIAGE.

Rape and seduction of an unbetrothed virgin are distinguished. A man who has seized (תפש) a maiden and forced her must pay her father fifty shekels (her marriage present) and take her to wife; he may never divorce her (Deut. 22:28-29). If he has seduced (פתה) her, he must also pay her marriage present, but her father may refuse to give her in marriage. If the seducer marries her, she is not guaranteed against subsequent divorce, presumably because she was a willing partner in the offense (Exod. 22:16-17—H 22:15-16).

*c. Incest.* The idea of what constituted a prohibited degree of kinship for sexual relations appears to have broadened during the course of biblical times (*see* § B2 *above*). Deut. 27:20, 22-23, curses the man who cohabits with his father's wife (=23:1), his paternal or maternal sister, or his mother-in-law. This list is obviously incomplete, and even the fuller enumeration of P (Lev. 18:6-18; 20:11-21) omits the union of father and daughter (CH 154; HL 189). The priestly law penalizes by the death of both parties (*a*) union with father's wife (Lev. 20:11), (*b*) with daughter-in-law—called תבל, "mismating" (vs. 12; RSV "incest") —and (*c*) with a woman and her mother—called זמה, "depravity" (RSV "wickedness"), and punished by burning (vs. 14). Other cases carry no legal penalty. Later law prescribed scourging for incest not punished by death, but imported several more relations into those laws applying the death penalty (see M. Mak. 3.1; Sanh. 9.1; *see* INCEST).

*d. Unnatural connection.* Sodomy and BESTIALITY, respectively termed תועבה, "abomination," and תבל, are punished by the death of both parties—including, in the latter case, the beast (Lev. 18:22-23; 20:13, 15-16). Contrast other Near Eastern laws: MAL A 20 punishes sodomy with sodomy and castration; HL punishes relations between father and son with death (189); it distinguishes bestiality with cattle, sheep, and pigs—which is subject to death (pardonable by the king)—from bestiality with horses and mules, which entails no punishment (187-88, 199; 200).

**4. Insubordination and treason.** The authority of parents has divine sanction (Exod. 20:12; Lev. 19:3). Striking them (Exod. 21:15) or contemning them (Exod. 21:17; Lev. 20:9; for the meaning of קלל, cf. the parallel Deut. 27:16) is punishable by death (CH 195 penalizes striking one's father by loss of the hand; note that in every biblical law both father and

mother are expressly mentioned). A son who defies his parents' discipline in pursuit of a dissolute life may be haled by them before the city elders; after being charged formally, he is stoned by the people (Deut. 21:18-21).

The authority of the supreme court of appeal that Deuteronomy establishes at the central sanctuary is enforced by the death penalty for all who disobey its decisions (17:8-13).

Exod. 22:28—H 22:27 forbids contemning a tribal chief. From the later application of the law to the king it may be inferred that the penalty for so doing was death (I Kings 21:10; cf. also Josh. 1:18).

Since the law corpora do not anticipate the new social and legal arrangements arising out of the establishment of the monarchy, crimes against the king —treason in the English sense—are not dealt with by them. The narratives, however, furnish valuable information regarding the Israelite concept of treason. It consists in: (*a*) "compassing or imagining the death of the king" (Amos 7:9-10; cf. I Kings 22:18-27; Jer. 32:1-5). Rival claimants to the throne seem to have been regarded as offenders under this head and automatically put to death, at least in the early monarchy (I Kings 1:21, 50; cf. Judg. 9:5; I Sam. 20:31; II Sam. 13:30). (*b*) Violating the king's wives: since the harem of a deceased king passed to his successor (II Sam. 12:8), cohabiting with a king's wives was *ipso facto* usurpation (II Sam. 16:21; I Kings 2:22). (*c*) Levying war against the king in his realm (II Sam. 15:12). (*d*) Adhering to the king's enemies and giving them aid and comfort (I Sam. 22:7-19). (*e*) Slaying the king's officer during the performance of his duty (I Kings 12:18-19). Contemning or reviling the king was a capital offense (II Sam. 16:5-9; I Kings 21:10).

**5. Perjury and defamation.** The law forbids bearing false reports and false witness (Exod. 20:16; 23: 1), and punishes the malicious witness with that penalty he had schemed to inflict upon his fellow (Deut. 19:16-21; cf. CH 1, 3-4). By later interpretation this form of talion applied only when the case had already been decided on the basis of the false testimony (Jos. Antiq. IV.viii.15; M. Mak. 1.6).

A husband who falsely alleges that his newlywed wife was not, as represented to him, a virgin (whose marriage present is fifty shekels [Deut. 22:29]) is whipped by the court of elders before whom the bride's father prosecutes him, and fined a hundred shekels—twice the amount he had sought to recover by his fraud. He may not divorce the woman thereafter (Deut. 22:13-19).

**6. Crimes against person. *a. Kidnaping.*** Practiced chiefly for sale into slavery (cf. Gen. 37:28; 40:15), the stealing of an Israelite for sale, even if the victim is still in the possession of the kidnaper, is punishable by death (Exod. 21:16; Deut. 24:7; cf. CH 14).

*b. Bodily injury.* For injury inflicted unpremeditatedly, upon a sudden heat of the passions, as when in a quarrel one man suddenly strikes the other with a stone or with his fist, indemnification for any resulting loss of income and physician's costs must be made (Exod. 21:18-19; cf. CH 206). The rule of talion in Lev. 24:19 ("When a man causes a disfigurement in his neighbor, as he has done it shall be done to him") refers to injuries inflicted maliciously and with premeditation, as is clear from the context (cf. vss. 17, 21) and from its application in Exod. 21: 23-25; Deut. 19:19-21. On the possibility of composition, *see* § D2 *below.*

A woman who comes to the aid of her husband who is being beaten in a fight, and seizes the privy parts of his opponent, loses her hand (Deut. 25:11-12; cf. MAL A 8).

A man who, while fighting another, strikes a pregnant woman and causes her to miscarry, but without further harm to herself, must indemnify the husband for the fetus, paying a sum fixed by him and approved by judges (Exod. 21:22; cf. CH 209, 211, 213; HL 17, 18; for the curious LXX version of Exod. 21: 22-23, making the culprit liable to death if the fetus was fully formed, cf. Philo *On the Special Laws* III. 108-9).

A slaveowner who injures the eye or tooth of his slave must set him free (Exod. 21:26-27). This law has no parallel in Near Eastern law for its humane interest in the slave as a person in his own right; contrast the interest of CH 199.

**7. Crimes against property.** *a. Damage.* One who authors or permits damage to property is at fault and must make full reparation if he personally did the damage (Lev. 24:18, 21*a*), or permitted it to occur through negligence (Exod. 21:33-34, 36; 22:5-6—H 22:4-5). When an ox causes damage through no fault of its owner—e.g., if it was not known to gore—the law divides the loss equally between the owner and the injured party (21:35; cf. LE 53).

*b. Theft and misappropriation.* Whoever has acquired the property of another without his consent and knowledge is considered a thief. It is immaterial to biblical law whether the property came into the culprit's possession legally or not (not so in Babylonia; contrast CH 6-13, 25, with 112, 120, 265). A bailee who has misappropriated goods entrusted to him is treated the same as the burglar and housebreaker: all pay double damages (Exod. 22:4, 7, 9—H 22:3, 6, 8). Theft of beasts is aggravated by subsequent slaughter or sale; in that case there is a fourfold penalty for sheep, and a fivefold for oxen, whose absence prevented the farmer from plowing (Exod. 22:1—H 21:37). If the thief cannot pay, he is sold into slavery, his price going to the injured party (22: 1*b*—H 22:2). On housebreaking and burglary, *see* § C2*d above.*

Here biblical law departs markedly from that of Babylonia and Assyria, where life and property are commensurable. The counterpart to the idea that life can be compensated for in pecuniary terms (*see* § C2*a above*) is capital punishment for theft (CH 9; MAL A 3). The exception of CH 8, punishing with ten- and thirtyfold damages, is perhaps only apparent since it adds: "If the thief does not have sufficient to make restitution, he shall be put to death."

*c. Robbery.* Taking property by force or intimidation (גזל; cf. Gen. 31:31; II Sam. 23:21) and withholding from another his rightful due (עשק; e.g., Mal. 3:5) are forbidden in the laws (Lev. 19:13; Deut. 24: 14-15). It is remarkable, however, that no penalty is prescribed for convicted offenders (CH 22 punishes robbery by death). Lev. 6:1-7—H 5:20-26; Num. 5: 5-8 deal with the voluntary restitution of property taken by robbery or fraud: it must be returned with the addition of a fifth of its value to its rightful

owner, and a guilt offering brought for atonement. The smallness of the penalty is probably to encourage voluntary surrender in these cases, where, owing to lack of evidence, or to the impotence of the victims—the victims of robbery and oppression are almost invariably poor and defenseless (Ps. 35:10; Isa. 3:14; Jer. 7:6; Amos 4:1)—legal means of recovery were of little avail. Later law required no more of the convicted robber than to make full restitution, the severer law of theft being explained thus: "While the robber treated man and God equally, the thief regarded man more than God, acting [in stealth] as if no heavenly eye saw, or heavenly ear heard" (Tosef. B. K. 7.1).

**D. MODES OF PUNISHMENT. 1. Capital.** The commonest form of capital punishment specified by the laws is stoning, whereby the whole community participated in "purging the evil out of Israel." It took place outside the city (Lev. 24:14; Deut. 22:24; I Kings 21:13; but cf. Deut. 22:21: "the door of her father's house"). The witnesses placed their hands on the head of the offender (Lev. 24:14; cf. Sus. 34), as it were transferring the guilt which lay on the whole community to the criminal, who thus partook of the nature of an expiatory offering (cf. Lev. 4:15; 16:21). They then cast the first stone, followed by the rest of the people (Deut. 17:7).

Death by burning is prescribed for two sexual offenses (Lev. 20:14; 21:9); in the story of Gen. 38:24 it is for harlotry. The latter passage indicates that execution took place outside the city. Later sources show that the victim was surrounded by fagots and burned alive (Jos. Antiq. IV.viii.23; M. Sanh. 7.2—the "inexpert court"). Persons slain as *ḥērem* were afterward burned (Josh. 7:25)—another echo of the cult (cf. Deut. 13:16—H 13:17).

Death by the sword is prescribed for the population of the apostate city (Deut. 13:15—H 13:16; cf. Exod. 32:27). Execution of idolatrous persons in the narratives takes the same form, its sacrificial or purgative character often explicit in the terminology (e.g., I Kings 18:40 [cf. Deut. 9:21]; II Kings 23:20). Presumably the sword was also the favored weapon of private execution (e.g., by the redeemer of blood [II Sam. 3:27]).

Beheading appears to have been the royal mode of executing persons offensive to the king (II Kings 6:31-32; cf. II Sam. 16:9). Later law prescribed it for the judicial execution of murderers (M. Sanh. 7.3; 9.1).

Shooting (with arrows) is mentioned once as a means of punishing those who trespassed on a sacred area (Exod. 19:13).

HANGING was not a form of execution, but a means of exposing the body of an executed criminal as a public warning (Deut. 21:22-23).

Mutilation of the body of an executed criminal was sometimes practiced (II Sam. 4:12).

Such unusual modes of execution as dismemberment (Dan. 2:5; cf. HL 166) and being thrown to beasts (Dan. 6:7—A 6:8) were not practiced in Israel.

**2. Corporal.** There are few specific corporal penalties prescribed in biblical law. Mutilation, various sorts of which are prescribed in Babylonian and Assyrian law (CH 192 [tongue]; 193 [eye]; 194 [breast]; 205 [ear]; MAL A 4 [nose and ears]; 9

[finger, lip]; 15 [castration and mutilation of whole face]), is specified once: the hand of a woman who has committed an indecent assault is cut off (Deut. 25:11-12).

For bodily injuries inflicted wilfully and with premeditation, talion is prescribed (*see* §C6 *above*). In the premonarchic, decentralized tribal polity which is presupposed by the laws, the duty of prosecuting personal injuries fell first upon the injured party or his kin. The talion rule of the Bible is directed to the private prosecutor, and aims at restricting his privilege to an exactly corresponding punishment. While talion is a principle common to Babylonian and Assyrian law as well, its application in the Bible differs in one respect: the idea of vicarious punishment, which was the outcome, in Babylonia and Assyria, of a rigorous legal logic, is rejected. Thus, in CH, a creditor who has so maltreated the distrained son of his debtor that he dies, must lose his own son (116); if a man struck the pregnant daughter of another so that she miscarried and died, his own daughter must be put to death (209-10); if through faulty construction a house collapses, killing the householder's son, the son of the builder who built that house must die (230). MAL A 50 prescribes that a man who has caused the wife of another to miscarry must surrender his wife to suffer correspondingly, and MAL A 55 penalizes the seducer by requiring him to deliver his wife to the seduced girl's father for prostitution. Biblical law rejects this mode of talion tacitly in Exod. 21:22-23, expressly in 21:31, eventually formulating its rejection in the generalized principle of Deut. 24:16.

Whether talion was ever a judicial penalty may be doubted. Even in the biblically revised form many cases suggest themselves in which the object of the rule—the infliction of an exactly equivalent punishment upon the wrongdoer—can scarcely have been attained by its literal application; as, e.g., the case of a man blind in one eye who either destroyed one eye of a man of sound vision, or had his sound eye destroyed by the latter. In other cases the difficulty of inflicting an equivalent harm must have been great— as, e.g., if the injury only partially incapacitated an organ of the victim, or if it was located close to a vital spot. In Assyria, where mutilation appears to have been commonly practiced, expert officials were attached to the courts to supervise it (MAL A 58), so that the latter obstacle to inflicting talion, at least, was not present. It is interesting, therefore, to note that MAL A 55 provides as well for the case where a literal vicarious talion cannot be carried out, substituting for it a pecuniary penalty. Since biblical law neither provides for a court executioner or mutilator, nor ever suggests a pecuniary substitute for cases in which literal talion is inapplicable, it does not seem seriously to contemplate the infliction of talion as a judicial punishment.

The three passages in the laws which speak of ransom indicate that, except for homicides, it was the practice to offer and accept a monetary composition in lieu of talion. These three passages in effect license composition for every injury short of homicide committed by a human being. Exod. 21:30 permits the negligent owner of a vicious, homicidal ox to ransom himself. Num. 35:32 forbids allowing the accidental homicide to ransom himself from banishment to the city of refuge, and vs. 31 forbids accepting ransom from a murderer in lieu of his life. The necessity for such limiting laws speaks for the common practice of composition, which the laws seek to check only in the area of homicide, and therefore treat of it only in this connection. That composition was permitted for crimes involving no bloodguilt appears to be self-understood, and was apparently widely practiced. Cf. Josephus' formulation of talion: "He that maims anyone, let him undergo the like himself . . . unless he that is maimed will accept money instead; for the law makes the sufferer the judge of the value of what he has suffered, and permits him to estimate it, unless he would be too severe" (Antiq. IV.viii.35; cf. Sifra at Lev. 20:7).

It remains to be said that, since biblical law recognizes self-help, an injured party that inflicted talion on its own was within its rights.

Scourging was a judicial penalty, the severity of which varied with the gravity of the offense. The maximum number of strokes is set by the law at forty (Deut. 25:1-3; for details *see* SCOURGING).

Imprisonment is not found as a punishment in biblical or early Near Eastern law. Accused persons were sometimes detained in custody pending clarification of their case (e.g., Lev. 24:12). Later, however, imprisonment was employed by the state to dispose of persons who were regarded as dangerous (Jer. 32:2-3; for further details *see* PRISON).

Sale into slavery is prescribed by the laws only for the thief who cannot pay multiple penalties (Exod. 22:1b—H 22:2b), though debt slavery was also known in Israel (II Kings 4:1; Neh. 5:5; cf. Lev. 25:39; and *see* DEBT; SLAVERY).

**3. Pecuniary.** Pecuniary penalties in biblical law are indemnificatory and exemplary; they are paid in every case to the injured party. Fines paid to the court or state are unknown. Indemnification must be made (*a*) for causing a miscarriage—assessed by the husband and approved by judges (Exod. 21:22); (*b*) for deflowering a virgin—her marriage present (fifty shekels of silver, to judge from Deut. 22:29), paid to her father (Exod. 22:16-17—H 22:15-16); (*c*) for violating a slave woman designated to marry a man—unspecified (Lev. 19:20); (*d*) for death caused by a vicious ox—a ransom paid in lieu of life by the negligent owner of the ox to the kin of the deceased at their determination (Exod. 21:30). Exemplary damages are the double, fourfold, and fivefold penalties for theft (Exod. 22:1-4, 9—H 21:37-22:3, 8), and the double amount of the marriage present paid to the father of the falsely defamed bride (Deut. 22:19).

**E. *CRIME AND PUNISHMENT IN THE NT.***
**1. General considerations.** The NT does not contain a corpus of criminal laws. While several sayings of Jesus touch upon points of biblical law, they do not themselves take the form of law, but of exhortation to saintly behavior (e.g., Matt. 5:21-32; note vs. 20). Jesus' pronouncement on talion is a case in point: what is rejected is far more than the literal application of "an eye for an eye and a tooth for a tooth," which, as suggested above, can hardly have been a judicial penalty even in ancient Israel. The Tannaitic understanding that monetary compensation alone is im-

plied (Mekilta at Exod. 21:23; M. B. K. 8.1) would be no less repugnant to Matt. 5:38-41. For the demand here is that the injured waive his rights to sue for reparations of any sort whatever. This saintly teaching is, of course, the very antithesis of a legal prescription. What substantive criminal and penal law appears in the NT is, then, a reflex of contemporary Jewish and Roman practice. Particularly the collisions of the central figures of the NT with Jewish and Roman authorities provide the materials with which we must deal.

To determine the legal situation reflected in these materials is at times a desperate task. The authors of the NT narratives were no more concerned than their OT counterparts with furnishing precise and comprehensive legal information. Not even the TRIAL OF JESUS and the multistaged trial of Paul, about which we seem to be relatively well informed, are free from obscurities at crucial moments of legal interest. Nevertheless, the stock of information on Jewish and Roman criminal law and procedure does illuminate the general background, if not all details, of the NT data on crime and punishment.

**2. Jewish criminal law in the NT.** Judea, since the year 6 under Roman procurators, continued to enjoy, as under Persian and Greek rule (cf. Ezra 7:25-26; Jos. Antiq. XII.iii.3), a considerable internal autonomy. Following the Herodian tyranny, "the government became an aristocracy, and the high priests were intrusted with a dominion over the nation" (Antiq. XX.x). Local jurisdiction was recognized over all matters involving Jewish law and custom. The authority of the high priest extended to the Jewish Dispersion as well (cf. Caesar's edict to the Sidonians [Antiq. XIV.x.2])—the presupposition of Acts 9:1-2. The extraordinary privilege granted to the communities of the Dispersion of exclusive competence in religious matters (cf. Acts 18:12-17) was probably conceived of as a delegation of high-priestly jurisdiction.

**a. Capital punishment.** The competence of Jewish authority to deal with capital offenses against Jewish law is a vexed question. Against John 18:31 (cf. Jos. Antiq. XX.ix.1) and a rabbinic tradition to the effect that *ca.* forty years before the destruction of the temple capital jurisdiction was taken from Jewish courts (cf. T.B. Abodah Zarah 8*b* and parallels), several instances of capital trials and executions by Jews without the intervention of Roman authority are on record: Peter's second trial (Acts 5:27 ff [note especially vs. 33]); Paul's attestation of the high priest's authority to execute (Acts 26:10); Tannaitic records of executions by stoning and burning (Tosef. Sanh. 10.11; M. Sanh. 7.2). From the account of Stephen's stoning (Acts 7:57-60) it is difficult to decide whether a lynching or a judicial execution took place. *See* STONING.

Lynching was recognized as a legitimate mode of punishing gross religious offenses (Philo *On the Special Laws* I.54-57; III.94-98; M. Sanh. 9.6), and was tolerated even in the Dispersion (III Macc. 7:10-14). Hence the legality, from the Jewish viewpoint, of the plots to slay Paul in Damascus (Acts 9:23-24) and Jerusalem (23:12-15), and the stoning at Lystra (14:19).

An unusual privilege gave the Jews the right to slay any foreigner, not excluding Roman citizens, who trespassed on the temple precinct (Jos. War VI.ii.4; for the Greek inscriptions to this effect, *see bibliography*). Whether a judicial execution or a lynching by outraged bystanders (cf. Acts 21:28-29) is meant cannot be determined.

The religious offenses for which the Jewish authorities prosecuted Jesus and his followers are not clearly defined. The "blasphemy" of which Jesus and Stephen are accused (Matt. 9:3; 26:65; John 10:33 ff; Acts 6:11), like that which Jesus imputes to his antagonists (Matt. 12:22-32), covers a far greater area of insult to God and religion than the concept of the Mishna (Sanh. 7.5; *see* § C1*b above; see also* BLASPHEMY). Christian belief is alleged by Paul to be the basis of his persecution by the Jews (Acts 26:19-23). On the basis of Tannaitic law it is not possible to account for the death penalty here involved.

**b. Corporal punishment.** The violation of biblical prohibitions not provided with a specific penalty was punished by Jewish law with thirty-nine stripes (Jos. Antiq. IV.viii.21; M. Mak. 3). To judge from the freedom with which flogging was dealt out, however, it appears to have served the Jewish authorities, as it did the Roman, as a general coercive measure (Matt. 10:17; Acts 5:40; 22:19; II Cor. 11:24; *see* SCOURGE).

Pending trial or execution, an offender might be detained in PRISON (cf. Acts 4:3; 5:18).

For various religious delicts the synagogal authorities had at their disposal the penalty of EXCOMMUNICATION (cf. Luke 6:22; John 9:22; 12:42; 16:2).

**3. Roman criminal law in the NT.** The procurator reserved jurisdiction in cases touching the public peace and order. His authority enters the scene when sedition, riot, or brigandage is involved. Theudas and Judas the Galilean (Acts 5:36-37) were prosecuted as inciting sedition (Jos. Antiq. XX.v.1; War II.viii.1), and Jos. Antiq. XVIII.v.2 gives a similar ground for Herod Antipas' execution of John the Baptist. Jesus was crucified by Pilate as "King of the Jews" (*see* INSCRIPTION ON THE CROSS), and his followers were viewed by the Jews also as belonging to the line of rebels against Rome (Acts 5:35-39). Cf. the ground of the tribune's arrest of Paul in Acts 21:38. While the procurator reserved the right to sentence and execute in such cases, it was up to the Jewish authorities to arrest, examine, and deliver to him persons dangerous to public order (Mark 14:43 ff; cf. Jos. War. II.xii.2; VI.v.3).

**a. Punishments.** The cruelest and most degrading form of capital punishment, applied by the Romans to slaves and the lower classes, was CRUCIFIXION, regularly aggravated by prior scourging. Beheading was done with the sword (Matt. 14:10), though the older, republican use of the ax persisted in the early empire (Rev. 20:4; cf. M. Sanh. 7.3). Next to death, the severest punishment was condemnation to lifelong work in the mines; since this involved being kept in fetters, it was often called *vincula*—the δεσμοί, "bonds" (RSV "imprisonment"), of Acts 23:29; 26:31. Municipal magistrates were empowered to scourge as a coercive measure in punishing minor disorders (Acts 16:22). Scourging was also employed to elicit information from noncitizens (Jos. Antiq. XV.viii.4; XVI.viii.1, 4; cf. Acts 22:24). Imprisonment, primarily employed for the detention of culprits pending trial or execution, served also as a coercive measure; it was aggravated by stocks and fetters (Acts 16:23-24).

**b. The importance of Roman citizenship.** Under the *lex Julia de vi publica*, enacted by Augustus, it was a crime to order that a Roman citizen be scourged or placed in prison. Being a Roman citizen, Paul enjoyed this immunity (Acts 22:25-29; cf. 16:37), though it was not always respected (cf. II Cor. 11:25; Jos. War II.xiv.9) and seems not at all to have inhibited Jewish authorities from scourging coreligionists for offenses under their jurisdiction (II Cor. 11: 24). In capital cases, a Roman citizen had the right to be tried, in the provinces, by the governor *in consilium* (cf. Acts 25:12; the council is composed of those listed in vs. 23). But he was privileged also to refuse this court and to appeal directly to the emperor in Rome. The precise application of the right of appeal to the case of Paul (25:11-12) is a complex legal problem. *See bibliography.*

**Bibliography.** Sources in English translation: H. St. J. Thackeray, Jos. Antiq. IV, Loeb Classical Library (1930). H. Danby, *The Mishnah* (1933). F. H. Colson, trans., Philo *On the Special Laws,* Loeb Classical Library (1937-38). J. Z. Lauterbach, *Mekilta* (1949). H. E. Goldin, *Hebrew Criminal Law and Procedure* (1952): translation of tractates Sanhedrin and Makkoth of the Mishna, with a copious rabbinic commentary. G. R. Driver and J. C. Miles, *The Assyrian Laws* (1935); *The Babylonian Laws* (2 vols.; 1952, 1955): detailed legal commentaries, comparing biblical and other Near Eastern law. J. B. Pritchard, ed., *ANET* (2nd ed., 1955), pp. 161-97.

OT: J. L. Saalschütz, *Das Mosaische Recht mit Berücksichtigung des späteren Jüdischen* (1848), II, 437-592, is still the best legal discussion. J. Wellhausen, "Arabisch-Israelitisch," in K. Binding, ed., *Zum ältesten Strafrecht der Kulturvölker; Fragen zur Rechtsvergleichung, gestellt von Theodor Mommsen* (1905), pp. 91-99. J. M. P. Smith, *The Origin and History of Hebrew Law* (1931). A. Alt, *Die Ursprünge des israelitischen Rechts* (1934; in *Kleine Schriften zur Geschichte des Volkes Israel,* I [1953], 278-332), is fundamental. A. Gulak, "Law, Jewish," *Encyclopaedia of the Social Sciences,* IX (1937), 218-25. D. Daube, *Studies in Biblical Law* (1937).

Special topics: H. Weyl, *Die Jüdischen Strafgesetze bei Flavius Josephus* (1900). D. Amram, "Retaliation and Compensation," *JQR,* N.S., II (1911-12), 191-211. R. P. Lagrange, "L'homicide d'après le code de Hammourabi et d'après la Bible," *RB,* XIII (1916), 440-71. E. R. Goodenough, *The Jurisprudence of the Jewish Courts in Egypt . . . as Described by Philo Judaeus* (1929); strongly contested by I. Heinemann, *Philons griechische und jüdische Bildung* (1932). D. Daube, "Error and Accident in the Bible," *Revue internationale des droits de l'antiquité,* II (1949), 189-214. P. J. Verdam, " 'On ne fera point mourir les enfants pour les pères' en droit biblique," *Revue internationale des droits de l'antiquité,* II (1949), 393-416. A. van Selms, "The Goring Ox in Babylonian and Biblical Law," *Archiv Orientální,* XVIII (1950), 321-30. W. Kornfeld, "L'adultère dans l'Orient antique," *RB,* LVII (1950), 92-109. M. Greenberg, "The Biblical Conception of Asylum," *JBL,* LXXVIII (1959), 125-32.

NT: T. Mommsen, "Die Rechtsverhältnisse des Apostels Paulus," *ZNW,* II (1901), 81-96. J. Juster, *Les Juifs dans l'empire romain* (1914), II, 127-82: the most comprehensive discussion of the relevant Jewish and Roman penal law. H. J. Cadbury, "Roman Law and the Trial of Paul," in F. J. Foakes-Jackson and K. Lake, eds., *The Beginnings of Christianity,* V (1933), 297-338. E. Bickermann, "Utilitas crucis, observations sur les récits du procès de Jésus . . . ," *RHR,* CXII (1935), 169-241: from the viewpoint of Roman provincial administration. H. Zucker, *Studien zur jüdischen Selbstverwaltung im Al-*

*tertum* (1936), 50-91: an excellent account of Roman and Jewish jurisdictions in NT times. The Greek temple inscription barring strangers is translated in A. Parrot, *The Temple of Jerusalem* (1957), p. 87; latest discussion by M. Schwabe in M. Avi-Yonah, ed., *Sepher Yerushalayim* (1956), pp. 358-61.

         M. GREENBERG

**CRIMSON** [תּוֹלָע, *lit.* worm *or* insert; שָׁנִי; כַּרְמִיל, *a* Pers. *loan word,* worm; LXX κόκκινος]. A red color of varying hues, extracted for dyeing from the bodies of female kermes or cochineal insects.

*See also* SCARLET; COLORS.     C. L. WICKWIRE

**CRIPPLE.** *See* DISEASE.

**CRISPING PIN.** KJV translation of חָרִיט (RSV HANDBAG) in Isa. 3:22. *See* BAG.

**CRISPUS** krĭs'pəs [Κρίσπος, *from* Lat., curly]. A Jew residing in Corinth (Acts 18:8); leader of the synagogue, who with all his household was baptized into the Christian faith, having been convinced by Paul's preaching that Jesus was the Christ. His was one of the few cases in which Paul personally baptized new believers (I Cor. 1:14). Tradition claims that he afterward became bishop of Aegina (Apostolic Constitutions, VII.46).     J. M. NORRIS

**CRITICISM.** *See* BIBLICAL CRITICISM.

**CROCODILE** [לִוְיָתָן] (Job. 41:1—H 40:25 RSV mg.); KJV-RSV LEVIATHAN. Any of various species of large carnivorous aquatic reptiles (of the order *Crocodilia*), with a long, pointed head, a lizardlike body, a long and powerful tail, and short legs.

The animal described in Job 41—H 40:25-41:26 is now commonly thought to be a crocodile. Actually vss. 1-11 contain little to identify the subject as a crocodile, and they could apply to any large sea animal, real or mythical. Vss. 12-34, however, reflect some knowledge of a crocodile's body, habits, and powers, though vss. 18-21 are hyperbolic and may represent local folklore. The crocodile is the largest of the extant reptiles, and it would certainly be the longest animal known to the Hebrews (Herodotus records [II.68] a length of seventeen cubits for the Egyptian species), which may explain vss. 33-34.

The author of Job must have heard of the crocodiles of Egypt (*Crocodilus niloticus*), and doubtless some of this hearsay would be similar to what is found in Herodotus (II.68-70). But much of his information on crocodiles probably came from Palestine itself. Strabo (XVI.27) refers to the town of Crocodeilopolis (S of Mount Carmel), which presumably owed its name to its crocodiles; and Pliny (V.17) mentions apparently the same place, as Crocodilon, while Tristram also records the capture of crocodiles in this area in the nineteenth century.

         W. S. McCULLOUGH

**CROCODILE, LAND.** *See* LAND CROCODILE.

**CROCUS** [חֲבַצֶּלֶת *ḥăbaṣṣeleth;* Akkad. *ḥabaṣillatu*]. A plant which blossoms abundantly. The true rose is clearly not intended. The Hebrew word appears in Isa. 35:1 in a figure of the blossoming desert (KJV

ROSE) and in a description of the bride in Song of S. 2:1 (ROSE; RSV mg. "crocus").

Several species of crocus are found in Bible lands, but the identification is widely disputed. Many scholars favor the narcissus (*N. tazetta*) on the basis of the Targ. The Akkadian cognate implies that the meadow saffron, genus *Colchicum*, also called "autumn crocus," may have been meant.

*See also* FLORA § A10; ROSE; SAFFRON.

**Bibliography.** H. N. and A. L. Moldenke, *Plants of the Bible* (1952), pp. 147-48, 234-35.          J. C. TREVER

**CROSS** [σταυρός]. Literally an upright stake, pale, or pole; in the plural, a palisade or stockade. When Paul writes of his "thorn in the flesh" (II Cor. 12:7), the word for "thorn" (σκόλοψ) is almost identical with σταυρός in meaning; but the latter is always the NT word for the cross of Christ.

As an instrument of execution, the cross was a stake sunk vertically in the ground. Often, but by no means always, a horizontal piece was attached to the vertical portion, sometimes at the top to give the shape of a "T"; sometimes just below the top, producing the form most familiar in Christian symbolism. Generally the condemned man was forced to bear his own cross, or the transverse part, to the place of execution. According to the Synoptic gospels, Simon of Cyrene was compelled to carry Jesus' cross for him. If Jesus was at this point too exhausted to bear his own load, this was from the merciless flogging he had received. Frequently an inscription was attached to a cross, to indicate the nature of the crime. *See* INSCRIPTION ON THE CROSS; CRUCIFIXION.

As a physical object, Jesus' cross is, of course, mentioned in all four gospels (Matt. 27:32 ff; Mark 15:21 ff; Luke 23:26; John 19:17 ff), and also at Phil. 2:8; Heb. 12:2. To the orthodox Jew it was inevitably a stumbling block or scandal (Gal. 5:11), for Christians declared that Israel's long-hoped-for Messiah had indeed come, only to be thus ignominiously executed at Roman hands. To Gentile pagans, likewise, such a proposition was foolishness. As Paul acknowledged, it could not be understood by worldly wisdom (I Cor. 1:17-18). So it became the occasion for persecuting the followers of Christ (Gal. 6:12). Precisely here, however, lay the paradox of Christian belief. Christ's death on the cross brought salvation (Col. 2:14; cf. Eph. 2:16), and hence was the basis for Christian hope (Col. 1:20). Therefore, it was, for Paul, the only ground on which he might boast (Gal. 6:14). Thus the cross, with all its offensiveness, became the supreme symbol of the new faith.

In the NT, as among later writers, this symbolic or metaphorical use of "cross" is far more frequent than are references to the physical instrument. Jesus himself seems to have been responsible for one metaphorical extension, using "the cross" to signify the suffering and death that his followers must be prepared to undergo (Matt. 10:38; 16:24; Mark 8:34; Luke 14:27; cf. also Mark 10:21; Luke 9:23). NT writers did not follow him in this particular usage, however. So starkly did Jesus' death loom in their minds that they seem to have shrunk from calling their own sufferings "crosses" (but see Gal. 2:20). This may be why, as noted above, Paul called his suffering, not a σταυρός, but a σκόλοψ. The σταυρός,

"cross," was peculiarly Jesus' own, and stood for the divine act which he alone had accomplished. Then if baptized Christians lived immoral lives, they became "enemies of the cross of Christ" (Phil. 3:18). Should they desert the faith, they would "crucify the Son of God on their own account and hold him up to contempt" (Heb. 6:6).

Of writers after the NT period, two deserve particular mention. Ignatius of Antioch (*ca.* A.D. 115) sought to refute two contemporary enemies of the Christian faith—viz., orthodox Judaism, and the so-called Docetism (δοκέω, "seem"), which asserted that Christ had not really come in the flesh but had only seemed to do so. Both groups, Ignatius maintained, were refuted by the facts of Jesus' life and passion. In particular, Docetism was, he held, disproved by the fact of Jesus' death on the cross.

In what is known as the Epistle of Barnabas (A.D. 130-60), it is noted that Abraham had 318 servants (Gen. 14:14). In the Greek alphabet, where letters also represented numbers, 318 is expressed as ΙΗΤ. Here, said the author of the epistle, is a matter of inexhaustible import: "ΙΗ" are the first two letters of Jesus' name (ΙΗΣΟΥΣ), while "Τ" is a picture of the cross. Therefore, Gen. 14:14 is, in reality, a prefiguring of Christ's death (Barn. 9.8). Such bizarre exegesis is, of course, unacceptable today. The conviction underlying it, however, has remained essential to Christianity since its inception—viz., that the cross of Christ was, in fact, the climax and fulfilment of all that OT religion had stood for.

*See also* CRUCIFIXION; TRIAL OF JESUS; DEATH OF CHRIST.          PIERSON PARKER

**CROW.** *See* RAVEN.

**CROWN** [נֵזֶר, *reserved for the royal and priestly crowns;* עֲטָרָה, *a general word, mainly poetic;* כֶּתֶר (Esther *only, for the Persian royal crown*); קָדְקֹד, *see below;* בֹּתֶרֶת, *usually* CAPITAL; KJV זֵר, *see* MOLDING; στέφανος (*alternately* WREATH)]. Apart from the architectural features mentioned above and the English idiom "crown of the head" (קָדְקֹד; Deut. 28:35; 33:16, 20; II Sam. 14:25; etc.), "crown" is reserved for the headdress symbolic of royal rank or of special merit or achievement. The OT refers mainly to the princely crown (*see* KING), the NT to the wreath given as a prize to a victorious athlete (*see* GAMES IN THE NT). *See also* DIADEM.

Two common headdresses, the cap or turban and the cloth band worn around the temples, evolved into crowns. Near Eastern art depicts a great variety of caplike crowns (*see* TURBAN), one of the most common being the conical headdress of Assyrian monarchs, a band of cloth wrapped repeatedly around the head in the manner of the modern turban. The headband developed in two directions. On the one hand it gave rise to the metal diadem, either simple in shape and without ornamentation, or more ornately formed, embossed with floral or geometric designs and set with precious stones. The great antiquity of this type of crown is attested by the discovery in a tomb at Jericho dating from *ca.* 2000 B.C. of a copper headband apparently belonging to an Amorite chieftain. Later examples have been discovered at numerous Palestinian sites. The turban and diadem were frequently combined into a composite crown. Persian kings followed this practice, and the blue cloth band of the Persian crown was adopted by the Hellenistic kings and called "diadem." The Ptolemaic and Seleucid kings wore a diadem with spikes (the radiant crown), of which the Crown of Thorns may have been an imitation.* The headband is the ancestor also of the garland of leaves or flowers given by the sports-minded Greeks and Romans to victorious athletes and sometimes to citizens of special note. Fig. CRO 53.

53. Royal crowns and headdresses: (1) red crown of Lower Egypt; (2) crown of Upper and Lower Egypt; (3) white crown of Upper Egypt; (4) Egyptian; (5) Assyrian; (6) Ptolemaic and Seleucid

The royal and priestly crowns of Israel are described by a word which means "dedication," "consecration" (נזר; used in this sense in Lev. 21:12; Num. 6:4, 9; etc.). They therefore signify not only the rank and authority of the wearer, but also the sacred nature of his office. In both cases the giving of the crown is associated with anointing (Exod. 29: 6-7; II Kings 11:12). The priestly crown, called the holy crown and engraved with the words "Holy to the Lord," was a plate of pure gold worn on the forehead and bound to the turban (KJV MITRE) by a blue lace (Exod. 28:36-37). Josephus (Antiq. III. vii.6) adds to this description of the priest's crown a three-tiered diadem worn over the turban around the nape of the neck and extending to the temples, with an elaborate floral decoration upon it. The crown, worn by the high priest only, symbolized his authority to intercede for the nation and to offer sacrifices in the Holy Place (Exod. 28:38).

It may be inferred from Ps. 21:3—H 21:4; Ezek. 21:26 that the royal crown was also a golden diadem, possibly worn over a turban. It was probably set with precious stones (Zech. 9:16; cf. the crown of Milcom [II Sam. 12:30], "their king"; cf. also Rev. 12:1). The crown symbolized the king's royal authority and special election to his office, and was accordingly worn by him when he sat on his throne and when he went to war (II Sam. 1:10). In the original form of the text the royal and high-priestly crowns were mentioned together in Zech. 6:11, but editing has made the passage in its present form refer only to the high priest's crown.

In more general usage the crown (עטרה) may be worn by the queen (Jer. 13:18), nobles (Esth. 8:15), or the bridegroom at his wedding (Song of S. 3:11). The last reference is probably to a garland of flowers worn on festive occasions (Ezek. 23:42). This word occurs often in poetic books as a metaphor for anything which confers honor or authority: gray hairs (Prov. 16:31), grandchildren (Prov. 17:6), a large and prosperous city (Isa. 28:1), a bountiful harvest (Ps. 65:11—H 65:12), wisdom or, ironically, folly (Prov. 14:24), the steadfast love of God, or even God himself (Ps. 103:4; Isa. 28:5).

The "crown royal" set upon the head of the king's horse in Esth. 6:8 KJV has been compared to the tall, crownlike head ornaments of horses depicted on Assyrian monuments, but the reference may be to the king's own crown (so RSV).

In the NT outside the book of Revelation "crown" (στέφανος) almost invariably refers to the garland, metaphorically used of eternal life as the prize for patient endurance (I Cor. 9:25; II Tim. 2:5); its wreathlike nature is clearly indicated in such phrases as "unfading crown of glory" (I Pet. 5:4). The golden royal crown of princely authority returns in Revelation as a possession of the elders (4:10), the rider of the white horse (6:2), the woman clothed with the sun (12:1), and the Son of man (14:14).

**Bibliography.** K. Galling, *Biblisches Reallexikon* (1937), pp. 126-27; A. G. Barrois, *Manuel d'Archéologie Biblique*, II (1953), 54-56. L. E. TOOMBS

**CROWN OF THORNS** [στέφανον ἐξ ἀκανθῶν or ἀκάνθινον στέφανον]. The circlet fashioned by Roman soldiers and forced down on Jesus' head as part of their derisive treatment, after Pilate had sentenced him to death. Officially Jesus was guilty of treason or rebellion, having claimed to be a king (*see* TRIAL OF JESUS). This act of the soldiers was only what might have been accorded anyone caught similarly in the toils of the Roman law. Luke, who consistently minimizes harshness toward both Jesus and his followers, does not mention it.

The word for "thorns," ἄκανθαι, means "briers." It is used figuratively in Jesus' teaching, always in a bad sense (Matt. 7:16; Mark 4:7, 18; cf. Heb. 6:8). *See* THISTLES. PIERSON PARKER

**CRUCIBLE** [מצרף, *from root* to refine]; KJV FINING POT. A melting pot, probably made of pottery, for refining silver. It is mentioned in parallel passages in Prov. 17:3; 27:21 ("The crucible is for silver, and the furnace is for gold"), in contexts alluding to the testing or judging of a man.

*See also* POTTERY § 3; SILVER § 2. H. G. MAY

*CRUCIFIXION. The act of putting to death by nailing or binding the victim to a CROSS or, sometimes, to a tree. The noun "crucifixion" does not occur in the NT, but the corresponding verb, "to crucify" (σταυρόω), appears frequently.

1. Crucifixion in general
  *a.* The public shame
  *b.* The torture

2. Jesus' crucifixion
3. The Crucifixion as a symbol

**1. Crucifixion in general.** The cruelty of this form of capital punishment lay in the public shame that was involved and in its slow physical torture.

*a. The public shame.* Partly as a warning to other potential offenders, the condemned man was made to carry his cross, or the transverse part, along the public roads and to the execution ground, which itself was nearly always in a public place. There he was stripped of all his clothing. Affixed to the cross, he could not care for his bodily needs, and was the object of taunts and indignities from passers-by.

*b. The torture.* Crucifixion damaged no vital part of the body. The victim, set astride a peg in the upright beam, was fastened to the cross by nails through the hands or wrists, and through the feet or above the heels. Ropes bound the shoulders or torso to the wooden frame. He was thus held immobile, unable to cope with heat or cold or insects. Death came slowly —often after many days—as the result of fatigue, cramped muscles, hunger, and thirst. Sometimes the victim was offered a drug to deaden the pain (Matt. 27:34; Mark 15:23).

Crucifixion had been practiced by the Phoenicians and Persians, and from them was taken over by Rome. Rome reserved the punishment for slaves and foreigners. Hence Jesus could be crucified, whereas Paul, who had Roman citizenship, would not have been. (When on rare occasions citizens were crucified—as by Verres in Sicily and by Galla in Spain— great indignation was felt among the Roman people.) In Palestine, crucifixion was used to punish robbery, tumult, and sedition. In the latter cases especially, it served as a public reminder of the Jews' servitude to the foreign power. Crosses were a familiar sight in Galilee and hence provided a poignant metaphor for Christian discipleship (Matt. 16:24; Mark 10:21; Luke 9:23).

**2. Jesus' crucifixion.** All four gospels record that Jesus foretold his own death, but only Matthew says that he knew it would be by crucifixion (Matt. 20:19; 26:2), and that he foresaw the same fate for some of his followers (Matt. 23:34).

Jesus' crucifixion is recounted in Matt. 27; Mark 15; Luke 23; John 19, and is many times referred to elsewhere in the NT (e.g., Acts 2:36; 4:10; I Cor. 2:8; II Cor. 13:4; Gal. 3:1; Rev. 11:8). None of these dwells, however, on the physical details that interest a modern. Even the statements that Jesus died on a tree (Acts 5:30; 10:39) should probably be taken figuratively, a tree being roughly suggested by the cross's shape. The exact spot of the execution is not known (*see* GOLGOTHA), though it was evidently beside one of the main roads leading into Jerusalem. Jesus refused the drink offered to deaden his pain. Two other men were put to death at the same time. These, or at least one of them, joined in the derision heaped on Jesus (Matt. 27:44; Mark 15:32; Luke 23:39)—perhaps in the forlorn hope of gaining some favor by siding at last with the rulers. A sign, indicating the crime for which he was condemned, was placed on Jesus' cross (*see* INSCRIPTION ON THE CROSS), but nothing is said of similar signs on the other two.

The next day was a Jewish holy day. So, the Fourth Gospel says, the Roman authorities permitted the victims to be removed from the crosses at evening, their legs being first broken to assure that they did not escape. When the executioners came to Jesus, they saw that he was already dead. This raises the question, How did he die so quickly? The spear thrust, which only John records, is there said to have been made after he died. The familiar suggestion that he died of a broken heart depends on a medically dubious explanation of the "blood and water" of John 19:34—and the latter was written, not with a physiological, but with a theological purpose. Far more probably, Jesus' end had been hastened by the scourging. Roman scourging was so severe that victims often died under it. For one charged, as Jesus was, with sedition, it would have been merciless.

The Synoptics say that at Jesus' death there was a supernatural darkness, and that the temple veil was rent in two. Matthew adds an earthquake and bursting rocks, and corpses walking about Jerusalem. John says nothing of any of this.

**3. The Crucifixion as a symbol.** Death by crucifixion brought Jesus into public disrepute. It placed him under an ancient curse, "for it is written, 'Cursed be every one who hangs on a tree' " (Gal. 3:13; cf. Deut. 21:23). This provided the greatest obstacle in the subsequent effort to convert Jews to the new faith. Nothing in the OT or in Jewish lore had prepared them for the thought that the Messiah should be thus handled. To many Jews, the Christian claim was a shocking blasphemy.

To Christians, however, the Crucifixion was the most intense demonstration of Christ's love and power, and the symbol of the Christian's own union with his Lord. To become his follower meant to crucify one's old and sinful self (Rom. 6:6; Gal. 2:20; 5:24). Or, with a changed figure, ungodliness itself had been put to death by the Crucifixion (Gal. 6:14), so that the Christian was now free to live in Christ alone. *See also* TRIAL OF JESUS.

PIERSON PARKER

**CRUSE.** A small, elongated pottery jug *ca.* four to six inches tall, used to hold olive oil. It is referred to in the episode of Elijah's visit to the widow of Zarephath, when he asks for food (צפחת, I Kings 17: 12-16). In the KJV of I Sam. 26:11-16 (צפחת, RSV "jar") the reference is to a pottery canteen. In II Kings 2:20 (צלחית), the RSV "bowl" is a better translation. J. L. KELSO

**CRYPTOGRAPHY** krĭp tŏg′rə fĭ. *See* ATHBASH.

**CRYSTAL.** A quartz, nearly transparent, either colorless or slightly tinged. "Crystal" is the translation of the following terms:

*a)* גביש, *gābhîsh* (cf. אלגביש, "hail"; Arabic *gibs*, "gypsum"; Akkadian *gibšu*, "a mass"; LXX γαβείς); KJV PEARLS. It is mentioned with coral and pearls(?) in the evaluation of wisdom (Job 28:18).

*b)* קרח (cf. Akkad. *qarḥu*, "ice"; LXX κρύσταλλος; Vulg. *crystallus*). It is used to describe the clearness of the sky (Ezek. 1:22, where the RSV, with the LXX, omits "terrible"; cf. KJV). It is elsewhere translated "the cold," "frost," "ice."

*c)* Κρύσταλλος, a simile for "clearness." It is used

to describe the sea of glass (Rev. 4:6) and the river of life (Rev. 22:1).

*d*) Κρυσταλλίξω, "to be as crystal." A participle form, translated "clear as crystal," describes the jasper-like radiance of the New Jerusalem (Rev. 21:11).

*See also* JEWELS AND PRECIOUS STONES § 2.

W. E. STAPLES

**CUB** kŭb [כוב] (Ezek. 30:5 RSV mg.); KJV CHUB. A place mentioned in connection with Cush, Libya, and Lydia, and generally regarded as an error for כוב, LIBYA (so RSV). The LXX, whose rendering of this verse differs from the Hebrew in several particulars, mentions the Libyans at this point.

T. O. LAMBDIN

**CUBIT** kū'bĭt. A unit of measurement based on the length from elbow to tip of middle finger, eighteen inches or a little more. *See* WEIGHTS AND MEASURES § D4*a*.

**CUCKOO.** KJV translation of שחף (RSV SEA GULL). "Cuckoo" refers to any of a family (Cuculidae) of mostly small birds, of which two species, according to Tristram, visit Palestine in the summer, the Common Cuckoo (*Cuculus canorus canorus*) and the Great Spotted Cuckoo (*Clamator glandarius*). שחף, however, is deemed unclean in the OT presumably because it is either raptorial or carrion-eating; and as the cuckoo is an insect-eater, this would appear to eliminate "cuckoo" as a possible meaning for שחף.

W. S. McCULLOUGH

**CUCUMBER** [קשאה, *qiššū'â;* מקשה, *miqšâ;* Akkad. *qiššu;* Arab. *qiṭṭa;* Punic κισσου]. A vegetable or fruit of the genus *Cucumis*. During the wilderness wanderings the Israelites longed for the fish, *qiššū'îm*, melons, leeks, onions, and garlic they had eaten in Egypt (Num. 11:5). Zohary (*see* FLORA § 3*e*) claims that קשאה referred to the muskmelon (*Cucumis melo* L.) rather than the cucumber. The long list of linguistic evidences, beginning with the LXX (σικυος) would tend to argue for the cucumber (*Cucumis sativus* L., or *Cucumis chate* L., the hairy, elongated variety), despite the absence of early Egyptian references to it.

The noun of place, based on the same word, is found in Isa. 1:8 in a vision of destroyed Jerusalem, "like a lodge in a cucumber field [מקשה]." It is also used in Jer. 10:5 depicting the worthlessness of idols, "like scarecrows in a cucumber field" (KJV "They are upright as the palm tree"; cf. Bar. 6:70—G 6:69; *see* PALM TREE).

*See also* AGRICULTURE; FLORA §§ A3*d-e;* FOOD; LODGE; MELON; SCARECROW.

**Bibliography.** I. Löw, *Die Flora der Juden,* vol. 1, pt. 2 (1928), pp. 530-35; H. N. and A. L. Moldenke, *Plants of the Bible* (1952), pp. 80-81, 88. J. C. TREVER

**CULT.** *See* WORSHIP.

**CUMMIN** [כמון, *kammōn;* κύμινον; Ugar. *kmn, and most Semitic languages*]. The caraway-like seed of the *Cuminum cyminum* L., an herb of the carrot family mentioned with DILL.* Though not common in Bible

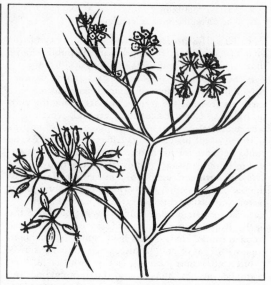

54. Cummin

lands today, the seed was apparently much used in ancient times as a condiment for seasoning foods. Isaiah portrays (28:23-29) in vivid poetry the work of the farmer, including planting and threshing cummin (vss. 25, 27). In Matt. 23:23 (cf. Luke 11:42) cummin is included with MINT and dill in Jesus' criticism of the particularism of the Pharisees, who fail to show adequate concern for the more important matters in human behavior (cf. Mic. 6:8). Deut. 14: 22-23 (cf. Lev. 27:30) prescribes the tithing of grain, wine, oil, and firstlings of the flock, and the Pharisaic Mishna (Ma'as. IV.5) defines "grain" to include dill and cummin. Fig. CUM 54.

*See also* FLORA § A6*d;* ANISE; SPICES.

**Bibliography.** I. Löw, *Die Flora der Juden,* III (1924), 435-39; H. N. and A. L. Moldenke, *Plants of the Bible* (1952), p. 89. J. C. TREVER

**CUN** kŭn [כון; Lat. *Cunnae*] (I Chr. 18:8); KJV CHUN. A Syrian town from which David took much bronze. The parallel in II Sam. 8:8 has BEROTHAI.

**CUNEIFORM** kū nē'ɔ fôrm [Lat. *cuneus,* wedge]. The wedge-shaped syllabic signs impressed on CLAY TABLETS with a stylus or carved on stone.* Originally pictographic, the signs soon were simplified and stylized. Invented by the Sumerians, the script passed to the Akkadians, Hurrians, Hittites, and Elamites. Other cuneiform scripts were developed for Old Persian and Ugaritic. Fig. UGA 3.

*See also* WRITING AND WRITING MATERIALS.

R. J. WILLIAMS

**CUP** [אגן, גביע, כום, כים, סף; ποτήριον]. The cup of Bible times ran in two general forms. One was similar to our cup and was made both with and without a handle. The handled cup also served as a dipper (Fig. POT 63, no. 3*a*). The more common cup, however, was a shallow bowl which came in various forms and sizes. Joseph possessed a silver cup used for DIVINATION (Gen. 44:2-5). The LAMPSTAND had in its branches "cups" made like almonds, each with "capital" and flower (Exod. 25:31-35).

The cup was widely used in figurative language. It was symbolic of the kind of life experience which God the Host pours out for his world. For the saints there was the cup of the blessings of God (Pss. 23:5; 116:13). For the wicked there was the wine cup of the wrath of God (Pss. 11:6; 75:8—H 75:9; Isa. 51: 17, 22; Jer. 25:15; 49:12; Hab. 2:15-16). Babylon was the golden wine cup in the Lord's hand from which all the nations drank (Jer. 51:7). Samaria's cup of horror and desolation was her fate, and Jerusalem must drink of it (Ezek. 23:31-33). Similarly, Jerusalem might be pictured as a cup of reeling to all its enemies (Zech. 12:2). The cup of Jesus was the cup of suffering (Matt. 20:22-23). The cup of the wrath of God appears also in Rev. 14:10; 16:19; 17: 4; 18:6. The unique use of "cup" is in connection with the LORD'S SUPPER.

The Lord might be spoken of as the cup of the faithful (Ps. 16:5). The "cup of salvation" (Ps. 116: 13) may be the libation of wine in the temple rites, symbolic of the Lord's saving help. In Jer. 16:7 the "cup of consolation" is perhaps the cup of wine presented to the mourner at the completion of the fast. The cup of the Lord's Supper is called the "cup of blessing," a term used for the third of the cups drunk at the Passover, and is contrasted with the "cup of demons" (I Cor. 10:16-21). J. L. KELSO

**CUPBEARER** [משקה, one who gives drink; LXX οἰνοχόος]. An official who serves the king wine and enjoys his confidence. Pharaoh's cupbearer is called a BUTLER.

Fear of intrigue made this a position of peculiar trust. Loyalty was a prime requisite. Solomon's cupbearers were part of the entourage which amazed the Queen of Sheba (I Kings 10:5; II Chr. 9:4). They may be the messengers of Assyria called RAB-SHAKEH

55. An Assyrian cupbearer

who stood before Hezekiah to challenge Israel. Palace reliefs of Assyria show the importance of the cupbearer in relation to other retainers of the king.* Nehemiah was a cupbearer to the Persian king (Neh. 1:11; 2:1). That a foreigner could attain such a high place is testimony both to the freedom of Persia and to the astuteness of Nehemiah. Herod the great had a EUNUCH as his cupbearer (Jos. Antiq. XV.vii.4; XVI.viii.1). Fig. CUP 55. C. U. WOLF

**CURDS;** KJV BUTTER. The usual translation of חמאה and its variants. The modern equivalent is leban, prepared by churning fresh milk in a goatskin containing leftover clots from the previous supply. Thus in Prov. 30:33 we read that "pressing milk produces curds."

Curds are a part of the ordinary diet of the Near East. Abraham offers them to the three men (Gen. 18:8); Sisera receives them from Jael (Judg. 5:25); and they are brought to David at Mahanaim (II Sam. 17:29). Similarly, Jeshurun will receive from Yahweh all manner of good things, including "curds from the herd" (Deut. 32:14). And Zophar notes that the wicked man

> will not look upon the rivers,
> the streams flowing with honey and curds
> (Job 20:17).

In Isa. 7:15 the honey and curds to be eaten by the child Immanuel probably represent, not the food of the gods, but the food of poverty—a nomadic diet. Vs. 22, however, which is probably not a part of the original oracle, returns to the use of curds as figurative for material abundance.

*Bibliography.* G. Fohrer. "Zu Jes. 7₁₄ im Zusammenhang von Jes. 7₁₀₋₂₂," *ZAW*, LXVIII (1956), 54-56. J. F. ROSS

**CURSE** [אלה, מארה, קללה; ἀρά, κατάρα]. The expression of a wish that evil may befall another; a malediction. It found a wide variety of uses in Israelite society and was a phenomenon universal in Israel's contemporary world.

Among those cultural institutions exhibiting the use of malediction as a protective device may be noted the contractual agreement, most notably the international agreement or treaty (e.g., *ANET* 203-5). The curses were designed to protect the terms of contract by being directed at the future violator of the treaty. In the OT this appears in two forms: (*a*) following the election of a sovereign, reflected in Israel's acceptance of the suzerainty of Yahweh (Deut. 27:15-26; 28:15-19, 20-36), and in the trees' acceptance of the suzerainty of the bramble (Judg. 9:15); and (*b*) the agreement among the independent tribes of Israel, gathered in amphictyonic assembly, to bar intermarriage with the tribe of Benjamin (Judg. 21:18). Also displaying such security measures was the class of texts known as royal inscriptions (e.g., *ANET* 267*b*), to which were appended maledictions leveled at any who should alter or destroy the inscription. Though no Hebrew royal inscription bearing maledictions has been recovered, the OT has preserved an edict of Darius the Persian monarch, ending with a curse similar in style and purport to those known from elsewhere (Ezra 6:12; cf. Saul's prohibition to his troops in the midst of his military victory: I Sam. 14:24, 28). Tombs also, on occasion, were protected by means of curses aimed at any who might violate or desecrate them (e.g., *ANET* 504-5). That this curse type found employment in Israel is now affirmed by the discovery of an inscription on the tomb of an Israelite royal officer containing a curse (*IEJ*, III [1953], 137-52). Joshua hoped to prevent the rebuilding of Jericho by laying a curse upon its future founder (Josh. 6:26). Curses were further pronounced upon oneself in an effort to protect or ensure the truth and reliability of assertions concerning actions in the past or the present (Num. 5:19-22; Job 31:7-8, 9-10, 19-22, 38-40; Ps. 7:4-6), or promises regarding the future (Ps. 137:5-6). *See* OATH.

As a retributive or punitive measure, curses are found to have been leveled against murderers (Gen. 4:11-12; 49:7; II Sam. 3:29) or against the land, the scene of the homicide (II Sam. 1:21); against sons by their fathers for sexual offenses (Gen. 9:25-27; 49:4); and served, furthermore, as explanation for enigmatic physiological or environmental peculiarities: the ancestor or prototype of those exhibiting such abnormalities was reckoned as having been cursed by God (e.g., the serpent, which, unlike all other creatures, must crawl on its belly [Gen. 3:14]; woman, who experiences pain in childbirth [vs. 16]; and man, who must exert himself to wring sustenance from the earth [vss. 17-19]), or by some ancient hero (Josh. 9:23). In utter depression and despair the Hebrew poet could give vent to his feelings in a curse against his day of birth (Job 3:3-10; Jer. 20:14-18). Lastly, curses were employed against enemies who might in the future harm one (e.g., II Sam. 18:32; Job 27:7; Dan. 4:16), had already hurt, or were currently discomfiting one (e.g., Pss. 35:4-8, 26; 40:15-16; 109:6-15, 17-19, 29; Jer. 11:20; 12:3; 17:18), or who threatened the national safety (e.g., Pss. 79:6-12; 83: 10-18; 129:5-7; Jer. 10:25). Curses thus served to castigate and chastise, to protect, and to punish, and were employed in all situations for which other protective or punitive measures were either lacking or inadequate. This is confirmed, in part, by David, who, having cursed Joab for his murder of Abner, confessed his inability to deal with the murderer in any other way (II Sam. 3:39).

The distinctive and distinguishing trait of Hebrew maledictions lies in the manner of curse formulation. In general, a clear difference may be remarked between "East" and "West" (including Hebrew) Semitic curses. Whereas East Semitic (Akkadian) maledictions were formulated in a religio-literary tradition which sought divine approval and execution, importuning a god or gods through imprecation, West Semitic curses were composed in a tradition which relied, primarily, not upon deity, but upon the power of the word. Hebrew shared the general West Semitic preference for constructions in which the agent of the curse remained undesignated, and for verbs in passive forms. Characteristically and specifically Hebraic is the use of the *Qal* passive participle ארור, "Cursed be . . . !" The significance of this distinction between East and West Semitic curse formulations is that in the former, reliance is placed upon deity for the execution of the desired effect, whereas in the latter, in the absence of any indica-

tion of curse agency, the reliance is upon the power inherent within the curse itself.

Against two in the OT curses are never cited: God and David. That God *might* be cursed appears evident from Exod. 22:28—H 22:27; Isa. 8:21 (cf. Job 2:9), and was grounds for capital punishment (I Kings 21:13). Though David is twice said to have been cursed (by Goliath in I Sam. 17:43; by Shimei in II Sam. 16:5-7), the words of the curses are not quoted (Shimei's "Begone, begone, you man of blood . . . ," may not be construed as a curse, since it would hardly deserve David's description of it as a "grievous curse" [I Kings 2:8], and is moreover comparable to no known biblical or extrabiblical curse, either in form or in content). The concern in refraining from quoting these was the protection of the Davidic dynasty; for a curse, it was feared, might come to fruition in future generations (I Kings 2:8-9).

All the more remarkable, therefore, is the occasional disregard shown this device: Ezekiel rebuked the "rebellious house" for Zedekiah's having "despised the oath and broke[n] his covenant" with the king of Babylon (Ezek. 17:11-21); Hiel of Bethel, in the days of Ahab, rebuilt Jericho and suffered the consequences of Joshua's curse (I Kings 16:34); and one need only recall the general prophetic criticism of Israel for breaking its covenant with the Lord (e.g., Jer. 34:8 ff; Amos 2:6-8). It may be that under pressure political or other necessities might well outweigh religious niceties. Nevertheless, the reluctance evident in Hebrew literature to permit a curse to be leveled at God or at David, the necessary circumlocution designed and made available to the ostracized tribe of Benjamin whereby it might procure wives from its fellow tribes of Israel without, thereby, having the latter suffer the effects of their curse (Judg. 21:16-23), and the frequent abbreviation of the OATH from an original self-curse to an oath formula in which all but the most meager traces of the curse have been excised, constitute eloquent testimony to the fear and veneration accorded malediction.

*See also* ACCURSED; ANATHEMA; BLESSINGS AND CURSINGS; DEVOTED THINGS; EXCOMMUNICATION; OATHS.

*Bibliography.* J. Pedersen, *Der Eid bei den Semiten* (1914), pp. 64-118; S. Mowinckel, Psalmenstudien, V: *Segen und Fluch in Israels Kult und Psalmdichtung* (1924), 1-4, 61-135; J. Hempel, "Die israelitischen Anschauungen von Segen und Fluch im Lichte altorientalischer Parallelen," *ZDMG*, N.F. IV (1925), 20-110; J. Pedersen, *Israel*, I-II (1926), 437-52; H. Gunkel, *Einleitung in die Psalmen* (1933), pp. 304-9; S. H. Blank, "The Curse, the Blasphemy, the Spell, and the Oath," *HUCA*, vol. XXIII, no. 1 (1950/51), pp. 73-95; A. G. Herbert and N. H. Snaith, "A Study of the Words 'Curse' and 'Righteousness,' " *The Bible Translator*, vol. III, no. 3 (1952), pp. 111-14; N. Avigan, "The Epitaph of a Royal Steward from Siloam Village," *IEJ*, III (1953), 137-52; J. Scharbert, *Solidarität in Segen und Fluch im AT und in seiner Umwelt* (1958); "'Fluchen' und 'Segnen' im AT," *Bibl.*, XXXIX (1958), 1-26. S. GEVIRTZ

**CURTAIN** [יְרִיעָה (*alternately* TENT), *from* יָרַע, to quiver; דַּק (Isa. 40:22), *probably* a thin veil; KJV מָסָךְ (Num. 3:26; RSV SCREEN); καταπέτασμα]. Normally the fabric of which tents were made. In most instances "curtain" appears in parallel with "tent"

and is synonymous with it (Song of S. 1:5; Isa. 54:2; Jer. 4:20; 10:20; 49:29; Hab. 3:7). The tabernacle in which the ark was to be carried was made of ten curtains measuring twenty-eight by four cubits (Exod. 26:2; etc.; see TABERNACLE). This tradition may be mirrored in the tent (KJV "curtains") in which the ark of God was kept (II Sam. 7:2; I Chr. 17:1). The tent curtain is a figurative description of the sky in Isa. 40:22, where Yahweh "stretches out the heavens like a curtain" (cf. Ps. 104:2). In the NT the "curtain" is always the curtain of the temple, which covered the MOST HOLY PLACE (see also VEIL OF THE TEMPLE). In Hebrews the curtain which covered the inner shrine is a figure of Christ's flesh (10:20), which is the way by which Christians enter the sanctuary of faith (6:19).                E. M. GOOD

## CURTAIN OF THE TEMPLE [καταπέτασμα].
The curtain which separated the Most Holy Place from the rest of the temple. The curtain of the temple was torn in two, from top to bottom, at the moment of Jesus' death (Matt. 27:51; Mark 15:38; Luke 23:45).

See also VEIL OF THE TEMPLE.                E. M. GOOD

\*CUSH kōōsh [כוש; LXX, Aq., Symm., and Theod. Χουσὶ υἱοῦ Ἰεμενί]. **1.** A Benjaminite whose solitary reference in the title of Ps. 7 permits us at least to infer that he was a calumnious foe of David and that his slanderous words were considered by the later liturgists, who attached the superscription to the psalm, to form the setting of the composition.

E. R. DALGLISH

**2.** An ancient name of the territory S of Egypt, corresponding roughly to the present Sudan; more often called ETHIOPIA.

## CUSHAN kōō'shăn [כושן] (Hab. 3:7). A name used
as a parallel to Midian. It may be an older and poetical name of Midian, based on the presence of tribes descended from CUSH. It is probable, therefore, that the word כשית ("Cushite"), applied to the wife of Moses (Num. 12:1), does not mean "Ethiopian," but rather refers to the Midianitess, Zipporah.                S. COHEN

## CUSHAN-RISHATHAIM kōō'shăn rĭsh'ə thā'əm
[כושן רשעתים, Cushan of double wickedness(?)]; KJV CHUSHAN-RISHATHAIM. The name—or possibly a disfigurement of the name—of the king of ARAM-NAHARAIM who was the first oppressor of the Israelites mentioned in the book of Judges (3:8-10). His eight-year oppression was ended by the military victory of the first judge, OTHNIEL.

The meaning of the unusual form of this name has received no satisfactory solution. CUSHAN, although by some scholars understood as referring either to the Cushites in Ethiopia or to the Kassites of Babylonia, is most likely related to a Midianite tribe near Edom (Hab. 3:7). The an ending is like that of a number of Edomite tribal names (Gen. 36: 26-28). It may be that by an oblique reference to both Cush, son of Ham, and the hated Edomites and Midianites, the Deuteronomic editor, from whom this story probably comes, means to debase the unknown

real name. The dual form Rishathaim, deliberately rhyming with Naharaim, and meaning "double wickedness," is an epithet denouncing this foreign conqueror. This play on words is similar to the "shame" intended to be cast by the names Ishbosheth for ISHBAAL and Mephibosheth for MERIBAAL.

The identity of this king is uncertain. Because he was defeated by a S Palestinian hero, Othniel, some have understood Cushan-rishathaim to have been an Edomite chieftain, assuming "Aram" as an error for "Edom" and Rishathaim as perhaps "chief of the Temanites." Others have identified him with a fourteenth-century-B.C. Mitannian ruler or with a Hittite king or his Syrian vassal. His name may be reflected in a N Syrian district called Qusana-ruma, mentioned in a list of Ramses III. Possibly he was a powerful foreign ruler named Irsu from the Upper Euphrates region, who invaded Egypt shortly before 1200 B.C. and was expelled by Ramses III's father, Set-nakht, founder of the Twentieth Dynasty.

***Bibliography.*** E. Taeubler, "Cushan-Rishathaim," *HUCA,* XX (1947), 137-42; R. T. O'Callaghan, *Aram Naharaim* (1948), pp. 122-23, 139-42; W. F. Albright, *Archaeology and the Religion of Israel* (1953), pp. 110-11, 205; A. Malamat, "Cushan Rishathaim and the Decline of the Near East Around 1200 B.C.," *JNES,* XIII (1954), 231-42; J. Bright, *A History of Israel* (1959), pp. 156-57.                C. F. KRAFT

**CUSHI** kōōsh'ī [כושי, Cushite]. **1.** Great-grandfather of Jehudi, a prince in Jehoiakim's court (Jer. 36:14).

**2.** The father of the prophet Zephaniah (Zeph. 1:1).

**3.** KJV translation in II Sam. 18:21-32 (RSV THE CUSHITE) of the name of the man who carried the news of Absalom's defeat and death from Joab to David. He was perhaps a Negro slave or a mercenary, and, as an alien, preferable to Ahimaaz as the bearer of the tragic news.                J. M. WARD

**CUSHION** [προσκεφάλαιον] (Mark 4:38); KJV PILLOW. A regular part of the furnishings of a boat.                S. A. CARTLEDGE

**CUSTODIAN** [παιδαγωγός, boy guider]; KJV INSTRUCTOR (I Cor. 4:15); SCHOOLMASTER (Gal. 3:24-25). A slave who attended a boy, took him to school, etc., until he was of age—i.e., sixteen years old. This meaning has been shown to be the common one in koine Greek and is found in classical Greek, where the term might also refer to the slave's function as a tutor. The word does not occur in the LXX.

Paul in Gal. 3:24-25 uses the term figuratively of the law (see LAW IN THE NT) to imply the inferior status of those living under it. The figure is introduced in vs. 23 by the related idea of guardianship (cf. Gal. 4:2 ff; see GUARDIAN): "We were confined [ἐφρουρούμεθα, 'guarded'] under the law, . . . so that the law was our custodian until Christ came . . . . But now that faith has come, we are no longer under a custodian." While this rendering achieves consistency and gives the general sense of the passage, it may lose the full force of εἰς Χριστόν, which probably has here something more than only temporal force ("until Christ came"). The custodian would seem not only to guard, but also in a sense to guide, "to Christ." In spite of the negative and temporary function assigned to it in Pauline thought, the law is in itself holy and good (Rom. 7:12, 16), as such serving to convict men of sin and to bring them to Christ. There is here doubtless also some lingering influence of the Jewish conception of Torah as a mediator between man and God.

In Jewish sources the term παιδαγωγός is found as a loan word in rabbinic literature (פדגוגא or פדגוג), but is apparently never applied to the law. In IV Macc. 5:34, however, the law is addressed by Eleazar as παιδευτὰ νόμε ("teacher-law"). One may here compare references to Moses as a teacher par excellence.

In I Cor. 4:15, Paul somewhat differently uses the same Greek word to contrast himself as the spiritual father of the Corinthian Christians with the many other "guides" (KJV "instructors") which they have "in Christ."

*Bibliography.* E. D. Burton, *Galatians,* ICC (1920), pp. 200-201; H. L. Strack and P. Billerbeck, *Kommentar zum NT aus Talmud und Midrasch,* III (1926), 339-40, 557; J. S. Calloway, "Paul's Letter to the Galatians and Plato's *Lysis,*" *JBL,* LXVII (1948), 353-55; S. Sandmel, *A Jewish Understanding of the NT* (1956), ch. VIII.                           A. WIKGREN

**CUTH, CUTHAH** kōͦth, —ə [כותה, כות; Assyrian-Babylonian *Kūtuna, Kūtû*]. An ancient N Babylonian city the ruins of which are located at Tell Ibrahim NE of Babylon. It was famous as a center for the cult of Nergal, king of the underworld. According to II Kings 17:24, 30, Sargon II of Assyria, after taking Samaria and leading its inhabitants off in captivity (721 B.C.), repopulated the city with foreigners. Among these was a contingent from Cuthah, who brought the cult of Nergal with them to their new home.                                             T. JACOBSEN

**CUTHA** kōͦth'ə [Κουθα (A); B *omits*] (I Esd. 5:32); KJV COUTHA kōͦ'thə. Head of a family of temple servants who returned with Zerubbabel. The name is omitted in the parallels Ezra 2:52; Neh. 7:54.
                                             C. T. FRITSCH

**CUTTING LOCUST;** KJV PALMERWORM. See LOCUST § 1*d.*

**CUTTINGS IN THE FLESH.** *See* MUTILATION.

**CYAMON** sī'ə mən [Κυαμών] (Jth. 7:3). An area "which faces Esdraelon"; possibly a corruption of "JOKNEAM."                                       C. T. FRITSCH

**CYMBAL.** *See* MUSICAL INSTRUMENTS § B1*b.*

**CYPRESS** [תאשור, *te'aššûr* (alternately PINE), Ugar. *tišrm;* ברוש, *berôš* (alternately PINE); KJV תרזה, *tirzâ* (RSV "holm tree"), *see below;* κυπάρισσος]. The earliest occurrence of this word is on a fourteenth-century tablet at Ugarit (120:7) in an inventory list along with ALMUG.

The תאשור is mentioned in Isa. 41:19; 60:13 with other trees in figures of God's transformation of Pal-

estine. The KJV translates this word "box tree"; the Amer. Trans. and the AJA use "larch"; the RSV translates "pine" (also in the emended Ezek. 27:6). Moffatt uses "cypress" (*Cupressus sempervirens* var. *horizontalis* Mill., Gord.), along with several others (*see* FLORA § A9*e*), for linguistic and other reasons. A final solution seems remote.

ברוש is usually translated "cypress," but *see* PINE.

In Ezek. 27:6 בת אשרים (KJV "company of the ASHURITES") is generally recognized as incorrectly divided for בתאשרים, "with cypress wood" (RSV "of pines").

The KJV OT uses "cypress" only for תרזה in Isa. 44:14. This reference might be to the slender cypress, *Cupressus sempervirens* var. *pyramidalis* (but *see* HOLM TREE). The KJV, with the RSV, uses "cypress" in Ecclus. 24:13; 50:10 (*see* OIL TREE).

Many consider the עצי גפר, *'aṣê gōpher* ("gopher wood") of Noah's ark (Gen. 6:14) to refer to cypress wood, since it was used extensively in shipbuilding in ancient times (*cf.* FLORA § A8*b*), but the word remains obscure.

*See also* BOX TREE; FIR; ASSYRIA AND BABYLONIA.

*Bibliography.* I. Löw, *Die Flora der Juden,* III (1924), 26-33; H. N. and A. L. Moldenke, *Plants of the Bible* (1952), pp. 89-91, 62-64.                                      J. C. TREVER

\***CYPRUS** sī'prəs [כתים, *kittîm* (Isa. 23:1, 12; Jer. 2: 10; Ezek. 27:6; *elsewhere* KITTIM kĭt'ĭm [*see also* KITTIM]; KJV CHITTIM); κύπρος]. A Mediterranean island situated *ca.* forty-one miles from the coast of Asia Minor and sixty miles from Syria. In both prehistoric and historic times Cyprus was in close relationship with Syria and Palestine.

The oldest attested name for Cyprus is Alashia,

which occurs in cuneiform texts from Mari (eighteenth century B.C.), Khattushash, Ugarit, and Tell el-Amarna (fourteenth-thirteenth centuries B.C.), in Egyptian sources as *A-ra-sa,* and in the OT as ELISHA. The name κύπρος occurs in the *Iliad* (XI.21) and the *Odyssey* (IV.83; VIII.362; XVII.442; etc.). The name Iadnan/Iatnan is used in the Assyrian inscriptions from the late eighth and seventh centuries B.C. Kittim, a name based on Kition (Citium), a city colonized by the Phoenicians, is used for the whole island in the OT.

Archaeological finds and textual references make it apparent that already in the Middle Bronze Age (*ca.* 1800) trade between Cyprus (Alashia) and the mainland—Syria and Palestine—and Egypt flourished. Evidence for this trade during the Late Bronze Age on Cyprus (1500-1100) has increased with the excavations at Ras Shamra (Syria) and Enkomi (Cyprus). Cypriote white ware (milk bowl) has been found as imports in many parts of the Levant and the Aegean world. It has been found at Lachish, Tell el-Amarna, Atchana, Troy, etc. Cyprus also was in close contact with the Mycenean world. Mycenean pottery has been found in abundance on Cyprus, and there is considerable proof of Mycenean colonization of Cyprus during this period. Cyprus in turn became the base for export of Cypro-Mycenean (Late Helladic III) wares to Syria and Palestine. Such imports—based-ring ware and wishbone-handled bowls are the main types—and locally made imitations are found at many Late Bronze Age sites in Palestine (LB II A, B, 1300-1200). UGARIT was under strong Cypriote influence and served as a port of entry for Cypriote imports. It is most probable that there was a colony of Cypriote merchants at Minet el-Beida, Ugarit's harbor town. Tablets in a variety of the Cypro-Minoan script have been found there. Similar tablets, as yet undeciphered, and in an unknown language, have also been found on Cyprus, especially at Enkomi. They date from *ca.* 1500-1100. From *ca.* 700-200 a modified offshoot of the same type of script—called the "Cypriote syllabary" (deciphered in the 1870's)—is used to write both Greek and the Eteocypriote language. The latter, found especially at Amathus, can be read, but not understood.

It was as a source for copper that Cyprus was famous in the ancient world. Legend made Cinyras of Cyprus father of coppermining; and to Pliny, Cyprus is "where there was the first invention of copper." The Mari economic archives have affirmed the importation of copper from Cyprus (Alashia) already in the eighteenth century. Both the Egyptians and the Hittites imported Cypriote copper (Tell el-Amarna letters; Boghazköy archives), and copper ingots from Enkomi have been found at Ugarit. In the *Odyssey*, Cyprus is the source of copper (I.184). During the Amarna Age, Cyprus was raided by Lukku (Lycians?), as the king of Cyprus complained in a letter to Pharaoh. Hittite rulers like Hattusilis exiled dissident subjects there. Cyprus was spared the ravages of the Dorian invasion that destroyed Mycenae and strongly affected nearby Rhodes. The Cypriote Greeks spoke an Achaean pre-Doric Greek. It has been claimed, on the basis of the excavations at Enkomi, that Cyprus was invaded by the "People of the Sea" (*see* PHILISTINES) before their unsuccessful assault upon Egypt, but proof for this is lacking. Few facts concerning the island are available for the next three hundred years, the "Cypriote dark ages."

During the eleventh century, it may be garnered from the Wen-Amon report, Cyprus was independent. The tenth brought the Phoenicians, who colonized Cyprus and spread from there to the shores of the W Mediterranean. Testimony of Phoenician rule at this early period is limited. A Phoenician funerary inscription from the ninth century has been found; and Hiram, king of Tyre in 738, is known from the dedication on bowls from Monti Sinoas. Phoenician inscriptions first become plentiful in the fourth and third centuries. The Phoenicians founded strong outposts at first in seacoast ports on the E side of the island, like Kition (modern Larnaka), which remained until the fourth century the strongest Phoenician post in the island. OT passages such as Isa. 23:1, 12; Ezek. 27:6 attest the close connection of the Tyrians and Sidonians with Kittim. To Jeremiah it was a familiar designation for the West (2:10).

During the late eighth century and the seventh century the Assyrians, under Sargon, Sennacherib, and Esarhaddon, controlled most of Cyprus. Sargon boasted of the seven rulers from whom he collected tribute and had an inscribed statue of himself, which was found in 1845, set up in Kition. Sennacherib maintained his rule over the area; Luli, king of Sidon, did not find it a safe refuge from Assyrian might. His successor, Esarhaddon, provided us, in his prism, with a list of ten of the important cities of Cyprus and their kings. Among those cities known from the historic period whose identification seems positive are Idalion, Khytroi, Soli, Paphos, Salamis, Kurion, Tamassos, Ledron. The names of the kings have not been as positively identified. Two—Eteander and Pylagoras/Pythagoras—are probably Greek, the other Eteocypriote. None of the names is Semitic. Kition, missing on this list, was probably once again under the rule of Tyre, hence already vassal to Assyria.

With the decline of Assyria, Egyptian influence grew in Cyprus. Apries and Amasis attacked Cyprus, according to the Greek historians, and archaeology has borne out the rule of the latter on the island. The Cypriotes aided Cyrus in his expedition against Babylon and were rewarded with the right to be ruled by their own kings rather than by Persian governors as were the other parts of the fifth satrapy of *ebir nari,* "across the river."

Cyprus was the W seaward limit of Persian expansion. The Cypriotes participated in the Ionian revolt against Persia but were defeated (499-498). The high point of Greek influence in Cyprus during this period is the reign of Euagoras I of Salamis (*ca.* 411-373). The Phoenicians, whose main center was Kition, conquered or colonized various other cities such as Idalion and Tamassos. In some cities like Amathus the native "Eteocypriote" element was strong.

After the Battle of Issus (333), the kings of the city-states joined Alexander, and Cyprus became part of the Hellenistic world. After some dispute as to the fate of the island among Alexander's successors, it was from 294 to 58 B.C. under Egyptian rule and supplied silver, wood for shipbuilding, and grain to the Ptolemides. There were Jews on the island from the time of Ptolemy I, if not earlier. According to I Macc. 15:23, Cyprus was one of the many lands to which were sent copies of the letter which the Roman consul in 139-138 wrote to Ptolemy Euergetes II, urging that the Jewish settlers should be well treated. At the time of John Hyrcanus, as we are informed by Josephus, the Jews living in Egypt and Cyprus were in a flourishing state (Antiq. XIV.x.4). In 58 B.C., Cyprus was annexed by Rome and was joined with Cilicia for administrative purposes. From a remark of Philo's (*Legatio ad Gaium* 28) and the references to Cyprus in Acts, it is clear that there was a large community spread throughout the island in the first century A.D. Joseph surnamed Barnabas was a native of Cyprus and an early convert to Christianity (Acts 4:36). After the persecution which followed the martyrdom of Stephen, some of the dispersed traveled as far as Cyprus, preaching to the Jews, and some converts from Cyprus preached to Greeks at Antioch (11:19-20). Paul and Barnabas preached together in Cyprus and visited such leading cities as Salamis and Paphos while traversing the whole island. It was at Paphos that they encountered the magician Bar-Jesus (13:4-12). Barnabas visited Cyprus again for missionary work, accompanied this time by Mark (15: 39). Paul, although he passed the island twice again, is not reported to have revisited it (21:3; 27:4).

The Jews on the island rebelled against the Romans in A.D. 116-17. This revolt led to their massacre and banishment from the island. It is possible that these events affected the growth of Christianity on Cyprus, since only after Constantine did it become the religion of a majority of Cypriotes.

**Bibliography.** E. Oberhummer, "Kypros," in Pauly-Wissowa, *Realenzyklopädie*, XII (1924), 59-117. S. Casson, *Ancient Cyprus* (1937); *Swedish Cyprus Expedition*, vols. I-IV (1934-38). G. Hill, *A History of Cyprus* I (1949). F. H. Stubbings, *Mycenean Pottery from the Levant* (1951). C. F. A. Schaeffer, *Enkomi-Alesia* I (1952).    J. C. GREENFIELD

**CYRENE** sī rē′nĭ [Κυρήνη]; CYRENIANS —ənz. A Greek city on the N coast of Africa; capital of Cyrenaica.

Cyrene was founded *ca.* 630 B.C. by Dorian Greeks from the islands Thera and Crete (Herodotus IV. 150 ff). It received reinforcements of Peloponnesian settlers and became a prosperous city of Greeks living among the Libyans. Cyrene was ruled by a dynasty of kings, the Battiads, until the middle of the fifth century B.C. Its wealth was mostly based on agriculture. Herodotus records that three crops were gathered in one year (IV.199). The export of silphium, a plant in high demand as spice and medicine, was a royal monopoly. This plant occurs as the badge of Cyrene on its coins.

In the fourth century B.C., Cyrene was a democracy and acquired fame as the seat of a school of philosophers. The city submitted to Alexander in 331, and thus later became part of Ptolemy's kingdom. Bequeathed to Rome in 96 B.C., it was declared free; but after some local strife Cyrenaica became a Roman province and was united with Crete.

In Hellenistic and Roman times a large part of the population of Cyrene consisted of Greek-speaking Jews who were sent as settlers by the Ptolemies and enjoyed equal rights. Simon (Matt. 27:32; Mark 15: 21) was a member of this group; so were Lucius the prophet of Antioch (Acts 13:1) and possibly Stephen, who was attacked in the synagogue to which Cyrenians and Alexandrians belonged (Acts 6:9). Cyrenians were prominent among the Jews in Jerusalem and elsewhere abroad (Acts 2:10).

The Jewish revolt under Vespasian had its repercussions in Cyrene, but the major outbreak occurred in A.D. 115-16, when the pagan monuments of the city were burned and smashed, and over 200,000 inhabitants reputedly were killed in the rioting (Dio Cassius 68.32). Hadrian restored the buildings of the city, as is recorded in many inscriptions. The prosperity of Cyrene was declining rapidly, however, as a result of careless exploitation of the soil. The silphium supply was exhausted by Nero's time.

The monuments of Cyrene were explored in the nineteenth century and again by the Italians before the Second World War. The major shrine is the archaic temple of Apollo, rebuilt several times and transformed into a Christian church in the fourth century A.D. Many other temples, as well as a building for the cult of the Roman emperors, baths, and a theater, have been identified.

**Bibliography.** A. H. M. Jones, *The Cities of the Eastern Roman Provinces* (1937), pp. 351-64; A. Rowe, *A History of Ancient Cyrenaica* (1948).    M. J. MELLINK

**CYRENIUS.** KJV form of QUIRINIUS.

**CYRIL OF JERUSALEM, TWENTIETH DISCOURSE OF** sĭr′əl [Κύριλλος]. A Coptic (Sahidic) rhapsody containing a version of the ASSUMPTION OF THE VIRGIN, as well as other legendary details of the Virgin's early life and death.

**Bibliography.** E. A. W. Budge, *Miscellaneous Coptic Texts* (1915).    M. S. ENSLIN

**CYRUS** sī′rəs [Heb.-Aram. כורש; Old Pers. *kûruš*; Elam. *ku-ruš;* Akkad. *ku-ra-aš;* κῦρος]. A Persian king, founder of the Achaemenian dynasty and the Persian Empire. Fig. CYR 56.

According to Herodotus (I.107), Cyrus (II) was the son of Cambyses (I), ruler of the unified territories of Paršumaš-Anšan and Pārsa, and Mandane, daughter of the Median king Astyages. The ancestor of Cyrus' house is Achaimenes (Achaemenes; Old Persian *haxāmaniš*, Greek ᾽Αχαιμένης; *see* PERSIA § D3), as stated in a short inscription from Pasargadae: "I am Cyrus, the king, an Achaemenian."

Several years after succeeding his father, Cyrus turned against Astyages (550). Deserted by his own vassals, Astyages was defeated, and Cyrus entered Ecbatana. The leadership over the possessions of the Median kings (Assyria, Mesopotamia, Syria, Armenia, Cappadocia) now passed to Cyrus "the Great." In the following years he marched against and defeated Croesus, king of Lydia, and captured Sardes, Lydia, and the Greek cities on the coast of Asia Minor. The precise extent of his conquests in the East can only be guessed, but it is certain that he was in control of the vast area between the Oxus River in the E and the Aegean Sea in the W at

Courtesy of the Oriental Institute, the University of Chicago

56. Tomb of Cyrus at Pasargadae in Iran, built of limestone blocks united by iron ties

the time of his attack against NABONIDUS and
Babylon in 539. The Nabonidus Chronicle tells the
story as follows: "In the month of Tashritu, when
Cyrus attacked the army of Akkad in Opis on the
Tigris, the inhabitants of Akkad revolted, but he
(Nabonidus) massacred the confused inhabitants.
The 14th day, Sippar was seized without battle.
Nabonidus fled. The 16th day . . . the army of Cyrus
entered Babylon without battle. Afterwards Naboni-
dus was arrested in Babylon when he returned
(there)" (*ANET* 306).[1]

Cyrus, then, proclaimed himself "king of the
world, great king, legitimate king, king of Babylon,
king of Sumer and Akkad, king of the four rims (of
the earth), son of Cambyses, great king, king of
Anshan, grandson of Cyrus, great king, king of Anshan, descendant of Teispes, great king, king of
Anshan, of a family (which) always (exercised) kingship" (*ANET* 316),[1] and, cast in the role of a merciful
liberator, he restored Marduk to his former position
of eminence and dignity. He also "returned to [the]
sacred cities on the other side of the Tigris, the sanctuaries of which have been ruins for a long time, the
images which (used) to live therein and established
for them permanent sanctuaries, . . . gathered all
their (former) inhabitants and returned (to them)
their habitations" (*ANET* 316).[1]

By the fall of Babylon the awareness of the Hebrews of the political and military power of Cyrus,
the "Lord's anointed" (Isa. 45:1), within the frame-

[1] From James B. Pritchard, *Ancient Near Eastern Texts* (Princeton
University Press; rev. ed., 1955).

work of the prophetic tradition of the coming of
God's empire and the expected restoration of Israel
(Isa. 44:28; see in general chs. 35; 40–55), was
alerted and got a partial confirmation. The Aramaic
decree (Ezra 6:3-5) on the rebuilding of the temple in
Jerusalem (still controversial in details), issued in the
first year of King Cyrus (538), fits into the general
picture of a policy of tolerance and wisdom practiced
by Cyrus. The context in which the decree occurs is
an exchange of correspondence between King Darius
and the satrap of Syria-Palestine on the permissibility
of the reconstruction of the temple (Ezra 5:6–6:12).
Darius quoted the Cyrus document, which was found
in the archives of Achmetha-Ecbatana (*see* ECBATANA)
and granted the permission on its strength. It seems
the decree was incorporated considerably later in the
Chronicler's account of the repatriation (Ezra 1:2-4).
According to Ezra 6:15, the temple was actually finished on the third day of Adar in the sixth year of
King Darius (spring of 515).

A tendency toward idealization of Cyrus' portrait
is manifest in Herodotus' qualification of him as a
"father" to his people (III.89), his statement that nobody would have dared to compare himself with Cyrus
(III.160), and Aeschylus' picture of Cyrus as an ideal
monarch (*Persae* 768-69).

Before leaving on his campaign against Queen
Tomyris and the Massagetae (Herodotus I.201-4),
which resulted in his death (529), Cyrus designated
his son Cambyses as his successor. Of this last campaign Herodotus writes: "The reasons which drove
and urged him were of more than one kind, first his
birth, the belief that he was more than a man, secondly the good fortune which had been his in his
campaigns" (I.204).

In the book of Daniel, Daniel is pictured as retaining his official position until the first year of Cyrus
(1:21), and the final vision of Daniel is dated to the
third year of Cyrus (10:1). Cyrus is perhaps the
"anointed one" of Dan. 9:26.

*Bibliography.* General: In addition to the bibliography
under PERSIA, see the chapter "Founder Cyrus" in A. T. Olmstead, *History of the Persian Empire* (1948), pp. 34-58.

On the literary history of the Aramaic passages in Ezra
4:7–6:18, see, e.g., M. Noth, *Überlieferungsgeschichtliche Studien
I* (1943), pp. 151 ff.

On Herodotus' account of Cyrus' life and reign (I.95-216),
see F. H. Weissbach, "Kyros," Pauly-Wissowa, *Realencyclopädie
der klassischen Altertumswissenschaft,* Supplement Band IV
(1924), 1129-66. For an analysis of the Greek author's sources,
see F. Jacoby, *Griechische Historiker* (1956), pp. 423-26.

M. J. DRESDEN

**D.** A symbol used to designate two biblical MSS, BEZAE and CLAROMONTANUS. *See* TEXT, NT.

**D (DEUTERONOMIST)** dōō'tə rŏn'ə mĭst, dū'—. The designation of one of the principal literary sources or strata of the PENTATEUCH. The Deuteronomist was the editor or compiler of this source, which is roughly coextensive with the book of DEUTERONOMY.

**DABAREH.** KJV form of DABERATH in Josh. 21:28.

**DABBESHETH** dăb'ə shĕth [דבשת, hump] (Josh. 19:11); KJV DABBASHETH. A border town in Zebulun. Although its exact location is unknown, the context suggests that it should probably be identified with one of the sites near Jokneam, perhaps Tell esh-Shemman.

*Bibliography.* F.-M. Abel, *Géographie de la Palestine,* II (1938), 301.　　　　　　　　　　　G. W. VAN BEEK

**DABERATH** dăb'ə răth [דברת]; KJV DABAREH —rə in Josh. 21:28. A Levitical town in Issachar (Josh. 21:28; I Chr. 6:72—H 6:57), situated on the border between Issachar and Zebulun (Josh. 19:13— H 19:12). "Daberath" should be read also for MT "Rabbith," with LXX B, in the list of towns in Issachar (Josh. 19:20).

It is located at Deburiyeh, W of Mount Tabor.

*Bibliography.* W. F. Albright, "The Topography of the Tribe of Issachar," *ZAW* (1926), pp. 230-31; F.-M. Abel, *Géographie de la Palestine,* II (1938), 301.

　　　　　　　　　　　　　　　　　　　G. W. VAN BEEK

**DABRIA** dăb'rĭ ə [Lat.] (II Esd. 14:24). One of five scribes whom Ezra was bidden to take with him, "because they are trained to write rapidly."

　　　　　　　　　　　　　　　　　　　　J. C. SWAIM

**DACOBI.** KJV Apoc. form of AKKUB 2.

**DAGGER.** *See* WEAPONS AND IMPLEMENTS OF WAR.

**DAGON** dā'gŏn [דגן, corn]. A god associated with the Philistines (I Sam. 31:10; see I Chr. 10:10) in Gaza (Judg. 16:23) and in Ashdod (I Sam. 5:2-7),

where he had a temple in which the Philistines deposited the ark after its capture, and which was still used in the Hasmonean period, being destroyed by Jonathan, the brother of Judas Maccabeus in 147 B.C. (I Macc. 10:83-84).

The cult of Dagon is attested among the Semites of the Near East long before the Philistine invasion —Dagon occurs as an element in theophoric names from the Amorite period in Mesopotamia a millennium before (cf. Dagan-takala, the chief of an unknown locality in Palestine in the Amarna Tablets). His cult was well established at Ras Shamra, where his temple rivaled that of Baal. It is the opinion of C. F. A. Schaeffer that both temples date from *ca.* 2000 B.C.

In the mythological texts from Ras Shamra describing the vicissitudes of BAAL as a dying and rising vegetation-deity, Baal is termed the "son of Dagon." This title may reflect a certain stage in the development of the conception of Baal—i.e., Hadad (*see* HADADRIMMON), the Amorite god of winter storms and rain—to that of the vegetation he stimulates. The name Dagon is almost certainly connected with the Semitic common noun for corn (דגן), as Philo of Byblos in his work on Phoenician religion implies. The relative seniority of Dagon is implied in Philo's statement that he was with El, who is the senior god in the Ras Shamra texts, the son of heaven and earth. His functions as a vegetation-god, however, appear to have been transferred to Baal by the middle of the second millennium. Dagon, however, continued to be worshiped independently at Ras Shamra, and provision for his cult is attested in offering lists, where he appears with—but generally after—El, the senior god of the Canaanite pantheon, and Baal, the most active deity, and in two *ex voto* inscriptions—neither of which, however, gives any indication of the nature of the god or his cult.

In the obviously corrupt passage I Sam. 5:4, רק נשאר דגן עליו ("only the trunk of Dagon was left to him"), Wellhausen proposed to read רק נשאר דגו עליו ("only his fishy part was left on him"). The association of Dagon with a fish goes back at least as early as Jerome (*ca.* A.D. 400), and the conception of the god as half fish goes back to David Kimchi (*ca.* A.D. 1200), both reflecting popular etymology unsupported by any known facts. The passage in I Sam. 5:4 may be emended on the basis of the LXX to רק נשאר גוו עליו ("only his back was left on him").

Other centers of the cult of Dagon in Palestine may have been at Beth-dagon, mentioned in Josh. 15:41 in the orbit of Judah; possibly Bit-Daganna (modern Beit Dajan five miles SE of Jaffa), mentioned with Jaffa in Sennacherib's annals; Bethdagon in Asher (Josh. 19:27); and Beit Dajan on the E edge of the Mukhneh plain just E of Nablus.

*Bibliography.* R. A. S. Macalister, *The Philistines, Their History and Civilization* (1914), pp. 99-114; S. A. Cook, *The Religion of Ancient Palestine in the Light of Archaeology* (1930), pp. 170-71; R. Dussaud, *Les découvertes de Ras Shamra (Ugarit) et l'AT* (1941), pp. 104-6; A. S. Kapelrud, *Baal in the Ras Shamra Texts* (1952), pp. 52-56, 64-66; W. F. Albright, *Archaeology and the Religion of Israel* (1953), pp. 74, 106.

　　　　　　　　　　　　　　　　　　　　J. GRAY

**DAISAN.** KJV Apoc. form of REZIN.

**DALAIAH.** KJV form of DELAIAH in I Chr. 3:24.

**DALETH** dä'lĭth (Heb. dä'lĕth) [ד, d (*Dāleth*)]. The fourth letter of the Hebrew ALPHABET as placed in the KJV at the head of the fourth section of the acrostic psalm, Ps. 119, where each verse of this section of the psalm begins with this letter.

**DALILA** də lī'lə. Douay Version form of DELILAH.

**DALMANUTHA** dăl'mə nōō'thə [Δαλμανουθά] (Mark 8:10). A place of uncertain location along the W shore of the Sea of Galilee.

The word occurs in the best Greek MSS. Following the feeding of the four thousand, it is said that Jesus embarked with his disciples and crossed to the "district of Dalmanutha." Since there is some acceptable MS evidence for MAGADAN or MAGDALA at this point, and since these two names also appear as variants in the parallel passage in Matt. 15:39, but Dalmanutha does not, there is great difficulty in establishing the name of the place in the original text. The word is not found in other ancient sources and may be a textual error, even though it is read in the best MSS.

Dalmanutha and Magdala (or Magadan) may have been names for the same place or names of two places in the same area, but Dalmanutha was so little known or used that only this reference to it has survived.

*Bibliography.* G. Dalman, *Die Worte Jesu* (1930), I, 52-53. B. Hjerl-Hansen, "Dalmanutha," *RB*, LIII (1946), 372-84.

D. C. PELLETT

**DALMATIA** dăl mā'shə, —shĭ ə [ἡ Δαλματία] (II Tim. 4:10). The S part of ILLYRICUM.

In the long process of the establishment of their authority over Illyria the Romans found the Dalmatians among their most stubborn opponents. A Roman embassy under Gaius Fannius (157/156 B.C.) was mistreated by them (Polybius XXXII.13), and in the subsequent war Marcius Figulus burned the Dalmatian capital, Delminium. In 119 B.C., Caecilius Metellus marched against the Dalmatians and wintered among them at Salona; in 50 and 48 B.C., armies of Caesar and of Gabinius were defeated; by 33 B.C., Octavian completed a subjugation of the Dalmatians which required several years (Appian *Illyrian Wars* 11-12, 28). Again in A.D. 6-8 a Dalmatian revolt, led by a certain Bato, was put down by Tiberius (Dio LV.xxix-xxxiv). According to Strabo (VII.315), the Dalmatians redistributed their land every seven years, and made no use of coined money.

*Bibliography.* Patsch, "Delmatae," *Pauly-Wissowa*, vol. IV (1901), cols. 2448-55.

J. FINEGAN

**DALPHON** dăl'fŏn [דלפון] (Esth. 9:7). One of the ten sons of Haman who were put to death by the Jews.

**DAMARIS** dăm'ə rĭs [Δάμαρις] (Acts 17:34). A woman of Athens who heard Paul's speech before the AREOPAGUS and believed, along with DIONYSIUS and some others. The name Damaris, hitherto unknown, may be a variant for Damalis ("heifer"), a fairly common name; but Damarion is also known. Codex D (fifth century) omits reference to Damaris, while E (seventh century) applies "esteemed" (τιμία) to her. Luke knew of honorable women (Acts 13:50; 17:12) but makes no claim about Damaris. Chrysostom mistakenly names her as the wife of Dionysius (*On the Priesthood* IV.7).

D. M. BECK

**DAMASCENE** dăm'ə sēn. The region of Damascus famous for its fertility, which is caused by the River Barada. The Ghuta is the name of the real oasis, and the district stretching toward the semiarid steppe is called Merj. In the region there are a number of ancient mounds showing its importance in ancient times.

A. HALDAR

**DAMASCUS** də măs'kəs [דמשק, דומשק (II Kings 16:10), דרמשק (II Chr. 16:2; 24:23; 28:5, 23); Akkad. *Dimišqi;* Amarna *Dimašqa, Dumašqa, Timašgi;* Arab. *Dimišq, Dimašq, Dimišq aš-Šām*]. A city of SYRIA (Aram). The present city, capital of modern Syria, is situated under the E slopes of Anti-lebanon, with the Mount of Hermon in the SW.

The region of Damascus is an oasis watered by a system of rivers and canals. Damascus itself is situated on the Nahr Barada (River Abana) coming from Anti-lebanon, and S of the town the Nahr el-A'waj (River Pharpar) flows eastward. Both these rivers disappear in the semiarid country to the E (*see* DAMASCENE). Damascus has always played an important role as a center of commerce and religion because of its situation where, since time immemorial, the most important military and commercial routes have met.

Damascus is mentioned several times in the OT; at that time the town was the capital of the Aramean (Syrian) kingdom (cf. Gen. 14:15; 15:2; I Kings 11: 24; 15:18; 19:15; 20:34; II Kings 8:7, 9; 14:28; 16: 10-12; Isa. 7:8).

The earliest occurrence of the name of Damascus is found in an inscription of Thut-mose III (sixteenth century). In the vicinity of Damascus there are a number of important tells—i.e., mounds—in which the remains of ancient towns are buried. This shows that in the early periods there were several centers of settlement, and it is not certain that the present town was the main center—e.g., in the first half of the second millennium. Since the region of Damascus is the fertile valley of Nahr Barada, opening eastward toward the semiarid country, from which enemies have come more than once, it was necessary to have defense against them. *Ca.* nine miles E of Damascus one fortified town was situated on the Nahr Barada (its remains are now hidden in Tell es-Salihiyeh; *see* HOBAH, where a large town was situated in the Old Babylonian period, *ca.* eighteenth-seventeenth centuries). *Ca.* nine miles SW of Damascus another big mound (Deir Habiyeh) is witness of another center of habitation in the Old Babylonian period.

In the Amarna age (*see* TELL EL-AMARNA) Damascus was the center of an important Amorite kingdom, whose ruler seems to have played a leading role in the efforts to get rid of the Egyptian domination. During that period there were apparently connections between the region of Damascus and the

Mycenean world, to judge from the discovery of pieces of Mycenean pottery at Tell es-Salihiyeh (in the Museum of Damascus). At the end of the second millennium, Damascus was the capital of the important Aramean kingdom, which for some time was powerful enough to compete with the Assyrians. The Arameans conquered the town after the downfall of the Hittite kingdom *ca.* 1200 B.C., and during the united and divided Hebrew monarchies Damascus was the rival of Jerusalem and Samaria (i.e., Judah and Israel). In II Kings 5:12 we are reminded of this fact, when Naaman was told to wash himself in Jordan and answered Elisha that the rivers of Damascus were "better than all the waters of Israel." King David was victorious in his war against Damascus and made it tributary (II Sam. 8:5-6; I Chr. 18:5 ff). During the reign of Solomon, Damascus was conquered by Reson of Aram-Zobah, and he made himself independent of the Israelites (I Kings 11:23 ff). Tabrimmon of Damascus was the ally of Abijam of Judah against Israel (see I Kings 15:19). His son Ben-hadad I (900-875) was allied to Baasha of Israel, but afterward made a league with Asa of Judah (I Kings 15:18 ff). Ben-hadad II and his son Hadadezer made war against Ahab of Israel, who was killed in the battle at Ramoth-gilead (853; I Kings 22). Ben-hadad III ruled for two years and was then killed by Hazael (843-797; II Kings 8:7-15), who was followed by Ben-hadad IV. This king was victorious against Israel, conquered almost the whole territory of Israel, and besieged Samaria (II Kings 6:24 ff). Through the intervening of Elisha, we are told, the siege was raised. Jeroboam II of Israel restored the power of his country (II Kings 14:28).

In the meantime, Damascus had to fight also against Assyria. If the kingdom of Damascus was to keep its position, it was necessary to prevent the Assyrians from being successful in their efforts in the W. Of importance in this connection is the Syro-Ephraimite War (734), when Rezin of Damascus and Pekah of Israel made war against Ahaz of Judah to force him to join them in the war against Assyria. Isaiah warned King Ahaz, but in spite of the warning he relied upon Assyria. The outcome of the war was that Assyria under Tiglath-pileser conquered Damascus in the year of 733/32 (*ANET* 282-83). Rezin himself was killed (II Kings 16:9), as the prophet Isaiah had prophesied (Isa. 7:4 ff; 8:1 ff; 17:1 ff). Because of these events, Damascus lost its position as the capital of a flourishing kingdom and after that was merely the center of a province under foreign rulers. Afterward the Assyrians, the Babylonians, the Persians, and finally Alexander conquered the town (*see* ASSYRIA AND BABYLONIA). Through Roman policy, Damascus became the capital of an independent Nabatean kingdom (85 B.C.). The ruler was Aretas III. In 65 B.C. the Romans conquered Syria, and Damascus came under a Nabatean governor. When Paul came to Damascus (Acts 9:2 ff), Damascus was ruled by Aretas IV. At that time there were numerous Jews and also a Christian group (Acts 9:2; 22:5-6, 10-11; 26:12; cf. Josephus). The Roman emperor Trajan joined the town to the Roman province of Syria.

During the development of the following centuries,

the population of Damascus was Christianized. The famous Church of Saint John Baptist was begun by the Emperor Theodosius and completed by Arcadius. It was built on the site of an earlier temple of Hadad, the ancient West Semitic storm-god.

*Bibliography.* A. von Kremer, *Topographie von Damaskus* (2 vols.; 1854-55). R. Hartmann, *Enzyklopaedie des Islam,* I (1908-13), 941-49. H. von Kiesling, *Damaskus. Altes und Neues aus Syrien* (1919). C. Watzinger and K. Wulzinger, *Damaskus die antike Stadt und die islamische Stadt* (2 vols.; 1921-24). E. Honigmann, *Historische Topographie von Nordsyrien im Altertum,* ZDPV, 46 (1923), 149-93; 47 (1924), 1-64; J. Sauvaget, *Les monuments historiques de Damas* (1932); Esquisse d'une histoire de la ville de Damas, *Revue des études islamiques,* 8 (1934), 421 ff. A. HALDAR

**DAMASCUS, COVENANT OF.** The abbreviated title of a sectarian Jewish community known from remains of its writings, which are usually called "ZADOKITE FRAGMENTS." In them the community calls itself the "New Covenant in the Land of Damascus" (6:19; 8:21; cf. 20:12). It flourished in the time of Jesus and belonged to the ESSENES, as has been proved by the fact that fragments of this writing have been found in caves IV and VI near Khirbet Qumran and from the content of the DEAD SEA SCROLLS themselves. O. BETZ

**DAMN, DAMNABLE, DAMNATION.** *See* CONDEMNATION.

**DAN** dăn [דן (God) judges; *originally a proper name, a shortened perf ct (verbal) form*]; DANITE dăn′īt [דני]. 1. The fifth son of Jacob, and the *heros eponymos* of the tribe of Dan. Born of Rachel's personal maid Bilhah (Gen. 30:1-6), Dan was the full brother of Naphtali, therefore always named along with him in the lists (Gen. 35:25; 46:23; Exod. 1:4; separated by mistake in I Chr. 2:2).

Dan's inferior reputation as half-caste, as well as the special relationship to Rachel, is explained by the history of the tribe. At first Dan attempted to settle in the area W of Benjamin. In Judg. 1, an old reliable source, named by Alt the "negative inventory of possessions," vss. 34-35 list as cities which the Danites could not conquer Aijalon (Yalo), Harheres (probably = Beth-shemesh Tell er-Rumeileh), and Shaalbim. The Danites attempted, therefore, to establish themselves in the Shephelah, but they could not hold out. The "Amorites" not only did not permit them to come down into the plain, but even forced them up into the mountains. Obviously the Danites had entered too far into what was really Canaanite-settled territory. What is related about the Danite Samson (Judg. 13:2 ff) fits in with this. The point of departure for his ventures, which also led him down into the plain of the Philistines, was Mahaneh-dan (vs. 25). The Danites, therefore, had only a fortified camp, not a settlement at all; and this camp lay between Zorah and Eshtaol, thus between two more Canaanite cities. The list of towns in Josh. 19:40-46, which extends the Danite settlement area in this region far into the maritime plain, is taken from a larger list, from an inventory of the kingdom of Judah at the time of Josiah, and it contributes nothing to the history of the tribe of Dan. In the system of border descriptions which originated in the period of the judges itself and was worked into the book of Joshua, Dan is significantly missing.

Therefore, the tradition in Judg. 17–18, which shows Dan in search of a new opportunity for settlement, is to be given credence. The Danite scouts traversed the country as far as the source of the Jordan. There they found a city, Laish, whose area was well suited to their purposes. It was connected neither with the Sidonians in the W nor with the Arameans (read אֲרָם) in the E (18:7, 28). They succeeded in conquering the isolated city. It was renamed Dan after the ancestral Dan (Josh. 19:47; Judg. 18:29). It is explicitly reported that the tribe set forth with six hundred men (Judg. 18:11); apparently this was the entire levy. Dan was a small tribe. But now Dan grew into the character of a Canaanite city-state; the tribe became half-caste. If one considers in addition its fringe location in the extreme N, one understands why it no longer played a role in the history of Israel. But it furnishes an interesting example of the fact that everything was by no means finished with the first settlement, but that the process of taking possession of the land was of longer duration and of varying fortune.

The course of Dan's history, as outlined above, is also reflected in the oldest poetry. In the Song of Deborah, Dan is reprimanded because it did not show an interest in the common Israelite cause, but lingered with the ships as a stranger (Judg. 5:17). Are the ships of the inhabitants of Tyre or those of Joppa meant? In the Blessing of Jacob we read:

> Dan shall judge [judges] his people
> as one of the tribes of Israel
> (Gen. 49:16).

This could be correctly interpreted as a wish—in analogy with what follows. But even if one does not transform the indicative into a jussive, the verse seems to reveal the fact that the autonomy of Dan was, nevertheless, felt to be a problem in the circle of the amphictyony. This points to the period of residence in the S. The saying in the Blessing of Moses (Deut. 33:22), on the other hand, clearly assumes that Dan is in the N, for Dan is compared to the young lion which leaps forth from Bashan—i.e., probably, who attacks the trade caravans to and from Damascus.

In the more recent literature Dan appears primarily in lists. In this connection the sequence in which Dan appears is interesting. In the Priestly Code, Dan is usually the third from the last, before the Zilpah tribe of Asher and Naphtali, the other Bilhah tribe (Num. 1:38-39; 2:25-26; 7:66-71; 10:25; 26:42-43); in the list of the scouts (13:12) Gad, the other Zilpah tribe, is added; in the list of the leaders of the tribes (1:12) the same Gad is even inserted ahead of Naphtali. A geographical principle is discernible only in Num. 34:22, where of the 9½ W tribes in the commission for the division of the land, the fourth place, immediately after Benjamin, is allotted to Dan. For the same reason Dan always appears in the fifth place after Benjamin and Ephraim (Josh. 21:5, 23-24; I Chr. 6:61, 69—H 6:46, 54) in the lists of the Levite cities. In Deut. 27:13, Dan—with his brother—belongs, as the final pair, to the group which must speak the curse from Mount Ebal.

In Ezek. 48:1, Dan, in remembrance of its previous geographical situation, has allotted to it the most northerly strip; in vs. 32 the third E gate is called the "gate of Dan," so that Dan appears as the sixth directly after the Rachel group and far removed from Naphtali as the twelfth, but—with regard to the position of the gates—diagonally across from Naphtali. In the two lists of Chronicles, which show a peculiar structure (cf. I Chr. 2:1 ff), Dan ranks, in one instance, between Naphtali and Asher at the end of an exclusively W Jordan series of twelve (12:36); in the other instance it is at the end of another series of twelve, but separated from Naphtali by the Rachel group (similar to 2:2).

Individuals who belonged to the tribe of Dan were Oholiab, Bezelel's co-worker in the construction of the tabernacle (Exod. 31:6; 35:34; 38:23); also Huramabi, likewise an artist, from Tyre but the son of a Danite woman (II Chr. 2:13; according to I Kings 7:13-14 his mother stemmed from Naphtali); and, finally, the blasphemer of Lev. 24:11, who, at least on his mother's side, had Danite blood in his veins. The last two are probably not chance examples of the fact that the Danites were susceptible to the intermingling of blood. In the case of the Egyptian father of the one, the S sojourn of the tribe of Dan is thought of; in the case of the Phoenician father of the other, the later residence in the N.

For the territory of Dan, *see* Tribes, Territories of, § D9a. *See* the bibliography under Asher.

K. Elliger

* **2. A city in the extreme N of Palestine to which the Danites migrated (Judg. 18).**

Dan is identified with Tell el-Qadi (the "mound of the judge"), a site located at the S foot of Mount Hermon, at the source of the Nahr Leddan, one of the major headwaters of the Jordan River. It overlooks the Huleh Plain several hundred feet below, and guards the important trade route which links Tyre with Damascus.

The mound itself is quadrangular and measures 500-600 yards in length. Its E end is higher than the W, and perhaps marks the location of the original town. Although the mound has not been excavated, surface explorations have shown that it was occupied throughout the Bronze Age (*ca.* 3000-1200) and in Iron II (*ca.* 900-600).

During the Canaanite period, the city was known as Laish, according to Judg. 18:7, 14, 27, 29, and to the list of towns conquered by Thut-mose III of Egypt (fifteenth century B.C.), in which it is spelled *Ra-wi-sa* (no. 31 in the list). A variant name, Leshem, is also preserved in Josh. 19:47. After the Danites abandoned their original territorial allotment—probably as a result of Philistine pressure—they migrated to the N and captured Laish, renaming it Dan (Judg. 18). Dan was one of the two cities in Israel in which Jeroboam established a Yahweh sanctuary complete with a golden calf, following the division of the kingdom (I Kings 12:29); the sanctuary survived the thorough religious revolution of Jehu (II Kings 10:29). Early in the ninth century, it was one of the N Israelite cities taken by Ben-hadad of Damascus at the instigation of Asa of Judah (I Kings 15:20=II Chr. 16:4). Elsewhere in the OT, the city is frequently mentioned in the phrase "from Dan to Beer-sheba" as the northernmost point of Israelite territory.

**Bibliography.** W. F. Albright, "The Jordan Valley in the Bronze Age," *AASOR*, VI (1926), 16-18; J. Garstang, *The Foundations of Bible History* (1931), pp. 103, 246-47. J. B. Pritchard, ed., *ANET* (2nd ed., 1955), pp. 242, 329.

G. W. Van Beek

**DANCING.** The harmonious and rhythmic movement of the body in sheer exuberance of spirit and bodily health, in practiced mime, or in conscious devoted joy before God. As in all religions of antiquity, the dance has its place in Israelite life and worship.

Different types of movement seem to be represented by the principal words used to describe dancing in the OT. רקד means "skip about," and the verb is used in three separate tenses of gay and merry movement—e.g., of children (Job 21:11). כרר in the participle, *Pilpel*, מכרכר, "dancing, whirling about" (II Sam. 6:14, 16), is used of David's long and whirling dance before the ark. In II Sam. 6:16 the word is used synonymously with the *Pi'el* of פזז, which means "to show agility" and "to leap in dancing." חול (חיל) denotes "whirl, dance, writhe"; the nouns, masculine and feminine, from this root describe the dance as the joyous opposite of mourning (Ps. 30:12), as an act of praise to Yahweh (149:3; 150:4), and as accompanied by timbrel and other instruments and by singing. It is graceful and beautiful (Song of S. 7:1) and can be idolatrous (Exod. 32:19). Occasionally שחק, "laugh, make sport, jest," is used of singing and dancing (Judg. 16:25; I Sam. 18:7), and these performed before the Lord as in II Sam. 6:5=I Chr. 13:8; II Sam. 6:21; I Chr. 15:29.

In the NT ὀρχέομαι is used of Herodias' daughter's dancing (Mark 6:22; Matt. 14:6) and of innocent dancing (Matt. 11:17; Luke 7:32). The prodigal son heard a company of dancers, on his return (Luke 15:25). Herodias' daughter's artistic dancing is, of course, another matter, for it was designed to captivate and further the ends of the dancer. Of such dancing there is little in the Bible (but cf. Eccl. 3:4).

It is clear that dancing was a prominent feature

2. Dancing-scene relief from a tomb at Saqqarah: nude girls beat clappers, women beat drums, and men march with raised arms (Sixth Dynasty, 2350-2200 B.C.)

3. Wall painting from a tomb at Thebes: two nude girls dance to music, musicians have ointment jars on their heads (fifteenth century B.C.).

in religious Feasts, and may be implicit in the meaning of חג, "festival, pilgrimage." At times it is specifically mentioned. Ancient religion was joyous, and the sanctuaries were the scenes and the festivals the occasions of rejoicing before God, so that dancing would be an inevitable and normal part of worship. There is little reference to dancing in the Bible, but the references that occur show that it was virtually as frequent as mourning and that it was an activity so common as not to require special mention.

Yet certain dances are mentioned, and these obviously are mentioned for important reasons. Israel's deliverance at the Sea of Reeds is celebrated by dancing with singing and instruments (Exod. 15:20; cf. Isa. 30:29). For other occasions see I Sam. 18:6; 21:11; 29:5; 30:16. Cf. Abel-meholah—"dancing meadow" (Judg. 7:22; I Kings 4:12; etc.). Perhaps Passover included a limping dance connected with the threshold. Yahweh's annual feast at Shiloh featured vineyard dancing by the maidens (Judg. 21:16-24). David, dressed as a priest, danced before the ark (II Sam. 6). Idolatrous dancing is mentioned in the golden-calf story (Exod. 32:19), and at Carmel (I Kings 18:26); in the latter passage calling on the name of Baal is linked with a limping dance (cf. Pss. 149:3; 150:4). Similarly, evidence of dancing on the fifteenth of Abib, on the Day of Atonement, on the day before and during the Feast of Tabernacles, in post-OT times may preserve practices from OT times.

There is comparatively little mention of dancing in the Psalms, but enough to show that it was a legitimate part of the worship. There is, however, some reference to processions (e.g., Ps. 68:24-27, where the order of the procession is also described; cf. "thy goings," or "thy processions," in vs. 24). Other psalms also make reference to or imply processions. Thus Pss. 24 (especially vss. 7-10); 26:6-7; 29:2; 42:4; 45:14-15; 47:5; 48:12-14; 84:5-7; 87:7; 89:15; 95:

1. Girls perform with acrobatic dancing; from a necropolis of Memphis at Saqqarah

1-2; 100:2, 4; 109:30; 110:3; 118:19-29 (cf. "festal procession" in vs. 27); 122:1-5; 132:8-10; 149:1-4; 150 include the most obvious passages, though by no means exhaust the possible references. Such processions, being mainly occasions of triumph and of joy, would inevitably include acts of dancing or rhythmic religious movement. It is generally accepted that II Sam. 6; Ps. 132 are closely related, the history as the founding legend, and the psalm as the liturgical celebration, probably of annual occurrence. If this relation be true, then the dance of II Sam. 6:14-15 may be implied in vss. 8-10 of the psalm. In that event the procession of Ps. 132:8-10 would include a dance. Figs. DAN 1-3; MUS 92.

*Bibliography.* H. Kees, *Der Opfertanz des ägyptischen Königs* (1912); W. O. E. Oesterley, *The Sacred Dance* (1923); P. D. Magriel, *A Bibliography of Dancing* (1936), pp. 26-35, 39-43; J. Pedersen, *Israel*, III-IV (1940), Index under "Dance, cultic," p. 759; W. Sorell, "Israel and the Dance," in D. D. Runes, ed., *The Hebrew Impact on Western Civilization* (1951), pp. 505-11.                                    G. HENTON DAVIES

**DANIEL** dăn'yəl [דניאל]. The book now appearing in English versions as the fourth of the prophetic writings contained in the OT; also, the man of the same name, with whom the book is mostly concerned; also, the name of an ancient figure referred to in Ezek. 14:14; 28:3, where the *Kethibh* is דנאל, Dan'el, but *Qere* is דניאל, Daniel. Other occurrences of the name are for a son of David (I Chr. 3:1—text dubious) and for a priest of the house of Ithamar (Ezra 8:2; Neh. 10:6). The last two occurrences attest the fact that the name was current among the Jews in the postexilic period.

1. The man
2. The book
    *a.* Contents
    *b.* Place in canon
    *c.* Language, text, and versions
    *d.* Unity
    *e.* Historical problems
    *f.* Date and style of composition
    *g.* The Additions to Daniel
    *h.* Purpose of composition and abiding worth
Bibliography

**1. The man.** The Ugaritic literature (*see* UGARIT) has provided in the *Aqht* legend* the story of a King Dnil, which name may be vocalized as Danel or Daniel. He is said as king to dispense justice:

> He judges the case of the widow,
> And judicates the cause of the fatherless.

His name means "God has judged," so that wisdom would appear to be a significant element in the character, though the *Aqht* legend does not itself draw this out. Ezek. 14:14 links a man Daniel with Noah and Job, and the reference is obviously to an ancient figure considered to be, like the other two, prediluvian. Daniel is cited here for his righteousness, rather than his wisdom. But in Ezek. 28:3 Tyre is mocked because she thought herself "wiser than Daniel." Thus we may take it that there was a Phoenician-Canaanite tradition concerning a king who in some stories not preserved for us had a reputation for uprightness of character and surpassing wisdom. This tradition presumably accounts for the occurrence of the name as Enoch's father-in-law (Jub. 4:20). Fig. UGA 11.

The relation of this legendary figure to the central figure of the book of Daniel is not certain, but the probability is that the author was acquainted with a number of stories about him, which had already shifted their location in space and time to Babylon and the Neo-Babylonian period, and the new home of wisdom (*see* CHALDEA). For a similar shift of period and location, cf. the British cycle concerning King Arthur. The occurrence of the name Daniel in I Enoch 6:7 suggests a variant development whereby the original wisdom figure became angelic, first

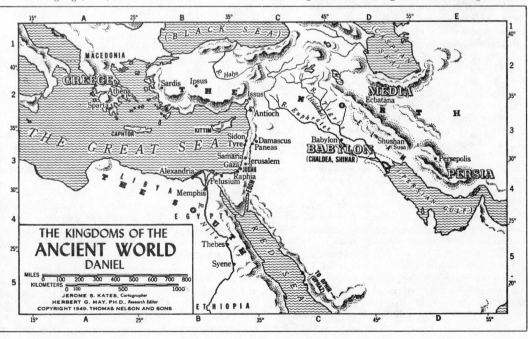

THE KINGDOMS OF THE
**ANCIENT WORLD**
DANIEL

MILES 0 100 200 300 400 500 600 700 800
KILOMETERS 0 100 500 1000

JEROME S. KATES, Cartographer
HERBERT G. MAY, PH.D., Research Editor
COPYRIGHT 1949. THOMAS NELSON AND SONS

doubtless in a good sense, and then later in a bad sense. In our author's hands (*see* § 2*f below*), Daniel becomes a young Jew, who is loyal to his ancestral religion and who is made by divine inspiration wiser than all the sages of Mesopotamia. This combination of wisdom and righteousness enables him to receive the visionary revelations which form the latter part of the book. The older traditions make no reference to the other outstanding characteristics of the hero of the book Daniel, which are his unshakable faith in God and courage of the highest order in the face of persecution. These we may consider to be bestowed upon the character by the author of our present book.

**2. The book. a. Contents.** The book divides into two parts. Chs. 1–6 contain six stories, five of which concern Daniel, and one his three friends Shadrach, Meshach, and Abednego. In these stories Daniel is introduced in the third person. The stories are: (*a*) Daniel and his friends loyal to their religion in matters of food; (*b*) the King's dream concerning an image interpreted by Daniel; (*c*) the three friends cast into the furnace for refusing to worship an image: (*d*) Nebuchadnezzar's madness prophesied by Daniel; (*e*) the writing on the wall at Belshazzar's feast interpreted by Daniel (*see* MENE, MENE, TEKEL, AND PARSIN); (*f*) Daniel cast into a lions' den for refusing to recognize Darius the Mede as a god.

In the second part Daniel receives four visions. In the first of these visions Daniel is introduced in the third person (7:1) and tells of his experience in the first (7:2-28); in the other three he writes in the first person (chs. 8–12), but at the beginning of the third vision he is briefly mentioned in the third person again (10:1). Thus the change from third person to first is unobtrusively effected with great skill. We shall consider the implication of this fact in § 2*d below.*

The first vision is of the four beasts. Daniel sees four beasts arise from the sea (i.e., the nations of mankind) in turn. They typify four world empires. On the fourth beast arises a horn which represents a monarch who makes large boasts; but then follows a judgment-theophany, the beast is destroyed, and a fifth kingdom typified by a human figure (*see* SON OF MAN) is established by God as an everlasting dominion. This last is the kingdom of God incorporated in the people of Israel. In the exposition of the vision it is said that the saints will be delivered into the hand of the last king of the fourth beast for "a time, times [a plural but traditionally taken as dual; see Rev. 11:2-3; 13:5], and half a time"—which apparently means three and a half years.

The second vision is of the ram and the he-goat. A ram with two horns is destroyed by a furious he-goat, which then sprouts four horns, from one of which a little horn sprouts. This again is the blasphemous and persecuting monarch, who intermits the daily sacrifice in the temple for a period of 2,300 mornings and evenings (i.e., 1,150 days), but it is foretold that he will be broken "by no human hand."

The third vision is of the seventy weeks. Daniel is let into the secret that the seventy years which Jeremiah prophesied as the duration of the Exile actually means seventy weeks of years (i.e., 490), and the history of Israel from the rebuilding of Jerusalem onward is sketched in terms of an initial period of seven weeks, a further period of sixty-two weeks, and then the last week, which is ushered in by the death of "an anointed one." During this last week the "prince who is to come" shall cause sacrifice and oblation to cease for half a week (i.e., three and a half years), until the decreed end comes upon him.

The final vision is of the revelation of the angel. Daniel is told by an angelic being what the history of Israel is to be from the time of the Persian Empire to the rise of the Greek Empire under Alexander and his successors, and the rivalries of the "king of the south" and the "king of the north" are detailed in cryptic terms until the current king of the north succeeds in conquering Egypt. Hearing of trouble in the East, he turns to march thither, but as he comes up again through the Holy Land, he meets his end there. The time until the end of these wonders is solemnly asseverated as a time, times, and half a time.

We may note here that the image of the King's dream has four component metals which accord with the four beasts of ch. 7, and typify four empires. During the time of the last empire, a stone not cut by human hand smites the image and destroys it, and then itself becomes a mountain and fills the whole earth. This is explained by Daniel as an everlasting kingdom which God himself will establish.

The usual explanation is that the four kingdoms of these visions are the four world empires of Babylon, Media, Persia, and Greece. The he-goat of the second vision is Alexander, and the "king of the south" and the "king of the north" in the fourth vision are the Ptolemaic and Seleucid dynasties of Egypt and Syria, while the boasting horn of the first vision, the blasphemous little horn of the second, the "prince who shall come" of the third, and the furious "king of the north" of the fourth vision all typify Antiochus Epiphanes, who persecuted the Jews from 168 onward and sought to destroy Judaism in its ancestral home. For further discussion, however, *see below.*

Stories 1-4 are set in the reign of Nebuchadnezzar, story 5 in the reign of Belshazzar, story 6 in the reign of Darius the Mede. Vision 1 is set in the first year of the reign of Belshazzar, vision 2 in his third year, vision 3 in the first year of Darius the Mede, and vision 4 in the third year of Cyrus. Thus the stories and visions are in a chronological order, but the visions commence before the stories end.

**b. Place in canon.** When the OT canon was fixed at the Synod of Jamnia, *ca.* A.D. 90, Daniel was included in the Writings or third section—not in the Prophets or second section. The reason for this was that the second section had come to be regarded as closed since *ca.* 200 B.C., and the Synod was only concerned to adjudicate on the contents of the still fluid third section. The attempt to show that Daniel was originally among the Prophets fails on the evidence of the Talmud (B.B. 15*a*). That Daniel was widely recognized as scripture from the second and first centuries B.C. onward can be in no doubt. Ecclesiasticus (*ca.* 180 B.C.) omits Daniel from its list of Israel's great men, but there is a clear relationship between passages in Daniel and I Enoch (e.g., I Enoch 14:18-22; Dan. 7:9-10), and while both may be dependent on a common source (in this case in part Ezek. 1), the strong likelihood is that I Enoch is borrowing from Daniel. Since I Enoch (*see* ENOCH, BOOK OF) is basically a pre-Christian book, this would·argue for the popularity of Daniel and in some degree for its authority in the pre-Christian period. I Macc. 2:59-60 (after 135 B.C.) refers to Daniel and his three friends by name, and a florilegium of passages and commentary from Qumran (Q4) refers, like Matt. 24:15, to "Daniel the prophet." Josephus retells the story of Daniel at length in Antiq. X.x-xi. Thus the evidence is that the book was not known or quoted before 160 B.C. but was known and revered from the middle of the second century B.C. onward and was regarded as scripture at least by the second half of the first century A.D. Those who have tried to prove the existence of the book before the beginning of the second century B.C. have not succeeded in gaining widespread support for their views. Its late emergence alone can explain why in the Hebrew Bible the book is in the Writings and not among the Prophets.

Orthodox Judaism has evinced only a moderate enthusiasm for the book, partly because of its attempt to calculate the time of the end, and partly because of the general Jewish reaction against apocalyptic; but the Christian church has never been in any doubt as to its prophetic character and value. When the Greek-speaking Jews responsible for the LXX rearranged the order of the books, from the Hebrew tripartite division (Law, Prophecy, Writings), they placed Daniel among the prophets—after Ezekiel and before the Twelve; this position the book has retained in English versions and Christian versions generally. *See* CANON OF THE OT.

*c. Language, text, and versions.* 1:1–2:4*a* is in Hebrew; 2:4*b*–7:28 is in Aramaic; and chs. 8–12 are in Hebrew. Whether the whole book was originally in one language or the other has been strongly disputed. The views most canvassed are (*a*) that of Dalman, Torrey, Montgomery, and others—that the stories existed first as a complete work on their own, written in Aramaic, and the visions were written later in Hebrew; a redactor brought the two halves together by translating the first story into Hebrew and the first vision into Aramaic; (*b*) that of Lenormant, Bevan, and others—that the whole book was written in Hebrew but chs. 2–7 were lost and the lacuna made up from an Aramaic translation; (*c*) that of Charles—that the book was written in Aramaic and the first chapter and the last four were done into Hebrew with the idea of commending the work to Jewish piety. Rowley suggests that the stories were issued first as separate pieces in the popular language and that the author changed to Hebrew when he began to issue other pieces of less popular interest and designed for more distinctively religious groups. This change may, however, be linked to a noticeable growth in apocalyptic interest as the book progresses. The first chapter was translated into Hebrew when the pieces were collected to form a book.

The Greek translation called the SEPTUAGINT has come down to us in one MS only, that of Codex Chisianus, copied perhaps in the eleventh century (so Swete; Pfeiffer says ninth). It was displaced in the affections of the Christian church by Theodotion's translation, and the two texts are now often printed together. The LXX is more periphrastic and contains numerous expansions apart from the Additions (*see* § 2*g below*), and this was doubtless the cause of its rejection in favor of Theod. But pre-Theod. readings occur in the NT and the early fathers which have led to the theory that side by side with the LXX there existed another translation more faithful to the Hebrew, and that Theod. is a revision of this text rather than a new version (but cf. Montgomery [*bibliography*], p. 46; Roberts [*bibliography*], p. 123). The other important witnesses to the LXX text are the Chester-Beatty Papyri (second-fourth centuries A.D.; 3:72–6:18; 7:1–8:27) and the Syro-Hexaplaric version (*see* TEXT, OT). For the value of OL, Syr., and Vulg. versions, cf. Montgomery (*bibliography*), pp. 43-44, 55-56. As a general judgment drawn in broad terms, it may be said that the Hebrew-Aramaic text (MT) is in good condition and that the LXX and other versions do not lead us to think that it has been gravely corrupted. We may add to this the testimony of the Qumran MSS. The following portions have been reported: (1Q) 1:10-17; 2:2-6; 3:22-30; (6Q) 10:8-16; 11:33-36; and (4Q) "a sizeable proportion of the book of Daniel . . . in three relatively well-preserved MSS." F. M. Cross comments: "The text of Daniel in these [4Q] scrolls conforms closely to later Massoretic tradition; there are to be found, however, some rare variants which side with the Alexandrian Greek against MT and Theod." (cf. *BA* cited below).

When we turn to consider the character of the Hebrew and Aramaic, the question arises whether the language can give any clue to the date of composition. In this connection we must also note the significant presence of a number of Persian and Greek loan-words (*see* MUSICAL INSTRUMENTS for "bagpipe"). S. R. Driver (*see bibliography*) puts his conclusions very succinctly: "The verdict of the language of Daniel is thus clear. The *Persian* words presuppose a period after the Persian empire had been well established; the Greek words *demand*, the Hebrew *supports* and the Aramaic *permits*, a date *after the conquest of Palestine by Alexander the Great* (B.C. 332)." Rowley's careful study of OT Aramaic sought to substantiate that part of the claim, but Bentzen rightly says that since later studies have cast serious doubts on the possibility of distinguishing in the older manner between Eastern and Western branches of the language, the Aramaic had better be left out of the discussion. H. L. Ginsberg's theory of Court Aramaic as the universal and dateless super dialect of that language and the one in which Daniel was written, certainly makes this the wiser course to adopt. As far as the Greek is concerned, Montgomery points out that we must allow for the influence of cultures being more widespread and at an earlier date than we would at first presume, and that Driver lacks his usual caution in saying that the Greek words "demand" a date later than Alexander. Nevertheless, Driver was sufficiently cautious about the Aramaic if not about the Greek, and Montgomery, as well as Bentzen, supports his general conclusion. A further small point is that the term "Chaldean" (*see* CHALDEA) is used in this book as a synonym for "soothsayers"; it had acquired this meaning by the second century B.C., but such usage was foreign to it in the sixth. We may sum the matter up by saying that while the linguistic evidence is not strong enough to rule out the bare possibility of the book's being a product of sixth-century Babylon, nevertheless it does make it extremely unlikely.

*d. Unity.* The book divides itself into two halves, stories (chs. 1–6) and visions (chs. 7–12). The vivid simplicity of the first part considered over against the complicated obscurity of the second, together with the human interest of the one and the apocalyptic character of the other, has led many scholars to see the book as a composite work. Further, part of the book is in the third person and part in the first, and part is in Aramaic and part in Hebrew. It is not surprising, therefore, that theories of composite authorship have arisen, but what is significant is that there is no agreement as to how the book should be divided. We are confronted with a bewildering variety of partitions, which range from Spinoza in the seventeenth century (1–7; 8–12) and Isaac Newton in the eighteenth century (1–6; 7–12) to Bertholdt at the beginning of the nineteenth century (nine authors!), to Barton at its close (three authors and two other contributors), and in the twentieth to Torrey (1–6 third century B.C.; 7–12 Maccabean) and to Hölscher (1–6 third century B.C.; 7 a later appendix; 8–12 Maccabean). Montgomery and Bentzen both hold to the prior origin of the stories, and both assign them to the third century approximately, though the latter suggests that they may have had only an oral, not a literary, pre-existence. Rowley ("Unity of Daniel"), on the other hand, vigorously repudiates all divisive theories, pointing to the lack of agreement among the dividers as a significant consideration—they cannot find the lines of demarcation because no such lines exist. The fact that the division between stories and visions, the division between Aramaic and Hebrew, and the division between third- and first-person passages do not coincide, calls for the recognition that the book is the work of one man, who changed his method and style of working but who, nevertheless, produced a literary unity. Rowley stresses the significance of the stories with regard to the second-century persecution of the Jews, showing that they are so pertinent to that situation that they must have been constructed with it in view. When we add to this that the message of the second story is acknowledged by almost all authorities to be in essence the same as that of the first of the visions, so that stories and visions are securely tied together, and when we note that the visions also clearly relate to the time of the Antiochene persecutions, the case for the unity of the book becomes overwhelming. Some traditional material was probably available centering around the name Daniel, and having its milieu in Babylon, whence it acquired a certain Babylonian coloring, but the stories were evidently selected and thoroughly reshaped by one author with a very definite purpose in mind, and he was responsible for the visions also.

*e. Historical problems.* Certain sections of Daniel are carefully dated by regnal years as follows: third Jehoiakim, the siege of Jerusalem (1:1); second Nebuchadnezzar, the dream of the great image (2:1); first Belshazzar, the vision of the four beasts (7:1); third Belshazzar, the vision of the ram and the he-goat (8:1); first Darius the Mede, the vision concern-

ing the seventy weeks (9:1); third Cyrus, the vision concerning the "king of the north" (10:1). Thus the succession of regnal authority in Babylon is detailed as Nebuchadnezzar, Belshazzar, Darius the Mede, Cyrus. It is stated that Nebuchadnezzar was Belshazzar's father and that Darius the Mede received the kingdom from Belshazzar (5:2, 31). 6:29 LXX states that Darius died and that Cyrus took "his kingdom." Further, in third Cyrus, the angel can refer to first Darius as in the past (11:1). There can then be no doubt that this is the succession of kings the author accepted.

But these statements do not accord with our own knowledge of the history of this period. The publication of fresh Babylonian material by Wiseman makes it quite clear that Nebuchadnezzar could not have visited Jerusalem at the very earliest until after the Battle of Carchemish in 605 and almost certainly not until 597. Even if we allow an earlier, unrecorded visit, the siege of Jerusalem is definitely dated as having ended on 2 Adar (March 16), 597, after a siege of less than three months. Jehoiakim had then reigned eleven years (II Kings 23:36). How then can Dan. 1:1 say the siege was in his third year? Our author evidently thought that Jehoiakim had been Nebuchadnezzar's vassal from the beginning of his reign, so that a rebellion "after three years" (II Kings 24:1) could have been in his third year, but we know that he had previously been Pharaoh Neco's vassal (II Kings 23:34). Further, Jehoiakim was not given into Nebuchadnezzar's hand as 1:2 states; he died in Palestine, and it was his son Jehoiachin whom Nebuchadnezzar took to Babylon (II Kings 24:12). The author of Daniel appears to have followed the untrustworthy account of II Chr. 36:6. Another difficulty arises in that we are told that Nebuchadnezzar deported certain Judeans and commanded that some, among whom were Daniel and his friends, were to be trained in the wisdom of the "Chaldeans" for three years (1:5). At the end of that time (1:18) Daniel and his friends graduated at the top of the class; yet in 2:1 ff we find Daniel fully operative "in the second year" of Nebuchadnezzar's reign. As a result of his prowess he is made ruler over the whole province of Babylon (2:48), yet a year later he graduates. Still another difficulty is that in ch. 4 Nebuchadnezzar is said to have suffered banishment from Babylon because of madness, apparently for seven years. We can find no trace of this extraordinary event in any other record, though the argument from silence is, of course, never very strong. It now appears probable that in the original tradition the king in question was Nabonidus.

But the major problems of the book center around three other matters: the kingship of Belshazzar, the identity of Darius the Mede, and the succession of empires. The historicity of Belshazzar is no longer in doubt: he was the son of Nabonidus, the last of the neo-Babylonian monarchs. He was not, it is true, Nebuchadnezzar's son (5:2). The succession ran: Nabopolassar (626-605), Nebuchadnezzar (605-562), Amel-Marduk (562-559), Neriglissar (559-555), Labashi-Marduk (556), Nabonidus (556-539); and since Nabonidus was a Babylonian and not a Chaldean, who came to the throne as a result of a palace revolution, Belshazzar's descent from Nebuchadnezzar even through his mother (as has been suggested) is unlikely, quite apart from actual sonship. On the other hand, it is now established that he was coregnant with his father and could be properly termed king (*ANET* 313*b*). But it must be remarked that Dan. 5 gives no hint that he is not the supreme and sole monarch, for the term "third" in vs. 7 must mean after King Belshazzar and his queen mother, mentioned in vs. 10. The capture of Babylon by Cyrus' troops is an event so overlaid with legend that it is fruitless to argue for or against the historicity of the assertion that "that very night [he] was slain" (5:30; for details see Cyrus Cylinder, *ANET* 315*b;* Nabonidus Chronicle, Barton [*bibliography*], p. 482; Herod. I.191; Xenophon *Cyropaedia* VII.5; and discussion in Montgomery [*bibliography*], pp. 68-69. Also note Dougherty [*bibliography*], p. 180). The *Nabonidus Chronicle* and the *Cyrus Cylinder* are Persian interpretations of the fall of Babylon which glorify Cyrus and vilify Nabonidus.

The identity of Darius the Mede is the crucial problem. History tells of Darius I (Hystaspes) and of Darius II and III, but they were very decidedly Persians, not Medes, and in any case came after Cyrus, not before him. The only possibility is that Darius the Mede is known to history by some other name. Rowley in *Darius the Mede* has patiently explored the various identifications which have been proposed: Astyages, the Median king whom Cyrus overthrew about the same time that Nabonidus came to the throne (and who therefore antedates Belshazzar considerably); Cambyses, who was coregnant with his father for a brief period after the fall of Babylon (but who was certainly not a Mede, nor sixty-two years of age in 539); Gobryas, Cyrus' general who took command of Babylon before his master arrived (but he was either an Assyrian, which probably means Babylonian, or a Persian; the one thing he could not have been was a Mede, since Herodotus records his indignation that "we Persians" should be ruled by a Mede in the person of pseudo-Merdis; and he was never a king); Cyaxares, son of Astyages according to Xenophon (but he was certainly never king of Babylon, and the inscriptions show that Astyages was the last Median king and that Cyaxares is in fact a figment of Herodotus' imagination). In any case, there remains the simple fact that none of these men was ever called Darius. Rowley also shows that the biblical spelling of the name (*see* DARIUS THE MEDE) is not significant, since it merely perpetuates the spelling used in Aramaic during the reign of Darius Hystaspes, though other spellings became current in reigns of the two later kings of that name. The really conclusive fact, however, is that Dougherty gives two series of dated Babylonian tablets, the one referring to Nabonidus' last (seventeenth) regnal year and the other to Cyrus' first year, and the two series overlap by two months. This definitely rules out any possibility that "Darius the Mede" can have succeeded Belshazzar and preceded Cyrus.

The third problem has now to be considered: the existence of a Median Empire. Both the dream of Nebuchadnezzar in ch. 2 and the vision of the four beasts in ch. 7 purport to give a prediction by Daniel of the history of the Near East following the times of Nebuchadnezzar, and it is foretold that four world empires will arise successively. The fourth is clearly the Greek Empire of Alexander and the Successors, and the little horn is Antiochus Epiphanes. Then the one before the Greek must be the Persian, and the first is, of course, the Neo-Babylonian, and the second can only be the empire of "Darius the Mede." But as this Darius never existed, so, too, no Median Empire interposed its control over Babylon between the Neo-Babylonian and the Persian hegemonies. For the Median Empire had become the Medo-Persian Empire by the act of Cyrus himself at least sixteen years before he displaced Nabonidus as king in Babylon. It is, however, possible to interpret the succession of empires as "Neo-Babylonia, Persia, Greece, Rome," and this view is as old as II Esd. 12:10 ff, but, as Rowley points out, the author is aware that to make the fourth kingdom the Roman is not true to the original scheme (cf. II Esd. 10:12: "But it was not expounded unto [Daniel] as I now expound it unto thee"). The reason for so reading the succession is plain—Daniel lists four kingdoms following which the kingdom of God is to come. But the Greek hegemony passed away and the promised kingdom had not come, so the fourth was then reinterpreted as the Roman, to buoy up deferred hopes. But when that also passed and still the kingdom did not come, there was no longer any point in suppressing the fact that for the author the fourth kingdom was the Greek Empire. Nevertheless, the fourth kingdom has been interpreted as the Greco-Roman Empire, or the Holy Roman Empire, and even the Papacy, in attempts to avoid the recognition that the book prophesies the coming of God's kingdom following on the demise of the Greek power. But the twin stumbling blocks upon which all other interpretations trip are that the four kingdoms cannot be made to stretch from Neo-Babylonian times until now, even though the kingdom has not yet come in the sense the book requires, and that no other historical person fits the character of the little horn as does Antiochus Epiphanes, of whom the characterization is singularly apt. Therefore, the fourth empire is the Greek, and this means the second is the Median. For the fifth kingdom *see* SON OF MAN; KINGDOM OF GOD.

Thus we are left with a siege of Jerusalem by Nebuchadnezzar in Jehoiakim's third year; with a strange discrepancy in the career of Daniel during Nebuchadnezzar's reign, and an unlikely seven-year banishment of that monarch; with Belshazzar portrayed as absolute monarch when at best he was only coregnant; with Darius the Mede, who never existed; and with a Median Empire which passed away sixteen or so years before our author chronicles its overthrow.

*f. Date and style of composition.* The historical problems thus presented by the book raise the questions, What manner or style of book is this and when was it composed? Since the book is written in part in the first person, the composition purports to be contemporary with the events narrated, or at least not later in origin by more than the human life span. Further, if we accept the book as a unity, this is true of the parts written in the third person. Yet the book is not known until the middle of the second century B.C. The author is apparently aware that his work will not circulate until long after the times of which he is writing, for in 12:9 an angel commands that the revelation to Daniel is to be kept secret until the "time of the end." This means that the period at which the book was allowed to circulate was evidently thought by someone to be the "time of the end." The possibilities are therefore two: (*a*) that the composition of the book is contemporary with the events it narrates and has been hidden away in some esoteric group and that under the impression that the time of the second century B.C. was the decisive period with which the book is concerned; it was published in the first half of that century; (*b*) that it was written in the second century B.C. under the guise of being composed some four hundred years earlier. We may note that if *a* is the right view, then the peculiar pertinence of the book to the second century B.C. was recognized at that time, so that by far the oldest testimony we have to the significance of the book relates it firmly to the events of the second century; and that if, on the other hand, *b* is correct, then again we are led to the second century B.C. as the period against which the book is to be set if its significance is to be grasped. Either way, the events of Jewish history from 180 B.C. onward are of the greatest importance for the understanding of the book.

In support of the first view, there is the clear testimony of the book—its use of the first person, its elaborate system of dating the events, the provision for its late appearance. Further, there is tradition—Daniel was accepted, as we have seen, at Qumran and by the NT writers as "the prophet" and by the rabbis at Jamnia as a sixth-century work; and, apart from the neo-Platonist Porphyry (third century A.D.), tradition in both its Jewish and its Christian streams unhesitatingly testifies to the book as contemporary with its chief character and written by him. This unanimity of acceptance was not broken until the first criticisms arose from Spinoza and Sir Isaac Newton in the seventeenth and eighteenth centuries, and these were followed by others until the late eighteenth and early nineteenth centuries, when the modern pseudepigraphical view of the book emerged in the work of Eichhorn (*Einleitung* [1783]) and Bertholdt (*Commentary* [1806]). For many, however, the main argument for accepting the sixth-century origin of the book is what seems to them the disastrous results of accepting the other alternative—that the book is a dishonest production which, although in the Bible, claims to be what in fact it is not, and at the best can only be described as a "pious fraud." To this conclusion we must return later (*see* § *2h below*). Nevertheless, the evidence must be fairly weighed, not ruled out of court, and we must consider what are the arguments for the second view.

At once there arise the discrepancies within the book itself. Daniel becomes "ruler over the whole province of Babylon" (2:48) a year before he graduates. Also it is said in 1:21 that he continued until the first year of Cyrus; but in fact he is recorded as having a vision in Cyrus' third year. Further, in 8:14 the cessation of daily sacrifice is to last 2,300 mornings and evenings (i.e., 1,150 days = 3 solar years and 35 days, or 3 lunar years and 88 days), but in 7:25 the estimate is 3½ years, and in 9:27 it is half a week

of years, which is again 3½ years. In 12:11 the estimated period is 1,290 days and in the next verse 1,335 days. These variations are hard to explain if the book is an inerrantly inspired prophecy by Daniel of the events far ahead of his time. They become more understandable if the author is writing a number of separate pieces in the midst of Antiochus' persecution, and is making his estimate after the setting up of the altar to Zeus Olympios (*see* ABOMINATION THAT MAKES DESOLATE) and is thus operating with an advancing *terminus a quo* and a fixed *terminus ad quem*. Even so, it indicates a change of estimate at least once in the process. (Interpolation must also be reckoned with.) The other discrepancies are also easily explained if the writer sent out his pieces at differing times—serial-writers like Charles Dickens have been known to fall into similar errors. But if the book is the inerrant record of historic fact, they are quite inexplicable.

Turning to the discrepancies between the historical record in Daniel and our own knowledge of history, we need to note that when ordinary bills of sale such as Dougherty records were being dated as "seventeenth Nabonidus" or "first Cyrus," or when the Chaldean Chronicle was being composed as an official document, there could be no possible reason for using false dates. The evidence of bills of sale and royal annals and inscriptions on such matters as dates of accession are as nearly unimpeachable witnesses as this world is likely to afford. Yet it is just these which wreck any attempt to find room for Darius the Mede and a Median Empire between the reigns of Nabonidus and Cyrus. To these we must add that Jehoiakim was not besieged in his third year according to biblical evidence, and that we cannot credit a high Babylonian official (such as Daniel is depicted to be) with ignorance of Belshazzar's true status as his father's representative. Further, it is at least difficult to believe that Nebuchadnezzar could have been absent from his throne for seven years without our having some knowledge of it. Moreover, Nebuchadnezzar is represented as converted to faith in Daniel's God, and Darius issues a decree "to all the peoples, nations, and languages that dwell in all the earth" that all men are to fear Daniel's God as the living God, and yet we have no other echo of these momentous conversions. But the decisive point is that if the book was written by Daniel in the sixth century, he must have known the true succession of power in Babylon, and he must have falsified it for his own purposes; if, on the other hand, it is a second-century product, all these mistakes could at least have been due to honest error. We do not save Daniel's veracity by confining him to the sixth century. But if we accept the work as a second-century production, consisting of pieces issued at first separately and later gathered (whether by the original writer or by another) into a book, the change of language can be accounted for (*see* § *2c above*) as can also change of person from third to first, while the discrepancies between one story and another and the variance of the estimated length of cessation of sacrifice become intelligible, and the errors in historical record may be seen as the mistakes of a man who has a faulty knowledge of events which took place some four hundred years before his own time.

It has also been suggested that he did know the facts but deliberately departed from them because the idea of four kingdoms was traditional and the Assyrian Empire was unsuitable for his schematic purpose. The other major testimony is that of the linguists. The implication of S. R. Driver's judgment in this matter is inescapable. Thus the weight of evidence—internal, historical, and linguistic—forces us to the conclusion that the book of Daniel was not merely published, but was also written, fairly late in the Greek period.

But once we have reached this conclusion, further data become available. The author knows about the "abomination that makes desolate," and if the book is not prophecy, then his knowledge must arise from the fact that the setting up of the altar has already taken place; but he makes several estimates of the duration of the cessation of sacrifice, which therefore has not yet been resumed. Therefore, he wrote between December 17(?), 167 (I Macc. 1:54), and the corresponding date in 164 (I Macc. 4:52). Further, in 11:22-45 he records the history of Antiochus' reign, including the persecution, and the revolt of Judas (the "little help" of vs. 34), but at vs. 40 a third and successful campaign by Antiochus Epiphanes against Egypt is recorded and then his death in the Holy Land itself. As there was no third such campaign, and as Antiochus died in the East, we may take it that history passes into prophecy at vs. 40 and that this point is the moment of the writer's own date—after Judas' revolt and before Antiochus' death (i.e., between 166 and 163), and nearer the former terminus. Thus we can determine the date of the book as *ca.* 166-165 B.C.

This conclusion forces us to face the charge that the book, in that it purports to be written in the sixth century B.C., is nothing more nor less than a "pious fraud." Before doing so, we deal with the one outstanding literary question.

*g. The Additions.* The Greek versions (both LXX and Theod.) and the versions derived from the Greek (notably the Vulg.) contain material not found in the Hebrew-Aramaic MT. They are: (*a*) The Prayer of Azariah and the Song of the Three Children. This is inserted after 3:23 and records the prayer and praise of the Hebrews while they were in the furnace. The Song contains the familiar Benedicite of the Christian church. (*b*) The Story of Susanna, which tells how a young Jewish matron was falsely accused of adultery and cleared by Daniel's intervention. (*c*) The stories concerning Bel and the Dragon; in these Daniel shows the false character of the gods which Cyrus worshiped and is instrumental in their destruction. The latter two Additions (*b* and *c*) follow at the end of canonical Daniel. In the English Apoc., all three are printed as separate compositions, each of one chapter. There has been much discussion whether these Additions were originally written in Greek or in either Hebrew or Aramaic. With regard to *a* we must differentiate between 3:24-25 (vss. 1-2) and 3:46-51 (vss. 23-28), which are prose introductory narratives, and 3:26-45 (vss. 3-22) and 3:52-90 (vss. 29-68), which are liturgical compositions in verse. The probability is that the Addition had a Semitic original and that the prose was in Aramaic to conform with the rest of the story, but if, as is likely, the

liturgical passages had a previous separate existence, they were probably in Hebrew. With regard to *b* and *c,* it is unlikely that they were first written in Greek, but the literary evidence (despite the presence of a pun, which has been held since the third century A.D. to require a Greek original, but which could, of course, have been an apt introduction of a translator) does not allow of any clear decision. We may regard all three as expansions of the original book rather than as legitimate parts of it. If, however, some of the stories of Dan. 1-6 were circulating in an amorphous oral state around the ancient name Daniel, then these stories may well be part of that tradition and may represent some of the material our author rejected as not particularly suited to his purpose. This is particularly likely of Susanna and of Bel, in which Daniel is shown as resourceful and shrewd, quite in the tradition of the ancient wisdom figure. Once our author circulated his own new-fashioned stories, some of the floating tradition might well appeal to some of his readers as too good to be left out, and in Egyptian-Jewish circles, if not elsewhere, they were added to the book. The liturgical compositions were doubtless added from the same pious motives as were responsible for the psalms in Jonah and in Habakkuk and Isa. 38 (cf. II Kings 20). They were felt to be good compositions and not inappropriate to the occasion and therefore were included. (We may note that some scholars have been inclined to take the same view of the prayer in 9:4-19, but there is no evidence to support this suggestion.) We need not seek for esoteric meanings in these Additions; they are simple folk tales which rejoice in the victory of virtue over deceit and in Jewish shrewdness over Gentile stupidity. J. T. Milik has reported from Qumran Cave IV three MSS in Aramaic in which Daniel is recounting Hebrew history before a king, but their fragmentary character allows little to be said at this stage, other than that they are another witness to the popularity of the figure of Daniel in eschatologically minded groups. Milik tentatively names them Pseudo-Daniel (*a, b,* and *c*).

*h. Purpose of composition and abiding worth.* When the book is read against the background of the persecution instituted by Antiochus Epiphanes (*see* ANTIOCHUS 4), the purpose of both parts, stories and visions, becomes clear. Whatever was the nature of the traditional material he took over, the author evidently reshaped the stories to have a relevance for his own day. Antiochus was trying to stamp out all distinctively Jewish practices and as a test required the Jews to eat the nonkosher pork; Daniel and his friends refused to defile themselves with nonkosher food, and they prospered greatly. Antiochus set up an altar and commanded the worship of Zeus; the Three Children refused to worship just such an image, were thrown into the fire, and yet emerged triumphant. Antiochus thought himself a god but was thought by others to be a little mad, and Nebuchadnezzar was brought down by madness from just such heights of *hubris* to a God-fearing humility. Antiochus despoiled the temple; Belshazzar, who also desecrated the temple vessels, was summarily destroyed. Antiochus claimed to be divine, and Daniel, who refused to recognize similar claims made on behalf of

Darius, was flung into the den of lions and yet was kept safe by God. The parallels are too many and too exact to be fortuitous, and the message for the writer's contemporaries was too clear to be overlooked by them—be courageous and remain loyal, and God will deliver you also!

But the persecution was intense, and many had to pay the price of martyrdom. Some further message than a mere exhortation to courage and loyalty was necessary. Our writer found it in the new teaching of apocalyptic (*see* APOCALYPTICISM). It offered two immense boons. First, a deterministic development of the prophetic idea that history is controlled by God. There is a fixed span of time allotted by him to the powers of evil, and the initiated have been let into the secret as to when this time will be fulfilled. Our writer believes that he has this secret and that therefore he can foretell the time of the End. In his visions he communicates his conviction that it will not be long delayed—in fact, it is to come 3½ years from the date of the cessation of temple sacrifice. Using the apocalyptic device of history disguised as prophecy, he puts into Daniel's mouth an account of the period between his lifetime and the writer's own, and then continues it to cover the next two or three years —which continuation is the writer's actual prophecy of events shortly to take place. This prophecy must have come to the Jews of the day as a message of glorious reassurance and of hope. That it was clothed in the weird dress of apocalyptic vision was the mere accident of the writer's times, and in any case gave his words the authority which, in an age in which inspiration was held to have ceased, it alone could give. *See* INSPIRATION AND REVELATION.

The second great boon was that apocalyptic held out to men brought up on the grim Sheol doctrine (*see* SHEOL) the prize of a life in a world to come (12: 2-3, 13). Armed with this, a man could face martyrdom not only with courage but also with triumphant hope (II Macc. 7:9). The purpose of the book, then, is clear: it was to meet the urgent need of the Jewish people in the face of the Antiochene persecution.

But if a writing is to be regarded as scripture, it must have a relevance not only for its own age but also for every age. The book of Daniel needs none to plead its cause on this count. It speaks for itself and has done so for two thousand years and will continue to do so as long as there are men to read it. Its noble call for the oft-forgotten virtue of courage will meet with a response wherever men are faced with the final challenge—disloyalty or death. But courage in the decisive hour can come only to those who have practiced loyalty in the smaller choices of life. Daniel is a book for character-training as well as for crisis. Further, its insistence that time too is the creature of God, and that all history is under his sovereign will, is a lesson that mankind can never be allowed to forget. It is a magnificent exposition of what faith in God means. And again, if we find Daniel's promise of eternal life only a first meager adumbration of the fuller doctrine of the Christian gospel, nevertheless no book in the whole of scripture reveals so clearly the truth of Paul's words: "If in this life only we have hoped in Christ, we are of all men most to be pitied" (I Cor. 15:19 RSV mg.). For in Daniel we are reminded how grim is man's situation when he thinks that his brief life span here must encompass his whole destiny.

Even in that matter where Daniel is so grievously in error, the book serves us most usefully, for it is of the very greatest importance to the church that the whole wearisome business of "biblical arithmetic" and eschatological calculation should have been tried so sincerely and found to be a false path. The author of Daniel tried to calculate the time of the end and failed, and his failure is part of holy scripture to remind all lesser men to heed the warning of Jesus: "Of that day or that hour no one knows, not even the angels in heaven, nor the Son, but only the Father" (Mark 13:32).

Nor is the book rightly to be accused of being merely a "pious fraud." We forget that our standards of judgment in matters of authorship, plagiarism, pseudonymity, and interpolation are not those of the ancient world, but are largely the creation of printing press, which fixes a text unalterably, and the necessary economics of the publishing trade, which can be carried on only if copyright is respected; our standards on these matters are not absolute ethical criteria. Our author played fair by the standards of his day, for he did not create his message, but received it from the tradition of the apocalyptic movement. This tradition he handed on through the medium of the character he had created, Daniel, and, unhampered by our ideas of identity and authorship, gave his message in all good faith to those who stood in sore need of it. He little guessed that this same message would feed the faith of the people of God in many an age until the Eschaton which he foretold should at last come.

*See also* APOCALYPTICISM.

**Bibliography.** Commentaries: J. A. Montgomery, *Daniel,* ICC (1927); R. H. Charles, *Daniel* (1929); E. J. Young, *The Prophecy of Daniel* (1949); A. Bentzen, *Daniel,* HAT (2nd ed., 1952).

Special studies: H. B. Swete, *Introduction to the OT in Greek* (1900); R. D. Wilson, "The Book of Daniel and the Canon," *PTR,* 13 (1915), 352 ff; R. P. Dougherty, *Nabonidus and Belshazzar* (1929); C. H. Gordon, *Ugaritic Literature* (1929), p. 88; H. L. Ginsberg, "Aramaic Dialect Problems," *AJSL,* L (1933-34), 1 ff; H. H. Rowley, *Darius the Mede* (1935); G. A. Barton, *Archeology and the Bible* (7th ed., 1937); H. H. Rowley, *Relevance of Apocalyptic* (1944); H. L. Ginsberg, *Studies in Daniel* (1948); R. H. Pfeiffer, *History of NT Times with an Introduction to the Apoc.* (1949); H. H. Rowley, *Aramaic of the OT* (1949); M. Noth, "Noah, Daniel and Job in Ezechiel XIV," *Vetus Testamentum* (1951), pp. 251 ff; B. J. Roberts, *OT Text and Versions* (1951); S. B. Frost, *OT Apocalyptic* (1952); H. H. Rowley, "Unity of Daniel," *The Servant of the Lord* (1952); J. C. Dancy, *Commentary on I Maccabees* (1954); D. Barthélemy and J. T. Milik, *Discoveries in the Judean Desert,* I (1955), 150-52; J. B. Pritchard, *ANET* (2nd ed., 1955); P. Benoit, "Editing the MS Fragments from Qumran," *BA,* vol. XIX (1956), pt. 4, pp. 75 ff (= *RB,* LXIII [1956], 49 ff); S. R. Driver, *Introduction to the Literature of the OT* (reprinted 1956); J. T. Milik, "Prière de Nabonide," *RB,* LXIII (1956), 407; D. J. Wiseman, *Chronicles of Chaldean Kings* (1956); D. N. Freedman, "The Prayer of Nabonidus," *BASOR,* no. 145 (Feb., 1957), pp. 31-32. S. B. FROST

**DANITES.** See DAN 1.

**DAN-JAAN** dăn jā′ən. KJV translation of דָּנָה יַּעַן, the name of a town in N Palestine visited by David's census takers (II Sam. 24:6). The town referred to here is almost certainly DAN (2), but textual corruption (cf. the unintelligible reading of LXX B) precludes a satisfactory reading. The RSV follows one widely accepted emendation: "They came to Dan, and from Dan they went . . . ." Others prefer to read: "They came to Dan and to Ijon."

**Bibliography.** J. Wellhausen, *Der Text der Bücher Samuelis* (1871), p. 218; A. Klostermann, *Die Bücher Samuelis und der Könige,* in Kurzgefasster Kommentar (1887), p. 256.

G. W. VAN BEEK

**DANNAH** dăn'ə [דנה, stronghold; LXX Ρεννα] (Josh. 15:49). A village of Judah in the hill-country district of Debir; possibly to be identified with Deir esh-Shemsh or Simya.

**DAPHNE** dăf'nĭ [Δάφνη] (II Macc. 4:33). A magnificent place near ANTIOCH; famous for its temple of Apollo and right of asylum. The former high priest ONIAS in the Maccabean period came here for refuge, and from here was enticed to his doom.

*See also* MENELAUS.

N. TURNER

**DAPPLED** [ברדים, *plural adjective, related to* ברד, *hail*]; KJV GRISLED. A term referring to the color of certain horses mentioned in Zech. 6:3, 6. It indicates "mottled," "spotted," or perhaps "dappled gray" (vs. 3) horses. Cf. Gen. 31:10, 12.

*See also* COLORS.

C. L. WICKWIRE

**DARDA** där'də [דרדע] (I Kings 4:31—H 5:11). Alternately: DARA där'ə [דרע] (I Chr. 2:6, where, however, some Hebrew MSS and some MSS of the LXX, Syr., and Targ. read דרדע). One of the sons of Zerah, son of Judah. He was proverbial for his wisdom, which was surpassed only by Solomon's, and he is also included among the ancient musicians as one of the "sons of Mahol"—i.e., "members of the orchestral guild."

**Bibliography.** W. F. Albright, *Archaeology and the Religion of Israel* (3rd ed., 1953), pp. 127-28, 210.

E. R. DALGLISH

**DARIC** där'ĭk [אדרכן, דרכמון; LXX δαρεικός] (I Chr. 29:7; Ezra 2:69; 8:27; Neh. 7:70-72); KJV DRAM drăm. A Persian gold coin of 8.424 grams. It is the first coin mentioned in the Bible. The name "daric" is presumably derived from "Darius"—i.e., the Persian king DARIUS (1) the Great. But it is possible that it is of a much older source and comes from the Assyrian *darag mana* ( = 1/60 of the mina). It seems that in the Persian period each gold coin was called a daric, as this name is already used in the Bible in connection with Cyrus (Ezra 2:69) and with King David (I Chr. 29:7), which is an anachronism. *See also* MONEY.

H. HAMBURGER

**DARIUS** də rī'əs [Heb.-Aram. דריוש, דריוהוש, דריוש; Old Pers. *dārayava(h)uš,* he who upholds the good; Elam. *da-ri-ia-ma-u-iš;* Akkad. *da-ri-ia-muš;* Δαρεῖος]. 1. Darius I, the Great (522-486 B.C.).* Cambyses II (529-522) died during a period of political unrest in Persia which had resulted from the fact that the "Magian" (Old Persian *maguš*) Gaumata, who claimed to be Bardiya (Σμέρδις), the murdered brother of Cambyses, had made a strong bid for the throne. Darius (born in 550), son of

Hystaspes (Old Persian *vištāspa;* Ὑστάσπης), gives an account of his fight for the succession in the famous Inscription of Behistun, which appears on the surface of a gorge in the cliff which rises on the left side of the main caravan route leading from Baghdad to Teheran, *ca.* sixty-five miles from Hamadan.* His struggle, with the help of his six companions (Behistun Inscription IV, ll. 80-86), against Gaumata and leaders of revolts in other parts of the Empire ended in the consolidation of his possessions, which, after further campaigns extended from Sogdiana in the NE to Libya in the W and from Thracia in the NW to India (Old Persian *hi(n)du;* modern Sind) in the E. In 513(?) Darius embarked upon an unsuccessful campaign against the Scythians and crossed the Danube, with the intention to turn around the Black Sea and, perhaps, the Caspian Sea as well. The close contact between Persia and continental Greece led to the Ionian Revolt (499-493),

Courtesy of the Oriental Institute, the University of Chicago

4. King Darius I seated on his throne, with his son Xerxes standing behind him; from Persepolis

Courtesy of George C. Cameron, American Schools of Oriental Research and the University of Michigan

5. Relief and inscription of Darius on the cliff at Behistun in Iran, in three languages—Old Persian, Elamite, and Akkadian

which in its turn resulted in the expedition against Greece and the defeat of the Persian army at Marathon (490). Several years before his death (486) Darius designated his son XERXES as his successor. Figs. DAR 4; XER 1; DAR 5; AHU 6; INS 10.

A glimpse at Darius' conviction in matters of religion and ethics is provided by the still rather puzzling contents of the Naqš-i Rustam B inscription. His policy on the same subject with regard to the peoples of his empire is shown by two of his decrees. The first is a royal decree, which was later inscribed on stone, to the official Gadatas in the region of Magnesia on the River Maeander in Asia Minor. In it Gadatas is urged not to levy taxes from the officials of the Apollo temple nor to force them to cultivate profane soil. The other is his decree to cease obstruction and to promote the reconstruction of the temple in Jerusalem (Ezra 6:6-12; cf. Hag. 1:1-2).

"Darius king of Persia" (Ezra 4:5, 24; 6:1) and "Darius the Persian" (Neh. 12:22), whose reign is mentioned in connection with the registration of certain priests, both seem to refer to Darius I.

"Darius the Mede," however, who is mentioned in Dan. 5:31 (see also Dan. 6:1, 25; 11:1) as the successor to Belshazzar, and "Darius, the son of Ahasuerus, by birth a Mede, who became king over the realm of the Chaldeans" (Dan. 9:1), are most likely the result of wrong or wrongly interpreted information. *See* DANIEL.

**2.** Darius II (423-404 B.C.), son of Artaxerxes I (*see* ARTAXERXES), known as Nothus. His position in the W part of his empire was strengthened by the Peloponnesian War (431-404), which tied the hands of Athens and induced Sparta to solicit Persian help. The disastrous Athenian expedition against Sicily (413) provided Tissaphernes, satrap of Lydia, with the opportunity to reoccupy Lydia. Court intrigues inspired by Parysatis, the wife of Darius, in favor of her son Cyrus, caused Tissaphernes to be relieved from his post and nullified the results of his policy.

Frequent references to Darius II, mostly in the dates of the documents, occur in the Aramaic Papyri. The so-called Passover Papyrus is one of them. In it Arsames (ארשם), satrap of Egypt, is ordered as follows: [" '*Authorize a festival of unleavened bread for the* Jew]ish [garrison].' *So do you count* fou[rteen days of the month of Nisan and] obs[erve *the passover*], and from the 15th to the 21st day of [Nisan observe the festival of unleavened bread]" (*ANET* 491).

**3.** Darius III (336-330 B.C.), known as Codomannus, according to Justinus (X.3.3 ff). He suffered repeated defeats against Alexander's Macedonian armies (Granicus [334], Issus [333], Gaugamela [331]) and was finally murdered by Bessus, satrap of Bactria.

The desperate struggle of the last Achaemenian king against the Macedonian conqueror is referred to in I Macc. 1:1-8; see also the "fourth" king of Persia in Dan. 11:2. *See* ALEXANDER 1.

*Bibliography.* "Dareios" in Pauly-Wissowa, *Realencyclopädie der klassischen Altertumswissenschaft*, vol. IV, pt. 2 (1901), pp. 2184-2212. P. J. Junge, *Darius I, König der Perser* (1944).

For references to Darius II in the Aramaic documents, *see:* A. Cowley, *Aramaic Papyri of the Fifth Century B.C.* (1923), no. 21, p. 282. E. G. Kraeling, *The Brooklyn Museum Aramaic Papyri* (1953), p. 305.

The text of the Gadatas inscription is to be found in G. Dittenberger, *Sylloge Inscriptionum Graecarum*, I (3rd ed., 1915-1924), 22. For a translation, see C. J. Ogden in G. W. Botsford and E. G. Sihler, *Hellenic Civilization* (1915), p. 162. For a discussion, see E. Meyer, *Die Entstehung des Judentums* (1896), pp. 19 ff.

*See also* the bibliography under PERSIA, HISTORY AND RELIGION OF. M. J. DRESDEN

**DARIUS THE MEDE** [דריוש, Old Pers. *Darayva'ush;* דריוהוש *and* דריהוש, *later forms attested by papyri from reigns of Darius II and III;* ד׳המדי, D. *ham-mādhî* (Dan. 11:1); Aram. ד׳מדיא, D' *mādhāy'a*, (Dan. 6:1), *some MSS give* (kethibh) *mādhāyâ'* , (qere) *mādhā'â*]. A king of Babylon mentioned in the book of Daniel only,

who is said to have followed Belshazzar and preceded Cyrus (LXX 6:29), being then sixty-two years old. He had at least a "first year," and divided the kingdom into 120 satrapies, over which he appointed three presidents, of whom Daniel was one. On historical difficulties arising and for bibliography, *see* DANIEL. S. B. FROST

**DARKNESS.** *See* LIGHT.

**DARKON** där'kŏn [דרקון, rough, *or* stern(?)] (Ezra 2:56; Neh. 7:58). Head of a family of "sons of Solomon's servants" (*see* NETHINIM) returning from exile with Zerubbabel. *Cf.* LOZON (I Esd. 5:33).

*Bibliography.* M. Noth, *Die israelitischen Personennamen* (1928), p. 225. H. H. GUTHRIE, JR.

**DART** [מסע, שבט; KJV חץ (Prov. 7:23; RSV *more correctly* "arrow"), שלח (II Chr. 32:5; RSV *better* "weapon"), תח (Job 41:29—H 41:21; RSV *better* "club"); βέλος; KJV βολίς (Heb. 12:20), *see below*)]. A short pointed weapon used for thrusting.

Joab used three darts (שבטים, lit. "rods"; II Sam. 18:14), probably better "pointed rods," to kill Absalom.

In Heb. 12:20 the phrase "or thrust through with a dart" is rightly omitted in the RSV as being a textual gloss.

According to I Macc. 6:51, darts (RSV "arrows") were mechanically hurled. These may well have been wrapped in inflammable materials and ignited (cf. Eph. 6:16). J. W. WEVERS

**DATES.** The fruit of the palm tree, *Phoenix dactylifera* L. The only biblical reference to dates is in a metaphor extolling the bride in Song of S. 7:7—H 7:8, where אשכלות, "clusters," refers to the manner in which the dates grow. The following verse reflects the method of picking dates. The KJV mg. of II Chr. 31:5 suggests "dates" instead of "honey" for דבש, *debhaš* (Arabic *dibsh* refers to date honey).

That dates formed a staple food in ancient times there is no question, for the palm tree is frequently mentioned. The absence of references to the fruit in the Bible must be pure coincidence.

*See also* AGRICULTURE; FLORA § A2h; FOOD; HONEY; PALM TREE. J. C. TREVER

**DATHAN** dā'thən [דתן; *cf.* Akkad. *datnu,* strong]. Leader, with his brother ABIRAM (1), of a revolt against the authority of Moses; son of Eliab, a Reubenite (Num. 16:1, 12, 24-25, 27; 26:9; Deut. 11:6; Ps. 106:17; Ecclus. 45:18).

The accounts of two revolts against Mosaic leadership of the wandering Israelite tribes have been woven together in Num. 16. One account deals with a protest led by Korah against the religious prerogatives of Moses and Aaron; the other, with a protest voiced by Dathan and Abiram against Moses' alleged usurpation of princely authority over the community (vss. 1b-2a, 12-15, 25-26, 27b-34). This allegation against Moses is joined with disenchantment that he has been able to secure only the wilderness and not an "inheritance of fields and vineyards" for those who fled Egypt with him. The vindication of Moses' commission as one sent by Yahweh "to do all these works" is obtained by appeal to Yahweh.

As a result of divine action Dathan, Abiram, their families and goods are swallowed up by the earth. Thus the narrative assumes that the challenge to the structure of authority within the Israelite community is of direct concern to Yahweh, who "creates something new" (vs. 30) in order to meet the challenge.

*Bibliography.* M. Noth, *Die israelitischen Personennamen* (1928), pp. 68-75, 145, 225; W. Eichrodt, *Theologie des ATs,* II (2nd ed., 1948), 83-84.      R. F. JOHNSON

**DATHEMA** dăth′ə mə [Δάθεμα] (I Macc. 5:9). A fortress in Gilead to which the Jews repaired and in which they were besieged by the Syrians and relieved by JUDAS MACCABEUS. It may be the modern Remtheh (for the Syr. of I Macc. 5:9 reads "Rametha"), or Dameh (for some think that the Syr. may be an error for "Damtha").

*Bibliography.* G. A. Smith, *The Historical Geography of the Holy Land* (25th ed., 1931), p. 616.      N. TURNER

**DAUGHTER-IN-LAW.** An alternate translation of כלה and νύμφη, both of which are used also for "bride."

Incestuous relations with a man's daughter-in-law are forbidden (Lev. 18:15); death is the penalty for both if this law is broken (20:12). The daughter-in-law belonged to the family group and migrated with it to a new land (Gen. 11:31). The meaning "bride" identifies the status of daughter-in-law during the period of the betrothal and marriage transaction.

*See also* FAMILY; INCEST; MARRIAGE.

     O. J. BAAB

**DAVID** dā′vĭd [דוד]. The second king of Israel (1000-962 B.C.).

1. Sources
2. Name and family
3. Early stories
4. Fugitive
5. King at Hebron
6. King at Jerusalem
7. Estimate
Bibliography

**1. Sources.** The main sources are the books of SAMUEL and I Kings 1-2 (*see* KINGS, I AND II, § 1), paralleled, with significant omissions and additions, in I Chr. 11-29 (*see* CHRONICLES, I AND II). Many of the materials of Samuel and Kings are contemporary, or nearly so, with the times of David—notably the court records of II Sam. 9-20—and are manifestly some of the most authentic historical writings of the OT.

**2. Name and family.** The name David occurs nearly eight hundred times in the OT, *ca.* sixty times in the NT. The term *dawidum* occurs more than a score of times in the Mari Texts, but it probably has nothing to do with the name of David, as formerly thought. The Alalakh Tablet (6.37) is not clear. The only unequivocal parallel is found in the archives of Khafajah. For studies of the Mari Texts, *see bibliography.*

Tradition is unanimous in attesting David's Judean origin. He was a member of the Bethlehemite family of Jesse, who was himself reckoned in the late genealogy of Ruth as the grandson of Boaz and Ruth (Ruth 4:18-22). Hence Moabite blood flowed in his veins, and this fact was apparently not forgotten in later days (I Sam. 22:3-4), though afterward David dealt severely with the Moabites (II Sam. 8:2). David had at least six brothers and two sisters (I Chr. 2:13-16). I Sam. 16:10-11; 17:12 report eight sons for Jesse. The family tree of Jesse (Diagram 1) illustrates the situation (the sources are the relevant passages of I Samuel and I Chronicles as indicated).

David's family is far more complicated, as may be understood from the circumstances of his life and the customs of the age. Diagrams 2-3 attempt to present the facts as gathered from the several narratives of the Bible.

**3. Early stories.** The stories of David's growing fame are in some respects embellished by later, idealizing elements, but there is no reason to doubt their

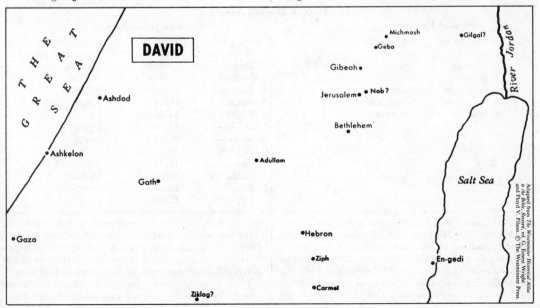

DAVID

Michmash ·   · Gilgal?
· Geba
Gibeah ·
Jerusalem ·   · Nob?
Bethlehem ·
Ashdod ·
· Adullam
Ashkelon ·
Gath ·
Salt Sea
· Gaza
· Hebron
· Ziph
En-gedi ·
Ziklag?
· Carmel

THE GREAT SEA

River Jordan

DIAGRAM 1

## Family of Jesse

Boaz and Ruth (Ruth 4:18-22)

Obed

Jesse

| Eliab (I Sam. 16:6-9) or Elihu (I Chr. 27:18) | Abinadab (I Sam. 16:6-9) | Shammah (I Sam. 16:6-9) or Shimeah (II Sam. 13:3) or Shimei (II Sam. 21:21) | Nethanel (I Chr. 2:13-16) | Raddai (I Chr. 2:13-16) | Ozem (I Chr. 2:13-16) | David (I Sam. 16:6-13) | Zeruiah (I Chr. 2:16) | Abigail (I Chr. 2:17) |
|---|---|---|---|---|---|---|---|---|

Amasa (I Chr. 2:17)

Joab (I Chr. 2:16)    Abishai (I Chr. 2:16)    Asahel (I Chr. 2:16)

DIAGRAM 2

## David's Wives and Sons

| Michal (I Sam. 18:27) | Abigail (I Sam. 25:42) | Ahinoam (I Sam. 25:43) | Maacah (I Chr. 3:2) | Haggith (I Chr. 3:2) | Abital (I Chr. 3:3) | Eglah (I Chr. 3:3) | Bath-shua/Bathsheba (I Chr. 3:5) | Others |
|---|---|---|---|---|---|---|---|---|
| | Daniel (I Chr. 3:1) | Amnon (I Chr. 3:1) | Absalom (I Chr. 3:2) | Adonijah (I Chr. 3:2) | Shephatiah (I Chr. 3:3) | Ithream (I Chr. 3:3) | Shimea/Shammua Shobab Nathan Solomon (II Sam. 5:14; I Chr. 3:5) | Ibhar Elishua/Elishama Nogah Nepheg Japhia Elishama Beelida/Eliada Eliphelet/Elpelet (II Sam. 5:14; I Chr. 3:6-8; 14:4-7) |

DIAGRAM 3

## The Lists of David's Sons

| Born at Hebron | | Born at Jerusalem | | |
|---|---|---|---|---|
| *II Sam. 3:2-5* | *I Chr. 3:1-4* | *II Sam. 5:14* | *I Chr. 3:5-9* | *I Chr. 14:4-7* |
| 1. Amnon | Amnon | 1. Shammua | Shimea | Shammua |
| 2. Chileab | Daniel | 2. Shobab | Shobab | Shobab |
| 3. Absalom | Absalom | 3. Nathan | Nathan | Nathan |
| 4. Adonijah | Adonijah | 4. Solomon | Solomon | Solomon |
| 5. Shephatiah | Shephatiah | 5. Ibhar | Ibhar | Ibhar |
| 6. Ithream | Ithream | 6. Elishua | Elishama | Elishua |
| | | 7. —— | Eliphelet | Elpelet |
| | | 8. —— | Nogah | Nogah |
| | | 9. Nepheg | Nepheg | Nepheg |
| | | 10. Japhia | Japhia | Japhia |
| | | 11. Elishama | Elishama | Elishama |
| | | 12. Eliada | Eliada | Beeliada |
| | | 13. Eliphelet | Eliphelet | Eliphelet |

essential correctness. David was a gifted and many-sided personality. In fact, there are many indications that he possessed charismatic qualities.

He comes to the attention of the biblical narrator first in connection with Saul's disobedience during the Amalekite campaign, when Saul was rejected in favor of a "neighbor of yours, who is better than you" (I Sam. 15:28). Samuel went to Bethlehem to carry out his commission to select Saul's successor. There he was directed to the family of Jesse, whom he invited to a sacrifice. After the purification and sacrifice Samuel requested an introduction to the sons of Jesse. One, however—David—happened not to be present, because he was tending the flock that day.

This was the one whom the Lord had chosen to be king. When he arrived, Samuel "anointed him in the midst of his brothers" (I Sam. 16:13), whereupon "the Spirit of the LORD came mightily upon David." This particular story is generally regarded as legendary and centers in Samuel rather than David. The connection of David with the family of Jesse, the anointing by Samuel, and the reference to the Spirit of the Lord are certainly authentic.

I Sam. 16:14-23 follows logically and most naturally on the Amalekite episode of I Sam. 15. Because of Samuel's rejection, Saul became melancholy. To soothe the troubled mind of the king, a skilful player on lyre or harp was suggested. Saul assented to the proposal, and one of his servants forthwith recommended the son of Jesse. Evidently David's ability as a gifted musician was well known at the royal court. He is depicted as one "skilful in playing, a man of valor, a man of war, prudent in speech, and a man of good presence" (I Sam. 16:18), which pretty well sums up the character of David at this time. Arriving at court, he at once became the personal attendant of the king, who thought very highly of him. In fact, he made him one of his armor-bearers. By virtue of its position and its tenor, this appears the most likely story of David's introduction to royal circles.

The Goliath tale is probably secondary. It has David coming to the notice of Saul through the heroic feat of the slaying of the Philistine giant.* The Philistines and Israelites were encamped *ca.* eighteen miles SW of Jerusalem, between Azekah and Soco, at a place called Ephes-dammim, the location of which is unknown today. On the side of the enemy was a giant from Gath, the place of giants (I Chr. 20:4-8), who was dressed like a Homeric warrior. Each day he challenged the army of Israel to send one of its men to fight him in single combat. The boldness of the challenge threw Saul and his followers into panic. In the meantime, David was sent across the hills by his father to bring provisions for his three older brothers who had taken service in the army of Saul. Soon after arriving at the battle scene, he heard the taunt of the Philistine and offered to accept his challenge, to the disgust of Eliab, his oldest brother. Others of the army also ridiculed David's offer. Finally, someone brought word to Saul. Again David repeated his willingness to fight the giant. The king reminded him of his lack of experience as against that of Goliath, who had been a "man of war from his youth" (I Sam. 17:33). David replied that he, as a shepherd, had often contended with lions and bears which tried to molest the flock. At last Saul was persuaded and permitted him to proceed. David could not bear the armor Saul wanted to provide for him, choosing instead to fight in his own way. The Philistine was insulted when he saw the Bethlehem youth with his staff and sling, but he soon felt the sting of the pebble so accurately delivered by David. The shepherd was champion; Goliath lay dead. In the ensuing battle the Philistines were routed. David was not known by name, according to our story (I Sam. 17:53-58). Fig. SLI 68.

*See* map "Palestine: I Samuel 16–31, Saul and David," under SAUL.

Again, there may be legendary elements in this narrative, but there can be no doubt about the Philistine struggle and the service of David's brothers in Saul's army. Nor can there be any inherent improbability that the daring youth from Bethlehem performed some heroic exploit. But whether this was how he came to the attention of Saul is another matter. One thing is certain, however: that the two stories of his coming to the notice of Saul were so firmly established in the tradition that neither could be suppressed in favor of the other.

In any case, David's rise to fame was extraordinary. He was so successful in his service and so discreet in his actions that the king soon put him in charge of a group of soldiers, to the complete satisfaction of the people and the officials of the court. On their return from a campaign against the old enemy, they were welcomed home by a group of women celebrating their victory with the fateful song:

> Saul has slain his thousands,
> And David his ten thousands (I Sam. 18:7;
> cf. 21:11; 29:5).

These lines attest the popularity of David, whether it was achieved by some heroic deed or in the ordinary course of resistance against the foe. The disturbed mind of Saul could not bear such extravagant praise for the man who had so recently come to his court. With the virtual curse of Samuel resting upon him, he now felt himself slipping and, as we learn later (I Sam. 19:22), must have sensed somehow an alliance between the old prophet and the young man who was succeeding all too well. Henceforth he tried his best to put David out of the way.

Saul's attempt to pin David to the wall with his spear is explained as a seizure of an "evil spirit from God" (I Sam. 18:10). Twice David is reported to have escaped (18:11); this made the king even more suspicious and probably envious. The more successful David was, the more frustrated Saul became (18:15). He thought of giving his older daughter, Merab, to David as wife, then changed his mind (18:17, 19). But when Michal fell in love with David, Saul took advantage of the situation by requiring a dowry of a hundred Philistine foreskins—hoping that this once he might succeed in confronting the young upstart with an impossible task or that David might be killed by the Philistines (18:21; cf. vs. 17*b*). Again success crowned David's efforts, only to fan to white heat the persecution complex of the king. Every time David went out against the enemy, he returned in triumph (18:30).

At the request of David, Jonathan pleaded with his father on his behalf. Saul promised by oath that David should not be put to death, but the very sight of the man of success impelled the king to violate his vow, so that he sent his police to take David from his quarters. David might have met his doom then and there had not Michal plotted his escape. The partisanship of his own children for David so enraged Saul that he pursued him to Naioth in Ramah (19:22), seeking his life. But David fled from Ramah before he arrived. David now saw, after another demonstration of the king's attitude (ch. 20), that life at the court was impossible, and so he left Gibeah permanently.

There is no reason to doubt the general sequence of events related in chs. 18–20. So far David's conduct remained beyond reproach. That he conducted local skirmishes with the Philistines cannot be questioned; neither can the growing deterioration of the relationship between him and Saul. His marriage to Michal also appears quite certain.

Before we follow David's career as an outlaw, it is necessary to pause a moment over his relations with the crown prince, Jonathan. There are numerous references to their friendship in the books of Samuel. From their first meeting they developed a relationship which was to last beyond the death of Jonathan. They entered into a covenant of friendship (18:1-5) ratified by Jonathan's gift of personal military equipment. This covenant was further strengthened by Jonathan's plea for David (19:2-10), his assistance in ascertaining the mind of his father toward David and informing him accordingly (ch. 20), and the renewal of the covenant between them at Horesh (23:16-18). For the most part, the initiative appears to have been taken by Jonathan, perhaps because of his position as son of the king. That their friendship was more than fictional may be seen from David's lament (II Sam. 1:17-27) and his concern later for Mephibosheth, Jonathan's son (II Sam. 9).

**4. The fugitive (I Sam. 21-27; 30).** The only avenue of escape from the clutches of Saul was to seek refuge with the Philistines, who were powerful enough to protect him. On the way he stopped at Nob, where, by his clever deception of Ahimelech the priest, he acquired provisions for the flight (I Sam. 21:1-9), which ended with his taking refuge with Achish, the tyrant of Gath. The Philistines, including Achish, were suspicious of David and possibly a bit resentful because of his success against them. Feigning madness, David contrived to get himself out of what might at the moment have proved an untoward incident.

From Gath, David fled to Adullam, present Tell esh-Sheikh Madhkur, some dozen miles NE of Gath, where he gathered about him "everyone who was in distress, and every one who was in debt, and every one who was discontented" (22:2). He became their *condottiere* and advocate, and they in turn formed the nucleus of his later troop of professional soldiers. From Adullam he went to Mizpeh in Moab to entrust his aged parents into the hands of the king of Moab (22:3-4), where they were out of reach of Saul. At the word of God he returned to the forest of Hereth (unknown, but somewhere in S Judah).

While there, David was informed of a Philistine raid against Keilah ca. fourteen miles E of Gath. After some hesitation (23:3), he and his men drove the Philistines away and took a quantity of booty. Saul soon heard about David's adventure at Keilah and set out to find him. In the meantime David, having discovered that the citizens would not protect him from Saul, fled to the desert of Ziph, some ten miles S of Keilah (23:13-23). Informers from Ziph told Saul of David's whereabouts, and he was once more compelled to flee, this time to the desert around Maon, S of Ziph, where he was almost trapped by the forces of the king (23:26-28). From there David withdrew to Engedi (24:1 ff), midway down the W shore of the Dead Sea.* Again loyalists were not slow in bringing the news of David's new hide-out to Saul, who at once went in search of him. On this campaign the king fell into the hands of the fugitive, who spared his life because he had sworn he would not lay hands on the Lord's anointed one. Fig. ENG 28.

After Saul's departure David again turned westward to the desert of Maon. At the sheep-shearing festival he sent messengers to a rich man named Nabal at Carmel (ch. 25), a city ca. five miles S of Ziph (cf. Josh. 15:55), requesting a gift in return for his protection of his interests. When Nabal refused, David prepared for action. Dire consequences for Nabal were averted only by the swift action of his servants and his wife, Abigail (25:18-19). After Nabal's death David married Abigail (25:40-42). He also married another wife, whose name was Ahinoam, from Jezreel, whose location is uncertain, but which was near Ziph. In the meantime, Saul had married David's wife Michal to Palti (25:44).

Once more Saul is said to have pursued David in the region of Ziph, only to fall into the power of the latter, who again spared his life. Most scholars regard this story (ch. 26) as parallel with that related in ch. 24. In any case, David could no longer feel secure among his own people and so sought protection from the Philistines at Gath.

David had by this time quite a coterie of followers, which might have become burdensome to Achish had he not, at David's request, given David a place where he might fend for himself. Ziklag, which was to be his center of operations until he took up residence at Hebron, was ca. fifteen miles SW of Hebron and seventeen miles SE of Gath, possibly to be identified with the present Tell el-Khuweilfeh. This was one of the most significant steps in David's whole outlaw life. The gathering of a host of followers owing allegiance to no one but himself now was about to pay off, for at Ziklag he became the founder of a small dynasty which served to launch him on his further efforts to procure the throne of Israel. But more than that, he utilized the time to root out opposing elements in the S area of Judah and thus consolidated a large portion of Judah itself under himself (I Sam. 27:8). With the booty he enriched and equipped himself and his followers for the next adventure, which had to wait until the death of Saul. By his movements against the dissidents on the borders of Judah he hoodwinked Achish (27:12).

Matters went on in this fashion for two years (29:3), when the Philistines decided to strike another blow against Israel, this time with David's help or at least with him in inactive status. Had it not been for the concerted opposition of the other Philistine kings, David might have found himself in a precarious position. But by their opposition they unwittingly played into his hands. As things stood, he was permitted to continue his activity around Ziklag, notably a punitive raid against the Amalekites (ch. 30), who had taken advantage of David's absence and had themselves victimized the chief and his followers by a destructive foray. After his return with much booty, he distributed some to the elders of Judah, in whose territory he had operated before. This was an astute move designed to win them over and possibly to quell criticism of him for having gone over to the Philistines.

David's Ziklag period, therefore, enabled him to gain supplies for the next step, to wipe out opponents on the borders of Judah, to organize his forces for action when the time was propitious, and to strengthen his hand with his Judean brethren. The "kingdom" of Ziklag marked the second stage on his way to the throne of Judah, the first being his collection of personal followers. The important fact in these stages was the personal position occupied by David. The conquered areas owed allegiance to no one but David. His followers were also bound to him personally, not to a place or to a group of elders or even to a religious institution.

**5. King at Hebron (II Sam. 1:1–5:5).** Soon after his return from his punitive expedition against the Amalekites, news reached David of the defeat of Israel at Gilboa and the death of Saul and Jonathan. Curiously enough, the very one who brought the news to him was the one who had obeyed the last command of his sovereign to slay him in his confused state before he could fall into the hands of his enemies. While David could not really have been surprised at the news, he acted very diplomatically by immediately going into mourning and dispatching the Amalekite messenger who was responsible for relieving the king. In addition he composed one of the finest odes on friendship that has ever been written (II Sam. 1:17-27). It celebrated the virtues of Saul and extolled the prowess of both Saul and Jonathan. This composition doubtless had much to do with the tradition which ascribes many psalms to David. That he was a gifted musician and a composer of songs can hardly be questioned. I Sam. 16:18 describes him as ידע נגן and נבון דבר—i.e., one who knows how to play instruments and who is clever with words. This tradition is supported by the lamentation which is almost universally conceded to have been composed by David. But he hardly wrote all the seventy-three psalms which are ascribed to him in the titles thereto.

David lost no time in marching northward in Judah after an inquiry of the oracle of the Lord. He took up residence in the old center at Hebron,* where the men of Judah anointed him king over their territory (II Sam. 2:4). This evidently marked simply the formalization of a relation which already existed. David had proved himself by his exploits in the desert, and while he was resident at Ziklag, the Lord had approved him by directing him to go to Hebron (2:1), where the elders of Judah entered into a virtual covenant with him. Here were all the fundamentals required for establishing David in office—demonstration of prowess, divine approval, and popular assent represented by the act of the people of Judah. Fig. HEB 12.

His first act as king of Judah was to send a congratulatory message to Jabesh-gilead for performing funeral rites for Saul and to inform them that he had been anointed king of Judah, suggesting between the lines that, since their king was no longer alive, they follow suit. But Abner, Saul's field marshal, had to be reckoned with. He had set up Ish-bosheth, Saul's son, as successor to his father at Mahanaim (2:8-10). This was a purely arbitrary act without divine sanction, but since it was the custom in surrounding nations and since no one else was available, the Israelites probably assented. Sooner or later the forces of Ish-bosheth and David were bound to come into collision. They met in the border area at Gibeon, and Abner and his army were routed by Joab (2:12-17) after a bitter battle. Abner himself was chased from the field by Joab's brother Asahel, whom he

struck down with his spear (2:18-23); thus began a blood feud between Joab and Abner, which finally ended in Abner's paying the penalty (3:27). Though this battle was brought to an end by mutual agreement, border troubles continued (3:1). David's position became stronger, while that of Ish-bosheth was gradually losing strength and face.

Just then there was a serious altercation between Abner and the man he had placed on Saul's throne. The difficulty ostensibly was occasioned by Abner's dealings with one of Saul's concubines, which pointed up Abner's ambitions: "Abner was making himself strong in the house of Saul" (3:6). The position of Abner is clearly reflected by the fact that Ish-bosheth could do nothing when Abner threatened to deliver the kingdom to David. Abner was the *de facto* executor of Saul's kingdom and as such immediately undertook arrangements with David to deliver to him the political estate of his former king. Here again the Davidic genius displayed itself, and circumstances played into his hands. He did not make overtures to Abner but allowed him to initiate proceedings which led to the transfer of the throne to David. Moreover, David, having been approached by Abner, was in position to lay down certain terms favorable to himself which at the same time were not detrimental to the pride of Abner or Israel.

Ish-bosheth had by now demonstrated his incapacity to maintain Israel against the rising star of David, while David had definitely shown his ability by uniting all Judah under his rule. The further link in the chain which David was forging, therefore, was the demand for the return of Michal. As the king's son-in-law he was in a better situation to press his rights or at least to present a more convincing front. Abner had already persuaded the elders of Israel, especially those from Benjamin, to agree to his proposed action, on the grounds of David's being the Lord's choice to deliver them from the Philistines and of previous proposals made by some of the Israel tribes (3:17-19). So he was well prepared to negotiate with David at Hebron. But just when the stipulations agreed upon were about to be consummated, Joab carried out his revenge upon Abner for the slaying of his brother Asahel (3:27), and David's well-laid plans were placed in jeopardy. Had he not taken decisive measures to display his innocence, the whole plan might have fallen through. All the movements of David so far show clearly that he had thought out well his course of action and would permit nothing to interfere with its realization.

Again circumstances intervened to overcome the obstacles placed in his way by the rash act of Joab. When news of Abner's death reached Ish-bosheth, both he and his followers, realizing the extent of their loss, were utterly disheartened. Ish-bosheth was helpless. David waited. Then two leaders of guerrilla bands from Beeroth murdered Ish-bosheth during his noonday siesta. The basis for their deed is not clear, but it can be said with considerable certainty that David had nothing to do with it, for when they brought Ish-bosheth's head to him, he rewarded them with death (4:9-12), just as he had done with the Amalekite who brought him news of Saul's death, and he gave honorable burial to Ish-bosheth's head in the grave of Abner at Hebron.

There remained now no legitimate successor of

Saul except the lame and therefore impossible Mephibosheth, the son of Jonathan. David's claim as son-in-law of the king was thus unimpeachable, though there is no indication that he pressed it openly. The elders of Israel did the only thing possible under the circumstances. They made their way to Hebron and formally carried through the agreement made by Abner. By his adroit conduct in connection with the deaths of Saul, Jonathan, Abner, and Ish-bosheth, David won the approbation of Israel. By his skilful diplomacy at Ziklag, recognized by the people of Judah in making him king, he had shown his fitness to rule over Israel also; the Spirit of the Lord was with him. This was sufficient: "Then all the tribes of Israel came to David at Hebron, and said, 'Behold, we are your bone and flesh. In times past, when Saul was king over us, it was you that led out and brought in Israel; and the LORD said to you, "You shall be shepherd of my people Israel, and you shall be prince over Israel" ' " (5:1-2: cf. I Chr. 11:1-2). A covenant was made, and David was forthwith anointed king over Israel.

It is to be observed that the people of Judah had no part in this transaction. They had already acted (2:4), and there was no need to repeat this act in conjunction with Israel. David was now king of Judah and king of Israel, but not of a so-called united kingdom. David's rule was paratactic—i.e., he in his person became ruler over both kingdoms. He was the only uniting principle; the kingdoms themselves were not united into a superstate; they remained as they had been before.

For 7½ years David remained at Hebron, at first as king of Judah and then as king of Israel, for Ish-bosheth reigned for only two years (2:10). He had now achieved apparently the major points of his plan, though there was yet much to be done by way of consolidation of his gains and establishment of his personal position. He was possessed by the genius of doing one thing at a time, and he held steadfastly to this course. Complications were bound to arise, but at each stage he was prepared and capable of dealing with them by virtue of his increasing power and prestige.

**6. King at Jerusalem (II Sam. 5:6-I Kings 2:11).** David's first step after becoming king of Israel was to move his residence from the capital of Judah to the extraterritorial city of Jerusalem, which up until now had remained in the hands of the Jebusites. Its location on the borders of the two kingdoms made it ideal for David's purposes. Moreover, it was neutral ground and so would not arouse jealousy on the part of either Judah or Israel. The fortress could be entered only through the water shaft (II Sam. 5:8), which was scaled by Joab (I Chr. 11:6); after this the inhabitants capitulated. The capture of Jerusalem added one more precious jewel to David's diadem. He never incorporated the city into either kingdom; it remained outside the regal system apparently throughout the period of the kingdom of Judah. David was now not only king of Judah and Israel, but also master of Jerusalem by right of conquest. He fortified the city and took up residence in the citadel. He built up the city "from the Millo inward" (II Sam. 5:9; I Chr. 11:8; *see* MILLO 1). He further contracted with Hiram, king of Tyre, with whom he

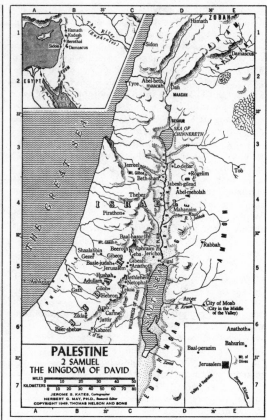

PALESTINE
2 SAMUEL
THE KINGDOM OF DAVID

MILES
0    10    20    30    40    50
KILOMETERS
0  10  20  30  40  50  60  70  80

JEROME S. KATES, Cartographer
HERBERT G. MAY, PH.D., Research Editor
COPYRIGHT 1949, THOMAS NELSON AND SONS

entered into a treaty, for cedar wood, carpenters, and stonecutters to construct a palace for himself and probably quarters for his coterie. This activity was not accomplished at one stroke; it doubtless took some time to finish the building project as planned.

Evidently the Philistines were slow in reacting against the rapidly expanding power of David; at least, this is the conclusion indicated when the venture against Jerusalem is put after the Philistine uprising. It may be also that they had no objection to his moves so long as he did not engage in any militant forays against them or attempt to fortify his seat of government. It must be remembered that he was still regarded as a vassal of the Philistines, and they probably maintained their confidence in him at the behest of Achish (I Sam. 27:12), believing him to be still basically unacceptable to Israel because of his earlier defection. Consequently, since his operations were limited to the territory of Israel and Judah, they let him alone. On the other hand, it is possible that they took action against David as soon as they learned of his anointing by the elders of Israel, which made him the successor of Saul, their old enemy, and obligated him to carry on the program of defense and expansion of Israel to their disadvantage.

However this may be, David was compelled to deal with them on two, apparently not too widely separated, occasions. His rule over both Judah and Israel was bound to hamper their trade routes into the central highland, which they now undertook to defend. The first battle took place in the Valley of Rephaim just to the SW of Jerusalem at Baqa, which lies across the Bethlehem road. The new king defeated them at a place called Baal-perazim (II Sam. 5:20-21). Perhaps the Philistines had misjudged the strength of David or their forces had been mustered too hastily and improperly deployed. But David knew every inch of the land and was perfectly acquainted with the Philistine tactics, having lived among them and having fought them earlier under Saul. Experience had shown that the Philistines would not give up with one attempt. Once more they appeared in the Valley of Rephaim (II Sam. 5:22-25), this time better prepared to checkmate the army of David. The latter attacked them from the rear and not only drove them away from Jerusalem but pursued them northwestward by the way of Gibeon, down the Valley of Aijalon as far as Gezer, *ca.* twenty miles W of his capital.

This defeat ended his major open conflict with the Philistines and turned the tables on them. David now changed positions with them, and they became his vassals, though there is no indication that he disrupted their internal organization. He did not even add their city-states to Judah or Israel; he simply permitted their tyrants to govern them as vassals so long as they did not attempt hostile acts outside their boundaries. The areas which originally belonged to Israel or Judah were doubtless taken over and incorporated in the respective territories. Thus the king bound the Philistine city-states to himself in a personal union, as he did those other small states in the coastal plain ruled over by them.

The next major diplomatic stroke was David's handling of the religious problem, which, so far as Israel was concerned, was a sore spot during most of the time Saul was king. Saul had paid no attention whatever to the old national-religious symbol of the ark, which after its return by the Philistines was housed at Kiriath-jearim (I Sam. 7:1-2). He had also laid violent hands on the priests at Nob after they had unwittingly offended him by assisting David in his escape (I Sam. 21:1-9; 22:9-19). David resolved to make amends by bringing the ark to Jerusalem, thereby strengthening his bonds with the priesthood and at the same time keeping them near enough to be under constant surveillance. He thus returned to the primitive religious tradition of the twelve tribes— the only move so far made by him toward unity of the two kingdoms. The first attempt to bring the ark into Jerusalem had been unsuccessful (II Sam. 6:3-11), and it was placed in the house of Obed-edom, where it remained for a time. But later it was successfully brought into the city and placed in a tent especially constructed for it. David's conduct (II Sam. 6:16) during the ceremony of transferring it to Jerusalem is characteristic of his enthusiasm for the Lord, and it reflects his charismatic qualities. Michal's attitude (6:20) indicates either lack of respect for the ark in the royal family of Saul, because of its neglect, or progression away from conservative tradition.

Not only did David thus bring to his capital the sacred symbol of Israel and combine the religious with the political elements there, but he went even further. He included the priests in his official family (II Sam. 8:17-18; 20:25-26). Henceforth Davidsburg became the holy city, the city of the Lord. So well was David's plan conceived and carried out that he

ever after retained the support of the religious authorities.

Many regard all of II Sam. 7 as a later midrash. But there is undoubtedly some early material in it. That David should have desired to build a house for the ark is what might be expected. Just why his plan was not carried through is unknown. It may have been because he was too busy with wars (I Kings 5:3; I Chr. 28:3), or because his plans were too elaborate for immediate execution, or because he felt the time was not ripe to break with the old tabernacle tradition which he had just employed with the Israelite priesthood to win the support of the religious elements of his kingdoms. The prayer of David (II Sam. 7:18-29) is also early, for the most part, and has to do with the perpetuation of his dynasty. The chapter combines two elements, the desire to build the house of the Lord and the promise of the continuity of the Davidic dynasty. But the chief significance of the chapter in connection with David is its emphasis on the traditional combination of the religion and politics in his kingdom.

*See* map "Palestine: I Chronicles, the Kingdom of David," under CHRONICLES, I AND II.

The main conquests of David fell in the early period of his reign. The chief sources are II Sam. 8:1-14; 10; 11:1; and the parallels in I Chr. 18–20. The order in which his wars took place is uncertain. The reference to the Philistines in I Chr. 18:1 must be to his two battles with them in the Valley of Rephaim (II Sam. 5:17-25; *see above*). Moab was the next to feel the thrust of his power. Nothing specific is known about this war, apart from the fact that David was probably more ruthless in his punishment of the Moabites than in punishing any other people (II Sam. 8:2). No reason is given for his cruelty, but it may be that the Moabites took advantage of some occasion when David was occupied elsewhere to further their interests. After punishing their army, he laid them under tribute and became their overlord. Otherwise their kingdom remained as it had been before.

The Aramean wars are associated, at least in part, with the campaign against Ammon. Saul's expedition succeeded for a time in holding the Ammonites in check. David now sent a delegation of his men to Hanun, son of Nahash, king of Ammon, to bear his condolence on the death of his father. The men were taken as spies and humiliated (II Sam. 10:3-5). This precipitated a crisis, and preparations were speedily made on both sides for a showdown. The Ammonites called in their Aramean allies to assist them. Four separate Aramean states are mentioned: Zobah, the largest of these, was located in the Antilibanus region N of Damascus; Rehob was somewhere near Dan; (Ish)tob near Lake Huleh; and Maacah to the NE of Lake Huleh.

The genius of Joab asserted itself, with the result that the Arameans fled and the Ammonites retired to their stronghold. Hadadezer, king of Zobah, however, summoned his allies in another challenge to David (10:15-19). The battle took place at Helam (vs. 16) N of Gilead. The Arameans were roundly defeated, their chariots captured, their horses hamstrung, and their commander, Shobach, mortally wounded. The result was a treaty of peace under which they became subjects of David, whose governing officials were domiciled at Damascus. It is likely that these Aramean states were drawn together into a kind of province whose administrative seat was Damascus. In addition to this more or less organized group of states, the kingdom of Hamath under King Toi (תֹעִי; I Chr. 18:9-10) concluded a treaty of friendship with David, whom he evidently regarded as his savior (II Sam. 8:10). In the defeat of Hadadezer and by the treaty with Toi, David derived much booty (II Sam. 8:7-8, 10), which he brought to Jerusalem.

David's rule now extended as far N as Hamath and in an eastwardly direction to the Euphrates, though the borders between Zobah and the great river were indefinite. The Aramean states were under David directly but were in charge of one of his officials.

The Ammonite campaign continued, perhaps on a lesser scale, for a time, with Joab engaged in marauding activity. Finally Joab laid the capital under siege. When it was about to capitulate, David himself was called to the scene (II Sam. 12:26-31), so that he might have the prestige of victory. Hence Ammon became Davidic territory with David ostensibly as king.

Edom was attacked after the Aramean campaign —for what reason, is not stated (II Sam. 8:13-14; I Kings 11:15-16), but possibly because the Edomites took advantage of David's engagements elsewhere to carry on razzias against Israelite towns in the border regions. The battle took place in the Valley of Salt and ended as all the other battles of David, in complete victory. Joab spent six months in further ravaging the country and visiting dreadful cruelty upon its male population. Edom then was taken over and garrisoned by David.

David was now the undisputed master from Egypt to the Euphrates. He was king of Judah, king of Israel, king of Jerusalem, king of Ammon, king of the Canaanite states incorporated into Judah and Israel, the ruler by governors over the Aramean states and Edom, and chief of Moab. He was bound by treaty with Tyre and Hamath. Thus he was the most powerful ruler in the world of his day. His success was due in large part to the fact that there was no formidable power elsewhere in the world in the early tenth century. The twenty-first Egyptian dynasty (1085-945) was ruled by priest kings; in Mesopotamia there was also no strong power (Tiglath-pileser II, 966-935, was a weakling), though the Assyrians were pushing the Arameans out of Aram Naharaim into the W desert of Syria, whence David came into collision with them. Nor was there a strong state in Asia Minor comparable to that of the Neo-Hittite Empire two centuries earlier.

David's affair with Bathsheba (II Sam. 11:1–12:25), one of the best known incidents in his life, occurred during the last phase of the Ammonite campaign. For some reason the king did not accompany the army to Rabbath Ammon but remained at Jerusalem. One evening while he was walking about on the roof of his palace, his passions were aroused when he saw Bathsheba bathing. He immediately sent for her. Presently she found herself with child. Her husband, Uriah the Hittite, one of David's mercenaries,

was with Joab at Rabbah. He was summoned home at once in the hope that scandal might be averted. But Uriah was too much a man of conscience to enjoy himself at home while his associates were in the field. When David saw that his plans were thus thwarted, he sent Uriah back to Joab with his own death warrant. Joab carried out the orders of the king, and so Uriah was slain and David was free to marry his widow. If David had hoped thereby to avoid censure, he was mistaken, for his court prophet Nathan (see NATHAN 2) was aware of the situation. He did not hesitate to bring the word of the Lord to the king, and it was not a pleasant one. According to the writer of II Sam. 12:7-10, David's sin did not consist of adultery but of appropriating the wife of another man after having had him murdered. David's reaction to the stern word of the prophet was one of repentance and submission to the judgment of the Lord. The child died, but sometime later another was born to Bathsheba. His name was Jedidiah, better known as Solomon (II Sam. 12:24-25). The affair with Bathsheba marked the beginning of the decline of David, the zenith of whose power and success was reached in the capture of Rabbath Ammon.

The conquests of David brought immense wealth and luxury to Jerusalem. Moreover, they kept David away from his family much of the time. It has been said that the man who knew all the arts of war and diplomacy could not control his own family. But this was, in all probability, due more to circumstances than to inability. The family feud between Amnon and Absalom over the latter's sister, Tamar, originated in uncontrolled passion and ended in tragedy (II Sam. 13:1-14, 29). David was deeply troubled, but it was too late (vss. 30-36). Absalom was exiled for three years to Geshur (vss. 37-38), W of the Sea of Galilee, to live with Talmai, his grandfather (I Chr. 3:2). Absalom was the beloved son (II Sam. 13:39; 18:33-19:4), perhaps because he was the crown prince, and his father longed for his return but could not see his way clear to recall him. Joab, sensing the desire of David, contrived a way to get him back (II Sam. 14:1-20). But for two years (14:28) Absalom lived apart and did not come into the presence of the king, until he himself took the initiative by inducing Joab to intercede for him. The result was a happy reunion (14:33).

This rather lengthy story of Absalom's return and reconciliation is used by the narrator as an introduction to Absalom's revolt (II Sam. 15:1–19:8). David was, no doubt, immersed in other affairs of state, and he was growing old, so that he could no longer attend to local matters. Absalom, being quite aggressive, gathered a group of sympathizers, provided for himself a bodyguard, and began to capitalize on the manifest discontent of dissident individuals. He may also have been aware of the promise of the kingdom to Solomon, and so he may have planned to usurp what was rightfully his as crown prince. He carried on in this way for some time (15:7). Finally, under the pretense of going to fulfil a vow made during his exile at Geshur, he obtained permission from David to proceed to Hebron (vss. 7-9), where he had himself proclaimed king (vss. 10 ff).

News of the revolt stunned the king, who gave orders to his officials to prepare posthaste for evacuation of the city. The fact that David saw the seriousness of the uprising so quickly may point to some knowledge of the strength of his opponents. Just how formidable it was may be judged from the fact that David could count only on his "servants"—i.e., his officials and his standing army (15:18). While many of the people were sympathetic to David, they were, for the most part, unable to do anything effective, perhaps because Absalom had lured their leaders to Hebron with him (15:11). The religious officials did remain loyal but were sent back, in all likelihood because they could aid him better there than in his immediate company. At the last moment, David had enough of his old sagacity left to plot subversion against Absalom from within the city. This is shown by his urging Hushai to remain to nullify the counsel of Ahithophel and by his suggestion that he had the support of the priests (15:34-36). Ziba's message about Mephibosheth (16:1-4) may have more in it than appears on the surface. It may indicate that Israel was backing Absalom and that in so doing Mephibosheth had hoped to gain something for himself. The Shimei incident (16:5-14) points up the fact that not all the people of Israel wholeheartedly supported David, even during the early portion of his reign.

Within the city Absalom seems to have been in undisputed control, and to attest it publicly, he openly entered the harem. Meanwhile, Hushai succeeded in defeating the counsel of Ahithophel with respect to the rapid pursuit of David, so that David was able to get across the Jordan before Absalom had time to collect his forces (17:1-23). But Absalom took up the pursuit, with Amasa as his commander (vs. 25).

David had taken up residence at Mahanaim, the old seat of Ish-bosheth, where he was supplied amply by his friends who remained loyal. When the forces of Absalom appeared, David took charge of the strategy to be employed by Joab, though he did not participate personally in the ensuing battle (18:3). His orders to the army were to spare Absalom; but this was not to be, for Joab saw to it, when the opportunity came, that the rebel was punished. The battle went against Absalom, and his army was cut to shreds. "All Israel fled every one to his own home" (18:17; 19:8). Tradition has perhaps inflated the king's grief over the death of his son, but it certainly rings true to his character as portrayed elsewhere. At the insistence of Joab, David was at last persuaded to accept the situation and show his gratitude to those who had so loyally supported him and saved his kingdom (19:5-8).

Here it is necessary to consider briefly the political implications of Absalom's uprising. Alt is of the opinion that only Israel was involved on the side of the rebel and that Judah remained neutral. The term "all Israel" (17:11; 18:17; 19:8; etc.) is taken as an exaggeration, as may be seen from 20:2, where a clear distinction is drawn between "all the men of Israel" and "the men of Judah." Furthermore, there are the summons sent by David to the "elders of Judah" to welcome him back to Jerusalem (19:11-16) and the loud protestations of support on the part of the "men of Israel" and the "men of Judah" (19:40-43). On the whole, these deductions appear to be correct. Israel was conscious of its identity; so was Judah. And, on a broad basis, they continued to maintain their independent loyalties. But several other factors are to be taken into account:

Absalom made Amasa, David's nephew (I Chr. 2:17), his commander, though in this act he may merely have imitated his father, who had made Joab, his nephew and Amasa's cousin, the commander-in-chief. The reticence of the people of Judah in welcoming David back to Jerusalem is susceptible of another interpretation. Then there is the statement in II Sam. 19:40 that "all the people of Judah, and also half the people of Israel, brought the king on his way," which would seem to indicate that not all Israel was in rebellion against David. Again, there is the welcome the king received from Barzillai in Transjordan in the most crucial stage of the rebellion. The whole episode clearly demonstrates one of the weaknesses of David's empire—i.e., the lack of effective organization (*see below*). It also illustrates the fact that local loyalties cannot usually be overcome by the kind of personal union exemplified in the Davidic pattern. Actually David divided the kingdom instead of uniting it firmly.

Among the first to beg forgiveness of David was Shimei (19:16-23), who had cursed him and his servants as they fled from Jerusalem before Absalom (16:5-14). David's characteristic magnanimity displayed itself in the pardon granted Shimei, though Abishai wanted to put the scoundrel to death. Next came Mephibosheth with the excuse that he had been deceived by his servant (19:24-30). The king was apparently not quite sure of Mephibosheth, since he commanded that Saul's patrimony be divided with Ziba. The attitude of Barzillai was a welcome contrast (17:27-29; 19:31-39); he was one of those who provided for David and his men at Mahanaim and who now came to bid him farewell as he was about to recross the Jordan on his way back to Jerusalem.

That the state of affairs did not return to "normalcy" after the Absalom fiasco is shown by the abortive move of Sheba the Benjamite, who tried to rally Israel against David (20:1-22). David really compromised with the followers of Absalom by appointing Amasa as commander of the army in place of Joab. So Amasa was delegated to put down the uprising of Sheba, but since his heart was not in the project—another instance of the growing disunity—Joab seized the initiative, treacherously stabbed Amasa, and with the assistance of the wise woman of Abel-beth-maacah, brought back victory.

David, who had learned something in the course of all the hard and bitter struggle to retain his kingdom, now took steps toward a better organization of the territories of Israel and Judah. The appendix of II Samuel (chs. 21-24) is devoted, for the most part, to this problem. Much of the early period of his reign was occupied with war and conquest, which sapped his vigor to such an extent that not much thought could be devoted to matters of building for the future. Discontent and rebellion and the complex question of succession accentuated the necessity for a more stable order. David probably came to realize that personal union was not enough to hold together his vast empire. It will be recalled that after he became king of Judah and king of Israel, he did not add subsequently conquered territory to either of these kingdoms, except such cities or areas as traditionally were included in their respective borders. Rather, he maintained each unit separately by binding it to himself as king or by ruling it through governors. The lists show beyond doubt that his officials were not bound to either kingdom but to him personally and that in the early period their duty was to assist him in war and in the maintenance of his military establishment.

Among his men of war were the four who slew giants (21:15-22); the famous three who also performed mighty deeds (23:8-17), especially slipping through the Philistine lines to bring water from the well at Bethlehem to David at Adullam; and the Thirty (23:18-39), who were modeled after Egyptian parallels. The age of the list of the Thirty is shown by the presence of the name of Asahel, brother of Joab, who was slain by Abner in the first collision between the armies of David and Ish-bosheth (2:23). Then there were the Cherethites and the Pelethites (II Sam. 8:18; 15:18; 20:7, 23; I Kings 1:38, 44), probably Cretans and Philistines, who formed the bodyguard of the king. Joab was the commander of the army, and Benaiah was in charge of the bodyguard (II Sam. 8:18; 20:23). Thus David had a well-organized fighting force developed over a long period of time, and its effectiveness may be judged by the results of his conquests.

But there were other officials (see lists in II Sam. 8:16-18; 20:23-25) in David's governing body. The *corvée*, or forced labor, was introduced again under David. II Samuel lists Adoram as the chief of the tribute bureau, which probably has nothing to do with forced labor (cf. LXX φόρος). But in II Sam. 12:31 =I Chr. 20:3, we read that David "brought forth the people who were in it [the Ammonites in Rabbah], and set them to labor with saws and iron picks and iron axes, and made them toil at the brick-kilns; and thus he did to all the cities of the Ammonites." The Edomites became David's slaves (II Sam. 8:14) and were doubtless included in the forced-labor battalions of the king and his officials. Glueck calls attention to the huge copper and iron smelting furnaces and refineries at Ezion-geber (present Elath at the head of the Gulf of Aqabah), which were manned by slaves. It is quite possible that Ezion-geber fell into the hands of David in the campaign against Edom and that it was merely transmitted to Solomon in the normal course of inheritance. There is thus ample evidence for some forced labor under David.

The fact that there was an official over the tribute points to some organization also along this line. Then there were the recorder or remembrancer (מזכיר) and the scribe (ספר), both of whom belonged to the most important segment of the officialdom of David. In addition to these civil officers were the priests, Zadok and Abiathar, who were over the state cult, while the king himself had a private confessor (II Sam. 20:25-26). There were also the prophets, Nathan and Gad, who were more or less attached to the court. All these officials and others with other functions show that there was a growing body of high-ranking officers which was necessitated by the expanding power and interests of the king. That it was more than haphazard is shown by the Egyptian pattern followed by David.

That the situation demanded still further consolidation is shown by the two rebellions with which he had to cope. It is possible that these uprisings were the result of an attempt to restrict tribal autonomy, since they were instigated solely by groups within the kingdoms of Judah and Israel. On the other hand, it may be that they compelled a rethinking of the relatively loose organization prevalent before it was impressed upon the king and his near associates that something more had to be done either to satisfy or to obviate the discontent, or to hold the dissidents in check.

However this may be, the beginnings of a tighter organization are evident in the decision to take a census (II Sam. 24; I Chr. 21). Joab was the chief of the census takers. The outline of territory covered (II Sam. 24:5-7) is significant. They began in Transjordan at Aroer on the Arnon River, then moved N to Jazer in the tribal territory of Gad and on into Gilead. From there they went N as far as Kadesh (on the Orontes), then S to Dan and across to Sidon and Tyre and the neighboring Canaanite and Hivvite (Hurrian) centers. To the S they went as far as Beer-sheba and its surroundings. Since Adoram was the chief of the tax bureau (II Sam. 20:24), it is likely that the census was undertaken for fiscal as well as for administrative purposes. The list of David's officials in II Sam. 8:15-18 does not include the officer in charge of the tribute.

Two misfortunes occurred at the time of the census. One has to do with famine (II Sam. 21:1-14) and the other with pestilence (24:15 ff). The former is connected with the complaint of the Gibeonites whom Saul had put to death and whose blood had not been avenged. For the purpose of vengeance David handed over to them two sons and five grandsons of Saul, thus sparing Mephibosheth, Jonathan's son. To atone in part for this act, he brought the remains of Saul and Jonathan from Jabesh in Gilead, reclaimed the bodies of those who had been hanged by the Gibeonites, and accorded all of them an honorable burial "in the tomb of Kish" (21:14). The second misfortune occurred in the wake of the census. It consisted of a devastating pestilence which was finally stayed at the threshing floor of Araunah. The conservatives attributed the plague to the "sin" of the census. Both stories are somehow related, but the details escape us at the present. In any event, here is a definite conflict between the older Yahwists and the innovation introduced by the king.

The last days of David were beset with further difficulties in relation to the succession. This time the trouble was caused by Adonijah (I Kings 1:5 ff), the next in line (II Sam. 3:4) for the throne after the death of Absalom. Aware of the promise made by David to Bathsheba that her son should be his successor, Adonijah thus took steps prematurely to secure his rights. He followed the pattern of Absalom by providing for himself the accouterments of a crown prince and then by entering into negotiations with Joab, David's commander, and Abiathar, one of the priests. But he had not reckoned with the most powerful forces behind the scenes at the time—with Zadok, Nathan, Benaiah, and David's mercenaries; and Joab had lost too much favor to make up for such a formidable opposition. Nevertheless, at the appointed time, probably a New Year's festival, Adonijah had himself proclaimed king at En-rogel. Only his partisans had been invited, which included "all his brothers, the king's sons, and all the royal officials of Judah" (I Kings 1:9). Absalom's followers were mostly Israelites; Adonijah, on the other hand, drew upon the people of Judah and upon those who were closest to his father (e.g., Joab).

The chief opponent of Adonijah's move was evidently the prophet Nathan, who, with the connivance of Bathsheba, set in motion the movement to have Solomon anointed (I Kings 1:11-40). He sent Bathsheba to the sickbed of the king to remind him of his promise (vs. 17) and plead her case for her son. When she left the presence of the king, Nathan, by previous arrangement, appeared to tell the king of the usurpation of Adonijah and to inquire whether this was really his will (vss. 24, 27). The fact that Nathan, Zadok, Benaiah, and Solomon had, for obvious reasons, not been invited, rightly seemed ominous in the sight of both Bathsheba and Nathan. The arguments of the prophet and of the favored wife won the day; for the king vowed that he would fulfil his promise with respect to Solomon that very day (vss. 29-30). Immediate arrangements were made for the ceremony of investiture, which David was too ill and feeble to witness. So Solomon was anointed officially by Zadok and Nathan and set on David's mule, the sign of royalty. The royal bodyguard was there to take over. When the trumpet sounded, the people acclaimed Solomon the new king. The word of David had thus settled the problem of succession at one stroke.

Adonijah saw at once that his cause was lost, for the word of the king was too strong for him to resist. He was granted his life by Solomon but kept under constant surveillance. Not until he asked for Abishag did he forfeit his life. With Adonijah went Joab and Abiathar. David's last will called for the avenging of Abner and Amasa (I Kings 2:5) by the death of Joab. Shimei, who had so violently cursed David in his flight from Absalom but was judiciously spared by the king at the time, also was marked for death. Hence there would be removed any possible revolt at the beginning of Solomon's reign. David's experience stood him in good stead, or perhaps it was the prudence of his advisers.

After a forty-year reign over Judah and a thirty-three-year reign over Israel, David died. The Chronicler says: "He died in a good old age, full of days, riches, and honor" (I Chr. 29:28), which is literally true, with the exception of honor.

**7. Estimate.** David's early life had certainly been filled with honor. His dignified demeanor at the court of Saul is beyond reproach. The way he handled himself when his life was in grave danger could win him nothing but praise, though there may be some editorial embellishment or idealization in some of the material. But there is enough truth elsewhere in the tradition to substantiate these claims. Not once did David attempt reprisal against Saul or indirectly against his house. He was consistently loyal to his king, even when he sought refuge with the Philistines, whom he endeavored to curb at every opportunity in favor of his own people. So long as he remained with Saul, he faithfully fulfilled his obligations, though fortune more than once smiled upon him. On at least one occasion, perhaps two, he could

have slain his master. The weight (honor) of his actions won him respect on all sides.

With this honor he combined a rare quality of diplomacy. His sojourn with the Philistines was directed in such a way as to aid himself and his people rather than the enemy. In so doing he reflected a keen perception of destiny for himself and Israel as a whole, and thereby he revealed a kind of charismatic quality, which tended to increase as time progressed. While the enemy was busy elsewhere, David gradually subdued the border areas of S Judah and attached to his little kingdom at Ziklag a growing array of subject cities and territories in the guise of putting down marauders and winning material support for himself and his followers. When the time came for him to proceed to Hebron, most of Judah was strongly united behind him.

Then there was the way in which he dealt with his brethren from the N. His lament over the death of Saul and Jonathan and his treatment of the messenger who brought him word of their death set the standard for his subsequent relations with Abner and Ish-bosheth, which cannot have been altogether deceptive. Again, there was his provision for Mephibosheth, Jonathan's son, which was not withdrawn after Absalom's rebellion, in which he participated, possibly unwittingly. The selection of Jerusalem, a Jebusite city, which belonged neither to Judah nor to Israel, as his capital and the way he administered it was another master stroke of diplomacy. Such acts show David's cleverness and astuteness in handling difficult situations.

That David was a great warrior is shown not only by his numerous conquests but also in the way he organized and deployed his forces. Some of his methods he undoubtedly learned from the Philistines; others he derived from his own ingenuity—e.g., the attack on the Philistines from the rear (II Sam. 5:23), the management of the campaign against Ammon, the defeat of the Arameans under Hadadezer and his allies, and the arrangement of his forces against the army of Absalom (18:2). These all portray the excellence of his generalship. The Chronicler rightly says: "The fame of David went out into all lands, and the LORD brought the fear of him upon all nations" (I Chr. 14:17).

David's shrewdness as a politician is demonstrated by the personal unions he formed with Judah, Israel, Jerusalem, and Ammon and by the personal allegiance he demanded of the other territories he conquered. In his own nations he maintained tribal autonomy throughout most of his reign; in the latter period he attempted to check tribal extravagances by planning a better organization, which was carried out under Solomon. In all his specifically political moves he did not neglect the religious authorities, as Saul had done. He restored the ancient symbol of the ark, the darling of the conservative groups, and brought into play once more the virtually abandoned Israelite priesthood. Henceforth religion played a vital role in every major move made by the king.

That David was a deeply religious man is confirmed by every stratum of the tradition of his kingdom. Nothing was undertaken without inquiring of the Lord, and the priests or prophets crop up everywhere. The external display of emotion on the removal of the ark to Jerusalem, which disgusted Michal, is indicative of his personal devotion and furnishes a fine insight into the psychological aspects of his personality. The story of his ready repentance when confronted by the prophet Nathan in connection with the Bathsheba affair fits in quite well with this incident, although it may have been somewhat expanded by the narrator. His reaction to the remonstrance of God concerning the sin of the census follows the same pattern.

Over and over again the stories of David tell us that he was a poet and musician of note. It is certain that he was the author of the lament over Saul and Jonathan (II Sam. 1:19-27) and a priori there is no reason why II Sam. 23:1-7 (his last words) should not be attributed to him. II Sam. 22 is more doubtful, but the arguments in favor of Davidic authorship outweigh those against it. And since there was no clear differentiation between poet and musician, there can be no valid objection to ascribing to David poetic pieces. That he was a musician is well established. He was brought to the court of Saul because he could play instruments (I Sam. 16:23), and when the ark was taken to Jerusalem, he was among those who were "making merry before the Lord with all their might, with songs and lyres and harps and tambourines and castanets and cymbals" (II Sam. 6:5). The text of Amos 6:5 is not beyond dispute, but the words "like David" do reflect the tradition current when Amos was edited. Then there is the tradition of the Chronicler that David not only planned and made preparations for the construction of the temple (I Chr. 22–23) but that he was responsible for the organization of the staff of temple personnel, including the musical guilds (I Chr. 24–26). This tradition no longer appears so impossible as it was once thought.

Finally, David was a great organizer. This is demonstrated in the development of his military machine and in his plan for the reorganization of his vast territories in line with needs revealed by the several rebellions toward the end of his reign. He was responsible for the allotment of the Levitical cities in Josh. 21 = I Chr. 6:54-81, and probably for the six cities of asylum included among them, which were intended to alleviate the problem of tribal feuds and make for a more orderly system of administration.

*Bibliography.* G. Beer, *Saul, David, Salomo* (1906). R. Kittel, *Geschichte des Volkes Israel* (7th ed., 1925), II, 102-41. L. Rost, *Die Überlieferung von der Thronnachfolge Davids* (1926). R. Kittel, *Great Men and Movements in Israel* (1929), ch. 6. A. Alt, *Die Staatenbildung der Israeliten in Palästina* (1930); "Das Königtum in Israel and Juda," *Vetus Testamentum*, I, 2-22. O. Eissfeldt, *Die Komposition der Samuelisbücher* (1931). A. T. Olmstead, *History of Palestine and Syria* (1931), ch. 21. T. H. Robinson, *A History of Israel* (1932), vol. I, ch. 10. J. M. P. Smith, "The Character of David," *JBL*, 52 (1933), pp. 1-11. K. Elliger, "Die dreissig Helden," *Palästinajahrbuch*, 31 (1935), pp. 29-75. F. James, *Personalities of the OT* (1939), ch. 7. R. de Vaux, "Titres et fonctionnaires égyptiens à la cour de David et Salomon," *RB*, 48 (1939), pp. 394-405. J. Begrich, "Sofer und Mazkir," *ZAW*, 58 (1940/41), pp. 1-29. J. Bright, "The Age of King David," *Union Seminary Review*, vol. 53, no. 2 (1942), pp. 87-109. W. F. Albright, *Archaeology and the Religion of Israel* (1942); *From the Stone Age to Christianity* (2nd ed., 1946); "The Biblical Period" (The Biblical Colloquium; 1950), reprint from L. Finkelstein, ed., *The Jews: Their History, Culture and Religion.* M. Noth, *Geschichte Israels* (1950), pp. 155-77. A. C. Welch, *Kings and Prophets of Israel* (1952). A. Alt, "Das Grossreich Davids," *Kleine Schriften zur Geschichte Israels,* II (1953), 66-75. E. Meyer, *Geschichte des Altertums* (3rd ed., 1953), vol. II, pt. 2, pp. 248-62. G. E. Wright, *Biblical Archaeology* (1957), ch. 8.

On the Mari Texts, see now: J. Kupper, *Les nomades en Mésopotamie au temps des rois de Mari* (1957), pp. 60-62. H. Tadmor, "Historical Implications of the Current Rendering of Akkadian *daku*," *JNES,* 17 (1958), 129 ff.

J. M. MYERS

*DAVID, CITY OF [עִיר דּוֹד]. The name given to the fortified city of the Jebusites (*see* JEBUS), after the capture by David. Hence "city of David" is used as a synonym for the stronghold of ZION (II Sam. 5:7, 9; I Chr. 11:5, 7; I Kings 8:1; II Chr. 5:2). There is no longer any doubt concerning the identification of the city of David with the triangular hill wedged between the valleys of the TYROPOEON and the KIDRON, and overlooking the gardens and pools of SILOAM (II Chr. 32:30). The narrative of the conquest suggests that David entered the town by surprise, presumably by climbing through the water shaft by means of which the inhabitants drew the water from the underground spring of GIHON (II Sam. 5:7-8; *cf.* WATERWORKS). David established his residence within the perimeter of the city. Some additional fortifications were built under his reign and the reign of his successors, particularly to the N. *See* MILLO § 1; OPHEL.

The city of David retained its distinct identity after Jerusalem had outgrown its original boundaries. Nehemiah's account of the postexilic restoration and dedication of the walls mentions a few well-known monuments or features of the city—e.g., the FOUNTAIN GATE (Neh. 2:14; 3:15; 12:37); the STAIRS OF THE CITY OF DAVID (Neh. 3:15; 12:37); the sepulchres of David (Neh. 3:16; *see* TOMBS OF THE KINGS); the house of David (Neh. 12:37); the house of the mighty men (Neh. 3:16); and eventually the WATER GATE (Neh. 3:26; 12:37). Several of these landmarks have been identified with various degrees of probability in the course of excavations conducted by R. Weill in 1913-14 and 1923-24. The excavations conducted by G. Duncan and S. Macalister in 1923-25 have failed to fix with certainty the N boundary of the city of David. The existence of a fortified gate opening to the W into the Tyropoeon has been ascertained by J. W. Crowfoot in 1927. *See* JERUSALEM.

Josephus, failing to visualize the growth of Jerusalem through the centuries of its history, generally identified the city of David with the whole of Jerusalem as he knew it, with the confusing result that he localized the "Castle" (φρούριον) of David (War V.iv.1), with the higher hill to the W of the Tyropoeon. This hill, partly for reasons of religious symbolism, has become the Christian Zion. *See* map under JERUSALEM.

*Bibliography.* G. A. Smith, *Jerusalem,* I (1907), 134-69. H. Vincent, *Jérusalem Antique* (1912), pp. 142-46. G. Dalman, *Jerusalem und sein Gelände* (1930), pp. 127-30. R. Weill, *La Cité de David,* vol. I (1920); vol. II (1947). J. Simons, *Jerusalem in the OT* (1952), pp. 60-64.                      G. A. BARROIS

**DAWN, THE** [שַׁחַר; ἀνατολή (Luke 1:78)]. A common noun usually rendered in the KJV as MORNING, and occasionally as DAYSPRING (e.g., Job 38:12; Luke 1:78). This is a secondary usage, as שׁחר is primarily the name of the Amorite god manifest in the Venus Star at dawn (*see* SHAHAR). The references to the "eyelids of the morning dawn" in Job 3:9; 41:18 reflect this primary sense of שחר.

For bibliography, *see* SHAHAR.                    J. GRAY

**DAY** [יום; ἡμέρα, *adverbially* σήμερον, this day; KJV *inexactly* אור (Judg. 16:2; Job 26:10), light; KJV *incorrectly* תמול (I Sam. 21:5)].

A division of time. There are three principal uses of the term:

*a*) The time of daylight, from sunrise to sunset, as contrasted to NIGHT (Gen. 1:5; 8:22; Acts 20:31; etc). The day in this sense was divided into morning, noon, and evening (cf. Ps. 55:17). Before the NT era there was no division of the day into hours, although Neh. 9:3 speaks of fourths of a day. Usual designations of periods in the day were sunrise, the heat of the day, the cool of the day, sunset, etc. In the NT the day as the period of light (*see* LIGHT AND DARKNESS) becomes symbolic of salvation and righteousness (John 11:9; Rom. 13:12-13). In I Thess. 5:5, 8, Christians are called sons of the day, and in II Pet. 1:19 faith is likened to the coming of the day. Apocalyptic writings such as Rev. 21:25 envisage perpetual day in the state of perfection (cf. I Enoch 58:6).

*b*) The civil day, a space of twenty-four hours, extending from sunrise to sunrise or from sunset to sunset (Gen. 7:24; Job 3:6; Luke 9:37; Acts 21:26; etc.; as opposed to an hour, Matt. 25:13; as opposed to hours, months, seasons, and years, Gal. 4:10; Rev. 9:15). It would appear that the early Hebrews reckoned the civil day from one dawn to the next, as would naturally follow from its simplest meaning (*see above;* cf. Num. 11:32; Judg. 19:5-9; also the common expression "day(s) and night(s)," in Exod. 24:18, etc.). Gradually, however, they began to count from sunset to sunset, in accordance with the rising importance of their lunar festivals (cf. Gen. 1:5 ff; Exod. 12:18; Lev. 23:32; Esth. 4:16; Isa. 27:3; Dan. 8:14; II Cor. 11:25; Jos. War IV.ix.12). Among the Hebrews none of the days of the week except the sabbath was named. In the NT the weekdays have numbers (cf. Luke 24:1). Because parts of days could be counted as wholes, "after three days" (Mark 8:31) refers to the entire period of Jesus' burial.

*c*) Loosely, the period of an action or state of being. Thus "in the day that" means "when" in Gen. 2:4; Lev. 14:2; etc. One's lifetime or reign is his "days" (Gen. 26:1; I Kings 10:21; cf. Heb. 5:7). There is a "day of trouble" (Ps. 20:1), a "day of God's wrath" (Job 20:28), the messianic day (John 8:56), a "day of salvation" (II Cor. 6:2), and an "evil day" (Eph. 6:13). A day in this sense can be the time of a notable battle, judgment, disaster, or deliverance (Deut. 16:3; Ps. 137:7; Isa. 9:4; Ezek. 30:9; etc.). Similar is the diverse terminology of eschatology, such as "in that day," "in the latter days," the "day of the Lord," etc. *See* DAY OF CHRIST; DAY OF JUDGMENT; DAY OF THE LORD.

In addition to these uses of "day," the term is employed inexactly in such expressions as "dawn of day," "break of day," "a great while before day" (Mark 1:35), "when the day was now far spent" (Mark 6:35 KJV), "the next day," "four days" (John 11:39), none of which involves יום or ἡμέρα.

S. J. DE VRIES

**DAY OF ATONEMENT.** *See* ATONEMENT, DAY OF.

**DAY OF CHRIST** [ἡμέρα Χριστοῦ]. In certain OT prophetic passages the "Day of Yahweh" is mentioned (e.g., Isa. 2:12; 13:6 ff; Joel 1:15; 2:31 [quoted in Acts 2:20]; Amos 5:18; Zeph. 1:7 ff; Zech. 14:1; Mal. 4:5). This will, as a rule, be an awful day of divine retribution, vengeance, destruction, and judgment. This prophetic concept was taken over into Jewish APOCALYPTICISM: God would bring this evil age to a catastrophic end involving a final divine judgment. In a few instances the Messiah, not God, would be the judge. *See* DAY OF JUDGMENT.

The phrase "Day of God" (ἡμέρα τοῦ Θεοῦ) appears but twice in the NT, each time in an apocalyptic framework. In II Pet. 3:12 the fiery destruction of heaven and earth at the end of this age is called the Day of God. In Rev. 16:14 the "great day of God the Almighty" is the time set for the Battle of Armageddon, shortly before the end of this present age.

When the SEPTUAGINT translation of the OT into Greek was made, the Hebrew word for "Yahweh" was not transliterated; instead, the Greek word for "Lord" (κύριος) was substituted. Hence, in the LXX the "Day of Yahweh" becomes the DAY OF THE LORD.

Since the early Christians called Jesus, as well as God, "Lord," it was but natural that the "Day of the Lord" (as they found the phrase in their Greek Scriptures) came to be understood as Christ's day. E.g., in I Cor. 5:5 Paul handed a sinful man over to Satan for the destruction of his flesh, that he might be saved on the Day of the Lord. For Paul the Day of the Lord is the second coming of Jesus Christ from heaven with destructive power, as is stated in I Thess. 5:2-3. Actually, this identification is specific in II Thess. 2:1-2, where the second advent of the Lord Jesus Christ is called the Day of the Lord, as is true of II Pet. 3:10 (cf. vs. 4).

In I Cor. 1:8 the coming of Jesus Christ, which was so ardently hoped for, is explicitly called the "day of our Lord Jesus Christ"; in II Cor. 1:14 it is the "day of the Lord Jesus," and in Phil. 1:6 it is termed the "day of Jesus Christ." In but two places (Phil. 1:10; 2:16) do we find the shorter term, the "day of Christ."

An analogous phrase is the day when the Son of man will be revealed and the wicked destroyed (Luke 17:30; cf. vs. 24)—i.e., the day when Jesus Christ will appear in his second advent as the heavenly Son of man. Elsewhere in the NT the Day of Christ is referred to as "the Day" (II Tim. 1:12, 18; 4:8; Heb. 10:25), as the "day of visitation" (I Pet. 2:12), and as the "day of judgment" (II Pet. 2:9; I John 4:17).

The Day of God and the Day of the Lord (i.e., of Jesus) were not always clearly differentiated; in II Pet. 3:10, 12, they are practically equated. Similarly, in Rom. 2:16 Paul refers to the day when God will judge the secrets of men through the agency of Jesus Christ.                    M. RIST

**DAY OF JUDGMENT.** In late Judaism and in the NT, the dividing act of the final drama between the old and the new aeon, bringing God's just judgment upon all men. As distinguished from the natural events or historical developments considered now and then in earthly life as divine punishment or deliverance which may be regarded as preliminary stages of the final judgment, the eschatological day of judgment denotes a universal forensic act of God or of a representative authorized by him for that purpose, which concerns both the living and the dead (who have been resurrected to be judged).

This highly developed apocalyptic expectation does not appear in the OT, or only in hints at the fringe. God's final intervention is, to be sure, often described here and there in forensic categories in order to explain the justice of his action. God has a legal contest with the nations or with Israel: he is accuser, witness, and judge in one person (Isa. 1:2, 18; 3:13 ff; 51:5; 66:15-16; Jer. 2; Hos. 4:1 ff; 5:1, 5, 9; 12:3; Mic. 1:2 ff; 6:1 ff; Zeph. 3:8; Mal. 3:5; cf. also Pss. 50; 76; 82; 96; 98). Nevertheless, in the descriptions of the impending decisive "day" (*see* DAY OF THE LORD) the natural catastrophes and the horrors of war, which Yahweh (for the deliverance of his own) brings upon his enemies, predominate throughout. Most heavily interspersed with forensic concepts is the description of the eschatological argument of Yahweh with the nations in Joel 3—H 4; cf. vs. 12:

> Let the nations bestir themselves,
> and come up to the valley of Jehoshaphat
> [i.e., "Yahweh judges"];
> for there I will sit to judge
> all the nations round about.

(*See* JEHOSHAPHAT, VALLEY OF.) Cf. also vs. 14:

> Multitudes, multitudes,
> in the valley of decision!
> For the day of the LORD is near
> in the valley of decision.

(*See* DECISION, VALLEY OF.) The idea of individual judgment of each single human being, which also presupposes the idea of resurrection of the dead, is still lacking. This concept appears for the first time in Dan. 12:1-3 (cf. also the court scene of Dan. 7:9 ff): "Many of those who sleep in the dust of the earth shall awake, some to everlasting life, and some to shame and everlasting contempt" (vs. 2).

*See also* DAY OF CHRIST; ESCHATOLOGY OF THE OT; ESCHATOLOGY OF THE APOC. AND PSEUDEP.; ESCHATOLOGY OF THE NT; WRATH OF GOD.

**Bibliography.** B. Gemser, "The Rîb- or controversy-pattern in Hebrew mentality," *Supplements to Vetus Testamentum*, III (1955), 120-37; S. Mowinckel, *He that cometh* (1956).

E. JENNI

*DAY OF THE LORD [יום יהוה; ἡμέρα κυρίου]; DAY OF GOD [ἡ τοῦ θεοῦ ἡμέρα] (II Pet. 3:10, 12). One of the designations of the impending decisive intervention of God in the prophetic anticipation of the future (*see* ESCHATOLOGY OF THE OT). The expression יום יהוה ("day of Yahweh," more frequently with a mark of characterization as to purport, such as "day of the wrath of Yahweh," sometimes also simply "that day") probably finds its explanation in the Hebrew practice of designating decisive events of history as "days" (e.g., Isa. 9:4—H 9:3: "day of Midian"; cf. Judg. 7:25). *See* TIME § A1a. For the early Christian way of understanding this OT expression, *see* DAY OF CHRIST.

The oldest passage in the OT in which the "day of the LORD" occurs is Amos 5:18-20:

> Woe to you who desire the day of the LORD!
> Why would you have the day of the LORD?
> It is darkness, and not light;
>
> . . . . . . . . . . . . . . . . . . .
>
> Is not the day of the LORD darkness, and not light,
> and gloom with no brightness in it?

It follows from this passage that Amos did not originate the concept of the Day of the Lord, but rather found it already in the popular belief. But he definitely opposes the idea that this day, for which they were longing as a day of light, would mean salvation for Israel. According to his prophecy, it will be a day of misfortune and darkness for Israel. This does not in itself constitute a decisive change in the concept of the Day of the Lord; for the coming of the Lord on his day includes both, from the start: disaster and judgment for the enemies of the Lord, but salvation and deliverance for the remnant faithful to the Lord (*see* REMNANT; ESCHATOLOGY OF THE OT § 1*b*). Amos opposes his contemporaries only with regard to the question as to which aspect of the Day of the Lord would really come to pass for them. Because of their apostasy they have become enemies of the Lord and therefore are now in the same rank with the other enemies of the Lord (Amos 1–2), whereas at other times they expected the judgment of the Lord to fall only upon the foreign nations. Thus the prophecy of Amos (cf. also 6:3; 8:9) makes a break with the average piety in Israel, which in its self-assurance imagined it had the Lord on its side. That he too knew, in addition, a meaning of salvation in "that day" is probably indicated by Amos 9:11.

In the pre-exilic prophecy the proclamation of the Day of the Lord occurs, furthermore, in the prophecy of disaster. Isa. 2:9 ff reveals the universal character of the terrible Day of the Lord:

> The LORD of hosts has a day
> against all that is proud and lofty.
>
> . . . . . . . . . . . . . . . . . . .
>
> And the haughtiness of man shall be humbled.
>
> . . . . . . . . . . . . . . . . . . .
>
> And men shall enter the caves of the rocks
> and the holes of the ground,
> from before the terror of the LORD,
> and from the glory of his majesty,
> when he rises to terrify the earth (vss. 12, 17, 19; cf. 22:5).

The description of the universal and oppressively near Day of the Lord is most detailed with Zephaniah, who for this very reason has been called the prophet of the Day of the Lord (1:7 ff, 14 ff; 2:2-3; 3:8). Cosmic and political terrors, natural catastrophes, and events of war are here united into the impressive picture which has furnished the model for the medieval sentence: *Dies irae dies illa:*

> The great day of the LORD is near,
> near and hastening fast;
> the sound of the day of the LORD is bitter,
> the mighty man cries aloud there.
> A day of wrath is that day,
> a day of distress and anguish,
> a day of ruin and devastation,
> a day of darkness and gloom,
> a day of clouds and thick darkness,
> a day of trumpet blast and battle cry

against the fortified cities
and against the lofty battlements (1:14-16).

The dull monotony of these sentences, with their uncanny repetition, has an even more immediate effect in the original text.

In the prophecy of doom directed against Israel before the catastrophe of 587 the conceptual complex of the Day of the Lord—disregarding less clear allusions—occurs once more in Ezek. 7:7, 10, 12. Here it is combined with the proclamation of the "end."

Looking back upon the catastrophe of 587, one can speak of the Day of the Lord as having arrived (Lam. 1:21; Ezek. 34:12). But soon "Day of the Lord" is again used in the eschatological sense; though now, in harmony with the general trend of prophecy, it turns again from the prophecy of doom to the prophecy of salvation. The transition is brought about with regard to both matter and time in the passages in which the universal threats of the Day of the Lord are directed specifically against individual hostile nations—e.g., Isa. 13:6, 9, 13 (Babylon); 34:8; 63:4 (Edom); Jer. 46:10 (Egypt); 47:4 (the Philistines); Ezek. 30:3 (Egypt and its allies); Obad. 15 (Edom). The "day of vengeance of our God" will "comfort all who mourn" (Isa. 61:2). It brings the destruction of the Godless, but purification and salvation for those who fear God, who are prepared for the "great and terrible day of the LORD" by the sending of the prophet Elijah (Mal. 3:2; 4:1, 5—H 3:19, 23). In Joel 1-2 a plague of grasshoppers is considered as a sign of the nearness of the Day of the Lord, which calls for repentance (1:15; 2:1-2, 11). The eschatological descriptions become more and more detailed. The heavenly bodies are darkened when the time for final judgment comes upon the nations (3:14-15—H 4:14-15); but in Jerusalem there is salvation for those who call upon the name of the Lord (2:32—H 3:4; 3:18—H 4:18). Similar, but even more comprehensive, is the picture painted in Zech. 12-14. More than a dozen times we find the stereotyped phrase "on that day"; once, "a day of the LORD" (14:1).

In the late Jewish literature, which no longer uses the name Yahweh, the expression "day of the LORD" disappears, but not the idea it expresses—the day of the great last judgment at the end of this aeon. Only rarely is there any mention of the Day of God in continuation of the old terminology (II Bar. 48:47; 49:2: "Thy day"; 55:6: "day of the Mighty One"); also, expressions such as "day of the Messiah" and the like have scarcely come into use.

In the NT, on the other hand, the linguistic usage of the OT has a more pronounced aftereffect. The end of the world is called "day of the Lord" and "day of God"; and the final battle in Rev. 16:14 is called the "great day of God the Almighty." The day is carried over to the parousia of the Messiah in Luke 17:24: "For as the lightning flashes and lights up the sky from one side to the other, so will the Son of man be in his day" (cf. also John 8:56: "my day"). In the case of Paul the day of the last judgment is, in harmony with the eschatology of the NT (see ESCHATOLOGY OF THE NT), in closest association with the parousia of Christ. He speaks of the "day of the Lord" (I Thess. 5:2; II Thess. 2:2), of the "day of our Lord Jesus Christ" (I Cor. 1:8; 5:5; II Cor. 1:14),

or simply of the "day of Jesus Christ" (Phil. 1:6, 10; 2:16).

*Bibliography.* H. Gressmann, "Der Messias," *Forschungen zur Religion und Literatur des Alten und Neuen Testaments,* XLIII (1929); R. Volz, *Die Eschatologie der jüdischen Gemeinde im neutestamentlichen Zeitalter* (1934), pp. 163-65; P. A. Munch, "The Expression *bajjôm hahu'*, Is It an Eschatological Terminus Technicus?" *Avhandlinger utgitt av Det Norske Videnskaps-Akademi i Oslo* (1936); L. Černý, *The Day of Yahweh and Some Relevant Problems* (1948); V. Maag, *Text, Wortschatz und Begriffswelt des Buches Amos* (1951), pp. 246-52; S. Mowinckel, *He That Cometh* (1956; see Index); G. von Rad, "The Origin of the Concept of the Day of Yahweh," *Journal of Semitic Studies,* IV (1959), 97-108.    E. JENNI

**DAY'S JOURNEY** [מהלך יום, דרך יום; ἡμέρας ὁδός]. The Bible mentions a day's journey (Num. 11:31; I Kings 19:4; Jonah 3:4; Luke 2:44), three days' journey (Gen. 30:36; Exod. 3:18; 5:3; 8:27; Num. 10:33; Jonah 3:3), and seven days' journey (Gen. 31:23; II Kings 3:9). Evidently the distance was not exact; it would depend on the nature of the ground traversed and the kind of person making the journey. Presumably a day's journey was between eighteen and twenty-five miles. *See* WEIGHTS AND MEASURES § 4d.
    O. R. SELLERS

**DAYSMAN** dāz'mən. KJV translation of מוכיח (RSV UMPIRE).

**DAY STAR** [הילל, bright one]; KJV LUCIFER loo'sə fər. A designation of the king of Babylon in the taunt song in Isa. 14:12, where the pretensions of the bright Day Star to rise higher than all the stars, "to sit on the mount of assembly," to "ascend above the heights of the clouds," are disappointed, and the "bright one," who is obviously a deity, is obliged to come down to earth. This passage seems to reflect an episode in the Baal myth known from the Ras Shamra Texts. There, when Baal, whose seat is Mount Sapon, is in eclipse in the dry summer season, the question of a substitute on his vacant throne is raised, and Athtar, the Venus-star, is proposed. He is, however, too small to fill the throne and must come down to the earth and reign "god of it all."

*Bibliography.* G. B. Gray, *Commentary on Isaiah I-XXVII,* ICC (1912), pp. 255-56; C. H. Gordon, *Ugaritic Literature* (1949), p. 44 (translation of the Ras Shamra text). *See also* the bibliography under SHAHAR.    J. GRAY

**DAY-STAR.** KJV translation of φωσφόρος (RSV MORNING STAR) in II Pet. 1:19.

**DEACON** [διάκονος, servant, attendant, minister]. A title, since apostolic times, of one of the major orders of ministers in the church (*see* MINISTRY, CHRISTIAN). Its institution is commonly related to the account in Acts 6:1-6 of the selection and ordination of the SEVEN, to assist the Twelve in the distribution of charitable provisions to the Hellenist widows. But the author of Acts does not use the noun "deacon" of these men, but rather the verb διακονεῖν to describe their function of "serving tables." The word "deacon" does not occur in Acts; but one of the Seven, Philip, is called an EVANGELIST in Acts 21:8.

A more likely indication of the office is in Phil. 1:1, where Paul addresses the "bishops and deacons" with the whole church in Philippi. Since this letter was a note of thanks for material assistance sent to Paul by the Philippians, it is reasonable to suppose that he mentions in the address those ministers who were particularly responsible for collecting and sending the offering for his needs. Otherwise, the word διάκονος is used by Paul to describe his fellow workers and assistants in evangelizing—of Timothy (I Thess. 3:2; cf. I Tim. 4:6), Tychicus (Col. 4:7; cf. Eph. 6:21), and Epaphras (Col. 1:7). Paul also uses the term in describing his own ministry (I Cor. 3:5; II Cor. 3:6; 6:4; 11:15, 23; Col. 1:23, 25; cf. Eph. 3: 7), or the ministry of Christ (Rom. 15:8; Gal. 2:17), or even that of civil magistrates (Rom. 13:4). For the meaning of the feminine use of the word (Rom. 16: 1), *see* DEACONESS.

References to deacons in the literature of the post-apostolic age are abundant, and afford clear and precise indications of their rank and duties within the hierarchy of the church's ministry: I Tim. 3:8-13; I Clem. 42; Did. 15.1; Ign. Eph. 2.1; Ign. Magn. 2.1; 6.1; 13.1; Ign. Trall. 2.3; 3.1; 7.2; Ign. Phila. pref.; 4.1; 7.1; 10.1-2; 11.1; Ign. Smyr. 8.1; 10.1; 12.2; Ign. Polyc. 6.1; Polyc. Phil. 5.2-3; Herm. Vis. III.5.1; Herm. Sim. XXVI.2. In addition to these notices, one should consult the directions for the ordination of deacons in Hippolytus' *Apostolic Tradition* 9, and other regulations concerning their duties (21, 23-25, 30), for these also represent ancient custom. The deacon ranked third, after bishops and elders, in the ordained ministry. He was distinctly the bishop's assistant, being ordained by the bishop alone and serving him in his liturgical and pastoral duties.

At the Eucharist, the deacons received the offerings of the people and assisted in the administration of the elements of communion. At a later time the deacons had the exclusive right of reading the gospel lection at the Eucharistic assembly. They sought out and visited the sick, the poor and indigent—especially widows and orphans and prisoners, informed the bishop of their needs, and carried to them the alms of the church. According to Justin Martyr (Apol. I.67) they took the consecrated sacrament to those who were unavoidably absent from the Eucharistic celebration. In the light of these duties, the qualifications of character for the deacon's office, outlined in I Tim. 3:8-13, are pertinent, since his constant visitations among the people and his responsibilities with the church's material offerings provided many temptations to himself and his family for gossip, greed, slander, and intemperance.

Attempts to find prototypes of the diaconate in Jewish or pagan sources are but partially successful. There is some analogy in liturgical, though not in pastoral, functions, between the Christian deacon and the *ḥazzan* (ὑπερέτης) who assisted the ruler of a Jewish synagogue. Both in the LXX and in classical Greek writers, the word "deacon" has a secular sense —of servants, messengers, and civil officials. Josephus and Epictetus, however, sometimes employ the word in reference to a "servant" of God. Numerous pagan cult inscriptions list "deacons" among their officers, but without a fixed technical meaning. In most cases the close association of the term with "boys" and "cooks" suggests the functions of waiters or menial servants.

Without doubt, the church's diaconate was developed in response to specific needs within the corporate life of the church itself. But its inspiration was no less the example of Christ himself, who "came not to be served but to serve" (Mark 10:45 and parallels). The idea of service (διακονία) and serving (διακονεῖν), with particular illustration from service at table, underlies all of Jesus' teaching about his own ministry and that of his disciples after him (cf. Matt. 25:44; Luke 12:37; John 12:26; and esp. Matt. 20:26-28; 23:11; Mark 9:35; 10:43; Luke 22:26-27). In this sense, the diaconate is the foundation of all ministry in the church.

*Bibliography.* W. Lowrie, *The Church and Its Organization in Primitive and Catholic Times* (1904), especially pp. 371-83; H. Lietzmann, "Zur altchristlichen Verfassungsgeschichte," *Zeitschrift für wissenschaftliche Theologie*, LV (1914), 97-153; H. B. Swete, ed., *Essays on the Early History of the Church and the Ministry* (2nd ed., 1921), pp. 57-92; K. E. Kirk, ed., *The Apostolic Ministry* (1946), pp. 142-50, 216-27, 243-53; H. W. Beyer in *TWNT*, II, 88-93. *See also bibliographies* under BISHOP; MINISTRY, CHRISTIAN.      M. H. SHEPHERD, JR.

**DEACONESS; KJV SERVANT.** The word used to translate διάκονος in Rom. 16:1, where Paul mentions Phoebe as a διάκονος of the church at Cenchreae. In no place does the NT describe a ministerial order of deaconesses, but because of this reference it is commonly assumed that such an order existed from apostolic times. Whether the term bears in this instance a technical sense, or only a more general meaning of service, cannot be certainly determined. The problem is similar to Paul's mention of "deacons" in Phil. 1:1 (*see* DEACON). Greater ambiguity surrounds the mention of women in I Tim. 3:11 within a context describing a deacon's qualifications. The passage may refer merely to the wives of deacons (so KJV); but some interpreters take it as a reference to deaconesses. Also obscure is the relation of deaconesses to the order of widows (*see* WIDOW), as denoted in I Tim. 5:9-10.

A clearer indication of the existence of the office in the early years of the second century is provided by the report of Pliny the Younger, governor of Bithynia in 112, to the Emperor Trajan with respect to his investigation of the Christians. Pliny says that he had put to torture two Christian handmaidens who are called deaconesses (*ancillis quae ministrae dicebantur;* Epistle X.97). References to deaconesses in Christian literature of the second and third centuries are remarkably rare. The Syrian *Didascalia* (ch. 16, ed. Connolly, pp. 146-48) of the late third century gives an excellent summary of their functions: (*a*) to assist at the baptism of women, especially in the act of anointing, and (*b*) "to go into the houses of the heathen where there are believing women, and to visit those who are sick, and to minister to them in that of which they have need, and to bathe those who have begun to recover from sickness."

Our chief sources about the order of deaconesses derive from the Church Orders and conciliar decrees of the fourth-fifth centuries. The order does not appear to have been in existence in the church at Rome.

*Bibliography.* C. Robinson, *The Ministry of Deaconesses* (1898); H. Leclercq, "Diaconesse," *Dictionnaire d'archéologie chrétienne et de liturgie*, IV, 725-33; A. Kalsbach, "Die altkirchliche Einrichtung der Diakonissen bis zu ihrem Erlöschen," *Römische Quartalschrift*, Supplement 22 (1926); J. Knox on Rom. 16:1 in *IB*, IX (1954), 654-55; and F. D. Gealy on I Tim. 3:11 in *IB*, XI (1955), 417-18.      M. H. SHEPHERD, JR.

# DEAD, ABODE OF THE.

The teachers and prophets of Israel discountenanced necromancy and occult speculation (Deut. 18:11; Ps. 106:28; Isa. 8:19). "The secret things," says the Law, "belong to the LORD our God; [only] the things that are revealed belong to us" (Deut. 29:29). Consequently the OT offers no formal doctrine concerning the destination and fate of the dead; all that it says on the subject belongs to the domain of popular lore. The NT, though more specific about rewards and punishments in the ultimate Day of Judgment, is likewise vague and undogmatic about the preliminary abode of the dead in general.

1. The Hebrew concept
2. Parallels in ancient Near Eastern cultures
3. OT terminology
4. In the NT
5. Personification
6. The abode of the dead and hell
Bibliography

**1. The Hebrew concept.** Like all other ancient peoples, the Hebrews believed that the dead, though ending earthly life, did not relinquish existence per se. Somewhere, in a region outside the earth but accessible to God (Job 26:6; Ps. 139:8; Amos 9:2), they lingered on, oblivious of their former lives (Ps. 88:12—H 88:13), bereft of all mundane pleasures (Ecclus. 14:16), freed at last from the "sick fatigue" of the flesh (Job 3:17), yet at the same time divorced from empirical experience of God's presence (Ps. 88:6), and hence with nothing for which to thank or praise him (Pss. 6:5; 30:9; 88:12-13; 115:17; Isa. 38:18; Ecclus. 17:27-28). This region was usually located under the earth (Num. 16:30), in the lower part of the cosmic ocean (Job 26:7), beneath the roots of the mountains (Jonah 2:6); but there was also an alternative view (Enoch 22:1-5) which placed it in the W, where the sun goes down. Described as the final "synagogue of all living" (Job 30:23; cf. Enoch 22:3), it is variously depicted as a dark, chaotic realm (Job 10:20-21), characterized by a grim silence (Pss. 94:17; 115:17), or as a city with gates (Job 38:17; Isa. 38:10; cf. Wisd. Sol. 16:13; Ecclus. 51:9; Matt. 16:18).

The denizens of this realm are usually styled REPHAIM, a term which recurs in Ugaritic and Phoenician texts, but which is of quite uncertain etymology and meaning. They apparently retain their earthly ranks (Isa. 14:9-10; Ezek. 32:21, 24), but are described as "weary" (Job 3:17) and "without strength" (Ps. 88:4—H 88:5)—expressions comparable with the Egyptian "weary of heart" (*wrd 'ib*) as a euphemism for "the dead" and with Homer's description of the infernal phantoms in *Odyssey* XI. 474-75. A particular feature of their plight is that they suffer constant thirst (Isa. 5:13).

Although the way to the abode of the dead was a one-way street (Job 16:22), individual spirits could be evoked for consultation (I Sam. 28:13). In this aspect, they were termed *'elōhîm*, "numina," an infernal visitor to the earth being known as *'ôbh*, "revenant" (cf. Arabic *āba*, "return").

**2. Parallels in ancient Near Eastern cultures.** Almost every detail of the foregoing picture can be paralleled from Mesopotamian and Canaanite literature, showing that the biblical writers were simply drawing on traditional Semitic folklore and not inventing any new and original conceptions. *See bibliography* § 2.

Likewise in Akkadian texts, the abode of the dead is portrayed as a subterranean realm (*erṣitu*, "earth"), sometimes also located under the waters or in the W, and regarded as a city with gates. There too it is represented as a region of darkness (*bît ikliti*, "house of darkness"), and the way thither admits of no return. And there too, as in many ancient and primitive cultures, its inhabitants are characterized as suffering constant thirst—dwelling, as the expression goes, in a "field of thirst." *See bibliography* § 3.

Similarly, in the mythological poems from Ras Shamra Ugarit, the domain of death (*Môt*) lies under the earth, beneath the mountains (II AB, viii, 1-7), and it is described as a city (*qrt;* ib., 11; I\* AB, ii, 15), whose lord is obliged to feed on mud and to drink it "by cupful and barrel-full" (I\* AB, i, 19-22).

**3. OT terminology.** The realm of the dead is designated in the OT by several names. Most of them, however, are simply special applications of common nouns, and these too can be exactly paralleled in Mesopotamian texts:

*a)* שחת, "the Ditch" (RSV "the Pit"; Job 33:18; Pss. 16:10; 30:9—H 30:10; Isa. 38:17; 51:14; Jonah 2:6—H 2:7; cf. Akkadian *šuttu*). The ancient versions, however, prefer to derive this name from שחת, "corrupt" (cf. LXX διαφθορά, φθορά; Vulg. *corruptio, interitus;* Syr. חבלא).

*b)* בור, "the Pit" (Pss. 28:1; 88:4, 6—H 88:5, 7; Isa. 14:15; 38:18; Ezek. 32:18; etc.; cf. Akkadian *būru*).

*c)* מות, "(realm of) Death" (Job 28:22; 30:23; 38:17; Pss. 6:5—H 6:6; 9:13—H 9:14; Prov. 7:27; cf. Akkadian *bît mûti*, "house of death"; CT XVIII, 30, rev. 28-30). In Ps. 22:15—H 22:16 this is styled more precisely עפר מות, "the dust of death," and this expression too finds an exact parallel in Akkadian (*eprat mûti*).

*d)* ארץ, "the earth" (Exod. 15:12; Ps. 71:20; Jonah 2:6—H 2:7; etc.; cf. Akkadian *erṣitu* in this sense and Ugaritic *'rṣ* [e.g., II AB, viii, 9]). Sometimes the more precise expression ארץ תחתית, "the nethermost earth" (RSV "the nether world") is employed (e.g., Ezek. 31:14), and to this corresponds the Akkadian *erṣitu šaplitu*, the lowest of the three layers of the EARTH, regarded as that in which the dead dwelt.

*e)* אבדון, "Perdition" (RSV "Abaddon"; Job 26:6; 28:22; Ps. 88:11—H 88:12; Prov. 15:11; 27:20; cf. Rev. 9:1).

There is, however, one special term which has the full force of a proper name—viz., "Sheol" (שאול). It is used sixty-six times, but it does not occur (except as a loan word from Hebrew) in any other Semitic language. Its etymology, and hence its precise meaning, is disputed. The most plausible view is that it derives from the root שאל, "ask, inquire," and was originally applied to the realm of the dead as the place whence oracles were sought from them. In support of this is the fact that the verb in question is, indeed, used in the OT in connection with (forbidden) necromantic practices (Deut. 18:11; I Chr. 10:13), while the cognate Akkadian *ša'ilu* denotes "one who consults spirits," and South Arabic *m-s-'-l* sometimes means "oracle." The term would, of course, have been a survival from pagan antiquity. (Older attempts to connect "Sheol" with שעל, "be concave"— i.e., the Hollow—or with Arabic *sahal,* "soft ground," are philologically precarious.) The LXX usually renders ᾅδης, "Hades." *See bibliography* § 4.

**4. In the NT.** In the NT the abode of the dead is invariably called "Hades" (ᾅδης; Matt. 11:23; 16: 18; Luke 10:15; 16:23; Acts 2:27, 31; Rev. 1:18; 20: 13-14), and nothing is added to the OT descriptions of it.

**5. Personification.** The abode of the dead (Sheol) is sometimes personified as an insatiable demon with wide-open throat or gaping jaws (Prov. 1:12; Isa. 5: 14; Hab. 2:5). This picture recurs in the mythological texts from Ras Shamra–Ugarit (I* AB, i, 1-3), and is common also to many other cultures. It survives also in medieval pictures of hell. *See bibliography* § 5.

In Canaanite mythology, the nether pit (*ḥ-r;* cf. חור, Arabic *ḥaur,* and Akkadian *ḥurru* as a name of the nether world) was personified as the god Ḥaurân, who is known to us from the Ugaritic texts, from several references in Egyptian literature, and from a Canaanite incantation of the eighth century B.C. from Arslan Tash. This name survives in the OT in Beth-horon (Josh. 16:5). *See bibliography* § 6.

**6. The abode of the dead and hell.** Nowhere in the OT is the abode of the dead regarded as a place of punishment or torment. The concept of an infernal "hell" developed in Israel only during the Hellenistic period, probably under the influence of Iranian ideas (*see* ABYSS; GEHENNA). It first appears in Enoch, but even in this compilation there are several passages (e.g., 10:2; 22; 102:5) in which a clear distinction is drawn between the abode of the dead in general and the place of damnation, to which the wicked among them will be eventually consigned; while Jesus ben Sirach finds it necessary to protest explicitly that "there is no [correction of life] in Hades" (Ecclus. 41:4). The same distinction is preserved in the NT (cf. especially Rev. 20:13-14), except only in Luke 16:23, where the rich man of the parable is depicted as being in torment "in Hades." Here, however, the use of the word "Hades" may reflect contemporary Greek idiom, rather than be a rendering of "Sheol" or represent an evolution of Semitic ideas. Indeed, it is to be observed that in II Pet. 2:4 the verb ταρταρόω, "send to Tartarus," is deliberately coined to denote the dispatch of the rebel angels to the infernal realm of punishment. At the same time, it cannot be denied that this differentiation did, indeed, tend to become blurred (cf. Wisd. Sol. 3:10-14; 4:10-19; 5:1; Jos. War II.viii.11, 14), in much the same way that the Greek "Hades" ended up as a virtual synonym of the originally distinct "Tartarus." This, however, should be regarded as a confusion, rather than an evolutionary coalescence, of two distinct concepts, for even in later Jewish thought the abode of the dead and the place of torment are clearly differentiated.

*Bibliography.* 1. General studies: F. Schwally, *Das Leben nach dem Tode* (1892); G. Beer, "Der biblische Hades," *Holtzmann Festschrift* (1902), pp. 3-29; A. Lods, *La croyance à la vie future et le culte des morts dans l'antiquité israélite* (1906); P. Dhorme, "La séjour des morts chez les Babyloniens et les Hébreux," *RB,* IV (1908), 59-78; A. Bertholet, "Zu den babylonischen und israelitischen Unterweltsvorstellungen," *Paul Haupt Volume* (1926), pp. 8-18.

2. For Mesopotamian parallels to OT descriptions and names of the nether world, see: E. Ebeling, *Tod und Leben nach den Vorstellungen der Babylonier* (1931); K. Tallquist, *Sumerisch-akkadische Namen der Totenwelt* (1934).

3. On the thirst of the dead, see: T. H. Gaster, *Thespis* (1950), p. 188.

4. On Sheol as "the place of inquiry," see: M. Jastrow, *AJSL,* XIV (1897), 165-70.

5. On Ḥorôn, see: W. F. Albright, *BASOR,* no. 84 (1941), pp. 7-12.

6. On the jaws of the nether world, see: T. H. Gaster, *Thespis* (1950), p. 189. T. H. GASTER

**DEAD SEA.** The name by which the Western world commonly designates the remarkable salt lake situated at the mouth of the Jordan River.

1. Name
2. Physical features
   *a.* Nature of the water
   *b.* E and W shores
   *c.* Lisan
   *d.* S embayment
   *e.* Jebel Usdum
   *f.* Es-Sebkha
   *g.* General effect
Bibliography

**1. Name.** The most frequent and probably the most ancient biblical term for the lake is "Salt Sea" (Gen. 14:3; Num. 34:3, 12; Deut. 3:17; Josh. 3:16; 12:3; 15:2, 5; 18:19). This name appears only in the Hexateuch; and, although the additional designation "Sea of the Arabah" (KJV "Plain") appears several times in this section of biblical literature (Deut. 3:17; 4:49; Josh. 3:16; 12:3), in all but one such passage (Deut. 4:49) the previous name accompanies it in an explanatory equation. In II Kings 14:25, also, the latter name appears independently and without such an explanation. The "Eastern Sea" is a third biblical designation which appears in certain rather late prophetic passages (Ezek. 47:18; Joel 2:20; Zech. 14: 8) by way of indicating the lake's position on the E boundary of the territory of ancient Israel.

The NT makes no reference to the Dead Sea under any of its various designations. Extrabiblical literature of approximately the same period, however, supplements the multiplicity of the lake's various names. II Esd. 5:7 and Jos. Antiq. V.i.22 refer to it as the "Sea (or Lake) of Sodom"; Pliny (Nat. Hist. V.15.15), Diodorus Siculus (*Bibliotheke* II.48; XIX.98) and Josephus (War IV.vii.2) employ the term "Sea of Asphalt" or "Asphaltitis." The name "Dead Sea" seems to have been introduced into Greek and Latin usage in the second century A.D. by Pausanias and Justin. Modern Arabic ascribes to the lake the name *Bahr Lut,* "Sea of Lot."

**2. Physical features.** The Dead Sea begins at the mouth of the Jordan River and extends southward— occupying fifty-three miles of the deepest part of a great rift-valley and constituting a natural reservoir

6. Ghor 'Asal, the narrow plain at the foot of the Moabite mountains on the E side of the Dead Sea

7. The Dead Sea, with the Negeb mountains in the foreground

for the reception of the Jordan's waters. It is oblong in general outline, the regularity of its contour being interrupted only by a large peninsula two thirds of the way down the E shore. At its widest point it reaches approximately ten miles and is enclosed on both E and W by steep, rocky cliffs. Occasional terraces of marl and ancient, eroded beaches serve as reminders of the sea's Pleistocene precursor. This great reservoir is open at the ends—the rift-valley of which it is a part ascending gradually both N and S from the level of the lake in its depths. The surface of the sea is 1,292 feet below the level of the Mediterranean, making it the lowest region of the earth's surface, and soundings of the water's depth indicate that in its NE section the lake floor plunges yet another 1,300 feet and more into the bosom of the earth. Figs. DEA 6-7.

*a. Nature of the water.* Though the Dead Sea receives the waters of the Jordan, and of several small streams entering along its E shore, it has no outlet. Such is the heat and aridity of its sub-sea-level situation, however, that evaporation of the captive waters keeps pace with its intake—resulting in an ever-increasing concentration of solid materials. Though this evaporation is the responsible agent in the action, the volcanic origin of elements of the sea's drainage basin, salt and sulphur deposits near its shores, mineral-laden springs in its vicinity, and the fact that the present Dead Sea is the residue of a mid-Pleistocene salt lake of much greater proportions—all have contributed to a degree of salinity that is no less amazing than its geographical situation. Its being twenty-five per cent solids gives it approximately five times the concentration of the ocean and makes it the world's densest large body of water. The principal mineral compounds involved are the chlorides of

magnesium, sodium, calcium, and potassium, plus magnesium bromide. These salts constitute the chief mineral resource of the region round about and, to some extent, have been commercially extracted at both the N and the S end of the lake. Since the specific gravity of the water exceeds that of the human body, attempts at swimming in it can be both amazing and amusing experiences. One bobs about on its surface like a cork and, standing erect, will hardly sink to the shoulders. The water is bitter and distasteful to the mouth, disconcertingly painful to the eyes, oily to the touch, and a certain and speedy reminder of all abrasions of the skin. Bathing in its waters should be followed by a fresh-water rinse to remove the irritating salt film deposited on the body. The oily sheen of its salinity is even visible when viewed close at hand and in the proper angle of the sun's rays. From the surrounding hills, however, with the rising or setting sun over one's shoulder, it takes on a deep and beautiful blue, deceptively suggestive of refreshment which it does not afford.

All forms of marine life find it impossible to exist in the Dead Sea's briny depths. Though fish are occasionally found in brackish pools a few feet from the shore line or at the mouths of incoming streams of fresh water, even salt-water varieties quickly succumb when exposed to the lethal concentration of the lake's main body. Because of this the notion has been prevalent in the past that the surrounding land area was also incapable of supporting life. This is quite incorrect. Both vegetation and animal life are found near its shores, especially near valley mouths and springs of fresh water, and in the plain along the SE shore vegetation is both abundant and luxuriant.

*b. E and W shores.* Steep, barren hills enclose the sea on either side, rising to a maximum of approximately 2,500 feet above the shore line on the W and as much as 500 feet higher on the E. The E mountain wall is often precipitous, plunging directly into the sea and permitting of no passage along its forbidding foot. This compact face of Moab is seamed by several gorges—the most spectacular being the Arnon—through which plateau streams plunge downward to debouch into the sea. Callirhoe and Machaerus are sites of interest near the NE shore. In the mineral-laden hot waters of the former, Herod vainly sought relief from his fatal malady; and in the remote and isolated fortress of the latter, Antipas had John the Baptist beheaded.

The broken Judean hills on the W are more terraced and receding, generally permitting a track to parallel the shore line between cliff base and gravel beach. This shore of the lake, with the Judean wilderness at its back, has not a single stream coursing through it to the sea. However, two copious springs beside this W shore form oases of green along a brown and barren strand. One of these, 'Ain Feshkha, near the NW corner of the sea, adjoined the Qumran community which produced the Dead Sea Scrolls. The second, about midway of the W shore, was Engedi, near which David fled for refuge from the jealous hand of Saul (I Sam. 23:29) and whose pleasant vineyards are mentioned in an ancient canticle of love (Song of S. 1:14).

Ten miles farther S, on a commanding crag rising

two thousand feet above the sea, is the site of the incredibly strong Maccabean-Herodian fortress of Masada. Here, following the Roman destruction of Jerusalem, the Jews staged their last desperate resistance—finally, in A.D. 73, taking their own lives in preference to surrender (Jos. War VII.ix.1).

*c. Lisan.* Directly across from Masada and two thirds of the way down the E coast of the sea a broad peninsula juts outward—at one point reaching within two miles of the W shore. The course of an ancient road across the peninsula suggests that a ford crossed the adjacent strait in the Roman period, and both travelers' observations and recent Arab tradition indicate that fordings were still possible in the first half of the nineteenth century. This peninsula, though called El-Lisan ("the tongue"), is shaped like a boot with the toe pointed northward. The forty- to sixty-foot cliffs of this nine-mile plateau of gray-white marl rise sheer like a glacier advancing into the sea.

*d. S embayment.* S of Lisan is a large, shallow embayment having a maximum depth of only fifteen feet and becoming progressively shallower as one proceeds southward or toward the E or W shores.

Bordering this embayment all along its E shore is a broad, fertile plain watered by five small streams (the southernmost being the biblical Zered) cascading out of the adjacent hills. That the level of the sea has been steadily increasing and the area of this plain correspondingly diminishing is indicated by the statements of classical writers, the Roman ford from Lisan to the W shore, recent observations of submerged trees extending on the E as much as one mile from the present coast of the embayment, and various published observations and measurements made since the early part of the nineteenth century. In this connection, it has been maintained on the basis of competent authority that the area of the S embayment increased by fully one third in the hundred-year span between the first quarters of the nineteenth and twentieth centuries. It is probable, therefore, that all or most of the sea S of Lisan was once a plain and that here were located the five CITIES OF THE PLAIN and the nearby Vale of Siddim, which is characterized as containing bitumen pits (Gen. 14: 10). The presence of bituminous materials in and about the sea has been known since ancient times, and both classical and modern writers speak of the rising of chunks of the material to the surface of the lake. It is particularly in the area now occupied by the S embayment that this phenomenon—usually associated with an earthquake—occurs.

*e. Jebel Usdum.* Extending for more than five miles along the SW shore of the embayment is a hundred-foot stratum of crystalline salt surmounted by layers of marly clay and limestone cap rock—the entire mass being known as Jebel Usdum ("Mount of Sodom"). Not only is the name associated with the Cities of the Plain, but the caverned and creviced salt stratum seems to have repeatedly produced a pinnacle to which tradition has pointed when relating the story of Lot's wife and the pillar of salt (Gen. 19:26).

*f. Es-Sebkha.* At its S extremity the Dead Sea slopes almost imperceptibly into a flat and barren plain of white and glistening salt marsh known as es-Sebkha. During periods of flood the lake encroaches upon it, then receding, leaves it an impassable sea of mud. This land, "possessed by nettles and salt pits, and a waste for ever" (Zeph. 2:9), extends some eight miles southward until terminated by the cliffs of 'Ain Khaneizir. From this point onward the great rift-valley is known as the Arabah.

*g. General effect.* The otherworldly appearance of the Dead Sea's deep and barren basin often inspires awe and wonder in the minds of those who view it. It did the same for biblical writers, for both its history and its appearance made of it an apt symbol of the devastation and barrenness visited upon those who despised the law of God. On the other hand, such was the prophetic understanding of God's creative and redemptive care that Ezekiel could envision even such a region refreshed and recreated by the life-giving stream issuing forth from beneath the temple (Ezek. 47:1-12). As an inspiration to meditation on the relation of the present to the future life, this otherworldly setting was unexcelled. It is not surprising, therefore, that a company of Essenes chose a site on its shores to establish a community of contemplation.

*Bibliography.* W. F. Lynch, *The Dead Sea and the Jordan* (1852). G. A. Smith, *The Historical Geography of the Holy Land* (11th ed., 1904), pp. 499-516. F.-M. Abel, *Géographie de la Palestine*, I (1933), 176-78, 192-98, 498-505. J. P. Harland, "Sodom and Gomorrah: I. The Location of the Cities of the Plain," *BA*, V (May, 1942), 17-32; "Sodom and Gomorrah: II. The Destruction of the Cities of the Plain," *BA*, VI (Sept., 1943), 41-54. D. Baly, *The Geography of the Bible* (1957), pp. 202-10.                    W. H. MORTON

\*DEAD SEA SCROLLS. The writings of an Essene community (*see* ESSENES) which were discovered in 1947 near the Dead Sea.\* These scrolls and the fragments found with them represent the most important find of MSS bearing on the Bible, the Jewish religion, and the beginnings of Christianity. Fig. DEA 8.

1. The discoveries of the MSS
2. The external dating of the MSS
3. The excavations at Khirbet Qumran
4. Biblical and apocryphal writings
5. The writings of the sect and their content
   *a.* The Pesharim: the history
   *b.* The Manual of Discipline: the holy life
   *c.* The War Scroll: the holy war
   *d.* The Hodayoth: the praise of God
   *e.* The apocryphal writings: the hope
6. Conclusions
Bibliography

**1. The discoveries of the MSS.** The exact date and circumstances of the famous find are uncertain. In February or March, 1947, Muhammad adh-Dhib (i.e., "the Wolf"), a young Bedouin fellow of the Ta'amireh tribe, searching for a lost goat, entered one of the caves in the cliffs of the W coast of the Dead Sea, 8½ miles S of Jericho.\* There he discovered jars, mostly 25.5-29.5 inches high and almost 10 inches wide, which contained leather scrolls wrapped in linen cloth. First they were offered at Bethlehem for twenty pounds to a dealer who refused to pay this price. After some time, five of these scrolls were bought by the archbishop of the Syrian Orthodox Monastery at Jerusalem, Mar Athanasius Samuel, and three by E. Sukenik at the Hebrew University at Jerusalem. In 1954 Sukenik's son, Y. Yadin, bought the five scrolls from the archbishop for $250,000, so that all these scrolls are now in the possession of the state of Israel. Fig. DEA 9.

Early in 1948, by the time the high age and value of the scrolls had been recognized, the war between the Arabs and the Israelis made a scientific investigation of the cave impossible. Such an investigation was later carried out from February 15 to March 5, 1949,

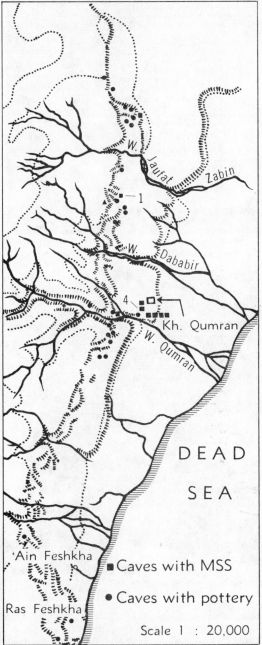

From Milik, *Ten Years of Discovery in the Wilderness of Judaea* (London: SCM Press, 1959; U.S.A.: Alec R. Allenson, Inc.)

8. The Qumran area, showing caves wherein pottery and MSS have been found

by Lankester Harding of the Department of Antiquities in Jordan and R. de Vaux of the Ecole Biblique. Several hundred fragments of biblical books, apocrypha, and unknown writings were found. The amount of jar sherds indicated that the cave had been used to conceal a library of about two hundred scrolls. This library may have been discovered previously. Eusebius reports that Origenes (A.D. 185-254) had used a Greek translation of the Psalms which was found in a jar near Jericho (Euseb. Hist. 6.16). In the year 800 the Nestorian patriarch Timothy I tells in a letter that a shepherd found a "little house of books" near Jericho. The Karaite Ḳirḳisani, in a work on Jewish sects (973), mentions the Magharites, whose books had been found in a cave (*maghar*).

On account of the war in Palestine, Archbishop Athanasius brought his five scrolls to the United States (1948). They were published by M. Burrows with the assistance of J. C. Trever and W. H.

Courtesy of Otto Betz

9. A Ta'amireh Bedouin in the wilderness of Judah

Brownlee. The first volume (1950) contains the plates and the transcription of two scrolls, one a complete book of the prophet Isaiah (1QIs^a)* and the other a commentary on the first chapters of Habakkuk (1QpHab). The second volume (1951) reproduces two smaller scrolls which formed a "Manual of Discipline" (1QS). The last of the five scrolls, believed to be an apocalypse of Lamech, could not be opened at that time. Fig. DEA 10.

In September, 1948, E. Sukenik published his first volume on the MSS and followed it in 1950 by a second one. Both, however, contain only some of the well-preserved portions in his scrolls. After Sukenik's death his son Y. Yadin finished the edition of the complete scrolls in 1954 under the title *Osar Hamegilloth Hagenusoth* ("the treasury of the hidden scrolls"). It includes another Isaiah scroll (1QIs^b), a scroll which describes the eschatological War of the Children of Light and the Children of Darkness (1QM), and four parts of a collection of thanksgiving psalms (1QH). In 1956, together with N. Avigad, Y. Yadin published the so-called Lamech apocalypse, which meanwhile had been opened in the Hebrew University and turned out to be a midrash on some chapters in Genesis. Therefore, it was entitled *A*

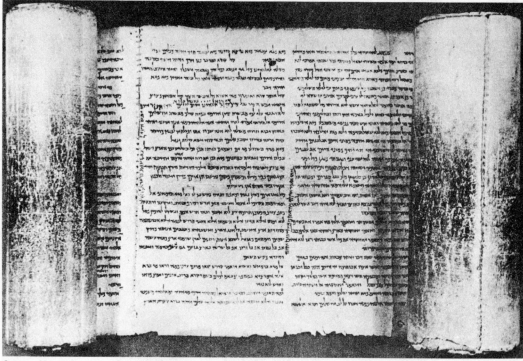

Courtesy of John C. Trever

10. Scroll of Isaiah (1QIs^a), from Cave I in the vicinity of Khirbet Qumran

*Genesis-apocryphon.* The fragments of Cave I were published in 1955 by D. Barthélemy and J. T. Milik in a volume entitled *Qumran Cave I.*

At the end of the summer of 1951 some Ta'amireh tribesmen offered new fragments which they had found in two caves of the Wadi Murabba'at,* *ca.* eleven miles S of the famous Qumran cave and two miles W of the Dead Sea.* Early in 1952 an expedition excavated these caves, which had also been used for hiding places in different ages. They contained biblical MSS of a strictly Masoretic type, among them a scroll of the minor prophets and a papyrus palimpsest of the eighth century B.C. Most revealing for the conditions during the Second Jewish Revolt against Rome (A.D. 132-35), to which most of these writings belong, are some letters on papyrus in Hebrew. Two of them are signed by Simon Bar Cocheba, the leader of this revolt, and others are dated at the time "of the deliverance of Israel by the ministry of Simon Bar Cocheba, the prince of Israel." Pl. XXX*c;* Figs. DEA 11; CAV 20.

Other fragments, which were discovered at Khirbet Mird, 2½ miles NE of the famous monastery Mar Saba, belong to a later date. The biblical documents, written in Greek and in Palestinian Aramaic, come from the fifth-eighth centuries A.D. At a place still unknown were found in July, 1952, Nabatean and Jewish papyri and a fragmentary Greek text of the minor prophets.

While the documents of Wadi Murabba'at and Khirbet Mird are not directly related to those from the cave near Qumran, other caves in the Qumran region supplied the Bedouins with new MSS. An expedition in March, 1952, found remains of pottery in

Courtesy of William L. Reed

11. View of a cave at Murabba'at

thirty-seven caves, some of which also yielded MSS. Cave II (2Q), situated a short distance S of Cave I, contained biblical and apocryphal fragments, among them a portion of the book of Jubilees and an Aramaic document describing the New Jerusalem; and Cave III (3Q), *ca.* a mile N of Cave I, besides 274 frag-

Courtesy of Otto Betz

12. View of Cave IV and Wadi Qumran

Courtesy of the Palestine Archaeological Museum, Jerusalem, Jordan

13. Dr. John Strugnell working on fragments from Cave IV in the scrollery of the Palestine Archaeological Museum

ments in Aramaic and Hebrew, contained two copper scrolls. Cave IV (4Q),* located just opposite and W of Khirbet Qumran, was discovered by the Bedouins in September, 1952.* It offered by far the greatest wealth of fragments: of all biblical books except Esther, of many apocryphal writings, both known and unknown, of commentaries, liturgical texts, and other writings of the sect. Caves V (5Q) and VI (6Q), both in the vicinity of Qumran, yielded smaller finds, as did Caves VII-X, which were discovered during 1955 in the sides of the marl terrace of Khirbet Qumran. All these fragments have been gathered in the Palestine Museum of Jerusalem, where they are being cleaned, ordered, and edited by an international group of scholars.* Later, Cave XI, not far from Cave III, was found, containing several relatively complete scrolls. Pl. XXXIIc; Figs. DEA 12-13; Pl. XXXIb.

The most mysterious among these finds were the two copper scrolls. Originally they were three strips of copper, riveted together and measuring as a whole 7.8 feet. The material was so much oxidized that the scrolls could not be unrolled but had to be cut into strips. This was done at the Manchester College of Technology (1956-57) under the guidance of J. M. Allegro. Both scrolls together have twelve columns. As K. G. Kuhn had suggested after an examination

of the letters which stood out in relief on the back, the scrolls give a list of treasures and the places where they were hidden. In view of the enormous quantity of precious metals, Kuhn thinks of the temple treasury.

2. The external dating of the MSS. The language of most of these writings is the OT Hebrew. Only a few terms of the Mishnaic Hebrew are used; however, four fragments found in Cave IV show elements of the Mishnaic grammar, like frequent participles or the relative particle sh.

The MSS were written in a beautiful hand by learned scribes. They used the hairside of the animal skins and ruled them with horizontal lines for writing and with vertical lines to fix the margins. The script closely resembles that of the Nash Papyrus (second century B.C.) or of inscriptions on ossuaries found near Jerusalem. To fix the date of the scrolls, Albright, Trever, Birnbaum, Sukenik, and others used paleographical evidence, which pointed to the second or first century B.C. The sherds of the jars belong to the end of the Hellenistic period, which is about the same time. The carboactivity of the flaxen covers of the scrolls converged on A.D. 33 and, with a margin of two hundred years more or less, to the time between 168 B.C. and A.D. 233.

3. The excavations at Khirbet Qumran. But all these observations are not sufficient for an exact dating of the scrolls. More determining for it were the excavations at Khirbet Qumran.* The khirbet ("ruin"), situated on a terrace at the foot of the mountain ca. two miles N of the 'Ain Feshkha* and a half mile S of Cave I, was erroneously held to be the ancient site of Gomorrah or a military outpost of the Romans.* The findings at the caves drew more attention to the site until it was excavated in different campaigns by R. de Vaux and L. Harding: (a) November 24-December 12, 1951; (b) February 9-April 24, 1953; (c) February 13-April 14, 1954; (d) February 2-April 6, 1955; (e) February 18-March 28, 1956. These excavations disclosed the ruins of a large fortified monastery, which served as the center of the sect. The following periods of settlement can be distinguished:

a) The site was a rather large city in the eighth-seventh centuries B.C. M. Noth has identified it with 'ir hammélaḥ ("city of the salt [sea]"), mentioned in Josh. 15:62, in a list from the time of King Josiah (639-609 B.C.).

b) This OT city was abandoned at the end of the sixth century and used again under the Hasmonean high priest John Hyrcanus (134-104 B.C.).

c) During the first century B.C. the site was rebuilt and enlarged by the sectarians. In the winter an impressive water system conducted the water from a waterfall in the W by a stone aqueduct into channels and large cisterns. In some of them large steps were railed off for the different classes of the sect to use in the ritual of purification.* A large rectangular hall at the S, measuring approximately 73.8 by 14.7 feet, was used for the holy assemblies and the common prayers and sessions, and also must have been the refectory,* since a chamber connected with it contained several hundred bowls, plates, and also cups and jars. Remarkable signs of the life within these walls are the remains of the workshops for the craftsmen:* the pottery, the forge, the grain mill, the bakery,

Courtesy of Otto Betz

14. The Qumran region: in the middle the plateau of the monastery; in the background the cliffs of the caves

From *Atlas of the Bible* (Thomas Nelson & Sons Limited)

15. Khirbet Qumran; the arrow points to the excavated site.

Courtesy of Otto Betz

16. Staircase into one of the cisterns, probably used for the ritual of purification

Courtesy of Otto Betz

17. The refectory of the community at Khirbet Qumran

Courtesy of Otto Betz

18. Workshops of the community at Khirbet Qumran

and the laundry. The monastery was fortified by walls and a strong tower in the NW. S of the tower was the scriptorium, indicated by a long, narrow table, a bench, and two inkwells. These remains illustrate the wealth of activity among the sectarians.* They were holy men and holy warriors, industrious workers and writers. S of the monastery was their cemetery, with more than a thousand graves.* The dead were buried without any ornamental objects. Among the skeletons were several female ones.

*d*) The monastery was considerably destroyed by an earthquake, no doubt in 31 B.C. (Jos. War I.xix.3; Antiq. XV.v.2). The place must have been abandoned until the death of Herod the Great (4 B.C.).

*e*) Then the sect rebuilt and used the site again. Their flourishing life came to an end under military impact. The sect probably defended the monastery bravely, so that the enemy set fire to it. No doubt, this took place in A.D. 68, when the Tenth Roman Legion marched against Jericho (Jos. War IV.viii.1-2; II.viii.10).

*f*) After the destruction the site was used partially by Roman troops and afterward by Jewish revolutionaries.

This entire sequence of occupation is verified by the series of coins found there, dating from Hyrcanus I (135-104 B.C.) until the Second Jewish Revolt (A.D. 132-35). The pottery of the monastery is of the same type as that in the caves, and the content of the scrolls points to a community whose way of living fits a monastery of that kind.

An auxiliary of the monastery existed at 'Ain Feshkha, where a large wall enclosed buildings of the same date as in Qumran. They comprised the agricultural center from which the sect worked an irrigated strip of farm and orchard along the Dead Sea; herded its cattle; and stored, manufactured, and distributed their produce for its own use.

Pls. XXVIIIc; XXXIIb; Figs. DEA 14-19; BUR 57.

**4. Biblical and apocryphal writings.** The largest copies of OT MSS are the two Isaiah scrolls of Cave I (1QIsᵃ and 1QIsᵇ). 1QIsᵃ contains the complete

Hebrew text of Isaiah and 1QIsᵇ about one third of it. The first of these scrolls, with fifty-four columns on seventeen sheets, is 24 feet long and 10.2 inches high. It is the largest and best preserved of all, and was written in the second-first century B.C. Much older are fragments of Leviticus in the same Old Hebrew script in which the other Dead Sea Scrolls sometimes express the holy name of God. They are followed by fragments of Samuel (third century B.C.). From the distribution of the fragments, it is clear that the favorite biblical books of the sect were Deuteronomy, the Psalms, Isaiah, and Genesis. These fragments also give a very complicated picture of the

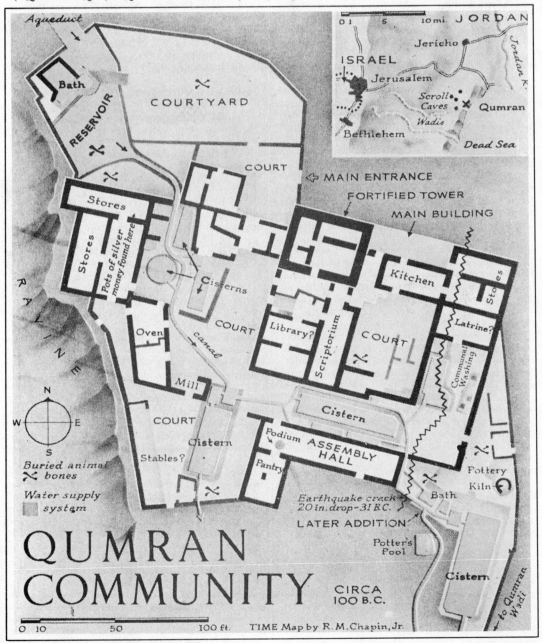

*Time* map by R. M. Chapin, Jr.; copyright Time Inc., 1957

19. Plan of the settlement at Khirbet Qumran

text tradition. A diversity of text forms appears. Some of the MSS are close to the MT, as 1QIs[b], while the fragments of I and II Samuel (4Q) are much closer to the Hebrew original of the LXX. There must also have been MSS at Qumran which were more in accordance with the Samar. and those of a mixed type (*see* VERSIONS, ANCIENT). However, a trend toward a standard form of the text is noticeable, and the MSS of the Wadi Murabba'at, which belong to the first half of the second century A.D., all represent the MT and show that at this time the development had come to an end. *See* TEXT, OT.

The caves also presented fragments in Hebrew and Aramaic of apocryphal and pseudepigraphal writings, which until now were known only in translations—Latin, Greek, Syriac, Ethiopic, and others (*see* APOCRYPHA). One fragment of 6Q corresponds to the text of the Hebrew book of Ecclesiasticus found sixty years ago in the Synagogue of Old Cairo, and this cave also offered fragments from the book of Tobit in Hebrew and Aramaic. The book of Jubilees was used by the sect in several copies; parts I and III-V of the book of Enoch (*see* ENOCH, BOOK OF); the Testament of Levi; and the Rule of the New Covenant in the Land of Damascus (*see* ZADOKITE FRAGMENTS). But there are other fragments of apocryphal writings which are unknown to us. This leads to the following suggestions: (*a*) some of the Apoc., which until now could not be related to a distinct religious group, must be attributed to the Essenes of Qumran; (*b*) the book of Enoch is a collection of writings which were used separately; the sect probably did not know the famous second part of this book, which contains the visions of the Son of man; (*c*) except for the Testament of Levi, the Testaments of the Twelve Patriarchs were not found either; they were written afterward by another author; (*d*) there must have existed a lot of other apocryphal writings centered around figures like Noah, the patriarchs, and Moses.

The sect also produced commentaries on books or passages of the Bible. Among them were midrashim like Jubilees, which paraphrase the text, and besides them *Pesharim*, a type of commentary peculiar to the sect. In the latter the text of the prophets like Isaiah, Micah, Nahum, Habakkuk, and Zephaniah is written phrase by phrase, whereby each phrase is followed by an explanation of "its meaning" (*pesharô*) and referred to the history of the sect. The outstanding example of the midrashim is the Genesis Apocryphon, of the *Pesharim* the Habakkuk commentary.

A new literary form appears in the florilegia—i.e., collections of biblical texts—and in the testimonia, proof texts for a distinct idea. 4Q offers a florilegium with passages from Exodus, II Samuel, Isaiah, Amos, Psalms, and Daniel, and a testimonium of messianic texts (Deut. 5:28-29 with Deut. 18:18-19; Num. 24: 15-17; Deut. 33:8-11). The phylacteries found in 4Q contain larger biblical portions than those prescribed by the rabbis.

Among the writings which characterize the order and represent the life of the sect may be distinguished the following groups: (*a*) the rules (*Serakhim*), as the Manual of Discipline and the War Scroll; (*b*) the hymns, among which the *Hodayoth* (Thanksgiving

Psalms) are the most notable; (*c*) liturgical writings, as the Blessings (1QSb); (*d*) sapiental writings and books for esoteric teaching. Some of these literary forms can be found together in one book, as in the Manual of Discipline, which has a dogmatical section and ends with a long hymn.

**5. The writings of the sect. *a. The Pesharim: the history.*** The Habakkuk *Pesher* has thirteen columns of eighteen lines each and is now 4.6 feet long and 5.1 inches high. Its biblical passages differ from the MT in about sixty cases.

The *Pesher* throws light on the history of the sect, since important events and problems of it are related to Habakkuk's prophecies. They can be summarized in the following groups: (*a*) the controversy between the "Right-Teacher" and the "Wicked Priest" (1.1-2, 10; 6.12-12.10); (*b*) God's judgment upon the people (2.10*b*-6.12); (*c*) God's judgment upon the nations (12.10-13.4).

Hab. 1:4, where the wicked and the righteous are mentioned, is used to introduce the two opponents. The Right-Teacher, a priest (2.8), who is sent by God to tell the future to this last generation (2.7)—i.e., the impending judgment of God upon his people (2.10). This prophetic message comes from God himself (2.2-3), but is mediated through the Scriptures—i.e., the prophecy of Habakkuk (2.9-10; 7.1-5). The Right-Teacher understands even more of it than the prophet (7.2). He knows the coming of the end and also that this coming tarries (7.7). He has found men who believed him (8.1-3) and with them established a community (9.10), which represents a new covenant (2.3, if the lacuna may be thus restored). Its members will survive the imminent catastrophe safely because of their loyalty to the Torah (7.10-12) and their faith in the Right-Teacher (8.1-3).

However, his message and claims are rejected by the Wicked Priest and his followers (2.6-7). This Wicked Priest must be the high priest at Jerusalem, for he carries the "true name" and is ruling in Israel (8.8-10). But he became haughty, forsook God's commandments out of his lust for wealth and booty, and defiled his holy service (8.10-13). He also persecuted the Right-Teacher and violated him "at the body of his flesh" (9.1-2). The conflict, in which a party called the "House of Absalom" was neutral (5.9-11), reached its height at the Day of Atonement, when the Wicked Priest proceeded to "swallow up" and to banish(?) the Right-Teacher and to cause his followers to stumble (11.4). But God's judgment will reach all the evildoers: the Wicked Priest (10.3-5) must have already fallen into the hands of his enemies (9.9-11), the priests of Jerusalem will lose all their unjust wealth at the hand of the "Kittim" (9.6), and the whole nation will be devastated by the same Kittim (2.10-6.12).

Who are these Kittim? In the OT the name is used for the people of Cyprus (Gen. 10:4; Isa. 23:1, 12; Jer. 2:10; Ezek. 27:6), for the Greeks (I Macc. 1:1; 8:5), and probably for the Romans (Num. 24:24; Dan. 11:30). The Kittim of the *Pesher* are mighty conquerors (2.12-15; 3.4-6), coming "from the coasts of the sea" (3.10-11). Their rulers follow each other "by the counsel of a guilty house" (4.11), and they themselves sacrifice to their standards (6.3-5).

There are only two possibilities: the Kittim of this

*Pesher* are the Greeks—i.e., the Seleucids—or they are the Romans. The description of the power and the military success of this terrible foe fits the Romans better. Their army was well known to the sect, as the War Scroll implies. The worship of the standards applies to Roman soldiers (Jos. War VI.vi.1), and the "guilty house" probably means the Roman Senate.

Many theories have been suggested for the identification of the Right-Teacher and the Wicked Priest. Since the excavations at Qumran, post-Christian theories cannot be defended any longer. If we look for such a conflict in the middle of the second century B.C., the invasion of Antiochus IV and his Hellenizing zeal suggests itself; if in the middle of the first century, the decline of the Hasmonean dynasty and Pompey's conquest of Jerusalem stand out. The first period, chosen by Reicke, Rowley, Stauffer, Bardtke, *et al.,* offers more suitable names for the two opponents: the orthodox high priest Onias III for the Right-Teacher; the Hellenizers Jason, Menelaus, Alcimus, for the Wicked Priest; and the Tobiads for the House of Absalom. The second, vouchsafed by Dupont-Sommer and followed by Gossens, Dhorme, Kahle, and to some extent by Elliger, does not provide a name for the Right-Teacher but does suggests men like Hyrcanus II or his brother Aristobulus II as wicked priests. It is also difficult to decide whether the Right-Teacher was killed by the Wicked Priest or only tortured and exiled, and also whether he was regarded as a divine being and expected to rise again.

Fragments of other *Pesharim* mention the struggle of these two opponents. According to the *Pesher* of Ps. 37, the Right-Teacher was instituted by God to build up his congregation (2.15-16), which will inherit the Mount of the Height of Israel—i.e., occupy the holy city and its temple (2.10-11). If the lacuna is filled out correctly, the Wicked Priest was sent to kill the Right-Teacher and to slay the upright of the Way (vss. 32-33). In fragments of a Nahum *Pesher* appear for the first time the proper names of men who are known to us from secular history. Demetrius, "king of Javan," tried to enter Jerusalem on behalf of the council of the "Seekers-after-Smooth-Things." Besides him is mentioned an Antiochus, who is most probably Antiochus Epiphanes. Demetrius seems to be the Syrian king Demetrius III (Eucaerus), who reigned at Damascus and was called upon for help by the Pharisees against their despotic king Alexander Janneus (103-76 B.C.). Demetrius defeated Janneus but was suddenly deserted by most of the rebels and withdrew from the country (1QM 1.95). Janneus took a terrible revenge on the remaining enemies, crucifying eight hundred of them at Jerusalem (Jos. War. I.iv.6). The *Pesher* probably refers to this awful deed when it tells that the "Lion of Wrath" hung up men alive and remarks that such a thing had never been done before in Israel. The Nahum *Pesher* describes the priests of Jerusalem gathering wealth as in the Habakkuk *Pesher,* where they appear in the company of the Wicked Priest. Thus one can draw the conclusion that the high priest and king, Alexander Janneus, is meant as the Wicked Priest.

**b. The Manual of Discipline: the holy life.** This scroll, measuring 6.1 feet by 9.4 inches, has eleven columns of twenty-six lines each. The beginning of this writing is missing, and therefore its true title is unknown. It probably was *Sérekh Hayyaḥadh*, "Rule of the Community." M. Burrows has called it "Manual of Discipline." The importance of this scroll is shown by the fact that fragments of eleven MSS have been found. The oldest of them, which presents a rather archaic script, should be dated, according to F. M. Cross, at the very beginning of the first century B.C. The scroll prescribes: (*a*) the rules and the liturgy of the covenant (1.1-3.12); (*b*) the doctrine of the community (3.13-4.26); (*c*) the admission (5.1-6.23); (*d*) the penal code (6.24-7.25); (*e*) the holy life in the world of evil (8.1-9.26); (*f*) the praise of God (10.1-11.22). The community claims to represent the true covenant of God. Everyone who joined the sect had to enter the covenant with all the members who renewed their obligation to it. This ceremony, held probably every year at Pentecost (cf. Jub. 6:17), follows the pattern of the covenant ceremonies in the OT (cols. 1-2). The basic rules of the community, given in the introduction of the Manual (1.1-15), were accepted as the foundation of the covenant. Most characteristic are the blessings and the curses. The blessing takes its form from the Aaronitic blessing (Num. 6:24-26), and the curse against the hypocrite from Deut. 29:18-19. But these passages are interpreted according to the eschatology of the sect.

With this first section should be connected the order for those "who are willing to return from sin" —i.e., to enter the sect (5.1). They have to bind themselves by an oath to the Torah as it is interpreted by the chief authorities of the sect, the Zadokite priests and the laymen (5.7-10). Only the sect's interpretation of the Law, which was acquired after strenuous research (5.11-12), is true. This form of obedience made it impossible to share a common life with the Jews. Therefore, the members of this covenant had to separate themselves into the wilderness, where they prepared the way of God by searching in the Law and living according to the new revelation (8.12-16). No other scroll emphasizes so strongly the necessity of separation. The Manual discloses the strictest form of Essene life, since it was written for the close brotherhood at Qumran.

Its life was a holy one, whose holiness was expressed by: (*a*) obedient fulfilment of the laws of the brotherhood; (*b*) holy ceremonies such as ritual baths and the common meals; (*c*) economic purity; and (*d*) chastity.

Everyone who entered the sect was considered to be unclean in regard to his knowledge, strength, and property (*see* CLEAN AND UNCLEAN). All these capacities and resources had to be purified by the truth of God's commandments so that one could lead a perfect life (1.11-13). It was only gradually that one could reach this goal, by going from one degree of purity to the other after severe examinations. For two to three years one was a novitiate (cf. Jos. War II.vii.7). After a first examination by the overseer (6.14) and a period of instruction, the novitiate was admitted to the covenant (6.15). In it he had to live according to the law of this covenant—i.e., the Torah and the rules which the sect derived from it. Obedience to the law purifies the conduct of life, and the penal code of the sect condemns both moral and ritual transgressions as defiling the holy community (6.24–7.25). After one year of probation he was examined by the general assembly and allowed to participate in the "purification of the Many" (6.16-17). This rite, which was performed daily in one of the large cisterns at Qumran, foreshadowed the great and final lustration of the elect by God himself (4.20-22). It had two aspects: through it the body is washed by water and the heart cleansed by the Holy Spirit (3.2-9). Ritual purity was completed by economic purity in that the property of the proselyte was taken over and his work devoted to the sect (6.19). Its communistic order must be derived from priestly zeal: just as the priestly tribe of Levi had no share in the promised land, because God himself was their "inheritance" (Ezek. 44:28), so every member of the community lived from the holy property of God and did his work under an overseer (6.20). After a third year of perfect life the novitiate was admitted to the most sacred rite, the "drink," which probably was followed by the general assembly (6.22-23). From then on, he took his seat in the sessions of the sect and voted on all affairs of the community. The procedure of these sessions is given in 6.8-13, whereby the hierarchical order of the sect (priests, Levites or elders, and laymen) is highly respected. Within his order every man received an annual rank according to his knowledge and practice of the Torah. It fixed his place in the holy army (2.22-23) and also in the sacred meals. These meals can be compared to the offerings and the sacrificial meals in the sanctuary, for the table of the community (6.4) was at the same time the table of the Lord. The sect did not reject animal sacrifice in general, but prayers and a perfect life were regarded as suitable substitutes (9.4-5).

The life of the sect is marked by the prayers. They were held every day in the morning and in the evening (10.1, 10), before and after work, and in battle array (10.13-14); and the Manual closes with a long hymn. The times of worship differed from those of the Jews outside. This can be seen from the calendar, which indicates the pattern of holy times during the course of the day and the year (10.1-8).

The agencies of administration are quite the same as those in the ZADOKITE FRAGMENTS. Besides the general assembly there was a council of twelve laymen and three priests which represented the perfect nucleus of the holy community (8.1-4).

The zeal for a holy and separate life was reinforced by eschatological expectations and a dualistic world view. Both belong together. They are described in the first section "for the wise man" (3.13-4.26). In order to explain the existence of evil, the sect teaches that the world is dominated by two spirits, the spirit of light and the spirit of darkness (3.20-25). Both are created by God (3.25) and act according to his plan; but each of them represents the head of a realm of angels and men, and also a moral power struggling in every man's heart (4.23). By predestination of God each man belongs to one of these dominions (3.15-17). In spite of this, the moral struggle goes on until the forces of evil will be extinguished in God's final judgment, and the elect will be unified with the angels in one perfect community (4.20-22). Since the Children of Light too

will be tempted by sin and plagues until that date (3.21-24), the theory of predestination does not exclude an appeal for moral struggle. Therefore, the dogmatical section contains a catalogue of virtues and vices and the rewards and punishments corresponding to them (4.2-14). In view of the problem of living a holy life in the midst of unclean men, some regulations are given in the second section "for the wise man" (9.12-26).

In 1950 some large fragments were bought which belonged to the end of the Manual, although they differ in content. The first part (1QSa) is a rule (sérekh) for the "congregation of Israel at the end of days" (1.1), called 'ēdhâ instead of yáḥadh. The rule mentions wives and children (1.4); it prescribes the age of marrying for a man, the rights of his wife (1.9-11), and also the education of the children and young people (1.6-16). This indicates that the rule was written mainly for the second order of the sect. Quite unique is the eschatological outlook. Thus the assemblies, described in the second part of the rule, point to the messianic age. The first begins mobilization for the holy war, which requires three days of purification and chastity (1.25-26) and a clean and perfect body (2.5-9; cf. 1QM 7.5-7; Deut. 23:9-15). The second assembly is the holy meal (2.11-22). The Messiah of Israel participates in it, seated, however, after the priests and their head, who is probably to be identified with the Messiah of Aaron (2.12, 19). Every meal of the sect gave a foretaste of the messianic banquet. Even the group of ten follows this pattern (2.21-22).

The second part is a collection of blessings (1QSb). It consists of six columns which are in a very fragmentary condition. These blessings were probably not performed in a ritual but were written to illustrate the eschatological reward as an encouragement to the "wise man." Each of them describes the receiver and his dignity before it gives the blessing for his faithfulness. The messianic banquet order is retained also: the invocation blesses the faithful ones in general (1.1 ff); then follow the blessings for the high priest (1.21 ff), the priests (3.22 ff), and the "prince of the congregation" (5.20 ff)—i.e., the Messiah of Israel. This collection of benedictions seems to have a counterpart in maledictions whose fragments were found in Cave IV.

*c. The War Scroll: the holy war.* The scroll in its present state is 9.5 feet long and 6.2 inches high. It contains 18½ columns of 16-18 lines each. 4Q has yielded four fragmentary copies of this scroll. Fig. DEA 20.

The War Scroll gives the plan for the final war between the Children of Light and the Children of Darkness, who represent the forces of good and evil. This holy war ends with God's final judgment and has two aspects, a moral and a national one. The description is strongly influenced by the traditions of the holy war in the OT and of the Maccabean uprising against the Seleucids, by apocalyptic visions like the war against Gog and Magog (Ezek. 38–39), and by the pattern of contemporaneous Roman warfare.

The scroll is a collection of rather different materials. The first part (cols. 1-9) gives the rules for equipment and tactics; the second contains mostly

20. Parchment of scroll 1QM, "War of the Sons of Light and the Sons of Darkness"

exhortations and prayers (cols. 10-19). After a prologue which provides a survey on the whole war (col. 1), there follow the order for the service at the sanctuary (2.1-6) and a time table for the different campaigns of this war (2.6-14). The next chapter is concerned with the use of the trumpets (3.1-11) and standards (3.12-4.14), 5.3-6.6 give a detailed description of the weapons for the heavy-armed soldiers of the phalanx (5.3-16) and the troops fighting between them (6.1-6). 6.7-16 prescribes equipment and age of the cavalry, 6.17-7.7 ability and purity of the army in general. In 7.9-9.9 the duties during the battle itself are told: the functions of the priests and Levites who lead the war, and the movements of the troops according to the signals of the trumpets. 9.10-15 describes special formations for crushing and pursuing the enemy.

9.17-14.15 presents the exhortations and prayers for the different stages of the war, pointing to God's promises—Deut. 20:2-4 (10.3-5) and Num. 10:9 (10.6-8) are quoted—to his might in creation and in Israel's history (11.1-17), and to the heavenly army which will bring help (12.1-10). A battle song (12.10-17), a benediction and curse (13.1-5), and a hymn of victory (14.2-17) conclude this part.

Cols. 15-19 delineate the different stages of the war against the Kittim. Each stage is characterized by an admonition. In the first round the Children of Light are the victors (15.1-16.9), in the second they are defeated (16.10-17.9), in the third they are finally triumphant (17.10-18.9). The end of the scroll is missing; col. 19 is parallel to 12.7-16.

The sect already lives in holy camps, which must be free from any kind of sexual impurity and human excrements (1QM7.6-7; cf. Deut. 23:14; Jos. War II.vii.9). The war, which lasts forty years, is directed against all the nations of the biblical world. Six years are spent against Israel's enemies in the neighborhood: Edom, Moab, Ammon, the Philistines, and

above all the "Kittim of Assur" (1.1-2; 2.9; cf. Ps. 83:6-9), and twenty-nine years are needed for the remote nations the "Kittim of Egypt" and the "kings of the North" (1.4; cf. Dan. 11:41-44); these are listed separately according to Gen. 10:22-23 (2.10-14). Five years are sabbatical years, in which any kind of mobilization of warfare is forbidden (2.8-9). The strong sabbatical discipline even in wartime reminds us of the Maccabees (cf. I Macc. 6:53-54; Jos. Antiq. XIII.vii.1), as also the solemn ceremony held at the sanctuary (2.1-6; cf. I Macc. 3:46-60) and the confident awaiting of help from heaven (I Macc. 3:18-22; cf. also the list of OT victories in 1QM 11 with I Macc. 4:9, 30; 7:41; II Macc. 12:15). The Children of Light, represented by the tribes of Levi, Judah, and Benjamin (1.2), are "God's people" (3:13), his elect (3.2), and holy warriors (4.9-11), who win by God's help alone (3.5, 9). This conviction is strongly expressed in the signals and the inscription on the trumpets (3-4).

On the other hand, the equipment and tactics of this army are realistic and modern. The weapons like shield, sword, and javelin correspond to the Roman *scutum, gladius, hasta,* and the Qumran phalanx to the Roman legion. The formations of Roman tactics like the *cuneus* (wedge formation), the *forfax* (scissors formation), and the *testudo* (tortoise) are used (9.10-15). The total army has 28,000 men of infantry and 6,000 men of cavalry (9.4; 6.10-11). It has three kinds of participants: (*a*) the line troops, (*b*) the camp troops, (*c*) the priests and Levites. The phalanx is arranged in three columns of heavy-armed infantry, each of which forms seven lines of 1,000 men (5.3). Between the seven lines of the middle column stand seven other lines of special infantry which fight from the vacant spaces ("battle doors") in the front line, shooting war darts and using their spears (6.1-6). The cavalry attacks on the wings of the phalanx, 1,400 mixed among the infantry (6.9) and 1,400 fighting as pure cavalry units (6.10-11); 3,200 are stationed at the camp (6.9).

It is remarkable that there are no polemics against Israel in general or distinct groups in this scroll. This is due to the fact that the sect uses the tradition of Israel's holy war in the OT. But "Israel" here too means the elect of this nation—i.e., the Children of Light, who live now in the "exile of the wilderness" (1.2), partially dispersed in the "wilderness of the nations" (1.3), and partially in the "wilderness of Jerusalem" (1.3)—i.e., at Qumran.

The use of the sanctuary reveals the sectarian calendar, since the twenty-six offices of the priests (2.2) correspond to the fifty-two weeks of the solar system, while the Jews had only twenty-four offices.

The scroll was written in the second half of the first century B.C., as it shows a comparison of the military data given in it with the nature of the Roman army at that time. A possible influence of the scroll is to be seen in Josephus' report on the mobilization of a Jewish army in Galilee (War II.xx.6-8), whereby OT traditions and the Roman example are combined in a similar way.

***d. The Hodayoth: the praise of God.*** The scroll 1QH was found in two separate parts: the first contains three sheets of four columns each; the second amounts to about twenty detached fragments.* The sheets of the scroll, which are badly damaged, are unusually high, having thirty-five to forty-one lines each. The collection was written by two scribes. Cave IV contained fragments of five MSS of Hodayoth, which help to fill up some lacunas in the scroll and also show that the order of the psalms was variable. Fig. DEA 21.

Courtesy of the Israel Office of Information, New York

21. Column from scroll 1QH (*Hodayoth*), a collection of thanksgiving psalms, from Cave I

Almost every one of these psalms is introduced by the formula "I shall praise Thee, my Lord," which is quite typical for a thanksgiving hymn.

A clear order or progress of thought is hard to discern. By way of introduction the first hymn describes the overwhelming power of the almighty God which is manifest in his creation, and in contrast the weakness and impurity of man. This is also the general theme of these hymns. It depicts the affliction which the force of evil instigates against the people of God. The psalms of cols. 2-6 describe these terrible attacks in various pictures. The psalmist compares himself to a banner in the midst of battle (2.11-13), a fortress

surrounded and assaulted by enemies (2.20-30; 3.7), a wife in her birth pangs (3.7-12), a ship in the depth (3.6), and a man threatened by lions (5.7). All these dramatic scenes refer to the controversy of the pious members of the sect with their Jewish opponents. These are wrong teachers (4.9-10) and creatures of Belial, while the speaker himself is an exponent of God's truth and power. He seems to be persecuted, driven out from his country like a bird from his nest; even his friends and relatives have rejected and insulted him (4.8-9). He also is afflicted by troubles unloosed by former followers, for he tells that strife and discord, murmuring and complaint, arose from those who had eaten his bread and adhered to his council (5.22-26).

The speaker must be a teacher of the sect. He is not only the representative of God but also of his community, and the attacks of the satanic powers are directed against it in a similar way. The community too is compared to a fortress which God himself has built upon a rock, impregnable against attacking warriors of evil (6.25-39). It originated with the teacher. The members of the community are his spiritual children, whom he brings to light out of the eschatological woes (1QH 3.7-12) and feeds as a nurse does her babes (7.20-22). As God is his father, in place of his parents according to the flesh (9.29-32), so the teacher becomes a father of the faithful ones (7.20). The creative power is God's holy spirit, which changes man completely. While the speaker in these psalms is weak and sinful in his physical nature (1QH 1.21-22), he appears as a strong fortress when he is endowed with the holy spirit (7.6-10). This miracle which he has experienced in his own existence leads him again and again to express his joy and thankfulness.

The eschatological hope is strong in these psalms. The community can be seen already as a segment of paradise, as trees of life standing by living waters (8.5-7). At the same time the catastrophe at the end of days is vividly portrayed (3.26-36).

*e. The apocryphal writings: the hope.* The Genesis Apocryphon, written in Aramaic, was held to be an apocalypse of Lamech until it was opened at the Hebrew University. It was severely damaged, most probably because it was not put in a jar. The scroll consists of four sheets with a total length of 9.28 feet and a height of approximately 1 foot. It has twenty-two columns of thirty-four to thirty-seven lines each. However, most of these columns are in a very fragmentary condition. The apocryphon represents a type of free and speculative exegesis of a biblical text. Its style resembles that of the book of Jubilees and of Daniel. The scroll is composed of several apocalypses. In the first (cols. 1-5) Lamech is the central figure, in the second (cols. 6-15) Noah. After a report on the division of the world (cols. 16-17) there follows an apocalypse of Abraham (cols. 18-22). The heroes of these apocalypses speak themselves. They usually paraphrase the biblical text. At some points they tell new legendary stories which explain the motives of their actions in the Bible. The patriarchs live rather close to the sphere of God. This is certainly the reason for the sect's speculative research in their lives. Since the *eschaton* goes back to the glory of the primeval age, the righteous of the remote past become great examples for the righteous of the last generation—i.e., the members of the sect. Thus the angelic beauty and splendor of the young Noah—col. 2 is to be connected with Enoch 106:7—is an image of the glory of the reborn righteous in the messianic age. For the women of the sect the ideal is Sarah, whose beauty is highly praised by Pharaoh's courtiers (20:1-7; cf. Joseph and Asenath 14, 18-19). Eschatological significance is given to Abraham's dream of the two trees, which are symbols for Abraham and Sarah (col. 19; cf. 1QH 8.4-15, where the members of the sect are compared to trees standing in the Paradise). Besides Ps. 92:13, both Ezek. 31 and Dan. 4 have influenced this story. Dan. 4 provides the background for a story in which the Babylonian king Nabonidus tells his sickness, his dream, and his conversion and healing by Daniel. Fragments of it were found in 4Q. All these apocalyptic stories are written to encourage the afflicted pious ones, that they might remain faithful while awaiting the wonderful life in the messianic age.

This age brings the fulfilment of history. The sect's concept of history is more fully described in the ZADOKITE FRAGMENTS.* God himself carries on the work of salvation, but he uses chosen instruments: (a) the prophet who prepares the way as a second Moses and Elijah; (b) the Messiah from Aaron, the Right-Teacher of the last period of revelation; (c) the Messiah of Israel, the victorious fighter (1QS 9.11). The twofold messianic office was certainly derived from the concept of the two anointed in Zech. 4:14. It developed out of heated protest against the usurpation of both titles, that of king and that of high priest, by the Hasmoneans. This trinity of saviors is depicted. by a group of messianic testimonia in which Deut. 18:18 refers to the prophet, Num. 24:15-17 to the Messiah from Israel-Judah, and Deut. 33:8-11 to the Messiah from Aaron. The function of the prophet and forerunner was probably fulfilled by the Right-Teacher, since the Zadokite Fragments, after the teacher's death, only wait for the coming of the two Messiahs (cf. CDC 20.14). The task of the Messiah from Israel is best described in 1QSb 5, according to which he fulfils the prophecies of Num. 24:17; Gen. 49:8-10; Isa. 11. But he will obey the spiritual guide—i.e., the Messiah of Aaron, whose mission is told in Test. Levi 18. When the Messiah of Israel has defeated God's enemies on earth, the Messiah of Aaron will establish his holy community. This takes place in a New Jerusalem, which is described in several fragments (2Q; 5Q). The messianic functions are already taken over, to some extent, by the members of the sect. They all study the Law like the Right-Teacher; they are all holy warriors like the Messiah of Israel; they all perform the holy service for God as the Messiah of Aaron will do. But they have to do this during the continuous attacks of Belial in the time of evil. Fig. ZAD 1.

The figure of the Son of man, which contradicts the messianic hope of the sect, seemingly was not used, as is indicated by the fact that section II of Enoch is missing. Probably the sect interpreted Dan. 7 in a collective way, regarding itself as those who shall judge and rule the world after the final victory (cf. Dan. 7:18-27 with 1QS 8.5-6; 9.6-7).

**6. Conclusions.** The history of the sect can be sketched only with great caution. It has its religious origin in the HASIDIM, the pious ones, an orthodox group which successfully opposed the Hellenizing tendencies in Judaism. The conflict reached its height under Antiochus Epiphanes (175-163 B.C.) and was ended by the victory of the orthodox party in the Maccabean wars (see MACCABEES). But in the second half of the second century B.C. the coalition between the Maccabean-Hasmonean rulers and the pious ones broke up, and the latter split off into different groups. Josephus mentions three religious parties under John Hyrcanus (134-103 B.C.; Antiq. XIII.x.6) and an Essene prophet with his disciples under Aristobul I (104-103 B.C.; War I.iii.5). Their criticism was directed against the connection of high priesthood and political power in the hands of the Hasmoneans (Antiq. XIII.x.5). Moreover, the Zadokite priesthood could not regard them as legitimate high priests. These tensions led to a revolt of the pious ones against King Alexander Janneus (103-76 B.C.). If Janneus was the Wicked Priest who persecuted the Right-Teacher, the exodus of the sect can be connected with the flight of eight thousand men under his reign (War I.iv.6). Some of them probably went to the "Land of Damascus"—i.e., the Hauran region—others settled at Qumran. There they could survive the conquest of Jerusalem by Pompey (63 B.C.) and the end of the Hasmonean dynasty. HEROD the Great is reported to have held the Essenes in high esteem, and this, no doubt, was because of their anti-Hasmonean attitude. The Essene sympathies for Herod can be seen in the story of the Essene Manaemos, who prophesied to the young boy Herod that he would become king of the Jews (Antiq. XV. x.4-5). Since the monastery at Qumran was destroyed by an earthquake in 31 B.C., the Essenes probably dispersed throughout the country and may have lived also in Jerusalem under Herod's protection. But they were certainly hated by the Pharisees, who disliked the Idumean Herod and differed in their interpretation of the Scriptures. After Herod's death the Essenes withdrew to Qumran again and lived there until A.D. 68, when the monastery was destroyed. After this catastrophe some of the Essenes became Jewish Christians, who were later called Ebionites.

There is no doubt that the community of the scrolls formed a part of the ESSENES. This is proved by a comparison of the scrolls with the reports on the Essenes given by Philo, Josephus, and Pliny, of which the best is Jos. War II.viii.12-13. The main difference between the authentic writings of this religious group and the description of these historians is that while the first reveal the religious motives and feelings of the sect, the latter mainly tell its structural system to the Hellenistic reader. From this outline its main features, like the eschatology, the holy war, and the roots of the holy life, cannot be recognized.

The relations between the scrolls and the NT writings will emerge within the next few years. This will be a very fruitful task. John the Baptist, e.g., was certainly a kind of Essene, and since Jesus was baptized by John and took over his mission, he too must have been closely related with this group. This can be seen in certain striking features of his life: the fact that he was unmarried, his sharp attitude toward money and the rich, his conflict with the Pharisees and the Sadducees over against the silence of the gospels on the Essenes. Some of his words can be better understood from the writings of Qumran, and in his mission traces of the three eschatological offices of the sect can be seen. It is highly probable that some of his disciples came from the Essenes, more likely from those living outside Qumran. The early Christian community at Jerusalem shows Essene features which were afterward preserved by the Ebionites. The Dositheans at Samaria are probably to be related with the Essenes. Eventually the Karaites in the Middle Ages were influenced by their writings.

*Bibliography.* Texts: E. L. Sukenik, *Megilloth Genusoth*, I (1948); II (1950). M. Burrows, *The Dead Sea Scrolls of St. Mark's Monastery*, I: The Isaiah MS and the Habakkuk Commentary (1950); II: plates and transcription of the Manual of Discipline (1951). E. L. Sukenik, *Osar Hamegilloth Hagenusoth* (1954), contains 1QIs[b], 1QM, 1QH; English trans.: *The Dead Sea Scrolls of the Hebrew University* (1955). D. Barthélemy and J. T. Milik, *Qumran Cave I*, Discoveries in the Judaean Desert, I (1955), contains the fragments of Cave I (text, trans., notes); the series will be continued. N. Avigad and Y. Yadin, *A Genesisapocryphon* (1956).

Monographs: Until 1956 about 1,500 books and articles had appeared which are related to the Dead Sea Scrolls. General surveys with translations of some texts: A. Dupont-Sommer, *Aperçus préliminaires* (1950). G. Molin, *Die Söhne des Lichts* (1952). A. Dupont-Sommer, *Nouveaux aperçus* (1953). M. Burrows, *The Dead Sea Scrolls* (1956). T. H. Gaster, *The Dead Sea Scriptures in English Translation* (1956). M. Burrows, *More Light on the Dead Sea Scrolls* (1958). F. M. Cross, Jr., *The Ancient Library of Qumran and Modern Biblical Studies* (1958). Monographs on single scrolls: K. Elliger, *Studien zum Habakkuk-Kommentar* (1953). Y. Yadin, *Megillath Milḥamaeth bₐne 'or*, etc. (War Scroll; 1955). J. Licht, *Megillath Hahodayoth* (1957). P. Wonberg-Møller, *The Manual of Discipline* (1957).

Special studies: K. Stendahl, *The Scrolls and the NT* (1957). R. de Vaux, "Fouilles de Khirbet Qumran," *RB*, LXIII (1956), 533-77; LXVI (1959), 225-55.　　　O. Betz

**DEAFNESS.** *See* Disease.

*DEATH. The teaching of the Bible on the subject of death assumes various aspects, because beliefs have changed in the course of history.

1. As the normal end of life
2. The opposite of life
3. A force of destruction
4. Death and Yahweh
Bibliography

**1. As the normal end of life.** This view is found in both the ancient and more recent portions of the OT. A human life, arrived at its full maturity, is plucked like a ripe stalk at harvest time (Job 5:26). After a happy old age, man, "full of years," is "gathered to his people" (Gen. 15:15; 28:8; 35:29; Judg. 8:32; I Chr. 23:1; 29:28; II Chr. 24:15; Job 42:17). Arrived at the end of his life, man goes the way of all earthly creatures (Josh. 23:14; I Kings 2:2; Job 30:23).

Viewed in this perspective, what follows death is scarcely important. According to certain texts, it even seems that the end of life was thought to mean the end of all existence (II Sam. 14:14; Job 7:21; Ps. 39:13—H 39:14). It was most commonly believed that the dead continued to exist in Sheol or in the family

sepulchre, but that this was a nondynamic existence, destined to end in a relatively brief period of time. However, certain conditions had to be fulfilled if death were to be thought of as the end of existence: (a) The normal life span must be attained—120 years, according to Gen. 6:3; 70 years, according to Ps. 90:10. (b) The deceased must leave children to perpetuate his name and on whom he perhaps bestows a testament or words of blessing. This, however, does not imply ancestor worship. (c) The dead person must be buried in a sepulchre, for it is necessary to avoid any possibility of his taking revenge and upsetting the equilibrium between the world of the living and that of the dead. The absence of one of these conditions—e.g., when one died in the prime of life (Isa. 38:10), or childless (II Sam. 18:18)—made death a problem which Israelitic faith endeavored to resolve.

**2. The opposite of life.** Since life is characterized by the נפש, it is natural that death should sometimes be represented as the disappearance of this *nephesh* (Gen. 35:18; I Kings 17:21; Jer. 15:9; Jonah 4:3). The "departure" of the *nephesh* must be viewed as a figure of speech, for it does not continue to exist independently of the body, but dies with it (Num. 31:19; Judg. 16:30; Ezek. 13:19). No biblical text authorizes the statement that the "soul" is separated from the body at the moment of death. The רוח, "spirit," which makes man a living being (cf. Gen. 2:7), and which he loses at death, is not, properly speaking, an anthropological reality, but a gift of God which returns to him at the time of death (Eccl. 12:7). The stoppage of breath, the loss of all movement and of all capacity for relations with others, all make death appear to be the opposite of life. Deprived of life and separated from the world of the living, the dead person becomes impure (Num. 9:6; 19:11, 16, 18; 31:19), and contact with him must be avoided. The deceased and all things related to him consequently took on an aspect of mystery. In general, this mystery was shunned, but it was also the source of certain popular beliefs attributing superior power and knowledge to the dead.

**3. A force of destruction.** As faith meditated on the problem of death, its destructive aspect became dominant. A premature death was thought to be a punishment meted out by a hostile power. This was not at first considered to be the power of Yahweh, since he is at various times asked to snatch his followers from the hand, the prison, or the net of death (Pss. 18:6; 116:3). Such images may be reminiscent of a time when the kingdom of the dead had its own divinities, perhaps Sheol or Mot, the latter being clearly associated with death in the Ugaritic texts. In the OT these divinities are reduced to the rank of images (Jer. 9:21—H 9:20; Hos. 13:7), or inferior powers, angels of death (Exod. 12:23; II Sam. 24:16; Job 33:22), or demons (Ps. 91:5 ff).

Never in biblical texts is the power of death exercised without the control of God. If he permits and uses this power, he does so because the sin of man has rendered death inevitable and has given it its "sting" (I Cor. 15:56). The apostle Paul sums this up: "The wages of sin is death" (Rom. 6:23). The Yahwist narrator of Gen. 2–3 attempts to resolve the problem of the relationship of sin and death, and does so in a way which makes it necessary to modify Paul's categorical statement: since man is created of perishable matter, his natural condition is mortality (Gen. 3:19). Israel shares this belief with all the Semitic peoples. It is expressed, e.g., in the declaration of Siduri to Gilgamesh: "When the gods created humanity, they established death for mankind; they kept life in their own hands" (Tablet X,iii,3-4; *ANET* 90). The myth of the tree of life indicates, however, that the boundary between the two domains was not an absolute one. Had man persevered in obedience to God by respecting the divine commands, God would have reserved the right to change man's condition and to grant him immortality as a favor. Man's disobedience irremediably destroyed this possibility, and thenceforth death, which until that time had been virtual, became an actuality for him.

It may therefore be said that the change brought about by sin has less bearing on the nature of man than on the altered perspective of his existence. Prior to his fall, man does not think of death, either because he is unaware of its existence or because he is not affected by it. Afterward, on the contrary, his entire existence is placed under the sign of death. Thus man's labor and woman's childbearing carry with them an odor of death. However, the OT never expresses the idea that the Fall had irremediably corrupted human nature. Sin is not viewed as a fatality hanging over mankind; man remains free and capable of choice. If he chooses disobedience, he takes the way leading to death (Deut. 30:19). On the other hand, the mortal nature of man creates in him a propensity for evil (Pss. 78:39; 103:10; 143:2; Isa. 57: 16), so that death may be called at once a consequence and a cause of sin.

In thus defining the domain of death, one sees that the power of death is further manifested in all lessening of the vital force. The most important example of this is illness, for to be ill is to be in the hold of death and already really in Sheol. The psalms celebrating recovery from illness as a victory over death must be interpreted in a realistic rather than a symbolic sense (Pss. 9:13—H 9:14; 30:3—H 30:4; etc.; Luke 15:24). Illness and other calamities, such as war, are thought to be, like death, a consequence of sin. This concept, however, was shown to be unduly rigid (cf. Job and Jesus). Falling into the power of death does not mean passing beyond the limits of Yahweh's authority; he employs the forces of death to punish those who have voluntarily turned from him. All tendency toward dualism has been overcome. At the most, one might speak of a dualist monism by virtue of which Yahweh dispenses the opposing powers of life and death (Deut. 32:39; I Sam. 2:6; Isa. 45:7).

**4. Death and Yahweh.** In certain texts which apparently reflect the oldest concept of death, existence in the dwelling place of the dead is represented as entirely independent of Yahweh. Sheol is the region where praise of God is impossible (Isa. 38:18), where even the recollection of God has been annihilated (Pss. 6:5—H 6:6; 28:1; 30:9—H 30:10; 88:12; 115: 17), and where one falls into the hands of other powers than Yahweh. Amos already affirms, however, that the power of Yahweh extends to Sheol (Amos 9:2; cf. Ps. 139:7 ff). He controls the forces of death and uses them to serve his holy will (Hos. 13: 14). The entry of Yahweh into the domain of death not only allowed him to dispose of the power of death, but ultimately led to conflict between him and death. Death could not exist as a destructive force beside the living God without raising the question of his omnipotence. Life had to absorb death (cf. II Cor. 5:4).

The descriptions of the realm of the dead and existence there feel the repercussion of this extension of power to Yahweh. The ancient belief in the end of all existence at death or in a miserable afterlife in Sheol gives way to an increased interest in the status of the dead. The belief in the impurity of the dead does not prevent the living from taking pains with sepulchres, as is shown by the great hypogeums cut out of the rock, beginning with the postexilic period. Here the dead are no longer treated as anonymous—their individuality is kept. References are no longer made to the wretchedness of the inhabitants of the realm of the dead, doomed to nourish themselves on dust. Instead, texts refer to the sleep of the dead (Job 14:10-12; Pss. 3:5—H 3:4; 4:8—H 4:9; 13:3—H 13:4; 22:29—H 22:30 [reading ישני for דשני]; 90:5; Isa. 26:19; Jer. 51:39, 57; Dan. 12:2; John 11:11; Acts 7: 60; I Thess. 5:10).

It was not always concluded by analogy that death is a provisional state of being, for certain texts consider the sleep of death to be eternal (Jer. 51:39, 57). At least the idea had begun to develop, and in Dan. 12:2 the text shifts easily from the mention of sleep to that of resurrection. This image at all events proves an attenuation of the horror inspired by death, and it is not forbidden to suppose that the sleep of death may have been considered, like the sleep of dreams, to be the occasion of a more intimate communion with God.

The hope of a lessening of the power of death and even of its disappearance (mention of this is first made in Isa. 25:8), develops toward a resurrection of the dead rather than toward a superhuman or divine power of the dead. The two passages in the OT where the designation אלהים is given to the dead (I Sam. 28:13; Isa. 8:19), do not express an authentically Yahwist belief. Similarly, attributing to the dead superior knowledge or the power to cure illness (Lev. 19:31; 20:6; Deut. 18:11; I Sam. 28:3, 9) is not in line with true Israelitic doctrine, even if this idea was much in favor at certain periods. General opinion held that "a living dog is better than a dead lion" (Eccl. 9:4), and the hope of RESURRECTION had as a corollary the horror inspired by death. The affirmation of the triumph of life over death represents the main line of thought of the OT as well as of the NT, and the resurrection of Jesus Christ is the definitive manifestation of the power of the living God (Mark 12:24 ff). *See also* IMMORTALITY; PEACE IN THE OT.

*Bibliography.* F. Schwally, *Das Leben nach dem Tode nach den Vorstellungen des alten Israel und des Judentums* (1892). R. H. Charles, *A Critical History of the Doctrine of a Future Life in Israel and in Judaism* (1899). A. Lods, *La croyance à la vie future et le culte des morts dans l'antiquité israélite* (1906). A. Bertholet, *Die israelitischen Vorstellungen vom Zustande nach dem Tode* (2nd ed., 1914). G. Quell, *Die Auffassung des Todes in Israel* (1925). E. Ebeling, *Leben und Tod nach den Vorstellungen der Babylonier* (1931). J. Pedersen, *Israel, Its Life and Culture*, vols. I-II (1926); vols. III-IV (1940). P. H. Menoud, *Le sort des trépassés* (1945). E. F. Sutcliffe, *The OT and the Future Life* (1946). C. Barth, *Die Errettung vom Tode in den individuellen Klage- und Dankliedern des AT* (1947). A. R. Johnson, *The Vitality of the Individual in the Thought of Ancient Israel* (1949). O. Schilling, *Der Jenseitsgedanke im AT* (1951). R. Martin-Achard, *De la mort à la résurrection d'après l'AT* (1956), especially the Bibliography.     E. Jacob

**DEATH, SECOND** [ὁ δεύτερος θάνατος]. This expression—limited to Revelation—is defined by John in symbolic terms as the "lake that burns with fire and brimstone" (Rev. 21:8; cf. 20:14). But its clearer definition in John's usage appears from its being set over against the "crown of life" promised to those who suffer the physical death of martyrdom (2:10-11), and further from the suggestion that he who is "holy" or truly sanctified, having shared in the "first resurrection" to newness of life, will not experience it (20:6). *See* Holiness.

Second death is, therefore, the opposite of that life lived in the presence of God which is promised believers in Rev. 21:3-4; 22:3-5. "Death and Hades" experience this second death (20:14), along with those whose names are not "found written in the book of life" (vs. 15). The expression is rabbinic (cf. Jer. Targ., Deut. 33:6; Jer. 51:39) and in Philo (cf. *On Rewards and Punishments* II.419).     J. W. Bowman

**DEATH OF CHRIST.** The central event in the history of redemption.

1. The historicity of the saving event
2. The sources as interpretation and history
3. The facts of Jesus' execution
4. The meaning of his death to himself
5. Interpretations from within Judaism
6. Interpretations from the Resurrection
   *a.* The center of the history of redemption
   *b.* The fulfilment of the OT
   *c.* Expiation for sin
   *d.* A cosmic event
   *e.* Victory over death
   *f.* A call for discipleship in suffering
Bibliography

**1. The historicity of the saving event.** From the very beginning, the unanimous conviction of the Christian church has been that the death of Jesus Christ is the center of the whole history of redemption. The godly Jew awaited, and is still today awaiting, the central event in the history of redemption from the future. On the other hand, the Christian knows that God has definitively spoken in an event of the past, specifically in the death of Jesus, which took place at a definite time and a definite place. A historically verifiable event stands at the beginning of Christianity, not just a "doctrine" for which some confirmation must be sought belatedly in history. According to the NT, the way a person thinks about the death of Jesus of Nazareth determines salvation and distinguishes faith from unbelief. But this faith has also its own history. Only the experience of the resurrected one, the Lord whom God had exalted above all powers and authorities (Phil. 2:9 ff), opened the eyes of the profoundly disillusioned disciples. Without Easter, Jesus' death would be no more than one among many deaths, and would soon have ceased to be discussed. It was the Resurrection which was

the point of departure for real reflection on the meaning of Jesus' death. Therefore, in the NT, Jesus' death and resurrection belong closely together, and we do well not to lose sight of this connection as the presupposition of Christian thought.

**2. The sources as interpretation and history.** This is already true with regard to the sources which report Jesus' death. The detailed presentations of the Synoptic gospels (Mark 14-15; Matt. 26-27; Luke 22-23) and the Gospel of John (chs. 18-19) show quite clearly that the Easter faith participated heavily in the formation of the tradition. The evangelists do not describe situations of the past as historians; rather, they desire to pass on the message of salvation as preachers who themselves have experienced salvation. However, this in no way hinders one from using their reports also as sources for reconstructing the historical event. The death of Jesus is an event within the sphere of verifiable history, and therefore accessible to the observation of historians.

**3. The facts of Jesus' execution.** Jesus died a criminal's death on the cross, the gallows of that time. Even non-Christian sources know about it (Tac. Ann. XV.44; Jos. Antiq. XVIII.iii.3). The Jewish aristocracy bears the main moral responsibility for his end, and the Christians have always made a point of accentuating strongly this guilt of the Jews—this tendency is noticeable in the Synoptic gospels, especially Matthew and Mark, just as it is in Paul (I Thess. 2:14-15), in the Petrine sermons of Acts (2:23; 3:14; 4:10), in the Epistle of Barnabas, etc., on down to the time of the Jewish persecutions in the Middle Ages. Yet the juristic responsibility is borne by the Roman occupation forces: the trial, death sentence, and execution are based on Roman procedure. Jesus was condemned by the Romans as a Zealot, a political agitator. The denunciation before the governor Pontius Pilate (A.D. 26-36) was, of course, made by the highest Jewish authorities, who saw themselves challenged by Jesus' "signs and mighty deeds" (Mark 11:15 ff and parallels; John 11:47 ff). It was this body which first examined the dangerous *mesith*, or "misleader," before he was turned over to the Roman court, in order to establish the accusation, not to carry out the juristic condemnation (so Luke and especially John, who perhaps had at his disposal especially good sources for the passion narrative).

According to Luke 23:2, the Jewish leaders accused him before Pilate of instigating tax evasion (cf. Mark 12:13-17 and parallels). This must have sufficed for the Romans, for it was precisely this which they regarded as characteristic of the Zealot movement. Similarly the titulus, the official explanation placed at the top of the cross (Mark 15:26 and parallels; John 19:19 ff), says nothing other than that the person crucified was a political criminal, a Zealot, like many others executed before and after him (cf. Luke 13:1; Jos. Antiq. XVIII; XX; etc.). However, Jesus was no Zealot. To be sure, he was obliged during his whole ministry to deal with the Zealot movement; indeed, Zealots were among his disciples, as can be deduced from the names: Simon "the Cananaean" means Simon "the Zealot" (cf. Mark 3:18; Luke 6:15); Judas "Iscariot" probably comes from "sicarius," meaning "Zealot" (cf. Acts

21:38); Simon Peter "Bar-Jona" probably means Simon Peter "the Terrorist"; perhaps the two sons of Zebedee were also Zealots. But Jesus' rejection of the Zealots' program is only too clearly attested (Mark 12:17 and parallels; Matt. 11:12; John 10:8 ff). It was precisely he who had occasion again and again to reject the Zealots' messianic ideal for himself as *the* satanic temptation (Matt. 4:9-10; 26:53; Mark 8:33), who was condemned and crucified as a Zealot.

The date of this execution can no longer be established historically with any certainty. The only point of certainty is that it took place on a Friday at the time of Passover. For the date it is better to assume, with the Gospel of John (19:14), the fourteenth of Nisan, the day before the first main feast day of Passover week, rather than the feast day itself. The year of Jesus' death is most likely 33, for in that year the first day of Passover coincided with a sabbath. (But *see* CHRONOLOGY OF THE NT for other opinions.)

**4. The meaning of his death to himself.** Jesus accepted this death quite intentionally. He knew nothing about "life ending in failure." For him, the death he anticipated stood at the center of his sense of vocation. The voice from heaven at the Baptism (Mark 1:11 and parallels = Isa. 42:1) designates the moment when it became clear to him that his task was to accept the office of the *Ebed Jahwe* of Isa. 52-53: As the Suffering Servant (*see* SERVANT OF THE LORD) of God he should expiate by his death the sins of Israel and, in addition, the sins of all men. From now on, he sees his path set out before him: he who calls himself SON OF MAN and thus applies to himself one of the loftiest Jewish honorific titles will have to "suffer." Consequently, when Jesus speaks of his baptism, the idea of suffering always lurks in the background (Mark 10:38; Luke 12:50). His teaching always circles around this point (Mark 8:31 and parallels; 9:31; 10:33-34, 45), although he is not even understood by his disciples (Mark 8:33; Luke 24:31).

Outwardly it was the "turn toward Jerusalem" (Mark 10:32 and parallels) which brought about the decision. It was a decision especially because death, which thereby became certain for Jesus, did not at all come as a friend: he saw in it really the "last enemy" (I Cor. 15:26), which he must fight strenuously (Mark 14:32 ff and parallels; 15:34 = Matt. 27:46; Heb. 5:7). But it happened as a consequence of his vocation, to which he chose to be obedient. He was led by the plan of salvation of the Father, with whom he knew himself to be united as "Son of God" in a unique way. His death was to be the climax to which all God's saving action led. This is the meaning of the Johannine Christ's saying on the cross: "It is finished" (John 19:30).

**5. Interpretations from within Judaism.** For Jesus' disciples the end of the Master meant at first the factual collapse of all hope. The more they saw in him the Messiah of Israel, the more his infamous death must have appeared a *scandalon* to them as Jews (cf. I Cor. 1:18), for the concept of a suffering Messiah is foreign to Jewish thinking. Of course, there was still the possibility of understanding Jesus' death in analogy to the usual fate of the prophet, who is despised and killed (cf. Matt. 13:57; 23:37; I Thess. 2:15). Traces of this interpretation are found in Luke 24:19, and then especially in heretical Jew-

ish Christianity, where Jesus was regarded as the prophet of the end of time. They could also look upon the crucified as one of the many suffering righteous ones of Israel, who in every age are led by God in the path of humiliation, and whose death effects expiation in God's sight (cf. IV Macc. 6:29). Actually there was in the earliest community such an interpretation of the death of Christ: In old traditions he is designated, in view of his path of suffering, the "Righteous One" (Acts 3:14; 7:52; 22:14; I Pet. 3:18), and the strong connection of the passion narrative to the OT psalms portraying the suffering of the righteous one points in the same direction. Finally, the responsible Jewish leaders seem to have feared a third possibility—namely, that Jesus could have been venerated by his followers on the basis of his crucifixion as a martyr to the national cause, a Zealot witnessing in his blood (Matt. 27:64). Yet the reaction of the disciples to the occurrence (Mark 14:50 = Matt. 26:56; Mark 14:66 ff and parallels), their at least partial dispersion into Galilee (Mark 14:28; 16:7), show that they at first stood helpless before the event of Jesus' death. This confirms again the fact that Jesus' position between the fronts did not make it possible for him during his lifetime to eliminate in the circle of his followers (and much less among his opponents and the Romans!) the Zealots' false messianic concepts.

**6. Interpretations from the Resurrection. a. The center of the history of redemption.** Only the appearances of the resurrected one opened the way for a "Christian" interpretation of the death of Jesus. We must again emphasize that reflection developed here along with the occurrence, that it had its point of departure wholly in the experience—not the other way around. Jesus resurrected, living, and clearly leading his community as the exalted Lord, placed his death in a new light when seen in retrospect. God had publicly taken sides with the crucified (cf. Acts 2:24; 3:15; 4:10; 5:31)! Consequently, Jesus' death had to be evaluated as an act in God's history of redemption. Of course, the joy of Easter dominated completely the thinking of the earliest community, but such a statement is to a certain extent one-sided, for in the thinking of the first Christians the Easter faith had its effect precisely with regard to the understanding of Jesus' death. Only in this way is it comprehensible that from the very beginning the Christian community saw the death of Jesus located at the center of the history of redemption. This did not become an emphasis first with Paul. To be sure, Paul presents the first comprehensive orientation of all of theological thought toward the death of Jesus and its saving significance; the "word of the cross" is for him a technical term for Christian preaching as a whole (cf. I Cor. 1:18). Yet the same tendency can already be noted in the early Synoptic tradition. The passion narrative is the oldest formulated portion of the tradition, and the whole composition of the gospels is oriented to the Passion. The Cross is from the very beginning the goal and climax (cf. Mark 3:6; Matt. 1:21); and the "hour" of which John is always talking and toward which the life of Jesus moves (John 2:4; 7:6; 8:20; 12:23; 13:1; 17:1) is the hour of the Cross.

*b. The fulfilment of the OT.* According to Luke

24:25 ff, 44 ff, the resurrected one opened the eyes of his disciples to the significance of his passion by pointing to the OT. In any case, it is certain that the holy scripture of the Old Covenant contributed decisively to the interpretation of Jesus' death in the early Christian community. OT history, which was understood completely as prophetic history (cf. Rom. 15:4; I Cor. 10:6, 11), supplied to a large extent the categories under which one could understand Jesus' death. The insistence that he "must" die is based on the conviction that the ancient promises must have eschatological fulfilment (cf. Matt. 26:31; Luke 22: 37; 24:7, 26-27, 44-45; John 3:14). Such "theology of the early community" does not, to be sure, float in the air. The earthly Jesus had already carried through the appeal to the OT to interpret his death, and the community after Easter could here connect itself directly with his thought. The Gospel of John points explicitly to this connection by speaking of the disciples' "recollection," which opened to them in retrospect the meaning of Jesus' discourses (John 12:16), and which is brought about by the Spirit in them (John 14:26; 15:25-26). We must always take into consideration this double root of the early Christian interpretation of Jesus' death: the OT and the preaching of the earthly Jesus, who himself appealed to the OT. This is true in exemplary fashion with regard to what was doubtless one of the earliest christological explanations, perhaps circulating in Petrine circles, in terms of the "Suffering Servant" (Acts 3:13, 26; 4:25, 30; 8:26 ff). If the early community saw in Jesus' death the fulfilment of the saving action of the OT Servant of God from Isa. 53, as we can assume with certainty, then the community was at the same time taking over Jesus' own interpretation (*see § 4 above*).

**c. Expiation for sin.** Then the community also shared Jesus' view of the decisive significance of this death: He, the Son of man, who dies on the cross in fulfilling the function of the Servant of God, effects vicariously EXPIATION for the sins of men (cf. Mark 10: 45). He effects expiation for sins, since only because of sin is the history of redemption necessary at all. Paul was not the first to introduce the connection of Jesus' death for sin into the theological thinking of primitive Christianity, as is demonstrated by the ancient kerygma of the community quoted in I Cor. 15:3: Jesus Christ died "for our sins in accordance with the scriptures" (cf. Acts 10:43). But precisely in this brief formula the other root of primitive Christian thought becomes visible again: faith in the expiatory death of Jesus for sins has its basis in scripture. In fact, the appeal to OT thinking has profoundly molded this most important aspect in the interpretation of Jesus' death. The term "for" in I Cor. 15:3, which recalls quite strongly the term "for" in Isa. 53, is the key word for the interpretation of Jesus' death as vicarious expiatory suffering, a key word which runs through all of primitive Christian preaching. It occurs already in the primitive Christian Eucharistic liturgy, which is built upon Jesus' last meal ("for you" [I Cor. 11:24; Luke 22:19]; "for many" [Mark 14:24; Matt. 26:28]). Then it occurs especially in Paul (Rom. 4:25; 5:8; 8:34; II Cor. 5:14-15, 21; Gal. 1:4; 2:20; 3:13; Eph. 5:2; I Thess. 5:10; etc.), in the Pastorals (I Tim. 2:6; Tit. 2:14),

the Catholic letters (I Pet. 2:21; 3:18), and the Johannine literature (John 10:11; 11:50 ff; 15:13; I John 2:2; 3:16a; 4:10). But in addition, a quantity of OT and Jewish terms and concepts present themselves, to illuminate anew again and again the interpretation of Jesus' death as an expiatory act for the sins of the world.

"Juristic" terminology in the stricter sense emphasizes with regard to Jesus' death the legal act through which the situation of the sinful creature before God was basically reordered. Here belong the interpretations of Jesus' death as "ransom" (Rom. 3:24-25; I Cor. 6:20; 7:23; I Tim. 2:6; I Pet. 1:18; Rev. 1:5; cf. Mark 10:45), and also the whole complex of concepts forming the Pauline doctrine of JUSTIFICATION, which is rooted in the event of the Cross (Rom. 3:24-25; 4:24-25; 5:9-10; II Cor. 5:21).

Closely related to this is the cultic terminology which describes the legal act of expiation in OT sacrificial concepts. Jesus' death appears as an expiatory sacrifice (Rom. 3:25), a Passover sacrifice (I Cor. 5:7), or in general as a "sacrifice" (Eph. 5:2) for sins. Especially the Letter to the Hebrews makes the sacrificial idea fruitful as an interpretation of Jesus' death. Jesus is here both sacrificer and sacrifice; his sacrifice is valid once for all (Heb. 7:27; 9:12, 25 ff; 10:10 ff).

The idea of the sacrifice offered to expiate sins is also the basis of the picture of the lamb, which is clearly oriented to Isa. 53:7 (cf. Acts 8:32; I Pet. 1: 19). It plays an especially large role in the Johannine literature. In the Gospel of John, Jesus dies in the moment when the Passover lambs are slaughtered in the temple (John 19:14): he himself is the true Passover lamb who bears the sins of the world (John 1:29; 19:36). Also, in Revelation the crucified is mentioned again and again as the Lamb.

OT sacrificial language is also the origin of speaking of Christ's blood, which, like the OT expiatory rites, is poured out for the forgiveness of sins (cf. Acts 20:29; Rom. 3:25; 5:9; Eph. 1:7; 2:13; Col. 1:20; I Pet. 1:2, 19; I John 1:7; Rev. 1:5). The interpretation of Jesus' death as an expiatory death has found here a visible expression which later had a strong influence, especially in the various forms of mystical union with Christ. This usage could build on the fact that, according to the tradition, Jesus himself used the same expression with the cup at the Last Supper in interpreting his death (Mark 14:24: "blood of the covenant," based upon Exod. 24:8). Paul was therefore right in carrying through the consistent anchoring of the Eucharist in the death of Christ (I Cor. 10:16; 11:23 ff), perhaps as a protection against all too excessive and fanatical practices at the primitive Christian Lord's Supper, just as he also united primitive Christian baptism with the Cross (Rom. 6:4 ff), in dependence upon Jesus' own understanding.

**d. A cosmic event.** The interpretation of Jesus' death attained a further dimension in the post-Easter community, which prayed to the exalted Lord (I Cor. 16:22; Rev. 22:20; cf. II Cor. 12:8): this death is also the decisive act of a cosmic event. The Cross signifies victory over the powers hostile to God. Jesus had already taken up very early the struggle with them (cf. Mark 1:12 and parallels; 1:34; etc.), and his "mighty acts"—exorcisms, healings, and raising the dead—were held by the primitive community to be anticipatory signs of his victory on the cross, although according to Gnostic Hellenistic speculation the powers did not recognize him (Ign. Eph. 19.1; cf. I Cor. 2:6 ff). The statement about the victory over the powers, which left its imprint especially through the numerous quotations of Ps. 110 (e.g., I Cor. 15: 25; Heb. 10:13; Acts 2:34; Mark 12:36; Matt. 22:44; Luke 20:42), appears, indeed, to have had a firm place in the confession (Phil. 2:10; I Pet. 3:22; Mark 16:19). In the confessionlike psalm quoted in Phil. 2:6 ff, this victory of Jesus is put in direct causal relation to his death: *"Therefore* [because he humbled himself even unto the death on the cross] God has highly exalted him."

Jesus' death is the turning point also of the whole cosmic process. The passion narrative in the Synoptics suggests this by presenting the whole of nature as affected by Jesus' death (Mark 15:33 and parallels; Matt. 27:51), and Col. 1:20 provides the theological explanation: through the blood of Christ's cross the universe is reconciled with God. Nothing is excepted from the saving effect of Christ's death. According to the common primitive Christian viewpoint, the Cross opens the way for the history of redemption to move from the "one" to the "many," from limited applicability to universality (Mark 10:45 = Matt. 20:28; Mark 14:24 and parallels). Paul provided the most closely reasoned basis for the universality of the Cross. It is revealed to him in view of the universality of sin, under which all have fallen (Rom. 3:6, 19; I Cor. 6:2; 11:32); accordingly Christ died for all (Rom. 8:32; II Cor. 5:14). Limitations which were formerly valid must now fall away: Jews and Gentiles share in redemption (Rom. 11:32; Gal. 3:27; cf. Luke 24:47). Christ is the end of the law, which belongs on the side of sin and death (Rom. 7:5-6; 10:4). The ingenious presentation in Rom. 5:12 ff is here especially full of significance: as in Adam all men stand under God's judgment, so in Christ, the second Adam, all are included in the saving will of God (Rom. 5:15).

*e. Victory over death.* It is especially death which is included among the subjugated powers (cf. Rom. 8: 38). It is a central affirmation of the NT that Christ took away the power of death. His death is generally understood as the victorious struggle against the demonic power of death, which is often personified (cf. Acts 2:24; I Cor. 15:45-46; Rev. 6:8), against the "last enemy" (I Cor. 15:26; Rev. 20:14), whose power, however, is already broken (II Tim. 1:10). The NT knows of no optimistic view of death as a "friend" which frees the soul from the bonds of the body. Such an understanding is excluded by the view of death as the terrible consequence of sin (so already in Judaism; then especially in Paul [Rom. 1:32; 6: 7 ff, 16]; also Jas. 1:15; John 8:24]. Here is the connection, for primitive Christian thinking, between Jesus' expiatory death and his victory over death. If death is the consequence of sin, then expiation for sin is needed to break death's power at the roots. Jesus' entrance into the sphere of sin's curse (II Cor. 5:21; Gal. 3:13-14; Rom. 8:3) was the presupposition of his victory. Once sin is overcome, then death has lost the basis of its power (Rom. 6:7 ff). The Son of man has from now on the keys of death and Hades (Rev. 1:18).

All believers are drawn into Jesus' victory over death; since the triumph of the "first fruits of those who have fallen asleep" (I Cor. 15:20), death has lost its sting (I Cor. 15:55). John can speak in strong words of "eternal life," which is already assured the believers here on earth since Christ's death and resurrection (John 3:36; 5:24; 6:47). Paul likes to use for baptism the figure of "dying and rising with Christ" (Rom. 6:3; Gal. 6:14; Col. 2:20; II Tim. 2:11), to describe the Christian's participation in the central saving event. And also in this context the idea of the first and second Adam plays a role, for Paul uses this idea to anchor his interpretation of death very firmly in the saving occurrence of the old covenant and its fulfilment (I Cor. 15:45 ff).

*f. A call for discipleship in suffering.* The individual Christian who believes in the expiatory death of Jesus Christ sees himself in the NT constantly called upon to "follow" Jesus. This call to discipleship means, first of all, discipleship in suffering. Jesus himself already prepared his disciples for sharing with him the fate of being persecuted and suffering. The meaning of the well-known saying about bearing one's cross (Mark 8:34-35 and parallels; similarly Matt. 10:38; John 12:25-26) seems to have been originally that the disciple is to accept for himself the same fate of death as did the master (Mark 10:38-39; Luke 14:26-27; John 15:20). The early church sometimes made a one-sided principle out of it: only the "martyr" who gives his life for Christ's name (cf. Mark 13:13; Acts 15:26; 21:13) can really count as a disciple of Jesus. The tendency to reserve the concept of "witness" for the witness in one's blood is already noticeable in the NT (Acts 22:20; Rev. 2:13; 12:11). Jesus' death is the prototype and model for the death of his disciples, even down to the details. The martyrdom of Stephen in Acts 6–7 reveals clearly the influence of the passion narrative, and traces of the assimilation of the disciple's suffering to the form of the Lord's suffering are often detected elsewhere (cf. Luke 23:26 with Mark 15:21; further Matt. 10:17 ff; John 15:18 ff; 21:18-19; Acts 21:13; II Cor. 12:7-8).

To be sure, the way in which, e.g., Paul speaks of showing the suffering of Christ in his body (I Cor. 15:31; II Cor. 4:10; Gal. 6:17) suggests that the saying about bearing one's cross has a much broader significance for the Christian: his whole life is discipleship in suffering. The Lukan form of the saying (Luke 9:23), which speaks of bearing one's cross *daily,* is already guided by this idea (cf. further Acts 9:16; I Pet. 4:13; for Paul also I Thess. 1:6). Here is where Christian parenesis begins, for which purposes the suffering and dying Christ is the great example one is to emulate: in humility (Phil. 2:5 ff), selflessness (Rom. 15:3), endurance (Heb. 12:1 ff), patience (I Pet. 2:20 ff), love (John 15:13). Even the exhortations of the Pauline "mysticism of suffering," which play a large role in later asceticism, are fed from the idea of Christ's death: e.g., the call to put to death the flesh (Rom. 8:13), to crucify the old self (Rom. 6: 6; Gal. 5:24; Col. 3:5). In hard times the thought of the Lord's death has again and again been the source of comfort for Christians of all generations: "A disciple is not above his teacher, nor a servant above his master" (Matt. 10:24; cf. Luke 6:40; John 13:16).

On this subject, *see also* CHRIST, CHRISTOLOGY.

**Bibliography.** J. Denney, *The Death of Christ* (1903); V. Taylor, *The Atonement in NT Teaching* (1940); J. Knox, *The Death of Christ* (1957). O. CULLMANN

**DEATH OF JOSEPH.** *See* JOSEPH THE CARPENTER, HISTORY OF.

**DEBIR** dē'bər [דביר, back part(?); דבר, remote village(?)]. Alternately (3 *below*): LO-DEBAR lō dē'bər [לא דבר (II Sam. 17:27; Amos 6:13), לו דבר (II Sam. 9:4-5)]. **1.** A king of Eglon, SW of Jerusalem (Josh. 10:3). He was one of five confederate kings in the Amorite coalition that attempted to halt Joshua's invasion. R. F. JOHNSON

**\* 2.** A Canaanite royal city in the S Judean hill country, in the Negeb (Josh. 10:38; 12:13). Though the topographically satisfactory sites of Zahariyeh (twelve miles S of Hebron), Khirbet Rabud, Khirbet Zanuta, and Khirbet Tarrameh (all in the same vicinity) have been proposed, until suitable archaeological evidence to the contrary appears, the preferred location for Debir is Tell Beit Mirsim, *ca.* eleven miles SW of Hebron. Fig. DEB 22.

Courtesy of the American Schools of Oriental Research

22. Debir (modern Tell Beit Mirsim) from the N

The Canaanite city was sacked by Joshua. At the time it was occupied by the Anakim (Josh. 11:21). It was either initially captured by the Calebites under Joshua or recaptured by them after only a temporary conquest by Joshua's forces (Josh. 15:15-17; Judg. 1:11-15).

In the administrative reorganization of Judah, it became the district capital of the southernmost hill-country district (Josh. 15:49); it was also one of the Levitical cities (Josh. 21:15; I Chr. 6:58—H 6:43). The earlier name for Debir was Kiriath-sepher, "city of the scribe" (Josh. 15:15, 49, where it is incorrectly copied as "Kiriath-sannah" [cf. LXX]; Judg. 1:11-12).

The site of Tell Beit Mirsim was partially excavated in four campaigns by W. F. Albright (1926-32). Like BETH-SHEMESH, Debir was first settled in Early Bronze IV (or IIIB, twenty-third to twenty-first centuries B.C.) and was finally destroyed in 587 B.C. The Middle Bronze I city, set in a sparsely populated countryside, was possibly visited by Abraham as one of the nomadic and seminomadic groups common in this period. During this and the subsequent (Middle Bronze II) period, Egypt dominated the land. The city was destroyed when the Hyksos assumed the rule (during the early stages of which, Jacob and his family may have migrated to Egypt) and when the Hyksos were overthrown. A typical *terre pisée* (beaten earth) wall (built early in the period) protected the prosperous Hyksos city. Well-built houses, metalwork, ivory and bone inlays, and stonework, all of excellent quality, attest to the prosperity resulting from its location on busy trade routes.

This and the following Late Bronze occupation (after a lag of several generations following the destruction of the Hyksos city) were marked by great unrest. The latter city, a poor relation of its prosperous predecessor, was probably the Canaanite royal city captured by Joshua in the late thirteenth century and destroyed in a holocaust so violent that it left ashes three feet thick in some places (cf. Josh. 10:38).

After being almost immediately rebuilt by the Israelites, it came under Philistine influence in the mid-twelfth century and was destroyed by them *ca.* a century later after the Battle of Ebenezer (I Sam. 4). Shortly after his defeat of the Philistines and as a measure against further invasion, David strengthened Debir's fortifications with a typical casemate wall and gateway, as at Beth-shemesh. Shishak destroyed this city in 918 B.C. (I Kings 14:25-28; II Chr. 12:9 ff).

The fortifications were probably not rebuilt until the time of Asa (*ca.* 913-873; cf. I Kings 15:23; II Chr. 14:6-7). The city, a center for a textile dyeing industry (Fig. DYE 39), flourished, reaching the height of its prosperity during the eighth century. It was probably attacked by Sennacherib in 701 B.C. and in the next century suffered two more partial destructions. The city began to decline sharply in the closing decades of the seventh century and was destroyed by Nebuchadnezzar in 587 B.C. in a violent conflagration. It was not rebuilt.

**Bibliography.** W. F. Albright, *The Archaeology of Palestine and the Bible* (1932); *The Excavation of Tell Beit Mirsim, AASOR*, vol. XII (1930-31); vol. XIII (1931-32); vol. XVII (1936-37); vols. XXI-XXII (1941-43); *The Archaeology of Palestine* (1954). K. Galling, "Zur Lokalisierung von Debir," *ZDPV*, 70 (1954), 135-41.

**3.** A place on Judah's N boundary (Josh. 15:7), possibly Togheret ed-Debr, the "pass of Debir," near Tal'at ed-Damm (*see* ADUMMIM) between Jerusalem and Jericho. The Wadi Dabr is the NE boundary of the Buqe'ah (Valley of Achor); the Joshua reference may well refer to this wadi. V. R. GOLD

**4.** A city of Gad, located in the E part of Gilead (Josh. 13:26). Mephibosheth, the lame son of Jonathan, lived there after the royal family fled to Gilead on the defeat of Israel at Mount Gilboa, and was the guest of Machir, the son of Amiel; David recalled him from there and made him his pensioner (II Sam. 9:4-13). Later on, when David himself was a fugitive, the same Machir was one of those who furnished his troops with provisions (II Sam. 17:27). Apparently Debir (Lo-debar) fell into the hands of the Arameans during their wars with Israel and was recovered by Jeroboam II, for Amos has a sarcastic reference to "you who rejoice in Lo-debar [*lô' dhᵉbhār*]" (Amos 6:13), in which the vowels are deliberately altered to read "a thing of nought" (*lô' dhābhār*). The site has not been identified. S. COHEN

**DEBORAH** dĕb'ə rə [דבורה, bee]; KJV Apoc. DEBORA. **1.** Rebekah's nurse and lifelong companion (Gen. 35:8; cf. 24:59).

**2.** One of the early "judges" or charismatic leaders

of ancient Israel. The title "prophetess" (Judg. 4:4) probably refers to this quality of inspiration by the Spirit of God (cf. 6:34; 11:29; 14:6). She was an outstanding person, able to arouse the scattered tribes of Israel to a sense of unity and loyalty to Yahweh in their early struggles against the Canaanites. This sense of religious unity was of crucial importance for the establishment and continuing life of the nation Israel.

The Song of Deborah (Judg. 5:2-31), which celebrates her achievement, is one of the oldest examples of Hebrew literature still in existence. It is the one contemporary source of any length from this period (twelfth century B.C.), and is therefore of unparalleled importance for the study of early Hebrew literature, history, and religion. It is a magnificent poem, containing some of the same forms of poetic parallelism that are found in the ancient Canaanite texts from Ugarit (cf. Judg. 5:3, 7; C. H. Gordon, *Ugaritic Handbook* [1947], Baal and Anat 51, V.94-97; 76, II.26-28). It shows the Hebrews still isolated in the hill country of Palestine, not yet united in any lasting tribal organization, and just now able to challenge Canaanite control of the fertile plains and trade routes (Judg. 5:6, 13-18). Itself a song of victory in war, it brings alive the ancient attitudes toward God, the war God of Israel, coming to fight against his enemies with storm and torrent (vss. 4, 20-21). Judg. 4:2-24 gives a later, prose account of these same events.

**3.** The grandmother of Tobit, and the one who brought him up after the death of his father (Tob. 1:8). She must have instructed the boy with conspicuous success, to judge from Tobit's later piety.

D. HARVEY

**DEBT, DEBTOR.** Rules and customs relative to debts and credit in ancient Palestine are known to us through anecdotes or proverbs recorded in the Bible, and through the legislative sections of the Pentateuch, which aim at codifying usages common among the Semites, or at condemning practices deemed contrary to the spirit of the religion of Yahweh. These condemnations were never fully effective, and they rather testify to the continuance of the abuses they strived to eradicate.

**1. Loans the common cause of debts.** The imposition of a considerable INTEREST added or to be added to the principal to be repaid, which had become common practice among the Semites since the beginning of the second millennium, was discouraged and even condemned by the earliest legislative sections of the Pentateuch, possibly in accordance with the older tribal customs of the nomads; fellow members of the clan ought to be helped free of interest, and without regard for personal profit; hence their debt remains a simple one (Exod. 22:25). Later sections condemned anew the taking of interest (Lev. 25:36-37; Deut. 23:19-20). The lending of silver, chattel, or produce may not give occasion to charging interest, unless the borrower is a non-Israelite.

Violations of the law in these matters, however, were frequent, and the practice of lending to Israelites at rates of interest which we would regard as exorbitant had become a social plague, by making the situation of debtors practically hopeless. Such

violations were vehemently condemned by the prophets. Ezekiel and Nehemiah call their contemporaries back to a strict observance of the law (Ezek. 18:8, 13, 17; 22:12; Neh. 5:6-13), while the author of Proverbs remarks wryly that riches acquired by usury are essentially unstable, and shall not profit their owner in the long run (Prov. 28:8).

The etymology of the common Hebrew word for "interest," נֶשֶׁךְ (*neshek*), from a verb meaning "to bite," seems to imply a manner of imposing the interest in advance, as if the borrower agreed to repay, e.g., sixty shekels, while receiving only forty shekels from the lender. נֶשֶׁךְ is consistently used in Exodus and Deuteronomy, while Leviticus and Ezekiel use תַּרְבִּית or מַרְבִּית (lit. "increase"), whereby the borrower pledged himself to repay the loan integrally, plus the interest as agreed. The Hebrew תַּרְבִּית is generally rendered both in the KJV and the RSV by "increase," while נֶשֶׁךְ is interpreted by the RSV as "interest" and by the KJV as "usury." It should be remembered here that the English term "usury," in the language of early English translators, was not so pejorative as it sounds today. The translators, however, were perfectly aware of the prohibitions formally expressed in the Law and the Prophets, and of the sad fact that moneylenders of all times had been charging interest at abusive rates, so that some medieval theologians had condemned, at least in theory, the practice of lending money for interest. In Babylon a common rate of interest for loans of produce was one third of the loan—i.e., 33 1/3 per cent per annum—whereas the interest on money was only one fifth—i.e., 20 per cent. Neo-Babylonian contracts show that the rate had been subsequently reduced uniformly to one fifth. The documents of Nuzi often fail to specify the rate of interest; some tablets, however, mention an interest rate as high as one half of the loan—i.e., 50 per cent. Interest rates were not expressed on a percentage basis, but by an absolute indication of value, or by a numerical fraction of the capital.

**2. Pledges and sureties.** Lenders and creditors were protected against the failure of debtors to repay by a system of guaranties which had developed spontaneously throughout Western Asia, and which the Israelites adopted in its broad outline, with a few modifications required by the moral ideal of Yahwism. At the time of taking the loan, or of contracting a debt, the borrower or debtor surrendered a piece of movable property into the hands of the creditor or lender (נֹשֶׁא, *nôshê*). The Hebrew language uses the following terms for various kinds of pledges: usually חֲבֹל (*ḥabhôl*) *and* עֲבוֹט (*'abhôṭ*); once עֲבָטִים (*'abhṭîṭ*; Hab. 2:6); also עֵרָבוֹן (*'ērābhôn;* Gen. 38:17-18, 20). In the majority of cases, the PLEDGE is to be considered as an objective token of the debtor's intention to pay off his debt, capital and interest. According to Deut. 24:10-11, the creditor is not permitted to enter the house of the debtor to take the pledge, but he must receive it at the door, before witnesses, from the debtor's hand. Objects indispensable for daily living may not be taken as pledges (Deut. 24:6). Similarly, a cloak or garment temporarily offered as pledge has to be returned before nightfall, probably until a definitive arrangement is agreed upon (Exod. 22:26-27; Deut. 24:12-13).

It is possible and even likely that the חבל or עבוט pledges, which seem to have but a token value, were at first complementary of a more primitive type of contract, of which Yahwistic ethics generally disap-'proved. The debtor pledged to place his son, daughter, or slave at the disposal of the creditor, in case of insolvency. The value of the labor performed by the person thus engaged would be credited against the interest, and perhaps the principal, of the debt. This was tantamount to slavery for debts, and the law strived at reducing the evils of the system by prescribing the periodical liberation of Hebrew slaves or of persons held on account of unsatisfied debts (*see* SLAVERY; SABBATICAL YEAR; JUBILEE, YEAR OF). In spite of the legal restrictions, the entire system of pledges and sureties was recklessly abused by the Israelites. In the time of Nehemiah, some Jews whose lands and vineyards were heavily mortgaged had to give away their sons and daughters as sureties (Neh. 5:2-3).

A borrower or debtor could also have a third party, usually a rich or generous friend, assume responsibility for him and become his SURETY. The book of Proverbs cautions Israelites against the imprudence of standing surety for others, especially strangers (Prov. 6:1; 11:15; 17:18; 20:16; 22:26; 27:13).

**3. Debts and debtors in the NT.** There are in the teachings of Jesus references to debts, pledges, loans, and the like, given for the sake of illustration, and which ought not to be interpreted always as rigorously as paragraphs of law. The parable of the wicked servant (Matt. 18:23-35) mentions the jailing of an insolvent debtor (cf. Matt. 5:25-26; Luke 12: 58-59). This is to be understood against the background of Hellenistic jurisprudence and of Roman law, rather than of the Semitic practice of holding a person as surety. Hellenistic papyri contain several cases of men thrown in jail for debts. In Rome, the creditor could be authorized by the magistrate to seize an insolvent debtor and set him to work or keep him in chains. The idea was to force the debtor to sell out whatever property he might have secretly retained, that he might pay off, or to have the debtor's relatives or friends acquit the debt, or to apply the value of the labor furnished under compulsion against the debt. The practice of jailing an insolvent debtor, however, had been abolished, at least officially, in Roman Egypt, except in the case of debts to the king or the state. Legal expressions for debts, sureties, etc., are used figuratively in the NT, as, e.g., the debt contracted by one who has offended his neighbor and "sinned" against him; hence, in the Lord's Prayer, "debts" (τὰ ὀφειλήματα; Matt. 6:12) are synonymous with "sins" (τὰς ἀμαρτίας; Luke 11:4). The theological statement in Heb. 7:22, that Jesus was made the "surety [ἔγγυος] of a better covenant," ought to be understood against the background of Israelite and Jewish usage (*see* § 2 *above*).

*Bibliography.* Concerning sanctions against defaulting debtors in the Hellenistic and Roman periods, see E. Cuq, *Manuel des Institutions Juridiques des Romains* (1917). A. Deissmann, *Light from the Ancient East* (1927), p. 270. E. Cuq, *Etudes sur le Droit Babylonien* (1929), pp. 255 ff. D. Cross, *Movable Property in the Nuzi Documents* (1937), p. 5. H. M. Weill, "Gage et Cautionnement dans la Bible," *Archives du Droit Oriental*, II (1938). G. A. Barrois, *Manuel d'Archéologie Biblique*, II (1953), 217-21, 212-13 (on slavery for debts), 222-23 (on liberation of pledges). H. Levy, "On Some Old Assyrian Cereal Names," *JAOS*, LXVII (1955), 201-4 (containing information on short-term loans of grain).　　　　　G. A. BARROIS

**DECALOGUE.** *See* TEN COMMANDMENTS.

**DECAPOLIS** dǐ kăp'ə lǐs [Δεκάπολις, ten cities]. A federation of Greek cities in Palestine, originally ten in number, mentioned in the Bible only in the gospels (Matt. 4:25; Mark 5:20; 7:31).

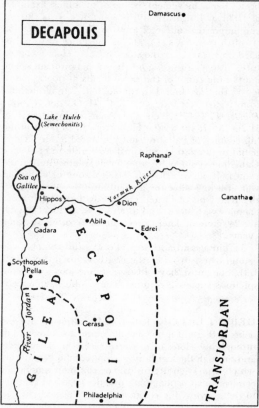

**1. Origin.** After the death of Alexander the Great (323 B.C.) and following his example, his successors established many Greek cities in the Near East. Some were apparently established in Palestine by the veterans of Alexander's army, for two of the cities, Pella and Dion, bear Macedonian names. After Alexander, the Seleucids of Syria and the Ptolemies of Egypt continued to found and rebuild Greek cities in Palestine. Some of these were on the sites of older Semitic cities, but many were new foundations. These were typical of the Greek cities in the East and attracted many Greek-speaking immigrants. They were striking examples and centers of Greek culture and so became strongholds for the pagans against the indigenous Semitic peoples, such as the Jews. Four cities of the Decapolis—Gadara, Scythopolis, Pella, and Abila—were already important in 218 B.C. (Polybius V.70-71; Jos. Antiq. XII.iii.3). These Greek cities formed the heart of the opposition to the Maccabean Revolt and to the later Hasmonean rulers (168-164). The Jews had captured and controlled many of them when the Romans arrived in Palestine.

Jewish independence ended with the appearance of the Roman army led by Pompey (64-63), which brought a new era to Palestine and its Greek cities. In his reorganization Pompey recognized the vigorous part which these Greek cities could play in Rome's plans to stabilize the East. They could provide ready-built fortresses against the various Semitic tribes which constantly threatened any alien rule. At the same time, they would provide centers for the spread of Greco-Roman culture, and so strengthen the Roman position. These cities were filled with people who welcomed the coming of Rome and who could be trusted to further her interests. Pompey's reorganization also severely restricted Jewish rule in Transjordan.

Josephus summarizes this by saying that Pompey removed these cities from Jewish rule and restored them to their own citizens under the province of Syria (Jos. Antiq. XIV.iv.4; War I.vii.7). The importance of this for these cities is indicated by the fact that many of them promptly issued coins which dated a new era with the coming of Pompey. The Greek cities were free, provided they remained loyal to Rome, paid the required taxes, and supplied the needed military service. Since these cities were on the frontier and must provide their own defenses, it was natural that they should band together in a league for mutual protection and profit, a practice permitted elsewhere in the Roman Empire.

The "Decapolis" or "Ten Cities" was the name given to this loose federation which was founded to protect themselves, the trade routes, and the interests of Rome. There is no specific mention of the origin of the league, but the term "Decapolis" does not appear until the first century A.D. The formation of it certainly took place no earlier than the reorganization of Pompey (64-63 B.C.), and possibly not until the death of Herod the Great (4 B.C.), for some of these cities had been transferred to his rule. By the time of Jesus, "Decapolis" was a well-known term and indicated a specific region. Josephus (ca. A.D. 75) also provides evidence that the term was in common use in his day (War III.ix.7).

**2. In the first century A.D.** The earliest list of the Decapolis is that provided by Pliny (ca. 75), who states that most agree on these ten: Scythopolis, Hippo, Gadara, Pella, Philadelphia, Galasa (Gerasa), Dion, Canatha, Damascus, and Raphana (Nat. Hist. V.xvi.74). Josephus gives no list, but he seems to exclude Damascus when he speaks of Scythopolis as the greatest city of the Decapolis (War III.ix.7).

Even though the location of some of these cities is uncertain, there can be little doubt as to the extent of the "region of the Decapolis" (τὰ ὅρια Δεκαπόλεως; Mark 7:31; cf. Pliny Nat. Hist. V.xvi.74: *decapolitana regio*). At its greatest extent the region formed a rough triangle with the W apex at Scythopolis, the N at Damascus, and the S at Philadelphia. The heart of the region was thus the Gilead of the OT. Although a distinct territory, it was not necessarily solid, for Pliny speaks of it as interpenetrated by tetrarchies.

The location of all these indicates their strategic importance, for they were along or near the chief trade routes and military highways which fanned out from Scythopolis eastward toward the desert.

Each of these cities was independent and bound to the others only in a loose federation. Each had its own council, controlled its surrounding territory and villages, and possessed the right of coinage and asylum. They could negotiate relations with one another, yet all were regarded as part of the province of Syria.

In the first century A.D. they were thriving cities; each was equipped with the usual buildings of a Greek city in the Roman Empire: a colonnaded street, a forum, baths, an amphitheater and at least one theater, temples, an aqueduct, and tombs. At a later date some of these cities had Christian basilicas. Each would have its own colorful festivals and games. The high degree of culture is indicated by the literary figures who came from this area, such as Theodorus, Menippus, Meleager, and Philodemus, who were all from Gadara.

**3. Location of sites.** Scythopolis is the Beth-shan of the OT and the modern Beisan. It was the only one of the cities W of the Jordan, but it was in a strategic position to guard the main highway which came down through the Plain of Esdraelon to cross the Jordan at the fords S of the Sea of Galilee. Josephus calls Scythopolis the largest of the Decapolis, perhaps indicating that it was the capital (War III.ix.7). The site was excavated by the University of Pennsylvania in 1921-33.

Across the Jordan and seven miles to the SE is the site of Pella, now known as Khirbet Fahil. The site has not been excavated except for soundings in 1933 and 1958. Gadara was ca. fifteen miles N-NE of Pella. Extensive remains are visible on the site, which is now called Um Qeis. Eight miles farther N and ca. four miles from the Sea of Galilee is the probable site of Hippo or Hippos, also called Susitha, the modern Qal'at el-Husn, which is near Fiq. Hippos guarded the road to Damascus. These three were all in strategic positions and so important that Eusebius could speak of the Decapolis as the territory around them (Jerome *De Situ et Nom. Loc. Hebr.* 199).

Deep in the mountains of Gilead and twenty-one miles SE of Pella was Gerasa.* The extensive ruins of this city, now called Jerash, are the best preserved and the most impressive in all Transjordan. The site has been partially excavated and restored in seasons from 1925 to 1935. Twenty-four miles S of Gerasa was Philadelphia, the modern Amman and the Rab-

23. Theater and forum at Jerash, city of the Decapolis

bah of the OT. Some ruins are visible.* Philadelphia was at the extreme S limit of the Decapolis. Figs. DEC 23; RAB 2.

The location of Dion is uncertain. It may be Tell el-Ash'ari, *ca.* twenty miles NE of Gadara and N of the Yarmuk River. An alternate site is Tell el-Husn, twenty miles SE of Gadara and S of the Yarmuk. Raphana was *ca.* thirty miles NE from Tell el-Husn, a site now called er-Rafeh. This is probably the Raphon of I Macc. 5:37. Canatha, now called Qanawat or Qanat, but in OT times called Kenath (Num. 32:42), was the most easterly city and lay *ca.* thirty miles SE of Raphana and at the edge of the desert. *Ca.* fifty miles to the N of Raphana and beyond the Decapolis proper was the most N member of the league, Damascus. Its inclusion is a witness to its importance as a military and commercial center.

The most important of the later lists is that of the geographer Ptolemy of the second century A.D. He replaces Raphana with Abila, probably Tell Abil, S of the Yarmuk, and adds the following eight cities, most of which lay to the N toward Damascus: Kanata (to be distinguished from Canatha), Kapitolias, Edrei, Bosra, Abila Lysanius, Heliopolis, Hina, and Saana. It was in the second century during the reign of the Antonines (138-93) that the cities of the Decapolis reached their peak.

*Bibliography.* G. A. Smith, *Historical Geography of the Holy Land* (1896), ch. 28: "Greece Over Jordan: The Decapolis"; A. Rowe, *Topography and History of Beth-Shan* (1930); M. A. Rostovtzeff, *Caravan Cities* (1932); F.-M. Abel, *Géographie de la Palestine*, II (1938), 145 ff, 234 ff; C. H. Kraeling, ed., *Gerasa—City of the Decapolis* (1938); R. W. Funk and H. N. Richardson, "The 1958 Sounding at Pella," *BA*, XXI (1958), 82-96.       D. C. PELLETT

**DECISION, VALLEY OF** [עמק החרוץ; κοιλὰς τῆς δίκης]. The name given in the book of JOEL (3:14—H 4:14) to the place where Yahweh's judgment or decision falls upon the heathen nations assembled for the eschatological assault on Jerusalem (cf. Ezek. 38-39; Zeph. 3:8). It is synonymous with the Valley of Jehoshaphat—i.e., "Yahweh judges" (Joel 3:2, 12—H 4:2, 12; *see* JEHOSHAPHAT, VALLEY OF) and has been traditionally identified with the valley of the KIDRON. Some, following Calvin, connect vs. 14 with vs. 13 and translate "valley of threshing" (cf. חרוץ in Isa. 28:27; Amos 1:3).       W. NEIL

**DECK** [קרש] (Ezek. 27:6); KJV BENCHES; in Gen. 6:16 תחתים שנים שלשים is translated "lower, second, and third decks" (KJV "stories"). A platform extending from side to side on a ship, serving as a covering for the space below and as a floor. Decks on early ships were often only fore and aft, because of the necessity of accommodating rowers, but a merchant ship equipped with sails might have a full-length deck.

The meaning of Ezek. 27:6*b* is not clear, one of the doubtful words being קרש. This noun, which occurs in the description of the tabernacle (Exod. 26:15, etc.), seems to mean "board" or "frame," and it is only the nautical context of Ezek. 27:1-9 which supports the meaning "deck" in vs. 6: "deck . . . inlaid with ivory" (*see* INLAY: SHIPS AND SAILING). "Prow" has also been suggested for this word.

Noah's ark had three decks (Gen. 6:16). For a three-decked ship (a warship), see *ANEP* 106.       W. S. McCULLOUGH

**DECREE** [אסר, גזרה, דת, חק, חקק, חקה, מעם; δόγμα]. A public declaration or proclamation, normally set up in writing. In Isa. 10:1 the prophet refers to unjust laws, probably inscribed on stone by command of the Judean king. In later OT books (Daniel, Esther, Ezra) decrees are frequently referred to, no doubt as a result of their widespread use under the Persian Empire.

*See also* LAW IN THE OT; LAW IN THE NT.       W. J. HARRELSON

\***DEDAN** dē'dən [דדן]; DEDANITES —də nīts. An important commercial people which lived in NW Arabia, probably in the neighborhood of Khaibar, el-Ula, and el-Hijr (Medain Salih), not far from Teima, W of which are ruins called Daidan. Their derivation is variously given in the Bible, either as descendants of Raamah son of Cush (Gen. 10:7; I Chr. 1:9) or as the offspring of Jokshan son of Abraham and Keturah (Gen. 25:3; I Chr. 1:32). In both these cases Dedan and Sheba are regarded as brothers. This would indicate a mixed origin, as well as a wide-ranging activity along the length and breadth of the Arabian Peninsula.

The caravans of Dedan are mentioned in the Prophets (Isa. 21:13; Ezek. 38:13); in the former passage they and the caravans of Tema are warned to come to the aid of the fugitives from Kedar, a country N of them. They are reported as supplying Tyre with saddlecloths for riding (Ezek. 27:20; KJV "precious clothes for chariots"). The mention of the "sons of Dedan" in vs. 15 of the same chapter is obviously superfluous, and this should be emended to "Rhodians" (LXX, followed by RSV, "men of Rhodes"). There are also two references to a Dedan in connection with oracles against Edom (Jer. 49:8; Ezek. 25:13). Since it does not appear that Edom ever extended its territory so far to the SE, this was apparently a settlement of Dedanites in that country.       S. COHEN

**DEDICATION, FEAST OF** [חנכה (*ḥanukkah*), dedication, consecration; ὁ ἐγκαινισμός (I Macc. 4:56); ὁ καθαρισμός (II Macc. 10:5)]. A general term for a dedicatory celebration (Num. 7:10, of an offering; II Chr. 7:9, of the altar in Solomon's temple; Neh. 12:27, of the wall of Jerusalem; Ps. 30:1, of the temple); specifically, the feast of rededication of the temple, inaugurated by Judas Maccabeus (I Macc. 4:56; II Macc. 10:5; cf. φῶτα in Jos. War XII.vii.7).

Festive celebrations of dedication in Israel, especially in relation to the temple, probably date back to the era of Solomon (I Kings 8). However, it was the reconsecration of the temple in 165 B.C. by Judas the Maccabee, following its desecration by the Greeks, and particularly the dedication of the new altar (I Macc. 4:53), that occasioned the establishment of the annual Feast of Dedication, commonly known today as Hanukkah (I Macc. 4:59).

The feast lasts eight days, a fact sometimes associated with Hezekiah's purification of the temple (II Chr. 29:17). It is celebrated in winter, beginning on the twenty-fifth of the month Chislev (John 10:22-23). Its proximity to the winter solstice has figured prominently in discussions about its possible pagan origins; but Jewish tradition rather emphatically associates the date with the precise anniversary of the dedication (I Macc. 4:54; II Macc. 10:3; Jos. Antiq. XII.vii.6).

The feast is alternately known as Lights, since the ceremonial lighting of eight candles, an additional one on each day of the feast, has figured prominently in the observance, especially since the destruction of the temple. In the Babylonian Talmud a legend about a very small quantity of temple oil that burned miraculously long, until new oil could be consecrated, serves as a warrant for the practice. In the days of the temple the joyous celebration featured the singing of the Hallel and was in some ways modeled on Booths (II Macc. 1:9; 10:6 ff). Though not a feast prescribed by the law, Hanukkah has been observed without interruption and in very recent times has come to exert a greater religious influence.

**Bibliography.** O. S. Rankin, *The Origins of the Festival of Hanukkah* (1930); S. Zeitlin, "Hanukkah; Origin and Its Significance," *JQR*, 29 (1938-39), 1-31.      J. C. RYLAARSDAM

**DEEP, THE** [תהום; LXX ἄβυσσος, abyss; *alternately* πόντος, sea (Exod. 15:5); κύματα, billows (Exod. 15:8)]. A term which refers chiefly to the primeval ocean or to the waters of the Exodus (*see* WATER). The myth of CREATION is always in the background (Gen. 49:25; Deut. 33:13; Hab. 3:10).

**1. In Mesopotamian literature.** The Hebrew word is related to the Akkadian TIAMAT, the name of the goddess who was the dragon of the deep slain by MARDUK in the creation epic Enuma Éliš (*see* COSMOGONY). This theogony, which was apparently recited at the New Year's Festival at Babylon, began:

> When on high the heaven had not been named,
> Firm ground below had not been called by name,
> Naught but primordial Apsu, their begetter,
> (And) Mummu-Tiamat, she who bore them all
> (*ANET* 60 ff).[1]

Soon a bitter strife arose between Apsu (fresh water), Tiamat (the salt waters), and the gods their descendants. The god Ea managed to overthrow and slay Apsu, whereupon Tiamat spawned a brood of monsters to help her (cf. Job 9:13), gave the tablets of fate to Kingu her lover (cf. Enoch 81:1-3; 103:2; Rev. 5:1-8), and prepared for battle with the gods. They were dismayed, until Marduk, son of Ea, was found willing to fight her. When Tiamat opened her mouth to consume him, Marduk drove in the four winds to distend her belly, and slew her with an arrow. He split the huge body like a shellfish (flatfish?) and used half to create the sky, ordering the stars and moon. As a reward, the other gods gave him the tablets of destiny and built Babylon and the temple for Marduk, Esagila.

**2. In the Ugaritic literature.** The term is used:
*a*) Of El's dwelling place, to which various gods go

> Towards El of the Sources of the Two Floods [*nhrm*]
> In the midst of the headwaters of the Two Oceans [*thmtm*]
> (*ANET* 133; Gordon 51:IV;22, 2 Aqht:VI;48, 49:16,
>    2 Aqht:VI;12, 129:4, p. 166; translations in
>    *ANET* 133, 152, 140, 152, 129, respectively).[1]

*b*) Of the secret love message which Baal sends to Anath:

> Message of Puissant Baal,
> . . . . . . . . .
> Speech of tree and whisper of stone,
> Converse of heaven with earth,
> E'en of the deeps [*thmt*] with the stars
>    (*ANET* 136; Gordon 'nt:III:22,
>       'nt:IV:61).[1]

*c*) Simply of the ocean, beside which El lives, "edge of the sea [*yam*] and . . . edge of the ocean [*thm*]" (Gordon 52:30; translation from T. H. Gaster, *Thespis*, p. 249: "The Poem of Dawn and Sunset," B III).

*d*) Most interestingly in Daniel's prediction of drought:

> Seven years shall Baal fail,
>    Eight the Rider of the Clouds.
> No dew,
>    No rain;
> No welling-up of the deep [*šr'. thmtm*],
>    No sweetness of Baal's voice
>       (*ANET* 153; Gordon 1 Aqht:
>       45; and note the suggested
>       emendation on II Sam. 1:21,
>       which the RSV has adopted).[1]

**3. In the OT.** The word תהום designates:

*a*) Most frequently, the primeval waters of Creation, in which the mythical background has been suppressed, or at least in which it is not prominent (see Gen. 1:2, the basic text). Note especially the use in Job 38:16, 30; Ps. 104:6; Prov. 8:24, 27-28. Less clear are Pss. 33:7; 36:6; 78:15 (in the wider context of the Exodus); Amos 7:4.

*b*) The waters of the Exodus, which God controls for Israel (Exod. 15:5, 8 [note the unusual phrase: "The deeps congealed in the heart of the sea"]; Ps. 106:9; Isa. 63:13).

*c*) The FLOOD, a reversal of Creation (Gen. 7:11; 8:2; Prov. 3:20).

*d*) Sometimes simply deep waters, normally impassable to men and horses (Ps. 135:6); in a good sense, waters which irrigate the land (Deut. 8:7 [note RSV "springs"!]; Ezek. 31:4; cf. 34:18); storms at sea (Ps. 107:26; cf. vs. 24); the deep and the great waters which are to cover the island of Tyre (Ezek. 26:19; cf. 27:34).

*e*) The depths of the earth, apparently without reference to water (Ps. 71:20; cf. 95:4); related is the use in the individual laments of the psalmists (Ps. 42:7; Jonah 2:5; cf. Pss. 69:2, 14-15; 88:6; 130:1; Jonah 2:3 of the waters through which one must pass to arrive at the underworld).

*f*) Survivals of the myth of a primeval struggle between Yahweh and the forces of chaos—though in such passages other terms are preferred, like "Rahab," "Leviathan," and "Dragon," to refer to the sea monster which is subdued (Gen. 49:25; Deut. 33:13: "the deep that couches beneath"; Ps. 77:16; Hab. 3:10: the mountains and the deep are terrified at the approach of God; Job 28:14; neither Sea [ים] nor Deep [תהום] acknowledges the presence of Wisdom; Ps. 148:7: the Dragons [תנינים] and all deeps are exhorted to praise Yahweh; Leviathan makes the deep to boil like a pot [Job 41:31], so that one would

---

[1] J. B. Pritchard, ed., *Ancient Near Eastern Texts* (Princeton University Press; rev. ed., 1955).

[1] J. B. Pritchard, ed., *Ancient Near Eastern Texts* (Princeton University Press; rev. ed., 1955).

think it to be hoary [vs. 32], in the long description of that monster; and finally, much of the myth terminology is used in Isa. 51:9-10:

Was it not thou that didst cut Rahab in pieces,
that didst pierce the dragon?
Was it not thou that didst dry up the sea [יָם, without the article],
the waters of the great deep [מֵי תְהוֹם רַבָּה];
that didst make the depths of the sea [מַעֲמַקִּים] a way for the redeemed to pass over?—

the myth has been placed in the context of the Exodus).

It is likely that the TEMPLE at Jerusalem was related closely to the creation myth, as were similar temples of chief gods of pantheons at the key cities of Eridu and Babylon (*see* BRAZEN SEA). It is well known that the temple on Mount Zion was thought to be the summit and center of the earth. Moreover, the rock on which the temple was founded is related to the Deep. The Mishna (Parah III.3) states that the temple stood over against (מִפְּנֵי) the תְּהוֹם, whereas a Targ. (Ps.-Jon. to Exod. 28:30) says that the temple rock closes the "mouth of the תְּהוֹם." It is possible that the victory of Yahweh over the primeval waters and his subjugation of them under the temple rock at the time of Creation may be referred to in Ps. 29 and elsewhere.

**Bibliography.** H. Gunkel, *Schöpfung und Chaos in Urzeit und Endzeit* (1895). A. J. Wensinck, *The Ocean in the Literature of the Western Semites* (1918). S. H. Hooke, ed., *Myth and Ritual* (1933), pp. 40-67; *The Labyrinth* (1935). T. H. Gaster, *Thespis* (1950), pp. 145-51, 225-56. J. B. Pritchard, ed., *ANET* (2nd ed., 1955), pp. 60-72. S. H. Hooke, ed., *Myth, Ritual and Kingship* (1958). P. Reymond, *L'Eau, sa vie, et sa signification dans l'AT* (1958), pp. 167-98.                J. J. JACKSON

**DEER.** Among the true ruminants (*pecora*) is the deer family (Cervidae), distinguished outwardly by the peculiar horns or antlers, borne only by the males (except in reindeer) and shed annually. The family consists of two subfamilies, the Moschinae and the Cervinae, the latter having no fewer than nineteen subgroups. It is claimed (*see* FAUNA § A2*e*iv) that at least three of these subgroups were known in biblical Palestine—viz., the Red Deer (*cervus elaphus*), the Fallow Deer (*dama*), and the Roe Deer (*capreolus*). It is, however, impossible to determine precisely the meanings of the various Hebrews words in the OT which appear to refer to deer; the OT writers themselves may have been rather casual in their use of such terms. Possibly אַיָּל ("hart") was the general name for any kind of deer, and it may have been applied more particularly to the Red Deer. *See* DOE; FALLOW DEER; FAWN; HART; HIND; ROE; ROEBUCK.
                                    W. S. MCCULLOUGH

**DEFILE** [*Pi'el and Niph'al of* טמא, make unclean, make oneself unclean (Lev. 11:43; Num. 5:3); *of* גאל, pollute (Dan. 1:8); *and of* חלל, *properly* PROFANE, *in* Ezek. 28:7; κοινόω, make COMMON (Mark 7:15, 18); μιαίνω, stain (Jude 1:8); μολύνω, make filthy (Rev. 14:4)]. Literally and precisely, to make ethically or ritually unclean. *See* CLEAN AND UNCLEAN.
                                    L. E. TOOMBS

**DEGREES, SONG OF.** KJV translation of the title of Pss. 120-34, שִׁיר הַמַּעֲלוֹת RSV ASCENTS, SONG OF;

cf. LXX ᾠδὴ τῶν ἀναβαθμῶν). The degrees were understood to be the steps leading from the women's to the men's court in the Second Temple; on these steps the Levites sang these psalms, according to M. Middoth 2.5.                J. HEMPEL

**DEHAVITES** dĭ hā'vīts. KJV translation of דְּהָוֵא in Ezra 4:9. According to this interpretation, the word refers to one of the groups which signed the letter sent by the inhabitants of Samaria to Artaxerxes to protest the rebuilding of Jerusalem. They have been identified with the Daoi (Herodotus I.125), a Persian tribe whose original home was near the Caspian Sea (Strabo XI.7). Probably, however, this verse should be read: "the men of Susa, that is [pointing דְּהָוֵא as *dihû'*], the Elamites" (so RSV, with the LXX). A glossator's identification of the men of Susa was later mispointed, creating a new "tribe."
                                    R. W. CORNEY

**DEKAR.** KJV form of Deker. *See* BEN-DEKER.

**DELAIAH** dĭ lā'yə [דְּלָיָה, דְּלָיָהוּ, Y draws up (*i.e.,* saves)]; KJV DALAIAH də— in I Chr. 3:24; LADAN lā'dən [Λαδαν, Δαλαν] in I Esd. 5:37. 1. A priest under David (I Chr. 24:18).

2. One of Jehoiakim's officers (Jer. 36:12, 25).

3. Head of a family which returned with Zerubbabel (Ezra 2:60; Neh. 7:62; I Esd. 5:37).

4. A descendant of David through Zerubbabel (I Chr. 3:24).

5. Father of a contemporary of Nehemiah (Neh. 6:10).

**Bibliography.** M. Noth, *Die Israelitische Personennamen* (1928), p. 180.                H. H. GUTHRIE, JR.

**DELILAH** dĭ lī'lə [דְּלִילָה; *from* דלל, cf. Arab. *dallatum*, flirt]. A woman of Sorek, probably a Philistine, beloved by Samson (Judg. 16:4-22). When Samson, the hero of the tribe of Dan, repeatedly worsted the Philistines, they offered Delilah a large sum of money to "entice him, and see wherein his great strength" lay (vs. 5). After putting her off three times, Samson finally told Delilah the secret of his strength—his hair, which had never been cut (vs. 7; cf. 13:2-5). She then betrayed him to the Philistines, so that they were able to seize and imprison him.                D. HARVEY

**DELIVERER, THE.** The principal theme of the Bible is God's deliverance of mankind from the power of sin, death, and Satan through his action in Jesus Christ; and this mighty deliverance is foreshadowed in the history of God's people Israel by his deliverance of them from such disasters as Egyptian bondage or Babylonian exile. But the English words "deliverer" and "deliverance" are not very frequent in our English versions of the Bible, the idea of deliverance being more usually expressed by other words, particularly "salvation," "redemption," and their cognates. *See* REDEEM; SALVATION.

The word "deliverer" occurs nine times in the OT. The three occurrences in Judges (3:9, 15; 18:28) refer to human deliverers sent by God, such as the "judges" themselves; the other OT passages (II Sam. 22:2; Pss. 18:2; 40:17; 70:5; 140:7; 144:2) refer to God as Deliverer. The basic idea is that of the *go'el* or "next of kin," whose duty it is to succor his kinsman in distress, to redeem him from slavery, etc. Thus, God raises up deliverers from his people when they suffer oppression or stand in danger (Judg. 3:9, 15); but, far more daringly than this, the Israelites advanced to a conception of God as not merely sending, but actually himself becoming, their Deliverer: "I have seen the affliction of my people . . . ; and I have come down to deliver them out of the hand of the Egyptians" (Exod. 3:7-8). It is in this sense that the psalmist (in the passages cited above) thinks of God as himself the Deliverer of Israel.

In the NT, Jesus is never called "deliverer" or "redeemer." In Acts 7:35, Moses is called "deliverer." The Greek word is λυτρωτής ("ransomer," "redeemer," "liberator"), and this is its only occurrence in the NT. In Rom. 11:26, Paul quotes from Isa. 59:20: "The Deliverer will come from Zion"; the Greek is ὁ ῥυόμενος, as in the LXX.

The idea of deliverance is, of course, central to the proclamation of the NT, but the actual word is found only twice in the English versions of the NT. At Luke 4:18 the KJV has "to preach deliverance to the captives" (ἄφεσις); at Heb. 11:35 the ERV and the ASV have "others were tortured, not accepting their deliverance" (ἀπολύτρωσις); in both cases the RSV has "release." The rarity of the English word is, however, of no particular significance, because by means of a variety of synonyms the Bible teaches that God is a God of deliverance; in the words of the ERV-ASV of Ps. 68:20: "God is unto us a God of deliverances." We acknowledge this truth every time we pray: "Deliver us from evil" (Matt. 6:13).

ALAN RICHARDSON

**DELOS** dē'lŏs [Δῆλος]; KJV DELUS dē'lǝs. A small Greek island in the Aegean Sea, three miles long and one mile wide, sacred to the god Apollo. It was important enough in ancient times to have become the rival of Athens, and during the last two centuries B.C. it became a great harbor and center of trade in the Mediterranean. It became a Roman possession, part of the province of ACHAIA, peopled largely with Roman traders after the Greek inhabitants fled to the mainland *ca.* 167, when the island was punished by Rome. After that, Rome made Delos a free port, and RHODES and CORINTH, the commercial rivals, suffered in consequence.

When SIMON MACCABEUS sent envoys to Rome in 138-137 B.C., the consul Lucius is said to have sent

From Olmstead, *History of the Persian Empire* (The University of Chicago Press)
24. Theater and shore at Delos

From Sukenik, *Ancient Synagogues in Palestine and Greece* (The British Academy, Schweich Lectures, 1930); courtesy of the Hebrew University, Jerusalem, Israel
25. General view of the synagogue at Delos

letters to various states, including Delos, with instructions not to fight against or injure the Jews (I Macc. 15:16-23). Probably there were a great number of Jews settled there. In the next century Delos largely lost its wealth and power when it was captured by Mithridates in his war against Rome. Even after its restoration to Rome the island did not recover its former prosperity; Rome preferred to trade directly with the East for her slaves and other merchandise, and not, as formerly, through Delos.

Figs. DEL 24-25. N. TURNER

**DELUGE.** *See* FLOOD.

**DELUS.** KJV form of DELOS.

**DEMAS** dē'mǝs [Δημᾶς, *a shortened form of* Δημήτριος(?) *or* Δήμαρχος(?) *or* Δημάρατος(?)]. **1.** A coworker of Paul. In Philem. 24, Paul refers to Demas and others as "fellow workers" who send greetings. Demas is also mentioned in Col. 4:14 as sending greetings. In II Tim. 4:10 Timothy is asked to come to Paul because Demas, "in love with this present world," has deserted him and gone to Thessalonica. Demas has been identified by some with Demetrius of III John 12.

*Bibliography.* J. Chapman, *JTS*, V (1904), 357-68, 517-34.
B. H. THROCKMORTON, JR.

**2.** Alternate name of DYSMAS.

**DEMETRIUS** dǐ mē'trǐ ǝs [Δημήτριος; דמיטרום]. **1.** Demetrius Poliorcetes (died 283), son of Antigonus. He was defeated by Ptolemy I at Gaza in 312 B.C.

*Bibliography.* R. H. Pfeiffer, *History of NT Times* (1949), pp. 8, 129.

**2.** Demetrius I, Soter, Syrian king *ca.* 162-151 B.C. When Seleucus IV succeeded to the Syrian throne of his brother Antiochus III, the Great, his son Demetrius I was sent to Rome as a hostage (in place of Antiochus IV). Seleucus was assassinated, and Antiochus IV, Epiphanes, became the ruler. Nevertheless, Demetrius was not released. Learning of the death of Antiochus IV, Demetrius asked for his freedom, but the Roman Senate refused. He then escaped, with the aid of Polybius, in the early summer of 162 B.C. (Polybius 31). He had learned that the people were not favorable toward Lysias, Antiochus' general. Demetrius proclaimed himself king of Syria and killed Antiochus V, Eupator, the young son of Antiochus Epiphanes, and also the general Lysias, in the late summer (I Macc. 7:1-4). Alcimus, the incumbent high priest, accused Judas Maccabeus before Demetrius, who thereupon sent Bacchides with armed expeditions to take revenge upon the Judeans.

Judas Maccabeus then made a treaty with Rome, and Demetrius was warned about the atrocities he perpetrated on the Jews. A second time Demetrius sent General Nicanor to exterminate the people, but on the thirteenth day of Adar (152 B.C.) Nicanor's army was routed (I Macc. 7:26 ff). When Demetrius heard that Nicanor had fallen, he again sent Bacchides and Alcimus the high priest to rout the Jews. In this battle Judas Maccabeus fell (9:1 ff).

When Alexander Balas was battling Demetrius, the latter sent a letter to Jonathan (the Hasmonean) seeking peace with him and giving him authority. But Alexander Balas, hearing of this, appointed Jonathan high priest. Demetrius was distressed in this anticipation and wrote to Jonathan, asking for continued friendship, freeing the people from poll and crown taxes. He promised them many concessions, to obey their own laws, granting them immunity on the holidays. He even suggested giving Ptolemais (Acra) to the sanctuary of Jerusalem as a gift—but this was in the hands of Alexander Balas. He also declared that the citadel in Jerusalem and three districts from Samaria be given over to the high priest and that the temple be regarded as an asylum. But Jonathan did not trust him; he rather favored Alexander Balas. The latter fought with Demetrius and finally prevailed over him. Demetrius' horse fell in a swamp, and there Demetrius was killed in 151 B.C. (I Macc. 10:50; Jos. Antiq. XIII.iii.4).

*Bibliography.* R. H. Pfeiffer, *History of NT Times* (1949), pp. 16 ff; S. Tedesche and S. Zeitlin, *The First Book of Maccabees* (1950), pp. 173-77, 261.

**3.** Demetrius II, Nicator (146-139 B.C.), son of Demetrius I. He came from Crete to Syria, and Alexander Balas was disturbed. Demetrius appointed Apollonius as governor of Syria to subject Judea, and the latter provoked Jonathan to battle with him. But the Judeans—Jonathan and Simon—defeated him. Meanwhile Alexander Balas had become the son-in-law of Ptolemy Philometor VI of Egypt. The latter discovered that his son-in-law plotted against him, and, accordingly, he sent envoys to King Demetrius asking for a pact and promising him that he would reign over his father's kingdom. Demetrius II made an alliance with Ptolemy and received Cleopatra as wife. In 147-146 B.C., Demetrius became king of Syria (I Macc. 11 ff).

Hearing of Jonathan's siege of Jerusalem, Demetrius II asked him to meet him at Ptolemais and confirmed upon him the high priesthood. Jonathan did not lift the siege; however, instead of punishing him, Demetrius II conferred upon him the title "friend of the king." In a letter Demetrius II reaffirmed the privileges granted by his father, Demetrius I, and exempted from dues all Jews who sent sacrifices to Jerusalem.

Seeing that the land was at peace, Demetrius released his soldiers, except the mercenaries, but the people turned against him. (Justin says they had contempt because of his slothfulness. Livy speaks of Demetrius' cruelty.) Seeing the helpless situation of Demetrius II, Jonathan asked that he remove the Syrian garrison in Jerusalem. Demetrius agreed and asked for Jewish troops to help fight Trypho of Syria.

Thus it came about that the Jews aided Demetrius II in Syria. But Demetrius II again proved false; he did not keep his promises and became estranged from Jonathan. Demetrius sent an army against Jonathan, but Jonathan became master of the entire country, including Damascus. Meanwhile, Trypho, by ensnaring Jonathan, killed him. Thereafter Trypho, knowing of Demetrius' cruelty, proclaimed, as his guardian, the infant son of Alexander Balas, Antiochus VI, as king.

While Trypho and Demetrius were battling, Simon the Hasmonean appealed to Demetrius II to make peace and recognize Judea as an independent state. Demetrius sent a letter confirming independence. Later Demetrius marched to Media to persuade them to help him make war against Trypho. There he was captured, exhibited as a warning, but later kindly treated by King Arsaces of Persia (Mithradates I), founder of the Persian army; and he married his sister.

While Demetrius II was in captivity in Persia, the Romans did not recognize Trypho. They also delayed recognition of Antiochus VI, brother of Demetrius, as king of Syria, thus bringing confusion into the Seleucid Dynasty.

*Bibliography.* E. Schürer, *History of the Jewish People in the Time of Jesus Christ* (1891), div. 1, vol. I, pp. 244 ff. R. H. Pfeiffer, *History of NT Times* (1949), pp. 17 ff.

**4.** Demetrius III, Eucerus, son of Antiochus Grypos. He came to the aid of the Pharisees against Alexander Janneus (88 B.C.). The Pharisees turned from him later, however, out of sentiment, to aid their own Jewish king. Some scholars see a historic allusion to him in the Dead Sea Scroll commentary on Nahum, referring to him as "[Deme]trius, the Greek king who attempted to enter Jerusalem at the advice of 'those who seek flattery.'" The first part of the name is missing.

*Bibliography.* Jos. Antiq. XIII.xiii.5. For Nahum text, see J. M. Allegro, *JBL*, LXXV (1956), 90.

**5.** An Alexandrian Jewish historian who deals with biblical chronology, seeking to show the antiquity of Israel. Josephus regards him as a pagan. Only fragments of his work remain, quoted by Josephus.

*Bibliography.* R. H. Pfeiffer, *History of NT Times* (1949), p. 200.

**6.** Demetrius of Phalerum. He was head of the library at Alexandria, according to the Letter of Aristeas. He induced Ptolemy II to obtain the translation of the Bible for the museum.

*Bibliography.* R. H. Pfeiffer, *History of NT Times* (1949), p. 224.                                        S. B. HOENIG

**7.** A Christian leader who enjoyed the full confidence of John the Elder and was recommended by him in III John 12.

**8.** A silversmith at Ephesus who provoked a riot

against Paul on the ground that his Christian preaching was interfering with the sale of silver shrines of Artemis, the patron goddess of the city (Acts 19:24, 38). Any attempts to show that this Demetrius and 7 *above* are the same person, or to equate them with DEMAS, are based purely on conjecture.

F. W. GINGRICH

\*DEMON, DEMONOLOGY. In considering the question of demonology in the Bible, it must be borne in mind at the outset that the modern definition of a demon as a devil, or malign spirit, is the result only of a long development. As used by ancient writers, the word often means something far different; while, on the other hand, many of the figures of ancient belief that are today blanketed by this general designation actually bore quite distinctive names and were of a quite different character.

In the original sense, a demon may be defined broadly as an anonymous god—i.e., as a personification of one or another of those vaguer, less identifiable powers and influences that were believed to operate alongside the major deities and to condition particular circumstances and experiences. In Homer, e.g., "demon" (δαίμων) and "god" (θεός) are virtually interchangeable (*see bibliography* § 3); while the Iranian term *daeva*, which came to be appropriated to evil spirits, meant properly "spirit" in general. Such demons can be beneficent as well as harmful; indeed, where they are the latter, Homer often characterizes them expressly as noxious or bad (e.g., *Odyssey* V.396; X.64; XXIV.129); while the Babylonians and Assyrians speak similarly of both good and evil "demons" (*šēdu damqu* and *šēdu limnu; see bibliography* § 4).

To preserve the essential distinction between the original and the later meanings of the term, the Greek spelling, *daimon,* will herein be used for the original meaning.

A. In the OT
  1. Daimonism
    *a.* Daimon
    *b.* Spirit
  2. Demoniacal possession
  3. "Demons" as a generic term
  4. Specific demons
    *a.* Lilith
    *b.* Resheph
    *c.* The midday demon
    *d.* The vampire
    *e.* The "faery arrow"
    *f.* The "terror in the night"
    *g.* Catastrophe (*Débher*)
    *h.* Qeṭeb
    *i.* The seven evil spirits
    *j.* The "king of terrors"
    *k.* Azazel
  5. The habitat of demons
  6. Aversion of demons
B. In the Apoc. and the Pseudep.
C. In the NT
  1. Pagan deities as demons
  2. Demons as noxious spirits
  3. Expulsion of demons
  4. Names of demons
Bibliography

**A. *IN THE OT.* 1. Daimonism. *a. Daimon.*** The Hebrew equivalent of "demon" (*daimon*) in the original sense is simply אל or אלהים (*'elōhîm*), commonly rendered "god." Thus, when an inspired man is termed "a man of *'elōhîm* (e.g., Deut. 33:1; I Sam. 2:27; 9:6; I Kings 13:1; 17:18; II Kings 4:7; Ps. 90:1), the meaning is virtually the same as when a Greek says that a sudden flash of insight or the recognition of an omen, or the like, is due to a θεός (god) or a *daimon* (e.g., *Odyssey* IX.339; XV.172; XIX.10, 138). The Hebrew turn of expression is, in fact, paralleled exactly in Hittite, where "man of the gods" (*siunan antuhsas*) means something like "seer," and where a verb formed from the noun "god" (viz., *siuniyant-*) means "inspire" (*see bibliography* § 5; and cf. Greek ἔνθεος). Similarly, when Rachel declares, at the birth of Naphtali, that she has been wrestling with her sister Leah "with the wrestlings of *'elōhîm*" (נפתולי אלהים; Gen. 30:8), what she means is that she has been struggling with her as if possessed by a daimon. And when Balaam makes his ability to prophesy dependent on an encounter with an *'elōhîm* (Num. 22:38; 23:3 [LXX, Samar.], 4), what he envisages is likewise possession by such a being (*see bibliography* § 6). By the same token, the use, in the Mari and Amarna texts and in other documents of the second millennium B.C., of the plural *ilāni,* "gods," as an alternative to the singular *ilu,* "god," reflects, *au fond,* the primitive notion that "the divine" may be conceived as a congress of daimons ("they," "the powers that be") no less than as a single cosmic entity.

***b. Spirit.*** The power that is thus represented as a personal being can be represented also as an impersonal "influence," or spirit; for this reason daimons and spirits usually exist side by side in the primitive mind as alternative expressions of the same thing. In the OT, however—standing, as it does, at a considerable distance from the primitive—a certain fusion of the two concepts has already been effected, the spirit (רוח) being always regarded as itself emanating from a daimon (אלהים). Thus if, in one idiom, the impulse to prophesy is attributed to encounter with an *'elōhîm,* or daimon (Num. 23:4), in another it is ascribed to the spirit of such a daimon, which besets, or alights upon (צלח) an individual (Num. 24:2; I Sam. 10:10; 19:23). Similarly, sickness or indisposition, which in one idiom is described as "seizure" (אחז) by a daimon (II Sam. 1:9), is said in another to be produced by an evil "spirit of a daimon" (רוח אלהים רעה), sent by Yahweh (I Sam. 16:15-16, 23). Again, guidance through danger, which, in one idiom, is portrayed as the work of a personal angel—i.e., a daimon (Exod. 23:23; 32:23)—is envisaged in another as that of a spirit (Isa. 63:14; cf. Ps. 143:10). And a "gifted" man, such as would be described by Homer as "daimonic" (δαιμόνιος), is a man "filled with the spirit of an *'elōhîm*" (cf. Exod. 31:3; 35:31).

It must be recognized, however, that the word "spirit" is used in two senses. On the one hand stands the notion of spirit as identical with breath. Since the breath escapes from the body at death, the primitive mind concludes that it is but the physical manifestation of something that can exist independently of it and that simply takes up temporary lodging within it as its vital principle and the determinant of its personality. This in turn breeds the notion of "unembodied personalities," which spirits, as alternatives to daimons, really are.

On the other hand, however, the word "spirit" also carries the meaning of "wind"; and the notion of spirits that operate on human affairs arises also from the analogy of winds that blow where they list and that can waft either good or evil toward men. The idea is well illustrated by our own phrase "the winds of fortune," but it is attested specifically in the ancient Near East by the Akkadian expressions "good wind" (*šarku ṭabu*) and "bad wind" (*šarku limnu*) in the sense respectively of "blessing" and "misfortune" (*see bibliography* § 7), and by the widespread oriental belief that diseases are borne by the winds (*see bibliography* § 8).

With the development of monotheism—i.e., when the idea of a single cosmic deity supersedes that of a congress of controlling powers—daimons and spirits tend to become subordinated to that central figure and regarded as his ministers or "angels" (envoys); or else they coalesce into a single "holy spirit" which emanates from him, represents the totality of his ergative powers, and serves to diffuse his personality throughout the world of his creation.

**2. Demoniacal possession.** From the standpoint of religious psychology, daimonism represents an externalization of human experiences. Feelings and sensations, moods and impulses, even physical conditions, which might otherwise be described as obtaining autonomously *within* a man, are portrayed, on this basis, as outer forces working *upon* him. Aspiration becomes inspiration; ecstasy, rapture (i.e., a state of being "seized"); insight, revelation. Emotion becomes, so to speak, *im*motion; that which is *pro*jected out of the self, that which is *in*jected into it; the flight of imagination, a flight inward, not outward, an invasion rather than an escape. In the language of daimonism, therefore, all such experiences are represented as visitations—i.e., as actions of an external power, rather than as internal psychic states. In this idiom, e.g., an ecstatic is not a man who leaps (lit., "stands") outside his normalcy, but one upon whom a spirit has leapt (צלח; e.g., Judg. 14:6; I Sam. 10:6; 11:6). Terror is not something that issues out of a man's inner self, but something by which that inner self is seized or gripped (אחז; e.g., Exod. 15:14; Job 21:6; Ps. 48:7; Isa. 33:14). Excitement is not a spontaneous psychic spasm, but a blow from an external spirit (פעם; Judg. 13:25; Ps. 77:5). Disease is not an organic disorder but is due to the bearing down of a daimonic hand (יד יהוה; Exod. 9:3; cf. Sumerian ŠU DINGIR.RA; Akkadian *qât ili*, in the sense of "demonic assault"), or again to "seizure" (II Sam. 1:9; cf. also Talmud Shab. 151*b;* Yom. 83*a*, 84*a;* Akkadian demon *Aḫḫazu*).

A particularly arresting illustration of this concept is afforded by the description, in Isa. 53:4, of the diseased and disfigured "suffering servant" as "one struck by an *'elōhîm* [מכה אלהים; RSV 'smitten by God'] and afflicted." The expression finds a perfect parallel in Hittite, where the term *siuniyahh-*, formed from the noun *siunas*, "god," means "to be visited with sickness"; and likewise in the Arabic *majnun* (lit., "jinn-struck"), in the sense of "demented." Indeed, when we ourselves speak of a man as stricken by disease or as awe-struck or love-struck, we are

employing, albeit unconsciously, the essential language of daimonism; the daimon is the assumed striker.

Basically, of course, this distinction between the objective and the subjective approaches to experience amounts only to looking at the same thing from opposite ends of the mental telescope. It is a formal, rather than a substantive, distinction; and the primitive mind is, indeed, by no means unable to turn the telescope the other way around. Accordingly, there is often a perceptible undercurrent of ambiguity in speaking of spirits, and, with the progressive refinement of religious thought and psychological insight, these tend more and more to be transformed from outright external agents to mere personifications of inward psychic states. In other words, men begin to speak of the troubled spirit rather than of the spirit that troubles. This ambiguity, or rather ambivalence of expression, is especially evident in the Bible, where it is not always absolutely clear whether the spirit is envisaged as that which operates or that which is operated upon.

**3. "Demons" as a generic term.** In the LXX and the Vulg., and hence in our English versions, the term "demons" (δαιμόνια, *daemonia, daemones*) is used to render the Hebrew words שדים (Deut. 32:17; Ps. 106:37) and שעירים (Lev. 17:7; II Chr. 11:15 [Vulg.; but LXX μάταια]), which denote objects of pagan worship. In all cases, these are mentioned as being actually cultivated by recalcitrant Israelites. It is probable, therefore, that to the translators the term δαιμόνια ("demons") meant in such contexts more than merely "heathen deities," and was intended to convey at the same time the opprobrious nuance of "bogeys." The Hebrew words, however, possess a specific rather than a generic sense.

*a*) שד, though it became in postbiblical Hebrew a common term for "malign spirit," is simply the Akkadian *šêdu,* "protective (or adverse) daimon," usually represented as a winged bull or colossus.

*b*) שעירים means properly "hairy ones" and refers to a particular class of genies or sprites, analogous to the hirsute demons with which Arabic popular fancy peoples desert places and ruins (*see bibliography* § 9)—a notion which finds a further parallel in the Teutonic *scrat* (*see bibliography* § 9*a*).

(The ancient versions see a further reference to these demonic beings in Isa. 13:21; 34:14, where they are said to gambol in desolate cities; while KJV-RSV even go so far as there to render "satyrs." Since, however, the word is conjoined with "ostriches," "wild beasts" and "hyenas" [if also with LILITH], it is at least equally probable that the prophet was using it in the normal sense of "wild goats" or "he-goats," as rendered by some translators.)

**4. Specific demons.** Concerning demons in the modern sense—viz., as malign spiritual beings—two fundamental considerations must first be mentioned:

*a*) Demons often survive as figures of speech (e.g., "gremlins") long after they have ceased to be figures of belief. Accordingly, the mention of a demon's name in a scriptural text is no automatic testimony to living belief in him.

*b*) Although demons are not in themselves personifications of evils, but only of the forces supposed to cause them, they tend often to be named for those evils (e.g., the Mesopotamian *Ṭiû,* "Headache"), and this renders it difficult to determine in particular contexts whether a word is being used as a common noun or as the name of a corresponding demon. In such an expression, e.g., as "Cramp has seized me" (אחזני השבץ; II Sam. 1:9; RSV "Anguish has seized me"), it is a delicate matter to decide whether "cramp" is to be understood physically or as the name of a demon, albeit attenuated to a mere figure of speech.

A number of specific demons known from other ancient Near Eastern sources or identifiable from parallels in other cultures are, indeed, mentioned in the OT. All the references to them occur, however, in poetic passages, and it is therefore open to question whether they are really anything more than mere figures of speech—traditional *façons de parler.*

*a. Lilith* (לילית; LXX ὀνοκένταυρος; Vulg. *Lamia;* "the night hag"; Isa. 34:14). Lilith is the Akkadian *lilītu,* female counterpart of a type of demon called *lilû.* In Mesopotamian texts she appears primarily as the *succuba,* who tempts men in sexual dreams, and she is quite distinct from the child-stealing hag, who is known as Lamashtu. As early, however, as the eighth century B.C.—as attested by a Canaanite magical plaque from Arslan Tash in the Plain of Seruj—the two tended to be confused in the popular mind; and Lilith became, as in later Jewish folklore, an analogue of the classical Lamia, Empousa, and Gello, and of such figures of European belief as Frau Holle, Berchta, and the like (*see bibliography* § 10). She is depicted by Isaiah as haunting desolate places in company with such unclean birds as the kite, pelican, and owl, and with such ghoulish beasts as wildcats and jackals. The association with winged creatures finds a parallel in the widespread identification of the child-stealing beldam with the screech owl (Latin *strix;* cf. Ovid *Fasti* VI.131-36). In the Arslan Tash Inscription she is styled "the flying one" (עפתא), and in later Jewish folklore is known also as Broxa, which is the Portuguese *broxa,* "nightjar," and as P-ṭ-r-ô-t-â (פטרותא), which is the Greek πτερωτή, "winged." Similarly, her association with ghoulish beasts is well illustrated by the fact that on the aforementioned plaque from Arslan Tash she is, indeed, portrayed also as a wolf swallowing a child, while in Akkadian texts the analogous Lamashtu is called "she-wolf" (*barbarat*), and in ancient Greece the child-stealing witch was sometimes known as Mormolukeion—i.e., "Bogey-*wolf*" (Aristophanes *Thesmophoriazusae* 417; Plato *Phaedo* 77E).

The name derives from the Sumerian *lil,* "wind" (cf. "spirit"), and has no connection with ליל, "night," as was formerly supposed.

*b. Resheph* (רשף; Deut. 32:24; Pss. 76:3—H 76:4; 78:48; Song of S. 8:6; Hab. 3:5). Resheph (Rašāp[?]) was the Canaanite god of plague and pestilence, and is attested in native documents from Mari, Ugarit, Zenjirli, Karatepe, Cyprus, and Carthage from *ca.* 1800 B.C. until 350 B.C., and in Egyptian sources dating back to the Late Middle Kingdom. In the Ugaritic Poem of K-r-t (A i, 18-19), a violent death is described as "being ingathered by Rašap" (*yitsp Ršp*); while in a description of one of his campaigns, Amen-hotep II boasts that he "strode across the stream with the fury of a Rašap" (*ANET* 245b). The god is associated both on Egyptian stele (*ANEP*

473) and in the Ugaritic texts (*RŠ* 1929, i.7; iii.6; Krt B, ii.6) with the war-goddess 'Anat, and in late Phoenician-Greek bilingual inscriptions from Cyprus is equated with Apollo, doubtless in the latter's role as a plague-god (cf. *Iliad* I.43-54).

In Hab. 3:5 Resheph is paired with *Débher,* "Catastrophe" (*see* § A4g *below*), as an attendant upon Yahweh when the latter takes to the warpath. The picture is based on the ancient notion that major gods are escorted by two divine bodyguards. Homer, e.g., describes both Arês and Phoibos as being flanked by the demons Deimos, "Dread," and Phobos, "Fear" (*Iliad* IV.440; XV.119); while in the Babylonian story of the Flood (Gilgamesh 11.100), Adad is similarly attended by Šullat and Ḥaniš (*see bibliography* § 11). Analogous also are the pair Tras ("tremor") and Strakh ("terror") of modern Bohemian folklore (*see bibliography* § 12).

The name Resheph seems sometimes to be used by metonymy in the sense of "searing flame." In Ps. 78:48, Yahweh is said to have delivered the livestock of the Egyptians to hail and their cattle to "the Resephs" (LXX τῷ πυρί; Vulg. *igni;* cf. Egyptian *ršpw*); and in Song of S. 8:6 the flames of love are described as "fiery Reshephs" (Vulg. *lampades*). By similar metonymy, whizzing arrows are pictured in Ps. 76:3—H 76:4 as "Reshephs of the bow"—i.e., virtually, "demon shafts." This is perhaps illustrated by the Egyptian expression *ḥpš bn ršf* ("spear, son of Resheph"), denoting a lance (G. Michaelidis, *ASAE* 47 [1947], 47-73).

Lastly, in Job 5:7 occurs the statement that man is born to trouble, "and the sons of Resheph fly aloft" (ובני רשף יגביהו עוף). This is commonly rendered: "as the sparks fly upward," but the rendering distorts the true sense. What the poet is really saying, in the language of a traditional proverb, is that man is beset with trouble from all quarters; not only does it seem to spring from the very dust and sprout from the very soil (vs. 6: כי לא יצא מעפר און [cf. Amarna *kî lâ*] ומאדמה לא[=כילא] יצמח עמל, but over his head the demonic coterie of Resheph seems ever to be hovering. The reference is to the fact that plague-gods are often represented as birds of carrion. Nergal, the Mesopotamian counterpart of Resheph, e.g., is portrayed with a vulture's head. (It is such a concept that the LXX evidently had in mind when they rendered "sons of Resheph" as "fledglings of the vulture" [νεοσσοὶ γυπός]—an interpretation adopted substantially by Aq., Symm., Vulg., Syr., and Targ. The same notion also underlies the translation of Resheph [רשף] by "birds," which is adopted by LXX, Vulg., and Targ. Jon. in Deut. 32:24.)

The name Resheph is best explained by the Akkadian *rašbu* and *rašubbu,* "frightful," an epithet applied to several gods, including·(significantly) Girra, the god of fire and pestilence (Maqlu, II.109; III. 182). It is believed that the word meant originally "glowing," or perhaps "flickering" (*see bibliography* § 13), and this would readily account for the use of the name as a synonym for "fire."

The versions represent variant traditions concerning the interpretation of the term, adhering in some cases to the association of Resheph with winged creatures, in others with fire, and in yet others resorting to mere paraphrase. Especially curious is the LXX rendering of Hab. 3:5: ויצא רשף לרגליו ("and Resheph went forth at his feet") as: "and he will go forth with his feet in fetters" (καὶ ἐξελεύσετοι ἐν πεδίλοις οἱ πόδες αὐτοῦ). This, it may be suggested, is due to fanciful combination of the word with the verbal root represented by Arabic *rasāfa,* "to walk with hobbled feet."

Besides these clear cases there are several passages of the OT which may likewise contain references to demons but where the possibility can less certainly be eliminated that the relevant terms are not simply common nouns, without personification. Such more "ambiguous" demons are the following:

*c. The midday demon* (קטב ישוד צהרים; LXX δαιμόνιον μεσήμβρινον [reading וישד צהרים]; Vulg. *daemonium meridianum;* "the destruction that wastes at noonday"; Ps. 91:6). This is the demon responsible for the overpowering noonday heat, which can cause sunstroke or dizzy spells. Such a demon was recognized also in ancient Greece, where it was popularly identified with Pan (Theocritus I.15) or with Artemis-Hecate (Lucian *Philopseudês* 22). It is likewise recognized in modern Greece, in Italy, among Slavonic peoples, in Teutonic folklore, and in many other parts of the world. *See bibliography* § 14.

*d. The vampire* (עלוקה; Prov. 30:15). The Hebrew original of Prov. 30:15 speaks of a creature who has two (LXX; Syr. three) greedy and insatiable daughters. The cognate Arabic, Aramaic, and Syriac words mean "leech, limpet" (from עלק, "cling"), and this rendering is adopted by the LXX (βδέλλη), the Vulg. (*Sanguisugae*), and the English versions. In Arabic, however, the word *'Aulaq* also bears the specific meaning of "vampire, ghoul"; and the reference to the two (or three) greedy daughters enhances the probability that there is here an allusion to such a demon.

*e. The "faery arrow"* (חץ; Job 6:4; 34:6; Ps. 91:5). Throughout antiquity, disease and misfortune were attributed to the loosing of demonic shafts. In the *Iliad* (I.43-52), Apollo inflicts plague by shooting his darts. In Vedic lore, the arrow of Jara, "Old Age," kills the hero Krishna. In the Eddas and English folklore, a sick person is described as "elf-shot"; and in Germany, sudden pain ("stitch") in the side is known as *Hexenschuss,* or "witches' shot" (*see bibliography* § 15). In a Phoenician inscription from Kition, Cyprus (341 B.C.), the plague-god Resheph is styled "Resheph of the arrow" (רשף חץ), being probably assimilated to the "far-darting" Apollo (ἐκήβολος) of the Greeks (*see bibliography* § 16), doubtless in the latter's role of plague-god. It is therefore eminently probable that the "arrow that flies by day," mentioned in Ps. 91:5, is the name of a demon, or at least alludes to a form of demonic assault.

*f. The "terror in the night."* In Ps. 91:5, "terror of the night" (פחד לילה; LXX φόβος νυκτερινός; Vulg. *timor nocturnus*) is conjoined with the "arrow that flies by day" and the "pestilence that stalks in darkness," and may therefore be regarded, like them, as a specific demon, analogous to the Akkadian *muttalik muši,* "night-stalker."

In Song of S. 3:8, men who escort a bridegroom to his wedding are said to go armed against "alarms by night" (מפחד בלילות; LXX ἀπὸ θάμβους ἐν νυξίν; Vulg. *propter timores nocturnos*). If this is not to be understood in a purely general sense, it may com-

port with the fairly universal custom of regarding the escorts of bride and groom as a bodyguard against hovering demons. Often, in fact, they shoot arrows, fire shots, or crack whips to keep the fell spirits at bay (*see bibliography* § 17). In this case, the allusion might be to a kind of kobold or hobgoblin.

*g. Catastrophe* (דבר, *Débher*). In accordance with what has been said above (§ A4*b*) about the belief that divine attendants accompany major gods on their expeditions, it is probable that when Habakkuk speaks (3:5) of *Débher's* marching along with Resheph at the side of Yahweh, he is not using the word as a common noun but in a personified sense, as the name of a demon. Similarly, when *Débher* that "stalks in darkness" is associated, in Ps. 91:5-6, with the "faery arrow" and the midday demon, it is probable that it is again personified.

The name *Débher* derives from a root meaning properly "cast prone" (cf. Pss. 18:48; 47:4; cf. also Akkadian *duppuru,* "thrust forward"), and is thus an approximate parallel to Greek καταστροφή, "catastrophe." (The conventional rendering, "pestilence," is inaccurate.)

*h. Qeteb* (קטב). This demon is conjoined in Deut. 32:24 (LXX ὀπισθότων) with Resheph; while in both Ps. 91:6 (LXX σύμπτωμα); Hos. 13:14 (LXX κέντρον) the word stands parallel, as a common noun, to *débher,* "catastrophe." The name derives from the root קטב (cognate, קטף), "cut off," and thus finds an interesting parallel in that of Namtar—from Sumerian *tar,* "cut"—the Mesopotamian demon of plague and henchman of Nergal.

In Isa. 28:2 the champion (or, with LXX, the wrath) of Yahweh is likened to a "storm of hail, a *qeteb*-like [RSV 'destroying'] tempest," whence it may perhaps be concluded that the demon was regarded primarily as a personification of the searing stormwind (*see bibliography* § 18).

(In both Deut. 32:24; Hos. 13:14, the Vulg. renders *morsus,* "bite," perhaps identifying the word with Aramaic קטם.)

*i. The seven evil spirits.* In the great commination of Deut. 28–29, the Israelites are warned (28:22) that if they disobey the commandments of Yahweh, he will smite them with "consumption, and with fever, inflammation, and fiery heat, and with drought, and with blasting, and with mildew; they shall pursue you until you perish." The fact that seven disasters are here enumerated, and that they are represented as pursuing the recalcitrants, strongly suggests an allusion—if only by way of literary figure—to the familiar seven demons of plague and pestilence mentioned ubiquitously in Mesopotamian literature and regarded expressly as the agents of Irra, god of disease. These demons, it may be added, survive in modern Syriac magical texts (*see bibliography* § 19).

*j. The "king of terrors"* (מלך בלהות). In Job 18:14 it is said of the wicked:

> He is torn from the tent in which he trusted,
> and is brought to the king of terrors.

(The Hebrew of the second line of this quotation is: ותצעדהו למלך בלהות. The LXX, reading ותצערהו, renders: σχοίη δε αὐτὸν ἀνάγκη αἰτίᾳ βασιλικῇ; the Vulg., reading בלות, renders: *et calcet super eum, quasi rex, interitus.*) Here the words "king of terrors" are best understood as a folkloristic allusion to the demonic king of the nether world. This may be pertinently illustrated by the fact that Nergal, the lord of that realm in Babylonian mythology, is indeed styled "King of the Terrible Place" (*Lugal-ḫus-ki-a*), and the realm itself "the terrible house" (*eš ḫuluḥ; see bibliography* § 20). Comparable also is the description of Pluto (Dis) as *rex tremendus* in Vergil *Georgica* IV.469. By this interpretation, it may be added, the real point of the verse becomes clear; the word rendered "is brought" (lit., "Thou mayest as well bring him") properly refers to solemn and ceremonious procession (cf. II Sam. 6:13; cf. especially Jer. 10:5); hence, what is implied is that the wicked man, hoping ever for social advancement, finds himself in the end indeed "presented at court"—but at the court of Hades!

*k. Azazel.* In Lev. 16:8, 10, 26, the scapegoat dispatched on the Day of Atonement is said to be consigned "to עֲזָאזֵל." Most modern commentators, and a few medieval ones (e.g., Menahem ibn Saruk) take this to be the name of a demon inhabiting the desert. This interpretation, however, is open to question. On the whole subject, *see* AZAZEL.

**5. The habitat of demons.** Demons inhabit waste places and ruins. One of their favorite haunts is the desert (Lev. 16:10; Isa. 13:21; 33:14; *see bibliography*). The idea recurs in Mesopotamian sources (e.g., Utukkê Limnûti Tablets, III.29, 36), and likewise in pre-Islamic Arabic folklore. In the Ugaritic texts, demonic animals appointed by El to lure Baal to his doom are born in the desert (Ras Shamra 75, i.20-32), and in Iranian belief, the evil spirits (*daevas*) are sometimes said to haunt the wild regions of Gilan and Mazanderan (*Vendidad* VIII.31-32). Similarly, in the NT (Matt. 12:43; Luke 4:1-2), Satan tempts Jesus in the wilderness; and the basic notion is, in fact, fairly universal (*see bibliography* § 21). The idea is rooted, of course, in the peril, eeriness, and unpredictability of life in the wilderness—a situation which, in terms of daimonism, makes it the natural abode of the powers that harass mankind. But there is also another factor: in ancient Semitic folklore, desert and sea were regarded as symbols of primordial chaos (*see bibliography* § 22). Accordingly, since daimons necessarily existed before the present cosmos was organized, desert and sea were commonly regarded as their natural habitat.

In accordance with this widespread belief, it has been suggested (*see bibliography* § 23) that in Job 5:23:

You shall be in league with the stones of the field,
 and the beasts of the field shall be at peace with you,

the Hebrew words for "stones of the field"—viz., אַבְנֵי הַשָּׂדֶה—should be emended to the very similar אַדְנֵי הַשָּׂדֶה, *"lords* of the field," in reference to the demonic spirits of the wild.

**6. Aversion of demons.** Certain of the cultic usages of the Hebrews seem to go back to primitive measures for averting demons. Thus, the bells on the robe of the high priest, the tinkling of which prevented his death when he entered the holy of holies (Exod. 28:35), have been plausibly explained as a relic of the world-wide practice of forefending evil spirits by means of noise, especially the ringing of bells (*see bibliography* § 24). Analogous would be the blowing of the ram's horn at the beginning of the month and on sacred occasions (*see bibliography* § 25).

The fumigation performed by the high priest on the Day of Atonement (Lev. 16:12-13) was probably also, in origin, an apotropaic device to expel demons at the beginning of the agricultural year; for this is the standard procedure in many parts of the world (*see bibliography* § 26). Note especially that it is by such means that the demon Asmodeus is exorcised in the book of Tobit (6:7).

To the same order, too, belongs the practice of smearing doorpost and lintel with sacrificial blood at the beginning of the barley harvest in spring (Exod. 12:7). To be sure, the practice was rationalized by the Israelites (or by the codifiers of their law) on historical lines, but even in this later rationalization it was still remembered that the primary purpose was to avert the entry of the demon of plague into the home (vs. 13). The sacrificial blood was, in all probability, a token of the commensal bond which united god and community and the display of which therefore served to guarantee his protection and scare away hostile spirits. The usage has extensive parallels among modern Bedouin tribes, as also among the Druzes and Nosairis and among the Kurds living near Ain Kalife. It likewise forms part of the statutory New Year rites in Madagascar (*see bibliography* § 27).

Again, the practice of wearing a blue cord on the hem of one's garment (Num. 15:38), though reinterpreted in the Israelitic legislation, was, in all likelihood, originally an apotropaic device against demons; for blue is credited with this power in many parts of the world. In the Hittite-Hurrian story of Kessi (*KUB* XVII.1; XXXIII.121), that hero's mother gives him blue wool to carry as an amulet on a hunting expedition (III.25). Similarly, in some parts of Germany, the lock of the door is bound with blue threads after the birth of a child, to prevent the entry of evil spirits. *See bibliography* § 28.

Lastly, the commandment to bind the words of God upon the hand, and to let them be as "frontlets" (טוֹטָפוֹת) between the eyes, and to place them also on the doorposts (מְזוּזוֹת) of houses and on gates (Deut. 6:8; 11:19), doubtless alludes—if only figuratively (cf. Exod. 13:16; Prov. 7:3)—to the widespread custom of wearing amuletic fillets (cf. Aramaic טוֹטַפְתָּא, "bracelet") and of affixing inscriptions against demons at the entrances of houses (see Driver, ICC, on Deut. 6:8), The LXX, conscious of this reference, significantly renders טוֹטָפוֹת ("frontlets") by φυλακτήρια—i.e., amulets.

**B. *IN THE APOC. AND THE PSEUDEP.*** During the postexilic and intertestamental periods, the conception of demons, as of angels (*see* ANGEL), was greatly influenced by the infiltration of Iranian ideas. The principal effect of this was to turn the daimons into devils—i.e., to transform them from anonymous gods into distinctive forces of evil, whose function was not only to inflict misfortune and disaster but also deliberately to seduce mankind from an ordered and profitable mode of life. In classic Mazdean doctrine, the world, though ultimately subject to the supreme god, Ahura-Mazda, is in actual fact a battleground between the adherents of the Good Mind and those of his rival, the Spirit of Perversity and Deception; and for all practical purposes, demons (*daevas*) are the spiritual legions and ministers of the latter. They are said, in fact, to be the offspring of the Evil Mind (Yasna 30.5; 32.3) and to be in compact with the archfiend, Angra Mainyu (30.6).

Popular Judaism adopted this picture by thinking of daimons as a distinct order of malign spirits, subject to SATAN, or BELIAL, and destined ultimately to be overthrown by Yahweh and his partisans as a prelude to the "renewal of the world," or the new creation. The idea is articulated most clearly in the Testaments of the Twelve Patriarchs (Test. Asher 1:9; 6:2; Test. Benj. 5:2; Test. Dan 1:6-7; Test. Iss. 4:4; Test. Judah 13:3; 14:2; Test. Levi 19:1; Test. Naph. 2:6; 3:1; Test. Reuben 4:7; Test. Simeon 5:3; Test. Zeb. 9:8) and in the Dead Sea Scrolls. A passage in the Manual of Discipline (III.22-24), e.g., states explicitly that all mortal plagues and tribulations stem from the Spirit of Perversity (רוח העול=the Iranian Druj), and that the "spirits in his lot" (רוחי גורלו=the Iranian daevas) are bent ever on causing the sons of light and righteousness (בני אור and בני צדק=the Iranian ashavanō) to stumble (cf. also 1QS IV.12-13). In similar vein, the book of Jubilees speaks (10:1-14; 11:1-5; 19:28) of the power of Mastemah, the genius of hostility, and likewise (1:20) of the archfiend Beliar (i.e., Belial), who dominates men and seeks ever to "obstruct" them. Elsewhere—e.g., in the Dead Sea Hymns (fragments IV.6; XLV.3)—these fell beings are designated "satans"—i.e., obstructors (שטן), or "corruptors" (משחית); and in the War of the Sons of Light and the Sons of Darkness their final discomfiture, along with that of their overlord and of their earthly confederates (=the Iranian dregvanots), is luridly described.

This popular conception had, however, to face competition at the hands of the "orthodox" tradition, which saw in even such qualified dualism a challenge to the monotheistic supremacy of Yahweh. Orthodoxy, for its part, felt obliged to furnish an alternative explanation of the ills to which flesh and spirit are heirs; and this it did by means of two variant theories. The one theory substituted for the distinct and rival hosts of Satan (or Belial) a special order of "angels of destruction" (מלאכי חבלה), who were themselves the emissaries of Yahweh, appointed by him to execute condign punishment on sinners and heathen. They were known also as "agents of vengeance," and were identified with the controlling genii of adverse natural phenomena. Ecclus. 39:28-31 depicts them, e.g., as the agents of fire, hail, famine, and death (or plague; cf. Aramaic מותנא), and, according to the Genizah Hebrew and the Syriac versions, as stored by God in promptuaries "against the time when they are needed." So, too, in Test. Levi 3:2, fire, snow, and ice are described as "spirits of retribution, for vengeance upon men."

The other theory, presented most fully in Enoch, turned the devils into apostatic angels, ministers of Yahweh who had rebelled against him, descended to earth, and wrought mischief among men (cf. Gen. 6:1-4; Ezek. 28:13-17) and who, by reason at once of their disobedience and of the pollution which they had encountered, had disqualified themselves from restoration to the courts of heaven. Their ultimate fate, it was said, would be destruction in fire.

Moreover, in order more closely to align the concept with traditional, "normative" teaching, the ringleader of the demons was identified explicitly with

an OT character. The favorite candidates for this role were: (a) SATAN, "the Obstructor," already familiar from the book of Job and the prophecies of Zechariah, and a neat Jewish substitute for the Iranian Druj; (b) Mastemah (משטמה), a personification of the Hebrew term for "hostility, obstruction," employed in Hos. 9:7; (c) BELIAL, a word which occurs frequently in OT in the sense of "worthless"; and (d) AZAZEL (variously transmogrified), the desert demon—as the name was interpreted—of the Atonement ritual (Lev. 16:8, 10, 23).

In the book of Tobit (3:8, 17), a specific demon named Asmodeus is named as a kind of male counterpart of the succuba. This name recurs in the Babylonian Talmud (Pes. 110a) and in later Jewish literature, but it is uncertain whether it is simply a concoction from the Hebrew sh-m-d, "destroy, blight," and thus a mere variant of the demonic name Shamedon, which appears in Palestinian midrashim, or whether it represents an Iranian *Aeshma daeva—i.e., the well-known Iranian demon Aeshma.

**C. IN THE NT.** The NT conception of demons is, in general, identical with that which obtains in the apocryphal and pseudepigraphic literature, the Dead Sea Scrolls, and the earlier strata of the Talmud. The existence of demons, as agents of all manner of ills, is taken for granted. They continue to be regarded as the ministers of Satan or Belial (also called BEELZEBUL [Matt. 10:25; 12:24, 27; Mark 3:22; Luke 11:15, 18-19]), and they are destined, as in Enoch, to discomfiture in a final conflict with the forces of righteousness, and thereafter to punishment in eternal fire. There is, however, an important advance on earlier ideas concerning man's relations with them. As in Iranian teaching and in the Dead Sea Scrolls, the faithful, it is held, belong necessarily to the "children of light" and are thus part of the army of God, supported by him and his angels against the princes of darkness. But they are armed also by the special redemptive power communicated to his apostles by the incarnate God. The authority of the Godhead, with which he was himself invested when he walked among them as the Son of man, is transmitted by grace to those diffusers of his message; and the unclean spirits must needs obey it, once it is invoked against them. Moreover, the subjection of men to demons is itself merely the result of their own refusal to accept such redemption and of their own obstinate disobedience of God's law.

The term δαιμόνια ("demons"), it should be added, is employed in the NT in all the various senses discussed above.

**1. Pagan deities as demons.** In a few passages (Acts 17:18; I Cor. 10:20; Rev. 9:20), δαιμόνια means simply "pagan deities." A particularly interesting example of this usage occurs in I Cor. 10:20, where the faithful are admonished that they who partake of the Lord's table cannot also partake of the "table of demons." That the word here means "pagan deities," rather than "devils," is shown clearly by the fact that the expression is simply an extension in a general sense of the prophet Isaiah's more specific allusion (65:11) to apostates who "forsake the LORD" and "set a table for Gad" (RSV "Fortune"), the Canaanite god of fortune. The word "Gad," it may be added, is actually rendered δαιμόνιον by the LXX.

Nevertheless, the question may be raised—even if it cannot be answered—whether in such contexts δαιμόνια is merely a pejorative term ("bogeys") or indeed implies—as the church tended subsequently to interpret it—a distinct order of suprahuman beings, opposed to the rule of God, but courted and cultivated by the heathen.

**2. Demons as noxious spirits.** More commonly, the term δαιμόνια is used to denote "unclean spirits" (πνεύματα ἀκάθαρτα; cf. Luke 8:29; Acts 5:16; 8:7; etc.)—analogous to the Talmudic "spirit of catalepsy" (רוח צרדה; Pes. 111b), "spirit of delirium" (רוח חזזית; J.T. Yom. 45b), or "spirit of melancholy" (רוח קרדיקוס [καρδιακός]; J.T. Giṭ. 48c)—which "enter into" a man (Luke 8:30; cf. Jos. War VIII.vi.3), "trouble" (ὀχλεῖν; Acts 5:16) or "overtake" him (καταλαμβάνειν; Mark 9:18), or which a man "possesses" (ἔχειν; Luke 4:33), and which produce in him disorders either physical (Matt. 4:24; 8:16, 28; 9:32; 12:22; Mark 9:18; Luke 11:14; 13:11) or psychic (Matt. 11:18; Luke 4:33; John 10:19-21). No very clear distinction is drawn between the "demoniac" (δαιμονιζόμενος) and the diseased, though it is perhaps significant that in some passages (Matt. 4:24; Mark 1:32; Acts 5:16; 8:7; 10:38) the former is, indeed, specified *in addition to* the latter. (In Matt. 4:24; 17:15, an epileptic is described as "moon-struck, lunatic" [σεληνιαζόμενος], but this harks back to ancient notions concerning the physical influence of the moon, and, though usually so classified, does not really belong within the category of demonology.)

**3. Expulsion of demons.** Demons are expelled primarily by invoking against them the superior name of God (Matt. 7:22). This, of course, is standard practice everywhere and is rooted in the notion that the name is not simply a verbal appellation but an integral part of the personality, and hence of the power and "virtue," of him who bears it (*see bibliography* § 29). It is particularly well illustrated in our field by the Jewish popular practice of beginning magical incantations against demons with the words: "I conjure you by the Name" (אשביע עליך בשם) and of wearing amulets inscribed therewith. The idea is anticipated in Ps. 118:12, where the loyal Israelite "mows down" his enemies by the name of Yahweh (בשם יהוה כי אמילם), and in Ps. 20:7—H 20:6, where he is said, on going into battle, to employ that name as a figurative banner—(ובשם אלהינו נדגול)—a passage misread and misinterpreted in both LXX and RSV!). Moreover, the words of the priestly benediction (Num. 6:27): "They [shall] put my name upon the people of Israel, and I will bless them," were anciently interpreted—as they still are by the Samaritans (*see bibliography* § 30)—as referring to its amuletic properties.

On the other hand, it should be noted—though the fact may be purely accidental—that the verb "exorcise" (ἐξορκίζειν)—i.e., "expel by conjuration"—is itself nowhere employed in the NT to describe Jesus' casting out of demons; and the corresponding noun (ἐξορκισταί) is applied only in an opprobrious sense to certain itinerant shamans who attempted to do so by invoking his name (Acts 19:13).

**4. Names of demons.** The only names of demons mentioned in the NT are those of the "prince of the devils" himself—viz., SATAN; BELIAL; BEELZEBUL. The Destroyer (ὁ ὀλοθρευτής), to whom allusion is

made in I Cor. 10:10, is an avenging angel, not a malign spirit. The name is an exact rendering of the המשחית of II Sam. 24:16 ("the angel who was working destruction"), the corresponding verb שחת being commonly so translated by the LXX. Similarly, APOLLYON or ABADDON, the prince of the abyss (Rev. 8:11), is an angel, not a demon; the distinction is that an angel is an agent of, not a rebel against, the power of God.

*Bibliography.* 1. General: H. Duhm, *Die bösen Geister des ATs* (1903). J. A. Montgomery, *Aramaic Incantation Texts from Nippur* (1903). R. C. Thompson, *Semitic Magic* (1908). J. Tamborino, *De antiquorum daemonismo* (1908-9). G. A. Barton, "The Origin of the Names of Angels and Demons in the Extra-canonical Apocalyptic Literature to 100 A.D.," *JBL*, XXXI (1912), 156-67. I. Scheftelowitz, *Altpalästinensischer Bauernglaube* (1925). T. Canaan, *Dämonenglaube im Lande der Bibel* (1929). H. Kaupel, *Die Dämonen im AT* (1930). W. Bold, *Die antidämonischen Abwehrmächte in der Theologie des Spätjudentums* (1938). J. Trachtenberg, *Jewish Magic and Superstition* (1939). F. Heitmüller, *Engel und Dämonen: eine Bibelstudie* (1948). E. Langton, *Essentials of Demonology* (1949). T. H. Gaster, *The Holy and the Profane* (1955).

2. Concerning particular demons: W. O. E. Oesterley, "The Demonology of the OT Illustrated by Ps. 91," *Exp.* (1907), pp. 132-51. S. Landersdorfer, "Das daemonium meridianum," *BZ*, XVIII (1929), 294-300. B. Challois, "Les démons de midi," *RHR*, CXV (1937), 142-73; CXVI (1938), 54-63. A. Caquot, "Sur quelques démons de l'AT," *Semitica*, VI (1956), 53-68 (on Resheph, Qeṭeb, and Debher).

3. On Homer's use of δαίμων and θεός: M. Nilsson, *ARW*, XXII (1924), 363 ff; E. R. Dodds, *The Greeks and the Irrational* (reprinted 1957), pp. 11-13.

4. On good and evil demons in Babylonian religion: J. Morgenstern, *The Doctrine of Sin in the Babylonian Religion* (1905), p. 23.

5. On the Hittite use of "god" and "inspire": H. Ehelolf, *ZA*, N.F. IX (1936), 180.

6. On the OT idea of *'elōhîm* as daimon: K. Beth, *ZAW*, XXXVI (1916), 128-86. P. Kleinert, *Baudissin Festschrift* (1918), pp. 261-84. H. Kruse, *Verbum Domini*, XXVII (1949), 278-86.

7. On the Akkadian idea of "good wind" and "bad wind": S. Langdon, *The Epic of Creation* (1923), on VII.15.

8. On the widespread oriental belief that diseases are borne by the winds: R. Corso, *Rivista di Antropologia*, XXII (1917-18), 80. I. Zoller, *Rivista di Antropologia*, XXVII (1926), 9-10. T. Fish, *Iraq*, VI (1939), 184.

9. On the Arabic hirsute demons: W. R. Smith, *The Religion of the Semites* (2nd ed., 1894), p. 120. J. Wellhausen, *Reste des arabischen Heidentums* (2nd ed., 1897), p. 139.

9a. On the Teutonic *scrat:* J. Grimm, *Teutonic Mythology* (trans. F. Stallybrass; 1883), pp. 478-79.

10. On Lilith analogies: T. H. Gaster, *Orientalia*, XI (1942), 41-79.

11. On Šullat and Ḥaniš: I. J. Gelb, *Archiv Orientální*, XVIII (1950), 189-98.

12. On Tras and Strakh: J. Grimm, *Teutonic Mythology* (trans. F. Stallybrass; 1883), p. 801.

13. On the meaning of the word "Resheph": P. Jensen, *KUB*, VI/i, 570. S. Langdon, *JRAS* (1921), p. 573.

14. On the midday demon in the literature of various peoples: K. Schwenk, *Die Mythologie der Slawen* (1853), p. 319 (Slavonic). B. Schmidt, *Das Volksleben der Neugriechen* (1871), pp. 94-96 (Greek). K. Haberland, *Zeitschrift für Völkerpsychologie*, XIII (1882), 313. J. Grimm, *Deutsche Mythologie* (4th ed., 1875-88), II, 114 (Teutonic). T. Trede, *Das Heidentum in der römischen Kirche* (1889-91), IV, 362 (Italian).

15. On *Hexenschuss:* J. Grimm, *Teutonic Mythology* (trans. F. Stallybrass; 1883), pp. 25, 443, 846, 1182, 1244. S. Eitrem, *Papyri Osloenses,* I (1925), 52.

16. On "Resheph of the arrow": G. A. Cooke, *A Text-Book of North-Semitic Inscriptions* (1903), pp. 55, 57.

17. On the custom of protecting a bride and groom from

hovering demons: H. Oldenberg, *Die Religion des Vedas* (1894), p. 271. P. Sartori, *Sitte und Brauch* (1910-14), I, 92. H. Granquist, *Marriage Conditions in a Palestinian Village*, vol. II (1914), p. 90, note 1. E. Crawley, *The Mystic Rose* (2nd ed., 1927), II, 37-38. T. H. Gaster, *JBL*, LXXIV (1955), 243.

18. On Qeteb as a personification of the stormwind: A. Caquot, *Semitica*, VI (1956), 53-68.

19. On the seven demons of plague, (*a*) in Mesopotamian literature: C. F. Jean, *Revue Asiatique*, XXI (1924), 98. Myth of Irra, II, i.20-21. (*b*) In modern Syriac magical texts: H. Gollancz, ed., *The Book of Protection* (1912), p. lxxi.

20. On Nergal, the "king of terrors" in Babylonian mythology: E. Ebeling, *Tod und Leben nach den Vorstellungen der Babylonier* (1931), no. 65, 14.

21. On the habitat of demons: H. Duhm, *Die bösen Geister des ATs* (1904), pp. 46-48. In Mesopotamian sources: R. C. Thompson, *The Devils and Evil Spirits of Babylonia* (1903), I.5; R.5; etc.; K. 4347, obv. ii, 50-51 = S. Langdon, *AJSL*, XXVIII (1911), 222. In pre-Islamic Arabic folklore: J. Wellhausen, *Reste des arabischen Heidentums* (2nd ed., 1897), pp. 135-40. In the Ugaritic texts: T. H. Gaster, *Thespis* (1950), p. 220. In later Jewish literature: L. Ginzberg, *Legends of the Jews* (1904-26), V, 322. In various other references: John Milton, *Comus*, lines 207-9. H. Yule, *The Book of Marco Polo* (2nd ed., 1875), vol. I, p. xxxix; ch. 57. A. Smythe-Palmer, *Babylonian Influences on the Bible* (1897), pp. 72-75.

22. On desert and sea as symbols of primordial chaos: A. J. Wensinck, *The Ocean in the Literature of the Western Semites* (1918), p. 53. A. Haldar, *The Notion of the Desert in Sumero-Akkadian and West Semitic Religions* (1950).

23. On the "stones of the field" in Job 5:23: G. Beer, *Zeitschrift für die AT Wissenschaft* XXXIII (1915), 63. Cf. Rashi *in loc.*

24. On bells as a means of averting evil spirits: S. Eitrem, *Papyri Osloenses*, I (1925), 142. J. G. Frazer, *Folk-lore in the OT* (one-vol. ed.; 1927), pp. 417-19. F. X. Dölger, *Antike und Christentum*, IV (1934), 233-42.

25. On the ram's horn as a means of averting evil spirits: A. Eberharter, *Zeitschrift für katholische Theologie*, LII (1928), 492-518.

26. On fumigation as a means of averting evil spirits: K. Frank, *Babylonische Beschwörungsreliefs* (1908), p. 44. S. Seligmann, *Der böse Blick* (1910), I, 318. A. Wiedemann, *Das alte Aegypten* (1920), p. 154.

27. On the custom of averting hostile spirits with sacrificial blood, (*a*) as practiced among the Druzes and Nosairis and among the Kurds living near Ain Kalife: S. L. Curtiss, *Primitive Semitic Religion Today* (1902), pp. 181-91. E. Eitrem, *Papyri Osloenses*, I (1925), 60. (*b*) As a part of the New Year rites in Madagascar: G. A. Shaw, *Journal of Transactions of the Victoria Institute*, XX (1887), 516.

28. On the power of blue in averting demons: H. Gressmann, *Palästinas Erdgeruch* (1909), p. 8. E. C. Sykes, *Persia and Its People* (1910), p. 336. On the use of blue in the Hittite story of Kessi: T. H. Gaster, *The Oldest Stories in the World* (1952), pp. 147, 154.

29. On the power of the name of God in expelling demons: B. Jacob, *Im Namen Gottes* (1903). J. G. Frazer, *The Golden Bough*, II (1913), 318-90. S. Eitrem, *Papyri Osloenses*, I (1925), 98.

30. On the Samaritan interpretation of Num. 6:27: T. H. Gaster, *Orientalia*, XI (1942), 71. T. H. GASTER

**DEMONIAC** dĭ mō'nĭ ăk [δαιμονιζόμενος]. One possessed by a DEMON. The term does not appear in the LXX, Josephus uses it only once (Antiq. VIII. ii.5), and rabbinism knows no corresponding expression. The term appears thirteen times in the NT (two additional times in MS D, in Luke 8:35; Acts 19:14), and it is translated "demoniac" seven times (Matt. 4:24; 8:28, 33; 9:32; 12:22; Mark 5:15-16), "possessed with/by a demon" five times (Matt. 8:16; 15:22; Mark 1:32; 5:18; Luke 8:36), and "one who has a demon" once (John 10:21).

Such a condition may be associated with a form of mental sickness (cf. Mark 5:15; Luke 8:35). Demoniacs were a class of persons healed by Jesus. They are to be distinguished from the physically ill (Matt. 4:24; 8:16; Mark 1:32), although the condition sometimes influenced such physical ailments as dumbness and blindness (Matt. 9:32; 12:22).

The most important NT reference is to the Gerasene demoniac (Matt. 8:28-34; Mark 5:1-20; Luke 8:26-39). Mark and Luke refer to a single demoniac; Matthew refers to two. The pericope especially serves to show the power of Jesus over all uncleanness and demonic might. In the Orient knowing the name of a person meant power over him, but for the demons such recognition of Jesus was their doom. Thus a demoniac is made to testify to Jesus as the Son of God. P. L. HAMMER

**DEMOPHON** dĕm'ə fŏn [Δημοφῶν] (II Macc. 12:2). One of the Palestinian district governors (στρατηγοί) in Maccabean times. He and his fellow governors, Timothy, Apollonius, and Hieronymus, "would not let [the citizens] live quietly and in peace."

J. C. SWAIM

**DEN OF LIONS** [גֹּב אֲרָיוָתָא]. A term used several times in Dan. 6, with variant forms of גֹּב and often with the word for "lions" understood. Cf. . . . . כְּפִיר מִמְּעֹנָתוּ, "a young lion [cry out] from his den" (Amos 3:4); מְעֹון אֲרָיֹות, "the lions' den" (KJV "dwelling"; Nah. 2:11—H 2:12); also Job 37:8; 38:40; Ps. 104: 22; Song of S. 4:8; Nah. 2:12—H 2:13.

The most famous OT story of a den of lions is in Dan. 6. In keeping with a favorite notion of ancient justice, Daniel's accusers and their families were cast into the pit once Daniel had been removed alive (vs. 24).

The lions' den, particularly in a more natural setting, was used metaphorically to represent Nineveh (Nah. 2:11-12), to suggest the grandeur and power of God's creation (Job 38:39-41), and to remind man that even such beasts are fed by God and live in ways which he has established (Ps. 104:21-22). *See also* LION. H. F. BECK

**DENARIUS** dĭ nâr'ĭ əs [δηνάριον]; KJV PENNY. A Roman silver coin, 3.8 grams, coined from 268

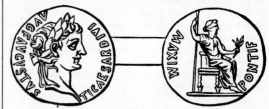

26. A denarius, showing the head of Tiberius

B.C. until the time of Septimius Severus; the most frequently mentioned coin in the NT. It was a day's pay for a laborer (Matt. 20:2, 9-10, 13). Fig. DEN 26. *See also* MONEY.

**DENY** [ἀρνέομαι, ἀπαρνέομαι, ἀντιλέγω]. In addition to its general sense (cf. Acts 4:16), "deny" has these special uses: **1.** Denying Christ, in contrast to confessing him (Matt. 10:32-33). The Jerusalemites "denied the Holy and Righteous One" before Pilate (Acts 3:13-14). Peter was guilty of lip-denial when he declared he did not know him (Mark 14:66 ff and parallels), but his heart remained unsworn and his situation was retrievable, whereas those who deny Christ in heart will be disowned by the Son of man (Matt. 10:33 = Luke 12:9; cf. II Tim. 2:12; Tit. 1:16; Jude 4 = II Pet. 2:1). In I Tim. 5:8 KJV a Christian who fails to maintain his dependents has "denied the faith"; the same phrase in Rev. 2:13 denotes wavering under persecution (cf. Rev. 3:8). To deny the power of godliness (II Tim. 3:5) is to make a lip-profession of Christianity with no corresponding reality. In I John 2:22-23 denying the Father and the Son implies a denial of Christ's real humanity (cf. I John 4:2-3).

2. Denying oneself (Matt. 16:24 = Mark 8:34 = Luke 9:23) means the renunciation of all self-interest and personal ambition in unreserved commitment to Christ, just as he "emptied himself" in his incarnation and crucifixion (Phil. 2:7-8). But note: God "cannot deny himself" (II Tim. 2:13)—i.e., he is always true to his character and promise.

F. F. BRUCE

**DEPOSIT.** Something committed to the charge of another. It may be for safekeeping (cf. Isa. 10:28), or it may be as a guarantee of security against a DEBT.

The law of deposit in the OT is in Exod. 22:7-13 (cf. Jos. Antiq. IV.viii.38). The laws are classified by the kind of deposit left: either money and goods or animals. The OATH and SIN OFFERING are involved in the deposit (Lev. 6:2-4). The deposit may be stored in a TREASURY, as in II Macc. 3:10-15. The Greek of the LXX emphasizes a special trust in which honesty is primary (II Macc. 9:25). So the gospel is a special deposit or "trust" granted to the disciples (I Tim. 6:20; II Tim. 1:12, 14).

C. U. WOLF

**DEPTHS.** The translation of three distinct Hebrew words:

*a*) מצולה, the depths of the sea (Exod. 15:5; Neh. 9:11; Ps. 68:22—H 68:23; Mic. 7:19) or the bed of a river (Zech. 10:11). The word has been variously combined with צלל II (Exod. 15:10; cf. Akkadian *ṣalālu;* Arabic *ṣalla*), "sink"; צלל I (I Sam. 3:11; Jer. 19:3; etc.; cf. Arabic *ṣalla*), "tingle, ring, gurgle(?)," *sensu*, "swirling waters"; and Syrian Arabic *miṣwal*, "deep basin, trough." In Ps. 88:6—H 88:7, where the term stands parallel to "depths of the Pit," the LXX and the Syr. read, by transposition of letters, בצלמות, "in deep darkness," but the following: "Thou dost overwhelm me with all thy waves" (vs. 7—H vs. 8) supports the MT.

*b*) תחתית, "the lowest parts"—i.e., of the earth (Pss. 63:9—H 63:10; 139:15; Isa. 44:23). The term has been compared with the Akkadian *šaplāti*, "nether regions," similarly employed. *See* DEAD, ABODE OF THE.

*c*) ירכה (Isa. 14:15; Ezek. 32:23). The term often means "the uttermost reaches" (e.g., Ps. 48:2—H 48:3; Isa. 14:13; Jer. 6:22; Ezek. 38:6). However, in Akkadian, the corresponding *arkatu* is, indeed, sometimes synonymous with *išdu*, "foundation," being

written with the same ideogram (ÚR); and it is probable that in the passages cited this is the meaning.

In Rom. 8:39 ("Nor height, nor depth, nor anything else in all creation, will be able to separate us from the love of God in Christ Jesus our Lord"), it has been suggested that both "depth" (βάθος) and "height" (ὕψωμα) are astronomical terms, denoting respectively the celestial space beneath the horizon when the stars ascend, and the closest approximation of a star to the zenith (*see bibliography*). There is, however, no exact parallel to the use of the Greek word βάθος in this sense.

*Bibliography.* H. Lietzmann, *Handbuch* (1907), vol. II, p. 75, note 1.

T. H. GASTER

**DEPUTY** [נצב (I Kings 22:48); פחה, סגן (Jer. 51:28; CAPTAIN *in* II Kings 18:24; GOVERNOR *in* Esth. 8:9; 9:3); KJV ἀνθύπατος (RSV PROCONSUL)]. A person appointed to act for another; a viceregent.

**DERBE** dûr'bĭ [Δέρβη]. A city in the central part of S Asia Minor.

Derbe is a town in the district of Lycaonia, a plateau in the central part of S Anatolia, of which ICONIUM is the leading city. Iconium, however, was a Phrygian center, whereas Derbe and LYSTRA were inhabited by a population speaking a separate language, Lycaonian (Acts 14:11).

Little specific history is known for the town of Derbe. It must have been somewhat Hellenized in the time of Hellenistic penetration in Asia Minor. In the first century B.C. it acquired a certain fame as the residence of Antipater, a chieftain who ruled a small principality which included Lystra and Laranda. He was on good terms with Cicero (*Ad Familiares* XIII.73), but others refer to him as a brigand (Strabo XI.535). Antipater was defeated and ousted from his land by Amyntas, king of Galatia, after whose death in 25 B.C. the political allegiance of Derbe shifted several times. At first it was part of the Roman province of Galatia; but in the first century A.D. the city belonged temporarily to the Cilician kingdom of Antiochus IV of Commagene, who seems to have given the city a special epithet in honor of the Emperor Claudius. On second-century coins the name of the city appears as Clau(dia) Derb(e) (or Claudioderbe).

Derbe acquired its present fame as a place twice

visited by Paul, who on his first journey (Acts 14:6, 20) made many disciples at Derbe, and on his second journey passed through Derbe (16:1) on his way from Cilicia to Lystra. One of Paul's disciples from Derbe was Gaius, who accompanied him on the journey from Corinth to Macedonia and Asia (20:4).

The exact location of Derbe was long a matter of dispute. It now seems to have been settled in favor of the site of Kerti Hüyük, a medium-sized habitation mound *ca.* fifteen miles to the N-NE of Laranda-Karaman. At Kerti Hüyük a dedicatory inscription by the council and people of Derbe was found, honoring Antoninus Pius in A.D. 157. This site was inhabited in the Iron Age and during the Hellenistic and Roman periods, but apparently was entirely abandoned and forgotten in medieval times.

*Bibliography.* W. M. Ramsay, *The Historical Geography of Asia Minor* (1890), pp. 336-37; M. Ballance, "The Site of Derbe; A New Inscription," *Anatolian Studies,* VII (1957), 147-51.    M. J. MELLINK

**DESCENT. 1.** Ancestry, lineage. In this sense the following words are used:

*a)* זרע (Ezra 2:59; Neh. 7:61; elsewhere "children," "offspring," "race," "seed").

*b)* ערב, "mixed company," translated "of foreign descent" in Neh. 13:3.

*c)* Ἀγενεαλόγητος, "without descent" (Heb. 7:3 KJV; RSV "without GENEALOGY").

In Heb. 7:16 the RSV supplies "descent" where there is no corresponding word in the Greek.

**2.** A mountain pass (מורד; κατάβασις). *See* ASCENT.

L. E. TOOMBS

**DESCENT INTO HADES** hā′dēz [ירד שאולה; LXX καταβαίνειν εἰς ᾅδου]. The traditional biblical view of the experience of one's "shade" at death and burial (*see* SHEOL); also, the depth of Christ's humiliation, the turning point to his exaltation. The creedal phrase (*descendit ad inferna* [*inferos*]; κατελθόντα εἰς τὰ κατώτατα [καταχθόνια]) is not used of Christ in the NT, but the idea develops out of the proclamation of his death and his resurrection "from the dead." This derivation from the kerygma is the basis of the idea's "apostolicity" and the key to its theologically valid meaning.

**1. In the history of religion.** A descent into Hades by a divinity or hero is in antiquity a common myth of solar origin. It is recounted of the Sumerian divinity Inanna early in the second millennium B.C.; is taken over into Semitic lore in the Akkadian descent of Ishtar; comprises the last of the labors of Hercules; recurs in the Hellenistic mystery religions—e.g., of Persephone and Orpheus; has a classical literary heritage from Homer via Vergil to Dante; provides the pattern for the Gnostic redeemer's victory over the world of darkness; takes on Jewish garb in the apocryphal book of ENOCH; and pours into apocryphal Christian literature, as Peter's vision of the tortures of hell in the Apocalypse of Peter, and as Christ's harrowing of hell in the Gospel of Nicodemus (*see* NICODEMUS, GOSPEL OF). This broad tradition of mythology provides less the origin and meaning of the NT idea of Christ's descent into Hades than the vehicle of its development and the cause of its degeneration.

**2. In the NT.** *a. As the resurrection "from the dead."* In NT times the OT view that all the dead go to Sheol had only begun to be replaced by the view that the righteous go to PARADISE. Those holding the older view could assume that a descent into Hades was implied in the reality of Christ's death. A deliverance from Hades was for them latent in the kerygma's standard assertion that he rose "from the dead" (ἐκ νεκρῶν; Acts 3:15; 4:2, 10; 10:41; 13:30, 34; 17:31; Rom. [1:4]; 4:24; 6:4, 9; 10:7, 9; I Cor. 15:12, 20; Gal. 1:1; Eph. 1:20; Col. 1:18; 2:12; I Thess. 1:10; II Tim. 2:8; Heb. 13:20; I Pet. 1:3, 21). The original idea of rising from among the dead (see Ps. 88:5, 10, LXX)—i.e., from their abode—was usually dormant in the NT, until some stimulus focused attention upon it and thereby determined the direction of its interpretation. Often the stimulus was the conviction that Christ's resurrection "from the dead" was "according to the scriptures" (Luke 24:46; John 2:22; 20:9; Acts 17:2-3; I Cor. 15:4; etc.). Since "from the dead" does not occur in the LXX, the connection was established by appeal to the OT category of a deliverance from Sheol. These OT proof texts are the origin of the explicit idea of Christ's descent into Hades.

In Rom. 10:6-10, Paul uses Ps. 71 to interpret Deut. 30:11-14 in terms of the kerygma. When Deuteronomy uses two rhetorical questions merely to express the impossible, Paul goes to considerable effort to show that they are literally answered by the proclamation of Christ's incarnation and resurrection from the dead. He associates "Thou broughtest me up again from the abyss of the earth" in Ps. 71:20 (LXX) with the kerygma's "resurrection from the dead" (Rom. 10:9) to produce the expression "to bring Christ up from the dead" (vs. 7)—i.e., from the "abyss." This rephrasing of the kerygma answers the second rhetorical question of Deuteronomy: "Who will go over to the other side of the sea?" (LXX). The latter is rephrased in terms of another idiom for the impossible: "Who will descend into the abyss?" This substitution would seem justified by the close association of the sea with the abyss (cf. in the NT: Luke 8:31 with 8:33; Rev. 11:7 with 13:1; and Rom. 10:7 with Matt. 12:40). The ABYSS designated the waters below, and soon led to an association of baptism's "descent into the water" with the descent into Hades (I Pet. 3:19-21; Barn. 11; Shepherd of Hermas, Sim. IX.16; Odes of Solomon).

Jesus' original saying in Matt. 12:40 did not clarify the "sign of Jonah," but Q associated this saying with another dealing with Jonah's "kerygma." Matthew's customary effort to show the explicit reference of scripture to Jesus was guided by the fact that the early church interpreted Jesus and his kerygma (Mark 8:31; 9:31; 10:33-34 and parallels) in terms of his death and resurrection "from the dead" as a sign (Luke 2:34-35; John 2:18-22), while Judaism associated Jonah and his message with his deliverance from the fish as a sign. Since Sheol was sometimes represented as a sea monster (III Bar. 5: "His belly is Hades"), and this association had already been carried through in the case of Jonah by the insertion of a psalm describing a descent into Sheol (Jonah 2:2-9), Matthew simply completed the parallel to Jonah by stating in the case of Jesus the sojourn in Hades implicit in the kerygma. (Cf. Odes of Solomon 42: "Hades saw me and became ill, death spit me up and many with me.") The word "Hades" is replaced by the designation of its location, "the heart of the earth," language adapted from the psalm to express formally the parallel to "the belly of the whale."

From Luke 24:46 it is apparent that behind Luke there stood a tradition of Christian exegesis to support the "resurrection from the dead." The direction which this research took is visible in Acts 2:24, where "from the dead" is replaced by "having loosed the pangs of death." This expression is from the LXX of Pss. 18:4; 116:3, where it is parallel to "pangs of Hades" and "dangers of Hades," and from II Sam. 22:6, where it is the LXX translation of "cords of Sheol." This allusion to Hades is explicit in the other occurrence of this exegetical tradition in Polyc. Phil. 1.2 ("Whom God raised, having loosed the pangs of Hades"); as well as in the early textual variant to Acts 2:24, reading "pangs of Hades." Now when Acts 2:24 uses this motif to introduce Ps. 16, and in the application of the psalm points to the phrase "Thou wilt not abandon my soul to [in?] Hades," it is clear that the allusion to Hades is the common factor in the testimonia underlying Acts 2:24-32, in which context Ps. 16 could have been interpreted as a deliverance from within Hades, rather than as an avoidance of Hades (the rabbinic exegesis). Luke has partially obscured all this by reading only "pangs of death," for his own view is that Jesus was not "abandoned" by God (Luke 23:46 replaces Mark 15:34), but went to Paradise (Luke 23:43; 16:19-31). In Acts 13:34-37 Luke obscures completely the exegetical tradition by returning "having loosed the pangs of death" to "from the dead," and finding the point of contact with Ps. 16 exclusively in terms of "corruption," so as to associate "from the dead" with the tomb (vss. 29-30; cf. Luke 24:5; Acts 2:29). Yet the meaning of Christ's deliverance from Hades (in the exegetical tradition), from the personified power of death (in Acts 2:24*b*), and from the corruption of the tomb (in Acts 13:29-37) is the same: he overcame death.

*b. The beginnings of further development.* The paradox of Christ's victory in death was early interpreted as a conflict with the hostile spirit-world forces, who in their ignorance (I Cor. 2:6-8; I Pet. 1:12) dug their own graves by putting him to death. Thus Christ's victory could be expressed either as their subjugation (Eph. 1:21-22; Phil. 2:10; Col. 1:20; 2:15; I Pet. 3:22) or as their awful enlightenment (I Tim. 3:16; Ign. Eph. 19; Trall. 9.1; Just. Dial. 36, 85; Ascension of Isa. 9–11; Iren. Demon. of Ap. Teaching 84; Pistis Sophia 7 ff; etc.). When the universality of Christ's victory was not expressed by the listing of the various designations for the spirits he overcame, it could be indicated spatially, in terms of a three-story cosmos (which might suggest a descent into Hades; see Phil. 2:10; Ign. Trall. 9 [cf. the two recensions]), or in terms of a two-story cosmos (which might associate his victory with his ascension; see Col. 1:20; Polyc. Phil. 2.1; Matt. 28:18). Even the latter alternative would not exclude the motif of Christ's visit to Hades (Eph. 4:8), since Hades, Gehenna, the prison of fallen angels, or the

abode of evil spirits was often located in one of the lower of the seven heavens (Isa. 24:21-22; II Enoch 7, 10, 18, 29; III Bar. 4-5; Ascension of Isa. 10–11; Acts of John 114; Acts of Thomas 148; Acts of Philip 144). In I Pet. 3:19-20 Christ's victorious revelation before the spirit world is expanded beyond the cryptic phrase "seen by angels" (I Tim. 3:16), when the author applies to Christ the idea of I Enoch 12 ff, where Enoch goes to Hades and proclaims final judgment to the fallen angels who married the daughters of men and produced not only the godless generation destroyed by the flood, but also the evil spirit world of paganism.

Since Jesus' victory over death in its original eschatological setting was seen as the "first fruits of those who have fallen asleep" (I Cor. 15:20), he was brought into direct relation with the fate of the dead (Rom. 14:9), and received the title "judge of the living and the dead" (Acts 10:42; II Tim. 4:1; I Pet. 4:5; Barn. 7.2; Polyc. Phil. 2.1; II Clem. 1.1). The same idea finds expression with direct reference to Hades: "I died, and behold I am alive for evermore, and I have the keys of Death and Hades" (Rev. 1:18; cf. Matt. 16:18). The future destruction of personified Death (I Cor. 15:26, 54) is held by Heb. 2:14; II Tim. 1:10; Barn. 5.6; Justin I.63.16 to have been already realized by Christ. It is this background which leads I Pet. 4:6 to shift slightly the motif of a revelation before the spirit world to a "preaching of the gospel to the dead, that though judged according to men in the flesh, they might live according to God in the spirit" (orig. tr.; cf. Matt. 27:51-53; John 5:19-29; Heb. 12:23). From the second century onward, the primary purpose seen in Christ's descent was to rescue the pre-Christian saints from Hades into heaven (Ign. Magn. 9.2; Justin I.72; Odes of Solomon; etc.). This secondary view of Christ's descent made it no longer possible for Christians to conceive of the godly as going to Hades, and thus removed from Western thought the OT view of the afterlife out of which the idea of Christ's descent originally arose (see Tertullian *On the Soul* 55).

Just as the Hades motif could occur apart from the descent motif, the descent itself could also be connected with the earth rather than with Hades, by the application to Christ of the current Hellenistic terminology (in the NT: Acts 14:11) of a savior's descent from heaven and ASCENSION back to heaven (John 3:13, etc.). This is the meaning of Eph. 4:8-10, where the argument to prove that Jesus (not Moses) is the one who "ascended on high" in Ps. 68:19 consists in declaring that the one ascending to heaven must previously have descended from heaven to earth; since Christ's descent is conceded, the ascent of the psalm should be attributed to him. The descent here is not to Hades, for the Incarnation is meant, and Ephesians presupposes a two-story cosmos of heaven and earth; the passage through Hades is part of the ascent (Eph. 4:8; cf. 2:2; 6:12). "The lower parts of the earth," formed in parallelism to "far above all the heavens" to express the depth of the humiliation, would in a Gnostic environment be an intelligible allusion to the earth (Iren. Her. V.31.2), where Hades motifs occur in designating the earth (cf. John 3:31; 8:23; Acts 2:19).

**3. In creedal formulations.** The descent motif is preserved in creedal formulations, first, as the descent from heaven at the Incarnation. Apelles' creed began: "[We believe] that Christ descended from the power above . . . ," and this was typical of Gnostic systems (see Iren. Her. III.11.3). But the motif recurs also in creedal formulations by Tertullian, Bishop Hymenaeus of Jerusalem, Lucian of Antioch, etc., finally attaining permanent status in the Nicene

27. Descent into Hades; from an early painting in a Roman catacomb

Creed: "He descended from heaven and became flesh." The motif occurs as the descent into Hades first at the somewhat Arian synods of Sirmium, Niké, and Constantinople in A.D. 359-60. It was introduced into the old Roman creed at Aquileia by the time of Rufinus (ca. 400), whence it moved into France and Spain. Consequently the "descent into Hades" entered into the Athanasian and Apostles' creeds codified in this period, and shared in the general acceptance which these creeds attained under Carolingian auspices. Fig. DES 27.

*Bibliography.* K. Gschwind, *Die Niederfahrt Christi in die Unterwelt* (1911); G. Wetter, "Der Gottessohn ist vom Himmel gekommen," *"Der Sohn Gottes"* (1916), pp. 82-101; R. Ganschinietz, "Katabasis," *Pauly's Real-Encyclopädie der klassischen Altertumswissenschaft,* X, 2 (1919), cols. 2359-2449; H. Diels, "Himmels- und Höllenfahrten von Homer bis Dante," *Neue Jahrbücher für das klassische Altertum,* XXV (1922), 239-53; J. A. MacCulloch, *The Harrowing of Hell* (1930); J. Kroll, *Gott und Hölle* (1932); W. L. Knox, "The Descent of the Redeemer," *St. Paul and the Church of the Gentiles* (1939), pp. 220-26; B. Reicke, *The Disobedient Spirits and Christian Baptism* (1946); W. Bieder, *Die Vorstellung von der Höllenfahrt Jesu Christi* (1949); H. Bietenhard, "Jesu Abstieg vom Himmel," *Die himmlische Welt im Urchristentum und Spätjudentum* (1951), pp. 82-86.                    J. M. ROBINSON

\*DESERT. The translation of several different words (*see below*), often used interchangeably with "WILDERNESS." As can frequently be determined by a study of the context of scriptural references containing these terms, in the light of geographical data, "desert" is more descriptive than "wilderness." In the following passages, the KJV uses "wilderness" and the RSV "desert": I Chr. 5:9; Job 38:26; Pss. 78:17; 106:9; 107:33; Isa. 42:11; 50:2; Matt. 15:33; Luke 8:29; etc. However, archaeological exploration has demonstrated that so-called desert regions were not entirely uncultivated or uninhabited. They included pasture lands, plains, and oases where springs and occasional rains plus careful water conservation made possible the building of villages and the maintaining of important caravan routes. The great deserts of Syria and Arabia were not unknown to biblical men, but those in the Transjordan Plateau, near the Dead Sea, and in the Sinai Peninsula are the ones most frequently mentioned.

The following words are translated "desert" or "wilderness":

*a*) מדבר (LXX usually ἔρημος; cf. Ugaritic *mdbr;* Akkadian *madbaru, mudbaru*) occurs 270 times in the OT. The etymology is uncertain; a root meaning "to drive" cattle has been proposed.

OT usage indicates several facts about מדבר. It was a place of pastures (Ps. 65:13; Jer. 23:10; Joel 2:22) and flocks (I Sam. 17:28). It was frequently a term designating large, defined areas such as the Arabian or the Sinai deserts (Gen. 14:6; Num. 14:16; Judg. 11:22). מדבר also indicated barren or uncultivated regions near such places as EDOM (II Kings 3:8); MOAB (Num. 21:11); BEER-SHEBA (Gen. 21:14); GIBEON (II Sam. 2:24); ENGEDI (I Sam. 24:1); DAMASCUS (I Kings 19:15); and several places in the Sinai Desert (*see* WILDERNESS). Cities in the מדבר are named (Josh. 15:61-62) and also resting places (Jer. 9:2—H 9:1; a "wayfarers' lodging place"). Among the creatures living in the מדבר are wild asses (Job 24:5), jackals (Mal. 1:3; KJV "dragons"), vultures (Ps. 102:6—H 102:7; KJV "pelican"), and ostriches (Lam. 4:3). It was also a place of thorns (Judg. 8:7) and pits (Gen. 37:22).

The barren character of the מדבר is further illustrated by its use with such expressions as a "land not sown" (Jer. 2:2) and a place "in which there is no man" (Job. 38:26), and in parallelism with the "howling waste of the wilderness" (Deut. 32:10).

מדבר is also used in a figurative sense. In the MT of Isa. 21:1 the expression "the oracle concerning the wilderness of the sea" (משא מדבר ים) is usually interpreted to mean that the desert is like a stormy and desolate sea. However, the LXX omits "sea," and the Dead Sea Scroll Isaiah (1QIsᵃ) omits both מדבר and "sea," and reads דברים ("words"). Although the title of the oracle is enigmatic, the mention of מדבר later in vs. 1 implies that it is a place of whirlwinds and a terrible land. Hence, the term is used to describe the desolate state of a nation defeated by her enemies (Jer. 22:6; Hos. 2:3—H 2:5). But the Lord's power extends over the desert (Ps. 107:35), and prophets found in it places of theophany (I Kings 19:4).

*b*) ערבה, an arid or remote region, is translated variously as "wilderness" and "desert" (Isa. 33:9; 35:1, 6; 40:3; 51:3), often paralleled with מדבר. ערבה with the article is rendered by the RSV as a place name (*see* ARABAH) designating the region of the Jordan Valley N of the Dead Sea and the depression extending to the Gulf of Aqabah (Deut. 1:1, 7; 3:17; Josh. 11:16; etc.). When the term is used with Jericho and Moab, it refers to the desertlike plains in the region (Num. 22:1; 26:3; Josh. 4:13; II Kings 25:5; etc.). The phrase "wolf from the desert" in Jer. 5:6 (KJV "wolf of the evenings") alludes to the destruction in store for those who disobey the Lord.

*c*) ישימון, ישימן, is a desert region (Deut. 32:10; Ps. 68:7—H 68:8), and often appears also in parallel with מדבר (Pss. 78:40; 106:14; 107:4; Isa. 43:19-20). When used with the article, it is a place name (*see* JESHIMON) mentioned in connection with Ziph and Maon (I Sam. 23:19, 24; 26:1, 3) and possibly referring also to the region in the Jordan Valley N of the Dead Sea (Num. 21:20; 23:28; KJV "Jeshimon," mg. "wilderness"; RSV "desert," mg. "Jeshimon").

*d*) חרבה has been translated "desert" (KJV: Ps. 102:6—H 102:7; Isa. 48:21; Ezek. 13:4; RSV: Isa. 48:21 only). Because the term refers to places of desolation or ruins, waste places, it is usually so rendered (Lev. 26:33; Isa. 5:17; Ezek. 36:10, 33; etc.), and as such had nothing to do with desert regions but with ruined cities or places which had been destroyed and could be rebuilt.

*e*) ציה is translated "desert" in Ps. 78:17 (KJV "wilderness"); although when used with "land" (ארץ), it is usually rendered "dry" or "parched" (Isa. 41:18; Jer. 51:43; Ezek. 19:13; Hos. 2:3—H 2:5). The term is used with מדבר and ערבה (Jer. 50:12) and with מדבר (Isa. 35:1), and is descriptive of waterless regions.

*f*) תהו, meaning "empty" or "vain" (I Sam. 12:21), is sometimes rendered "waste" (Deut. 32:10; Job 6:18; 12:24; Ps. 107:40) and as such denotes an empty or trackless area like the desert.

*g*) Ἔρημος, ἐρημία, are terms used in the NT and the LXX (Gen. 14:6; Judg. 11:22; II Sam. 2:24; cf. IV Macc. 18:8 for reference to demons of the desert) for "wilderness," "desert," or "lonely place." In the NT, except in the case of the "wilderness of Judea" (Matt. 3:1), particular desert regions are not identified. The RSV translates "lonely place" (ἔρημον τόπον; Matt. 14:13, 15; Mark 1:35; 6:31-32, 35; Luke 4:42; 9:12; KJV usually "desert place"), thus taking account of the geographical setting, which did not necessarily involve a desert region. Elsewhere the terms are translated variously "wilderness" and "desert" by both KJV and RSV (Matt. 15:33; 24:26; Mark 8:4; Luke 5:16; 8:29; John 6:31; Acts 8:26: "desert road"; Heb. 11:38) where the terms refer to lonely regions visited as places of retreat and prayer.

W. L. REED

**DESIGN. 1.** מעשה חשב (Exod. 39:3; KJV WORK). The work of a technician.

**2.** לחשב כל־מחשבת (II Chr. 2:14—H 2:13; KJV DEVICE). The verb means "to plan, contrive, create, a work requiring skill." The noun, which is used in this passage, indicates "skilled work."

**3.** את־תרעת המן (Esth. 8:3; KJV MISCHIEF). An evil scheme.

*See also* CRAFTS; METALLURGY; EMBROIDERY AND NEEDLEWORK.      J. M. MYERS

**DESIRE.** A word used in the Bible to cover a wide range of human wants, emotions, and cravings. It can describe everything from simple requests to sexual longing, from hunger for God to craving for gold. Occasionally desires are ascribed to God. Usually man's desires stand under the scrutiny of God.

**1. Terminology of desire in the Bible.** The OT uses several words for desire: שאל, "to request" (Deut. 18:16); בקש, "to seek" (Exod. 10:11); even the simple אמר, "to say" (Esth. 2:13). Usually the verb is חמד, אוה, or חפצ, with an infrequent use of חשק (Deut. 21:11). Acute longing is described as נשא נפש, a lifting up of the self (Jer. 44:14). The nouns are formed from the same roots, although אבויסה (Eccl. 12:5), רצון (II Chr. 15:15; Ps. 145:16, 19), and תשוקה (Gen. 3:16; 4:7; Song of S. 7:10) are also nominally employed.

In the NT, ἐπιθυμέω is the common verb, ἐπιθυμία

the noun, for "desire." However, θέλω, "to wish," with its noun, θέλημα, is also so translated, as are ζηλόω, "to desire earnestly," "to pursue"; ὀρέγομαι, "to reach after"; and ἱμείρομαι, "to long for." Once (Rom. 10:1) εὐδοκία is used nominally.

**2. In the OT.** There are human desires which are treated in the OT as natural to man's being (Deut. 18:6; I Kings 10:13; Ps. 107:30). Included among these are hunger (Ps. 145:16; Mic. 7:1), sexual desire (Deut. 21:11; Ps. 45:11; Song of S. 7:10; Gen. 3:16), and delight in the beautiful and the good (I Sam. 9:20; Prov. 3:15; 8:11; 19:22; Isa. 53:2; Ezek. 23:6, 12, 23). The Hebrew never saw asceticism as a part of the good life. He enjoyed life in all its fulness. He reveled in the beautiful, in long life (Ps. 34:12), in friends (Ps. 133; Prov. 19:22), in prosperity (Ps. 19:10), in the love of a good wife (Ps. 128; Ezek. 24: 16), in a house full of children (Ps. 128). For him, God had created a world which was "very good" (Gen. 1:31), and the Hebrew took advantage of it (Eccl. 2:10).

Nevertheless, the desires of the Hebrew stood under the judgment of his God. From the first, desire was to be subject to obedience—obedience to the will of Yahweh (Gen. 3; cf. vs. 6). And he who knew the true fulfilment of his desires was he who relied on the Lord (II Sam. 23:5; II Chr. 15:15; Pss. 21:2; 34: 12 ff; 37:4; 145:19; Prov. 10:24; 11:23; 13:12, 19). To him the meek could turn for justice (Ps. 10:17). Only in him could one like Job find satisfaction (Job 13:3). Thus the final object of the desire of the pious Hebrew was Yahweh himself (Isa. 26:9). The temple on Zion was the delight of Israel's eyes (Ezek. 24:21, 25). Yahweh's name was the desire of her soul (Isa. 26:8; cf. Neh. 1:11). His commandments were better than gold (Ps. 19:10). Communion with him was the ultimate good (Ps. 73:25). Wisdom was better than all desire (Prov. 3:15; 8:11), and the beginning of wisdom was the fear of the Lord (Prov. 1:7).

Over against the desire of the pious stood the desire of the wicked, whose object was, not God, but evil (Prov. 21:10; Mic. 7:3). The desires of the wicked were ungoverned, covetous, lustful (Deut. 5: 21; 7:25). He cursed Yahweh (Ps. 10:3) and shunned knowledge of him (Job 21:14). He preyed on the pious (Ps. 140:8) and sought only self (Prov. 13:4; 21:25; 23:6-8). His companionship was to be avoided (Prov. 24:1). His desires would come to nought (Ps. 112:10). Indeed, he was destined to lose even desire and life itself (Eccl. 12:5).

Yet seemingly religious desires had their limits. Those who piously looked forward to the day of the Lord's final triumph and judgment were warned that their self-righteous security would be destroyed by Yahweh (Amos 5:18; cf. Jer. 17:16). For Yahweh, too, had desires—not for outward religiosity (Pss. 40:6; 51:16; Hos. 6:6), but for inner obedience to his will, for steadfast love (Hos. 6:6), for truth (Ps. 51:6), for loyalty to his covenant. This one thought, obedience, with its concomitants of thankfulness and praise, formed the context of Hebrew desire.

**3. In the NT.** The situation is similar in the NT. Rarely (Luke 5:39; 8:20; 15:16; 16:21; 23:8; Gal. 4:20; 6:13; I Tim. 1:7) is any human desire treated as morally indifferent. Rather, most desires fall into one of two categories: those which are evil, lustful, covetous, ungoverned, and those which are commensurate with the new life in Christ. Among the former we find the desire for material possessions (Jas. 4:2), for wealth (Acts 20:33), for licentious sexual practices (Matt. 5:28; Rom. 1:24; Gal, 5:24; I Thess. 4:5; II Pet. 2:10). However, not all evil desires are catalogued. The NT speaks, not so much of sins, but of sin, of the nature of the old life apart from Christ, of life lived outside the Spirit and therefore contrary to the will of God (Rom. 6:12; 13:14; Gal. 5:16; Eph. 4:22; I Pet. 1:14; 4:2). Such a life, which is ruled totally by the desires of the flesh, of the old Adam (Rom. 6:12; Eph. 2:3; 4:22; Tit. 3:3), is to be put aside when the Christian enters into the new life in Christ (Rom. 13:14; Gal. 5:24; Col. 3:5; Tit. 2:12; I Pet. 2:11; I John 2:16). By the grace of God in Christ, the Christian is made a new being (Tit. 2:12). The desires of the world no longer hold him in bondage (II Pet. 1:4). He becomes a slave, not to passion, but to the Lord.

The Christian, then, is to take on new desires—desires commensurate with his new life. He is to "earnestly desire the higher gifts" (I Cor. 12:31) of prophecy, of teaching, of healing, but above all of faith, of hope (cf. Heb. 6:11), and of love (I Cor. 13). His desire is to be for full Christian fellowship (I Thess. 2:8, 17; cf. Luke 22:15) and for Christ. Indeed, his true home is not earth but heaven (Heb. 11: 16; cf. I Pet. 2:11), and his ultimate desire is to be with his Lord (Phil. 1:23), who is the perfecter and end of all desire.                                    E. R. ACHTEMEIER

**DESOLATING SACRILEGE.** *See* ABOMINATION THAT MAKES DESOLATE.

**DESSAU** dĕs'ô [Λεσσαού (A), Δεεσαου (V^vid)] (II Macc. 14:16). A town in Judea where Nicanor and the Jews met in battle.                  C. T. FRITSCH

**DESTINY.** 1. The translation of מני, the name of a pagan deity (Isa. 65:11). *See* MENI.

2. One's lot, appointed end, or FATE. Among the ancient Hebrews the destiny of the individual was bound up with that of the group, whether clan, tribe, or nation. There was no clear-cut conception of life after death. Hence one fulfilled his destiny by maintaining a right relation with, and furthering the interests and fate of, the social unit to which he belonged, which included a right relation and obedience to its God. Chief among the OT emphases were keeping covenant and obedience to the divine law (cf. Exod. 19:5; Deut. 4:1-8; 5:28-33; Ps. 25:10).

Israel's destiny was to be the people of God, to tell of his mighty acts (Pss. 96:3; 106:8; 145:4, 11-12), and to be a blessing to the nations (Gen. 12:2; Zech. 8:23; cf. Isa. 43:21). Beginning with the exilic period, there was an increasing emphasis on the individual's responsibility for his own destiny (cf. Ezek. 18). However, the Jews tenaciously relied upon Abrahamic descent to guarantee their future (cf. Luke 3:8; John 8:33, 39).

During the intertestamental period a more elaborate eschatology was developed, including a doctrine of individual resurrection, and one's destiny became determined by good works according to a system of merits and demerits. In the NT the destiny of the individual depends on his relationship to Jesus Christ

and adherence to his teaching (Acts 16:31; I John 2:3; 3:21-24).

*Bibliography.* J. Hempel, *Gott und Mensch im AT* (2nd ed., 1936), p. 192; H. H. Rowley, *The Faith of Israel* (1956), pp. 79-123.                                    V. H. KOOY

**DESTROY NOT.** *See* MUSIC.

**DESTROYER, THE** [המשחית; ὁ ὀλοθρεύων, ὁ ὀλοθρευτής, ὀλεθρεύων, ὀλεθρευτής]. A term used in Exod. 12:23 (cf. Heb. 11:28); I Cor. 10:10 to designate a superhuman agent of destruction. In the Exodus passage the reference is clearly to an angelic agent of Yahweh (*see* ANGEL). The meaning in I Cor. 10:10 is less clear. Is Paul referring to such an angel or to SATAN? (*See also* DEMON.) If the reference is to a destroying angel, is the designation a general term or a specific title? The rabbis sometimes used משחית as the title for a single angel of destruction among others similarly named. They also thought of God's mercy and wrath as being put into effect by opposing groups of angels (cf. II Sam. 24:16; I Chr. 21:15; II Cor. 12:7). On the other hand, the role of Satan was enlarged by postexilic Judaism (*see* DUALISM), and he was presented as an agent of destruction under God's control (Wisd. Sol. 2:24; John 8:44; Heb. 2: 14). Paul speaks in similar vein (II Cor. 12:7; I Thess. 2:18), and in I Cor. 5:5 combines σατανᾶς with ὄλεθρος (cf. I Thess. 5:3; II Thess. 1:9; I Tim. 6:9).

Apart from this special usage, "destroyer" as commonly understood appears in Job 15:21; Isa. 49:17; Jer. 4:7; 22:7 (שחת). It also appears five times in the KJV alone, and sixteen times in the RSV alone, thirteen of the latter as a translation of שדד (cf. Isa. 16:4; 21:2; Jer. 6:26; 48:8; 51:53). The LXX exhibits great variety but uses most often some form of ὄλεθρος or ταλαιπωρία.

*Bibliography.* M. Dibelius, *Die Geisterwelt im Glauben des Paulus* (1909), pp. 43-45. Contrast H. L. Strack and P. Billerbeck, *Kommentar zum NT aus Talmud und Midrasch,* III (1926), 412-16.                                    I. W. BATDORF

**DESTROYING LOCUST; KJV CATERPILLAR.** *See* LOCUST § 1*d*.

**DESTRUCTION, CITY OF.** KJV translation of עיר החרם (RSV "city of the sun") in Isa. 19:18. *See* HELIOPOLIS.

**DESTRUCTION, DEVOTED TO.** *See* DEVOTED.

**DETAINED BEFORE THE LORD** [נעצר לפני יהוה]. Confined at the sanctuary, in custody of the priests(?), for some religious purpose.

The exact meaning of this phrase is uncertain. The biblical reference (I Sam. 21:7) is to DOEG the Edomite, whom David, in his flight from Saul, met at the sanctuary at Nob. The phrase is from the same religious terminology and root as the word "taboo" (עצר; cf. Neh. 6:10; Jer. 36:5). It probably signifies "under a taboo," or "excluded from the cult." It is possible Doeg was undergoing some rite of purification, or fulfilling some vow. (Men were also detained at the sanctuary for suspected leprosy; cf. Lev. 13:4, 11, 31.) However, he may have been simply a visitor at the sanctuary, sitting in a consecrated position, so as to be strengthened by its holiness.

*Bibliography.* H. P. Smith, *Samuel,* ICC (1899), pp. 199-200; W. R. Smith, *The Religion of the Semites* (3rd ed., 1927), pp. 455-56; J. Pedersen, *Israel,* III-IV (1947), 273, 450-51, 514.

V. H. Kooy

**DEUEL** dōō′əl [דְּעוּאֵל, *see below*]. The father of Eliasaph, who was the leader of Gad in the wilderness (Num. 1:14; 7:42, 47; 10:20). In Num. 2:14 the father of Eliasaph is named Reuel, although some MSS read "Deuel." The LXX Ραγουηλ and the Syr. rendering both support a spelling with an initial letter "r." It has been suggested that the obscure first syllable of the name Deuel may be a derivative of the verb יָדַע, "know."

*Bibliography.* M. Noth, *Die israelitischen Personennamen* (1928), p. 241; L. Koehler, *Lexicon in VT Libros* (1953), p. 215.

R. F. Johnson

**DEUTERONOMY** dōō′tə rŏn′ə mĭ, dū′— [δευτερο-νόμιον]. The fifth book in the OT canon. It has no name in the MT. The Hebrew Bibles named it after its first clause: אֵלֶּה הַדְּבָרִים, "These are the words . . . ." The name which has now become universal has come into use since the time of the LXX—on the basis of a misunderstanding, to be sure, for the Hebrew text of Deut. 17:18, to which the translation δευτερονόμιον goes back, speaks, not of a "repetition of the law," but of a "copy," a "duplicate," of the Torah. *See* Law in the OT. *See* map "Egypt and Sinai: Exodus to Deuteronomy," under Exodus, Book of.

1. Contents
2. Critical literary analysis
3. The Book of the Covenant and Deuteronomy
4. Materials peculiar to Deuteronomy
5. A collection of sermons
6. Origin
7. Theology
8. King Josiah and Deuteronomy
Bibliography

**1. Contents.** Deuteronomy is a farewell address by Moses. After an introduction (1:1-5), which endeavors to fix the time and the place of this great address, the first part begins in 1:6. Moses recapitulates the events between the departure from Sinai and the arrival in the land E of the Jordan (spies, defeat at Hormah, the conquering of Sihon of Heshbon and of Og of Bashan, the occupation of the whole territory E of the Jordan). Beginning with 4:1, the subject of the address changes: Moses admonishes obedience to the "statutes and the ordinances." Titles are brought in once more in 4:44-49; and after a new beginning in 5:1, Moses relates the events on Sinai, especially how Israel was unable to listen to the voice of Yahweh and how Moses received the revelation of Yahweh's will instead. Now, however, he passes on the message he received at that time (5:29–6:3). The great exhortation follows. It is an urgent appeal for loyalty, for gratitude, and for obedience in view of the imminent settlement in Canaan and its dangers (6:4–11:32). Beginning with ch. 12, the form and the content of the address change: Moses turns to the communication of individual legal regulations. The long series of these transmittals begins with rules for worship (altar law, apostasy, unclean animals; chs.

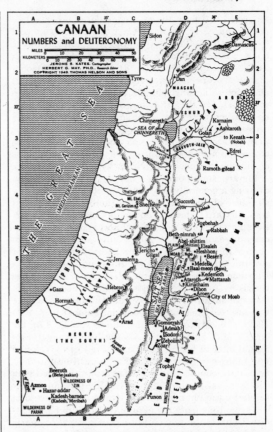

**CANAAN**
NUMBERS and DEUTERONOMY
MILES
KILOMETERS
JEROME S. KATES, *Cartographer*
HERBERT G. MAY, PH.D., *Research Editor*
COPYRIGHT 1949, THOMAS NELSON AND SONS

12–14). It continues with other legal prescriptions (the Year of Release, the bondage of debtors, feasts; 15:1–16:17) and the regulation of the offices (judges, king, priests, prophets; 16:18–18:22). From ch. 19 on, no plan can be distinguished in the arrangement. Regulations concerning cities of refuge, laws of war, statements of family rights and of a general humanitarian nature, follow one another in indiscriminate succession (chs. 19–25). The series ends with a formula of commitment to the covenant (26:16-19). Ch. 27 breaks with the scheme somewhat, for it gives directions for the building of an altar on Mount Ebal and for a ceremonial of blessing and cursing between Mount Ebal and Mount Gerizim. The thread of ch. 26 is continued in the great proclamation of blessings and curses in chs. 28–30. Ch. 31 reports the appointment of Joshua and the writing down of "this law." Then follows the Song of Moses (ch. 32) and Moses' blessing of the people of Israel (ch. 33); in conclusion, ch. 34 gives an account of his death on Mount Nebo.

**2. Critical literary analysis.** The knowledge that Deuteronomy is, generally speaking, not to be equated with a Hexateuch source document—i.e., that it is to be considered an independent literary document—goes back to De Wette's *Dissertatio critica* of 1805. This knowledge was, to be sure, even at that time not absolutely new; but De Wette is the pioneer in methodical-scientific analysis of Deuteronomy. This analysis has the advantage over that of the sources JE and P insofar as source D is present exclusively in the book of Deuteronomy and did not have to be separated first from the entanglement of other source documents (*see* BIBLICAL CRITICISM, HISTORY OF; PENTATEUCH). The portion of other sources in the book of Deuteronomy is minimal (4:41-43; 32:38-52; 34:1*a*, 7-9=P; 34:1*b*-6=JE). It was also soon evident that the two poetic texts, the Song of Moses (ch. 32) and Moses' blessing (ch. 33), have nothing to do with source D. On the other hand, the text which is to be ascribed to source D makes a very irregular impression (cf. the "titles" in 1:1; 4:44 ff; 6:1; 12:1), so that the assumption of a not uncomplicated process of development suggests itself immediately in the case of this source document. Nevertheless, analysis from a literary standpoint has not as yet succeeded in drawing a generally convincing picture of the literary structure of source D. Without doubt, it was a great step forward when, around the beginning of the twentieth century, Steuernagel and Staerk, independently of each other, could point out the constant change in the form of address and separate an older stratum which used the singular pronoun from a later one which used the plural. Actually this change is striking, and there are not a few instances in which one can say with certainty that the plural passage was inserted later into the singular context (e.g., 9:7-10:11; 20:2-4; 29:1-29—H 28:69-29:28). On the other hand, this analysis, which Steuernagel presented later in his *Kommentar* (2nd ed., 1923), found few followers, because it led to superfine and artificial distinctions. This was, of course, connected with the fact that Steuernagel was guided by no means solely by the change in number, but also started at the same time from the assumption that our present-day Deuteronomy is composed of several formerly independent "editions" of the original Deuteronomy, each of which was already provided with a parenetic introduction. But the plural edition, which Steuernagel extracted, probably never existed by itself. The assumption of several parallel editions is altogether improbable; one would probably do better to explain the composite nature of Deuteronomy from the point of view of a completion hypothesis—hence, in the sense of a subsequent gradual expansion and elaboration of an original Deuteronomy. One scholar believes, to be sure, on the basis of a penetrating analysis, that Deut. 12-18 must be interpreted as a combination of two codices. Moreover, if the assertion should be correct that Deut. 1-3(4) is to be regarded as the beginning of the Deuteronomic historical work and has nothing at all to do with source D, then the theory of the various editions of Deuteronomy would be completely without foundation; for Deut. 1-3 was still regarded by Steuernagel as the introductory address of one edition of Deuteronomy.

Still another lesson from the history of the Deuteronomic investigation is that in the search for the original Deuteronomy one must disregard the account in II Kings 22-23 completely. One scholar attempted in an exaggerated fashion to determine the content and scope of the original Deuteronomy from the point of view of the events related there. However, even if Deuteronomy did influence history at the time of Josiah, it is, nevertheless, not to be assumed that it had achieved its full effect; moreover, Josiah may have gone beyond Deuteronomy in his measures (*see* § 6 *below*). Finally, also, the view, which seems ob-

vious at first glance and has been advocated often—from J. Wellhausen to R. Pfeiffer—that the original Deuteronomy is to be sought only within chs. 12-26, must be termed unsatisfactory; for the section chs. 12-26 cannot be designated as the real "codex" as opposed to the "introduction" (chs. 6-11), since the characteristic signs (change of number, parenetic style) are to be found in chs. 6-11 as well as in chs. 12-26; and, besides, chs. 12-26 are something quite different from a "codex." *See* § 5 *below*.

Obviously the zeal for literary analysis has flagged for a long time. The realization is growing that with the aid of the purely literary critical method one can get at the actual complexity of Deuteronomy only to a limited extent because the strata which are present, without a doubt, point, not to literary processes, but to a preliterary process of slow enrichment of the original mass of tradition. Thus the oft-repeated laborious attempt to untangle the original Deuteronomy (which was at the same time, possibly, considered to be identical with the Josiah Codex) by literary analysis was the pursuit of a phantom. Therefore investigation—apart from that concerned with the final literary form which Deuteronomy eventually assumed, which has not yet been satisfactorily solved—has recently turned to examination of the many individual traditional materials, which have been collected in Deuteronomy, with regard to their characteristic features of form and content and especially as to their particular place in life. This task is by no means finished even today. *See* § 3 *below*.

**3. The Book of the Covenant and Deuteronomy.** Even if Moses could be regarded as the author of Deuteronomy, this analytical work on Deuteronomy would still have to be done. However, since Deuteronomy—from the first sentence on ("beyond the Jordan")—shows that the position of the speaker is the Palestine W of the Jordan, and since, in point of time, many of the arrangements provided for in Deuteronomy suggest composition after the time of Moses, the time in which and for which Deuteronomy was produced must be determined first of all with the aid of this analysis. The first point of refer-

| Table 1 | |
|---|---|
| Exodus | Deuteronomy |
| 21:1-11 | =15:12-18 |
| 21:12-14 | =19:1-3 |
| 21:16 | =24:7 |
| 22:15-16 | =22:28-29 |
| 22:20-23 | =24:17-22 |
| 22:24 | =23:20-21 |
| 22:25-26 | =24:10-13 |
| 22:28-29 | =26:1-11; 15:19-23 |
| 22:30 | =14:3-21 |
| 23:1 | =19:16-21 |
| 23:2-3, 6-8 | =16:18-20 |
| 23:4-5 | =22:1-4 |
| 23:9 | =24:17-18 |
| 23:10-11 | =15:1-11 |
| 23:12 | =5:14-15 |
| 23:13 | =6:13 |
| 23:14-17 | =1:1-17 |
| 23:19*a* | =26:2-10 |
| 23:19*b* | =14:21*b* |

ence in establishing Deuteronomy with regard to time —but also theologically—is afforded by a comparison with the Book of the Covenant (*see* COVENANT, BOOK OF THE), for a great number of the legal materials in the Book of the Covenant reappear in Deuteronomy, frequently, to be sure, in a characteristically changed form. *See* Table 1.

One can conceive of this circle of mutually corresponding passages as being smaller; one can also conceive of it as being still larger. In either case it becomes clear how great the stock of legal materials is which Deuteronomy has in common with the Book of the Covenant. Whether one must draw from this the conclusion that Deuteronomy wanted to take the place of the Book of the Covenant and wished itself —no longer the Book of the Covenant—to be looked upon as the authentic revelation of Sinai, is not so certain: for if Deuteronomy were traced back to the Book of the Covenant so directly, the question would still remain as to why it then passed over and omitted so large a portion of the regulations of the Book of the Covenant—it is a matter of about fifty per cent, after all. It would also be conceivable, indeed, that Deuteronomy was derived from a legal collection unknown to us, which in its turn had many materials in common with the Book of the Covenant. In such a collection also, however, many of those things would possibly be contained which are now found in Deuteronomy only and not in the Book of the Covenant (concerning this special material, *see* § 4 *below*). It is easy to see that in the majority of the cases in which a comparison of the versions is possible at all, that of Deuteronomy proves to be definitely the younger, and that of the Book of the Covenant the older.

The "Hebrew law" in Exod. 21:1 ff had assumed the case of the purchase of a Hebrew slave (עבד עברי) and fixed the duration of his service; Deut. 15:12 ff, on the other hand, deals with the enslavement of a man who was formerly free and probably also was a landowner himself, who had been forced to give himself up to debtor's bondage for economic reasons. In this case the initiative comes from him and not, as in Exod. 21:1, from the master of the slave. A further difference lies in the fact that, according to Deut. 15: 12 ff, it is also possible for a woman to enter into debtor's bondage. This must be connected with a change in the conditions of holding property; in the meantime, women had also acquired the right to inherit property (cf. II Kings 8:3) and could get into the same situation as a male landowner (*see* SLAVERY). In the Book of the Covenant the law of the Year of Release (שמטה; *see* RELEASE, YEAR OF) is a religious regulation which applies exclusively to agrarian life (Exod. 23:10-11). There it is a question of letting the fields lie fallow temporarily, not for economic or social-charitable reasons, but for religious reasons; it was a matter of demonstrating by the practice Yahweh's original ownership of the soil (cf. Lev. 25:23). Such a custom could be practiced particularly in the old days of Israel, when agriculture was not yet the only source of income but was only carried on as a supplement to the raising of stock. Deut. 15:1 ff is different. The old religious terminology is retained, to be sure (שמטה ליהוה), but the custom has changed decidedly in that the legal effectiveness of the "re-

lease" has been extended to debtor's law; by this time it is financial values which are subject to the law of release—thus, perhaps, loans which someone had to assume in order to save his economic position. In the case of the Hebrew law, as also in the law of the Year of Release, it is perfectly clear that, compared with the Book of the Covenant, Deuteronomy reflects a considerably advanced stage with respect to economic history. The use of money—which was still in its primitive beginnings in the earlier days of Israel— has in the meantime become more complex. If one is to assign the Book of the Covenant to the period between the immigration and the organization of the states, then this means that one must surely go down as far as the period of the kings with Deuteronomy.

**4. Materials peculiar to Deuteronomy.** The materials in Deuteronomy for which there is no equivalent of any kind to be found in the Book of the Covenant are very diverse and also obviously date from various periods. The stipulation as to how to proceed in the case of a murder (*see* CRIMES AND PUNISHMENTS § C2*a*), the perpetrator of which is unknown (Deut. 21:1-9), bears all the marks of an early age. Just as the קהל or Assembly law (23:2-9) in its original form, it must go back to the time before Israel was organized as a state. However, viewed as a whole—only the more important can be mentioned here—these materials cannot be very old. In Deut. 13 three regulations directed against cases of deliberate apostasy from the belief in Yahweh (vss. 1-5—H 2-6, 6-11—H 7-12, 12-18—H 13-19) are grouped together. The first assumes that the initiative for this came from a "prophet." Such a proposal, however, can only have emanated from a prophetic class which was already badly demoralized by the Canaanitic syncretism; moreover, the נביאים at the time of Samuel did not yet generally have such a prominent position in the life of the people, at all (*see* PROPHET). The third provision is revealing, for it assumes that the initiative for apostasy came from a city. Such a thing actually lay within the realm of possibility, but again, to be sure, not before the period of the kings; for one would, in this case, necessarily think first of all such towns as those which lay outside the old colonial domain of the former tribal confederacy and which were incorporated into the kingdom of Israel only in the course of intermittent extension of the boundaries under David. In these cities, which during the long period of their Canaanitic history were politically independent and in which the belief in Yahweh had probably never really taken root, it was possible for the old feeling of independence to awaken even during the time of the Israelitic kings, especially in a period in which the Yahweh cult itself was already undermined and lacking in vigor. An especially characteristic kind of material peculiar to Deuteronomy is the so-called "laws of war"—namely, a regulation concerning exemption from military service (20:1-9), two laws concerning the besieging of cities (vss. 10-18, 19-20), and one concerning camp sanitation (23:9-14—H 23:10-15). It is difficult to date the last one: probably it is the oldest of this group. Deut. 20:1-9 has obviously been revised (vss. 2-4 constitute the most recent stratum); its basic element is found in the words of the officers in vss. 5-7 (*see* WAR, IDEAS OF). These officers

(שטרים; *see* OFFICER), however, were royal officials who were responsible for military affairs and recruitment for military service. As certainly as the particular regulations according to which individuals were excluded from military service date from a very early period in the waging of war, just as certainly does even the oldest stratum in Deuteronomy not date from before the period of the kings (Deut. 20:1-9). The same applies to the laws concerning the besieging of cities, which certainly presuppose an advanced technique of siege (20:20). Deuteronomy also contains a law pertaining to the KING (17:14-20). The most striking thing about this is the almost exclusively negative tendency, for the law is concerned primarily with restricting the power and functions of the king. It does not give a picture of the office of a king in Israel, but merely a picture of the king as he should not be, for which the picture of King Solomon in Deuteronomy probably served as a model.

The demand for centralization of worship (*see* WORSHIP IN THE OT) in the "place which the LORD your God will choose" has always been regarded as the most important peculiarity of Deuteronomy as compared with the Book of the Covenant; and this demand was certainly new at the time of Deuteronomy. On the other hand, however, it is not true that all parts of Deuteronomy take this demand, which was revolutionary for its time, for granted. There are not a few laws in Deuteronomy which seem to be completely unaware of this demand for centralization. There are only six larger units which were enacted explicitly on this assumption: the altar law (ch. 12); the law on tithing (14:22-29; *see* TITHE); the law of the FIRST-BORN, (15:19-23); the law of the feasts (ch. 16; *see* FEASTS AND FASTS); the law of the court in Jerusalem (17:8-13); and the law of the priests (18: 1-8; *see* PRIESTS AND LEVITES). There is, in addition, the law of ASYLUM (19:1-13), which makes new arrangements for the system of sanctuary after the abolition of the many shrines. The altar law is divided into three decrees, each of which independently adds to the demand for centralization (12:1-7, 8-12, 13-19 [20-29]); only the third is written in the singular, and it is probably the oldest. The first one contrasts the new demand for *one* altar with the custom of the neighboring Canaanites; the second contrasts it with the custom heretofore practiced by Israel itself. The lawgiver, therefore, is aware that he is demanding something utterly new in his time. Nevertheless, one must question whether the centralization of worship was something so completely new in the religious history of Israel. In the time of the judges, when Israel was a sacred alliance of tribes, the ARK OF THE COVENANT—ultimately in Shiloh— was, after all, the religious center to which the tribes traveled on the great pilgrimages. In the extreme manner in which Deuteronomy demands centralization, so that no sacrifices whatever are permitted except those which are made in places chosen by Yahweh, and so that even the firstlings and the tithes can be offered only at Yahweh's one place of worship, it was, to be sure, unknown in that earlier period. But that early period was also not in the utmost danger of losing the special character of its worship of Yahweh, as was the Israel of Deuteronomy. The immediate consequence of this demand of Deuteronomy

naturally had to be a great purging of the popular religious life; but the lawgiver faces up to this secularization. He even strives to give a helping hand to the people in this secular life of every day and to keep Yahweh before their eyes even there. Especially drastic was the new regulation for the prevailing custom of the PASSOVER, which was celebrated as a feast by local family units. Deuteronomy breaks with it also in that it transforms the Passover into a pilgrimage feast which is to be celebrated at the common place of worship by the slaughter of cattle and sheep. This regulation of the Passover is, to be sure, complicated still more by the fact that the old Israelitic Feast of the Passover was combined with the Feast of Unleavened Bread, which was originally Canaanitic (16:1 ff).

**5. A collection of sermons.** The analysis of the individual materials contained in Deuteronomy must now be supplemented by an investigation of their peculiarity with regard to form. In the Book of the Covenant the two basic forms of the old Israelitic legal maxims may be found, the conditional and the apodictic, usually still in classic purity (*see* LAW IN THE OT). The conditional legal maxims—introduced by "assuming that," and continued by "if"—belong in the local courts at the gate where justice was administered by the elders in all disputes such as might come up in peasant and petty bourgeois circles (cf. Ruth 4:1). The statements in apodictic form, on the other hand, are derived from the cult. They are, in a much more literal sense, the law of God, because they were proclaimed to the congregation in a setting of the observance of divine worship and were acknowledged by the acclamation of the congregation (cf. Deut. 27:14 ff). This liturgical origin also explains the fact that the apodictic statements, as a rule, do not appear singly but rather in the form of series of prohibitions (Exod. 20:2 ff; 21:12, 15-17; Lev. 19:9-10, 11-12, 13-18). Such series of commandments or fragments of series are also found in Deuteronomy. Deut. 23:2-8 deals with membership in or exclusion from the religious congregation. In 16:21–17:1 there are three apodictic prohibitions of a religious nature; in 16:19, also three prohibitions which forbid any partiality in the administration of justice. Above all, however, the Decalogue (*see* TEN COMMANDMENTS) and the Dodecalogue of Shechem must be mentioned (Deut. 5:6-18; 27:15-26). The number of conditional legal maxims in Deuteronomy is likewise large (e.g., 21:15-17, 18-22; 22:13-29; 24:1-4; 25:1-3, 5-10).

But the characteristic feature of Deuteronomy is not these two forms of law in their original form, but larger and more complex units which, in each instance, first require a special analysis. The law on the firstlings (15:19-22) begins with a sentence which can be recognized without difficulty as an old apodictic commandment; vss. 20-22, on the other hand, are an interpretation of the regulation by which the old legal maxim is explained in the light of the demand for centralization. This interpretation does not, however, proceed in technical legal terms; it is, rather, a personal address; it is a sort of sermon, in any case, information for the layman. Similar, but still more complicated in structure, is the unit on the Year of Release (15:1-11). Here, too, a statement of apodictic divine law, on which everything which follows is based, stands at the beginning. In vss. 2 ff ("This is the manner of the release . . .") an explanation is offered; this time it is an exact legal interpretation. But from here on to the end the preacher again has the floor, for these words of admonition, of warning, of promise, which lay this commandment very personally on the conscience of the hearer, can only be labeled a sermon. This structure is also found in the decree concerning debtor's bondage (vss. 12-18), except that here the old legal maxim, which is then expanded homiletically, is not a statement of apodictic law but of conditional law. Here, too, it is not simply a matter of obeying the commandments; but time and again there is an appeal to sentiment (cf. vs. 18: "It shall not seem hard to you, when you let him go free from you"). The preacher tries to arouse the right spirit, in which the old laws are to be observed. In the case of the Passover decree it is again an old apodictic statement from which the explanation proceeds (16:1). However, in addition to these parenetic elaborations which refer to an old statement of sacred tradition, there are others, in which there is no old legal maxim discernible from which the exhortation might proceed. To these belong, e.g., the law concerning the king (17: 14-20) or the prohibition of Canaanitic prophecy and the promise of a prophet like Moses (18:9-22) and the regulation concerning the CITY OF REFUGE (19: 1 ff). In these cases the lack of old legal maxims is not surprising, since no regulations concerning kings, prophets, or cities of refuge could be found in the old religious tradition of the period before Israel became a state. These broadly expansive parenetic units are, therefore, the characteristic feature of the Deuteronomic presentation of the law, and for this reason it would be an improper designation if one were to call Deut. 12–26 a "corpus" (or body of laws), for what is genuinely juridical is completely absorbed into the parenetic material. It would be better to speak of "preached commandments." Anyone who speaks of a "codex" would, therefore, only mean the old legal materials which were developed by Deuteronomy in the form of sermons. But is it certain, then, that they ever did constitute a complete codex? To be sure, the degree of this homiletic expansion in Deut. 12–26 is not uniform. Beginning with ch. 23, this parenetic permeation diminishes perceptibly, and the material changes more and more into a succession of many minor individual regulations, which by this time have little or nothing of the parenetic style. This suggests the possibility that Deuteronomy was expanded at an early stage by all kinds of legal materials which, however, were no longer homiletically reshaped in the same fashion.

Analysis of the history of the form of Deut. 6–11 yields another result. Here, too, we find a number of parenetic units hung together which can usually be separated from one another relatively easily. They are not, however, as in chs. 12–26, exhortatory compositions which each make a certain religious or legal regulation binding; instead, they are exhortatory compositions which, in a very general way, call for obedience to the "statutes and the ordinances which I set before you this day." It has long since been surmised that these parenetic compositions were connected with a proclamation of the law so that they should be considered as speeches which preceded a liturgical recitation of the divine commandments or formed a setting for them (*see* the work of A. Klostermann in the *bibliography*). Thus the section 7:1-15 clearly falls into two parts. In the first part, vss. 1-11, with an eye on Canaanitic religious practices and on the danger of intermingling, a call is issued for obedience to the commandments "which I command you this day." The second part, on the other hand, speaks of the blessing which Yahweh will bestow upon men, animals, and fields if Israel continues to be obedient to these commandments. This section, by the way, is closely related to the promise of blessing in 28:3-6, which is essentially much more strictly liturgical in style. Thus it is very obvious that 7:1-15 was originally something like a liturgical formula for exhortation and the promise of blessing which made a setting for a liturgical proclamation of the law: vss. 1-11 introduce it; vss. 12-15 conclude it. This liturgical sequence (exhortation, commandments, blessing and curse) is repeated, indeed, on a larger scale in the arrangement of the book of Deuteronomy. The sequence of its individual sections (exhortation: chs. 6-11; statement of the law: 12–26:15; commitment to the covenant: 26:16-19; blessing and curse: chs. 28–30) can surely not be considered an arbitrarily selected literary arrangement. Here, too, there is reflected a liturgical ceremony, the framework of a religious celebration in the center of which was the proclamation of the commandments and the commitment of Israel to the intent of Yahweh's law.

Within the parenetic units of chs. 6–11 there are, however, several which have nothing to do with the proclamation of the law. Thus, e.g., 7:16-25 revolves around the military subjugation of the peoples of Canaan, around the admonition to be fearless, and around the warning against appropriating the things which were accursed (חרם). The situation is very similar in the case of 9:1-6 and also of 31:3-8. Here it is a question of speeches which were made to the army before a war. That it is a matter not merely of a literary fiction but of an actual form of literature—namely, the war sermon—can be gathered from the law of war (20:1 ff), which in its most recent stratum also provides for an address to the troops by a priest (vss. 2-4). These war sermons are important in the determination of the origin and composition of Deuteronomy. *See* § 6 *below*.

**6. Origin.** After what has been said so far, the question of the authorship of Deuteronomy can, to begin with, only be expressed thus: The representatives of this practice of sermonizing gave Deuteronomy —from the first to the last sentence—this characteristic stamp, peculiar to it, with respect to phraseology. They were concerned with actualizing the old religious and legal traditions for their own time. We sense, in the urgency of their sermons, that those to whom they addressed themselves had already nearly outgrown the old Israelitic regulations. This explains the importunate, occasionally imploring, manner of speech and the attempt to grip the listeners very personally in order to impress the divine commandments on their consciences. If, in this respect, a certain monotony in Deuteronomy—at least with regard to its phraseology—has justifiably been mentioned, in any case, one may not overlook the very broad nature of the content, the diversity of the subjects preached about. Alongside homiletic presentations of old apodictic legal maxims one finds those which represent the conditional legal regulations. Those preachers are concerned with the arrangement of festivals, with the institution of kingship, as well as with the support of the priests, the stipulations of the holy war, and the laws concerning marriage and the family. Who were the men to whom the entire sacred and legal material of their tradition was equally available and who could claim for themselves the authority for such an arbitrary interpretation of these old materials? They cannot have been laymen, but must have been men who held a religious office. The ease with which they go back and forth between materials of the most varied origin at once points to a relatively advanced period in the history of Israelitic traditions. The only passage within the historical tradition of the OT which can be of assistance here is the description of the reading of the law of the God of heaven, which Ezra arranged (Neh. 8:1 ff; *see* EZRA AND NEHEMIAH, BOOKS OF); for the chronicler reports that at the same time the Levites instructed the people in the law, in that they interpreted what was read. In point of time, the evidence probably lies well before the period of time which can seriously come into consideration for the dating of Deuteronomy, but if such interpretive activity—exactly what we are looking for, from the point of view of Deuteronomy—is known in the fifth century, then there is certainly a possibility that the Levites also engaged in this activity even earlier (*see* PRIESTS AND LEVITES). There is, however, still another indication that the preachers of Deuteronomy should be sought in the priestly-Levite circles: according to the law of war (Deut. 20: 1 ff) a priest was to make a speech before the beginning of the battle. The outline of the address which is attributed to him (vss. 3-4) corresponds exactly to the sermons of war which are also found elsewhere in Deuteronomy. However, the texts which refer to war are not merely one part of Deuteronomy among others; on the contrary, all of Deuteronomy is influenced by a decidedly warlike spirit, which pervades the parenetic (chs. 6–11) and the legal portions (chs. 12–26) equally (cf. 6:18; 7:1-2; 11:23 ff; 12:29; 19:1; 20:16; etc.). In this very respect Deuteronomy differs markedly from the Book of the Covenant, the Holiness Code, or the Priestly Code. Therefore, the question as to the origin and the authors of Deuteronomy is tantamount to the other question as to who the representatives of this militant piety were. To be sure, it is also possible to consider Deuteronomy the exponent of a more intellectual-literary current, hence as the theoretical-theological project of a literary group. But one should raise the question first, however, as to whether Deuteronomy cannot be explained precisely on the basis of its characteristically warlike impression by a specific situation in the history of Israel.

Whereas Israel in the period before its statehood waged its wars by a general levy, the conscription of free peasants, the kings changed over more and more to carrying on their wars with mercenaries or professional soldiers. *Ca.* 701, to be sure, the political existence of Judah was destroyed by Sennacherib. Not only were extensive territories of the old kingdom of Judah assigned to the Philistines; but the Assyrian probably also, as was generally his custom in dealing with subjugated peoples, took the mercenaries and the specialized warriors who fought from chariots over into his own military force. If JOSIAH, after this catastrophe, wished to make himself politically independent, he had to fall back upon the old method of procedure, conscription of the free peasants; for the building of an effective mercenary force was much too expensive for the empty coffers of the state. Actually it can be proved by a series of statements from the historical work of Deuteronomy and Chronicles that Josiah in his striving for political expansion did go back to this ancient form of military organization (*see* the work of E. Junge in the *bibliography*). Since Deuteronomy must be connected anyway with the events under Josiah, it is natural to connect the warlike spirit of Deuteronomy, which emerged so abruptly, with this reorganization. Up until that time politics and waging war had been a concern of the king and his officials, officers, and mercenaries. With the calling out of the militia, forces suddenly came into a central position which had been excluded for centuries: old traditions from the holy wars, as they were waged in the days before statehood, came alive again and were adapted in a makeshift fashion to the demands of the new age. It is to be assumed that the Levites, in particular, were the representatives of this warlike revival. Prophetic circles may also have had a part in it, for Deuteronomy shows prophetic influences here and there. However, the prophetic coefficient in Deuteronomy should probably be credited to a greater degree to the general ideas and conceptions which were characteristic of the religious life and thought of this whole period. The supporters, spokesmen, and expositors of the old traditions which are gathered together in Deuteronomy were hardly prophets, but Levites.

If, then, Deuteronomy had gone into effect in the kingdom of Judah under Josiah, this does not mean that it must therefore be considered a specifically Judaic tradition. On the contrary, there are indications which point to an origin in the N kingdom. The demarcation with respect to the Canaanitic worship of Baal and the struggle against religious syncretism which runs through all parts of Deuteronomy fits, according to everything we know, much better into the situation in the kingdom of Israel than into that of Judah. Moreover, there is the fact that Deuteronomy also addresses itself to "all of Israel" and that this Israel tradition had its home in the N kingdom, while in Jerusalem and Judah, as can be seen, e.g., from Isaiah, a tradition built around Zion and David was cherished. Also the Deuteronomic law of the king points much more to the kingdom of Israel with respect to constitutionality, because it speaks of a free choice of the kings and even considers the election of a foreigner possible. Especially significant are the points of agreement between Deuteronomy and the prophet Hosea, whose polemic against kingship (3:4; 8:4, 10; 13:11) coincides with the negative point of view of Deuteronomy (Deut. 17:14 ff). Likewise, the demand that they love Yahweh (Deut. 6:5 and repeatedly) probably is more or less closely connected with the message of Hosea, although one may not imagine a direct, possibly literary, dependence. The

Shechem chapter (Deut. 27), the position of which in Deuteronomy is problematic in any case, would also not appear to be an incomprehensible foreign element in Deuteronomy if Deuteronomy is interpreted from the point of view of the N Israelitic tradition. If these considerations prove valid, one must think of N Israelitic sanctuary (Shechem or Bethel?) as the place of origin of Deuteronomy and must fix its date in the century before 621. There are no legitimate reasons for going back still further. The question as to whether the sacred and legal regulations which are basic for Deuteronomy are N Israelitic, and whether their homiletic treatment first took place under Josiah, suggests itself, naturally; but it is hard to decide.

**7. Theology.** If Deuteronomy were a code of law, it would scarcely be possible to speak of a "theology" of Deuteronomy. However, since it must be understood to be the result of a far-reaching homiletic activity, the attempt can also be made to establish the basic thought of this Levitic sermon and the theological accomplishment which is behind it. The fact that Deuteronomy does not represent a unit, either from a literary point of view or from the point of view of the history of tradition, is only a minor obstacle in this attempt, because even the more recent portions do not differ appreciably from the older with regard to their theology. Above all, the fact that Deuteronomy considers itself a great authentic compilation of the belief and statutes of Israel demands such a breakdown of its contents. Nothing is to be added and nothing taken away from it (12:32—H 13:1; cf. 4:2): this means that Deuteronomy was already claiming something like canonical validity. As a matter of fact, almost all the sacred traditions alive at that time were brought together in one big whole in Deuteronomy. But one may not assume that Deuteronomy seeks to fix the doctrine of Israel in a form valid for all time—there never was such a thing in Israel. Deuteronomy does claim to be the word of Moses to Israel for a specific hour of its history, and therefore presents its message aggressively, in that it never for a moment loses sight of its religious opponent, the Canaanitic natural religion.

The most varied traditions, the belief in election (of a chosen people), the tradition of the patriarchs, the traditions of Moses and the revelation of God on Mount Sinai, and many other things have been fused in Deuteronomy into a unit of such encyclopedic scope and of such a rigid theological uniformity as was never again possible for the faith of Israel. One does justice to the significance of this theological accomplishment only if one understands that there had never been such a compilation of the traditions of all Israel at all before Deuteronomy. Formerly the individual Israelite lived in obligation to one of the holy places and to the regulations and traditions practiced there. Deuteronomy, however, is in earnest with its belief in the indivisible Yahweh (6:4), who can be worshiped in only one sacred place by one Israel. Deuteronomy injected this understanding into a period in which everything, the political as well as the religious existence of Israel, was in complete dissolution. The demand for a centralization of worship is surely much less a religio-political measure than a theological consequence which resulted from the con-

ception of one Israel before the one Yahweh. To this Israel, Yahweh granted the Torah through Moses. Before Deuteronomy, "Torah" in Israel meant the individual priestly decision, a short statement with which the priests perhaps answered the question of a layman—usually concerning "clean or unclean" (Deut. 33:10; Hos. 4:1-2, 6; Hag. 2:11 ff). Deuteronomy uses the word "Torah" in a new sense—namely, as the sum of all the revelations of the will of Yahweh, which finally constitute an indivisible unit (Deut. 4:3; 17:19; 30:10). The knowledge that the whole direction of history and the many religious and legal traditions of Israel represent only parts of one unique self-revelation of Yahweh was of greatest significance for the faith of those who came later. To this Israel, Yahweh had promised the land of Canaan as a hereditary possession (נחלה). Again there is a new linguistic usage: until now one spoke of the inheritance of kinsfolk (Gen. 31:14; Num. 16:14; Josh. 24:28 ff) or of that of a tribe (Josh. 13:7, 14; 14:9, 13-14), and in this sense it is a question of a religious concept of genuine legal significance. When Deuteronomy spoke of the נחלה of Israel, the term no longer had a legal, but only a religious, significance. In this inheritance Yahweh will bestow upon his people all conceivable blessings (Deut. 12:7; 15:6, 14; 16:10; 28:2), and they will enjoy rest from all enemies round about (12:9; 25:19). The blessings of salvation, toward which the people of whom Moses took leave are moving, are completely of this world and to a large extent of a material nature. With this derivation of all natural blessings which serve to support a people, however, Deuteronomy victoriously concluded a long and fluctuating battle between the natural religion of the Canaanites and the belief in Yahweh. Yahweh, sovereign not only in the shaping of history, is also the unique dispenser of every blessing of the earth, which hitherto had been the domain of Baal. The constitution according to which Israel is to live in the Promised Land is more nearly one of an ideal amphictyony than that of a state with a king. The Israel of Deuteronomy is no state, but a great religious community; and the Deuteronomic law of the king makes it clear enough that Israel, in the opinion of Deuteronomy, will not have lost anything if it is not ruled by a king "like all the nations that are round about" (17:14).

Thus Deuteronomy is the word of Moses to an Israel which is in a very advanced hour of its history. This Israel, which outwardly no longer resembles in any respect the one which was once on Horeb—it has kings, prophets, and is even acquainted with false prophets!—comes once more under the sovereignty of Yahweh, in order to be claimed by him as his people—as a "holy people" (7:6; 14:2, 21; 26:19; 28:9). It would be wrong, however, to regard "this Torah" as law in the theological sense of the word (*see* LAW IN THE OT); Deuteronomy does not demand that Israel earn its salvation by obedience. On the contrary, the election, the laying claim to Israel, has taken place before Israel had a chance to prove itself before God; only then does the demand that the commandments be kept follow. It is also significant that Deuteronomy derives the obedience of Israel from gratitude (ch. 8). Especially characteristic for the sequence election-obedience is 27:9-10: "Keep silence and hear, O Israel: this day you have become the people of the LORD your God. You shall therefore obey the voice of the LORD your God, keeping his commandments and his statutes, which I command you this day." The historical point in which Deuteronomy sets this great speech by Moses, which must be interpreted as an explanation of the Decalogue (5:26 ff), is "on the other side of the Jordan," in the land of Moab, thus between the election of Israel to be the people of Yahweh and the receiving of the gifts of the promise. However, great concern extends all through Deuteronomy lest Israel, even after it was chosen by Yahweh, might forfeit its salvation. With this theological claim Deuteronomy also passed over into the late period of the kings, not as a historical document from a time long past, but as Yahweh's claim on and promise to Israel. Then, however, one cannot avoid the assumption that this period also must have regarded itself as still being between the election and the fulfilment of the great promises—i.e., as a generation which, although it had already lived in Canaan for centuries, was nevertheless still waiting for the final fulfilment of Yahweh's promise.

**8. King Josiah and Deuteronomy.** Investigation of Deuteronomy began when the close connection between Deuteronomy and the reforms of King Josiah was pointed out, and for a long time the road to Deuteronomy led through II Kings 22–23. In the process the mutual relationships were undoubtedly overestimated, and it would be jumping to conclusions to seek simply to interpret Deuteronomy from the point of view of Josiah and Josiah on the basis of Deuteronomy. Deuteronomy is a product of the theology of this period; accordingly, in spite of all its propensity for the practical, it also undeniably has a theoretical spirit. Not without some justification, it has actually been called Utopian. King Josiah, on the other hand, certainly did not get all his impulses for action from Deuteronomy. The rapid collapse of the Assyrian Empire must have encouraged him to throw off feudal service and, accordingly, to free himself also from the worship of the Assyrian national gods. It is improbable that all measures along this line were inspired by Deuteronomy. And if Josiah should have thought of restoring the kingdom of David, then, indeed, there is no connection with Deuteronomy, which is so far removed from the sacred traditions of Jerusalem. On the other hand, Josiah's action against the places of worship of Yahweh in the country and against the places of worship of Canaanitic deities is not to be understood on the basis of the political demands of this period (II Kings 23:8, 10, 13-15), nor can the special celebration of the Passover (vss. 21-23). However, it is understandable that a document such as Deuteronomy could not be used as the program for the religious reform of a Judaic king without being affected to some extent. It was inevitable that the king in his actions would go beyond Deuteronomy to some extent and, also to some extent, lag behind it. One case in which a regulation provided for in Deuteronomy (18:6 ff) could not be carried out in practice is noted in the account of the reform itself (II Kings 23:9).

*Bibliography.* A. Klostermann, *Der Pentateuch* (1907), p. 246. A. C. Welch, *The Code of Deuteronomy* (1924). F. Horst, *Das Privilegrecht Jahwes* (1930). A. C. Welch, *The Framework of Deuteronomy* (1932). E. Junge, *Der Wiederaufbau des Heerwesens des Reiches Juda unter Josia* (1937). C. A. Simpson, "A Study of Deut. 12–18," *ATR* (1952), pp. 247 ff. A. Alt, "Die Ursprünge des israelitischen Rechts," *Kleine Schriften zur Geschichte des Volkes Israel* (1953), I, 278 ff; "Die Heimat des Deuteronomiums, II, 250 ff. G. von Rad, *Studies in Deuteronomy* (1953).

G. VON RAD

**DEVIL** [διάβολος, slanderer, calumniator]. A word which relates to several terms in the OT, the later Jewish writings, and the NT. The LXX translates שׂטן with διάβολος. The NT uses both διάβολος and the transliterated σατανᾶς without any basic differentiation. Interesting to note is the use only of σατανᾶς in the undisputed letters of Paul and only of διάβολος in the disputed letters and in the Johannine Gospel and letters.

The OT term has its origin in Hebrew judicial terminology as the "adversary," especially in the sense of the accuser at court (Zech 3:1). Israel's enemies have from God a special function as her accusers (I Kings 11:14). In Job 1:6-12, SATAN is Job's accuser before God, working in behalf of God and in no sense as a demonic power. However, the original judicial content is transcended as Satan becomes the worker of Job's misfortunes and in I Chr. 21:1 the inciter to evil. These later developments may be due to Persian or Babylonian influence, but a metaphysical dualism does not appear in the OT.

In some of the later Jewish writings the term is associated with evil desire (*see* DEMON), fallen angels (*see* ANGEL), and the angel of DEATH, but these are secondary. The central understanding of the term is of one who destroys the relationship between God and men, especially Israel, by leading men to sin, accusing them before God, and seeking to thwart God's plans. It is to be emphasized, however, that the term is not identified with the ruler of this world.

In the NT the term (only "διάβολος" passages cited) is understood as the singular and supernatural adversary of God, the tempter and seducer of men (Matt. 4:1 ff; 13:39; Luke 4:1 ff; 8:12; John 13:2; Acts 10:38; Eph. 4:27; 6:11; I Tim. 3:6-7; II Tim. 2: 26; Jas. 4:7; I Pet. 5:8). One under his power can be called a devil or the devil's child (John 6:70; 8:44; I John 3:8, 10). In his hands is the power of death (Heb. 2:14). Although he is the ruler of this world, Christ brings his defeat (Matt. 25:31; Jude 9; Rev. 2:10; 12:9, 12; 20:2, 10; cf. John 12:31; 14:30; 16:11; II Cor. 4:4). Without the use of διάβολος, the original OT emphasis as "accuser" appears overtly in Rev. 12:10 (κατήγωρ) and as a presupposition in Rom. 8:33-34. As an adjective διάβολος appears in II Tim. 3:3, 11; Tit. 2:3; and the verb διαβαλλεῖν appears in Luke 16:1. *See also* ABADDON; APOLLYON; BEELZEBUL; BELIAL; DRAGON; EVIL ONE; LION; LUCIFER; SERPENT.

*Bibliography.* R. Bultmann, *Theologie des Neuen Testaments* (1954), pp. 363, 493; G. F. Moore, *Judaism,* I (1954), 191, 406-7, 492-93.

P. L. HAMMER

**DEVOTED.** The basic meaning of the noun חרם (ḥērem) and the verb החרים, commonly rendered "devoted thing(s)" and "devote" respectively, is connected with the idea of holiness, exclusion, separation, taboo. The root is used in all the Semitic languages to denote things forbidden to common use: cf. Arabic *ḥarām,* used of the sacred precincts of Mecca, Medina, and Jerusalem; *ḥarīm,* the area forbidden to all except the husband and eunuchs; and Akkadian *ḥarimtu,* "sacred prostitute." Clothing worn at the circuit of the Qa'aba are *ḥarīm* and may not be worn or sold. In Lev. 27:28 a person or thing devoted to the deity is excluded from private use, for "every devoted thing is most holy to the LORD." The *ḥērem* is especially connected with warfare. In hope of victory a vow was made devoting all spoils, animate and inanimate, to the deity (Num. 21:2-4). The unmitigated *ḥērem* required the slaughter of everything that breathes (Deut. 20:16) and the destruction of everything destructible. Things inflammable were burned (Deut. 7:25-26), but noncombustible precious metals might be taken into the sanctuary treasury (Josh. 6:24). None of the devoted things could be appropriated for private use (Deut. 13:17). By the extension of this principle, every devoted thing became the property of the priests (Lev. 27:21; Num. 18:14; Ezek. 44:29). Achan's sin in this regard brought upon all Israel the curse of the devoted thing, which could be removed only by the extermination of the sinner and his household (Josh. 7:11-15, 25). No person devoted might be spared or ransomed (Lev. 27:29). The destruction of Jericho is a vivid example of complete devotion of a city (Josh. 6:18 ff). The barbarity of the *ḥērem* was mitigated by exempting women and children (Num. 31:7-12, 17-18; Deut. 21:10-14), and particularly young virgins (Judg. 21:11-12). Cattle and sheep also might be saved (Deut. 2:34); but this was not condoned by the purist, even when the pretext was that they were to be sacrificed to the Lord (I Sam. 15:9, 21). The enemy king especially was regarded as a prime candidate for devotion, and failure to execute him brought divine disfavor (I Sam. 15:24-33; I Kings 20:42).

The Canaanites were devoted to destruction (Deut. 7:1-3; 20:16-18; Josh. 2:10; 6:17), in order that Israel might not be seduced into idolatry. Joshua is credited with accomplishing their wholesale extermination (Josh. 10:1, 28-40; 11:11-21). Actually this was only wishful thinking of a later time, and it is admitted that the Israelites were unable to carry out the destruction (I Kings 9:21). An idolatrous Israelite city was to be treated the same as the Canaanites (Deut. 13:12-18). Anyone who sacrificed to a god other than the Lord merited destruction (Exod. 22:20), though it is doubtful that such a penalty was often exacted.

In the postexilic period the *ḥērem* was no longer applied as a military measure, but certain aspects of it were adapted as a means of eliminating undesirable elements from the community. When Ezra attempted to close the ranks of the returned exiles against the heathen influence of the people of the land (*see* AM HA'AREZ), those who refused to cooperate had their property devoted—i.e., confiscated —and they themselves were expelled from the community (Ezra 10:8). Thus the *ḥērem* became a means of ecclesiastical discipline, by expropriation and EXCOMMUNICATION.

The idea of the *ḥērem* persisted in apocalyptic thought. The enemies of Israel, the heathen nations, collectively symbolized by Edom, are doomed (devoted) to slaughter (Isa. 34:2, 5). The heathen will be threshed by Zion and their wealth devoted to the Lord (Mic. 4:13; cf. Hag. 2:6-7). Horror and revulsion against the *ḥērem,* and fear of it, also persisted (Mal. 4:6); in the new Jerusalem (Zech. 14:11) and the heavenly Jerusalem (Rev. 22:3) there will be no more *ḥērem,* or curse.

*See also* ANATHEMA; BLESSINGS AND CURSINGS.

*Bibliography.* H. J. Strack and P. Billerbeck, *Handkommentar,* IV (1928), 293-333; L. Brun, *Segen und Fluch im Urchristentum* (1931); F.-M. Abel, "L'anathème de Jéricho et la maison de Rahab," *RB,* 57 (1950), 321-30; H. Stieglecker, "Härte und Grausamkeit im AT," *Theologisch-Praktische Quartalschrift,* 98 (1950), 9-30.  M. H. POPE

**DEVOUT** [צדיק (Isa. 57:1; KJV MERCIFUL); εὐλαβής; εὐσεβής (GODLY *in* II Pet. 2:9); σεβόμενος, *participial form of* σέβω, to worship]. In the OT passage, a synonym for "righteous"; in the NT, "reverent, pious, devoted to the cult or to worship." In Acts, σέβω is used only in reference to the worship of pagans, some of whom may have had a loose connection with the synagogue.

*See also* WORSHIP IN NT TIMES, CHRISTIAN.

B. H. THROCKMORTON, JR.

**DEW** [טל; LXX *and* Apoc. δρόσος]. Condensation of water vapor from air cooled by contact with ground or objects which have lost sufficient heat by radiation during the night. This occurs chiefly during clear, calm nights when temperature drops markedly and the air is moist. Dew is important for vegetation in Palestine because it is at its maximum during the almost rainless four months of summer. It is heaviest on the coast W of Beersheba, in the Plain of Esdraelon, and at the sources of the Jordan beneath the slopes of Hermon (Ps. 133:3). It soon evaporates (Exod. 16:14) as the heat of the sun increases (Hos. 6:4). Dew was believed to fall imperceptibly (II Sam. 17:12) from the sky (Zech. 8:12) or the highest clouds (Prov. 3:20).

As a figure of speech "dew" represents abundant fruitfulness (Gen. 27:28), refreshment and renewing (Ps. 110:3; Hos. 14:5—H 14:6), what is beyond man's powers (Mic. 5:7—H 5:6), a silent coming (II Sam. 17:12), impermanence (Hos. 13:3), and exposure (Song of S. 5:2).

*See also* PALESTINE, CLIMATE OF.

*Bibliography.* D. Ashbel, *Bio-Climatic Atlas of Israel* (n.d.), pp. 51-55; D. Baly, *The Geography of the Bible* (1957) pp. 43-45.  R. B. Y. SCOTT

**DIADEM** [צניף (Isa. 62:3; TURBAN *in* Job 29:14), *from verb* to wrap, wind; צפירה (Isa. 28:5); KJV מצנפת (RSV TURBAN; Ezek. 21:6); διάδημα (KJV CROWN)]. A wreathlike crown. A turban bound to the head by a cloth or metal band was a characteristic type of CROWN in the ancient world; hence "turban" or "miter" is more accurately descriptive of the royal headdress of the OT period. The Greeks called the blue band of the Persian crown a diadem; and when the Hellenistic kings adopted a wreathlike crown as their royal emblem, the name "diadem" was applied to it. A diadem, therefore, is properly a royal crown in distinction from the garland given for special merit or attainment (στέφανος; cf. I Cor. 9:25; II Tim. 4:8; Jas. 1:12; etc.), although the distinction is not always rigidly maintained.

"Diadem" is used metaphorically in two ways. In

the new age the Lord will be a crown of glory and a diadem of beauty to the remnant of his people (Isa. 28:5), and Zion will be a crown of beauty and a royal diadem in the hand of the Lord (Isa. 62:3). In John's visions the great red dragon bore a diadem on each of its seven heads (Rev. 12:3) and the beast from the sea a diadem on each of its ten horns (Rev. 13:1), and the figure on the white horse (the conquering Christ) had many diadems on his head (Rev. 19:12).

L. E. TOOMBS

**DIAL** [מַעֲלוֹת] (II Kings 20:11; Isa. 38:8); KJV SUN DIAL (Isa. 38:8). A device for measuring time, ascribed to Ahaz and employed by Isaiah for giving Hezekiah the sign of the sun's shadow returning.

Sun dials of several types were employed by the peoples of the ancient Near East. Herodotus (II.109) mentioned that the Babylonians had been using an instrument with twelve hour-gradations. It is not certain which type Ahaz used. The word מַעֲלוֹת may have a variety of meanings, and is used in the above passages for both the "dial" itself and the "steps" (KJV "degrees") which marked the passing hours.

Many exegetes have followed the Targ. and the Vulg. in the view that Ahaz' dial was a special instrument of the Babylonian type with an indicator and hour-gradations. The LXX, Jos. Antiq. X.ii.1, the Syr., and most recent scholarship have agreed, however, that it consisted of a stairway whose steps marked the time of day as the shadow of a nearby object passed over them. It is now known that the Egyptians used a device of this type. Readings in the Qumran texts tend to confirm this view.

*Bibliography.* J. A. Montgomery and H. S. Gehman, *Kings,* ICC (1951), p. 508; S. Iwry, "The Qumrân Isaiah and the End of the Dial of Ahaz," *BASOR,* 147 (Oct., 1957), 30-33; Y. Yadin, "Ma‘aloth 'Aḥaz," *Jerusalem Society for Palestine Exploration and Antiquities* (1958), pp. 91-96 (in Hebrew).

S. J. DE VRIES

**DIAMOND** [יַהֲלֹם, *from* הלם, to smite, LXX *and* Vulg. jasper; שָׁמִיר (Jer. 17:1), *see* ADAMANT]. A crystallized native carbon. For יַהֲלֹם (Exod. 28:18; 39:11) the versions seem to indicate a colored stone. *See* JASPER.

**DIANA** dī ăn'ə. *See* ARTEMIS.

**DIASPORA** dī ăs'pə rə [διασπορά]. A general term to indicate the widespread settlement of Jews outside Palestine. *See* DISPERSION; EXILE.

**DIATESSARON** dī'ə tĕs'ə rŏn. A harmony of the four gospels prepared *ca.* A.D. 170 by Tatian. *See* VERSIONS, ANCIENT, § 4a.

**DIBLAIM** dĭb'lĭ əm [דִּבְלַיִם, lump of figs, raisin cakes] (Hos. 1:3). The father of Hosea's wife Gomer. It has sometimes been suggested that the name is figurative—i.e., "Gomer the daughter of raisin cakes" —as an allusion to her harlotry, since raisin cakes were employed in fertility-cult rites in the ancient world.

J. M. WARD

**DIBLATH.** KJV form of RIBLAH in Ezek. 6:14.

**DIBLATHAIM.** *See* BETH-DIBLATHAIM.

**DIBON** dī'bŏn [דִּיבֹן, דִּיבוֹן, דִּימוֹן] (Isa. 15:9; KJV DIMON)]. Alternately: DIBON-GAD dī'bŏn găd' (Num. 33:45-46). **1.** A city of Moab; modern Dhiban, thirteen miles E of the Dead Sea and three miles N of the Arnon River. Eusebius (Onom. 76.17 ff) knew the site but placed the name in the desert.

The city of Dibon was taken by Sihon king of the Amorites. It was taken from him by Israel and allotted to Gad (Num. 21:23-30; 32:3, 34; apparently counted as belonging to Gilead in 32:29 [but to Reuben in Josh. 13:17]; named Dibon-gad in 33:45 [cf. Josh. 13:9]). It was probably subjugated by Eglon king of Moab (Judg. 3:12-14) and possibly freed by Ehud (vss. 15-30), but almost certainly by David (II Sam. 8:2).

"Dibon" occurs in the oracles of Isaiah and Jeremiah against Moab (Isa. 15:1-9; Jer. 48:18, 22). In Isa. 15:2 "the house and Dibon" (הַבַּיִת וְדִיבֹן; KJV "Bajith, and . . . Dibon") is perhaps a corruption of "daughter of Dibon" (so RSV; בַּת דִּיבֹן; cf. Targ. and Syr.). In Isa. 15:9 the phrase "waters of Dimon" may perhaps, with the Dead Sea Scroll of Isaiah (1QIs[a]) and the Vulg., be read "waters of Dibon" (so RSV).

The famous MOABITE STONE, discovered at Dibon in 1868, supplements and corrects the record. Doubtless when the Israelite kingdom was divided, the Moabites regained their independence.* But, according to the inscription, Omri of N Israel recovered control of Moab and retained it for "forty years," collecting a tribute of "a hundred thousand lambs, and the wool of a hundred thousand rams" (II Kings 3: 4). But Mesha restored Moab's independence and carried his conquests farther N (cf. II Kings 3:4-27). In the Moabite Stone, Mesha refers to making "this high place to Chemosh in Qarhah" and describes at length his buildings at Qarhah. He calls himself a Dibonite and praises the obedience of Dibon and its fifty chiefs. Was Qarhah a new capital at some unidentified site (later abandoned), or was it a new and temporary name for one of the two mounds at Dhiban? The question cannot now be answered. The imposing buildings on the mound suggest the latter alternative. Fig. MOA 66.

Of two mounds at Dibon, the S one is occupied by the present village. The one on the N, which is the more easily defensible because of wadies about it, and which, therefore, probably preserves the remains of Mesha's buildings, is fortunately unoccupied. The American School of Oriental Research at Jerusalem, through its directors, has undertaken the excavation of the promising site.* Preliminary reports from 1950-56 indicate the general outline of the city's history. Evidence of an Early Bronze Age level of occupation has been found, but none of the Middle or Late Bronze Age—quite in keeping with the results of Nelson Glueck's surface surveys. In other words there was only a nomad population in this area from 2100 to 1300. Fig. DIB 28.

Soundings have discovered some ten feet of Iron Age occupation, including from five to ten feet of rich Moabite remains; and the Nabatean levels are especially productive.

The earliest excavation discovered five (or four) city walls. One was built over by some of the others, but never bonded into any, and its crude construction suggested the Early Bronze Age. A tower, simi-

Courtesy of A. D. Tushingham

28. Ancient Dibon in Moab during the 1953 excavations

larly free-standing, was judged to be even earlier. A second wall, battered (not perpendicular), may be only a facing for wall no. 1. The heaviest wall (no. 3), 7.5-10.8 feet thick and built of large, well-squared blocks, is thought to belong to Mesha's time. A fourth wall, also battered, was built over wall no. 1. A fifth (upright) wall, of roughly cut stone, must have been built in Arab time, since the fill in the early tower, which was crossed by this last wall, included potsherds from Early Bronze to Arab times. Figs. BUR 56; 59.

In the SE sections of the mound a complex of buildings centered on a structure which was marked as Nabatean by the diagonal dressing of the outer surface of the walls. Little above the foundations remains, but these were deeply laid and solidly built. This structure was incorporated into a Roman building that was longer and had a higher floor level than the Nabatean structure, and heavier walls that were faced with well-dressed blocks. It was probably a Roman temple built over a Nabatean sanctuary. Later a Byzantine church was built beside it, using one of its walls, and domed Christian tombs were constructed in the Roman building.

A date for a Roman tower (not yet located) is given by an inscription "at the order of Claudius Capitolinus" and dated in the year 557, which, assuming the Seleucid era, sets the erection of the building in A.D. 245-46. If the word πύργος, "tower," is correctly read in the inscription, as appears probable, the structure intended is a Roman defense, presumably erected against Arab inroads. To the Roman period also belongs a typical Roman bath.

A Carbon[14] test of carbonized grain found in the Iron Age levels has given a date of 2815 B.P., or 858 B.C., ± 165 years (1023-693). The median date falls with remarkable agreement into the period determined by the pottery finds, which had previously been set by W. F. Albright and Roland de Vaux at 850 B.C. The grain in question was probably wheat, but too highly carbonized for the species to be determined. Presumably it was חטה, "WHEAT," frequently mentioned in the OT.

The discovery of such grain recalls the well-known fact that Moab was not only famous for sheep and goats (cf. II Kings 3:4), but also as a land of wheat and barley, the "breadbasket" of W Palestine. It was traditionally a land to which Palestinians resorted in time of famine (Ruth 1:1). Further comparison of its culture with that of the Hebrews in the Iron Age and the Nabatean period, the Hellenistic Roman Age, should contribute to the Hebrew-Jewish history.

**Bibliography.** R. E. Murphy, "A Fragment of an Early Moabite Inscription from Dibon," *BASOR*, no. 125 (1952), pp. 20-23. A. D. Tushingham, "Excavations at Dibon in Moab, 1952-53," *BASOR*, no. 133 (1954), pp. 6-25; "An Inscription from the Roman Imperial Period from Dhiban," *BASOR*, no. 138 (1955), pp. 29-33.     C. C. McCown

**2.** A town in the Negeb, in a list of towns outside Jerusalem settled by the Jews (Neh. 11:25); same as Dimonah.

**DIBRI** dĭb′rī [דברי, wordy(?)] (Lev. 24:11). A member of the tribe of Dan; grandfather of the man stoned in the wilderness for blaspheming "the Name" of God. The name of the blasphemer has been forgotten, although his descent from an Israelite mother and an Egyptian father is remembered.

**Bibliography.** M. Noth, *Die israelitischen Personennamen* (1928), p. 240.     R. F. Johnson

\***DIDACHE** dĭd′ə kĭ [διδαχή, teaching]. The oldest known document of a class denoted as "Church Orders," containing directives for catechetical instruction, worship, and ministry. In the single extant MS of the work, which was transcribed in 1056, it bears the title "Teaching of the Twelve Apostles," with a subtitle: "The Lord's Teaching to the Heathen by the Twelve Apostles." This text was discovered in 1873, and published ten years later, by Philotheus Bryennius in the library of the Jerusalem Patriarchate at Constantinople. The MS also contained texts of the Pseudo Epistle of Barnabas and the two epistles attributed to Clement of Rome. The Didache is undoubtedly the "Teachings of the Apostles" recorded by Eusebius (Hist. III.25.4) among the NT apocrypha. The earliest citation of the Didache (or possibly of one of its sources) is in Clement of Alexandria (Misc. I.20,100), who quotes 3:5 as scripture. The relative date of the Didache, its provenance, textual history, and significance, have to date been occasion of considerable disagreement among scholars; and no solution of these problems has yet received a widely accepted consensus.

The Didache, like all Church Orders, is a compilation from various sources. The contribution of its editor, apart from his selection and arrangement of his materials, consisted only of a few retouches and connecting links. Thus the date and provenance of the compiler are not the same necessarily as those of his sources; and it may well be that some of the materials of the Didache, as many critics maintain, derive from the apostolic age. The problem is particularly illuminated by the first section of the Didache (chs. 1-6), a collection of moral precepts and commandments illustrative of "two ways, one of life, and one of death."

The pattern of ethical instruction according to "two ways" was a basic method of Jewish catechesis (e.g., Ps. 1:6; Prov. 4:18-19; Jer. 21:8; Test. Asher 1:3; 1QS IV; Philo *On the Special Laws* IV.108; cf. Matt. 7:13-14). This Jewish pattern of teaching—whether in an oral or a written source—must have been adapted by an early Christian teacher for instruction of Gentile converts; for it is utilized as an exposition of the two chief commandments (cf. Matt. 22:37-39; Mark 12:30-31) and the "Golden Rule" (in negative form; cf. Western text of Acts 15:20).

In addition to Did. 1–6, two other recensions of this Christian formulation of the "two ways" are extant: (a) chs. 18–20 of the Pseudo Epistle of Barnabas (see BARNABAS, EPISTLE OF), in which the arrangement of the material is quite different from that of the Didache; and (b) a Latin version of the late second or third centuries, extant in two MSS, that is very close to the Greek Didache in both order of contents and text.

Despite the efforts of many critics to relate these three recensions in some scheme of interdependence, the simplest explanation is that all three stem from a common original. A revealing indication of the Jewish or Jewish Christian source of the "two ways" is the citation of Ps. 37:11 (cf. Matt. 5:5) in Did. 3: 7: "The meek shall inherit the land," where the reading of the Latin version is: "The meek shall inherit the holy land." (The phrase is absent from Pseudo-Barnabas.) There is nothing in the "two ways" material that would be unacceptable to a Jew. But the compiler of the Greek Didache has enlarged the teaching by an interpolation (1:3-6) of precepts drawn from distinctly Christian sources: Synoptic sayings similar to Matt. 5:39-44; Luke 6:30-33; I Pet. 2:11; Hermas Mandates 2:4-6; and an unknown apocryphon. And he has rounded off the instruction by the accommodating advice (6:2): "If you can bear the whole yoke of the Lord, you will be perfect; but if you cannot, do what you can."

The Didachist connects his "two ways" source to his Church Order material by making it a catechesis prior to baptism. In ch. 7 he directs that baptism be administered in the triune name, and, if possible, in running, cold water. Affusion is allowed if the supply of water is limited. A fast of one or two days before baptism is enjoined. The mention of fasting leads him, in ch. 8, to recommend that Christians fast on Wednesdays and Fridays, in distinction to the fasts of the "hypocrites" (i.e., the Pharisees) on Mondays and Thursdays. The Lord's Prayer (in a form very similar to that in Matthew—and with a concluding doxology) is to be recited three times a day.

Chs. 9–10 provide forms of thanksgiving before and after the common meals of the church. These forms are Christian versions of Jewish Benedictions (berakoth). The unbaptized are to be excluded from this "Eucharist," as it is called. But many critics believe that the prayers are designed for AGAPE meals, not the Lord's Supper, since they contain no reference to the Last Supper nor any identification of the bread and the cup with the body and blood of the Lord.

The notice that "prophets are to give thanks as they wish," rather than use the prescribed forms, leads the Didachist in chs. 11–13 to a discussion of how the churches are to receive, test, and provide for inspired ministers ("apostles and prophets") that may happen to visit their communities. The tests are not theological—which suggests that the problem of false prophets was not due to heresy—but ethical. Presumably the churches addressed had been afflicted with charlatans, who exploited their supposedly spiritual gifts for selfish, material subsistence. Chs. 14–15 direct the regular celebration of the Eucharist on the Lord's Day, and the appointment of "bishops and deacons worthy of the Lord" to provide this ministry in case "prophets and teachers" are lacking. The Eucharist is denoted as a "sacrifice," a fulfilment of the prophecy of Mal. 1:11, 14. Mutual confession of sins is enjoined before participation in the Eucharist.

A final chapter (16) is an apocalyptic admonition with respect to the signs of the coming of the Lord. The Didachist has made up his materials for this conclusion from Matt. 24; I Thess. 4:16; II Thess. 2:9; and the Pseudo Epistle of Barnabas 4:9. This chapter is probably not derived from a Church Order source, but is a compilation of the editor after the manner of his interpolation in 1:3-6.

In five instances, the Church Order material of the Didache refers as its authority to what the Lord commanded (8:2) or said (9:2) in the gospel, or to an ordinance of the gospel (11:3), or "as you have in the gospel" (15:3-4). In each case, the closest gospel parallel is to be found in Matthew. This circumstance, added to the close similarity of the ministries described in the Didache with those denoted at Antioch in Acts 13:1 ff, has persuaded most critics that the Church Order source is of Syrian provenance. This hypothesis seems supported also by internal evidence: the recognition of possible scarcity of running water, the reference to grain sown upon the mountains in the prayers, and the economic conditions presupposed by the directives concerning the offering of first fruits to the prophets (bread, wine, oil, money, clothes). The date of this Syrian Church Order would thus be later than Matthew, but prior to the acceptance of the fourfold gospel canon—i.e., the latter part of the first or the early years of the second century.

The editor who combined the "two ways" and the Church Order to form the Greek Didache probably worked toward the middle of the second century. He was probably not a Montanist, as some critics maintain; for though he admired prophets, he was no less wary of them. His use of Pseudo Barnabas and Hermas in free combination with his NT sources suggests that he flourished in Egypt, the only area where these two documents enjoyed anything like canonical authority. We have noted that Clement of Alexandria possibly cited the Didache as scripture, and the document was much used by Egyptian authors and compilers of the fourth and fifth centuries. Outside Egypt, the only notable use of the Didache was by the fourth-century Syrian compiler of the Apostolic Constitutions (VII.1-32).

Since Bryennius' discovery of the eleventh-century MS of the Didache, two papyri fragments of the text have come to light: a fourth-century Greek papyrus from Oxyrhynchus, containing 1:3-4; 2:7-3:2; and a fifth-century Coptic papyrus in the British Museum, of 10:3b–12:2a. The latter includes, following the thanksgivings at meals, a prayer for the blessing of the oil of unction (cf. Jas. 5:14).

**Bibliography.** The literature on the Didache is very extensive. For texts, translations, commentaries, see the bibliography under APOSTOLIC FATHERS. The most recent commentary, with exhaustive bibliography, is J.-P. Audet, *La Didachè, Instructions des Apôtres* (1958).

Select studies: A. Harnack, *Die Apostellehre und die jüdischen beiden Wege* (1886); J. A. Robinson, *Barnabas, Hermas and the*

*Didache* (1920); M. Dibelius, "Die Mahl-Gebete der Didache," *ZNTW*, XXXVII (1938), 32-41; F. E. Vokes, *The Riddle of the Didache* (1938); W. Telfer, "The 'Plot' of the Didache," *JTS*, XLV (1944), 141-51; E. J. Goodspeed, "The Didache, Barnabas and the Doctrina," *ATR*, XXVII (1945), 228-47; S. E. Johnson, "A Subsidiary Motive for the Writing of the Didache," *Munera Studiosa* (1946); R. Glover, "The Didache's Quotations and the Synoptic Gospels," *NTS*, V (1958), 12-29.

*See also* the bibliography under LORD'S SUPPER; MINISTRY, CHRISTIAN; TEACHING IN THE EARLY CHURCH.

M. H. SHEPHERD, JR.

**DIDRACHMA** dī drăk'mə [δίδραχμον, double drachma]. A Greek silver coin of the value of two drachmas, but no longer issued at the time of the NT. A didrachma was the sum of the sacred tribute which had to be paid to the temple annually by each Jew. Therefore this tribute was called simply δίδραχμον (Matt. 17:24), which the RSV translates "half-shekel tax" because its value corresponded to a half shekel (KJV "tribute money").

*See also* PIECE OF MONEY.          H. HAMBURGER

**DIDYMUS** dĭd'ə məs [Δίδυμος, twofold, twin]; RSV THE TWIN. An alternative designation for the apostle Thomas (John 11:16; 20:24; 21:2); probably his name among Greek-speaking Christians.

In the papyri it appears in the plural as a common noun (meaning "twins") and as a proper name. *See* THOMAS.

*Bibliography.* J. R. Harris, *The Twelve Apostles* (1927), pp. 23-27; J. H. Moulton and G. Milligan, *The Vocabulary of the Greek NT* (1914-29), p. 159.          E. P. BLAIR

**DIKLAH** dĭk'lə [דִּקְלָה, palm grove]. A son of Joktan, and hence the name of an Arabian locality (Gen. 10:27; I Chr. 1:21). It was probably an oasis, and has been plausibly, though not definitely, identified with the Phoinikon of Procopius and located at the S end of the Wadi Sirhan.          S. COHEN

**DILEAN** dĭl'ĭ ən [דִּלְעָן, promontory(?)] (Josh. 15:38). A village of Judah in the Shephelah district of Lachish. There is no agreement on the location.

**DILL** [קֶצַח, *qeṣaḥ* (Isa. 28:25, 27; KJV FITCHES), *cf.* Ugar. *qṣḥ*(?), Arab. *qazḥa;* ἄνηθον (Matt. 23:23; KJV ANISE)]. The occurrence of this word with CUMMIN clearly indicates a kind of seed used as a condiment or seasoning. Botanists agree with this identification for ἄνηθον in Matt. 23:23, the true dill being *Anethum graveolens* L., which resembles parsley and is cultivated for its aromatic, brownish, oval-shaped seed, not unlike caraway. Much used for flavoring foods, it is also valued for its carminative medicinal values. In rabbinic sources (Ma'as. IV.5) "dill" (שֶׁבֶת, *shebheth*)—stem, leaves, and seeds—is mentioned as subject to the tithe, as indicated by Matt. 23:23 (cf. Deut. 14:23; Luke 11:42).

Identification of the Hebrew קֶצַח with dill in Isa. 28:25, 27, is opposed by botanists, who claim it refers to *Nigella sativa* L., commonly called "nutmeg flower" (no relation to the nutmeg tree) or "black cummin." Support for this latter identification is found in the LXX use of μελάνθιον, identified with this herb, as well as the Arabic use of *qazḥa* for it, and the fact that the treatment of its seeds during the harvest is exactly as described in Isa. 28:27. *Qeṣaḥ,* "black cummin," in rabbinic literature (e.g., Ber. 40*a*) is distinguished from *shebheth,* "dill" (*see above*).

*See also* FLORA § A6*c;* ANISE; FITCHES; SPICE.

Pl. XVI*a*.

*Bibliography.* H. N. and A. L. Moldenke, *Plants of the Bible* (1952), pp. 46, 152-53.          J. C. TREVER

**DIMNAH** dĭm'nə [דִּמְנָה] (Josh. 21:35). A Levitical town in the territory of Zebulun; same as RIMMON 3.

**DIMON** dī'mən [דִּימוֹן] (Isa. 15:9 KJV). The RSV follows the Dead Sea Scrolls in reading "Dibon" (*see* DIBON 1). Some suggest that "Dibon" was deliberately altered to "Dimon" to furnish a play on the sound of the word "blood" (Hebrew *dam*). In this case, the "waters of Dibon" would probably be the Arnon. Those who disagree with this reading point out that (*a*) Dibon has already been mentioned in vs. 2, and no other location is mentioned twice in this chapter; (*b*) Dibon does not stand on a large stream (it is removed from the Arnon both by distance and by elevation), and Isa. 15:9 speaks of the "waters of Dibon."

A possible identification is with MADMEN, whose initial *mem* could be a dittography. In this case, the location may be Khirbet Dimneh, 2½ miles NW of Rabbah.          E. D. GROHMAN

**DIMONAH** dī mō'nə [דִּימוֹנָה] (Josh. 15:22). A town in the Negeb, near Edom; a part of the territory allotted to the tribe of Judah. Dimonah is mentioned in a list of cities in the far S, centered in Beer-sheba (Josh. 15:21-32). It may be the same city as DIBON, occupied after the return from exile (Neh. 11:25).          E. D. GROHMAN

**DINAH** dī'nə [דִּינָה, *perhaps* rights controversy]. Daughter of Leah and Jacob (Gen. 30:21; 46:15).

Only in Gen. 34 (a composite narrative with traditions preserved by J, E, and P) does Dinah play any role in the OT. In the vicinity of the city of Shechem, Dinah was raped by one of its residents, who was also named Shechem and whose father was Hamor the Hivite. Shechem wanted to marry Dinah, so Hamor, speaking for his son and the whole city, proposed to Jacob and his sons that the marriage be permitted and that a social and commercial covenant be made between the two peoples. The outrage against Dinah was bitterly resented by Jacob's sons, and especially by Simeon and Levi, two of her full brothers. The sons slyly agreed to the covenant, provided that the Shechemites consent to circumcision. Taking advantage of its inhabitants' postoperative weakness, Simeon and Levi attacked the city and slew Hamor and Shechem. After their brothers had joined in the plunder of Shechem, Jacob reproved them, since their action had imperiled his safety (cf. Gen. 49:5-7).

That this story reflects an incident in the premonarchical relations between the city of SHECHEM and the Hebrews, particularly SIMEON and LEVI, is generally agreed; but its exact nature is disputed. The part that Dinah, either as an individual or as a clan, might have had in it is also quite uncertain.

M. NEWMAN

**DINAITES** dī'nə īts. KJV translation of דיניא (RSV JUDGES), one of the groups associated with REHUM (Ezra 4:9) in the complaint to Artaxerxes regarding the rebuilding of Jerusalem by the returned exiles (vss. 8-23). The word is not a gentilic but an official title, as in the LXX (Lucianic recensions). These judges are frequently mentioned in the Aramaic papyri, and both Herodotus and Josephus describe them briefly.

Bibliography. Herodotus *History* III.31; Jos. Antiq. XI.ii.1; A. Cowley, *Aramaic Papyri of the Fifith Century B.C.* (1923), pp. 16, 18, 22-23, 99-100. R. F. SCHNELL

**DINHABAH** dĭn'hə bə [דנהבה]. The city of the Edomite king Bela son of Beor (Gen. 36:32; I Chr. 1:43). Various conjectures have been made as to its location, but none seems demonstrable.

**DINNER.** The noon meal in biblical times. *See* MEALS § 1.

**DIOGNETUS, LETTER TO** dī'əg nē'təs ['Επιστολή πρὸς Διόγνητον]. An apologetic Christian writing in a highly rhetorical and somewhat artificial style, of uncertain date but probably not earlier than the third century A.D. It is usually included among the APOSTOLIC FATHERS, although its purpose and literary character would place it more naturally among the early apologists. Both the writer and the person addressed are unknown. There is no indication of any important influence of the writing in the ancient church. It is best known perhaps for its simile of the Christians as being to the world what the soul is to the body, and for its statement that the Christians are a third "race"—the others being, of course, the pagans and the Jews. The last two of the twelve chapters of the work are obviously by another hand, also unknown.

Bibliography. The best text and modern discussion, with translation, is in H. G. Meecham, *The Epistle to Diognetus* (1949). J. KNOX

**DIONYSIA** dī'ə nĭsh'ĭ ə, —nĭzh'ə [Διονύσια, festival of Dionysus]. A festival in honor of the god Dionysus (later Bacchus), a vegetation-deity. It celebrated the return of life in spring, after the long sleep of winter, and by means of sympathetic magic attempted to secure fertility. Therefore, it was often accompanied by drunken excesses, sexual license, and the tearing to pieces of a human or animal victim, symbolizing the god, and the burying of the flesh. In Attica the lesser Dionysia was held in the villages in December; the greater Dionysia was held in the city and was accompanied by the comedies and tragedies of the great dramatists, and by long processions of the people wearing ivy. Antiochus Epiphanes (*see* ANTIOCHUS 4) compelled the Jews to join these processions when he introduced the Dionysia into Coele-Syria (II Macc. 6:7). N. TURNER

**DIONYSIUS** dī'ə nĭsh'əs, —ĭ əs [Διονύσιος]. A frequent Greek name related to Dionysus (Roman Bacchus), a Greek god of vegetation, later of wine and of drama. In the NT, an Athenian, a member of the AREOPAGUS, who was converted with Damaris and others by Paul's preaching (Acts 17:34). Belief by this prominent official illustrates Luke's interest in the conversion of men of position (13:12; 19:31; 26:32; 28:7), since an Areopagite belonged to a small, aristocratic, powerful governmental group. Paul's speech in the Areopagus at Athens met various responses, but some men such as Dionysius joined him and accepted the faith.

Little is known of Dionysius. Codex D adds "prominent" (εὐσχήμον) to his name. Eusebius (Hist. III.4.11; IV.23.3) repeats information now both accepted and questioned, from another Dionysius, bishop of Corinth (*ca*. A.D. 175), that the Areopagite became the first bishop of Athens.

Vast but pseudonymous influence from Dionysius began in the fifth century, when an anonymous Syrian churchman attached the name of Dionysius to his own influential writings. This mystical theology, uniting Christian and Neoplatonic thought, is known in part from four treatises and some letters, purportedly from the first century. Many medieval theologians from the ninth century onward wrote commentaries and expounded the thought of this Pseudo-Dionysius. Dionysius' fame led to his mistaken identification (ninth century) with the first bishop of France (third century) or Saint Denys, martyr and patron of France. D. M. BECK

**DIONYSUS** dī'ə nī'səs [Διόνυσος]. A vegetation-deity of Thraco-Phrygian origin, worshiped by orgiastic rites of singular crudeness and brutality. He won a growing place in the religious life of Greece, and later of Italy, in the teeth of strong opposition. He was generally known to the Romans by his Greek cult title of Bacchus; they also called his great festival Bacchanalia, for the Greek Dionysia. Among the Greeks and Romans he was known chiefly as the god of the vine; like other vegetation gods, he was also the center of a mystery cult and admitted his initiates to participation in the divine nature. The orgies of the primitive cult were conventionalized in the Greek world, and at the Attic festival of the Greater Dionysia. The Attic drama was evolved out of the dances and music of the religious rites. In the Hellenistic age, his worship was widely extended through the kingdoms ruled by the successors of Alexander, and was actively promoted by the kings themselves; artists, musicians, and craftsmen were often organized in private religious societies devoted to Dionysus.

The god is mentioned in the Bible only in II and III Maccabees: Antiochus Epiphanes forces the Jews to walk in the procession of Dionysus, carrying his sacred ivy, at the festival of the Dionysia (II Macc. 6:7); Nicanor threatens to destroy the temple and erect a sanctuary to Dionysus on its site (II Macc. 14:33); and Ptolemy Philopator orders Jews to be branded with the ivy leaf of Dionysus, who was the patron of the Macedonian dynasty (III Macc. 2:29). F. W. BEARE

**DIOSCORINTHIUS** dī'əs kə rĭn'thĭ əs [Διοσκορίνθιος]. The name of a month in the dating of Lysias' letter to the Jews in 165-164 B.C., according to II Macc. 11:21. Perhaps the reference is to the first month of the Macedonian calendar, *Dios*, which Josephus identifies with the Jewish month

Marcheshvan (Antiq. I.iii.3)—late November–early December—but the additional κορίνθιος is inexplicable. The reading *Dioscoridos* is also found in some Latin MSS, but this is not known to be the name of a month. Many editors prefer a variant Latin reading *Dioscurus*, which is known to be the third month of the Cretan year. This may have been the name of an intercalary month in the Macedonian calendar, corresponding to a position just before Nisan (April) in the Jewish calendar. Others conjecture that the name is a corruption of *Dystros*, corresponding to the Jewish month Adar (March). On the whole, the reading *Dioscurus* appears preferable.

**Bibliography.** F.-M. Abel, *Les livres des Maccabées* (1949), pp. 427-28.        E. W. SAUNDERS

**DIOTREPHES** dī ŏt′rə fēz [Διοτρέφης]. An early Christian known only from the unfavorable comment in III John 9 that he "likes to put himself first, does not acknowledge" the authority of "the elder," who writes that letter. *See* JOHN, LETTERS OF.

**DIPHATH** dī′făth [דיפת] (I Chr. 1:6). Same as RIPHATH.

**DIRECTIONS.** *See* ORIENTATION.

**DIRGE.** *See* MUSIC.

**DISCERNING OF SPIRITS.** *See* SPIRITS, DISTINGUISHING.

**DISCHARGE** [זוב]; KJV ISSUE. The normal Pentateuchal designation of gonorrhea. The Levitical regulations for controlling this ancient scourge of humanity are among the earliest on record. Caused by the *Neisserian gonorrheae* (gonococcus), the disease is a highly infectious, acute inflammation of the mucous membrane of the genital tract. The discharge of Lev. 15:19 ff includes menstruation.

       R. K. HARRISON

**DISCIPLE** [μαθητής, *from* μανθάνω, learn; תלמיד, *from* למד, and Latin *discipulus, from discere, are close equivalents;* μαθήτρια *(feminine;* Acts 9:36)]. A learner or pupil; one who accepts and follows a given doctrine or teacher.

**1. OT use.** At I Chr. 25:8, תלמיד becomes "scholar" in the KJV, "pupil" in the RSV. At Isa. 8:16, however, the closely related למד is rendered "disciple" in both versions. Like Jesus, Isaiah saw that his message had been rejected by his people. He therefore determined to entrust it to selected disciples who should keep and proclaim it.

**2. NT use.** In later times *talmidim* meant disciples of the rabbis, whose studies resulted in the TALMUD. Yet the Talmud itself speaks of five *talmidim* of Jesus (Sanh. 43*a*).

Contrary to popular belief, "disciple" is not, in the NT, a specific designation for one of the Twelve. The word occurs about 260 times in the gospels and Acts, but nowhere else in the NT. It is employed in various ways:

*a*) To designate an adherent of almost any great leader or movement. Thus we read of disciples of Moses (John 9:28); of the Pharisees (Matt. 22:16;

Mark 2:18); and perhaps of Paul (Acts 9:25), though here the MS evidence is conflicting. Disciples of John the Baptist are mentioned a dozen times, and in all four gospels. At John 1:35 ff, two of these leave John for Jesus when they hear John call Jesus the Lamb of God. John's disciples remain active, however (Mark 2:18 ff; Luke 11:1), even after their leader is jailed (Matt. 11:2; Mark 6:29). Jesus' own followers are usually called, not "the," but "his" disciples, as though to distinguish them from other like groups.

*b*) As the most frequent and general term for believers in Christ. The word is so used twenty-two times in Acts, as compared with four instances of "saint," two of "Christian," and one of "Nazarene" used in this sense (Acts 24:5; see Acts 6:1-2, 7; 9:10, 26; 11:26; 15:10; 16:1). ·

Of over 230 instances of the term in the gospels, about 90 per cent either are not limited to the Twelve at all, or else do not make clear whether these or some larger group is indicated (e.g., Matt. 8:21; Mark 3:7; Luke 6:13; 19:37). At Luke 6:17, the RSV follows the best MSS in reading "great crowd of his disciples," whereas the KJV, based on a later and inferior text, omits "great" and changes "crowd" to "company." This illustrates the tendency, in later times, to limit "disciple" to one of the inner group.

John is especially concerned to stress the inclusiveness of the term. From the beginning, we are told, Jesus had numerous disciples in Judea (John 1:35-50; 7:3; 8:30-31; 9:27-28; 11:54). These included some of his chief followers, and were to be found particularly among Jewish leaders (John 12:42; 19:38-39). The differentiation of disciples from the Twelve is very clear at John 6:66-67. This has undoubted bearing upon the identity of the "other disciple" or the "disciple whom Jesus loved." *See* JOHN, GOSPEL OF.

*c*) Referring specifically to one or more of the Twelve. This occurs some two dozen times (e.g., Luke 9:54; John 6:8; 12:4), more than half of which are in Matthew; and Matthew is the only NT book to speak of "twelve disciples" (Matt. 10:1; 11:1; 20:17). While Mark never limits the term in this way, its author does occasionally seem to think of a small group, who appear in a boat (Mark 6:45; 8:10), or "in the house" (Mark 7:17; 10:10), or talking with Jesus "privately" (Mark 4:34; 9:28). At the most, such restrictions upon the word are exceptional. Its common meaning for the early Christians was that of *b above*. This continued to be true in the second century. Even Irenaeus, who called the author of the Fourth Gospel *"the* disciple," never applied this phrase to any other; he, too, used "disciple" as equivalent to "Christian."

**3. In the singular.** The singular form of the word never occurs in Mark. It is frequent in John, always in reference to a particular person. In Matthew and Luke, it appears only on Jesus' lips. There it is in teachings about the nature of discipleship. The disciple cannot escape the calumny that has befallen his Master (Matt. 10:24-25). He must be prepared to forego home, kindred, and possessions for Christ's sake (Luke 14:26, 33), and to carry his cross (Luke 14:27). If he lives in Christlike selflessness, he will be recompensed (Matt. 10:42). Indeed, full discipleship and full Christlikeness are the same thing (Luke 6:40). *See also* MASTER; RABBI.        PIERSON PARKER

**DISCIPLE WHOM JESUS LOVED.** *See* BELOVED DISCIPLE.

**DISCIPLINE.** In the Bible discipline is closely associated with training, instruction, and knowledge on the one hand, and with reproof, correction, and punishment on the other hand. Its natural application is in the sphere of child training, but in the religious context it has been expanded in its range of meaning to include God's corrective measures in the life of men and nations. Its theological bearing is seen in the interpretation of dire happenings as God's disciplinary measures in love.

**1. In the OT.** In the OT the usual terms are יָסַר, "to chasten, correct, punish," and מוּסָר, "chastisement, discipline, instruction." A term of similar meaning is תּוֹכַחַת, "correction, chastisement, reproof." The Greek equivalent in the LXX for יָסַר is παιδεύω; and for מוּסָר, παιδεία. The changes in the history of English translation for παιδεία may be illustrated in Eph. 6:4: KJV "nurture," ERV-ASV "chastening," and RSV "discipline."

The OT context for this "discipline" is the family and the process of education in the family. The Israelites did not believe in "education without tears"; at least, they professed not to spare the rod. To the words of father and mother chastisement was added (Deut. 21:18); children were trained on the theory that "the rod of discipline drives [folly] far from [a child]" (Prov. 22:15).

Out of the family context this discipline sometimes meant pure punishment: "My father chastised you with whips, but I will chastise you with scorpions" (I Kings 12:11, 14; cf. Deut. 22:18).

On the other hand, some uses of this discipline implied simple instruction and correction. The father carried responsibility for the education of his son in the traditions of the chosen people (cf. Deut. 6:20 ff) and in the commandments of the law.

There was an easy transference from this discipline of the family to the discipline of God: "As a man disciplines his son, the Lord your God disciplines you" (Deut. 8:5b). Happy, then, is the man whom God chastens and teaches by dire adversity, for God deals with him as with a son (cf. Job 5:17; Ps. 94:12). Such chastisement was a proof of fatherly love (Prov. 13: 24). This severe discipline was meted out to the nation or the nations, and it was for punishment of sin, for correction, or for instruction. Here, too, this chastisement, no matter how severe, was to be accepted as evidence of God's enduring love. However, the psalmist did pray:

> O Lord, rebuke me not in thy anger,
>   nor chasten me in thy wrath
>       (Ps. 6:1).

**2. In the Apoc.** In the Apoc. this discipline is still heavy-handed; whips and scourges appear as synonymous with discipline (Ecclus. 22:6; 23:2; Sirach counsels masters not to hesitate to make the side of a slave to bleed). Wisdom as personified in Ecclesiasticus is the author of this discipline (4:17), though at times she torments a man.

The religious point of view can make the difference between disastrous calamity and remedial, saving discipline. To the world the souls of the righteous appear to be undergoing punishment, but they should know that God is testing them and disciplining them (Wisd. Sol. 3:4-7), and in the end they will be found worthy (cf. Wisd. Sol. 11:10). The author of II Maccabees personally urges his readers not to take the apparent disasters as calamities; the punishments are designed to discipline the people (6:12).

**3. In the NT.** In the NT use of παιδεία, "discipline," and παιδεύω, "to instruct, educate, discipline," the Jewish tradition comes in contact with the broader educational ideal of Greece. In the world of the Greeks these terms were applied to the household training of children and also to man's training to take his place in the culture of the world—with little emphasis on chastisement. In the NT the education of Moses is described in such terms in Acts 7: 22, an education in all the wisdom of the Egyptians. Paul's education at the feet of Gamaliel is put in the same terms.

The old idea of pure punishment crops up in Jesus' scourging at the hand of Pilate (Luke 23:16: παιδεύσας) or in the apostles' chastisement (II Cor. 6:9). By contrast, the absence of painful discipline is reflected in II Tim. 2:25: the Lord's servant corrects his opponents with gentleness.

The author of the Letter to the Hebrews in ch. 12 returns to the OT analogy of the father's disciplining his son as applying to God's use of trial and hardship for man's own good, and he cites the familiar passage in Prov. 3:11-12. The troubles that befall God's people are therefore to be understood as signs and instruments of his fatherly training. Even Satan could exercise a wholesome, disciplinary role in the case of certain blasphemers, Hymenaeus and Alexander (I Tim. 1:20; cf. I Cor. 5:5).

The milder sense of "reproof" appears in some phases of this Christian discipline, and its purpose is sometimes to bring to repentance (Rev. 3:19).

Christian education in the home is the picture in Eph. 6:4: "Fathers, do not provoke your children to anger, but bring them up in the discipline and instruction of the Lord" (cf. Col. 3:21). Education here is not just painful discipline; it is training by act, example, and word.

The content of this Christian education in the church was to be found in the Didache. So Apollos was trained in the way of the Lord (Acts 18:25). But the church and its leaders at the same time exercised a discipline to reprove and correct improper conduct or abuses in its fellowship—e.g., at Corinth or at Antioch.

Paul is an example of one who could take hardships and adversities and transmute them into godly discipline. So he accepted the "thorn in the flesh" (II Cor. 12:7). He considered his dire experiences, described in II Cor. 4:7-15, as "slight momentary affliction" which works an "eternal weight of glory."

*Bibliography.* W. W. Jaeger, *Paideia: the Ideals of Greek Culture* (trans. G. Highet; 1943-45).                P. E. DAVIES

**DISCOURSE OF CYRIL OF JERUSALEM, TWENTIETH.** *See* CYRIL OF JERUSALEM, TWENTIETH DISCOURSE OF.

**DISCOURSE OF SAINT JOHN THE DIVINE.** A Greek version of the ASSUMPTION OF THE VIRGIN.

**DISCOURSE OF THEODOSIUS** thē'ɔ dō'shĭ ɔs. A Coptic (Bohairic) version of the ASSUMPTION OF THE VIRGIN.

*Bibliography.* For a comprehensive summary, see M. R. James, *The Apocryphal NT* (1924), pp. 198-201.

**DISCRETION AND PRUDENCE.** The capacity to determine what is appropriate on a given occasion, or what will gain a desired end. The words appear together only three times (Prov. 1:4; 8:12; Dan. 2:14) and appear individually chiefly in the wisdom literature. They are intimately related to the idea of the knowledge of God, representing the fruit of instruction, as tact, discrimination, good taste, shrewdness, and are seen as necessary for leading a good life and avoiding evil.

"Discretion" is used variously to translate מַעַם (lit., "to examine by tasting"; figuratively, "to discern what is appropriate or in good taste"; cf. I Sam. 25: 33; Prov. 11:22; Dan. 2:14); הַשְׂכִּיל ("to act circumspectly"; I Chr. 22:12; II Chr. 2:12; Ezra 8:18; Prov. 19:11); and מְזִמָּה ("to devise"), the power to decide one's course, in a good sense (Prov. 1:4; 2:11; 3:21; 5:2; plural in 8:12; 14:17).

"Discretion" is often found in combination with "wisdom" (Prov. 3:21; 5:2), "understanding" (I Chr. 22:12; II Chr. 2:12; Prov. 2:11), and "knowledge" (Prov. 1:4; 5:2; 8:12). It may represent "tact" (as in the case of Abigail's soothing the ire of David; I Sam. 25:33). It enables one to keep the law of Yahweh (I Chr. 22:12), to avoid the way of evil (Prov. 2: 11), and to walk securely (Prov. 3:21). Where the plural is used, it may represent "witty inventions" (Prov. 8:12) or "wicked devices" (Prov. 14:17), as in the KJV (cf. Job 21:27; Ps. 10:2, 4; Prov. 12:2; 24:8).

"Prudence" (עָרְמָה) is derived from עָרַם, "to be crafty," and is used in the wisdom literature only in a good sense, signifying "shrewdness," the ability to keep oneself from being misled. The word is predicated of the serpent in Gen. 3:1, and appears in a bad sense in Exod. 21:14; Josh. 9:4. In the NT "prudence" is used to translate φρόνησις ("understanding," especially knowledge and love of the will of God; Eph. 1:8 KJV) and φρονίμως ("wisely"; Luke 16:8). In the etymological sense of "foresight," φρόνησις does not appear in the NT, although there is some reflection of this significance in Luke 16:8.

Prudence is taught to the simple, the unlearned, whose minds are open, but who are without a guide and easily led astray. Prudence (as "shrewdness") would seem to combine the "wisdom of the serpent with the innocence of the dove" (cf. Matt. 10:16).

*Bibliography.* C. H. Toy, *Proverbs*, ICC (2nd ed., 1914), p. 7; J. Lindblom, "Wisdom in the OT Prophets," in M. Noth and D. W. Thomas, eds., *Wisdom in Israel and in the Ancient Near East* (1955), p. 199.      V. H. KOOY

**DISCUS** [δίσκος, quoit]. A Greek game, introduced among the Jews by the high priest JASON in the Maccabean period, as part of his general process of Hellenization. According to II Macc. 4:7-17, the "ungodly" Jason received authority from the Syrian king Antiochus Epiphanes (*see* ANTIOCHUS 4), to set up a Greek gymnasium and to form youth clubs for exercising therein. The high priest and his colleagues are said to have been more zealous to attend the dis-

plays in the palaestra, including especially the throwing of the discus, than to attend to their duties at the altar.

The discus itself, the object from which the game was named, was a flat circular plate of wood, stone, or metal, quite heavy. The game consisted in each player's attempting to throw this farther than his competitors. It was often hurled a hundred feet or more. The method is well illustrated by the famous statue of the Discus Thrower by the Greek sculptor Myron.

*See also* GYMNASIUM.      N. TURNER

**DISEASE.** Physiological and psychological diseases may involve a degeneration of, or morbid change in, any of the bodily tissues; the perversion of physical or mental functions; or an abnormal condition of the body or mind which may be lengthy or of short duration. Because pathogenic organisms are parasitic in nature, disease may be defined as the product of a relationship between associating organisms in which one exhibits structural or functional degeneration from the norm because of the activity of the other. Diseases due to imbalance of bodily chemistry are not strictly parasitic in nature, however.

1. Ancient pathological concepts
2. Biblical concepts of the etiology of disease
3. Diseases of the OT
4. Diseases of the NT
5. Demon-possession
6. The death of Jesus
Bibliography

**1. Ancient pathological concepts.** Among primitive races, disease was either regarded as the result of hostile magic gaining a hold upon a person, or else its incidence was ascribed to the violation of a taboo. In either event a background of magic, sorcery, and witchcraft was presupposed where cases of intractable sickness were encountered, and such remedial measures as were undertaken inevitably involved the shaman, or medicine man. It was his function to divine the supernatural cause of the disease, and attempt to banish it by the use of spells, charms, drugs, and incantations. In Neolithic times it was widely believed that epilepsy, insanity, and certain neurotic manifestations were caused by the presence of a demonic force in the head of the sufferer. In order to release the imprisoned demon, an operation known as trephining or trepanning was performed by the priest-magician. A circular groove was scraped in the skull by means of a flint, and this procedure was continued until the disc of bone thus isolated could be lifted out. One skull exhibited no fewer than five such holes, probably indicating that the victim, a woman, was an epileptic. This formidable surgical procedure was apparently confined to Western Europe, although three trephined skulls were uncovered in a cistern when Lachish was excavated in 1936. Fig. DIS 29.

The pathological concepts of the ancient Babylonians were governed to a large extent by the profoundly superstitious nature of these ancient peoples. While certain simple diseased conditions were attributed to natural causes, the majority, including some

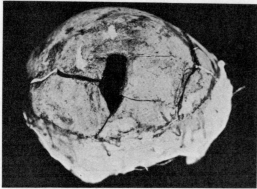

Courtesy of *Man* magazine

29. Three trephined skulls, uncovered in a cistern at
Lachish (late eighth century B.C.)

accidents, were taken to be visitations from the
demonic forces which inhabited the underworld. It
was commonly believed that these evil spirits gained
access to the inside of the body through the apertures
of the head, and as a countermeasure, charms, amulets, necklaces, and nose ornaments were employed
to restrict their depredations. It was from this form
of prophylaxis that subsequent decorative articles of
feminine adornment took their rise. Certain of the
medical tablets recovered from Babylonia attributed
the occurrence of specific diseases to the "hand of
Ishtar," or some other member of the Babylonian
pantheon. The "hand of a ghost" was also recognized
as an etiological factor in sickness.

Although the ancient Egyptians were far less superstitious and considerably healthier than their
Mesopotamian counterparts, they too subscribed to a
demonic theory of the origin of disease. Once an evil
spirit had possessed a man and brought about a
characteristic form of pathology, the aid of magic
was needed to effect a cure. It was therefore the
function of the priest-physician to determine the real
nature of the possessing spirit, to expel it by means of
incantations, magical formulas, charms, and the like,
and to repair the damage sustained by the individual
by means of a medical prescription.

Not all diseases were regarded as the product of
demonic activity, however, as the Edwin Smith surgical papyrus, published by J. H. Breasted in 1930,
clearly indicates. Such contingencies as injuries, surgical accidents, or wounds sustained in battle were
held to be rational in origin, and were treated accordingly by a variety of sensible empirical surgical
procedures.

**2. Biblical concepts of the etiology of disease.**
The general view of the OT writers is that disease
is sent by God as a punishment for transgression or
as an expression of his wrath (cf. Exod. 4:11; Deut.
32:39). Other views ascribed the origin of disease to
the work of the adversary (Job 2:7), or to what were
called spirits of dumbness (Mark 9:17) or uncleanness (Mark 9:25). Jealousy on the part of others (Job
5:2) and self-indulgence (Ecclus. 37:30-31) were also
held to be causes of disease. The penal concept of
sickness survived into NT times, as illustrated by the
case of the congenitally blind man (John 9:2). In the
light of these observations it is scarcely surprising
that the Bible does not encourage a purely naturalistic theory of the incidence of disease. On the contrary, holy scripture consistently implies that there is
a persistent psychic element which must be taken
into account in any consideration of the factors which
have contributed to the rise of characteristic forms
of pathology.

Estimations of the etiology of disease, particularly
in the writings of the OT, have not infrequently been
related by medical historians and biblical scholars
alike to the ancient system of humoral interaction.
According to this theory, bodily health was governed
by the quantitative balance and functional interaction of four fluids or humors, consisting of blood,
phlegm, yellow bile (choler), and black bile (melan-
choler). A preponderance of one or more of these
substances in the body was held to produce characteristic diseases, which were accompanied by certain
changes in the personality. Thus an individual in
whom phlegm, the heavy humor, was most prominent was considered to be calm, apathetic, or self-
restrained. If these qualities of character were evident
in a person, they were held to be caused by this
specific imbalance of humoral secretions.

In the OT, however, a rather different principle
is in view. The Hebrews never subscribed to the
Egyptian concept of substances being channeled to
various parts of the body by a series of internal
canals or conduits. Instead, they tended to concur
in the traditional practice of assigning emotional
functions and attributes to specific organs of the body
as distinct from, but operating in conjunction with,
their normal physiological activity.

Thus the heart, while functioning in its characteristic physical manner, was also regarded as the locale
of intelligence, mind, and will. Deficiencies of motive
or deranged states of the mind were often expressed
in terms of cardiac dysfunction or pathology, so that,
e.g., the divine challenge to Israel to obtain a "new
heart" (Ezek. 18:31) was in effect an appeal for the
operation of more lofty motives and spiritual values
(*see* HEART). This tacit recognition of the relationship
between emotional states and the functioning of
bodily organs to produce abnormal physical or mental conditions is characteristic of the biblical writers
generally.

The expression "bowels of mercies" (cf. Col. 3:12
KJV) has preserved in a forceful manner the conviction that a connection existed between a specific
emotional state and the operation of particular physical organs. It has remained for modern psychosomatic medical research to demonstrate clinically the
empirical truths appreciated for so many centuries,

and to show beyond reasonable doubt the intimate connection between emotional states and pathological changes in bodily tissues. With this in view, it is legitimate to disavow any but the most casual connection between the ancient system of humoral pathology and the thought of the biblical writers regarding the relationship of the emotions to bodily functioning. Instead, the scriptural authors may be regarded as antedating by their empirical insights the more systematized observations of modern psychosomatic medicine.

When Jesus interrogated those who came to him for healing, he did so in order to obtain a picture of the disease situation from the standpoint of the sufferer or his relatives. When a degree of faith had been elicited, Jesus proceeded, not merely to treat the physical or mental affliction, but to direct his therapy at the deepest levels of the human spirit. He envisaged much of disease as the result of evil operative within the recesses of the mind, though he was by no means unaware of the place which the conflict between individual and environment occupies in the causation of illness. There can be no doubt that Jesus regarded disease as one manifestation of evil within human experience, and as such it came under the judgment which was to be meted out to all the "works of the devil" (cf. I John 3:8; see HEALING).

**3. Diseases of the OT.** Difficulties of diagnosis loom large when the nature of most OT pathological conditions is under consideration. It is seldom that diseases are described with such care as those contained in Lev. 13, and where symptoms are encountered, the oriental manner of recording them presents many difficulties for the Western scientific mind. The. problem is not made any easier by the uncertainty which exists concerning the nature of those diseases which flourished in the ancient Near East. Without doubt, afflictions such as dysentery, malaria, the enteric fevers, leprosy, tuberculosis, and the like were present then as now, probably in greater proportions. Smallpox, bubonic plague, and other epidemic diseases were undoubtedly commoner in antiquity than at the present time. Quite obviously it would be unreasonable to expect the Bible to mention more than a few of the diseases which were prevalent at the time, since in any event the references to diseased conditions were nearly always incidental to some other, more important aim of the particular narrative in which the pathology is mentioned.

In the OT, the words "disease," "sickness," and sometimes "illness," together with their cognates "diseased," "sick," and "ill," are employed chiefly to translate the noun חֳלִי, "sickness," and its cognates, which derive from the verb חלה, "to be weak" (cf. Akkadian *halu*, "sickness," "grief"; Aramaic חלא, "to suffer"). In the NT the word "sickness" is generally used for the rendering of νόσος, μαλακία, and ἀσθένεια. Often the simple concept of "sickness" is modified by the addition of another phrase—e.g., "sick and . . . at the point of death" (II Chr. 32:24) or "sick and had recovered" (Isa. 39:1). The term "plague" either may imply some particular epidemic, or, if used in a general sense, is to be taken as equivalent to "sickness." Figurative references to disease were common among OT writers (e.g., Job 6:4; Ps. 91:6).

Of the more commonly found specific diseases, ophthalmic afflictions (*see* BLINDNESS) were prominent in antiquity. They were the result of a variety of causes including climatic factors, infection by flies, considerations of heredity, senility, and other factors. Blindness itself was regarded as a divine visitation (Exod. 4:11), and able to be cured only by God. *Ophthalmia neonatorum,* a severe purulent conjunctivitis found in newborn infants as a result of venereal infection, frequently causes a permanent opacity of the cornea if left untreated, and was probably the cause of much of the congenital blindness which occurred in ancient Palestine.

The most careful account of ophthalmic disease which has survived from Jewish sources was that which described the afflictions of TOBIT. The ailment in question was apparently albugo, a dense white opacity of the cornea which was distinguished among the ancients from nubecula (a faint corneal cloudiness) and macula (a moderately dense corneal opacity). At the present day ophthalmia is the general cause of such a condition. Tobit was healed subsequent to an application of fish gall to the white tissue (Tob. 11:4 ff), which appears to indicate an attempt at pigmentation of the opacity.

A temporary form of blindness without any apparent lesions of the eyes (amaurosis) overtook the Syrian soldiers at the behest of Elisha (II Kings 6:18). In this instance the affliction served as a punishment, and was removed after a short time. In the light of the variety of collyria (eyewashes) contained in the Ebers papyrus from Egypt (*ca.* 1500 B.C.), it is interesting to note that the Pentateuchal hygienic enactments nowhere are concerned with ocular care.

Deficiencies of hearing were apparently fairly common in antiquity, though whether they were due to lesions of the cerebral cortex, disease of the internal ear, or to other causes is unknown. Deaf-mutes—i.e., those unable either to hear or to speak—were not unknown in Bible times also. Persons deprived of the use of a limb, or crippled in other respects, formed a permanent part of the Hebrew population in antiquity. Sometimes this affliction was congenital, where an individual was born with one leg shorter than the other. Not infrequently, however, it was the result of surgical accident, or of diseases such as poliomyelitis. The left-handed were also considered as cripples, being spoken of as "impeded on the right side" (Judg. 3:15; 20:16; LXX ἀμφοτεροδέξιος). *See* LAME.

The incidence of carious spinal vertebrae disqualified a man from the priesthood (Lev. 21:20), as did supernumerary fingers or toes. The latter were mentioned (II Sam. 21:20; I Chr. 20:6) in connection with a giant who possessed six fingers and six toes on each side. The unusual stature of this individual was probably the result of an anterior pituitary tumor, which may also have been the case with Goliath of Gath.

The affliction which Jacob suffered after his encounter with the divine messenger (Gen. 32:22-32) may perhaps be capable of interpretation in modern terms. The narrative seems to imply that as a result of the contortions of wrestling, he was suddenly struck with severe sciatica, which caused him to limp painfully thereafter. Subluxation of the head of the femur (cf. Gen. 32:25) is probably an incorrect interpretation of the symptoms presented. Perhaps a prolapsed intervertebral disc was the cause of the disability.

The widespread nature of infantile disease received but scant notice in the OT. The infant son of Bathsheba (II Sam. 12:15) became ill shortly after birth, and died of an unspecified disease seven days later. The child born to the Shunammite woman (II Kings 4:18-37) became suddenly ill one summer when he was perhaps about seven years of age, and died within five hours. Cerebral symptoms alone are mentioned in the narrative, which might indicate an attack of heatstroke, cerebral malaria, or meningitis, among other possibilities. The son of the widow at Zarephath (I Kings 17:17) succumbed to an unspecified fatal affliction of short duration, which may have been of a similar nature.

The narrative describing the death of Nabal (I Sam. 25:36-38) indicates that he was probably a chronic alcoholic whose state of cerebral arteriosclerosis was such that he suffered an apoplectic seizure on learning what David had purposed to do to him. After being in a comatose condition for about nine days, he died without regaining consciousness.

The disease from which Job suffered has been a matter of considerable speculation for many centuries. Beginning suddenly, it assumed a chronic nature and was irritating without actually immobilizing the sufferer. His body was affected by an eruption described as "boils," which attacked the soles of his feet and the crown of his head. His facial appearance was altered, and his sores became infested with maggots (myiasis). Neurasthenia, lassitude, and myasthenia also characterized his affliction. The plantar "boils" may perhaps have been the pustules of smallpox, while the facial disfiguration could have resulted from the more acute confluent smallpox. However, it is improbable that a patient suffering from the confluent variety of variola would want to engage in ordinary conversation, much less in closely reasoned theological discussion. Other suggestions are that the "boils" constituted a secondary manifestation of treponematosis, that they were a chronic form of Delhi boil, or that they characterized herpetiform dermatitis, impetigo, or frambesia. The most that can be said is that, on the basis of the evidence presented, smallpox as the disease in question is unlikely. Job's psychological picture may well indicate that his affliction was psychogenic in nature and had nothing to do with Hansen's disease. *See* BOIL.

Cutaneous diseases have always been common in oriental countries, and accordingly they receive some notice in the OT. The "itch" of the head and neck (Lev. 13:30) was a form of ringworm, while the TETTER of Lev. 13:39 was probably vitiligo. The "scabs" of Lev. 21:20 constituted the symptoms of some itching disease such as ringworm, while the "scurvy" (Lev. 21:20 KJV; Deut. 28:27) was possibly a variant form of favus or some other fungus disease. The instructions for the diagnosis of LEPROSY as contained in Lev. 13 also take cognizance of skin afflictions other than the result of infection by Hansen's bacillus.

The dread scourge of bubonic plague (*see* PLAGUE) is described most fully in I Sam. 5-6, which records the sudden incidence of the epidemic, its transmission along lines of human communication, the principal symptom of inguinal buboes, the presence of dead rodents, and the heavy mortality which accompanied the disease. Although bubonic plague was not endemic in Palestine, it may have been the means by which the forces of Sennacherib were decimated (II Kings 19:35).

Some of the pathological conditions which terminated the lives of certain kings can probably be recognized. David succumbed to old age, and there is no ground for assuming that he was afflicted with general paralysis of the insane, as some authors have maintained. King Asa suffered from diseased feet, which some scholars have interpreted as gout. (It will also be observed that the Hebrews used the word "feet" as a euphemism for the sexual organs.) According to II Chr. 16:12-13, his ailment lasted for two years and then terminated fatally, which might indicate that it was a case of senile gangrene. This seems to be confirmed by the use of scents and fumigants during the interment, though this practice also obtained for other funerary circumstances. King Uzziah died of leprosy (II Chr. 26:21), which seems to have been the true Hansen's disease, while Jehoram suffered from a painful intestinal ailment for the last two years of his life (II Chr. 21:18-19). From all indications it would appear that he had been suffering from some form of diarrhea, which may have been that of amoebic dysentery with concomitant sloughing of the intestines. The terminal event was evidently marked by a massive prolapse of the rectum.

The occurrence of paralysis is seldom mentioned in the OT, but there are two cases which merit comment. The sudden paralysis which Jeroboam sustained (I Kings 13:4) was an instance of brachial monoplegia, in which there is paralysis of one side of the face or of one limb only, in this case the arm. Where the condition occurs at the present, it is usually caused by cerebral embolism or hemorrhage. The temporary or permanent nature of the paralysis is generally determined by the precise location and extent of the hemorrhage.

In Zech. 11:17, a curse was invoked upon the worthless shepherd, one result of which would be that his arm would shrivel up completely. This is apparently a reference to locomotor ataxia, a disease of the spinal cord resulting in chronic progressive sclerosis of the posterior spinal nerve roots and accompanying structures. It is generally the result of syphilitic infection, and the disease normally commences in middle age. An ataxic condition in which there is marked diminution of muscular co-ordinating power is followed by paralysis. Atrophy of the optic nerve (cf. Zech. 11:17*b*) may take place at an early stage of the disease. Locomotor ataxia may pursue a chronic course, or it may have a rapid fatal termination.

The OT contains very few references to actual insanity or mental disease as such, despite its prevalence in the ancient Near East. The manner in which David feigned madness (I Sam. 21:12-15) appears to have been convincing, since it secured his dismissal from the presence of Achish king of Gath. Throughout the East, madmen were regarded as having a peculiar relationship with a possessing deity or demon, and in consequence were left strictly alone by the rest of the populace. The mental pathology of SAUL is that of the paranoid schizophrenic (see MADNESS), with all the marks of characteristic personality deterioration. The insanity which overtook Nebuchadnezzar and which was tactfully described in the book of Daniel (4:19 ff) is of particular interest because of its genuine nature and its comparative rarity. In general psychiatric terms he would be regarded as suffering from paranoia, a mental disorder characterized by systematized delusions and normally independent of other symptoms of mental imbalance. More specifically, his delusions took the form of boanthropy, a rare condition in which Nebuchadnezzar imagined himself to be an animal and acted accordingly. Lycanthropy (cf. "werewolf") is another form of this monomania. (In recent years one patient who was afflicted with boanthropy, a physically healthy young man, was known to live entirely on grass, winter and summer, and to crouch on all fours while plucking and eating it.)

As might well be expected, contemporary accounts of this dramatic reverse in the personal fortunes of the mighty empire builder are almost nonexistent, and it was only some centuries later that garbled versions of the account in Daniel, which is probably contemporary, began to emerge. Berossus (third century B.C.), a Babylonian priest, has preserved one such account. Of the inscriptions which emerged from the reign of Nebuchadnezzar, one was translated by Sir Henry Rawlinson as follows: "For four years the seat of my kingdom in my city . . . did not rejoice my heart. In all my dominions I did not build a high place of power, the precious treasures of my kingdom I did not lay out. In the worship of Merodach my lord, the joy of my heart in Babylon, the city of my sovereignty, I did not sing his praises and I did not furnish his altars; nor did I clear out the canals." Possibly this inscription refers to the period of his insanity, when he was shunned by friend and enemy alike (see MADNESS). Syncope or fainting resulting from shock or other emotional factors was recorded in the case of several OT personages, including Jacob (Gen. 45:26), Eli (I Sam. 4:18), Saul (I Sam. 28:20), and Daniel (Dan. 8:27). A state of trance overtook Abraham (Gen. 15:12), while the stupor of fatigue was present in the case of Sisera (Judg. 4:21), Saul (I Sam. 26:12), and Jonah (Jonah 1:5).

The OT has recorded a number of diseases, some of them fatal, whose precise nature is obscure. Abijah, son of Jeroboam, died in infancy of an unspecified ailment (I Kings 14:17), while Elisha became ill in his ninetieth year and died shortly afterward (II Kings 13:14). Ben-hadad, king of Syria, fell ill shortly before his death at the hands of Hazael (II Kings 8:14-15), and the wife of Ezekiel succumbed quite suddenly to an unnamed disease (Ezek. 24:16).

Some instances of parturition having a fatal termination are found in the OT. The dystocia of Rachel (Gen. 35:16-18) may have been occasioned in part by constitutional weakness, whereas the death of the wife of Phinehas (I Sam. 4:19) resulted from the shock which initiated premature labor. See MEDICINE.

Febrile diseases (see FEVER) were common in Palestine in Bible days. The most familiar were malaria, typhoid, paratyphoid, and diseases conveyed by milk. Malaria was endemic in a number of areas of ancient Canaan, including the Lebanon, the Jordan Valley, Jerusalem, and the environs of the Sea of Galilee. Bubonic plague, universally dreaded in the ancient world, was marked by a high fever, as were pneumonic plague, smallpox, sunstroke, typhus, erysipelas, and eruptive fevers, all of which doubtless occurred to some extent in ancient Palestine.

Records of the latter days of Antiochus Epiphanes (II Macc. 9:5-27) indicate the presence of a number of symptoms, the chief of which were severe abdominal pain, loss of weight, the presence of parasitic worms, and putrefacience. These, combined with the fatal nature of the disease, seem to indicate that the affliction was intestinal cancer. See ANTIOCHUS 4.

**4. Diseases of the NT.** As part of the healing ministry of Jesus, a considerable number of widely differing diseases were encountered and cured. Blindness, leprosy, paralysis, physical infirmity, and mental affliction all came within the scope of his beneficent activity. The incidence of BLINDNESS was dealt with as befitted the condition or circumstances of the patient. The blind man at Beth-saida was healed by stages (Mark 8:22-26) after being anointed with saliva. He appears to have been congenitally blind, unlike the beggar Bartimaeus (Mark 10:46-52; cf. Matt. 20:29-34), who asked to regain his sight. The latter may have been influenced psychologically by the presence of an expectant crowd. What occasioned the blindness of those who were healed is never stated, but in cases of acquired blindness, climatic, environmental, hygienic, and psychosomatic considerations must be taken into account as etiological factors.

The nature of the LEPROSY which Jesus healed is again obscure, but it may have been vitiligo rather than the true Hansen's disease. The mechanism of suggestion which Jesus employed (cf. Mark 1:40-44 and parallels; Luke 17:11-19) as part of the cure suggests that the skin affliction was actually psychogenic in nature, resulting from emotional conflict in the subconscious mind. If this was actually the case, resentment would most probably be one of the reactions involved. Luke furnishes a more detailed clinical description of one of the lepers healed by Jesus (5:12) when he speaks of him as πλήρης λέπρας, thereby indicating an advanced stage of the disease. On the other hand, the ten lepers are simply described as λεπροί without any further portrayal of their condition.

The gospels record several instances of paralysis which, from the rather general descriptions furnished by the evangelists, give every indication of resulting from organic disease of the central nervous system. The Capernaum paralytic (Matt. 9:2; Mark 2:3) is described by the more technical word παραλελυμένος in the Third Gospel (Luke 5:18 ff), and was evidently paraplegic. His condition may have resulted from compression myelitis occasioned either by an accident earlier in life or by a bony lesion. In any event, organic changes would have taken place in the spinal cord, and it is improbable that they would have been initiated by factors of a psychic nature such as conversion hysteria, which would transmute an emotional state of guilt or conflict into physical symptoms of paralysis or blindness.

The servant of the centurion (Matt. 8:5-13; Luke 7:1-10) was acutely ill with a serious form of paralysis. Luke, who invariably employs medical terminology as a regular part of his clinical descriptions, points out the moribund condition of the patient (7:2). The disease has been described in terms of tetanus, progressive paralysis, and acute spinal meningitis, but probably the best diagnosis is that of acute ascending paralysis, with concomitant myelitis.

The man with the withered hand (Matt. 12:9-13; Mark 3:1-5; Luke 6:6-10) may have suffered from anterior poliomyelitis as a youth. If, however, the term ξηρός indicates a degeneration of the small muscles of the hand only, the man may have been afflicted with amyotrophic lateral sclerosis. The suggestion content of Jesus' treatment indicated the patient's need for deep psychotherapy. The absence of detailed description precludes an estimate of the place which emotional factors had in the progress of the disease. The ailment which had afflicted Aeneas for eight years (Acts 9:33) is of uncertain character, although paraplegia is the most probable diagnosis.

The impotent man at Beth-zatha (John 5:2) has been regarded as the victim of locomotor ataxia, paraplegia, or disseminated sclerosis. However, the narrative seems to indicate that he had suffered from anterior poliomyelitis as a child.

Peter's mother-in-law (Matt. 8:14-16; Mark 1:29-31; Luke 4:38-39) had probably succumbed to some form of malaria (*see* FEVER). Perhaps Jesus employed suggestive mechanisms in therapy to lower the temperature (Luke 4:39).

The psychogenic nature of certain other NT diseases seems evident from the circumstances under which they arose. Zechariah (Luke 1:11-64) sustained a severe emotional shock which resulted in hysterical aphonia and deafness. This combination is unusual, though by no means impossible, for recent psychosomatic investigation has brought to light accredited instances of individuals becoming aphonic and deaf periodically because of the interaction of emotional conflict within the personality. In such cases the onset of the syndrome is precipitated by shock or severe strain. The same may be said of the amaurosis sustained by Paul (Acts 9:8), which was clearly the result of severe emotional conflict. Indeed, the dramatic nature of Paul's conversion, requiring as it did a complete reversal of his earlier outlook on life, was characterized by profound emotional overtones. With a change in his "point of view," to express the psychic situation in the organ language of the eyes, it would not be unreasonable to expect some temporary disturbance in ocular function. Thus his amaurosis was the psychosomatic expression of his mental and spiritual inability to see his way clearly. Medical literature contains many accounts of psychogenic amblyopia and amaurosis, and of cures by means of suggestion (cf. Acts 9:17). A temporary amaurosis also overtook Elymas (Acts 13:10-11), where profound emotional factors of guilt, fear, and resentment combined to produce the condition of amblyopia and amaurosis. Luke describes this syndrome by means of the term ἀχλύς καὶ σκότος (vs. 10). *See* BLINDNESS.

The woman with hemorrhage (Matt. 9:20-22; Mark 5:25-34; Luke 8:43-48) may have been suffering from menorrhagia, dysmenorrhea, or more probably from a uterine fibroid. The ceremonial uncleanness occasioned by the discharge prevented her from participating in her religious duties, and she had gone to considerable lengths to be healed before she met Jesus.

The restoration of the daughter of Jairus, which followed the healing of the woman with hemorrhage, is described by Luke in contemporary clinical style which takes account of the stages of recovery, whereas Matthew and Mark write from a different standpoint. The exact nature of the illness which had overtaken the girl is unknown, but she appears to have been comatose when Jesus and the disciples arrived.

Medical language common to Galen and Hippocrates is employed by Luke (13:11-13) to describe the healing of spondylitis deformans in a woman. This condition is characterized by nodular deposits at the edges of the intervertebral discs of the spinal column and subsequent ossification of the ligaments. When bony ankylosis of the joint spaces occurs, the spine becomes kyphosed and rigid, assuming a characteristic appearance. Some writers think that the woman was afflicted with psychogenic paraplegia, but this diagnosis is highly questionable. *See* MEDICINE.

The illness which afflicted the nobleman's son (John 4:46-53) is difficult to assess, except that it was a febrile condition, possibly cerebral malaria. Death from diseases of an unspecified nature was recorded in the case of Lazarus (John 11:11-44) and the son of the widow at Nain (Luke 7:11-15). The suggestion that the latter was in a cataleptic or comatose condition, and not actually dead, does not accord with the opinions of eyewitnesses, and appears unlikely.

The healing of the deaf-mute, recorded only by Mark (7:32-35), followed the symbolic use of saliva and digital contact to stimulate the confidence of the sufferer. This appeal to senses other than the auditory was an attempt to communicate the purpose of the general activity, and thus provoke expectancy and faith. To what extent deep emotional conflicts were responsible for the condition of the deaf-mute is uncertain. Psychosomatic deafness and aphonia occurring simultaneously have been reported in medical literature.

The only instance of ὑδρωπικός in the NT occurs in the Lukan (14:2) account of the dropsical man healed by Christ. Dropsy (hydrops) constitutes an abnormal effusion of watery fluid into bodily cavities or tissues (especially in the feet and legs), and is symptomatic of disease elsewhere. It is generally described in relationship to its location—e.g., ascites (abdomen) and hydrothorax (chest). Whether the man concerned was suffering from some physical disease which was marked by terminal dropsy (e.g., cancer, heart or kidney disease) or not is difficult to determine. Some writers have suggested that he was afflicted with angioneurotic edema, in which edematous swellings occur at intervals in the skin and subcutaneous tissues. This ailment is generally neurotic in origin, and is probably an allergic reaction. Whether the term ὑδρωπικός would cover such an affliction adequately is uncertain.

The dramatic death of Ananias and Sapphira (Acts 5:1-11) obviously involved powerful emotional reactions, guilt being prominent. Probably both succumbed primarily to shock, the terminal event constituting some such form of cardiac involvement as coronary thrombosis.

The congenitally lame man at the Beautiful Gate (Acts 3:10) may have been afflicted with cyllosis or a malformation akin to *spina bifida*. A crippled person healed by Paul at Lystra (Acts 14:8-10) may have been afflicted similarly. The evidence for both these cases is scanty, although the former was spoken of as manifesting structural weakness of the ankles and feet. *See* LAME.

Luke traces the appropriate stages of recovery in the restoration to life of Tabitha (Acts 9:40-41) according to the best Greek medical traditions. His account of the last days of Herod Agrippa (Acts 12:21-23) involves the use of an unusual compound term, σκωληκόβρωτος. The Greek roots of this designation were used of intestinal worms and human myiasis (σκώληξ), and of the consuming of bodily tissue by disease (βιβρώσκειν). Agrippa had probably suffered intestinal obstruction, perhaps because of the presence and activity of parasitic worms, and may have died from perforation of the bowel, with resultant peritonitis. Parasitic worms sometimes leave the body after the individual has died, and this may have been the reason for their mention in the Lukan account. On the other hand, they could have been voided while Agrippa was still alive. *See* AGRIPPA.

When Paul lodged with Publius on Malta (Acts 28:7-9), he laid his hands on his host's sick father and healed him. The ailing man was apparently, suffering from dysentery and an accompanying febrile condition which may have been of a malarial nature (*see* FEVER). However, the fever itself may have constituted one symptom of the dysentery, especially if it was a fulminating case of bacillary dysentery. This condition is caused by the presence of a species of Shigella bacilli, and is marked by considerable pain, tenesmus, evacuation of blood and mucous, and membranous, catarrhal, or necrotic inflammation of the colon. Death ensues quickly in fulminating cases. The severity of the fever was indicated by the plural form of the word (πυρετοῖς) in a manner typical of the Greek medical writers. In Hippocrates, Galen, Areteus, and others, πυρετός was often found in association with δυσεντερία to describe a specific pathological condition, and Luke may have followed the same general procedure.

**5. Demon-possession.** Allusions to mental pathology in the NT appear to exhibit little in the way of recognizable internal subdivision. Some differentiation seems to have been attempted between the diseases which were thought of in terms of epilepsy and lunacy on the one hand, while on the other there existed a group which included neurasthenic conditions and that variety of pathology known as demon-possession. Some centuries before the birth of Christ, the Jews forsook the etiological pronouncements of the OT and encouraged the belief, long held in Babylonia, Egypt, and elsewhere, that possession by disease demons was the cause of sickness in general, and of insanity in particular. Even though the epileptic and the moon-struck were sometimes dis-tinguished from the demon-possessed, the underlying thought tended to attribute the same etiological factors to both varieties of mental affliction. Questions of terminology are important considerations in this matter, since the point at issue is the interpretation of NT terms rather than their rejection in favor of more modern designations, many of which are equally meaningless to the user.

The epileptic boy (Matt. 17:14-18; Mark 9:14-27; Luke 9:37-42), whose healing was closely linked with his father's faith, is described by Matthew as "moon-struck" (σεληνιάζεται). The RSV translation, "epileptic," apart from describing one of the symptoms, affords no greater understanding of the pathology than Matthew's term. There are numerous forms of epilepsy; the disease may be of a hereditary type, or may result from a cerebral tumor, an apoplectic stroke, or some injury to the brain. Single attacks of epilepsy can also be precipitated by emotional conflicts, and if a sudden shock were to produce cerebral vasoconstriction with a rapid diminution of oxygen in the brain, an epileptiform seizure would follow. Very little is known of the etiology of genuine epilepsy, and in consequence it is difficult to distinguish between the classical convulsive disease and emotional or glandular disturbances which may simulate it. In the case of the epileptic boy, therefore, it is virtually impossible to say whether he was suffering from true congenital epilepsy, or from emotional disturbance in the subconscious mind resulting in epileptiform attacks. Because of this it would be quite arbitrary to assume that "demon-possession" was nothing more than a folk designation for epilepsy. While Mark appears to describe a case of idiopathic epilepsy, he and the other evangelists also imply that something besides ordinary epilepsy was involved. *See* EPILEPSY.

Although more is said elsewhere regarding demon-possession (*see* DEMON), some comment appears desirable here also. Among other cases, those of the Syrophoenician's daughter (Matt. 15:22; Mark 7:25), the Gerasene (Matt. 8:28; Mark 5:2; Luke 8:27) and Capernaum (Mark 1:23; Luke 4:33) demoniacs, the blind and dumb demoniac (Matt. 12:22; Luke 11:14), and the maiden with divinatory insight (Acts 16:16) were held to be the result of spirit-possession. Evidences of a survival into modern times of biblical demon-possession have been described by some medical and other missionaries. Frequently found in the Far East, the phenomenon assumed the form of characteristic personality-possession, and when the individuals were exorcised, they led normal, healthy lives thereafter. Among such races, demon-possession was placed in a category *sui generis*, and was thereby distinguished from other diseases. Similarly, in Bible times there were evidently some particular symptom which enabled demon-possession to be recognized and differentiated from other afflictions such as fever, blindness, and lameness. The determining factor was probably evidence of suicidal impulses.

Many cases of demon-possession would undoubtedly be designated by other, scarcely more meaningful terms in modern psychiatry. On the other hand, it is extremely doubtful if the language used by the Gadarene demoniac, e.g., which implies the functioning of a separate personality speaking through the mouth of the sufferer, is ever heard in a modern mental hospital.

Whether demon-possession can be explained in terms of the "id" gaining control over the entire personality as the result of mental disease or imbalance is difficult to say. At all events, the solution evidently seems to transcend the purely physical realm of existence. Jesus saw sin lurking in the background of every possessed person who confronted him, indicating that there was a profound spiritual involvement to be reckoned with and remedied. The nature and function of the forces of good and evil which are rooted in the human personality are obscure, making the solution to the problem of demon-possession one of great difficulty.

**6. The death of Jesus.** The physical causes underlying the death of Jesus on Calvary (*see* CRUCIFIXION) have been the subject of medical comment. Speculation commenced with the opinions of Stroud in 1874, that the terminal event in the Crucifixion was cardiac rupture. According to this view, Jesus died of a broken heart both literally and figuratively, and this theory has gained widespread currency. Others, however, have held that the exudation from the spear thrust indicated that Jesus was only in a fainting condition, from which he speedily recovered when taken down from the cross. Still further explanations of the terminal event have included asphyxia, thirst, exhaustion, and loss of blood.

The passion narratives are unequivocal in showing that the experience of the agony, trial, and crucifixion was one of intense emotional strain, involving as it did a crisis in the spiritual destiny of humanity. Compared with this consideration, the physical aspect of the Crucifixion is almost trivial, but it is important insofar as it confirms the intensity of the spiritual experience. The "bloody sweat"—i.e., perspiration tinged with blood—is a rare phenomenon noted occasionally from the time of Aristotle, and appearing under conditions of extreme mental strain.

The actual cause of death does not seem to have been either thirst, hunger, loss of blood, or exhaustion. Cardiac rupture is rare, and generally affects the seriously ill only. Coronary thrombosis is also unlikely, in view of the generally accepted age of Jesus at his death. Asphyxia caused by respiratory impairment due to muscular cramp, is less probable than cardiac failure resulting from the blood sinking into the lower part of the body. The most probable cause of Jesus' death seems to be the incidence of acute dilation of the stomach. The spear thrust would doubtless release accumulated watery fluid under such circumstances, and perhaps some venous blood.

*Bibliography.* H. P. Newsholme, *Health, Disease and Integration* (1929); F. Fenner, *Die Krankheit im NT* (1930); R. R. Willcox, "Venereal Disease in the Bible," *British Journal of Venereal Disease,* XXV (1949), 28 ff; C. R. Smith, *A Physician Examines the Bible* (1950); L. D. Weatherhead, *Psychology, Religion and Healing* (rev. ed., 1954), pp. 51-108; R. K. Harrison, "A Christian Interpretation of Disease," *The Churchman,* vol. LXII, no. 4 (1953), pp. 220-27; A. R. Short, *The Bible and Modern Medicine* (1953), pp. 47-123; L. Köhler, *Hebrew Man* (1956), pp. 46-60.                    R. K. HARRISON

**DISH.** *See* POTTERY; VESSELS.

**DISHAN** dī′shăn [דִּישָׁן; LXX Ρεισων, Δαισων]. The seventh son of Seir (Gen. 36:21; I Chr. 1:38); a native Horite clan chief in Edom (Gen. 36:30). Confusion exists with Dishon.

**DISHON** dī′shŏn [דִּישֹׁן, דִּישָׁן, דִּשֹׁן, mountain goat(?); *cf.* Deut. 14:5]. **1.** The fifth son of Seir (Gen. 36:21 [LXX Δησων]; I Chr. 1:38); a native Horite clan chief (אַלּוּף דִּשֹׁן, or "the clan chief *of* Dishon") in Edom (Gen. 36:26, 30; I Chr. 1:41*b*). For "Dishon" in I Chr. 1:42 read, with Gen. 36:28, "Dishan" (so RSV).

**2.** Son of the Horite clan chief Anah, and grandson of Seir (Gen. 36:25; I Chr. 1:41*a* [LXX Δαισων]).                    L. HICKS

**DISHONOR.** *See* SHAME.

**DISMAS.** An alternate form of DYSMAS.

**DISOBEDIENCE.** *See* OBEDIENCE.

**DISPERSION** [διασπορά, *see* § 1*b below*]. A general term to indicate the widespread settlement of Jews outside Palestine from the time of the EXILE through the Greek and Roman periods. Many Jews themselves, especially Zionists, use the terms "Dispersion," "Diaspora," and "Galuth" (Yiddish—Goless), to apply to the settled residence of Jews outside the state of Israel today.

1. Terminology
  *a.* In Hebrew
  *b.* In Greek
2. Origins and causes
3. Areas and extent
4. Importance and significance
Bibliography

**1. Terminology. *a. In Hebrew.*** The Hebrew nouns גּוֹלָה and גָּלוּת and the Aramaic גָּלוּתָא may mean "dispersion" as well as "EXILE." The noun גּוֹלָה in rabbinical literature frequently means "dispersion" ('A.Z. 30*b;* Sanh. 38*a*), as well as גָּלוּת (Ab. 1:11; Ber. 56*a*) and גָּלוּתָא (Suk. 31*a*). Other Hebrew words such as נדח (Neh. 1:9; Isa. 11:12), זרה (Ezek. 36:19), נפץ (Isa. 11:12), פוץ (Jer. 25:34; Ezek. 36:19; Zeph. 3:10), פזר and פרד (Esth. 3:8) are also translated "dispersed" or "dispersion."

***b. In Greek.*** The word διασπορά frequently translates the above Hebrew words in the LXX (Neh. 1:9; Ps. 147:2—G 146:2). The cognate Greek verb is διασπείρειν, "to disperse" (Esth. 3:8). It is used for נצר, "the preserved of Israel," in Isa. 49:6. In Deut. 28:25; Jer. 34:17—G 41:17 it translates זעוה (זְוָעָה ?). In Jer. 13:14 the reading should probably be διαφθορά. Διασπορά may mean "the dispersed" (II Macc. 1:27; Pss. Sol. 8:28; John 7:35) or the place where they are dispersed (Jth. 5:19; Test. Asher 7:2; Jas. 1:1; I Pet. 1:1). Παροικία (*see* EXILE) may mean the place of dispersion (Ezra 8:35; III Macc. 7:19; Wisd. Sol. 19:10; Acts 13:17) or more figuratively consignment to earthly life as a pilgrimage or sojourn (Ps. 119:54—G 118:54; I Pet. 1:17; II Clem. 5:1; *cf.* Rom. 7:23; Heb. 11:13).

**2. Origins and causes.** There is no period in Israelite or Jewish history when it may be said with absolute certainty, except by *a priori* argument, that all the Jews or their predecessors (*see* JEW) were at home in Palestine. There were two principal causes of resettlement in antiquity: commerce and war. The great expansion of the United Monarchy under David and Solomon sent Jews into varied parts of Asia and Africa, both as government colonists and administrators and as private tradesmen (II Sam. 8; I Kings 4; cf. Deut. 17:16; I Kings 20:34), many of whom undoubtedly settled permanently. Trade itself undoubtedly dates from the beginnings of Israelite history and alone would have been enough to initiate a sizable dispersion. An early possible deportation of prisoners of war occurs in the reigns of Rehoboam and Jeroboam I (*ca.* 918 B.C.) when SHISHAK of Egypt invaded Judah (I Kings 14:25-28; II Chr. 12:1-12). However, the greatest cause of dispersion and the historical turning point for speaking of the Dispersion were the Assyrian and Babylonian exiles. *See* EXILE.

**3. Areas and extent.*** Outside Palestine, Babylonia was the area most densely settled by Jews in the Greco-Roman period. Testimony to the extent of Jewish settlement in Babylonia is in the fact that the authoritative successors to the great Tannaim or Palestinian sages were the Babylonian Amoraim (interpreters), and that the Babylonian Talmud is considered the official interpretation of the Mishna. *See* TALMUD. Fig. DIS 30.

The Dispersion in Egypt was next in importance. The fact that within the aging Jeremiah's own lifetime he ministered in Egypt to the Jews at Migdol, Tahpanhes, Memphis, and in the land of Pathros (Jer. 44:1) is sufficient indication that there had been a sizable Jewish population before he arrived. The ELEPHANTINE PAPYRI of the fifth century B.C. and other archaeological materials give ample evidence of comparatively early and well-settled Jewish settlements in Egypt. Philo Judeus (20 B.C.–A.D. 40) reports that the Jews in Alexandria numbered one million, constituting one eighth the population and two of the five quarters of the city (*In Flaccum* 6, 8).

The full extent of the Dispersion can be envisaged from Philo's listing (*Legatio Ad Caium* 36) of such far-flung places as Egypt, Phoenicia, Syria, Coele-Syria, Pamphylia, Cilicia, Asia Minor as far as Bithynia and the remotest corners of the Pontus; in Europe, Thessaly, Boeotia, Macedonia, Aetolia, Attica, Argos, Corinth and the "fairest parts" of the Peloponnesus; the islands of Euboea, Cyprus, and Crete; and almost all the countries beyond the Euphrates, in "all the satrapies which contain fruitful land" (cf. Esth. 3:8). But many Jews continued to pay the half-shekel tax for maintenance of the Jerusalem temple and, indeed, traveled at great distances to participate in the great festivals there. At the Feast of Weeks or Pentecost, recorded in Acts 2:9-11, Jews came from Parthia, Media, Persia, Mesopotamia, Judea, Cappadocia, the Pontus, Asia, Phrygia, Pamphylia, Egypt, parts of Libya, Cyrene, Rome, Crete, and Arabia. The Letter of James is addressed to the twelve tribes in the Dispersion (cf. John 7:35), and I Peter to the exiles in Pontus, Galatia, Cappadocia, Asia, and Bithynia. Strabo (first century B.C.) said there was no city to which Jews had not come (Jos. Antiq. XIV.vii.2). The Jewish author of the third book of the Sybilline Oracles (3.271) says: "Every land is full of thee and every sea" (cf. I Macc. 15:15).

**4. Importance and significance.** It seems reasonable to assume that the Dispersion gave birth to the SYNAGOGUE. Jeremiah's advice to the Babylonian exiles to pray to Yahweh in captivity (Jer. 29:7) was ample enough incentive to instigate houses of prayer and study outside Palestine. Neither Yahwism nor

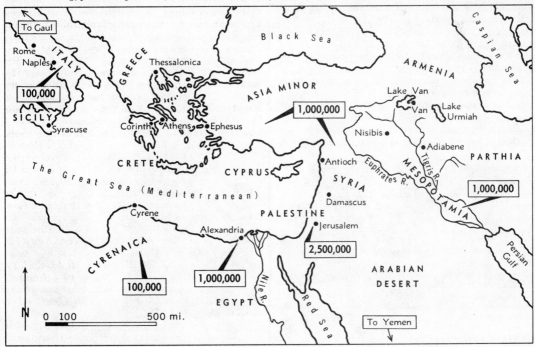

Published by the Jewish Publication Society of America

30. Map showing the dispersion of the Jews in the first century of the Christian era

Judaism has ever held belief in a located deity. Moses' own faith is evident in the question: "Is it not in thy going with us, so that we are distinct, I and thy people, from all other people that are upon the face of the earth?" (Exod. 33:16). Nor was this faith limited to expression in one language. By the second century B.C. the Jews in Alexandria were able to read the Scriptures in Greek (*see* SEPTUAGINT). Throughout the Roman Empire until the fourth century A.D., Judaism was a *religio licita*, recognized and tolerated wherever practiced. It was respected and its adherents for the most part admired. The Dispersion was, indeed, the vehicle for God's light to the nations (Isa. 49:6). The early rapid spread of Christianity must ultimately be explained by the remarkable historical faith of Judaism, which knew not time or space.

*Bibliography.* T. Reinach, "Diaspora," *The Jewish Encyclopedia*, IV (1903), 559-74; J. Juster, *Les Juifs dans l'empire romain* (2 vols.; 1914); G. F. Moore, *Judaism* (3 vols.; 1927-30); E. J. Bickerman, "The Historical Foundations of Postbiblical Judaism," in L. Finkelstein, ed., *The Jews*, I (1949), 70-114; S. Grayzel, "Scattered Israel," *A History of the Jews* (1952), pp. 137-53; E. R. Goodenough, *Jewish Symbols in the Greco-Roman Period*, vol. II (1953); J. B. Pritchard, ed., *ANET* (2nd ed., 1955), pp. 263-64, 491-92.　　J. A. SANDERS

**DISTAFF** [כִּישׁוֹר]; KJV SPINDLE. A stick used to hold prepared fibers from which thread is spun. Thread could also be spun from fibers held in the hand or pocket, and, as represented in Egyptian tomb paintings, from prepared fibers wound up in the form of a ball or placed in a round container. The term כִּישׁוֹר is found only in Prov. 31:19, and its meaning is plausibly derived from the context: "She stretches forth her hand to the כִּישׁוֹר in order to pull fibers for spinning" is doubtless the sense of the first line. The second line informs that "her hands hold the spindle" (פֶּלֶךְ; Akkadian *pilakku*, "spindle"; cf. Arabic *pallaka*, "be round"). The spindle was properly held in the hands. The KJV translates the first term "spindle" and the second "distaff," but the reversal of the two in the RSV is more accurate. *See* CLOTH.

The spindle is a round stick made of wood, bone, ivory, or metal, tapering at one or both ends, with a whorl or round disk (also made of various materials) mounted closer to one end, on which spun thread is wound; with the invention of the suspended-spindle method of spinning, a hook or notch was provided at the whorl end as a means of holding the thread while the spindle was not in the hands. The spindle probably takes its name from the round whorl. Fig. DIS 31.

In addition to Prov. 31:19, "spindle" occurs in II Sam. 3:29, where the LXX interprets פֶּלֶךְ as "staff" (KJV). The notion that spinning is effeminate (for women and old men) is widespread in the Near East, however, so that "spindle" is appropriate in the context (Aq. and Symm. ἄτρακτον, "spindle").

*Bibliography.* S. R. Driver, *Notes on the Hebrew Text and the Topography of the Books of Samuel* (1913), pp. 250-51; L. Klebs, *Die Reliefs und Malereien des mittleren Reiches* (1922), pp. 125-27; G. Dalman, *Arbeit und Sitte*, V (1937), 49-52; C. Singer *et al.*, eds., *A History of Technology* (1954), pp. 424-25, 434, 437-38, and pl. 13A.　　R. W. FUNK

**DISTRIBUTION OF GOODS.** *See* COMMUNITY OF GOODS.

**DISTRICT.** A geographical area either general in designation or specific in reference. In Neh. 3:9, 12-18 (פֶּלֶךְ), the reference is to specific areas of the city of Jerusalem; and in Matt. 2:22; 15:21; 16:13; Mark 8:10; Acts 16:12 (μερίς, μέρος) the reference is to specific, though larger, areas: the districts of Galilee, Tyre and Sidon, Caesarea Philippi, Dalmanutha, and Macedonia. However, where the designation is general, as in the expression "in all that region," other terms are used: גָּלִיל, גְּלִילָה, γῆ, ὅριον (cf. תְּרוּמָה in Ezek. 45:1).　　J. A. SANDERS

**DIVES** dī'vēz [Lat., rich]. The name traditionally given to the rich man in Jesus' parable (Luke 16:19-31) of the rich man and Lazarus (*see* LAZARUS AND DIVES). From the Vulg. translation, *homo quidam erat dives*, "there was a certain rich man," there resulted in medieval times the idea that *dives* was the name of the nameless man. In the third century such names as Nineve and Finaeus were given to him.

*Bibliography.* L. T. Lefort, "Le nom du mauvais riche et la tradition copte," *ZNW*, 37 (1939), 65-72.　　D. M. BECK

**\*DIVINATION.** A form of communication with the higher powers. Divination to elicit answers to definite inquiries was widely practiced in antiquity. The Babylonians, who traced back the system of foretelling future events by signs to the antediluvian king Enmeduranki of Sippar, were the first to develop the

Courtesy of Editions des Musées Nationaux, Paris

31. Woman holding spindle and wool, with attendant; stone relief from Susa

Courtesy of the American Schools of Oriental Research

32. Two parts of a broken clay model of an animal's liver bearing cuneiform inscriptions for the use of temple diviners; from Hazor (fifteenth century B.C.)

art of soothsaying to an almost semiscientific discipline.

The objects from which omens were derived may be classified as (a) natural phenomena and (b) manmade phenomena. To the first category belong primarily the observation of the heavenly bodies (astrology); the inspection of the liver of a sacrificial animal (hepatoscopy); and, to a lesser degree, sudden and unexpected storms, peculiar formations of clouds, birth monstrosities among men and animals, appearances and disappearances of snakes, the disconsolate howlings or unnatural actions of dogs, nightmarish dreams, etc. To the second category, called "voluntary divination," because deliberately produced for the purpose of soothsaying, belong such actions as the pouring of oil into a basin of water and then observing the bubbles and rings formed in the receptacle, the shooting of arrows, the casting of lots, necromancy, etc.

The main field of divination in which the Babylonians excelled and for which they were famous in classical antiquity (cf. Dan. 1:4; 2:4, 10; 5:7, 11, where the name Chaldeans [כשדים] is synonymous with "magicians") was hepatoscopy. A highly trained and carefully selected group of priests, called *bārû*, "diviners" (lit., "seers, inspectors"), were in charge of this vital function. The liver was considered the seat

33. A model liver, without inscriptions; from Megiddo (1350-1150 B.C.)

of the blood and hence of life itself. On the basis of this belief the Mesopotamians, by some inscrutable process of reasoning, identified the liver of the sacrificial sheep with the gods and therefore deemed it a proper vehicle by which to divine the will and the intentions of the higher powers. (For similar views that the liver was the seat of life and thus often used in the sense of "heart, mind," cf. the Ugaritic Epic of Baal, where it is stated of the goddess Anath that "her liver [kbd] swells with laughter, her heart fills up with joy, Anath's liver exults" [ANET 136a]; Lam. 2:11, where Jerusalem is portrayed as a mother whose "heart [כבד; lit., 'liver'] is poured out in grief"; Prov. 7:23, where נפש, "life, soul," is used as a parallel to כבד, "liver.") For the purpose of divination the liver was carefully mapped out and divided into numerous sections, and each one given a name such as "front surface," "finger," "mouth," etc. The

officiating *bārû*-priest had to undergo an elaborate ceremonial process consisting of washing and anointing himself and donning clean garments in order to be ritually pure. Great care was also taken regarding the place and time of the sacrifice. Figs. DIV 32-34.

The large collections of liver omens, prepared in the *bārû*-academies attached to the temples, from practically all periods of Babylonian and Assyrian history prove the great importance that was assigned to this branch of divination. (According to several texts from Mari, a *bārû*-priest was attached to each army contingent [cf. *Archives royales de Mari*, II, no. 22; III, no. 80]; the texts from Chagar-Bazar mention the existence of a *bīt bārî*, "diviners' college.") Before any decisive action was undertaken, such as a declaration of war, the conclusion of a peace treaty, the erection of a temple, a *bārû*-priest was called upon to sacrifice a sheep and to inspect its liver in order to determine whether the gods were favorably or unfavorably disposed toward the impending procedure.

Unlike astrology, which was the exclusive prerogative of the state, hepatoscopy was also made use of by the common people for their individual needs (cf. the composition "I Will Praise the Lord of Wisdom," *ANET* 434b, in which the patient complains that the diviner through divination did not discern the nature of his sickness). Divination based on the flight of birds was unknown in Babylonia. The only reference to augury is found in an inscription from Alalakh, Syria. King Idrimi (middle of the second millennium B.C.) reports that he had released a number of birds with the aim of obtaining an omen.

The OT terms קסם, נחש, and מעונן are commonly translated by "divination," "augury," or "soothsayer." (With the exception of Josh. 13:22; Prov. 16:10; Ezek. 21:22, קסם is uniformly rendered "divination"; נחש is translated "divination," "enchantment," "augury," "omens"; and מעונן, "soothsaying," but also "sorcerer" and "diviner.") The primary meanings of these words are uncertain (קסם is derived from Arabic *qasama*, "to cut, divide," and hence "to distribute by casting lots"; נחש has the meaning "to observe signs," and hence "to interpret omens"; מעונן has its cognates in Ugaritic '*nn* and Arabic '*anna*, "to appear, to present oneself," and hence "to cause to appear, to raise"). But whatever the original meanings of these words were, they have acquired a wider connotation in the OT, and they stand for the various practices of foretelling the future by the aid of artificial means—in sharp contrast to inspired prophecy. Deut. 18:14-15 succinctly expresses the difference between these two types: "For these nations, which you are about to dispossess, give heed to soothsayers [מעוננים] and to diviners [קסמים]; but as for you, the LORD your God has not allowed you so to do. The Lord your God will raise up for you a prophet [נביא] like me from among you, from your brethren—him you shall heed." The diviners and soothsayers are like false prophets (Ezek. 13:19; 22:28; Mic. 3:7, 11); their pronouncements are "lying divinations" (Isa. 44:25; Jer. 14:14; 27:9-10; Ezek. 12:24; Zech. 10:2; etc.); and, according to Isa. 44:25; Jer. 50:36, they themselves are "liars" (בדים). It is the Canaanites, the Philistines, and, among the nations outside the borders of Palestine, the Egyptians and the Babylonians who resort to this practice (cf.

Gen. 30:27; Num. 22:7; 24:1; Josh. 13:22; I Sam. 6:2; Isa. 2:6; Ezek. 21:21—H 21:26; etc.). Divination is, as all other magical activities, forbidden to Israel (Lev. 19:26; Deut. 18:11—H 18:10), and the prophets are tireless in their uphill struggle to uproot this evil among the people.

34. Clay model of a sheep's liver with a cuneiform inscription, containing omens and magical texts used by diviners; from First Dynasty of Babylon (*ca.* 1830-1530 B.C.)

The objects used and the technique employed by the Canaanite and Israelite diviners are nowhere described in detail. Isa. 44:25 uses the term "liars" (ברים) who employ "omens" (אתות) as a parallel to "diviners" (קסמים), thus showing that the soothsayers made use of omens in their manipulations (cf. Gen. 30:27; Num. 24:1; I Kings 20:33, where the word נחש has the connotation of "omen"). Balaam "the diviner," who was hired to curse Israel, asked Balak to build for him seven altars, on which he sacrificed bulls and rams. After having repeated the same performance several times and failed to achieve his purpose, Balaam exclaimed:

> There is no enchantment against Jacob,
> no divination against Israel
>      (Num. 23:23).

He finally gave up the whole affair and refused to do what he had done before—namely, "to meet with omens" (24:1). Though it is not explicitly stated in the text, the use of the terms נחש, נחשים, and קסם in conjunction with sacrifices might suggest that Balaam attempted by means of hepatoscopy to ascertain whether the Moabite army would be successful in the battle against Israel (cf. the role played by the *bârû* in the military expeditions at Mari, mentioned above). Joseph, in Egypt, divined by means of pouring a liquid into a cup (Gen. 44:5). I Sam. 15:23 clearly proves that the shades of the dead served as mediums for divination. Ezekiel (21:21-22—H 21:26-27) informs us that the king of Babylonia stood at the parting of two ways and used a threefold rite of divination: he shook the arrows, he consulted the TERAPHIM, and he looked at the liver. It is quite

likely that some of the objects ascribed by Ezekiel as having been used by Nebuchadnezzar were actually part of the paraphernalia of the Palestinian diviners. The use of the teraphim for divination purposes seems to be alluded to in Hos. 3:4 (where it is preceded by אפוד, an oracle-giving object); Zech. 10:2. For a possible reference to belomancy in Israel, Hos. 4:12 may be quoted:

> My people inquire of a thing of wood,
> and their staff gives them oracles.

The shooting of arrows by Jonathan to indicate to David the disposition of Saul shows that this practice was known, although the incident as told in I Sam. 20 lacks any allusion to its original divinatory character. From the reference in Isa. 57:3 to the "sons of the sorceress" (בני ענה; taking the word בני in the sense of "members" of a guild), it would seem that the Palestinian soothsayers were, like the Babylonian *bârû*-priests, organized as a professional group. The place name "the Diviners' Oak" (אלון מעוננים) in Judg. 9:37 would indicate that these practitioners tended to concentrate in certain localities.

The only direct reference to divination in the NT is found in Acts 16:16-19. The passage tells of the appearance of a slave girl at Philippi "who had a spirit of divination and brought her owners much gain by soothsaying." Paul considered her possessed, and after he had driven the spirit out of her body, the girl ceased to divine, and her master lost a source of income.

*Bibliography.* M. Jastrow, *Aspects of Religious Belief and Practice in Babylonia and Assyria* (1911), Lectures III-IV; A. Guillaume, *Prophecy and Divination* (1938); M. Rutten, "Trentedeux modèles de foies en argile inscrits, provenant de Tell-Hariri (Mari)," *RA*, 35 (1938), 36-70; G. Contenau, *La divination chez les Assyriens et les Babyloniens* (1940), with extensive bibliography.      I. MENDELSOHN

*DIVINERS' OAK [אלון מעוננים]; KJV PLAIN OF MEONENIM mē ŏn'ɔ nĭm. A tree near Shechem, by way of which men were coming toward the city (Judg. 9:37). The KJV translation "plain" is incorrect. *Meʻônenîm* is a participle meaning "diviners" or "soothsayers." There is a possible connection with the oak of MOREH, near Shechem (Gen. 12:6; cf. 35:4). It is probable that the place was one where a sacred tree was located and divination practiced.

     W. L. REED

**DIVINITY OF CHRIST.** The idea or doctrine that Jesus Christ is divine or belongs to the divine order. A distinction is sometimes drawn between the deity of Christ—i.e., the idea that he is fully God—and an idea which would ascribe to him a place in the divine order and a unique relationship to God while failing to affirm his full deity. The theology which became "orthodox" and was accepted by the Catholic church in the fifth century insisted that Christ was God. The Gospel of John makes such an assertion in 1:1, unless θεός is taken as an adjective; in 10:34-36 it defends the idea that Christ can be called God, and in 20:28 Thomas addresses him as "my Lord and my God!" When Paul, in Col. 2:9, says that in Christ "the whole fulness of deity dwells bodily," he comes close to the doctrine. It is not quite certain whether the phrase in Tit. 2:13 should be translated the "glory of our great God and Savior Jesus Christ" (RSV) or the "glory of the great God and our Savior Jesus Christ" (RSV mg.).

Whenever the NT refers to Jesus as Son of God, it asserts his divinity in some sense (*see* SON OF GOD; CHRIST), for the term regularly refers to some characteristics in which Christ is like God and unlike other men. Nearly every part of the NT speaks of Jesus as Son of God. Since the term "Christ," as used by early Christians, included the ideas of Son of God; SON OF MAN; and LORD, the divinity of Christ can be regarded as a universal doctrine of the NT. It can be argued that most NT writers in speaking of Christ as Son of God mean substantially what the later church meant when it spoke of Jesus as God, but avoided the language used by John, because they held firmly to the HUMANITY OF CHRIST as well as his divinity, and wished to avoid any charge that they believed in more than one God. It should also be remembered that the issues raised in the second and later centuries were not dreamed of by the early Christians.

The two writers with the highest Christology, Paul and the author of the Fourth Gospel, take pains to assert that in some sense the Son is subordinate to the Father. Thus John says that the Son can do nothing of himself but only what he sees the Father doing (John 5:19), and that he seeks the will of him who sent him (5:30). Paul holds that at the end Christ will relinquish the kingdom to God the Father (I Cor. 15:24) and will be subject to him (15:28). Similarly in the book of Revelation the messianic reign comes to an end (20:6-7).

The divinity of Christ, however, continues without end. Is it also without beginning? According to the Fourth Gospel, the Logos was in the beginning with God (John 1:2). In Hebrews also it is said that the *aeons* (ages or worlds) were made through the Son (1:2), and other language of this passage suggests the eternality of the Son. A similar idea must lie behind the statements of Paul that through Christ all things in the heavens and on earth were created (Col. 1:16) and that he originally existed in the form of God (ἐν μορφῇ θεοῦ ὑπάρχων; Phil. 2:6). A problem is, however, raised by Col. 1:15, which calls him πρωτότοκος πάσης κτίσεως. Does this mean that he is the first to have been created?

A further question arising from the Pauline letters is whether Paul thought of Christ as possessing or exercising the attributes of divinity during his earthly ministry. The christological passage in Philippians asserts that Christ "emptied himself," taking upon himself the form of a slave (Phil. 2:7; *see* KENOSIS), and elsewhere Paul emphasizes Jesus' submission to human conditions (e.g., II Cor. 13:4; Gal. 4:4).

Most of the NT books do not reflect such speculations at all. In the case of the Gospel of Mark, it can be asked whether the evangelist believed that Jesus became Son of God at his baptism, or that he had always been Son of God and was at this time marked out for his public ministry. In the gospels of Matthew and Luke, Jesus is presumably Son of God from the moment of his conception, but there is no way to discover whether any of the Synoptics had the idea of the pre-existence of the Son of God.   S. E. JOHNSON

**\*DIVORCE** [כריתות (KJV *alternately* DIVORCE-MENT); ἀποστάσιον (KJV DIVORCEMENT)]. Divorce was generally permitted, largely on the initiative of the husband. However, there is recognition that a concubine could desert her husband under certain conditions (Exod. 21:11). In an Egyptian Jewish colony a Jewish bride had the right to obtain a divorce. *See bibliography.*

When a man divorced his wife, he wrote her a "bill of divorce," a certificate of divorce, and then sent her away (Deut. 24:1-4; cf. Isa. 50:1; Jer. 3:8; Matt. 19:7; Mark 10:4). This procedure was enacted by Moses because of the hardness of man's heart (Matt. 19:8). A simple form of such a decree may be found:

> She is not my wife,
> and I am not her husband
> (Hos. 2:2).

A loosely defined reason for divorce is that a man finds "some indecency" in his wife (Deut. 24:1); the Hillel school viewed this as a general term, and the Shammai school took it to mean adultery only. Joseph decided to divorce Mary when he thought her guilty of adultery (Matt. 1:19; cf. Matt. 19:9; Mark 10:2-9, 11-12). Divorce could be effected for religious reasons (Ezra 10:3, 44; cf. Deut. 7:3; but see I Cor. 7:12-13, 15). Childlessness was a common reason for both divorce and multiple marriages (Mal. 2:15; Code of Hammurabi; *see bibliography*).

A divorced wife might be reinstated (Isa. 54:6); but if she married another, the husband would not take her back (Deut. 24:1-4; Jer. 3:1). To marry a divorced woman is adultery (Matt. 5:32; Mark 10: 11-12; Luke 16:18). If a man puts away his wife, having falsely charged her with unchastity, he must take her back (Deut. 22:19); and when a man is required to marry a girl he has seduced, he may not divorce her (vs. 29). If a man has taken a slave as a wife, by taking another wife he may not divorce the first.

*See also* BILL; MARRIAGE; SEX; WOMAN.

*Bibliography.* C. W. Johns, *Babylonian and Assyrian Laws, Contracts, and Letters* (1904); R. H. Charles, *Teaching of the NT on Divorce* (1921); A. E. Cowley, *Aramaic Papyri of the Fifth Century B.C.* (1923), p. 45; J. Paterson, "Divorce and Desertion in the OT," *JBL*, LI (1932), 161-70; S. E. Johnson, *Jesus' Teaching on Divorce* (1945).   O. J. BAAB

**DIZAHAB** dĭz'ə hăb [דיזהב, that which has gold]. A place E of the Arabah, listed among others to fix the locality in which Moses delivered his farewell address (Deut. 1:1; cf. Mezahab in Gen. 36:39).

The present location is unknown. The suggestion of Minet edh-Dhahab, due E of Sinai, is out of the question, since it is not in the area of the other known places in the list, nor is it a suitable camping site. Since geologists suggest the only likely place to find gold in this region is in the crystalline rocks E of the Arabah, the other suggestion of edh-Dheibeh, E of Heshbon, near Qasr el-Mwaqqar, is better from the point of view of location; but again, it is not a good camp site.

*Bibliography.* F.-M. Abel, *Géographie de la Palestine*, II (1938), 307.   V. R. GOLD

DO NOT DESTROY. *See* MUSIC.

DOCETISM dŏs'ə tĭz'əm, dō'sə— [*from* δοκέω, to seem]. A type of doctrine, prevalent in certain sections of the church in NT times and later, to the effect that Christ had not come in the flesh. The doctrine might take the form of a denial that the humanity of Jesus was more than an appearance—he only seemed to have a physical body—or it might consist in the teaching that the divine Christ came into, or upon, the human Jesus, perhaps at his baptism, and withdrew from him before the Crucifixion, at no time being really identified with him. This kind of teaching presupposed a dualistic view of the world according to which it would have been impossible for a divine being to assume human flesh. Since there was no doubt of Jesus' divinity, the reality of his humanity was questioned or denied. Docetism was characteristic of gnostic systems generally (*see* GNOSTICISM) and is being combatted in the Prologue of the Fourth Gospel and in the Johannine letters (*see* JOHN, GOSPEL OF; JOHN, LETTERS OF). A good example of docetic teaching is the Acts of John (*see* JOHN, ACTS OF). This kind of doctrine came very early to be regarded as heretical.                  J. KNOX

DOCTOR [νομοδιδάσκαλος; *also* διδάσκαλος (Luke 2:46 KJV; RSV TEACHER)]. Alternately: TEACHER OF THE LAW; KJV DOCTOR OF THE LAW (Luke 5:17; Acts 5:34). The term νομοδιδάσκαλος occurs only in Christian writings, though Plutarch (*Cato Major* XX) has νομοδιδάκτης. In Acts 5:34 the former word is applied to GAMALIEL (1), who belonged to the liberal school of Hillel and is said to have been teacher to Saul of Tarsus (Acts 22:3). Luke 5:17 states that, in the house where Jesus healed the paralytic, many doctors of the law were seated, having "come from every village of Galilee and Judea and from Jerusalem." This is hyperbole, though based on Mark 2:2, 6. From vs. 21, it is clear that Luke's "doctors" were scribes (*see* SCRIBE). In both Luke and Acts, therefore, the term clearly signifies those who were expert in the Mosaic law; and the same is true of the later patristic writings.

In I Tim. 1:7, on the other hand, the expression means *false* teachers, or would-be teachers, of the law. These are grouped with those who "occupy themselves with myths and endless genealogies [=emanations?] . . . , speculations . . . , vain discussion." The passage (I Tim. 1:3 ff) reads like a description of the Gnostic heresy that plagued the church in the second century and possibly in the first (*see* GNOSTICISM). This coupling of Gnosticism with a false Judaism is made also by Irenaeus (*ca.* A.D. 180). Gnostics, he says, equate the Genesis stories with their own doctrines of the Tetrad, the Ogdoad, Sophia, and Ialdabaoth (*Her.* I.18.30). Likewise Ignatius of Antioch (*ca.* A.D. 115), in writing to the Magnesians and to the Philadelphians, lumps Gnostic and Jewish opponents of the faith together, and refutes both with arguments from the life and passion of Christ. Even Paul, in Galatians, is fighting two errors which, he seems to say, come from the same group: a false imposition of Mosaic law on Christian converts, and a false enlightenment that has led to moral laxity (Gal. .1:7 ff; 3:1; 4:3-9; 5:13). The latter came to be a frequent Christian complaint against

Gnosticism. Thus the false doctors of I Timothy may provide one more connecting link between these two early enemies of Christian orthodoxy.

                                        PIERSON PARKER

DOCTRINA ADDAEI dŏk trē'nə ă dē'ī [of Addaeus, *the Latinized form of the* Syr. *Addai, commonly equated with* Thaddaeus]. *See* ABGARUS, EPISTLES OF CHRIST AND.

DOCTRINE. *See* TEACHING.

DOCUMENTS. In its classic form the Documentary Hypothesis reckoned with four literary sources as the primary constituents of the PENTATEUCH or HEXATEUCH. Arranged in chronological sequence, these are J (for Jehovist or Yahwist), E (for Elohist), D (for Deuteronomist), and P (for Priest or Priestly Document).

J, the oldest of the Pentateuchal sources, has been commonly assigned to the tenth-ninth centuries B.C., and regarded as a product of the Jerusalem court during the age of David or Solomon, or the early decades of the S kingdom (*Judah*), in contrast with the E Document, which has been associated with the N kingdom (*Ephraim*). As the principal narrative source, J carries the story from the Garden of Eden (beginning at Gen. 2:4*b*, after the P account of Creation in Gen. 1:1–2:4*a*) through the patriarchal history in GENESIS. It continues in EXODUS and NUMBERS (Leviticus is all P), recounting the story of the deliverance from Egypt, the wanderings in the wilderness, and the conquest of Transjordan. Whether J carries beyond the book of Numbers is a matter of dispute. The usual view is that the death of Moses (Deut. 34) belongs to this source, and it may also include parts of Joshua, thus completing the account of the Conquest. Some scholars even trace J into the books of Samuel, finding its climax and conclusion in the triumphs of David (which fulfil the promises made to the fathers; cf. Gen. 15:18-21, etc.).

E is the second narrative source, in general paralleling and supplementing J. It is in more fragmentary condition than J, and its limits are even more difficult to determine. E has been dated in the ninth-eighth centuries. JE, the combination of J and E, was the work of an editor or redactor, R$_{JE}$. His activity has been plausibly assigned to the period after the fall of Samaria (722/21 B.C.)—i.e., eighth-seventh centuries.

D is to be found chiefly in the book of DEUTERONOMY, though the occurrence of "Deuteronomic" expressions has been noted in other books of the Pentateuch. The Book of the Law, discovered in the temple in the eighteenth year of Josiah (622 B.C.), has been identified with the legal code in Deut. 12–26; 28 (possibly also chs. 5–11). The framing of this code has been dated in the seventh century, while the compilation of the present book of Deuteronomy has been placed somewhat later. An editor combined JE and D not earlier than the sixth century, according to this view.

The final document, P, was compiled by a priestly editor from surviving temple records during the Exile (sixth-fifth centuries). P is the principal technical source of the Pentateuch, consisting of little more than a series of lists and tables containing genealogical and liturgical data, and running from Gen. 1:1 through the book of Numbers. There is little, if any, sign of P in Deuteronomy. Whether P occurs in Joshua is a matter of dispute, though there is considerable P-type material—e.g., the lists of tribal boundaries (chs. 13 ff). A priestly redactor (R$_{JEDP}$) combined P with JED, using P as the framework and distributing the other sources through it. This compilation of the Pentateuch substantially as it has come down to us occurred during the Exile, and was complete by the end of the fifth century at the latest. Ezra has been thought to have brought the Pentateuch (or at least P) with him from Babylon to Jerusalem.

Modern study of the documents has resulted in some important shifts in perspective and conclusions, though the general pattern remains the same. There is no longer the same certainty about the documents themselves. The neat four-source theory has disintegrated into a variety of multiple-source theories, or some form of the Fragmentary Hypothesis, while behind the literary process stands oral tradition and its transmission. Scholars have demonstrated the composite nature of the sources (J$_1$, J$_2$, E$_1$, E$_2$, etc.), and it is now customary to speak of literary strata rather than documents. The very existence of E as a separate source has been questioned, and efforts have been made to dissolve it into a series of addenda.

Working in the other direction, a ground-source (G) has been identified behind the narratives of the Tetrateuch (Genesis–Numbers). Originally oral and poetic in character, G may actually have been reduced to writing; it probably dates to the period of the judges or the United Monarchy at the latest (i.e., eleventh-tenth centuries), and may represent the official tradition of Israel, preserved at the central sanctuary and recited at the amphictyonic festivals. J and E would then be regarded as independent prose abstracts derived from G, while JE is a compendium preserving only parts of J and E, which must have been much more alike than now appears.

D has been disconnected from the other books of the Pentateuch, and regarded rather as the first part of the Deuteronomic history (extending through Joshua, Judges, Samuel, and Kings). The legal code in Deuteronomy has been traced back to a northern provenience, and a ninth-eighth-century date. The other legal codes likewise have been recognized as separate sources, later incorporated into the Pentateuchal documents.

The status of P as an independent document has also been questioned. Reviving an older view, some scholars regard the Priestly writer as the redactor (R$_{JEDP}$) of the Pentateuch. He wove together the older narratives with archival material at his disposal, and attached the book of Deuteronomy as a conclusion to the story of Moses and Israel, the revelation at Sinai, and the tabernacle in the wilderness.

*Bibliography.* Standard treatments of the subject are to be found in S. R. Driver, *Introduction to the Literature of the OT* (9th ed., rev., 1913); R. H. Pfeiffer, *Introduction to the OT* (2nd ed., 1949). For a survey of recent developments see C. R. North, "Pentateuchal Criticism," *The OT and Modern Study* (1951), pp. 48-83. O. Eissfeldt, *Einleitung in das AT* (2nd ed., 1956), is best of all. D. N. FREEDMAN

**DOCUS.** KJV form of DOK.

**DODAI.** Alternate form of DODO 2.

**DODANIM** dō'də nĭm [דדנים]. A people mentioned in Gen. 10:4 and in some Hebrew MSS of I Chr. 1:7. This name is often emended to RODANIM, "Rhodians." Connections have been proposed with "Dedan" (Gen. 10:7) and cuneiform "Danunites," but they are phonetically improbable.

C. H. GORDON

**DODAVAHU** dō'də vā'hū [דודוהו, beloved of Yahu] (II Chr. 20:37); KJV DODAVAH dō'də və. The father of an obscure prophet, Eliezer. The name, of which DODO is probably an abbreviation, may have been suggested to the Chronicler by "Eleazar the son of Dodo" in II Sam. 23:9. J. M. WARD

**DODO** dō'dō [דודו, דדו]. Alternately: DODAI dō'dī [דדי, דודי] (II Sam. 23:9 *Kethibh;* I Chr. 27:4).
**1.** Grandfather of Tola, one of the minor judges in early Israelite history from the tribe of Issachar (Judg. 10:1).
**2.** An Ahohite; the father of Eleazar, who was among the Mighty Men in the high command of David known as the "Three" (II Sam. 23:9; I Chr. 11:12). According to I Chr. 27:4, Dodai or, more probably, his son Eleazar—since the words "Eleazar the son of" appear to have fallen out of the text—was the officer in charge of the division of the Davidic militia for the second month.
**3.** A Bethlehemite, the father of Elhanan, one of the Mighty Men of David known as the "Thirty" (II Sam. 23:24; I Chr. 11:26). E. R. DALGLISH

**DOE** [יעלה, *feminine of* יעל, *see* WILD GOAT] (Prov. 5:19); KJV ROE. The female of the deer and of allied animals, and sometimes of the hare, but not of the Red Deer. *See* HIND.

Both "doe" and "roe" in Prov. 5:19 appear to be mistranslations. The text is "a (female) wild goat of grace," which means "a graceful wild goat"; this seems an unusual epithet for a wife, but it may have been an acceptable term of endearment.

W. S. McCULLOUGH

**DOEG** dō'ĭg [דואג; דאג; דוֹיג]. An Edomite, the chief of Saul's herdsmen (runners?), who at the instance of Saul executed the priests of Nob. Doeg was at the sanctuary at Nob, "detained before Yahweh" for some ceremonial obligation, when David arrived there in his flight from Saul (I Sam. 21:7—H 21:8). Misrepresenting the true nature of his visit, David obtained from the priest Ahimelech provisions, the sword of Goliath, and an oracle of Yahweh. When Doeg rejoined his master at Gibeah, he informed the king what he had witnessed. Summoning all the priestly house of Ahimelech to his court at Gibeah, Saul accused them of treason in providing aid to the king's enemy. Ahimelech did not deny that he had given to the king's son-in-law his wonted assistance but asseverated that he knew nothing of the present rupture between the king and David. Notwithstanding the solemn protests of innocence, Saul commanded his bodyguard to slay the priests as conspirators against the crown. When the bodyguard refused to execute the king's order, Doeg assumed the invidious command and slew eighty-five defenseless priests (I Sam. 22:11-18).

The historical notice in the superscription of Ps. 52, which reads: "A Maskil of David, when Doeg, the Edomite, came and told Saul, 'David has come to the house of Ahimelech,' " merely indicates that this incident in the life of David was considered by the later liturgists, who attached the superscription to the psalm, to form the setting of the composition.

E. R. DALGLISH

**DOG** [כֶּלֶב, *cf.* Ugar. *klb,* Phoen. כלב, Akkad. *kalbu,* Arab. *kalb;* κυνάριον (Matt. 15:26-27; Mark 7:27-28), *diminutive of* κύων (Matt. 7:6; *etc.*] A domesticated carnivorous digitigrade mammal (*canis familiaris*) of the family Canidae (which includes dogs, wolves, jackals, and foxes).

**1. Literal usage.** The dog was domesticated some millenniums before Israel's history began. A canine skull of the Middle Stone (Mesolithic) Age was found at Wadi el-Mugharah apparently indicating domestication, as also remains of a dog found in both pottery and prepottery Neolithic levels at Jericho. The dog is a common animal in the Bible. The biblical writers, however, seem unfamiliar with any kind of warm personal relationship between a dog and its master such as Pliny describes (Nat. Hist. VIII. 61(40); cf. Tob. 5:16; 11:4), although the references in Matt. 15:26-27; Mark 7:27-28 (where not much importance should be attached to the use of the diminutive, κυνάριον) imply that some dogs had access to the eating quarters of a home. The dogs of the Bible, except for those just mentioned and the sheep dogs of Job 30:1, appear to have been the scavenger sort, which haunted the streets and refuse dumps of the towns and which were generally considered to be unclean and vicious. The biblical data do not permit any conclusions about the breeds of dog which were known, although a study of the representation of dogs in Egyptian and Mesopotamian art would presumably shed light on this question.

We read of dogs' drinking with the tongue (Judg. 7:5); of their growling (Exod. 11:7; cf. Jth. 11:19); of their unwelcome attention at times (Luke 16:21); of their reaction to a playful gesture (Prov. 26:17); of their returning to their own vomit (Prov. 26:11; II Pet. 2:22); of their eating of animal flesh, including what is unclean (Exod. 22:31; cf. M. Bek. 5.6), and even of human flesh (I Kings 14:11; 16:4; 21: 19, 23-24; 22:38; II Kings 9:10, 36; Ps. 68:23—H 68:24; Jer. 15:3). Despite such habits, a live dog (over against a dead lion) is used in Eccl. 9:4 to emphasize the advantage of life over death. In the Mishna there are references to a house dog's bite (B.K. 5.3), the chaining of a dog reared in a house (7.7), a mad dog (Yom. 8.6), and feeding dogs with meat (Ned. 4.3; Hullin 4.2).

**2. Dogs as sacrificial offerings.** Isa. 66:3 ("he who breaks a dog's neck") seems to point to a non-Yahwistic cultic act in which a dog was sacrificed. The references, however, to illustrate such an act in the ancient world are rather meager (*see bibliography*); there is, in fact, no decisive evidence for dog sacrifice either in ancient Mesopotamia or in Egypt, al-

though dogs were honored in the latter region, as is illustrated by the hundreds of mummified dogs which have been uncovered. The great Egyptian mortuary god, Anubis, was usually represented either by a human figure with a jackal's (or possibly dog's) head, or by a jackal (or dog) couchant; and some misunderstood echo of this practice may lie behind the references in Isaiah. More probably, the author is citing the dog, as he does the swine in the next line, as an unclean animal, illustrative of the generally unclean sacrifices of the non-Hebrew world.

**3. Figurative usage.** "Dog" is a term of contempt applied to a man (I Sam. 17:43; in excessive humility, II Kings 8:13); cf. the same usage in the Lachish Ostraca (*see bibliography*). Presumably "dog's head" (II Sam. 3:8) has a similar meaning. "Dogs" in Matt. 15:26; Mark 7:27 would appear to designate non-Jews. The isolated saying in Matt. 7:6 (which may be an old proverb) is without an appropriate context, and its significance is therefore obscure, but the "dogs" to which it alludes seem to be unworthy or unappreciative persons, whether Jew or Gentile; Did. 9:5 interprets the term as the unbaptized.

A "dead dog" represents a worthless object (I Sam. 24:14—H 24:15; II Sam. 9:8; 16:9).

An enemy may be called a "dog"; the term is applied by the psalmists to their own opponents (Pss. 22:16, 20—H 22:17, 21; 59:6, 14—H 59:7, 15), in Enoch 89:41-50 to Israel's enemies.

"Dog" also designates the wicked: in Isa. 56:10-11 the reference is to Israel's religious leaders, possibly the prophets of the day, who are not performing their duty aright and are withal excessively greedy; in Phil. 3:2; Rev. 22:15 the allusion is to workers of evil, possibly in the former case to a Judaistic party within the church.

In Deut. 23:18—H 23:19 "dog" means a male temple prostitute; the Mishna, however, takes the word literally (Tem. 6.3).

**Bibliography.** W. R. Smith, *The Religion of the Semites* (3rd ed., 1927), pp. 291-92, 596, on dog sacrifice; H. Torczyner, *The Lachish Letters* (1938), letters 2:4, 5:4, etc.; F. E. Zeuner, "Dog and Cat in the Neolithic of Jericho," *PEQ* (1958), pp. 44 ff.

W. S. McCULLOUGH

**DOK** dŏk [Δώκ]; KJV DOCUS dō′kəs. Dagon, in Jos. Antiq. XIII.viii.1. The small fortress in which SIMON MACCABEUS met his death in 135 B.C. Simon and two of his sons, while under the influence of wine, were murdered here by Simon's son-in-law Ptolemy. The fort is said to have been built by Ptolemy (I Macc. 16:15). It is probably the modern 'Ain Duq, a fountain a mile or two NW of Jericho.

N. TURNER

*DOLMENS dŏl′mĕnz. Ancient monuments consisting of several large stones in the form of one or more chambers, surmounted by a larger stone, called the capstone. They are found in many parts of the world, including Southern Asia, Southern Russia, and a long crescent extending through North Africa, Malta, Portugal, Spain, France, Britain, and the W part of Scandinavia. Archaeologists are of the opinion that they were erected as burial chambers and that in many cases they must have originally been heaped about with earth, which has disappeared in the course of the centuries.

Courtesy of Nelson Glueck

35. Double-chambered dolmen in Transjordan in the foothills eastward of Tell ed-Damiyeh (Adam)

Such dolmens have been found by the thousands in the W part of the Transjordan region, especially on the slopes leading down to the Jordan Valley and the Dead Sea. There are only a few in W Palestine. They are both single and double-chambered (Fig. DOL 35). No contemporary pottery of any sort has been found in them, and they are evidently the work of people of the Neolithic period, perhaps as early as the sixth millennium B.C. and certainly not later than the fourth. The amount of labor involved in the erection of these tombs points to a large and well-organized agricultural civilization in the Jordan Valley and the areas to the E in the Neolithic period. It is probable that the presence of dolmens in Palestine gave rise to the legends of the "mighty men that were of old" (Gen. 6:4) and of the ANAKIM and the REPHAIM.

S. COHEN

*DOMINION. 1. The translation of several words implying "mastery": (a) רדה ("trample"); (b) משל, ממשלה, ממשל ("rule"); (c) שלט שלטן ("to have power over"); (d) κυριεύω ("to be master"); (e) κράτος ("power"; used only in doxologies); (f) ἐξουσία ("authority"); (g) βασιλείαν ("kingship"). The word expresses the sovereign rule of God, political power (either the rule, the power of governing, or the realm governed), man's mastery over nature, and sin's grip on man. For the Hebrews, ultimate dominion belonged to God (Job 25:2; Ps. 22:28). At times it was shared by man over nature (Gen. 1:26; Ps. 8:6); by the king, as the Lord's Anointed (cf. Ps. 2:7), over the nation or nations; and by the saints of the Most High in the eschaton (cf. Dan. 7:14, 27). The term often implies authority or power gained by conquest (Num. 24:19; Judg. 14:4; I Kings 4:24; Neh. 9:28; Pss. 19:13; 119:133). Authors of both the OT and the NT speak in glowing terms of the eternal dominion of God (Ps. 72:8; Dan. 4:3; Zech. 9:10; and the doxologies I Tim. 6:16; I Pet. 4:11; 5:11; Jude 25; Rev. 1:6).

2. The translation of κυριότης (Eph. 1:21; Col. 1:16; Jude 8[?]), meaning an order of angels(?). Dominion appears to be one of the highest ranks of angels, along with θρόνοι (cf. Test. Levi 3:8). These were probably originally pagan deities, considered by the Hebrews as part of the divine council (Ps. 89:6) and regarded as superintending the affairs of the nations (Deut. 32:8; Isa. 24:21; Dan. 10:13; Ecclus. 17:17). In Col. 1:16 Paul uses the term in a good sense, but such beings are usually referred to as requiring to be overcome (cf. Rom. 8:38; I Cor. 15:24; Eph. 6:12; Col. 2:15). *See also* ANGEL; POWER; PRINCIPALITY.

*Bibliography.* J. B. Lightfoot, *St. Paul's Epistles to the Colossians and to Philemon* (1912), pp. 150-53; O. Cullmann, *The State in the NT* (1956), pp. 95-114.        V. H. KOOY

**DOMITIAN** də mĭsh'ən. Titus Flavius Domitianus, son of VESPASIAN and successor of his older brother TITUS as Roman emperor (A.D. 81-96). Born in 51, he was in Rome at the time of Vitellius' murder in 69 and escaped from the Capitol only by wearing Isiac vestments. As emperor he rebuilt the temple of Isis.

When his father became emperor, it was planned that the throne should go first to Titus and then to Domitian, but because of Titus' distrust of Domitian he was given no real authority until he came to rule in the year 81.

His reign became increasingly autocratic, especially during and after the year 89, when a dangerous revolt in Germany was put down and astrologers and philosophers critical of the regime were expelled from Rome. Trials for sedition became frequent. At some point between 85 and 89, courtiers and court poets had begun to address the emperor as "Master and God," and ultimately, as Dio Chrysostom (Or. XLV.1) says: "All Greeks and barbarians called him a god." In the year 95 the emperor became suspicious of his niece's husband, Flavius Clemens, whose two young sons were to have inherited the throne. Clemens was accused of "godlessness" and put to death; his wife, Flavia Domitilla, was exiled. Many others were indicted on the same charge and on that of following Jewish customs. At least in part, the latter charge was initiated because of Domitian's need for money. Since 70 the Jewish temple tax had been paid to Rome. The Emperor was anxious to enforce payment by proselytes as well as by those born Jews. In this connection he may well have investigated the Christians, since at least some of them were close to Judaism. Flavia Domitilla may have been a Christian, since a woman of that name later gave a cemetery to the Roman Christian community. But whatever persecution of Christians may have taken place (probably reflected or largely anticipated in the book of REVELATION), it was incidental to the whole "reign of terror" characteristic of Domitian's last years. In 96 his wife took part in the last of a series of plots against him, and he was murdered.

To portray Domitian simply as an autocrat is to neglect his achievements for the Empire, even though most of these came early in his reign. He was aware of the difficulty of defending the N frontier, especially between the Rhine and the Danube, and advanced a line of forts roughly fifty miles beyond the line established by Vespasian; the new defenses were completed by his successors. He also fought along the Danube, in Dacia (85-89), and in Pannonia (92). At

Rome he tried to enforce an Augustan standard of public morality and refused to accept bequests from testators who had children. In 92 he published an economic edict intended to increase wheat production at the expense of wine; to this measure (later rescinded) there may be an allusion in Rev. 6:6. Yet all his merits were obliterated by his encouragement of informers after 89 and by his self-deification (cf. Suetonius *Domitian* XIII).

Fig. DOM 36.

Courtesy of the American Numismatic Society

36. Roman coin showing head of Domitian

*Bibliography.* S. Gsell, *Essai sur le règne de l'empereur Domitien* (1894); B. W. Henderson, *Five Roman Emperors* (1927). R. M. GRANT

**DOOR.** דַּל (Ps. 141:3), דֶּלֶת (Isa. 26:20), and דֶּלֶת (*deleth*) are the swinging door set in sockets; the pictorial representation is the letter *daleth* in the early Semitic alphabet. Doors plated with metal (II Chr. 4:9, 22) were fastened with metal hinge pivots. סַף, "door" in the KJV, is better "threshold" in the RSV, except in II Chr. 23:4, where it is "gate." The *hithpolel* participle, הִסְתּוֹפֵף, of the denominative verb in Ps. 84:10—H 84:11 is "doorkeeper." פֶּתַח is the opening in the wall, in which might be a single or double דֶּלֶת. The lintel was a horizontal beam above; jambs were at the side. שַׁעַר in Exod. 35:17; Job 38: 17 is "door" in the KJV, but properly "gate" in the RSV. So the participle of the denominative verb, שׁוֹעֵר, is "doorkeeper" in the KJV (I Chr. 15:23) and "gatekeeper" in the RSV. בַּיִת in I Kings 14:17 KJV is given its regular meaning, "house," in the RSV.

In the NT and the LXX, θύρα is used for the swinging door, as in Matt. 6:6, and for the opening, as in Matt. 27:60. It is also used metaphorically, as in John 10:7: "I am the door"; Acts 14:27: "door of faith." Θυρωρός is a doorkeeper (John 18:16).

*See also* ARCHITECTURE; HOUSE; SOCKET.

O. R. SELLERS

**DOORKEEPER** [שׁוֹעֵר, תֵּרָע; θυρωρός]; KJV often PORTER. One who guards a door. There were special gatekeepers for the ark (I Chr. 15:23-24). They also watched the threshold of the temple (II Kings 22:4) and collected money from the people (*see* PRIESTS AND LEVITES § C3). Eunuchs acted as doorkeepers in the palace of Persian kings (Esth. 2: 21; *see* EUNUCH). Sometimes women kept the door (II Sam. 4:6; John 18:16-17). This relatively humble task would be a joy for any servant in the house of the Lord (הִסְתּוֹפֵף, "to stand at the threshold, to be a doorkeeper"; Ps. 84:10). C. U. WOLF

**DOPHKAH** dŏf'kə [דָּפְקָה] (Num. 33:12). The first stopping place of the Israelites after they left the wilderness of Sin. It is usually identified with the Egyptian mining center at Serabit el-Khadim in Sinai.

*Bibliography.* G. E. Wright, *Biblical Archaeology* (1957), p. 64. For Serabit el-Khadim, see W. M. F. Petrie, *Researches in Sinai* (1906); R. F. Starr and R. F. Butin, *Excavations and Protosinaitic Inscriptions at Serabit el-Khadem* (1936).

J. L. MIHELIC

\***DOR** dôr [דֹּאר, דּוֹר]; KJV Apoc. DORA dôr'ə [Δῶρα]. A city on the Mediterranean seacoast S of Mount Carmel. NAPHATH-DOR (Josh. 12:23; I Kings 4:11) and NAPHOTH-DOR (Josh. 11:2) are probably the same city.

The city is located at the small harbor town of et-Tanturah, near which excavations were conducted by the British School of Archaeology in 1923-24, when it was found that the site was occupied for many centuries beginning in the Late Bronze Age (1500-1200 B.C.). The remains of what was once a strong building, now called el-Burj, have been described as a possible tower which guarded the small bay just to the S in Canaanite and later times.

The king of Dor was a member of the coalition of Canaanite kings defeated by Joshua (Josh. 11:2; 12: 23; cf. I Chr. 7:29). Joshua's victory was apparently a temporary one (Judg. 1:27). The city was probably in Solomon's fourth administrative district, and its chief officer, Ben-abinadab, was married to one of Solomon's daughters (I Kings 4:11).

Extrabiblical references (*see below*) to Dor indicate that it was an important coastal town for many centuries. It appears in the Egyptian story of Wen-Amon as a place visited by him during his journey to Phoenicia. The city was probably occupied by the Tjeker, who migrated with the Philistines in the twelfth century B.C. Dor was being besieged by Antiochus Sidetes (139/138-129), who employed infantry, cavalry, and ships for the siege; he finally forced Trypho, who had rejected Simon's offer of assistance, to flee by ship (I Macc. 15:12-13, 25). According to Josephus, Apollo was worshiped at Dor by the Gentiles who inhabited the city (Apion II.x). Dor was granted autonomy by Pompey in 64 B.C.

*Bibliography.* G. Dahl, *Materials for the History of Dor*, Transactions of the Connecticut Academy of Arts and Sciences, XX (1915), 1-131; W. F. Albright, "The Administrative Divisions of Israel and Judah," *JPOS,* V (1925), 31-32.

W. L. REED

**DORCAS** dôr'kəs [Δορκάς; Aram. טְבִיתָא, Tabitha, gazelle, *a feminine name favored by both Greeks and Jews*]. A woman disciple at JOPPA who was full of charitable works; she fell sick, died, and was raised from the dead by PETER after he was urgently summoned from Lydda, nine miles distant (Acts 9:36-42). Dorcas is named "disciple" (μαθήτρια—the feminine is used only here in the NT, but the second-century Gospel of Peter applies it to Mary Magdalene), which could mean an actual adherent of Jesus (cf. Mark 15:40; Luke 8:2) or a Christian, probably the latter. Her death left widows weeping as they showed garments which she had made. Her influence continues in later Dorcas Societies of church women devoted to good works.

The raising of Dorcas is notable because it is the first of such miracles by an apostle (Matt. 10:8; Acts 20:9-10), and because it resulted in winning many believers. Luke probably found this narrative in the early traditions of the Palestinian church and reported it, believing such an event was both possible and probable—a confidence accepted and wondered at today. *See* MIRACLE.                    D. M. BECK

**DORYMENES** dôr ĭm'ə nēz [Δορυμένης; Vulg. Dorymini]. The father of Ptolemy Macron, who, with Nicanor and Gorgias, "mighty men among the friends of the king," were chosen by Lysias to lead an army "into the land of Judah and destroy it" (I Macc. 3:38). Menelaus, though facing defeat, promised a large sum of money to Ptolemy son of Dorymenes (II Macc. 4:45). II Macc. 10:12 may refer to another Ptolemy.                    J. C. SWAIM

**DOSITHEUS** dō sĭth'ĭ əs [Δοσίθεος]. **1.** A captain under Judas Maccabeus; troops commanded by him and Sosipater captured Timothy and the stronghold he held; they did not, however, keep Timothy a prisoner (II Macc. 12:19, 24-25).
**2.** A cavalryman of great strength; one of Bacenor's men. He sought to take Gorgias alive, but was thwarted by a wound inflicted on him by a Thracian horseman (II Macc. 12:35).
**3.** A Jew given high military post by Ptolemy Philopator and Cleopatra; Josephus (Apion II.v) relates that "Onias and Dositheus, both Jews whose names are laughed at by Apion, were the generals of their whole army" (cf. III Macc. 1:3).
**4.** A man claiming to be a priest and Levite who, with his son Ptolemy, carried down to Egypt Mordecai's letter regarding the Feast of Purim (Add. Esth. 11:1).                    J. C. SWAIM

**DOSITHEUS, APOCALYPSE OF.** A Gnostic work in Coptic discovered at Chenoboskion (*see* APOCRYPHA, NT), but not yet published or adequately studied. It appears to be one of a group of apocalypses attributed in some remove to the Great Seth. Since this writing bears the subtitle "The Three Great Steles of Seth," a provisional query has been raised as to whether this material was not earlier engraved on stone and hidden against the time of discovery, and whether Dositheus, scarcely the famous Samaritan teacher, was not the "discoverer"—i.e., interpreter.                    M. S. ENSLIN

**DOT** [κεραία, *see below*] (Matt. 5:18; Luke 16:17); KJV TITTLE. The most minute detail. The NT passages lay stress upon the eternal and immutable character of every detail of the Torah. This emphasis is frequent in late Judaism, especially in the rabbinic writings. *See also* IOTA.
The traditional rendering, "tittle," goes back to Wyclif and Tyndale's "title" (Latin *titulus*), of which it is a variant spelling. Originally used of a sign of abbreviation, it came to designate any distinguishing mark. The Greek word means "horn," "projection," "antenna," "apex of a letter," etc., and is found in Greek writers, sometimes associated with the word "syllables," with reference to something small or trivial. In the gospels κεραία is usually taken to represent a Hebrew expression used of "hornlike" marks, made perhaps to distinguish letters, or of ornamental strokes on letters. In Hebrew these are called "crowns," "thorns," or "points." Differences of opinion exist, however, regarding these explanations. *See* WRITING AND WRITING MATERIALS.

A. WIKGREN

**DOTHAN** dō'thən [דתן, דתין, *cf. locative* דתניה (Gen. 37:17), Egyp. *Tutayana;* Δωθαΐμ, Δωταια, Δωτεα]; KJV Apoc. DOTHAIM dō'thī əm. A city which Eusebius (Onom. 76.13) locates twelve Roman miles N of Sebastia. It was rediscovered by Van de Velde in 1851, and its modern name is Tell Dotha.
Here Joseph, after passing through Shechem, found his brothers who threw him into a well and later sold him to Ishmaelites following the ancient caravan route over the Plain of Dothan toward Egypt (Gen. 37:17). The king of Syria laid siege to the city in an attempt to seize Elisha, according to II Kings 6:13 ff. In Jth. 4:6 (also 3:9 in some MSS; cf. RSV) Dothan serves to identify an area, "Esdraelon opposite the plain near Dothan." In Jth. 7:3 the army of Holofernes spread out over Dothan as far as BALBAIM.
Tell Dotha had long been regarded as a tempting archaeological site. Excavations were begun in 1953 under the sponsorship of Wheaton College (Illinois) and directed by Joseph E. Free. The excavations fully confirm occupation during all the periods documented by written data, and more.
The attractive and commodious site was occupied from the end of the Chalcolithic Age (*ca.* 3000 B.C.) down through the Hellenistic Roman period. Byzantine-Christian remains are barely mentioned in the preliminary accounts thus far published. On the surface was Arabic material. But early remains are abundant.
The isolated mound, which rises to nearly 1,000 feet above sea level, stands *ca.* 175 feet above the Dothan Plain. Its top covers *ca.* 10 acres, the occupied slopes 15 more. Intact Middle Bronze Age (*ca.* 2000-1500 B.C.) jars were found on the lower slope within 16 inches of the surface. A heavy Early Bronze Age (*ca.* 3000-2000 B.C.) wall appeared *ca.* 50 feet from the top. As found, it rose to a height of 16 feet. The outside face was perpendicular, but inside it flaired from *ca.* 9-foot thickness at the top to *ca.* 11 feet at the bottom. Its stones were small and flat, apparently not differing greatly from those of Jericho four thousand years earlier. Steps of the same material 13 feet wide led from low on the mound to a gate area at the base of the wall. Seven different levels were found in the Early Bronze millennium.
Farther up the slope at the crest of the tell, the great Middle Bronze Age wall of the city was found. In the 30 feet of debris within it, the first four levels of occupation were the Iron Age I and II (*ca.* 1200-700), Late Bronze (*ca.* 1500-1200)—an important period—and two in the Middle Bronze Age. Occupation was more or less continuous, with periodic destructions and rebuildings. To the earliest Middle Bronze stratum belongs an infant burial in a jar found under a heavy wall. It is dated by a Tell el-Yehudiyeh juglet and other items in the pottery deposit.

An extremely ugly, many-handled bowl, of which four handles end in stylized animal heads, distinguished Iron I (*ca.* 1200-900). An orange Cypriot juglet decorated with concentric circles, portions of two Astarte plaques, and other objects linked ancient Dothan with other cities of the era. A street averaging 4 feet in width and continuing into Iron II was uncovered to a length of 111 feet.

Courtesy of Herbert G. May

37. Dothan (Tell Dotha), from the W

In Iron Age deposits was another jar burial of an infant, a human skeleton of a man evidently killed on the spot, and a bowl of thin, hard Assyrian "palace ware." On the center of the tell was a considerable area of Hellenistic and Roman remains culminating in an acropolis in which was a domestic building of twenty-five rooms opening on a large court.

Thus the mound offers a fairly complete conspectus of Palestinian culture from 3000 B.C. to A.D. 300 or 400.

Fig. DOT 37. C. C. McCowN

**DOUAY VERSION** dōō′ā, dōō ā′. The official Roman Catholic English Bible (1609-10). By 1540 Roman Catholic leaders complained of the lack of a Catholic translation of the Bible in English. William Allen, Oxford scholar and cardinal, in 1578 urged the English Catholic University at Douay, France, to translate the official Latin Bible into English. Gregory Martin, also an Oxford graduate, completed the NT translation in 1582. The school had fled to Rheims, hence "Rheims NT." In 1593 the school returned to Douay, where the OT was completed, but publication was delayed till 1609-10 because of lack of funds. The Douay Version is a translation of the Vulg., although the translators seem to have used the Geneva Bible and to have made occasional reference to Greek and Hebrew originals. The Preface clearly states the reasons for the translation, chief among which is the existence of heretical versions. The Rheims NT influenced the translators of the KJV, especially in the use of Latin terms.

*See also* VERSIONS, ENGLISH, § 6.

J. R. BRANTON

**DOUBLE-MINDED** [סעפים (KJV VAIN THOUGHTS); δίψυχος]. A term denoting an uncertain and wavering state of mind. It implies skepticism and doubt, instability, unsettledness, perhaps even deceitfulness.

The word סעפים (Ps. 119:113) means more particularly "divided" (cf. I Kings 18:21), and probably implies half-Israelite and half-heathen.

In the NT and some of the Fathers (Jas. 1:7-8; 4:8; Herm. Mand. 9:6; Apostolic Constitutions 7:11;

cf. Ign. *Hero* 7) δίψυχος (lit., "double-souled"), a term first appearing in Christian writings, is related to doubt and wavering in prayer. It indicates a vacillating between faith and the world (Jas. 1:7-8; 4:8); or a doubt, springing from lack of faith (Apostolic Constitutions 7:11) or a feeling of unworthiness (Herm. Mand. 9:6), as to whether God will answer prayer. Such an attitude results in prayers' going unanswered. In I Clement the term denotes those who, as Lot's wife, distrust the power of God (11:2), or those who have lost faith that God's purpose will be accomplished and Jesus will soon appear (23:3). It is a similar lack of faith and dedication which Jesus decries in those who try to serve two masters (Matt. 6:24; cf. Luke 16:13).

*Bibliography.* E. D. Starbuck, "Doublemindedness," *HERE,* IV (1912), 860-62; J. H. Ropes, *James,* ICC (1948), 143.

V. H. KOOY

**DOUBLE-TONGUED** [δίλογος]. A word of uncertain meaning, occurring only in I Tim. 3:8. The Greek root suggests "repetition" or "to repeat." One suggested translation is "not untruthful"—i.e. (in the I Timothy passage), deacons are always to tell the truth. The meaning "double-tongued" suggests insincerity and lack of integrity. It is doubtful that the writer exhorted deacons simply not to repeat themselves. The Greek word was perhaps coined from the Latin *bilinguis,* which means, not only speaking two languages, but also "hypocritical," "deceitful."

*Bibliography.* B. S. Easton, *The Pastoral Epistles* (1947), p. 130. B. H. THROCKMORTON, JR.

**DOUGH** [בצק; KJV עריסה, *see below;* φύραμα]. A mixture of flour (or meal) with water (or olive oil), kneaded in a wooden basin, or kneading trough (Exod. 12:34, 39; II Sam. 13:8; Jer. 7:18; Hos. 7:4; Rom. 11:16; I Cor. 5:6-7). The usual cereals for dough were barley and wheat, although at times spelt, oats, and rye were also used (cf. Sifre Num. 15:21). Into the kneaded dough a bit of leaven (dough left to sour from the previous baking) was placed in the making of leavened BREAD.

In the NT "dough" is used figuratively to represent the converted state (I Cor. 5:6-7), and the nation Israel (Rom. 11:16).

The obscure word עריסה, translated "dough" in the KJV (Num. 15:20-21; Neh. 10:37; Ezek. 44:30), has been supposed to denote either COARSE MEAL (so RSV) or a porridge made of coarse meal. But it may well mean simply "dough," implying the offering of first fruit was required of the kneading trough as well as of the threshing floor. Paul seems to have understood it in this sense (Rom. 11:16), as also the rabbis (Challah 1.1, 5, 7; 2.1).

*Bibliography.* J. Wellhausen, *Prolegomena to the History of Israel* (trans. J. S. Black and A. Menzies; 1885), p. 158; P. Haupt, *Numbers* (1900), p. 50; E. W. Heaton, *Everyday Life in OT Times* (1956), p. 82. V. H. KOOY

**DOVE** [יונה, *see* PIGEON; חרייונים (II Kings 6:25), *presumably* dung, חרי, *or* חרא, of doves; יונים, *see below;* περιστερά, *see* PIGEON]. A term rather loosely applied to many of the smaller species of pigeon; usually used in a figure of speech. The moaning of the dove supplies a metaphor in Isa. 38:14; 59:11; Ezek. 7:

16; Nah. 2:7—H 2:8. Its powers of flight are referred to in Ps. 55:6—H 55:7 (and possibly Hos. 11:11), its nesting in rocks in Jer. 48:28, its colors in Ps. 68:13 —H 68:14, and its eyes in Song of S. 1:15; 4:1; 5: 12. Its loyalty to its mate and its gentleness make it a fitting epithet for a loved one (Song of S. 2: 14; 5:2; 6:9), and it serves as a symbol of innocence in Matt. 10:16; a less favorable view of this bird is expressed in Hos. 7:11. In Ps. 74:19 the psalmist uses "dove" to designate Israel. The appearance of "dove" in the title of Ps. 56 ("The Dove on Far-off Terebinths") has not been satisfactorily explained. The reference in Isa. 60:8 has been taken to be to a dovecot.

The meaning of "dove's dung" (II Kings 6:25) is uncertain. While such dung may have been used for fuel or fertilizer, it is improbable that it served as food (Josephus claims that it was used as salt; Antiq. IX.iv). In Syriac ḥrûthâ means both "excrement" and "buttocks," which suggests that the OT reference may be to some hind part of the dove not usually considered palatable. See DOVE'S DUNG.

In the gospels the Spirit of God, which came upon Jesus after his baptism, is said to have descended "like a dove" (Matt. 3:16; Mark 1:10; Luke 3:22; John 1:32). The source of this symbolism can only be surmised, but probably it lies in Jewish thought, scriptural and otherwise. Thus we have the "hovering" of the Spirit of God in Gen. 1:2; the role which the dove played in the flood tradition (Gen. 8:8-12); the acceptability of pigeons and doves as bird offerings; the proverbial gentleness of these birds (Matt. 10:16); Philo's interpretation of the dove as a symbol of virtue and reason (*Questions and Answers on Genesis* II.39-44; III.3); the Targum's interpretation of the "voice of the turtledove" in Song of S. 2:12 as the "voice of the Holy Spirit of redemption"; Rabbi Jose's statement in the Talmud (Ber. 3a): "I heard a divine voice [*bath qôl*] cooing like a dove."

*See also* FAUNA § B6a. W. S. McCULLOUGH

## DOVE ON FAR-OFF TEREBINTHS. See MUSIC.

**DOVE'S DUNG** [*Kethibh* חריונים, *perhaps* חרי יונים, *from* חרא *or* חרי, dung; *Qere* דביונים; *cf.* Aram. דיבא, flux]. During the siege of Samaria, this material was sold at exorbitant prices, one fourth kab (approximately one half pint) for five shekels of silver (II Kings 6:25; *see* WEIGHTS AND MEASURES). Jos. War V.xiii.7 mentions cattle dung as food during the siege of Jerusalem (A.D. 66-70), and Vergil and other classical authors also note the use of such material as food under dire circumstances. That it was used as salt seems insufficient explanation. Some commentators, following the lead of Bochart (*Hierozoicon* I, 42), suggest the comparison of an Arabic herb named sparrow dung, but a parallel Hebrew plant has not been found. E. M. GOOD

**DOWRY** [זבד; שלוח (KJV PRESENT); KJV מהר (RSV MARRIAGE PRESENT)]. Ordinarily, the property a wife brought to her husband in marriage. This might take the form of a gift of the father to his daughter when she was about to be married. But in bargaining with Jacob for his daughter Dinah, Shechem said he would give whatever was requested

as "marriage present" (KJV "dowry") and gift (Gen. 34:12). The meaning of the crucial word here, מתן, is uncertain, although it probably derives from the verb נתן, "to give."

In the early period it is probable that the father gave the bride a maidservant as a dowry (Gen. 16: 1; 24:61; 29:24, 29). Over the maidservants referred to in these passages the husbands appeared to have had no control. When Laban's daughters complained that their father had been using up the money given for them, they may have had their dowry in mind (Gen. 31:15). Examples of dowries to daughters include a gift of springs of water (Josh. 15:18-19; Judg. 1:14-15), and of a city by the pharaoh when his daughter married Solomon (I Kings 9:16). The idea of a gift shows that MARRIAGE was not simply by purchase, for the wife could hold property in her own right. O. J. BAAB

**DOXOLOGY** dŏks ŏl'ə jĭ [δοξολογία, *from* δόξα, glory, *and* λόγος, utterance]. A formula for expressing praise to God. As early as in the J document of the Pentateuch, God's deeds are "blessed" (ברוך; εὐλογητός; Gen. 24:27; Exod. 18:10; *see* BLESSINGS AND CURSES). In the Jewish service these BLESSINGS were recited at the end of hymns (I Chr. 16:36; Pss. 41:13; 72:18; 89:52; 106:48; cf. 150:1-6), at the end of the single benedictions of a longer prayer—e.g., the Amida—or even after every mention of God's name. They are connected with the cups of wine in the Pesach ritual (Ber. 49a) and with the building of the booths in the Feast of Tabernacles (Suk. 46a). Sometimes they are found too at the beginning of a prayer (I Chr. 29:10; Dan. 2:20; Luke 1:68; cf. II Cor. 1:3; Eph. 1:3; I Pet. 1:3). They protect the speaker from God's punishments of men's sin (Rom. 1:25; II Cor. 11:31).

Another form of the doxology starts Ps. 29: the exhortation to "ascribe the LORD glory [כבוד; δόξα] and strength" and "the glory of his name" (vss. 1b, 2a; cf. Bar. 2:18; *see* GLORY), later enlarged by "for ever and ever" at the end of prayers (e.g., Prayer Man. 15) or books (IV Macc. 18:24).

The object of the doxology in the Christian (even the pre-Pauline) congregations was God, seldom Christ (cf. Rom. 9:5; Rev. 5:12), but it was sometimes "through the Son" (e.g., Rom. 16:27; I Pet. 4:11), "in the Holy Spirit" (Prayers of Serapion). This formula was changed, in opposition to Arianism, into "and to the Son and to the Holy Spirit." The doxologies at the end of the Christian prayers (I Clem. 61), especially in the Eucharistic service, are deeply influenced by Luke 2:14.

**Bibliography.** E. von der Goltz, *Das Gebet in der ältesten Christenheit* (1901). G. F. Moore, in F. Cabrol and H. Leclerq, eds., *Dictionnaire d'Archéologie Chrétienne et de Liturgie*, IV (1921), 1526 ff; *Judaism*, I (1927). L. G. Champion, *Benedictions and Doxologies in the Epistles of Paul* (1935). H. Schauss, *The Jewish Festivals from Their Beginnings to Our Own Day* (1938). J. A. Jungmann, *Missarum Solemnia*, I (1948). G. Rietschel, *Lehrbuch der Liturgik*, I (2nd ed., ed. P. Graff, 1951). J. HEMPEL

**DRACHMA** drăk'mə [δραχμή]. The unit of silver coinage of Greece; weight 4.3 grams. At the time of the NT it was equated with the Roman denarius, which was therefore called "drachma" by the Greek world; and the word is translated "silver coin" (Luke 15:8-9; KJV "piece of silver").　　　　H. Hamburger

**DRAGNET** [חרם] (Ezek. 32:3); KJV NET. A NET to be dragged along the bottom of a river or on the ground. Pharaoh of Egypt, under the figure of a sea or river dragon, would be caught in a dragnet.

**DRAGON.** In several poetic passages of the OT reference is made to a primordial combat between Yahweh and a draconic monster, variously styled LEVIATHAN (Job 3:8; Ps. 74:14; Isa. 27:1); RAHAB (Job 9:13; 26:12; Ps. 89:10—H 89:11); *Yam*—i.e., "sea" (Job 7:12; Hab. 3:8); *Nahar*—i.e., "stream" (Ps. 93:3 [plural נהרות]; Hab. 3:8 [plural נהרים]); *Tānnîn*—i.e., "sea monster" (Job 7:12; Ps. 74:13; Isa. 51:9); and *Bashan*—i.e., "sea serpent" (Ps. 68:22—H 68:23; cf. Ugaritic *btn*, Akkadian *bašmu*). Moreover, in accordance with the idea that all primordial conditions will be repeated before the "new creation" which is to follow the collapse of the present world order, the renewed fight against the Dragon (temporarily loosed from his bonds) also plays a role in Jewish eschatological speculation (cf. Isa. 27:1; Rev. 20:2; II Esd. 6:52; II Bar. 29:3-8; Palestinian Targ. Num. 9:26-27; B.B. 74a-75a; Shab. 30b; Keth. 111b).

On the significance of the myth, and on its numerous parallels in ancient Near Eastern and other literatures, *see* COSMOGONY §§ A2d, D2b.

"Dragon" is also used in the KJV as the translation of תנין, even in nonmythological contexts (e.g., Gen. 1:21; Ps. 148:7), but the RSV correctly substitutes "sea monster."　　　　T. H. GASTER

**DRAGON WELL.** KJV translation of עין התנין (RSV JACKAL'S WELL).

**DRAM.** KJV form of DARIC.

**DRAMA.** *See* MYTH; JOB; SONG OF SONGS.

**DRAWERS OF WATER** [שאבי־מים]. One of the lowest classes of SERVANT. But such servitude was to be preferred to death. Voluntary SLAVERY, as well as the defeat of enemies like the Gibeonites, might produce drawers of water (Josh. 9:21, 23, 27). Women drew water from the well as part of their domestic chores (Gen. 24:11, etc.). Young men also might draw water in connection with their other duties (Ruth 2:9). But the lowliness is clearly indicated in Deut. 29:11, where these drawers of water are least in the listing of the covenanting people (vs. 10).

*See also* HEWERS OF WOOD.　　　　C. U. WOLF

**DREAD, DREADFUL.** *See* FEAR.

**DREAM** [חלום, חלם; ἐνύπνιον, ὄναρ]; **DREAMER** [חלום, חלם; ἐνυπνιάζομαι]. Dreams, or "visions of the night," were considered in the ancient Near East as messages emanating from supernatural powers, and great importance was attached to their contents and interpretation (as evidenced by the compilation of "dream books" in Mesopotamia and Egypt). On a lower level, frightful and nightmarish dreams experienced by ordinary people were ascribed to the machinations of sorcerers and evil spirits. On a higher level, dreams experienced by kings or priests were conceived to be a vehicle by which the gods made known their intentions.

As a means of communication between gods and men, kings sometimes tried to induce dreams by passing the night in a temple in the hope of receiving a revelation in a night vision. This method is known as incubation-dreams. Typical examples of such sought-for visions are reported from Babylonia (e.g., the dreams of Gudea and Tammuz), and from Ugarit (e.g., the dream of King Keret). Solomon's dream at Gibeon (I Kings 3:4-15; II Chr. 1:3-12) belongs to the same pattern. For examples of unintentional incubation-dreams—i.e., when an individual chances to sleep in a holy place and becomes the recipient of a message dream without having consciously sought one—see Jacob's dream at Bethel (Gen. 28:11 ff), his "vision of the night" at Beersheba (Gen. 46:1-4), and Samuel's experience while asleep in the sanctuary at Shiloh (I Sam. 3).

The dreams reported in the Bible may be classified typologically as (*a*) simple dreams, in which announcements are delivered in plain language (cf. Gen. 20:3, 6-7; 31:10-13, 24; I Kings 3:5 ff; Matt. 1:20; 2:12; Acts 9:10); and (*b*) symbolic dreams, which, in many cases, could be resolved by professional interpreters only (cf. Gen. 37:5-10; 40:5 ff; 41: 1 ff; Dan. 2). The OT recognizes one source of dreams: all night visions proceed from God, and his assistance is sought in interpreting them (cf. Gen. 40:8; 41:16; Dan. 2:19-23). Dreams are one of the legitimate channels by which God reveals his will to chosen individuals (cf. Job 33:15-16), to kings (cf. I Sam. 28:6), and to prophets (cf. Num. 12:6). Joel (2:28—H 3:1) looked forward to the day when

> your sons and your daughters shall prophesy,
> your old men shall dream dreams,
> and your young men shall see visions.

The false prophets based the veracity of their pronouncements on the claim that they were the recipients of divine dreams (cf. Jer. 23:32; 27:9), but to the true prophets these were "lying dreams" giving "empty consolation" (cf. Zech. 10:2), and Deut. 13:1-5—H 13:2-6 prescribes the death penalty for any spurious "dreamer of dreams." While great weight was generally attached to dreams, it was at the same time assumed that some night visions were of no consequence (cf. Job 20:8; Ps. 73:20; Eccl. 5:7—H 5:6; Isa. 29:8), and a person prone to dreaming was mockingly referred to as a "master of dreams" (cf. Gen. 37:19).

The words חלום, "dream," and חזון or חזיון, "vision," are sometimes mentioned together (cf. Job 20:8; 33:15; Isa. 29:7); the roots of both mean "to see" (for the former see C. H. Gordon, *Ugaritic Handbook* (2nd ed., 1947), p. 228, no. 674). The terms used for "interpreting dreams" are Hebrew פתר, Aramaic פשר, and once Hebrew שבר (Judg. 7:15). The first two words (cf. Akkadian *paṭāru* and *pašāru*) mean "to dissolve, to analyze," and the root of the latter denotes, literally, "to break up."

*Bibliography.* J. Obermann, "How Daniel Was Blessed with a Son: an Incubation Scene in Ugarit," *JAOS,* supplement no.

6 (1946); E. L. Ehrlich, *Der Traum im AT*, BZAW, vol. 73 (1953); A. L. Oppenheim, *The Interpretation of Dreams in the Ancient Near East with a Translation of an Assyrian Dream Book*, Transactions of the American Philosophical Society, N.S., vol. 46, pt. 3 (1956). I. MENDELSOHN

## DRESS AND ORNAMENTS.

A. Men
 1. Terms for garments in general
 2. Undergarments
 3. Types of outer garments
  *a.* Coat, robe, mantle
  *b.* Mantle of distinction
  *c.* Girdle, belt, sash
 4. Headgear
 5. Footwear
 6. Ornaments
B. Women
 1. Terms for garments in general
 2. Undergarments
 3. Types of outer garments
 4. Headgear
 5. Footwear
 6. Ornaments
Bibliography

**A. MEN. 1. Terms for garments in general.** One of the general terms for "garment" or "clothes" is מדו, מד. In Lev. 6:10—H 6:3 ("garment") it refers to the linen garment of the high priest (cf. Ps. 133:2). Its general character may be seen from Judg. 3:16; I Sam. 4:12 ("clothes"), while in I Sam. 17:38-39; 18:4 ("armor") it appears to be used in the narrow sense of "soldiers' dress." That it was a long, robelike garment is indicated in II Sam. 10:4 = I Chr. 19:4 ("garment").

The most widely used term (some two hundred times) is בגד, whose meaning appears in Lev. 6:27 —H 6:20; 14:55, which refer to any whole garment. Its general character may be determined by the fact that it was used also to describe a cover-cloth (for the ark [Num. 4:6-9]; for a bed [I Sam. 19:13; I Kings 1:1]). It is also used of robes of kings (Judg. 8:26; II Sam. 13:31; I Kings 22:10, 30; etc.) and of the high priest (Exod. 28:2 ff) and also of the garments of prisoners of war (II Kings 25:29; Jer. 52: 33). There were both outer garments (II Kings 7:15) and inner garments (Ezra 9:3, 5; Ezek. 26:16). There were cultic garments (Exod. 28:2), mourning garments (II Sam. 14:2), and royal garments. Garments might be made either of linen or of wool, but not of a mixture of the two (Lev. 19:19; Deut. 22:11).

Another general term for "garment" is שמלה, "something wrapped around," "mantle." With such a cloth the sons of Noah covered his nakedness (Gen. 9:23); the people cast in it their offerings for Gideon's ephod (Judg. 8:25); and the sword of Goliath was wrapped in it (I Sam. 21:9—H 21:10). It designates the clothing of the wanderers (Deut. 8:4), of the sojourner (Deut. 10:18), and of the ordinary person (Deut. 22:3), as well as the best clothes of Ruth (Ruth 3:3). It was the dress of the poor (of burlap [Ecclus. 40:4]) by day and his cover by night (Exod. 22:26). As such it was simply a large sheet or cloth wrapped around the body. That it was probably all of one piece is demonstrated from the שלמה (a cognate or related word), torn in pieces by the prophet (I Kings 11:29-30; "garment"). The שמלה was first a wrapper and then came to mean "clothes" in a more general sense.

Another general term is כסות, whose broadest meaning is "covering," particularly of the poor (Exod. 21:10; 22:26; Deut. 22:12; Job 24:7; 26:6; 31:19; rendered variously "clothing," "cloak," "garment," "covering").

Of גלום, "clothes," we know nothing more than that they were a valuable article of trade (Ezek. 27:24).

The ἱμάτιον of the NT (Matt. 17:2; 27:31, 35; etc.; "garment," "robe") was probably an oblong piece of cloth worn as an outer garment ("cloak") over the χιτών ("coat"), with which it formed the main items of clothing at the time (Matt. 5:40; Luke 6:29). For a more general meaning of the word, see Matt. 9:16; Mark 2:21; Luke 5:36 ("garment"). Of similar nature was the περιβόλαιον (Heb. 1:12; "mantle"), though in I Cor. 11:15 ("covering") it doubtless means "veil." Ἐπενδύτης in John 21:7 is a general word for wearing apparel ("clothes"; KJV "coat").

**2. Undergarments.** All the terms above apply to clothes generally or, usually, to the outer garment in particular. Along with them there were undergarments, for which there are some more or less general terms that do not detail either specific forms or usages beyond the fact that they were undergarments.

The most widely used word for such garments is כתנת ("coat," "robe," "tunic," "garment"), which was a long- or half-sleeved shirtlike garb reaching to the ankles (Gen. 37:3, 23, 31-35). The famous Beni-hasan painting is a good illustration of such garments (Fig. JOS 29) which were worn by both men and women. They are of varied colors, though two of them are white. They are draped over one shoulder, leaving the other shoulder bare, and they reach to a point slightly below the knees. Those of the women are apparently of the same general style but are somewhat longer. The first biblical mention of the כתנת is in Gen. 3:21, where Yahweh is said to have made for Adam and Eve such "garments" (KJV "coats") of skins. Hushai (II Sam. 15:32) had such a garment, as did Shebna (Isa. 22: 21). The mention of a collared tunic in Job 30:18 points to a baglike garment with apertures for head and arms. Women wore it as well as men (II Sam. 13:18-19; Song of S. 5:3). It was an important item in the wardrobe of the priests (Exod. 28:4, 39-40; 29:5, 8; 39:27; 40:14; Lev. 8:7, 13; 10:5; 16:4; Ezra 2:69; Neh. 7:70, 72—H 7:69, 71; the RSV uses "coat" for some of the references to priests, except in II Sam. 15:32, but the KJV uses "coat" more frequently). Generally wool was the material from which the tunic was made, especially for the poor, though linen was used for that of priests and some others.

The χιτών of Matt. 5:40; Luke 6:29 ("coat") was also an undergarment (cf. Matt. 10:10; Mark 6:9; Luke 9:3; "tunic"). This was the seamless tunic of Jesus (John 19:23) for which the soldiers cast lots. The garment rent by the high priest (Mark 14:63; "mantle"; KJV "clothes") was such a tunic, though in Matt. 26:65 it is referred to as ἱμάτια ("robes"; KJV "clothes"). Josephus describes the official garment of the high priest as a tunic, χιτών (Antiq. III.vii.2, 4).

Another undergarment was the סדין, "linen garment" (Judg. 14:12-13; Prov. 31:24; Isa. 3:23). The midrash catalogues it among the men's clothing. In the NT, σινδών appears as a piece of cloth used as a sheet or shroud for the dead (Matt. 27:59; Mark 15:46; Luke 23:53). The "young man" who followed Jesus (Mark 14:51-52) was clothed only with a σινδών, obviously only a cloth wrapped around his body.

The waistcloth or loincloth (אזור) was still another undergarment. Elijah had one of leather (II Kings 1:8; "girdle"). It was worn next to the skin (Jer. 13; "waistcloth"; KJV "girdle") and loosened at night (Isa. 5:27), though apparently not removed entirely (cf. Isa. 11:5). This was the forerunner of the כתנת, as may be seen from the angular wrapper worn by the Syrian tribute-bearers depicted on Egyptian monuments.

Breeches or drawers (מכנסי בד) are mentioned only in connection with priestly vestments and were designed to cover the naked body "from the loins to the thighs" (Exod. 28:42; "linen breeches"). They were made of linen (Exod. 39:28; cf. Ecclus. 45:8) and were used in connection with the removal of the ashes of the burnt offering from the altar (Lev. 6:10 —H 6:3) and by the high priest on the Day of Atonement (Lev. 16:4). According to the Ezekielian order (44:18), the Levitical priests were to wear them when on duty. Josephus calls these breeches ἀναξυρίδες (Antiq. III.vii.1), a term used by Herodotus (1.71; 3.87; 7.61) to describe the customary drawers of the Persians. See *Syria*, XVII (1936), 249 and pl. 46, 1, fig. 10; XVIII (1937), 4-31.

The term סרבל (Dan. 3:21, 27; "mantle," "tunic"; KJV "coat," "hose") is of uncertain meaning.

**3. Types of outer garments. *a. Coat, robe, mantle.*** "Coat," "robe," and "mantle" are all used to translate מעיל, which was obviously an outer garment and part of the dress wardrobe of men. Samuel's mother made one each year for her son (I Sam. 2:19), and he is on significant occasions described as wearing one (I Sam. 15:27; 28:14). Saul (I Sam. 24:4, 11—H 24:6, 12) and Jonathan (I Sam. 18:4) wore one, as did David on the occasion of the transfer of the ark to Jerusalem (I Chr. 15:27). Ezekiel (26:16) refers to the robes and embroidered garments of the princes of the sea. (For figurative use, see Job 29:14; Ps. 109: 29; Isa. 59:17; 61:10.) This was the garment rent in times of distress (Ezra 9:3, 5; Job 1:20; 2:12). The word is used to designate the garment which was worn with the priestly ephod (Exod. 28:31 ff; 29:5; 39:22 ff). The ephod was put on over the מעיל (Lev. 8:7). Women also had such garments, as we know from II Sam. 13:18, where the כתנת פסים ("long robe with sleeves"; KJV "coat of many colors") is described as the מעילים ("robes") of the virgin daughters of the king (*see* CLOTH § 6). In a general way the מעיל corresponds to the *qumbaz* of modern Palestine (see Dalman, *Arbeit und Sitte*, V, fig. 58), a long, loosely fitting robe worn over all other garments. In ancient times it was probably sleeveless.

The linen ephod (בד אפוד) of Samuel (I Sam. 2: 19), of the priests (I Sam. 22:18; Hos. 3:4), and of David (II Sam. 6:14) was not the high-priestly vestment, but a simple white linen priestly robe.

For soldiers' dress, *see* COAT OF MAIL.

***b. Mantle of distinction.*** Kings and prophets wore, in addition to other garments, a mantle (אדרת). The king of Nineveh (Jonah 3:6) wore his as a robe of state. Such a mantle was one of the objects coveted and stolen by Achan (Josh. 7:21, 24). Elijah also had one of them, and it played a very important role in his activities (I Kings 19:13, 19; II Kings 2:8, 13-14). According to Zechariah (13:4), it was the sign of the prophetic office. It was made of animal hair; goat's hair is implied in Gen. 25:25, and the mantle of John the Baptist was of camel's hair (Matt. 3:4; Mark 1: 6). The robe put on Jesus as a mockery was the Roman soldier's mantle, simulating that of royalty (Matt. 27:28, 31; Mark 15:17, 20; John 19:2, 5).

Cf. also Herod's robe (Acts 12:21) and the στολή of Philip (I Macc. 6:15)—this is the term used to render אדרת in Jonah 3:6. According to the NT, the στολή was worn by men of rank, as, e.g., the scribes (Mark 12:38; Luke 20:46); by the young man who sat at the head of the empty tomb (Mark 16:5); by the returned prodigal (Luke 15:22); and by the martyrs (Rev. 6:11) and the redeemed (Rev. 7:9, 13). *See* MANTLE; ROBE for other words so translated.

***c. Girdle, belt, sash.*** For warmth and maneuverability the flowing garments required a girdle (חגור, חגורה).* This was especially true of the soldier, whose BELT was worn over his regular garb and was used to carry his sword (II Sam. 20:8). It was apparently a long folded cloth of wool, which had other uses— e.g., to hold money or other valuables (Matt. 10:9; Mark 6:8). Fig. DRE 38.

From Kurt Galling, *Biblisches Reallexikon* (Tübingen: J. C. B. Mohr)

38. Girdles worn in biblical times: (1-2) from Egypt; (3) from Lachish

There was also the linen sash (אבנט, "girdle") of the priest (Exod. 28:4, 39; 29:9; 39:29; Lev. 8:7, 13; 16:4) or of officials (Isa. 22:21). It was of special significance as an insigne of office.

The מזח, "belt" (Ps. 109:19), and מזיח, "belt" (Job 12:21), were girdles of a peculiar type. The ζώνη, "girdle," of the NT (especially Acts 21:11; Rev. 1:13; 15:6) was a long folded sash used to hold in the flowing robes and as a money belt.

**4. Headgear.** Mention of headgear, except for special occasions, is relatively rare in the Bible. There was the פאר, which applied to a headdress for women, a turban of priests, and headgear for others, especially a bridegroom. It was put aside in times of mourning.

The מצנפת, "turban," was worn by the high priest and was made of linen. A different kind of turban, מגבעה (*see* CAP), was worn by the ordinary priests. *See* TURBAN.

The hats of Dan. 3:21 are too uncertain for comment.

Soldiers wore protective helmets (כובע; κόρυς; περικεφαλαία).

The prayer covering of I Cor. 11 is nondescript.

The monuments show mostly Syrians and Palestinians with simple headbands or conical-shaped strip caps (*ANEP* 46-47, 52, 61, 355).

Closely related to headgear is the styling of HAIR and BEARD. *See also* VEIL.

**5. Footwear.** An essential item of normal dress was shoes or sandals (II Chr. 28:15; Ezek. 24:17, 23; Luke 15:22; Acts 12:8). In times of mourning or on holy ground they were removed (Exod. 3:5; Josh. 5:15; Ezek. 24:17, 23; Acts 7:33). The fact that they could be mended (Josh. 9:5, 13) and that the shoes of the Israelites are said not to have worn out during the wilderness wanderings (Deut. 29:5) indicates the almost universal practice of wearing shoes. The monuments depict different types of footwear made of leather and fastened to the foot around the ankle with leather straps. Shoes are not mentioned in the catalogue of priestly vestments.

For further discussion, *see* SANDALS AND SHOES.

**6. Ornaments.** One of the special ornaments for men was the finger ring (טבעת) which signified rank (Gen. 41:42; Esth. 3:10, 12; 8:2, 8, 10, 12; I Macc. 6:15).

Related to it was the seal ring (חותם) which bore the name of the wearer and was carried on a cord around the neck (Gen. 38:18). It could also be worn on the hand (Jer. 22:24). This was the σφραγίς of the NT (Rom. 4:11; I Cor. 9:2; II Tim. 2:19; Rev. 5:1 ff; 6:1 ff; 7:2; 8:1; 9:4), where, however, the term is used figuratively. It was used to seal documents, hence the figure. The δακτίλιος of Esth. 8:8, 10 LXX; Dan. 6:17 Theod.; Luke 15:22 has the same general meaning but was also used as an article of luxury. *See* SEALS AND SCARABS.

The נזם, "ring," was also worn by men (Job 42: 11) but was a characteristic ornament of Ishmaelites (Judg. 8:24-26; "earring"). Their kings were adorned with crescent-shaped amulets (שהרנים; Judg. 8:21, 26) and eardrops (נטפה; Judg. 8:26).

Saul wore an armlet (אצעדה; II Sam. 1:10), and excavations of tombs in Palestine indicate that both armlets and bracelets (צמיד) were common.

Apart from the personal items just named, there were doubtless others of a more general character which belong in the category of the jewel chest—e.g., מגדנות, "choice gifts" (cf. Gen. 24:53; II Chr. 21:3; 32:23; Ezra 1:6), and פנינים, CORAL. *See* JEWELS AND JEWELRY. For special insignia, *see* CROWN; DIADEM.

**B. WOMEN. 1. Terms for garments in general.** The same general terms are used for women's clothing as for men's: לבוש, "what is put on" (Ps. 45:14; Prov. 31:22); מלבוש, "what is put on" (Ezek. 16:13); בגד, "garment" (Gen. 38:14, 19; Deut. 24:17; II Sam. 14:2; II Kings 11:14; etc.); שמלה, "clothes" (Deut. 21:13; Ruth 3:3; etc.); ἱμάτιον, "garment" (Jth. 8:5; Acts 9:39; I Tim. 2:9; I Pet. 3:3). "Widow's garments" (Gen. 38:14) are specifically mentioned; cf. Jth. 8:5; 10:3, where the "garments of widowhood" were probably sackcloth.

**2. Undergarments.** Women also wore the long undergarment called כתנת, as may be seen from II Sam. 13:18 ff; Song of S. 5:3. It was probably made of wool or linen. The Beni-hasan painting shows women wearing such garments slung over the right shoulder and extending farther up around the neck than the men's garment.* They were longer than those worn by men and more varied in color. Fig. JOS 29.

**3. Types of outer garments.** The woman depicted on a Megiddo ivory is dressed in a long robe decorated with fringes (*ANEP* 125). Naturally a girdle was part of women's clothing, though it is mentioned only in Isa. 3:24. Ruth 3:15; Isa. 3:22 speak of a mantle or cloak which could be used as a carrier—e.g., of grain.

**4. Headgear.** For headgear women wore a פאר, "headdress" (Isa. 3:20); צניפה, "turban" (Isa. 3:23); צעיף, veil for covering the face (Gen. 24:65; 38:14, 19); and רדיד, veil for the upper part of the body (Song of S. 5:7; Isa. 3:23). An especially elegant headdress was the μίτρα, "tiara" or "diadem" (Jth. 10:3; 16:8; Bar. 5:2). *See also* HAIR.

**5. Footwear.** The Bible has little to say about women's footwear. The sandaled feet of the maiden are graceful (Song of S. 7:1—H 7:2), and Judith put on sandals to attract the eyes (10:4; 16:9). The bride, according to Ezek. 16:10, was shod with fine leather sandals. The Beni-hasan painting shows Palestinian women wearing brown shoes with a white border around the top.

Fig. SAN 22.

**6. Ornaments.** One of the most complicated subjects dealing with the dress of women is that of ornaments. Brides and other ladies on festival occasions wore ornaments (עדי; lit., "shining, glittering objects"; II Sam. 1:24; Isa. 49:18; 61:10; Jer. 2:32; Ezek. 16: 11, 13; 23:40). כלי, "jewels," were of silver or gold (Gen. 24:53; Num. 31:50; cf. also I Tim. 2:9; I Pet. 3:3). The best description of bridal attire is in Ezek. 16:10-13.

The NECKLACE was much desired, and sometimes, as we know from tombs of Egypt and Mesopotamia, was quite elaborate and complex. For other items of women's ornaments, *see* ANKLET; BRACELET; EARRING; FRONTLETS; NOSE RING; RING 1, 5.

The identity of the קשרים ("sash" [Isa. 3:20; KJV "headband"]; "attire" [Jer. 2:32]) is not certain.

The text of the myth, "The Descent of Ishtar into the Underworld" (*ANET* 107-9), provides a good idea of women's clothing in Mesopotamia.

J. M. MYERS

**DRESSER OF SYCAMORE TREES** [בולס] (Amos 7:14). This term seems to refer to one engaged in the process of pruning or nipping back the trees for better yields of fruit. AMOS apparently claims that he is not of prophetic line, but is a layman called by God to testify.

C. U. WOLF

**DRIED GRAPES** [ענבים יבשים]. Grapes dried in the sun, listed as food forbidden to a Nazirite (Num. 6:3). *See also* RAISIN; RAISIN-CAKES.

**DRINK.** In biblical times the chief liquids consumed by man were WINE; MILK; WATER (cf. Ecclus. 39:26, where all three are mentioned as elements necessary for life). In addition to these, VINEGAR was used as a thirst-quenching beverage. Of course, drink as such is not condemned in either the OT or the NT (*see* DRUNKENNESS); Moses and the elders eat and drink before God on Mount Sinai (Exod. 24:9-11), and only the ungodly withhold drink from the thirsty (Isa. 32:6). Furthermore, Jesus refers to his gospel as "water welling up to eternal life" (John 4:14) and to his blood as "drink indeed" (John 6:55). Nevertheless, although Koheleth claims that there is nothing better for a man than to eat, drink, and take pleasure in his work (Eccl. 2:24; 3:13; 5:18—H 5:17; cf. 8:15), Paul says that "the kingdom of God does not mean food and drink but righteousness and peace and joy in the Holy Spirit" (Rom. 14:17).

*See also* FOOD; STRONG DRINK.　　　J. F. ROSS

**DRINK OFFERING.** *See* SACRIFICE AND OFFERINGS § A2*b*i-ii.

**DROMEDARY** [כרכרות (Isa. 66:20; KJV SWIFT BEAST), *meaning uncertain;* KJV בכרה (Isa. 60:6; Jer. 2:23; RSV YOUNG CAMEL), *cf.* Arab. *bakr,* young camel; רכש (I Kings 4:28—H 5:8; RSV SWIFT STEED), *cf.* Syr. *rakšā,* horse; רמך (Esth. 8:10; RSV BRED FROM THE ROYAL STUD), *cf.* Arab. *ramakah,* mare]. A swift riding CAMEL belonging to the Arabian (one-humped) species (*Camelus Dromedarius*).

Since the time of Aristotle the distinction has been made between the two-humped Bactrian camel and the one-humped Arabian camel (*Historia Animalium* 499*a* [II.1]). Within the latter group there is a further division between the burden-bearing camel and the riding camel, the latter being commonly known as the dromedary.

In I Sam. 30:17 the Amalekites who escaped on camels from David's attack presumably did so on fast riding animals; the same type of camel may be referred to in Isa. 66:20, where "dromedary" is the translation.

*Bibliography.* For swift camels ridden by Arabians, see Herodotus VII.86. For the view that all Arabian camels ought to be designated dromedaries, see R. J. Forbes, *Studies in Ancient Technology,* II (1955), 187-208.　　W. S. McCULLOUGH

**DROPSY.** The translation of ὑδρωπικός (Luke 14:2), a term which was widely used by medical practitioners from Hippocrates onward. This condition is a symptom rather than a disease, but its relationship to the progress of specific pathology is such that it is always indicative of advanced organic disease. Dropsy constitutes a disproportionate effusion of watery fluid into the tissues or cavities of the body, and is described technically according to its location, as *ascites* (abdominal dropsy), *hydrothorax* (pleural cavity) *hydropericardium* (cardiac dropsy), *edema* (feet and legs), etc. In Luke 14:2 the condition probably accompanied either cardiac, renal, or hepatic disease.

R. K. HARRISON

**DROSS** [סיג (*Kethibh* סוג; Ezek. 22:18); *otherwise plural,* סיגים]. The impurities of metals, particularly of silver, which accumulate in the smelting furnace (Prov. 25: 4). Silver "turned to dross" is an outcome of debased morals, as dross is generally in the OT a symbol of moral decay (Isa. 1:22; Ezek. 22:18-19; cf. Ps. 119: 119).

Prov. 26:23, translated literally "silver of dross cov-

ering an earthen vessel," makes little sense, and it is suggested that כסף סיגים, "silver dross," be read כספסיגים, "as glaze," with Ugaritic *spsg,* "glaze" (so RSV).

*Bibliography.* W. F. Albright, *BASOR,* 98 (1945), 24-25; H. L. Ginzberg, *BASOR,* 98 (1945), 21, note 55.

I. BEN-DOR

**DROUGHT** [בצרת, חרב (KJV SWORD *in* Deut. 28:22 *with* MT), ציה, חרבון (KJV DRY), תלאבות (KJV GREAT DROUGHT); ἀβροχία]. Disastrous consequences of shortage of rain, which in a dry year (Jer. 17:8) may fall to half the barely sufficient normal. Since surface water is relatively scarce, a prolonged complete drought (I Kings 17:1; Jas. 5:17) would have made Palestine almost uninhabitable. In addition to partial failure of the winter rains, the Bible refers to the regular summer drought, which lasts four months (Ps. 32:4); to the dessicating effect of the EAST WIND (Hos. 13:15); and to the desert areas, where rainfall is minimal (Luke 11:24).

*See also* PALESTINE, CLIMATE OF.

R. B. Y. SCOTT

**DRUNKENNESS.** Wine was not banned in Israel. It was not only valued for giving pleasure and banishing sorrow (Judg. 9:13; Ps. 104:15; Prov. 31:6-7); it had a place in the sacrificial meal (Deut. 14:26; cf. I Sam. 1:9, 12-16; Amos 2:8). Drinking to intoxication (שכרון [only figuratively]; Jer. 13:13; Ezek. 23: 33), however, was a disgrace, and the exemplary stories of the drunkenness of Noah (Gen. 9:20-27) and Lot (19:31-38) serve to show to what immoral uses the drunkard (שכור) exposes himself. Drunkenness is associated with licentiousness in Hos. 4:11, 18 (cf. II Sam. 11:13). Drunkenness is related of wealthy Nabal (I Sam. 25:36), and of the kings Elah (I Kings 16:9), Ben-hadad (20:16), and Ahasuerus (Esth. 1:10). The wisdom writers disapprove of it on utilitarian grounds (Prov. 20:1; 21:17; 23:20-21, 29-35); the prophets condemn it in the leaders of the people for causing moral blindness (Isa. 5:11-12; 28: 7 ff; 56:11-12; Amos 6:6; cf. Prov. 31:4-5).

The charge brought against the insubordinate son by his parents epitomizes his corruption in the phrase: "He is a glutton and a drunkard [סובא]" (Deut. 21:20). Priests must not take any strong drink while on duty in the sanctuary (Lev. 10:8-9).

In the NT, too, drunkenness (μέθη [Rom. 13:13]; οἰνοφλυγία [I Pet. 4:3]) is associated with debauchery and Gentile depravity. A bishop may not be intemperate (πάροινος; I Tim. 3:3; Tit. 1:7). Drunkards (μέθυσος) will not inherit the kingdom of God (I Cor. 6:10; Gal. 5:21), nor are they to be tolerated within the Christian community (I Cor. 5:11-13).

*See also* WINE AND STRONG DRINK.

M. GREENBERG

**DRUSILLA** drŏŏ sĭl′ə [Δρούσιλλα]. The third and youngest daughter of Agrippa I, king of Judea (*Antiq.* XVIII.v.4). She was probably born in A.D. 38 (XIX.ix.1). She had been engaged to marry an Epiphanes, prince of Commogene; but the marriage did not take place because Epiphanes, though he had promised Agrippa I to embrace Judaism, changed his mind and refused to become converted.

Later on, her brother Agrippa II arranged for her marriage to Azizus, king of Emesa, who consented to be circumcised (*ca.* A.D. 53).

When FELIX was procurator of Judea (A.D. 52-60), he saw Drusilla and fell in love with her. Josephus relates that Felix sent to her a friend, Simon of Cyprus, a Jew, who prevailed upon Drusilla to transgress the Jewish law and marry Felix. She bore him a son named Agrippa, who perished in the eruption of Vesuvius in 79.

The account of Acts 23:24–24:27 includes a mention of Drusilla.

*See also* HEROD (FAMILY) § H8.

*Bibliography.* Jos. Antiq. XX.vii.1-2; E. Schürer, *A History of the Jewish People in the Time of Jesus Christ* (1881), div. 1, vol. II, pp. 176-77.                   S. SANDMEL

**DUALISM.** A term used since the beginning of the eighteenth century for two different systems of thought. One, which may be called cosmic dualism, is apparently derived from the Zoroastrian belief in two essentially equal and opposing gods, in conflict with each other: Ahriman, the god and cause of all evil and wickedness; and Ormazd, the god of all good and righteousness. The present evil age is under Ahriman; the future age of righteousness will be under Ormazd. The righteous, who resist the god of evil, will be recompensed in the age to come. This type of dualism provides a satisfactory solution of the problem of evil.

A second type of dualism, the metaphysical, is concerned with the quite incompatible natures of body and soul, as the Pythagorean and Orphic religions taught and Plato and other philosophers believed. According to this teaching, not only was the body much inferior to the soul, which was pre-existent in heaven, but it was the prison house and sepulchre of the soul, imprisoning it and defiling it as well. Salvation consisted of effecting the permanent release of the soul from the body. This was accomplished in part by mortifying the body and depriving it through ascetic practices and disciplines, and in part by mystic religious rites. Numerous reincarnations, with repetitions of the disciplines and rites, were necessary before the soul would be permanently freed from the body so that it might dwell forever in the heavenly realms. Associated with this view was the belief that the world of matter was itself imperfect, if not evil, and the world of spirit perfect and good.

There are few, if any, traces of the cosmic dualism of two opposing forces—one good, the other evil—in pre-exilic Judaism. Instead, the monotheistic doctrine was strongly maintained; Yahweh, the creator and governor of the world and of mankind, was directly or indirectly responsible for all evil, as well as for all good. To be sure, there were evidences of popular beliefs in evil spirits, but these were kept in the background. SATAN, if mentioned at all, was an agent of God, not his equal, not his opponent.

However, in the exilic and postexilic periods Satan (or his equivalent) became the opponent of both God and man. He was not merely the tempter of man, but was also his oppressor and the cause of sin and wickedness. Accompanying this dualism, with its source in Persian religion, was a growing acceptance of the eschatological pattern of two ages: the present one evil, since it was ruled by Satan, and the future to be good, for it would be governed by God (*see* ESCHATOLOGY OF THE OT; APOCALYPTICISM). However, in no case was the dualism as marked as in Zoroastrianism; Yahweh is actually in control; Satan and evil exist only because God for his own purposes is permitting them to do so for a while.

Save in Hellenistic Judaism (Philo, e.g.), the metaphysical dualism of spirit and flesh hardly appears in Judaism. Since Yahweh was all-powerful and wise, as well as good, the world which he had created, with its contents (including the human body), was also good and designed for man's use and enjoyment. Asceticism was the exception, not the rule. As belief in a meaningful existence beyond the grave developed, there came an acceptance of the doctrine of the physical RESURRECTION of the body from Sheol so that it might be reunited with the soul. To be sure, man was created with two impulses—one good, the other evil—but this was as far as dualistic thinking went in Jewish anthropology.

Christianity inherited its cosmic dualism from Judaism. There was a general, though not complete, acceptance of a belief in Satan as an independent personification of evil; in two ages, the first evil, the second to be good; and in the physical resurrection of the FLESH. This dualism reaches its height in Revelation. Moreover, through its Hellenistic heritage Christianity also acquired a belief in a metaphysical dualism, which Paul, e.g., combined with cosmic dualism. For him the body of flesh, with its desires, was evil, and the cause of both sin and death. He accepted the belief in the resurrection; however, the resurrected body was not of flesh and blood, but had been transformed into a spiritual body, for flesh and blood could not inherit the kingdom of God.

Christian GNOSTICISM apparently inherited its metaphysical dualism from Hellenistic sources. The world of matter, created by an inferior or evil creator god, was inherently evil, but the realm of spirit was good. Man was a pre-existent good soul that was imprisoned and defiled by a material body. Redemption consisted—as in certain Hellenistic religions—in the release of the soul from its prison house through ascetic practices and mystic rites, which in Gnosticism involved the reception of a secret, saving Gnosis. Gnosticism, however, seems to have allowed for but one incarnation. This metaphysical dualism as accepted by Christianity prepared the way for Christian asceticism and monasticism.            M. RIST

**DUKE.** The KJV translation of אַלּוּף, נָשִׂיא (RSV CHIEF), and στρατηγός (I Macc. 10:65; RSV GENERAL). "Duke" was not a title in KJV times but was used to refer to a PRINCE or ruler of a family or TRIBE.

**DULCIMER (SHAWM).** *See* MUSICAL INSTRUMENTS.

**DUMAH** dōō′mə [דוּמָה]. **1.** A son of Ishmael, and the presumed ancestor of an Arabian tribe (Gen. 25:14; I Chr. 1:30). There are a number of places in Arabia which bear this name, but the one that seems to fit the biblical reference is Dumat al-Ghandal (now called el-Jof), an oasis located halfway between the head of the Gulf of Aqaba and the head of the Persian Gulf. It seems to be the same as the *Adummatu* which was destroyed by Sennacherib and Esarhaddon of Assyria, and the *Adummu* which was conquered by Nabonidus of Babylonia in his expedition against Tema.

&#42; **2.** A city in the mountains of Judah (Josh. 15:52). According to the *Onomasticon,* there was a village of this name seventeen miles from Eleutheropolis (Beit Jibrin); this is the same as the modern el-Dome, six miles SW of Hebron.

**3.** A name which occurs only in Isa. 21:11: "The oracle concerning Dumah" (משא דומה). Since the next words refer to Seir, it is evident that the reference is to Edom, and the LXX actually renders the word as "Edom." It is possible that "Edom" (אדום) was the original reading and that one א was lost by a scribal error; or else, as "Dumah" can also mean "silence," the word refers to the enigmatic nature of this oracle, which really gives no answer at all to the proposed query.                     S. COHEN

**DUMBNESS.** An inability to speak or vocalize, whether because of functional or organic causes. *See* DISEASE.

**DUNG** [גלל, גל, צאה, דמן, פרש, *see below*]. Animal, bird, or human excrement, often used for manure or for FUEL. גל, גלל, is translated as both human and animal excrement. צאה is used generally for filth but for human excrement as well (II Kings 18:27; Ezek. 4:12). דמן refers to corpses lying on the ground as offal (II Kings 9:37; Jer. 8:2). פרש is used in the priestly legislation for the fecal matter in the intestines of recently slaughtered animals.

In ancient times, as today in Palestine, dung was gathered dried and used for fuel (Ezek. 4:12, 15) when wood and charcoal were scarce. Collected in a dunghill or dung pit, it was mixed with straw and used to fertilize plants (Isa. 25:10). The priestly legislation specifically required the burning of the dung in the intestines of a sacrificial animal at a point outside the camp (Exod. 29:14; Lev. 4:11; Num. 19:5).

The term "dung" was also used symbolically to indicate the degraded end to which a person or nation might come (II Kings 9:37; Ps. 83:10—H 83: 11; Jer. 8:2; 9:22—H 9:21; Zeph. 1:17). It might also be put on the face as a sign of extreme humiliation (Mal. 2:3).

In Nehemiah's account of the inspection, reconstruction, and dedication of the walls of Jerusalem, reference is made to the DUNG GATE (שער השפת, שער האשפת; Neh. 2:13; 3:13-14; 12:31). Most scholars locate this gate in the S wall near or at the SW corner. It probably marks the place where refuse in general was thrown.

A reference to the high cost of pigeon dung during Ben-hadad's siege of Samaria is found in II Kings 6: 25, but the lack of knowledge as to the use of pigeon dung complicates the interpretation.

*Bibliography.* M. Burrows, *AASOR,* XIV (1934), 115-40; J. Montgomery, *The Books of Kings* (1951), pp. 385, 407.
                              H. N. RICHARDSON

**DUNG GATE** [שער האשפת, שער השפת (Neh. 3:13)]; KJV DUNG PORT in Neh. 2:13. A gate of Jerusalem, leading into the Valley of Hinnom (*see* HINNOM, VALLEY OF THE SON OF); restored by Nehemiah (Neh. 3:14; 12:31). Josephus calls it "Gate of the Essenes" (War V.iv.2).

*See* map under NEHEMIAH; *see also* JERUSALEM § 7*b*.
                              G. A. BARROIS

**DUNGEON** [בור, pit; בית הבור (Exod. 12:29; Jer. 37: 16; *cf.* Zech. 9:11), house of the pit; מסגר (Isa. 42:7; PRISON *in* Ps. 142:7—H 142:8; Isa. 24:22), *from* סגר, to shut up, close]. The primary meaning "pit" for בור suggests that it was a sunken room, perhaps a dry well (cf. Jer. 38:6 [a pit or cistern which had no water], and vss. 7, 9-11, 13). This is also the figure which is used in Isa. 42:7, where the verb הוציא intimates "bringing up out of the dungeon" (מסגר).

*See also* PRISON; PIT; CRIMES AND PUNISHMENTS.
                              E. M. GOOD

**DURA** do͞or′ə [דורא] (Dan. 3:1). A valley in the province of Babylon. Since proximity to the city of Babylon is implied, earlier identifications (based on Polybius V.48 and Ammianus Marcellinus XXV.6) as N of Babylon and E of the Tigris, or as the well-known Dura of the Euphrates 270 miles NW of Babylon, are unlikely. More probable is Oppert's suggestion of Tulul Dura, a few miles S of Babylon. But Dura (Akkadian *dûru,* "circuit," "wall," "walled place") is a common place name in ancient Mesopotamia, and the identification, if indeed at all precise in the mind of the author of DANIEL, must remain uncertain.

*Bibliography.* J. Oppert, *Expédition scientifique en Mésopotamie,* I (1863), 238 ff.                     S. B. FROST

**DUST** [אבק, דקק, עפר, שחק; κονιορτός, χόος]. Generally "dust," "dirt," "clay"; but the significant use of עפר occurs in the dominant OT view that man is an earthy creature animated by the breath of God. Of dust man was made (Gen. 2:7*a;* 18:27*b;* Job 4:19; Ps. 103:14; cf. I Cor. 15:47-49), and to dust he returns (Gen. 3:19*b;* Job 10:9; 34:14-15; Ps. 104:29*b*).

*See* ADAM (MAN) § 1*b;* DEATH; MAN, NATURE OF, IN THE OT, § 3.                     L. HICKS

**DWARF** [דק, *from* דקק, crush, be fine] (Lev. 21:20). One category of those physically disqualified from the ministry of sacrifice; either one with defective eyesight (so LXX, Vulg., and context) or preferably one who is withered (paralyzed, consumptive?). The word is elsewhere translated "gaunt," "thin," "small."
                              G. HENTON DAVIES

**DWELLING PLACE.** The translation of a number of words, with little consistency in the KJV, RSV, and other versions. The dwelling place may be occupied by human beings (Hab. 1:6), animals (Jer. 9:11), or God (II Chr. 30:27). Figuratively God is called a dwelling place (Ps. 90:1). "Dwelling place" has been used to translate the following:

*a)* מושב (Num. 24:21; I Chr. 6:54; KJV "habitation" in Gen. 36:43), related to the verb ישב, "sit," "dwell."

*b)* מקום שבת (I Kings 8:30; II Chr. 6:21).

*c)* מכון שבת (I Kings 8:39-49; II Chr. 6:30-39).

*d*) מעון (II Chr. 36:15; Ps. 90:1; "habitation" in II Chr. 30:27; "haunt" in Jer. 51:37), from the root עון, "dwell."

*e*) The feminine מעונה (Ps. 76:2—H 76:3; KJV "refuge" in Deut. 33:27).

*f*) משכן (from שכן, "dwell"), the common word for "TABERNACLE," applied to the structure built during the Exodus. In some passages where reference is not to this structure (Pss. 49:11—H 49:12; 74:7) both the RSV and the KJV use "dwelling place," but elsewhere there are variations. In Jer. 30:18; 51:30 the KJV has "dwelling place" and the RSV "dwelling," while in Job 39:6; Ps. 87:2 the RSV has "dwelling place" and the KJV "dwelling." In Hab. 1:6 the KJV has "dwelling place" and the RSV "habitation," while in Ps. 132:5 the RSV has "dwelling place" and the KJV "habitation."

*g*) אהל (Job. 8:22; Ps. 52:5—H 52:7; RSV TENT).

*h*) מושבותיכם (Ezek. 6:6; KJV "in all your dwelling places"; RSV "wherever you dwell").

*i*) מכון (Isa. 18:4; RSV "dwelling"), from the root כון, "be firm, established." כל מכון (Isa. 4:5) is "every dwelling place" in the KJV and "the whole site" in the RSV.

*j*) נוה (Ps. 79:7; RSV HABITATION), which generally refers to a pasture.

*k*) Κατοικητήριον (Eph. 2:22; Rev. 18:2; KJV "habitation").

*l*) Ἀστατοῦμεν (I Cor. 4:11; KJV "have no certain dwelling place"; RSV "are homeless"), from ἀστατέω, "wander about."

*See also* HOME.                                 O. R. SELLERS

**DYEING.** Dyeing is an ancient art and played a necessary and important role in the lives of Palestinians throughout the biblical period. Although the process is not mentioned in the Bible, dyed stuffs often are (Exod. 35:6, 23, 25, 35; Judg. 5:30; Mark 15:17; Acts 16:14; etc.). What specifically the Israelites learned of the process from neighbors to the S and the N is unknown, but Solomon is reported to have requested of Hiram of Tyre a man skilled "in purple, crimson, and blue fabrics" (II Chr. 2:7; cf. 3:14); the Phoenicians apparently guarded the secret of making purple from mollusks so that the rest of the ancient world had to purchase from them.

Dyeing was carried on in centers which presumably represented the concentration of a guild (cf. I Chr. 2:55; 4:21). The juxtaposition of physical factors such as grazing land for herds of sheep and goats and an abundant supply of water helped determine the location of these centers. It has been learned from excavations that the major industry at Tell Beit Mirsim (*see* DEBIR) was dyeing and weaving. Dye plants on a smaller scale were also found at GEZER; BETH-SHEMESH; Tell en-Nasbeh (ancient MIZPAH?); and BETH-ZUR. According to rabbinic traditions a Magadala on the Jarmuk was a dyeing center, and Luz near Shechem produced "blue stuffs." *See* CLOTH § 3*b*.

The dyeing operation itself is not well known from antiquity, but significant data regarding equipment and organization have been collected at various sites. At Tell Beit Mirsim* an estimated thirty homes devoted rooms roughly ten by twenty feet to dyeing, showing that it was a domestic, but well-organized,

industry. The installations excavated (six or seven in number) share a basic plan: each room was arranged with two round stone vats with small openings on top and retrieving drains around the rims; masonry basins and benches were constructed be-

Courtesy of the Oriental Institute, the University of Chicago
39. Dye plant at Tell Beit Mirsim

tween or in front of the vats. Occasionally an additional jar-vat was set into the bench. Additional storage jars containing lime or potash—for fixing the dyes—stood close by. As the size of the mouth of the vats indicates, thread rather than the woven fabric was dyed, from which multicolored cloth could be woven. The normal process required two baths, after which the dye was carefully squeezed out and saved. The dyed thread was then laid out to dry. The cold-bath process seems to have been employed in Palestine, but the Egyptians may have used the hot-bath method. Fig. DYE 39.

Similar Iron Age installations were found at Beth-shemesh and Tell en-Nasbeh, although, in the latter case, a single vat with the small opening in the top and no benches seem to have been characteristic. A Hellenistic dye plant of considerable proportions found at Gezer indicates that the fundamental arrangement had been altered little in the intervening centuries; an illuminating difference is the concentration of three dyeing rooms in a single building, indicating consolidation of the physical plant. Stone vats have given way to large masonry tanks in the shape of bathtubs; the pair in each room is accompanied by the same open vats and benches nearby. A furnace in the cellar of this establishment points to the use of hot dyes. A comparable, though less elaborate, dye plant appeared in the Hellenistic level at Beth-zur. Scattered throughout the city, moreover, were smaller, single stepped-baths which may have been connected with dyeing or may have been used for laundry or bathing. The rooms with two tanks, open vats, and benches at both Gezer and Beth-zur, however, are best understood in connection with dyeing.

**Bibliography.** R. A. S. Macalister, *Gezer,* I (1912), 223-28. L. Klebs, *Die Reliefs und Malereien des mittleren Reiches* (1922), pp. 123-24, Fig. 89; *Die Reliefs und Malereien des neuen Reiches* (1932), pp. 181-82, Fig. 115 (illustrations from Egyptian tomb paints). O. R. Sellers, *Citadel of Beth-zur* (1933), pp. 16-19, pl. II. G. Dalman, *Arbeit und Sitte in Palästina,* V (1937), 70-89. E. Grant and G. E. Wright, *'Ain Shems Excavations,* vol. IV (1938), pls. XVIII-XXI; V (1939), 73, 75. W. F. Albright, *Tell Beit Mirsim*, vol. III (*AASOR*, vols. XXI-XXII; 1941-43), pp. 55-62, pls. 11*b*, 51*c-d*, 52, 53. C. C. McCown, *Tell en-Nasbeh*, vol. I (1947), p. 256, fig. 67, pl. 97. C. Singer *et al.*, eds., *A History of Technology* (1954), pp. 245-50.

R. W. FUNK

**DYSENTERY** [δυσεντερία] (Acts 28:8); KJV BLOODY FLUX. A painful, inflamed condition of the colon, with tenesmus and evacuations of blood and mucus. Bacillary and amoebic dysentery are the most common varieties. Dysentery may be acute, chronic, epidemic, or sporadic.

*See also* DISEASE; FEVER.       R. K. HARRISON

**DYSMAS** dĭz′məs. Alternately: DISMAS; DEMAS dē′məs; TITUS tī′təs. A name given to the penitent thief in the apocryphal stories prompted by Luke 23: 39-43, his unrepentant companion being usually called GESTAS. Garish stories of Dysmas' kindness to the infant Jesus, the infant's prediction of his crucifixion and instant admittance to paradise, and the fulfilment of this promise are found in such apocrypha as the Arabic Gospel of the Infancy (*see* INFANCY GOSPELS) and the Acts of Pilate (*see* PILATE, ACTS OF). As the *bonus* or *evangelicus latro* ("thief"), he received much attention from the Greek and Latin fathers, and eventual sainthood (Saint Latro). He is commemorated in the Roman church on March 25, in the Greek church on March 23, and in the Syrian and Mesopotamian church on the ninth day after Good Friday.

*Bibliography.* M. S. Enslin, "Hagiographic Mistletoe," *JR*, vol. XXV, no. 1 (Jan., 1945), pp. 10-24.     M. S. ENSLIN

# MAPS

MAP I

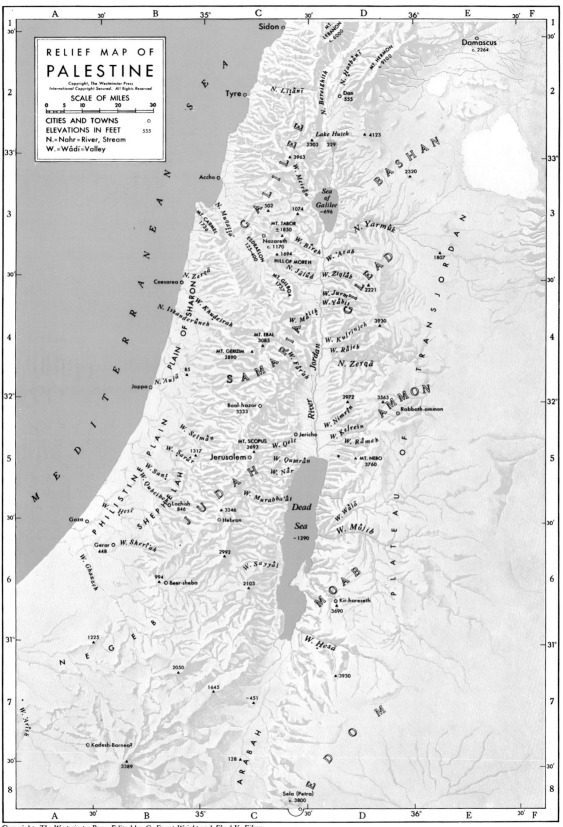

RELIEF MAP OF
# PALESTINE
Copyright, The Westminster Press
International Copyright Secured. All Rights Reserved

SCALE OF MILES
0 5 10 20 30

CITIES AND TOWNS ○
ELEVATIONS IN FEET 555
N.=Nahr=River, Stream
W.=Wâdi=Valley

MAP II

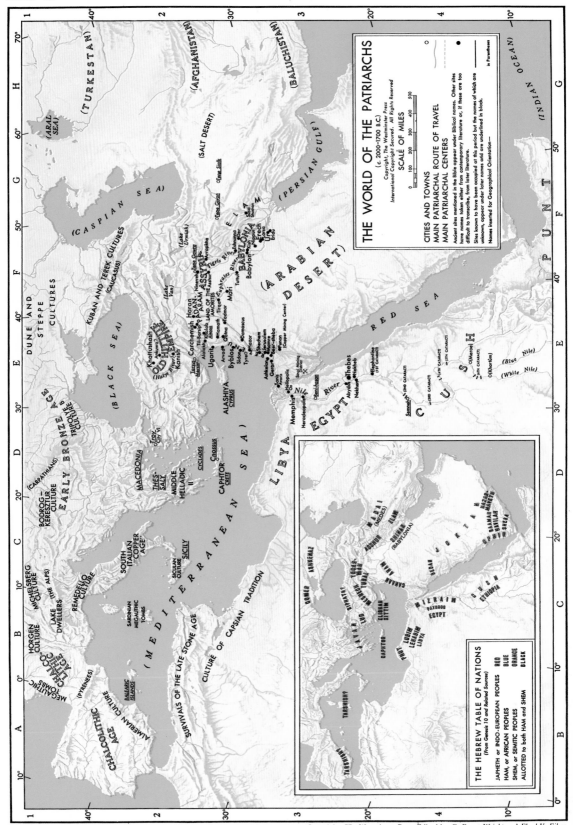

THE WORLD OF THE PATRIARCHS

(c. 2000–1700 B.C.)

Copyright, The Westminster Press
International Copyright Secured. All Rights Reserved

SCALE OF MILES

0   100   200   300   400   500

CITIES AND TOWNS

MAIN PATRIARCHAL ROUTE OF TRAVEL

MAIN PATRIARCHAL CENTERS

Names inserted for Geographical Orientation—

Ancient sites mentioned in the Bible appear under Biblical names. Other sites have names taken either from contemporary literature or, if these are too difficult to transcribe, from later literature.

Sites known to have been occupied at this period but the names of which are unknown, appear under later names and are underlined in block.

in Parentheses

THE HEBREW TABLE OF NATIONS

(From Genesis 10 and Related Sources)

JAPHETH or INDO-EUROPEAN PEOPLES    RED
HAM, or AFRICAN PEOPLES    BLUE
SHEM, or SEMITIC PEOPLES    ORANGE
ALLOTTED to both HAM and SHEM    BLACK

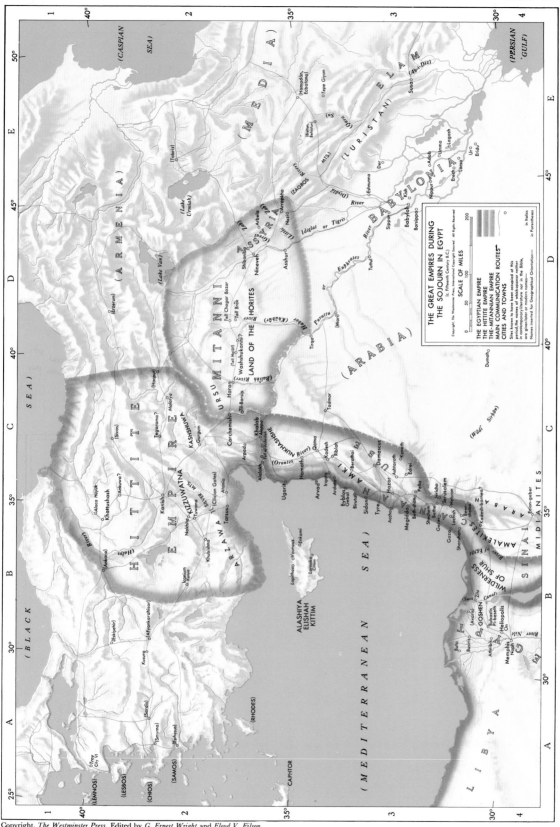

MAP III

THE GREAT EMPIRES DURING
THE SOJOURN IN EGYPT
(c. Fifteenth Century B.C.)

Copyright, The Westminster Press, International Copyright Secured. All Rights Reserved

SCALE OF MILES

THE EGYPTIAN EMPIRE
THE HITTITE EMPIRE
THE MITANNIAN EMPIRE
MAIN COMMUNICATION ROUTES
CITIES AND TOWNS

Sites known to have been occupied at this
period, the names of which appear neither
in contemporary literature nor in the Bible,
are given later or modern names—
Names inserted for Geographical Orientation—

# MAP IV

THE LAND OF
## CANAAN
BEFORE THE
ISRAELITE
CONQUEST

Copyright, The Westminster Press
International Copyright Secured. All Rights Reserved

SCALE OF MILES

0   5   10   15   20   25   30

BOUNDARIES
UNCERTAIN
BOUNDARIES
○ CITIES AND TOWNS
ROADS

MAP V

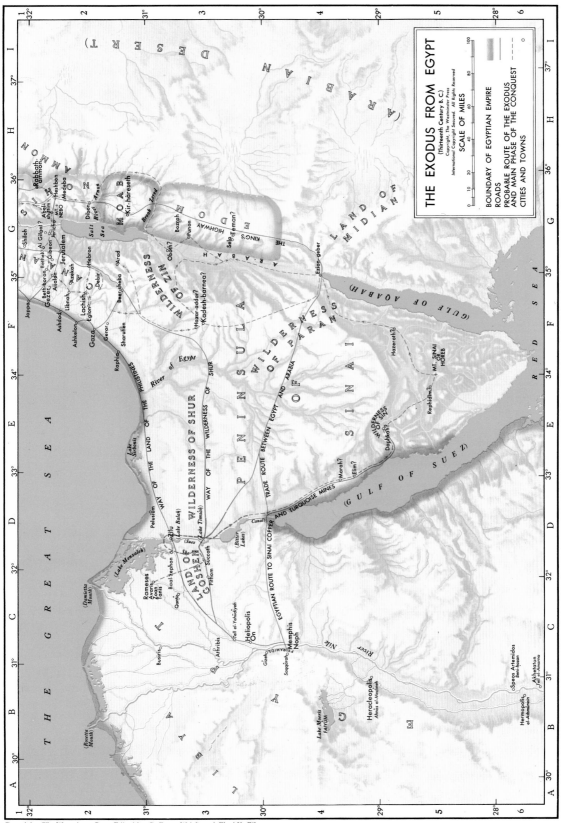

## THE EXODUS FROM EGYPT

(Thirteenth Century B.C.)

SCALE OF MILES

BOUNDARY OF EGYPTIAN EMPIRE
ROADS
PROBABLE ROUTE OF THE EXODUS
AND MAIN PHASE OF THE CONQUEST
CITIES AND TOWNS

Copyright, *The Westminster Press*. Edited by *G. Ernest Wright* and *Floyd V. Filson*.

# MAP VI

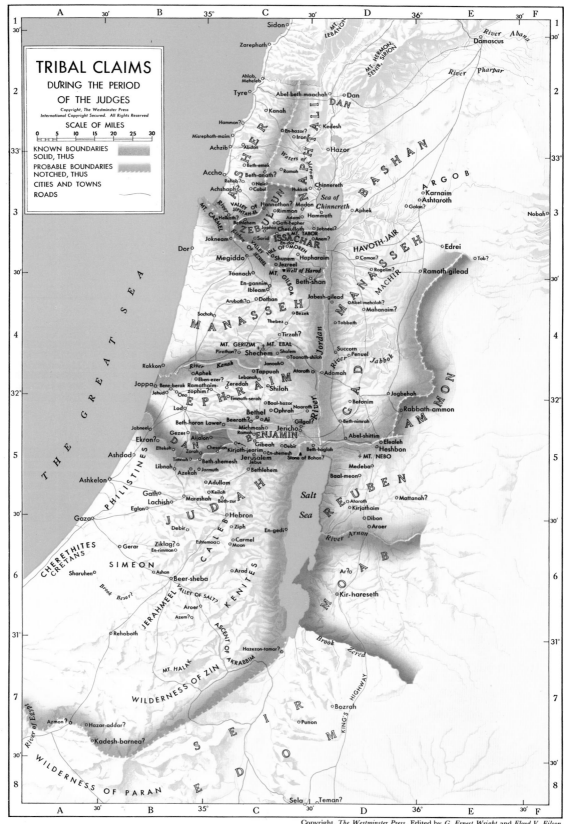

## TRIBAL CLAIMS
### DURING THE PERIOD
### OF THE JUDGES

SCALE OF MILES

0  5  10  15  20  25  30

KNOWN BOUNDARIES
SOLID, THUS

PROBABLE BOUNDARIES
NOTCHED, THUS

CITIES AND TOWNS

ROADS

MAP VII

CYPRUS

THE GREAT SEA

PHOENICIA

MT. LEBANON

MT. HERMON

ISRAEL

PHILISTIA

JUDAH

GESHUR

MAACHAH

ZOBAH

AMMON

MOAB

EDOM

(ARABIAN DESERT)

Hamath

Arvad

Tadmor

Kadesh

Riblah

Chun

Zedad

Hazar-enan?

Byblos
Gebal

Berothai

Helbon

Sidon

Damascus

Ijon?

Abel

Dan

Tyre

Accho

Cabul

Ashtaroth

Nobah

Dor

Megiddo

Edrei

Ramoth-gilead

Salcah

Mahanaim?

Shechem

Adamah

Joppa

Bethel

Rabbath-ammon
Rabbah

Ashdod

Jerusalem

Heshbon

Medeba

Ashkelon

Gath

Hebron

Dibon

Gaza

Lachish

Salt
Sea

Gerar

Beer-sheba

Ar?

Kir-hareseth

Bozrah

Punon

Kadesh-barnea?

River of Egypt

Sela

Teman?

Ezion-geber

IX, VIII, X, IV, V, III, VII, VI, I, XII, XI, II

THE EMPIRE OF DAVID
AND SOLOMON
(c. 1000-930 B.C.)
Copyright, The Westminster Press
International Copyright Secured. All Rights Reserved

SCALE OF MILES
0   10   20        40        60

BOUNDARY OF THE EMPIRE
INDEPENDENT PHILISTIA AND PHOENICIA
ADMINISTRATIVE DISTRICTS OF SOLOMON
TERRITORY CONQUERED BY DAVID
CITIES AND TOWNS                      o

MAP VIII

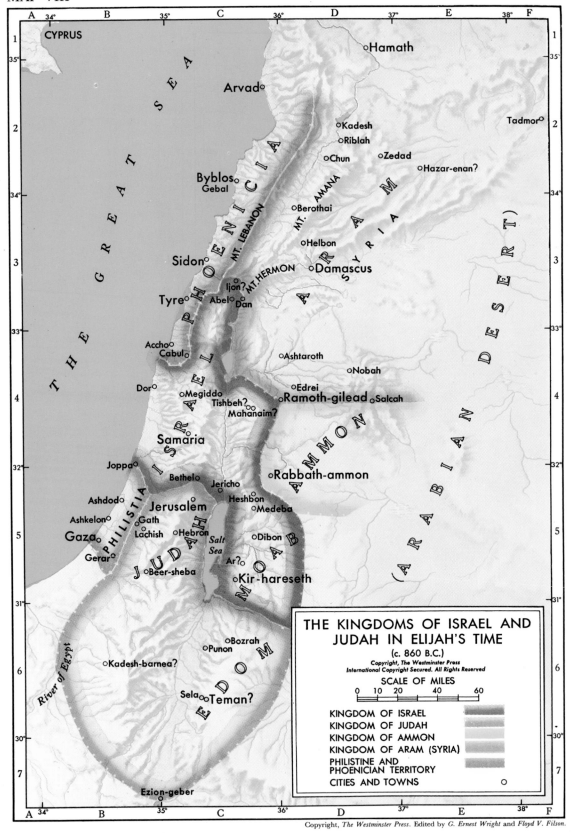

CYPRUS

oHamath

Arvad o

THE GREAT SEA

oKadesh
oRiblah
Chun o
oZedad
oHazar-enan?

Byblos
Gebal

oBerothai

PHOENICIA
MT. LEBANON
MT. AMANA
ARAM
SYRIA

oHelbon

Sidon o
MT. HERMON
Ijon? o
Abel o Dan
oDamascus

Tyre o

Accho o
Cabul o

Dor o
oMegiddo
Tishbeh? o o
Mahanaim? o

oAshtaroth
oNobah
oEdrei
Ramoth-gilead o oSalcah

ISRAEL

AMMON

Samaria

Joppa o

Bethel o
Jericho o
Rabbath-ammon o

Ashdod o
Jerusalem
Heshbon o
oMedeba

Ashkelon o
o Gath
Lachish o
Hebron o
Salt
Sea
oDibon

Gaza o
JUDAH
Ar? o
MOAB

Gerar o
Beer-sheba o
Kir-hareseth

PHILISTIA

(ARABIAN DESERT)

River of Egypt

oBozrah
Punon o
o Kadesh-barnea?

EDOM

Sela o
Teman?

Ezion-geber

**THE KINGDOMS OF ISRAEL AND
JUDAH IN ELIJAH'S TIME**
(c. 860 B.C.)
Copyright, The Westminster Press
International Copyright Secured. All Rights Reserved
SCALE OF MILES
0  10  20    40        60

KINGDOM OF ISRAEL
KINGDOM OF JUDAH
KINGDOM OF AMMON
KINGDOM OF ARAM (SYRIA)
PHILISTINE AND
PHOENICIAN TERRITORY
CITIES AND TOWNS        o

MAP IX

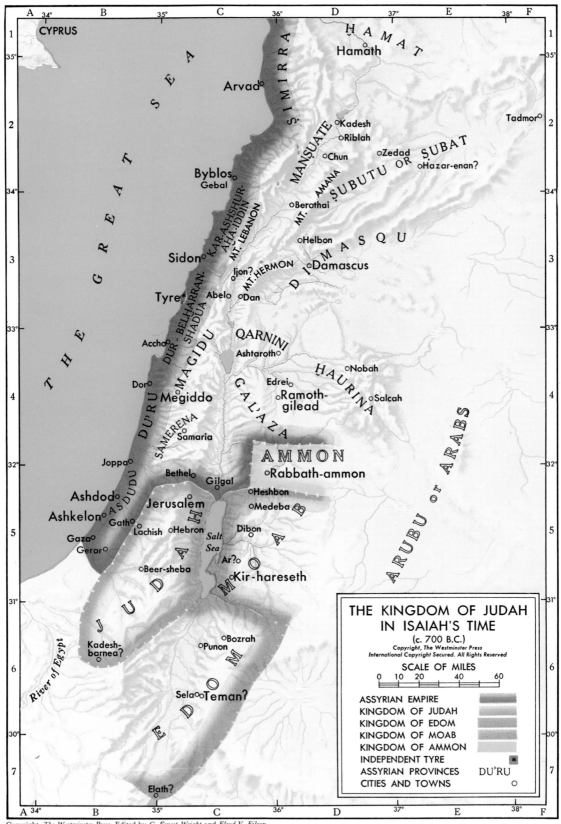

THE GREAT SEA

CYPRUS

HAMAT
Hamath

ȘIMIRRA

Arvad

MANSUATE

Kadesh
Riblah
Chun
Zedad
Hazar-enan?

MT. AMANA

ȘUBUTU OR ȘUBAT

Tadmor

Byblos
Gebal

Berothai

Helbon

KARAȘHSHUR-AIJA-IDDIN

DIMASQU

MT. LEBANON

Sidon

Ijon?
MT. HERMON

Damascus

Tyre
Abelo
Dan

DUR-BELHARRAN-SHADUA

Accho
QARNINI

Ashtaroth

Nobah

HAURINA

DU'RU
Doro

MAGIDU

Edrei
Ramoth-gilead

Salcah

Megiddo

GAL'AZA

SAMERENA
Samaria

Joppa

AMMON
Rabbath-ammon

ARUBU OR ARABS

Bethel
Gilgal

Heshbon
Medeba

Ashdod
Ashkelon
Gath

ASBUDU

Jerusalem

M O A B

Gaza
Gerar

Lachish
Hebron

Salt Sea

Dibon

JUDAH

Beer-sheba

Ar?

Kir-hareseth

River of Egypt

Kadesh-barnea?

Bozrah
Punon

E D O M

Sela
Teman?

Elath?

THE KINGDOM OF JUDAH
IN ISAIAH'S TIME
(c. 700 B.C.)
Copyright, The Westminster Press
International Copyright Secured. All Rights Reserved

SCALE OF MILES
0  10  20    40      60

ASSYRIAN EMPIRE
KINGDOM OF JUDAH
KINGDOM OF EDOM
KINGDOM OF MOAB
KINGDOM OF AMMON
INDEPENDENT TYRE            *
ASSYRIAN PROVINCES        DU'RU
CITIES AND TOWNS            o

## MAP X

**CYPRUS**

THE GREAT SEA

Hamath

Arvad
ARVAD

HAMATH

Tadmor

Tripolis
TRIPOLIS

Riblah
Chun

Zedad

Hazar-enan?

Byblos
Gebal
BYBLOS

ROYAL PARK

MASSYAS

MT. AMANA

Berothai

Helbon

Sidon
SIDON

Ijon?
MT. HERMON

Damascus

Tyre
TYRE

Abel
Dan

GELIL
HA-GOIM

QARNAIM

Accho

Ashtaroth

HAURAN

Nobah

Dor
DOR

Ramoth-
gilead

Edrei

Salcah

SAMARIA

GILEAD

Samaria

AMMON

Joppa

Bethel

Rabbath-ammon

Ashdod
ASHDOD

JUDAH

Jerusalem

Heshbon

Medeba

Ashkelon

Beth-zur

Gaza

Lachish

Hebron

Salt
Sea

Gerar

IDUMAEA

MOAB

Beer-sheba

(ARABIAN DESERT)

ARABS

River of Egypt

Kadesh-barnea?

Elath?

### THE PROVINCE OF JUDAH
### IN NEHEMIAH'S TIME
#### (c. 440 B.C.)

#### SCALE OF MILES

0   10   20   40   60

BOUNDARY OF THE
PERSIAN EMPIRE

PROVINCES OF THE
FIFTH PERSIAN SATRAPY

CITIES AND TOWNS          ○

MAP XI

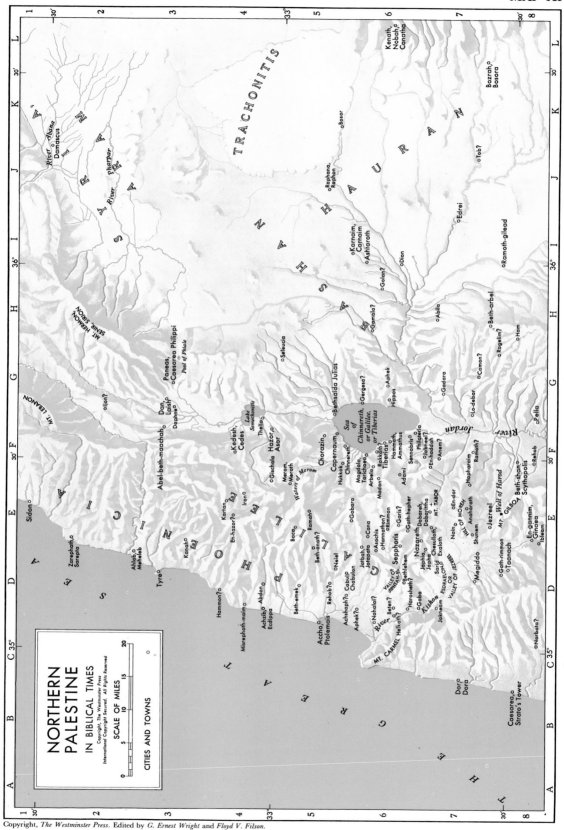

NORTHERN
PALESTINE
IN BIBLICAL TIMES

Copyright, The Westminster Press
International Copyright Secured. All Rights Reserved

SCALE OF MILES

CITIES AND TOWNS

MAP XII

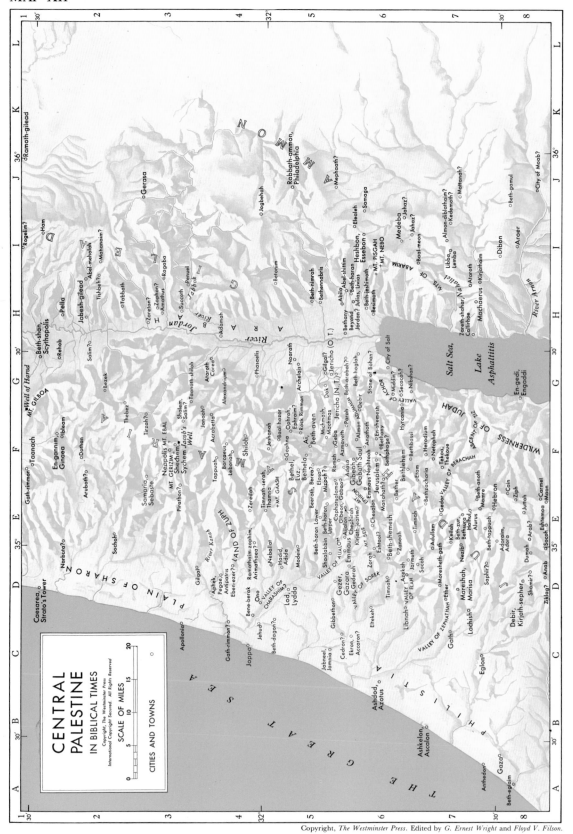

CENTRAL PALESTINE
IN BIBLICAL TIMES

SCALE OF MILES

0  5  10  15  20

CITIES AND TOWNS   o

MAP XIII

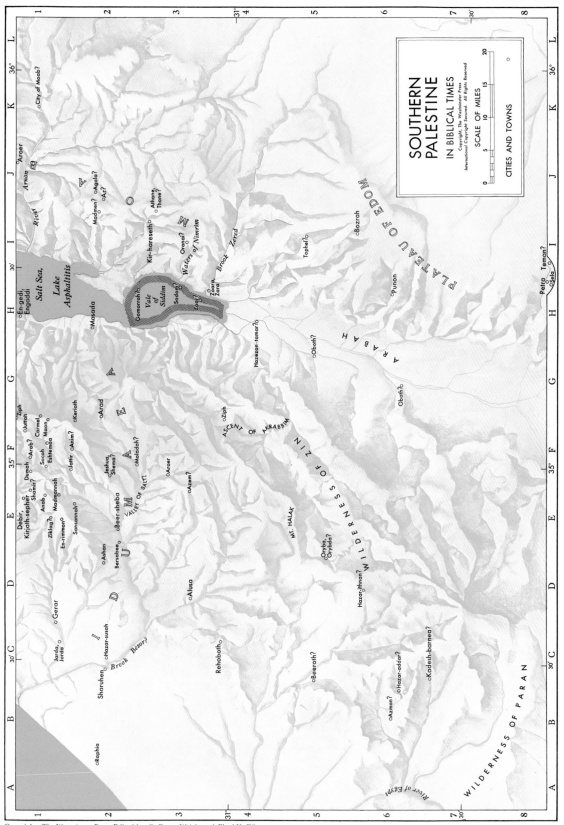

SOUTHERN
PALESTINE
IN BIBLICAL TIMES
Copyright, The Westminster Press
International Copyright Secured. All Rights Reserved

SCALE OF MILES
0    5    10    15    20

CITIES AND TOWNS    ○

MAP XIV

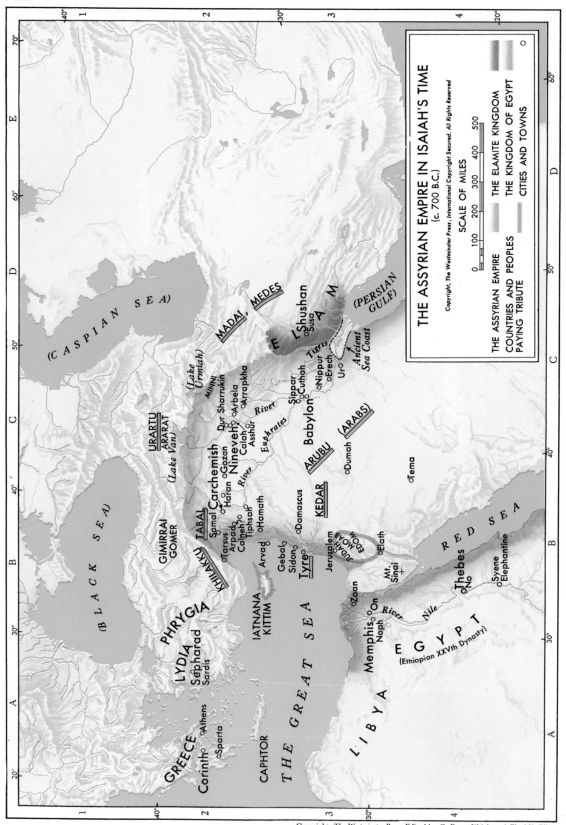

THE ASSYRIAN EMPIRE IN ISAIAH'S TIME
(c. 700 B.C.)

SCALE OF MILES

0  100  200  300  400  500

THE ASSYRIAN EMPIRE
COUNTRIES AND PEOPLES
PAYING TRIBUTE

THE ELAMITE KINGDOM
THE KINGDOM OF EGYPT
CITIES AND TOWNS

(CASPIAN SEA)

(BLACK SEA)

GREECE
Corinth
Athens
Sparta

CAPHTOR

LYDIA
Sepharad
Sardis

PHRYGIA

GIMIRRAI
GOMER

KHILAKKU

TABAL

URARTU
ARARAT
(Lake Van)

(Lake Urmiah)

MINNI

MADAI, MEDES

ELAM
Shushan
Susa

(PERSIAN GULF)

Tigris

Ancient Sea Coast

Nippur
Cuthah
Erech
Ur

Sippar
Babylon

(ARABS)

ARUBU

Dumah

KEDAR

Tema

Dur Sharrukin
Gozan
Arbela
Arrapkha
Nineveh
Calah
Asshur

Carchemish
Haran

River

Euphrates

River

Samal
Tarsus
Arpad
Calneh
Tiphsah
Hamath

Damascus

Arvad
Gebal
Sidon
Tyre

Jerusalem
JUDAH
MOAB
EDOM
Elath

Mt. Sinai

RED SEA

Thebes
No

Syene
Elephantine

IATNANA
KITTIM

THE GREAT SEA

Zoan
On
Memphis
Noph
River
Nile

LIBYA

EGYPT
(Ethiopian XXVth Dynasty)

MAP XV

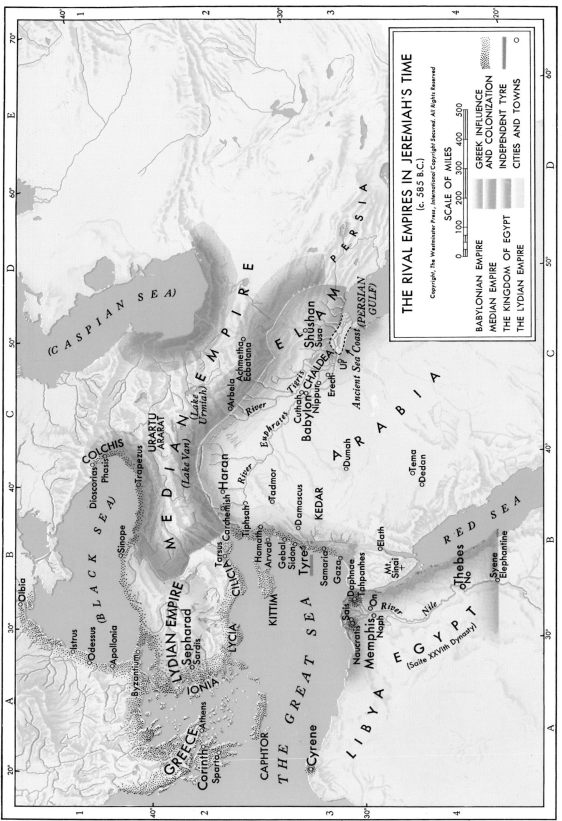

THE RIVAL EMPIRES IN JEREMIAH'S TIME
(c. 585 B.C.)

SCALE OF MILES

0   100   200   300   400   500

BABYLONIAN EMPIRE

MEDIAN EMPIRE

THE KINGDOM OF EGYPT

THE LYDIAN EMPIRE

GREEK INFLUENCE AND COLONIZATION

INDEPENDENT TYRE

○ CITIES AND TOWNS

(CASPIAN SEA)

BLACK SEA

THE GREAT SEA

RED SEA

MEDIAN EMPIRE

ELAM

PERSIA

CHALDEA

ARABIA

EGYPT (Saite XXVIth Dynasty)

LIBYA

GREECE

IONIA

LYDIAN EMPIRE

LYCIA

CILICIA

KITTIM

CAPHTOR

COLCHIS

URARTU ARART

KEDAR

Olbia
Istrus
Odessus
Apollonia
Byzantium
Sepharad
Sardis
Corinth
Athens
Sparta
Cyrene
Dioscorias
Phasis
Trapezus
Sinope
Tarsus
Carchemish
Haran
Tiphsah
Hamath
Arvad
Gebal
Sidon
Tyre
Samaria
Gaza
Damascus
Tadmor
Dumah
Tema
Dedan
Arbela
Achmetha Ecbatana
(Lake Urmiah)
(Lake Van)
Shushan Susa
Babylon
Cuthah
Nippur
Erech
Ur
Elath
Mt. Sinai
Daphnae
Tahpanhes
Sais
Naucratis
On
Noph Memphis
Thebes No
Syene Elephantine
Nile River
Euphrates River
Tigris River

Ancient Sea Coast (PERSIAN GULF)

MAP XVI

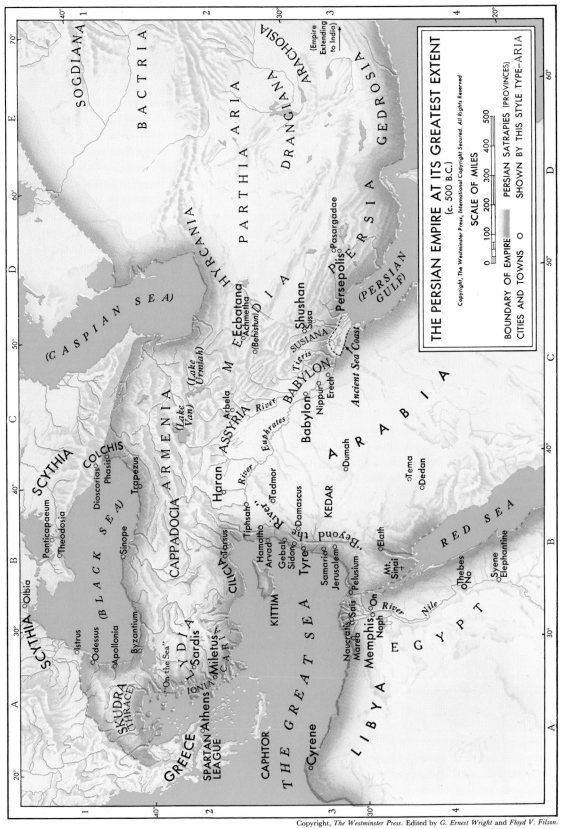

### THE PERSIAN EMPIRE AT ITS GREATEST EXTENT
(c. 500 B.C.)

Copyright, The Westminster Press, International Copyright Secured. All Rights Reserved

SCALE OF MILES

0   100   200   300   400   500

BOUNDARY OF EMPIRE ——  PERSIAN SATRAPIES (PROVINCES)
CITIES AND TOWNS  o       SHOWN BY THIS STYLE TYPE–ARIA

MAP XVII

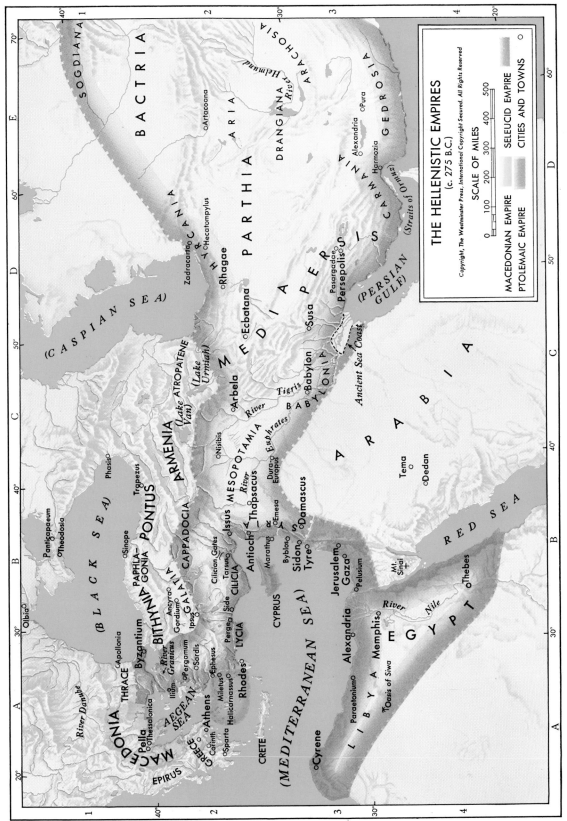

THE HELLENISTIC EMPIRES
(c. 275 B.C.)

Copyright, The Westminster Press, International Copyright Secured. All Rights Reserved

SCALE OF MILES

0   100   200   300   400   500

MACEDONIAN EMPIRE

PTOLEMAIC EMPIRE

SELEUCID EMPIRE

CITIES AND TOWNS   o

MAP XVIII

## PALESTINE
### IN THE
### MACCABEAN PERIOD
#### (168-63 B.C.)

(SEA)
Sidon
PHOENICIA
MT. LIBANUS
MT. HERMON
Damascus
Tyre
Cedes
Asor
GAULANITIS
Seleucia
Ptolemais
GALILEE
Raphon
Bosor
Carnaim
Cana
Tarichaea
Asochis
Arbela
Gamala?
Sepphoris
Hippos
Dion
Philoteria
MT. CARMEL
Dora
Gadara
Bosora
Bostra
Strato's Tower
SAMARIA
Scythopolis
GALAADITIS
Pella
Samaria
Asophon?
Gerasa
Apollonia
Pharathon?
Amathus
Ragaba
Antipatris
Sichem
PERAEA
Joppa
Corea
Alexandrium
Lydda
Modein
Gophna
Philadelphia
Elasa
Aphairema?
Jamnia
Gazara
Berea
Cedron?
Caphar-
Machmas
Dok
Accaron?
salama
Adasa
Jericho
Massepha?
Samaga
Azotus
Jerusalem
JUDAEA
Hyrcania
Medeba
Ascalon
Bethzacharia
Bethbassi
Libba
Marisa
Bethsura
Lemba
Anthedon
Adora
Hebron
Machaerus
Gaza
Adoreus
(Dead
IDUMAEA
Sea)
MOABITIS
Raphia
Agala?
Athone?
Alusa
Thone?
Oronai?
Zoara
Zara
MEDITERRANEAN
Oryba?
Orybda?
N
A
B
A
T
A
E
A
Petra

### SCALE OF MILES

0  5  10    20      30

BOUNDARY LINE SHOWS MAXIMUM
EXTENT OF MACCABEAN KINGDOM
UNDER ALEXANDER JANNAEUS
(103-76 B.C.)

KINGDOM OF
ALEXANDER JANNAEUS

FREE CITY - - -

CITIES AND TOWNS  ○

MAP XIX

## PALESTINE
### UNDER
### HEROD THE GREAT
### (40-4 B.C.)

Copyright, The Westminster Press
International Copyright Secured.   All Rights Reserved

SCALE OF MILES

0   5   10      20      30

KINGDOM OF
HEROD THE GREAT
DECAPOLIS
FREE CITY
CITIES AND TOWNS

MAP XX

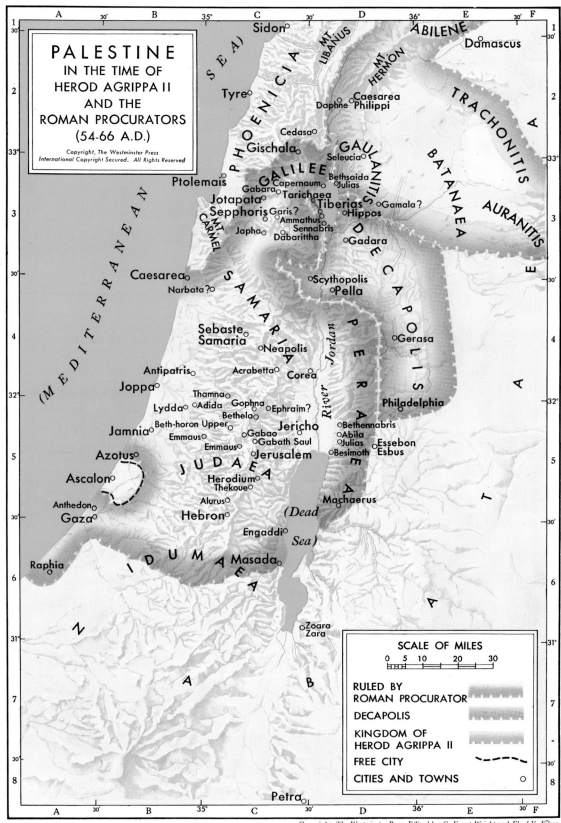

# PALESTINE
## IN THE TIME OF
## HEROD AGRIPPA II
## AND THE
## ROMAN PROCURATORS
### (54-66 A.D.)

Sidon

Damascus

ABILENE

(SEA)

MT LIBANUS

MT HERMON

Tyre

Caesarea
Daphne Philippi

TRACHONITIS

Cedasa

Gischala

PHOENICIA

GAULANITIS

Seleucia

BATANAEA

AURANITIS

Ptolemais

GALILEE

Bethsaida
Julias

Capernaum

Gabara

Tarichaea

Gamala?

Jotapata

Tiberias

Hippos

Sepphoris

Garis?

Ammathus

Japha

Sennabris

Dabarittha

MT. CARMEL

Gadara

DECAPOLIS

Caesarea

Scythopolis

Narbata?

Pella

SAMARIA

River Jordan

Sebaste
Samaria

Gerasa

PERAEA

Neapolis

Antipatris

Acrabetta

Corea

Joppa

Philadelphia

Thamna

Lydda

Adida

Gophna

Ephraim?

Bethela

Beth-horon Upper

Jericho

Bethennabris

Jamnia

Gabao

Abila
Julias

Essebon

Emmaus

Gabath Saul

Besimoth

Esbus

Azotus

Emmaus

Jerusalem

JUDAEA

Ascalon

Herodium
Thekoue

Anthedon

Alurus

Machaerus

Gaza

Hebron

(Dead

Engaddi

Sea)

Raphia

IDUMAEA

Masada

N

Zoara
Zara

A

B

(MEDITERRANEAN

Petra

## SCALE OF MILES

0  5  10    20    30

RULED BY
ROMAN PROCURATOR

DECAPOLIS

KINGDOM OF
HEROD AGRIPPA II

FREE CITY

CITIES AND TOWNS    ○

MAP XXI

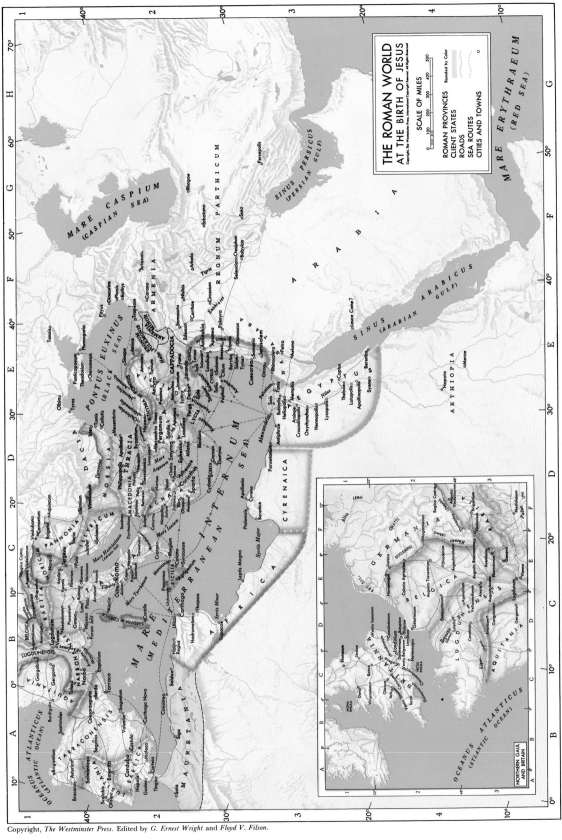

MAP XXII

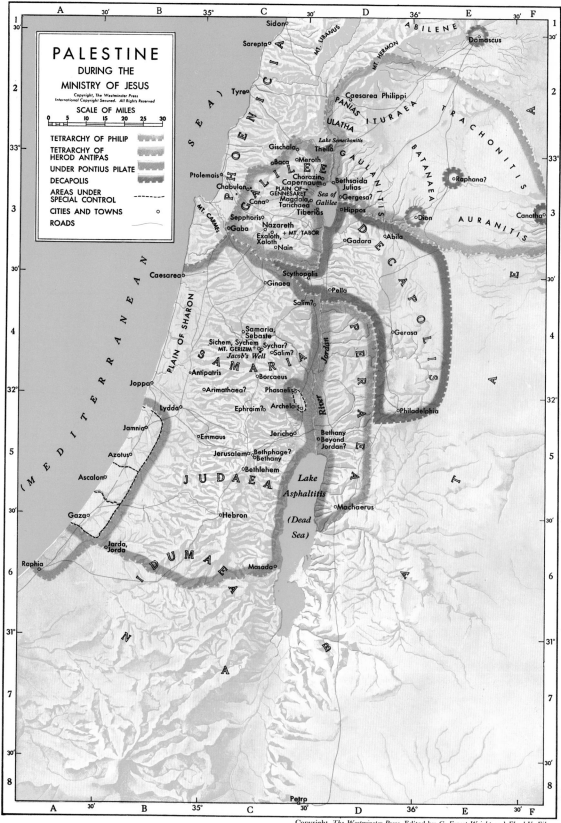

PALESTINE
DURING THE
MINISTRY OF JESUS

Copyright, The Westminster Press
International Copyright Secured. All Rights Reserved

SCALE OF MILES

0    5    10   15   20   25   30

TETRARCHY OF PHILIP
TETRARCHY OF
HEROD ANTIPAS
UNDER PONTIUS PILATE
DECAPOLIS
AREAS UNDER
SPECIAL CONTROL
CITIES AND TOWNS            o
ROADS

Copyright, *The Westminster Press*. Edited by *G. Ernest Wright* and *Floyd V. Filson*.

MAP XXIII

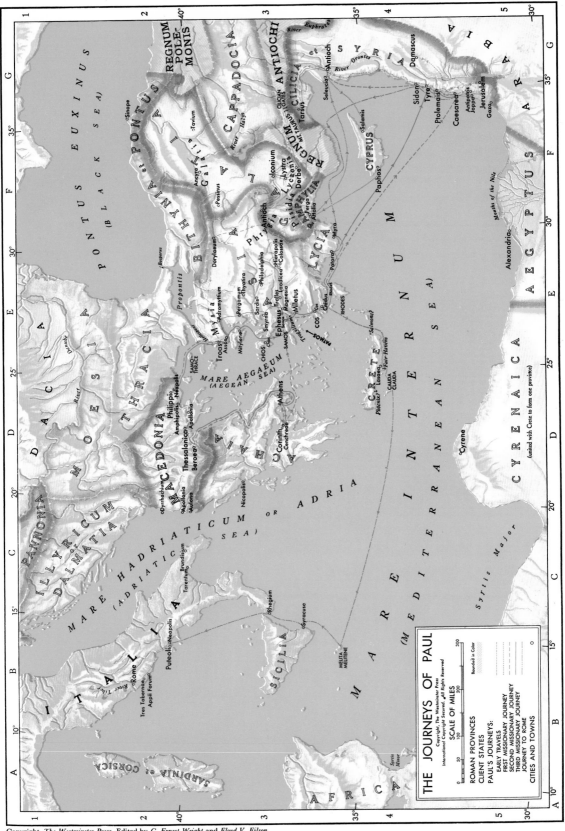

### THE JOURNEYS OF PAUL

Copyright, The Westminster Press. All Rights Reserved
International Copyright Secured.

SCALE OF MILES

ROMAN PROVINCES
CLIENT STATES
PAUL'S JOURNEYS:
   EARLY TRAVELS
   FIRST MISSIONARY JOURNEY
   SECOND MISSIONARY JOURNEY
   THIRD MISSIONARY JOURNEY
   JOURNEY TO ROME
   CITIES AND TOWNS

MAP XXIV

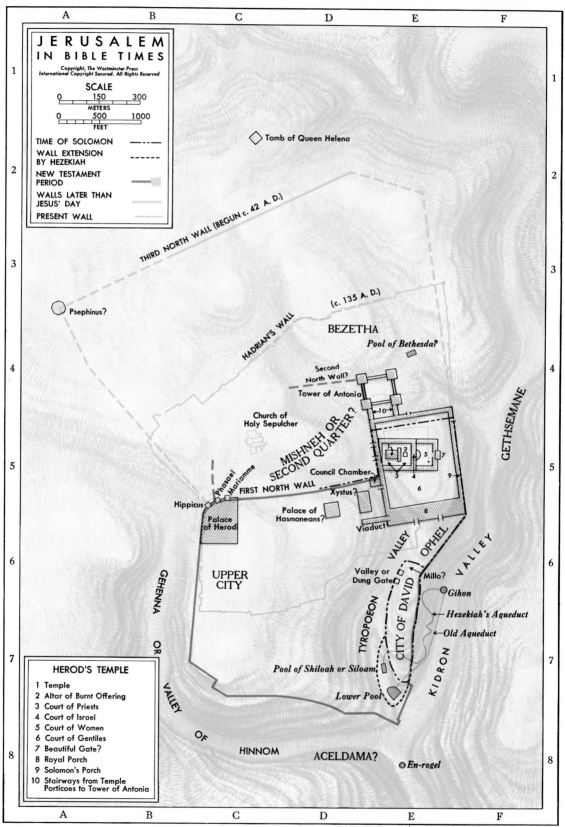

**JERUSALEM IN BIBLE TIMES**

Copyright, The Westminster Press
International Copyright Secured. All Rights Reserved

SCALE

0    150    300
METERS

0    500    1000
FEET

| | |
|---|---|
| TIME OF SOLOMON | —·—·— |
| WALL EXTENSION BY HEZEKIAH | — — — |
| NEW TESTAMENT PERIOD | |
| WALLS LATER THAN JESUS' DAY | |
| PRESENT WALL | |

Tomb of Queen Helena

THIRD NORTH WALL (BEGUN c. 42 A.D.)

Psephinus?

HADRIAN'S WALL

(c. 135 A.D.)

BEZETHA

Pool of Bethesda?

Second North Wall?

Tower of Antonia

Church of Holy Sepulcher

MISHNEH OR SECOND QUARTER?

Council Chamber

Phasael
Mariamme

FIRST NORTH WALL

Xystus?

Hippicus

Palace of Herod

Palace of Hasmoneans?

Viaduct

UPPER CITY

GEHENNA OR

VALLEY

OF

HINNOM

ACELDAMA?

En-rogel

TYROPOEON VALLEY

Valley or Dung Gate

CITY OF DAVID

OPHEL

Millo?

Gihon

Hezekiah's Aqueduct

Old Aqueduct

KIDRON VALLEY

GETHSEMANE

Pool of Shiloah or Siloam

Lower Pool

**HEROD'S TEMPLE**

1 Temple
2 Altar of Burnt Offering
3 Court of Priests
4 Court of Israel
5 Court of Women
6 Court of Gentiles
7 Beautiful Gate?
8 Royal Porch
9 Solomon's Porch
10 Stairways from Temple Porticoes to Tower of Antonia

# THE OLD TESTAMENT

| | |
|---|---|
| Genesis | Song of Solomon |
| Exodus | Isaiah |
| Leviticus | Jeremiah |
| Numbers | Lamentations |
| Deuteronomy | Ezekiel |
| Joshua | Daniel |
| Judges | Hosea |
| Ruth | Joel |
| I and II Samuel | Amos |
| I and II Kings | Obadiah |
| I and II Chronicles | Jonah |
| Ezra | Micah |
| Nehemiah | Nahum |
| Esther | Habakkuk |
| Job | Zephaniah |
| Psalms | Haggai |
| Proverbs | Zechariah |
| Ecclesiastes | Malachi |

# THE APOCRYPHA

I and II Esdras
Tobit
Judith
Additions to Esther
Wisdom of Solomon
Ecclesiasticus (Wisdom of Jesus
     the Son of Sirach)
Baruch
Letter of Jeremiah
Prayer of Azariah
Song of the Three Young Men
Susanna
Bel and the Dragon
Prayer of Manasseh
I and II Maccabees